43rd EDITION

CAMRA's GOOD BEER GUIDE

2016

Edited by Roger Protz

Head of Publishing Simon Hall
Project Managers Emma Haines, Susannah Lord
Assistant Editors Ione Brown, Simon Tuite
Project Assistance Katie Button, Julie Hudson, Iain Loe, Emma Porrett
Sales & Marketing David Birkett

CAMRA BOOKS

Contents

The Pubs

The Breweries

Indexes & Further Information

Special thanks to 175,000 CAMRA members who carried out research for the pub entries; the Campaign's Regional Directors and Area Organisers, who co-ordinated the pub entries; the Campaign's Brewery Liaison Officers and Brewery Liaison Coordinators, who carried out research for the brewery entries; Paul Moorhouse for assembling the beer tasting notes; Michael Slaughter for advising on heritage pubs; Alex Presland for technical support; Nik Antona and Abi Newton for assistance co-ordinating the brewery entries; the publicans, breweries and others who kindly contributed their photographs; and CAMRA's National Executive for their support.

Thanks also to the following at CAMRA head office: Lauren Anderson, Richard Ashton, Steven Brooks, Jill Burder, Caroline Clerembaux, David Cooper, John Cottrell, Neil Cox, Helen Curnow, Gillian Dale, Aaron Dobbing, Rob Ferguson, Nick Forshaw, Gary Fowler, Anita Gibson, Faye Grima, Ganesh Gudka, Ellie Hudspith, Jamie Hughes, Benedict Hume, Nicole Hyams, Paul Kelly, Ayo Kila, Chris Lewis, Katie McKelliget, Jonathan Mail, Jay Norton, Marilyn O'Donoghue, Tim Page, Rachel Rissbrook, Emily Ryans, Gregory Rycroft, Nicky Shipp, Barnaby Smith, Tom Stainer, Ron Stocks, Claire-Michelle Taverner-Pearson, Neil Walker, Liz Wickham.

Photo credits: [Key: t = top; b = bottom; c=centre; l = left; r = right] p4: Cath Harries; p5: Sheffield Tap; p8: (b) Carlsberggroup.com; p9: (t) Baylis Media Ltd; p10: (l) Flickr/Ewan Munro, (r) Adam Thomas; p11: (t) Steve Weemes/Hertfordshire Mercury; p14: Jonathan Kemp; p15: Roger Protz; p16: (l) Roger Protz, (r) Fred Samuel; p18: (l) Layla Parry-Hide, (r) Josh Muldoon; p24: (l) Tom Stainer, (r) Valentyn Volkov/shutterstock; p25: (l) photowind/shutterstock, (r) Tom Stainer; p26 (b) Cath Harries; p683: Matt Balls; p1009: Roger Protz

Maps & illustrations: Cover illustration: © Claire Rollet; illustration p25: Mark Walker, MW Digital Graphics; Pubs section maps: David and Morag Perrot, PerroCarto.

Production: Cover and colour pages design: Keith Holmes, Thames Street Studio; database, typesetting and indexes: AMA Dataset Ltd, Preston.

Printed and bound in the UK by William Clowes, Beccles, Suffolk.

Typeset in Stag and Dax.

Published by the Campaign for Real Ale Ltd, 230 Hatfield Road, St Albans, Herts, AL1 4LW.
www.camra.org.uk

 ISBN 978-1-85249-327-1

About the Good Beer Guide

It's far more than just a pub guide

If you need to know where to find a good pub serving good beer, then let this guide be your constant companion. It's far more than just a pub guide – it directs you to breweries, their ales as well as the essential outlets in towns and rural areas where you can enjoy them.

More than just a pub guide

Pubs are the central core of the Guide, the essential outlets for real ale. But the *Good Beer Guide* has always walked tall on two feet, with its Breweries section complementing the pub listings by detailing all the producers of cask beer and their regular ales. As well as listing some 4,500 of the finest outlets for real ale and the ever-growing number of breweries, we also look at the threats to the pub and good beer and the spirited fight-back by consumers and publicans: see the Introduction on pages 6–9.

Comprehensive Breweries section

The *Good Beer Guide* includes a comprehensive listing of all British breweries and their core beers. Breweries are monitored on a regular basis and each brewery is visited by CAMRA members, who speak to the brewer and check on the beers being produced before reporting to the Guide. As soon as a new brewery comes on stream, a liaison officer will be appointed to make sure the Breweries section of the Guide is updated every year and readers are aware of the increased choice available.

Democratically selected entries

The way in which pubs are chosen is equally meticulous and unique. Much of CAMRA's 175,000-plus membership is involved and those members who cannot be active or attend regular meetings are invited to recommend pubs via email or branch websites. Branch areas are broken down into local sections so pubs can be monitored regularly. The quality of beer in each pub is checked using a meticulous 'beer scoring' system. Special branch meetings are convened once a year where short-lists are presented and then members vote on the final selection for the Guide.

Regular inspections

The entries in most pub guides are chosen either by small editorial teams or by members of the public, whose recommendations are not necessarily checked. On the other hand, every pub that appears in this Guide has been visited regularly, often weekly, by CAMRA members. We offer full entries, with no unchecked 'lucky dip' sections of pubs sent in at random. Readers' recommendations are passed to local CAMRA branches, who take this feedback on board during their survey work.

It's not only about quality beer

The key driving force of the Guide – beer quality – has not changed over 43 years. However, the Guide also takes account of the history and architecture of pubs and such important aspects as food, family and disabled facilities, gardens, special events such as mini-beer festivals, and even the standard of the toilets. CAMRA volunteers are called on to be minor essayists, describing in detail all aspects of the pubs they choose. We know, from the feedback we receive, that users of the Guide need full information about pubs before embarking on journeys to visit them.

Town & country pubs

In addition to full descriptions, users want a good spread of pubs. Unlike some guides that concentrate on rural pubs, we recognise that most people live in towns and cities and expect a good selection of pubs in those areas. But we don't neglect suburban and country pubs: on the contrary, CAMRA campaigns for the survival of rural pubs that are often vital hubs of their isolated communities.

We are at pains to ensure that all areas of the country are covered. Each county or region has an allocation of pubs based on a scientific calculation of population, number of licensed premises and the level of 'tourist penetration'. As a result, the Guide's reach is unparalleled.

The *Good Beer Guide* celebrates Britain's pubs and cask-conditioned real ale

Proudly independent

Unlike many of our competitors, all entries are free. CAMRA is a proudly independent organisation and there are no hidden costs of appearing in the *Good Beer Guide*. CAMRA is a broad church and the Guide reflects that by choosing pubs across a wide spectrum that will appeal to people from all walks of life, regardless of income and background.

Keeping up to date

The Campaign has more than 200 branches. Each branch surveys the pubs in its area and monitors not only the quality of the cask beer in each one but also watches for change of ownership or management that could affect the range of ale on offer and the overall standard of the pub. In addition, branch officers liaise frequently with breweries in their areas and keep a close eye on the local brewing scene.

There is a cynical saying in the publishing world that all guide books are out of date as soon as they appear. That's not the case with the *Good Beer Guide*. Thanks to modern technology, the Guide is checked and re-checked many times before publication. Checking doesn't stop there: both CAMRA's national website and its monthly newspaper *What's Brewing* publish regular information and updates about the Guide, including pubs that have closed or where beer quality has declined. These changes are also reflected in the Good Beer Guide Mobile app that, along with an e-book and sat-nav POI file, give readers access to the Guide in many different formats (see p1013). This regular checking, along with the pubs and breweries databases underpinning the Guide, means that CAMRA and the *Good Beer Guide* share an unrivalled electronic storehouse of information about pubs and breweries.

Additional resources

There are limits to the size of the *Good Beer Guide*. We believe – thanks to our members' efforts and the recommendations sent in by readers – that we offer a choice of the very best pubs throughout the country. But the Guide is complemented by other resources, including local pub guides produced by CAMRA branches and available at beer festivals, local outlets and www.camra.org.uk/books and the online www.whatpub.com – CAMRA's official guide to all known real ale outlets in the country.

National Beer Scoring Scheme

Pubs are selected for the Guide by CAMRA branches who use the scores submitted by members to help them identify places that serve consistently good beer. The scheme uses a 0–5 scale that can be submitted online. Any CAMRA member can submit a beer score by going to CAMRA's online pub guide **www.whatpub.com**, logging in as a member and selecting 'Submit Beer Scores'.

Reader updates & feedback

You can keep your copy of the Guide up to date by visiting the *Good Beer Guide* area of the CAMRA website: **www.camra.org.uk/gbg**. Click on 'Updates to GBG 2016' where you will find information about changes to pubs and breweries.

The Guide is keen to hear from readers. If you wish to recommend a pub or feel that one you have visited fell below your expectations, then we would like to know. Please use the Readers' Recommendations and Have Your Say forms at the back of the book or contact the editor at **gbgeditor@camra.org.uk**.

CAMRA's GOOD BEER GUIDE

Introduction

The unstoppable rise of real ale

Real ale is on a roll. It's the outstanding success story in an industry that's clawing its way back to growth after the disastrous years of heavy taxes and the 'beer duty escalator' imposed by government in 2008.

More and more consumers, concerned about value-for-money, the quality of ingredients used in brewing, and 'provenance' – where a beer is brewed – are switching to the certainties of cask-conditioned ale. Real ale is shedding its image of a drink for older people. Statistics show that women and younger people are among the keenest drinkers of naturally made beer.

- Figures produced by the British Beer & Pub Association (BBPA) show that in 2012 sales of real ale stood at 2,204,000 barrels. By 2014, the figure increased to 2,248,000 barrels.
- The 2014 annual Cask Report, written by Pete Brown and published by Cask Marque, said sales of real ale outperformed the total on-trade beer market (beer sold in pubs, clubs, bars and other licensed premises) by 4.5%.
- One in six pints of beer in a pub is now cask ale. 634 million pints are consumed a year at a time when old-style keg beers – such 'smooth' beers as John Smith's and Tetley's – are in rapid decline.
- The Cask Report says that cask beer sales are greater than those of all other keg ales – smooth-flow and craft keg – combined.
- The BBPA's analysis of beer sales in the first quarter of 2015 showed real ale's upward trend was continuing. While standard beer – up to 4% alcohol – is still the most popular form, premium ale is enjoying a boom. In February 2015, sales of premium real ale were up 5.1% compared to the previous year.

Beer revival

The beer revival is spectacular and shows the support beer enjoys among the drinking public. Between 2008 and 2013, beer sales fell by a catastrophic 24% as a result of the Beer Duty Escalator that automatically increased duty on beer with every annual Budget. In that five year period, duty increased by 42% and 6.7 million fewer pints a day were consumed. 7,000 pubs closed and an estimated 58,000 jobs disappeared.

The escalator was killed off in 2013 thanks to an e-petition to parliament organised by CAMRA. More than 100,000 people signed the petition, which sparked a debate in parliament in which MPs on all sides of the House argued the case for ending the escalator. It was duly consigned to the scrapheap by Chancellor George Osborne in his Budget that year, along with a penny cut in duty.

The Chancellor followed that in 2014 and 2015 with further penny cuts in duty. These measures, brought in as a result of consumer activity in the form of petitions, rallies and demonstrations, has brought draught beer back into growth, with real ale leading the pack.

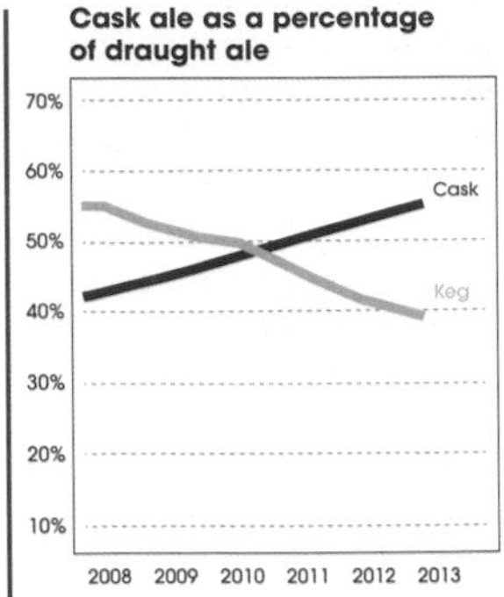

'On the up': The 2014 Cask Report shows cask ale continuing to grow its market share at the expense of keg ale

Three Cheers to the beer tax hat-trick!

Three successive cuts in beer duty by Chancellor George Osborne have helped drive real ale's revival

Brewery boom goes on

The reductions in duty have undoubtedly fuelled the continued and astonishing increase in the number of breweries operating in Britain. There are now around 1,400 breweries busily mashing, boiling and fermenting, the biggest number since the 1930s and 40s. 204 breweries have started up since the last edition of the Guide and choice for drinkers has been transformed in many parts of the country.

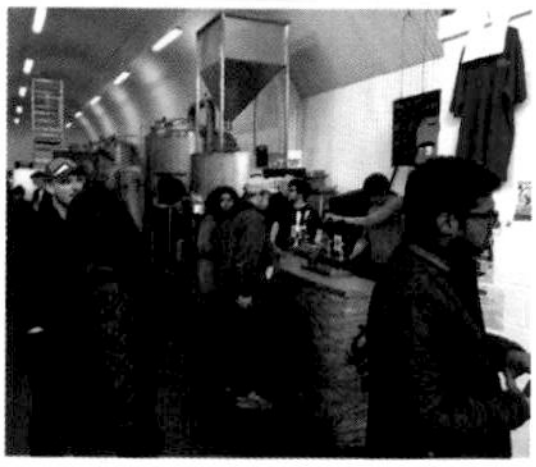

Southwark Brewery, one of the many breweries on the Bermondsey 'Beer Mile' in South London that is open to the drinking public at weekends

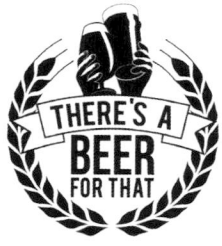

London is the most remarkable success story. When CAMRA was founded in the early 1970s it described London as a 'beer desert' as a result of the small number of breweries in the capital and the paucity of choice. Today there are 70 London breweries, compared to 51 recorded in 2014. There are so many packed into areas such as Bermondsey in the south-east and Hackney in the east that weekend 'brewery crawls' have become a popular part of the drinking scene.

Along with growth has come an undreamt of explosion of choice for drinkers throughout the country. The first *Good Beer Guide*, published in 1974, listed some 40 operating breweries, most of them producing just two beer styles, Mild and Bitter. While Bitter remains the most popular style today – and long may this iconic and uniquely British beer continue to be so – it has been joined by a cornucopia of new styles. Today, drinkers are confronted by the delights of Golden Ale, Porters, Stouts, IPAs, fruit beers, beers aged in wine and whisky casks and even beers made in the medieval fashion with the addition of herbs and spices.

No historic occasion, such as the signing of Magna Carta and the Battle of Waterloo, is allowed to pass without special beers being brewed to mark the event. And as we show on page 1009, Britain has opened its doors to such scintillating Belgian styles as Old Brown, Sour, Saison and spiced wheat beers. American, Australian, Czech, Belgian, German and Polish beers are found throughout Britain, with many featured at CAMRA beer festivals.

Some Belgian and Italian brewers are producing their interpretations of India Pale Ale and this style, which England gave to the world in the 19th century, has truly gone global and is now the most popular type of beer brewed by America's 3,700 craft breweries.

At home, the beer revolution means there is an ale for every mood, season and occasion. The revolution is underscored by brewers and consumers, including CAMRA, who have joined forces in the Beer Alliance to proclaim the joys and pleasures of beer, with beer-and-food matching suggestions. The alliance's work includes a series of high-profile TV advertisements.

THERE'S A BEER FOR THAT

BACKED BY BRITAIN'S BEER ALLIANCE

CAMRA has joined forces with brewers, pub companies and other industry organisations to form Britain's Beer Alliance. The 'There's a Beer for That' campaign promotes the pleasure of beer drinking through TV advertisements and other high-profile publicity

Tackling the pubcos

Beer choice is restricted in many pubs and particular parts of the country as a result of the grip exercised by some of the largest pub companies or 'pubcos'. As a result of energetic lobbying by CAMRA and publicans' organisations, Members of Parliament were made aware of the way in which giant pubcos are able to charge their tenants exorbitant rents and restrict beer choice by supplying beers only from their approved lists, a system known as 'the tie'.

Two key decisions were made as a result of a debate on pub companies in parliament during the final days of the Coalition Government:

- Pubco tenants would be allowed at various points during their tenancies to choose a Market Rent Option (MRO). When a publican opts to pay an agreed higher rent to the pub-owning company, he or she will be allowed to buy beers free of the tie. The option to go free of the tie will be provided to tied tenants of the large pub companies at each rent review, which must occur at least every five years, and also when an existing agreement is renewed.

- The appointment of a Pub Adjudicator, in effect an ombudsman for pubs, who will intervene and settle disputes between publicans and their pubco landlords. The adjudicator will be able to set the market rate for a rent when an MRO is disputed and will insist that pub companies act in a fair and lawful manner. The adjudicator will also make sure that tenants who choose to remain within the tie are not worse off than those who go free of tie.

These welcome reforms will take time to work through the system. The Pub Adjudicator had not been appointed when the *Good Beer Guide* went to press while the legislation that will bring in the Market Rent Option won't come into effect until April 2016. A Pubs Code, a piece of secondary legislation, has yet to be agreed and is likely to spark a further spate of vigorous lobbying by all interested parties.

Vigilance is needed to make sure there is no watering down of these changes. The pubcos, some big pub-owning breweries and their trade body the BBPA are vehemently opposed to the MRO option as they are against any relaxation of the tie that will weaken their ability to control the supply and choice of beer. They may put pressure on the new government to revise the legislation. It's also essential the Pub Adjudicator is a genuinely free and independent official who has no links to any pub companies or breweries.

CAMRA will continue to stress that the MRO will transform the pub trade, enabling tenant publicans to run viable businesses, invest in their pubs and offer a better range of beer at keener prices.

Keeping an eye on tax and prices

In spite of the welcome reductions in beer duty, Britain remains one of the most heavily taxed countries in the European Union. As a result, beer prices in pubs remain high, forcing many people, especially those on lower incomes, to buy cheaper beer from supermarkets. CAMRA will continue to put pressure on the government to continue to reduce duty to the levels that existed before the introduction of the duty escalator in 2008.

Brewers must play fair with customers. In January 2015, three of the country's biggest producers, Carlsberg, Heineken and Molson Coors, increased wholesale prices of their beers by 5p a pint, which led to a 12p a pint retail increase at the bar. The brewers blamed the increase on rising costs – an argument that was considered risible by suppliers.

Robin Appel Associates, leading grain merchants in Wiltshire, said prices of malting barley had 'fallen dramatically' over the previous 12 months while the British Hop Association said prices were so low that many farmers couldn't make a profit.

Mike Rowlands of Guardian Leisure said there was no justification for brewers increasing prices by around 12p a pint. He said most brewers' operating costs had fallen between 2014 and 2015.

The big brewers are not the only offenders. Beer prices remain high, often shockingly so, in many parts of the country – London and the South-east in particular. The GoEuro Price Index reported in June 2015 that beer prices in London were double those in Liverpool. Some 'new

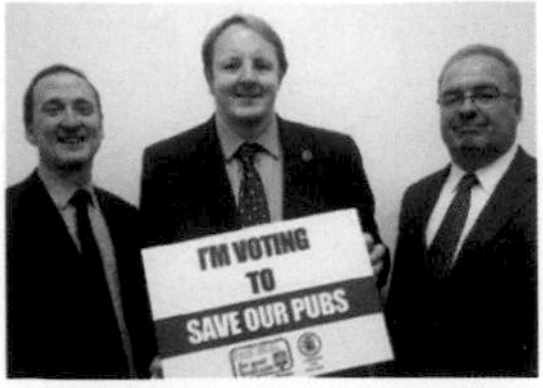

In November 2014, CAMRA lobbied MPs to pledge their support ahead of a crucial parliamentary debate on pubco reform. (From left: campaigner and licensee Simon Clarke, former Shadow Pubs Minister Toby Perkins, and CAMRA Chief Executive Tim Page)

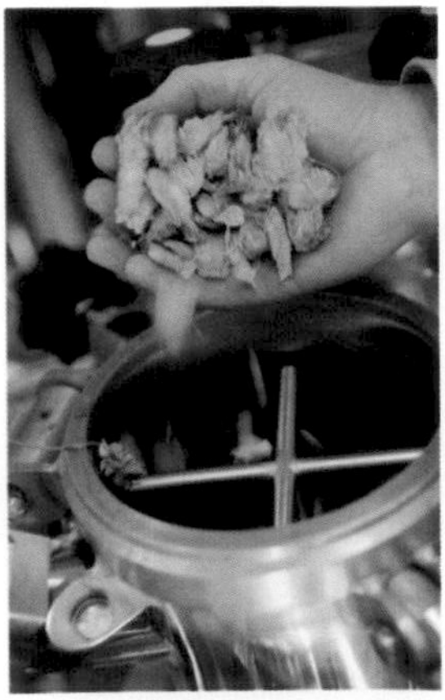

Whole hops being added to a brew. Some large brewing groups have increased the wholesale prices of their beers but have also driven down the makrket prices for hops and barley making it difficult for farmers to make a profit

wave' brewers, as well as traditional producers, charge high prices, especially for new 'craft keg' beers, which are not more expensive to make and yet can cost up to 80p a pint more than a cask ale.

Drinkers are being penalised by the growing practice of charging higher prices for beer sold in half pint glasses. One bar in Manchester in 2015 was found to charge £3.95 for a pint but £2.15 – the equivalent of £4.30 – for a half. It's now customary to charge a 50p supplement for a half pint – scarcely the way to encourage sensible and moderate drinking.

Excessive prices and profiteering drive drinkers into supermarkets that offer cut-price alcohol as a result of the deep discounts they demand from their suppliers. The result is to undermine the pub and its ability to attract customers from all social groups and incomes.

Saving pubs

We report on the campaign to save pubs and the often nefarious role of pubcos in closing viable outlets on pages 10 and 11. Central to the campaign is the ability of drinkers within a community to band together and have a threatened pub listed as an ACV – Asset of Community Value. CAMRA will continue to argue the case for listing pubs and will urge government to extend existing legislation in order that all pubs under threat are subject to rigorous planning permission with procedures.

The Guide is aware that some publicans are not happy with ACVs as they feel being listed would restrict their ability to change, develop and expand their businesses. CAMRA is sensitive to their views but will point out that pubs play such a vital role in communities that local people have the right to be consulted when a pub is under threat.

The Campaign will also stress the benefits of pubs to the well-being of the nation. In an increasingly fragmented society, pubs offer one of the last outlets where people can gather to enjoy good conversation as well as good beer. Pubs are vital hubs for social activity, sponsoring sports teams, running beer festivals and supporting charities.

There is a powerful link between real ale and pubs, too. Cask beer reaches perfection not in the brewery but in the pub cellar. We need pubs to allow our national treasure – real ale – to continue its great revival and its growing popularity among the British people: women and men, young and old, and from all backgrounds and incomes.

Drinkers in the borough of Windsor and Maidenhead lobbying the council to demand that the Golden Harp pub be listed as an Asset of Community Value

ACVs enable a pub closure or sale to be put on hold while local people attempt to save it

In 2015, Roger Protz was given a Lifetime Achievement Award by SIBA – the Society of Independent Brewers – for his 'Outstanding Contribution to the British Brewing Industry'.

The great British pub

Our locals at risk

More and more people are joining forces to save local pubs for their communities. At the same time, new 'pop-up pubs' and beer bars are widening drinkers' choice of venues and their enjoyment.

The destruction of the Great British Pub continues apace. Giant pub companies sell off popular locals to property developers to turn into houses or supermarkets. Pubs that are involved in a dispute between owners and customers mysteriously burn down or are bulldozed to the ground without planning permission.

But efforts are now being intensified to save an institution that's not only locked into our history and heritage but is also admired throughout the world.

'Asset of Community Value' neatly sums up the role of the pub. It's more than just a place for a drink – it's the sticking plaster that holds communities together. In an age when so many attractions keep people indoors, the pub is one of the last places where people can meet for good conversation and discussion while enjoying a beer. Pubs play other important roles in local communities. Charities, for example, rely on pubs to raise support for their causes: more than £10 million is raised every year. Many pubs help young musicians to kick-start their careers, others offer facilities for actors, writers and poets to present their work to the public.

With pubs closing at a rate of around 30 a week, CAMRA is intensifying its activities to save and protect endangered locals. There's now a solid bedrock of legislation to protect pubs, and CAMRA has developed helpful information in the form of a website and a special pack for publicans.

Assets of Community Value (ACVs) were introduced by the Localism Act of 2011 to enable communities to protect vital assets, including pubs. The granting of ACV status by a local authority effectively lists a pub and brings in a cooling-off period to stop the closure, destruction or change of use going ahead. This period gives local people the opportunity to raise the money to buy a threatened pub from its owner and run it themselves, often in the form of a co-operative. There are now 35 pubs in Britain run as co-ops and 12 more were in the pipeline in 2015. The Plunkett Foundation, which helps save pubs, shops and other local enterprises from closure, has been at the forefront of this campaign.

By the autumn of 2015, there were over 800 pubs in England protected by ACVs, and that number is expected to increase. Different legislation applies in Scotland and CAMRA has urged the Welsh Assembly to bring in ACV powers in Wales. CAMRA's aim is to get 3,000 pubs listed.

New government legislation in 2015 extended planning protection to pubs that are listed as ACVs. This means that a listed pub will become the subject of a full planning application if the owner wants to sell or demolish it.

The Carlton Tavern in Maida Vale, North-West London, was the only pub in its street to survive the WWII Blitz. But it didn't survive an onslaught from bulldozers early one morning in April 2015. The pub originally built by London brewer Charrington was just two days away from being listed by Historic England when the property developer who wanted to turn it into flats laid waste to it. Westminster Council instructed the developer to restore the pub 'brick by brick', but as he is based in Israel legal experts think it unlikely the Carlton will ever rise again.

The Sailor Boy in Hitchin, Hertfordshire, was an Enterprise Inns pub that the group sold to a property developer to turn into a convenience store. Following pressure from the local CAMRA branch, the council listed the premises as an ACV. But early one morning in May 2015, fire-fighters were called to a blaze at the Sailor Boy, which was badly damaged and will not re-open as a pub. CAMRA

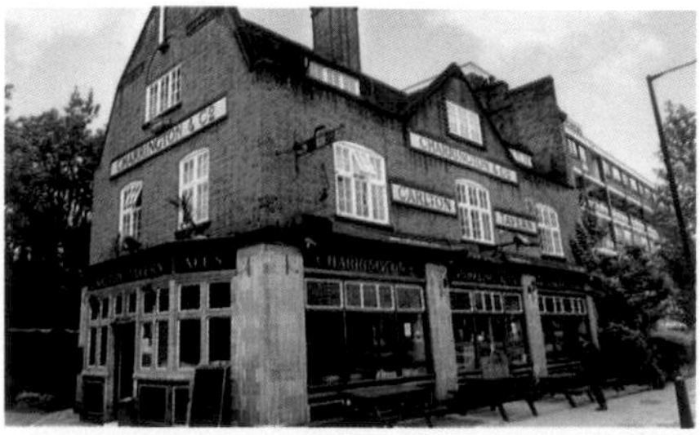

The Carlton Tavern, Maida Vale, London, was bulldozed days before being listed by English Heritage

Sailor Boy, Hitchin – badly damaged by fire after being listed as an ACV

branch pub preservation officer Malcolm Chapman (pictured above) said there are now no pubs left in the Walsworth area of the town and people will have to travel into Hitchin town centre for a drink.

Adapting to survive

Traditional pubs may be closing but a new type of outlet for beer is growing at a rate of knots. Known colloquially as 'pop-up pubs' and officially as micropubs, they are based in buildings originally designed for other purposes but now offer a wide choice of beers for drinkers.

Martyn Hillier opened the first micropub in Herne, Kent, in 2005. It's called the Butcher's Arms, named after a butcher's shop that closed in 1995. The pub has room for 10 people sitting and 20 standing, with beer stored in the former butcher's cold store. Martyn, who was named CAMRA's Campaigner of the Year in 2015, spent a total of £5,000 on turning the shop into a pub.

As he doesn't have to pay business rates or VAT, he can offer beer at sharp prices. A pint of Dark Star Hophead, for example, costs £3. Even Fuller's strong ESB weighs in at just £3.75.

Inspired by Martyn's initiative, micropubs spread rapidly across Kent. There are two in neighbouring Herne Bay, three in Margate and four in Dover. But now they are popping up across the country, as far north as Northumbria, across into Lancashire, and down into Wales and the West Country. There were expected to be 200 micropubs operating by the end of 2015 and the owners have their own organisation, the Micropub Association: **www.micropubassociation.co.uk**.

The drinking scene is also being enlivened by outlets that offer a relaxed café bar atmosphere and a wide range of beer, including real ale, modern keg beers and imported beers in bottle and on draught from other countries, with Belgian beers often making a strong appearance.

Bristol has the Beer Emporium set in three tunnels, the Canteen on the ground floor of an office block, and No.1 Harbourside, a diner alongside the floating harbour. Manchester offers Bar Fringe, a Belgian-style café, the Cask Bar, which despite the name, concentrates on imported beers, and the Soup Kitchen with a wide-ranging choice of beers from near and far.

The Euston Tap, in a stone lodge that fronts Euston Station in London, has been a pacesetter in new-style bars, with up to 27 draught beers pumped to taps set in the wall, and offering American beers as well as British and European ones.

So don't write off the British pub – but new ones may be far removed from the traditional image of the Dog & Duck.

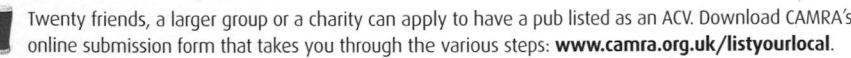

Martyn Hillier opened the first micropub, the Butchers Arms in Herne, Kent, in 2005

How to save your local

- Twenty friends, a larger group or a charity can apply to have a pub listed as an ACV. Download CAMRA's online submission form that takes you through the various steps: **www.camra.org.uk/listyourlocal**.
- An information pack for publicans explaining the role of ACVs and their benefits to those running pubs and their communities is available from the same website.

If you have any further queries about the system and its benefits, send an email to: **ACV@CAMRA.org.uk**

Pub of the Year

Gloucestershire pub named as the best in Britain

The Salutation Inn, a rural free house in the small village of Ham, Gloucestershire, was named CAMRA's National Pub of the Year in 2015 – a remarkable achievement, as it's the first pub the landlord has ever run.

Former business analyst Peter Tiley had never even pulled a pint when he decided to quit his job in London and follow his love of beer to take over the Salutation Inn – known as the Sally – with his wife Claire. Eleven months later the pub had won its local CAMRA branch competition, then the whole region, finally making it through to the final four and then being named National Pub of the Year.

'For the Sally to have won this award is beyond our wildest dreams,' Peter said. 'We count ourselves unbelievably lucky to have a brilliant team who are so passionate and dedicated as well as a community of locals who have given so much support. It's these people who have made the pub what it is today.'

The award-wining Salutation Inn – officially the best pub in Britain (see page 178)

The Salutation was popular with the judges as a result of a superb selection of beer and homely feel. One judge said: 'What struck me most was the welcome, as if I were being invited into a private house as a friend.'

CAMRA's Abigail Newton said that being named Pub of the Year is a major achievement for any landlord. 'What Peter and Claire have done in the short time they have been running the pub is nothing short of staggering and goes to show that passion, enthusiasm and a real love of beer are hugely important when running a pub. They have taken what was already a great pub and made it truly exceptional, beating off more than 50,000 other landlords across the UK,' she added.

CAMRA's National Pub of the Year competition considers all the criteria that make for a good pub. The competition is judged by the Campaign's 172,000-plus members. Each branch selects its top pub. The branch winners are entered into 16 regional competitions, with the regional winners battling it out to reach the final stages of the competition. Look out for the 🏆 symbol against pub entries in the Guide and see 'Award-winning pubs' on pages 1005-6 for the winning branch pubs.

The three other finalists in the 2015 competition were:

Freshfield, Formby, Merseyside (see page 340)
There's a strong emphasis on the community in this Greene King pub where the landlord is allowed to offer up to 10 guest beers as well as Greene King staples. It has a good reputation for food and local action saved a fine stone-flagged floor that was under threat of removal.

Harewood Arms, Broadbottom, Greater Manchester (see page 321)
The Green Mill Brewery is based in the cellar of the pub, which forms the brewery tap. As well as the house ales, there are continental beers while an open fire adds to the warm welcome given to visitors. There's a colourful garden for use in warmer weather.

Windmill, Sevenoaks Weald, Kent (see page 231)
There's a strong emphasis on locally-brewed ales in the Windmill, along with guest beers from further afield. Such dark beers as porter and stout are frequently available. The pub has wooden settles, a log-burning stove and etched windows.

Club of the Year
Yorkshire club wins top award

Wortley Men's Club in South Yorkshire beat off competition from 28,000 clubs in the UK to win CAMRA's prestigious Club of the Year award for 2015.

Wortley Men's Club, South Yorkshire is CAMRA's Club of the Year, 2015 (see page 553)

The club – which admits women members as well as men – is at the heart of an attractive village and is a timber-framed building with, inside, ornate ceilings, a plush lounge and large games room. Beer comes from local breweries and steward Nigel Pickering says cask ale was introduced with just one pump in 1997 but 'now we have four pumps and our annual beer festival offers 40 beers.'

The club is at the heart of a small village and is active in the community. It holds events with local firms and the church, including a brass band competition.

The competition's organiser, John Holland, said: 'Wortley Men's Club deserves this prestigious award. It's not only a beautiful building but the steward's commitment to quality ale and the welcome you receive are second to none. CAMRA members are free to visit.'

The Club of the Year competition is run by CAMRA in conjunction with the journal *Club Mirror* to find the best real ale clubs in the country. One of the criteria for entry into the competition is that clubs must admit CAMRA members, both men and women. A number of the best real ale clubs feature in the *Good Beer Guide* alongside recommended pubs. As well as admitting CAMRA members, many will also admit non-members carrying a copy of this book. See individual entries for more information.

The three other finalists in the 2015 competition were:

Appleton Thorn Village Hall, Appleton Thorn, Cheshire
(see page 70)
This previous winner of the national title is housed in the former village school. It offers a members' lounge as well as a large function room that stages quizzes, live music and an annual beer festival. As many as seven cask beers are available.

Cheltenham Motor Club, Cheltenham, Gloucestershire
(see page 175)
The former Crown pub is now a club and won the CAMRA national title in 2013. It offers beers from Salopian and Stroud breweries with guest ales from other micros and holds two beer festivals every year.

Poole Ex-Servicemen's Club, Poole, Dorset
The club has a large bar and an upstairs function room that houses a skittle alley and pool tables. The bar serves three cask ales, with Exmoor Ale as a regular and guests drawn from breweries in the South-west and West Country. There's live music on Saturday evenings and Sky Sports shows most major events.

Beer destinations

Discovering the best beer towns in the UK

Many of Britain's industrial towns and cities have been transformed in recent years. Today they are centres of modern commerce and learning, with high-tech enterprises and new-style universities. The beer-drinking scene reflects the change, with traditional pubs nestling alongside micropubs and modern bars, many with their own in-house breweries. The *Good Beer Guide* looks at four cities that have risen to the challenge of appealing to beer lovers of all ages and backgrounds.

Glasgow

Edinburgh may be Scotland's capital but Glasgow is the country's biggest city, the fourth largest in the UK. Based on the banks of the River Clyde, Glasgow had a long industrial history based on shipbuilding and heavy engineering. The wealth created by these industries enabled the city to invest in education – Glasgow University dates from the 15th century – art galleries and museums. A massive programme of urban renewal over several decades has seen a switch to modern light industry, with satellite towns and suburbs dubbed – with typical Glaswegian dry humour – 'Silicon Glen'. Today Lonely Planet lists Glasgow as one of the world's top tourist attractions and visitors will find a fine choice of pubs to enhance the pleasures of their tours.

Babbity Bowster, 16-18 Blackfriars Street, is a brilliant interpretation of an 18th-century coffee house, based in the stylish Merchant City and named after an ancient Scottish dance. Folk music is omnipresent while Scotland's Auld Alliance with France is marked with both food with a French tilt and a boules piste in the garden. Large windows, stripped-wood floors and a blazing fire in winter add to the charm, along with beers from Caledonian and Fyne Ales and other Scottish breweries.

Nearby, the Blackfriars at 36 Bell Street is a café bar with some Pre-Raphaelite flourishes and regular live music and a comedy club. There are large bowed windows and plenty of seating at wooden tables, where generous helpings of food, including haggis, are served. As well as cask ales from Alechemy and Kelburn, there's also a large offering of bottled beers, including Belgian lambic.

The Clockwork Beer Company, Cathcart Road, is a long-standing brewpub that's well placed for Hampden Park. Good-value food is served but the main point of interest lies with the home-brewed beers that include Amber, Cartside Red, Lager and Oregon IPA. Some of the beers are cask conditioned in the usual fashion, others come from a tank system that retains natural carbon dioxide from fermentation: no applied CO_2 is used to serve them. There are also guest beers from Scottish independents, including Loch Lomond and Stewart.

Inn Deep, 445 Great Western Road, is in the Hillhead area of the city and is built into arches along the river, close to Kelvin Bridge. As well as music hosted by DJs, the pub offers something rare and highly acceptable: spoken-word events on Tuesday. Williams Brothers of Alloa, famous for their Fraoch heather ale, often supply their beers, along with offerings from south of the border.

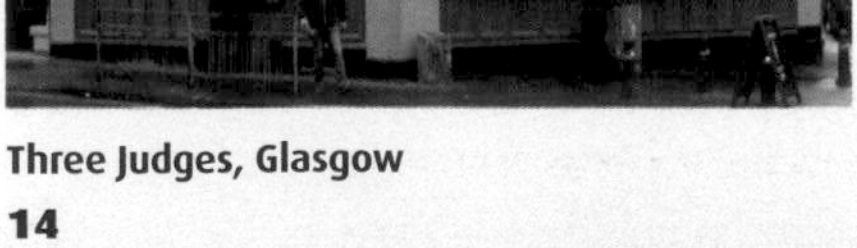

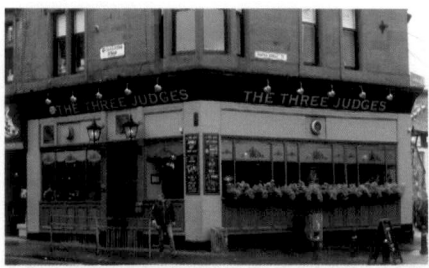

Three Judges, Glasgow

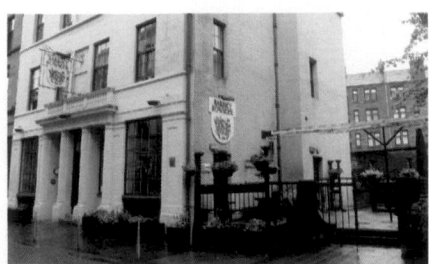

Babbity Bowster, Glasgow

No beer-and-pub lover visiting Glasgow can afford to miss the Three Judges on Dumbarton Road, over the road from Partick station. The pub flew the real ale flag in the dog days of fizzy beer, when Scotland's infamous 'Big Two', Tennents and Scottish & Newcastle, concentrated on keg and lager. The vast collection of beer mats shows the 2,000 or more cask beers that have been served in the tenement bar, which has many framed awards from the local branch of CAMRA. You will find Caledonian Deuchar's IPA and up to eight other beers on tap.

For more Glasgow pubs, see pages 648 – 650

Liverpool

Liverpool stands on the great Mersey River and will be forever synonymous with shipping and the great liners of Cunard and White Star, the latter with its tragic Titanic associations. Ships still ply their trade on the Mersey but the city is much changed. Liverpool One is a regenerated area with smart restaurants and clubs while the waterside, including the Albert Dock and Pier Head, is a Unesco World Heritage Site. It's in the Britannia Vaults area of the Albert Dock that you'll find the Beatles Story, which traces the rise and rise of the Fab Four: just follow the Japanese tourists!

The pub scene is vibrant. If you arrive by train at the main station, just cross the road to the Crown Hotel, 43 Lime Street, a Grade II-listed shrine to Art Nouveau with an exterior proclaiming its links to the long-defunct Walkers of Warrington brewery. The interior is packed with wood panelling, ornate ceilings and an impressive dome above a staircase. The regular beers are from Greene King but many guest ales are on offer.

Close to the Albert Dock, the aptly named Baltic Fleet (33 Wapping) serves beer from the Wapping microbrewery in the cellar. This is another listed pub, designed on the 'flat iron' principle. As well as the house beer and guests, you can tuck into a plate of scouse, a type of stew that gave its name to the locals and their dialect.

As Liverpool is the point of departure for the Isle of Man, it's fitting that the island's Okell's Brewery should have a pub in the city. The Fly in the Loaf (Hardman Street) is in a former bakery that advertised there were 'no flies in the bread'. As well as Okell's range of beers, there's excellent food with – naturally – freshly baked bread from the Baltic Bakehouse.

The Roscoe Head, 24 Roscoe Street, is a must-visit pub, one of a diminishing number that has been in every edition of this Guide. It's been run by the same family for more than 30 years and it commemorates the work of William Roscoe, who campaigned against the slave trade. It serves Jennings and Tetley's bitters and guest beers.

For more Liverpool pubs, see pages 341 – 344

Newcastle upon Tyne

Newcastle and Gateshead, on either side of the Tyne, are linked as 'NewcastleGateshead' by their authorities to spearhead the regeneration of this key area of the North-east. It's their respective quaysides that stress the dynamic changes from an area associated with coal mining and shipbuilding to one based on modern retailing. From Newcastle's Quayside you can view at close hand Norman Foster's new Sage music centre across the river and decide whether it complements the skyline or is a hideous carbuncle.

In Gateshead, the Central, Half Moon Lane, is a wedge-shaped, listed pub that was the first in the Head of Steam chain, now owned by Cameron's Brewery in Hartlepool. Standing alongside the railway track, it's decked out with age of steam paintings by local artist Arthur E Gills. The pub rambles over four floors and the main bar is boosted by a snug, a games room, a large area for live music and a room being converted into a whisky bar. Beers are from artisan breweries, including Anarchy.

On Newcastle's Quayside, the Hop & Cleaver, 40 Sandhill, based in a former Jacobean timber-framed building, is a new addition to the eating and drinking scene. Owned by Ladhar Leisure, it brings a touch of America to the North-east with a smokehouse concept of barbecued meats – though there are veggie options. The sprawl of rooms, with beams and standing timbers, has many intimate areas and an in-house brewery with a 2½ barrel kit that produces Quayside Pale, Black Beard Stout, India Red and Pearl Harbour.

Fly in the Loaf, Liverpool

Low Lights Tavern, Newcastle upon Tyne

Bacchus, 125 Westgate Road, one of the Sir John Fitzgerald chain of pubs, in sharp distinction to the Hop & Cleaver, pays homage to Art Deco, with an interior decked out like a stately liner of the 1920s. Don't miss the toilets reached by a broad staircase. Photographs recall the great industries of Tyneside's past. Guest beers rotate at a dizzying pace on nine handpumps on the sumptuous mahogany bar.

The Cumberland Arms, James Place Street, Byker, is a splendid traditional ale house overlooking the Ouseburn Valley with seating on a terrace and spacious bars inside. Live music and beer festivals are regular features, and among the many ales and ciders you'll find beers from the North Alchemy brewery next door. This brings a wholly new concept to the term 'micro'. Brothers-in-law Carl Kennedy and Andy Aitchison brew on a 1.6-barrel kit inside a form shipping container – how very Tyneside! They produce eight beers, unfined and unfiltered, including Baltic Sour, Late Hopped Ale and Marmalade and Assam Tea IPA.

Nearby, the Cluny, with its wedge-shaped roof (36 Lime Street), is pub, music venue and art gallery rolled into one. It's a former whisky warehouse that's been a pub since 1998 and has a large open-plan main bar with beers from Durham, Mordue and Roosters.

If you're feeling peckish, the Low Lights Tavern, Brewhouse Bank, North Shields, is an old fishermen's pub, that serves beers from Three Kings and Cameron's and the now rare Draught Bass, and offers a range of Desperate Dan-sized home-made pies, one of which will keep you going for a good 48 hours.

For more Tyneside pubs, see pages 468 – 475

Swansea

Swansea is best known today as the birthplace of Dylan Thomas: his home in Uplands, where he wrote most of his poetry and prose, has been preserved and is open for visits but you can raise a glass to his memory in any of the city's pubs. As he wrote in *Portrait of the Artist as a Young Dog,* 'I liked the taste of beer, its live, white lather, its brass-bright depths, the sudden world through the wet brown walls of the glass, the tilted rush to the lips and the slow swallowing down to the lapping belly, the salt on the tongue, the foam at the corners.' Swansea was once bigger than Cardiff, its position on the South Wales coast making it an ideal place for commercial shipping. Its major industry was copper smelting, earning the city the nickname of 'Copperopolis'. Now Swansea's main sources of income come from modern commerce, retailing and tourism. It's a major sporting city, with Premier League football and top rugby clubs.

The No Sign Bar at 56 Wind Street claims to be one of Dylan Thomas's regular haunts, but it's not alone in this respect. The ancient hostelry dates from the late 17th century and its design reflects architectural changes over the centuries. The name comes from an old licensing requirement that forced all pubs to have inn signs, but this venue at the time was a wine bar, not a pub, and didn't qualify. It has standing timbers and wingback chairs, with live music played in the Vaults. There's a restaurant for good food and four beers are available, usually including one from Cwrw Madoc. Thomas and other artists and writers formed the Kardomah Club that met regularly in the No Sign, though they took the name from a café where they drank... coffee.

Continuing the poetic theme, the Queen's Hotel in Gloucester Place, is close to the Dylan Thomas Museum as well as the City and National Waterfront museums. The pub is decorated with photos of Swansea's maritime past and specialises in live music and quizzes. It serves Theakston's Best and Old Peculier, rare for the area.

Wetherspoon, with its usual beady eye for local history, commemorates another local industry in the Potters Wheel in the Kingsway, in the city centre. Casks are arranged on a back-bar stillage and there's a strong commitment to local independent brewers, though the main handpumped beers come from Brains and Greene King. There's a Real Ale information board with news of forthcoming beers along with the usual Spoons' good-value pub grub.

For more Swansea pubs, see page 584

Cluny, Newcastle upon Tyne

Queen's Hotel, Swansea

CAMRA beer festivals

Spreading the real ale message

The Campaign for Real Ale's beer festivals – totalling more than 200 a year throughout the UK – are first and foremost about pleasure for beer drinkers. They also act as vital shop windows for independent brewers and display the tremendous choice of beers now available from around 1,400 producers.

CAMRA beer festivals also make an important contribution to the economy. £3.5 million is spent every year buying beer and cider from producers and the festivals boost trade in the towns and cities where they are held. The Great British Beer Festival, held in London in August, contributes a remarkable £10 million to the capital as around 55,000 people flock to Olympia, stay in hotels, eat in restaurants, use public and private transport, and take the opportunity to visit theatres, cinemas and museums.

While the festivals are staffed solely by CAMRA volunteers, they have become highly professional events. They have to meet the strict requirements of Health & Safety legislation and the volunteers need special training. It's not just a case of ordering beer and opening the doors to the public. Real ale is a living, breathing product and it needs careful handling and time to 'drop bright' before it's ready to serve.

CAMRA's annual showcase event, the Great British Beer Festival, is held at Olympia, London each August

As a result of the importance of the festivals, CAMRA has invested to ensure that beer is served in tip-top condition. The quality of the end product – the beer in your glass – is essential. Volunteers attend an annual training course to learn all the skills needed to run a successful event. Cellar management is vital to serve beer at the correct temperature, aided by modern cooling equipment. Bar staff are taught how to pour the perfect pint while other volunteers are trained to order beer, cider and food, book live entertainers, run bookshops and product stalls, and prepare publicity material and handle the local media.

Visitors to the festivals listed in the next two pages can be assured of a warm welcome and cool beer. Depending on the size of the event, there may be special seasonal ales, hot and cold food, live music and, where possible, facilities for families.

Festivals are the main way in which CAMRA attracts new members to its ranks. And they also play an important campaigning role, championing local beers and breweries. For example, in 2015, the festival in Burton-on-Trent launched Draught Burton Ale, a beer axed by Carlsberg but revived by the local Burton Bridge Brewery. Casks of DBA were emptied in a few hours and pubs in both Burton and Derby clamoured for supplies.

CAMRA's beer festivals underscore the British pub by emphasising today's great range of beers.

CAMRA festivals are run by volunteers who are trained to serve the perfect pint

CAMRA's beer festivals through the year

JANUARY
Atherton – Bent & Bongs Beer Bash
Cambridge – Winter
Colchester – Winter
Ely
Exeter – Winter
Manchester
Salisbury – Winter

FEBRUARY
Derby – National Winter Ales
Chappel – Winter
Chelmsford – Winter
Chesterfield
Darlington – Spring
Dorchester
Dover – White Cliffs Winter
Ely – Winter
Fleetwood
Gosport – Winter
Hucknall
Jersey – Winter
Liverpool
Luton
Pendle
Redditch
Stevenage
Stockton – Ale & Arty
Tewkesbury – Winter

MARCH
Bradford
Bristol
Bromley
Burton upon Trent
Brighton – Sussex
Horsham
Leeds
Leicester
London Drinker
Loughborough
St Neots – Booze on the Ouse
Seascale
Thanet
Walsall
Wigan
Winchester

APRIL
Bath
Bexley
Bolton
Bury St Edmunds – East Anglian
Chippenham
Coventry
Doncaster
Farnham
Glenrothes – Kingdom of Fife
Gloucester
Hull
Isle of Man
Larbert – Falkirk
Maldon
Mansfield
New Mills
Newcastle upon Tyne
Oldham
Paisley
Stourbridge

MAY
Banbury
Barnsley
Cambridge
Clitheroe
Colchester
Dewsbury
Halifax
Kidderminster
Kingston
Lincoln
Macclesfield
Newark
Newport (Gwent)
Reading
Skipton
Wrexham – North Wales
Yapton
Yaxley – East Anglia

JUNE
Aberdeen
Braintree
Bromsgrove
Glasgow
Greater Manchester Cider & Perry Festival
Hitchin
Ipswich
Lewes – South Downs
Old Harlow – Gibberd Garden
Rugby
St Ives (Cornwall)
Salisbury
Southampton
Stockport
Stratford-Upon-Avon
Tenterden – Kent & East Sussex Railway
Thurrock
Wolverhampton

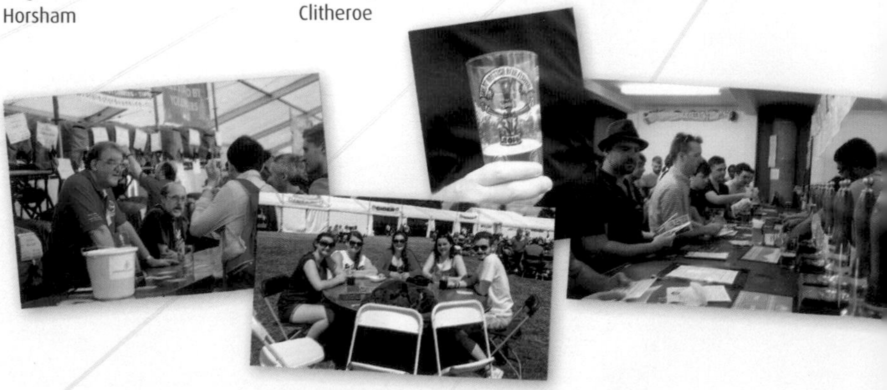

JULY
Bishops Stortford
Canterbury – Kent
Chelmsford – Summer
Chorlton
Derby
Devizes
Ealing
Edinburgh – Scottish
Hereford – Beer on the Wye
Maidenhead
Market Bosworth – Rail Ale
Plymouth
Stafford
Stowmarket
Winchcombe – Cotswold
Woodcote – Steam Fair
Wyke Regis – Wykefest

AUGUST
London – Great British
Clacton-on-Sea
Darlington
Durham
Grantham
Harbury
Manchester – National Cycling Centre
Peterborough
Swansea
Worcester

SEPTEMBER
Barnsley
Belper – Amber Valley
Bridgnorth – Severn Valley
Bromley
Burnley
Cannock
Chappel
Cockermouth – Taste Cumbria (Jennings)
Crewe – Rail Ale
East Malling (Kent)
Faversham – Hop
Hinckley
Jersey
Melton Mowbray
Minehead (West Somerset Railway)
Morecambe
Moreton-in Marsh – North Cotswolds
Portsmouth
St Albans
St Helens
Scunthorpe
Tamworth
Ulverston
Westmorland
York

OCTOBER
Alloa
Ascot
Basingstoke – Hampshire Octoberfest
Bedford
Birmingham
Carmarthen
Cambridge – Octoberfest
Cardiff – Great Welsh
Chesterfield – Market
Eastbourne
Egremont (Cumbria)
Falmouth
Gainsborough
Huddersfield – Oktoberfest
Kendal – Westmorland
Louth
Lytham
Milton Keynes
Norwich
Nottingham
Oxford
Poole
Redhill
Richmond (North Yorkshire)
Sheffield
Solihull
South Woodham Ferrers
Southport
Spa Valley Railway (West Kent)
St Ives (Cambs) – Booze on the Ouse
Stoke-on-Trent – Potteries
Sunderland
Swindon
Troon – Ayrshire
Twickenham
Wakefield
Weymouth
Woolston – Southampton
Worthing

NOVEMBER
Belfast
Carlisle
Chester – Cheshire
Dudley
Grimsby
Heathrow
Keighley
Saltburn
Shrewsbury
Wantage
Watford
Woking

DECEMBER
Harwich & Dovercourt Bay
London – Pig's Ear

Pipers. Britain's tastiest crisps?

It goes (almost) without saying that if you're reading this Guide you're a lover of fine beer. A lover not just of the taste of beer but also passionate about its ingredients, its heritage, the way it's made, kept and served, and the places it's enjoyed.

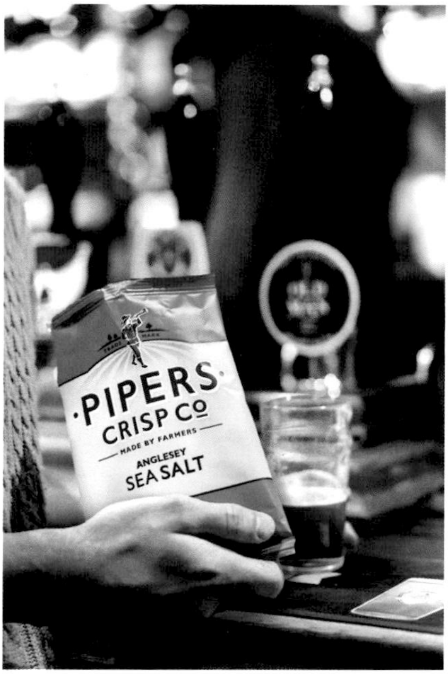

In fact, you probably care about *all* the food and drink you consume, valuing quality, taste and authenticity above all else. So you'll certainly be choosing your pub snacks with the same care as you choose your beer. For you, crisps need to have real 'bite'; crunchy without being too hard; a rich golden colour, with natural variations from the hand-cooking process; and please, no bland, ever-changing 'flavours of the month' – just a full-bodied, distinctive, mature taste.

Here at Pipers Crisps we've been making 'crisps as they should taste' since we started the company in 2004. We endeavour to make Britain's tastiest crisps; crisps to enjoy alongside the finest beers in the UK's best pubs. We think we're succeeding, but there's no need to take our word for it. There are plenty of independent commendations; our crisps have won 22 Gold Great Taste Awards since 2007; for the last three years we've been voted Best Brand in Savoury Snacks by readers of Fine Food Digest; and The Independent recently decided we were the best 'Posh Crisps'!

How do we do it? Just like good beer, there's a combination of factors at work to ensure a consistently great product. It's not just about our background as farmers, although this is important. Nor is it just about the specialist producers we've chosen to make our tasty flavours, though they too are key. It's also about why and how we select our potatoes; the oil we fry them in; and the cooking skills we apply. Finally it's about the passion and knowledge we apply to combine all these factors to deliver the best-tasting crisps in Britain.

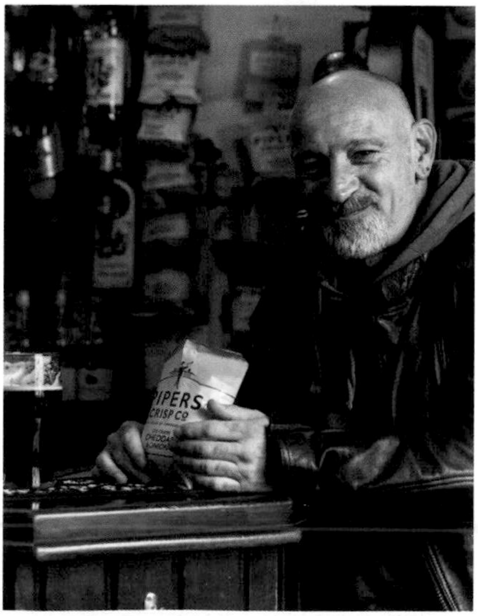

We also like to keep Pipers Crisps a touch 'exclusive'; that's why you won't find Pipers Crisps in major supermarket chains. We're fanatical about our quality and reputation so we prefer it when the people selling our crisps are similarly avid about our product. That's why you will find us in the best retailers, delicatessens, farm shops, food halls and, of course, in some of the finest pubs in the UK.

We appreciate that not every pub currently stocks Pipers, and that some *Good Beer Guide* readers may find it difficult to find our crisps in their favourite pubs. We've long been a supporter of CAMRA and attend many of their events and festivals every year. You've probably seen us at the Great British Beer Festival, which Pipers have helped to sponsor on a number of occasions. If you've had a chance to sample our crisps and agree that we make Britain's tastiest crisps, why not ask your local to stock Pipers Crisps?

Pipers Crisps... crisps as they should taste.

All about beer

Real ale *is* craft beer

A bar at London's Paddington Station called the Beer House sums up a conundrum facing the brewing industry. It offers travellers 'Craft Beer and Cask Ale'. The casual observer could conclude that real ale is not a craft product, to the consternation of the craftsmen and women who labour hard to brew it. The *Good Beer Guide* has no doubt that real ale is a craft product.

But the word has become both a catch-all and a source of dispute. Large and even global brewers claim today to make craft beer. And for a small number of brewers, the term means 'anything but real ale' in the mistaken belief that younger drinkers don't want to touch beer that comes out of a handpump and a cask – ignoring the proven fact that the biggest swing to real ale is among young drinkers.

The problem with 'craft beer' is that it has no industry definition. CAMRA's annual conference has agreed that 'while real ale is craft beer, not all craft beer is real ale' – an attitude that reaches out to all artisan brewers. The Campaign appreciates that not all outlets for beer are suitable for storing and serving cask-conditioned beer and there is room in the market for new types of beer called 'craft keg'.

Modern keg beers have little in common with the beers of the 1960s and 70s, such as Red Barrel and Double Diamond, which gave rise to CAMRA's consumer backlash. Modern keg beers are filtered but not always pasteurised and, while served colder than real ale, are not heavily carbonated. Several new beer festivals in Britain offer a range of craft keg beers but not exclusively so: some offer cask ale as well. Any events that encourage people to sample the pleasures of good beer are to be welcomed.

A London bar that points to the confusion surrounding 'craft beer'

But in spite of the sound and fury generated by one or two craft keg brewers, it's important to keep its support in proportion. It's a small niche and the big success story of recent years is cask-conditioned real ale.

The *Good Beer Guide* remains committed to real ale not because we're hidebound but because we believe it's a beer style that's not only rooted in Britain's heritage and traditions but one that also offers the finest drinking experience for pubgoers. It's not a beer of the past but the beer of the moment.

Real ale reaches out to drinkers who seek beers made naturally from the finest ingredients. It's possible to make something called 'beer' with rice, maize and corn syrup, and flavoured with green juice squeezed from pulverised hops. The world's biggest beer brand even lists rice before barley malt on its label. But cask beer brewers prefer to use the finest malting barley along with hops left in their natural state.

Consumers are increasingly concerned by the way food and drink are made. They don't want products trunked half-way round the world and stuffed with preservatives to keep them in edible or drinkable condition. Neither are they impressed by dubious advertising that masks the fact that a 'Belgian' lager is brewed in Wales and 'Australian' and 'French' ones are manufactured in Manchester. Drinkers seek confirmation that their beers are made locally from ingredients grown by farmers who use the finest forms of husbandry.

Thanks to the work of such companies as Warminster Maltings in Wiltshire and Branthill Farm in Norfolk, it's now possible to trace where barley is grown, down to the precise fields where it's harvested (see the reference to Maris Otter barley in *How Beer is Brewed*, pages 23-26). Hop growers are developing new varieties that require fewer agri-chemicals and allow natural predators such as ladybirds to kill the mites that attack the plants.

As pub entry after pub entry in this Guide proves, more and more publicans are opting for a good range of local cask beers. Their efforts are underscored by CAMRA's LocAle scheme that encourages publicans to source some of their beers from breweries within a 30-mile radius and reduce carbon footprints as a result. For more information on the scheme see www.camra.org.uk/locale.

The finished product is a beer that's neither filtered nor pasteurised and is pulled to the pub bar without the use of applied gas pressure. In all its forms – from the palest pale ale to the blackest stout – it's the perfection of beer and the best of British.

Both old and new styles bring fresh pleasure to the beer scene

Britain's pubs and beer festivals are awash with a vast array of tempting and even challenging types of beer. Today you will find beers made with the addition of fruits, herbs, chocolate, coffee, ginger, lemon grass, pumpkin, coriander and even chilli peppers. But without doubt the beer style that is making waves is a revival from the 19th century – India Pale Ale or IPA for short.

In its hey-day, it was a truly revolutionary beer: long before golden lager, it was the first pale beer, made possible by the industrial revolution. Paler malts, better-quality hops and an improved scientific understanding of water, yeast and fermentation combined to produce a beer ideally suited for export to 'the Raj' in the blistering climate of the Indian sub-continent.

IPA's impact was both dramatic and brief. By the end of the 19th century it had been maginalised in colonial countries by new golden lager beers served cold with the aid of ice while in Britain strong IPAs were replaced by lower-strength pale ales. In recent years, however, brewers on both sides of the Atlantic have discovered a passion for this almost-lost style. With greater strength than pale ale or bitter and more heavily hopped, IPA offers the complex flavours many discerning drinkers demand today.

Scores of British brewers have added their interpretations of IPA to their portfolios while India Pale Ale has become the most popular style produced by American craft brewers.

On a smaller but no less fascinating level, both brewers and publicans are experimenting with 'beer from the wood'. For several years, a number of brewers have experimented with storing beer in casks sourced from wine and whisky producers. There's no doubt that beers served from oak vessels that previously held Bourbon, Cognac, single malt whisky and wine have new depths of aroma and flavour. A more recent development has seen beer stored in freshly made casks that allow the oak, smoke and vanilla flavours of the wood to permeate the beer. Two pubs in West Yorkshire, the Junction in Castleford and the Duck & Drake in Leeds, specialise in serving beers from the wood and will offer the same beer in both metal and oak casks in order that drinkers can test and taste the difference.

Neil Midgley, landlord of the Junction, orders new casks from the White Rose Cooperage in Wetherby and takes them to breweries as far south as Chiltern in Buckinghamshire to have them filled with beer. He stages an annual 'beer from the wood' festival in his pub.

A growing number of breweries listed in the Guide describe their beers as suitable for vegetarians and vegans. Others say their beers are not fined. Finings are traditionally made from fish swim bladders and the glutinous liquid created (called isinglass) is added to casks of beer as they leave the brewery. The finings attract yeast and proteins and drag them to the base of the cask, leaving clear beer above. Some breweries, such as Marble in Manchester, have replaced isinglass with other clearing agents such as silica, while others prefer not to use finings at all and serve their beers naturally cloudy.

How beer is brewed

Barley is beer's building block. Other grain can be used and many brewers blend in small amounts of wheat or oats and even rye, but barley is the preferred grain because it works in perfect harmony with hops and yeast.

But barley has to be turned into malt before brewing can begin. Once it's harvested, the grain is taken to a maltings where it's steeped in water to absorb moisture, then spread on heated floors or inside rotating drums where it starts to germinate. Once germination is under way, the grain is transferred to an oven known as a kiln. Heat dries the grain and, depending on the temperature, produces pale or darker malts.

All beer, regardless of colour, is made mainly from pale malt as it has the highest level of enzymes – natural chemical catalysts – that are

Gerry Condell, Bath Ales head brewer

crucial to the brewing process. Higher temperatures produce brown, black and chocolate malts used for colour and flavour in darker beers. Roasted barley, which is not malted, is often featured in stouts while a method similar to toffee-making produces specialist crystal malts for colour and flavour. Depending on the mix of malts, the grain will give aromas and flavours similar to Horlicks, Ovaltine, oatmeal biscuits, Ryvita, almonds and other nuts, honey, butterscotch, caramel, tobacco and vanilla.

Hops: the vital seasoning

The annual harvest also produces beer's other key ingredient: hops. In common with grain, hops need good soil, in this case loamy or sandy soil that retains a good supply of water. Kent, Herefordshire and Worcestershire are the main hop-growing counties of England. Hops grow at great speed in the spring and summer and once harvested they are dried by warm air in special sheds or oast houses.

Hops contain acids, oils and resins that deliver bitterness to beer along with fragrant aromas of spice, pepper, grass, cedar wood and citrus fruit. The oils and tannins in the plant help stabilise beer and prevent infection. English hops are prized for their spice and pepper notes. Fuggles and Goldings are the best-known traditional varieties but new hops have been introduced in recent years, including First Gold, Boadicea, Endeavour and Jester: the last two have been bred to give the aromas and flavours of grapefruit, mango and tropical fruits demanded by many modern brewers.

The brewing process

When malt reaches the brewery, it's ground in a mill into a powder called grist. Grist and pure hot water flow into the mash tun, where the porridge-like mixture of grain and water starts the brewing process. Pure water can come from springs, bore holes or from the public supply. It will be thoroughly filtered, and brewers often add such sulphates as gypsum and magnesium to enhance the flavours of malt and hops. The mixture is left to stand in the mash tun for some two hours and during that time enzymes in the malt convert the remaining starch into fermentable sugar.

When starch conversion is complete, the brewer and his team will run the sweet extract, called wort, to a second vessel, the copper, where it's vigorously boiled with hops. The hops are usually added in stages: at the start of the boil, half way through and just before the end, in order to extract the maximum aroma and bitterness from the plants.

The copper boil lasts between 1½ and 2 hours. The hopped wort is passed through a cooler to lower the temperature and is then pumped to fermenting vessels. These can be open or closed, upright or horizontal, but it's here that the liquid starts the conversion to alcohol with the aid of yeast. Yeast is a fungus that feeds on sugary liquids. Every brewery has its own yeast culture that gives an important 'house' character to the beer.

Ale fermentation is rapid and lasts for a week – it's a method known as 'warm fermentation' to distinguish it from the cold fermentation method used to make genuine lager. Yeast converts malt sugar into alcohol and carbon dioxide and creates a dense, rocky blanket on top of the liquid. It also produces natural chemical compounds called esters that give off aromas reminiscent of apples, oranges, pear drops, banana, liquorice, molasses and, in especially strong beers, fresh leather. These add to the complexity of the finished beer.

Eventually the yeast will be overcome by the alcohol it has created and the yeast blanket is skimmed from the vessel. The beer will rest for several days in conditioning tanks to mature and to purge unwanted rough alcohols and esters.

The big divide

Then comes the major divide in the world of brewing. One route leads to filtered, pasteurised and carbonated beer. The other creates Britain's great contribution to the world of beer: cask-conditioned ale. Cask ale is unique as it's not finished in the brewery but in the pub cellar. From conditioning tanks, it's racked into casks.

Beer is made from just four key ingredients:

1 HOPS: There are around two dozen hop varieties in England, ranging from the Golding and the Fuggle, first grown in the 18th and 19th centuries, to more modern ones, such as Boadicea and Endeavour. Hops can be used in the brewery either as whole flowers or ground and compressed into pellets.

2 WATER: Pure water, called 'liquor' by brewers, can come from springs, bore holes or from the public supply. It will be thoroughly filtered, and brewers often add such sulphates as gypsum and magnesium to enhance the flavours of malt and hops.

Finings are added to clear the beer. Additional hops may be placed in the casks for extra aroma and flavour and brewing sugar can be added to encourage a strong secondary fermentation.

The beer that reaches the pub cellar is said to be 'still working' as remaining yeast turns the final sugars into alcohol and CO_2. Casks have to be vented to allow the natural gas to escape. A cask has two openings: a bung at the flat end where a tap is inserted to serve the beer; and a shive hole on top. A soft porous peg of wood, a spile, is knocked into the shive, enabling some of the CO_2 to escape. As fermentation dies down, the soft spile is replaced after 24 hours by a hard one that leaves some gas in the cask: this gives the beer its natural sparkle, known as 'condition'.

Inside the cask, finings sink to the floor, attracting yeast and proteins in suspension. The publican will draw off small samples of the beer and when he or she is satisfied it has 'dropped bright', plastic tubes or 'lines' are attached to the tap and the beer is drawn by a suction pump activated by a handpump on the bar. The recommended serving temperature for real ale is 11 or 12°C. Some golden summer beers are served between 8 and 10 degrees and they may go through a special cooler below the bar. New methods of storing and serving real ale are described on page 26.

The brewing process

No two breweries are identical. Some will use open fermenters, others more modern closed conical vessels. Yeast is added to the fermenter to turn malt sugar into alcohol, and often to casks to encourage a secondary fermentation in the pub cellar. Hops are added during the copper boil but may also be added to the fermenter and even casks to enhance hop aroma.

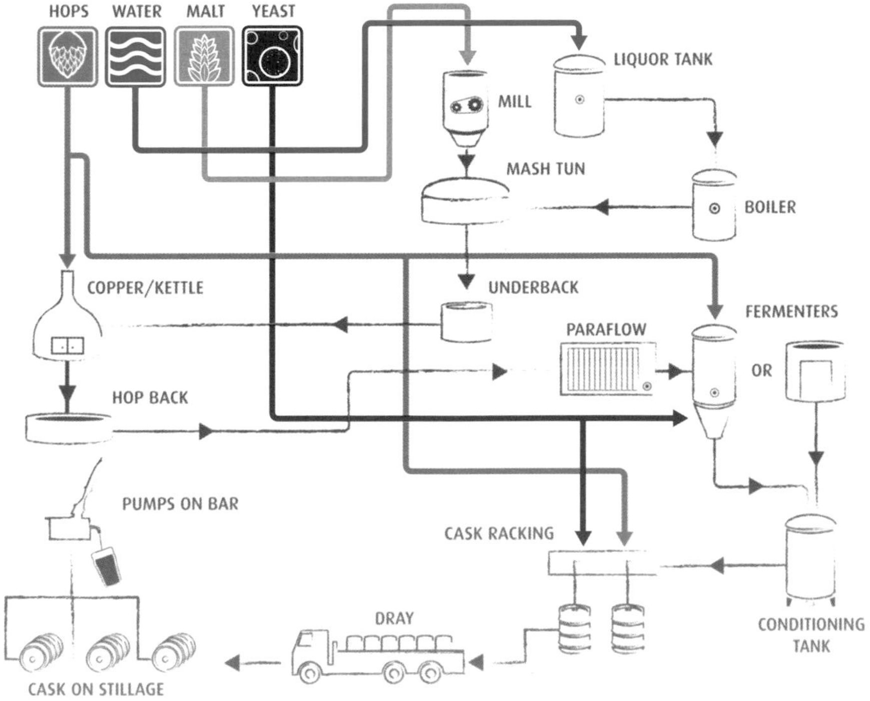

3 MALT: Maltsters steep barley in water to absorb moisture, then spread it on heated floors or inside rotating drums where it starts to germinate. Once germination is under way, the grain is transferred to an oven known as a kiln. Heat dries the grain and, depending on the temperature, produces pale or darker malts.

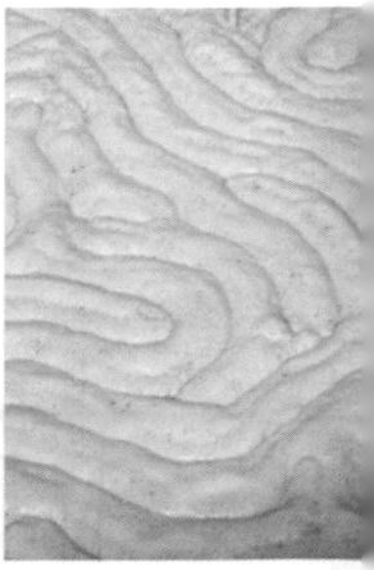

4 YEAST: Yeast is a type of fungus that feeds on sugary liquids. Every brewery will have its own yeast culture that's carefully guarded and stored, as it gives its own important 'house character' to the beer. Brewers keep samples of their yeast cultures in a special bank in Norwich in case they need a fresh supply.

50 years of Maris Otter barley

Between the years 2000 and 2013, nine of the 14 winners of CAMRA's annual Champion Beer of Britain award were made with a barley variety called Maris Otter. It suggests that Maris Otter is a rather special grain, yet in 1990 it was de-listed by big farmers and maltsters and faced extinction. It's survived because of its popularity with artisan brewers, and in 2015 a festival was staged in Norwich to celebrate the grain's 50th anniversary, with a range of beer brewed only with that variety.

Maris Otter was first grown in Norfolk in 1965 and rapidly became popular as a result of the fine sugary 'extract' it produced in the brewery and its rich biscuit flavour. It was de-listed when new 'high-yielding' varieties were developed, which meant they produced more grain per acre – a classic case of 'never mind the quality, feel the width'.

Maris Otter survived when two companies, H Banham in Norfolk and Warminster in Wiltshire, bought the rights to the grain. Today it's produced by the traditional floor malting system and is supplied to small brewers in both Britain and the United States.

Barley farmer Teddy Maufe at Branthill Farm in Norfolk and Warminster Maltings in Wiltshire have both developed a 'grain to glass' system that enables brewers to trace the farm and even the actual field where a particular batch of the grain is grown and harvested.

Teddy Maufe, Maris Otter farmer, Norfolk

New methods of packaging

The growing interest in good beer has seen it move from traditional pubs to new venues, such as bars, restaurants and micropubs. Many of these outlets lack cellars where beer can be stored and served in the conventional manner. As a result, a number of breweries are now using one-trip 'key kegs' that take up little space, can be kept close to the bar if the temperature is controlled, and remove the need for the breweries to pick up the empties.

As the name suggests, a key keg is designed for modern keg beers. It's made up of a plastic container that looks like a large brown urn. Inside a sterile bag holds the beer. Keg beers are filtered and the kegs are connected to gas cylinders at the point of delivery, with the gas replacing the beer as it's served.

As a result of small venues asking for real ale, key kegs now have a variant called a key cask. The principle is the same, with the beer inside a bag in the container, but the gas – either carbon dioxide or oxygen – sits in a second bag on top of the beer. When the serving tap is turned, beer is displaced as the bag of gas pushes down. As the gas does not come into contact with the beer, which is neither filtered nor pasteurised and contains live yeast, key casks are acceptable to CAMRA. The system is similar, though on a smaller scale, to the one used by the Zerodegrees brewpubs (see Breweries section) where the live beer is stored in large tanks under bags of air that drive the beer to the bar. The fact that both bars and breweries are using key casks and tanks stresses the growing demand for real ale in modern outlets.

A Zerodegrees bar where live beer is stored and served from tanks without extraneous gas

Beer appreciation

We can increase our appreciation of beer by sampling and tasting. Gently swirl the liquid in the glass to release the aroma or the 'nose' and discover the malt, hop and fruit notes that emerge. Allow the beer to trickle over the tongue, which picks up bitterness, sweetness and salt, and enjoy the palate or 'mouthfeel' as the beer coats the cheeks. Finally, the beer passes down the back of the throat in what is known as the 'finish'.

On the nose you may find a rich biscuit or Ovaltine-like malt character. Hops will add their own distinctive note. English hops deliver a restrained spicy, peppery, earthy, wood and resinous note. American hops are renowned for their profound citrus notes, with grapefruit to the fore. German hops are called 'noble' varieties and offer cedar wood, mint, pine kernels and lemon zest. New Zealand hops have a vinous fruit character. One leading variety, Nelson Sauvin, is so called as a result of flavours similar to Sauvignon wine.

Fruit may be detected and this comes from both hops and yeast. A sulphur or salty note is derived from the water, which will have had sulphates added to replicate the famous salty waters of Burton-on-Trent, home of classic pale ale brewing.

In the mouth, the malt may have a delicious juicy note while hop bitterness will build, balancing any fruitiness. Finally the finish should combine all the elements of malt, hops and fruit into a satisfying, dry finale. The flavour characteristics of a particular beer will depend on its style: see the Classic beer styles section that follows. Suffice it to say that a Mild Ale will offer a pronounced malt and caramel note, with restrained bitterness, while Bitters and IPAs will have a robust hop character, Porters and Stouts a roasted and toasted grain note, while Barley Wines are fruity and vinous, and Old Ales will often have a slight hint of sourness allied to ripe malt, gentle hops and notes of leather and tobacco.

Tasting beer can be carried out in the home but greater appreciation will emerge if a group of people take part – and there's no better place to do it than in a pub. Many pubs now stage regular beer festivals, with a wide choice of beers available. If festivals are not held in your local but it has a good range on the bar, ask whether a room or part of the bar could be set aside for a tasting event.

Glasses should be either half-pint beer glasses or the large ones used for red wine. You will need fresh water and a supply of crackers to allow tasters to clean their palates between beers.

Scoring sheets add to the enjoyment of the event, especially if you want to name a 'best beer'. The sheets should be divided into marks out of 10 for appearance, aroma, palate and finish. Usually, not more than six beers are judged in a single event.

Depending on the availability of beer, you could base a tasting round just one style, such as Mild, Bitter or Porter & Stout. However, it's unlikely that many pubs would have six versions of a single style, so it's best to have a mixed event. It's advisable to work up from the lowest strength: it would be difficult to judge a Mild after a Barley Wine.

Marks for appearance will be based on the clarity of the beer when the glass is held up to the light. Does it have a good head of foam, which indicates the beer has what brewers call 'condition'. The absence of foam means the beer is flat. Some beers, such as wheat beers, are designed to have a cloudy appearance, and this should be borne in mind when marking.

Marks for aroma will be based on the appeal of the beer as it's sniffed. Is there a good balance of malt, hops and fruit or is the beer overly malty or, conversely, too bitter? If you are judging bitter beers, including IPA, then expect to find the balance tilted towards hops and bitterness. Palate is based on the appeal of the beer in the mouth: you would mark down for cloying sweetness or harsh bitterness, and give higher marks when both characteristics are in balance. Finally, the finish: is the beer harmonious as it passes over the back of the tongue and down the throat, well-balanced between malt, hops and fruit, ending neither too malty nor too bitter. Again, marks in this section will be guided by the style of beer: you would expect a roasted grain character from a Stout or Porter.

If it's not possible to organise a tasting event of your own, bear in mind that many CAMRA festivals stage beer tastings, often hosted by experts in the field. Check out the festivals listed in this Guide (see pages 18–19).

Britain's classic beer styles

Think of British beer and most people think of Bitter. In spite of the arrival of many new styles, Bitter is still beer drinkers' favourite tipple. Until the 1950s, Mild Ale matched Bitter in popularity but then went into steep decline, though it's now making a comeback, with many small brewers including it in their portfolios. Older styles, such as genuine IPAs, Porters and Stouts, have reappeared, while Golden Ale, fruit beer and wheat beer provide further choice for drinkers. In this briefing, **Roger Protz** gives an indication of some of the great beers available in British pubs and recommends some of his favourite versions of each style.

Porter & Stout

Porter was a London beer that created the first commercial brewing industry in the world in the early 18th century. Its name came from its popularity with London porters, who needed calories to help sustain them in their hard manual labour. The origins of the beer are disputed but the most recent research suggests that Porter, first called 'Entire', was blended in the brewery from pale, mild and aged or 'stale' beer. The strongest version of Porter was called Stout Porter, later shortened to just Stout.

Porter and Stout were exported from London to the rest of the British Isles and, as a result, Arthur Guinness built his own Porter brewery in Dublin. During World War One, when the British government stopped brewers from using heavily roasted malts in order to divert energy to the arms industry, Guinness and other Irish brewers came to dominate the market. In recent years, Porter and Stout have returned to popularity in Britain, the United States and Australasia, with brewers digging into old recipe books to create genuine versions of the style.

Look for a jet-black colour and expect a dark and roasted grain character with burnt fruit, espresso or cappuccino coffee, liquorice and molasses. The beer should have a deep bitterness to balance the richness of malt and fruit.

Roger's Round
Elland 1872 Porter
Leatherbritches Porter
Moonshine Nightwatch Porter

Mild

Mild developed in the 18th and 19th centuries as drinkers started to demand a slightly sweeter and less aggressively hopped beer than Porter. Mild Ale was drunk primarily by industrial and agricultural workers, who needed to refresh themselves after long hours of arduous labour. Early Milds were much stronger than modern versions, which tend to fall into the 3 – 3.5% category, though the likes of Rudgate are among brewers bringing strength back to the style. Mild is usually dark brown in colour, owing to the use of well-roasted malts or roasted barley, though there are paler versions such as Banks's Mild and Timothy Taylor's Golden Best. Look for a rich malty aroma and flavour, with hints of dark fruit, chocolate, coffee and caramel, with a gentle underpinning of hop bitterness.

Roger's Round
Castle Rock Black Gold
Rhymney Dark
Strathaven Craigmill Mild

Old Ale

Old Ale is another style from the 18th century, stored for many months or even years in wooden vessels where the beer picked up some lactic sourness from wild yeasts and tannins in the wood. As a result of the sour taste, it was dubbed 'stale' by drinkers and the beer was one of the components of the early Porters. In recent years, Old Ale has made a return to popularity, owing primarily to the success of such beers as

Theakston's Old Peculier and Gales' Prize Old Ale. Contrary to expectations, Old Ales do not have to be especially strong and can be no more than 4% alcohol. Neither do they have to be dark: Old Ale can be pale and bursting with lush malt, tart fruit and spicy hops. Darker versions will have a more profound malt character, with powerful hints of roasted grain, dark fruit, polished leather and fresh tobacco. The hallmark of the style is a lengthy period of maturation, often in bottle rather than cask.

Roger's Round

Ballard's Wassail
Moor Old Freddy Walker
Palmer's Tally Ho!

Barley Wine

Barley Wine dates from the 18th and 19th centuries when England was often at war with France and it was the duty of patriots, usually from the upper classes, to drink ale rather than French claret. Barley Wine had to be strong – often between 10% and 12% – and was stored for as long as 18 months or two years. Fuller's Vintage Ale (8.5%) is a bottle-conditioned version of its Golden Pride and is brewed with four different varieties of malts and hops every year. Expect massive sweet malt and ripe fruit of the pear drop, mandarin orange and lemon type, with chocolate and coffee if darker malts are used. Hop rates are generous and produce bitterness and peppery, grassy and floral notes.

Roger's Round

Darwin Extinction Ale
Kinver Over the Edge
Lees Moonraker

IPA

India Pale Ale changed the face of brewing in the 19th century. The new technologies of the Industrial Revolution enabled brewers to use pale malts to design beers that were pale bronze in colour. The first 'India Ales' were brewed in London and were probably based on October Beers that were matured for many months and were ideally suited to a long sea journey to India. But London was soon eclipsed by Burton-on-Trent with its spring waters rich in minerals that brought out the fullest flavours of malt and hops. 19th-century IPAs were high in both alcohol and hops to keep them in good condition during the journey to the colonies. Its life span was brief, driven out of Africa and India by German lager beer. But the style has made a big comeback in recent years and is now made in abundance in Britain, Down Under and the United States. Look for a big peppery hop aroma and palate balanced by juicy malt and tart citrus fruit.

Roger's Round

Beowulf IPA
Marble Lagonda IPA
Tiny Rebel Urban IPA

Burton Ale

As the name suggests, the origins of Burton Ale lie in Burton-on-Trent, but the style became so popular in the 18th and 19th centuries that most brewers had a 'Burton' in their portfolio, and the expression 'gone for a Burton' entered the English language. Bass in Burton at one time had six different versions of the beer, ranging from 6% to 11.5%: the strongest versions were exported to Russia and the Baltic States.

In the 20th century, Burton was overtaken in popularity by Pale Ale and Bitter but it was revived with great success in the late 1970s with the launch of Ind Coope Draught Burton Ale. When Allied Breweries broke up, the beer was owned by Carlsberg, who stopped production in 2015. But the style has been recreated by Burton Bridge Brewery in its home town. Other versions of the style exist under different names: Young's Winter Warmer was originally called Burton. Bass No 1, brewed occasionally, is called a barley wine but is in fact the last remaining version of a Bass Burton Ale. Look for a bright amber colour, a rich malt and fruit character underscored by a solid resinous and cedar wood hop note.

Roger's Round

Burton Bridge Draught Burton Ale
Latimer Burton Best
Young's Winter Warmer

Pale Ale

According to a legend in the 19th century, when a sailing ship bound for India with a cargo of IPA foundered off the coast at Liverpool, the casks were brought ashore and news of both the colour and taste of Pale Ale spread throughout the country. IPAs were brewed for the domestic market as a result, but the Burton brewers were keen to produce versions with lower alcohol and hop rates and which didn't need months to mature. The spread of the railway system allowed brewers in Burton to move beer around the country at speed and Pale Ale was dubbed 'the beer of the railway age' as a result. The clamour for Pale Ale was so great that brewers from London, Liverpool and Manchester opened second breweries in Burton to make use of the mineral-rich water to make their own versions of the style. From the early 20th century, Bitter began to overtake Pale Ale in popularity and as a result Pale Ale became mainly a bottled product. A true pale ale should be different to Bitter, similar in colour and style to IPA and brewed without the addition of coloured malts. It should have a spicy/resinous aroma and palate with biscuit malt and tart fruit from the hops. Many beers called Bitter today should properly be labelled Pale Ale.

Roger's Round
Highland Pale Ale
Redemption Pale Ale
Slaughterhouse Pale Ale

Bitter

At the turn of the 19th and 20th centuries, brewers built large estates of 'tied' pubs and they moved away from beers stored for months or years and developed 'running beers' that could be served after a few days of conditioning in pub cellars. Bitter was a new type of running beer: it developed from Pale Ale but was usually copper coloured or deep bronze owing to the use of slightly darker malts, such as crystal, that gave the beer fullness of palate. Best is a stronger version of Bitter but there is considerable crossover. Bitter falls into the 3.4 – 3.9% band while Best Bitter is 4% upwards, though a number of brewers call their ordinary Bitter 'best'. A further development of the style comes in the shape of strong Bitter of 5% or more: Fuller's ESB and Greene King Abbot are well-known examples. With ordinary Bitter, look for spicy, peppery and grassy hop character, a powerful bitterness, tangy fruit and juicy/nutty malt. With best and strong Bitters, malt and fruit character will tend to dominate but hop aroma and bitterness are still crucial to the style, often achieved by 'late hopping' during the copper boil or by adding additional hops to casks as they leave the brewery.

Roger's Round
Harvey's Sussex Best Bitter
Otter Bitter
Purple Moose Glaslyn Ale

Golden Ale

Golden Ales have become so popular with both drinkers and brewers of all sizes that the style now has its own category in the annual Champion Beer of Britain competition. Exmoor Gold, Hop Back Summer Lightning and Rooster's Yankee started the trend in the early 1980s and other brewers quickly followed in a rush to wean younger drinkers from mass-produced lager to the pleasures of cask ale. The style is different to Pale Ale in two critical ways: Golden Ale is paler, often brewed with lager malt or specially produced low-colour ale malt and, as a result, hops are allowed to give full expression, balancing sappy malt with luscious fruit, floral, herbal, spicy and resinous notes.

While brewers of Pale Ale tend to use such traditional English hop varieties as Fuggles and Goldings, imported hops from North America, the Czech Republic, Germany, Slovenia and New Zealand give radically different notes to Golden Ale. As a result these beers offer a new and exciting drinking experience. They are often served colder than draught Bitter and some brewers, such as Fuller's, have installed special cooling devices to ensure the beer reaches the glass at an acceptably refreshing temperature.

Roger's Round
Brewster's Hophead
Castle Rock Elsie Mo
Fyne Jarl

Wheat Beer

Wheat beer is a style closely associated with Bavaria and Belgium and its popularity in Britain has encouraged many brewers to add wheat beers to their portfolios. The title is something of a misnomer

as all 'wheat beers' are a blend of malted barley as well as wheat, as the latter grain is difficult to brew with and needs the addition of barley, which acts as a natural filter during the mashing stage. But wheat, if used with special yeast cultures developed for brewing the style, gives distinctive aromas and flavours, such as clove, banana and bubblegum, that make it a complex and refreshing beer. The Belgian version of wheat beer often has the addition of herbs and spices, such as milled coriander seeds and orange peel – a habit that dates back to medieval times.

Roger's Round
Little Valley Hebden's Wheat
Offbeat Way Out Wheat
Otley 07 Weissen

Fruit/Speciality Beers

Brewers endlessly search for new flavours to reach out to a wider audience for their beers. The popularity in Britain of Belgian fruit beers has not gone unnoticed and now many domestic brewers are using fruit in their beer. Others have gone the extra mile and add honey, herbs, heather, spice and even spirits – brandy and rum feature in a number of speciality beers, while beers matured in Bourbon, whisky and Cognac casks has become a major development in both this country and the United States. It's important to dispel the belief that fruit and honey beers are sweet: the ingredients add new dimensions to the brewing process and are highly fermentable, with the result that beers that use the likes of cherries or raspberries are dry and quenching rather than cloying.

Roger's Round
Bartram's Grozet
Humpty Dumpty Lemon & Ginger
Saltaire Triple Chocoholic

Scottish Beers

Historically, Scottish beers tend to be darker and maltier than beers south of the border, the reflection of a colder climate where beer needs to be nourishing. It's an urban myth, though, that Scottish beers are less heavily hopped than English ones. The classic traditional styles are Light, Heavy and Export, which are not dissimilar to Mild, Bitter and IPA. They are also known as 60, 70 and 80 Shilling ales from a 19th-century system of invoicing beers according to strength. A 'Wee Heavy' or 90 Shilling Ale, now rare, is the Scottish equivalent of barley wine. Many of the newer brewers in Scotland are producing beers lighter in colour and with pronounced hop character.

Roger's Round
Cairngorm Stag
Inveralmond Lia Fail
Stewart 80/-

Only accept perfect pints

Remember, you're the consumer, forking out a high price for beer, so don't be afraid to take your pint back to the bar if:

- Your beer is either too warm or too cold. Real ale should be served cool – around 11–12°C. It's a myth that it should be served at room temperature. Warm beer tastes bad, as the temperature creates unpleasant off flavours. But bear in mind that some Golden Ales are meant to be served at a lower temperature than other styles.
- Your beer smells of acetone, vinegar or stale bread.
- The pint has no head, is totally flat and out of condition.
- It's not only flat but hazy and has yeast particles or protein floating in the liquid.

If you get the response 'Real ale is meant to be warm and cloudy', invite the publican to join the 21st century. If the offending pub has a Cask Marque plaque, get in touch with Cask Marque. Otherwise, let us know at the *Good Beer Guide* – **camragbgeditor@camra.org.uk**.

And please go back to the bar if you are served a short measure – less than a pint (or half-pint) of liquid in the glass. Drinkers lose millions of pounds a year as a result of short measures. It's an outrageous rip-off. CAMRA beer festivals serve beer in oversize glasses that ensure drinkers always get the amount of beer they have paid for. Most pub owners refuse to use oversize glasses, preferring brim-measure glasses that allow them consistently to serve short measures. It's a scandal. Don't put up with it.

CAMRA's Beers of the Year

The beers listed below are CAMRA's Beers of the Year. They were short-listed for the 2015 Champion Beer of Britain competition, held at the Great British Beer Festival in August, or the Champion Winter Beer of Britain competition, held in February that year. Each beer was found by a panel of trained CAMRA judges to be consistently outstanding in its category and they all receive a 🍺 against their entry in the Breweries section. In the Champion Beer of Britain finals, the best beers from each category in both competitions are judged together to decide the overall national winner. For the full results visit **www.camra.orh.uk/cbob**.

BEST BITTERS

An Teallach, Crofters Pale Ale
Barngates, Tag Lag
Blue Monkey, Sanctuary
Brains, Rev James
Brewster's, Hop A Doodle Doo
Church End, What the Fox's Hat
Colchester, No. 1
Green Jack, Trawlerboys Best Bitter
Hawkshead, Lakeland Gold
Highland, Scapa Special
Hogs Back, TEA
Plain, Innspiration
Salopian, Darwins Origin
Saltaire, Blonde
Surrey Hills, Shere Drop
Timothy Taylor, Landlord
Tintagel, Arthur's Ale
Tiny Rebel, Cwtch

BITTERS

Acorn, Barnsley Bitter
Born in the Borders, Game Bird
Brecon, Three Beacons
Buntingford, Twitchell
Butcombe, Matthew Pale Ale
Hawkshead, Bitter
Holden's, Black Country Bitter
Houston, APA
Nottingham, Rock Ale Bitter Beer
Otter, Bitter
Pheasantry, Best Bitter
Purple Moose, Cwrw Madog/Madog's Ale
Salopian, Shropshire Gold
Surrey Hills, Ranmore
Timothy Taylor, Boltmaker
Triple fff, Alton's Pride
Wolf, RAF Collection Battle of Britain
Yates, Bitter

BARLEY WINES & STRONG ALES

Adnams, Tally Ho
Darwin, Extinction Ale
Kinver, Over the Edge
Lees, Moonraker
Oakleaf, Blake's Heaven
Orkney, Skull Splitter
Parish, Baz's Bonce Blower
Tiny Rebel, Hadouken
Wessex, Beast of Zeals

GOLDEN ALES

Acorn, Barnsley Gold
Adnams, Explorer
Blue Monkey, Infinity
Dark Star, Hophead
Hawkshead, Cumbrian Five Hop
Kelburn, Jaguar
Salopian, Oracle
Skinner's, Porthleven
Tiny Rebel, Fubar

MILDS

Branscombe Vale, Mild
Brentwood, Marvellous Maple Mild
Byatt's, XK Dark
Double Top, Nelson Mild
Great Orme, Welsh Black
Rudgate, Ruby Mild
Strands, Pied Piper
Triple fff, Pressed Rat & Warthog
Williams, Black

OLD ALES & STRONG MILDS

Adnams, Old Ale
Broughs, Superior
Castle Rock, Midnight Owl
Dark Star, Original
Kelburn, Dark Moor
Leeds, Midnight Bell
Purple Moose, Ochr Tywyll y Mws/Dark Side of the Moose
Ramsbury, Deerhunter
Ulverston, Fra Diavolo

PORTERS

Bath, Festivity
Blakemere, Deep Dark Secret
Blythe, Johnsons
Elland, 1872 Porter
Facer's, North Star Porter
Fuller's, London Porter
Red Fox, Black Fox Porter
Welbeck Abbey, Portland Black

SPECIALITY BEERS

Cromarty, Red Rocker
Green Jack, Orange Wheat Beer
Hanlons, Port Stout
Kissingate, Black Cherry Mild
Leatherbritches, Lemongrass & Ginger
RedWillow, Smokeless
Saltaire, Triple Chocoholic
Titanic, Plum Porter
Zerodegrees (Cardiff), Pilsner

STOUTS

Ascot, Anastasia's Exile Stout
Dancing Duck, Dark Drake
Dent, T'owd Tup
Enville, Gothic
Green Jack, Lurcher Stout
Heart of Wales, Welsh Black
Highland, Sneeky Wee Orkney Stout
Magic Rock, Dark Arts
Plain, Inncognito

STRONG BITTERS

Cairngorm, Wildcat
Coniston, K7
Dark Star, Revelation
Grain, India Pale Ale
Ilkley, Lotus IPA
Raw, Grey Ghost IPA
Salopian, Golden Thread
St Austell, HSD
Tiny Rebel, Urban IPA

REAL ALE IN A BOTTLE

8 Sail, Damson Porter
Acorn, Gorlovka Imperial Stout
Bartrams, Comrade Bill Bartram's Egalitarian Anti Imperialist Soviet Stout
Beowulf, Dark Raven
Blueball, Gold Digger
Brecon, Gold Beacons
Bristol Beer Factory, Southville Hop
Castle Rock, Elsie Mo
Coniston, Bluebird Bitter
Elland, 1872 Porter
Fuller's, 1845
Fyne, Sublime Stout
Fyne, Superior IPA
Harveys, Imperial Extra Double Stout
Hobsons, Old Henry
Hook Norton, Double Stout
Humpty Dumpty, Broadland Sunrise
Leatherbritches, Hairy Helmet
Marble, Lagonda IPA
Moor, Revival
Mordue, IPA
Otley, 09 Blonde
Otley, 10 Oxymoron
Rebel, Bal Maiden
Stewart, Radical Road
Woodforde's, Wherry
Wye Valley, Butty Bach

CHAMPION WINTER BEER OF BRITAIN
Elland, 1872 Porter

CHAMPION BEER OF BRITAIN 2015
Tiny Rebel, Cwtch

The Pubs

Crown Hotel, Liverpool, Merseyside (p342)

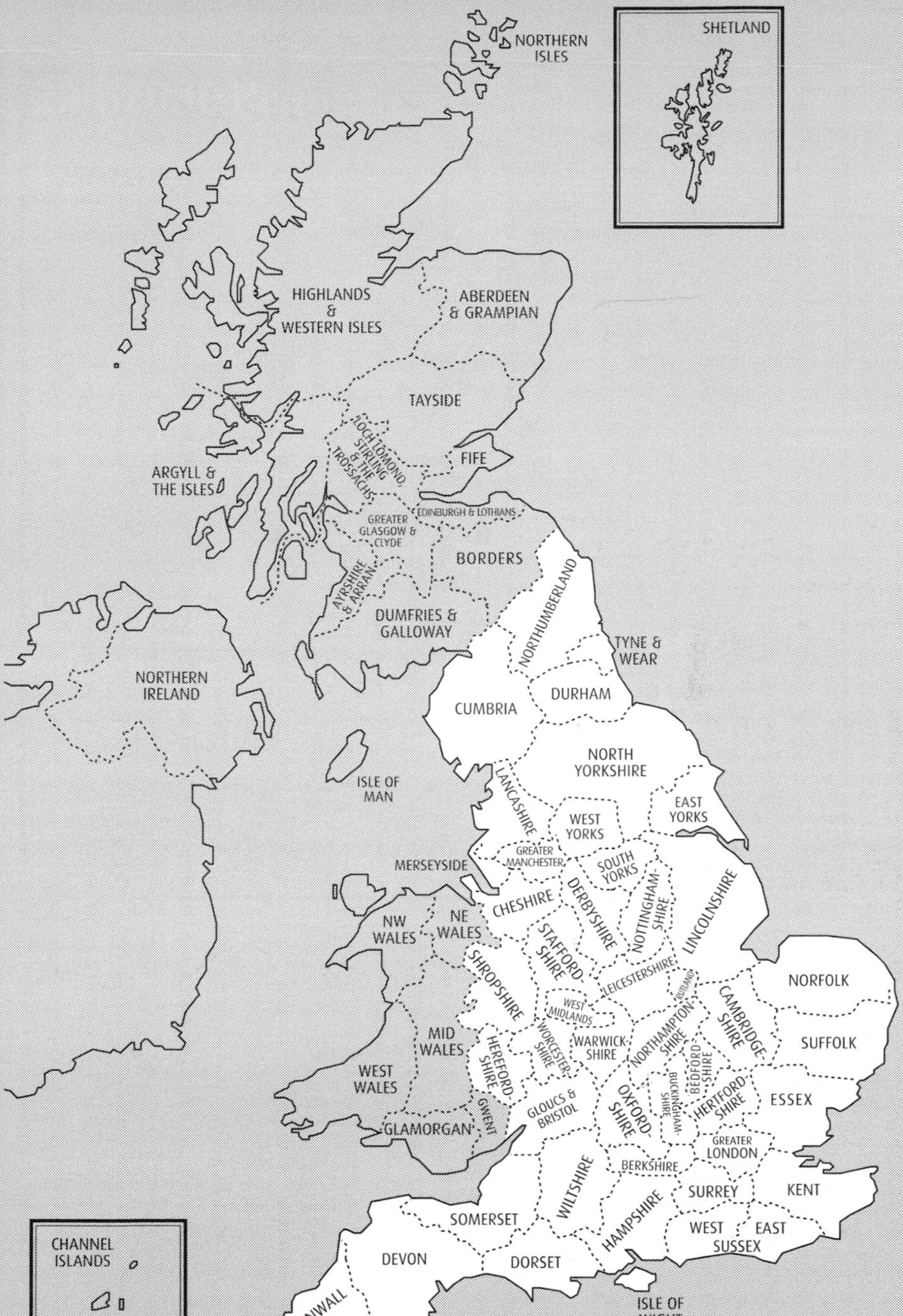
SHETLAND
NORTHERN ISLES
HIGHLANDS & WESTERN ISLES
ABERDEEN & GRAMPIAN
TAYSIDE
LOCH LOMOND, STIRLING & THE TROSSACHS
FIFE
ARGYLL & THE ISLES
EDINBURGH & LOTHIANS
GREATER GLASGOW & CLYDE
BORDERS
AYRSHIRE & ARRAN
DUMFRIES & GALLOWAY
NORTHUMBERLAND
TYNE & WEAR
NORTHERN IRELAND
CUMBRIA
DURHAM
NORTH YORKSHIRE
ISLE OF MAN
LANCASHIRE
EAST YORKS
WEST YORKS
GREATER MANCHESTER
SOUTH YORKS
MERSEYSIDE
CHESHIRE
DERBYSHIRE
NOTTINGHAMSHIRE
LINCOLNSHIRE
NW WALES
NE WALES
STAFFORDSHIRE
SHROPSHIRE
LEICESTERSHIRE
RUTLAND
NORFOLK
WEST MIDLANDS
CAMBRIDGESHIRE
MID WALES
HEREFORDSHIRE
WORCESTERSHIRE
WARWICKSHIRE
NORTHAMPTONSHIRE
BEDFORDSHIRE
SUFFOLK
WEST WALES
BUCKINGHAMSHIRE
HERTFORDSHIRE
ESSEX
GLOUCS & BRISTOL
OXFORDSHIRE
GWENT
GLAMORGAN
GREATER LONDON
BERKSHIRE
WILTSHIRE
SURREY
KENT
SOMERSET
HAMPSHIRE
WEST SUSSEX
EAST SUSSEX
CHANNEL ISLANDS
DEVON
DORSET
CORNWALL
ISLE OF WIGHT

England

Ampthill

Albion

36 Dunstable Street, MK45 2JT

11.30-11 ☎ (01525) 634857

B&T Shefford Bitter, Golden Fox, Dragon Slayer; Everards Tiger Best Bitter; 7 changing beers H

An award-winning, narrow-fronted Victorian pub with one large bar and 12 handpumps serving a range of local B&T beers as well as Everards Tiger and seven constantly changing ales mainly from microbreweries. Two real ciders and a perry are also available. Beer and cider festivals are held at least annually. Filled rolls are served at lunchtimes. There is a cosy patio garden at the rear. English music nights feature once a month on a Wednesday evening. Twice CAMRA Bedfordshire Pub of the Year.

Arlesey

Vicars Inn

68 Church Lane, SG15 6UX

5-midnight; 12-4, 7-midnight Sat & Sun

☎ (01462) 731215

Wells Eagle IPA; 1 changing beer H

Friendly village local situated just a few minutes from the railway station and bus stop. The front bar features some local historical pictures and hosts the dominoes and cribbage teams, who enjoy sandwiches or cheese and biscuits provided by the landlady. At the bar, the regular Eagle IPA is supported by an ever-changing low gravity guest ale. To the rear is a large comfortable lounge bar and a function room, beyond is an enclosed child-friendly garden. Q P (72,97)

Bedford

Bedford Arms

2 Bromham Road, MK40 2QA (opp HM Prison)

12-midnight ☎ (01234) 214656

thebedfordarmsbedford.co.uk

Courage Directors; Wells Bombardier; Young's Bitter, Special; 3 changing beers H

A Charles Wells Speciality Beer House offering three regularly changing guest beers and a changing guest cider as well as four regulars from Charles Wells. A typical pub lunch menu is served daily except Sunday. There is live jazz on Monday evenings and Sunday afternoons, local bands on Sunday evenings, traditional music on the first Thursday of the month and an open mic acoustic session on the second Tuesday evening. A book club meets on the second Thursday of the month.

Burnaby Arms

66 Stanley Street, MK41 7RU (Prime Ministers area N of town centre)

5-11 (midnight Fri); 4-midnight Sat; 2-10.30 Sun

☎ (01234) 330056

Courage Directors; Wells Eagle IPA; Young's London Gold; 2 changing beers H

This two-room street corner pub has rapidly become a hub of the local community. It hosts a fortnightly quiz while the darts team plays weekly. Hot pies and toasted sandwiches are available daily and the monthly pie night is well patronised. Monthly music evenings and Sunday jazz afternoons are also popular. Throughout the year there are other special events including a new beer festival in early April. Local CAMRA Town Pub of the Year 2014. Q (10)

Castle

17 Newnham Street, MK40 3JR

12-11 (midnight Thu); 11.30-midnight Fri; 11-midnight Sat

(01234) 353295 castlebedford.co.uk

Courage Directors; Wells Eagle IPA; Young's Bitter, London Gold, Special; 2 changing beers H

A recently refurbished two-bar pub with a pleasant walled patio garden. Lunches are served daily, and evening meals weekdays only. Current guest beers with tasting notes are listed on the website. Peacock Auction Rooms and Bedford Rugby Club are close by. A guest house behind the pub provides five en-suite letting bedrooms. Charles Wells Pub of the Year 2014 and local CAMRA Most Improved Pub 2015. P (4,5,7)

Devonshire Arms L

32 Dudley Street, MK40 3TB (1 mile E of town centre S of A4280)

5 (4 Fri)-11; 12-11 Sat; 12-10.30 Sun (01234) 359329

devonshirearmsbedford.co.uk

Courage Directors; Wells Eagle IPA; Young's London Gold, Special; 2 changing beers H

Pleasant Victorian LocAle pub in a residential area. Guest and seasonal ales are mainly from Charles Wells, the two ciders and perry are from Westons. Pub festivals are held each year. The front bar has bare floorboards and an open fire, while there is a separate rear bar. The garden has a gazebo for smokers and a no-smoking paved area. A good range of wines is sold by the glass or bottle. Local CAMRA Pub of the Year 2013. Q (4)

Three Cups L

45 Newnham Street, MK40 3JR (200yds S of A4280 near rugby ground)

11-11 (midnight Fri & Sat); 12-10.30 Sun

(01234) 352153

4 changing beers H

Comfortable inn dating from the 1770s, now a Greene King Local Hero pub offering local microbrewery beers. These include at least two from White Park Brewery, whose owner holds the lease. Tasting thirds are available for all beers. Locally sourced home-cooked lunches are served. The old wood panelling helps retain some of the pub's original character. Situated five minutes from the town centre and close to Bedford Blues rugby ground. Local CAMRA Town Pub of the Year 2015. P (4,5,7)

Wellington Arms L

40-42 Wellington Street, MK40 2JX (off A6 N of town centre)

12-11 (10.30 Sun) (01234) 308033

thewelly.wix.com/bedford

Adnams Southwold Bitter; B&T Shefford Bitter; Draught Bass; 9 changing beers H

Winner of many awards, this street-corner local operated by B&T Brewery offers a wide selection of ever-changing regional and microbrewery beers from 12 handpumps. A rotating range of ciders is served from two handpumps. Draught Belgian and Dutch beers plus a wide range of bottled Belgian beers are also available. There is a courtyard for drinkers and smokers. A friendly pub with a mixed clientele, it can get very busy on Friday and Saturday evenings.

Biggleswade

Golden Pheasant L

71 High Street, SG18 0JH

12-11.30 (midnight Fri); 11-midnight Sat; 1-11.30 Sun

(01767) 313653 goldenpheasantpub.co.uk

Wells Eagle IPA; 5 changing beers H

Straightforward town-centre alehouse a stone's throw from buses, trains and busy shoppers. Six handpumps cover a range of styles and strengths, often embracing mild and porter among local beers and more distant microbrewery offerings. Franklin's Cider from nearby Dunton is usually one of the two or three available, but otherwise the focus is on freshness, not familiarity. Weekly meat raffles, a monthly quiz and carol services at Christmas rightly suggest this is a pub well integrated into the town's everyday life.

Q

New Inn Ale House & Kitchen

Market Square, SG18 8AS

9am-11.30 (1am Thu); 7am-1am Fri & Sat

(01767) 222938

Greene King IPA; 7 changing beers H

Formerly an 18th-century coaching inn, this is now a thriving one-bar town-centre pub. It has comfortable seating and large-screen TVs for sport, particularly live rugby. Outside, the patio and pavement seating are popular during warmer months. The Local Hero-themed bar features three Greene King monthly specials plus four rotating guest ales free of the tie, some locally produced. Several real ciders come from Thistly Cross. The pub opens early for breakfast with bar service from 10am. Q

Wheatsheaf

5 Lawrence Road, SG18 0LS

11-4, 7-11.30; 11-midnight Fri & Sat; 12-11 Sun

(01767) 222220

Greene King IPA; 2 changing beers H

Part of Hawthorn Leisure's estate, this back-street pub continues to serve excellent ales at competitive prices through its three handpumps. Simply but comfortably furnished with benches, tables and chairs, entertainment includes dominoes, cribbage and friendly chat, with darts available for the more athletic. Sport is screened but does not detract from other pub activities. The spacious rear garden is a delightful spot in which to enjoy a drink on warm evenings.

REAL ALE BREWERIES

B&T Shefford
Charles Wells Bedford
Leighton Buzzard Leighton Buzzard (NEW)
Potton Potton
White Park Cranfield

Bolnhurst

Plough

Kimbolton Road, MK44 2EX (on B660 S of village) TL088587

closed Mon; 12-3, 6.30-11; 12-3 Sun (01234) 376274

bolnhurst.com

3 changing beers [H]

Award-winning pub-restaurant dating back to Tudor times, offering excellent food and beer. The main bar features a wood-burning stove, and a second room is set aside for diners and functions. Up to three real ales are available, usually including one from Adnams and one from a local microbrewery. Outside is a large garden with decking beside a small pond. The pub is closed from Christmas until the second week of January each year. **Q P**

Broom

Cock ★

23 High Street, SG18 9NA

12-11 (10 Sun) (01767) 314411

thecockatbroom.co.uk

Sharp's Doom Bar; 3 changing beers [G]

A classic Grade II-listed freehouse, with a nationally important historic pub interior. It has flagstone floors throughout the many cosy rooms and several fireplaces. Up to four ales are served direct from the cellar, as there is no bar, plus local Potton Press ciders. Pub games are played including Northants skittles. The pub has a strong community focus and offers a variety of events including live music, quizzes, barbecues and mini beer festivals. Locally sourced pub food is served daily.

Q P

Clophill

Stone Jug

10 Back Street, MK45 4BY (500yds off A6 at N end of village) TL083381

12-3.30, 6-11; 12-11 Fri & Sat; 12-10.30 Sun

(01525) 860526 stonejug.co.uk

B&T Shefford Bitter; Otter Amber; 3 changing beers [H]

Originally three 16th-century cottages, this popular village local has an L-shaped bar that serves two drinking areas and a family/function room. Excellent home-made lunches are available Tuesday to Saturday. The three guest beers are often from local breweries, the cider is Westons. Picnic benches at the front and a rear patio garden offer space for outdoor drinking in fine weather. Parking can be difficult at busy times. Local CAMRA Pub of the Year 2014. **Q P** (44,81)

Dunstable

Gary Cooper

Grove Park, Court Drive, LU5 4GP

9am-midnight (2am Fri); 8am-2am Sat; 8am-midnight Sun

(01582) 471452

Adnams Broadside; Greene King Abbot; Ruddles Best Bitter; 7 changing beers [H]

This modern Wetherspoon bar is named after the famous Hollywood star who attended the local grammar school between 1910 and 1913. It offers a selection of up to seven guest ales, often local. The large and airy bar also serves good-value meals. Situated in Grove Park leisure area, its patio overlooks the Grove House gardens with buses stopping opposite. It tends to be busy on Friday and Saturday nights. Be prepared for a long hike to the upstairs loos.

Globe

43 Winfield Street, LU6 1LS

12-11 (midnight Fri & Sat); 12-10.30 Sun

(01582) 512300

B&T Shefford Bitter, Black Dragon Mild, Edwin Taylor's Extra Stout, SOD; Everards Tiger Best Bitter; 5 changing beers [H]

Popular beer destination and community local where 13 handpumps feature a range of B&T beers, five ever-changing microbrewery ales, a real cider and a perry. More than 20 Belgian beers are also available. Bare boards, bar stools, breweriana and a famous plank at the end of the bar create a traditional town pub atmosphere buzzing with conversation. Acoustic music night is Tuesday. Regular beer festivals are hosted. Former Bedfordshire and local CAMRA Pub of the Year.

Q

Pheasant Inn

208 West Street, LU6 1NX

11-11 (11.30 Fri & Sat); 12-11.30 Sun (01582) 662706

the-pheasant-inn-dunstable.co.uk

Courage Directors; Sharp's Doom Bar; 4 changing beers [H]

Pub plus hotel/B&B, located just out of the town centre, with a large main bar and a large function room selling six real ales. Traditional pub games are played and all major sports are screened via Sky and BT Sport TVs. Outside are a covered and heated front smoking area, rear garden, large umbrellas and a car park. Free curry is served on Friday and free pizza on Saturday evenings (drinks must be purchased). An annual beer festival is hosted and live music on occasion.

P (31)

Victoria

69 West Street, LU6 1ST

11-11.30 (midnight Fri & Sat); 12-midnight Sun

(01582) 662682 victoriapub.co.uk

House beer (by Tring); 3 changing beers [H]

Popular town-centre pub with four ales usually on offer including a house beer, Victoria Bitter, from Tring Brewery. The varying guest ales are from micro and regional breweries, one of which is sold at a reduced rate Monday-Friday. Good-value food is available until early evening Monday-Saturday, and Sunday lunchtimes. Darts, dominoes and crib are popular and televised sport features in the bar. Beer festivals are held several times a year. There is a separate function room available.

(34,61)

Dunton

March Hare

34 High Street, SG18 8RN

6-11 (midnight Thu); 12-midnight Fri & Sat; 12-10.30 Sun

(01767) 448093 duntonvillage.org.uk/pub/home.htm

4 changing beers [H]

Relaxed village local run by a beer enthusiast who takes pride in his craft and serves a meticulous, first-rate pint. Local CAMRA Rural Pub of 2015, with regular beer and cider festivals, it often serves Wells and Buntingford beers as well as Franklin's ciders made 200 yards away. Pub attractions include a community shop, folk music sessions on the first Tuesday of the month and occasional themed food nights. Warmed plates and cutlery can be provided for those wanting to order an evening takeaway. Q🐴❀♣🍎🚻🚌(188)🐾📶

Felmersham

Sun 🏆 Ⓛ

Grange Road, MK43 7EU

⏲ 4 (3.30 Fri)-11; 12-11 Sat; 12-10 Sun ☎ (01234) 781355
🌐 thesuninn-felmersham.com

Wells Eagle IPA; 2 changing beers Ⓗ

Pretty, thatched community local reopened as a family-owned free house in 2013. Guest beers are changed weekly and normally include at least one from a local microbrewery. The pub has a family-friendly rear garden and is convenient for visits to the historic parish church and a waterfowl nature reserve just across the river. Beer festivals are held once or twice a year. Local CAMRA Pub of the Year 2015. 🐴❀♣P🚌(50)🐾📶

Flitton

Jolly Coopers Ⓛ

Wardhedges, MK45 5ED

⏲ 12-3 (not Mon), 5.30-11.30; 12-midnight Sat; 12-10.30 Sun
☎ (01525) 303648 🌐 jollycoopersflitton.co.uk

Wells Eagle IPA; 2 changing beers Ⓗ

In the hamlet of Wardhedges at the east end of Flitton, the landlord and lady take obvious pride in this wonderful country community pub. Two ever-changing and varied guest ales are available alongside the regular Eagle. Traditional British food is served in the bar and restaurant, with a choice of menus. There is a large garden to the rear and a patio with spectacular floral displays in the summer months. Dogs are welcome in the impressively flagstoned bar. 🐴❀◐♿♣P🐾📶

Harlington

Carpenters Arms

Sundon Road, LU5 6LS

⏲ 12-3.30, 6-midnight; 12-midnight Fri-Sun
☎ (01525) 872384 🌐 thecarpentersarmsharlington.com

Greene King IPA; Woodforde's Wherry; 2 changing beers Ⓗ

Situated in the heart of Harlington, this low beamed watch-your-head traditional village pub was first licensed in 1790 and has listings of landlords from then until the present day. The current landlord is a local who has always lived in the village. Two regular beers and two changing guests are available. Food is reasonably priced with generous helpings. The railway station and occasional bus service along with a range of country walks make this a popular stop-off.
Q🐴❀◐♿⇌♣P🚌(X42)🐾📶

Old Sun

34 Sundon Road, LU5 6LS

⏲ 2 (12 Fri & Sat)-11; 12-11.30 Sun ☎ (01525) 877330

Harveys Sussex Best Bitter; St Austell Trelawny, Tribute; 1 changing beer Ⓗ

With three regular ales and one or two guests, this traditional, half-timbered pub dates back to 1785 and the building to the 1740s. Tuesday is steak night, Thursday is pie night and Friday evening is for fish and chips. There are two separate bars with a side room and outdoor seating plus a children's play area. Situated just a short walk from the main-line rail station. Q❀◑⇌♣P🚌(X42)🐾📶

Heath & Reach

Axe & Compass Ⓛ

Leighton Road, LU7 0AA

⏲ 12-midnight ☎ (01525) 237394
🌐 theaxeandcompass.co.uk

4 changing beers Ⓗ

This village community pub has been a free house since 2014. The older front bar, with its low beams, is a lounge and dining area while the rear public bar has gaming machines, a pool table and TV. The large garden includes a children's play area. Regular beers are from Tring and Leighton Buzzard Brewing Co, and guests often come from local breweries such as White Park, XT and Concrete Cow. Accommodation is available in a separate lodge. 🐴❀🛏◐♣P🚌(150)🐾📶

Henlow

Engineers Arms 🏆 Ⓛ

68 High Street, SG16 6AA

⏲ 12-midnight (1am Fri & Sat) ☎ (01462) 812284
🌐 engineersarms.co.uk

8 changing beers Ⓗ

Popular free house offering at least eight ever-changing real ales and sometimes two more served straight from wooden barrels. Up to eight ciders often include local producers Dunton and Potton Press. The front bar features historical pictures and breweriana; the back room has wide-screen TVs for live sport and pub games including darts and Northants skittles. Occasional live music and disco evenings are hosted. The Octoberfest offers 100 real ales and a winterfest showcases 30 ciders and perries. Local CAMRA Pub of the Year 2015. 🐴❀⛺♣🍎🚌(71,188)🐾📶

Houghton Conquest

Knife & Cleaver Ⓛ

The Grove, MK45 3LA (opp parish church)

⏲ 7am-midnight (7 Sun) ☎ (01234) 930789
🌐 theknifeandcleaver.com

Courage Best Bitter, Directors; Wells Eagle IPA; 1 changing beer Ⓗ

A smart pub/restaurant with accommodation, reopened by Charles Wells in January 2012 and run by licensees who previously operated a restaurant in France. Quality meals are made with fresh locally sourced ingredients. The nine en-suite bedrooms are housed in a separate block behind the secluded family-friendly rear garden. Awarded an AA gold award for food 2013 and 2014.
🐴❀🛏◐♿P🚌(42)📶

Leighton Buzzard

Black Lion 🏆

20 High Street, LU7 1EA

⏲ 12-11 (midnight Fri & Sat); 12-10.30 Sun
☎ (01525) 853725

Draught Bass; Nethergate Suffolk County Best Bitter; Oakham Bishops Farewell; 5 changing beers Ⓗ

With 17th-century origins and under new management since early 2014, this is now a traditional alehouse, the atmosphere enhanced by exposed beams, wooden floors and an open fire. Eight handpumps often feature ales from local microbreweries including Tring, Leighton Buzzard and XT. Eighty bottled continental beers and eight guest real ciders are also available. There is a large paved garden. No food is served but bring-your-own cold lunches are welcome. Local CAMRA Pub of the Year 2015. Q❀♣🍎🚌🐾

Golden Bell

5 Church Square, LU7 1AE
⏲ 10-11.30 (midnight Fri & Sat); 11-11 Sun
☎ (01525) 373330 🌐 thegoldenbell.co.uk
4 changing beers Ⓗ
Dating from the 18th-century and with Grade II listing, this lively and welcoming community local has a single bar with low-beamed ceilings and sofas at one end. Food, using ingredients from local suppliers, is served throughout opening hours. Beers might include Adnams Broadside, Sharp's Doom Bar, Taylor Landlord or Tetley Golden Bell Bitter from four handpumps and one gravity dispense. Sport is shown on four large screens, one in the landscaped garden where a bar operates in summer. 🐎❀◑♣P🚌📶

Red Lion

1 North Street, LU7 1EF
⏲ 10-11 (midnight Fri & Sat); 11-11 Sun ☎ (01525) 374350
Banks's Bitter; Greene King Abbot; 1 changing beer Ⓗ
This 17th-century building is a town centre institution. An old-fashioned pub with old-fashioned values, the manager of 20 years provides a warm welcome. The public bar offers all of the traditional pub games; the main bar resembles a living room with comfy chairs, a large fish tank, TV screen and the pub's dogs wandering around. As well as the well-kept ales there is Westons Old Rosie cider plus a selection of Irish and Scottish single malt whiskies. ♣🍎🚌🐾📶

Swan Hotel 𝕃

50 High Street, LU7 1EA
⏲ 6am (7am Mon & Sat)-midnight; 7am-11.30 Sun
☎ (01525) 380170
Adnams Broadside; Greene King Abbot; Ruddles Best Bitter; Sharp's Doom Bar; 5 changing beers Ⓗ
Dating from the 17th century, this former coaching inn has been renovated by Wetherspoon. With good-value food and 39 guest rooms, the Swan is busy and bustling for much of the week. Friendly staff operate one long bar serving two rooms, a conservatory and a courtyard. Guest beers regularly come from local microbreweries such as Tring, Vale, Concrete Cow and Oxfordshire, and real cider is available in the summer months. Families are welcome until 10pm. Events include beer festivals twice a year. Q🐎🛏◑♿🍎🚌📶

Luton

Bricklayers Arms

High Town Road, LU2 0DD
⏲ 12-11 (midnight Fri & Sat); 12-10.30 Sun
☎ (01582) 611017 🌐 bricklayersarmsluton.co.uk
Batemans XB; 5 changing beers Ⓗ
The six busy handpumps serve a choice of light, amber or dark beers from an ever-changing range of guest ales from local and national breweries, often including a mild and an Oakham brew, with draught Belgian beers also available. This quirky town-centre pub has been run by the same landlady for 30 years. It is popular with Hatters fans on match days, with TVs in both bars. Quiz night is Monday. Two changing real ciders are always available. ❀⇌♣🍎📶

English Rose

46 Old Bedford Road, LU2 7PA
⏲ 1 (4 Mon)-11; 12-11 Fri-Sun ☎ (01582) 723889
4 changing beers Ⓗ
Traditional one-room, CAMRA-friendly, street-corner pub which serves 500-600 different ales per year. A pub since 1845, it was originally called the Rabbit – this area was then called Coney Heath, coney being the old word for rabbit. In 1919 this was one of four pubs in which the dissidents met before marching into town and eventually burning down the town hall. A stalwart CAMRA supporter, it plays a part in the Luton Beer and Cider Festival. ❀♿⇌♣🍎🚌(24,25)

London Hatter

46 Park Street, LU1 3ET
⏲ 8am-11 (1am Fri & Sat) ☎ (01582) 390920
Adnams Broadside; Greene King Abbot; Ruddles Best Bitter; 3 changing beers Ⓗ
Tasteful Wetherspoon conversion of a former nightclub at the university end of town, opened in 2011. Guest ales greet you on the first few pumps and the others dispense the regular beers. One real cider is usually available on draught plus one or two ciders or perries from boxes in the fridge. The smart interior caters more for dining than partying, and local history, in pictures, adorns the walls. A supporter of the CLIC Sargent charity.
Q🐎◑♿⇌🍎📶

Wigmore Arms 𝕃

Wigmore Lane, LU2 9XG
⏲ 11 (10 Sat & Sun)-11 ☎ (01582) 417343
Wells Bombardier; 3 changing beers Ⓗ
Lively and large modern two-bar pub in a residential area of Luton next to Asda. Beer festivals are held in April and October each year. The interior has a comfortable lounge with a dining area where food is served. The sports bar has two large HD screens and 3D TV showing sport and the Luton Town channel. Live music features fortnightly on Saturdays. A large function room is available.
🐎◑♿♣P📶

Moggerhanger

Guinea

Bedford Road, MK44 3RG
⏲ 12-11 (midnight Fri & Sat); 12-10.30 Sun
☎ (01767) 640388 🌐 guineamoggerhanger.co.uk
Wells Eagle IPA; Young's Bitter; 2 changing beers Ⓗ
Large 18th-century village pub with beamed ceilings in a prominent position on the main road in the heart of the village. There is a garden at the front and car parks at the side and rear. The main bar has a spacious drinking area and an area beyond for diners. A separate games bar has hood skittles. Freshly prepared food is available every day (not Sun eve). Q🐎❀◑♿♣P🚌(73,188)🐾📶

Potton

Rising Sun 𝕃

11 Everton Road, SG19 2PA
⏲ 12-3, 5-11 (midnight Fri); 12-midnight Sat & Sun
☎ (01767) 260231 🌐 risingsunpotton.co.uk
Wells Eagle IPA, Bombardier; 6 changing beers Ⓗ
Licensed as a beer house in 1836, this spacious beamed pub is popular with both diners and drinkers. A good choice of eight ales is available, mainly from the Wells group, including Young's,

Courage and McEwan's plus two or three guest beers. The interior features several distinct areas as well as an upstairs room with a west-facing roof terrace. Irregular Performers and Pints music gigs are hosted and beer festivals are held each year in May and October. ⬤⚾◑♣P🍴(188,190)🐾📶

Renhold

Polhill Arms

25 Wilden Road, MK41 0JP (at Salph End)
⬤ 12 (4.30 Mon)-11; 12-10.30 Sun ☎ (01234) 771398
🌐 polhillarms.co.uk
Greene King IPA; Hardys & Hansons Olde Trip; 3 changing beers Ⓗ
One-bar family-friendly village local with a welcoming atmosphere and large garden, play area and restaurant. An interesting collection of pub and brewery artefacts is displayed, as well as R101 airship memorabilia. Traditional pub food is served, including fish and chips (no food Sun or Mon eves). Live entertainment and quiz nights feature regularly, with darts and skittles also played. Three guest beers are usually available, with two real ciders in the winter months increasing to four in the summer.
⬤⚾◑♣●P🍴(27)🐾📶

Riseley

Fox & Hounds

High Street, MK44 1DT
⬤ 11.30-11 (11.30 Fri & Sat); 12-10.30 Sun
☎ (01234) 709714 🌐 foxandhoundsriseley.co.uk
Courage Directors; Wells Eagle IPA; 1 changing beer Ⓗ
Originally a 16th-century farmhouse and attached cottage, the building was converted into a beer house in the 19th century. Refurbishment in the 1990s revealed a priest's hiding hole. A more recent facelift brought a new look butcher's counter, steak flame grill, bar and restaurant. The Riseley Room to the right of the bar can be reserved for parties. The large, lawned garden includes a covered patio with heaters.
Q⬤⚾◑♿P🍴(28)🐾📶

Salford

Red Lion Hotel Ⓛ

Wavendon Road, MK17 8AZ (2 miles N of M1 jct 13)
SP934389
⬤ 11-2, 6-11; 12-2.30, 6-10 Sun ☎ (01908) 583117
🌐 redlionhotel.eu
Wells Eagle IPA, Bombardier Ⓗ
Friendly, traditional country hotel serving a fine choice of home-cooked food in the bar and restaurant. The cosy bar is heated by an open fire in winter and offers a selection of interesting board games. The large garden includes a covered area and a secure children's playground. Six rooms are available for overnight accommodation. A quiet pub and village but convenient for access to the motorway. Q⬤⚾🛏◑♿♣P📶

Sandy

Sir William Peel Ⓛ

39 High Street, SG19 1AG
⬤ 12 (11 Sat)-midnight; 12-10.30 Sun ☎ (01767) 680607
🌐 sirwilliampeel.webs.com
Batemans XB; 3 changing beers Ⓗ

Flower-basket bedecked pub with outdoor seating front and rear. Named after the hero whose picture and potted history are displayed inside, the interior also features a unique mirror advertising the Old Stables Brewery which used to operate behind the pub. Live music is hosted occasionally and there is a regular monthly quiz. Popular beer and cider festivals are held in April and July respectively. The three guest beers always include one from Oakham. Regular ciders are usually from the Westons range. ⬤⚾≈♣●P🍴(73,188)🐾📶

Sharnbrook

Swan With Two Nicks

High Street, MK44 1PF
⬤ 12-3, 6 (5 Fri & Sat)-11; 12-6 Sun ☎ (01234) 781585
🌐 swanwith2nicks.co.uk
Wells Eagle IPA; Young's London Gold; 2 changing beers Ⓗ
Friendly village pub with a rear courtyard and patio garden. Home-cooked quality lunches and evening meals are served (no food Sun eve), using locally sourced ingredients where possible and including daily specials. A selection of award-winning wines is also available by the glass or bottle. This is a good base for many local walks and nature reserves near the River Great Ouse.
⬤⚾◑P🍴(25,26,50)🐾📶

Shefford

Brewery Tap

14 North Bridge Street, SG17 5DH
⬤ 11.30-11; 12-10.30 Sun ☎ (01462) 628448
B&T Shefford Bitter, Shefford Dark Mild, Dragon Slayer; Everards Tiger Best Bitter; 2 changing beers Ⓗ
Renamed by the nearby B&T Brewery in 1996, the Tap is primarily a drinkers' pub, offering four regular ales plus two guests which are usually stronger beers. Breweriana decorates an open-plan interior divided into two distinct areas with a family room at the rear. Lunchtime pies and rolls are available. Darts, dominoes and cribbage teams are supported, as is a golf society. The rear patio garden is heated on cool evenings. Car park access is through the archway beside the pub.
⬤⚾♣P🍴(71,72)🐾

Souldrop

Bedford Arms Ⓛ

High Street, MK44 1EY (½ mile W of A6)
⬤ closed Mon; 12-3, 6-11; 12-midnight Fri & Sat; 12-10 Sun
☎ (01234) 781384
Black Sheep Best Bitter; Greene King IPA; 3 changing beers Ⓗ
Large village pub created partly from a 17th-century hop and ale house. Guest beers are often from local microbreweries, the cider is from Saxby's and nearby producer Evershed. The restaurant has a central open fireplace and offers traditional pub favourites prepared to order, with daily specials and a roast on Sunday. A games room with skittles runs off the main bar. The spacious garden with pétanque is popular with families in summer. Local CAMRA Country Pub of the Year 2013. ⬤⚾◑♿♣●P🍴(26)🐾📶

Stanbridge

Five Bells

Station Road, LU7 9JF
⏲ 11-11 (11.30 Sat); 12-10.30 Sun ☎ (01525) 210224
🌐 fivebellsstanbridge.co.uk
Fuller's London Pride; Gale's Seafarers Ale; 2 changing beers Ⓗ
A Fuller's-owned country pub with wooden floors, two real fires, a cosy snug and mind-your-head beams. A separate 80-seater restaurant in the 18th-century wing offers good-quality food and is available for weddings and functions. The building is set in extensive and attractive grounds and named after the nearby church which had five bells but subsequently acquired a sixth. Guest ales are usually from Fuller's/Gale's and may occasionally come from a local microbrewery.
🐴❀◐◑♿♣P🚌(70)🐾📶

Toddington

Cuckoo Ⓛ

Market Square, LU5 6QJ
⏲ 3-11 (midnight Fri); 12-midnight Sat; 12-3 Sun ☎ 07871 600442 🌐 thecuckoo.pub
7 changing beers Ⓗ
Located in the old town hall, this 15th-century Grade II-listed building has a main bar, separate lounge with comfy chairs and an upstairs function room. The bar features a selection of real ales and ciders with a strong local leaning along with a range of unusual keg beers (not real ale). There is no TV and no music, just convivial conversation and good beer and cider. A limited range of high-quality pub snacks is available. Q♣🍎🚌(42,E)🐾

Oddfellows Arms

2 Congar Lane, LU5 6BP
⏲ 5 (1 Sat & Sun)-11 ☎ (01525) 872021
Adnams Broadside; Fuller's London Pride; 2 changing beers Ⓗ
Attractive 700-year-old two-bar pub facing the village green with a heavily beamed bar featuring a vast collection of pump clips. It has a separate games room with a pool table. With two regular real ales and a wide selection on the two guest handpumps there is always plenty of choice. The regular real cider is Westons Old Rosie and there is often an alternative. The patio garden is popular in summer and has shelter for smokers.
♣🍎🚌(42,E)🐾📶

Totternhoe

Old Farm Inn

16 Church Road, LU6 1RE
⏲ 5-midnight Mon; 12-3, 5-11; 12-midnight Sat; 12-11 Sun
☎ (01582) 674053 🌐 oldfarminndunstable.co.uk
Fuller's London Pride, ESB; 2 changing beers Ⓗ
Located in the conservation area of Church End Totternhoe, this charming village pub boasts two inglenooks. The public bar with its low boarded ceiling is where you will find good conversation and where traditional pub games are played. Dogs are welcome in the front bar and there is a child-friendly garden. Monday is folk music night. Tasty home-cooked food is served (booking advised) including popular Sunday roasts (no food Mon or Sun eves). Beer festivals are held in May and August. Q🐴❀◐◑♿♣🍎P🚌(61)🐾📶

Whipsnade

Old Hunters Lodge Ⓛ

The Crossroads, LU6 2LN
⏲ 11.30-2.30 (3 Fri & Sat), 6-11; 12-11 Sun
☎ (01582) 872228 🌐 old-hunters.com
Greene King Abbot; Tring Brock Bitter; 1 changing beer Ⓗ
A beautiful 15th-century thatched inn set on the outskirts of Whipsnade village close to the world renowned Whipsnade Zoo. The cosy main bar, warmed by a log fire, includes soft seating as well as traditional dining tables. The side bar retains many old features such as the inglenook fireplace. Separate restaurant areas may be used as function rooms. The picturesque front garden makes a lovely area for summer dining and drinking. Six guest rooms include a bridal suite.
Q🐴❀🛏◐◑P🚌(X31)🐾📶

Wootton

Chequers Ⓛ

Hall End, MK43 9HP (NW edge of village) SP001457
⏲ 12-11 ☎ (01234) 930464 🌐 chequerswootton.co.uk
Wells Eagle IPA; 2 changing beers Ⓗ
Originally a farmhouse, this handsome old free house retains a wealth of heavy wooden beams and period features. A wide range of guest beers is offered, often from local microbreweries. An interesting, quality menu is served in the restaurant and good-value bar food is available throughout the pub (no food Sun eve). The large, pleasant garden is popular in fine weather.
Q🐴❀◐◑♿♣P🚌(68)🐾📶

Wrestlingworth

Chequers Ⓛ

43 High Street, SG19 2EP
⏲ 5-10.30 Mon; 12-3, 5-11; 12-midnight Fri & Sat; 12-10.30 Sun ☎ (01767) 631818 🌐 chequersfreehouse.co.uk
Adnams Southwold Bitter; 3 changing beers Ⓗ
Friendly country pub in a picturesque 17th-century building, with one long room featuring several open fires and a cosy inglenook. The three guest ales often include one from nearby Buntingford. Wholesome home-cooked food is offered and there are regular specials nights (no food Sun eve). For the sporting-minded the pub offers a pétanque court, a dartboard and a Sky Sports screen, usually on silent. Local CAMRA Most Improved Pub of 2015.
Q🐴❀◐◑♣P🚌(188)🐾📶

Public transport information

Leave the car behind and travel to the pub by bus, train or tram

Using public transport is an excellent way to get to the pub, but many people use it irregularly, and systems can be slightly different from place to place. So, below are some useful websites and phone numbers where you can find all the information you might need.

Combined travel information

The national **Traveline** system gives information on all rail and local bus services throughout England, Scotland and Wales. Calls are put through to a local call centre and if necessary your call will be switched through to a more relevant one. There are also services for mobiles, including a next-bus text service and smart-phone app. The website offers other services including timetables and a journey planner with mapping:

- 0871 200 22 33
  www.traveline.org.uk

The **Transport Direct** website uniquely offers information for door-to-door travel by public transport, bicycle and car around England, Scotland and Wales. The site provides street-level mapping of transport stops and stations, places and addresses and can generate route maps for various types of journeys:

- **www.transportdirect.info**

LONDON

In London use Traveline or **Transport for London (TfL)** travel services. TfL provides information and route planning for all of London's transport networks, including London Underground and Overground, Docklands Light Railway, National Rail, buses, River Buses, Tramlink, Barclays Cycles and cycle routes. Detailed ticketing information helps you find the most cost effective ways to travel in London. There are also live departure boards, service and traffic updates; mobile services and more:

- 020 7222 1234
  www.tfl.gov.uk

Train travel

National Rail Enquiries covers the whole of Great Britain's rail network and provides service information, ticketing, online journey planning and other information.

- 08457 48 49 50
  www.nationalrail.co.uk

Coach travel

The two main UK coach companies are **National Express** and **Scottish Citylink**. Between them, they serve everywhere from Cornwall to the Highlands. Their websites offer timetables, journey planning, ticketing and route mapping, along with other useful information.

- National Express: 08717 81 81 81
  www.nationalexpress.com

- Scottish Citylink: 08705 50 50 50
  www.citylink.co.uk

Northern Ireland & islands

For travel outside mainland Britain but within the area of this Guide, information is available from the following companies:

NORTHERN IRELAND

- Translink: 028 9066 6630
  www.translink.co.uk

ISLE OF MAN

- Isle of Man Transport: 01624 662 525
  www.iombusandrail.info

JERSEY

- Liberty Bus: 01534 828 555
  www.libertybus.je

GUERNSEY

- Island Coachways: 01481 720 210
  www.buses.gg

Public transport symbols in the Guide

Pub entries in the Guide include helpful symbols to show if there are stations and/ or bus routes close to a pub. There are symbols for railway stations (⇌); tram or light rail stations (🚊); London Underground, Overground or DLR stations (⊖); and bus routes (🚌). See the 'Key to symbols' on the inside front cover for more details.

BERKSHIRE

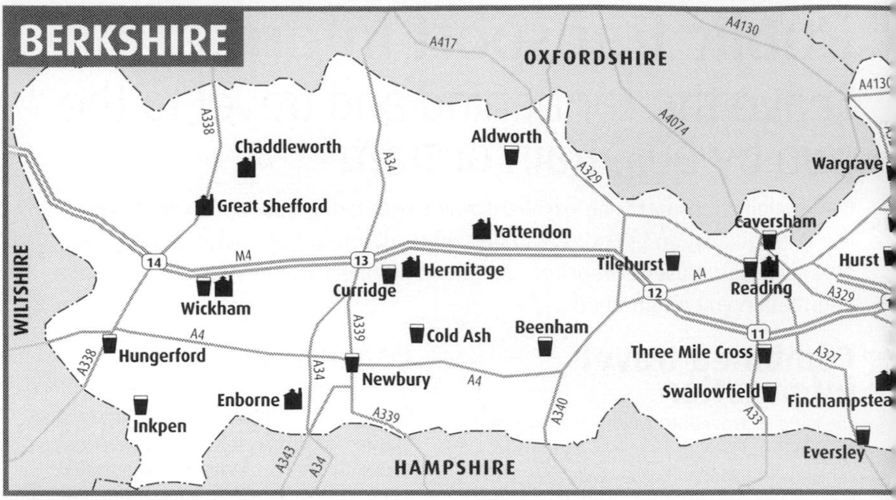

Aldworth

Bell Inn ★ 🄻

Bell Lane, RG8 9SE (250yds off B4009)
✪ closed Mon; 11-3, 6-11; 12-3, 7-10.30 Sun
☎ (01635) 578272
Arkell's 3B, Kingsdown; West Berkshire Maggs' Magnificent Mild; house beer (by West Berkshire); 2 changing beers (sourced locally; often West Berkshire) 🄷
Adjoinng a cricket ground and excellent for walking on the Berkshire Downs, this is an unspoilt gem of a pub with a sunny garden. In the same ownership since the 19th century, it is famed for its hot filled rolls and its unique ale, Old Tyler. It has an unspoilt historic interior. Formerly national, regional and branch CAMRA Pub of the Year, it sells Tutts Clump and Lilley's ciders. Q❀♣P

Ascot

Duke of Edinburgh

Woodside Road, Woodside, SL4 2DP SU928709
✪ 11-11; 12-6.30 Sun ☎ (01344) 882736
⊕ thedukeofedinburgh.com
Arkell's Wiltshire Gold, 3B, Kingsdown; 1 changing beer (sourced regionally) 🄷
Although a distant outpost of Arkell's Brewery, a good selection of its ales is always available including seasonal beers such as Noel and Moonlight. Less than a mile from Ascot Racecourse, it is a lively place on race days. Good food can be enjoyed in the restaurant, bar or large well-kept garden. Sports events are screened (on low volume) in the bar area where football memorabilia is on prominent display. ❀♿P

Beenham

Six Bells 🏆 🄻

The Green, RG7 5NX (at Bucklebury end of main road through village)
✪ 12-2.30 (not Mon), 6-11; 12-2.30, 6.30-11 Sat; 12-3, 6.30-10.30 Sun ☎ (0118) 971 3368 ⊕ thesixbells.co.uk
West Berkshire Good Old Boy; 2 changing beers 🄷
This quintessential English village pub meets the needs of locals and travellers alike. The name commemorates the recasting of the parish church bells after the 1794 fire. Two cosy bars, delightfully decorated with items from around the world, provide comfortable seating and ample tables for diners. Four guest bedrooms, conference facilities and a chance to explore miles of local footpaths help make this a popular destination.
Q❀▲P (104)

Bracknell

Cannie Man 🄻

Bywood, Hanworth, RG12 7RF
✪ 12-11 (11.30 Fri & Sat); 12-10.30 Sun ☎ (01344) 307620
Fuller's London Pride; 3 changing beers (often Brains, Sharp's, West Berkshire) 🄷
Four handpumps serve an ever-changing range here, which always includes a LocAle, session beer and a guest. The pub supports darts, pool and football teams as well as sponsoring local charitable and community events. Sport is screened on TV and live entertainment hosted every Friday and Saturday. This is a great example of a well-run estate pub. ♣P (100)

Old Manor 🄻

Grenville Place, RG12 1BP
✪ 8am-midnight (1am Fri & Sat) ☎ (01344) 304490
Greene King Abbot; Loddon Hoppit; Ruddles Best Bitter; 5 changing beers 🄷
Visitors to this former manor house should explore the fascinating rooms and alcoves in the original Tudor building that make this well-frequented Wetherspoon establishment so unique. The pub offers up to eight well-kept real ales including at least one LocAle plus a real cider. Good pub grub is served at competitive prices. The back bar and Monk's Room can be reserved for events.
Q♿P

Caversham

Fox & Hounds 🏆 🄻

51 Gosbrook Road, RG4 8BN
✪ 12-midnight (11 Sun) ☎ 07540 816293
⊕ foxandhoundscaversham.co.uk
8 changing beers (sourced nationally; often Dark Star, Oakham, Triple fff) 🄷

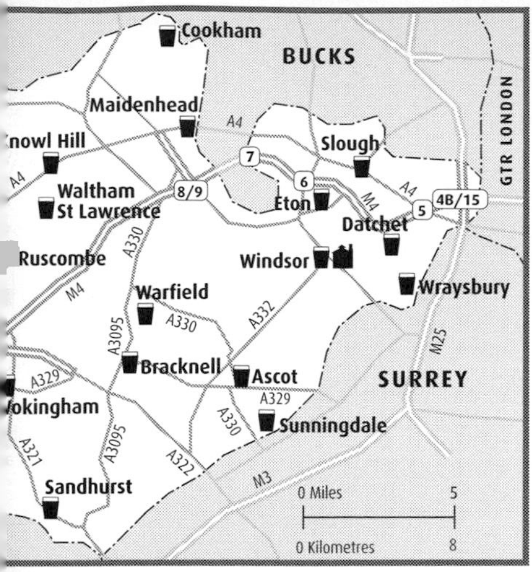

The landlord is a former brewer and offers up to eight real ales from microbreweries, together with a choice of real cider and perry from local producers. Football and other sports are often shown on TV, with darts and pool on offer in the bar. Quiz night is Thursday. Food is restricted to the popular Sunday roasts.
P (25,28,800)

Grosvenor

Kidmore Road, RG4 7NH
11.30-11 (midnight Fri; 11.30 Sat; 10.30 Sun)
(0118) 947 4643
Brakspear Bitter; Fuller's London Pride; Sharp's Doom Bar; 2 changing beers Ⓗ
The smartly decorated interior provides plenty of room for both drinking and dining. Five real ales are available, often including two from microbreweries, and pub food is served all day until 10pm. Cask Ale Club on Monday offers discounted real ales. Cash prizes are the draw at quiz nights on Sunday and Wednesday.
♣P (22)

Cold Ash

Castle Inn

Cold Ash Hill, RG18 9PS
11.30-11.30 (midnight Fri & Sat; 11 Sun)
(01635) 863232 thecastleatcoldash.co.uk
Courage Best Bitter; Fuller's London Pride; Sharp's Doom Bar; West Berkshire Good Old Boy; 2 changing beers (sourced nationally) Ⓗ
A 19th-century inn that has benefited from a recent tasteful refurbishment, and is known for its good food and popular pensioners' weekday lunches. As well as the regular beers, including a local brew from West Berkshire Brewery, it serves two guests and a real cider. Monday is quiz night and a meat raffle is held on Friday.
♣P (101)

Cookham

Bounty

Cock Marsh, SL8 5RG (over railway bridge from Bourne End or walk along Cookham towpath) SU890872
12-11 (01628) 520056 thebountypub.com
Rebellion IPA, Mutiny; 1 changing beer (sourced locally; often Rebellion) Ⓗ
Located on National Trust's Cock Marsh between Cookham village and Bourne End, this quirky, characterful pub is only accessible on foot or by boat. Dogs, walkers and children are made welcome. Bar billiards can be played while listening to '60s music. Live events feature throughout the summer, including the Mikron Theatre. Summer weekends can be busy. Note that opening hours are reduced in winter – noon-dusk weekends only. (Bourne End)♣

Old Swan Uppers

The Pound, SL6 9QE
11.30-midnight (10.30 Mon; 11 Tue & Wed); 12-10.30 Sun
(01628) 523573 theoldswanuppers.co.uk
Butcombe Bitter; Courage Best Bitter; Fuller's London Pride; 2 changing beers Ⓗ
Friendly, cosy pub with flagstone floors and a wood-burning stove. The front bar accommodates drinkers, with a separate restaurant and lounge to the rear. Choose from a traditional pub menu (burgers, fish and chips, pies, steaks) or a tapas-style menu with a selection of around 20 plates.
P (37)

Curridge

Bunk Inn

Kiln Drive, RG18 9DS
11-11; 11-10.30 Sun (01635) 200400
thebunkinn.co.uk
Upham Tipster, Punter, Stakes; 1 changing beer (sourced regionally; often Upham) Ⓗ
A charming, traditional village pub dating from the 1700s which gained its name as a result of local workers bunking off to visit the pub. Head chef Lewis Spreadbury's carefully crafted seasonal menus offer traditional pub classics and more refined dining, well matched by a range of tasty Upham ales. Not far from Newbury racecourse and Highclere Castle, the pub's nine warm and stylish rooms provide the perfect base to explore the Berkshire Downs. P

Datchet

Royal Stag

The Green, SL3 9JH (next to church)
11-midnight (01753) 584231
Fuller's London Pride; Windsor & Eton Guardsman, Conqueror; 1 changing beer Ⓗ
The pub is reputed to be the oldest house in the village – ring counting of roof timbers dates it to 1494. The three regular beers are supplemented by Windsor & Eton seasonals. The front is for drinking

REAL ALE BREWERIES

Binghams Ruscombe
Butts Great Shefford
Dickens Reading (NEW)
Hermitage Hermitage
Hop King Reading (NEW)
Indigenous Chaddleworth (NEW)
INNformal Wickham (NEW)
Siren Craft Finchampstead
Two Cocks Enborne
West Berkshire Yattendon
Windsor & Eton Windsor
Zerodegrees Reading

and the restaurant, to the rear, serves home-made food. Outside is a large patio-style seating area. Quiz night is Tuesday. Q🚸❀◑≋P🚌(60)🐾📶

Eton

Watermans Arms 🄻
Brocas Street, SL4 6BW
⌚ 12-11.30 (midnight Sat); 12-11 Sun ☎ (01753) 861001
🌐 watermans-eton.com
House beer (by Caledonian); changing beers 🄷
Situated close to the River Thames and Eton Bridge, this welcoming and cosy pub serves up to eight ales, usually including a beer from a local microbrewery plus Harveys Best, Brakspear Bitter and something from Cornwall. The interior decor is a mixture of tartan wallpaper and rowing memorabilia. Food is served daily – the Sunday roast is recommended. The courtyard garden is popular on summer evenings.
❀◑≋(Windsor & Eton Riverside)●🚌(60)🐾

Eversley

Tally Ho 🄻
Fleet Hill, RG27 0RR (on A327 at jct of B3348 Fleet Hill)
⌚ 10.30-11 (10.30 Sun) ☎ (0118) 973 2134
🌐 tallyho.hcpr.co.uk
4 changing beers (sourced regionally) 🄷
Nestled just north of the River Blackwater on the Berks/Hants border, this pub has a pleasant riverside garden with trestle tables and children's play equipment. An ideal spot for outdoor dining in good weather. A focus on upmarket pub food makes it busy at weekends. The bar area, paved with ceramic tiles, leads to a timber-floored seating area furnished with antique-style furniture and rugs. The pub is determinedly proud of its four handpumps offering up to three LocAles from the likes of Andwell, Loddon and Longdog. Ample parking is available. Q🚸❀◑♿P🚌🐾📶

Hungerford

Hungerford Club
3 The Croft, RG17 0HY (on foot via Church Lane, by road via Church St and Croft Rd)
⌚ 12-3, 7-11 (10.30 Sun) ☎ (01488) 682357
🌐 hungerford-club.co.uk
Fuller's London Pride; 1 changing beer (sourced nationally) 🄷
A friendly sports and social club, home to tennis and bowls club members. Snooker, billiards and other indoor games are also played. There is a comfortable lounge where you can enjoy your beer and engage in conversation with club members. Cold filled rolls are available Saturday lunchtimes. A beer festival is held every August bank holiday. Show this Guide or your CAMRA membership card to gain entry. ❀≋♣P🚌🐾📶

John o' Gaunt 🄻
Bridge Street, RG17 0EG
⌚ 11-11 (midnight Fri & Sat); 12-10.30 Sun
☎ (01488) 683535 🌐 john-o-gaunt-hungerford.co.uk
6 changing beers (often Loddon, Two Cocks) 🄷
Reopened in 2013, this 16th-century listed building retains many original features. One of the beers is brewed at its sister pub in Wickham. The ales are supplemented by four real ciders. Additionally, some 80 bottled beers from around the world are stocked, 50 of which are Belgian. Quality seasonal and locally sourced food is available lunchtimes, evenings and all day Sunday.
Q🚸❀◑≋♣●P🚌🐾📶

Hurst

Castle Inn 🄻
Church Hill, RG10 0SJ
⌚ 12-3 (not Mon), 5.30-11; 12-11 Sat & Sun
☎ (0118) 934 0034 🌐 castlehurst.co.uk
Binghams Twyford Tipple; 2 changing beers 🄷
Parts of the Castle Inn, owned by the church opposite, date back to the 10th century. A free house, it provides both good beer and good food. Two guest beers are served rotating between local and national breweries. The food menu changes every couple of months. Access to the garden is between the pub and the neighbouring bowling green. May close early on Monday evenings.
Q🚸❀◑P🚌(129)🐾📶

Inkpen

Swan Inn 🄻
Craven Road, Lower Green, RG17 9DX
⌚ 12-2.30, 7-11; 12-11 Sat; 12-4 Sun ☎ (01488) 668326
🌐 theswaninn-organics.co.uk
Butts Jester, Traditional; 1 changing beer (often Butts) 🄷
A splendid traditional rural inn situated deep in the countryside. The proprietor of 18 years produces excellent home-made organic food and serves local Butts organic beer – the pub acts as the brewery tap. Cosy tables are arranged on different levels. There is also a separate restaurant and 10 quality bedrooms, all en-suite. Quiz nights and darts alternate every Thursday. An extensive terraced patio to the front of the pub is popular.
Q🚸❀🛏◑♿♣P🚌(3)🐾📶

Knowl Hill

Bird in Hand 🄻
Bath Road, RG10 9UP (on A4 between Reading and Maidenhead)
⌚ 11-11; 12-10.30 Sun ☎ (01628) 826622
🌐 birdinhand.co.uk
5 changing beers 🄷
A warm welcome from the friendly staff is guaranteed at this historic country inn, with parts dating back to the 14th century. Local breweries such as Ascot, Vale and Binghams are well supported. The spacious, multi-roomed areas with oak panelling and a generous Inglenook log fire add to the comfortable and unhurried atmosphere. Good-quality food is served throughout the day. In summer, the well-kept beer garden comes into its own. Q🚸❀🛏◑♿P🚌(127)🐾📶

Maidenhead

Bear 🄻
8-10 High Street, SL6 1QJ
⌚ 8am-midnight (11 Sun) ☎ (01628) 763030
Greene King Abbot; Sharp's Doom Bar; 5 changing beers 🄷
A short walk from the town hall, this large Wetherspoon venue, formerly a coaching inn, was refurbished in 2009. It has an open-plan bar with several different seating areas. A spiral staircase leads to an upper floor with an additional bar and comfy sofas. The 10 handpumps dispense up to

five guest ales, many from local breweries. Two or three ciders are often available, including Mr Whiteheads.

Grenfell Arms

22 Oldfield Road, SL6 1TW

10-midnight; 11-11 Sun ☎ (01628) 620705

Greene King IPA, IPA Gold; Morland Old Speckled Hen; 5 changing beers H

A welcoming wood-panelled two-room pub a short walk from the town centre and the Thames, offering eight handpumps on the bar. Two real ciders are available, normally Orchard Pig and Hogan's. The pub opens at 8am for breakfast followed by traditional pub food lunchtimes and evenings. Accommodation is available in eight recently refurnished bedrooms.
Q P

Newbury

Hatchet Inn

12 Market Place, RG14 5BD

7am-midnight (1am Fri & Sat) ☎ (01635) 277560

Fuller's London Pride; Greene King Abbot; Ruddles Best Bitter; changing beers (often Ramsbury, Two Cocks, Wild Weather) H

This JD Wetherspoon pub, located in the market place close to Newbury Corn Exchange, opened in July 2011 after extensive refurbishment. The large interior has several seating areas, with TV only in the front bar. Beers from local breweries such as Ramsbury, Two Cocks and Wild Weather are available. Ideally positioned for public transport links. Q P

King Charles Tavern

54 Cheap Street, RG14 5BX

11.30-midnight (1am Thu-Sat); 12-11 Sun

☎ (01635) 36695 kctavern.com

8 changing beers (sourced nationally; often Butts, Two Cocks, West Berkshire) H

Recently refurbished and under new management, this welcoming town-centre pub is known as the KC or KCT. It has three separate drinking areas surrounding the central bar. Note the 1950s map of Newbury on the ceiling of the main bar. Handy for the rail and bus stations.

Newbury

137 Bartholomew Street, RG14 5HB

12-midnight (11 Mon); 10-1am Fri & Sat; 10-11 Sun

☎ (01635) 49000 thenewburypub.co.uk

Two Cocks 1643 Cavalier, 1643 Roundhead; West Berkshire Good Old Boy; 2 changing beers (often West Berkshire) H

Launched in 2012, this town-centre gastro-pub has enjoyed great success. Renowned for its food, it also welcomes drinkers to its comfortable bar areas and, in all weathers, to its 'hidden' roof terrace. Real ale is not available in the upstairs bar so buy your pint before climbing the narrow back stairs.
Q

Reading

Alehouse

2 Broad Street, RG1 2BH

11-11; 12-10.30 Sun ☎ (0118) 950 8119

the-alehouse-reading.co.uk

8 changing beers H

The Alehouse has a unique and quirky atmosphere – it is the perfect antidote to town-centre bars. The pub champions many microbreweries (local and further afield), with various pumpclips festooning the walls and ceiling as evidence. This is the only pub in Reading that serves mead, as well as an excellent range of cider and perry. CAMRA branch Cider Pub of the Year 2014.

Greyfriar of Reading

53 Greyfriars Road, RG1 1PA

12-11 (midnight Fri & Sat); 12-6 Sun ☎ (0118) 958 0560

thegreyfriarreading.co.uk

6 changing beers H

A pub that came back from a long period of closure, now enjoying a new lease of life under independent ownership. An ever-changing range of six real ales from microbreweries plus unusual keg beers and a variety of craft gins are on offer. Regular events include quiz nights, film nights and tap takeovers. Easily accessible from the station main entrance.

Hop Leaf

163-165 Southampton Street, RG1 2QZ

12-11.30 (12.30am Fri & Sat) ☎ (0118) 931 4700

Hop Back Redsell's EKG, Citra, Crop Circle, Summer Lightning; 2 changing beers (often Hop Back) H

This traditional local offers pub games such as bar billiards, crib and backgammon, and hosts regular competitions. It also has a pinball machine. The pub stocks six Hop Back beers plus a selection of ciders and perries. Fans of classic rock will enjoy the landlord's choice in music. A variety of pub snacks is available and a good range of daily newspapers is provided. (5,6,11)

Nag's Head

5 Russell Street, RG1 7XD

12-11 (midnight Fri); 11-midnight Sat ☎ 07765 880137

nagsheadreading.com

12 changing beers H

The Nag's has established itself as a premier ale and cider venue, winning the local CAMRA branch Pub of the Year award multiple times. Pies and baguettes are available during the week, with a roast on Sundays. An eclectic mix of bottled beers is stocked. Numerous board games are available above the (tuned and working) upright piano which is next to the popular dartboard. The pub gets busy on Reading FC match days.
(West) P

Queen's Head

54 Christchurch Road, RG2 7AZ

12-11 ☎ (0118) 986 3040 queensheadreading.com

3 changing beers H

A delightful old building close to the university's Whiteknights campus, 50 yards from the Shinfield Road entrance. Recently refurbished, it has an oriental theme and is decorated with unusual furniture and artefacts, mainly from Thailand. There is an emphasis on high-quality but good-value Thai and British food. Three real ales are available, often with a local slant. (21,21a)

Zerodegrees

9 Bridge Street, RG1 2LR

12-midnight (11 Sun) ☎ (0118) 959 7959

zerodegrees.co.uk/reading

Zerodegrees Wheat Ale, Black Lager, Pale Ale, Pilsner A**; 1 changing beer (often Zerodegrees)** H

Real ale continental style, brewed on-site by Andrei, an Italian brewer; the stainless steel brewing plant, visible from the bar, is very much a feature of the establishment. Beer is served chilled, unfiltered and unpasteurised, direct from conditioning tanks. Interesting seasonal beers often include Mango. Italian-style food is served all day. Outside is a small terrace. ❀◑♿⇌▯🚌

Ruscombe

Royal Oak 𝕃

Ruscombe Lane, RG10 9JN (on B3024 E out of Twyford)
⌚ 12-3, 6-11 (not Mon eve); 12-4 Sun ☎ (0118) 934 5190
🌐 burattas.co.uk
Fuller's London Pride; 2 changing beers (often Binghams) Ⓗ
This spacious open-plan pub is naturally divided between comfortable seating areas and space for dining, with a bright conservatory overlooking the beautifully kept garden. The interior is furnished and decorated with quirky objects and antiques, most available to buy. The pub (also known as Buratta's) is noted for its food, but welcomes drinkers with a fine range of wines and three beers. **Q**❀◑⇌(Twyford)**P**🚌(127)

Sandhurst

Rose & Crown 𝕃

108 High Street, GU47 8HA (on A321, 7 mins' walk W of Sandhurst railway station)
⌚ 12-11 (midnight Fri & Sat); 12-10.30 Sun
☎ (01252) 878938 🌐 roseandcrownsandhurst.info
Otter Bitter; 6 changing beers (sourced nationally) Ⓗ
The pub is renowned for an ever-changing selection of six ales – five nationals plus one LocAle at a reduced price. Beer festivals are held quarterly. Sunday lunch is popular, with booking essential. Live music plays on Friday or Saturday nights. Sport TVs with the volume kept low enable lively bar-side chatter. The pub attracts many visitors and a good cross-section of the community. Children and dogs most welcome. Local CAMRA Branch Pub of the Year 2014. 🐴❀◑⇌♣**P**🚌(194)🐾ᯤ

Slough

Red Cow 𝕃

140 Albert Street, SL1 2AU
⌚ 12-11 (12.30am Fri & Sat) ☎ (01753) 522614
🌐 redcowpub.co.uk
2 changing beers (sourced locally; often Ascot, Twickenham, Vale) Ⓗ
A picturesque 17th-century listed building with two rooms separated by the large original fireplace. The room to the left is very traditional while the other room is decorated and furnished in a more contemporary style, and has a pool table and dartboard. There are normally two LocAle beers available. Food is served until 7pm, Sunday roast until 4pm. There is often live music on Saturdays. 🐴❀◑♣**P**🚌(78,81)🐾ᯤ

Rose & Crown 𝕃

312 High Street, SL1 1NB
⌚ 11-midnight ☎ (01753) 521114
🌐 roseandcrownslough.co.uk
House beer (by Vale); 2 changing beers Ⓗ
Small pub, at the quiet end of the High Street, with a good local feel. It has a front bar and a smaller rear bar, both with plenty of TVs to allow uninterrupted Sky sports viewing. The three handpumps offer a constantly changing selection of well-kept ales, including the pub's house ale, brewed by Vale. A covered area outside at the back offers comfy sofas, wood-burning stoves and another TV. On Sunday there is a free barbecue with a selection of meats. ❀♣🚌🐾ᯤ

Sunningdale

Nag's Head

28 High Street, SL5 0NG (behind church) SU954676
⌚ 12-11 (11.30 Fri & Sat); 12-10.30 Sun ☎ (01344) 622725
🌐 nagsheadsunningdale.co.uk
Harveys Sussex Best Bitter; 3 changing beers (often Harveys) Ⓗ
This newly refurbished Harveys pub now has a contemporary feel while retaining the charm of a traditional pub, with areas where drinkers and diners may find their own space. Good home-cooked food is served weekday evenings and all day at weekends. The chef uses locally sourced ingredients whenever possible, and the menu changes regularly. Sporting events are shown on two large screens in the bar. Real cider is available from a box. Outside there is a large garden and a patio area. **Q**❀◗♿●**P**🚌(01)🐾ᯤ

Royal Oak 𝕃

19 Station Road, SL5 0QL
⌚ 12-11 ☎ (01344) 623625
Greene King IPA; house beer (by Hardys & Hansons); 4 changing beers (often Binghams, Rebellion, Windsor & Eton) Ⓗ
A friendly, much-improved village pub. The enthusiastic landlord puts great emphasis on well-kept beer, with strong support for CAMRA's LocAle campaign. He makes good use of Greene King's Local Heroes scheme, offering two GK beers and four guests (usually three LocAle). Simple pub food is served at lunchtimes. One bar has a TV for sport. A large collection of card and board games is freely available in the bar. There is a large enclosed garden behind the pub. **Q**🐴❀◐♿♣**P**🚌🐾

Swallowfield

Crown 𝕃

The Street, RG7 1QZ
⌚ 12-2.30 (not Mon), 5.30-11; 12-11.30 Sat; 12-10.30 Sun
☎ (0118) 988 3260 🌐 thecrownswallowfield.co.uk
Fuller's London Pride; 1 changing beer Ⓗ
An early 18th-century building now established as a genuine family-run, independent business. It is off the beaten track in a rural village location. A good range of pub favourites is on the menu, including vegetarian choices. The large L-shaped main bar is complemented by two smaller rooms, with pictures and maps of old Swallowfield adorning the walls. Community focused, children, dogs and walkers are all welcome. An ideal spot to start or finish a country walk.
🐴❀◑♿♣●**P**🚌(72,82)🐾

Three Mile Cross

Swan 𝕃

Basingstoke Road, RG7 1AT
⌚ 11-1, 2-11; 11-3, 7-11 Sat; 11-4 Sun ☎ (0118) 988 3674
Fuller's London Pride; Loddon Hoppit; Timothy Taylor Boltmaker, Landlord; 1 changing beer Ⓗ

This Grade II-listed 17th-century inn has been occupied by the current licensees for over 30 years. The nearest pub to the Madejski Stadium, the Swan has a large rugby/football crowd on match days. Hearty, locally produced home-cooked food is served. Look out for the inglenook fireplace. P (72,82)

Tilehurst

Butchers Arms

9 Lower Armour Road, RG31 6HH

11-11 (midnight Fri & Sat); 12-11 Sun ☎ (0118) 942 4313

Sharp's Doom Bar; West Berkshire Good Old Boy; 1 changing beer [H]

Traditional two-bar back-street local. Although thoroughly refurbished inside and out, this is still very much a locals' pub. The landlord comes with an ale pedigree from the Row Barge in Guildford. It currently offers pubco beers plus Good Old Boy from West Berks, but intends to expand with another pump and support more smaller breweries as the volume builds. Real cider is available. Outside is a large lawned rear garden. P (33)

Fox & Hounds

116 City Road, RG31 5SB

11.30-11; 12-10.30 Sun ☎ (0118) 942 2982

Fuller's London Pride; Sharp's Doom Bar [H]**; 1 changing beer** [H]/[G]

Friendly hostelry with a country-pub feel near the western edge of Tilehurst. Garry and Julie the licensees offer a fishing club, barbecues, beer festivals and other events throughout the year at this community local. A large conservatory has been added at the rear, creating a light airy space for dining and drinking. Guest beers are often served from gravity casks kept in the kitchen. P (33)

Royal Oak

69 Westwood Glen, RG31 5NW

2-11; 12-midnight Fri & Sat; 12-11 Sun ☎ (0118) 941 6056

theroyaloak-tilehurst.co.uk

4 changing beers [H]

Perched at the summit of a steep driveway and pre-dating most of the surrounding suburban housing, the pub has been greatly improved by the present landlord and family. The building is a traditional 'bitsa' with all sorts of phases of building, so one bar has you towering above the bar staff while the other bar is ground level. P (33)

Waltham St Lawrence

Bell

The Street, RG10 0JJ

12-3, 5-11; 12-11 Sat; 12-10.30 Sun ☎ (0118) 934 1788

thebellwalthamstlawrence.co.uk

Loddon Hoppit; 4 changing beers [H]

A cosy, village-owned locals' pub that dates back to the 14th century. It offers a wide selection of real ales, mainly locally sourced, plus eight ciders and perries served from the cellar, alongside high-quality food, also locally sourced where possible. Log fires in winter and a good-sized beer garden for those sunny summer days complete the idyll. A gem of a country inn. Q (4)

Warfield

New Leathern Bottle

Jealotts Hill, RG42 6ET (on A3095 Bracknell-Maidenhead road)

12-10.30 (11 Fri & Sat) ☎ (01344) 421282

newleathernbottle.co.uk

3 changing beers (often Rebellion, St Austell, Windsor & Eton) [H]

A genuine locals' pub serving wholesome home-made food with large portions at competitive prices. Friday is steak night – the locally sourced meat is excellent value. The real ales include three ever-changing beers, at least one a LocAle, alongside one or more handpumped real ciders. The pub has a large garden with plenty of seating and extensive fenced-off play equipment. There is a separate smoking area and ample parking. Q P

Wargrave

Wargrave & District Snooker Club

Woodclyffe Hostel, Church Street, RG10 8EP

7-11; closed Sat & Sun ☎ (0118) 940 3508

1 changing beer [H]

The club opens weekday evenings and shares the building with the local library. The regularly changing beers reflect members' recommendations, with two on in the winter months and one in the summer. Bar billiards, darts, chess, cards and books are available. The TV's default is off. Show this Guide or a CAMRA membership card for entry (£3 fee to use the snooker tables). Winner of CAMRA branch Club of the Year for several years. (850)

Wickham

Five Bells

Baydon Road, RG20 8HH

12-3, 5-11; 12-11 Sat; 12-10.30 Sun ☎ (01488) 657300

fivebellswickham.co.uk

9 changing beers (sourced regionally; often Siren, Two Cocks, Vale) [H]

The INNformal brewery tap, this popular thatched inn was awarded 2014 CAMRA Central Southern region Pub of the Year. Brewery activity can be viewed from the large back garden. The nine ales and eight ciders are all available as thirds. Home-cooked food includes hand-made pizzas, pies and sandwiches with chips. Live music plays every Sunday afternoon. Q P

Windsor

Acre

Donnelly House, Victoria Street, SL4 1EN

11-11 (midnight Fri & Sat); 12-10.30 Sun ☎ (01753) 841083 theacrewindsor.com

Windsor & Eton Guardsman; 2 changing beers [H]

Formerly the Liberal Club but now a free house open to all. The name refers to the adjacent Bachelors Acre. Three ales are on offer, with Windsor & Eton's Guardsman a permanent feature and two regularly changing guests. Live music is hosted every Saturday night plus an open mic night on the first Monday of the month. Two screens show live sporting events and there are excellent facilities for darts. Two function rooms are available for hire. (Windsor & Eton Central) (77)

Alma

61 Springfield Road, SL4 3PP
🕓 3-11.30 (12.30am Fri); 12-12.30am Sat; 12-11 Sun
☎ (01753) 840515 🌐 innthealma.co.uk
Fuller's London Pride; Sharp's Doom Bar; 1 changing beer Ⓗ
Street-corner pub about 15 minutes' walk from the town centre. An eclectic mix of antiques and collectables can be found inside. It has reputedly the largest beer garden of any pub in Windsor, with a covered area for smokers and those wishing to shelter from the changeable English weather. A children's play area has recently been added. Sunday roasts are popular.
Q❀(16,701)

Carpenters Arms

4 Market Street, SL4 1PB
🕓 11-11 (midnight Fri & Sat) ☎ (01753) 863739
Fuller's London Pride; St Austell Nicholson's Pale Ale; Sharp's Doom Bar; 5 changing beers Ⓗ
Situated on a narrow cobbled street close to the castle, this excellent Nicholson's pub has been voted local CAMRA Pub of the Year several times. The elegantly decorated interior is on three levels, the lowest reputedly housing a passageway to the Castle. Ashby's Brewery tiles are retained on the floor by the entrance, harking back to the pub's former owners. Three regular beers are supplemented by five interesting guests, usually including something dark.
⇌(Windsor & Eton Central)(71,702)

Vansittart Arms Ⓛ

105 Vansittart Road, SL4 5DD
🕓 12-11 (11.30 Thu; midnight Fri); 10.30-midnight Sat; 10.30-11 Sun ☎ (01753) 865988
🌐 vansittartarmswindsor.co.uk
Fuller's London Pride, ESB; Gale's Seafarers Ale; 1 changing beer Ⓗ
Known to all as the Vanni, this popular and well-run Fuller's pub is worth the 10-minute walk from the town centre. The ale range includes the current seasonal beer and often a beer not from Fuller's. There is a separate pool room which has a small book swap library and a good selection of daily newspapers. Sport, particularly rugby, is keenly followed and the large garden is available to hire for functions.
❀⇌(Windsor & Eton Central)(71,702)

Windlesora Ⓛ

11 William Street, SL4 1BB
🕓 8am-midnight (1am Fri & Sat) ☎ (01753) 754050
Greene King IPA; 4 changing beers (sourced locally; often Adnams, Sharp's) Ⓗ
A relatively quiet pub during the day, tucked off Peascod Street, this Wetherspoon is named from the old Saxon word which became Windsor. The enthusiastic manager makes an effort to stock beers from local micros, including Windsor & Eton and Binghams, and displays a map showing their location. Recently the handpumps have increased from five to 10, with more real ale to come as demand increases. There is seating outside at the front of the building.
Q&⇌(Windsor & Eton Central)(77)

Wokingham

Crispin Ⓛ

45 Denmark Street, RG40 2AY (from the town centre 150 yards down Denmark Street)
🕓 2-11; 12-midnight Fri & Sat; 12-10.30 Sun
☎ (0118) 978 0309 🌐 crispinpub.co.uk
4 changing beers Ⓗ
Reputedly one of the oldest pubs in Wokingham. It usually offers three to five constantly changing ales including local beers from breweries such as Hogs Back and Loddon. Hot bar snacks (sausages, roast potatoes, Yorkshire puddings) are served only on Sundays. At other times customers may bring in food from local takeaways to eat with a drink. The pub hosts a darts team. Perudo, Poker and Aunt Sally (in summer) are also played.
❀⇌♣P(89,90)

Queen's Head 🏆 Ⓛ

23 The Terrace, RG40 1BP
🕓 12-11 (12.30am Fri & Sat); 12-10.30 Sun
☎ (0118) 978 1221
Greene King Abbot, IPA Reserve; house beer (by Hardys & Hansons); 3 changing beers (sourced locally; often Loddon, Vale, West Berkshire) Ⓗ
A sign describes this as a 15th-century timber cruck-framed inn, but nowadays it is a Greene King Local Heroes pub serving three GK beers plus three ales from local breweries. Beer paddles with three third-pints make it easier to sample several different ales. The real fire creates a cosy feel in winter. In summer there is a surprisingly large rear garden with a covered area and seating on the south-facing front terrace. The pub serves food only on specials night – see the noticeboard.
❀⇌♣(99,151)

White Horse

Easthampstead Road, RG40 3AF (1 mile S of town centre)
🕓 12-11 (6 Sun) ☎ (0118) 979 7402
🌐 whitehorsewokingham.co.uk
Greene King IPA, Abbot; 1 changing beer Ⓗ
Country pub with a relaxed atmosphere, with views across the fields. Since taking over in 2011, Peter and Natalie have improved the beer quality and expanded the food menu. Ingredients are sourced from selected independent producers. Staff and locals offer a friendly welcome to all. A recent winner of the Wokingham Times Pub of the Year award. Q❀&♣P

Wraysbury

Perseverance

2 High Street, TW19 5DB
🕓 12-11 (9 Sun) ☎ (01784) 482375 🌐 thepercy.co.uk
Sharp's Doom Bar; 3 changing beers Ⓗ
Comfortable pub with several seating areas. The larger front room has soft sofas, a piano and an inglenook fireplace with a real log fire. Another seating area, again with an open fire, leads to the rear dining area, which has well-stocked bookshelves. To the rear of the building is a delightful garden. Three guest ales are always varied and sourced from some of the more interesting breweries around the country. Regular beer festivals are held. Quiz night is Thursday.
Q❀♣P(60,305)

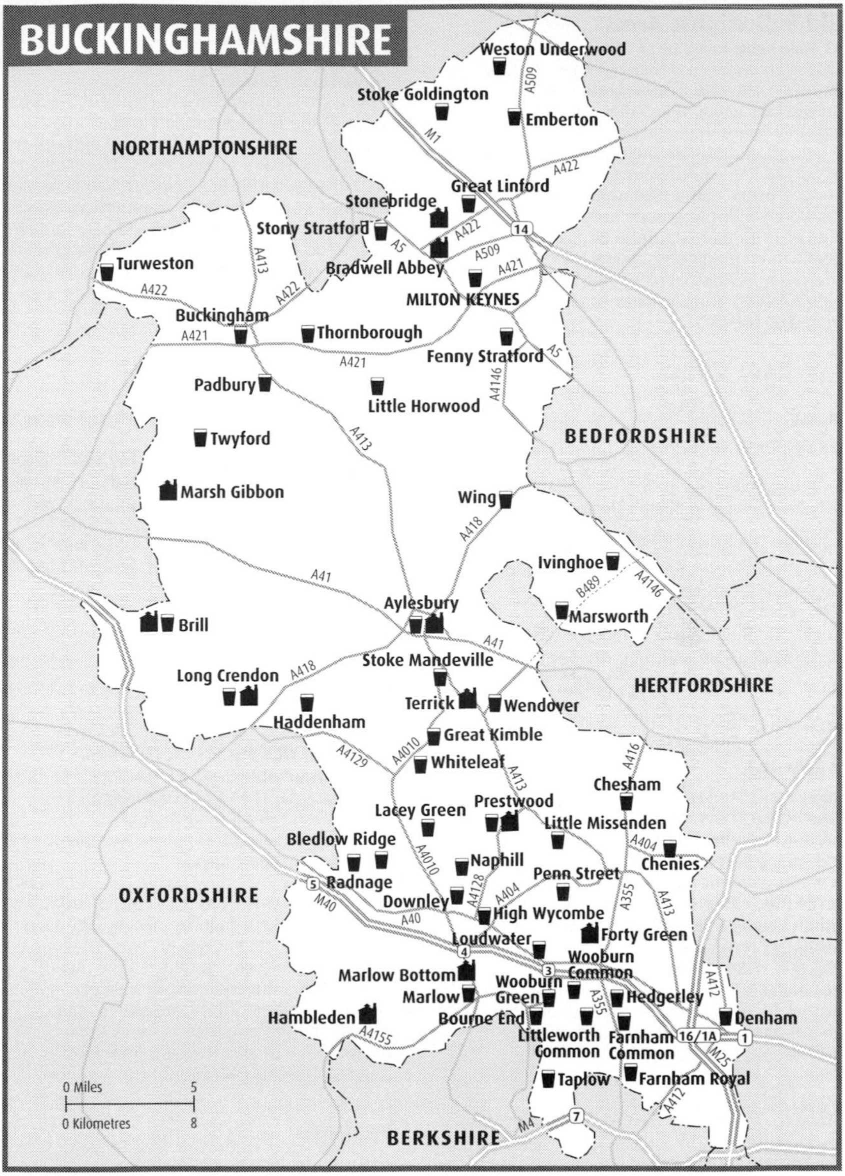

Aylesbury

Farmers' Bar at King's Head

King's Head Passage, Market Square, HP20 2RW
11-11; 12-10.30 Sun (01296) 718812
farmersbar.co.uk
Chiltern Beechwood Bitter, Black, Pale Ale; 1 changing beer
When Chiltern Brewery took over the running of the Farmers' Bar for the National Trust, it became the first bar in the country to be no-smoking and free from piped music. Dating from circa 1455, this is the oldest courtyard inn in England and was donated by the Rothschild family in 1924. Ales are often used in cooking and lunches are prepared using ingredients from local suppliers. A former local CAMRA Pub of the Year. Q

Hop Pole Inn

83 Bicester Road, HP19 9AZ (near Gatehouse Industrial Area)
11-11 (midnight Fri & Sat); 11-10.30 Sun
(01296) 482129 hoppolepub.com
Aylesbury Pure Gold; Vale Best IPA, Gravitas; 7 changing beers
'Aylesbury's Permanent Beer Festival' is home to the Aylesbury Brewhouse and shop which opened in 2011. The individual brews feature regularly in the pub, but may not last very long. This is Vale's sister brewery – the pub is the brewery's main outlet, featuring Vale beers plus a selection from other small brewers. A friendly welcome and good food (no food Mon) add to the attraction. Children are welcome until 9pm if dining.

Old Millwrights Arms

83 Millwrights Road, HP21 7SN

12-11 (midnight Fri); 9am-midnight Sat; 12-11 Sun
(01296) 488161 oldmillwrightsarms.co.uk

Greene King Abbot, IPA; 5 changing beers H

Recently refurbished, the pub has nine handpumps offering four ales from the Greene King stable and, as part of the Local Heroes scheme, five locally brewed beers. Pump takeovers from one of many local breweries are regular events. The open-plan interior is divided into three distinct areas with ample room for diners to enjoy the excellent food. There is a pleasant outdoor area to the rear of the pub. A loyalty scheme gives you your eighth pint free.

Bledlow Ridge

Boot

Chinnor Road, HP14 4AW

closed Mon; 11-3, 5-11; 12-7 Sun (01494) 481499
theboot-bledlowridge.co.uk

Rebellion Smuggler; Sharp's Doom Bar; 1 changing beer H

Recently refurbished by Andy and Emma, this is a family-friendly, modern village pub and diner. Situated in the heart of the picturesque Chiltern Hills, the Boot offers local ales, fresh, locally produced food and a huge garden where well-behaved dogs are welcome. Sunday lunch is always busy – book ahead.

Bourne End

Garibaldi

Bourne End, SL8 5EE

Closed Mon; 12-15, 17.30-22 Tue-Thu; 12-midnight Fri-Sat; 12:00-21:30 Sun (01628) 522092 garibaldipub.co.uk

3 changing beers H

A warm welcome awaits at this traditional pub, saved from closure when it was bought by the local community in 2013. The L-shaped bar has a mixture of comfy sofas and tables and chairs, plus a real fire, TV screen and dartboard. There are three handpumps, at least one dispensing beer from the nearby Rebellion brewery. A small outside terrace affords views across fields at the rear.
(Bourne End) P (37)

Brill

Pointer

27 Church Street, HP18 9RT

12-11 (midnight Fri & Sat); 12-10.30 Sun
(01844) 238339 thepointerbrill.co.uk

Vale Pale Ale; XT Four; 2 changing beers H

More than a destination diner, this free house is also a must-visit ale house, thanks to the skilled cellarwoman. XT Pointer from five miles away and Vale VPA from Brill are always available, complemented by a stout or porter and another guest ale to ensure a reliable selection from the four handpumps. The pub supports the Brill beer festival in August. An open-walled kitchen produces wonderful, locally sourced food served in the vaulted dining room. Q

Buckingham

Mitre

2 Mitre Street, MK18 1DW

5-11 (midnight Fri); 12-midnight Sat; 12-10.30 Sun
(01280) 813080 themitre.org.uk

Banks's Bitter; 4 changing beers (sourced nationally; often Marston's, Oakham) H

Charming small pub out of the centre of town but well worth the walk. The oldest pub in Buckingham, it has a wonderful, cosy atmosphere with a real open fire in the winter. The landlord offers a changing selection of interesting beers and always tries to have at least one from Oakham. Outside, there is a large garden and patio area for smokers. Local CAMRA branch Pub of the Year 2015. P

Woolpack

57 Well Street, MK18 1EP

11-11 (midnight Fri & Sat); 12-10.30 Sun
(01280) 817972

Brains The Rev James; Sharp's Doom Bar; 2 changing beers H

Just out of the town centre, this busy pub is nicely modernised but retains many old features and has a riverside garden. Four handpumps serve two regular beers and guest ales from the SIBA list. Freshly cooked food is available, made with local produce where possible. Children are welcome in the large back room. Parking nearby can be awkward. Beer festivals are held from time to time. Q

Chenies

Red Lion

Latimer Road, WD3 6ED (off A404 between Chorleywood and Little Chalfont)

11-2.30, 5.30-11; 11-11 Sat; 12-10.30 Sun
(01923) 282722 redlionchenies.co.uk

Vale Best IPA; Wadworth 6X; house beer (by Rebellion); 1 changing beer H

This excellent 16th-century village pub, set in great walking country, lives up to its description as an autarchic, or independent, free house. The long-serving landlord does things his way. The food is high quality (there are no chips on the menu) and good value, and there is a comfortable dining room to the rear. However, this is a pub first and foremost, and the emphasis is firmly upon excellent ales – at least two are from local breweries. Q P (336)

Chesham

Black Cat

Lycrome Road, Lye Green, HP5 3LF (off A416) SP977034

9am-2.30, 5-11 (7 Mon); 9am-11 Sat; 12-10 Sun
(01494) 773966 blackcatchesham.co.uk

REAL ALE BREWERIES

Aylesbury Aylesbury
Britannia Forty Green (brewing suspended)
Bucks Star Stonebridge (NEW)
Chiltern Terrick
Concrete Cow Bradwell Abbey
Malt Prestwood
Old Luxters Hambleden
Oxfordshire Ales Marsh Gibbon
Rebellion Marlow Bottom
Vale Brill
XT Long Crendon

Timothy Taylor Landlord; Young's Bitter; 1 changing beer (sourced nationally; often Brains, Fuller's, Young's) Ⓗ
Welcoming, cosy, single-bar pub decorated with a collection of pumpclips and plenty of black cat memorabilia. Games players are well catered for with darts, quiz, dominoes and crib played on various evenings. Generous portions of traditional food are available in both the bar and the back room which doubles as a dining area. Families are welcome and the spacious garden has a play area. Breakfast is served 9am-noon (no food Sun and Mon eves). Q ⑬ ⑤ ✿ ◗ ♣ P ♫ (730) ❀ ᾧ

Chesham Brewery Shop Ⓛ

8 Market Square, HP5 1ES
✪ 12-8 (9 Fri); 10-9 Sat; 12-6 Sun ☎ (01494) 754857
4 changing beers (sourced nationally; often Red Squirrel) Ⓟ
This is a new venture from the Red Squirrel Brewery. Among the vast array of bottled beers you will find a selection of ales served by air pressure from taps mounted on a tiled wall. The licence here allows customers to purchase beers at the bar for consumption on the premises, and there are benches and bar stools for this purpose. The friendly and knowledgeable staff are happy to advise on the beer styles that are available.
Q ⊖ ♿ ♫

Queen's Head Ⓛ

120 Church Street, HP5 1JD (in old town) SP956013
✪ 12-11 Mon-Wed (midnight Thu & Fri); 11-midnight Sat; 11-10.30 Sun ☎ (01494) 778690
⊕ queensheadchesham.co.uk
Brakspear Bitter; Fuller's London Pride, ESB; 1 changing beer (sourced regionally; often Fuller's) Ⓗ
First licensed in 1759, this welcoming, traditional, two-bar pub is next to the River Chess in the old part of town. The public bar retains many original fittings while the larger saloon was formerly four rooms. Seasonal beer festivals take place and a quiz night on Thursday. Thai food and pub meals are served in both bars and the separate restaurant, which is open in the evening. Outside is a heated courtyard. ⑤ ✿ ◗ ㄴ ⊖ ♿ P 🐾 ❀ ᾧ

Denham

Green Man Ⓛ

Village Road, UB9 5BH
✪ 11-11 ☎ (01895) 832760 ⊕ greenmandenham.com
Fuller's London Pride; Greene King IPA; Rebellion Smuggler; 1 changing beer Ⓗ
This free-of-tie, friendly pub has just been sympathetically refurbished and is popular with diners, families and drinkers alike. The front bar has beams, a real fire and flagged floors, opening out into a large conservatory and well-tended beer garden. There are four real ales and tempting menus. Historic Denham is a picturesque rural village within the M25 boundary, a pleasant stroll from the Colne Valley Country Park Visitor Centre.
⑤ ✿ ◗ ⇌ ♣ ♫ (581) ❀ ᾧ

Downley

Le De Spencers Arms

The Common, HP13 5YQ (across common from village on flint track beyond the end of Plomer Green Lane)
✪ 12-11 (midnight Fri & Sat); 12-10.30 Sun
☎ (01494) 535317 ⊕ ledespencersarms.co.uk

Fuller's ESB, London Pride; 2 changing beers Ⓗ
Named after Francis Dashwood, the notorious 15th Baron le Despencer, whose family still owns the surrounding estate, this traditional village pub on Downley Common offers four real ales, good wines and home-cooked food. Quiz nights, music nights, beer and food events add to the attraction of this cosy flint inn. Situated just a quarter of a mile by road or across the common from the village hall bus stop, it is popular with walkers and cyclists.
❀ ◗ ♣ P ♫ (31) ❀ ᾧ

Emberton

Bell & Bear Ⓛ

12 High Street, MK46 5DH
✪ closed Mon; 12-2.30, 5-11; 12-8 Sun ☎ (01234) 711565
⊕ bellandbear.net
Marston's Burton Bitter; 3 changing beers Ⓗ
A small independent family-run free house serving a variety of interesting beers and wonderful food. The landlord is a self-confessed foodie and real ale fan. The interesting old Grade II-listed building provides a long bar, a cosy snug and a restaurant. Particularly busy in summer and at weekends, book ahead if dining. Joint Cider Pub of the Year.
Q ⑤ ✿ ◗ ▲ ♣ ♿ P ♫ (21) ❀ ᾧ

Farnham Common

Stag & Hounds Ⓛ

18 The Broadway, SL2 3QQ
✪ 12-11 (1am Fri & Sat) ☎ (01753) 647716
Greene King IPA Gold; Morland Old Golden Hen; 8 changing beers Ⓗ
Cosy one-room pub with comfy sofas and beer casks as stools. The cellar can be viewed through a window near the side entrance. Ten beers are generally available, five from local and national microbreweries and five from the Greene King stable. There is also a good selection of ciders and bottled beers from around the world. A beer bat serves three third-pint glasses allowing a good number of ales to be tasted. The TV is only in use for major sporting events.
Q ⑤ ✿ ◗ ㄴ ♣ ♿ P ♫ (X74) ᾧ

Farnham Royal

Emperor Ⓛ

Blackpond Lane, SL2 3EG SU959842
✪ 12-11 (midnight Fri & Sat); 12-10.30 Sun
☎ (01753) 643006 ⊕ theemperorfarnhamcommon.co.uk
Fuller's London Pride; 3 changing beers (sourced locally; often Andwells, Rebellion, Windsor & Eton) Ⓗ
An old pub, but with a contemporary air about it. The front area, furnished with comfy seating and many cushions, is perfect for relaxing with a pint, and there is a cosy lower area with plenty of tables. To the rear is a room dedicated to dining. Outside is a pleasant garden and covered seating area. Live music is hosted monthly on a Saturday. Supplementing the London Pride are two or three constantly changing ales. No food is served Sunday evening. Q ⑤ ✿ ◗ P ♫ (X74) ❀ ᾧ

Great Kimble

Swan Ⓛ

Grove Lane, HP17 9TR
✪ 12-3.30, 5-11; 12-3.30, 7-10.30 Sun ☎ (01844) 275288
⊕ kimbleswan.co.uk

3 changing beers [H]
Set in prime walking and cycling country at the foot of the Chilterns, the Swan is a traditional, family-run village local. Facing onto the village green, the 18th-century pub offers a warm welcome to visitors and also serves as a community hub, staging regular live music events and quizzes. It is a committed supporter of LocAle, offering a rotating selection from nearby breweries on two of its handpumps. The food menu features fresh home-cooked food with ingredients sourced from local suppliers.
Q❀⇆◑♿⇌(Little Kimble)♣P🚌(300)🐾📶

Haddenham

Rising Sun [L]
9 Thame Road, HP17 8EN
⏲ 12-2.30, 5-11; 12-1am Fri & Sat; 12-10.30 Sun
☎ (01844) 291744
3 changing beers
The Riser continues to be the best ale house in the neighbourhood with its ever-changing selection of LocAles and guest beers. With pumpclips adorning the ceiling, the intellectuals in 'Compost Corner', who are banned from discussing religion, politics and hedge-laying, can mull over pints gone by as they flavour Rob's latest offering. All ales are served straight from the cask from the cellar immediately behind the bar. Truly a jewel in Haddenham's crown, this is a friendly haven for regulars and visitors alike.
❀⇌(Haddenham & Thame Parkway)♣🍎🚌(280)🐾📶

Hedgerley

White Horse 🏆 [L]
Village Lane, SL2 3UY (in old village, near church)
⏲ 11-2.30, 5-11; 11-11 Sat; 12-10.30 Sun ☎ (01753) 643225
Rebellion IPA; changing beers [G]
CAMRA branch Pub of the Year on numerous occasions, this village local has an impressive range of real ales. Rebellion IPA is complemented by one from Oakham or Mallinson's plus a further six from microbreweries. A draught Belgian beer and three real ciders are also available. This classic pub has a well-tended garden and a heated, covered patio area. Regular beer festivals are held – the largest is over the Whitsun weekend and is a must for real ale enthusiasts. Q🐴❀◐♣🍎P🐾

High Wycombe

Bootlegger
3 Amersham Hill, HP13 6NQ
⏲ 4-11; 12-midnight Thu-Sat; 12-11 Sun ☎ (01494) 525457
🌐 thebootleggerpub.co.uk
Rebellion IPA; 7 changing beers [H]
Recently refurbished ale house directly opposite the railway station. The front bar was extended by removing a wall to provide improved customer access to the handpumps. Bearing left from the entrance is another small room with comfortable armchairs. Outside is a large secluded garden with decking. There is a comprehensive beer menu containing tasting notes for the 300 craft and speciality beers and ciders sourced worldwide. The bottled beers are in glass-fronted chiller cabinets.
❀♿⇌🍎🚌🐾📶

Ivinghoe

Rose & Crown [L]
Vicarage Lane, LU7 9EQ
⏲ 12 (5 Mon & Tue)-11 ☎ (01296) 668472
🌐 roseandcrownivinghoe.com
Chiltern Beechwood Bitter; Skinner's Betty Stogs; 4 changing beers (sourced nationally; often Haresfoot, Sharp's, Skinner's) [H]
Hidden away but clearly signposted, this is a traditional country pub with a surprisingly large and modern interior featuring an open fire and slate floors. A free house, it offers a good choice of regular beers and guests including those from local and national breweries. There is a quiet restaurant area to the rear leading to a covered courtyard patio. The pub is popular with walkers and cyclists. Reasonably priced traditional British food is served Wednesday-Sunday. Q🐴❀◑⛺🚌(61)🐾📶

Lacey Green

Pink & Lily
Pink Road, HP27 0RJ
⏲ 12-midnight (10 Sun) ☎ (01494) 489857 🌐 pink-lily.com
Sharp's Doom Bar; 3 changing beers [H]
This 300-year-old historic pub, where World War One poet Rupert Brooke was a regular, has flourished since reopening in 2013. It is a free house offering fine food and four real ales, including three guests from local breweries. The garden includes heated outdoor dining, a barbecue and a children's play area. A games room is available for adults and children. Muddy boots and (well-behaved) dogs are welcome.
Q🐴❀◑♿♣P🐾📶

Whip Inn
Pink Road, HP27 0PG
⏲ 11-11 (midnight Fri & Sat); 12-10.30 Sun
☎ (01844) 344060 🌐 thewhipinn.co.uk
6 changing beers
High in the Chilterns, easily accessible by bus, and popular with real ale fans, ramblers and cyclists, this pub is renowned for its variety of ales. It has six handpumps serving more than 900 different beers per annum, from local breweries, other micros and nationals. It also offers three real ciders and holds regular beer festivals. An excellent range of reasonably priced food is on offer. There is an attractive enclosed garden overlooking the Lacey Green Windmill. Q❀◑♣🍎P🚌(300)🐾📶

Little Horwood

Shoulder of Mutton
Church Street, MK17 0PF
⏲ 12-2.30 (not Mon), 6-11.30; 12-midnight Fri-Sun
☎ (01296) 713703 🌐 theshoulderofmutton.org.uk
Sharp's Doom Bar; Young's Bitter; 1 changing beer (sourced nationally; often Wychwood) [H]
This local country pub attracts visitors from nearby towns and villages for its friendly atmosphere and extremely good, reasonably priced food. The old building, dating back to 1468, has not been overly restored, retaining its original atmosphere. Darts nights are hosted and in the summer beer festivals and children's days are held in the large garden.
Q🐴❀◑♿♣P🚌🐾📶

Little Missenden

Crown Inn

HP7 0RD (off A413, between Amersham and Gt Missenden)
⏲ 11-2.30, 6-11; 12-3, 7-10.30 Sun ☎ (01494) 862571
🌐 the-crown-little-missenden.co.uk
Adnams Southwold Bitter; St Austell Tribute; 2 changing beers (sourced locally; often Harveys, Rebellion, Vale) Ⓗ
Popular with tourists, walkers and locals, this pub has been run by the same family for almost 100 years and a warm welcome continues to be provided by successive generations. It has featured in the Guide continuously for over 25 years. Real ales are rotated regularly, so it is wise to check beforehand if you want a particular beer. There are now three double/twin en-suite rooms available.
Q❀🛏◐♣🍎P🚌(177)🐾📶

Littleworth Common

Blackwood Arms

Common Lane, SL1 8PP SU 937863
⏲ closed Mon; 12-11 (9 Sun) ☎ (01753) 645672
🌐 theblackwoodarms.net
Brakspear Bitter, Oxford Gold; Wychwood Hobgoblin; 3 changing beers Ⓗ
A delightful Victorian country pub brought back to life by an enthusiastic couple after a long period of closure. Close to Burnham Beeches and popular with walkers and diners, it has a roaring fire in winter and an attractive garden with plenty of seating for the summer. Three guest ales are on offer – one from the Marston's Group plus two free of tie. Dog- and horse-friendly, hay is provided. Note the pub closes at 7pm on winter Sundays.
Q🐎❀◐◑🍎P🐾📶

Long Crendon

Eight Bells L

51 High Street, HP18 9AL
⏲ 12 (10 Sat & Sun)-11 ☎ (01844) 208244 🌐 8bellspub.com
Ringwood Best Bitter; XT Four; 2 changing beers Ⓗ
The Eight Bells was refurbished internally in 2014, but retains the charm and character of a village pub. It is renowned for slaking the thirst of ale aficionados – XT Four from less than a mile away and Ringwood Bitter are permanent fixtures on two of the four handpumps, joined by guest ales from across the country. Long Crendon Manor cider is also an attraction, and diners come from near and far for the local produce. Beer festivals are held over the Easter weekend and August bank holiday.
Q❀◐◑♣🍎P🚌(110)🐾📶

Loudwater

General Havelock

114 Kingsmead Road, HP11 1HZ
⏲ 12-2.30, 5.30-11; 12-11 Fri & Sat; 12-10.30 Sun
☎ (01494) 520391 🌐 generalhavelock.co.uk
Fuller's ESB, London Pride; Gale's Seafarers Ale; 3 changing beers Ⓗ
In its 26th consecutive year in the Guide and run by the same family since Fuller's acquired it in 1986, the General Havelock remains popular with all ages. The interior has an eclectic selection of bric-a-brac and antiques. Six ales are available at all times including a range of seasonals and guests. Meals are served lunchtimes (not Sat) and Friday evenings. The pub has a cosy feel in winter while the garden makes for a peaceful haven in summer.
❀◐♣P🚌(35)🐾📶

Marlow

Royal British Legion

Station Approach, SL7 1NT (50yds from train station)
⏲ 7-11; 11-3, 7-midnight Fri & Sat; 11-4 Sun
☎ (01628) 486659 🌐 rblmarlow.co.uk/index.html
Jennings Bitter; 5 changing beers Ⓗ
Effectively a free house, this friendly RBL members' club offers four handpumped ales from four independent breweries, with a Derbyshire beer usually among the selection. Home of the Marlow Jazz Club, music features regularly on a Saturday night. Pool, darts and crib are encouraged. The recently refurbished hall is for hire. Show a CAMRA membership card or copy of the Guide for entry. CAMRA Regional Club of the Year 2014.
❀♿🚆(Marlow)♣🍎P🚌

Three Horseshoes L

Wycombe Road, Burroughs Grove, SL7 3RA
⏲ 11.30-3, 5-11; 11.30-11 Fri & Sat; 12-5.30 Sun
☎ (01628) 483109
Rebellion IPA, Mild, Mutiny, Smuggler; 2 changing beers Ⓗ
A large open-plan pub a short bus ride from both High Wycombe and Marlow. The extensive specials board, open fires and pleasant garden make this a popular destination for diners, drinkers and families. Close proximity to the Rebellion Beer Company means the six Rebellion ales are always in great condition. Q❀◐◑P🚌(800,850)🐾

Marsworth

Red Lion L

90 Vicarage Road, HP23 4LU (opp church)
⏲ 11-3, 5-11; 11-11 Sat; 12-10.30 Sun ☎ (01296) 668366
🌐 redlionmarsworth.co.uk
Fuller's London Pride; 5 changing beers Ⓗ
An excellent, traditional village pub dating from the 17th century, close to the Grand Union Canal. The interior is on two levels – the comfortable upstairs lounge has a small restaurant serving generous home-cooked food, while the beer-focused public bar has a real coal fire and a games area with bar billiards, darts and shove-ha'penny, where children are allowed. There is seating in front of the pub and behind is an attractive garden and covered patio.
Q🐎❀◐◑♣🍎P🚌(164,167)🐾📶

Milton Keynes

Slug & Lettuce

1 Savoy Crescent, MK9 3PU
⏲ 11-11; 10-2am Fri & Sat; 12-10.30 Sun ☎ (01908) 395147
🌐 slugandlettuce.co.uk/milton_keynes
Timothy Taylor Landlord; house beer (by Greene King); 1 changing beer (sourced nationally) Ⓗ
A busy city-centre pub serving the renowned Theatre district in central Milton Keynes. It is part of the vibrant night life in the area, along with many nightclubs and chain restaurants. Entertainment includes a weekly disco for disabled people and events celebrating major sporting fixtures such as the Rugby World Cup. Although this is a large venue with plenty of room, it can still be full at weekends. ◐◑♿🚌📶

Milton Keynes: Fenny Stratford

Red Lion

11 Lock View Lane, Simpson Road, MK1 1BY
12-11 (midnight Fri & Sat); 12-10.30 Sun
☎ (01908) 372317
Hook Norton Hooky; Oakham JHB; 1 changing beer [H]
Tucked alongside a lock on the Grand Union Canal, this Grade II-listed gem promises friendly conversation with a real ale enthusiast landlord and a rolling choice of up to three ales, selected to contrast in style and strength. Every Friday there is a new and interesting guest ale and real cider is now also on offer. There is a main bar with TV and pool, a quieter lounge and a lock-side garden. Within walking distance of Stadium MK.
❀⇌♣P🚌🐾

Milton Keynes: Great Linford

Black Horse

Wolverton Road, MK14 5AJ
11-11 (10.30 Sun) ☎ (01908) 398461
theblackhorsegreatlinford.co.uk
Everards Tiger; Harviestoun Bitter & Twisted [H]
This is a popular waterside pub with extensive beer gardens. The focus is mainly on food but drinkers are welcome. It has been refurbished in recent years following a fire and aims to look like an authentic old pub. Beer festivals are hosted regularly. The decked dining area overlooking the Grand Union Canal is busy in good weather.
❀♿P🚌🐾

Milton Keynes: Stony Stratford

White Horse

49 High Street, MK11 1AA
2-11 ☎ (01908) 567082 rockinghorsenights.com
Sharp's Doom Bar; 1 changing beer (often XT) [H]
This small pub has only one bar. The building, with its coach arch to the side, probably dates back to the 18th century. Along with the regular beer, a guest ale is available from one of three local breweries. The pub hosts live bands on most Friday or Saturday nights and has large TVs for sports coverage. It can get busy during music events and when showing major sports fixtures. Q♣🚌🐾

Naphill

Wheel

100 Main Road, HP14 4QA
12 (4.30 Mon)-11; 12-10.30 Sun ☎ (01494) 562210
thewheelnaphill.com
Greene King IPA, IPA Reserve; 2 changing beers [H]
Traditional 18th-century village pub in the heart of the Chilterns. It offers four excellent cask ales, including two regularly changing guests, and good quality, home-cooked pub meals. Two bars and a large dining area are available for all – walkers, cyclists and families – dogs and muddy boots welcome too. There is a large garden at the front and a secluded, smoker-friendly courtyard at the rear. Two large beer festivals are held each year.
Q❀♣P🚌(300)🐾

Padbury

New Inn

London Road, MK18 2AW (on A413 Buckingham-Aylesbury road)
5-11 Mon, Tue & Thu; closed Wed; 5-midnight Fri; 11-midnight Sat; 11-10 Sun ☎ (01280) 813173
Hook Norton Hooky Gold; 1 changing beer (sourced locally) [H]
This free house has three linked bars which blend old architecture and modern design, plus a smart dining room and a pleasant garden. Run by the third generation of the same family, it has retained its original genuine character but provides modern facilities. The landlord offers an interesting selection of different beers on two of the pumps. The ales and food are always of excellent quality, featuring LocAles and local produce where possible. Q❀🚌

Penn Street

Squirrel

HP7 0PX
12 (5 Mon)-11; 12-1am Fri; 12-10.30 Sun
☎ (01494) 711291 thesquirrelpub.co.uk
Rebellion IPA; 4 changing beers (sourced locally; often Tring, Vale, XT) [H]
The change at this village local over the last few years has been outstanding. Hard-working licensees have created a wonderful haven of great beer and food. The main improvement is the beer range – the row of handpumps will bring joy to any ale lover, with mostly local beers alongside guests from farther afield, plus real cider. The large award-winning garden is great for families. A beer festival with over 100 different ales is held in July in conjunction with another village pub.
❀P🚌(1)🐾

Prestwood

Green Man

2 High Street, HP16 9EB (on A4128 near Great Missenden)
12-midnight (1am Fri & Sat); 12-10.30 Sun
☎ (01494) 890074
Greene King IPA; St Austell Tribute; Sharp's Doom Bar [H]
This establishment is the local boozer to go to for a good selection of quality beers sourced from far and wide, served in excellent condition. In the two bars, darts, crib and dominoes are played occasionally and lively conversation is particularly boisterous late afternoon. There is a front patio for smokers and a rear garden. Great Missenden is a mile away, with small independent shops in the high street and the Roald Dahl Museum.
❀♿♣P🚌(48)🐾

Radnage

Crown

City Road, HP14 4DW
11-3, 5-midnight; 11-midnight Wed-Sun
☎ (01494) 482301 crownradnage.co.uk
Rebellion IPA [G]**; 2 changing beers** [H]
The Crown is nestled in the picturesque Chiltern village of Radnage, a five-minute drive from junction 5 of the M40. It is a family-friendly pub with a large garden and modern accommodation, offering a warm welcome and an open fire in winter. The pleasant one-room bar has a choice of local real ales and local ciders, all gravity dispensed. Home-cooked seasonal food is recommended. ❀♿🐾

Stoke Goldington

Lamb

High Street, MK16 8NR

5-11 Mon; 12-11; 12-7 Sun ☎ (01908) 551233

🌐 thelambatstokegoldington.co.uk

Sharp's Doom Bar; Tring Side Pocket for a Toad; 2 changing beers (sourced regionally) Ⓗ

The village is picture postcard-perfect and the Lamb is at its heart – a welcoming, friendly free house with a fine choice of unfailingly excellent beer, often including a LocAle, real cider and superb, generously portioned food. The pub has a separate cosy bar, a less formal dining room, a restaurant and a large garden with a stage area used for live music events. Joint Cider Pub of the Year. Q

Stoke Mandeville

Bull

5 Risborough Road, HP22 5UP

12-11 (midnight Fri & Sat) ☎ (01296) 613632

🌐 thebullstokemandeville.co.uk

Chiltern Pale Ale; Sharp's Doom Bar; 1 changing beer Ⓗ

Reopened in May 2012 as a free house, this small two-bar family-run village pub, situated on a main road, is well served by buses and trains. The public bar at the front is popular with locals, especially those who gather to watch football on TV, while the comfortable lounge bar at the back tends to be quieter. The large secure garden with seating is popular, especially in summer.

Q ⇌ P (300)

Taplow

Oak & Saw 🄻

Rectory Road, SL6 0ET

4-9.30 Mon; 12-11 (midnight Fri); 12-10.30 Sun

☎ (01628) 604074 🌐 oakandsaw.co.uk

Brakspear Bitter; Fuller's London Pride; 1 changing beer Ⓗ

Situated opposite the village green and church in an idyllic setting, this pub offers good pub food and three real ales including the monthly Rebellion. A large decked patio to the rear is great in the summer. The popular steak evening every Saturday includes a free bottle of wine. There are quizzes on the second and fourth Sundays of the month. Outside is a covered smoking area. Dogs are allowed in the non-dining area. P

Thornborough

Two Brewers 🄻

Bridge Street, MK18 2DN

12-2 (not Mon, Tue & Thu), 6-11; 12-2, 5-11 Sat; 11.15-3, 7-10 Sun ☎ (01280) 812020

Hook Norton Hooky Gold; St Austell Tribute; 1 changing beer Ⓗ

Everyone's idea of an old country pub, run by the same friendly landlord for almost 30 years. Set in a tranquil village, it has a cosy snug with an inglenook fireplace and a larger main bar with a wood-burning stove, pool tables and darts. OAPs get half-price drinks on Wednesday lunchtimes.

Q P

Turweston

Stratton Arms

Main Street, NN13 5JX

12-11 (midnight Sat & Sun) ☎ (01280) 704956

Sharp's Doom Bar; Timothy Taylor Golden Best, Landlord; 2 changing beers Ⓗ

This lovely old pub within a quiet village has retained all its original features, including a horseshoe-shaped bar. It has extensive lawns with marquees and barbecues in summer. There is a TV for sport but the volume is low. Diners are advised to book in advance. Q P

Twyford

Crown Inn

The Square, MK18 4EG

4 (12 Fri-Sun)-11.30 ☎ (01296) 730216

🌐 thecrowntwyford.co.uk

1 changing beer

Freehold locals' pub central to the life of the village. Once one of three pubs in Twyford, the landlady, Joan, has seen the others decline and close. The Crown is a deceptively large brick building opposite the village hall. A spacious bar area leads through to an even larger lounge/ function area. One frequently changing beer is served from the cask, with seven different beers usually on offer during the week.

P (16)

Wendover

King & Queen

17 South Street, HP22 6EF

11-11 (midnight Fri & Sat); 11-10.30 Sun

☎ (01296) 623272

Fuller's Discovery, London Pride; 1 changing beer Ⓗ

The pub is situated just off the High Street within easy reach of the station and has been refurbished without losing its original character. It has three rooms, one a restaurant serving good food. There is an impressive map of the local countryside on the wall in one room. A wood fire helps to provide a warm winter welcome for cold ramblers returning after walking on the nearby Chiltern Hills. A former Aylesbury Vale District Council Pub of the Year.

Q ⇌ (Chiltern Railways) P

Pack Horse

29 Tring Road, HP22 6NR

12-11 (midnight Fri & Sat) ☎ (01296) 622075

Fuller's London Pride; Gale's Seafarers Ale; 1 changing beer Ⓗ

Small, friendly village pub dating from 1769 and situated at the end of a terrace of thatched houses known as Anne Boleyn Cottages. On the Ridgeway Path, it has been owned by the same family for over 50 years. They also run the White Swan, another Fuller's pub in the village that deserves a visit. The wall above the bar is decorated with RAF squadron badges, denoting connections with nearby RAF Halton. The pub runs men's and women's darts, dominoes and cribbage teams.

⇌

Weston Underwood

Cowpers Oak 🄻

High Street, MK46 5JS

⏲ 12-3, 5.30-11; 12-midnight Sat; 12-9 Sun
☎ (01234) 711382 🌐 cowpersoak.co.uk
Sharp's Doom Bar; Woodforde's Wherry; 2 changing beers (often Concrete Cow, Tring) 🄷
This charming pub in the quiet village of Western Underwood is a peaceful place to come for a quiet drink or a meal. It is friendly and welcoming to all including drinkers, diners and families, managing to balance all requirements due to its layout. The old building has been sympathetically restored with stone floors and wonderful open fireplaces. The large garden is often used for events and community activities and has children's play equipment. ❀◑P🚌🐾📶

Whiteleaf

Red Lion

Upper Icknield Way, HP27 0LL (hilly side of A4010 at Monks Risborough)
⏲ closed Mon; 12-3, 5-11; 12-11 Sat; 12-10.30 Sun
☎ (01844) 344476 🌐 theredlionwhiteleaf.co.uk
Sharp's Doom Bar; 2 changing beers 🄷
Set in an attractive village on the slopes of the Chilterns, close to the Ridgeway, the Red Lion is a family-run 17th-century free house. Visitors are greeted by an open fire in winter and a pleasant beer garden in summer. The pub offers a rotating selection of real ales, many from local breweries, and brews its own ale to celebrate the nearby Kop Hill Climb vintage car event in September. It holds an annual beer festival.
Q❀🛏◑♿P🚌(300)🐾📶

Wing

Queen's Head 🄻

9 High Street, LU7 0NS
⏲ closed Mon; 11.30-3, 5.30-11; 11.30-midnight Fri & Sat; 12-10.30 Sun ☎ (01296) 688268
🌐 thequeensheadwing.co.uk
Wells Bombardier; Young's Bitter; 2 changing beers 🄷
A 16th-century village-centre free house with a comfortable public bar and restaurant. LocAle accredited, guests are from nearby Tring, Vale, Hopping Mad or other micros. The restaurant at the rear has a well-deserved reputation. Log fires in winter months enhance the welcoming atmosphere and the pub is TV-free. A large garden has a patio and a covered, heated smoking area. There is ample car parking. ❀◑♿P🚌(100,150)

Wooburn Common

Royal Standard 🏆

Wooburn Common Road, HP10 0JS (follow signs to Odds Farm)
⏲ 12-11 (10.30 Sun) ☎ (01628) 521121
🌐 theroyalstandard.biz
Caledonian Deuchars IPA 🄷**; Hop Back Summer Lightning** 🄶**; St Austell Tribute; 7 changing beers** 🄷
Ever-popular semi-rural pub with a congenial ambience in the bar, catering for diners and discerning drinkers alike. Ten real ales, five direct from the cask, alongside many real ciders, make this venue an important flagship pub in the area. There is always at least one dark beer on offer, either a stout, porter or dark mild. Two beer festivals are held, one over the May Day weekend, the other on the last weekend in October. Quiz night is the second Monday of the month.
Q❀◑♿🍎P🐾📶

Wooburn Green

Queen & Albert

24 The Green, HP10 0EJ
⏲ 12-midnight (10.30 Sun) ☎ (01628) 523098
Rebellion IPA, Smuggler; 1 changing beer 🄷
Wonderful little inn overlooking Wooburn Green. Recently refurbished, the space at the front is a traditional drinkers' area, complete with a fire in cooler months. A large function room to the rear provides an ample area for dining, and can be booked for functions throughout the year. A family-run pub, children are welcome, with games in the garden in the summer. Sunday lunches are recommended. ❀🛏◑♿🚌🐾

Old Millwrights Arms, Aylesbury (Photo: Katie Button)

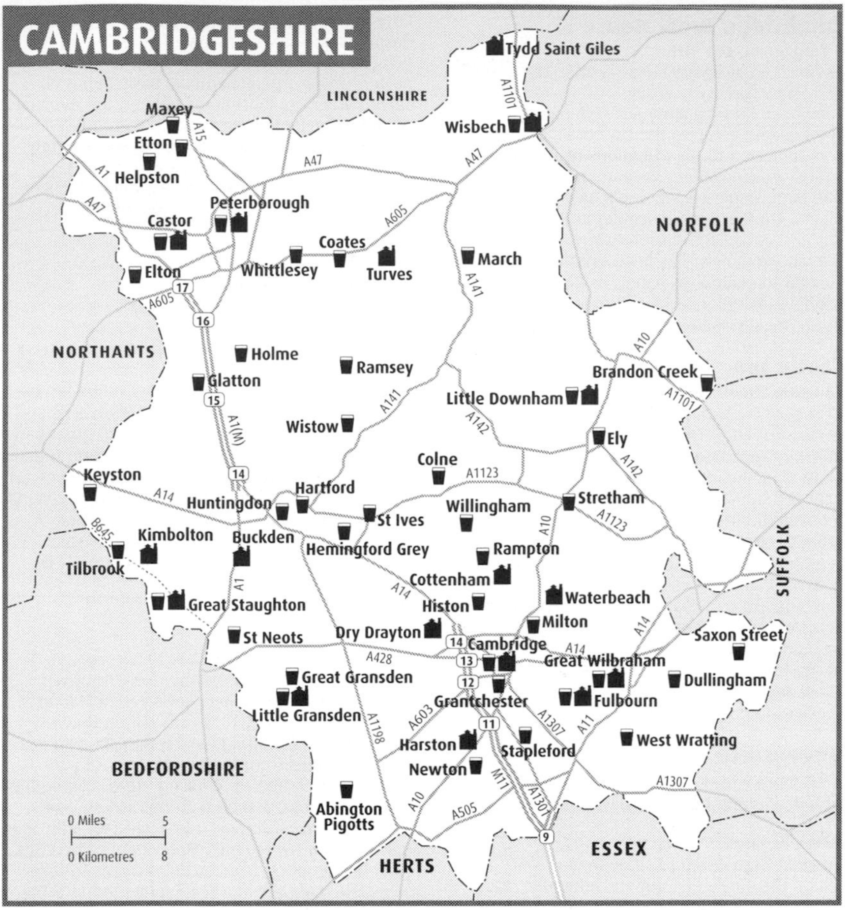

Abington Pigotts

Pig & Abbot

High Street, SG8 0SD (off A505 through Litlington)
12-3, 6-11; 12-11 Sat; 12-10.30 Sun ☎ (01763) 853515
pigandabbot.co.uk
Adnams Southwold Bitter; Fuller's London Pride; 2 changing beers Ⓗ
Located in a surprisingly remote part of the south Cambridgeshire countryside, this Queen Anne-period pub offers a warm welcome. The interior has exposed oak beams and two fires, including a large inglenook featuring a wood-burning stove. A comfortable restaurant offers traditional pub food, specialising in fresh fish and chips, steak and kidney puddings and pies. Two guest beers are stocked, often sourced from Burton Bridge, Humpty Dumpty, Mighty Oak, Timothy Taylor or Woodforde's. Q❀◐♣P🐾

Brandon Creek

Ship

Brandon Creek Bridge, PE38 0PP
12-11 ☎ (01353) 676228 theshipbrandoncreek.co.uk
5 changing beers (sourced locally; often Milton, Two Rivers) Ⓗ
A country pub in a riverside location, set in a striking fork where the Great Ouse meets the Little Ouse on the Cambridgeshire/Norfolk border. It has a comfortable bar, snug, restaurant and outdoor seating area overlooking the water. Up to five beers and one cider are available as well as unusual local spirits. Locally sourced food is served lunchtimes and evenings including gluten-free dishes. Live music plays every Friday night and three beer festivals are held during the year.
❀◐P🐾

Cambridge

Cambridge Blue

85 Gwydir Street, CB1 2LG
12 (11 Sat)-11; 12-10.30 Sun ☎ (01223) 471680
the-cambridgeblue.co.uk
12 changing beers Ⓗ/Ⓖ
Busy single-bar pub with seating in three areas and a large garden. Breweriana and pumpclips from the hundreds of different beers served over the years provide the decoration. Beers are from handpumps or the taproom. A huge selection of bottled beers, a number of ciders and perries plus mead are also on offer. Beer festivals are held in February, June and October. Wholesome home-cooked food using locally sourced ingredients is available all day. A former CAMRA Cambridge and Cambridgeshire Pub of the Year. Q❀◐♣(Citi2)🐾

Cambridge Brew House

1 King Street, CB1 1LH

9am-11.30; 10-midnight Fri & Sat (01223) 855185

thecambridgebrewhouse.com

Cambridge Brewing Misty River; changing beers

The building occupies the side of King Street that was subjected to the attentions of the Brutalist school of architecture. Recently refurbished with one large single bar, the right side is mainly for diners. There is further seating in two rooms upstairs. An on-site microbrewery, Cambridge Brewing Company, has been installed and can be viewed through glass panels in the bar. Six handpumps sell its own and other breweries' beers, mainly sourced locally.

Castle Inn

38 Castle Street, CB3 0AJ

11.30-11 (11.30 Fri & Sat); 12-11 Sun (01223) 353194

thecastleinncambridge.com

Adnams Lighthouse, Southwold Bitter, Explorer, Ghost Ship, Broadside; 4 changing beers

Acquired by Adnams in 1994 and respectfully renovated, the Castle is family run and offers a great selection of the brewery's own beers, plus its seasonal offerings and two or more changing guests. Originally two buildings, they have been combined to create a number of separate drinking areas on two floors, including a downstairs snug. To the rear is a suntrap garden next to the mound of the long-gone castle. Excellent food is served every session, including a wide selection of specials. Q (B)

Devonshire Arms

1 Devonshire Road, CB1 2BH

12-11 (midnight Fri & Sat); 12-10.30 Sun

(01223) 316610 individualpubs.co.uk/devonshire

Milton Pegasus; 7 changing beers

Rescued from decline and opened in 2010 as Milton Brewery's first pub in Cambridge, the building has been impressively renovated, with front and rear drinking areas offering a mixture of wooden booths and larger tables. Generally five Milton beers are available and up to three changing guests, plus two real ciders, a selection of Belgian bottled beers and Moravka unpasteurised lager. Good-quality food is on offer every session (no food Sun eve), including pizzas cooked in a stone bake oven. A wood-burning stove warms the back room in winter. Q (Citi2)

Elm Tree

16a Orchard Street, CB1 1JT

11-11; 12-10.30 Sun (01223) 502632

theelmtreecambridge.co.uk

B&T Edwin Taylor's Extra Stout; Young's Bitter; 10 changing beers

This relaxed back-street pub is decorated with brewery memorabilia and quirky bric-a-brac plus recent photographs. The single-bar interior has a long narrow seating area extending to the back. Ten handpumps dispense three changing ales from B&T and Wells & Young's, the remainder being used for guest ales from myriad breweries. A cider or perry is also served. There is a printed menu of more than 150 bottled Belgian beers, and occasional beer tastings.

Flying Pig

106 Hills Road, CB2 1LQ

12-11 (midnight Fri); 7-11 Sat & Sun (01223) 354623

Crouch Vale Brewers Gold; 6 changing beers

Cosy and friendly L-shaped pub with a local feel despite being on a main road. The walls and ceiling are adorned with an eclectic collection of old posters and pig paraphernalia. Basic pub grub is served weekday lunchtimes only. In the evenings the intimate lighting is enhanced by candles on the tables. Beers from local breweries are regularly available, as well as specialist keg beers. Live acoustic music features some evenings. Local branch Pub of the Year 2013.

Free Press

7 Prospect Row, CB1 1DU

12-11; 12-10.30 Sun (01223) 368337

freepresspub.com

Greene King XX Mild, IPA, Abbot; 4 changing beers (often Greene King)

Intimate, friendly pub named after a temperance movement newspaper that lasted for just one edition. It serves high-quality food and great beer, including the rare XX Mild. Guests are from Greene King's seasonal and guest lists. A pub for over 120 years, only the tiny snug remains from the original building – the rest is a loving reconstruction. A walled garden is at the rear. Food is served, including snacks for dogs. Q

Haymakers

54 High Street, CB4 1NG

12-11 (midnight Fri & Sat); 12-10.30 Sun

(01223) 311077 individualpubs.co.uk/haymakers

Milton Pegasus; 4 changing beers (often Milton)

Reopened in April 2013, this is Milton Brewery's second pub in Cambridge and is popular with locals and employees from the nearby science park. There are a number of drinking areas – one either side of the door, a snug with bar access, and another room off to one side. Eight real ales, four real ciders or perries plus Moravka unpasteurised lager are on offer. Food includes pizzas to take away. The car park has been converted into the largest pub cycle park in Cambridge, leaving a few spaces for cars. Local branch's Most Improved (City) Pub in 2014. P (Citi2)

Kingston Arms

33 Kingston Street, CB1 2NU

12-3, 5-11; 11-midnight Fri & Sat; 11-11 Sun

(01223) 319414 kingston-arms.co.uk

REAL ALE BREWERIES

Bexar County Peterborough
BlackBar Harston
Calverley's Cambridge
Cambridge Cambridge
Castor Castor
Crafty Beers Great Wilbraham
Draycott Buckden
Elgood's Wisbech
Fellows Cottenham
Lord Conrad's Dry Drayton
Mile Tree Wisbech
Milton Waterbeach
Moonshine Fulbourn
Oakham Peterborough
Red Great Staughton
Son of Sid Little Gransden
Three Blind Mice Little Downham
Tinshed Kimbolton (NEW)
Tydd Steam Tydd Saint Giles
Xtreme Turves

Crouch Vale Brewers Gold; Hop Back Summer Lightning; Oakham JHB; Thornbridge Jaipur IPA; Timothy Taylor Landlord; Woodforde's Wherry; 4 changing beers Ⓗ
Classic side-street pub just off Mill Road. Twelve handpumps serve regular and changing guest beers, usually including a dark beer, plus two ciders or perries. A large selection of Belgian and other bottled beers is stocked, and beer festivals are held in the warmer months. Food is available at all sessions with breakfast from 11am at weekends. The walled garden has canopies and heaters and is popular all year round. Recession beer and food is offered at bargain prices.
Q❀◑⇌♣●🚌(Citi2)🐾📶

Live & Let Live

40 Mawson Road, CB1 2EA
11.30-2.30, 5.30 (6 Sat)-11; 12-2.30, 7-11 Sun
☎ (01223) 460261
Oakham Citra; 4 changing beers Ⓗ
Wood panelling and railway and beer memorabilia add to the atmosphere at this discreet corner local just off Mill Road. The single bar has a small snug to the rear. The beer range usually includes an additional Oakham (frequently Green Devil) and often a mild or stout. Two ciders are also offered. There is an outstanding collection of rums from around the world, and occasional rum festivals. Food is restricted to snacks – the pork pies and Scotch eggs are excellent. Q⇌♣●🚌(Citi2)🐾

Maypole 𝕃

20a Portugal Place, CB5 8AF
11.30-midnight (2am Fri & Sat); 12-11.30 Sun
☎ (01223) 352999 🌐 maypolefreehouse.co.uk
16 changing beers Ⓗ
The Castiglione family have run this city-centre pub for over 30 years and bought the freehold from Punch Taverns in 2009. It has since become a showcase for quality beers and won Vincent Castiglione the CAMRA branch's first Real Ale Champion award in 2010. It offers up to 16 beers, including LocAles, with micros predominating. There are two rooms downstairs, a large function room upstairs and a large partly covered patio at the front. Food focuses on home-cooked Italian dishes. ❀◑♿●🚌(Citi5,Citi6)📶

Mill 🏆 𝕃

14 Mill Lane, CB2 1RX
11-11 (midnight Thu-Sat) ☎ (01223) 311829
🌐 themillpubcambridge.co.uk
6 changing beers Ⓗ
Set in a honeypot location next to the Mill Pond, the building has been recently refurbished – improvements include an especially attractive wood-panelled side room. The bar has eight handpumps, including one for cider. There is a strong commitment to locally brewed beers, including those brewed at sister pub the Cambridge Brew House. An Adnams beer is generally available, and a polypin of local cider often sits behind the bar. Local CAMRA branch's LocAle (City) winner in 2014 and its Pub of the Year 2015.
Q◑●🐾

Pint Shop

10 Peas Hill, CB2 3PN
12-11 (midnight Fri & Sat) ☎ (01223) 352293
🌐 pintshop.co.uk
6 changing beers Ⓗ
Formerly the university pensions office, the building has been extensively refurbished with multiple areas across two floors providing a variety of drinking and dining areas. Six changing real ales are joined by 10 keg beers from the UK and the rest of the world. The terraced patio garden is no-smoking – a separate smokers' alley is provided. Food is upmarket, with home-made cold bar snacks available at all times. ❀◑♿🚌

Castor

Prince of Wales Feathers 𝕃

38 Peterborough Road, PE5 7AL
12-11.30 (1am Fri & Sat); 12-midnight Sun
☎ (01733) 380222 🌐 princeofwalesfeathers.co.uk
Adnams Broadside; Woodforde's Wherry Ⓗ**; 5 changing beers** Ⓗ/Ⓖ
This 17th-century stone-built inn has an open-plan layout with the bar in the centre and different areas for dining, pool, darts and television. There are seven real ales including one served from the cellar, and an ever-changing real cider and perry available at all times. Lunches are served daily, evening meals weekdays only. Live music is hosted every Saturday and a quiz night on Sunday. Outside there are two areas for drinkers with benches and parasols. ❀◑♣●🚌(9)🐾

Coates

Vine 𝕃

4 South Green, PE7 2BJ
3-11; 12-midnight Fri & Sat; 12-10.30 Sun
☎ (01733) 840343 🌐 vinefreehouse.wordpress.com
3 changing beers Ⓗ
Lively bar/lounge and separate restaurant with its own bar. In the summer of 2013 a private investor secured ownership of the pub from Charles Wells to make it officially a free house, now fully refurbished, including a new kitchen. Meals are served lunchtimes and evenings, and breakfast on Saturdays. The varying beer list includes a LocAle. The large outdoor area includes several pétanque terrains. Local buses pass in front of the building.
Q❀◑P🚌(33,701)🐾📶

Colne

Green Man 𝕃

1 East Street, PE28 3LZ
12-2.30 (not Mon), 5-11; 12-11 Fri-Sun ☎ (01487) 840368
🌐 greenmancolne.co.uk
Oakham Inferno; Sharp's Doom Bar; 3 changing beers (sourced locally; often Elgood's, Star) Ⓗ
Picturesque 17th-century village local in an old Fenland fruit growing area. The corrugated roof covers an original thatch. This busy, friendly pub provides a public bar with pool, darts and TV, and a warm, sociable lounge with a modern dining area extension serving good food. Quiz nights feature fortnightly. Outside, the garden has a children's play area and hosts barbecues in summer. There is camping nearby at Earith Lakes.
❀◑⛺♣P🚌(21,22)🐾📶

Dullingham

Boot

18 Brinkley Road, CB8 9UW
11.30-2.30, 5-11; 11.30-11.30 Sat; 11.30-10.30 Sun
☎ (01638) 507327

Adnams Southwold Bitter; Greene King IPA; 2 changing beers [H]
Greene King tried to close this traditional village inn as non-viable in 2000 but it was rescued by a villager and is now a vibrant and welcoming community local where something is always going on. It supports darts, crib and pétanque teams, and hosts regular live music and beer festivals twice a year. Simple, good-value grub is served lunchtimes (no food Sun), plus fish and chips on Wednesday evenings. Children are welcome until 8pm. Situated around a mile from Dulllingham railway station. ❀◑♣P🐾

Elton

Crown Inn Ⓛ
8 Duck Street, PE8 6RQ
🕐 12 (5 Mon)-11 ☎ (01832) 280232 🌐 thecrowninn.org
Greene King IPA; Phipps NBC India Pale Ale; 3 changing beers [H]
This 16th-century stone-built thatched pub has a main bar, a small dining area to the front and a restaurant to the rear. Six real ales are usually on offer via handpump including the house beer, Golden Crown Ale, brewed by Tydd Steam. There is a dedicated handpump for real cider. No bar food is served on Saturday evening or Sunday. Note the unusual cartoons and drawings on the walls to the toilets. Five-star B&B accommodation is available. ❀🛏◑🍎P🚌(24,X4)🐾📶

Ely

Prince Albert 🏆 Ⓛ
62 Silver Street, CB7 4JF (opp cathedral car park)
🕐 11-11.30; 12-10.30 Sun ☎ (01353) 663494
Greene King XX Mild, IPA, Abbot; 5 changing beers [H]
A classic small back-street local, just a short walk from historic Ely Cathedral. This was once the officers' mess for the local militia. It has 10 handpumps offering up to five guest beers and a guest cider, and is a rare outlet for XX Mild. Recent refurbishment has created a restaurant area for fine dining. No music, TV or fruit machines distract from the pleasant bar-room banter. The staff and locals are welcoming. Q❀◑♿🚆🍎🚌🐾📶

Townhouse Pub Ⓛ
60-64 Market Street, CB7 4LS (near Ely Museum)
🕐 11-11 (1.30am Fri & Sat); 12-11 Sun ☎ (01353) 664338
🌐 thetownhousepub.co.uk
4 changing beers (often Buntingford, Three Blind Mice) [H]
A former Georgian town house, Grade II-listed, this is now a modern bar with a spacious conservatory and enclosed garden. The five handpumps serve a range of ever-changing guest ales, sourced from local breweries, including the local Three Blind Mice, plus a real cider. A popular annual beer festival is held in July. DJs play from 9pm on Friday and Saturday evenings and there is live music on Sunday afternoons. ❀◑🍎🚌

Etton

Golden Pheasant Ⓛ
1 Main Road, PE6 7DA
🕐 12-2.30 (not Mon), 5-11; 12-11 Fri-Sun ☎ (01733) 252387
🌐 thegoldenpheasant.net
Adnams Broadside; Greene King Abbot; 3 changing beers (often Grainstore, Star, Woodforde's) [H]
An impressive stone-built Grade II-listed former manor house, now boasting five handpumps dispensing two permanent and three changing (mostly local) beers in the newly redesigned, bigger bar. There is a separate restaurant, ample parking, a large garden and children's play area. A permanent marquee with bar caters for functions of up to 150. The pub is a meeting place for several local groups and on the Green Wheel cycle route from Peterborough. It hosts an annual beer festival in spring. A former CAMRA Gold Award winner. Q❀◑♿♣🍎P🚌(22)

Fulbourn

Six Bells
9 High Street, CB21 5DH
🕐 11-2.30, 5-midnight; 11.30-2am Fri; 12-2am Sat; 12-11 Sun
☎ (01223) 880244 🌐 thesixbellsfulbourn.co.uk
Adnams Southwold Bitter, Broadside; Greene King IPA; Woodforde's Wherry; 2 changing beers [H]
Traditional thatched village pub, previously a coaching inn. The main bar has low ceilings, a real fire and many cosy corners. The food is locally sourced and home cooked, served in the bar and separate dining room (no food Sun or Mon eves). The function room hosts a trad jazz club on the first and third Wednesdays of the month. For the warmer months, there is one of the largest beer gardens in the area. A regular in the Guide. 🔥❀◑♿♣🍎P🚌(Citi1,Citi3)🐾📶

Glatton

Addison Arms Ⓛ
Sawtry Road, PE28 5RZ
🕐 11-3, 5-11; 11-11 Fri-Sun ☎ (01487) 830410
🌐 addisonarms.co.uk
Adnams Broadside; house beer (by Digfield) [H]**; 2 changing beers (sourced locally; often Grainstore, Nene Valley)** [H]/[G]
Grade II-listed pub built at the start of the 18th century and named after the playwright and politician Joseph Addison (co-founder of the Spectator), who was a relative of the first landlord. The pub offers at least three real ales and a real cider, with a focus on local producers. Food is prepared from fresh locally sourced supplies. A thriving quiz is held on Sunday night. The house beer Addison Ale is Digfield Shacklebush. Q🔥❀◑♿⛺♣🍎P🚌(46)🐾📶

Grantchester

Green Man Ⓛ
59 High Street, CB3 9NF
🕐 11-11; 12-10 Sun ☎ (01223) 844669
🌐 thegreenmangrantchester.co.uk
4 changing beers [G]
Five-hundred-year-old single-bar pub, complete with oak beams, under the current enthusiastic ownership since reopening in 2009. Home-made food using local ingredients is served lunchtimes and evenings, all day Saturday and Sunday. A separate restaurant area caters for wedding receptions and parties. Beers are often sourced from regional microbreweries, including local breweries. A cider and a perry are usually available. An extensive beer garden leads towards Grantchester Meadows by the River Cam, accessible by punt. Q🔥❀◑🍎P🚌(18)🐾

Great Gransden

Crown & Cushion

2 West Street, SG19 3AT
⏲ closed Mon; 5.30 (4 Fri; 12 Sat)-11; 12-10 Sun
☎ (01767) 677214 🌐 crownandcushion.com
3 changing beers (sourced regionally; often Adnams) 🄷
Picture-postcard village inn with a thatched roof and oak beams, believed to date partly from the 16th century. The lounge/dining area features a large fireplace with a wood-burning stove. This busy pub has much to offer including live music on Wednesdays and Thursdays. An interesting menu focusing on Indonesian cuisine is available Friday evening to Sunday and at other times by prior arrangement. **Q🐴❀◐⛺♣P🚌📶**

Great Staughton

White Hart

56 The Highway, PE19 5DA (on B645)
⏲ 12-2.30, 4-11 (midnight Fri); 12-11 Sat & Sun
☎ (01480) 861131 🌐 whitehartgreatstaughton.co.uk
Batemans XB, XXXB; 1 changing beer 🄷
Passing through the narrow entrance to this fine former coaching inn takes you back to the days of horse-drawn coaches. The small building, dating from 1630, has been extended and altered, but still warrants a Grade II-listing. The interior comprises a main bar, a small room at the front and a restaurant at the rear. Traditional pub food is served 12-2.30pm, 6-9pm Thursday-Saturday and 12-3pm Sunday. **Q🐴❀◐P🚌**(156)**🐾📶**

Great Wilbraham

Carpenters Arms 🄻

10 High Sreet, CB21 5JD
⏲ 11.30-3, 6.30-11; closed Tue; 11.30-3 Sun
☎ (01223) 882093 🌐 carpentersarmsgastropub.co.uk
Crafty Beers Carpenter's Cask; 2 changing beers 🄷
Parts of the building date back to the 17th century. The public bar serves up to three real ales including one or two of its own brews – it has its own microbrewery in the old stables at the rear - and occasional guests. Traditional pub food is on offer as well as a menu reflecting the owners' previous experience running an award-winning restaurant in France. The bar billiards table is in regular use. Local CAMRA branch's LocAle (Rural) winner in 2014. **❀◐♿♣P📶**

Hartford

King of the Belgians 🄻

27 Main Street, PE29 1XU
⏲ 11-11 (midnight Fri & Sat); 12-10.30 Sun
☎ (01480) 52030 🌐 kingofthebelgians.com
4 changing beers (sourced regionally; often Batemans, Elgood's, Great Oakley) 🄷
A 16th-century inn in a picturesque setting. This genuine community pub actively supports local charities and hosts an annual beer festival and a family fun day. An ever-changing selection of four real ales and ciders is available, and good-value food including Sunday roasts and take-away pizza. Oak beams and a copper-topped bar characterise the public bar. There is a separate dining area. Entertainment includes regular quizzes, games nights and an open mic night on the first Monday of the month. **🐴❀◐♣🍎P🚌🐾📶**

Helpston

Bluebell 🄻

10 Woodgate, PE6 7ED
⏲ 11-3 (not Mon), 5-11; 11-11 Sat; 12-10.30 Sun
☎ (01733) 252394 🌐 bluebellhelpston.pub
Fuller's London Pride; house beer (by Star); 2 changing beers (often Adnams, Nene Valley) 🄷
Quiet 17th-century stone village pub with its main entrance at the side. It has two wood-panelled bars, a number of dining areas, and a snug named after local poet John Clare. The beer range includes Fuller's London Pride and 10 Woodgate Bitter, a house beer brewed by Star Brewery, plus two rotating guests from breweries around the country. Good-value food is served lunchtimes and evenings. **Q🐴❀◐♿🍎P🚌**(201)**🐾📶**

Hemingford Grey

Cock 🄻

47 High Street, PE28 9BJ (off A14, SE of Huntingdon)
⏲ 11.30-3, 6-11; 11.30-11 Sat; 12-10.30 Sun
☎ (01480) 463609 🌐 cambscuisine.com
Brewsters Hophead; Elgood's Cambridge Bitter; Great Oakley Wagtail; 1 changing beer 🄷
This village inn and restaurant has won local, regional and national awards. The cosy interior has recently been refurbished to provide more comfortable facilities and is popular with locals who enjoy the well-kept locally sourced beers and real Cromwell cider produced in the village. The separate restaurant features an extensive fish board, meat, game and excellent home-made sausages (booking essential at all times). During the summer, occasional beer festivals are held in the beer garden. **Q❀◐♿⛺P🚌**(5)**🐾📶**

Histon

Red Lion

27 High Street, CB24 9JD
⏲ 10.30-11 (midnight Fri); 12-11 Sun ☎ (01223) 564437
🌐 theredlionhiston.co.uk
Adnams Ghost Ship; Batemans Black & White; Lacons Falcon Ale; Oakham Bishops Farewell; Tring Side Pocket for a Toad 🄷
The two bars of this free house are adorned with a wonderful collection of breweriana and historic photos. The left-hand bar has recently been extended and has a TV. The beer range includes Belgian and German beers on draught, guest beers including a mild, plus a selection of continental bottled beers. A regular cider, perry and guest cider are also available. Breakfast is served from 10.30am on Saturday. Two beer festivals are held each year – an Easter aperitif, then the main event in September. Cambridge CAMRA branch Dark Beer Pub 2014. **🐴❀◐♿♣🍎P🚌**(Citi8)**📶**

Holme

Admiral Wells 🄻

41 Station Road, PE7 3PH (jct of B660 and Yaxley Rd)
⏲ 11-2.30, 5-11; 11.30-11 Sat; 11.30-10.30 Sun
☎ (01487) 831214 🌐 admiralwells.co.uk
Adnams Southwold Bitter, Broadside; Digfield Shacklebush; Oakham JHB; 2 changing beers 🄷
Victorian inn named after one of Nelson's pall bearers and officially built on the lowest land in Britain. It has two drinking areas in a modern contemporary style, and a function room at the

rear. Next to the old Holme railway station, and the East Coast mainline, the walls are adorned with photographs from steam railway days. Up to six real ales are usually available and a cider in summer. The pub serves excellent food. Quiz night is Tuesday. Q♞❀◖◗♿♣●P🐾ᯤ

Huntingdon

Falcon 𝕃

Market Hill, PE29 3NR
⌚ 11-11
Marston's Old Empire; Nobby's Best; Potbelly Pigs Do Fly; 12 changing beers (often Great Oakley, Nene Valley, Potbelly) [H]
Steeped in local history, the Falcon reopened in December 2014 after a six-year closure and a lengthy campaign by local community groups. This 16th-century former coaching inn is said to be the site of Oliver Cromwell's recruiting station and the gates from the Market Square were once the entrance to Huntingdon Prison. An ever-changing selection of beers is served from up to 15 handpumps, along with a range of real ciders.
Q♞❀◖⇌♣●🚌🐾

Old Bridge Hotel 𝕃

1 High Street, PE29 3TQ (at S end of High St on ring road, by river)
⌚ 11-11; 12-10.30 Sun ☎ (01480) 424300
🌐 huntsbridge.com
Adnams Southwold Bitter; 2 changing beers (often Hart Family Brewers, Nene Valley) [H]
A handsome ivy-clad 18th-century building set in a prominent position on the banks of the River Great Ouse. Diners can enjoy imaginative, high-quality food in the terrace restaurant or on the covered patio, while drinkers can relax in the bar or lounge area. The award-winning Old Bridge Wine Shop offers wine tasting as a diversion and there is an emphasis on local and regional beers. The bus station is a short walk away.
Q♞❀🛏◖◗♿P🚌🐾ᯤ

Keyston

Pheasant 𝕃

Loop Road, PE28 0RE (on B663, 1 mile S of A14, E of Thrapston)
⌚ closed Mon; 12-3, 6-11; 12-11 Fri & Sat; 12-5 Sun
☎ (01832) 710241 🌐 thepheasant-keyston.co.uk
Adnams Southwold Bitter; 2 changing beers (sourced locally; often Nene Valley, Digfield) [H]
The village is named after Ketil's Stone, probably an Anglo-Saxon boundary marker. Created from a row of thatched cottages in an idyllic setting, the pub offers high-quality food, fine wines and cask ales. There is a splendid lounge bar and three dining areas. Regularly changing guest beers are offered, usually from Nene Valley or Digfield. One of the few pubs still in the Guide that featured in the original 1972 edition. Q♞❀◖◗P🐾ᯤ

Little Downham

Plough

106 Main Street, CB6 2SX (W end of village)
⌚ 12-3 (not Mon), 6-11; 12-midnight Fri & Sat; 12-3, 6-10.30 Sun ☎ (01353) 698297
3 changing beers (often Adnams, Oakham, Woodforde's) [H]
An early-Victorian Grade II-listed pub, well preserved in character and charm. Two cask-conditioned ales are served, increasing to three in summer, often sourced from East Anglian breweries. The pub serves Thai cuisine, also available to take away. An annual beer festival is held in early September. Open all day at weekends if busy – children are welcome until 9pm.
❀◖◗♣P🚌(125)

Little Gransden

Chequers 𝕃

71 Main Road, SG19 3DW
⌚ 12-2, 7-11; 12-11 Fri & Sat; 12-6, 7-10.30 Sun
☎ (01767) 677348 🌐 chequersgransden.co.uk
4 changing beers (sourced locally) [H]
Village pub owned and run by the same family for over 60 years and in this Guide for 20. The unspoilt middle bar, with its wooden benches and roaring fire, is a favourite spot to catch up on the local gossip. The pub's Son of Sid brewhouse supplies the pub and local beer festivals. Fish and chips are a highlight on Friday night (booking essential). Pickled Pig cider is nearly always available. Winner of numerous CAMRA awards. Q❀◗●P🚂🚌🐾ᯤ

March

Rose & Crown 𝕃

41 St Peters Road, PE15 9NA
⌚ 12-11 (11.30 Thu; midnight Fri & Sat) ☎ (01354) 652077
St Austell Trelawny; 5 changing beers [H]
Traditional family-run community free house, over 150 years old. The two-room interior features low beams and a real fire. The range of up to six ales is mainly sourced from micros, often including an Oakham ale and beers from the West Country. Perry is permanently on handpump plus other ciders. A beer fest is held at Easter. High-quality food is served evenings and lunchtimes. Thursday is quiz night and there is occasionally live music on Saturdays. Q❀◖◗●P🚌(33,46)

Ship Inn 𝕃

1 Nene Parade, PE15 8TD
⌚ 11-11 (12.30am Fri & Sat); 11-10.30 Sun
☎ (01354) 607878
Tydd Steam Barn Ale; Woodforde's Wherry; 3 changing beers [H]
Thatched Grade II-listed riverside pub built in 1680 with extensive riverside moorings. The unusual carved wood beams are said to have fallen off a barge during the building of Ely Cathedral. Reopened in March 2010 as a free house, after a major refit, it has a friendly and welcoming atmosphere and a large collection of pumpclips. Note the quaint wobbly floor and wall leading to the toilets and to a small games room. A Guide regular since 2012. Q❀♿♣●🚌(33,46)🐾ᯤ

Maxey

Blue Bell 𝕃

39 High Street, PE6 9EE
⌚ 5.30 (1 Sat)-11.30; 12-11.30 Sun ☎ (01778) 348182
Abbeydale Absolution; Fuller's London Pride, ESB; Oakham Bishops Farewell; 6 changing beers [H]
This multi award-winning stone-built free house has been run by the same landlord for over 12 years. Originally a barn, it was converted many years ago and reflects the rural setting in which it is

found. Paraphernalia of countryside living adorn the walls and shelves of the two-roomed interior. Nine handpumps dispense a range of ales from large and small breweries from far and wide. A popular meeting place for groups including birdwatchers and golfers. Q❀♣P🖳(22,413)😺🗢

Milton

Jolly Brewers Ⓛ
5 Fen Road, CB24 6AD
✪ 12-midnight (1am Fri); 12-10.30 Sun ☎ (01223) 863895
🌐 jollybrewersmilton.co.uk
Elgood's Cambridge Bitter; Greene King IPA; Milton Pegasus; 2 changing beers Ⓗ
Refurbished pub and restaurant reopened in 2012, after a closure of many years. A timber-framed building dating back to 1700, it had its own brewery until 1925. There is a small, well-furnished bar to the left of the entrance, with the restaurant to the right. The rear of the building has a courtyard that includes a seating area, children's playground and B&B accommodation (four en-suite rooms). Guest beers include ales from the local Milton Brewery. ⏃❀🛏🕪●P🖳(9)😺

Newton

Queen's Head
CB22 7PG
✪ 11.30-2.30, 6-11; 12-2.30, 7-10.30 Sun ☎ (01223) 870436
Adnams Southwold Bitter, Broadside; 2 changing beers Ⓖ
This village local is one of a handful to have appeared in every edition of the Guide. The list of landlords since 1729, displayed on the wall in the simply furnished public bar, has just 18 entries. The cosy lounge has a welcoming fire in the colder months. Simple but excellent food centres on soup and sandwiches. Guest beers are often Adnams seasonals. The King and Kaiser are reputed to have stopped here for a pint in the early 1900s. Q🕪🅰♣●P🖳(31)

Peterborough

Brewery Tap Ⓛ
80 Westgate, PE1 2AA
✪ 12-11 (2am Fri & Sat); 12-10.30 Sun ☎ (01733) 358500
🌐 thebrewery-tap.com
Oakham JHB, Inferno, Citra, Scarlet Macaw, Bishops Farewell; 4 changing beers Ⓗ
Housed in a former 1930s labour exchange, this claims to be one of Europe's largest brewpubs. The small brewery can be seen through large windows, where limited editions of beers are brewed. The 12 ales usually on offer are mainly from the Oakham range. A mezzanine floor area with some brewing artefacts is incorporated in the pub's modern design. Authentic Thai food is served. Entertainment includes live music. Close to bus and rail stations. 🕪🚆●P🖳🗢

Charters Ⓛ
Town Bridge, PE1 1FP (down steps at Town Bridge)
✪ 12-11 (midnight Fri & Sat); 12-10.30 Sun
☎ (01733) 315700 🌐 charters-bar.com
Oakham JHB, Inferno, Citra, Bishops Farewell; 6 changing beers Ⓗ/Ⓖ
The converted Dutch grain barge from circa 1907 sits on the River Nene near the city centre. An oriental restaurant is on the upper deck and food is

also served in the bar. A large garden with a marquee, bar and landing stage for boats is popular in summer. Up to 12 beers are on offer plus cider. Live music plays some weekends, in summer outside the pub. Busy on football match days. Close to the Nene Valley Railway. ❀🕪♣●P🖳😺🗢

Coalheavers Arms
5 Park Street, Fletton, PE2 9BH
✪ 12-2 (not Mon-Wed), 5-11; 12-11 Fri & Sat; 12-10.30 Sun
☎ (01733) 565664 🌐 individualpubs.co.uk/coalheavers
Milton Justinian, Sparta; 4 changing beers Ⓗ
This friendly one-roomed back-street community pub dates back to the 1850s. Bombers Drop, the house beer, is one of the Milton beers on offer, alongside up to four guest ales. Cider, Belgian bottled beers and an English unpasteurised lager are also stocked. Home-made pies are available all week, and fresh rolls on Friday. Beer festivals are held in spring and autumn and the large garden is popular with families in the summer. A free quiz is hosted on Sunday nights. Busy on football match days. Q⏃❀♣●🕮🖳😺🗢

Dragon Ⓛ
Hodgson Centre, Hodgson Avenue, Werrington, PE4 5EG
✪ 4-11.30; 12-midnight Fri & Sat; 12-11 Sun
☎ (01733) 578088 🌐 thedragon-werrington.co.uk
6 changing beers Ⓗ
A community pub that opened in 1988 and home to four darts teams, three pool teams and a crib team. Live music or karaoke is hosted on Friday and Saturday nights, and a quiz on Sundays. League poker is played on Mondays, Wednesdays and Thursdays. There are six real ales and an annual beer festival. Children are welcome. A former CAMRA local branch Gold Award winner. ❀♿♣P🖳(1)

Draper's Arms Ⓛ
29-31 Cowgate, PE1 1LZ
✪ 8am-midnight (1am Fri & Sat) ☎ (01733) 847570
Greene King Abbot; Woodforde's Wherry; 8 changing beers (sourced locally) Ⓗ
A converted former draper's shop dating from circa 1899, one of two Wetherspoon pubs in the city. The spacious split interior includes more intimate wood-panelled areas. The beers, often from local microbreweries, are dispensed through 10 handpumps. Food is served all day and regular beer and wine festivals are held throughout the year. Quiz night is Wednesday. A regular top 10-listed real ale pub within the Wetherspoon chain. Close to bus and rail stations. Q⏃🕪♿🚆🚆🖳🗢

Hand & Heart 🏆 ★ Ⓛ
12 Highbury Street, PE1 3BE
✪ 3-11.30 (midnight Fri); 12-midnight Sat; 12-11.30 Sun
☎ (01733) 564653
5 changing beers (sourced regionally) Ⓗ
This 1930s back-street pub features in CAMRA's National Inventory of Historic Pub Interiors for its unspoilt interior. There is a main bar to the front and a quiet room to the rear connected by a drinking corridor. Five handpumps often feature some hard-to-find real ales. The large garden has a bar and stage used for beer festivals and music events. Live music plays on the second Thursday of the month and a cheese club is held on the last Thursday. Local CAMRA Pub of the Year 2015. Q❀♣🖳(1)😺

Palmerston Arms 🄻

82 Oundle Road, PE2 9PA (on main A605 road S of city centre)

⏲ 3 (12 Fri & Sat)-midnight; 12-11 Sun ☎ (01733) 565865

🌐 palmerston-arms.co.uk

Batemans Black & White, XXXB 🄶; Castle Rock Harvest Pale; Oakham Citra 🄷/🄶; 10 changing beers 🄶

Popular 400-year-old listed stone-built locals' pub. Owned by Batemans, three of its beers are rotated alongside nine or more changing ales, including some from Oakham. Traditional cider, perries and an extensive range of malt whiskies are also available. Most beers are served straight from the cellar which can be seen through a large glass window. Rolls and a variety of snacks tempt customers. Live music features most weekends and occasional psychology nights. Busy on football match days. ❀♣🍎🚌(1,24)🐾📶

Ploughman 🄻

1 Staniland Way, Werrington, PE4 6NA

⏲ 2-11; 12-midnight Fri & Sat; 12-11 Sun ☎ (01733) 327696

🌐 theploughman-werrington.co.uk

10 changing beers 🄷

This rejuvenated two-roomed community pub has been brought to the forefront of the city's real ale outlets by the enthusiastic licensee. Ten handpumps serve beers from breweries both local and from afar. An annual beer festival is held early in July. Many activities are hosted including charity events and live music at weekends. Part of the pub was converted into community tea rooms, which open at 10am on some days. Local CAMRA branch Pub of the Year in 2014. ❀♣P🚌(1,22)

Rampton

Black Horse

6 High Street, CB24 8QE

⏲ closed Mon; 6-11; 12-4 Sun ☎ (01954) 251867

Changing beers 🄷

Former Greene King pub that has been a free house for some time. At least one of the beers is likely to be a local ale, and all are guaranteed to be interesting. Beers can be served in third-pint glasses if you are not sure what to try. The interior comprises two bars separated by an archway. Both are smart and comfortable, with the left side mainly for diners. There is a large garden to the rear and car parking either side. 🐴❀◗♿♣P🐾

Ramsey

Jolly Sailor 🄻

43 Great Whyte, PE26 1HH

⏲ 11-11 ☎ (01487) 813388 🌐 jollysailorramsey.co.uk

Greene King Abbot; St Austell Tribute; Sharp's Doom Bar; 2 changing beers 🄷

This Grade II-listed building has been a pub for over 400 years. The three linked rooms feature wooden beams which date from various periods as the pub has been extended over the years. On the walls are pictures and artefacts depicting Ramsey history. A friendly and welcoming venue which attracts a varied clientele of all ages, it hosts occasional charity nights plus acoustic music sessions. Guest beers are available at the weekend. Good-value home-cooked food is served.

Q❀◐◗♿♣P🚌(31)📶

St Ives

Royal Oak 🄻

13 Crown Street, PE27 5EB

⏲ 11-11 (2am Fri & Sat); 12-midnight Sun ☎ (01480) 462586

Oakham Inferno; Sharp's Doom Bar; Wychwood Hobgoblin; 3 changing beers 🄷

Busy town-centre pub, one of a number of historic listed inns in the town, whose most famous inhabitant was Oliver Cromwell. Despite the date 1502 over the door, most of the building is 18th century. The room layout and character were happily preserved in a sensitive renovation in the 1990s. A changing choice of three guest beers, several ciders and perries and a range of whiskies keep the customers happy. Card nights and live music are hosted. 🐴♿♣🍎🚌🐾📶

St Neots

Hog & Partridge

25 Russell Street, PE19 1BA

⏲ closed Mon; 6.30-11 Tue; closed Wed; 6-12.30am Thu; 4-12.30am Fri; 12-12.30am Sat; 1-7 Sun ☎ 07951 785678

🌐 hogandpartridge.co.uk

Batemans Black & White 🄷; 4 changing beers 🄷/🄶

A small, traditional back-street pub with the comfortable feel of a lounge bar. Up to five guest beers are offered, usually including two from Batemans and the rest focusing on local microbreweries. Also available are two real ciders, Trappist beers on tap and a good range of UK and foreign bottled beers and ciders. Tapas are served Thursday-Saturday evenings.

Q🐴❀◗♣🍎P🚆🚌(X5)🐾📶

Olde Sun

11 Huntingdon Street, PE19 1BL

⏲ 12-11 ☎ (01480) 216863 🌐 yeoldesun.moonfruit.com

Woodforde's Wherry; 5 changing beers (often Adnams, Elgood's, Woodforde's) 🄷

Low-beamed and cosy traditional town-centre pub with two large inglenook fireplaces, three bar areas, a dining area and a secluded patio. The jukebox is zoned allowing quiet areas for conversation. Shove-ha'penny and bar billiards are played. Five constantly changing guest beers come from various regional breweries including Adnams, Elgood's, Marston's, Thwaites and Woodforde's. A mild and other dark beers are usually among the range. Good home-cooked food includes a menu of traditional pub fare and blackboard specials.

❀◐◗♣🍎🚌(X5)🐾

Pig 'n' Falcon 🄻

9 New Street, PE19 1AE (behind Barretts department store)

⏲ 11-midnight (2.30am Fri & Sat) ☎ 07951 785678

🌐 pignfalcon.co.uk

Batemans Black & White, Gold; Greene King IPA 🄷, Abbot 🄶; Potbelly Best 🄷; 5 changing beers 🄶

Busy town-centre free house with up to eight real ales and four real ciders, focusing on microbreweries and unusual beers including milds, porters and stouts. It also has a good range of bottled ciders and UK and foreign bottled beers including Trappist ales. Four beer festivals are held each year. Live blues and rock nights are hosted on Wednesday, Friday, Saturday and Sunday. Outside is a large and imaginative covered and heated beer garden. 🐴❀♣🍎🚆🚌(X5)🐾📶

Saxon Street

Reindeer

62 The Street, CB8 9RS

5-11 Fri & Sat only winter; 5-11 Mon & Fri; 2-11 Sat; 2-6 Sun summer ☎ (01638) 731138

5 changing beers (often Pitfield) H/G

Brick and flint-built former Tolly pub reopened in 2013 by the current licensee, who was the founder of Pitfield Brewery, and whose beers appear regularly on the bar. A large selection of bottled beers is also available. The single room has a large and diverse collection of pub memorabilia and breweriana, ranging from cigarette cards to pub signs, all of which are available to buy. Note that opening hours are limited. Q❀♿P

Stapleford

Three Horseshoes

2 Church Street, CB22 5DS

12-2.30, 5-11; 12-midnight Fri & Sat; 12-10.30 Sun ☎ (01223) 503402

Woodforde's Wherry; 6 changing beers H

Extensively altered and refurbished, the pub has reverted to its former name. The interior has three areas: the main bar with pool table, a small games room to the left and a large room to the right with access to the garden. The new management also run the Cambridge Blue in Cambridge, and follow a similar formula here. There are eight handpumps and a selection of bottled beers, with an emphasis on Belgian brews. Occasional beer festivals are hosted. Local CAMRA branch's Most Improved (Rural) Pub in 2014.
❀♿≠(Shelford)♣P🚌(Citi7)

Stretham

Lazy Otter

Cambridge Road, CB6 3RU

8am (9am Sat)-11; 9am-9 Sun ☎ (01353) 649780
lazy-otter.co.uk

5 changing beers (sourced locally; often Milton) H

Spacious free house situated on the banks of the River Great Ouse with a large bar area and extensive restaurant serving locally sourced food. Up to five real ales are usually sold, including a house beer. There are plenty of outside tables and a children's play area. A beer festival is held annually and there are regular themed food events. Conveniently accessed by riverside footpath for walkers and cyclists, and there are moorings available if visiting by boat.
❀P

Tilbrook

White Horse L

High Street, PE28 0JP

12 (5.30 Mon)-11 ☎ (01480) 860764
whitehorsetilbrook.com

Wells Eagle IPA, Bombardier; Young's Bitter; 1 changing beer (sourced nationally) H

Two-roomed village pub partly dating back to 1735 and surrounded by large gardens and open fields. The public bar, furnished with sofas and bar stools, provides darts and hood skittles, and there is a large lounge, dining area and bright conservatory with further seating. Locally sourced food includes the popular Sunday lunches. The garden has swings and slides for children and a petting zoo featuring ducks, chickens, sheep, goats and a goose. Look for the artistic posters in the ladies' and gents'.
❀Λ♣P🚌(150)

West Wratting

Chestnut Tree

1 Mill Road, CB21 5LT

12-3, 5.30-11.30; 12-midnight Fri & Sat; 12-10.30 Sun ☎ (01223) 290384 chestnuttreepub.co.uk

Greene King IPA; 3 changing beers H

Welcoming two-bar locals' pub with ample car parking and an attractive rear garden. The public bar, with dark wood furniture and red upholstery, has an extension with a pool table. The saloon bar is used more for dining. The pub hosts darts and pool teams and also has a small lending library. Acquired by the present owners from Greene King in 2012, it is now free of tie – the guest beers are mainly from microbreweries, including local suppliers. A changing real cider is also available. Local CAMRA branch Pub of the Year 2014.
Q❀♣P🚌(19)

Whittlesey

Boat Inn L

2 Ramsey Road, PE7 1DR

4 (11 Fri-Sun)-midnight ☎ (01733) 202488
quinnboatinn.wordpress.com

Elgood's Cambridge Bitter, Golden Newt; 1 changing beer G

This 11th-century inn is mentioned in the Domesday Book. It attracts locals, anglers and visitors, who all receive a warm welcome. The lounge has an unusual boat-shaped bar and hosts a whisky club on the second Friday of the month. Up to five traditional ciders and perries supplement the real ales, mainly served direct from the cask. Open mic music nights are occasional Tuesdays and Fridays. Outside is a pétanque terrain. Good-value accommodation is offered. Closing times can vary as the pub has a 24-hour licence.
❀♿♣P🚌(31,33)

Hubs Place

No.1, 12 Market Place, PE7 1AB

12-midnight (1am Fri & Sat) ☎ (01733) 204199
hubs-place.co.uk

Fuller's London Pride; 1 changing beer H

Pleasant and comfortable bar opened by a lottery winner in 2010. Formerly solicitors' offices, it has three rooms refurbished in a cream and red colour scheme, plus a large patio to the rear. The guest ale is usually from Woodforde's and other real ales may be available on special occasions such as the Whittlesea Straw Bear Festival. Closed all day Monday and Tuesday and Wednesday afternoons in winter. ❀♿♣🚌

Letter B L

53-57 Church Street, PE7 1DE

5-11; 3.30-midnight Fri; 12-midnight Sat; 12-11 Sun ☎ (01733) 206975 theletterbpublichouse.co.uk

Tydd Steam Barn Ale; 3 changing beers H

A friendly and welcoming community pub dating back more than 200 years. It was called the Bee for a while but has now reverted to the Letter B – said to be so named because there were so many pubs in Whittlesey they ran out of names. Beer festivals take place in January (Straw Bear weekend) and in the spring. Up to 10 ciders and perries are available. Quiz nights are held on alternate Tuesdays and Sundays, and popular charity events are hosted. A former winner of CAMRA Gold Awards and local branch and county Pub of the Year. Q❀🛏♣🍎🚌🐾📶

Willingham

Bank Micropub

High Street, CB24 5ES

closed Mon; 6-10 Tue; 5.30-11 (10 Wed); closed Sun

☎ (01954) 260331 thebankmicropub.co.uk

6 changing beers Ⓖ

Part of the growing micropub movement, the Bank was converted from a former village bank branch. Although not a full-sized pub, 'micro' is perhaps a misnomer here. The space has been well used, with an L-shaped drinking area around a shortish bar that, together with some of the furniture, was rescued from a closed pub and renovated. Photographs of local interest adorn the walls. Between three and six real ales are usually available, with local beers featuring strongly. Q🍎🚌(Citi5)

Duke of Wellington

55 Church Street, CB24 5HS

12-3, 5-11 (11.30 Thu & Fri); 12-11.30 Sat; 12-10.30 Sun

☎ (01954) 261622 dukeofwellington-willingham.co.uk

Greene King XX Mild Ⓖ, IPA; 3 changing beers Ⓗ

This attractive, low-ceilinged village local makes the most of its exposed beams and three open fires to create a relaxed, rustic feel. The main bar has big scrubbed tables, bare-boarded floors and candelabras, plus a dining area set aside. The small public bar sports an unusual colour scheme. Excellent home-cooked food majors on pies and salads. Unusually, most real ales are dispensed either by handpump or directly from the cask at the customer's request – this is a rare outlet for the delicious Greene King Mild. Quiz night is Sunday. ❀◐◑♣P🚌(Citi5)

Wisbech

Red Lion Ⓛ

32 North Brink, PE13 1JR

11.30-3, 6 (5 Fri)-11; 11.30-3, 7-midnight Sat; 12-11 Sun

☎ (01945) 582022

Elgood's Black Dog, Cambridge Bitter; 2 changing beers Ⓗ

The Red Lion has a bar to the front and a dining room to the rear. The main access is via a side passage which links the North Brink Road to the rear car park and patio area. It is a friendly and comfortable pub which caters for drinkers and diners equally well. Up to four ales are served via handpump in the bar, usually coming from the pub's owners, Elgood's. There is home-cooked food throughout the week, with the Friday-evening special being fish and chips. Q❀◐◑♿♣P🚌(X1)📶

Wistow

Three Horseshoes

Mill Road, PE28 2QQ

6-10 Mon; 12-3, 6-11; 12-10 Sat; 12-4 Sun

☎ (01487) 822270

Adnams Southwold Bitter, Ghost Ship Ⓗ

Multi-roomed brick and thatch 18th-century inn opposite the village church. Though always a pub, the building has evolved over time – part was once a blacksmith's and it provided accommodation for workers employed in church rebuilding work in the 18th century. Traditional pub food is available daily. A quiz is held once a month. Families are welcome in both bars and there is a covered smoking area outside. ❀◐◑♿⛺♣P🚌(30)📶

Queen's Head, Newton (Photo: Katie Button)

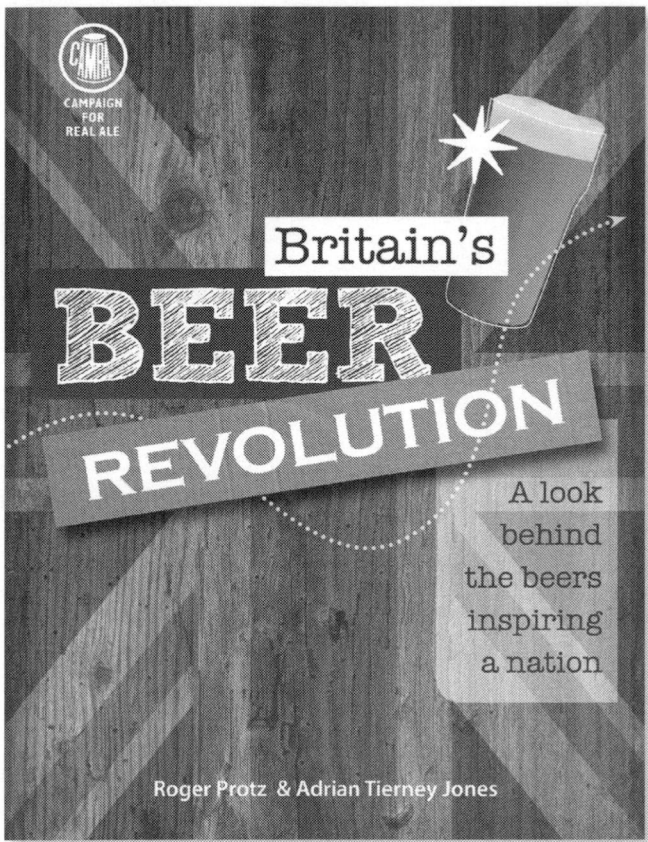

CHESHIRE

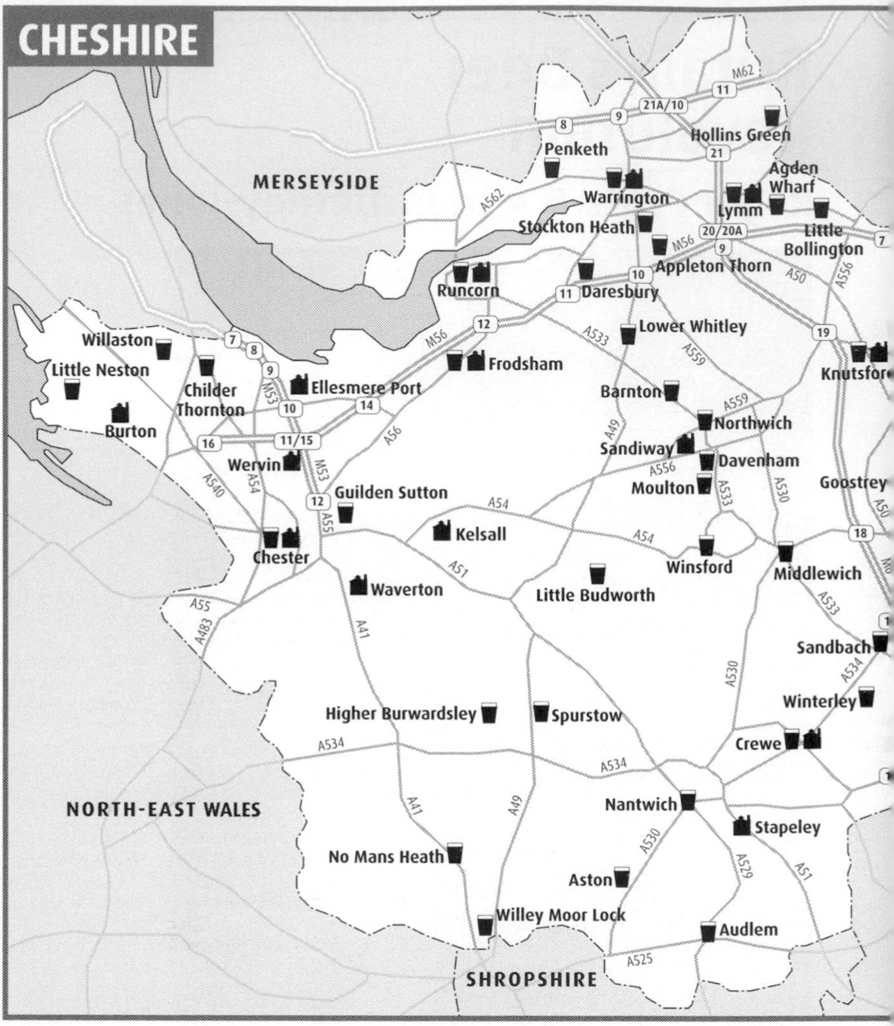

Agden Wharf

Barn Owl 𝕃

Warrington Lane, WA13 0SW (on Bridgewater Canal, off A56)

12-11 ☎ (01925) 752020 thebarnowlinn.co.uk

Thwaites Original, Wainwright, Lancaster Bomber; 4 changing beers (sourced regionally) Ⓗ

Situated alongside the Bridgewater Canal, the Barn Owl is popular with canal trippers as well as locals, and customers enjoy views across the Cheshire countryside. Three regular beers are complemented by up to four guest ales, sourced mainly from independent breweries. Renowned for its food as well as its ale, freshly cooked meals are made with mainly local produce. P

Alsager

Lodge 𝕃

88 Crewe Road, ST7 2JA (at crossroads where Crewe Rd meets Station Rd)

4-11 (midnight Fri); 2-midnight Sat; 2-11 Sun

☎ (01270) 873669

8 changing beers (sourced regionally) Ⓗ

Large, two-roomed pub with eight ever-changing guest ales, sourced equally from regional breweries and local microbreweries. It also has occasional beers from its own brewery, a two-and-a-half-barrel plant called Goodall's, located on site. The large beer garden at the back can be busy in summer. The pub is well served by local transport and there is a public car park at the rear.

QP(20)

Appleton Thorn

Appleton Thorn Village Hall

Stretton Road, WA4 4RT

closed Mon-Wed; 7.30-11.30; 1-4, 7.30-10.30 Sun

☎ (01925) 261187 appletonthornvillagehall.co.uk

7 changing beers (sourced nationally) Ⓗ

This multi award-winning club, a previous winner of CAMRA National Club of the Year, has a large function room, with pool room off, and a smaller lounge. A central bar serves both rooms, with up to seven ever-changing beers and several ciders and perries. An annual beer festival is held in October,

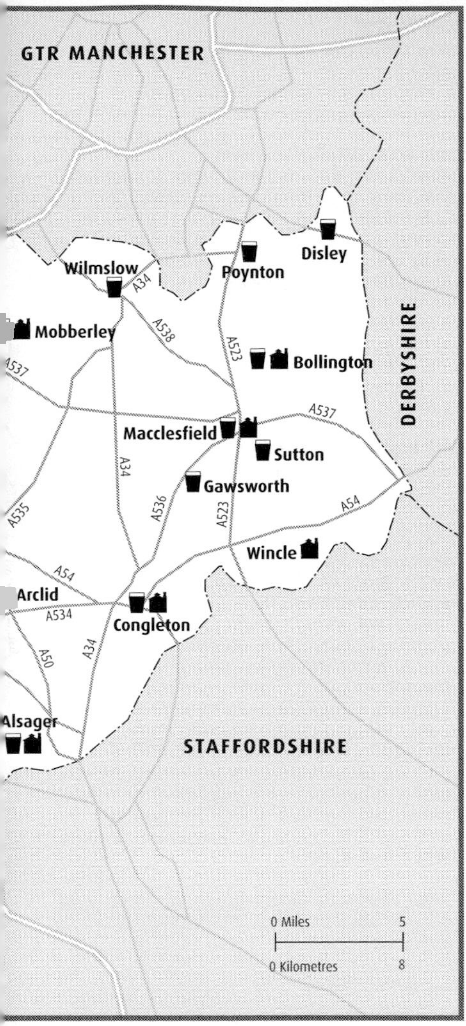

as well as regular live music and quizzes. Light lunches are served Sundays 1-3pm only.
Q P (8E)

Aston

Bhurtpore

Wrenbury Road, CW5 8DQ

12-2.30, 6.30-11.30; 12-midnight Fri & Sat; 12-11 Sun
(01270) 780917 bhurtpore.co.uk

11 changing beers (sourced regionally)

Featuring in the Guide for a 23rd consecutive year, this is a pub worth searching out. It offers a fabulous range of ales plus two ciders, frequently from local producers. Live acoustic music features every third Tuesday and sometimes on a Sunday evening. There are four distinct drinking areas plus an excellent restaurant specialising in curries.
Q P (72)

Audlem

Lord Combermere

The Square, CW3 0AQ

12-midnight (01270) 812277
thelordcombermere.co.uk

Greene King IPA; Timothy Taylor Landlord; Wells Bombardier; 3 changing beers (sourced regionally; often Salopian, Tatton, Wincle)

This modern, airy, open-plan pub, full of natural light, is a friendly hub in the centre of the town. There are two rooms available for dining at one end, a TV area at the other, and an attractive bar in between. The food menu offers a full gluten-free range of dishes. Tuesday is quiz night, live music plays on Thursday and/or Sunday.
P (73)

Barnton

Barnton Cricket Club

Broomsedge, Townfield Lane, CW8 4QL (200yds from A533 via Stoneheyes Lane)

6.30-11.30 (11 Wed; 12.30am Thu; midnight Fri); 4-midnight Sat; 12-11 Sun (01606) 77702
barntoncc.co.uk

Hancock's HB; M&B Brew XI; 3 changing beers (sourced nationally; often Brimstage, Scarborough, Tatton)

CAMRA National Club of the Year in 2014, this popular and multi award-winning club provides many real ales sourced from microbreweries from all over the country. CAMRA members are welcome. A beer festival is held every November. Food is available Wednesday to Saturday evenings, plus Sunday lunchtime. P (4,46)

Bollington

Poachers Inn

95 Ingersley Road, SK10 5RE

12-2 (not Mon), 5.30-11; 12-11 Sun (01625) 572086
thepoachers.org

Storm Beauforts Ale; Weetwood Old Dog Bitter; 3 changing beers (sourced regionally)

Friendly and welcoming family-run community free house near the Gritstone Trail with two regular beers and three rotating guests. Internally divided into comfortable seating and dining areas, it has a real coal fire in winter and a suntrap rear garden for the summer months. The licensee enthusiastically supports local breweries, including nearby Happy Valley. Real cider is also on handpump, with world beers in bottles. Well-regarded, good-value, home-prepared food is sourced locally. Events include Wednesday pie night and a monthly quiz for local charities. P (10,392)

Vale Inn

29-31 Adlington Road, SK10 5JT

12-2.30, 5-11; 12-11 Fri & Sat; 12-10.30 Sun
(01625) 575147 valeinn.co.uk

6 changing beers (sourced locally)

Terraced, family-run free house dating from the 1890s. The brewery tap for Bollington Brewing Company, it features five to six of its beers, an occasional guest and two real ciders/perries. Excellent home-cooked food is available. The pub is popular with the local community, walkers and bikers using the nearby canal and Middlewood Way footpath. The beer garden overlooking the cricket ground is a perfect place to enjoy a pint while listening to the sound of leather on willow.
P (10,392)

Chester

Brewery Tap L

52-54 Lower Bridge Street, CH1 1RU
⏲ 12-11 (10.30 Sun) ☎ (01244) 340999 🌐 the-tap.co.uk
7 changing beers (sourced nationally) H
Occupying a Jacobean great hall, the building is a former winner of CAMRA's Heritage Conservation and Conversion to Pub Use award. Food is inventive, freshly prepared and locally sourced. Seven ales are available, with the brewery's own Spitting Feathers beers complemented by a range of guests including many from other local microbreweries. Q◑♣●🚌🐾📶

Cellar 🏆

19-21 City Road, CH1 3AE
⏲ 4-1am (2.30am Fri); 12-2.30am Sat; 12-midnight Sun
☎ (01244) 318950 🌐 thecellarchester.co.uk
5 changing beers (sourced nationally; often Marble, Oakham) H
Friendly, modern bar which is actually at street level despite the name. Five changing, always interesting, nationally sourced beers are served in top condition by enthusiastic, knowledgeable staff. Live music and TV sport feature regularly, particularly at weekends. Locally sourced pies and Scotch eggs are available, with free bacon sandwiches on Sundays. A winner of several recent CAMRA branch awards including Pub of the Year. Dogs are welcome except Friday and Saturday nights when the bar can be busy. ⇌●🚌🐾📶

Cross Keys

2 Duke Street, CH1 1RP
⏲ closed Mon; 12-11 (10.30 Sun) ☎ (01244) 344460
🌐 crosskeyschester.co.uk
Joule's Blonde, Pale Ale, Slumbering Monk; 2 changing beers (sourced nationally; often Joule's, Oakham, Thornbridge) H
Attractive Victorian red-brick building, featuring a stylish interior with etched mirrors, oak floors, wood panelling and a log fire. Specially commissioned stained-glass windows depict other hostelries in the Joule's estate. A large upstairs room (the Slaughtered Lamb) is available for functions. A small beer terrace in front of the building catches the afternoon sun. One guest ale complements the one seasonal and three permanent beers. Food is available Wednesday to Sunday. Live Irish music nights are held on the second and fourth Wednesdays of the month.
🐎❀◑●🚌📶

Lodge Bar

8-10 Hoole Road, Hoole, CH2 3NH
⏲ 11-11 (midnight Fri & Sat) ☎ (01244) 324971
🌐 lodgebar.co.uk
3 changing beers (sourced nationally; often Abbeydale, Rudgate, Salopian) H
Modern lounge-style bar, part of the Bawn Lodge Hotel, situated half a mile from Chester railway station in the suburb of Hoole. The bar at the entrance leads to intimate alcove seating and a large side lounge. Three handpumps serve a varied and interesting range of ales at competitive prices. Good-value food is available all day. The large beer garden is popular in the summer. One of very few pubs where traditional bagatelle is played.
🐎❀🛏◑♿⇌♣P🚌(9,21,X30)📶

Mill Hotel L

Milton Street, CH1 3NF (canalside, east of inner ring road)
⏲ 10-midnight ☎ (01244) 350035 🌐 millhotel.com
Copper Dragon Golden Pippin; Weetwood Best Bitter; house beer (by Coach House); changing beers (often Castle Rock, Salopian, Titanic) H
Former corn mill located next to the Shropshire Union Canal, close to the railway station. Three regular beers plus six guest beers are available including a mild. Ciders are available on the bar and by request from the cellar. A full range of lunchtime and evening meals is served in the bar, with more formal dining in the restaurant. Sport fans are well catered for with three large screens, and there is live jazz music on Monday nights. Canal cruises are available every day on the hotel's own restaurant cruiser. 🐎🛏◑♿⇌●P🚌📶

Old Harkers Arms L

1 Russell Street, CH3 5AL (down steps off City Rd to canal towpath)
⏲ 11.30 (12 Sun)-11 ☎ (01244) 344525
🌐 harkersarms-chester.co.uk
Fuller's London Pride; Weetwood Cheshire Cat; house beer (by Phoenix); 6 changing beers (sourced nationally; often Derby, Hawkshead) H
Upmarket pub converted from the ground floor of a former Victorian canalside warehouse. Timber flooring, traditional wooden furniture and cast iron pillars provide an insight to its former use. Blackboards list real ales with tasting notes – usually nine are available including a selection of bitters, stouts, milds or porters. Many are from local breweries. Ciders and perries are listed separately and served from the cellar. Food is served all day (booking advised for busy weekend periods). Outside, there is a seating area alongside the canal.
Q❀◑♿⇌♣●🚌🐾📶

REAL ALE BREWERIES

4Ts Runcorn
Beartown Congleton
Beer Refinery Wervin (NEW)
Blakemere Sandiway
Blueball Frodsham
Bollington Bollington
Borough Arms Crewe (brewing suspended)
Britman Burton
Cheshire Brew Brothers Ellesmere Port
Cheshire Brewhouse Congleton
Coach House Warrington
Frodsham Frodsham
Front Row Congleton
Goodall's Alsager
Happy Valley Bollington
Lymm Lymm
Merlin Arclid
Mobberley Mobberley
Norton Runcorn
Offbeat Crewe
Pied Bull Chester
Redball Chester
RedWillow Macclesfield
Spitting Feathers Waverton
Storm Macclesfield
Tatton Knutsford
Tipsy Angel Warrington
Weetwood Kelsall
Wincle Wincle
Woodlands Stapeley

Olde Cottage Inn

34-36 Brook Street, CH1 3DZ
4-11 (midnight Fri); 2-midnight Sat ☎ (01244) 324065
oldecottagechester.co.uk
Timothy Taylor Boltmaker; 3 changing beers (sourced nationally)
Welcoming traditional community hostelry on a popular eating and drinking street between the city centre and railway station. Two long parallel rooms are served by a central bar. The pub boasts a bagatelle table, a game rarely seen outside Chester, and many sport trophies are on display. There is a real fire in colder weather. The beers are competitively priced with various loyalty and discount schemes offered. Wednesday is quiz night.

Pied Bull

57 Northgate Street, CH1 2HQ
10-11 (midnight Fri & Sat) ☎ (01244) 325829
piedbull.co.uk
Adnams Broadside; house beer (by Pied Bull); 2 changing beers (sourced nationally; often Blackjack, Ossett, Waen)
Home to the only microbrewery inside the city walls, this historic pub attracts a lively mix of locals and visitors. Up to three of the six cask ales on offer come from the range of 12 regular house brews. The knowledgeable staff organise occasional beer festivals, often in association with other northern breweries. Thursday sees a competitive quiz. High-quality pub food, made with locally sourced ingredients, is available all day. A loyalty discount is available, and dogs are allowed in the area by the entrance.

Piper

Pipers Lane, Hoole, CH2 3LS (adjacent to A41)
12-11 (midnight Fri & Sat) ☎ (01244) 322093
piperpub.co.uk
Sharp's Doom Bar; 3 changing beers (sourced nationally; often Liverpool Organic, Peerless)
Located on the outskirts of Hoole, this is a modern pub with an open-plan interior discernibly split between drinkers and diners. There are three rotating guest beers, usually from local microbreweries. Sports fans are well catered for with large-screen TVs. Meals are served all day until 9.30pm (7.30pm Sun). A pub quiz is held on Sunday and a poker evening on Thursday. A patio at the front provides covered outdoor seating. Within easy reach of buses from the city centre.
P

Telford's Warehouse

Canal Basin, Tower Wharf, CH1 4EZ (just off city walls)
12-12.30am (11 Mon & Tue); 12-2am Fri & Sat
☎ (01244) 390090 telfordswarehousechester.com
Salopian Oracle; Thwaites Original; Weetwood Cheshire Cat; 3 changing beers (sourced nationally; often Derby, Tatton, Three Tuns)
Impressive converted Georgian warehouse with original features, industrial artefacts, a glass frontage and a popular seating area overlooking the canal basin. Three regular ales are available plus a varied range of guests, usually seasonal and often local. A specialised live music venue, admission charges may apply. It hosts regular salsa/Latin dance classes and open mic sessions. A beer festival is held every October. Quality food is available and families are welcome upstairs.
P (1A)

Childer Thornton

White Lion

New Road, CH66 5PU (off A41 between Great Sutton and Hooton)
11.30-11.30 (11 Sun) ☎ (0151) 339 3402
whitelionchilderthornton.co.uk
Thwaites Original, Wainwright, Lancaster Bomber; 2 changing beers
No stranger to the Guide, this splendidly convivial local lies tucked away from nearby main roads and makes for a wonderful oasis from life's stresses and strains. Small and cosy throughout, it features the tiniest of snugs, a bar warmed by a logburner, a quieter adjoining side room and a tasteful, unobtrusive dining area. Outside, there are a front patio and tidy, lawned rear garden for warmer days. Although a Thwaites tied house, guest ales do appear. P (1,2)

Congleton

Barley Hops

2 Swan Bank, CW12 1AH
closed Mon; 12-8 (10 Fri); 10-8 Sat; 12-6 Sun
☎ (01260) 270164 barleyhops.co.uk
3 changing beers (sourced locally)
A recent addition to Congleton's growing beer scene, this former shop now doubles as a well-stocked bottled beer specialist and single-room micropub with three handpumps serving mainly local beers. It also offers locally produced bottled ciders and some wines. A free pint or bottle of beer is given for every 10 purchased. Occasional beer tasting sessions offer a further excuse to visit.
Q (38,42)

Queen's Head Hotel

Park Lane, CW12 3DE
12-midnight (1am Fri & Sat) ☎ (01260) 272546
queensheadhotel.org.uk
Black Sheep Best Bitter; Draught Bass; Greene King Abbot; Joule's Pale Ale; 4 changing beers (sourced regionally)
Improvements continue with a new covered smoking area outside and upgrades to the B&B accommodation. This community pub supports pool and darts teams, a girls' football team and boules in summer. A pub quiz and poker night feature weekly. The creative kitchen offers a good range of food at sensible prices.
P (99)

Young Pretender

30-34 Lawton Street, CW12 1RS
12-midnight (1am Thu-Sat) ☎ (01260) 273277
youngpretenderbeerparlour.co.uk
5 changing beers (sourced locally)
Cheshire CAMRA Pub of the Year 2014, this pub goes from strength to strength. Its ever-changing range of five cask beers, complemented by an array of keg and bottled beers, is only part of its appeal. At the heart of the community, it plays host to a wide variety of local groups as well as offering regular live music, films and quizzes.
P

Crewe

Borough Arms

33 Earle Street, CW1 2BG (on Earle St railway bridge, entrance up steps in adjoining Thomas St)
5 (12 Fri & Sat)-11; 12-10.30 Sun ☎ None

9 changing beers (sourced nationally; often Dark Star, Fyne Ales, Oakham)
This friendly town-centre pub has been supplying Crewe with an excellent range of quality ales and draught Belgian beers for some years now. The upstairs is a comfortable split-level arrangement, and there is a large room downstairs leading out to the beer garden. Downstairs is also home to the Borough Arms Brewery, which operates infrequently. Nine handpumps feature constantly changing real ales, mainly light in style but often including one or two dark beers. P

Gaffers Row

48 Victoria Street, CW1 2JE (opp Les's Fish Bar)
8am-11 (midnight Thu; 1am Fri & Sat) (01270) 503820
Greene King Abbot; Ruddles Best Bitter; 6 changing beers (sourced nationally)
A busy town-centre establishment, this Wetherspoon pub opened in 2003 in a former furniture showroom. The interior is mainly open plan with a large bar and family area. Two TV screens show news channels with subtitles throughout the day. It has 10 handpumps with a good range of six rotating guest ales from local and national breweries.

Hops

Prince Albert Street, CW1 2DF (opp Lifestyle Centre)
11 (5 Mon)-11; 12-11 Sun (01270) 211100
House beer (by Townhouse); 5 changing beers (sourced regionally)
Welcoming family-run free house where six handpumps dispense a wide range of real ales, including a stout or porter. Up to six real ciders and perries are also available. A downstairs wall displays images of old Crewe while another extols the delights of the extensive Belgian bottled beers available. There is a large room upstairs and a paved patio out front, popular on sunny summer days. A regular meeting place for the South Cheshire Motorcycle Club. Q

Daresbury

Ring O' Bells

Chester Road, WA4 4AJ
11-11; 12-10.30 Sun (01925) 740256
ringobells-daresbury.co.uk
Butcombe Adam Henson's Rare Breed; Robinsons Unicorn; 1 changing beer (sourced locally)
A welcome return to the Guide for this multi-roomed pub, which once served as the local parish courtroom. Now very much a food-oriented establishment, it has four handpumps, one serving a local beer. Opposite the pub is Daresbury parish church where Charles Dodgson – better known as Lewis Carroll – was the son of the curate. Memorabilia can be seen in the pub.
P (X30)

Davenham

Davenham Cricket Club

Butchers' Stile, Hartford Road, CW9 8JG
4.30-7.30 (11 Wed; 8.30 Fri); 5.30-11 Sat; 1.30-7.30 Sun
(01606) 48922 davenhamcc.co.uk
3 changing beers (sourced locally; often Beartown, Brimstage, Mobberley)
This is a community cricket club located in an idyllic country setting in a small village. The recently redeveloped clubhouse provides enhanced facilities including an extension to the lounge area. Three handpumps serve real ale from locally sourced breweries. The club stages an annual beer festival each spring. During the cricket season opening hours are extended. The local golf society and football teams are catered for. Families and CAMRA members all welcome. P

Disley

White Lion

135 Buxton Road, SK12 2HA
12 (6.30 Mon)-11; 12-12.30am Fri & Sat
(01663) 762800
8 changing beers
Originally the red house that gave the name to the adjacent side road, this pub is now painted white. Eight ever-changing real ales are on offer, many from micros and all selected from SIBA member breweries. The contemporary interior is open plan apart from a separate dog room. A comprehensive menu is served until 9pm (no food Mon). Situated on the A6 towards the eastern end of the village, a short walk from Peak Forest Canal (bridge 26).
P (199)

Frodsham

Cholmondeley Arms

12 Church Street, WA6 7EB
12-11 (2am Fri & Sat); 12-1am Sun (01928) 733052
3 changing beers (often Jennings, Marston's, Wychwood)
Cosy, friendly Marston's group pub now under new management and recently refurbished. The landlord has renewed the focus on real ale with over 130 different beers sold during his first 21 months' stewardship. Three seasonal beer festivals are held annually and include many beers from outside Marston's listings. Home-cooked lunches are prepared by the landlord's wife – the steak and stout pie is a local favourite.

Helter Skelter

31 Church Street, WA6 6PN
11-11.30 (midnight Fri & Sat); 12-11 Sun
(01928) 733361 helterskelter-frodsham.co.uk
Weetwood Best Bitter; 7 changing beers (sourced nationally; often Ossett, Phoenix, Purple Moose)
Regular local CAMRA branch award-winner and Pub of the Year 2014, this single-roomed bar offers eight handpumps serving a budget-priced local bitter and an ever-changing beer range sourced mainly from local and national micros. A guest cider and a selection of imported bottled beers are also available. Excellent home-cooked food is served in the bar or upstairs restaurant. An informal folk band plays upstairs on Sunday evenings.

Gawsworth

Harrington Arms ★

Church Lane, SK11 9RR (off A536)
12-3, 5-11.30 (midnight Fri); 12-11.30 Sat; 12-11 Sun
(01260) 223325
Robinsons Dizzy Blonde, Unicorn; 2 changing beers (sourced locally)
Situated in open countryside, close to the Tudor manor house Gawsworth Hall, this superb Grade II-listed former farmhouse has lost none of its character, securing a place on CAMRA's National

Inventory of Historic Pub Interiors. Several small rooms with simple wooden tables and chairs, warmed by open fires in winter, provide a comfortable retreat. There is a patio and garden to escape to in the summer. Home-cooked food is served lunchtimes and evenings. A former CAMRA branch Pub of the Year. Q🐴❀◑♿♣🚌(38)🐾📶

Goostrey

Crown

111 Main Road, CW4 8PE (E end of village)
⏲ 12-11.30 ☎ (01477) 532128 🌐 thecrowngoostrey.co.uk
Jennings Cumberland Ale; Weetwood Best Bitter, Cheshire Cat; 2 changing beers (sourced locally) Ⓗ
Refurbished by a small local pub company in 2012, the Crown combines a strong community presence with a reputation for good quality food. The pub retains its public bar, accessed from the main bar, with four other distinct areas, including a conservatory, in which to choose a seat. Two real fires add warmth in winter. Beers from Cheshire or Yorkshire usually feature among the guests.
Q🐴❀◑♿⇌P🚌(319)🐾📶

Guilden Sutton

Bird in Hand

Church Lane, CH3 7EW (off Station Lane)
⏲ 12-2, 5-11; 12-11 Fri & Sat; 12-10.30 Sun
☎ (01244) 301753
3 changing beers (sourced regionally; often Brimstage, Peerless, Purple Moose) Ⓗ
Situated along a secluded lane on the edge of the village, the pub is popular with walkers tackling the Longster Trail, and racks outside cater for cyclists using the nearby Millennium Greenway. Four handpumps usually serve three beers, with four at weekends. For warmer weather there are picnic tables at the front and a beer garden to the side. Closed Monday-Wednesday afternoons in winter. Q❀◑⛺P🚌(27)

Higher Burwardsley

Pheasant Inn Ⓛ

Barracks Lane, CH3 9PF
⏲ 11-11; 12-10.30 Sun ☎ (01829) 770434
🌐 thepheasantinn.co.uk
Weetwood Best Bitter, Eastgate Ale; 2 changing beers (sourced locally) Ⓗ
Charming 300-year-old inn nestled high up the Peckforton Hills with stunning views over the Cheshire plain to the Welsh hills. Popular with walkers on the Sandstone Trail and visitors to the nearby candle workshops, two Weetwood beers are usually on offer and two guest ales. Quality locally sourced food is served in the main bar and separate dining room. Accommodation is in 12 en-suite rooms. Q🐴❀🛏◑♿P🐾📶

Hollins Green

Black Swan

Manchester Road, WA3 6LA
⏲ 12-11 (11.30 Tue & Wed; midnight Thu; 12.30am Fri & Sat); 12-11.15 Sun ☎ (0161) 222 4444 🌐 theblackswan.co.uk
6 changing beers (sourced locally; often Boggart Hole Clough, Dunham Massey) Ⓗ
Old coaching inn much enlarged a few years ago adding accommodation and function rooms. A balance between food and drink is achieved with a quality menu complementing the cask ales that make this a haven for local drinkers. Very much the centre of the local community, it offers a wide range of occasionally quirky and often innovative events. The extensive garden has a duck pond, barbecue and play area. Quiz nights are Wednesday, Thursday and Sunday. A former local CAMRA branch Community Pub of the Year.
Q🐴❀🛏◑♿⛺♣P🚌(100)📶

Knutsford

Lord Eldon Ⓛ

27 Tatton Street, WA16 6AD
⏲ 11-11 (midnight Fri & Sat); 12-10.30 Sun
☎ (01565) 652261
Tetley Bitter; 2 changing beers (sourced nationally) Ⓗ
This 300-year-old Grade II-listed pub has an attractive exterior with a sundial and hanging baskets. Surprisingly spacious, it has a bar with a real fire and three further rooms. A popular local, the sociable atmosphere is evident when darts or dominoes are in progress. Live music plays twice a week and a quiz is held weekly. One guest ale is often a Cheshire LocAle while the Tetley is reduced in price before 7pm on weekdays.
Q🐴❀⇌♣🚌🐾📶

Little Bollington

Swan with Two Nicks 🏆 Ⓛ

Park Lane, WA14 4TJ (signposted off A56)
⏲ 12-11 (10.30 Sun) ☎ (0161) 928 2914
🌐 swanwithtwonicks.co.uk
2 changing beers (sourced locally) Ⓗ
Welcoming country pub on the fringes of the Dunham Massey National Trust property. The interior is rustic and comprises several rooms with a central bar. Local beers feature on the seven beer engines, two usually from Dunham Massey Brewery. The house beer, Swan with Two Nicks, is from Coach House. There is a varied food offering including gluten-free dishes available all day until 9pm (8pm Sun), served throughout the pub and restaurant. Handy for canal boaters. 🐴❀◑P🚌🐾

Little Budworth

Egerton Arms

Pinfold Lane, CW6 9BS
⏲ closed Mon; 12-11; 11-1am Fri & Sat ☎ (01829) 760424
🌐 egerton-arms.co.uk
Thwaites Original; 5 changing beers (sourced locally; often Big Hand, Brimstage, Dunham Massey) Ⓗ
Knowledgeable, enthusiastic and friendly staff contribute to a convivial atmosphere that makes drinking and dining such a pleasant experience at this unspoilt country pub, reopened in 2013 after a four-year closure. A range of continental lagers on draught is available plus a selection of bottled world beers. The pub holds regular live music sessions, themed events and beer festivals. Watch cricket from the beer garden or take a short stroll to nearby Budworth Common or Oulton Park Circuit.
🐴❀◑⛺♣🍎P🗑🐾📶

Little Neston

Harp

19 Quayside, CH64 0TB (turn left at bottom of Marshlands Rd, pub is 300yds on left overlooking marshes)

🕐 12-11 (10.30 Sun) ☎ (0151) 336 6980
Holt Bitter; Peerless Triple Blonde; Timothy Taylor Landlord; 2 changing beers (sourced regionally) Ⓗ
A former coal miners' inn near the site of Neston Colliery which closed in 1927. Converted from two cottages, it has a public bar with a real fire in winter and a basic lounge. In a glorious location on the new Deeside to Neston part of the national cycle network, the pub overlooks the Dee Marshes and North Wales, with a garden and a drinking area abutting the edge of the marshes. Q🐴✿P🐾

Lower Whitley

Chetwode Arms

Street Lane, WA4 4EN (just off A49)
🕐 5-11; 1-8 Sun ☎ (01925) 640044 🌐 chetwode-arms.co.uk
4 changing beers (sourced nationally; often Adnams, Sharp's) Ⓗ
Welcoming Grade II-listed former coaching inn, where locals gather in the cosy bar snug. Seasonal beers are sourced locally or regionally, with cider from a Shepton Mallet hog. There are some small, private rooms for dining, with a wide choice of fresh fish, British and exotic meats cooked at your table on hot rocks. Outside is a bowling green and covered beer garden. The pub is used for traction engine rallies and by local hunts. Winter opening times may be shorter. Q✿◐◑●P🐾📶

Lymm

Brewery Tap 𝕃

18 Bridgewater Street, WA13 0AB
🕐 12-11 (midnight Fri & Sat); 12-10.30 Sun
☎ (01925) 755451 🌐 lymmbrewing.co.uk
Lymm Bitter, Bridgewater Blonde; 5 changing beers (sourced locally) Ⓗ
A modern venue opened in 2013 in the red-brick former post office near the canal. The well-lit bar is complemented by a tastefully decorated front room with subdued lighting, comfy armchairs and a wood-fired stove. Five guest ales are often either from the microbrewery under the pub or nearby Dunham Massey. Two rotating real ciders are also available. No food is served but you can bring your own pies and sandwiches from the deli next door. 🐴✿♿♣●🚌(5,35)🐾📶

Macclesfield

Park Tavern 𝕃

158 Park Lane, SK11 6UB
🕐 4-11; 12-midnight Fri & Sat; 12-10.30 Sun
☎ (01625) 667846 🌐 park-tavern.co.uk
Bollington Long Hop, Best; 4 changing beers (sourced locally) Ⓗ
Just outside the town centre, this pub is a must on any Macclesfield visit. One of three owned by Bollington Brewing, it has a modern interior with separate rooms and drinking areas. It holds numerous events including quizzes and a monthly science discussion group, Sci Bar, and has its own cinema/function room upstairs. A roast dinner is served on the first Sunday of the month. 🐴✿⇄♣●🚌(2,3,38)🐾📶

RedWillow 𝕃

32A Park Green, SK11 7NA
🕐 closed Mon; 4-11 Tue & Wed (midnight Thu); 12-midnight Fri & Sat; 12-10.30 Sun ☎ (01625) 503253
🌐 redwillowbar.com
RedWillow Headless; 4 changing beers (sourced regionally) Ⓗ
Formerly a shop, this bar was opened in 2013 by the eponymous local brewery. The sensitive conversion has retained the original windows and parquet flooring which offer an interesting contrast to the copper styling of the bar servery and light fixtures. Five handpumps dispense RedWillow beers and a rotation of other national microbrewery beers. A further handpump offers a changing real cider. Pizzas and cheese/charcuterie boards are available until 9pm (7pm Fri and Sat). 🐴◐◑♿⇄●🚌🐾

Waters Green Tavern 𝕃

96 Waters Green, SK11 6LH
🕐 12-3, 5-11; 12-4, 7-11 Sat; 12-4, 7-10.30 Sun
☎ (01625) 422653
7 changing beers (sourced regionally) Ⓗ
Multi award-winning free house, recently improved, close to rail and bus stations, serving a varying range of up to seven ales, usually from northern breweries, mainly pale beers but with a dark beer at weekends in winter. Real cider/perry is also available and excellent home-cooked lunches are served (no food Sun). The pub has two distinct seating areas, one with a real fire, and a pool room. ✿◐⇄♣●🚌🐾📶

Wharf 𝕃

107 Brook Street, SK11 7AW
🕐 12-11.30 (midnight Fri & Sat) ☎ (01625) 261879
🌐 thewharfmacc.co.uk
St Austell Cornish Best Bitter; 4 changing beers (sourced locally) Ⓗ
Friendly multi award-winning free house popular with the local community. The landlord, a committed beer enthusiast, owns the Brewtique bottle shop in Macclesfield centre selling worldwide beers. The Wharf has four constantly changing guest beers, always including a dark variety, plus one draught cider. The interior comprises a cosy, secluded fireside area with newspapers, books and games and a more open space for darts, skittles, pool, quizzes, wide-screen TV and live music on Fridays. 🐴✿⇄♣●🚌(1,58)🐾📶

Middlewich

White Bear Hotel 𝕃

Wheelock Street, CW10 9AG
🕐 11-11 (midnight Fri & Sat) ☎ (01606) 837666
🌐 thewhitebearmiddlewich.co.uk
4 changing beers (sourced locally) Ⓗ
This establishment, situated in the centre of Middlewich, reopened in 2011, refurbished by the Milestone Pub Company. Now a free house, it has a rotating range of four reasonably priced real ales and a traditional cider on handpump. It shows all the major sporting events and on the first Sunday of the month hosts a Cheshire folk music night. 🐴✿🛏◐◑●P🚌🐾📶

Mobberley

Bull's Head 𝕃

Mill Lane, WA16 7HX
🕐 12-10.30 (11 Wed & Thu; midnight Fri & Sat)
☎ (01565) 873395 🌐 thebullsheadpub.co.uk
Weetwood Cheshire Cat; 7 changing beers (sourced regionally) Ⓗ

At this excellent country inn the cobbles outside are a promise of the delights within – three open fires, stone floors, candlelit tables, low beams, exposed brick and an old back-to-back fireplace. Much of the good, freshly cooked food is locally sourced, as of course are the seven Cheshire real ales. Each handpump has tasting notes and tasters are provided to help you decide. The house beers are by Weetwood. ❀◑♿♣●P🚌(88)🐾

Moulton

Lion Hotel 🏆 L

74 Main Road, CW9 8PB

5-11 (midnight Fri); 2-midnight Sat; 2-11 Sun

☎ (01606) 606049

Timothy Taylor Boltmaker, Landlord; 3 changing beers (sourced locally; often Cheshire Brewhouse, Hornbeam, Merlin) H

Allcomers are welcome at this friendly pub, set in the centre of the village, which has a real locals' feel. Regular events include quiz nights and music/themed events, with a complimentary cheeseboard on Friday evenings. Darts and pool teams compete, and a book exchange and board games are available. There are two seating areas outside for warmer weather. Children are welcome until 8pm. Local CAMRA Pub of the Year 2015. ❀♣P🚌🐾

Nantwich

Black Lion

29 Welsh Row, CW5 5ED (on Welsh Row, opp Cheshire Cat)

12-3 (not Mon), 5-11; 12-11 Sat; 12-10.30 Sun

☎ (01270) 628711 blacklion-nantwich.co.uk

Weetwood Best Bitter, Cheshire Cat, Old Dog Bitter; 3 changing beers (sourced regionally) H

A traditional inn dating from the 17th century, this black-and-white fronted pub stands among the historic buildings of Welsh Row. The beautiful plaster and wooden-beamed interior boasts the requisite bowed walls and creaking floorboards. An open fire welcomes you into an open-plan area which in the past would have been three separate rooms. There is a dining area upstairs, an additional small room with a pot-bellied stove for heating and a covered beer garden to the side. Q❀◑⇌♣●🚌🐾

No Mans Heath

Wheatsheaf

Chester Road, SY14 8DY (just off A41, 4 miles N of Whitchurch)

12-2.30 (not Mon), 5.15-11; 12-2.30, 5.15-midnight Fri & Sat; 12-3, 5.15-11 Sun ☎ (01948) 820337

pubwheatsheaf.co.uk

Facer's North Star Porter, Sunny Bitter; 1 changing beer H

Situated just off the A41 four miles north of Whitchurch, this 18th-century free house is handy for the Sandstone Trail and Cheshire Cycleway Route 70. Food is largely home-made with vegetarian, vegan and gluten-free options. This is a popular dining pub but customers just wanting a drink are equally welcome. Board games are available. There are gardens to the side and rear. Gluten-free beer is often available and a guest when trade permits. Dogs are permitted outside food service times. ❀◑♿♣P🚌(41,41A)

Northwich

Penny Black L

110 Witton Street, CW9 5AB

8am-midnight (1am Fri & Sat) ☎ (01606) 42029

Greene King Abbot; Ruddles Best Bitter; 9 changing beers (sourced nationally; often Beartown, Peerless, Phoenix) H

Dating from 1914, this Grade II-listed former post office has been transformed into a large and mainly open-plan pub. LocAle-accredited, Cheshire-brewed beers are often to be found on the bar in this former local CAMRA Pub of the Year. At least one darker beer, mild, stout or porter, is often on the bar. The car park is behind the pub off Meadow Street immediately after the Royal Mail sorting office. Q❀◑♿⇌●P🚌(2,289)

Penketh

Ferry Tavern

Station Road, WA5 2UJ (near yacht marina)

12-3, 5.30-11 (11.30 Fri); 12-11.30 Sat; 12-10.30 Sun

☎ (01925) 791117 theferrytavern.com

6 changing beers (sourced nationally) H

Could this be the original ferry across the Mersey? The pub has been serving customers for over 250 years. From the car park, cross the railway line and bridge over the St Helens Canal near the Fiddlers Ferry Power Station and yacht marina or, like many walkers, cyclists and horse riders, branch off the Transpennine Trail. Six handpumps change beers frequently, complemented by an enormous range of whiskies. The famous fish and chips are served on Friday, Saturday and Sunday. ❀♿●P🚌(32)🐾

Poynton

Cask Tavern

42 Park Lane, SK12 1RE

4-11; 12-midnight Fri & Sat; 12-10.30 Sun

☎ (01625) 875157 casktavern.co.uk

Bollington Long Hop, Best, Dinner Ale; 2 changing beers H

One of three Bollington Brewery taps in Cheshire showcasing the range of its beers and a couple of guests. A locally brewed lager, Moravka, is also available. A mecca for real ale drinkers, national brands are conspicuous by their absence. The one-roomed pub has comfortable seating areas, with two more outside. The upstairs area is used for meetings by local groups. A regular clientele has developed but a warm welcome is assured to all visitors. Q❀♿♣●🚌(P101,392,393)🐾

Runcorn

Lion Hotel

100 Greenway Road, WA7 5AG

5-11 (midnight Fri); 12-midnight Sat; 12-10.30 Sun

☎ (01928) 574129

2 changing beers H

Now enjoying a third year in the Guide, this former Greenall's pub shows what can be done to bring pubs up to modern-day standards and give them a new lease of life. What was once a two-roomed keg pub is now a bright, airy place with a horseshoe bar featuring four handpumps. Beers change regularly. The pub is just 200 yards from Runcorn main-line station and ½ mile from the main Old Town bus station. ⇌🚌(10)

Norton Arms
125-127 Main Street, WA7 2AD
12-11 (midnight Fri & Sat) (01928) 567642
thenortonarms.co.uk
4 changing beers (sourced nationally)
This is the second year in the Guide for this two-roomed, Grade II, oak-beamed pub in the centre of Halton village. It has recently shown its dedication to cask ale by increasing the number of handpumps from two to four. Third-pint taster glasses are available. Quiz nights, live music and open mic nights all feature. Food is sourced locally. P

Prospect
70 Weston Road, WA7 4LD
12-11 (10.30 Sun) (01928) 561280
folkattheprospect.co.uk
Adnams Broadside; Timothy Taylor Landlord; 2 changing beers
On the outskirts of Weston village with fine views across the Mersey estuary, this traditional two-roomed pub has three handpumps for ale and one for cider. The pub prides itself on sourcing local produce for its meals and commits to local businesses whenever possible. It is also the venue for a busy folk club. Winner of numerous awards including local CAMRA Pub of the Year 2015. P (3A,3B,3C)

Sandbach

Beer Emporium
8 Welles Street, CW11 1GT (off Hightown roundabout)
12-7 Mon; 10-7 (10 Thu & Fri); 12-4 Sun
(01270) 760113 thebeeremporium.com
4 changing beers (sourced regionally)
An independently run bar, with four ever-changing handpulls and an esoteric choice of bottled ales, including bottle-conditioned continental beers and cider. The emporium is located in a former butcher's shop – externally the original façade has been maintained, while inside the old tiling is still in place. The seating area has recently been extended, with additional seating in a rear room. Keen home brewers meet here on the first Thursday of the month. Q (37,38)

Spurstow

Yew Tree
Long Lane, CW6 9RD (at jct of Long Lane and Bunbury Lane)
12-11 (10.30 Sun) (01829) 260274
theyewtreebunbury.com
Stonehouse Station Bitter; changing beers (sourced regionally)
This part black-and-white-fronted building is a multi award-winning dining pub with a number of rooms in various sizes. The horseshoe-shaped bar has between five and 10 handpumps in use depending on the time of year. Regular beer festivals are hosted and it is popular with many community groups. A bit off the main highway, this pub is a must-visit. P

> Bread is the staff of life, but beer is life itself. **Traditional**

Stockton Heath

Costello's Bar
23 Walton Road, WA4 6NJ
12-11 (midnight Fri & Sat); 12-10.30 Sun
(01925) 600910 costellosbar.co.uk
Dunham Massey Big Tree Bitter; Lymm Bridgewater Blonde; 5 changing beers (sourced locally)
Relaxed, modern real ale bar owned and run by Dunham Massey Brewing Co. The bar has seven handpumps for cask ale, five rotating and two mainstays. All real ale is provided by Dunham Massey and Lymm Brewing. There is always at least one dark beer, one mild and one strong ale on tap. The sister bar to Costello's in Altrincham. Q

Sutton

Church House
Church Lane, SK11 0DS
12-midnight (01260) 252436
Banks's Bitter; Robinsons Unicorn; 3 changing beers (sourced regionally)
This popular, comfortable village pub is a favourite with cyclists and walkers. Two regular ales plus three guests are always available, often local. Good home-cooked food is served daily, both daytimes and evenings. The interior comprises three separate seating areas, warmed by a real fire in winter. At the rear of the pub is a children's play area and covered seating. There is a large car park to the side and camping nearby. P (14)

Warrington

Looking Glass
41-43 Buttermarket Street, WA1 2LY
8am-midnight (1am Fri & Sat) (01925) 405030
Greene King Abbot; Ruddles Best Bitter; house beer (by Coach House); 5 changing beers (sourced nationally; often Peerless)
Warrington's newer Wetherspoon venue is located on the edge of the pedestrianised town centre. There is a balcony with its own bar, a pleasant outdoor seating area and a CAMRA corner. Jabberwocky is brewed especially for the pub by Coach House, and an interesting selection of guest ales is usually on offer. Meet the Brewer events are sometimes held. Q (Central)

Lower Angel
27 Buttermarket Street, WA1 2LY
11-11 (midnight Fri); 11-12.30am Sat; 12-10 Sun
(01925) 653326
Tipsy Angel Angelic Mild; 6 changing beers (sourced nationally)
The Angel is an unspoilt gem in the pedestrianised centre of Warrington, a remnant of the former Walkers Brewery in the town, whose memorabilia adorn the walls. A rear beer garden complements the two rooms – a traditional vault and a lounge. Behind the pub is the Tipsy Angel Brewery whose beers often count among the six guest ales, mainly from independent breweries, as well as the regular mild. A real cider is available in the spring and summer. (Central)

Tavern
25 Church Street, WA1 2SS
2-midnight (1am Fri & Sat); 12-midnight Sun 07917 730184

8 changing beers (sourced nationally) Ⓗ
The tap for 4T's Brewery, this single-roomed pub offers up to eight ever-changing beers and two real cider/perries. Sport features regularly on the many TV screens, with different games shown on different screens. A covered rear area also has TV screens and plentiful seating. The pub gets very busy when rugby league matches are on TV or when Warrington Wolves are at home. Bottled ciders, perries and Belgian beers are also available. ❀⇌(Central)♣●▯🚌🐾ᯤ

Willaston

Nag's Head

Hooton Road, CH64 1SJ
⏲ 11-11 (midnight Fri & Sat); 11-10.30 Sun
☎ (0151) 328 0808 🌐 thenagswillaston.co.uk
Wells Bombardier; 2 changing beers (sourced nationally; often Otter, York) Ⓗ
Opposite the green of this historic village, the Nag's Head is a friendly local at the heart of the community. Refurbished extensively in 2011, it has areas appealing to different tastes, with warm, relaxing surroundings and real fires in winter. Good food is available all day ranging from light bites to full meals. Popular with locals, tourists and walkers from the nearby Wirral Country Park footpath. Q❀◑♣P🚌(272)🐾ᯤ

Willey Moor Lock

Willey Moor Lock Tavern

Tarporley Road, SY13 4HF (400yds off A49)
⏲ 12-2.30, 6-11 (10.30 Sun) ☎ (01948) 663274
🌐 willeymoorlock.co.uk
6 changing beers (sourced nationally) Ⓗ
This family-run free house is a former lock-keeper's cottage, reached from the car park by a footbridge over the Llangollen Canal. The pub is popular with boaters and walkers on the Sandstone Trail, especially in the summer. Outside seating is available by the canal and in the attractive beer garden. Three changing beers increase to six in summer, with at least one from a local micro. Q❀◑ÅP🐾ᯤ

Wilmslow

Bollin Fee 🄻

6-12 Swan Street, SK9 1HE (two mins' walk from station)
⏲ 8am-midnight (1am Fri & Sat) ☎ (01625) 441850
Greene King Abbot; Sharp's Doom Bar; Thornbridge Jaipur IPA; 5 changing beers (sourced regionally) Ⓗ
Open-plan, stylish Wetherspoon pub attracting a wide clientele. An extensive lounge area with a mix of table formats surrounds the central airy bar area. Up to eight handpumps are in use dispensing a varying beer choice, typically with up to six guest beers including at least two LocAles. Food is served 8am-11pm. ❀◑♿⇌♣●🚌🐾ᯤ

Old Dancer 🄻

16 Grove Street, SK9 1DR (on main pedestrianised shopping street)
⏲ 12-midnight (1am Fri & Sat) ☎ (01625) 530775
🌐 theolddancer.co.uk
5 changing beers (sourced locally) Ⓗ
This lively café-bar, recently opened, was previously a lap-dancing club, hence the name. Furnished mainly with simple wooden tables set on boarded floors, the walls are decorated with striking handpainted murals with a dance theme. Six handpumps serve an interesting range of beers including LocAles. Food includes a selection of award-winning pies. There are weekly live music, film and quiz nights and a monthly book club and science night. ❀◑♿⇌🚌🐾ᯤ

Winsford

No. 4

Over Square, CW7 2LS (on roundabout at S end of Delamere St)
⏲ 4-11; 12-midnight Fri & Sat; 12-10.30 Sun
☎ (01606) 550835
4 changing beers (sourced regionally; often Merlin, Partners, Salopian) Ⓗ
A unique bar in Winsford, No. 4 prides itself on its four ever-changing cask beers. Victorian awnings give shelter to a pavement area at the front which is popular during the summer. There is also an upstairs seating area providing a quieter setting when there is live music downstairs (fortnightly at weekends). Complimentary bar snacks for both customers and dogs are standard. ❀♿🚌🐾ᯤ

Queen's Arms

Dene Drive, CW7 1AT (opp Winsford Cross shopping centre)
⏲ 8am-midnight (1am Fri & Sat); 9am-11 Sun
☎ (01606) 595350
Greene King Abbot; Ruddles Best Bitter; 4 changing beers (sourced regionally) Ⓗ
Classic Wetherspoon pub in central Winsford, close to the bus stop and taxi rank. There are muted TV screens at both ends, and comfortable seating and dining areas. An extensive patio area with decking at the front is popular in summer. In addition to the Wetherspoon national beer festivals, Queen's hosts monthly Meet the Brewer sessions and an annual Battle of the Brewers challenge. A good range of ever-changing guest beers is on offer, and a suggestion box for customers to list their preferences. Q❀◑♿●P🚌(31,29,37)ᯤ

Winterley

Foresters Arms 🄻

473 Crewe Road, CW11 4RF
⏲ 4.30 (12 Sat)-11; 12-10.30 Sun ☎ None
Lees Manchester Pale Ale; Wood Shropshire Lad; 5 changing beers (sourced regionally) Ⓗ
Welcoming, popular village pub, formerly four Victorian cottages, with low beams and a long narrow bar. Fireplaces at both ends of the pub are decorated with relief wood carvings reflecting the pub's name, and fires are always lit in winter – a most welcoming sight for visitors. Excellent home-made food is available Wednesday to Sunday. Three beer festivals are held each year, in June, July and August. Q❀◗♣P🚌(37,38)🐾ᯤ

There can't be a good living where there is not good drinking. **Benjamin Franklin**

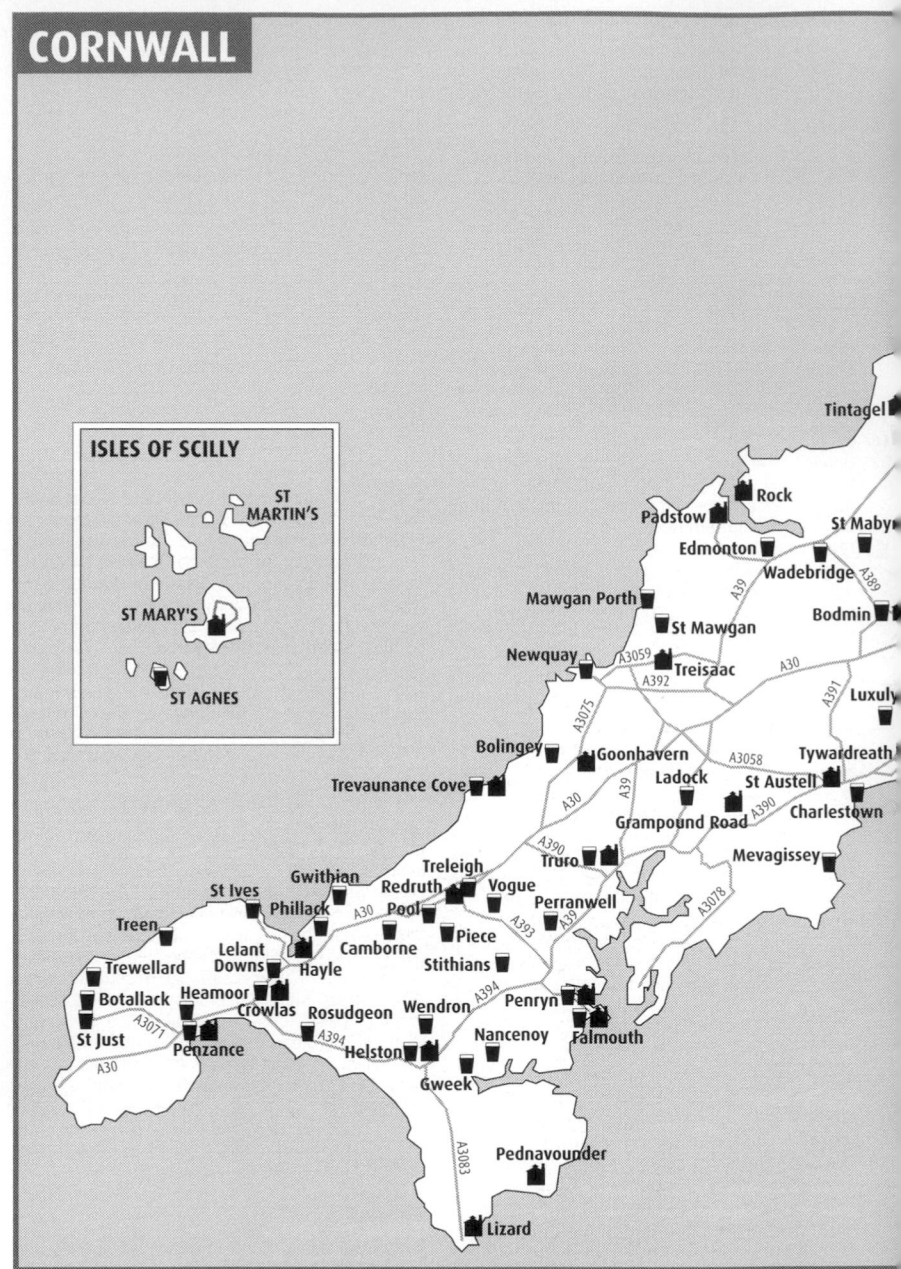

CORNWALL

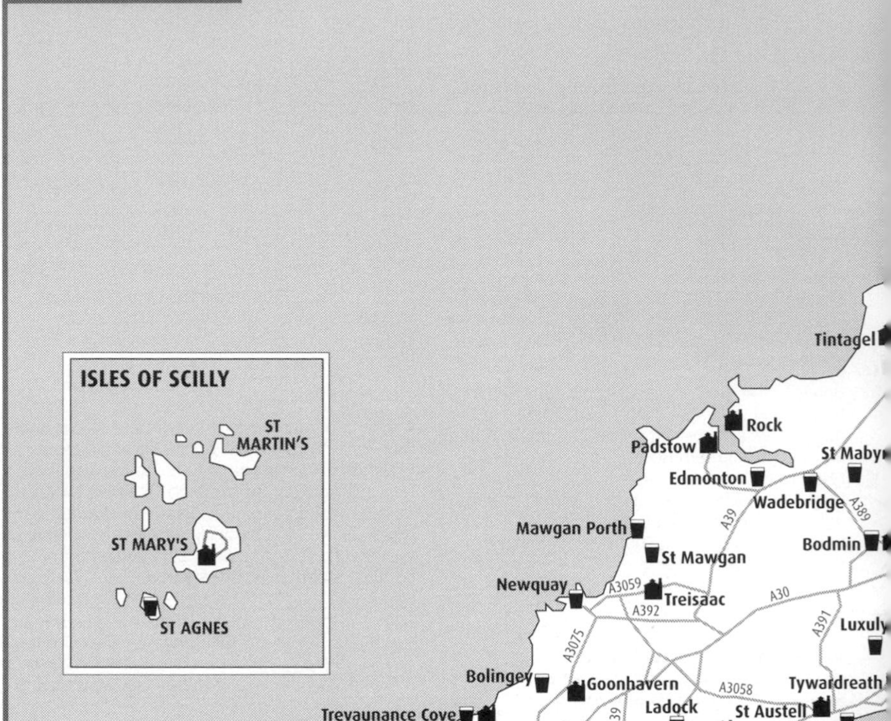

Altarnun

Rising Sun 🄻

PL15 7SN (off A30, 2 miles NW of Five Lanes village) SX215825

12-2.30, 5.30-11; 12-11 Sat; 12-10.30 Sun

☎ (01566) 86636 therisingsuninn.co.uk

Penpont St Nonna's, Shipwreck Coast; Skinner's Betty Stogs; 2 changing beers 🄷

An inn for 150 years, this characterful building on the outskirts of Altarnun is a thriving community pub and tap for nearby Penpont Brewery. The interior is cosy and warm, with beamed ceilings, an open fireplace, and antique guns and various pictures on the walls. Deceptively spacious, there is ample seating in the bar, plus two small annexes for pool and drinkers, and a separate restaurant. Outside is a large patio and grassed area for games. Food is home cooked with locally sourced ingredients. Q

Blisland

Blisland Inn 🄻

The Green, PL30 4JF (off A30 NE of Bodmin) SX100732

11.30-11; 12-10.30 Sun ☎ (01208) 850739

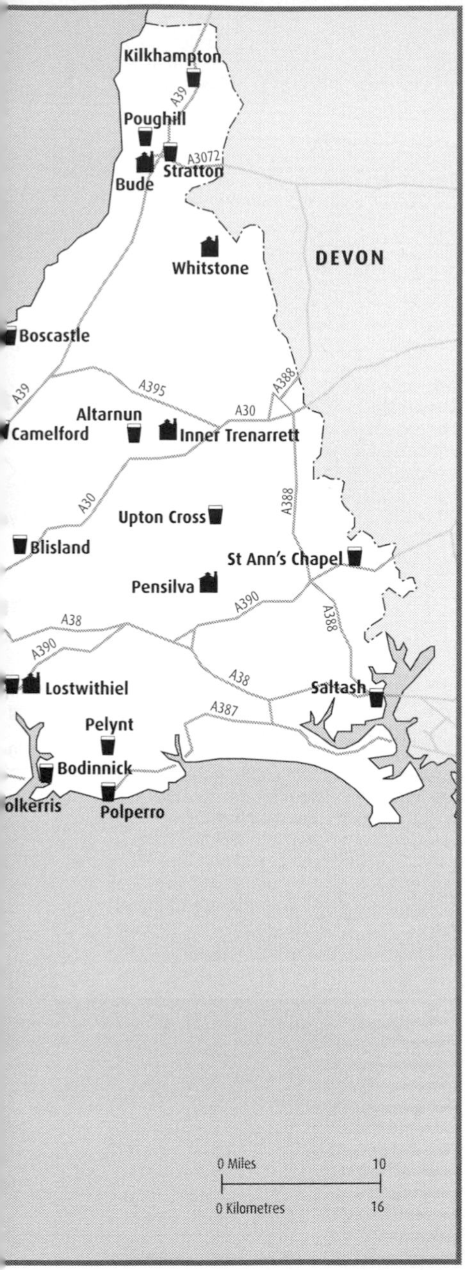

6 changing beers Ⓗ/Ⓖ
Friendly rural community inn by the village green and a former CAMRA National Pub of the Year, this establishment retains its reputation as a real ale centre of excellence on the edge of Bodmin Moor. It has served over 3,000 different real ales over the years, and usually has six or seven beers available, at least two brewed locally. The draught cider range includes more unusual varieties and changes frequently. Freshly prepared food is made with local produce. Popular with walkers and cyclists, and well-behaved children and dogs are all welcome. Q🚸❀◑⛺♣🍎🍺🐾

Bodinnick

Old Ferry Inn

PL23 1LX (next to Ferry)
🕘 10-midnight ☎ (01726) 870237 🌐 oldferryinn.co.uk
Sharp's Cornish Coaster, Own; 2 changing beers Ⓗ
Unspoilt 400-year-old pub in a scenic village location, overlooking the Fowey River and near Bodinnick Ferry. The lounge has a slate floor and is full of nautical artefacts, memorabilia and antique photographs of the area. A separate family room has one wall of the bedrock into which the inn is built, while the upstairs terrace and dining room afford great views over the river. Parking is up the hill through an archway. Draught cider is from Haye Farm. Q🚸❀🛏◑⛺🍎P🚌(24)🐾📶

Bodmin

Chapel an Gansblydhen 🄻

Fore Street, PL31 2HR
🕘 8am-midnight (11 Sun) ☎ (01208) 261730
Greene King Abbot; Ruddles Best Bitter; Sharp's Doom Bar; 4 changing beers Ⓗ
This busy town-centre pub has been beautifully converted from a former Methodist chapel, with many original features restored or retained. Four real ales are on offer, mostly from Cornish microbreweries, with two draught ciders also available. The pub pioneered the Wetherspoon Ale Club which meets every Wednesday and includes events such as Meet the Brewer evenings, tutored tastings and beer quizzes. Two beer festivals and a real cider festival are held annually, and a popular quiz night each Sunday. 🚸❀◑⛺♣🍎🚌📶

Hole in the Wall 🏆 🄻

16 Crockwell Street, PL31 2DS
🕘 12-11 (10.30 Sun) ☎ (01208) 72397
Sharp's Doom Bar; Skinner's Betty Stogs; 2 changing beers Ⓗ
Popular locals' pub built in the 18th century as a debtors' prison. The pub can be accessed direct from the public car park or through a secluded leafy garden featuring a hop bine, stream and stuffed lion. The single bar, which is divided by archways, displays a large and eclectic collection of antiques and military memorabilia, while a comfortable adjacent conservatory houses the TV. The Lion's Den restaurant upstairs offers a good menu prepared with local produce.
Q❀◑♿⛺♣🍎🚌🐾📶

Bolingey

Bolingey Inn 🄻

Penwartha Road, TR6 0DH (near B3284) SW763532
🕘 11-midnight (1am Fri & Sat); 12-11 Sun ☎ (01872) 571626
Sharp's Doom Bar; 3 changing beers Ⓗ
Delightfully located in a village backwater within reasonable walking distance of Perranporth and its hotels, caravan sites and sandy beach, this pub offers a warm welcome, the locals soon engaging you in conversation in the wood-floored bar, warmed by an open fire in winter. The carpeted L-shaped lounge is furnished with tables suitable for dining – food is home-cooked using local produce where possible. Four beers are offered throughout the year, boosted by beer festivals in April, August and October. Q❀◑⛺♣P🐾📶

Boscastle

Napoleon Inn

High Street, PL35 0BD
11 (12 winter)-11 ☎ (01840) 250204
napoleoninn.co.uk
St Austell Trelawny, Tribute, HSD G
This whitewashed stone inn dating from the 16th century in upper Boscastle is reputedly haunted. Several drinking areas on different levels cluster around a central bar featuring gravity dispense. One bar is simply furnished with settles, tables, chairs and a dartboard. The larger beamed lounge comprises four areas including a separate restaurant and family bar with TV sport. The third beer is usually Cornish Best or Trelawny, with a fourth in summer. Local singers perform on Tuesdays, a band on Friday nights February-December, and summer Wednesdays.
Q ♣P (595)

Botallack

Queen's Arms

TR19 7QG (just off Lands End-St Ives road)
12-11.30 (12.30am Fri & Sat) ☎ (01736) 788318
queensarms-botallack.co.uk
Sharp's Doom Bar; Skinner's Heligan Honey; 2 changing beers H
Popular with coast path walkers, this charming family-friendly free house offers a warm welcome to all. Situated in the heart of tin-mining country, its cosy single-bar interior features an open fire and several distinct drinking and dining areas, with a family room at the rear. Its homely decor depicts old local mining scenes. Up to four ales are offered, usually from Cornish breweries. Imaginative meals are served daily. A popular August beer festival is held annually in the rear beer garden.
Q P (10,300)

Camborne

John Francis Bassett

21 Commercial Street, TR14 8JZ
8am-midnight (1am Fri & Sat) ☎ (01209) 721720
Cornish Crown Red IPA; Greene King Abbot; Ruddles Best Bitter; Sharp's Doom Bar; 5 changing beers H
Town-centre Wetherspoon pub, in the former market house built by the architect William Bond in 1866. Previous uses of the building have included a cinema, night club and a pub called the Corn Exchange. Named after a prominent former local mine owner, it is a large, airy, open-plan venue with high ceilings, tall windows and a single long bar offering an impressive selection of guest beers and a wide variety of meals served all day until 11pm. Q

Camelford

Masons Arms

11 Market Place, PL32 9PB (on A39)
11-midnight ☎ (01840) 213309
St Austell Trelawny, Tribute, Proper Job H
Unpretentious two-room town-centre pub with open stone walls and low beamed ceilings. The public bar is floored in tiles and wood, the separate lounge with flagstones, and the whole is decorated with an eclectic collection of old toys, long-vanished domestic products, bottles, banknotes and sheet music, among other artefacts. The garden overlooks an early stage of the River Camel. Home-cooked meals include a selection of fresh fish. The beer choice reduces to two in winter. A proper locals' pub. Q ♣ (584,595)

Charlestown

Harbourside Inn

Charlestown Road, PL25 3NJ (on harbour front)
11-11 (midnight Fri & Sat); 12-11 Sun ☎ (01726) 68051
pierhousehotel.com
Draught Bass; St Austell Tribute; Sharp's Doom Bar; Skinner's Betty Stogs; 2 changing beers H
Former harbourside warehouse whose extensive glass frontage affords a view of the tall ships moored in the historic harbour nearby. The one-bar, split-level interior features exposed stonework and mixed slate and wood flooring, with wooden furnishings throughout. Up to seven ales are on offer, mainly from Cornish breweries – one of the changing ales is normally from Skinner's. Locally sourced good-value meals are served throughout the day. Live music plays on Saturday evenings and popular sporting events are screened on TV.
(24)

Crowlas

Star Inn

TR20 8DX (on A30, 5 miles E of Penzance)
11.30-11; 12-10.30 Sun ☎ (01736) 740375
Penzance Mild, Crowlas Bitter, Potion No. 9, Brisons Bitter; 3 changing beers H
Cornwall CAMRA Pub of the Year several times in recent years, this impressive red-brick roadside free house is an ale-drinkers' paradise. The single long bar is festooned with handpumps, dispensing an ever-changing range of real ales from the pub's own brewhouse plus beers from the around the country. A real locals' pub where beer quality reigns supreme and conversation abounds.
Q ♣P (17,18)

REAL ALE BREWERIES

Ales of Scilly St Mary's
Atlantic Treisaac
Black Flag Goonhavern
Black Rock Falmouth
Blue Anchor Helston
Bude Bude
Castle Lostwithiel
Coastal Redruth
Cornish Chough Lizard
Cornish Crown Penzance
Driftwood Trevaunance Cove
Granite Rock Penryn
Harbour Bodmin
Hardhead Pensilva (brewing suspended)
Keltek Redruth
Lizard Pednavounder
Longhill Whitstone
Padstow Padstow
Paradise Hayle
Penpont Inner Trenarrett
Penzance Crowlas
Rebel Penryn
Sharp's Rock
Skinner's Truro
St Austell St Austell
Tintagel Tintagel
Wooden Hand Grampound Road

Edmonton

Quarryman Inn

PL27 7JA (just off A39 near Royal Cornwall showground)
12-11 ☎ (01208) 816444 thequarryman.co.uk
4 changing beers H
Mobile phones are prohibited at this convivial family-friendly free house where banter and conversation thrive. Its comfortable interior divides into slate-floored public bar, carpeted lounge and separate dining area. The eclectic decor includes local art. The ever-changing beer menu offers four quality ales, usually including one each from Otter and Skinner's breweries. First-rate cuisine features locally sourced produce. Dogs are allowed in the public bar only. Located near the county showground, a diversion to this popular pub rewards the effort well.
Q P (555,594)

Falmouth

'Front

Custom House Quay, TR11 3JT
11-11.30 (midnight Fri & Sat); 11-11 Sun ☎ 07593 811734
6 changing beers H/G
A dimly-lit interior, bare wooden floors and a vaulted ceiling characterise this cellar-style single bar on the quay overlooking Falmouth docks, a former finalist in CAMRA's national Pub of the Year competition. Ten handpumps offer a selection of microbrewery beers, ciders and perries from Cornwall and elsewhere. Entertainment most evenings includes a Breton folk music night, and the pub attracts strolling singers during various shanty festivals held in the town. No food, but you may bring your own. (Town)

Beerwolf Books

3-4 Bells Court, TR11 3AZ (up a side alley off main shopping street)
10-midnight; 11-11 Sun ☎ (01326) 618474
beerwolfbooks.com
Penzance Potion No. 9; 5 changing beers H
At the top of a wooden staircase you are faced with a bookshop, but turn right for the bar displaying an impressive array of handpumps dispensing an ever-changing beer choice from microbreweries nationwide, plus four ciders and perry. The basic wood-floored interior is furnished with second-hand tables, chairs and a couple of sofas near the fire. An eclectic mix of ornaments adorns the beams, and a ping-pong table occasionally appears for the sporty. No food, but you may bring your own. Q (Town)

Boathouse

Trevethan Hill, TR11 2AG (top of High Street)
12-11 (midnight Thu-Sat) ☎ (01326) 315425
4 changing beers H
Multi-level locals' pub on the corner of two steep hills on the edge of the town centre. Bare wooden floors, a decked balcony and porthole windows give the impression of being on board a boat, and there are fantastic views over Falmouth inner harbour. The real ales change frequently, at least two locally brewed. An interesting and varied food menu uses as much locally sourced produce as possible, all freshly cooked (booking advised for Sunday lunch). Live entertainment features most weekends. (Town)

Seven Stars ★

The Moor, TR11 3QA
11-11; 12-10.30 Sun ☎ (01326) 312111
Draught Bass; St Austell Proper Job; Sharp's Atlantic, Special; Skinner's River Cottage EPA, Porthleven; 1 changing beer G
Grade II-listed and on CAMRA's National Inventory of Historic Pub Interiors, the pub's taproom at the front links via a corridor with the original bottle and jug hatch to a snug at the rear. Beers are drawn straight from the cask and served over a somewhat warped bar top. The pub is popular with locals, and conversation provides the entertainment. Food is limited to the occasional sandwich or when the locals organise a pasty competition – but you can eat your own food on the benches outside.
Q (Town)

Gweek

Black Swan

TR12 6TU
11-11.30 (midnight Fri & Sat); 12-11.30 Sun
☎ (01326) 221502 blackswangweek.co.uk
St Austell Tribute; Sharp's Doom Bar, Atlantic; Skinner's Betty Stogs; 1 changing beer H
Lively village pub with a spacious L-shaped bar and half-wood walls topped with exposed stonework. An airy slate-floored dining room is up a few steps to the left, with ample seating on either side and warmed by a stove in winter. A bay window overlooks the outside seating area and offers views to the harbour. There is also a pool table and TV. The car park is on a higher level behind the pub.
P (35)

Gwithian

Red River Inn

1 Prosper Hill, TR27 5BW
closed Mon; 12-2, 5.30-11; 12-11 Sat & Sun winter; 12-11 summer ☎ (01736) 753223 red-river-inn.com
Sharp's Own; 4 changing beers H
This thriving family-friendly and community-oriented free house is well worth seeking out. Named after the nearby river, its pleasant single-bar interior features wooden flooring and furnishings throughout. There are separate dining areas, and wood-burning stoves add winter warmth. The quiet, relaxing ambience allows conversation to thrive. Quality meals are served daily, made using locally sourced produce. Up to five real ales are offered, three generally from Cornish breweries. Live music plays every Saturday evening and a popular Easter beer festival is held.
P

Heamoor

Sportsman's Arms

Bolitho Road, TR18 3EH (on B3312)
12-midnight (11 Mon & Tue); 12-11 Sun
☎ (01736) 362831 sportsmanspenzance.com
3 changing beers H
Family- and dog-friendly village local on the outskirts of Penzance, principally a drinkers' pub although food is available daily except Monday. The large L-shaped bar area is carpeted throughout and tastefully decorated with modern furniture. Three real ales are usually on offer - though there may be less choice during quieter periods – always including one Cornish brew and others sourced

from various microbreweries. To the left beyond the bar is a small extension which hosts the pool table. (10,10A)

Helston

Blue Anchor

50 Coinagehall Street, TR13 8EL
10am-1am (1.30am Sat) (01326) 562821
spingoales.com
Blue Anchor Flora Daze, Jubilee IPA [H], **Ben's Stout** [G], **Spingo Middle, Spingo Special** [H]
One of the oldest home-brewing pubs in Britain. Originally a monks' rest house which produced a strong honey-based mead, it now brews a variety of Spingo ales to traditional recipes. With well-worn stone floors throughout, several cosy rooms adjoin a central arched alleyway, including two bars, one with a real fire. There is a skittle alley and garden seating area to the rear, each with its own bar. A mural of local patrons features in the front bar. Q (2,36,37)

Kilkhampton

New Inn

EX23 9QN
11-11 (01288) 321488
Dartmoor Legend; Sharp's Own; 1 changing beer [H]
Spacious 15th-century village pub on three levels: a quiet front bar where conversation dominates, a busy middle bar with dartboard and TV, and an old skittle alley deep in the back. The bar itself is constructed of old bricks and timber beams, with a polished wooden top. The interior makes extensive use of recycled materials and is furnished with wooden tables, settles and other pew-style seating. A guest beer from a local brewery appears in summer; the cider is from Somerset.
Q P (219,319)

Ladock

Falmouth Arms

TR2 4PG
12-2, 5 (6 Sun)-11 (01726) 882319
thefalmoutharms.co.uk
St Austell Tribute; Tintagel Cornwall's Pride; 1 changing beer [H]
Welcoming 17th-century village pub and thriving free house in the heart of Cornwall. The main bar has a wood-burning stove and is decorated with horse brasses, historic photographs and copper and brass jugs; there is also an overflow bar and separate restaurant. Past the bar is a meeting room that houses the community library with access to the county library service. A selection of wooden puzzles is available. Locally sourced ingredients are used to prepare the fresh home-cooked meals.
P

Lelant Downs

Watermill Inn

Old Coach Road, TR27 6LQ (off A3074, on secondary St Ives road)
12-11 (01736) 757912
Sharp's Doom Bar; Skinner's Betty Stogs; 2 changing beers [H]
In attractive surroundings near Lelant Saltings station, this former 18th-century mill house is now a family-friendly two-storey free house. The comfortable traditional single bar incorporates part of the original watermill complete with millstones, and is divided into drinking and dining areas. Up to four real ales and a creative food menu are offered. A stylish evenings-only restaurant is upstairs in the former mill loft. Annual June and November beer festivals are staged in the beer garden. Live music plays on Friday nights.
Q (Lelant Saltings)P (14)

Lostwithiel

Globe Inn

3 North Street, PL22 0EG (near railway station, town side of bridge)
12-11 (midnight Fri & Sat) (01208) 872501
globeinn.com
Otter Ale; Sharp's Doom Bar; Skinner's Betty Stogs; 1 changing beer [H]
Nestling in the streets of an old stannary town near the railway station, this cosy 13th-century free house is definitely worth visiting. Its rather rambling interior accommodates a single bar with several drinking and dining areas, an intimate stylish restaurant to the rear, and a sheltered suntrap patio. Up to four beers, generally from microbreweries, feature on the varying beer menu. An imaginative cuisine prepared from local seasonal produce features daily specials including game. All accommodation is en suite.
Q

Luxulyan

King's Arms

Bridges, PL30 5EF SW048580
11-11 (midnight Fri & Sat) (01726) 850202
St Austell Trelawny, Tribute, Proper Job, HSD; 1 changing beer [H]
Typical Cornish granite community pub, locally known as Bridges, offering a friendly welcome to both locals and visitors. Its single large L-shaped room hosts both drinking and dining – the pub offers breakfast from 8.30am in summer, Sunday roasts and a take-away service. Meats come from the local butcher and fish from the local fisherman. The King's can be reached via the beautiful Luxulyan Valley, which still shows many remnants of the area's industrial past. The nearby railway station is on the local Rail Ale Trail.
P (101)

Mawgan Porth

Merrymoor

TR8 4BA (beside B3276 coast road, opp beach)
10-11.30 (01637) 860258 merrymoorinn.com
St Austell Tribute; Sharp's Doom Bar, Own; 1 changing beer [H]
Atmospheric pub run by the same family since 1961. The interior comprises a spacious main bar with picture windows overlooking the beach just 50 yards away, a separate family room and a large beer garden. Locally sourced food is cooked on the premises, with a carvery on Sundays. This pub is at the heart of the local community and raises large sums for charity every year. Accommodation is in seven en-suite rooms, and there is ample parking.
Q P (556)

Mevagissey

Fountain Inn
3 Cliff Street, PL26 6QH
⏲ 11-midnight (11.30 Sun) ☎ (01726) 842320
St Austell Tribute, HSD Ⓗ
Friendly two-bar 15th-century inn near the harbour, with slate-flagged floors, exposed stone walls and low-beamed ceilings. The decor includes historic photographs and paintings of old Mevagissey. The back Smugglers Bar once housed a pilchard press – a glass plate in the floor covers the former fish-oil sump, which also served as a store for contraband. The menu offers a range of home-cooked dishes wherever possible. Nearby buses connect with St Austell and the Lost Gardens of Heligan. Q♞🛏◐♿▲♣🚌(24,525)📶

Nancenoy

Trengilly Wartha Inn Ⓛ
TR11 5RP (off B3291 near Constantine) SW732283
⏲ 11-3.15, 6-11 winter; 11-3.15, 6-11; 12-midnight Sat summer ☎ (01326) 340332 🌐 trengilly.co.uk
Penzance Potion No. 9; 3 changing beers Ⓗ
Versatile inn in extensive grounds including a lake, set in an isolated steeply wooded valley – the pub's name means 'settlement above the trees'. Originally a farmhouse, it has a variety of furniture and rooms, the wood-beamed bar displaying pictures by local artists. A conservatory extension serves as the family room. The real ales are mainly from local microbreweries, with cider appearing in summer. A wide-ranging and imaginative fresh-food menu uses mostly fresh local produce.
Q♞❀🛏◐♣●P🐾📶

Newquay

Red Lion
North Quay Hill, TR7 1HE (NW of town centre)
⏲ 11-11 (midnight Fri & Sat) ☎ (01637) 872195
🌐 redlionnewquay.co.uk
Sharp's Doom Bar, Special; Skinner's Betty Stogs, Cornish Knocker; 1 changing beer Ⓗ
Deceptively spacious open-plan pub overlooking the harbour on the north-western edge of the town centre, affording panoramic views through picture windows. The bar offers a central log fire, pool table and dartboard, and large-screen TVs on the walls often featuring surfing videos. There is a mid-week quiz, and live music Friday and Saturday nights. The number of changing beers increases to two in summer, with a CAMRA member discount on all real ales. ♞❀◐♿▲♣P🚌🐾📶

Towan Blystra Ⓛ
Cliff Road, TR7 1SG
⏲ 8am-midnight (1am Fri & Sat) ☎ (01637) 852970
Greene King Abbot; Ruddles Best Bitter; 5 changing beers Ⓗ
Conveniently situated on the main street a short walk from the railway station, hotels and beaches, this Wetherspoon shop conversion has a partitioned interior offering some privacy to drinkers. The walls are adorned with pictures of old Newquay, Towan Blystra being the town's former name before the arrival of the railway and tourism. The beers are mostly selected from Cornish microbreweries. A narrow drinking terrace overlooks the street. Disabled access is via an alley off Springfield Road at the rear.
Q♞❀◐♿▲⇌♣●🚌📶

Pelynt

Jubilee Inn
Jubilee Hill, PL13 2JZ (on B3359)
⏲ 12-11 ☎ (01503) 220312 🌐 jubilee-inn.co.uk
St Austell Trelawny, Tribute, Proper Job, HSD Ⓗ
Welcoming 17th-century village inn in a former farmhouse, originally called the Axe, but renamed in 1887 for Queen Victoria's Golden Jubilee. Inside are oak-beamed ceilings, antique furniture, a Delabole slate floor, a wood-panelled bar with a huge burnished copper hood, plus a collection of jubilee and other royalty-related memorabilia. An extensive menu features locally sourced produce. One of the regular brews may occasionally be replaced by a St Austell seasonal beer, and in winter the beer range is usually reduced.
Q♞❀🛏◐♿▲P🚌(573)🐾📶

Penryn

Seven Stars
73 The Terrace, TR10 8EL
⏲ 11 (12 Sun)-11 ☎ (01326) 373573
Blue Anchor Spingo Middle; 4 changing beers Ⓗ
The nearest Penryn has to an alehouse, with a narrow frontage that belies its spacious interior. Run by a jovial Dutchman, this single-bar pub is decorated with foreign cash, postcards and beer-related clippings. The spacious interior has a raised drinking annexe to the rear, dominated by a large ship's wheel. The pub is home to Penryn Community Theatre, which entertains with plays and pantos. Live music also features occasionally. Changing beers are usually from nearby Rebel or other Cornish microbreweries. ❀⇌●🚌

Penzance

Crown Ⓛ
Victoria Square, TR18 2EP
⏲ 12-11.30 ☎ (01736) 351070 🌐 thecrownpenzance.co.uk
Cornish Crown Mousehole, Causeway, SPA; 1 changing beer Ⓗ
Locals' pub by a Victorian residential square off the town centre, and Cornish Crown Brewery tap – the beer selection may vary according to availability. Essentially a one-room pub, it is tidily furnished with upholstered window bench seats and a huge mirror covering one wall, though there is a cosy two-table snug to the rear, available for an intimate drink. You may bring your own food. Outside there is a small patio for drinkers. Live entertainment features on Mondays, and a quiz on Tuesdays. Q❀▲⇌♣🚌🐾📶

Perranwell

Royal Oak Ⓛ
TR3 7PX
⏲ 11-3, 6-11 ☎ (01872) 863175
St Austell Tribute; Sharp's Doom Bar; Skinner's Betty Stogs; 1 changing beer Ⓗ
Small and sociable 18th-century cottage-style village pub with an emphasis on good food. Most of the tables are set for meals, but don't be put off – drinkers are equally welcome. Booking for meals is advisable however, especially in the evenings. The beers listed may vary occasionally – the single changing beer is usually from another local brewery. Q❀◐⇌●P🚌(36,46)🐾

Phillack

Bucket of Blood

14 Churchtown Road, TR27 5AE

12-2.30 (not Mon-Wed), 6-11; 12-4, 7-11 Sun winter; 12-2.30, 5.30-11; 11.30-3, 5.30-midnight Fri & Sat; 12-4, 5.30-11 Sun summer (01736) 752378

bucketofblood.co.uk

St Austell Tribute, Proper Job, HSD

Historic, reputedly haunted pub near Hayle Towans. The quiet, comfortable single-bar room divides into cosy drinking and dining areas. An open fire, slate flooring, low-beamed ceilings and wooden furnishings including settles add to the atmosphere and character. Tribute and HSD are regulars while other St Austell beers vary, with a fourth sometimes added in summer. Meals are served Easter-October. Named after a local gory legend, the pub's decor includes local scenes, ships' wheels and a mural depicting St Ives Bay. Q P

Piece

Countryman Inn

Carnkie, TR16 6SG (on Four Lanes-Pool road) SW679398

11-11 (midnight Sat); 12-11 Sun (01209) 215960

Courage Best Bitter, Directors; Sharp's Doom Bar, Own; Skinner's Heligan Honey; Theakston Old Peculier; 1 changing beer

Once a grocery shop for the miners, now a lively community pub set high among old copper mines near the distinctive landmark of Carn Brea. The larger of the two bars is dominated by a granite fireplace and massive cast-iron, coal-fired cooking range, the smaller room is more public bar in style and welcomes families. The pub hosts entertainment most nights, and on Sunday lunchtimes there is a raffle in support of local charities. P(442)

Polkerris

Rashleigh Inn

PL24 2TL (off A3082 Par-Fowey road) SX093521

11-11 (01726) 813991

therashleighinnpolkerris.co.uk

Otter Bitter; Skinner's Betty Stogs; Timothy Taylor Landlord; 3 changing beers

Known as 'the inn on the beach', this former 18th-century pilchard boathouse is now an excellent family-run free house overlooking a sheltered beach near the Saints Way footpath, and on the South West Coastal Path. The atmospheric interior features exposed stonework, wooden flooring, beamed ceilings, open fires and a splendid slate-topped bar. Up to six ales are available, and quality meals are served in the bar and restaurant. The bay windows and terrace offer panoramic views of St Austell Bay. Q P

Polperro

Blue Peter Inn

Quay Road, PL13 2QZ (W side of harbour)

11-11 (10.30 Sun) (01503) 272743

thebluepeterinn.yolasite.com

St Austell Tribute; 4 changing beers

Named after the naval flag, this friendly inn is reached up a flight of steps near the quay, and is the only pub with a sea view in the village. In summer it offers up to five ales, mainly from Cornwall and Devon, and a varied menu of home-cooked dishes includes breakfast from 8am. Featuring low beams, wooden floors, unusual souvenirs and work by local artists, the pub is popular with locals, fishermen and visitors to the area.

Crumplehorn Inn

The Old Mill, Crumplehorn, PL13 2RJ (on A387, top of town)

11-11; 12-10.30 Sun (01503) 272348

crumplehorn-inn.co.uk

St Austell Tribute; Sharp's Doom Bar; Tintagel Castle Gold, Harbour Special

Once a mill and mentioned in the Domesday Book, this 14th-century inn at the entrance to the village still has a working waterwheel outside. The split-level bar has three comfortable areas with low ceilings and flagstone floors, and a spacious patio by the millstream offers large umbrellas as sunshades. A varied menu includes locally caught fish. Accommodation is B&B or self catering. In summer catch the milk float tram down to the harbour from the nearby public car park. Q P(481,572,573)

Pool

Plume of Feathers

Fore Street, TR15 3PF (on A3047)

11.30-11.30; 12-midnight Sat; 12-10.30 Sun (01209) 713513

3 changing beers

Cosy old granite inn with low beams and several drinking areas around a central bar. There is a separate restaurant and a sandwich take-away bar. The ever-changing beer range comes mainly from Cornish and South-West microbreweries, with three brews always available, and occasional cider. Family-friendly, with an outdoor play area, it is also a meeting place for clubs. Once used as a mortuary for a local mining disaster, the pub is home to two ghosts. No food on Sunday evenings. Q P(14,18)

Poughill

Preston Gate Inn

Poughill Road, EX23 9ET (just outside Bude, on Sandymouth Bay road)

11-11 (midnight Fri & Sat) (01288) 354017

prestongateinn.co.uk

Tintagel Cornwall's Pride; 3 changing beers

Originally two cottages, this cosy 16th-century building became a village pub in 1983. The spacious U-shaped room hosts the dartboard at one end of the bar; the other, roomier, end has more seating and a roaring log fire in winter. Conversation rules here, and the pub supports darts and quiz teams. Meals include monthly theme nights (booking is advised). The beer range may be reduced in winter and the cider varies. The name Preston comes from the Cornish word for priest. Q P(128)

Rosudgeon

Falmouth Packet

TR20 9QE (on A394 Penzance-Helston road)

12-3, 5.30-11; 12-7 Sun winter; 12-11 summer (01736) 762240 falmouthpacketinn.co.uk

Penzance Potion No. 9; 3 changing beers

Named after the Falmouth Packet Company, operator of fast-moving ships supplying the former Empire, one of the last captains of the shipping company retired and bought this former coach house in the 1850s. Now a single-roomed community-oriented pub, it houses an L-shaped bar and adjacent restaurant specialising in fine food and good ale, plus a conservatory with a pool table. An open fire, exposed stonework, slate floors and wooden furnishings add character. A self-catering holiday let is available.
Q⚘❀🛏◑♿▲♣●P🚌(2)🐾📶

St Agnes (Isles of Scilly)

Turk's Head

TR22 0PL (close to the quay)
⏲ 10.30-11 ☎ (01720) 422434
St Austell Tribute; 2 changing beers Ⓗ
Near the jetty, this busy pub's beamed front bar displays an interesting hat collection; an adjacent small room is for quieter drinking and dining. The beer garden offers unrivalled scenic views, and you can watch your boat back to St Mary's approaching. Tribute is the house beer, badged as Turk's Ale – guest ales are from Ales of Scilly, Skinner's or Sharp's. Real ciders are varied. Order lunchtime pasties early. If you are planning a winter visit, check opening hours first. **Q⚘❀◑▲♣●🐾📶**

St Ann's Chapel

Rifle Volunteer Inn

PL18 9HL (on A390)
⏲ 11.30-11 ☎ (01822) 833038 🌐 theriflevolunteer.co.uk
Dartmoor Legend; Sharp's Doom Bar; 1 changing beer Ⓗ
Former mine captain's house, converted to a coaching inn during the mid-19th century. The main bar has been extended to accommodate a conservatory, popular with diners for the views of the garden. Meals are made using locally sourced ingredients as far as possible. A separate public bar caters for the more dedicated drinker, with a pool table and dartboard. The changing beer is usually Cornish. The pub offers panoramic views across the Tamar Valley and is in good walking country.
Q⚘❀◑♿♣P🚌(79)📶

St Ives

Castle Inn

16 Fore Street, TR26 1AB
⏲ 11 (12 Sun)-11 ☎ (01736) 796833
🌐 castleinn-stives.co.uk
Sharp's Own Ⓗ**; 6 changing beers** Ⓗ/Ⓖ
Busy town-centre pub, thought to have once been the offices of the Union Castle shipping line. Relaxing and welcoming, its single-bar interior is full of character with numerous nautical artefacts reflecting the pub's maritime history. Popular with a wide mix of locals, it offers up to seven ales in summer, with an interesting combination of local and national brews. The draught cider varies. Good pub food is available, though the emphasis is more on the beer. **Q⚘◑▲⇌♣●🚌🐾📶**

St Just

Star Inn

1 Fore Street, TR19 7LL
⏲ 11.30-midnight (11.30 Sun) ☎ (01736) 788767
🌐 thestarinn-stjust.co.uk
St Austell Cornish Best Bitter, Tribute, Proper Job Ⓗ
Ever-popular 18th-century granite inn, reputedly the oldest in town, its atmospheric single-bar interior reflecting a long association with tin mining and the sea. Celtic flags adorn the beamed ceilings, with wooden furnishings and an open fire creating character and warmth; a separate snug functions as a meeting or family room. Up to five St Austell ales are served, but no food – this is a proper drinkers' pub, a timeless place where conversation and singing are the primary entertainments. **Q⚘❀♿▲♣🚌(10,300)🐾**

St Mabyn

St Mabyn Inn

Churchtown, PL30 3BA
⏲ 12-midnight (11 Sun) ☎ (01208) 841266
Sharp's Doom Bar, Special; 2 changing beers Ⓗ
Welcoming village-centre free house next to the church and recently tastefully refurbished. Full of character and well worth seeking out, the pub accommodates a single bar, games room and well-appointed restaurant. Wooden furnishings include settles, stained-glass partitions and windows. A collection of Toby jugs and horse brasses adds interest. With four ales on offer and conversation flourishing, the pub's popularity continues to grow. Local produce features strongly on an ever-changing menu. To the rear is an attractive beer garden. **Q⚘❀◑♿▲♣●P🐾**

St Mawgan

Falcon Inn 𝕃

TR8 4EP (near Newquay airport)
⏲ 11-3, 5.30-11 (midnight Fri & Sat); 12-11 Sun winter; 11-11 (midnight Fri & Sat); 12-11 Sun summer ☎ (01637) 860225
🌐 thefalconinnstmawgan.co.uk
4 changing beers Ⓗ
Located in the Lanherne Valley near Newquay airport, this picturesque and charming 16th-century free house is worth seeking out. Its cosy, relaxed interior features a single bar with a large open hearth and an adjoining stylish restaurant. The extensive well-kept garden is ideal for alfresco drinking and dining. Four ales, one always local, are available from an ever-changing range. Excellent-quality home-cooked food is served daily. The pub is central to all local events and an annual July beer festival. **Q⚘❀🛏◑▲♣P🚌(556)🐾📶**

Saltash

Union Inn

Tamar Street, PL12 4EL (on waterfront, beneath bridges)
⏲ 11-11; 12-10.30 Sun ☎ (01752) 844770
Dartmoor Legend, Jail Ale; Sharp's Doom Bar Ⓗ**; 1 changing beer** Ⓖ
The frontage of this riverside local, overlooked by the Tamar bridges, is strikingly painted as a union flag. The single bar offers a selection of real ales and an ever-changing guest beer, usually on gravity from the cellar. The draught cider is Sam's Devon Dry. Tables outside overlook the river. Live music is hosted on Tuesday evenings and at the weekend. Tamar Street used to be known as Pickle Cock Alley, as shellfish were sold through open windows. **Q❀⇌♣●P🚌🐾**

Stithians

Seven Stars Inn
Church Road, TR3 7DH
⏲ 12-11 (midnight Fri & Sat) ☎ (01209) 860003
🌐 sevenstarsstithians.net
St Austell Trelawny, Tribute; 1 changing beer Ⓗ
A lively cottage-style local, located in the centre of the village. It is used by a broad cross-section of the community and supports local events and sports teams. The pub was originally purpose-built as a farmhouse extension to serve the drinking needs of tin miners at the end of the 19th century. The original bar and lounge (note the adjacent twin doors) have been merged into one L-shaped drinking/dining area, with a later extension added towards the rear. The ever-changing guest beer is usually from a microbrewery.
Q🐴❀◑♣🚌(36,442)🐾📶

Stratton

King's Arms Ⓛ
Howells Road, EX23 9BX (on A3072)
⏲ 12-11 ☎ (01288) 352396 🌐 kingsarmsstratton.com
Sharp's Doom Bar; Tintagel Cornwall's Pride; 2 changing beers Ⓗ
Popular locals' local in the heart of this ancient market town, a 17th-century former coaching inn whose name reflects the town's loyalties after the Civil War. The pub has many original features including two simply furnished bars, with well-worn Delabole slate flagstone and wooden floors. During renovation work, a small bread oven was exposed in the lounge. The two changing beers usually include one from a Cornish brewery and one from Devon. Four letting rooms are available, one of them en suite. Q❀🛏◑♿♣🍎P🚌🐾

Treen (Zennor)

Gurnard's Head Ⓛ
Zennor, TR26 3DE (on B3306, Lands End-St Ives coast road)
⏲ 10-11.30 ☎ (01736) 796928 🌐 gurnardshead.co.uk
St Austell Tribute; 3 changing beers Ⓗ
This impressive free house draws custom from near and far, enjoying a well-earned reputation for fine ales and excellent cuisine. The characterful, extensive interior comprises a spacious single bar, cosy snug and stylish dining room. Comfy sofas and wooden furnishings create a relaxing atmosphere, the decor featuring local art. Up to four local ales are offered, and the locally sourced food menu changes daily. On Wednesday evenings, beer prices are substantially discounted during Ale & Games Club events. Q🐴❀🛏◑♿⛺🍎P🚌(7)🐾📶

Treleigh

Treleigh Arms Ⓛ
Basset Road, TR16 4AY (beside old Redruth bypass)
⏲ 11-11 ☎ (01209) 315095 🌐 treleigharms.com
Draught Bass; Sharp's Doom Bar; Skinner's Betty Stogs; 1 changing beer Ⓗ
Expect warm, friendly service at this granite-built pub east of Redruth. The large, comfortable bar room features exposed stone walls and a woodburner. The emphasis is on Cornish ales, with real cider in summer. A separate dining room offers mainly locally produced food including gluten-free and vegetarian menus, plus speciality coffee and locally grown tea. Well-behaved dogs are welcome. No TV or games machines. Quiz night is Tuesday, and pétanque is available.
Q❀◑⛺♣🍎P🐾📶

Trevaunance Cove

Driftwood Spars Ⓛ
Quay Road, TR5 0RT
⏲ 11-11 (1am Fri & Sat) ☎ (01872) 552428
🌐 driftwoodspars.com
Driftwood Blackheads Mild, Red Mission, Lou's Brew, Alfie's Revenge; Sharp's Doom Bar; 2 changing beers Ⓗ
Outstanding coastal free house, nautically-themed, with three different bars, a sea-view restaurant specialising in fish, and a sun terrace. Vibrant and family-friendly, it is also a popular wedding venue. The listed beers from the Driftwood range are indicative and can vary. Two separate beer gardens and ample parking adjoin the pub. March and May beer festivals are held, including tutored tasting sessions. With live music in one bar and occasional live theatre, this pub is a must-visit.
Q🐴❀🛏◑♿⛺🍎P🚌🐾📶

Trewellard

Trewellard Arms Ⓛ
Trewellard Road, TR19 7TA (on B3318/B3306 jct)
⏲ 12-11 (midnight Sat) ☎ (01736) 788634
🌐 goodpubfoodlandsend.co.uk
6 changing beers Ⓗ
Easily accessible by bus, this award-winning and welcoming family-run free house offers a comfortable and homely atmosphere. Formerly the Geevor tin mine owner's residence, its cosy interior accommodates a spacious open-beamed single bar with dining area and secluded cellar seating. Up to six ales are on offer (four in winter) from an ever-changing beer menu. Good-value home-cooked meals are served. Outside is a patio beer garden and spacious car park. A beer festival is held each May. 🐴❀◑⛺♣🍎P🚌(7,10,10A)🐾📶

Truro

Old Ale House Ⓛ
7 Quay Street, TR1 2HD
⏲ 11-11 (midnight Mon & Fri; 1am Sat); 12-10.30 Sun
☎ (01872) 271122 🌐 old-ale-house.co.uk
Skinner's River Cottage EPA, Betty Stogs, Lushingtons, Cornish Knocker, Porthleven Ⓗ**; 3 changing beers** Ⓗ/Ⓖ
Near the bus station, this two-storey city-centre pub is Skinner's brewery tap. Its lower floor forms the atmospheric main bar, with wooden pillars, flooring and furnishings, a beamed ceiling and yesteryear artefacts adding to the atmosphere. The pub offers 13 ales and eight ciders plus free monkey nuts. Upstairs is the more intimate, stylish Hop Store restaurant and bar with an interesting menu created in partnership with the River Cottage organisation. Live music plays on Friday and Saturday evenings. Q◑⛺🚆🍎🚌🐾📶

Tywardreath

New Inn Ⓛ
Fore Street, PL24 2QP
⏲ 12-11 ☎ (01726) 813901

Draught Bass Ⓖ; St Austell Trelawny, Tribute, Proper Job Ⓗ; 1 changing beer Ⓖ
Classic village pub, built in the mid-18th century by mine owners, and a perfect example of a community local. Groups meet here regularly, and fêtes are held in the extensive gardens. Although tied to a brewery, the landlord serves a guest beer, as well as Draught Bass, which the pub is covenanted to sell in perpetuity. Pub games, good conversation and regular live music provide the entertainment. Cornwall CAMRA Village Pub of the Year in 2015. Q≈(Par)P(24)

Upton Cross

Caradon Inn

PL14 5AZ (on B3254)
5-11 (7 Mon); 12-3 Sun ☎ (01579) 364066
Butcombe Bitter; Sharp's Doom Bar; 1 changing beer Ⓗ
This friendly slate-built and ivy-clad 17th-century country inn near the Sterts open-air theatre attracts both local and passing trade, enjoying a reputation for decent beer and good-value food including fresh fish and local Cornish steaks (but no food Sun and Mon). Both the public and lounge bars have stone walls and slate or stone floors. Live music features at times. Accommodation is in two en-suite rooms. Daytime buses between Liskeard and Rilla Mill pass nearby.
QP(236)

Vogue

Star Inn

St Day, TR16 5NP (on St Day-Redruth road)
12-midnight (1am Fri & Sat); 11-11 Sun
☎ (01209) 820242 starinnvogue.biz
4 changing beers Ⓗ
Enterprising licensees maintain an interesting beer range for a diverse range of customers, encouraging a strong community focus by hosting a county library, hairdressing salon and meeting place for village events. The pub's homely interior has a bar for drinking and dining, with a quiet lounge and restaurant also available when weekend entertainment takes over. Good home-cooked food daily includes popular Sunday lunches (booking advisable) and a professional chef's evening menu. A charity beer and music festival is held in June. P(47)

Wadebridge

Ship Inn

Gonvena Hill, PL27 6DF (across bridge from town centre)
12-2, 5-11; 12-10 Sun ☎ (01208) 813845
shipinnwadebridge.co.uk
Sharp's Doom Bar, Atlantic; 1 changing beer Ⓗ
Traditional 16th-century coaching inn over the river. Recently refurbished, this award-winning pub has a beamed ceiling, wooden floor and fine leaded front window, offering a welcoming, relaxing atmosphere. On three levels, it is surprisingly extensive inside, with a main bar adjoined by a split-level, well-appointed restaurant leading to a suntrap deck and courtyard seating. The guest ale is generally from a local microbrewery, and the food is locally sourced. Probably the best pub in town.
QP

Wendron

New Inn

Redruth Road, TR13 0EA (on B3297)
12-3, 6-11 (10.30 Sun) ☎ (01326) 572683
3 changing beers Ⓗ
Sitting opposite the village church, this cosy, welcoming country pub caters for locals and visitors alike. Paintings of hunting scenes and horses adorn the Cornish stone walls, while a lovely wood carving of the four horsemen of the apocalypse resides above the fireplace. The restaurant is accessed through the bar, with food prepared by the landlady and her daughter. The bar, faced and topped in wood, sports three handpumps dispensing a Skinner's beer and other local brews. Real cider is occasionally sold.
QP(36,37)

Driftwood Spars, Trevaunance Cove

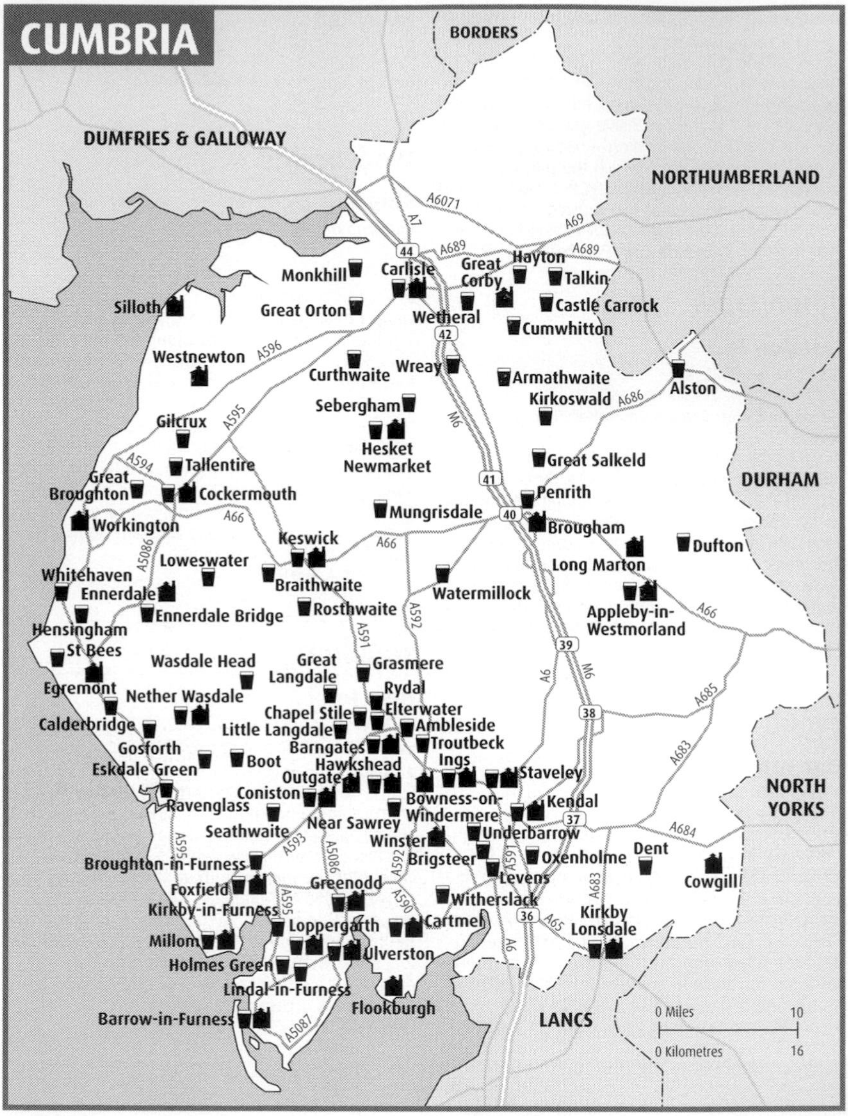

Alston

Cumberland Inn

Townfoot, CA9 3HX

12-11 (01434) 381875 alstoncumberlandhotel.co.uk

Yates Bitter; 3 changing beers

A family-run 19th-century inn overlooking the South Tyne river. It is close to both the Coast-to-Coast cycle route and the Pennine Way, and serves as an ideal base to explore Alston, the highest market town in England. The house beer is Yates Bitter, with guest beers from Hesket Newmarket, Allendale, High House Farm and Mordue breweries, as well as further afield. Old Rosie and occasional Cumbrian ciders and perry are also stocked. Voted Local CAMRA Cider Pub of the Year 2013 & 2014. Q P

Ambleside

Queen's Hotel

Market Place, LA22 9BU

10-11.45 (015394) 32206

queenshotelambleside.com

Coniston Bluebird Bitter; Cumbrian Legendary Ales Langdale, Loweswater Gold; Hawkshead Windermere Pale; Jennings Cumberland Ale; Yates Bitter

Town-centre hotel with a large bar and dining area, the separate Victoria's Restaurant on the ground floor and a cellar bar beneath. It is popular with locals and visitors for the quality of the beers – it is Cask Marque accredited – and its location in the centre of the Lake District. Buses run to several villages and towns with tourist attractions and fine walking opportunities.

Appleby-in-Westmorland

Midland Hotel

25 Clifford Street, CA16 6TS

closed Mon; 11.30 (5 Tue & Wed)-11 ☎ (017683) 51524

themidlandhotelappleby.co.uk

3 changing beers Ⓗ

Set in the beautiful Eden Valley between the Lake District National Park and the Yorkshire Dales National Park, the pub is adjacent to the town station on the Settle & Carlisle railway. The Midland has been extensively refurbished and much improved, now having a light, modern feel. Three handpumps offer beers from both local and national microbreweries. Real cider and perry are often available. Excellent locally sourced food is served in this former local CAMRA Pub of the Year. ≠P(563)

Armathwaite

Fox & Pheasant

CA4 9PY

11-11 ☎ (016974) 72400 foxandpheasantinn.co.uk

Robinsons Dizzy Blonde, Cumbria Way, Unicorn; 1 changing beer (sourced nationally; often Robinsons) Ⓗ

Atmospheric 17th-century coaching inn overlooking the River Eden. The main bar has a flagstone floor and inglenook fireplace. The former stables have been converted into a bar and dining area. Original wooden beams, exposed stonework and stable stalls all add to the ambience. Friendly, welcoming service is assured. Booking is recommended if dining. The guest beer is the Robinsons seasonal beer. P

Barngates

Drunken Duck Inn

LA22 0NG (signed off B5286 Hawkshead-Ambleside road) NY351013

11.30-11; 12-10.30 Sun ☎ (015394) 36347

drunkenduckinn.co.uk

Barngates Cat Nap, Cracker, Tag Lag; 1 changing beer Ⓗ

Home of Barngates Brewery, the Duck always serves six of the nine beers brewed here. The bar has been extensively renovated to create a pleasing mix of local and modern styles. Lunchtime bar meals, and the à la carte menu in the dining-room in the evening, are of an exceptionally high standard. The outside seating area at the front offers magnificent views of the fells to the north-east. Q P

Barrow-in-Furness

Furness Railway

76-80 Abbey Road, LA14 1PQ

8am-midnight (1am Fri & Sat) ☎ (01229) 820818

Courage Directors; Greene King Abbot; Ruddles Best Bitter; 5 changing beers Ⓗ

On the ground floor of the old central Co-op department store, divided into four distinct drinking areas, the pub is a fine example of early 20th-century commercial architecture and a credit to Wetherspoon, who have given this building a new lease of life. It can be busy throughout the day but particularly at weekends, when it is a popular starting point for the town-centre circuit. Good-value food is served all day. ≠

King's Arms

Quarry Brow, Hawcoat, LA14 4HY

5.30-11; 4-midnight Fri; 12.30-midnight Sat; 1-11 Sun

☎ (01229) 828137

6 changing beers Ⓗ

Popular local pub selling mainly from local micros, including Barngates, Bowness Bay, Copper Dragon, Cumberland, Cumbrian Legendary Ales and Kirkby Lonsdale. A beer menu on a chalkboard lists forthcoming attractions. The pub, which has been on these premises since the 1860s, has just been extensively and tastefully extended and renovated. It features an open bar with adjacent separate rooms. You will always receive a warm welcome from the friendly staff. Dogs are allowed in one of the rooms. Q(1,6,X6)

Boot

Brook House Inn

CA19 1TG (200yds walk from Dalegarth Station – La'al Ratty)

9am-11 ☎ (019467) 23288 brookhouseinn.co.uk

Cumbrian Legendary Ales Langdale; Hawkshead Bitter; 6 changing beers Ⓗ

In the heart of the western Lake District in the beautiful Eskdale Valley, close to the terminus of the Ravenglass and Eskdale narrow gauge railway, this popular family-run tourist pub is renowned for good food and a wide range of well-kept cask ales. Together with other nearby pubs in the valley, the

REAL ALE BREWERIES

Abraham Thompson Barrow-in-Furness
Appleby Appleby-in-Westmorland (NEW)
Barngates Barngates
Beckstones Millom
Blackbeck Egremont
Bowness Bay Winster
Brewshine Kendal
Carlisle Carlisle
Chadwick's Kendal (NEW)
Coniston Coniston
Cumberland Great Corby
Cumbrian Legendary Hawkshead
Dent Cowgill
Derwent Silloth
Eden Brougham
Ennerdale Ennerdale
Fell Flookburgh
Foxfield Foxfield
Greenodd Greenodd
Hardknott Millom
Hawkshead Staveley
Healey's Loppergarth
Hesket Newmarket Hesket Newmarket
Jennings Cockermouth
Kendal Kendal
Keswick Keswick
Kirkby Lonsdale Kirkby Lonsdale
Strands Nether Wasdale
Stringers Ulverston
Tarn Hows Outgate (NEW)
Tirril Long Marton
Tractor Shed Workington
Ulverston Ulverston
Unsworth's Yard Cartmel
Watermill Ings
Wild Boar Bowness-on-Windermere
Winster Valley Winster
Yates Westnewton

Brook House Inn provides the focal point for an annual beer festival held in June. Local CAMRA Pub of the Year 2015.
Q🐴❀🛏◑◐♿⛺≹(Dalegarth)🍎P🐾ᯤ

Woolpack Inn 𝕃

CA19 1TH (¾ mile E of village on approach to Hardknott Pass) SD192011
✪ 9am-11 ☎ (019467) 2328 🌐 woolpack.co.uk
Hardknott Continuum; Jennings Cumberland Ale; Theakston Best Bitter; 6 changing beers 🄷
Iconic Lakeland pub on the approach to Hardknott Pass, surrounded by stunning scenery, just under a mile from Dalegarth station. This popular family-run pub is renowned for good food and well-kept cask ales, attracting families and tourists. A lounge and walkers' bar offer an attractive mix of traditional and modern styles with wood-burning stoves in both areas. The Woolpack participates in the annual Boot beer festival held in June. Well worth a visit along with other nearby pubs in the Eskdale Valley. Q🐴❀🛏◑◐⛺🍎P🐾ᯤ

Braithwaite

Coledale Inn 𝕃

CA12 5TN (at top of village, off Whinlatter road)
✪ 11-11; 12-10.30 Sun ☎ (017687) 78272
🌐 coledale-inn.co.uk
Yates Bitter; 3 changing beers 🄷
A venue that started life as a woollen and then a pencil mill, it retains its 19th-century character in the Victorian and Georgian bars and elegant rooms. In a peaceful hillside position above Braithwaite village, it is well sited both for touring in the Lakes and for active outdoor activities. Paths lead directly up to the fells from the large beer garden.
Q🐴❀🛏◑◐♿⛺♣P🚌(X5,77A)🐾ᯤ

Middle Ruddings Country Inn 𝕃

CA12 5RY (W end of village, on jct for Thornthwaite/Gallery off A66)
✪ 10.30-11.30; 10.30-10.30 Sun ☎ (017687) 78436
🌐 middle-ruddings.co.uk
3 changing beers 🄷
This inn, run by a family passionate about both real ale and food, offers beers predominantly from Cumbrian breweries, changing with every cask. Up to eight ciders are also on offer plus a selection of unusual bottled Cumbrian ales. The pub has won several awards including local CAMRA branch Pub of the Year 2013. It hosts annual beer lovers' and cider lovers' dinners. Restaurant and bar meals are fresh-cooked using local produce where possible. There are great views of Skiddaw from the conservatory. Q🐴❀🛏◑◐♿⛺🍎P🗑🚌(X5)🐾ᯤ

Brigsteer

Wheatsheaf Inn

LA8 8AN
✪ 10-11; 10-10.30 Sun ☎ (015395) 68254
🌐 thewheatsheafbrigsteer.co.uk
Hawkshead Bitter; Thwaites Wainwright; 2 changing beers 🄷
Delightfully refurbished inn restored inside and out to a high standard, with patios and terraced gardens giving stunning streamside views, while internally several small rooms and the main bar all maintain a tasteful and comfortable rural appeal. The pub is on popular cycle routes, and walkers and dogs are welcome. Q🐴❀◑◐♿P🐾ᯤ

Broughton-in-Furness

Manor Arms 𝕃

The Square, LA20 6HY
✪ 12-11.30 (midnight Fri & Sat); 12-11 Sun
☎ (01229) 716286 🌐 manorarmsthesquare.co.uk
Hawkshead Windermere Pale; Yates Bitter; 4 changing beers 🄷
An outstanding free house owned by the Varty family for more than 26 years. It is the winner of numerous CAMRA awards, including Cumbria CAMRA Pub of the Year 2013. A comprehensive, frequently changing choice of up to eight real ales is served in a range of styles to suit all tastes. Six traditional ciders and perries are available. A mini beer festival is held every day.
Q🐴🛏♣🍎🗑🚌🐾ᯤ

Calderbridge

Stanley Arms Hotel

CA20 1DN (on A595)
✪ 12-11 ☎ (01946) 841235 🌐 stanleyarmshotel.com
Cumbrian Legendary Ales Loweswater Gold; Thwaites Wainwright; 2 changing beers 🄷
Small village hotel, just inside the Lake District National Park, with a superb beer garden alongside the River Calder – the hotel has full fishing rights. The two guest ales are usually from Cumbrian breweries. Hearty meals, freshly cooked with locally sourced ingredients where possible, are served in the two-room bar and dining room. A function room is available for group meetings. Local attractions include the riverside walk past the ruins of 12th-century Calder Abbey.
Q🐴❀🛏◑◐♣P🚌(X6)🐾ᯤ

Carlisle

King's Head Inn 𝕃

Fisher Street, CA3 8RF
✪ 10-11; 11-midnight Sat; 12-11 Sun
🌐 kingsheadcarlisle.co.uk
Yates Bitter; 3 changing beers 🄷
An excellent city centre pub, winner of many CAMRA awards, serving Yates Bitter and a range of guest ales from four handpumps. Pictures of old Carlisle adorn the internal walls and outside is an explanation of why the city is not in the Domesday Book. Good-value meals are served at lunchtime. Children and dogs are not allowed. The covered outdoor courtyard has a large-screen TV and regularly features live music. Local CAMRA City Pub of the Year 2013. ❀◑≹♣🍎🚌ᯤ

Milbourne Arms

150 Milbourne Street, CA2 5XB
✪ 12-11 ☎ (01228) 541194
2 changing beers (sourced regionally; often Allendale) 🄷
Former State Management pub which, when built in 1853, served the thriving surrounding textile industry. It is now owned by the the only remaining textile producer, Linton Tweeds, and is the only surviving pub in the Denton Holme area. The single room interior is cosy and welcoming with a central bar and is home to thriving darts, pool and football teams. It is 12 minutes' walk from Carlisle train station and on local bus routes. One changing beer is from the Allendale Brewery range. 🐴◑◐♿≹P🚌🐾

Moo Bar L

5 Devonshire Street, CA3 8LG
12-midnight ☎ (01228) 317273 moo-bar.com
Changing beers H
Opened in November 2014 in central Carlisle, this bar has rapidly established itself as a beer-lover's heaven. Twenty-four handpumps and 16 keg taps await the drinker's pleasure, featuring an ever-changing range of beers heavily biased towards Cumbrian breweries, as well as regional, national and international ales. There is also an extensive range of interesting world bottled beers. Although generally a quiet pub it does have live music every Monday evening, with other occasional music nights. Q

Spinners Arms L

Cummersdale, CA2 6BD
6 (5 Fri; 12 Sat & Sun)-midnight ☎ (01228) 532928
thespinnersarms.org.uk
Carlisle Spun Gold, Flaxen, Magic Number, Oatmeal Stout; 1 changing beer (sourced locally; often Carlisle) H
Cosy family-friendly hostelry, an original Redfern pub with unique and original features. Less than half a mile from Carlisle's south-western boundary, it is close to the Cumbrian Way and National Cycle Route 7, which run alongside the picturesque river Caldew. There is regular live music, with Irish music sessions every first and third Wednesday. Children are welcome until 9pm and well-behaved dogs are permitted. The pub is the home of the Carlisle Brewing Co, showcasing its beers on five pumps.
P (75)

Woodrow Wilson L

48 Botchergate, CA1 1QS
8am-midnight (12.30am Fri & Sat) ☎ (01228) 819942
Cumberland Corby Ale; Greene King Abbot; Jennings Sneck Lifter; Marston's Old Empire; Ruddles Best Bitter; Sharp's Doom Bar; 6 changing beers H
A Wetherspoon pub in a refurbished Co-op building named after the former US president, whose mother was born in the city. Up to 12 handpumps offer the largest range of real ales to be found in Carlisle, usually including many LocAle beers. Food is served all day till 10pm. At the rear there is a spacious outdoor seating area, heated patio and smokers' area. Children are welcome in some areas until 8pm. Five minutes' walk from the railway station and city centre. P

Cartmel

King's Arms L

The Square, LA11 6QB
10-1am ☎ (015395) 33246 thekingsarmscartmel.com
Hawkshead Windermere Pale, Bitter; 3 changing beers H
There has been a drinking establishment on this site, near Cartmel Priory, for 900 years. This recently refurbished pub serves good-value home-made locally sourced food in both the bar and the Paddock Restaurant overlooking the River Eea. If you arrive by car, park at the racecourse and walk through the village (100 yards). The outdoor area, overlooking the square, is popular in summer. The railway stations at Grange and Cark are linked by an infrequent bus to Cartmel (not Sat or Sun).
(530,532)

Castle Carrock

Duke of Cumberland L

Castle Carrock, CA8 9LU
12-11.30 (midnight Fri & Sat) ☎ (01228) 670341
thedukeofcumberlandinn.com
2 changing beers (sourced nationally; often Derwent, Hesket Newmarket) H
At the heart of this charming local village, the Duke reopened in 2009 and is now successfully re-established. A local following also sees it as the centre for the annual Marr Folk Festival in July. At the foot of the northern Pennines, it is ideally located for outdoor activity enthusiasts, who can enjoy real ale from local breweries and sample the home-made food which has a growing reputation. The layout separates the games/TV area from the dining area. P

Chapel Stile

Wainwrights' Inn

LA22 9JH
11.30-11; 12-11 Sun ☎ (015394) 38088
langdale.co.uk/dine/wainwrights
Jennings Cumberland Ale, Sneck Lifter; 4 changing beers H
Originally a farmhouse near the former gunpowder works before becoming a hotel, it was converted in the late '80s to a pub, now well known for its location in one of the most popular Lakeland valleys, its quality of service and its variety of real ales. The stone-flagged bar area – where customers with dogs are welcome – has, in addition to its regular beers, four guests which are usually from Cumbrian or small northern breweries.
P (516)

Cockermouth

Castle Bar

14 Market Place, CA13 9NQ
11-11; 11.30-11 Sun ☎ (01900) 829904
Cumbrian Legendary Ales Loweswater Gold; Jennings Bitter; 3 changing beers H
Busy gastro-pub in the town's marketplace with a modern interior that retains many historic features of this fine old building. The ground floor has a bar with five handpumps serving mainly Cumbrian ales. There is a restaurant on the first floor and a relaxing second-floor room with comfy leather sofas. The terraced courtyard beer garden is popular in summer. Large TV screens show sport. Private functions for family celebrations and events can be held here. (X4,X5,600)

Swan Inn L

52-56 Kirkgate, CA13 9PH
6-11.30; 5.30-12.30am Fri; 12-12.30am Sat; 12-11 Sun
☎ (01900) 822425
Jennings Bitter, Cumberland Ale, Cocker Hoop; 2 changing beers H
One of the oldest inns in Cockermouth with a flagged floor and exposed beams. Opposite a cobbled Georgian part of town, this open-plan pub is a free house well supported by the locals, offering beer from the local Jennings Brewery as well as from further afield. Is used as a meeting venue by a number of local groups, and supports quiz teams and a monthly folk music session.
Q (X4,X5,600)

Coniston

Black Bull Inn & Hotel

The Lake District, LA21 8DU

8.30am-11 ☎ (015394) 41335 blackbullconiston.co.uk

Coniston Oliver's Light Ale, Bluebird Bitter, Bluebird Premium XB, Old Man Ale, Special Oatmeal Stout, No.9 Barley Wine

This 16th-century coaching inn serves good food in traditional and comfortable surroundings. The taphouse for the on-site Coniston Brewing Company, six regular beers are supplemented by others from the brewery on a rotation basis. The spacious bar and lounge are always well frequented by tourists in this hugely popular area. The outside seating area is perfect for the summer months, in a spectacular location near Coniston Old Man. **Q P** (X12,505)

Cumwhitton

Pheasant Inn

CA8 9EX

closed Mon; 6-11 ☎ (01228) 560102 pheasantinncumwhitton.co.uk

3 changing beers (sourced nationally; often Ennerdale)

Partly dating from the 17th century, this pub has a well-deserved reputation for excellent food using fresh local ingredients, but retains that good pub welcome for the thirsty visitor in for a pint. There are three handpumps with a changing range of real ales. The venue has won several CAMRA awards, proudly displayed in the bar alongside a water jug collection. Quiz nights are held every second week. **Q ♣P**

Curthwaite

Royal Oak

CA7 8BG

12-2, 5-11; 12-2, 5-10.30 Sun ☎ (01228) 710219

3 changing beers

The Royal Oak is a popular, welcoming, traditional country inn less than a mile south of Thursby, fairly regularly served by public transport. The pub has a well-deserved reputation for excellent food, with an emphasis on local produce. Three changing real ales are available and these are usually sourced from local breweries including Carlisle, Cumberland, Eden, Hesket Newmarket and Jennings. **♣P**

Dent

George & Dragon

Main Street, LA10 5QL

12-11 (midnight Fri & Sat); 12-10.30 Sun ☎ (015396) 25256 thegeorgeanddragondent.co.uk

Dent Golden Fleece, Station Porter, Aviator, Ramsbottom Strong Ale, Kamikaze, T'Owd Tup

The Dent Brewery tap showcases its own beers plus different real ciders – it was runner-up in the CAMRA national Cider and Perry Pub of the Year competition. The mahogany-panelled walls are increasingly covered with awards for both the pub and brewery. Set on the cobbled main street of this attractive village, the pub has two bars that welcome all. It has a separate games room and downstairs dining room. There is a local bus on Wednesdays and Saturdays. **Q ♣ P** (564a)

Dufton

Stag Inn

CA16 6DB

12-3 (not Mon & Tue), 6-11 (midnight Fri); 12-midnight Sat; 12-11 Sun ☎ (017683) 51608 thestagdufton.co.uk

4 changing beers

Fellside pub in a picturesque village on the Pennine Way. It has two bar areas with open fires and four changing local ales, with one from Eden Brewery always on tap. Imaginative food is served; the separate dining room affords views to the Pike. There is a popular beer festival each August. Walkers and tourists join the locals to enjoy the craic in this dog-friendly pub, with gardens front and back. **Q P**

Elterwater

Britannia Inn

LA22 9HP

10-11 ☎ (015394) 37210 britinn.co.uk

Coniston Bluebird Bitter; Eden Gold; 4 changing beers

A traditional Lakeland pub overlooking the village green. The small bar is to the right of the hallway, with the dining room off to the left, and the flagged back bar to the rear. Seven handpulls dispense the permanent beers plus the house beer brewed in the style of Taylor's Landlord by Coniston Brewery, and the mainly Cumbrian guest ales. Dogs, children, muddy boots and dripping waterproofs are always welcome here. **Q P** (516)

Ennerdale Bridge

Fox & Hounds Inn

CA23 3AR

closed Mon; 11-11 (11.30 Fri & Sat) ☎ (01946) 861373 foxandhoundsinn.org

Ennerdale Darkest, Wild Ennerdale; 1 changing beer

A popular first (or last) destination on Wainwright's Coast-to-Coast walk, with ready access to the heart of wild Ennerdale, this community-run traditional Lakeland inn, with one small bus per week and no mobile phone signal, enjoys a sense of remoteness. Up to five West Cumbrian beers are offered, mostly from Ennerdale Brewery, just two miles away. The cosy bars have welcoming fires, and quality freshly prepared dishes are sourced locally and provide hearty fare. Walkers, cyclists and dogs are welcome. **Q P**

Eskdale Green

George IV Inn

CA19 1TS (400yds E of Outward Bound Centre)

11-midnight (1am Fri & Sat) ☎ (019467) 23470 kinggeorge-eskdale.co.uk

6 changing beers

At the crossroads between Birker Moor and the glorious Eskdale Valley, amid beautiful scenery, this popular tourist and community pub with oak beams and flagged floors is renowned for its pub food and range of well-kept cask ales. The inn runs its own beer festival in the peak tourist period although, with up to nine beers regularly available, it could be argued that there is a continuous beer festival here anyway. Mountain Goat buses run in high season. **Q P**

Foxfield

Prince of Wales

LA20 6BX

closed Mon & Tue; 2.45-11 Wed & Thu; 11.45-11 Fri & Sat; 12-10.30 Sun ☎ (01229) 716238

princeofwalesfoxfield.co.uk

Foxfield Dark Mild; 6 changing beers

This splendid pub is testament to what is achievable through passion and hard work – the Prince of Wales was voted local CAMRA Pub of the Year in 2014. The guest ales come from the pub's two house breweries – Foxfield and Tigertops – plus others nationwide. Beers will always include a mild. Beer and cider festivals twice a year are an added bonus. Excellent accommodation includes a superb breakfast. Bus and rail stops are outside. Q ♿ ♣ P (7)

Gilcrux

Barn Bistro

CA7 2QX (5 miles N of Cockermouth off A595)

closed Mon; 12-11 ☎ (016973) 23289 barnbistro.co.uk

Jennings Bitter; 3 changing beers

Four miles from Aspatria, the village of Gilcrux hosts a pub and this restaurant-bar, with its growing reputation for excellent ales and locally sourced food. Renamed and reopened in July 2010, it is still known to some as the Beeches (being next to the Beeches caravan park). The mainstay Jennings Bitter is the landlord's favourite, and two other handpumps showcase Cumbria's many other breweries, with over 100 different brews served in the Barn's first three years. Q P

Gosforth

Gosforth Hall Inn

Wasdale Road, CA20 1AZ (from A595 follow road signed to Wasdale)

3 (12 Sat)-midnight; 12-midnight Sun ☎ (019467) 25322

gosforthhall.co.uk

Yates Golden Ale; 2 changing beers

A mid 17th-century Grade II-listed building set in attractive surroundings at the edge of this west Lakeland village close to Wasdale. The lounge reputedly has the widest hearth in England. In winter there are real fires in both bar and lounge. Accommodation in the main building has recently been extensively refurbished. The menu is changed every two days but always features a selection of the landlord's home-made pies. Q ♿ ♣ P

Grasmere

Tweedies Bar (Dale Lodge Hotel)

Langdale Road, LA22 9SW

12-11 (midnight Fri & Sat) ☎ (015394) 35300

tweediesbargrasmere.co.uk

7 changing beers

Popular with locals and tourists alike, this large bar is part of Dale Lodge Hotel, situated in the middle of Grasmere. Up to 10 changing beers are available, with three or four ales from local breweries always present. The main bar with a stone-flagged floor and welcoming wood-burning stove has a side room leading off. A quiz night is held on Thursdays and there is live music at weekends; an annual beer festival takes place in September. P (555,599)

Great Broughton

Punch Bowl Inn

19 Main Street, CA13 0YJ

closed Mon-Wed; 8-11 Thu; 6-11 Fri & Sat; 12-3, 6-11 Sun

☎ (01900) 267070

2 changing beers

Originally a coaching inn, this 17th-century venue is now a community pub. Very much for drinkers, it is run by a committee that includes a number of CAMRA members. It has two handpumps serving beer from a choice of three Cumbrian breweries, usually one light and one dark. The bar is adorned with sporting memorabilia and a selection of water jugs, and has darts, dominoes and quiz teams. Q P (35,77)

Great Langdale

Old Dungeon Ghyll Hotel

LA22 9JY

11-11; 11-10.30 Sun ☎ (015394) 37272 odg.co.uk

Black Sheep Ale; Cumbrian Legendary Ales Esthwaite Bitter; Jennings Cumberland Ale; Theakston Old Peculier; Yates Bitter; 2 changing beers

Part of the hotel, set in the magnificent Langdale Valley, this is a traditional walkers' and climbers' bar – there is a separate bar for residents. An old range in the main bar has a welcoming real fire, much needed after a long day on the fells in winter. There is always a good selection of local ales, with several guest beers in the summer months. Two annual charity folk festivals are popular. Q P (516)

Great Orton

Wellington Inn

CA5 6LZ

closed Mon & Tue; 12-2, 6-11; 12-3, 6-11.30 Sun

☎ (01228) 710775

thewellingtongreatorton.robinsonsbrewery.com

Robinsons Dizzy Blonde, Trooper

Set in a quiet village, this is an attractive country inn. Good-value meals use local ingredients including meat from the renowned nearby butcher. Two handpumps serve ales from the Robinsons beer range as well as seasonal beers. Live music is being reintroduced here, with open mic nights on an occasional basis. There is space for 10 touring caravans on the adjacent campsite. Q ♿ ♣ P

Great Salkeld

Highland Drove

CA11 9NA

12-2.30 (not Mon), 6-11; 12-midnight Sat

☎ (01768) 898349 highland-drove.co.uk

Theakston Black Bull Bitter; house beer (by Eden); 1 changing beer

Just off the main road through this attractive village, everything here is of a high standard. Entering the exceptionally well-stocked bar, there is a lounge and a games room either side with the award-winning Kyloes restaurant upstairs, all with well-chosen decor featuring exposed timber and brickwork embellished with Highland-style soft furnishings, brass and copper ornaments. Excellent food is available every day and themed nights have recently been introduced. Watch out for the Highland cows! ♿ ♣

Greenodd

Ship

Main Street, LA12 7QZ
closed Mon; 5-11 (12.30am Fri); 12-midnight Sat ☎ 07782 655294
Greenodd Blonde, Citra, Best Bitter; 4 changing beers
A traditional village inn attracting a good mix of locals and visitors. Five handpumps offer a selection from the range of 12 beers brewed by Greenodd Brewery at the back of the building, and the occasional guest ale. The open plan interior features slate floors, stone walls, exposed beams and open fires, with a separate quiet room to the rear. An intriguing range of pizzas is available in the evenings. P (X6)

Hawkshead

King's Arms Hotel

The Square, LA22 0NZ
11 (12 Sun)-midnight ☎ (015394) 36372
kingsarmshawkshead.co.uk
Cumbrian Legendary Ales Loweswater Gold; Hawkshead Bitter; 2 changing beers
Popular 500-year-old inn with an open fire and traditional beamed ceilings, one of which is held up by a life-size monarch, hand carved by local artist Jimmy (The Whistle) Whitworth. There is a separate dining room and bar area and the outside seating area fronts onto the village square. Occasional live music plays. Ales are predominantly sourced locally. (505)

Red Lion

The Square, LA22 0NS
12-11; 12-10.30 Sun ☎ (015394) 36213
redlionhawkshead.co.uk
Hawkshead Bitter, Lakeland Gold, Lakeland Lager; Jennings Cumberland Ale; 2 changing beers
In the centre of a popular village, this pub offers a genuine welcome and a comfortable and quiet atmosphere. The warm fire and friendly staff make this a great place to relax after a day on the fells or visiting the local attractions. Hawkshead beers are always on offer along with other local ales, often including those from new brewer Tarn Hows. These can also be enjoyed in the popular beer garden, especially in the summer months. P

Hayton

Stone Inn

CA8 9HR
12-2, 5.30-11 (midnight Fri); 12-midnight Sat; 12-10.30 Sun ☎ (01228) 670896 stoneinnhayton.co.uk
Thwaites Original; 2 changing beers (sourced nationally; often Hadrian Border)
A traditional family-run community hostelry in the village of Hayton, home to the local leek club. There is an upstairs dining room which can be hired for small gatherings. Admire a fine pair of 1904 Christ Church boat club oars adorning one wall and ask to see the CAMRA mirror. There are two changing ales, often from a local brewery, as well as the regular Thwaites Original bitter.
P

Hensingham

Lowther Arms

18 Ribton Moorside, CA28 8PU
12-3, 6.30-11; 12-2; 7-10.30 Sun ☎ (01946) 63609
Cumberland Corby Ale; Cumbrian Legendary Ales Loweswater Pale Ale; 1 changing beer
A mile from Whitehaven town centre, this real community pub has good views overlooking the town. Renovated in early 2015, it still retains its stone walls, with a real fire in winter. To the right of the main bar area is a separate room with a big screen for sport and also pub games. It is more dedicated to food but the central area around the bar is great for drinkers. P (31)

Hesket Newmarket

Old Crown Inn

CA7 8JG
12 (5 Mon)-midnight; 12-10.30 Sun ☎ (016974) 78288
theoldcrownpub.co.uk
Hesket Newmarket Blencathra Bitter, Haystacks, Black Sail, Helvellyn Gold, High Pike, Doris' 90th Birthday Ale
Sitting in the heart of this lovely fellside village, the Old Crown is a showcase for the Hesket Newmarket Brewery, which is immediately behind the pub. It is well known as the first co-operatively owned pub in the country and is popular with locals and visitors alike, with Prince Charles and Sir Chris Bonington among its supporters. Closed Monday to Thursday afternoons in winter, with no meals on winter Mondays. Q

Holmes Green

Black Dog Inn

Broughton Road, LA15 8JP (from Dalton 1 mile past South Lakes Wildlife Park) SD233761
closed Mon; 4 (3 Fri & Sat)-midnight; 12-9 Sun ☎ 07715 447326
Abbeydale Moonshine; Cumbrian Legendary Ales Loweswater Gold; Hawkshead Windermere Pale; 5 changing beers
With five real ales on offer, a warm welcome awaits from the landlord and locals alike. This former coaching inn with two real fires, quarry-tiled floor, rustic beams and an outdoor decked seating area has plenty of character. Live music features most Saturdays, plus open mic nights and music festivals (Dog Fest!). Abraham Thompson beer is served when available, but Mr Thompson is always in the pub – can you spot him? Quality food is served Thursday, Saturday evening and Sunday lunchtime (booking advisable). Q P

Ings

Watermill Inn

LA8 9PY
11-11; 11-10.30 Sun ☎ (01539) 821309
watermillinn.co.uk
Coniston Bluebird Bitter; Theakston Old Peculier; Watermill Collie Wobbles, A Bit'er Ruff, Isle of Dogs, Wruff Night; 6 changing beers
An award-winning family-owned pub and brewery with a relaxed and friendly atmosphere, serving up to 16 real ales including those brewed on site. There is also an extensive range of foreign bottled beers. The two separate bars are served from a central counter, and viewing windows look into

both the cellar and brewery. A wide selection of meals is served daily until 9pm, while dogs are provided with biscuits and water.
Q☆★☕◑&★♥P🚌 (555) ☀ 🐾

Kendal

Castle Inn
Castle Street, LA9 7AA
☼ 11.30-midnight (1am Fri & Sat); 12.30-11.30 Sun
☎ (01539) 729983 ⊕ castleinnkendal.webs.com
Cumbrian Legendary Ales Loweswater Gold; Hawkshead Bitter; Sharp's Doom Bar; Tetley Bitter; Timothy Taylor Landlord; 1 changing beer 🅗
A popular local pub which is also welcoming to visitors. The central bar serves several areas. The lounge to the left has a fine fish tank set into the side wall, and the bar area to the right has a dartboard. Up a step is the adjoining games area with pool table. Good-value, quickly served lunches, especially the Sunday roast, are a popular feature. Close to the town centre and the ruins of Kendal castle. ☆★◑&★★🚌 (43) ☀ 🐾

Rifleman's Arms 🅛
4 Greenside, LA9 4LD
☼ 6.30 (4.30 Fri)-midnight; 12-midnight Sat & Sun
☎ (01539) 723224
Greene King Abbot; 4 changing beers 🅗
A true community pub on the edge of town with the Vaux motif still etched on the windows. Numerous local groups meet here, with popular live folk music sessions on Thursdays. It has a quiet atmosphere, with a Sunday quiz and traditional pub games. There are always five real ales on offer including local beers. The pub looks out onto a pleasant green and is often involved with events taking place there. Q☆★🚌 (44,48) 🐾

Keswick

Dog & Gun 🅛
2 Lake Road, CA12 5BT
☼ 12-11.30 ☎ (017687) 73463
Keswick Park Your Thirst, Thirst Quencher, Thirst Celebration; 2 changing beers 🅗
Newly refurbished with a more modern interior, but still with the appeal of old Keswick and the Lakes. On a popular route between the town centre and Derwentwater lake, the pub is usually busy, and is famed for its Hungarian goulash, as well as the largely local beers. Frequently full of dogs, they are catered for with a special menu and also doggy bags. A weather forecast is kindly provided for those looking to scale the nearby fells.
☆◑&🚌 (X4,X5,555) ☀ 🐾

Kirkby Lonsdale

Orange Tree 🅛
9 Fairbank, LA6 2BD
☼ 11-11 (midnight Fri & Sat) ☎ (015242) 71716
⊕ theorangetreehotel.co.uk
Kirkby Lonsdale Tiffin Gold, Ruskins Bitter, Monumental Blonde, Jubilee Stout, Westmorland Pale Ale; 3 changing beers 🅗
The Kirkby Lonsdale Brewery tap is just up the road from the church in this lovely market town. Friendly, enthusiastic staff ensure a warm welcome here. The front bar has old photographs and rugby prints, and there is a separate dining area to the rear, where good wholesome meals are served,

with most ingredients from local suppliers. There are always Kirkby Lonsdale beers on, and up to three guest ales. ☆★◑♣♥🚌 (567) ☀ 🐾

Kirkby-in-Furness

Burlington Inn 🅛
Askew Gate Brow, LA17 7TF
☼ 4-midnight (1am Fri); 2-1am Sat; 12-midnight Sun
☎ (01229) 889039
Beckstones Barley Juice; 4 changing beers 🅗
Busy roadside inn on a crossroads at the centre of the village, named after the slate quarry situated on the hills above and the reason for the village's existence. Three handpumps dispense a varied selection of local and other ales. Food is served Wednesday to Saturday evenings and Sunday lunchtime only. Several separate drinking areas make this a cosy atmospheric pub. The dining room at the rear has pleasant views over the Duddon Estuary to the fells beyond. No trains Sunday.
☆★◑╪P🚌 🐾

Kirkoswald

Fetherston Arms
The Square, CA10 1DQ
☼ 2 (5.30 Mon & Tue)-midnight; 12-midnight Sat & Sun
☎ (01768) 898284 ⊕ fetherston-arms.com
Theakston Best Bitter; 3 changing beers (sourced nationally; often Allendale, Hesket Newmarket) 🅗
In the centre of this historic village, extensive alterations and the friendly enthusiasm of the family owners have helped convert this into a truly outstanding pub. The Fethers has a deservedly excellent reputation for its food. Three changing real ales are available from breweries such as Allendale and Hesket Newmarket. Although the village is not on a bus route, it is a 20-minute stroll from Lazonby station on the Carlisle-Settle line. Check opening hours in winter. Q☆★◑♥🐾 ☀ 🐾

Levens

Hare & Hounds Inn
LA8 8PN
☼ 12-11; 12-10.30 Sun ☎ (015395) 60004
⊕ hareandhoundslevens.co.uk
Bowness Bay Swan Blonde; 4 changing beers 🅗
Popular village local with two bars, just off the A590 in a quiet part of the Lake District National Park. The multi-roomed pub, a 16th-century coaching inn with several low beams to be aware of, supports mainly local breweries. There is a raised outdoor seating area at the front looking out over the surrounding countryside.
Q☆★◑&P🚌 (555,552,X35) 🐾

Lindal-in-Furness

Railway Inn 🅛
6 London Road, LA12 0LL
☼ closed Mon & Tue; 5-11 Wed & Thu; 4-11.30 Fri; 5-11.30 Sat; 12-7 Sun ☎ (01229) 462889
4 changing beers 🅗
A welcoming open-plan, single-room pub with a beamed ceiling and slate floor. At one end is a comfortable lounge area with a woodburner. Adding to the character is a centrally positioned bar made from old church pews, with up to five handpumps active, and a local beer always available. Food is served including popular Sunday

lunches (booking advisable). Visitors are also welcome at the quiz night on Thursday.
❀◑🖪 (6,6A) ✿

Little Langdale

Three Shires Hotel
LA22 9NZ
✪ 11-11; 12-10.30 Sun ☎ (015394) 37215
⊕ threeshiresinn.co.uk
Coniston Old Man Ale; Cumbrian Legendary Ales Loweswater Gold; Hawkshead Windermere Pale; Jennings Cumberland Ale Ⓗ
A family-run village pub popular both with tourists and the local population of this quieter Lakeland valley. The main bar has a slate-flagged floor, with a small snug to the side where muddy boots are not permitted. A good selection of malt whiskies is available. There are superb views of the southern fells from the front of the pub, and the much photographed Slater Bridge is a short walk away.
Q ➳ ✿🖿◑ 㐄P✿

Loppergarth

Wellington Inn Ⓛ
Main Street, LA12 0JL (1 mile from A590 between Lindal and Pennington)
✪ 6-11 (1am Fri & Sat); closed Sun ☎ (01229) 582388
4 changing beers Ⓗ
Superb village local with its own microbrewery – Healey's – a custom-made stainless steel plant which is viewable from the games room. Four handpumps, occasionally five, primarily dispense Healey's beers. These include an award-winning blonde, a golden bitter, a traditional darker best bitter, a superb mild and occasional specials. Wood-burning stoves make this a cosy pub with games, books and good conversation. There is a quiz on alternate Saturdays. Well-behaved dogs on leads are welcome. ➳✿♣●🍴✿ 🎵

Loweswater

Kirkstile Inn Ⓛ
CA13 0RU (off B5289, S from Cockermouth, through Lorton) NY140210
✪ 11-11; 11-10.30 Sun ☎ (01900) 85219 ⊕ kirkstile.com
Cumbrian Legendary Ales Esthwaite Bitter, Langdale, Grasmoor Dark Ale, Loweswater Gold; 1 changing beer Ⓗ
Providing food and shelter since Tudor times, the pub is a short stroll from Loweswater and Crummock lakes. It has six handpumps, two seating areas and a reputation for food (it can get busy at mealtimes). It is the brewery tap for Cumbrian Legendary Ales, creator of 2011 Champion Golden Ale of Britain, Loweswater Gold. There is an outside seating area with stunning views of the surrounding fells.
Q ➳ ✿🖿◑ 㐄P🖪✿

Millom

Bear on the Square Ⓛ
2 St George's Terrace, LA18 4DB
✪ 10-11 (midnight Fri; 1am Sat) ☎ (01229) 771911
⊕ bearonthesquare.co.uk
6 changing beers Ⓗ
With toys and games for children, and easy parking on the street, this is a new pub and a brave venture in what was previously almost a beer desert. An

excellent choice of real ales is available, sourced from a wide range of breweries. There is also a good selection of bottles ranging from English specialist beers to interesting continental ones if you cannot find anything on the bar to suit, or just want to be adventurous. An excellent food menu is available featuring local suppliers. ➳◑🍴♣✿🎵

Monkhill

Drovers Rest
CA5 6DB
✪ 12-11 ☎ (01228) 576141
4 changing beers Ⓗ
A traditional country pub close to the popular Hadrian's Wall path with a strong community focus. Although opened up, the interior still has the feel of three distinct rooms. The bar area is cosy and welcoming, with a roaring fire in winter. Some interesting historic State Management Scheme documents adorn the walls. The Drovers is an oasis for lots of different and sometimes obscure (for the area) real ales. CAMRA Solway branch Pub of the Year 2015. ➳✿◑ ▲♣P🖪 (93)✿

Mungrisdale

Mill Inn
CA11 0XR
✪ 11-11; 12-11 Sun ☎ (017687) 79632 ⊕ the-millinn.co.uk
Robinsons Dizzy Blonde, Cumbria Way, Trooper; 1 changing beer (sourced nationally; often Robinsons) Ⓗ
A former 17th-century coaching inn, not to be confused with the hotel next door. Ideally located for both low- and high-level walking in the beautiful Lake District, it has stunning views down the valley. Food is all freshly prepared using local produce and is home made. Award-winning pies are a speciality. A bar menu is available all day, with evening meals 6-9pm. A range of Robinsons ales is dispensed from the four handpumps.
Q ➳ ✿🖿◑ ♣P✿

Near Sawrey

Tower Bank Arms Ⓛ
LA22 0LF (on B5285 2 miles S of Hawkshead)
✪ 12-11; 12-10.30 Sun ☎ (015394) 36334
⊕ towerbankarms.co.uk
Barngates Cat Nap; Hawkshead Bitter, Brodie's Prime; 2 changing beers Ⓗ
All the features of a 17th-century Lakeland inn are found here: slate floor, oak beams and an open fire set in a range. It is next to Beatrix Potter's home, Hill Top. Food of a high standard is served in the bar and restaurant. Children and dogs are welcome. Beers are sourced (very) locally, and cider and perry are available. The Cross Lakes Experience bus serves the pub in summer. Afternoon opening may be variable in winter – phone to check.
Q ➳ ✿🖿◑ ♣P🖪✿ 🎵

Nether Wasdale

Strands Inn Ⓛ
CA20 1ET
✪ 11-11; 11-10.30 Sun ☎ (019467) 26237
⊕ thestrandsinn.com
Strands Pied Piper, Brown Bitter, Low Flyer, Irresponsibly, T'errmmm-inator Ⓗ

This inn, originally a 17th-century post house, sits at the entrance to Wasdale, famed for its view of England's deepest lake and highest mountains. Five beers are regularly offered, chosen from over 20 produced by the inn's microbrewery, which also brews its own cider. A range of these beers is available in bottle. The annual beer festival in May usually attracts a troupe of morris dancers. There is an open mic night on the first Wednesday of every month. Q P

Oxenholme

Station Inn

LA9 7RF

12-midnight; 12-11 Sun (01539) 724094

stationinnoxenholme.co.uk

Hawkshead Bitter; Moorhouse's Blond Witch; 2 changing beers

Originally a farmhouse on the edge of Kendal, in a beautiful rural setting, it lies near the mainline railway station. Outside, there is a large garden complete with crazy golf and a large children's play area. The recently refurbished main bar serves an extensive menu offering many local ingredients along with daily specials. The inn is close to one of the Coast-to-Coast cycle routes. There is hard standing for caravans on site.
Q P (41,41A,564)

Penrith

Moo Bar

52 King Street, CA11 7AY

12-12.30am 07832 475910

6 changing beers

A small and intimate venue in the centre of Penrith on three floors which was only turned into a pub in 2012. Since then it has rapidly built up a reputation for serving a changing range of beers. There is always a variety of local ales and others from further afield. Small brewery keg beers are also offered and real cider is often available. There is a large choice of bottled beers from around the world. (646)

Ravenglass

Ratty Arms

CA18 1SN

11-midnight; 12-midnight Sun (01229) 717676

rattyarms.co.uk

Jennings Bitter; Theakston Best Bitter; Yates Bitter; 3 changing beers

A cosy family-run pub in this coastal hamlet, historically a Roman port. Its railway theme reflects the conversion from station buildings at the junction of the West Coast mainline and the La'al Ratty, a narrow gauge train that runs deep into Upper Eskdale, with more good pubs, high fells and Roman remains to explore. Up to six real ales are offered in summer, usually from West Cumbrian breweries. Good locally sourced pub food is served all day. Q P (6)

Rosthwaite

Scafell Hotel

Borrowdale, CA12 5XB (on B5289)

12-11; 12-10.30 Sun (017687) 77208 scafell.co.uk

Copper Dragon Best Bitter; Jennings Bitter, Cumberland Ale, Sneck Lifter; 2 changing beers

Open all year round, the Riverside Bar is positioned to the left of the main hotel building, which is six miles south of Keswick, on the Borrowdale road. In good weather enjoy the garden and its mountain views. For the rest of the time a roaring coal fire helps welcome walkers, cyclists (it is on the Coast-to-Coast and Cumbrian Way routes), fell runners and drinkers. Six handpumps offer mainly Cumbrian beers, especially Jennings.
P (78)

Rydal

Badger Bar (Glen Rothay Hotel)

LA22 9LR

11-11; 11-10.30 Sun (015394) 34500

theglenrothay.co.uk

Barngates Goodhew's Dry Stout; 4 changing beers

A very popular bar, part of the Glen Rothay Hotel, on the main road between Ambleside and Grasmere. Situated almost directly opposite Rydal Water and Loughrigg Terrace, it is a haven for walkers and visitors alike. The four changing guest ales are mainly Cumbrian beers; the Goodhew's Stout has become the only stout on the bar. The bar offers good-value meals, especially the lunches. Q P (555,599)

St Bees

Manor

Main Street, CA27 0DE

12 (4 Mon)-11; 12-10.30 Sun (01946) 820587

manorhousestbees.co.uk

St Austell Tribute; 3 changing beers

Grade I-listed 17th-century building popular with tourists and locals alike. Nearby is the station for the beautifully scenic Cumbrian Coastal Railway, running between seas and cliffs, with views of mountains (Sca Fell, Great Gable), rivers, tidal lagoons and wildlife reserves. Also close by are the ancient St Bees Priory from about 1120, with its legendary Willis organ, melodious Gillett bells and extensive history displays, St Bees Head and beach, and the start of the 192-mile Coast-to-Coast walk. Dogs are allowed in the public bar only.
P (6)

Seathwaite

Newfield Inn

Seathwaite, Duddon Valley, LA20 6ED SD228960

11-11 (01229) 716208 newfieldinn.co.uk

1 changing beer

A 17th-century free house in the Duddon Valley, Wordsworth's favourite area, an oasis for fell walkers and travellers passing through this secluded and peaceful valley. Note the unique banded slate floor in the bar. Good food is served all day and steaks are a speciality. The spacious beer garden has excellent views towards the South Lakeland Fells. Accommodation is in two self-catering flats. Q P

Sebergham

Sour Nook Inn

Sour Nook, CA5 7DY

11-11; closed Wed; 12-10.30 Sun (016974) 76242

sournookinn.co.uk

House beer (by Tetley); 2 changing beers

On the B5305 on the southern edge of the village, this pub has a Tack Room bar, a pool/darts room, a function room and restaurant. Food is locally sourced and reasonably priced. The area tractor group meets here on a regular basis, and the local fells pensioner group meets fortnightly for lunch. At least one guest ale from the local Hesket Newmarket Brewery is usually available in addition to Sour Nook (Tetley Bitter). ♘✿◑♿♣●P🐾

Staveley

Beer Hall

Mill Yard, LA8 9LR

12-6 (5 Mon; 11 Fri & Sat); 12-8 Sun ☎ (01539) 825260

Hawkshead Windermere Pale, Bitter, Red, Lakeland Gold, Brodie's Prime, Cumbrian Five Hop H

The two-storey brewery tap next door to the brewery – on both floors there is a mix of comfy sofas and solid wooden furniture. The food menu now includes a good selection of tapas to complement the Hawkshead beers. Spring and summer beer festivals are held, with up to 60 beers to sample. The beer shop has a range of bottled Hawkshead and foreign beers. CAMRA members and train users get a 10 per cent discount. Q♘✿◑♿▲≋♣P🚌(555)🐾

Talkin

Blacksmiths Arms

CA8 1LE

12-3, 6-11 ☎ (016977) 3452

Yates Bitter; 3 changing beers H

Since taking over in 1997, the owners have made this probably the most popular pub in the vicinity. The winning formula includes four real ales, a superbly stocked bar, friendly efficient staff, no TV and meticulous attention to detail. Set on the edge of an Area of Outstanding Natural Beauty, with a golf course and country park within two miles and plenty of other outdoor activities available locally, the pub attracts visitors from far outside the North Cumbria area. Q♘✿🛏◑♿♣P

Tallentire

Bush Inn

CA13 0PT

closed Mon; 6-midnight; 12-2, 7-11 Sun

☎ (01900) 823707

3 changing beers H

A good old-fashioned pub that often serves at least one ale from a Cumbrian brewery. The hub of the community and home of the cricket team, it hosts a traditional music session on the last Wednesday of the month. With its exposed beams, stone floor and wood-burning stove, the pub also has an exterior sensitive to the character of the village. Well-behaved dogs are welcome. Food is served in a separate restaurant Sunday lunchtimes and Thursday to Saturday evenings. Q◑

Troutbeck

Mortal Man

LA23 1PL (nr Windermere)

10.30-midnight ☎ (015394) 33193

🌐 themortalman.co.uk

Coniston Bluebird Bitter; Cumbrian Legendary Ales Loweswater Gold; Hawkshead Bitter; Hesket Newmarket Haystacks; 1 changing beer H

An unspoilt pub within the hotel, popular with locals and walkers and comprising a main bar, several smaller dining areas and a large well-appointed garden. The bar and garden have spectacular views of the Troutbeck Valley down to Windermere and the surrounding fells. A good range of local ales is available all year round, with guest beers in summer.
♘✿🛏◑▲●P🚌(517)🐾

Ulverston

Devonshire Arms

Braddyll Terrace, Victoria Road, LA12 0DH (next to railway bridge in town centre)

4-11; 12-midnight Fri & Sat; 12-11 Sun ☎ (01229) 582537

5 changing beers H

Conveniently situated between the bus and train station, the Dev is a real locals' pub with a welcoming atmosphere. Three TVs provide comprehensive sports coverage, while there is still plenty of room for banter around the bar or more intimate conversation in the comfortable seating areas. Outside tables are popular, especially in summer, and solar panels provide supplementary power. An informal quiz is held every other Sunday and a pool table and two dartboards add to the entertainment. There is a local bus service.
♘✿♿▲≋♣P🚌🐾

Mill

Mill Street, LA12 7EB

11-11 (midnight Fri & Sat); 11-10.30 Sun

☎ (01229) 581384

Lancaster Amber, Blonde, Black, Red; 6 changing beers H

A converted flour mill in a town-centre location with many interesting features, including a restored waterwheel. The main bar has 10 handpulls dispensing six guest beers, always including a dark brew, alongside the Lancaster Brewery range. There are two wood-burning stoves, a first-floor outdoor terrace, and seating outside at the front. Quality food is popular, served in the bar, and there is an upstairs restaurant (booking recommended). An open mic session takes place every Wednesday. Dogs are allowed in the bar area. ♘✿◑♿▲≋🚌🐾

Old Friends

49 Soutergate, LA12 7ES

4-11; 2-midnight Fri; 12-midnight Sat; 12-10.30 Sun

☎ (01229) 208195

5 changing beers H

Welcoming town pub, recently bought from Robinsons, about 200 yards uphill from the town centre. Two changing beers from the Robinsons range are supplemented by three ales from local brewers. No food is available except on Sunday lunchtime 12-2pm (booking recommended). A popular quiz is held every Tuesday evening. The beer garden is wonderful. Q♘✿▲≋🚌🐾

Stan Laurel Inn

31 The Ellers, LA12 0AB

7-11 Mon; 12-2.30, 6-11 (midnight Fri & Sat); 12-11.30 Sun

☎ (01229) 582814 🌐 thestanlaurel.co.uk

Thwaites Original; 2 changing beers H

Just off the centre of Stan Laurel's home town, the Stan offers a warm welcome to locals and visitors alike. Six handpulls serve a variety of mainly locally brewed beers. Excellent-value quality food is available throughout the week (no food Mon).

Adjacent to the bar is a large room with pool and darts, and a smaller room primarily used by diners. In winter a log-burning stove adds to the pub's comfortable ambience. Well-behaved dogs are welcome. Q❀⇌◑Å≷♣P (6,X6)

Swan Inn

Swan Street, LA12 7JX

3.30-11; 12-midnight Fri-Sun ☎ (01229) 582519

7 changing beers H

On the edge of the town centre overlooking the A590, the pub has an open-plan feel yet there are three distinct drinking areas for darts, TV or just good conversation by the fire. Live music features on Wednesdays, while a central jukebox allows all genres of music to be played. BT Sport shows the major events and a Sunday night quiz rounds off the entertainment. A large beer garden behind the pub is popular in summer. ❀♿Å♣ (6,X6)

Underbarrow

Punch Bowl Inn

LA8 8HQ

12-3, 6-11; closed Tue; 12-11 Sat & Sun

☎ (015395) 68234 punch-bowl-inn.co.uk

3 changing beers H

Traditional village inn on a scenic route between Kendal and Windermere. The flagstone-floored main bar includes large leather sofas around an inglenook fireplace. The pub is popular with locals, walkers and their dogs, and those who love good beer and food. There are separate dining and function rooms. Happy hour is 4-7pm on Wednesday, and a summer beer festival is held in the grounds each June. There is free local radius transport home for diners. Q❀◑♿♣P

Wasdale Head

Wasdale Head Inn

CA20 1EX (at head of Wasdale, 9 miles from A595)

11-11; 12-10.30 Sun ☎ (019467) 26229 wasdale.com

7 changing beers H

In summer, sit outside this historic pub, home of the original World's Biggest Liar contest, enjoying peace and views. In winter, sit by the fire, admiring the 19th-century pioneer rock climbers' gear, photographed on the crags, while enjoying some of the seven Cumbrian ales or real cider, and tasty home-cooked, local food. Nearby are Wastwater (England's deepest lake), Sca Fell (England's tallest mountain), the Pike and Great Gable (England's smallest church), with its memorials to fallen climbers, and lots of sheep!
Q❀◑♿Å♣P

Watermillock

Brackenrigg Inn

CA11 0LP (on A592)

12-11; 12-10.30 Sun ☎ (017684) 86206

brackenrigginn.co.uk

Cumbrian Legendary Ales Loweswater Gold; 5 changing beers H

A large roadside inn with outstanding views of Ullswater and the north-eastern Lake District fells. Very welcoming, it attracts locals and tourists with a friendly atmosphere and real fires. There are distinct areas for both drinking and dining. The landlord keeps three guest ales in winter and up to seven in the summer, mainly from local breweries, with plans for an on-site brewery to open this year. There is a great range of locally sourced food and cheeses. Q❀◑♿ÅP (108)

Wetheral

Wheatsheaf Inn

CA4 8HD

12-11 (midnight Fri & Sat); 12-11.30 Sun

☎ (01228) 560686 wheatsheafwetheral.co.uk

3 changing beers (sourced nationally; often Cumberland, Robinsons) H

Early 19th-century village pub, just a few minutes' walk from the village green and railway station. Deservedly popular with locals and visitors, three cask ales are usually available from both local and national breweries. Good-value bar meals are served Wednesday to Sunday. It is a local CAMRA award winner. The regular Tuesday quiz nights are very well supported. ❀◑≷♣P (75)

Whitehaven

Vagabond

9 Marlborough Street, Harbourside, CA28 7LL

12-3 (not Mon-Fri), 5-11 (midnight Fri); 12-3 Sun ☎ 07734 839547/07518 018465

4 changing beers H

Two-storey, wooden-floored pub, close to the historic harbour – the upper floor is used for dining, parties or meetings. It serves superb food, locally sourced and cooked. It has limited opening hours at the moment – mainly evenings and weekends. Closure on Sundays from 3pm will be reviewed as trade and staff build up. Beers, mostly from Cumbria micros, are constantly changing and are not usually available anywhere else in the town. Beer prices are on the lower side. Q◑♿≷

Witherslack

Derby Arms Hotel

LA11 6RH

12-11 ☎ (015395) 52207

Thwaites Wainwright H

Since being reopened by the Witherslack Community Land Trust, this pub has remained very much a local hub complete with a community-owned shop. A large room with open fires is entered from the front door, with dining space in the adjoining rooms. A snug and games room, which provide a village focus, are at the rear. The house beer, Jolly Boys, is brewed by Cumbrian Legendary Ales. ❀◑♿ÅP (X6)

Wreay

Plough Inn

CA4 0RL

12-3 (not Mon & Tue), 5.30-11.30 ☎ (016974) 75770

Cumberland Corby Ale; Hawkshead Lakeland Gold; 1 changing beer H

Tastefully modernised pub dating back to 1786, sat in the heart of this picturesque village, just five miles south of Carlisle. Excellent locally sourced food is served in the split-level bar and dining area, with two cask ales from Cumbrian breweries usually on tap. The village guardians continue to use it as a meeting place – their display of clay pipes can be seen inside. Quiz night is Monday and acoustic night is Tuesday. Q❀◑♿P

DERBYSHIRE

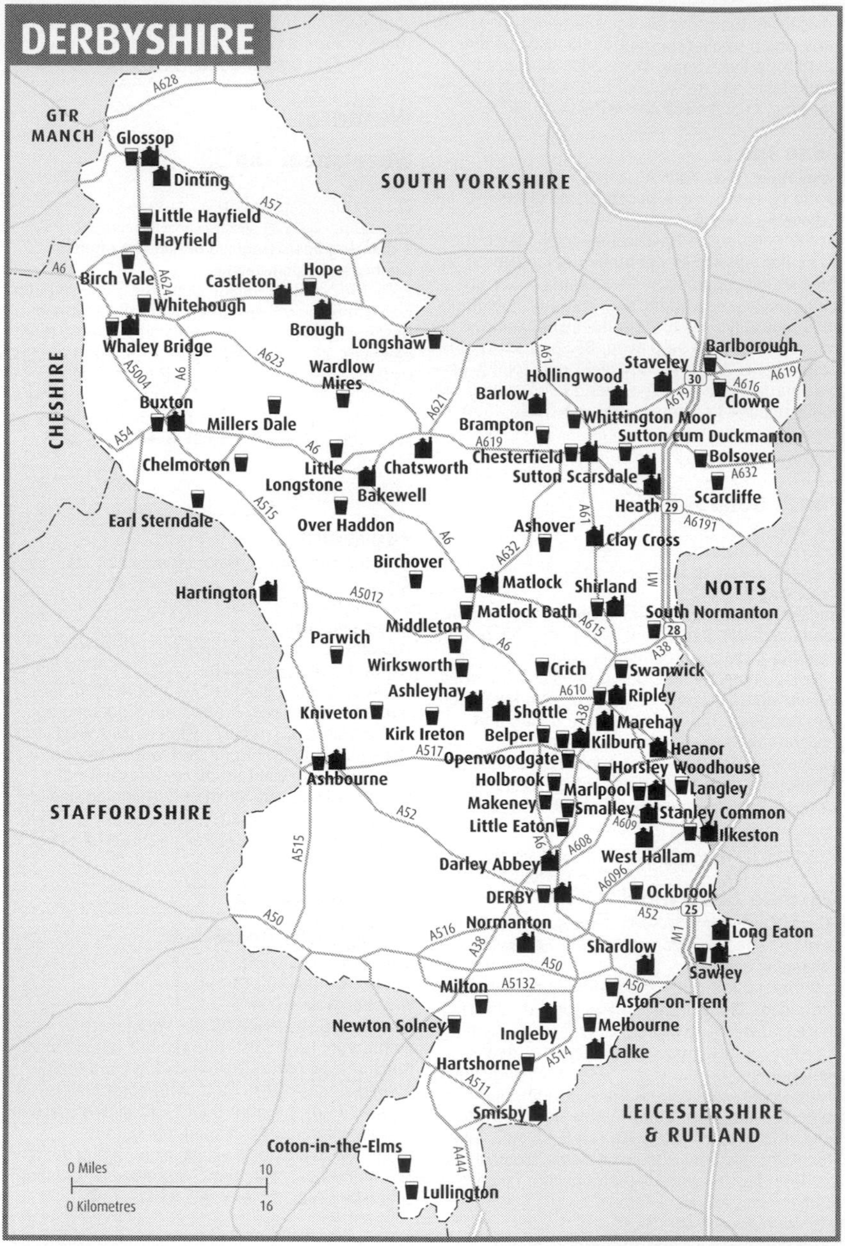

Ashbourne

Smith's Tavern 🏆

36 St John Street, DE6 1GH

12-11 (midnight Fri & Sat) ☎ (01335) 300809

Banks's Sunbeam; Marston's Pedigree New World Pale Ale, Pedigree; Ringwood Fortyniner; 1 changing beer Ⓗ

Small, highly traditional town-centre pub, assuring a friendly atmosphere and the warmest of welcomes. Up to seven real ales are available from the Marston's portfolio of beers. The landlord makes the widest possible selection, and he is also allowed one free choice guest ale, served at weekends, always from a local brewery. Darts is popular here. Voted local CAMRA Pub of the Year for the third successive year in 2015. Q♣🚌🐾📶

Ashover

Old Poets' Corner 🏆 L

Butts Road, S45 0EW (downhill from church)

12-11 ☎ (01246) 590888 🌐 oldpoets.co.uk

Ashover Poets' Tipple, Butts Pale Ale; changing beers Ⓗ

Home of the award-winning Ashover Brewery, this large Brewers' Tudor pub is a frequent local CAMRA Pub of the Year. The staff welcome walkers and dogs and provide excellent food and beer. Choose from up to 10 beers, including from Ashover, along with a range of guest ales, traditional ciders, bottled Belgian beers and country wines. The pub hosts three beer festivals a year, weekly quizzes and live music. Q❀⇌◐◑♿♣●P🚌(63,64)🐾

Aston-on-Trent

Malt 🄻

14 The Green, DE72 2AA
⏲ 12-11 (midnight Fri & Sat) ☎ (01332) 792256
🌐 themaltpubaston.co.uk
Draught Bass; Marston's Pedigree; Sharp's Doom Bar; 3 changing beers (often Dancing Duck) 🄷
The Tudor exterior makes this pub stand out from the other properties just off the main road in the centre of Aston-on-Trent. A traditional village pub, it has two rooms, with oak panelling in one and beams throughout both, giving it a cosy and stylish atmosphere. A cheery welcome awaits families, dogs and walkers. It is popular for meals, and there is a choice of six beers with an emphasis on local brews from the Derby and Nottingham areas.
Q⚇❀◐◑♣P🚌🐾📶

Barlborough

Royal Oak 🄻

High Street, S43 4EU
⏲ 12-3, 5-midnight; 12-midnight Fri & Sat; 12-8 Sun
☎ (01246) 570818 🌐 royaloakbarlborough.co.uk
Changing beers 🄷
Within half a mile of M1 junction 30, this pub is ideal for passing motorists and locals alike. The venue was completely refurbished in 2011 to create a traditional village pub with a contemporary twist. The three areas – restaurant, lounge and bar – provide a variety of options, from traditional British cuisine in the restaurant to a bar snack in the main bar or lounge.
⚇❀◐◑♣●P🚌🐾📶

Belper

Arkwright's Real Ale Bar 🄻

5 Campbell Street, DE56 1AP
⏲ 4-11; 12-11 Sat & Sun ☎ (01773) 823117
🌐 arkwrightsbar.com
Marston's Pedigree; 6 changing beers 🄷
Situated below the Strutt Club in the centre of town, Arkwright's is a modern, friendly, one-roomed bar regularly serving six real ales sourced from local breweries and a good selection of ciders and perries. Popular with local drinkers, it offers good-quality snacks throughout the day. The TV is turned on only for major sporting events and this, coupled with a 'no under-14s' rule, ensures a quiet and relaxing environment for adults to enjoy a pint or two. A discount is available to CAMRA members.
Q♿⇌♣●🚌🐾

Birch Vale

Printers Arms

Thornsett Road, SK22 1AZ (in village of Thornsett)
⏲ 4.30-11.30 (midnight Fri); 12-12.30am Sat; 12-9 Sun
☎ (01663) 744650
5 changing beers (sourced nationally; often Storm) 🄷
Refurbished and modernised friendly village local, with accommodation and a well-maintained children's play area, overlooking the Sett Valley. A free house, it has a changing range of five ales offered at competitive pricing for the area, normally including one from the Storm Brewery range. It is well known for the excellent value early evening Meals Plus a Pint deal, available Monday to Friday. The pub is very much the centre of the local community. Darts and pool are popular here.
⚇❀⇌◑♣P🚌(62)🐾📶

Birchover

Druid Inn 🏆 🄻

Main Street, DE4 2BL

REAL ALE BREWERIES

Amber Ripley
Ashleyhay Ashleyhay (NEW)
Ashover Clay Cross
Barlow Barlow
Bottle Brook Kilburn
Brampton Chesterfield
Brunswick Derby
Bumpmill Shirland
Buxton Buxton
Coppice Side Heanor
Dancing Duck Derby
Derby Derby
Derventio Darley Abbey
Draycott Shardlow (NEW)
Falstaff Derby: Normanton
Frontier Derby (NEW)
Globe Glossop
Hartshorns Derby
Haywood Bad Ram Ashbourne
Heath Village Heath
Hope Valley Castleton
Howard Town Glossop
Instant Karma Clay Cross
Intrepid Brough (NEW)
John Thompson Ingleby
Landlocked Ripley (NEW)
Leadmill Heanor
Leatherbritches Smisby
Little Bush Marehay (NEW)
Marlpool Marlpool
Matlock Wolds Farm Matlock (NEW)
Mercian Buxton
Middle Earth Derby
Mouselow Farm Dinting
Mr Grundy's Derby
Muirhouse Ilkeston
North Star Ilkeston
Nutbrook Stanley Common/West Hallam
Old Sawley Sawley
Peak Chatsworth
Pentrich Ripley (NEW)
Pigeon Fishers Hollingwood
Raw Staveley
Rowditch Derby
Shiny Derby
Shottle Farm Shottle
Songbird Long Eaton
Spire Sutton Scarsdale
Tap House Smisby
Thornbridge Bakewell
Titan Derby
Tollgate Calke
Townes Staveley
Wentwell Derby
Whaley Bridge Whaley Bridge
Whim Hartington

☼ 12 (6 Mon)-midnight; 12-10.30 Sun ☎ (01629) 653836
⊕ druidinnbirchover.co.uk
5 changing beers (sourced regionally; often Abbeydale, Oakham, Sarah Hughes) ⊞
Traditional country free house with the main room featuring open fires at either end. The landlord and landlady are passionate about beer, with the central bar offering five real ales, usually from breweries that include Abbeydale, Blue Monkey, Oakham and Sarah Hughes. The pub has a mixed clientele of locals and tourists visiting the Peak District National Park. Excellent home-cooked food is served in both the bar and separate restaurant. Q ⌂ 🏠 ⌂ ◑ ♿ Å P 🚌 (172) ❀ 🛜

Bolsover

Fidlers Rest ⅃

Craggs Road, S44 6BQ (just off A632, Bolsover Hill)
☼ 5-11; 12-11 Sat & Sun ☎ (01246) 828300
1 changing beer (often Dukeries, Spire, Welbeck Abbey) ⊞
A pub with a modern interior and a view through the floor into the original cellar. It has panoramic views of Bolsover Castle, extending across to the Peak District, from the seating area outside. The inn is named after Peter Fidler, the Bolsover-born explorer who mapped the Canadian wilderness for the Hudson Bay Company. Live artists occasionally perform here. 🏠 🏠 ♣ ● 🚌 (82,83) ❀ 🛜

Brampton

Real Ale Corner ⅃

415 Chatsworth Road, S40 3AD
☼ closed Mon; 1 (3 Tue; 11 Fri & Sat)-7; 1-5 Sun
☎ (01246) 202111
2 changing beers (often Ashover, Barlow, Shiny) ⊞
A bottle shop with a pub feel, it has two real ales to drink while browsing the 115 bottles of beer, nine ciders and wines. The seating area is extended to the outside, much like a small local. It offers a CAMRA-friendly home delivery service within five miles, gift vouchers and gift packs, or you can just enjoy a drink here in a warm and welcoming atmosphere. Q ❀ ● 🚌 ❀

Tap House ⅃

318 Chatsworth Road, S40 2BY
☼ 4-11; 12-midnight Fri & Sat; 12-11 Sun ☎ (01246) 234731
⊕ thetaphouse.co.uk
Thwaites Lancaster Bomber; house beer (by Barlow); 6 changing beers ⊞
A Thwaites project pub run in conjunction with Barlow Brewery, opened in February 2014 following refurbishment. Music can be heard in the main bar monthly – see the pub's Facebook page or adverts inside for dates and details. A quiet room is available to the rear, and there is a covered area outside. Hot and cold snacks are served along with hot roast cobs on Sunday. ❀ ◑ ● 🚌 ❀ 🛜

Tramway Tavern ⅃

192 Chatsworth Road, S40 2AT
☼ 4-11; 12-midnight Fri & Sat; 12-11 Sun ☎ (01246) 200111
⊕ tramwaytavern.co.uk
Brampton Golden Bud, Best; Everards Tiger; 5 changing beers ⊞
Local CAMRA Pub of the Year 2014, this is the Brampton Brewery tap. There are eight handpulls on the bar: four Brampton, one Everards and three guests. It also has a selection of Belgian and world beers along with traditional ciders and perries. Regular themed nights are held. An area is dedicated to pictures and history of the old Chesterfield tram service that once passed by, and there is an outdoor courtyard to the rear. ❀ ● 🚌 🛜

Buxton

Buxton Tap House ⅃

11-16 The Old Court House, George Street, SK17 6AT
☼ 10-midnight (1am Fri & Sat) ☎ (01298) 214085
Buxton SPA, Dark Nights; 3 changing beers (sourced nationally; often Buxton) ⊞
The Tap House is at the rear of the crescent in Buxton's café quarter, close to the opera house and the Dome. The tap for Buxton Brewery, it has five handpumps serving a range of the brewery's beers. SPA and Dark Nights are usually on, with three others. Draught cider comes from Pure North. A variety of food is on offer, ranging from baguettes to burgers Monday-Saturday and a traditional roast on Sunday. ❀ ◑ ♿ ⇌ ● 🍴 🚌 ❀ 🛜

Cheshire Cheese

37-39 High Street, SK17 6HA
☼ 12-11 (midnight Fri & Sat) ☎ (01298) 212453
Everards Tiger; Titanic Steerage, Iceberg, White Star, Plum Porter, Captain Smith's; 3 changing beers (sourced nationally; often Titanic) ⊞
A double-fronted building of considerable age that, after refurbishment, reopened under the management of Titanic in autumn 2013. The pub is essentially open plan but split into several distinct areas. Low ceilings with original beams add to the cosy atmosphere. There is a quiet area at one end which features an open fire. The bar boasts an impressive array of 10 handpulls serving a range of Titanic beers and guests. Thursday is pie night. Q ⌂ ❀ ◑ ♿ Å ♣ ● P 🚌 (199) ❀ 🛜

Chelmorton

Church Inn

Main Street, SK17 9SL
☼ 12-3, 6-11; 12-11 Fri-Sun ☎ (01298) 85319
⊕ thechurchinn.co.uk
Adnams Southwold Bitter; Marston's Burton Bitter, Pedigree; 5 changing beers (sourced nationally; often Abbeydale, Storm, Thornbridge) ⊞
Set in beautiful surroundings opposite the local church, this traditional village pub caters both for locals and walkers. The main room is laid out for dining and good home-cooked food is on offer; however, a cosy pub atmosphere is maintained, with a low ceiling and real fire. Guest beers are usually from local micros. There is an excellent patio area outside. Parking is available at the end of the road in front of the pub. Monday is quiz night. Q ❀ ⇌ ◑ Å ❀ 🛜

Chesterfield

Chesterfield Alehouse ⅃

37 West Bars, S40 1AG
☼ 12-10 ⊕ chesterfieldalehouse.co.uk
6 changing beers (often Abbeydale, Ashover, Raw) ⊞
Chesterfield's first micropub is a few minutes' walk from the historic marketplace. Previously a furniture shop, the split-level bar has a small seating area leading up a few steps to the serving area, where you will find six regularly changing beers; a stout or a porter are ever-present.

Traditional pub snacks including local pork pies are on offer, with a popular free cheese night every Tuesday evening. A growing range of bottled world beers, wines and 12 ciders are served by knowledgeable staff. Q♿♣●

Chesterfield Arms

Newbold Road, S41 7PH

4 (12 Thu)-11; 12-11.30 Fri & Sat; 12-11 Sun
(01246) 236634

Everards Tiger; 9 changing beers (often Abbeydale, Thornbridge, Brown Ales) H

Oak-clad walls, open fires and hop-strewn bars create a relaxing ambience here. Ten real ales, often from microbreweries, are on the bar, including the pub's own Brown Ales. A log-burning stove heats the barn, which opens at weekends with additional beers and hosts beer festivals. Conservatory doors open up on warm evenings, extending the outdoor seating area.
Q♿●P(10)

Market Pub

95 New Square, S40 1AH

11-11 (midnight Fri & Sat) (01246) 273641
themarketpub.co.uk

Greene King Abbot; Kelham Island Easy Rider; Timothy Taylor Landlord; 5 changing beers (often Chantry, Copper Dragon, Thornbridge) H

Popular, friendly town-centre pub in the historic market square. It has eight handpulled real ales and ciders, an extensive wine list and 100-plus whiskies. Quality home-cooked food is made with locally sourced produce. Regular events take place such as murder mysteries, gourmet food nights, wine and whisky tastings, a general knowledge quiz on Thursdays, a film and music quiz on Sundays, and occasional live music. ♣●

Royal Oak

1 The Shambles, S40 1PX (town centre)

11.30-11; 12-11 Sun (01246) 239588
royaloak-shambles.com

Bradfield Farmers Blonde; Draught Bass; Sharp's Doom Bar; Shepherd Neame Spitfire; Theakston Old Peculier; 1 changing beer (often Oakham) H

Reputed rest house of the Knights Templars and documented as an inn from 1722. It comprises two buildings of differing period and character, the older top bar dating to the 16th century. The lower room has a more modern feel, with a TV and a retro video game. Background music plays throughout. Food is served 11.30-7pm Monday-Saturday and 12-5pm Sunday. ♿

Rutland Arms

23 Stephenson Place, S40 1XL

12-11.30 (12.30am Thu-Sat); 12-11 Sun
(01246) 205857

Greene King Abbot; Sharp's Doom Bar; Thornbridge Jaipur IPA; 5 changing beers (often Leeds, Oakham, Titanic) H

Popular town-centre pub under the famous Crooked Spire parish church. It has the appearance of two buildings joined together, with a partly castellated roofline. Inside, it has two areas divided by steps. The beers vary far and wide, and there are two guest ciders. The food, especially roasts, are recommended and are good value. There are occasional beer festivals, a screen for sport, and piped music. ●

White Swan

16 St Mary's Gate, S41 7TJ

12-midnight (1am Fri & Sat) (01246) 229570

Greene King Abbot; house beer (by Raw); 10 changing beers (often Ashover, Raw, Whim) H

Affectionately known as the Mucky Duck, this popular pub is in sight of the famous Crooked Spire parish church. A spacious all-in-one room, it is the Raw Brewing Company's tied house, with continually changing guest beers and an impressive selection of bottled beers and real ciders. Home-made food is served all day, including light bites 12-3pm, and two-for-one burgers on Tuesdays and Sunday lunchtimes. An upstairs function room can be hired.
♿●P

Clowne

Centre

Recreation Close, Villa Park, S43 4PL

7-11 (01246) 819546

3 changing beers H

A council-run community centre widely used by the locals for functions. The Rock and Blues Club has live bands every Sunday and there is a popular quiz night on Tuesday, with free food. The venue is well cared for, with a relaxed and friendly atmosphere, and it has a beer festival in May. There is a Timothy Taylor changing house beer, plus guests. Ample car parking is available. ♿P(53,77,79)

Coton-in-the-Elms

Black Horse

17 Burton Road, DE12 8HJ

4-11 (midnight Fri); 1-midnight Sat; 12-10.30 Sun
(01283) 762947 theblackhorsederbyshire.co.uk

Draught Bass; Joule's Pale Ale; Marston's Pedigree; 1 changing beer (sourced regionally; often Church End, Gates Burton, Tollgate) H

This Guide regular of some 30 years ago was revived in 2009 as a lively and popular free house after more than a decade of neglect. Tastefully renovated with extensive use of wood, the bright and airy main room is divided into bar and lounge areas by glass-topped wood partitions. A small snug, served through a hatch, features a bar billiards table. A guest beer often comes from a local microbrewery, and real cider is Woody's. Quiz night is Tuesday and occasional live music plays on Sunday. ♣●P(22)

Crich

Cliff Inn

Town End, DE4 5DP (150yds from Crich Tramway Village)

5-midnight; 12-midnight Sat & Sun (01773) 852444

Buxton Moor Top; Dancing Duck Ay Up; Sharp's Doom Bar; 2 changing beers (sourced locally; often Abbeydale, Bradfield) H

Traditional gritstone free house at the top of the village just below the National Tramway Museum. Built about 1800, the two rooms are largely unchanged since the 1960s. There are logburners in both rooms and a quarry-tiled floor in the taproom. Of the five handpumps, four normally dispense LocAles. Home-made food is served Tuesday-Friday evenings and weekend lunchtimes.
Q♣P(140,142)

Derby

Alexandra Hotel

203 Siddals Road, DE1 2QE

12-11 (midnight Fri); 11-midnight Sat ☎ (01332) 293993

alexandrahotelderby.co.uk

Castle Rock Harvest Pale; 6 changing beers ℍ

The Alex is a Castle Rock pub serving two or three of its beers and up to five guest ales, including a mild and a stout/porter. There are also more than 50 UK and continental bottled beers of varying styles. The bar is adorned with railway memorabilia, and the lounge with breweriana. A Class 37 locomotive cab resides in the car park. This hostelry was the birthplace of Derby CAMRA in 1974 and was voted local CAMRA Pub of the Year 2015. Q P

Babington Arms

11-13 Babington Lane, DE1 1TA

8am-midnight (1am Fri & Sat) ☎ (01332) 383647

Greene King Abbot; Marston's Burton Bitter, Pedigree; 13 changing beers ℍ

A Wetherspoon pub converted from a furniture showroom and close to the city centre. It boasts a huge range of real ales, many from local microbreweries, and typically has five ciders on handpump/gravity dispense. The back end of the large bar has some half-partitioned banquette seating and caters for family eating. At the front of the pub there is a small fenced-off area where outdoor drinkers can have a smoke and watch the hustle and bustle of Babington Lane.
Q

Bell & Castle

92-96 Burton Road, DE1 1TG

12-midnight (1am Fri & Sat) ☎ (01332) 209808

bellandcastle.co.uk

5 changing beers ℍ

Converted from a row of cottages close to the city centre, this welcoming pub has been refurbished with modern decor. There are four open-plan areas and a separate meeting room. The largest area is used particularly for meals, including stone-baked pizzas. The bar has a changing choice of up to five guest beers from microbreweries, plus cider on handpump. For a pub so near the city, the large garden at the rear is an unexpected delight.

Brunswick Inn

1 Railway Terrace, DE1 2RU

11-11 (11.30 Fri & Sat); 12-10.30 Sun ☎ (01332) 290677

brunswickderby.co.uk

Everards Beacon Bitter, Tiger; Timothy Taylor Landlord; 13 changing beers (often Brunswick) ℍ

Originally part of the railway village, the pub was closed in 1974 and fell into disrepair. Rescued and restored, it opened as Derby's first multiple-choice real ale house in 1987. A purpose-built brewery was added in 1991, and it has since become one of the best known free houses in the country. Although owned by Everards, its range of up to 16 real ales includes at least six from the in-house brewery. Busy on Derby County match days.
Q P

Coach & Horses

Mansfield Road, DE1 3RF

12-midnight (1am Sat) ☎ (01332) 258901

Draught Bass; Exmoor Gold; 2 changing beers ℍ

Welcoming pub in Little Chester, the oldest part of Derby, dating back to Roman times. Focused on the local community, there is a games room for pool and darts. Events include popular Sunday night quizzes, support for local charities, and a book exchange. The pub has a team in the local skittles league. The two guest beers are from the SIBA range. There's live music on bank holidays, with a larger range of beers. P

Exeter Arms

13 Exeter Place, DE1 2EU

12-11 (11.30 Wed & Thu; midnight Fri & Sat); 12-10.30 Sun ☎ (01332) 605323 exeterarms.co.uk

Dancing Duck Ay Up, Dark Drake; Marston's Pedigree; 4 changing beers ℍ

A remarkable transformation in recent times by the licensees and Dancing Duck Brewery earned the pub local CAMRA Pub of the Year 2013. The Ex simply oozes old-world charm and features a small bar with open fire, partitioned lounges and a wooden-settled snug with an old-fashioned range. The adjoining atmospheric cottage dating from about 1815 has been incorporated into the pub. There is a quiz on Monday evening and live music every Saturday evening in summer.
P

Falstaff

74 Silverhill Road, DE23 6UJ

12-11 (midnight Fri & Sat) ☎ (01332) 342902

falstaffbrewery.co.uk

Falstaff Fist Full of Hops, Phoenix, Smiling Assassin; 1 changing beer ℍ

A 20-minute walk from the city centre rewards you with this atmospheric and reputedly haunted free house. Originally a coaching inn before the neighbourhood was built up, it is now the Falstaff Brewery tap, and has long been the best real ale house in the Normanton area of Derby. The rear lounge is a shrine to Offiler's Brewery, with a display of memorabilia. Other collectables can be viewed throughout the games room and second bar room. Q

Five Lamps

25 Duffield Road, DE1 3BH

12-11 (midnight Fri & Sat) ☎ (01332) 348730

fivelampsderby.co.uk

Everards Tiger; Oakham Citra; Peak Ales Chatsworth Gold; Thornbridge Jaipur IPA; Whim Hartington IPA; 8 changing beers ℍ

Since it reopened in 2010, the pub has gone from strength to strength thanks to the dedication of the licensees and staff. Fourteen handpumps showcase many local ales from breweries such as Derby, Buxton, Peak and Whim. The Lamps is essentially open plan, but has many little nooks and crannies giving it a homely feel. It has been tastefully refurbished with wood panelling and leather seating in a traditional style. P

Flowerpot

23-25 King Street, DE1 3DZ

12-11 (11.30 Wed & Thu; 12.30am Fri & Sat)

☎ (01332) 204955 flowerpotderby.co.uk

Frontier Gold Rush; Oakham Bishops Farewell; Whim Hartington IPA; house beer (by Black Iris); 4 changing beers ℍ/𝔾

Dating from around 1800 but much expanded from its original premises, this vibrant pub reaches back from the roadside frontage and divides into several interlinking rooms. One room provides the stage for regular live bands and another has a glass cellar wall revealing rows of stillaged casks, which can be seen from the bar and from the road outside. At least eight real ales are offered and it is now the home of the Frontier Brewery. Good en-suite accommodation is available.

Furnace Inn

Duke Street, DE1 3BX

4 (12 Fri & Sat)-midnight; 12-11 Sun (01332) 385981

6 changing beers H

Since it reopened in 2012 this pub has transformed itself into a real ale mecca, culminating in local CAMRA Pub of the Year 2014. A former Hardys & Hansons pub, it is now the tap for the Shiny Brewing Company. Up to eight real ales and three ciders/perries are served, plus guest beers from all over. There are two distinct open-plan rooms with a central bar. Open-mic, poker and cheese nights feature, with regular beer festivals held throughout the year. Q

Golden Eagle

55 Agard Street, DE1 1DZ

12-midnight; 12-11.30 Sun

Morland Old Golden Hen; 5 changing beers H

Completely refurbished by the Titan Brewery, this is now its brewery tap. The pub's original name has also been restored after many changes. A mural on the outside pays homage to Derby history. Inside, the single room has a wooden floor throughout. It is comfortable and welcoming, with a table next to the bar for newspapers and local interest books. The upstairs function room hosts a poker night on Sunday and there is live acoustic music every Thursday evening. P

Greyhound

76 Friar Gate, DE1 1FN

12-11 (midnight Thu; 1am Fri); 11-1am Sat; 11-11 Sun

(01332) 344155 greyhound-dbc.co.uk

Derby Business As Usual; 8 changing beers H

An old coaching inn that has been restored to a high standard by Derby Brewing Company, the Greyhound has a roofed terrace (open in summer) as well as a walled beer garden which are a boon in fine weather. Modern art adorns the walls in this vibrant establishment which caters for a mixed clientele. Up to seven beers from the Derby range and up to three guests are on offer as well as a real cider.

Horse & Groom

48 Elms Street, DE1 3HN

12-11 horseandgroomderby.co.uk

Draught Bass; 3 changing beers H

The Tudor exterior makes this pub stand out from the other properties just off the main road in the centre of the village. A traditional two-roomed pub, it has oak panelling in one room and beams throughout, which gives it a cosy and stylish atmosphere. A cheery welcome awaits families, dogs and walkers. It is popular for meals, and there is a choice of six beers with an emphasis on local brews from the Derby and Nottingham areas.

Little Chester Ale House

4a Chester Green Road, DE1 3SF

3-10.30; 12-11 Fri & Sat; 12-10.30 Sun 07900 475755

4 changing beers H

Derby's first micropub achieved local CAMRA City Pub of the Year runner-up in 2014. On the edge of a tree-lined conservation area, the pub is in the historic Little Chester part of the city, site of Roman Derventio, where two ancient wells can still been seen nearby. This former shop has one small main room with a passageway leading to a tiny rear room. It has four changing beers, including at least one from the local Wentwell Brewery, the pub's owner. Q

Old Bell Hotel

Sadler Gate, DE1 3NQ

12-11 (1am Fri); 11-1am Sat (01332) 723090

Draught Bass; 3 changing beers H

One of Derby's best-loved pubs continues to be restored to its former magnificence. Discerning drinkers seek out the Tudor Bar to the rear, which was a men-only bar until 1975. This 18th-century coaching inn is a welcome oasis in Sadler Gate, a premier shopping street in the Cathedral Quarter. The exterior Tudor-style half-timbering and the Tudor Bar with its courtyard for alfresco drinking were added in 1929.

Peacock Inn

87 Nottingham Road, DE1 3QS

11-11 (midnight Fri & Sat); 12-10.30 Sun

(01332) 583308

Draught Bass G**; Marston's Pedigree; Whim Arbor Light; house beer (by Leatherbritches); 5 changing beers** H

Attractive 18th-century stone-built roadside pub that used to be a staging post on the main coach road out of Derby, which ran alongside the old Derby Canal. Two rooms on different levels are divided by a central bar, featuring wooden floors, stove burners, photos of old Derby and Derby County memorabilia. Up to nine real ales and two ciders and/or perries feature; beer festivals are held in the large, covered garden area to the rear. Q

Rowditch Inn

246 Uttoxeter New Road, DE22 3LL

12-2 (not Mon-Fri), 7-11 (01332) 343123

Marston's Pedigree; 2 changing beers (often Rowditch) H

Welcoming roadside hostelry with an unexpectedly deep interior that divides into two bar areas and a small snug. There is a display cabinet of pub memorabilia, and the pumpclips adorning the walls testify to myriad guest ales. Downstairs, at the rear, the garden is a peaceful haven in warmer weather. The output of the pub's brewery is almost exclusively consumed on the premises. Well worth the walk or the five-minute bus ride from the city centre. Q

Silk Mill Cider & Ale House

19 Full Street, DE1 3AF

12-11 (midnight Fri & Sat); 12-10.30 Sun

(01332) 349160 thesilkmillderby.co.uk

Dancing Duck Ay Up; Draught Bass; 5 changing beers H

Handsome stone-faced building named after the historic silk mill nearby, which marks the start of the Derwent Valley World Heritage Trail. To the right of the entrance is the Offilers' lounge with a cosy real fire, ideal for drinkers. There is a dedicated dining area to the rear of pub – booking is recommended at peak times. The central bar has nine handpumps shared between real ales and ciders. Quirky decorative ornaments and fittings are used throughout.

Earl Sterndale

Quiet Woman
SK17 0BU (off B5053)
⏲ 7 (4 Sat)-11; 5-11 Sun ☎ (01298) 83211
Jennings Dark Mild; Marston's Burton Bitter; 4 changing beers (sourced nationally; often Marston's, Wincle) Ⓗ
Unspoilt basic local with an unusual name and sign, set in the heart of the Peak District National Park, opposite the church and village green. A low-beamed room has a real fire on the left and a small bar to the right. There is a separate games room with a pool table. Local fresh eggs and traditional pork pies can be purchased at the bar. The pub offers its own selection of bottle-conditioned beers from Leek Brewery. **Q**🐴✿▲♣**P**🚌(442)

Glossop

Crown Inn ★
142 Victoria Street, SK13 8JF (on Hayfield Rd out of town centre)
⏲ 5 (12 Fri & Sat)-11; 12-10.30 Sun ☎ (01457) 862824
Samuel Smith Old Brewery Bitter Ⓗ
End-of-terrace local, a few minutes from the town centre and railway station, built in 1846 and acquired by the brewery in 1977. The interior of the pub is listed by CAMRA as being of Outstanding National Historic Importance. A curved bar serves two snugs, each with a real fire in winter, and a pool/games room. Pictures of bygone Glossop add to the traditional character. Prices are keen. An enclosed outdoor drinking area is provided in the rear yard. **Q**✿♿⇌♣🚌(390)🐾

Queen's Arms
1 Shepley Street, SK13 7RZ
⏲ 12-midnight ☎ (01457) 853005
🌐 queens-arms-hotel-old-glossop.co.uk
Holt Bitter; Morland Old Speckled Hen; Robinsons Unicorn; Thornbridge Jaipur IPA; Thwaites Wainwright; 3 changing beers Ⓗ
Increasingly popular pub in the original heart of Glossop – now Old Glossop – an ideal stopping-off point for walkers from the hill-walking areas close by who can drink, eat and stay here. It is well used by locals and visitors from far and wide. The excellent beer range is lovingly cherished by an exceptional cellarman. Upstairs is the popular Coriander Indian restaurant and takeaway. Regular music events are held on Tuesday and Saturday evenings. Coach parties welcome by appointment.
🐴✿🛏◐◑♿▯🚌(390)🐾📶

Star Inn
2 Howard Street, SK13 7DD (next to railway station)
⏲ 4-11; 2-midnight Fri; 12-midnight Sat; 12-10.30 Sun
☎ (01457) 853072
Timothy Taylor Landlord; changing beers Ⓗ
A highly popular town centre pub, run by a dedicated CAMRA member, adjacent to the railway station. The large, comfortable main room, where conversation predominates, has a tiled and wooden floor and is complemented by a smaller room to the rear. Guest beers are mainly from local microbreweries, and real draught cider is available. Regular beer and cider festivals are held throughout the year. The pub is an ideal starting point for walking within the Dark Peak area.
Q⇌🍎**P**🚌📶

Hartshorne

Admiral Rodney Inn
65 Main Street, DE11 7ES (on A514)
⏲ 6-11; 5.30-11.30 Fri; 4-11 Sat; 12-midnight Sun
☎ (01283) 216482
Exmoor Gold; Marston's Pedigree; 4 changing beers (sourced nationally; often Cottage, Derby, Fuller's) Ⓗ
A traditional village pub dating back to the early 19th century, rebuilt and extended in the late 20th century to provide an open-plan L-shaped drinking area while retaining the original oak beams in the former snug. Up to four guest beers are available, usually from SIBA members. The Cheese Society meets here on the first Monday of the month, a quiz night takes place on Friday, and karaoke on Sunday. The grounds include a cricket pitch, home of Hartshorne Cricket Club; Saturday opening hours are 12-midnight during the season.
🐴✿♿♣**P**🚌(61)🐾📶

Hayfield

George
14 Church Street, SK22 2JE
⏲ 11.45-11 (11.30 Fri & Sat); 12-11 Sun ☎ (01663) 743691
🌐 georgehotelhayfield.co.uk
Banks's Bitter; 3 changing beers Ⓗ
Rambling stone-built 16th-century pub, located in the village centre, originally a mail house; the Derby Militia was formed here in 1808. In addition to the handpulled ales, Thatchers Heritage cider is available. The interior includes stained-glass mullioned windows and a magnificent cast-iron range fireplace with a real fire in winter. Two comfortable lounges, a cosy bar area and a separate dining room are complemented by a function room. Hikers and cyclists are welcome. Close to Hayfield bus station.
✿🛏◐◑▲🍎**P**🚌(358,61)📶

Royal Hotel
Market Street, SK22 2EP
⏲ 11-11 ☎ (01663) 742721 🌐 theroyalhayfield.co.uk
Thwaites Original, Wainwright; house beer (by Happy Valley); 2 changing beers Ⓗ
An imposing stone pub near the church, cricket ground and River Sett. The interior boasts oak panels and pews, creating a relaxing atmosphere; real fires burn in winter. Guest beers from local micros are always on the bar and an annual beer festival is hosted in October. A restaurant and function room complete the facilities, with food available all day in summer. The village is the base for many leisure activities in the Dark Peak and was the birthplace of actor Arthur Lowe.
Q🐴✿🛏◐◑♿▲**P**🚌(61,358)📶

Holbrook

Dead Poets Inn
38 Chapel Street, DE56 0TQ
⏲ 12-2.30, 5-11; 12-11 Fri-Sun ☎ (01332) 780301
🌐 socialserenity.co.uk
Draught Bass; Greene King Abbot; Marston's Pedigree; Oakham Citra; 5 changing beers Ⓗ
This stone village inn was built in 1800 and was formerly known as the Cross Keys. The place has a charming old-worldly atmosphere and is popular with locals. There is a delightful snug and the main bar has high-backed pews, low ceilings, stone-flagged floors, a real fire and an inglenook fireplace. There is a welcoming, recently

refurbished, conservatory area to the rear, which is bright in summer and warm in winter. A great destination in any season.
Q P (138,71)

Hope

Cheshire Cheese Inn

Edale Road, S33 6ZF
closed Mon; 12-3, 6-11; 12-11 Sat; 12-9 Sun
(01433) 620381 thecheshirecheeseinn.co.uk
Bradfield Farmers Blonde; 3 changing beers (sourced locally; often Bradfield, Peak Ales) H
A cosy country inn dating from 1578 with an open-plan bar area and a smaller room at a lower level that was probably originally used to house animals, but now is mainly used as a dining area. It is situated in good walking country but has limited parking, and the road outside is narrow. The pub can arrange outdoor activities for guests.
Q P

Horsley Woodhouse

Old Oak Inn

176 Main Street, DE7 6AW (on A609)
4 (3 Thu & Fri; 12 Sat)-11; 12-10.30 Sun (01332) 881299
Leadmill Old Oak Bitter, Fluffer; changing beers (often Leadmill) H
Taphouse for the Leadmill Brewery, the Old Oak features an extensive variety of Leadmill beers, plus a couple of guests. This traditional pub boasts four rooms of differing character, some with open fires. At weekends drinkers can enjoy the RuRAD bar which is effectively a mini beer festival offering ales from the cask from breweries near and far alongside the more local Leadmill and Bottle Brook beers. Homely, welcoming and excellent value for money, this roadside tavern is well worth a visit.
Q P

Ilkeston

Brewery Tap

24 South Street, DE7 5QE
12-11 (0115) 837 6886 muirhousebrewery.co.uk
4 changing beers (sourced nationally; often Muirhouse) H
Established micropub without jukeboxes or gambling machines, simply a place where you can appreciate quality beers and enjoy a friendly conversation. There are two rotating ales direct from its award-winning Muirhouse Brewery, plus two guest beers and two real ciders to choose from. Only pre-packed snacks are available, but cobs and pies can be purchased from the adjacent deli and eaten on the premises. Children are allowed up to 8pm. A loyalty card is available.
Q

Dewdrop

24 Station Road, DE7 5TE
4 (3 Fri; 12 Sat)-11; 12-10.30 Sun (0115) 932 9684
Oakham Bishops Farewell; changing beers (often Acorn, Blue Monkey, Castle Rock) H
A friendly, multi-roomed Victorian free house on the outskirts of town. The cosy lounge with real fire is adorned with awards and mirrors. There is also a bar with a pool table and a classic jukebox, and a quieter family room. Dogs are allowed in the bar and lobby. There are two ciders, Westons Old Rosie and Vintage Organic. Hearty cobs are made to order. Outside there is a covered, heated smoking area. The railway station is due to open in 2016.
Q

Observatory

14A Market Place, DE7 5QA
8am-11 (midnight Fri & Sat) (0115) 932 8040
Adnams Broadside; Greene King Abbot; Oakham Citra; Ruddles Best Bitter; 4 changing beers (often Exmoor) H
Overlooking the marketplace, this glass-fronted converted supermarket is a well-run Wetherspoon, named in recognition of John Flamsteed, the first Astronomer Royal, who lived locally. The ground floor has a large bar and the toilets, while upstairs is a smaller drinking and dining area. There is a roof terrace which is also the smoking zone. The pub is a short walk from all bus routes into Ilkeston.
Q

Spanish Bar

76 South Street, DE7 5QJ
10-11 (midnight Fri & Sat); 10.30-11 Sun
(0115) 930 8666
Jennings Cumberland Ale; Whim Hartington IPA; 3 changing beers H
Close to the town centre, this community pub attracts all age groups. The main bar has a logburner and is furnished with an array of comfortable chairs. A second room which is open at busier times has a large-screen TV showing all major sports events. The pub has darts, dominoes and skittle teams. Outside there is an exceptional summer flower display, heated skittle alley and a covered smoking shelter. An annual beer festival is hosted. Q

Kilburn

Hunter Arms

Church Street, DE56 0LU
2-11; 12-midnight Fri-Sun (01332) 781518
Marston's Pedigree; Oakham Bishops Farewell; Timothy Taylor Landlord; 6 changing beers (often Blue Monkey, Dancing Duck, Thornbridge) H
Built in 1879 and named after the owners of nearby Kilburn Hall, the pub was rescued from closure in 2009 and has since become a popular, friendly local serving good beer. It has a pleasant opened-out interior with a welcoming fire, TV and free Wi-Fi. The separate Old Slaughterhouse cider bar features 10-14 ciders and perries. Light food is served Tuesday to Saturday only. A large function room is available upstairs. Q P

Kirk Ireton

Barley Mow Inn

Main Street, DE6 3JP (off B5023) SK266501
12-2, 7-11; 12-2, 7-10.30 Sun (01335) 370306
Whim Hartington IPA; 3 changing beers G
Set in a charming village overlooking Ecclesbourne Valley, this gabled Jacobean building houses an old-fashioned down-to-earth pub, of the type that is increasingly hard to find. Several interconnecting rooms of different character have low beams, mullioned windows and well-worn woodwork, and there is a welcoming open fire in the main bar. A small serving hatch reveals a stillage with up to six gravity beers. Local breweries such as Blue Monkey, Dancing Duck, Burton Bridge, Thornbridge and Peak Ales often feature. Q

Kniveton

Red Lion

Main Street, DE6 1JH

✪ 12-11 (midnight Fri & Sat); 12-10.30 Sun

☎ (01335) 345554

Marston's Pedigree; Sharp's Doom Bar; 1 changing beer Ⓗ

Attractive stone pub exactly in the middle of this small village, serving a good range of beers, mainly from established regionals, but occasionally with a local brewery offering. It has friendly and welcoming staff, and a good range of food with several different speciality nights such as pie nights and curry nights. Awarded Most Improved Pub in the local CAMRA awards for 2014.
🛏🍴◑♣P🐾🐶🛜

Langley

Butchers Arms Ⓛ

127 Hands Road, Heanor, DE75 7HB

✪ 4 (3 Fri & Sat)-midnight; 12-midnight Sun ☎ 07790 305682

Coppice Side Nottingham Blonde, Owd Miner; 6 changing beers (often Bottle Brook, Coppice Side, Leadmill) Ⓗ

The Butchers Arms is a traditional local establishment run by the local Coppice Side and Leadmill breweries; their beers feature, as do those of Bottle Brook Brewery. It has a large car park and beer gardens to the front and rear. The pub was awarded local CAMRA Pub of the Year in 2014. The main bar is simply furnished and has a log-burning fire. No jukebox or gaming machines interfere with the conversation.
Q🛏🍴🚆(Langley Mill)♣🍺P🐾🐶

Little Eaton

Queen's Head Ⓛ

131 Alfreton Road, DE21 5DF

✪ 12-11; 11-midnight Fri & Sat; 11-11 Sun

☎ (01332) 986065 ⊕ queenshead-dbc.co.uk

Derby Business As Usual, Dashingly Dark; Everards Tiger, Original; 6 changing beers Ⓗ

Historic Derbyshire stone inn in Little Eaton village boasting some original features, including low-beamed ceilings. The main entrance has been renovated and the bar relocated to create a welcoming and stylish interior, with an attractive patio garden to one side for warmer summer days. There are normally nine real ales including five from Derby Brewing Company. The menu selection includes home-made locally sourced food, all prepared and cooked on site. 🛏🍴◑🐾🍺P🐾🐶🛜

Little Hayfield

Lantern Pike

45 Glossop Road, SK22 2NG (10 mins' walk from Hayfield towards Glossop)

✪ 12-3 (not Mon), 5-11; 12-11 Sat & Sun ☎ (01663) 747590

⊕ lanternpikeinn.co.uk

Timothy Taylor Landlord; 1 changing beer Ⓗ

Picturesque ivy-clad pub nestling in a small hamlet within the Dark Peak area. The comfortable, traditional lounge bar, with a real fire in winter, connects to separate informal dining areas. There is a traditional pub menu featuring home-made dishes, with specialist lunches on Sundays. Coronation Street originator Tony Warren once lived nearby and wrote early episodes of the soap while in the pub. There are superb views from the rear patio area. Hikers are welcome.
🐶🍴◑P🏠(61)🛜

Little Longstone

Packhorse Inn

Main Street, DE45 1NN

✪ 12-3, 5-11; 12-11 Sat & Sun ☎ (01629) 640471

⊕ packhorselongstone.co.uk

Black Sheep Best Bitter; Thornbridge Wild Swan, Lord Marples, Jaipur IPA; 2 changing beers Ⓗ

A small pub that began life as two miners' cottages, but which has been welcoming drinkers since 1787. Just a short walk from stunning views of Monsal Head, dogs and walkers are welcome. Fresh local produce is a passion, an ethos also extended to the beers, which always include a choice from the nearby Thornbridge Brewery. There is a pleasant beer garden, and food is served all day at weekends. 🛏🐶◑▲♣🏠(173)🐾🛜

Longshaw

Grouse

S11 7TZ

✪ 12-3, 6-11; 12-11 Sat & Sun ☎ (01433) 630423

⊕ thegrouseinn-derbyshire.co.uk

Banks's Bitter; Marston's EPA, Pedigree; 1 changing beer (often Banks's) Ⓗ

In the same family for the past 51 years, this free house stands in isolation on bleak moorland south-west of Sheffield, and is a welcome refuge for walkers as well as climbers from the nearby Fraggatt Edge. The comfortable lounge and bar are at the front, with a separate room at the rear reached through the conservatory in which vines manage to grow. The accommodation is a self-catering holiday flat. No food Monday evenings.
Q🛏🐶🍴◑&P🏠🐶

Lullington

Colvile Arms

Main Street, DE12 8EG (centre of village)

✪ 6-11; 12-3, 7-11 Sun ☎ (01827) 373212

⊕ colvilearms.co.uk

Draught Bass; Marston's Pedigree; 1 changing beer (sourced regionally; often Blue Monkey, Holden's, Thwaites) Ⓗ

Leased from the Lullington Estate, the seat of the Colvile family until the early 1900s, this popular 18th-century free house is at the heart of an attractive hamlet at the southern tip of the county. The public bar comprises an adjoining hallway and snug, each featuring high-backed settles with wood panelling. The bar and a comfortable lounge are situated on opposite sides of a central serving area. A second lounge/function room overlooks the beer garden and lawn. Q🐾♣P🐶🛜

Makeney

Holly Bush 🍺 ★

Holly Bush Lane, DE56 0RX

✪ 12-11; 12-10.30 Sun ☎ (01332) 841729

⊕ hollybushinnmakeney.co.uk

Fuller's London Pride; Greene King Abbot; Marston's Pedigree Ⓗ; Ruddles County Ⓖ; Timothy Taylor Landlord; 3 changing beers Ⓗ

Local CAMRA 2015 Pub of the Year, the Holly Bush is an excellent late 17th-century Grade II-listed pub with character. Once a farmhouse and brewery on the Strutt Estate, the building stood on the main Derby turnpike before the new road opened in 1818. Dick Turpin reputedly drank here. The inn has a nationally important historic pub interior, including various hideaway slabbed-floor rooms, warmed in winter by welcoming fires. Bar snacks are served all day, every day. Walkers, families and dogs are all welcome. Q❄✿Ⓓ&♣●P🚌🐾🛜

Marlpool

Marlpool Ale House Ⓛ
5 Breach Road, Heanor, DE75 7NJ
✪ closed Mon-Thu; 2-10 Fri; 12-10 Sat & Sun
☎ (01773) 711285 ⊕ marlpoolbrewing.co.uk
Marlpool Blind Boris, Otters Pocket, Scratty Ratty Ⓗ; 5 changing beers (sourced regionally; often Marlpool) Ⓗ/Ⓖ
Micropub and brewery tap for the Marlpool Brewery. Formerly a butchers' shop, it comprises a cosy bar area, a room at the rear with a wood-burning stove and an outside seating area. The bar is a pulpit from a Methodist chapel, now adorned with four handpumps. Further ales and ciders are brought from the cellar, normally providing a choice of eight in total. The small size encourages conversation. Opening hours are restricted but include all bank holidays. Q✿●🚌🐾

Matlock

MoCa Bar Ⓛ
77 Dale Road, DE4 3LT
✪ 11-11 (1am Fri & Sat) ☎ (01629) 583973
7 changing beers (sourced locally; often Thornbridge, Abbeydale, Blue Monkey) Ⓗ
Modern single-room bar with a sophisticated big-city café feel, with wooden floors and chunky pine furniture. Comfortable seating includes a large window area and a decked terrace at the rear. Open plan and urbane, with music memorabilia adorning the walls, the MoCa Bar has seven handpulls featuring ales from dedicated breweries Abbeydale, Blue Monkey, Brampton, Dancing Duck, Kelham Island, Oakham and Thornbridge. There is a reduction in the price of real ales Monday-Wednesday. ❄✿Ⓓ≠🚌🐾🛜

Thorn Tree Inn
48 Jackson Road, DE4 3JQ (up Bank Rd, left into Smedley St, 2nd right up Smith Rd, 1st left)
✪ 12-2 (not Mon), 5-11.30; 12-midnight Fri & Sat; 12-11.30 Sun ☎ (01629) 580295 ⊕ thorntreeatmatlock.co.uk
Draught Bass; Ruddles Best Bitter; Timothy Taylor Landlord; 4 changing beers (sourced nationally; often Castle Rock, Oakham, Thornbridge) Ⓗ
Perched high above Matlock town, this traditional two-roomed pub enjoys beautiful views from the heated patio area. Children and dogs are welcome although cat-swinging is not recommended due to the compact nature of the establishment. Reputedly, a haunted wall clock hangs in the lounge where regulars, ramblers and real ale enthusiasts convene to enjoy the atmosphere. Three permanent real ales are complemented by four changing guests. Home-made food is served Tuesday-Friday lunchtimes, pie night is Wednesday 6-8pm, and Sunday lunch is served from 5pm. Q✿Ⓓ≠♣🍴🚌🐾🛜

Matlock Bath

Fishpond Ⓛ
204 South Parade, DE4 3NR
✪ 11-midnight; 11-11 Sun ☎ (01629) 55006
⊕ thefishpondmatlockbath.co.uk
Changing beers Ⓗ
At the south end of this historic spa town and set into the limestone cliff face, this recently refurbished free house has not lost any of its traditional character. Woodburners bookend the cavernous interior, adding to the congenial atmosphere. The varied selection of ales and ciders has a strong focus on LocAle, and is complemented by an interesting menu featuring artisan bread from the venue's own bakery. It regularly hosts live music and comedy plus special events. ❄✿Ⓓ&≠●P🚌🐾🛜

Melbourne

Blue Bell Inn Ⓛ
53 Church Street, DE73 8EJ
✪ 11-11; 11.30-10.30 Sun ☎ (01332) 865764
⊕ thebluebellinnmelbourne.co.uk
Shardlow Reverend Eaton; 3 changing beers Ⓗ
The brewery tap for Shardlow Brewery offers a range of its beers including Reverend Eaton, with guests coming mainly from local breweries. Real cider is sold and there are two beer festivals each year. Run on traditional lines, the bar has a sporting emphasis and the restaurant serves traditional pub fare. The place is popular with walkers and is well located for visitors to Melbourne Hall and the 12th-century Norman parish church. ✿Ⓓ♣●🚌🐾🛜

Middleton

Nelson Arms
The Green, Main Street, DE4 4LU
✪ 5 (12 Sat)-midnight; 12-11 Sun ☎ (01629) 825154
⊕ nelsonarmsmiddleton.co.uk
Marston's Pedigree; 2 changing beers Ⓗ
Friendly family-owned free house at the top of the village. A small, comfortable bar is to the left as you enter; a large beamed room to the right has a welcoming fire and an interesting array of pictures, artefacts and curious ornaments that adorn the walls. A separate pool/function/family room is to the rear of the pub, as is an outdoor drinking area. Real cider complements the choice of two guest ales. ❄✿🏠&♣●P🚌🐾🛜

Millers Dale

Angler's Rest 🍷 Ⓛ
SK17 8SN
✪ 12-3, 6.30-11; 12-midnight Sat; 12-9 Sun
☎ (01298) 871323 ⊕ theanglersrest.co.uk
Adnams Southwold Bitter; Storm Silk of Amnesia; 2 changing beers (sourced locally; often Intrepid) Ⓗ
Ivy-clad inn dating from 1753 on the banks of the River Wye, handy for the spectacular walk along the Monsal Trail. It is a multi-room establishment including a cosy lounge with a real fire and a comfortable dining area. Walking boots and dogs are welcome in the hikers' bar. Good, traditional pub food is served daily and the guest beers are mostly LocAle. Accommodation is in a self-catering apartment. Q❄✿Ⓓ▲♣●P🚌(65)🐾

Milton

Swan Inn
49 Main Street, DE65 6EF
11-4 (3 Mon & Wed), 6-11; 11-10.30 Sun
(01283) 703188 theswaninnmilton.co.uk
Marston's Pedigree; Sharp's Doom Bar; 1 changing beer H
Free house serving highly praised ale including at least one guest beer, often from a local microbrewery. There is a fine display of railway memorabilia in the bar and the pub has mini beer festivals. Excellent home-cooked food is on offer and the restaurant operates as the Cygnets Tearoom during the day. The pub, in a small village just over a mile's walk from the nearest bus route through Repton, is well worth a visit. ❀◑♿P

Newton Solney

Brickmakers Arms
9 Main Street, DE15 0SJ (on B5008; opp jct with Trent Lane)
5-11; 12-11 Sat & Sun (01283) 703170
Burton Bridge Golden Delicious, Bitter, Porter, Stairway to Heaven; Timothy Taylor Landlord H
Acquired by the Burton Bridge Brewery in 2011, this comfortable, cosy local is at the end of an 18th-century terrace of cottages; it was converted into a pub in the early 19th century for workers at a nearby brickworks. Internally, it features a narrow central bar leading at one end to a room served through a hatch, and at the opposite end to an impressive oak-panelled room. A hallway houses a small library. Quiz night is Monday, bingo Tuesday. Q❀♣P(V3)

Ockbrook

Cross Keys
Green Lane, DE72 3SE
12-midnight (11.30 Sun) (01332) 662308
crosskeys-ockbrook.co.uk
Marston's Pedigree; Sharp's Doom Bar; Tetley Mild; 2 changing beers H
A traditional village pub with a quirky character, offering a selection of five real ales and one real cider. The bar has a low-beamed ceiling, darts playing area, several screens for TV sport and a woodburner for the winter months. Events include karaoke evenings and theme nights. Home-made food includes stone-baked pizza. Outside there is a small terrace with seating at the front and a small enclosed garden and play area to the side.
❀◑♣P

Royal Oak L
55 Green Lane, DE72 3SE
11.30-3, 5-11.30; 11.30-11.30 Sat; 12-11.30 Sun
(01332) 662378 royaloakockbrook.com
Draught Bass; 4 changing beers H
Attractive 18th-century pub with a number of small rooms. Run by the Wilson family since Coronation year, they have brought about many improvements while retaining the original character and features. Excellent home-cooked food is served every lunchtime and Monday to Friday evenings. A large function room allows the pub to host many community and public events including live music and open mic nights. Outside there are two pleasant gardens, one with an enclosed play area for children.
Q❀◑♿♣P

Openwoodgate

Black Bull's Head
2 Kilburn Lane, DE56 0SF
12-11; 12-10.30 Sun 07860 757741
blackbullshead.com
Draught Bass; Greene King Abbot; Oakham Bishops Farewell; 6 changing beers (often Blue Monkey, Castle Rock, Dancing Duck) H
Two-roomed former Greene King pub, now a free house, offering a warm welcome in comfortable surroundings. Walls are adorned with historic photographs and newspaper clippings of local and national interest, with one wall dedicated to the RAF. The pub serves many real ales and ciders and there are more available in the separate rustic Bedlam Bar, open Friday-Sunday. The Black Bull's Head was local CAMRA Pub of the Year in both 2013 and 2014. Q♿♣P(6.4,6.X)

Over Haddon

Lathkil Hotel L
School Lane, DE45 1JE
11-11; 12-10.30 Sun (01629) 812501 lathkil.co.uk
Everards Tiger; 4 changing beers H
A pub overlooking a masterpiece of Peak District scenery, marvellous in any weather. Walking in, one side is an old-fashioned bar room with a real fire and oak beams, while the larger room opposite is where diners enjoy superb home-cooked meals, again with a log-burning fire. The covered beer garden is the perfect place to while away summer evenings with a pint. Dogs are welcome in the bar, but walkers should remove their boots at the door.
Q❀◑ΛP(178)

Parwich

Sycamore Inn
DE6 1QL (nr church) SK187543
12-2, 7 (6 Thu & Fri)-11; 12-11 Sat & Sun
(01335) 390212
Robinsons Double Hop, Old Tom H
A true village hub in the centre of a picturesque and remote-feeling village, although only 15 minutes' drive from Ashbourne. The landlady took on the village store a few years back and runs it from a side room off the bar corridor, as well as serving beers from Robinsons, including Old Tom when in season. It has a small single-room bar, although there are side rooms in use occasionally. It regularly features highly in the local CAMRA Pub of the Year awards. Q❀◑Λ♣P

Ripley

Beehive Inn
151 Peasehill, DE5 3JN
5-midnight (1am Fri); 3-1am Sat; 4-midnight Sun
(01773) 749593
8 changing beers H
On the edge of town, this three-roomed free house is a hub for local rugby and pub league teams. The separate Honeypot Bar at the top of the beer garden is popular, serving up to four real ales and several ciders and perries (check with pub for opening times). Landlocked and Pentrich brewing companies both brew on the premises and their beers feature regularly in the Honeypot.
Q❀♿♣P

Red Lion
Market Place, DE5 3BS
🟢 8am-midnight (1am Fri & Sat) ☎ (01773) 512875
Adnams Broadside; Greene King Abbot; Ruddles Best Bitter; 6 changing beers Ⓗ
A former Home Ales pub built in the 1960s and easily identified by the large red lion rampant on the frontage. It faces the Victorian Ripley town hall and marketplace, and is at the centre of a vibrant, well-pubbed market town. A busy Wetherspoon outlet, the venue serves a large selection of guest beers and good-quality wines. Food is available all day. The pub will redeem Wetherspoon CAMRA discount vouchers. Q❀⏣◐❶⟁♿♣P🕮🖵🔊

Talbot Taphouse Ⓛ
1 Butterley Hill, DE5 3LT
🟢 5-11; 3-11.30 Fri; 2-midnight Sat; 12-11 Sun
☎ (01773) 742626 ⊕ amberales.co.uk/brewerytap
Amber Barnes Wallis, Derbyshire Gold, Original Black Stout; changing beers Ⓗ
The eye-catching Amber Ales Brewery tap occupies a flat-iron site and is handily situated between Ripley town centre and the Midland Railway heritage centre. Renovated in 2009, the Victorian former Shipstone's house is blissfully free of music and TV, instead preferring the sounds of conversation, laughter and the traditional games of bar billiards and table skittles. Recognised for innovation in brewing, Amber Ales often tests experimental brews as well as serving regular local favourites. A friendly pub with excellent beer, it is well worth a visit. Q♣♠P🖵(91,92)❀

Sawley

Nag's Head Inn
Wilne Road, NG10 3AL
🟢 11-11 (midnight Fri & Sat); 12-11 Sun ☎ (0115) 973 2983
⊕ sawleypub.wix.com/nagshead
Marston's Burton Bitter, Pedigree; 1 changing beer Ⓗ
Early 19th-century inn close to the River Trent and Sawley marina. This is a traditional Marston's local, often lively and with a good community spirit. The bar, with a low-beamed ceiling and flagstoned floor, and warmed by a wood-burning stove in winter, has a homely, intimate feel. Good-value home-cooked food is available lunchtimes and early evenings (no food Sun).
❀⏣◐♿≷(Long Eaton)♣P🖵❀

Scarcliffe

Horse & Groom
Mansfield Road, S44 6SU
🟢 12-11 ☎ (01246) 823152
Black Sheep Best Bitter; Greene King Abbot; Morland Old Golden Hen; Sharp's Doom Bar; 2 changing beers Ⓗ

> What is your best – your very best – ale a glass?' 'Twopence-halfpenny,' says the landlord, 'is the price of the genuine Stunning Ale.' 'Then,' says I, producing the money, 'Just draw me a glass of the Genuine Stunning, if you please, with a good head to it.'
>
> **Charles Dickens, David Copperfield**

Over 500 years old, this hostelry has two rooms, one of which is a mobile phone-free main bar. Owned by the same family for the last 16 years, it is now run by the daughter, to high standards. The locally made pork pies should be tried. Accommodation is available on-site in a couple of cottages. There is car parking to the front and a bus stop right outside. ❀⛉P

Shirland

Shoulder of Mutton Ⓛ
Hallfieldgate Lane, DE55 6AA (on B6013, Wessington-Shirland crossroads)
🟢 5-11; closed Tue; 12-11 Fri & Sat; 12-10.30 Sun
☎ (01773) 834992
3 changing beers Ⓗ
Eclectic, 16th-century traditional drinking den, nestling on the edge of Amber Valley. The beer garden offers spectacular views and sunsets. It is a true free house, where real people enjoy real ale from small breweries; there is no beer list on the wall because the ales change daily. The regular customers are drawn from far and wide, fuelling the unique, easy atmosphere created by the irrepressible landlord and landlady. Dogs and hikers are welcome. Check out the teacups.
Q❀▲♣P❀🔊

Smalley

Bell Ⓛ
35 Main Road, DE7 6EF (on A608)
🟢 12-2.30, 5-11; 11.30-11 Fri-Sun ☎ (01332) 880635
⊕ thebellsmalley.co.uk
Abbeydale Moonshine; Marston's Pedigree; Sharp's Doom Bar; 2 changing beers Ⓗ
Near Shipley Country Park, this mid 19th-century inn has three rooms in which brewing and other memorabilia adorn the walls. A drinkers' pub, it serves three regular beers plus guests, but is also renowned for food, with a good and varied menu including daily home-made specials (no food Sun eves). Accommodation is in three self-catering apartments in converted stables, and there is a large attractive garden. Weekday opening hours may be extended in the summer. Quiz night is Wednesday. Q❀⛉◐P🖵🔊

South Normanton

Clock Inn
107 Market Street, DE55 2AA
🟢 4-11 (midnight Fri); 12-midnight Sat; 12-11 Sun
☎ (01773) 811396 ⊕ theclockinn.co.uk
Jennings Cumberland Ale; Peak Ales Swift Nick; 1 changing beer Ⓗ
A multiple-roomed pub, with a central bar serving both lounge and public bar areas. It has a pleasant lawn and garden to the rear with seating and a covered smoking area. Sky Sports and BT Sport are shown in both rooms on large projection screens. Look out for the Clocktober Fest. Dogs are welcome in one of the rooms.
❀⏣≷(Alfreton)♣P🖵(9.1,9.2)❀🔊

Devonshire Arms ♟
137 Market Street, DE55 2AA (from M1 jct 28 take B6019; at first mini-roundabout turn right into Market St)
🟢 12-midnight ☎ (01773) 810748
5 changing beers Ⓗ

A genuine free house which offers up to five real ales and three real ciders/perries. Home-cooked food, including daily specials, is available every day except Sunday, when a very popular Sunday carvery is offered. Vegetarians, vegans and coeliacs are all catered for. Sky Sports and BT Sports are shown on up to four big screens. Local CAMRA branch Pub of the Year for the last seven years.
◑◐♿♣●P🚌(9.1,9.2)🐾📶

Sutton cum Duckmanton

Arkwright Arms 🄻

Chesterfield Road, S44 5JG (on A632 between Chesterfield and Bolsover)

🕐 11-11 (midnight Fri & Sat); 11-10.30 Sun

☎ (01246) 232053 🌐 arkwrightarms.co.uk

Greene King Abbot; Whim Arbor Light; changing beers 🄷

Brewers' Tudor-fronted free house. A changing range of 10 guest ales, many from local micros, is complemented by 12 ciders and four perries. Beer festivals are held at Easter and bank holidays, with mini events throughout the year. Quality food is served until 8pm Monday to Saturday, and until 3pm Sunday. The spacious beer garden has play equipment for children. It is a winner of numerous local CAMRA awards, including Cider Pub of the Year and Pub of the Year.
❀◑◐▲♣●P🚌(81,82,83)🐾

Swanwick

Steampacket Inn

Derby Road, DE55 1AB

🕐 2.30-11; 2-midnight Fri; 12-midnight Sat; 12-11 Sun

☎ (01773) 607771

5 changing beers (often Blue Monkey, Derby, Nottingham) 🄷

A friendly and welcoming ex-Shipstone's pub in the centre of Swanwick. Popular with locals, the Steampacket boasts an excellent and constantly changing range of real ales and ciders, many of them from local microbreweries. A lively pub at the weekends, it hosts regular live music and week-night quizzes, and features a real fire in winter and outdoor tables in summer. Local CAMRA 2014 Cider Pub of the Year. CAMRA members receive a discount. ♿♣●P🚌(9.1,9.2)🐾📶

Wardlow Mires

Three Stags' Heads ★

SK17 8RW (jct A623/B6465)

🕐 closed Mon-Thu; 7-11 Fri; 11-11 Sat; 12-10.30 Sun

☎ (01298) 872268

Abbeydale Brimstone, Absolution; house beer (by Abbeydale); 2 changing beers (often Abbeydale) 🄷

A quaint 300-year-old pub comprising two small rooms with stone-flagged floors and low ceilings. Unspoilt, it is one of the few pubs in the area identified by CAMRA as one of Britain's best Real Heritage Pubs. An ancient range warms the bar and the house dogs – the house beer, Black Lurcher, is named after one of them. The food is locally sourced, with game a speciality in season.
Q❀◑◐▲●P🚌(173)🐾

Whaley Bridge

Shepherds Arms

7 Old Road, SK23 7HR

🕐 3-midnight; 2-midnight Sat & Sun ☎ (01663) 732840

Marston's Burton Bitter, Pedigree; 3 changing beers 🄷

A little gem nestling close to the centre of the village, this attractive, whitewashed, stone-built pub has been preserved unspoilt, conveying the feel of the farmhouse it once was. The unchanged taproom is a delight, with open fire, flagged floor and scrubbed table tops. Additionally, there is a comfortable lounge with an open fire in winter. The changing guest beers are selected from the Marston's range. In lovely walking country, hikers are welcome. Q❀⇌♣P🚌(199,61)

Whitehough

Old Hall Inn 🏆 🄻

Chinley, SK23 6EJ (in village, 750yds off B6062)

🕐 12-midnight ☎ (01663) 750529 🌐 old-hall-inn.co.uk

Marston's Burton Bitter; changing beers 🄷

The 14th-century Whitehough Hall forms part of this quintessential country inn, which has won the Great British Pub award for best cask outlet in the region for several years and is a regular entry in this Guide. Eight ales, including seven varying guests from quality local micros, complement those available at the adjacent Paper Mill Inn (under the same ownership). A popular menu features dishes using local produce. Well-attended beer festivals run in September and February.
❀◑◐▲⇌(Chinley)●P🚌(189,190)🐾📶

Whittington Moor

Beer Parlour 🄻

1 King Street North, S41 9BA

🕐 4-11; 12-midnight Sat; 1-10 Sun ☎ 07870 693411

🌐 the-beer-parlour.co.uk

8 changing beers (often Double Top, Thornbridge, Timothy Taylor) 🄷

Originally a bottle beer shop with a few handpumps, it has moved into larger premises. It is now a rustic one-roomed bar with a warm, friendly feel, with comfy seating giving it a real micropub feel. A choice of eight real ales, cider and foreign beers is offered. Winner of a CAMRA award, you can opt to take a beer home too. Q♿●🚌🐾

Wirksworth

Royal Oak 🄻

North End, DE4 4FG

🕐 8-11.30 (midnight Fri & Sat); 12-3, 8-11 Sun

☎ (01629) 823000

Draught Bass; Timothy Taylor Landlord; Whim Hartington IPA; 2 changing beers 🄷

Excellent, ultra-traditional local near the marketplace, highlighted at night by rows of fairy lights. The bar features old pictures of local interest and there is also a pool room and smoking grotto. The Oak enjoys a long-standing reputation for Draught Bass, and always serves at least five ales, including a LocAle. The Ecclesbourne Valley Railway visitor attraction is close by, and this former lead mining town is an architectural gem with much to interest the historian. Q❀♣🚌🐾📶

Many entries in the Guide refer to pubs' support for CAMRA's LocAle scheme. The 𝕃 symbol is used where a pub has LocAle accreditation. The aim of the scheme is to get publicans to stock at least one cask beer that comes from a local brewery no further than 20 miles away. It also encourages publicans to use the Beerflex scheme run by SIBA, the Society of Independent Brewers (see p957). SIBA members deliver direct to pubs in their localities instead of going through the central warehouses of pub-owning companies.

The aim is a simple one: to cut down on 'beer miles'. Research by CAMRA shows that food and drink transport accounts for 25 per cent of all HGV vehicle miles in Britain. Taking into account the miles that ingredients have travelled on top of distribution journeys, an imported lager produced by a multi-national brewery could have notched up more than 24,000 'beer miles' by the time it reaches a pub.

Supporters of LocAle point out that £10 spent on locally-supplied goods generates £25 for the local economy. Keeping trade local helps enterprises, creates more economic activity and jobs, and makes other services more viable. The scheme also generates consumer support for local breweries.

Support for LocAle has grown at a rapid pace since it was created in 2007. It's been embraced by pubs and CAMRA branches throughout England and has now crossed the borders into Scotland and Wales.

For more information, see the CAMRA website www.camra.org.uk and type 'locale' into the search window.

What is CAMRA LocAle?

- An initiative that promotes pubs which sell locally-brewed real ale.
- The scheme builds on a growing consumer demand for quality local produce and an increased awareness of 'green' issues.

Everyone benefits from local pubs stocking locally brewed real ale...

- Public houses, as stocking local real ales can increase pub visits
- Consumers, who enjoy greater beer choice and locally brewed beer
- Local brewers, who gain from increased sales and get better feedback from consumers
- The local economy, because more money is spent and retained in the local economy
- The environment, due to fewer 'beer miles' resulting in less road congestion and pollution
- Tourism, due to an increased sense of local identity and pride – let's celebrate what makes our locality different.

DEVON

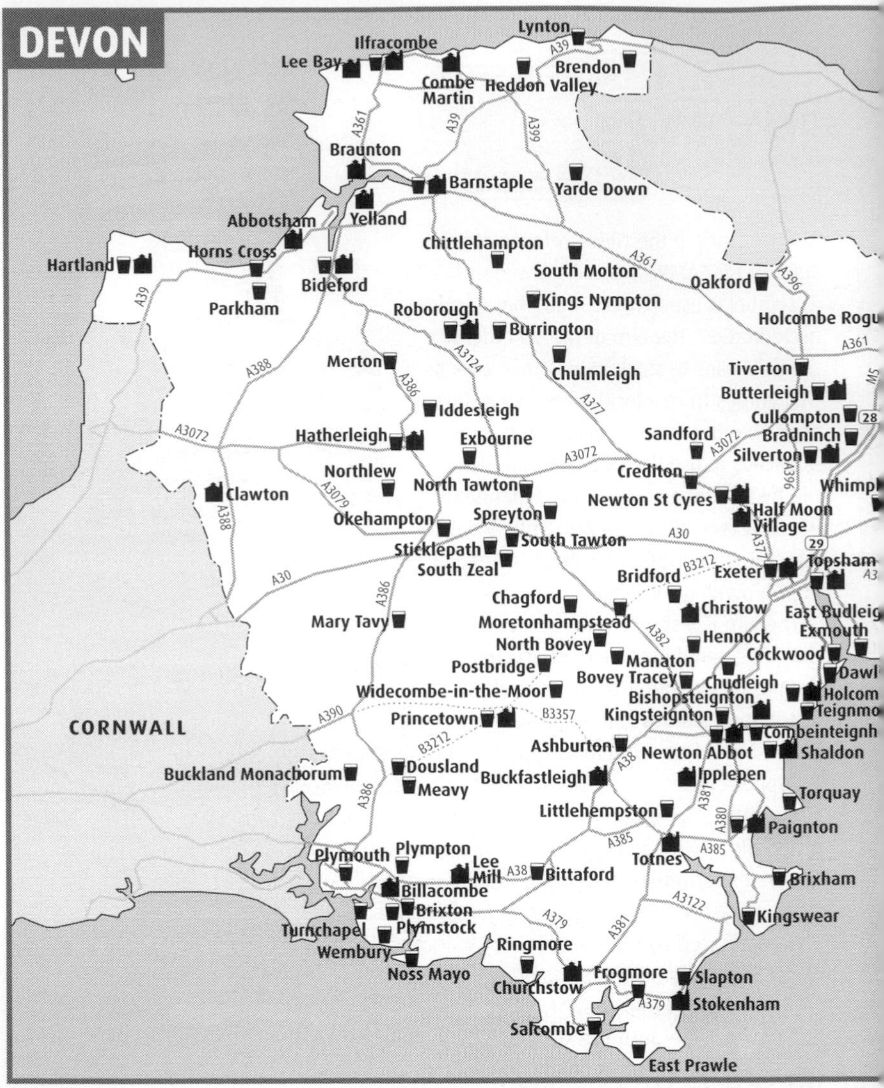

Ashburton

Exeter Inn L
26 West Street, TQ13 7DU (on main road through centre of Ashburton, opp church)
☼ 11-2.30, 5-11 (midnight Fri & Sat); 12-3, 7-10.30 Sun
☎ (01364) 652013
Dartmoor IPA, Legend Ⓗ
This friendly local is the oldest pub in Ashburton, built in 1131, with additions in the 17th century. It originally housed the workers constructing the church that stands opposite, and was also used by Sir Francis Drake on his journeys to London. Either side of the entrance hallway are seated drinking areas that lead to the L-shaped main bar, which is rustic and wood-panelled, and has a canopy. The smaller bar and seating area at the rear are served via a small hatch and counter. Local Thompstone's cider is also on sale.
Q☜⊛◑♣●🚌(88,X38)🐾🛜

Ashill

Ashill Inn
EX15 3NL ST0866411384
☼ 12-2.30 (not Mon), 5.30-11.30; 12-4, 6.30-10.30 Sun
☎ (01884) 840506 ⊕ ashillinndevon.co.uk
Otter Bitter; 2 changing beers (sourced locally) Ⓗ
A Grade II-listed pub, built in 1835, located down narrow lanes in the Culm Valley. It is a charming small venue with a cosy bar and a recently extended restaurant area to one side. The comfortable bar serves local south-west brewery ales. Good-value food is available, with produce sourced mainly from local farms. Live music and special events are often featured. Sandford Orchard Old Kirton real cider is served. Q⊛◑♣●🐾🛜

Barnstaple

Corner House
108 Boutport Street, EX31 1SY

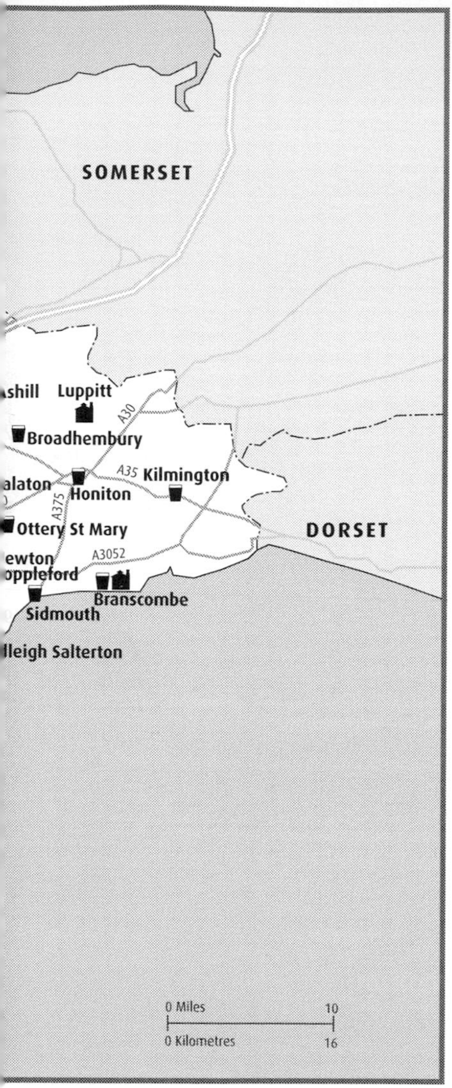

11-11; 12-10.30 Sun ☎ (01271) 343528

Draught Bass; St Austell Tribute; 1 changing beer Ⓗ

Built on the site of the old East Gate to the town, this popular and friendly pub is notable for its 1930s wood-panelled interior. A proud supporter of the town's rugby club, it can get busy during international matches. The highly competitive Barnstaple Open Shove-ha'penny Championship is held here, while the back bar is a meeting place for many local clubs and organisations.

Bideford

Appledore Inn

Chingswell Street, EX39 2NF

11-11; 12-10.30 Sun ☎ (01237) 476956

appledoreinnbideford.co.uk

Jollyboat Grenville's Renown; Sharp's Doom Bar, Own; 1 changing beer Ⓗ

Friendly, family-run pub, close to Bideford football ground, with a single bar and restaurant to the side. Four real ales are usually available, occasionally joined by a fifth served from the cask. Good-quality authentic Thai food is on the menu daily noon-9pm. The bar area displays an interesting selection of photos and prints of old Bideford, and witty philosophical messages on chalkboards above the bar. Q

Bittaford

Horse & Groom

Exeter Road, PL21 0EL

12-11 (midnight Fri & Sat) ☎ (01752) 892358

Dartmoor Jail Ale; house beer (by Hunters); 4 changing beers (sourced locally) Ⓗ

A family-owned pub run by a real ale enthusiast. Good home-cooked food is served in the separate dining area and six pumps deliver the beers in the long bar - Jail Ale and Horse & Groom Ale being the regulars. The other pumps offer ales predominantly from local breweries in south Devon and Cornwall. Real ciders are also served. CAMRA members receive a discount, and there is a quiz night on Fridays. A summer beer festival is held on the first weekend of July supporting local charities. Third-pint tapas are available.
Q P

REAL ALE BREWERIES

Barum Barnstaple
Bays Paignton
Beer Engine Newton St Cyres
Big Rabbit Butterleigh (NEW)
Black Tor Christow
Branscombe Vale Branscombe
Braunton Braunton (NEW)
Bridgetown Totnes
Clearwater Bideford
Country Life Abbotsham
Dartmoor Princetown
Devon Earth Buckfastleigh
Exe Valley Silverton
Exeter Exeter
Fat Pig Exeter
Forge Hartland
Grampus Lee Bay (NEW)
GT Braunton (NEW)
Hanlons Half Moon Village
Holsworthy Clawton
Hunters Ipplepen
Isca Holcombe
Jollyboat Bideford
Madrigal Combe Martin (NEW)
New Lion Totnes
Noss Beer Works Lee Mill
Occasional Silverton (NEW)
Otter Luppitt
Platform 5 Newton Abbot
Quercus Churchstow
Red Rock Bishopsteignton
South Hams Stokenham
Summerskills Billacombe
Tally Ho! Hatherleigh (NEW)
Tavy Ales Roborough
Teignworthy Newton Abbot
Topsham Topsham
Totnes Totnes (NEW)
Two Beach Shaldon
Wizard Ilfracombe
Yelland Manor Yelland

Bovey Tracey

Cromwell Arms

Fore Street, TQ13 9AE

11-11 (11.30 Fri & Sat); 12-11 Sun (01626) 833473

thecromwellarms.co.uk

St Austell Tribute; house beer (by St Austell); 2 changing beers H

A 17th-century inn in the centre of Bovey Tracey with 14 letting bedrooms and good access to Dartmoor. There is one large drinking area with two sections showing beams and exposed stonework, as well as a dining area and a separate restaurant. At the rear is both a pleasant garden with a large wisteria-covered smokers' retreat and a car park. Children are welcome in the restaurant and lounge. Up to five real ales are available.

Q P (39,178,271)

Bradninch

Olde White Lion

26 High Street, EX5 4QL

4 (12 Fri-Sun)-midnight (01392) 881263

yeoldewhitelion.co.uk

Dartmoor Best; Otter Amber, Ale; 1 changing beer (sourced regionally) H

A friendly family-run locals' pub which caters for everyone. It offers up to four real ales and good-value home-cooked food, using locally sourced produce where possible, is available evenings. A traditional roast is served on Sundays from March to December. Popular music nights feature, there is a folk club on the first Tuesday of the month, and an annual music festival in June. Westons Old Rosie cider is available.

Q P (1,1A,1B)

Branscombe

Fountain Head Inn

EX12 3BG (in main street 1 mile S of A3052)

11-3, 6-11; 12-3, 6-10.30 Sun (01297) 680359

fountainheadinn.com

Branscombe Vale Branoc, Summa That; house beer (by Branscombe Vale); 1 changing beer (sourced locally) H

Popular with walkers, this neat 500-year-old pub is at the west end of the long straggly village in a beautiful coastal valley. It retains wood-panelled walls and flagstone floors, with an inglenook fireplace. A beer festival is held on the nearest weekend to the longest day. The guest beer is from Branscombe Vale or another local brewery; the cider is Branscombe Vale Pip. Good-value home-cooked food is served. Dogs are welcome, as are children (but not in the bar).

Q P (899)

Brendon

Staghunters Inn

EX35 6PS SS767481

12-11 (01598) 741222 staghunters.com

St Austell Trelawny, Proper Job; 2 changing beers G

The Staghunters dispenses all its beers direct from the cask. The regular St Austell ales are often joined by guests from the local Exmoor and Cotleigh breweries. A wide range of locally sourced food is also available. The inn has an attractive restaurant, 14 well-appointed rooms and a 13th-century chapel which can be used as a private dining room. Popular with walkers, the pub welcomes dogs and allows them to stay overnight for a nominal charge. **Q P**

Bridford

Bridford Inn

EX6 7HT

12-11 (midnight Sat & Sun) (01647) 252250

bridfordinn.co.uk

Dartmoor Jail Ale; 3 changing beers (sourced regionally) H

A 17th-century Devon longhouse within the Dartmoor National Park, converted to a pub in 1968 and now housing a village shop. It has a spacious open-plan interior for both drinkers and diners, with old oak beams and an inglenook fireplace complete with an old bread oven and woodburner. Freshly home-cooked quality food is served to order. Outside there is a beer garden with picnic tables and stunning views. Traditional ciders from Devon and Somerset producers are always to be had. **Q P** (360,361)

Brixham

Queen's Arms

31 Station Hill, TQ5 8BN (from Brixham library go up Church Hill East then Station Hill)

4-11; 2-midnight Fri; 12-midnight Sat; 12-11 Sun

(01803) 852074 thequeensarmsbrixham.co.uk

9 changing beers (sourced nationally; often Hunters, Oakham, Teignworthy) H

Friendly end-of-terrace pub off the beaten track but worth seeking out. There is a charity beer festival in December with over 20 ales. The pub has live music at weekends and supports many community activities. One ale each from Hunters and Oakham take up two of the six handpumps; the others can be sourced countrywide but are mainly from Devon. Limited food is served – a Sunday roast and a Monday meal deal. Local CAMRA Pub of the Year 2014. (17,17A)

Vigilance

5 Bolton Street, TQ5 9DE

8am-midnight (01803) 850489

Dartmoor Jail Ale; Greene King Abbot; Ruddles Best Bitter; Sharp's Doom Bar; 4 changing beers H

Town-centre Wetherspoon pub named after the last sailing ketch built in Brixham's Upham shipyard in 1926, now fully restored and moored in the harbour. Local, mostly nautical, prints adorn the walls, and an imposing old ship's figurehead looks down on customers from its wall mounting. Food is served 8am-11pm. The pub holds various beer, cider and wine festivals throughout the year. Gwynt y Ddraig Black Dragon cider is stocked.

(12,15,16)

Brixton

Foxhound Inn

PL8 2AH

11-11 (midnight Fri & Sat); 12-11 Sun (01752) 880271

foxhoundinn.co.uk

Courage Best Bitter; 4 changing beers (sourced nationally; often Cottage, Dartmoor, Summerskills) H

An 18th-century former coaching house in a rural village just east of Plymouth, well served by a frequent daytime bus service. The pub has two separate bars and a small restaurant. Traditional

English meals are on the menu daily, featuring locally sourced ingredients. Look out for Red Coat, an ale crafted by the landlord, among four guest ales. A monthly charity quiz night is held. Local CAMRA Country Pub of The Year runner-up 2015.
Q🐴◐▲♣●P🚌(93,94)🐾

Broadhembury

Drewe Arms

EX14 3NF
⏲ 12-11; 12-10.30 Sun ☎ (01404) 841267
🌐 drewearmsinn.co.uk
Bays Topsail; Branscombe Vale Summa That; Exeter Avocet; Otter Ale; 2 changing beers (sourced locally) [H]
A Grade II-listed 16th-century thatched pub with a secluded garden, set in a picturesque estate village within the Blackdown Hills. This is a friendly and welcoming family-run venue, with the emphasis on local real ales and produce. Good-value food is served lunchtimes and evenings Monday to Saturday, and lunchtimes on Sunday. A takeaway menu is always available. The pub holds an annual beer festival over the Easter weekend.
Q🐴❀◐▲♣●P🐾📶

Buckland Monachorum

Drake Manor Inn [L]

The Village, PL20 7NA
⏲ 11.30-2.30, 6.30-11; 11.30-11.30 Fri & Sat; 12-11 Sun
☎ (01822) 853892 🌐 drakemanorinn.co.uk
Dartmoor Jail Ale; Sharp's Doom Bar; 1 changing beer (sourced regionally; often Otter) [H]
Cosy and friendly pub dating from the 16th century, nestling between the church and the stream in a pleasant village on the edge of Dartmoor. It is renowned for its friendly atmosphere and attracts a regular local clientele. The inviting traditional interior features an intimate meeting area, a public bar and a restaurant area in which to sample the good food. The tranquil garden is a relaxing suntrap. Good-value food is served both lunchtimes and evenings. Q🐴❀◐♣●🚌(55)🐾📶

Budleigh Salterton

Salterton Arms [L]

22 Chapel Street, EX9 6LX
⏲ 11-11.30; 12-11 Sun ☎ (01395) 445048
Dartmoor Jail Ale; Otter Ale; Sharp's Doom Bar; 1 changing beer [H]
A local pub with an interior of Cotswold stone floors and bare wood. A large variety of meals is available, served in the main bar and the upstairs mezzanine area. The three TVs in the bar are well spaced apart and occasionally show different sporting events. In addition to the regular beers there is a continually changing guest ale. Euchre is played and the local ukulele group meets on Monday evenings. ◐♿♣🚌(157,357)🐾📶

Burrington

Portsmouth Arms

EX37 9ND (on A377 approx 4 miles S of Umberleigh)
⏲ 4-11; 12-11 Fri-Sun ☎ (01769) 561117
Otter Bitter [H]**; 1 changing beer** [G]
With a welcoming farmhouse-style atmosphere, this former coaching inn in the heart of the Taw Valley is an ideal base for walkers, fishermen and those exploring the surroundings. The front bar area has oak beams and a log fire, while there are attractive views across the river from the peaceful, decked rear veranda. The pub serves well-sourced local food every day until 9pm. There is good accommodation and ample parking. Well-behaved children and dogs welcome.
Q🐴❀🛏◐⇌♣P🐾📶

Butterleigh

Butterleigh Inn [L]

The Green, EX15 1PN (opp church) SS9746108212
⏲ 12-2.30 (not Mon), 6-11; 12-2.30, 6-midnight Fri & Sat; 12-3 Sun ☎ (01884) 855433 🌐 butterleighinn.co.uk
Cotleigh Tawny Owl; Dartmoor IPA; Otter Ale; 1 changing beer [H]
Situated in this small, quaint village, the Butterleigh is an excellent country pub with a mixed clientele creating a great atmosphere with diverse conversation. Good-value home-cooked food is served lunchtimes and evenings Tuesday to Saturday, with a carvery Sunday lunchtime. There is always a choice of four real ales, one a LocAle, plus Sandford Orchards Devon Scrumpy, Winkleigh Sam's Medium and a rotating guest cider. There is a main bar, lounge and a modern dining room.
Q🐴❀🛏◐♿♣●P🐾📶

Chagford

Globe Inn [L]

9 High Street, TQ13 8AJ
⏲ 11-11.30 (midnight Fri & Sat); 12-10.30 Sun
☎ (01647) 433485 🌐 theglobeinnchagford.co.uk
Dartmoor IPA; Otter Bitter; 1 changing beer (sourced regionally) [H]
Overlooking the parish church in this historic stannary town, the Globe was once a coaching inn and coopery. It has evolved into a focal point for the town, providing good food, music evenings, a cinema club and numerous other events and functions. It has a splendid traditional public bar and another separate bar and restaurant, both with big open fires. A small courtyard is at the rear and a car park is nearby. The ciders are Westons Old Rosie and Winkleigh Cider.
🐴❀🛏◐●🚌(173,178,671)🐾📶

Sandy Park Inn [L]

Sandy Park, TQ13 8JW (on A382 Moretonhampstead-Whiddon Down road)
⏲ 11-11 summer; 11 (4 Mon & Tue)-11 winter; 12-10.30 Sun
☎ (01647) 433267 🌐 sandyparkinn.co.uk
Dartmoor Jail Ale; Otter Bitter; 1 changing beer (sourced regionally) [H]
A thatched free house, thought to be 17th century. The small bar has a large open fireplace, ancient beams, a stone floor and high-backed wooden bench seating. Beyond is a small snug set around a large table. There is a separate room beyond the front door, and a small car park at the front with steps to the garden. Good home-cooked meals are served (no food Sun eves or Mon). The cider is Westons Old Rosie. Castle Drogo (NT), Fingle Bridge and Chagford are nearby.
🐴❀🛏◐●P🚌(173,178,671)🐾📶

Chittlehampton

Bell Inn 🅛

The Square, EX37 9QL (opp St Hieritha's parish church)
SS636254
✪ 11-3, 6-midnight; 11-midnight Fri & Sat; 12-11 Sun
☎ (01769) 540368 ⊕ thebellatchittlehampton.co.uk
Exmoor Ale; Otter Bitter; St Austell Tribute; 5
changing beers Ⓗ
A well-run village local which has been in the same
family for more than 30 years. It offers a fine
selection of real ales, with four on handpump and
usually four more on gravity. Good-value home-
cooked food is served, both in the bar and the
adjoining restaurant area. The relatively new skittle
alley/games room doubles as a function room.
Well-behaved children and dogs are welcome.
🛏🏵🕪♣P🖳(658,859)🐾🍴🛜

Chudleigh

Bishop Lacy Inn 🅛

Fore Street, TQ13 0HY
✪ 12-midnight (1am Fri & Sat) ☎ (01626) 854585
3 changing beers (sourced regionally) Ⓗ
A Grade II-listed building opposite the church,
named after the bishop responsible for the town's
first water supply. You can be sure of a warm
welcome from an ebullient landlady and Sambuca
the dog here. The pub specialises in local Devon
beers and excellent home cooking. The left-hand
bar is dominated by a magnificent fireplace which
was used for hanging hams and is now incredibly
only half its original size. The inn is reputedly
haunted by a white lady and a monk.
🛏🕪⚓♣🖳(39,182)🐾🍴🛜

Chulmleigh

Old Court House

South Molton Street, EX18 7BW
✪ 11-11 ☎ (01769) 580045 ⊕ oldcourthouseinn.co.uk
Dartmoor IPA; Exmoor Ale; 1 changing beer Ⓗ
A warm welcome awaits at this historic locals' pub
which dates back to the 1600s. There are usually
three real ales on offer, together with a local cider.
Good home-cooked food is served in the separate
restaurant, which is to the rear of the bar. A CAMRA
discount of 10p per pint is available to members.
The popular Thursday evening quiz night supports
local charities. 🛏🏵🛺🕪♿♣🖳(377)🐾🛜

Cockwood

Anchor Inn 🅛

EX6 8RA (just off A379, outside Starcross, next to
harbour) SX9756480692
✪ 11-11; 11.30-10.30 Sun ☎ (01626) 890203
⊕ anchorinncockwood.com
Otter Ale; 5 changing beers (sourced nationally) Ⓗ
On picturesque Cockwood harbour, this 450-year-
old inn and former seaman's mission has many old
settles, timber panelling, low beams and snugs,
with an impressive display of old nautical
memorabilia. It has an extensive award-winning
seafood menu, with mussels a speciality. Up to five
ales are usually offered. Haunted by a friendly
ghost and his dog, this is a really atmospheric
Devon gem. Close to the main GWR line, it is a
steam train spotters' paradise. Parking is limited,
the bus stop is over the bridge.
Q🛏🏵🕪♿⚓♣P🖳(2)🐾

Ship Inn

Church Road, EX6 8NU (just off A379, outside Starcross)
✪ 11-11; 12-10.30 Sun ☎ (01626) 890373
⊕ shipinncockwood.co.uk
Dartmoor Jail Ale; Exmoor Ale; St Austell Tribute; 2
changing beers (sourced nationally) Ⓗ
A busy family-run pub, close to the picturesque
harbour at Cockwood, with a large beer garden
with views of the estuary, and a log fire in winter.
Popular with drinkers and diners alike, it offers a
choice of three regular ales and usually two
rotating guests. and has an excellent food menu.
Meals are prepared with local produce where
possible including a varied choice of locally caught
fish. The bus stops 100 yards across the bridge.
Q🛏🏵🕪⚓ΛP🖳(2)🐾🛜

Combeinteignhead

Wild Goose 🅛

TQ12 4RA (between Newton Abbot and Shaldon on S
side of river)
✪ 11-3, 5.30-11; 12-3, 7-11 Sun ☎ (01626) 872241
⊕ thewildgooseinn.co.uk
Changing beers (sourced regionally) Ⓗ
Charming 17th-century pub and restaurant with a
cosy and welcoming atmosphere. A changing
range of ales and continental beers is offered
alongside traditional cider from various producers,
mainly in the south-west. Food is sourced locally.
Friday night music is eclectic but good, while the
Saturday night quiz is popular. An attractive garden
at the rear abuts a 14th-century red sandstone
church. Two holiday cottages can be rented.
🛏🏵🛺⚓Λ♣●P🖳🐾

Crediton

Crediton Inn 🅛

28a Mill Street, EX17 1EZ (near A377 and station)
✪ 10-11; 12-3, 7-10.30 Sun ☎ (01363) 772882
⊕ crediton-inn.co.uk
Hanlons Yellowhammer; changing beers Ⓗ
The framed deeds date this inn to 1878, the
windows etched with the ancient town seal. It is a
genuine free house, well supported by the locals.
The handpumps have increased to 10, served by
local breweries, with an ale festival in November.
The skittle alley doubles as a function room. Good
home-cooked food is available at weekends, with
snacks and renowned Scotch eggs at other times.
The bubbly owner is the longest-serving landlady
in Crediton. 🕪≢♣P🖳(5,51,315)🐾🛜

Cullompton

Pony & Trap 🅛

10 Exeter Hill, EX15 1DJ (on B3181 S of town)
✪ 12-2, 5-11.30; 12-5, 8-11 Sun ☎ (01884) 34182
⊕ ponyandtrapcullompton.co.uk
Dartmoor IPA; Jail Ale; Otter Bitter; Ringwood Best
Bitter; 2 changing beers Ⓗ
A traditional local with a good atmosphere and a
mixed clientele. It has a smart interior featuring a
logburner, making it cosy in winter; flowers and
ornaments give it a homely feel. Up to eight real
ales are on offer. Food is served Tuesday-Sunday
lunchtimes, and evenings on request in advance.
There is a garden and seating area. Live music
features once a month and pub games are played.
Local CAMRA branch Pub of the Year 2014.
Q🏵🕪♣🖳(1)🐾

Dawlish

Gresham House Inn
1 Commercial Road, EX7 9HU
12-11.30 (midnight Fri & Sat) ☎ (01626) 864061
greshamhouseinn.co.uk
Teignworthy Gun Dog; 1 changing beer [H]
Formerly the Laffin Pig, the pub changed back to the Gresham House Inn, its original name, in 2011. It is a four-storey property built circa 1850, now family-run, with two double en-suite B&B guest rooms on the first floor. There are usually two real ales on tap, sometimes three, one from Teignworthy, plus real cider.
Q

Dousland

Burrator Inn
PL20 6NP
11-11 (12.30am Sat); 12-11 Sun ☎ (01822) 853121
theburratorinn.com
Dartmoor IPA, Jail Ale; St Austell Tribute; Sharp's Doom Bar [H]
Substantial pub on the road between Yelverton and Princetown, close to the picturesque Burrator Reservoir. Several rooms offer a pool table, two dartboards and a separate dining room. Home-made food and pies are produced from local suppliers and served all day. There is ample parking and a large enclosed beer garden with a children's play area. A beer festival is held annually in September, while a Sunday quiz night, live music and other entertainment feature regularly.
Q P (55,98)

East Budleigh

Sir Walter Raleigh Inn
22 High Street, EX9 7ED (off B3178 opp Hayes Lane)
12-2.30, 6-11; 12-2.30, 7-10.30 Sun ☎ (01395) 442510
sirwalterraleighinn.co.uk
4 changing beers (sourced regionally) [H]
Set in the middle of the delightful village of East Budleigh, the birthplace of Sir Walter Raleigh, this free house is a truly welcoming 16th-century country inn. Good-quality pub food is served lunchtimes and evenings, and four real ales and a real cider are usually available. Originally two cottages, it was then converted into a Jacobean-style pub, retaining the original wooden beams throughout. This gem is well worth a visit for good-quality real ale. Q (157)

East Prawle

Pig's Nose Inn
TQ7 2BY
12-3, 6-11 ☎ (01548) 511209 pigsnoseinn.co.uk
Otter Bitter [G]**; South Hams Devon Pride** [H]/[G]**, Eddystone; 1 changing beer** [G]
A much-loved 500-year-old smugglers' inn on the village green which attracts birdwatchers and coast path walkers. The maritime-themed interior is cluttered and quirky. Gravity beers are racked behind the bar and home-cooked locally sourced food is served. Children and dogs are welcome and have their own menus. Occasional live music events are held in a hall adjoining the pub. Children's games are available, and knitting for adults. Closed Sunday evenings in winter.
Q

Exbourne

Red Lion
High Street, EX20 3RY (200yds N of jct with A3072)
SS602018
12-11 ☎ (01837) 851551 theredlionexbourne.co.uk
Dartmoor IPA, Legend; 1 changing beer [G]
Set in the foothills of Dartmoor, this 2014 CAMRA branch Pub of the Year is a traditional Devon local serving real ales from Dartmoor Brewery together with additional guest beers. All ales, as well as the cider from nearby Sam's, are served on gravity. The bar has no handpumps of any description as the landlord refuses to serve draught lager. Food, much of which is supplied by local farmers, is served throughout the day. Live music features monthly.
Q P (318,631,648)

Exeter

Fat Pig
2 John Street, EX1 1BL (behind Fore St)
5 (12 Sat)-11; 12-5 Sun ☎ (01392) 437217
fatpig-exeter.co.uk
Changing beers (sourced locally) [H]
Formerly the Coachmakers Arms, this Victorian corner local has been brought back to life as a traditional pub, featuring a range of locally sourced food, including the pub's own pork and sausages from its herd of rare-breed pigs. In addition to making its own cider, it is also a brewpub producing a wide range of styles for its three pubs. There are malt whisky evenings, a Monday quiz night and home-brew competitions.
Q (Central)

George's Meeting House
38 South Street, EX1 1ED
8am-midnight (1am Fri & Sat) ☎ (01392) 454250
Dartmoor Jail Ale; Greene King Abbot; changing beers [H]
Formerly George's Meeting, this pub is listed as having special interest as an unaltered 18th-century building, a Unitarian chapel dating from 1760 and named after King George III. There are lovely stained glass windows, upstairs galleries and even a pulpit in situ. Nicely converted by Wetherspoon, it opened in January 2005, and is popular both lunchtimes and evenings. Food is served all day, and a good range of real ales is always available. Real ciders come from Sandfords and Orchard Pig. Q (Central)

Hour Glass Inn
21 Melbourne Street, St Leonard's, EX2 4AU (approx 300yds from Exeter Quayside)
12-3 (not Mon), 5-11 (midnight Sat); 12-10.30 Sun
☎ (01392) 258722
Changing beers [H]
A traditional pub in the back streets of Exeter, in the hub of the local area close to the quay and about five minutes' walk from the main city centre. The pub has two restaurants and a bar, serving contemporary and continental food. It is very traditional in its features, with a mixture of live entertainment including light theatre and music, which has proved popular with its eclectic group of customers. Q (S,T)

Imperial
New North Road, St David's, EX4 4AH
9am-midnight (1am Fri & Sat) ☎ (01392) 434050

Greene King Abbot [H]; Ruddles Best Bitter [H]/[G]; changing beers [H]
Large Wetherspoon pub, opened in 1996, near the university, with public transport close by. Its large sunny garden offers plenty of tables and seating. Ten beers are usually on offer, plus guest ales, often from local breweries. Good-value food is served all day. Built in 1810 as Elmfield House, then changed to the Imperial Hotel in 1923, its attractive architecture and orangery are still there to be enjoyed. Beer festivals are regularly held throughout the year, with some showcasing local breweries.
Q🐎❀◑♿🚆(St David's)🍎P🚌(D,50)📶

Mill on the Exe
Bonhay Road, St David's, EX4 3AB
🕔 10.30-11 ☎ (01392) 214464 🌐 millontheexe.co.uk
St Austell Tribute, Proper Job; 2 changing beers (sourced regionally) [H]
A beautiful riverside pub, formerly a paper mill, with a welcoming and vibrant atmosphere. It has two floors with a bar on each, serving two regular St Austell ales and usually two guests, one of which may not be a St Austell beer, plus a range of bottled beers. Quality home-cooked food is served noon-9pm daily. The large garden has stunning views of Blackaller Weir. Children and dogs are welcome, and there are three log fires.
❀◑♿🚆(St Thomas)P🚌🐾📶

Oddfellows
60 New North Road, EX4 4EP (just off High St)
🕔 12-3 (not Mon-Wed), 5-11; 12-1am Fri & Sat; 12-8 Sun ☎ (01392) 209050 🌐 theoddfellowsbar.co.uk
St Austell Tribute, Proper Job [H]; 1 changing beer [H]/[G]
The narrow frontage at the end of a Victorian terrace belies a deep interior and features the original Victorian conservatory. Its cellar benefits from backing onto the old Roman city wall. A friendly gastro-style bar with a varied clientele, it is divided into small areas and alcoves, with sofas and rustic furniture. It has weekly acoustic music and open mic evenings. The open kitchen allows you to watch your food being cooked.
Q🐎◑🚆(Central)🍺🚌🐾📶

Royal Oak 🄻
79-81 Fore Street, Heavitree, EX1 2RN
🕔 11.30-11 (midnight Fri & Sat); 12-4, 7-11 Sun ☎ (01392) 254121 🌐 heavitreeroyaloak.co.uk
Otter Amber, Ale; Young's Bitter; 3 changing beers [H]
Traditional family-run pub on several bus routes, with ample parking nearby. Three regular ales plus three guests are usually on offer. Good-value pub food is served lunchtimes, with a traditional roast on Sunday; no food is served evenings, except for a steak/fish night on Thursday. With a large comfortable main bar and smaller side room, the pub has a real community feel, while remaining welcoming to visitors. It has front and rear beer gardens with a covered smoking area.
🐎❀◑♣🚌🐾

Exmouth

Bicton Inn 🄻
5 Bicton Street, EX8 2RU (in town centre)
🕔 11-midnight ☎ (01395) 272589 🌐 bictoninn.co.uk
Branscombe Vale Branoc; Dartmoor Jail Ale; Hanlons Port Stout; Wadworth 6X; 3 changing beers [H]
A friendly and popular back-street local offering good beer and chat. Traditional games are played such as darts, pool and euchre, and regular live music events are featured. Up to seven real ales and one real cider are normally on offer, usually including several LocAles. The snug is available for small gatherings and meetings. Three annual beer festivals are held, in March, July and October.
🐎🚆♣🍎🚌🐾📶

First & Last Inn 🄻
10 Church Street, EX8 1PE (off B3178 Rolle St)
🕔 11-11 (11.30 Sat); 12-10.30 Sun ☎ (01395) 263275
Courage Directors; Otter Ale; Teignworthy Neap Tide [H]; 2 changing beers [H]/[G]
Victorian pub near the town centre with a public car park opposite. It is a genuine free house, with three distinct drinking areas and an outside patio with heated awnings. Games include pool and darts, and there is a skittle alley. Televised sport is prominent. Two or three guest beers are sold, usually from the West Country, and Green Valley, Old Rosie and Thatchers Dry ciders. Well-behaved dogs are welcome. ❀♿🚆♣🍎🚌(57,157)🐾

Grapevine
2 Victoria Road, EX8 1DL
🕔 4-11; 12-midnight Fri & Sat; 12-11 Sun ☎ (01395) 222208 🌐 thegrapevineexmouth.com
Exeter Avocet; changing beers [H]
A stylish free house with a continental café ambience which stocks a changing range of real British beers – over 100 different ales featured last year – along with continental lagers and bottled beers. Green Valley Cyder is also sold. The excellent food with a regularly changing plat du jour makes the pub an ideal place for people looking for something special. Monday is quiz night, Friday features live music, and an informal chess club has started on Tuesdays. ❀◑♿🚆🍎🚌(57,97)🐾📶

Grove
Esplanade, EX8 1BJ (on the seafront)
🕔 11-11; 12-10.30 Sun ☎ (01395) 272101 🌐 groveexmouth.com
Wells Bombardier; Young's Bitter, Special; changing beers [H]
A large Wells & Young's house at the western end of the esplanade, a 10-15-minute walk from the town centre, which has good bus and train links. Food is served 12-10pm daily. There is an upstairs bar which has good views across the bay and Exe estuary. Families are welcome, and the large beer garden is popular during the summer months. A quiz is held every Thursday evening. 🐎❀◑♿🚆🐾

Frogmore

Globe Inn
TQ7 2NR
🕔 12-2.30 (not Mon), 6-11; 12-2.30, 6-10.30 Sun ☎ (01548) 531351 🌐 theglobeinn.co.uk
Otter Bitter, Ale; Skinner's Betty Stogs [H]
Close to the head of the Frogmore Creek, the pub is accessible by car, bus or boat. First licensed in 1857, the building is of stone with timber beams, and has an inglenook fireplace with a logburner, oak floors, old settles, settees and an assortment of other furniture. Leading off from the bar is a separate games room with a pool table and dartboard. A terrace and garden are at the rear.
Q🐎❀🛏◑♿♣P🚌(93)🐾📶

Hartland

Hartland Quay Hotel

EX39 6DU (drive through Stoke and stop when you reach the sea!)

11-11 (01237) 441218 hartlandquayhotel.com

Dartmoor Legend; St Austell Tribute; 1 changing beer

This is so much more than a good pub. The bar, in the 400-year-old stable block, is filled with interesting historical artefacts. In a designated Area of Natural Beauty, the stunning views from Hartland Quay make this a venue you will return to many times. Walk the coastal path, watch seals and dolphins, see the sun disappear over the horizon, and enjoy the vast panorama from Lundy Island to Cornwall, all while enjoying a well-kept pint or two. Q P

Hatherleigh

Tally Ho!

14 Market Street, EX20 3JN (opp church)

12 (11 Tue)-11; 12-1am Fri & Sat (01837) 810306

tallyhohatherleigh.co.uk

Clearwater Devon Dympsy; St Austell Tribute; 1 changing beer

Single-bar 15th-century inn, characterised by an olde-worlde look, with exposed beams and log fires. The three real ales are significantly reduced on Tuesday market day 11am-3pm. Special prices also apply 3pm-6pm on weekdays. Good-quality food made with local produce is served in the bar and separate dining room. Outside there is a pleasant garden with a covered smoking area from where the vessels from the old Tally Ho! Brewery can be viewed. (118,51)

Heddon Valley

Hunters Inn

Heddon Valley, EX31 4PY (signed from A39 north of Parracombe, continue down country lane for a few miles) SS655481

10-11 (01598) 763230 thehuntersinnexmoor.co.uk

Exmoor Ale, Gold, Stag, Beast; 2 changing beers

Set in the heart of the Heddon Valley, this unique pub was designed to attract tourists in the early 20th century in the guise of a Swiss chalet. The setting, which includes strutting peacocks, is matched by the beer quality and range, with regular beers from Exmoor, as well as its own Heddon Valley Ales. Sam's Medium cider is available, as too are light bites and an à la carte menu. Q P

Hennock

Palk Arms

TQ13 9QB

12-2.30 (not Tue-Fri), 5-11; 12-9.30 Sun

(01626) 836584 theonlypalkarms.co.uk

Teignworthy Gun Dog; 2 changing beers

This reputedly haunted 16th-century free house is in a small village high above the Teign Valley, and from the pub's back dining room there are spectacular views over the valley and across to the Haldon Moors. The public bar is at the front and has a lovely wood-burning stove in the winter months. The lounge is comfortable and cosy, with settees and armchairs, and leads to the dining room. Q (361)

Holcombe

Smugglers Inn

27 Teignmouth Road, EX7 0LA (on A379 between Dawlish and Teignmouth)

11-11 (01626) 862301 thesmugglersinn.net

Dartmoor Legend; Teignworthy Reel Ale; 1 changing beer

With splendid coastal views, this roadside free house has an excellent reputation. Good food is served lunchtimes and evenings, including a popular carvery. There are two regular ales and one varying guest. The bar area has a wood-burning stove. The outside spaces, including a separate smokers' canopy, are popular throughout the seasons. A mini beer festival is held towards the end of January, and regular entertainment is hosted. There is a car park and buses pass the door. P (2)

Holcombe Rogus

Prince of Wales Inn

TA21 0PN ST0594518833

5.30-10 Mon; 12-3, 5.30-11; 12-midnight Sat; 12-10 Sun

(01823) 672070 theprinceofwales-uk.com

Otter Bitter; Sharp's Doom Bar; 2 changing beers (sourced regionally)

A 19th-century country pub, close to the Grand Western Canal on the Somerset border. The area is popular with walkers and cyclists. The bar features unusual cash register handpumps. Varied home-cooked food, with a carvery on Sundays, is served, and regular food-themed nights feature. A large cylindrical log-burning stove heats the pub in winter. There is a darts and pool area. An attractive walled garden is popular in summer. Up to four real ales are usually on offer. Q P

Honiton

Star Inn

33 New Street, EX14 1BS

8am-midnight (1am Fri & Sat) (01404) 541940

Dartmoor Jail Ale; 9 changing beers

A former town pub, one of the oldest licensed inns in Honiton, tastefully renovated and reopened by Wetherspoon in 2013. Three regular real ales are usually available - Dartmoor Jail Ale and one from Exmoor and Hunters on rotation through their ranges. Up to seven guests can be on offer, sometimes more, plus real cider. Good-value food is served all day. This is a welcome addition to the town. Q

Horns Cross

Coach & Horses

EX39 5DH (on A39 between Bideford and Clovelly)

11-2.30 (not Mon), 5-11; 11-11 Sat; 12-9.30 Sun

(01237) 451214 thebestpubindevon.co.uk

Exmoor Stag; Forge Rev Hawker; Sharp's Doom Bar; 2 changing beers

Up to five real ales are served in this friendly 17th-century roadside inn. There is a single bar and dining area, a separate pool room and three en-suite B&B rooms. Ideally placed for exploring the local North Devon coast, it lies close to Peppercombe beach. Good-quality food is sourced from local suppliers and a value-for-money lunchtime menu is available during the week. Q P (319)

Iddesleigh

Duke of York

EX19 8BG (off B3217 next to church) SS570083
✪ 11-11; 12-10.30 Sun ☎ (01837) 810253
🌐 dukeofyorkdevon.co.uk
Adnams Broadside; Bays Topsail; 1 changing beer [G]
Close to the Tarka Trail, River Torridge and Stafford Moor Fishery, this atmospheric 15th-century inn has old beams, inglenook fires and a friendly, homely atmosphere. There are eight en-suite rooms for visitors and the Duke hosts shooting parties during the season. Well-behaved children and dogs are welcome in this rural gem, where village resident Michael Morpurgo was inspired to write his famous book, War Horse. A courtesy bus services local B&Bs and nearby villages.
Q🐎❀🛏◐◑Å♣🍎🚌(648)🐾📶

Ilfracombe

Ship & Pilot 𝕃

10 Broad Street, EX34 9EE
✪ 11-midnight; 11-11.30 Sun ☎ (01271) 863562
Draught Bass [G]**; St Austell Trelawny; 4 changing beers** [H]
It is difficult to miss this thriving and friendly pub which is bright yellow and backs onto the harbour. There is usually a choice of six ales, mainly from West Country breweries, together with three ciders and a perry. Only bar snacks are available, although customers are welcome to bring in their own food if buying a drink or two. Local CAMRA Pub of the Year 2013 and Cider Pub of the Year in 2013 and 2014. 🐎♿Å♣🍎🚌(21,21A,300)🐾📶

Kilmington

Old Inn 𝕃

EX13 7RB
✪ 11-3, 6-11; 12-3, 7-10.30 Sun ☎ (01297) 32096
🌐 oldinnkilmington.co.uk
Branscombe Vale Branoc; Otter Bitter; 2 changing beers [H]
Thatched 16th-century inn on the A35. The Cricketers bar, a lounge with a log fire and a restaurant area are complemented by a suntrap patio and raised lawn. Food, served lunchtimes and evenings (except Sun eve), is sourced locally – including good mussels – and many specials are changed daily. Beer festivals are held at the end of May, August and bonfire night in November, as well as regular themed nights. A loyalty card system operates. Q🐎❀◐◑ÅP🚌(4)🐾📶

Kings Nympton

Grove Inn 𝕃

EX37 9ST SS683194
✪ 12-3 (not Mon), 6-11; 12-4, 7-10 Sun ☎ (01769) 580406
🌐 thegroveinn.co.uk
Exmoor Ale [G]**; 3 changing beers** [H]
A 17th-century, Grade II-listed thatched pub with good local trade. Four real ales are kept, two of which are on stillage, together with a local cider. Award-winning food is served in the dining area adjacent to the bar. There is a CAMRA discount scheme and the bar also offers a collection of over 65 single malts from around the world. Children and dogs are welcome, both in the pub and the self-catering cottage nearby.
Q🐎❀🛏◐◑♣🍎P🐾📶

Kingsteignton

Sandygate Inn

Sandygate, TQ12 3PU
✪ 5-9 Mon; 12-3, 5 (4.30 Fri)-11; 12-midnight Sat; 12-11 Sun
☎ (01626) 354679 🌐 sandygateinn.com
Otter Ale; 2 changing beers (sourced regionally) [H]
A warm and friendly old village pub. The lounge bar has beamed ceilings and a large open fireplace – if you sit beside it, it is up to you to put the logs on! The public bar is small and cosy with a TV. There is also a small family room and a comfortable dining room. At the rear of the premises is a large walled garden; a patio area with seating is to the front. Q🐎❀◐◑♿≋♣🍎P🚌(2,X64,79)🐾

Kingswear

Ship Inn 𝕃

Higher Street, TQ6 0AG
✪ 12-3, 6-midnight; 12-midnight Sat & Sun
☎ (01803) 752348
Adnams Southwold Bitter; Otter Ale; St Austell Trelawny; 3 changing beers (sourced regionally; often Otter) [H]
A Guide entry for the past 10 years, this is a typical Devon village inn set in a 15th-century building. The Ship has an enviable reputation for quality ales and excellent food, especially fish and seafood. It supports community projects, sponsors the rowing team and hosts live music on the patio in summer overlooking the River Dart. You will receive a warm welcome at this comfortable family-run pub. Beer festivals are held during Dartmouth food and sailing festivals. Q🐎❀◐◑≋♣🚌(18,18A,120)🐾

Littlehempston

Tally Ho 𝕃

TQ9 6LY SX813627
✪ closed Mon; 11-3, 5.30-11; 12-10.30 Sun
☎ (01803) 862316 🌐 tallyhoinn.co.uk
3 changing beers (sourced locally) [H]
South Devon's first community-owned pub opened for business in 2014, having been closed for over three years. It is a traditional village inn and dates back many centuries. The interior is olde worlde, with black timber beams, columns and panelling, both natural and painted thick stone walls, and three open fireplaces, one with a wood-burning stove. At the rear of the premises is an enclosed beer garden which leads to the car park.
Q🐎❀◐◑ÅP🚌(177,X64)🐾📶

Lynton

Sandrock Hotel 𝕃

Longmead, EX35 6DH
✪ 11-11 (midnight Fri & Sat); 12-10.30 Sun
☎ (01598) 752000
Exmoor Ale, Stag; 2 changing beers [H]
A detached Edwardian hotel and pub retaining many original features. Located in a lovely part of Lynton on the road to the Valley of the Rocks, it provides a great base from which to explore the picturesque local area. An excellent selection of local beers and cider, together with good-value pub grub, is available. The large wood-burning stove adds to the atmosphere in the bar, while there is a pleasant rear beer garden to enjoy in summer. Q🐎❀🛏◐◑♿♣🍎P⊟🚌(310,309)🐾📶

Manaton

Kestor Inn

TQ13 9UF (on main road through village)
11-11 ☎ (01647) 221626 kestorinn.com
Dartmoor Best [H]**, Legend** [H]/[G]**; 1 changing beer (sourced locally)** [H]
Spacious local village inn on Dartmoor with a large open-plan L-shaped bar with plenty of seating, including alcoves. There is also a separate pool room and a long dining room, which can be used for functions. It has a friendly atmosphere, and a good selection of local real ales is on offer. The lobby area of the pub has been turned into a small shop selling basic items, and a book exchange scheme is in operation. Sam's Medium Cider is sold. Q P (271,671)

Mary Tavy

Mary Tavy Inn

Lane Head, PL19 9PN
12-2.30, 6-11; 12-2.30, 5-midnight Fri; 12-11 Sat & Sun
☎ (01822) 810326 themarytavyinn.co.uk
Dartmoor IPA, Jail Ale; St Austell Proper Job; 1 changing beer (sourced nationally) [H]
A traditional roadside inn where families, visitors and locals are welcome. The popular bar area accommodates pool, darts, TV, a large fire and up to four real ales. This is complemented by a spacious restaurant and garden with views to Dartmoor. Music nights, charity events, a Sunday carvery and a bank holiday beer festival feature in the pub's calendar. Modern B&B accommodation is available in the adjacent building. The pub closes on Mondays and weekend afternoons in the winter. Q P (118)

Meavy

Royal Oak Inn

PL20 6PJ (on village green)
11-11; 11-10.30 Sun ☎ (01822) 852944
royaloakinn.org.uk
Dartmoor IPA, Jail Ale; 2 changing beers (sourced regionally; often Summerskills) [H]
An iconic English village inn dating from the 16th century, next to the church and overlooking the green where the eponymous tree stands. The lounge has a restaurant serving home-cooked food, complemented by an eclectic wine list. Up to four local ales figure prominently. The public bar provides a return to its history and agricultural roots – flagstone floor, large open fire and photos of times past. It does a good cider range. Local CAMRA branch Country Pub of the Year and Cider/Perry Pub of the Year runner-up 2015.
Q (56)

Merton

Malt Scoop Inn

EX20 3EA (on A386, 7 miles S of Great Torrington)
SS527121
12-3, 6-midnight; 12-1am Fri & Sat; 12-10.30 Sun
☎ (01805) 603924 themaltscoop.co.uk
St Austell Cornish Best Bitter, Tribute, HSD [H]
A 19th-century coaching inn originally part of a farm dating from the 1700s. The horseshoe-shaped bar, with inglenook fireplace, leads through to an adjoining restaurant. The pub tends to concentrate on beers from St Austell, together with a local cider in summer. Modern British food is mainly from nearby suppliers. The pub is reputed to have two resident ghosts, which perhaps goes some way to explaining the regular psychic meetings held here. Q P (118)

Moretonhampstead

Union Inn

10 Ford Street, TQ13 8LN (on A382)
11-11; 12-10.30 Sun ☎ (01647) 440199
theunioninn.co.uk
Fuller's London Pride; Red Rock Lighthouse IPA, Red Rock, Break Water [H]
Traditional 16th-century village-centre free house with a beamed and panelled bar; the adjoining pool room displays old photographs of the village. The function room has its own bar and skittle alley and is reached via a corridor displaying artefacts relating to the inn's history. Red Rock beers are given house names. Good-value home-cooked food is served, with a carvery Sunday lunchtimes. There is outside seating on the decking next to the small car park. P

Newton Abbot

Teign Cellars

67 East Street, TQ12 2JR
10.30-11 (midnight Fri & Sat); 11-11 Sun
☎ (01626) 332991 teigncellars.co.uk
4 changing beers (sourced nationally) [H]/[G]
A wonderful reincarnation of what was previously the Green Man. It was used by paupers from the workhouse opposite in the 19th century to pick oakum, and has one bar, wooden flooring and walls adorned by beer mats, posters and mirrors. Four draught beers are served, often of the unusual kind, including hoppy and unfined types, plus one good-value beer from either Bays or Teignworthy. Eight real ciders are also kept, some from local producers Hunt's and Reddaway's, and there are 170 bottled beers at the bar or in the shop behind. The food is superb. Q

Wolborough Inn

55 Wolborough Street, TQ12 1JQ
11.30-midnight ☎ (01626) 334511
Sharp's Doom Bar [H]**; Teignworthy Reel Ale** [G]**; 3 changing beers (sourced nationally)** [H]/[G]
Single-bar pub with two interesting glass windows to the right of the entrance, etched with the name of the now defunct Starkey Knight & Ford brewery, with the addition of the wording Gold Medal Ales and Tiverton Ales respectively. With its beamed ceilings and simple decor, and furnished with an assortment of tables and seating, it retains an air of relaxed homeliness. Lunchtime meals are traditional home-cooked quality pub grub, with filled rolls sometimes available in the evening.
Q

Newton Poppleford

Cannon Inn

High Street, EX10 0DW
11-2.30, 6-11; 11-midnight Thu-Sat; 12-10.30 Sun
☎ (01395) 568266 pubindevon.com
Bays Topsail; 2 changing beers [G]
A cheery welcome awaits you at this two-bar pub, with dining tables in the lounge bar and restaurant, and bar stools for those who wish to sit and watch

the action. Real ales are served by gravity from stillage behind the bar. This is a friendly locals' pub but with a busy passing trade. Good-value home-cooked food is served lunchtimes and evenings. There are two gardens and a skittle alley; dogs are allowed in the lounge bar.
P (52,157)

Newton St Cyres

Beer Engine

EX5 5AX (beside railway station N of A377)
11-11; 12-10.30 Sun (01392) 851282
thebeerengine.co.uk
Beer Engine Rail Ale, Silver Bullet, Piston Bitter, Sleeper Heavy
A Georgian pub, built in 1850, on the Exeter to Barnstaple Tarka Line. Popular with drinkers and diners alike, it is frequented by locals, visitors and the cricket team. The dining area adjoining the bar serves its own bread made with beer yeast, along with locally sourced food, available lunchtimes and evenings. The pub brews its own ales whose names, like the pictures and old pub signs, have a railway theme. Q P

Crown & Sceptre

EX5 5DA
11-11.30 (midnight Fri & Sat); 11.30-11 Sun
(01392) 851278 crownandsceptre.biz
3 changing beers (sourced locally)
Today's Crown & Sceptre was rebuilt in 1964, replacing the old thatched pub destroyed by fire in 1962. This centrally located village venue is truly the hub of the community. Local pool and darts teams are supported, and various charity events are featured, including a duck race on the Shuttern Brook which flows through the beer garden. Home-made meals are available as well as bar snacks. Five handpumps offer two or three ales, one usually from Otter, plus a real cider.
P (50)

North Bovey

Ring of Bells Inn

TQ13 8RB
10-11 (01647) 440375 ringofbells.net
Dartmoor IPA; 1 changing beer (sourced regionally)
Thatched 13th-century Dartmoor inn situated in an idyllic village with its ancient parish church and tree-lined village green. The pub has a wonderful interior which includes a 15th-century arched door frame, oak doors, low ceilings with beams, open fireplaces and a grandfather clock built into a wall. Food is sourced locally where possible and the lunchtime and evening menus change daily. Five well-appointed en-suite rooms are available on a B&B basis. Q

North Tawton

Railway Inn

Whiddon Down Road, EX20 2BE (1 mile S of town, just off A3124) SS666000
12-3, 6-11; 12-3, 7-10.30 Sun (01837) 82789
therailwaynorthtawton.co.uk
Teignworthy Reel Ale; 1 changing beer
Next to the former North Tawton station (closed in 1971), the Railway has numerous old station photos and memorabilia in evidence. This traditional single-bar local is well worth seeking out, with a warm welcome always assured. The regular Reel Ale from Teignworthy is joined by guest ales from other West Country breweries, together with a real cider in summer. The dining room is popular in the evening (no food Thu), with light meals served at lunchtime. Guide dogs only.
Q P (51,315,318)

Northlew

Green Dragon

EX20 3NN
12-2, 6-11.30 (2am Fri & Sat); 12-2, 6-11 Sun
(01409) 221228
Dartmoor IPA; Holsworthy Ales Muck 'n' Straw; Otter Bitter; 1 changing beer
Set at the heart of the village of Northlew, the Green Dragon offers three regular real ales from Devon breweries and an occasional guest. There are frequent themed food nights and beer festivals take place periodically. This historic 18th-century inn is the hub of the community and, with its wooden beams, snug interior and an inviting inglenook fireplace to be found blazing away in winter, a warm welcome awaits.
P (631)

Noss Mayo

Ship Inn

PL8 1EW
10.30-11; 10.30-10.30 Sun (01752) 872387
nossmayo.com
Dartmoor Jail Ale; Noss Beer Works Church Ledge; St Austell Tribute; 1 changing beer (sourced locally)
Popular with ramblers and seafarers alike, this fine pub is on an inlet of the Yealm Estuary. It is an ideal start/finish point for a walk to enjoy the breathtaking river and sea views along the route of Lord Revelstoke's Drive. If sailing, ring ahead to ascertain the tide times and mooring availability. Food is available all day until 9.30pm. There is no bus service in the evenings or on Sundays. A former CAMRA branch Pub of the Year.
Q P (93,94)

Oakford

Red Lion Hotel

Rookery Hill, EX16 9ES SS9101521336
closed Mon; 12-3 (not Tue & Wed), 6-11; 12-3, 6-midnight Fri & Sat; 12-8 Sun (01398) 351592
redlionoakford.co.uk
Otter Bitter, Amber; 1 changing beer
A welcoming free house, set in a quiet village in undulating countryside on the fringes of Exmoor. The area around Oakford is renowned for shooting, fishing and walking. The bar has a cosy atmosphere, with two or three real ales on offer. Good-value wholesome food is served (it is advisable to book ahead). Beer festivals are sometimes held. A small car park and garden area can be found across the road, and overnight en-suite accommodation is available. Opening hours vary in summer. Q P (307)

Okehampton

Plymouth Inn

26 West Street, EX20 1HH (W end of town)
11-11 (midnight Fri & Sat) (01837) 53633

Black Tor Pride of Dartmoor; 2 changing beers Ⓗ
Near the centre of an old market town, this 17th-century coaching inn has the feel of a friendly village local. The ales are usually from West Country brewers and a local cider is also kept. Two popular beer festivals are held each year, one coinciding with the Ten Tors Challenge in May, the other with the Baring-Gould Folk Festival in October. Reasonably priced, locally sourced meals and snacks are served. ♘❀◑♣P🚌(X9,510)🐾

Ottery St Mary

Volunteer Inn

Broad Street, EX11 1BZ
⌚ 12-11; 12-10.30 Sun ☎ (01404) 814060
⊕ thevolunteerinn-ottery.co.uk
Otter Bitter, Ale; 2 changing beers (sourced regionally) Ⓖ
In the centre of the town, this is a lively venue, popular with younger customers and families. All real ales, mainly from south-west breweries, are served by gravity. Good-value home-cooked pub food is available seven days a week, including a traditional Sunday roast. A newly refurbished courtyard leads to a small beer garden at the rear of the pub. There is also a small restaurant.
♘❀◑♿♣🚌🐾📶

Paignton

Henry's Bar 🄻

53 Torbay Road, TQ4 6AJ
⌚ 11-11 (midnight Fri & Sat) ☎ (01803) 551190
Dartmoor IPA; Sharp's Doom Bar; 2 changing beers (sourced nationally; often Exmoor) Ⓗ
Splendid traditional-style pub situated between gift shops and arcades, on the street running from the bus and railway stations to the beach. The venue is welcoming and family-friendly, and the beers reasonably priced. On handpump there are three regular beers, one guest and Sam's traditional cider, plus various bottles and polyboxes. Home-cooked, wholesome and fairly priced food is served all day until 9pm, with a highly regarded roast on Sunday. ♘◑⇌🍎🚌🐾📶

Isaac Merritt 🄻

54-58 Torquay Road, TQ3 3AA
⌚ 8am-midnight ☎ (01803) 556066
Dartmoor Jail Ale; Greene King Abbot; Ruddles Best Bitter; changing beers (often Hanlons, Hunters, Teignworthy) Ⓗ
Community-oriented Wetherspoon pub just five minutes' walk from both the bus and railway stations, popular with locals and visitors alike. It has a well-deserved reputation for an extensive range of quality handpumped real ales plus various ciders in bottles and polyboxes. The interior is themed around Isaac Merritt Singer, the inventor of the Singer sewing machine. It has seated alcoves, a separate family dining area, a covered/heated smokers' area and good disabled access.
Q♘❀◑♿⇌🍎🚌📶

Parkham

Bell Inn 🄻

Rectory Lane, EX39 5PL (1 mile S of A39 at Horns Cross) SS387212
⌚ 12-2 (not Fri), 5-11; 5.30-midnight Sat; 12-3, 6-midnight Sun ☎ (01237) 451201 ⊕ thebellinnparkham.co.uk
Otter Ale; Sharp's Doom Bar; 2 changing beers Ⓗ
Originally a forge and two cottages, this cosy 13th-century thatched free house generally has up to four real ales on tap, one of which is usually from a local north Devon brewery. Locally produced food, served in either the bar area or the raised dining room, is available at lunchtimes and evenings every day. Spit roasts are a popular feature in summer and a well-attended beer festival is held most years in either June or July.
♘❀◑♣🍎P🚌(372)🐾

Plymouth

Brass Monkey 🄻

12-14 Royal Parade, PL1 1DS
⌚ 9am-11 (midnight Wed-Sat); 9am-7 Sun
☎ (01752) 260442 ⊕ thebrassmonkeyplymouth.co.uk
House beer (by Hunters); changing beers (sourced nationally) Ⓗ
Typical modern bustling pub with a wide clientele. It serves up to eight real ales and two real ciders, including two house beers brewed by Hunters. Beers include some national favourites and others from Devon and Cornwall. Good-value family meals are also available. The pub is conveniently situated in the city centre, with easy access to shopping, buses, The Hoe and The Barbican. Several TVs are balanced by photographs of pre-war Plymouth. Ale festivals are held throughout the year. ♘◑♿⇌🍎🚌📶

Britannia Inn 🄻

2 Wolseley Road, Milehouse, PL2 3BH
⌚ 8am-midnight (1am Fri & Sat) ☎ (01752) 607596
Dartmoor Jail Ale; Greene King Abbot; Ruddles Best Bitter; Sharp's Doom Bar; changing beers (sourced nationally; often Bays, Fuller's, Summerskills) Ⓗ
A large, vibrant hostelry built in the 1830s which retained its name when it became a Wetherspoon in 1999, close to the football ground (it can get busy on match days). There are 10 pumps, one of which always dispenses a real cider. Opposite the main bus depot, it is on numerous bus routes from the train station and city centre. This is a community-oriented pub. ♘❀◑♿🍎🚌🐾📶

Dolphin Hotel

14 The Barbican, PL1 2LS
⌚ 10-11 (midnight Thu-Sat); 11-11 Sun ☎ (01752) 660876
Draught Bass; St Austell Tribute; 6 changing beers (sourced regionally; often Sharp's, Skinner's) Ⓖ
A Plymouth institution, this unpretentious hostelry is steeped in history. Its character is charming, with tiled floors, well-used wooden benches and a traditional open fire, all creating the perfect ambience. The walls are adorned with works by a local artist, the late Beryl Cook, who painted many of the characters she encountered in the Dolphin. Up to eight ales are all dispensed by gravity from the cask. Local CAMRA City Pub of the Year runner-up 2015. 🍎🚌(25)🐾

Fawn Private Members Club 🄻

39 Prospect Street, Greenbank, PL4 8NY
⌚ 3 (2 Fri)-11; 12-11 Sat & Sun ☎ (01752) 226385
Bays Topsail; 4 changing beers (sourced regionally; often Cotleigh, St Austell, Teignworthy) Ⓗ
The club is named after HMS Fawn, now scrapped. CAMRA members are welcome with a membership card; regular visitors will be required to join. The club is popular for rugby and other televised sports, and supports multiple darts and euchre teams. Four

guest ales from the local area are generally served, as well as a rotating range of local cider from Countryman. The covered smoking area is on the patio. Local CAMRA branch Club of the Year 2015.

Ferry House Inn

888 Wolseley Road, Saltash Passage, PL5 1LA

12-midnight (01752) 361063 ferryhouseinn.com

Dartmoor Jail Ale; Draught Bass; Sharp's Doom Bar; 1 changing beer (sourced regionally)

A picturesque community inn beside the River Tamar where you can be sure of a warm welcome. Four real ales are served. There are seven en-suite rooms on a new third floor, with a decking area at the front giving spectacular views of the Tamar bridges. Good home-cooked food is dished up daily. Both bars display photos dating back to the turn of the 20th century, showing IK Brunel's railway bridge and the Saltash foot ferry. (St Budeaux) (13)

Fortescue Hotel

37 Mutley Plain, PL4 6JQ

11-midnight; 12-11 Sun (01752) 660673

Bays Devon Dumpling; St Austell Proper Job; Skinner's Betty Stogs; 5 changing beers (sourced nationally; often Cornish Crown, Hunters, South Hams)

The landlord is a real ale enthusiast and the bar has nine handpumps serving a constantly changing range of ales, with one dedicated to real cider. Several local beers are always available, and up to seven real ciders/perries. There is a long main bar, a cellar bar and a beer garden. Traditional roasts are served on Sundays only, washed down with Spingo beer. Local CAMRA branch Pub of the Year 2013-2015.

Lord High Admiral

33 Stonehouse Street, Stonehouse, PL1 3PE

11-11; 12-10.30 Sun (01752) 256881

St Austell Tribute, HSD; 1 changing beer (sourced regionally)

Friendly community pub not far off Union Street in an area of the city undergoing regeneration. It is close to Millbay ferry port, not far from Royal William Yard and across the road from a highly rated restaurant. Diners having a drink before or after their meal mix happily with locals. It is advisable to book for Sunday lunch, which is the main food offering, although sandwiches are available in the daytime. (3,21,21A)

Lounge

7 Stopford Place, Devonport, PL1 4QT

11.30-3 (not Mon), 6-11; 11.30-3, 5.30-midnight Fri; 11.30-11 Sat; 12-11 Sun (01752) 561330

Draught Bass; 2 changing beers (sourced regionally; often Skinner's, Teignworthy)

Located in a quiet residential area, this street-corner local is near Devonport Park, and offers a warm welcome. The wood-panelled bar is comfortable and relaxing, although it may be busy at times with Plymouth Albion RFC's ground nearby. One weaker, one stronger than the regular Bass is the rule for guest beers, with lighter and darker brews also alternating. A secluded garden at the front offers a retreat for smokers.
Q (Devonport) (32,34)

Mannamead

61 Mutley Plain, PL4 6JH

8am-midnight (1am Fri & Sat) (01752) 825610

Dartmoor Jail Ale; Greene King Abbot; Ruddles Best Bitter; changing beers (sourced nationally; often Dartmoor, Summerskills, Tavy Ales)

A Wetherspoon establishment converted from a former NatWest bank. A wide range of ales from near and far can be found, with at least two local brews usually on the pumps. There is also a good range of real cider and perry. Beer and cider festivals take place several times a year, plus a Devon ale festival. Brewery showcase events are also held, featuring a large number of beers from local breweries.

Minerva Inn

31 Looe Street, Barbican, PL4 0EA

11.30-11.30 (midnight Wed; 12.30am Thu & Fri); 12-12.30am Sat; 1-10.30 Sun (01752) 223047 minervainn.co.uk

St Austell Trelawny, Tribute; 2 changing beers (sourced nationally)

Plymouth's oldest pub, dating from circa 1540, within easy walking distance of the city centre and the historic Barbican. The pub has a long and narrow bar, leading through to a cosy seating area at the rear. Two guest beers are supplemented by spring and autumn beer festivals, where beer could, and does, come from all over the country. Live music takes place Thursday-Sunday evenings and Sunday lunchtimes. The pub benefits from a varied clientele.

Nowhere Inn

21 Gilwell Street, PL4 8BU

4 (6 Sat)-3am; 7-midnight Sun (01752) 670592

St Austell Tribute; house beer (by Noss Beer Works); 3 changing beers (sourced locally; often Noss Beer Works, Summerskills, Tavy Ales)

Old-fashioned back-street hostelry tucked away in the midst of the student campus, near the city centre. There is usually one mainstream beer, supplemented by three varying guest beers, one of which is always LocAle, plus a cider. The pub is frequented by an eclectic variety of patrons, from students to elderly locals. Quiz night is Monday and live music features on Thursday, with beer festivals held twice annually.

Prince Maurice

3 Church Hill, Eggbuckland, PL6 5RJ

11-3, 6-11; 11-11 Fri & Sat; 12-10.30 Sun (01752) 771515

Dartmoor Jail Ale; Hanlons Stormstay; St Austell Tribute, HSD; Sharp's Doom Bar; Summerskills Best Bitter; 2 changing beers (sourced locally)

There is very much a village feel to this four-times local CAMRA Pub of the Year, which sits between the church and village green. It is named after the royalist general, the king's nephew, who had his headquarters nearby during the siege of Plymouth in the Civil War. Up to eight beers are on offer. Two log fires keep you warm in winter, adding to the ambience. Food is not available at weekends.
P (28,28A,28B)

Thistle Park Tavern

32 Commercial Road, Coxside, PL4 0LE

12-midnight (01752) 204890 thistlepark.com

South Hams Devon Pride, Eddystone; 2 changing beers (sourced nationally)

Brewery tap for the South Hams Brewery which, as Sutton, was next door. There is a roof garden and an excellent Thai restaurant upstairs. Biltong is available at the bar. Up to four real ales are on tap, supplemented by Thatchers Cheddar Valley cider. The pub can be accessed across the swing bridge from the Barbican (closes at 9.30pm) and is close to the National Marine Aquarium. Live music often features at the weekend. (14)

Waterloo Inn

30 Waterloo Street, Stoke, PL1 5RS

10-midnight; 11-11 Sun (01752) 550090

Hunters Best; Skinner's Betty Stogs; 1 changing beer (sourced regionally; often Sharp's)

Built circa 1890, this back-street locals' pub is a well-kept secret within the Stoke area of the city. Up to four different ales a week keep the ale fans happy. There are two main seating areas within the open-plan establishment, which also has a large and airy conservatory and a partially covered beer garden. The pub supports a number of pool and darts teams. It is one of the few venues in the western side of the city to serve real ale.
(Devonport) (32)

Plympton

London Inn

8 Church Road, Plympton St Maurice, PL7 1NH

12-11 (midnight Fri & Sat) (01752) 657045

Changing beers (sourced regionally; often Bays, Dartmoor, Skinner's)

A friendly 16th-century hostelry next to the church, and the epitome of a typical village inn. The cosy lounge bar is adorned with a large collection of Royal Naval memorabilia, while the public bar boasts a pool table, dartboard and TVs for sports enthusiasts. Up to eight real ales are on offer, supplemented by several real ciders, and regular beer festivals are held. The pub is allegedly haunted by Captain Hinds. Q P

Union Inn

17 Underwood Road, PL7 1SY

4-11 (11.30 Fri); 2-midnight Sat; 12-11 Sun
(01752) 336756 unioninnplympton.com

4 changing beers (sourced nationally; often Exeter, Summerskills, Tintagel)

A traditional, cosy, 19th-century inn, this family-run community venue offers a warm welcome to all who enter. The landlord's passion for ale is evident, with up to four changing beers providing a year-round beer festival. There are also four real ciders served on gravity. All meals are freshly prepared using local produce (booking is advisable). Lunchtime meals are only available on Sundays. Dogs on leads are welcome. CAMRA branch Cider Pub of the Year 2013 runner-up.
Q P (20,21,21A)

Plymstock

Morley Arms

4 Billacombe Road, PL9 7HP (E end of Laira Bridge)

11.30-2.30, 5-11; 12-9 Sun (01752) 401191
morleyarms.co.uk

Morland Old Speckled Hen; Sharp's Doom Bar; 3 changing beers (sourced nationally; often Brains, Fuller's, Theakston)

Built in 1824 to house the men working on the original Laira Bridge, the building was later converted into a pub. Most of the rooms have been opened out, but retain the original wall beams, giving a cosy feel to a spacious interior. There are open fires in winter. Home-cooked food is served which has an excellent local reputation, and up to five ales are available. Acoustic music takes place on Sunday afternoons. P

Postbridge

Warren House Inn

Postbridge, Postbridge, PL20 6TA (on the B3212 between Postbridge and Bennett's Cross)

11-5 Mon & Tue; 11-10 Wed & Thu; 11-11 Fri & Sat; 11-10.30 Sun (01822) 880208 warrenhouseinn.co.uk

Otter Ale; Summerskills Best Bitter; 2 changing beers (sourced regionally; often Butcombe, Teignworthy)

Isolated and exposed at 1,425 feet above sea level, this is one of the highest pubs in England. The interior features exposed beams, wood panelling, rustic benches and tables and the famous fire. All food menus offer home-cooked dishes using locally sourced ingredients. There is a large family room, and tables outside give breathtaking views over the moors. Countryman cider is available; guest beers vary. The pub is open all day in summer.
Q P (98;82summer only)

Princetown

Plume of Feathers Inn

Plymouth Hill, PL20 6QQ

10.30-11 (midnight Fri & Sat) (01822) 890240
theplumeoffeathersdartmoor.co.uk

Dartmoor Best, Jail Ale; St Austell Tribute; 3 changing beers (sourced regionally; often Bays, Otter, Tavy Ales)

Princetown's oldest building (1785) features granite walls, slate floors and slate-topped tables. A later addition is the large family/function room with its own bar. Food is served all day, with a carvery in the family room weekend lunchtimes. There is ample outdoor seating on the spacious patio, a children's play area, a large car park, campsite and a camping barn on site. Three local ales complement the three regulars. The bus service from Tavistock is infrequent.
Q P (98)

Ringmore

Journey's End Inn

TQ7 4HL

12-3, 6-11; 12-11 Sat & Sun (01548) 810205
journeysendinn.co.uk

4 changing beers (sourced locally; often Bays, Dartmoor, Teignworthy)

A 13th-century inn that takes its name from R.C. Sherriff's famous play, which he started to write while staying here. More recently, it is the real Who'd Have Thought It in John Simes's first Dream Factory novel. It comprises several rooms on different levels. Up to four real ales are on offer and a cider, all from Devon. There is a changing food menu daily which caters for children. The car park is at the top of the hill, 200 yards away.
P

Roborough

New Inn

West Road, EX19 8SY SS575170

12-3 (not Mon & Tue), 5-11; 12-midnight Fri & Sat; 12-11 Sun (01805) 603247 thenewinnroborough.co.uk

Teignworthy Gun Dog; 2 changing beers

Quaint 16th-century thatched inn nestling in the heart of the village and frequented by locals and visitors who support the many activities here. It has a warm, friendly atmosphere, with a lovely fire in colder months and a superb south-facing patio with views of the countryside to enjoy in the summer. The menu is interesting, including home-made ice cream and bread, and the range of ciders and perries is outstanding. Q🐴❀◑◐♣P🚌🐾📶

Salcombe

Victoria Inn

Fore Street, TQ8 8BU

🕘 11-11 ☎ (01548) 842604 🌐 victoriainn-salcombe.co.uk

St Austell Tribute, Proper Job; house beer (by St Austell) H

In the heart of Salcombe, the pub won a Tenant of the Year award from St Austell Brewery in 2014. It has a friendly atmosphere, good, knowledgeable staff and is extremely popular for food. The décor features slate floors, low beams and a huge log fire. The upstairs restaurant is cosy, bright and modern and leads to a pretty beer garden. Dogs are welcome and have their own menu, with the proceeds going to a hearing dogs charity. 🐴❀🛏◑◐▲🚌(606,X64)🐾📶

Sandford

Lamb Inn

The Square, EX17 4LW

🕘 10.30-11 ☎ (01363) 773676 🌐 lambinnsandford.co.uk

Otter Bitter; changing beers H

A traditional 16th-century free house in the village centre with a warm, welcoming atmosphere. It is well supported by locals and visitors alike, offering award-winning food, West Country ales and Sandford Orchards cider. Skittles is played four nights a week in the alley-cum-cinema-cum-conference venue. There are open mic music and comedy evenings. Accommodation is available and children and dogs are welcome. It is frequented by the village football, squash and cricket teams. Q🐴❀🛏◑◐♿♣🍎🚌(369)🐾📶

Shaldon

Clifford Arms 🄻

34 Fore Street, TQ14 0DE

🕘 11-2.30, 5-11 (11.30 Fri & Sat); 11.30-3, 5.30-10.30 Sun ☎ (01626) 872311

Dartmoor IPA; Two Beach Oarsome Ale; 2 changing beers (sourced regionally) H

In the centre of a pretty coastal village, this 18th-century pub has an attractive modern interior and a warming log fire. The guest and seasonal beers are usually from West Country breweries. The restaurant at the rear serves good-quality food daily and leads out onto a sunny, decked patio. Special menus are available on modern jazz evenings on Mondays, monthly lunchtime jazz sessions, and numerous charity events. Q🐴❀◑◐🍎🚌(11)

Shaldon Conservative Club 🄻

Dagmar Street, TQ14 0DU

🕘 12-3, 5-11; 12-11 Sat & Sun ☎ (01626) 873667

Teignworthy Reel Ale; 1 changing beer (sourced regionally) H

In the centre of the village, the club offers two real ales and a real cider at reasonable prices. The single bar has comfortable seating and is home to snooker, darts and euchre teams. At the hub of the community, it hosts charity fundraising events, wakes and private parties. Live music features regularly and includes open mic nights. Televised rugby is popular. CAMRA members are welcome with a membership card. ♿♣🍎🚉🚌(11)📶

Sidmouth

Balfour Arms

26 Woolbrook Road, Woolbrook, EX10 9UZ

🕘 12-11 (midnight Fri & Sat); 12-10.30 Sun ☎ (01395) 512993

Otter Bitter; Sharp's Doom Bar, Atlantic; 1 changing beer H

Built in the 1930s and named after Lord Balfour, this is a locals' pub and very much part of the local community of Woolbrook, the area of Sidmouth in which the pub is situated, about a mile from the seafront. It has had a mixed history, but has now settled down under an eager landlord. Good-value home-cooked food is served, and up to four real ales are usually on offer. The pub welcomes families and dogs. Buses stop outside. Q🐴❀◑◐♿♣P🚌(52,157)🐾📶

Silverton

Lamb Inn 🄻

Fore Street, EX5 4HZ

🕘 11.30-2.30, 6-midnight; 11.30-midnight Sat; 12-11 Sun ☎ (01392) 860272 🌐 thelambinnsilverton.co.uk

Exe Valley Dob's Best Bitter; Otter Ale; 1 changing beer (sourced regionally) G

Popular family-run village pub with stone floors, stripped timber, old pine furniture and a large open real fire. A fine display of old pumpclips is a reminder of the long list of previous guest beers. Three ales are served by gravity from a temperature-controlled stillage behind the bar, at competitive prices. There is a function room and skittle alley. Good-value home-cooked food is served lunchtimes and evenings, plus a popular Sunday roast. Q🐴❀◑◐♿♣🍎🚌(55B)🐾📶

Slapton

Queen's Arms 🄻

TQ7 2PN

🕘 12-3, 6-11; 12-3, 7-10.30 Sun ☎ (01548) 580800 🌐 queensarmsslapton.co.uk

Dartmoor Jail Ale; Otter Bright, Ale; 1 changing beer (sourced regionally) H

A hearty welcome awaits at this 14th-century village-centre pub. Numerous photographs depicting the WWII evacuation adorn the walls. A flower-filled garden with patios is at the rear and children and dogs are welcome. An extensive menu is available with daily specials; the chef is renowned for his home-made pies. During winter Sunday roasts are served (booking advisable). A takeaway food service is offered and an open fire adds warmth in the cold weather. Q🐴❀◑◐▲♣🍎P🚌(93)🐾📶

South Molton

Town Arms Hotel 🄻

124 East Street, EX36 3BU (100yds E of town square)

🕘 11-midnight (1am Fri); 12-midnight Sun ☎ (01769) 572531

Exmoor Ale; Sharp's Doom Bar; 1 changing beer [H]
A good example of a north Devon market town local, this popular main-street pub has a strong commitment to real ale, and a CAMRA discount scheme has been in operation here for several years. Although no cooked food is served, good-value filled rolls are usually on offer. The pub can get quite lively on occasions, particularly on Thursday market day. Well-behaved dogs are welcome. 🛏♿⛺♣●P🚌(X7,155)🐾📶

South Tawton

Seven Stars ⅬL

Fore Street, EX20 2LW
⏲ closed Mon; 12-3, 6-11; 12-11 Fri & Sat; 12-10.30 Sun
☎ (01837) 849377 🌐 thesevenstarssouthtawton.co.uk
Dartmoor IPA; Holsworthy Ales Original [G]**; 1 changing beer** [H]
In the centre of a pretty and unspoilt village on the edge of Dartmoor, this creeper-clad Victorian pub is a delight to visit, with a wonderful Art Deco theme. Antiques sales are held here every two months but, if you like something, make an offer. The two regular beers are joined by a guest ale at weekends. The food menu changes weekly and is based on locally sourced seasonal ingredients. A barbecue in the garden/courtyard can be booked for use. Q🐴❀◑⛺♣🚌🐾📶

South Zeal

King's Arms ⅬL

EX20 2JP SX649936
⏲ 12-11 ☎ (01837) 840300 🌐 thekingsarmssouthzeal.com
Dartmoor IPA, Legend; 2 changing beers [H]
Thatched 14th-century village local which was once a cider house. The long single bar has four handpumps in use all year round, with two regularly changing guest ales usually from West Country brewers. Good food is served lunchtimes and evenings every day. The pub is a popular meeting place, particularly during the Dartmoor Folk Festival in August. Regular live music sessions are held throughout the year. Well-behaved children and dogs are welcome.
Q🐴❀◑♿⛺♣●P🚌(178)🐾📶

Oxenham Arms ⅬL

EX20 2JT (lower end of village)
⏲ 12-3, 6-11; 12-3, 6-10.30 Sun ☎ (01837) 840244
🌐 theoxenhamarms.co.uk
4 changing beers [H]
The Oxenham was built as an early 13th-century monastery, into which the prehistoric standing stone, to be seen in the small lounge behind the bar, was incorporated. Later an imposing manor house, it now has the unspoilt atmosphere of an old country inn, with low beams, flagged floors, open fires and mullion windows. Two guest beers, usually from local breweries, join the particularly good Oxy Ale and Merry Monk house beers. An excellent beer festival is held in August.
Q🐴❀🛏◑♿⛺♣●P🚌(178)🐾📶

Beer makes you feel the way you ought to feel without beer. **Henry Lawson**

Spreyton

Tom Cobley Tavern 🏆 ⅬL

EX17 5AL (off A3124 in village) SX6986096761
⏲ 6.30-11 Mon; 12-3, 6-11 (1am Fri & Sat); 12-4, 7-11 Sun
☎ (01647) 231314 🌐 tomcobleytavern.co.uk
Changing beers [H]/[G]
A choice of 14 real ales, all from West Country brewers, together with real ciders and delicious home-cooked food, make this a gem of a pub. It was a finalist for CAMRA National Pub of the Year in 2012, testifying that this is a true community pub. Children are welcome and the garden is a delight on warm sunny days. Six comfortable guest rooms are available. A warm and friendly hostelry.
Q❀🛏◑♣●P🐾

Sticklepath

Taw River Inn ⅬL

EX20 2NW (on old A30 through village) SX642941
⏲ 12-midnight; 12-11 Sun ☎ (01837) 840377
🌐 tawriver.co.uk
Dartmoor IPA, Legend; St Austell Tribute; 1 changing beer [H]
A 17th-century manor house, this friendly and relaxed oak-beamed pub is popular with locals and visitors alike. Set in an attractive village on the edge of Dartmoor, it is ideally situated for exploring the area or visiting the Finch Foundry Museum (National Trust) opposite. The varied real ales are reasonably priced and good-value pub food is served in both the bar area and adjacent dining room. Families and dogs are welcome.
🐴❀◑♣●P🚌(X9)🐾📶

Talaton

Talaton Inn ⅬL

EX5 2RQ
⏲ closed Mon; 12-3, 7-11 ☎ (01404) 822214
🌐 talatoninn.com
Otter Bitter, Amber; 1 changing beer (sourced regionally) [H]
A popular 16th-century free house in the ancient village of Talaton, mentioned in the Domesday Book, offering up to three real ales, usually from south-west breweries. Good-value traditional pub food, using local produce where possible, is served lunchtimes and evenings (no food Mon and Sun eve; booking essential Tue eve). Regular theme nights are hosted and traditional games are played. There is a large car park, and plenty of seating outside, including a smokers' shelter.
Q🐴❀◑♿⛺♣P🚌(382)🐾📶

Teignmouth

Brass Monkey ⅬL

Hollands Road, TQ14 8SR
⏲ 11-midnight; 12-11 Sun ☎ (01626) 773961
St Austell Tribute, 1913 Cornish Stout [H]
This pub was the Half Moon in a previous incarnation. The longstanding and award-winning licensees offer a warm welcome at this community-oriented establishment with a strong local following. It has one simple bar, with sporting events shown on TV screens, a Tuesday quiz and Friday/Saturday night karaoke. Halfway between the railway station and the bus bays, it is both an unofficial waiting room and an excellent retreat from the nearby town centre. Q♿⇌♣🚌(2,11)🐾

ENGLAND

Tiverton

Courtenay's

10 Newport Street, EX16 6NH
12-11 (midnight Fri & Sat); 12-10.30 Sun
Otter Amber; 4 changing beers (sourced regionally) [G]
A micropub that opened in 2012 in a former pet shop and is named after the family who lived at the nearby Tiverton castle. There are four casks of ale plus four real ciders set up behind the compact wooden bar. Two ales are usually supplied by Otter and Hunters breweries. A small carpeted area is off to one side of the bar. Toilet facilities are limited.

Topsham

Bridge Inn ★

Bridge Hill, EX3 0QQ
12-2, 6-10.30 (11 Fri & Sat); 12-2, 7-10.30 Sun
(01392) 873862 cheffers.co.uk
Branscombe Vale Branoc; changing beers [G]
Historic, cosy, 16th-century inn run by six generations of the same family since 1897, with a varying range of ales from local breweries and further afield. This hostelry is a delight for fans of real ale, in a traditional setting overlooking the banks of the River Clyst. The inn was visited by the Queen in 1998. Nine beers are usually available, all dispensed by gravity straight from the cellar. Snacks are served lunchtimes and until 8.30pm in the evening. **Q P** (57,T)

Torquay

Hole in the Wall

6 Park Lane, TQ1 2AU
12-midnight (01803) 200755
holeinthewalltorquay.co.uk
Butcombe Bitter; Dartmoor Best; Otter Bitter; Shepherd Neame Spitfire; 4 changing beers [H]
Close to, but tucked away from, the harbour, this is Torquay's oldest inn (circa 1540). A real ale haven with beamed ceilings and cobbled floors, it is popular with holidaymakers and seafarers as well as businessmen and locals. The narrow passageway outside is adorned with award-winning floral displays and makes a pleasant alfresco drinking area. A busy and roomy restaurant serves highly regarded food. Dogs on leads are welcome. Live music features on Tuesdays, Thursdays and Sundays. **P**

Turnchapel

Clovelly Bay Inn

1 Boringdon Road, PL9 9TB
12-3 (not Mon-Thu), 6-11; 12-4, 7-10.30 Sun
(01752) 402765 clovellybayinn.co.uk
5 changing beers (sourced nationally; often Bays, Skinner's) [H]/[G]
Family-run free house nestled in a picturesque village on the South-West Coastal Path. The landlord has a passion for quality real ales and ciders, with up to five on offer. The pub holds a variety of festivals throughout the year, with an emphasis on local produce and a willingness to source beers and ciders from further afield. It is also renowned for its wonderful food. Accommodation is popular with tourists and walkers. (2)

Wembury

Odd Wheel

Knighton Road, PL9 0JD
12-3, 5-midnight; 12-midnight Sat & Sun
(01752) 863052 theoddwheel.co.uk
Dartmoor Jail Ale; St Austell Tribute; Sharp's Doom Bar; 3 changing beers (sourced regionally) [H]
Friendly country pub tastefully refurbished several years ago, at the northern end of this picturesque village. Three regular beers and up to three guests are on offer, mainly from Devon and Cornwall. Regular beer festivals are held. The pub is a short distance from many walking routes including the South-West Coastal Path. Food is served daily, with ingredients from local suppliers. Outside, there is a terraced garden and play area for children. **P** (48)

Whimple

New Fountain Inn

Church Road, EX5 2TA
12-2 (not Mon), 6.30-11; 12-3, 6.30-11 Sat; 12-3, 7-10.30 Sun (01404) 822350
Teignworthy Reel Ale; 2 changing beers [G]
Converted from cottages in about 1890, this pub has changed little over the years, although modern toilets were added in an extension to one of the bars in 2009. The other bar retains many original features including a real fire in winter. In this genuine free house the handpumps are decorative – ale is fetched from the cellar. Good-value home-cooked food is served. The village heritage centre in the car park is worth visiting. **Q P**

Widecombe-in-the-Moor

Rugglestone Inn

TQ13 7TF (¼ mile from centre of village)
11.30-3, 6-11.30; 11.30-3, 5-midnight Fri; 11.30-midnight Sat; 12-11 Sun (01364) 621327 rugglestoneinn.co.uk
Dartmoor Legend; house beer (by Teignworthy); 2 changing beers (sourced regionally) [G]
Unspoilt pub in a splendid Dartmoor setting. This Grade II-listed building was converted to an inn back in 1832. The stone-flagged bar area has seating, with beer also served through a hatch in the passageway. An open fire warms the lounge. A wide selection of home-cooked food is available. Across the stream is a large grassed seating area. The house beer is from Teignworthy and local farm cider is sold. The car park is just down the road. **Q P**

Yarde Down

Poltimore Arms

EX36 3HA (2 miles E of Brayford on jct with unclassified road from South Molton to Simonsbath) SS725356
7-11 (01598) 710381 poltimorearms.co.uk
Exmoor Ale; Otter Bitter; 1 changing beer [G]
Still powered by generator – there is no mains electricity – this pub is an old coaching inn dating from the 13th century. It retains many original features and is thought to be haunted by a friendly ghost. Three real ales are usually on tap and good-quality food is served Thursday-Sunday in the atmospheric restaurant. An attractive shop and gallery is also run from the premises. Set in glorious Exmoor countryside, it is well worth seeking out. **Q P**

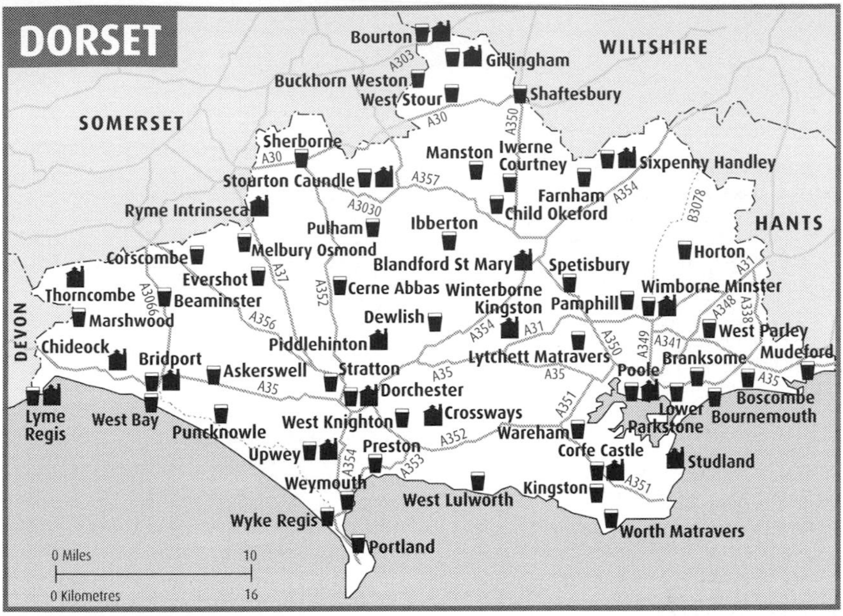

Askerswell

Spyway Inn

DT2 9EP

12-3, 6-11 ☎ (01308) 485250 spyway-inn.co.uk

Otter Bitter, Ale; 1 changing beer (sourced regionally) G

Family-friendly 16th-century smugglers' inn perched on a hill outside Askerswell on the road to Eggardon Hill fort. From March to October there is usually a guest beer and local cider on draught as well as the Otter beers on gravity. The lounge bar has beams and a woodburner; a further bar has tables for dining. The menu features dishes made with locally produced ingredients. The garden is popular with locals, walkers and dog owners, and has a play area for families. Q P

Beaminster

Greyhound

11 The Square, DT8 3AW

11-3, 6-11; 11-11 Fri & Sat; 12-11 Sun ☎ (01308) 862496

greyhoundbeaminster.co.uk

Palmers Copper Ale, Best Bitter; 1 changing beer H

Friendly pub in the town square, dating from the 1700s, popular with locals. The floor of the main bar is half carpeted and half stone, the bar is warmed by a real fire, and there is a snug at the back. The third handpump alternates between Palmers 200 and Dorset Gold in summer and Palmers 200 and Tally Ho! in winter. Home-cooked food includes daily specials and different theme nights on weekdays. Open all day Monday to Saturday in summer. (40,53)

Boscombe

Chaplin's & Cellar Bar

529 Christchurch Road, BH1 4AG

11 (12 Sun)-midnight ☎ (01202) 251953

chaplins-bar.co.uk

7 changing beers (sourced nationally; often Vibrant Forest) H/G

This bar, restaurant and live music venue was local CAMRA Pub of the Year in 2013. The upstairs Chaplin's Bar is decorated with memorabilia and shows silent films. Here there is locally sourced (usually organic) food and one beer. The artfully decorated Cellar Bar opens at 4pm weekdays, noon Saturday and Sunday, with live music and up to six well-chosen ales. The garden at the rear is full of quirky and amusing decorations and hosts four festivals annually.

Bournemouth

Cricketers Arms

41 Windham Road, BH1 4RN

11-11; 12-10.30 Sun ☎ (01202) 551589

Fuller's London Pride; 2 changing beers (sourced nationally; often Hook Norton) H

Bournemouth's oldest public house, dating from 1847. The pub once had stables and a boxing gym where former world champion Freddie Mills trained. The gym is incorporated into the main bar area which retains many interesting original features. This pub, at the heart of the community, offers two ever-changing guest beers and real cider straight from the box. It hosts an annual beer festival. There is occasional live entertainment, quiz night on Tuesday, games on Thursday and lunches served at weekends. P

Moon in the Square

4-8 Exeter Road, BH2 5AQ

7am-midnight (1am Fri & Sat; 11 Sun) ☎ (01202) 652090

Greene King Abbot; Ruddles Best Bitter; house beer (by Sixpenny); 8 changing beers (sourced nationally) H

Opened in 1994, this large Wetherspoon pub is handy for the town's shopping area, lower gardens and seafront. It has two bars over two floors and pavement tables. The lower bar is divided into three areas with the right side popular with family diners. The smaller upper bar is quieter, serving mainly local beers and cider on gravity, and has a rooftop patio. The pub is a favourite with hen and stag parties, and can get lively at weekends. Q

Bourton

White Lion

High Street, SP8 5AT

11.30-11; 12-10.30 Sun (01747) 840866

whitelionbourton.co.uk

Otter Amber; 1 changing beer (sourced nationally; often Ruddles, Timothy Taylor)

The White Lion is a traditional inn dating from 1763. Originally separate rooms, the cosy flagstoned bar has been opened out but there is always a quiet corner to be found. It has a small, intimate restaurant and, to the rear, a large beer garden. Either Thatchers Original or Rich's is served on the cider handpump. The pub is set back from the B3081 with parking opposite as well as in the car park. P (158)

Branksome

Branksome Railway Hotel

429 Poole Road, BH12 1DQ

11-11; 12-10.30 Sun (01202) 769555

Hop Back Summer Lightning; Timothy Taylor Landlord; 2 changing beers (sourced nationally; often Burning Sky, Vibrant Forest)

A Victorian railway hotel dating from 1894 opposite Branksome station on the Waterloo to Weymouth line, also on the main bus routes between Poole and Bournemouth. A large, open-plan interior is divided into three areas with a real-flame fire in two of them. Up to two guest beers are chosen by local CAMRA members, often including a dark ale. Live major sporting events are shown and there is occasional live music at weekends. Six en-suite bedrooms are available. P

Bridport

Crown Inn

56 West Bay Road, DT6 4AX

11.30-11 (1am Fri & Sat); 11.30-10.30 Sun (01308) 422037

Palmers Copper Ale, Best Bitter, Dorset Gold, 200, Tally Ho!

Welcoming traditional single-bar establishment on the A35 roundabout between Bridport and West Bay. A popular locals' pub, but families, parties and tourists are also made to feel at home. Good food is served daily (noon-9pm). Large TV screens show sports and there is a thriving live music scene at weekends. The full range of Palmers beers is served throughout the year. The pub has a beer garden and a large car park. P

Ropemakers Arms

36 West Street, DT6 3QP

10-11 (12.30am Fri & Sat); 12-5 Sun (01308) 421255

theropemakers.com

Palmers Copper Ale, Best Bitter, 200; 1 changing beer

Deceptively large pub situated in the centre of town serving the full range of Palmers ales, with Dorset Gold alternating with the seasonal beers. The interior has lots of separate themed areas decorated with memorabilia and local history. Outside is a large partially covered courtyard at the rear; disabled access is via the back door. Quality home-cooked food is made using locally sourced ingredients. Live music plays on Friday and Saturday evenings. Closes around 3pm on winter Sundays.

Tiger Inn

14-16 Barrack Street, DT6 3LY

12-11 (midnight Fri & Sat) (01308) 427543

tigerinnbridport.co.uk

Sharp's Doom Bar; 5 changing beers (sourced nationally; often Butcombe, Fuller's, Hop Back)

Busy and popular Victorian back-street pub offering six real ales including five guests. The single bar has two distinct areas, with TV for major sporting events, pub games and a skittle alley. There is a pleasant garden and a separate covered courtyard. Close to the town centre but tucked away, the Tiger is worth seeking out. Look out for the rare Groves Brewery etched window. B&B is offered in seven en-suite rooms.

Buckhorn Weston

Stapleton Arms

Church Hill, SP8 5HS (between A303 and A30) ST75652462

11-3, 6-11; 11-11 Sat & Sun (01963) 370396

thestapletonarms.com

Butcombe Bitter; Moor Beer Revival; 2 changing beers

Imposing village pub with a large car park and secluded garden. The two guest beers often reflect the seasons and are frequently from local breweries. Excellent food is served as well as classic bar snacks such as hand-made pork pies, Scotch eggs and chutney. Children, dogs and muddy boots are welcome. Modern en-suite accommodation completes the Drink, Eat, Sleep motto. Q P

Cerne Abbas

Giant Inn

24 Long Street, DT2 7JF

12-2.30, 6-11; 12-11 Sat; 12-10.30 Sun (01300) 341441

thegiantinncerneabbas.co.uk

REAL ALE BREWERIES

Blackmore Stourton Caundle
Bournemouth Poole
Brewhouse & Kitchen Dorchester
Brewhouse & Kitchen Poole (NEW)
Cerne Abbas Chideock (NEW)
Corfe Castle Corfe Castle
Dorset Crossways
DT Upwey
Eight Arch Wimborne Minster (NEW)
Gyle 59 Thorncombe
Hall and Woodhouse (Badger) Blandford St Mary
Isle of Purbeck Studland
King Alfred Bourton
Lyme Regis Lyme Regis
Palmers Bridport
Piddle Piddlehinton
Sixpenny Sixpenny Handley
Small Paul's Gillingham
Sunny Republic Winterborne Kingston
Wriggle Valley Ryme Intrinseca (NEW)

St Austell Tribute; 3 changing beers (sourced regionally; often Cerne Abbas, Dorset, Yeovil) Ⓗ
Situated within the centre of the village and often full of locals, visitors can be assured of a warm and friendly welcome. The exterior frontage is Victorian while internally an original 15th-century fireplace has been retained. Home-cooked food is served alongside a good selection of up to four real ales from Dorset and the West Country, including one from the Cerne Abbas Brewery. Skittles and darts are regularly played. Definitely worth popping into on the way to the Cerne Giant.
Q👪◐◑♿♣🚌(X11)🐾📶

Child Okeford

Saxon Inn

Gold Hill, DT11 8HD
🕒 12-3, 6-11 ☎ (01258) 860310 🌐 saxoninn.co.uk
Butcombe Bitter; Otter Bitter; 4 changing beers (sourced regionally) Ⓗ
Local CAMRA Rural Pub of the Year, this 300-year-old inn retains rustic charm despite significant extension following the conversion from cottages in the 1950s. The bar area is cosy with tables and chairs around a log fire. There are two distinct dining areas and a garden for alfresco dining. A varied menu of quality home-cooked food is available, including vegetarian options. The pub also offers B&B and is an ideal base for exploring rural Dorset. Q👪❀🛏◐◑♣P🐾📶

Corfe Castle

Royal British Legion Club

70 East Street, BH20 5EQ (off A351)
🕒 12-2.30, 6-11; 12-11 Sat & Sun ☎ (01929) 480591
Ringwood Best Bitter; Timothy Taylor Landlord; 1 changing beer (sourced nationally) Ⓗ
Built in Purbeck stone, this welcoming club has a bar area with upholstered bench seating, wooden tables and chairs. Major sporting events are shown on TV, and darts, shove-ha'penny and occasional live music are played. Filled rolls are available all day. An upstairs meeting room can be hired. The garden is fantastic in summer, with a boules court and views over the Purbecks. Show a CAMRA membership card or a copy of the Guide for entry.
❀♣P🚌(40)

Corscombe

Fox Inn

DT2 0NS
🕒 closed Mon & Tue; 12-2, 7-11; 12-8.30 Sun
☎ (01935) 892381 🌐 foxinncorscombe.com
Sharp's Doom Bar; 3 changing beers (sourced locally; often Dorset, Wriggle Valley, Yeovil) Ⓗ
Traditional family-run inn in ramblers' countryside with a thatched roof and an unspoilt interior including a slate bar, flagstone floors and lovely old inglenook fireplaces. Dining is in the conservatory, with menus that appeal to all ages and feature local seasonal produce. This free house serves three changing guest beers along with two real ciders. The pub hosts many events including regular live music. Q👪❀◐◑♣🍎P🐾📶

Dewlish

Oak at Dewlish

DT2 7ND
🕒 11.30-2.30, 6-11; 12-2.30, 7-11 Sun ☎ (01258) 837352
🌐 oakpub.co.uk
3 changing beers (sourced regionally; often Butcombe, Cotleigh, Dartmoor) Ⓗ
Unpretentious village inn with three ever-changing ales sourced mainly from the West Country. The horseshoe-shaped bar has a dining area and opens onto a patio and large garden. To the rear is a separate room with a pool table. A varied food menu offers good home-cooked dishes made using local produce. Two B&B rooms and self-catering accommodation are available in an adjacent converted coach house. Dogs and children are welcome. Q👪❀🛏◐◑♣🍎🚌(311)🐾

Dorchester

Blue Raddle

9 Church Street, DT1 1JN
🕒 11.30-3 (not Mon), 6.30-11; 12-3, 7-10.30 Sun
☎ (01305) 267762 🌐 blueraddle.co.uk
Butcombe Adam Henson's Rare Breed; Cerne Abbas Ale; Fuller's London Pride; St Austell Trelawny, Tribute Ⓗ
Popular, genuine, town-centre free house with friendly staff and an enthusiastic landlord. In addition to the regular beers, occasional guest ales and local ciders are also on offer. Good locally sourced food is served lunchtimes (Wed-Sat) and evenings (Thu-Sat). The pub takes part in local events and hosts regular folk music sessions. Piped comedy shows and Private Eye are available in the conveniences. Children are not permitted.
◐◑⇌(West)♣🍎🚌🐾📶

Brewhouse & Kitchen Ⓛ

17 Weymouth Avenue, DT1 1QY
🕒 11-11 (12.30am Fri & Sat); 12-10.30 Sun
☎ (01305) 265551 🌐 brewhouseandkitchen.com
Brewhouse & Kitchen Station Masters Ale, Nine Stones, Crickmay, Judge Jeffreys, Cerne Abbas Giant; 2 changing beers Ⓗ
Brewpub in the former stationmaster's house. Tastefully refurbished, extended and reopened in 2014, it has separate bar, lounge and restaurant areas. The microbrewery is fully on display in the bar. A large range of home-brews and one local cider are on eight handpumps. Food is served seven days a week including brunch from 9am at weekends. It hosts occasional live music and offers brewing experience days. Close to Dorchester South station, so why not break your journey for a pint? 👪❀◐◑♿⇌(South)♣🍎P🚌🐾📶

Tom Browns Ⓛ

47 High East Street, DT1 1HU
🕒 11-11 (midnight Fri & Sat); 12-11 Sun ☎ (01305) 264020
Dorset Tom Browns, Yachtsman, Durdle Door; 5 changing beers (sourced locally) Ⓗ
Formerly home to the Goldfinch Brewery, this is now the Dorset Brewing Company tap. The full range of Goldfinch/DBC ales rotates around the eight handpumps, alongside a local cider. Refurbished but retaining the feel of a town-centre alehouse, the pub hosts regular live music and other events, and has a skittle alley/function room. Food includes award-winning pies. The large riverside garden is ideal for lazy pints in the sun.
👪❀◐♣🍎🚌🐾📶

Evershot

Acorn Inn Hotel Ⓛ
28 Fore Street, DT2 0JW
✪ 11-11; 12-11 Sun ☎ (01305) 262360 ⊕ acorn-inn.co.uk
3 changing beers (sourced locally; often Dorset, Otter, Yeovil) Ⓗ
Small, attractive 16th-century hotel mentioned in Thomas Hardy's Tess of the d'Urbervilles as the Sow and Acorn. The large flagstoned village bar at the back has a wood-burning stove. A smaller bar and restaurant are at the front. Two ales and often a third are sold, along with a local cider in the summer. The skittle alley can be hired for functions. Winner of a Taste of the West Gold Award 2014 and Dorset Tourism Gold Award.
❄☆✿♿◖♣♠P🚲(212)🐾❀🛜

Farnham

Museum Ⓛ
DT11 8DE (off A354)
✪ 12-11 ☎ (01725) 516261 ⊕ museuminn.co.uk
Sixpenny 6D Best Bitter, Gold; 2 changing beers (sourced regionally) Ⓗ
Set in tranquil Dorset countryside, this 17th-century part-thatched country inn has a cosy, intimate feel. Refurbished in 2012, the interior is open plan but divided into four distinct areas. Some original features remain including the flagstone floor in the bar area, large inglenook and window seat. The pub is predominately food oriented but welcoming to those who just want beer. Excellent locally sourced food is served all day. Beers tend to be from the local Sixpenny Handley Brewery.
Q❄☆✿♿◖♿P🐾❀

Gillingham

Phoenix
High Street, SP8 4AW
✪ 10-3, 6-11 (not Mon eve); 10-11 Fri; 11-midnight Sat; 11-3, 6-11 Sun ☎ (01747) 823277
Sharp's Doom Bar, Atlantic Ⓗ
Originally built in the 15th century as a coaching inn with its own brewery and stables, it was rebuilt following a fire in the 17th century and renamed the Phoenix. It has an open-plan layout with a dining area to one side serving good-value pub grub. Guest beers occasionally supplement the regulars. There are two public car parks within walking distance. ◖⇄🚲(158)🐾❀🛜

Horton

Drusilla's Inn
Wigbeth, BH21 7JH
✪ 10-11 ☎ (01258) 840297 ⊕ drusillasinn.co.uk
Flack Manor Flack's Double Drop; Ringwood Best Bitter; 1 changing beer (sourced regionally) Ⓗ
Attractive thatched pub with leaded windows and olde worlde charm, offering views over the rolling Dorset countryside and Horton Folly. Decorated with brasses and rural prints, and with an inglenook fireplace and logburner, it has a traditional atmosphere. An ideal place for stopping off or making your destination, it has a secure garden and play area. Excellent ales, delicious meals and friendly, welcoming staff make this a pub to return to. Accommodation is offered in stylish traditional Dorset shepherds' huts.
Q❄☆✿♿◖P🐾

Ibberton

Crown Inn Ⓛ
Church Lane, DT11 0EN
✪ 12-3 (not Mon), 6-11; 12-3 Sun ☎ (01258) 817448
Butcombe Bitter; Palmers Copper Ale; 1 changing beer Ⓗ
A rural hideaway, this tranquil 16th-century inn retains original flagstone flooring, oak doors and an inglenook fireplace. In summer the lawned garden, with babbling brook, is a delight. The pub is located in the heart of Ibberton, a picturesque village mentioned in the Domesday Book, with one of only three churches in the county dedicated to St Eustace, and is an ideal starting point for walkers on the Wessex Ridgeway. In winter it opens evenings only Tuesday, Wednesday and Thursday and afternoons only on Sunday. Q❄☆✿◖P

Iwerne Courtney (Shroton)

Cricketers
Main Street, DT11 8QD (off A350 N of Stourpaine)
✪ 12-3, 6-11; 12-10.30 Sun ☎ (01258) 860421
⊕ thecricketersshroton.co.uk
Butcombe Bitter; 3 changing beers (sourced nationally) Ⓗ
Situated in the picturesque north-east Dorset village of Shroton, and convenient for walks around Hambledon Hill, the Cricketers is a community pub popular with locals, cricketers and tourists alike. An L-shaped central bar serves a bustling drinking area and a dining area at the rear. An extensive menu offers both local specialties and traditional pub food. In the summer the tranquil garden is popular, while the winter months can be enjoyed by the warm and cosy woodburner. Q❄☆✿◖P🚲(X9)🛜

Kingston

Scott Arms
West Street, BH20 5LH
✪ 11-11 ☎ (01929) 480270 ⊕ thescottarms.com
Dorset Jurassic; Ringwood Best Bitter; 2 changing beers (sourced nationally) Ⓗ
The pub dates back to 1787 but became the Scott Arms after the Second World War, named after John Scott, first Earl of Eldon. Views of the romantic ruins of Corfe Castle and Poole Harbour beyond can be enjoyed from the garden. Myriad rooms, on split levels, are heated by a log fire in winter. Locally sourced home-cooked food is available in addition to well-chosen ales and locally produced Joe's Cider. Q❄☆✿♿◖♣♠P🚲(40,44)🐾

Lower Parkstone

Bermuda Triangle
10 Parr Street, BH14 0JY
✪ 12-3, 5-11; 12-midnight Fri & Sat; 12-11 Sun ☎ (01202) 748047
4 changing beers (sourced nationally) Ⓗ
A busy pub decorated on a Bermuda Triangle theme. The single-room bar is on three levels, with wall and ceiling displays of artefacts relating to ships and planes, including maps, newspaper cuttings, and ship and aircraft fittings. Run by the same owner for 25 years, the bar has four handpumps offering an ever-changing range of ales sourced locally and across the UK, as well as speciality lagers and foreign beers.
❀⇄(Parkstone)♠P🚲(M1,1B)

ENGLAND

Poole Ex-Servicemen's (RBL) Club

66 North Road, BH14 0LY
⏲ 6-11 Mon & Tue; 12-3, 6-midnight; 12-midnight Fri-Sun
☎ (01202) 744515
4 changing beers (sourced nationally) [H]
Voted by CAMRA as one of the top four clubs in the UK, and local CAMRA Club of the Year 2013 and 2014, this RBL-affiliated club offers four ever-changing ales and real cider, and holds three beer festivals a year in May, August and November. A real community club with live entertainment at weekends and regular sporting events, it has a vibrant and friendly atmosphere. Visitors are welcome with a CAMRA membership card or copy of the Guide.
♨❀◐♿⇌(Parkstone)♣●P▯🚌(M2,1B,1C)📶

Lyme Regis

Lyme Regis Brewery Tap L

Mill Lane, DT7 3PU
⏲ 10 (11 Sat & Sun)-5 ☎ (01297) 444354
🌐 lymeregisbrewery.com
3 changing beers (sourced locally) [H]/[G]
Formerly named the Town Mill Brewery, the compact shop sells a selection of draught beers from the brewery in an outside courtyard situated in the Town Mill complex. There is limited seating available. The brewing equipment for the four barrel plant is on display, with the brewing process explained on information boards. Increased demand has now led to some beers being brewed off-site. A locally sourced real cider is available in the summer. Closes 4pm winter weekends.
Q❀●🚌(X31,X53)

Volunteer L

31 Broad Street, DT7 3QE
⏲ 11-11 (10.30 Sun) ☎ (01297) 442214 🌐 thevoli.co.uk
St Austell Tribute [H]**; house beer (by Branscombe Vale)** [G]**; 2 changing beers (sourced regionally; often Exmoor, Otter, Sharp's)** [H]
Old two-room pub in the heart of this historic town, close to the seafront, and popular with locals. Dogs are welcome in the main bar and children in the refurbished left-hand room – both these rooms are warmed by real fires. Food is served at weekends only in the winter. Buses heading easterly stop right outside the door. Q♨◐◑🚌(X31,X53)🐾📶

Lytchett Matravers

Rose & Crown

178 Wareham Road, BH16 6DT
⏲ 12-11 (midnight Fri & Sat); 12-10.30 Sun
☎ (01202) 625325 🌐 roseandcrownlytchett.co.uk
Sharp's Doom Bar; 2 changing beers (sourced nationally) [H]
The Rose & Crown is a welcoming, friendly, two-bar free house. Doom Bar is the regular beer, along with up to three guest ales often from local breweries, and there is also real cider on handpump. The public bar has an open fire and a dartboard. Excellent home-cooked food is available. The garden displays hanging baskets and a set of stocks. The pub hosts regular comedy and live music nights, and beer and cider festivals during the summer months.
♨❀◐◑♿⛺♣●P🚌(X8,10)🐾📶

Manston

Plough Inn

Shaftesbury Road, DT10 1HB (on B3091 2 miles NE of Sturminster Newton) ST81351611
⏲ 11.30-2.30, 6-11; 12-3 Sun ☎ (01258) 472484
Fuller's London Pride; Palmers Copper Ale; Sharp's Doom Bar; Timothy Taylor Landlord; 1 changing beer [H]
This 450-year-old stone-built country inn has a single large bar with oak beams and unique plaster decorations on the ceiling and bar front, thought to be harvest fertility symbols. There is a large conservatory dining area, a covered patio, a large garden complete with pétanque rink and a campsite. Live music plays every Saturday night. The annual beer festival is in May.
♨❀◐◑♿⛺♣P🚌(309)🐾

Marshwood

Bottle Inn

DT6 5QJ (on B3165 near Devon border)
⏲ 12-10.30 ☎ (01297) 678484 🌐 bottle-inn.net
6 changing beers (sourced nationally; often Crouch Vale, Downton, Yeovil) [H]
A 16th-century thatched pub situated on the Dorset/Devon border. The single bar serves two rooms, with a family room and skittle alley at the rear. A large garden overlooks the Marshwood Vale. Six continuously changing local and nationally sourced ales are served along with around 10 ciders and perries, plus a range of foreign bottled beers. The pub holds a nettle eating competition in June incorporating a beer festival. Local CAMRA Pub of the Year 2014. Q♨❀◐◑⛺♣●P🐾📶

Melbury Osmond

Rest & Welcome L

Yeovil Road, DT2 0NF (on A37 Yeovil-Dorchester road)
⏲ 11-11; 12-10 Sun ☎ (01935) 83248
3 changing beers (sourced locally; often Cerne Abbas, Plain, Wriggle Valley) [H]/[G]
Split-level, two-roomed roadside pub on a main Dorset artery offering a welcome break to all visitors. There is a choice of three changing local or regional beers with at least one served direct from the cask, and one or two real ciders. The home-cooked food is locally sourced. TVs show rugby and Formula 1, and the skittle alley doubles as a function room. ♨❀◐◑♣●P🚌(212)🐾📶

Mudeford

Ship in Distress

66 Stanpit, BH23 3NA
⏲ 11-11 (10.30 Sun) ☎ (01202) 485123
🌐 ship-in-distress.co.uk
Ringwood Best Bitter; 3 changing beers (sourced regionally; often Dartmoor, Dorset, St Austell) [H]
Friendly and comfortable hostelry with a long heritage, formerly a haunt for smugglers, situated near the historic harbour and Stanpit Marsh. Interesting old photographs of the area and seafaring memorabilia adorn the interior. Bar snacks are available and a separate restaurant specialises in seafood. There is pleasant outdoor seating including a heated patio with a nautical theme. The selection of well-chosen guest ales rotates constantly. Q❀◐◑♿♣P🚌(1c)📶

Pamphill

Vine Inn ★

Vine Hill, BH21 4EE (off B3082)
⏲ 11-3, 7-10.30 (11 Thu-Sat); 12-3, 7-10.30 Sun
☎ (01202) 882259
2 changing beers (sourced regionally) Ⓗ/Ⓖ
Run by the same family since 1900, this house has been identified by CAMRA as having a nationally important historic interior, and is a multi award-winning gem. A small public bar gives access to an upstairs family room, and there is also a cosy lounge. The garden is a pleasant suntrap, perfect for enjoying the two ever-changing ales or the ciders from Purbeck or Westons. Sandwiches and ploughman's are available at lunchtimes. Kingston Lacy house is nearby on the B3082.
Q❀♣🍎P🐾

Poole

Blue Boar

29 Market Close, BH15 1NE
⏲ 12-11 (midnight Fri & Sat) ☎ (01202) 682247
🌐 blueboarpoole.co.uk
Fuller's London Pride, ESB; Gale's Seafarers Ale; 1 changing beer (sourced nationally) Ⓗ
Popular Fuller's pub, located near the town centre, with four handpumps – the guest beer often not from the Fuller's range. The good-value home-cooked food is worthwhile investigating, but note that service finishes early on Sunday for the quiz. Pictures and artefacts around the L-shaped bar follow a military or local theme. The cellar bar, a converted air raid shelter, offers an interesting alternative, with occasional live music at weekends. An excellent first-floor function room is available for hire. ❀◐⇌🍎🚌(9,52)🐾📶

Brewhouse

68 High Street, BH15 1DA
⏲ 11-11; 11.30-10.30 Sun ☎ (01202) 685288
Milk Street Beer; 3 changing beers (sourced nationally; often Dark Star, Milk Street) Ⓗ
Popular, bustling town-centre local owned by the Milk Street Brewery of Frome. The split-level interior has a bar at street level with two pool tables at the rear. Beers include Mermaid, which is almost exclusively brewed for the people of Poole, along with two other Milk Street beers and one well-chosen guest, as well as real cider served from the cellar on gravity. You can sit out front and watch the world go by, or enjoy peace on the rear patio. ❀⇌♣🍎🚌🐾📶

Rope & Anchor

4 Sarum Street, BH15 1JW
⏲ 12-11 ☎ (01202) 675677
Wadworth Henry's IPA Ⓖ**, Horizon** Ⓗ**, 6X** Ⓖ**, Swordfish; 1 changing beer (sourced nationally)** Ⓗ
In an old cobbled alley off historic Poole Quay, this Wadworth house offers up to six real ales and an extensive home-cooked food menu, with locally caught fish a speciality. There is a comfortable bar-side seating area perfect for conversation and a tabled area for dining; outside, the rear patio is a real suntrap. A perfect pub for escaping the bustle on the quay, or for taking a break from shopping on the nearby High Street. ❀◐♿⇌🚌(1)🐾📶

Portland

George Inn

133 Reforne, Easton, DT5 2AP
⏲ 12-11 ☎ (01305) 820011 🌐 thegeorgeinn.org
3 changing beers (sourced nationally; often Harviestoun, Skinner's, Titanic) Ⓗ/Ⓖ
A friendly, family-oriented local dating from the mid-18th century. It has four separate bar and dining areas, and a large enclosed beer garden. Food is available daily Wednesday-Sunday. The substantial Sunday roasts are popular, as is the Thursday evening curry and quiz. There are usually three ales on offer, on both handpump and gravity, which are constantly rotated. A popular beer festival is held annually around St George's Day.
❀◐🍎🚌(1)🐾📶

Royal British Legion

3 High Street, Fortuneswell, DT5 1JQ
⏲ 11.45-3, 7.30 (7 Thu)-11; 11.45-3, 6.30-11.15 Fri; 11.30-11.30 Sat; 12-4, 7.30-11 Sun ☎ (01305) 821207
Exmoor Ale; 2 changing beers (sourced regionally; often Dartmoor, Piddle, St Austell) Ⓗ
Popular members' club with a large downstairs bar serving three ales on handpump. There is a pool table, snooker table and skittle alley. Sky and BT sport are screened showing all major events. The upstairs function room is available for hire. Live music features most weekends, and meat and alcohol raffles on Sunday lunchtime. Show your CAMRA membership card to be signed in as a guest. ♣P🚌(1)📶

Preston

Spice Ship

240 Preston Road, DT3 6BJ
⏲ 11.30 (11 Sun)-11 ☎ (01305) 834651 🌐 spiceship.co.uk
Ringwood Best Bitter; Sharp's Doom Bar; Timothy Taylor Landlord; 1 changing beer (sourced regionally; often Butcombe, St Austell, Sharp's) Ⓗ
Family-friendly Grade II-listed coaching house with wood panelling, low beams and a central bar separating the restaurant from the bar area, where screens show televised sport. The restaurant, which serves good-quality food from an à la carte menu, adjoins a covered, elevated patio overlooking a large beer garden with children's play area. Thursday is curry night and live music plays most Fridays. Car parking and overnight accommodation are available.
Q❀🛏◐⛺♣P🚌(4A,X53)🐾📶

Pulham

Halsey Arms

DT2 7DZ
⏲ 11.30-2, 6-11; 11.30-11 Sat & Sun ☎ (01258) 817344
Ringwood Best Bitter; 2 changing beers (sourced nationally; often Purity, St Austell, West Berkshire) Ⓗ
Welcoming pub with a snug and main bar, popular with diners on a Sunday lunchtime. Home-cooked and locally sourced food is served in the restaurant, and bar snacks are available. Outside is a beer garden with children's play area. Live music and quizzes take place throughout the month, and weddings and conferences are catered for in the function room. Closing time can vary.
Q❀🛏◐♿⛺♣🍎P🚌(307)🐾📶

Puncknowle

Crown 🄻

Church Street, DT2 9BN
11-10.30 (11 Fri & Sat); 11-10 Sun ☎ (01308) 897711
thecrowninndorset.co.uk
Palmers Best Bitter; 2 changing beers 🄷
Attractive thatched inn with an extensive menu including vegetarian dishes, plus pizzas to eat in or take away. The two bars are comfortably furnished and heated by three log fires; there is also a comfortable family room. The two changing beers are from Palmers, and there is a real cider in summer. A small village shop in an old store room at the rear of the building stocks a wide range of basic provisions. Opening hours vary in winter. The village name is pronounced 'Punnel'.
Q❀🛏◑◗⛺♣●P🐾📶

Shaftesbury

Fountain Inn

2 Breach Lane, Enmore Green, SP7 8NB
12-2.30, 6-11; 12-11 Sun ☎ (01747) 852062
3 changing beers 🄷
Built in the 1750s as a coaching inn, the pub was a place for wealthy coach passengers to quench their thirst while they waited for extra horses to be added to the existing team to enable them to make the steep climb up Tout Hill into Shaftesbury. The Fountain has recently won Best Pub in the Taste of Dorset Awards. ◑◗P🚌🐾

Sherborne

Digby Tap

Cooks Lane, DT9 3NS
11 (12 Sun)-11 ☎ (01935) 813148 digbytap.co.uk
4 changing beers (sourced regionally; often Bath Ales, Otter, Teignworthy) 🄷
The Digby Tap is an institution in west Dorset. Hidden away between the railway station and the beautiful abbey church, it is well worth seeking out. The owners of 17 years have retained the old character and atmosphere, with four separate drinking areas, pine panelling, flagstone floors, old beams, settles and three fireplaces. Four beers, mostly from the West Country, offer superb value, as does the excellent lunchtime pub food.
Q❀◑♿⇌♣🚌🐾

Sixpenny Handley

Sixpenny Tap

The Dairy Building, Manor Farm, SP5 5NU (turn off B3018 on to unclassified road ¼ mile S of village, signed behind farm buildings) ST99811663
closed Mon & Tue; 4.30-6 Wed & Thu; 4-6.30 Fri; 11.30-1 Sat; closed Sun ☎ (01725) 726006 sixpennybrewery.co.uk
Sixpenny 6D Best Bitter, 106 Jack FM Ale, Gold, IPA 🄷**;**
1 changing beer (often Sixpenny) 🄷/🄶
This is a bar attached to the brewhouse which doubles as the brewery shop. Seasonal and occasional ales are often available. Opening hours are restricted owing to the terms of the lease but the pub is popular and busy. The beers are available direct from the cask or by handpump, by the glass or in take-home disposable containers.
❀⛺P🚌(184)🐾

Spetisbury

Woodpecker

High Street, DT11 9DJ (A350)
12-3, 6-11; 12-3, 7-10.30 Sun ☎ (01258) 452658
woodpeckerspetisbury.co.uk
Hop Back Summer Lightning; 3 changing beers (sourced regionally; often Butcombe, Otter) 🄷
Imposing and comfortable village free house and recent winner of local CAMRA Rural Pub of the Year. This open-plan pub offers three ever-changing ales from the surrounding area, three real ciders and three perries. Good-quality food is available (no food Sun and Mon eves). Bar billiards and shove-ha'penny can be played. The spacious garden, home to an annual cider festival, is perfect for whiling away an afternoon. The pub is handy for the Blandford to Sturminster Newton Trailway.
❀◑◗⛺♣●P🚌(X8)🐾

Stourton Caundle

Trooper

Golden Hill, DT10 2JW (1½ miles E of A357) ST71491495
closed Mon; 12-2 (2.30 Sat), 7-11; 12-3.30, 7-11 Sun
☎ (01963) 362405 thetrooperinn.co.uk
2 changing beers 🄷
Stone-built, single-room community pub with a separate function room/skittle alley. There is an attached camping and caravan site and children's play area next to the beer garden. Good food is available lunchtimes and early evenings including a popular Friday fish and chips night. There are two changing ales and a farmhouse cider, with beers from the pub's own brewery when available. An annual beer festival is held in the spring. Dogs and walkers are welcome. CAMRA Regional Pub of the Year 2013. Q❀◑◗⛺♣●P🐾

Stratton

Saxon Arms

20 The Square, DT2 9WG
11-2.30, 5.30-11; 11-midnight Fri & Sat; 12-midnight Sun
☎ (01305) 260020 thesaxon-stratton.co.uk
Butcombe Bitter; Timothy Taylor Landlord; 2 changing beers (sourced nationally; often Fuller's, Otter, St Austell) 🄷
A thatched, stone and flint country pub built in 2001 overlooking the village hall and green. This welcoming and homely free house offers four real ales and serves good locally sourced food. A proper local supporting the community, it is also popular with visitors from further afield. Staff are friendly and knowledgeable. Dogs are welcome, but not in the main restaurant area.
Q❀◑◗♿●P🚌(212)🐾📶

Upwey

Royal Standard 🄻

700 Dorchester Road, DT3 5LA
11.30-3, 5.30-11; 11-midnight Sat; 12-11 Sun
☎ (01305) 812558 theroyalstandardupwey.co.uk
Yeovil Star Gazer; 3 changing beers (sourced regionally; often Plain, Sixpenny, Sunny Republic) 🄷
Situated on the outskirts of Weymouth, the pub is popular with locals and visitors for the excellent real ales, ciders and food. The U-shaped wood-panelled bar has a cosy lounge on one side and an area with tall tables and stools on the other. The on-site microbrewery occasionally supplies DT3 and

DT4 ales, and the pub hosts an annual beer festival and sausage/cider festival. Open all day Monday-Friday in the summer holidays. No food on Mondays. Q🚼❀◐♣●P🚌(10)🐾

Wareham

King's Arms

41 North Street, BH20 4AD

⏲ 11.30-11 ☎ (01929) 552503 🌐 kingsarmswareham.co.uk

Ringwood Best Bitter, Fortyniner; 2 changing beers (sourced regionally; often Bath Ales, Otter, St Austell) Ⓗ

A traditional thatched inn on the main street which has its roots in the 1500s and survived the great fire of 1762. This multi-roomed establishment has a flagstone-floored public bar, real fire, a drinking corridor and one room exclusively for dining. To the rear is a large garden with a covered area for smokers. A good range of reasonably priced home-cooked food is served. A range of guest beers is available, usually sourced from the West Country. Q❀◐⇌●P🚌(40,X53)🐾

Quay Inn

The Quay, BH20 4LP

⏲ 8am-midnight (1am Fri & Sat) ☎ (01929) 552735

🌐 thequayinn.com

3 changing beers (sourced nationally; often Isle of Purbeck, Ringwood, Timothy Taylor) Ⓗ

Historic 18th-century gem of a pub overlooking the picturesque Wareham quayside and River Frome. The open fire adds a cosy warmth in winter, while the walled garden to the rear offers a secluded summer retreat. Three ales are complemented by locally sourced ciders, and the extensive menu including steaks and seafood provides sustenance for the hungry. Live music features most weekends. B&B is offered with views from the rooms across the rolling Purbecks.

🚼❀🛏◐▲●P🚌(40,X53)🐾

West Bay

Quarterdeck Tavern

Durbeyfield Guest House, DT6 4EL

⏲ 12-midnight ☎ (01308) 423307

🌐 durbeyfieldguesthouse.com

St Austell Tribute; Sharp's Doom Bar Ⓗ

The Quarterdeck is the bar of the Durbeyfield Guest House but non-residents – both locals and tourists – are welcome and usually outnumber residents. There are just two handpumps but both beers are excellent. A wide range of food is listed on the blackboard, served in the bar or separate dining room. There are occasional food-themed events. The large garden is popular in summer.

❀🛏◐♣P🚌(X53,253)🐾📶

West Knighton

New Inn

DT2 8PE

⏲ 11.30-3 (not Mon), 5.30-11; 12-3, 5.30-10.30 Sun

☎ (01305) 852349 🌐 newinnwestknighton.co.uk

Bath Ales Gem; Sharp's Doom Bar Ⓗ

English Heritage listed public house situated in a peaceful village. The New Inn has been serving the village since 1851 and was extended in 2013 to increase the size of the restaurant and the number of letting rooms to eight. Home-cooked food is served lunchtimes and evenings, using local ingredients where possible, with a popular carvery on Sundays. A skittle alley/function room is available. Q🚼❀🛏◐♿♣●P🚌(101)🐾📶

West Lulworth

Castle Inn 𝕃

Main Road, BH20 5RN

⏲ 12-10 ☎ (01929) 400311

🌐 thecastleinn-lulworthcove.co.uk

Palmers Best Bitter Ⓗ**; 4 changing beers (sourced locally)** Ⓗ/Ⓖ

CAMRA Cider Pub of the Year 2015. This enchanting 16th-century thatched inn, close to Lulworth Cove, has two comfortable bars, one with a low ceiling, both beamed. Up to six mostly local ales and 45 or more ciders and perries are served alongside an extensive menu of good-value home-made dishes in generous portions. At the rear is a tiered garden with a giant chess set; inside there is a selection of board games. The inn has 15 bedrooms, 14 en-suite. Q❀🛏◐♣●P🚌(103)🐾

West Parley

Owls Nest

196 Christchuch Road, BH22 8SS

⏲ 12-3 (not Mon), 5-11; 11.30-3, 6-midnight Sat; 12-3, 6-10 Sun ☎ (01202) 572793 🌐 theowlsnest-westparley.com

Otter Bitter; 3 changing beers (sourced regionally) Ⓗ

Traditional family-run free house, with beamed ceilings and a wood-burning stove helping to create a warm welcome and comfortable ambience. An Irish music session on the first Thursday of the month and Stan's Blues Jam on the last Wednesday are popular. The annual winter pie and ale festival boasts home-made pies – steak and ale a speciality – and over 20 ales, mainly sourced locally. But Richard and Jacqui never need an excuse to put on a mini beer and music festival at any time of the year. Q🚼◐♿P🚌(13,57)🐾📶

West Stour

Ship Inn

SP8 5RP

⏲ 12-3, 6-11; 12-11 Sun ☎ (01747) 838640

🌐 shipinn-dorset.com

3 changing beers Ⓗ

Once a coaching inn, this popular roadside pub has views across the Blackmore Vale. The public bar features a flagstone floor, while the separate restaurant area is light and airy with stripped oak floorboards. There is a patio and large garden to the rear. This friendly pub is renowned for superb home-cooked food (no meals Sun eve) and comfortable accommodation. Three changing beers are always available and a beer festival is held in July. Dogs are welcome in the bar.

Q❀🛏◐♣●P🐾

Weymouth

Boot Inn

High West Street, DT4 8JH

⏲ 11-11 (midnight Fri & Sat); 12-11 Sun ☎ (01305) 770327

🌐 bootweymouth.co.uk

Marston's Old Empire; Ringwood Best Bitter, Fortyniner; 7 changing beers (sourced nationally; often Banks's, Jennings, Wychwood) Ⓗ

Weymouth's oldest pub has a single bar area leading to rooms at both ends, warmed by two roaring fires in winter. Up to 10 beers are served, the regulars supplemented by regional beers from Marston's and elsewhere. Cheddar Valley cider is also on offer. Large pork pies are always available, and on Sunday lunchtimes there is a free banquet, with the fare provided by both landlord and customers. Live music plays on Tuesdays, and a quiz is hosted on Wednesdays. A conversation-dominated venue, free from TV and background music. Q❀♣●▣❀

Globe Inn

24 East Street, DT4 8BN
11-1am (midnight Sun) ☎ (01305) 786061
Dartmoor Jail Ale; St Austell Tribute, Proper Job; Sharp's Doom Bar; 2 changing beers (sourced regionally; often Clearwater, Flack Manor, Palmers) H
A free house with a friendly welcome, tucked away on a street corner, just 30 yards from the iconic harbourside. The Globe is only a short distance from the town centre, beach and esplanade, and offers a distinct change from the packed waterside. A separate games room has a pool table, darts and pub games. A fun quiz is held on Sunday afternoons.

Royal Oak 🏆

Custom House Quay, DT4 8AW
11 (10 Fri-Sun)-midnight ☎ (01305) 761343
Dorset Jurassic; 3 changing beers H
Situated right on Weymouth's picturesque harbourside, this pub is linked to the larger Rendezvous pub/club next door which also provides the meals. Inside, though, it is very different. A wood-beamed (and uneven) floor fronts a long single bar, furnished with rustic and variable seating. There is no TV or piped music. Four Dorset Brewing Company beers are on at any time, with ciders from Dorset and neighbouring counties. Seating outside overlooks the harbour. Local CAMRA Pub of the Year 2015. Q

Wimborne Minster

Green Man

1 Victoria Road, BH21 1EN
10-11.30 (1.30am Fri & Sat) ☎ (01202) 881021
greenmanwimborne.com
Wadworth Henry's IPA, 6X, Swordfish H
An 18th-century one bar inn with four small open-plan drinking areas and a patio where games are played. The front of the pub is noted for its summer floral displays, watched over by a red telephone box and a plaque marking the spot where the town pond once was. Excellent food is served lunchtimes only. Live music features on a Friday night, karaoke monthly on Saturdays. Watch you do not step on the green man as you enter the pub.
QP

Man in the Wall

10 West Borough, BH21 1NF
8am-midnight (1am Fri & Sat) ☎ (01202) 639800
Fuller's London Pride; Greene King Abbot; Ruddles Best Bitter; house beer (by Sixpenny); 4 changing beers (sourced nationally) H
A tiled entrance hallway leads to a large bar area where there is plenty of seating; the walls are adorned with artefacts relating to the area, from the pictures in the cosy front snug to the map of the Wessex region on the wall near the bar. Arched windows provide a view of the world outside, while the large garden is somewhere to relax on a warm summer afternoon. Do look out for the man in the wall. Q

Taphouse 🏆

11 West Borough, BH21 1LT
12 (11 Fri-Sun)-11 ☎ (01202) 911200
Sharp's Doom Bar; 5 changing beers (sourced nationally) G
Close to the town centre, this small, cosy, wood-panelled pub is popular with locals. The centrepiece is a long hardwood bar, with beer displayed on a stillage behind. Up to six beers are offered during the week and 12 on weekends and busy periods. The selection is ever-changing, with much of it sourced locally. A convivial and lively hostelry, especially on Sunday afternoons when live music is hosted. Local CAMRA Pub of the Year.
Q

Worth Matravers

Square & Compass ★

Weston Road, BH19 3LF (off B3069)
12-11 ☎ (01929) 439229 squareandcompasspub.co.uk
Palmers Copper Ale; 3 changing beers (sourced regionally) G
A real gem, this multi award-winning pub with a nationally important historic interior has appeared in every edition of the Guide and has been in the same family since 1907. Two rooms either side of a serving hatch convey an impression that little has changed over the years. The sea-facing garden offers fantastic views across the Purbecks, and fossils are displayed in the small adjacent museum. Pasties are available along with home-made cider. Beer and cider festivals are held in October and November respectively. In the winter the pub closes 3-6pm. Q(44)

Wyke Regis

Wyke Smugglers

76 Portland Road, DT4 9AB
12-midnight (1am Fri & Sat) ☎ (01305) 760010
thewykesmugglers.com
St Austell Proper Job; 2 changing beers (sourced regionally) H
A large, lively local hosting many community pastimes. Live music features on most Friday and Saturday nights, when it can be busy. The menu offers good-quality locally sourced pub food, served in the main dining area which is warmed by a woodburner. Guest beers are mainly from the Punch Cask range. The large skittle alley doubles as a function room, and is home to a pool table. A beer and cider festival is held in July.
P

Keep your Good Beer Guide up to date by visiting the CAMRA website **camra.org.uk**, then Good Beer Guide, then Updates.

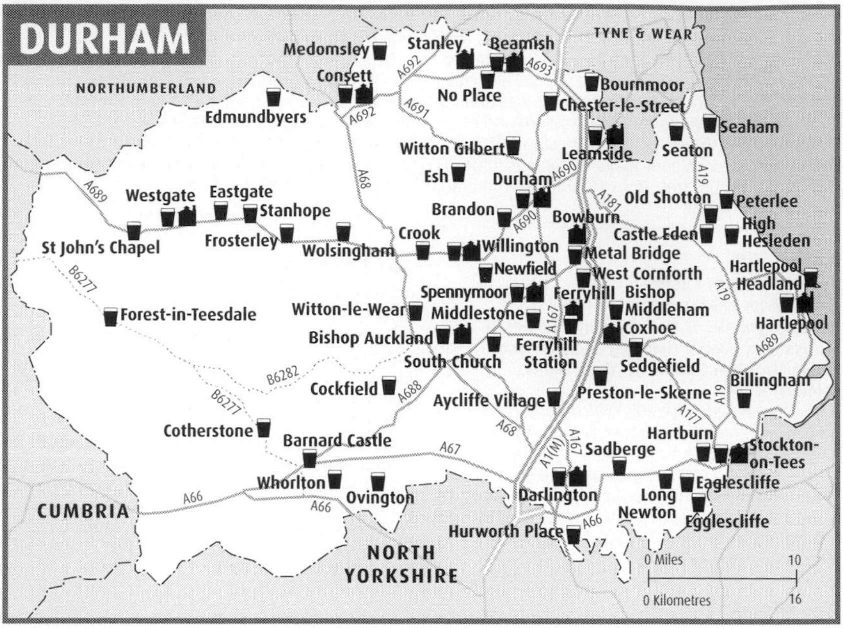

Co Durham incorporates part of the former county of Cleveland

Aycliffe Village

County

13 The Green, DL5 6LX

12-3, 6-11; 12-11 Sun ☎ (01325) 312273

thecountyaycliffevillage.com

4 changing beers H

Overlooking the award-winning green in a picturesque village, this attractive cream-coloured country free house was originally three 17th-century cottages. It is now open plan with the bar and three dining areas unified by bright modern decor, complemented by older beams and log fireplaces. The current owners took over in 2008 and have a passion to marry good food with excellent beers. Up to four guests come from northern micros. Sunday is quiz night. There is accommodation in seven rooms. Q P

Barnard Castle

Golden Lion

30 Market Place, DL12 8NB

12-11 (midnight Fri & Sat) ☎ (01833) 690295

Marston's New World Pale Ale, Pedigree; Wychwood Hobgoblin; 3 changing beers H

A friendly and welcoming pub in the centre of Barnard Castle – the tall chequered-front building is built partly into the castle ditch. Dating back to 1679, it is the town's oldest pub. It has a quirky layout with a central bar serving two rooms, one with an open fire. Run by CAMRA members, it offers good-value food. Real ale and real cider are £2.50 a pint to CAMRA members. (75,76)

Old Well Inn L

21 The Bank, DL12 8PH

12-11 ☎ (01833) 690130 theoldwellinn.co.uk

Timothy Taylor Landlord; 4 changing beers H

The boundary of this 17th-century town-centre inn incorporates part of the medieval castle wall. The pub has a cosy front bar and a comfortable lounge, a separate restaurant and an airy conservatory, plus an enclosed beer garden. At least five beers are available including four guests from local micros. Excellent food is served daily and there is accommodation in 10 rooms. Two 10-day beer festivals are held at Easter and in October. The Castle Players meet here. Q (75,76)

Beamish

Stables Bar & Restaurant L

Beamish Hall Country House Hotel, DH9 0YB

11-11 (midnight Fri & Sat); 11-10.30 Sun

☎ (01207) 288750 beamish-hall.co.uk/stables

Stables Beamish Hall Best Bitter, Old Miner Tommy, Bobby Dazzler, Silver Buckles, Beamish Burn, Bell Tower H

REAL ALE BREWERIES

Black Paw Bishop Auckland
Blackhill Stanley
Camerons Hartlepool
Consett Ale Works Consett
Crafty Pint Darlington
Durham Bowburn
Gambling Man Willington
George Samuel Spennymoor
Hill Island Durham
Just A Minute Spennymoor
Leamside Leamside
Schoolhouse Darlington (NEW)
Sonnet 43 Coxhoe
Stables Beamish
Stockton Stockton on Tees (NEW)
Village Brewer: Brew Twenty2 Darlington (NEW)
Weard'ALE Westgate
Yard of Ale Ferryhill

ENGLAND

The Stables is attached to Beamish Hall Country House Hotel, and has its own microbrewery. Stone floors, old beams, solid furniture and crackling log fires in winter help to create a relaxing environment. Outside is a courtyard seating area and, behind the pub, an extended play area for children. Beer festivals are hosted in September and January. The pub is also a popular live music venue. An extensive menu of locally produced food is served. Q🛏❀◐◑♿P

Billingham

Greenholme Catholic Club

37 Wolviston Road, TS23 2RU (on E side of old A19, just S of Roseberry Road roundabout, next to bus stop)
7-midnight (2am Fri); 12.30-2am Sat; 12-midnight Sun
☎ (01642) 901143 billinghamcatholicclub.webs.com
3 changing beers H
This Victorian mansion and former school is a friendly private members' club, renowned locally for its vibrant R&B/rock scene, where a genuine welcome awaits CAMRA members. Dedicated and enthusiastic volunteers ensure that the club's reputation for serving 150 different beers annually continues. Three ales, three ciders and a perry are normally on offer, with up to 10 beers available during regular beer/music festivals, held during bank holiday weekends. A recent local CAMRA branch Club of the Year. ❀♿♣●P🚉🚌(35,36)🐾

Bishop Auckland

Bay Horse

38-40 Fore Bondgate, DL14 7PE (50yds N of bus station)
11-11 (1am Fri & Sat); 12-11 Sun ☎ (01388) 609765
bayhorse-pub.co.uk
Timothy Taylor Landlord; 1 changing beer H
At the heart of Bishop's pub scene since 1530, this welcoming hostelry is a haven from the shops during the week, and a joyfully boisterous place on a weekend, with Friday live bands and Saturday-night karaoke. It retains its roots as a long-established, proper pub, with televised sports and pub games. Durham CAMRA Town Cider Pub of the Year runner-up 2015. ❀♿♣●🚌

Pollards

104 Etherley Lane, DL14 6TU (400yds W of railway station)
12-2, 5.30-11; 12-3, 6-11 Sun ☎ (01388) 603539
thepollardsinn.co.uk
Jennings Cumberland Ale; Marston's Pedigree; 5 changing beers H
Four separate but linked drinking areas form the main part of this bright and comfortable pub on the edge of town, with a large restaurant to the rear. A popular quiz is hosted on Sunday evening, with supper included. Pollards has a reputation for good food, served lunchtimes and evenings, including the renowned Sunday carvery. A genuine pub offering seven ales and good conversation.
Q🛏❀◐◑♿⇌♣P

Bishop Middleham

Cross Keys L

9 High Street, DL17 9AR (1 mile from A177)
12 (5 Mon)-11 ☎ (01740) 651231 crosskeyspub.net
3 changing beers H
A busy family-run village pub with a good reputation for food. It has a bar with a real fire, a lounge and a large restaurant at the back. The pub is opposite the remains of Fosters Brewery which closed in 1913 and may well have been its tap house. The village has a series of walks through beautiful countryside and to the ruins of Bishop Middleham Castle. Q🛏❀◐◑♣🐾

Bournmoor

Dun Cow L

Primrose Hill, DH4 6DY
12-11 ☎ (0191) 385 2631 theduncowbournmoor.co.uk
2 changing beers H
Welcoming 18th-century pub, reputedly haunted by an oft-seen Grey Lady ghost. It offers a varying beer range, good-value pub food served in the lounge and bar, and an à la carte menu in the Lambton restaurant. There is also a large function room. The pub is family-friendly, with extensive gardens. Beer festivals showcasing local ales are held in March and October. Music festivals on the first Saturday in June and last in September feature local folk and rock bands. 🛏❀◐◑●P🐾📶

Brandon

Morley Wood

Winchester Drive, DH7 8UG (near corner of Winchester Drive and Scripton Gill Rd)
12-11 ☎ (0191) 447 5995 themorleywood.co.uk
Black Sheep Best Bitter; Timothy Taylor Landlord H
Large, modern, family-focused pub serving excellent ales and a selection of reasonably priced food. It has a lively atmosphere and ample comfortable seating. Activities include pool, darts and dominoes. Live music plays occasionally on Friday or Saturday nights and there is a pub quiz on Thursdays. Outside, there is a good-sized enclosed beer garden and ample parking including a dedicated disabled parking bay.
🛏❀◐◑♿♣P🚌(46)🐾📶

Castle Eden

Castle Eden Inn L

Stockton Road, TS27 4SD
11-11 ☎ (01429) 835137 castleedeninn.com
Timothy Taylor Landlord; 3 changing beers H
Castle Eden village is famous for the former Castle Eden Brewery. This refurbished old coaching inn has a large bar offering a good selection of ales. The lounge has a spacious and comfortable seating area. Quality food featuring local produce is served in the bar, lounge or the more formal restaurant. There is also a private function room. 🛏❀◐◑P

Chester-le-Street

Butchers Arms

Middle Chare, DH3 3QD (off Front St on left from Market Place)
11-11 (midnight Fri & Sat) ☎ (0191) 388 3605
butchersarms.org.uk
Jennings Cumberland Ale; Marston's Pedigree; 5 changing beers H
A cosy pub in the centre of town acknowledged for the quality and quantity of its beers – the landlady has now increased the number of cask ales to seven. The pub is also noted for its food, with home cooking a speciality – Sunday lunches are

popular and good value. Teas and coffees are also served. Convenient for the railway station and all buses through the town. Quiz night is Tuesday.
Q ➤ ✿ ♿ ⏰ ⊆ ⇔ ♣ ⊞ (21) ☮

Chester-le-Street Cricket Club ⓛ
Ropery Lane, DH3 3PF
❂ 11-11 (midnight Fri-Sun) ☎ (0191) 388 3684
⊕ chesterlestreet-cc.com
Cumberland Corby Ale; 1 changing beer Ⓗ
A splendid club house with two main rooms downstairs and an area outside for warm-weather drinking – all with fine views over the cricket ground. Sandwiches and pies are available from the bar on most days. Functions for up to 100 people (including wheelchair users) can be accommodated in the well-appointed function room on the first floor. Local CAMRA Club of the Year or runner-up on many occasions – winner for 2015. ➤ ⏰ ♿ ⇔ P ⊞ (21) ☮ 🛜

Lambton Worm ⓛ
North Road, DH3 4AJ
❂ 11.30-11 (midnight Fri & Sat); 12-10.30 Sun
☎ (0191) 387 1162 ⊕ thelambton.com
Sonnet 43 Steam Beer, Blonde Beer, Bourbon Milk Stout, India Pale Ale, American Pale Ale; 2 changing beers Ⓗ
Sonnet 43 Brew House tap with a bar at the front and gastro restaurant at the back matching traditional English food with Sonnet 43 beers. Experimental and limited edition beers are offered here alongside the core range, complemented by guest ales from regional microbreweries. A relaxed ambience, friendly staff, spacious bar area and plenty of tucked-away niches for seating including a patio add to the enjoyment. Accommodation in 14 boutique B&B rooms is a recent addition.
➤ ✿ ⏰ ⓘ P ⊞ (21) 🛜

Smiths Arms ⓛ
Forge Lane, Castle Dene, DH3 4HE NZ299507
❂ 4-11; 12-midnight Fri & Sat; 12-11 Sun ☎ (0191) 385 7559
⊕ smithsarms-lumley.co.uk
7 changing beers Ⓗ
Somewhat off the beaten track, this traditional pub has a small cosy bar with an open fire, a room for pool and darts, and a larger lounge also with an open fire. Good home-cooked food is served in the Castle Dene restaurant on the first floor. Up to seven real ales are sourced by the landlord, always including LocAle. The pub is reputed to be haunted.
➤ ⓘ ♿ ♣ P ⊞ (71,78) ☮ 🛜

Cockfield

Queen's Head
106 Front Street, DL13 5AA
❂ 5 (11 Sat)-11; 12-11 Sun ☎ (01388) 710981
2 changing beers Ⓗ
This cosy, welcoming and popular pub is right next to the bus stop at the north end of the village, and serves two constantly changing beers from the Marston's range. It is open plan but with various seating areas, as well as tables outside at the front of the building. Bar staff will happily ask your opinion on the beers, and chat about which ones have been popular. A proper community local, handy for the historic Cockfield Fell and associated industrial archaeology. Q ✿ ♣ P ⊞ (6,8)

Consett

Company Row ⓛ
Victoria Road, DH8 5BQ
❂ 8am-11 ☎ (01207) 585600
Greene King Abbot; Ruddles Best Bitter; 5 changing beers Ⓗ
Modern pub named after the rows of houses built by the Derwent Iron Company for its workers which were mostly demolished in the mid-1920s. This spacious and well-decorated Wetherspoon establishment is a real asset to Consett town centre. An excellent beer selection and good food make this social pub popular with a wide clientele of all ages. Alcohol is served from 9am.
➤ ✿ ⓘ ♿ ♣ ● ⊞ 🛜

Grey Horse ⓛ
115 Sherburn Terrace, DH8 6NE
❂ 12-12.30am (midnight Mon & Tue); 12-midnight Sun
☎ (01207) 502585 ⊕ thegreyhorse.co.uk
Consett Steel Town Bitter, White Hot, Red Dust; 4 changing beers Ⓗ
Traditional pub dating back to 1848. The interior comprises a lounge and an L-shaped bar, with a wood-beamed ceiling. Consett Ale Works Brewery is located at the rear. Beer festivals are held twice a year, live entertainment is hosted on Thursday and a quiz on Wednesday. The coast-to-coast cycle route is close by. There is some bench seating outside at the front of the pub. ✿ ♿ ● ⊞ 🛜

Cotherstone

Red Lion ⓛ
Main Street, DL12 9QE
❂ 12-3 (not Mon-Fri), 7-11; 12-4, 7-10.30 Sun
☎ (01833) 650236 ⊕ theredlionhotel.blogspot.com
Yorkshire Dales Rowan Tree; 3 changing beers Ⓗ
An 18th-century Grade II-listed coaching inn, built in stone and set in an idyllic village. Simply furnished, this homely local with two open fires has changed little since the '60s. There is no TV, jukebox or one-armed bandit, just good beer and conversation. Children, dogs and clean boots are welcome. Local CAMRA Community Pub of the Year, the venue is used by various local clubs, and the small garden is a suntrap. Guest beers regularly come from Mithril Ales. ➤ ✿ ♣ ● 🛜

Crook

Horse Shoe ⓛ
4 Church Street, DL15 9BG
❂ 8am-midnight ☎ (01388) 744980
Greene King Abbot; Ruddles Best Bitter; 6 changing beers Ⓗ
Formerly a pub and butcher's shop, with a nod to its previous use in the metal bar top. This Wetherspoon refurbishment has four interlinked drinking areas making up the main part of the pub, with a pleasant patio to the side. Local history is reflected in the decor, with a surprise at the top of the stairs in the shape of old mining equipment.
➤ ✿ ⓘ ● ⊞ (1) 🛜

Darlington

Darlington Snooker Club ⓛ
1 Corporation Road, DL3 6AE (corner of Northgate)
❂ 12-11; 11-1am Sat; 11-11 Sun ☎ (01325) 241388
4 changing beers Ⓗ

First-floor, family-run and family-oriented private snooker club which in 2015 celebrated its centenary. Four guest beers from micros countrywide are stocked. A cosy, comfortable TV lounge is available for those not playing on one of the 10 top-quality snooker tables. Twice-yearly, the club plays host to a professional celebrity, and two beer festivals are held annually. Frequently voted CAMRA Regional Club of the Year, and a finalist for National Club in 2014, it welcomes CAMRA members on production of a membership card or copy of this Guide. ⛀◐≉●

Half Moon Ⓛ
130 Northgate, DL1 1QS
✪ 12 (5 Wed)-11 ☎ (01325) 469965 🌐 thecraftypint.co.uk
7 changing beers Ⓗ
Across the ring road from the town centre, this local reopened in 2013 as a relaxed and welcoming real ale pub following a long period of closure. The seven guest beers include ones from micros unusual for the area as well as from the on-site Crafty Pint nano brewery. You have a choice of two ciders. The Crafty Pint bottled beer shop is also incorporated here, offering a large selection of bottled beers from regional micros. ⛀❀♿♣●🐾

Number Twenty 2 Ⓛ
22 Coniscliffe Road, DL3 7RG
✪ 12-11 (9 Mon); closed Sun ☎ (01325) 354590
🌐 villagebrewer.co.uk/our-pubs/number-twenty-2
Village White Boar, Bull, Old Raby; 10 changing beers Ⓗ
Town-centre ale house with a passion for cask beer and winner of many CAMRA awards. Ales are dispensed from 16 handpumps, alongside two real ciders and a stout or porter, and 10 draught European beers. Huge curved windows, stained-glass panels and a high ceiling give the interior an airy, spacious feel. To the rear is the in-house nano distillery and microbrewery producing gin, vodka and fine ale. Sandwiches and snacks are available throughout the day. Home of Village Brewer beers, commissioned from Hambleton by the licensee. Q⛀◐♿●📶

Old Vic Ⓛ
95a Victoria Road, DL1 5JQ (200yds down from Victoria Rd entrance of train station)
✪ 11.30 (1 Sun)-11 ☎ 07984 574332
🌐 theoldvicdarlington.co.uk
4 changing beers Ⓗ
This upstairs pub, formerly the Victoria Social Club, is situated on the corner of Victoria Road and Backhouse Street – perfect for a pint on the way to or from the train station. Once you have negotiated the stairs you are welcomed by an enthusiastic landlady. Up to four real ales are on offer in a good range of styles, sourced from local breweries including Mithril and Truefit. Up to three real ciders are also available. CAMRA branch Cider Pub winner for 2015. ≉♣●🚌(14,14A)🐾📶

Old Yard Tapas Bar
98 Bondgate, DL3 7JY
✪ 11-11; 12-10.30 Sun ☎ (01325) 467385 🌐 tapasbar.co.uk
John Smith's Bitter; Theakston Old Peculier; 4 changing beers Ⓗ
Interesting mixture of a bar and Mediterranean taverna offering real ales alongside a fascinating blend of international wines and spirits in a friendly setting. Four guest beers are sourced anywhere from local micros to brewers countrywide, with an extra two added from Thursday onwards. Although this is a thriving restaurant you are more than welcome to pop in for a pint and tapas. The pavement café is popular in good weather. TV is for sport only. Q❀◐▶📶

Quakerhouse 🏆 Ⓛ
2 Mechanics Yard, DL3 7QF (off High Row)
✪ 11 (12 Sun)-midnight ☎ (01325) 245052
🌐 quakerhouse.co.uk
10 changing beers Ⓗ
Twelve times local CAMRA Town Pub of the Year and North-East Pub of the Year 2013, this gem of a hostelry is located in one of the town's historic yards. The lively bar offers 10 handpulled guest beers from local and regional breweries and Old Rosie cider. A popular music venue, it caters for all tastes from acoustic to rock, with live music every Wednesday and other nights too. Entry is free to all music events. ❀♿♣●P🚌🐾📶

Tanners Hall
63-64 Skinnergate, DL3 7LL
✪ 8am-midnight (1am Sat) ☎ (01325) 369939
Greene King Abbot; Ruddles Best Bitter; 7 changing beers Ⓗ
A popular Wetherspoon town pub named after the local leather trade that dominated the town in the 18th century. Its 12 handpumps provide a good selection of real ales including up to nine guests, often from local micros. A large interior provides plenty of space for holding its own beer festivals and Meet The Brewer nights as well as the chain's national events. Reasonably priced food is served until 11pm, with a 20 per cent discount for CAMRA members. Q⛀❀◐▶📶

Voodoo Café Ⓛ
Skinnergate, DL3 7LX
✪ 10-11.45 (5 Mon); 9am-11.45 Wed; 12-5 Sun
☎ (01325) 467555 🌐 voodoocafe.co.uk
2 changing beers Ⓗ
Mexican/South American-themed café which stocks a large range of bottled beers from around the world. Downstairs is a colourful, simply furnished bar area, serving handpulled beers from local microbreweries, usually at least one light and one dark. Upstairs is the vibrant main restaurant. During warmer weather there is seating out on the street. There is a 50p discount on a pint for CAMRA members. Also a popular Latin dance venue where salsa lessons are given, and often open late. ⛀❀◐▶♿≉

Durham

Bishop Langley Ⓛ
Framwellgate Bridge, North Road, DH1 4PW
✪ 12-11 (midnight Fri & Sat) ☎ (0191) 386 4779
🌐 bishoplangleydurham.co.uk
Sharp's Doom Bar; 4 changing beers Ⓗ
This is a popular city-centre gastro-pub with a large roof terrace looking out onto the River Wear and the Cathedral. There is a good selection of changing cask ales alongside the regular Doom Bar. The pub is open until late each evening, and offers a 50p discount on a pint and 10 per cent off food to CAMRA members. Acoustic singers perform on Fridays or Saturdays. ⛀❀◐▶≉●🚌(20,64)📶

Colpitts Hotel
Colpitts Terrace, DH1 4EG
✪ 2 (12 Thu-Sat)-11; 12-10.30 Sun ☎ (0191) 386 9913

Samuel Smith Old Brewery Bitter
An unspoilt gem, this late-Victorian pub has changed little since it was first built. Occupying a corner site, the building has an unusual A-shape with three rooms: a cosy snug, pool room and the comfortable main bar partially divided by a fireplace. Like all Samuel Smith pubs, the noise comes from conversation not jukebox or games machines. There is a quiz on Tuesday evenings. This is a must-visit hostelry for anyone who appreciates pubs as they used to be. Q

Court Inn
Court Lane, DH1 3AW
11-11 (midnight Fri & Sat) (0191) 384 7350
courtinn.co.uk
Timothy Taylor Landlord; 5 changing beers
Up to six real ales are on offer here at any one time as well as two real ciders, with a CAMRA discount available (although not on Timothy Taylor). A wide selection of food is served until 10.15pm daily. The décor reflects the location of the pub near the city's Crown Courts, with exposed brickwork and original artwork. The pub is popular with students and prison staff and offers a warm welcome to all visitors to the area. (6)

Half Moon Inn
86 New Elvet, DH1 3AQ
11-11 (midnight Fri & Sat); 12-11 Sun (0191) 374 1918
thehalfmooninndurham.co.uk
Draught Bass; Durham White Gold; Greene King IPA; Timothy Taylor Landlord; 2 changing beers
Popular city-centre pub named after the crescent-shaped bar that runs from the front room through to the lounge area. The interior is traditional decor throughout and interesting photos of the pub at the beginning of the 20th century are on display. It has a large beer garden next to the river and is a friendly venue with a relaxed atmosphere, offering a good selection of real ales to locals and visitors to the city. (6)

Head of Steam
Reform Place, DH1 4RZ (through archway from North Rd)
12-11 (1am Fri & Sat) (0191) 383 2173
3 changing beers
A popular open-plan modern pub over two floors. As well as real ale it offers an extensive choice of bottled European beers and a range of real ciders. High-quality food is prepared on the premises, and the pub often holds special events featuring a wide choice of ales and ciders. During the day, the pub is family-friendly. One floor can be reserved for private functions. Ownership changed in 2013, when it was purchased by Camerons Brewery. Q

John Duck
91A Claypath, DH1 1RG
12-11 (midnight Fri & Sat) (0191) 374 1114
5 changing beers
A busy city alehouse offering a wide selection of real ales and cider. There are multiple screens for sporting events and a popular quiz held on Thursday evenings. Live music features on Friday nights and the weekend atmosphere is lively. This pub is in the same Durham City pub group as Ye Old Elm Tree. It was voted local CAMRA Town Cider Pub of the Year in 2014 and 2015.

Market Tavern
27 Market Place, DH1 3NJ
11-midnight (1am Fri & Sat); 11-11 Sun
(0191) 386 2069
5 changing beers
Situated in Durham's historic Market Place, this single-roomed, L-shaped bar offers a good selection of five local and national cask ales and one real cider. Refurbished in 2013, while keeping its traditional wooden alehouse appearance, this is one of the most improved venues in town. Good food is served up to 10pm and friendly staff offer a warm welcome to both the regular and casual visitor. Q

New Inn
29 Church Street, DH1 3DN (corner of A177 and Church St)
11-11 (midnight Sat); 12-11 Sun (0191) 384 7308
3 changing beers
Located opposite the main campus of Durham University, this pub is popular with locals and university students alike. It is open until midnight on weekdays during term time. Darts, dominoes and shove-ha'penny are available, and all major sporting events are shown on TV. Good pub grub is served. Look out for the Thursday-night quiz in term time and the popular annual beer festival in March. The pub has its own New Inn Ale, brewed by Camerons. P(6,X12)

Old Elm Tree
12 Crossgate, DH1 4PS
11.30-11 (midnight Fri & Sat) (0191) 386 4621
Wychwood Hobgoblin; 4 changing beers
This is one of Durham's oldest inns, dating back to at least 1600, and is reputed to have two ghosts. The interior comprises an L-shaped bar and a top room linked by stairs. A friendly pub, it attracts a good mix including locals, students and visitors to the city. Enjoy a wide range of excellent home-cooked food, the Wednesday quiz (arrive early), and a folk group on Mondays and Tuesdays. Local CAMRA branch Town Pub of the Year 2015. QP

Tap & Spile
Front Street, Framwellgate Moor, DH1 5EE
12-3 (not Mon-Fri), 6-11; 12-3, 7-10.30 Sun
(0191) 386 5451
8 changing beers
One of the last survivors of the old Camerons chain, the inn has two bars at one side while the other side can be partitioned into two. Families are welcome in the side room until 9pm. A local CAMRA award winner, it has a varied selection of ales from near and far, with eight constantly changing handpumps. Folk music nights are a weekly event on Thursdays at 8.30pm and there is a quiz on Wednesdays at 9pm. P(21)

Victoria Inn ★
86 Hallgarth Street, DH1 3AS
11.45-11; 12-2, 7-10.30 Sun (0191) 386 5269
victoriainn-durhamcity.co.uk
Big Lamp Bitter; Wylam Gold Tankard; 3 changing beers
This Grade II-listed Victorian pub remains almost unaltered since it was built in 1899. The quaint decor, coal fires, cosy snug and genuine Victorian cash drawer help create an olde-worlde feel. Ales are mainly from local breweries and a wide selection of single malt whiskies and whiskeys is

on offer. No meals are served but toasties are available. Voted local CAMRA Pub of the Year for the eighth time in 2014, it is popular with locals, students and visitors to the city.
Q🐴🛏♣🍎P🚌(21)🐾ᯤ

Eaglescliffe

Cleveland Bay

718 Yarm Road, TS16 0JE (jct of A67 and A135)
⏲ 11-1am ☎ (01642) 780275 🌐 clevelandbay.co.uk
Timothy Taylor Landlord; 3 changing beers Ⓗ
Popular locals' pub under the stewardship of an enthusiastic licensee who has established an enviable reputation for serving a fine range of premium bitters, in oversized glasses, as well as a free Sunday lunch. The main bar, with four handpumps, has two TVs for sport, while there is also a quieter lounge and a function room where live bands play on Friday evenings. Third-of-a-pint glasses and tasting notes are available. A former CAMRA branch Community Pub of the Year.
Q❀♿⇌(Eaglescliffe/Yarm)♣P🛈🚌(7,17)🐾ᯤ

Eastgate

Cross Keys 🄻

DL13 2HW (on A689)
⏲ 5 (12 Sat)-midnight (1am Fri & Sat); 12-midnight Sun
☎ (01388) 517234 🌐 crosskeyseastgate.co.uk
Allendale Wagtail Best Bitter Ⓗ
Ancient building with a pleasant interior right next to the main road up Weardale. A restaurant provides relaxed dining, while the bar is comfortable and welcoming. Popular with holidaymakers and locals, the ceiling here is adorned with tankards and there are tables to the front of the pub. A second Allendale beer is occasionally sold. Q🐴❀🛏◐◑⛺♣P🚌(101)🐾

Edmundbyers

Punch Bowl 🄻

DH8 9NL (2½ miles W of A68)
⏲ 11-11; 12-10.30 Sun ☎ (01207) 255545
🌐 thepunchbowlinn.info
3 changing beers Ⓗ
Lovely rural location close to Derwent reservoir – fishing permits can be arranged. Three handpumps dispense an ever-changing range of local ales. The three comfortable rooms are smartly furnished, with roaring log fires in the winter months. The pub has a separate room that serves as a comfortable and attractive tea room as well as a delicatessen and shop. Quiz night is Thursday.
Q🐴❀🛏◐◑♿P🚌(773)🐾ᯤ

Egglescliffe

Pot & Glass

Church Road, TS16 9DQ (300yds E of A167, opp parish church)
⏲ 12-2 (not Mon & Tue), 6-11; 5.30-midnight Fri; 12-midnight Sat; 12-11 Sun ☎ (01642) 651009
Black Sheep Best Bitter; Caledonian Deuchars IPA; Draught Bass; 4 changing beers Ⓗ
A previous local CAMRA branch award winner, this cosy, old-fashioned and multi-roomed 17th-century village local is situated in a quiet cul-de-sac opposite the parish church. Former licensee and cabinet maker Charlie Abbey, whose last resting place overlooks the pub, fashioned the ornate bar fronts from old country furniture. Tasting notes are available for the seven handpumps, which include four guest beers. Outside is a large south-facing garden. Themed food evenings complement the good-value home-cooked food.
Q🐴❀◐◑♿⇌(Eaglescliffe/Yarm)♣P🚌(7,17)

Esh

Cross Keys 🄻

Front Street, DH7 9QR (3 miles W of A691 via Langley Park)
⏲ closed Mon; 12-midnight ☎ (0191) 373 1279
Big Lamp Prince Bishop Ale; Black Sheep Best Bitter; 3 changing beers Ⓗ
A pleasant 18th-century pub in a picturesque village offering a varied food menu including vegetarian and children's choices. A comfortable locals' bar is complemented by a lounge/restaurant overlooking the Browney Valley. Delft racks display porcelain artefacts, some of which portray the old village. The village is commonly known as Old Esh to distinguish it from nearby Esh Winning. A good selection of beers always includes some from local breweries.
Q🐴❀◐◑♿♣P🚌(52,725)ᯤ

Ferryhill Station

Surtees Arms 🏆 🄻

Chilton Lane, DL17 0DH
⏲ 4-11; 12-midnight Sat; 12-11 Sun ☎ (01740) 655724
🌐 thesurteesarms.co.uk
Yard of Ale Surtees Gold, Black as Owt Stout, One Foot in the Yard; 2 changing beers Ⓗ
Traditional multi-roomed pub serving locally and nationally sourced ales and ciders as well as beers from the on-site Yard of Ale Brewery (est 2008). Annual beer festivals are held in the summer and at Halloween. Live music and charity nights are regular events. Lunches are served on Sunday only. Local CAMRA branch Country Pub of the Year 2015.
Q🐴❀⛺🍎P🐾ᯤ

Forest-in-Teesdale

Langdon Beck Hotel

DL12 0XP (on B6277, 8 miles NW of Middleton in Teesdale)
⏲ closed Mon winter; 11 (12 Sun)-10.30 ☎ (01833) 622267
🌐 langdonbeckhotel.com
Jarrow Rivet Catcher; Ringwood Best Bitter Ⓗ
Known as the Sportsman's Rest in the early 1800s, this pub is situated in the North Pennines, three miles from the spectacular High Force and Cauldron Snout waterfalls and close to the Pennine Way. The welcoming inn has long been a destination for walkers, fishermen and those seeking hospitality in scenic and peaceful surroundings, whether staying overnight or just long enough to enjoy the excellent food and drink. A beer festival is held over the late May bank holiday weekend.
Q🐴❀🛏◐◑♿⛺♣🍎P🐾

Frosterley

Black Bull 🄻

Bridge End, DL13 2SL
⏲ closed Mon-Wed; 11-11; 11-5 Sun ☎ (01388) 527784
🌐 blackbullfrosterley.com
4 changing beers Ⓗ

A truly unique, family-run pub next to the Weardale Railway and river, with four guest ales usually from local brewers, and up to four ciders and perries. Bare boards, stone flags featuring Frosterley marble, all manner of artefacts and antique furniture create a wonderful ambience. It offers high-quality, locally sourced food, and music, plays and story-telling. The outbuilding houses a peal of bells, visited by enthusiasts from far and wide. Q❀◑♿♣●P🚌(101)

Hartburn

Parkwood Hotel

64-66 Darlington Road, TS18 5ER (on A67, 1m SW of Stockton town centre)

12-11 (midnight Fri & Sat) ☎ (01642) 587933

parkwoodhotel.co.uk

Camerons Strongarm; Greene King Abbot; 3 changing beers Ⓗ

This magnificent red-brick Victorian building, circa 1865, with its imposing porch, tiled hallway, staircase and public rooms, and set in its own grounds, is the former home of the Ropner family – shipbuilders, ship owners and civic benefactors. A local CAMRA branch award winner, two regular beers are supplemented by three guests. The ciders are Westons Old Rosie or Thatchers Traditional Scrumpy. Outdoors there is a pagoda providing shelter for smokers, and well-kept gardens. Six high-quality en-suite bedrooms are available. Q❀◑P🚌(6,87)🐾

Hartlepool

Brewery Tap

Stockton Street, TS24 7QY (on A689 in front of Camerons Brewery)

11-4; closed Sun ☎ (01429) 852000

cameronsbrewery.com

Camerons IPA, Strongarm, Gold Bullion Ⓗ

When Camerons Brewery discovered it owned a somewhat derelict pub, the former Stranton's future was secured – it was converted into the brewery tap. Now in its 12th successful year, there has recently been a busy period of celebrations for both the 150th anniversary of the brewery together with the 60th anniversary of Strongarm, the brewery's flagship brand. Brewery tours start from here (for which there is a small charge). Meetings and conferences, evening opening and other social events can be arranged. ♿≋P🚌(1,36)🐾

Causeway

Vicarage Gardens, Stranton, TS24 7QT (beside Camerons Brewery)

11.30-11 (11.30 Thu; midnight Fri & Sat); 11-11 Sun ☎ (01429) 273954

Banks's Bitter; Camerons Strongarm; 3 changing beers Ⓗ

Marvellous multi-roomed, red-brick Victorian building, dating from 1862 and Camerons' unofficial brewery tap for more than a century. The Causeway is now owned by Marston's, though the sales of Strongarm remain huge. It even gets a mention in Hansard for the quality of its Strongarm. Three guest beers are sourced from the Marston's stable. The licensee hosts an eclectic mix of live music most evenings, while Tuesday is quiz night. Good-value bar snacks are available. A CAMRA multi award-winner. ◑♿≋🚌(1,36)🐾

Jackson's Arms

Tower Street, TS24 7HH (100yds S of railway and bus stations)

12-midnight (2am Fri & Sat) ☎ (01429) 862413

Wychwood Hobgoblin; 2 changing beers Ⓗ

A friendly and warm welcome awaits you at this traditional, largely unaltered, street-corner local. It is ideally situated close to the bus station and the Northern Rail/Grand Central railway station, with easy access to Hartlepool United football ground and the thriving marina area. There are two busy bars, one for convivial conversation, the second for pool and darts. An upstairs function room is also available. Three handpumps serve over 100 different premium beers annually, sourced from throughout the country. ♿≋♣🚌🐾

King John's Tavern

1 South Road, TS26 9HD (at NW corner of the market)

8am-midnight (1am Fri & Sat) ☎ (01429) 274388

7 changing beers Ⓗ

Converted from a market place furniture shop, this Wetherspoon outlet is named after King John, who in 1201 granted the town the right to hold markets. It offers the chain's nationally contracted beers alongside locally sourced guests. Real cider is also available. Beer festivals, Meet the Brewer events, a January sale and celebrations of saints' days are all regular events. There is a large, sunny patio; however, with onshore north-easterly winds, it is advisable to wrap up well, even in the middle of summer. ❀◑♿≋●🚌

Rat Race Ale House 🏆

Hartlepool Rail Station, Station Approach, TS24 7ED (on Platform 1)

closed Mon; 12.02-2.15, 4.02-8.15; 12.02-9 Sat; closed Sun ☎ 07903 479378 ratracealehouse.co.uk

4 changing beers Ⓗ

Recent CAMRA regional Cider Pub winner and current local branch Pub of the Year, the station's former newsagent's is now a beer lovers' paradise, with more than 200 different beers, ciders and perries served annually. Its opening/closing times coincide with the arrival/departure of the local coast trains. No fizzy lager/beer, no spirits/alcopops, no TV/jukebox, no one-arm bandit/quiz machine, no bar. During the last seven years, more than 1,200 different beers have been served direct to the table by the licensee himself. Perfect. Q♿≋♣●🚌

Hartlepool Headland

Globe

Northgate, TS24 0LJ (on headland, towards the Fish Quay in Old Hartlepool)

11.30 (11 Sun)-11 ☎ (01429) 860097

Camerons Strongarm Ⓗ

Opposite the port that was once bustling with fishing boats, coal staithes and pit props, this family-run, friendly community pub, comprising a main public bar and a smaller quieter lounge, is under the stewardship of licensees now celebrating 30 years of service to the trade. The posh ladies' loo could win prizes apparently. The price of the Strongarm (ask for a Hartlepool Head), reflects the pub's freehold status – savings negotiated with Camerons passed on to the customer. Q♿♣🚌(7.)

High Hesleden

Ship Inn

Mickle Hill Road, TS27 4QD (signed from B1281, between A19 and Blackhall)
⌚ closed Mon; 12-3 (not Tue-Fri), 6-11; 12-9 Sun
☎ (01429) 836453 🌐 theshipinn.net
7 changing beers 🄷
Now in its 15th year of continual family ownership, complete satisfaction is guaranteed at this nautically themed rural gem. The landlord serves seven ever-changing locally sourced real beers. His wife runs the superb restaurant offering top-quality food at reasonable prices, including mid-week early-doors two-course specials. Six motel-style chalets provide highly recommended good-value accommodation. There are stupendous coastal views from the well-kept gardens. Closes for a week in January for the owners' annual holiday. A recent CAMRA Regional Pub of the Year.
Q🛋❀🛏◑♿P🚌(206)

Hurworth Place

Comet 🄻

16 Tees View, DL2 2DH
⌚ closed Tue & Wed; 12-2.30 (not Mon), 5.30-11; 12-9 Sun
☎ (01325) 722228 🌐 thecometathurworth.co.uk
Daleside Old Leg Over; Village White Boar; Wall's County Town Gun Dog Bitter 🄷
Formerly a coaching house on the old A1, this local country pub overlooks the River Tees where it passes under the historic Croft bridge, marking the border with Yorkshire. This friendly hostelry has three separate rooms, two with open fires. The walls and shelves are covered with quirky objets d'art, many pictures and ornaments. Home-cooked meals are served Thursday to Sunday (not Sun eve). Entertainment features on some Saturday nights. 🛋◑♿♣P🚌(12,12A)📶

Leamside

Three Horseshoes 🄻

Pit House Lane, DH4 6QQ (½ mile N of A690, just outside West Rainton)
⌚ 11-11 ☎ (0191) 584 2394
🌐 threehorseshoesleamside.co.uk
Leamside Adventure, Alexandrina, Brockwell; Timothy Taylor Landlord; 4 changing beers 🄷
A country pub with an excellent restaurant (the Back Room – booking advisable). The traditional bar has open fires in winter and a large TV for sport. The attached Leamside Brewery provides up to five real ales, with Timothy Taylor Landlord always available. The Leamside beers are named after local geographical features, with a map in the corner of the room pointing out their location. The pub is home to local cycle and clay pigeon clubs.
Q🛋❀◑♿🍎P🐾📶

Long Newton

Vane Arms

Darlington Road, TS21 1DB (W end of village, close to A66 jct)
⌚ 12-2 (not Mon), 5-11; 12-2, 5-midnight Fri & Sat; 12-11 Sun
☎ (01642) 580401 🌐 vanearms.com
4 changing beers 🄷
This picturesque village pub, comprising a public bar and restaurant, was left abandoned for 898 days before a local couple, new to the trade, bought the freehold. Now well into their third 898-day period of tenure, they have established an enviable reputation for serving five microbrewery sourced beers, together with freshly home-made and reasonably priced top-quality restaurant meals. There is a superb south-facing outdoor drinking space. Various community events are hosted and four newly refurbished en-suite letting bedrooms are available. No jukebox or gaming machines.
Q🛋❀🛏◑♿♣P🚉🚌(88)📶

Medomsley

Royal Oak 🄻

7 Manor Road, DH8 6QN
⌚ 11.30-3, 5.30-11; 11-11 Sat; 12-11 Sun ☎ (01207) 560336
🌐 homeeditor.wix.com/the-royal-oak
Hadrian Border Tyneside Blonde; 2 changing beers 🄷
The Royal Oak is a traditional country-style pub which has been refurbished to create a warm, welcoming country feel. It has a large bar with a selection of seating including soft sofas and leather chairs, and plenty of dining space. Outside, there is a large, attractive garden at the back and ample parking to the front. An excellent, friendly local, it offers a rotation of excellent beers as well as good food. Quiz night is Sunday. Q🛋❀◑♿P🚌🐾📶

Metal Bridge

Old Mill Hotel 🄻

Thinford Road, DH6 5NX (off A1M jct 61, follow signs on A177)
⌚ 12-11 (10.30 Sun) ☎ (01740) 652928
🌐 oldmilldurham.co.uk
4 changing beers 🄷
Originally built as a paper mill in 1813, this spacious inn is now the venue of choice for discerning locals and visitors alike. It offers good-quality food and well-kept ales – four handpumps serve an ever-changing range, with the nearby Durham Brewery often supplying one of the beers. The food menu is extensive, with daily specials written on a board above the bar. Larger groups are welcome in the conservatory. Accommodation is of a high standard, with all rooms en-suite.
Q🛋🛏◑P

Middlestone

Ship Inn 🄻

Low Road, DL14 8AB (between Coundon and Kirk Merrington)
⌚ 4 (12 Fri-Sun)-11 ☎ (01388) 810904
6 changing beers 🄷
Regular drinkers come from far and wide to the Ship. It has a bar room divided into three areas with an open fire, and a large function room upstairs which is the location for twice-yearly beer festivals. The rooftop patio has spectacular views, and there is always an event either in the offing or taking place. Various pieces of Vaux memorabilia are on display – one of the many subjects of conversation. Sunday lunches are popular. Durham CAMRA Country Pub winner 2014, runner-up 2015.
Q🛋❀◑♿♣🍎P🐾

Newfield

Newfield Inn 🄻

Front Street, DH2 2SP
⌚ 4 (12 Sat & Sun)-11.30 ☎ (0191) 370 0565

Maxim Ward's Best Bitter; 2 changing beers H
A friendly two-roomed pub in the centre of the village, now owned by Maxim Brewery from nearby Houghton-le-Spring, with two of its beers and a guest available. The pub offers accommodation, fortnightly live music, quiz nights and televised football. Families are welcome and there is a beer garden. ♣P

No Place

Beamish Mary Inn L

DH9 0QH (follow signs to No Place off A693 from Chester-le-Street to Stanley)
12-11 (10.30 Sun) ☎ (0191) 370 0237
beamishmaryinn.co.uk
Big Lamp Sunny Daze, Lamplight Bitter; Consett White Hot, Red Dust; 5 changing beers H
This pub, full of character, is well respected for its warm welcome, generously portioned pub grub and ample selection of real ale. Accommodation is available including twin, double and family rooms. The location is handy for visitors to the nearby world-renowned Beamish Open Air Museum. Owned by the owner of Consett Ale Works, its beers are now included among the range of LocAles. A former local CAMRA Pub of the Year.
Q P (8,78)

Old Shotton

Royal George L

The Village, SR8 2ND
11-11 (midnight Fri & Sat); 11-10.30 Sun
☎ (0191) 586 6500 royalgeorgeoldshotton.co.uk
Leamside Adventure, Alexandrina; Timothy Taylor Landlord; 2 changing beers H
Pub and restaurant situated on the old village green, reopened after a major refurbishment of a virtually derelict establishment in March 2014. The bar has been reinstated as well as a larger lounge and restaurant area. Owned by the Leamside Ale Company, at least two of its beers are on handpump. Traditional pub grub and bar snacks are available. Q P

Ovington

Four Alls L

The Green, DL11 7BP (2 miles S of Winston & A67)
7 (6 Fri)-11; 3-11 Sat; closed Sun ☎ (01833) 627302
thefouralls-teesdale.co.uk
2 changing beers H
Friendly 18th-century inn opposite the village green in what is known as 'the maypole village'. A Victorian sign denotes the four alls: 'I govern all (queen), I fight for all (soldier), I pray for all (parson), I pay for all (farmer).' The pub has a hop-adorned bar, games room and restaurant serving excellent value food. Two real ales are on offer, at least one from local Mithril Ales. Comfortable country inn accommodation is available in seven rooms in a lovely setting. A Thai evening is held every last Friday and Saturday of the month.
Q ♣P

Peterlee

Five Quarter

Units 3B-3C, Hailsham Place, SR8 1AB
8am-11 (midnight Fri & Sat) ☎ (0191) 518 5880
5 changing beers H
This well-presented Wetherspoon bar provides an oasis of real ale in an area not renowned for it. The pub is situated in the town's shopping centre and good food is always available. Nearby is Horden which at one time boasted the biggest pit in Britain, where miners worked the High Main, Yard and Five Quarter seams – from where the pub took its name, reflecting the area's coal-mining heritage. P

Preston-le-Skerne

Blacksmiths Arms

Ricknall Lane, DL5 6JH (1 mile E of A167 at Gretna Green)
closed Mon; 11.30-2; 6 (6.30 winter)-11; 12-10.30 Sun
☎ (01325) 314873 blacksmithsarms-pls.co.uk
3 changing beers H
Welcoming free house known locally as the Hammers, in a rural location near Newton Aycliffe. A long corridor separates the bar, restaurant and a beamed lounge furnished in farmhouse style. The pub has an excellent reputation for home-cooked food and up to three guest beers are available, sourced mainly from local micros. A former local CAMRA Rural Pub of the Year, it even has a helicopter landing pad.

Sadberge

Buck Inn L

Middleton Road, DL2 1RR
12-11 (10 Sun winter) ☎ (01325) 335307
thebuckinnsadberge.co.uk
Black Sheep Best Bitter; Sonnet 43 Steam Beer, Blonde Beer; 1 changing beer H
Friendly traditional English pub overlooking the green in an attractive village setting, named after George Buck, a benevolent 18th-century landowner. It has two bars, one mainly for dining, a beer garden at the rear and benches and tables in front. A range of good food is served lunchtimes and evenings. The beer choice supports local micros. The village sits atop a hill in a popular walking area. P (20)

St John's Chapel

Blue Bell Inn L

Hood Street, DL13 1QJ
5 (12 Sat & Sun)-1am ☎ (01388) 537256
2 changing beers H
Originally a pair of terraced cottages, the Blue Bell is a friendly and cosy pub with a bar across the front of the building leading to a small pool room, and garden to the rear. Situated right on the A689, it serves the local community and those who holiday in Upper Weardale. Pub games are popular and there are plenty of books to choose from.
Q ♣ (101)

Seaham

Crow's Nest

Featherbed, East Shore Village, North Road, SR7 7XR
11.30 (9am Sat)-11; 9am-10.30 Sun ☎ (0191) 581 4927
crowsnestpub.co.uk
Banks's Bitter; Marston's Pedigree; Wychwood Hobgoblin; 3 changing beers H
A light and airy pub from the Marston's group with an excellent position on Seaham seafront at the head of East Shore Village. The site was originally

part of Vane Tempest pit. The pub reopened in December 2013 after major refurbishment, with six handpumps. A cask platter can be ordered with three one-third pints. It opens at 9am at weekends for breakfast (no alcohol sold until 11am), and offers an extensive food menu including a weekend carvery. P (202,238)

Seaton

Dun Cow

The Village, SR7 0NA

4 (5 winter)-midnight; 12-midnight Fri-Sun

(0191) 513 1133

4 changing beers H

Excellent, friendly, unspoiled inn on the village green comprising public bar and lounge areas. A pub for good conversation or a game of darts, the TV is only turned on for special events. No meals are served but toasties are always available. The guest beer selection changes but usually includes two light and two dark beers to satisfy all tastes. Regular busker and acoustic music nights feature here. P (238)

Sedgefield

Dun Cow

43 Front Street, TS21 3AT

11-3, 6-11; 11-11 Sat; 12-10.30 Sun (01740) 620894

duncowinn.co.uk

Black Sheep Best Bitter; Theakston Best Bitter; 2 changing beers H

Run by the same landlord for nearly 40 years, this large and comfortable 18th-century inn has an excellent county-wide reputation for good food. It was the scene of a historic George Bush and Tony Blair lunch in 2003. There are three bars including a farmers' bar-cum-snug and restaurant. Four real ales are always available including at least one local beer. Q P (X1)

South Church

Red Alligator

Auckland Road, DL14 6SP

12-2.30, 5.30-10.30 (11.30 Sat); 11.30-3 Sun

(01388) 605644

2 changing beers H

A mile from the centre of Bishop Auckland, this smart local has a bright feel and a good reputation for food. There is a spacious L-shaped bar across the front and a small dining room/snug to the rear. The eponymous Grand National winner was trained just across the road. Two beers are generally on offer. Q P (1,5)

Spennymoor

Grand Electric Hall

Cheapside, DL16 6DJ

8am-midnight (1am Fri & Sat) (01388) 825470

Greene King Abbot; Ruddles Best Bitter; 6 changing beers H

A Wetherspoon conversion of a former cinema and bingo hall, this is a bright, spacious pub with film-themed decor and fittings. It is in the centre of town and boasts a large patio drinking area to the front which can be quite a suntrap in the summer months. Alcohol is served from 9am. (6,21)

> Beer: a high and mighty liquor.
> **Julius Caesar**

Stanhope

Bonny Moorhen

Market Place, DL13 2TS

11-11.30 (01388) 528214

thebonnymoorhenstanhope.co.uk

4 changing beers H

Busy pub next to the church in the market place, with a lively bar that has a pool table, and a separate lounge. Convenient for the coast-to-coast cycleway, it is popular with locals and holidaymakers. TVs screen sport, and there is live music at weekends plus occasional beer festivals. (101)

Stockton-on-Tees

Golden Smog

1 Hambletonian Yard, TS18 1DS (in a ginnel between the High St and West Row)

2 (12 Sat)-10 (01642) 385022

4 changing beers H

The town's first micropub, complete with a huge Belgian twist, is located in a ginnel leading west off the main drag and named after the environmental conditions that recently prevailed on Teesside. Four real beers, real ciders and real perry are available alongside an impressive range of Belgian beers, some familiar, most not so familiar, served in matching glasses in the continental way. Q (Stockton/Thornaby)

Sun Inn

2 Knowles Street, TS18 1SU (off High Street)

11-11; 12-10.30 Sun (01642) 611461

Draught Bass H

This popular traditional town-centre drinkers' pub is reputed to sell more Draught Bass than any other pub in the country – a gallon of Bass is pulled for each pint of lager. The pub supports darts, football teams and various charitable causes. At weekends, R&B bands feature in the back lounge, while on Mondays it has been home to the famous Stockton Folk Club for the last 45 years. The clock in the bar deliberately runs fast. (Stockton/Thornaby)

Thomas Sheraton

4 Bridge Road, TS18 3BW (at S end of High St)

8am-midnight (11 Sun) (01642) 606134

7 changing beers H

This previous CAMRA branch Pub of the Year is a fine Wetherspoon conversion of the Victorian law courts and named after one of the country's great Georgian cabinet makers, born in the town in 1751. The interior comprises several dining/drinking areas, together with a balcony and an upstairs patio. As well as the nationally contracted beers, it offers a range of guest beers, usually locally sourced. Real cider is also on handpump. Meet the Brewer events, beer festivals, a January sale and celebrations of various saints' days are all hosted. Q (Stockton/Thornaby)

West Cornforth

Square & Compass

7 The Green, DL17 9JQ (off Coxhoe-W Cornforth road)

⏲ 7 (5 Fri)-11; 12-11 Sat & Sun ☎ (01740) 653050
3 changing beers Ⓗ
A proper drinking pub and friendly local on the village green in the old part of Doggy (the village's local nickname). It has sold real ale for over 30 years and always offers at least one local beer among its three guests. It hosts darts, dominoes and chess clubs. The pub has good views over to Wear Valley and Durham City. ❀♣P🐾

Westgate

Hare & Hounds Ⓛ

24 Front Street, DL13 1RX
⏲ closed Mon; 12-3.30 (not Tue-Fri), 6.30-11; 12-3.30, 6.30-9 Sun ☎ (01388) 517212
🌐 hareandhoundswestgate.blogspot.co.uk
Weard'Ale Challenger, Gold, Fell Over, Dark Nights; 2 changing beers Ⓗ
The pub is situated on the main road up Weardale, with the river at the bottom of the garden. The spacious stone-flagged bar is partially fitted out with furniture and other items salvaged from the former village chapel, and the restaurant has a patio overlooking the Wear. Catch up on the local news over a pint brewed only a few feet below you, while watching the pub's poultry in the rear garden. Food is locally sourced, including the famous Sunday carvery. Local CAMRA branch Country Pub of the Year runner-up in 2015.
Q❀◗♿Å♣P🚌(101)

Whorlton

Fernaville's Rest Ⓛ

The Green, DL12 8XD (1 mile S of A67)
⏲ 12-11 (11.45 Sat) ☎ (01833) 627341 🌐 fernavilles.com
4 changing beers Ⓗ
Grade II-listed Teesdale country inn that retains its traditional features and charm, in a quintessential English village surrounded by riverside walks and a welcome stop for ramblers. Whether you are treating yourself to a break, sampling some of the country fare, or simply popping in to try some of the excellent cask ales from north-east micros, including Wylam, local Mithril, Hadrian & Borders, you will be warmly welcomed and looked after. Stay in the pub or in the shepherds' huts out back.
❀🛏◐◗♣P🐾📶

Willington

Black Horse

42 Low Willington, DL15 0BD
⏲ 6 (12 Sat & Sun)-11 ☎ 07727 280196
2 changing beers Ⓗ
Tastefully refurbished to provide a spacious, open-plan pub while maintaining separate drinking areas. Beers are often from local brewers, pub games are regularly played, and sport is popular on the large screens. Local car clubs use the Black Horse as a base, and the pub enthusiastically supports the local ladies' football team. Handily placed between Durham and Weardale.
♣P🚌(50,46)

Witton Gilbert

Glendenning Arms

Front Street, DH7 6SY (off A691 bypass)
⏲ 4 (12 Sat & Sun)-11 ☎ (0191) 371 0316
Black Sheep Best Bitter; 1 changing beer Ⓗ
A typical village community local and Guide regular with a small, comfortable lounge and a lively, welcoming bar with a real open fire. The bar is attractively decorated in a contemporary style and still sports the original Vaux 1970s red and white handpulls. The lounge remains more traditional. The pub runs darts, dominoes and football teams. Classic car and motorcycle clubs meet here monthly. Situated on the village main road, with ample parking. Q❀♣P🚌(14,X25)🐾📶

Witton-le-Wear

Dun Cow

19 High Street, DL14 0AY
⏲ 6 (1 Sat)-11; 12-11 Sun ☎ (01388) 488294
3 changing beers Ⓗ
Dating from 1799, this comfortable and welcoming pub is set back from the road through the village. The single room has an open fire at both ends, one guarded by a sleeping fox who always seems to have just closed his eyes, and the other by an impressive set of horns. There are benches to the left of the bar, and seating outside offering pleasant views. The decor is completed by some interesting football memorabilia. Q❀♣P

Wolsingham

Black Lion Ⓛ

21 Meadhope Street, DL13 3EN (50yds N of Market Place)
⏲ 6.30 (6 Fri)-11; 12-11 Sat; 12-10.30 Sun
☎ (01388) 527772
4 changing beers Ⓗ
Hidden away a minute from the Market Place, this friendly, comfortable gem is a great place to relax. An open fire features in the single, open-plan room, with a pool table to the rear and a bar with TV sport to the front. Regular beer festivals are held in the suntrap garden at the rear, and local charities benefit from the efforts of the pub. Ask for the cider menu, as more than six can be on offer. North-East Cider Pub of the Year 2013 and local branch Country Cider Pub of the Year 2013-2015.
Q❀♿♣🍎🚌(101)🐾📶

Store of good ale

Though it was but about the middle of August, and in some places the harvest hardly got in, we saw the mountains covered with snow, and felt the cold very acute and piercing but we found, as in all these northern counties, the people had a happy way of mixing the warm and the cold together; for store of good ale which flows plentifully in the most mountainous parts of this country seem abundantly to make up for all the inclemencies of the season, or difficulties of travelling.

Daniel Defoe, A Tour through the Whole Island of Great Britain, 1726

Cyclops Beer – the key to beer tasting

There are thousands of real ales in this copy of the *Good Beer Guide* – more than ever given the increasing number of British breweries. This is a welcome development but how do you know which ones you're going to enjoy the most? You don't often know what a beer will taste like from its name alone or from the pump clip, so do you take a risk and hope for the best, or stick to those beers and breweries that you know and trust?

A beer tasting scheme called Cyclops was set up in 2006 to help beer drinkers find their way through the myriad tastes and flavours that we find in real ale. Run by members of the beer industry, including CAMRA, Cyclops can help inform your decision with its simple tasting notes which are available for over 2,200 British beers. Cyclops tasting notes tell you how a beer will look, smell and taste, and how bitter and sweet it is. You can also see at a glance its beer style, colour and ABV.

Almost 400 breweries have signed up to be accredited by Cyclops since its inception. Those breweries are indicated in the Breweries section by the symbol.

Cyclops tasting notes are increasingly used in pubs around the UK. You can find them on beer mats, chalkboards, glasses as well as brewery websites and even in some supermarkets. Many pubs and breweries also use them to train staff as they take the jargon out of beer descriptions. If you use Cyclops tasting notes you will develop an understanding of your favourite tastes and flavours in real ale; you may discover that you're a Hop Head if your bitter rating is always 5/5, or a Sweet Tooth, or you may prefer a well-balanced beer if you enjoy a real ale with both bitter and sweet, malty flavours. You can then find more beers with similar profiles and develop an awareness of what, to you, makes a great beer.

You can find the ever-growing number of Cyclops tasting notes at **www.cyclopsbeer.co.uk**. We hope you enjoy your voyage of discovery using Cyclops Beer.

Cyclops® Beer

Discover your beer sense

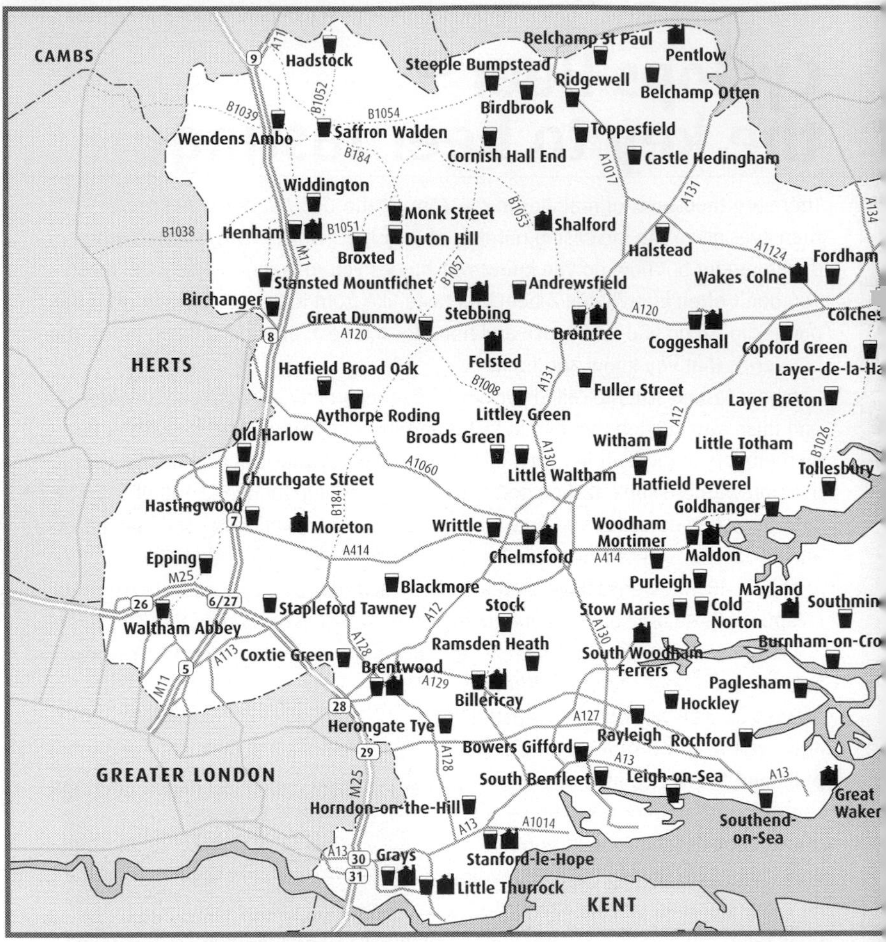

Andrewsfield Airfield

Milli-bar

Saling Road, CM6 3TH (accessed by track beside runway, near Stebbing Green) TL689448

8.30am-9pm ☎ (01371) 981900 andrewsfield.com/bar

Bishop Nick Ridley's Rite H

Local private airfield with a small grass strip, dominated by single-engine Cessna aircraft. The café/bar manager is keen on local supply and has installed Ridley's Rite from Bishop Nick's Brewery as his sole ale. There is also a range of bottled beers from Bishop Nick's. The flying school offers everything from trial lessons up to commercial pilot's licence instruction. The public are welcomed here. **Q P**

Aythorpe Roding

Axe & Compasses

Dunmow Road, CM6 1PP (on B184 5 miles SW of Dunmow) TL594154

12-11 (midnight Sat); 12-10 Sun ☎ (01279) 876648

theaxeandcompasses.co.uk

Adnams Broadside; Sharp's Doom Bar H**; 3 changing beers (sourced regionally)** G

An 18th-century thatched pub in open countryside, frequented by a mixed clientele of drinkers, diners and local farming folk. Good beer and food are always on offer, with friendly and efficient service. The food is high quality and locally sourced, with seasonal deals. In winter there is a log fire and on fine days the garden gives views across the fields to the windmill. Quizzes and themed nights are popular. **Q P** (17,18)

Belchamp Otten

Red Lion

Fowes Lane, CO10 7BQ (on small single track lane, signed by duck pond) TL799415

12-3, 5.30-11; closed Tue; 12-11 Fri & Sat; 12-7 Sun

☎ (01787) 278301 ottenredlion.co.uk

Adnams Southwold Bitter; 2 changing beers (sourced nationally) H

Lovely local pub hidden away in the smallest of the Belchamps. The owners provide a warm welcome, with an open fire in winter. There is local artwork here for sale. Pub games include bar billiards and darts. Live music is scheduled on the last Saturday of the month in summertime. Wholesome home-cooked food is available lunchtimes and evenings, and to take away too (no food Mon and Tue). There are excellent views, good walks and cycle rides from here. **P**

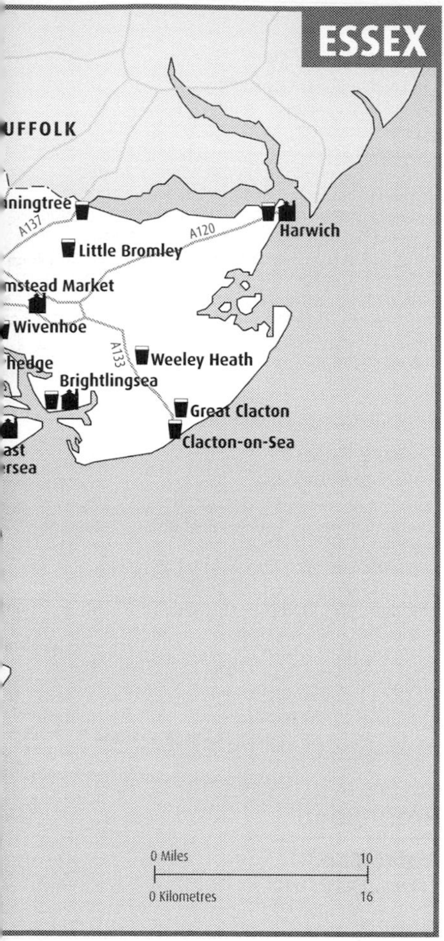

Belchamp St Paul

Half Moon

Cole Green, CO10 7DP TL792423
12-3, 6-11; 12-11 Sat & Sun ☎ (01787) 277402
halfmoonbelchamp.co.uk
Greene King IPA; 2 changing beers (sourced nationally) Ⓗ
Beautiful, warm and friendly thatched rural inn dating from about 1685, opposite the village green. Three beers are on tap and guest beers change regularly. The venue is popular with locals and has an excellent choice of bar and restaurant meals (no food Sun eve). Outside there is a separate smoking area and chickens in the back garden. The pub provided one of the locations for the first Lovejoy TV series. Q❀◑♣P

Billericay

Blue Boar

39 High Street, CM12 9BA
8am-11 ☎ (01277) 655552
Greene King Abbot; Ruddles Best Bitter; 5 changing beers Ⓗ
An often-busy Wetherspoon pub situated in Billericay High Street. Five changing real ales are served, some from local breweries such as Brentwood and Maldon, and two real ciders. Occasional sports fixtures are shown on TV but no music is played. There is a designated family area where children are permitted up to 8pm, and a seating area outside for drinking and smoking. A Pay & Display car park is at the rear, and train station and bus stops nearby.
Q❀◑♿⇌●P🚌(100)

Coach & Horses

36 Chapel Street, CM12 9LU
11-11; 10-11 Sat; 12-10 Sun ☎ (01277) 622873
thecoachandhorses.org
Sharp's Doom Bar; Wibblers Dengie IPA; 3 changing beers Ⓗ
Close to the High Street, this welcoming one-bar pub with an inviting atmosphere is a regular in this Guide. Guest beers, from the Gray's portfolio, change weekly. Good-quality, home-made food is available lunchtimes and evenings, with a curry night on Wednesdays (including Thai and Goan). The bar and food service is efficient and friendly. The walls are adorned with prints and decorative plates, and a collection of jugs hangs from the ceiling. There is BT Sport for rugby and football matches. Q❀◑⇌●P🚌(100)

Railway

1 High Street, CM12 9BE
12-11 (midnight Fri & Sat) ☎ (01277) 652173
Greene King IPA; Woodforde's Wherry; 3 changing beers Ⓗ
Friendly, old-fashioned pub with a welcoming atmosphere and the tagline 'No.1 in the High Street' (not least because of its address). The guest beers are updated regularly on Facebook. It hosts live music twice a month and on bank holidays, and regular charity events. This community-oriented pub has three darts teams and sponsors a local rugby team. It has traditional bar games including shove-ha'penny with real ha'pennies. A small beer garden is outside, and an open fire indoors. ❀⇌♣P

REAL ALE BREWERIES

Billericay Billericay (NEW)
Bishop Nick Braintree
Brentwood Brentwood
Brightlingsea Brightlingsea
Colchester Wakes Colne
Crouch Vale South Woodham Ferrers
Deverell's Little Thurrock (Grays)
Dominion Moreton
Felstar Felsted
George's Great Wakering
Hart of Stebbing Stebbing
Harwich Town Harwich
Hope Stanford-le-Hope
Maldon Maldon
Mersea Island East Mersea
Mighty Oak Maldon
Mr Majolica Grays (NEW)
Nethergate Pentlow
Railway Tavern Brightlingsea
Red Fox Coggeshall
Round Tower Chelmsford
Saffron Henham
Shalford Shalford
Sticklegs Elmstead Market
Wibblers Mayland

Birchanger

Birchanger Sports & Social Club

229 Birchanger Lane, CM23 5QJ

🕒 7-11 Mon, Tue & Thu; 11.30-2.30, 6-11 Wed; 11.30-11 Fri & Sat; 12-10.30 Sun ☎ (01279) 813441 🌐 birchangerclub.com

3 changing beers (sourced nationally) Ⓗ

A friendly, busy social club where CAMRA members are welcome to drink as guests. Beers change frequently, usually with one guest staying for a month or two. Many matches and events are hosted here and the club can get busy. It is home to football, cricket, bowls, darts, crib and snooker teams, and holds regular quizzes, bingo and bottle draws. Local CAMRA branch Club of the Year 2014 and 2015 and East Anglian Club of the Year 2014. 🐴❀◐♿♣🍎P🚌(7,7A)🐾

Birdbrook

Plough 🄻

The Street, CO9 4BJ

🕒 6-11; 4-midnight Fri; 12-midnight Sat; 12-10.30 Sun ☎ (01440) 788066

Greene King IPA; 2 changing beers (sourced locally; often Mighty Oak) Ⓗ

The Plough is the central focus of the village, and the family owners run a shop and the library too. The interior has low ceilings and is divided into three rooms – a games room, the bar area and the restaurant. The owners are extending, having added new toilets behind the main building, and have brought this pub back to being a successful business. A new thatched roof is expected to be fitted soon. ❀◐♣P🐾

Blackmore

Leather Bottle

The Green, CM4 0RL

🕒 11-11 (midnight Fri & Sat) ☎ (01277) 821891 🌐 theleatherbottle.net

Adnams Southwold Bitter, Broadside; Sharp's Doom Bar; 1 changing beer Ⓗ

Large village pub with a smallish flagstone-floored snug with comfortable seating and a real fire in winter. Four real ales and a cider are always on tap. Most of the pub is taken up by a high-quality restaurant, serving freshly cooked local produce. A conservatory leads to an enclosed garden with picnic tables. ❀◐🍎P🚌(32)🐾

Bowers Gifford

Gun

London Road, SS13 2DU (on old A13)

🕒 11-10 (11 Thu; midnight Fri & Sat); 12-10 Sun ☎ (01268) 551506 🌐 thegunpub.co.uk

Sharp's Doom Bar; 3 changing beers Ⓗ

Community pub with a friendly and inviting atmosphere for all age groups. At least one real cider is served, usually two. Beer festivals are held each year in May and August. Lots of events take place here, including pub outings and rock & roll bingo for charity. Good-value pub classics and Sunday roasts are served. It has won several awards for customer service. Well-behaved children are permitted until 9pm, and dogs are welcome on leads in the garden with water provided. 🐴❀◐♿🍎P

Braintree

King William IV

114 London Road, CM77 7PU

🕒 3 (12 Fri-Sun)-midnight ☎ (01376) 567755 🌐 kingwilliamiv.co.uk

4 changing beers Ⓖ

Warm and friendly freehouse serving an ever-changing range of four to five real ales, usually featuring some from Essex microbreweries. Three or four ciders are also available. The interior comprises a main bar and a small back bar with a dartboard. Outside, the large patio and extensive gardens are used to host many events throughout the year including beer festivals and music events. This is a traditional drinking pub with no hot food. ❀♣🍎P🚌(70,352)🐾

Picture Palace

Fairfield Road, CM7 3HA

🕒 8am-11.30 (1.30am Fri & Sat) ☎ (01376) 550255

Greene King Abbot; Ruddles Best Bitter; 4 changing beers Ⓗ

Originally a cinema, the Picture Palace was built in 1912 and replaced by the Embassy in 1930. This spacious pub retains the character of a picture house. The floor slopes down to the long curved bar at the front where the stage used to be, with a large TV screen above it, and some eye-catching Art Deco installations. Additional TVs give a choice of channels. It trades as a Lloyds No.1 bar. Close to the bus and train stations. **Q**🐴◐♿⇌🍎🚌📶

Brentwood

Rising Sun 🄻

144 Ongar Road, CM15 9DJ (on A128, at Western Rd jct)

🕒 3-11.30 (midnight Fri); 12-midnight Sat; 12-10.30 Sun ☎ (01277) 213749

Fuller's London Pride; Sharp's Cornish Coaster; Timothy Taylor Landlord; 2 changing beers Ⓗ

Great community local with five real ales. Charity quizzes are held on Monday evenings and there are frequent darts matches in the public bar, as well as occasional chess evenings. There are three regular beers plus one from Brentwood Brewery and a guest which can be from anywhere. Framed prints of the local area decorate the walls. Outside there is a covered, heated patio and a smokers' area. **Q**❀♿♣P🚌(21,71,72)🐾

Brightlingsea

Railway Tavern 🄻

58 Station Road, CO7 0DT

🕒 4 (5 winter)-10; 3-11 Fri; 12-11 Sat; 12-3, 7-10.30 Sun

Crouch Vale Essex Boys Best Bitter; 2 changing beers Ⓗ

This friendly, basic local pub has made over 20 entries in the Guide. It is a place to enjoy a really fine pint of real ale and conversation with the locals, but with no frills attached. It always serves at least one real cider and often beers from its own brewery. Community-friendly, a number of music events are held throughout the year, often showcasing local bands. Please note that no children are allowed. **Q**🍎🚌(78,79,87)

Broads Green

Walnut Tree

CM3 1DT (off B1008 at Ash Tree corner, signed Great Waltham, after ¼ mile turn left into Larks Lane, continue ¾ mile) TL694125

✪ 12-11 ☎ (01245) 360222

Timothy Taylor Landlord; Young's Bitter; 1 changing beer Ⓖ

Handsome Victorian pub overlooking the green. The front door opens into what was the bottle and jug, now a small snug. To the left is the wood-panelled public bar, little changed since 1888. To the right is the more modern saloon bar. Outside is seating in front of the pub, a children's play area and a large garden. There is no food, the landlord preferring to focus on his beers and maintaining a traditional atmosphere. Q❀♣P🐾

Broxted

Prince of Wales 𝕃

Brick End, CM6 2BJ

✪ closed Mon; 12-11 (midnight Fri & Sat) ☎ (01279) 850256

🌐 princeofwalesbroxted.co.uk

Greene King IPA; 5 changing beers (sourced nationally) Ⓗ

In the south of Broxted, this former Charrington's pub, for many years in the doldrums, has been transformed into a welcoming community venue after the current landlords took over in 2011. It has a comfortable split-level bar, an adjoining room with two woodburners and a large conservatory. Generously proportioned pub grub is on offer, mostly locally sourced. Up to five guest beers are served, with LocAle from Bishop Nick. There is a small garden to the rear. CAMRA branch Pub of the Year 2014. Q❀◑P🚌(5)

Burnham-on-Crouch

New Welcome Sailor

Station Road, CM0 8HF

✪ 12-11 ☎ (01621) 784778

Dark Star Hophead; Sharp's Doom Bar; Wibblers Dengie IPA; 1 changing beer (sourced locally) Ⓗ

Only 400 yards from the railway station, this Gray's pub is a comfortable, tidy and welcoming community local. No food is served. The single-roomed inn offers a range of traditional games such as table skittles and shove-ha'penny, and two darts teams play in the local league. There is a spacious function room at the rear. The guest ale, available in summer only, is often from one of the local microbreweries, and the cider is Westons Rosie's Pig. ❀≠♣●P🚌🐾

Queen's Head

26 Providence, CM0 8JU

✪ 2 (5 Mon)-11; 12-11 Fri-Sun ☎ (01621) 784825

Dark Star Hophead; house beer (by Wibblers); 2 changing beers (sourced regionally) Ⓗ

Friendly Gray's house tucked away in a narrow side street just off Burnham High Street. It is a spacious single-roomed pub with an attractive courtyard at the rear. Thatchers Cheddar Valley cider, a perry and an interesting selection of Belgian bottled beers are available alongside the ales. The huffers (Essex baps) are baked on the premises; the landlord also cooks some flavoursome curries (including Caribbean curried goat). Beer festivals are held over the late May and August bank holiday weekends. ❀◑♣●🚌(31X)🐾

Castle Hedingham

Bell 𝕃

10 St James Street, CO9 3EJ

✪ 12-3, 6-11; 12-midnight Fri & Sat; 12-11 Sun

☎ (01787) 460350 🌐 hedinghambell.co.uk

Adnams Southwold Bitter; Mighty Oak IPA, Maldon Gold; 1 changing beer (sourced nationally) Ⓖ

Fifteenth century Gray's-owned coaching inn with small rooms for drinking and dining alongside two main bars. Beer is dispensed from the cask and summer and winter beer festivals are held. Jazz is played lunchtimes on the last Sunday of the month, local musicians play on Friday evenings and Sunday is quiz night. Locally sourced food includes Turkish specials prepared in a wood-fired stone oven, and on Monday evenings there is a barbecue fish menu. Q❀◑Å♣●P🚌(89)🐾

Chelmsford

Ale House

24-26 Viaduct Road, CM1 1TS

✪ 11-11 (midnight Fri & Sat); 12-10.30 Sun

☎ (01245) 260535 🌐 the-ale-house-chelmsford.co.uk

12 changing beers Ⓗ

In the style of a continental ale house, this pub is situated under three railway arches beneath Chelmsford station. There are 12 real ales, with the changing range always including dark and stronger beers, and 12 real ciders. There are also imported German lagers on tap and a wide range of bottled beers from around the world. Food is limited to pies and pickled eggs. A mini beer festival is held on the last weekend of every other month.
♿≠●🚌

Globe

65 Rainsford Road, CM1 2QJ

✪ 11-11 (midnight Fri & Sat); 12-11 Sun ☎ (01245) 350232

6 changing beers Ⓗ

Completely renovated pub, trading as John Barras, selling real ale and craft beers. An imposing timbered building, it has seating outside at the front surrounded by hedges and flowers. Separate bays inside mean that sports enthusiasts can watch TV while others enjoy conversation over a drink or a meal. Varied entertainment is offered, with league poker every Monday, cash poker on Wednesday, a quiz every Sunday, and a Jack the Joker raffle on Friday. ❀◑♿≠♣P🚌(46,51)

Oddfellows Arms

195 Springfield Road, CM2 6JP

✪ 12-11 (midnight Thu-Sat) ☎ (01245) 490514

🌐 theoddfellowsarms.com

Mighty Oak Maldon Gold; Sharp's Atlantic; Wibblers Dengie IPA; 2 changing beers Ⓗ

Refurbished in 2012, this pub has a modern wood interior but maintains the feel of a local. There is a large U-shaped bar area with a back room containing a pool table, leading out to the garden/smoking area. Beer festivals are held annually. There is sports TV coverage, monthly live music and poker nights Tuesday and Wednesday. An extensive home-made food menu is served lunchtimes and evenings weekdays, and all day at weekends up to 9pm. ❀◑♣P🚌(54,56a,71c)

Orange Tree 🏆

Lower Anchor Street, CM2 0AS

✪ 12-11 (11.30 Fri & Sat) ☎ (01245) 262664 🌐 the-ot.com

Dark Star Hophead [G]; Mighty Oak Oscar Wilde; Plain Sheep Dip; Skinner's Betty Stogs [H]; 4 changing beers [G]
The Orange Tree is one of the best real ale pubs in Chelmsford and was voted local CAMRA Pub of the Year in 2014 and 2015. A place for conversation and meeting friends, it has a public bar plus a large saloon bar. The guest beers, served from handpump or on gravity, usually include a stout or porter, and the cider is often Westons Family Reserve. Food is available lunchtimes, with a roast on Sunday, and Thursday is steak and curry night. Q P

Queen's Head
30 Lower Anchor Street, CM2 0AS
12-11 (11.30 Fri & Sat) (01245) 265181
queensheadchelmsford.co.uk
Crouch Vale Essex Boys Best Bitter, Brewers Gold; 5 changing beers [H]
Crouch Vale Brewery's only pub, the Queen's Head sells three of its beers permanently, with four guests which may include a Crouch Vale seasonal and always include a dark beer. The Victorian L-shaped pub has bare-board flooring and comfortable bench seating. Two fires make it cosy in winter. This popular local can be busy when there is a match at the nearby county cricket ground. The Essex Beard Club meets here once a year in February. Q P

Railway Tavern
63 Duke Street, CM1 1LW
10-11 (11.30 Fri & Sat); 11-6 Sun (01245) 280679
Greene King Abbot; Mighty Oak IPA; Sharp's Special; Woodforde's Wherry; 4 changing beers [H]
A Tardis-like corner pub right outside Chelmsford station, more visible now due to nearby redevelopment. Not surprisingly, a railway theme dominates. Long and narrow, it has banks of handpumps at opposite ends of the central bar counter, with a TV at one end for sporting events and seating towards the rear laid out like a railway carriage. There is a small garden where you can listen to the station announcements. It does a good range of quality lunchtime meals.

Ship
18 Broomfield Road, CM1 1SW
10-11 (1am Fri & Sat); 12-11 Sun (01245) 265961
theshipchelmsford.co.uk
Greene King IPA, Abbot; 4 changing beers [H]
Traditional medium-sized pub with a comfortable interior and some outside seating in front. The decor is nautical, with dark-brown panelling, portholes, masts, rope, rigging and other maritime artefacts. A wide range of food is offered including daily specials. There is a jukebox but no live music on a regular basis. Sport is shown on the TV. Close to rail and bus stations, it has a public car park at the rear.

Churchgate Street

Queen's Head
26 Churchgate Street, Old Harlow, CM17 0JT
12-11.30; 12-9 Sun (01279) 427266
tqhchurchgatest.co.uk
Adnams Southwold Bitter, Broadside; Crouch Vale Essex Boys Best Bitter, Brewers Gold [H]; 1 changing beer [H]/[G]
Originally an early-Tudor building, with wooden beams spanning a spacious interior dating from 1515, it is believed that it has been a pub since around 1750. It is in Old Harlow, from which Harlow (the new town) took its name. The smaller side bar has a fire in winter and a range of food is served lunchtimes and evenings. There are regular quizzes, special events and cocktail evenings, and the occasional barbecue in summer.
Q P (7)

Clacton-on-Sea

Moon & Starfish
1 Marine Parade East, CO15 1PT
8am-11 (12.30am Fri & Sat) (01255) 222998
Greene King Abbot; Ruddles Best Bitter; 7 changing beers [H]
The only Wetherspoon pub in the Tendring District, conveniently situated opposite Clacton's famous pier and therefore affording excellent views of the Clacton Carnival and Clacton Air Show, held every August. In common with other Wetherspoon pubs it has two beer festivals, held in April and October, and a cider festival, held in July. Food is served daily. Q

Old Lifeboat House
39 Marine Parade East, CO15 6AD
11-11; 12-10.30 Sun (01255) 476799
5 changing beers [H]
A friendly family-run pub close to the seafront and town centre, popular with locals and visitors. Voted local CAMRA Pub of the Year 2013 and 2014, there are usually six ciders and perries available and five real ales that change as often as the tides – there is always something to please everyone. Freshly made home-cooked meals are served lunchtime and evening on Wednesdays. Beer festivals are held twice yearly at the end of April and October.
P

Coggeshall

Chapel Inn
4 Market Hill, CO6 1TS
11-midnight; 12-10.30 Sun (01376) 561655
thechapelinn.com
Adnams Ghost Ship; Sharp's Doom Bar; Woodforde's Wherry; 2 changing beers [H]
Market-square pub, built on the site of an old chapel. Separated beamed drinking areas give an indication of its age (it was first licensed in 1554). It hosts a popular quiz on Sundays and prides itself on good food and well-kept ales. Relatively new to the Guide, its place is well earned. It advertises live music on some weekends but can otherwise be a nice quiet place to drink or dine. Closing time may vary slightly on a day-to-day basis. P (70)

Colchester

Ale House
82 Butt Road, CO3 3DA
3-11; 12-midnight Fri; 12-11 Sat; 12-10 Sun
(01206) 573464
6 changing beers [H]
A friendly free house and runner-up Colchester CAMRA Town Pub of the Year 2015, with a large bar and comfortable seating. The changing selection of real ales, many from local breweries, includes four that are gravity fed from casks on the back bar. At least one dark ale and real ciders are always available. It has a lovely walled garden at

the rear. Features include a well-established darts team, a rare bar billiards table, cribbage and BT Sport. Quiz night is the third Wednesday of the month. 🐎❀⇌(Town)♣🍎🐾📶

Bricklayers

27 Bergholt Road, CO4 5AA

⌚ 11-3, 5.30-11; 11-midnight Fri; 11-11 Sat; 12-7 Sun ☎ (01206) 852008

Adnams Southwold Bitter, Broadside; 7 changing beers Ⓗ

Close to the station, this Adnams pub serves up to eight ales, with a variety of guests as well as Adnams regular and seasonal ranges. Up to four real ciders are kept, with Crones always on. A large lounge bar is complemented by a traditional public bar containing a pool table and dartboard, plus a large beer garden with cycle racks. Excellent home-cooked food is available at lunchtimes (no food Sat), with a great-value roast on Sunday. Q◖⇌(North)🍎P🚌

Britannia Gurkha Restaurant & Bar Ⓛ

42 Meyrick Crescent, CO2 7QY

⌚ 3.30-11; 2-midnight Fri; 12-midnight Sat & Sun ☎ (01206) 76100 🌐 britanniagurkharestaurant.co.uk

Colchester Metropolis, Colchester No. 1; 1 changing beer Ⓗ

Free house pub and restaurant owned and run by a Ghurka family. It has a friendly traditional bar area with pool table, darts, a large-screen TV showing major sporting events, and regular live music nights. Fascinating Gurkha memorabilia adorns the walls, some featuring the owner himself. The separate restaurant is cosy and relaxed, serving delicious home-cooked Nepalese cuisine at reasonable prices. It is popular, so booking is advisable. Regular barbecues are held during the summer, and takeaway food is available most evenings. 🐎❀◗♿⇌(Town)♣P🚌(63,8,67)🐾📶

British Grenadier Ⓛ

67 Military Road, CO1 2AP

⌚ 5-11.45; 12-midnight Fri & Sat; 12-11.45 Sun ☎ 07832 215118

4 changing beers Ⓗ

This former Adnams-tied, LocAle and Apple-accredited pub has been a regular in the Guide for more than 10 years, winning numerous awards during this time. There is a varied range of local, regional and national beers delivered from four handpumps. This two-bar Victorian hostelry has a small back bar dominated by a pool table, while the larger main bar is heated by a large open fire in colder months. ❀♿⇌(Town)♣🍎▯🚌(6,61,66)

Live & Let Live Ⓛ

12 Millers Lane, CO3 0PS

⌚ 12-11 (midnight Fri & Sat) ☎ (01206) 574071 🌐 theliveandletlive.co.uk

5 changing beers Ⓗ

Traditional, welcoming local with a quiet, homely saloon bar and a separate public bar that offers sports TV, darts, pool and a comprehensive jukebox. The landlord takes considerable pride in the condition of his ales as well as offering them at pleasantly low prices. These mostly local beers are available in take-out containers. A menu of traditional, good-value, home-cooked food is available and in summer and winter there are highly popular Sausage and Beer festivals. 🐎❀◖◗♿♣P🚌(65,70,71)🐾📶

Odd One Out Ⓛ

28 Mersea Road, CO2 7ET

⌚ 4.30-11; 12-11 Fri & Sat; 12-10.30 Sun ☎ (01206) 513958

Mauldons Silver Adder; 6 changing beers Ⓗ

The Oddie was opened by the current landlord 30 years ago as Colchester's original real ale house. Up to seven local, regional and national ales are on tap, at least one of which will be dark. Four real ciders are also on offer and the Oddie is the current local CAMRA branch Cider Pub of the Year. This welcoming traditional corner pub has two well-tended fires and is an ideal place to relax, free from music, TV and fruit machines. There is a garden area to the rear. Q❀⇌(Town)🍎🚌(8,67,175)🐾

Playhouse

4 St John's Street, CO2 7AA

⌚ 8am-midnight (1am Fri & Sat) ☎ (01206) 571003

Greene King Abbot; Ruddles Best Bitter; 7 changing beers Ⓗ

Always busy, with a mixed clientele, the Playhouse is Colchester's only Wetherspoon pub. An ever-changing selection of fine ales is always available in the unique setting of this converted Victorian music theatre. The original box seats and ornately decorated dress circle survive intact, while the auditorium and stage area are set for eating and drinking. With easy access for the disabled and all the features of a large bustling Wetherspoon, this is a place to meet and enjoy something new. 🐎◖◗♿⇌(Town)🍎🚌📶

Purple Dog

42 Eld Lane, CO1 1LS

⌚ 11-11 (1am Thu); 10-1am Fri; 10-2am Sat; 11.30-10.30 Sun ☎ (01206) 564995

Adnams Ghost Ship, Broadside; Sharp's Doom Bar; 3 changing beers Ⓗ

A place of refreshment since 1687 and still popular with younger folk, shoppers and ale enthusiasts. A single bar serves various drinking and dining areas and a sunny courtyard. Up to six ales on handpump and a guest on gravity are available, plus excellent food and a range of drinks to please everyone. The pub hosts seasonal beer festivals and monthly music nights and quizzes. A fine modern venue in a historic building, in the heart of Britain's oldest recorded town. 🐎❀◖◗⇌(Town)📶

Victoria Inn 🏆 Ⓛ

10 North Station Road, CO1 1RB

⌚ 12-11 (midnight Fri & Sat); 2-11 Sun ☎ (01206) 514510 🌐 victoriainncolchester.co.uk

House beer (by Colchester); 4 changing beers Ⓗ

Welcoming pub, which was regional CAMRA Pub of the Year 2014 and local Pub of the Year 2015. Five ales are on handpump from local and national breweries, including Yorkshire Blonde exclusively brewed for the Vic by Colchester Brewery, and often a dark ale. Nine real ciders are also on offer. It features an unusual bottle-top bar and a large courtyard area which hosts the annual beer festival. Live music plays on Sundays, and there is a varied jukebox. ❀⇌(North)♣🍎🚌🐾📶

Cold Norton

Norton

54 Latchingdon Road, CM3 6JB

⌚ 4.30 (12 Thu)-11; 12-midnight Fri & Sat; 12-11 Sun ☎ (01621) 826948 🌐 savethenorton.org

4 changing beers (sourced nationally) Ⓗ

A friendly and welcoming village pub, rescued from closure in 2009 by a committee of local people, who have recently purchased it outright. The pub has a vibrant mix of community events including live music, open mic and local walks. The pub's annual beer festival is in early May, with a cider festival in September. Real ciders from Abrahalls and Gwatkins are served. Good locally-sourced food is available in the attractive restaurant lunchtimes and Thursday-Saturday evenings. 🐴❀◑♿♣🍎P🚆🚌🐾📶

Copford Green

Alma 𝕃

School Road, CO6 1BZ

12-3, 5-11 (midnight Fri); 12-midnight Sat; 12-11 Sun ☎ (01206) 210607 🌐 thealma.org.uk

Greene King IPA, Abbot; Red Fox Hunter's Gold; 1 changing beer Ⓗ

Attractive 16th-century village pub offering Greene King and guest beers, with a large bar with various seating areas. The garden was voted in the top three rural community pubs in north-east Essex. The late-spring bank holiday beer festival has over 20 beers on offer. Home-cooked food is available lunchtimes and evenings Wednesday-Saturday, plus a popular Sunday roast. Quiz night is every first Thursday and the pub features an open fire, sports TV, darts and pool. Q🐴❀◑♿♣P🐾📶

Cornish Hall End

Horse & Groom 🏆 𝕃

B1057, CM7 4HF TL683366

closed Mon; 12-midnight ☎ (01799) 586306 🌐 thehorseandgroom.org

Greene King IPA, Abbot; St Austell Tribute; 3 changing beers (sourced nationally) Ⓗ

A pleasant village pub opposite the parish church with a restaurant and garden. It runs beer festivals and events and is a warm and friendly place, with beers that change frequently. Good food includes special lunches, carveries and fish and chips nights (always popular so book ahead). It is the social centre of this village, supporting many charities too. Local CAMRA Pub of the Year 2015. Q🐴❀◑♣P🐾📶

Coxtie Green

White Horse 𝕃

173 Coxtie Green Road, CM14 5PX (1 mile W of A128, at jct with Mores Lane) TQ564959

11.30-11 (midnight Fri & Sat); 12-10.30 Sun ☎ (01277) 372410 🌐 whitehorsebrentwood.co.uk

Fuller's London Pride; Greene King Abbot, IPA Reserve; 7 changing beers Ⓗ

Pleasant country free house with an extended comfortable saloon bar leading through to the public bar with a dartboard and large TV. The 10 handpumps dispense at least four beers from Brentwood Brewery, three regulars and four guests. The pub is badged as the Brentwood Brewery tap. The large garden has a children's play area and hosts a beer festival in early July. The local bus service is limited but reliable. ❀◑♿♣🍎P🚌(71,72)🐾

Duton Hill

Three Horseshoes 𝕃

CM6 2DX (1 mile W of B184) TL606268

12-2.30 (not Mon-Thu), 6-11; 12-3, 6-11 Sat; 12-3, 7-10.30 Sun ☎ (01371) 870681

Mighty Oak Captain Bob; 2 changing beers (sourced nationally) Ⓗ

Cosy village local with a garden, wildlife pond and terrace overlooking the Chelmer Valley and farmland. The landlord hosts a weekend of open-air theatre in July. A millennium beacon in the garden, breweriana and a remarkable collection of Butlins memorabilia are features. A beer festival is held on a spring bank holiday in the Duton Hill Den. Look for the pub sign depicting a famous painting, Our Blacksmith, by a former local resident Sir George Clausen. 🐴❀♿♣P🚌(313)

Epping

Forest Gate Inn

111 Bell Common, CM16 4DZ

10-2.30, 5-11; 12-3.30, 6.30-10.30 Sun ☎ (01992) 572312 🌐 haywardsrestaurant.co.uk

Adnams Southwold Bitter, Broadside; Bishop Nick Ridley's Rite Ⓗ**; 2 changing beers** Ⓗ/Ⓖ

On the edge of Epping Forest, a mile from Epping Underground station, this is an old-fashioned pub in a 17th-century building with low ceilings and flag floors. It is frequented by locals, walkers and their dogs. Bar snacks are available in the pub and full meals in the new adjacent Haywards restaurant. Another recent addition is the B&B with four rooms. The pub concentrates on real ale in a traditional setting, with a large seating area outside at the front. Q🐴❀🛏◑🍎P🚌(213,541)🐾📶

Fordham

Three Horseshoes 𝕃

Church Road, CO6 3NJ

closed Mon; 12-3, 5-11; 12-midnight Sat; 12-8 Sun ☎ (01206) 240195 🌐 threehorseshoes-fordham.co.uk

3 changing beers Ⓗ

Welcoming 16th-century village local, whose heavily timbered interior has a lovely brick fireplace and comfy sofas. Three Horseshoes Bitter is brewed by Red Fox, and the guest ales are quite often from local micros. In the separate dining area a reasonably priced menu of local home-cooked food is available lunchtimes and evenings. A beer festival is held in October, a folk night once a month and also cribbage evenings. 🐴❀◑P🚌(80,88A,88)🐾

Fuller Street

Square & Compasses

CM3 2BB TL748161

11-11; 12-midnight Sat; 12-11 Sun ☎ (01245) 361477 🌐 thesquareandcompasses.co.uk

3 changing beers Ⓖ

A 17th-century free house known locally as the Stokehole. Set in attractive countryside and handy for the Essex Way long-distance footpath, this is a small, well-looked-after country pub. There are exposed beams throughout, with two wood-burning stoves in inglenook fireplaces. Old local woodworking tools adorn the Taproom Bar. Up to four real ales and Westons cider and perry are served. Fresh locally sourced home-cooked food is available daily including game from the surrounding estates (no food Sun eves).

Goldhanger

Chequers

The Square, CM9 8AS

11-11; 12-10.30 Sun (01621) 788203

thechequersgoldhanger.co.uk

Adnams Ghost Ship; Crouch Vale Brewers Gold; Sharp's Doom Bar; Young's Bitter; 2 changing beers (sourced nationally) H

Delightful 15th-century pub in a pretty village near the River Blackwater. It boasts several timbered rooms including a snug and a games room with bar billiards. There are real fires in two of the bars in winter. In the summer the enclosed courtyard is a pleasant suntrap. Beer festivals are held in March and September. The pub is popular with walkers, birdwatchers and other visitors who are keen to sample excellent food from an extensive menu. Q P (95)

Grays

Theobald Arms

141 Argent Street, RM17 6HR

11-11 (midnight Fri & Sat); 12-11 Sun (01375) 372253

4 changing beers H

Genuine, traditional pub with a public bar that has an unusual hexagonal pool table. The changing selection of four guest beers features local independent breweries, and a range of British bottled beers is also stocked. Regular St George's weekend and summer beer festivals are held in the old stables and on the rear enclosed patio. Lunchtime meals are served Monday-Friday. Darts and cards are played. A former local CAMRA Pub of the Year. P

White Hart

Argent Street, RM17 6HR

12-11.30 (midnight Fri & Sat); 12-11 Sun

(01375) 373319 whitehartgrays.co.uk

Crouch Vale Brewers Gold; house beer (by Sharp's); 3 changing beers H

Traditional local just outside the town centre, rejuvenated since it was taken over in 2006. Two regular ales, including the house beer, White Hart Ale (3.8%), are supplemented by three guests (one usually dark) and a selection of bottled Belgian beers. Good-value meals are served weekday lunchtimes. There is a meeting/function room and a large, secluded beer garden. Live music is a feature most Saturdays. The pub supports pool and darts teams, and TV sport is screened. Local CAMRA Pub of the Year 2015. P

Great Clacton

Ship Inn

2 Valley Road, CO15 4AR

12-11 (1am Fri & Sat); 12-10.30 Sun (01255) 475889

shipinnclacton.co.uk

Adnams Ghost Ship; Sharp's Doom Bar; Wells Bombardier H

Completely refurbished in autumn 2013, this pub has been transformed by new landlord and landlady Dave and Donna into a growing community venue, popular with local real ale drinkers. As well as live sport shown at one end of the pub, the other end offers a quieter section for drinkers and diners. Regular entertainment is provided at weekends. Promotions are often available on drinks and food. If it has been a while since you have last been here, a visit is recommended. P

Great Dunmow

Angel & Harp

Church End, CM6 2AD

9am-11 (11.30 Fri & Sat); 9am-10.30 Sun

(01371) 859259 angelandharp.co.uk

Nethergate IPA; 2 changing beers (sourced regionally) H

A refurbished pub and restaurant with a substantial garden area, patio, function room and a large car park. Local ales regularly feature as guest beers alongside the Nethergate IPA. Occasional beer festivals are hosted, usually at Easter and in September. This pub is on the north-east side of Great Dunmow and accommodates families and large parties, although the drinking area around the bar is small. Q P

Hadstock

King's Head

Linton Road, CB21 4NU TL559449

12-2 (not Mon), 5-11 (midnight Fri); 12-midnight Sat; 12-8 Sun (01223) 894550 kingsheadhadstock.co.uk

Mighty Oak Captain Bob; 2 changing beers (sourced regionally) H

This is an old traditional village pub with good locally supplied home-cooked food and excellent beers from nearby breweries. The pub is in the centre of the village, has a garden at the rear and is popular with walkers and cyclists. Pensioners' meals are available Tuesday-Friday lunchtimes, curry night is Wednesday and Feed for a Fiver is on Saturday lunchtimes. A Community Benefit Society (see the Kingsheadfriends website) wants to purchase the pub to prevent its closure. Q P

Halstead

Three Pigeons

6 Mount Hill, CO9 1AA

4.30-11.30; 12-midnight Fri & Sat; 12.30-11 Sun

(01787) 274392

3 changing beers H

A friendly place with wooden floors, beams and a real fire. It comprises two separate drinking areas plus a well-maintained garden which hosts its popular yearly beer festival. There is a large-screen TV for watching football. The pub made its first appearance in the 2015 Guide and offers three varying guest ales, with a focus on local brewers. A traditional meat raffle is held every Sunday. P (88)

Harwich

Alma Inn

25 Kings Head Street, CO12 3EE

12-11 (midnight Fri & Sat) (01255) 318681

almaharwich.co.uk

Adnams Southwold Bitter, Broadside; 3 changing beers H

Vibrant freehold pub that offers a wide choice of Adnams ales, varying guests from near and far, real cider and a huge range of wines and spirits. Fresh food cooked in-house featuring locally sourced and caught produce can be eaten in the bar areas or the dining room. Recently refurbished B&B rooms are available for a stopover in the heart of historic Harwich. Do not miss a visit to this busy pub just a stone's throw from the quayside.
🐎❀🛏◑≹(Town)🍎🚌🐾

New Bell Inn L

Outpart Eastward, CO12 3EN
⏲ 11-3, 7-11 (5-midnight Fri & Sat); 12-11 (12-4, 7-11 winter) Sun ☎ (01255) 503545
Greene King IPA; Mighty Oak Oscar Wilde; 3 changing beers Ⓗ
A true community pub, offering a choice of real ale and wholesome lunchtime food. Always buzzing with conversation, the front bar is the place to enjoy some local banter while the back offers a quieter area for eating and drinking and leads to a modest walled garden. An essential stop on a tour of the historic old town, the pub is a hub for many local events including the Harwich Festival of the Arts and the Sausage Festival. Q❀◐≹(Town)P🚌

Hastingwood

Rainbow & Dove

Hastingwood Road, CM17 9JX
⏲ 11.30-3, 6-11 (not Mon eve); 12.30-3, 6-11 Sat; 12-3.30 Sun ☎ (01279) 415419 🌐 rainbowanddove.com
4 changing beers (sourced locally; often Adnams, Bishop Nick, Mauldons) Ⓗ
The owners bought this venue in 2009 from Punch and have turned it into a thriving pub. Originally a 16th-century farmhouse, it is Grade II-listed with many original beams. It was an inn during the Civil War, used by Parliamentarian troops, and has several small rooms. Mainly a restaurant, there is limited seating for drinkers at weekends. A large barn set in the extensive garden is used for functions and a September beer festival.
Q🐎❀◑P🐾

Hatfield Broad Oak

Cock Inn

High Street, CM22 7HF
⏲ 12-11 (midnight Fri & Sat); 12-10.30 Sun
☎ (01279) 718306 🌐 thecockinn-hatfieldbroadoak.co.uk
Adnams Southwold Bitter; Wells Eagle IPA; Woodforde's Wherry; 1 changing beer (sourced regionally) Ⓗ
Close to Hatfield Forest and popular with walkers, this is a real village local in a picturesque location. The building is a 16th-century coaching inn decorated in a rustic yet elegant style. You can get freshly made food, with good-quality ingredients, locally sourced where possible, and sensibly priced. A second bar has a dartboard and satellite TV; a third room is a quiet area although it is occasionally used by large groups. Q🐎◐P🚌(5,7,347)📶

Hatfield Peverel

Wheatsheaf

The Green, CM3 2JF
⏲ 12-11; 12-9 (10.30 summer) Sun ☎ (01245) 380330
🌐 thewheatsheaf-pub.com
Greene King IPA; 3 changing beers Ⓗ
Traditional country pub with one bar and a restaurant serving locally sourced, home-cooked food. It holds four beer festivals a year in a barn behind the pub, at Easter, early May bank holiday, August bank holiday and Christmas. There is a quiz on the second Monday of every month. These events raise funds for the Helen Rollason cancer charity. A Caravan Club site is adjacent (booking necessary). The pub is a 20-minute walk from Hatfield Peverel station.
Q🐎❀◑♿♣P🚌(73)🐾📶

Henham

Cock Inn L

Church Street, CM22 6AL (1 mile off B1051) TL545286
⏲ 12-3, 5-11; 12-midnight Fri & Sat; 12-10 Sun
☎ (01279) 850347 🌐 thecockinnhenham.co.uk
Greene King IPA; Sharp's Doom Bar; 2 changing beers (sourced nationally) Ⓗ
Traditional village pub opposite the church, with outdoor seating at the front and a garden at the rear. The snug has a large TV where major sporting events are screened, and a large separate dining room is next to the bar. The Saffron Brewery is 100 yards away and one of its beers is normally available here. There is a quiz night the first Monday of the month. A special dish of the day is served weekday lunchtimes (no food Sun eves).
Q🐎❀◑P🚌(7,7a)🐾📶

Herongate Tye

Olde Dog Inn L

129 Billericay Road, CM13 3SD (E of A128) TQ641909
⏲ 11.30 (12 Sat)-11; 12-10.30 Sun ☎ (01277) 810337
🌐 theoldedoginn.co.uk
Crouch Vale Brewers Gold; Greene King Abbot Ⓗ**; 3 changing beers** Ⓖ
This 17th-century weatherboarded inn with traditional decor is family owned and run. It keeps a variety of real ales, with three varying guest beers from countrywide microbreweries, along with more established national brands and its own Olde Dog IPA, brewed locally. A traditional cider is also offered. Food is served at the bar or in the separate restaurant area lunchtimes and evenings. Fish and chips are available to take away.
❀◑♿🍎P

Hockley

White Hart

274 Main Road, Hawkwell, SS5 4NS
⏲ 11-11; 12-10.30 Sun ☎ (01702) 203438
🌐 whitehartockley.co.uk
3 changing beers Ⓗ
A well-established, friendly local dating from the 18th century, facing the village green. The pub is community oriented and supportive of local charities through its quiz nights and music events. Up to three changing guest ales are served. Lunchtime food is available all week, including roasts on Sunday, with evening meals served Tuesday-Saturday. There is a large rear garden with seating and a patio area, plus picnic tables at the front. A beer festival is held every spring.
🐎❀◑≹P🚌(7,8)📶

Horndon-on-the-Hill

Bell Inn

High Road, SS17 8LD (almost opp Woolmarket)
11-11; 12-10.30 Sun (01375) 642463 bell-inn.co.uk
Crouch Vale Brewers Gold; Greene King IPA; Sharp's Doom Bar; 2 changing beers H
Popular 15th-century coaching inn with beamed bars featuring wood panelling and carvings, run by the same family since 1938. Note the hot cross bun collection – a bun has been added every Good Friday for more than 100 years. Three regular beers plus two guests are on tap, including ales from Essex breweries. The award-winning restaurant is open daily, lunchtimes and evenings, and gourmet nights are a highlight (booking is advisable). Accommodation is available in 27 bedrooms.
Q P (374)

Layer Breton

Hare & Hounds

Crayes Green, CO2 0PN
9am-midnight; 10-midnight Sun (01206) 330459
thehareandhound.co.uk
Adnams Southwold Bitter; Greene King IPA, Abbot; 2 changing beers H
Pleasant community pub with separate drinking and dining areas. The bar area has a welcoming real fire and also sells newspapers and some grocery items. Outside is a large car park and an area with camping and accommodation. Three beer festivals are held each year including one for St George's Day, a quiz night on the first Wednesday and live music on the last Friday of each month. A good-value menu of home-cooked food is served, with sausage rolls and Cornish pasties available all day.
P (92)

Layer-de-la-Haye

Layer Fox L

2 Malting Green Road, CO2 0JH
9am-11 (midnight Fri & Sat); 9am-10.30 Sun
(01206) 738723 thelayerfox.co.uk
Red Fox Bitter; 4 changing beers H
On the picturesque village crossroads, this is a large, friendly village pub at the heart of the community, with several comfortable drinking and dining areas on different levels. There are four handpumps delivering a variety of real ales, many of them from local breweries. Quality food is served daily from a varied menu, with curry nights and Sunday roasts; the pub has its own delicatessen counter, paypoint and cash machine. Accommodation is available in the Sleepy Fox B&B chalets next door. Q P (50)

Leigh-on-Sea

Crooked Billet

51 High Street, Old Leigh, SS9 2EP
12-11; 12-10.30 Sun (01702) 480289
Adnams Southwold Bitter; Sharp's Doom Bar; St Austell Nicholson's Pale Ale; 2 changing beers H
Situated in Old Leigh fishing village, overlooking the Thames Estuary, this 16th-century pub has two small bars with bare floorboards and beamed ceilings. The walls are decorated with local village and fishing pictures. Beer sampling evenings take place monthly and a charity beer festival is held yearly. There is a small garden to one side and a larger seating area to the front, which is shared with a seafood merchant. Ten minutes' walk from Leigh Station, and popular in the summer.

Elms L

1060 London Road, SS9 3ND (on A13)
8am-midnight (1am Fri & Sat); 8am-11 Sun
(01702) 474687
Greene King Abbot; Ruddles Best Bitter; 7 changing beers H
Old coaching inn converted by Wetherspoon into a large, open pub decorated with old photos of the local area. Breakfast is available until noon, with main meals and snacks until 11pm. Children are admitted until 9pm. Seven changing guest ales and up to three real ciders are served. There is no music but there are fruit machines and muted TVs. Outside is a hedged front garden and a paved, heated and covered area for smokers. P

Mayflower L

5-6 High Street, Old Leigh, SS9 2EN
11-11; 12-11 Sun (01702) 478535
mayfloweroldleigh.com
Crouch Vale Brewers Gold; George's Cockleboats; 3 changing beers H
Local CAMRA Pub of the Year 2014 and 2015, this single-bar hostelry is unusual in that it adjoins a fish and chip restaurant. The popular menu, unsurprisingly, consists mainly of fish dishes. Two permanent Essex ales, including one from local brewer George's, are served, with up to three guest ales, usually from East Anglia. One wall depicts the Pilgrim Fathers' passenger manifest of those who sailed on the Mayflower. The pub has a drinking/smoking terrace with views across the estuary. P

Little Bromley

Haywain

Bentley Road, CO11 2PL
closed Mon; 12-2.30 (not Tue), 6-10.30 (11 Fri & Sat); 12-5 Sun (01206) 390004 thehaywain.co.uk
Adnams Southwold Bitter; 2 changing beers H
Twice local CAMRA Pub of the Year, this 18th-century roadside pub is the centre of village life and hosts many local events. Adnams Southwold Bitter and two locally-sourced guest ales are the norm. Landlady Dawn supplies diners with generous portions of home-made and largely locally sourced food, including a number of vegetarian dishes. The Sunday roasts are legendary. The rear function room with its own bar is available for private functions.
Q P (2)

Little Thurrock

Ship

16 Dock Road, RM17 6ES (on A126)
12-11 (midnight Fri & Sat); 12-10.30 Sun
(01375) 371121 theshiplittlethurrock.co.uk
Wadworth 6X; 3 changing beers H
Since being taken over in 2011, this pub has been rejuvenated and now offers one regular beer and three guests. A separate restaurant serves good-value food, with a popular carvery on Thursdays and Sundays – booking is recommended for Sunday lunches. A large, secluded, south-facing garden is

available at the rear of the building. Live bands perform three times a month – check out the A-board at the front of the pub.
(22A,66)

Traitors' Gate

40-42 Broadway, RM17 6EW (on A126)
12-11 (midnight Fri & Sat); 12-10.30 Sun
(01375) 372628
Greene King Abbot; 5 changing beers H
This pub was taken over in autumn 2013 and is now the tap for Deverell's Brewery. Six handpumps deliver a rotating selection of Deverell's beers, plus other guest beers, with an emphasis on Essex breweries. Look for the chalkboard above the bar listing current and forthcoming beers. Live music alternates on Thursdays with an open mic night, and there are live bands most Fridays and Saturdays. Local CAMRA Pub of the Year 2014.
(22A,66)

Little Totham

Swan

School Road, CM9 8JL
12-11; 12-10.30 Sun (01621) 331713
Crouch Vale Brewers Gold; Mighty Oak Oscar Wilde, Captain Bob; Red Fox IPA; Sharp's Doom Bar; house beer (by Red Fox); 2 changing beers (sourced nationally) G
Making a welcome return to the Guide after several years' absence is this cosy and friendly cottage-style village pub, which is being restored to its former glory by new, enthusiastic owners. It boasts large inglenook fireplaces, a public bar with a dartboard, an attractive restaurant area and an enclosed front garden. Good locally sourced food is served at lunchtimes. Beer and cider festivals are held in June and December. CAMRA National Pub of the Year 2002 and 2005. P

Little Waltham

White Hart Inn

107 The Street, CM3 3NY
9am-11 (11.30 Fri & Sat); 9am-10.30 Sun
(01245) 360205 whitehartessex.co.uk
4 changing beers H
Village pub revived as a popular gastro-pub, which still welcomes those who just want a drink. Grade II-listed, the outside has been attractively refurbished while a complete renovation has produced a modern, light and airy interior, with two areas reserved for dining. Five handpumps normally supply four beers and one cider, with at least one beer from Adnams and two from local breweries. Meals start at 9am with breakfast.
Q P (70,352)

Littley Green

Compasses

CM3 1BU
12-3, 5.30-11.30 Mon-Wed; 12-11.30 (01245) 362308
compasseslittleygreen.co.uk
Bishop Nick Ridley's Rite; Skinner's Betty Stogs; 2 changing beers G
Formerly Ridley's Brewery tap, this is a picturesque Victorian country pub in a quiet hamlet. A wood-panelled bar has benches around the walls and tiled floor. Beers are drawn direct from casks in the half-cellar. Renowned filled huffers (giant baps) are available lunchtimes and evenings, plus other traditional dishes. There are seats and tables outside and in the large gardens. Five high-quality rooms are available in a modern annexe. CAMRA Essex Pub of the Year 2013.
Q P

Maldon

Carpenters' Arms

33 Gate Street, CM9 5QF
11-11 (01621) 859896
thecarpentersarmsmaldon.co.uk
Adnams Southwold Bitter; Sharp's Special; 4 changing beers (sourced nationally) H
Voted local CAMRA Pub of the Year and Cider Pub of the Year 2015, this welcoming back-street establishment at the top end of historic Maldon has flourished since the current landlord took over in 2013. The pub has a convivial community feel, with thriving darts and dominoes teams. Beer and cider festivals are held annually. It was originally the brewery tap for the now defunct Gray's (Maldon) Brewery around the corner. The Maldon Brewing Company's brewery/shop is close by.
Q

Manningtree

Red Lion

42 South Street, CO11 1BG
12-3, 5-11 (midnight Fri); 12-midnight Sat; 12-11 Sun
(01206) 391880 redlionmanningtree.co.uk
Adnams Southwold Bitter; 2 changing beers H
Up South Street from the Manningtree Ox, this local gem is Manningtree's oldest pub and will be newly refurbished for 2016. Landlord Tom took the pub on in 2012 and this is its second year in the Guide. Three or four real ales, Adnams Southwold and guests, are the norm. No food is served but menus, cutlery and crockery are provided for those ordering from local takeaways. Observer Food Monthly Awards Place to Drink runner-up 2013 and 2014.

Monk Street

Farmhouse Inn

CM6 2NR (off B184, 2 miles S of Thaxted) TL614288
11-11 (midnight Fri & Sat); 11-10.30 Sun
(01371) 830864 farmhouseinn.org
Greene King IPA; 2 changing beers (sourced locally) H
Built in the 16th century, this former Dunmow Brewery pub has been enlarged to incorporate a restaurant and accommodation; the bar is in the original part of the building. The quiet hamlet of Monk Street overlooks the Chelmer Valley, two miles from historic Thaxted. A disused well in the garden supplied the hamlet with water during World War II. The pub has a rear patio, front garden and a top field. Draught cider from Westons is usually sold. Q P (313)

Old Harlow

Crown

40 Market Street, CM17 0AQ
12-11 (midnight Sat); 12-10.30 Sun (01279) 301380
Greene King IPA, Abbot; 4 changing beers (sourced locally; often Greene King) H

A former coaching inn, this 16th-century building retains many original beams. The smaller part of the pub was a grocer's shop until about 20 years ago. When removing the connecting wall, a 17th-century floral wall painting was discovered in the side room and preserved. The Crown is a favourite meeting place for a varied clientele and the large garden is popular in summer. The tenants pride themselves on a TV-free pub and host occasional acoustic afternoons. ◑♿≢(Harlow Mill)🚌🐾🏠 ?

Paglesham

Punch Bowl
Church End, SS4 2DP
🕭 11.30-11 (10 Mon); 12-10 Sun ☎ (01702) 258376
Adnams Southwold Bitter; 3 changing beers Ⓗ
Sixteenth-century building clad in white Essex board with a single low-beamed bar. It has been a pub since the 1800s and is said to have been used by the notorious local smuggler William Blyth. His reputed exploits include drinking two glasses of wine in the Punch Bowl, then eating the glasses (not allowed now!). A small cosy restaurant next to the bar serves excellent, reasonably priced food. Picnic tables are to the front of the pub. Q ➷ ⊛ ◑ P

Purleigh

Bell
The Street, CM3 6QJ
🕭 closed Mon; 11.30-3, 6-11; 12-4, 6-11 Sat; 12-6 Sun
☎ (01621) 828348 ∰ purleighbell.co.uk
Adnams Southwold Bitter; Mighty Oak Captain Bob; 2 changing beers (sourced regionally) Ⓗ
With commanding views of the Blackwater Estuary from its hilltop location, this 14th-century village pub provides a warm welcome. There is a large inglenook fireplace with an open fire, two heavily beamed seating areas and a hop-decorated bar. It has a good reputation locally for its excellent food. The pub hosts a wide range of activities for the local community such as movie nights, book clubs, art exhibitions and darts matches. The Prince of Wales visited in 2014. Q ⊛ ◑ ♣ P 🐾 ?

Ramsden Heath

Fox & Hounds
Church Road, CM11 1PW
🕭 12-11 ☎ (01268) 711625
5 changing beers Ⓗ
Large community local with a friendly atmosphere. A real fire during winter gives added warmth to the welcome. There are no permanent beers, but up to five changing guest ales, often from Mighty Oak and Turners, with an emphasis on smaller breweries. It has stillage for two beers on gravity. A huge garden at the rear is popular during the summer, and is used for occasional beer festivals. Sporting events are shown on TV. ➷ ⊛ P 🐾 ?

Rayleigh

Roebuck
138 High Street, SS6 7BU
🕭 9am-midnight (1am Fri & Sat) ☎ (01268) 748430
Fuller's London Pride; Greene King Abbot; Ruddles Best Bitter; 5 changing beers Ⓗ
Friendly Wetherspoon pub in the High Street with a varied selection of guest ales from around the UK – as well as Westons Mulled and Wyld Wood cider on

draught. Families are welcome in a sectioned-off area. Breakfast is served 8am-midday, the main menu 9am-11pm. There are patio areas to the front and side for smoking and drinking, with heaters for when it gets cold.
➷ ⊛ ◑ ≢ ♿ 🚌 (1,8,9) ?

Ridgewell

White Horse Inn Ⓛ
Mill Road, CO9 4SG (on A1017) TL735408
🕭 12-11 (5 Mon & Tue) ☎ (01440) 785532
∰ ridgewellwhitehorse.com
Mighty Oak Oscar Wilde; 3 changing beers (sourced nationally) Ⓖ
Set in a pretty village which was home to the American 381st Heavy Bomb Group during WWII. At least one dark beer is always available here, and annual beer festivals are held in early March and early August on the patio behind the pub. As well as a choice of excellent real ale and food, the pub offers 4-star accommodation and an interesting selection of good-quality wines to suit a variety of tastes. Q ➷ ⊛ 🏠 ◑ ♿ ♣ P 🚌 (1,89B,89X) 🐾 ?

Rochford

Golden Lion Ⓛ
35 North Street, SS4 1AB
🕭 11-midnight (1am Fri & Sat) ☎ (01702) 545487
∰ goldenlionrochford.co.uk
Adnams Southwold Bitter; Greene King Abbot; Mighty Oak Maldon Gold; 3 changing beers Ⓗ
This weatherboarded free house is a long-standing Guide entry within the town-centre conservation area. The small, 16th-century, traditional Essex building features stained-glass windows and a fireplace with a logburner. Seven ales are always available including three changing guests, one usually a dark beer, from local micros. Three ciders are also served, one from Essex. There is a pretty patio garden to the rear with a vintage petrol pump water feature. Licensed until 2am, it holds two beer festivals each year. ⊛ ≢ ♣ 🚌 🚌 (7,8,60) 🐾

Rowhedge

Olde Albion
High Street, CO5 7ES
🕭 12-3 (not Mon), 5-11; 12-11 Thu-Sat; 12-10.30 Sun
☎ (01206) 728972 ∰ yeoldealbion.co.uk
4 changing beers Ⓗ
Friendly, one-bar, split-level pub on Rowhedge waterfront. The lower area has bench seating and a logburner, the higher bar area has more seating and tables; sailing artefacts decorate the pub throughout. There is a changing range of four quality real ales and the pub hosts annual beer festivals on St George's Day, Halloween, and to coincide with the Rowhedge Regatta. Riverside seating offers picturesque views along the Colne towards Wivenhoe. ⊛ ♣ ● 🚌 (66) 🐾

Saffron Walden

King's Arms
10 Market Hill, CB10 1HQ
🕭 12-midnight (11 Mon; 12.30am Fri & Sat); 12-11 Sun
☎ (01799) 522768 ∰ thekingsarmssaffronwalden.co.uk
Adnams Broadside; Oakham JHB; Sharp's Doom Bar; Woodforde's Wherry; 1 changing beer (sourced nationally) Ⓗ

Venerable multi-roomed pub, just off the market square (market days are Tuesday and Saturday). Five handpumps feature four regular beers and one guest, which is often a mild in winter. There is live music at weekends, acoustic music on Thursdays and a monthly quiz. Log fires are welcoming in winter and there is a pleasant patio for alfresco dining and drinking in summer. Food is served lunchtimes and some evenings. Q⚭❀◐●P⊟❦ᯤ

Old English Gentleman

11 Gold Street, CB10 1EJ (E of B184/B1052 jct)
⌚ 11-midnight (11 Mon; 1am Fri & Sat); 11-11 Sun
☎ (01799) 523595 ⊕ oldenglishgentleman.com
Adnams Southwold Bitter; Woodforde's Wherry; 2 changing beers (sourced nationally) 🄷
An 18th-century town-centre pub with log fires and a welcoming atmosphere. It serves a selection of guest ales and an extensive menu of bar food and sandwiches. Traditional roasts and chef's specials are available on Sunday in the bar and dining area, where works of art are displayed. There is a heated patio at the rear. Saffron Walden is busy on Tuesday and Saturday market days. ⚭❀◐⊟❦ᯤ

South Benfleet

South Benfleet Social Club 𝕃

8 Vicarage Hill, SS7 1PB
⌚ 12-11 (midnight Fri & Sat) ☎ (01268) 206159
3 changing beers 🄷
All members of the family are welcome at this friendly and spacious club. CAMRA members just need to show their membership card or a copy of this Guide for entry. Two beer festivals are held each year, and other events include a family day and barbecues in summer, a quiz night on Thursdays and pool on Tuesdays. Live music plays most Saturday evenings, a function room is available, and there is BT Vision/Sky TV for football and other sports. Bar snacks are available all day. ⚭❀◐♿⇌(Benfleet)●P⊟ᯤ

Southend-on-Sea

Last Post 𝕃

Weston Road, SS1 1AS
⌚ 8am-midnight (1am Fri & Sat) ☎ (01702) 431682
Greene King Abbot; Ruddles Best Bitter; Sharp's Doom Bar; 7 changing beers 🄷
Large Wetherspoon pub converted from the old post office, close to two railway stations and the bus station. There are two bars serving up to seven changing real ales and three permanent ones. Local breweries often represented are George's and Wibblers. Up to six real ciders are on sale – the pub was local CAMRA Cider Pub of the Year 2015. There are plans for guest rooms and a new outside drinking area. Q⚭◐◑♿⇌(Central/Victoria)●⊟ᯤ

Olde Trout Tavern 𝕃

56 London Road, SS1 1NX
⌚ 11-11; 12-11 Sun ☎ (01702) 337000
⊕ theoldtrout.webs.com
George's Trout Ale; 3 changing beers 🄷
This modern town hostelry is within walking distance of Southend High Street and both mainline railway stations. The house beer, George's Trout Ale, is from the local brewery. Two guest ales are served (three at weekends and on Southend United match days), together with Westons Rosie's Pig on draught. Hot meals and snacks are available lunchtimes. A quiz night is held fortnightly on Sundays. An interesting selection of clocks adorns the walls. Local CAMRA Pub of the Year 2013. Q◐⇌(Victoria/Central)●⊟ᯤ

Southminster

Station Arms

39 Station Road, CM0 7EW
⌚ 12-2.30, 6 (5.30 Fri)-11; 2-11 Sat; 12-4, 7-10.30 Sun
☎ (01621) 772225 ⊕ thestationarms.co.uk
Adnams Southwold Bitter; 4 changing beers (sourced locally) 🄷
This friendly weatherboarded pub, with a cosy interior and open fire in winter, has appeared in every edition of the Guide for a quarter of a century. The sheltered courtyard is a great place to relax in fine weather. Westons Rosie's Pig cider is served. Live music includes a monthly folk club plus a blues night every third Saturday of the month. Occasional mini beer festivals are held, often with a barbecue, in the courtyard. Q❀⇌♣●⊟

Stanford-le-Hope

Rising Sun 𝕃

Church Hill, SS17 0EU (opp church and near A1014)
⌚ 3-10.30 Mon; 12-midnight (10.30 Tue; 11 Wed; 11.30 Thu); 11-10.30 Sun ☎ (01375) 671097
4 changing beers 🄷
Much-improved two-bar town pub in the shadow of the church. The four guest beers are mainly from independent breweries, including LocAles, and up to three ciders or perries are stocked. Freshly prepared, locally sourced Sunday lunches are served 12-4.30pm in the back bar. Beer festivals are held in spring, summer and winter. Live music takes place regularly and a back bar is available for private functions. Local CAMRA Pub of the Year 2013. ❀◐⇌♣●P⊟(100,200,374)ᯤ

Stansted Mountfitchet

Rose & Crown

31 Bentfield Green, CM24 8HX (mile W of B1383) TL505256
⌚ closed Mon; 6-11 Tue; 12-3, 6-11 Wed & Thu; 12-11 Fri & Sat; 12-9 Sun ☎ (01279) 812107
3 changing beers (sourced nationally) 🄷
Family-run Victorian pub near a duckpond, on the edge of a small hamlet. This free house has been modernised to provide one large bar but retains the atmosphere of a village inn and is popular with locals. Home-cooked food made from locally sourced produce is served (no meals Sunday eve). Guest beers are often from local breweries. The smoking area is covered and heated. Children and dogs welcome. ⚭❀◐◑♣P⊟(7,7a)❦ᯤ

Stapleford Tawney

Moletrap

Tawney Common, CM16 7PU TL500013
⌚ 11.30-2.30, 6-11; 12-3, 7-10.30 Sun ☎ (01992) 522394
⊕ themoletrap.co.uk
Fuller's London Pride; 3 changing beers 🄷
A 200-year-old pub in a remote location in beautiful countryside. It offers a wide selection of varying guest ales, usually including one dark beer, and serves good-value home-cooked food (no food Sun or Mon eves). There is a cosy bar with a real fire. Well-behaved children are welcome; dogs at

the landlord's discretion. It has plenty of outside seating and an extensive beer garden with amazing views of the countryside. Though it can be difficult to locate, it is well worth the effort.
Q P

Stebbing

White Hart

High Street, CM6 3SQ

11-3, 5-11; 11-11 Sat; 12-10.30 Sun (01371) 856383
hartofstebbingbrewery.co.uk

Hart of Stebbing Hart IPA; Wells Eagle IPA; 1 changing beer (sourced nationally)

A 15th-century timbered inn in a picturesque village, featuring exposed beams, an open fire, eclectic collections from chamber pots to cigarette cards, an old red post box on an interior wall, and a section of exposed lath and plaster wall behind a glass screen. The Hart of Stebbing microbrewery is in the garage, producing beers currently only available here and at beer festivals. Good-value food is served daily. There is a patio and a covered, heated gazebo. Q P (16)

Steeple Bumpstead

Fox & Hounds

3 Chapel Street, CB9 7DQ

12-3, 5-11; 12-midnight Fri & Sat; 12-11 Sun
(01440) 731810 foxinsteeple.co.uk

Greene King IPA; 3 changing beers (sourced nationally)

A 500-year-old pub with a main bar warmed by an open fire, two other rooms used mainly for dining and a rear courtyard garden. Four beers are on offer from local and national breweries. The locally-sourced food ranges from bar snacks to a full à la carte menu. Live music plays on occasional Friday evenings, and quiz nights feature on some Sundays. Reduced-price beer and wine and free cheese are on offer on Wednesday evenings, with steak nights on Thursdays.
Q P (18)

Stock

Hoop

High Street, CM4 9BD

11-11; 12-10.30 Sun (01277) 841137 thehoop.co.uk

Adnams Southwold Bitter; 3 changing beers

This 450-year-old weatherboarded inn welcomes drinkers and diners alike. The heavily-beamed pub, with two fires, has lots of character and has appeared in this Guide for over 20 years. One of the three guest beers is often a local Essex brew, and a cider or perry is usually available. Home-made food is served in the bar lunchtimes and evenings weekdays, 12-9.30pm Saturday and 12-5pm Sunday. A quiz is held monthly and a popular beer festival takes place over a May bank holiday.
Q (100)

Stow Maries

Prince of Wales

Woodham Road, CM3 6SA

11-11 (midnight Fri & Sat); 12-10.30 Sun
(01621) 828971 prince-stowmaries.net

Hop Back Summer Lightning; Mighty Oak Captain Bob; 3 changing beers (sourced nationally)

This legendary weatherboarded pub boasts several characterful drinking areas, all with real fires, and an old bread oven used for baking pizzas on Thursday nights in the winter. There is an extensive garden, courtyard and terrace for outside drinking. Good food using local produce is served. A major comedy event with stars from the Edinburgh Fringe is held on the last Saturday in July, and a firework extravaganza takes place on the last Saturday in October. Q P (593)

Tollesbury

King's Head

1 High Street, CM9 8RG

12-11 (midnight Fri & Sat); 12-10.30 Sun
(01621) 869203

Bishop Nick Ridley's Rite; house beer (by Colchester); 3 changing beers (sourced nationally)

The owner of this thriving free house has been here for a quarter of a century. Pictures reflecting village history adorn the walls. There are lots of community connections, from providing hospitality for the Tollesbury v East Coast Old Gaffers' small boat event to the Tollesbury Cake Off. The pub also hosts darts and pool teams, poker and quizzes on Tuesday and Wednesday nights and live music on the second Tuesday of the month. Food is available Friday lunchtimes only. Q P

Toppesfield

Green Man

Church Lane, CO9 4DR

4-midnight; 12-1am Fri & Sat; 12-midnight Sun
(01787) 237418 thegreenmantoppesfield.co.uk

Bishop Nick Ridley's Rite; Greene King IPA; 2 changing beers (sourced regionally)

Village community-owned pub now run by locals. Darts and pool are available in the public bar and there are beer festivals and events throughout the year. Special meals are served on Thursday evenings; Sunday lunches need to be booked as they are popular. There are plans to set up a community-owned brewery at the pub, to be called Pumphouse Brewery, which will be one of the first in the UK to be owned and run by a local community. Q P

Waltham Abbey

Woodbine Inn

Honey Lane, EN9 3QT

11.30-11 (2am Fri & Sat); 11.30-10.30 Sun
(01992) 713050 thewoodbine.co.uk

Dominion Woodbine Racer; Greene King Abbot; Mighty Oak Captain Bob; 3 changing beers (sourced regionally)

Local CAMRA Pub of the Year 2015 and Cider Pub of the Year 2014. Situated in Epping Forest and close to junction 26 of the M25, the pub is ideally located. The new restaurant is a great addition, though the pub concentrates on real ale. Up to six local ciders are normally on sale. It caters for many locals and walkers. Guest beers are from local breweries, including the house beer. The food is home-made from local suppliers, with home-cooked ham and sausages as specialities. The Ale Sampling Society meets here monthly.
P (250,251)

Weeley Heath

White Hart 🏆

Clacton Road, CO16 9ED (on B1441)

⏲ 12-2.30, 4-11 (10 Mon); 12-11 Fri & Sat; 12-10.30 Sun

☎ (01255) 830384

2 changing beers Ⓗ

A typical community-focused local, consistently serving good-quality beer, the White Hart is a regular in the Guide. It hosts pool and darts teams and has its own Sunday league football team. A popular sportsman's pub, it screens Sky TV and BT Sport, with different events shown on various TV screens. It also has a real ale club. The garden has a covered patio for smokers. Local CAMRA Pub of the Year 2015. ❀▲♣●P🚌(2,76)

Wendens Ambo

Bell

Royston Road, CB11 4JY (on B1039)

⏲ 5-10 Mon; 11.30 (12 Tue)-2.30, 5-10.30; 12-11 Fri & Sat; 12-10.30 Sun ☎ (01799) 540382

Oakham JHB; Woodforde's Wherry; 2 changing beers (sourced nationally) Ⓗ

Country pub in a picturesque village, serving traditional, locally sourced pub food. A chalkboard features forthcoming guest ales. There is a large garden, a terrace with seating and tables, a pétanque pitch and children's play apparatus. A charity fundraising event is held with a beer festival over the summer bank holiday weekend. Dogs, walkers and cyclists are welcome here. Q🐴❀◐◑⇌(Audley End)●P🚌(59,301)🐾

Widdington

Fleur de Lys

High Street, CB11 3SG TL538316

⏲ 12-3 (not Mon), 6-11; 12-11.30 Fri & Sat; 12-10.30 Sun

☎ (01799) 543280 🌐 thefleurdelys.co.uk

Adnams Southwold Bitter; Sharp's Doom Bar; 2 changing beers (sourced nationally) Ⓗ

Rumours of a ghost abound at this welcoming 400-year-old village local, which boasts a large open fireplace and beams. The games room has a pool table, foosball table and dartboard. This was the first pub to be saved from closure by the North-West Essex branch of CAMRA after the branch's formation. Quality meals are offered made with fresh local ingredients. The source of the River Cam and Prior's Hall Barn are both nearby. Q❀◐◑♿♣P🚌(301)🐾

Witham

Battesford Court

100-102 Newland Street, CM8 1AH

⏲ 8am-11 ☎ (01376) 504080

Greene King Abbot; Ruddles Best Bitter; 6 changing beers Ⓗ

Large Wetherspoon conversion of a former hotel. The 16th-century building was previously the courthouse of the manor of Battesford. It has distinct areas, with wood panelling and oak beams, including a family area. Four to six guest beers are served, including something local, usually from Nethergate or Shalford, plus up to four ciders and perries from Westons, Sandford Orchard and Gwynt y Ddraig. The usual Wetherspoon's food offering is available. Q🐴❀◐◑♿●P🚌(71,90,131)📶

Wivenhoe

Black Buoy

Black Buoy Hill, CO7 9BS

⏲ 11-11; 12-10.30 Sun ☎ (01206) 822425

🌐 blackbuoy.co.uk

Adnams Southwold Bitter; Colchester No. 1; 5 changing beers Ⓗ

Local CAMRA Rural Pub of the Year winner, this is a community-owned hostelry with bar, lounge and restaurant areas. The main bar area has high-level seating and an open fire. It serves six real ales, wines and spirits. The restaurant area has views to the River Colne. The pub hosts nights for local musicians and an open mic night. There is a large garden to the rear and secure bike racks next to the car park. 🐴❀🛏◐◑⇌P🚌(62)🐾📶

Horse & Groom

55 The Cross, CO7 9QL

⏲ 10.30-3, 5.30 (6 Sat)-11; 12-4.30, 7-11 Sun

☎ (01206) 824928

Adnams Southwold Bitter, Broadside; 2 changing beers Ⓗ

Friendly Adnams local with separate saloon and public bar areas. The landlord and landlady have been here for over 25 years. A selection of books is available to browse with your pint. There is a well-used dartboard and the pub hosts five teams. A varied menu of home-made food is served lunchtimes (not Sun) including (unusually) a Thursday roast. There is a large garden to the rear, and a frequent bus service to and from Colchester passes the door. Q🐴❀◐◑♣P🚌🐾

Woodham Mortimer

Hurdlemakers Arms

Post Office Road, CM9 6ST

⏲ 12-11; 12-9 Sun ☎ (01245) 225169

🌐 hurdlemakersarms.co.uk

5 changing beers (sourced locally) Ⓗ

A 400-year-old, traditional, friendly Gray's country pub with a good reputation for well-kept local ales and excellent home-cooked food, served daily. Three ciders including Wibblers Dengie Dry and a perry are available. Various monthly events are held including quiz nights. It boasts a spacious beer garden with a barbecue, children's play area, a small barn and a marquee for hire. The pub is popular with walkers, cyclists, locals and families. An annual beer festival is held in June. 🐴❀◐◑♿♣●P🚏🚌🐾📶

Writtle

Wheatsheaf

70 The Green, CM1 3DU

⏲ 11-11.30 (midnight Fri & Sat); 12-11 Sun

☎ (01245) 420672

Adnams Southwold Bitter; Camerons Strongarm; Maldon Drop of Nelson's Blood Ⓗ**; Mighty Oak Oscar Wilde** Ⓖ**, Maldon Gold; Wibblers Dengie IPA** Ⓗ**; 2 changing beers** Ⓖ

Good old-fashioned village pub built in 1813 with a small public bar, an equally compact lounge and a covered patio by the road. It is a long-time favourite of the local CAMRA branch. The atmosphere is generally quiet, with the TV switched on only for occasional sporting events. Traditional pub grub is served Tuesday-Saturday lunchtimes. Note the old Gray's sign in the public bar. Q◐♣P🚌(45)

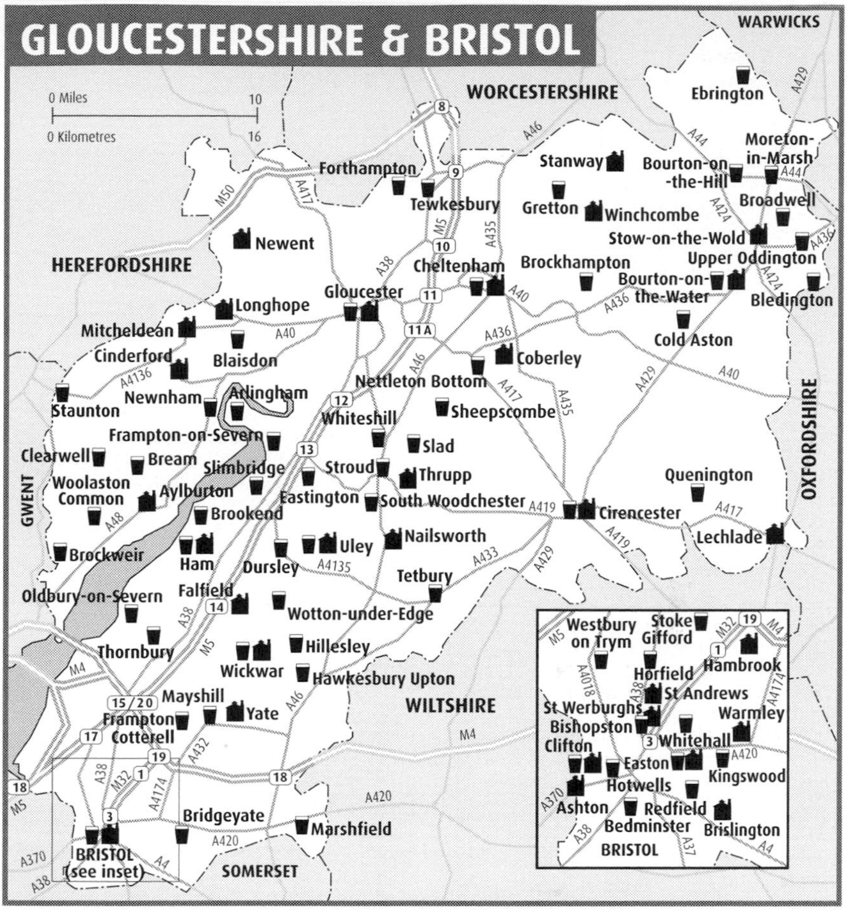

Arlingham

Red Lion 🄻

High Street, GL2 7JH

⏲ 12-3 (not Mon), 6-11; 12-11.30 Fri & Sat

☎ (01452) 740700 🌐 redlionarlingham.co.uk

Uley Bitter; 3 changing beers 🄷

This community hub was reopened in November 2013 after the locals purchased it at auction from Enterprise. Some elements of the lovely building date from the 17th century. It has gained a name for its home-cooked meals, with an extensive choice of dishes. An extra guest ale (not LocAle) is usually available at busier times. A wonderful starting point for circular walks around the village – look for the attractive tiled pub sign. Gloucester CAMRA rural Pub of the Year 2015.

Q🛝❀◐◑⛺♣P🐾📶

Blaisdon

Red Hart 🄻

GL17 0AH (centre of village, signed from A4136 E of Longhope or N of A48)

⏲ 12-3, 6-11; 12-3, 7-11 Sun ☎ (01452) 830477

🌐 redhartinn.co.uk

Young's Bitter; 3 changing beers 🄷

In a charming village, this lovely old building has flagstones in the bar, a cracking fireplace and a plethora of memorabilia. Guest ales are often LocAle, with a local cider or perry always available from Severn Cider. The restaurant extension means that this pub is food-oriented at busy times, so be prepared to mix it with a rack of lamb, not to mention free-range children, if dining encroaches into the bar area. There is a lovely large garden for families. 🛝❀◐◑♿⛺♣🍎P🐾

Bledington

King's Head 🄻

The Green, OX7 6XQ (off B4450 on village green)

⏲ 12-3, 6-11 ☎ (01608) 658365 🌐 kingsheadinn.net

Brakspear Oxford Gold; Butcombe Adam Henson's Rare Breed; Hook Norton 12 Days 🄷

Delightful, 16th-century, stone-built inn overlooking the village green. The pub has original old beams, an open inglenook log fire and high-back settles. This free house, with 12 comfortable letting rooms, is famous for its wide range of ale and food. The guest beers are selected from local brewers in Gloucestershire and Oxfordshire. Bledington is about four miles from Stow-on-the-Wold. There are good local walks to nearby villages, with Kingham station close by. CAMRA award winner and again finalist in 2015 Pub of the Year. Q🛝❀🛏◐◑⇌(Kingham)♣P

Bourton-on-the-Hill

Horse & Groom

GL56 9AQ (on A44 at top of hill)
11-2.30, 6.30-11 ☎ (01386) 700413
horseandgroom.info
Goff's Jouster; Prescott Hill Climb H
Grade II-listed Georgian stone inn, family-run since 2005. It serves three local real ales – Goff's and two guests – alongside award-winning contemporary food in an attractive dining area. The light and airy bar with an open fire has been tastefully modernised. Ideal for visits to nearby Moreton-in-Marsh and Batsford Arboretum, the pub has five en-suite rooms. The delightful sheltered garden has plenty of seating and stunning views over the Cotswold countryside. CAMRA runner-up Pub of the Year 2015. P

Bourton-on-the-Water

Mousetrap Inn

Lansdowne, GL54 2AR (300yds W of village centre)
11.30-3, 6-11; 12-3, 6-11 Sun ☎ (01451) 820579
mousetrap-inn.co.uk
Butcombe Adam Henson's Rare Breed; Hook Norton Old Hooky; Stroud Budding H
Attractive, traditional Cotswold-stone free house run by the same family for several years, in the quieter Landsdowne part of Bourton but convenient for the centre. It has a large dining area with a feature fireplace. Three regular local beers are on offer, alongside friendly service and good-value home-cooked meals. A patio area in front of the pub with tables and hanging baskets provides a suntrap in the summer. This popular pub has 10 good-value en-suite rooms.
Q P (801,855)

Bream

Rising Sun

High Street, GL15 6JF (opp war memorial)
SO6032305812
4.30 (6 Mon)-midnight; 12-midnight Sat; 12-3, 6.30-midnight Sun ☎ (01594) 564555
Butcombe Bitter; St Austell Tribute; 1 changing beer H
This spacious 300-year-old stone-built pub with spectacular views of the forest is an interesting visit. The building houses a friendly main bar with overspill into adjoining rooms including a large function room and separate bar. Food can be served by arrangement. The enclosed garden with seating is pleasant in the summer. With accommodation, a central forest location and a warm welcome for all, this is a popular base for visitors. P (23)

Bridgeyate

Hollybush

29 Bath Road, BS30 5JP
12-11; 12-10.30 Sun ☎ (0117) 239 5879
Bath Ales Gem; 4 changing beers H
This 19th-century roadside inn on the A4175 between Bridgeyate and Oldland Common reopened in March 2014 after being closed for several years. Home-cooked local seasonal produce is produced on-site in an open-plan kitchen in one of the two dining areas. The central bar has six handpumps dispensing four guest ales, including some from local breweries such as Bath Ales, and a changing real cider from Orchard Pig. At the front of the pub is a pleasant patio area.
Q P (35,42)

Bristol

Bank Tavern

8 John Street, BS1 2HR (take the lane next to the arcade on All Saints St)
12-midnight (1am Thu-Sat) ☎ (0117) 930 4691
banktavern.com
4 changing beers H
Popular, compact, one-bar pub, in the city centre yet well hidden away. The four beers are often from microbrewers from the South-West and can be of any style. Two real ciders change constantly. Quirky humour and many varied events define the pub, a great alternative to the more predictable establishments all around. Live music features on Wednesdays and Thursdays. Look out for the summer fête and Christmas party. Quality food is served 12-4pm (booking advisable Sunday).
(40,41,42)

Barley Mow

39 Barton Road, BS2 0LF (400yds from rear exit of Temple Meads station over footbridge)
12-11 (11.30 Fri & Sat); 12-10 Sun ☎ (0117) 930 4709
barleymowbristol.com
8 changing beers (often Bristol Beer Factory) H
Completely refurbished in early 2013 and now relaunched as Bristol Beer Factory's flagship pub.

REAL ALE BREWERIES

Arbor Bristol: Easton
Ashley Down Bristol: St Andrews
Bath Bristol: Warmley
Battledown Cheltenham
Bespoke Mitcheldean
Brewhouse & Kitchen Bristol: Clifton (NEW)
Bristol Beer Factory Bristol: Ashton
Ciren Cirencester
Combined Brewers Falfield (NEW)
Corinium Cirencester
Cotswold Bourton-on-the-Water
Cotswold Lion Coberley
Donnington Stow-on-the-Wold
Force Cirencester
Freeminer Cinderford
Gloucester Gloucester
Goff's Winchcombe
Great Western Bristol: Hambrook
Halfpenny Lechlade
Hillside Longhope
Incredible Bristol: Brislington (NEW)
Moor Bristol
Nailsworth Nailsworth
New Bristol Bristol
Prescott Cheltenham
Rocket Science Yate
Stanway Stanway
Stroud Thrupp
Terrace Aylburton
Tiley's Ham (NEW)
Towles' Bristol: Easton
Uley Uley
Whittingtons Newent
Wickwar Wickwar
Wiper and True Bristol: St Werburghs
Zerodegrees Bristol

Eight handpulls offer two from the brewery plus six different guests from only the highest-quality UK breweries. There is also an extensive bottled beer list and regular beer-related events are hosted. A small range of frequently changing quality meals is available lunchtimes and evenings, with Sunday roasts 12-5pm. A short walk from Temple Meads station. ❀◑◐⇌(Temple Meads)●⊟(506)🐾ᯤ

Beer Emporium

13-15 Kings Street, BS1 4EF

✪ 4 (12 Fri)-2am; 11-2am Sat; 12-midnight Sun

☎ (0117) 379 0333 ⊕ thebeeremporium.net

12 changing beers Ⓗ

A beer cellar bar opened in July 2013 and set in three tunnels – one containing the bar and seating, one for seating only, and the third housing the kitchens. A lift makes it all accessible. Up to 12 changing real ales are served plus keg beers and a wide range of world bottled beers – a new bottle shop has opened just inside the entrance. Regular beer-related events feature. Quality food is offered all day plus brunch at weekends. ◑◐♿⊟ᯤ

Bell

16-18 Hillgrove Street, BS2 8JT (just off Jamaica St)

✪ 12-midnight (1am Fri); 3-1am Sat; 1-midnight Sun

☎ (0117) 909 6612 ⊕ bell.butcombe.com

Butcombe Bitter, Gold; Fuller's London Pride; 1 changing beer (often Butcombe) Ⓗ

Pleasant, eclectic, two-roomed pub where DJs often spin their discs from 10pm in the back room. Friday evenings attract drinkers on their way to nearby clubs, while local workers are regular customers for the lunchtime food. Sunday lunches (served 1-4pm) are popular too. A surprising feature is the pleasant rear garden with a patio, which is heated in colder weather. Local art on the wood-panelled walls adds a bohemian feel. There is a dartboard in the back room.
❀◑⇌(Montpelier)⊟(5,12,70)🐾ᯤ

Bridge Inn

16 Passage Street, BS2 0JF

✪ 12-11 (1am Fri & Sat); 2-11 Sun ☎ (0117) 929 0942

Dark Star Hophead, American Pale Ale; 2 changing beers Ⓗ

Tiny pub by the river bridge and not too far from the station, yet only a short walk from the city centre. Music industry memorabilia features, along with a selection of board games, occasional live music and free Wi-Fi. Guest beers are adventurous, with two from high-quality microbreweries. Lunch is served 12-3pm weekdays only. Outside tables increase capacity in good weather. It now stocks a range of UK and US bottled beers plus around 50 Scottish single malt whiskies.
❀◑⇌(Temple Meads)♣⊟🐾ᯤ

Cornubia

142 Temple Street, BS1 6EN

✪ 11-11.30; 12-8 Sun (closed Sun winter)

☎ (0117) 925 4415 ⊕ thecornubia.co.uk

8 changing beers Ⓗ

A cosy small pub with two linked rooms adorned with much patriotic memorabilia as well as countless pumpclips. Eight real ales are on the bar, plus changing ciders in spring and summer. A small but interesting range of speciality bottled beers is also stocked. You can enjoy a large number of board games and books here. Live blues takes place on Thursday evenings, when anyone can come along and jam, and live bands on some Saturdays. The outside area with a boules piste has been enclosed, developed and expanded in recent years. ❀⇌(Temple Meads)♣●⊟(1,2,50)🐾ᯤ

Gryphon

41 Colston Street, BS1 5AP

✪ 1 (3 Mon)-11; 1-1am Fri & Sat; 6-11 Sun ☎ 07894 239567

6 changing beers Ⓗ

A shrine to dark beer and great rock/heavy metal music. Posters, guitars and many pumpclips adorn the walls. Triangular in shape, due to its corner plot, and just a few yards uphill from the Colston Hall, it has six handpumps dispensing rapidly changing brews, many dark and often strong. Live bands sometimes play upstairs and beer festivals are in March and September. Food is served evenings Tuesday-Saturday. It may open earlier on Sundays. Children and dogs are admitted at the licensee's discretion. ◑◐⊟🐾ᯤ

Hillgrove Porter Stores

53 Hillgrove Street North, BS2 8LT

✪ 4-midnight (1am Fri); 2-1am Sat; 2-midnight Sun

☎ (0117) 924 9818

Dawkins Bristol Blonde; 7 changing beers (often Dawkins) Ⓗ

The first of the Dawkins Taverns, this is the brainchild of a local entrepreneur who also bought Matthews Brewery in 2009. The interior is horseshoe-shaped, with a lounge area hidden behind the bar, and a pleasant patio. An excellent community pub, it usually dispenses up to seven guest ales, including dark beers and rare styles, plus up to two changing traditional ciders. There are occasional beer festivals. Live music features on the first and third Wednesday and the second Thursday of each month.
❀◐⇌(Montpelier)●⊟(5,12,70)🐾

No.1 Harbourside

1 Canons Road, BS1 5UH

✪ 10-midnight (11 Mon; 1am Fri & Sat); 10-11 Sun

☎ (0117) 929 1100 ⊕ no1harbourside.co.uk

5 changing beers (often Bristol Beer Factory, Arbor) Ⓗ

Refurbished pub/diner on the covered walkway on the quayside of the floating harbour. With early opening, it is ideal for morning coffee, snacking or a cheeky early beer. Five handpumps usually feature two Bristol Beer Factory beers and three guests, many from Arbor, supplemented by a good selection of bottled beers and changing ciders. Food is served all day and there are some tables outside. Free live music takes place late evenings Wednesday to Saturday. ❀◑◐♿●⊟ᯤ

Seven Stars

1 Thomas Lane, BS1 6JG (just off Victoria St)

✪ 12-11; 12-10.30 Sun ☎ (0117) 927 2845 ⊕ 7stars.co.uk

8 changing beers Ⓗ

Many who live miles away call this small free house their local. It has a pool table, a rock-oriented jukebox and outdoor seating. Eight pumps dispense a full range of styles and strengths, plus ciders and perries. Quality acoustic acts play on weekend afternoons. Beeriodicals are held on the first Monday to Thursday of every month, with 20 beers from a different county each time. Anti-slavery campaigner Thomas Clarkson used this establishment as a base during his research into the trade. ❀⇌(Temple Meads)♣●⊟(1,2,51)🐾ᯤ

Small Bar

31 King Street, BS1 4DZ

🕐 12-12.30am (1am Fri & Sat); 12-midnight Sun ☎ 07592 203470 🌐 thebigbeerco.com/small-bar
8 changing beers Ⓗ
Opened in late 2013, this bar specialises in great beer – up to eight on cask, and a huge bottle list. Not really small, it has three rooms – the upstairs one features comfy sofas and a small library. The small brew kit on-site is used to test brew recipes for Left Hand Giant brewery, which are then brewed elsewhere. Quality food is available most times when open. Unusually, the beer is served in third, half or two-thirds of a pint measures only.
Q❀◑🍎🚌🐾📶

Three Tuns
78 St George's Road, BS1 5UR (300yds from Bristol Cathedral towards Hotwells)
🕐 12-11 (midnight Fri & Sat); 12-10.30 Sun
☎ (0117) 907 0690 🌐 the3tuns.com
7 changing beers (often Arbor) Ⓗ
Though no longer in the direct control of Arbor Ales, the pub still showcases many of its beers. This independent inn has seven pumps dispensing the full range of beer styles, with two or three from Arbor and the rest from top-rated British brewers, plus many unusual bottled beers and several ciders. The L-shaped interior has scrubbed wooden tables and mixed seating, plus a covered, heated rear patio. A small range of high-quality bar food is served. It hosts occasional beer festivals.
❀🍎🚌🐾📶

Volunteer Tavern
9 New Street, BS2 9DX (close to Cabot Circus car park)
🕐 12-11 (midnight Fri & Sat) ☎ (0117) 955 8498
🌐 volunteertavern.co.uk
8 changing beers Ⓗ
Tucked away in a side street, the Volunteer is close to Cabot Circus shops and convenient for Old Market and its bus interchange. Dating from 1670 and listed, it reopened in 2011 and has quickly become popular on the local scene. It always serves eight changing beers including dark brews, plus two changing ciders. Regular beer festivals, with 25-plus ales, take place, as do live music events. It has a large enclosed paved garden. Food is served every day and is hugely popular on Sundays (book ahead). ❀◑🍎🚌🐾📶

Bristol: Bedminster

Hare
51 North Street, BS3 1EN
🕐 5-11; 4-midnight Fri; 3-midnight Sat; 3-11 Sun
☎ (0117) 966 5740 🌐 theharepub.co.uk
3 changing beers (often New Bristol, Twisted Oak) Ⓗ
Formerly the Full Moon, this building has been a pub since at least 1822. Three changing guest beers are sold which are often unusual in this area, and it regularly features brews from New Bristol and Box Steam breweries. The compact bar attracts a mixed clientele, many of them relatively young. A steep flight of stairs leads to a rear garden/patio area above the pub which is used for barbecues in the summer. Bar snacks are available. It has no connection with Bath Ales, despite the name.
❀⇌🍎🚌(24)🐾

Spotted Cow
139 North Street, BS3 1EZ
🕐 12-midnight (1am Thu & Fri); 11-1am Sat; 11-midnight Sun
☎ (0117) 963 4433 🌐 thespottedcowbristol.com
Bath Ales Gem; Butcombe Gold; 3 changing beers (often Arbor, Tiny Rebel) Ⓗ
Two-bar pub for a while called 139 Degrees North. An original Georges and Co Ltd sign is still prominent over the entrance. It was taken over in late 2014 by the people who run the Christmas Steps in central Bristol. Guest beers usually come from independents such as Tiny Rebel and Arbor Ales. A pleasant refurbishment has given it a chilled atmosphere, with mood music played at a non-intrusive volume. It has a sizeable garden.
❀◑🚌(24)📶

Steam Crane
4-6 North Street, BS3 1HT
🕐 5-11 Mon & Tue; 12-midnight; 12-11 Sun
☎ (0117) 953 1446 🌐 thesteamcrane.co.uk
6 changing beers Ⓗ
Reopened with a new name, new owners and a new image in January 2014, this alehouse offers six varying real ales, with prices for each beer clearly displayed on a chalkboard. A selection of bottled beers is also stocked. The large open-plan interior has a selection of comfy sofas scattered among various pieces of furniture, giving it a retro and vintage feel. There are regular music events including an open jazz jam session. At the rear is a good-sized patio. 🐴❀◑⇌🚌(X5,24,777A)

Windmill
14 Windmill Hill, BS3 4LU (100yds uphill from Bedminster station)
🕐 12-11 (midnight Fri & Sat); 12-10.30 Sun
☎ (0117) 963 5440
Bath Ales Gem; 2 changing beers Ⓗ
With pastel colours and wooden flooring throughout, the pub is on two levels, with a family room on the lower area where children are welcome until 8pm. There are two changing guest ales, as well as real cider and foreign bottled beers. Good food is served all day until 9.30pm and Sunday roasts too. An old 1970s jukebox features. Outside is a small patio area to the front.
🐴❀◑⇌🍎🚌(75,76,77)🐾📶

Bristol: Bishopston

Prince of Wales
5 Gloucester Road, BS7 8AA
🕐 12-midnight (1am Fri & Sat) ☎ (0117) 924 5552
🌐 powbristol.co.uk
Bath Ales Gem; Butcombe Gold; Otter Amber; 3 changing beers (sourced regionally) Ⓗ
A pub with a beautiful frontage just up from the Arches, and a popular outdoor area at the rear. As you enter, a U-shaped bar serves two linked drinking areas. It has a mixture of tiled flooring and floorboards throughout, with comfortable leather-back settles. Guest beers are regionally sourced and the nearby Ashley Down Brewery often features. The pub offers an extensive food menu. Handy for the shops of Gloucester Road and the restaurants of Zetland Road.
🐴❀◑⇌(Montpelier)♣🍎🚌(12,19,71)🐾📶

Bristol: Clifton

Eldon House
6 Lower Clifton Hill, BS8 1BT (off top of Jacobs Wells Road)
🕐 5-11.30; 12-1am Fri & Sat; 12-11 Sun ☎ (0117) 922 1271
🌐 theeldonhouse.com

Bath Ales Special Pale Ale, Gem; 3 changing beers (often Bristol Beer Factory) H
A tasteful extension in 2009 has not detracted from the traditional look and feel of this cosy end-of-terrace pub, which lies close to the busy Clifton Triangle area. Get off a bus near the top of Park Street and head a short way down Jacobs Wells Road. The four or five beers include guests from well-chosen independent brewers, often local, occasionally from further afield. Good-quality food is served daily and Sunday roasts are popular. Many events are hosted. (1,2,8)

Hope & Anchor

38 Jacobs Wells Road, BS8 1DR (between Anchor Rd and top of Park St)
12-11 ☎ (0117) 929 2987 hopebristol.com
6 changing beers H
Popular and friendly pub offering up to six changing microbrewery real ales in a range of strengths and styles, generally including a dark ale and varying real ciders. Food is served all day every day (until 9.30pm). On summer days the secluded terraced garden up some steep steps at the rear can be pleasant. Expect beer festivals, probably three a year, tying in with those of its sister pub, the Volunteer Tavern in St Judes. Street parking is limited.

Portcullis

3 Wellington Terrace, BS8 4LE (close to Clifton side of suspension bridge)
4.30 (12 Sat)-11; 12-10.30 Sun ☎ (0117) 908 5536
Dawkins Bristol Blonde, Bristol Best; changing beers (often Dawkins) H
A pub since 1821, rescued by Dawkins in 2008, with a downstairs bar and a quieter upstairs lounge (also used for functions) with a supply of board games. Seven handpumps usually dispense three or four Dawkins beers and a range of interesting guests from other micros. All styles and strengths are showcased. Real ciders and good-value tapas-style nibbles are usually available. Several mini beer and cider festivals a year take place. The rear garden is accessed from upstairs.
Q (8,9,505)

Victoria

2 Southleigh Road, BS8 2BH (off St Pauls Rd)
4 (12 Sat)-11; 12-10.30 Sun ☎ (0117) 974 5675
Dawkins Bristol Blonde, Bristol Best; 4 changing beers (often Dawkins) H
Small 19th-century, Grade II-listed Dawkins' tavern, tucked away just off the bottom of Whiteladies Road next to the Clifton Lido. Six pumps offer changing independent beers and ciders, always including two or more from Dawkins Brewery. An ever-increasing stock of bottled Belgian beers is also available. The walls are adorned with pumpclips and brewery mirrors, plus an amusing collection of obsolete keg fonts on a mantelpiece. Regular events, including beer festivals and quizzes, are held. Parking close by is difficult.
(Clifton Down) (1,2,9)

Bristol: Easton

Plough

223 Easton Road, BS5 0EG
4-midnight; 2-2am Fri; 12-2am Sat; 12-midnight Sun
☎ (0117) 955 8556
4 changing beers (sourced locally) H
Popular and lively street-corner pub with a young and cosmopolitan clientele. There is a pool table, several large screens for TV sport, and a stage for live acts in the back room. An easy-to-miss door leads to a rear patio/smoking area that tends to be extremely busy and has two further screens on which to watch sport. Four handpumps dispense a varied range of interesting beers, mainly from local brewers. (Lawrence Hill)

Bristol: Horfield

Annexe

Seymour Road, BS7 9EQ (directly behind Sportsman pub near county cricket ground)
11.30-3, 5-11.30; 11.30-11.30 Sat; 12-11 Sun
☎ (0117) 949 3931
Otter Amber; St Austell Tribute; Sharp's Doom Bar; Timothy Taylor Landlord; Wye Valley HPA; 2 changing beers H
Community pub not far from the Memorial Stadium, which means it can be busy on match days. Inside is a converted skittle alley and a large conservatory/family room to one side. Several TVs show live sport, including one on the partially covered patio outside. Good wholesome food is served, including quality pizzas, available until 10pm. No dogs are allowed, even on the patio. It serves one or two guest beers which can be fairly adventurous. (12,19,71)

Bristol: Hotwells

Bag of Nails

141 St Georges Road, BS1 5UW (5 mins' walk from cathedral towards Hotwells)
4 (12 Fri & Sat)-11; 12-10.30 Sun
8 changing beers H
Small, gas-lit terraced free house dating from the 1860s, serving up to eight changing beers from both small or new brewers from all over, including local micros. It also has over 100 bottled beers, a real cider, occasional beer festivals, and a policy of no children or 'idiot pub crawls'. The interior features terracotta colours, sultry wallpaper, portholes in the floor, pub cats roaming free and eclectic music from a proper record player.
(55,352,354)

Grain Barge

Mardyke Wharf, Hotwell Road, BS8 4RU (moored on the opp bank to the SS Great Britain)
12-11 (11.30 Fri & Sat) ☎ (0117) 929 9347
grainbarge.co.uk
Bristol Beer Factory Nova, Seven, Sunrise; 2 changing beers H
Easily accessed on foot, by bus or ferry, this moored boat was built in 1936 and converted into a floating pub by Bristol Beer Factory in 2007, with great views of the SS Great Britain, the floating harbour, and passing boats from the two top decks. Popular themed food nights are held every Wednesday and Thursday. The kitchen is open lunchtimes and evenings. A downstairs bar and function room are available, with live music on Fridays.

Merchants Arms

5 Merchants Road, BS8 4PZ
4-11; 12-11 Fri-Sun ☎ (0117) 907 3047
Bath Ales Special Pale Ale, Gem, Barnsey; 1 changing beer H

One of the earliest Bath Ales tied houses but now a free house, it still usually has three Bath Ales beers on, plus a guest beer, often from a South-West brewer. Pies and rolls are usually available. Both its rooms are furnished with dark wood seating. In the small back bar, chess, draughts, Othello, cribbage, dominoes and other games can be played. There is a small free car park 50 yards behind the pub.
Q♣🚌🐾📶

Bristol: Redfield

Old Stillage

145-147 Church Road, BS5 9LA (on A420)
12-11 (12.30am Thu; 1.30am Fri & Sat)
☎ (0117) 939 4079
Arbor Motueka; 2 changing beers (sourced locally; often Arbor)
Though no longer connected directly to Arbor Ales, it offers four changing Arbor beers and a seasonal Arbor or guest ale. A bistro/cafe, with a disabled toilet, has been added to the side of the main pub and food is served regularly. Known for its Sunday roasts, booking is advisable. There is a pool table, a dartboard and a large rear patio. It is a community pub and music venue, with BT Sport and a comprehensive jukebox. Dogs are welcome in the garden. ❀◑♿⇌(Lawrence Hill)♣🚌(37,42,43)

Bristol: Westbury on Trym

Prince of Wales

84 Stoke Lane, BS9 3SP (off the A4018, 5 mins' walk from village centre)
11-11 (midnight Fri); 12-10.30 Sun ☎ (0117) 962 3715
Butcombe Bitter, Gold; Fuller's London Pride; 3 changing beers (often Butcombe)
Busy Butcombe-owned pub on the edge of Westbury village, with a magnificent exterior and a friendly, welcoming feel inside and a number of drinking areas. Up to seven real ales are served including Butcombe seasonal beers and some from larger regional brewers. Meals are served lunchtimes only Monday-Saturday 12-2pm. Conversation dominates except when major rugby fixtures are shown on a drop-down large screen. There is a large garden and patio at the rear. Children are welcome until 7pm. Q❀◑🚌(1)📶

Victoria

20 Chock Lane, BS9 3EX (in small lane behind churchyard)
12-2.30, 6-11; 12-3, 7-10.30 Sun ☎ (0117) 950 0441
thevictoriapub.co.uk
Wadworth Henry's IPA, Horizon, 6X; 3 changing beers (often Wadworth)
Once a courthouse, this traditional and welcoming Wadworth-owned pub has been in the Guide for many years. A raised garden to the rear is a suntrap in summer. Pictures of Westbury as a village adorn the walls. Popular home-cooked food is available lunchtimes and evenings (no food Sunday evening). Entertainment includes quizzes, themed meals and regular pub outings. Various societies meet here. Bonus card offers are now available if you provide your email address.
Q❀◑🚌(1,520)🐾📶

Bristol: Whitehall

Red Lion

206 Whitehall Road, BS5 9BP
2-12.30am (3am Fri); 12-3am Sat; 12-midnight Sun
☎ (0117) 329 1316 theredlionbs5.co.uk
4 changing beers
Built at the beginning of the 20th century and rescued from closure in 2012, this basic pub has a bar, lounge, pool table and darts. There is a log-burning fire, and a beer garden to the rear. The real ales change regularly, with a minimum of three on at any time, often from local microbreweries. At least one dark beer is usually on the bar, plus two real ciders, one of which is Black Dragon. Regular live music plays in the bar area.
❀⇌(Lawrence Hill)♣🚌(6,7)🐾📶

Broadwell

Fox Inn

The Green, GL56 0UF (off A429 Fosse Way)
11-2.30, 6-11; 12-3, 7-10.30 Sun ☎ (01451) 870909
Donnington BB, SBA; 1 changing beer (sourced locally; often Donnington)
Attractive stone-built hostelry overlooking the village green. The Donnington beers, brewed only a few miles away, are well kept, attractively priced and popular with visitors. A family-run local, it offers good company and quality good-value home-cooked food. There are flagstoned floors in the bar area, jugs hanging from the beams and Aunt Sally in the garden. At the back is a camping and caravan site. Ideally placed for local walks and Stow-on-the-Wold. A CAMRA award-winner.
Q❀◑Å♣P🚌🐾

Brockhampton

Craven Arms

Kingsbury Street, GL54 5XQ (off A436 in a cul-de-sac in centre of village)
12-3, 6-11 ☎ (01242) 820410 thecravenarms.co.uk
Butcombe Bitter; Otter Bitter; 1 changing beer
Spacious 17th-century free house set in an attractive hillside village with truly outstanding views and local walks. It has a bar area with an open fire and an excellent dining room, separated by church-style stone windows. Three carefully selected beers are well kept by the owner-chef. A regular local CAMRA award winner (Pub of the Year runner-up for 2015), this is a properly managed gem, run by a friendly family who organise functions for locals each month. There are two letting rooms. Q❀◑Å♣P🐾📶

Brockweir

Brockweir Inn

Mill Hill, NP16 7NG (off A466, over bridge)
12-2.30, 6-11; 12-11 Sat & Sun ☎ (01291) 689548
thebrockweirinn.co.uk
Butcombe Bitter; 3 changing beers
Blessed with two cosy bars of differing character, both a symphony of stone, this quirky and much-loved hostelry generates a convivial, warm and calming atmosphere. There is a small dining area to the rear, and a popular community games room upstairs (with a book swap scheme) available for meetings and functions. Outside is an intriguing walled garden, a beautiful suntrap for those wanting to relax away from hectic modernity. An undervalued and veritable gem of the Wye Valley.
Q❀◑Å♣P

Brookend

Lammastide Inn L

Old Brookend, GL13 9SF (off B4066, nr Berkeley)
SO6842202062
12-3, 7 (6 Fri)-midnight; 12-midnight Sat; 12-11 Sun
(01453) 811337 lammastideinn.co.uk
Draught Bass; Wye Valley Bitter; 2 changing beers H
Single-bar pub built in 1932. It has an imposing main bar with a raised seating area in the bay window, otherwise the pub, garden and toilets are accessible by wheelchair. The ample dining area serves freshly home-cooked food all week. The large garden is equipped with children's play equipment and has great views towards the River Severn and Forest of Dean. It opens at 6pm on Monday and Tuesday to serve takeaway fish and chips. Well-behaved dogs are welcome.
QP

Cheltenham

Bank House

15-21 Clarence Street, GL50 3JL
7am-midnight (1am Fri & Sat) (01242) 240940
Greene King Abbot; Purity Mad Goose; Ruddles Best Bitter; 7 changing beers H
Large town-centre Wetherspoon pub on two floors in a former bank. The building retains many fine architectural features, the upper floor taking the form of a gallery with a cosy library area and views over the floor below. Ten ales are generally dispensed, with the three regular beers also available from the upper floor bar. As with many Wetherspoons, the internal wall decor provides interesting facts about the building and other local history. Q

Charlton Kings Club

21 Church Street, Charlton Kings, GL53 8AP (opp church)
12-3, 6-11; 11.30-3, 6-midnight Fri; 12-midnight Sat; 12-11 Sun (01242) 525511 charltonkingsclub.co.uk
Butcombe Bitter; 3 changing beers (often Butcombe, Hop Kettle, Oakham) H
Popular village club in the heart of Charlton Kings with a large lounge, separate bar and a skittle alley on the ground floor, plus a large function room and snooker room upstairs. Regular live music is a feature upstairs (Vonnies Blues Club) and also in the main lounge. Four varied beers are served, generally at least one from Butcombe, with guests usually from the region. A beer festival is held annually in November. Occasional visits by card-carrying CAMRA members are free (otherwise there is a small fee). P(B,P,Q)

Cheltenham Motor Club L

Upper Park Street, GL52 6SA (first right off Hales Rd from London Rd lights, 100yds on right; pedestrian access from A40 via Crown Passage opp Sandford Mill Rd jct)
6-midnight (1am Fri); 12-1am Sat; 7-midnight Sun
(01242) 522590 cheltmc.com
Moor Beer Hoppiness; Stroud Tom Long; 3 changing beers H
Visitors are welcome at this friendly club just east of the town centre in the former Crown pub. It was CAMRA national Club of the Year in 2013 and has won multiple county and regional awards. Three changing ales from microbreweries across the country complement the regulars, plus Thatchers cider. Two beer festivals are held annually (one in September for charity, one on New Year's Eve), and regular Meet the Brewer evenings prove popular. Home to local league quiz, darts and pool teams. QP(B,51)

Jolly Brewmaster L

39 Painswick Road, GL50 2EZ (off A40 Suffolk Rd between Suffolk and Tivoli, 200yds S along Painswick Rd)
2.30 (12 Fri & Sat)-11; 12-10.30 Sun (01242) 772261
7 changing beers (sourced nationally; often Bespoke, Moor Beer, Severn Vale) H
A frequent local CAMRA Pub of the Year, the pub's seven handpumps feature a changing range of ales, alongside six ciders including Black Rat perry and cider and Gwynt y Ddraig Black Dragon. This busy, friendly community hub has original etched windows, a horseshoe bar and an open fire. The attractive courtyard garden is popular in the summer, and hosts regular barbecues. Weekly quiz and music nights are held. Q(10,94)

Moran's Eating House

123-129 Bath Road, GL53 7LS (appox ½ mile from centre at town end of Bath Rd shopping area)
10-11; closed Sun (01242) 581481
moranseatinghouse.co.uk
2 changing beers (often Purity, Timothy Taylor, Wye Valley) H
Highly regarded as a restaurant, the separate attractive bar is popular for socialising, and currently serves two ales. The beer choice varies daily, featuring interesting brews generally from the region, although Timothy Taylor beers are frequent guests. The interesting bar menu includes tapas and platters, and speciality sandwiches and home-made cakes are served in the afternoons. There is a pleasant conservatory to the rear and covered outdoor seating at the front.
Q(F,46)

Royal Union Inn L

37 Hatherley Street, GL50 2TT (from Westal Green roundabout bus stop on A40 take Andover Rd for 100yds, turn right in to Hatherley St; pub is 50yds on left)
4-11; 12-midnight Fri & Sat; 11-11 Sun (01242) 519098
theroyalunion.com
7 changing beers (often Great Western, Hook Norton, Sharp's) H
A cosy corner local, just 10 minutes' walk from the rail station, with a contemporary dining and drinking area. A wide range of single malts and wines is offered along with up to seven ales sourced nationally. A real cider, often Pheasant Plucker, is also generally stocked. Food is served 6-10pm Tuesday-Saturday, with brunch only on Sundays. Regular live acoustic or jazz music and quiz nights feature. Q(94,94U)

Sandford Park Alehouse L

20 High Street, GL50 1DZ (E end of High St)
12-midnight (11 Mon & Tue); 12-11 Sun
(01242) 574517 spalehouse.co.uk
Oakham Citra; Purity Mad Goose; Wye Valley Butty Bach; 6 changing beers H
Local CAMRA Pub of the Year 2014 and 2015, this smart new alehouse has a U-shaped main bar area complete with bar billiards, a cosy front snug with a wood-burning stove, and a large south-facing patio/garden. A function room/lounge with TV sport is on the first floor. Ten handpumps feature constantly changing ales from microbreweries sourced nationally, plus a cider (see pub website). There are also 16 speciality lagers and other beers.
Q(B,P,Q)

Strand L

40-42 High Street, GL50 1EE (at E end of High St)
⚙ 12-11 (midnight Fri); 10-midnight Sat; 12-10.30 Sun
☎ (01242) 511848 🌐 strandpub.co.uk
5 changing beers H
Modern, comfortable pub offering five beers generally from the region including at least one from a featured brewery of the month, and a cider. Good-value food is served daily (12-2.30, 6-9pm Monday-Friday; 12-9pm Saturday; 12-5pm Sun), with a gourmet burger night on Wednesday. An upstairs function room is available for hire, along with a cellar bar, home to live comedy and music nights. The large garden and patio provide a pleasant outdoor drinking area. ❀◖◗🍎🚌🐾📶

Cirencester

Corinium Hotel L

12 Gloucester Street, GL7 2DG (off A435 to N of town centre)
⚙ 11-11; 11-10.30 Sun ☎ (01285) 659711
🌐 coriniumhotel.co.uk
Wickwar Cotswold Way; 3 changing beers H
An agreeable 2-star hotel with a discreet frontage entered via an attractive, narrow courtyard; this leads to a slightly idiosyncratic interior, with a comfortable lounge area complete with woodburner. The varying thickness and layout of the walls hint at its heritage as an Elizabethan wool-merchant's house. The guest ales include at least one LocAle. A modern vestibule leads into a smart dining room and the popular, pleasant suntrap of a garden at the rear of the premises.
❀🛏◖◗♿P🚌🐾📶

Drillman's Arms L

34 Gloucester Road, GL7 2JY (on old A417, 200yds from A435 jct)
⚙ 11-2.30, 5.30-midnight; 11-midnight Sat; 12-4.30, 7-11 Sun ☎ (01285) 653892
Sharp's Doom Bar; 3 changing beers H
A lively Georgian inn perched beside a busy road, with a warm, convivial lounge with woodburner, a pub games-dominated public bar and a popular, busy skittle alley. Run by the same landlady for over 20 years, this free house features low-beamed ceilings, horse brasses, brewery pictures and cracking beer. Fresh flowers grace the immaculate toilets. Well-priced standard pub fare is served, lunchtimes only. It has a summer beer festival, and live music on Saturday evenings. There is outside seating plus a small car park at the front. ❀◖⛺♣P🐾📶

Marlborough Arms L

1 Sheep Street, GL7 1QW
⚙ 12-midnight ☎ (07748 185261)
🌐 marlborougharms.co.uk
Box Steam Piston Broke; North Cotswold Windrush Ale; 6 changing beers H
Opposite the old GWR Station, and local CAMRA Cider Pub of the Year, this lovely, wooden-floored pub is a real ale haven. Offering eight beers from regionals and microbreweries (it is a rare outlet for Corinium Ales), it also has a plethora of interesting boxed ciders. Brewery memorabilia adorn the walls, with pews and a deep-set fireplace adding character. The ceiling is disappearing behind the encroaching pumpclip collection. The small patio at the rear is used for barbecues during beer festivals.
◖♣🍎🐾📶

Clearwell

Lamb Inn L

The Cross, Newland Road, GL16 8JU (towards W end of village) SO5704508170
⚙ closed Mon & Tue; 12-3 (not Wed & Thu), 6-11; 12-4, 7-10.30 Sun ☎ (01594) 835441
Wye Valley Bitter; 3 changing beers G
Former iron miners' pub, and over 200 years old. It is a wonderful village local with two bars: a tidy snug warmed by an open log fire, and a main bar with large, attractive settles alongside long tables flanking the woodburner, providing plenty of room for families and groups. The beer selection is indicated on the defunct handpumps, as all the ales are straight from the cask in the cellar behind the bar. Most of the beers are from local brewers.
Q❀♿⛺♣P🐾

Cold Aston

Plough Inn 🏆 L

GL54 3BN
⚙ 12-3 (not Mon), 6-11; 12-11 Fri-Sun ☎ (01451) 822602
🌐 coldastonplough.com
Cotswold Spring Stunner H**; Prescott Hill Climb; Stroud Budding** G**; 1 changing beer** H
A transformed stone-flagged country pub high in the Cotswolds. The attractive village went by the name of Aston Blank as far back as the Domesday Book. It was reopened in May 2013 by new owners, with three luxury letting bedrooms in an innovative internal extension of the original 17th-century cottage. The emphasis is on real ale and good, interesting food. Look out for three local beers from award-winning Gloucester Brewers, two of them served directly from the cask. Local CAMRA Pub of the Year 2014 and 2015.
Q🐎❀🛏◖◗♿⛺♣P🐾

Dursley

Old Spot Inn L

2 Hill Road, GL11 4JQ (by bus station and free car park)
⚙ 11-11; 12-11 Sun ☎ (01453) 542870 🌐 oldspotinn.co.uk
Uley Old Ric; 7 changing beers H
Dating from 1776, this free house serves up to seven independent ales. Named after the Gloucestershire Old Spot pig, a porcine theme blends with the extensive brewery memorabilia, low ceilings, log fires and welcoming staff to create a convivial atmosphere. The attractive garden has a heated and covered area. Wholesome, freshly prepared dishes complement the pub's enthusiasm for real ale (food is served 12-6pm). On the Cotswold Way, it is popular with walkers, and hosts regular Meet the Brewer evenings.
Q🐎❀◖♿🍎🚌🐾📶

Eastington

Old Badger Inn L

Alkerton Road, Spring Hill, GL10 3AT
⚙ 12-11; 12-10.30 Sun ☎ (01453) 822892
🌐 oldbadgerinn.co.uk
Moles Tap Bitter; 4 changing beers H
Formerly the Victoria, the pub was rescued, renovated and reopened as a free house after being closed by Punch Taverns in 2010. The large single bar features a wood-burning stove, with smaller rooms on either side plus a restaurant area. The walls are covered with brewery and other

memorabilia. Outside there is a covered and heated patio and a large garden with a children's play area. Dog-friendly: quarry-tiled floors, water bowls and a biscuit await every four-legged visitor. Q (61,401)

Ebrington

Ebrington Arms

GL55 6NH (centre of village by green)
12-11 (01386) 593223 theebringtonarms.co.uk
Prescott Hill Climb; Stroud Organic Ale; 3 changing beers
A 17th-century Cotswold stone-built pub in a beautiful village with excellent walks, family-run and with enthusiastic staff. The cosy bar has a lovely open fireplace and six handpumps, with three dispensing the pub's own Yubby ales and three others usually from Gloucestershire. It does an excellent range of food from local suppliers, and is open seven days a week, offering five en-suite rooms, one with a four-poster. A regular CAMRA award winner and a Pub of the Year finalist in 2015. QP

Forthampton

Lower Lode Inn

GL19 4RE (follow sign to Forthampton from A438 Tewkesbury to Ledbury road) SO8788231809
12-midnight (2am Fri & Sat); 12-11 Sun
(01684) 293224 lowerlodeinn.co.uk
Sharp's Doom Bar; 4 changing beers
Blessed with views across the River Severn to Tewkesbury Abbey, this attractive 15th-century brick-built inn, with its three acres of lawns, is a popular stopover for boats and is a camping and caravan club hideaway site. Some stained glass is noteworthy, although the fireplace dominates if you have battled flooded approach roads in winter. It hosts a beer festival in September, and a small ferry operates from the Tewkesbury side from Easter to mid-September. Day fishing is available, plus en-suite accommodation. QP

Frampton Cotterell

Rising Sun

43 Ryecroft Road, BS36 2HN
11.30-11.30 (midnight Fri & Sat); 12-11 Sun
(01454) 772330 risingsunframpton.co.uk
Draught Bass; Great Western Maiden Voyage, Classic Gold; 2 changing beers (often Great Western)
Brewery tap for the Great Western Brewery, an excellent free house owned by the same family for many years. At least two Great Western beers and at least one guest are available. The three-roomed interior comprises the main bar, a small snug, and a conservatory/restaurant. Food is served all day (until 8pm Sun). There is also a skittle alley and function room, and an enclosed child-safe beer garden. The pub has featured in almost every edition of this Guide. QP (81,82)

Frampton-on-Severn

Three Horseshoes

The Green, GL2 7DY (off B4071)
11.30-2, 5.30-11 (1am Fri); 11.30-1am Sat; 11.30-2, 5.30-10 Sun (01452) 742100 threehorseshoespub.co.uk
Sharp's Doom Bar; Timothy Taylor Landlord; Uley Bitter
Atmospheric 19th-century community pub built by a farrier at the south end of England's longest village green. The food is home cooked, featuring the unique 3-Shu pie which is freshly baked to order. The two bars have coal fires; dogs are welcome in the flagstoned public bar, and children are permitted until 8.30pm. Evening jamming sessions are popular (especially folk music) as are pasty baking competitions, conker contests and veggie Olympics. A double boules court hosts annual championships. Q

Gloucester

Dick Whittington

100, Westgate Street, GL1 2PE
11-midnight; 11-2am Fri & Sat; 12-11 Sun
(01452) 502039 thedickwhittington.co.uk
Olde Swan Original; Sharp's Doom Bar; St George's Dragons Blood; 5 changing beers
The imposing 18th-century brick façade of this Grade I-listed building hides a 15th-century structure that was the Whittington family town house until 1546. The Victorian-style bar dominates the spacious medieval interior. A few LocAle ales complement those from further afield. Good food is served 12-9pm (12-4pm, 6-8pm on Sun). The spacious Black Cat cellar bar is available for concerts and private functions, and a patio/garden permits summer drinking in the shadow of the adjacent church. (Gloucester)

Fountain Inn

53 Westgate Street, GL1 2NW
11-11 (midnight Fri & Sat); 12-11 Sun (01452) 522562
Bristol Beer Factory Independence; Dartmoor Jail Ale; St Austell Tribute; 3 changing beers (sourced regionally)
Busy 17th-century inn on the site of an alehouse known to have existed in 1216. A passage leads from Westgate Street into a courtyard that is ablaze with flowers in the summer. The Cathedral Bar has a panelled ceiling and carved stone fireplace. The Orange Room serves as an overflow area or a room for private functions, and there is a separate function room upstairs. It offers a LocAle beer and a good food menu, especially popular on match days. Q

King Edward VII

47 Old Cheltenham Road, Longlevens, GL2 0AN
11.30-11 (midnight Thu-Sat) (01452) 381273
Bath Ales Gem; Butcombe Bitter; Wadworth 6X; 3 changing beers
Red-brick pub built in 1907 by Mitchells & Butlers and renamed after Edward VII's visit to Gloucester in 1909. This large, popular community asset was given a total refit in 2001, featuring some practical modern styling, a large, central bar layout, and retaining the real fire. The menu choices go down well with the locals. Changing guest ales are sourced from the Ember Inns cask list (CAMRA members receive a discount). An attractive garden graces the front. P (94)

Linden Tree

73-75 Bristol Road, GL1 5SN (on A430, S of docks)
11.30-2.30 (not Mon), 6-11; 11.30-11.30 Fri & Sat; 12-11 Sun (01452) 527869 lindentreegloucester.co.uk

Wadworth Henry's IPA, Horizon, 6X, Swordfish, Bishops Tipple; 1 changing beer (sourced regionally) Ⓗ
An end property of a Grade II-listed Georgian terrace, with a country feel inside. A popular drinking spot, it has beamed ceilings, exposed stone walls (of questionable origin), an open log fire with unusual canopy, carriage lamps – even a carriage wheel as a seating area boundary. A skittle alley opens up to create extra space. Substantial home-made meals (no food Sat & Sun eves) and bargain accommodation are offered, and there is a small patio in front. The guest ale is from Family Brewers. Q❀🛏◑♣P🚌(12)📶

Pelican Inn 🄻
4 St Mary's Street, GL1 2QR (WNW of cathedral)
🕒 11-11.30 ☎ (01452) 387877
Wye Valley Bitter, HPA, Butty Bach, Dorothy Goodbody's Wholesome Stout; 2 changing beers (sourced locally) Ⓗ
So named because people believe that some of its beams could have come from Drake's Golden Hind, which began life as the Pelican, this busy two-room establishment was rescued and refurbished by Wye Valley Brewery in 2012. The single bar is dominated by conversation and a large fire. The ciders and perry come from Herefordshire. Local CAMRA Pub of the Year once again, it hosts two beer festivals annually. There is an attractive patio area at the rear. Q❀♿⇌♣🍎🐾📶

Gretton

Royal Oak 🄻
Gretton Road, GL54 5EP (E end of the village, 1½ miles from Winchcombe)
🕒 11-11; 12-10.30 Sun ☎ (01242) 604999
🌐 royaloakgretton.co.uk
Marston's EPA; Ramsbury Gold; Wye Valley HPA; 2 changing beers Ⓗ
A warm welcome is assured from the local owners of this popular Cotswold pub set in two acres. All the regular beers are from local breweries or Marston's. Home-cooked food can be eaten in the L-shaped bar or the conservatory with its outstanding views across the Vale of Evesham. The Royal Oak dates from about 1830 and the large garden includes a children's play area and a tennis court. The Gloucestershire-Warwickshire railway runs past the garden. 🔥❀◑♿♣P🐾

Ham

Salutation Inn 🏆 🄻
Ham Green, GL13 9QH (from Berkeley take road signed to Jenner Museum)
🕒 12-2.30 (not Mon), 5-11; 12-11 Sat; 12-10.30 Sun
☎ (01453) 810284 🌐 the-sally-at-ham.com
Butcombe Bitter; 4 changing beers Ⓗ
CAMRA National Pub of the Year in 2015, this cracking rural free house and brew pub is in the Severn Valley within walking distance of the Jenner Museum, Berkeley Castle and its deer park. The landlord, a CAMRA member, keeps an inspired selection of ales and eight real ciders and perries. The pub has two cosy bars with a log fire and a skittles alley. Food is served lunchtimes and occasional evenings only. Live folk music and piano singalongs regularly feature, and shove-ha'penny and skittles are played. Q🔥❀◑♿♣🍎P🐾📶

Hawkesbury Upton

Beaufort Arms 🄻
High Street, GL9 1AU (off A46, 6 miles N of M4 jct 18)
🕒 12-11; 12-10.30 Sun ☎ (01454) 238217
🌐 beaufortarms.com
Bath Ales Special Pale Ale; Bristol Beer Factory Seven; 3 changing beers Ⓗ
Grade II-listed Cotswold stone free house, built in 1602, close to the historic Somerset Monument. It has separate public and lounge bars, a dining room and skittle alley/function room, and contains an ever-increasing plethora of ancient brewery and local memorabilia. Up to five ales and traditional cider are available on handpump. It has an attractive garden with a barbecue, used for local community activities. A great bunch of regulars assure a warm welcome. Q🔥❀◑♿♣🍎P🚌🐾📶

Hillesley

Fleece Inn 🄻
Chapel Lane, GL12 7RD (between Wotton-under-Edge and Hawkesbury Upton)
🕒 11-11 (midnight Fri & Sat) ☎ (01453) 520003
🌐 thefleeceinnhillesley.com
Butcombe Bitter; 3 changing beers Ⓗ
An attractive 17th-century whitewashed pub owned by the community. It has a single bar with a separate lounge/dining room and a snug area. An extensive food menu is mainly sourced from local produce. CAMRA members receive a 10 per cent discount on real ales, which are mainly from local micros. Thatchers Heritage cider is on handpump. Children are welcome and the garden has a safe play area with limited access to the large car park. Q🔥❀◑🍎P🚌📶

Kingswood

King's Arms 🄻
16 High Street, BS15 4AB
🕒 12-11 ☎ (0117) 961 2351
Cheddar Gorge Best; 2 changing beers Ⓗ
Traditional pub that recently became a free house in an area short of real ale-friendly outlets. The building is Grade II-listed and was once a coaching inn. There is a recessed games area and a very large patio and garden area to the rear. The young owner/landlord is a real ale enthusiast and tries to offer interesting guest beers of all styles – one or two at a time, plus bottle conditioned beers, often from local breweries. 🔥❀♣🍎🚉🚌(6,17,42)🐾📶

Marshfield

Catherine Wheel
39 High Street, SN14 8LR
🕒 12-11 ☎ (01225) 892220 🌐 thecatherinewheel.co.uk
Butcombe Bitter; Cotswold Spring Stunner; Sharp's Doom Bar; 1 changing beer (sourced locally) Ⓗ
Impressive mainly 17th-century building in a large yet quiet village on the edge of the Cotswolds, but close to Georgian Bath and ideally situated for a number of tourist attractions in three counties, as well as the city of Bristol. An owner-managed free house, there are several dining areas in addition to the bar, and three letting rooms.
Q🔥❀🛏◑♿🍎P🚌🐾📶

Mayshill

New Inn

Badminton Road, BS36 2NT (on A432 between Coalpit Heath and Nibley)
11.45-3, 5.30-10.30 (11 Wed & Thu); 11.45-11 Fri & Sat; 12-10 Sun (01454) 773161 newinn-mayshill.co.uk
Timothy Taylor Landlord; 2 changing beers (sourced nationally)
A 17th-century inn hugely popular for its food, including gluten-free options (booking is advised). The three guest beers are from far and wide – one usually dark – plus a traditional cider. The main bar is warmed by a real fire in winter, and the rear area serves as a restaurant. Children are welcome until 8.45pm. The garden, with play area, is pleasant in summer. **QP**(46,47,81)

Moreton-in-Marsh

Inn on the Marsh

Stow Road, GL56 0DW (on A429, at S end of town)
12-2.30, 7-11 (01608) 650709
Marston's Burton Bitter, Pedigree; 1 changing beer (often Ringwood)
This charming pub is a rare outlet in the area for Marston's beers and guest ales such as Ringwood. Next to a duck pond, the former bakery features woven hanging baskets. There is a comfortable locals' bar and a large, attractive conservatory and dining area suitable for parties. The garden area is secluded, with nesting sites for the resident ducks who swim on the pond next door. One of the best pubs in Moreton, with an attentive landlord and an annual beer festival. **QP**

Nettleton Bottom

Golden Heart

Birdlip, GL4 8LA (on A417)
10.30-11 (01242) 870261 thegoldenheart.co.uk
Brakspear Bitter; Cotswold Lion Best in Show; Otter Bitter; 4 changing beers
A welcome oasis beside the single-carriageway section of the Gloucester to Swindon road, this 400-year-old Cotswold free house retains most of its original features, although adjoining cottages have been absorbed to create extra rooms. The small bar, almost hidden beyond a huge open fireplace, overlooks a stone-paved patio and garden abutting a cow pasture. The finest local produce contributes to the award-winning, yet reasonably priced, dishes. There are two en-suite guest bedrooms. **QP**

Newnham

Railway Inn

Station Road, GL14 1DA (turn off A48 at clock tower)
12-midnight (01594) 516317
Butcombe Bitter; Wickwar Brand Oak Bitter; 3 changing beers
This friendly community hub is a joy to visit, with railway memorabilia adorning the walls, flagstoned floors, warm fires and a large beer garden. County CAMRA Cider Pub of the Year again, it keeps 15 ciders and perries in the cellar and 30-plus bottled real ciders. Local cider producers drink here and love explaining their craft to visitors. One beer is always a LocAle. Live music features most weekends, and a quiz on Thursdays. There is an Indian restaurant upstairs.

Oldbury-on-Severn

Anchor Inn

Church Road, BS35 1QA
11.30-2.30, 6-11; 11.30-11 Sat; 12-10.30 Sun
(01454) 413331 anchor-inn-oldbury.co.uk
Butcombe Bitter; Draught Bass; St Austell Trelawny; 1 changing beer
A lovely village local set by a tributary of the River Severn. There is a traditional public bar to the right, and a comfortable lounge through the main entrance. A bright restaurant sits at the rear, and the extensive garden has mature trees for shelter, with a pétanque piste at the far end. The guest beer is served from Thursday until it runs out. Children are welcome in the garden and dining room. **QP**

Quenington

Keepers Arms

Church Road, GL7 5BL (from Fairford turn right at village green)
12-11 (01285) 750349 thekeepersarms.co.uk
3 changing beers
Formerly a gamekeeper's cottage, this wonderful community local has been transformed into a modern hostelry by the landlord. Dogs, children, cricketers, cyclists and ramblers are welcome in both the refurbished oak bar and the petite front garden. The unpretentious menus help fill both dining areas (no food Mon or Tue), with regular theme nights and quizzes proving popular. Two fireplaces give a pleasant glow in winter. Three swish en-suite rooms helped the pub win TV's Four in a Bed programme. **P**

Sheepscombe

Butchers Arms

GL6 7RH (signed off A46 N of Painswick and off B4070 N of Slad) SO8911610434
11.30-3, 6.30 (6 Fri)-11; 11.30-11 Sat; 12-10.30 Sun
(01452) 812113 butchers-arms.co.uk
Prescott Hill Climb; 2 changing beers
Handsome 17th-century Cotswold-stone pub overlooking a wooded valley. Its inn sign, a painted three-dimensional carving of a butcher quaffing ale while tethered to a pig, is world famous. In 2014 the lean-to outdoor toilets metamorphosed into a new bar, seamlessly executed in reclaimed stone and Welsh oak. This complements a quality inter-war refurbishment that added the generous bay windows and porch. A wood-burning stove offers warmth in winter, while the forecourt tables and sloping side garden are suntraps in summer. **QP**

Slad

Woolpack

GL6 7QA (on B4070)
12-midnight (01452) 813429 thewoolpackslad.com
Stroud Budding; Uley Bitter, Old Spot Prize Strong Ale, Pig's Ear Strong Beer; 1 changing beer
Popular 17th-century inn made famous by Cider With Rosie (author Laurie Lee was a regular all his life). Just one-room deep, the pub offers superb views over the Slad Valley, and has been thoughtfully restored; the built-in dark wooden settles in the end rooms are modern. The bar runs the length of the building, extending into all four

rooms. Monday is pizza night, prepared on the hob in the revolutionary oven designed by the pub's owner, Daniel Chadwick. Q☺🛏🌳🍴♣♠♥☕🎵🛜

Slimbridge

Tudor Arms 🗅

Shepherd's Patch, GL2 7BP (from A38 1 mile beyond Slimbridge village)
✪ 11-11 ☎ (01453) 890306 ⊕ thetudorarms.co.uk
Palmers Dorset Gold; Uley Bitter, Pig's Ear Strong Beer; Wadworth 6X; Wye Valley HPA; 1 changing beer Ⓗ

First licensed in the early 1800s when the Gloucester & Sharpness Canal was being dug, this large free house, owned and run by the family, has two bars and five dining areas plus a skittle alley and games room. A modern lodge alongside offers accommodation for visitors to the Wildfowl and Wetlands Trust site. Serving some cracking home-cooked food, plus a range of 10 ciders and perries, this lovely pub gets quite busy. There is a separate caravan and camping site at the back.
Q☺🌳🚳🍴♿▲♣♠♥P🛜

South Woodchester

Ram Inn 🗅

Station Road, GL5 5EL (signed off A46) SO8395202189
✪ 11-11; 12-10.30 Sun ☎ (01453) 873329
Butcombe Adam Henson's Rare Breed; Flying Monk Elmers; Otter Amber; 3 changing beers Ⓗ

Much-altered and extended 400-year-old Cotswold-stone inn tucked into the hillside, commanding fine views over the Nailsworth Valley towards Amberley and Minchinhampton Common from a suntrap front terrace. Inside, three inter-connecting rooms (one with a log fire) are grouped around a long stone-built bar. Popular with locals and visitors alike, it is in superb walking country near Woodchester Mansion. Beers are competitively priced. It has an extensive car park at the front on two levels. Local CAMRA Cider Pub of the Year. Q☺🌳🍴♿♣♠♥P🚌(40,63)🐾🛜

Staunton

White Horse Inn 🗅

Monmouth Road, GL16 8PA (on A4136)
✪ closed Mon; 6.30-11 Tue; 12-3, 6-11 Wed-Fri; 12-11 Sat; 12-4 Sun ☎ (01594) 834001 ⊕ whitehorseinnstaunton.co.uk
3 changing beers Ⓗ

Billed as the last inn in England, on the main road between Gloucester and Monmouth, this welcoming hostelry has taken on many aspects of a village shop as well. There are welcoming wood-burning stoves in both the bar and dining areas. The food is home cooked from fresh, locally sourced ingredients wherever possible. With the rear of the pub filled with groceries and other household essentials, the lovely, spacious garden comes into its own. Q☺🌳🍴♿P🐾🛜

Stoke Gifford

Beaufort Arms

55 North Road, BS34 8PB
✪ 11.30-11 (midnight Fri & Sat) ☎ (0117) 969 5471
Bath Ales Gem; Butcombe Bitter; Sharp's Doom Bar; 7 changing beers Ⓗ

An Ember Inns acquisition from Harvester, it has recently increased the number of real ales. There is just the one bar, although its many-roomed past as a Harvester is apparent in the division of the drinking areas. It is a comfortable pub in a pleasant location opposite the village green, yet only a few minutes' walk from Parkway station. Children are welcome and the 73 bus from Bristol Centre stops close by. Quiz nights are every Wednesday (general knowledge) and Sunday (music). 🌳🍴♿🚆(Parkway)♥P🚌(18,73,81)🛜

Stroud

Ale House 🗅

9 John Street, GL5 2HA (opp Cornhill farmers' market)
✪ 12-3, 5-11; 12-midnight Fri; 10.30-midnight Sat; 12-11 Sun
☎ (01453) 755447
Cotswold Lion Golden Fleece; Dark Star Hophead; Stroud Budding; 6 changing beers Ⓗ

Built in 1837 for the Poor Law Guardians, this Grade II-listed building hosts an all-year-round beer festival. The bar occupies the double-height top-lit former boardroom, where an adventurous range of guest beers from the likes of Brass Castle, Burning Sky, Downton, Marble and Oakham (plus a cider and perry) are dispensed from a bank of 12 handpumps. Opposite is a blazing log fire. Two smaller rooms adjoin this principal space. Home-made curries are a speciality. Local CAMRA Pub of the Year. Q☺🌳🍴♿🚆🚌🐾🛜

Crown & Sceptre 🗅

98 Horns Road, GL5 1EG
✪ 3-11; 12-11 Fri-Sun ☎ (01453) 762588
⊕ crownandsceptrestroud.com
Stroud Budding; Uley Bitter, Pig's Ear Strong Beer; 1 changing beer Ⓗ

This lively back-street boozer is at the heart of its local community – a genuine free house where Blue Anchor beers are regular guests. An eclectic mix of framed prints and posters graces the walls. A large oak table in a side room is popular with local groups, including Knit and Knatter. The pub also has its own motorcycle society. Football, rugby and cricket matches are screened in the back bar. A terrace to the rear offers panoramic views over Stroud. 🌳🌞♥P🚌(8,227)🐾🛜

Prince Albert 🗅

Rodborough Hill, GL5 3SS (corner of Walkley Hill)
✪ 4-11.30 (12.30am Thu & Fri); 12-12.30am Sat; 12-10.30 Sun ☎ (01453) 755600 ⊕ theprincealbertstroud.co.uk
Otter Bitter; Stroud Budding; Timothy Taylor Landlord; 3 changing beers Ⓗ

This lively, cosmopolitan, stone-built pub below Rodborough Common is simultaneously bohemian, homely and welcoming, with a reputation for live music. The single bar boasts an eclectic mix of furniture, fittings and memorabilia – the walls covered with film and music posters – and a log fire. The pub hosts a May beer festival, exhibitions and stand-up comedy. Some events are ticketed (phone or check website). Friday is pizza night, on other nights you are welcome to bring your own food or phone for a takeaway. 🌳🌞♥♠♥🐾🛜

Tetbury

Royal Oak 🗅

1 Cirencester Road, GL8 8EY (on B4067)
✪ 11-11 (11.30 Fri & Sat); 12-11 Sun ☎ (01666) 500021
⊕ theroyaloaktetbury.co.uk
Bath Ales Gem; Stroud Tom Long; 3 changing beers Ⓗ

Local CAMRA Pub of the Year, its clever design options make this totally renovated pub feel so modern that it is almost traditional. The expanse of wooden surfaces provides a welcoming feel, with a small fireplace adding warmth. Six handpumps include Severn Cider and a vegan ale from Moor – chosen to match the vegan menu option. The one-pot food option is popular, especially on quiz nights. Upstairs dining rooms and six letting rooms are available, with acoustic music on Sunday evenings.

Tewkesbury

Berkeley Arms

8 Church Street, GL20 5PA (between Tewkesbury Cross and the abbey on old A38)

10-11 (01684) 290555

Wadworth Henry's IPA, 6X, Swordfish; 2 changing beers

A 15th-century half-timbered Grade II inn, just off Tewkesbury Cross. At the rear, a barn – believed to be the oldest non-ecclesiastical building in this historic town – is used for dining in the summer and serves as a meeting room year round. The two-bar pub offers good-value food daily – of particular note are the landlord's home-baked steak and ale pies. Live music is performed on Saturday evenings. Buses to Cheltenham and Gloucester stop close by.
Q (41)

Nottingham Arms

129 High Street, GL20 5JU (on A38 in town centre)

11-11 (01684) 276346

St Austell Tribute; Sharp's Doom Bar; Wye Valley HPA, Butty Bach

Fourteenth-century town-centre hostelry with two welcoming rooms, a public bar at the front and the restaurant behind, with timber predominating. Framed photographs of old Tewkesbury adorn the walls. It is getting noticed for its excellent, well-priced contemporary cuisine, served lunchtimes and evenings. Knowledgeable staff will happily tell you about the resident ghosts. Live music takes place most Sunday evenings, and Thursday is quiz night. Westons Old Rosie cider is on the bar.

Royal Hop Pole

94 Church Street, GL20 5RS (centre of town between abbey and cross)

7am-11 (01684) 274039

Great Western Old Higby; Greene King IPA; Hook Norton Old Hooky; Ruddles County; 4 changing beers

This well-known landmark is an amalgamation of historic buildings from the 15th and 18th centuries. It has been known as the Royal Hop Pole since it was visited in September 1891 by Princess Mary of Teck (Queen Mary, Royal Consort of George V). The pub is mentioned in the Pickwick Papers. Purchased by Wetherspoon, it reopened in 2008. There is wood-panelling on almost every wall of this spacious, multi-roomed drinking establishment, with a large patio and garden area at the rear. Q P (41,42,72)

Theoc House

85 Barton Street, GL20 5PY (on A438, 50yds from the cross)

8.30am-11 (01684) 296562 theochouse.co.uk

3 changing beers

This popular town-centre hostelry is a blend of pub, café and coffee lounge. The owners have succeeded in creating a relaxed atmosphere, opening all day to serve good-value breakfast, brunch and evening meals. Two real ales are regularly available, usually a bitter and a stout. Quiz night is Sunday, while jazz evenings are the second and fourth Wednesdays of the month. Upstairs there is an atmospheric function room which can seat up to 80 in comfort.
Q P (42)

Tudor House Hotel

51 High Street, GL20 5BH

11-11 (01684) 297755 relaxinnztewkesbury.co.uk

Butcombe Bitter; Sharp's Doom Bar; 3 changing beers

This delightful Tudor building, the childhood home of author John Moore, oozes charm and dignity. Cromwell's Bar offers a selection of fine ales. Pub meals are served in the bar, with more upmarket cuisine available in either the Mayor's Parlour or Court Room. Two outdoor areas provide relaxed places to watch the boats on the river behind the pub, and you can enjoy a quiet drink in the Secret Garden. A coffee shop offers lighter refreshments.
Q P

White Bear

Bredon Road, GL20 5BU (off N end of High St)

10-midnight (01684) 296614

Sadler's Peaky Blinder; Sharp's Doom Bar; 3 changing beers

Local CAMRA Pub of the Year, this good-value, family-run inn on the north-western edge of the town centre attracts a varied clientele. Handily situated close to the marina, it is popular with river users. The open-plan L-shaped bar offers room to play pool, cribbage and darts, and there is also a skittle alley. Live music features every Sunday evening. Guest beers change frequently and are usually from smaller breweries; three traditional perries and ciders, often from Thatchers, are also offered. P

Thornbury

Anchor Inn

Gloucester Road, Lower Morton, BS35 1JY

11-11 (01454) 281375 theanchorthornbury.co.uk

Draught Bass; 5 changing beers

Licensed since 1695 and the second oldest pub in Thornbury, this friendly, traditional inn has one regular beer and five changing guests, mostly of low to medium strength, with occasional milds, plus a real cider. Good home-cooked food is served daily. There are two large rooms, one with a central fireplace. The pub has its own darts, crib, dominoes and cricket teams and an angling syndicate. The garden includes a boules piste and children's play area. P

Hawkes House

St Mary Street, BS35 2AB

8.30am-11 (01454) 417621 hawkeshouse.co.uk

3 changing beers

In the pedestrian district of Thornbury, the building was refurbished and reopened in October 2013 as a free house/cafe/bar. The three guest beers, one pale, one brown and one dark, are from breweries within 20 miles or so of Thornbury. Coffee, continental lagers and home-cooked food are available throughout the day from 8.30am. The pub is decorated with bookshelves populated with old and interesting books and board games.

Uley

Old Crown

17, The Green, GL11 5SN (on B4066 at top end of village)

12-11 (01453) 860502 theoldcrownuley.co.uk

Uley Bitter, Pig's Ear Strong Beer; 3 changing beers [H]

An attractive 17th-century whitewashed coaching inn, situated towards the upper end of an attractive village close to the Cotswold Way. The pub has a pleasant, walled garden with magnificent views of the Cotswold hills, and is popular with passing walkers. The low-beamed single bar has a welcoming fire. The beers are sourced mainly from microbreweries. The pub offers four en-suite double bedrooms and food is available. There is a covered smoking area. **Q P**

Upper Oddington

Horse & Groom

GL56 0XH (top of village signed off A436 E of Stow)

12-3, 5.30-11 (01451) 830584

horseandgroom.uk.com

Prescott Hill Climb; Wye Valley Bitter, HPA; 1 changing beer [H]

A warm welcome awaits at this attractive 16th-century inn run by attentive licensees, a winner of CAMRA awards and a finalist again in 2015. It has an extended bar area for locals, with its own sitting room linked by a real open log fire in an inglenook setting. Wye Valley beer is on the bar, with weekly changing guests from Gloucestershire brewers. Outside there is an attractive garden and patio area and a large car park. Set in good walking country close to Stow, it has eight letting bedrooms.

Q P

Whiteshill

Star Inn

Main Road, Star Green, GL6 6AE

5-11; 12-11.30 Fri & Sat; 12-11 Sun (01453) 765321

the-star-inn-whiteshill.co.uk

Bath GEM; Otter Amber; Purity Pure Ubu; 4 changing beers [G]

The Grade II-listed Cotswold-stone exterior of this 17th-century inn belies a comprehensively modernised interior – the new state-of-the-art toilets were opened by the local MP. The bar features a large inglenook fireplace with a wood-burning stove, slate floors, and two oak drinking counters that divide the space. Up to four beers (fewer earlier in the week) are served, including Bath, Cottage, Moles and Otter, from a stillage directly behind the bar. The TV prioritises rugby.

Q P (63,63A)

Wickwar

Buthay

15 High Street, GL12 8NE (close to traffic lights)

closed Mon; 12-11 (midnight Fri & Sat) (01454) 299083

thebuthay.com

3 changing beers [H]

Family-run 16th-century coaching inn attracting a varied clientele into its welcoming single-bar main drinking area, complete with log fire. The large dining room specialises in authentic Italian food cooked fresh to order by Roberto. There is a skittles alley/function room and to the rear is a large enclosed garden with a well-equipped children's play area. Dogs are welcome in the bar area.

P

Woolaston Common

Rising Sun

The Common, GL15 6NU (1 mile off A48 at Woolaston) SO5901500924

12-2.30, 6.30-11; 12-3, 6.30-midnight Sat

(01594) 529282

Butcombe Bitter; Wye Valley Bitter; 1 changing beer [H]

Off the beaten track, this attractive 350-year-old stone-built pub has gorgeous views over the Forest of Dean. The welcoming main bar has an open fire and a small snug, both displaying part of the landlord's large collection of framed banknotes. Featuring in local guides to walks of the forest, the varied menu of good home-cooked food is popular with ramblers (no food Mon and Tue lunchtimes). Some great locals make for a convivial atmosphere. Local CAMRA Pub of the Year 2015.

Q P

Wotton-under-Edge

Falcon Inn

20 Church Street, GL12 7HB

12-11.30; 12-11 Sun (01453) 521894

Great Western Maiden Voyage [G]**; Stroud Tom Long; 2 changing beers** [H]

A free house built in 1659 in this historic market town, the interior has rooms on several levels. The cosy single bar has an open fire and leads to a snug with a flagstone floor. The dining area specialises in locally sourced food and the steaks come from the family farm situated a mile away. The beers are selected by customer vote from brewers within a 25-mile radius. This hostelry is popular with walkers travelling the Cotswold Way.

Royal Oak Inn

3-5 Haw Street, GL12 7AG (on B4060, top of town)

12-midnight (01453) 844366

theroyaloakwotton.com

Cotswold Spring Codger; Fuller's London Pride; Wye Valley HPA; 1 changing beer [H]

A large coaching inn with a friendly atmosphere, complete with two comfortable bars, both with open fires, plus a large dining room. There is a full-size snooker table upstairs which is very popular. This establishment supports the local community and welcomes walkers using the Cotswold Way. At the rear is a car park and enclosed garden containing a well-equipped children's play area, originally occupied by stables, a pigsty and poultry house. **Q P**

A fine beer may be judged with only a sip, but it's better to be thoroughly sure.
Czech proverb

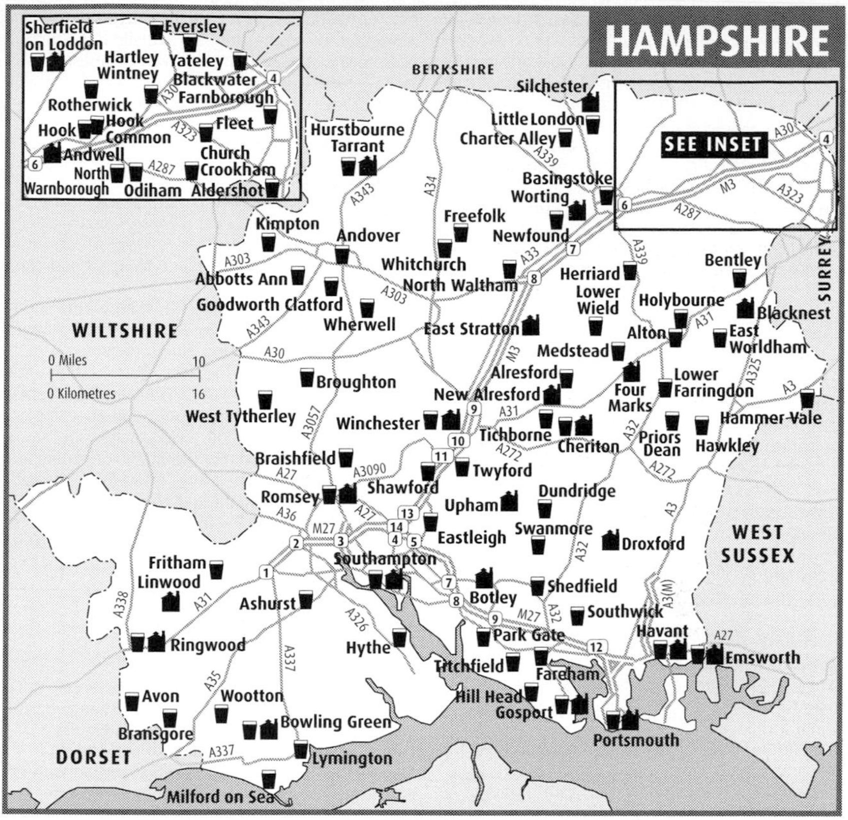

Abbotts Ann

Eagle Inn

Duck Street, SP11 7BG

11.30-11; 12-10.30 Sun (01264) 710339

theeagleinn.wordpress.com

Bowman Wallops Wood; 3 changing beers (sourced locally)

In a picturesque village just two miles south west of Andover, this pub is at the heart of the community, with numerous events organised. Friendly conversation rules the house. The regular from Bowman is supplemented by three changing beers, often from local breweries. A beer festival with live music is held each summer. The public bar features pool and there is a skittle alley at the rear. Locally sourced food is served. No food Tuesday and Sunday evenings. P (87)

Aldershot

White Lion

20 Lower Farnham Road, GU12 4EA (200yds from A331/A323 jct)

1-11 (10.30 Mon; midnight Fri); 12-midnight Sat; 12-10.30 Sun (01252) 323832

Triple fff Alton's Pride, Moondance; 2 changing beers (sourced regionally)

A traditional back-street two-bar pub, opened by 1857 and one of the oldest pubs in Aldershot. Cut-down church pews, a real fire, jukebox and dartboard are in the main bar. The back bar is generally quieter. Owned by Triple fff, it showcases the brewery's beers, often with a guest. Pub dog Millie welcomes away fans when Aldershot Town are home. The A5 Scooter Club meet here on Sundays, with a pub quiz and rock & roll bingo alternating on Thursdays. (3,20,46)

Alresford

Horse & Groom

2 Broad Street, SO24 9AQ

10.30-11; 11.30-10.30 Sun (01962) 734809

horse-and-groom-alresford.co.uk

Fuller's London Pride; Gales Seafarers Ale; 3 changing beers (sourced nationally)

A splendid wrought-iron sign above the entrance advertises the pub's presence. The building dates from the 17th century and is one of many listed buildings in the aptly named street. The public area – bright, airy, beamed and with much exposed brick – contains three real fires; it comprises several discrete areas, all served from a central bar, and a nicely separated, comfortable dining room. Local produce, including Alresford trout and the area's famed watercress, features. Handy for the Watercress Line preserved railway. (64,C41,C42)

Alton

Eight Bells

Church Street, GU34 2DA (across road from St Lawrence Church)

11-11; 12-10.30 Sun (01420) 82417

Bowman Swift One; Sharp's Doom Bar; 3 changing beers (sourced nationally) Ⓗ
Free house, dating from circa 1640, just outside the town centre, with St Lawrence Church, site of the Civil War Battle of Alton, just across the road. It has an original oak-beamed interior with a main bar and a smaller drinking area, plus a restored listed smoking shelter incorporating a 17th-century well in a secluded paved garden. Sandwiches and soup and a roll are available Monday to Saturday from 12.30pm. Look out for Nigel's not-so-secret beer festival following the late summer holiday. Q❀◐⇌🚌(13,38,64)🐾

George 🏆
Butts Road, GU34 1LH
⏲ 11-11; 11-10.30 Sun ☎ (01420) 82331
🌐 thegeorgealton.co.uk
Sharp's Doom Bar, Atlantic; 3 changing beers Ⓗ
Grade II-listed hostelry that dates from 1745, also the courthouse famed for the trial of the murderer of Sweet Fanny Adams. Previously the Duke's Head, it is back under Jason and Suzie's stewardship, who run a friendly local with two regular beers and three guest ales from the SIBA list. Excellent snacks and main meals to suit all tastes are on offer. Music plays on the first Sunday of the month. 🐴❀◐◑P🚌(64)🐾📶

Railway Arms Ⓛ
26 Anstey Road, GU34 2RB (opp Station Rd)
⏲ 12-11; 11-midnight Fri & Sat ☎ (01420) 82218
Triple fff Alton's Pride, Moondance, Comfortably Numb; 2 changing beers Ⓗ
Friendly pub close to the Watercress Line and mainline station. Owned by Triple fff Brewery, its beers are supplemented by ales from a host of micros. Bottled cider is from Mr Whitehead's. A rear function room, with its own bar, is available for hire. The patio area, designed with a traditional railway theme, incorporates a covered smoking area. There are tables outside at the front under a striking sculpture of a steam locomotive. Well-behaved dogs and CAMRA members are welcome. ❀⇌♣🚌(64,65)🐾

Andover

John Russell Fox
10 High Street, SP10 1NY
⏲ 7am-midnight (1am Fri & Sat) ☎ (01264) 320920
Greene King Abbot; Ruddles Best Bitter; 8 changing beers Ⓗ
A High Street JD Wetherspoon pub in former offices of the Andover Advertiser, founded by John Russell Fox. The first edition of the paper was produced here in 1858. A large entrance area leads to the bar with 10 handpumps. References to printing and newspapers adorn the pub. A separate raised seating and dining area is to the rear where families are welcomed. Note the Time Ring set in the pavement outside. ◐◑♿🍎P🚌📶

Town Mills
20 Bridge Street, SP10 1BL
⏲ 11-12.30am ☎ (01264) 332540 🌐 thetownmills.co.uk
Wadworth Henry's IPA, 6X; 2 changing beers (often Wadworth) Ⓗ
Although in the town centre, this pub is located in an historic mill with a working water wheel. There are several separate areas for dining and drinking, including a comfy lounge upstairs. Pub games are also played upstairs, and a well-supported quiz is held on Wednesday evenings. The riverside garden is popular in summer months. Usually three to four beers are available from Wadworth's guest list. 🐴❀◐◑♿♣P🚌🐾📶

Ashurst

Forest Inn Ⓛ
Lyndhurst Road, SO40 7DU (on A35, E end of village)
⏲ 11.30-11.30; 12-10.30 Sun ☎ (023) 8029 3071
🌐 forest-inn.co.uk
Ringwood Best Bitter, Fortyniner; Sharp's Doom Bar; 3 changing beers Ⓗ
Look out for a bungalow-like building on the south side of the A35, some way east of Ashurst village. Inside, a large lounge and dining room are separated by a double fireplace. Outside, there are fine views of the New Forest National Park from the garden. The pub has a good reputation for varied home-cooked food, with smaller portions often available. In summer the three core beers are supplemented by three more, often local beers. Friday is live music night and there is a quiz on Sundays. 🐴❀◐◑⛺♣P🚌(6)🐾📶

Avon

Tyrrell's Ford Country Inn Ⓛ
Ringwood Road, BH23 7BQ (on B3347, halfway between Ringwood and Christchurch)
⏲ 10.30-11 ☎ (01425) 672646 🌐 tyrrellsford.co.uk
Ringwood Best Bitter; Wadworth 6X; 1 changing beer (sourced locally; often Flack Manor, Goddards) Ⓗ
Former country residence of Lord and Lady Manners in an attractive woodland setting with an expansive lawn, a large patio area and sought-after accommodation. The cosy bar area serves three ales and excellent-value meals. It often gets visited by classic car clubs, when their vehicles, be they Morgans or Ferraris, are respectfully parked on

REAL ALE BREWERIES

Alfred's Winchester
Andwell Andwell
Betteridge's Hurstbourne Tarrant (NEW)
Botley Botley
Bowman Droxford
Brewhouse & Kitchen Portsmouth
CrackleRock Botley
Dancing Man Southampton
Emsworth Emsworth (brewing suspended)
Flack Manor Romsey
Flowerpots Cheriton
Fulflood Arms Winchester
Havant Havant
Hop Art Blacknest (NEW)
Irving Portsmouth
Itchen Valley New Alresford
Longdog Worting
Mash East Stratton
Oakleaf Gosport
Queen Inn Winchester
Red Cat Winchester
Red Shoot Linwood
Ringwood Ringwood
Rusty Prop Romsey (NEW)
Sherfield Village Sherfield on Loddon
Triple fff Four Marks
Upham Upham
Vibrant Forest Bowling Green
Wild Weather Ales Silchester

the lawn. It is close to the Avon Valley Path and features a minstrels' gallery, candlelit restaurant and open fires, and offers many board games to entertain the young and young at heart.
Q☺❀⇌◑◗♣P🐾≈

Basingstoke

Basingstoke Sports & Social Club

Fairfields Road, RG21 3DR (S end of town)
✪ 12-3, 5-11; 12-11 Fri & Sat; 12-10.30 Sun
☎ (01256) 331646 🌐 basingstoke-sports-club.co.uk
Fuller's London Pride; Gales Seafarers Ale; 2 changing beers (often Andwells, Longdog) H
Founded in 1865 by local brewery owner and entrepreneur Col John May, the club is home to cricket, rugby, football and squash. Widescreen TV in the bar is dedicated to sports events. A full programme of social activities is held throughout the year and the clubhouse and grounds are available for hire. The grounds are currently home to the annual Hampshire OctoberFest. CAMRA members are welcome as are members of the public. Opening hours are flexible when sporting fixtures are held. North Hampshire CAMRA Club of the Year 2015. ☺❀◑◗♣●P▯⊟🐾≈

Maidenhead Inn

17 Winchester Street, RG21 7ED (at top of town)
✪ 7am-midnight (1am Fri & Sat) ☎ (01256) 316030
Greene King Abbot; Loddon Forbury Lion; Ruddles Best Bitter; 5 changing beers H
Formerly home to a building society and on the site of an inn of the same name, this JD Wetherspoon pub is in the sometimes lively Top of Town area, with five pumps dispensing local and guest ales. Beers from local breweries such as Andwell's, Longdog, Wild Weather and Loddon regularly feature. A dining area at the front leads to the compact bar, with further seating to the rear over two levels, complemented by a courtyard beer garden to the rear. ☺❀◑◗♿⇌●⊟≈

Queen's Arms

Bunnian Place, RG21 7JE (100yds E of railway station)
✪ 11-11 (midnight Fri & Sat) ☎ (01256) 465488
Courage Best Bitter; Sharp's Doom Bar; 3 changing beers H
Just outside the main shopping area, this cosy pub is handy for all transport links. It attracts a wide-ranging clientele of all ages from all walks of life, and is a regular port of call for rail commuters. The choice of up to three guest beers is imaginative and the turnaround can be swift. Good-value home-cooked food is served lunchtimes and evenings. During warmer weather the shady courtyard garden at the rear is a popular attraction.
Q❀◑◗⇌P⊟≈

Bentley

Star L

Main Road, GU10 5LW
✪ 9am-midnight; 11-midnight Sat; 11-11 Sun
☎ (01420) 23184 🌐 thestarinnbentley.co.uk
Sharp's Doom Bar; Triple fff Moondance; 1 changing beer H
Following an extensive refurbishment, this pub now has a pleasant imbibers' environment. From the station follow signs to Bentley Village or local footpaths. The 65 bus stops nearby (outside, from the Alton direction). It opens at 9am for breakfast and is licensed from 11.30am. A varying beer range is offered, often from local breweries. There is a premium for half pints – check the price board above the bar. Excellent food is served, much of it locally sourced – the licensee is also a local farmer.
Q☺❀◑◗P⊟(65)🐾≈

Blackwater

Mr Bumble L

19 London Road, GU17 9AP
✪ 12-11 (midnight Fri); 11-midnight Sat; 12-10.30 Sun
☎ (01276) 32691
Fuller's London Pride; 3 changing beers (sourced nationally; often Downton, Windsor & Eton) H
Busy pub in the centre of Blackwater near the station, a bus route and local shops. London Pride is the regular beer, available alongside up to three other real ales, including LocAles. Stout and porter are popular in the winter months. There is a large bar for drinking and conversation, while a smaller bar leads to the pool room, with three tables. This opens onto the patio and smoking area. Live music features Thursday and Saturday. ⇌♣P⊟(3)≈

Bowling Green

Wheel Inn L

Sway Road, SO41 8LJ (2 miles NW of Lymington)
✪ 12-midnight (11 Tue; 1am Fri & Sat) ☎ (01590) 676122
🌐 thewheelinnpub.co.uk
Ringwood Best Bitter; 2 changing beers (sourced locally; often Red Cat, Vibrant Forest) H
Pleasant little Victorian country pub, set in the middle of a triangle of roads, which has in the past been both a pottery and a blacksmith's. It serves mostly local ales, some of them darker and of higher strength than is usual in this day. It still has two bars, the lounge now mainly acting as a restaurant serving Thai food from Tuesday to Sunday, and bank holidays, while the public bar has music, a pool table and TV.
Q☺❀◑◗♿Å♣P⊟(X2)🐾≈

Braishfield

Dog & Crook L

Crook Hill, SO51 0QB (S edge of village)
✪ 11.30-11 summer; 11.30-3, 5.30-11; 11.30-11 Fri-Sun winter ☎ (01794) 368530 🌐 dogandcrook.co.uk
Ringwood Best Bitter; Sharp's Doom Bar; 1 changing beer (sourced locally; often Bowman, Itchen Valley, Triple fff) H
Well-established village pub with a restaurant and a large garden. Three beers are on handpumps, at least one always from a local brewery. Excellent home-cooked food and bar snacks are served every day, both lunchtimes and evenings (not Sun). There is no jukebox or sports TV, but sport is sometimes shown on terrestrial TV. Cribbage and darts are played and alternate Tuesdays are quiz nights. The famous Hillier Arboretum is nearby.
Q☺❀◑◗♣P🐾≈

Wheatsheaf L

Braishfield Road, SO51 0QE
✪ 11.30-11; 12-10.30 Sun ☎ (01794) 368652
🌐 thewheatsheafbraishfield.co.uk
Flack Manor Flack's Double Drop; Sharp's Doom Bar; St Austell Tribute; 1 changing beer (sourced nationally) H

The Wheatsheaf is a neat, cream-painted brick house in southern Braishfield. Inside, the single bar serves several linked areas including a dining room and a small games annexe with pool and bar skittles. The bare brick and wood décor plus mismatched furniture create a homely feel. The menu has adventurous, often fishy, specials, and good-quality wine. The Newport Session Players entertain on Thursdays. A large open garden looks onto fields and wooded hills. Hillier Arboretum is nearby. Q🐎❀◑◐♿♣P🐾ᯤ

Bransgore

Three Tuns

Ringwood Road, BH23 8JH (between Burley Rd and Harrow Rd)

⌚ 11-11; 11.30-11 Sat; 12-10.30 Sun ☎ (01425) 672232

🌐 threetunsinn.com

Otter Bitter; Ringwood Best Bitter, Fortyniner; 2 changing beers Ⓗ

Attractive 17th-century listed and thatched building, originally a farmhouse, at the southern end of the village. Inside, a central lounge joins a dining room and a cosy snug; a satisfactory arrangement for both drinkers and diners. Nice touches include newspapers, beer descriptions over the bar, and weekly events posters. The menu is well regarded, with imaginative specials. Outside, a large patio and a barn are used for various events and functions, both with peaceful rural views. Pétanque is played.
Q🐎❀◑◐♿⛺P🚆🚌(125,175)🐾ᯤ

Broughton

Tally Ho!

High Street, SO20 8AA

⌚ 12-11 (midnight Fri & Sat); 12-10.30 Sun

☎ (01794) 301280 🌐 thetallyhobroughton.co.uk

Ringwood Best Bitter; Sharp's Doom Bar; 3 changing beers (sourced regionally) Ⓗ

Village pub opposite the church with a modern interior and popular with local drinkers. The guest beers tend to be from Dorset or Somerset and draught cider is usually available. A beer and cider festival is held over the August bank holiday. Upmarket pub food is served but drinkers are welcome in the main bar. The beer garden has play equipment for children and dogs are welcome too.
🐎❀◑◐⛺♣●🐾ᯤ

Charter Alley

White Hart 𝕃

White Hart Lane, RG26 5QA (1 mile W of A340, opp turning for Little London)

⌚ 7-11 Mon; 12-2.30, 5.30 (7 Tue)-11; 6.30-11 Sat; 12-4 Sun

☎ (01256) 850048 🌐 whitehartcharteralley.com

Triple fff Moondance; 5 changing beers Ⓗ

Cosy inn, built in 1819, the epicentre of this rural village, where allcomers are assured of a friendly greeting. Welcoming features include log fires, oak beams and a capacious restaurant, serving a variety of quality food and home-made pies. The breweriana-decorated main bar has six pumps dispensing an array of ales that changes so frequently that an email notification service is available by subscription. It has been a stalwart Guide entry for over 20 years. No food on Monday.
Q❀🛏◑◐P🐾ᯤ

Cheriton

Flowerpots Inn 🏆 𝕃

Brandy Mount, SO24 0QQ (½ mile N of A272 between Winchester and Petersfield) SU581283

⌚ 12-2.30 (3 Sat), 6-11; 12-3, 7-10.30 Sun

☎ (01962) 771318 🌐 flowerpots.f2s.com

Flowerpots Perridge Pale, Bitter, Goodens Gold; 1 changing beer (sourced locally) Ⓖ

Lovely 1800s-built village pub, with two separate bars, including an open log fire and a glass-covered well in the public bar. It sells three regular ales and sometimes one seasonal, all served by gravity and all from its own brewery across the car park. Home-cooked food is served daily, but not Sunday evening. Adding to the charm, converted stables provide accommodation all year round (two double B&B rooms), making this an ideal setting for a restful vacation. Q❀🛏◑◐ ●P🚌(67)🐾

Church Crookham

Fox & Hounds

71 Crookham Road, GU51 5NP

⌚ 12-11 (midnight Fri) ☎ (01252) 663686

🌐 foxandhoundschurchcrookham.co.uk

Caledonian Flying Scotsman; Courage Best Bitter; Fuller's London Pride; 1 changing beer Ⓗ

A welcoming open-plan pub, alongside the Basingstoke Canal, with four distinct seating areas. Traditional home-cooked food is served daily. There is even a dining area especially for dog walkers and their dogs. The garden and play area are a delight on warmer days. A lovely wood-panelled darts area and lots of historic pub photos can be seen. Live music features every Friday and a pub quiz is held once a fortnight on a Tuesday.
🐎❀◑◐♿♣P🚌(72)🐾ᯤ

Tweseldown 𝕃

Beacon Hill Road, GU52 8DY (on B3013 between Fleet and Farnham)

⌚ 11-11.30 (midnight Fri & Sat); 11-11 Sun

☎ (01252) 613976 🌐 thetweseldown.co.uk

Fuller's London Pride; Sharp's Doom Bar; Triple fff Alton's Pride; 1 changing beer Ⓗ

Country pub in a great walking area close to Tweseldown Racecourse, which hosted the 1948 Olympic equestrian events. The separate public bar has pool, darts, a jukebox and fruit machines. There is also a comfortable saloon bar where an extensive and varied home-made food menu is served, and a large barn function room/restaurant. The pub is adorned with interesting horse racing memorabilia. A LocAle from the Triple fff brewery is always available. 🐎❀◑◐♿♣P🚌(72)🐾ᯤ

Dundridge

Hampshire Bowman 𝕃

Dundridge Lane, SO32 1GD (1½ miles E of B3035) SU578184

⌚ 12-11 (midnight Fri); 12-10.30 Sun ☎ (01489) 892940

🌐 hampshirebowman.com

Bowman Swift One; Oakleaf Quercus Folium; 3 changing beers Ⓖ

A free house that has something for everyone. Aside from great local beers, served directly from the cask, there is good freshly prepared food daily. For families there is a pleasant outdoor play area. A number of great walks in the surrounding countryside can be enjoyed and dogs are welcome in the pub too. A beer festival is held on the last weekend in July and numerous other charity events take place throughout the year. Q P

East Worldham

Three Horseshoes

Cakers Lane, GU34 3AE

11.30-3, 5.30-10.30; 11.30-11 Sat; 11.30-8 Sun

(01420) 83211 threehorseshoesalton.co.uk

Fuller's London Pride; Gales Seafarers Ale, HSB; 1 changing beer H

Once a Gales house and a former coaching inn, part of the building dates back over 300 years and is allegedly haunted. Mine hosts John and Gill are rapidly gaining an excellent reputation for their high quality locally sourced food as well as their ales. Very much a community pub, it is the place to go to for information about local events. Quiz night is the last Thursday of the month, and special events are hosted on the last Saturday of the month – murder mystery and the like. Q P (13)

Eastleigh

Wagon Works

28 Southampton Road, SO50 9FJ

7am-midnight (1am Fri & Sat) (023) 8062 2670

Greene King Abbot; Itchen Valley Pure Gold; Ruddles Best Bitter; Sharp's Doom Bar; 5 changing beers H

Smaller than most Wetherspoon houses, this cosy corner pub is an ideal place to wait for a train as it is directly opposite the railway station. Food is served all day from 7am and alcohol from 9am. There is a good-sized paved area at the rear of the pub which is a suntrap in the summer months, and it has a heated, covered seating area. Guest beers are often from local breweries and one handpump always serves cider. Q

Emsworth

Coal Exchange

21 South Street, PO10 7EG

10.30-3, 5.30-11; 10.30-midnight Fri & Sat; 12-11 Sun

(01243) 375866 thecoalexchange.co.uk

Butcombe Bitter; Fuller's London Pride; Gales Seafarers Ale, HSB; 2 changing beers H

A short walk from Emsworth harbour, this pub has a somewhat unusual (for a former Gales pub) green-tiled frontage. The harbour is no longer commercial so the pub is no longer a trading place for local farmers exchanging produce for coal delivered by sea. The award-winning lunchtime food is complemented with themed evening options. The pub is also a good starting or ending point for walks along the edge of the harbour. (700)

Eversley

Golden Pot L

Reading Road, RG27 0NB

12-11; 12-3.30 Sun (0118) 973 2104

golden-pot.co.uk

3 changing beers H

Picture-postcard village pub that was formerly two red-brick cottages dating back to the 18th century. The pub is supplied by 14 different microbreweries on rotation, eight of which are local, including Andwell, Siren and Longdog. High-quality wholesome food is served, which is also available in small-plate options. There are tables and chairs plus comfortable sofa areas. Another delightful feature is the Snug and Vineyard garden at the rear of the pub. Opening hours may vary on midweek evenings. Q P

Fareham

Crown L

40 West Street, PO16 0JW

7am-midnight (1am Fri & Sat) (01329) 241750

Greene King Abbot; Ruddles Best Bitter; 3 changing beers H

Town-centre Wetherspoon situated in a former brewery in a pedestrianised street, convenient for the bus station and shopping centre. Wall-mounted portraits with brief histories of famous local figures add to the cosy atmosphere. The three guest beers normally include one from a local brewery, and the occasional US guest beer (brewed in the UK). Near each handpump is a mini Kilner jar showing the beer colour. Real cider is available occasionally.

Delme Arms

1 Cams Hill, PO16 8QY

11-11 (midnight Fri & Sat); 12-11 Sun (01329) 232638

Sharp's Doom Bar; 2 changing beers (sourced regionally) G

On the eastern outskirts of Fareham, the Delme Arms reopened in 2014 under new management and free of tie. There is a main bar area with sports TV, and up a few stairs is a quiet bar which can be hired for functions. The guest beer range often includes ales from local breweries. A beer festival is held over the spring bank holiday weekend. Food is served all day on Saturdays and until 6pm on Sundays. Q P

Lord Arthur Lee

100-108 West Street, PO16 0EP

8-11 (midnight Fri & Sat) (01329) 280447

Greene King Abbot; Ruddles Best Bitter; Sharp's Doom Bar; 5 changing beers H

A popular, typically spacious Wetherspoon pub close to the bus and rail stations. The walls are lined with photos and historical details of the pub's namesake and other locals. The family area is often popular at lunchtimes. Three regular ales and five guest beers are offered, many selected from local breweries. Occasional beer festivals boost the choice. The usual Wetherspoon food is always available.

Farnborough

Prince of Wales L

184 Rectory Road, GU14 8AL

11.30-2.30, 5.30-11; 11.30-11 Fri & Sat; 12-10.30 Sun

(01252) 545578 theprinceinfarnborough.co.uk

Dark Star Hophead; Fuller's London Pride; Hop Back Summer Lightning; Ringwood Fortyniner; Young's Bitter; 5 changing beers H

Featuring in the Guide for over 30 years, this cosy, freehold pub is well known to beer lovers throughout the area, and was again the local CAMRA Pub of the Year in 2014. Of the 10 cask ales, five are guests, including one lower-priced monthly session ale, and local beers. It is popular for lunches, Monday evening pie night, Friday evening fish night, and an annual beer festival in

October. The pub is around the corner from Farnborough North station.
❀◑⇌(North)P🚌(41)🐾📶

Tilly Shilling

Unit 2-5 Victoria Road, GU14 7PG
✪ 7am-midnight (1am Fri & Sat) ☎ (01252) 893560
Greene King Abbot; Ruddles Best Bitter; 5 changing beers [H]
Town-centre aero-themed pub named after an engineer at the nearby RAE factory who designed a major improvement to the Merlin engines that powered many RAF fighter planes during WWII. The large rectangular open-plan lounge features a glass frontage that opens in good weather, extending the pub out onto the pavement. Ten handpumps leave plenty of space for regular and ever-changing guest beers. Real cider is available from polypins at the end of the bar. Alcohol is served from 9am. 🐴◑♿⇌🍎🚌📶

Fleet

Prince Arthur [L]

238 Fleet Road, GU51 4BX
✪ 8am-midnight (1am Fri & Sat) ☎ (01252) 622660
Greene King Abbot; Ruddles Best Bitter; house beer (by Longdog); 4 changing beers [H]
Wetherspoon pub in a former grocery store, named after Prince Arthur, Duke of Connaught, who lived in Fleet when he was commander of the nearby Aldershot Garrison. Beer festivals take place approximately every other month, in addition to the national Wetherspoon festivals, some featuring LocAles and others beers from further afield. In addition to the ales a locally produced cider is available on handpump. Q🐴❀◑♿🍎🚌(72)📶

Freefolk

Watership Down Inn [L]

Freefolk Priors, RG28 7NJ (just off B3400)
✪ 12-3, 6-11; 12-11.30 Fri & Sat; 12-9.30 Sun
☎ (01256) 892254 🌐 watershipdowninn.com
5 changing beers (sourced locally) [H]
Built in 1840, in the Upper Test Valley, this place is still affectionately known locally as the Jerry, for reasons that are as varied as the ales. The pub is named in honour of local author Richard Adams' book, set in the downland to the north of the pub. Outside there is an extensive garden, patio and family area. A beer festival is held each year and occasional live music and themed food evenings are featured. CAMRA North Hampshire Pub of the Year 2015. Q🐴❀🛏◑P🚌(76,86)🐾📶

Fritham

Royal Oak [L]

SO43 7HJ (W end of village no through road)
✪ 11-3, 6-11; 11-11 Sat; 12-10.30 Sun ☎ (023) 8081 2606
Bowman Wallops Wood; Flack Manor Flack's Double Drop; Ringwood Best Bitter; 4 changing beers (sourced locally; often Keystone, Stonehenge, Vibrant Forest) [G]
One of the New Forest's treasures. A front bar leads through to several interconnected back rooms, where bare boards, low beams, log fires and wainscoted and colourwashed walls make the very essence of a rural inn. It is a welcoming haven for walkers, cyclists, equestrians (facilities provided) and dog lovers. The seven gravity-dispensed ales may include one brewed in Fritham. Excellent, simple lunches utilise much local produce. A vast tabled garden area also houses three high-grade rentable shepherd's bothies. Q🐴❀🛏◐🐾

Goodworth Clatford

Clatford Arms

Village Street, SP11 7RN
✪ 12-2.30 (not Mon & Tue), 5.30-11 (11.30 Thu; midnight Fri); 12-midnight Sat; 12-11 Sun ☎ (01264) 363298
Flack Manor Flack's Double Drop; 3 changing beers (sourced locally) [H]
A refurbished traditional local pub maintaining a village atmosphere, but in a modern style. One end of the pub has a large-screen TV and games, while the other has a pleasant dining area. There is a strong sporting theme, with pool, darts and cribbage teams as well as a golf society. Four beers are served, mainly from local breweries. A good food menu uses much local produce. There is a large garden to the rear with a pétanque rink for a game of boules. Q🐴❀◑♣P🚌(15)🐾📶

Gosport

Brewpot [L]

11A/B North Cross Street, PO12 1BE
✪ closed Sun & Mon; 12-5 (6 Wed & Thu; 7 Fri); 11-7 Sat
☎ (023) 9252 2746
Oakleaf Hole Hearted; 2 changing beers [G]
The retail outlet of the nearby Oakleaf Brewery, this bar and off-licence is a short walk from the Gosport ferry and local buses. Three Oakleaf beers are on tap and casks of beer can be ordered for home consumption. There is a large range of bottled beers from Oakleaf and other regional breweries and a limited range of foreign beers and bottled ciders. Pies and pasties are also available. The venue is occasionally used to launch new beers, usually on Friday afternoons. Q♿♣🚌

Junction Tavern

1 Leesland Road, Camden Town, PO12 3ND
✪ 12-midnight; 12-11 Sun ☎ (023) 9258 5140
🌐 junctiontavern.com
3 changing beers (sourced regionally) [H]
Relatively small pub on the site of Brockhurst Junction on the dismantled Fareham to Gosport railway line, now a cycle track and footpath. In addition to three varied real ales, there are several real ciders from Countryman and Farmer Jims, plus Lilley's Bee Sting Still Perry. Beer festivals take place over the Easter weekend and a weekend in late summer. ❀♣🍎🚌(E1)

Queen's Hotel

143 Queens Road, Forton, PO12 1LG
✪ 11.30-2.30 (not Mon-Thu), 5-11.30; 11.30-11.30 Sat; 12-3, 7-11 Sun ☎ 07974 031671
Ringwood Fortyniner; 4 changing beers (often Oakleaf, Titanic, White Horse) [H]
Award-winning free house with over 30 years in this Guide, which is sought after by locals and visitors from all over the country. The focal point of the bar is a real fire with a carved wood surround. Beers from local breweries appear from time to time and JJ's Suicider is the regular cider. An annual beer festival takes place in October. Snacks are served on Friday lunchtimes. ❀♣🍎🚌

Hammer Vale

Prince of Wales
Hammer Lane, GU27 1QH (enter Hammer Lane from Haslemere end, due to width restriction at Liphook end)
⏲ 11-11; 12-11 Sun ☎ (01428) 652600
Fuller's London Pride; Gales HSB; 1 changing beer 🄷
Although tucked away, this pub is well worth a visit to sample the Pride, HSB and the occasional Fuller's guest. It has a huge outside seating area and is well sited for walkers and campers. Nick and Heidi serve excellent meals and the lunchtime baguettes will hit the spot. There are many stories (mostly apocryphal) as to how such a large 1927-built roadhouse was sited away from the main road. Check the stained-glass windows, one for Amey's of Petersfield. Q🐴❀◐◑♿▲♣P🐾📶

Hartley Wintney

Waggon & Horses
High Street, RG27 8NY
⏲ 11-11 (midnight Fri & Sat); 12-11 Sun ☎ (01252) 842119
Courage Best Bitter; Gales HSB; 2 changing beers (sourced nationally) 🄷
A village pub whose landlord of over 30 years has won several local CAMRA awards. HSB and Courage Best are regularly served alongside changing guest beers. The pub's lively public bar contrasts with a quieter lounge. Tables outside on the pavement enable guests to enjoy the atmosphere of the village, renowned for its antique shops. At the rear is a pleasant courtyard garden and a heated, covered smokers' area. Food is served lunchtimes only, but not Sundays. Q❀◐♿🍎🚌(72)🐾

Havant

Robin Hood
6 Homewell, PO9 1EE
⏲ 11-11; 12-10.30 Sun ☎ (023) 9248 2779
🌐 robin-hood-havant.co.uk
Fuller's London Pride; Gales Seafarers Ale, HSB; 1 changing beer 🄷
Originally this 18th-century pub was more like someone's front room, and had no keg beer – it has expanded considerably. The bar is divided into two areas – the front has bare flagstones and the rear is carpeted, with comfortable seating. Outside, there is a small garden and smoking area. The low beams, open fireplaces and cosy interior add to the appeal of this somewhat hidden gem in the centre of town. ❀◐⇌🚌🐾

Hawkley

Hawkley Inn
Pococks Lane, GU33 6NE
⏲ 12-3, 5-11; 12-11 Sat; 12-10.30 Sun ☎ (01730) 827205
Dark Star Hophead; Hop Back Summer Lightning; Sharp's Doom Bar; 4 changing beers 🄷
A genuine free house, popular with locals and passers-by alike. The present landlord has refurbished the interior tastefully, adding a personal touch while respecting the locals' wishes, creating a warm, welcoming ambience that proves difficult to tear yourself away from. It is gaining a reputation for quality food, with a steak night each Monday, although the landlord insists that real ale is the hub of the business. A beer festival is held each May. B&B accommodation is available.
🐴❀🛏◐◑🐾

Herriard

Fur & Feathers 🄻
Back Lane, RG25 2PN (on old Basingstoke-Alton road, parallel to A339)
⏲ closed Mon; 12-3, 5-11; 12-11 Fri & Sat; 12-6 Sun
☎ (01256) 384170 🌐 thefurandfeathers.co.uk
Sharp's Doom Bar; 3 changing beers (sourced locally) 🄷
Victorian ale house originally built for local farmworkers in 1880, now an open-plan family-run free house with a central bar area. The three guest beers are often from local breweries, including Hogs Back, Flack Manor, Longdog and Red Cat. The two dining areas either side of the bar area provide a pleasant atmosphere in which to enjoy the mouthwatering locally sourced menu. If dining, booking in advance is recommended, but a quiet pint can be enjoyed at any time.
Q❀◐◑♿P🚌(13X)📶

Hill Head

Crofton 🄻
48 Crofton Lane, PO14 3QF
⏲ 11-11; 12-10.30 Sun ☎ (01329) 314222
🌐 thecrofton.co.uk
Oakleaf Hole Hearted; Sharp's Doom Bar; 4 changing beers (sourced nationally) 🄷
One of the more successful Punch Taverns outlets, which resulted in the premises being extended in 2012. Beers from SIBA breweries are on tap in addition to those from the Punch portfolio, plus Westons Old Rosie Scrumpy cider. The popular function room with skittle alley gets booked up well in advance. A small beer festival takes place on St George's Day, and a larger weekend festival in November. Home-cooked food is served all day every day. Q🐴❀◐◑♿♣🍎P🚌(21)

Holybourne

Queen's Head
London Road, GU34 4EG
⏲ 12-11 (12.30am Fri & Sat); 12-10.30 Sun ☎ (01420) 86331
🌐 queensheadalton.co.uk
Greene King IPA; Hardys & Hansons Bitter; 2 changing beers 🄷
Traditional, friendly pub offering an interesting selection from the Greene King range and occasionally another guest ale. The Queen's comprises three refurbished rooms plus a covered and heated smoking area. Home-made hearty food is served daily featuring the pub's famous pies. There is regular live music throughout the year, with the charity music and beer event, Altonbury, on the first Saturday in July. An extensive beer garden features a children's play area and dogs are permitted on a short lead. Happy hour is Monday-Friday 4.30-6.30pm. Q🐴❀◐◑♣P🚌(65)🐾📶

Hook

White Hart Hotel
London Road, RG27 9DZ (next to Hook Texaco garage)
⏲ 11-11; 12-10.30 Sun ☎ (01256) 762462
Sharp's Doom Bar; 2 changing beers 🄷
You will always get a warm welcome at the White Hart, a 16th-century coaching inn. It has a spacious bar area, oak beams and some nooks where you can sit. Near the bar it gets busy with softly piped music and TVs showing sport; the opposite end is

much quieter and ideal for enjoying a meal. There is an extensive beer garden to the side and a large car park behind. The bus service is daytime only. ❀🛏◑◑≹P🚌(13)🐾📶

Hook Common

Crooked Billet

London Road, RG27 9EH

⏲ 11.30-3, 6-midnight; 11.30-midnight Sat; 12-11 Sun
☎ (01256) 762118 🌐 thecrookedbilletpub.co.uk

Courage Best Bitter; Sharp's Doom Bar; 2 changing beers (sourced nationally) [H]

The Crooked Billet is situated on the London Road just outside Hook and has been a free house under the same ownership for 28 years. In the summer you can enjoy the pleasant riverside garden or the air-conditioned bars, restaurant or snug. In winter, warm up around one of the traditional log fires. Good food and ales are always on sale here. An annual beer and rock music festival is held over the August bank holiday weekend. Q❀◑◑P🐾

Hurstbourne Tarrant

George & Dragon

The Square, SP11 0AA

⏲ 8am-11; 11-9 Sun ☎ (01264) 736277
🌐 georgeanddragon.com

Betteridge's HBT; Upham Punter; West Berkshire Good Old Boy; 3 changing beers (sourced regionally) [H]

There has probably been an inn here since the 11th century, with present parts dating from the 16th century. It has recently reopened after a long closure and is now comprehensively restored with flagstone flooring, original oak beams and oak woodburners. There is a warm and cosy atmosphere for relaxation indoors, with an outdoor patio suntrap. Look out for the historic post holes above the fireplace. There are cycle racks outside at the front. Sunday evening food is pizzas only. Betteridge's HBT beer is brewed just along the road. Q🔥❀🛏◑◑♿P🚌(7)🐾📶

Hythe

Ebenezers [L]

18A Pylewell Road, SO45 6AR

⏲ 11-2.30, 5.30-11; 11-11.30 Fri & Sat; 12-11 Sun
☎ (023) 8020 7799

Flack Manor Flack's Double Drop; Greene King Abbot; 2 changing beers (sourced locally; often Bowman, Flowerpots, Vibrant Forest) [H]

Delightful little single-storey bar, built in 1845 as a chapel and previously used as a school, flour store and furniture store. Now the venue serves some of the best local ales in the area. The open-plan bar's traditional feel encourages good conversation, with a warm welcome from friendly bar staff. Home-made pub grub is available lunchtime and evenings. Outside are large covered and uncovered dining/smoking areas. Nearby is the world's oldest working pier railway. Q❀◑◑♿🍎🚌(8,9)📶

Kimpton

Welcome Stranger

Kimpton Down, SP11 8PG

⏲ 12-4, 7-11 ☎ (01264) 772444
🌐 thewelcomestranger.co.uk

Wadworth 6X; 2 changing beers (sourced regionally) [H]

A traditional beamed family pub in a lovely country setting. The interior is a mix of old alongside new, with a games room with pool and darts, and a cellar for events. The garden offers a selection of games for young children, and a separate sheltered smoking area. The focus is on real ale, with fast-moving guest beers. A weekly meat draw is held on Sunday afternoons. Regular music events take place, including a monthly open mic night. Q🔥❀♣P🐾

Little London

Plough Inn 🏆

Silchester Road, RG26 5EP

⏲ 12-3, 5.30 (6 Fri & Sat)-11; 12-3, 7-10.30 Sun
☎ (01256) 850628

Palmers Dorset Gold; Ringwood Best Bitter; 2 changing beers (sourced regionally; often Andwells, Branscombe Vale, Stonehenge) [G]

Excellent traditional village pub and recent CAMRA Regional Pub of the Year. Enjoy beer gravity-fed from casks behind the bar and sit in front of a log fire or in the peaceful garden. A good range of baguettes is available (no food Sun eve). Very popular with locals and also visitors to Pamber Forest and the nearby Roman remains in Silchester. Q🔥❀♣P🚌(14)🐾

Lower Farringdon

Golden Pheasant [L]

Fareham Road, GU34 3DJ (at Farringdon crossroads on A32)

⏲ 12-11; 12-10.30 Sun ☎ (01420) 588255

Courage Best Bitter; Hogs Back HBB, TEA; 3 changing beers (sourced locally; often Flowerpots) [H]

Free house serving up to six cask ales, with Hogs Back HBB badged as Pheasant Ale. Mine host is renowned in the local area for his excellent food, locally sourced, including diabetic ice cream. Candlelit dining to piano accompaniment features every third Friday (booking required). Fresh fish is available daily. The first Sunday in the month is Curry Club (from Odiham Spice) after 6.30pm. There is a large bar area, a separate dining room and ample parking outside. Q🔥❀◑◑♣🍎P🐾

Lower Wield

Yew Tree [L]

SO24 9RX SU636398

⏲ closed Mon; 12-3, 6-11; 12-10.30 Sun ☎ (01256) 389224
🌐 the-yewtree.org.uk

Triple fff Alton's Pride; 1 changing beer (sourced locally) [H]

Out-of-the-way rural local set in picturesque rolling Hampshire countryside, with an old yew tree growing outside (hence the name), on a quiet lane opposite the local cricket pitch. The house beer is Triple fff Alton's Pride and the guest normally comes from a local brewery. All real ales are sold at a reasonable price. The pub has a separate dining area where locally renowned, good value food is served. The nearest bus stop is Medstead, 1½ miles away. Q❀◑◑P

Lymington

Borough Arms

39 Avenue Road, SO41 9GP (on B3054, N edge of town centre)
⏲ 5-11 Mon & Wed; 5-10.30 Tue; 12-2, 4-11 Thu; 12-2, 4-1am Fri; 12-1am Sat; 12-10.30 Sun ☎ (01590) 672814
Ringwood Fortyniner; 2 changing beers (sourced regionally; often Andwells, Flack Manor, Itchen Valley) Ⓗ
Intimate, family-run locals' pub with a jukebox, gaming machines, pool table and dartboard. A separate area enables quiet conversation. It has a spacious car park and is close to St Barbe's Museum, the community centre, high street and town hall. Features are stained-glass windows, a real fire and a curious pub cat. Occasional terrestrial and Freeview sporting events are shown on TV in the central bar area. Support for local breweries is shown by the changing guest ale selection.
Q❀⇌(Town)♣●P🚌📶

Six Bells Ⓛ

48 St Thomas Street, SO41 9ND (top of high street)
⏲ 8am-11 (midnight Fri & Sat) ☎ (01590) 689990
Greene King Abbot; Ruddles Best Bitter; Sharp's Doom Bar; Vibrant Forest Flying Saucer; 2 changing beers (sourced locally; often Vibrant Forest) Ⓗ
This Wetherspoon pub has been a furniture shop and kitchenware store. The name reflects a pub that once stood nearby and was the headquarters of the bell-ringers from St Thomas' Church next door. Double glass doors lead into a reasonably sized seating area, with flame-effect gas fire, plus a disabled toilet; curved stone steps bring you up to the servery and bar, unfortunately not wheelchair accessible. Through the bar, exits lead to outside dining and smoking areas.
Q♨❀◐◑⇌(Town)●🚌📶

Medstead

Castle of Comfort

Castle Street, GU34 5LU
⏲ 12-11; 12-10.30 Sun ☎ (01420) 562112
🌐 castleofcomfortmedstead.co.uk
St Austell Tribute; Sharp's Doom Bar; 1 changing beer Ⓗ
Set back from Castle Street, with a huge frontage and car park, this is a two-bar local and a village hub. The pub is now under the wing of Susannah, one half of the successful duo responsible for the George at Alton – she is revitalising this country inn without spoiling any part of it. Excellent food is on offer, with a similar menu to the George, and cooked to order. Q♨❀◐◑P🐾📶

Milford on Sea

Red Lion

32 High Street, SO41 0QD
⏲ 11.30-2.30, 6-11 (11.30 Fri); 11.30-11.30 Sat; 12-7 Sun
☎ (01590) 642236 🌐 theredlionmilford.co.uk
Ringwood Best Bitter; 1 changing beer Ⓗ
Attractive, homely but spacious locals' pub in a vibrant village, handy for the beach and the community centre. There is a small car park at the rear but free parking in the village after 6pm. Traditional pub food is served, with daily specials. Occasional live bands play, with a pianist on the second Sunday of the month and a Tuesday music quiz. The bar is on a split level, with a side room and a separate, unobtrusive games area, and a large garden to the rear. The beer range increases in summer. One real cider should always be available. Q♨❀🛏◐◑♿⛺♣●P🚌(X1)🐾📶

Newfound

Fox

Andover Road, RG23 7HH
⏲ 12-11.30; 12-10.30 Sun ☎ (01256) 780493
🌐 foxnewfound.co.uk
Fuller's London Pride; Gales HSB; 1 changing beer (sourced nationally; often Fuller's) Ⓗ
A warm and welcoming local pub set in wonderful countryside, with a large garden. It is a member of several pub leagues, playing pool, dominoes and crib. Regular quiz nights, live music and themed buffet nights are held. There is a separate dining area, pool room and function room containing a skittle alley. Excellent home-cooked meals are served, including Caribbean specialities. Two permanent beers from Fuller's are available, plus either a Fuller's seasonal or one from its guest list.
♨❀◐◑♿♣P🚌(11,76,86)📶

North Waltham

Fox Ⓛ

Popham Lane, RG25 2BE (off Frog Lane, between village and A30, M3 jct 7)
⏲ 11-11 (midnight Fri & Sat); 12-10.30 Sun
☎ (01256) 397288 🌐 thefoxpub.wordpress.com
Brakspear Bitter; Sharp's Doom Bar; West Berkshire Good Old Boy; 1 changing beer Ⓗ
Lovely traditional country pub on the edge of the village and overlooking extensive farmland. The pub is divided into two – a popular restaurant and a public bar where food is also served (booking advisable). Outside is an extensive beer garden and a children's adventure play area. The Ushers signage remains on the rear of the pub. Themed food events are arranged. Q♨❀◐◑♿P🐾📶

North Warnborough

Mill House Ⓛ

Hook Road, RG29 1ET
⏲ 11-11 ☎ (01256) 702953 🌐 millhouse-hook.co.uk
Brunning & Price Original; Hogs Back TEA; 4 changing beers (sourced regionally) Ⓗ
Listed as one of eight mills of Odiham in the Domesday Book, current sections are 17th-century additions, and it was last used as a corn mill in 1895. Most recently a restaurant, it is now under Brunning & Price ownership. It has a central bar area, separate dining areas and a lower level view of the waterwheel and restaurant. The area surrounding the mill pond fed from the Whitewater provides pleasant seating linking the function barn and parking. Q♨❀◐◑♿P🚌(13)🐾📶

Odiham

Odiham & Greywell Cricket Club Ⓛ

King Street, RG29 1NF (approx ¾ mile along King Street from village centre) SU751462
⏲ 5-10 (9 Wed); 1-10 Sat; 1-9 Sun ☎ (01256) 703749
Andwells Gold Muddler, King John; 1 changing beer (sourced locally) Ⓗ
The first recorded match at this club, set in countryside just south of the village, was in 1764, making it one of the oldest cricket clubs in the country. The timber building closed in 2011

following a fire, and the new well-appointed replacement opened in August 2013 with a single modern lounge bar with three handpumps, normally serving two Andwell beers and a guest. Although a private club, CAMRA members and visitors are welcome. Check for seasonal opening times. Local CAMRA Club of the Year 2014.
♿P

Park Gate

Village Inn
67 Botley Road, SO31 1AZ
11.30-11 (midnight Fri & Sat) ☎ (01489) 573223
Ringwood Best Bitter; Sharp's Doom Bar; 3 changing beers Ⓗ
The Village Inn was for many years keg only, but then reopened as a gastro-pub with a good selection of real ales. Although the beer range is limited to the Ember Inns portfolio, the three guest beers are normally of varying styles from interesting breweries, and tasting notes are available. Food is served all day until 10pm. Occasional live music takes place.
♿ P (28,28A)

Portsmouth

Artillery Arms
Hester Road, Milton, PO4 8HB
12-11.30 (midnight Fri & Sat) ☎ (023) 9273 3610
Bowman Swift One; Fuller's London Pride; Ringwood Fortyniner; 3 changing beers Ⓗ
Tucked away in the back streets of Portsmouth, this pub is a real find and one to tick off on a visit to the city. There are two different bar areas and a large garden at the rear with plenty of seating. Close to Fratton Park football ground, pool and darts teams compete weekly and food is served on match days and Sundays. A good selection of regional ales is to be found all year round. ♣P

Barley Mow
39 Castle Road, Southsea, PO5 3DE
12 (11 Sat)-midnight; 12-11 Sun ☎ (023) 9282 3492
barleymowsouthsea.com
Fuller's London Pride; Gales HSB; 6 changing beers Ⓗ
Friendly two-bar community pub offering a selection of eight ales including a mild, stout or porter, as well as Old Rosie cider. There is an impressive array of events including live music, meat raffles, quizzes, pool, darts, golf teams, bar billiards, chess league and monthly druid moots – all listed on the pub's website. The garden is a real gem, with some hidden treasures, and has won awards in its own right. Children are welcome until 8pm. ♣

Brewhouse & Kitchen
26 Guildhall Walk, Landport, PO1 2DD
10-11 ☎ (023) 9289 1340 brewhouseandkitchen.com
Brewhouse & Kitchen Mucky Duck, Sexton, George Anson, Guildhall, Crafty; 1 changing beer Ⓗ
One of the closest pubs to Portsmouth & Southsea train station, this is an ideal place to meet to plan the day ahead when arriving in the city. The ales are all brewed on-site by the 2.5 barrel plant that greets you as you walk in. Food is served 10am-9pm. A true LocAle pub in the city centre.
♿(Portsmouth & Southsea)

Bridge Tavern
54 East Street, Old Portsmouth, PO1 2JJ
11-11; 12-10.30 Sun ☎ (023) 9275 2992
bridge-tavern-portsmouth.co.uk
Fuller's London Pride; Gales Seafarers Ale, HSB; 1 changing beer (often Fuller's) Ⓗ
Named after the old swing bridge that once spanned the Camber Docks, this is the last survivor of some 14 pubs in East Street. One side of the building is decorated with a large mural depicting Old Portsmouth in days gone by. The single bar is divided into several areas and is complemented by an outside drinking area that overlooks the fishing fleet. It is not surprising therefore that fish features heavily on the menu. (16,19)

Eldon Arms
11-17 Eldon Street, Southsea, PO5 4BS
12-11 (midnight Fri & Sat) ☎ (023) 9229 7963
Fuller's London Pride; 1 changing beer Ⓗ
A traditional tiled exterior belies an expansive interior, as the building encompasses the neighbouring cottage. Pub games can be enjoyed here including pool, bar billiards, darts, dominoes and crib, along with a selection of board games. Real ales include local guests. This is a community-based, student-friendly pub with a mixed clientele. Food is served, with a carvery on Sunday.
(Portsmouth & Southsea)♣ (15)

Golden Eagle
1 Delamere Road, Southsea, PO4 0JA
3-midnight (1am Fri); 12-1am Sat; 12-11 Sun
☎ (023) 9282 1658
Fuller's London Pride; Gales Seafarers Ale, HSB; 2 changing beers Ⓗ
A large local hidden in the back streets of Southsea but only a short walk from Albert Road. The larger carpeted front bar hosts live music every weekend featuring bands from both near and far. The back bar has bare boards with a pool table. To the rear is a small garden. When there is a band playing, do not be surprised if the landlord offers you a child's musical instrument to play. A quiz is held every Thursday. (Fratton)♣

Hole in the Wall
Great Southsea Street, Southsea, PO5 3BY
4-11; 12-midnight Fri; 2-11 Sat & Sun ☎ (023) 9229 8085
theholeinthewallpub.co.uk
Oakleaf Hole Hearted Ⓖ; 10 changing beers Ⓗ
A traditional, friendly local pub serving an excellent range of well-kept real ales. It is off the beaten track in an old part of town, and offers simple, good-value food including speciality local sausages and meat puddings. The decor has nicely worn floorboards, dark pews and wood panelling, old photographs and prints on the walls, with hundreds of pumpclips on the ceiling, and there is a little snug behind the bar. Daily papers are available. A quiz night is held on Thursdays. Local CAMRA Pub of the Year 2015. (7,15)

Lawrence Arms
63 Lawrence Road, Southsea, PO5 1NU
2-11.30 (12.30am Fri); 11-12.30am Sat; 11-11 Sun
☎ (023) 9282 1280 lawrence-arms-portsmouth.co.uk
Sharp's Doom Bar; 3 changing beers (often Irving) Ⓗ
Dating back to 1887, this street-corner pub's exterior retains some traditional tiles and lanterns. Inside, the L-shaped bar faces a large lounge area. Very much a friendly community pub, there are darts, pool and football teams, weekly meat

raffles, quizzes and themed days. Guest ales are Irving seasonals, another local beer plus one other. A good cider selection is also on sale, with Westons plus boxed and bottled ciders; up to 20 in the summer. Food includes tasty gourmet toasties.
❀⇌♣●⊟(2,18,20)

Leopold Tavern L
154 Albert Road, Southsea, PO4 0JT
12 (11 Sat)-midnight; 12-11 Sun ☎ (023) 9282 9748
leopoldtavern.co.uk
Dark Star Hophead, American Pale Ale; 8 changing beers H
A former Portsmouth & Brighton United Breweries pub, it is spacious and divided into three drinking areas served by a single bar. There is also a small patio garden which is overlooked by the pub's own Tardis. It has 10 handpumps, usually serving five choices from local breweries and five from further afield. It also offers over 100 bottled beers from around the world and several ciders and perries. A popular quiz is held on Monday evenings.
Q❀●⊟(2,20)

Lord Palmerston L
84-90 Palmerston Road, Southsea, PO5 3PT
8-midnight (1.30am Fri & Sat) ☎ (023) 9272 8000
Fuller's London Pride; Greene King Abbot; 8 changing beers H
Large Lloyds No.1 bar in a busy shopping area. The landlord is a firm supporter of LocAle, with as many as six available at any time, served on a rota basis; there is also a range of ciders. Food is available all day from 8am. This local is close to many bus routes and just yards from Southsea Common and the beach. It is popular with families throughout the day. A DJ plays on Friday and Saturday night, when it can get noisy.

Northcote Hotel L
35 Francis Avenue, Southsea, PO4 0HL
11-midnight (1am Fri & Sat); 12-midnight Sun
☎ (023) 9282 8852 northcotehotel.co.uk
Hop Back Summer Lightning; Irving Invincible; Timothy Taylor Landlord; Wadworth 6X H
An ornate ex-Pike Spicer pub which sits imposingly on the corner of Northcote Road and Francis Avenue, with two bars and a large heated patio garden. The public bar has a raised area with a dartboard and the lounge is decorated with photos and memorabilia of Laurel and Hardy, the Marx Brothers and Basil Rathbone in his famous role as Sherlock Holmes. The cider is Lilley's Pheasant Plucker. ❀♣●⊟(2,20)

Old Customs House
Gunwharf Quays, Gunwharf, PO1 3TY
9am-11.30 Mon & Tue (midnight Wed & Thu; 12.30am Fri; 1.30am Sat); 9am-11 Sun ☎ (023) 9283 2333
theoldcustomshouse.com
Fuller's London Pride, ESB; Gales Seafarers Ale, HSB; 1 changing beer (often Fuller's) H
Proclaiming itself the only traditional pub in the Gunwharf Quays retail complex, this Grade II-listed building retains the layout of the former naval offices of HMS Vernon. There is a heated rear patio area and seating at the front which is ideal for people-watching during the summer. The pub is open all day for food, including breakfast, and a number of the food dishes include local ales in their recipes. ❀⇌(Harbour)⊟

Old House at Home
104 Locksway Road, Milton, PO4 8JR
12-11.30 (11 Mon; 1am Fri & Sat); 12-11 Sun
☎ (023) 9273 2606
Adnams Ghost Ship; Sharp's Doom Bar; 3 changing beers H
Lively community local with high aspirations. The spacious public bar, furnished with tables, chairs and comfy sofas, offers a selection of changing real ales and real ciders – it is a former local CAMRA Cider Pub of the Year. An unusual menu includes English tapas. Live music features every weekend. Live sport is televised on large screens in the main bar, while the separate lounge bar is used for functions, clubs and associations. The pub is home to darts, pool and even a rugby team.
❀♣●P⊟

Pembroke
20 Pembroke Road, Old Portsmouth, PO1 2NR
10-midnight (1am Fri & Sat); 12-4, 7-11 Sun
☎ (023) 9282 3961
Draught Bass; Fuller's London Pride; Greene King Abbot H
Dating back to 1711, and under this name since 1900, this single-room pub reflects its street-corner aspect with an L-shaped bar decorated with naval memorabilia. A rare place to find a good pint of Bass, it is well worth seeking out, just a short distance from the cathedral. It is home to a darts team and hosts live music at weekends and occasionally during the week. Hand-made rolls are available behind the bar. ♣⊟

Phoenix
13 Duncan Road, Southsea, PO5 2QU
10-midnight (1am Fri & Sat); 12-midnight Sun
☎ (023) 9282 1189
3 changing beers H
A classic community local, this is a small two-bar pub close to Albert Road. The venue has a close association with the nearby Kings Theatre and the lounge bar is adorned with photos of those who have appeared there – including a signed one of the great Spike Milligan. Next to the lounge is a quirky patio garden and a separate games room which was once part of the old Dock End brewery. Many games are available, including Space Invaders. The ciders/perries change regularly.
❀♣●⊟(2,20)

Rose in June L
102 Milton Road, Milton, PO3 6AR
12-midnight (1am Fri & Sat) ☎ (023) 9282 4191
theroseinjune.co.uk
Ballards Midhurst Mild; Downton Quadhop; Gales HSB; Irving Frigate; Ringwood Best Bitter; Thwaites Lancaster Bomber; 2 changing beers H
About 10 minutes' walk from Fratton Park, this two-bar pub is popular with football fans. It hosts plenty of events including a quiz night on Thursday, pool and darts matches, occasional comedy nights and a curry night on the first Wednesday of the month. The extensive garden has a play area and holds barbecues and a popular summer beer festival. Ciders include Cheddar Valley, Weston's Rosie's Pig and Perry. The yearly winter festival is very enjoyable. ●⊟(2,17,21)

Sir Loin of Beef
152 Highland Road, Eastney, PO4 9NH
11-11.30 (midnight Fri & Sat); 12-11.30 Sun
☎ (023) 9282 0115

8 changing beers H
Large single-bar pub with an almost Mediterranean-style café feel. The walls are decorated with submarine paraphernalia and a klaxon is used to call time. A good selection of bottle-conditioned ales is also stocked to supplement the eight fine ales on draught. The pub hosts a quiz night every Thursday, live entertainment Sunday lunchtimes and the ever-popular meat raffle. ▲🖩(1,2,17)

Priors Dean

White Horse
GU32 1DA
✪ 12-11 ☎ (01420) 588387 ∰ pubwithnoname.co.uk
Butcombe Bitter; Fuller's London Pride; Ringwood Best Bitter, Fortyniner; 6 changing beers H
Difficult to find but well worth the effort, this imposing, white former farmhouse continues to be a real ale haven. Two bars, one dedicated to local war poet Edward Thomas, plus a separate dining area, strike a fine balance between rustic, old world charm and modern hospitality. Good, homely food is served at lunchtime and in the evening all week, and all day at weekends. Beer festivals are held in June and December. Camping is available in summer in a field next to the pub.
🕭❀🛏🍸🖐P🛜

Ringwood

Railway Hotel
35 Hightown Road, BH24 1NQ (off Christchurch Rd) SU152048
✪ 11.30-11; 12-10 Sun ☎ (01425) 473701
∰ ringwoodrailway.com
4 changing beers H
Friendly two-bar traditional pub with a cosy snug at the rear, leading to a tidy child-friendly enclosed beer garden. The pub derives its name from the nearby station (now demolished) which is reflected in the railwayana, pictures, maps and photos adorning the public bar. The lounge has interesting old pews and chairs with more photographs. Home-cooked traditional food is served, including Sunday roast. Four changing ales are on tap, three from the Admiral list and one from SIBA. Q🕭❀🍸▲♣P🖩(RG2)🐾🛜

Romsey

Old House at Home
62 Love Lane, SO51 8DE (NE of town centre, adjoining Waitrose car park)
✪ 11-11 (11.30 Fri & Sat); 12-10.30 Sun ☎ (01794) 513175
∰ theoldhouseathomeromsey.co.uk
Fuller's London Pride; Gales Seafarers Ale, HSB; 2 changing beers (often Fuller's) H
Romsey's only thatched pub, a Guide entry since 2005, ceased to be a home-brew house in the early 20th century, and was then owned successively by Hammertons, Charrington and Gales. The three comfortable areas within include a cosy little restaurant, and two wood-burning stoves contribute to the heating. Outside, a heated patio leads to a gravelled, planted garden. Local ingredients are favoured in the cooking, and snacks are available throughout the afternoon. Live acoustic music plays on Mondays. No under-18s after 9pm. 🕭❀🍸⇌P🖩🐾🛜

Rotherwick

Coach & Horses
The Street, RG27 9BG
✪ closed Mon; 12-3, 5-11; 12-11 Sat; 12-6 Sun
☎ (01256) 768976 ∰ coachandhorses-rotherwick.co.uk
Badger First Call, Tanglefoot; 1 changing beer (sourced regionally) H
Unspoilt, unpretentious village pub set in stunning countryside. The friendly staff and locals offer a warm welcome and good old-fashioned hospitality every time. It boasts a lovely south-facing garden to the rear, overlooking tranquil farmland and, in cold weather, a large open fireplace and two wood-burning stoves. Badger ales are always available on handpump, including a changing seasonal ale. The menu is sourced using local suppliers where possible. Q🕭❀🍸🖐P🛜

Shawford

Bridge Inn
Shawford Road, SO21 2BP
✪ 12-11; 12-10 Sun ☎ (01962) 713171
4 changing beers (often Flack Manor, Red Cat, Sharp's) H
Large Chef & Brewer pub close to Shawford railway station. The ale range is continuously changing but four are usually available at one time. Local breweries are favoured. The large terraced beer garden next to the Itchen Navigation has seating for 200 and can be busy on a sunny weekend. The pub is suitable for wheelchair users and is popular with walkers, cyclists, families and dog owners. 🕭❀🍸&⇌🖐P🖩(1,E2)🐾🛜

Shedfield

Wheatsheaf Inn L
Botley Road, SO32 2JG (on A334)
✪ 12-11; 12-10.30 Sun ☎ (01329) 833024
Flowerpots Perridge Pale, Bitter, Goodens Gold; 2 changing beers (sourced locally; often Goddards, Itchen Valley, Stonehenge) G
Popular two-bar roadside pub between Botley and Wickham, serving mainly Flowerpots beer directly from casks behind the bar. Two other usually local beers are also available plus a choice of Westons real ciders. Good home-cooked food is served lunchtimes and Tuesday and Wednesday evenings. Live blues, jazz or folk music features on most Saturday evenings and a meat draw every Sunday. Darts and dominoes are played in the public bar. Q❀🍸♣🖐P🖩(69)🐾🛜

Sherfield on Loddon

White Hart
Reading Road, RG27 0BT
✪ 11-11 (midnight Fri & Sat); 12-11 Sun ☎ (01256) 882280
∰ whitehartsherfield.com
Wells Bombardier; Young's Bitter, Special; 2 changing beers (often Courage) H
Traditional 17th-century village inn opposite the village green and serving Young's beers and often a couple of guest ales and cider. The pub retains its oak beams and brick fireplaces and there are quiet cosy corners for conversation. The large and popular restaurant area has regular themed food events. The pub often runs events such as hog roasts and barbecues and is popular with families. Q🕭❀🍸&🖐P🖩(14)🐾🛜

Southampton

Bitter Virtue L

70 Cambridge Road, SO14 6US (jct with Alma Rd)
closed Mon; 10.30-8.30; 10.30-2 Sun ☎ (023) 8055 4881
bittervirtue.co.uk
2 changing beers (sourced regionally; often Red Cat, Siren, Vibrant Forest) G
Off-licence that is an Aladdin's cave for world beer enthusiasts, stocking over 500 differing bottled ales, many of them bottle-conditioned. Two or more draught beers and cider, stillaged at the rear, are available for carry-outs. An array of brewery-branded glasses, T-shirts, books and memorabilia is also on offer. You will often find a rare one-off brew you have never seen before – the knowledgeable staff are always willing to advise.

Butcher's Hook

7 Manor Farm Road, SO18 1NN
closed Mon & Tue; 6 (4 Fri; 1 Sat)-11; 2-10 Sun ☎ 07912 092928
4 changing beers (sourced nationally) G
The Butcher's Hook is a micropub in a converted shop, originally a butcher's, serving four changing cask beers and a good selection of bottled beers. The compact interior makes a lively and sociable drinking environment, especially at weekends. There is no bar as such and service is standing up at the stillage. Please check for the latest opening hours, events and beer availability as these do vary. Closed last Sunday evening of the month for ticketed music events.
Q (Bitterne) (7,16)

Giddy Bridge L

10-16A London Road, SO15 2AE
8am-11.30 ☎ (023) 8033 6346
Greene King Abbot; Ruddles Best Bitter; 6 changing beers (sourced nationally) H
Wetherspoon pub on the edge of the city centre, previously a furniture shop. It has a large single bar on the ground floor with additional seating upstairs, and an unusual, secluded roof terrace for when it is sunny. Covered tables and chairs are also outside on the pavement. Food is served all day, alcohol from 9am. The large range of guest beers is often from local breweries, and there are two draught ciders. Close to Southampton Solent University and the law courts. Q

Guide Dog L

38 Earl's Road, SO14 6SF
12-11; 12-10.30 Sun ☎ (023) 8022 5642
theguidedogsouthampton.co.uk
Flowerpots Goodens Gold; Fuller's ESB; 8 changing beers (sourced regionally; often Dark Star, Oakleaf, Triple fff) H
Welcoming side-street pub with the emphasis firmly on real ale and good company. A long array of handpumps offers the thirsty visitor an exciting range of brews, mostly local but also from further afield. Just a 15-minute walk from St Mary's Stadium, it makes a handy base for discerning Saints and away fans on match days. No meals, but filled rolls and pickled eggs are usually available from the bar. Local CAMRA Pub of the Year 2014.
(7,16,U6)

Hop Inn L

Woodmill Lane, SO18 2PH
12 (11 Sat)-11; 12-10.30 Sun ☎ (023) 8055 7723
Bowman Swift One; Gales HSB; Sharp's Doom Bar H
Good urban local in a residential area by Bitterne's Riverside Park, this 1930s pub has two bars with separate entrances. The exterior of the building is adorned with flowerboxes, winning three gold medals in the 2014 Southampton in Bloom competition. The lounge bar, divided by a central fireplace, is decorated with pictures and china ornaments. The more modern-style public bar houses bar games and a jukebox. The first Sunday of each month features a quiz and Wednesday is curry night. P (7,12,16)

Junction Inn L

21 Priory Road, SO17 2JZ
12-11 (midnight Fri & Sat) ☎ (023) 8058 4486
thejunction-inn.co.uk
Greene King XX Mild, IPA, Abbot; 5 changing beers H
This Greene King Local Hero pub, specialising in cask ales, is a popular community local with a range of eight beers, including the rarely seen Mild. Freshly cooked traditional meals are served, including Sunday roasts and dishes from a specials board. Live music is on the first Saturday of the month, a weekly quiz on Fridays, and ukulele jam sessions Wednesdays. There are three darts and two crib teams and a bar billiard table. Saints' St Mary's Stadium is a 15-minute walk away along the Itchen Boardwalk.
(St Denys) (7,16)

Obelisk Hotel

108 Obelisk Road, SO19 9DP (jct with Bedford Avenue)
3-11; 12-midnight Fri & Sat; 12-11 Sun ☎ (023) 8044 4271
obeliskhotel.co.uk
Draught Bass; Ringwood Best Bitter; Sharp's Doom Bar; 2 changing beers (sourced nationally; often Purity) H
Imposing street-corner local set in the quiet streets behind Woolston High Street. There is a public bar with a pool table and a smaller lounge, a function room and a south-facing beer garden. The welcoming landlord runs quizzes and meat draws, there is live music and karaoke each week, and TVs show football in each of the bars. The Obelisk Hotel and road are named after a memorial to Charles Fox, Whig politician, in nearby Mayfield Park.
(Woolston) P

Platform Tavern L

Town Quay, SO14 2NY
12-11 (midnight Thu); 11.30-midnight Fri; 12-midnight Sat ☎ (023) 8033 7232 platformtavern.com
Fuller's London Pride; Gales Seafarers Ale; 4 changing beers (sourced locally; often Dancing Man) H
Home of the Dancing Man microbrewery, with up to three of its beers usually available. The Platform's two rooms are separated by a ragged slate archway. Interior decoration includes African art, batik, musical instruments, news of the Titanic, and part of the ancient town walls. Food is high quality and good value. Live music features Thursday to Saturday evenings and Sunday lunchtimes. It hosts a winter ales festival in November and a cider fest at Easter. The closest pub to Southampton's ferry terminals.
(U1,U6)

Rockstone L

63 Onslow Road, SO14 0JL
11-midnight (1am Fri & Sat) ☎ (023) 8063 7256
therockstone.co.uk

7 changing beers (sourced regionally; often Dark Star, Flack Manor, Sunny Republic) H
Dating from the 1840s and prominently located in the Bevois Valley area, a deserved reputation has been established for this hostelry's varied range of cask ales and ciders, many from local breweries and sometimes sporting house names. It also offers probably the widest selection of rums, bourbons and whiskies locally. The renowned, generously portioned burgers are not to be missed. Several beer and cider festivals are held annually in conjunction with themed music events.
ᗢ☾◗●▯⊟(7,16,U6)🐾ᯤ

South Western Arms ⅃

38-40 Adelaide Road, SO17 2HW
⊙ 12-11 (midnight Fri & Sat) ☎ (023) 8032 4542
Bowman Yumi; 9 changing beers (sourced nationally) H
Single bar, corner pub with a seating area on the ground floor and more seating, a pool table and table football on the gallery upstairs. It is so close to St Denys station that it is almost on the platform! The walled garden, with its covered smoking area, is a suntrap in the summer. Nine ales are usually available plus one cider and up to 20 foreign bottled beers – Nellie's Nob, the house beer, is Bowman's Yumi. Two beer festivals are held each year. A pizza van stops outside Wednesday-Saturday. Qᗢ❀◗⇌(St Denys)♣●P⊟(7,16)🐾ᯤ

Talking Heads

320 Portswood Road, SO17 2TD
⊙ 6 (5 Fri & Sat)-1am; 2-1am Sun ☎ (023) 8067 8446
⊕ thetalkingheads.co.uk
Longdog Kismet, Lamplight Porter; Red Cat Prowler Pale, Red Cat Best; 2 changing beers (sourced locally) H
Popular combined pub and late-closing music and comedy venue near the university. The front public bar has a variety of upholstered chairs giving it a laid-back atmosphere. The beer range emphasis is on local breweries. There is no food, but the Frying Druid food van can be found in the car park most nights. A full monthly list of gigs is available. Note that opening and closing times can be trade/event-dependent and event entrance charges may apply. ᗢ♣P⊟(2,5,U6)🐾ᯤ

Waterloo Arms ⅃

101 Waterloo Road, SO15 3BS
⊙ 12-11 (midnight Fri & Sat) ☎ (023) 8022 0022
Downton New Forest Ale, IPA; Hop Back Golden Best, Crop Circle, Entire Stout, Summer Lightning; 2 changing beers (sourced nationally) H
The Waterloo Arms has been a Hop Back pub for over 20 years and currently boasts eight handpumps on the bar. The T-shaped pub has two Roman brick fireplaces, and many upholstered benches and stools to sit on while enjoying the ales. The 1920s building has a mock-Tudor façade and a more modern conservatory (available for functions) at the rear, which leads to the paved garden. ❀☾◗⇌(Millbrook)♣⊟🐾ᯤ

Wellington Arms ⅃

56 Park Road, SO15 3DE (on corner of Park Rd and Mansion Rd)
⊙ 12-11.30 (12.30am Fri & Sat) ☎ (023) 8022 0356
Fuller's London Pride, ESB; 9 changing beers (sourced locally; often Bowman, Oakleaf, Triple fff) H
The Wellington Arms has been a pub since circa 1850, and is decorated with tankards and Iron Duke memorabilia, linking to its name. The settle seating and fire in the front bar make it a cosy place to enjoy an ale in winter. The rear bar area leads through to the garden. Eleven handpumps serve two permanent and up to nine, predominantly local, changing beers. It is the only consulate of Redonda. A popular quiz is held on Thursdays.
❀⊟🐾ᯤ

Southwick

Golden Lion ⅃

High Street, PO17 6EB
⊙ 12-3, 5.30-11; 12-midnight Sat; 12-7 Sun
☎ (023) 9221 0437
Suthwyk Old Dick, Skew Sunshine Ale; 2 changing beers (sourced locally) H
Historic free house in a village that is still privately owned. The D-Day landings were partially planned by Montgomery and Eisenhower in the back bar. In the car park is the old brewhouse museum and the house beer is named after Old Dick, the last brewer. The award-winning food can be enjoyed in the bar or in the separate dining room. Tuesday is jazz night. Guest beers usually come from within 30 miles. Qᗢ❀☾◗♣●P🐾

Swanmore

Rising Sun ⅃

Droxford Road, SO32 2PS
⊙ 11.30-3, 6-11; 12-3, 6-10.30 Sun ☎ (01489) 896663
⊕ risingsunswanmore.co.uk
Sharp's Doom Bar; 3 changing beers (sourced locally) H
A 17th-century coaching inn with large fireplaces, oak beams and an exceptional red-brick vaulted ceiling in part of the restaurant. This family-run pub serves a good selection of mainly local ales. In early 2015 it started brewing in-house as Sunset Brewery – early brews show good promise. It has a large well-maintained garden with facilities for children and there is lots of parking. Good-quality food is available daily. Qᗢ❀☾◗P▯🐾

Tichborne

Tichborne Arms

SO24 0NA (1¼ mile S from B3047 Alresford Rd jct)
SU571304
⊙ 11.45-3, 6-10.30 (11 Wed & Thu; midnight Fri); 12-11.30 Sat; 12-7.30 Sun ☎ (01962) 733760 ⊕ tichbornearms.co.uk
Palmers Copper Ale; 2 changing beers (sourced locally) G
A delightful thatched village inn with a cosy wood-panelled public bar offering traditional pub games including darts and shove-ha'penny. The second and larger rustic bar has a welcoming wood-burning stove and daily newspapers for the walkers, cyclists – the bar can provide a puncture repair kit – and locals. The garden has an attractive covered patio and dogs are welcomed by the three resident canines. A seasonal menu changes daily (no food Sun eve). Motorhome stopovers are welcome. Cider is available in summer only.
Qᗢ❀☾◗♣●P🐾ᯤ

Titchfield

Queen's Head ⅃

13 High Street, PO14 4AQ

⌚ 12-11 (10.30 Mon; 11.30 Fri); 11-11.30 Sat; 11-11 Sun
☎ (01329) 842154 🌐 queenshead-titchfield.co.uk
4 changing beers (often Flack Manor, Irving, Oakleaf) H
A 17th-century listed pub, with a homely bar and open fire. Four regularly rotated ales are mainly from local breweries. Home-made, locally sourced food, including sausages from a nearby butcher, and a gluten-free menu, is served in the bar. A separate restaurant is open Friday and Saturday evenings and Sunday lunchtimes. A quiz and meat raffle are held every Sunday evening. Upstairs, a function room caters for events such as weddings, theme nights and discos. **Q**❀◑◐**P**🚌(X4)🐾📶

Wheatsheaf L

1 East Street, PO14 4AD
⌚ 12-11 (midnight Fri & Sat) ☎ (01329) 842965
🌐 wheatsheaftitchfield.co.uk
Flowerpots Bitter; Palmers Best Bitter; 3 changing beers H
Popular village free house, renowned for its friendly atmosphere, excellent ales and high-quality food. The cosy bar, with its real fire and adjacent snug, is a great place to catch up with local gossip. Food is served daily in the bar and separate restaurant (times may vary). Curries headline on Monday evening, steaks on Tuesday and roasts feature every Sunday. The first Monday of each month is folk music night, and a beer festival is held every summer and winter.
Q❀◑◐♿●**P**🚌(X4)🐾

Twyford

Phoenix Inn L

High Street, SO21 1RF
⌚ 11.30-2.30, 6-11; 11.30-11 Fri & Sat; 12-10.30 Sun
☎ (01962) 713322 🌐 thephoenixinn.co.uk
Flowerpots Bitter; Hardys & Hansons Bitter; 6 changing beers H
Traditional 17th-century coaching inn tastefully modernised to become a single-bar pub, run by the same family for over 30 years. Four local ales are sold along with four from Greene King, focusing on its guest beers. Traditional pub food is served, with themed food nights Tuesday to Thursday. Occasional live music and quiz nights take place. A popular function room with skittle alley is at the rear, with two patio areas outside. A loyalty card gives every 10th beer free. ❀◑◐♣**P**🚌(69,E1)📶

West Tytherley

Black Horse L

North Lane, SP5 1NF
⌚ closed Mon-Wed; 12-3, 6-11; 12-7.30 Sun
☎ (01794) 340308 🌐 theblackhorsepublichouse.co.uk
Hop Back Golden Best; 3 changing beers (sourced locally; often Bowman, Palmers, Red Cat) H
A gem of a village pub. Dating from the early 17th century, it expanded over the years to become a fully fledged coaching inn; the stables are now the skittle alley and function room. It is Grade II-listed with a special mention of the magnificent carved wood fireplace – dating from 1680, it was moved from the nearby Norman Court to a new part of the pub in 1830. The interesting menu features locally sourced produce such as venison and buffalo. The pub closes for the owners' annual holidays.
Q❀◑◐♣●**P**🚌(37)🐾📶

Wherwell

White Lion

Winchester Road, SP11 7JF
⌚ 11-11 ☎ (01264) 860317 🌐 thewhitelionwherwell.co.uk
Flowerpots Bitter; Sharp's Doom Bar; Timothy Taylor Landlord; 1 changing beer H
Pleasant former coaching inn at the centre of a historic and idyllic thatched village alongside the River Test, world famous for its trout fishing. The venue was built in 1611 and hit by a cannon ball in the Civil War, which still hangs on the bar today. Now the pub is used by the village community and walkers on the Test Valley Way. It opens for breakfast to non-residents and lunch hampers are available. Closed 3-5pm in winter.
Q❀◑◐**P**🚌(15)🐾📶

Whitchurch

Prince Regent L

104 London Road, RG28 7LT
⌚ 12-11 ☎ (01256) 892179
Hop Back Summer Lightning; 1 changing beer (sourced regionally) H
The pub up the hill is a single-bar local free house on the edge of the town, overlooking the higher reaches of the Test Valley. Local conversation takes pride of place among a mixed clientele. There is an excellent jukebox, a pool table and sports TV, with an emphasis on football matches. It is a good start for walks into the countryside. Live music features occasionally. ♣**P**🚌(76,86)🐾

Winchester

Black Boy L

1 Wharf Hill, SO23 9NQ (just off Chesil St, B3404)
⌚ 12-11 (midnight Fri & Sat); 12-10.30 Sun
☎ (01962) 861754 🌐 theblackboypub.com
Alfred's Saxon Bronze; Flowerpots Bitter; 3 changing beers (sourced locally; often Andwells, Bowman, Hop Back) H
Old, rambling building where six rooms, on differing levels, are interconnected and surround an island bar. Eclectic and eccentric décor abounds with a treasure trove of surprises, from tradesmen's tools to a farmhouse kitchen and serious taxidermy. Pub food is served daily and for more formal dining the Black Rat restaurant opposite is in the same ownership. The beer range emphasises local small breweries. Ten double en-suite rooms are available in the attached Black Hole B&B. **Q**❀🛏◑◐●🚌(4)🐾📶

Fulflood Arms L

28 Cheriton Road, SO22 5EF (take Western Rd off Stockbridge Rd)
⌚ 12-2.30, 4.30-11; 12-midnight Fri & Sat; 12-11 Sun
☎ (01962) 842996 🌐 thefulfloodarms.com
Greene King IPA; Red Cat Prowler Pale; 7 changing beers (sourced locally; often Flowerpots, Red Cat) H
In a residential conservation area, the dark-green tiled façade and etched windows show this 19th-century pub's former Winchester Brewery ownership. Inside, a makeover has produced a smart and comfy single bar (note the city map on the ceiling). Quizzes, special events and a loyalty card scheme attract an enthusiastic local following. Up to seven beers, many local, often include one from the pub's own tiny microbrewery. Newspapers are provided. There are patios outside for drinkers, front and rear. **Q**≋♣●🚌(4)📶

Hyde Tavern [L]

57 Hyde Street, SO23 7DY
🕐 12.30-2 (not Mon-Wed), 5-11; 5-midnight Fri; 12-midnight Sat; 12-11 Sun ☎ (01962) 862592
Flowerpots Bitter; Harveys Sussex Best Bitter [H]; 4 changing beers (sourced locally) [G]
Small, medieval and timber-framed, dominated by twin gables, this is an unspoilt pub lying below street level (beware low ceilings and undulating floors). The main bar leads into a cosy rear area and a cellar bar which hosts meetings of writers, storytellers and other groups. Up to six beers, some on gravity, many local and including a dark beer and a cider, are usually available. No food is served, but customers may order takeaways. Live folk music takes place on Saturday evenings. The pub has a delightful secluded garden.
Q❀⇌🍎🚌(67)🐾📶

Old Vine [L]

8 Great Minster Street, SO23 9HA (opp cathedral green)
🕐 11-11; 11-10.30 Sun ☎ (01962) 854616
🌐 oldvinewinchester.com
Ringwood Best Bitter; 3 changing beers (sourced locally; often Alfred's) [H]
Grade II-listed 18th-century inn covered in vine, opposite the cathedral green and the city museum (rear entrance in Little Minster Street), in the area known as The Square. It boasts an oak-beamed bar, a conservatory/garden room at the rear and medieval cellars that are said to be haunted. Its four handpulls dispense mainly local ales. A curtain separates the pub from the restaurant serving award-winning food, much made from local produce. There is 4-star en-suite accommodation.
Q❀🛏◑♣🚌(1,69)🐾📶

St James Tavern

3 Romsey Road, SO22 5BE (on main Romsey road)
🕐 12-11; 12-midnight Fri; 11-midnight Sat; 11-10.30 Sun ☎ (01962) 861288 🌐 saintjamestavernwinchester.co.uk
Wadworth Henry's IPA, Horizon, 6X, Swordfish; 1 changing beer (sourced nationally) [H]
Acutely-angled, end-of-terrace pub on a steep hill close to the hospital. The main L-shaped bar has light oak panelling, bare floorboards and a raised area with tables and settles for dining. Outside, a smart rear patio is ideal for small groups. Newspapers and board games are provided. Home-cooked food is served daily (not Sun eve), with interesting specials and themes, and a brunch club at the weekend. Quiz night is Tuesday. The cider is Westons Old Rosie. Q🚼❀◑⇌♣🍎🚌🐾📶

Wykeham Arms

75 Kingsgate Street, SO23 9PE (just outside the city's ancient Kingsgate)
🕐 11-11 ☎ (01962) 853834
🌐 wykehamarmswinchester.co.uk
Flowerpots Goodens Gold; Fuller's London Pride; Gales Seafarers Ale, HSB; 1 changing beer [H]
A Georgian inn dating from 1755, now owned by Fuller's, in the city's most historic area betwixt cathedral and college. Several interlinked rooms, all crammed with memorabilia, are served from a central bar. Furnishings include old school desks, and Nelsoniana abounds. Although a Fuller's pub, a Flowerpots beer is nearly always present. This civilised hostelry for conversationalists features in almost every known guide book and also offers 14 highly-rated rooms, an extensive food service and over 20 wines sold by the glass.
Q🛏◑🚌(1,69)🐾📶

Wootton

Rising Sun [L]

Bashley Common Road, BH25 5SF (on B3058, 1½ miles SE of A35)
🕐 10-11; 10-10.30 Sun ☎ (01425) 610360
Flack Manor Flack's Double Drop; Morland Old Speckled Hen; 1 changing beer [H]
Prominent roadside pub on the edge of open forest, within easy reach of the A35. It caters for visitors of all eras, with equine tethering posts and electric car charging points. There is ample seating and a large, separate family room leading to an enclosed adventure playground. It features many attractive stained-glass windows, and artefacts including old photos of celebrated forest folk. Value-for-money meals are served from an extensive menu 11.30am-9.30pm daily. The guest ale is often from a smaller West Country or lesser-known brewer. Q🚼❀◑♿P🚌(C32,C33)🐾📶

Yateley

Dog & Partridge

105 Reading Road, GU46 7LR
🕐 12-11 (midnight Fri & Sat); 12-10.30 Sun ☎ (01252) 870648 🌐 dogandpartridgeyateley.co.uk
St Austell Tribute; Theakston Best Bitter; Wadworth 6X; 1 changing beer [H]
This friendly open-plan pub reopened in July 2014 after major refurbishment. The new owners have an excellent reputation for serving quality real ales and home-made locally sourced food – their Sunday lunches are already legendary (booking essential). A beer festival is held in the summer, a quiz night every Thursday and live music Saturday. A golf society, pool, darts and Aunt Sally teams are hosted. It is the former HQ of the Official Monster Raving Loony Party, whose leader was landlord for 10 years. 🚼❀◑♿♣P🚌(3)🐾📶

The soul of beer

Brewers call barley malt the 'soul of beer'. While a great deal of attention has been rightly paid to hops in recent years, the role of malt in brewing must not be ignored. Malt contains starch that is converted to a special form of sugar known as maltose during the brewing process. It is maltose that is attacked by yeast during fermentation and turned into alcohol and carbon dioxide. Other grains can be used in brewing, notably wheat. But barley malt is the preferred grain as it gives a delightful biscuity/cracker/Ovaltine note to beer. Unlike wheat, barley has a husk that works as a natural filter during the first stage of brewing, known as the mash. Cereals such as rice and corn/maize are widely used by global producers of mass-market lagers, but craft brewers avoid them.

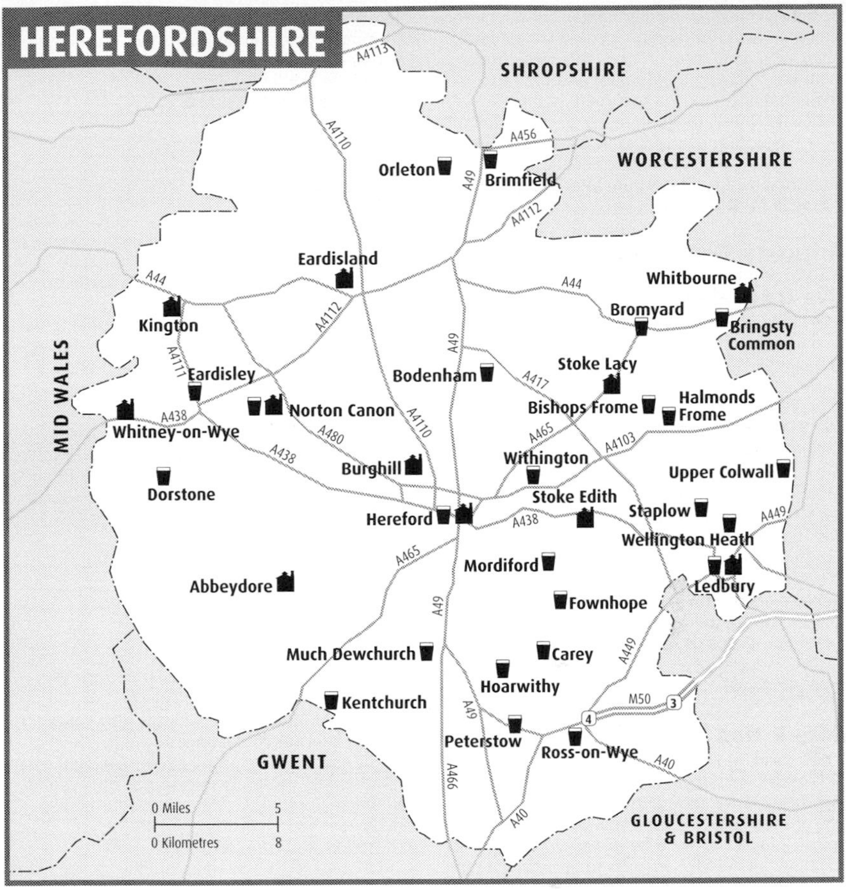

Bishops Frome

Green Dragon L

WR6 5BP (just off B4214)

5-11; 4-11.30 Fri; 12-11.30 Sat; 12-4, 7-10.30 Sun

(01885) 490607 thegreendragoninn.com

Purple Moose Cwrw Eryri (Snowdonia Ale); Theakston Best Bitter; Timothy Taylor Golden Best; Wye Valley Butty Bach; 2 changing beers (sourced locally; often Otter) H

Characterful 17th-century inn which lies at the heart of the community. A regular award winner, including Herefordshire CAMRA Cider Pub of the Year 2014, the bar has six handpumps offering a range of beers plus ciders and perries. Bar meals are served Saturday and Sunday lunchtimes and Tuesday-Saturday evenings. A beer festival is held in June. **Q**P

Bodenham

England's Gate Inn L

HR1 3HU (just off A417)

12-11 (10.30 Sun) (01568) 797286

englandsgate.co.uk

Hobsons Best Bitter; Wye Valley HPA, Butty Bach; 1 changing beer (sourced locally) H

This 16th-century black and white inn has been opened out internally and extensively modernised but retains the fine original timbers and flagstone floor. The guest beer is usually from a local brewery. The pub enjoys a loyal following for its excellent and affordable range of food including traditional roasts on Sundays. Letting rooms are in the newly converted coach house. A beer and sausage festival is held in July.

P(426)

Brimfield

Roebuck L

SY8 4NE (just E of A49 and S of A456)

12-2.30 (not Mon), 6-11; 12-3, 7-11 (not eve winter) Sun

(01584) 711827

Hobsons Best Bitter; 2 changing beers H

REAL ALE BREWERIES

Arrow Kington
Golden Valley Abbeydore (NEW)
Hereford Hereford
Jones the Brewer Whitney-on-Wye
Ledbury Ledbury
Mulberry Duck Burghill
Odyssey Whitbourne (NEW)
Saxon City Stoke Edith (brewing suspended)
Shoes Norton Canon
Simpsons Eardisland
Wobbly Hereford
Wye Valley Stoke Lacy

Previously a fine dining destination, but now firmly refocused as a community-oriented village local, albeit with good food on offer. The large front room has interesting old maps, and the more traditional oak-panelled rear room is the restaurant. Meals range from bar snacks to full à la carte – all locally sourced, with guest beers from local breweries. Community credentials are confirmed by the village store attached to the pub. Q⛵❀◑◗ÅP🐾📶

Bringsty Common

Live & Let Live 🄻

WR6 5UW (off A44, at cat & mouse sign follow right-hand track down onto common) SO699547

✪ closed Mon; 12-2.30, 6-11; 12-11 Fri & Sat; 12-7 Sun winter; 12-11 (10.30 Sun) summer ☎ (01886) 821462

🌐 liveandletlive-bringsty.co.uk

Wye Valley Butty Bach; 2 changing beers 🄷

A real survivor, the Live was saved from conversion into a house following a long-running campaign by locals and CAMRA, and an outstanding renovation has transformed this isolated Grade II-listed ex-cider house. Off a track on the common, and Herefordshire's only thatched pub, it features exquisite exposed timbers, flagstone floors, a fine fireplace and numerous oak settles. Quality locally sourced food is enjoyed in the bar and upstairs restaurant. Q⛵❀◑◗ÅP🚌(420)🐾

Bromyard

Rose & Lion 🄻

5 New Road, HR7 4AJ

✪ 11-11 ☎ (01885) 482381

Wye Valley Bitter, HPA, Butty Bach 🄷

One of the expanding Wye Valley estate, the Rosie enjoys a loyal following by locals, and is never anything but friendly. The two small original rooms are complemented by a further bar to the rear plus an annexe with fully equipped disabled toilets and a pleasant garden. It acts as a venue for live folk music on Sunday nights. Q❀♿♣P🚆🚌(420)🐾

Carey

Cottage of Content 🄻

HR2 6NG

✪ closed Mon & winter Tue; 12-2, 6-10.30 (11 Fri & Sat); 12-3 Sun ☎ (01432) 840242 🌐 cottageofcontent.co.uk

Hobsons Best Bitter; Wye Valley Butty Bach 🄷

A beautiful part black-and-white building with parts dating from 1485. There are two bars and a separate restaurant. Booking is advised at most times for the freshly prepared bar meals at lunchtime and à la carte in the evening. There is a large garden to the rear. Local cider is from Ross-on-Wye and Carey Organic. Q⛵❀🛏◑◗🍎P🐾

Dorstone

Pandy Inn 🄻

HR3 6AN (signed off B4348; opp village green)

✪ 12-3 (not Mon), 6-11; 12-11 Sat; 12-3, 6.30-10.30 Sun ☎ (01981) 550273 🌐 pandyinn.co.uk

Three Tuns XXX; Wye Valley Butty Bach 🄷

Although opened out, the interior here has a welcoming feel with discrete areas, a huge fireplace, timber-framing and exposed stone walls. The garden includes a children's play area. The pub caters equally for drinkers and diners, with an interesting range of dishes, including vegetarian. Accommodation is in an impressive eco-house at the rear. Gwatkins and nearby Pips cider is available in bottles.
Q⛵❀🛏◑◗🍎P🚌(39,39A)🐾📶

Eardisley

Tram Inn 🄻

HR3 6PG (on A4111, in village)

✪ closed Mon; 12-3, 6-midnight (12.30am Fri & Sat); 12-3, 7-10.30 Sun ☎ (01544) 327251 🌐 thetraminn.co.uk

Hobsons Best Bitter; Wye Valley Butty Bach; 1 changing beer 🄷

Grade II-listed black and white half-timbered inn taking its name from a long-gone horse-drawn tramway. The cosy bar (complete with original floor tiles and woodwork) contrasts with a larger bar with panelled walls and grand bay window, and a simple games room to the rear. Traditional, locally sourced freshly made pub meals are served and Sunday roasts (no food Sunday eve). Draught Dunkertons and bottled Orgasmic and Gwatkins ciders are also stocked.
Q❀◑◗Å♣🍎P🚌(446,462)🐾📶

Fownhope

New Inn 🄻

HR1 4PE (on B4224)

✪ 12-3, 6-midnight; 11-midnight Sat; 12-midnight Sun ☎ (01432) 860350 🌐 thenewinnfownhope.co.uk

Hobsons Best Bitter; house beer (by Wye Valley); 1 changing beer (often Hobsons) 🄷

A single room with exposed beams and light decor is divided into more discrete spaces by a central, bare-brick fireplace. Typical pub food is served Monday-Saturday lunchtimes, with fish and chips, pies, steaks and curry on various evenings. A Sunday roast is also served monthly. Jam sessions and quiz evenings are held regularly. Fownhope Football Club use the pub as a base.
⛵❀◑◗♿Å♣P🚌(454)🐾

Halmonds Frome

Majors Arms 🄻

WR6 5AX (¾ mile N of A4103 at Bishops Frome) SO675481

✪ 5 (4 Fri; 3 Sat; 12 Sun)-11 ☎ (01531) 640261

🌐 themajorsonsnailsbank.weebly.com

Purity Pure Gold; Wye Valley Bitter; 1 changing beer 🄷

Housed in an isolated old cider mill, this small and simple locals' pub has a basic bar area with bare stone walls and a large woodburner. An archway leads through to a larger room, with a patio that affords probably the best view from a pub in the county, particularly at sunset. Live music is hosted occasionally. Local Henney's Still Cider is available. Food is not normally served, but can be arranged for events. ⛵❀Å♣🍎P🐾📶

Hereford

Barrels 🄻

69 St Owen Street, HR1 2JQ

✪ 11-11.30 (midnight Fri & Sat); 12-11.30 Sun ☎ (01432) 274968

Wye Valley Bitter, HPA, Dorothy Goodbody's Golden Ale, Butty Bach; 1 changing beer (often Wye Valley) 🄷

Winner of Herefordshire CAMRA Pub of the Year six times, it is first and foremost a community pub. No food and no gimmicks here, but tons of character across five different bars. The cobbled courtyard to the rear hosts a charity beer and music festival each August bank holiday weekend. With the TV only turned on for major sports events, this is a pub where conversation and good times always hold sway.

Beer in Hand

136 Eign Street, HR4 0AP

5-10.30 Mon; 12 (4 Tue & Wed)-11; 12-10.30 Sun

beerinhand.co.uk

12 changing beers (often Odyssey, Purity) G

Herefordshire's first micropub was converted from a launderette in 2013, and by 2014 was named Herefordshire CAMRA Pub of the Year. With an impressive chilled racking system, it typically sells up to a dozen ales and 10 mainly local ciders and perries. Meals are served Thursday to Sunday – booking is recommended via the website. A quiz is held the first Wednesday and a jam session the last Tuesday of the month. Q

Hoarwithy

New Harp Inn

HR2 6QH

12-3, 6-11.30; 11.30-midnight Fri-Sun (01432) 840900

thenewharpinn.co.uk

Wye Valley Butty Bach; 3 changing beers (sourced locally; often Bespoke, Ludlow, Wood) H

Close by the River Wye, and with a brook running through the garden, this friendly pub comprises one long bar room with a stone floor and light modern decor, with a village shop (and post office on Monday) at one end, plus a large alfresco dining area. Home-prepared food ranges from bar snacks to full à la carte. Ales come from regional and local microbreweries, and a good selection of bottled beers is stocked. P(37)

Kentchurch

Bridge Inn

HR2 0BY (on B4347)

closed Tue; 12-2 (not Mon), 6-10; 12-2, 6-11 Fri & Sat; 12-4 Sun (01981) 240408 bridgeinnkentchurch.co.uk

Otter Bitter; 2 changing beers (often Wye Valley) H

Beautifully situated on the banks of the River Monnow, close to the Welsh border, the building probably dates from the 14th century. It comprises a welcoming single front bar, plus a restaurant with excellent views, and boasts riverside gardens and a pétanque piste. The freshly prepared food ranges from bar snacks to full meals. Guest beers are from regional and local breweries, with local Ty Gwyn cider in summer. Q P

Ledbury

Prince of Wales

Church Lane, HR8 1DL

11-11 (10.30 Sun) (01531) 632250 powledbury.com

Butcombe Bitter; Hobsons Best Bitter; Ledbury Bitter; Otter Bitter; Wye Valley HPA, Butty Bach; 1 changing beer H

Set in a delightful cobbled alley leading up to an imposing church, this 16th-century timber-framed pub boasts two bars and a discrete alcove where a folk jam session is held each Wednesday evening. Westons draught cider is stocked, together with an extensive range of foreign beers, both draught and bottled. The bar meals are excellent value, with roasts on Sunday.

Mordiford

Moon Inn

HR1 4LW (on B4224)

12-3 (not Mon), 6-midnight; 12-midnight Sat & Sun

(01432) 873067 moonatmordiford.com

Otter Amber; Timothy Taylor Landlord; Wells Bombardier; 2 changing beers H

A half-timbered and much-altered two-bar roadside village inn, the Moon started life as a farmhouse over 400 years ago. Popular among locals and with families tripping out from Hereford, it benefits from its proximity to the Mordiford Loop – a well-known local walk – as well as the Rivers Lugg and Wye. Traditional locally sourced pub food is served. Quiz night is every Tuesday.

P(453)

Much Dewchurch

Black Swan

HR2 8DJ (on B4348)

12 (11.30 Sat)-3, 5.30-11; 12-4, 6-10.30 Sun

(01981) 540295

Timothy Taylor Landlord; 2 changing beers (often Butcombe, Three Tuns) H

Possibly the oldest pub in Herefordshire, this delightful 15th-century heavily beamed village inn has its own priest hole. The small lounge leads into the dining room with an open fire, and the separate public bar with flagstone floors leads to a pool and darts room. Home-prepared, mainly locally sourced food is available every session. The guest beers are typically from regional breweries. Draught Westons cider and perry are available, together with bottles from other local cider makers. Thursday is folk night. P

Norton Canon

Three Horseshoes

HR4 7BH (on A480)

closed Mon & Tue; 12-3 Wed; 7-11; 12-3, 7-11 Sun

(01544) 318375

Shoes Norton Ale, Canon Bitter, Peploe's Tipple, Farrier's Ale H

Early-Victorian red-brick roadside pub of timeless rural character, home to the Shoes Brewery at the rear of the premises. It is one of only a handful of pubs to still have a shooting gallery. A friendly atmosphere always pervades, with a small but loyal following. The cosy and comfortable lounge, furnished with an eclectic collection of old chairs and sofas, contrasts with a more traditional public bar. Q P(461,462)

Orleton

Baker's Arms

SY8 4JB (on B4361)

12 (6 Mon)-11 (01584) 831686

Hobsons Twisted Spire, Best Bitter; Ludlow Boiling Well; Wood Shropshire Lass, Beauty; 1 changing beer (sourced locally) H

A 17th-century roadside pub, recently reopened after comprehensive refurbishment. To the left is the lounge with a restaurant to the rear, while to the right is the public bar – the snug – and behind that a games room with pool and darts. Two woodburners supplement the ground-source central heating. Food includes home-baked bread from the on-site bakery – hence the pub's new name. Horses are welcome, with a hitching bar and trough in the car park. Happy hour is Tuesday-Friday 5-6pm. ♘❀◐♣P🚌(490)🐾

Boot Inn 𝕃
SY8 4HN (off B4361)
⏲ 12-3, 5.30-11; 12-11.30 Sat; 12-11 Sun ☎ (01568) 780228
🌐 thebootinnorleton.co.uk
Hobsons Best Bitter; 1 changing beer (sourced locally; often Wye Valley, Ludlow, Three Tuns) Ⓗ
A comfortable and welcoming 16th-century black-and-white village pub with a large inglenook fireplace and original oak beams. A charity quiz is held monthly on each second Tuesday in winter and a beer and cider festival in July in the large beer garden. The home-prepared food ranges from bar snacks to interesting gourmet meals. Walkers are welcome, with the Mortimer Trail passing about a mile away, and the bus stops right outside. Q♘❀◐▲●P🚌(490)🐾📶

Peterstow

Red Lion 𝕃
Winters Cross, HR9 6LH (on A49, just NW of village)
⏲ 12 (5 Mon)-11 ☎ (01989) 730546
🌐 redlionpeterstow.co.uk
Hobsons Best Bitter; Wye Valley Bitter, Butty Bach; 1 changing beer (often Butcombe, Timothy Taylor, Wye Valley) Ⓗ
A single bar serves extensive drinking and dining areas including a large roadside conservatory. Home-prepared food ranges from bar snacks, including lighter options, to full meals. Guest beers are from local micros or regional breweries. Outside is an adventure playground for children. A charity quiz is held on the first Monday of the month. The regular Hereford-Gloucester bus service stops outside. ♘❀◐▲♣●P🚌(32)🐾📶

Ross-on-Wye

Mail Rooms
Gloucester Road, HR9 5BS
⏲ 8am-midnight (1am Fri & Sat) ☎ (01989) 760920
Greene King Abbot; Ruddles Best Bitter; 5 changing beers Ⓗ
Behind the fine red-brick and stone façade of what was once the main post office is this single-bar Wetherspoon conversion. Good-value food is served all day, including a children's menu. Two regular beers are complemented by up to five guests from a diverse range of breweries, plus two Westons ciders. Local beer and cider festivals are a feature. Alcohol is served from 9am.
Q♘❀◐♿●🚌(32,33)📶

Staplow

Oak Inn 𝕃
HR8 1NP (on B4214)
⏲ 12-11 (10.30 Sun) ☎ (01531) 640954
🌐 oakinnstaplow.co.uk
Bathams Best Bitter; Ledbury Bitter; Wye Valley Bitter; 1 changing beer Ⓗ
A stylishly renovated and well-run roadside country inn with exceptional food, good beer and quality accommodation overlooking nearby hop yards. A contemporary public area neatly divides into three: a reception bar area with modern sofas and low tables, a snug and a main dining area featuring an open kitchen. At the rear is a further room with scrubbed tables. Such is the reputation of the Oak that booking ahead is essential for both food and accommodation. Q♘❀🛏◐♿P🚌(417)🐾📶

Upper Colwall

Chase Inn 𝕃
Chase Road, WR13 6DJ (off B4218, turning at upper hairpin bend signed British Camp) SO766431
⏲ 12-3, 5-11; 12-11 Sat; 12-10.30 Sun ☎ (01684) 540276
Bathams Best Bitter; 3 changing beers (often Ledbury, Malvern Hills, Wood) Ⓗ
Lovely two-bar free house tucked away in a quiet wooded backwater on the western slopes of the Malvern Hills. Popular with walkers as well as regulars, it comprises a small lounge for dining (booking advised at weekends) and a long narrow public bar for drinking and genteel conversation. The delightful, manicured rear garden commands views across Herefordshire to the Welsh Hills. A beer festival is held each June, and a cider festival in October. Q♘❀◐♣●P▯🚌(675)🐾📶

Wellington Heath

Farmers Arms 𝕃
Horse Road, HR8 1LS (E of B4214)
⏲ closed Mon; 12-3, 5.30-11; 12-11 Sat; 12-10 Sun
☎ (01531) 634776 🌐 farmersarmswellingtonheath.co.uk
Otter Amber; Wye Valley Butty Bach; 1 changing beer Ⓗ
The bar and main dining area are in the original 18th-century building and on either side are more modern extensions housing a games room with pool table and restaurant/function room, all recently refurbished in a light and fresh style. The food offer covers a wide range from burgers and pub classics to steaks and speciality dishes, locally sourced where possible. ♘❀◐♿♣P🚌(675)🐾📶

Withington

Cross Keys 𝕃
HR1 3NN (on A465 in Withington Marsh)
⏲ 5 (12 Sat)-11; 12-10.30 Sun ☎ (01432) 820616
Otter Ale; Wye Valley Butty Bach; house beer (by Wye Valley); 1 changing beer Ⓗ
Run by the same landlord for over 40 years, here a long single bar divides either side of a central servery into two drinking areas, with original beams, exposed stonework and comfortable bench seating, bookended by two woodburners. A folk jam session is held on the last Thursday of the month. Filled rolls are available on Saturday only. Q♘❀▲♣P🚌(420)🐾

> Where village statesmen talked with looks profound
> And news much older than the ale went round.
> **Alfred, Lord Tennyson**

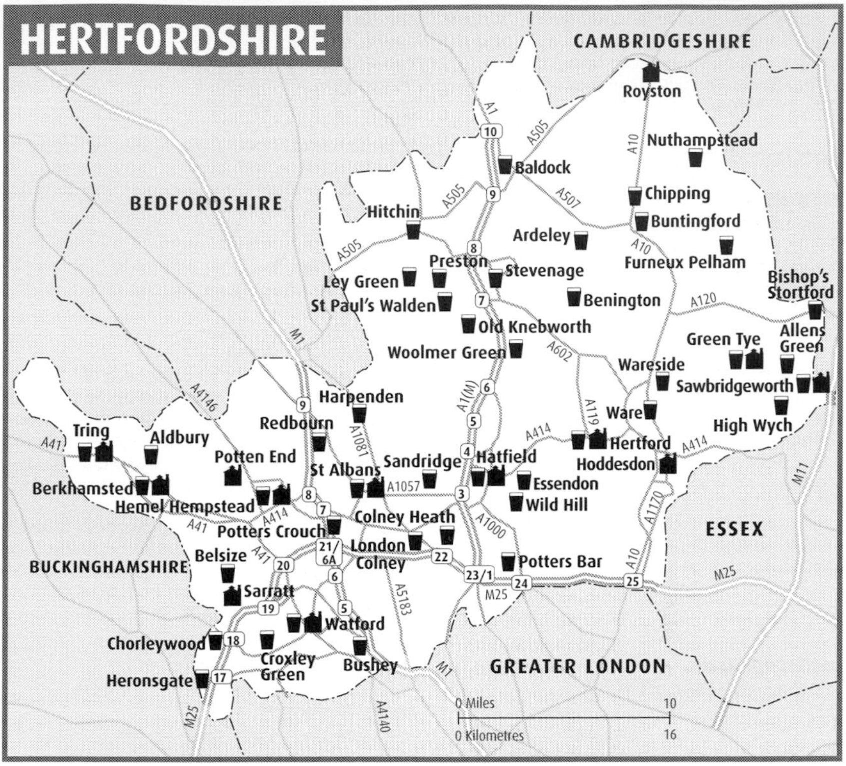

Aldbury

Valiant Trooper 𝕃

Trooper Road, HP23 5RW

⏲ 11-11 (10.30 Sun) ☎ (01442) 851203

🌐 valianttrooper.co.uk

Chiltern Beechwood Bitter; Fuller's London Pride; Tring Side Pocket for a Toad; 2 changing beers (sourced locally; often Dark Star, Tring, Vale) Ⓗ

Situated in an area of outstanding natural beauty, this 17th-century pub has featured in the Guide for many years. Its quality real ale and good food, prepared with locally sourced ingredients, plus the separate restaurant and bar snacks make it a must-visit for all. The log-burning fires in the winter together with the large garden and children's play area in the summer makes this pub worthy of a visit at any time of year. Your host, Mr Ed, welcomes everyone, both regular and newcomers, in the same jovial manner.
Q🐎❀◑♿♣🍎P🚌(30,31)🐾📶

Allens Green

Queen's Head 𝕃

CM21 0LS TL455170

⏲ 12-2.30 (not Mon & Tue), 5-11; 12-10.30 Sun

☎ (01279) 723393 🌐 qhpub.co.uk

Mighty Oak Maldon Gold Ⓗ**; Shepherd Neame Spitfire; 2 changing beers (sourced locally)** Ⓗ/Ⓖ

A popular village inn, well worth seeking out for a constantly changing range of around four beers. On the third weekend of every month and over bank holiday weekends mini beer festivals are held that use gravity stillage to bring up the number of beers to 10 or 12. Hot snacks are available unless the pub is busy. CAMRA branch Pub of the Year in six of the past 10 years, and Hertfordshire Cider Pub of the Year 2014. Q❀♿🍎P🐾📶

Ardeley

Jolly Waggoner

SG2 7AH (off B1037 between Walkern and Cottered)

⏲ 12-11.30 (12.30am Fri & Sat) ☎ (01438) 861350

🌐 jollywaggoner.co.uk

Buntingford Highwayman; 2 changing beers Ⓗ

This 16th-century pub was once farmworkers' cottages. Now managed by the nearby Church Farm, the Jolly Waggoner has a reputation for fine food, most of it sourced from the farm itself or local suppliers. Real ale is sourced locally too, from Buntingford, Red Squirrel and Nethergate. Regular events include speciality food evenings, guest landlords, and a beer festival in August.
🐎❀◑♿♣P🐾📶

Baldock

Orange Tree 🏆 𝕃

Norton Road, SG7 5AW

⏲ 12-2.30, 4.30-11; 12-midnight Thu-Sat; 12-10.30 Sun

☎ (01462) 892341 🌐 theorangetreebaldock.com

Greene King XX Mild, IPA, Abbot; 7 changing beers Ⓗ

Local CAMRA Pub of the Year and Cider Pub of the Year 2015. This Grade II-listed pub is not a typical Greene King house. Three regular beers include XX Mild, and there are 10 guests from small brewers including two from the award-winning Buntingford Brewery. Add to this four real ciders from local Apple Cottage, voted East Anglia Regional Cider Producer of the Year 2015. Good home-made food

is served here. Sport TV shows international Rugby Union. Entertainment includes quiz night on a Tuesday, folk music on Wednesday, and it participates in the Balstock festival.
♉❀◐◑♿⇌♣●P🚌(94)🐾📶

Belsize

Plough

Dunny Lane, WD3 4NP
⚙ 12-11 (10.30 Sun) ☎ (01923) 262261
🌐 theploughatbelsize.co.uk
Greene King IPA; St Austell Tribute; 1 changing beer Ⓗ
This free house was purpose built for the Kings Langley Brewery in the early-19th century. Located in the hamlet of Belsize between Chipperfield and Sarratt, it is a traditional English country pub with low oak-beamed ceilings, open log fires, a restaurant and a pleasant garden. Lunches are served daily and evening meals Wednesday-Saturday. Two regular beers are available with the remaining handpump an optional surprise. There is a convenient bus stop, but unfortunately no evening or Sunday service.
Q❀◐◑♿♣P🚌(352)🐾📶

Benington

Lordship Arms

42 Whempstead Road, SG2 7BX
⚙ 12-3, 6-11 (not Mon eve); 12-3, 7-11 Sun
☎ (01438) 869665 🌐 lordshiparms.com
Black Sheep Best Bitter; Crouch Vale Brewers Gold; Timothy Taylor Landlord; 6 changing beers Ⓗ
Single-room pub situated at the southern end of the village with a fantastic 22 years in this Guide. The tidy bar is decorated with telephone memorabilia – even some of the handpumps are modelled on telephones. A well-maintained garden sports superb floral displays in the summer. Good-quality sandwiches and bar snacks are available at lunchtimes. Classic car club meetings are held in the summer. A repeat winner of local and county CAMRA Pub of the Year awards.
Q❀◐P▯🚌(384)📶

Berkhamsted

Crown 𝕃

145 High Street, HP4 3HH
⚙ 8am-midnight (1am Fri & Sat) ☎ (01442) 863993
Greene King IPA, Abbot; Sharp's Doom Bar; 4 changing beers (sourced locally; often Red Squirrel, Tring, Vale) Ⓗ
First recorded as the Crown in the 18th century, the pub is now a classic Wetherspoon venue, popular with a variety of locals, especially on Friday and Saturday nights. A large pub divided into several sections, some areas are traditional with wooden panelling and a fireplace – others have a more modern and spacious feel. There is a small patio garden outside. The Crown stocks a good range of local and regional guest beers.
♉❀◐◑♿⇌●🚌(500)📶

Lamb 𝕃

277 High Street, HP4 1AJ
⚙ 12-11.30 (12.30am Fri & Sat) ☎ (01442) 862615
Adnams Ghost Ship; Fuller's London Pride; Tring Side Pocket for a Toad, Ridgeway Ⓗ
This friendly pub is over 300 years old. It has a narrow section in front of the bar connecting the two sides and a small beer garden to the rear. Old photographs of the town, wood panelling and a log fire contribute to the traditional atmosphere. Raffles and games are regularly hosted to raise funds for charity. Food is available some weekday lunchtimes along with frequent curry and rib nights. Occasionally there is a guest beer served from the cask. ❀◐♿⇌♣🚌(500,501)🐾📶

Rising Sun 🏆 𝕃

1 Canal Side, George Street, HP4 2EG (at lock 55 on Grand Union Canal)
⚙ 3-11 (midnight Thu); 12-midnight Fri & Sat; 12-10.30 Sun
☎ (01442) 864913 🌐 theriserberko.net
House beer (by Tring); 4 changing beers Ⓗ
Frequently voted local CAMRA Pub of the Year, this friendly and popular canalside pub boasts an ever-changing range of four national guest beers as well as around 17 guest ciders served straight from the cask. It also stocks a wide range of liqueurs, spirits, snuff and cigars as well as a renowned ploughman's. The Riser offers regular beer festivals as well as gastro nights, quizzes and a cheese club. A CAMRA members' discount is available. Dogs and hikers are welcome.
Q♉❀◐⇌♣●🚌(500,501)🐾📶

Bishop's Stortford

Jolly Brewers

170 South Street, CM23 3BQ
⚙ 12-midnight ☎ (01279) 836055
Timothy Taylor Landlord; 4 changing beers (sourced nationally; often Fuller's, Sharp's) Ⓗ
Community-based pub on the edge of the town centre, originally waggishly named the Teetotallers. It has a comfortable lounge bar and a sports-oriented bar used by several darts and pool teams and equipped with a large satellite TV. A local golf society is based here. Food is available weekday lunchtimes only. The accommodation (bed only, no breakfast) is ideal for Stansted Airport and a 24-hour bus service stops outside the pub.
Q❀🛏◐♿⇌♣P🚌(308,510,511)📶

Star 𝕃

7 Bridge Street, CM23 2JU
⚙ 11-midnight (2am Fri); 12-2am Sat; 12-6 Sun
☎ (01279) 654211 🌐 thestar-bishopsstortford.co.uk
3 changing beers (sourced regionally; often Adnams) Ⓗ

REAL ALE BREWERIES

3 Brewers Hatfield
Ash Valley Green Tye
Broxbourne Hoddesdon
Buntingford Royston
Haresfoot Berkhamsted
McMullen Hertford
Mix Hemel Hempstead
Old Cross Hertford
Paradigm Sarratt (NEW)
Pope's Yard Watford
Red Squirrel Potten End
Sawbridgeworth Sawbridgeworth
That Little Brewery St Albans
Tring Tring
Verulam St Albans

A 17th-century town-centre pub catering for all ages. It is busy on Friday and Saturday evenings with a young crowd. Tuesday is quiz night. A quiet pint can be enjoyed on other evenings and at lunchtimes. Reasonably priced traditional pub food is freshly prepared throughout the day. Additionally pizzas are made to order at any time. ❀◐◑⇌🚌ᯤ

Buntingford

Crown

17 High Street, SG9 9AB

⏲ 12-midnight; 6-11 Tue ☎ (01763) 271422

St Austell Trelawny; Thwaites Wainwright; 1 changing beer Ⓗ

Town-centre pub with a large front bar, cosy back bar and function room. Outside are a covered patio and a secluded garden. Although the emphasis is on drinking, there are regular themed speciality food nights and traditional fish and chips on Thursday and Friday (book ahead for food). Crossword fans find the large collection of dictionaries and reference books useful, and every six weeks gents' haircuts are available.
Q♘❀◐◑🚌(331,700)🐾

Bushey

Swan

25 Park Road, WD23 3EE

⏲ 11-11; 12-10.30 Sun ☎ (020) 8950 2256

🌐 swanpubbushey.co.uk

Greene King Abbot; Sharp's Doom Bar; Timothy Taylor Landlord; Young's Bitter Ⓗ

Situated in a quiet residential road off Bushey High Street, this small single-bar pub offers a warm and friendly welcome. Walls are adorned with photos of sporting achievements, life in the village and a plaque commemorating the pub's entry in the first 10 editions of the Guide. Four regular ales are offered and reasonably priced toasties and rolls are available all day. Two real fires create a cosy feel. The Ladies is in the back garden. ❀♣🚌🐾ᯤ

Chipping

Countryman

Ermine Street, SG9 0PG TL356319

⏲ closed Mon-Thu; 12-11 Fri & Sat; 12-10.30 Sun

☎ (01763) 272721

3 changing beers Ⓗ

Built in 1663 and a pub since 1760, the Countryman is a one-bar, split-level pub. The interior boasts some well-executed carvings on the bar front, an impressive fireplace and some obscure agricultural implements. Three changing real ales and a cider (in summer) are usually available. This is a pub where social networking happens in the bar. Note the restricted opening hours. Q♘❀●P🚌(331)🐾

Chorleywood

Rose & Crown L

Common Road, WD3 5LW

⏲ 11.30-3, 5.30-11; 11.30-11.30 Sat; 12-9 Sun

☎ (01923) 283841 🌐 roseandcrownchorleywood.co.uk

Fuller's London Pride; Young's Bitter; 2 changing beers Ⓗ

Dating from the mid-18th century, this is a friendly one-bar pub opposite the common with a separate, popular restaurant (booking often necessary). Guest beers are usually fairly local, but beers from brewers further afield, such as Loose Cannon, do appear. The homely drinking area can get crowded, and may operate as a restaurant overspill in the evenings. Children are not allowed in the bar. Note the unusual metal pub sign.
❀◐◑⇌⊖♣P🚌(336)🐾ᯤ

Colney Heath

Crooked Billet L

88 High Street, AL4 0NP

⏲ 11.30-2.30, 4.30-11; 11.30-11 Fri; 12-11 Sat; 12-10.30 Sun

☎ (01727) 822128

Tring Side Pocket for a Toad; 3 changing beers Ⓗ

Popular and friendly cottage-style village pub dating back over 200 years. A genuine free house, it stocks three to five guest beers from national, regional and microbreweries. A wide selection of good-value home-made food is served lunchtimes and Friday and Saturday evenings. Summer barbecues and Saturday events feature occasionally. This is a favourite stop-off for walkers on the many local footpaths. Families are welcome in the bar until 9pm and in the large garden where there is play equipment. ♘❀◐◑♣P🚌(304)🐾

Croxley Green

Sportsman 🏆 L

2 Scots Hill, WD3 3AD (at A412 jct with the green)

⏲ 12-11 (10.30 Sun) ☎ (01923) 443360

Fuller's ESB; Sharp's Doom Bar; 6 changing beers Ⓗ

A friendly, family-run pub focusing on real ale, with a selection of up to eight on offer plus a real cider during the warmer months. Tasting racks of six ales are available to help you choose. Beers are sourced from throughout the country but with an emphasis on local and London breweries. The pub supports various community activities including occasional live music, beer festivals, quizzes, darts teams, pool, a book club and a jazz club.
❀♣P▯🚌(320,324)

Essendon

Candlestick L

West End Lane, AL9 6BA (accessed from Essendon village or Wild Hill village, each under 1 mile) TL262083

⏲ closed Mon; 12-11; 12-8 Sun ☎ (01707) 261322

🌐 thecandlestickpub.co.uk

Young's Bitter; 2 changing beers Ⓗ

A remote country pub/restaurant where good food features strongly at lunchtime and during the evening. It is popular with walkers and cyclists, who are rewarded with two guest ales from Hertfordshire brewers. Originally called the Chequers, the pub became known as the Candlestick because of the habit of a previous landlord who took the sole candle to the cellar when collecting the beer, leaving customers in the dark. Now a friendly, well-lit, free house.
♘❀◐◑P🐾

Furneux Pelham

Brewery Tap L

Barleycroft End, SG9 0LL

⏲ closed Mon; 12-3, 5-11 (11.45 Fri); 12-11.45 Sat; 12-9 Sun

☎ (01279) 777604 🌐 brewerytapfp.co.uk

Buntingford Highwayman; Greene King IPA; 1 changing beer Ⓗ

A former Greene King pub, now under new management as a free house. It is situated just across the road from the site of the old Rayments of Pelham Brewery, closed by Greene King in 1987. Brewery memorabilia is displayed in the bar. There is something for everyone here, with good home-cooked food, Sky and BT sport, live music and a pleasant garden with children's play area and livestock to look at. Popular with walking and cycling groups. ⛂❀◑♿P🚌(20)🐾📶

Green Tye

Prince of Wales Ⓛ

SG10 6JP (Green Tye is signed but, as there are many country turnings, sat-nav is recommended) TL444184
✪ 12-3, 5.30-11; 12-11 Sat; 12-9.30 Sun ☎ (01279) 842139
🌐 thepow.co.uk
Ash Valley Prince of Wales IPA; Wadworth Henry's IPA; 3 changing beers (sourced locally; often Ash Valley) Ⓗ
A traditional and friendly village local, whether you are a walker, cyclist, dog owner or just plain thirsty. Landlord and owner Rob has recently established the Ash Valley Brewery at the back of the pub, making the Prince of Wales its brewery tap. Food ranges from sandwiches to great-value traditional pub grub. There is a small garden for fine weather. Beer festivals with a barbecue and entertainment are held in May and September.
Q⛂❀◐♿●P🐾📶

Harpenden

Cross Keys Ⓛ

39 High Street, AL5 2SD (opp war memorial)
✪ 11.30-11; 12-10.30 Sun ☎ (01582) 763989
🌐 cross-keys-harpenden.co.uk
Rebellion IPA; Timothy Taylor Landlord; Tring Ridgeway Ⓗ
Tucked in among the shops in the town centre, this two-bar pub has retained its traditional charm with a rare fine pewter bar top and flagstone floors. The original oak-beamed ceiling has tankards from past and present customers hanging from it. In spring and summer enjoy your pint in the secluded, attractive rear garden, and in autumn or winter relax in front of the saloon bar's fire. Traditional home-cooked lunches are served Monday to Saturday. Q⛂❀◐♿⇌♣🚌🐾📶

Harpenden Arms

188 High Street, AL5 2TR (corner of High St and Station Rd)
✪ 11-11 (midnight Fri-Sun) ☎ (01582) 461113
🌐 harpenden-arms.co.uk
Fuller's London Pride, ESB; Gale's Seafarers Ale; 1 changing beer Ⓗ
Overlooking Harpenden Common, this imposing Victorian pub, formerly the Railway Hotel, adopted its present name in the 1960s. The exterior retains some original features and inside the open-plan bar dispenses four Fuller's beers. The landlord is a Fuller's Master Cellarman and has won the competition three times outright. Sky Sports is shown on TV but, except for major events, the sound is kept low, allowing customers to enjoy the convivial conversational atmosphere. A Thai restaurant is attached. ❀◑⇌🚌🐾📶

Hatfield

Horse & Groom

21 Park Street, AL9 5AT
✪ 11.30-11 (midnight Fri & Sat); 12-10.30 Sun
☎ (01707) 264765
Black Sheep Best Bitter; Greene King Abbot; 3 changing beers Ⓗ
In the heart of Old Hatfield, this allegedly haunted, 16th-century, Grade II-listed former timber-framed and later brick-clad building is also thought to house a priest hole. The pub serves up to five real ales and hosts three beer festivals a year. Tuesday is bangers and mash night and Saturday is chilli and rice night – purchase an ale for a free portion. Hatfield railway and bus stations are just a few minutes' walk away.
Q⛂❀◑⇌♣🚌(300,301,724)🐾

Hemel Hempstead

Full House Ⓛ

128 Marlowes, HP1 1EZ
✪ 8am-midnight (1am Fri & Sat) ☎ (01442) 265512
Greene King IPA, Abbot; Sharp's Doom Bar; 6 changing beers (sourced nationally; often Concrete Cow, Nethergate, Oldershaw) Ⓗ
This former cinema and bingo hall (hence the name) is spacious, with plenty of seating, and decorations reminiscent of its history. Consistent quality and an ever-widening range of changing beers make this pub a worthy new entry. The regular cider from the box is Westons Old Rosie, plus one other. Food is served all day. Regular beer festivals, Meet the Brewer events and occasional brewery trips are hosted. As a nod to its past, films are often shown on a Sunday evening.
Q⛂◑♿●🚌📶

Heronsgate

Land of Liberty, Peace & Plenty Ⓛ

Long Lane, WD3 5BS TQ023949
✪ 12-11 (midnight Fri & Sat) ☎ (01923) 282226
🌐 landoflibertypub.com
10 changing beers Ⓗ
Welcoming pub close to the M25 with historic connections to the Chartists who had a short-lived rural community nearby. Popular with walkers, cyclists, locals and real ale enthusiasts, up to 10 beers are offered, all from microbreweries, in a range of styles and strengths. Real ciders, a perry and a wide range of whiskies are also offered. Beer festivals, tastings and other regular events are held throughout the year. Bar snacks are available all day. Outside is a pavilion for families.
❀♣●P🗑🚌(R2)🐾📶

Hertford

Black Horse Ⓛ

29-31 West Street, SG13 8EZ
✪ 12-11 (midnight Wed & Thu; 1am Fri & Sat); 12-10.30 Sun
☎ (01992) 583630 🌐 theblackhorse.biz
6 changing beers Ⓗ
Community-focused timbered free house, dating from 1642 and situated in one of Hertford's most attractive streets, near the start of the Cole Green Way. The well-kept garden includes a separate safe children's play area. The interesting food menu features game and the pub has its own bakery. Handy for Hertford Town FC supporters, the pub has

a rugby team affiliated to the RFU. CAMRA members enjoy a discount on real ales from near and far. ≈(East/North)

Duncombe Arms

24 Railway Street, SG14 1BA
11-11 (11.30 Thu; midnight Fri & Sat); 11-10.30 Sun
(01992) 581445
Greene King IPA, Abbot; 3 changing beers H
A welcoming single-bar town-centre pub with a comfortable modern feel, plenty of outside drinking space and an enticing selection of guest beers alongside standard Greene King options. It hosts two mini beer festivals every year and a separate cider festival, in addition to a well-established quiz on Thursdays and folk music and poker sessions on Mondays. Meals are available all day, with sandwich and burger deals proving popular. Thomas Slingsby Duncombe was MP for Hertford in the 1830s. ≈(East)

Hertford Club

Lombard House, Bull Plain, SG14 1DT
12-3 (not Mon & Tue), 5-11; 12-11 Fri; 11-11 Sat; 12-8 Sun
(01992) 421422 thehertford.club
3 changing beers H
Dating from the 15th century with later additions, Lombard House, on the River Lea, was built as an English Hall House and is one of the oldest buildings in Hertford. It has been the home of the private Hertford Club since 1878. CAMRA members are welcome and may be signed in on production of a membership card. You will find three ever-changing beers and real cider, which in summer can be enjoyed in the delightful walled garden.
Q≈(East)

Old Barge

2 The Folly, SG14 1QD (ask for Folly Island)
11-11 (midnight Fri & Sat); 12-11 Sun (01992) 581871
theoldbarge.com
Sharp's Doom Bar; St Austell Tribute; 4 changing beers H
A free house on Folly Island pleasantly situated canalside on the River Lee, offering not only a good selection of beers – often including a dark mild, stout or porter – but also a range of ciders and perries. Locally sourced home-cooked food is served all day. Regular beer festivals are hosted, as well as a popular Sunday night quiz and a music quiz every last Thursday of the month. Look out for the annual duck race and the children's crayfish festival held in August. ≈(East)

Old Cross Tavern L

8 St Andrew Street, SG14 1JA
4.30-11; 12-midnight Fri & Sat; 12-10.30 Sun
(01992) 583133
Old Cross Gertcha!; Timothy Taylor Landlord; 4 changing beers H
Superb town free house offering a friendly welcome. Up to eight real ales, usually including a dark beer of some distinction, come from brewers large and small, including the pub's own microbrewery, and there is a fine choice of Belgian bottle-conditioned beers. Two beer festivals are held each year – one over the spring bank holiday, the other in October. No TV or music here, just good old-fashioned conversation. Home-made pork pies are available. Q≈(North)

White Horse

33 Castle Street, SG14 1HH
12-midnight 07450 273294
Adnams Southwold Bitter; Butcombe Bitter; Fuller's London Pride, ESB; Gale's Seafarers Ale; 5 changing beers H
Charming old timber-framed building with two bars and extra rooms upstairs, popular with community groups. One room has a bar billiards table and there are family rooms where children are welcome. The Horse is a pub for conversation and is a must-visit for real ale fans in Hertford, with up to 10 beers available including a wide Fuller's range and additional guests. Two beer festivals are held each year. Thursday is tapas night and Sunday roasts are served during the cooler months. Dogs are welcome, even the resident canine pub dog ghost. Q≈(East)

High Wych

Rising Sun

High Wych Road, CM21 0HZ
12-2.30 (not Tue), 5.30-11; 12-2.30, 6-11 Sat; 12-3, 7-10.30 Sun (01279) 724099
Courage Best Bitter; Mighty Oak Maldon Gold; Woodforde's Wherry; 2 changing beers G
This friendly village local has never used handpumps – a range of four or five beers is served on gravity, often from East Anglian breweries. Although recently refurbished, the original character of the building has been preserved, with a stone floor, attractive fireplace and wood panelling. Popular with locals and walkers, it holds a monthly quiz and an annual vegetable competition. Parking is in the village hall car park opposite. QP(347)

Hitchin

Half Moon L

57 Queen Street, SG4 9TZ
12-midnight (1am Fri & Sat); 12-11 Sun
(01462) 452448 thehalfmoonhitchin.co.uk
Adnams Southwold Bitter; Young's Bitter; 6 changing beers H
Split-level one-bar pub dating from 1748, once owned by Hitchin brewer W&S Lucas. It sells two regular beers and six guests often from local breweries, plus two ciders, a perry and four guests. Home-prepared meals and tapas are served daily. Monthly quiz nights and speciality food events are popular in this friendly community pub. Cribbage is played during the summer. A former Hertfordshire CAMRA Pub of the Year. P

Nightingale L

Nightingale Road, SG5 1RL
2.30 (3 Mon)-11; 12-midnight Thu-Sat; 12-10.30 Sun
(01462) 457448
Tring Colley's Dog; 4 changing beers H
Community pub hosting darts, pool, dominoes and cricket teams. Tring Colley's Dog is a permanent fixture, alongside four SIBA guest ales and a real cider. Thursday is open mic night and live music plays on some Saturdays. Behind the pub is a large patio area complete with pond and goldfish. Those interested in local brewing history should note the Fordham's Ales & Stout sign in the brickwork on the front of the pub. ≈P

Radcliffe Arms L

31 Walsworth Road, SG4 9ST

⏲ 9am-11 (midnight Sat); 9am-4 Sun ☎ (01462) 456111
🌐 radcliffearms.com
Buntingford Twitchell; 1 changing beer [H]
This independent gastro-pub continues to go from strength to strength. While much of the interior is given over to dining, there is a bar area open to drinkers which sports two handpumps, usually dispensing LocAle beers from Buntingford Brewery or occasional guest beers sourced via Buntingford. An eclectic range of lagers and fruit beers and an extensive wine list are also offered, and a good choice of excellent food. ❀◐♿≷P⊟🐾📶

Ley Green

Plough

Plough Lane, SG4 8LA (look for brown pub signs at each end of Plough Lane) TL162243
⏲ 4-11 Mon & Tue; 12-midnight (11 Wed); 12-10.30 Sun
☎ (01438) 871394
Greene King IPA, Abbot; 1 changing beer [H]
An ale house as far back as 1846, this warm and friendly traditional pub is set in rolling farming country. The large patio has idyllic views across the Beds/Herts countryside – look for the red kites. All are welcome to join in the acoustic music sessions on Tuesday evenings. The snug bar is available for small functions and hot and cold snacks are served throughout the week. A popular stop-off for walkers and cyclists, it features in local guides to the area, but it can be hard to find – if you get lost ask a friendly local. ❀◐♣P🚌(88)🐾📶

London Colney

Bull

Barnet Road, AL2 1QU
⏲ 12-11 (midnight Thu-Sat) ☎ (01727) 823160
🌐 thebullatlondoncolney.co.uk
Black Sheep Best Bitter; St Austell Trelawny [H]**; 2 changing beers** [G]
Lovely old 17th-century timbered building near the River Colne with a cosy lounge and original fireplace, offering a range of real ales. The large public bar features darts, pool and TV. Evening events include live music on Saturday and a quiz on Sunday. Good-value home-made meals are served Monday-Saturday lunchtimes. Wednesday is food night with curry evenings held monthly. There is a children's play area outside. ❀◖♣●P🚌🐾📶

Nuthampstead

Woodman

Stocking Lane, SG8 8NB
⏲ 4-7 Mon; 11.30-11; 12-7 Sun ☎ (01763) 848328
🌐 thewoodman-inn.co.uk
Buntingford Twitchell; Greene King IPA; 1 changing beer [G]
Seventeenth-century free house with an L-shaped bar and a wonderful open fire. The restaurant offers à la carte meals as well as house specials and snacks (no food Mon or Sun eves). Beer is dispensed by gravity from casks behind the bar. The TV is restricted to major sports events. During WWII the USAF 398th Bomber Group was based nearby and much memorabilia is displayed here. Regular entertainment includes quarterly comedy nights, monthly quizzes and aviation lectures. Functions can be catered for in the marquee in the garden. Q❀🛏◐♣P🐾📶

Old Knebworth

Lytton Arms

Park Lane, SG3 6QB
⏲ 11-11 (midnight Fri & Sat); 12-10.30 Sun
☎ (01438) 812312 🌐 lyttonarms.co.uk
Adnams Southwold Bitter; Dark Star Hophead; Mighty Oak Maldon Gold; Sharp's Doom Bar; 6 changing beers [H]
Nineteenth-century pub next to the Knebworth House estate, built for Hawkes & Company of Bishop's Stortford whose original logo can be seen in the wrought ironwork of the pub sign. Four house beers are supplemented by a changing mix of ales from regional and microbrewers. Good home-made food is served daily. Outside is a decked patio and garden. Live music is a highlight on Friday evenings. ❀◐♣P🚌(44,45)🐾

Potters Bar

Old Manor

Wyllyotts Place, Darkes Lane, EN6 2JD (opp Wyllyotts Centre)
⏲ 11-11 (midnight Fri & Sat); 12-10.30 Sun
☎ (01707) 650674 🌐 the-old-manor.co.uk
Caledonian Deuchars IPA; Fuller's London Pride; Oakham Inferno; 2 changing beers [H]
Popular dining and drinking venue near the railway station, frequented by all age groups. Dating from the 13th century, the building is the surviving part of an old manor house and opened as a pub in its present form in 2000. The large adjoining galleried restaurant offers an extensive menu. The pub is busy before and after events at the theatre/leisure centre opposite. The walls display a collection of photos of bygone Potters Bar. ❀◐♿≷P🚌🐾📶

Potters Crouch

Holly Bush

Bedmond Lane, AL2 3NN (jct of Potters Crouch Lane and Ragged Hall Lane) TL116052
⏲ 12-2.30, 6-11; 12-3, 7-10.30 Sun ☎ (01727) 851792
🌐 thehollybushpub.co.uk
Fuller's London Pride, ESB; Gale's Seafarers Ale [H]
An attractive early 17th-century pub in rural surroundings, beautifully and tastefully furnished to a high standard, with large oak tables, antique dressers and period chairs. Spotless throughout, there are no jukeboxes, slot machines or TVs to disturb customers in any of the three separate drinking areas. The food menu is not extensive but is high quality. Well-behaved children are welcome. The garden is ideal in summer.
Q❀◐♿P🚌(300,301)

Preston

Red Lion [L]

The Green, SG4 7UD TL180247
⏲ 12-2.30 (3.30 Sat), 5.30-11; 12-3.30, 7-10.30 Sun
☎ (01462) 459585 🌐 theredlionpreston.co.uk
3 changing beers [H]
This attractive free house on the village green is the first community-owned pub in Great Britain. It offers an ever-changing list of beers, many from small breweries. Ray and Jo prepare fresh home-made food using locally sourced ingredients where possible. The pub hosts the village cricket teams and fundraises for charity.
Q❀◐♣●P🚌(88)🐾📶

Redbourn

Cricketers

East Common, AL3 7ND
12-11 (midnight Fri & Sat); 12-10.30 Sun
(01582) 620612 thecricketersofredbourn.co.uk
Greene King IPA; Sharp's Doom Bar; 3 changing beers
Redbourn's only free house, dating back to 1725. Five real ales and a cider are always available and the food is excellent. The pub is opposite Redbourn's common and historic cricket pitch, making it the perfect setting for a drink on a sunny summer's day. In winter a wood-burning stove creates a cosy atmosphere. Summer beer festivals showcasing local beers are held in marquees erected in the car park. Quiz nights feature regularly, raising funds for local organisations.
Q P (34,46,657)

St Albans

Blacksmiths Arms

56 St Peters Street, AL1 3HG
11-11 (12.30am Fri & Sat); 12-10.30 Sun
(01727) 868845 blacksmitharms.co.uk
Morland Old Speckled Hen; Sharp's Doom Bar; 6 changing beers
A large and welcoming town-centre pub with an open-plan bar, featuring two regular ales and six changing guests including beers from local breweries. The pub has a friendly and lively feel, with live music on Friday and Saturday evenings. Regular real ale festivals are held during the year in the main bar and in the extensive garden which features a yurt, available for private parties. Good-quality reasonably priced meals are served throughout the day. Families with children are welcome until 7pm. (City)

Boot Inn

4 Market Place, AL3 5DG
12-midnight (12.45am Fri & Sat); 12-11.30 Sun
(01727) 857533 thebootstalbans.com
7 changing beers
Situated in the centre of the city, this one-bar pub has a welcoming atmosphere. It can be busy on weekend evenings and during Wednesday and Saturday market days. The clock tower and Abbey are nearby and Verulamium Park is a short walk. The bar features a real fire, exposed beams, low ceilings and wood flooring. Families are welcome until 6pm. Real ciders are available alongside a changing range of ales. Live music plays on Wednesday and Sunday evenings. Speciality food events are held on Tuesdays.
(Abbey)

Farriers Arms

32-34 Lower Dagnall Street, AL3 4PT (off A5183 Verulam Rd)
12-2.30 (not Mon & Tue), 5.30-11; 12-11 Sat; 12-10.30 Sun
(01727) 851025
McMullen Country Bitter; St Austell Tribute; 2 changing beers
Originally a grocer's and butcher's shop, the building was converted to a pub in the 1920s. The Farriers is a classic back-street local, becoming a free house in 2013 – it is the only pub in the city never to have forsaken real ale. A plaque outside commemorates the first meeting of the Hertfordshire branch of CAMRA. The split-level interior has an area fronting the bar for stand-up drinking, darts and cards, and a back room with comfortable seating. Sport is shown on TV. Parking can be difficult.

Garibaldi

61 Albert Street, AL1 1RT
12 (2.30 Mon)-11; 12-11.30 Thu; 12-midnight Fri & Sat; 12-10 Sun (01727) 894745 garibaldistalbans.co.uk
Fuller's London Pride, ESB; Gale's Seafarers Ale, HSB; 1 changing beer
Larger inside than its frontage suggests, this is a classic example of a quality back-street local in the heart of Sopwell. Named after the 19th-century Italian patriot, the Garibaldi offers an extensive range of Fuller's ales and excellent home-cooked food, with a fine Sunday roast particularly recommended. Regular live music on Saturdays, quizzes, darts, food nights and charity events give the place a homely, community feel. Awarded Most Improved Pub by the local CAMRA branch in 2014. (Abbey)

Lower Red Lion

34-36 Fishpool Street, AL3 4RX
12-11 (10.30 Sun) (01727) 855669
thelowerredlion.co.uk
Dark Star Hophead; Tring Kotuku; 3 changing beers
Both bars in this classic pub have plenty of character and history. Located in a conservation area between the city centre and the site of Roman Verulamium, the pub stands in one of St Albans' most picturesque streets. The Lower Red was an early champion of the real ale revival movement and has featured a good range of beers ever since. One handpump dispenses real cider. There are regular beer festivals and quality home-made food is served daily. Q P

Mermaid

98 Hatfield Road, AL1 3RL
12-midnight (11 Mon & Tue); 12-10.30 Sun
(01727) 568912
Oakham Citra; 5 changing beers
Located between the main railway station and the city centre, this friendly free house has one bar with bare-board flooring. Customers are welcomed by six real ales, at least a dozen ciders and perries, and a wide range of Belgian beers. Try the six mixed thirds of cider, perry or ale. The pub has received several CAMRA cider awards in recent years. Wetherspoon CAMRA vouchers are accepted. Live music features on Wednesday nights and there are regular quizzes. Mind the outward-opening front door!
(City) P (601,602,655)

Olde Fighting Cocks

16 Abbey Mill Lane, AL3 4HE
12-11 (midnight Fri & Sat); 12-10.30 Sun
(01727) 869152 yeoldefightingcocks.co.uk
Harviestoun Bitter & Twisted; Purity Pure Ubu; 6 changing beers
The pub stakes a claim to be the oldest in the country, dating from the late-8th century, though the current building was completed in 1485. Original features include timbers, low ceilings, interesting nooks and crannies, and a bread oven next to one of the fireplaces. Today the pub caters for tourists visiting the Abbey and the nearby Roman remains in Verulamium Park, offering real ales from across Britain. Parking nearby is a challenge – perhaps take a pleasant walk through the park.

White Hart Tap

4 Keyfield Terrace, AL1 1QJ

🕚 11 (12 Sun)-11 ☎ (01727) 860974 🌐 whiteharttap.co.uk

Castle Rock Harvest Pale; Fuller's London Pride; Sharp's Doom Bar; Timothy Taylor Landlord; 3 changing beers Ⓗ

Welcoming, one-bar, back-street local with four regular beers and three guests. Good-value, home-prepared food, featuring fresh vegetables from the pub's own allotment, are served every lunchtime and Monday-Saturday evenings, with fish and chips on Fridays and roasts on Sundays. Quiz night is Wednesday. Live music plays occasionally on Saturdays. Outside is a large garden and separate heated, covered smoking area. Barbecues are held in summer and beer festivals throughout the year. A public car park is opposite.
❀◐◑⇌(Abbey/City)♣🚬🚌🐾📶

St Paul's Walden

Strathmore Arms 🄻

London Road, SG4 8BT TL193222

🕚 6-11 Mon; 12-2.30, 5-11; 12-11 Fri & Sat; 12-10.30 Sun

☎ (01438) 871654 🌐 thestrathmorearms.co.uk

5 changing beers Ⓗ

This pub on the Bowes-Lyon estate caters for drinkers and lunchtime diners. Obscure breweries are a speciality on the ever-changing rota of guest beers. The house ale is by Buntingford Brewery. Unusual bottled beers are also available along with a real cider and perry. The pub is well known locally for charity fundraising and hosts regular beer festivals. It boasts a full collection of Good Beer Guides from 1976 onwards. A former local CAMRA Pub of the Year and Community Pub of the Year. **Q**❀◐◑♣P🚌(304)🐾📶

Sandridge

Rose & Crown 🄻

24 High Street, AL4 9DA

🕚 11-11; 12-10.30 Sun ☎ (01727) 859739

🌐 roseandcrownpubsandridge.co.uk

Tring Ridgeway; Young's Special; 2 changing beers Ⓗ

A 17th-century inn with oak beams, an inglenook fireplace and several areas for drinking and dining. The pub was reopened in September 2010 following major renovation work, and has been tastefully modernised, enhancing its traditional features with additional seating and dining areas. There is a large car park to the rear and a garden where barbecues are regularly held. A popular beer festival is hosted in summer.
Q❀◐◑♿♣P🚌(304,305,657)🐾📶

Sawbridgeworth

Gate 🄻

81 London Road, CM21 9JJ

🕚 11.30-2.30, 5.30-11 Mon; 11.30-2.30 Tue; 11.30-2 Wed; 11.30-2.30 Thu; 11.30-11 Fri & Sat; 12-11 Sun

☎ (01279) 722313 🌐 thegatepub.weebly.com

Sawbridgeworth Gold; 6 changing beers (often Sawbridgeworth) Ⓗ

A lively hostelry with a huge collection of pumpclips adorning the beams. It is sport-oriented with several satellite TV screens, and is home to numerous pub teams. A range of up to six beers is offered, typically three from the small Sawbridgeworth Brewery at the back of the building and three guests. Beer festivals are held over the Easter and August bank holiday weekends. No dogs allowed.
❀◐♿♣P🚌(509,510,511)

Old Bell

38 Bell Street, CM21 9AN

🕚 11-11 (1am Fri & Sat); 12-11 Sun ☎ (01279) 721050

Adnams Broadside; Woodforde's Wherry; 1 changing beer (sourced nationally; often Thwaites) Ⓗ

This 16th-century timber-framed pub boasts many exposed beams in the main bar. Situated among Bell Street's traditional village shops, it is cosy and friendly. There is a side bar where food is served and in the summer a popular courtyard and sunny garden which includes a children's play area. A quiz is held every Sunday evening and a ukulele jam session every Tuesday evening. Real cider and perry are always available.
❀◐◑♿🍎P🚌(509,510,511)🐾📶

Stevenage

Our Mutual Friend

Broadwater Crescent, SG2 8EH

🕚 12-11 (11.30 Fri & Sat) ☎ (01438) 312282

🌐 omfpub.co.uk

6 changing beers Ⓗ

Thriving community pub on the south side of Stevenage serving an ever-changing selection of cask beer. Ten or more real ciders and perries are also offered and regular beer festivals are held throughout the year. Since it was rescued from the cask ale graveyard back in 2002, the pub has appeared in the last 13 editions of the Guide and is a winner of many local CAMRA awards including Pub of the Year. It can be busy on Stevenage FC match days. **Q**◐♣🍎P🚬🚌(4,5)🐾📶

Tring

Anchor 🄻

73 Western Road, HP23 4BH

🕚 12-11 (11.30 Fri & Sat) ☎ (01442) 823280

Greene King IPA; Ruddles County; Tring Side Pocket for a Toad; 3 changing beers (sourced nationally; often St Austell) Ⓗ

Situated a 10-minute walk west of the town centre, this welcoming pub has a spacious bar with tall tables in the front bay windows and plenty more seating around the room. The front bar area has quirky wall decoration featuring wine crates and reclaimed door and floor timbers. Pictures of local interest and TVs for sporting events adorn the walls. Fresh filled rolls made with local bread from the bakery opposite are available from the bar.
❀◐♣🚌(61,500,501)🐾📶

Castle 🄻

Park Road, HP23 6BN (around corner from Natural History Museum)

🕚 3-11; 12-11.30 Fri & Sat; 12-11 Sun ☎ (01442) 823552

Vale Wychert Ale, Special; 1 changing beer (sourced locally; often Tring) Ⓗ

This friendly Victorian corner pub is on the southern edge of the town. A thriving local, it is owned by Vale Brewery and the guest beer is predominantly from Tring Brewery. A genuine single-roomed drinkers' pub, it has comfortable, upholstered bench seating and TVs for sport. No food is served. The attractive rear courtyard has some covered seating. Home to two darts teams. ❀♣🐾📶

King's Arms 🄻

King Street, HP23 6BE SP921111

12-2.30, 5.30-11.30; 12-3, 5-11.30 Fri; 12-11.30 Sat & Sun

☎ (01442) 823318 kingsarmstring.co.uk

Tring Moongazing; 5 changing beers (sourced nationally; often Leighton Buzzard, Vale, XT) Ⓗ

This local back-street favourite is now well established under new ownership, staying with the tried-and-tested formula of good beer and food in equal measure. A Tring beer is regularly available plus five ever-changing guests, mostly from local breweries. The single-room interior is warmed by a real fire in winter and the rear courtyard with outdoor heaters adds another dimension. A beer festival is held every August bank holiday weekend. Q (64,500,501)

Ware

Crooked Billet 🏆

140 Musley Hill, SG12 7NL

5.30-11.30 (midnight Fri); 12-midnight Sat; 12-11.30 Sun

☎ (01920) 462516

4 changing beers Ⓗ

Stuart and Sue have presided over the Billet for more than 20 years. Since the pub was acquired by Admiral Taverns it has stocked more than 500 different ales, fully utilising the local SIBA Direct Delivery Scheme to provide an ever-changing range of four or five ales, always including a mild, porter or stout. Two beer and cider festivals are held each year. This gem of a community pub has two small bars featuring TV sport, pool and darts – Carlisle United and Ware FC fans are assured of a warm welcome. (395)

Wareside

Chequers

Ware Road, SG12 7QY (on B1004)

12-3, 6-11; 12-4, 6.30-10.30 Sun ☎ (01920) 467010

Buntingford Highwayman; 2 changing beers (sourced regionally; often Adnams) Ⓗ

A rural free house dating from the 15th century, the Chequers was originally a coaching inn and has three distinct bars plus a restaurant. Food is home made and reasonably priced, and includes many vegetarian options. Walkers and cyclists are welcome, making this a popular base for a ramble. No machines, no music and no swearing.

Q P (M3,M4)

Watford

West Herts Sports Club

8 Park Avenue, WD18 7HP (S of A412, near town hall)

4-11 (11.30 Fri); 10-11 Sat; 10-10.30 Sun

☎ (01923) 229239 westhertssports.co.uk

Young's Bitter; 4 changing beers Ⓗ

This comfortable members' bar is a multiple winner of CAMRA East Anglian Club of the Year. Up to four regularly changing guest beers are on offer. The bar is tastefully decorated with sporting memorabilia, and major sporting events are screened. A separate function room, home of the Watford Beer Festival, is available to hire. Show a CAMRA membership card or a copy of this Guide to gain entry up to four times a year.

P

Wild Hill

Woodman

45 Wildhill Road, AL9 6EA (between A1000 and B158) TL264068

11.30-2.30, 5.30-11; 12-2.30, 7-10.30 Sun

☎ (01707) 642618

Greene King IPA, Abbot; 4 changing beers Ⓗ

Winner of local CAMRA Pub of the Year 10 times and Hertfordshire Pub of the Year three times, this excellent unpretentious village hostelry extends a warm welcome to a loyal and varied clientele of all ages. Six beers are available including four guests from regional and microbreweries, usually one from Hertfordshire. Good pub grub is served lunchtimes (no food Sun). The large garden is ideal in summer. An all-round superb pub – but look out for God's Waiting Room. P

Woolmer Green

Chequers 🄻

16 London Road, SG3 6JP (on B197)

12 (4 Mon)-11; 12-8.30 Sun ☎ (01438) 813216

benicksatthechequers.co.uk

Young's Bitter; 2 changing beers Ⓗ

Large inn on the Great North Road at the southern end of the village with an open-plan bar warmed by a real fire during the cooler months. Cask ale is popular, with high quality compensating for the limited range. Good-quality home-made food featuring fresh ingredients is served daily (no food Monday), with fantastic-value home-made pies on Wednesday and Saturday. Take time to discover the secret zoo in the garden.

P (300,301)

Beer not brandy

Before brandy, which has now become common and solid in every little alehouse, came to England in such quantities as it now doth, we drank good strong beer and ale, and all laborious people (which are the greater part of the kingdom), their bodies requiring after hard labour some strong drink to refresh them, did therefore every morning and evening used to drink a pot of ale or a flagon of strong beer, which greatly helped the promotion of our grains and did them no great prejudice; it hindereth not their work, neither did it take away their senses nor cost them much money, whereas the prohibition of brandy would prevent the destruction of his majesty's subjects, many of whom have been killed by drinking thereof, if not agreeing with their constitution.

Petition to the House of Commons, 1673

ISLE OF WIGHT

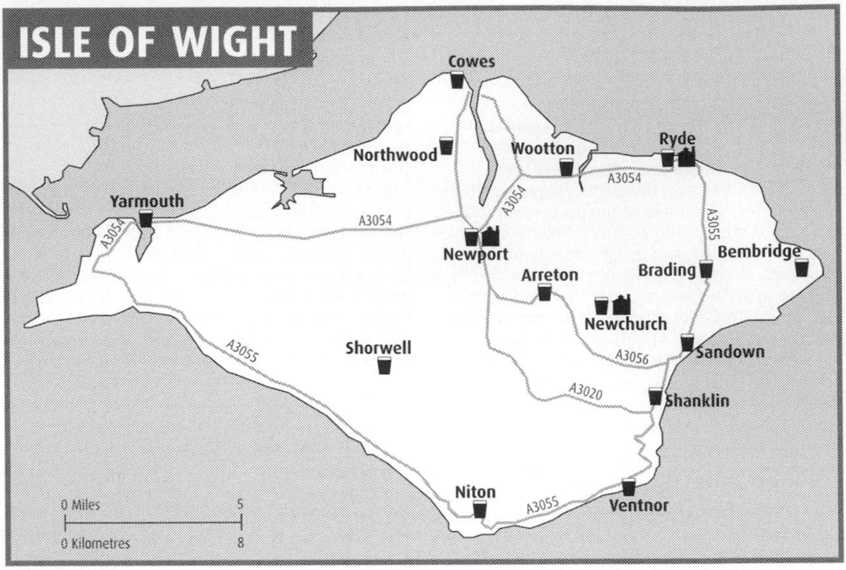

Arreton

Dairyman's Daughter

Main Road, PO30 3AA SZ53258680
10-11 (10.30 Sun) (01983) 539361
thedairymansdaughter.com
Goddards Fuggle-Dee-Dum; Ringwood Best Bitter, Fortyniner; house beer (by Ringwood); 1 changing beer (sourced nationally; often Andwell) H
A hugely popular museum, gift, craft and pub experience on the site of the once massive Arreton Barn. As well as five real ales there is a large selection of Island bottled beers in the old brewery. The full menu is served from 6pm but there is plenty to tempt you throughout the day from a cream tea to snacks. Adjacent is the 11th-century church of St George, the carp pond, the Maritime Museum and the dairyman's daughter's grave. P (8)

Bembridge

Old Village Inn

61 High Street, PO35 5SF
12-11 (01983) 872616
Brakspear Bitter; Courage Directors; 4 changing beers (sourced nationally; often Black Sheep, Greene King, Wells) H
The Old Village Steak & Ale House is the latest addition to the Bembridge scene, specialising in local meat and fish dishes. A fine choice of real ales, ciders including Old Rosie and selected wines are served in a refined and relaxed atmosphere. Food is available lunchtimes and evenings. Live music plays on occasional Fridays and a popular quiz is held on the first Monday of the month. There is a patio area to the rear and a pétanque terrain. Q P (8)

Brading

Yarbridge Inn

Yarbridge, PO36 0AA (on Brading-Sandown road) SZ60448642
11-11 (01983) 405585
Sharp's Doom Bar; 3 changing beers (sourced nationally; often Wadworth, Yates') H
Previously known as the Anglers, this is a pleasant single-bar pub with a changing range of four beers. The dining area offers a fixed menu plus specials board and a choice of roasts on Sunday. Outside is a safe area for children and a paved area with parasols. Live music is hosted occasionally. Sunday roast is a firm favourite and booking is advisable. Q P (2,3)

Cowes

Anchor Inn

1 High Street, PO31 7SA (opp Sainsbury's)
11-11 (midnight Fri & Sat); 12-10.30 Sun
(01983) 292823 theanchorcowes.co.uk
Caledonian Deuchars IPA; Fuller's London Pride; Goddards Fuggle-Dee-Dum; 2 changing beers (sourced nationally; often St Austell, West Berkshire, Wychwood) H
This High Street pub, originally the Trumpeters back in 1704, is close to the Marina, tempting visiting yachtsmen for their first pint ashore. The recent conversion has integrated the stables and created a pleasant beer garden. A good selection of beer is on offer, including one Island ale and two guests. A varied food menu is available, served in prodigious quantities. Frequent live entertainment is provided. Accommodation is in seven comfortable rooms. (1)

Kingston Arms

176 Newport Road, PO31 7PS
11-2.30, 6-11; 11-11 Fri & Sat; 12-4, 7-10.30 Sun
(01983) 293393
Andwells King John; 2 changing beers (sourced nationally; often Goddards, Wadworth) H

REAL ALE BREWERIES

Goddards Ryde
Island Newport
Yates' Newchurch

On the main road out of Cowes towards Newport, you cannot miss the imposing building that is the Kingston Arms. This is a friendly family and locals' pub situated near the yachting centre. It offers a lively public bar with darts and pool, a pétanque terrain and any variety of game that takes your fancy. A free house, the beer range is always in good order, usually including one local and two guest ales. Q❀♣P(1)

Union Inn

Watch House Lane, PO31 7QH (just off the Parade)
11-midnight; 12-10.30 Sun ☎ (01983) 293163
unioninncowes.co.uk
Fuller's London Pride; Gale's Seafarers Ale, HSB; 1 changing beer (sourced regionally; often Fuller's) H
A haven for yachting enthusiasts, locals and holidaymakers, one three-sided bar serves the lounge, snug, dining area and airy conservatory. A roaring fire in winter adds to the cosy atmosphere. Delicious family meals are on the menu, with portions for children and ingredients sourced from local suppliers. A popular quiz is held on Wednesday evenings. The pub may close at 11pm but frequently stays open later. There is pay parking on the Parade 25 yards away, free later in the day. Q(1)

Newchurch

Pointer Inn

High Street, PO36 0NN (next to church)
11-11; 12-10.30 Sun ☎ (01983) 865202
pointernewchurch.co.uk
Fuller's London Pride; Gale's HSB; 2 changing beers (sourced nationally; often Fuller's, Gale's) H
Ancient village local where families are welcome. The home-cooked food is prepared by a chef with a vast experience of Island trade (booking is essential) and served until 9.30pm (9pm Sun). A highchair and toys are always available for children. The large garden has a pétanque terrain and a covered area for smokers. Awards include Fuller's Best Country/Village Pub and a Certificate of Excellence by Trip Advisor.
Q❀♣P(23)

Newport

Bargeman's Rest L

Little London Quay, PO30 5BS (signed from dual carriageway)
10.30-11; 12-10.30 Sun ☎ (01983) 525828
bargemansrest.com
Goddards Fuggle-Dee-Dum; Ringwood Best Bitter, Fortyniner; 4 changing beers (sourced nationally; often Brakspear, Marston's) H
This massive locally owned pub has been an animal feed store and a sail and rigging loft for the barge fleet that used to use the river. The huge bar is divided into intimate drinking areas and the nautical memorabilia, decor and ambience are all you could hope for in a traditional, well-seasoned pub. The outdoor drinking area is only a few feet from the bustling River Medina. Beer and food are consistently good and the range varied. Live entertainment features on most nights.
❀P

Prince of Wales

36 South Street, PO30 1JE (opp bus station)
10.30-11; 12-10.30 Sun ☎ (01983) 525026
Fuller's London Pride; Morland Old Speckled Hen; 1 changing beer (sourced nationally; often Adnams, Ringwood, Wychwood) H
Excellent mock-Tudor single-bar local that has earned a fine reputation for its ale, with up to three beers from the Punch list. Old Rosie cider is also on handpump. On a street corner opposite the bus station and Morrisons, this is very much a locals' pub that retains the feel of a public bar. It stages an annual beer festival and has a good games following. Food includes good wholesome sandwiches, pies and mother's home-baked specials. A real gem. ♣

Niton

Buddle L

St Catherines Road, Niton Undercliff, PO38 2NE (follow signs to St Catherine's Lighthouse) SZ50207580
11-10.30 (11.30 Fri & Sat); 12-10.30 Sun
☎ (01983) 730243
Sharp's Doom Bar; Yates' Wight Old Ale; house beer (by Yates'); 3 changing beers (sourced nationally; often Black Sheep, Fuller's) H
This 16th-century inn was built as a farmhouse and reputedly became a smugglers' inn during the 18th century. Extensively refurbished, it retains the ancient flagstones and beams, inglenook fireplace and many interesting photographs. A popular destination dining pub, offering good locally sourced food, it also has a strong real ale following, with six ales available. Situated near the lighthouse, the pub has many links to Trinity House. Q❀♣P(6)

Northwood

Travellers Joy L

85 Pallance Road, PO31 8LS (on Northwood-Porchfield road) SZ48009360
12-11 (midnight Thu-Sat) ☎ (01983) 298024
thetravellersjoy.co.uk
Goddards Wight Squirrel; Island Wight Gold; 6 changing beers (sourced nationally; often Andwells, St Austell, Theakston) H
Offering one of the best choices of cask ale on the island, this long-standing old country inn was the Island's first beer exhibition house. Up to seven varied and interesting ales rotate to supplement the Island's Wight Gold. A real cider, Biddenden Bushels, is also available. A good range of home-cooked food is served lunchtimes and evenings. The pub is a thriving venue for real ale followers, the local community and visitors seeking a friendly and amenable base. Q❀♣P(1)

Ryde

Castle Inn

164 High Street, PO36 8HY
10 (11 Sun)-11.30 ☎ (01983) 613684
Fuller's London Pride, ESB; Gale's HSB H
This large public house, a fine building standing proud at the junction with the High Street, was opened in 1850 by Thomas Vanner who operated the Ryde to Newport stagecoach. Owing to its impressive etched windows it is Grade II-listed, which may have saved it from demolition or conversion in the mid-'80s. It has enjoyed a long-standing reputation for its ales – HSB is its best seller and is always in wonderful condition.
❀≠(Esplanade)♣

Railway 🍺 Ⓛ

68 St Johns Road, PO33 2RT (by station)

⊘ 12 (3 Mon & Tue)-midnight; 12-11 Sat & Sun

☎ (01983) 566651

Morland Old Golden Hen; Timothy Taylor Landlord; 4 changing beers (sourced nationally; often Adnams, Goddards) Ⓗ

This pleasant town local has seen several changes of ownership over the past few years before becoming a free house. The new owner refurbished it to a high standard, while retaining flagstone floors, beams and plenty of wood. Note the Ginkgo biloba tree in the garden, a species whose ancestry can be traced back over 200 million years. The handy train station is yards away, bringing visitors from Portsmouth in search of quality real ale. Bottled gluten-free ale and lager are now available. ⛟☺☂⇌(St Johns Road)♣🚆(2,3,8)☺

Simeon Arms Ⓛ

21 Simeon Street, PO33 1JG (short walk from Canoe Lake)

⊘ 11-11 (11.30 Mon & Thu; midnight Fri & Sat); 12-11.30 Sun

☎ (01983) 614954

Courage Directors; Goddards Ale of Wight; 1 changing beer (sourced nationally; often Goddards) Ⓗ

Thriving yet unlikely gem tucked away in a Ryde back street with a Tardis-like interior and annexed function hall. The pub is immensely popular with the local community who come to participate in various leagues including shove-ha'penny, darts, crib and pool, and pétanque on the enormous floodlit terrain in summer. You can always expect to find a local ale. Live music plays on Saturday and Sunday nights. The smoking area outside is heated and covered. ⛟☺⇌(St John's Road)♣🚆 🛜

Sandown

Castle Inn Ⓛ

12-14 Fitzroy Street, PO36 8HY (off High Street)

⊘ 11-11 (midnight Fri); 10.30-midnight Sat & Sun

☎ (01983) 403169 ⊕ sandowncastle.co.uk

Young's Special; 4 changing beers (sourced locally; often Wadworth, Yates') Ⓗ

The Castle is an excellent town free house and locals' pub with crib and two darts teams. Six real ales are offered including the best from local breweries. There is a children's room at the back and a patio for warm weather. The TV is not allowed to intrude, but is turned on for special occasions. Happy hour is popular, as is the Sunday quiz. Beer festivals are held several times a year, usually featuring local ales and cider. Q⛟☺☂⇌♣●🚆(3,8)☺🛜

Shanklin

Chine Inn Ⓛ

1 Chine Hill, PO37 6BW (up hill at end of Esplanade)

⊘ closed Mon; 11.30-11; 12-10.30 Sun ☎ (01983) 865880

Timothy Taylor Landlord Ⓖ; house beer (by Sharp's); 2 changing beers (sourced nationally; often Adnams, Kelham Island) Ⓗ

This inn, which has stood since 1621, must be one of the oldest pubs with a licence on the Island. Completely refurbished, it has retained its original charm, with magnificent views of the bay. Live music is hosted on Saturday night and Sunday afternoon. The Chine Inn ghosts – a girl in blue and an old man in the corner – have been seen by small

children. Ask to see the opening hours notice. Winter hours vary – check before travelling. Q⛟☺⊕●🚆(2,3)☺

King Harry's Bar

6 Church Road, PO37 6NU (on edge of Old Village towards Ventnor)

⊘ 11-midnight; 12-10.30 Sun ☎ (01983) 863119

⊕ kingharrysbar.co.uk

Fuller's ESB; 3 changing beers (sourced nationally; often Fuller's, Island, Young's) Ⓗ

Charming 19th-century thatched property with two established Tudor bars, restaurants, decked gardens and the Chine walk, plus car parking front and rear. Up to three guest beers are offered, chosen for their originality, and Thatchers Traditional cider. Food is served in the summer months commencing Easter – the long-established Henry VIII kitchen specialises in steaks to die for. Function facilities and entertainment are also provided. Accommodation is available. Winter opening hours vary. Q⛟☺☂⊕🍴⊕▲♣●P🚪🚆(3,2)☺

Shorwell

Crown Inn Ⓛ

Walkers Lane, PO30 3JZ

⊘ 10.30-11; 11.30-11 Sun ☎ (01983) 740293

⊕ crowninnshorwell.co.uk

Adnams Broadside; Goddards Fuggle-Dee-Dum; Sharp's Doom Bar; 3 changing beers (sourced nationally; often Fuller's, Robinsons, St Austell) Ⓗ

Expansive 300-year-old hostelry in the picturesque village of Shorwell with a central multi-sided bar and traditional bar areas. It offers a range of up to six beers and a good home-cooked pub menu all day prepared by head chef Paul Hayward. The pub has a trout stream running through the garden, ducks in abundance to keep the children amused, and plenty of car parking. The real ale range is reduced to four during the winter months. Q⛟☺☂⊕♣P🚆(12)☺🛜

Ventnor

Perks

46 High Street, PO38 1LT

⊘ 9am (10 Sun)-midnight ☎ (01983) 857446

⊕ perksofventnor.com

Draught Bass Ⓗ

Perks is one of those gems that happen infrequently, offering one beer, plenty of wine, good service and sensible prices. A great collection of memorabilia reflects the pub's Best of British theme. A second beer, from Yates', may be added at weekends. Owner Graham Perks has spent 25 years running a succession of bars in Ventnor and knows what the customer wants – pleasant surroundings, good company and a tipple to suit the most discerning palate. Q☺⊕☂●🚆(3,6)☺

Volunteer Ⓛ

30 Victoria Street, PO38 1ES (50yds from bus terminal)

⊘ 11-11.30 (midnight Fri & Sat); 12-10.30 Sun

☎ (01983) 852537

Courage Best Bitter; 4 changing beers (sourced nationally; often Exmoor, Sharp's) Ⓗ

Built in 1866, the Volunteer is one of the smallest pubs on the island. A former winner of local CAMRA Pub of the Year, up to six beers are available including an occasional local brew. No chips, no children, no fruit machines, no video games – just a pure adult drinking house and one of the few places where you can still play rings and enjoy a traditional games night. Live music is hosted on Sunday afternoon. Westons Old Rosie cider is available. **Q♣🍎🚌** (3,6)🐾

Wootton

Cedars

2 Station Road, PO33 4QU (top of village by traffic lights)
🕐 11-11; 12-10.30 Sun ☎ (01983) 882593
🌐 cedarsisleofwight.co.uk
Fuller's London Pride; Gale's HSB; 1 changing beer (sourced nationally; often Fuller's, Gale's) Ⓗ
Late-Victorian two-bar village local set in a prominent position at the top of Wootton High Street. Curiously, although a large pub, it has one of the smallest front doors on the island. An extensive food menu is available and the friendly bar staff ensure a good atmosphere. There is a children's room and a large garden with a play area. Smokers are spoilt – the outdoor smoking area is adapted from a beautiful Victorian outbuilding. Close to the steam railway station. **Q❀◑♿⇌♣P🚌** (4,9)🐾 📶

Yarmouth

King's Head 𝕃

Quay Street, PO41 0PB (opp ferry terminal)
🕐 11-11 ☎ (01983) 760351
Sharp's Doom Bar; Timothy Taylor Landlord; 1 changing beer (sourced locally; often Yates') Ⓗ
Ancient 16th-century town pub with a big open fire, interesting collection of old Island prints and local photographs. Stone floors, low ceilings and cosy corners in abundance help to create an intimate atmosphere. Home-cooked food includes fresh fish and daily specials. A handy place to wait for the Yarmouth-Lymington ferry, it offers recently refurbished accommodation. Westons Old Rosie cider is available. **❀🛏◑🍎🚌** (7)🐾 📶

Union Inn, Cowes

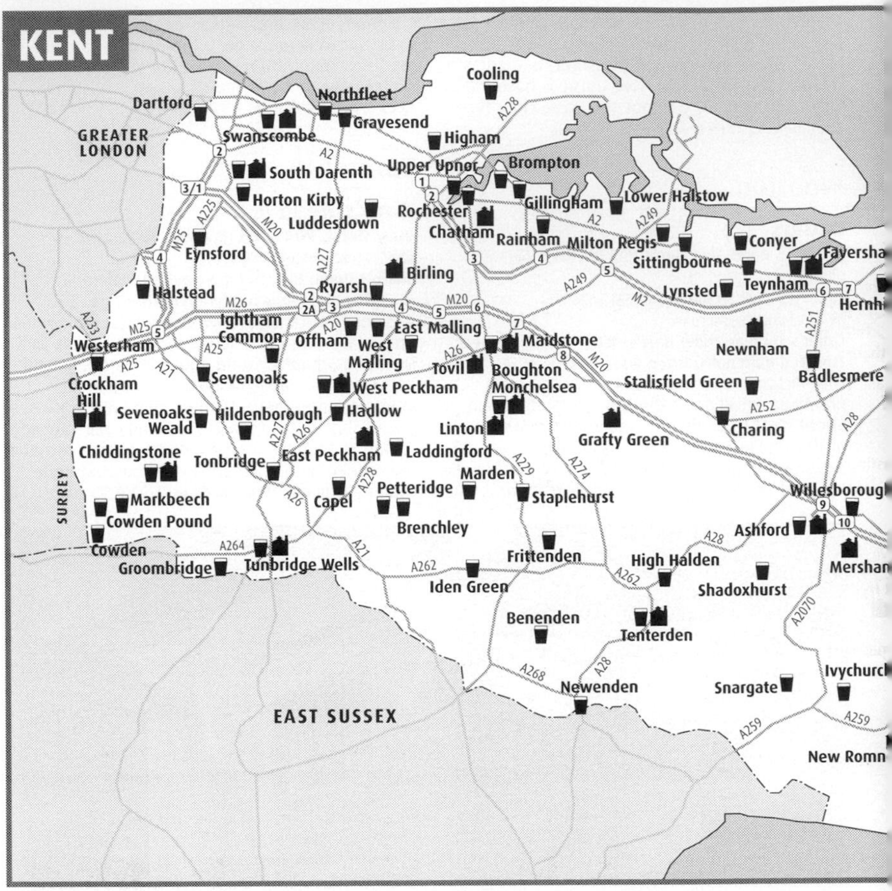

Ashford

County Hotel

10 High Street, TN24 8TD

8am-11 (midnight Thu; 1am Fri & Sat) ☎ (01233) 646891

Greene King Abbot; Ruddles Best Bitter; 4 changing beers Ⓗ

A spacious Wetherspoon pub in the town centre. This 18th-century red brick building has seven bays, a tile-hung top storey and two bars with three separate seating areas; note the distinctive metal statue. Up to two real ciders are dispensed from polypins in the fridge. Food is served daily 8am-10pm. Children are allowed in the dining area until 9pm. ❀◐♿⇌(International)P

Badlesmere

Red Lion

Ashford Road, ME13 0NX (on main A251 Faversham to Ashford road)

12-11 (9 Mon; midnight Fri & Sat); 12-7 Sun

☎ (01233) 740320 redlionbadlesmere.co.uk

3 changing beers (sourced regionally; often Millis, Ramsgate, Shepherd Neame) Ⓗ

Traditional country pub built in 1546, with many public bridleways and footpaths nearby. The selection of ales often includes local beers from Kent micros. The pub offers home-cooked food and can cater for functions. There is regular live music from local bands. Camping facilities are available in the pub's own paddock. The 666 bus runs during the daytime (not Sun). ❀◐♣P(666)

Barfrestone

Wrong Turn

Pie Factory Road, CT15 7JG (2 miles from Barfrestone jct off A2) TR261503

closed Mon & Tue; 3-8 Wed; 12-9 Thu; 12-10 Fri & Sat; 12-8 Sun ☎ 07522 554118

3 changing beers Ⓖ

Along a quiet country lane, at the bottom of a gravel drive, this rural micropub is housed in a converted artist's studio. The interior is homely, with wooden tables, a sideboard and a stove. A good range of real ales is offered, largely from Kent microbreweries, plus real ciders from Kentish Pip and Westons, a choice of wines and a bottled lager. Snacks are available including pork pies, Scotch eggs and quiche. Opening times may vary from October to March. It has a pleasant patio and garden. Q❀♿♣P

Benenden

Bull Ⓛ

The Street, TN17 4DE

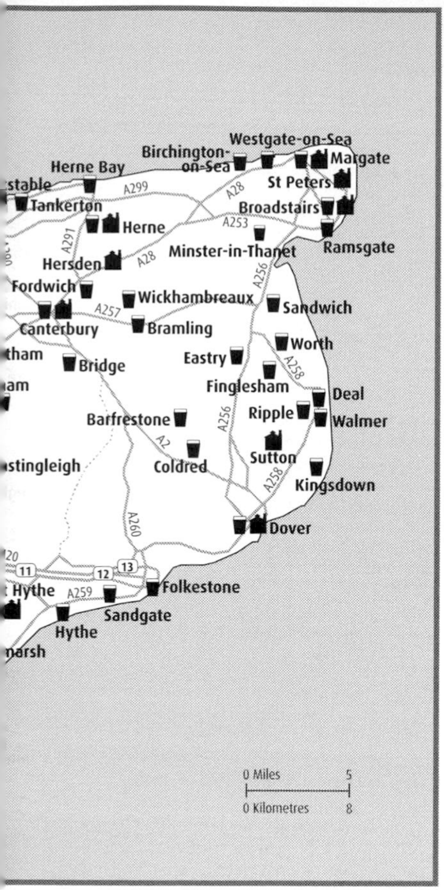

⏲ 12-midnight ☎ (01580) 240054
🌐 thebullatbenenden.co.uk
Dark Star Hophead; Harveys Sussex Best Bitter; Larkins Traditional Ale; 1 changing beer (sourced locally; often Long Man, Old Dairy, Shepherd Neame) H
Large, genuine free house dating back to the early 17th century next to the village green. Wooden floors and exposed oak beams are visible throughout and a large inglenook fireplace is in the public bar. Good food is prepared using locally grown produce, available in both the public bar and the separate restaurant. Booking is advisable for the Sunday lunchtime carvery (with different sittings in the public bar and restaurant). Live music is hosted most Sunday afternoons once dining has finished. Q❀◑♣●P🚌(297)🐾📶

Birchington-on-Sea

Wheel Alehouse

60 Station Road, CT7 9RA
⏲ closed Mon; 12-2, 5-9; 12-2 Sun ☎ 07826 130927
🌐 thewheelalehouse.co.uk
4 changing beers G
Converted from a shop, this pub has been a welcome addition to the village's beer scene. A nautical theme runs throughout. The beers are served direct from the cask from a temperature-controlled stillage room behind a small bar counter. At the rear is a steep flight of stairs leading up to the Upper Deck, where toilets and further seating can be found. Q≋●🚌(33,34)🐾

Boughton Monchelsea

Cock Inn L

Heath Road, ME17 4JD TQ776512
⏲ 11-11; 12-10.30 Sun ☎ (01622) 743166
Shepherd Neame Master Brew; 3 changing beers (sourced nationally; often St Austell, Shepherd Neame) H
A 16th-century coaching inn built to provide lodgings for Canterbury pilgrims, full of character, with oak beams and an inglenook fireplace. A varied menu complemented by real ales is served in both the bar and restaurant (no food Sun eves). There is a large patio area. Darts and board games are available. Situated near the Greensand Way, walkers are welcome. Q❀◑♣P🐾

Bramling

Haywain L

Canterbury Road, CT3 1NB
⏲ 7-11 Mon; 12-3, 6-11; 12-4 Sun ☎ (01227) 720676
🌐 thehaywainbramling.co.uk
Fuller's London Pride; Wells Bombardier; 2 changing beers (sourced nationally; often Goacher's, Ramsgate, Whitstable) H
Traditional and friendly country pub with hanging hop bines and assorted curios. Mondays feature a quiz night, Wednesday evenings cribbage. There is a cheese club on the last Sunday of the month and a jazz evening on the last Tuesday. An annual beer festival is hosted over the spring bank holiday

REAL ALE BREWERIES

Canterbury Ales Chartham
Canterbury Brewers Canterbury
Caveman Swanscombe
Farriers Arms Mersham
Four Candles St Peters (NEW)
G2 Ashford
Goacher's Tovil
Goody Herne
Hop Fuzz West Hythe
Hopdaemon Newnham
Isla Vale Margate (NEW)
Kent Birling
Larkins Chiddingstone
Mad Cat Faversham
Maidstone Maidstone
Millis South Darenth
Musket Linton
Nelson Chatham
Old Dairy Tenterden
Pig & Porter Tunbridge Wells
Ramsgate Broadstairs
Ripple Steam Sutton
Rockin' Robin Boughton Monchelsea
Romney Marsh New Romney (NEW)
Shepherd Neame Faversham
Swan West Peckham
Tír Dhá Ghlas Dover
Tonbridge East Peckham
Turnstone Whitstable (NEW)
Wantsum Hersden
Westerham Crockham Hill
Whitstable Grafty Green

weekend in a marquee in the attractive garden. The guest beers and the ingredients for the food tend to be sourced locally. No food Mondays.
Q❀◑♣P🚌(13,14)🐾

Brenchley

Halfway House 𝕃
Horsmonden Road, TN12 7AX (½ mile SE of village)
⏲ 11-11; 11-10.30 Sun ☎ (01892) 722526
🌐 halfwayhousebrenchley.co.uk
Goacher's Fine Light Ale; Skinner's Betty Stogs; Tonbridge Rustic; Westerham 1965 Special Bitter Ale; changing beers (sourced locally; often Goacher's, Larkins, Whitstable) [G]
Ever-popular 17th-century rural free house serving good-value beers direct from the cask, and Kentish Chiddingstone cider. The rustic interior features farming and woodland memorabilia hanging from exposed timbers. Chalkboards around the log fire display meal choices. The extensive rear garden includes an area with covered seating, dedicated for families and children, which comes into its own on Whitsun and August bank holidays when festivals are held featuring up to 75 ales.
Q🐎❀🛏◑♣🍎P🚌(297)🐾

Bridge

White Horse Inn 𝕃
53 High Street, CT4 5LA
⏲ closed Mon; 12-11; 12-10 Sun ☎ (01227) 830845
🌐 whitehorsebridge.co.uk
Ringwood Best Bitter; Timothy Taylor Landlord [H]**; 2 changing beers (sourced nationally; often Ramsgate)** [H]/[G]
Sixteenth-century coaching inn with superb oak beams and two large fireplaces. There is plenty of space both for drinkers and diners, and a large garden at the rear. An interesting range of gins and vodkas as well as the beer is on offer. Food is freshly prepared using ingredients that are mainly sourced locally; the specials board reflects this and varies depending on what is in season.
🐎❀◑P🚌(17,89)🐾📶

Broadstairs

Brown Jug
Ramsgate Road, Dumpton, CT10 2EW
⏲ 6-11; 1.30-11.30 Sat; 12-11 Sun ☎ (01843) 862788
3 changing beers (often Hardys & Hansons, Morland) [H]
A pub with shuttered, leaded windows and a flint façade dating back to 1795, when it was called the Queen's Arms Tap, though the building is said to be much older. Its current name was mentioned on documents in 1814, when it was reputed to have been used as an officer's billet during the Napoleonic wars. It smacks of old world charm. There are eight pétanque pistes in the garden and on alternate Monday evenings there is a writers' circle. Regular quiz nights are held.
Q❀🚆(Dumpton Park)♣P🚌(Loop,39)🐾

Thirty-Nine Steps Alehouse
5 Charlotte Street, CT10 1LR
⏲ 12-11
4 changing beers [G]
A former shop now operating as one of Thanet's many micropubs, tastefully converted with heavy wooden high tables and bench seating. The frequently changing beers are dispensed from a glass-fronted cooled stillage cabinet behind the bar. The enthusiastic and knowledgeable landlord is keen to source interesting and unusual brews from around the country, and the place has become a popular destination for discerning local ale drinkers, as well as offering a pleasant alternative for the town's tourists.
Q🐎🚆🍎🚌(56)🐾

Yard of Ale 🏆
61 Church Street, St Peter's, CT10 2TU
⏲ 5-11; 12-11 Sat & Sun ☎ 07792 042993
3 changing beers [G]
The former stable block of the adjacent funeral directors, housing a gem of a micropub. Decorated with old riding equipment, it retains much of the building's unique character, including the original flagstone floor. Seating varies from high stools to bales of straw, and there is a wood-burning stove for the colder months. The pleasant outdoor seating area is a wonderful suntrap in summer. Ale and cider are served from a small adjacent room, or through the window to the outdoor area. Local CAMRA branch Pub of the Year 2015.
Q❀🍎🚌(Loop)🐾

Brompton

King George V 𝕃
1 Prospect Row, ME7 5AL
⏲ 12-11; 12-10.30 Sun ☎ (01634) 842418 🌐 kgvpub.com
Old Dairy Red Top; house beer (by Mad Cat); 3 changing beers (sourced locally; often Goody Ales, Old Dairy, Whitstable) [H]
Historic 17th-century free house on the Saxon Shore Way featuring military memorabilia. It has three connected areas and a covered and heated area for smokers in the garden. Guest ales come from local Kent microbreweries, plus a wide variety of Belgian beers, malt whiskies, rums and ciders. Food is served every lunchtime, as well as evenings Tuesday-Saturday, with themed pizza (except Sun), curry, tapas and steak nights. Sunday roasts are popular. Four guest rooms are available.
🐎❀🛏◑♣🍎🚌(101,182)📶

Burmarsh

Shepherd & Crook 𝕃
Shear Way, TN29 0JJ (signed from A259) TR101320
⏲ closed Tue; 12-11 (10 Mon); 12-4 Sun ☎ (01303) 872336
🌐 shepherdandcrook.co.uk
House beer (by Old Dairy); 2 changing beers [H]
A friendly family-run free house on the Romney Marsh Cycle Route. The pub has a separate dining room and a single bar where ring the bull can be played. Frequently changing guest ales are always on tap. Traditional home-cooked English food, utilising local ingredients where possible, is available lunchtimes and evenings (no food Tue and Sun eves). The interesting adjacent medieval church has a Norman doorway within a 16th-century porch and is well worth a visit.
Q🐎❀◑⛺♣🍎🚌🐾📶

Canterbury

Dolphin 🄻

17 St Radigund's Street, CT1 2AA
⏲ 12-11 (midnight Thu-Sat) ☎ (01227) 455963
🌐 thedolphincanterbury.co.uk
Sharp's Doom Bar; 2 changing beers (sourced nationally; often Castle Rock, Hopdaemon, Timothy Taylor) 🄷
Friendly local decorated with 1950s-1970s memorabilia and free of TV screens. Good pub food in generous portions is served daily, with roasts on Sundays. There is a comprehensive collection of board games. The attractive verandah is popular with diners, and there is a large suntrap garden. Two of the handpumps serve cider, and a changing range of local and regional beers is on the other pumps. The pub may close on Mondays and opening hours vary from month to month (see website for times). ⚘❀◑⇌(West)●ᯤ

Eight Bells

34 London Road, CT2 8LN
⏲ 3-11; 12-midnight Fri & Sat; 12-10.30 Sun
☎ (01227) 454794
Young's Bitter, Special 🄷
Small, traditional local dating from 1708 and rebuilt in 1902, retaining the original embossed windows and decorated with memorabilia. There is live music fortnightly on Fridays and a quiz, usually on the last Wednesday of the month. Five darts teams play every week and their trophies are on display. Food is served only on Sunday lunchtimes. It has an attractive small walled garden and a comfortable heated smoking area. ❀◐⇌(West)♣⊟(3,6)🐾ᯤ

New Inn

19 Havelock Street, CT1 1NP (off ring road near St Augustine's Abbey)
⏲ 12-2, 5-11; 12-midnight Fri & Sat; 12-2.30, 6-11 Sun
☎ (01227) 464584 🌐 newinncanterbury.co.uk
6 changing beers (sourced nationally; often Adnams, Dark Star, Kent) 🄷
Victorian back-street terraced house only a few minutes' walk from the cathedral, St Augustine's Abbey and the bus station. The main bar has a cosy woodburner, a wooden floor and a jukebox. At the back is a long, bright conservatory where there are newspapers to browse over your pint, and a range of board games. Beer festivals are held on the Whitsun and August bank holiday weekends. Disabled access is through the attractive garden via Old Ruttington Lane. ⚘❀♿♣●⊟🐾

Unicorn 🄻

61 St Dunstan's Street, CT2 8BS
⏲ 11.30-11 (midnight Fri & Sat) ☎ (01227) 463187
🌐 unicorninn.com
Sharp's Doom Bar; Shepherd Neame Master Brew; 2 changing beers (sourced nationally; often Hopdaemon, Ramsgate, Timothy Taylor) 🄷
Comfortable 1604 pub near the historic Westgate, with an attractive suntrap garden. Bar billiards is played and a quiz, set by regular customers, is held weekly on Sunday evening. One of the guest beers is usually from one of several Kent microbreweries, and beer updates are posted on Twitter. Food is good value, with a two meals for £10 special offer on selected meals (no food Sun eve). Sporting events are televised (not Sky) unobtrusively.
Q⚘❀◑⇌(West)♣●⊟(3,4,6)🐾ᯤ

Capel

Dovecote Inn

Alders Road, TN12 6SU (½ mile W of A228)
⏲ 12-3 (not Mon), 5.30-11; 12-10.30 Sun ☎ (01892) 835966
🌐 dovecote-capel.co.uk
Gales HSB; Harveys Sussex Best Bitter; 3 changing beers (sourced locally; often Musket, Salopian, Tonbridge) 🄶
In the hamlet of Capel, this rural pub offers a good range of ales and plenty of room in which to relax. Excellent beers are served along with Westons Old Rosie cider to complement the cosy ambience and local feel. The pub has a good reputation for food and attention to customer service. Inside there are low-beamed ceilings and walls decked with local memorabilia and rural artefacts. Outside there is an appealing summertime patio, extensive garden space for children and car parking.
Q⚘❀◑♿♣●P⊟(6A)ᯤ

Charing

Bowl Inn

Egg Hill Road, TN27 0HG (signed from A20 and A251)
⏲ 12-11 (midnight Fri & Sat) ☎ (01233) 712256
🌐 bowlinn.co.uk
Sharp's Doom Bar; 3 changing beers (sourced locally; often Hopdaemon, Wantsum, Whitstable) 🄷
A 16th-century free house on the top of the North Downs in an Area of Outstanding Natural Beauty. A large inglenook fire warms the bar and there is a spacious garden and a covered and heated sun terrace. The pub is a popular stop-off point for walkers and cyclists and offers five rooms. Quirky features, such as the boar behind the bar, add character. It holds an annual beer festival with live music in the summer. ⚘❀🛏◑♿⛺P⊟🐾ᯤ

Chiddingstone

Castle Inn 🄻

TN8 7AH (turn off B2027 1 mile W of Penshurst station)
⏲ 10-11; 12-10.30 Sun ☎ (01892) 870247
🌐 castleinn-kent.co.uk
Larkins Traditional Ale; 2 changing beers (sourced locally; often Long Man, Whitstable) 🄷
Despite a profusion of clocks, this impressive stone inn is timeless. The long building accommodates a number of distinct areas, from rustic public bar to comfy dining rooms. The Castle is the perfect place to sample ales from the Larkins Brewery along the road, and a refreshment stop for visitors to the stunning village of Chiddingstone, Hever Castle and nearby Penshurst Place. In winter a fire and wood-burning stove keep out the chill. An attractive courtyard garden is popular on balmier days.
Q⚘❀◑♣🐾ᯤ

Coldred

Carpenters Arms 🏆 🄻

The Green, CT15 5AJ
⏲ 5-9; 6-11 Fri & Sat; 7-11 Sun ☎ (01304) 830190
4 changing beers 🄷/🄶
Overlooking the village green and duck pond, this 18th-century two-roomed pub is a real gem and well worth seeking out. It has been in the Fagg family for over 100 years, and largely unchanged in

the last 50 years – the centre of the community where conversation is king. Up to four real ales are served alongside a real cider. The pub hosts regular community events including quizzes and vegetable competitions. A beer festival is held in June. CAMRA branch Pub of the Year 2015. Q常❀♣●P🐾≋

Conyer

Ship

Conyer Quay, ME9 9HR

12-3, 6-11 (midnight Fri); 10-11.30 Sat; 10-9.30 Sun

☎ (01795) 520881 ⊕ shipinnconyer.co.uk

Shepherd Neame Master Brew; 3 changing beers (sourced locally; often Mad Cat, Old Dairy) Ⓗ

An 18th-century creekside pub with a nautically themed interior. Bare floorboards and scrubbed pine tables add rustic charm and a real fire adds character. The pub is popular with walkers and cyclists and is located on the Saxon Shore Way. It is a 20-minute walk from Teynham train station. Food is served in the main bar and in an upstairs dining room. A small courtyard garden overlooks the creek. Q❀◐◑♣P🚌(344,345,346)🐾≋

Cooling

Horseshoe & Castle 🄻

Main Road, ME3 8DJ

12-3 (not Mon), 5.30-11; 11.30-11 Wed-Sat; 12-11 Sun

☎ (01634) 221691 ⊕ horseshoeandcastle.com

Shepherd Neame Master Brew; 1 changing beer (sourced locally) Ⓗ

Village local, with the same welcoming landlord for the last 26 years, on the Hoo Peninsula, which is well known for birdlife. The restaurant specialises in seafood (closed Mon). This free house is near a ruined castle and the local church, whose graveyard is believed to have been the inspiration for the opening chapter of Charles Dickens' book Great Expectations, where Pip meets the convict Magwitch. Good-quality accommodation is available. Q❀🛏◐◑♿♣P🐾

Cowden

Fountain

30 High Street, TN8 7JG (1 mile W of B2026)

12-3, 6-midnight; 12-11 Sun ☎ (01342) 850528

⊕ fountain-cowden.com

Harveys IPA, Sussex Best Bitter; 1 changing beer (sourced locally; often Harveys) Ⓗ

Harveys-owned village pub with a strong community focus hosting a golf society, darts team, cricket club and an annual outing to Ascot races. Good traditional English fare is served in generous portions (book for Sunday roasts). A light, spacious conservatory overlooks the pleasant garden which incorporates a shelter beautifully decorated with a mural depicting Cowden scenes. The railway station nearby makes the Fountain an attractive refreshment stop for walkers and cyclists.
❀◐◑♣P🚌(234)🐾≋

Cowden Pound

Queen's Arms ★ 🄻

Hartfield Road, TN8 5NP (on B2026 halfway between Edenbridge and A264)

5-10.30 (7 Wed & Thu; 9 Fri); 12-2.30 Sun

Larkins Traditional Ale Ⓗ**; 1 changing beer (sourced locally; often Larkins)** Ⓖ

Owned and operated by a local family, this is one of only three Kent pubs with a nationally important historic interior, featuring one of the last remaining totally unspoilt public bars dating from the Victorian era. Local Larkins Trad, supplemented by a seasonal cask on the counter, can be enjoyed alongside friendly locals in the ambience of the pub's old-world charm, with open fires in both bars in winter. Note the No Lager sign and till.
Q♣P🄱🐾

Crockham Hill

Royal Oak 🄻

Main Road, TN8 6RD (on B2026 jct with B269)

12-3, 5-11 (midnight Fri); 12-11 Sat; 12-10.30 Sun

☎ (01732) 866335 ⊕ royaloakcrockhamhill.co.uk

Westerham Finchcocks Original; 3 changing beers (sourced locally; often Westerham) Ⓗ

One of only two Westerham Brewery pubs, offering a selection from its portfolio, with third-pint tasters to help you choose. Recent sympathetic refurbishment has retained the feel of the 16th- and 18th-century bar areas, featuring stone-mullioned and leaded windows. The smart and comfortable furnishings are enhanced by the amusing Tottering cartoons donated by Country Life artist Annie Tempest which adorn the walls. Serving good home-cooked meals, this is a convenient refreshment destination for walkers, cyclists and visitors to Winston Churchill's home, Chartwell. Q❀◐◑P🚌(236)≋

Dartford

Dartford Working Men's Club 🄻

Essex Road, DA1 2AU

11-11; 12-10.30 Sun ☎ (01322) 223646

⊕ dartfordwm.club

Courage Best Bitter; Shepherd Neame Spitfire Ⓗ/Ⓖ**; changing beers (sourced nationally; often Caveman)** Ⓗ

This modern CIU club boasts a selection of 15 ales on handpump, plus ciders on gravity. The ales come from various micros and regional breweries countrywide, with over 400 different beers served each year. The club is also home to the BBC award-winning Dartford Folk Club, meeting on Tuesday nights. Up to four beer festivals are held each year. CAMRA members and guests can be signed in on entry. ❀◐◑♿⇌●🚌≋

Ivy Leaf 🄻

72 Darenth Road, DA1 1LS

12-11; 12-10.30 Sun ☎ (01322) 220993

Sharp's Doom Bar; Wells Bombardier; 4 changing beers Ⓗ

Brewers' Tudor suburban pub having a large single bar with two real fires. The Fastrack B bus stops opposite and the pub is between the town centre and Dartford football ground. Up to four guest ales from various regional brewers are served with at least one from a local brewer. Home-made food and sandwiches are available at lunchtime. The garden has a covered smoking area. Live music features on Thursday and Saturday evenings and there is an open quiz on Sunday evening.
❀◐⇌P🚌(B)

Malt Shovel
3 Darenth Road, DA1 1LP
12 (3 Mon)-11; 12-midnight Sat ☎ (01322) 224381
St Austell Tribute; Young's Bitter, Special; 2 changing beers Ⓗ
Country pub owned by Young's, just outside the town centre, dating from 1673. It has two bars, with the low-ceilinged taproom featuring an 1880s Dartford Brewery mirror. The large conservatory, attached to the main bar, leads to a beer garden with views across Dartford. The Fastrack B bus stop is just down the hill and other bus stops are nearby. Food is served, except Mondays, and barbecues are hosted in the summer. An open quiz night takes place every Monday. P

Deal

Just Reproach Ⓛ
14 King Street, CT14 6HX
12-2, 5-9 (11 Fri); 12-3.30, 5-11 Sat; 12-4 Sun
4 changing beers Ⓖ
One of Kent's first micropubs, opened in 2011, right in the town centre. The welcoming ambience, high benches and table service make for friendly interaction, and the notice on the wall explaining the pub's name is a guaranteed conversation starter. It serves excellent-quality beers, with the emphasis on local breweries, and ciders from Kent Cider, plus wine and soft drinks. No keg or spirits, and no food, music or TV. Do not let your mobile phone ring, whatever you do! Q

Ship Inn Ⓛ
141 Middle Street, CT14 6JZ
11-midnight; 12-midnight Sun ☎ (01304) 372222
Dark Star Hophead, American Pale Ale; Ramsgate Gadds' No.7 Bitter Ale, Gadds' No.5 Best Bitter Ale; 1 changing beer Ⓗ
Traditional, unspoilt, back-street pub in Deal's historic conservation area, just off the seafront. The interior has a nautical theme, with a dark, cosy atmosphere. The main bar, with its five handpumps, always features a good range of ales, and the comfortable lounge area has an open fire in winter. There is a rear snug with a staircase leading to the garden and covered smoking area. The pub is just 10 minutes' walk from the town centre.

Dover

Eight Bells Ⓛ
19 Cannon Street, CT16 1BZ
8am-midnight ☎ (01304) 205030
Adnams Broadside; Fuller's London Pride; Sharp's Doom Bar; 9 changing beers Ⓗ
Probably selling more real ale than any other Wetherspoon in south-east Kent, this bustling pub is celebrating its seventh year in the Guide. Located on Dover's main shopping street, it was once a cinema and its name is linked to the Dover parish church opposite. The large open-plan single-room interior includes a raised restaurant area. Twelve handpumps adorn the long bar, with 10 normally in use, featuring at least one Kent microbrewery. Outdoor seating overlooks the pedestrian precinct.

Louis Armstrong Ⓛ
58 Maison Dieu Road, CT16 1RA
2-11; 7-11 Sun ☎ (01304) 204759
Hopdaemon Skrimshander IPA; 3 changing beers Ⓗ
Renowned music venue and down-to-earth local on Dover's one-way system, about five minutes' walk from the town centre, with an L-shaped bar with stage and music posters and a mirror running the full length of the end wall. It has an attractive, secluded garden. Beers are mainly from Kent micros. Music takes place at weekends, with jazz on Sundays, and there are occasional music and beer festivals. On Wednesdays there is good-value food, and real ale at £2.50 a pint. A large public car park is opposite. Easily accessible by bus.

Mash Tun Ⓛ
3 Bench Street, CT16 1JH
closed Mon & Tue; 12-10 Wed-Sat; 12-4 Sun
☎ (01304) 219590
House beer (by Hopdaemon); 4 changing beers Ⓖ
Extremely comfortable micropub on the southern edge of Dover's shopping precinct, owned and managed by former CAMRA Pub of the Year winners. The furnishings – sofa, cosy armchairs, tables and chairs – give the place a homely feel. The bar is a 200-year-old former church pulpit. A constantly changing selection of ales and ciders, priced according to their strength, is dispensed from the temperature-controlled cellar room. No food, but superb nibbles on Sunday. Kent Cider Pub of the Year 2015.

Rack of Ale Ⓛ
7 Park Place, CT16 1DF
12-10.30; 1-10.30 Sun ☎ 07703 059201 rackofale.co.uk
4 changing beers Ⓖ
Opened in October 2013, this was the first of Dover's range of micropubs. A modern one-roomed venue with simple but quirky decor, it encourages conversation, reading a paper or playing pub games while enjoying a pint or two of real ale. The selection includes beers from Kent microbreweries and cider from Kentish Pip. A rack of three one-third pint glasses is available. Live folk music features occasionally. Opening hours can be flexible, depending on how busy it is.
Q

East Malling

King & Queen Ⓛ
1 New Road, ME19 6DD
11 (12 Sat)-11; 12-6.30 Sun ☎ (01732) 842752
kingandqueeneastmalling.co.uk
Harveys Sussex Best Bitter; Musket Fife and Drum; 2 changing beers (sourced nationally; often Black Sheep, Hook Norton, Kent) Ⓗ
A 16th-century beamed inn noted for the quality of its restaurant menu and traditional bar snacks, served all day. At either end of the main bar there are quieter rooms, and the garden is pleasant in summer. Two beers change regularly and supplement the permanent beers. Quiz nights and occasional music or comedy nights take place on Sunday evenings, for which the pub stays open later. Accommodation is available at the rear with three well-appointed rooms.
Q P (58)

Eastry

Five Bells

The Cross, CT13 0HX
⚙ 11-11.30 (1am Fri & Sat) ☎ (01304) 611188
🌐 thefivebellseastry.com
Greene King IPA; 1 changing beer [H]
Traditional community pub in the heart of the village, well served by local buses, with a comfortable lounge bar and a public bar with pool, darts and TV sport. The old fire station, with historic memorabilia, is used as a function room/restaurant. The busy calendar features live music, quiz nights, poker evenings and an Easter beer festival. Home-made food is served all day, with an excellent-value two-course lunchtime menu Monday-Friday. The suntrap patio has a children's play area and pétanque pitch.
❀🛏◐▲♣P🚌(14,87,88)🐾

Eynsford

Five Bells

High Street, DA4 0AB
⚙ 4 (12 Sat)-11; 12-10.30 Sun ☎ (01322) 863135
Courage Best Bitter; Harveys Sussex Best Bitter; Oakham JHB; 1 changing beer (sourced regionally; often Long Man) [H]
Popular pub in the heart of an attractive village. The public bar retains a traditional atmosphere with wooden tables and a wood-burning fire; the dartboard is in the comfortable separate saloon bar. The changing guest beer comes from an independent brewery. Quiz night is the third Thursday of the month. It has a pleasant garden to the rear and a small car park. Food is not served here but try its larger sister pub, the Malt Shovel, nearby. Q❀♣P🚌(421,429)🐾

Faversham

Bear Inn

3 Market Place, ME13 7AG
⚙ 10.30-11; 12-10.30 Sun ☎ (01795) 532668
Shepherd Neame Master Brew; 1 changing beer (sourced nationally; often Shepherd Neame) [H]
A 16th-century pub in Faversham's historic market square, attracting visitors to Faversham and locals alike. The traditional interior has three separate bar areas running the length of the building. It often features the seasonal Shepherd Neame beer, and serves a popular lunchtime menu. A general knowledge quiz is held on the last Monday of the month. A small number of tables out the front are ideal in good weather. Q◐⇌♣🚌🐾

Elephant [L]

31 The Mall, ME13 8JN
⚙ closed Mon; 3 (12 Sat)-11; 12-7 Sun ☎ (01795) 590157
5 changing beers (sourced regionally; often Dark Star, Mighty Oak, Rother Valley) [H]
Award-winning pub close to the railway station, with a well-cared-for Flint & Sons of Canterbury fascia. Beers frequently include rarer styles, such as milds and porters, mainly from microbreweries. Local real cider, usually from Kent Cider Company or Dudda's Tun, is delivered by handpump. The interior benefits from partitioned seating areas in the upper part, and it has a log fire and a large enclosed garden. Regular music nights take place. Children are welcome. A house beer, from Hopdaemon, is often on the bar.
❀⇌♣🍎🚌🐾

Shipwrights Arms [L]

Hollowshore, ME13 7TU (over 1 mile N of Faversham at confluence of Faversham and Oare creeks) TR017636
⚙ 11-3 Mon-Wed; 12-3, 6-10; 11-11 Sat; 12-6 Sun
☎ (01795) 590088 🌐 theshipwrightsathollowshore.co.uk
Goacher's Special/House Ale; 3 changing beers (sourced locally; often Goacher's, Wantsum, Whitstable) [G]
A remote 300-year-old family-run free house with a jolly, welcoming, old-style landlord —a good place to relax after a 45-minute walk across the marshes from Faversham. The interior of the wooden-clad building reflects its nautical heritage, with many ornaments and pictures on display or tucked into nooks and crannies. The large garden at the rear is open spring to autumn, with outside seating at the front in all seasons. It has extended opening hours in summer, but in severe winter weather telephone to check opening times.
Q❀◐♣P🐾

Vaults Cask & Kitchen [L]

75 Preston Street, ME13 8PA
⚙ 11-11 ☎ (01795) 591817 🌐 theoldwinevaults.com
House beer (by Mad Cat); 4 changing beers (sourced nationally; often Caledonian, Cottage, Otter) [H]
A 16th-century town-centre pub with two bars and a large beer garden. The small front bar has traditional pub games such as skittles, bar billiards and darts, the large back bar has an extensive area that can accommodate private parties. An interesting selection of good-quality food is served. Regular events such as quiz and curry nights, live music and beer and cider festivals take place. Up to two ciders, such as Dudda's Tun, are available.
❀◐⇌🍎🚌🐾

Finglesham

Crown Inn [L]

The Street, CT14 0NA
⚙ 12-11; 12-10 Sun ☎ (01304) 612555
🌐 thecrownatfinglesham.co.uk
Dark Star Hophead; 2 changing beers [H]
Traditional village pub with wooden floors and a real fire offering a warm welcome and a friendly atmosphere. Real ales include one from a local microbrewery. Freshly cooked home-made food is served lunchtimes and evenings, all day Friday and Saturday, with a traditional roast on Sunday and barbecues in summer. Eat in the bar or the restaurant, which opens onto the pleasant garden. There is a children's play area, bat and trap, occasional live music, pool and darts to keep the pub busy. Winter opening hours may be slightly shorter. ❀◐▲♣P🐾

Folkestone

Chambers [L]

Radnor Chambers, Cheriton Place, CT20 2BB
⚙ 12-11 (1am Fri & Sat); closed Sun ☎ (01303) 223333
🌐 pubfolkestone.co.uk
Adnams Lighthouse; 4 changing beers [H]
A spacious cellar bar beneath a licensed coffee shop, providing beers from local breweries and at least two real ciders. A beer festival is held over

the Easter weekend. Food includes Mexican, European and daily specials (no food Mon and Fri eves). There is a disco on Fridays and a quiz on the first Sunday of the month. No entry for under-18s unless dining. ◑⇌(Central)●▣

East Cliff Tavern

13-15 East Cliff, CT19 6BU (from harbour, up hill straight past Lifeboat PH and 2nd right; from Dover Rd looking S, turn left at Raglan, first left, down hill, footpath across railway – no trains – pub is in front of you)

5-11; 12-11 Sat & Sun ☎ (01303) 251132

2 changing beers H

Friendly terraced back-street local, near a footpath across the railway line, just a short walk from the harbour. The main bar is to the right and there are usually two beers, often from local breweries, with Biddenden cider on gravity behind the bar. Old photographs of Folkestone decorate the walls and community events include weekly raffles. There is a TV in the saloon bar. Opening hours may vary, check if making a special visit. Q❀▲♣●🐾

Firkin Ale House L

18 Cheriton Place, CT20 2AZ

12-9 (10 Fri & Sat); 12-4 Sun ☎ 07894 068432

firkinalehouse.co.uk

4 changing beers G

Folkestone's first micropub, with up to four cask beers, at least one from a Kent microbrewery. No lager, alcopops or spirits are sold but it does have a limited wine selection. Kentish cheeses and basic bar snacks are served. No music or pub games feature here, only good company and conversation, making it a place to enjoy a drink and relax in good company. Mobile phones are prohibited and their usage incurs a minimum £1 donation to charity. CAMRA branch Pub of the Year 2014. Q⇌(Central)●▣

Fordwich

Fordwich Arms L

King Street, CT2 0DB

11-11 (midnight Fri & Sat); 12-11 Sun ☎ (01227) 710444

fordwicharms.co.uk

Adnams Southwold Bitter; Sharp's Doom Bar; Shepherd Neame Master Brew; 1 changing beer (sourced nationally; often Brains, Draught Bass) H

Classic 1930s building, opposite the tiny town hall in England's smallest town, overlooking the River Stour. The large bar has a lovely open fireplace and there is a separate oak-panelled dining room (no food Sun eves). Themed food evenings, including the popular pudding club, usually take place on the second Wednesday of the month (booking essential). A folk club meets every second and fourth Sunday night, and there is live jazz in the garden once a month on summer Sunday afternoons. Q❀◑♿⇌(Sturry)P▣(4,6,8)🐾ᯤ

Frittenden

Bell & Jorrocks 🏆

Biddenden Road, TN17 2EJ TQ815412

12 (11 Sat)-11; 12-10.30 Sun ☎ (01580) 852415

thebellandjorrocks.co.uk

Harveys Sussex Best Bitter; Woodforde's Wherry; 2 changing beers (sourced nationally; often Dark Star, Rother Valley, Tonbridge) H

Village pub dating from the 18th century, very much the centre of the local community. Good pub grub is offered Wednesday to Sunday, with children's menus, a specials board and excellent Sunday lunches. Among the historical memorabilia is a propeller blade from a German Heinkel bomber shot down just outside the village in 1940. The efficient wood-burning stove helps to create a friendly atmosphere. An annual beer festival is held in old stables at the rear. Local CAMRA branch Pub of the Year for 2015. ☺❀◑▲♣🐾ᯤ

Gillingham

Barge

63 Layfield Road, ME7 2QY

7 (4 Fri)-11; 12-11 Sat & Sun ☎ (01634) 850485

thebargepub.co.uk

2 changing beers (sourced nationally) H

A welcome return to the Guide for this atmospheric pub a short walk from the town centre. It is candlelit-only in the evenings which, combined with the Life Below Decks mural, creates a unique environment. Well renowned locally, music plays a large part at this venue, with a monthly jam night and regular live acts. Its large garden with a decked smoking area offers views of the estuary. A beer from the local Nelson brewery is usually on the bar. ❀♣●

Frog & Toad

38 Burnt Oak Terrace, ME7 1DR

2-11; 12-11 Fri-Sun ☎ (01634) 852231

Fuller's London Pride; 1 changing beer (sourced regionally) H

Typical back-street local among housing, previously three-times winner of the local CAMRA Pub of the Year title, and only 10 minutes' walk from the railway station. The guest beer is usually from Cottage and cider on draught is Magic Bus. A large patio garden area at the rear has bench tables and seats, along with an outside bar. The pub hosts several beer festivals, mostly over bank holidays, throughout the year. Q❀⇌♣●▣🐾

Past & Present L

2 Skinner Street, ME7 1HD

12-11 (7 Mon & Tue; 6 Wed; 9 Thu); 12-4 Sun

3 changing beers (sourced regionally) G

Medway's first micropub and voted joint winner of Cider Pub of the Year 2015 by local CAMRA. A minimum of three real ales is always on, dispensed from a temperature-controlled room. Three third-pint tasters are offered for the same price as a pint. An array of photographs of closed Gillingham pubs (the Past) and Kent micropubs (the Present) are on display. The service here is friendly. A rear decked patio area with awning doubles as a smoking area. No admittance after 10pm on Friday and Saturday evenings. Q☺❀⇌♣●▣🐾

Will Adams

73 Saxton Street, ME7 5EG

12.30-4 (not Mon-Fri), 7-11; 12.30-3, 8-11 Sun

☎ (01634) 575902

3 changing beers (sourced nationally; often Dark Star, Oakham, St Austell) H

A real ale oasis for 20 years, serving two to three guest ales along with cider and perry, including Old Rosie. Pete welcomes both home and away fans on Gillingham FC home games, the pub typically opening early and getting busy. Will Adams was a

mariner born in Gillingham who opened up Japan to the West and became a Samurai, this being the theme of the mural on the pub's walls.
❀◐≠♣●🚌(116,176)🐾📶

Gravesend

Compass Alehouse L
7 Manor Road, DA12 1AA
⌚ closed Mon; 12-2 (not Tue & Wed), 5-9; 12-2, 5-10 Fri; 1-4 Sun ☎ 07873 918545
4 changing beers (sourced locally; often Caveman) G
Micropub opened in autumn 2014 in a former estate agents', seating 18 in a small front room plus standing in an overflow area. Up to four real ales are sold, at least one from a Kentish brewery, with occasional collaborations with Caveman Brewery to produce special beers. Four ciders are available from Kent producers. Convivial conversation is paramount but talking on mobile phones is outlawed, with a fine for charity. Water is always available for our canine friends.
Q🐴❀♿≠●🍺🚌🐾

Rum Puncheon L
87 West Street, DA11 0BL (by Gravesend-Tilbury ferry)
⌚ 11-11; 11-10.30 Sun ☎ (01474) 353434
🌐 rumpuncheon.co.uk
8 changing beers (sourced nationally; often Adnams, Box Steam, Westerham) H
Heritage riverside building near the town pier, with views of the Thames from the rear terrace and garden. The pub has two upstairs function rooms with a bar, and an elegant main bar with chandeliers and a log fire. Real ales rotate frequently and include Kentish beers. Quiz night is the last Wednesday of the month. Home-cooked meals are served every lunchtime, with tapas on Friday and Saturday evenings. No TV or machines, just relaxing background music at times and atmospheric live music occasionally.
Q🐴❀◐◑♿≠♣P🚌🐾

Ship & Lobster L
Mark Lane, Denton, DA12 2QB (E of town; follow Ordnance Rd, Norfolk Rd into Mark Lane)
⌚ 11-11 ☎ (01474) 324571 🌐 shipandlobster.co.uk
3 changing beers (sourced locally; often Goody Ales, Hackney, Hop Stuff) H
Historic building reputed to be the Ship in Dickens' Great Expectations. Situated on the riverfront in an industrial area to the east of town and also on the Saxon Shore Way, it is popular with walkers and anglers. There is a raised outside drinking area on the sea wall with views of the Thames. The pub itself exudes a nautical theme. ❀◐●P🐾

Three Daws
7 Town Pier, DA11 0BJ
⌚ 11-11; 12-11 Sun ☎ (01474) 566869 🌐 threedaws.co.uk
5 changing beers (sourced nationally; often Millis, Truman's) H
Attractive riverside pub next to the town pier with historic smuggling connections. The bar is upstairs in the old landlord's accommodation and divided into a number of small rooms and alcoves, with a bar billiards table and a separate function room. The walls are decorated with photos and drawings of old scenes and maritime themes. Live music is hosted most Fridays. The extensive menu uses listed local ingredients where possible; the beers served are also generally local. 🐴❀◐◑≠♣🚌📶

Windmill Tavern
45 Shrubbery Road, DA12 1JW
⌚ 12-11 (midnight Fri & Sat) ☎ (01474) 352242
Greene King IPA; Sharp's Doom Bar; Shepherd Neame Master Brew; 3 changing beers (sourced locally; often Musket, Tonbridge, Truman's) H
Lovely early 18th-century building in the Windmill Hill area of town, 10 minutes' walk from the station. The excellent choice of bars includes a large lounge, a small cosy room and a lively bar with darts, TV, a log fire and newspapers. A attractive large garden leads onto a small park with a bowls green and public tennis courts. A marquee in the garden is used for functions in summer. Beer festivals are a new feature. Food is available lunchtimes and occasional evenings.
Q🐴❀◐♿♣P🚌(495,496,498)

Groombridge

Crown Inn L
Groombridge Hill, TN3 9QH (on village green)
⌚ 11-11; 12-10.30 Sun ☎ (01892) 864742
🌐 thecrowngroombridge.com
Black Cat Original; Harveys Sussex Best Bitter; Larkins Traditional Ale H
Beautiful free house overlooking the village green and close to Groombridge Place and the Spa Valley Railway. A cosy and welcoming atmosphere prevails in winter, enhanced by a fire in the inglenook. There is a choice of outdoor seating to the rear and on the sunny front terrace. Renowned for food, booking is advisable for Sunday lunches. Walkers on various nearby long-distance trails may benefit from five B&B rooms. An additional ale is often available in summer. Closes 9pm on winter Sundays. Q🐴❀🛏◐◑⛺♣P🚌(291)🐾📶

Hadlow

Two Brewers
Maidstone Road, TN11 0DN (on A26)
⌚ 12-2.30, 5-midnight; 12-midnight Wed & Thu summer; 12-1am Fri & Sat; 12-11.30 Sun ☎ (01732) 850267
🌐 thetwobrewershadlow.co.uk
Harveys Sussex XX Mild Ale, IPA, Sussex Best Bitter; 2 changing beers (sourced regionally; often Harveys, Sharp's) H
The only surviving pub serving real ale in this large, pretty village, in the hands of Harveys Brewery for a decade and a perfect place to enjoy an extensive range of its ales. This well-run roadside pub is very much a community focus for quality beer, food and friendly chat. Archive photographs and beer bottles reflect Hadlow's history including the former maltings, with the IPA still badged as Hadlow Bitter in tribute. Escape the traffic in the secluded rear garden. 🐴❀◐◑♿♣P🚌(7,77)🐾📶

Halstead

Rose & Crown
Otford Lane, TN14 7EA
⌚ 12-11.30 ☎ (01959) 533120
🌐 roseandcrownhalstead.co.uk
Larkins Traditional Ale; house beer (by Elgood); 4 changing beers (sourced nationally; often Hogs Back, Sharp's, Westerham) H
Grade II-listed flint-built pub, close to the North Downs Way, with easy access by bus from

Orpington to the north and Sevenoaks to the south. Choose from the lively public bar, relaxed lounge with log fire, or the annexe housing a tea room and restaurant. It is popular for good-value home-cooked food, especially the Sunday lunch. The rear garden contains a children's play area and covered patio and barbecue, where a beer and jazz festival is held in summer. ⛭❀◐◑♣P🚌(402,R5)🐾📶

Hastingleigh

Bowl Inn 🄻

The Street, TN25 5HU TR095449

⏲ closed Mon; 5-9 Tue & Wed; 5-10 Thu & Fri; 12-10 Sat; 12-9 Sun ☎ (01233) 750354 🌐 thebowlonline.co.uk

3 changing beers 🄷

This lovingly restored listed village building retains many period features including a taproom, used for playing pool, and is free from jukebox and games machines. Quiz night is Tuesday. A beer festival is held on the August bank holiday Monday. Excellent sandwiches and baguettes are available weekends. The lovely garden has a tame European eagle owl. **Q⛭❀◐♣🍎P**

Herne

Butcher's Arms 🄻

29A Herne Street, CT6 7HL (opp church)

⏲ closed Mon; 12-1.30, 6-9; 12-2 Sun ☎ (01227) 371000 🌐 micropub.co.uk

Adnams Broadside; Dark Star Hophead; Old Dairy Copper Top; 2 changing beers (sourced nationally; often Adnams, Ramsgate) 🄶

Britain's first micropub, opened in 2005, is a real ale gem and the inspiration for other micropubs. Once a butcher's shop, it still has the original chopping tables, and has seating for 10 customers and standing room for 20 – the compact drinking area ensuring lively banter. Customers can also buy beer to drink at home. Snack food includes local Ashmore cheeses. The pub has won many CAMRA awards and the landlord was voted one of CAMRA's top 40 campaigners. **Q🚌**(4,6)🐾

Herne Bay

Bouncing Barrel 🄻

20 Bank Street, CT6 5EA

⏲ closed Mon; 12-2, 6-9 (11 Sat); 12-2 Sun ☎ 07777 630685

4 changing beers (sourced nationally; often Goody Ales, Old Dairy, Ramsgate) 🄶

Friendly welcoming micropub with bench seating for 20 customers around old workshop tables. The beer range changes regularly and normally includes up to five beers, mainly from microbreweries, generally at least one from a Kent brewery. Local cheeses and other snacks are also served. The pub is named after the bombs used in the Dambuster raids, which were tested off the coast nearby. The pub has a mural of a bomber flying past the Reculver Towers. **Q⛭♿♣🍎🚌🐾**

Firkin Frog 🄻

157 Station Road, CT6 5QA

⏲ 12-3 (not Mon), 5-9; closed Sun ☎ 07460 895527

4 changing beers 🄶

The bar of this micropub has comfortable seating, and the ceiling is decorated with English county flags. There is a small snug where children are welcome and board games can be played. Up to five beers may be served, with at least one Kentish microbrew alongside local and regional ales. Bar snacks include a fine cheese board, pork pies and Scotch eggs. There is a monthly quiz and a curry night. Charity fundraising includes fining mobile phone users. **Q⛭❀⇌♣🍎🚌**(4,6)🐾

Hernhill

Red Lion

Crockham Lane, ME13 9JR

⏲ 11.30-11; 12-10.30 Sun ☎ (01227) 751207

🌐 theredlion.org

Shepherd Neame Master Brew; 3 changing beers (sourced nationally; often Adnams, Sharp's, Westerham) 🄷

A picturesque 14th-century pub near Mount Ephraim Gardens and close to Faversham. The traditional interior has great character. Benches at the front overlook the village green and the large rear beer garden has a children's play area. A range of traditional meals is available, including seasonal specials. The area around Hernhill has a rich history, including an association with the Rebel Army of Sir William Courtney. ⛭❀◐◑P🐾📶

High Halden

Chequers on the Green 🄻

Ashford Road, TN26 3LP (on A28 between Ashford and Tenterden)

⏲ 11-11; 12-10.30 Sun ☎ (01233) 850503

🌐 chequersonthegreen.com

Harveys Sussex Best Bitter; Old Dairy Red Top 🄷

The pub is known to have been used by smugglers such as the Hawkhurst, Cranbrook and Aldington gangs who were active in the 18th century. The name originates from the fact that the villagers paid their taxes in the pub. Fully refurbished in 2013 and converted into a restaurant serving good-quality food all day, it retains a separate drinking area and patio. **Q⛭❀◐◑♿🍎P🚌**(2)🐾

Higham

Gardeners Arms 🄻

2 Forge Lane, ME3 7AS

⏲ 11-11; 12-11 Sun ☎ (01474) 823901

🌐 gardenersarmshigham.com

Shepherd Neame Master Brew, Kent's Best, Spitfire, Bishops Finger; 1 changing beer 🄷

Quiet pub in Upper Higham with a clock that goes backwards. It has two bars, one with a restaurant, the other with a large TV for showing major sporting fixtures. A full range of Shepherd Neame ales is available. The food in the restaurant is sourced locally and represents good value. The garden is secluded, with a raised patio which backs onto a small car park. **Q❀🛏◐◑♿♣P🚌**(136)🐾📶

Hildenborough

Plough 🄻

Leigh Road, TN11 9AJ (½ mile S of Hildenborough at Powdermills)

⏲ closed Mon; 12-3, 6-11; 12-5 Sun ☎ (01732) 832149

🌐 theploughatleigh.com

Tonbridge Copper Nob; 2 changing beers (sourced locally; often Old Dairy, Rockin' Robin, Westerham) Ⓗ
Idyllic 16th-century inn which ticks all the boxes – low-beamed ceilings festooned with hops, a huge open-sided fire, good food and local ales. In addition there is a large, pretty streamside garden with a children's play area. In warmer months the pub stays open all day. The landlord is keen to support Kentish beers, occasionally with a cask on the bar. Real cider may also be on tap. The magnificent adjacent Great Barn can be booked for wedding receptions and parties.
Q ❀ ◐ ♣ P (210)

Horton Kirby

Bull

Lombard Street, DA4 9DF
12-11; 12-10.30 Sun ☎ (01322) 869253
Dark Star Hophead; Goody Ales Genesis; Oakham Citra; 3 changing beers (sourced regionally; often Kent, Rudgate) Ⓗ
Friendly one-bar local with a large garden affording views across the Darent Valley, 15 minutes' walk by public footpath across fields from Farningham Road railway station. The landlord is a member of the Oakham Oakademy cellarmanship award scheme. Food is served at lunchtimes, except Monday. Cribbage is played on Tuesday evenings, darts on Wednesdays and poker on Thursdays.
❀ ◐ ♣ (414)

Hythe

Potting Shed 𝕃

160A High Street, CT21 5JR
closed Mon; 12-6 Tue (7 Wed & Thu; 9 Fri & Sat); 12-4 Sun ☎ 07780 877226
4 changing beers (sourced nationally; often Hop Fuzz) Ⓖ
A former café that has been converted into an micro-alehouse retaining the original high service counter. At the Folkestone end of Hythe High Street, it serves an interesting range of ales from around the country including at least one local Kentish beer. Ciders are also on gravity, and one ale is through a handpump. Limited bar snacks are available. A good place to enjoy a drink and interesting conversation. ❀

Three Mariners 𝕃

37 Windmill Street, CT21 6BH
4-10 Mon; 12-11 (midnight Fri & Sat); 12-10.30 Sun ☎ (01303) 260406
Young's Bitter; 4 changing beers Ⓗ
Hidden away in a side street, not far from the Royal Military Canal, this refurbished traditional pub is well worth visiting. Friendly staff and local customers are always happy to have a chat with you. No food is served – customers come for the quality and selection of real ales on offer, which may be enjoyed in the bar or in an outside area that is partly heated and popular with smokers.
❀ ♣

Iden Green

Peacock

Goudhurst Road, TN17 2PB (1½ miles E of Goudhurst at A262/B2085 jct)
12-11 ☎ (01580) 211233 peacockgoudhurst.co.uk
Shepherd Neame Master Brew, Kent's Best, Bishops Finger; 1 changing beer (sourced regionally; often Shepherd Neame) Ⓗ
Situated in the Weald of Kent, this Shepherd Neame pub serves its ales superbly. Dating back to 1397, it is steeped in character. The tenants offer fantastic locally sourced food, with fish and chips a particular favourite. Close to Sissinghurst and Bodiam castles, it is an ideal stop-off. Morris men have met here for many years and are regulars on the events calendar. A refreshingly traditional country pub. Q ❀ ◐ ♿ P (297)

Ightham Common

Old House ★

Redwell Lane, Redwell, TN15 9EE (½ mile SW of Ightham village, between A25 and A227) TQ590558
7-11 (9 Mon & Tue); 12-3, 7-11 Sat & Sun
☎ (01732) 886077
6 changing beers (sourced regionally; often Fyne Ales, Long Man) Ⓖ
Kentish red-brick, tile-hung cottage, with no pub sign, located in a narrow, isolated country lane. The public bar features a wood-panelled counter, parquet flooring and an imposing inglenook fireplace. The parlour bar is a quiet haven. Up to six rotating beers are dispensed from a chilled tap room, always including at least one bitter, a golden ale and a dark beer, from a vast range of regional breweries, and real cider is available. CAMRA-designated Nationally Important Historic Interior.
Q ❀ Å ♣ P

Ivychurch

Bell Inn

Ashford Road, TN29 0AL (signed from A2070 between Brenzett and Hamstreet) TR028275
12-11; 12-10.30 Sun ☎ (01797) 344355
thebellinnromneymarsh.co.uk
St Austell Trelawny; Sharp's Doom Bar; 4 changing beers Ⓗ
Like many Marsh pubs, where a warm welcome awaits, this is adjacent to the church. It is popular for its excellent ales and ciders as well as the selection of food. The licensees have achieved an enviable reputation for the establishment, frequently gaining the honour of the CAMRA branch Pub of the Year, most recently in 2013. Well worth finding, it was once the centre of the Romney Marsh Owlers (smugglers).
❀ ◐ ♿ ♣ P

Kingsdown

King's Head

Upper Street, CT14 8BJ
5-11; 12-3, 6-11 Sat; 12-10.30 Sun ☎ (01304) 373915
kingsheadkingsdown.co.uk
Greene King IPA; 2 changing beers Ⓗ
Traditional 18th-century village pub, a short walk uphill from the sea, with three beamed bars around a central counter. The back bar opens onto a dining area and spacious family room. A quiet rear courtyard includes a skittle alley and covered smoking area. Local historic photographs adorn the wall and the frosted glass front door advertises the long-closed local brewery, Thompsons of Walmer.

Lunch is served at the weekend, with a roast on Sunday. A popular quiz night takes place on Tuesday. (82)

Laddingford

Chequers

The Street, ME18 6BP TQ689481
12-3, 5-11; 12-11 Sat & Sun (01622) 871266
chequersladdingford.co.uk
Adnams Southwold Bitter; 3 changing beers (sourced nationally; often Otter, Young's) H
Attractive, community-spirited, oak-beamed pub, dating from the 15th century, with one double letting room. A warm welcome is assured in the simply furnished bar and split-level dining area. Food theme nights include Sausage Thursdays and Pie Days on the first Tuesdays and Wednesdays of the month. A beer festival is held in late April. It has a large rear garden with children's play equipment. Buses stop outside and Beltring Halt railway station is a 20-minute walk.
QP(23,26)

Lower Halstow

Three Tuns

The Street, ME9 7DY
12-11 (midnight Fri & Sat); 12-10.30 Sun
(01795) 842840 thethreetunsrestaurant.co.uk
Goacher's Real Mild Ale; Millis Kentish Best; 2 changing beers (sourced locally; often Caveman, Hop Fuzz, Wantsum) H
True family village pub with a friendly, cheerful atmosphere and lively conversation. The owners actively support real ale, offering mainly Kentish ales and several local ciders, including Dudda's Tun. It has a good reputation for food, winning many awards. Two beer festivals are held each year during the summer bank holiday and in December. A log fire, sofa seating, brick walls and beams add character. It has a large garden with streamside decking. P(327)

Luddesdown

Cock Inn

Henley Street, DA13 0XB (1 mile SE of Sole St station) TQ664672
12-11; 12-10.30 Sun (01474) 814208
cockluddesdowne.com
Adnams Lighthouse, Southwold Bitter, Broadside; Goacher's Real Mild Ale; Musket Trigger, Cock & Stock; St Austell Trelawny; 2 changing beers (sourced regionally; often Truman's) H
Traditional rural free house dating from 1713 and under the same ownership since 1984, with cosy rooms, log fires and a conservatory. It stocks an extensive range of real ales and quality German beers. It has a peaceful, child-free atmosphere, dedicated to conversation, traditional games and relaxation, surrounded by fascinating curios, memorabilia and photographs on walls and in cabinets. A function room hosts many clubs and societies. The pleasant garden has a heated smoking area. Local CAMRA branch Pub of the Year 2015. QP

Lynsted

Black Lion

The Street, ME9 0RJ
11-3, 6-11; 12-3, 7-10.30 Sun (01795) 521229
Goacher's Real Mild Ale, Fine Light Ale, Best Dark Ale; 1 changing beer (sourced locally; often Goacher's) H
Welcoming village local frequented by discerning drinkers and popular with walkers. Although a free house, it offers four Goacher's beers, including rarely seen occasionals such as Old Ale and Imperial Stout. The characterful and jovial landlord holds court with a cluster of regulars and always has a story to tell. The pub has a large garden, bar billiards and is full of pub memorabilia. Home-made meals are served. QP(345)

Maidstone

Flower Pot

96 Sandling Road, ME14 2RJ
12 (11 Sat)-11; 12-10.30 Sun (01622) 757705
flowerpotpub.com
Goacher's Gold Star Strong Ale; 8 changing beers (sourced nationally; often Dark Star, Maidstone, Oakham) H
Split-level street-corner free house, a must-visit when in Maidstone. The upper bar has nine handpumps with the ales mainly coming from microbreweries. Up to four ciders are served directly from the cask. The lower bar has a pool table and there are screens showing the beers on offer, along with the price. Maidstone United football ground is nearby. Music nights are every other Saturday and a jam night on Tuesday, while beer festivals take place twice yearly.
(East)(101,155)

Olde Thirsty Pig

4a Knightrider Street, ME15 6LP
12 (4 Mon)-1am; 12-2am Fri; 12-3am Sat
(01622) 299283 yeoldethirstypig.com
4 changing beers (sourced locally; often Mad Cat, Musket, Rockin' Robin) H
A 15th-century street-corner local that is Grade II-listed, with original beams throughout. Beware of low ceilings and doorways, especially upstairs where the floor slopes. Four handpumps dispense ales, mainly from Kent microbreweries, and there is an array of bottled beers including several foreign ones. Another room has more comfortable chairs while directly above that is a meeting room. Outside is a heated and covered courtyard area. A free jukebox is provided.

Pilot

25 Upper Stone Street, ME15 6EU (on A229 southbound to Hastings)
6-11 (midnight Sat); 12.30-11 Sun (01622) 691162
Harveys Sussex XX Mild Ale, Sussex Best Bitter, Armada Ale; 3 changing beers (often Harveys) H
Maidstone's country pub in the town, this is a welcoming 16th-century, Grade II-listed inn with a beamed interior and inglenook fireplaces. Bands play Saturday evenings and Sunday afternoons, with a quiz in the evening. Jam nights are held monthly on a Wednesday and alternate between acoustic and electric. Darts is played and at the rear there is a pétanque piste and two covered smoking areas. Westons Old Rosie cider is sold.

Society Rooms

Brenchley House, Week Street, ME14 1RF

🕐 7am-midnight (1am Fri & Sat) ☎ (01622) 350910

Adnams Broadside; Greene King Abbot; Ruddles Best Bitter; 7 changing beers (sourced nationally; often Wantsum, Westerham) Ⓗ

A spacious Wetherspoon pub situated in a former newspaper printing works, on the ground floor of a five-storey office block. The mainly glass external walls allow panoramic views of the pedestrian shopping street alongside. The large covered outside space is split into smoking and no-smoking areas. The name refers to William Shipley, founder of the Royal Society of Arts and the Maidstone Society for Promoting Useful Knowledge, who is buried nearby. Food is served 7am-11pm. Q🐴❀◑◐♿⇌(East)♣🍎🚌(101,155)📶

Marden

Marden Village Club Ⓛ

Albion Road, TN12 9DT

🕐 12-3 (not Mon-Fri), 6-11; 12-3, 7-10.30 Sun

☎ (01622) 831427 🌐 mardenvillageclub.co.uk

Shepherd Neame Master Brew; 3 changing beers (sourced nationally; often Kent, Ramsgate, Rockin' Robin) Ⓗ

Four real ales are offered at this local CAMRA award-winning club; three change regularly and are generally from local microbreweries. The club is the community hub, with live entertainment on Saturday evenings. Many members live locally and follow the football and rugby shown on Sky TV, and are involved in the club's snooker and darts teams; others simply enjoy the friendly ambience. CAMRA members are welcome but regular visitors will be required to join. 🐴♿⇌♣🍎🚌(26,27)📶

Stile Bridge Ⓛ

Staplehurst Road, TN12 9BH (on A229 just before jct with B2079)

🕐 11-11; 11-8 Sun ☎ (01622) 831236

🌐 thestilebridge.co.uk

Goacher's House Ale; 4 changing beers (sourced nationally; often Musket, Pig & Porter) Ⓗ

A warm welcome awaits at this roadside hostelry. Pub and drinking memorabilia abound, and the interior provides a good mixture of drinking and dining areas. A large enclosed garden/patio at the rear is useful in summer. Ales from microbreweries are on offer, as well as a good selection of continental and US beers and lagers. The food menu is popular. Live music and comedy feature several times each year. CAMRA branch Pub of the Year 2014. ❀◑◐P🚌(5)

Margate

Ales of the Unexpected

105 Canterbury Road, CT9 5AX

🕐 12-3, 5-10; 12-3.30 Sun ☎ 07958 647753

3 changing beers Ⓖ

A micropub located in a former fishmonger's, in a row of shops in the Westbrook district of town. The front seating area has various tables and chairs and is decorated with maps of the UK and the world. The serving counter is in a rear room, decorated with pumpclips of the various ales served since the pub opened in 2013, beyond which is a separate temperature-controlled cold room where the beers are kept. Q⇌🍎🚌🐾

Markbeech

Kentish Horse

Cow Lane, TN8 5NT

🕐 12-11; 12-10.30 Sun ☎ (01342) 850493

🌐 kentishhorsemarkbeech.co.uk

Harveys Sussex Best Bitter; Larkins Traditional Ale; 1 changing beer (sourced locally; often Larkins) Ⓗ

The pub and adjacent church form the heart of this rural village. Located high on the Weald, the spacious garden, which incorporates a large children's play area, affords fine views towards the Ashdown Forest. Despite its apparent isolation, Cowden railway station is only 20 minutes' walk away, and a limited bus service connects the village with Edenbridge and Tunbridge Wells. Home-cooked food is served (no food Mon and Sun eves) and larger parties can be catered for in the dining room. 🐴❀◑◐P🚌(234)🐾

Milton Regis

Three Hats

93 High Street, ME10 2AR

🕐 12-11; 12-10.30 Sun ☎ (01795) 427645

4 changing beers (sourced nationally; often Banks's, Dartmoor, St Austell) Ⓗ

Popular and friendly local in historic Milton Regis. The open-plan interior has low beams and a large lounge bar area. The landlord serves a selection of national beers from the Enterprise range, including ales rarely available in this part of Kent from breweries such as Windsor & Eton. Beer festivals are held occasionally. The pub hosts a number of darts teams and stages regular charity events. CAMRA branch Pub of the Year 2013 and 2014. 🐴❀◑🚌(347)🐾📶

Minster-in-Thanet

Minster & Monkton Royal British Legion Club

Clements House, 61 Augustine Road, CT12 4DH

🕐 11-11 (midnight Fri & Sat); 12-11 Sun ☎ (01843) 821471

Courage Best Bitter; 2 changing beers Ⓗ

Friendly and spacious British Legion club comprising a main bar, side room and separate bar with plenty of naval memorabilia for all to enjoy. Darts and pool can be played, with bingo, quizzes and other social events regularly planned. Guest beers are often from the local Ramsgate Brewery. The beer sells quickly. Entry is permitted on production of a CAMRA membership card, the current Guide or the phone app. 🐴❀◑♿🚌(11,38A,42)📶

Newenden

White Hart

Rye Road, TN18 5PN (on A268) TQ834273

🕐 11-11; 12-11 Sun ☎ (01797) 252166

🌐 thewhitehartnewenden.co.uk

Harveys Sussex Best Bitter; Rother Valley Level Best; changing beers Ⓗ

This historic 16th-century weatherboarded building includes old oak-beamed bars and an inglenook fireplace. The pub provides good-quality home-cooked food and has six en suite rooms. Conveniently situated for the Kent & East Sussex

Railway and several National Trust properties, it is in an ideal location for exploring the Rother Valley.
P

Northfleet

Campbell Arms
1 Campbell Road, DA11 0JZ
12-11 (1am Fri & Sat); 12-10.30 Sun
3 changing beers
Edwardian corner local, near the shops at Perry Street, within walking distance of Gravesend town centre and railway station. The real ales are normally from small breweries, but few are under 4.5% ABV. Real cider is always available. There is a ladies' darts team and dominoes is also played. Summer barbecues and occasional live music features. An interesting collection of old photographs above the bar are nearly all of the surrounding area. (Gravesend)

Olde Coach & Horses Inn
25 The Hill, DA11 9EU
12-11; 12-10.30 Sun (01474) 395088
yeoldecoachandhorses.com
3 changing beers (sourced regionally; often Moorhouse's, Robinsons, Timothy Taylor)
An attractive former coaching inn, dating back to 1665, only 10 minutes' walk from Northfleet station. Expect a warm welcome in this small one-bar pub, with no gaming machines, TVs or jukebox. In winter the open fire adds to the cosy ambience. The kitchen has been updated, and good home-cooked food is served all day and early evening (booking is recommended for Sunday lunch). Westons cider is always available. Q

Offham

King's Arms
Teston Road, ME19 5NR
12-midnight (01732) 845208
kingsarmsoffham.co.uk
6 changing beers (sourced nationally; often Kent, Musket, Tonbridge)
Originally two 16th-century farm cottages, but now two drinking areas and a restaurant. A former sports bar has been refurbished to make a drinking space with a variety of games. It enjoys a warm atmosphere, with ales from Kent microbreweries such as Ramsgate among many others. The pub holds beer festivals periodically and has live music monthly. Home-made pies are a speciality and it serves up Thai food on Friday and Saturday evenings, plus roasts every Sunday.
Q P (70)

Petham

Chequers
Stone Street, CT4 5PW
12-3 (not Mon), 6-11; 12-4, 7-10.30 Sun
(01227) 700734
Dark Star Hophead; Oakham Citra; 3 changing beers (sourced nationally; often Dark Star, Old Dairy, Sharp's)
On the Roman road from Canterbury to Hythe, the Chequers was built in 1898. The bar area has comfortable leather sofas. A spacious dining area and restaurant is at the back, with a tempting menu including a popular carvery on Sunday lunchtime and Wednesday evening. Darts and bar billiards are played. Up to six beers are served at busy times. A green hop festival is planned for October. P (620,18)

Petteridge

Hopbine
Petteridge Lane, TN12 7NE (1 mile W of Brenchley)
12-2.30, 5-11; 12-11 Fri-Sun (01892) 722561
Long Man Best Bitter; Tonbridge Traditional Ale; 1 changing beer (sourced locally; often Tonbridge)
Attractive and friendly weatherboarded building perched on a hilly corner in a quiet hamlet, though accessible by a nearby bus route. The central log fire adds to the homely atmosphere within. The home-prepared food menu features pizzas prominently (no food Mon or Tue lunchtime). Formerly a Hall & Woodhouse pub, it is now in private ownership. The cider is from Orchard Pig. Additional seating is available in the newly constructed rear terraced garden.
P (296,297)

Rainham

Three Sisters
Otterham Quay Lane, ME8 8QR (jct B2009, Lower Rainham Road and Otterham Quay Lane)
1-midnight (2am Fri); 12-2am Sat; 12-midnight Sun
(01634) 231991 threesistersrainham.com
Goacher's Gold Star Strong Ale; house beer (by Mad Cat); 2 changing beers (sourced nationally)
Welcoming country pub, on the eastern edge of the Medway towns, only a short distance from the Saxon Shore Way. Sandwiches are made to order and Pukka Pies are normally available at all sessions. There is a pool table and dartboard in a side bar. Occasional live music features, usually on a Friday evening. Beer festivals are held during the year in a separate function room. Ales are discounted on Mondays 1-7.30pm.
P (327)

Ramsgate

Artillery Arms
36 Westcliff Road, CT11 9JS
12-11; 12-midnight Fri-Sun (01843) 853202
Changing beers
Celebrated and popular alehouse a short walk from the town which attracts a diverse clientèle. The lower bar area has stairs leading to an upper area with more seating. The landlord maintains a long tradition of stocking a carefully considered range of real ales. Doom Bar is the house bitter, but other handpumps serve a selection of beers from Kent and beyond. Interesting old painted windows depict battle scenes and the theme is continued with displays of other militaria.

Conqueror Alehouse
4c Grange Road, CT11 9LR
closed Mon; 11.30-2.30, 5.30-9.30; 12-3 Sun 07890 203282 conqueror-alehouse.co.uk
3 changing beers
Welcoming micropub with room for about 20 customers, offering a cosy and pleasant music- and TV-free environment. Opened in a former retail

outlet, it has three changing real ales, served straight from the cask, as well as a local cider and perry. It is named after a two-funnelled paddle steamer which operated excursions from the town in the early 1900s, pictures of which adorn the walls. A finalist CAMRA National Pub of the Year in 2013. Q⛺♣🍎🚌(Loop,34,9)🐾

Hovelling Boat

12 York Street, CT11 9DS

⏲ 11.30-9.30 (11 Fri & Sat); 12-4 Sun ☎ 07974 613030

🌐 hovellingboatinn.co.uk

4 changing beers G

Sympathetic shop conversion micropub, opened Easter 2013, which was to have had another name until the landlord discovered it had originally been the Hovelling Boat pub that ceased trading in 1909. It has a handy town-centre location, with exposed brickwork displaying breweriana. Four changing beers from Kent and beyond are served at customers' tables by friendly staff. It has proved to be a welcome addition to the burgeoning real ale scene in Ramsgate. Cold snacks, tea and coffee are also available. Q🐴❀🍎🚌🐾

Rose of England

97 High Street, CT11 9RH

⏲ 12 (11 Fri & Sat)-11; 11.30-10.30 Sun ☎ (01843) 586273

2 changing beers (often Ramsgate) H

Friendly free house, on the edge of the town centre, family-run for over 20 years. Standing slightly back from the road, the pub dates back to 1779 when it was known as the Rose and Crown, receiving its present name in 1957. As well as the main bar it has a snug and pool room. The walls boast plenty of old pictures, curios and memorabilia including a number of vintage arcade machines. Q🐴❀♣🐾

Ripple

Plough Inn L

Church Lane, CT14 8JH TR348498

⏲ 12-11 ☎ (01304) 360209 🌐 theploughripple.co.uk

Fuller's ESB; 3 changing beers H

Welcoming and unpretentious village local surrounded by rolling countryside. With an open fire in winter and comfortable seating, the pub is popular with walkers and families alike. It is Cask Marque-accredited. Beers from the nearby Ripple Steam Brewery and Fuller's feature alongside two rotating guests. There is a quiz night on the second Wednesday of the month, vintage/classic car events with a barbecue on the last Sunday, and locally caught fresh fish and chips on Fridays. Dogs on leads welcome. ❀🛏◐◑⛺♣P🐾📶

Rochester

Britannia Bar Café L

376 High Street, ME1 1DJ (½ mile E of railway station)

⏲ 10-11 (9 Mon); 12-9 Sun ☎ (01634) 815204

🌐 britannia-bar-cafe.co.uk

Goacher's Fine Light Ale; 2 changing beers (sourced nationally) H

Situated between Rochester and Chatham railway stations, customers will find excellent service in this combination of a traditional English public house and a continental café bar. Breakfast and an extensive lunchtime menu are served, with a traditional roast offered on Sundays, and fish and chips on Thursday evenings. The stylish bar leads to a small walled garden at the rear, full of flowers in bloom in the summer months. No jukebox or fruit machines. Q❀◐◑⇌(Chatham)🚌

Coopers Arms

10 St Margaret Street, ME1 1TL

⏲ 12-11 (midnight Fri & Sat) ☎ (01634) 404298

🌐 thecoopersarms.co.uk

Courage Best Bitter; Young's Special; 5 changing beers (sourced regionally) H

A one-minute walk past Rochester castle and cathedral brings you to a building dating from 1199, which has been used as an inn since 1543. Despite many changes over the years the inn retains its original charm and character. There is a legend of a ghost who appears once a year during November. Sunday roasts are on the menu here. The well-kept garden area is popular on sunny days. ❀◐⇌🚌

Good Intent

3 John Street, ME1 1YL

⏲ 12-midnight ☎ (01634) 843118

3 changing beers (sourced regionally) G

Back-street pub which has a gravity-fed system dispensing up to three beers. The casks are clearly visible in the public bar, which has a pool table and a large-screen TV for major sporting fixtures. The back bar is accessed via a garden gate and has a much quieter atmosphere. A monthly quiz is held, as well as live music events. There are regular beer festivals. Q❀⇌♣🍎P🚌

Man of Kent L

6-8 John Street, ME1 1YN (200yds off A2 from bottom of Star Hill)

⏲ 3-11; 12-midnight Fri; 12.30-midnight Sat ☎ 07772 214315

Goacher's Fine Light Ale, Gold Star Strong Ale; 9 changing beers (sourced locally) H

The real ales come from Kent microbreweries only. An extensive range of Kent ciders and wines is also stocked, while a number of Belgian and German beers are available both on draught and in bottles. Live music features on Wednesdays and Thursdays, a jam night on Sunday and a ukulele jam night on the first Tuesday. A quiz night is held on the third Tuesday. An enclosed garden allows for a quieter drinking area. ❀⇌🍎🍺🚌📶

Who'd Ha' Thought It

9 Baker Street, ME1 3DN

⏲ 12-11.30 (midnight Fri & Sat) ☎ (01634) 830144

🌐 whodha.co.uk

3 changing beers (sourced nationally) H

Back-street local, off Rochester's Maidstone Road. A friendly free house, it has a wood-panelled bar, log fire, two TVs with satellite sport and a separate snug bar. A range of events is held, including live music and a monthly charity quiz evening. The family- and dog-friendly garden holds barbecues and beer festivals. The bar snacks include rolls and pizzas. 🐴❀♣🚌(134,155)🐾📶

Ryarsh

Duke of Wellington L

The Street, ME19 5LS

⏲ 11-11; 12-10.30 Sun ☎ (01732) 842318

🌐 dukeofwellingtonryarsh.com

Harveys Sussex Best Bitter; Westerham Grasshopper Kentish Bitter; 2 changing beers (sourced nationally; often Caledonian, Kent) Ⓗ
A 16th-century pub in the village centre, welcoming to ramblers. When entering, the main bar is to the left and the restaurant is to the right, featuring a varied menu plus Sunday roasts. Fireplaces in both bars provide winter warmth. A large covered and heated patio opens onto the garden and pétanque piste. At the front, an enclosed area with tables provides a safe area for children. A popular music evening is held monthly on a Thursday. Q ➠ ✿⓪ ♣ P ☐ (58) ✿ ☎

Sandgate

Earl of Clarendon
Brewers Hill, CT20 3DH (25yds up footpath off A259 from seafront between Seabrook and Sandgate)
✪ 12-11 (midnight Fri & Sat) ☎ (01303) 248684
4 changing beers (sourced nationally) Ⓗ
This ex-Mackeson and Shepherd Neame pub became a free house in 2009. It was originally built as a hotel and provided refreshment to troops, as it is on a path between Shorncliff Camp and the sea. Beers from all over Great Britain feature on the bar. Live music takes place monthly during the summer. Tasty pub grub is served every day, and there is bar billiards and sport on two screens. ➠ ⓪ ♣ ☐ ✿

Ship Inn Ⓛ
65 Sandgate High Street, CT20 3AH (on A259)
✪ 11-11.30 (12.30am Fri & Sat) ☎ (01303) 248525
Dark Star Hophead; Greene King IPA, Abbot; Hop Back Summer Lightning; Hopdaemon Incubus; Long Man Brewery Old Man Ⓗ; 2 changing beers Ⓖ
Narrow pub on a corner facing onto the High Street, partly dating from 1798, with a front bar and a back room, plus a restaurant with sea views and an upstairs top deck for drinkers, both added in 2010. Nautical maps and pictures featured on the walls reflect the landlord's naval and military interests. Biddenden and guest ciders are always available and an August bank holiday beer festival is held. 🛏⓪ ✿ ☐

Sandwich

Crispin Inn Ⓛ
4 High Street, CT13 9EA
✪ 11-11; 12-10.30 Sun ☎ (01304) 621967
⊕ sandwichpubs.co.uk
Adnams Broadside; Sharp's Doom Bar; house beer (by Mad Cat); 2 changing beers Ⓗ
Ancient low-beamed house alongside the medieval Barbican, by the old toll bridge. Its low ceilings and wooden beams foster a nice easy-going ambience. Relax in the comfortable lounge or the back courtyard overlooking the river – not to be missed on a summer's day. Real cider is from Westons or Thatchers. A good range of home-cooked food and bar snacks is usually available. Regular live music events are held.
➠ ✿⓪ ▲ ♣ ✿ ☐ ✿ ☎

Red Cow Ⓛ
12 Moat Sole, CT13 9AU
✪ 11-midnight (11 winter) ☎ (01304) 613399
6 changing beers Ⓗ
Historically, this pub was a watering hole for cattle market traders in years gone by, hence the red cow

on the front. Tiled floors and exposed beams give it a comfortable and traditional country pub ambience. Up to six ales are on tap, one usually from the Foundry Brewery. The cider is from Broomfield. Everyone is catered for, with areas for drinkers, diners and bar billiards players, and a pleasant suntrap garden. It can be lively, but also a haven for chess players at quieter times.
➠ ✿⓪ ▲ ⤚ ♣ ✿ P ☐ ✿ ☎

Sevenoaks

Anchor
32 London Road, TN13 1AS
✪ 11-3, 6-11; 10.30-11 Fri; 10.30-4.30, 7-11 Sat; 12-11 Sun
☎ (01732) 454898 ⊕ anchorsevenoaks.co.uk
Harveys Sussex Best Bitter; Sharp's Doom Bar; 1 changing beer (sourced nationally) Ⓗ
Town centre community pub that is always buzzing with conversation often instigated by cheerful Barry, a landlord of over 30 years standing. High-quality real ales and good keenly priced traditional pub food (no food Sun) are enjoyed by loyal local customers, shoppers and patrons of the nearby Stag theatre and cinema. Guest beers may include a dark ale. Other draws include quiz and poker evenings and live blues and open mic events most Wednesday nights. ⓪ ♣ ☐ ✿

White Hart Ⓛ
Tonbridge Road, TN13 1SG (1 mile S of town centre)
✪ 11.30-11; 12-10.30 Sun ☎ (01732) 452022
⊕ whitehart-sevenoaks.co.uk
Harveys Sussex Best Bitter; Old Dairy Blue Top; house beer (by Phoenix); 3 changing beers (sourced nationally; often Timothy Taylor, Westerham, Whitstable) Ⓗ
Sprawling but cosy coaching inn with four fireplaces, many alcoves and subdued lighting, exposed brickwork, beams, wooden flooring and a bright conservatory at the rear, adjacent to an attractive landscaped garden. Although popular for artisan food, drinkers are welcome, with beer tasting notes displayed on a chalkboard opposite the bar and third-pint samplers available. Real cider is from alternating Kent cideries. Look out for food, beer and cider festivals organised through the year. Q ➠ ✿⓪ ♿ ♣ ✿ P ☐ (401,402) ✿ ☎

Sevenoaks Weald

Windmill ♥ Ⓛ
1 Windmill Road, TN14 6PN
✪ 12 (5 Mon)-11 ☎ (01732) 463330
Larkins Traditional Ale; 5 changing beers (sourced nationally; often Goacher's, Salopian, Sambrook's) Ⓗ
Passionate attention to customer service and the all-inclusive atmosphere in this reborn village pub led to its inclusion in the final four of the CAMRA National Pub of the Year 2015 contest, and it was local branch Pub of the Year again for 2015. Beers are a range of styles and strengths, and the ciders are from Biddenden, Chiddingstone and Double Vision, all available in third-pint taster bats. The choice of top-quality food is imaginative and consequently booking is advisable. The tasteful interior leads through to a pleasant patio garden.
Q ➠ ✿⓪ ▲ ♣ ✿ ☐ ☐ (401,402) ✿ ☎

Shadoxhurst

King's Head 𝕃
Woodchurch Road, TN26 1LQ
⌚ closed Mon; 11.30-3, 6-11; 11.30-4, 6-11 Sun
☎ (01233) 732243
Shepherd Neame Master Brew, Spitfire; 3 changing beers (sourced nationally; often Shepherd Neame) Ⓗ
Shadoxhurst dates from the 13th century and has a parish church with lancet windows. The many footpaths and woods around the area offer plenty of interesting walks. The building dates back in part to 1580 and retains some fine architectural features, notably the old porch with the family crest of the original owners. A spacious typical country pub with historic charm, it caters for both the local community and visitors.
♨❀◑◗♿▲♣P🚌(2A)🐾

Sittingbourne

Paper Mill 🏆 𝕃
2 Charlotte Street, ME10 2JN (N of railway station, at corner of Church St and Charlotte St)
⌚ 12-2 (not Mon-Thu), 5-9; 12-9 Sat; 12-6 Sun ☎ 07927 073584 🌐 thepapermillmicropub.co.uk
Goacher's Real Mild Ale; 2 changing beers (sourced locally; often Goacher's, Kent, Wantsum) Ⓖ
The first micropub to open in Swale, close to Sittingbourne town centre and railway station. The Paper Mill has one room with bench seating around four large wooden tables. Local beers feature alongside national ones such as Blue Monkey and Redwillow and there is a range of Dudda's Tun ciders available. Occasional events such as food tasting and pub quizzes take place. Opening hours are flexible with advance notice. Local CAMRA branch Pub of the Year for 2015.
Q♨⇌♣●▯🚌(334,347)🐾

Summoner
Units 1-3, Bell Shopping Centre, High Street, ME10 4AY
⌚ 8am-midnight; 8am-1am Fri ☎ (01795) 410158
Greene King Abbot; Ruddles Best Bitter; 3 changing beers (sourced nationally; often Cotleigh, Wantsum, Whitstable) Ⓗ
Town-centre Wetherspoon, popular with a wide variety of customers. The pub has a large open-plan area, with more private booths on a raised platform. The Summoner is a character in Chaucer's Canterbury Tales, who promises to 'telle tales of friars, ere I come to Sittingbourne'. In medieval times, the town was on the pilgrim's route to Canterbury. The range of guest beers often includes local ales with an occasional cask cider.
Q♨◑◗⇌●🚌📶

Snargate

Red Lion 🏆 ★ 𝕃
TN29 9UQ (on B2080, 1 mile NW of Brenzett) TQ990285
⌚ closed Mon; 12-3, 7-11; 12-3, 7-10.30 Sun
☎ (01797) 344648
4 changing beers Ⓖ
Unspoilt 16th-century smugglers' pub in the same family for over 100 years and universally known as Doris's. Decorated with posters from the 1940s and the Women's Land Army, it has a nationally important historic pub interior. Up to five guest beers, always including at least one from Goacher's, are to be had. A beer festival is held in June with a mini festival in October. Basic snacks are available. Local CAMRA branch Pub of the Year for 2015. Q❀♣●P🚌(11,11B)🐾

South Darenth

Queen 𝕃
58-62 New Road, DA4 9AR
⌚ 2-11; 12-11.30 Sat; 12-10.30 Sun ☎ (01322) 862430
Fuller's ESB; Kent Session Pale; 2 changing beers (sourced regionally; often Dark Star, Hook Norton) Ⓗ
Friendly back-street local within walking distance of Farningham Road station, once serving the nearby former paper mill, now a housing development. Extended in 1988 to absorb a former shop, it has two bars, one adorned with memorabilia of London football teams, and there is a pool table and jukebox. It is a genuine free house, promoting beers from Kent Brewery and other suppliers. Free bar food is available Sunday lunchtimes, and children are welcome until 8.30pm. It has a garden/patio with a covered area.
♨❀◑♣●🚌(414)🐾📶

Stalisfield Green

Plough Inn 𝕃
Stalisfield Road, ME13 0HY
⌚ closed Mon; 12-3, 6 (5 Fri)-11; 10.30-11 Sat; 12-6 Sun
☎ (01795) 890256 🌐 theploughinnstalisfield.co.uk
3 changing beers (sourced locally; often Hopdaemon, Musket, Old Dairy) Ⓗ
Grade II-listed family-run country pub serving local beers, wines and cider and located high on the North Downs. Two miles from Charing and the A20, the Plough has wonderful views over farmland and is popular with walkers and cyclists. It has a seasonal and constantly changing food menu with ingredients sourced locally whenever possible. Biddenden Bushels cider is sold on handpump. A family-friendly garden is well frequented in the summer. The real fire adds great character.
Q♨❀◑◗♿▲●P🚌(660)🐾

Staplehurst

Lord Raglan 𝕃
Chart Hill Road, TN12 0DE (½ mile N of A229 at Cross at Hand) TQ786472
⌚ 12-3, 6.30-11; closed Sun ☎ (01622) 843747
Goacher's Fine Light Ale; Harveys Sussex Best Bitter; 1 changing beer (sourced locally; often Musket, Tonbridge, Westerham) Ⓗ
A long-standing entry, this popular and unspoilt free house retains the atmosphere of a country pub from bygone days. The bar is hung with hops and warmed by two log fires and a stove. The large orchard garden catches the evening sun. Excellent snacks and full meals are always available. The guest beer changes regularly and local Double Vision cider is sold. Well-behaved children and dogs are welcome. The nearest bus stop is on the A229. Q❀◑◗●P🐾

Swanscombe

George & Dragon L
1 London Road, DA10 0LQ
✪ 12 (4 Mon & Tue)-11; 12-10.30 Sun ☎ (01322) 386440
🌐 georgedragonswanscombe.co.uk
Wells Bombardier; 8 changing beers (sourced nationally; often Caveman) Ⓗ
Enterprising Victorian coaching inn, now a destination for real ale and good food. A horseshoe-shaped bar supports nine handpumps, and there are local ciders, an interesting cabinet with whiskies, and bottled beers from UK and international brewers. The restaurant is open Wednesday-Saturday lunchtimes and evenings, plus Sunday lunchtime for the recommended roasts. The Caveman Brewery is located in the cellar. Ebbsfleet United football club is close by. Local CAMRA Pub of the Year 2013 and 2014.
🏵️🛏️◖🍺⬥♣●P🚃🐾🛜

Tankerton

Tankerton Arms L
139B Tankerton Road, CT5 2AW
✪ closed Mon; 12-2, 5-9 (11 Fri); 12-11 Sat; 12-3 Sun ☎ 07532 025626 🌐 thetankertonarms.co.uk
4 changing beers (sourced locally; often Ripple Steam, Tonbridge, Wantsum) Ⓖ
Friendly micropub with a firm policy of supporting Kent microbreweries, situated among Tankerton's small shops. The pleasant, airy room is lined with high wooden tables which encourage conversation among customers. Mobile phones are banned. The walls are adorned with hop bines and pictures featuring Thames sailing barges and the sea forts. Food is restricted to local Ashmore cheeses and Scotch eggs from the butcher's shop opposite. There is some seating outdoors on the tree-shaded pavement. Q🏵️♣●🚃(4,6)🐾

Tenterden

Woolpack Hotel L
26 High Street, TN30 6AP (on A28 in centre of town)
✪ 11-11.30 (12.30am Sat); 11-10 Sun ☎ (01580) 388501
🌐 thewoolly.com
Harveys Sussex Best Bitter; Timothy Taylor Golden Best; 2 changing beers (sourced nationally; often Old Dairy) Ⓗ
Early 15th-century red-tiled coaching inn that was originally the mayor's parlour where the magistrates' court also met. In the meantime smugglers were sitting in the back room for their trading. The pub name refers to the business that brought so much prosperity to this part of Kent. Excellent bar and restaurant food is served, sourced from the landlord's local farm. Quiz night is Monday. A good place to stay for a short break in Tenterden. Q🛏️🛏️◖🍺♣●P🚃🐾🛜

Teynham

Swan L
78 London Road, ME9 9QH (on A2)
✪ 4-midnight; 12-midnight Sat & Sun ☎ (01795) 521218
2 changing beers (sourced locally; often Mad Cat, Wantsum, Whitstable) Ⓗ

Large roadside pub on the A2, just over half a mile from Teynham railway station. The real ales are often from Kent microbreweries. Two real ciders are also available, usually from Dudda's Tun. The pub hosts darts teams, shows sporting events and has occasional live music. The large function room, which can be hired, is home to the pub's annual beer festival. Good home-cooked food is served early evenings and weekend lunchtimes.
🛏️🏵️◖●P🚃(7,333)🐾

Tonbridge

Humphrey Bean
94 High Street, TN9 1AP
✪ 7am-midnight (1am Fri & Sat); 8am-midnight Sun
☎ (01732) 773850
Adnams Broadside; Greene King IPA, Abbot; Ruddles Best Bitter; 6 changing beers (sourced locally; often Dark Star, Westerham, Whitstable) Ⓗ
Large town-centre pub with an open and airy feel thanks to the skylights that give it lots of natural light. The extensive and pleasant beer garden has attractive views of the river and castle. It is named after the landlord of a pub called the Logger Heads which stood on the site before 1908, but was more recently converted from a post office by Wetherspoon. Its real ale commitment is demonstrated by single-brewery showcase events. Two Westons ciders are served, plus guests in summer. Q🛏️🏵️◖♿🍺●P🚃🛜

Tunbridge Wells

Bedford L
2 High Street, TN1 1UX
✪ 12-11 (midnight Fri & Sat); 12-9.30 Sun
☎ (01892) 510133 🌐 thebedfordtw.co.uk
Greene King IPA, Abbot; 7 changing beers (sourced locally; often Long Man, Old Dairy, Tonbridge) Ⓗ
Corner pub, a stone's throw from the railway station on the cusp of the historic High Street and Pantiles area. This ale drinkers' paradise has a changing selection, with beers from near and far displayed on the rather appropriate Arrivals and Departures boards. Real cider such as Thistly Cross is served. The atmosphere is lively, sometimes raucous, but always friendly. Food ranges from quality snacks to Sunday lunches. The adjacent Bedford Beer Cave sells local bottled beers.
🛏️◖🍺♣●🚃🐾🛜

Fuggles Beer Café
28 Grosvenor Road, TN1 2AP
✪ 11.30-11; 12-9.30 Sun ☎ (01892) 457739
🌐 fugglesbeercafe.co.uk
Tonbridge Copper Nob; 4 changing beers (sourced nationally) Ⓗ
Opened in 2013 in former shop premises, this venue combines the best elements of a British pub and a continental café-style bar. The narrow glass frontage leads to a deep open-plan bar room. Wooden flooring is complemented by candlelit tables, stools, chairs and comfy sofas. Beer and cider come from local and distant producers, together with an extensive range of craft keg and bottled beers from the UK and Belgium. No full meals are served, but you can get British charcuterie and cheeses. ◖🍺●🚃🐾🛜

Grove Tavern 𝕃
19 Berkeley Road, TN1 1YR
12-midnight ☎ (01892) 526549
Harveys Sussex Best Bitter; Timothy Taylor Landlord; 2 changing beers (sourced nationally; often Kent, Thwaites) Ⓗ
Just off the High Street, this traditional pub is close to train and bus routes and in the labyrinth of paved or cobbled twittens and narrow roads in Grove Village. It is a venue for often lively and topical conversation, pub games, screened sports events or just for relaxing in the homely atmosphere. There is a real fire in winter. Good ales and packet snacks are served, while water and biscuits are usually available for dogs.

Mount Edgcumbe
The Common, TN4 8BX
11-11 (11.30 Thu-Sat); 12-10.30 Sun ☎ (01892) 618854
themountedgcumbe.com
Harveys Sussex Best Bitter; Long Man Long Blonde; 2 changing beers (sourced locally; often Kent, Tonbridge) Ⓗ
Recently refurbished Georgian house among the trees and rocks and the only licensed building on the common. Excellent food and beer can be enjoyed in the modern dining area overlooking the terraced garden and common. In the bar area, complete with sandstone cave, a warm and relaxed atmosphere pervades and walkers with dogs are welcome. Situated close to the county border, both Kent and Sussex beers are well represented. Rooms are available to hire for private functions. P

Royal Oak 𝕃
92 Prospect Road, TN2 4SY
12-11; 12-10.30 Sun ☎ (01892) 542546
Harveys Sussex Best Bitter; 5 changing beers (sourced locally; often Cottage, Larkins, Whitstable) Ⓗ
Homely and comfortable pub a short stroll away from the busy town centre. Beers are mainly from Kent, Sussex and London breweries, plus a cider in summer. Occasional beer and cider festivals are held. The Oak reaches out to the local community by offering a range of activities from live music, quizzes and film nights through to darts, and it has a rare bar billiards table.
P(6,285)

Upper Upnor

King's Arms
2 High Street, ME2 4XG
11.30-11; 12-11 Sun ☎ (01634) 717490
kingsarmsupnor.co.uk
Adnams Southwold Bitter; 4 changing beers (sourced regionally) Ⓗ
Set at the far end of the scenic cobbled High Street, leading to the River Medway and an historic castle, this village inn is the current local CAMRA branch Pub of the Year, the fourth time it has won. The beers on offer frequently include a mild or stout, plus cider and perry, and a good range of bottled beers from around the world. It has an off-licence and a good reputation for the quality of its food.
QP(197)

Walmer

Berry 𝕃
23 Canada Road, CT14 7EQ
11 (2 Tue; 12 Thu)-11.30; 11.30-11 Sun
☎ (01304) 362411 theberrywalmer.co.uk
Dark Star American Pale Ale; Harveys Sussex Best Bitter; 9 changing beers Ⓗ
A beer lover's paradise, this back-street local has won multiple CAMRA awards, and offers up to 11 beers, six ciders and perries, and six beers on KeyKeg from Time & Tide and other leading breweries such as Kernel. The knowledgeable and friendly landlord holds three real ale festivals a year, including a Green Hop festival in October, and a cider festival. Entertainment includes darts, pool, a monthly quiz and occasional live music. CAMRA branch Pub of the Year for seven years.

Lighthouse 𝕃
50 The Strand, CT14 7DX
closed Mon-Wed; 5 (12 Sat)-11; 12-10 Sun
☎ (01304) 366031 thelighthousedeal.co.uk
3 changing beers Ⓖ
With an enviable position overlooking Walmer Green and the sea, this pub is a leading music venue hosting the best of local talent and beyond. Entry is via a revolving door which can be opened wide for wheelchair access. Beers are from nearby breweries including Ripple Steam, Wantsum and Time & Tide, and a range of ciders is available, often from Kentish Pip. Pie and mash is served afternoons and early evenings with reggae roast on Sunday. There is a small front patio.

West Malling

Bull 𝕃
1 High Street, ME19 6QH
12-2.30, 4-11; 12-11 Fri & Sat; 12-10.30 Sun
☎ (01732) 842753 thebullinnwestmalling.com
Timothy Taylor Landlord; Young's Bitter; 6 changing beers (sourced nationally; often Goacher's, Harveys, Musket) Ⓗ
At the north end of the village, by the railway line, you will find this hospitable free house. The owner has undertaken considerable renovation and decoration but preserved the character with wood panels, hops on the beams and a log fire. Local cider is on handpump. Good pub meals are served in the bar, but the left side is mainly for diners.
Q(72,151)

West Peckham

Swan on the Green
The Village Green, ME18 5JW (near church) TQ644525
11-3, 6-8.30 Mon (11 Tue & Wed; 11.30 Fri); 11-4, 6-11 Sat; 12-7 Sun ☎ (01622) 812271 swan-on-the-green.co.uk
Swan Fuggles Pale, Trumpeter Best, Cygnet, Bewick Swan; 1 changing beer (sourced locally; often Swan) Ⓗ
As its name implies, the Swan is quite literally part of the village green. Tables and benches outside perfectly complement the location and customers drift onto the green. The on-site microbrewery supplies all the real ales and the food has a fine reputation. The interior is fresh and inviting with a wooden floor, matching stripped-pine tables and

an open double-sided fire. The nearest bus stop is an easy one-mile walk down the lane from Mereworth School. Q🐴❀◑P🐾📶

Westerham

Grasshopper on the Green

The Green, TN16 1AS

⏲ 10-11 (midnight Fri & Sat); 10-10.30 Sun

☎ (01959) 562926 🌐 grasshopperonthegreen.co.uk

Courage Best Bitter; Harveys Sussex Best Bitter; Timothy Taylor Landlord; 3 changing beers (sourced locally; often Adnams, Westerham) Ⓗ

Former coaching station enjoying an enviable position facing the green, which gets its name from the insect on the crest of the Tudor owners of the manor of Westerham. Three bars cater for a varied clientele, with the rear room housing a log fire. A comprehensive menu includes breakfast and light bites. The first-floor restaurant provides more dining space. Outdoor table seating is available for people-watching on the green or in the peaceful rear garden. 🐴❀◑♣P🚌(246,401)🐾📶

Westgate-on-Sea

Bake & Alehouse

21 St Mildred's Road, CT8 8RE

⏲ closed Mon; 12-2, 5.30-9; 12-2 Sun ☎ 07581 468797

🌐 bakeandalehouse.co.uk

4 changing beers Ⓖ

One of the earliest of the burgeoning number of micropubs in this part of east Kent. A former baker's shop, it has been sensitively managed to create an intimate and friendly community atmosphere, and has room for around 20 people. Four ales, predominantly Kentish, and real cider are normally available. Food comprises local pork pies and cheese, which seems to keep regulars and visitors alike satisfied. Q≹♣🍎🚌(8,8A,35)🐾

Whitstable

Black Dog

66 High Street, CT5 1BB

⏲ 12-11.30 (midnight Thu-Sat)

Dark Star Hophead; 4 changing beers (sourced nationally; often Kent, Oakham, Triple fff) Ⓖ

This attractive town centre micropub has a Victorian decor with a twist. There are five constantly changing real ales from local and regional breweries, and six local ciders and perries from Dudda's Tun and Kentish Pip. The handpumps on the bar counter are for decoration only; the beers are gravity dispensed from the cooled cellar room. Food is Scotch eggs and pies from local producers. There is occasional live music from local folk singers and morris dancers. Q≹🍎🚌(4,5,6)🐾

New Inn Ⓛ

30 Woodlawn Street, CT5 1HG

⏲ 3-11 (midnight Fri); 12-midnight Sat; 12-10 Sun

☎ (01227) 264746

Shepherd Neame Master Brew; 1 changing beer (sourced locally; often Shepherd Neame) Ⓗ

Dating from 1860, this is a typical Whitstable back-street pub, not far from the harbour and shopping area. The etched windows hint at the original layout of several small bars, now a long narrow bar and a cosy area further back. The small snug has a collection of board games. There is a good selection of gins and malt whiskies, and an interesting choice of snacks. Live music nights feature occasionally. 🐴≹♣🚌🐾📶

Ship Centurion 🏆 Ⓛ

111 High Street, CT5 1AY

⏲ 11-11; 12-7 Sun ☎ (01227) 264740

Adnams Southwold Bitter; Young's Bitter; 2 changing beers (sourced nationally; often Elgood) Ⓗ

Friendly, traditional town-centre pub and local CAMRA branch Pub of the Year for 2015. Colourful hanging baskets add to its charm in summer. Pictures of Whitstable adorn the bar. A mild is always served along with a local Kentish beer. Home-cooked bar food includes authentic German dishes, with schnitzel on Saturdays (no food Sun). Live music plays on Thursday evenings and Friday lunchtimes. There is a summer cider festival and an October beer festival. ◑≹🚌(4,5,6)🐾📶

Wickhambreaux

Rose Inn

The Green, CT3 1RQ

⏲ 12-11; 12-10.30 Sun ☎ (01227) 721763

🌐 theroseinnwickhambreaux.co.uk

Greene King IPA; 2 changing beers Ⓗ

Situated in a lovely village, the Rose dates back around 700 years. It has oak beams and hanging hops. The friendly bar has an open fire, and the dining area has a huge fireplace. One guest beer is from a Kent brewery. Events include a quiz night on the third Tuesday of each month and various beer festivals. There is a bar in the garden on summer weekends. The pub may close on Mondays in winter. Q🐴❀◑♣🍎P🚌(11)🐾📶

Willesborough

Blacksmith's Arms

84 The Street, TN24 0NA

⏲ 12-11 (midnight Fri & Sat); 12-11.30 Sun

☎ (01233) 623975 🌐 blacksmithsarmsashford.co.uk

Fuller's London Pride; 2 changing beers Ⓗ

This 18th-century, Grade II-listed, family-friendly pub on the outskirts of Ashford offers a range of cask ales, wines and a changing menu. It has a large terraced garden and children's play area, and is ideally situated just off the M20 for a break on the way to the channel ports, or to unwind if you are visiting the area. 🐴❀◑♿♣P🚌🐾

Worth

Blue Pigeons Ⓛ

The Street, CT14 0DE

⏲ 12-10 (11 Fri & Sat); 12-9 Sun ☎ (01304) 613233

🌐 thebluepigeons.co.uk

3 changing beers Ⓗ

An imposing Georgian building opposite St Nicholas' Church. The front door leads into the main bar area, wooden floored and decorated in neutral colours. There are three real ales, with one from a Kent brewery, typically Rockin' Robin or Canterbury Ales. A varied menu of home-made food is on offer in the bar and the vaulted restaurant. The rear patio overlooks a large garden, with gazebo and climbing frame.
🐴❀🛏◑P🚌(13A)🐾📶

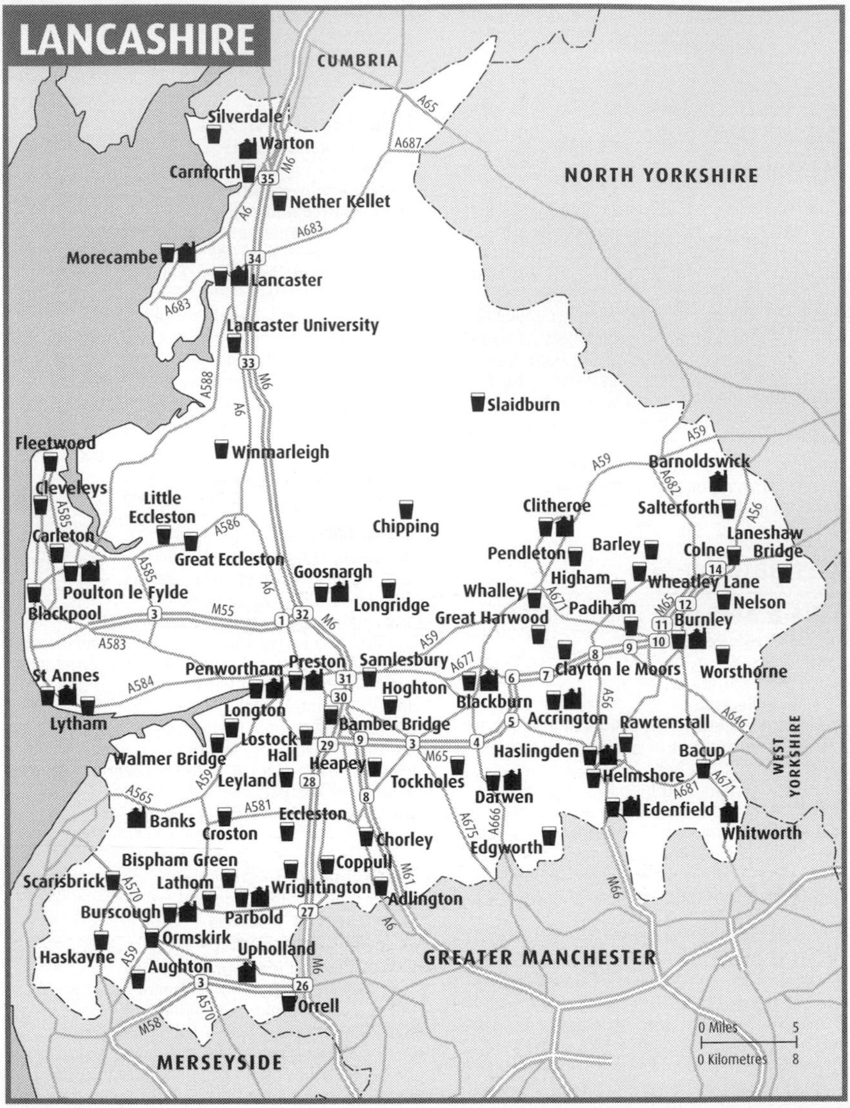

Please note that Thwaites of Blackburn sold its beer brands and brewing rights to the Marston's group in 2015. With the exception of small-run beers brewed on Thwaites's micro plant, all the main Thwaites beers are now brewed and supplied by Marston's. See Breweries section, p921.

Accrington

Commercial Hotel 🄻

1 Church Street, BB5 2EN

8am-midnight (1am Fri & Sat) ☎ (01254) 300140

Greene King Abbot; Ruddles Best Bitter; 8 changing beers Ⓗ

An open-plan pub in the Wetherspoon tradition, the Commercial contains many local features with more than a nod to the local Tiffany glass collection. It is adjacent to the bus station and markets and only a short walk from the railway station. The pub supports LocAle, with eight of the 10 handpumps given over to guest ales, alongside two ciders. Q❀◑♿⇌🚌

Grants

1 Manchester Road, BB5 2BQ

12-11 ☎ (01254) 393938 🌐 grantsbar.co.uk

12 changing beers Ⓗ

A large, imposing building on the edge of the town centre, tastefully refurbished in 2009 in a distinct modern style and attracting a wide clientele. It is home to the Big Clock Brewery, which can be viewed from the main drinking area. At least six Big Clock ales are available at any time, with the rest of the handpulls serving other micro beers. Third-pint glasses are available, served on a wooden platter. Tapas-style snacks are available lunchtimes and early evening. ◑⇌P🚌

Peel Park Hotel L
Turkey Street, BB5 6EW
✪ 12-11.30; 12-10.30 Sun ☎ (01254) 235830
Tetley Bitter; 5 changing beers ⓗ
A true traditional free house tucked away from the main road, situated opposite the old Accrington Stanley football ground. The main bar is a large open front room divided into two sections. There is a separate small pool room leading to a function room which is available to hire. Outside is a pleasant suntrap garden. Light snacks are served at all times although there is no menu – orders are taken at the bar. ⛀❀◐⇌P🚌(23)

Adlington

Spinners Arms L
23 Church Street, PR7 4EX
✪ 12-11 (midnight Fri & Sat); 12-10.30 Sun
☎ (01257) 483331
Moorhouse's Pride of Pendle; Timothy Taylor Dark Mild; 5 changing beers (sourced regionally) ⓗ
The pub is known as the Bottom Spinners to differentiate it from the other Spinners Arms in the village. Welcoming and friendly, a single bar serves three seating areas and there is a pleasant outdoor drinking area to the front. It has no pool table or gaming machine, just an open log fire. The bar menu offers home-cooked food with weekend specials. Five alternating guest beers, often from local breweries, are on handpump. Small functions are catered for. ⛀◐⇌P🚌(3)🐾ᯤ

Aughton

Derby Arms L
Prescot Road, L39 6TA (on B5197 at Bowkers Green between Ormskirk and Kirkby)
✪ 12-11 (1am Fri); 9am-1am Sat ☎ (01695) 422237
Tetley Mild, Bitter; 3 changing beers (often Burscough, Moorhouse's, Problem Child) ⓗ
Friendly country pub between Ormskirk and Kirkby with a long CAMRA award-winning heritage. The interior is intimate, with many small nooks and crannies. A changing choice of beers is dispensed from the three guest handpumps, sourced from any local or national brewery. The pub hosts quiz nights on Tuesdays and Thursdays and holds regular charity events. Excellent-value food is available, with breakfast served on Saturdays from 9am. Q⛀❀◐♣P🐾ᯤ

Dog & Gun
233 Long Lane, L39 5BU
✪ 4-midnight; 12-midnight Sat & Sun ☎ (01695) 423303
Banks's Bitter; Marston's Pedigree; 3 changing beers ⓗ
A genuine community pub dating from 1891 with an interior that retains an intimacy unspoilt by the modern planner. Two rooms, one with a real fire, are set around a central bar, with ales served from five handpulls. The pub still has a bowling green supporting up to six teams, and also hosts darts matches and regular quiz nights. There are outside drinking areas both to the front and rear of the building adorned with excellent floral displays. Live football is shown during week. ⛀♿⇌♣P🐾ᯤ

Bacup

Crown Inn
19 Greave Road, OL13 9HQ
✪ 5-midnight (1am Sat); 12-midnight Sun
☎ (01706) 873982
Pictish Brewers Gold; 3 changing beers ⓗ
The Crown is a traditional country pub with flagged floors throughout. A welcoming coal fire adds to the warm atmosphere at the bar. There are always three guest beers, usually from local breweries. Food is served, both snacks and main meals, from 5pm daily. Wednesdays and Sundays are quiz nights. A function room, accommodating up to 35 people, is available on the second floor. There is also a beer garden for those long summer evenings. Q⛀❀◗♿♣P🚌(465)

Bamber Bridge

Withy Arms L
Station Road, PR5 6QP
✪ 11-midnight (1am Fri); 10.30-1am Sat; 10.30-midnight Sun
☎ (01772) 697706 🌐 withyarms.com
House beer (by Thwaites); 5 changing beers (often Moorhouse's, Prospect) ⓗ
On the main crossroads and 15 minutes' walk from the railway station, this pub was reopened in 2011 after being bought by a local business for the office space. The open-plan bar has a slightly continental feel and there is an impressive bar counter with six handpumps. Guest beers are usually from local breweries. Quiz night is Tuesday. ⛀❀◐⇌P🚌ᯤ

Barley

Pendle Inn L
Barley Lane, BB12 9JX
✪ 11-11; 12-10 Sun ☎ (01282) 614808 🌐 pendle-inn.co.uk
6 changing beers ⓗ
A large pub in the centre of Barley village, popular with walkers ascending Pendle Hill. Muddy boots and dogs are welcome. The pub frontage retains many original features and there is a large dining conservatory to the rear. All front rooms have log

REAL ALE BREWERIES
Arkwright's Preston
Barlick Barnoldswick
Big Clock Accrington
Bishop's Crook Penwortham
Bluestone Whitworth
Borough Lancaster
Bowland Clitheroe
Burscough Burscough
Chapel Street Poulton-le-Fylde
Cross Bay Morecambe
Edenfield Edenfield (NEW)
Fuzzy Duck Poulton-le-Fylde
Goosnargh Goosnargh
Hart of Preston Preston
Hopstar Darwen
Lancaster Lancaster
Lytham St Annes
Moonstone Burnley
Moorhouse's Burnley
Old School Warton
Parker Banks
Problem Child Parbold
Reedley Hallows Burnley
Rossendale Haslingden
Three B's Blackburn
Thwaites Blackburn
Wellcross Upholland
Worsthorne Burnley

fires. There is a lovely central oak bar with six cask ales. CAMRA members receive a discount. Accommodation is available. Q P

Bispham Green

Eagle & Child

Malt Kiln Lane, L40 3SG

12-11; 12-10.30 Sun (01257) 462297

7 changing beers H

An 18th-century pub with eight handpumps showcasing local ales – Southport Carousel is always available and a variety of guest ales can come from AllGates, Prospect and Moorhouse's. This busy country pub is the Lancashire Dining Pub of the Year for the fifth time – diners are advised to book early for a table. The beer garden, with its wildlife area and great views, hosts a beer festival on the May bank holiday. Quiz night is every Monday. P

Blackburn

Black Bull

Brokenstone Road, BB3 0LL

closed Mon & Tue; 4-11 (midnight Fri); 12-midnight Sat; 12-10.30 Sun (01254) 664771 threebsbrewery.co.uk

8 changing beers H

The Bull is a real ale drinker's mecca. A good 25 minutes' walk up from Blackburn Rovers Stadium builds up a thirst. This award-winning pub, home of Three B's Brewery, has an incredible range of permanent beers courtesy of Robert and Wendy. An eclectic clientele patronises this pub – walkers, farmers, ageing hippies, young folk, old folk, folk musicians and others. Visit this pub before you pop your clogs. Q P

Hare & Hounds

78 Lammack Road, BB1 8LA

4-midnight; 12.30-midnight Sat & Sun (01254) 690762

5 changing beers H

Rescued from the jaws of oblivion by the current landlord and backed by a passionate local community, this is the last remaining purpose-built Dalton's pub in the country. Adjacent to Pleckgate and Lammack playing fields, it is the meeting place for local sports teams including women's netball and hockey. It has been restored to a two-storey venue and the number of handpumps increased from one to five. Live music plays on Fridays and Saturdays. P (5)

Blackpool

Auctioneer

235-237 Lytham Road, FY1 6ET

8am-12.30am (01253) 346412

Greene King Abbot; Ruddles Best Bitter; 8 changing beers H

Now in its 15th year, this Wetherspoon establishment, with its recently refurbished, cosy, community-pub feel, has an outside rear drinking area and, because of a café licence, tables at the front. It is handy for the football ground – home and away supporters are most welcome. It can get busy in the summer months with visitors from the local hotels and Waterloo Road shopping area. Up to eight guest beers are served and two ciders are usually available in polypins.
Q (South) (10,11,68)

Blackpool Cricket Club

Barlow Crescent, West Park Drive, FY3 9EQ (follow signs to Stanley Park)

4.30-11; 2.30-midnight Fri; 12-midnight Sat; 12-11 Sun (01253) 393347 blackpoolcricket.co.uk

Thwaites Wainwright; 4 changing beers (often Lytham, Reedley Hallows) H

Part of Stanley Park, the club hosts local sports teams who play on the nearby pitches. Large-screen TVs show all sports events and an upstairs room is available for social events. The club has its own squash courts and holds quiz and entertainment nights. It is the local CAMRA branch Club of the Year, and home of the Bass Appreciation Society locally. Dogs are permitted outside food service times. It holds an annual beer festival. P (4,16,61)

Layton Rakes

17-25 Market Street, FY1 1ET

8am-midnight (1am Fri & Sat) (01253) 743710

Greene King Abbot; Ruddles Best Bitter; 7 changing beers H

Town-centre pub, close to the town hall, with excellent, friendly staff. It offers a range of excellent beers and boasts plenty of choice, changing on a regular basis. There is a quieter upper floor and a large open roof terrace, both with their own bar and serving different cask ales. Music is played on the ground floor on a Friday and Saturday evening. Q (North)

Pump & Truncheon

13 Bonny Street, FY1 5AR

11 (10 Fri & Sat)-midnight; 12-11 Sun (01253) 624099 thepumpandtruncheon.co.uk

6 changing beers (often Acorn, Clark's, Cross Bay) H

Situated behind Tussauds on Blackpool's Golden Mile, this delightfully old-fashioned pub boasts up to six different guest ales and a range of ciders/perries. The licensee is a keen cask enthusiast and this shows in the quality of his ales. The wood-panelled decor has a strong police theme, doubtless inspired by the pub's proximity to the local nick. (1,10,11)

Rose & Crown

20-24 Corporation Street, FY1 1EJ

10.30-11; 11-11 Sun (01253) 299821 roseandcrownblackpool.co.uk

Thwaites Wainwright; 1 changing beer H

Town-centre pub, close to the Grand Theatre. It has an open-plan, multi-level ground floor with covered and heated outdoor seating areas surrounding the building. Background music is played but at a level that allows conversation. Food is served all day, with the menu offering standard pub fare (discounted for OAPs and children). Live sports events are shown.
(North)

Burnley

Bridge Bier Huis

2 Bank Parade, BB11 1UH

closed Mon & Tue; 12-midnight (1am Fri & Sat); 12-11 Sun (01282) 411304 thebridgebierhuis.co.uk

Moorhouse's Premier Bitter; 4 changing beers H

A multi award-winning true free house with a large open-plan bar that has a logburner and small snug to one side. It offers mainly microbrewery beers alongside a changing real cider. More than 60 foreign bottled beers are sold plus seven foreign beers on tap including rare German brews. Wednesday is quiz night. Live music is hosted on occasional weekends. This welcoming pub opens at 5pm on Tuesday evenings if Burnley FC is playing at home. (Central)

Ighten Leigh Social Club

389 Padiham Road, BB12 6SZ

closed Mon-Wed; 7-11 Thu; 3-11.45 Fri; 12.30-11.45 Sat; 12.30-11 Sun (01282) 422306

4 changing beers

Large friendly club in its own grounds with a dedicated real ale bar. It has a car park and outside smoking area, and a Sky Sports TV viewing area to the front. It boasts a pool table, large and small snooker tables and a darts area. Thursday is quiz night, with live music every Friday to Sunday. There is a large function room upstairs that caters for every occasion. Non-members are charged 50p entry at weekends. ♣P(26,152)

Rifle Volunteer

1 Smalley Street, BB11 3HH

2-11; 12-11 Sat; 12-10.30 Sun (01282) 453839

Draught Bass; 2 changing beers

The Vols is an award-winning pub and a rare outlet in this area for the iconic Draught Bass. This free house is a supreme example of a street-corner local. No jukebox disturbs the quiet ambience of this friendly pub where the emphasis is on good beer and conversation. The Gents has a rare example of the Burnley-manufactured Ducketts urinals. Q♣P(483)

Talbot

65 Church Street, BB11 2RU

5-midnight; 4-1am Fri; 12-1am Sat; 12-midnight Sun (01282) 412074

Copper Dragon Golden Pippin; Holt Bitter; Moorhouse's Premier Bitter; 5 changing beers

A warm welcome awaits you at this free house dating back to the 1800s. The licensee is a keen real ale enthusiast and supporter of local breweries. Live bands feature every weekend. There are two pool tables plus a large-screen TV for sports fans. Four en-suite rooms are available for guests, who also have use of the private car park. (Central)♣P(4,5,X43)

Burscough

Hop Vine

Liverpool Road North, L40 4BY (on A59)

10.30-midnight (12.30am Fri & Sat); 10.30-11 Sun (01704) 893799 thehopvine.co.uk

Burscough Mere Blonde; house beer (by Burscough); 7 changing beers (often George Wright, Phoenix, Timothy Taylor)

Spacious former coaching house that is now a thriving community brewpub renowned for its friendly atmosphere and popular for its exceptional ale and food. The classic country pub interior has wood-panelling and characterful wood flooring throughout, and is decorated with historic local maps, photographs and vintage bottled ales. The award-winning Burscough Brewery operates from the attractive floral courtyard at the rear. Catering for all age groups, it offers great-value meals, live music and twice-yearly beer festivals. (Bridge)P

Carleton

Castle Gardens

Poulton Road, FY6 7NH

11.30-11 (midnight Fri & Sat); 12-11 Sun (01253) 890015

Brakspear Bitter; Moorhouse's Pendle Witches Brew; Thwaites Wainwright; 3 changing beers

Situated roughly halfway between Poulton and Bispham, there has been a hostelry on this site since about 1750. It is a popular place that successfully combines being a food-led destination pub and a local community venue. A weekly quiz is held. A range of six ales including three changing guests is available. There is a pleasant outdoor area to the side of the pub. P(14,16,87)

Carnforth

Snug

Unit 6, Carnforth Gateway Building, LA5 9TR (at N end of former mainline up platform)

closed Mon; 12-2, 5-9; 12.30-3 Sun (01524) 735677 thesnugmicropub.blogspot.co.uk

5 changing beers

A micropub both in the sense of being very small and also of being minimalist in concept. The only drinks are ale, cider, wine and soft drinks, the only food light snacks, the only sounds conversation and the roar of passing trains. The decor is similarly stripped back – painted walls, bare floorboards and chunky tall tables. The eye is naturally drawn to a beautiful glazed wooden cabinet where all the drinks are stored. Parking is in the station car park (a charge applies). Q♣(5,55,555)

Chipping

Tillotsons Arms

18 Talbot Street, PR3 2QE

closed Mon; 12-3, 5-midnight Tue, Wed & Fri; 4-midnight Thu; 12-midnight Sat; 12-11 Sun (01995) 61568 thetillotsonsarms.co.uk

4 changing beers

In a picturesque village in the Forest of Bowland, this two-roomed, beamed pub built in 1836 offers between two and four beers, often from micros, with Copper Dragon and Hawkshead featuring regularly. With two real fires and a garden at the rear, it welcomes children and dogs, and is a popular stop-off for walkers exploring the countryside. Locally sourced home-cooked food is served in generous portions lunchtimes and evenings, all day at weekends. The current licensee, Curly Neary, is the great grandson of Jeremiah Joy, who was licensee of the pub in 1897. Q♣P(4)

Chorley

Crown

46-48 Chapel Street, PR7 1BW

11-midnight; 12-11 Sun 07552 092176

House beer (by Fuzzy Duck); 4 changing beers (sourced locally; often AllGates, Bowland, Lancaster)

Newly refurbished and reopened in February 2014 following two years of closure, the pub features an impressive bar counter and bar-back, together with contemporary seating in a mainly open-plan layout. A cosy area to the side of the bar and a small lounge offer more privacy. Two TVs screen live sport but do not intrude. Five handpumps provide a changing array of beers, mainly from local microbreweries. Live music plays every Friday evening. ☺&≠🖳🐾🛈🏠

Potters Arms 🅛

42 Brooke Street, PR7 3BY (next to Morrisons)
☉ 3-11.30 (midnight Fri); 12-4, 7-midnight Sat; 12-11 Sun
☎ (01257) 267954
Black Sheep Best Bitter; Three B's Doff Cocker; 1 changing beer 🅗
Small, friendly free house named after the owners, at the bottom of Brooke Street alongside the railway bridge. The central bar serves two games areas, while two comfortable lounges are popular with locals and visitors alike. The pub displays a fine selection of photographs from the world of music, as well as vintage local scenes. Regular darts and dominoes nights are well attended and the chip butties go down a treat. The smoking area is covered. ≠♣P🖳(1,1A,2)

Railway

20 Steeley Lane, PR6 0RD (under subway from train station)
☉ 12-midnight (1am Fri & Sat) ☎ (01257) 671541
Banks's Sunbeam; Jennings Cumberland Ale; Wychwood Hobgoblin; 2 changing beers 🅗
Adjacent to the railway station and 100 yards from the bus station, this is a community local that offers a changing range of up to five real ales from the Marston's portfolio. A single corner bar serves different drinking areas and a separate pool alcove. Darts, dominoes and pool are popular with the locals, along with seasonal music festivals, Saturday night concerts and occasional Friday music nights. ❀≠♣🖳🛈

Shepherds Hall Ale House 🅛

67 Chapel Street, PR7 1BS
☉ closed Mon; 2-10 (11 Fri); 12-11 Sat; 2-9 Sun ☎ 07850 393482
⊕ shepherdshallalehouse.wordpress.com
5 changing beers (sourced nationally) 🅗
Formerly a shop, the building has been tastefully converted and utilises fittings from other closed pubs in the town, the bar coming from Harry's Bar and the tables from the Tut 'n' Shive. Like most micropubs there is no food, TV or music, and the drinks range is limited to real ale, cider, bottled beers, wine and soft drinks. The changing beers come mainly from microbreweries across the country, although a LocAle or two should normally be expected. Q≠●🖳🐾

Clayton le Moors

Forts Arms

1 Lower Barnes Street, BB5 5TA
☉ 4-11; 2-1am Fri & Sat; 2-11 Sun ☎ (01254) 433713
6 changing beers 🅗
Partially opened out in a modern style, the pub also boasts a function suite. Of the six changing beers, at least one is from Snaggletooth Brewery and the others come from micros nationwide. Four beer festivals are held each year with around 25 beers, all served through handpumps. A regular bus service terminates across the road (daytime only). P🖳(1,6,7)

Cleveleys

Jolly Tars

154-158 Victoria Road, FY5 3NE
☉ 8am-midnight (12.30am Thu-Sat) ☎ (01253) 856042
9 changing beers 🅗
This JD Wetherspoon house is in the middle of Cleveleys town centre by the main shopping area and down the road from the beach. It is decorated with blown glasswork and photos of Cleveleys between the wars. There are several booths in this community-focused venue which, unusually for a Wetherspoon pub, is all on one level. Regional and national beers are generally on offer from a range of constantly rotating guest ales. ☺❀◐&🖳●🖳🐾🛈

Clitheroe

New Inn

22 Parson Lane, BB7 2JN
☉ 11-11; 12-11 Sun ☎ (01200) 423312
Coach House Gunpowder Mild, Farrier's Best Bitter; Moorhouse's Premier Bitter, Pride of Pendle; 7 changing beers 🅗
A friendly, old-fashioned gem of a pub found just off the high street in the shadow of Clitheroe Castle. In addition to the snug rooms and cosy bar area there is a large beer garden at the back and seating out the front. The choice of ales is remarkable, with Postlethwaite and Blueberry regularly featuring from the Coach House Brewery. Traditional Irish music sessions are held every second Sunday afternoon in the back room. Q❀≠🖳🐾

Colne

Admiral Lord Rodney 🍷 🅛

Mill Green, BB8 0TA
☉ 4-midnight (2am Fri); 1-2am Sat; 1-midnight Sun
☎ (01282) 862217 ⊕ thelordrodney.co.uk
7 changing beers 🅗
A much-loved community pub in Colne's old South Valley area, set out in three rooms, with up to nine constantly changing beers, mainly from local breweries. Regular live entertainment takes place during the evenings, plus local history and art displays. It has recently been refurbished, with open fires and flagged floors, plus outdoor seating with a separate smokers' area. Q☺❀◐≠♣🐾

Coppull

Red Herring

Mill Lane, PR7 5AN
☉ 3-11; 12-11.30 Fri & Sat; 12-11 Sun ☎ (01257) 470130
5 changing beers 🅗
Real ale pub in the former offices of the next-door mill. It was converted to a pub some years ago – the bar area comprises a large single room plus an extension. Up to five beers, mainly from micros, are usually on handpump. TV sports fans are catered for, as are anglers who use the pond opposite. The pub hosts regular music nights and barbecues, and has a large first-floor function room. ☺❀&♣P🖳(362)🐾🛈

Croston

Crown

80 Station Road, PR26 9RN

12-11; 10-11 Sat & Sun ☎ (01772) 972785
crowncroston.co.uk
Thwaites Original; 4 changing beers (sourced nationally) H
A traditional open-plan village pub with a large garden to the rear where boules can be played. The guest ales are from the Thwaites 1807 Cask Club range, with an emphasis on the beers from its microbrewery. You can get third-of-a-pint taster trays. The front door into the bar has glass engraved with the logo of Massey's Burnley Brewery. Q P

Wheatsheaf L
Town Road, PR26 9RA
12-11 (midnight Fri); 10-midnight Sat; 10-11 Sun
☎ (01772) 600370 wheatsheaf-croston.com
5 changing beers (often Hawkshead) H
On the main road and overlooking the village green, this recently refurbished pub has a contemporary feel. It has one distinct area for dining as well as one for comfortable drinking, with sofas and chairs. The large patio area to the front is also used to hold an annual beer festival during October. Up to five varying ales are served, sourced from the SIBA list. Live music features on either Friday or Saturday nights twice a month.
P (7,112)

Darwen

Number 39 L
39-41 Bridge Street, BB3 2AA
12-midnight ☎ 07849 369798 hopstarbrewery.co.uk
Hopstar Dizzy Danny Ale, Dark Knight, Smokey Joe's Black Beer; 2 changing beers H
Number 39 is the brewery tap for Hopstar Brewery, and an award-winning pub – CAMRA Cider Pub of the Year 2015 – serving championship ales, ciders and continental beers. There is an apple and cheese event every Sunday and regular live music. A true community asset, it serves the full Hopstar range plus a changing choice of local, regional and national beers. Darwen is a popular destination for real ale enthusiasts and Number 39 is arguably the leader of the pack. (1,2)

Old Chapel
Railway Road, BB3 2RG
8am-11 (midnight Fri & Sat) ☎ (01254) 778700
8 changing beers H
The Old Chapel is a Wetherspoon conversion of an old Methodist chapel, hence the name. Inside there is a spectacular open staircase leading to a balcony seating area. The usual wide selection of real ale and food is on offer, and there is plenty of seating with quieter areas away from the main bar.

Eccleston

Original Farmers Arms
Towngate, PR7 5QS
12-midnight; 12-11.30 Sun ☎ (01257) 451594
originalfarmersarms.co.uk
Black Sheep Best Bitter; Robinsons Dizzy Blonde; Thwaites Wainwright; Timothy Taylor Landlord; 2 changing beers H
This white-painted village pub has expanded over the years into the cottage next door, adding a substantial dining area. However, the original part of the building is still mainly used for drinking. The changing guest beers are predominantly sourced from local breweries large and small. Meals are served throughout the day, seven days a week, and there is accommodation in four good-value guest rooms. P (113,347)

Edenfield

Rostron Arms
1 Market Place, BL0 0JZ
12-9 ☎ (01706) 821756
Edenfield Old Red Dog; 3 changing beers H
Large stone-built pub overlooking both Scout Moor and Dearden Moor. Built in the 19th century, it was one of three coaching inns in Edenfield. There are five handpumps, and it is home to the Edenfield Brewery (Magic Village Ales) – the house beers are produced on the premises at the rear of the pub. There is a large bar area and a pool room. The Rostron has both a darts and a pool team.
P (482,483,484)

Edgworth

White Horse L
2-4 Bury Road, BL7 0AY
5-11 Mon & Tue; 12-3, 5-midnight; 12-midnight Fri & Sat; 12-11 Sun ☎ (01204) 852929
Bank Top Flat Cap; Moorhouse's Pendle Witches Brew; Thwaites Wainwright; Timothy Taylor Landlord; 2 changing beers H
The name of this particular White Horse has heraldic origins dating back to the 18th century – white being the colour of peace and the horse representing steadiness (a plaque outside explains more). Situated prominently at the Bolton-Bury crossroads, this venue is a large corner building with an impressively decorated interior. The exquisite cuisine pulls in locals and tourists alike, who can also enjoy an excellent choice of mainly local ales. Q P

Fleetwood

Steamer
Queens Terrace, FY7 6BT
12 (11 Tue & Thu)-11; 11-1am Fri; 12-1am Sat
☎ (01253) 681001
8 changing beers H
A former coaching inn dating from 1842, this is one of Fleetwood's oldest surviving pubs, still with a mahogany and Spanish teak bar. Up to eight guest beers and real cider are available. Handy for Fleetwood market, bar snacks are served on market days. The pub has both pool and dominoes teams, and hosts live bands on Friday and Saturday evenings, plus a singer and singalong Tuesday lunchtime.

Strawberry Gardens L
Poulton Road, FY7 6TF (on A587)
11-12.30am (1am Fri & Sat) ☎ (01253) 771991
strawberrygardensfleetwood.co.uk
Brakspear Oxford Gold; Marston's Pedigree New World Pale Ale; changing beers H
Free house with up to 14 beers and Old Rosie cider plus one other. It is home to the Fleetwood Folk Club, two racing pigeon clubs and crown green bowling teams, and holds a beer festival at the end of May. Food is served daily from noon. Darts, dominoes and pool can be played. Dogs on leads are permitted in the vaults. Away fans are

welcome when playing Fleetwood Town. A former winner of the local CAMRA Pub and Cider Pub of the Year. ❀◐◑♿🚉♣🍎P🚌(14,74,84)🐾📶

Thomas Drummond

London Street, FY7 6JE

⏲ 8am-11 (midnight Thu-Sat) ☎ (01253) 775020

Greene King Abbot; Ruddles Best Bitter; 8 changing beers Ⓗ

This Wetherspoon pub, named after the builder who helped construct the town, also displays details of the town's founder, Sir Peter Hesketh Fleetwood, and architect Decimus Burton. Food is served daily 8am-11pm, and children are welcome until 9pm. Eight guest beers, which come from an extensive list and are constantly rotated, are on tap. Two rotating draught ciders are also on offer. Three beer festivals and two cider festivals are held each year. Q🐴❀◐◑♿🚉🍎🚌(1,14,74)📶

Goosnargh

Horn's Inn ★ 𝕃

Horns Lane, PR3 2FJ (corner of Inglewhite Rd, 2 miles NE of village)

⏲ 11.30-3 (not Mon), 6-11; 12-9 Sun ☎ (01772) 865230

🌐 hornsinn.co.uk

Goosnargh Bit o' Blonde, Gold; 1 changing beer (sourced locally) Ⓗ

Dating from 1782 and close to the Forest of Bowland, this venue has five rooms including a rare snug, one of only three in the country – customers sit behind a bar counter while staff serve from the same area. The beers are brewed by the landlord in a small outbuilding, with two or three changing Goosnargh beers available alongside occasional guests. It serves up good food using locally sourced ingredients. Accommodation is in a converted barn at the rear. Lancashire CAMRA Pub of the Year 2014. Q❀🛏◐◑⛺P📶

Great Eccleston

White Bull Hotel

The Square, PR3 0ZB

⏲ 11-midnight; 12-11.30 Sun ☎ (01995) 670203

Black Sheep Best Bitter; Everards Tiger; 4 changing beers Ⓗ

Historic coaching inn in the heart of the village, family-friendly and welcoming, with flagged floors and an unspoilt atmosphere. A real local, it has a games room with pool, darts and the usual pub games, and three quieter rooms for conversation, drinking and dining. Locally sourced home-cooked food is good quality and excellent value. Interesting guest ales come from breweries on the SIBA list. There is free public parking in front of the pub. Q🐴❀◐◑♿♣P🚌(42,76,80)🐾📶

Great Harwood

Victoria ★ 𝕃

St Johns Street, BB6 7EP

⏲ 3.30 (12 Fri & Sat)-midnight; 12-10.30 Sun

☎ (01254) 885210

Bowland Gold; 7 changing beers Ⓗ

An excellent community pub, this stunning early-Edwardian, multi-roomed establishment features extensive period tiling, wood panels and etched windows. The central horseshoe bar serves the main bar area. A comfortable lounge, small snug and good-sized pool and darts rooms lead off from a tiled corridor. Northern beers feature regularly including Hopstar, Goose Eye, Ossett and Salamander. The pub hosts an annual beer festival in autumn and offers cask cider in summer. Q❀♣🚌(6,7)🐾

Haskayne

Ship Inn

6 Rosemary Lane, L39 7JP (just off A5147 at King's Arms)

⏲ 12-11 ☎ (01704) 840077 🌐 Theshipinnhaskayne.co.uk

Lees Manchester Pale Ale, Bitter; 1 changing beer (often Lees) Ⓗ

In a rural location on the Leeds and Liverpool Canal just off the A5147, the Ship Inn has fantastic views, and boasts a large garden with a children's play area and a patio. It also has its own moorings on the canal for use by patrons. The pub was one of the first on the canal, dating back to the 1750s, and retains many original features, such as an old cooking range, inside. Q🐴❀◐◑♿P🚌🐾📶

Haslingden

Griffin Inn 𝕃

86 Hud Rake, BB4 5AF

⏲ 2-midnight; 12-2am Fri & Sat; 12-midnight Sun

☎ (01706) 214021

Rossendale Hameldon Bitter, Glen Top Bitter, Ale, Halo Pale, Pitch Porter, Sunshine; 1 changing beer Ⓗ

The Griffin, Rossendale CAMRA Pub of the Year 2015, is a jewel in the crown of east Lancashire, a thriving community venue and a drinking and social experience not to be missed. Rossendale Brewery, based at the pub premises, operates an eight-barrel plant with a maximum of seven beers in production at any given time. All the beers are excellent. The pub hosts regular events catering for different interests, including Spanish conversation, a curry night and live music.
Q♿♣🍎🚌(464,X41)🐾📶

Heapey

Top Lock

Copthurst Lane, PR6 8LT (by Leeds and Liverpool Canal at Johnson's Hillock)

⏲ 11-11; 11-10.30 Sun ☎ (01257) 263376

9 changing beers (sourced nationally) Ⓗ

Popular canalside pub with a large single room, at the top of the Johnson's Hillock locks. Nine real ales are served including a mild and a stout or porter, mainly from micros but always including beers from Coniston and Timothy Taylor. Up to three ciders are on gravity. Curry night is Tuesday, fish and chips on Wednesday, Monday is quiz night, with live music most Thursdays. An annual beer festival is held in October with up to 100 real ales. Q🐴❀◐◑🍎P📺🚌(24)

Helmshore

Robin Hood Inn 𝕃

280 Holcombe Road, BB4 4NP

⏲ 4-11; 12-11 Fri-Sun ☎ (01706) 213180

Hydes Original Bitter; 3 changing beers Ⓗ

The Robin Hood is a small stone-built, traditional country pub with flagged floors throughout. The façade still has four of the original etched windows from Glentop Brewery. Although the interior has been opened up, it still has the feel of three small separate rooms, warmed by two coal fires in the winter months. Steps to the side of the building lead to a small terraced garden and smoking area overlooking the Helmshore Textile Museum. Quiz night is Thursday. Q (11)

Higham

Four Alls Inn

Higham Hall Road, BB12 9EZ

12-2.30 (not Mon), 5-11; 12-11 Sat & Sun

(01282) 778063 fourallsinn.co.uk

Copper Dragon Golden Pippin; Moorhouse's Pride of Pendle; 2 changing beers H

Popular village pub dating from 1792 with three distinct areas – a bar, taproom and dining room. The taproom has a pool table, jukebox and large-screen TV. The pub sign shows a clergyman (I pray for all), king (I govern for all), soldier (I fight for all) and worker (I pay for all). The Foursmen Society meets monthly; the pub also claims to be the HQ of the Balloon Juice Co of Higham.

P (65)

Hoghton

Boar's Head

Blackburn Old Road, PR5 0RX (on A675 just N of Hoghton Tower)

12-11; 12-10.30 Sun (01254) 852272

boarsheadhoghton.co.uk

Cross Bay Sunset Blonde Bitter; Jennings Bitter; 2 changing beers (sourced locally) H

Recently refurbished 16th-century stone-built pub. The smart bar area has a slate floor while the dining area is carpeted and on split levels. The emphasis is on food, but drinkers are welcome in the bar area and in the adjoining lounge. An extensive food menu is offered, from sandwiches to full meals. The two changing guest beers tend to come from smaller breweries. P (152)

Lancaster

Bobbin

8 Chapel Street, LA1 1HH

11-midnight (1am Thu-Sat) (01524) 32606

thebobbinlancaster.co.uk

Coniston Bluebird Bitter; York Guzzler; 4 changing beers H

Large, part 18th-century, mainly Victorian pub, entirely open plan but still divided by raised areas and pillars, with a vaguely Edwardian decor. It is handy for the bus station, and frequented by a goth/metal crowd (but they are by no means the only customers). Musically, it has an extremely eclectic jukebox, open mic night on Mondays, and live music Thursdays and some Fridays. There is a quiz on Sundays.

Borough

3 Dalton Square, LA1 1PP (near town hall)

12-11.30 (12.30am Fri); 11-12.30am Sat; 11-11.30 Sun

(01524) 64170 theboroughlancaster.co.uk

Borough Pale, Bitter, Wintertime Dark; 4 changing beers H

An upmarket town house built in 1824 but with a Victorian frontage, this pub succeeds in appealing both to food lovers and ale aficionados. The front area resembles a gentlemen's club, with deep-buttoned chairs and chandeliers, the back room is a restaurant and the bar is in a passage between them. Outside is a sheltered patio with a covered smoking area, and there is a brewery in the cellar. A comedy club takes place on Sunday evenings. Wintertime Dark is replaced by Summertime Dark in the summer.

Merchant's

27 Castle Hill, LA1 1YN

11.30-11 (12.30am Fri); 11-12.30am Sat (01524) 66466

merchants1688.co.uk

8 changing beers H

Converted wine merchant's cellars built in 1688 with an extensive outdoor drinking space. Inside, the main drinking areas are in three separate tunnels, with a fourth forming the entrance and bar area. One tunnel is now a restaurant, another is used for functions as required. Quiz night is Sunday. Look for the stoneware bottles used in the construction of the cellar walls. The house beer, Castle Blonde, is brewed by Old School. Many board games are available. Live music features every Saturday evening.

Sun

63 Church Street, LA1 1ET

11-midnight; 11.30-1am Fri; 11-1am Sat; 11-11.30 Sun

(01524) 66006 thesunhotelandbar.co.uk

Lancaster Amber, Blonde, Black, Red; Thwaites Wainwright; 4 changing beers H

The decor combines a mixture of exposed stonework, wood-panelling and solid furniture, with ambient candlelight in the evenings. The original pub has open space for vertical drinking, the extension is mostly furnished with old dining tables. Some original features remain, including stone fireplaces (one with a wood-burning stove) and a well. The pub is the primary outlet for Lancaster Brewery in the city. Outside is a peaceful courtyard. Breakfast is available from 7.30am (later at weekends).

Tap House

2 Gage Street, LA1 1UH

12-midnight (1am Fri & Sat); 12-11 Sun

(01524) 842232 taphouselancaster.co.uk

Hawkshead Windermere Pale; 3 changing beers H

The Tap House describes itself as a world beer shrine, but sells plenty of British beer alongside the imports. It is a small, 19th-century, street-corner pub completely refurbished in 2012 with some bare brickwork, a lot of visible wood (including old beer casks incorporated into the furnishings) and a white and grey decor. It has a small beer library, monthly beer events and a quiz on Mondays.

Three Mariners

Bridge Lane, LA1 1EE (near Parksafe car park entrance)

11-midnight (1am Fri & Sat) (01524) 388957

thethreemarinerslancaster.co.uk

Everards Beacon Bitter; Hawkshead Windermere Pale; York Guzzler; 3 changing beers H

Commonly claimed to be the oldest pub in Lancaster, the Three Mariners certainly looks old, inside as well as out, but it has suffered some rebuilding and had a comprehensive revamp in 2004. The cellar is excavated at first-floor level. The pub is now a popular watering hole with a thriving local clientele, but with limited parking. Home-cooked, reasonably priced food is served. Live music includes blue-grass Wednesday and folk on the first Friday of the month. Beacon is sold as Mariner's Gold. Q

White Cross

Quarry Road, LA1 4XT (behind town hall, on canal towpath)
11.30-11 (12.30am Fri & Sat); 12-11 Sun (01524) 33999
thewhitecross.co.uk
Copper Dragon Golden Pippin; Sharp's Doom Bar; Theakston Old Peculier; Timothy Taylor Landlord; 13 changing beers
A modern 1988 renovation of an old canalside warehouse with an open-plan interior and a light airy feel. French windows open onto extensive canalside seating. There is a Tuesday quiz and an annual Beer & Pie Festival in April. The pub stands in the corner of an extensive complex of Victorian textile mills, now converted to other uses. It has the appearance of a circuit pub, but much of the custom comes from either the residential area up the hill or from nearby workplaces including the adult college. P

Yorkshire House

2 Parliament Street, LA1 1DB (opp Greyhound bridge)
7-midnight (1am Thu & Fri); 2-1am Sat; 7-11.30 Sun
(01524) 64679 theyorkshirehouse.co.uk
Coniston Bluebird Bitter; Everards Tiger; 2 changing beers
A former 18th-century coaching inn, now one of Lancaster's music venues, with a great jukebox and bands playing Fridays, Saturdays and some Sundays in the big room upstairs. The mix of ages, friendly service and intimate drinking spaces, including a cosy corner with a wood-burning stove, help to explain this pub's appeal. One handpump dispenses Westons perry and cider on rotation. A quiz is held on the first Sunday of the month. The sheltered courtyard garden is recommended throughout the year.

Lancaster University

Graduate College Bar

Bailrigg, LA2 0PF (on pedestrian square in Alexandra Park; graduate college is signposted)
7 (5 Fri)-11; 5-11.30 Sat; 8-11 Sun (01524) 592824
4 changing beers
The graduate college bar is much pubbier and attracts a higher age range than the usual student watering hole. The choice of beer is good, with eight handpumps, and it hosts a beer fest in June. Curry night is Friday, while open mic night alternates with live bands on Thursday. The university bars all have alternative names – this one for some reason is Herdwick. Reduced hours in vacations. (3,4)

Laneshaw Bridge

Emmott Arms

Keighley Road, BB8 7HX
11.45-10 (midnight Thu-Sat) (01282) 864889
the-emmott-arms.co.uk
Lancaster Blonde; Tetley Bitter; 2 changing beers
A traditional cosy country pub set in the heart of the village, with wooden floorboards, real log fires and a beer garden. The main room is for dining and has an open fire. There is an area for drinkers near the central bar and a separate, quiet front room. Easily accessible by bus from Keighley or Colne.
Q P (25)

Lathom

Ring o' Bells

Ring o' Bells Lane, L40 5TF (about 500yds from A5209 on road between Burscough and Parbold)
11-11 (midnight Fri); 10-11 Sun (01704) 893157
Thwaites Original, Wainwright; 3 changing beers (often Dunscar Bridge, George Wright, Thwaites)
Impressive country pub in large rural grounds along the Leeds and Liverpool Canal about a 20-minute walk from Burscough village. Reopened in 2011 by a local pubco, the huge split-level interior boasts stone and wood floors with separate locals' and family areas. Six handpumps dispense beers from Thwaites and other local breweries and two serve rotating ciders from Gwynt y Ddraig. The food is well priced and beef is locally sourced. An upstairs private room is available, plus canal moorings.
Q P (3A,337)

Leyland

Leyland Lion

60 Hough Lane, PR25 2SA
8am-11.30 (12.30am Fri & Sat) (01772) 643990
Adnams Broadside; Ruddles Best Bitter; house beer (by Moorhouse's); 8 changing beers
Opened in 2011, this conversion of a town-centre post office is smaller than most Wetherspoon establishments. A central log fire is also unusual for this operator. The pub's name commemorates one of the buses that made this town famous, and which were built a few yards up the road – it is handy for the Commercial Vehicle Museum. Nine guest beers are usually on tap, often coming from local breweries, plus a real cider. The house beer, Leyland Lion, is brewed by Moorhouse's.
(109,111,113)

Market Ale House

33 Hough Lane, PR25 2SB
closed Mon; 2-10; 12-11 Sat; 2-8 Sun (01772) 623363
6 changing beers (sourced locally)
Leyland's smallest pub opened in 2013 in former shop premises. It is the area's first micropub and is at the entrance to the former Leyland Motors North Works, which now serves as the town's market hall. Six changing beers come predominantly from local breweries. Changing ciders, wine and a few spirits are also served. Food is limited to Lancashire cheeses and pork pies. In summer tables are put out on the wide pavement to create an alfresco drinking area. Q (109,111,113)

Withy Arms

3 Worden Lane, PR25 3EL (opp Fox & Lion near Tesco)
12-11 (01772) 301969 withyarms.com/leyland
House beer (by Thwaites); 5 changing beers
Previously known as the Roebuck, this hostelry reopened in 2013 as the Withy Arms. Closely modelled on its sister pub in Bamber Bridge, it is an attractive open-plan venue with a wine-bar feel. The five changing guest beers often come from local breweries. There is a surprisingly large beer garden at the rear with open and covered areas, which hosts three annual beer festivals.
(109,111,113)

Little Eccleston

Cartford Inn

Cartford Lane, PR3 0YP

⏲ 12-2 (not Mon), 5.30-9 (10 Fri & Sat); 12.30-8.30 Sun
☎ (01995) 670166 🌐 thecartfordinn.co.uk
Hawkshead Lakeland Gold; Moorhouse's Pride of Pendle; Theakston Old Peculier; house beer (by Bowland) Ⓗ
Originally a 17th-century coaching inn, the pub is set in an idyllic location at the heart of rural Lancashire but less than a 10-minute drive from the M55. A multi award-winning pub, restaurant and boutique hotel, the bar alcoves allow for informal dining while the River Lounge boasts panoramic riverscape views. A range of four cask beers is available, usually including a dark beer, along with a variety of draught continental lagers, bottled beers and ciders. ❀♿P🐾

Longridge

Corporation Arms
Lower Road, PR3 2YJ (nr B5243/B6245 jct)
⏲ 11-midnight (1am Fri & Sat); 12-10.30 Sun
☎ (01772) 782644 🌐 corporationarms.com
4 changing beers Ⓗ
A substantial 18th-century stone-built inn close to the Longridge Reservoirs on the road to Ribchester, handy for local walks. This free house has a reputation for excellent ale, food, service and accommodation. Four handpumps serve beers from local breweries, with Bowland, Copper Dragon and Moorhouse's among the favourites. Real cider is usually available during the summer months. There is an annual beer festival on the spring bank holiday weekend. Q❀♿▲P🚌(5,35)

Towneley Arms
41 Berry Lane, PR3 3JP
⏲ 11-11 (1am Fri & Sat); 12-11 Sun ☎ (01772) 782219
🌐 towneleyarms.co.uk
4 changing beers (sourced nationally) Ⓗ
Large, fully refurbished pub on the main street. Food is served all day from a seasonally changing menu, while the pub has a good reputation for real ale, with four handpumps offering a variety of up to 16 different ales each week. There is a quiz night on Wednesdays and live music and entertainment at weekends. The Towneley has a friendly feel about it and welcomes families and dogs.
❀♿♣P🚌🐾

Longton

Dolphin Ⓛ
Marsh Lane, PR4 5JY
⏲ 12-11 ☎ (01772) 612032
4 changing beers (sourced locally) Ⓗ
Isolated country pub at the end of a lane on Longton Marsh. The handpumps are in the wood-floored public bar, and there is a comfortable lounge and a restaurant in the rear conservatory. A large and varied menu covers everything from sandwiches to man-versus-food challenges. Up to four real ales are on offer from a varying selection, with an emphasis on local micros, often including a mild or dark beer. A cider is also stocked. Evening closing is flexible dependent on trade.
❀♿P🐾

Lostock Hall

Anchor
Croston Road, PR5 5LA (300yds from B5254 alongside Preston-Blackburn railway line)
⏲ 4.30-11.30 (midnight Fri); 12-midnight Sat; 1-11.30 Sun
☎ (01772) 335637 🌐 theanchorinnlostockhall.co.uk
5 changing beers (sourced nationally) Ⓗ
Just a short distance from the Tardy Gate shopping area, this friendly community pub offers five changing cask ales from the Heineken Discover Cask range, with LocAle beers often available. In May and September it holds a beer festival in marquees on a large grassy area next to the pub. A traditional roast is served on Sundays only, 3-5pm.
Q❀♿≹♣P🚌(111,113)

Lytham

County Hotel Ⓛ
1 Church Road, FY8 5LH
⏲ 11-11 (midnight Fri & Sat); 12-11 Sun ☎ (01253) 795128
🌐 thecountylytham.co.uk
Moorhouse's Pendle Witches Brew; 4 changing beers Ⓗ
Located close to the edge of town, this listed pub, with its inviting atmosphere, is ideal for families, especially at weekends, and is well supported by locals and visitors alike. With its cool feel and superb dining facility, you can watch your 100 per cent fresh dough pizza being prepared in front of you in the open kitchen. Some drinkers just come to sample the wide choice of real ales from local and regional brewers. Comfortable en-suite rooms are available for those staying over.
Q❀♿≹P🚌(7,11,68)

Railway Hotel
Station Road, FY8 5DH (next to fire station on B5259)
⏲ 8am-midnight ☎ (01253) 797250
Fuller's London Pride; Ruddles Best Bitter; house beer (by Moorhouse's); 5 changing beers Ⓗ
When Wetherspoon acquired this pub they revived its original Victorian name. It has a bright, new-look interior on different levels, with four distinct themed areas featuring golf, railways and old photos of Lytham's halcyon days as a tourist resort. There is a small beer garden at the front with a separate smoking area, and another small drinking area at the side. The C&S Ale harks back to a long-defunct local brewery. Limited parking is at rear.
Q❀♿≹P🚌(7,11,68)

Taps 🏆 Ⓛ
12 Henry Street, FY8 5LE
⏲ 11-11 (midnight Fri & Sat) ☎ (01253) 736226
🌐 thetaps.net
Greene King IPA; Morland Old Speckled Hen; 8 changing beers Ⓗ
Traditional wooden-floored, bare-walled pub, refurbished in summer 2015, with an enthusiastic national following. Ten beers, always including a dark mild, with guests from independent brewers, alongside two ciders, are served by a friendly and knowledgeable staff. The venue hosts darts and dominoes teams and supports the local lifeboat. Home-cooked food is served lunchtimes, and there are always locally sourced pies. It has a heated outside seating area and a real fire in winter. It was voted CAMRA branch Pub of the Year 2015 among many other awards. Q❀♿≹♣🚌(7,11,68)

Morecambe

Eric Bartholomew
10 Euston Road, LA4 5DD
⏲ 8am-11 (midnight Fri & Sat) ☎ (01524) 405860

Greene King Abbot; Ruddles Best Bitter; 4 changing beers 🄷
Opened in April 2004, this Wetherspoon pub is dedicated to Eric Morecambe (born Eric Bartholomew). Near the seafront, it functions on two levels, with an upstairs lounge and dining area. The long bar services an open-plan room with pictures of 19th-century Morecambe and artwork with a Morecambe and Wise theme. There is some outside seating at the front for smokers but no drinking is allowed. Close to shops and a public car park. Q◑◐♿⇌🍏🚌ᯤ

Royal 🄻

257 Marine Road Central, LA4 4BJ
✪ 12-11 ☎ (01524) 416668
🌐 theroyalbarhotelmorecambe.co.uk
3 changing beers 🄷
The Royal, built around 1850, is a survivor from Edwardian Morecambe, though far from intact. Although renovated and refurbished in 2012, the remaining original features were treated with respect. A single bar room, stretching from the handsome bay window that overlooks the bay and Eric Morecambe statue to the back windows, is complemented by an upstairs room variously used for dining or functions. Steak night is Thursday, and there is live music Thursday (acoustic) to Sunday. The house beer is from an unknown source.
❀🛏◑◐⇌🚌(4,6)ᯤ

York

87 Lancaster Road, LA4 5QH (where B5321 crosses railway)
✪ 12-midnight ☎ (01524) 425353
Everards Beacon Bitter; 2 changing beers 🄷
Large Victorian community pub on the edge of the town centre with several rooms and some original plasterwork ceilings. It is the headquarters of Morecambe Royal British Legion. On Morecambe FC match days away fans relax with the locals in this football-friendly pub – check out the display of football scarves in the back room. A large function room (with catering if required) and a recently opened patio complete the picture. A quiz takes place on Thursdays. All ales are £2 a pint on Tuesdays, Everards Beacon is sold as York Bitter.
❀🛏◑◐♣P🚌ᯤ

Nelson

Shooters Arms

Southfield Lane, BB10 3RJ
✪ 3 (12 Thu)-midnight; 12-1am Fri & Sat; 12-midnight Sun
☎ (01282) 614153
4 changing beers 🄷
In a picturesque spot between Burnley and Nelson, this cosy little pub, parts of which date back to 1660, has had something of a facelift in the last two years. As a Thwaites house all four handpulls serve the brewery's beers, including a rotating seasonal ale. Sky Sports is shown on a large screen, and live entertainment features regularly. Pool and darts facilities are available. ❀◑◐P🚌(6)🐾

Nether Kellet

Limeburners Arms

32 Main Road, LA6 1EP
✪ closed Mon; 7.45-11 Tue-Sat; 4-11 Sun ☎ (01524) 732916
1 changing beer 🄷
The building here dates from the early 19th century. Once, within living memory, most country pubs were like this – no food, no jukebox, plain and simply furnished. Minor improvements have not changed the character of the place. Unsurprisingly, most of the customers are locals – the landlord himself is a local farmer whose family have run the pub for 80 years. The old photographs in the bar are a rewarding study. Opens 2pm in summer.
Q❀⛺♣P🚌(51)🐾

Ormskirk

Court Leet

4 Wheatsheaf Walk, L39 2XA
✪ 8am-12.30am (1am Thu-Sat) ☎ (01695) 579803
Greene King 1799; Ruddles Best Bitter; 10 changing beers (often Cross Bay, Moorhouse's, Weetwood) 🄷
Opened in 2014, this Wetherspoon pub is in the centre of Ormskirk in a small courtyard area off Burscough Street. It has a large open-plan main bar area fitted out in a contemporary style. Virtually the entire upper floor is taken up by a fully exposed terrace which includes a no-smoking section. It is thought the pub occupies the site where the court leet met, which was responsible for running the town's affairs until 1876. A lift is available.
☕❀◑◐♿⇌🍏🚌ᯤ

Cricketers 🏆 🄻

24 Chapel Street, L39 4QF
✪ 12-midnight; 12-11 Sun ☎ (01695) 571123
🌐 thecricketers-ormskirk.co.uk
Thwaites Nutty Black, Wainwright; 3 changing beers (often George Wright, Old School, Prospect) 🄷
Offering an extensive range of real ales from a selection of local breweries, the refurbished Cricketers provides a warm and cosy bar area and a stunning beer garden. It is close to Ormskirk Cricket Club and the walls are adorned with memorabilia including team photos from the local club that date back to the early 1900s. Quality home-cooked food, from pub classics to chef's specials, using ingredients from local suppliers, is served daily, with exclusive food and drink offers Monday-Saturday 12-6pm. ◑◐♿⇌🚌(375,385)

Hop Inn Bier Shoppe 🄻

12 Burscough Street, L39 2ER
✪ 11-11 ☎ (01695) 575907
House beer (by Burscough); 3 changing beers (often Burscough, First Chop Brewing Arm, George Wright) 🄷
A former shop that has been custom-converted into a plush Belgian-style single-room bar. It features an extensive range of foreign bottled beers (Lambic, Trappist, fruit beers) which can be perused on beautiful menus or in tasteful wall-mounted cabinets. The bar serves authentic foreign lagers and four real ales, including beers from nearby Burscough Brewery. A Bavarian night, a quiz during the week and live music at weekends make this a popular venue. No TV or games.
Q⇌🍏🗑🚌ᯤ

Orrell

Delph Tavern

Tontine Road, WN5 8UJ (just under ½ mile from station)
✪ 11.30-midnight (12.30am Fri & Sat); 12-11.30 Sun
☎ (01695) 622239
4 changing beers 🄷

A real community pub frequented by a mixed clientele and occasional visitors taking advantage of the varied tasty pub grub on offer, served in a pleasant separate dining area. Evening events cover a broad range of activities including pool, darts, TV sport on several large screens, quizzes and live music. The pub offers a wide range of local ales and the bar area can get quite busy. There is a small outside seating area. ⚲✿❶&≢♣P☂

Padiham

Hare & Hounds Ⓛ
58 West Street, BB12 8JD
✪ 4-11; 12-midnight Sat; 12-10.30 Sun ☎ (01282) 545308
6 changing beers Ⓗ
An award-winning true free house rescued from pub company mismanagement, now thriving and selling an excellent choice of beers alongside a changing real cider. Two rooms front the large bar, with a large separate room to one side where beer festivals are held. There are real fires in the main lounge and side room. A large beer garden to the rear and a small seating area to the front complete this great pub. ⚲✿&♣●P🖳(27,152)🐾

Parbold

Wayfarer Inn Ⓛ
1-3 Alder Lane, WN8 7NL
✪ 12-midnight (1.30am Fri & Sat) ☎ (01257) 464600
⊕ wayfarerparbold.co.uk
Problem Child Rapscallion, Good Spankin'; 4 changing beers Ⓗ
At least two of the Problem Child beers, brewed on site, are always available, plus a range of local ales and a real cider. Popular for food, diners can choose from the bar, restaurant and Italian menus served in the pub and restaurant areas. Built in the 1700s but with a modern extension, there are low beamed ceilings with cosy nooks and crannies. The pub is popular in the summer, with outside seating, and close to the Leeds and Liverpool Canal and Parbold Hill with its panoramic views.
Q⚲✿❶&≢●P🖳🐾☂

Windmill Hotel Ⓛ
3 Mill Lane, WN8 7NW
✪ 12-11 (11.30 Fri & Sat); 12-10.30 Sun ☎ (01257) 462935
⊕ thewindmillatparbold.co.uk
Southport Golden Sands; 5 changing beers (sourced nationally) Ⓗ
A former grain store to the adjacent Windmill, parts of the building date back to 1794. Clean lines in the interior design complement period furniture in keeping with the building's history. Two open fires provide a warm welcome for drinkers, diners, bargees and walkers. The bar serves mainly beers from Prospect and George Wright breweries. A separate snug to the right of the doorway features delightful carved animals in the wooden panels. Unfortunately this pub has no disabled access.
Q⚲✿≢●P🖳

Pendleton

Swan with Two Necks Ⓛ
Main Street, BB7 1PT
✪ 12-2.30 (not Mon), 6-11; 12-11 Sat & Sun
☎ (01200) 423112 ⊕ swanwithtwonecks.co.uk
4 changing beers Ⓗ

An outstanding community pub in the centre of Pendleton run by two CAMRA members. The many awards they have won include the prestigious CAMRA National Pub of the Year 2014. Four handpulls serve a varying selection of guest beers. Mild and strong ales are often available and a real cider is also on handpull. The home-cooked food is excellent and there are monthly themed food evenings. Darts and dominoes dominate on Monday evenings. Q✿❶♣●P

Penwortham

Black Bull Inn
83 Pope Lane, PR1 9BA
✪ 11-11 (midnight Fri; 11.30 Sat); 12-11 Sun
☎ (01772) 752953 ⊕ blackbull-penwortham.co.uk
Greene King IPA; Theakston Lightfoot; 3 changing beers (sourced nationally) Ⓗ
Attractive cottage-style inn, dating back to the early-1800s, which has managed to retain a village-pub atmosphere despite its location in a well-populated area. On entering, a narrow passageway leads through to a central bar serving a number of drinking areas including a separate public bar. A friendly community pub, it hosts many social events including a popular Thursday quiz, and local charities are actively supported. Three guest beers are usually available. Sky and BT Sport are screened. Q✿♣P🖳(3,3A)🐾☂

Fleece Ⓛ
39 Liverpool Road, PR1 9XD
✪ 11.30-11 (midnight Thu & Sat; 12.30am Fri)
☎ (01772) 745561 ⊕ fleecepenwortham.co.uk
Tetley Bitter; house beer (by Hart); 3 changing beers (sourced nationally) Ⓗ
The Fleece is located next to Penwortham's most distinctive feature, the old water tower. This is a pub which from the front presents a cosy village-inn appearance, but which has been extensively modernised. The interior has been arranged to include a number of separate drinking and dining areas, while outside there is a large beer garden for use in the summer months. Food includes a good range of pub classics and a traditional roast on Sundays. The house ale, Fleeced, is a 3.9% ABV beer produced by Hart Brewery.
⚲✿❶&♣P🖳(2,3)

Poulton le Fylde

Old Town Hall
5 Church Street, FY6 7AP
✪ 11-11.30 (12.30am Fri & Sat); 12-11 Sun
☎ (01253) 892257
5 changing beers (often Cross Bay, Moorhouse's, Saltaire) Ⓗ
Originally a pub called the Bay Horse, the building was later used as the town hall and council offices. A changing range of five cask beers, mainly from Lancashire and Yorkshire brewers, is served. Several TVs show live sport, and the rear of the pub is decorated with football memorabilia. Live bands play every Saturday and some Fridays. A wine bar on the first floor is open on Fridays and Saturdays. &≢🖳🐾☂

Poulton Elk
22 Hardhorn Road, FY6 7SR
✪ 8am-midnight (1am Fri & Sat) ☎ (01253) 895265

Greene King Abbot; Ruddles Best Bitter; 8 changing beers
This pub, officially Wetherspoon's 900th outlet, has rapidly gained a reputation for the quality of its ales. Although mostly one large room, it has been split into several distinct smaller areas to give a cosier feeling. French doors open onto a popular terrace at the front of the pub. Its name relates to the finding of an approximately 13,500-year-old elk skeleton nearby – a spearpoint found with it provides the earliest evidence of people in north-west England.

Thatched House

30 Ball Street, FY6 7BG
11.30-11 (11.30 Thu); 11-midnight Fri & Sat; 12-11 Sun
☎ (01253) 891063 thatchedhousepoulton.co.uk
Chapel Street Brewhouse Blonde, Brewhouse Gold; Tetley Bitter; 6 changing beers
This 1910 mock-Tudor venue in the corner of the Norman churchyard in Poulton town centre replaced a much older, smaller pub that did have a thatched roof. Three or four beers from the range produced in the microbrewery in the former stable area are usually on the bar. Many pictures of sporting heroes and historic Poulton decorate wood-panelled walls. There are two wood-burning fires and one log fire. Regular beer festivals are held every season. Q P (2,2A)

Preston

Ale Emporium

53 Fylde Road, PR1 2XQ
12-11.30 (11 Mon; 12.30am Fri & Sat) ☎ (01772) 378290
8 changing beers (sourced regionally)
A free house serving eight guest beers from microbreweries. It has a comfortable single-room bar set back from Fylde Road at the side of the unrelated Ferret pub, and there is a pool table in the area behind the bar. Live music plays on Thursday and Saturday evenings, and an upstairs room is available for hire. An annual beer festival is staged in September and occasional Meet the Brewer nights are held. CAMRA branch Pub of the Year 2015.

Anderton Arms

Longsands Lane, Fulwood, PR2 9PS
11.30-11 (11.30 Wed & Thu; midnight Fri & Sat)
☎ (01772) 700104
Moorhouse's Pendle Witches Brew; Thwaites Wainwright; 3 changing beers
Welcoming, warm and friendly pub at the heart of the local community. Up to five real ales are selected from over 90 breweries from a seasonal cask menu that changes quarterly. Meals are served all day, and children are welcome if dining up to 8pm. All cask ales are at £2.49 a pint on Mondays, and bottles of wine are sold at a discount on Sundays from 5pm. There is a quiz night on Wednesday. P

Black Horse ★

166 Friargate, PR1 2EJ
10.30-11 (midnight Fri & Sat); 12-10.30 Sun
☎ (01772) 204855
Robinsons Dizzy Blonde, Cumbria Way, Unicorn, Trooper; 4 changing beers (sourced nationally)
Classic Grade II-listed pub in the main shopping area close to the historic open market. With its tiled bar and walls, and mosaic floor, it has a nationally important historic pub interior. The two front rooms, with log fires, are adorned with photos of old Preston. The famous hall of mirrors seating area is to the rear, and memorabilia of a previous landlord is displayed. Up to five Robinsons ales are on offer, with guest beers coming from various smaller breweries.

Continental

South Meadow Lane, PR1 8JP
12-11.15 (12.15am Fri & Sat) ☎ (01772) 499425
newcontinental.net
7 changing beers (sourced nationally)
Beside the River Ribble, the main railway line and Miller Park, the pub has a main bar area plus lounge with a real fire in winter, and a conservatory overlooking the garden. Live music and theatre regularly feature in a separate arts/events space that is also used for beer festivals. Seven microbrewery beers are on tap, including the house ale from Marble and a dark beer. Freshly cooked meals are served daily (no food Mon). A two-times winner of local CAMRA Pub of the Year. Q P (3A)

Grey Friar

144 Friargate, PR1 2EJ
8am-midnight (1am Fri & Sat) ☎ (01772) 558542
Exmoor Gold; Fuller's London Pride; Greene King Abbot; Ruddles Best Bitter; Theakston Old Peculier; 8 changing beers (sourced nationally)
Modern open-plan Wetherspoon establishment with raised areas to the side and rear. Preston's students and citizens, both young and old, appreciate the range of ales and food at good prices. The social mix creates a bustling atmosphere and the bar can get extremely busy at weekends. The pub plays an active role in local CAMRA recruiting. The guest beers vary in both style and strength, but frequently tend towards the stronger end of the scale. Alcohol is served from 9am daily.

Moorbrook

370 North Road, PR1 1RU
12-midnight ☎ (01772) 823302 themoorbrook.com
Thwaites Original; 6 changing beers (sourced nationally)
Now privately owned, this pub is where the West Lancashire CAMRA branch was formed over 40 years ago. It comprises a traditional-style wood-panelled bar with two rooms off, complete with William Morris wallpaper. The beer garden to the right is a suntrap. Up to five guest beers plus a house beer attract ale fans from far and wide. Traditional music plays on the last Wednesday of the month, plus other live acts on Thursdays. Good food includes speciality pies.

Old Black Bull

35 Friargate, PR1 2AT
10.30-11 (midnight Fri & Sat); 12-10.30 Sun
☎ (01772) 823397
10 changing beers (sourced nationally)
Mock-Tudor city-centre pub with a tiled exterior. A small front vault, a main bar with distinctive black and white floor tiles, and two comfortable lounge areas combine to make this a popular venue. There is also a patio to the rear. Live music plays on Saturday evenings and all televised sport is shown. Free of tie for cask beers, the guest ales come mainly from micros or small independent breweries. The two rebadged house beers are by Moorhouse's and Tetley.

Wellington

124 Tulketh Road, Ashton-on-Ribble, PR2 1AR

12-11; 12-12.30am Fri & Sat ☎ (01772) 726641

thewellington-tulketh.co.uk

Copper Dragon Golden Pippin; Jennings Cumberland Ale; 4 changing beers (sourced nationally) Ⓗ

Friendly end-of-terrace pub, both community and family oriented. A single main room in this recently redecorated venue has six handpumps; three white-handled ones serving pale or blonde beers, and three dark-handled ones serving darker ales. A pool and darts room is to the rear. Front entry is by a flight of steps, but there is level access at the side from Waterloo Terrace. Live music features on Friday and Saturday nights, and open mic every other Monday. (68)

Wheatsheaf

50 Water Lane, Ashton-on-Ribble, PR2 2NL

11-11 (11.30 Fri & Sat); 12-10.30 Sun ☎ (01772) 725917

5 changing beers (sourced nationally; often Moorhouse's) Ⓗ

This hostelry is a Victorian local on the way to Preston marina, a mile from the city centre, where beer prices are among the lowest in the area. Five guest beers include at least one from Moorhouse's, and third-pint tasting racks are available. It is big on TV sport, and live music plays Friday and Saturday nights. At least two beer festivals a year are held in a marquee at the rear. There is disabled access through the courtyard. (68,35)

Rawtenstall

Buffer Stops

Bury Road, BB4 6DD

11-9 (11 Fri); 10-11 Sat; 12-9 Sun ☎ (0161) 764 7790

Outstanding Piston Broke; 4 changing beers Ⓗ

Situated on the platform of the East Lancashire Railway, despite the small premises, the bar has a most impressive offer, with five handpumped real ales including a stout or porter. There is also a real cider plus a range of continental bottled beers. On warm summer evenings plenty of outside seating is available. Well patronised by locals and steam enthusiasts, the bar offers entertainment on the last Saturday of every month. Close to the Whitaker museum and dry ski slope. Q P

Craven Heifer

264 Burnley Road, BB4 8LA

4-midnight; 1-11 Sat & Sun ☎ (01706) 214757

Moorhouse's Premier Bitter, Pride of Pendle, Blond Witch Ⓗ

Originally two cottages, this is a stone-built two-roomed pub, part of which is over the Limy Water. There are six handpulls in this Moorhouse's tied house, offering the full range of the brewery's beers and an occasional guest ale. In winter a log-burning fire greets you in the main bar. The Pendle Witches Vintage Velo cycle race is hosted every Easter. Live entertainment features on Friday nights. (X43)

White Lion

72 Burnley Road, BB4 8EW

4.30 (4 Fri)-11; 12-midnight Sat; 1-11 Sun ☎ (01706) 213117

Black Sheep Best Bitter, Golden Sheep; Copper Dragon Golden Pippin; 1 changing beer Ⓗ

Since 1816 there has been a public house on this site. Formerly a row of cottages, it is now a substantial split-level pub. It serves a range of guest beers from microbreweries, including Reedley Hallows, Prospect, Acorn and Salamander. There is a weekly quiz night on Tuesdays and entertainment on Fridays and Saturdays. It also has a pools team. Nearby attractions include the East Lancashire Steam Railway, the museum and the dry ski slope. P (X43)

St Annes

Fifteens at St Annes

42 St Annes Road West, FY8 1RF

11-11 (midnight Fri & Sat); 12-11 Sun ☎ (01253) 725852

fifteensstannes.com

House beer (by Moorhouse's, Eden, Hawkshead); 4 changing beers Ⓗ

Styling itself 'The Best Little Pub in St Annes', the pub welcomes all with eight handpulls, guest beers from regional independent brewers, and a changing cider. There is a DJ Friday and Saturday night, sport on large-screen TVs, and an extensive music collection on the jukebox. By contrast, the vault is a cushioned haven of peace. CAMRA branch Cider Pub of the Year 2015, runner-up Pub of the Year, and St Annes Express Pub of the Year. Great coffee. (7,11,17)

Trawl Boat

36-38 Wood Street, FY8 1QR

8am-midnight (1am Fri & Sat) ☎ (01253) 783080

Greene King Abbot; Ruddles Best Bitter; 8 changing beers Ⓗ

Former solicitors' office, now a Wetherspoon pub, 400 yards from the seafront. With a varied clientele, it is busy at weekends. Dispensing up to eight changing guest beers, its tasteful decor and natural fire create a warm and friendly atmosphere. The designated area for families proves popular. A large outdoor drinking area is attractive in summer. Natural cider/perry comes in polypins. Handy for the shops and the railway station. Q (7,11,17)

Victoria

Church Road, FY8 3NE

12-11 (midnight Fri & Sat) ☎ (01253) 721041

6 changing beers (often Cross Bay, Lytham, Moorhouse's) Ⓗ

A local that has been recently refurbished in an elegant, modern style. It was saved from closure a couple of years ago by community action. There is a TV and a comfortable dining area. Good-quality reasonably priced food is served, however the focus is on real ale. P (11,68)

Salterforth

Anchor Inn

Salterforth Lane, BB18 5TT

12-11; 12-10.30 Sun ☎ (01282) 813186

Jennings Cumberland Ale; Thwaites Wainwright; Wells Bombardier Ⓗ

Popular old inn on the side of the Leeds and Liverpool Canal, with home-cooked food served lunchtimes and evenings plus all day Sunday. It is comfortably furnished, with a separate room to one side of the bar and a pool room through the lounge. The old cellar has stalactites and stalagmites formed by water seeping through the limestone. P (28,29)

Samlesbury

Nabs Head

Nabs Head Lane, PR5 0UQ
⏲ 12-3 (not Mon), 5-11; 12-3, 4.30-midnight Fri; 12-12.30am Sat; 12-11 Sun ☎ (01254) 851416 🌐 thenewnabshead.co.uk
Thwaites Original, Wainwright; 2 changing beers Ⓗ
Isolated two-roomed country pub in a picturesque setting with a central bar serving two distinct drinking areas. The guest beers are from the Daniel Thwaites 1807 Cask Club selection. There is an extensive food menu including lunchtime senior citizens' deals, with food from local suppliers wherever possible. Quiz night is Tuesday and open mic sessions take place monthly in winter. Sports TV is from BT and ESPN. Q🐎◑♣P🐾📶

New Hall Tavern 𝕃

Cuerdale Lane, PR5 0XA (on B6230, near jct 31 of the M6)
⏲ 12-11 (midnight Thu-Sat) ☎ (01772) 877942
Copper Dragon Best Bitter; changing beers Ⓗ
Situated on a crossroads, this pub has a large car park and a heated outdoor smoking area. The interior is divided by wood and glass panels, providing separate areas for dining. Up to six real ales are served, often from local micros. Home-cooked food is from local suppliers where possible. Old photos and prints give an insight into the history of the area, which includes nearby Samlesbury Hall. 🐎❀◑♿♣P🐾📶

Scarisbrick

Heatons Bridge Inn

2 Heatons Bridge Road, L40 8JG (on B5242 road by Leeds and Liverpool Canal)
⏲ 12-midnight ☎ (01704) 840549
Moorhouse's Black Cat; house beer (by Tetley); 1 changing beer (sourced regionally; often Moorhouse's) Ⓗ
Great traditional canalside pub dating from 1837, when it served as offices for the Leeds and Liverpool freight services, with separate areas and serving home-cooked food. Pillbox beer is often served to commemorate WWII – there is a lookout post outside – and military displays and classic bus services feature throughout the year, with themed beers for the occasion. This is a popular pub with families, walkers and cyclists, in an excellent rural setting and with a dining area in the garden. 🐎❀◑♿⛺♣🚌(375)🐾📶

Silverdale

Woodlands

Woodlands Drive, LA5 0RU
⏲ 5-11.30; 12-midnight Sat; 12-11.30 Sun
☎ (01524) 701655
4 changing beers Ⓗ
Large country house from circa 1878 on an elevated site, converted to a pub with only minimal alterations. The bar has a large fireplace and enjoys great views across Morecambe Bay. Beer pumps are in another room with a list of the four available ales on the wall facing the bar. Home-made sandwiches are served at weekends. A quiz is held on the last Sunday of the month and a beer festival with 30 ales in October. To phone the pub, please ring twice. Q🐎❀♣🍎P🚌(1,51)🐾

> **Cask beer sizes**
> Hogshead: 54 gallons
> Barrel: 36 gallons
> Kilderkin: 18 gallons
> Firkin: 9 gallons
> Pin: 4.5 gallons

Slaidburn

Hark to Bounty

Townend, BB7 3EP
⏲ 12-11 ☎ (01200) 446246 🌐 harktobounty.co.uk
Theakston Best Bitter, Old Peculier; 2 changing beers Ⓗ
In the centre of the village, this traditional country inn has nine en-suite bedrooms and is well placed to enjoy the Forest of Bowland Area of Outstanding Natural Beauty. The lounge with oak beams has a real fire and is a comfortable place to enjoy one of the four ales normally on handpump. Meals are served lunchtimes and evenings from a traditional home-cooked menu with a range of daily changing specials. Q🐎❀🛏◑♿⛺P🐾📶

Tockholes

Royal Arms 𝕃

Tockholes Road, Rydal Fold, BB3 0PA
⏲ 4-8 Mon; 12-11 ☎ (01254) 705373
4 changing beers Ⓗ
The Royal Arms is adjacent to Roddlesworth Visitors Centre and is surrounded by moors, woods and reservoirs. The pub is patronised both by local residents and walkers and is within easy walking distance of Darwen Tower. It is owned and run by the Tockholes Treacle Tarts, three local ladies. Isa, who was landlady from 2003 to 2010, returned in November 2013 and now manages the pub together with Ann and Sandra. Q🐎❀◑♣P🐾📶

Walmer Bridge

Walmer Bridge

Liverpool Old Road, PR4 5QE
⏲ 4-midnight; 1-midnight Sat & Sun ☎ (01772) 612296
3 changing beers Ⓗ
Village local comprising two rooms, for either of which you have to go through four doors to reach the bar. In the comfortable lounge photographs of bygone Walmer Bridge and Longton are displayed. The vault is popular with the sporting fraternity, while outside there is a large garden with a children's play area. Bingo is on Monday and quiz night is Thursday. Up to three changing beers are offered from the Punch portfolio, with an emphasis on pale and golden beer. 🐎❀♣P🚌(2,2A)🐾📶

Whalley

Dog Inn 𝕃

55 King Street, BB7 9SB
⏲ 11-11 (midnight Fri & Sat); 12-11 Sun ☎ (01254) 823009
🌐 dog-innwhalley.co.uk
6 changing beers Ⓗ
A much-loved traditional village pub, popular with visitors, walkers and regulars. A long wooden bar with brass handrail forms its heart, where the changing beers are predominantly from local breweries. Hunting and fishing paraphernalia adorn walls and windowsills, and there are various rooms with real fires, a pool room, darts and a small

function room. There are open mic nights, and dogs are welcome. The exterior and the pub sign were restyled recently, but the traditional interior is unchanged. A warm welcome and eccentric conversation is assured! (22,26,280)

Wheatley Lane

Old Sparrowhawk Inn

Wheatley Lane Road, BB12 9QG

12-11 ☎ (01282) 603034 thesparrowhawk.co.uk

Thwaites Original; 5 changing beers H

Up to six cask ales with four rotating regular local guest ales are on handpump here. On the edge of the Pendle Forest, the original building is thought to be a farmstead dating from the 17th century. It has oak-beamed ceilings, flagged floors and floorboards, and is famed for its stained-glass dome ceiling. Upstairs is a function room, and outside large gardens to the front and rear. QP

Winmarleigh

Patten Arms

Park Lane, PR3 0JU (on B5272 3 miles N of Garstang)

4-11; 12-midnight Sat; 12-10 Sun ☎ (01524) 791484

Thwaites Wainwright; 2 changing beers H

Genuine, isolated free house situated away from villages, yet enjoying regular local custom. This 19th-century Grade II-listed building has a single bar with a country-pub feel, high-backed bench seats and open fires. There is a separate restaurant, and terraced seating overlooking a bowling green. P

Worsthorne

Crooked Billet

1-3 Smith Street, BB10 3NQ

7 (6 Thu)-midnight; 4.30-1am Fri; 12-1am Sat; 12-12.30 Sun ☎ 07766 230175 crookedbilletworsthorne.co.uk

Tetley Bitter; Timothy Taylor Boltmaker, Landlord; 4 changing beers H

An award-winning village free house with a beautiful wood and glass horseshoe bar serving both the main lounge area and the snug. Guest beers are mainly from local microbreweries. Quiz nights are popular, as are Thai food nights. This pub is dog-friendly and has a large covered outdoor drinking area. QP (2)

Wrightington

White Lion

117 Mossy Lea Road, WN6 9RE

11-midnight ☎ (01257) 425977

thewhitelionlancs.co.uk

Banks's Bitter; Jennings Cumberland Ale; 6 changing beers H

Extremely popular country pub attracting many locals, with an excellent range of food and beers for diners and drinkers. Eight handpumps are in constant use dispensing two regular and six rotating beers from the Marston's guest range. It has a weekly quiz on Tuesday, a poker league on Thursday, and themed evenings are held in the restaurant. It is family-friendly, with a large garden area, and very community oriented, running the village scarecrow festival, snail racing plus seasonal events and brewery trips. QP (113)

Crooked Billet, Worsthorne

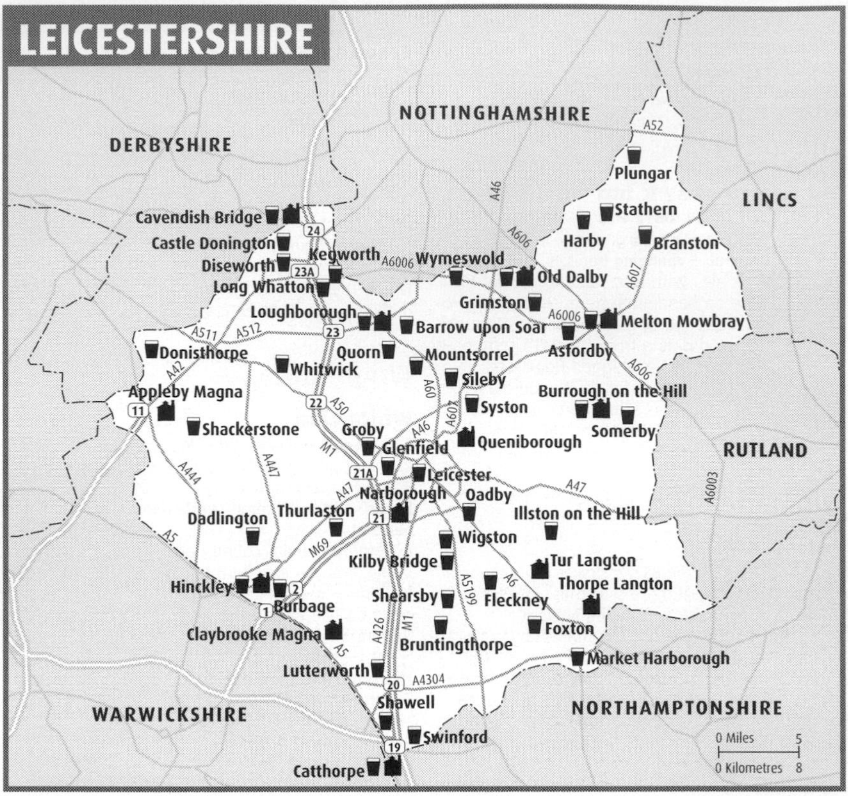

Asfordby

Horse Shoes

128 Main Street, LE14 3SA

12-11.30; 12-4.30, 7-11.45 Sat ☎ (01664) 813392

Batemans XB; 2 changing beers Ⓗ

A single-roomed pub located at the heart of the village, the Horse Shoes compensates for its plain and simple décor with a warm welcome for all. This community inn is home to male and female darts teams and also has a skittle alley. This is the only Batemans' house within the CAMRA branch area with at least two of the brewery's real ales available and usually a seasonal beer. There is a large garden at the rear. ❀♣(5)

Barrow upon Soar

Soar Bridge

29 Bridge Street, LE12 8PN

12 (4 Mon)-11; 12-10.30 Sun ☎ (01509) 412686

Everards Sunchaser Blonde, Tiger, Original; 3 changing beers Ⓗ

Situated next to the bridge that gave it its name, this pub is popular with walkers, boaters and drinkers. The large single-room interior divides into distinct areas, with a separate restaurant, function room and skittle alley. Outside there is a floodlit pétanque court, beer terrace and garden. Well-behaved dogs and children are welcome. Home-made food is available Tuesday to Sunday with a different theme each evening.
Q❀♣P(2,27)

Branston

Wheel

Main Street, NG32 1RU

closed Mon; 11-11; 12-10.30 Sun ☎ (01476) 870376
thewheelinnbranston.co.uk

Batemans XB; 2 changing beers Ⓗ

This attractive stone-built 18th-century pub houses a small bar with some seating and a larger restaurant area, sympathetically renovated. The deceptively large outdoor area is quiet and relaxing in the summer, with traditional outbuildings used to host festivals and regular live music. It boasts an extensive lunch and evening food menu using locally sourced ingredients where possible, including produce from the nearby Belvoir Estate. Cask cider is usually available on the bar. Vale of Belvoir CAMRA Leicestershire Pub of the Year 2012 and 2015. Q❀♣P

Bruntingthorpe

Plough

Main Street, LE17 5QE

4-11; 12-midnight Fri & Sat; 12-11 Sun ☎ (0116) 247 8300

Draught Bass; Greene King Abbot; St Austell Tribute; Theakston Best Bitter; 1 changing beer (sourced regionally) Ⓗ

Traditional village pub with a large public bar to the front and a games room to the rear leading to a pretty cottage garden. The earliest reference to this inn is recorded in the 1841 census but the building is obviously much older. It is thought to have originally been a terrace of cottages and, to this day, retains a cottagey character. Pictures on the walls are of the Vulcan Bomber, which has close associations with nearby Bruntingthorpe Aerodrome. Q❀♿♣P🐾

Burbage

Lime Kilns

Watling Street, LE10 3ED

12-3, 5.30-11; 12-11 Sat; 12-10.30 Sun ☎ (01455) 631158

Jennings Cocker Hoop; Marston's Burton Bitter, Pedigree; 1 changing beer H

Situated alongside the Ashby Canal and the A5, the pub was originally an 18th-century coaching inn. It offers free moorings, a large canalside beer garden and a children's play area. The first floor lounge has canal views and an open fire in winter. The guest beers change regularly and real ciders include Thatchers Traditional, Cheddar Valley and Heritage. Traditional food is served, with special deals including Monday curry night and pie and a pint on Wednesday. Q❀♿♣P

Burrough on the Hill

Grant's Free House

4 Main Street, LE14 2JQ

closed Mon; 12-3, 5-11; 12-11 Sat & Sun ☎ (01664) 452141

Oakham Citra; Parish PSB, Burrough Bitter H**, Baz's Bonce Blower** G**; 1 changing beer** H

Formerly a 16th-century inn known as the Stag & Hounds, Grant's Free House is firmly established as the home of the Parish Brewery which is located in an adjacent outbuilding. New licensees redecorated and refurbished the pub in 2013 and reopened the restaurant to the rear of the building. The bar is on two levels surrounding a central servery on three sides and a function room on the fourth. ❀♣P(113)

Castle Donington

Chequered Flag

32 Borough Street, DE74 2LA

closed Mon; 4-9.30 (10.30 Fri); 12-10.30 Sat; 12-3 Sun ☎ 07780 507926

Shardlow Reverend Eaton; 3 changing beers G

Newly opened micropub in Castle Donington with a motor racing theme. Four gravity real ales are dispensed from a small atmospherically controlled cool room behind the bar. Beers are usually from local microbreweries. Up to three real ciders are also served on gravity. There is no lager here. Stilton-topped award-winning local pork pies and pickles are available to enjoy with your beer. Q🐾

Catthorpe

Cherry Tree

Main Street, LE17 6DB

12-2.30, 5-11 (midnight Fri); 12-12.30am Sat; 12-11.30 Sun ☎ (01788) 860430 cherrytree-pub.co.uk

Jennings Bitter; 3 changing beers (sourced nationally; often Dow Bridge, Jennings, Marston's) H

Welcoming community free house popular with villagers and visitors. The single bar has an open fire at one end, a view of the cellar, and railway memorabilia adorning the walls. The adjoining games room hosts local teams and twice-yearly beer festivals. The excellent menu has an emphasis on local produce. One beer is always from Dow Bridge based in the village. Outside is a sun deck and a small south-facing garden overlooking the River Avon. Q❀♣P🐾

Cavendish Bridge

Old Crown

DE72 2HL (off A6)

11 (3 Mon)-11; 11-midnight Fri & Sat; 11-10.30 Sun ☎ (01332) 792392 oldcrownshardlow.co.uk

Banks's Sunbeam; Marston's EPA, Pedigree, Old Empire; 2 changing beers H

Coaching inn dating from the 17th century with the original oak-beamed ceiling displaying an extensive collection of old jugs. The cosy open-plan interior is divided into two areas with a large inglenook on the right. The walls are covered with pub mirrors, brewery signs and railway memorabilia, which even extend into the toilets. Good-value food includes fish and chips on Friday evening. Quiz night is Monday and live music features on Tuesday. A former local CAMRA branch Pub of the Year. ❀♣P🐾

Dadlington

Dog & Hedgehog

2 The Green, CV13 6JB

12-11 (5 Sun) ☎ (01455) 213151

House beer (by Tunnel) H

This friendly free house continues to build on its reputation for quality ales, as well as serving the best in locally produced food in its fine restaurant. Situated in a picturesque location, the terrace and beer garden overlook the Ashby Canal and site of the famous Battle of Bosworth (1485). The bar boasts three LocAles, all rebadged for the pub – Henry Tudor is Tunnel Nelson's Column, Dadlington Hamlet is Quartz Crystal and Bridge 30 is Elliswood Just One More. Q❀♿P(86)🐾

Diseworth

Plough

33 Hall Gate, DE74 2QJ

11.30-11 (midnight Fri & Sat); 12-10.30 Sun ☎ (01332) 810333 theploughdiseworth.com

Draught Bass; Greene King Abbot; Marston's Pedigree; Sharp's Doom Bar; 1 changing beer H

Situated in a village with many half-timbered buildings, this is a cosy, multi-roomed pub with parts dating back to the 13th century. Low-beamed ceilings and exposed brickwork are just some of the original features discovered during renovation work in the 1990s. There is an interesting display of old photographs of the area. Tasty home-made

REAL ALE BREWERIES

Belvoir Old Dalby
Charnwood Loughborough (NEW)
Dow Bridge Catthorpe
Elliswood Hinckley
Everards Narborough
Gas Dog Melton Mowbray
Golden Duck Appleby Magna
Langton Thorpe Langton
Parish Burrough on the Hill
Pig Pub Claybrooke Magna
Q Queniborough (NEW)
Shardlow Cavendish Bridge
Très Bien Tur Langton (NEW)

food is served. The spacious, well-presented beer garden is popular in summer. A former local CAMRA Village Pub of the Year. Q❀◑♿⛺●P🚌📶

Donisthorpe

Halfway House 🏆

65 Church Street, DE12 7PX

⏲ 12-11 (midnight Fri & Sat) ☎ (01530) 588783

🌐 halfwayhousedonisthorpe.com

Draught Bass; Marston's Pedigree; 3 changing beers H

Traditional dog-friendly village inn in the heart of Donisthorpe. Recently refurbished to a high standard, the it now comprises a public bar, lounge bar and a separate dining room, with beamed ceilings and a wood-burning fire. Home-made food is available Tuesday-Saturday. Three guest beers, one usually from Burton Bridge, can be served in a taster selection of three third-pint glasses. Local CAMRA village Pub of the Year in 2014 and branch winner in 2015. Q❀◑●P🚌🐾📶

Fleckney

Golden Shield L

46 Main Street, LE8 8AN

⏲ 4 (12 Wed & Thu)-11; 12-midnight Fri & Sat; 11.30-11 Sun ☎ (0116) 240 2366

Banks's Bitter; Greene King IPA, Abbot; Timothy Taylor Landlord; 2 changing beers (sourced nationally; often Bradfield, Church End, Theakston) H

Village pub in the heart of Leicestershire serving six real ales, including ever-changing LocAles, microbrewery and regional beers. Home-cooked and à la carte meals are available lunchtimes Wednesday-Sunday and evenings Tuesday-Saturday – Sunday lunches are always popular. A pétanque court is available and BT Sports regularly on TV. The annual beer festival in August is always well supported. ❀◑♣P🚌(44,49B)🐾📶

Foxton

Bridge 61 L

Bottom Lock, LE16 7RA

⏲ 10-11 ☎ (0116) 279 2285 🌐 foxtonboats.co.uk

Adnams Southwold Bitter; house beer (by Langton); 2 changing beers (sourced locally; often Langton) H

The smaller of the two pubs situated at the bottom of the famous flight of 10 Foxton locks, the two-roomed interior comprises a snug with a serving-hatch bar and a larger room with wide doors that open out onto the waterfront. The garden has barbecue facilities – an ideal spot for watching the boats pass by. The two guest beers are from the nearby Langton Brewery. Q❀◑♿P🐾

Glenfield

Forge Inn L

Main Street, LE3 8DG

⏲ 11 (12 Sat)-11; 12-10.30 Sun ☎ (0116) 287 1702

🌐 theforgeinn.co.uk

Everards Tiger, Original; 2 changing beers (sourced nationally) H

A village pub on the edge of Leicester with a friendly, welcoming atmosphere. Modern British food is available in the restaurant and snacks in the bar. Two guest beers are available alongside a changing cider, usually from a local producer. Quiz night is Sunday and a charity music festival is held in May. The pub has launched a 'bring back jugs' campaign which continues to be well received. Q❀◑♿●P🚌(40,94)📶

Grimston

Black Horse

3 Main Street, LE14 3BZ

⏲ 12-3, 6-11; 12-6 Sun ☎ (01664) 812358

🌐 theblackhorsegrimston.co.uk

Adnams Southwold Bitter; Marston's Pedigree; 2 changing beers H

Overlooking the village green, this single-room pub is divided into three sections on two separate levels, warmed by a real fire. It is busy both lunchtimes and evenings, with a reputation for good food and ale. Outside to the rear is a garden with patio heaters and a pétanque court which hosts local teams. Two regular and two guest real ales are usually available. A former local CAMRA branch Pub of the Year. ❀◑♣🚌(23)

Groby

Stamford Arms L

2 Leicester Road, LE6 0DJ

⏲ 10-11 ☎ (0116) 287 5616 🌐 stamfordarms.co.uk

Everards Beacon Bitter, Tiger, Original; house beer (by Everards); 3 changing beers (sourced nationally) H

At the heart of Groby and home of the Everard family until 1921, the main house has become a comfortable drinking area, while an annexe is now a large restaurant. The menu includes pizzas, pasta, tapas and more traditional fare. The house ale, Lady Jane, is brewed by Everards and complements the Everards cask ales and three guest ales. Beer and cider festivals are held during the year. B&B accommodation is available in a nearby 15th-century cottage. ❀🛏◑♿♣●P🚌🐾📶

Harby

Nag's Head

20 Main Street, LE14 4BN

⏲ 12-3 (not Mon), 4.30-11; 12-11 Sat & Sun ☎ (01949) 869629 🌐 nagsheadharby.com

Jennings Cumberland Ale; Ringwood Boondoggle; 1 changing beer H

The Nag's Head has experienced a new lease of life over the past year under the care of new landlords and is building a well-deserved reputation for good food and beer. A large, attractive, stone-built pub, it features a spacious beer garden and plenty of car parking. Food is served daily, lunchtimes and evenings. The bar is home to three well-kept beers, mainly from the Marston's stable. Live music is hosted regularly. ❀◑P🚌📶

Hinckley

Ashby Road Sports Club L

Hangmans Lane, LE10 3DA

⏲ 5 (7 Mon)-11; 12-11.30 Sat & Sun ☎ (01455) 615159

Sharp's Doom Bar; 2 changing beers H

A regular in the Guide since 2008 and frequently CAMRA branch Club of the Year, this private members' club welcomes CAMRA members. The stewardess has over 10 years' service. Sharp's Doom Bar is always available plus two changing guests, local and national, Wednesday-Sunday. Facilities include satellite TV for sport, traditional games, camping, caravanning and large function rooms for hire. The club has a large car park. (48,81A,158)

New Plough Inn

Leicester Road, LE10 1LS

4.45-11; 12-midnight Fri-Sun ☎ (01455) 615037

thenewploughinn.co.uk

Marston's Burton Bitter, Pedigree; 6 changing beers H

Victorian building with original wood settles, comfortable lounge areas and a traditional, cosy ambience, decorated with rugby memorabilia. Darts, dominoes and skittles are played in the games room. Outside is a sheltered beer garden and heated smokers' area. The landlady, a CAMRA member, runs a charity pub quiz on the last Thursday of the month and sponsors HRFC. A former Hinckley & Bosworth CAMRA Pub of the Year and Marston's Cask Ale Pub of the Year 2014 (South Region). P (159)

Queen's Head

Upper Bond Street, LE10 1RJ

5-11 (midnight Fri); 12-midnight Sat; 12-9 Sun ☎ 07887 770038 thequeensheadinn.co.uk

4 changing beers H

Award-winning family-run Victorian pub dating from 1809 and serving four ever-changing real ales. Sympathetically refurbished it retains many Victorian features in its four rooms, with open fires and a Victorian range in the snug. A cosy atmosphere and a warm welcome await. A regular in this Guide, it was local CAMRA Pub of the Year in 2013 and 2014 and runner-up Leicestershire, Northamptonshire & Rutland Pub of the Year 2014. Sorry, no children or pets. (48,158)

Illston on the Hill

Fox & Goose

Main Street, LE7 9EG

11.30 (6 Mon-Fri)-11; 11.30-9 Sun ☎ (0116) 259 6340

Everards Beacon Bitter, Tiger; 3 changing beers (sourced nationally; often Everards) H

Unique gem of a pub unscathed by the passage of time, featuring many artefacts including hunting scenes, McLachlan cartoons, farming tools and taxidermy exhibits. The cul-de-sac Main Street was once part of an ancient trackway used by drovers who sought their pleasures here. Local charities benefit from the proceeds of Onion Sunday, with judging of the annual onion-growing competition held here. The premises comprise a public bar, lounge bar and patio with garden furniture and planters. Q

Kegworth

Red Lion

24 High Street, DE74 2DA

11.30-11; 12-10.30 Sun ☎ (01509) 672466

redlionkegworth.com

Adnams Southwold Bitter; Castle Rock Harvest Pale; Draught Bass; Gale's HSB; Nutbrook Mild Side; 4 changing beers (sourced locally; often Milestone, Nutbrook) H

Georgian building standing on the 19th-century route of the A6, with four rooms served from one bar. There are bench seats and original features including coal fires. Eight cask ales and a real cider are offered plus a good selection of malt whiskies. Food is served every lunchtime and weekday evenings. Outside is a large car park and garden plus a pétanque court and children's play area. En-suite accommodation is available. A frequent winner of local CAMRA awards.
Q P

Kilby Bridge

Navigation

Welford Road, LE18 3TE

11.30-11.30 ☎ (0116) 288 2280

thenavigationatkilbybridge.co.uk

Adnams Broadside; Marston's Pedigree; Morland Old Speckled Hen; house beer (by Greene King) H

The hamlet of Kilby Bridge emerged around 1800 alongside the newly constructed Grand Union Canal. To meet the needs of bargees, two pubs were built – the Black Swan, which is long gone, and the Navigation. The interior comprises three adjoining areas – the public bar to the front with quarry-tiled floors and exposed ceiling joists, a lounge bar to the rear, and a dining room. Outside, across the car park, is a canalside patio with picnic tables. P (49B)

Leicester

Ale Wagon

27 Rutland Street, LE1 1RE

11-11; 7-10.30 Sun ☎ (0116) 262 3330 alewagon.co.uk

Hoskins HOB Bitter, IPA; 5 changing beers (sourced regionally; often Hoskins) H

Run by the Hoskins family, this city-centre pub with a 1930s interior, including an original oak staircase, has two rooms with tiled and parquet floors and a central bar. There is always a selection of Hoskins Brothers ales and guests available. The place is popular with visiting rugby fans and real ale drinkers. A function room is available to hire. Handy for the nearby Curve Theatre.

Black Horse

65 Narrow Lane, Aylestone, LE2 8NA

12-11 (midnight Fri & Sat) ☎ (0116) 283 7225

blackhorse-aylestone.co.uk

Everards Beacon Bitter, Tiger, Original; 4 changing beers (sourced nationally; often Brunswick, Titanic, York) H

Welcoming traditional Victorian pub with a distinctive bar servery in a village conservation area. Eight real ales are always available and home-cooked food is served lunchtimes and evenings Monday to Friday and all day at weekends. Coaches are welcome by prior arrangement. The skittle alley and function room can be hired and live music and comedy feature regularly. Beer festivals and community events are hosted. Quiz night is Sunday. There is a large beer garden and children's play area. Q

Black Horse

1 Foxon Street, Braunstone Gate, LE3 5LT

12-midnight (11 Sun) ☎ (0116) 254 0446

Everards Beacon Bitter, Sunchaser Blonde, Tiger, Original; 2 changing beers (sourced nationally) H

The only remaining traditional pub in a street of youth-oriented bars, with two rooms separated by a central bar. Comfortably furnished with practical furniture and wood-panelled walls, this is a genuine community venue. Live music is hosted four nights a week and Wednesday is quiz night.

The guest beers are sourced through Everards and the cider is Westons Old Rosie. A roof terrace for alfresco drinking was opened in 2015.

Criterion

44 Millstone Lane, LE1 5JN
12-11; closed Sun (0116) 262 5418
thecriterion.co.uk
Changing beers (sourced regionally; often Oakham, Sadler's, Shiny)
Two-roomed 1960s pub offering up to 12 guest ales from microbreweries and regionals. Beer festivals are held regularly, with many beers on gravity from the cellar. More than 70 international bottled beers are also stocked. Italian-style pizzas are available Monday to Saturday. Darts and dominoes are played in the front bar. A general knowledge quiz is hosted on Wednesdays, live music on Thursdays, some Fridays and Saturdays, and it is open some Sundays for special events. The pub is a venue for the Leicester Comedy Festival.

High Cross

103-105 High Street, LE1 4JB (400yds from Clock Tower)
8am-midnight; 9am-11 Sun (0116) 251 9218
Adnams Broadside; Grainstore Ten Fifty; Greene King Abbot; Ruddles Best Bitter; Sharp's Doom Bar; 4 changing beers (sourced nationally; often Grainstore, Langton, Oldershaw)
Named after the cross marking the centre of medieval Leicester, which was situated nearby, this is a Wetherspoon conversion of a former shop. The large L-shaped room has some changes of level to divide it into different areas. Guest beers usually include a mild and ales from local breweries. International guest brewers also feature and twice-yearly beer festivals as part of the chain's events.

King's Head

36 King Street, LE1 6RL
12-midnight (0116) 254 8240
thekingsleicester.co.uk
Black Country Bradley's Finest Golden, Pig on the Wall, Fireside; 5 changing beers (sourced nationally; often Great Central, Itchen Valley, Mallinsons)
A traditional one-room city-centre local owned by Black Country Ales. Ten handpulls serve five regularly changing guest ales and two varying ciders. Its open fire and roof terrace make it popular at any time of year, attracting real ale and cider enthusiasts as well as visitors to the local football and rugby grounds. Two changing specialist beers and a range of bottles are offered, and seasonal beer festivals are held. Sky and BT sports are screened. Access can also be gained from New Walk.

Old Horse

198 London Road, LE2 1NE
11-11.30 (midnight Fri & Sat); 11-11 Sun
(0116) 254 8384 oldhorseleicester.co.uk
Everards Beacon Bitter, Sunchaser Blonde, Tiger, Original; 3 changing beers (sourced nationally)
19th-century coaching inn, handy for dog walkers, students and sports supporters. New this year is a cider bar serving seven handpulled ciders. There are four monthly changing guest beers, and tasty and good-value food is served. Behind the pub is the largest pub garden in town complete with children's play equipment and pétanque court. Regular quiz nights, karaoke and other special events take place. Note the unique coffee table and coffin.

Pub

12 New Walk, LE1 6TF
12-11 (midnight Fri & Sat); 12-8 Sun
Changing beers (sourced regionally)
The Pub showcases a wide range of real ales, with up to 14 ever-changing guests, many from microbreweries. It also offers a good choice of continental draught and bottled beers. Home-cooked food is served Tuesday-Sunday. An annual beer festival is hosted and a pub quiz held on Wednesdays. The pub is home to rugby and football fans and the Leicester Morrismen. Live sport is shown. Discounts are available to CAMRA members and via a loyalty card.

Rutland & Derby

21 Millstone Lane, LE1 5JN
12-11 (1am Fri & Sat); closed Sun (0116) 262 3299
therutlandandderby.co.uk
Everards Sunchaser Blonde, Tiger; 2 changing beers (sourced nationally)
The pub entrance is close to the bar but a large open-plan room runs either side, and at the back is a smart block-paved backyard with a metallic spiral staircase leading to an astro-turfed roof terrace. Both the courtyard and roof terrace are furnished and heated. The menu features uncomplicated, ethically sourced pub food. Guest ales are from the Everards list.

Swan & Rushes

19 Infirmary Square, LE1 5WR
12-11 (midnight Thu-Sat); 12-11.30 Sun
(0116) 233 2452 swanandrushes.co.uk
Batemans XB; Oakham JHB, Bishops Farewell; 7 changing beers (sourced regionally; often Blue Monkey, Grainstore, Purity)
Comfortable, triangular, two-roomed pub in the city centre with a relaxed atmosphere, displaying breweriana and framed photos on the wall. Up to nine real ales are served plus a changing real cider and bottled beers including international classics. Several food-linked beer festivals are held each year plus cider and cheese events. Thursday is quiz night, open mic the second Wednesday of the month, and live bands play some Saturdays. Home-made pizzas are available.

Western

70 Western Road, LE3 0GA
12-midnight (1am Fri & Sat) (0116) 254 5287
Steamin' Billy Tipsy Fisherman, Bitter, Skydiver; 4 changing beers (sourced regionally; often Abbeydale, Charnwood, Leatherbritches)
Traditional local in a residential location close to football and rugby grounds on the edge of the city centre. The bar and lounge are popular with a mixed clientele of all ages. Up to four guest beers are available, mainly from microbreweries. Old pub signs decorate the pub and beer garden. There are regular music and beer festivals and the pub is home to a theatre upstairs.

Long Whatton

Royal Oak

26 The Green, LE12 5DB
12-11 (midnight Fri & Sat) (01509) 843694
theroyaloaklongwhatton.co.uk

Charnwood Vixen; Draught Bass; St Austell Tribute; 1 changing beer 🄷
Tastefully modernised, award-winning gastro-pub welcoming real ale drinkers and diners alike. The owners are passionate about their ales and are strong supporters of local breweries. Local produce also features in an interesting food menu. Convenient for East Midlands airport and Donington race circuit, AA 4-star accommodation is available in a separate building behind the pub. A former local CAMRA Village Pub of the Year.
Q❀🛏◐◑♿⛺●P🚌

Loughborough

Generous Briton

85 Ashby Road, LE11 3AB
⌚ 12-11 (midnight Fri & Sat) ☎ (01509) 263565
🌐 thegbpub.com
Draught Bass; Nottingham Legend; Oakham JHB; 4 changing beers 🄷
Reopened in 2011 as a genuine free house, the GB is ideally situated between the town centre and university. The traditional bar has a dartboard and features old local photographs, the lounge has a pool table and jukebox. Satellite sport is shown throughout. A limited food menu is available but customers are welcome to bring their own food. There is an enclosed beer garden to the rear and families are welcome until 7.45pm. Local CAMRA Town Pub 2013. ❀♣●🚌(126)📶

Organ Grinder

4 Woodgate, LE11 2TY
⌚ 12-11 (midnight Fri & Sat); 12-10.30 Sun
☎ (01509) 264008
Blue Monkey BG Sips, 99 Red Baboons, Infinity, Guerrilla; 4 changing beers (sourced locally; often Blue Monkey) 🄷
Previously known as the Pack Horse and bought by Blue Monkey in 2012, the building has received a top-to-bottom renovation, uncovering lots of interesting original features. The stable bar at the back reflects the pub's past life as a coaching inn. Eight cask ales are always available alongside Belgian bottled beers and a choice of two real ciders and a perry. Bar snacks include an interesting range of pork pies. CAMRA branch Pub of the Year 2013. 🐎❀●🚆🚌🐾📶

Swan in the Rushes

21 The Rushes, LE11 5BE
⌚ 11-11 (midnight Fri & Sat); 12-11 Sun ☎ (01509) 217014
Castle Rock Sheriff's Tipple, Harvest Pale, Elsie Mo; 7 changing beers (often Castle Rock, Charnwood) 🄷
Traditional three-room Castle Rock pub comprising a quiet, traditionally styled lounge, a contemporary dining room and a lively bar with a jukebox. A constantly changing range of up to seven guest beers always includes a mild. Real cider, perry, a wide selection of continental bottled and draught beers and a good choice of malt whiskies and country wines are also available. Upstairs is the Hop Loft function room and first floor terrace.
Q🐎❀◐◑♿⛺●P🚆🚌🐾📶

Tap & Mallet

36 Nottingham Road, LE11 1EU
⌚ 7 (5 Tue & Thu)-midnight; 12-midnight Sat; 3.30-midnight Sun ☎ None
Batemans Black & White, XB; 4 changing beers (sourced regionally; often Abbeydale, Oakham, Salopian) 🄷
Genuine free house specialising in beers from microbreweries not commonly found in the Loughborough area, plus seasonal brews from Abbeydale and Salopian. The large single-room interior is divided into two distinct drinking areas – a public bar with pool table, darts and board games, and a quieter lounge area that can be partitioned off for functions. Outside there is a large, secluded lawned garden, patio and pets' corner. Q❀⇌♣●🚌📶

White Hart

27 Churchgate, LE11 1UD
⌚ 11-midnight; 12-11 Sun ☎ (01509) 236976
Charnwood Salvation; Draught Bass; Timothy Taylor Landlord; 3 changing beers (sourced locally) 🄷
Reopened in 2013 as a free house after an extensive refurbishment, the pub has a secluded patio and beer garden to the rear. Regularly changing guest beers are often from local breweries such as Alchemist, Leatherbritches or Charnwood, with one dark and one light beer always available. Live music is hosted on Friday evenings and Sunday afternoons. Local CAMRA branch Most Improved Pub of 2013 and Town Pub 2014. ❀⇌●🚌🐾📶

Lutterworth

Fox

34 Rugby Road, LE17 4BN (400yds from Whittle roundabout)
⌚ 12 (5 Mon)-midnight; 12-1am Fri & Sat ☎ (01455) 550935
🌐 fox-lutterworth.co.uk
Draught Bass; Salopian Shropshire Gold; Sharp's Doom Bar; 1 changing beer 🄷
Situated at the southern end of the town close to the Sir Frank Whittle jet monument, this busy 18th-century pub has an open-plan L-shaped interior warmed by two open fires. Pub food is served lunchtimes, with Thai food available in the evening upstairs in the Sawasdee restaurant. Outside is a large landscaped award-winning garden and drinking area. Weekly quizzes are held on Tuesdays. ❀◐●P🚌🐾📶

Unicorn

29 Church Street, LE17 4AE (near church)
⌚ 10.30-11 (midnight Fri & Sat); 12-11 Sun
☎ (01455) 552486
Adnams Southwold Bitter; Draught Bass; Greene King IPA; 1 changing beer 🄷
Traditional town-centre, street-corner local with a black-and-white frontage, built in 1919 on the site of an 18th-century coach house. The large public bar with an open fire offers TV sports coverage and hosts darts, dominoes and skittles teams. A central fireplace divides the comfortable lounge, decorated with historic local photographs, from a small dining area. Lunchtime meals include vegetarian options. 🐎◐♣P🚌

Market Harborough

Admiral Nelson

49 Nelson Street, LE16 9AX
⌚ 12-2, 5-midnight; 12-midnight Fri & Sat; 12-11 Sun
Wells Eagle IPA, Bombardier; 1 changing beer (sourced regionally) 🄷
Welcoming, friendly locals' pub, built in 1900, a short stroll from the centre of the historic market town. Just off the beaten track, this pub is the

town's best-kept secret, offering a lounge with TV (where they like their rugby) and a bar with darts, pool, a jukebox and another TV. A function room is also available. Outside is a heated and covered smoking area with seating. Dogs are welcome. ❀◑♣P🐾≋

Cherry Tree

Church Walk, Little Bowden, LE16 8AE
12-2.30, 5-11; 12-11.30 Fri & Sat; 12-10.30 Sun
☎ (01858) 463525 🌐 thecherrytree-littlebowden.co.uk
Everards Beacon Bitter, Tiger, Original; 2 changing beers (sourced nationally) Ⓗ
Although the pub is situated in Little Bowden, it is very much a part of the Market Harborough community. A spacious building with low beams and a thatched roof, there are many alcoves and seating areas for drinkers and diners to choose from. Outside is a large garden with a children's play area. A beer festival is held over the August bank holiday. Guest beers are from the Everards list. No food Sunday or Monday evenings. ❀◑≹♣P🐾

Melton Mowbray

Boat

57 Burton Street, LE13 1AF
12 (5 Mon & Wed)-11.45; 11-11.45 Sat ☎ (01664) 500969
Hook Norton Hooky; Wells Bombardier; 2 changing beers Ⓗ
This traditional single-roomed pub takes its name from a canal basin that was once adjacent. The walls are decorated with old pictures of the town and a map of the old Melton-Oakham canal whose workers this establishment once served. The pub is always busy with mature drinkers and local darts teams, who enjoy good conversation with their pint. An open range gives plenty of warmth and adds to the atmosphere in winter. CAMRA branch Pub of the Year 2013. ≹♣🚌(5,5A)🐾≋

Kettleby Cross Ⓛ

Wilton Road, LE13 0UJ
7am-midnight ☎ (01664) 485310
Greene King Abbot; Ruddles Best Bitter; 6 changing beers Ⓗ
The Kettleby Cross is a Wetherspoon new-build, opened in 2007 as a flagship eco-pub complete with a prominent wind turbine on the roof. The building stands close to the bridge over the nearby River Eye and is named after the cross that once directed travellers in the direction of Ab Kettleby. The large single-room interior is on two levels. Dan the manager has a good commitment to local breweries and hosts an occasional local beer festival. Q◑♿≹P🚌(5,5A)≋

Noel's Arms Ⓛ

31 Burton Street, LE13 1AE
4-11 (11.45 Fri); 12-11.45 Sat; 12-7 Sun
☎ (01664) 562363
Sharp's Doom Bar; 3 changing beers Ⓗ
This popular single-room town pub became a free house in 2013 and shows a commendable commitment to real ale, with microbreweries featuring prominently. The Gas Dog Brewery is located to the rear of the building and its beers are occasionally available. A live music venue, including open mic sessions, the Noel's is busy on weekend evenings. CAMRA branch Pub of the Year 2014, a discount for CAMRA members is offered. ❀≹♣🍎🚌(5)🐾≋

Mountsorrel

Swan

10 Loughborough Road, LE12 7AT
12-2.30, 5.30-11; 12-11 Sat; 12-10.30 Sun
☎ (0116) 230 2340 🌐 the-swan-inn.eu
Black Sheep Best Bitter; Castle Rock Harvest Pale; 2 changing beers Ⓗ
Traditional 17th-century, Grade II-listed coaching inn entered via a narrow arch into a courtyard. The split-level interior has open fires, stone floors and low ceilings, and includes a small dining area with a polished wood floor. Good quality, interesting food is cooked to order, with the menu changing weekly and regular themed events. Outside is a long secluded riverside garden with moorings. A beer festival is hosted annually. Q❀◑P🚌🐾

Oadby

Cow & Plough

Gartree Road, LE2 2FB
11-11 ☎ (0116) 272 0852 🌐 steamin-billy.co.uk/cowplough
Fuller's London Pride; Steamin' Billy Bitter, Skydiver; 4 changing beers (sourced regionally; often Belvoir, Charnwood, Lincoln Green) Ⓗ
Situated in a former farm building with a conservatory, the pub is decked out with breweriana. It is home to Steamin' Billy beers, named after the owner's now departed Jack Russell who features on the logo and pumpclips. A mild is always available and real cider added in the summer months. An annual beer festival is held. Former dairy buildings house a renowned restaurant. Q❀◑♿♣🍎P🐾

Lord Keeper of the Great Seal

96-100 The Parade, LE2 5BF
7am-midnight ☎ (0116) 272 0957
Greene King Abbot; Ruddles Best Bitter; Theakston Best Bitter; 6 changing beers (sourced regionally) Ⓗ
Named after Sir Nathan Wright, a local landowner who held this position in the 17th century, this typical Wetherspoon conversion of a row of shops stands on the site of Sandhurst Infants School. It features pictures of old buildings and industries of Oadby and a varied library of books. Regular beer festivals and charity events are held. Families are welcome until 9pm. ❀◑♿🍎🚌(31,31A)≋

Old Dalby

Belvoir Alehouse Ⓛ

Station Road, LE14 3NQ
10-11; 12-6 Sun ☎ (01664) 823978
🌐 belvoiralehouse.co.uk
Belvoir Dark Horse, Whippling, Star Bitter, Beaver Bitter, Oatmeal Stout, Old Dalby Ⓗ
The brick-fronted Belvoir Alehouse on the outskirts of the village incorporates a bar, function room and visitors' centre, with brewery tours available by arrangement. The comfortable, spacious interior, filled with brewing artefacts, has a traditional bar area, with room for long-alley skittles and a bar billiards table. Two large internal windows provide views into the brewery. A full menu is served daily, with the focus on good wholesome food made with local produce. A former local CAMRA Pub of the Year. ❀◑♿♣P≋

Plungar

Anchor 𝕃

Granby Lane, NG13 0JJ

⏲ 12-3 (not Mon-Fri), 6-11; 12-10.30 Sun ☎ (01949) 860589

Oldershaw Barkston Bitter; 2 changing beers Ⓗ

This brick building in the middle of a small Leicestershire village dates from 1774 – it was at one time the local courtroom. The pub now houses a large bar and lounge area, a separate restaurant and a pool room. Outside is an attractive beer garden and seating area. The Anchor has developed a reputation for good food, using locally sourced ingredients, and serving quality cask ale – at least one but sometimes all beers are from local breweries. Q✿◖◗♿♣P🐾📶

Quorn

Royal Oak

2 High Street, LE12 8DT

⏲ 5.30-11 ☎ (01509) 413506

Charnwood Vixen; Timothy Taylor Landlord; 2 changing beers Ⓗ

Traditional village inn situated in the centre of the village. The building was originally three terraced cottages and has been an inn for around 160 years. The internal walls were removed long ago to open the pub up while retaining many original features including beamed ceilings, tiled floors and an open log fire. There is a sheltered, covered courtyard to the side. Q⛺🚌🐾

Shackerstone

Rising Sun 𝕃

Church Road, CV13 6NN

⏲ 12-2.30 (not Mon), 5.30-11; 11.30-11 Sat & Sun ☎ (01827) 880215 🌐 risingsunpub.com

Marston's Pedigree; Timothy Taylor Landlord; Wychwood Hobgoblin; 1 changing beer Ⓗ

This traditional family-owned free house is located in the heart of Shackerstone village near the Ashby Canal and the preserved Battlefield Railway. It has a wood-panelled bar serving traditional ales, a restaurant, pool room with Sky Sports, a family-friendly conservatory and an attractive garden. Popular with locals and visitors alike, the pub is renowned for the quality and variety of its ales and its good pub food – the ideal hub for visiting this rural part of Leicestershire. 🐴✿◖◗♿♣P🐾📶

Shawell

White Swan

Main Street, LE17 6AG (off roudabout on A5/A42)

⏲ closed Mon; 11-11.30; 12-6 Sun ☎ (01788) 860357 🌐 whiteswanshawell.co.uk

Church End Goats Milk; Dow Bridge Acris; 2 changing beers (sourced locally; often Hook Norton, Milestone) Ⓗ

This extensively refurbished village pub and restaurant has won a CAMRA pub design award. The main emphasis is on high-quality locally produced food, served in the restaurant (booking advisable). Drinkers are well cared for in the smartly appointed bar featuring stone tiling and wood panelling, and in the adjoining lounge with a wood-burning stove. There is a small patio area at the front and a larger walled garden at the rear. Q✿◖◗♿P🐾

Shearsby

Chandlers Arms 𝕃

Fenny Lane, LE17 6PL

⏲ closed Mon; 12-3 (not Tue), 6-11; 12-4, 6-11 Sat; 12-10.30 Sun ☎ (0116) 247 8384 🌐 chandlersatshearsby.co.uk

Dow Bridge Acris; 6 changing beers (sourced regionally) Ⓗ

Quintessential village inn with a big reputation – it has won the prestigious Leicester CAMRA Country Pub of the Year award for the past seven years, and was the first pub in the Leicester branch to sign up to CAMRA's LocAle scheme. Microbrewery beers are always on the bar, often locally sourced. The pub's name is a reminder of the building's original use as a tallow candlemaker's business. It has a public bar, dining room and a beer garden overlooking the village green from a high vantage point. ✿◖◗♣🍎🐾📶

Sileby

Free Trade

27 Cossington Road, LE12 7RW

⏲ 5 (11.30 Thu)-11; 11.30-midnight Fri & Sat; 12-11 Sun ☎ (01509) 814494 🌐 thefreetradeinn.co.uk

Everards Beacon Bitter, Tiger, Original; 3 changing beers Ⓗ

Sixteenth-century thatched pub with a resident ghost. The comfortable front lounge with low beams and lots of nooks and crannies leads to a more open area at the back, with plenty of room to get together after a rugby match. Three guest beers are always available as well as real cider and perry. Regular beer festivals and charity events are hosted throughout the year. Local CAMRA branch Pub of the Year 2014 and Leicestershire, Rutland & Northamptonshire Pub of the Year 2014.
🐴✿⇌♣🍎P🚌🐾📶

Horse & Trumpet

4 Barrow Road, LE12 7LP

⏲ 1-11 (midnight Fri & Sat); 12-11 Sun ☎ (01509) 812549

Steamin' Billy Tipsy Fisherman, Bitter, Skydiver; 2 changing beers Ⓗ

This multi-room pub with open fires has undergone a huge transformation since becoming part of the Steamin' Billy chain. Two guest beers plus a real cider and a perry are on handpump. No hot food is served although cobs are available, and there is a monthly curry club. Open mic nights are held weekly and jazz nights monthly. Well-behaved dogs are welcome in the bar and outside seating area. A function room is available.
Q✿⇌♣🍎P🚌(2)

Somerby

Stilton Cheese 🏆 𝕃

High Street,, LE14 2QB

⏲ 12-3, 6 (7 Sun)-11 ☎ (01664) 454394 🌐 stiltoncheeseinn.co.uk

Grainstore Ten Fifty; Marston's Burton Bitter; 3 changing beers Ⓗ

Late 16th-century pub built in local ironstone, as are most of the buildings in the village. The interior comprises two bars and a function room/ restaurant upstairs. Tall customers beware the wide range of pumpclips on the low beam above the bar. Look for the large stuffed pike and badger on the wall. An ideal place to stop off for lunch while walking the Leicestershire Round.
Q🐴✿🛏◖◗♣P🚌(113)📶

Stathern

Red Lion 𝕃

Red Lion Street, LE14 4HS
⊕ 12-3, 6-11; 12-11 Fri & Sat; 12-6 Sun ☎ (01949) 860868
🌐 theolivebranchpub.com
Fuller's London Pride; house beer (by Grainstore); 1 changing beer 🄷
Beautiful village pub dating from the 17th century, situated in the village of Stathern surrounded by the Belvoir Hills. Popular and highly rated for its food, it uses locally sourced ingredients where possible, including fruit, veg and herbs from the kitchen garden. Recent beer and food matching evenings have proved a success. The house beer is Red Lion Ale from Grainstore, and beers from Brewsters Brewery, which originated in the village, often feature. One of two excellent pubs in Stathern. Q❀◐◑P🚌🐾📶

Swinford

Chequers

High Street, LE17 6BL (near church)
⊕ 7-midnight Mon; 12-2.30, 6-midnight; 12-midnight Sat & Sun ☎ (01788) 860318 🌐 chequersswinford.co.uk
Adnams Southwold Bitter; 2 changing beers (sourced regionally; often Butcombe, Dow Bridge) 🄷
The hub of the community, this traditional friendly village pub has been run by the same family for 28 years. Catering for all ages, it offers good pub food including snacks, mains, a children's menu and specials board. For the summer months the large garden has play equipment and a marquee where the pub's summer beer festival is held. Nearby is the 16th-century Stanford Hall and its adjoining caravan park. 🐴❀◐◑⛺♣P🚌

Syston

Queen Victoria

76 High Street, LE7 1GQ
⊕ 4 (2 Wed; 12 Thu)-11; 12-midnight Fri & Sat; 12-10.30 Sun ☎ (0116) 260 5750
Everards Beacon Bitter, Tiger; 4 changing beers (sourced nationally; often Bath Ales, Brunswick, Greene King) 🄷
A former coach house, the building is 200 years old – Everards has traded here since 1922. The pub has several small rooms and a large garden at the rear. A separate restaurant carvery is accessed via the garden. Entertainment is hosted every other Saturday and a beer festival is held in the summer. Guest beers are sourced through Everards.
🐴❀◐◑P🚌📶

Syston & District Social Club

36 High Street, LE7 1GP
⊕ 4.30-11; 11.30-midnight Fri & Sat; 11.30-11 Sun ☎ (0116) 260 9086 🌐 systonsocial.co.uk
Banks's Mild, Bitter; 4 changing beers (sourced regionally) 🄷
This former pub is home to many local societies and sports clubs including darts, skittles, chess and crib. The large function room is available for hire. The range of six beers includes four regularly rotating guests, and beer festivals are held in February and June. Show a CAMRA membership card or copy of this Guide for entry. CAMRA East Midlands Club of the Year 2013.
🐴❀♿♣🚌(5,5A,6)🐾📶

Thurlaston

Elephant & Castle 𝕃

26 Main Street, LE9 7TP
⊕ 12-2.30 (not Mon & Tue), 6-11; 12-3, 6-11.30 Sat; 12-3, 7-10.30 Sun ☎ (01455) 888213
Everards Beacon Bitter, Tiger, Original; 2 changing beers 🄷
A regular in the Guide, this friendly inn is situated in the heart of the village. The pub's ales benefit from the landlord's national awards in cellarmanship. Three Everards beers and two guests are on offer plus two real ciders. The refurbished front lounge has a log burner, and to the rear is a restaurant/lounge. The landlady's home-made pies and good-value Sunday lunches are a treat. Outside is a children's play area and patio. Walking and cycling routes pass the pub.
Q🐴❀◐◑♿♣🍎P🚌(X55)🐾📶

Whitwick

Three Horseshoes ★

11 Leicester Road, LE67 5GN
⊕ 11-3, 6.30-11; 12-2, 7-10.30 Sun ☎ (01530) 837311
Draught Bass; Marston's Pedigree 🄷
Identified by CAMRA as having a nationally important historic pub interior, the Three Horseshoes is nicknamed Polly's after a former landlady, Polly Burton. The pub was originally two separate buildings but now has two rooms. To the left is a long bar with a quarry-tiled floor and open fires, wooden bench seating and pre-war fittings; to the right is a small similarly furnished snug. 🚌

Wigston

William Wygston

84 Leicester Road, LE18 1DR
⊕ 8am-midnight ☎ (0116) 288 8397
Adnams Broadside; Greene King Abbot; Ruddles Best Bitter; changing beers (sourced nationally) 🄷
Classic Wetherspoon establishment named after William Wygston (1456-1536), who was an extremely wealthy wool merchant, philanthropist, MP, and twice mayor of Leicester. This pub opened in 1997 in a former Kwiksave store which was itself part of a redevelopment, many years ago, that replaced terraced housing with retail outlets. The 1911 census records that the house previously on this site was occupied by an elderly widow and her spinster sister. The pub underwent extensive refurbishment throughout 2015. 🐴◐◑♿🍎🚌📶

Wymeswold

Three Crowns

45 Far Street, LE12 6TZ
⊕ 12-midnight ☎ (01509) 880153
🌐 threecrownswymeswold.co.uk
Adnams Southwold Bitter; Draught Bass; Sharp's Doom Bar; 1 changing beer 🄷
Late 18th-century pub standing opposite the church. This friendly village local features open fires, a beamed ceiling in the bar and a cosy split-level snug/lounge. Guest beers are usually from local breweries including Castle Rock, Belvoir or Nottingham. A good range of snacks and main meals is available lunchtimes and Thursday to Saturday evenings. A function room and skittle alley are available to hire. There is a regular daytime bus service. Q🐴❀◐◑♿⛺♣🍎P🚌🐾📶

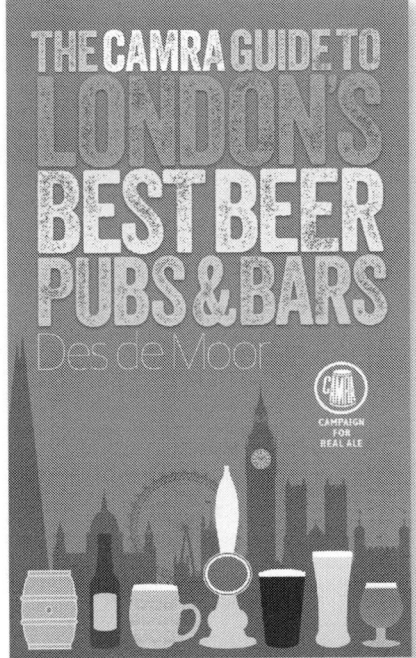

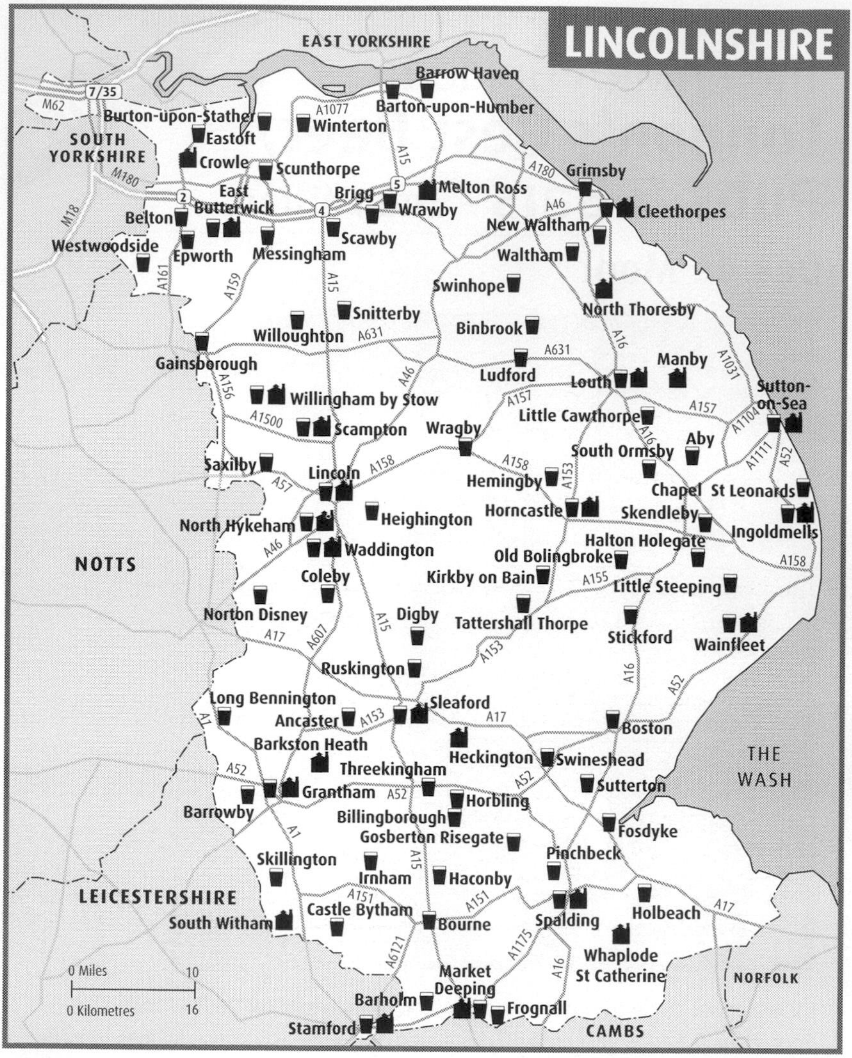

Aby

Railway Tavern

Main Road, LN13 0DR (off A16 via South Thoresby)
✪ 12-11.30 ☎ (01507) 480676
2 changing beers Ⓗ
A lovely rural pub which lies just outside the beautiful village of Aby. There is always a good selection of carefully chosen real ales along with a tasty home-cooked food menu. A real fire adds to the homely atmosphere at this welcoming hostelry. (Closed on Tuesdays during November, and between January and Easter.) ᗜ◑P🐾

Ancaster

Ancaster Social Club

Ermine Street, NG32 3PW
✪ 7 (12 Sat)-11; 12-10.30 Sun ☎ (01400) 230896
Wells Bombardier; 1 changing beer Ⓗ
This village club is home to numerous sporting teams and hosts local cup finals and events. Bombardier is supplemented by different guest ales. There is an airy conservatory and outside seating area overlooking the sports field. This excellent club has been voted local CAMRA Club of the Year 2013-2015, Lincolnshire Club of the Year 2014 and a regional finalist in 2014.
ᗜ❀♿⇌♣P🚌🐾ᯤ

Barholm

Five Horseshoes Ⓛ

PE9 4RA
✪ 4 (1 Sat)-11; 12-10.30 Sun ☎ (01778) 560238
Adnams Southwold Bitter; Oakham JHB; 4 changing beers (often Elland, Fuller's, St Austell) Ⓗ
An 18th-century stone-built country pub comprising two bars, two side rooms and a TV/pool room. A welcoming wood fire burns throughout the winter, and stuffed birds and enamelled adverts adorn the walls. Outside is a garden, children's play area and car park. Barbecues and music events are held during the summer. A changing range of beers from local and regional breweries is available, along with real

ciders. Pizzas are on the menu on Fridays. The pub supports the Macmillan Nurses charity.
Q🛏❀🍎P🐾

Barrow Haven

Haven Inn

Ferry Road, DN19 7EX (approx 1½ miles E of Barrow-upon-Humber)
11.30-11.30; 12-10 Sun ☎ (01469) 530247
thehaveninn.co.uk
Timothy Taylor Landlord; 2 changing beers (often Black Sheep, Great Newsome, Tom Wood's) Ⓗ
The Haven has been known as an inn for centuries and is renowned for its hospitality, food and comfortable lodgings. The entire pub was devastated by the tidal surge of December 2013, but reopened five months later and has retained its style and character, with a traditional beamed ceiling and open fire in the lounge and bar. The restaurant is well appointed, with a team of chefs who produce a varying menu and an extremely popular Sunday carvery.
🛏❀🛏◑♿Å⇌♣🍎P🚌(252)🐾📶

Barrowby

White Swan

Main Street, NG32 1BH
12-midnight (1am Fri & Sat) ☎ (01476) 562375
Adnams Southwold Bitter; Sharp's Doom Bar; 2 changing beers (often Fuller's, Wells) Ⓗ
Welcoming village local always worth visiting, close to the A1/A52. The cheerful landlord is an active CAMRA member and has been mine host for over 20 years. The pub boasts a comfortable lounge and a separate public bar where the friendly locals play darts or pool. There is a pleasant secluded garden area and a heated smoking shelter. As well as the regular beers, more than 100 different guests have been served over the past year. Q🛏❀◐♣P🚌🐾📶

Barton-upon-Humber

George Inn

George Street, DN18 5ES
12-11 (12.30am Fri & Sat) ☎ (01652) 636303
thegeorgebarton.co.uk
Black Sheep Best Bitter; 2 changing beers (often St Austell, Tom Wood's) Ⓗ
Large 17th-century coaching inn occupying a prominent position just off the marketplace and offering much-needed town-centre accommodation. Originally called the George & Dragon, it served Barton on the London to Hull route, but has also been used as an excise office, posting house and local government venue. The central bar serves several comfortable and spacious rooms. The Thursday evening quiz and Friday fish and chip specials are popular weekly events.
🛏🛏◑♿⇌P🚌(250,350,X1)🐾📶

Belton

Crown Inn 🅻

Church Lane, Churchtown, DN9 1PA (300 yds off High St behind parish church)
1-12.30am (1.30am Fri); 12-1.30am Sat; 12-midnight Sun
☎ (01427) 872834
Batemans XB; Bradfield Farmers Blonde; Brakspear Bitter; Glentworth Lightyear; Jennings Cocker Hoop; 1 changing beer (sourced locally; often Bradfield, Pheasantry) Ⓗ
Under the same ownership for six years, the licensee of this friendly village local prides himself on the quality and range of his ales. The pub supports a number of local sports teams as well as hosting quiz and theme nights, live music and a summer beer festival in the extensive garden. Winner of CAMRA district Pub of The Year in 2013. Give this little gem a visit – you will not be disappointed. 🛏❀♣🍎P▯🚌(399)🐾📶

Billingborough

Fortescue Arms

27 High Street, NG34 0QB
12-3, 5.30-11; 12-11 Sat & Sun ☎ (01529) 240228
fortescuearms.co.uk
Greene King IPA, Abbot; Timothy Taylor Landlord; 1 changing beer Ⓗ
Fine Grade II-listed inn with an interesting multi-roomed interior and a rustic feel, and a large patio to the rear. Quality home-cooked food is popular with diners, and guest beers are usually from micros. Nearby is the site of Sempringham Priory and its monument to Gwenllian, daughter of the Prince of Wales, who was confined to the priory in the 12th century. Stone from the priory was used to build part of the inn. Q🛏❀◑P

Binbrook

Plough

Market Place, LN8 6DE
12-11 (12.30am Fri & Sat) ☎ (01472) 398808
4 changing beers (sourced regionally; often Grafters, Horncastle Ales, Wentworth) Ⓗ
A Victorian pub in the heart of this Lincolnshire Wolds village which has been well maintained over

REAL ALE BREWERIES

8 Sail Heckington
Austendyke Spalding
Axholme Crowle
Bacchus Sutton-on-Sea
Batemans Wainfleet
Black Horse Louth
Blue Bell Whaplode St Catherine
Blue Cow South Witham
Brewster's Grantham
Cathedral Heights Lincoln
Cheeky Imp Waddington (NEW)
DarkTribe East Butterwick
Firehouse Manby
Fulstow Louth
Grafters Willingham by Stow
Greg's Scampton
Hopshackle Market Deeping
Horncastle Horncastle (NEW)
Leila Cottage Ingoldmells
Lincolnshire Lincoln (NEW)
Melbourn Stamford
Newby Wyke Grantham
Oldershaw Barkston Heath
Poachers North Hykeham
Riverside Wainfleet
Rowett North Thoresby (NEW)
Sleaford Sleaford
Star Market Deeping
Tom Wood's Melton Ross
Willy's Cleethorpes

the decades. Its aviation links to the nearby defunct airbase are proudly displayed on the walls, with pictures of Lightning jet planes which used to fly past. Home-cooked food is served regularly and is becoming much sought after. Live music can be heard most weekends. Dogs are welcome outside food service times. ♘❀◑♣P🚌(3)🐾

Boston

Eagle

144 West Street, PE21 8RE

🕒 11 (11.30 Thu)-11; 11-midnight Fri & Sat

☎ (01205) 361116

Castle Rock Black Gold, Harvest Pale, Preservation Fine Ale, Elsie Mo; changing beers 🄷

Part of the Castle Rock chain, the Eagle is known as the real ale pub of Boston. This two-roomed, friendly hostelry has an L-shaped bar with a large TV screen for big sports events. The small, cosy lounge has an open fire. The pub stocks a wide range of guest ales and at least one cider. A function room upstairs is home to Boston Folk Club. Thursday is quiz night – allegedly the hardest in town. Q❀♿⇌♣●🚌🐾

Golden Lion

46 High Street, PE21 8SP

🕒 6 (12 Thu)-midnight; 12-midnight Sat & Sun

☎ (01205) 352745

Brains The Rev James; Theakston Best Bitter; 1 changing beer (sourced nationally; often Wells) 🄷

Low-beamed ceilings and wood-panelling mark out this pub on the old High Street away from the main shopping thoroughfares. It serves a good range of beers, and has active traditional games teams. Old fishing boat nameplates hang above the bar as a reminder of the history of Boston as a fishing port. The pub was once owned by Hardys & Hansons and came into private hands in 2010. ❀⇌♣🚌

Moon under Water

6 High Street, PE21 8SH

🕒 9am-midnight ☎ (01205) 311911

Greene King Abbot; Ruddles Best Bitter; 4 changing beers 🄷

A large, lively town-centre Wetherspoon pub near the tidal section of the River Witham. Formerly a government building, an imposing staircase leads from the lounge up to the toilets. A spacious conservatory-style dining area is supplemented by a second child-friendly dining room adjacent to the lounge. The pub offers a good number of guest ales and a large range of continental bottled beers. Local history photographs and information boards highlight important people associated with Boston. ♘❀◑♿⇌●🚌

Bourne

Smith's 🄻

25 North Street, PE10 9AE

🕒 10-11 (midnight Fri & Sat); 11-11 Sun ☎ (01778) 426819

🌐 smithsofbourne.co.uk

Castle Rock Harvest Pale; Fuller's London Pride; 4 changing beers (often Hopshackle, Star, Titanic) 🄷

A successful conversion of an old grocery store into an atmospheric pub, with exposed red brick walls throughout. The building is a warren of interconnecting rooms spanning three floors. The main front bar serves six beers, mostly from independent brewers. Two ciders from Westons are usually available. Outside there is a large patio and beer garden with a children's play area. There is an annual beer festival in August and also an annual cider and sausage festival in September. Q❀◑♿♣●🚌🐾📶

Brigg

Nelthorpe Arms

1 Bridge Street, DN20 8LN

🕒 11-11; 12-11 Sun ☎ (01652) 653173

Greene King IPA, Abbot; 2 changing beers (often Black Sheep, Springhead, Thornbridge) 🄷

Town-centre pub that has undergone extensive refurbishment with a large, comfortable bar-cum-lounge and a separate snug, both with real fires. Traditionally styled, the bar area has leather armchairs and padded seating. Four handpulls dispense Greene King beers and a varied range of guests. An interesting selection of bottled beers is also available. A separate restaurant has recently opened and meals can be taken here lunchtimes and evenings Wednesday-Sunday. Beer festivals are also staged occasionally. ❀◑♿⇌P🚌(4)🐾📶

Yarborough Hunt 🄻

49 Bridge Street, DN20 8NS (across bridge from marketplace)

🕒 11-11 Sun-Wed; 10 (11 Fri)-midnight ☎ (01652) 658333

Tom Wood's Best Bitter, Lincoln Gold, Bomber County; 3 changing beers (often Greene King, Marston's, Milestone) 🄷

Former Sergeants Brewery tap built in the 1700s and retaining some original rustic features, now extended to include an extra room. It is simply furnished, with warming open fires in three rooms. Three Tom Wood's beers are generally available, supplemented by three guest beers and draught Westons Old Rosie cider, along with a good selection of bottled beers and ciders, plus a wide selection of malt whiskies and wines. No food is served, but customers can bring sandwiches and other cold food. Q♘❀♿⇌♣●🚌(4)🐾📶

Burton-upon-Stather

Ferry House Inn

Stather Road, DN15 9DT (follow campsite signs through village, down hill at church)

🕒 6-11; 12-11 Sat & Sun ☎ (01724) 721783

🌐 ferryhousepub.co.uk

2 changing beers (often Tom Wood's) 🄷

Friendly village local on the banks of the River Trent which has been in the same family for 55 years. The pub brews its own beer (check for availability) as well as offering a range of rotating guest ales, and is Cask Marque accredited. Real cider is also sold. An annual beer festival is generally held on the August bank holiday weekend. It has a large outdoor children's play area and hosts occasional live music. The pub is a popular meeting place for local heritage groups. Q♘❀▲♣●P🐾

Castle Bytham

Castle Inn 🄻

High Street, NG33 4RZ

🕒 5-midnight; 12-3, 6-11 Sun ☎ (01780) 410504

🌐 castleinnbytham.co.uk

Black Sheep Ale; Woodforde's Wherry; 2 changing beers (often Oldershaw, St Austell, Star) Ⓗ
This pub has been voted Country Pub 2015 by the local CAMRA branch. One of the original public houses in an historic village, this 17th-century gem has Star Brewery beers permanently on the bar along with regularly changing guest ales sourced both locally and nationally. A traditional cider is also on offer. An excellent menu of home-made food, cooked in a wood-fired stove in the bar, is available every evening and Sunday lunchtime. 🐴❀◐◑♣🍏🐾

Chapel St Leonards

Admiral Benbow

The Promenade, PE24 5BQ
🕐 10-7 (10.30 Fri & Sat); 10-8 Sun ☎ (01754) 871847
🌐 admiralbenbowbeachbar.webplus.net
Black Sheep Best Bitter; Kelham Island Pale Rider; 1 changing beer Ⓗ
A beach bar on the promenade – opening times and facilities are dependent on the weather and are limited in winter (please see the website for current times). Bar snacks and hot food are on offer. It has an outside seating area, the Hispaniola, on the newly refurbished boat deck. Picnic trays and plastic glasses to take out your favourite ale on to the beach are provided. Dogs are welcome on leads. ❀◐🐾

Cleethorpes

No.1 Pub

Railway Station, DN35 8AX
🕐 12-midnight (5 Mon; 1am Fri & Sat); 12-11 Sun
☎ (01472) 691707
Batemans XB, XXXB; 6 changing beers Ⓗ
A Victorian station building turned into a pub. It has a large main room on two tiers, with a few steps to the first bar. The quieter back room is filled with railway memorabilia and there is an annexe which looks out onto to the station platform. This theme is carried on throughout the pub. There is home-cooked food, and live music at weekends. 🐴❀◐◑≉♣🚌🐾📶

No.2 Refreshment Room

Station Approach, DN35 8AX
🕐 7-11.30 (1am Thu-Sat) ☎ 07905 375587
Hancock's HB; Rudgate Ruby Mild; Sharp's Doom Bar; 3 changing beers (sourced regionally; often Blue Monkey, Cottage, York) Ⓗ
A one-roomed bar on the station concourse which is bright and airy for its size. It is a draw for tourists in summer, but is also a friendly locals' pub with a good mix of changing ales and a real cider. A free buffet is provided on Sundays. Tuesday is dominoes night, Thursday has a quiz, and a beer festival is held each June. 🐴❀♿≉♣🍏🚌(3,4,5)🐾📶

Nottingham House 🏆

7 Seaview Street, DN35 8EU
🕐 12-11 (midnight Thu; 1am Fri & Sat) ☎ (01472) 505150
Tetley Mild, Bitter; Timothy Taylor Landlord; Wychwood Hobgoblin; 3 changing beers Ⓗ
Splendid three-roomed traditional pub. It has a standard public bar to the left, a comfortable lounge to the right, both with open fires, and a delightful snug with all-round banquette seating in the rear extension. An upstairs restaurant serves good-quality lunches Wednesday-Sunday, and evening meals Wednesday-Saturday. Food is also available in the bars. Local CAMRA branch Pub of the Year in 2014. Q🐴🛏◐◑≉🍏🚌(8,9,46)🐾📶

Willy's

17 High Cliff, DN35 8RQ
🕐 11-11 (midnight Thu; 2am Fri & Sat) ☎ (01472) 602145
Draught Bass; Willy's Original; 3 changing beers Ⓗ
One-roomed pub with a smaller function room above, enjoying fine views of the beach and over the River Humber. It tends to get busy in the summer season, with families and regulars popping in for the food, and it is the only place where you can sup a pint of Willy's produced in its own adjoining brewery. Thursday is curry night, where home-cooked dishes to rival some restaurants are served. At weekends it attracts clubgoers for the DJs. 🐴❀◐◑≉🍏🚌(8,9,46)🐾📶

Coleby

Tempest Arms

Hill Rise, LN5 0AG
🕐 12 (4 Mon)-11; 12-midnight Fri & Sat; 12-10.30 Sun
☎ (01522) 810258 🌐 thetempestcoleby.co.uk
Castle Rock Harvest Pale; St Austell HSD; 4 changing beers (sourced nationally; often Fuller's, Theakston, Thwaites) Ⓗ
Lovely village pub on the Viking Way with one of the best views of the Trent Valley. The central bar offers a friendly welcome and a chance to chat to the locals. Alternatively, sit in the comfortable lounge and drink, or why not eat in the aptly named Vista restaurant. Walkers and dogs are welcome. A quiz is held every other Thursday and the second Tuesday of each month is acoustic music evening. Q🐴❀◐◑🍏P🚌(1)🐾

Digby

Red Lion 🄻

3 North Street, LN4 3LZ
🕐 closed Mon; 11.30-3, 6-10.30; 11.30-11 Fri & Sat; 11.30-10 Sun ☎ (01526) 321686
4 changing beers (often Fuller's, Greene King, Pheasantry) Ⓗ
Next to the medieval stone Digby Cross, the pub is located in the heart of the village. The modern bar area provides a contrast to the low beamed ceiling running down the length of the pub. There is a separate games area at the end of the main bar, with a restaurant area on the right as you enter. There is no food service on Sunday evenings. 🐴❀◐◑♣P🚌📶

East Butterwick

Dog & Gun 🄻

High Street, DN17 3AJ (off A18 at Keadby Bridge, E bank)
🕐 5-11; 12-11 Sat & Sun ☎ (01724) 782324
DarkTribe Pieces of 8; 2 changing beers (often DarkTribe) Ⓗ
Village community pub alongside the River Trent. The three rooms are supplemented with a drinking area and picnic-style bench seating on the riverbank. Three beers from the house DarkTribe microbrewery are always on the bar, and occasional seasonal beers are also produced. Quiz night is Tuesday. During the warmer months motorsport meetings are held, including motorcycles and vintage cars. A nearby cycle club

has time trials in the summer, starting outside the pub, which is on a national cycle route.
≋❀♿♣P🚌(12)🐾

Eastoft

River Don Tavern

Sampson Street, DN17 4PQ (on A161 Goole-Gainsborough road)
✪ 3.30-11; 12-11 Sat & Sun ☎ (01724) 798040
🌐 riverdontavernandlodge.co.uk
2 changing beers (often Acorn, Roosters, Tom Wood's) Ⓗ
Traditionally styled village local on the main road through the village. Open plan in design, the bar serves two distinct drinking areas, one also used for dining. Evening meals are served throughout the week with a renowned carvery on Sunday. A rotating beer from Roosters is featured, plus other real ales from Yorkshire and Lincolnshire micros. A large orchard to the rear is set out with tables for alfresco drinking. Accommodation is available in four lodges at the back of the pub.
❀🛏◑♿♣●P🚌(356)🐾📶

Epworth

Old School Inn

10 Battle Green, DN9 1JT (off Station Rd)
✪ 12 (4 Mon & Tue)-11 ☎ (01427) 875835
🌐 theoldschoolinnepworth.co.uk
Brains The Rev James; Timothy Taylor Landlord; 2 changing beers (sourced nationally; often Sharp's, Tom Wood's, Wychwood) Ⓗ
Converted from a village schoolhouse in the 1980s, this pub was bought by a local family in 2012 and extensively refurbished. Now a free house, four cask ales are on offer, two of them regularly changing. It is notable for its high-quality meals. The pub won its first CAMRA award in spring 2015. The Old School Inn is well worth a visit.
≋❀◐◑♿●P🚌(399)📶

Fosdyke

Ship Inn

Moulton Washway, PE12 6LH
✪ 11.30-10 (11 Fri & Sat) ☎ (01205) 260764
🌐 shipinnfosdyke.co.uk
Adnams Southwold Bitter, Broadside; Batemans XB Ⓗ
Located just outside Fosdyke when travelling from Boston on the main A17 next to the bridge. As its name suggests, this former Batemans hostelry is dedicated to all things maritime – maps, photographs, charts and model ships of every description are in plentiful supply. The week's tide table is also detailed on a blackboard. The inn is near the busy Fosdyke Marina and boaters and landlubbers are well catered for, with excellent home-cooked food and a welcome cheer.
Q≋◐◑♿P🐾📶

Frognall

Goat 🄻

155 Spalding Road, PE6 8SA
✪ 12-3, 6-11.30; 12-11.30 Sat; 12-10.30 Sun
☎ (01778) 347629 🌐 thegoatfrognall.com
6 changing beers (often Batemans, Hopshackle, Star) Ⓗ
A food-oriented country pub with five dining areas and a drinking area at one end of the bar. Six handpumps serve a range of regional and microbrewery beers, including at least one LocAle and a strong ale. There are usually two real ciders from Westons on gravity. A large selection of malt whiskies is available, and a popular beer festival is held in the summer. The large garden has two separate play areas for children and toddlers.
Q≋❀◐◑♿●P🚆🚌(100)📶

Gainsborough

Blues Club

Northolme, North Street, DN21 2QW
✪ 7-midnight; 5-1am Fri; 12-1am Sat; 12-midnight Sun
☎ (01427) 613688
2 changing beers Ⓗ
The club has a bar area with several TVs showing sport, a quieter lounge and a large function room which hosts regular live entertainment (admission charges may apply). Two changing real ales are usually on tap and details of forthcoming beers can be emailed to customers on request. CAMRA guests are always welcome on production of a membership card or a copy of this Guide.
≋⇌(Central)♣🚌

Canute 🄻

12-14 Silver Street, DN21 2DP
✪ 9am-11 (midnight Thu; 1am Fri & Sat); 11-11 Sun
☎ (01427) 678715
Courage Best Bitter; 3 changing beers Ⓗ
A typical town-centre chain pub where Courage Best Bitter is a permanent feature. There are usually five real ales on, most from the larger national breweries such as Marston's and Greene King. Good-quality food is served until late and live sport is shown. Special events are catered for such as birthdays and anniversaries. The pub can be busy on Friday and Saturday nights.
≋◐◑♿⇌(Central)●🚌📶

Eight Jolly Brewers 🏆 🄻

Ship Court, DN21 2DW
✪ 11-midnight; 12-midnight Sun ☎ 07926 797767
Dukeries A Ray of Sunshine; 8 changing beers (often Glentworth) Ⓗ
A real ale haven, the pub has been in this Guide since 1995, and is based in a 300-year-old Grade II-listed building. Eight changing beers, at least one at a discounted price, are always on sale, many from northern micros, but new breweries from all areas feature. Real cider and continental bottled beers are also sold. Fortnightly Wednesday quiz nights take place, and quality live music every Thursday. Customers bring in food to share on Sunday lunchtimes. Q♿⇌(Central)●P🚌(200)

Elm Cottage 🄻

138 Church Street, DN21 2JU
✪ 11.30-midnight; 12-11.30 Sun ☎ 07590 806584
6 changing beers Ⓗ
The pub is close to Gainsborough Trinity's football ground and the Blues Club. There are six varying beers, some from the Marstons' portfolio, but microbrewery beers are frequently available. Good-value lunchtime food is served Tuesday-Sunday, and early evening meals Thursday and Friday. The pub is popular with local amateur sports teams. Weekly live music is featured.
Q≋◐◑♿⇌(Central)●P🚌🐾📶

Sweyn Forkbeard

22-24 Silver Street, DN21 2DP

8am-midnight ☎ (01427) 675000
Adnams Broadside; Ruddles Best Bitter; 3 changing beers Ⓗ
A town-centre Wetherspoon establishment that is making itself one of the must-do pubs in Gainsborough. Three rotating guest beers often include some oddities for this part of the country – customers can ask for their favourite beer and it often appears. The pub is named after the Danish King of England in 1013, whose son Canute is rumoured to have attempted to stop the Trent Aegir tidal bore at Gainsborough. Good-value food is served until 11pm. (Central)

Gosberton Risegate

Duke of York

106 Risegate Road, PE11 4EY
12 (6.30 Mon)-11; 11-3, 7-10.30 Sun ☎ (01775) 840193
Batemans XB; St Austell Tribute; 2 changing beers Ⓗ
A friendly pub and a long-standing entry in the Guide which has a deserved reputation for value-for-money beers and food. As well as the regular ales, guests come from a range of independent brewers. A wide choice of cooked food is available with portions to suit the largest appetite. Local community life is supported through charities, sports teams and other social events. Visitors can expect an enthusiastic welcome from the two pub dogs. P

Grantham

Chameleon Music Bar & Restaurant

15-16 Finkin Street, NG31 6QZ
4-11; 12-1am Fri; 12-2am Sat; 12-11 Sun
☎ (01476) 575863
Greene King Abbot; 2 changing beers (often Newby Wyke, Oldershaw) Ⓗ
This friendly music bar and steakhouse always supports the three local breweries Newby Wyke, Oldershaw and Brewster's. Locally sourced food is of a high quality and cooked to order. A music theme features throughout the bar. Children are welcome until 10pm. Live music takes place on a Friday and Saturday night, with light live music on occasional Saturday and Sunday lunchtimes. Every other Sunday is open mic night, which is popular.

Lord Harrowby

65 Dudley Road, NG31 9AB
3-11; 12-11 Sat & Sun ☎ (01476) 563515
Oldershaw Heavenly Blonde; 4 changing beers Ⓗ
An original back-street community pub with a separate bar and lounge area, one of the few remaining in town, and well worth a visit. It was voted Grantham Journal Pub of the Year 2015 by readers. The landlord is a CAMRA member and a real ale enthusiast, hosting two beer festivals a year. As well as Oldershaw Heavenly Blonde, there are four changing guest beers, one of which will not be found elsewhere locally. Q

Nobody Inn

9 North Street, NG31 6NU (opp Asda car park)
12-11 ☎ (01476) 565288
Newby Wyke Orsino; Wells Bombardier; 4 changing beers (often Newby Wyke) Ⓗ
Local CAMRA Pub of the Year for the second year running, this is a vibrant sports-oriented hostelry, especially busy at the weekend when showing live sporting events. It also has its own successful football team. A superb example of a well-run, independent town pub, it sells a range of six beers featuring award-winning LocAles from Newby Wyke. Trying to find the toilets might be harder than you think, with the hidden door, and watch out for the spider!

Tollemache Inn

17 St Peters Hill, NG31 6PY
8am-midnight (1am Fri & Sat) ☎ (01476) 594696
Adnams Broadside; Fuller's London Pride; Greene King Abbot; Purity Mad Goose; Ruddles Best Bitter; 5 changing beers (often Brewster's, Newby Wyke, Oldershaw) Ⓗ
This Wetherspoon pub was one of the first to be opened outside London. It occupies the old Co-op building and is a former CAMRA Pub of the Year. Ideally situated in the town centre and next to the museum and arts centre, it always has a large selection of national and guest ales. Especially noteworthy is that there is always one beer from each of Grantham's award-winning and renowned microbreweries – Brewster's, Newby Wyke and Oldershaw.

Grimsby

Barge

Riverhead, DN31 1NH
10-2am (11.30 Mon; midnight Wed); 10-11 Sun
☎ (01472) 340911 thebargegrimsby.co.uk
Wells Bombardier; Wychwood Hobgoblin Ⓗ
An established and much-loved pub in the heart of town. As the name suggests, it is a converted barge moored at the head of the River Freshney, with two regular beers and two regular sets of customers. Those visiting in the day tend to pop along for the fantastic home-cooked food, while those in the evening come for the loud jukebox and an even louder drinking environment. Monday is quiz night and Tuesday is student night.

Rose & Crown

Louth Road, DN33 2HR
11-11 (midnight Fri & Sat); 11.30-11 Sun
☎ (01472) 278517
Abbeydale Moonshine; Black Sheep Best Bitter; Draught Bass; 4 changing beers Ⓗ
A warm welcome awaits allcomers at this friendly, well-appointed Ember Inn. Visitors are greeted by the delightful sight of 10 handpumps serving wonderful ales, with a guarantee of a perfect pour. Monday is designated cask club day, when prices are reduced. There is a menu of excellent food, with promotions at all times. The large bar services several seating areas and there are two outside areas to accommodate smokers.
P(8,51)

Spiders Web

180 Carr Lane, DN32 8LN
12-11.30 (12.30am Thu-Sat) ☎ (01472) 692065
thespiderswebgy.co.uk
John Smith's Bitter; Timothy Taylor Landlord; 2 changing beers (sourced regionally; often Black Sheep, St Austell, Thwaites) Ⓗ
Three-roomed '50s-built community pub which holds regular music nights of varied genres, including live bands most weekends in the function room to the side. The lounge is furnished with

banquette seating and a real fire, while in the public bar games such as poker, darts and pool are played and there is a weekly quiz night. At the rear is a large grassed play area and provision for smoking. Q❀♣P🚌(4)🐾📶

Wheatsheaf

Bargate, DN34 5AD

11-11 (midnight Fri & Sat); 12-11 Sun ☎ (01472) 246821

Abbeydale Moonshine; Brakspear Bitter; 3 changing beers H

Within walking distance of town, this popular Ember Inn has five real ales and a guaranteed perfect pour. There is good-quality food to suit all tastes, with promotions at all times. Two bars serve the split-level layout with various seating areas. A function room is available and quizzes are held on Sunday and Thursday nights. There is a heated patio at the rear and a grassed area at the front, and both accommodate smokers. ❀◐♿P🚌📶

Haconby

Hare & Hounds

2 West Road, PE10 0UZ

12-2, 6-11 (10.30 Mon); 12-11 Sat; 12-10.30 Sun ☎ (01778) 570521

Marston's EPA; 1 changing beer (sourced nationally; often Jennings) H

Low-beamed pub and popular dining establishment built around 1600 with soft settees in the back room. Walking groups frequent the pub and there is live music on the first and second Sundays as well as the third Monday of the month. Guest ales are from the Marston's stables, with one changing regularly. Nearby is the Primitive Baptist Methodist Chapel, built in 1867, which must be one of the smallest in the land. Q❀◐♿♣P🐾

Halton Holegate

Bell Inn

Spilsby Road, PE23 5PA

12-3 (not Mon & Tue), 6-11 ; 12-3, 5-11 Thu & Fri; 12-11 Sat & Sun ☎ (01790) 753242 🌐 thebell.me.uk

3 changing beers H

A 16th-century country inn with low beamed ceilings set in a quiet village. Pictures of the Dambusters adorn the small, cosy lounge. The welcoming landlord has a keen interest in quality beers, and the three guests are often from small breweries within the county. No food is served Mondays or Tuesdays. A computer club meets on Sunday evenings. Q❀◐♣●P🐾

Heighington

Butcher & Beast

High Street, LN4 1JS

12-11; 12-10.30 Sun ☎ (01522) 790386

Batemans Black & White, XB, XXXB; 3 changing beers H

A Batemans village pub in an old stone building with picturesque hanging baskets and a large garden with pétanque. Inside is a real fire, and historic local photographs hang on the walls. The six handpumps offer changing guest beers, as well as a range of Batemans beers. Real ciders and rare malt whiskies are also to be had. There is an extensive food menu, with themed nights (steak, fish and curry), and roasts on Sundays. Q❀◐♣●P🚌(2)🐾📶

Hemingby

Coach & Horses L

Church Lane, LN9 5QF (1 mile from A158 at Baumber)

12-2 (not Mon & Tue), 6-11; 12-2, 7-11 Sat; 12-3, 7-10.30 Sun ☎ (01507) 578280

3 changing beers (sourced regionally; often Clark's, Horncastle Ales, Tom Wood's) H

Nestling under the Lincolnshire Wolds, next to the church, this 17th-century pub has been in the same hands for over 20 years. A games area is separated from the bar by a double-sided open fire. The three beers on the bar always include a mild and usually a local brew. Good, reasonably priced meals and proper coffee are available. Beware the low beams. Q❀◐Ă♣P🐾

Holbeach

Cask in Hand L

3 Boston Road South, PE12 7LR

12-10; 12-4, 6-10 Thu; 12-11 Fri & Sat ☎ 07469 185952

4 changing beers G

A 17th-century coaching inn now recently reopened as a micropub. Beers are served by gravity from a stillage behind the bar, and most are from local microbreweries. The licensee is a third-generation publican, his grandfather and father both having run pubs in Holbeach. There is a large collection of old beer mats on display, some foreign, and many advertising tobacco products. Open mic and entertainment takes place every second Sunday of the month. Discounts on beers Monday to Friday lunchtimes. Q❀♣●🚌(505)🐾📶

Horbling

Plough Inn

4 Spring Lane, NG34 0PF

11.30-2.30, 6.30-11.30; 11.30-midnight Fri & Sat; 12-10.30 Sun ☎ (01529) 240263 🌐 theploughinnhorblingltd.co.uk

Adnams Ghost Ship; 1 changing beer (sourced nationally; often Horncastle Ales) H

Low-beamed, true community pub, built in 1832 and owned by the parish, set in a quiet village. In addition to the lounge and bar, its snug is surely one of the smallest and most intimate of its kind. Beers are often from microbreweries and change regularly. Home-cooked meals are served in the bar and restaurant. Spring wells are a feature just a few yards down the lane. CAMRA local Pub of the Year 2012/13. ❀◐♿♣●P🐾

Horncastle

King's Head

16 Bull Ring, LN9 5HU

12-midnight (11 Mon; 2am Fri & Sat); 12-1am Sun ☎ (01507) 523360

Batemans XB; 2 changing beers (sourced locally; often Batemans) H

A comfortable and friendly pub with a single bar/lounge that accommodates two separate drinking areas. Three beers from Batemans are normally available. Unusually for this locality the building has a thatched roof, hence its local name, the Thatch. Reputedly the pub inspired an 00 gauge Hornby model, an example of which is displayed behind the bar. In summer the exterior is bedecked with hanging baskets and it has won the Batemans Floral Display competition. ❀🚌🐾📶

Ingoldmells

Countryman 🄻

Chapel Road, PE25 1ND

12-midnight ☎ (01754) 872268

home2.btconnect.com/countryman-ingoldmells

Leila Cottage Leila's Lazy Days, Ace Ale, Lincolnshire Life, Leila's One Off 🄷

The privately-owned Countryman appears to be a modern building but it incorporates the early 19th-century Leila Cottage, which gives its name to the brewery behind the pub. A notorious smuggler, James Waite, used to reside here when Ingoldmells was a wild and lonely place, but he certainly would not recognise the current holiday coast, with Skegness, Butlin's and Fantasy Island nearby. Information boards give brewery, pub and beer information for visitors. The pub is on northern bus routes from Skegness.

Irnham

Griffin Inn

15 Bulby Road, NG33 4JG

closed Mon & Tue; 11-3, 6-11; 12-3, 6-10.30 Sun ☎ (01476) 550201 thegriffinirnham.co.uk

Oakham JHB; 2 changing beers (often Batemans, Star) 🄷

The Griffin is a recently refurbished 200-year-old stone-built property with a bar area serving Oakham JHB and two changing and personally sourced microbrewery beers. Two separate dining rooms offer a wide selection of food from the traditional to the innovative. It was recently awarded 4 stars by Visit England. Spring/summer vintage and classic car evenings start on the first Wednesday of the month, April to September.
Q P

Kirkby on Bain

Ebrington Arms

Main Street, LN10 6YT

12-2 (not Mon), 6-11 ☎ (01526) 354560

ebringtonarms.com

Adnams Broadside; Batemans XB; Black Sheep Golden Sheep; Sharp's Doom Bar; 2 changing beers 🄷

Attractive country pub close to the River Bain and dating from 1610. World War II airmen used to slot coins into the ceiling beams to pay for beer when they returned from missions over Germany. Sadly, many of these coins are still in situ and make a unique memorial to the dead. The popular restaurant offers good food made with local produce (booking advised). There is a convenient caravan site within a mile of the pub.
Q P (65)

Lincoln

Adam & Eve Tavern

25 Lindum Road, LN2 1NT

12-11 (midnight Fri & Sat) ☎ (01522) 537108

adamandevelincoln.co.uk

Castle Rock Harvest Pale; Greene King Abbot; 2 changing beers 🄷

Sitting halfway up Lindum Hill, opposite the medieval Pottergate Arch and within sight of the cathedral, this pub claims to be Lincoln's oldest. It has the atmosphere of an old tavern, with low ceilings, open fires and doorways leading to many rooms off the large bar. But this is not a pub stuck in the past – it has live bands playing regularly, two screens showing sport, a weekly quiz, dartboard and a pool table. P

Dog & Bone 🏆

10 John Street, LN2 5BH

4.30-11; 12-11 Fri-Sun ☎ (01522) 522403

dogandbonelincoln.co.uk

Batemans XB, Gold; 4 changing beers 🄷

A traditional two-roomed pub tucked away a short walk from the city centre. Features include changing displays of artwork, a plentiful supply of games and an extensive book-swap library. It has a strong community following, with a craft group, cook-offs, quizzes, regular rambles, music and more. There is an outdoor room for groups, meals or meetings, and the garden is stunning. Home-cooked food is served Thursday and Friday evenings and Saturday lunchtimes. Local CAMRA Pub of the Year 2014. (4)

Golden Eagle

21 High Street, LN5 8BD

11-11 (11.30 Fri & Sat); 12-11 Sun ☎ (01522) 521058

Castle Rock Harvest Pale; Fuller's London Pride; 7 changing beers (sourced nationally; often Newby Wyke, Oldershaw, Pheasantry) 🄷

Formerly a coaching inn, this two-roomed establishment has up to nine ales. Broadoak Moonshine is the regular cider. A recent refurbishment has given the bar a more relaxed and rustic look. The lounge, with its logburner, is quiet and cosy, with old football programmes on display. Outside is a premier beer garden with sheltered seating, lights and heaters. Friday is quiz night, and occasional beer festivals and live music events take place. Food is served 12-7pm every day. Q P

Jolly Brewer 🄻

27 Broadgate, LN2 5AQ

12-11 (midnight Fri & Sat); 12-8 Sun ☎ (01522) 528583

jollybrewer.org

Tom Wood's Lincoln Gold; Welbeck Abbey Henrietta, Portland Black; 3 changing beers 🄷

A friendly and quirky pub, just a short walk from the town centre, serving an interesting range of beer and ciders. You will find it a pleasant place to relax and escape the bustle of town during the day and to enjoy the many live music events and quizzes in the evening. The Jolly Brewer has an pleasant beer garden which is both heated and sheltered, and is regarded as an excellent live music venue during the summer months.
P

Morning Star

11 Greetwell Gate, LN2 4AW

11-midnight; 12-11 Sun ☎ (01522) 527079

Draught Bass; Ruddles Best Bitter; Timothy Taylor Golden Best; Wells Bombardier; 2 changing beers (sourced regionally; often Brains, Castle Rock, Ossett) 🄷

An 18th-century pub close to Lincoln Cathedral and near bus stops on several routes. The cosy main bar, with an open fire, is usually buzzing with chatter and has pictures of old Lincoln on the walls. There is a small snug/back bar. Quiz night is Tuesday and there is occasional live music. The two guest beers change regularly. Q P

Strugglers Inn 🄻

83 Westgate, LN1 3BG

12-1am (11 Mon & Tue; midnight Wed); 12-11.30 Sun
(01522) 535023
Greene King Abbot; St Austell Tribute; Timothy Taylor Landlord; 6 changing beers (often Brewster's, Welbeck Abbey, Wentworth) H
Standing in the shadow of Lincoln Castle, the Struggs is a magnet for locals and visitors alike. The small main bar and even smaller snug are often crammed with drinkers in the evenings. The containers in the sunken garden are a riot of colour throughout the summer. Pumpclips festoon the walls, evidence of the wide variety of ales that has featured on the nine handpumps – over 550 in a single year. Filled bread rolls may be available.
Q(7,8)

Victoria
6 Union Road, LN1 3BJ
11-midnight (1am Fri & Sat); 12-midnight Sun
(01522) 541000
Batemans XB, Gold; Castle Rock Harvest Pale; Timothy Taylor Landlord; 4 changing beers H
Under the majestic shadow of Lincoln Castle, the Victoria certainly is not lacking atmosphere. You can be sure of a warm welcome and a relaxed atmosphere. The suntrap beer garden offers stunning views of the castle while the interior is in traditional style. It always has beautiful-quality cask ales, as well as superb real ciders and perries, and offers everything from hearty meals to light snacks. The pub hosts regular live music and quizzes. **Q**

West End Tap
108 Newland Street West, LN1 1PE
4-11.30 (12.30am Fri); 1-12.30am Sat; 3-11.30 Sun 07970 872530
5 changing beers (sourced nationally; often Adnams, Dark Star, Oakham) H
Tucked away in the west end of Lincoln, this little free house has not been open long but has a wonderful community atmosphere and knowledgeable staff. The beer garden is a suntrap and the pub welcomes dogs. Open mic, comedy and quiz nights are hosted monthly, as well as regular live bands and occasional beer-tasting evenings. It has a wide range of cask ales, international bottles and one real cider.

Wig & Mitre
30 Steep Hill, LN2 1LU
8.30am-11; 8.30am-9.30 Sun (01522) 535190
wigandmitre.com
Black Sheep Best Bitter; Everards Tiger; Oakham JHB; 1 changing beer H
Located in the city's historic cathedral quarter atop the appropriately named Steep Hill, the characterful 14th-century building has many rooms, making it perfect for parties, meetings or intimate get-togethers. Bars on both floors mean you are not traipsing up and down stairs carrying your pint. Mind your head on the low ceilings in parts of the building. Catering for drinkers and diners alike, it is popular for its themed dining evenings and Meet the Brewer nights. **Q**

Little Cawthorpe

Royal Oak Inn (Splash)
Watery Lane, LN11 8LZ (right off main road to Legbourne then left onto Buston Lane, through ford and turn left)
11-midnight (01507) 600750 royaloaksplash.co.uk
Black Sheep Best Bitter; Greene King IPA; 2 changing beers H
Known locally as the Splash because of the picturesque ford nearby, this 400-year-old inn is situated in its own large lawned gardens on the edge of the Lincolnshire Wolds near Louth. Four beers are regularly on the bar, and often a guest ale from a local brewery. Three restaurants cover most culinary requirements and themed evenings are popular. The en-suite rooms are often used by visitors to Cadwell Park or explorers of the Wolds.
P

Little Steeping

Eaves Inn
Main Road, PE23 5BL
closed Mon-Wed; 6.30-11 Thu-Sat; 12-4 Sun
(01754) 830639 theeavesinn.com
Batemans XB H
The Eaves is the only pub remaining in the Five Parishes. The restaurant serves good-quality, locally sourced food and attracts visitors from the surrounding area. The venue has maintained a good local feel, and the bar area with a log fire and comfortable chairs is a cosy place to spend time, with the staff often joining in with the conversation. It also has a camping and caravan site attached. **QP**

Long Bennington

Reindeer
22 Main Road, NG23 5EH
closed Mon; 11.30-3, 6-11; 12-4 Sun (01400) 281382
reindeerinn.co.uk
Adnams Southwold Bitter; Timothy Taylor Landlord; 1 changing beer (often Fuller's, St Austell, Wells) H
Delightful 18th-century village pub, run by the same landlady for over 30 years, with a cosy and welcoming public bar area where four beers are always available. The Reindeer has an excellent area-wide reputation for superb food, served in the dining room or in the comfortable lounge. At the front there is large outdoor drinking space with tables and umbrellas. Any journey up or down the A1 would benefit from a visit. **QP**

Louth

Brown Cow
133 Newmarket, LN11 9EG (top of Newmarket on jct with Church St)
5-11; 12-3 Fri; 12-11 Sat & Sun (01507) 605146
Black Sheep Best Bitter; Castle Rock Harvest Pale; Courage Directors; Fuller's London Pride; 1 changing beer H
Friendly town pub with a great atmosphere and, most importantly, great beer. A free quiz is held every Sunday night and the local folk club meets here on a Tuesday evening. The popular bistro serves traditional, home-cooked food, made with locally sourced products. Every Thursday is pie night, with a selection of different pies. Food is served Thursday to Sunday. The pub is a great community meeting place.
QP(51)

Gas Lamp Lounge L
13 Thames Street, LN11 7AD (bottom of Thames St by factories)

🕓 5-11; 12-11 Sat & Sun ☎ (01507) 607661
🌐 fulstowbrewery.com/News.html
Fulstow Common, Marsh Mild, Northway IPA; 1 changing beer Ⓗ
A unique pub, one of only 22 in the UK lit by gas lamps, with no music or bandits, just good pub traditions. It serves four regular beers from the upstairs brewery, plus one guest. Benches are set along the canalside for enjoying a drink during the summer, and inside you will find a roaring logburner to sit by in the winter months.
Q♿♣●**P**🚌🐾📶

Joseph Morton

Pawnshop Passage, LN11 9EZ (small alleyway off Mercer Row)
🕓 8am-midnight (1am Fri & Sat) ☎ (01507) 353700
Batemans XXXB; Greene King Abbot; Ruddles County; changing beers (sourced regionally; often Black Horse, Milestone) Ⓗ
A JD Wetherspoon establishment which opened in May 2011 in Louth town centre. The pub offers good-value food and a large selection of regional and national ales. The former warehouse was built between 1808 and 1834 and has cast-iron wall plates bearing the name of the local ironmonger, Joseph Morton. ❀◐♿●🚌(9,10,51)📶

Wheatsheaf

62 Westgate, LN11 9YD
🕓 11-11 ☎ (01507) 606262
Batemans XB; Black Sheep Ale; Brains Bitter; Thornbridge Jaipur IPA; 1 changing beer Ⓗ
Picturesque thatched-roof pub close to Louth's historic St James' Church, which has the tallest spire of any medieval parish church in England and is visible from miles around. The pub offers a good selection of real ales and a tasty home-made food menu. There is a lovely beer garden and the venue is a popular meeting place for walkers and ramblers. ◐♿**P**🐾

Ludford

White Hart 🏆 L

Magna Mile, LN8 6AD
🕓 closed Mon; 12-2 (not Tue-Thu), 6-11; 11-2, 6-11 Sat; 12-3.30, 7-11 Sun ☎ (01507) 313489
4 changing beers Ⓗ
A flagship ale pub – Mick and Jenny do their best to get as many beers behind the bar as possible and pride themselves on serving real ale from microbreweries. Formerly a coaching house dating from the 18th century, it is now a two-roomed, rural village inn, close to the Viking Way and popular with hikers and ramblers. Four different guest beers are offered. Meals are available lunchtimes and evenings. All food is home made using ingredients from local suppliers. **Q**🛏◐**P**

Market Deeping

Vine Inn L

19 Church Street, PE6 8AN
🕓 4-11; 12-11.30 Fri; 12-11 Sat & Sun ☎ (01778) 218622
Sharp's Doom Bar; house beer (by Wells); 3 changing beers (often Grainstore, Hopshackle, Star) Ⓗ
A free house since 2011, this small, friendly pub was once a Victorian school. The bar features oak beams and stone floors, with interesting mid 20th-century framed prints on all the walls. There is a large patio at the rear. Five handpumps dispense two regular beers and a changing range of mostly LocAle guests. Westons Rosie's Pig cider is served. Free nibbles are provided Sunday lunchtimes and early during the week. The TV is only used for major sporting events. ❀●**P**🚌(101)🐾📶

Messingham

Pooleys

46 High Street, DN17 3NT
🕓 closed Mon; 6-11; 7-11 Sun ☎ (01724) 762220
5 changing beers (often Batemans, Everards, Greene King) Ⓗ
Pooleys is a compact and tastefully rustic village local, only open in the evenings. Popular with local drinkers and visitors alike, the bar has five handpulled real ales and a selection of unusual keg beers plus many malt whiskies. It comprises three rooms, heated by log-burning stoves in the colder months. A smaller drinking area off the main room leads to a larger glass-roofed area where children are allowed until 9pm. **Q**♿🚌(100,103)🐾📶

New Waltham

Harvest Moon

Station Road, DN36 4QQ
🕓 11.30-11; 11-midnight Fri & Sat ☎ (01472) 824659
Brakspear Bitter; Tetley Bitter; York Yorkshire Terrier; 1 changing beer Ⓗ
A large, comfortably furnished Ember Inn with distinct areas, one of which is a dining space where children are welcome. Three permanent beers are on the bar and one seasonal, changed three-monthly, while food is available daily from midday, with vegetarians catered for. Low background music and occasional weekend live acts feature. Quiz nights are Sunday, Monday and Wednesday. Televised football is limited to one area and there is a heated smokers' space plus a secluded beer garden. A complete pub for all tastes.
❀◐♿♣**P**🚌(8)📶

North Hykeham

Centurion

Newark Road, LN6 8LB
🕓 11-11 (midnight Thu-Sat) ☎ (01522) 509814
Abbeydale Moonshine; Brakspear Bitter; Wells Bombardier; 5 changing beers Ⓗ
A modern, family-friendly pub in North Hykeham, a few miles south of Lincoln city centre. It is part of the Mitchell & Butlers Ember Inns brand. The place appeals to drinkers and diners alike, offering a good selection of national ales and international bottled beers, as well as food served until 10pm daily. Three quiz nights a week, along with regular food and drink offers, cement the pub's popularity within the local community.
❀◐♿⇌(Hykeham)♣**P**🚌(27,46)📶

Norton Disney

Green Man L

Main Street, LN6 9JU
🕓 12-3 (not Mon), 5.30-11; 10-11 Sat; 10-10 Sun ☎ (01522) 789804
3 changing beers (often Grafters, Oldershaw, Star) Ⓗ
In an idyllic village setting, this modern and cosy pub has a real fire, TV in the bar area and a separate dining area. There are three rotating ales, often from Lincolnshire breweries. Real ciders are

also offered, changing on a regular basis. Good-quality food is served lunchtimes and evenings, and includes vegetarian dishes. A large beer garden offering extensive views is at the rear. Q ⚲ ✿ ❀ ◑ ఉ ♣ ➽ P ✿ 🔊 🛜

Old Bolingbroke

Black Horse Inn

Moat Lane, PE23 4HH
✿ closed Mon; 8.30-11 Tue; 12-3, 7-11 ☎ (01790) 763388
Young's Bitter; 3 changing beers (sourced regionally; often Milestone, Wold Top) Ⓗ
In a splendid walking area, this fine old country inn has 14th-century origins but was largely rebuilt in 1930. Henry IV was born at nearby Bolingbroke Castle, which was besieged during the Civil War. Still part of the Duchy of Lancaster, the Black Horse is a great place to visit when exploring the Lincolnshire Wolds. Friday fish night is a speciality and there are other popular themed food nights. Lunchtime meals are available weekends only. Q ✿ ◑ ఉ ♣ ▲ ➽ P ✿ 🛜

Pinchbeck

Bull Inn

1 Knight Street, PE11 3RA
✿ 12-2.30, 5-11; 12-midnight Fri & Sat; 12-11 Sun
☎ (01775) 723022
John Smith's Bitter; Wadworth Henry's IPA; 1 changing beer Ⓗ
Welcoming, friendly village pub opposite the old stocks with two comfortable bars – the public bar with a log fire, and the lounge, used mainly for dining. A carved bull's head features on the long bar front, with the bar rail representing its horns. The pub has a reputation for good food, from bar snacks to meals in the upstairs restaurant, including weekend carveries. Guest beers often come from local micros. Quiz night is the second Tuesday of the month. ✿ ◑ ఉ P 🖂 (59,113) 🛜

Ruskington

Shoulder of Mutton

11 Church Street, NG34 9DU
✿ 12-11 ☎ (01526) 832220
John Smith's Bitter; Sharp's Doom Bar; 1 changing beer Ⓗ
A popular and thriving pub in the heart of the village which attracts customers of all ages. With its low wooden ceilings in its two main rooms it is probably one of the oldest buildings in the village and, reputedly, once housed a butcher's shop, hence the name. Although additions have been made in recent years they have not spoilt the essential character. There is a separate pool room. ✿ ఉ ≈ ♣ P 🖂 (31) ✿ 🛜

Saxilby

Anglers

65 High Street, LN1 2HA
✿ 11.30-11.30 (12.30am Fri & Sat); 12-11.30 Sun
☎ (01522) 702200
Caledonian Deuchars IPA; Theakston Best Bitter; 2 changing beers (often Brains) Ⓗ
Built as a hotel, this imposing building dates from the 1890s. At the heart of the village in more ways than one, the pub is home to pool, dominoes, crib and darts teams, and two golf societies. Regular

poker nights are held. The pool table is towards the rear and does not impinge on the main drinking area. The small lounge has old photographs of the village. Moorings on the historic Fossdyke Navigation are close by. ✿ ≈ ♣ P 🖂 (100,105) ✿ 🛜

Scampton

Dambusters Inn Ⓛ

23 High Street, LN1 2SD
✿ 5-7 Mon; 12-11 (midnight Fri & Sat); 12-10.30 Sun
☎ (01522) 731333 ⊕ dambustersinn.co.uk
Greg's Navigator, Aviator, Final Approach; Timothy Taylor Landlord; 2 changing beers Ⓗ
From the outside this is an unassuming country pub – walk inside and you will think you have entered a RAF museum. An entire wall is dedicated to the men of 617 Squadron, known as the Dambusters, after whom the pub is named. The tap to Greg's Brewery, it is popular with drinkers and diners alike. It is a peaceful hostelry, free of intrusive TVs or booming sound systems – the peace only interrupted by the roaring engines of the world-famous Red Arrows. Do not miss the artwork in the lavatories. Q ⚲ ✿ ◑ ➽ P 🖂 (103) ✿ 🛜

Scawby

Sutton Arms

10 West Street, DN20 9AN
✿ 11.30-midnight ☎ (01652) 652430
Theakston Best Bitter; 3 changing beers (often Axholme, Horncastle Ales, Milestone) Ⓗ
Comfortable village local renowned for its excellent food. A central bar serves an open-plan dining area and a separate dining room, with a small snug on one side which is used mostly for drinking. It has an extensive food menu plus daily specials available lunchtimes and evenings; steak night is Wednesday. Theakston Best Bitter is the regular beer, supplemented by three rotating guest ales – these have tasting notes displayed on the bar. Sunday is quiz night. ✿ ◑ P

Scunthorpe

Berkeley Hotel ★

Doncaster Road, DN15 7DS (½ mile from end of M181)
✿ 11.30-2.30, 5-11; 12-11 Fri & Sat; 12-10.30 Sun
☎ (01724) 842333 ⊕ theberkeleyscunthorpe.co.uk
Samuel Smith Old Brewery Bitter Ⓗ
Large 1930s Samuel Smith's pub and hotel. The landscaped front entrance, suitable for wheelchairs, leads to three rooms. The main lounge bar, with Art Deco interior, has a real fire; the second is a large eating/drinking/family room with a ballroom leading off, the latter used for functions. A side entrance provides access to the large public bar and rear beer garden. Eight guest rooms are available. The pub is five minutes' walk from Glanford Park football ground. Q ⚲ ✿ 🛏 ◑ ఉ ♣ ➽ P 🖂 (37,40) 🛜

Blue Bell

1-7 Oswald Road, DN15 7PU (at town centre crossroads)
✿ 8am-midnight (1am Sat) ☎ (01724) 863921
Greene King Abbot; Ruddles Best Bitter; 6 changing beers (often Acorn, Dark Star, Saltaire) Ⓗ
Popular Wetherspoon town centre pub with an open-plan layout on two levels. The upper level is a family and dining area with a guarded fire; the

lower level, also used for dining, has wooden and carpeted floors with a mix of high and low seating. The enclosed beer garden at the rear has a heated area for smokers. Six rotating guest beers are generally available plus real ciders. Beer festivals are held regularly, and the establishment has free Wi-Fi and a muted TV screen for sport/news. Food is served all day until 11pm. Q

Malt Shovel

219 Ashby High Street, DN16 2JP (in Ashby Broadway shopping area)
10-11 (midnight Fri & Sat); 12-11 Sun ☎ (01724) 843318
Exmoor Gold; Tom Wood's Best Bitter; 4 changing beers (often Acorn, Mallinsons, Oakham) [H]
Comfortably furnished single-room pub with a dining/drinking conservatory. The new management team promoted from within have retained enthusiasm for quality ales served in friendly surroundings. Oakham beers remain a permanent fixture alongside three regionally sourced, regularly changing guests and real ciders. The pub can get busy lunchtimes and early evening for good-value, home-cooked food. Quiz nights are Tuesday and Thursday, live music features on alternate Saturdays and a folk night monthly on Sunday. Members-only snooker facilities are available.

Skendleby

Blacksmiths Arms

Main Road, PE23 4QE
12-3 (not Mon), 5.30-11; 12-4 Sun ☎ (01754) 890662
Batemans XB; 2 changing beers [H]
A traditional country pub dating back to the 18th century, nestling on the south-east edge of the Lincolnshire Wolds. Ducking beneath the low door lintel, fortunately well-padded, you discover the gem of a small quarry-tiled snug, complete with range and settles, with the cellar visible through a glass panel behind the bar. The dining room at the rear incorporates the building's former well. There is also a separate restaurant and a conservatory. On the last Sunday of the month the pub opens 7pm-late with live music. Q P (96)

Skillington

Cross Swords

The Square, NG33 5HB
12-2 (not Mon), 7-11; 12-2, 6-11 Fri & Sat; 12-2 Sun ☎ (01476) 861132 thecross-swordsinn.co.uk
Draught Bass; Grainstore Steelback IPA; 1 changing beer (often Wells) [H]
Impressive stone-built pub dating from the early to mid 1800s. The current hosts, Harold and Linda, have owned the inn since 1991, with the ales on the bar from Grainstore Brewery and other LocAle brewers. Quality pub food is available daily and the pub boasts three letting cottages. Local CAMRA Country Pub of the Year 2014. P

Sleaford

Carre Arms Hotel

Mareham Lane, NG34 7JP
10-11 ☎ (01529) 303156 carrearmshotel.co.uk
3 changing beers [H]
A privately run hotel previously owned by Bass, adjacent to the Bass Sleaford maltings complex which is now awaiting a regeneration scheme. It has a comfortable bar area with two rooms, offering two or three real ales, normally from larger regional breweries, which change regularly. Draught cider is occasionally available on handpump. An extensive food menu is offered, served in the bar area or restaurant. There is a pleasant covered courtyard, ideal on inclement days. P

Packhorse Inn

7 Northgate, NG34 7BH
8am-midnight ☎ (01529) 308730
Greene King Abbot; Ruddles Best Bitter; 6 changing beers [H]
An 18th-century coaching inn on the London to Lincoln road that has had several names during its lifetime, reverting to the original name when taken over by Wetherspoon a few years ago. Despite being remodelled and now partly open plan, the pub retains an intimate atmosphere. As the Lion Hotel it hosted the inaugural dinner for the Sleaford Railway, an event that marked the beginning of the decline in coaching trade.
Q

Snitterby

Royal Oak

High Street, DN21 4TP (1½ miles from A15)
5-midnight; 12-midnight Sat; 12-9 Sun ☎ (01673) 818273
Adnams Lighthouse; Everards Tiger; Rooster's Buckeye [H]**; 5 changing beers (often Fuller's, Wold Top, Woodforde's)** [H]/[G]
Traditional family-run community pub in a village setting with up to eight real ales on – and more on bank holidays. During 2015 it has run a coastal beer trail with guest beers themed around a tour of the coastal counties of Britain. The comfortable, spacious interior is light and airy, with real fires. The outside seating area overlooks a stream and ford. Sky Sports is shown in the lounge and the pub features monthly pop-up pizza nights.
P

South Ormsby

Massingberd Arms

Brinkhill Road, LN11 8QS (1 mile off A16)
closed Mon; 12-2.30, 6-11; 12-11 Sun ☎ (01507) 480492
Thwaites Original; 1 changing beer [H]
A old, traditional country pub set in the heart of the Lincolnshire Wolds, a designated Area of Outstanding Natural Beauty. Home-cooked food is served here and a quiz for charity takes place every Wednesday night. The landlord has recently upgraded the dining room which now has a woodburner. A proper country hostelry in a beautiful location – walkers welcome.
Q P

Spalding

Ivy Wall

18-19 New Road, PE11 1DQ
8am-midnight (1am Fri & Sat) ☎ (01775) 719770
Greene King Abbot; Ruddles Best Bitter; Sharp's Doom Bar; Wychwood Hobgoblin; 4 changing beers [H]
The town-centre site on which this spacious modern pub now stands has had a variety of uses over the years, and used to be on the bank of the former Westlode River. Excavations during the rebuild in 2005 discovered an undercroft and cellar

from the late medieval period. There is a guest cider dispensed by gravity, and food is available all day. Photographs and archaeological finds are displayed on the wall.

Priors Oven

1 Sheep Market, PE11 1BH

closed Mon; 12-9 (10 Thu; midnight Fri & Sat)

6 changing beers

The first micropub to open in Lincolnshire. The building has quite a history and is believed to be 800 years old – it was originally the prison of the local priory. Its more recent use was as a bakery, and it acquired its current identity in mid-December 2013. As well as the ground floor bar with its domed ceiling, it has a comfortable lounge room accessed by a stone spiral staircase. Beers can be sampled in third-pint measures. Q

Red Lion Hotel

Market Place, PE11 1SU

10-midnight (01775) 722869

redlionhotel-spalding.co.uk

Draught Bass; Greene King Abbot; Wells Bombardier; 1 changing beer

Cosy and welcoming, this one-room traditional hotel bar is popular with locals and visitors. It overlooks the marketplace, with tables and chairs outside in fine weather. It is a regular entry in this Guide owing to its excellent range of cask ales, which the bar staff take great pride in serving in top condition. It is a rare outlet for Bass in the locality. P

Stamford

Green Man

29 Scotgate, PE9 2YQ

11-midnight; 12-midnight Sun (01780) 753598

Castle Rock Harvest Pale; Sharp's Doom Bar; 6 changing beers (often Blue Monkey, Kelham Island, Sheffield)

Dating from 1796, this stone-built former coaching inn has an L-shaped split-level bar warmed by a real fire. Up to eight ales, complemented by a good range of European bottled beers, are available. As many as seven ciders and perries, often from Broadoak, are on offer. Beer festivals are held at Easter and in September on the secluded patio, which boasts a mounting block from the days when visitors arrived on horseback. The pub has much beer memorabilia adorning the walls.
(201)

Jolly Brewer

1 Foundry Road, PE9 2PP

11-midnight; 12-11.30 Sun (01780) 755141

jollybrewer.com

Brewster's Marquis; Oakham JHB; 4 changing beers (often Grainstore, Magpie, Tydd Steam)

A stone-built inn dating from 1830, comprising an L-shaped room surrounding the bar and an adjoining small room that serves as a dining area. Outside is a large paved area with tables. The home-cooked food is locally sourced. The pub is home to pool, darts, crib and dominoes teams from the local community. Beers from six handpumps come from local and countrywide brewers. One handpump serves cider, usually Old Rosie. A good range of malt whiskies is available.
Q P (9,202)

Tobie Norris

12 Saint Pauls Street, PE9 2BE

11.30-11; 12-10.30 Sun (01780) 753800

tobienorris.com

Adnams Southwold Bitter; Castle Rock Harvest Pale; 3 changing beers (sourced regionally; often Adnams, Colchester, Moonshine)

The building, parts of which date back to 1280, was bought by Tobie Norris in 1617 and used as a bell foundry. A conversion into a pub from the former RAFA Club gained it CAMRA's Conversion to Pub Use Award in 2007. It is split into many small rooms with real fires, stone floors and low beams. Five handpumps serve beers from local and countrywide brewers, and two beer festivals are held each year. At least one real cider is always available. Q (202,203)

Stickford

Red Lion Inn

Church Road, PE22 8EP

closed Mon & Tue; 7-11; 4-11.30 Fri & Sat; 12-10.30 Sun (01205) 480395 redlionstickford.co.uk

Batemans XB; 1 changing beer

The inn's name is the most common in England, and frequently found hereabouts because it was a heraldic emblem of the 14th-century John of Gaunt, Earl of Lancaster, and Lord of the Manor at nearby Bolingbroke Castle. This cosy and friendly two-bar pub produces its own range of cider and holds an annual cider festival. Food is served evenings and Sunday lunchtimes using local produce, and all pies are home made. There are two en-suite letting bedrooms.
Q P (113)

Sutterton

Thatched Cottage

Pools Lane, PE20 2EZ

11.30-11.30 (01205) 460870

thatchedcottagerestaurant.co.uk

Batemans XB; Greene King 1799; Wells Bombardier

Thatched 17th-century listed building, a rarity in fen country, which was a private house until 1985. Although extended and modernised to the rear, the bar and separate dining-room exhibit a wealth of ancient timbers and inglenook fireplaces. Tall people beware! Behind the pub is a country farm store, and meat is butchered and cured on the premises. Outside is an area for giant chess, pétanque and quoits, together with a country park containing a natural burial ground and arboretum.
Q P (113)

Sutton on Sea

Bacchus Hotel

17 High Street, LN12 2EY

11-11 (01507) 441204 bacchushotel.co.uk

Bacchus Best Bitter, Blonde; Greene King Abbot; Ruddles Best Bitter

This hotel in the seaside resort of Sutton on Sea offers a range of ales, including those brewed by the adjoining brewery. The hotel accommodation has recently been upgraded and there is a comfortable bar, restaurant and function room. The pub hosts two beer festivals a year, usually in May and August, which attract people to the area.
Q P (9)

Swineshead

Pig & Whistle

Market Place, PE20 3LJ

⏲ 5.30 (12 Sat)-11; 12-4, 7.30-11 Sun ☎ (01205) 821381

Banks's Mild; Fuller's London Pride; 3 changing beers 🄷

Years ago the pub was called the Green Dragon – its fortunes gradually declined, it became run down and, despite a change of name, it eventually closed. Now the current owners have brought it back to life as a vibrant and thriving village local, successfully blending old and new to recreate a genuine community pub with an emphasis on beer and traditional pub games. Guest beers come from a wide range of breweries and the food comprises home-made pizzas and bar snacks.
❀◑♣●P🚌(K59)

Swinhope

Clickem Inn

Binbrook Road, LN8 6BS (2 miles N of Binbrook on B1203)

⏲ 12-3 (not Mon-Wed), 5-11; 12-11.30 Fri & Sat; 12-10.30 Sun ☎ (01472) 398253 🌐 clickem-inn.co.uk

Batemans XXXB; Timothy Taylor Landlord; house beer (by Batemans); 3 changing beers 🄷

Country pub in the picturesque Lincolnshire Wolds and a good stopping place for walkers and cyclists. The unusual name originates from the counting of sheep passing through a nearby clicking gate. Good home-cooked food is served in the bar and conservatory, while six handpumps feature beers from independent and regional breweries, including a house beer called Terry's Tipple (Batemans XB). A covered but unheated area outside is provided for smokers. Local CAMRA branch Country Pub of the Year 2014.
Q🐴❀◐◑♣●P📶

Tattershall Thorpe

Blue Bell Inn

Thorpe Road, LN4 4PE

⏲ closed Mon; 12-3, 6-11; 12-4 Sun ☎ (01526) 342206 🌐 bluebell-inn.com

Batemans XB; Thwaites Lancaster Bomber; Tom Wood's Bomber County; 2 changing beers 🄷

This ancient building, in a delightful location, has 13th-century origins and is one of Lincolnshire's oldest inns. It has a large open fire and beamed ceilings that are covered in signatures and photographs of airmen from World War II RAF squadrons who used the pub, including the 617 Dambusters and 627 Pathfinders. King Henry VIII reputedly visited the Blue Bell and there is a ghost in residence. Q🐴❀◐◑♿⛺♣P📶

Threekingham

Three Kings Inn

Saltersway, NG34 0AU

⏲ closed Mon; 12-3, 6-11; 12-3, 6-10.30 Sun ☎ (01529) 240249 🌐 thethreekingsinn.com

Draught Bass; Morland Old Speckled Hen; Timothy Taylor Landlord; 1 changing beer 🄷

A classic country inn with charm and character. Its bright and comfortable lounge bar with attractive rural prints, and panelled dining room serving locally-sourced food, are deservedly popular with locals and visitors. Guest beers are usually from independent brewers. There is a pleasant beer terrace and garden for summer months and a large function room. The pub's name refers to the slaying, by the Saxons, of three Danish chieftains in battle in 870 at nearby Stow; look for the effigies above the entrance. ❀◐◑⛺P🐾

Waddington

Three Horseshoes 🄻

High Street, LN5 9RF

⏲ 3 (2 Fri; 11 Sat)-11; 12-11 Sun ☎ (01522) 720448

John Smith's Bitter; 4 changing beers 🄷

Four frequently changing ales make this pub worth seeking out. The main bar area is usually busy and has one screen showing sport, although there is also a quieter side room. Both have real fires. Situated next to the church in the heart of the village, this pub has a strong community feel but still offers a warm welcome to visiting guests, especially any who can master their hook and ring pub game. 🐴❀♣🚌(1,13)🐾

Wainfleet

Batemans Brewery Visitor Centre 🄻

Salem Bridge Brewery, Mill Lane, PE24 4JE

⏲ 11.30-4; closed Jan & Mon bateman.co.uk

Batemans Black & White, XB, Gold, XXXB; 1 changing beer (sourced locally; often Batemans) 🄷

Visiting Batemans brewery provides the chance to experience the blend of Batemans' proud 140-plus years of craft brewing tradition with its forward-looking attitude. Mr George's Bar, within the attractive windmill, is the ideal venue to sample a range of the brewery's beers. Further entertainment is to be found with brewery tours, featuring the Theatre of Beers, and in the pleasant beer garden with its games. A good range of Lincolnshire food is served 12-2pm. Tours take place at 12.30pm and 2.30pm in summer, 2.30pm in winter. Q🐴❀◐♿⛺⇌♣P🚌(7)📶

Waltham

Tilted Barrel

2 Kirkgate, DN37 0LS

⏲ 10-11 (midnight Thu-Sat); 11-11 Sun ☎ (01472) 826887 🌐 tiltedbarrel.co.uk

Morland Old Speckled Hen; Tetley Bitter; Theakston Best Bitter; 1 changing beer (sourced regionally; often Batemans, Timothy Taylor) 🄷

A bustling local free house with a single bar warmed by a coal fire and period photographs on the walls. It has the look of a cosy country pub, with a paved terrace outside. Three permanent beers and a regularly changing one make for a varied, always well-kept, choice. Televised football and rugby are a major attraction. Food is served daily until 8pm in the bar. A visitor will immediately feel at home in this friendly and well cared for family pub. 🐴❀🛏◐◑♿♣P🚌(9)🐾📶

Westwoodside

Carpenter's Arms

Newbigg, DN9 2AT (on B1396)

⏲ 4 (2 Sat)-11.30; 12-10.30 Sun ☎ (01427) 752416

Brains The Rev James; Caledonian Deuchars IPA; 3 changing beers (sourced nationally; often Black Sheep, Greene King) 🄷

Popular village local which takes an active part in the community and has raised significant sums for charity. A regular in this Guide under the present licensees, the pub actively promotes cask ale. Up to five are available, often including beers from microbreweries. The Carps hosts a variety of local events and participates in the Haxey Hood game in January. ♣P

Willingham by Stow

Half Moon

23 High Street, DN21 5JZ

5-10.30 Mon; 12-2, 5-11 (midnight Thu & Fri); 12-midnight Sat; 12-10.30 Sun ☎ (01427) 788340 graftersbrewery.com

Grafters Moonlight, Traditional, Over the Moon, Darker Side of the Moon; 4 changing beers H

Home to Grafters Brewery, this popular village pub goes from strength to strength. It offers four changing Grafters beers, and four additional pumps serve rotating guests, mainly from micros. Seasonal beers are also sold when brewed. The renowned home-cooked fish and chips are a must, available lunchtimes and evenings Tuesday-Friday, all day Saturday, and Sunday lunchtime (booking recommended). Brewery tours, including food and a tasting session, can be arranged by appointment. Q♣

Willoughton

Stirrup Inn

1 Templefield Road, DN21 5RZ

5 (3 Sat)-midnight; 12-11.30 Sun ☎ (01427) 668270

Black Sheep Best Bitter; 1 changing beer H

Built from local Lincolnshire limestone, this hidden gem in an out-of-the-way location is well worth seeking out, and you can be sure of a warm welcome. The pub oozes character, with a roaring log fire in winter, and is popular with locals and folk from further afield. A choice of ales is always available, with Black Sheep Best Bitter a permanent fixture, accompanied by two changing guests. Pub quizzes are well supported and traditional pub games are played. QP

Winterton

George Hogg

25 Market Street, DN15 9PT

2-11 (midnight Fri); 9.30am-midnight Sat; 9.30am-11 Sun ☎ (01724) 732270 thegeorgehogg.co.uk

Batemans XB; Tom Wood's Best Bitter; York Guzzler; 1 changing beer H

Popular Grade II-listed marketplace pub and local CAMRA award winner. It has a large lounge/dining area and a separate public bar, both with real fires. Good-value locally sourced food is served, plus home-made snacks, including breakfast on Sunday from 9.30am. Guest beers are sourced locally. The pub has an annual beer festival, and is a meeting place for football teams and the local supporters' club. There is an upstairs restaurant and tea and coffee are available. Cask Marque accredited. Q♣P(350)

Wragby

Ivy

Market Place, LN8 5QU

12-12.30am (1am Sat) ☎ (01673) 858768

theivy.vpweb.co.uk

Black Sheep Best Bitter; Draught Bass; 1 changing beer H

A free house, recently renovated, located by the market square in a 17th-century building. The large bar retains the original beams and a woodburner in the fireplace. Up to four ales are available, and the bar also keeps gluten-free bottled beers. Two side rooms form the restaurant, with a menu featuring local produce. Upstairs are six B&B rooms. The pub's crib team plays in the local league, and there are weekly charity quiz nights.
QP(6,10)

Wrawby

Black Horse

Melton Road, DN20 8SL (roadside on A18)

12 (5.30 Mon)-midnight ☎ (01652) 652382

theblackhorsewrawby.com

2 changing beers (often Kelham Island, Marston's, Sharp's) H

Large roadside establishment, tastefully decorated in village-inn style, comprising a spacious lounge set out for dining and a comfortable bar complete with wood-burning fire. The central bar displays a collection of pumpclips from previously featured beers. Two real ales are on the bar, rotated from a range of around eight different beers. The bar menu and carvery are available lunchtimes and evenings. The pub has a large beer garden at the rear. P

Jolly Miller

Brigg Road, DN20 8RH (roadside on A18)

12-11; 11.30-midnight Fri; 11.30-1am Sat; 11.30-11 Sun ☎ (01652) 655658 jollymiller.co.uk

Greene King IPA; 2 changing beers (often Batemans, Greene King) H

Comfortable village inn styled as an eatery but offering a changing range of real ales. It has a large, well-appointed lounge set out for meals at one end, plus a games room with a pool table and sports TV. Outside is a large, covered dining area called Miller's Store. Extensive lunchtime and evening menus can be enjoyed here Monday-Saturday, plus Sunday lunches. It serves three real ales, two of which are rotating guest beers.
♣P

A quart a day keeps the doctor away

A judicious labourer would probably always have some ale in his house, and have small beer for the general drink. There is no reason why he should not keep Christmas as well as the farmer; and when he is mowing, reaping, or is at any other hard work, a quart, or three pints, of really good fat ale a-day is by no means too much.

William Cobbett, Cottage Economy, 1822

London index

***Shown on Inner London map**

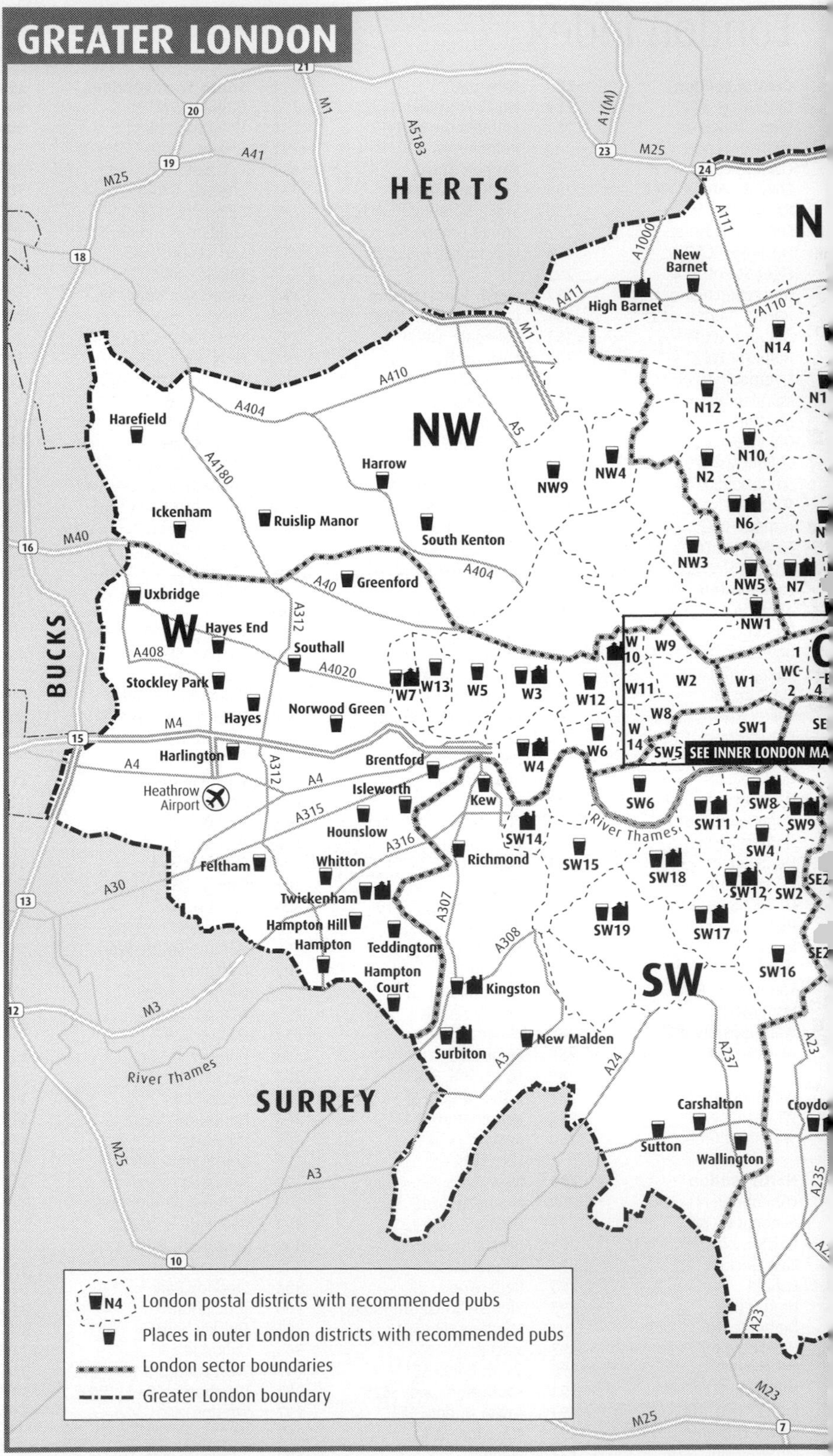
GREATER LONDON
HERTS
BUCKS
SURREY
NW
W
SW
N
Harefield
Ickenham
Ruislip Manor
Harrow
South Kenton
Greenford
Uxbridge
Hayes End
Southall
Stockley Park
Hayes
Norwood Green
Harlington
Heathrow Airport
Brentford
Isleworth
Hounslow
Feltham
Whitton
Twickenham
Hampton Hill
Hampton
Teddington
Hampton Court
Kew
Richmond
Kingston
Surbiton
New Malden
High Barnet
New Barnet
Carshalton
Sutton
Wallington
Croydon
NW9
NW4
NW3
NW5
NW1
N14
N12
N10
N2
N6
N7
N1
W13
W7
W5
W3
W12
W6
W4
W9
W2
W1
W 10
W11
W8
W 14
WC 1
WC 2
SW1
SW5
SW6
SW8
SW9
SW11
SW4
SW14
SW15
SW18
SW12
SW2
SW19
SW17
SW16
SEE INNER LONDON MA
River Thames
M25
M1
M40
M4
M3
A1(M)
A5183
A41
A1000
A411
A111
A110
A410
A404
A4180
A5
A40
A312
A408
A4020
A4
A315
A316
A30
A307
A308
A3
A24
A237
A23
A235
M23
21
20
19
23
24
18
16
15
13
12
10
7
London postal districts with recommended pubs
Places in outer London districts with recommended pubs
London sector boundaries
Greater London boundary

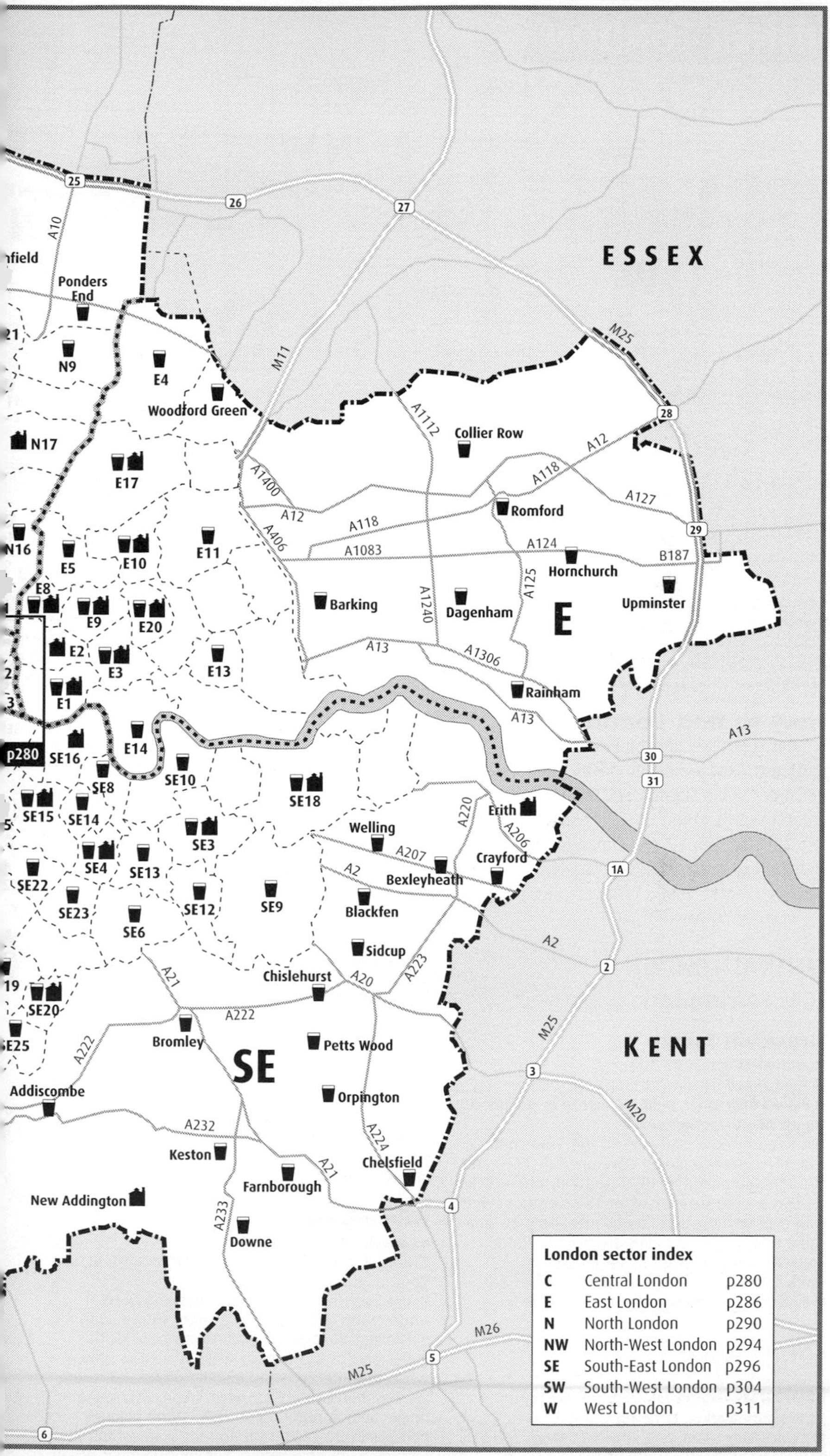
ESSEX
KENT
E
SE
Ponders End
N9
E4
Woodford Green
N17
E17
N16
E5
E10
E11
E8
E9
E20
E2
E3
E13
E1
E14
SE16
SE8
SE10
SE18
SE15
SE14
SE3
SE4
SE13
SE22
SE23
SE6
SE12
SE9
SE20
Collier Row
Romford
Hornchurch
Upminster
Barking
Dagenham
Rainham
Erith
Welling
Crayford
Bexleyheath
Blackfen
Sidcup
Chislehurst
Bromley
Petts Wood
Orpington
Addiscombe
Keston
Chelsfield
Farnborough
New Addington
Downe
p280

London sector index

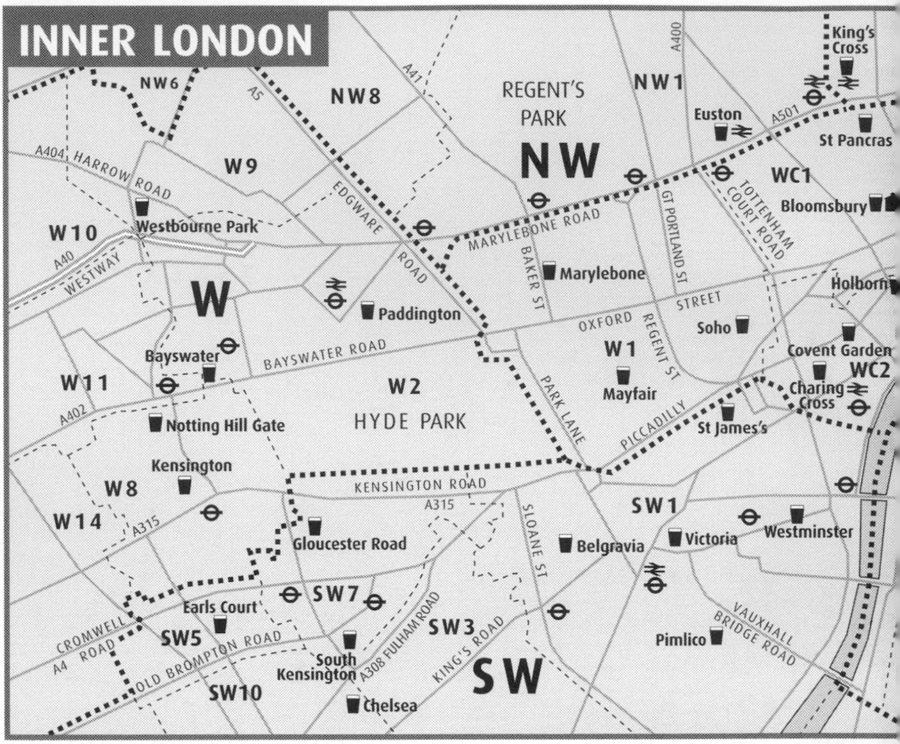

How to find London pubs

Greater London is divided into seven sectors: Central, East, North, North-West, South-East, South-West and West, reflecting postal boundaries. The Central sector includes the City (EC1 to EC4) and Holborn, Covent Garden and the Strand (WC1/2) plus W1, where pubs are listed in postal district order. In each of the other six sectors the pubs with London postcodes are listed first in postal district order (E1, E2 etc), followed by those in outer London districts, which are listed in alphabetical order (Barking, Chadwell Heath, etc) – see Greater London map. Postal district numbers can be found on every street name plate in the London postcode area.

CENTRAL LONDON

EC1: Farringdon

Jerusalem Tavern

55 Britton Street, EC1M 5UQ

11-11; closed Sat & Sun ☎ (020) 7490 4281

St Peter's Best Bitter, Mild, Organic Best, Organic Ale, Golden Ale, Grapefruit Beer A

This site can be traced back to the 14th century, with the current building developed in 1720 and the frontage added in 1810. The pub was opened in 1996 as a re-creation of an 18th-century tavern, with exposed wooden floorboards and panelling and a real fire. All the ales are from St Peter's Brewery and dispensed by air pressure. Sandwiches and a range of cooked dishes are available at lunchtime only. **Q**

EC1: Finsbury

Exmouth Arms

23 Exmouth Market, EC1R 4QL

11-midnight (1.30am Fri & Sat); 11-10.30 Sun

☎ (020) 3551 4772 exmoutharms.com

4 changing beers H

On the corner of Exmouth Market and Spa Field, this former Courage pub (see name and green tiling) was rebuilt in the early 20th century. It commemorates Viscount Exmouth, a naval officer in the French wars. Since its reopening a few years ago it has become well known for the range of its draught and other beers. The four handpumps normally dispense one or more from London breweries. Food, mainly sliders and seafood, is served all day.

(Farringdon) (Angel/Farringdon)

Wilmington

69 Rosebery Avenue, EC1R 4RL

8am-11 (midnight Fri); 9am-midnight Sat; 10-10.30 Sun

☎ (020) 7837 1384

House beer (by Greene King); changing beers H

Large 19th-century pub on a street corner, with the bar to the front and a dining area behind. The lower part of the outside walls is tiled in brown, while the interior is fashionably distressed. There are five handpumps for guest beers, while the house beer is named after two stone plaques perhaps representing the former Watney and Reid breweries, there is also a Watney's window. Meals

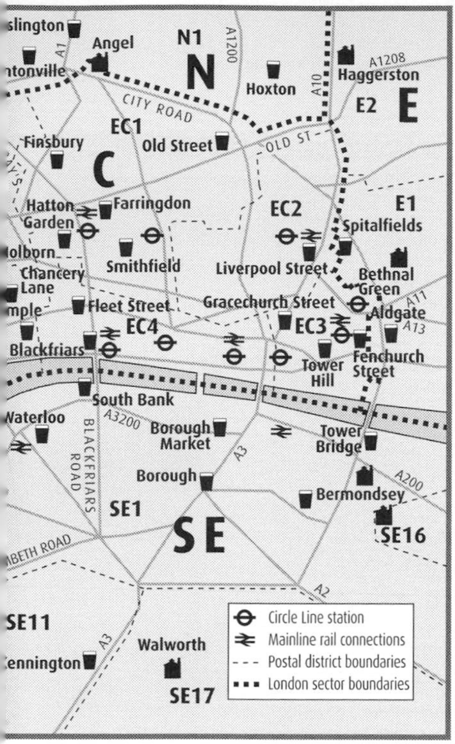

are served until 10pm Monday-Thursday, 10.30pm Friday and Saturday and 9.30pm Sunday.
◑♿⇌(Farringdon)⊖(Angel/Farringdon)🚌🐾📶

EC1: Hatton Garden

Craft Beer Co 🏆 L

82 Leather Lane, EC1N 7TR

⚙ 12-11 (10.30 Sun) ☎ 07530 211437

House beer (by Kent); changing beers H

This is the only pub in the City using lined glasses – just one of the changes introduced by Craft Beer Co since leasing it from Greene King three years ago. The choice of beers is vast, with 16 handpumps serving cask ales alone. Now thoroughly redecorated, a large Charrington mirror is on display along with the unusual ceiling mirror depicting a clock face, a reminder of the previous pub, the Clock House. The Scotch eggs and pork pies are recommended.
Q⇌⊖(Farringdon)🍎🥛🚌📶

Olde Mitre ★ L

1 Ely Court, Ely Place, EC1N 6SJ

⚙ 11-11; closed Sat & Sun ☎ (020) 7405 4751

Adnams Broadside; Fuller's London Pride; Gales Seafarers Ale; 3 changing beers (sourced regionally) H

Hidden away off Hatton Garden is one of London's pub gems, dating back to 1546. The current 18th-century building has a historic interior of national importance; the wood-panelled rear, with a small side room, is original. The small front bar is a later addition, complete with tree. There is also a small upstairs room with seating. Occasional beer festivals are held and it opens at weekends around the Great British Beer Festival. Bar snacks include toasties and pork pies.
Q⇌(City Thameslink)⊖(Chancery Lane/ Farringdon)♣🍎🚌🐾

EC1: Old Street

Masque Haunt L

168-172 Old Street, EC1V 9BP

⚙ 8am-11 (midnight Fri & Sat) ☎ (020) 7251 4195

Adnams Broadside; Greene King IPA, Abbot; Sharp's Doom Bar; 6 changing beers (sourced regionally) H

Large corner-shop Wetherspoon conversion divided into three, with a large raised dining area at the rear, seating at the front and the bar in the middle. Brewster Michaela White of Upstairs Brewing fame is one of its cellar team, looking after the excellent range of beers. Look out for special events as well as the usual ale festivals. Real cider is from a box in the fridge. Q🛋◑♿⇌⊖🍎🚌📶

Old Fountain L

3 Baldwin Street, EC1V 9NU

⚙ 11-11; 12-11 Sat & Sun ☎ (020) 7253 2970

🌐 oldfountain.co.uk

Fuller's London Pride; changing beers (sourced regionally) H

This Guide regular is unusual, with an entrance in two different streets and now a roof garden with two large tables and heated parasols for all-year enjoyment. The main reason to go to the pub is the cask beer, selected from local and special regional breweries. It also serves a wide range of bottled beers from local breweries and further afield. Check the website for details of special beer festivals. ❀◑⇌⊖♣🍎🚌📶

EC1: Smithfield

Old Red Cow L

71-72 Long Lane, EC1A 9EJ

⚙ 12-11 (midnight Fri & Sat); 12-10.30 Sun

☎ (020) 7726 2595 🌐 theoldredcow.com

4 changing beers (often Magic Rock, Redemption) H

A small pub near Smithfield market, decorated in a smart, contemporary style. It describes itself as a local beer house. As such, its four handpumps often dispense London beers such as Redemption, complemented by others from the likes of Bristol Beer Factory, Ilkley, Magic Rock, Redwillow and Roosters. Food ranges from Scotch eggs and sausage rolls through pies and burgers to sharing dishes. An upstairs bar is available to hire.
◑⇌(Farringdon)⊖(Barbican)🍎🚌📶

EC2: Liverpool Street

Magpie

12 New Street, EC2M 4TP

⚙ 11-11; 12-10 Sat; closed Sun ☎ (020) 7929 3889

Fuller's London Pride; St Austell Nicholson's Pale Ale; Sharp's Doom Bar; Truman's Runner; 6 changing beers (sourced regionally; often Adnams, Fuller's, Timothy Taylor) H

Opposite the Bishopsgate entrance to Liverpool Street station, behind the police station, here is a pub with 10 handpumps, two of them for local beers. It can become crowded in the evening rush hour, when the roadway outside is often pressed into service as an overspill, although many do not notice there is an upstairs restaurant renowned for its large pie meals. Family are allowed only on Saturday. Q🛋◑⇌⊖🍎🚌📶

EC3: Fenchurch Street

East India Arms

67 Fenchurch Street, EC3M 4BR

11.30-11; closed Sat & Sun ☎ (020) 7265 5121

Shepherd Neame Whitstable Bay, Kent's Best, Spitfire; 1 changing beer H

Close to Fenchurch Street Station, this small, award-winning Shepherd Neame house is a Grade II-listed red-brick building dating from the 1820s. Bare wooden floors and half-walled wood panelling, framed old photographs and welcoming customers contribute to a warm, friendly and traditional atmosphere, overseen by Bob, the long-serving landlord. The guest beer is usually a Sheps seasonal. ❀ ⇌ ⊖ (Aldgate/Tower Hill) 🚌 ᯤ

Peacock L

41 Minories, EC3N 1DT

12-midnight; closed Sat & Sun ☎ (020) 7488 3630

Butcombe Bitter; Windsor & Eton Guardsman; 2 changing beers (sourced regionally) H

In the corner of the Grade II-listed Ibex House, possibly the largest survivor of Streamline Moderne (a short-lived form of Art Deco), this pub is reputed to have been earmarked for Gestapo HQ had we lost World War II. Now a darts players' haven with seven dartboards and over 20 teams playing, it can get busy during darts nights. The landlord is passionate about real ale so check the guest beers and CAMRA social board.
⇌ ⊖ (Aldgate/Tower Gateway/Tower Hill) ♣ 🚌

EC3: Gracechurch Street

Crosse Keys

7-12 Gracechurch Street, EC3V 0DR

8am-11 (midnight Fri); 9am-10 Sat; 9am-8 Sun
☎ (020) 7623 4824

Fuller's London Pride; Greene King IPA; Sharp's Doom Bar; changing beers H

A palatial Wetherspoon pub that is a Mecca for real ale drinkers, with its own special festivals to watch out for besides the company's seasonal ones. There are 24 handpumps around the bar; look at the screens above showing the pump numbers and beers on offer. This pub comprises the large main entrance and slightly smaller area to the right, two smaller seating areas either side of the bar, and three convenient function rooms.
Q ♿ ⇌ (Cannon St) ⊖ (Bank/Monument) 🍎 🚌 ᯤ

EC3: Tower Hill

Draft House Seething

14-15 Seething Lane, EC3N 4AX

12-11; closed Sun ☎ (020) 7626 3360

Sambrook's Wandle Ale; 5 changing beers H

Part of the small Draft House chain, this large, open-plan pub has the bar along one side and the kitchen at the back, giving it a somewhat American diner style. There are six handpumps, one offering the special of the day selling at £2.75, and when it has gone it has gone. Food is served all day and a large screen shows sport while music plays at the same time. ◑ ♿ ⇌ (Fenchurch St) ⊖ 🚌 🐾 ᯤ

EC4: Blackfriars

Black Friar ★

174 Queen Victoria Street, EC4V 4EG

8am-11; 12-10.30 Sun ☎ (020) 7236 5474

St Austell Nicholson's Pale Ale; Sharp's Doom Bar; Truman's Runner; changing beers H

REAL ALE BREWERIES

Anspach & Hobday SE1: Bermondsey
Barnet High Barnet
Beavertown N17: Tottenham Hale
Belleville SW12: Wandsworth Common
Bexley Erith (NEW)
Big Smoke Surbiton (NEW)
Bloomsbury WC1: Bloomsbury (NEW)
Brew By Numbers SE16: Bermondsey
Brewhouse & Kitchen EC1: Angel (NEW)
Brewhouse & Kitchen N5: Highbury (NEW)
Brick SE15: Peckham
Brixton SW9: Brixton
Brockley SE4: Brockley
Brodie's E10: Leyton
By the Horns SW17: Summerstown
Canopy SE24: Herne Hill (NEW)
Clarkshaws SW9: Loughborough Junction
Crate E9: Hackney Wick
Cronx New Addington
Dragonfly W3: Acton
East London E10: Leyton
Essex Street WC2: Temple (NEW)
Five Points E8: Hackney Downs
Florence (A Head in a Hat) SE24: Herne Hill
Fourpure SE16: Bermondsey
Fuller's W4: Chiswick
Gipsy Hill SE27: West Norwood
Hackney E2: Haggerston
Hammerton N7: Barnsbury
Hop Stuff SE18: Woolwich
Howling Hops E9: Hackney Wick
Kernel SE16: Bermondsey
Kew SW14: East Sheen (NEW)
Laine @ Aeronaut W3: Acton
Laine @ Four Thieves SW11: Battersea (NEW)
Laine @ People's Park Tavern E9: Victoria Park
Late Knights SE20: Penge
Left Bank E17: Walthamstow (NEW)
London Beer Factory SE27: West Norwood
London Brewing N6: Highgate
Long Arm W5: South Ealing
Moncada W10: Kensal Town
Mondo SW8: South Lambeth (NEW)
Monkey Chews SW15: Peckham (NEW)
One Mile End E1: Whitechapel
Orbit SE17: Walworth (NEW)
Park Kingston (NEW)
Partizan SE16: South Bermondsey
Portobello W10: North Kensington
Pressure Drop E8: Hackney
Redchurch E2: Bethnal Green
Redemption N17: Tottenham
Rocky Head SW18: Southfields
Sambrook's SW11: Battersea
Signature Brew E10: Leyton
Southwark SE1: Bermondsey (NEW)
Sultan SW19: South Wimbledon (NEW)
Tap East E20: Stratford Westfield
Three Sods E2: Bethnal Green (NEW)
Truman's E3: Hackney Wick
Twickenham Twickenham
Volden Croydon (NEW)
Weird Beard W7: Hanwell
Wild Card E17: Walthamstow
Wimbledon SW19: Colliers Wood (NEW)
Zerodegrees SE3: Blackheath

Unique pub, occupying part of the site of a Dominican Friary, rebuilt in 1905 in an exuberant Art Nouveau style. Inside and out, especially in the back room, the daily life of the friars is celebrated in copper panels and figures on the marble and alabaster walls, some with appropriate mottoes. It has a nationally important historic pub interior, and is also Grade II* listed. Food is served all day, beginning with breakfast on weekdays.

EC4: Fleet Street

Old Bell

95 Fleet Street, EC4Y 1DH

10-11 (midnight Fri & Sat); 10-10.30 Sun

(020) 7583 0070

Sharp's Doom Bar; Truman's Runner; 4 changing beers

Now an M&B Nicholson's pub, it was said to have been first built for Wren, to cater for his masons rebuilding St Bride's Church after the 1666 fire. The crossed knife and fork in brass, set into the front threshold until the '80s, was considered to be a sign for the illiterate workmen. The back of the pub looks out on to St Bride's churchyard. Outside is a little smoking space and inside is a U-shaped bar and a semi-separate drinking area.

(City Thameslink)(Blackfriars)

WC1: Bloomsbury

Calthorpe Arms

252 Grays Inn Road, WC1X 8JR

11-11.30; 12-10.30 Sun (020) 7278 4732

Young's Bitter, Special; 2 changing beers (sourced nationally)

Unusual double doors lead into this single-bar corner local. With no music and an unobtrusive corner TV, it is easy either to strike up a conversation at a bar stool or take one of the tables along the sides for more privacy. The upstairs dining room opens for lunch (12-2.30pm) but can be booked at other times. Evening meals are served 6-9.30pm. Young's bottle-conditioned beers are stocked plus a Young's seasonal and a guest beer. There is pavement seating outside.

(Russell Sq)

Lamb

94 Lambs Conduit Street, WC1N 3LZ

12-11 (midnight Thu-Sat); 12-10.30 Sun

(020) 7405 0713

Courage Directors; Young's Bitter, London Gold, Special; 4 changing beers (sourced regionally)

Beautifully preserved and Grade II-listed, the Lamb has a historic interior of regional importance including a small snug and etched glass snob screens above the bar. The Empire Bar and restaurant are upstairs. The glorious Victorian history of the pub and area is commemorated by a working polyphon (predecessor to the gramophone). Among nine handpumps, at least four guest beers usually include one brewed for the pub by Redemption. At the back is a small walled garden. Q (Russell Sq)

Swan

7 Cosmo Place, WC1N 3AP

12-11 (midnight Fri & Sat); 12-10.30 Sun

(020) 7837 6223

Fuller's London Pride; St Austell Tribute; Westerham Taylor Walker 1730; 5 changing beers (sourced locally)

A family-oriented pub among the tourist hotels on Southampton Row, popular with visitors to Great Ormond Street Children's Hospital. There is a single long room, and tables in front on a pedestrian passage. Eight handpumps dispense three regular real ales and five guests, mainly from London breweries. Real cider is served on handpump in summer and during festivals. Pub grub and snacks are available until 10pm every day. It has a large-screen TV for live sports events.

Q (Russell Sq)

WC1: Holborn

Penderel's Oak

286-288 High Holborn, WC1V 7HJ

8am-11.30 (midnight Thu; 1am Fri & Sat); 10-11.30 Sun

(020) 7242 5669

Adnams Broadside; Fuller's London Pride; Greene King IPA, Abbot; Sharp's Doom Bar; 7 changing beers (sourced nationally)

Large, busy Wetherspoon pub offering up to six guest beers. Tables at the front lead to the bar and a raised seating area. There is also a back room and various settees and high stools; low-key lighting adds to the atmosphere. A cellar bar with screens for music is popular with younger visitors and available for hire; it opens later than the main bar. Food is served until 11pm; children are welcome until 7pm. A small walled garden is at the rear.

Q (Chancery Lane/Holborn)

WC1: St Pancras

Mabel's Tavern

9 Mabledon Place, WC1H 9AZ

11-11 (midnight Thu-Sat) (020) 7387 7739

Shepherd Neame Master Brew, Whitstable Bay, Spitfire, Bishops Finger; 1 changing beer (sourced regionally; often Shepherd Neame)

Originally owned by Whitbread and called the Kentish Arms (note the plaque high on the outside wall), the pub was renamed for landlady Mabel Macinelly, who is said to haunt these cosy premises. Up to the left of the bar is a snug, and a raised area at the back has a nice fireplace plus a large TV screen. Various prints and old photos adorn the walls. Food is served until 9.30pm. Seasonal beers come from the brewery. Handy for the British Library. (St Pancras)

Queen's Head

66 Acton Street, WC1X 9NB

12-midnight (11 Mon); 12-11 Sun (020) 7713 5772

queensheadlondon.com

3 changing beers (sourced nationally)

Narrow, late-Georgian premises with a single bar, a smoking patio at the rear and benches in front. The piano is used for jazz and blues on Thursdays. Guest beers are from microbreweries and include a dark beer. One handpump serves cider, with three more real ciders and a range of keg and bottled beers. Sharing platters of pub snacks are available at this comfortable locals' pub (with occasional tourists) off the Gray's Inn Road. Now home to a microbrewery. (St Pancras)

WC2: Chancery Lane

Seven Stars

53-54 Carey Street, WC2A 2JB

11-11; 12-11 Sat & Sun (020) 7242 8521

thesevenstars1602.co.uk

Adnams Southwold Bitter; 4 changing beers H

Dating from 1602 and formerly known as the League of Seven Stars, this pub has a regionally important historic interior. The bar, with its decorative Victorian bar-back, sits in the narrow space between two distinctive drinking areas, one of them named the Wig Box. The Royal Courts of Justice are nearby. The landlady favours Adnams beers as well as comforting food. The pub is also home to Ray Brown, the resident cat. Q

WC2: Charing Cross

Harp

47 Chandos Place, WC2N 4HS

10-11.30 (midnight Fri & Sat); 12-10.30 Sun

(020) 7836 0291

Dark Star Hophead, American Pale Ale; Fuller's London Pride; Sambrook's Wandle Ale; 6 changing beers H

Small, friendly, Fuller's pub which became a haven for beer choice when it was a free house run by the legendary Binnie Walsh. A fine range of real ales and ciders is offered. The narrow bar is adorned with mirrors and portraits. There is no intrusive music or TV, and a cosy upstairs room provides a refuge from the busy throng. A winner of numerous awards including, in 2010, the ultimate accolade, CAMRA National Pub of the Year.

Q

WC2: Covent Garden

Coach & Horses

42 Wellington Street, WC2E 7BD

11-11; 12-10.30 Sun (020) 7240 0553

Courage Best Bitter; Shepherd Neame Spitfire H

A small and traditional independent pub with a lot of Irish influence, very much used by locals but also some tourists. It has a fantastic collection of about 70 Irish whiskeys and Scotch whiskies. Food is served lunchtimes Monday to Saturday and sometimes on Sunday. There are photos of Gaelic football teams, and the sport of hurling also features, plus theatre posters. Note the beautiful front windows. Q

Cross Keys

31 Endell Street, WC2H 9BA

11-11 (020) 7836 5185 crosskeyscoventgarden.com

Brodie's Bethnal Green Bitter; house beer (by Brodie's); 2 changing beers (often Brodie's) H

Built in the mid-1840s when Endell (formerly Belton) Street was widened as part of clearing the St Giles' Rookery (slum). An ornate façade reveals a long, welcoming bar, subdued lighting, comfortable banquette seating and tables and chairs. A mix of copper kettles, pans, street signs, stuffed fish, framed pictures and photos, Beatles memorabilia and a fine Truman, Hanbury, Buxton & Co mirror adorns the walls. Families are welcome (over 12s only) until 7pm unless it is busy, but no dogs.

Salisbury ★

90 St Martin's Lane, WC2N 4AP

11-midnight (1am Fri); 12-1am Sat; 12-10.30 Sun

(020) 7836 5863

Fuller's London Pride; St Austell Tribute; Timothy Taylor Landlord; Westerham Taylor Walker 1730; 4 changing beers H

One of London's Victorian gems, Grade II-listed, licensed in 1694, and named the Coach and Horses until 1866. The nationally important historic interior is spectacular, with an island bar, cut and etched glass, large mirrors and Art Nouveau light fittings. The sign shows the Marquess of Salisbury, Prime Minister three times in the 19th century, whose family once owned the freehold. The pub featured in the 1961 film Victim.

(Charing Cross)(Leicester Sq)

White Swan

14 New Row, WC2N 4LF

10-11 (11.30 Sat); 12-10.30 Sun (020) 3077 1129

St Austell Nicholson's Pale Ale; Sharp's Doom Bar; Truman's Runner; 4 changing beers H

Once owned by the famous London banking firm Hoare & Co and formerly an O'Neills, this Grade II-listed building just a stone's throw from Covent Garden is now an M&B Nicholson's pub. It has eight handpumps and is popular with tourists. It has been tastefully refurbished with a small bar, limited seating in the bar area but with more room past a partition. The first-floor dining room can be booked for functions. Breakfast is served until noon except Sunday.

(Charing Cross)(Leicester Sq)

WC2: Holborn

Shakespeare's Head

Africa House, 64-68 Kingsway, WC2B 6BG

7am-midnight (1am Fri); 8am-1am Sat; 8am-midnight Sun

(020) 7404 8846

Fuller's London Pride; Greene King IPA, Abbot; 6 changing beers H

A large Wetherspoon bank conversion from 1998, named after a famous pub located nearby until that entire street (Wych Street) was demolished over 100 years ago. It is nearly always busy with shoppers, tourists, local office workers and students from the nearby London School of Economics during term time. A convenient place for a couple of pints after your cultural sojourn at the British Museum.

WC2: Temple

Devereux

20 Devereux Court, WC2R 3JJ

11-11; 12-8 Sat; closed Sun (020) 7583 4562

Fuller's London Pride; Sharp's Doom Bar; Truman's Runner; Westerham Taylor Walker 1730; 1 changing beer H

An attractive Grade II-listed pub built in 1844; part of the site was once the Grecian Coffee House. The comfortable lounge with wood panelling has a bar with five handpumps. Prints on the walls show local places of interest and historic figures, the judges and wigs reflecting its proximity to the law courts. Upstairs is a restaurant available for hire.

Q

W1: Marylebone

Carpenters Arms

12 Seymour Place, W1H 7NE

☼ 11-11; 12-10.30 Sun ☎ (020) 7723 1050
⊕ markettaverns.co.uk/the_carpenters_arms
Harveys Sussex Best Bitter; 5 changing beers (sourced nationally; often Marston's) Ⓗ
A sister pub to the Market Porter in Southwark but with a smaller range of beers, this is a friendly and welcoming haven from the bustle of Oxford Street. Many local people enjoy watching TV sport and playing darts in the rear alcove. It has had a sensitive refurbishment which preserved the wall tiling and floor mosaics. On the side wall is a display of woodworking tools. The food menu consists entirely of pork pies and Scotch eggs.
◐▶⊖(Marble Arch)➤🐾🛜

Golden Eagle
59 Marylebone Lane, W1U 2NY
☼ 12-11 (midnight Fri & Sat); 12-7 Sun ☎ (020) 7935 3228
Fuller's London Pride; St Austell Tribute; 2 changing beers Ⓗ
A welcome return to the Guide after a decade. Take a step back in time – this single-bar Victorian pub, first licensed in 1842 and rebuilt in 1890, is traditional in every way, albeit with a smart decor. There is a fine etched back-of-bar mirror and proper leaded windows. Piano singalongs on Tuesday, Thursday and Friday evenings complement the timeless atmosphere.
Q&⊖(Bond St)➤🐾

Gunmakers Ⓛ
33 Aybrook Street, W1U 4AP
☼ 11-11.30 (midnight Fri & Sat); 11-10.30 Sun
☎ (020) 7487 4937
St Austell Tribute; 3 changing beers Ⓗ
Formerly the Bricklayers Arms and then the Scottish-themed William Wallace, the pub here was originally licensed in 1791 and rebuilt 90 years later. It now comprises a large room with the bar towards the back, a corner nook seating about a dozen and an upstairs function room. Quiz night is on Monday, from 8pm. A wide selection of food includes vegetarian options. ◐▶⊖(Baker St)➤🐾🛜

W1: Mayfair

Clarence
4 Dover Street, W1S 4LB
☼ 10-11.30 (midnight Fri & Sat); 10-11 Sun
☎ (020) 7491 3607
Fuller's London Pride; St Austell Nicholson's Pale Ale; Sharp's Doom Bar; Windsor & Eton Knight of the Garter; 4 changing beers Ⓗ
Licensed in 1724 as the Coach & Horses and rebuilt in 1892 and 1953, the Duke of Clarence became King William IV in 1830. Its smallish frontage belies a much larger area extending back. It has a very convivial atmosphere after its refurbishment in 2012, with a pleasant, quieter upstairs bar. Keg cider is sold as well as real ale. The pub is located close to the famous Ritz hotel in Piccadilly.
◐▶⊖(Green Park)➤

Coach & Horses
5 Bruton Street, W1J 6PT
☼ 11.30-11; 12-8 Sat; 12-midnight Sun ☎ (020) 7629 4123
Brains SA Gold; Fuller's London Pride; 1 changing beer Ⓗ
An excellent refuge from the nearby Bond Street shopping area. First licensed in 1738, it was rebuilt in 1933 and has an imposing mock-Tudor exterior. Inside, the atmosphere is traditional, with wooden beams and panelling. Pictures on the walls feature

caricatures of 19th-century politicians and clerics. The small dining room with bar upstairs is available for private functions. Q◐▶&⊖(Green Park)➤

Windmill
6-8 Mill Street, W1S 2AZ
☼ 11-11; 12-7 Sat; closed Sun ☎ (020) 7491 8050
⊕ windmillmayfair.co.uk
Wells Bombardier; Young's Bitter, London Gold, Special; 3 changing beers Ⓗ
In adjoining buildings previously housing a nightclub and an escort agency, this pub has a well-furnished lounge, split into two sections, with wood panelling, decorative ceilings and a frieze. There is a restaurant on the first floor. Pies are a speciality; the Pie Club claims 6,000 members, who enjoy changing monthly specials such as beef and stilton. A new roof terrace has now been added.
Q◐▶⊖(Oxford Circus)➤🛜

W1: Soho

Argyll Arms ★
18 Argyll Street, W1F 7TP
☼ 8am-11.30 (midnight Fri & Sat); 12-10.30 Sun
☎ (020) 7734 6117
Fuller's London Pride; St Austell Nicholson's Pale Ale; Sharp's Doom Bar; 5 changing beers (sourced nationally) Ⓗ
Victorian M&B Nicholson's house that is Grade II*-listed and has a nationally important historic pub interior. Three snugs are separated by etched-glass partitions; note the remarkable Bass mirror. The bar-back is impressive, and adjacent is a rare survivor, a manager's office with etched glazing. The magnificent saloon is decorated with ornate mirrors. With eight of the 16 handpumps in regular use, enjoy guest ales from brewers such as Adnams, Harviestoun and Thwaites.
◐▶&⊖(Oxford Circus)➤🛜

Dog & Duck ★
18 Bateman Street, W1D 3AJ
☼ 10-11 ☎ (020) 7494 0697
Fuller's London Pride; St Austell Nicholson's Pale Ale; 4 changing beers Ⓗ
In the heart of Soho, this Grade II-listed Nicholson's pub, built in 1897, has a nationally important historic interior. An elaborate mosaic depicts dogs and ducks, and wonderful advertising mirrors adorn the walls. Guest beers may include Sambrook's Wandle and Orkney Dark Island. The upstairs Orwell Bar can be hired for functions. The pub is small and so popular, especially with media people, that it is not just smokers who have to drink outside.
◐▶⊖(Tottenham Court Rd)➤🛜

Lyric ★
37 Great Windmill Street, W1D 7LU
☼ 11-11.30 (midnight Fri & Sat); 12-10.30 Sun
☎ (020) 7434 0604 ⊕ lyricsoho.co.uk
8 changing beers Ⓗ
A welcome to the Guide for the first time for this small, independently owned bar just off Shaftesbury Avenue, popular with local trade. Bay-fronted with a tiled, panelled interior, it was originally two adjacent taverns, the Windmill and the Ham, which merged in the mid 18th century to form the Windmill and Ham, renamed in 1890 and rebuilt 16 years later. Cask beers may come from Brodie's, Dark Star, Magic Rock, Pressure Drop, Redemption and Thornbridge.
◐▶⊖(Piccadilly Circus)➤🛜

Queen's Head 𝕃
15 Denman Street, W1D 7HN
✪ 11-11.30 (midnight Fri & Sat); 12-10.30 Sun
☎ (020) 7437 1540 🌐 queensheadpiccadilly.com
Fuller's London Pride; Robinsons Trooper; Sambrook's Wandle; 2 changing beers Ⓗ
Free house dating from 1738, taking its name from Queen's Street, renamed Denman Street in 1862 in honour of a Lord Chief Justice born there. In the 1840s it was known as the Courier's Club, trading in wine, brandy and coal. Later, reduced in size, it became part of the Piccadilly Theatre site. With the main bar on the ground floor and more accommodation upstairs, it is most convenient for pre-theatre dining and drinks.
◐◑⊖(Piccadilly Circus)🚌🐾

EAST LONDON
E1: Aldgate

Dispensary
19A Leman Street, E1 8EN
✪ 11.30-11; closed Sat & Sun ☎ (020.) 7977 0486
🌐 thedispensarylondon.co.uk
5 changing beers (sourced regionally) Ⓗ
Dating from 1859, this Grade II-listed pub was originally the Eastern Dispensary Hospital. It opened as a pub/dining room in 2006 and was extensively refurbished in 2014. The number of ales on offer increases towards Friday. The bar is a pleasantly furnished designer space and the main room is high enough for a dining balcony above the drinking area. Function rooms are available. Local CAMRA's Pub of the Year in 2014.
Q◐◑⇌(Fenchurch St)⊖(Aldgate/Aldgate East)🚌🐾

E1: Spitalfields

Crown & Shuttle
226 Shoreditch High Street, E1 6PJ
✪ 11-11 (1am Thu-Sat); 11-10.30 Sun ☎ (020) 7375 2905
🌐 crownandshuttle.co.uk
Changing beers (sourced regionally) Ⓗ
Once a Truman's pub with an unsavoury reputation, it is now refurbished and a pleasant and welcoming venue with on-trend music. The stripped floors, bare brick walls and mismatched furniture reflect the area in which this establishment sits. The large, covered garden is used for outdoor drinking, and has a street food truck in the corner dispensing food.
❀◐◑⇌(Liverpool St)⊖(Shoreditch High St)🚌📶

Pride of Spitalfields
3 Heneage Street, E1 5LJ
✪ 10-1am (2am Fri & Sat); 10-midnight Sun
☎ (020) 7247 8933
Crouch Vale Brewers Gold; 3 changing beers (sourced regionally) Ⓗ
An East End institution, this unchanged boozer is close to the curry houses of Brick Lane, Petticoat Lane Sunday Market and the events and exhibitions in the Old Truman Brewery. There is one main bar and a small room off to one side. Both get crowded in the evening, when drinkers spill out on to the pavement. If it is not too busy you may see Lenny, the cat. Hot food and sandwiches are served lunchtimes.
◐⇌(Liverpool St)⊖(Aldgate East /Shoreditch High St)🚌

Williams Ale & Cider House 𝕃
22-24 Artillery Lane, E1 7LS
✪ 11-11 (midnight Thu-Sat); closed Sun ☎ (020) 7247 5163
🌐 williamsspitalfields.com
House beer (by Greene King); changing beers (sourced locally; often Crouch Vale, Hackney, Truman's) Ⓗ
Formerly a Whitbread establishment, this pub was called the Ship by the mid-1800s, and became the Williams in about 1980. The one main bar is separated into two areas by arches. Old beer posters decorate the walls. Rebranded by Greene King, it serves up to 14 beers, including some from local breweries. There is occasional live music, mainly on Saturdays. Westons cider is also stocked.
◐◑♿⇌⊖(Liverpool St)♣🍎🚌🐾📶

E1: Wapping

Turners Old Star
14 Watts Street, E1W 2QG
✪ 11-11 (1.30am Thu-Sat) ☎ (020) 7702 9199
🌐 turnersoldstar.co.uk
House beer (by Elgood's) Ⓗ
An 1830s one-bar pub at the rear of Wapping Green, once owned by the artist JMW Turner and run by his mistress Peggy Booth. A small beer festival is held annually to coincide with the Wapping Shindig on the green outside. The pub runs a darts team and has a well-used pool table. With occasional visits from Pearly Kings and Queens, this is a true East End community local.
🐴❀♿⊖🚌(100,D3)🐾📶

E1: Whitechapel

White Hart 𝕃
1-3 Mile End Road, E1 4TP
✪ 10.30-midnight ☎ (020) 7790 2894
6 changing beers (sourced locally) Ⓗ
A large, generous-hearted, one-bar pub, once decrepit but now extensively refurbished, close to Whitechapel Market and several infamous Kray-era East End pubs. During the rebuilding completed in 2014, a 3.5-barrel brewing plant was installed in the cellar, now turning out a wide selection of One Mile End beers in cask and keg. Since its reopening, this place has grown rapidly in popularity among locals, visitors and staff of the nearby Royal London Hospital.
◐◑⊖(Bethnal Green/Whitechapel)♣🍎🚌📶

E3: Bow

Eleanor Arms
460 Old Ford Road, E3 5JP
✪ 4-11; 12-11 Fri & Sat; 12-10.30 Sun ☎ (020) 8980 6992
🌐 eleanorarms.co.uk
Shepherd Neame Kent's Best, Amber Ale; 2 changing beers Ⓗ
Built in 1879, this pub was bought by Shepherd Neame in 1985. The present landlord has been here since 2008 and has won many awards in recognition of how well the pub is run. The bar separates the front and back rooms. The back bar has TV and a pool table; the front bar has a real fire in winter and hosts the first Thursday of the month quiz night and Sunday jazz (8-11pm).
🐴❀♿⊖(Bow Church/Bow Rd)🍎🚌(8)🐾📶

E4: Chingford

King's Ford Ⓛ
250-252 Chingford Mount Road, E4 8JL
✪ 8am-midnight (1am Fri & Sat) ☎ (020) 8523 9365
Adnams Broadside; Fuller's London Pride; Greene King Abbot; Ruddles Best Bitter; changing beers Ⓗ
Now there are 10 handpumps (four regular and six guest ales) the choice here is great. Converted by Wetherspoon from a furniture store, it has six alcoves/snugs where it is possible to enjoy a quiet talk with friends. The cellar manager is a real ale fan and CAMRA member. There are two beer festivals a year and Meet the Brewer evenings. Meals are served all day, and TVs are mute.
Q✿⊘◑⅋♿♣🚃🐾🛜

King's Head Ⓛ
2B Kings Head Hill, E4 7EA
✪ 12-11 (midnight Fri & Sat) ☎ (020) 8529 6283
⊕ thekingsheadchingford.co.uk
Fuller's London Pride; Morland Old Speckled Hen; St Austell Tribute; Sharp's Doom Bar; changing beers (sourced regionally) Ⓗ
A popular Stonegate pub in north Chingford. As well as the four regular ales, six more guest ales are on handpump, often from local breweries. The decor is a mix of modern and traditional, with different styles of seating, and a covered drinking area outside. A wide choice of food is served all day until 9pm. ✿◑●♿🚃

E5: Clapton

Anchor & Hope Ⓛ
15 High Hill Ferry, E5 9HG (800yds N of Lea Bridge Rd, along river path)
✪ 1 (12 Sat)-11; 12-10.30 Sun ☎ (020) 8806 1730
Fuller's London Pride, ESB; 2 changing beers (often Elgood's, Everards, Fuller's) Ⓗ
A small, friendly Fuller's pub beside the Lee Navigation. The clientele includes boaters, walkers, cyclists and a wide variety of locals. Benches and picnic tables along the towpath afford a view of the marshes opposite and the nearby railway line. A dartboard is available at the rear, and a fire at the front in winter. Occasional barbecues are held in summer. Note that service is cash only.
🍽✿◑♣🚃(393)🐾

Clapton Hart Ⓛ
231 Lower Clapton Road, E5 8EG
✪ 4-11; 12-midnight Thu; 12-1am Fri & Sat; 12-11 Sun
☎ (020) 8985 8124 ⊕ claptonhart.com
Changing beers (often Hackney, Otley, Siren) Ⓗ
With eight handpumps, this large multi-roomed Antic pub has one of its widest range of ales, usually from well-renowned microbreweries. Film nights are held on Mondays, quiz nights on Tuesdays and there is a DJ on Fridays. Decor is the distressed style with assorted furniture and bric-a-brac common among Antic pubs. Meet the Brewer nights are frequently held. TV is limited to major sporting events shown in the back room.
🍽✿◑⊖♣🚃🐾🛜

Crooked Billet Ⓛ
84 Upper Clapton Road, E5 9JP
✪ 4-11; 12-midnight Fri & Sat; 12-11 Sun ☎ (020) 8291 8649
⊕ e5crookedbillet.co.uk
Changing beers (often Dark Star, East London Brewing, Sambrook's) Ⓗ

A large establishment a stone's throw from Clapton station with a single U-shaped bar and much wood panelling. The old car park is now a garden and there is a patio with a ping-pong table, surrounded by wooden booths. The five changing ales are mostly London brewed. A popular pub for viewing major televised sport events. 🍽✿◑⅋⊖♣🚃🐾🛜

E8: Hackney

Cock Tavern Ⓛ
315 Mare Street, E8 1EJ
✪ 12-11 (1am Fri & Sat); 12-10.30 Sun ☎ (020) 8533 6369
8 changing beers (often Howling Hops) Ⓗ
A single-bar pub with a tiny back patio. A bare wood floor and wood panelling give the bar a traditional feel. Eight handpumps dispense at least five Howling Hops beers and changing guest ales. Eight varying ciders are also delivered on handpumps. Bar snacks are served. The main brewing operation has moved to Hackney Wick, but the original Howling Hops brewery remains downstairs for special brews and hosting guest brewers. Q✿⊖(Central/Downs)●🚃🐾🛜

Pembury Tavern
90 Amhurst Road, E8 1JH
✪ 12-11 (midnight Fri & Sat) ☎ (020) 8986 8597
Milton Minotaur, Pegasus, Nero, Cyclops; changing beers Ⓗ
This large one-room bar has 16 handpumps dispensing the Milton range of beers, varying guest ales and two different ciders. Bar billiards, pool and board games are played. Freshly made pizzas are served until 10pm and a full Italian menu 12-3pm and 6-9pm, with roasts only on Sundays served until 4pm. Monday is quiz night. Beer festivals are held at the start and end of summer.
Q🍽✿◑♿⊖(Central/Downs)♣●🚃🐾🛜

E8: Haggerston

Fox
372 Kingsland Road, E8 4DA
✪ 4 (12 Sat)-midnight; 12-11.30 Sun ☎ (020) 7254 8462
⊕ thefoxe8.com
Changing beers (sourced nationally; often Buxton, Kent, Redemption) Ⓗ
A pub has been on this site since the 18th century; this version was built in 1881. Once two bars, it is now open plan and was relaunched as a specialist ale house in 2012, complete with roof terrace. The changing range includes beers from local breweries; one brewery takes over on the last Thursday of each month. The pub stocks a big range of bottled beers, some bottle-conditioned.
🍽✿◑▲⊖♣🚃🐾🛜

E9: Hackney Wick

Crate Brewery & Pizzeria Ⓛ
Unit 7, White Building, Queen's Yard, White Post Lane, E9 5EN (down steps by canal bridge)
✪ 12-11 (midnight Fri & Sat) ☎ 07834 275687
⊕ cratebrewery.com
Crate Best Bitter, Stout; 2 changing beers (sourced regionally; often Crate) Ⓗ
A single bar in an old warehouse, opened in 2012. There is also a canalside terrace and a barge with beer (bottled, no cask). Pizza is available until an hour before closing. An ale from a regularly changing guest brewery is offered and usually a

real cider. No spirits are sold. The original on-site brewery is still in production, as is a larger brewery across the yard. (276,488)

E9: Homerton

Adam & Eve

155 Homerton High Street, E9 6AS

4-11 (midnight Thu); 12-1am Fri & Sat; 12-11 Sun

(020) 7985 1494 adamandevepub.com

Five Points Pale Ale; 5 changing beers (sourced locally; often Hackney)

Restored in 2014, this pub has kept many of its original features, especially the attractive Edwardian façade constructed from blue tiles with terracotta facing above. The interior has a main bar and kitchen at the rear. Six handpumps serve a range of cask beers from near and far, including some from Cornish breweries.

E10: Leyton

Leyton Orient Supporters Club

Matchroom Stadium, Oliver Road, E10 5NF

match days from 5.30; 12.30-6 Sat; closed Sun

(020) 8988 8288 orientsupporters.org

Mighty Oak Oscar Wilde; changing beers

Award-winning bar in the West stand of the ground run by volunteers and O's fans. Eight handpumps deliver a variety of ales, with a real cider also available. The bar is open before and after, but not during, matches and closing times vary. The club runs four brewery-themed nights during the season (please see website for details). Admission is by club/CAMRA membership card or show a copy of this Guide.

E11: Leytonstone

Red Lion

640 High Road Leytonstone, E11 3AA

12-11 (midnight Thu; 2am Fri & Sat) (020) 8988 2929

theredlionleytonstone.com

Changing beers (often Thornbridge)

A popular and traditional single-bar Antic pub with a large garden. On offer are 10 changing cask ales and a selection of over 60 bottled beers. A wide range of freshly cooked, home-made food is available (no food 3-6pm weekdays or Sun eves). There are seasonal beer festivals, DJs on Friday and Saturday evenings, live acoustic music on Sunday evenings, quiz nights on Mondays and cinema in the garden on some summer nights.
(257,W14)

E11: Wanstead

George

155-159 High Street, E11 2RL

8am-midnight (12.30am Fri & Sat) (020) 8989 2921

Fuller's London Pride; Greene King Abbot; Ruddles Best Bitter; Sharp's Doom Bar; 8 changing beers (sourced regionally)

This Victorian pub is a large, two-storey Wetherspoon free house. There are 12 handpumps on the main bar, with London Glider cider usually available, but no handpumps upstairs. The pub has etched windows with pictures of old Wanstead and famous Georges on the walls. A large dragon, fitted with smoke detector, hovers above the main bar and you can try out the large mythical creature chair. Q

E13: Plaistow

Black Lion

59-61 High Street, E13 0AD

11-11; 12-10.30 Sun (020) 8472 2351

blacklionplaistow.co.uk

Courage Best Bitter; 3 changing beers (often Mighty Oak, Sharp's)

An old coaching inn rebuilt in 1747. The smaller back bar is accessible by a separate door or through the end of the main bar. Next to the original cobbled courtyard, stables and outbuildings have been converted to a function room for hire and for when West Ham United are at home, serving two real ales from casks behind the bar. Up to six real ales are on offer. The landlord has been here for 29 years. P

E14: Crossharbour

George

114 Glengall Grove, E14 3ND

11-midnight (020) 7987 4433

Fuller's London Pride; Sharp's Doom Bar; Timothy Taylor Landlord; Young's Bitter

This Enterprise pub is a vibrant local with a historic interior of regional importance, rebuilt in the 1930s and keeping to the three-bar layout, plus a large conservatory and award-winning patio garden. Ma Baker's Bar is a cosy snug sandwiched between two larger bars, with prints and posters on the ceiling. The public bar is panelled and has a dartboard and plenty of seating; the lounge bar has the conservatory laid out for excellent dining.

E17: Walthamstow

Bell

617 Forest Road, E17 4NE

11-midnight (11 Mon; 1am Fri & Sat); 12-11 Sun

(020) 8523 2277 belle17.com

Sharp's Doom Bar; Timothy Taylor Landlord; 6 changing beers

Large Victorian pub built in 1900, refurbished and reopened in 2012 in its current format with two distinct areas; the rear bar has wood panelling. Six changing beers include local brews, and food is served all day. Quiz night is Tuesday, jazz the third Sunday of the month, bluegrass the second Wednesday and DJs Friday and Saturday evenings. Children are allowed until 8pm, after which it is over-21s only. Dogs are welcome, with water bowls and biscuits provided.
(Central)

Nag's Head

9 Orford Road, E17 9LP

12-11 (10.30 Sun) (020) 8520 9709

thenagsheade17.com

Redemption Trinity; St Austell Tribute; Timothy Taylor Landlord; 5 changing beers (sourced regionally)

Built in 1857, this is a good community pub in the centre of Walthamstow Village and a Guide regular since 2007, renowned for its regular Mild and its many guest beers. Neighbourhood activity includes art classes and wine tastings. Smoking is allowed in the large rear garden, where beer festivals are held. Food is cooked on-site and is described as modern British. Two minutes away are the 12th-century parish church and the oldest house in Walthamstow. (Central)(W12)

Olde Rose & Crown Ⓛ

53-55 Hoe Street, E17 4SA

☼ 10-11 (midnight Fri & Sat); 12-11 Sun ☎ (020) 8509 3880
⊕ yeolderoseandcrowntheatrepub.co.uk

Changing beers (often Crouch Vale, East London) Ⓗ

A large, friendly community pub with six handpumps serving changing beers from SIBA and local brewers; in addition, there are usually two ciders. Food is available alternate Mondays and Tuesday-Saturday with various pop-up restaurants, plus Sunday roasts. The theatre upstairs has frequent productions and the bar regularly has live music, and a 78s night on the second Wednesday of the month. Look out for special beer festivals. Alcohol is served from noon.

ॐ◖᯾⊖(Central)●➡❀≋

Wild Card Brewery Tap Bar

Unit 7, Ravenswood Industrial Estate, Shernhall Street, E17 9HQ

☼ closed Mon-Thu; 5-midnight Fri; 11-midnight Sat; 11-10 Sun ☎ 07890 588991 ⊕ wildcardbrewery.co.uk

Wild Card Ace of Spades Ⓗ**, Pale** Ⓗ**/**Ⓖ**, Jack of Clubs, King of Hearts** Ⓗ**; 2 changing beers** Ⓖ

Established in 2013, Wild Card moved in February 2014 to its current location, an industrial unit comprising an open brewery at one end and a spacious bar at the other, with extra seating outside. A small woodburner provides heating in the winter, and food stalls set up outside in the summer. There is also occasional music and DJs.

ॐ❀⊖(Central/Wood St)P➡(W12,W16)❀≋

E20: Westfield Stratford City

Tap East Ⓛ

Montfichet Road, 7 International Square, E20 1EE

☼ 11-11; 12-10 Sun ☎ (020) 8555 4467 ⊕ tapeast.co.uk

Tap East Tonic Ale, JWB; 4 changing beers (sourced regionally; often Tap East) Ⓗ

For many drinkers, this pub, with its brewery adjoining the bar, is the only reason to visit Westfield. It serves three of its own beers and three others, often from local breweries. Beer festivals featuring guest brewers are popular. Directly outside is Stratford International station, while the Queen Elizabeth Olympic Park is a short walk away. The pub supports the Royal Artillery Benevolent Fund, with collecting boxes. Food is served until 9pm, including pork pies and pizzas.

❀◖᯾≋⊖(Stratford/Stratford Intl)●➡

Barking

Barking Dog

61 Station Parade, IG11 8TU

☼ 8am-midnight ☎ (020) 8507 9109

Greene King Abbot; Ruddles Best Bitter; Sharp's Doom Bar; 6 changing beers Ⓗ

Busy town-centre Wetherspoon pub, popular with locals and passing commuters alike. An impressive 12 handpumps serve changing beers of varying types and strengths, plus two or three real ciders, including Westons Old Rosie and Gwynt y Ddraig Black Dragon, giving the best choice in the area. Food is served all day until 11pm; alcohol from 9am. Muted TV screens show rolling news and occasional sport. Framed prints portray local scenes and famous figures such as Captain Cook and Vera Lynn. ॐ◖᯾≋⊖●❀≋

Collier Row

Colley Rowe Inn

54-56 Collier Row Road, RM5 3PA (on B174)

☼ 9am-midnight (1am Fri & Sat) ☎ (01708) 760633

Fuller's London Pride; Greene King Abbot; Ruddles Best Bitter; 6 changing beers Ⓗ

A popular local, this typical Wetherspoon shop conversion has booths at the rear and a more open area at the front. A wall-mounted TV routinely shows horse racing silently during the day. Guest beers often come from Adnams, Oakham and Wibblers. Handpumps also dispense two real ciders such as Westons Old Rosie and Gwynt y Ddraig Black Dragon. The Colley is a 10-minute bus ride from Romford Station. Qॐ◖᯾᯾●➡≋

Dagenham

Eastbrook ★

Dagenham Road, RM10 7UP (near jct with Rainham Rd South)

☼ 11-11 (midnight Fri & Sat) ☎ (020) 8592 1873

2 changing beers Ⓗ

A Grade II*-listed 1930s pub with a nationally important historic interior. Eastbrook is a welcoming community local with a large function room/restaurant and two bars. The main bar is the Walnut Room with extensive panelling; the Oak Room, used for functions, can be visited on request. Beers are from the Brakspear range and change monthly. The pub is the local for Dagenham & Redbridge FC supporters. Football memorabilia adorns the walls. ❀⊠◖᯾P➡(103,174)❀≋

Hornchurch

JJ Moons

48-52 High Street, RM12 4UN (on A124)

☼ 8am-11.30 (12.30am Fri & Sat) ☎ (01708) 478410

Adnams Ghost Ship; Greene King Abbot; Ruddles Best Bitter; 6 changing beers Ⓗ

Busy Wetherspoon high street pub, popular with all age groups, featuring a changing selection of ales with an emphasis on breweries from London and the south-east. Watercolour paintings of local scenes provide the main decoration, with local interest panels to the rear of the pub. Families are welcome until 6pm. Alcohol is on sale from 9am. Local CAMRA branch Pub of the Year 2014. Qॐ◖᯾⊖●➡≋

Rainham

Phoenix

Broadway, RM13 9YW (near clock tower, station and new bus terminus)

☼ 11-11; 12-3, 7-11 Sun ☎ (01708) 553700
⊕ the-phoenix-hotel.com

Courage Directors; Greene King Abbot; John Smith's Bitter; Wells Bombardier; 1 changing beer Ⓗ

Busy, spacious town pub close to Rainham station and convenient for the RSPB Rainham Marshes nature reserve. It has a public bar with a dartboard, and a saloon for dining. There is poker on Wednesday, quizzes and live entertainment/music alternating on Thursday, then entertainment again on Saturday and Sunday. The large garden has three aviaries, animals and a barbecue area. Family fun days are held every bank holiday Monday. Accommodation comprises seven twin rooms, two doubles and one single room. ॐ❀⊠◖≋♣P➡

Romford

Golden Lion

2 High Street, RM1 1HR

⏲ 11-11 (1am Fri & Sat) ☎ (01708) 740081

Brains The Rev James; Sharp's Doom Bar; Theakston Old Peculier; 2 changing beers Ⓗ

Grade II-listed 15th-century building claiming to be the oldest public house in England that has been in continuous use as an inn. Elizabethan philopsopher Francis Bacon is listed as a former owner. The main bar area is dimly lit and the ceiling is supported by ancient wooden beams. TVs on two walls show sport, food is served in the public bar and upstairs restaurant area, and there is a patio outside at the rear. The real cider is normally Westons Old Rosie.
❀◑⇌⊖🍎🚌

Moon & Stars

99-103 South Street, RM1 1NX

⏲ 8am-midnight (12.30am Fri & Sat) ☎ (01708) 730117

Adnams Broadside; Greene King Abbot; Ruddles Best Bitter; 5 changing beers Ⓗ

Close to Romford station and buses, this Wetherspoon pub can get busy on Thursday and Friday evenings. Beers from Bath, Brewsters and Orkney breweries are among its changing guest beer range. Real ciders on gravity dispensed from cooled containers behind the bar are usually Old Rosie and Black Dragon. Children are allowed in the raised area at the rear of the pub until 6pm Friday and Saturday, later on other days. Alcohol is served after 9am, and food until 11pm.
Q🐴◑♿⇌⊖🍎🚌📶

Upminster

Huntsman & Hounds

2 Ockendon Road, Corbets Tey, RM14 2DN (on B1421)

⏲ 11-11 (midnight Fri & Sat) ☎ (01708) 221672

Adnams Broadside; Brakspear Bitter; Greene King Abbot; 2 changing beers Ⓗ

A much-extended local with a good real ale choice, including seasonal guest beer selected from numerous microbreweries. Real cider is occasionally available. There is a range of meat, seafood and vegetarian offerings throughout the day until 10pm, with a set price buffet and daily specials. Weekly quiz nights take place. It has a south-facing beer garden and a large car park. Dogs are welcome in the garden, but only assistance dogs are allowed in the pub.
🐴❀◑♿🍎P🚌(370)🐾📶

Woodford Green

Cricketers 🄻

299-301 High Road, IG8 9HQ (on A1099)

⏲ 11.30-11 (midnight Fri); 12-midnight Sat; 12-11 Sun

☎ (020) 8504 2734

McMullen AK, Cask Ale, Country Bitter; 1 changing beer Ⓗ

Warm and friendly, this two-bar local has a dartboard in the public bar and plaques in the saloon for all 18 first class cricket counties, together with photographs of former MP Sir Winston Churchill, whose statue stands on the green almost opposite. Good-value food is served Monday-Friday lunchtimes (with pensioners' specials Mon-Thu). There are picnic tables on the front patio and a covered smoking area with seats at the rear. Boules is sometimes played at the back.
Q❀◐♿♣P🚌(179,W13)🐾📶

Travellers Friend 🏆

496-498 High Road, Woodford Wells, IG8 0PN (on slip road off A104)

⏲ 12-midnight ☎ (020) 8504 2435

🌐 thetravellersfriendwoodford.co.uk

Courage Best Bitter; St Austell Tribute; Wells Bombardier; 3 changing beers Ⓗ

Owned by two local families, this friendly and comfortable local has a regionally important historic interior, with original oak-panelled walls and rare snob screens. As far as is known, the pub has never sold keg bitter. Behind is a large heated patio with a smoking area, plus a small, recently extended car park. There are picnic tables at the front and the side beer garden is now fully open. Perudo (a dice game) is played. Local CAMRA Pub of the Year 2015. Q❀♿♣🍎P🚌(20,179,W13)🐾📶

NORTH LONDON

N1: Canonbury

Hops & Glory 🄻

382 Essex Road, N1 3PF

⏲ 4.30-11 (midnight Thu); 12-2am Fri & Sat; 12-10.30 Sun

☎ (020) 7226 2277 🌐 hopsandglory.co.uk

Redemption Big Chief; Weird Beard Mariana Trench; 3 changing beers Ⓗ

Popular, privately owned free house offering a fine selection of cask beers and ciders. It has an open-plan public area with high ceiling and the usual Islington mix of unmatched tables, chairs and sofas. With a heated patio garden, it is family-friendly, and dogs and cyclists are welcome. Live piano music features on Thursdays. The in-house microbrewery now produces a saison and pale keg beer. The beers listed are likely to change regularly. 🐴❀◗⇌(Essex Rd)⊖🍎P🚌🐾📶

N1: Hoxton

Howl at the Moon 🄻

178 Hoxton Street, N1 5LH

⏲ 12-11 (1am Fri & Sat) ☎ (020) 7339 9221

🌐 hoxtoncrafthouse.com

Hackney Best Bitter; 4 changing beers (sourced nationally) Ⓗ

Pleasant conversion of a disused pub in a once run-down but now revived area. Five real ales are served from smaller breweries across the UK, with one real cider on tap plus two cider boxes behind the bar. A superb selection of music is played. Mixed seating consists of sofas and chairs around the bar and numerous interesting items adorn the walls. The friendly staff offer tastings. Real English food is served at a reasonable price. Live blues features on Friday. ❀◑⊖♣🍎🚌🐾📶

Wenlock Arms 🄻

26 Wenlock Road, N1 7TA

⏲ 12-11 (midnight Thu; 1am Fri & Sat) ☎ (020) 7608 3406

10 changing beers (sourced nationally) Ⓗ

Saved from closure by a vigorous local campaign, this free house has 10 handpumps featuring beers from all across the UK, concentrating on small and medium-sized breweries, usually including a mild ale. With up to six ciders and perries and a small snacks menu headlined by salt beef sandwiches, this is a truly welcoming street-corner local with an international reputation. Jazz is played in the bar on Thursday nights. 🐴◑♿⇌⊖(Old St)🍎🚌🐾📶

N1: Islington

Charles Lamb

16 Elia Street, N1 8DE

⊙ 12 (4 Mon & Tue)-11; 12-10.30 Sun ☎ (020) 7837 5040
🌐 thecharleslambpub.com

Dark Star Hophead; Windsor & Eton Windsor Knot; 2 changing beers (sourced regionally) [H]

Deservedly busy little two-roomed pub serving four real ales, all from independent brewers and occasional cask cider. Service is fast, friendly and efficient. There is also a worthwhile range of bottle-conditioned ales. Food is a point of pride, but all seating is available to non-diners. The decor is traditional, with bare floorboards. There is some outside seating in a quiet street. Close to Regent's Canal. ❀◑⊖(Angel)♣🚌🐾📶

New Rose L

84-86 Essex Road, N1 8LU

⊙ 12-11 (midnight Thu; 2am Fri & Sat; 10.30 Sun)
☎ (020) 7226 1082

Dark Star Hophead; 3 changing beers (sourced locally) [H]

Spacious and friendly place, traditional but quirky, in the heart of Islington. Alongside the regular beer is a changing range of three quality real ales, light through dark, such as Sambrook's or Windsor & Eton, and there are American bottled beers. A tempting menu of pub favourites is dished up, made using locally sourced ingredients – home-cooked pizzas are a speciality. Enjoy a pint in the small rear garden or on a bench at the front, or catch the big game on TV.
❀◑⇌(Essex Rd)🍎🚌🐾📶

N1: King's Cross

Parcel Yard

King's Cross Station, N1C 4AH

⊙ 8am-11; 9am-10.30 Sun ☎ (020) 7713 7258

Fuller's Chiswick Bitter, London Pride, Bengal Lancer, ESB; Gales HSB; 3 changing beers (sourced nationally) [H]

Large pub approached by stairs at the west end of the new concourse, converted from the former station parcel office. Used by local workers, commuters and for meetings, as well as bars on two levels there are semi-private rooms converted from offices (which can be booked) and an indoor balcony. The lower bar has 12 handpumps, the upstairs bar fewer. It has no music, minimal decor and rescued furniture. Breakfast is served until 11.45am, main meals 12-10pm. Disabled access is by lift, and there are no smoking facilities.
🐴❀◑♿⇌⊖(King's Cross/St Pancras)🚌📶

N1: Pentonville

Craft Beer Co

55 White Lion Street, N1 9PP

⊙ 4-11 (midnight Thu); 12-1am Fri & Sat; 12-10.30 Sun
☎ (020) 7278 4560

Kent Pale; 9 changing beers (sourced nationally) [H]

Multi-room pub with a wooden bar displaying 10 handpumps, all from independent brewers. Green curtains and a red carpet give some warmth to the main bar, which has two Victorian pillars, a wooden floor, raised tables and stools, all overseen by Winston Churchill. A cosy room, with settees and subtle lighting, is to the right as you enter, and there is a smaller room to the back. A small garden is to the side of the pub. ❀◑⊖(Angel)🚏🚌

N2: East Finchley

Bald Faced Stag

69 High Road, N2 8AB

⊙ 12-11 (midnight Fri & Sat) ☎ (020) 8442 1201
🌐 thebaldfacedstagn2.co.uk

Greene King IPA; 3 changing beers (sourced regionally; often Adnams, Sambrook's, Windsor & Eton) [H]

Just up the road from East Finchley underground, this recently refurbished pub has a large dining area and a second smaller area, both available to hire for functions. Meals are also served in the bar, which is over-21s only. The pub is popular with patrons from the nearby Phoenix cinema. Although part of a Greene King-owned chain, guest beers from local and regional breweries are always on offer. A selection of board games is available.
🐴❀◑⊖P🚌🐾📶

N4: Stroud Green

Old Dairy

1-3 Crouch Hill, N4 4AP

⊙ 12-11 (midnight Thu; 1am Fri & Sat); 12-10.30 Sun
☎ (020) 7263 3337 🌐 theolddairyn4.co.uk

Greene King IPA; 4 changing beers (sourced locally) [H]

Popular in the evenings, this is now a Greene King Metropolitan outlet. The outer walls on Crouch Hill feature decorations showing all of its previous dairy activities. The cavernous space is divided between a sit-down restaurant and two large rooms served by the bar (no food Mon lunchtime). A menu of British standards is common to both. Four or five ales include a house beer from Greene King, and a real cider is served in summer.
◑♿⊖(Crouch Hill)♣🚌(210,W3,W7)🐾📶

N5: Canonbury

Snooty Fox L

75 Grosvenor Avenue, N5 2NN

⊙ 4-11 (1am Fri); 12-1am Sat; 12-10.30 Sun
☎ (020) 7354 9532 🌐 snootyfoxlondon.co.uk

Otter Ale; 4 changing beers (sourced nationally) [H]

Vibrant, spacious pub with 1960s icons depicted throughout and a 45rpm jukebox giving a retro feel. The light, airy lounge leads to a small patio, a pleasant spot to enjoy one of up to four real ales and watch the world go by. There is an occasional DJ for music, and several seasonal beer festivals featuring up to 30 beers. Good modern British food is cooked to order, and roasts on Sundays (bookings welcome). Local CAMRA Pub of the Year 2014. ❀◑⊖🍎🚌

N6: Highgate

Bull L

13 North Hill, N6 4AB

⊙ 12-11 (midnight Fri); 9.30am-midnight Sat; 9.30am-11 Sun
☎ (020) 8341 0510 🌐 thebullhighgate.co.uk

London Brewing Company High Rise, Beer Street, Vista; 2 changing beers (sourced nationally) [H]

Home to the London Brewing Company, this brewpub has at least three of its regular beers on sale plus seasonal offerings or guests and a rotating cider. Rescued after serving as a restaurant for 15 years, it offers a fine menu with a dining area to the left, but is determined to attract beer drinkers from near and far into its remodelled bar area, which is just as you enter and to the right. There is an outside seating area on the front terrace. (143,603)

Duke's Head

16 Highgate High Street, N6 5JG
12-midnight (1am Thu-Sat); 12-11.30 Sun
(020) 8341 1310 thedukesheadhighgate.co.uk
Hammerton Oyster Stout; 9 changing beers (sourced nationally)
Former coaching inn with a courtyard, reopened as a specialist beer house offering a large range of real ales and ciders, changing regularly. Local brewer Hammerton is a permanent presence, but expect to find beers from around the country, such as Brodie's, Magic Rock, Moor, Siren and Burning Sky. Usually one mild, one porter/stout, a pale and a best bitter are listed on a chalkboard behind the bar. (210,271)

N7: Holloway

Coronet

338-346 Holloway Road, N7 6PA
8am-11 (midnight Fri-Sun) (020) 7609 5014
Fuller's London Pride; Greene King Abbot; 6 changing beers (sourced nationally)
Impressive Wetherspoon conversion of an old cinema, the Savoy, designed by William Glen and closed in 1983. It is now adorned with large prints of movie stars and former local entertainers, with an old projector the centrepiece of a raised dais towards the rear. There are frequently up to six guest ales, with single-brewery festivals at times. Expect plastic glasses and higher prices when Arsenal are playing at home. Tables (some under cover) are on the pavement and at the rear.
Q (Holloway Rd)

N9: Lower Edmonton

Beehive

24 Little Bury Street, N9 9JZ
12-11.30 (1am Fri & Sat); 12-11 Sun (020) 8360 4358
thebeehiveedmonton.co.uk
Adnams Southwold Bitter, Ghost Ship; Sharp's Doom Bar; 1 changing beer (sourced nationally; often Butcombe, Tetley)
Friendly community local tucked away in semi-detached suburbia. This imposing pub usually has four real ales, kept in top condition by the keen landlord. The all-through bar has a games area with pool and darts at one end and a dining area at the other, popular with a good mix of local customers. Quiz night is Tuesday and there is live music most Saturday evenings. Fresh daily specials as well as traditional pub grub are available lunch and evening. P (329,W8)

N10: Muswell Hill

John Baird

122 Fortis Green Road, N10 3HN
11-11 (midnight Fri & Sat); 12-10.30 Sun
(020) 8444 8830 thejohnbaird.co.uk
Brakspear Bitter; Sharp's Doom Bar; 4 changing beers (sourced nationally)
A mecca for real ale and cider fans in this part of north London, sporting up to six ales and a couple of ciders. One wing of this large pub is home to an excellent Thai restaurant, the other provides ample space for drinkers and those wanting to watch major sporting events in comfort. A sizeable smoking and drinking area is provided outside at the rear. Quiz night is Thursday. Children are allowed in the bar until 7pm and restaurant until 9pm.

N12: North Finchley

Bohemia

762-764 High Road, N12 9QH
12-11 (midnight Thu; 1am Fri & Sat); 12-10.30 Sun
(020) 8446 0294 thebohemia.co.uk
London Beer Street; 5 changing beers (sourced nationally; often Burning Sky, By the Horns, Hammerton)
A vibrant, friendly brewpub near Tally Ho, with daily community events culminating in Friday and Saturday boogie nights. Its own London Brewing Co real ales are brewed both on-site and at its sister pub in Highgate. These are supplemented by a changing range of guests ales and real cider. An interesting menu with a contemporary twist includes excellent sharing and buffet platters. Comfortable easy chairs in the front area create a relaxed atmosphere.
(Woodside Park) (125,263)

Elephant Inn

283 Ballards Lane, N12 8NR
11-11 (midnight Fri & Sat); 12-10.30 Sun
(020) 8343 6110
Fuller's London Pride, ESB; 2 changing beers (sourced locally; often Fuller's)
Formerly the Moss Hall Tavern, this fine wood-panelled pub with a U-shaped bar split into three distinct drinking areas has a quiet zone free of TV screens. Bar meals focus on Thai food; there is also an upstairs restaurant. The two guests and the wide range of bottled beers are usually from the Fuller's portfolio. Darts, dominoes and other pub games can be played here. Wooden seating under huge umbrellas on the front patio gives you somewhere to sit and watch traffic go by.
(West Finchley)

N13: Palmers Green

Alfred Herring

316-322 Green Lanes, N13 5TT
8am-11 (midnight Thu-Sat) (020) 3232 1083
Courage Directors; Greene King Abbot; Ruddles Best Bitter; 7 changing beers (sourced nationally; often Adnams, Redemption, Sambrook's)
A busy Wetherspoon shop conversion in the heart of the Green Lanes shops, opened in 2006, comprising a large open drinking and dining area with side booths. Six of the 10 handpumps offer a varying range, with the manager regularly obtaining beers from a wide list of London breweries. There is a resident darts team. The pub is named after a local First World War soldier who was awarded the Victoria Cross for his heroic action in France in 1918. Q (121,329,W6)

N14: Southgate

New Crown

80-84 Chase Side, N14 5PH
8am-11.30 (12.30am Fri & Sat) (020) 8882 8758
Adnams Broadside; Greene King IPA, Abbot; 7 changing beers (sourced nationally; often Jennings, Portobello)

This well-run Wetherspoon pub is close to the Tube and offers an attentive and efficient service. Formerly a Sainsbury's store, it has a large open-plan interior. A wonderful range of 10 ales with eight ever-changing guests is kept in good condition by the keen staff. The manager aims to have two ales from small local breweries at all times. It is good to see a dartboard in use. You can enjoy a beer from 9am after breakfast.
Q⚭◑♿⊖♣●🚌🐾📶

N16: Dalston Kingsland

Railway Tavern Ale House 🄻

2 St Jude Street, N16 8JT
⌚ 4-11; 12-midnight Fri & Sat; 12-10.30 Sun
☎ (020) 0011 1195
Adnams Southwold Bitter; Redemption Pale Ale; 4 changing beers (sourced nationally) 🄷
A gem of a pub well worth visiting, a stone's throw from bustling Dalston. It has six varied and interesting cask ales to suit all tastes, including one from Adnams and a LocAle, plus exceptional bottled beers such as Kernel. A tasty food menu and Sunday roasts complete the offering. It is full of quirky character, friendly, and a perfect venue to relax, away from the sports crowd, with good beer and good company.
◑♿⊖(Dalston Junction/Dalston Kingsland)🚌🐾📶

N16: Stoke Newington

Jolly Butchers 🄻

204 Stoke Newington High Street, N16 7HU
⌚ 4-midnight (1am Fri); 12-1am Sat; 12-11 Sun
☎ (020) 7241 2185 🌐 jollybutchers.co.uk
Five Points Pale Ale; King Beer Horsham Best Bitter; Moor Beer So'Hop; 3 changing beers (sourced nationally) 🄷
A classic Art Deco-style bar boasting elaborate ironwork and glass, with a lively modern feel and the enviable status of being a true free house. Nine handpumps offer six different real ales, usually from microbreweries, and three ciders or perries. The beers listed are examples of what might be found but the website provides up-to-date pouring information. The beer is complemented by great food on weekday evenings, all day at weekends.
❀◑⇌●🚌🐾📶

N21: Winchmore Hill

Dog & Duck

74 Hoppers Road, N21 3LH
⌚ 12-11.30 (12.30am Fri & Sat) ☎ (020) 8886 1987
🌐 doganddDuckwinchmorehill.co.uk
Fuller's London Pride; Greene King IPA; Timothy Taylor Landlord; Young's Bitter 🄷
Traditional small one-bar pub popular with football fans, although all sport is screened and it can get busy. The golfing fraternity is also well served, with a corner devoted to trophies and memorabilia. Other walls are adorned with pictures of local history. The patio-style walled garden at the rear has a covered area and welcomes dogs at quiet times. The pub has been in the Guide for 12 consecutive years, 25 years in total. ❀🚌(W9)🐾

Orange Tree

18 Highfield Road, N21 3HA
⌚ 12-midnight (12.30am Fri & Sat) ☎ (020) 8360 4853
Greene King IPA; Morland Old Speckled Hen; 4 changing beers (sourced nationally; often Belhaven, Redemption) 🄷
This old-fashioned back-street local, just yards from the New River walk, has been in the Guide since 1995. Originally a Taylor Walker venue with the old sign still hanging outside, it is now a well-established free house offering two guest ales alongside the permanent beers. Live sport is shown and one of the ales is often sport-related. Always welcoming, with friendly staff, it has two darts teams, a fortnightly quiz, and summer barbecues in the prize-winning garden. ⚭❀◑⇌♣P🚌(329)📶

Enfield

Moon under Water

115-117 Chase Side, EN2 6NN
⌚ 9am-11 (10.30 Sun) ☎ (020) 8366 9855
Greene King IPA, Abbot; 6 changing beers (sourced nationally; often Adnams, Brains, Nethergate) 🄷
Long-established Wetherspoon pub converted from a former dairy, within easy reach of both Enfield Chase and Gordon Hill stations. The L-shaped bar sports 10 handpumps, with real cider served from polypins. Look up while drinking and you will see exposed roof trusses, stained-glass windows and a mock balcony complete with library. The conservatory at the rear adds to its light and airy ambience. Popular with all age groups, children are welcome until 8.30pm.
⚭❀◑♿⇌(Chase)●P🚌(191,W9)📶

Wonder 🄻

1 Batley Road, EN2 0JG
⌚ 11-11 (midnight Fri & Sat); 12-11 Sun ☎ (020) 8363 0202
McMullen AK, Cask Ale, Country Bitter; 1 changing beer (sourced locally; often McMullen) 🄷
A great old-fashioned back-street local with a separate public bar with a real fire, dartboard, fruit machine and piano. The lounge area is quieter. It is a football-free pub, with music and entertainment – a honky tonk on Saturday evenings and Sunday afternoons, and a jam session on the last Wednesday of every month. A monthly newsletter confirms these and other events. Paved seated areas outside include heaters. Hot pies are served till sold out (mushy peas optional). Be warned, McMullen may start using sparklers.
Q❀◐♿⇌(Gordon Hill)♣P🚌(191,W8)📶

High Barnet

Black Horse

Wood Street, EN5 4HY
⌚ 12-midnight (1am Fri & Sat); 12-11 Sun
☎ (020) 8449 2230 🌐 blackhorsebarnet.co.uk
8 changing beers (sourced nationally; often Castle Rock, Milestone, Vale) 🄷
Drinkers are always made welcome in this dog-friendly bar and well-run restaurant with ample seating; a large garden overlooks the road. Barnet Brewery is located here and the landlord is proud to welcome visitors to the first microbrewery in Barnet. One or two of its brews will be available alongside a changing range of ales from around the country. The restaurant area may not be open some Fridays or Saturdays when live bands feature. On these occasions it is over-21s only.
⚭❀◑♿●🚌🐾📶

Olde Mitre Inne 🏆

58 High Street, EN5 5SJ

12-11 (1am Fri & Sat) ☎ (020) 8449 5701

Adnams Southwold Bitter; Greene King Abbot; Timothy Taylor Landlord; Tring Ridgeway; 4 changing beers (sourced nationally; often East London, Red Squirrel, Thwaites) H

Barnet's oldest coaching inn has won CAMRA's local Pub of the Year award many times for obvious reasons. A traditional pub, it has beams, exposed brickwork, wood panelling, open fires and friendly, attentive staff who serve an excellent pint from a range of ales selected from SIBA and national breweries – the understanding landlord lets the local CAMRA branch select one of them. There are many areas to drink and eat, also a courtyard garden with retractable roof and brick-built chiminea.

New Barnet

Railway Bell

13 East Barnet Road, EN4 8RR

8am-11 (midnight Fri & Sat) ☎ (020) 8449 1369

Courage Directors; Greene King IPA, Abbot; Ruddles Best Bitter; Sharp's Doom Bar; 6 changing beers (sourced nationally; often Adnams, Blindmans, Hook Norton) H

A recently refurbished Wetherspoon pub that was previously neither a shop nor a showroom. The large conservatory with open kitchen is bright and may remind you of your school refectory or the works canteen, but do not let that put you off. The changing guest beers often include ales from London breweries selected by the keen manager. A large patio to the side and back of the pub helpfully offers a no-smoking area.

Ponders End

Picture Palace L

Howard Hall, Lincoln Road, EN3 4AQ

9am-11 (midnight Fri & Sat) ☎ (020) 8344 9690

Adnams Broadside; Fuller's London Pride; Greene King Abbot; Ruddles Best Bitter; 4 changing beers (sourced nationally; often Redemption, Twickenham) H

Opened in 1913 as a cinema, this is now a popular Wetherspoon pub. The spacious hall maintains architectural features as well as fabulous murals of the likes of Charlie Chaplin and Laurel and Hardy high above the bar. Two smaller areas to the front and the side are quieter. Small TVs are on silent mode all day and a huge drop-down screen shows major sporting events. LocAle comes from London microbreweries and the current manager does not use sparklers. (Southbury)P

NORTH-WEST LONDON

NW1: Camden Town

Black Heart L

3 Greenland Place, NW1 0AP

3-11.30 (midnight Wed & Thu); 12-2am Fri & Sat; 12-11 Sun ☎ (020) 7428 9730 ourblackheart.com

2 changing beers H

Tucked away in a side street off the main drag, this is nonetheless a true Camden Town bar, with its exterior painted completely black and a large black heart hanging outside the only indication of its name. This rather stark view is offset by white lace curtains on large French doors opened wide in dry, warm weather. Essentially, it is a single bar with booths along one side, tables on the other, plenty of bar stools, a pool table and an impressive poster display.

Tapping the Admiral 🏆 L

77 Castle Road, NW1 8SU

12-midnight (11 Sun-Tue) ☎ (020) 7267 6118

tappingtheadmiral.co.uk

Adnams Ghost Ship; Dark Star Hophead; 6 changing beers (sourced nationally) H

A popular community pub where friendly and knowledgeable staff offer a warm welcome. Eight handpumps deliver up to six varying guest ales, mainly from local breweries. The menu is great British food, with good-value lunches. The heated and covered beer garden is well designed and a nice feature. There is a popular Wednesday night quiz and live sessions of traditional music on Thursday evenings. Local CAMRA 2013 and 2015 Pub of the Year.

Q (Kentish Town West)

NW1: Euston

Bree Louise L

69 Cobourg Street, NW1 2HH

11.30-11; 12-10.30 Sun ☎ (020) 7681 4930

thebreelouise.com

17 changing beers (sourced nationally) H/G

One-bar corner pub, busy with locals and Euston commuters. A cooled gravity stillage of up to 11 beers, complemented by six handpumps, provides a large, continually changing range from London and across the UK, alongside up to 11 ciders and perries. Regular beer festivals are held. Pumpclips festoon the ceiling. There is no music, just conversation, with occasional sport on TV (especially rugby, not football). Outdoor seating is on the pavement. Closing time may be later on weekdays. (Euston/Euston Sq)

Doric Arch L

Euston Station Colonnade, 1 Eversholt Street, NW1 2DN

11-11; 11-10.30 Sun ☎ (020) 7383 3359

Fuller's London Pride, ESB; 6 changing beers (sourced nationally) H

Up a flight of stairs, the pub's large picture windows allow for a view of the busy urban world below. Situated right next to Euston station, the bar is used extensively by commuters, aided by the train times screen. Guest beers are from other London breweries as well as from all across the UK. Toilets are at basement level. Excellent staff are helpful and informative about ale. Brewery and railway memorabilia adorn the walls. Food is served all day.

Euston Tap

West Lodge, 190 Euston Road, NW1 2EF

12-11.30; 12-10 Sun ☎ (020) 3137 8837

eustontap.com

8 changing beers (sourced nationally) H

Fronting the main station building, an impressive Grade II-listed Portland stone lodge, this is one of the few relics from the original 1830s station. Up to eight changing beers are pumped up to taps behind the bar. Space is limited but there is a large outside drinking area as well as seating (and the toilets) up a wrought-iron spiral staircase. The lodge opposite, the Cider Tap, opening at 3.30pm

(not Sun), features six real ciders. Food can be ordered from various takeaway menus.
✪⊜≋⊖(Euston/Euston Sq)●🚐😺🛜

Royal George 🄻
8-14 Eversholt Street, NW1 1DG
✪ 11-midnight (1am Fri & Sat); 12-11.30 Sun
☎ (020) 7387 2431
Fuller's London Pride; Westerham Taylor Walker 1730; 4 changing beers (sourced regionally) 🄷
Large pub built in 1939, Grade II-listed, arranged as interconnecting rooms facing the three street frontages, with a central bar. One side has an unusual fireplace with marquetry work on the surrounds. Right opposite Euston station, it is named after HMS Royal George, a flagship vessel for the Royal Navy in the 1800s. Local London beers are augmented by regional guests. Food is served daily until 11pm. ✪◑≋⊖🚐🛜

NW3: Hampstead

Duke of Hamilton 🄻
23 New End, NW3 1JD
✪ 12-11; 12-10.30 Sun ☎ (020) 7794 2068
⊕ thedukeofhamilton.com
Fuller's London Pride; 4 changing beers (sourced nationally) 🄷
An old favourite, saved from conversion into flats in 2010, this historic back-street pub serves a changing range of ales from across the UK. Named after a Civil War Royalist, it has been in the Guide for two decades, while its origins date back over 250 years. The main bar has a TV screen and quieter areas. The cellar is now a theatre, hosting music, plays and comedy. The front terrace is a particularly pleasant place to sit in warm weather.
🕭😺⊖♣🚐(268,603)😺🛜

NW4: Hendon

Greyhound
52 Church End, NW4 4JT
✪ 12-11 (midnight Fri & Sat) ☎ (020) 8457 9730
Young's Bitter, Special; 2 changing beers (sourced regionally; often Twickenham, Wells) 🄷
A short distance from Middlesex University and next door to St Mary's Church, a pub has been on this site since 1675 – the current building dates back to 1896. The landlord is keen on real ale and cider and up to four of each are regularly available. There are four separate comfortable seating areas, one is wood panelled and sometimes set out for dining. Photographs depict the pub and village through the years. Quiz nights are Monday and Thursday. Q🕭✪🚐◑♣●🚐😺🛜

NW5: Kentish Town

Grafton 🄻
20 Prince of Wales Road, NW5 3LG
✪ 12-11 (midnight Fri & Sat); 12-10.30 Sun
☎ (020) 7482 4466 ⊕ thegraftonnw5.co.uk
Sambrook's Wandle; Timothy Taylor Landlord; 5 changing beers (sourced locally) 🄷
Popular pub with beautiful Victorian features, combining a traditional feel with many contemporary touches and specialising in cask beer from local breweries. The spacious ground floor horseshoe bar is partly tiled, with ample seating. Upstairs is a bar/function room (no real ale) and an elegant, covered roof garden. A popular quiz is

hosted on Tuesday and occasional open-mic music nights take place. There are board games and a piano. The bar staff are friendly.
🕭✪◑⧖≋⊖(Kentish Town West)●🚐😺🛜

Lion & Unicorn 🄻
42-44 Gaisford Street, NW5 2ED
✪ 12-11; 12-10.30 Sun ☎ (020) 7267 2304
Young's Special; 3 changing beers 🄷
This popular community pub is a great favourite with its genuine homely feel, open fire and comfortable seating. Run by friendly management and staff as a Geronimo branded gastro-pub, it offers a good-quality cask ale range featuring several LocAle breweries. It has won local and regional awards for its front and back gardens. Above the pub is the Giant Olive Theatre.
Q🕭✪◑⧖≋⊖●🚐😺🛜

Pineapple 🄻
51 Leverton Street, NW5 2NX
✪ 12-11 (midnight Fri & Sat); 12-10.30 Sun
☎ (020) 7284 4631
Sharp's Doom Bar; 4 changing beers (sourced nationally) 🄷
An authentic, friendly community pub, saved from closure by the locals, Grade II-listed and with a regionally important historic interior, notable for its mirrors and splendid bar-back. The front bar, with comfortable seating around tables, leads through to an informal conservatory overlooking the patio garden. The food menu is Thai kitchen cuisine. LocAles can include beers from across London and, the pub being free of tie, the range changes regularly. Q🕭✪◑≋⊖●🚐😺🛜

Southampton Arms
139 Highgate Road, NW5 1LE
✪ 12-midnight ⊕ thesouthamptonarms.co.uk
11 changing beers (sourced nationally) 🄷
This pub does what it says on the sign outside – Ale, Cider, Meat. On and behind the bar, 18 handpumps serve almost equal amounts of cider and changing beers from microbreweries across the UK. Snacks include pork pies, cheese and meat baps. Music is played on vinyl only and the piano is in regular use. Down at the back is a secluded patio. ✪◑≋⊖(Gospel Oak/Kentish Town)●🚐

NW9: Colindale

Chandos Arms
31 Colindale Avenue, NW9 5DS
✪ 12 (4 Mon)-11; 12-1am Fri & Sat ☎ (020) 8200 0032
⊕ thechandosarms.com
Caledonian Deuchars IPA; 2 changing beers (sourced nationally; often Brains, Caledonian) 🄷
Reopened in 2013 to take advantage of the surge of new homes in the area, this friendly and warm community pub has become a real hit with the locals. Hot dog Mondays, two-for-£10 pizza Tuesdays, quiz night Wednesdays and folk or comedy club most Thursdays are just some of the events on offer. You may have to pay to enjoy live music on the occasional Saturday, but live jazz on the third Sunday of the month is free.
🕭✪◑●🚐😺🛜

Harefield

Old Orchard 🄻
Jacks Lane, UB9 6HJ (off Park Lane)

✪ 11.30-11; 11.30-10.30 Sun ☎ (01895) 822631
⊕ oldorchard-harefield.co.uk
Mighty Oak Oscar Wilde; Phoenix Arizona; Tring Side Pocket for a Toad; 3 changing beers (sourced locally; often Binghams, Oakham, Tring) ⓗ
This Brunning & Price establishment was once a country house before becoming a restaurant. Refurbished in 2010, the pub is lined with bookcases and pictures, has an unfussy array of mismatched tables and chairs, and offers three welcoming real fires in the colder months. The Original is brewed by Phoenix. There are commanding views of the Colne Valley from the terrace and beer garden. Ciders are Westons Old Rosie and Thatchers Cheddar Valley.
Q ☻ ❀ ◑ ㅎ ♣ ♠ P ☶ (U9) ❀ ☞

Harrow

Moon on the Hill
373-375 Station Road, HA1 2AW
✪ 8am-midnight (12.30am Fri & Sat) ☎ (020) 8863 3670
Adnams Broadside; Fuller's London Pride; Greene King Abbot; Ruddles Best Bitter; 3 changing beers (sourced locally; often Portobello, Twickenham) ⓗ
Small, busy Wetherspoon pub close to Harrow-on-the-Hill station and served by numerous bus routes. With food all day, it is popular with price-conscious regulars, office workers and students from the University of Westminster. The place gets extremely busy when there are sporting events on at nearby Wembley Stadium and plastic glasses may be used on these occasions. Alcohol is served from 9am. ☻ ◑ ㅎ ⇌ ⊖ (Harrow-on-the-Hill) ● ☶ ☞

Ickenham

Tichenham Inn
11 Swakeleys Road, UB10 8DF
✪ 8am-midnight (1am Fri & Sat) ☎ (01895) 678916
Fuller's London Pride; Greene King Abbot; Ruddles Best Bitter; Sharp's Doom Bar; 6 changing beers (sourced locally; often Twickenham) ⓗ
Small and friendly Wetherspoon pub converted from a garage with a strong local following. Food and beers are good value, with the usual chain promotions. The pub has its own occasional festivals with more guest ales in conjunction with other local Wetherspoon branches. Gwynt y Ddraig Black Dragon cider is served from a bag in a box in the fridge. Q ☻ ❀ ◑ ㅎ ⊖ ● ☶ (U1,U10) ❀ ☞

Ruislip Manor

J J Moons Ⓛ
12 Victoria Road, HA4 0AA
✪ 8am-midnight (1am Fri & Sat); 8am-11 Sun
☎ (01895) 622373
Courage Directors; Fuller's London Pride; Greene King Abbot; Ruddles Best Bitter; Sharp's Doom Bar; 5 changing beers ⓗ
A large Wetherspoon conversion conveniently located opposite the Tube station. Popular and often busy in the evening and at weekends, it has good-value food and beer and the usual daily special promotions. At the rear is an elevated section for dining, leading to a small garden patio, while the front has a partitioned-off smoking area on the street. Alcohol is served from 9am.
Q ☻ ❀ ◑ ㅎ ⊖ ● ☶ (114,398,H13) ☞

South Kenton

Windermere ★
Windermere Avenue, HA9 8QT
✪ 12-11.30 (12.30am Fri); 11-12.30am Sat; 11-11.30 Sun
☎ (020) 8904 7484 ⊕ windermerepub.com
Courage Best Bitter; 1 changing beer (sourced nationally; often Fuller's, Young's) ⓗ
Built in 1939 next to South Kenton station, this pub has a nationally important historic interior. It is a genuine community venue with three bars, although the public bar is now only used for functions. The saloon and lounge retain many original features including the large inner porches, bar counters, back-fittings, wall panelling and fireplaces. A quiz is held on alternate Thursdays and there is sometimes live entertainment. The guest beer is Fuller's London Pride or Young's Special. ☻ ❀ ⊖ ♣ P ☶ (223) ☞

SOUTH-EAST LONDON
SE1: Bermondsey

Simon the Tanner
231 Long Lane, SE1 4PR
✪ 12 (5 Mon)-11; 12-10.30 Sun ☎ (020) 7357 8740
⊕ simonthetanner.co.uk
Adnams Lighthouse; 3 changing beers (sourced nationally; often Siren, Southwark) ⓗ
In a quiet road just off busy Bermondsey Street, the Simon is a mid-terrace, modestly sized, Grade II-listed pub. Formerly a Shepherd Neame outlet, it is now a free house. The regularly changing real ales are often from London breweries. Real and mulled cider is also available. Food is a quality take on standard dishes like pies, burgers and soups, plus there is a roast on Sundays. A quiz is held on Tuesday evenings and live piano music every Wednesday. ☻ ◑ ⇌ ⊖ (London Bridge) ● ☶ ❀ ☞

SE1: Borough

Lord Clyde
27 Clennam Street, SE1 1ER
✪ 11 (12 Sat)-11; 12-6 Sun ☎ (020) 7407 3397
⊕ lordclyde.com
Adnams Southwold Bitter; Hogs Back TEA; Sharp's Doom Bar; Young's Bitter; 1 changing beer (sourced nationally) ⓗ
A Grade II-listed gem of a corner pub that has changed little since it was rebuilt in 1913, and well worth a visit to step back in time. Outside it retains lovely Truman's Brewery tilework, and the regionally important historic interior has traditional decor with comfortable seating and curtains over the doors. There is one main bar and a side room with its own serving hatch. The pub has been run by the same family for over 50 years.
◑ ⇌ (London Bridge) ⊖ ☶ ❀

Royal Oak
44 Tabard Street, SE1 4JU
✪ 11 (12 Sat)-11.30; 12-9 Sun ☎ (020) 7357 7173
Harveys Sussex XX Mild Ale, IPA, Sussex Best Bitter; 2 changing beers (sourced locally; often Fuller's, Harveys) ⓗ
A back-to-basics pub with charm and high standards, separated into two sections by the bar counter and an off-sales hatch. It was Harveys' first London tied house, but also offers a changing guest beer from Fuller's. You will be delighted with the attentive service, the extensive range of beers

including seasonal brews, and a large choice on the food menu often sourced from London markets. The proof is evident from the many regulars who come from miles around to spend time here. Q◐⇌(London Bridge)⊖♣●🚌

SE1: Borough Market

Market Porter

9 Stoney Street, SE1 9AA

6-8.30am, 11 (12 Sat)-11; 12-10.30 Sun

☎ (020) 7407 2495

Harveys Sussex Best Bitter H; 9 changing beers (sourced nationally) H/A

A classic market pub with rustic decor, on the edge of the famous Borough Market and retaining traditional early morning weekday opening hours. Up to 10 real ales are on tap plus three ciders, usually including a Westons. The vast array of pumpclips on the walls indicates the huge range of beers offered over the years. Popular with locals and visitors, it can get busy, with drinkers spilling out onto the street. An upstairs restaurant serves lunches. ◐⇌⊖(London Bridge)●🚌

Old King's Head

45 Borough High Street, SE1 1NA

11-midnight (1am Fri & Sat); 12-midnight Sun

☎ (020) 7407 1550 🌐 theoldkingshead.uk.com

Harveys Sussex Best Bitter; St Austell Tribute, Proper Job; Sharp's Doom Bar; Wells Bombardier H

Down a narrow, cobbled road off Borough High Street lies this traditional pub. The stained-glass windows hint at a bygone era and the pictures adorning the walls tell the story of a pub, and an area, that has a rich history. The layout inside is simple, with an L-shaped bar in one corner usually offering five or six real ales on handpump. The clientele is a mix of tourists, office workers and marketgoers. ◐♿⇌⊖(London Bridge)🚌

Rake

14 Winchester Walk, SE1 9AG

12 (11 Fri; 10 Sat)-11; 12-8 Sun ☎ (020) 7407 0557

3 changing beers (sourced nationally; often Dark Star, Oakham) H

A great, but tiny, destination pub. Its walls have over 200 messages from visiting brewers from around the globe, yet its bar is only 10 feet long. There are three real ales at a time plus an amazing selection of bottled beers. Light food is available and customers may, with permission, bring in food from nearby Borough Market. It can close early in winter months, so check to avoid disappointment. Q❀♿⇌⊖(London Bridge)🚌

Sheaf

24 Southwark Street, SE1 1TY

11-11 (midnight Fri); 12-midnight Sat; 12-10.30 Sun

☎ (020) 7407 9934

Fuller's London Pride; Young's Bitter; house beer (by Nethergate); 7 changing beers (sourced nationally) H

Beneath the old Hop Exchange, this pub is remarkably bright and airy for a basement bar and offers a retreat away from the bustle of the nearby market. The recent contemporary refurbishment contrasts with the more traditional surroundings of nearby establishments. Retro benches, stools and tables are complemented by modern partitioning and flat-screen TVs showing popular sport events. With 10 handpumps, up to seven guest ales are offered alongside the regulars, including the house Red Car Bitter. ◐⇌⊖(London Bridge)♣🚌🐾

SE1: South Bank

Doggett's Coat & Badge

1 Blackfriars Bridge, SE1 9UD

8am-11 (midnight Thu-Sat) ☎ (020) 7633 9081

St Austell Nicholson's Pale Ale; Sambrook's Junction; Sharp's Doom Bar; Truman's Runner; 6 changing beers (sourced nationally) H

A large, multi-level Nicholson's pub on the South Bank at the end of Blackfriars Bridge. The name refers to a 300-year-old amateur Thames boat race originally organised by actor Thomas Doggett, with the winner awarded a waterman's coat and silver badge. There are bars on the ground, second and third floors, plus a first-floor restaurant. The terrace overlooking the river and a covered beer garden at the rear are great places for outdoor drinking. ❀◐♿⇌(Blackfriars)⊖(Blackfriars/Southwark) 🚌

SE1: Tower Bridge

Draft House

206/208 Tower Bridge Road, SE1 2UP

12-11 (midnight Fri); 12-10 Sun ☎ (020) 7378 9995

Sambrook's Wandle; 3 changing beers (sourced nationally) H

Busy bar in the shadow of Tower Bridge, part of a small chain of London pubs focused on real ales. The main bar area has a fairly contemporary feel, whereas the restaurant area is more retro. As well as four real ales on handpump, there is a wide bottled range. One discounted cask beer is on the bar daily until it runs out. There is usually music playing. ◐⇌⊖(London Bridge)🚌🐾

SE1: Waterloo

King's Arms

25 Roupell Street, SE1 8TB

11-11; 12-10.30 Sun ☎ (020) 7207 0784

🌐 thekingsarmslondon.co.uk

Adnams Southwold Bitter; 8 changing beers (sourced nationally) H

On a back-street corner, here is a treasure worth seeking out. With two rooms separated by a central bar and seating at a premium, it is not unusual to find many people drinking in the street. The nine real ales usually include two or more from London brewers and at least one dark beer. The real cider is Snailsbank Tumbledown. To the rear is a Thai restaurant.

◐⇌(Waterloo/Waterloo East)⊖●🚌🐾

SE3: Blackheath

Hare & Billet

1a Eliot Cottages, Hare & Billet Road, SE3 0QJ

11-11 (midnight Thu-Sat); 12-10.30 Sun

☎ (020) 8852 2352 🌐 hareandbillet.com

Greene King IPA; house beer (by Greene King); 3 changing beers (sourced nationally; often Kent, Mordue, Portobello) H

This pub has the largest range in Blackheath, with eight real ales from a variety of breweries and real cider too. The interior has plenty of natural light, is not chic or trying too hard, and affords a nice view of the heath. In summer months plastic glasses are available for outside drinking. The seasonal food menu focuses on British dishes including pies, roasts and seafood. The pub is home to the Hare & Billet Pond Volunteers. ◐♿⇌●🚌🐾

SE4: Brockley

Brockley Barge

184 Brockley Road, SE4 2RR

8am-midnight ☎ (020) 8694 7690

Greene King Abbot; Ruddles Best Bitter; Sharp's Doom Bar; 4 changing beers (sourced nationally) H

Conveniently located in the heart of Brockley, these premises were reopened in 2000 by Wetherspoon, breathing new life into a pub whose previous incarnation had closed a few years earlier. The name harks back to the old Croydon Canal, replaced in 1836 by the present railway line. The spacious U-shaped interior has modern décor and large windows. There is a courtyard garden to one side. A mixed clientele of all ages reflects the area.

Q (171,172,484)

Talbot

2-4 Tyrwhitt Road, SE4 1QG

12-11 (midnight Fri & Sat); 11-10.30 Sun

☎ (020) 8692 2665 talbotpublichouse.com

Harveys Sussex Best Bitter; 4 changing beers (sourced nationally; often Brockley, Salopian) H

A fine Victorian suburban local on two floors, popular with all ages, families and dog owners. After changing hands in 2014, it was tastefully redecorated inside and out. Large windows help to make the interior light and airy. A series of murals, highlighted with gilt, decorates the walls. An extensive, upmarket menu caters for all including vegetarians and vegans, with daily specials and meal deals on Mondays. Regular live music, seasonal events and a weekly quiz take place.

Q (St Johns) (Elverson Rd)

SE5: Camberwell

Stormbird

25 Camberwell Church Street, SE5 8TR

4-midnight (1am Fri); 12-1am Sat; 12-midnight Sun

☎ (020) 7708 4460 thestormbirdpub.co.uk

Dark Star American Pale Ale; 3 changing beers (sourced nationally; often Dark Star, Magic Rock) H

This is the sister pub of the Hermit's Cave across the road and offers a slightly more contemporary feel, attracting a mixed but generally younger crowd. A huge range of beers of all types includes four real ales on handpump, other beers on tap and an extensive bottled beer selection, encompassing brews from the UK, continental Europe and the US. Draught beers are available in third-pint measures.

(Denmark Hill)

SE5: Denmark Hill

Fox on the Hill

149 Denmark Hill, SE5 8EH

8am-12.30am (1am Fri & Sat) ☎ (020) 7738 4756

Fuller's London Pride; Greene King Abbot; Ruddles Best Bitter; 5 changing beers (sourced locally; often By the Horns, Sambrook's) H

Spacious and welcoming Wetherspoon pub at the top of a fairly steep hill. Inside are a number of cosy, low-screened booths, while outside is a spacious rear garden, smokers' terrace and front lawn with picnic tables. Wall displays depict the history of the local area, including Victorian resident John Ruskin, after whom the nearby park is named. Up to five London guest beers are usually available in addition to the regulars. It hosts frequent Meet the Brewer events.

P

SE6: Catford

Catford Constitutional Club

Catford Broadway, SE6 4SP

4-midnight (11 Mon; 1am Fri); 12-midnight Sat; 12-11 Sun

☎ (020) 8613 7188 catfordconstitutionalclub.com

Adnams Lighthouse; Caledonian Deuchars IPA; Dark Star Partridge Best Bitter; 3 changing beers (sourced regionally) H

Located down a short, well-lit alley opposite Canadian Avenue, the former Conservative club closed in 1996 and reopened in November 2013, retaining many original features. The single bar and restaurant areas feature a large chandelier hanging from the bare rafters. A quirky assortment of old furniture, pictures, Private Eye covers and mirrors creates a unique atmosphere which could be described as shabby chic. A weekly pub quiz, monthly comedy and occasional film nights take place in a separate smaller room.

(Catford/Catford Bridge)

London & Rye

109 Rushey Green, SE6 4AF

8am-midnight ☎ (020) 8697 5028

Greene King Abbot; Morland Old Speckled Hen; Ruddles Best Bitter; 3 changing beers (sourced nationally; often Adnams, Weltons, Westerham) H

Converted by Wetherspoon from a former DIY shop in 2000, this pub takes its name from its location on the old coaching route between London and Rye in Kent. Displays feature historic figures with local connections, ranging from singer Tommy Steele to nursery education pioneers Rachel and Margaret McMillan, the statesman Herbert Morrison and the tragic love poet Ernest Dowson. Guest beers may come from microbreweries.

Q (Catford/Catford Bridge)

SE8: Deptford

Dog & Bell L

116 Prince Street, SE8 3JD

12-11.30 (midnight Fri & Sat) ☎ (020) 8692 5664

Fuller's London Pride; 5 changing beers (sourced nationally; often Clarkshaws, Dent, Old Dairy) H

Traditional and welcoming pub tucked away down a side street close to the centre of Deptford, a Guide stalwart offering six real ales, plus a selection of Belgian bottled beers, malt whiskies and simple, tasty meals. It has a lively bar, a real fire in winter and a mixed clientele including locals, cyclists and strollers along the nearby Thames Path. A quiz is held on Sunday evenings and a popular annual pickle festival takes place in November.

Q

Job Centre

120 Deptford High Street, SE8 4NS

4-11 (midnight Fri & Sat) ☎ (020) 8692 6859

jobcentredeptford.com

Caledonian Deuchars IPA; 4 changing beers (sourced regionally) H

A welcome addition by Antic to the fairly sparse Deptford pub scene, opened in 2014 and named after a former occupier of the premises. The spacious rectangular bar area has minimalist decor with bare concrete flooring and exposed ducts and pipework. Music is often playing from a twin-deck turntable. The beer range has a regional focus with various styles and strengths; there is also a cider on handpump. Food is supplied by a changing street-food vendor. (Bridge)

SE9: Eltham

Park Tavern

45 Passey Place, SE9 5DA

12-11 (020) 8850 3216 parktaverneltham.co.uk

8 changing beers (sourced regionally; often Otter, Sambrook's)

Traditional Victorian pub with the original tiled frontage and historic Truman's signage. The small interior has an impressive wooden L-shaped bar with stylish lamps and chandeliers. The etched windows have elegant drapes, and decorative plates and pictures line the walls. Jazz and light classical background music is played. There is a well-kept, heated rear garden and further seating to the front and side. Alongside the range of real ales an impressive selection of whiskies and wine is available. Q

SE10: East Greenwich

Pelton Arms

23-25 Pelton Road, SE10 9PQ

12-midnight (1am Fri & Sat); 12-11 Sun

(020) 8858 0572 peltonarms.com

Greene King IPA; St Austell Tribute; Wells Bombardier; 6 changing beers (sourced regionally; often Hop Stuff, Truman's, Westerham)

Popular and spacious back-street pub a short stroll from Greenwich town centre. The L-shaped bar is surrounded by an eclectic mix of furnishings and soft lighting, giving the place a cosy and welcoming feel. Community-oriented, it has varied live music four nights a week, a quiz on Tuesdays and the Pelton knitters get together on Wednesdays. Six varying guest ales are mainly from regional brewers, and a changing cider on handpump is often from Herefordshire. Five B&B rooms are available.
(Maze Hill)

SE11: Kennington

Mansion House

46 Kennington Park Road, SE11 4RS

12-midnight (1am Fri & Sat) (020) 7582 5599

oakalondon.com

Oakham JHB, Inferno, Citra; 3 changing beers (sourced regionally; often Oakham)

London's only pub run by Oakham Ales. Seven of its beers are usually available including a monthly special, a real cider and occasionally a guest beer. The pub is of contemporary design, with a glass frontage that can be opened during warm weather. A nice touch is the interior brass base of an old mash tun set into the floor. Staff are uniformed and service is taken seriously in both the bar area and the Oaka pan-Asian restaurant.
(Elephant & Castle)

SE12: Lee

Baring Hall Hotel

368 Baring Road, SE12 0DU

4-11 (midnight Fri); 12-midnight Sat; 12-11 Sun

(020) 8851 2184 baringhallhotel.com

Adnams Lighthouse; Caledonian Deuchars IPA; 4 changing beers (sourced nationally; often Hawkshead, Mantle, Sambrook's)

Designed in 1882 by renowned architect Ernest Newton and a rare example of his early work, this pub was saved from demolition by the efforts of the local community and pub company Antic, reopening in 2013. The interior decor makes a feature of the fire damage which had led to its closure in 2009. A cosy and welcoming island in a sea of suburbia, it is conveniently located opposite Grove Park station, offering a varying range of beer styles. (Grove Park)

SE13: Hither Green

Station Hotel

14 Staplehurst Road, SE13 5NB

12-11 (midnight Fri & Sat); 12-10.30 Sun

(020) 8463 0367 stationhotelhithergreen.co.uk

10 changing beers (sourced nationally)

A beautiful and imposing Victorian-style building dating from 1906, a stone's throw from Hither Green station and attracting a varied clientele. Since a comprehensive refurbishment in 2012, the interior is now open plan with tasteful contemporary decor. There is a spacious L-shaped bar at the front and a restaurant area to the rear. An impressive 11 handpumps offer up to 10 changing real ales plus real cider. It holds a regular quiz night. Q (273)

SE14: New Cross

Royal Albert

460 New Cross Road, SE14 6TJ

4-midnight (1am Fri); 12-1am Sat; 12-midnight Sun

(020) 8692 3737 royalalbertpub.com

Adnams Lighthouse; Dark Star Hophead; Sharp's Doom Bar; 4 changing beers (sourced regionally; often Brockley, Five Points, London Fields)

A cosy Antic pub with a relaxed, homely ambience and varied clientele. The decor includes original Victorian etched windows and mirrors, an L-shaped bar leading to the rear conservatory and an open-to-view kitchen. The front patio is popular for outside drinking. Guest beers have a mainly regional focus, sometimes showcasing newly opened microbreweries. The food includes seasonal dishes that change weekly. Monday is quiz night, there is a DJ on Friday evenings and live music on Sundays.
(Deptford Bridge/New Cross)

SE15: Nunhead

Ivy House

40 Stuart Road, SE15 3BE

12-11 (midnight Fri & Sat; 10.30 Sun) (020) 7277 8233

ivyhousenunhead.com

Five Points Pale Ale; 7 changing beers (sourced regionally; often Brockley, Hop Stuff, Truman's)

London's first co-operatively run pub, rescued from closure in 2012 by local community action. Designed by Truman's Brewery and a wonderful example of a 1930s so-called improved public house, it is Grade II-listed, with a regionally important historic interior retaining many original features and fittings. Its website records its 1970s pub rock history. Beers from Brockley and Truman's are usually on tap, with five other guest beers generally sourced from small London breweries. Local CAMRA Pub of the Year 2014.
Q (343,484)

Old Nun's Head

15 Nunhead Green, SE15 3QQ

12-11 (midnight Thu; 1am Fri & Sat); 12-10.30 Sun
(020) 7639 4007 theoldnunshead.co.uk
House beer (by King Beer); 5 changing beers (sourced locally; often Belleville, Clouded Minds, Gipsy Hill)
A large 1930s mock-Tudor community pub with a wood-panelled interior and a rear courtyard garden. Five changing guest ales are usually served, mainly sourced from London microbreweries, in addition to the Laine's Best house beer. The food menu varies throughout the week as the pub turns its kitchen over to different street food and other producers. Live comedy acts perform regularly and a quiz is held on Thursday evenings. (78,P12)

SE15: Peckham

Beer Rebellion

129 Queens Road, SE15 2ND
12-11
6 changing beers (sourced regionally; often Late Knights)
A micropub-style establishment in a former betting shop, one of a small group of bars run by the Late Knights microbrewery. Unlike a true micropub, this one stocks six real ales and two real ciders on handpump, has background music and allows mobile phones. Four of the ales are usually from Late Knights. The somewhat raw interior remains a work in progress and features light fittings made out of recycled Kilner jars.
(Queens Road)

SE18: Plumstead Common

Old Mill

1 Old Mill Road, SE18 1QG
12-11 (020) 3719 1499
6 changing beers (sourced nationally; often Bexley, Goddards, Hop Stuff)
On the north side of Plumstead Common, this pub was formerly an 18th-century windmill and the Grade II-listed tower still remains. The single L-shaped bar is sparsely furnished, with a pool table to the rear, leaving ample space for the frequent live music acts. Six real ales change frequently, with those from local and regional independent breweries predominating. One changing real cider is usually available. Lunchtime and evening meals are now served (except Wed).
(51,53,291)

SE18: Shooters Hill

Bull

151 Shooters Hill, SE18 3HP
1-11; 12.30-11.30 Fri & Sat; 12-10.30 Sun
(020) 8856 0691
Courage Best Bitter; 5 changing beers (sourced nationally; often Adnams, Purity, Sharp's)
Situated on the brow of a hill, this reputedly haunted Grade II-listed pub was rebuilt in 1881. It retains separate public and saloon bars with their own entrance doors from the street, and a central circular bar counter serving both rooms. The saloon bar is well appointed, whereas the public bar has a more basic appearance. There is a pool table, and occasional live music events are held. The licensee makes good use of the landlord's beer range.
(89,244,486)

SE19: Crystal Palace

Westow House

79 Westow Hill, SE19 1TX
12 (5.30 Mon)-midnight; 12-2am Fri & Sat; 12-11 Sun
(020) 8670 0654 westowhouse.com
Adnams Lighthouse; Dark Star Hophead; 6 changing beers (sourced nationally; often Hobsons, King Beer, Sharp's)
Prominent Victorian street-corner pub, although reduced in height by one storey following WWII bomb damage. Internal decor and furnishings are Antic's shabby chic with, in this case, a 1960s psychedelic feel. Outside at the front is a large seating area. Up to eight real ales include many from microbreweries, and there are ciders on handpump. Live music is hosted, often on Thursday evenings, and a quiz night on Tuesdays.

SE20: Penge

Moon & Stars

164-166 High Street, SE20 7QS
8am-11 (020) 8776 5680
Dark Star Hophead; Greene King Abbot; Kelham Island Pale Rider; Ringwood Fortyniner; Ruddles Best Bitter; changing beers
A popular high-street Wetherspoon pub with a large L-shaped bar, a raised seating area at the rear and many small alcoves suitable for small groups. The bar has 17 handpumps, normally offering some ales from London microbreweries including the nearby Late Knights, in a variety of beer styles. The pub hosts regular mini festivals and other beer-related events. (Kent House)

SE22: East Dulwich

East Dulwich Tavern

1 Lordship Lane, SE22 8EW
12-midnight (1am Fri & Sat) (020) 8693 1316
eastdulwichtavern.com
Adnams Lighthouse; Harveys Sussex Best Bitter; St Austell Tribute; Sharp's Doom Bar; 3 changing beers (sourced locally; often Crate, Gipsy Hill)
Spacious and popular Victorian corner pub sitting proudly at the head of Lordship Lane. Furnished in Antic's eclectic style, the interior includes an impressive tiled floor in the main bar area. Upstairs is a large function room, outside there is pavement seating at the front. In addition to seven real ales, there is usually real cider during summer months. It offers good-quality food and hosts monthly film club and jazz nights.

Flying Pig

58-60 East Dulwich Road, SE22 9AX
12-11 (020) 7732 7575 theflyingpiglondon.com
4 changing beers (sourced nationally)
A beer and barbecue bar in former restaurant premises with a small front bar, a large seating area and an open-to-view kitchen to the rear. There is also some outdoor seating on the front terrace. A large draught range includes four changing real ales on handpump, plus up to two real ciders in polypins. Various small breweries feature, as well as US and European brews.

Great Exhibition

193 Crystal Palace Road, SE22 9EP

12-11 (midnight Fri & Sat) (020) 8693 4968
greatexhibition.pub
House beer (by King Beer); 2 changing beers (sourced nationally)
Victorian pub, formerly known as the Crystal Palace Tavern, just off the main drag in East Dulwich. Although the historic two-bar layout no longer exists, some period features do remain. It is, however, an excellent contemporary pub, popular with the locals and providing plenty of outside space with a garden at the rear and an enclosed patio at the front. There are usually two changing real ales in addition to the house beer, Laine's Best, plus a cider.

SE23: Forest Hill

All Inn One
53 Perry Vale, SE23 2NE
12 (3 Mon)-11.30; 12-1.30am Fri & Sat
(020) 8699 3311 allinnone.org.uk
Brains SA; Caledonian Deuchars IPA; 2 changing beers (sourced nationally; often Gipsy Hill, Tiny Rebel)
Also known as the Foresters, this large red-brick pub is located behind Forest Hill rail station. The bar area is roomy, comfortable and open plan, with a C-shaped bar that extends through into the rear wood-panelled function room. A spacious garden with children's play equipment and smoking area is an oasis in the summer. There is live music twice monthly, plus a weekly quiz night on Wednesdays. The two regularly changing guest beers are often from local breweries.

Blythe Hill Tavern
319 Stanstead Road, SE23 1JB
11-11 (midnight Thu-Sun) (020) 8690 5176
Courage Best Bitter; Dark Star Hophead; Harveys Sussex Best Bitter; 2 changing beers (sourced nationally; often Dark Star, Hogs Back)
A Victorian corner pub with an interesting three-room interior of regional historic importance and 1920s panelling. This is a friendly local, rooted in the community, where the barmen wear traditional collar and tie. TV screens often show sports in two bars. The garden includes a children's play area and is abloom with flowers in summer. Quiz nights are Mondays from September to April, and traditional Irish music features on Thursdays. Local CAMRA Pub of the Year 2015.
(Catford/Catford Bridge)

SE25: South Norwood

Joiners' Arms
52 Woodside Green, SE25 5EU
11-11 (midnight Fri & Sat); 12-11 Sun (020) 8656 8180
Fuller's London Pride; Purity Mad Goose; Sharp's Doom Bar
A traditional local with a single bar comprising three distinct drinking areas: a small snug at one end, a seating space at the other, separated by the bar area. The interior is filled with brassware and other artefacts, giving a rural pub atmosphere. The pub has been run since 1973 by Croydon's now longest-serving landlady. Several screens provide sports coverage, and popular karaoke evenings are regularly held. Roast dinners are served on Sundays. (130,197,312)

Addiscombe

Claret Free House
5 Bingham Corner, Lower Addiscombe Road, CR0 7AA
11.30-11 (11.30 Thu; midnight Fri & Sat); 12-11 Sun
(020) 8656 7452
Palmers Best Bitter; 5 changing beers
Justly popular, this privately owned free house around the corner from the tram stop is now in its 28th year in this Guide. The small bar is decorated in mock-Tudor style. The house beer, Palmers Best Bitter, has sold over one million pints over the years. Five other rapidly changing ales, mainly from microbreweries, come from all over the UK. Beers on and coming next are shown on a unique board facing the bar. Cider is fetched from the cellar. (130,289,367)

Cricketers
47 Shirley Road, CR0 7ER
12-midnight (11 Sun) (020) 8655 3507
Harveys Sussex Best Bitter; Redemption Trinity; Sharp's Doom Bar; 2 changing beers
Popular traditional community pub having a single-room interior with two distinct areas. It has a comfortable lived-in atmosphere, with three real fires. Two changing beers come from the SIBA or Enterprise lists. Food is served all day until 7pm, and regular curry nights and quiz nights are held, along with beer festivals. Cider is normally available. Televised sport is an attraction, especially when local teams are playing.
P (130,289,367)

Bexleyheath

Robin Hood & Little John
78 Lion Road, DA6 8PF
11-3, 5.30 (7 Sat)-11; 12-4, 7-10.30 Sun
(020) 8303 1128 robinhoodbexleyheath.co.uk
Adnams Southwold Bitter, Broadside; Brains The Rev James; Fuller's London Pride; Harveys Sussex Best Bitter; Sharp's Doom Bar; 2 changing beers (sourced locally; often Bexley, Shepherd Neame, Westerham)
Back-street local dating from the 1830s when it was surrounded by fields. Eight real ales are on offer, mostly from independent breweries, including regular guest beers from the new Bexley Brewery. It has a reputation for its home-cooked food at lunchtimes (no food Sun) with Italian specials, which can be eaten at tables made from old Singer sewing machines. A regular CAMRA branch Pub of the Year and the London regional winner three times. Over-21s only. **Q** (B13)

Wrong 'Un
234-236 Broadway, DA6 8AS
8am-midnight (020) 8298 0439
Greene King Abbot; Ruddles Best Bitter; Sharp's Doom Bar; 5 changing beers
Bexleyheath's first Wetherspoon pub, opened in 1994 in a single-storey former furniture store. There are records of cricket being played locally since 1746, and the unusual pub name is an alternative expression for a googly. Westons Old Rosie cider is available. There are comfortable booths to sit in as well as an open-plan area. Alcohol is served from 9am, and food until 11pm daily. **Q**

Blackfen

George Staples
273 Blackfen Road, DA15 8PR
☼ 12-11 (midnight Thu-Sat) ☎ (020) 8850 3181
Shepherd Neame Whitstable Bay; 3 changing beers (sourced nationally; often Adnams) Ⓗ
Originally the Woodman, the pub was built in 1845 and was one of the first buildings in Blackfen. It was later demolished and rebuilt in 1931 when large-scale construction began in the area. Recently refurbished and renamed after the original landlord, it is now a comfortable and pleasant venue. Mirrors along one wall give the perception of a much larger space.
ᵹ❀◐♿P🚌(51,132)🛜

Bromley

Partridge
194 High Street, BR1 1HE
☼ 12-11.30 (12.30am Fri & Sat); 12-11 Sun
☎ (020) 8464 7656
Fuller's London Pride, ESB; Gales Seafarers Ale, HSB; 2 changing beers (sourced nationally; often Adnams, Butcombe, Fuller's) Ⓗ
A former NatWest bank, now a Fuller's Ale and Pie House, the building has retained many of its original features including the high ceilings and chandeliers. There are two small snug rooms in addition to the main bar. An extensive food menu includes vegetarian choices. The pub is popular with shoppers, those who like live music on a Saturday night, and sports fans who want to watch football and rugby. ᵹ❀◐♿⇌(North/South)🚌🐾

Red Lion
10 North Road, BR1 3LG
☼ 11-11; 12-11 Sun ☎ (020) 8460 2691
Greene King IPA, Abbot; Harveys Sussex Best Bitter; 2 changing beers (sourced nationally; often Black Sheep, Jennings, Oakham) Ⓗ
This little gem in the quiet back streets north of Bromley town centre has been a regular entry in this Guide for many years and is well worth seeking out. The pub retains many of its original features, including tiling, and has an extensive library of books dominating one wall.
Q❀◐⇌(North)♣🚌

Shortlands Tavern
5 Station Road, BR2 0EY
☼ 12-11.30 (midnight Fri & Sat); 12-11 Sun
☎ (020) 8466 0202 🌐 theshortlandstavern.com
4 changing beers Ⓗ
A fine, spacious pub at the heart of the local community and convenient for the station. It has several separate drinking areas including a snug and an upstairs room, plus a large garden. The management is committed to serving a wide variety of ales, with microbreweries normally well represented on the four handpumps. Regular events throughout the week include a book club, knitting circle and live music nights.
Q❀◐⇌(Shortlands)♣🚌(227,358,367)

Chelsfield

Five Bells
Church Road, BR6 7RE
☼ 11.30-11; 12-10.30 Sun ☎ (01689) 821044
🌐 thefivebells-chelsfieldvillage.co.uk
Courage Best Bitter; 3 changing beers (sourced nationally; often Butcombe, Pig & Porter, Tonbridge) Ⓗ
In the village centre, this popular and welcoming village pub still has a public bar. Around the corner, a separate entrance gives access to the saloon and dining area. A regular Guide entry for many years, with seven handpumps and also a cask on the bar, it holds beer festivals at Easter and in October. There is a small drinking area on the forecourt and a large garden. ᵹ❀◐♣P🚌(R3)🐾🛜

Chislehurst

Imperial Arms
1 Old Hill, BR7 5LZ
☼ 12-11 (11.30 Thu; midnight Fri & Sat; 10.30 Sun)
☎ (020) 3605 7899 🌐 imperialarms.co.uk
Harveys Sussex Best Bitter; Marston's Pedigree; Sharp's Doom Bar Ⓗ
This stylish and comfortable pub has now completed the final phase of its rejuvenation with the opening of a wine bar and function room in the rear courtyard. All the bars feature beamed ceilings and the Library Bar has wood panelling and a fireplace. There is live music at weekends and regular quiz nights. The Catherine Bar is named after the mistress of Napoleon III who stayed here when he was exiled to Chislehurst in 1870.
Qᵹ❀◐⇌🚌(162,269)🐾🛜

Crayford

Crayford Arms Ⓛ
37 Crayford High Street, DA1 4HH
☼ 12-11.30; 12-midnight Fri & Sat ☎ (01322) 555214
🌐 thecrayfordarms.com
Shepherd Neame Master Brew; 2 changing beers (sourced nationally; often St Austell, Shepherd Neame) Ⓗ
Two distinctive and separate drinking areas with comfortable seating greet you here, along with wood-panelled walls and an amazing chandelier consisting of brown beer bottles. Since the change of management in late 2013, the pub seems to have got its mojo back. It is buzzy, with live music on Saturdays, karaoke on Wednesdays, folk music once a month on a Thursday and an occasional musical (or otherwise) ad hoc outburst from the customers at other times. Quiz nights are on Sundays. Thatchers Heritage Cider is served.
ᵹ❀◐⇌♣🍎P🚌(96,428,492)🐾🛜

Croydon

Builders Arms
65 Leslie Park Road, CR0 6TP
☼ 12-11 (midnight Fri & Sat) ☎ (020) 8654 1803
Fuller's London Pride, ESB; 1 changing beer (sourced locally) Ⓗ
A back-street community local opened in the 19th century. The two bars each have their own character: the smaller public-style bar with large-screen TV sport and dartboard, and the larger saloon bar with comfortable seating and leading to a pleasant garden, with outdoor games available during the warmer months. Events include darts on Monday, quizzes on Tuesday and cribbage on Thursday. There is also a monthly blue-grass music night. The pub holds Fuller's Master Cellarman accreditation.
ᵹ❀◐♿⇌(East)🚊(Lebanon Rd)♣🚌🐾🛜

Dog & Bull
24 Surrey Street, CR0 1RG
11-11 (11.30 Fri & Sat); 12-10.30 Sun (020) 8667 9718
Young's Bitter, Special; 2 changing beers (sourced nationally)
Situated in the town's daily street market and recognised as Croydon's oldest pub, the building originated in the 16th century and was rebuilt in the 18th. The interior features a main room with an island bar, and there are two distinct adjoining rooms. The changing beers are often from local breweries. There is a pleasant walled garden where barbecues are held in the summer. An upstairs function room can be hired.
(East/West)(George St/Reeves Corner)

George
17-21 George Street, CR0 1LA
8am-midnight (1am Fri & Sat; midnight Sun)
(020) 8649 9077
Dark Star Hophead; Fuller's London Pride; Oakham JHB; Ruddles Best Bitter; Sharp's Doom Bar; Thornbridge Jaipur IPA; 9 changing beers (sourced nationally; often Surrey Hills, Tillingbourne)
Town-centre Wetherspoon pub with two bars and drinking areas. A changing range of guest beers both local and from further afield make this a destination for beer enthusiasts as well as shoppers and diners. The pub is named after an old coaching inn, demolished when Croydon was redeveloped. Dark Star beers are usually on the back bar, which does close early at the start of the week; customers may be asked to move to the front bar.
(East/West)(George St)

Green Dragon
58 High Street, CR0 1NA
10am-midnight (1am Fri & Sat); 12-10.30 Sun
(020) 8667 0684 thegreendragoncroydon.co.uk
Changing beers
Street-corner pub in former bank premises close to the upper end of Croydon's street market. Popular with all ages, it is quiet and friendly during the day but more lively in the evenings and at weekends. Music and other events take place upstairs. Six handpumps and two gravity casks dispense a changing range of beers. A collection of pumpclips on the upper walls is evidence of the huge range of beers dispensed in the past. Good-value pub food is on offer daily.
(East/West)(George St)

Oval Tavern
131 Oval Road, CR0 6BR
12-11 (midnight Fri & Sat); 12-10.30 Sun
(020) 8686 6023 theovalcroydon.co.uk
St Austell Tribute; 4 changing beers (sourced nationally; often Cronx, Robinsons, Timothy Taylor)
A popular back-street family pub with a good reputation for live music. Tasty home-made food is always available; the huge Scotch eggs and sausage rolls are especially recommended. Children and dogs are welcome and there is a large garden and barbecue area to the rear. The decor is unusual; the half-timbering creates an interesting interior with a rural atmosphere. Under new management since August 2013, the pub continues to improve and boost promotion of cask ale. (East)

Skylark
34-36 South End, CR0 1DP
8am-midnight (1am Fri & Sat) (020) 8649 9909
Dark Star Hophead; Fuller's London Pride; Greene King Abbot; Ruddles Best Bitter; Sharp's Doom Bar; Shepherd Neame Spitfire; 5 changing beers
Spacious Wetherspoon cinema conversion in the restaurant quarter to the south of the town centre. Wood-panelled walls and bookshelves in a raised seating area, together with an absence of TV screens, help to give a relaxed atmosphere. The internal decoration focuses in part on the history of London's first airport, in Croydon. There is always a good choice of ales, frequently local or from microbreweries. The upper floor can be reserved for groups or events. (South)

Spreadeagle
39-41 Katharine Street, CR0 1NX
11-11 (midnight Fri & Sat); 12-10.30 Sun
(020) 8781 1134
Fuller's London Pride, ESB; Gales HSB; 3 changing beers
Large street-corner pub in former bank premises next door to the old town hall. The impressive interior has lots of glass, mirrors and wood panelling. There are two upstairs function areas which are regularly used for film and theatrical performances. As well as beer from six handpumps, a range of Fuller's bottled beers and quality foreign bottled beers is on offer. The pub has Fuller's Master Cellarman accreditation. Quiz night is Sunday. (East)(George St)

Downe

Queen's Head
25 High Street, BR6 7US
12-11 (11.30 Fri & Sat); 12-10.30 Sun (01689) 852145
queensheaddowne.com
Harveys Sussex Best Bitter; Sharp's Doom Bar; 2 changing beers (sourced locally; often Cronx, Late Knights, Westerham)
A family-run classic village pub and former coaching stop dating back to 1565. The bar and dining rooms are full of old-world charm, with open fires and cosy sofas. The guest beers are mostly from local microbreweries and the menu uses many locally sourced ingredients. With an active darts team, the pub also hosts the local cricket club and golf society, and is popular with walkers and visitors to Charles Darwin's Down House. (146,R8)

Farnborough

Woodman
50 High Street, BR6 7BA
12-11 (10.30 Sun) (01689) 852663 thewoody.co.uk
Shepherd Neame Master Brew, Kent's Best, Spitfire; 1 changing beer (often Shepherd Neame)
A friendly village pub, popular with locals and handy for walkers using the nearby High Elms trail. The landlord is a real ale enthusiast and his beers include seasonal ales and a monthly non-Sheps guest. The Woody, as it is unofficially known, hosts a weekly quiz and various charity events. The pub has a large garden and is dog-friendly, with dog treats on offer. P(358,402)

Keston

Greyhound
Commonside, BR2 6BP

🕐 11-11; 12-10.30 Sun ☎ (01689) 856338
🌐 greyhoundkeston.co.uk
Adnams Southwold Bitter; Timothy Taylor Landlord; 2 changing beers [H]
A busy pub with a rural feel – it is located on the edge of Keston Common – but easily reached from Central Bromley. Various walking routes pass nearby. The pub is at the heart of Keston village life with a crowded calendar of local events. There is an extensive garden and two real fires in winter. The landlord is a real ale enthusiast who holds an annual beer festival in early April.
❀◑♣●P🚌(146,246)🐾

Orpington

Orpington Liberal Club [L]
7 Station Road, BR6 0RZ
🕐 8 (6 Fri)-11; 12-3, 7-11 Sat; 12-3, 8-10.30 Sun
☎ (01689) 820882 🌐 orpingtonliberalclub.co.uk
4 changing beers [H]
A free-of-tie club that has served over 200 different real ales a year, particularly focusing on microbreweries. Real cider and perry are always on the bar. It holds beer festivals twice a year and Meet the Brewer events, with regular live folk or blues music nights in a separate room. Winner of many local and regional CAMRA awards, the club was a CAMRA National Club of the Year finalist in 2014. A CAMRA or National Union of Liberal Clubs membership card is required for entry.
Q🐴❀⇌♣●P▯🚌🐾📶

Petts Wood

One Inn The Wood 🏆 [L]
209 Petts Wood Road, BR5 1LA
🕐 closed Mon; 12-2.30, 5-9.30 (11 Fri); 11.30-11 Sat; 12-3 Sun ☎ 07799 535982 🌐 oneinnthewood.co.uk
5 changing beers (sourced regionally; often Kent, Old Dairy, Tonbridge) [G]
A former wine bar that opened as the first micropub in the Bromley area in May 2014, with its wooden floor, bench seating and large woodland scene on one wall all adding to the country feel. A changing range of Kentish beers is served on gravity from a cold room with a glass fronted door; you can watch your pint being poured. Snacks include locally sourced cheeses, sausage rolls and crisps. Local CAMRA branch Pub of the Year in 2015.
Q🐴◑⇌●🚌🐾

Sovereign of the Seas [L]
109-111 Queensway, BR5 1DG
🕐 9am-11 (11.30 Fri & Sat) ☎ (01689) 891606
Greene King Abbot; Ruddles Best Bitter; Sharp's Doom Bar; 7 changing beers [H]
A large, popular Wetherspoon pub, centrally located in Petts Wood, which boasts 12 handpumps offering the regular ales alongside a changing range of guests and cider. A choice of seating includes alcoves to add a cosy feel. Local photos of historic interest adorn the walls, including one of the ship after which the pub is named. Another panel refers to the daylight saving time campaigner William Willett, a former local resident. There is an active community noticeboard.
🐴❀◑♿⇌●🚌📶

Sidcup

Tailor's Chalk
47-49 High Street, DA14 6ED
🕐 8am-11 ☎ (020) 8308 6880
Courage Best Bitter; Greene King IPA, Abbot; 2 changing beers [H]
In the middle of Sidcup's shopping parade, this more than usually compact Wetherspoon pub has lots of nooks and crannies. The large internal support pillars can make it seem fuller than it really is. Constantly changing guest ales often include some from local breweries. The news is always on the TV screen by the main door. ◑♿🚌📶

Welling

Door Hinge
11 Welling High Street, DA16 1TR
🕐 closed Mon; 3-9 (10 Fri); 12-10 Sat; 12-3 Sun ☎ 07956 845509 🌐 thedoorhinge.co.uk
3 changing beers [G]
London's first permanent micropub opened in March 2013 in part of a former electrical wholesalers, and is a welcome breath of fresh air on the local pub scene. At least three beers are usually available, dispensed from within a glass-fronted cold room. The cider comes from various sources. The cosy bar encourages conversation among strangers. It was 2014 local CAMRA branch and London Regional Pub of the Year winner. A handy stop-off for the nearby football ground.
Q●▯🚌🐾

New Cross Turnpike [L]
55 Bellegrove Road, DA16 3PB
🕐 8am-midnight (1am Fri) ☎ (020) 8304 1600
Greene King Abbot; Ruddles Best Bitter; Shepherd Neame Spitfire; 8 changing beers [H]
The New Cross turnpike here was one of many private toll roads. This attractive Wetherspoon pub on four levels, including a gallery and two patios, opened in 1998; it was previously a NatWest bank. Disabled access includes two wheelchair lifts and a ground-floor toilet. Up to eight guest ales are served and the management aims to ensure there are always some local beers among them. Alcohol is served from 9am, no admission after 11pm.
Q🐴❀◑♿⇌🚌📶

SOUTH-WEST LONDON

SW1: Belgravia

Antelope
22-24 Eaton Terrace, SW1W 8EZ
🕐 12-11 (11.30 Fri & Sat); 12-10 Sun ☎ (020) 7824 8512
Fuller's London Pride, Bengal Lancer, ESB; Gales Seafarers Ale [H]
Dating back to 1827, this pub is now operated by Fuller's after many years as a Nicholson's pub. Preserved original features include etched glass windows, a side room used as a snug, and the central bar. This is an upmarket house and the clientele consists mainly of local professionals. The pub plays cricket matches against the Churchill Arms in Notting Hill. The upstairs bar and side room can be hired for functions. Q🐴◑⊖(Sloane Sq)🚌

Star Tavern [L]
6 Belgrave Mews West, SW1X 8HT
🕐 11 (12 Sat)-11; 12-10.30 Sun ☎ (020) 7235 3019

Fuller's London Pride, ESB; Gales Seafarers Ale; 2 changing beers (often Fuller's) 🄷
Situated in a mews and near embassies, the Star is rich in the history of the powerful, famous and infamous; it is rumoured that the Great Train Robbery was planned here. Now a popular Fuller's pub, local residents, business people and embassy staff rub shoulders with casual visitors. Sometimes a special Fuller's beer can be found. The dining room is upstairs, also bookable for functions. This pub has featured in every edition of the Guide.
Q⊖(Hyde Park Corner/Knightsbridge)

SW1: Pimlico

Cask Pub & Kitchen

6 Charlwood Street, SW1V 2EE
12-11 (10.30 Sun) ☎ (020) 7630 7225
caskpubandkitchen.com
Dark Star Hophead; 9 changing beers 🄷
Formerly the Pimlico Tram, it was converted to a beer destination pub by owners who have since acquired and converted several more premises in the South-East. Ten handpumps serve real ales from many microbreweries such as Arbor Ales and Dark Star, and a vast range of bottled beers from the UK and around the world complements some unusual keg choices. Burgers feature on the weekday menu, with Sunday roasts until late afternoon. A top three CAMRA branch Pub of the Year 2013-2015. Q(Victoria)⊖

Jugged Hare

172 Vauxhall Bridge Road, SW1V 1DX
11-11; 12-10.30 Sun ☎ (020) 7828 1543
Fuller's London Pride, ESB; Gales Seafarers Ale; 1 changing beer (often Fuller's) 🄷
Formerly a NatWest bank, it was converted in 1996 to a Fuller's Ale & Pie House with the hallmark mahogany decor and chandeliers. The pub is supported by a loyal band of regulars, plus office workers and tourists enjoying the all-day food, including jugged hare pie. Both the back room and the balcony can be booked for functions.
(Victoria)⊖(Pimlico/Victoria)

SW1: St James's

Red Lion ★

2 Duke of York Street, SW1Y 6JP
11.30-11; closed Sun ☎ (020) 7321 0782
Fuller's Chiswick Bitter, London Pride, ESB; Gales Seafarers Ale; 1 changing beer (often Fuller's) 🄷
Close to the upmarket shops in Jermyn Street, this is a deservedly celebrated little gem. The Grade II-listed building dates from 1821 and was given a new frontage in 1871. It has a tiny but nationally important historic pub interior, with spectacular Victorian etched mirrors and glass. Visitors often spill out onto the pavement outside. Mind the precipitous steps down to the toilets. Food is served 12-3pm (4pm Sat).
⊖(Green Park/Piccadilly Circus)

SW1: Victoria

Cask & Glass

39 Palace Street, SW1E 5HN
11-11; 12-8 Sat; closed Sun ☎ (020) 7834 7630
Shepherd Neame Master Brew, Spitfire; 1 changing beer (often Shepherd Neame) 🄷
First licensed in 1862 as the Duke of Cambridge, this small, attractive one-room pub on the route between Buckingham Palace and Westminster Cathedral, adorned with flowers in summer, is a haven for tourists, office workers and local residents. The wood-panelled bar has pictures of local scenes and politicians. Look out for the bull's-eye windows and the two paintings of the pub on the way to the toilets. A cosy place for a pint after (or instead of) visiting the sights.
Q⊖(St James's Park/Victoria)

Wetherspoon's

Unit 5, Upper Concourse, Victoria Station, Terminus Place, SW1V 1JT
7-11 (midnight Fri & Sat) ☎ (020) 7931 0445
Fuller's London Pride, ESB; Greene King IPA, Abbot; 8 changing beers 🄷
Overlooking the station concourse and accessed mainly by escalators, this pub has recently been refurbished in a bright café-bar design. The interior features blue and cream tiling, two curved bars with marble-style tops and the welcome addition of banquettes along the opposite side. Two sets of six handpumps dispense four regular beers and eight changing guest ales. TV screens show times of train departures. Note that British Transport Police sometimes close the bar when football fans are due. Q⊖

SW1: Westminster

Buckingham Arms

62 Petty France, SW1H 9EU
11-11 (6 Sat) ☎ (020) 7222 3386
Wells Bombardier; Young's Bitter, Special; 1 changing beer (often Young's) 🄷
Said to have once been a hat shop, this pub opened in the 1720s as the Bell, was renamed the Black Horse in the 1740s, rebuilt in 1898 and renamed again in 1901. Substantially renovated in recent years, it has appeared in every edition of this Guide. With modern and traditional seats and tables, high and low, it draws civil servants, visitors and the occasional MP from the Houses of Parliament. ⊖(St James's Park)

Speaker

46 Great Peter Street, SW1P 2HA
12-11; closed Sat & Sun ☎ (020) 7222 1749
Timothy Taylor Landlord; Young's London Gold; 3 changing beers 🄷
This comfortable wood-panelled one-bar local dates from at least 1729 when it was the Castle, renamed Elephant & Castle around 1800, and the Speaker in 1999. This area was once known as the Devil's Acre, a notorious slum and next to the world's first public gas works. The pub, decorated with parliamentary caricatures, welcomes residents from local estates and workers from government offices and Channel 4, who enjoy the range of five beers and home-made food. There is no music or TV, and children are not allowed. Occasional beer festivals take place.
Q⊖(St James's Park)

SW2: Streatham Hill

Crown & Sceptre

2A Streatham Hill, SW2 4AH
9am-midnight (1am Fri & Sat) ☎ (020) 8671 0843

Greene King Abbot; Ruddles Best Bitter; Sharp's Doom Bar; changing beers (often Sambrook's)
A landmark building where the South Circular crosses the A23, this pub was the first Wetherspoon conversion in south-west London. A long-serving young manager and his team provide quick and efficient service, selling more cask beer than lager and offering a wide range of ale strengths and styles. Westons ciders are also on draught. Outside is the original Truman's façade and tiling; inside, the walls are decorated with unusual framed floral artwork.
Q P

SW4: Clapham

Craft Beer Co
128 Clapham Manor Street, SW4 6ED
4.30-11 (midnight Fri); 12-midnight Sat; 12-11 Sun
(020) 7622 2894
House beer (by Kent); changing beers
Formerly the Manor Arms, this is now the fifth Craft Beer Co pub. Ten handpumps serve the house ale alongside nine changing guest beers of different kinds from other microbreweries. Beer is priced according to its strength. A central square bar has high tables and stools at the front, with padded settles, tables and chairs to the sides and rear. The large garden is popular in good weather and for beer festivals.
(Common/High St/North)

Rose & Crown
2 The Polygon, SW4 0JG
3-11 (1am Fri); 12-1am Sat; 12-midnight Sun
(020) 7720 8265
Greene King IPA, St Edmunds, Abbot; 4 changing beers (often Dark Star, Greene King, Purity)
A friendly drinkers' pub that is going from strength to strength, the Greene King beers complemented by guests, often including Dark Star Hophead. The pub lies at the heart of Clapham's picturesque Old Town and is notable for its fine tiled Simonds façade. At less busy times you may get to meet Beyonce and Betty, the resident cats. Outside seating is available at the front in the newly refurbished pavement area.
(Common/High St)

SW5: Earl's Court

King's Head
17 Hogarth Place, SW5 0QT
11-11 (10.30 Sun) (020) 7373 5239
4 changing beers (often Portobello, Westerham)
Rebuilt in 1937, this pub is the oldest surviving licensed premises in this area, dating back to the 17th century. It is now a friendly corner pub off the busy Earl's Court Road, laid out in a modern style with a wooden floor and coloured tiling around the bar, comfortable sofa seating and high stools around tall tables. Quiz night is Monday and there is occasional live music on special days.
(West Brompton)

SW6: Fulham

Durell Arms
704 Fulham Road, SW6 5SB
12-11 (1am Fri & Sat) (020) 7736 3014
durellarmsfulham.com
4 changing beers (often Greene King)
A welcome new addition to the Guide, this spacious corner pub has an L-shaped drinking area. The large room to the rear, with mouldings and mirrors giving an air of Victorian decadence, and a big screen for sporting events, can be hired for functions. The pub serves a number of local ales such as Portobello and Truman's, and is popular on Sundays for an excellent roast.
(Parsons Green)

SW6: Parsons Green

White Horse
1-3 Parsons Green, SW6 4UL
9.30am-11.30 (midnight Thu-Sat) (020) 7736 2115
whitehorsesw6.com
Adnams Broadside; Oakham JHB; 4 changing beers (often Harveys)
A destination M&B (now Castle) pub which normally boasts five guest beers and a selection of international bottled beers. Regular beer and food matching events take place as well as four annual beer festivals, including the not-to-be-missed Old Ale Festival in late November, when the Coach House, usually reserved for dining, has a stillage. The pub can get busy when Chelsea FC are playing at home, but the upstairs area is a good place to escape the crowds. Q (22.424)

SW7: Gloucester Road

Queen's Arms
30 Queens Gate Mews, SW7 5QL
12-11 (10.30 Sun) (020) 7823 9293
thequeensarmskensington.co.uk
Fuller's London Pride; Sharp's Doom Bar; 6 changing beers
This lovely corner mews pub is well worth seeking out for its real ales and the large range of interesting bottled beers, malt whiskies and other spirits. Note the unusual curved doors. The L-shaped room features wood floors and panelling. The clientele reflects the location – well-heeled locals, students from Imperial College and musicians from, and visitors to, the nearby Albert Hall. The food menu and specials are of superior quality. Q

SW7: South Kensington

Anglesea Arms
15 Selwood Terrace, SW7 3QG
11-11; 12-10.30 Sun (020) 7373 7960
angleseaarms.com
Adnams Broadside; Greene King IPA; 4 changing beers (often Timothy Taylor)
A welcome return to the Guide for this real ale stalwart of CAMRA's early years, built in 1827 and now Grade II-listed. With hanging baskets and a terrace, it has the air of a country pub. The bar features a large Salt & Co brewery mirror and various paintings, prints, photographs and cartoons. Charles Dickens and Andrew Bonar Law were locals. Q

SW8: South Lambeth

Canton Arms
177 South Lambeth Road, SW8 1XP
11 (5 Mon)-11.30; 11-10.30 Sun (020) 7582 8710
cantonarms.com

Skinner's Betty Stogs Ⓖ; Timothy Taylor Golden Best; 2 changing beers Ⓗ
Styled as an ale and food house, this street-corner gastro-pub is highly regarded for its changing menu, but it retains a traditional drinking area at the front. The pub has bare wooden floorboards and is simply furnished throughout. The bar displays blackboards listing available real ales, wines and snacks, while the walls are adorned with mirrors and pumpclips. Attractive mullioned windows overlook a front terrace and the busy South Lambeth Road. Guest beers are often from Belleville or Red Squirrel. ❀◐⊖(Stockwell)🚌📶

SW9: Brixton

Trinity Arms
45 Trinity Gardens, SW9 8DR
⏲ 11-11 (midnight Fri); 12-midnight Sat; 12-11 Sun
☎ (020) 7274 4544
Young's Bitter, London Gold, Special; 1 changing beer (often Young's) Ⓗ
A friendly, traditional and comfortable pub tucked away in a quiet square off the busy Acre Lane and Brixton High Road, named after an ancient asylum nearby. Drinking areas are around three sides of a horseshoe-shaped bar and front patio. The garden at the rear features a wishing well and a covered smoking area. It is popular in the evening and busy on Brixton Academy nights. Real ale is a big attraction. Families are welcome until 7.30pm and food is served until 10pm. Q🐴❀◐⇌⊖♣🚌📶

SW10: Chelsea

Sporting Page Ⓛ
6 Camera Place, SW10 0BH
⏲ 11-11; 11-10.30 Sun ☎ (020) 7349 0455
6 changing beers (often Sharp's, Truman's) Ⓗ
Rebuilt in 1974 as the Red Anchor on the site of the Odell Arms (1856-1971) and renamed in 1989, the pub is now part of the small Food & Fuel London chain. It is a comfortable one-bar gastro-pub with a friendly feel. Six handpumps deliver real ales, often including locals such as Moncada. An interesting wine selection complements the food offering. Sporting-themed prints and memorabilia adorn the walls. Quiz night is Sunday. Q◐🍎🚌🐾

SW11: Clapham Junction

Beehive
197 St John's Hill, SW11 1TH
⏲ 12-midnight (1am Fri & Sat) ☎ (020) 7450 1756
🌐 beehiveclapham.com
Fuller's London Pride, ESB; Gales Seafarers Ale; 3 changing beers (often Fuller's) Ⓗ
Tasteful and elegant refurbishment and new management have revitalised this classic local. Some bench seating has been restored and a big screen shows major sporting events. The rear area is also now available for functions, and the food menu, although limited, is excellent. Blankets are thoughtfully supplied for guests who wish to sit outside. Look out for the wonderful framed housing survey map of south-west London dating from 1898 – before the Luftwaffe and 1970s town planners altered things somewhat.
🐴◐⇌⊖🚌🐾📶

Eagle Ale House 🏆 Ⓛ
104 Chatham Road, SW11 6HG
⏲ 4-11 Mon-Thu; 3-11 Fri; 12-11 Sat; 12-10.30 Sun
☎ (020) 7228 2328 🌐 eaglealehouse.co.uk
Surrey Hills Shere Drop; changing beers (sourced nationally; often Downton, Hackney, Pilgrim) Ⓗ
Situated a short uphill walk from Northcote Road, this traditional pub has a homely interior, local regulars and a friendly welcome for visitors and dogs. A place for lively conversation, it has been at the centre of the Fair Deal for Your Local campaign in recent years. Major sporting events are shown on three TV screens and there is a heated marquee in the garden. Local CAMRA Pub of the Year for 2012 and 2014. 🐴❀🚌(319,G1)🐾📶

Falcon ★ Ⓛ
2 St John's Hill, SW11 1RU
⏲ 10-11.30 (midnight Thu-Sat); 10-11 Sun
☎ (020) 7228 2076
Changing beers (often Sambrook's, Truman's) Ⓗ
This landmark building dating from 1887 has recently been fully refurbished, preserving a nationally important historic pub interior noteworthy for its island servery, screens, glasswork and the longest bar in the country. The wide range of ales from the Nicholson's list often includes dark beers and choices from London microbreweries. Thatchers or Westons ciders are also served on handpump. At the corner closest to Clapham Junction, it is nearly always busy, and the rear seating area is usually reserved for dining.
🐴◐⇌⊖🍎🚌🐾📶

Junction
36 St John's Hill, SW11 1SA
⏲ 11-11 (midnight Fri); 10-midnight Sat; 11-10.30 Sun
☎ (020) 7228 1708
Greene King IPA; Jennings Cumberland Ale; Westerham Taylor Walker 1730; 2 changing beers (sourced nationally; often Fuller's, Sambrook's, Thwaites) Ⓗ
Conveniently sited between the upper and lower entrances to Clapham Junction, the former Windsor Castle with its mock-Tudor exterior has been opened up with ample seating inside, leading to the rear patio (Platform 18). The walls are adorned with old photos of the railway. In taking over this Taylor Walker-branded pub from Spirit Group, Greene King is maintaining an attractive range of national and local beers to complement the appetising food menu. 🐴❀◐⇌⊖🚌📶

Powder Keg Diplomacy
147 St John's Hill, SW11 1TQ
⏲ 4-11; 10-midnight Sat; 10-10.30 Sun ☎ (020) 7450 6457
🌐 powderkegdiplomacy.co.uk
3 changing beers (sourced nationally; often Belleville, Five Points, Siren) Ⓗ
An immensely popular gastro-pub kitted out in colonial style. Three handpumps dispense real ale from innovative microbreweries, often from London, and Meet the Brewer events are held from time to time. About 50 bottled beers are stocked from around the world. The high-class but reasonably priced restaurant meals include a Sunday brunch. An exemplar for the future of the British pub. 🐴❀◐⇌⊖🚌🐾

SW12: Balham

Nightingale Ⓛ
97 Nightingale Lane, SW12 8NX
⏲ 12-midnight; 11-11 Sun ☎ (020) 8673 1637
🌐 thenightingalebalham.co.uk

Sambrook's Wandle Ale; Young's Bitter, Special; 1 changing beer (sourced locally) [H]
Tucked away among the grand houses of Nightingale Lane, this popular local has been sensitively refurbished recently and maintains high sales of draught beer, ensuring a good variety including seasonal offerings. It has a proud record of community fundraising including an annual charity walk to help raise money for Guide Dogs. Attentive and long-serving bar staff pride themselves on serving a quality pint. Local CAMRA Pub of the Year runner-up in 2014.
Q🐎❀◐♿⇌(Wandsworth Common)⊖(Clapham South)🚌(G1)🐾📶

SW15: Putney

Bricklayer's Arms
32 Waterman Street, SW15 1DD
⏲ 12-11; 12-10.30 Sun ☎ (020) 8789 0222
🌐 bricklayers-arms.co.uk
Changing beers (often Dark Star, Downton, West Berkshire) [H]
The oldest pub in Putney, dating from 1826, the Bricklayer's Arms is a rolling mini beer festival, with up to nine changing beers, often with several from the same brewery. It is a family-run community local. Shove-ha'penny and bar skittles are played and the pub runs a cricket team. Fulham FC supporters tend to reduce the beer range after home matches. Opening hours vary in the winter.
🐎❀⇌⊖(Putney Bridge)♣🚌🐾📶

SW16: Streatham

Railway [L]
2 Greyhound Lane, SW16 5SD
⏲ 12-11 (midnight Thu; 1am Fri & Sat) ☎ (020) 8769 9448
🌐 therailwaysw16.co.uk
5 changing beers (sourced locally; often Belleville, Sambrook's, Twickenham) [H]
Community pub with five handpumps serving London-brewed ales such as Redemption, complemented by a large selection of bottled local beers. The front bar has a high ceiling, large windows, low-level lighting and a wine-bar atmosphere. The rear bar hosts a comedy show on the last Sunday of the month and can otherwise be hired, and there are twice-monthly Saturday farmers' markets, quiz night Tuesdays, food nights and regular craft workshops. TV-free, dogs are welcome and children admitted until 7pm.
🐎❀◐♿⇌(Common)🚌(60,118)🐾📶

SW17: Tooting

Antelope
76 Mitcham Road, SW17 9NG
⏲ 4-11 (1am Fri); 12-1am Sat; 12-11 Sun
☎ (020) 8672 3888 🌐 theantelopepub.com
Adnams Lighthouse; 4 changing beers [H]
A large Victorian pub serving a frequently changing variety of ales and food all day, with Sunday roasts especially recommended. Wood panelling, candles and a real fire give a cosy feel to this friendly, welcoming pub, rescued from oblivion, refurbished and revived by Antic. It hosts a weekly quiz, occasional comedy nights and other special events. At the back is a huge separate room and there is also seating outside. You may find an unusual real cider here. 🐎❀◐♿⇌⊖(Broadway)🍎🚌🐾📶

King's Head ★
84 Upper Tooting Road, SW17 7PB
⏲ 12-midnight; 12-11 Sun ☎ (020) 8767 6708
Fuller's London Pride; 3 changing beers [H]
This local landmark has a nationally important historic pub interior dating from 1896 featuring wonderful cut and etched glass screens as well as tiling in the side passages. Real ale has made something of a comeback here, with three guest beers that may include one from the local By the Horns or Belleville breweries. In warmer months patrons may enjoy sitting on the front or rear patio.
🐎❀◐♿⊖(Bec/Broadway)P🚌🐾📶

SW18: Wandsworth

Cat's Back
86-88 Point Pleasant, SW18 1NN
⏲ 12-midnight (10.30 Sun & Mon) ☎ (020) 8617 3448
🌐 thecatsback.com
Harveys Sussex Best Bitter; 3 changing beers (sourced regionally) [H]
Harvey's long-awaited second London pub is an elegant, restrained refurbishment of a wonderful back-street local and a welcome survival from the mass development of luxury riverside apartments that now surround it. The pub offers live music (folk, jazz, classical) every Thursday, and a film show in the upstairs room each Wednesday at 8pm. If the pub and beer were not enough, the food here is excellent, with Sunday lunch cited by a major London paper as one of the 10 best in the capital. 🐎❀◐♿♣🚌(220,270,485)🐾📶

Grapes
39 Fairfield Street, SW18 1DX
⏲ 12-11 (midnight Fri & Sat) ☎ (020) 8874 3414
Young's Bitter, Special [H]
A gem of a street-corner local providing a haven of calm from the traffic on the manic Wandsworth one-way system. Always friendly and welcoming, the well-decorated bar offers unobtrusive TV sport and outside there is a heated patio for smokers and a suntrap secret garden for everyone. The pub serves excellent beer as well as good-value lunches during the week. A seasonal ale is occasionally on the bar.
🐎❀⇌(Wandsworth Town)🚌

Old Sergeant [L]
104 Garratt Lane, SW18 4DJ
⏲ 12-11 (midnight Fri & Sat) ☎ (020) 8874 4099
Sambrook's Wandle Ale; Young's Bitter, Special; 2 changing beers (sourced nationally) [H]
Selected as Best Community Pub of 2012, this friendly and impressively refurbished local has also been voted the best place to bring your dog for a drink. Table menus for the excellent food include an informative beer list. The John Young Room upstairs displays treasured memorabilia of the late chairman and the Wandsworth Brewery. Quiz night is Monday. Local CAMRA Pub of the Year runner-up for 2013. ❀◐♿🚌(44,270)🐾

SW19: South Wimbledon

Sultan
78 Norman Road, SW19 1BT
⏲ 12-11; 12-midnight Fri & Sat ☎ (020) 8544 9323
Hop Back GFB, Summer Lightning; 3 changing beers (often Downton, Hop Back) [H]

Traditional, well-run and sometimes lively corner local that welcomes those seeking Hop Back beers in its only tied house in London. The smaller bar, usually open in the evenings, has a dartboard, and a conservatory has recently been added along with a microbrewery intended for monthly specials. A beer club with reduced prices operates Monday 8-10pm and Wednesday 6-9pm. Other beers from the Hop Back range are available as well as seasonals and beers from Downton Brewery. ❀♿⇌(Haydons Rd)⊖(Colliers Wood/South Wimbledon)♣🚌 wifi

---

Trafalgar 🄻

23 High Path, SW19 2JY

12-11 ☎ (020) 8542 5342 🌐 trafalgarfreehouse.co.uk

Downton Quadhop; Surrey Hills Shere Drop; 3 changing beers (sourced nationally; often By the Horns, Binghams, Hop Stuff) Ⓗ

Friendly one-bar street-corner house with Nelson memorabilia, mostly carpeted and furnished with farmhouse chairs and tables, with painted matchboard for the bar and lower part of the walls. The main part of the pub dates from the 1860s, with the extension from 1906. A variety of bottled beers is on sale, including a good selection from Belgium. One guest cider, from suppliers such as Lilley's, is offered. Cold and hot snacks (pot meals) are served 12-10pm. Live music features at times. 🚋(Morden Rd)⊖♣🍎🚌🐾 wifi

SW19: Wimbledon

Hand in Hand 🄻

7 Crooked Billet, SW19 4RQ

11-11 (midnight Fri & Sat); 12-11 Sun ☎ (020) 8946 5720

Young's Bitter, Special; changing beers (often Young's) Ⓗ

Celebrated single-bar ale house on the edge of Wimbledon Common with separate drinking areas and a variety of seating. Three or more guest beers usually include at least one each from Sambrook's and Twickenham. Paddles of three third-pints are available. This is a great place to eat, with beer included in several recipes. There is poker on Mondays and a quiz on Tuesdays. Local CAMRA Pub of the Year 2013. Q🐴❀◐◑♿♣🚌(200)🐾

Carshalton

Hope 🏆 🄻

48 West Street, SM5 2PR

12-11; 12-10.30 Sun ☎ (020) 8240 1255

🌐 hopecarshalton.co.uk

Downton New Forest Ale; Windsor & Eton Knight of the Garter; 5 changing beers (sourced nationally; often Kent, Magic Rock, Siren) Ⓗ

Popular traditional local and community hub now fully owned by its customers. Great beers from the country's best breweries rotate at remarkable speed from seven handpumps, and monthly themed beer festivals offer many more, all available in lined pint, third and two-thirds glasses. With no music except traditional jam sessions and no machines, beer dominates here. Good lunches are served until 3pm and pot meals until 10pm. CAMRA regional Pub of the Year 2013 and runner-up 2014. Q🐴❀◐⇌♣🍎P🚂🚌🐾 wifi

---

Sun 🄻

4 North Street, SM5 2HU

12-11 (10.30 Mon; midnight Fri & Sat); 12-10.30 Sun ☎ (020) 8773 4549 🌐 thesuncarshalton.com

6 changing beers (sourced nationally; often Arbor, Brighton Bier Co, Rooster's) Ⓗ

A handsome and imposing Victorian pub, built as a railway hotel, the Sun was given a tasteful makeover several years ago and has not looked back since. Several distinct areas accommodate diners, with excellent food, and discerning drinkers, with a wide beer choice on six handpumps. In summer the large courtyard garden with its continental-style veranda is popular. Quiz night is Tuesday. The huge upstairs function room receives sunlight almost all day, hence the pub's name. 🐴❀◐◑⇌🚌🐾

Windsor Castle

378 Carshalton Road, SM5 3PT

11-11 (11.30 Fri & Sat); 12-10 Sun ☎ (020) 8669 1191

🌐 windsorcastlepub.com

Long Man Best Bitter; Shepherd Neame Kent's Best, Spitfire, Bishops Finger; 2 changing beers Ⓗ

Landmark crossroads pub west of the town centre, with a roomy wood-panelled bar containing a restaurant at one end. The pumpclips on the ceiling beams attest to the variety of ales served over the years. Outside, a partially covered courtyard gives access to both a garden and a separate function room. Events include live music on Saturdays and a beer festival in May. Restaurant meals and bar food are available (except Sun and Mon eves) including a Sunday carvery. ❀◐◑♿⇌(Beeches)🍎P🚌🐾 wifi

Kew

Tap on the Line

Kew Gardens Station, Station Parade, TW9 3PZ

8am (9am Sat)-11; 10-10.30 Sun ☎ (020) 8332 1162

🌐 tapontheline.co.uk

Fuller's London Pride; 5 changing beers (sourced nationally; often Butcombe, Fuller's, Windsor & Eton) Ⓗ

Acquired by Fuller's in 2012 and reopened after refurbishment in 2013, this is an attractive old building with oak-beamed ceilings, beside the station's eastbound platform. Its main features include an arched ornate conservatory atrium and floor-to-ceiling picture windows looking directly onto the railway. There is a popular outside seating area at the front. Six real ales normally include three or four from Fuller's and two guests from the local region. Food is served all day. 🐴❀◐◑⊖(Kew Gardens)🚌🐾 wifi

Kingston

King's Tun 🄻

153-157 Clarence Street, KT1 1QT

8am-midnight (1am Fri & Sat) ☎ (020) 8547 3827

Greene King IPA, Abbot; Sharp's Doom Bar; Thornbridge Jaipur IPA; 8 changing beers Ⓗ

Large Wetherspoon pub in a grand-looking building that was originally the Empire Theatre. It attracts allcomers during the day, with a younger crowd in the evenings, particularly on Friday and Saturday nights, when there is a disco from 9pm. A long bar runs along the rear, with two separate seating areas leading to the front. There is also a good-sized bar upstairs. Two Westons ciders plus six guest ciders are available. Alcohol is served from 9am. 🐴◐◑♿⇌🍎🚌 wifi

Willoughby Arms Ⓛ

47 Willoughby Road, KT2 6LN
❂ 10.30-midnight; 12-midnight Sun ☎ (020) 8546 4236
⊕ thewilloughbyarms.com
Fuller's London Pride; 9 changing beers (sourced nationally; often Surrey Hills, Twickenham, Weltons) Ⓗ
Friendly Victorian back-street local comprising a sports bar, with games and a large-screen TV, and a quieter lounge area. At least one of the changing beers is locally brewed. An upstairs function room, where the Yardbirds rehearsed in the '60s, can be hired. Pizzas and pies are cooked to order. Beer festivals are held around Valentine's Day, St George's Day and Halloween. The spacious garden includes a covered, heated and lit smoking area also with a large TV screen. Quiz night is Sunday.
Q❀&♣●🚐(371,K5)♣📶

Woody's Ⓛ

5 Ram Passage, High Street, KT1 1HH
❂ 11-11 (midnight Fri); 10-midnight Sat; 10-10.30 Sun
☎ (020) 8541 4984 ⊕ woodyspubco.com
2 changing beers (sourced locally; often Brightwater, Portobello, Twickenham) Ⓗ
An independent free house situated on the riverfront, Woody's is welcoming, family-friendly and a little quirky. It serves two real ales, at least one from a local brewery, plus a selection of craft keg beers. Table service is always available, even in the summer months when it can get busy. Locally sourced fresh food is served all day from noon (10am weekends) until 10pm (9pm Sun).
🦽❀◑&🚐📶

New Malden

Woodies ♟

Thetford Road, KT3 5DX
❂ 11-11; 12-10.30 Sun ☎ (020) 8949 5824
⊕ woodiesfreehouse.co.uk
Adnams Broadside; Fuller's London Pride, ESB; Young's Bitter; 3 changing beers Ⓗ
A former cricket pavilion, this free house is smothered internally with sporting and theatrical memorabilia. Three changing ales are usually sourced from small breweries, with details of forthcoming beers listed on the website. Thatchers Dry cider is also available. Home-cooked lunches are served daily, with a carvery on Sundays and weekend barbecues in summer. There is a veranda for the warmer months. A beer festival is held in August. Local CAMRA Pub of the Year for 2015 and five of the previous 10 years.
🦽❀◑&●P🚐(265)♣📶

Richmond

Roebuck

130 Richmond Hill, TW10 6RN
❂ 12-11 (midnight Fri & Sat); 12-10.30 Sun
☎ (020) 8948 2329
Fuller's London Pride; Westerham Taylor Walker 1730; 6 changing beers (sourced nationally; often Binghams, Downton, Surrey Hills) Ⓗ
Close to Richmond Park Gate, this 200-year-old pub overlooks the World Heritage view of Petersham Meadows and the River Thames. Air-conditioned and Taylor Walker-branded, it has two regular beers and six rotating guest beers on tap, as well as one real cider. There is an upstairs bar (open weekends only) and a large function room. The

outside terrace across the road can also be used by patrons. Food is available until 10pm.
🦽◑&●🚐(65,371)♣📶

Waterman's Arms

12 Water Lane, TW9 1TJ
❂ 12-11 (9 Sun) ☎ (020) 8940 2893
Twickenham Naked Ladies; Young's Bitter, Special; 1 changing beer (sourced regionally; often Twickenham, Young's) Ⓗ
One of the oldest pubs in Richmond, dating back to at least 1660 and rebuilt in 1898, tucked away down a side street leading to the river. Retaining its Victorian two-bar layout, it is cosy and full of character, wood-panelled throughout and with etched glass windows. In the 1950s it was a lunchtime stop for Swan Uppers en route from Blackfriars to Henley. Traditional pub food, Sunday lunches and Thai specials are served daily. A Monday music club meets upstairs.
Q🦽◑≠⊖🚐🐾♣

Surbiton

Antelope Ⓛ

87 Maple Road, KT6 4AW
❂ 12-11 (11.30 Fri & Sat); 12-10.30 Sun ☎ (020) 8399 5565
⊕ theantelope.co.uk
10 changing beers (sourced nationally; often Big Smoke) Ⓗ
A welcome addition to the local real ale scene. Behind the covered and heated back patio is the Big Smoke Brewery and at least three of its beers are usually on sale. It has a fairly spacious split-level L-shaped interior with a varnished wooden floor. Dark-wood panelling, grey painted walls and candles complete the decor, and there is a real fire in winter. Home-cooked food includes Sunday roasts. It gets very busy at weekends and most evenings, when thirsty commuters invade. There are five changing ciders. ❀◑≠●🚐📶

Lamb Ⓛ

73 Brighton Road, KT6 5NF
❂ 12-11 (midnight Thu-Sat) ☎ (020) 8390 9229
Hop Back Summer Lightning; Robinsons Trooper; Surrey Hills Ranmore Ale; 1 changing beer Ⓗ
A small, family-run free house at the heart of the local community. Built in 1850 and formerly divided into four separate rooms, it still retains the original horseshoe-shaped bar. The changing beer is from a microbrewery, sometimes local, or family brewer. Specialist cheeses are always available, with cheeseboards all day Friday to Sunday. Music and other events are regularly held throughout the year. Local CAMRA Pub of the Year 2012 and 2014.
🦽❀≠🚐📶

Sutton

Little Windsor

13 Greyhound Road, SM1 4BY
❂ 12-11.30 (midnight Fri & Sat); 12-11 Sun
☎ (020) 8643 2574
Fuller's London Pride, ESB; 2 changing beers Ⓗ
A small back-street corner venue located in the New Town area, east of Sutton town centre. The pub is popular with locals, especially in the evening and at weekends, and sport is shown on TV. The L-shaped bar leads to a heated covered terrace and garden. The food menu is offered at lunchtimes and in the evenings, and quizzes are held on

Sundays. Four-pint jugs of beer can be bought at a discount. Children are welcome until 9pm.

Moon on the Hill

5-9 Hill Road, SM1 1DZ

8am-midnight (1am Fri & Sat) (020) 8643 1202

Greene King Abbot; Ruddles Best Bitter; Sharp's Doom Bar; 7 changing beers (sourced regionally; often Dark Star, King Beer, Surrey Hills)

A Wetherspoon pub built into the side of a hill just off Sutton's main street. There are three levels: the bar at ground level, a lower level to the left with more seating, and an upper level at the rear catering mainly for diners and serving as the family area. The walls are decorated with pictures, drawings and illustrations depicting matters of local historic interest. There are two TV screens.

Robin Hood

52 West Street, SM1 1SH

11-11 (midnight Fri & Sat); 12-11 Sun (020) 8643 7584

robinhoodsutton.com

Young's Bitter, Special; 2 changing beers

Traditional English local with a single spacious L-shaped bar decorated with a good range of historic photographs of the area. Home-cooked food includes curries, vegetarian lasagne and burgers. There is a piano, and highchairs and baby-changing facilities are available. Upstairs is a large function room. Quiz night is every Monday, and cribbage is played on Tuesdays. Other events are hosted throughout the year, including some for charity. The pub is home to golf and darts teams.
(West Sutton)

Wallington

Wallington Arms

6-16 Woodcote Road, SM6 0NN

4-11 (midnight Thu & Fri); 12-midnight Sat; 12-11 Sun

wallingtonarms.com

Adnams Lighthouse; Sharp's Doom Bar; 4 changing beers (sourced nationally; often Purity, Sambrook's)

Nestling under the shelter of the railway station and reopened as an Antic venture in 2014, the pub is decorated in a shabby chic style. Six handpumps dispense national and local beers, and the management's enthusiastic approach extends to a good range of British and continental bottled beers and cider. The menu includes staple pub grub as well as gourmet dishes, and there are promotional days and prices for ale as well as food.

Whispering Moon

25 Ross Parade, SM6 8QF

6-11 (midnight Fri & Sat) (020) 8647 7020

Greene King Abbot; Ruddles Best Bitter; Young's Bitter; 5 changing beers (sourced nationally; often Adnams, Dark Star, Exmoor)

A popular, family-friendly Wetherspoon establishment in former cinema premises, where you can expect a warm welcome. Handy for the railway station, it has a single L-shaped bar with a raised dining section, and the decor includes historic photographs of the local area. You can use the book provided to express your preferences for guest ales, which the manager is keen to source from the local area.

WEST LONDON

W2: Bayswater

Champion

1 Wellington Terrace, W2 4LW

12-11 (midnight Fri & Sat); 12-10.30 Sun

(020) 7243 6054 thechampionpub.co.uk

Adnams Broadside; Windsor & Eton Knight of the Garter; 3 changing beers

Another M&B Castle pub entering the Guide for the first time. Built in 1838 and Grade II-listed, it was refurbished in 2004. In warm weather the front windows are usually opened. A plush basement area, available for functions, leads onto a sunken beer garden, with patio heaters in cold weather. This pub is the nearest to Kensington Palace, right opposite the security-protected road on the northern side of Kensington Gardens.
(Notting Hill Gate/Queensway)

W2: Paddington

Mad Bishop & Bear

1st Floor, Paddington Station, W2 1HB

8am-11; 10-10.30 Sun (020) 7402 2441

Fuller's Chiswick Bitter, London Pride, ESB; St Austell Tribute; 4 changing beers (sourced nationally; often Fuller's)

Above the shopping complex just behind the station concourse, the traditional pub interior features a long bar, mirrors, good prints and a rather grand chandelier, with train information screens and two TVs for sport. The raised area can be hired for events and there are café-style seats outside. It does not get too crowded, even in the rush hour. Note that the bar may close early if there are football crowds passing through. CAMRA branch Pub of the Year 2015.

Victoria ★

10A Strathearn Place, W2 2NH

11-11; 12-10.30 Sun (020) 7724 1191

Fuller's Chiswick Bitter, London Pride, Bengal Lancer, ESB; 1 changing beer (often Adnams)

There is plenty to admire in the nationally important historic interior of this Grade II-listed mid-Victorian inn, including ornately gilded mirrors above a crescent-shaped bar, painted tiles in wall niches and numerous portraits of Queen Victoria. The walls display cartoons, paperweights and a Silver Jubilee plate. A recessed area at the back is furnished with a leather bench seat. Upstairs, via a spiral staircase, there is a Library and Theatre Bar available for public use. Tuesday is quiz night.
Q (Lancaster Gate/Paddington)

W3: Acton

George & Dragon

183 High Street, W3 9DJ

12-11 (midnight Fri & Sat) (020) 8992 3712

dragonflybrewery.co.uk

Dragonfly 2 o'Clock Ordinary, Dark Matter, Early Doors

At the heart of the historic Acton Town centre, this Grade II-listed pub has three bars of real character. An atmospheric front bar, with a list of landlords dating back to 1759, leads through to a heritage bar with exposed original features, and a cavernous and stylish back room serves as the bar and Dragonfly brewery. Dragonfly's three regular

cask beers are served – a bitter, pale ale and stout – and usually two real ciders.
(Central)

Red Lion & Pineapple
281 High Street, W3 9BP
8am-midnight (1am Fri & Sat) (020) 8896 2248
Greene King IPA, Abbot; Sharp's Doom Bar; 5 changing beers H
A Wetherspoon pub formerly owned by Fuller's, originally two pubs which then combined, hence the unusual name and layout. The larger room is home to the circular bar, surrounded by red and black tiles. The windows are large, with etched and stained tops, and the walls are decorated with photographs of old Acton. The smaller room is mainly for diners and families. There are four guest ales during the week, five at weekends. Alcohol is served from 9am. Q (Town)

West London Trades Union Club
33-35 High Street, W3 6ND
7-midnight (020) 8992 4557 wltuc.com
2 changing beers (often Nelson) H
Small and friendly club, run as a co-operative, which combines excellent real ale with a busy cultural and social life. Two real ales are normally served from a variety of small independent breweries, and particularly from the ever-changing Nelson Brewery range. The Acton Community Theatre is upstairs, and the club hosts regular special events including summer barbecues in the courtyard. The local CAMRA branch is an associate member; show a CAMRA membership card or this Guide for entry. Q (Central)

W4: Chiswick

Fox & Hounds/Mawson Arms
110 Chiswick Lane South, W4 2QA
10.30-8; closed Sat & Sun (020) 8994 2936
Fuller's Chiswick Bitter, London Pride, Bengal Lancer, ESB; Gales Seafarers Ale; 1 changing beer (often Fuller's) H
On the corner of the Griffin Brewery and its de facto brewery tap, this Grade II*-listed pub is the start for the Fuller's brewery tour. The unusual double naming is a historical relic of separate licences needed for beer and spirits. The pub is well known for its quality food, which is served until 7pm. Brewery memorabilia on the walls include ancestral portraits of the Fuller, Smith and Turner families. It opens at weekends for functions only.
Q (190)

George IV
185 Chiswick High Road, W4 2DR
12-11 (1am Fri & Sat) (020) 8994 4624
Fuller's Chiswick Bitter, London Pride, ESB; 3 changing beers (sourced nationally; often Fuller's) H
There has been an inn here in the heart of Chiswick since 1777. The present inter-war pub had a substantial makeover in 2014, but is still reputed to have its own ghost, George. The Boston Room plays host to a variety of events including a comedy club, and is also available for private hire. There are eight real ale pumps. The current manageress has reached Master Cellarman status.
(Turnham Green)

Old Pack Horse
434 Chiswick High Road, W4 5TF
11-midnight (1am Thu; 2am Fri & Sat); 12-midnight Sun
(020) 8994 2872
Fuller's Chiswick Bitter, London Pride, ESB; 1 changing beer (sourced locally) H
A Grade II-listed corner pub last rebuilt in 1910 but claimed to date back to 1747. Refurbished recently, it has a beautiful frontage often featured in local photographs, and enjoys a view across Turnham Green. With ornate woodwork and glasswork, including some stained glass panels, it has a regionally important historic pub interior. Five drinking areas include a snug and a Thai restaurant towards the back. A bar sign refers to the long-gone Chiswick Empire, and walls display theatre memorabilia.
(Chiswick Park/Gunnersbury)

Tabard L
2 Bath Road, W4 1LW
12-11 (midnight Thu-Sat) (020) 8994 3492
Fuller's London Pride; Westerham Taylor Walker 1730; 7 changing beers (sourced regionally) H
The pub is Grade II* listed, dates back to 1880, and was built as part of the Bedford Park estate, the first London garden suburb. Notable features include the swing sign painted by TM Rooke, tiling by William de Morgan and Walter Crane, and Arts & Crafts mirrors and pictures. Ten handpumps serve a cider and mainly guest ales, presenting a permanent beer festival always including local beers. There is an intimate first-floor fringe theatre.
(Turnham Green)

W5: Ealing

Grove L
1 Ealing Green, W5 5QX
10-11; 11-10.30 Sun (020) 8567 2439
Greene King IPA; changing beers (sourced locally; often Sambrook's, Truman's, Vale) H
Large one-bar pub with many semi-private areas. Owned by Greene King, it focuses on local microbreweries such as Truman's, Sambrook's, Vale and Windsor & Eton. The food offer has also moved up a notch and there is a dedicated restaurant area. The large heated front and side gardens are popular. The pub holds regular beer festivals and Meet the Brewer events.
(Broadway)

Plough
297 Northfield Avenue, W5 4XB
11-midnight (1am Thu-Sat); 12-midnight Sun
(020) 8567 1416
Fuller's Chiswick Bitter, London Pride; 2 changing beers (sourced locally; often Fuller's) H
Popular with all ages and a real hub for the Little Ealing community, the pub has a children's playground and extensive garden, a restaurant area serving a quality menu, and an L-shaped front of house for adults only. A centre for the Ealing jazz scene, it features regular Monday and Thursday evening performances as well as fringe sessions for the summer Ealing jazz festival. Quiz night is every Tuesday. Charles Blondin, the Victorian tightrope walker, lived opposite.
(Northfields) P (E2,E3)

Questors Grapevine Bar L
12 Mattock Lane, W5 5BQ
7-11; 12-2.30, 7-10.30 Sun (020) 8567 0011
questors.org.uk
Fuller's London Pride; 2 changing beers H

A friendly theatre club bar near the centre of Ealing and Walpole Park run by enthusiastic volunteers. CAMRA members and Questors theatre ticket holders are also welcome. Guest beers include some from local breweries and the bar runs beer festivals and malt whisky tastings. Some books and the odd board game are available. Please note that credit or debit cards are not accepted at the bar.
Q (Broadway) P

Red Lion

13 St Marys Road, W5 5RA

12-11 (midnight Thu & Fri); 11-midnight Sat
(020) 8567 2541

Fuller's Chiswick Bitter, London Pride, ESB; 2 changing beers (sourced nationally; often Fuller's)

A splendid example of a traditional London pub, believed to be first recorded in local newspapers in the early 1700s and affectionately known as Stage 6, opposite Ealing Studios. Associated black and white photographs of TV and film stars are displayed with memorabilia of their films. The Lee family have maintained the real character of the pub. Excellent upmarket food is cooked to order, and there is a heated, covered patio at the rear.
Q (Broadway) (Broadway/South Ealing) (65)

Sir Michael Balcon

46-47 The Mall, W5 3TJ

8am-11.30 (midnight Fri & Sat) (020) 8799 2850

Greene King IPA, Abbot; Sharp's Doom Bar; 5 changing beers (often Adnams, Hogs Back, Sambrook's)

Located on the busy Uxbridge Road east of Ealing town centre, this became a Wetherspoon pub in 2008, named after the legendary film producer whose life and films form the basis of many of the wall displays. It is split level, with a raised area at the rear and a glass-covered area at the front for smokers. Alcohol is served from 9am.
Q (Broadway)

W6: Hammersmith

Andover Arms

57 Aldensley Road, W6 0DL

12-midnight; 12-11 Sun (020) 8748 2155

Fuller's Chiswick Bitter, London Pride; 2 changing beers (often Fuller's)

A frequent entry in this Guide, tucked away in the side streets of Hammersmith, this popular local is an enduring real ale champion. The kitchen offers a wide range of lunchtime and evening meals. There is a terrestrial TV for major sporting events, and traditional pub games such as dominoes are available. The venue holds regular quiz and live music nights. Guest ales are a recent innovation and drinkers can sup beers from brewers such as Brains or Long Man.
Q (Ravenscourt Park)

Dove

19 Upper Mall, W6 9TA

11-11; 12-10.30 Sun (020) 8748 9474

Fuller's London Pride, ESB; Gales Seafarers Ale; 1 changing beer (often Fuller's)

Traditional Fuller's pub overlooking the Thames and hence often crowded in summer. A Grade II-listed building with a regionally important historic interior, it holds the Guinness world record for the smallest bar area. Classic food with a twist is served every day; meals can take a little time to arrive at busy times but are worth the wait. The likes of Dylan Thomas, Ernest Hemingway and Alec Guinness have reputedly enjoyed a pint or two here.
(Hammersmith/Ravenscourt Park)

Plough & Harrow

120-124 King Street, W6 0QU

8am-11.30 (020) 8735 6020

Adnams Broadside; Fuller's London Pride; Greene King IPA, Abbot; Young's Special; 5 changing beers

On the site of an inn established in 1419, and more recently a Rolls-Royce showroom, the present light and airy Wetherspoon pub, on Hammersmith's King Street, dates from 2002. It has a mixture of stone and carpeted floors and a long metal-topped bar with 10 handpumps, half devoted to a changing range of guest ales, many from microbreweries. There are several no-smoking tables outside and standing room on a veranda by the side of the premises.
Q (Hammersmith/Ravenscourt Park)

Swan

46 Hammersmith Broadway, W6 0DZ

10-11 (midnight Fri & Sat); 10-10.30 Sun
(020) 8748 1043

Fuller's London Pride; Windsor & Eton Knight of the Garter; 5 changing beers (often St Austell)

Claimed to be on the site of the first coaching stop after leaving the City, wood predominates in this bustling M&B Nicholson's pub handily placed opposite Hammersmith Broadway. Ornate stairs lead to a first-floor restaurant and bar (and the toilets). It is well worth breaking your journey here to or from Heathrow airport. Guest beers are often from regional brewers such as Adnams, Elgood's and Thornbridge. Note the fine tessellated gables.

W7: Hanwell

Fox

Green Lane, W7 2PJ

11-11; 12-10.30 Sun (020) 8567 4021
thefoxpub.co.uk

Fuller's London Pride; Sharp's Cornish Coaster; Timothy Taylor Landlord; 2 changing beers

Wonderful back-street free house in the welcoming multicultural town of Hanwell, as popular with walkers, cyclists and other nearby canal users as with locals. A good range of beers, with changing guest ales from independent breweries, is complemented by excellent, inexpensive food, including a popular Sunday lunch (booking recommended). Beer festivals and occasional jazz are hosted. The Fox was local CAMRA Pub of the Year in 2013. P (195,E8)

Grosvenor

127 Oaklands Road, W7 2DT

12 (9am Fri)-11; 12-10.30 Sun (020) 8840 0007
thegrosvenorhanwell.co.uk

6 changing beers (sourced locally; often Sharp's, Truman's, Weird Beard)

A traditional back-street local, reopened under new ownership after a major refurbishment in 2014. Reconditioned tables are complemented by a variety of comfy seating. Six real ales are available during busy periods, and bottle-conditioned beers are also stocked from Weird Beard and the Sharp's Connoisseurs range. The cider is usually Westons

Old Rosie. A quiz takes place some Mondays, jazz alternate Tuesdays and the pub promotes local events.

W8: Kensington

Elephant & Castle

40 Holland Street, W8 4LT

11-11; 12-10.30 Sun (020) 7937 6382

St Austell Nicholson's Pale Ale; Sharp's Doom Bar; Truman's Runner; 2 changing beers (often Copper Dragon, Salopian)

Licensed in 1865 as a beer house in what were two adjacent houses, and tucked away north-east of the town hall, this cosy, wood-panelled pub is a welcome refuge from the bustle of Kensington High Street. There are strong journalistic connections – witness the notable framed newspapers in the back bar. Guest beers are from the wide-ranging Nicholson's portfolio and food is served all day. (High St Kensington)

W8: Notting Hill Gate

Churchill Arms

119 Kensington Church Street, W8 7LN

11-11 (midnight Thu-Sat); 12-10.30 Sun

(020) 7727 4242

Fuller's Chiswick Bitter, London Pride, ESB; 1 changing beer (often Fuller's)

Long-serving landlord Gerry keeps standards high at this multi award-winning pub with its regionally important historic interior. Churchillian and Irish memorabilia hang from the panelled ceiling, and plaques at the bar commemorate former drinkers. The Thai restaurant in the conservatory was one of the first in a London pub. Often busy, with drinkers standing on the pavement below the hanging flower baskets, it has regularly been a top three contender for the local CAMRA Pub of the Year.

Q

Uxbridge Arms

13 Uxbridge Street, W8 7TQ

12-11 (10.30 Sun) (020) 7727 7326

Fuller's London Pride; Harveys Sussex Best Bitter; St Austell Tribute

A world away from nearby Portobello Road, the manager Linda and her team run a great Enterprise pub, built as a beer house in 1836. Carpeted throughout, the bar has a welcoming appeal. The Lt Colonel's tunic has been part of the decor, together with the plates, for a number of years now.

Q

W9: Westbourne Park

Union Tavern

45 Woodfield Road, W9 2BA

12-11 (midnight Fri & Sat); 12-10.30 Sun

(020) 7286 1886

Fuller's London Pride, ESB; 3 changing beers

A radical departure by Fuller's, this is an unbranded beer house offering cask ales produced within 30 miles and, with the exception of one brewery, from London. The mainly young crowd enjoys reduced beer prices on Monday, a weekly quiz and Meet the Brewer events on the last Tuesday of the month. Good-value food is another plus, including traditional Sunday lunch. The canalside terrace comes into its own on a warm, sunny day.

W12: Shepherds Bush

Defector's Weld

170 Uxbridge Road, W12 8AA

12-midnight (2am Fri & Sat); 12-11 Sun

(020) 8749 0008 defectors-weld.com

Young's Bitter; 4 changing beers

Although recently acquired by Young's, the pub plans to continue offering rotating beers from local guest brewers including Moncada, Redemption, Sambrook's or Twickenham. The large horseshoe-shaped main bar has five handpumps and a mix of sofas, tables and chairs. An upstairs bar is available for hire. DJs play music Thursday to Sunday evenings (no admission after midnight Fri and Sat). Only home fans are allowed in on QPR match days, but card-carrying CAMRA members not wearing team colours are welcome.

Q (Shepherd's Bush Market)

W13: West Ealing

Forester ★

2 Leighton Road, W13 9EP

11-11.30 (midnight Wed & Thu; 1am Fri & Sat); 11-11 Sun

(020) 8567 1654

Fuller's London Pride, ESB; 4 changing beers (sourced nationally; often Fuller's)

Built in 1909 from designs by Nowell Parr for the Royal Brewery of Brentford and bought by Fuller's in 2012, this pub has a nationally important historic interior. Thai and English food are available daily except Sundays, when the traditional carvery is served until 6pm. Wednesdays are quiz nights and on Thursdays there are poker tournaments. Two guests beers are supplemented by two additional beers from Fuller's (often Gales HSB). Several beer festivals a year are held.

(Northfields) (E2,E3)

Brentford

Express Tavern

56 Kew Bridge Road, TW8 0EW

11-11 (midnight Fri & Sat); 12-11 Sun (020) 8560 8484

expresstavern.co.uk

Draught Bass; Haresfoot Lock Keeper's Launch Ale; 8 changing beers

A local landmark since the 1800s and with an interior of regional historic importance, the building retains illuminated external Bass signage, and Draught Bass is still on the bar. The Chiswick bar has 10 ale handpumps and a playable upright piano (music is also played from vinyl LPs), while the Saloon and Lounge bar has five ciders and perries on handpump. At the rear is a beer garden with a covered and heated area.

(Kew Bridge)

Magpie & Crown

128 High Street, TW8 8EW

12-midnight (1am Thu-Sat) (020) 8560 4570

6 changing beers

This mock-Tudor free house is a cosy haunt for locals and beer lovers. London breweries often feature among the eclectic range of six guest ales. Also on offer are a cider and a perry on handpump, and English, German and Belgian bottled beers, all served by enthusiastic and knowledgeable staff. There are paved areas with tables at the front and covered areas at the back. The food is freshly cooked, with roasts on Sunday.

Feltham

Moon on the Square

30 The Centre, High Street, TW13 4AU

8am-midnight (10.30 Sun) (020) 8893 1293

Courage Best Bitter; Greene King Abbot; Ruddles Best Bitter; changing beers

A real ale oasis that continues to flourish. The interior is early Wetherspoon, featuring wood panels and glass-partitioned booths, with pictures and local history panels. Eight real ales include continually varying guests, often local brews, with a bar-top gravity cask on tap during beer festivals in April and October. Westons cider is available. Food is served all day, alcohol from 9am. Children are welcome until 6pm.

Greenford

Black Horse

425 Oldfield Lane North, UB6 0AS

11.30-11 (midnight Thu-Sat); 12-11 Sun

(020) 8578 1384 blackhorsegreenford.co.uk

Fuller's London Pride, ESB; 1 changing beer (often Fuller's)

Large, tastefully refurbished, split-level pub close to mainline rail, Tube and bus routes, with a landscaped garden overlooking the Grand Union Canal. Bargees and walkers are frequent visitors; the canal used to deliver the beer here. Good food includes traditional Sunday lunches. There is TV, music – karaoke or jam night on Wednesdays and a live band once a month on Saturday – and a quiz on Thursday nights.

Q P (92,395)

Hampton

Jolly Coopers

16 High Street, TW12 2SJ

11-11 (midnight Fri & Sat); 12-10.30 Sun

(020) 8979 3384 squiffysrestaurant.co.uk

Caledonian Deuchars IPA; Courage Best Bitter; Hop Back Summer Lightning; 2 changing beers

A popular, traditional community pub proud of its heritage – a wooden wall panel lists landlords from 1727 to the present owners who took over in 1986. The small horseshoe bar features five handpumps. Walls are adorned with water jugs, old pub photographs and local memorabilia, including some coopers' tools. An extensive menu of tapas and traditional food including Sunday lunches is on offer, served in the bar, Squiffy's restaurant beyond and, weather permitting, on the sun patio outside.

Hampton Court

Mute Swan

3 Palace Gate, KT8 9BN

11-11 (midnight Fri & Sat); 11-10.30 Sun

(020) 8941 5959 muteswan.co.uk

House beer (by Phoenix); 5 changing beers (sourced regionally)

Opposite Hampton Court gates, this was previously a restaurant but following a complete makeover is now a modern, upmarket pub/restaurant. A number of rugs on the floor provide a calm ambience. Expect five cask ales from local or regional breweries. A good selection of food can be consumed either upstairs or in the main bar. Tables are provided outside during warmer months. There are no TV screens, gaming machines or intrusive music to spoil the civilised atmosphere of this welcome addition to the area.

Hampton Hill

Roebuck

72 Hampton Road, TW12 1JN

11-11 (11.30 Fri & Sat); 12-4, 7-10.30 Sun

(020) 8255 8133 roebuck-hamptonhill.co.uk

St Austell Tribute; Sambrook's Junction; Young's Bitter; 2 changing beers

A comfortable Victorian street-corner pub with screens dividing the single bar into various seating areas. The array of bric-a-brac and other displays (framed bank notes and military memorabilia, fishing rods, model seaplanes, a cigar store Indian and, of course, a wickerwork Harley-Davidson) is amazing but does not distract from the comfort of the pub. The small, award-winning garden has a gazebo for smokers and there is a garden room (available for hire) for cooler evenings.

Q (Fulwell)

Harlington

White Hart

158 High Street, UB3 5DP

11-11 (11.30 Thu; midnight Fri & Sat); 12-11 Sun

(020) 8759 9608

Fuller's London Pride, ESB; 1 changing beer (sourced locally; often Fuller's)

Large Grade II-listed Fuller's pub standing proud at the north end of the village. The single bar provides access to an open-plan area for sport on large TV screens, through to a seated area favoured by diners. The pub was refurbished in 2009 to improve facilities and create the open feel it now has. Regional history is the theme of the wall displays enjoyed by locals and visitors from Heathrow airport nearby. Quiz night is Thursday.

P

Hayes

Botwell Inn

25-29 Coldharbour Lane, UB3 3EB

8am-midnight (020) 8848 3112

Adnams Broadside; Greene King Abbot; Ruddles Best Bitter; Sharp's Doom Bar; 3 changing beers (sourced nationally; often Adnams, Nelson, Windsor & Eton)

A large Wetherspoon pub opened in 2000 following a shop conversion from furnishers Moore and Son, with several areas for dining and drinking. There is a fenced, paved area to the front and a patio at the rear with large parasols with heaters. Alongside the regular and guest beers, at least one Westons cider is available. Several beer festivals are held annually. Alcohol is served from 9am.

Q (Hayes & Harlington)

Hayes End

Angel ★

697 Uxbridge Road, UB4 8HX

11-midnight (1am Fri & Sat) (020) 8848 8020

angelpub.net

Fuller's Chiswick Bitter, London Pride; Gales HSB; 1 changing beer (sourced nationally; often Fuller's)

A real community local with a nationally important historic pub interior. The small saloon bar is quiet and the traditional atmosphere is maintained in

the larger public bar, which has a pool table annexe. The large back bar is mostly used for functions. The pub is in both darts and pool leagues and sponsors Hayes Angels football team. Regular events include jazz, film, jam, comedy nights and Sunday bingo. The pub was Grade II-listed in 2015.
Q❀◐♣P🚌🐾📶

Hounslow

Moon under Water
84-88 Staines Road, TW3 3LF (W end of High St)
⏲ 9am-12.30am (1am Fri & Sat) ☎ (020) 8572 7506
Greene King Abbot; Ruddles Best Bitter; Sharp's Doom Bar; 5 changing beers (sourced regionally) Ⓗ
A 1991 Wetherspoon shop conversion in original style, still displaying many local history panels and photos. It is a regular venue for the town's beer lovers, also attracting others from surrounding areas. Up to five guest ales are often locally sourced, with many more at festival times when all 12 handpumps are put to work. The cider is usually Westons Old Rosie, again with others during festivals. Children are welcome until 8.30pm.
Q❀◐◑♿⇌⊖(Central)🍎🚌📶

Isleworth

London Apprentice
62 Church Street, TW7 6BG
⏲ 11-11 (midnight Fri & Sat) ☎ (020) 8560 1915
🌐 thelondonapprentice.co.uk
Adnams Ghost Ship; Fuller's London Pride; 4 changing beers Ⓗ
Famous Grade-II listed former Isleworth Brewery riverside pub in old Isleworth, with a unique name and interesting history. The interior is classic traditional, although opened out, with an upstairs Riverview Room. The large patio has many tables with more on the riverbank. Four guest ales are regularly on offer, plus a cider, as well as excellent food. With music most Monday evenings, Thursday poker and a Sunday quiz, it is well worth the short walk from the nearest bus stop.
❀◐◑♿🍎P🚌(H37)

Norwood Green

Plough
Tentelow Lane, UB2 4LG
⏲ 11 (12 Sun)-midnight ☎ (020) 8574 7473
Fuller's London Pride; Gales Seafarers Ale; 2 changing beers (sourced nationally; often Fuller's) Ⓗ
A Grade II-listed 17th-century building with exposed wooden beams, low ceilings and a real fire. This is Fuller's oldest pub, acquired in 1816, and run by a splendid landlord who takes pride in the friendly service all customers receive. Traditional and some Italian food is served lunchtimes and evenings (excluding Mon). Country and folk music is played every Tuesday, and other genres of music some Fridays, most Saturdays and the odd Sunday. ❀◐◑♣🚌(120)🐾📶

Southall

Southall Conservative & Unionist Club 🄻
Fairlawn, High Street, UB1 3HB
⏲ 11.30-2.30, 7-11; 11.30-3, 6-11 Fri & Sat; 12-3, 7-10.30 Sun
☎ (020) 8574 0261
Rebellion IPA; 1 changing beer (often Rebellion) Ⓗ
This is virtually the last real ale outlet in Southall, and is to be found behind the former town hall. Show this Guide or a CAMRA membership card for access. It was completely refurbished to a high standard in early 2015. Lunches are served daily except Sundays, but this is a good place to visit either before or after eating in one of the numerous nearby Indian restaurants.
❀◐⇌♣P🚌📶

Stockley Park

White House
The Arena, Bennetsfield Road, UB11 1AA
⏲ 7am-10 (11 Thu-Sat) ☎ (020) 8589 7870
Fuller's London Pride; Sharp's Doom Bar; 2 changing beers Ⓗ
A fairly modern Lloyds No.1 bar set in a small commercial complex servicing the Stockley Park business community and golf course. A long bar/restaurant with a charming conservatory at the end leads out onto a decked area overlooking a small lake with several species of waterfowl, lovely on a nice summer's day. There is an outside patio with heaters and a large grassed area. A Westons cider is on handpump. Q❀◐◑♿🍎P🚌📶

Teddington

Masons Arms
41 Walpole Road, TW11 8PJ
⏲ 12-11 (11.30 Fri & Sat); 12-10.30 Sun ☎ (020) 8977 6521
🌐 the-masons-arms.co.uk
Sambrook's Junction; Tillingbourne AONB; 2 changing beers Ⓗ
Small back-street community free house with a uniquely friendly atmosphere, a beer-drinkers' haven as reflected in the array of bottles, pictures and pub memorabilia on display (including the infamous Watney's Party Seven). Carpeted and comfortable seating create a cosy atmosphere. The digital jukebox is a popular feature, and there is a log-burning stove, dartboard and a small secluded rear patio. Guest beers change frequently, coming from a wide range of independent brewers across the UK. ❀♿⇌♣🍎▯🚌

Twickenham

Aleksander
277/279 Richmond Road, TW1 2NP
⏲ 12-11 ☎ (020) 8892 6252 🌐 thealeksander.co.uk
Burning Sky Plateau; Oakham Citra; Timothy Taylor Boltmaker; 1 changing beer Ⓗ
Previously known as the Rising Sun, then the Marble Hill, this corner pub is now a free house. It is opposite Marble Hill Park, between Richmond and Twickenham, and well served by public transport, with buses stopping outside. Live music is a feature on Friday and Saturday. The food serving area and dining tables dominate half of the pub. The kitchen, which includes a wood-fired pizza oven, opens 12-10pm. There is a pleasant seating area outside and a small car park.
❀◐◑♿⇌(St Margarets)P🚌🐾📶

Prince Blucher
124 The Green, TW2 5AG
⏲ 11-11 (midnight Fri & Sat); 12-11 Sun ☎ (020) 8894 1824
Fuller's London Pride, ESB; Gales Seafarers Ale; 2 changing beers (often Fuller's) Ⓗ

Historic 19th-century inn, the first built on the newly enclosed Twickenham Green and the only pub in Britain still to pay homage to the Duke of Wellington's left flanker at Waterloo. Renovated in 2014, it has four separate bar areas and serves home-cooked food all day. In summertime it hosts barbecues and hog roasts in the ample child-friendly garden. The bare-boarded main bar has nine antique-style pump handles and unusual pumpclip fittings. Cornish Orchard cider is on handpump.
(Strawberry Hill) P

Rifleman

7 Fourth Cross Road, TW2 5EL
12 (2 Mon & Tue)-11; 12-10.30 Sun (020) 8893 3836
theriflemantwickenham.co.uk
Butcombe Bitter; Ringwood Best Bitter; Timothy Taylor Landlord; Twickenham Naked Ladies; Young's Bitter; 1 changing beer (sourced locally) H
Traditional Victorian pub commemorating riflemen billeted nearby in Napoleonic times. It benefits from a small beer garden, front patio and close proximity to seven bus routes. No main meals are served but toasties are available up to 7pm. On Thursdays it hosts a lively open mic night. Very much a community hub, it has board games, darts and TV sport. It is 15 minutes' walk from Twickenham stadium and Harlequins rugby clubs. Local CAMRA Pub of the Year 2014.
(Strawberry Hill) P

Sussex Arms

15 Staines Road, TW2 5BG
12-11; 12-10.30 Sun (020) 8894 7468
thesussexarmstwickenham.co.uk
Changing beers (often Twickenham) H
This traditional pub with two real fires has now become a firm favourite with beer lovers. Eighteen handpumps showcase Twickenham and other independent UK breweries, and six ciders and perries. Acoustic blues and Irish music feature regularly, as does recorded music from vinyl LPs. Food includes Anthea's famous pies. Every 10th pint of ale is free with the pub's loyalty card. CAMRA Greater London Cider Pub of the Year 2014, and local branch Pub of the Year 2013.
(Strawberry Hill)

White Swan

Riverside, TW1 3DN
11-11; 10-11 Sat; 11-10.30 Sun (020) 8744 2951
whiteswantwickenham.com
Fuller's London Pride; Sharp's Doom Bar; 3 changing beers H
A Grade II-listed building and award-winning traditional pub built in about 1690. Entry is via steps to the first floor, with real fires and walls covered with rugby and other memorabilia. A small veranda/balcony and a triclinium (three-sided room with window seats) afford views of the river and Eel Pie Island. There is a large beer garden opposite, right on the water's edge (tides permitting). Quiz night is Wednesday. A summer beer festival and an annual raft race are held.
Q

William Webb Ellis

24 London Road, TW1 3RR
9am-11 (020) 8744 4300
Adnams Broadside; Fuller's London Pride; Greene King IPA, Abbot; Sharp's Doom Bar; 6 changing beers H
Twelve handpumps with a good selection of local and regionally sourced beers are in constant use in this imaginative Wetherspoon conversion of a town centre Grade II-listed building that was for 100 years Twickenham's post office. The pub is large and spacious. The rear patio is open until 9pm, food is served all day and children are welcome until 8pm. A Monday ale club offers reduced prices and third-pint glasses.

Uxbridge

Good Yarn

132 High Street, UB8 1JX
8am-midnight (1am Fri & Sat) (01895) 239852
Fuller's London Pride; Greene King IPA, Abbot; Sharp's Doom Bar; 4 changing beers (sourced nationally; often Binghams, Oakham, Twickenham) H
Opened in 1994 in the former Pearson's menswear shop in the town centre – other than the narrow frontage, this is a typical Wetherspoon pub by day. In the evening loud music can feature, especially at weekends. The pub has a long narrow bar, the raised far end surrounded with shelves of old books. The walls of the front area display old framed advertisements for local businesses, and old local photographs can be found throughout. Alcohol is served from 9am.

Queen's Head L

54 Windsor Street, UB8 1AB
11-11 (midnight Fri & Sat); 12-10.30 Sun
(01895) 258750
Fuller's London Pride; changing beers (sourced locally; often Cotleigh, Twickenham, Windsor & Eton) H
A Grade II-listed mid 19th-century pub opposite the church, a few yards from the Tube station. Features and furnishings include bay windows, wooden floorboards, low ceilings and walls largely of exposed brick, and an irregularly shaped bar. It was the local CAMRA Pub of the Year in 2014 – the landlord proudly displays a certificate he received from the branch for the most improved beer range and for doing the most to promote real ale.

Whitton

Admiral Nelson

123 Nelson Road, TW2 7BB
11-11 (midnight Fri & Sat); 12-10.30 Sun
(020) 8894 9998
Fuller's Chiswick Bitter, London Pride, ESB; 2 changing beers (often Fuller's) H
A large landmark pub rebuilt in the 1930s, with a small patio area on the side. It stands in a prominent position on the crossroads at the end of the high street, and has both a Nelsonian and a rugby theme. Near to Twickenham Stadium and Twickenham Stoop, it is a haven for rugby fans on match days, with large TVs for sport, baby-changing facilities and its own ATM. Sunday is quiz night.

GREATER MANCHESTER

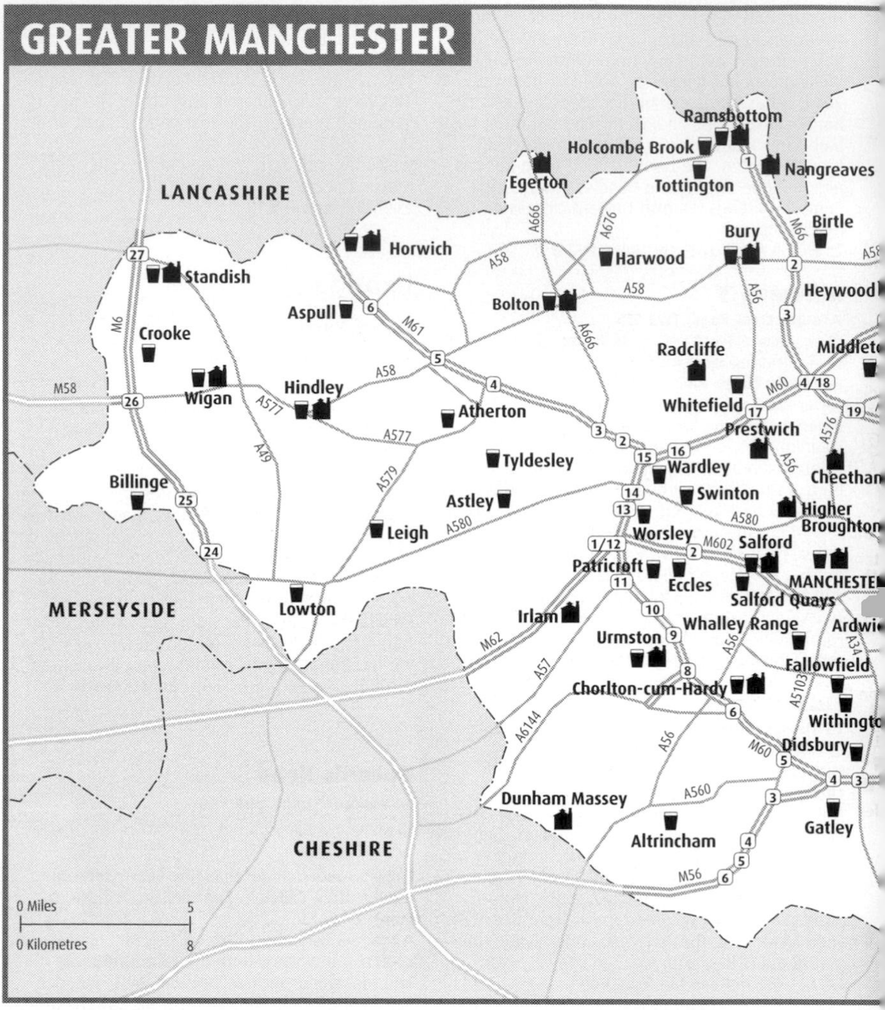

Altrincham

Costello's Bar

18 Goose Green, WA14 1DW (down pedestrian road opp jct of Stamford New Rd & Regent Rd)

12-11 (midnight Fri & Sat); 12-10.30 Sun

(0161) 929 0903 costellosbar.co.uk

7 changing beers (sourced locally)

Costello's is Dunham Massey Brewing Company's brewery tap, situated in Altrincham's attractive Goose Green behind the new hospital. The small bar has a modern feel and is popular with locals and visitors alike. The brewery has more than 25 different recipes and showcases them all in the bar over time on seven handpumps. A perry and three real ciders are also available. Local CAMRA Pub of the Year 2013.

Old Market Tavern

Old Market Place, WA14 4DN (on A56)

12-midnight (11 Mon & Tue); 12-11 Sun

(0161) 927 7062 omt123.co.uk

Caledonian Deuchars IPA; George Wright Northern Lights; Phoenix Arizona; Timothy Taylor Landlord; 5 changing beers (sourced locally) H

A large black and white former coaching inn, the Old Market Tavern is renowned for both its excellent range of real ales and live music. Eleven handpumps dispense up to six regular beers plus five guests from mostly local breweries. A large whiteboard lists the available beers. Real cider is also served in addition to a range of bottled beers. There is an open acoustic session on Thursday evenings and rock bands feature on Friday and Saturday evenings. Wednesday is quiz night.

Q

Pi

18 Shaws Road, WA14 1QU

11-11 (11.30 Wed & Thu; midnight Fri & Sat); 12-11 Sun

(0161) 929 9098 abarcalledpi.com

Tatton Blonde; 2 changing beers (sourced nationally) H

A sibling to Pi (Chorlton), this intimate bar arranged over two floors opened in 2012. Four handpumps serve three real ales and a guest cider or perry alongside world beers on draught and an extensive foreign bottle collection. Guest beers are sourced from microbreweries as well as from more established breweries including RedWillow,

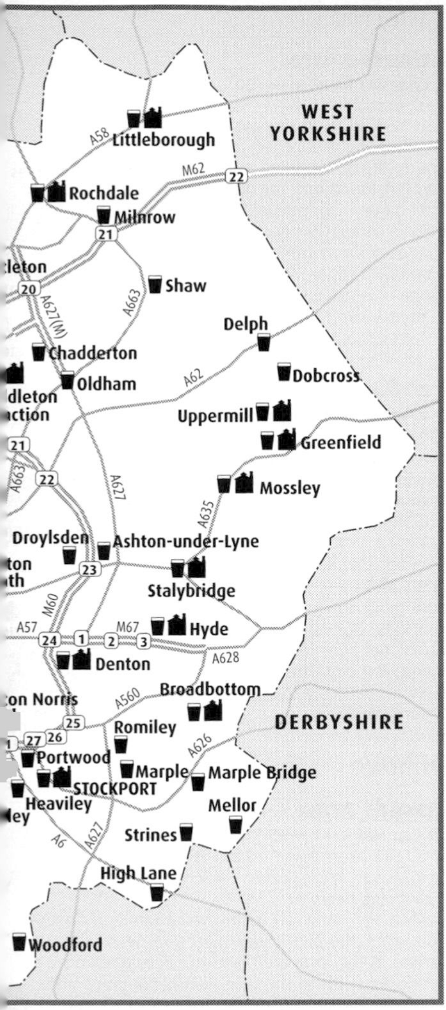

Dog & Pheasant

528 Oldham Road, OL7 9PQ

12-11 (11.30 Fri & Sat) ☎ (0161) 330 4894

Banks's Sunbeam; Jennings Dark Mild; Marston's Burton Bitter, Pedigree H; 2 changing beers H/G

Known as the Top Dog, this popular, friendly local near the Medlock Valley Country Park has been a regular Guide entry since 1992. It has a large bar serving three areas, plus another room at the front. The beer range is supplemented by two guest ales from the Marston's portfolio. A menu of good-

Saltaire and First Chop. Pieminister pies and mash are served until 11pm daily. Service is always friendly, with little touches such as complimentary peanuts, and blankets for those outside.
(Altrincham)

Ashton-under-Lyne

Ash Tree

9-11 Wellington Road, OL6 6DA

8am-midnight ☎ (0161) 339 9670

Greene King Abbot; Moorhouse's Blond Witch; Ruddles Best Bitter; changing beers (sourced nationally) H

Directly facing the Victorian Market Hall and square, this pub has become one of the premier real ale destinations in the town centre and is easily accessible by bus and train. Families are welcome in the lower level; above are the bar and lounge/dining area, leading to the rear entrance and outdoor smoking area. Wetherspoon's usual good value applies to the beers and food. Two real ale festivals are run each year. TVs have the sound turned off. P

REAL ALE BREWERIES

AllGates Wigan
Alphabet Manchester (NEW)
Bank Top Bolton
Beer Nouveau Prestwich (NEW)
Blackedge Horwich
Blackjack Manchester
Boggart Hole Clough Manchester: Newton Heath
Bootleg Chorlton-cum-Hardy
Brewsmith Ramsbottom (NEW)
Brightside Radcliffe
Chorlton Manchester (NEW)
Cloudwater Manchester (NEW)
Cryptic Stockport (NEW)
Deeply Vale Bury
Dunham Massey Dunham Massey
Dunscar Bridge Bolton
First Chop Salford
Five Oh Prestwich (NEW)
Fool Hardy Stockport: Heaton Norris
Green Mill Broadbottom
Greenfield Greenfield
Hay Rake Littleborough
Hogarths Bolton (NEW)
Holt Cheetham
Holy Well Egerton (NEW)
Hophurst Hindley (NEW)
Hornbeam Denton
Hydes Salford
Irwell Works Ramsbottom
Lees Middleton Junction
Leyden Nangreaves
Marble Manchester
Martland Mill Wigan (NEW)
Millstone Mossley
Outstanding Bury
Phoenix Heywood
Pictish Rochdale
Privateer Manchester: Ardwick
Prospect Standish
Quantum Stockport
Ramsbottom Craft Ramsbottom
Robinsons Stockport
Rtwo Dtoo Urmston
Runaway Manchester
Saddleworth Uppermill
Seven Bro7hers Salford (NEW)
Silver Street Bury
Six O'Clock Manchester
Squawk Manchester: Ardwick (NEW)
Star Inn Higher Broughton
Stockport Stockport (NEW)
Thirst Class Stockport (NEW)
Ticketybrew Stalybridge
Track Manchester (NEW)
Tweed Hyde (NEW)
Watts Brewing? Stockport (NEW)
Wilson Potter Middleton
Zymurgorium Irlam (NEW)

value food includes vegetarian options. Quiz night is Thursday. The pub is also home to a local hiking group called the Bog Trotters. ❀◐♿P🚌(409,419)

Aspull

Crown Hotel 𝕃

106 Wigan Road, New Springs, WN2 1DP

7-midnight (1am Fri); 2-1am Sat; 2-11 Sun

Prospect Gold Rush, Big John; 1 changing beer (sourced regionally) Ⓗ

Traditional free house just two miles from Wigan centre, close to Haigh Country Park. A real coal fire and woodburner add to the warm, welcoming ambience. Popular in the summer with canal users, opening hours can be variable. The licensee, Kent, offers an excellent range of local beers on up to three handpumps, and high-quality food is served. The pub is renowned for cabaret evenings on Friday and Saturday. Well worth a visit. Q❀◐♿♣P🐾

Gerrard Arms 𝕃

615 Bolton Road, WN2 1PZ

12 (4 Mon & Tue)-11; 12-midnight Fri & Sat ☎ (01942) 832346 thegerrard.com

Prospect Silver Tally; 3 changing beers Ⓗ

One-room, open-plan, cosy pub with a light and airy interior, comfortable seating and a good atmosphere. It has retained the original Boddington and Smoke Room windows. There are six handpumps, with Tetley and Prospect beers the regulars plus varying guests. Two TV screens show sport. Located on the edge of Borsdane Wood, a local nature reserve, it makes an ideal refreshment stop for walkers. Food is served lunchtimes and evenings, and all day at weekends. There is covered seating outside. Over-18s only. ❀◐♿P

Victoria 𝕃

50 Haigh Road, Haigh, WN2 1YA

4 (2 Sat & Sun)-midnight

AllGates Napoleon's Retreat; 3 changing beers Ⓗ

Traditional two-room local and AllGates Brewery's first pub in the now-popular local chain. The smart yet intimate lounge displays photographs depicting the history of Aspull and Haigh. Large screens cater for sports fans, although the TV in the lounge is rarely switched on. The pub is not far from Haigh Hall Country Park and halfway between Bolton Wanderers and Wigan Athletic football grounds. Guest beers come from AllGates and other microbreweries. There is a covered smoking area. Q♣●P🚌🐾

Astley

Old Boat House

Higher Green Lane, M29 7JB

12-midnight ☎ (01942) 883300

oldboathouseastley.co.uk

3 changing beers (sourced regionally; often Lancaster, Ruddles, Timothy Taylor) Ⓗ

On the towpath of the Bridgewater Canal, the pub is off Higher Green Lane. It was originally built with stabling for horses that pulled the barges. There is an old-fashioned taproom with pictures of the area past and present, and a spacious lounge with wood decor and big tables where you can spread the newspapers out. Good ales are served alongside excellent food. Live music features most weekends. ❀◐♣P🚌(551)🐾

Atherton

Atherton Arms

6 Tyldesley Road, M46 9DD

12-midnight ☎ (01942) 882885

Holt Mild, Bitter; 2 changing beers Ⓗ

Traditional public house with a great atmosphere and facilities, including a full-sized snooker table and function room. The pub is known for its superb beer garden, which has TV screens and heaters. The beer is competitively priced and promotions change on a monthly basis, with happy days Monday to Friday. Mid-week, the pub offers a wide range of entertainment. Fridays and Saturdays feature Steve's Karaoke and there is live entertainment on Sundays. ❀♿♣P🚌

Pendle Witch 🏆

2-4 Warburton Place, M46 0EQ

12-midnight ☎ (01942) 884537

Moorhouse's Black Cat, Premier Bitter, Pride of Pendle, Blond Witch, Pendle Witches Brew; 3 changing beers Ⓗ

A real gem hidden down a narrow alley. The entrance, part of a conservatory, leads to an open-plan bar that serves the full range of Moorhouse's beers plus up to two guests. The games area has a pool table and large-screen TV. Quiz night is Thursday, regular rock nights are hosted and occasional beer festivals are held. Food is served during the day. There is a well-kept garden for summer. Close to town-centre parking. ❀◐♿♣●P🚌

Billinge

Masons Arms

99 Carr Mill Road, WN5 7TY

2-11.30; 12-midnight Sat & Sun ☎ (01744) 603572

masonsarmsbillinge.co.uk

4 changing beers Ⓗ

Built in 1779 and run by the same family for over 200 years, the pub is well-placed for walking or cycling in the local area, and the beer garden overlooks fields to the rear. Five handpumps offer regularly changing guest beers to complement up to five changing real ciders. Folk and quiz nights are hosted mid-week. Sky Sports is screened but usually without the volume. The luxurious smoking shelter boasts a bison's head and logburner. ❀♿●P🐾

Birtle

Church Inn

Castle Hill Road, BL9 6UH (opp St John the Baptist Church)

closed Mon; 12-2.30, 5-midnight Tue & Wed; 12-midnight Thu-Sat; 12-2am Sun ☎ (0161) 764 2857

thechurchinnbirtle.co.uk

4 changing beers (sourced regionally; often Deeply Vale) Ⓗ

This is quite a large pub commanding terrific views due to its elevation. The interior is divided in two by the bar, with two rooms to the left for dining or drinking, and another room to the right for drinking leading to the restaurant. There is more than adequate seating outside. The building was formerly used as a law court – the condemned were led away for prompt punishment at the gallows in the barn still atop Gallows Hill. ❀◐♿P

Bolton

Alma Inn
152-154 Bradshawgate, BL2 1BA
12 (4 Mon)-11; 12-2am Fri & Sat; 4-11 Sun
(01204) 364113
3 changing beers (sourced nationally; often Jennings, Ringwood, Wychwood) H
Originally in the right-hand building, the pub was extended into next door, creating a split-level interior. There is one real cider on handpump and others may be available from different sources. There are some interesting decorative features – the old cast-iron range and even a tricycle hanging from one of the walls. The Alma is both a welcoming local pub and a venue for regular weekend gigs and music festivals, attracting rock and metal fans. (8,37,471)

Bank Top Brewery Tap
68-70 Belmont Road, Astley Bridge, BL1 7AN
12-11 (11.30 Fri & Sat) (01204) 302837
banktopbrewery.com
Bank Top Dark Mild, Flat Cap, Gold Digger, Old Slapper, Pavilion Pale Ale, Port o' Call; 1 changing beer (sourced nationally) H
This popular pub has eight handpumps reserved for beers from the Bank Top Brewery range, and there is always a beer from another brewery available. Up to six varying ciders are also on offer from this two-times winner of local CAMRA Cider Pub of the Year. The welcome is friendly and the service outstanding, with quiet background music, no TV, jukebox or fruit machine. There is a dartboard in the small vault and a large drinking area outside to the rear. (1,534,535)

Barristers Bar
2-4 Churchgate, BL1 1HJ (entrance is on Bradshawgate in passageway at rear of Swan Hotel)
12-1am (4am Fri & Sat) (01204) 365174
6 changing beers (sourced nationally; often Bank Top, Cross Bay, Moorhouse's) H
Barristers Bar is part of the Swan Hotel, a listed Grade II building dating from 1845. The bar's original wood-panelled interior has been retained and tastefully decorated to re-create a traditional pub atmosphere. Cask beers are usually from local breweries, supplemented by interesting guests from further afield, along with one real cider from Westons or Thatchers. There is live acoustic music most weekend evenings. A heated courtyard with tables is used as a smoking area. Disabled toilet facilities are available. (525,534,575)

Bob's Smithy
1448 Chorley Old Road, Heaton, BL1 7PX
12 (4.30 Mon & Tue)-11; 12-10.30 Sun (01204) 842622
bobs-smithy.com
Bank Top Flat Cap; Thwaites Wainwright; Timothy Taylor Boltmaker; 3 changing beers (sourced regionally; often Bowland, Hornbeam, Salamander) H
This comfortable hostelry on the edge of the moors has seating at the front to enjoy panoramic views over the south Lancashire plain. There is also a larger patio area at the rear. The pub is handy for walkers as well as visitors to the Macron Stadium two miles away. The inn is named after the blacksmith who allegedly spent more time in the pub than in his smithy across the road. Evening meals are served in the Old Forge restaurant (booking is recommended). P(125)

Bolton Ukrainian Social Club
99 Castle Street, BL2 1JP
3.30 (12 Sat & Sun)-11 (01204) 526038
3 changing beers (sourced locally; often Bank Top, Blackedge) H
Large, imposing building to the east of town with a comfortable and well-laid-out two-room bar. Two of the three handpumps dispense beers from Bank Top or Blackedge, and a guest from another local brewery features on the third one. The Bolton CAMRA annual beer festival is held here in April. The club is home to several societies including chess, brass band and bagpipes. Local CAMRA Club of the Year in 2013 and 2014.
QP(471,510,544)

Hen & Chickens
143 Deansgate, BL1 1EX
12-midnight; closed Sun (01204) 411099
Thwaites Nutty Black; 4 changing beers (sourced regionally) H
A traditional immaculately kept town-centre establishment, providing a friendly welcome to the thirsty customer. The interior, divided in two by a horseshoe-shaped bar, has recently been refurbished while retaining all its original charm and traditional features. A good cask offer is always available including the house beer, Clucking Mad, sourced from a secret brewery. A CAMRA members' discount, currently 50p a pint, is available on the three changing ales.
(501,480,534)

King's Head
52/54 Junction Road, Deane, BL3 4NA
3.30 (12 Sat & Sun)-11 (01204) 62609
Bank Top Flat Cap; Timothy Taylor Landlord H
A late-18th-century Grade II-listed building extended in the mid-19th century. Located near Deane parish church in the Deane Village conservation area, it is set back from the road with a two-tier car park, and is partially surrounded by woodland. The pub has three rooms, one with a cast-iron range and the others with low wood-beamed ceilings. QP(715)

Spinning Mule
Unit 2 Nelson Square, BL1 1JT
8am-midnight (1am Fri & Sat) (01204) 533339
Greene King Abbot; Ruddles Best Bitter; 10 changing beers (sourced nationally; often Moorhouse's) H
Opened in 1998, this large town-centre pub has an open-plan split-level interior with a separate comfortable dining area. It is named after Samuel Crompton's Mule, a revolutionary invention in cotton spinning that made Bolton famous worldwide. In 1862 a statue of Crompton was erected in the square in front of the pub. Ten ever-changing beers come from both local breweries and beyond, and one real cider is usually available from a varying source.
Q(125,526,534)

Broadbottom

Harewood Arms
2 Market Street, SK14 6AX
3-11 (midnight Fri); 2-midnight Sat; 2-11 Sun
(01457) 762500
Green Mill Gold, Stellar, Chief, Old Git; 2 changing beers H

Regional CAMRA Pub of the Year, the Harewood Arms has gone from strength to strength since it was bought by the current owners in 2013. The home of the Green Mill Brewery, it offers five regular Green Mill beers plus seasonals, guests and a rotating real cider. The bar has various seating areas and two real fires. For warmer days, there is a beer garden to the rear. The railway station is five minutes' walk and buses pass by.

Bury

Automatic Café & Malt Real Ale Bar

Derby Halls, 36 Market Street, BL9 0BW (just N of Bury Interchange)
10-11 (midnight Fri & Sat); 12-10.30 Sun
(0161) 763 9399 automaticcafe.com
4 changing beers (often Silver Street) H
This welcoming independent bar and restaurant shares the Derby Hall with two theatres. With the use of glass, the Malt Bar gives a complete view of the beer cellar and its small electric hoist and pulley system, and also provides an overspill at busy times for the dining area. Priority may be given to diners at lunchtime. In the evening it becomes a lovely, quiet, cosy space to enjoy a pint. Relaxed, safe and comfortable, this a popular choice for all. (Bolton St)

Black Bull

8-10 Lowercroft Road, Starling, BL8 2EY
12-midnight (1am Fri & Sat) (0161) 761 5961
theblackbullbury.co.uk
Thwaites Nutty Black, Original, Wainwright, Lancaster Bomber; 1 changing beer H
This family-run local offers a warm and friendly welcome to drinkers and diners alike. Winner of a number of Thwaites' brewery beer and cellar awards, it is also Cask Marque-accredited and takes great pride in serving the perfect pint. Guest beers are from the Thwaites' 1807 Cask Club range. Excellent meals are served daily, prepared using locally sourced top-quality produce. Booking is recommended as the pub's reputation creates a high demand for tables.
P(486,510)

Clarence

2 Silver Street, BL9 0EX
11-11; 12-11 Sun (0161) 464 7404 theclarence.co.uk
Silver St Brewing Co Session, One; 4 changing beers (sourced locally; often Silver St Brewing Co) H
The Clarence is an upmarket pub with four floors of brewery, real ale and real food. The building has been lovingly restored in great style, taking care to recreate the pub as it was. The basement houses the Silver Street brewery (and the loos), the ground floor has the central main bar with original floor tiles (which showed the bar's location), the restaurant is on the first floor, and the second floor contains a lounge and cocktail bar.
(Bolton Street)

Lamb Inn

533 Tottington Road, Woolfold, BL8 1UB
4.30-11; 5-midnight Fri; 1-midnight Sat; 1-10:30 Sun
(0161) 764 2714
Changing beers (often Deeply Vale, Phoenix, Ramsbottom Craft) H

Originally a coaching house dating back to 1831, this well-run local has an enviable reputation for being a friendly establishment. A warm welcome awaits all – regulars, visitors, young and old alike. The landlord is keen to promote local microbreweries, often Deeply Vale, Rammy Craft, Moorhouse's and Outstanding, and others on a less regular basis. Breweries from further afield also feature. A local real cider from Red Bank is available all year. P(468,469)

Robert Peel

10 Market Place, BL9 0LD
8am-midnight (1am Fri & Sat) (0161) 764 7287
Greene King Abbot; Ruddles Best Bitter; changing beers (often Brightside) H
Situated in Bury's cultural quarter, the Robert Peel is well-established, popular and has the largest open public area in Bury, with a mixture of tables and booths. This Wetherspoon pub bears the name of the local mill owner and MP whose son became Prime Minister and founded the modern police force. The decor also celebrates other local worthies including Richmal Crompton, the author of the Just William books. Ciders are from Gwynt y Ddraig, Westons and Thatchers.
(Bolton St)

Trackside Bar

Bolton Street Station, BL9 0EY (platform 2 on East Lancs Railway)
12-midnight Mon & Tue; 9am-12.30am (midnight Wed & Thu) (0161) 764 6461 eastlancsrailway.org.uk
Outstanding Piston Broke; changing beers H
A small buffet bar renowned for its range of nine ever-changing real ales and a house beer, Piston Broke, from Bury's Outstanding Brewery. The bar also stocks a selection of continental beers and malt whiskies together with between four and 10 real ciders/perries. There is a folk evening on the last Thursday of the month. A great venue for a drink while reliving the days of steam. Ample adjacent car parking is Pay & Display.
(Bolton St)P

Castleton

Blue Pits Inn

842 Manchester Road, OL11 2SP
12-midnight (01706) 632151
Lees Manchester Pale Ale, Bitter; 1 changing beer (sourced locally; often Lees) H
The Blue Pits is a welcoming, friendly local in a former railway building that was once used as a mortuary. The building was fully refurbished by Lees in 2013 and as a result the three distinct drinking areas now offer a much warmer environment. Cards and darts are played in the taproom, and sports fixtures are shown on screen. A regular quiz night is hosted and karaoke on Fridays. Of particular interest is the tiled mosaic of John Willie on the outside wall.
P

Chadderton

Rose of Lancaster

7 Haigh Lane, OL1 2TQ
11.30-11 (11.30 Fri & Sat); 12-11 Sun (0161) 624 3031
roseoflancaster.co.uk
Lees Brewer's Dark, Manchester Pale Ale, Bitter; 1 changing beer (sourced locally; often Lees) H

Attractively located adjacent to the Rochdale Canal and close to railway and bus links, the Rose is popular for its conservatory restaurant and its thriving separate vault for live sporting events. Additionally, the busy, convivial lounge attracts both drinkers and diners while friendly management and staff ensure a warm welcome to its varied clientele. The covered outside patio is a popular summer attraction. Look out for the chalkboard detailing the number of pints of real ale sold. ❀◐♿⇌(Mills Hill)♣P🚌(59,64)📶

Chorlton-cum-Hardy

Bar 🄻

533 Wilbraham Road, M21 0UE (opp Morrisons supermarket)

🕐 12-11.30 (midnight Thu; 12.30am Fri); 11.30-12.30am Sat; 11.30-11.30 Sun ☎ (0161) 861 7576 🌐 barchorlton.co.uk

Castle Rock Harvest Pale; Marble Ginger 5.1; 5 changing beers (sourced regionally) 🄷

The first of Chorlton's modern café bars and still going strong over 15 years later. Seven handpumps are split over two sections of the bar – in addition to the two regular beers there are up to five guests, with a focus on local breweries. Cider is available on handpump and box in the fridge. Hearty snacks including one-pots, hot dogs, soups and pies are served during the week and traditional roasts on Sundays. Quiz night is Monday. ❀◐♣🍎🚌🐾📶

Beech Inn

72 Beech Road, M21 9EG

🕐 4-11; 12-midnight Fri & Sat; 12-11 Sun ☎ (0161) 312 0309

Black Sheep Best Bitter; Copper Dragon Golden Pippin; Timothy Taylor Golden Best, Landlord; 5 changing beers (sourced nationally) 🄷

The Beech is one of Chorlton's few remaining traditional pubs. Recent changes have smartened up the pub and garden, which now houses the Hungry Gecko caravan from which a MasterChef finalist serves excellent Asian street food (largely Thai). Alternatively there are some bar snacks or the staff are happy for you to bring in your own food from one of the local takeaways. Live music features on Mondays and Wednesdays and traditional games such as bridge are played. Q❀◐♣🚌🐾📶

Dulcimer 🄻

567 Wilbraham Road, M21 0AE

🕐 4-12.30am (1.30am Fri); 12-1.30am Sat; 12-11.30 Sun ☎ (0161) 860 6444 🌐 dulcimer-bar.co.uk

Thwaites Wainwright; 4 changing beers (sourced nationally) 🄷

Popular bar/music venue in the centre of Chorlton with five cask ales and guests from local breweries including First Chop as well as from breweries further afield. The main bar has five handpumps and a rotating selection of three ciders and perries. The first-floor bar has live music events and may have one additional ale on at weekends. Food includes chilli, toasties, platters and pork pies. Quiz night is Monday. There is a small beer garden/smoking area to the rear. ❀♿🍎🚌📶

Font 🄻

115-117 Manchester Road, M21 9PG

🕐 11-12.30am (1am Fri & Sat) ☎ (0161) 871 2022 🌐 thefontbar.wordpress.com

8 changing beers (sourced nationally; often Mallinson's, RedWillow) 🄷

Vibrant bar in the Font family with eight cask ales and four ciders. Featuring breweries such as RedWillow, Magic Rock, Tickety Brew, Sunbeam and more, plus a wide range of bottles, there is plenty of choice. All draught beer is available in thirds, halves, two-thirds and pints. A small open kitchen serves excellent food including vegan and vegetarian-friendly options until 10pm daily. DJs provide the musical background on Fridays and Saturdays. Regular Meet the Brewer events are hosted. ❀◐🍎🚌🐾📶

Marble Beer House 🄻

57 Manchester Road, M21 9PW (just N of library)

🕐 12-11 (midnight Thu-Sat) ☎ (0161) 881 9206 🌐 marblebeers.com/beerhouse

Marble Pint, Manchester Bitter, Ginger 5.1; 2 changing beers (sourced nationally) 🄷

The opening of Marble Beer House heralded the start of a real ale revolution in Chorlton and its magic continues. Low key with simple lines, it is always welcoming – even down to the resident cat. The ales are a fine mix of light, dark, strong, pale and familiar and always on top form. Speciality snacks are available to complement the beers – of particular note are the Manchester Scotch Eggs, hand-made at the Marble Arch, served with home-made pickles and chutney. Q❀♣🍎🚌🐾

Parlour

60 Beech Road, M21 9EG

🕐 12-11.30 (1am Fri & Sat); 12-11 Sun ☎ (0161) 881 3871 🌐 theparlour.info

5 changing beers (sourced locally) 🄷

Laid back, café-style bar on the popular Beech Road strip, noted for its award-winning food and drink. There are five ales on pumps, one usually from RedWillow and the rest a changing range mostly from local breweries. At least one real cider and/or perry is always available. The Sunday roasts are popular so get there early! ❀◐🍎🚌🐾📶

Pi 🄻

99 Manchester Road, M21 9GA (opp Unicorn organic supermarket)

🕐 11-11 (12.30am Fri); 12-12.30am Sat; 12-11 Sun ☎ (0161) 882 0000 🌐 abarcalledpi.com

Tatton Blonde; 3 changing beers (sourced regionally) 🄷

Popular café bar to the north of Chorlton's main drag. Five handpumps serve four real ales and a guest cider or perry alongside a selection of 10 world beers on draught – no mainstream brands here. An impressive menu of 80 international bottled beers is also offered. Gourmet Pieminister pies with trimmings are served until 11pm daily. The service is always friendly – it is the little touches like complimentary peanuts and blankets for those sitting outside that make Pi stand out from the crowd. ❀◐🍎🚌🐾📶

Sedge Lynn 🄻

21A Manchester Road, M21 9PN (next to library)

🕐 8am-11 (midnight Fri & Sat) ☎ (0161) 860 0141

Greene King Abbot; Moorhouse's Blond Witch; Phoenix Wobbly Bob; Ruddles Best Bitter; 6 changing beers (sourced nationally) 🄷

Built by Norman Evans as a billiard hall for the temperance movement, this Grade II-listed building, with a barrelled roof and Art Deco styling, is well-worth a look. The managers aim to ensure there is a range of light to darker beers always available on the 10 handpumps, and ales from

Hawkshead, Brightside and Phoenix are well-represented among the guests. Winner of Wetherspoon's North-West regional Best Ale Pub 2015. Q ► ✿ ◑ ⓛ ⑆ ♿ ➡ 🖥 🌐

Crooke

Crooke Hall Inn ⓛ

Crooke Road, WN6 8LR
✪ 12-midnight ☎ (01942) 204451
AllGates California; 4 changing beers (sourced nationally) Ⓗ
This multi-roomed pub features beers from AllGates Brewery and a range of guests. The garden and children's play area at the rear overlook the Leeds-Liverpool Canal. Good food including an excellent vegetarian selection is served noon-8pm seven days a week, and children are welcome until 9pm. The Cellar Bar is available for functions and meetings. A ukulele club meets Wednesdays, folk night is Thursday. The pub also serves as a small village shop. Winner of local CAMRA Pub of the Year and Community Pub of the Year. ► ✿ ◑ P ♥ 🌐

Delph

Royal Oak (Th' Heights) ⓛ

Broad Lane, OL3 5TX (via Thame Lane, off main Delph-Denshaw road)
✪ closed Mon; 7 (5 Thu & Fri)-11; 12-7.30 Sun
☎ (01457) 874460
House beer (by Moorhouse's); 3 changing beers (sourced nationally; often Millstone) Ⓗ
Isolated 250-year-old stone-built pub on a packhorse route overlooking the Tame Valley. In a popular walking area, it benefits from outstanding views. The pub comprises a cosy bar and three rooms, each with an open fire. The refurbished side room boasts a hand-carved stone fireplace, while the comfortable snug has exposed beams and old photos of the inn. The house beer is from Moorhouse's and three changing guests include one from Millstone. A regular in the Guide for 24 consecutive years. Q ✿ P ♥ 🌐

Denton

Lowes Arms

301 Hyde Road, M34 3FF
✪ 12-11 ☎ (0161) 336 3064
4 changing beers (sourced locally; often Conwy) Ⓗ
Built in 1824 to serve the new Manchester Road, this thriving local has a reputation for quality beers and good-value food. Unusual for the area, the regular beers are from Conwy, alongside three varying ales, mainly from local micros. The comfortable lounge area to the left is the main food area. To the right is the vault, with a wooden floor and a pool table. The pub is home to local darts, dominoes and pool teams. ► ✿ ◑ ⓛ ♣ P 🖥 (201) ♥

Didsbury

Fletcher Moss

1 William Street, M20 6RQ (off Wilmslow Rd, A5145 via Albert Hill St)
✪ 12-11 (11.30 Thu; midnight Fri & Sat) ☎ (0161) 438 0073
Hydes Original Bitter, Hydes Finest; 4 changing beers (sourced nationally; often Hydes) Ⓗ

Named after the alderman who donated the nearby botanical gardens, this thriving community local attracts people of all ages and drinking tastes, all engaged in lively conversation. The front encompasses three traditional snugs, full of Hydes memorabilia and an extensive collection of porcelain teapots, while the rear opens up into a bright conservatory. Beyond that is a neat garden. A quiz features every Tuesday and acoustic music on alternate Mondays. Board games are available. The cider is Gwynt y Ddraig.
Q ✿ ◑ ⓛ ⑆ ♿ (Village) ● 🖥 (42,142) 🌐

Gateway

882 Wilmslow Road, M20 5PG (jct Kingsway)
✪ 8am-11.30 (midnight Fri & Sat); 9am-11.30 Sun
☎ (0161) 438 1700
Greene King Abbot; Ruddles Best Bitter; house beer (by Brightside); 5 changing beers Ⓗ
This large late-1930s roadhouse was acquired by Wetherspoon in 2011. The company has done an excellent job in improving the comfortable interior, with various areas surrounding an island bar. An enthusiastic manager and knowledgeable staff ensure both good beer and efficient service. A guest brewery is showcased each month, often a local brewery. The house beer comes from Brightside of Bury. Handily located for the nearby Parrs Wood Entertainment Centre and the public transport terminus.
Q ► ✿ ◑ ⇌ (East) ⓠ (East) ● P 🖥 (42,50) 🌐

Milson Rhodes

School Lane, M20 6RD (off Wilmslow Rd, A5145)
✪ 8am-11.30 (12.30am Fri & Sat) ☎ (0161) 446 4100
Greene King Abbot; Ruddles Best Bitter; 7 changing beers Ⓗ
Friendly Wetherspoon pub near Didsbury metro station, named after Dr Milson Rhodes who treated local people suffering from learning difficulties and epilepsy. The pub has a main bar downstairs and a slightly smaller upstairs room. There is more space outside in a drinking area at the front and on the balconies. Two regular beers plus seven guests and a different locally brewed house beer every six months are offered. Look for the regular beer and cider festivals. The pub can be busy with all age groups. Q ✿ ◑ ⓛ ⑆ ♿ (Village) ● P 🖥 (42,142) 🌐

Dobcross

Navigation Inn ⓛ

21-23 Wool Road, OL3 5NS
✪ 12-3, 5-11; 12-3.30, 5-midnight Fri; 12-11 Sat; 12-10.30 Sun ☎ (01457) 872418
Millstone Tiger Rut; 4 changing beers Ⓗ
A busy family-run watering hole for Huddersfield canal boaters and walkers, this stone-built pub of 1806 slaked the thirst of navvies cutting the Standedge Tunnel. It comprises an open-plan bar and L-shaped interior, with four handpumps offering ever-changing guest beers. The freshly prepared food is popular, with special offers Monday-Saturday and occasional themed evenings. Food events raise funds for local charities. It is a venue for the popular Saddleworth Rushcart Festival in August. Dog-friendly, and families are welcome at all times.
Q ► ✿ ◑ ⑆ P 🖥 (184,350) ♥ 🌐

Swan Inn (Top House)

The Square, OL3 5AA

12-2.30, 5-11 (midnight Fri); 12-11 Sat; 12-10.30 Sun
(01457) 873451 theswandobcross.com
Banks's Sunbeam; Jennings Cumberland Ale; Marston's Pedigree; 2 changing beers H
A focal point for the local community, this rejuvenated stone pub overlooks the attractive village square. Built in 1765, the building has been tastefully renovated with three separate rooms, each with an open fire. A home-cooked menu features dishes from around the world. The function room hosts entertainment including theatre, comedy and music. Annual events such as the Whit Friday Brass Band Contest, Rushcart Festival and Yanks Weekend are popular. Voted Marston's National Pub of the Year in 2013.
Q (184,353,354)

Droylsden

Beehive
145 Market Street, M43 7AR
12-11 (midnight Fri & Sat) (0161) 292 2302
1 changing beer (sourced locally) H
This lively two-room suburban community pub is close to the town centre and Droylsden FC. It has a small traditionally furnished public bar and a larger lounge on two levels. One handpull dispenses alternating beers from local micros including Hornbeam and Boggart Hole Clough. The lounge has brass ornaments, a quiz machine and free jukebox. There is a weekly Monday afternoon club with a singer and bingo, and quiz night is the first Monday of the month.

Eccles

Lamb Hotel ★
33 Regent Street, M30 0BP (opp Metrolink station)
11.30-11 (11.30 Sat); 12-11 Sun 07702 400292
Holt Mild, Bitter; 1 changing beer (sourced nationally; often Fuller's, Greene King, Thwaites) H
This Edwardian building is Grade II-listed and has been identified by CAMRA as having a nationally important historic pub interior, featuring carved wood, etched glass and ornate tiling. There is a large lobby surrounded by two smartly upholstered lounges, an L-shaped traditional vault and a billiards room with a full-size table. Friday and Sunday are karaoke nights and quiz night is Wednesday. The changing guest beer is from Holt's reciprocal agreement. P

Fallowfield

Friendship
353 Wilmslow Road, M14 6XS (on B5093, jct Egerton Rd)
12-11 (12.30am Fri & Sat) (0161) 224 5758
Hydes Light Mild/1863, Original Bitter, Hydes Finest; 8 changing beers (sourced nationally; often Hydes) H
Impressive Victorian mansion in a busy student area. Although it mainly caters for a younger crowd, it does attract a good mix of folk, especially when live sport is shown on the many TV screens. A large horseshoe bar serves a snug, lounge and the large rear extension – this latter area has created more space for the provision of popular pizzas and Italian food. Nine handpumps offer the Hydes range, as well as varying guest ales. The cider is Gwynt y Ddraig. A quiz is held weekly.
P (42,43)

Gatley

Horse & Farrier
144 Gatley Road, SK8 4AB (jct Church Rd)
11-11 (midnight Fri & Sat); 12-10.30 Sun
(0161) 428 2080
Hydes Light Mild/1863, Original Bitter, Hydes Finest; 5 changing beers (sourced nationally; often Hydes) H
Formed from three cottages, this former coaching inn is a Tudor-style, low-ceilinged, Hydes heritage house with a central bar that serves several rooms. Refurbished in early 2015, a new dining room with an orangery look and a beer garden to the front of the pub were added. The beer range has been extended to include four Hydes/Beer Studio beers plus four guests, and quarterly beer festivals are held. Live bands play at weekends. The cider is Gwynt y Ddraig. Q P (11,11A,44)

Greenfield

King William IV L
134 Chew Valley Road, OL3 7DD
12-midnight (01457) 873933
Black Sheep Best Bitter; Sharp's Doom Bar; Tetley Bitter; 3 changing beers (sourced locally; often Greenfield, Millstone) H
Stone pub comprising a central bar and two rooms, one with a wood-burning stove. A benched, cobbled forecourt out front is used for outdoor drinking and smoking. Six handpumps serve three LocAles including Greenfield and Millstone. Home-cooked food is served Thursday to Sunday until 8pm. The King Bill is the centre of village life, featuring in the annual August Rushcart Festival and Whit Friday brass band contest. It can get busy when live football is shown. Children and dogs are welcome. P (180,350)

Railway Inn L
11 Shaw Hall Bank Road, OL3 7JZ (opp station)
12-midnight (12.30am Thu & Fri); 11.30-12.30am Sat
(01457) 872307
Copper Dragon Golden Pippin; Millstone Tiger Rut; Theakston Old Peculier; Wells Bombardier; 2 changing beers H
Unspoilt pub comprising a central bar, lounge, games area and taproom with a log fire and old photos of Saddleworth. The Railway is a popular venue for all styles of live music on Thursday, Friday (unplugged night) and Sunday. It is also a stop-off on the Transpennine Real Ale Trail. In a picturesque area, the pub affords beautiful views across Chew Valley and is a great base for outdoor pursuits. Various ciders are served on gravity.
P (180,184,350)

Wellington Inn L
29 Chew Valley Road, OL3 7AF
3-9 Mon; 12 (3 Tue)-11; 12-9 Sun None
Greenfield Silver Owl; Nook Blond; Phoenix Arizona; Thwaites Nutty Black, Original, Wainwright; 1 changing beer H
Friendly village local on the end of a terrace, which became a privately owned free house in 2011. It has a small bar area, an open-plan room catering for diners and a separate sports room with Sky TV, cribbage and a dartboard. Good-value home-made food features pies, puddings and real chips, served on Tuesday and Wednesday evenings and all day Thursday to Sunday, with fish specials on Friday. A guest beer is sometimes available and real cider in summer. (180,350,353)

Harwood

House Without a Name Ⓛ

75 Lea Gate, BL2 3ET
⏲ 12-midnight (1am Fri & Sat) ☎ (01204) 433568
🌐 housewithoutaname.co.uk
Courage Best Bitter; Holt Bitter; St Austell Tribute; 3 changing beers (sourced regionally; often Lancaster, Moorhouse's, Outstanding) Ⓗ
Locally known as the No Name, this pub is a cosy terraced venue made from two cottages. It has been recently refurbished and sensitively modernised, with flagstone floors retained in some areas. On the left as you enter is a small bar, straight ahead is the lounge which now has a real fire. A blackboard lists the real ales on offer. Bands often play on Sunday evenings when the venue can be busy. ❀◑♣🚌(480,507)🐾📶

High Lane

Royal Oak

Buxton Road, SK6 8AY
⏲ 12-midnight ☎ (01663) 766827
Marston's Burton Bitter, Pedigree; 4 changing beers Ⓗ
This traditional inn is situated on the main A6 as it ascends from Stockport towards the Peak District and Lyme Park. It offers four guest beers from the Marston's portfolio in addition to the two regular Marston's beers. Food is served lunchtimes and evenings in the week and 12-6pm at weekends. Families are welcome and a dog-friendly room is available. The pub is home to crib, darts and pool league teams.
Q❀◑⇌(Middlewood)♣P🚌(199,394)🐾

Hindley

Hare & Hounds Ⓛ

31 Ladies Lane, WN2 2QA
⏲ 4 (2 Fri)-midnight; 12-midnight Sat & Sun
☎ (01942) 702227
AllGates Napoleon's Retreat, Pretoria; 3 changing beers Ⓗ
This small but traditional pub located between the railway station and town centre has a large cosy lounge and a distinct bar/vault area. The lounge displays pictures from bygone Hindley and has a large-screen TV for sport. This is an AllGates pub serving its own beers and a range of guests. Darts is popular here and both men's and women's teams play in the local league. Quiz night is Thursday. Q❀⇌♣🚌(559)📶

Holcombe Brook

Hare & Hounds Ⓛ

400 Bolton Road West, BL0 9RY (on A676 at jct with Longsight Rd)
⏲ 12-11 (midnight Thu-Sat) ☎ (01706) 822107
🌐 hare-and-hounds-bury.co.uk
10 changing beers Ⓗ
There has been an inn on this site for over 100 years and the multi award-winning venue has recently had a major refurbishment. Beer festivals are held throughout the year – the landlord sources ales from around the country, especially from new breweries. The pub has its own quiz team. Excellent food is served until 9pm. Local CAMRA Pub of the Year 2015. ❀◑♿♣P🚌(472,474)🐾📶

Horwich

Bank Top Brewery Ale House Ⓛ

36 Church Street, BL6 6AD
⏲ 12-11 (11.30 Fri & Sat) ☎ (01204) 693793
🌐 banktopbrewery.com
Bank Top Bad to the Bone, Dark Mild, Flat Cap, Gold Digger, Old Slapper, Port o' Call; 1 changing beer (sourced regionally) Ⓗ
This is Bank Top Brewery's second tied pub and is situated opposite Horwich parish church with excellent views of Rivington Pike. Formerly the Brown Cow, it has been refurbished to a high standard. A welcome addition to the Horwich real ale scene, it offers eight competitively priced beers from the Bank Top range plus one ever-changing guest. There are six varying real ciders or perries too. A good starting point for a pub crawl of Horwich. ❀🍎🚌(125)🐾

Crown Ⓛ

1 Chorley New Road, BL6 7QJ (on B6226)
⏲ 11-11 (midnight Fri & Sat); 12-11.30 Sun
☎ (01204) 693109
Holt Mild, IPA, Bitter, Two Hoots; 2 changing beers (sourced locally; often Bootleg) Ⓗ
A grand local landmark near Lever Park and the West Pennine Moors. A spacious pub with high ceilings and many original features, it has a separate pool and games room with its own bar where darts, dominoes and pool teams play. All sports are screened in the games room and other side rooms. Various artists provide entertainment on Sunday evenings. An ideal spot for a refreshing pint after a walk to Rivington Pike or around the nearby reservoirs. Q❀♿♣P🚌(125,575)📶

Old Original Bay Horse Ⓛ

206 Lee Lane, BL6 7JF
⏲ 2 (12 Sat & Sun)-midnight ☎ 07961 266095
Moorhouse's Pride of Pendle, Blond Witch; Ossett Silver King; Thwaites Wainwright; Wychwood Hobgoblin Ⓗ
A striking white-painted stone building dating back to the 19th century, known locally as the Long Pull. Originally a coach house, it has recently been tastefully refurbished and has retained the separate vault. There is live music on Friday and Saturday evenings. Sport features prominently on massive TV screens. Outside at the rear there is a sheltered patio area to enjoy on sunny days, with space for smokers. Handily placed for Lever Park and walks up to Rivington Pike.
❀♣P🚌(125,575)🐾📶

Victoria & Albert 🏆 Ⓛ

114 Lee Lane, BL6 7AF
⏲ 4-11 (midnight Fri); 2-midnight Sat; 2-11 Sun
☎ (01204) 770837 🌐 vicandalbert.co.uk
Holt Bitter; 6 changing beers (sourced nationally; often Blackedge, Marble, Moorhouse's) Ⓗ
Formerly the Albert Arms, the pub is situated across the road from Horwich Public Hall. Modernised in 2011 to a very standard, it is a comfortable lounge-style venue with three separate seating areas. There are six ever-changing beers in addition to the regulars – Abbeydale and Elland breweries often feature. The pub is handy for Lever Park and walks up to Rivington Pike. Over-21s only. Local CAMRA Pub of the Year 2013 and 2015. Q❀🍎🚌(125)

ENGLAND

Hyde

Cheshire Ring Hotel 𝕃

72-74 Manchester Road, SK14 2BJ

⌚ 4 (12 Sat)-11; 12-10.30 Sun ☎ 07917 055629

Beartown Kodiak Gold, Bearskinful, Polar Eclipse; 3 changing beers (often Beartown) Ⓗ

One of the oldest pubs in Hyde, the building was comprehensively overhauled several years ago by Beartown. Seven handpumps offer a range of Beartown ales and guests from micros, in addition to ciders, perries and continental beers. A selection of bottled beers is also stocked. Gentle background music plays. Home-made curries are available on Thursday evenings. Opening hours vary with the season – closing time may be earlier on Mondays and Tuesdays. 🛋❀⇌(Central)●P🚌(201)🐾

Godley Hall

Godley Hill, SK14 3BL

⌚ 4 (12 Fri-Sun)-midnight ☎ (0161) 368 4415

Sharp's Doom Bar; 1 changing beer Ⓗ

A converted farmhouse built in 1718 and used as an inn since 1830, this comfortable pub retains many original features. It is not easy to find but well-worth the effort and a warm and friendly welcome is assured. One or two guest beers are available, changing weekly and often from the Hornbeam range. There is wheelchair access through the main door but not to the toilets as the Grade II-listed building cannot be altered. Q❀◐◑⇌(Godley)P🚌(201,202)

Joshua Bradley

Stockport Road, SK14 5EZ

⌚ 11-11 (midnight Fri & Sat); 11-10.30 Sun

☎ (0161) 406 6776 🌐 thejoshuabradley.co.uk

Hydes Original Bitter; 3 changing beers (often Hydes) Ⓗ

Bar/restaurant, formerly a large house set in its own grounds, and named after a previous mayor of Hyde. While this is primarily a venue for dining and functions, the drinker is not forgotten. Beers from the Hydes range vary but should include at least one of the Hydes Studio ales in addition to two guests. There are regular live music events and a Monday quiz night. Booking for the restaurant is highly recommended. 🛋❀🛏◐◑♿P🚌📶

Sportsman Inn 𝕃

57 Mottram Road, SK14 2NN (exit of Morrisons car park)

⌚ 12-midnight ☎ (0161) 368 5000

Rossendale Floral Dance, Glen Top Bitter, Rossendale Ale, Halo Pale, Pitch Porter, Sunshine Ⓗ

This pub features regularly in the Guide, offering a full range of Rossendale Brewery ales plus a mild from Thwaites and real cider on a changing basis. Upstairs is a restaurant specialising in Cuban food and tapas. The pub is home to football, darts and pool teams and hosts matches for the local chess team. The rear patio includes a covered and heated smoking area. A former CAMRA pub of the region, it is popular with locals and retains its character. 🛋❀◐◑⇌(Newton for Hyde)♣●P🚌(201,202) 🐾📶

Leigh

George & Dragon

7 King Street, WN7 4LP

⌚ 11-11 (midnight Fri & Sat); 12-11 Sun ☎ (01942) 605214

2 changing beers Ⓗ

A pub with a Tudor façade in the centre of Leigh near the bus station serving a changing range of guest beers. Many TV screens show live Rugby League and football matches. There is a large outdoor seating area to the rear. No children are allowed and no food is served. ❀♿P🚌📶

Thomas Burke 𝕃

Leigh Road, WN7 1QR

⌚ 12-midnight ☎ (01942) 609144

Greene King Abbot; changing beers Ⓗ

Popular with all ages, this Wetherspoon pub is named after a renowned Leigh tenor, known as the Lancashire Caruso. The pub divides into three areas: the main long bar, a raised dining area and, in what was once a cinema foyer, lounge-style seating. Ten handpumps offer a changing range of beers from local and distant breweries. Q🛋❀◐◑♿🚌📶

White Lion 𝕃

6A Leigh Road, WN7 1QL

⌚ 12-midnight ☎ 07814 575883

AllGates California; 5 changing beers (often AllGates) Ⓗ

Fully refurbished and reopened in 2011, the White Lion is situated opposite the historic parish church just a few minutes' walk from Leigh's centre. A friendly town-centre pub, you can choose whether to enjoy the comfort of the main bar, bar games in the vault, or the quiet of the snug. Six handpumps dispense a selection of AllGates real ales plus guests, and draught Gwynt y Ddraig cider. Q❀♿♣●🚌(12,582)🐾📶

Littleborough

Red Lion 𝕃

6 Halifax Road, OL15 0HB

⌚ 2-midnight; 12.30-1am Fri & Sat; 1-midnight Sun

☎ (01706) 378195

Lees Bitter; Timothy Taylor Landlord; house beer (by Phoenix); changing beers (often Robinsons) Ⓗ

Detached stone-built pub, nestling between the railway and canal (yet older than both). Four distinct rooms, each different in character, include two for games and TV sport. The main room is large and homely, while the adjacent snug has comfortable high-backed chairs. Up to six guest beers supplement the two regulars, with a house beer from Phoenix. German and Belgian beers and lagers are available on draught, and traditional ciders from Thatchers and Westons. A jam session features on Wednesday and quiz night is Thursday. Q⇌♣●P🚌(528,590)🐾📶

White House 𝕃

Blackstone Edge, Halifax Road, OL15 0LG

⌚ 12-3, 6.30-midnight; 12.30-10.30 Sun ☎ (01706) 378456

🌐 thewhitehousepub.co.uk

Black Sheep Best Bitter; Theakston Best Bitter; 2 changing beers Ⓗ

Originally built in 1691 and named the Coach & Horses, the White House stands on the Pennine Way. At over 1,300ft it commands outstanding views over the local countryside. A family-run inn for 30 years, it offers a warm and friendly welcome to all, with two bars, both warmed by log fires. Four handpumps serve two regular and two guest beers, and a wide range of bottled beers, cider and wine is also stocked. An excellent food menu is available, served all day on Sunday. Q❀◐◑⛺P🚌(528)🐾📶

Lowton

Travellers Rest

443 Newton Road, WA3 1NZ
☼ 12-10.30 (midnight Fri & Sat) ☎ (01942) 293222
⊕ travellersrestlowton.com
Theakston Best Bitter; Thwaites Wainwright; 2 changing beers ⊞
Traditionally furnished pub/restaurant between Lowton and Newton-le-Willows with a cosy and relaxed atmosphere. The Travellers Rest has a number of seating areas and a separate dining room. There is a bar area to the right for drinkers, serving ales from Thwaites and Theakston. Outside is a large garden and car park.
Q✿❀◑♿P☲(34)♣

Manchester: City Centre

Angel

6 Angel Street, Collyhurst, M4 4BQ (off Rochdale Rd)
☼ 12-midnight (9 Sun) ☎ (0161) 833 4786
⊕ theangelmanchester.com
Bob's White Lion; 10 changing beers (sourced regionally; often Hawkshead, Liverpool Organic, Pictish) ⊞
A popular member of the Manchester real ale scene, serving a wide range of regional ales of all styles from 10 handpumps plus two real ciders on draught. Food is available until 9pm in the bar and upstairs in the small restaurant. The L-shaped main room has bare floorboards throughout and is warmed by real fires. A grand piano enhances the ambience. The beer garden at the front is popular – weather permitting. ❀◑⇌(Victoria)☲●☲♣☂

Bar Fringe

8 Swan Street, M4 5JN (close to jct with Oldham Rd)
☼ 12-midnight (12.30am Fri & Sat) ☎ (0161) 835 3815
5 changing beers ⊞
A regular Guide entry with five handpumps dispensing a changing range of beers from all over the country. It also keeps an extensive range of continental draught and bottled beers. The staff are friendly and knowledgeable. Free chilli is served on the first Sunday of the month. Quirky decor adorns the walls and there is a small garden at the back. Winner of CAMRA branch Cider Pub of the Year in 2015, three ciders are always available.
❀⇌(Victoria)☲●☲♣☂

Cask Bar

29 Liverpool Road, M3 4NQ
☼ 12-11; 12-midnight Fri & Sat; 12-10.30 Sun
☎ (0161) 819 2527 ⊕ caskmanc.co.uk
4 changing beers (sourced nationally) ⊞
Cask specialises in imported beers, with a number available on tap and a wider selection in bottles. The four real ale pumps tend to have at least one Pictish beer, often joined by a Hornbeam or a Phoenix. Sited just off the main Deansgate route, the bar has been in business for 12 years, with a friendly attitude, and is a relaxed sanctuary away from the centre of Manchester. Patrons may bring in their own food. ❀⇌(Deansgate)☲☲♣☂

Castle Hotel

66 Oldham Street, M4 1LE (near Warwick St)
☼ 12-1am (2am Fri & Sat) ☎ (0161) 237 9485
⊕ thecastlehotel.info
Robinsons Dizzy Blonde, Unicorn, Trooper; 5 changing beers (sourced regionally; often Great Heck, Titanic) ⊞

A Robinsons pub outside Stockport – the only one in the heart of Manchester. Four guest ales complement the four Robinsons beers. Despite the name this is not a hotel, it is a friendly and lively pub and becoming increasingly popular as a live entertainment venue. It has a small front room with a bar and jukebox and two larger rooms to the rear connected by a long corridor. The decor is splendid, especially the skylight in the back room. ✿❀⇌(Victoria)☲●☲☂

Crown & Kettle ♈

2 Oldham Road, M4 5FE (corner Great Ancoats St)
☼ 12-11 (midnight Fri & Sat); 12-10.30 Sun
☎ (0161) 236 2923
Ossett Silver King; 8 changing beers (sourced locally; often Tickety Brew, Track) ⊞
This Grade II-listed free house reopened in 2005 in co-operation with English Heritage after 16 years – note the fine and unusual ceiling. The central bar serves up to eight ever-changing real ales with an emphasis on local independent brewers. There is a large drinking area in front of the bar and a small vault and snug to the rear. The vault serves a wide range of traditional ciders. Locally produced pork pies are available. ❀⇌(Victoria)☲●☲♣☂

Font

7-9 New Wakefield Street, M1 5NP (off Oxford Rd by railway viaduct)
☼ 11-1am (12.30am Sun) ☎ (0161) 236 0944
⊕ fontbar.com
4 changing beers (sourced nationally) ⊞
Not far from the busy Oxford Road corridor and popular with students and non-students alike, the Font's four handpumps dispense beers from the likes of Arbor, Magic Rock, Blackjack and Burning Sky along with ales from upcoming local breweries. British, American and Belgian bottled beers are also stocked. Freshly cooked food is served 11-9pm (until 8pm Fri and Sat). DJs entertain in the evening when the pub gets busy. CAMRA members receive a 25 per cent discount on ales and cider. Branch CAMRA Cider Pub of the Year 2012/2013, three ciders are always available.
✿◑♿⇌(Oxford Rd)☲●☲♣☂

Grey Horse Inn

80 Portland Street, M1 4QX (jct Princess St)
☼ 11-midnight (1am Fri & Sat) ☎ (0161) 236 1874
Hydes Light Mild/1863, Original Bitter; 3 changing beers (sourced nationally; often Hydes) ⊞
A friendly old single-roomed pub, probably converted from early-19th-century weavers' cottages, and named after an act in the circus that used to winter in this block. It has a light, clean interior with tartan upholstered bench seating and stools, and a dark laminate floor around a small semi-circular bar. The walls are decorated with images of Manchester in bygone times. Certainly one of the smallest pubs in the city, it can get busy on match days when space is at a premium. ⇌(Oxford Rd)☲(St Peters Square)☲(1,3)♣☂

Knott Bar ♈ Ⓛ

374 Deansgate, M3 4LY
☼ 12-11.30 (midnight Thu; 12.30am Fri & Sat)
☎ (0161) 839 9229 ⊕ knottbar.co.uk
Castle Rock Harvest Pale; Marble Ginger 5.1; 4 changing beers (sourced nationally) ⊞
Award-winning pub famous for its real ales and an extensive range of foreign beers alongside British keg. Two regular ales and four guests come from

breweries including RedWillow, Magic Rock and Pictish. Real cider is also available from a box on the back bar (ignore the handpump serving non-real cider). Excellent transport links make this an ideal start/end point for a pub crawl. Meals are served until 8pm daily, with all food cooked fresh. Interesting vegetarian and vegan options are available. (Deansgate)

Marble Arch ★

73 Rochdale Road, Collyhurst, M4 4HY (corner Gould St)
12-11.30 (12.30am Sat); 12-midnight Sun
(0161) 832 5914 marblebeers.com/marble-arch
Marble Pint, Lagonda IPA, Chocolate Marble; 7 changing beers

The original home of Marble Beers is a 10-minute walk from Manchester city centre. Marble Beers are now brewed in a nearby railway arch with several available here alongside the regulars, further supplemented by two guest beers and a cider. This listed pub displays many interesting features including an imposing entrance and impressive ceiling mosaics. Good food is served throughout the day and there is a more modern back room primarily for dining, leading to the beer garden. Q (Victoria)

Micro Bar

Unit FC16, Arndale Market, M4 3AH (located in Arndale Food Market, off High St)
11-6; 12-5 Sun (0161) 277 9666
boggart-brewery.co.uk
Boggart Hole Clough Rum Porter; 3 changing beers

Friendly little bar owned by the Boggart Hole Clough Brewery. Two Boggart beers are always available and two guests. A good range of British and foreign bottled beers is also offered, to drink on or off the premises. The bar's location close to a variety of worldwide food outlets gives it possibly the most varied menu around. It has a friendly welcome and the ambience of a good local. (Victoria)

Molly House

26 Richmond Street, M1 3NB (jct Sackville St)
12-1am (midnight Mon & Tue; 2am Fri & Sat)
(0161) 237 9329 themollyhouse.com
Beartown Ginger Bear; 5 changing beers

A comfortable yet modern pub set in the heart of Manchester's Gay Village. It fast became a destination for the more discerning/older village devotees. The welcoming ground floor has a bar and small restaurant (tapas a speciality) as well as papers and a small library. The larger upper floor holds another bar, comfy sofas and a terrace smoking area where people congregate in fine weather. The beer range makes a point of specialising in local brewers' products including Hornbeam, Red Willow and others. (Oxford Rd) (1,3)

Paramount

33-35 Oxford Street, M1 4BH (jct Portland St)
7am-midnight (1am Fri & Sat) (0161) 233 1820
Moorhouse's Blond Witch; Robinsons Trooper; Thwaites Wainwright; house beer (by Elland); 6 changing beers

This large, busy Wetherspoon pub stands out owing to its extremely positive attitude to cask ale, offering many beers from local micros. It has a more relaxed atmosphere than similar city-centre pubs, with pictures of old theatres adorning the walls and new subdued lighting adding to the ambience. Named after the cinema that stood on the site in Manchester's old theatreland, it is handy for modern entertainment venues including the Palace Theatre, Bridgewater Hall and Manchester Central.
(Oxford Rd)(St Peters Square) (1,3)

Port St Beer House

39-41 Port Street, M1 2EQ (opp Brewer St)
closed Mon; 4 (2 Fri)-midnight; 12-1am Sat; 12-midnight Sun (0161) 237 9949 portstreetbeerhouse.co.uk
7 changing beers (sourced nationally; often Dark Star, Mad Hatter, Thornbridge)

Opened in 2011, this bar has become a mecca for beer lovers from far and wide. Its knowledgeable staff serve seven real ales plus an extensive selection of draught and bottled beers from the US, Belgium, Holland and beyond. Thornbridge and Dark Star breweries usually feature. Prices for bottled beers can be expensive but you pay for quality. Regular Meet the Brewer events are held. The toilets are on the first floor, where there is additional seating. (Piccadilly)

Salisbury Ale House

2 Wakefield Street, M1 5NE
12-1am (2am Thu-Sat) (0161) 236 5590
Caledonian Deuchars IPA, Edinburgh Castle 80/-; Courage Directors; Theakston Old Peculier; 5 changing beers (sourced nationally)

With a traditional tiled exterior, the Salisbury is on a sett-paved side-shoot to Oxford Road Station. It has long been renowned as a rock pub due to its excellent jukebox. It attracts an eclectic range of customers from mid-week suits to students and rockers. The ales come from a selection of breweries with a rapid turnover. Not for those looking for a quiet pub – this place is always buzzing. (Oxford Rd)

Sandbar

120-122 Grosvenor Street, Chorlton-on-Medlock, M1 7HL (off Oxford Rd A34/B5117 jct)
12-midnight (1am Thu; 2am Fri & Sat) (0161) 273 1552
sandbarmanchester.co.uk
Phoenix Arizona; house beer (by Privateer); 4 changing beers (sourced regionally; often Beartown)

Excellent conversion of 18th-century town houses into a quirky and bohemian bar. In the heart of Manchester's student land, the bar is popular both with students and university staff. Exhibitions of photographs and paintings adorn the walls and DJs do their thing at weekends. A good range of foreign beers complements the seven handpulled cask ales and changing guest cider, often from smaller producers. Beers from First Chop and Privateer usually feature, while a pizza menu is available all day.
(Oxford Rd) (50,197)

Vine Inn

42-44 Kennedy Street, M2 4BQ
12-11; 11-midnight Fri; 11-11 Sat; 11-10 Sun
(0161) 237 9740 thevineinn.wordpress.com
6 changing beers (sourced nationally)

Rumoured to have begun life as Manchester's oldest brothel, this traditional inn has an impressive tiled and stained-glass exterior. Extended over three levels inside, it is surprisingly spacious. The walls upstairs are adorned with images of old Manchester while downstairs there are old enamelled and painted signs. Darts, dominoes and board games are available. A downstairs room with a separate bar serves meals weekday lunchtimes and is available for hire evenings and weekends. ◐♿⇌(Oxford Rd)♫♣●🚌

Waterhouse Ⓛ

67-71 Princess Street, M2 4EG

⏲ 9am-midnight ☎ (0161) 200 5380

Greene King Abbot; Phoenix Wobbly Bob; Roosters Buckeye; Thwaites Wainwright; 5 changing beers (sourced nationally) Ⓗ

Standing adjacent to the town hall, this Wetherspoon outlet is unusual for the chain in that it has a split interior with several areas for drinking and dining. The four regular beers are complemented by an ever-changing range of six guest ales often from local micros. Meet the Brewer nights feature regularly and such is the relationship between the cellar team and local breweries that the pub often stocks beers that have been produced in collaboration between the two. Q🛏❀◐◑♿⇌(Oxford Rd)♫●🚌📶

Wharf Ⓛ

6 Slate Wharf, Castlefield, M15 4ST

⏲ 11-11 (midnight Fri & Sat); 11-10.30 Sun

☎ (0161) 220 2960

Brunning & Price Original; Thwaites Wainwright; Weetwood Cheshire Cat; 9 changing beers (sourced nationally) Ⓗ

Impressive pub with a large outdoor terrace overlooking the Castlefield Basin where the Bridgewater and Rochdale canals meet, making this a popular mooring point for leisure boaters. The bar boasts 12 handpumps, nine serving guest beers including one dedicated to a stout/porter and one dispensing a real cider. Food is a major attraction with meals served in the ground-floor bar area and the restaurant upstairs. Knowledgeable staff can advise on a wide range of wines and whiskies.
Q🛏❀◐◑♿⇌(Deansgate)♫♣●P🚌🐾📶

Marple

Railway

223 Stockport Road, SK6 3EN

⏲ 12-11 (10.30 Sun) ☎ (0161) 427 2146

Robinsons Dizzy Blonde, Unicorn; 1 changing beer (often Robinsons) Ⓗ

First opened in 1878, replacing a pub called the Gun Inn, this impressive hostelry has two airy rooms and an outside verandah and drinking area. Located close to Rose Hill Station, it is handy for rail commuters, and is also handily positioned for walkers and cyclists on the nearby Middlewood Way and Goyt Valley Way. Well-run with a friendly atmosphere, this is a very pleasant place to while away some time. ❀◐♿P🚌(383,384,358)

Marple Bridge

Norfolk Arms

2 Town Street, SK6 5DS

⏲ 12-11 (10.30 Sun) ☎ (0161) 427 8090

🌐 thenorfolkarms.co.uk

4 changing beers (sourced regionally; often Green Mill, Kelham Island, Moorhouse's) Ⓗ

A recently refurbished stone-built pub that sits in an attractive urban setting next to the Goyt river bridge. Comfortably furnished, it attracts a wide clientele by catering for all tastes. The atmosphere is warm and friendly with good-value food available and four real ales, usually from microbreweries. The beer range is a good addition to the choice in the area. Live music plays on Thursdays and occasional beer festivals are held in the summer. Well-served by public transport. ❀◐◑♿⇌(Marple)🚌(375,383,384)🐾

Mellor

Oddfellows Arms

73 Moor End Road, SK6 5PT

⏲ closed Mon; 4 (12 Fri-Sun)-11 ☎ (0161) 449 7826

🌐 oddfellowsmellor.com

Marston's Pedigree; 3 changing beers (sourced regionally) Ⓗ

This elegant stone-built pub is tucked away in a dip in the road in the old part of the village. The smart but traditional interior is enhanced by beams and flagged floors, with blazing real fires in winter. Guest beers are often sourced from micros such as Marble, Howard Town and Thornbridge. Sought-after food comes from a realistic menu with a gourmet twist. The 375 bus service passes the door but runs only infrequently. ❀◐◑♿▲P🚌(375)🐾

Middleton

Ring o' Bells

St Leonards Square, M24 6DJ

⏲ 5-midnight; 12-1am Fri & Sat; 12-midnight Sun

☎ (0161) 654 9245

Lees Manchester Pale Ale, Bitter; 1 changing beer (sourced locally; often Lees) Ⓗ

Situated by Jubilee Park and opposite the historic parish church, this old pub has a strong place in the community. It hosts an annual Maypole event on the May bank holiday Monday and a unique Pace Egg play on Easter Monday. Live music and quizzes are regular events. The Lees beers are complemented by seasonal ales. An upstairs function room features old collages made from butterflies. At the rear is a covered smoking area and beer garden. ❀◐♣P🚌🐾📶

Milnrow

Waggon Inn

35 Butterworth Hall, OL16 3PE

⏲ 12 (4 Mon & Tue)-midnight; 12-11 Sun ☎ (01706) 648313

Banks's Bitter; 2 changing beers Ⓗ

A true family hostelry welcoming young and old, the Waggon dates back to 1782 and with its mullioned windows has the appearance of a real village pub. The beer range, supplied by Marston's, with outside guest beers, changes monthly. A broad variety of live musical acts features at weekends, which draws a crowd. Wednesday is jam night. A quiz is also hosted on Thursday evenings. The pub is within walking distance of the Manchester Metro tramline. 🛏◐♫♣P🚌🐾📶

Mossley

Britannia Inn

217 Manchester Road, OL5 9AJ

⏲ 2-midnight; 12-1am Fri & Sat; 12-midnight Sun

☎ (01457) 832799

Marston's Burton Bitter; 5 changing beers Ⓗ

The Britannia's appearance dates from 1870 when the two cottages that formed the original beer house (called the Musicians' Arms) were enlarged. The building stands next to the erstwhile Britannia Mills – hence the name. Inside is a snug for dining and a games room with the bar area between them. There is a covered seating area outside at the front. Meals are served until 7.30pm (5pm Sun). Quiz night, on Sunday, is popular. (343,350)

Commercial Hotel

58 Manchester Road, OL5 0AA

12-11 (midnight Fri & Sat) ☎ (01457) 510518

Millstone Tiger Rut, Stout; 3 changing beers

The Commercial opened in 1831 and was enlarged around 1859. It was the first pub in bottom Mossley and initially catered for coach travellers and later for those arriving by rail. The Commi is a boisterous pub with bar areas, a pool room and a low stage. There is a pavement patio outside. Expect a live act or disco on Saturdays, an electronic interactive inter-pub quiz on Tuesdays and poker on Thursdays. Children are welcome until 8pm. (343,350)

Fleece

53 Stamford Street, OL5 0LN

12-midnight (1am Fri & Sat) ☎ (01457) 835487

Irwell Works Tin Plate, Copper Plate, Iron Plate; Thwaites Original (contract brewed); 4 changing beers

There has been a pub on this site since 1808, but it was not called the Fleece until 1819. In the 1870s one of the pub's more eccentric landlords used to organise lark singing contests. In the 20th century it became part of the Openshaw Brewery's estate, passing in succession, between 1957 and 1967, to Hope & Anchor (Sheffield), Northern Breweries and finally Bass Charrington. Today it is a free house. A cider or perry is always available. P (343,350)

Oldham

Ashton Arms

28-30 Clegg Street, OL1 1PL (rear of Town Square shopping centre)

11.30-11 (11.30 Fri & Sat); 11.30-8.30 Sun

☎ (0161) 630 9709

Changing beers

Extremely popular town-centre free house overlooking the new cinema complex, serving an excellent range of four to seven rotating beers from both new and long-established breweries. It specialises in local micros and LocAles with themed beer festivals throughout the year. Traditional cider/perry is available all year round and a good selection of Belgian and German bottled beers is stocked. Good-value food is served weekdays until 6pm (3pm Fri). The pub is 100 yards from Oldham Central tram stop.

Carrion Crow

271 Huddersfield Road, OL4 2RJ

12-midnight ☎ (0161) 633 4490

6 changing beers (often Banks's, Jennings, Marston's)

Multi award-winning former coaching inn dating from 1796, the Crow is the epitome of a superb community local. Six handpulls serve an extensive selection of ales from the Marston's range. Wholesome meals are made from local produce. The pub runs darts, football and quiz teams, and hosts a quiz night on Thursdays. There are quarterly beer festivals, trips to theatres and county cricket, an annual Christmas fair and St George's Day walk. A CAMRA discount is available Tuesday-Thursday. Local CAMRA branch Pub of the Year 2014. P

Royal Oak Hotel ★

178 Union Street, OL1 1EN

11 (12 Sun)-midnight ☎ (0161) 633 2642

Robinsons Cumbria Way, Unicorn, Trooper, Old Tom; 1 changing beer (sourced locally; often Robinsons)

An early-20th-century brick building with a quality refitting in 1928, including the addition of a splendid glazed servery and lots of wall tiling which remain to this day. The pub has kept a traditional multi-roomed layout with a pool room and a cosy snug. The landlord is an avid real ale fan. Robinsons Old Tom is usually available in winter. Tea, coffee and bar snacks are served throughout the day. Handy for the Mumps tram stop. Q

Up Steps Inn

17-23 High Street, OL1 3AJ (between shopping centre and Tommyfield Market)

8am-midnight ☎ (0161) 627 5001

Greene King Abbot; Ruddles Best Bitter; changing beers

Traditional town-centre Wetherspoon pub on the main shopping street near the bus station and market. There are usually two regular beers and six to eight rotating guests on offer, including several from local breweries under the LocAle scheme and also US Brewers range. The pub also hosts beer festivals showcasing different beers and ciders. Food is available all day from 8am, alcohol from 9am. Ciders are from Westons and Gwynt y Ddraig, with others at festival times.

Patricroft

Queen's Arms

Green Lane, M30 0SH (adjacent to railway station, up ramp opp James Nasmyth Way)

7 (5 Fri)-11; 12-11 Sat & Sun ☎ (0161) 789 2019

Thwaites Original; 1 changing beer

One of the world's first railway pubs, the Patricroft Tavern opened in 1828 in anticipation of the coming railway. Renamed in 1851 for Queen Victoria's visit, it remains unspoilt. A popular vault and large rear lounge are served by a central bar and on the right is an exquisite, secluded snug. The railway passes in front of the pub, which occupies a lofty position, five minutes' walk from the main A57 bus route. Q P (67,100)

Wangies

303 Liverpool Road, M30 0QN (corner of Fielding St)

2 (12 Sat 7 Sun)-11.30 ☎ (0161) 787 8995

3 changing beers (sourced nationally; often Marston's, Wychwood)

Originally the Oddfellows but known locally as Wangies, hence the name change. Up to three nationally sourced real ales are available and the pub attracts customers from far and wide. There are two lounges at the front, with two rear rooms where darts and pool are played. Live alternative music features frequently, with a DJ on a Friday. The pub can be noisy but is always friendly.

Ramsbottom

First Chop

43 Bolton Street, BL0 9HU

✪ 12 (4 Mon-Wed)-midnight ☎ (01706) 827722

4 changing beers (sourced regionally; often First Chop)

This friendly bar set over two floors has a passion for beer, food and music. It specialises in real ale and cider with four handpumps usually supplying two of its own beers plus ales from the north of England, alongside up to six real ciders. Food is locally sourced and home-prepared. Live music features regularly. The bar offers a buy-five-get-one-free card and CAMRA members receive a 20 per cent discount.
◑♿⇌(East Lancs)🍎🚌(472,474)🐾

Irwell Works Brewery Tap

Irwell Street, BL0 9YQ

✪ closed Mon; 12-11 ☎ (01706) 825091

🌐 irwellworksbrewery.co.uk

Irwell Works Tin Plate, Copper Plate, Richard Mason 1888, Steam Plate, Iron Plate; 5 changing beers (often Irwell Works)

The Irwell Works Brewery is situated in the former Irwell Steam, Tin, Copper and Iron Works foundry. The building was used as an engineering works until a few years ago. It now houses a six-barrel brewery above the entrance on Strang Street. A balcony was opened in spring 2015. The bar offers a minimum of seven beers and locally produced Ribble Valley Gold cider. Small plates of food are served at lunchtime. Brewery tours are available on request. ◐⇌(East Lancs)🍎🚉🚌(472,474)🐾

Major Hotel

158 Bolton Street, BL0 9JA

✪ 3-11 Mon & Tue; 12-midnight ☎ (01706) 826777

Bank Top Flat Cap; St Austell Tribute; 2 changing beers

Now in its eighth year under the current owners, the stone-built Major prides itself on being a traditional local, with a large logburner in the main lounge. The central bar features Sky TV, pool, darts and dominoes. Four real ales are sold, from local brews to those from further afield. Unpretentious and reasonably priced food is available, ranging from snacks to full meals. The pub is a short walk from the local steam railway and has a large car park adjacent.
♨❀◑⇌(East Lancs)♣P🚌(472,474)🐾📶

Rochdale

Baum 🏆

35 Toad Lane, OL12 0NU

✪ 11.30-11 (midnight Fri & Sat); 11.30-10.30 Sun

☎ (01706) 352186 🌐 thebaum.co.uk

Changing beers

A hidden gem within a conservation area, the Baum occupies part of the Rochdale Pioneer Museum building on an isolated part of Toad Lane, just south of the bypass. A split-level inn with old-world charm, the conservatory at the rear overlooks a large beer garden and smoking area. Friendly staff serve seven real ales, a cider, a large selection of worldwide bottled beers and continental lagers on draught. Good, reasonably priced fresh food is available daily until 9pm (6pm Sun). ♨❀◑🚊🍎🚌🐾📶

Cemetery Hotel ★

470 Bury Road, OL11 5EU (on B6222 Bury Rd)

✪ 12-11 (1am Thu-Sat) ☎ (01706) 645635

5 changing beers (often Phoenix)

Recognised by CAMRA as having a nationally important historic pub interior for its Edwardian decor. There are three separate rooms off the main bar area, impressive tiles and splendid mahogany seating areas in the front left room. Rochdale AFC is close by and the pub is popular on match days with one room displaying club memorabilia. Five real ales are always available, often seven at the weekend, always including three from Phoenix. The pub has a lively atmosphere despite being next to Rochdale Cemetery.
♨❀◑♣🍎P🚌(469,468)🐾📶

Flying Horse Hotel

37 Packer Street, OL16 1NJ

✪ 11-midnight (1am Fri & Sat); 12-midnight Sun

☎ (01706) 646412 🌐 theflyinghorsehotel.co.uk

Lees Bitter; changing beers (sourced locally; often Phoenix, Pictish, Wilson Potter)

Built in 1691 and rebuilt in 1926, this impressive Edwardian stone free house is situated in the Town Hall Square. The hotel features log fires, TV sport plus B&B accommodation. The food menu offers meat from the local butcher and pies made on the premises. A function room is available for hire and there is a heated outside smoking area. Live music plays most Thursdays, Fridays and Saturdays. Parking is free at weekends and after 3pm weekdays. 🛏◑⇌🚊🍎P🚌🐾📶

Healey Hotel

172 Shawclough Road, OL12 6LW

✪ 11.30-11.30 (midnight Fri & Sat); 12-11.30 Sun

☎ (01706) 645453

Robinsons Unicorn; 6 changing beers (often Robinsons)

The pub is situated close to Healey Dell Nature Reserve. A major enlargement and refit in 2013 has taken this always-excellent venue to a new level, while retaining the original tiling and bar. Three ever-changing guest beers complement the four Robinsons ales and a guest cider. The beer garden now has a decked and covered area, also used for smoking, plus a pétanque piste to the rear. Quality food is served until 9pm (6pm Sun).
Q❀◑♣🍎🚌(446,466)🐾📶

Regal Moon

The Butts, OL16 1HB

✪ 9am-midnight (1am Fri & Sat) ☎ (01706) 657434

Ruddles Best Bitter; Thwaites Wainwright; changing beers

A large and imposing former cinema in the town centre, handy for the tram and bus interchange. The pub divides into discrete drinking areas in an open-plan room. Eighteen handpumps dispense a wide variety of ales and ciders, with local and West Yorkshire microbreweries featured. The cider is usually from Westons with three rotating guests. The interior has been refurbished, but the mannequin organist remains on his perch above the bar. A patio to the rear is available for smokers.
Q♨◑♿🚊🍎🚌📶

Romiley

Platform One

6 Stockport Road, SK6 4BN

12-11 (10.30 Mon); 12-midnight Fri & Sat; 12-10.30 Sun
☎ (0161) 406 8686
Changing beers Ⓗ
The pub is situated adjacent to Romiley railway station within a conservation area close to the village centre. It opened in 2012 as a free house and wine bar following complete refurbishment. Six real ales are on offer, usually including beers from local micros such as Hornbeam and Redwillow, served from a large bar situated down the side of the mainly open-plan lower floor. A separate restaurant area named Platform 2 on the first floor serves food 12-8pm.

Salford

Eagle Inn
18 Collier Street, M3 7DW (opp Rolla St)
3-11 (1am Fri & Sat); 1-11 Sun ☎ (0161) 819 5002
Holt Bitter; 4 changing beers Ⓗ
This Grade II-listed building is a traditional, unspoilt, hidden gem and a great survivor in an area that has lost a lot of pubs. There is a vault to the left on entry and a small lobby leading to a lounge and back room with a piano. The central bar serves the vault and lobby. The cottage attached to the pub was recently converted into a lively music venue. Handy for Manchester Arena.
(Manchester Victoria)

New Oxford
11 Bexley Square, M3 6DB (corner of Browning St)
12-midnight ☎ (0161) 832 7082 thenewoxford.com
Changing beers Ⓗ
This multi award-winning two-room pub is an 1830 building with a modern interior. The highlight is the bar with its 20 handpumps, 17 for cask ales and three for cider. Add to this draught European beers and a selection of bottled Belgian beers and you have a beer drinkers' utopia. Ales change regularly but usually include at least one from Ossett and frequent beer festivals are held. Excellent home-cooked lunches are available noon-4pm Monday to Friday. (Central)

Salford Arms Hotel
146 Chapel Street, M3 6AF (corner Bloom St)
12-midnight (10.30 Sun) ☎ (0161) 288 8883
salfordarmshotel.co.uk
House beer (by Green Mill); 5 changing beers Ⓗ
Street-corner hotel reopened under new ownership in 2012. Now its five handpumps dispense an array of real ales from near and far, including a house beer from Green Mill Brewery. A side room to the right provides additional space when the main bar is busy. Various events are held including a popular quiz night, and good food is served lunchtimes and evenings until 9pm. Just across the road from Salford Central station.
(Central)

Salford Quays

Craftbrew
1 Lowry Plaza, The Quays, M50 3UB (opp Lowry Theatre and Gallery)
8am-11 (midnight Fri); 10-midnight Sat; 10-11 Sun ☎ None craftbrew-uk.com
3 changing beers (sourced regionally; often Brightside, Hawkshead) Ⓗ
Smart bar opened in 2013 on the ground floor of a modern black-clad office building. There are three real ales available, usually from Brightside and Hawkshead. A large Lowry-style mural dominates the single room, one half showing old and the other modern Salford. Freshly prepared food is good quality, attracting workers from nearby offices. There is a mixture of seating available – high, low and chesterfield.

Shaw

Shay Wake
4 Lane Ends, OL2 8EQ
8am-midnight (1am Fri & Sat) ☎ (01706) 889120
Greene King Abbot; Thwaites Wainwright; changing beers Ⓗ
A Wetherspoon outlet opened in 2011 featuring eight handpumps for real ale, with real ciders also available. With a pleasant interior décor, the bar is to the right alongside American diner-style bench seating. The pub has close ties to the local playhouse, offering discounted food to those attending performances. Beer festivals are held throughout the year. The pub's name is derived from the local dialect for shaw (shay) and holiday (wakes).

Stalybridge

Old Hunters Tavern
51 Acres Lane, SK15 2JR
12-midnight ☎ (0161) 303 9477
Robinsons Unicorn; 3 changing beers (often Robinsons) Ⓗ
Traditional characterful two-roomed pub, just outside the town centre, which appeals to all. The main room features unusual brass poles with circular shelves for holding pints, and there is a separate room off to one side. The ladies' Manchester log end darts team meets every Tuesday and the golf society meets monthly. Quiz night is Thursday. Regular football matches are shown in both main rooms. There is a covered, heated area outside for smokers. No food at weekends. P

Society Rooms
49 Grosvenor Street, SK15 2JN
8am-midnight ☎ (0161) 338 9740
Greene King Abbot; Ruddles Best Bitter; changing beers Ⓗ
Wetherspoon's pub named after the former Co-op store premises it occupies within the town centre. It features two elevated sections either side of the entrance and a typically large main area. Enthusiastic management and a strong focus on real ales (using 10 handpumps) have made this a favourite destination for local drinkers. Beer-oriented events such as Meet the Brewer nights, and beer requests by customers, have helped to boost this pub's reputation. Real ciders are always available.

Stalybridge Labour Club
Acres Lane, SK15 2JR
7.30-11.30; 2-midnight Fri; 12-midnight Sat & Sun
☎ (0161) 338 4796
5 changing beers (sourced locally) Ⓗ
A large well-appointed club close to Stalybridge town centre with a welcoming lounge, separate large function room available for hire, and a games room with a full-sized billiards table. Five constantly changing ales are generally available,

sourced mainly from local micros including Hornbeam, Howard Town and Mouselow Farm. Catering for functions is available on request. Show a copy of this Guide or a CAMRA membership card for entry. ♿P🚌

Station Buffet Bar ★

Stalybridge Railway Station, Platform 4, Rassbottom Street, SK15 1RF (access from station platform 4)
⌚ 11-11 (midnight Fri & Sat); 12-10.30 Sun
☎ (0161) 303 0007 🌐 stalybridgebuffetbar.co.uk
Changing beers Ⓗ
Featuring in many beer publications and on TV, this enduring Victorian gem is worth missing a train for. Sympathetic refurbishment has allowed expansion of the food menu which includes home-cooked meals and pies. Nine handpumps dispense a variety of beers, most locally sourced, plus at least one real cider or perry. A good range of bottled beers is also available. Events including live music and Meet the Brewer nights are held in the function room. Monday is quiz night.
Q◐◑♿⇌●P🚌

White House

1 Water Street, SK15 2AG
⌚ 12-11 (midnight Sat) ☎ (0161) 303 2154
Hydes Original Bitter; 5 changing beers Ⓗ
This popular pub close to both bus and rail stations is semi-open plan but retains four distinct drinking areas and a quiet corner can often be found even at busy times. Up to five ever-changing guest beers from micros and Hydes Studio complement the regular Original, and up to three real ciders are offered. Live music plays every Friday and a folk night is hosted every Thursday. Quiz night is Sunday. ◐⇌♣●P🚌🐾

Standish

Albion Ale House Ⓛ

12 High Street, WN6 0HL
⌚ 2-10 (11 Fri & Sat); 2-8 Sun ☎ 07411 081342
6 changing beers Ⓗ
High street microbar with a narrow frontage. The interior is bright and airy with a pine bar dominating the rear of the room, an attractive stone floor and comfortable modern furniture. This is a pleasant place to while away the hours with a pint and friends, and light bites are usually available. The pub is well-served by local bus services though nearby parking can be limited. Wheelchair-friendly with a disabled WC.
Q♨♿●🚌🐾

Silver Tally Ⓛ

41 Shevington Moor, WN6 0SQ
⌚ 12-11.30 ☎ (01257) 472733 🌐 silvertally.co.uk
Prospect Silver Tally; Thwaites Wainwright; 5 changing beers Ⓗ
The Silver Tally is the first pub to be run by Prospect Brewery and offers its own beers, a regular from Thwaites and real cider. It has a traditional feel about it while being contemporarily furnished. The interior divides into three distinct areas – for games, dining and drinking. Pub food favourites are of a high standard. Mini beer festivals are hosted a couple of times a year.
Q♨❀◐◑♿♣●P🚌(113)🐾📶

Standish Unity Club Ⓛ

Cross Street, WN6 0HQ
⌚ 7.30-11 (midnight Fri & Sat) ☎ (01257) 424007
🌐 standishunityclub.com
Prospect Silver Tally; 4 changing beers Ⓗ
Established over a decade ago, this is an independent, non profit-making club open to all. It has a comfortably furnished bar and function room with a separate pool/snooker room. A busy club with quizzes and pool, it is also a music venue and available for private functions. Prospect Unity Gold is a regular along with ales from many local breweries. The club hosts an annual beer festival and CAMRA members are welcome at all times. Local CAMRA Club of the Year 2013. Q♿♣●P🚌

Stockport: Centre

Arden Arms ★

23 Millgate, SK1 2LX (jct Corporation St)
⌚ 12-11 ☎ (0161) 480 2185
Robinsons Dizzy Blonde, Unicorn, Double Hop Ⓗ, Old Tom Ⓖ; 1 changing beer (sourced nationally; often Robinsons) Ⓗ
This Grade II-listed building close to Stockport market has a nationally important historic pub interior. The multi-roomed interior centres around one main serving area; to reach the rear snug you must walk through the bar. Many Victorian features remain and it is said that the cellar once served as a mortuary and still retains body niches in its walls. Evening meals are served Thursday-Saturday 6-9pm. A former CAMRA branch Pub of the Year, this is an unmissable gem. ♨❀◐◑♿♣🚌(300,384)📶

Bakers Vaults

Market Place, SK1 1ES (jct Vernon St)
⌚ 12-1am ☎ (0161) 480 9448
Robinsons Dizzy Blonde, Unicorn, Trooper; 5 changing beers (sourced nationally; often Robinsons) Ⓗ
This relaxed yet lively market house is an architecturally impressive space. Grade II-listed, it has a bohemian feel enhanced by high ceilings and arched windows, the decor a muted grey and dark blue. The spacious interior has the bar located towards the back and behind that a small lounge area with low leather sofas for those wishing to escape the hustle and bustle. One of the few Robinsons houses to offer guest beers.
❀◐◑⇌●🐾📶

Boar's Head

2 Vernon Street, Market Place, SK1 1TY (jct Market Place)
⌚ 11-11; 12-6.30 Sun ☎ (0161) 480 3978
Samuel Smith Old Brewery Bitter Ⓗ
A town-centre multi-roomed pub with a genuine, cosy feel. Owners Samuel Smith spent a fair sum restoring this pub to how it may once have looked. On entering, the bar runs to the left in the lobby, an open area to the right leads to a corner room, and two small rooms face the bar. Beyond this is a large function room with its own bar. Outside is a small, decked drinking area. Coal fires on winter days add warmth and ambience.
Q♨❀⇌🐾

Cocked Hat

2 Market Place, SK1 1EW (jct Churchgate opp St Mary's church)
⌚ 11-11 (1am Fri & Sat); 12-10.30 Sun ☎ (0161) 480 4446
6 changing beers Ⓗ
The former Pack Horse, rejuvenated in 2013 by new owners AtWill Pub Co. It now enjoys a healthy and buoyant trade with six changing guest ales

available, typically from micros within a 30-mile radius of Chester where AtWill is based. Tasting notes on blackboards help you pick the right ale. Traditional home-cooked meals are served 11-4pm Monday-Saturday, with roasts on Sundays until 4pm. Live music features every Friday and Saturday. ♉◐⇌●🚌(300)🐾📶

Crown Inn

154 Heaton Lane, SK4 1AR (jct King St W under viaduct)
⌚ 12-11 (10.30 Sun) ☎ (0161) 480 5850
Stockport Stock Porter; 9 changing beers Ⓗ
Situated in a dramatic location beneath Stockport's famous viaduct, the Crown continues to be one of the town's leading real ale destinations. Up to 16 guest beers feature, often including those from Stockport Brewing Co across the road. A mild, stout and/or porter and up to four guest ciders are always on tap. Four rooms with many original features radiate from the busy bar. Food is served until 3pm on weekdays, with pork pies usually available. Q❀◐⇌●P🚌(192)🐾📶

Robinsons Brewery Visitors Centre

Apsley Street, SK1 1YE (off Wellington St)
⌚ closed Mon; 10.30-6 (5 Sun) ☎ (0161) 612 4100
🌐 robinsonsvisitorscentre.co.uk
Robinsons Wizard, Dizzy Blonde, Unicorn, Trooper; 1 changing beer (sourced nationally; often Robinsons) Ⓗ
Since opening in March 2013 the Robinsons Visitor Centre (which incorporates a public bar) has gone from strength to strength and in 2015 won a gold award from Visit England. The reception area features a huge display of brewery memorabilia tracing Robinsons' history since 1838. Steps lead down to the bar to the right and a café to the left. The brewery's seasonal and one-off beers are usually premiered here.
Q♉◐♿⇌P🚌(300,314)📶

Swan with Two Necks ★

36 Princes Street, SK1 1RY (jct Hatton St)
⌚ 10.30-7 (11 Fri & Sat); 10.30-6 Sun ☎ (0161) 480 2341
Robinsons Unicorn, Old Tom; 1 changing beer (sourced nationally; often Robinsons) Ⓗ
Narrow-fronted with a mock-Tudor façade, the building was bought by Robinsons in 1924 and rejuvenated in 2008 by young licensees. It is impressively panelled in light oak throughout in familiar Robinsons style, with labelled doors to match. The front door leads to a vault, then the bustling bar corridor, beyond that a cosy snug with an attractive skylight, and at the rear a small lounge and diner. Outside is a compact, walled drinking area. Quality lunchtime meals are served Tuesday-Saturday. The cider is Westons Old Rosie.
♉❀◐⇌●🚌(300,330)🐾

Stockport: Edgeley

Armoury

31 Shaw Heath, Edgeley, SK3 8BD (on B5465, jct Greek St)
⌚ 1 (11 Sun & Mon)-midnight; 11-1am Fri & Sat ☎ 07931 621220
Robinsons Dizzy Blonde, Unicorn, Trooper; 1 changing beer (sourced nationally; often Robinsons) Ⓗ
Comfortable, recently refurbished, multi-roomed local with a strong community involvement and efficient friendly service. The pub caters for a varied clientele from sports watchers to darts teams (with two leagues often playing on the same night) to quiet bookworms alike. The lounge walls feature memorabilia of the Cheshire Regiment. There is a pleasant beer garden, quite a suntrap in summer months. Handy for the train station and football ground, the pub opens at 11am if Stockport County are at home.
Q♉❀♿⇌♣🚌(310,369)📶

Olde Vic

1 Chatham Street, Edgeley, SK3 9ED (jct Shaw Heath)
⌚ closed Mon; 5 (7 Sat & Sun)-midnight ☎ (0161) 480 2410
6 changing beers Ⓗ
Once visited, never forgotten. This gem of a local, containing a fascinating array of bric-a-brac, games and reading matter, hides behind a colourful exterior. However, a friendly and sometimes surprising welcome awaits. Landlord Steve will taunt you given the chance, while Jo acts as a foil with her warm and cheerful welcome. Six handpumps dispense a changing variety from micros far and near, building on the Olde Vic's history as Stockport's first pub to offer a continuous rotation. Last entry is 10.30pm.
Q❀⇌♣●🚌(310,369)🐾📶

Stockport: Heaton Norris

Hope Inn

118 Wellington Road North, Heaton Norris, SK4 2LL (to N of Belmont Way)
⌚ 12-11 (midnight Fri & Sat) ☎ (0161) 637 6191
🌐 thehopestockport.co.uk
Fool Hardy Rou Shou, Risky Blond, Reckless Danger; Outstanding 3.9, IPA; 8 changing beers (sourced nationally; often Fool Hardy) Ⓗ
A thorough refurbishment and installation of the new Fool Hardy Ales microbrewery has turned a dead duck into a gem – winning CAMRA branch Pub of the Year in 2014. Comprising two large rooms, to the right is the cask ale side with 12 handpumps serving at least four of the brewery's own beers, two regulars from Outstanding, plus changing guests; the left side is dedicated to foreign beers and real ciders. An extensive bottled beer range and beer festivals also feature.
Q❀◐♣●P🚌(22,192)🐾📶

Magnet 🏆

51 Wellington Road North, Heaton Norris, SK4 1HJ (jct Duke St)
⌚ 4 (12 Fri-Sun)-11 ☎ (0161) 429 6287
🌐 themagnetfreehouse.co.uk
Salopian Oracle; 9 changing beers Ⓗ
A focus on quality and choice gained the Magnet acclaim and it was awarded CAMRA local branch Pub of the Year in 2015. It boasts 14 handpumps for beer and a draught cider, complemented by a large foreign bottled range. There is a bustling vault to the left leading to a lower pool room, and a series of rooms separated by arched magnet doorways on the right. The beer terrace and function room upstairs provide extra space. Monday is cheese night. An in-house micro, Watts Brewing, opened in 2014.
Q♉❀⇌♣●P🚌(22,192)🐾📶

Nursery ★

258 Green Lane, Heaton Norris, SK4 2NA (off A6, jct Heaton Rd)
⌚ 11.30-11 (midnight Fri & Sat); 12-11 Sun
☎ (0161) 432 2044

Hydes Light Mild/1863, Owd Oak, Original Bitter, Hydes Finest; 5 changing beers (sourced nationally; often Hydes) Ⓗ
Now a Grade II-listed building, this former CAMRA National Pub of the Year is a classic, unspoilt 1930s pub with its own bowling green, hidden away in a pleasant suburb. The multi-roomed interior includes a traditional vault and a spacious wood-panelled lounge where lunchtime diners enjoy home-cooked food. Two changing guest beers are always available, and several beer festivals are held each year. Live music features on Tuesday, Thursday and weekend evenings.
❀◐♣P🚌(22,364)🐾

Railway

74-76 Wellington Road North, Heaton Norris, SK4 1HF (jct Georges Road)
12-midnight ☎ (0161) 477 3680
Holt Bitter; 4 changing beers Ⓗ
Welcoming multi-roomed pub on a busy main road. To the front are two lounges, one with a raised stage area for the frequent, and highly rated, live entertainment – jazz on Sunday and Tuesday, open mic on Friday and rockabilly the last Saturday of the month. The games room to the rear features darts – numerous teams are based here – and pool. The four guest beers are often from microbreweries and often rarely seen in other local pubs. ❀♣🚌(22,192)

Stockport: Heaviley

Fairway

137 Higher Hillgate, Heaviley, SK1 3HR (jct Longshut Lane)
closed Mon; 12-11 (midnight Fri & Sat); 12-10.30 Sun
☎ (0161) 474 1082
8 changing beers Ⓗ
Former Robinsons house, purchased and rejuvenated in 2012 by Stuart and Emma, who have a pedigree in running north-west pubs. It has a smart, modern interior, with a pleasant decor and lighting helping to create a warm and welcoming ambience. Outside is a neat smoking and drinking area. Eight constantly rotating cask beers, many from local micros, are available, plus an ever-changing cider. Good-quality meals are served lunchtimes and evenings. Local CAMRA branch Pub of the Year 2014 runner-up.
Q❀◐◑♿♣🚌(192,383)

Stockport: Portwood

Railway

1 Avenue Street, Portwood, SK1 2BZ (jct Gt Portwood St A560)
12-11 (10.30 Sun) ☎ (0161) 429 6062
Copper Dragon Golden Pippin; Moorhouse's Pride of Pendle; Outstanding Red, Blond; Pictish Brewers Gold; Rossendale Floral Dance; 5 changing beers Ⓗ
Bustling, street-corner house with 15 handpumps showcasing the ranges of Rossendale, Outstanding and Pictish breweries, plus guests. A changing mild and a real cider are always stocked, plus a wide selection of Belgian, German and other bottled beers. Occasional beer and cider festivals take place too. Note the model railway atop the bar canopy, alongside much railway-related memorabilia. A bar billiards table is regularly in use, while the outside yard is a suntrap in summer. A former local CAMRA Pub of the Year.
Q❀♣🚌(325,330)

Strines

Sportsman

105 Strines Road, SK6 7GE (on B6101)
12-3, 5-11; 12-11 Sat & Sun ☎ (0161) 427 2888
the-sportsman-pub.co.uk
Phoenix Spotland Gold; 4 changing beers (often AllGates, Howard Town, Pictish) Ⓗ
Splendid white pub standing alone overlooking the Goyt Valley, popular with local drinkers and diners. The comfortable lounge has large picture windows giving superb views over the wooded valley to the hills beyond. A monumental fireplace accommodates log fires in winter and there is a separate taproom. Five guest beers, mainly from micros, are available. Outside, a terrace and balcony are popular in summer and the pub is close to the Peak Forest Canal and Goyt Way Trail.
❀◐◑♿♣P🚌(62,358)🐾

Swinton

Park Inn

135-137 Worsley Road, M27 5SP (corner Shaftesbury Rd)
11-11 (midnight Fri & Sat) ☎ (0161) 793 1568
Holt Bitter; 2 changing beers Ⓗ
A smart and popular local, serving Holt beers since 1878, but extended slightly and given a mock-Tudor frontage. Two rooms on the right have been knocked into one, and there is a busy vault. A delightful tiny snug behind the bar has its own serving hatch. Many events are hosted – karaoke Saturday, poker Sunday and Tuesday, bingo Thursday, chat and chill Friday – and a motorcycle club meets on the first Wednesday of the month.
Q♣🚌🐾

Tottington

Dungeon Inn

9 Turton Road, BL8 4AW
5-11 (12.30am Fri); 2-1am Sat; 2-10.30 Sun
☎ (01204) 887068 thedungeontottington.co.uk
Thwaites Nutty Black, Original, Wainwright, Lancaster Bomber; 2 changing beers Ⓗ
A well-maintained example of an Edwardian Bury Brewery pub offering comfortable surroundings and a great ambience. Six handpumps feature Thwaites ales and guests, and an extensive range of wines is available by the glass. The open fire is an attraction during the winter while the south-facing beer garden is popular with locals and walkers alike during the summer months. All cask ales are reduced on Mondays and Dungeon Platters are served every day. Entertainment includes a weekly quiz night. Q❀♣P🚌🐾

Tyldesley

Mort Arms

235-237 Elliott Street, M29 8DG
12-midnight (1am Fri & Sat); 12-11 Sun ☎ (01942) 883481
Holt Bitter Ⓗ
From the façade to the interior, this 1930s pub is recognisable as a Holt's hostelry. The entrance has two etched doors directing you into the taproom or lounge, with a central bar serving both rooms. The taproom is a bright contrast and just how one should be. ❀♣🚌(32,12)

Uppermill

Cross Keys Inn

Running Hill Gate, OL3 6LW (off A670 up Church Rd)
12-midnight (01457) 874626 crosskeysinn.co.uk
Lees Brewer's Dark, Manchester Pale Ale, Bitter; 2 changing beers (sourced locally; often Lees) H
Overlooking Saddleworth Church, this attractive 18th-century stone building has exposed beams throughout. The public bar features a stone-flagged floor and Yorkshire range. Home-cooked food includes puddings, pies and real chips. Annual events including the Rushcart Festival and Wartime Weekend are popular. Outside is a children's play area and a covered, heated smoking area. Folk music plays on Wednesday and Sunday nights. The pub is the centre for Mountain Rescue and the Saddleworth Runners. A regular in the Guide for 40 years. Q P

Urmston

Steamhouse L

Station Road, M41 9SB
10-11 (1am Fri & Sat); 9am-11 Sun (0161) 748 6487
thesteamhouse.co.uk
6 changing beers (sourced nationally) H
A free house, the Steamhouse boasts eight handpumps. The on-site brewery, RtwoDtoo, is based in the pub's outbuildings and produces several beers. These feature on at least one handpump most of the time. An impressive range of bottled beers is also available, and occasionally real cider. This spacious and popular pub is located in the original (1872) railway station on the westbound platform of Urmston station. Expect to find a crowd around the bar on a Friday evening.
P

Wardley

Morning Star

520 Manchester Road, M27 9QW (opp Bagot St)
12-11 (11.30 Fri & Sat) 07827 850258
Holt Mild, Bitter; 1 changing beer H
This smart red-brick Joseph Holt pub built in 1890 is an extremely popular community venue. There is a traditional vault to the left of the central bar and a small lounge to the right, leading to a larger comfortable lounge with several TV screens. The pub can be busy when live football is screened. There is a quiz on Wednesday and entertainment at the weekends. A guest beer often features alongside the regulars.
(Moorside) P (36,37)

Whalley Range

Hillary Step L

199 Upper Chorlton Road, M16 0BH
4-11.30; 3-12.30am Fri; 12-12.30am Sat; 12-11.30 Sun
(0161) 881 1978 thehillarystep.co.uk
5 changing beers (sourced nationally; often Phoenix, Thornbridge, Thwaites) H
A modern bar in a small strip of shops and bars just north of Chorlton centre. Three handpumps are dedicated to Thwaites, Phoenix and Thornbridge breweries, with two more serving guest ales, alongside a good range of draught and bottled continental beers plus over 20 malt whiskies. Cheese boards and charcuterie snacks are popular, with a choice of other nibbles (olives, salami, nuts) also on offer. Live jazz features on Sunday evenings and a quiz the first Tuesday of the month. Children are not permitted.

Whitefield

Eagle & Child

Higher Lane, M45 7EY
12-11 (midnight Fri & Sat) 07827 850229
Holt Mild, IPA, Bitter, Two Hoots; 1 changing beer H
Traditional black-and-white-timbered double-fronted inn with a spacious lounge and a vault served by a central bar, plus a separate front room, ideal for meetings and private parties. Home to darts, dominoes and cribbage teams, it hosts live acts every Friday and a quiz-and-curry night fortnightly on a Tuesday. The pub is family-friendly and dogs are allowed on a lead in outside areas. A large floodlit bowling green is open April to September and is available for hire.
Q P (98,135)

Wigan

Anvil L

Dorning Street, WN1 1ND
11-11; 12-10.30 Sun (01942) 239444
AllGates California; 3 changing beers (sourced nationally) H
Popular town-centre pub with seven handpumps offering beers from the nearby AllGates Brewery, guest ales, a real cider, six draught continental beers and a range of bottled beers. The small snug features a 'wall of fame' displaying the pub's many awards. Several TV screens show sports action. Close to bus and railway access for the DW Stadium, the pub can be busy on match days. CAMRA Cider Pub of the Year 2014. Over-18s only.
(Wallgate & North Western)

Berkeley

27-29 Wallgate, WN1 1LD
11.30-11.30 (midnight Fri & Sat); 12.30-10.30 Sun
(01942) 242041
3 changing beers H
An attractive former coaching house in the busy Wallgate area, close to the rail stations. Sited on the corner of the infamous King Street, it attracts a younger clientele on weekend evenings. The large bar hosts a range of rotating guest beers. Food is served daily 12-7pm. Watch your favourite sporting event on the massive projector screen or one of the eight large flat-screen TVs. A first-floor function room is available for hire.

Doc's Symposium

85 Mesnes Street, WN1 1QJ
closed Mon-Wed; 12-11 Thu-Sat; 1-10.30 Sun 07472 063296
5 changing beers H
Voted local CAMRA New Cask Outlet 2014, this is the town's first micropub. It offers five real ales including local brews and a variety of European beers. With the interior's light and airy atmosphere and on-street seating outside, the pub has a continental feel. It also overlooks the beautiful Mesnes Park. June and Chris are well-respected Wigan landlords and visitors are guaranteed a warm welcome from them and their staff.
Q (Wallgate) P

John Bull Chophouse

2 Coopers Row, Market Place, WN1 1PQ
4.30-midnight; 12.30-3am Fri & Sat; 2-midnight Sun
☎ (01942) 242862
Thwaites Wainwright; 5 changing beers
This unique pub, run by the same family for over 40 years, is a must-visit if you are in Wigan. The building dates back over 300 years and has been cottages, stables and a slaughterhouse in the past. A popular two-floor town-centre venue, it is renowned for having the best pub jukebox for miles around, and a pool table upstairs. It offers ales on six handpumps, continental beers and a real cider. CAMRA Pub of the Year 2014.
❀≈(North West/Wallgate)

Raven Hotel

5 Wallgate, WN1 1LD
11-11 ☎ (01942) 239764 theravenwigan.com
5 changing beers
This superb example of an early-1900s commercial hotel was virtually derelict before a tasteful renovation in 2012, retaining and restoring many original features including panelling and windows. It is well worth a visit just for a look at the building and is especially cosy in winter with proper coal fires. A range of fine real ales, mainly from local breweries, is served from five handpumps. Good home-made pub food is available at a reasonable price. The bar has two unobtrusive TVs. A former CAMRA award winner.

Wigan Central

Arch No.1, Queen Street, WN3 4DY
12-11 (midnight Fri & Sat); 12-10.30 Sun
☎ (01942) 246425 wigancentral.bar
Prospect Nutty Slack; house beer (by Prospect); 5 changing beers (sourced nationally)
Customers are assured of a warm welcome at Wigan's newest real ale pub, situated in a mid-19th-century railway arch, owned by Prospect Brewery. With its railway-themed interior and live departure and arrival boards, it is a delight and has quite a cosy feel to it. The beers are sourced from all over and there is a continental bottled beer library for those wanting something different. Bar snacks are available. Visitors will not be disappointed. Q

Withington

Victoria

438 Wilmslow Road, M20 3BW (on B5093, jct Davenport Av)
11.30-11 (midnight Thu-Sat); 12-11 Sun
☎ (0161) 434 2600
Hydes Owd Oak, Original Bitter; 6 changing beers (sourced nationally; often Hydes)
A recent refurbishment has turned this once-ordinary pub into a thriving real ale venue, selling the full spread of Hydes' core range, Beer Studio beers, four guest ales and two rotating ciders (usually from Westons). The large single-roomed interior is partitioned into separate spaces, belying the building's true size. Very much a community pub, the Victoria is popular with all ages. Look out for occasional beer festivals, live bands, quizzes and a regular disco night. (42,43)

Woodford

Davenport Arms (Thief's Neck)

550 Chester Road, SK7 1PS (on A5102, jct Church Lane)
11-11; 12-10.30 Sun ☎ (0161) 439 2435
Robinsons Dizzy Blonde, Unicorn, Old Tom; 1 changing beer (sourced nationally; often Robinsons)
This characterful red-brick farmhouse-style hostelry received a smart refurbishment in 2014 but retains a multi-roomed feel with real fires in winter. This is the pub's 29th consecutive year in the Guide, and the licence has now been in the same family for 80 years. Excellent food is mostly home made, with some adventurous specials. Outside, the spacious forecourt and attractive garden, set well-away from the road, are popular in summer, with impressive floral displays on show.
P (157,X57)

Worsley

Barton Arms

2 Stablefold, M28 2ED (off Barton Rd)
11.30-11 ☎ (0161) 728 6157
Black Sheep Best Bitter; Thwaites Original, Wainwright; 6 changing beers
Built in a traditional style, this is in fact quite a modern pub and very comfortable. It is situated close to the centre of Worsley village and next to the Bridgewater Canal. The enthusiastic management have built up cask ale sales progressively over the past few years. It serves three regular and up to six guest ales from the varied Ember Inns cask ale list, usually including a dark ale. Good food is available daily until 10pm.
P (33,68)

Worsley Old Hall

Worsley Park, M28 2QT (off Walkden Rd)
10.30-11 (10.30 Sun) ☎ (0161) 703 8706
Brunning & Price Original; house beer (by Facer's); 4 changing beers
Worsley Old Hall is a Grade II-listed country house pub built in the 16th and 17th centuries, full of character and historic features. Set in extensive grounds, there is plenty of space for alfresco drinking and dining. Fine food is served all day, every day, and six excellent real ales and two ciders are always available. Once the home of the Duke of Bridgewater, the Old Hall is close to the heart of the village and the picturesque Bridgewater Canal. P

Noted ales

At one time or another nearly every county town in England of any size has been noted for its beers or ales. Yorkshire claims not only stingo but also Hull and North Allerton ales whilst Nottingham, Lichfield, Derby, Oxford and Burton have almost branded their ales. During the eighteenth century the fame of Dorchester beer almost equalled the popularity of London porter. **Frank A. King, Beer Has a History, 1947**

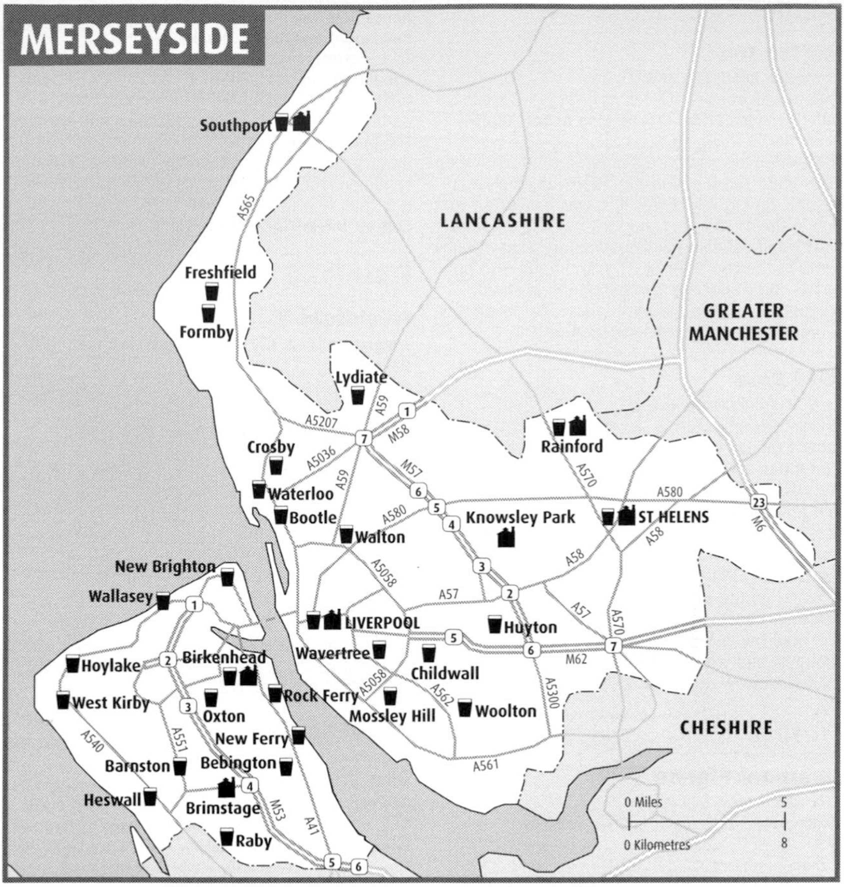

Barnston

Fox & Hounds

107 Barnston Road, CH61 1BW (on A551)
11-11; 12-10.30 Sun ☎ (0151) 648 7685
the-fox-hounds.co.uk
Brimstage Trappers Hat Bitter; Theakston Best Bitter, Old Peculier; Timothy Taylor Landlord; 2 changing beers (sourced nationally) Ⓗ
Village pub with a bar, lounge and snug full of bric-a-brac, local photos and other memorabilia. The lounge, converted from tea rooms, is quiet with no music or games machines. The pub retains its original character, with real fires in the bar and snug. The stone courtyard is a profusion of colour in the summer. Good food is available including fish dish of the day, daily specials and traditional Sunday roasts (no evening meals Mon). The real cider is Rosie's Triple D. Q❀◑♿♣P (77)

Bebington

Rose & Crown

57 The Village, CH63 7PL
12-midnight (1am Fri & Sat) ☎ (0151) 643 1312
the-ro.se
Thwaites Nutty Black, Original, Wainwright, Lancaster Bomber Ⓗ
Former coaching inn built in 1732, adjacent to Mayer Park and now a thriving suburban pub with a bar and games room. Satellite TV sport is prominent and a popular quiz is hosted on Sunday night. Nearby is Port Sunlight Village, founded by William Hesketh Lever in 1888 to house his soap factory workers. In the village is the Lady Lever Art Gallery, home to one of the most beautiful collections of art in the country.
⇌(Port Sunlight)♣P (410,487)

Birkenhead

Gallagher's Pub & Barber's Shop 🏆

20 Chester Street, CH41 5DQ
12 (4 Mon)-11; 12-midnight Fri; 11.30-midnight Sat; 12-midnight Sun ☎ (0151) 649 9095
gallagherspubwirral.com
Brimstage Trappers Hat Bitter; 5 changing beers (sourced regionally; often Hawkshead, Rat, Salopian) Ⓗ
Multi award-winning genuine free house close to the famous Mersey ferries, resurrected after closure and refurbished in 2010 by a former Irish Guardsman as a unique pub with barber's shop. The interior is decorated with a fascinating range of military memorabilia and a collection of shipping images. The pub runs a green hop beer festival in autumn. Good-value meals are served lunchtimes (no food Sun or Mon) and early evening Friday and Saturday only. ❀◑⇌(Hamilton Sq)

Bootle

Merton Inn

42 Merton Road, L20 3BW

8am-midnight (1am Fri & Sat) (0151) 934 7790

Fuller's London Pride; Greene King Abbot; Sharp's Doom Bar; 5 changing beers

The Merton Inn was once a hotel created when two villas were combined in the 1930s. Used as a hospital during World War II, it was converted to a pub in the 1970s. This spacious multi-level venue, with wood panelling and subdued lighting, retains some of the character of its villa origins. The pub boasts some specially commissioned abstract paintings depicting the local landscape. Alcohol is served from 9am. (Oriel Rd)P

Wild Rose

2a & 1b Triad Centre, L20 3ET

8am-midnight (1am Fri & Sat) (0151) 922 0828

Fuller's London Pride; Greene King Abbot; Ruddles Best Bitter; Sharp's Doom Bar; 4 changing beers

The name of this large, open-plan Wetherspoon pub relates to a reference made by William Gladstone, the 19th-century prime minister and MP for Liverpool, who spent part of his childhood on Merseyside. He recollected: 'I have seen wild roses growing on the very ground which is now the centre of Bootle.' The pub, located at the base of the Triad tower block, is popular with locals, shoppers and workers alike.
(New Strand)

Crosby

Liverpool Pigeon

14 Endbutt Lane, L23 0TR

closed Mon; 4 (12 Sat)-9; 12-5 Sun None

liverpoolpigeon.co.uk

5 changing beers

Merseyside's pioneering micropub is a fine example of the type, with real ales, ciders and British and European bottled beers available. The cask beers will usually include a local brew and often a dark beer such as a stout or porter. Locally made pies are available at the bar. The Liverpool Pigeon is named after an extinct bird from Polynesia – long may this one live. Liverpool CAMRA Pub of the Year 2014. Q

Stamps Bar

5 Crown Buildings, L23 5SR

12-11 (midnight Fri & Sat) (0151) 286 2662

stampsbar.co.uk

6 changing beers (often Stamps)

Stamps is a true community pub attracting a wide mix of people who come for the great range of real ales, cider, food and live music. The pub supports many local and national charities and hosts a number of activities including art classes on Monday, a ukulele band on Tuesday and a quiz night on Wednesday. Live music features Friday to Sunday. Not sure which beer to try? Get three third-pints for the price of one.

Formby

Sparrowhawk

Southport Old Road, L37 0AB (just off Formby bypass near Woodvale traffic lights)

10.30-10.45 (01704) 882350

sparrowhawk-formby.co.uk

House beer (by Phoenix); 3 changing beers (often Bowland, Hawkshead, Titanic)

The Sparrowhawk is a Brunning & Price pub situated between Southport and Formby. It was built as the dower house to the nearby Formby Hall and is set in five acres of woodlands and gardens. The pub is open plan with an emphasis on food but up to six real ales are always available in excellent condition. The bus stop at Woodvale traffic lights is less than five minutes' walk away.
Q P(47,49,X2)

Freshfield

Freshfield

1 Massams Lane, L37 7BD (5 mins' walk from train station)

11-11 (midnight Fri & Sat); 10-11 Sun (01704) 874871

freshfield-liverpool.co.uk

Greene King IPA, Abbot; Ruddles Best Bitter; 11 changing beers

Predominantly a drinkers' pub but with a good restaurant in house, the beer choice here is enlightened, with independent breweries to the fore and local ales well supported. At least one real cider is also always on offer. Engaging staff enhance the visitor experience, with Friday and Saturday nights always busy. Dogs on leads are welcome in the bar area and well-behaved children are tolerated. CAMRA regional Pub of the Year winner 2013 and 2014 and national finalist in 2014. P

Heswall

Dee View Inn

Dee View Road, CH60 0DH

12-midnight (11 Sun) (0151) 345 9165

Brimstage Trappers Hat Bitter; Fuller's London Pride; Timothy Taylor Landlord; Wells Bombardier; 2 changing beers (sourced nationally)

Homely, characterful local built in the late-1800s, offering a warm welcome and a friendly ambience. It sits on a hairpin bend by the war memorial and famous mirror, with views over the Dee Estuary and close to the Wirral Way path. A popular and entertaining weekly quiz is held on Tuesday night and live music is a frequent attraction. Traditional home-cooked food is served and children are welcome if dining. P

Hoylake

Ship Inn

Market Street, CH47 3BB

12-11.30 (12.30am Fri & Sat) (0151) 632 4319

Brimstage Trappers Hat Bitter; St Austell Tribute; Salopian Shropshire Gold; Timothy Taylor Landlord;

REAL ALE BREWERIES

Brimstage Brimstage
Connoisseur St Helens (NEW)
George Wright Rainford
Liverpool Craft Liverpool
Liverpool Organic Liverpool
Mad Hatter Liverpool
Melwood Knowsley Park
Peerless Birkenhead
Southport Southport
Stamps Liverpool
Wapping Liverpool

Wells Bombardier; 4 changing beers (sourced nationally)
Popular town-centre pub set back from the busy main shopping street, first licensed in 1754 (recent testing has dated the building to 1730). Although modernised in recent years, with a single L-shaped bar area, the old wood beams remain in the back lounge. Good-value bar meals are served every lunchtime and Monday-Friday evenings. Live music plays on Saturday and Sunday evenings. The large, secluded garden at the rear has a pond.
P (38,83)

Huyton

Barker's Brewery
Archway Road, L36 9UJ
8am-11 (midnight Fri & Sat) (0151) 482 4500
Adnams Broadside; Fuller's London Pride; Ruddles Best Bitter; Sharp's Doom Bar; changing beers
A large, airy Wetherspoon pub with a traditional feel, popular with local office workers and families in the early evening. A good beer selection means at least one local and one dark beer are always available. The pub is on the site of the old Huyton Brewery, founded in 1825 and managed by the Barker family over four generations until 1925. The main dining area leads to the beer garden at the rear. Alcohol is served from 9am.
Q P

Liverpool: Childwall

Childwall Abbey
Childwall Abbey Road, L16 5EY
11-11 (midnight Fri & Sat); 12-11 Sun (0151) 722 5293
childwallabbeyhotelpub.co.uk
Jennings Cumberland Ale; Wychwood Hobgoblin; 1 changing beer (sourced nationally)
An imposing buiding opposite Childwall Church. The bar area is popular with drinkers and three other rooms are mainly used for dining. Tables with umbrellas are outside by the bowling green and bike stands are provided. Cask ale is reduced in price after 8pm on Tuesdays. Food is served until 9pm (6pm weekends). Seven en-suite rooms are available. Q P

Childwall Fiveways
179 Queens Drive, L15 6XS
8am-11.30 (0151) 738 2100
Fuller's London Pride; Greene King Abbot; Sharp's Doom Bar; 4 changing beers (often Titanic)
A former Higsons tied house, this large single-roomed pub opened as a Wetherspoon in 2010. Located in a leafy suburb, it has good motorway and public transport links. The refurbished interior is decorated with wood panelling, and outside there is a beer garden. A popular establishment, it can get busy, especially at weekends.
P

Liverpool: City Centre

Abbey
85-89 Hanover Street, L1 3DZ
11-11 (0151) 708 5688
Changing beers (often Copper Dragon, Peerless)
A large venue with plenty of seating in various arrangements. Most major sporting events are shown live so the pub can get busy, especially in the evening. A private function area is available to book. Good-value food is served and one local beer is usually among the range of ales. A discount is available on production of a CAMRA membership card. (Central)

Augustus John
Peach Street, L3 5TX (off Brownlow Hill)
11.30 (12 Sat)-11; closed Sun (0151) 794 5507
4 changing beers
Opened in 1901 and run by the University of Liverpool, the Augustus John is an open-plan pub popular with students, lecturers and locals. Up to four guest beers are available alongside a large number of ciders – the pub is a former local and regional CAMRA Cider Pub of the Year. Pizza is served at all times, sport is shown and there is a jukebox. Closed over Christmas and New Year.

Baltic Fleet
33 Wapping, L1 8DQ
12 (11 Sat & Sun)-11 (0151) 709 3116
balticfleetpubliverpool.com
3 changing beers
Liverpool's only brewpub, this Grade II-listed building is located near the Albert Dock. It has a distinctive flat-iron shape and is decorated with a nautical theme. Real ale and cider are dispensed from seven handpumps, with a mix of the pub's own Wapping Brewery beers and occasional changing guests. Home-cooked scouse is available from lunchtime until it runs out. The existence of tunnels in the cellar has led to speculation that the pub's history may involve smuggling and press gangs. (James St)

Belvedere
8 Sugnall Street, L7 7EB (off Falkner St)
12-11 (0151) 709 0303
4 changing beers
Tucked away in the Georgian area of the city, close to the famous Philharmonic Hall and frequented by its orchestra members, this small two-roomed pub is a free house serving four rotating beers mainly from local microbreweries. Redeemed from closure for housing development in 2006, this Grade II-listed building retains original fixtures and interesting etched-glass features. It is a pub with a mixed local clientele, where various small groups meet and good conversation thrives. Q

Blackburne Pub & Eatery
24 Catharine Street, L8 7NL
11.30 (9am Sat & Sun)-midnight (0151) 709 9159
theblackburne.co.uk
3 changing beers (sourced locally; often Liverpool Organic, Salopian)
A popular, open-plan pub in the heart of the Georgian Quarter at the edge of the city centre. One end concentrates on food, but the other end is good for a beer or real cider from one of four handpumps, always including a LocAle. The outside sign shows this was once a Higsons pub. Breakfast is served at weekends and food is available until 9.30pm. The boutique hotel above has seven rooms. Q

Clove Hitch
23 Hope Street, L1 9BQ
4.30-11 (10 Mon); 12-midnight Fri & Sat; 12-10 Sun
(0151) 709 6574 theclovehitch.com
4 changing beers (sourced locally; often Liverpool Craft)

The ground floor restaurant has a small bar area and garden, and downstairs is the basement bar, the No 23 Club, providing more drinking space and possibly a different ale choice. Beers are sourced from the Liverpool Craft Brewery – a mixture of its own brews and swaps from other smaller breweries. Near to the Everyman Theatre, Philharmonic Hall and other cultural venues. ✿◑⇌(Central)●🚌ᯤ

Crown Hotel ★

43 Lime Street, L1 1JQ

⏲ 11-11 ☎ (0151) 707 6027 🌐 thecrownliverpool.co.uk

Greene King IPA; 3 changing beers Ⓗ

With a nationally important historic interior this is a recent CAMRA heritage pub and recent branch Pub of Renaissance. The Grade II-listed building is noticeable for its Walkers Ales Warrington frieze. Its two downstairs rooms retain many original features including the ornate plasterwork and wood panelling. Food is served daily downstairs and on the upper floor. Close to Lime Street station and public transport links. ♘◑⇌(Lime St)🚌ᯤ

Dispensary 𝕃

87 Renshaw Street, L1 2SP

⏲ 12-11 (midnight Fri & Sat) ☎ (0151) 709 2160

George Wright Mild; changing beers (often Hawkshead, Titanic) Ⓗ

The licensee's impeccable attention to beer quality is renowned at this lively city pub, making it a haven for real ale drinkers of all ages. Seven handpumps serve an ever-changing choice of interesting microbrewery beers, offering a good range in terms of both style and strength. A regular local beer, Mark's Mild, commemorates the much-missed barman who died in 2012. The attractive bar area has Victorian features, and there is a raised wood-panelled area to the rear. ⇌(Central)🚌

Fly in the Loaf

Hardman Street, L1 9AS

⏲ 12-11 (midnight Fri & Sat) ☎ (0151) 708 0817

Okells Bitter; 7 changing beers (often Okells) Ⓗ

A former bakery, the name comes from the slogan 'no flies in the loaf'. Owned by Isle of Man brewer Okells, it serves four of its beers alongside a changing range of guests from around the country, many from microbreweries, and a good selection of foreign beers. Recently refurbished, the spacious interior has a light, airy frontage with contrasting wood-panelled areas towards the rear. There is an attractive on-street drinking area at the front and a function room upstairs. ◑♿⇌(Central)🚌(86)ᯤ

Globe

17 Cases Street, L1 1HW (opp Central station)

⏲ 11-11; 12-10.30 Sun ☎ (0151) 707 0067

Sharp's Doom Bar; Thwaites Wainwright; Timothy Taylor Landlord; 2 changing beers (sourced nationally) Ⓗ

Small traditional pub where long-serving Kitty McNicholas was awarded Bar Person of the Year in 2014. The pub is a buzz of lively conversation and attracts regulars from all over the city, with visitors also made to feel at home. In the small back room a brass plaque commemorates the inaugural meeting of CAMRA Merseyside and 40th year celebrations were held here in 2014. The sloping floor in the bar area is legendary. ⇌(Central)🚌

Grapes 𝕃

60 Roscoe Street, L1 9DW

⏲ 12 (2.30 Mon)-12.30am; 12-1.30am Fri & Sat

☎ (0151) 709 3977 🌐 thegrapesliverpool.co.uk

Changing beers Ⓗ

This corner local dates back to 1804 and retains its original Mellors signage outside. There is a total of nine handpumps, with a large number of beers coming from local microbreweries such as Mad Hatter and Liverpool Craft. The cosy beer garden at the rear is popular with smokers. Live jazz features every Sunday night from 9pm. Home-cooked Thai and Lao food is available. ✿◑⇌(Central)🚌(82,84,C1)

Lime Kiln 𝕃 ✔

Fleet Street, L1 4NR (500yds from Central station, 200yds from bus route)

⏲ 9am-1am (2am Thu-Sat) ☎ (0151) 702 6810

Ruddles Best Bitter; 10 changing beers Ⓗ

From first impressions the decor and layout may not appear to offer much for the real ale drinker, but looks can be deceiving. Thanks to significant commitment by the management real ale is well catered for, with at least one local beer usually on tap. In the trendy Concert Square area, it is a peaceful haven during the day. A Victorian warehouse once occupied the site, home to manufacturing chemists from the early-1900s into the 1950s. There is a separate smoking area. ♘◑♿⇌(Central)●ᯤ

Lion Tavern ★ 𝕃

67 Moorfields, L2 2BP

⏲ 11 (12 Sun)-midnight ☎ (0151) 236 1734

Young's Bitter; 6 changing beers Ⓗ

Named after the locomotive that worked the Liverpool to Manchester railway, the Lion features exquisite artwork plus intricately etched and stained glass. The building is Grade II-listed and has a nationally important historic interior. Regular society meetings and occasional Meet the Brewer events take place. Lunchtime food is served and speciality pork pies are available at all times. The house beer, brewed by George Wright, is the Lion Returns, and the cider is from Westons. ⇌(Moorfields)●🚌

Peter Kavanagh's ★

2-6 Egerton Street, L8 7LY (off Catharine St)

⏲ 12-midnight (1am Fri & Sat) ☎ (0151) 709 3443

Greene King Abbot; 4 changing beers (sourced locally) Ⓗ

Having a nationally important historic interior this pub in the Georgian area of Liverpool is well worth seeking out. The original pub at No.2 has murals by Eric Robinson on the walls of the two snugs and fine stained-glass windows with wooden shutters. The benches have carved armrests thought to be caricatures of Peter Kavanagh, the licensee for 53 years until 1950. These features were not adversely affected when the pub was expanded, first in 1964 into No.4, then in 1977 into No.6. Up to four rotating guest beers are available, usually from smaller breweries in the region. Q◑🚌

Richmond Hotel 𝕃

32 Williamson Street, L1 1EB

⏲ 10-11; 11-midnight Fri-Sun ☎ (0151) 709 2614

Draught Bass; changing beers Ⓗ

Lively family-run pub in a pedestrianised shopping area, offering up to three guest ales from local and

regional breweries. Formerly a Bass house, the original Bass mirror remains. More than 50 malt whiskies are usually available, sports fixtures are shown and there are occasional beer festivals and Meet the Brewer events. The pub sign, simply saying Richmond Pub, depicts World War II veteran Paddy Golden, a much missed regular and one of the first to land on the Normandy beaches.
⛟♿≹(Central)🚌

Roscoe Head

24 Roscoe Street, L1 2SX
11.30 (12 Sun)-midnight ☎ (0151) 709 4365
Tetley Bitter; 5 changing beers (sourced regionally) Ⓗ
One of the Magnificent Five pubs that have been in every edition of the Guide. This is a cosy four-roomed pub where conversation and the appreciation of real ale rule. Run by members of the same family for over 30 years, the name commemorates William Roscoe, a leading campaigner against the slave trade. Six handpumps feature Tetley Bitter and five changing guests, mostly from small breweries from the Finest Cask or SIBA lists. Home-cooked food is served Monday-Friday lunchtimes.
Q◐≹(Central)♣🚌

Ship & Mitre 🄻

133 Dale Street, L2 2JH (by Birkenhead Tunnel)
10-11 (midnight Thu-Sat) ☎ (0151) 236 0859
Changing beers Ⓗ
A 1930s Art Deco pub partly hidden by the Queensway tunnel entrance and the Churchill Way flyover. Its name is a combination of two previous incarnations, the Flagship and the Mitre. Fifteen handpulls serve an ever-changing array of beers and real ciders, with the friendly, knowledgeable staff always willing to make a recommendation. There is also an impressive range of world beers. Beer and cider festivals are hosted throughout the year. ◐◑♿≹(Moorfields)♣●🚌🐾

Thomas Rigby's

23-25 Dale Street, L2 2EZ
11.30-11 (10.30 Sun) ☎ (0151) 236 3269
Okells Manx Pale Ale, Bitter, Dr Okell's IPA; 3 changing beers Ⓗ
This multi-roomed, Grade II-listed building, bearing the name of wine and spirit dealer Thomas Rigby, now supplies an extensive world beer range on draught and in bottles. Three beers on handpump come from the pub's owner, Okells Brewery, the others are regularly changing guests. Good-value food is served until early evening, including specials, with one room offering a friendly and efficient table service. There is a courtyard for outdoor drinking. ◐◑≹(Moorfields)

Vernon Arms 🄻

69 Dale Street, L2 2HJ
11.45-11.30 (12.30am Fri & Sat) ☎ (0151) 236 6132
Boggart Hole Clough Rum Porter; Brains Rev James; 3 changing beers Ⓗ
Situated close to the business district, the Vernon retains the feel of a street-corner local. The single long-roomed bar serves three drinking areas including a back room with frosted-glass windows advertising the Liverpool Brewing Company which used to serve the pub. The main bar has wood panelling, several large columns and a small snug area. The regular Boggart Rum Porter is popular with many, and real cider on handpull is unusual for the city centre. Q◐≹(Moorfields)●🚌

Liverpool: Mossley Hill

Pi

106 Rose Lane, L18 8AG
11-11 (11.30 Fri & Sat) ☎ (0151) 222 0443
pi-roselane.co.uk
Tatton Blonde; 2 changing beers (sourced regionally) Ⓗ
A café-style bar in premises that was previously a shop, near to Mossley Hill railway station. The guest beers are from smaller breweries in the region. A number of foreign beers are also on tap and dozens of bottled beers are stocked. A simple hot-food menu – real pies with sides – is available all day. The extension into the shop next door has provided more space. ◐◑≹●🚌(61,80)

Liverpool: Walton

Raven 🄻

72-74 Walton Vale, L9 2BU
8am-midnight (1am Fri & Sat) ☎ (0151) 524 1255
Fuller's London Pride; Greene King Abbot; Ruddles Best Bitter; Sharp's Doom Bar; 5 changing beers Ⓗ
An open-plan Wetherspoon pub, popular with locals, particularly at weekends. It is themed on Edgar Allan Poe's The Raven, after a local, James William Carling, produced illustrations for the famous poem in the late-19th century. Born in 1857, Carling became a pavement artist at the age of five, later went to America, and is buried in Walton Cemetery. Aintree, the home of the world-famous Grand National, is less than a mile away. Alcohol is served from 9am.
◐◑♿≹(Orrell Park)🚌

Liverpool: Wavertree

Richmond Tavern 🄻

23A Church Road, L15 9EA
11.30-11 (midnight Thu-Sat) ☎ (0151) 733 9025
Liverpool Organic 24 Carat Gold; Thwaites Wainwright; 4 changing beers Ⓗ
A modern pub near the famous Penny Lane, operated by Ember Inns. Food may appear to be dominant, but drinkers are welcome. The guest beer list is revised each season, with the beers listed on the drinks menu. Traditional pub food including seasonal specials is served until 10pm. Quiz nights are Monday, Wednesday and Sunday.
❀◐◑♿P🚌

Willowbank

329 Smithdown Road, L15 3JA
12-11 (11.30 Wed & Thu; midnight Fri & Sat)
☎ (0151) 733 5782
Greene King Abbot; Tetley Bitter; 4 changing beers Ⓗ
Vibrant traditional multi-room pub with the original public bar dating back to when it was a Walkers establishment. Popular with students, it hosts regular events including a quiz night. Up to eight ever-changing guest beers are on offer as well as Westons Old Rosie cider. Real ale night is Tuesday and occasional beer festivals are hosted.
◐◑●P🚌

Liverpool: Woolton

Gardeners Arms

101 Vale Road, L25 7RW
4 (2 Fri)-11.30; 12-11.30 Sat; 12-11 Sun
☎ (0151) 428 1443

Greene King IPA; Timothy Taylor Landlord; 4 changing beers Ⓗ
Friendly, one-room, community village pub situated over the hill from Woolton village and separated from Menlove Avenue by blocks of flats. It now serves evening food in the form of a curry club. A popular quiz is held on Tuesday evening, and live music hosted monthly. Sky Sports is shown. There are numerous sports teams based at the pub. Q◗🚌🐾📶

Lydiate

Scotch Piper ★

Southport Road, L31 4HD
⏲ 12 (4 Mon; 2 Tue)-midnight; 12-10.30 Sun
☎ (0151) 526 2207
House beer (by Marston's); 2 changing beers (often 2 Guests) Ⓗ
The medieval, cruck-framed, Grade II-listed Scotch Piper is a thatched and whitewashed building just north of Lydiate. The entrance opens into a traditional bar with a servery on the left. A passage to the right leads to a further two rooms, the middle one with original woodwork. The end room, added later, is less rustic but retains some upholstered bench seating. The toilets are outside. The house beer is Piper 1320, from Marston's.
Q♨❀♣P🚌(300)🐾📶

New Brighton

Master Mariner Ⓛ

Union Terrace, Marine Promenade, CH45 2JT
⏲ 8am-midnight (1am Thu-Sat) ☎ (0151) 346 8950
Greene King Abbot; Ruddles Best Bitter; changing beers (sourced nationally; often Peerless) Ⓗ
Modern Wetherspoon pub with a bright, airy interior on two floors, a balcony above giving excellent views over Liverpool Bay and Fort Perch Rock, and a large sea-facing beer garden. Situated on Marine Promenade, close to local amenities including the Floral Pavilion theatre and opposite a new cinema complex, the pub is proving popular both with locals and visitors to the resort.
♨❀◖◗⇌🚌📶

Stage Door Tap

Queen's Royal, Marine Promenade, CH45 2JT
⏲ 10.30-11 (10.30 Sun) ☎ (0151) 691 0101
🌐 thequeensroyal.com
6 changing beers (sourced regionally; often Hawkshead, Phoenix, Weetwood) Ⓗ
A bright, airy, modern bar in the Queen's Royal Hotel, an imposing Victorian building close to the Floral Pavilion theatre with which it is now associated. In a seafront location overlooking Marine Promenade, this free house is popular with both locals and day trippers. The enclosed drinking area outside affords superb views over Liverpool Bay. Snacks are served in the bar daily until 9pm and good-value hot meals including breakfast from 7.30am. ❀🛏◖◗♿⇌🚌📶

Stanley's Cask

212 Rake Lane, CH45 1JP
⏲ 11-midnight (11 Mon); 11-11 Wed ☎ (0151) 691 1093
5 changing beers (sourced nationally; often Brains, Caledonian, Robinsons) Ⓗ
This ever-popular local continues to thrive, due in no small part to the landlady who has a track record for serving good beer. The five guest ales on offer often include seasonal beers from regional breweries. A traditional, single-roomed community local, it hosts various sports teams, quiz nights and regular live music including rock, blues and folk.
❀♿♣🚌(410,433)🐾📶

New Ferry

Freddie's Club Ⓛ

36 Stanley Road, CH62 5AS
⏲ 7 (5 Fri & Sat)-11; 12-11 Sun
Brimstage Trappers Hat Bitter; 1 changing beer (sourced locally; often Brimstage) Ⓗ
A popular social club, formerly a Conservative Club, converted into a comfortable lounge bar with adjoining snooker room with two full-size tables. It is situated in a residential street just a short walk from New Ferry shopping centre. There is regular live entertainment. A former local CAMRA Club of the Year, show a CAMRA membership card or a current copy of the Guide for entry.
Q❀♿⇌(Bebington)♣P🚌(1,41,42)

John Masefield

70-72 New Chester Road, CH62 5AD
⏲ 8am-midnight (11.30 Fri & Sat) ☎ (0151) 644 4250
Greene King Abbot; Ruddles Best Bitter; 4 changing beers (sourced nationally; often Coach House, Frodsham, Peerless) Ⓗ
Comfortable open-plan Wetherspoon pub in a former bicycle shop in the main shopping area. Named after a former poet laureate with local links, controversy surrounded the opening when locals suggested that the portrait on the pub's sign looked more like Adolf Hitler – judge for yourself. The pub features Wetherspoon's meal deals, a Wednesday night quiz and regular vintage bus pub trips. The real cider is usually from Gwynt y Ddraig.
♨❀◖◗♿⇌(Bebington)🍎🚌📶

Oxton

Caernarvon Castle

Bidston Road, CH43 2JZ
⏲ 11-11.30 (12.30am Fri & Sat) ☎ (0151) 652 2831
Greene King IPA, Abbot; Morland Old Speckled Hen; 4 changing beers (sourced nationally; often Peerless) Ⓗ
Large, pleasant pub on a busy road next to St Saviour Church. It was built in 1954 by Birkenhead Brewery on the site of the original Caernarvon Castle pub which was destroyed by bombing in World War II. The patio area is ideal for alfresco dining and drinking and is very popular as it catches the sun for most of the day.
Q♨❀◖◗♿P🚌(12,293)📶

Oxton Bar & Kitchen

2 Claughton Firs, CH43 5TQ
⏲ 12-11.30 (11 Mon & Tue); 12-11 Sun ☎ (0151) 651 2535
🌐 oxtonbar.co.uk
Brimstage Trappers Hat Bitter; 2 changing beers (sourced locally; often Liverpool Organic, Peerless) Ⓗ
Situated in the centre of attractive Oxton village among shops, bars and restaurants, this former John Smith's pub built in 1969 has been tastefully converted into a smart, comfortable, single-room lounge bar. There is a strong emphasis on quality food, ranging from sandwiches and snacks to full meals, available daily until 9.30pm (9pm Sun). Guest beers are usually all from local microbreweries. ♨❀◖◗P🚌(90,492/495)📶

Raby

Wheatsheaf Inn 𝕃

Raby Mere Road, CH63 4JH
11.30-11 (midnight Fri & Sat); 11.30-10.30 Sun
☎ (0151) 336 3416 wheatsheaf-cowshed.co.uk
Brimstage Trappers Hat Bitter; Tetley Bitter; Thwaites Original, Wainwright; 5 changing beers (sourced regionally) Ⓗ
An inn for 350 years, this is Wirral's oldest pub. The thatched building was rebuilt following a fire in 1611 and is reputed to be haunted by Charlotte, who died here. The walls are decorated with old photographs of Raby. The bar has nine handpumps serving two rooms and a restaurant in a converted cowshed. Lunch is served in the bar until 2pm, then snacks until 5pm. The restaurant is open evenings Tuesday-Saturday. **Q**P(84,85)

Rainford

Star Inn 𝕃

Church Road, WA11 8PX
11-11; 12-10 Sun ☎ (01744) 882639
Coach House Postlethwaite; changing beers Ⓗ
Situated towards the edge of the village of Rainford, the pub has a cosy lounge and a restaurant to the rear. Beers are sourced from local microbreweries, always including a dark brew. The comfortable bar is at the front of the building. Meals are served Wednesday to Sunday in the restaurant to the rear. **P**

Rock Ferry

Refreshment Rooms

Bedford Road East, CH42 1LS (off B5136, take Rock Lane East, then 4th right and over bridge)
12-11 (1am Fri & Sat) ☎ (0151) 644 5893
refreshmentrooms.info
House beer (by Lees); 4 changing beers (sourced locally; often Liverpool Organic, Peerless) Ⓗ
Refurbished and reopened in 2012 under its original name, the pub was built in the 1880s for ferry passengers to Liverpool. Although the ferry terminal is long gone, this off-the-beaten-track establishment is well worth seeking out, with excellent views over the Mersey. One central bar services two rooms. The house beer, HMS Conway, is from Lees and the cider is from Rosie's. Excellent-quality reasonably priced food is served daily until 9pm. Live music features every Friday evening. (1,2)

St Helens

Brown Edge

Nutgrove Road, Nutgrove, WA9 5JR
1-12.30am ☎ (0151) 426 5078
Banks's Sunbeam; Marston's Pedigree; 2 changing beers Ⓗ
On the main road between St Helens and Rainhill, this is an attractive suburban pub. It has two main areas – a public bar at the front of the building with pub games such as darts and live sport on TV, and a comfortable lounge at the rear leading to a bowling green. Live bands and beer festivals are hosted at various times of the year.
(Thatto Heath)**P**

Cricketers Arms 🏆 𝕃

Peter Street, WA10 2EB
2-11; 12-1am Fri & Sat; 12-11 Sun ☎ (01744) 361846
Changing beers (sourced locally) Ⓗ
Now in new hands, the Cricketers has established itself as an excellent cask ale pub. Eleven handpumps on the bar dispense beers from local microbreweries. Situated on the edge of the town centre, this friendly local community venue hosts darts and pool teams. Entertainment is offered at the weekend. St Helens CAMRA Pub of the Year for the last two years. **P**

Market Tavern

Bridge Street, WA10 1NW
11-11 ☎ (01744) 757313
Changing beers Ⓗ
This large town-centre pub with an imposing façade has recently reopened after a lengthy period of closure. The spacious interior has many TV screens catering for sport, particularly football and Rugby League. An extensive range of competitively priced real ales is on offer, often sourced from local micros. (Central)

News Room

Duke Street, WA10 2JG
5-11; 4-midnight Fri; 1-midnight Sat; 1-11 Sun
☎ (01744) 322129
George Wright Pipe Dream; 1 changing beer (sourced locally) Ⓗ
A small, stylish bar among the many keg-only bars on Duke Street. It is a recent convert to real ale – two ales are now offered from local microbreweries. It also offers many different Belgian and foreign bottled beers. With a vibrant and cosy atmosphere, the bar is often busy, particularly at weekends.

Phoenix 𝕃

Canal Street, WA10 3LL
2-11; 12-1am Fri & Sat; 12-11 Sun ☎ (01744) 751890
Changing beers Ⓗ
Built in 1903, the pub has its name in mosaic tiles on an outer wall, and a mosaic tile floor. A community local, the smallish bar is home to pool, darts and dominoes, and the spacious lounge is more comfortable. Up to six beers are available, mostly from local microbreweries. Sky Sports is shown on numerous TVs. Music dominates, with karaoke on Friday night and live Irish bands on Saturday. A yard at the back has been converted into a heated smoking area. (Central)

Sefton

Baldwin Street, WA10 1QA
11-11 (3am Fri & Sat) ☎ (01744) 22065
Brains Bitter; 3 changing beers (sourced nationally) Ⓗ
This town-centre local is basically one large room with a long bar down one side offering four beers, usually including one from George Wright Brewery in nearby Rainford. Real ale sales have increased significantly over recent years. There is a large function room upstairs and bands often appear at the pub. Good-value food is offered.
(Central)

Turk's Head 𝕃

Morley Street, WA10 2DQ
2-11; 12-12.30am Sat & Sun ☎ (01744) 751289
Changing beers Ⓗ
A short distance from town, this popular pub was a previous CAMRA National Pub of the Year runner-up. Half-timbered, with etched-glass windows, it

was built in the 1870s by Ellis Warde Brewery. It offers a constantly changing beer range, with 12 handpulls in use over the weekend, six at other times. Draught and bottled continental beers are also stocked. Thursday is curry and jazz night, and on Tuesday night there is a free quiz. Darts and dominoes are played. ◖●♣♠

Southport

Barons Bar

239 Lord Street, PR8 1NZ (within Scarisbrick Hotel)
✪ 11-11 (12.30am Fri & Sat) ☎ (01704) 534000
Moorhouse's Pride of Pendle; Tetley Bitter; house beer (by Moorhouse's); 10 changing beers (sourced regionally; often Cottage, Lytham, Moorhouse's) Ⓗ
An ornate baronial-style bar set within the Scarisbrick Hotel complex, now with a front lounge with chairs, tables and comfy settees overlooking the town's famous Lord Street. The bar has been championing real ale in Southport for many years and offers a wide selection, both local and national. One real cider is also stocked.
Q ⏰ ❁ ⊜ 🍴 ♿ ≈ ● 🚍 ♣

Barrel House Ⓛ

42 Liverpool Road, Birkdale, PR8 4AY
✪ 10-10 ☎ (01704) 566601
3 changing beers (often Liverpool Organic, Parker, Southport) Ⓗ
The Barrel House is a brand new micropub, opened in May 2014. A former newsagent's and still selling daily papers, it owes its existence to the new Sainsbury's that opened across the road – the owners felt that if they couldn't compete, they'd change their business. Totally refurbished with attractive decor and lighting, it is now an Aladdin's cave of wonderful bottled beers, wines, loose-leaf teas and speciality coffees. It also offers two real ales on handpumps, usually from local breweries such as Parker and Burscough.
Q ❁ ♿ ≈ (Birkdale) 🚍 (49,X2) ♣ 🐾 ?

Guest House

16 Union Street, PR9 0QE
✪ 11.30-11 (11.30 Fri & Sat); 12-10.30 Sun
☎ (01704) 537660 ⊕ guesthouse-southport.blogspot.com
Adnams Southwold Bitter; Caledonian Deuchars IPA; Jennings Cumberland Ale; Ruddles Best Bitter; Theakston Traditional Mild, Best Bitter; 1 changing beer (often Moorhouse's) Ⓗ
Close to the station and Lord Street, this listed building sports an impressive frontage and interior with three separate wood-panelled drinking areas. A quiet, traditional pub, the bar has 11 handpumps, one serving a local micro beer, and stocks a wide range of malt whiskies. There is seating outside at the front and a courtyard area to the rear. A Thursday quiz night and acoustic folk club on the first and third Mondays of the month attract a mixed clientele. Q ❁ ◖● ≈ 🚍

Inn Beer Shop

657 Lord Street, PR9 0AW
✪ 12-10.30; 11-11 Fri & Sat ☎ (01704) 533054
Southport Sandgrounder Bitter, Golden Sands; 2 changing beers (sourced locally; often Southport) Ⓗ
Friendly café bar offering a huge selection of local, national and foreign bottled beers for takeaway or consumption on the premises. The bar now sports a second handpump and serves real ciders and draught foreign lagers. The interior is lined with bottles and continental-style seating, leading to a

comfy area with games. Snacks and a tea/coffee service with cakes are available throughout the day. Outside seating is on Lord Street. The bar can get busy at weekends. ≈ ♣ ● 🚍 🐾 ?

Sir Henry Segrave Ⓛ

93-97 Lord Street, PR8 1RH (on A565, S end of Lord St)
✪ 8am-midnight ☎ (01704) 530217
Greene King Abbot; Moorhouse's Pendle Witches Brew; Phoenix Wobbly Bob; Ruddles Best Bitter; Thwaites Wainwright; changing beers (often Coach House, Lytham, Saltaire) Ⓗ
Named after the former land speed world record holder who used to race on Southport flats, this is a spacious Wetherspoon pub with an attractive 19th-century exterior. The manager is a strong supporter of real ale and runs regular beer festival trips and occasional Meet the Brewer evenings. The 12 handpumps offer the best all-round choice of microbrewery beers in Southport – regular orders are placed with Phoenix, Saltaire, Titanic and Hawkshead. There is outside seating on Lord Street.
⏰ ◖● ♿ ≈ ● 🚍 ?

Tap & Bottles

19A Cambridge Walk, PR8 1EN
✪ 12-11 (midnight Fri & Sat); 12-10.30 Sun
☎ (01704) 544322
3 changing beers (often AllGates, George Wright, Southport) Ⓗ
The Tap & Bottles is a new micropub situated in the arcade between Chapel Street and Lord Street next to the Atkinson Centre. It offers a choice of four real ales from virtually any brewery, though with a preference for beers from north-west England. A huge bottled selection is also stocked. There is a cosy seating area upstairs with benches and tables. A small tapas menu is available all day.
Q ⏰ ❁ ≈ ● 🐾 ?

Willow Grove Ⓛ

387-389 Lord Street, PR9 0AG (on A565)
✪ 8am-midnight ☎ (01704) 517830
Greene King Abbot Ⓗ/Ⓖ; Ruddles Best Bitter; Thwaites Wainwright; changing beers (often Moorhouse's, Phoenix, Robinsons) Ⓗ
The Willow Grove is now a Wetherspoon pub with much more emphasis on real ale and food. A quiet establishment, it is situated on Lord Street opposite the impressive 1920s war memorial. The interior is L-shaped with a long bar offering 10 handpumps with a choice of beers sourced from breweries ranging from the local Parker to other micros to nationals. It offers a mixture of chairs, tables and comfy settees. ⏰ ◖● ♿ ≈ ● 🚍 ?

Zetland

53 Zetland Street, PR9 0RH
✪ 12-11.30 (midnight Fri & Sat) ☎ (01704) 808404
⊕ zetlandhotelsouthport.co.uk
Jennings Cumberland Ale; 2 changing beers (sourced nationally; often Brakspear, Ringwood, Wychwood) Ⓗ
Situated in a residential area just 10 minutes from Lord Street, the Zetland is a local community hostelry offering amazingly low-priced home-cooked food in a friendly atmosphere. The pub shows live sport and hosts bowling competitions, with one of the finest crown green facilities in the north-west. A large pub with several side rooms, it offers excellent buffets and can cater for parties of up to 100. ⏰ ❁ ◖● ♣ P 🚍 (46,49) 🐾 ?

Wallasey

Cheshire Cheese 🄻

2 Wallasey Village, CH44 2DH

✪ 12-11 (midnight Fri & Sat) ☎ (0151) 638 3641

Wells Bombardier; 3 changing beers (sourced locally; often Liverpool Organic) Ⓗ

The current building dates from 1885 but a pub was on this site as early as 1561. This friendly local has a separate bar and snug, with the handpumps in the lounge. The guest beers usually include a local ale. Outside is a walled garden where regular beer festivals are held. Excellent home-cooked meals are served until 6.30pm (4pm Sun). Quiz nights are Monday and Wednesday, and the pub is home to a golf society and football, darts and bowls teams. Q ➸ ❀ ◐ ≈ (Village) ♣ 🚍 (124,423) ❀

Waterloo

Old Bank 🄻

34 South Road, L22 5PE

✪ 11-midnight (11 Mon-Wed) ☎ (0151) 928 7020

⊕ theoldbankwaterloo.co.uk

4 changing beers Ⓗ

Four handpumps dispense a range of beers, both local and from across the North-West. A quiet oasis on weekday afternoons, the pub is a hive of activity most evenings and weekends, with a strong commitment to live music and football. Music memorabilia adorn the walls, and a book swap library and games are available. A courtyard at the back of the pub provides an outdoor drinking area for warmer days, and the marina and beach are nearby. ❀ ≈ (Waterloo) ♣ 🚍 (53) ❀ 🛜

Queen's Picture House 🄻

47-49 South Road, L22 5PE

✪ 9am-11 (11.30 Fri & Sat) ☎ (0151) 949 2070

Fuller's London Pride; Greene King Abbot; Ruddles Best Bitter; Sharp's Doom Bar; changing beers Ⓗ

Named after a cinema that once graced this site, the Queen's Picture House is a typical Wetherspoon refurbishment with decor reflecting local events and people, particularly the local White Star Line, Titanic connections and local aviation pioneers. The main room and bar area offer various seating alternatives. An area to the right of the entrance is a dining space ideal for families and groups. Satellite TV is silent. ➸ ❀ ◐ ᵹ ≈ ● 🚍 🛜

Stamps Too 🄻

99 South Road, L22 0LR (opp Waterloo station)

✪ 12-11 (midnight Fri & Sat) ☎ (0151) 280 0035

5 changing beers (sourced locally; often Liverpool Organic) Ⓗ

Liverpool CAMRA branch Pub of the Year in 2013 and its original accredited LocAle pub. This friendly open-plan venue, where lively banter often prevails at the bar, is the haunt both of real ale enthusiasts and live music fans. Five handpumps serve mainly local beers, from Liverpool Organic, Brimstage, Southport and AllGates in particular, with occasional beers from further afield – a sixth handpump dispenses real cider. Bands and local musicians feature Thursday through to Sunday. ᵹ ≈ ● 🚍 (53) ❀ 🛜

Volunteer Canteen ★ 🄻

45 East Street, L22 8QR

✪ 2-11; 12-midnight Fri & Sat; 12-10.30 Sun

☎ (0151) 928 4676

4 changing beers (often Liverpool Organic) Ⓗ

A cosy traditional pub housed in a Grade II-listed terraced building, the Volly, as it is locally known, still provides a table service. Nestling in the back streets of Waterloo, the pub dates back to 1871 and, until the 1980s, was owned by Higsons, evidence of which can be seen etched into its windows. Small breweries around Merseyside and north Wales often supply guest ales. Pies, pate, olives and a variety of nuts are served at all times. Q ❀ ≈ ♣ 🚍 (53,53A) ❀ 🛜

West Kirby

West Kirby Tap 🄻

Grange Road, CH48 4DY

✪ 11-11 ☎ (0151) 625 0350 ⊕ westkirbytap.co.uk

7 changing beers (sourced locally; often Spitting Feathers) Ⓗ

Refurbished and reopened by Spitting Feathers brewery in 2014, this smart, modern bar features wood panelling, bare brick walls and a high ceiling. The single bar has a small raised area and a couple of discrete spaces. It is close to West Kirby's shops and transport connections, a short walk to the beach and convenient for trekkers to Hilbre Island. Eight handpumps dispense a varying range of beers plus a changing real cider. ➸ ◐ ᵹ ≈ ● 🚍 ❀ 🛜

What is real ale?

Real ale is also known as cask-conditioned beer or simply cask beer. In the brewery, the beer is neither filtered nor pasteurised. It still contains sufficient yeast and sugar for it to continue to ferment and mature in the cask. Once it has reached the pub cellar, it has to be laid down for maturation to continue, and for yeast and protein to settle at the bottom of the cask. Some real ale also has extra hops added as the cask is filled, a process known as dry hopping for increased flavour and aroma. Cask beer is best served at a cellar temperature of 11-12 degrees C, although some stronger ales can benefit from being served a little warmer. Each cask has two holes, in one of which a tap is inserted and is connected to tubes or lines that enable the beer to be drawn to the bar. The other hole, on top of the cask, enables some carbon dioxide produced during secondary fermentation to escape. It is vital that some gas, which gives the beer its natural sparkle or condition, is kept within the cask: the escape of gas is controlled by inserting porous wooden pegs called spiles into the spile hole. Real ale is a living product and must be consumed within three or four days of a cask being tapped as oxidation develops.

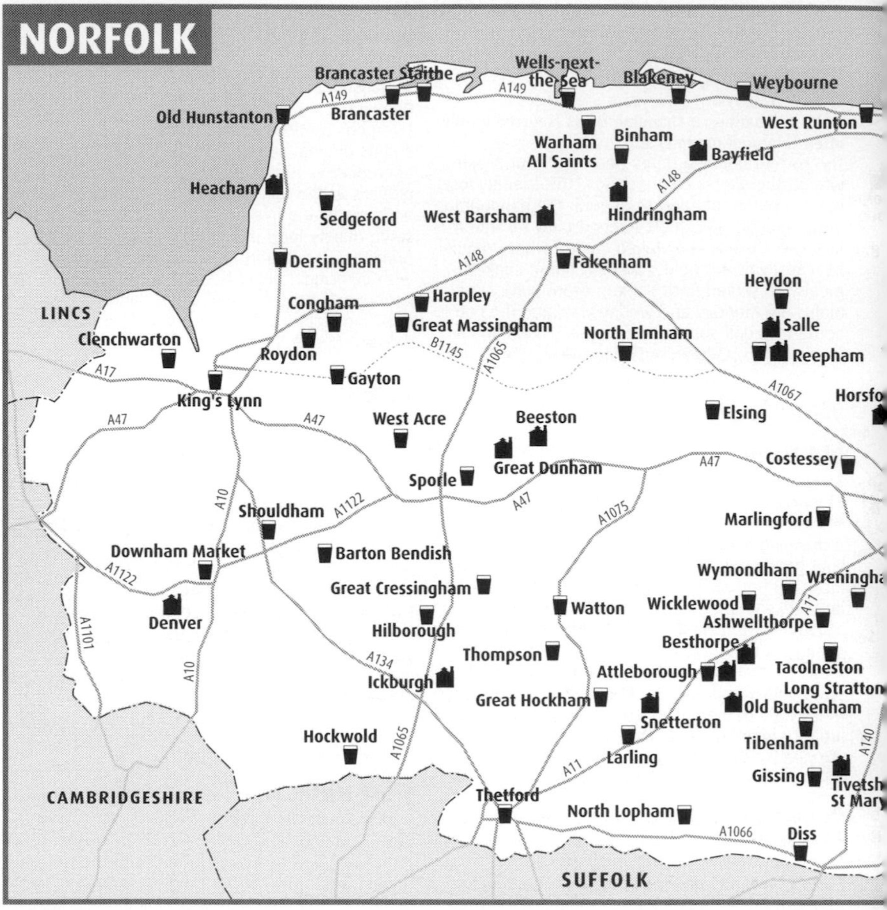

Ashwellthorpe

King's Head

The Turnpike, Norwich Road, NR16 1EL (on B1113)
12-11 (10.30 Mon & Tue) ☎ (01508) 489419
kingsheadashwellthorpe.co.uk
3 changing beers Ⓗ
A traditional family-run country pub with a spacious L-shaped bar interior and a dining area adjacent. Round to one side of the main bar, overlooking the large back garden, is a games area with a pool table and dartboard which is guarded by a parrot. There is an interesting range of up to three rotating beers, plus real cider. Good-quality home-cooked food is offered at very reasonable prices. ❀⇔◑♣●P

Attleborough

London Tavern Ⓛ

Church Street, NR17 2AH
11-11 (1.30 Fri & Sat) ☎ (01953) 457415
6 changing beers Ⓗ
Town-centre pub where families and dogs are welcome. The beer range is always different, with up to six real ales on offer. There is usually one beer from the on-site Taylor's of Attleborough Brewery which came on stream in 2014. The other five come from all over the UK. The pub has a dining room and serves breakfast and lunch every day. A beer festival takes place over the August bank holiday weekend. ❀◑♿⇌P🐾

Banningham

Crown Inn Ⓛ

Colby Road, NR11 7DY (N of B1145, 1 mile E of A140)
12-2.30, 6-11 (12.30am Fri); 12-12.30am Sat; 12-11 Sun
☎ (01263) 733534
Greene King IPA, Abbot; 2 changing beers Ⓗ
Traditional 17th-century free house with a welcoming atmosphere, an original beamed interior and a log fire. Two regular real ales and two guests (three in summer) are on offer. The pub has a first-class reputation for fine cuisine using local produce served in a superb new restaurant area open to the kitchen. There is a patio, garden and barbecue area for summer dining. Events include quiz nights and jazz on Sundays. Overlooking the village green, this is a popular and friendly pub. Q❀◑♿▲♣P🚌(18)🐾

Barton Bendish

Berney Arms

Church Road, PE33 9GF
12-11 (10 Sun) ☎ (01366) 347995
theberneyarms.co.uk

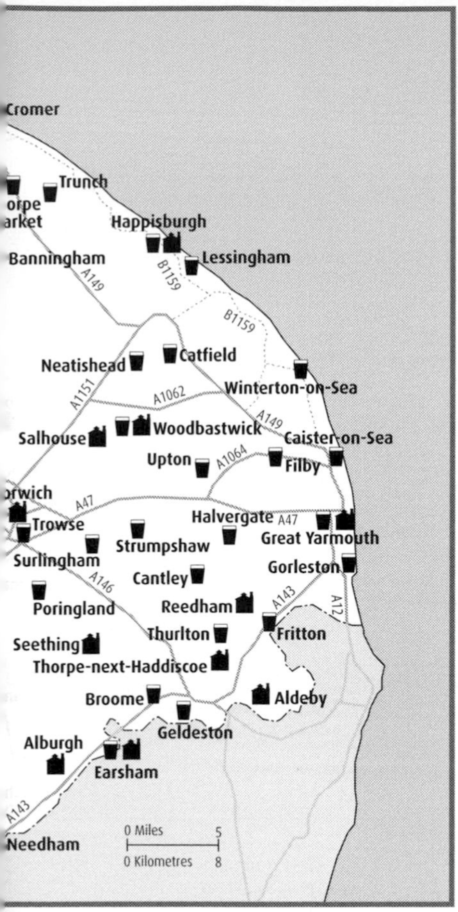

Adnams Southwold Bitter, Broadside; 2 changing beers

A smart village local with a bar and dining room. The beers are from Adnams and usually include seasonal ales. The food is a step up from normal pub food, but good value on the specials menu. There is a large garden area and accommodation is offered in the converted stable block. Look out for the interesting pictures in the bar. Q P

Binham

Chequers Inn

Front Street, NR21 0AL (on B1388)

12-3, 6-11; 12-11 Sat & Sun (01328) 830297

binhamchequers.co.uk

Adnams Southwold Bitter; Norfolk Brewhouse Moon Gazer Golden Ale; 2 changing beers

An old village pub, the Chequers is a tremendously popular place both with locals and visitors and has a lively atmosphere. Since the ownership changed in 2013 the bar has been redecorated, and children and dogs are now welcome. The menu comprises a range of good wholesome fare (including vegetarian) at reasonable prices. The range of beers may have altered, but the quality has not diminished – the new owners are keen, enthusiastic and experienced.
Q P (46)

Blakeney

King's Arms

Westgate Street, NR25 7NQ

9.30am-11; 12-10.30 Sun (01263) 740341

blakeneykingsarms.co.uk

Woodforde's Wherry; 4 changing beers

Situated close to the harbour in one of Norfolk's most picturesque coastal villages, this old building was originally three fishermen's cottages. The interior comprises a series of interconnecting rooms, and there is a large garden to one side. Around five to six real ales are dispensed either by handpump or gravity, including at least one from Woodforde's. Cooked breakfasts are now served 9.30-11.30am, which is handy for campers and walkers. Children and dogs are welcome and en-suite accommodation is offered.
Q P (3)

Brancaster

Ship Hotel

Main Road, PE31 8AP

8am-11 (01485) 210333 shiphotelnorfolk.co.uk

Jo C's Norfolk Kiwi, Bitter Old Bustard, Knot Just Another IPA

A Flying Kiwi inn located on the north Norfolk coast with two bars, serving local ales from Jo C's brewery. There is a large restaurant and beer garden. Accommodation is available in nine en-suite rooms, two of which make a family suite. Takeaway fish and chips can be ordered at the bar seven days a week. Restored in 2010, the building has kept much of the original history in design and decor. P

REAL ALE BREWERIES

All Day Salle (NEW)
Beeston Beeston
Buffy's Tivetshall St Mary
Chalk Hill Norwich
Dancing Men Happisburgh (NEW)
Elmtree Snetterton
Fat Cat Norwich
Fox Heacham
Golden Triangle Norwich
Grain Alburgh
Humpty Dumpty Reedham
Iceni Ickburgh
Jo C's West Barsham
Lacons Great Yarmouth
Norfolk Hindringham
Opa Hay's Aldeby
Panther Reepham
People's Thorpe-next-Haddiscoe (NEW)
Poppyland Cromer
Redwell Norwich
S&P Horsford
Stumptail Great Dunham
Taylors Attleborough
Tindall Seething
Tipples Salhouse
Tombstone Great Yarmouth
Two Rivers Denver
Wagtail Old Buckenham
Waveney Earsham
Why Not Norwich
Winter's Norwich
Wolf Besthorpe
Woodforde's Woodbastwick
Yetman's Bayfield

Brancaster Staithe

Jolly Sailors
Main Road, PE31 8BJ
⏲ 11-11; 12-10.30 Sun ☎ (01485) 210314
🌐 jollysailorsbrancaster.co.uk
Adnams Broadside; Brancaster Best; Woodforde's Wherry; 1 changing beer [H]
A cosy inn with several small drinking areas and two dining rooms, convenient for the Norfolk coast path and Brancaster Staithe harbour. It welcomes families and dogs, and has a garden, play area and ice cream hut. Brancaster beers are produced by a local brewery to the pub's recipes and at least one is always available. Food offerings include local seafood and stone-baked pizza, with the oven visible from the bar. Coasthopper buses stop outside. Q≿❀◐◑♿⛺♣P🚌(2)🐾📶

Broome

Artichoke [L]
162 Yarmouth Road, NR35 2NZ (just off A143, on road through village)
⏲ closed Mon; 12-3, 5-11; 12-midnight Sat
☎ (01986) 893325
Adnams Southwold Bitter [H]**, Broadside; Lacons Legacy** [G]**; Mauldons Micawber's Mild** [H]**; 6 changing beers** [G]
A community-oriented village local made special by the people who run it. Delicious home-cooked food is served lunchtimes and evenings, which can be eaten in the separate dining area, the main bar near a roaring log fire, or in the garden in summer. A range of up to 10 beers is offered, with emphasis on local ales dispensed either by handpump in the bar or by gravity from the taproom. The pub has around 100 malt whiskies. Open all day Tuesday-Friday April-September.
Q≿❀◐◑♿⛺🍎P🚌(580,588)🐾📶

Caister-on-Sea

Never Turn Back
Manor Road, NR30 5HG (to N of lifeboat station)
⏲ 12.30-11; 12-10.30 Sun ☎ (01493) 722697
Marston's Pedigree; 1 changing beer [H]
The saying 'Caister men never turn back' was coined following an ill-fated RNLI rescue during a severe storm in 1901 in which nine lifeboatmen were lost. The story is displayed on the wall inside. Only a short stretch of marram grass separates the pub and the sea wall. There are two pleasant bars and a large garden. The building is in best Lacons' 1930s style. There is one beer available in the winter but two in the summer. ≿❀◐◑♿⛺♣🍎P🐾

Cantley

Cock Tavern
Manor Road, NR13 3JQ (1½ miles N of village centre)
⏲ 11-3, 6-11.30 ☎ (01493) 700895
Adnams Southwold Bitter; 4 changing beers [H]
A roadside pub that serves a large rural catchment area, not just the nearby village of Cantley. Although a popular food venue (booking advisable) it retains the feel and atmosphere of a real pub, helped by the traditional decor. There are several themed food nights weekly, and a quiz night on Mondays. Its wide range of reasonably priced ales make it well worth the detour off the usual Broads tourist trail. ≿◐◑♣P🚌(730)🐾

Catfield

Crown Inn [L]
The Street, NR29 5AA
⏲ 12-2.30, 7 (5 Fri)-11; 12-3, 7-midnight Sat; 12-3, 7-10.30 Sun ☎ (01692) 580128
Greene King IPA; 3 changing beers [H]
Formerly a Lacons house, this 300-year-old village inn, with its real fire in winter, is a real focus for village life. There is an interesting selection of guest beers from local microbreweries. The food has an Italian accent, but traditional offerings are also featured, and fresh local ingredients used where possible. There is a separate function/dining room and a secluded garden for summer. Accommodation is available in a detached building that was once the doctor's surgery.
≿❀🛏◐◑🍎P🚌(12/12A)🐾📶

Clenchwarton

Victory Inn [L]
243 Main Road, PE34 4AQ
⏲ 12-11 (10.30 Sun) ☎ (01553) 775668
Elgood's Cambridge Bitter; 3 changing beers [H]
A thriving village local with a bar and a dining room where you can try the good-value hearty pub food. There is also a garden and smoking area. The Elgood's beers, which include a house brew, are complemented by a couple of guest ales. Look out for special events such as the quiz night on the first Wednesday of the month and the occasional beer festival. ≿❀◐◑♣🍎P🚌(505)🐾📶

Congham

Anvil Inn
St Andrews Lane, PE32 1DU (off B1153)
⏲ 12-3, 6-11.30; 12-11.30 Sun ☎ (01485) 600625
🌐 anvilcongham.co.uk
3 changing beers [H]
Recently refurbished pub a little off the beaten track, but worthwhile finding for its great home-made food. The bar is set in a large open-plan area and has three handpumps for the changing beers. Food is served in the bar area and a separate restaurant. Regular pub quizzes, charity bingo nights and live music make this a popular venue. A small campsite at the rear of the pub is a welcome new feature. Closed Mondays in winter.
❀◐◑♿⛺♣P📶

Costessey

Bush
58 The Street, NR8 5DD (¼ mile from post office in direction of Drayton)
⏲ 12-3, 6.30-11; 12-4, 6.30-11.30 Fri; 12-11.30 Sat; 12-5, 7-11.30 Sun ☎ (01603) 747227
Woodforde's Wherry; 2 changing beers [H]
Village pub dating back to the 19th century and once frequented by the artist Alfred Munnings. Inside, it has been modernised yet retains a wood-beamed ceiling. The interior is divided into two bars, one with a dartboard – the pub has its own darts team – the other with a large open fire. Outside there is a large beer garden leading down to the river, an unexpected delight in the summer. Disabled access is via the garden door.
Q≿❀♣P🚌(23A)🐾

Dersingham

Coach & Horses 🏆

77 Manor Road, PE31 6LN
12-11.30 ☎ (01485) 540391 🌐 thecoachpub.com
Woodforde's Wherry; 3 changing beers H
CAMRA Norfolk Pub of the Year 2014 and local branch Pub of the Year 2015. This busy 19th-century carrstone inn close to Sandringham offers one constant ale plus three varying guests at reasonable prices. It is popular for home-made traditional meals. Entertainment includes quiz nights, a piano, pool table and live music on Friday nights and some Sundays. The large garden has a children's play area. There are three en-suite B&B rooms. An October beer festival features around 20 real ales plus five real ciders.
Q P (11,10)

Diss

Waterfront Inn

43 Mere Street, IP22 4AG (just off A1066 past Aldi)
11-11 (midnight Fri & Sat) ☎ (01379) 652695
Greene King IPA; 4 changing beers (often Greene King) H
A 17th-century beamed single-bar pub in the centre of Diss owned by Greene King. Doors lead to a large decked area with tables and sofas overlooking the ancient six-acre Diss Mere. A well-kept range of Greene King seasonal and guest ales is on sale. A full refurbishment is planned which will see all ales dispensed by gravity from casks on the bar.

Downham Market

Railway Arms

Platform 1, Railway Station, Railway Road, PE38 9EN
(entrance on platform remains open when station office is closed)
10-12.10, 3.30-5.30 (9 Thu); 10-10.30 Fri; 10-12, 6-10.30 Sat; 12-2.30 Sun ☎ (01366) 386636 🌐 railway-arms.co.uk
2 changing beers G
A cosy micropub on the platform at Downham Market railway station, with two beers from around the country and, sometimes, more local breweries. The winner of CAMRA National Cider Pub of the Year 2013, typically at least five ciders/perries are available. The ciders come from national and local producers, usually including nearby Pickled Pig. Telephone ahead to check opening hours if you are travelling a long way.
Q P

Earsham

Queen's Head 🏆 L

Station Road, NR35 2TS (just W of Bungay)
12-11; 12-10.30 Sun ☎ (01986) 892623
Waveney East Coast Mild, Lightweight; 2 changing beers (sourced locally; often Green Jack, Waveney) H
On the Norfolk-Suffolk border near Bungay, this busy 17th-century locals' pub has a large front garden overlooking the village green. The main bar has a flagstone floor, wooden beams and a large fireplace with a roaring fire in winter. It is home to the Waveney Brewing Co. There is a separate dining area serving food at lunchtimes (not Mon and Tue). The landlord has owned the pub since 2000. Four ales and at least one real cider are usually sold. P (580)

Elsing

Mermaid Inn

Church Street, NR20 3EA
12-3, 7 (6 Fri & Sat)-11; 12.30-10.30 Sun
☎ (01362) 637640
Adnams Broadside; Woodforde's Wherry G**; 2 changing beers** H
A 17th-century pub opposite the village church. The large single room has a log-burning fire at one end and a pool table at the other. Guest ales are mainly, though not exclusively, from local brewers, typically Humpty Dumpty and Batemans, and are dispensed by gravity. The menu features curries, steaks and pie specials. Books and pub games are available for patrons' use, and the 12-mile Wensum Way walk passes the door. Lined glasses are available on request. P

Fakenham

Bull L

41 Bridge Street, NR21 9AG
10-11; 11-11 Sun ☎ (01328) 853410
Woodforde's Wherry; 3 changing beers H
Close to the marketplace, this modern local offers a warm welcome with its bright decor and open fire. The Bull has a long single bar and a range of comfortable seating options. Meals are served every lunchtime, with a roast on Sundays, and Wednesday evening is steak night. As well as the Woodforde's Wherry it tries to have another Norfolk ale available. Accommodation is offered in four comfortable en-suite bedrooms.

Filby

King's Head L

Main Road, NR29 3HY
12-11; 12-midnight Sun ☎ (01493) 733948
3 changing beers H
Filby is renowned for its superb summer floral displays, which are everywhere. The pub was originally owned by Lowestoft brewer Morse before it was taken over by Morgans. Now it is a free house, standing at the eastern end of the village set back a little from the road, with two bars serving local beers and good food.
P

Fritton

Decoy Tavern

Beccles Road, NR31 9AB
11-11 ☎ (01493) 488277
2 changing beers H
Cosy country free house set back from the main Beccles to Yarmouth road. It is close to Fritton Lake and about a mile from Broads moorings on the River Waveney at St Olaves, and has a play area for children. There is a wide range of home-cooked meals available. The beer selection varies but there will usually be two or three locally sourced ales. Note the collection of framed Lacon's beer labels on the wall. The current landlords have been here for 26 years. P (80/81)

Gayton

Crown Inn

Lynn Road, PE32 1PA (on B1145)

☼ 12-11 ☎ (01553) 636252
Greene King XX Mild, IPA, Abbot; Morland Old Speckled Hen; 1 changing beer Ⓗ
Originating from the 13th century, the Crown Inn combines a charming historic feel with a friendly atmosphere. It is a rare outlet for the XX dark mild and also offers an interesting guest beer on occasion. There are several drinking areas and an outside patio with attractive flowerbeds. The restaurant serves locally sourced food including game dishes and a popular Sunday carvery. Q❀🛏◑♿⛺♣P🚌(48)🐾

Geldeston

Locks Inn 🄻
Locks Lane, NR34 0HW (around 800yds along track from Station Rd; use postcode NR34 0HS for your sat nav)
☼ 12-11; 9am-11 Sat ☎ (01508) 518414
6 changing beers Ⓗ
Situated on the north bank of the River Waveney, the pub is accessed by a long meandering track between dykes and marshes. The small main bar has low ceiling beams and a clay floor, with candlelight adding atmosphere. A good range of ales, often from local micros, is supplemented by real ciders and perries. Live music features in summer. The pub is closed Monday-Wednesday, and liable to flood, in winter. Q❀◑♣🍎P🐾

Gissing

Crown Inn
Lower Street, IP22 5UJ
☼ 11.30-2.30, 6.30-midnight (1am Fri); 11.30-1am Sat; 12-midnight Sun ☎ (01379) 677718 🌐 gissingcrown.co.uk
Adnams Southwold Bitter; 4 changing beers (sourced nationally; often Courage, Fat Cat, Greene King) Ⓖ
There is a friendly atmosphere in this tucked-away, oak-beamed 18th-century pub near the church with its ancient Saxon round tower. Quiz nights take place every Wednesday and curry nights on the first Wednesday of the month. There is a heated smokers' shelter outside. Dogs are welcome but not in the restaurant. It is worth navigating the narrow lanes to find this pub, which mainly offers national beers usually accompanied by at least one local ale.
Q🐴❀◑♿♣P🚌🐾📶

Gorleston

New Entertainer
80 Pier Plain, NR31 6PG
☼ 12-11 ☎ (01493) 300022
Greene King IPA; 7 changing beers Ⓗ
Fairly close to the north end of the seafront, this traditional street-corner local with a curved frontage has an interesting design and layout. There is always a fine choice of beers on offer, including up to eight guests, many locally brewed, and draught ciders on handpump. The customers are as widely varied as the beer. This dedicated free house is well worth seeking out – please note that the main entrance is at what appears to be the back of the pub. ◐♣🍎🐾📶

Great Cressingham

Windmill Inn
Water End, IP25 6NN (off A1065 S of Swaffham)
☼ 11-11 ☎ (01760) 756232 🌐 oldewindmillinn.co.uk
Adnams Southwold Bitter, Broadside; Greene King IPA; 2 changing beers Ⓗ
Run by a local family since 1956, the Windmill features rooms of every shape and size including a conservatory. A rolling list of guest beers keeps you on your toes and real cider is an increasingly popular feature. The food ranges from great-value lunches to real sophistication, all masterminded by Chef (daughter of the family). A range of games is available and popular music nights are held. Modern accommodation is on offer plus a caravan site opposite. Q🐴❀🛏◑♿⛺♣P🐾

Great Hockham

Eagle 🄻
Harling Road, IP24 1NP
☼ 12-2.30, 6-11; 12-midnight Fri & Sat; 12-10.30 Sun
☎ (01953) 498893 🌐 hockhameagle.com
Adnams Southwold Bitter; Greene King Abbot; Morland Old Speckled Hen; Woodforde's Wherry; 2 changing beers Ⓗ
Dating from the 1850s, this large family and dog-friendly pub is set in a picturesque village close to Thetford Forest. Two bars divided by an open fire serve five real ales on handpump and food is served Friday to Sunday. Outdoor seating is provided at the front and in an enclosed brickweave courtyard at the rear. The pub hosts four pool teams and a darts team in addition to a fortnightly quiz and other regular events.
🐴❀◑♣P🗑🚌(Yes)🐾📶

Great Massingham

Dabbling Duck 🄻
11 Abbey Road, PE32 2HN
☼ 12-11; 12-10.30 Sun ☎ (01485) 520827
🌐 thedabblingduck.co.uk
Adnams Broadside; Beeston Worth the Wait; Woodforde's Wherry; 1 changing beer Ⓗ
Set between two ponds at the heart of a lovely village, the pub features bar areas with roaring fires in the winter and a garden to enjoy in the summer. With ample room for those who wish to try one of the five or six beers on offer, there is also a popular restaurant (booking is recommended). There is accommodation in six rooms, and guides featuring details of local walks are available from the bar. 🐴❀🛏◑♣P🐾📶

Great Yarmouth

Mariners 🄻
69 Howard Street South, NR30 1LN (behind both Palmers and Star Hotel)
☼ 11-11 ☎ (01493) 332299
8 changing beers Ⓗ
Traditional two-bar pub in the town centre, this venue stocks up to eight ales and eight real ciders/perries – visitors could be excused for thinking that a beer festival is always in progress, given the range and choice from all over the country. However, regular beer festivals are held throughout the year, including one at Easter, and another when the town's maritime festival is held in early September. Most local buses stop nearby. Q🐴❀◐⛺≠♣🍎P🐾📶

Red Herring 🄻
24-25 Havelock Road, NR30 3HQ (Havelock Rd is off St Peters St and at the back of the Time & Tide Museum)

🕔 12-3, 6-midnight; 12-midnight Sat & Sun
☎ (01493) 853384
3 changing beers Ⓗ
Back-street corner local close to the award-winning Time & Tide Museum and spectacular sections of medieval town wall. There is a nice, relaxed, comfortable atmosphere and the pool table and TV are tucked away in a room separated from the bar by folding doors. There are plenty of photos of Old Yarmouth during the herring fishing days when the town was invaded by many Scottish herring boats. The cider is Westons Old Rosie. ♣🍎

St John's Head Ⓛ
58 North Quay, NR30 1JB
🕔 12-midnight; closed Sun ☎ (01493) 843443
Elgood's Cambridge Bitter; 2 changing beers Ⓗ
In one of the oldest areas of the town, this former Lacons Brewery pub is reputed to be built on land confiscated from monks of the Carmelite order. A single bar houses a large TV screen for live sport, and the pub is busy on match days. There is a pool table in one area, plus a smoking shelter which is minimalist but heated on a pay-per-use basis. Q✿♿⛺≋♣P🐾📶

Halvergate

Red Lion
Marsh Road, NR13 3QB
🕔 12-2 (not Mon), 6-11 (midnight Fri & Sat); 12-2.30, 9-midnight Sun ☎ (01493) 700317
2 changing beers Ⓗ
An 18th-century thatched marshland pub on the Weavers Way long distance footpath. This refreshingly traditional local is the only survivor in a village that once had three pubs. It offers a warm welcome and a blazing fire on winter days. The clientele is an eclectic mix of locals, walkers and those seeking a quiet pub with good company. In winter it may be advisable to ring ahead at lunchtimes. Q✿◗♿♣P🐾

Happisburgh

Hill House
The Hill, NR12 0PW (off B1159, behind church)
🕔 12-3, 7-11 Mon-Wed; 12-11 ☎ (01692) 650004
🌐 hillhouseinn.co.uk
6 changing beers Ⓗ
A 16th-century inn close to the sea in an attractive coastal north Norfolk village. This rural retreat was a favourite with author Sir Arthur Conan Doyle in the late 19th century. The pub usually offers a range of around six real ales, mostly from local brewers. Hot meals are served lunchtimes and evenings. The pub hosts a mid-summer beer festival each June that showcases over 100 real ales and attracts visitors from far outside the local area. Q✿🛏◖◗⛺♣P🐾

Harpley

Rose & Crown
Nethergate Street, PE31 6TW
🕔 closed Mon; 12-3.30 (not Tue), 6.30-10.30; 12-5 Sun
☎ (01485) 521807
Woodforde's Wherry; 2 changing beers Ⓗ
Just off the A148 King's Lynn to Fakenham Road, this attractive 17th-century pub offers guest ales from local breweries. It features open bar areas with a stylish and comfortable feel and has log fires in winter, while outside is an enclosed beer garden for summer drinking. There is an extensive menu serving excellent food, including one of the best Sunday roasts in the area. The unspoilt village provides pleasant walks and is close to Houghton Hall. Q🐴✿◖◗P🚌(X8)🐾📶

Heydon

Earle Arms
The Street, NR11 6AD
🕔 closed Mon; 12-3, 6-11; 12-11 Sun ☎ (01263) 587376
Adnams Southwold Bitter; 2 changing beers Ⓗ
Lovely 16th-century former coaching inn opposite the green, in the centre of a privately owned picture-postcard village that is often used as a film location. The bar is mainly candlelit, with a welcoming atmosphere and a log fire in winter; it also has an interesting collection of horse-racing memorabilia. The food is seasonal and locally sourced, cooked to order and of the highest quality – booking is advisable. Real cider is available in the summer. One guest beer is from Woodforde's. Q🛏◖◗♣🍎P📶

Hilborough

Swan Ⓛ
Brandon Road, IP26 5BW
🕔 11-11; 12-10.30 Sun ☎ (01760) 657380
🌐 hilboroughswan.co.uk
5 changing beers Ⓗ
The 17th-century Swan is an ideal stop-off, sitting directly alongside the A1065 which runs through Hillborough. It features a good range of local ales (mainly Elmtree, Humpty Dumpty and Beeston) from five handpumps. It maintains a friendly local atmosphere – the landlady comes from a long line of village gamekeepers – with excellent home-made food. There is a popular carvery on Sundays. Accommodation is available. Q✿🛏◖◗♣P

Hockwold

Red Lion
114 Main Street, IP26 4NB
🕔 12-2.30, 6 (5 Fri)-11; 11-11 Sat; 12-10.30 Sun
☎ (01842) 829728
House beer (by Ruddles); 2 changing beers (often Adnams, Greene King, Woodforde's) Ⓗ
Traditional, friendly village pub set on a green. The Red Lion was refurbished and reopened as a free house in 2012. It has a smart but comfortable interior – see how many toby jugs you can spot. A good selection of home-made food is served all week, with a carvery on Sunday. There are regular, well-supported quizzes and darts matches. Outside is a spacious garden with plenty of seating. 🐴✿◖◗♣P🐾

King's Lynn

Lattice House
Chapel Street, PE30 1EG
🕔 8-11 ☎ (01553) 769585
7 changing beers Ⓗ
Many of the typical Wetherspoon features such as the all-day food and competitive prices will be familiar, but this building has been a pub for centuries and the wealth of architectural details is a real treat. There are no TV screens, lots of rooms and three bars. Events such as Meet the Brewer

evenings demonstrate a commitment to good beer. There is a public (pay) car park next to the pub. Q☙◐≈●🏠

Live & Let Live ⓛ
18 Windsor Road, PE30 5PL (off London Rd near Catholic church)
☼ 11-10.30 (11 Fri & Sat) ☎ (01553) 764990
5 changing beers ⊞
Busy traditional locals' pub just off London Road. It has a small cosy lounge bar and a larger public bar with a TV screen. The public bar is also occasionally the venue for live music. Five beers are available, including a mild (rare for the area) and something stronger, often featuring local brews. Real cider, including Westons, is available. ≈●

Stuart House Hotel
35 Goodwins Road, PE30 5QX (up gravel drive off Goodwins Rd)
☼ 6-11 ☎ (01553) 772169 ⊕ stuart-house-hotel.co.uk
3 changing beers ⊞
A hotel bar down a gravel drive not far from The Walks park and football ground, and about half a mile from the station. The two or three beers are usually from larger regional breweries. There is an annual beer festival around the last week in July and various other events through the year. Note that the bar is closed at lunchtime except by arrangement. ❀⌁≈P🏠

Larling

Angel
NR16 2QU (1 mile SW from Snetterton racetrack, just off A11)
☼ 10-midnight; 11-11 Sun ☎ (01953) 717963
⊕ larlingangel.co.uk
Adnams Southwold Bitter ⊞
Multiple Norfolk CAMRA Pub of the Year winner, the Angel is a must-visit, and famous locally for the summer beer festival featuring more than 70 ales. Five real ales are on handpump; the choice is always eclectic, one is always a mild, and there are over 100 whiskies. The friendly atmosphere is enjoyed by locals, passers-by, campers and rallyists who use the Angel's campsite. Real fires keep you warm in winter. There is also a dining room which boasts excellent home-made fare.
Q☙❀⌁◐&ÅP🏠

Lessingham

Star Inn ⓛ
Star Hill, NR12 0DN (just off main B1159, on corner of High Rd and Star Hill)
☼ 12-3 (not Mon), 6-11 ☎ (01692) 580510
Adnams Southwold Bitter; Buffy's Bitter; Woodforde's Once Bittern; 1 changing beer Ⓖ
Excellent village local that serves excellent beers to regulars from near and far, and has a relaxed, welcoming atmosphere. It is near the north-east Norfolk coast and convenient for those visiting nearby East Ruston Old Vicarage Garden. The large beer garden is perfect for summer drinking. The regular cider is Westons Old Rosie, and there are up to two others. Bar snacks and freshly prepared high-quality lunches and dinners are available daily (no food Mon and Sun eve). A beer festival is held in August. Closed all day Monday in winter.
Q❀◐Å●P🚍(34,36)🌸

Long Stratton

Swan Hotel
The Street, NR15 2XG
☼ 11-2.30, 6-11; 11-11 Fri; 11.30-11 Sat; 12-10.30 Sun
☎ (01508) 530200
Fuller's London Pride; 2 changing beers (sourced locally; often Buffy's, Green Jack, Wolf) ⊞
Large 500-year-old former coaching inn on the busy A140 south of Norwich in the centre of the village, reported to have a resident ghost. Two bars serve one regular beer and changing guest ales, mainly local. It is a community-led pub supporting local football teams. Check availability of food before visiting, but there are many food outlets close by. The bus stop is right outside the pub.
☙◐&♣P🚍🌸

Marlingford

Bell
Bawburgh Road, NR9 5HX
☼ 5.30-11 Mon; 12-2.30, 5-11 (midnight Fri); 12-midnight Sat; 12-10 Sun ☎ (01603) 880263
Woodforde's Wherry; 2 changing beers ⊞
Friendly, family-run one-room village pub with a function room and large restaurant, serving a freshly cooked and locally sourced menu. Tastefully refurbished and extended, with an ancient brick fireplace, three ales are usually served here, one often from outside Norfolk. There is a large enclosed rear garden with a children's play area, and a pleasant patio in front. ☙❀◐&P

Neatishead

White Horse ⓛ
The Street, NR12 8AD (S of A1151 Hoveton-Stalham road)
☼ 11-11; 12-10.30 Sun ☎ (01692) 630828
7 changing beers ⊞
Tastefully refurbished Broadland village pub retaining many original features in a modern design, with log fires in three separate drinking areas. The enthusiastic landlord keeps seven real ales from across the UK that change frequently. Beer festivals are held in spring and autumn, and the staff are knowledgeable about beer choice. Excellent, good-value food is home prepared with local produce. The new restaurant area is split-level and cosy. A short walk away from moorings to this beer lovers' haven. Q❀◐&Å♣P🌸🏠

Needham

Red Lion
117 High Road, IP20 9LG
☼ closed Mon; 12-3, 6 (5.30 Fri)-10.30; 12-5 Sun
☎ (01379) 853930 ⊕ theredlionneedham.co.uk
3 changing beers (often Grain, Greene King, Shortts Farm) ⊞
Oak-beamed, family-run and Grade II-listed pub with a separate restaurant and a real fire. It is child-friendly, with a large car park and garden together with an outdoor dining area. Generous portions of home-cooked food make this a busy pub during mealtimes. It is looking to install a Caravan Club site in the grounds. The pub also sells fresh local eggs and Christmas trees. Usually at least one Greene King/Ruddles/Morland beer is on sale together with at least one other mainly local ale.
Q☙❀◐&♣🚍(80/81)

North Elmham

Railway Hotel L

40 Station Road, NR20 5HH
11.30-midnight ☎ (01362) 668300
3 changing beers H
A fine example of a rural community pub, set in central Norfolk. A rotating choice of ales is available – the range favours local brewers such as Wolf, Panther and Beeston. There is an adjacent function room that hosts many music events. Home-cooked meals, using mainly locally sourced ingredients, are available. The pub now offers B&B and has a campsite at the rear. Restored steam trains run occasionally on the nearby Mid-Norfolk Railway. Q

North Lopham

King's Head

16 The Street, IP22 2NE (2 miles N of A1066)
11.30-3 (not Mon), 5-11; 11.30-midnight Sat; 12-10.30 Sun
☎ (01379) 688007 lophamkingshead.co.uk
Adnams Southwold Bitter; Woodforde's Wherry; 1 changing beer (sourced nationally; often Elmtree) H
Timber-framed and thatched 16th-century pub set back from the main road through the village. There are two bars – the public bar has a pool table and an inglenook fireplace, the comfortable saloon/dining room has a woodburner. The guest ale varies but is usually over 4% ABV. A discounted guest ale on Saturday sells quickly. Food is served Wednesday-Saturday lunchtimes and evenings, plus Sunday lunch. The pub has a crazy golf course with free club and ball hire. Letting rooms and Wi-Fi coming soon. Q P

Norwich

Alexandra Tavern

16 Stafford Street, NR2 3BB (on corner of Stafford St and Gladstone St, off Dereham Rd)
12-11 (midnight Thu); 10.30-midnight Fri & Sat
☎ (01603) 627772
Chalk Hill Tap Bitter, CHB, Gold; 2 changing beers H
Popular, bustling and friendly, this pub is a little gem found just outside the city centre. The interior is brightly decorated, with the walls featuring pictures and articles about the landlord's charity achievements. The bar regularly serves three Chalk Hill Brewery beers as well as guest ales, along with a good variety of food including a soup menu. There is a pool table, dartboard and lots of board games to choose from.

Beehive L

30 Leopold Road, NR4 7PJ
12-11 (midnight Fri & Sat) ☎ (01603) 451628
Green Jack Golden Best; Oakham Bishops Farewell; 3 changing beers H
This two-bar pub is popular with the local community and serves up to five guest ales, mainly from East Anglia. It is home to several sporting teams and hosts a well-attended weekly quiz on Wednesdays. The annual beer festival is held in the first week of July and regular charity barbecues feature during the summer months in the rear garden/patio area. Food is served lunchtimes only.
Q P

Coachmakers Arms

9 St Stephens Road, NR1 3SP
11-11; 12-10.30 Sun ☎ (01603) 662080
coachmakers-arms-norwich.co.uk
Greene King Abbot H; Wolf Golden Jackal G; 2 changing beers H
This popular city-centre hostelry is a free house with a range of ales dispensed by gravity. Dating from the 17th century, the allegedly haunted former coaching inn stands on the site of an old asylum. A spacious courtyard converted into a large drinking area complements a garden patio. Inside there is a large L-shaped beamed bar and also a function room. Unobtrusive Sky TV combines well with a dartboard for sports fans.

Earlham Arms L

41 Earlham Road, NR2 3AD
11-11 (11.30 Thu; midnight Fri & Sat); 9am-10.30 Sun
☎ (01603) 622993
Jo C's Norfolk Kiwi, Bitter Old Bustard, Knot Just Another IPA; 8 changing beers H
A large, lively pub with great food. It is welcoming and oozes hospitality from the attentive staff. Beers from Jo C's Norfolk Ale are always available alongside up to 12 guests from Norfolk and Suffolk, both on handpump and on gravity from the cellar. The large bar combines with the dining area and drinkers and diners merge well. Excellent and good-value bar snacks and tapas are to be had, which in summer can be enjoyed outside in the large enclosed garden. Q P

Eaton Cottage L

75 Mount Pleasant, NR2 2DQ
12-11 (midnight Fri & Sat) ☎ (01603) 453048
Wolf Golden Jackal; 5 changing beers H
A large and friendly local pub close to the shops in the Golden Triangle, with a number of seating areas inside and out, serving an interesting variety of ales from local breweries such as Elmtree and Wolf, plus beers from other UK breweries large and small. Sport is shown on TV but the screens do not dominate (except in one small area). There is also a pleasant pergola-covered patio to one side of the pub. (25)

Fat Cat L

49 West End Street, NR2 4NA
12-11 (midnight Fri); 11-midnight Sat; 11-11 Sun
☎ (01603) 624364
Adnams Southwold Bitter; Crouch Vale Yakima Gold; Fat Cat Bitter; Fuller's ESB; Kelham Island Pale Rider; Timothy Taylor Landlord H; 16 changing beers G
An outstanding example of what a real ale pub should be, with excellent service, ales from the Fat Cat range, plus around 10 regular and 20 guest beers from all over the UK, including many dark and stronger ales, real ciders, and foreign beers on draught and in bottle. These complement the brewery memorabilia around the pub. Food is limited to excellent-value rolls and pies. It is a beer lover's paradise that no visitor to Norwich should miss, and has been CAMRA National Pub of the Year twice. Q

Fat Cat & Canary L

101 Thorpe Road, NR1 1TR
12-11 (midnight Fri); 11-midnight Sat ☎ (01603) 432393
Fat Cat Bitter, Hell Cat, Honey Cat, Marmalade Cat, Wild Cat; 7 changing beers H
One of three in the Norwich-based Fat Cat mini-chain, about 1½ miles from the centre of the city, the pub serves most of the Fat Cat Brewery's ales, and various guests from around the UK, together

with continental beers and real ciders. There is a small TV to the rear of the main bar, a large car park and terraces front and back, the latter being heated. Home-made rolls are available.
P (54B,123,124)

Fat Cat Tap

98/100 Lawson Road, NR3 4LF
12-11 (midnight Fri); 11-midnight Sat; 11-11 Sun
(01603) 413153
Adnams Southwold Bitter; Fat Cat Bitter, Honey Cat [H], Marmalade Cat [G]; Harviestoun Bitter & Twisted [H]; 9 changing beers [G]
The Tap has blossomed since becoming the northernmost of the three Fat Cats and, as the name suggests, it is the home of the Fat Cat Brewery. The single drinking area showcases extensive breweriana, and the impressive bar hosts a selection of beers and ciders on gravity and handpump, complemented by a worldwide selection of bottled beers. Closing time is indicated by a set of traffic lights suspended from the ceiling. Live music features twice a week and there is a challenging quiz fortnightly.
Q P (11,11A)

Gatehouse

391 Dereham Road, NR5 8QJ
12-11 (midnight Sat) (01603) 620340
Grain Oak; Greene King IPA [H], Abbot; Woodforde's Wherry [G]; 1 changing beer [H]
Two miles west of Norwich city centre, this quirky 19th-century traditional pub was built on the site of an old toll house. Four excellently kept, and excellent-value, real ales are dispensed by handpump and gravity. The interior consists of two oak-panelled bars and there is a roaring log fire in winter. It has a large garden that backs on to the River Wensum. There is music most nights – usually Irish and folk – with occasional guest musicians.
Q P (19,20)

Jubilee

26 St Leonards Road, NR1 4BL
12-11 (midnight Fri & Sat) (01603) 618734
Greene King IPA; Woodforde's Wherry, Sundew, Nelson's Revenge; 2 changing beers [H]
An attractive Victorian corner pub with a warm welcome. There is a choice of two bars and a comfortable conservatory and enclosed patio garden. Many of the ales are local and this is also reflected in the range of lagers available. This popular venue is at the heart of the community and caters for all tastes, from sports fans to those who enjoy local history talks, and has a village feel while being within easy reach of the city centre. Occasional pop-up street food fairs are held.

King's Arms

22 Hall Road, NR1 3HQ
11-3, 5-11; 11-11.30 Fri & Sat; 12-11 Sun
(01603) 766361
Batemans XB, XXXB; Beeston Worth the Wait; Hop Back Summer Lightning; 6 changing beers [H]
A friendly Batemans house to the south of the city serving an extensive range of guest ales to complement the Batemans beers, usually including a stout or porter. Food is served on Sundays and match days, but at other times the pub allows customers to bring their own food from various nearby takeaways (plates and condiments provided). It has monthly quiz nights, poker evenings and live music, and Westons Old Rosie cider is often available. Busy on match days.
Q

King's Head

42 Magdalen Street, NR3 1JE
12-11 (midnight Fri & Sat) (01603) 620468
Woodforde's Nelson's Revenge; 8 changing beers [H]
Award-winning pub that offers many quality real ales, but no keg beers at all. The beers are mainly from Norfolk-area microbreweries, but selected ales from around the country put in an appearance. The house beer, KHB, is brewed by Winter's. A range of continental bottled beers is stocked, plus draught Kingfisher cider. The pub plays host to the Norwich bar billiards league, with the table situated in the rear drinking area, and often has fresh eggs and local honey for sale.
Q

Murderers

2-8 Timber Hill, NR1 3LB
10-11.30; 12-10.30 Sun (01603) 621447
themurderers.co.uk
Sharp's Doom Bar; Woodforde's Wherry; 6 changing beers [H]
This is a large multi-level establishment dating back to 1530 with an attached café-bar (open lunchtimes only). The traditional city-centre pub has been family owned for 30 years. A free house, up to 10 ales from micros around the country are stocked, including the house beer brewed by Coors. Popular with shoppers and office workers during the day, it has a younger profile in the evening. A 19th-century landlord convicted of murdering his wife has given the pub its name – the history adorns the walls inside.

Number 12

12 Farmers Avenue, NR1 3JX
11.30-11.30; 12-4 Sun (01603) 611135
Sharp's Doom Bar; Woodforde's Wherry; 1 changing beer [H]
A 250-year-old building on the old Cattlemarket in the centre of the city, beside Norwich Castle. For most of that time known as the Plough, then Le Rouen (celebrating Norwich's twin city in Normandy), the pub was renamed Number 12 in 2008. Now refurbished inside and out in a modern style, it retains beams and brickwork. There are three ales on the bar, and a mix of pub grub and contemporary dishes on the menu.

Plasterers Arms

43 Cowgate, NR3 1SZ
12-midnight (1 Fri & Sat) (01603) 387525
Oakham JHB; 10 changing beers [H]
Smart and friendly traditional corner local with a range of local and national microbrewery beers from around the country. Occasional themed beer tasting events are held. Live music from local bands features on most Sundays and Tuesday evenings, and a quiz every Monday. Food is provided by Voodoo Daddy pizzas, cooked to order.
Q

Plough

58 St Benedict Street, NR2 4AR
12-11 (midnight Fri & Sat) (01603) 661384
5 changing beers [H]
Popular pub in one of the city's oldest areas near the Norwich Arts Centre. As the Grain Brewery tap, it offers the full range of ales and the occasional

guest. The two-bar interior is fairly small, with wooden chairs and tables, and a roaring log fire in winter. The large Mediterranean-style courtyard garden is a fine place to while away a summer's evening. Excellent cocktails and spirits are also available, along with Vicky's special sausage pie, and barbecues in summer. ❀♣●🐾📶

Red Lion 𝕃

79 Bishopgate, NR1 4AA

⏲ 11-11 ☎ (01603) 620154

Grain Redwood Ⓗ

A pretty riverside pub, less than 10 minutes' walk from the station, which boasts a great range of up to six local ales, excellent food including pizza from a wood-fired oven, and a fine view over the river and Norwich's oldest bridge. A gas-effect fire makes for a cosy feel on a winter's evening, but equally tables on the edge of the river in the summer are a great asset.
ᗢ❀◐◗⇌P🚌(19,20,24)🐾📶

Reindeer 𝕃

10 Dereham Road, NR2 4AY

⏲ closed Mon; 12-11 (midnight Sat); 12-10 Sun
☎ (01603) 612995

Elgood's Cambridge Bitter; 9 changing beers Ⓗ

Spacious single-roomed public house serving a selection from Elgood's range plus interesting ales from across the country. The excellent and varied food includes gourmet bar snacks and roasts on Sundays. The original home of Wolf Brewery, the former brewing room is now a separate dining area and function room. Patio decking at the rear, and benches at the front, provide for outdoor drinking in summer.
Qᗢ❀◐◗♿♣●P🚌(21,22)🐾📶

Rose

235 Queens Road, NR1 3AE

⏲ 3-11; 12-midnight Fri & Sat; 12-10.30 Sun
☎ (01603) 767713

Adnams Ghost Ship; Oakham JHB; 4 changing beers Ⓗ

A friendly community and family-based free house, within easy reach of the city centre, with a refurbished modernist interior. This pub is growing in popularity. It hosts music and open mic nights, quizzes and charity events, plus regular beer festivals and occasional beer and food matching evenings. There is an excellent beer range from interesting local and non-local microbreweries, and a huge selection of foreign bottled beers. It has a pool table and screens for football. A loyalty scheme is in operation. ❀◐◗♿♣🐾📶

Trafford Arms 𝕃

61 Grove Road, NR1 3RL

⏲ 11-11 ☎ (01603) 628466

Adnams Southwold Bitter; Tetley Bitter; Winter's Mild; 8 changing beers Ⓗ

Close to the city centre, a warm welcome is assured at this public house run by the same licensees for over 20 years. A wide range of beers is available, usually including a mild, and Kingfisher Farm cider. Excellent home-cooked food is available, with pie, curry and fish evenings each week. Monthly quiz nights are popular. A former CAMRA Pub of the Year, the annual Valentine's beer festival is one of the biggest in the country, with 70-plus ales. Q◐◗♣●🚌(9,17)📶

Vine 𝕃

7 Dove Street, NR2 1DE

⏲ 11-11; closed Sun ☎ (01603) 627362

Oakham JHB; 3 changing beers Ⓗ

Just off the marketplace, Norwich's smallest pub is a gem in the heart of the city, serving up to four quality ales plus traditional Thai cuisine in a winning combination. The restaurant is upstairs, although customers often eat downstairs in the bar area. The pub boasts a range of bottled ciders and world beers. Extra tables and chairs are set outside in the pedestrianised street. Beer festivals held in January and City of Ale week are highlights. Q◐◗♣

White Lion

73 Oak Street, NR3 3AQ

⏲ 12-11; 12-10.30 Sun ☎ (01603) 632333

Milton Dionysus, Justinian, Marcus Aurelius, Pegasus, Sparta; 3 changing beers Ⓗ

Award-winning pub with a real fire serving a range of over 20 ciders and perries, plus beers from the Milton Brewery, and two or three guests from non-local microbreweries. The food is varied and excellent value – check the daily specials menu. An annual beer festival is held in the autumn, there are monthly folk evenings, and bar billiards and darts are played. Q◐◗♣●🐾📶

Wig & Pen 𝕃

6 St Martin at Palace Plain, NR3 1RN

⏲ 11.30 (midnight Fri & Sat); 11.30-6.30 Sun
☎ (01603) 625891

Adnams Southwold Bitter; Humpty Dumpty Little Sharpie; Woodforde's Bure Gold; 3 changing beers Ⓗ

Pretty, beamed, 17th-century free house with a spacious patio, immediately opposite the Bishop's Palace and with an impressive view of Norwich Cathedral spire. Three permanent ales and three guests are always on tap, usually including two local beers. The small back room can be used for meetings. Good-quality food is available lunchtimes and evenings. The pub is a short walk from Tombland, where there are bus stands for several bus routes, and is an ideal starting or stopping place for a walk along the river.
Q❀◐◗♿📶

Old Hunstanton

Ancient Mariner

6 Golf Course Road, PE36 6JJ (within Le Strange Arms Hotel complex)

⏲ 11-11 ☎ (01485) 534411

Adnams Southwold Bitter, Broadside; 3 changing beers Ⓗ

Adjoining the Le Strange Arms Hotel, this popular pub was formerly the old barns and stables and includes a family room and restaurants. At least four ales are available and live music nights are held every month. A large beer garden offers direct access to the beach and, as Old Hunstanton is on the east coast facing west, there are superb views of spectacular sunsets over the sea from the decking at the rear. Qᗢ❀🛏◐◗♿P🚂🚌(2)🐾📶

Poringland

Royal Oak 𝕃

44 The Street, NR14 7JT

⏲ 11 (midnight Fri & Sat); 12-11 Sun ☎ (01508) 493734

🌐 poringlandroyaloak.co.uk

Sharp's Doom Bar; Woodforde's Bure Gold, Wherry; 12 changing beers Ⓗ

A comfortable country pub with welcoming bar staff. The interior is divided into several small seating areas, one of which features memorabilia of the former RAF radar station which was situated nearby. A good selection of local real ales is stocked, supplemented by others from around the country, plus real ciders from Westons. There is a themed tea room from 10-4pm, hot food in the evenings, and at other times customers are welcome to bring in fish and chips from the shop next door. No dogs allowed, even in the garden. Q❀♣●P⊡🚌(87,88)📶

Reepham

King's Arms [L]

Market Place, NR10 4JJ

⏲ 11.30-3, 5.30-11; 11.30-11 Sat; 12-10.30 Sun ☎ (01603) 870345

Adnams Southwold Bitter; Greene King Abbot; Panther Golden Panther; Woodforde's Wherry, Once Bittern; 1 changing beer [H]

A former coaching inn dating back to 1667, situated in the picturesque square of this small market town. Extended sympathetically in the 1990s, original beams, Norfolk brickwork and open fires have been retained, providing several drinking and dining areas. At least one ale from the local Panther Brewery is always on handpump. The comprehensive menu is mostly sourced from nearby suppliers. Jazz bands play in the rear courtyard on summer Sundays, and there is a bar billiards table. Q🐎◐◑♣🐾

Roydon

Union Jack

30 Station Road, PE32 1AW (off A148)

⏲ 12 (4 Tue-Thu)-midnight ☎ 07771 660439

4 changing beers [H]

Popular with locals, this traditional village has twice been local CAMRA Pub of the Year. Four handpumps dispense a variety of ales, and beer festivals held over the Easter and August bank holidays usually feature local breweries. It offers live music each month, regular bingo and quizzes, and weekly support for darts, crib and dominoes. ❀♣P🚌(48)🐾

Sedgeford

King William IV

Heacham Road, PE36 5LU (off B1454)

⏲ 11 (4 Mon)-11; 12-10.30 Sun ☎ (01485) 571765 🌐 thekingwilliamsedgeford.co.uk

Adnams Southwold Bitter; Greene King Abbot; Woodforde's Wherry; 2 changing beers [H]

A large well-appointed village pub, popular for the locally produced food. Known by the locals as the King Willie, it has an excellent reputation for quality food but still retains a pub atmosphere that attracts local drinkers. There are two bars and a restaurant divided into four areas. A large garden at the rear has a superb outdoor covered drinking/dining area. Nine luxury rooms are available. Q🐎❀🛏◐◑♿P🐾

Shouldham

King's Arms

The Green, PE33 0BY

⏲ 12-3 (not Wed & Thu), 4.30-11; 12-3, 5-11 Fri; 12-11.30 Sat; 12-10.30 Sun ☎ (01366) 347410 🌐 kingsarmsshouldham.co.uk

2 changing beers [G]

A community-owned pub which offers something for the whole village. There is a volunteer-run café open from 9.30am during the day, and a diverse series of events ranging from poetry evenings and philosophy nights to music and quizzes. The beers are served on gravity into oversized glasses and usually come from small local breweries. No food on Monday or Tuesday. 🐎❀◐◑●P⊡🐾📶

Sporle

Peddars Inn [L]

70 The Street, PE32 2DR

⏲ closed Mon; 12-3 (not Tue), 6-10.30; 12-3, 6-11 Fri; 2-11 Sat; 12-6 Sun ☎ (01760) 788101 🌐 thepeddarsinn.com

Adnams Southwold Bitter; 2 changing beers [H]

A real village local with lots going on, such as music and quiz nights. There is a comfortable bar with a log fire for winter, a conservatory for those who wish to eat, and local guest beers. Note that the pub is closed on Monday, and there is no food on Tuesday. Close to the Peddars Way long distance footpath. 🐎❀◐◑P🐾📶

Strumpshaw

Shoulder of Mutton

9 Norwich Road, NR13 4NT (on Brundall-Lingwood road)

⏲ 11-midnight; 12-11 Sun ☎ (01603) 712274

Adnams Southwold Bitter; 4 changing beers [H]

Traditional 18th-century village centre pub, set back from the main road, with a public bar and pool table. Pétanque is played in the area at the rear. There is a covered, heated smoking area. It is within walking distance of the RSPB nature reserve. Beers come from a variety of East Anglian breweries. An extensive choice of freshly prepared meals using local produce is served in the separate restaurant. 🐎❀◐◑♿⛺♣P🚌(17A)🐾📶

Surlingham

Ferry House [L]

Ferry Road, NR14 7AR (follow signs to Surlingham Ferry; from Bramerton Rd continue on to Pratts Hill, keep left at the fork; Pratts Hill turns slightly left and becomes Ferry Rd) TG314067

⏲ 11-11 ☎ (01508) 538659

Adnams Broadside; Humpty Dumpty Little Sharpie; Woodforde's Wherry; 1 changing beer [H]

Sited on the banks of the River Yare, this rambling and characterful country inn is popular with boaters and walkers. The pub provides free mooring for boaters, and electrical hook-ups and water are available. The spacious interior has a large brick fireplace in the centre of the room. Three cask ales are always on plus an occasional guest in high summer. High-quality home-cooked food is served all day. Live music and quiz nights feature occasionally. 🐎❀◐◑♿♣P🐾

Tacolneston

Pelican Inn [L]

136 Norwich Road, NR16 1AL (on B1113)

⏲ 5-11; 12-2, 6-11 Sat; 12-4 Sun ☎ (01508) 489521

4 changing beers [H]

A former roadside coaching inn dating from the 17th century with an old sprawling interior and lots of different drinking areas. The bar has timber beams, a stone floor and a large open fire; four handpumps supply a rotating range of real ales, mostly from local brewers. There is a separate restaurant at the rear, and a bottle shop selling beers, mostly from local micros. The large garden has a decked area, and there are five en-suite rooms. Q🐴❀🛏◐◑♣P🚌(10A)📶

Thetford

Black Horse

64 Magdalen Street, IP24 2BP

⏲ 11-11; 12-11 Sun ☎ (01842) 762717

Adnams Southwold Bitter; Greene King IPA; Woodforde's Wherry; 2 changing beers Ⓗ

The Horse is just a few yards from the centre of Thetford and has been transformed by a new husband and wife management team. Five handpumps are now in use, with two reserved for interesting guest beers. It is divided into three areas: the bar in one, a popular dining area, and a darts zone – very important to the teams it supports. There is a varied menu of good food so you will not go hungry. A welcome return to the Guide. ❀◐◑♿⇌P

Red Lion Ⓛ

Market Place, IP24 2AL

⏲ 8am-11 (1am Fri & Sat) ☎ (01842) 757210

Adnams Broadside; Greene King IPA, Abbot; 3 changing beers Ⓗ

Now approaching three years as a Wetherspoon pub, the Red Lion is a large town-centre establishment sitting on the market square made famous as a location for Dad's Army. The town hall is also worth a visit. The standard Wetherspoon beers are accompanied by three guests. The venue has a range of drinking and dining areas decorated in typical style, with plenty of information on local history and attractions. It was once a Lacons house. 🐴❀◐◑⇌📶

Thompson

Chequers Inn

Griston Road, IP24 1PX (turn at the big tree)

⏲ 12-3, 6.30-11; 11.30-11 Sun ☎ (01953) 483360

🌐 thompsonchequers.co.uk

Greene King IPA, IPA Gold; Woodforde's Wherry Ⓗ

A 16th-century beauty, featuring a steep thatched roof and timber-framed interior. As you go into the bar remember people were shorter 500 years ago. With exceptional food, there are two rooms for dining and a small area and one small room for drinking. A beer outside is preferable on sunny days. Guest beers come from Wolf. It has separate apartment-style accommodation. 🐴❀🛏◐◑♿P

Thorpe Market

Gunton Arms Ⓛ

Cromer Road, NR11 8TZ (on W of A149 Cromer-North Walsham road, SE of Thorpe Market; look for hanging sign, lit at night)

⏲ 12-11; 12-10.30 Sun ☎ (01263) 832010

Adnams Southwold Bitter, Broadside; Woodforde's Wherry; 1 changing beer Ⓗ

This award-winning inn, in the beautiful grounds of Gunton Park with its deer herd, features tasteful decor, comfortable furnishings and log fires in winter. Well-kept East Anglian ales predominate, with regular guests. The first-class restaurant has some dishes cooked in the vaulted main dining room. Accommodation is sumptuous – most rooms overlook the restored parklands and deer. Interesting art and artefacts abound for the connoisseur. A beer festival is held in summer. Q❀🛏◐◑♿♣P🚌(4)🐾📶

Thurlton

Queen's Head Ⓛ

Beccles Road, NR14 6RJ

⏲ 6 (7 Mon)-11; 5-midnight Fri; 12-midnight Sat; 12-9 Sun ☎ (01508) 548667

4 changing beers Ⓗ

Community-owned pub run by locals Jem and Kathy. Four real ales are on offer including beers exclusively brewed at the nearby associated People's Brewery. Grain and Lacons brews are regularly available, plus a selection from other breweries. The pub is family- and dog-friendly, with children allowed in the bar, while the village play area is to the rear. Regular live music takes place on Saturdays. It has a cosy log fire in winter and a beer festival at Easter. 🐴❀♿♣P🚌(577)🐾📶

Tibenham

Greyhound

The Street, NR16 1PZ (300yds from church)

⏲ 12-3 (not Tue), 6.30 (6 Fri)-midnight; 12-midnight Sat & Sun ☎ (01379) 677676 🌐 the-greyhound-tibenham.co.uk

Adnams Southwold Bitter, Ghost Ship; Fuller's London Pride; 2 changing beers (sourced nationally; often Black Sheep, Fuller's, Shepherd Neame) Ⓗ

Friendly local community pub in the heart of the south Norfolk countryside offering beers from Adnams and Fuller's plus rotating guests. The interior has many old beams and comprises a lounge, bar area and a small games room with pool table. There is a large car park and a four-acre field at the rear which hosts many transport-themed events throughout the summer season. The field provides an ideal base for campers and caravanners, complete with electric hook-ups. Q🐴❀◑♿⛺♣P🐾

Trowse

White Horse Inn

The Street, NR14 8ST

⏲ 11-3, 5.30-11; 11.30-11 Fri & Sat; 12-10.30 Sun ☎ (01603) 622341

Crouch Vale Brewers Gold; 2 changing beers Ⓗ

First mentioned in 1836, this ex-Watney's pub was formerly on the busy Norwich-Lowestoft main road. Since Trowse Newton was bypassed, the pub now commands a central position in this quiet village, overlooking the green, which has a children's playground. With a comfortable carpeted dark-wood interior, split into three areas, the pub has a contemporary feel. Popular with office staff at lunchtimes and locals in the evening, there is also a separate function room for hire. ❀◐◑♿P🚌(587)📶

Trunch

Crown
Front Street, NR28 0AH (opp parish church)
☼ 11.45-3 (not Mon), 5.30-11 (midnight Wed); 12-11 Sat
☎ (01263) 722341
Batemans XB; Greene King IPA; 3 changing beers Ⓗ
Set in the middle of a charming north Norfolk village with fine old flint cottages, close to the coast, the Crown, Batemans' only pub in the area, offers an excellent choice of beers and a friendly atmosphere. A Batemans seasonal beer is always stocked, as well as two guests, and the cider is from Westons. A quiz night is held on the second Tuesday every month. Dogs are welcome in the bar. The pub may close early on weekday evenings – ring ahead to check. Q❀❀◑&♣P⊟(5,34)❀ ≋

Upton

White Horse Ⓛ
17 Chapel Road, NR13 6BT (about 10 mins' walk from moorings at Upton Dyke)
☼ 12-midnight ☎ (01493) 750696
Woodforde's Wherry; 3 changing beers Ⓗ
Traditional broadland pub, taken over and renovated in 2012. The pub is owned by the local community, with residents purchasing shares and having a stake in its future. Beers are all from local breweries, including some gems from Humpty Dumpty and St Peters, among others. A community shop is due to open shortly in converted stables. Fish and chips (also to take away) on Friday are a local institution. Closed Mondays in winter.
⧖❀◑&♣P≋

Warham All Saints

Three Horseshoes
69 The Street, NR23 1NL (2 miles SE of Wells)
☼ 12-2.30 (3 Sat & Sun), 6-11 ☎ (01328) 710547
Woodforde's Wherry Ⓖ; **2 changing beers** Ⓗ
A real pub in every sense of the word, with the perfect atmosphere for a quiet drink and conversation. The interior comprises three connected rooms filled with a fascinating collection of antiques and pictures, including the traditional game of Norfolk twister. In winter months customers can warm themselves by a log fire in the main bar. The beer garden provides a quiet haven in the summer. The pub is renowned for good traditional cooking, featuring soups, pies and puddings. Q⧖❀⇆◑&♣♦P❀

Watton

Willow House Ⓛ
2 High Street, IP25 6AE
☼ 10.30-11.30 (midnight Sat); 12-3 Sun ☎ (01953) 881181
⊕ thewillowhouse.co.uk
3 changing beers Ⓗ
The beautiful Willow House is a thatched, 16th-century, Grade II-listed building and was the only survivor of the town fire in 1679. It offers a range of drinking and dining areas, all with beams and low ceilings, and is dog-friendly. It hosts history-themed events and has introduced beer tasting sessions featuring local brewers. A full menu is available and accommodation can be provided.
❀◑P❀≋

Wells-next-the-Sea

Albatros
The Quay, NR23 1AT
☼ 12-11 ☎ 07979 087228
Woodforde's Wherry, Nelson's Revenge; 2 changing beers Ⓖ
Possibly one of the Guide's most unusual entries, the Albatros is a 19th-century Dutch North Sea clipper, permanently moored on the quayside of Wells harbour. The bar is in the hold of the ship and is adorned with nautical memorabilia, including many shipping maps. It sells up to four Woodforde's beers on gravity. Dutch pancakes are a speciality, and live bands perform each Friday and Saturday night, as well as Sunday afternoons in high season. Q⇆♣⊟(2,3)

Crown Hotel
The Buttlands, NR23 1EX
☼ 12-11 ☎ (01328) 710209
Adnams Southwold Bitter; Jo C's Norfolk Kiwi; 2 changing beers Ⓗ
A former coaching inn whose interior has been much modernised, overlooking the picturesque Buttlands Green. Inside are a bar and two restaurants, one of which looks out over the rear garden. Despite the light, airy, modern feel, a sense of history remains about the place, and old photographs of the hotel are all around the bar. There are usually two beers from local East Barsham-based Jo C's brewery, plus up to two rotating guest ales. ❀⇆◑▲⊟(2,3)≋

West Acre

Stag Ⓛ
Low Road, PE32 1TR
☼ closed Mon; 12-3, 6.30 (5 Fri)-11 ☎ (01760) 755395
⊕ westacrestag.co.uk
3 changing beers Ⓗ
A cosy pub that is well worth finding at the east end of picturesque West Acre, popular with locals, walkers, cyclists and riders. It is a strong supporter of local ales, maintaining a high standard of three varying beers and hosting excellent beer festivals. There is a popular quiz night monthly on a Sunday. The restaurant serves a variety of great-value freshly prepared meals using locally sourced ingredients. Q❀◑&▲♣P⊟

West Runton

Village Inn Ⓛ
Water Lane, NR27 9QP
☼ 11-11; 12-11 Sun ☎ (01263) 838000
Adnams Ghost Ship; Grain Oak; Wolf Golden Jackal; 1 changing beer Ⓗ
A large pub a short distance from the station and the beach, set in pleasant gardens in the centre of this quiet coastal village. Up to six well-kept and mostly local ales are stocked and rotated. Excellent home-cooked meals can be enjoyed in the dining areas or outside, where there is plenty of seating in the spacious gardens. In the 1970s major rock bands such as Deep Purple played secret gigs at the Pavilion (sadly now demolished) which was at the rear of the pub. Q⧖❀◑&⇆⊟(3)

Weybourne

Ship Inn

The Street, NR25 7SZ

12-3, 6-11; 11-midnight Fri & Sat; 11-11 Sun

(01263) 588721

Woodforde's Wherry; 3 changing beers

In the heart of this attractive north Norfolk coastal village, the Ship has up to six cask ales from local brewers including Woodforde's, Humpty Dumpty, Beeston, Brewhouse, Wolf, Grain and Panther, plus a range of bottled beers. Home-cooked food is available lunchtimes and evenings. There is a monthly quiz night, and the Coasthopper bus stops outside. The pleasant enclosed garden is popular in summer. Close to the Muckleburgh Collection of military vehicles. P(3)

Wicklewood

Cherry Tree

116 High Street, NR18 9QA

5-11; 12-midnight Sat; 12-11 Sun (01953) 606962

Buffy's Polly's Folly, Norwegian Blue, Ale

A Buffy's tied house, with all the beers coming from the brewery's range. The pub has three distinct areas – the bar, a lounge separated from the bar by a chimney, and a dining room. The bar counter is formed from naturally curved planks of solid oak, so take care when putting down your glass. Home-cooked food is served at all sessions, including a range of pies with imaginative fillings. A quiz night is held on the first Wednesday of the month. P

Winterton-on-Sea

Fisherman's Return

The Lane, NR29 4BN (N of B1159, close to coast)

11-11 summer; 11-3, 5-10.30 Mon-Fri winter; 12-10.30 Sun (01493) 393305

Adnams Southwold Bitter; Woodforde's Wherry; 2 changing beers

Popular 17th-century brick and flint-faced pub at the heart of a thriving Norfolk coastal village. The bar retains many original features. Four ales include the house beer from Greene King and two guests. The pub is renowned for excellent, home-prepared food using local produce when available; meals may be enjoyed in the bar or the high-quality restaurant extension completed in 2015. Five en-suite rooms and a cottage can be booked all year round. Five minutes' walk from the beach and close to the Norfolk Broads.
P

Woodbastwick

Fur & Feather Inn

Slad Lane, NR13 6HQ

10-10 (11 Fri & Sat) (01603) 720003

8 changing beers

Converted from a row of three cottages, this large open-plan pub is largely food oriented while offering customers the full range of beers from the adjoining Woodforde's Brewery. A tour of the brewery can be arranged in advance and combined with a meal. In summer the large garden provides an excellent area for a drink. The rare Norfolk Nip is occasionally available, usually as a bottle-conditioned strong ale, which is much prized locally. P

Wreningham

Bird in Hand

Church Road, NR16 1BJ

12-11; 11.45-11 Sun (01508) 489438

Adnams Broadside; Oakham JHB; Sharp's Doom Bar; Woodforde's Wherry

A friendly family-run free house. The original bar of this roadside pub has been converted into the Victorian Dining Room and large extensions have been made to the side and rear of the building. Situated close to Lotus Cars, the bar displays Lotus racing memorabilia among rural items and old photos of the village. Occasional quiz nights are held, as are regular acoustic music nights. There is a large car park to the side of building, and a pleasant garden area. Q P

Wymondham

Feathers Inn

13 Town Green, NR18 0PN

11-2.30, 7-11; 11-2.30, 6-midnight Fri; 12-2.30, 9-11 Sun

(01953) 605675

Adnams Southwold Bitter; Fuller's London Pride; Greene King Abbot; 2 changing beers

The Feathers dates from the 18th century. The interior consists of two main drinking areas with alcoves served by one bar. The alcoves and walls are adorned with postcard collections, enamel signs and farming and rural memorabilia, including an old bike. There is a large well-furnished patio garden at the rear, and good-value food is served lunchtime and evenings. A folk evening takes place on the last Sunday of each month. Feathers Tickler is the popular house beer.
Q (14,15)

Green Dragon

6 Church Street, NR18 0PH (between Market St and Wymondham Abbey)

12-11 (midnight Fri & Sat); 12-10.30 Sun

(01953) 607907

4 changing beers

Half-timbered inn with an interior of historical interest, formerly a medieval merchant's shop converted in the 16th century. One bar serves two downstairs areas and a snug. An upstairs bar is a recent addition. The interior retains many original beamed timbers and there are medieval carved figures in the mantelpiece over a large fireplace. The rotating range of four real ales is mostly sourced from local breweries, and two excellent beer festivals are hosted.
Q (14,15)

We would like to hear from you. If you think a pub not listed in the Guide is worthy of consideration, please let us know. Send us the name, full address and phone number (if known). If a pub in the Guide has given poor service, we would also like to know. Write to: Good Beer Guide, CAMRA, 230 Hatfield Road, St Albans, Herts, AL1 4LW; or email: **gbgeditor@camra.org.uk**

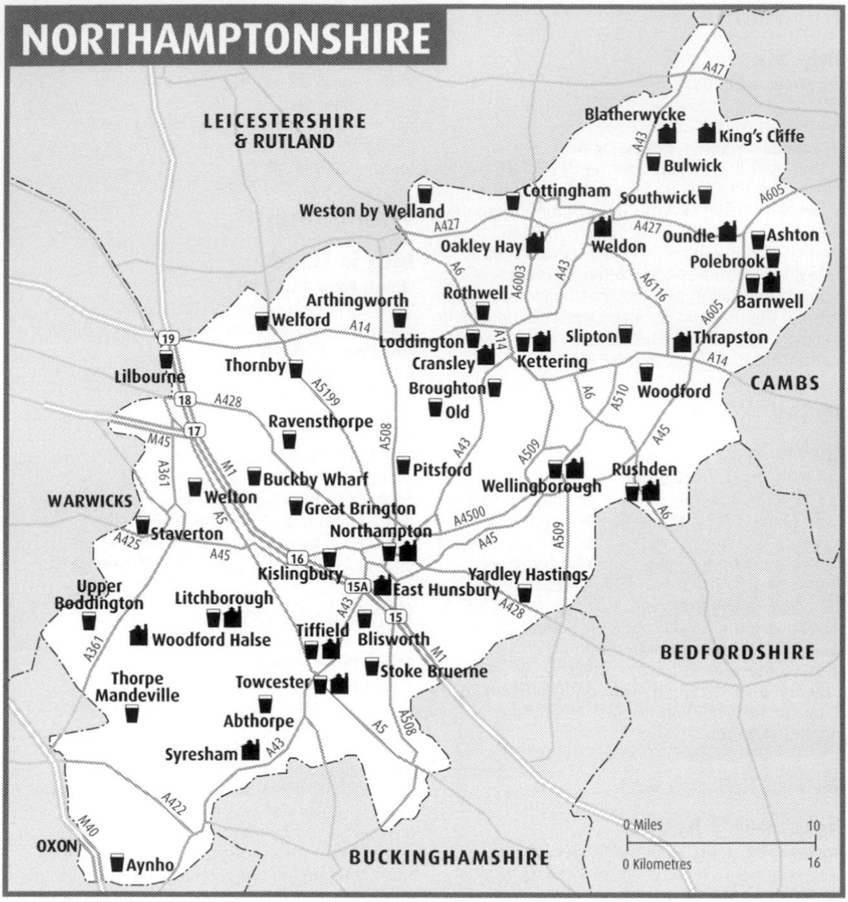

Abthorpe

New Inn 🄻

Silver Street, NN12 8QR

12-2.30 (not Mon & Tue), 6-11; 12-11.30 Fri & Sat; 12-10.30 Sun ☎ (01327) 857306 🌐 newinnabthorpe.co.uk

Hook Norton Hooky Mild, Hooky, Old Hooky; 2 changing beers 🄷

A tranquil country hostelry, hidden up a cul-de-sac off the corner of the village green. This mellow sandstone local, with its inglenook fireplace and low-beamed ceilings, is well worth searching out. Welcoming to visitors and locals alike, it offers high-quality meals cooked to order and served from the open kitchen, with much of the food locally sourced, including meat from the owner's farm. Hook Norton seasonal beers feature as guests. **Q🐴❀◐◑♣P🚌🐾📶**

Arthingworth

Bull's Head 🄻

Kelmarsh Road, LE16 8JZ

11-11 ☎ (01858) 525637 🌐 thebullsheadonline.co.uk

Everards Original; Thwaites Original; 2 changing beers (sourced locally) 🄷

A former farmhouse dating from the 19th century built from red brick. The pub has an opened-up bar with several cosy drinking areas and a restaurant to the front serving home-cooked fresh food from local producers. Popular with ramblers and cyclists, this is an ideal place to finish a walk in the local area, or stay over in one of the annexe rooms. A beer festival is held over the Whitsun bank holiday on the suntrap patio. Two regular guest ales are kept, sparklers removed on request.
Q🐴❀🛏◐◑♿♣P🐾📶

Ashton

Chequered Skipper 🄻

The Green, PE8 5LD

11.30-3, 6-11.30; 11.30-11 Sat & Sun ☎ (01832) 273494 🌐 chequeredskipper.co.uk

Brewsters Hophead; 2 changing beers 🄷

A thatched, stone-built pub renamed in the 1960s after a rare butterfly and rearranged internally in 1997 after a fire. It overlooks the green at the centre of the Rothschild's model village of Ashton. There are a number of rooms including a large function room used for an annual beer festival in the summer. The pub serves traditional food made with produce sourced locally as far as possible.
Q❀◐◑♿P🚌🐾📶

Aynho

Great Western Arms 🄻

Station Road, OX17 3BP (on B4031)

✪ 11-11 ☎ (01869) 338288 ⊕ great-westernarms.co.uk
Hook Norton Hooky, Lion, Old Hooky; 1 changing beer (sourced regionally) Ⓗ
This ivy-clad traditional inn is situated on the Northants and Oxfordshire borders and is between the former Great Western Railway and Oxford Canal. The pub is full of Great Western Railway memorabilia – photos past and present of both the railway and the canal adorn the walls. Renowned for its food, this is a popular venue for a relaxed Sunday lunch – outdoor seating alongside the canal is pleasant in the summer. Accommodation is offered in four rooms. ☎✪🛏◐👩‍🦽&♿P☐

Barnwell

Montagu Arms Ⓛ
PE8 5PH
✪ 12-3 (not Mon), 6-11; 12-11 Sat; 12-10.30 Sun
☎ (01832) 273726
Adnams Southwold Bitter; 3 changing beers Ⓗ
Overlooking Barnwell, this 16th-century stone-built inn has a public bar at the front and large restaurant to the rear. The bar area is traditionally decorated with large original exposed beams on the ceiling and walls. The car park is behind the inn and accessed via the village hall entrance. Also at the rear is a large play and camping area. There is disabled access from the rear to the restaurant only. Q☎✪◐👩‍🦽&♣♿P☐✿

Blisworth

Walnut Tree Ⓛ
21 Station Road, NN7 3DS
✪ 10-11 (midnight Fri; 1am Sat) ☎ (01604) 859551
⊕ walnut-tree.co.uk
Great Oakley Wagtail; Phipps NBC India Pale Ale; 2 changing beers (sourced regionally) Ⓗ
An award-winning family-run hotel and bar offering four ales and fresh cooking. The bar features leather padded chairs, comfy sofas and an open fireplace, and there is a separate quieter lounge. Situated just outside the historic village of Blisworth, the hotel is not far from Bridge 49 on the Grand Union Canal. A variety of monthly entertainment is provided including comedy, jazz, folk, blue-grass, rock and acoustic nights, as well as regular quiz nights. ☎✪◐&P☐(8,89)🔊

Broughton

Red Lion Ⓛ
7 High Street, NN14 1NF (off A43)
✪ 12-2 (not Mon), 5-11; 12-midnight Fri & Sat; 12-11 Sun
☎ (01536) 790239 ⊕ redlionbroughton.co.uk
St Austell Tribute; changing beers (often Julian Church) Ⓗ
Community-focused 18th-century ironstone pub with three main rooms – bar, lounge and open-plan dining area. Six changing ales are on offer plus two beer festivals a year. On the bar are two totem poles listing coming beers. A dark ale fan, the landlady ensures that a mild, porter or stout is always on the bar to accompany the home-cooked, locally produced food. Many unusual social events are hosted. The pub was local CAMRA Rural Pub of the Year 2013 and 2014. Q✪◐&♣♿P☐(39)✿

Buckby Wharf

New Inn
Watling Street West, NN6 7PW
✪ 12-11 (10.30 Sun) ☎ (01327) 844747
Marston's Pedigree; Wychwood Hobgoblin; 3 changing beers Ⓗ
A roadside pub standing alongside the A5 and Grand Union Canal with the locks forming part of the small gravelled garden to the rear. Dating back to the 1600s in parts, the interior features a central L-shaped bar serving a patchwork of different areas. The decor includes canal-related pots and pans. Situated alongside the canal, the pub comes into its own in the summer when the number of guest beers increases to three. ☎✪◐&♣♿P

Bulwick

Queen's Head Ⓛ
Main Street, NN17 3DY
✪ closed Mon; 12-3, 6-11; 12-7 Sun ☎ (01780) 450272
⊕ thequeensheadbulwick.co.uk
Digfield Barnwell Bitter; Oakham JHB; Shepherd Neame Spitfire; 2 changing beers Ⓗ
Seventeenth-century stone pub with a Collyweston slate roof on the main street opposite the church. Access is via a small back door through the patio and dining area at the rear. Inside, the single bar has five handpumps serving a range of ever-changing beers, often from local micros. There are a number of interconnecting dining areas. The high-quality locally sourced food is thoroughly recommended (booking advisable). Winner of CAMRA local branch Pub of the Year 2013. Q✪◐♣♿P☎🔊

Cottingham

Spread Eagle Ⓛ
1 High Street, LE16 8XL
✪ 12-11 (midnight Fri & Sat) ☎ (01536) 772038
⊕ thespreadeaglepub.co.uk
Sharp's Doom Bar; 3 changing beers (sourced locally; often Potbelly) Ⓗ

REAL ALE BREWERIES
Brigstock Kettering
Copper Kettle Rushden
Cotton End Northampton (NEW)
Cranky Cobbler Northampton (NEW)
Digfield Barnwell
Frog Island Northampton
Great Oakley Tiffield
Gun Dog Woodford Halse
Hart Family Wellingborough
Hunsbury Craft East Hunsbury
Julian Church Cransley
King's Cliffe King's Cliffe
Maule Northampton (NEW)
Merrimen Litchborough
Nene Valley Oundle
Nobby's Thrapston
Phipps Northampton
Potbelly Kettering
Rockingham Blatherwycke
Shoulder of Mutton Weldon (NEW)
Silverstone Syresham
Tom Smith Oakley Hay
Towcester Mill Towcester
Whistling Kite Kettering

A warm welcome to the Guide for this popular pub under new ownership for two years. The large lounge with the bar and a tiered area provides space for dining, while a separate bar serves as a busy games room. The owner is a former butcher and a multitude of affordable steak dishes is the speciality here. Weekly themed nights include steak, curry and steak and ale. A changing Potbelly beer is always on.

Great Brington

Althorp Coaching Inn (Fox & Hounds) 𝕃

Main Street, NN7 4JA

11-midnight; 12-11 Sun (01604) 770651

althorp-coaching-inn.co.uk

Greene King IPA; Hook Norton Old Hooky; Phipps NBC India Pale Ale; St Austell Tribute; 4 changing beers

Lovely thatched country pub dating back to 1765 close to Althorp House, home of the Spencer family. The interior features flagstone floors and a lounge with a large inglenook fireplace and oak beams. Outside is a courtyard, barn and enclosed garden. Excellent food is served in the bar and separate restaurant. Up to four guest ales are available. A beer festival is held in August. The pub is often busy, especially on Monday quiz night. Happy hour is 5-7pm daily with 50p off a pint.
Q P

Kettering

Alexandra Arms 𝕃

39 Victoria Street, NN16 0BU

2-11.30; 12-midnight Fri & Sat; 12-11 Sun

(01536) 522730

Changing beers

Traditional town-centre street-corner local where you will always find a beer from an unknown brewery. The new landlord searches out interesting beers and breweries, and over 9,000 different beers from over 800 breweries have been served here on 14 handpumps over a period of 12 years. Two opened-out rooms contain a piano and settee, with the walls covered in breweriana and pumpclips. The rear bar has a TV and Northants skittles. The patio area at the back features an aviary. Q

Three Cocks 𝕃

48 Lower Street, NN16 8DJ (opp Morrisons)

12-11.30 (11 Sun) 07909 698798

Mighty Oak Maldon Gold, Kings; 5 changing beers (often Full Mash, Grainstore, Hop Studio)

A pleasant edge-of-town pub with an L-shaped servery at the centre supplying two main bar areas furnished with comfortable armchairs and high-backed stools. On an upper level is a games area featuring Northants skittles and darts. Well-filled cobs are available to accompany the great beer choice. Beer festivals are held four times a year in the rear function room over the solstice and equinox weekends. Q

Kislingbury

Sun Inn 𝕃

Mill Road, NN7 4BB

12-2, 5-11; 12-11 Sat; 12-10.30 Sun (01604) 833571

thesuninnkislingbury.co.uk

Greene King IPA; Hoggleys Northamptonshire Bitter; St Austell Tribute; 1 changing beer

A pretty thatched village pub dating from 1866 with four cosy areas inside with low beams and church pew seating. Threatened with closure, it was purchased by three village couples in 2013. The walls are adorned with toby jugs and pub memorabilia, helping to create an olde-worlde atmosphere. Good-value meals are served in the evenings. There is a small car park to the front of the pub. A local CAMRA branch award winner.
Q P (D3)

Lilbourne

Head of Steam

10 Station Road, CV23 0SX

5-11.30; 12-3, 5-midnight Fri; 12-midnight Sat; 12-11 Sun

(01788) 860166 headofsteam.weebly.com

Dow Bridge Ratae'd; 3 changing beers (sourced regionally; often Bradfield, Phipps NBC, Salopian)

Welcoming community free house opened in 2014 at the centre of the village. The pub has two rooms and a large garden. The beer range includes local ales from Dow Bridge Brewery and rotating guests from all types and sizes of brewery across the UK. Music-free, this is an ideal venue for friendly conversation and socialising. Locally sourced pies and cheese boards are available. Folk guitar nights feature occasionally. A local CAMRA branch award winner. Q P

Litchborough

Old Red Lion 𝕃

4 Banbury Road, NN12 8JF (opp church)

12-11 (10.30 Sun) (01327) 830064

oldredlionlitchborough.co.uk

Great Oakley Wagtail; 2 changing beers (sourced locally)

A traditional four-roomed stone-built village pub worth seeking out. The bar area has flagstone flooring and seats inside the large inviting inglenook. The snug to the rear of the bar is a comfy casual room with double doors leading to a courtyard. An extension houses a restaurant and a shop selling local farm produce. A wide range of locally brewed bottled beers is stocked, with Merrimen Brewery a short distance away. Popular with walkers and cyclists on the Knightly Way.
Q P

Loddington

Hare at Loddington 𝕃

5 Main Street, NN14 1LA

12-3, 5.30-11; 12-midnight Sat & Sun (01536) 710337

thehareatloddington.com

Greene King Abbot; Sharp's Doom Bar; Wells Bombardier; 1 changing beer (sourced regionally; often Goff's)

Set in a conservation area, the Hare is a listed building in this picturesque village built from local ironstone. It stands in the middle of the Main Street surrounded by listed houses. Now more open plan, it has retained four areas – three are spread around the central bar and the fourth is a dining space where home-cooked food made using local produce can be enjoyed. The guest beer is often from an established microbrewery.
Q P

Northampton

Lamplighter

66 Overstone Road, The Mounts, NN1 3JS
12-midnight (1am Fri & Sat); 12-11 Sun
(01604) 631125 thelamplighter.co.uk
Phipps NBC India Pale Ale; Vale Pale Ale; 4 changing beers (sourced locally) H
A traditional street-corner pub just off the town centre attracting young and old alike. Four changing guest beers are from established micros, along with a selection of bottled beers. Home-cooked food is served until 9pm (7pm weekends) and children are welcome during meal times. There is a roaring fire in the bar and a heated courtyard for the colder seasons. The pub hosts open mic and quiz nights, a disco on Fridays and live music on Saturdays. Local CAMRA Pub of the Year 2013.

Malt Shovel Tavern

121 Bridge Street, NN1 1QF
11.30-3, 5-11; 11.30-11 Fri & Sat; 12-10.30 Sun
(01604) 234212 maltshoveltavern.com
Frog Island Natterjack; Fuller's London Pride; Oakham Bishops Farewell; 10 changing beers (sourced locally) H
Just off the town centre, this popular pub has won many awards including local CAMRA Pub of the Year on numerous occasions. Breweriana features everywhere. A range of 13 beers is available with 10 changing guests. Real cider, LocAle and Belgian draught and bottled beers are also on offer. Two beer festivals with live music are held each year, and blues bands play on Wednesday nights. The pub has a strong rugby following. Home-made lunches are served Monday-Saturday. Well worth a visit.

Olde England

199 Kettering Road, The Mounts, NN1 4BP
12-midnight (11 Mon); 12-11 Sun 07742 069768
theoldeengland.com
Great Oakley Wagtail G**, Wot's Occurring; Potbelly Bellowhead Hedonism; St Austell Trelawny; Vale Gravitas; changing beers** H
A converted end of terrace Victorian building on three floors with bars on two. The ground and first floors have a medieval theme and solid fuel burners. The cellar bar has a contemporary style and is more intimate. Over 20 beers from local micros and regional breweries are served by gravity and handpump as well as 20 ciders. Various board games, cards and dominoes are provided. Quiz night is Wednesday, live folk music is Thursday. No food on Sunday. Winner of Northants Food & Drink Town Community Pub.
Q

Queen Adelaide

50 Manor Road, Kingsthorpe, NN2 6QJ (off A5199)
11-11.30; 12-10.30 Sun (01604) 714524
queenadelaide.com
Adnams Southwold Bitter, Broadside; Nobby's Guilsborough Gold; St Austell Tribute; 2 changing beers H
This friendly, well-established local in Kingsthorpe village is an 18th-century listed stone building with low beams and an uneven floor in the main bar, a small snug with leather sofas, and a lounge bar to the rear. Up to four guest beers are available, often from local microbreweries. A beer festival is held in early September. The Sunday roasts are exceptional (booking advised). A popular pub for rugby followers, it was local CAMRA Pub of the Year for 2014. P

Road to Morocco

Bridgwater Drive, Abington Vale, NN3 3AG
12-11 (midnight Fri & Sat); 12-10.30 Sun
(01604) 632899
Greene King IPA, Abbot; Theakston Old Peculier; 4 changing beers (sourced regionally) H
A 1960s brick-built estate pub with a Moorish theme in some of the décor reflecting the pub's name, run by an enthusiastic landlord. There are two connected but distinctly different rooms. The bar area, where darts and pool are played, is quite lively, particularly when TV sport is on. The homely lounge is generally the quieter area of the pub. Quiz night is Tuesday. P (5)

Wheatsheaf

126 Dallington Road, Dallington, NN5 7HN
12 (4 Mon)-11; 12-5 Sun (01604) 758871
wheatsheafdallington.co.uk
Everards Beacon Bitter, Sunchaser Blonde, Tiger; 3 changing beers H
An attractive stone and thatched two-roomed pub with an unspoilt frontage tucked away in the conservation area of Dallington opposite the 13th-century village church. The bar has a partly flagstoned floor and the lounge/dining room is a large, quiet area with many photos of old Dallington on the walls. Live music features in the bar on Saturday nights and open mic on alternate Sundays. Up to three guest ales and two real ciders are available. P (7)

Wig & Pen

19 St Giles Street, NN1 1JA
10 (11 Sat)-11; 12-10.30 Sun (01604) 622178
thewigandpennorthampton.com
Adnams Ghost Ship; Elgood's Black Dog; Fuller's London Pride; Greene King IPA; 8 changing beers (sourced locally) H
A 300-year-old town-centre pub near the town hall and reputedly haunted by a young girl. A long L-shaped bar counter serves up to nine guest ales, cider and a wide range of bottled beers. A retractable cover provides shelter in the garden, where jazz bands play on Tuesday nights and live bands on Sunday afternoons. Good home-cooked food features locally sourced ingredients. A former local CAMRA Pub of the Year, it offers 10 per cent discount on ales to CAMRA members.

Old

White Horse

Walgrave Road, NN6 9QX
closed Mon; 12-3, 5-11; 12-11 Sat; 12-7 Sun
(01604) 781297 whitehorseold.co.uk
3 changing beers (often Phipps NBC, Whistling Kite) H
In Old, voted Best Small Village in Northamptonshire in 2012, this is a contemporary country pub comprising three opened-out rooms with polished wooden floors and a small snug towards the rear. The relatively small food menu offers interesting, quality home-cooked seasonal lunches and evening meals, from pub classics to house specials. Monthly live music and quiz nights, and a weekly Tuesday pie night, make this venue always worth a visit. Three local ales feature.
Q P

Pitsford

Griffin (L)

25 High Street, NN6 9AD (off A508)
🕓 6-11; 5-midnight Fri; 6-midnight Sat; 12-2.30, 7-11 Sun
☎ (01604) 880346 🌐 griffinpitsford.co.uk
Greene King Abbot; Potbelly Beijing Black; St Austell Tribute; 1 changing beer (sourced locally) (H)
Formerly cottages, this Grade II-listed 17th-century ironstone pub has a piecemeal exterior. Family run and owned, it has a comfortable charm about it and has retained most of its original character. The interior is festooned with fascinating artefacts in both the cosy bar room and larger lounges to the rear. The guest beer is often from Potbelly. Quiz night is Sunday. Ideally situated for Pitsford Reservoir and Brixworth Country Park. Q♿P🚌🐾📶

Polebrook

King's Arms (L)

Kings Arms Lane, PE8 5LW
🕓 12-3, 6-11; 12-11 Sat & Sun ☎ (01832) 272363
🌐 thekingsarms-polebrook.co.uk
Digfield Fools Nook, Barnwell Bitter; 3 changing beers (H)
This traditional stone-built thatched inn can be accessed from doors at the front and rear. The interior is open plan with a main bar, three areas for diners and a small garden. Third-pint glasses are available to allow customers to sample a wider variety of beer. An annual themed beer festival is held mid-September and there are regular food and beer pairing evenings. Free tapas happy hour is every Monday 6-7pm. Q❀◐◑♿♣P🚌🐾📶

Ravensthorpe

Chequers

Church Lane, NN6 8ER (off A428 opp church)
🕓 11.30-3, 6-midnight; 11.30-midnight Sat & Sun
☎ (01604) 770379 🌐 chequersravensthorpe.co.uk
Oakham JHB; Sharp's Doom Bar; Thwaites Original; 2 changing beers (H)
The hosts have enjoyed more than 25 years at this friendly pub which attracts locals, walkers and fishermen alike. A long-standing Guide entry, the brick-built Grade II-listed free house has an L-shaped bar and a restaurant to the rear serving excellent home-cooked food. There is a collection of jugs on the beams, and bank notes on the half-panelled walls. Outside is a children's adventure play area and a separate building for Northants skittles. 🐴❀◐◑♿♣P🐾📶

Rothwell

Rowell Charter Inn

Sun Hill, NN14 6AB
🕓 12-11 (midnight Sat); 12-10.30 Sun ☎ (01536) 710453
🌐 rowellcharter.com
Batemans XB; Phipps NBC Diamond Ale; Wychwood Hobgoblin; 1 changing beer (H)
Ironstone pub dating from 1642 with many rooms added in a piecemeal fashion resulting in different levels with low door lintels and ceilings. The name commemorates the granting of the Charter by King John in 1204 to hold a market and fair in the town each year. Preceding the annual beer festival the Bailiff of Rothwell rides out and reads a proclamation. Five beers and two ciders prove popular. Q❀♣🍎P🚌(19,X43)🐾📶

Woolpack (L)

Market Hill, NN14 6BW
🕓 2-10 (1am Fri & Sat) ☎ (01536) 710284
Grainstore Red Kite; Phipps NBC India Pale Ale; Wells Bombardier; 3 changing beers (sourced locally) (H)
A 17th-century ironstone inn with three low-beamed open-plan rooms. It is believed to be the site where wool was sold on the medieval market following the granting of the 1204 Charter. The games room features a pool table while an L-shaped bar and lounge are to the rear. The landlady has turned this pub around, increasing the number of changing guest beers to three, often from Grainstore and Julian Church. A CAMRA award winner. Q🐴❀◐◑♣P🚌(19,X43)🐾

Rushden

Rushden Historical Transport Society (L)

Station Approach, NN10 0AW (on ring road)
🕓 6 (7.30 Mon & Tue)-11; 4.30-11 Fri; 12-11 Sat & Sun
☎ (01933) 318988 🌐 rhts.co.uk
Phipps NBC India Pale Ale; Salopian Golden Thread; 5 changing beers (sourced locally) (H)
Former Midland Railway station serving seven real ales including a dark beer. The bar walls are adorned with enamel advertising panels and railway photos plus many CAMRA awards. On the platform, carriages provide a meeting room, Northants skittles and a buffet. Numerous open days are held in the summer, with steam and diesel train trips. A beer festival is hosted in September. Day membership is £1 except on open days. Q🐴❀♿♣🍎🚌(X46,M50)🐾

Slipton

Samuel Pepys (L)

Slipton Lane, NN14 3AR
🕓 12-3, 5-11; 12-11 Sat; 12-7 Sun ☎ (01832) 731739
🌐 samuel-pepys.com
Digfield Fools Nook (H)**; 3 changing beers (sourced locally)** (H)/(G)
Set in a picturesque thatched village, this lovely 16th-century ironstone pub has a low-beamed and brick-floored traditional bar to the front where locals and visitors can chat or relax in cosy armchairs in front of a real fire. The stone-built dining/lounge bar and the conservatory restaurant are decorated and furnished in a smart modern style. Three guest beers often come from local micros, with Nene Valley always featured, and in summer a real cider is also available. No food Sunday evening. Q❀◐◑♿P🚌🐾📶

Southwick

Shuckburgh Arms (L)

Main Street, PE8 5BL
🕓 closed Mon; 12 (4 Tue)-11; 10-11 Sat; 10-8 Sun
☎ (01832) 272044 🌐 shuckburghpub.co.uk
Brewsters Hophead; Nene Valley Bitter (H)/(G)**; 3 changing beers** (H)
Adjacent to the village hall and cricket pitch, this thatched stone-built pub has a front bar and side room. Outside there is a covered patio area with bar, large enclosed garden and car park. In 2014 the local villagers bought the lease and refurbished the interior. Quiz night is every Wednesday and live blue-grass music features on the third Thursday of

the month. A traditional menu is served most lunchtimes and evenings. Opens early at the weekend for breakfast only. Q❀◑♿⛺♣P🚌🐾📶

Staverton

Countryman 🄻

Daventry Road, NN11 6JH (on A425 just outside village)
⏲ 12-3, 6-11 (10.30 Mon); 12-10 Sun ☎ (01327) 311815
🌐 thecountrymanstaverton.co.uk
3 changing beers (sourced locally) 🄷
Formerly the New Inn, the Countryman is the last remaining of three pubs in this lovely village. The L-shaped bar, with wood beams throughout, serves four areas, some set aside for diners, and an open hearth fire between the spaces provides some seclusion. The enthusiastic landlord offers a wide choice of reasonably priced food, sourced locally whenever possible. The three changing guest beers are listed on the website and always include a locally brewed beer. Q❀◑♿P🚌(66)📶

Stoke Bruerne

Boat Inn

Shutlanger Road, NN12 7SB
⏲ 9am-11 ☎ (01604) 862428 🌐 boatinn.co.uk
Jennings Cumberland Ale; Marston's Pedigree, Old Empire; Wychwood Hobgoblin 🄷
Situated on the banks of the Grand Union Canal opposite the National Canal Museum and next to the locks, the Boat Inn has been owned by the same family since 1877. The long narrow pub has a wonderful tap bar and interconnecting rooms with canal views, open fires, original stone floors and window seats, while an adjoining room has Northants skittles. A canal boat is available for parties to hire. The cider is Thatchers Heritage. Opens for breakfast at 9am.
Q🐎❀◑♿♣🍎P🚌(86)🐾📶

Thornby

Red Lion 🄻

Welford Road, NN6 8SJ (on A5199)
⏲ 12-11 (10.30 Sun) ☎ (01604) 740238
🌐 redlionthornby.co.uk
6 changing beers (sourced locally) 🄷
An impressive whitewashed village pub dating back more than 400 years. The compact bar has two drinking areas with a wood-burning open fire in the lounge. A motley collection of beer tankards, steins and framed photos is displayed throughout. To the rear is the restaurant, which occupies two linked rooms, one heavily beamed. Six guest beers are usually from local breweries including Oakham and Dow Bridge. A beer festival is held in late July/August. Q🐎❀🛏◑♿P🚌🐾📶

Thorpe Mandeville

Three Conies 🄻

Banbury Lane, OX17 2EX (on edge of village)
⏲ 10-midnight ☎ (01295) 711025
Hook Norton Hooky, Lion, Old Hooky; 1 changing beer 🄷
This local ironstone building dates back to the 17th century, when it was a drovers' inn. The beamed bar has open fires at both ends. Noted for its meals, it opens at 10am for coffee, and there is a separate restaurant with a vaulted ceiling offering a full menu including Aberdeen Angus steaks. The pub hosts an annual beer festival and a cider festival, and is home to a Northants Skittles team.
Q◑♣🍎P🚌🐾

Tiffield

George at Tiffield 🄻

21 High Street North, NN12 8AD
⏲ 12-3, 6-11; 7-11 Tue; 12-midnight Sat; 12-7 Sun
☎ (01327) 350527 🌐 thegeorgeattiffield.co.uk
Great Oakley Wot's Occurring, Tiffield Thunderbolt; Vale Pale Ale; 2 changing beers (sourced locally) 🄷
A true community pub dating from the 16th century with Victorian and more modern additions. It has a cosy bar, games room with Northants skittles and back room restaurant which can be booked for small functions. It is the tap for Great Oakley Brewery, just outside the village, and also offers two changing guest ales. Two annual beer festivals are hosted at Easter and in October. Northamptonshire Food & Drink Awards 2012/13 Rural Community Pub of the Year.
Q❀◑♿⛺♣P🗑🐾

Towcester

Towcester Mill Brewery Tap 🄻

Chantry Lane, NN12 6AD
⏲ 11-3, 5-11; 11-11 Sat; 12-7 Sun ☎ (01327) 437060
🌐 towcestermillbrewery.co.uk
Towcester Mill Mill Race, Bell Ringer, Black Fire; 3 changing beers (sourced locally) 🄷
Popular and welcoming brewery tap in a historic mill dating from 1794, straddling the old mill race and adjacent to Bury Munt on which the town's fort once stood. The bar retains many original features including beams, stonework and a wooden floor. A large garden runs alongside the mill stream with views of the original mill workings. Three rotating guest ales are sourced from other local breweries and eight ciders are available. Beer festivals feature in June and September.
Q🐎❀♿♣🍎P🚌🐾📶

Upper Boddington

Plough 🄻

Warwick Road, NN11 6DH
⏲ 5.30-11; 5-midnight Fri; 12-midnight Sat; 12-10.30 Sun
☎ (01327) 260364 🌐 ploughinnboddington.co.uk
Greene King IPA; Shepherd Neame Spitfire; 2 changing beers (sourced regionally) 🄷
Early 18th-century stone-built and thatched village pub with a small bar with flagstone floors. The entrance lobby on two levels leads to a small lounge, formerly two small rooms, which has a small modern counter and a working Raeburn cooker, and a dining room. Stone and plaster walls and low wood beams feature in more interconnected rooms to the rear, including a snug with leather settees. Q🐎🛏◑⛺P🐾📶

Welford

Wharf Inn 🄻

NN6 6JQ (on A5199 by canal basin)
⏲ 12-11 ☎ (01858) 575075 🌐 wharfinn.co.uk
Grainstore Ten Fifty; Marston's Pedigree; Oakham Bishops Farewell; 3 changing beers (sourced locally) 🄷
Originally dating back to the 1800s, this 1980s red-brick inn conversion is next to the canal basin

where several walks can be started. The pub is popular with narrowboaters, walkers and locals alike. Inside is a small bottom bar, while up a couple of steps is the main bar, with an inglenook separating the drinking area from the restaurant. Six handpulls offer an Oakham beer and others from established micros. Food is served all day at the weekend. Q P

Wellingborough

Coach & Horses

17 Oxford Street, NN8 4HY (800yds from Market Square)

12-11 (9 Mon); 12-6 Sun (01933) 441848

coachandhorseswellingborough.co.uk

Changing beers

Town-centre local with an enthusiastic landlord fully committed to offering a constantly changing choice of 12 beers and 12 ciders, including two or more local ales. The single L-shaped room has cosy corners, and lots of breweriana adorning the bar and walls. Traditional home-cooked food is served (no food Sun eve, Mon and Tue), now including 40 different pies. A pub quiz is hosted on alternate Wednesdays. A former local CAMRA Regional Pub of the Year runner-up. (X4,X46)

Golden Lion

19 Sheep Street, NN8 1BN

12-11 (midnight Fri); 11-midnight Sat (01933) 223206

thegoldenlionwellingborough.co.uk

Adnams Ghost Ship; Fuller's London Pride; St Austell Tribute; 2 changing beers (sourced regionally)

This magnificent historic Grade II-listed Tudor building dates from 1540 and is one of the oldest buildings in the area. The restaurant/dining room, known as The Hall, has a vaulted ceiling, exposed beams and minstrels' gallery. Visitors can also relax in the comfortable lounge area with open fires in the winter and outdoor seating for clement days. Up to seven guest beers are served. Q

Old Grammarians

46 Oxford Street, NN8 4JH (opp Morrisons car park)

12-11 (11.30 Fri); 11.30-11 Sat; 12-10.30 Sun

(01933) 226188 wellingborough-ogs.org

Courage Directors; Oakham JHB; Young's Bitter; 4 changing beers (sourced locally)

Established in 1934 as a rugby club, this is now a flourishing sports and social club. Close to Wellingborough town centre, it has a large main bar, spacious function room and sports bar featuring Sky Sports on a large plasma screen. The club hosts several events each month, including fun quiz nights, bingo and live artists. Happy hour is 6.30-7.30pm. Non-members must be signed in. P (X4,X46)

Welton

White Horse

High Street, NN11 2JP (off A361 betwen Rugby and Daventry)

12-2.30 (not Mon & Tue), 5-11; 12-midnight Fri & Sat; 12-11 Sun (01327) 702820 thewhitehorsewelton.co.uk

Adnams Southwold Bitter; Oakham Bishops Farewell; Purity Pure Gold; 1 changing beer

Charming 17th-century country pub heated with woodburners. It has two bars on split levels – the public bar where skittles and darts are played and a traditional beamed lounge leading to the restaurant. A large canopied patio overlooks the garden. Traditional locally produced ciders are served. Live bands play in the garden during the summer. Children and dogs are welcome. A former local CAMRA award winner. Q P

Weston by Welland

Wheel & Compass

Valley Road, LE16 8HZ

12-11 (01858) 565864 thewheelandcompass.co.uk

Greene King Abbot; Marston's Burton Bitter, Pedigree; St Austell Tribute; Sharp's Doom Bar; 1 changing beer

A rural pub in the picturesque Welland Valley with a cosy bar/lounge and a large extended dining room. An outside drinking area offers good views and is an ideal playground for children. The pub is a popular stop-off for walkers on the Jurassic Way which runs close by. It now offers a local beer alongside the regulars. Q P (67)

Woodford

Duke's Arms

83 High Street, NN14 4HE (off A510)

12-11 (01832) 732224

Digfield Fools Nook; Greene King Abbot; 6 changing beers

Originally a 17th-century manor, the pub was renamed in honour of the Duke of Wellington who was a frequent visitor to the village. Overlooking the green, it has a split main bar, lounge, rear games room with 3D TV and an upstairs restaurant. Very much a community-focused pub, it holds a Whitsun bank holiday beer festival and August bank holiday music festival, plus an open mic night on Thursday, disco and karaoke on Friday and acoustic session on Sunday night. Traditional pub food is available alongside pizza and chilli. P (16)

Yardley Hastings

Rose & Crown

4 Northampton Road, NN7 1EX

12 (5 Mon)-11; 12-11.30 Fri & Sat; 12-10 Sun

(01604) 696276 roseandcrownbistro.co.uk

Greene King IPA, Abbot; Phipps NBC India Pale Ale; house beer (by Hart Family Brewers); 2 changing beers (sourced locally)

A lovely ironstone pub extensively refurbished in the 1980s. It retains stone-flagged floors and beamed ceilings throughout, and has a small drinking area in the bay window. The emphasis is on traditional home cooking with a daily changing menu. Regular live music events range from jazz to rock to blues. The landscaped gardens are wonderful in summer. The house beer is from Hart Family. Northamptonshire Food & Drink Award Food Pub of the Year 2013/14. P (41)

I never drink water. I'm afraid it will become habit-forming. **W C Fields**

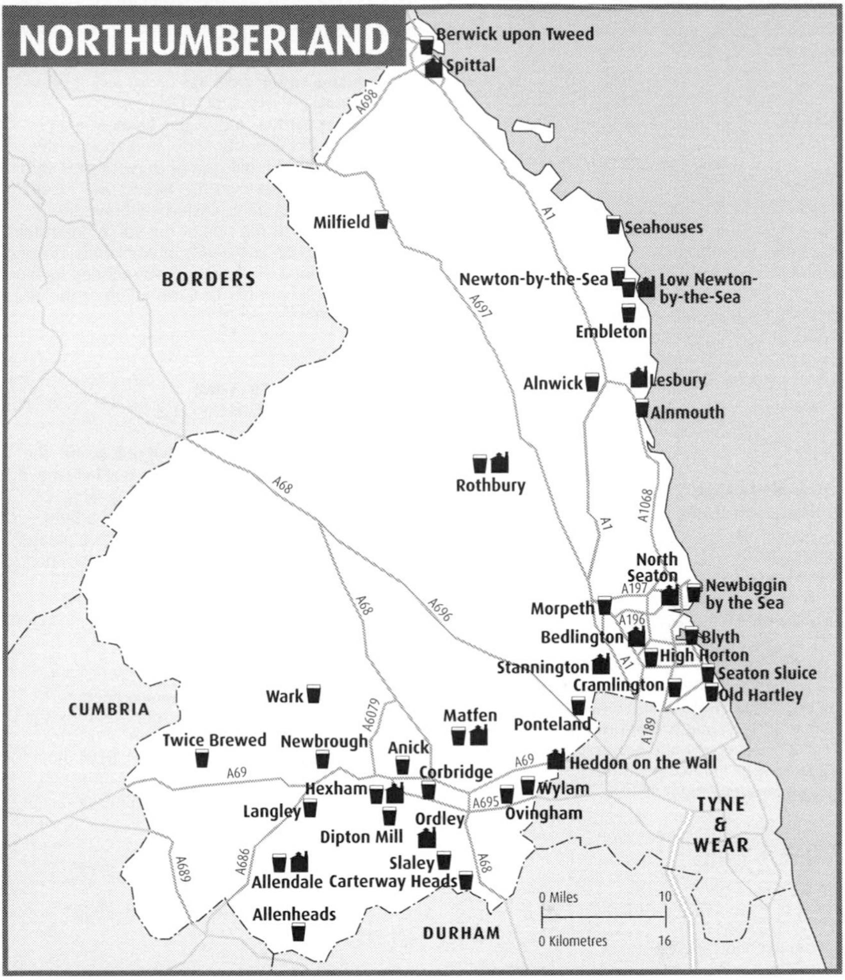

Allendale

Golden Lion Hotel 𝕃

Market Place, NE47 9BD

✪ 12-1.30am (1am Wed); 12-2.30am Fri-Sun
☎ (01434) 683225 🌐 goldenlionhotel.net

Timothy Taylor Landlord; Wylam Gold Tankard; 3 changing beers Ⓗ

Friendly and hospitable pub in the centre of town, patronised by locals and tourists. Interior walls are adorned with photographs of the annual tar barrel procession, an experience in itself, and local landscapes. Allendale's local choir practises here on Tuesday evening, and live Irish music plays on the last Wednesday of the month. With two regular beers and three guests, there is always plenty of choice of local ales. Home-cooked food is served and the pub has a late licence at weekends.
❀🛏◑🚌(688)🐾

Allenheads

Allenheads Inn 𝕃

NE47 9HJ

✪ 4 (12 Sat)-11; 12-10.30 Sun ☎ (01434) 685200
🌐 allenheadsinn.co.uk

Black Sheep Best Bitter; Mordue Northumbrian Blonde; 4 changing beers Ⓗ

Superb 18th-century rural inn with a public bar with log fire, games room and dining room. On the Coast-to-Coast cycle route it is popular with cyclists, ramblers and tourists. Good bar meals are available at reasonable prices. Originally the home of Sir Thomas Wentworth, the premises are bedecked with memorabilia from a bygone age. The pub will open early on request for coach parties and rambling groups. 🐴❀🛏◑♣P🚌(688)🐾

REAL ALE BREWERIES

Acton North Seaton
Allendale Allendale
Anarchy Stannington
Bear Claw Spittal
Bondgate Hexham
Coquetdale Rothbury
Hexhamshire Ordley
High House Farm Matfen
Northumberland Bedlington
Ship Inn Low Newton-by-the-Sea
VIP Lesbury
Wylam Heddon on the Wall

Alnmouth

Red Lion Inn

22 Northumberland Street, NE66 2RJ
11-midnight ☎ (01665) 830584 redlionalnmouth.com
Black Sheep Best Bitter; 3 changing beers H
Charming family-run, 18th-century coaching inn with a cosy lounge bar with attractive woodwork. Well patronised by tourists and locals, panoramic views across the Aln Estuary can be enjoyed from the decked area at the bottom of the garden. Occasional live music plays - in the open air in summer. Guest beers usually include one local and two interesting brews from further afield. An annual beer festival is held in October. Open for breakfast from 9am and excellent en-suite B&B accommodation is available.
Q❀P(X18)

Alnwick

John Bull Inn 🏆 L

12 Howick Street, NE66 1UY
12-3 (not Mon-Fri), 7-11; 12-3, 7-10.30 Sun
☎ (01665) 602055 john-bull-inn.co.uk
5 changing beers H
Many times local CAMRA Pub of the Year winner, this 180-year-old inn thrives on its reputation as a back-street boozer. The passionate landlord offers a wide range of cask-conditioned ales at varying ABVs, real cider, the widest range of bottled Belgian beers in the county and over 120 single malt whiskies. A darts team competes in the local league and the pub upholds the north-east tradition of an annual leek show. There is a cheese club on Saturday night. Q❀♣(X15,X18)

Tanners Arms L

2-4 Hotspur Place, NE66 1QF
5-11 (midnight Fri); 12-midnight Sat; 12-10.30 Sun
☎ (01665) 602553
6 changing beers H
Ivy-covered stone-built pub just off Bondgate Without and a short distance from Alnwick Garden. The rustic single room has a flagstone floor, tree beer shelf and warming real fire in winter. Acoustic music nights feature regularly and open mic on the last Friday of the month. The ever-changing real ales frequently come from north-eastern and Scottish Borders microbreweries.
♣(X15,X18)

Anick

Rat Inn

NE46 4LN (follow sign at Hexham A69 roundabout)
12-3, 6-11; 12-11 Sat; 12-10.30 Sun ☎ (01434) 602814
theratinn.com
Timothy Taylor Landlord; 5 changing beers H
Superb 1750 country inn with spectacular views across Tyne Valley. The pub has a welcoming and friendly feel to it, with an open log fire and chamber pots hanging from the ceiling. It has an excellent local reputation for good food prepared with locally sourced ingredients and appears in several food guides. The first Thursday of the month is singers'/poetry night. Bottled beers are stocked to complement the handpumped ales. Well worth the short taxi ride from Hexham rail station. Q❀♣P

Berwick upon Tweed

Barrels Ale House

59-61 Bridge Street, TD15 1ES (in old part of Berwick)
12-midnight (11.30 Sun) ☎ (01289) 308013
Jarrow Rivet Catcher; 4 changing beers H
There is an Old Curiosity Shop-ambience to this pub, located in the old part of Berwick next to the original road bridge over the Tweed. The excellent real ale no doubt helps customers brave the 'dentist's chair' at the side of the bar. A downstairs bar is used by DJs and bands at weekends. Outside is a unique open drinking area surrounded by high walls. A former winner of CAMRA Pub of the Year awards. ❀

Curfew

46a Bridge Street, TD15 1AQ
12-9 (11 Fri-Sun) ☎ 07842 912268
4 changing beers H
A recent addition to the Berwick pub scene, the town's first micropub is located up a small lane, off Bridge Street, which opens out into a large courtyard. It has a small bar area with a bottle fridge to one side. The courtyard makes a pleasant drinking area in summer. The cellar is in the shed at the top of the yard. Q❀

Pilot

31 Low Greens, TD15 1LZ
12 (11 Sat)-midnight; 12-11 Sun ☎ (01289) 304214
Caledonian Deuchars IPA; 2 changing beers H
Well patronised by locals and sought out by train trippers who have heard about this gem. The stone-built end-of-terrace pub dates from the 19th century and has a regionally important historic interior. It retains the original small room layout and boasts several nautical artefacts over 100 years old. The pub runs a darts team and hosts music nights. The bar staff are welcoming and friendly.
❀♣

Blyth

Wallaw L

14 Union Street, NE24 2DX
8am-midnight (1am Fri & Sat) ☎ (01670) 356830
Greene King Abbot; Ruddles County; 7 changing beers H
This recently opened free house is a former picture house and Wetherspoon have kept the name and Art Deco theme. Note the original projector in the entrance and seating and layout on the balcony (not open to the public). The pub aims to serve real ale of the highest quality from its 10 handpumps and welcomes suggestions for guest ales. Alcohol is available from 9am. Q❀

Carterway Heads

Manor House Inn

DH8 9LX (on A68 S of Corbridge)
11 (12 Mon)-11; 11-11.30 Thu; 12-10.30 Sun
☎ (01207) 255268 themanorhouseinn.com
Morland Old Speckled Hen; 3 changing beers H
Warm and hospitable country inn with three open fires and plenty of tables. A double-glazed window in the bar wall allows customers to view the well-maintained cellar. Proper home-cooked food is on offer and is popular with both tourists and locals. Excellent accommodation is available. Derwent Reservoir is nearby. ❀♣P

Corbridge

Angel Inn
Main Street, NE45 5LA
11 (12 Sun)-11 (01434) 632119
theangelofcorbridge.com
Cumberland Corby Ale; Hadrian Border Tyneside Blonde; 3 changing beers
Superb former 1726 coaching inn located on the main road with good transport links. Seven handpulls adorn the bar and a wonderful selection of malt whiskies is also kept. Family-friendly and with a reputation for good food, the pub is popular with tourists, ramblers and locals. A separate lounge area has comfy leather seating and outside is a relaxed seating area. The town has strong links with the Romans and Hadrian's Wall is nearby.
Q P (10,685)

Dyvels Inn
Station Road, NE45 5AY (30yds from station next to Tynedale Rugby Club)
12-11 (01434) 633633 thedyvelsinn.co.uk
4 changing beers
Situated next to Corbridge station, this country pub is cosy in winter yet light and airy in summer. It has a public bar, a pool room to the rear leading to a secluded area outside, and a popular meeting room. Food is served throughout, but check availability first on Mondays January to March. Three letting rooms are an ideal base for exploring this lovely town and the many country walks on the doorstep. P (10,685)

Cramlington

John the Clerk of Cramlington
2 Village Road, NE23 1DN
8am-midnight (11 Mon-Wed) (01670) 707060
Greene King Abbot; Ruddles Best Bitter; 5 changing beers
A pleasant modern open-plan conversion of the former Travellers Rest pub located in the heart of Cramlington village, opened by Wetherspoon in 2013. Now a firm favourite with Cramlington's drinkers, it has one long bar to the left on entering the pub and a large seating area to the right.

Plough
Middle Farm Buildings, NE23 1DN
11-11 (midnight Fri & Sat); 12-11 Sun (01670) 737633
theploughcramlington.co.uk
Cullercoats Jack the Devil; Harviestoun Bitter & Twisted; 5 changing beers
Converted farm buildings in the old village make up this Sir John Fitzgerald outlet, which is arranged in the style of a traditional pub with separate bar and lounge areas. Alongside the core range of local beers, an excellent range of ales from local microbreweries is on continual rotation, backed by a commitment to sourcing the best ales from across the UK. Under-18s are permitted in bar areas daytime only, but families are always welcome in the function room upstairs.
Q P (X5,X10,X11)

Dipton Mill

Dipton Mill Inn
Dipton Mill Road, NE46 1YA
12-2.30, 6-11; 12-3 Sun (01434) 606577
diptonmill.co.uk
Hexhamshire Devil's Elbow, Shire Bitter, Blackhall English Stout, Devil's Water, Whapweasel, Old Humbug
This small inn is the tap for Hexhamshire Brewery. Blackhall English Stout has proved so popular with drinkers that it has ousted the Guinness. To complement the ales there is great home-cooked food – Saturday is curry night. A cosy atmosphere and warm welcome make this pub well worth seeking out. The large garden has a stream running through it and there is plenty of countryside to explore. Q P

Embleton

Greys Inn
Stanley Terrace, NE66 3UZ
12-11 (10.30 Sun) (01665) 576983
6 changing beers
Pleasant, traditional pub in a lovely seaside hamlet, just a short walk to a wonderful beach. It has three open fires and a framed 1904 grocery list hangs on the wall. The pub is an excellent venue to enjoy a bite to eat washed down with a locally sourced real ale, sitting outside on the superb patio in good weather. It is home to a ladies' darts team, clay pigeon club and golf club. (501)

Hexham

Tannery
22 Gilesgate, NE46 3QD
12-midnight (01434) 605537
6 changing beers
This local hostelry has been taken over by an established landlord from Newcastle with a vision to serve the best beers, ciders, whiskies and gins alongside a menu of meats, cheeses and snacks sourced from small producers in the region. The pub is divided into two distinct bars – the public bar serves six real ales including one LocAle while the lounge offers up to 12 real ciders, six on handpull and six on gravity.

High Horton

Three Horse Shoes
Hathery Lane, NE24 4HF (off A189 N of Cramlington, follow A192) NZ277793
11-11 (midnight Fri & Sat); 12-11 Sun (01670) 822410
threehorseshoes-horton.co.uk
Greene King Abbot; 7 changing beers
Extended former coaching inn at the highest point in the Blyth Valley, with views of the Northumberland coast. The pub is open plan with distinct bar and dining areas plus a conservatory. Dedicated to real ale, there are regular beer festivals. Ten guest ales are sourced from local microbreweries and from further afield. An extensive range of meals and snacks is available lunchtimes and evenings, all day Friday-Sunday. Licensed for weddings and civil ceremonies.
P (X5)

Langley

Carts Bog Inn
NE47 5NW (3 miles off A69 on A686 to Alston)
closed Mon; 12-2.30 (2 Wed), 5-11; 12-11 Sat; 12-10.30 Sun (01434) 684338 cartsbog.co.uk
3 changing beers

Excellent rural pub serving the Langley community and tourists. The building dates from 1730 and was built on the site of an ancient brewery (circa 1521). Carts really did get bogged down here. A large open fire divides the two-room interior and the walls proudly display pictures of bygone days. Good locally sourced food including meat from a nearby farm is served (booking essential for Sunday lunch). Three real ales from local breweries are usually available, and a beer festival is held in August. Home to three quoits teams.
Q **P** (688)

Low Newton-by-the-Sea

Ship Inn

Newton Square, NE66 3EL (off B1340 between Seahouses and Craster)
11-11; 12-10.30 Sun (01665) 576262
shipinnnewton.co.uk
Ship Inn Sandcastles at Dawn, Sea Coal, Sea Dog, Sea Wheat, Ship Hop Ale H
Nestling in the corner of a three-sided square of former fishermen's cottages only a few yards from the beach, this small pub is often busy with beer drinkers seeking ales from the in-house microbrewery. The excellent menu uses fresh local ingredients. The pub is a short walk from the public car park at the top of the hill. Opening times may vary in winter so phone ahead if travelling any distance. **Q**

Matfen

High House Farm Visitor Centre

NE20 0RG
closed Wed; 10.30-9 (5 Mon & Tue); 10.30-5 Sun
(01661) 886192 highhousefarmbrewery.co.uk
High House Farm Auld Hemp, Nel's Best, Matfen Magic; 1 changing beer H
All real ales are sourced from the brewery, with tours available (book ahead). The visitor centre includes an award-winning restaurant offering a daytime menu, evening meals and Sunday lunches. A tearoom in a converted barn complements the traditional ambience. There is a children's play area outside. Situated one-and-a-half miles from the Military Road and not far from the Roman wall, it has a caravan and camping field. Licensed for weddings and popular for wedding receptions. **Q** **P**

Milfield

Red Lion Inn

Main Road, NE71 6JD
11-2, 5-11; 11-11 Sat & Sun (01668) 216224
redlionmilfield.co.uk
Black Sheep Best Bitter; 2 changing beers H
A true local pub at the heart of the village, just eight miles inside the border, dating back to the mid-1700s. Rescued by the current licensee from the tight grip of Scottish & Newcastle, the Red Lion is a proper free house, with many varied guest beers served through the third handpump. Freshly prepared food is available, with blackboards proudly displaying where the local produce is sourced. Home to the local leek-growing club.
Q **P** (267)

Morpeth

Black Bull

47 Bridge Street, NE61 1PE
9am-11 (midnight Fri & Sat); 9am-10.30 Sun
(01670) 512089
Anarchy Blonde Star; Caledonian Deuchars IPA; Sharp's Doom Bar; 3 changing beers H
Recently renovated pub in the town centre that looks deceptively small from the outside. Six handpulls currently serve two regular beers from the Heineken list, Anarchy Brew Co's Blonde Star, and up to three often locally sourced guests. There is a dedicated fridge for craft beers, including some bottle-conditioned from Anarchy. Food is served 9am-9pm daily, made with local ingredients as far as possible. (X14,X15,X18)

Electrical Wizard

11 New Market, NE61 1PS
8am-11 (01670) 500640
Greene King Abbot; Ruddles County; 4 changing beers H
Formerly a cinema, this pub was refurbished by JD Wetherspoon in 2011 to a high standard. It is named after Dr Walford Bodie, the 'Electrical Wizard' who entertained packed audiences in these premises in the cinema's early years. Interesting electrical sculptures and pictures of old Morpeth adorn the walls and there is comfortable seating throughout. The pub participates in an annual local beer festival along with other Wetherspoons in Northumberland.

Newbiggin by the Sea

Queen's Head

7 High Street, NE64 6AT
10-midnight (01670) 817293
2 changing beers H
Single-room building with the bar, lounge and snug all together. Rebuilt in 1909, some Edwardian features have been retained, including the curved bar counter. The pub sells competitively priced real ales at advantageous opening times and displays an ever-growing, impressive collection of guest beer pumpclips on the walls. One beer is usually available, two on Fridays, varying weekly. This no-nonsense pub is popular with locals and visitors alike.

Newbrough

Red Lion

Stanegate Road, NE47 5AR
12-11 (10.30 Sun) (01434) 674226
redlionnewbrough.co.uk
3 changing beers H
The road outside was first laid down by the Romans back in 71AD, long before Hadrian's Wall was built. The building reputedly dates back to the 13th century, featuring many flagstones and beams plus much old stonework. Popular with cyclists, Route 72 of the National Cycle Network runs alongside and the pub operates a pick-up, drop-off luggage service. Opening hours and food service are liable to change in winter. An ale from a local brewery is always available.
P (683)

Newton-by-the-Sea

Joiners Arms

Town Square, NE66 3EA (on B1340)
12-11 (10.30 Sun) (01665) 576112 joiners-arms.com
Hadrian Border Tyneside Blonde; 1 changing beer H
Situated in a pleasant Northumbrian hamlet with a small picturesque green opposite its outdoor seating area, this 18th-century former manor house has been tastefully restored and refurbished following closure for two years. The house ale, St Mary's, is named after the local church and for every pint sold a donation is made towards its upkeep. The five en-suite bedrooms are fitted out to a high standard. P (X18)

Old Hartley

Delaval Arms L

NE26 4RL (jct of A193/B1325 S of Seaton Sluice)
12-2.30, 4.30-10.30; 12-11 Fri-Sun winter; 12-11 summer
(0191) 237 0489 thedelavalarms.wordpress.com
4 changing beers H
Multi-roomed Grade II-listed building dating from 1748, with a listed WWI water storage tower (part of Roberts Battery) behind the beer garden. It is the first pub in Northumberland for those following the coastal route. Good-quality, affordable meals complement the beer, with guest ales coming from local micros. To the left as you enter there is a room served through a hatch from the bar and to the right a room where children are welcome.
Q P (308,309)

Ovingham

Bridge End Inn L

West Road, NE42 6BN
4 (12 Sat)-11.30; 12-3.30, 7-11 Sun (01661) 832219
thebridgeendinn.co.uk
Tetley Bitter; Timothy Taylor Landlord; Wylam Gold Tankard, Collingwood; 1 changing beer H
Superb traditional family-run hostelry with the same licensee for more than 38 years. The back door opens onto the village green. A popular stop-off for day trippers including Whistle Stops visitors, children are welcome until 9pm. Access to the pub from Prudhoe is over a bridge via a pedestrian walkway. Folk night is the third Wednesday of the month. An allotment club meets monthly. Visitors are made welcome by the friendly pub regulars.
Q (Prudhoe) P (X84,686)

Ponteland

Blackbird L

North Road, NE20 9UH
12-11 (midnight Fri & Sat) (01661) 822684
4 changing beers H
This pub goes back over 500 years – part of the building is the remains of Ponteland Castle. A blend of old and new, the Blackbird is central to village life, with a good mixed clientele. An annual New Year's Day wheelbarrow race starts and finishes at the pub. Two local beers are always available as well as two nationally sourced guest ales.
P (X77,X78)

> What care I how time advances: I am drinking ale today. **Edgar Allan Poe**

Rothbury

Queen's Head

Townfoot, NE65 7SR
11-1am (midnight Sun) (01669) 620470
queensheadrothbury.com
4 changing beers H
Friendly hotel dating from 1756 on the main street, popular with locals, tourists and ramblers. Live folk music features on the first Tuesday and last Thursday of the month (there is a charge and it often sells out). The hotel has pool and darts teams competing in local leagues. Four guest beers come from the SIBA Direct Delivery Scheme and Punch Finest Cask. All bedrooms are en suite. There is an hourly bus service. P (14,X14)

Seahouses

Olde Ship Hotel

7-9 Main Street, NE68 7RD
11 (12 Sun)-11 (01665) 720200 seahouses.co.uk
Black Sheep Best Bitter; Courage Directors; Hadrian Border Farne Island Pale Ale; Morland Old Speckled Hen; Ruddles County; Theakston Best Bitter; 2 changing beers H
This 1745 farmhouse was converted to the licensed trade in 1812 and still has a regionally important historic pub interior. Family-owned since 1910, the pub has three quality bars adorned with a veritable treasure trove of 19th and 20th century maritime memorabilia. Fully residential, it offers an interesting menu of fish, fresh crab meals and snacks although, unusually, no chips are served.
Q P (501)

Seaton Sluice

King's Arms

The Harbour, NE26 4RD (on cliff top E of main road)
12-11 (11.30 Fri & Sat); 12-10.30 Sun (0191) 237 0275
thekingsarms-ne.co.uk
Caledonian Deuchars IPA; Greene King Abbot; 3 changing beers H
Traditional pub dating from the 1700s, sitting majestically next to the man-made harbour constructed by the famous Delaval family. The pub is set back from the road, with extensive views of the beautiful beach at Seaton Sluice. It has an excellent reputation for good food made using local ingredients (booking is advised). There are five handpulls dispensing a range of nationally sourced ales. Live bands play on Sunday evening.
Q P (308,309)

Melton Constable

Beresford Road, NE26 4QL
12-11 (10.30 Sun) (0191) 237 7741
themeltonconstable.co.uk
Black Sheep Best Bitter; Morland Old Speckled Hen; Thwaites Wainwright; Wychwood Hobgoblin; 2 changing beers H
Large roadside pub a few minutes' walk from the beach and local history sights. It is named after the southern seat of Lord Hastings, a member of the Delaval family – Delaval Hall is close by. The pub hosts a late-night fishing club and the BSA owners' club on the first and third Thursdays of the month. Tuesday is steak night, Wednesday is quiz night, Sunday evening features live music.
P (308,309,X4)

Slaley

Travellers Rest

NE46 1TT (on B6306 1 mile N of village)
✪ 12-11 (10.30 Sun) ☎ (01434) 673231
🌐 travellersrestslaley.com
Black Sheep Best Bitter; Caledonian Deuchars IPA; 1 changing beer Ⓗ
Former farmhouse dating from the 16th century, licensed for over 150 years. The pub has an excellent reputation for good food and accommodation. The bar has a large open fire, stone flag floor and comfortable furniture. Children are welcome and there is a safe play area alongside. Note the beautiful wine rack skilfully carved from a large piece of wood. The pub is typically quiet. The mobile phone signal is poor, which is not unusual for this rural area, but there is Wi-Fi. 🐴❀🛏◐♿♣🍎P🐾📶

Twice Brewed

Twice Brewed Inn

Miltary Road, Bardon Mill, NE47 7AN (on B6318)
✪ 11-11 (10.30 Sun) ☎ (01434) 344534
🌐 twicebrewedinn.co.uk
5 changing beers Ⓗ
Superb remote inn close to Hadrian's Wall, patronised by tourists and ramblers. It has its own well supplying water. Yates Twice Brewed Bitter is the house beer and a range of bottled beers named Beers of the World is kept. The pub is home to two quoits teams. The inn acts as a rural transport interchange and has full disabled access and 16 bedrooms, seven en suite.
Q🐴❀🛏◐♿▲P🚌(185,681)📶

Wark

Battlesteads Hotel 🄻

NE48 3LS
✪ 11-11; 12-10.30 Sun ☎ (01434) 230209
🌐 battlesteads.com
5 changing beers Ⓗ
Well-appointed 1747 former farmhouse with a superb rear walled garden, restaurant, large conservatory and accommodation. The five handpulls offer an excellent choice of beers all in tip-top condition. Ingredients for the quality food menu are sourced locally from a 25-mile radius. Ground-floor accommodation is available with disabled access. Future developments include a walking book based on the pub. Handy for the PlusBus via Hexham Rail Station.
🐴❀🛏◐♿P🚌(880)🐾

Wylam

Black Bull 🄻

Main Street, NE41 8AB
✪ 4 (12 Sat & Sun)-11 ☎ (01661) 853112
🌐 blackbull-wylam.co.uk
Wylam Gold Tankard; 6 changing beers Ⓗ
Cheerful pub with a friendly landlord and staff located on the main street in Wylam, popular with the locals. Real ale is now available on six handpulls, the beers mainly sourced from the nearby Wylam Brewery. Food includes local home-cooked specialities, steak night on Wednesday, fish night on Friday and curry night on the last Thursday of the month. Regular themed nights are hosted, many raising funds for charities. Nearby is Wylam Waggonway, a popular walk that passes George Stephenson's cottage. 🛏◐≋♣🐾

Boathouse Inn 🄻

Station Road, NE41 8HR
✪ 11-11 (midnight Sat); 12-10.30 Sun ☎ (01661) 853431
🌐 theboathousewylam.com
7 changing beers Ⓗ
Superb two-roomed pub with 15 handpulls, three dedicated to cider, with more ciders served from the cellar. Beers are sourced locally and nationwide, and on bank holidays themed beer festivals are held. Toasties and sandwiches are available during the day. The pub is a popular stopping-off point for Whistle Stops II travellers. Fifteen CAMRA awards cover one wall. Alternate Tuesdays are buskers' nights. Q🐴❀≋♣🍎P🐾📶

LocAle

A growing number of entries in the guide refer to pubs supporting the LocAle system. This was devised by CAMRA members in Nottingham and is now in widespread use in England, Wales, Scotland and Northern Ireland. The aim is to encourage publicans to stock at least one cask beer that comes from a local brewery – the distance between pub and brewery varies but is now generally accepted to be not more than 30 miles. The scheme also encourages publicans to use Beerflex, the direct delivery scheme run by SIBA, the Society of Independent Brewers. SIBA members deliver direct to pubs in their localities rather than going through the central warehouses of pub-owning companies. The overall aim of LocAle is to cut down on beer miles. Research by CAMRA shows that food and drink transport accounts for 25 per cent of all HGV vehicle miles in Britain. Taking into account the miles that ingredients have travelled on top of distribution journeys, an imported lager produced by a multi-national brewery could have notched up more than 24,000 beer miles by the time it reaches a pub. £10 spent on locally-supplied goods generates £25 for local economies. Keeping trade local helps enterprises, creates more economic activity and jobs, and makes other services more viable. The scheme also generates consumer support for local breweries. Pubs that support the LocAle scheme receive a special window sticker.
For more information, see the CAMRA website: **www.camra.org.uk**

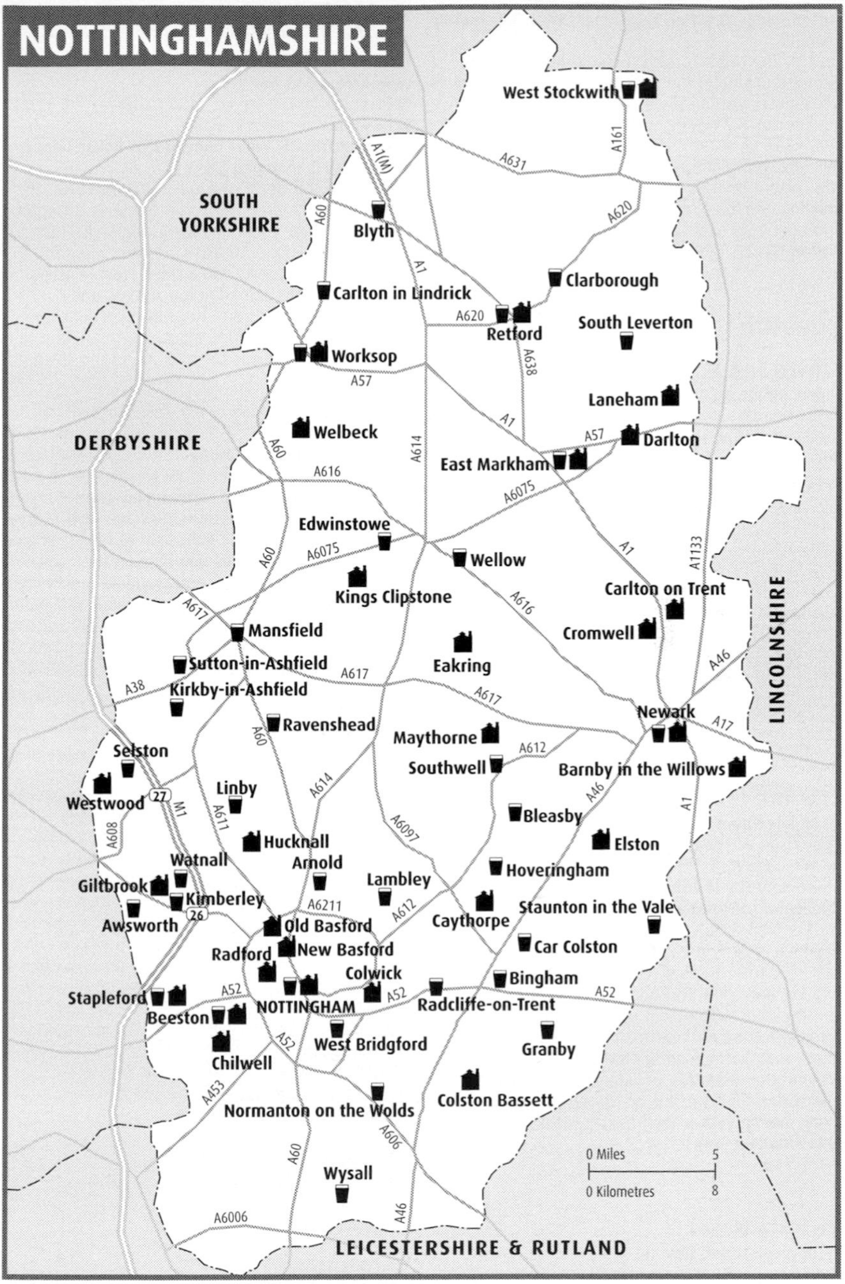

Arnold

Robin Hood & Little John

1 Church Street, NG5 8FD (on corner of Cross St)

12-11 (midnight Fri & Sat); 12-10.30 Sun

(0115) 920 1054 therobinhoodandlittlejohn.co.uk

Everards Tiger; Lincoln Green Marion, Hood, Sherwood, Tuck; 11 changing beers (often Lincoln Green)

A two-room Project William refurbishment with Lincoln Green and Everards Brewery. The bar features memorabilia of Home Ales. The lounge has details of the pub's history and that of the local area. A rear courtyard is a suntrap with seating and a long alley skittles room. As well as the 10 real ale pumps, a real cider wall behind the bar features eight taps dispensing real ciders from small local producers and further afield. **Q**

Awsworth

Gate Inn

Main Street, NG16 2RN

12-midnight (0115) 932 9821

Burton Bridge XL Bitter; Shipstones Bitter; 5 changing beers 🄷
Sold by the pub's former owners, having been deemed unviable, the Gate reopened in 2010 as a free house and quickly established itself as a quality real ale outlet, winning LocAle Pub of the Year in 2013. A truly welcoming and friendly local, this late 19th-century inn has a bar and a lounge. The current owners are gradually renovating the building and have recently refurbished the bar area and added an extension and an outside courtyard.
♿♣🍎P🚌(27,TBR1)🐾

Beeston

Crown Inn 🄻
Church Street, NG9 1FY
12-11.30 (11 Sun) ☎ (0115) 925 4738
🌐 brownales.co.uk/crown-inn
Brown Ales The Hustler, Gladiator; Draught Bass; Everards Sunchaser Blonde, Tiger; Leatherbritches Scoundrel; 8 changing beers 🄷
A genuine community-oriented pub, this 19th-century Grade II-listed alehouse was formerly a Hardys & Hansons pub and then restored by Everards. Up to 14 ales and several real ciders and perries are served at this former East Midlands CAMRA Pub of the Year. It has a cosy atmosphere with five distinct drinking areas including a snug and three-seat 'confessional'. The beer garden outside is regularly home to events. Snacks are available daily. Q❀♿⇌♣🍎P🚌🐾📶

Star Inn 🄻
22 Middle Street, NG9 1FX
12-11 (midnight Fri & Sat) ☎ (0115) 854 5320
🌐 starbeeston.co.uk
House beer (by Muirhouse); 9 changing beers (often Caledonian, Theakston) 🄷
Former Shipstone's pub still with the branded front windows, restored beyond its former glory. Visitors may recognise the bar, which featured in both Auf Wiedersehen, Pet and Boon. The decor is tasteful and minimal with three separate rooms inside complemented by a permanent marquee, sports room and spacious garden outside. Ten cask ales are on offer alongside a wide selection of whiskies and wines. Families are welcome during the day. Meals are served as well as bar snacks.
Q🐴❀🛏◐♿⇌♣P🚌🐾📶

Victoria Hotel 🄻
85 Dovecote Lane, NG9 1JG
10.30-11 (midnight Fri & Sat); 12-11 Sun
☎ (0115) 925 4049 🌐 victoriabeeston.co.uk
Castle Rock Harvest Pale; Everards Tiger; Timothy Taylor Boltmaker; changing beers (often Holden's) 🄷
A restored Victorian masterpiece with mass appeal. Up to 16 real ales are joined by real ciders and perries, an extensive whisky list and wine menu, along with a well-established food menu. Two distinct bars are complemented by a dining area and ample outside heated and smoke-free seating. VicFest is hosted in July in addition to beer festivals throughout the year. CAMRA and NUS discounts are available Sunday-Thursday and a taster tray of three third-pints is on offer all week.
Q❀◐♿⇌🍎P🚌🐾

Bingham

Horse & Plough
Long Acre, NG13 8AF
11-11 (11.30 Fri & Sat); 12-10.30 Sun ☎ (01949) 839313
🌐 horseandploughbingham.com
St Austell Tribute; Wells Bombardier; house beer (by Batemans); 3 changing beers 🄷
Situated in the heart of a busy market town, this warm, friendly, one-room free house is a former Methodist chapel and has a cottage-style interior and flagstone floor. Six cask ales are served including three guests and a cider. Freshly prepared food is available weekday lunchtimes and evenings in the bar, and the first-floor à la carte restaurant offers a varied seasonal menu. The pub has long been a focus for cask ale in the town.
◐♿⇌🚌🐾📶

White Lion
Nottingham Road, NG13 8AT
11 (11.30 Sun)-11 ☎ (01949) 875541
Jennings Cumberland Ale; 3 changing beers 🄷
The White Lion is your typical local pub, with a loyal following of regulars. It serves up to four cask ales and the landlady involves drinkers in the choice of beers. Good-value meals are available lunchtimes and evenings. The pub is home to pool and darts teams and hosts a popular quiz night every Sunday. The bar houses a large screen showing all major games on Sky Sports. There is a large car park plus a good-sized decked area for outdoor drinking. Local CAMRA branch Pub of the Year 2014.
❀◐♿⇌♣P🚌

REAL ALE BREWERIES
Alcazar Nottingham: Old Basford
Beeston Hop Beeston (NEW)
Black Iris Nottingham: New Basford
Blue Monkey Giltbrook
Castle Rock Nottingham
Caythorpe Caythorpe
Copthorne Darlton
Double Top Worksop
Dukeries Worksop
Flipside Colwick
Full Mash Stapleford
Funfair Elston
Grafton Worksop
Hale's Worksop (NEW)
Handley's Barnby in the Willows
Idle West Stockwith
Idle Valley Retford (NEW)
Kings Clipstone Kings Clipstone
Lincoln Green Hucknall
Magpie Nottingham
Mallard Maythorne
Maypole Eakring
Medieval Colston Bassett (brewing suspended)
Milestone Cromwell
Naked Brewer Westwood
Navigation Nottingham
Newark Newark
Nottingham Nottingham: Radford
Pheasantry East Markham
Reality Nottingham: Chilwell
Robin Hood Nottingham: New Basford
Scribbler's Stapleford
Springhead Laneham
Tom Herrick's Carlton on Trent (NEW)
Totally Brewed Nottingham
Welbeck Abbey Welbeck

Bleasby

Waggon & Horses

Gipsy Lane, NG14 7GG

12-2 (not Mon-Wed), 5-11; 12-midnight Sat; 12-11 Sun (01636) 830283

Blue Monkey BG Sips; Sharp's Doom Bar; 4 changing beers (sourced locally)

Thriving village free house offering six real ales, featuring award-winning Blue Monkey beers alongside others from micros. Real cider is also kept. This is a true village pub overlooking the church and green with no gimmicks or electronic games, just good conversation and banter. To the rear is a conservatory and a small restaurant. Well worth finding in a lovely Trent Valley village close to Southwell Minster and races. Walkers with muddy boots and dogs with muddy paws all welcome. QP

Blyth

Red Hart

Bawtry Road, S81 8HG (opp church)

2.30-11.30 Mon; 11.30-midnight (01909) 591221

redhart.co.uk

Sharp's Doom Bar; 3 changing beers

An attractive village pub in the centre of Blyth with a reasonably large lounge, traditional taproom and an attractive dining room. The walls in the lounge are decorated with photographs and paintings from nearby locations. Food is served daily in both the lounge and dining room. The Red Hart is a recent CAMRA award winner and runs an annual beer festival. QP(25,29)

Car Colston

Royal Oak

The Green, NG13 8JE

11.30-3, 5.30-11; 11.30-11 Fri & Sat; 12-10.30 Sun (01949) 20247

Marston's EPA, Burton Bitter; Ringwood Best Bitter; 1 changing beer

This impressive country inn is situated on one of England's largest village greens. The recently refurbished two-room interior includes a lounge and restaurant on one side and bar with comfortable seating on the other. The bar's vaulted brickwork ceiling is a legacy from the building's life as a hosiery factory. Good-quality, traditional food is served lunchtimes and evenings. There is a skittle alley to the rear, beer garden and camping facilities. The landlord maintains his 100 per cent record for entries in the Guide. P

Carlton in Lindrick

Grey Horses Inn

The Cross, S81 9EW (centre of old village)

12 (11 Sun)-11 (01909) 730252 greyhorsesinn.com

Welbeck Abbey Red Feather; 4 changing beers

The Grey Horses is the brewery tap for Welbeck Brewery and is situated in the heart of the village within the conservation area. It has a front bar accessible from the street where locals gather to play cards and dominoes, and a large lounge bar area. It holds beer festivals in conjunction with the Welbeck Abbey Brewery featuring ales on up to 12 handpulls as well as cider and perry. Muddy boots and dogs are welcome in the taproom. QP(21,22)

Clarborough

King's Arms

Main Street, DN22 9LN

12-midnight (01777) 708845

Dukeries A Ray of Sunshine; 2 changing beers

A quiet and pleasant village inn situated three miles from Retford offering three changing ales, some from local breweries. Food is served in the bar and a separate restaurant. A warm welcome is assured from Mags and Chris at this CAMRA award-winning pub. A car boot sale is held in the car park on Saturdays. QP(10)

East Markham

Pheasantry Brewery

High Brecks Farm, Lincoln Road, NG22 0SN

closed Mon; 11-10.30 (11 Wed-Sat) (01777) 870572

pheasantrybrewery.co.uk

Pheasantry Best Bitter, Pale Ale, Dark Ale, Dancing Dragonfly

Restaurant café and bar adjacent to the Pheasantry microbrewery. Set in excellent surroundings, this is a great location for families as there is an outside play area. Mark is always willing to talk about his beers and tours of the brewery are available. P

Queen's Hotel

High Street, NG22 0RE

12 (2 Mon)-11 (01777) 870288

queenshoteleastmarkham.co.uk

Everards Sunchaser Blonde, Tiger, Original; Truman's Runner; 2 changing beers

Situated on the village main street, this cosy public house has a friendly atmosphere enhanced by an open fire in winter. A single bar serves the lounge, pool room and dining area. Food ranges from hot and cold snacks to full home-cooked meals. There is a large garden area at the rear where you can enjoy a drink on a warm summer's day. Local CAMRA Pub of the Year for 2013. QP(36,37)

Edwinstowe

Black Swan

High Street, NG21 9QR

12-11 (12.30am Fri & Sat) (01623) 822598

5 changing beers (often Blue Monkey, Castle Rock, Kings Clipstone)

A traditional cask ale pub located on the High Street in this pretty village, featuring old pictures of Edwinstowe on the walls. A range of five real ales is usually available along with real cider. Local breweries are often represented including Castle Rock, Nottingham, Blue Monkey, Welbeck Abbey and the nearby Kings Clipstone. Three letting rooms are available above the pub. QP

Forest Lodge

2-4 Church Street, NG21 9QA

11.30-3, 5.30 (5 Fri)-11; 12-3, 6-10.30 Sun (01623) 824443

Wells Bombardier; house beer (by Welbeck Abbey); 2 changing beers

Owned and run by a family for the past 11 years, this inn is situated in the heart of Sherwood Forest. It offers a range of ever-changing guest beers, sourced from both local breweries and further afield. The house beer is supplied by the local Welbeck Abbey Brewery and the high-class

restaurant offers a wide choice of daily specials, featuring locally sourced produce wherever possible. Private functions can be catered for. Accommodation is 4-star AA rated.
Q P (14,15,SA)

Granby

Marquis of Granby

Dragon Street, NG13 9PN
4-11 (midnight Fri); 12-midnight Sat; 12-11 Sun
(01949) 859517
Brewster's Hophead, Marquis; 4 changing beers [H]
Believed to be the original Marquis of Granby, dating back to 1760 or earlier, this small two-roomed pub is now the brewery tap for Brewster's. York stone floors complement the yew bar tops and wood-beamed rooms, period wallpaper features throughout and the lounge has a welcoming open fire in winter months. Guest beers served alongside the Brewster's range usually come from microbreweries, and include a mild, stout or porter. Fish and chips night is Friday.
P

Hoveringham

Reindeer

Main Street, NG14 7JR
closed Mon; 5-11.30 Tue; 12-midnight; 12-8.30 Sun
(0115) 966 3629 thereindeerinn.com
Black Sheep Best Bitter; Castle Rock Harvest Pale; 3 changing beers [H]
Genuine free house in a pleasant country village with traditional beams and a log fire for cold winter nights. A central servery divides the bar and restaurant areas of the pub. Excellent ales are offered alongside a good range of home-cooked food including vegetarian and vegan choices. The outside drinking area is served through the pub window and overlooks the village cricket pitch for those who like the sound of leather on willow as they drink. Q P (103)

Kimberley

White Lion

74 Swingate, NG16 2PQ
4 (12 Fri-Sun)-11.30 (0115) 938 3193
whitelionswingate.co.uk
Castle Rock Black Gold, Harvest Pale; Sharp's Doom Bar [H]**; 8 changing beers** [H]/[G]
Two-roomed true free house in a residential area, acquired in 2013 and refurbished with a modern décor. Seven cask beers, mainly from local microbreweries, are served via handpump from the central bar. Up to 11 further beers are available on gravity from a permanent stillage housed in a separate room. Sandwiches are provided on request. There is a spacious garden for warmer weather. Q P (TB27)

Kirkby-in-Ashfield

Regent

Kingsway, NG17 7BQ
8am-midnight (1am Fri & Sat) (01623) 687630
Courage Directors; Greene King Abbot; Ruddles Best Bitter; Shepherd Neame Spitfire; Wychwood Hobgoblin; house beer (by Funfair); 4 changing beers [H]
Formerly the Regency cinema on the corner of Kingsway, this is a classic Wetherspoon conversion. There is a big emphasis on cask ales here, with up to 10 available at any one time, including a house beer brewed exclusively for the pub by Funfair. The usual excellent-value range of Wetherspoon meals is served all day every day. Families are welcome.

Lambley

Woodlark Inn

Church Street, NG4 4QB
12-midnight (0115) 931 2535
Castle Rock Harvest Pale; Samuel Smith Old Brewery Bitter; Timothy Taylor Landlord; 1 changing beer [H]
Tucked away on the edge of the village just past the church, this delightful red-brick local is a quiet pub mercifully free of electronic machines, making the art of conversation a delight. A roaring coal fire greets you on cold winter nights. The bare brick and beamed bar is welcoming and dog-friendly while the comfortable lounge has a justifiable reputation for home cooking (booking is recommended, even at lunchtime). The downstairs steak bar opens Fridays and Saturdays from 7pm.
Q P (NCT47)

Linby

Horse & Groom

12A Main Street, NG15 8AE
12-11 (10.30 Sun) (0115) 963 3334
thehorseandgroom-linby.co.uk
Morland Old Speckled Hen; 3 changing beers (often Lincoln Green) [H]
This traditional village pub has four separate rooms – two cosy snugs with wood-panelled walls and faded prints on the wall, a green room with settees, and a larger room with a feature fireplace. There is also a conservatory at the rear with a tiled floor and stools. To the rear is a tea room and restaurant, open daily 8am-5pm. A choice of six real ales, including local brews, and a real cider is offered. Q P (TB141)

Mansfield

Beer Shack

46 White Hart Street, NG18 1DG
12-2.30 (not Mon), 5-10; 12-2, 4-10.30 Fri; 12-10.30 Sat; closed Sun 07810 120805
5 changing beers [H]
Micropub with a single room downstairs with a full-length bar and two further small rooms upstairs with additional seating. Five handpulled beers and 12 real ciders are usually available alongside wine, soft drinks and bar snacks. Well-behaved dogs on leads are welcome. There are no TVs or gambling machines and mobile phone calls should be taken outside. Q

Bold Forester

Botany Avenue, NG18 5NF
11-11.30 (12.30am Fri & Sat); 12-11.30 Sun
(01623) 623970
Greene King IPA, Abbot; Hardys & Hansons Olde Trip; Morland Old Speckled Hen; 6 changing beers [H]
Hungry Horse-branded split-level pub and restaurant, run by the same landlord for more than 15 years. A wide choice of real ales is available, usually including six from Greene King and up to six

guests. Food is served all day until 9pm. The spacious open-plan interior has large-screen TVs showing all major live sport. There is a covered smoking area outside with a TV.
♿ ♣ P

Brown Cow

31 Ratcliffe Gate, NG18 2JA
12-11 (midnight Fri & Sat) (01623) 645854
Everards Tiger; 9 changing beers (often Raw)
Tasteful refurbishment of a former run-down pub by the owners, Everards Brewery, and operated by Raw Brewery under the award-winning Project William scheme. It has two bar areas and a function room upstairs. A range of up to 12 real ales is offered as well a selection of world bottled beers and real ciders. Car parking is available to the side of the building. Q P

Court House

Market Place, NG18 1HX (next to town hall)
9am-11 (midnight Fri & Sat) (01623) 412720
Greene King Abbot; Ruddles Best Bitter; changing beers
A friendly community pub in the town centre overlooking the marketplace. It offers a range of at least five cask ales, often from local microbreweries including Lincoln Green and Milestone, plus two real ciders. The usual excellent-value Wetherspoon meals are served every day until 11pm and families are welcome. A winner of numerous local branch CAMRA awards.
Q ♿

Il Rosso

180 Nottingham Road, NG18 4AF
8am-11 (midnight Fri & Sat) (01623) 623031
ilrosso.co.uk
Castle Rock Harvest Pale; Timothy Taylor Landlord; 3 changing beers
Busy modern venue offering up to three real ales. The restaurant serves a wide range of Italian meals as well as tapas and seafood specials alongside a range of traditional English dishes all day every day, starting with breakfast from 8am. Pizzas can be ordered to take away. The outdoor terrace has a retractable roof making it ideal for all seasons. Live music is hosted including acoustic and jazz nights. Sky Sports is shown on TV. P

Olde White Lion

White Lion Yard, NG18 1AF (off Church St)
11-11 07449 922821
8 changing beers
This real ale and real cider bar is situated in a natural cave, with another bar upstairs, in the White Lion Yard development, with a history that dates back to the 15th century. Up to eight real ales are available, all sourced from microbreweries and served on gravity dispense, and some real ciders and perries. As this pub is in a cave it can be cool in the evenings. Q

Railway Inn

9 Station Street, NG18 1EF
11-11 (01623) 623086
3 changing beers
A true community pub close to both the railway and bus stations. The main bar offers three constantly changing real ales. At least one LocAle features regularly, and real cider and bottled beer are also available. In addition to the main bar are two quiet rooms popular with diners. Home-cooked food is served all day at reasonable prices. Look out for the music nights held once a month. Outside there is a small walled garden and smoking area. CAMRA branch Pub of the Year 2015.
Q

Widow Frost

41 Leeming Street, NG18 1NB
8am-midnight (1am Fri & Sat) (01623) 666790
Greene King Abbot; Ruddles Best Bitter; changing beers
This spacious open-plan pub not far from the town centre gets busy, especially at weekends. The full range of Wetherspoon meals is served all day every day, with a separate family dining area. Up to six real ales are available, plus two real ciders. Winner of numerous local branch CAMRA awards, Meet the Brewer events are held here.
Q ♿

Newark

Just Beer Micropub

32A Castle Gate, NG24 1BG (in Swan & Salmon Yard)
1-11; 12-midnight Fri & Sat; 12-10 Sun 07983 993747
justbeermicropub.biz
4 changing beers
One-bar pub featuring real ale and cider, opened in 2010 by four local beer enthusiasts. Four ever-changing ales are usually available, all from microbreweries, with an emphasis on one-offs and new breweries. Two real ciders and a limited range of wines and soft drinks are offered but no keg, bottles or spirits. Food includes local pork pies, bar snacks and pickled eggs. Traditional pub games are played. Newark CAMRA Pub of the Year 2013 and 2014. Q ♿ (Castle) ♣

Organ Grinder

21 Portland Street, NG24 4XF
12-11 (01636) 671768
Blue Monkey Marmoset, BG Sips, 99 Red Baboons, Infinity, Guerilla; 2 changing beers
Completely refurbished after a short period of closure and renamed in April 2014, this is a no-nonsense drinkers' pub. The main bar has seven handpumps, and there is a separate room at the rear and a small outside, partly weatherproofed, garden/smoking area at the back. There are plans to introduce a limited choice of cold savoury snacks. ♣

Oscar's Inn

105 Balderton Gate, NG24 1RY
12-3, 5-11; 12-2am Fri & Sat; 12-11 Sun
(01636) 918130
Dark Star Espresso; Purple Moose Cwrw Madog; Thornbridge Jaipur IPA; 3 changing beers
New to the real ale scene, this pub has had a change of ownership and was reopened as Oscar's Inn in 2014. Situated close to the town, it has two separate rooms with tastefully furnished areas for drinking and dining. Oscar Wilde quotes are everywhere. Entertainment nights feature regularly at weekends. The pub is renowned for its legendary 15-inch square pizzas.
P (1,2,3A)

Prince Rupert

46 Stodman Street, NG24 1AW
11-midnight (1am Fri & Sat); 12-midnight Sun
(01636) 918121 theprincerupert.co.uk

Brains Rev James; Newark Norwegian Blue; Oakham JHB; 4 changing beers 🄷
This Grade II-listed building dates back to 1452 and has been lovingly restored. It has several rooms and snugs both downstairs and up – where the beamed, vaulted ceiling of the original Wealden House can be seen. Six handpumps dispense an ever-changing range of ales plus a real cider. An extensive food menu is available. Live music is a frequent attraction. A former local CAMRA Pub of the Year. Q❀◑⇌(Castle)●🚌🐾📶

Vaults Cider & Ale House

14 North Gate, NG24 1EZ
⏲ 11-3, 5-midnight (11 Mon & Tue); 11-midnight Sat; 11-11 Sun ☎ (01636) 678953 🌐 thevaultsnewark.co.uk
Oakham Citra; 3 changing beers 🄷
Located in the cellar of an easily missed building set back from North Gate, entry to the pub is via external steps leading up, then descending into the bar. Enthusiastic private owners offer an extensive range of ciders through handpumps and boxes, and eight real ales via handpumps on the bar counter. The food menu is based on local produce. Entertainment including live music features regularly. A CAMRA discount is offered on real ales, ciders and perries. ◑⇌(Castle)●P🚌🐾

Normanton on the Wolds

Plough Inn 𝕃

Old Melton Road, NG12 5NN (off A606 Melton Road)
⏲ 11-11 (midnight Fri & Sat); 12-11 Sun ☎ (0115) 937 2401
🌐 theploughatnormanton.co.uk
Black Sheep Best Bitter; Castle Rock Harvest Pale; Fuller's London Pride; Wells Bombardier; 1 changing beer 🄷
Traditional dining pub in an ivy-clad brick building, situated on the main street of this well-heeled sleepy village. Inside, to the right is a comfortable lounge bar area with a real fire, while to the left is a smaller bar linked to the restaurant through an archway. Outside is a huge garden hosting many events in the summer including a beer festival.
Q♨❀◑♿♣P🚌(19)🐾📶

Nottingham: Central

Canalhouse 𝕃

48-52 Canal Street, NG1 7EH
⏲ 11-11 (midnight Thu); 11-1am Fri & Sat; 11-10.30 Sun
☎ (0115) 955 5060 🌐 thecanalhouse.co.uk
Castle Rock Harvest Pale, Preservation Fine Ale; 6 changing beers (often Castle Rock) 🄷
A modern Waterways warehouse conversion. The canal to the rear runs inside the pub, where up to two narrowboats are moored. A good selection of real ales, real ciders and perries is complemented by quality world beers both on tap and in bottles. The pub has hosted the Champion Beer of Nottinghamshire competition for the past three years in the first-floor function room. Outside is a spacious covered patio overlooking the canal, which is popular on sunny summer days.
❀◑♿⇌🚊●P🚌🐾📶

Crafty Crow 𝕃

102 Friar Lane, NG1 6EB
⏲ 11-11 (midnight Fri & Sat) ☎ (0115) 837 1992
🌐 craftycrownotts.co.uk
Changing beers (often Magpie) 🄷
Magpie Brewery's first pub is a modern 2014 refurbishment with up to 10 handpulls serving microbrewery beers, a variety of real ciders and specialist keg beers. Maintaining its green ethos throughout, drinks and food are British and locally sourced where possible and the majority of fittings are recycled or home made, with birds from the crow family featuring strongly. Look for all the quirky twists throughout the building. Situated on two levels, a side entrance leads directly to all facilities. ◑♿⇌🚊●🚌🐾📶

Falcon Inn 𝕃

1 Alfreton Road, NG7 3JE
⏲ 5-11 (10 Mon); 12-11 Fri & Sat; 12-10 Sun
☎ (0115) 924 4635 🌐 thefalconinn.co.uk
5 changing beers (often Lincoln Green) 🄷
Established in 1853, this prominently positioned pub in the centre of Canning Circus was acquired and extensively refurbished in 2013. The pub has two small rooms, with a function room/restaurant area upstairs. Eight handpumps offer a selection of mainly local ales, always including a dark beer, and one real cider. Meals are served on Fridays and Sundays only, although large parties can be catered for at other times by prior arrangement, otherwise bar snacks are available. Q◐♣●🚌

Hand & Heart 𝕃

65 Derby Road, NG1 5BA
⏲ 12-midnight (11 Mon); 12-1am Fri & Sat; 12-11 Sun
☎ (0115) 958 2456 🌐 thehandandheart.co.uk
Maypole Little Weed; 7 changing beers (sourced locally; often Dancing Duck) 🄷
The modern frontage and bar area hide the age of this pub – there are sandstone caves to the rear where there is space for dining. A high-quality menu of both food and beer is offered, with eight (mostly local) beers on handpump, together with three real ciders or perries. Upstairs is a separate room and bar available for functions, along with a partially covered terrace overlooking the busy street below. Live music features on Sundays and Thursdays. ❀◑●🚌🐾📶

King William IV

6 Eyre Street, Sneinton, NG2 4PB
⏲ 12 (2 Mon)-11; 11-11 Sat; 12-10.30 Sun
☎ (0115) 958 9864
Oakham JHB, Bishops Farewell; changing beers 🄷
Nicknamed the King Billy, this cosy Victorian gem nestling on the edge of town now boasts a delightful rooftop terrace. A family-run free house that oozes charm and character, it is a haven for real ale drinkers, with a choice of seven microbrewery ales from near and far, as well as a cider. Occasional live music and televised sports feature. A fine selection of rolls is available. A stone's throw from the Capital FM Arena.
Q❀🚊♣●🚌(NCT43)🐾📶

Malt Cross 𝕃

16 St James's Street, NG1 6FE
⏲ 11-11 (midnight Fri & Sat); 11-9 Sun ☎ (0115) 941 1048
🌐 maltcross.com
5 changing beers (often Brewster's) 🄷
This Grade II-listed former Victorian music hall, built by Edwin Hill in 1877, is owned by a charitable trust. It was extensively restored in 2014 following Heritage Lottery funding which opened up two lower floors, including caves once inhabited by Carmelite monks. An upstairs gallery overlooks the ground floor area from all sides. The guest beers

are often from local microbreweries. Monday is quiz night and live music plays on Tuesday evenings. Food is served until 9pm.

Newshouse

123 Canal Street, NG1 7HB

12-11 (midnight Fri & Sat) (0115) 952 3061

Castle Rock Harvest Pale; changing beers (sourced locally)

In times past, newspapers would be read out here to inform the illiterate of elections at home and military victories overseas, hence the name. The walls of both the lounge and bar are covered with framed front pages of local newspapers showing headlines stretching back over many years. The public bar has a large TV screen, dartboard, bar billiards and table skittles. Light lunches are served Monday-Saturday with snacks at all times. Caythorpe beers are regularly among the guests.

Organ Grinder

21 Alfreton Road, Canning Circus, NG7 3JE

12-11 (11.30 Thu; midnight Fri & Sat) (0115) 970 0630

Blue Monkey BG Sips, 99 Red Baboons, Infinity, Guerrilla; Sharp's Doom Bar; 4 changing beers (sourced locally; often Blue Monkey)

Previously the Red Lion, this pub was bought and refurbished by Blue Monkey Brewery. The single-room, multi-level pub boasts a wood-burning fire. To the rear is a small courtyard leading to a raised decked area and first floor function room (where a TV is occasionally in use). The full Blue Monkey range of beers is offered, as well as three real ciders or perries. No meals, but bar snacks such as Scotch eggs and pork pies are sold.
(NCT77,78,TBR1)

Sir John Borlase Warren

1 Ilkeston Road, NG7 3GD

12-11.30 (11 Sun) (0115) 988 1889

Draught Bass; Everards Tiger; Nottingham Extra Pale Ale; 6 changing beers (often Brown Ales)

An Everards Project William pub with Brown Ales, this establishment reopened in 2014. It is situated in the centre of Canning Circus with views across the city. The furnishings are a comfortable mix of chairs and sofas. The lower bar area can be hired for private parties. It has a roof patio and a secluded, enclosed pub garden. Beers are sourced from breweries local and country-wide. Bar snacks are available including pork pies and sausage rolls.
Q

Vat & Fiddle

Queens Bridge Road, NG2 1NB

11-11 (midnight Thu-Sat) (0115) 985 0611

Castle Rock Sheriff's Tipple, Black Gold, Harvest Pale, Preservation Fine Ale, Elsie Mo, Screech Owl; 6 changing beers

Brewery tap for the adjacent Castle Rock Brewery, a minute's walk from the station. Twelve handpumps serve the Castle Rock range, with guests from local and new breweries completing the selection. The seated area to the front is the perfect spot to admire the Art Deco frontage and floral displays in summer. Hot food is served all week, with roasts on Sundays. Brewery tours operate Monday-Saturday (book ahead), and end in Golding's Room which opened in 2011.
Q

Nottingham: East

Bread & Bitter

153-155 Woodthorpe Drive, Mapperley, NG3 5JL

10-11 (midnight Thu-Sat); 11-11 Sun (0115) 960 7541

Castle Rock Black Gold, Harvest Pale, Preservation Fine Ale, Elsie Mo, Screech Owl; Fuller's London Pride; changing beers

Castle Rock pub built in 2007 on the premises of the old Judge's bakery on Mapperley Top. The original baker's oven fronts are still embedded in an inside wall, giving the place a warm and welcoming feel. The pub started a revival of real ale outlets in Mapperley. Twelve beers including a mild and rotating guests are available, along with an extensive foreign bottled beer list. Food is all home cooked and varies frequently – look for the specials board. Q

Willowbrook

13 Main Road, Gedling, NG4 3HQ

10-11 (midnight Fri); 9am-midnight Sat; 9am-11 Sun
(0115) 987 8596

Castle Rock Sheriff's Tipple, Harvest Pale, Preservation Fine Ale, Elsie Mo, Screech Owl; changing beers

Formerly a club, the building was converted into a pub at the end of 2013 and has 14 handpumps. Castle Rock ales supplement four guest beers and four real ciders, always including a stout or porter. A small side dining room and entrance lounge lead to the bar fronting a corridor that opens to a rear room. Off this, patio doors lead to a secluded paved outdoor area. Diners can enjoy a good food menu and daily specials.

Nottingham: North

Gladstone Hotel

45 Loscoe Road, Carrington, NG5 2AW

5-11 (midnight Thu); 4-midnight Fri; 12-midnight Sat; 12-11 Sun (0115) 912 9994

Castle Rock Harvest Pale; Fuller's London Pride; Oakham Bishops Farewell; Timothy Taylor Landlord; 2 changing beers

This friendly back-street local sits in the middle of a Victorian terrace, just north of Nottingham, with memorabilia decorating the walls in the bar alongside traditional bar games. The lounge features old brasswork, ornaments, pictures and a large collection of books, with drinkers encouraged to browse. Outside, the secluded garden offers a haven in summer, winning many a Nottingham in Bloom award. The function room has hosted the Carrington Folk Club for more than 25 years, meeting each Wednesday.

Horse & Groom

462 Radford Road, New Basford, NG7 7EA

4-11 (11.30 Fri); 11-11.30 Sat; 12-11.30 Sun
(0115) 970 3777 horseandgroombasford.com

Castle Rock Harvest Pale; changing beers

Friendly and popular inn, sitting in the shadow of the defunct Shipstone's Brewery. The pub has a cosy lounge with a real fire and a separate open-plan taproom area where you will find nine handpumps serving mainly microbrewery beers. The range always include a mild, at least one local guest beer and a real cider. Wheelchair access to the spacious function room and the raised area by the bar is via a ramp towards the rear.
Q (L12,L13,L14)

Nottingham: West

Johnson Arms

59 Abbey Street, Lenton, NG7 2NZ
12-midnight (11 Fri); 4-11 Sat (0115) 978 6355
johnsonarms.co.uk
Adnams Southwold Bitter; Sharp's Doom Bar; 4 changing beers
Popular pub close to the University of Nottingham and QMC hospital. This former Shipstone's house retains the original etched windows, complemented by a green-tiled frontage. Beers are largely from local breweries and traditional home-cooked food includes JA burgers. Highlights include beer festivals, Johnsonbury, Eurovision night, various screened sporting events and the local seasonal ale trails. The beer garden, with a pétanque court, is not to be missed. Q (NCT13)

Plough Inn

17 St Peter's Street, Radford, NG7 3EN
12-11 (midnight Thu-Sat) (0115) 970 2615
Nottingham Rock Ale Bitter Beer, Rock Ale Mild Beer, Legend, Extra Pale Ale; 2 changing beers (often Nottingham)
Linked with the old Nottingham Brewery since 1887, the Plough is now the brewery tap for the revived company. A full range of Nottingham beers is served, four regular and four rotating. The present building, a 1932 two-room house with a central servery, is largely unchanged. Attracting regulars from a wide area, this 'village pub in the city' has retained its local feel in a period of rapid change, offering real fires, an outside skittle alley and a popular quiz night. Q P

Radcliffe-on-Trent

Chestnut

Main Road, NG12 2BE
12 (5 Mon & Tue)-11; 12-11.30 Fri & Sat
(0115) 933 1994 horsechestnutradcliffe.com
Castle Rock Harvest Pale; Fuller's London Pride; St Austell Tribute; 4 changing beers (often Brewster's)
Well-regarded, cask beer-led village pub with a smart 1920s-style décor. Originally the Cliffe Inn, following a major refurbishment in 2006 it became the Horse Chestnut and in 2015 simply the Chestnut. Seven reasonably priced real ales are served including ever-changing guests, always including a beer from Brewster's. Quality home-made food, ranging from stone-baked pizzas to classic British dishes, is served in a relaxed, casual atmosphere. P

Ravenshead

Larch Farm

2 Mansfield Road, NG15 9HA
12-11 (10.30 Mon); 11.30-11 Sat (01623) 491987
Timothy Taylor Landlord; 2 changing beers
This converted farm building is situated at a busy crossroads on the main road between Nottingham and Mansfield. Three real ales are on offer at all times alongside home-cooked meals lunchtimes and evenings. A popular destination with a large garden in the area that used to be the farmyard, it gets especially busy on weekend lunchtimes. B&B accommodation is available. Q P

Retford

BeerHeadZ

3 Town Hall Yard, DN22 6DU (off Market Square to rear of 10 Green Bottles)
1 (11 Thu)-11; 11-midnight Fri & Sat; 12-10 Sun
(01777) 949631 beerheadz.biz
4 changing beers
This is a quiet and friendly pub offering four rotating guest beers and two ciders. The beer is always in excellent condition and served in over-sized glasses so you can be sure of a full pint. There are no fonts dispensing lagers and smooth flows. A recent local CAMRA award winner. Q

Brick & Tile Inn

81 Moorgate, DN22 6RR
1-5 (not Mon-Fri), 7-11; 1-4, 7-11 Sun (01777) 703681
2 changing beers
A quiet pub on the main road between Retford and Gainsborough. There is always a choice of two real ales here – one a light beer and the other dark, usually from local breweries Idle, Springhead and Milestone. B&B is available in two twin and two single rooms. A recent local CAMRA award winner. Q P

Rum Runner

Wharf Road, DN22 6EN (opp Little Theatre)
12-midnight (1am Fri & Sat) (01777) 860788
Batemans XB; Castle Rock Harvest Pale; 3 changing beers (sourced regionally)
Formerly home to the now-closed Broadstone Brewery, the interior comprises a long room warmed by a real fire and a second room with its own serving hatch through to the bar, which can be used for meetings. A quiz is held on Wednesday evening, frequent music nights are hosted and mini beer festivals are a regular feature. Outside is a large enclosed beer garden. The gates at the back of the pub are a work of art. A former CAMRA award winner. Q

Selston

Horse & Jockey

Church Lane, NG16 6FB
12-3.30, 5-midnight; 12-4, 7-1am Sun (01773) 781012
Greene King Abbot; Timothy Taylor Landlord; 3 changing beers (often St Austell)
A true drinkers' gem dating from 1664 with wooden bench seating, large open fires and flagstone floors. Up to six real ales are available, two served from the jug including a LocAle. A real cider or perry is also always kept. Quiz night is Sunday and folk night Wednesday. Look out for Selstock Beer & Music Festival in July. A winner of many CAMRA awards including local branch Pub of the Year 2014. Q P (90,331)

South Leverton

Olde Plough Inn

Town Street, DN22 0BT (opp village hall)
5 (4 Sat)-midnight; 2-midnight Sun (01427) 880323
2 changing beers (sourced regionally)
You could drive through South Leverton and not see this pub opposite the village hall, but then you would miss out on a little gem. Some of the seating appears to be old church pews. This small, friendly local is a genuine, old-fashioned hostelry and well worth a visit – visitors are always made welcome. Q P

Southwell

Final Whistle 🏆

Station Road, NG25 0ET

12-11.30 (11 Sun) ☎ (01636) 813094

Everards Beacon Bitter; Fuller's London Pride; changing beers (often Brown Ales) H

Previously known as the Newcastle Arms, this pub was extensively modified and reopened under its new name in 2011. Owing to its proximity to the former railway, there is a railway theme throughout. Even the outdoor drinking area is complete with railway lines and station fixtures and fittings. Inside, there are three main drinking areas with attractive alcoves, wood panelling, settles and real fires. Bar snacks are available. Quizzes are held weekly on a Tuesday and Sunday. (28,29,100)

Old Coach House L

69 Easthorpe, NG25 0HY

5 (4 Fri)-midnight; 2-midnight Sat; 12-midnight Sun ☎ (01636) 813289

Black Sheep Best Bitter; Oakham Citra; 4 changing beers H

Built around the 17th century, the pub has been refurbished and has five open areas with oak beams and three real fires including a cast-iron range. There is live jazz one Sunday a month, regular music festivals and a quiz night every Sunday. A CAMRA discount is offered. (28,29,100)

Stapleford

Horse & Jockey L

20 Nottingham Road, NG9 8AA

12-11 (midnight Fri & Sat) ☎ (0115) 875 9655 horseandjockeystapleford.co.uk

Full Mash Horse & Jockey; 9 changing beers H

Known locally as the Jockey, the pub was refurbished and turned into a traditional ale house in 2012. It offers a choice of 10 ever-changing real ales, including five LocAles, plus local ciders and a range of whiskies. There are two rooms on split levels, each with a different feel. Pictures of local landmarks decorate the pub alongside water jugs for whisky. There is no music, TV (other than for major sporting events) or games machines. CAMRA national Pub of the Year finalist 2013. Q P (4,15,18)

Staunton in the Vale

Staunton Arms L

NG13 9PE

12-11; 11-midnight Fri & Sat; 11-10 Sun ☎ (01400) 281218 stauntonarms.co.uk

Castle Rock Harvest Pale; Draught Bass; 1 changing beer H

Two-hundred-year-old listed pub in the far north of the Vale of Belvoir, carefully restored to retain its original character. The large bar offers comfortable seating for drinkers and diners, with a further separate raised restaurant area. The venue serves freshly prepared meals lunchtimes and evenings and has built a reputation for good food. Three cask beers, one always a LocAle, are on the bar. Mini festivals are held regularly, with upcoming events publicised on the website. CAMRA branch Pub of the Year 2013. Q P

Sutton-in-Ashfield

Masons Arms L

Unwin Road, NG17 4NB

12-11 ☎ (01623) 610421 themasonsarmspub.co.uk

2 changing beers H

A thriving community pub with a lounge and public bar served from a central bar dispensing two ever-changing real ales – one a LocAle – and a real cider. Darts and dominoes are popular. A conservatory has been added at the rear leading to the garden and smoking area. Mini beer festivals are held twice a year. Q P

Watnall

Queen's Head L

40 Main Road, NG16 1HT

12-11; 11.30-midnight Thu-Sat; 11.30-11 Sun ☎ (0115) 938 6774 queensheadwatnall.co.uk

Adnams Broadside; Everards Tiger, Original; 3 changing beers (often Lincoln Green, York) H

A 17th-century rural gem with a lounge/dining space, a small snug hidden behind the bar and an unusual area with a grandfather clock. The extensive garden has children's play equipment and a marquee, making the pub popular all year. The internal fittings around the bar are original, and photos of locals adorn the walls. Home-cooked English food is served all day. The pub is reputedly haunted. Occasional beer festivals and live music feature. Q P

Wellow

Olde Red Lion L

Eakring Road, NG22 0EG (opp maypole)

12-11 ☎ (01623) 861000

Maypole Wellow Gold; Welbeck Abbey Red Feather; Wells Bombardier; 2 changing beers H

This 400-year-old village pub is situated opposite the village green with its maypole and participates in a large event on May Day. The traditional wood-beamed interior includes a restaurant, lounge and bar areas with photographs and maps depicting the history of the village. Three real ales are available and food is good value. Close to both Sherwood Forest and Clumber Park. Q P

West Bridgford

Poppy & Pint L

Pierrepont Road, NG2 5DX

9.30am (10 Sun)-11 ☎ (0115) 981 9995

Castle Rock Sheriff's Tipple, Black Gold, Harvest Pale, Preservation Fine Ale, Elsie Mo, Screech Owl; 6 changing beers H

Former British Legion Club converted in 2011 to become a Castle Rock pub and café. It has a large main bar with a raised area and a family area with a café bar (children welcome until 9pm). A large upstairs function room features a folk club and the beer garden overlooks a bowling green. Twelve handpumps dispense Castle Rock beers plus guests, often from new breweries. There are usually two real ciders and excellent food is served. P

Stratford Haven L

2 Stratford Road, NG2 6BA

11-11 (midnight Fri & Sat); 12-11 Sun ☎ (0115) 982 5981

Adnams Broadside; Batemans XB; Castle Rock Harvest Pale, Elsie Mo, Screech Owl; 4 changing beers Ⓗ
A former pet shop, the pub has a single narrow bar with a larger seating area at the back and a secluded snug to one side. Up to 12 cask ales plus a cider are available at any one time, including LocAles from owner Castle Rock's portfolio. A wide food selection includes curry night on Monday and pie night on Tuesday. Sunday is silent quiz night and new brew day is the first Thursday of the month. Q❀◑&♣♠🖂🕮☕〒

Trent Bridge Inn ℓ
2 Radcliffe Road, NG2 6AA
❂ 8am-midnight ☎ (0115) 977 8940
Adnams Broadside; Greene King Abbot; Marston's Pedigree; Nottingham Rock Ale Mild Beer, Trent Bridge Inn Ale; Ruddles Best Bitter; 6 changing beers Ⓗ
This large, prominent, 1890s corner pub reopened in 2011 under the Wetherspoon banner to much acclaim. A number of interconnected, wood-panelled rooms include cosy booths, comfy sofas, an open fireplace and an array of mainly cricket-themed sporting memorabilia. Pleasant staff will be happy to pull a sample of one of the 12 real ales and two real ciders usually available from several bars, including those in the function rooms. 🕭◑&♠P🖂〒

West Stockwith

White Hart ℓ
Main Street, DN10 4EY (opp church and car park)
❂ 11-11 ☎ (01427) 892672
Idle Golden Crown, Dog, Sod, Black & Tan, Black Abbot, Landlord; 1 changing beer Ⓗ
Small country pub with a little garden overlooking the River Trent, Chesterfield Canal and West Stockwith Marina. One bar serves the through bar, lounge and dining area. In 2014 a new dining room was added. The Idle Brewery is situated in outbuildings at the side of the pub and the range of five real ales usually includes three from Idle. The area is especially busy during the summer, due to the canal and river traffic. 🕭❀◑&▲♣♠P🖂(97)☕

Worksop

Grafton Hotel ℓ
157-161 Gateford Road, S80 1UQ (town)
❂ 3 (12 Fri-Sun)-midnight ☎ (01909) 530470
Grafton Lady Julia, Lady Catherine, Apricot Jungle, Black Abbots, Coco Loco, Dark Lady; changing beers Ⓗ
The brewery tap for the Grafton Brewing Company, at least three of its beers are always on tap at reasonable prices as well as guests from other local

breweries. A lively community pub, it has a spacious bar area and a restaurant serving good-value food. It is situated close to the railway station and Worksop Town Football Club and offers good accommodation. A former local CAMRA branch award winner. 🕭❀🖂◑&≈♣♠🖂🚐🖂☕〒

Mallard ℓ
Station Approach, S81 7AG (just off railway platform)
❂ 12 (5 Mon; 4.15 Tue)-11; 11.30-11 Fri; 11-11 Sat; 12-10.30 Sun ☎ 07973 521824
Double Top Shanghai Bitter, Adonis; 3 changing beers Ⓗ
Formerly the Worksop station buffet, the Mallard is situated within the railway station buildings, with access from the car park. The pub offers a warm welcome as well as four real ales usually including one from the Double Top Brewery, a selection of foreign bottled beers and country fruit wines. A further room downstairs is used for special occasions such as the four beer festivals the pub holds each year. Double Top Brewery tours are available by prior arrangement. Q🕭≈♣♠P🖂☕

Unicorn ℓ
37 Bridge Street, S80 1DA (opp Queen's Head)
❂ 10-11.30 (1am Sat); 12-11.30 Sun ☎ (01909) 537011
3 changing beers (sourced locally) Ⓗ
Town-centre pub offering up to three handpulled LocAles and one real cider. Refurbished during the summer of 2013 in a traditional style, its comfortable surroundings attract a more mature clientele. Offering good customer service and value for money, a wide range of drinks is served. &♣♠🖂☕

Wysall

Plough ℓ
Main Street, Keyworth Road, NG12 5QQ
❂ 12-midnight ☎ (01509) 880339
Draught Bass; Greene King Abbot; Timothy Taylor Landlord; 3 changing beers Ⓗ
A busy country pub dating back more than 150 years, and for the past 14 years owned by the same family. This pleasantly updated village free house retains many period features and much original character, with an attractive beer garden at the front. A sensibly priced menu of traditional home-cooked pub favourites is available at lunchtime. Dogs are welcome after 2.30pm when food service is finished. There is a separate area for pool, and a quiz is hosted on Tuesday. Q❀◑♣P🖂(863)☕〒

Choosing pubs

CAMRA members and branches choose the pubs listed in the Good Beer Guide. There is no payment for entry, and pubs are inspected on a regular basis by personal visits; publicans are not sent a questionnaire once a year, as is the case with some pub guides. CAMRA branches monitor all the pubs in their areas, and the choice of pubs for the guide is often the result of democratic vote at branch meetings. However, recommendations from readers are welcomed and will be passed on to the relevant branch. Write to: Good Beer Guide, CAMRA, 230 Hatfield Road, St Albans, Hertfordshire, AL1 4LW; or send an email to: gbgeditor@camra.org.uk

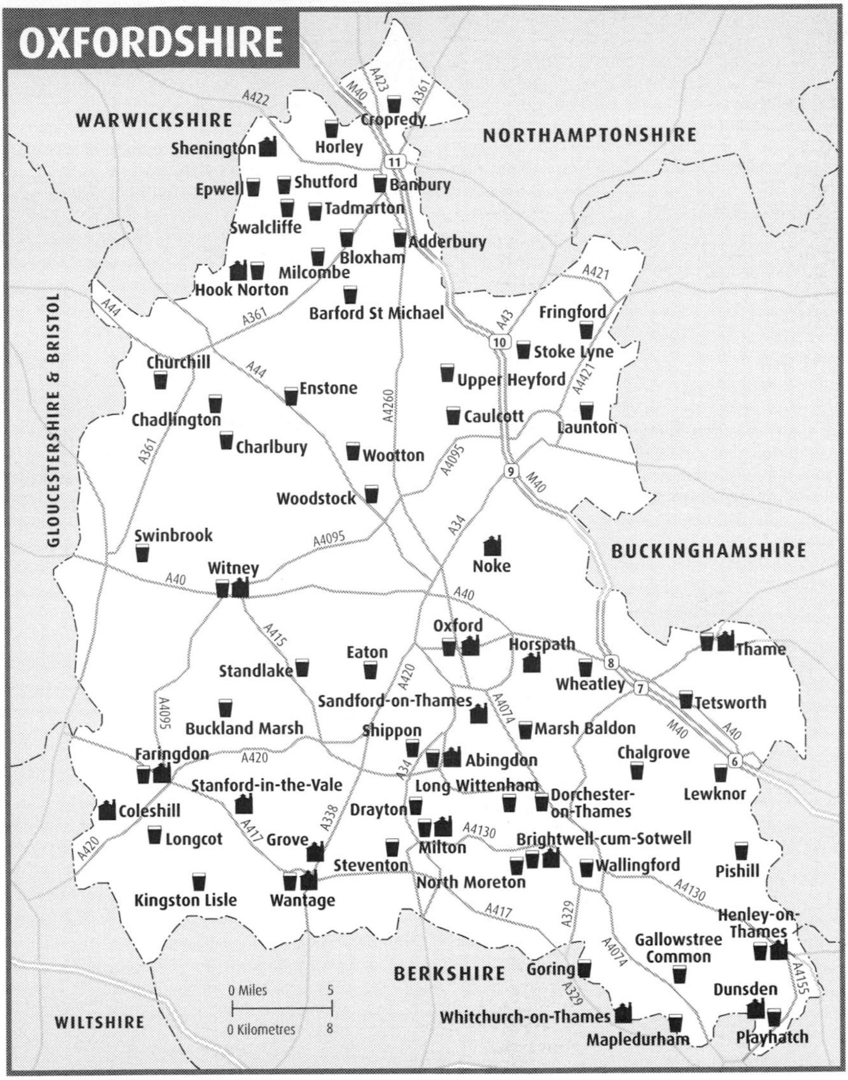

Abingdon

Brewery Tap

40-42 Ock Street, OX14 5BZ

11-11.30 (1am Fri & Sat); 12-11.30 Sun ☎ (01235) 521655
thebrewerytap.net

Loose Cannon Abingdon Bridge; Morland Original Bitter; 4 changing beers (sourced nationally; often Gun Dog, Oakham, Salopian)

Morland created a tap for its brewery in 1993 from three Grade II-listed town houses. The brewery is no more but the pub, run by the same family since it opened, has thrived. There are four regularly changing guest beers, including local ales not from Greene King's list. Three beer festivals are held a year. Good home-cooked food is available every lunchtime and evenings except Sunday. A former local CAMRA Town and Village Pub of the Year.

Q

King's Head & Bell

10 East St Helen Street, OX14 5EA

12-11 (midnight Thu-Sat); 12-10.30 Sun
☎ (01235) 525362 kingsheadandbell-abingdon.com

4 changing beers (sourced nationally; often Adnams, Box Steam, Hook Norton)

Dating back to before 1554 as the Bell and for some time a coaching inn, the pub has been much renovated and restored but retains traces of its historic origins. Although Charles I visited Abingdon there is no evidence he used the Bell. There are a number of rooms for drinking and dining, and two meeting rooms upstairs available for hire, one with a bar. Outside is a pleasant garden in the old courtyard. The food is home cooked using ingredients sourced from local farms and shops.

Nag's Head on the Thames

The Bridge, OX14 3HX

12-10; 11-11 Sat & Sun ☎ (01235) 524516
thenagsheadonthethames.co.uk

Loddon Ferryman's Gold; Loose Cannon Abingdon Bridge; Sharp's Doom Bar; house beer (by

Caledonian); 4 changing beers (sourced nationally; often Plain, Springhead, Two Cocks)
Set on an island right on Abingdon Bridge, the pub is split over two levels with a large garden area next to the river and lovely views of the countryside and the town's historic buildings. A free house, it offers eight regularly changing beers, mostly local. The house beer is Nag's Island Ale (4.1 % ABV). Good food is available all day. Live music plays at weekends and some weekdays. Salter's Steamers cruises from Oxford pass by in summer. Local CAMRA Town and Village Pub of the Year 2013 and 2014.

Adderbury

Bell Inn

High Street, OX17 3LS
12-3, 6-11; 12-3, 5-midnight Fri; 12-midnight Sat; 12-10.30 Sun (01295) 810338 thebelladderbury.co.uk
Hook Norton Hooky, Lion, Old Hooky; 1 changing beer (sourced locally; often Hook Norton)
Situated in the centre of this attractive ironstone village with its folk and morris dancing heritage, this Hook Norton public house has been restored to the heart of the community by Chris and Sandra. It has four comfortable rooms – two wood panelled, one with an inglenook fireplace and another decorated with murals of village morris dancers – and there is an attractive patio with Aunt Sally in the summer. Well-kept Hooky ales and freshly cooked food add to the appeal.
Q (81,90,S4)

Banbury

Easington

135 Bloxham Road, OX16 9JU
11.30-11 (midnight Fri & Sat) (01295) 254276
Brakspear Bitter; Hook Norton Old Hooky; 6 changing beers (sourced nationally)
Recently refurbished, welcoming, spacious road house in the Ember Inns stable. Good-value food is served all day and there is a quiet dining space where families are welcome. The drinking area is divided into alcoves which gives more of a multi-room feel to the space. Eight ales are normally available from 11 handpumps, and you are welcome to try before you buy. Monday is cask night, offering discounted ales, and weekly quizzes are held. P (488)

White Horse

50-52 North Bar Street, OX16 0TH
12-11 (10.30 Mon; midnight Fri & Sat); 12-10.30 Sun (01295) 277484 thewhitehorsebanbury.co.uk
Everards Tiger; 9 changing beers (sourced nationally; often Brains, Charnwood, Cornish Crown)
A warm and welcoming traditional alehouse in the heart of Banbury, the White Horse features an extensive range of up to 10 quality ales on its large L-shaped bar. Home-made dishes based on locally sourced ingredients are freshly cooked to order. Facilities include a courtyard area and real fires in the front bar. Regular events, such as pig and horse racing and a weekly pub quiz, are organised.
Q P

Barford St Michael

George Inn

Lower Street, OX15 0RH (off B4031)
7-11; 1-5 Sun (01869) 338226
2 changing beers (sourced nationally)
This quirky thatched free house dates from 1679. Landlord Martin, ably assisted by Dillon the labrador, provides a friendly welcome and a changing range of ales plus ciders from Westons and others. No food is served, but customers may bring their own or order in takeaways. A beer festival is sometimes held in summer. Weddings and functions are catered for in a marquee in the garden. Opening hours can vary to suit visitors on request. Q P (90)

Bloxham

Elephant & Castle

Humber Street, OX15 4LZ (off A361)
10-3, 6 (5 Fri)-11; 10-11 Sat; 12-11 Sun
(01295) 720383 bloxhampub.co.uk
Hook Norton Hooky; 2 changing beers (sourced nationally; often Hook Norton)
Run by the Finch family for 40 years, this 17th-century coaching inn seems to face the wrong way as the turnpike once ran through the car park and its carriage entrance. More historic features including a bread oven and photographs of old Bloxham lie inside, where a warm welcome awaits. Two Hooky beers and one guest are served, plus eight or so ciders and perries. Home-made food is served at lunchtimes (not Sun). Live music plays on the last Saturday of the month.
P (488,489)

Brightwell-cum-Sotwell

Red Lion

Brightwell Street, OX10 0RT (off A4130)
12-3, 6-11; 12-9 Sun (01491) 837373 redlion.biz
Loddon Hoppit; West Berkshire Good Old Boy; 2 changing beers (sourced nationally)
A traditional half-timbered thatched inn, dating from the 16th century, with a comfortable bar featuring wood beams and exposed brick leading to a restaurant area off to one side. The beers are usually from local breweries, and good-quality reasonably priced pub food is served all sessions (no food Mon and Sun eve). There is a choice of two ciders from local producer Tutts Clump. Jazz

REAL ALE BREWERIES

Adkin Wantage
Appleford Brightwell-cum-Sotwell
Bell Street Henley-on-Thames
Bellinger's Grove
Brakspear Witney
Cats Shenington
Faringdon Faringdon
Fisher Noke
Hen House Whitchurch-on-Thames
Hook Norton Hook Norton
LAM Sandford-on-Thames (NEW)
Loddon Dunsden
Loose Cannon Abingdon
Lovebeer Milton (NEW)
Old Bog Oxford
Old Forge Coleshill
Shotover Horspath
Thame Thame
Turpin Hook Norton
White Horse Stanford-in-the-Vale
Wychwood Witney

evenings and charity quiz nights are held monthly. A popular pub in a quiet village.
🍺🐕◖❢&🖶P🖵(131,X2)🐾🛜

Buckland Marsh

Trout Inn at Tadpole Bridge L
SN7 8RF
🕐 11.30-3, 6-11; 11-11 Fri & Sat; 12-10.30 Sun
☎ (01367) 870382 ⊕ trout-inn.co.uk
Ramsbury Bitter; Young's Bitter; 2 changing beers (sourced nationally) 🅗
Located in an idyllic setting by the upper reaches of the Thames, this former toll house for the adjacent ancient bridge has a light interior and contains much woodwork. It features stuffed fish in glass cases reflecting the popularity of this stretch of the river with anglers. Although there is an emphasis on food, for which the pub is acclaimed, it retains a pub feel with two regular ales supplemented by two changing guests. Q🍺🐕❢⇄◖❢&P🐾🛜

Caulcott

Horse & Groom
Lower Heyford Road, OX25 4ND
🕐 closed Mon; 12-3, 6-11; 12-3, 7-10.30 Sun
☎ (01869) 343257 ⊕ horseandgroomcaulcott.co.uk
White Horse Bitter; 3 changing beers (sourced nationally) 🅗
A small pub with a big welcome, this genuine free house offers one regular and three guest ales, often from local micros or Cornish brewers. The French landlord/chef serves excellent food and booking is recommended, especially for the Thursday steak night and Sunday lunches. The Bastille Day beer festival weekend is not to be missed. A good-sized garden is popular in summer. No dogs are permitted inside. Car parking is available nearby. A former local CAMRA Pub of the Year. Q🍺🐕❢◖P🛜

Chadlington

Tite Inn
Mill End, OX7 3NY
🕐 11.30-11 (10.30 Sun) ☎ (01608) 676910
⊕ thetiteinn.co.uk
Sharp's Doom Bar; 2 changing beers (sourced nationally; often Timothy Taylor, Vale, Wye Valley) 🅗
Welcoming community pub serving one regular and two ever-changing guest ales together with Westons Old Rosie cider on handpump. The pub name is taken from the old Oxfordshire dialect for 'spring' – water runs under the pub and through the beautiful hillside garden, an idyllic setting for a summer evening pint. Inside you can relax in comfortable surroundings and there is a logburner for colder nights. Excellent affordable food is served in the bar and restaurant.
🍺🐕❢▲❢P🖵(S3,X9)🐾🛜

Chalgrove

Red Lion L
115 High Street, OX44 7SS
🕐 11-3, 6-midnight (1.30am Fri & Sat); 12-11 Sun
☎ (01865) 890625 ⊕ redlionchalgrove.co.uk
Butcombe Bitter; Fuller's London Pride; 3 changing beers (sourced nationally; often Rebellion, West Berkshire) 🅗

Church-owned village local, run by a friendly husband and wife team, both trained chefs. The three guest beers are usually from small breweries such as Rebellion and West Berks. Good food is a speciality at this picturesque 16th-century inn. The interior is divided into several distinct areas and the pub is used by a wide cross-section of the community. You can drink outside in both front and rear gardens, while a real fire awaits inside in the winter months. Real Hitchcox cider is usually available in bottles. Q🍺🐕❢◖&❢P🖵(101,T1)🐾🛜

Charlbury

Rose & Crown
Market Street, OX7 3PL
🕐 12-11 (1am Fri); 11-1am Sat ☎ (01608) 810103
⊕ roseandcrown.charlbury.com
Ramsbury Bitter; 7 changing beers (sourced nationally; often Dark Star, Kelham Island, Salopian) 🅗
This traditional wet sales-only alehouse boasts one of the best beer selections in the area with eight handpumps serving quality beers from micros and regional breweries. Visit the pubby front bar or smart recently refurbished back bar on Mondays and enjoy a pint of real ale for £2.50. Live music is held fortnightly on Saturday evenings and there is an annual beer festival in January. The pub has featured in the Guide for 29 consecutive years.
🍺🐕❢▲⇄❢❢🖵(C1,S3,X9)🐾🛜

Churchill

Chequers
Church Road, OX7 6NJ
🕐 12-midnight ☎ (01608) 659393
⊕ thechequerschurchill.co.uk
Hook Norton Hooky; Sharp's Atlantic; 4 changing beers (sourced nationally; often Otter, Stroud) 🅗
Attractive 18th-century stone-built pub with later additions and extensions situated opposite the village church. Inside, exposed beams and stone-flagged and bare-wood floors abound in the many different areas, together with interesting and quirky items of decoration. Good food features heavily, but the drinker is far from forgotten, with the bar supporting six handpumps and an impressive brushed metal tube with an array of taps for beers and ciders. Children and dogs are welcome. 🍺🐕❢◖&❢❢P🖵🐾🛜

Cropredy

Brasenose Arms
Station Road, OX17 1PW
🕐 12-midnight (1.30am Fri & Sat) ☎ (01295) 750244
⊕ brasenosearms.com
Adnams Broadside; Hook Norton Hooky; 2 changing beers (sourced nationally; often York) 🅗
The Ward family from South Africa, with little previous experience of cask ale, transformed this outlet in six months. The pub's reputation for the condition and quality of its beers has doubled both footfall and the number of handpumps dispensing beers from the Enterprise list. It is here that the founding members of Fairport Convention met in the 1970s to plan a music festival, Fairport's Cropredy Convention – now in its 38th year, it attracts thousands of visitors every August.
🍺🐕❢⇄◖❢P🖵(277)🐾🛜

Dorchester-on-Thames

George Hotel

High Street, OX10 7HH (opp Abbey church lychgate)
11-midnight (01865) 340404
thegeorgedorchester.co.uk
Brakspear Bitter; Sharp's Doom Bar; Wadworth 6X; 1 changing beer (sourced locally)
Built in 1495, this coaching inn is one of the oldest in the country. It is situated in this historic village opposite Dorchester Abbey and museum, close to the River Thames. The friendly locals' front bar, lounge and restaurant are complete with oak beams and inglenook fireplaces. Liaan, the landlord, is passionate about serving real ale in perfect condition. Three regular and one guest ale are always available and are discounted by £1 per pint 5-7pm every day. Q P

Drayton

Wheatsheaf

3 The Green, OX14 4JA (jct of B4017 and B4016)
5-11 Mon; 12-3, 5.30-11.30; 12-6 Sun (01235) 531485
Draught Bass; 1 changing beer (sourced nationally)
The pub has a cosy interior with two front rooms and a small dining area to the rear which leads to the garden. It is furnished with antique chairs and tables and decorated with framed prints of horse racing and other traditional sports. Two beers are available, one usually Bass and the other selected from Dayla's guest list. The pub is active in the county Aunt Sally league, competing with other local pub teams. (34,X1,X2)

Eaton

Eight Bells

OX13 5PR
closed Mon; 12-3, 7-11; 12-11 Fri-Sun (01865) 862261
Loose Cannon Abingdon Bridge; 3 changing beers (sourced regionally)
The Eight Bells is a cream-coloured cottage-style brick building in the centre of the hamlet, to which extensions have been added over the years. Inside is a no-frills public bar with wooden benches and tables and a larger, simply furnished lounge bar, which leads to the restaurant/function room. Four beers from local breweries and further afield are available. Q P (66)

Enstone

Harrow

The Drive, OX7 4NF
10-11 (10.30 Sun) (01608) 678852 the-harrow.co.uk
Hook Norton Hooky; house beer (by Cats); 4 changing beers (sourced regionally)
Free house on a bend of the A44 at the northern end of the village, with ample parking. This is a meandering pub with a separate restaurant to the rear, where there always seems to be something going on, and a cosy front bar. Six handpumps dispense up to four guests mainly from local breweries, a guest Belgian ale and one real cider, making up an impressive offering. The house beer is Pride of Enstone (4.1% ABV). Dogs are welcomed with water and treats. Q P (S3)

Epwell

Chandlers Arms

Sibford Road, OX15 6LH
10-11 (01295) 780153 chandlersarms.com
Hook Norton Hooky; 1 changing beer (sourced nationally; often Shepherd Neame)
At the heart of the village, Peter and Assumpta offer a friendly welcome to all visitors. Opening at 10am every day, the pub is a welcoming venue for an early-morning coffee and a read of the papers as well as a bar and restaurant. Two handpumped ales are available all year round. The garden is a tranquil area for a summer evening tipple. Walkers are welcome but due to the small bar area dogs must remain outside. P (50A)

Faringdon

Swan

1 Park Road, SN7 7BP
4.30-midnight; 3.30-2am Fri; 12-2am Sat; 12-midnight Sun
(01367) 241480
Faringdon Folly Ale; 5 changing beers (sourced regionally)
The Swan was completely renovated in 2010. Up to six real ales are always available including a selection from the on-site Faringdon Brewery plus a wide choice sourced locally and further afield. Third-pint glasses are available for the unsure. Live music and folk jamming sessions keep the ever-increasing regular clientele entertained. Pub games include bar billiards, table skittles, bagatelle and many more. Q (66,67)

Fringford

Butchers Arms

Main Street, OX27 8EB
12-11 (01869) 277363
thebutchersarmsfringford.com
Black Sheep Best Bitter; Hook Norton Hooky; Sharp's Doom Bar
Pretty 18th-century country pub in beautiful village surroundings. A large well-decorated bar area serves three ales from handpumps, and there is a spacious separate restaurant available for parties. Excellent traditional food is available daily, with a well-priced, good-quality roast served in generous portions on Sundays (reservations recommended on all days). To the front is a large paved seating area popular in summer. (8,37)

Gallowstree Common

Reformation

Horsepond Road, RG4 9BP
closed Mon; 12-3, 5.30-11; 12-4, 6-11 Sat; 12-5 Sun
(0118) 972 3126 therefpub.com
Brakspear Bitter; 2 changing beers (sourced nationally; often Bell Street, Brakspear, Wychwood)
A traditional ale drinkers' local with a bar, dining room and conservatory. The two changing beers are usually seasonal ales from the Brakspear Pub Co approved list, and often include those from Bell Street (Brakspear Pub Co's own microbrewery). Home-cooked traditional pub food is given a modern presentation, with much of the produce sourced locally. The pub hosts events including live music, beer festivals and the famous Tractor Runs where vintage tractors do a tour of local pubs with

passengers travelling in open trailers. The enclosed garden has a children's play area.
Q🍼❀◐◑⛺♣P🚌🐾

Goring

Miller of Mansfield 𝕃

High Street, RG8 9AW (on B4009)
🕐 12-11 (10.30 Sun) ☎ (01491) 872829
🌐 millerofmansfield.com
Hook Norton Hooky; West Berkshire Good Old Boy Ⓗ
Attractive 18th-century coaching inn, overlooking the memorial gardens and close to the Thames, offering the warmest of welcomes and popular with locals and visitors alike. The cosy interior has three distinct areas, two enhanced by open fires during colder months. Top-quality food is served lunchtimes and evenings. A guest ale may occasionally be on alongside the two regular beers. There is a light and airy restaurant to the rear and luxury bedrooms are available.
Q🍼❀🛏◐◑⇌(Goring & Streatley)🚌(134,135) 🐾📶

Henley-on-Thames

Bird in Hand

61 Greys Road, RG9 1SB
🕐 12-2, 5-11; 12-11 Sat; 12-10.30 Sun ☎ (01491) 575775
Brakspear Bitter; Fuller's London Pride; Hook Norton Hooky Mild; 2 changing beers (sourced nationally; often Loddon, Rebellion, West Berkshire) Ⓗ
The Bird is a genuine community local, run by the same couple for more than 20 years. Two ever-changing guest beers, often from local micros, complement the three regulars. The pub hosts darts and cribbage teams, and regular quiz nights. The family room leads to a delightful rear garden with a pond and aviary, popular in summer. TVs show sporting events. A frequent winner of local CAMRA Pub of the Year and a regular in the Guide.
Q🍼❀⛺⇌♣🚌(145,151,154)🐾📶

Hook Norton

Pear Tree Inn 𝕃

Scotland End, OX15 5NU
🕐 12-11 (midnight Fri & Sat) ☎ (01608) 737482
🌐 thepeartreehooky.com
Hook Norton Hooky Mild, Hooky, Lion, Old Hooky; 1 changing beer (sourced locally; often Hook Norton) Ⓗ
With a single beamed bar, this pretty inn serves as the brewery tap for Hook Norton's nearby Grade II-listed Victorian tower brewery. The landlord has won numerous awards including local CAMRA Pub of the Year and was chairman of the local CAMRA branch prior to this tenancy. A child-friendly garden hosts Aunt Sally in summer. Three bedrooms (dogs welcome) provide an ideal base for brewery tours and for exploring this attractive ironstone village and nearby Cotswolds.
Q🍼❀🛏◐◑♿⛺♣P🚌(488)🐾📶

Horley

Red Lion 🏆 𝕃

Hornton Lane, OX15 6BQ
🕐 closed Mon; 6-11; 12-6 Sun ☎ (01295) 730427
Hook Norton Hooky; Purity Mad Goose; Sharp's Doom Bar Ⓗ
A traditional village pub at the heart and focal point of the community offering a friendly welcome to visitors, well-behaved dogs and walkers. The garden is a tranquil spot for a summer evening's tipple. Three handpumped ales are available. The annual beer festival around St George's Day has become a must for locals and visitors alike. Darts and dominoes are played, and a TV shows live sporting events. A traditional wet sales-only hostelry. Local branch Pub of the Year 2015.
❀♣🚌(504)🐾

Kingston Lisle

Blowing Stone Inn 𝕃

OX12 9QL
🕐 12-midnight (2am Fri & Sat) ☎ (01367) 820288
🌐 theblowingstone.co.uk
Morland Original Bitter; Sharp's Doom Bar; 2 changing beers (sourced nationally; often Ramsbury) Ⓗ
Large, friendly, relaxed free house in the shadow of Uffington White Horse. The building was totally refurbished in 2009 and the bars now feature contemporary decor and modern, comfortable furnishings. There is a separate conservatory, a large beer garden and an award-winning restaurant. A good mixture of locals and diners frequent the pub. Two regular ales are supplemented by two changing guests, usually from local breweries.
🍼❀◐◑♿⛺♣🍏P🚌(67,X47)🐾📶

Launton

Black Bull

52 West End, OX26 5DG
🕐 closed Tue; 12-11 ☎ (01869) 253656
🌐 blackbull-launton.co.uk
Hook Norton Hooky; St Austell Tribute; 1 changing beer (sourced nationally) Ⓗ
This is a cosy traditional village pub, the interior featuring some novel seating fashioned from beer barrels. A separate pool room sits alongside the main bar area. Three real ales are available on handpump. Freshly cooked food makes this a popular destination for diners. To the rear is a good-sized garden, quite a suntrap in summer months, with a patio area and a bar for parties and functions. 🍼❀◐◑♿♣P🚌(S5)🐾📶

Bull Inn

Bicester Road, OX26 5DQ
🕐 12-11 (midnight Fri & Sat) ☎ (01869) 248158
🌐 thebullinnbicester.co.uk
Greene King IPA; 2 changing beers (sourced nationally) Ⓗ
A partially thatched building with a garden and a large car park, on the crossroads at the heart of the village. The decor is modern yet retains original features such as beams and a real fire. Historic photos of the village adorn the walls. Traditional tabletop pub games are located near the bar. One regular plus two ever-changing guest ales are sold, plus bottled specialist beer. A separate room has tables for dining. 🍼❀◐◑♿♣P🚌(S5)🐾

Lewknor

Leathern Bottle

1 High Street, OX49 5TW (off B4009 near M40 jct 6)
🕐 11-2.30 (3 Sat), 5.30-11; 12-3, 7-10.30 Sun
☎ (01844) 351482 🌐 theleathernbottle.co.uk

Brakspear Bitter; Marston's Pedigree; 1 changing beer (sourced nationally) Ⓗ
This classic 17th-century inn has featured in all but one edition of the Guide. The pub has a reputation for great ale and good home-cooked pub food featuring locally sourced meats, alongside woodburners, a warm welcome and a family-friendly garden. Popular with walkers from the nearby Ridgeway, it is easily reached by car, or a short walk from the Oxford Tube and the airline coach stop at junction 6. The guest beer comes from the Brakspear Pub Co approved list.
Q ⑤ ⊛ ◑ ⑤ ♣ P ⊟ ❀ ☋

Long Wittenham

Plough Ⓛ
24 High Street, OX14 4QH
✪ 12-11 ☎ (01865) 407738 ⊕ theploughinnlw.co.uk
Butcombe Bitter; 2 changing beers (sourced regionally; often Loose Cannon, West Berkshire) Ⓗ
The Plough is Grade II-listed and dates back to the 17th century – you may need to duck when you enter the bar to avoid the wooden beams overhead. There are two cosy bars and a restaurant. Beyond the children's play area, the long garden stretches down to the River Thames – a delightful place in summer. Ever-changing guest ales are sourced from breweries and microbreweries in the South-East. On weekdays 5-7pm there is 30p off a pint.
⑤ ⊛ ⋈ ◑ ▲ ♣ P ⊟ (97) ❀ ☋

Longcot

King & Queen Ⓛ
Shrivenham Road, SN7 7TL
✪ 12-2 (not Mon), 5-11; 12-2.30, 5-11 Sat; 12-2.30, 5-10.30 Sun ☎ (01793) 784348 ⊕ longcotkingandqueen.com
Loose Cannon Gunners Gold; 2 changing beers (sourced nationally; often Oakham, Ramsbury, XT) Ⓗ
This pub enjoys one of the best views of White Horse Hill and the famous 3,000-year-old white horse. The interior comprises an extensive, open-plan drinking area and to one side a restaurant serving organic meat and local produce. The bar has a good selection of beers from local breweries and two ciders on handpump. In 2014 it was awarded Best Traditional Pub in the Oxfordshire Restaurant Awards.
Q ⑤ ⊛ ⋈ ◑ ⑤ ▲ ♣ ● P ⊟ (65,66) ❀ ☋

Mapledurham

Packhorse Ⓛ
Woodcote Road, RG4 7UG (on A4074)
✪ 11.30-11; 12-10.30 Sun ☎ (0118) 972 2140
Loddon Hoppit; 3 changing beers (sourced locally) Ⓗ
Originally a farm on the Mapledurham House estate dating from the 1600s, this Brunning & Price establishment is now a cosy pub and restaurant. The low-beamed bar has ample seating for drinkers and usually features local microbrewery beers. The larger restaurant area is furnished with bookcases and numerous prints and has a wide-ranging good-value menu. A large secluded garden at the rear has a shaded seating area overlooking fields. There is 50p off a pint 5-7pm weekdays.
Q ⑤ ⊛ ◑ ⑤ ♣ P ⊟ (X39,X40) ❀ ☋

Marsh Baldon

Seven Stars on the Green
The Green, OX44 9LP
✪ 12-11 (midnight Fri & Sat); 12-10 Sun ☎ (01865) 343337
⊕ sevenstarsonthegreen.co.uk
Fuller's London Pride; 4 changing beers (sourced locally; often Loddon, Shotover, White Horse) Ⓗ
This establishment reopened as a community-owned pub in 2013 with the main bar room refurbished and a new function room/restaurant. It sits on a village green that claims to be the largest in Europe. Three local ales are always available and food is served all day including extensive gluten-free options. Family- and dog-friendly, it hosts many community events. There is only one bus a day to the village (Tue, Thu & Sat only), so you will need to walk from Nuneham Courtenay.
Q ⑤ ⊛ ◑ ⑤ P ⊟ ❀ ☋

Milcombe

Horse & Groom
Main Road, OX15 4RS
✪ 12-3, 6-11; 12-5 Sun ☎ (01295) 722142
⊕ thehorseandgroominn.co.uk
3 changing beers (sourced nationally; often Black Sheep) Ⓗ
Welcoming 17th-century coaching inn on the edge of the village constructed from local stone and warmed by a log fire in the inglenook fireplace. The bar has a flagstone floor, traditional furnishing and three handpumps serving regularly changing ales. To the rear is a more contemporary dining room offering a regularly changing locally sourced menu. Outside is an attractive patio area. An ideal place to end a walk, with both children and dogs welcome. Q ⊛ ⋈ ◑ ⑤ ▲ ♣ ● P ⊟ (488) ❀ ☋

Milton

Plum Pudding ▼ Ⓛ
44 High Street, OX14 4EJ
✪ 11.30-2.30, 5-11; 11.30-11.30 Fri & Sat; 12-10 (4 winter) Sun ☎ (01235) 834443 ⊕ theplumpuddingmilton.co.uk
Brakspear Oxford Gold; Loose Cannon Abingdon Bridge; house beer (by Ringwood); 1 changing beer (sourced nationally) Ⓗ
Plum Pudding actually refers to the Oxford Sandy and Black pig, one of the older and rarer British breeds, so it is no surprise to see pork featuring on the menu here. Owned by Mandy and Jez, who have an excellent record of running Guide pubs, this is a great village local, close to the thriving Milton Business Park. Plum Pudding Best Bitter (3.8% ABV) is the house beer. Regular live music is hosted, and two beer festivals each year. Local CAMRA Pub of the Year 2015. ⑤ ⊛ ◑ ♣ ● P ⊟ ❀ ☋

North Moreton

Bear at Home Ⓛ
High Street, OX11 9AT (off A4130)
✪ 12-3, 6-11; 12-11 Sat; 12-10 Sun ☎ (01235) 811311
⊕ bear-at-home.co.uk
Timothy Taylor Landlord; house beer (by West Berkshire); 2 changing beers (sourced locally) Ⓗ
Friendly village local dating back to the 15th century. The main bar features sofas, an open fire and plenty of tables for diners to enjoy the excellent pub food. The four handpumps deliver a range of mostly local ales including Bear Beer (4%

ABV), brewed exclusively for the pub by West Berkshire. The Bear adjoins the village cricket ground where matches are played most summer weekends. A four-day beer and cricket festival is held at the end of July. ❀◑ ▲♣P🚌(95,131)🐾📶

Oxford

Chequers

130a High Street, OX1 4DH

🕒 11-11.30 (10.30 Sun) ☎ (01865) 727463

Brakspear Bitter, Oxford Gold; St Austell Nicholson's Pale Ale; 7 changing beers (sourced nationally; often Purity, Red Squirrel, Saltaire) Ⓗ

Down a narrow medieval passageway off the High Street, the Chequers is Grade II-listed, much of it dating back to the early-16th century when it was converted from a moneylender's tenement to a tavern, hence the name. Note the fine carvings, windows and the ceiling in the lower bar. Tasting notes are provided for all real ales including any frequently changing guest beers, and interesting food is available. A cobbled courtyard provides alfresco drinking, dining and smoking facilities. Q❀◑⇌🍎🚌

Gardener's Arms

39 Plantation Road, Walton Manor, OX2 6JE

🕒 12-2.30 (not Mon & Tue), 5-midnight; 12-11 Sun

☎ (01865) 559814 🌐 thegarden-oxford.co.uk

Brakspear Bitter; 3 changing beers (sourced regionally; often Loose Cannon, White Horse, Wychwood) Ⓗ

Cosy pub down a narrow street off Woodstock Road. The small bar opens up to a spacious dining area, once two rooms, serving some of the finest vegetarian food in the city (with some vegan food available). At the rear is a large and pleasant garden, as well as the outside toilets and another small lounge. A popular and relaxing place to eat and drink. Weekly quiz night is Sunday. Q🛋❀◑♣🍎🚌🐾

Grapes

7 George Street, OX1 2AT

🕒 11-11.30 (12.30am Fri & Sat) ☎ (01865) 793380

Bath Ales Gem, Golden Hare, Barnsey; 3 changing beers (sourced nationally; often Dark Star, Oakham, Wild Weather) Ⓗ

First built in 1820 and rebuilt in 1879, this is a rare Victorian pub in the city centre – its traditional exterior stands out from the surrounding chain bars and restaurants. Some original tiling remains in the entrance. There is one narrow, panelled room with the bar on one side and seating on the other, divided by glazed timber screens. The only outlet for Bath Ales in Oxfordshire, it also has specialist ales from Beerd and Siren Craft. Q◑♿⇌🍎🚌🐾📶

Lamb & Flag

12 St Giles, OX1 3JS

🕒 12-11 (10.30 Sun) ☎ (01865) 515787

Palmers Best Bitter; Skinner's Betty Stogs; Theakston Old Peculier; house beer (by Palmers); 3 changing beers (sourced nationally; often Big Hand, Tring, XT) Ⓗ

Grade II-listed building run by St John's College as a free house. Some of the profits from the pub support student scholarships. Beers from the South-West feature – the house beer Lamb & Flag Gold (4.5% ABV) is brewed by Palmers of Bridport. Two real ciders or perries are always available and beer festivals are held three or four times a year. It is believed to be the setting for the inn in Thomas Hardy's novel Jude the Obscure and has other literary links. Q🛋◑🍎🚌

Masons Arms 🏆 L

2 Quarry School Place, Headington Quarry, OX3 8LH

🕒 5 (7 Mon)-11; 12-11 Sat; 12-4, 7-10.30 Sun

☎ (01865) 764579 🌐 themasonsarmshq.co.uk

Black Sheep Best Bitter; Dark Star Hophead; Rebellion Mutiny; 2 changing beers (sourced regionally) Ⓗ

Family-run community pub full of character, hosting many pub games leagues, including bar billiards and Aunt Sally. The guest ales are varied and regularly come from the Old Bog Brewery (named after the original purpose of the building behind the pub where it is located). A range of local and foreign bottled beers is stocked. The pub is home to the Headington beer festival in September. A heated decking area and garden lead to the function room. Events include twice-monthly music nights. Local branch Pub of the Year 2015. 🛋❀♣🍎P🚌(H2)🐾📶

Rose & Crown L

14 North Parade Avenue, OX2 6LX (½ mile N of city centre, off Banbury Road)

🕒 11-midnight (1am Fri & Sat); 12-midnight Sun

☎ (01865) 510551 🌐 roseandcrownoxford.com

Adnams Southwold Bitter; Hook Norton Old Hooky; Shotover Trinity; 1 changing beer (sourced nationally) Ⓗ

Now a free house, this popular Victorian local on a vibrant north Oxford street is a time capsule with two small rooms and many original features. No intrusive music or mobile phones are permitted. A friendly community pub with books and local business cards to peruse, children are welcome until 5pm. Landlords Andrew and Debbie celebrated 30 years here in 2013 and its fame has even spread to Everest – see the photo on the wall. To the rear is a heated, covered patio. Q🛋❀◑♣🚌📶

Royal Blenheim L

13 St Ebbes Street, OX1 1PT

🕒 11-11 (11.30 Wed & Thu; midnight Fri & Sat; 10.30 Sun)

☎ (01865) 242355 🌐 royalblenheim.co.uk

White Horse Bitter, Village Idiot, Wayland Smithy; 7 changing beers (sourced nationally; often Everards, Isle of Purbeck, Titanic) Ⓗ

Street-corner, single-room, Victorian pub with a bright, airy interior, next to the Museum of Modern Art. Built in 1889 on the site of two earlier pubs, the original Royal Blenheim was a stagecoach. The pub is owned by Everards but leased to the White Horse Brewery. Ten handpumps dispense a full range of White Horse beers, plus guests (including one from Everards) and a real cider. Good food includes vegetarian and gluten-free options on the menu. ◑♿⇌♣🍎🚌📶

St Aldates Tavern L

108 St Aldate's, OX1 1BU

🕒 11.30-11 (midnight Thu & Fri); 11-midnight Sat

☎ (01865) 241185 🌐 staldatestavernoxford.co.uk

6 changing beers (sourced nationally; often Box Steam, Dark Star, XT) Ⓗ

Refurbished for its reopening in 2012, this friendly pub in the centre of Oxford features up to six real ales with at least two from local breweries such as XT and Hook Norton. Good-quality, freshly cooked food is served lunchtimes and evenings (all day at weekends) using locally sourced ingredients where possible. There is an attractive function room upstairs, available to hire, with its own bar and toilets. ◐≋🚌🐾📶

White Hart

12 St Andrew's Road, Headington, OX3 9DL
12-11 (midnight Fri & Sat) ☎ (01865) 761737
Everards Sunchaser Blonde, Tiger; 3 changing beers (sourced nationally; often Brunswick, Everards, York) Ⓗ
This friendly 17th-century establishment is located in the picturesque, Cotswold-stone area of Old Headington opposite the 12th-century church of St Andrew. In the 16th century it was an alehouse/brothel run by the notorious Joan of Headington (see the framed poem on the wall). To the rear is a large and attractive walled garden, home to the spring beer festival. The food is traditional and home-made, with pies a speciality. Local CAMRA City Pub of the Year 2013. ❀◐PΒ🐾📶

Pishill

Crown Inn

RG9 6HH (on B480) SU724900
12-3, 6-11; 12-3 Sun ☎ (01491) 638364
thecrowninnpishill.co.uk
Brakspear Bitter; 1 changing beer (sourced nationally; often Otter, Rebellion, Vale) Ⓗ
Quintessential high-quality English country pub overlooking Stonor Valley in the Chilterns. This 15th-century brick and flint former coaching inn boasts a plethora of wood beams, exposed brickwork and log fires. A small front bar leads to larger rooms primarily used by diners. In the grounds stands a beautifully renovated 400-year-old thatched barn used for functions, including a beer festival each September, and an en-suite self-catering cottage, converted from a 200-year-old stable block. Q❀◐P🐾📶

Playhatch

Flowing Spring

Henley Road, RG4 9RB (on A4155)
closed Mon; 12-3, 5-midnight; 12-midnight Sat & Sun
☎ (0118) 969 9878 theflowingspringpub.co.uk
Fuller's London Pride, ESB; Gale's Seafarers Ale; 1 changing beer (sourced nationally) Ⓗ
Sociable 18th-century country pub on the edge of the Chilterns featuring Fuller's ales, plus a changing guest from the Fuller's list. It serves home-made food with gluten-free, dairy-free, vegetarian and vegan options. Events include monthly unplugged nights, live jazz nights, stand-up comedy, story-telling, murder mysteries, an annual ferret show and beer and cider festivals in the summer and autumn. The pub has many weird and wonderful artefacts, particularly in the soft-furnished Quirky Corner. The pleasant covered balcony and large riverside garden are ideal for summer.
❀◐♣P🚌(800)🐾📶

Shippon

Prince of Wales

60 Barrow Road, OX13 6JQ (off A415, NW of Abingdon)
6-11 Mon; 11-11.30; 12-11 Sun ☎ (01235) 538546
princeofwalesshippon.co.uk
Loose Cannon Abingdon Bridge; Shotover Prospect; Skinner's Betty Stogs; Timothy Taylor Landlord; 3 changing beers (sourced nationally) Ⓗ

At the centre of the village, this traditional country pub is rumoured to be haunted. It has two large rooms, both with log fires – one dominating the lounge – and a separate function room. An ever-changing menu of English food is available alongside a large selection of malt whiskies and ciders. The pub hosts regular beer and cider festivals and traditional jazz and folk music evenings. All visitors are welcome including walkers, cyclists and dogs.
Q❀◐♣P🚌(4)🐾📶

Shutford

George & Dragon

Church Lane, OX15 6PG
12-2.30 (not Mon-Thu), 6-11; 12-11 Sat; 12-10.30 Sun
☎ (01295) 780320 thegeorgeanddragon.com
5 changing beers (sourced nationally; often Fuller's, Hook Norton, Turpin) Ⓗ
Friendly 13th-century village pub nestling into the hillside beside the church. The welcoming, well-stocked bar, with inglenook fireplace and tiled floor, offers five real ales, two from Hook Norton and three guests often including another local brew. Good home-cooked food made with local ingredients is served in the restaurant. Traditional pub games are played, including darts and Aunt Sally. There is a beer garden and a separate TV room with Sky and BT Sport.
Q❀◐♣🚌(269)

Standlake

Black Horse

High Street, OX29 7RH
11-3, 6-11; 11-midnight Sat & Sun ☎ (01865) 300307
blackhorsestandlake.co.uk
Hook Norton Hooky; 2 changing beers (sourced nationally; often Black Sheep, Caledonian) Ⓗ
The Black Horse has been a pub since 1761 and the building is even older. Once owned by Lincoln College, it is a typical low-beamed stone inn. There is a small bar with a dining room adjoining, and a separate back room. In summer a marquee in the garden provides more covered space. The pub has earned a good reputation for its food – a mix of pub classics and specials, with ingredients sourced locally as far as possible, especially fish.
Q❀◐♣P🚌(18,X15)🐾📶

Steventon

North Star ★

2 Stocks Lane, OX13 6SG (end of Causeway off B4017)
closed Mon; 5 (3 Fri)-11; 12-11 Sat; 12-10.30 Sun
Loose Cannon Abingdon Bridge; Morland Original Bitter; 1 changing beer (sourced nationally) Ⓖ
Identified by CAMRA as having a historic interior of national importance, the pub is situated next to The Causeway, a listed ancient monument. Inside are two bars, one with three settles around an open fireplace, and a separate function room. Beers are served through a stable door or hatch. Popular with locals and visitors, it hosts many village clubs and social events. Q❀♣P🚌(X2)🐾

Stoke Lyne

Peyton Arms

OX27 8SD
closed Mon; 12-2, 5-11; 12-7 Sat & Sun ☎ (01869) 345285

Hook Norton Hooky, Old Hooky Ⓖ
Enter here and step back in time. Two Hook Norton ales are served through a hatch direct from the casks and simple filled rolls are usually available. The pub is popular with locals, walkers and others looking for quality ales and great conversation, however the bar area is for adults only – children are allowed in the garden but dogs are not permitted. Two miles from the M40 junction 10, call ahead for opening hours during the week.
Q❀P🚌(37,81)

Swalcliffe

Stag's Head

The Green, OX15 5EJ
⏲ 11-2.30, 5-11 (not Tue eve); 11-11 Sat; 12-10 Sun
☎ (01295) 788660 🌐 the-stags-head.co.uk
Wye Valley Butty Bach; 2 changing beers (sourced nationally; often Black Sheep, XT) Ⓗ
Traditional thatched 15th-century pub close to the village church. Inside you can sample up to three real ales while enjoying the warmth of the cosy woodburner in winter, or in summer relax in the attractive beer garden with its wonderful views across the countryside. Good food is available, and a Greek night is hosted once a month with music and dancing. Walkers, children and dogs are welcome. An ideal place to unwind with the newspaper and a pint. **🔥❀🛏◐◑P🚌**(50A)🐾📶

Swinbrook

Swan Inn

OX18 4DY
⏲ 11-11 (11.30 Fri); 11.30-11.30 Sat; 12-10.30 Sun
☎ (01993) 823339 🌐 theswanswinbrook.co.uk
Hook Norton Hooky; 2 changing beers (sourced nationally) Ⓗ
Nestling beside the River Windrush, this 18th-century inn oozes Cotswolds charm. Outside walls are bedecked with wisteria while inside photographs illustrate the pub's rich heritage and connection with the Mitford sisters. Now devotees of Downton Abbey flock here recognising it as a location featuring in series two. Three handpumps dispense quality real ales and its locally sourced menu has a good reputation. Dogs are welcome in the bar area and attractive garden.
Q❀🛏◐◑♿P🚌(V17,V20,V21)🐾📶

Tadmarton

Lampet Arms

Main Street, OX15 5TB
⏲ 12-2, 4.30-11; 11-11 Sat; 12-5 Sun ☎ (01295) 780070
Hook Norton Hooky; 3 changing beers (sourced nationally) Ⓗ
This friendly local was built in the Victorian era as the village railway tavern, but the railway never arrived. Today locals, visitors and walkers are all warmly welcomed. Home-cooked food is served, four ales are on handpump and one cider is always available. This pleasant village pub offers three letting rooms plus a function room, and TV for major sporting events. Coffee mornings help make this a focal point for the village.
🔥🛏◐◑♣🍎P🚌(50A)🐾📶

Tetsworth

Old Red Lion

40 High Street, OX9 7AS
⏲ 10-10 (midnight Fri); 10-6 Sun ☎ (01844) 281274
🌐 theoldredliontetsworth.co.uk
Vale Best Bitter; White Horse Bitter; XT Four Ⓗ
The Old Red Lion is situated at the Oxford end of the quiet village of Tetsworth, opposite the village green. It has a warm and friendly atmosphere with a cosy log fire in winter and serves three well-kept real ales from various local breweries. Traditional pub food is available in the bar all day and in the more formal restaurant. The pub also serves as the village shop. **Q❀◐◑♿♣🍎P🚌**(124,275)🐾📶

Thame

Cross Keys Ⓛ

East Street, OX9 3JS
⏲ 12-2, 5-11; 12-11 Sat; 12-10.30 Sun ☎ (01844) 218202
XT Four; 6 changing beers (sourced nationally) Ⓗ
Once almost lost forever, this pub was saved by the current tenants, who have transformed it into a drinkers' local. Peter and Trudi always offer a warm welcome to all. Serving an ever-changing range of ales and ciders, local brews feature alongside beers from around the country. At busy times, it is not uncommon for beers to change during the evening, especially those brewed by Peter in the one-barrel Thame Brewery at the rear of the pub. Check Twitter for unusual beers, but be warned, they will go quickly. Local branch Cider Pub of the Year 2015. **Q❀♣🍎🚌**(280)🐾📶

James Figg

21 Cornmarket, OX9 2BL
⏲ 11-11; 12-10.30 Sun ☎ (01844) 260166
🌐 thejamesfiggthame.co.uk
Purity Mad Goose; Sharp's Doom Bar; Vale Best Bitter; 1 changing beer (sourced nationally) Ⓗ
Former 17th-century coaching inn with an early Georgian front. The long wooden-floored interior offers a choice of bars on the left or right as you enter, with dried hops hanging from the ceiling. To the rear is a larger room complete with sofas and a beer garden beyond. Previously the Abingdon Arms, the pub is now renamed after Thame's very own 18th-century undefeated boxing champion of England – sporting prints adorn the walls. Nibbles are usually available on the bar. **Q❀◐◑♣P🚌**🐾

Upper Heyford

Barley Mow

Somerton Road, OX25 5LB
⏲ 12-2.30 (3 Sat), 5-11; 12-3, 7-9 Sun ☎ (01869) 232300
🌐 barley-mow-upper-heyford.co.uk
Fuller's Chiswick Bitter, London Pride; 1 changing beer (sourced nationally) Ⓗ
A traditional family-run, community-focused local on the main road through the village. This popular venue is family-friendly and a warm welcome is assured. Both the landlord and landlady are Fuller's Master Cellarmen – the guest beer is a Fuller's seasonal or sourced locally. There is a large open bar area where you will often find locals playing darts and a separate dining area serving home-made food cooked to order. Aunt Sally can be played in the garden.
🔥❀◐◑♿♣P🚌(25A,90)🐾📶

Wallingford

Dolphin

2 St Marys Street, OX10 0EL
8am-11.30 (1am Fri & Sat); 9am-11.30 Sun
(01491) 837377 thedollyinwally.co.uk
Greene King IPA; Morland Original Bitter; house beer (by Greene King); 2 changing beers (sourced nationally) [H]
Situated on a pedestrian street off the main square of this market town, this establishment features live music, karaoke, disco and TV sport. Traditional pub food is served all day until 9pm (no food Sun and Mon eve) and the breakfasts are said to be the best in the area. Alcohol is served from 10am every day. The house beer is the Dolly (3.9% ABV). Entry on Friday and Saturday is before 11.15pm.
P

Wantage

Royal Oak

Newbury Street, OX12 8DF (S of Market Square)
5.30-11; 12-2.30, 7-11 Sat; 12-2, 7.30-10.30 Sun
(01235) 763129 royaloakwantage.co.uk
Wadworth 6X; West Berkshire Maggs' Magnificent Mild, Dr Hexter's Healer; 8 changing beers (sourced nationally) [G]
This multi award-winning street-corner pub is a mecca for the discerning drinker and a meeting place for many local clubs. Photographs of ships bearing the pub's name adorn the walls. The lounge bar features wrought-iron trelliswork covered in pumpclips. The pub is the primary outlet for West Berkshire ales in the area – one beer carries landlord Paul Hexter's name – together with 30-plus ciders and perries. All the beers are served direct from the cask. A former national finalist CAMRA Pub of the Year, national CAMRA Cider and Perry Pub of the Year, and local branch Pub of the Year 2015. Q

Wheatley

Cricketer's Arms

38 Littleworth, OX33 1TR
12-3 (not Tue-Thu), 6-11; 12-11 Fri; 12-2.30, 6-11 Sat; 12-4, 7-10.30 Sun (01865) 872738
cricketers-arms.co.uk
Hook Norton Hooky; 2 changing beers (sourced locally) [H]
Friendly, family-run free house – all three cask ales are from local breweries including frequent darker ales. A range of local bottled beers is also available and real cider. Great-value home-cooked food is served, locally sourced wherever possible, and there are themed nights. Beer and sausage festivals are held in February and September. Popular with walkers, and dogs and children are welcome. A former local CAMRA Town and Village Pub of the Year. Q P (103,104)

Witney

Eagle Tavern

22 Corn Street, OX28 6BL
11-3, 5-midnight (2am Fri); 11-2am Sat; 12-midnight Sun
(01993) 700121
Hook Norton Hooky, Lion, Old Hooky; Wychwood Hobgoblin; 1 changing beer (sourced locally; often Hook Norton) [H]
The landlord has been running pubs in Corn Street for 25 years, this one for 10, and has won Hook Norton Pub of the Year and Best-Kept Beer and Cellar on several occasions. This wood-panelled and stone-floored building has also been local CAMRA Town and Country Pub of the Year twice. Friendly locals, welcoming staff and quality beer all add up to a must-visit pub. Wychwood Brewery is just around the corner. (S1,S2)

New Inn

111 Corn Street, OX28 6AU
5-midnight; 12-1am Sat; 12-midnight Sun
(01993) 703807
Black Sheep Best Bitter; Sharp's Doom Bar; Timothy Taylor Landlord; Tring Side Pocket for a Toad; 2 changing beers (sourced locally) [H]
Just out of the town centre, this old, traditional pub has an excellent choice of six real ales, including two guests from microbreweries. It can be quiet midweek but is always busy when major rugby tournaments are televised. There is seating around the bar, where you can engage in a full and frank exchange of views with the friendly locals. There is live music on Saturday nights and a jazz jam on the third Sunday evening of the month.
P (S1,S2)

Woodstock

Black Prince

2 Manor Road, OX20 1XJ
12-11 (01993) 811530
theblackprincewoodstock.com
Hook Norton Hooky; St Austell Trelawny; 2 changing beers (sourced nationally) [H]
Historic and pleasant 16th-century pub with an attractive riverside setting by the River Glyme, opposite Blenheim Palace. There is a terrace with seating for warmer days, from where you can watch the yearly Mock Mayor ceremony or the June Duck Race. Inside, there are ancient fireplaces, stone walls and a suit of armour. Ever-changing ales and fresh well-cooked snacks and meals are available at reasonable prices. Aunt Sally is played and families, walkers and well-behaved dogs are welcome. P (S3,W12)

Wootton

Killingworth Castle

Glympton Road, OX20 1EJ
9am-11 (01993) 811401 thekillingworthcastle.com
4 changing beers (sourced locally) [H]
This former Morland tied house has a fine plaque on the front wall to prove its history. The handpumps usually feature house beers supplied by sister company Yubberton Brewing (Yubby, Goldie and Yawnie) but a guest is always available too. The food has won awards locally and the care taken in the kitchen is replicated behind the bar. The bar room, with its warming wood-burning stove, is a lively place where Aunt Sally teams mix with diners. Q P (W12)

I think now would be a good time for a beer.
Franklin Delano Roosevelt, 15 December 1933, on the day Prohibition ended

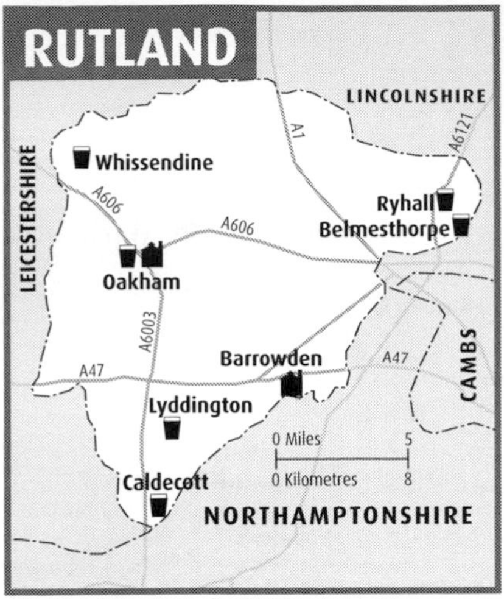

Belmesthorpe

Blue Bell 𝕃

Shepherds Walk, PE9 4JG

12-2.30 (not Mon), 6-11; 12-2, 5-11 Fri; 12-11.30 Sat; 12-11 Sun ☎ (01780) 753081

Abbeydale Absolution; Greene King IPA; Oakham Bishops Farewell; 3 changing beers (often Abbeydale, Grainstore) Ⓗ

The Blue Bell is a historic village pub. Low ceilings, a roaring fire and stone walls are part of its charm. Six handpulls offer a wide range of well-kept guest beers, including at least one LocAle and real cider. Dogs on leads are welcome in the bar area. Good honest home-made pub food is available Tuesday-Sunday lunchtimes (booking advisable). Rutland CAMRA Pub of the Year 2013.
Q❀◑♿⛺♣●P🐾

Caldecott

Plough Inn

16 Main Street, LE16 8RS

11-3.30 (not Mon-Fri), 6-11 ☎ (01536) 770284

Grainstore Rutland Bitter; Langton Angler; 2 changing beers Ⓗ

Attractive sandstone-built pub on the village green with a welcoming, traditional, open-plan interior incorporating a bar area, restaurant and a relaxing snug. There is a large garden to the rear and a front terrace. Q❀◑♿⛺P🚌🐾

Lyddington

Old White Hart

51 Main Street, LE15 9LR

10 (12 Sat)-11; 12-4, 7-10.30 Sun ☎ (01572) 821703

oldwhitehart.co.uk

Greene King IPA; Nene Valley Bitter; house beer (by Grainstore) Ⓗ

Charming and attractive country inn set among the sandstone cottages of Lyddington, a rural conservation village surrounded by the slopes of the Welland Valley. The 17th-century building has retained its original beamed ceilings, stone walls and open fires, and boasts well-stocked gardens. One of the few owner-run traditional country pubs remaining in the area, Stuart and Holly have been landlords for 18 years. ❀🛏◑♿♣P

Oakham

Grainstore Brewery Tap

Station Approach, LE15 6EA

11-11 (midnight Fri); 9am-midnight Sat; 9am-11 Sun ☎ (01572) 770065 grainstorebrewery.com

Grainstore Rutland Bitter, Rutland Panther, Cooking, Triple B, GB Best, Ten Fifty; 3 changing beers (often Grainstore) Ⓗ

A pub and brewery in a small, cleverly converted warehouse over four floors, retaining some original features. Brewery tours are available but must be booked in advance. There are 10 handpumps – the beer range always includes a mild. Home-made food is served at lunchtimes. Live bands feature regularly. An annual beer festival is held over the August bank holiday. Q◐♿⇌♣●P🚌🐾

Three Crowns

42 Northgate, LE15 6QS

3-11; 12-midnight Fri & Sat; 12-11 Sun ☎ (01572) 770779

Steamin' Billy Tipsy Fisherman, Bitter, 1485; 1 changing beer (often Batemans) Ⓗ

Purchased by Steamin' Billy and extensively refurbished prior to reopening in 2013, this pub appeared in the first edition of the Guide in 1972. Many events are held here, from live music to quiz nights and karaoke. The pub participates in the Oakham Ale Trail in conjunction with the annual CAMRA beer festival in June. No food is served but snacks are available. Q❀♿⇌♣●🚌🐾

Ryhall

Green Dragon 🏆

The Square, PE9 4HH

5 (12 Fri-Sun)-11 ☎ (01780) 751999

thegreendragonryhall.co.uk

Greene King IPA; Oakham Bishops Farewell; 2 changing beers (often Oakham, Penpont) Ⓗ

Former Melbourne's stone-built pub in the heart of the village. The main building is Grade II-listed and dates back to the 17th century, with low ceilings and nooks and crannies adding to the cosy ambience. Superb home-cooked meals are served including pizzas cooked in the pizza oven. A beer from the new Star Brewery is often available. Rutland CAMRA Pub of the Year 2015.
Q❀◑♣🚌(202)🐾

Whissendine

White Lion

Main Street, LE15 7ET

12-11 (10.30 Sun) ☎ (01664) 474233

whitelioninn.com

Everards Tiger, Original; changing beers (often Brunswick, Wood Farm) Ⓗ

Recently refurbished Everards pub next to the village brook with a restaurant and accommodation in eight bedrooms. There are 11 handpumps but some are only in use for special events. Real cider is always available. The landlord is a member of the Magic Circle and regularly entertains guests with his close-up magic.
Q❀🛏◑⛺♣●🚌

REAL ALE BREWERIES

Barrowden Barrowden
Grainstore Oakham

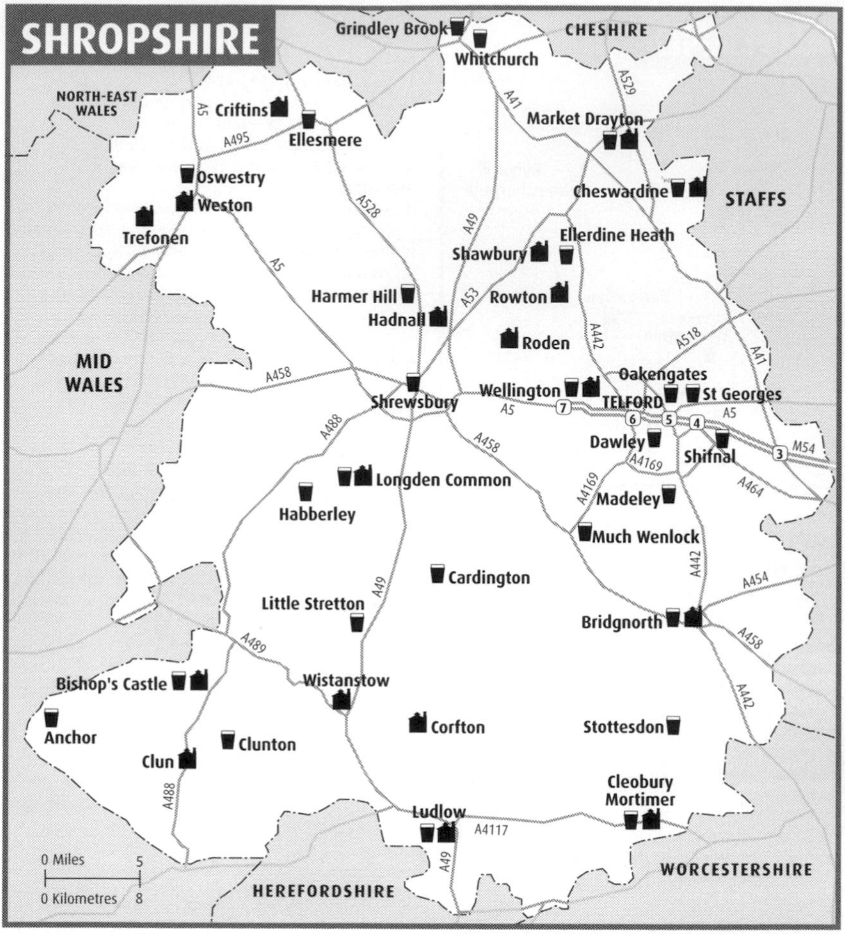

Anchor

Anchor

SY7 8PR (on B4368 Clun-Abermule road)
✪ 7-11; 12-2.30 Sun ☎ (01686) 670900
Hobsons Best Bitter; Six Bells Big Nev's Ⓗ
The pub is 1,300 feet above sea level at the head of the Clun Valley in the most remote part of Shropshire, and close to the Welsh border. The bar room has a wood-burning stove and a pool table, with another cosy room on the other side of the bar. Opening hours can vary by arrangement. The Anchor features in a Mary Webb novel, Seven for a Secret, as the Mermaid's Rest. **Q🍎P🐾**

Bishops Castle

Six Bells 🄻

Church Street, SY9 5AA
✪ 12-2.30 (not Mon), 5-11; 12-11 Sat & Sun
☎ (01588) 638930 🌐 sixbellsbrewery.co.uk
4 changing beers Ⓗ
The tap for the Six Bells Brewery, re-established on the site of the original brewery which closed in the early 1900s. A friendly place and full of character, it has a wood-beamed and stone-walled bar. Three regular and one seasonal Six Bells beer are on handpump, plus cider in summer. The lounge doubles as a dining room (no food Mon and Sun and Tue eves). The pub participates in the town's beer festival in July, with around 20 ales available. Sunday hours may vary. **Q❀◑▲♣🍎🚌(5)🐾**

REAL ALE BREWERIES

Big Shed Shawbury (NEW)
Chapel Criftins
Clipper Bridgnorth (brewing suspended)
Clun Clun
Corvedale Corfton
Dickensian Roden
Hobsons Cleobury Mortimer
Hop & Stagger Bridgnorth
Joule's Market Drayton
Lion's Tale Cheswardine
Longden Longden Common
Ludlow Ludlow
Offa's Dyke Trefonen
Rowton Rowton
Salopian Hadnall
Six Bells Bishop's Castle
Stonehouse Weston
Three Tuns Bishop's Castle
Wood Wistanstow
Wrekin Telford: Wellington

Bridgnorth

Black Boy 🏆
58 Cartway, WV16 4BG
12-11 ☎ (01746) 766497
5 changing beers (sourced nationally; often Greene King, Sadler's, Three Tuns) Ⓗ
First licensed in 1790, this recently refurbished pub stands on historic Cartway linking High Town with the quayside. The enthusiastic landlord and knowledgeable staff can advise on a range of ales delivered from five handpumps, mainly from Greene King but also from a choice of other breweries. A real cider is also always available. The patio affords views over the River Severn and Bridgnorth landscape. ❀≋(SVR)♣●🚌🐾📶

King's Head Ⓛ
3 Whitburn Street, High Town, WV16 4QN
11-11 (midnight Fri & Sat); 12-10.30 Sun
☎ (01746) 762141 🌐 kingsheadandstablebar.co.uk
Hobsons Twisted Spire, Town Crier; 2 changing beers (sourced locally; often Ludlow, Wye Valley) Ⓗ
A Grade II-listed 16th-century coaching inn complete with timber beams, flagstone floor, leaded windows and roaring log fires in winter. This bustling bar, popular with drinkers and diners, has two regular and two guest beers. An extensive food menu, with daily blackboard specials, uses locally sourced produce. The Stable Bar, to the rear, is open evenings. The courtyard is a perfect location on a warm summer evening.
❀◐♿≋(SVR)🚌🐾📶

Old Castle Ⓛ
10/11 West Castle Street, WV16 4AB (between SVR and town centre)
11.30-11 (10.30 Sun) ☎ (01746) 711420
🌐 oldcastlebridgnorth.co.uk
Hobsons Town Crier; Sharp's Doom Bar; Thwaites Lancaster Bomber; Wye Valley HPA Ⓗ
A popular pub dating from the 1600s, set between the Severn Valley Railway and the town centre. Good tasty meals are served in the dining area at the front, lunchtimes and evenings. The bar has four handpumps serving local and regional real ales. This leads to a conservatory/games room, with pool table and dartboard, and a small function room. The back garden has lovely views over part of Bridgnorth, an ideal spot for dining on a nice summer's day.
❀◐♿≋(SVR)♣🚌(436,890)🐾📶

Railwayman's Arms Ⓛ
Severn Valley Railway Station, Hollybush Road, WV16 5DT (follow signs for SVR, pub is on Platform 1)
11.30 (11 Fri & Sat)-11; 11.30-10.30 Sun
☎ (01746) 760920 🌐 svr.co.uk
Bathams Best Bitter; Hobsons Mild, Best Bitter, Town Crier; house beer (by Bewdley); 3 changing beers (sourced nationally) Ⓗ
Eight handpumps dispense a selection of local and national real ales, with two for cider and a perry in summer. The landlord is proud of his cellarmanship and serves a good pint of real ale – the number of pints sold each week is on display. The bars are full of railway memorabilia, and the platform is the perfect place to soak up the atmosphere of a steam railway. Q❀≋(SVR)●P🚌🐾📶

White Lion Ⓛ
3 West Castle Street, WV16 4AB (between town centre and Severn Valley Railway)
11-11; 12-10.30 Sun ☎ (01746) 763962
🌐 whitelionbridgnorth.co.uk
Hop & Stagger Simpson's Original, Golden Wander; Ludlow Gold; house beer (by Hop & Stagger); 2 changing beers (sourced nationally) Ⓗ
A warm welcome awaits locals and visitors to this 18th-century inn, with six handpumps offering home brews plus local and national beers. Sam and Bob have converted a room in the grounds into the Hop & Stagger brewery, producing a good selection of beers. A range of hot and cold snacks is available including home-made Scotch eggs. A folk club, quizzes and music all feature here.
Q❀🛏◐≋(SVR)♣●🚌(436,890)🐾📶

Cardington

Royal Oak
SY6 7JZ
closed Mon; 12-2.30, 6-11; 12-11 Sat & Sun
☎ (01694) 771266 🌐 at-the-oak.com
Ludlow Best; Sharp's Doom Bar; 2 changing beers (sourced locally) Ⓗ
Ancient 15th-century free house in a conservation village. Reputedly the oldest continuously licensed pub in Shropshire, it retains the character of a country pub. The low-beamed bar has a roaring fire in winter in a vast inglenook fireplace. The dining room has exposed old beams and studwork. Guest beers are mainly from local breweries. The menu includes Fidget Pie, made to a Shropshire recipe that has been handed down from landlord to landlord. Closed Sunday evenings in winter.
Q❀◐⛺♣●P🚌(540)🐾📶

Cheswardine

Red Lion
High Street, TF9 2RS
7-10.30 Mon; 6 (5 Thu & Fri; 4 Sat)-11; 12-3, 7-10.30 Sun
☎ (01630) 661234
Lion's Tale Blooming Blonde, Lionbru, Chesbrewnette; Marston's Burton Bitter Ⓗ
This three-room village pub with real fires has a relaxed ambience ideal for drinkers looking for a peaceful pint. The one exception is Irish/folk night on the second Tuesday of each month. A winter brew is available November to January and more than 130 whiskies are stocked. Note the unique folding front door. Within walking distance of bridge 52 on the Shropshire Union Canal. Q❀♿P

Cleobury Mortimer

King's Arms Ⓛ
6 Church Street, DY14 8BS
10-11.30 (12.30am Thu-Sat); 10-11 Sun
☎ (01299) 271954 🌐 kingsarms-cleobury.co.uk
Hobsons Mild, Twisted Spire, Best Bitter, Town Crier; 1 changing beer (sourced locally; often Hobsons) Ⓗ
Situated in 'the gateway to the Shropshire Hills', opposite the twisted spire of St Mary's Church, this 15th-century pub is the brewery tap for Hobsons' award-winning beers. The full range of the brewery's cask ales is often available. With deep leather sofas, a log fire and complimentary newspapers, the pub is busy throughout the day. Food service starts with breakfast from 10am. Accommodation is provided in four refurbished en-suite guest rooms. ❀🛏◐♿♣🚌🐾📶

Clunton

Crown 🄻
SY7 0HU
⏲ 4 (5 Tue)-11; 12-midnight Fri & Sat; 12-11 Sun
☎ (01588) 660265 🌐 crowninnclunton.co.uk
Hobsons Best Bitter; Stonehouse Station Bitter; 1 changing beer 🄷
Set in AE Housman country, the Clun Valley is a designated area of outstanding natural beauty. This genuine, community-owned inn, now run by a local family, has three rooms including a smart restaurant. It hosts a popular fish and chips night every Wednesday, including takeaways, and an acoustic folk night on the third Wednesday of the month. The Crown takes part in the annual Clun Valley Beer Festival. **Q❀◐◑♣●P🚌**(745,860)

Ellerdine Heath

Royal Oak 🄻
Hazles Road, TF6 6RL (2 miles off A442 towards A53) SJ603226
⏲ 12-11 ☎ (01939) 250300
Hobsons Best Bitter; Purity Pure Gold; Wye Valley HPA; 3 changing beers (often Rowton, Salopian) 🄷
'The Tiddly' is a popular, friendly, rural community pub beloved by locals, visitors, families and dogs. Three regular beers are available alongside up to three guests and a real cider. Open fires warm the cosy bar and dining room, which serves locally produced food Wednesday-Sunday. A folk night is hosted every third Tuesday of the month and a cider festival the last Saturday in July. Language groups meet Monday and Tuesday lunchtimes.
Q🐴❀◐◑♿⛺♣●P🐾📶

Ellesmere

White Hart 🄻
Birch Road, SY12 0ET
⏲ 3 (1 Sat & Sun)-11 ☎ (01691) 624653
Salopian Shropshire Gold; 3 changing beers 🄷
A Grade II-listed building of the early Jacobean period, once owned by the Border Brewery of Wrexham. The interior comprises a public bar and a lounge, and features a wealth of exposed timber, but with some later alterations. Outside, the drinking area to the rear has a tented gazebo. The three guest beers include offerings from local breweries. Further down Birch Road is the marina on the Llangollen Canal. **❀P🚌**(53,63,208)**🐾**

Grindley Brook

Horse & Jockey 🄻
SY13 4QJ
⏲ 12-11 (11.30 Fri & Sat) ☎ (01948) 662723
5 changing beers (sourced nationally; often Cheshire Brew Brothers, Phoenix, Wood) 🄷
The 19th-century core of the pub is quite small, but over time the interior has been extended considerably and is now a welcoming and attractive place. There are various nooks and crannies serving different purposes, all tastefully done, with extensive use of reclaimed timber and quality furnishings. While the emphasis is on dining, there is ample provision for drinkers. Outside is a lawned area with children's play equipment. Strategically placed close to the Shropshire Union Canal and Cheshire's Sandstone Trail. **🐴❀◐◑♿⛺♣P🚌**(41)**🐾📶**

Habberley

Mytton Arms 🄻
SY5 0TP
⏲ 4 (12 Fri-Sun)-11 ☎ (01743) 792490
Hobsons Best Bitter; Three Tuns XXX; 2 changing beers (sourced locally) 🄷
Situated in a small village on the edge of the South Shropshire Hills and somewhat off the beaten track, this popular pub is worth seeking out. There are four low-beamed rooms and a friendly rustic atmosphere – beer and conversation predominate. Outside are seats to the front, and a paved area with a vine-covered pergola to the side. A well-known local character and pub regular features on the inn sign. The South Shropshire Hills shuttle bus provides transport in summer. **Q❀♣●P🚌🐾**

Harmer Hill

Red Castle
SY4 3EB
⏲ 12-4, 6-midnight; 12-midnight Fri-Sun ☎ (01939) 291071
Hobsons Mild, Best Bitter; Stonehouse Station Bitter; 1 changing beer 🄷
A successful village local, under the same ownership for some 20 years. There are two public rooms, the larger one very much for dining. The community aspect is reflected in the stock of books (including some for children) and videos, participation in the local darts league, and a substantial amount of money raised for charity. Smokers will need to be persistent in seeking out the smoking area, the route being rather obscure.
🐴❀🛏◐◑♿♣P🚌(501)**🐾📶**

Little Stretton

Green Dragon
Ludlow Road, SY6 6RE (on B5477 S of Church Stretton near jct A49)
⏲ 11.30-11.30 ☎ (01694) 722925
🌐 greendragonlittlestretton.co.uk
Wye Valley Butty Bach; 3 changing beers (sourced locally) 🄷
This pub is picturesquely located – the Long Mynd lies behind and Ragleth Hill to the front – and is popular with walkers. Inside, the L-shaped room has a comfortable drinking area with a wood-burning stove at one end, and a restaurant at the other. Three guest beers are on offer and one handpump is dedicated to cask cider or sometimes a cask perry. The Shrewsbury-Ludlow bus stops outside. **❀◐◑♣●P🚌**(435)**🐾📶**

Longden Common

Red Lion 🄻
SY5 8AE
⏲ 5.30 (12 Sat)-11; 12-10 Sun ☎ (01743) 718889
🌐 theredlionlongden.co.uk
Longden Golden Arrow, Sawn Off, Spire Dancer 🄷
A free house since 2009, the Red Lion is home to the Longden Brewery which first started brewing in 2013. It is sufficiently spacious to be able to cater for both diners and drinkers. There are three public areas – a public bar, a snug and a conservatory to the rear providing dining space. The large garden is home to free-range ducks and chickens. The brewery is housed in a converted barn to the right of the pub and had its capacity extended in 2014.
🐴❀◐◑P🚌(546)**🐾**

Ludlow

Queen's Ⓛ
113 Lower Galdeford, SY8 1RU (just off town centre, opp Co-op)
🕑 12-11 (midnight Fri & Sat); 12-10.30 Sun
☎ (01584) 879177 ⊕ thequeensludlow.com
Hobsons Best Bitter; Ludlow Gold; Wye Valley Butty Bach; 1 changing beer (sourced locally) Ⓗ
Named after Queen Victoria, this is a popular pub and café bar with a decent range of local ales. Look out for the guest beer offered at a competitive price. The light and airy L-shaped bar has three distinct areas, with dining down a short flight of steps. Home-made traditional food is served in the bar as well as the restaurant, with local produce a proud boast. The large enclosed patio garden enjoys views toward Ludford. The monthly quiz is very popular. 🏚🍴◑ᬜ♿♣🚌😺🛜

Railway Shed Ⓛ
Station Drive, SY8 2PQ
🕑 10-5 (6 Fri; 4 Sat); closed Sun ☎ (01584) 873291
⊕ theludlowbrewingcompany.co.uk
Ludlow Best, Gold, Black Knight, Boiling Well, Stairway Ⓗ
Brewery and bar/lounge located in a converted railway shed, and handy for the railway station. It is open during the day with extensive off sales, and brewery visits are welcome. Occasional public and private evening functions are hosted including beer festivals and live music. The spacious venue has comfortable seating and impressive oak benches and tables spread over two levels, all overlooking the modern brewing plant. State-of-the-art underfloor heating, recycled rainwater, low-energy lighting and solar panels make for energy efficiency. Q🏚♿≈●P🚌(722,435,292)😺🛜

Market Drayton

Clive & Coffyne
6 Shropshire Street, TF9 3BY
🕑 5-11 (midnight Fri); 12-midnight Sat; 12-11 Sun
☎ (01630) 652272
Big Shed Brewery Sentinel Amber Ale, Engineers Best; Hancocks HB; 1 changing beer (sourced locally; often Rowton, Wood) Ⓗ
A town-centre Tudor house pub that was built in 1753 and named after Market Drayton's famous son Sir Robert Clive (of India) and a French recipe for mutton pie that was once served. The Clive, as it is known locally, is one of only three free houses in the town and serves local real ales from the Big Shed brewery in Shawbury, and Engineers Best and Sentinel Amber, as well as a number of other local beers. 🛒🏚◑♿●P🚌😺🛜

Red Lion Ⓛ
Great Hales Street, TF9 1JP
🕑 11-11 (midnight Fri & Sat) ☎ (01630) 652602
⊕ joulesbrewery.co.uk
Joule's Blonde, Pale Ale, Slumbering Monk; 1 changing beer (sourced locally; often Joule's) Ⓗ
Formerly a coaching inn, the pub is now the Joule's brewery tap. Built in 1623, it has an illuminated well in the main bar. The brewers' hall or 'mouse room' is a Robert Thompson-inspired function room featuring carved mice. Log fires and oak beams help to create a comfortable atmosphere. Locally sourced food can be enjoyed from an extensive menu, to complement the range of Joule's ales. Q🛒🏚◑♿♣P🚌😺🛜

Sandbrook Vaults
4 Shropshire Street, TF9 3BY
🕑 5-11 (midnight Thu; 1am Fri); 12-1am Sat; 1-11 Sun
☎ (01630) 478405 ⊕ joulesbrewery.co.uk
Joule's Blonde, Pale Ale, Slumbering Monk Ⓗ
You are guaranteed a warm welcome from the landlord in this Joule's pub, with the familiar eye-catching Joule's interior. Well-kept beers are served from the local brewery. It also offers free hot food at weekends to customers, but requests an optional donation to charity. The pub holds regular high-quality live acoustic music nights on Thursdays and Sundays, featuring good regional bands. Well worth a visit. 🛒🏚♿♣🚌😺🛜

Much Wenlock

George & Dragon
2 High Street, TF13 6AA
🕑 12-midnight; 12-11 Sun ☎ (01952) 727312
⊕ thegeorgedragon.co.uk
Greene King Abbot; Hobsons Town Crier; St Austell Tribute; 2 changing beers Ⓗ
A bar and snug restaurant is hidden behind an attractive but unassuming frontage, dating from 1714. This market-town local welcomes regulars and visitors alike. Three regular ales and two guests, which change weekly, are all on handpull. The cosy, alcove restaurant bases its excellent menu on local produce (no eve meals Sun or Wed and it is advisable to book Fri and Sat eves). Every effort is made to accommodate wheelchairs within the limits of the aged building.
Q🛒◑P🚌(88,436)😺🛜

Oswestry

Black Lion
Salop Road, SY11 2RJ (just past Homebase on left, entering town)
🕑 5 (4.30 Fri)-11; 12-11 Sat & Sun ☎ (01691) 652745
⊕ blacklionoswestry.co.uk
Wells Bombardier; 2 changing beers Ⓗ
This friendly pub with a relaxed atmosphere is the perfect place to enjoy a well-kept pint. The guest beer is sourced from a local brewery and not usually available elsewhere in town. The central bar divides the pub from the lounge at the front and the public bar and games area to the rear. New and enthusiastic management arrived in May 2013. Look out for the Black Lion Real Ale Club promotions that are sometimes available.
Q🛒🏚♣P🚌😺

Oak Ⓛ
Church Street, SY11 2SZ
🕑 12 (11.30 Sat & Sun)-midnight ☎ (01691) 659254
Draught Bass; Salopian Shropshire Gold; Stonehouse Station Bitter, Cambrian Gold; 1 changing beer Ⓗ
An early-18th-century listed building opposite the parish church, formerly the coach house of the hotel next door. It has a public bar at the front and a larger, comfortable lounge at the back with TV screens for sports events. The lounge is accessed via a passage that runs down the side, which also leads to a covered area outside.
🛒🏚♣🚌(54,71,72)😺🛜

Shifnal

Plough Ⓛ
26 Broadway, TF11 8AZ

🕐 12 (4.30 Mon)-11; 12-10.30 Sun ☎ (01952) 463118
🌐 artybars.co.uk
Hobsons Best Bitter; Three Tuns Mild, 1642 Bitter; 5 changing beers (sourced locally; often Broughs, Rowton) Ⓗ
Cosy family-run 17th-century free house boasting eight ales and two ciders, mainly local. A good range of home-made pub food is served (no food Mon). A weekly quiz is held each Wednesday night, and live Irish music features on the first Monday of the month. Local artists' work is exhibited and available to buy. A large function room can be hired. Outside is a heated smoking area and a vast suntrap beer garden.
🐴❀◐◑≈●⊟(891,892)🐾

White Hart 𝕃
High Street, TF11 8BH
🕐 12-11 ☎ (01952) 461161
Enville Ale; Greene King Abbot; Holden's Black Country Mild; Salopian Shropshire Gold; Wye Valley HPA, Butty Bach; 2 changing beers Ⓗ
Historic timber-framed free house with a family beer garden and sunny patio off the lounge bar. With 21 consecutive years in the Guide, the pub has received many CAMRA awards as well as consistent top marks in Cask Marque inspections. Home-cooked food is available lunchtimes Monday-Saturday. A friendly community local, it supports darts and dominoes teams. A hanging basket competition features in summer. The car park is large. Q❀◐≈♣P⊟

Shrewsbury

Admiral Benbow 𝕃
24 Swan Hill, SY1 1NF (just off main square)
🕐 5 (12 Sat)-11; 7-10.30 Sun ☎ (01743) 244423
🌐 theadmiralbenbowpub.co.uk/wp
Longden Sawn Off; Ludlow Gold; Salopian Hop Twister; Six Bells Cloud Nine; Slater's Top Totty; 2 changing beers (often Wrekin, Wye Valley) Ⓗ
Spacious free house offering a range of Shropshire and Herefordshire beers – often including a brew from Titanic – plus a selection of ciders from Rosie's including Black Bart, Wicked Wasp and Triple. A good choice of Belgian beers is also offered. A small room off the bar can be used for private functions, and there is a seating and smoking area outside at the rear. Children are not permitted.
Q❀≈♣●⊟

Bricklayers Arms
Copthorne Road, SY3 8NL
🕐 12 (4 Mon-Wed)-midnight ☎ (01743) 366032
🌐 joulesbrewery.co.uk
Joule's Blonde, Pale Ale, Slumbering Monk; 1 changing beer (often Joule's) Ⓗ
Built by Bass in the 1930s and acquired by Joule's Brewery in 2009, this is a comfortable two-roomed local situated on a prominent street corner. The major part of the pub consists of two open areas with a small enclosed room on the car park side. The side wall of this room illustrates several examples of brickwork bonding, so is quite educational – it is the Bricklayers Arms after all!
🐴❀◐◑♣●P⊟🐾

Coach & Horses
Swan Hill, SY1 1NF
🕐 11.30-midnight (12.30am Fri & Sat); 12-11.30 Sun
☎ (01743) 365661 🌐 odleyinns.co.uk/coach-horses
Salopian Shropshire Gold, Oracle; Stonehouse Station Bitter; 3 changing beers Ⓗ
Set in a quiet street off the main shopping area, the Coach & Horses provides a peaceful haven, with magnificent floral displays in summer. Victorian in style, it has a wood-panelled bar, a small side snug area and a large lounge where meals are served lunchtimes and evenings. Bar snacks are available at lunchtimes. Cheddar Valley cider is sold on handpull. Q◐◑♿≈●⊟🐾📶

Dolphin 𝕃
48 St Michaels Street, SY1 2EZ (nr station)
🕐 opening hours vary ☎ (01743) 247005
🌐 thedolphinalehouse.com
Joule's Blonde, Pale Ale, Slumbering Monk; 2 changing beers Ⓗ
A sympathetic refurbishment has retained a traditional atmosphere, with wooden floors, internal gas lighting and open fires. A pub for the community, folk music is hosted on the first and third Thursdays of the month, quiz and open mic sessions on the second and fourth Thursdays. A cider, often Westons, is served. Newspapers are usually available. Q❀◐◑≈♣●⊟(24,64,511)🐾📶

Montgomery's Tower 𝕃
Lower Claremont Bank, SY1 1RT
🕐 8am-midnight (1am Wed & Thu; 2am Fri & Sat)
☎ (01743) 239080
Salopian Shropshire Gold; Wood Shropshire Lad; 5 changing beers (often Chapel, Titanic) Ⓗ
Close to the Quarry Park and handy for Theatre Severn, this Lloyds No.1 offers a choice of two bars. To the left is a large open area rich in natural light, with a smoking area to the rear. The bar to the right provides quieter surroundings and subdued lighting, except on Fridays and Saturdays when there is a DJ. Gwynt y Ddraig cider is usually available. Food is served 9am-11pm.
🐴❀◐◑♿≈●⊟📶

Nag's Head 𝕃
22 Wyle Cop, SY1 1XB
🕐 11.30-midnight (1am Fri & Sat); 12-midnight Sun
☎ (01743) 362455
Hobsons Best Bitter; Sharp's Doom Bar; Timothy Taylor Landlord; Wye Valley HPA; 1 changing beer (often Moorhouse's) Ⓗ
Situated on the historic Wyle Cop, the main features of this timber-framed building are best appreciated externally – particularly the upper-storey jettying and to the rear the timber remnants of a 14th-century hall house including a screened passage which provided protection from draughts (and now offers shelter for smokers). The old-style interior has remained unaltered for many years. The pub is said to be haunted and features on the Shrewsbury Ghost Trail. ❀≈♣⊟

Prince of Wales 🏆 𝕃
30 Bynner Street, Belle Vue, SY3 7NZ
🕐 5 (12 Fri-Sun)-midnight ☎ (01743) 343301
🌐 princeofwaleshotel.co.uk
Greene King IPA; St Austell Tribute; Salopian Golden Thread; Thwaites Wainwright; 1 changing beer Ⓗ
Welcoming two-roomed community pub with a heated smoking shelter and a large suntrap deck adjoining a bowling green. Darts, dominoes and bowls teams abound. Beer festivals take place each year in February and May. Shrewsbury Town FC memorabilia adorn the building both inside and out, with some of the seating from the old Gay

Meadow ground skirting the bowling green. Meals are served Friday to Sunday lunchtimes. (27)

Salopian Bar

Smithfield Road, SY1 1PW

11-11 (midnight Wed, Fri & Sat) (01743) 351505

thesalopianbar.co.uk

Oakham Citra; Salopian Oracle; Stonehouse Station Bitter; 5 changing beers (often Oakham, Salopian) H

The bar's dedicated management strives to increase the beer, cider and perry range to satisfy public demand. Regular cider and perry is provided by Westons and Thatchers, and an impressive range of Belgian and American bottled beer is also sold. Coverage of major sports events is shown on large-screen TVs. A regular winner of local CAMRA branch Pub of the Year awards including 2013 and 2014.

Three Fishes

Fish Street, SY1 1UR

11.30-3, 5-11; 11.30-11.30 Fri & Sat; 12-10.30 Sun

(01743) 344793 realaleshrewsbury.co.uk

Sharp's Doom Bar; Stonehouse Station Bitter; Three Tuns Stout; Timothy Taylor Landlord; 2 changing beers H

In the shadow of two churches within the maze of streets and passageways in the town's medieval quarter. Freshly prepared food is available at lunchtimes and early evenings Monday-Saturday. The pub offers a range of up to six local and national ales, usually including some dark beers, and a choice of real ciders and perries. A former local CAMRA Pub of the Year. Q

Vaults

16 Castle Gates, SY1 2AB

12-11 (2am Fri & Sat) (01743) 358807

the-vaults.co.uk

Hobsons Town Crier; Stonehouse Station Bitter; 1 changing beer H

Situated in a prominent position adjacent to the railway station and a few minutes' walk from the town centre, this free house is part of Shrewsbury's vibrant weekend entertainment scene. It has an open-plan layout with separate seating areas, and for the summer there is a courtyard and roof garden in the shadow of the castle. The guest beer is usually from a local brewery.

Woodman

32 Coton Hill, SY1 2DZ

4 (12 Sat & Sun)-midnight (01743) 351007

Salopian Shropshire Gold, Oracle; Wye Valley Butty Bach; changing beers H

Half-brick and half-timbered black and white corner pub, originally built in the 1800s, destroyed by fire in 1923, and rebuilt in 1925. The building is reputedly haunted by the ex-landlady who died in the fire. The wonderful oak-panelled lounge has two real log fires and traditional settles, and the separate bar has the original stone-tiled flooring, wooden seating, log fire and listed leaded windows. The courtyard has a heated smoking area and seating. Q (501,576)

Stottesdon

Fighting Cocks

1 High Street, DY14 8TZ

6-midnight; 5-1am Fri; 12-midnight Sat; 12-10.30 Sun

(01746) 718270

Hobsons Mild, Twisted Spire, Best Bitter; 2 changing beers (sourced locally; often Ludlow, Three Tuns, Wye Valley) H

A traditional pub in the heart of south Shropshire, first licensed in 1830. Alongside locally brewed Hobsons beers, it now offers two guest ales. The traditional bar room, warmed by a log fire, leads to one of two dining rooms. Live music is hosted most Saturday nights with an open mic night monthly. It holds an Apple Day in October and a beer festival in November. A community pub, there are facilities for meetings as well as a local shop. Local CAMRA Rural Pub of the Year 2014. Q P

Telford: Dawley

Elephant & Castle

1 High Street, TF4 2ET

5-10; 4-11 Fri-Sun (01952) 506412

elephantdawley.net

Hobsons Twisted Spire; Joule's Pale Ale; 12 changing beers (sourced nationally) H

Extensive Grade-II listed landmark free house, restored to exacting standards. Features include 16th-century beams, oak bars, a conservatory and an expansive suntrap garden, plus meeting rooms for parties and societies. Cask beers are dispensed from 12 cooled handpumps plus two more in a separate large function room. Adjacent to the Station Road car park in Dawley centre, it is half a mile from Telford Steam Railway and three miles from Ironbridge Gorge. Sister pub to the Crown Inn, Oakengates, joint beer festivals are hosted the first weekends in May and October. Q

Telford: Madeley

All Nations

20 Coalport Road, TF7 5DP (signed off Legges Way, opp Blists Hill Museum)

12-11.30 (01952) 585747

Hobsons Twisted Spire; 3 changing beers (sourced locally; often Broughs, Hobsons, Ludlow) H

Historic brewhouse with a welcome and friendly atmosphere, offering four real ales and a cider, along with freshly made bar snacks. The famous brewhouse is currently undergoing refurbishment, but a Broughs beer is available. A cosy logburner warms the pub in winter, and there is a beer garden for milder weather. The TV is only turned on for Rugby Union matches. The Monday quiz is a must. Q P

Telford: Oakengates

Crown Inn

Market Street, TF2 6EA

12-11 (01952) 610888

Hobsons Twisted Spire, Best Bitter; 10 changing beers (sourced nationally; often Burton Bridge, Joule's, Wood) H

Traditional three-roomed inn with an oak bar and floor. Ten ever-changing guest ales plus a cider are on handpull, and a wide range of continental beers and single malt whiskies is also kept. There is always something going on: live bands, acoustic and blues evenings, quizzes, comedy and curry nights. Beer festivals with 34 handpulls are held on the first weekends of May and October. Cask-Marque listed, it has won various pub awards. P

Old Fighting Cocks 🅛

48 Market Street, TF2 6DU

✪ 12-11 ☎ (01952) 615607

Everards Tiger; Wrekin Pale Ale, Ironbridge Gold; changing beers Ⓗ

Four-roomed pub including a cosy snug at the rear, warmed by real fires. Originally a coaching inn, it was refurbished under the Everards Project William scheme, it holds beer festivals in May and November in conjunction with the nearby Station Hotel. Bring your own food – plates and cutlery provided. Upstairs a 32-seat cinema is available for hire. Q☺🕭ቋ&≒♣●🚌🐾☎

Station Hotel 🅛

42 Market Street, TF2 6DU

✪ 10 (11.30 Sun)-11 ☎ (01952) 612949

Changing beers Ⓗ

A basic town pub that has featured in the Guide for many years. The landlord specialises in beers from Yorkshire, but also sources locally and nationally. There is a real fire in the front room where drinkers can enjoy home-made bar snacks. Wednesday curry night is now legendary. Beer festivals are held in May and November along with the Old Fighting Cocks nearby. Do not miss the Belgian beer festival. Q☺≒♣●🚌🐾☎

Telford: St Georges

Saint Georges Sports & Social Club

Church Road, TF2 9LU

✪ 7-11; 6-midnight Fri; 12-1am Sat; 12-midnight Sun
☎ (01952) 612911 ⊕ stgeorgesclub.co.uk

Banks's Mild, Bitter, Sunbeam; Wye Valley HPA; 3 changing beers Ⓗ

Large, comfortable community sports and social club featuring an open-plan bar with a view of the sports field. A regular winner of the local CAMRA branch Club of the Year, it offers four permanent and up to three changing real ales, mostly sourced from Shropshire. Bar food is available including a roast on Sundays. There is also a large community hall with a small private bar which hosts community focused events and entertainment. Card-carrying CAMRA members are always welcome. 🕭☺◑♣●P🚌(33,481)☎

Telford: Wellington

Cock Hotel 🅛

148 Hollyhead Road, TF1 2DL

✪ 4 (12 Thu)-11.30; 12-11.45 Fri & Sat; 12-11 Sun
☎ (01952) 244954 ⊕ cockhotel.co.uk

Hobsons Mild, Best Bitter; 5 changing beers (sourced regionally; often Backyard, Holden's) Ⓗ

This much-loved multi award-winning 18th-century Grade II-listed coaching inn has four distinct drinking areas, plus a semi-covered courtyard which doubles as a smoking area. All areas are served from the main bar, the hop-festooned Wrekin Tap. Eight handpulls, one dispensing cider, offer a changing selection, usually from local breweries; a comprehensive international bottle list is also available. No music, just the hum of good conversation and customers ordering another beer. Q☺🖾◑♣●P🚌🐾☎

Pheasant Inn 🅛

54 Market Street, TF1 1DT

✪ 11-midnight; 12-11.30 Sun ☎ (01952) 260683

Everards Tiger; Wrekin Ironbridge Gold; 4 changing beers (sourced nationally) Ⓗ

Reopened in May 2014 after major refurbishment, an adjacent outbuilding is the new home of the old Ironbridge Brewery, now operating under the name of the Wrekin Brewing Company. The bar has nine handpulls, three used for cider, with all the keg fonts on the back wall. Opens for tea and coffee at 10am on market days – Tuesday, Thursday, Friday and Saturday. Q☺&≒●🚌🐾

Railway Inn

42-44 Mill Bank, TF1 1SD

✪ 4.30 (11 Fri-Sun)-11 ☎ (01952) 259212

Wye Valley HPA, Butty Bach; 2 changing beers (sourced locally; often Hobsons, Salopian) Ⓗ

This terrace-row pub has been the focus of the community for years. Recently refurbished, it retains a multi-room look even though it is now more open-plan in design. Sports screens now adorn the walls, and live music features every Sunday. It is home to a host of sports teams. Lower priced ales are on offer all day Tuesday to Thursday. Q🕭☺♣P🚌(44,55)☎

William Withering 🅛

43-45 New Street, TF1 1LU

✪ 8am-midnight (1am Fri & Sat) ☎ (01952) 642800

Greene King Abbot; Ruddles Best Bitter; Salopian Shropshire Gold; 5 changing beers (sourced nationally) Ⓗ

Named after a local physician and geologist, this large open-plan pub features an interior providing a mix of period 1700s and typical modern Wetherspoon decor. Three regular ales are complemented by five constantly changing beers from up and down the country, with a focus on ales from the local area. Four ciders are usually served but there can be as many as six. Good-value food is served in a relaxed atmosphere from 8am-11pm. 🕭☺◑&≒●🚌☎

Whitchurch

Black Bear 🅛

High Street, SY13 1AZ

✪ 12-3, 6-11; 12-11 Sat; 12-10.30 Sun ☎ (01948) 663800
⊕ blackbearpub.co.uk

6 changing beers Ⓗ

This tastefully renovated black and white corner pub lies opposite the historic St Alkmund's church. The ornate bar has six handpulls serving a range of guest beers from both local and lesser-known national microbreweries. Cider is served on gravity. The pub has two separate dining areas offering locally sourced home-cooked food from an ever-changing menu. Q☺◑●P🚌🐾

A glass of bitter beer or pale ale, taken with the principal meal of the day, does more good and less harm than any medicine the physician can prescribe. **Dr Carpenter, 1750**

Finings, gluten and other problems for drinkers

A number of brewers are now producing vegetarian and gluten-free beers

The *Good Beer Guide* is frequently asked for advice from readers on such matters as beers suitable for vegetarians, vegans and those that are gluten-free.

It may be surprising to many to learn that most real ales are not strictly vegetarian. This is because of finings, which are used to clarify beer. Traditionally, finings are made from fish swim bladders, usually from cod. The bladders are boiled and the glutinous liquid, called isinglass, is then added to casks as they leave the brewery or in the pub cellar. By a natural chemical reaction, these finings attract yeast and protein in the beer and drag them to the base of the cask, leaving clear beer above.

It's important to stress that the sediment in a cask is well below the level of the serving tap and isinglass should not be present in the glass. Even so, many vegetarians will not drink beer fined in this way.

Although isinglass is still far and away the most effective and fastest method of clearing real ale, a growing number of brewers are now choosing to use vegetarian alternatives. One such brewery is Marble Brewery in Manchester, which uses silica gel and is perfectly happy with the results. The Moor Brewery in Bristol does not fine its beers at all, as head brewer Justin Hawke says he believes the process strips some of the flavour from beer. He allows his beers to 'drop bright' naturally.

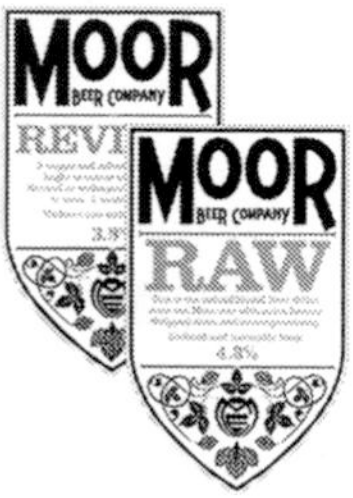

Vegans and vegetarians thinking of switching to keg beer instead should be warned that many of these beers are also produced using isinglass. Usually safer alternatives are bottle-conditioned beers. Vegans also have to avoid beers made with the addition of honey.

Gluten-free beers are sought by coeliacs who suffer from stomach and other ailments as a result of drinking beer which, usually, contains gluten derived from cereals: primarily barley and wheat. Wheat is the main problem as barley has a lower level of gluten and can be used in moderation in gluten-free beers. For a beer to be declared gluten-free the level of gluten must be less than 20 parts per million.

Brewers producing gluten-free beers include Wold Top Brewery in Yorkshire, which brews Against the Grain that's made from lager malt and maize. The beer is usually bottled but can be available in cask for selected customers. The main producer of gluten-free beers is Greens, founded by coeliac Derek Green. His beers are brewed by De Proef in Belgium but are available in selected supermarkets in the UK: see **www.glutenfreebeers.co.uk**. There are no draught beers but a number of the products are bottle conditioned, including Discovery, Amber, Dark and Blond. Other gluten-free producers include Hambleton, Hepworth and St Peter's.

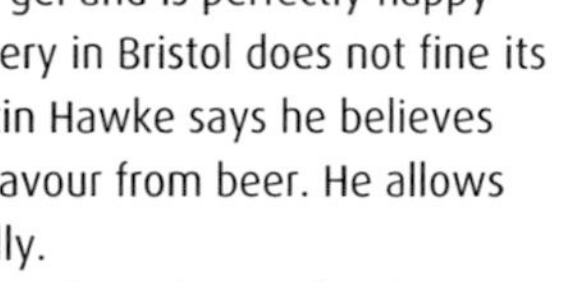

SOMERSET

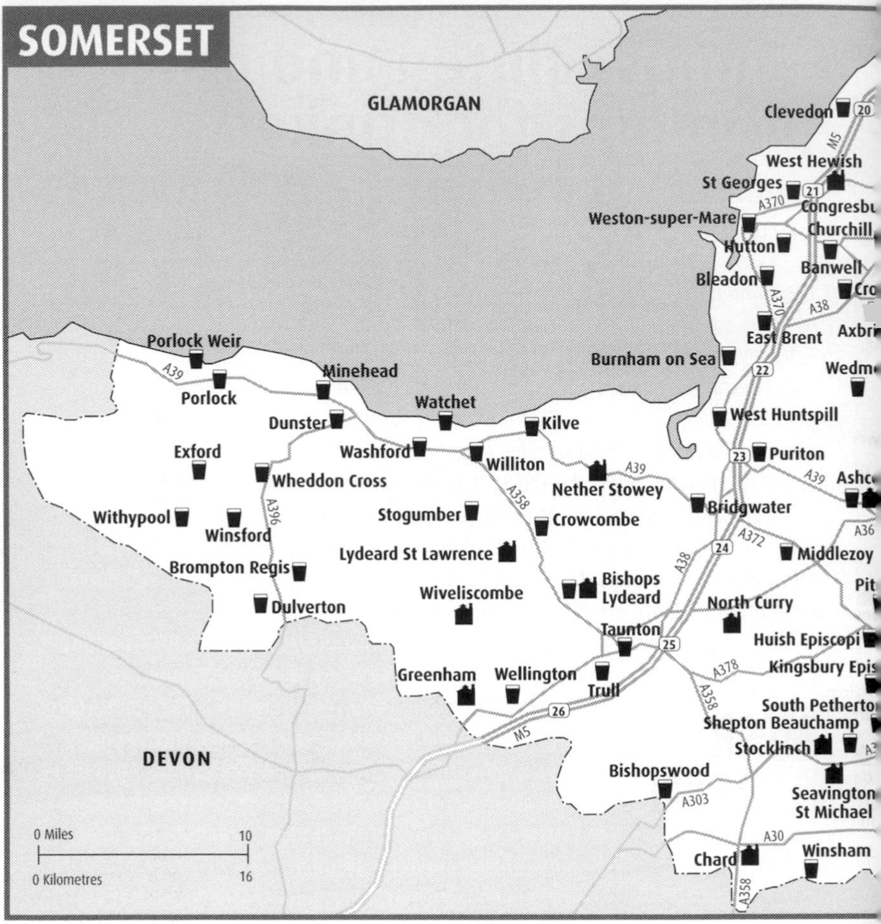

Ash

Bell Inn

3 Main Street, TA12 6NS

12-11.30 (1am Fri & Sat); 12-10 Sun ☎ (01935) 822727

thebellinnash.co.uk

4 changing beers (sourced locally) Ⓗ

Lively local pub offering a traditional, inviting and relaxed atmosphere with a changing choice of up to four, mainly Somerset, ales on handpumps, and Old Rosie cider. Good home-cooked seasonal food is served. The function room and skittle alley with its own bar and disabled access can cater for up to 180 people. Full of rustic charm, there is an inglenook fireplace and lots of belfry oddments adorning the walls, and a large garden and ample parking outside. Q P (N9,N9A)

Ashcott

Ring o' Bells

16 High Street, TA7 9PZ

12-2.30, 7-11; 12-2.30, 7-10.30 Sun ☎ (01458) 210232

ringobells.com

2 changing beers (often RCH, Teignworthy) Ⓗ

An 18th-century family-run free house, comprising three traditional areas on split levels with a separate restaurant. Old beams and fireplaces provide a warm ambience. There is a contrasting modern skittle alley and function room at the rear and an enclosed garden. Two or three real ales are on the bar, mainly from local microbreweries. Good home-cooked food is served, with meals and ales available for take-away. Close to Ham Wall and Shapwick Heath nature reserves.
P (29,37)

Axbridge

Lamb

The Square, BS26 2AP

11.30-11 (midnight Fri & Sat); 12-10.30 Sun

☎ (01934) 732253

Butcombe Bitter; 2 changing beers (often Butcombe) Ⓗ

Butcombe-owned Grade II-listed coaching house in the village square. The National Trust's medieval King John's Hunting Lodge lies directly opposite. There is a large low-beamed bar and several smaller, quieter areas leading off it. Outside drinking spaces are to the front and rear. Lunchtime and evening meals are served (not Sun eve). Butcombe seasonals are occasionally replaced by a guest beer and the cider is Thatchers. The Weston to Wells 26 and 126 buses stop nearby during the day. Q

Banwell

Bell Inn

1 The Square, BS29 6BL

5-11 ☎ (01934) 822330

Butcombe Bitter; 2 changing beers (often St Austell) Ⓗ

This village pub is being slowly and lovingly restored after years of neglect. The guest beer is sometimes joined by a second brew. A real fire warms the front bar and there is a small patio for alfresco drinking. There is a quiz on Thursdays, occasional live music, and board games are available. Despite the address, the pub is on a blind right-angled bend on the busy main road, so extra care is needed outside. Banwell Castle is nearby. ❀♣🚌(26,126,134)🐾 ᯤ

Batcombe

Three Horseshoes Inn

BA4 6HE (off Back Lane) ST69023908

11-3, 6-11; 11-11 Sat; 12-10.30 Sun ☎ (01749) 850359

thethreehorseshoesinn.co.uk

Butcombe Bitter; 2 changing beers Ⓗ

The Three Horseshoes is a 400-year-old country pub which has a spacious bar with an inglenook fireplace and beamed ceiling, a stunning dining room with a vaulted ceiling, and a lawned garden overlooked by the church tower. Open to all, it welcomes drinkers, foodies, walkers, children (with colouring books and games, to keep them entertained) and dogs. The local cider is from Rich's. Q❀🛏◐🍎P

Bath

Bath Brew House

14 James Street West, BA1 2BX

11-midnight (1am Thu-Sat); 11-11 Sun ☎ (01225) 805609

thebathbrewhouse.com

James Street Gladiator, Emperor; 5 changing beers (sourced regionally; often Arbor, Bristol Beer Factory, Wild Beer) Ⓗ

A major refurbishment in 2013 saw the former Midland Hotel transformed into a City Pub Company brewpub. The on-site James Street Brewery produces two regular beers, the refreshing and malty Gladiator (3.9%) and the hoppier, citrussy Emperor (4.4%), and rotating seasonal beers. Four guests, usually from nearby micros, are complemented by four craft beers. An L-shaped bar leads to a dining area and beer garden. The upstairs room hosts TV sport, quizzes, comedy and so on. ❀◐♿⇌(Spa)🍎🚌🐾ᯤ

Bell

103 Walcot Street, BA1 5BW

11.30-11; 12-10.30 Sun ☎ (01225) 460426

thebellinnbath.co.uk

Abbey Bellringer; Bath Ales Gem; Butcombe Bitter; Hop Back Summer Lightning; RCH Pitchfork; Stonehenge Danish Dynamite; 2 changing beers (sourced regionally; often Bristol Beer Factory, Goff's, Great Western) Ⓗ

Owned by 536 of its regulars, fans and staff following a community buy-out in 2013, the Bell has seven real ales plus two varied guests from micros near and far. Live music is a mainstay, with bands playing Monday and Wednesday evenings and Sunday lunchtimes and, in the separate Love Lounge to the rear, you will find open mic nights on Thursday evenings. Features include bar

REAL ALE BREWERIES

Abbey Bath
Black Bear Wiveliscombe (NEW)
Blindmans Leighton
Butcombe Wrington
Cheddar Cheddar
Cotleigh Wiveliscombe
Cottage Lovington
Dawkins Timsbury
Exmoor Wiveliscombe
Glastonbury Somerton
James Street Bath
Kubla Lydeard St Lawrence
Masters Greenham (brewing suspended)
Milk Street Frome
North Curry North Curry
Odcombe Odcombe
Quantock Bishops Lydeard
RCH West Hewish
Stocklinch Stocklinch
Stowey Nether Stowey
Tapstone Chard (NEW)
Twisted Oak Wrington
Wild Beer Evercreech
Windy Seavington St Michael
Yeovil Yeovil

billiards, board games and even a tiny launderette. At the rear is a walled garden with covered seating. ❀♣🍎🚌🐾📶

Coeur de Lion

17 Northumberland Place, BA1 5AR
⏲ 11-11.30 (12.30am Sat); 12-11 Sun ☎ (01225) 463568
🌐 coeur-de-lion.co.uk
Abbey Bellringer; 2 changing beers (sourced nationally; often Abbey, St Austell, Sharp's) [H]
In a passageway opposite the guildhall in the centre of town, this pub claims to be the smallest in Bath. With just four tables in the small bar, this may well be true. Traditional pub food is served at lunchtime. Seating capacity is increased in summer by placing tables outside. There is also an upstairs room used mainly for food. The pub's unique feature is the fine stained-glass window that forms its frontage. **Q**🛋◐⇌(Spa)🚌

Garrick's Head

8 St John's Place, Saw Close, BA1 1ET
⏲ 12-11 (midnight Thu-Sat); 12-10.30 Sun
☎ (01225) 318368 🌐 garricksheadpub.com
4 changing beers (sourced regionally; often Clearwater, Cotleigh, Three Daggers) [H]
A theatre pub for over 200 years but originally the town house of Beau Nash, Bath's 18th-century Master of Ceremonies, this local is reputedly the most haunted pub in the city. Four guest ales are on tap, mostly from regional micros, including some rarities. Traditional food sourced from local ingredients is served lunchtimes and evenings. Tables in the pedestrianised area outside are ideally placed for watching the world go by.
◐◑🚌🐾📶

Hop Pole

7 Albion Buildings, Upper Bristol Road, BA1 3AR
⏲ 12-11 (midnight Fri & Sat) ☎ (01225) 446327
Bath Ales Special Pale Ale, Gem; 2 changing beers (sourced nationally; often Bath Ales, Oakham) [H]
A Bath Ales pub a half-mile west of the city centre, close to Royal Victoria Park and the River Avon. Four beers from Bath Ales, plus an occasional guest, are on handpump. The enclosed and spacious beer garden is popular with families. Food is served all day Monday-Saturday, and until 8pm on Sunday. Home-made bar snacks – nuts, pork scratchings and Scotch eggs – are also on offer.
Q❀◐◑♿⇌(Oldfield Park)🍎🚌🐾📶

Old Green Tree ★

12 Green Street, BA1 2JZ
⏲ 11-11; 12-3 Sun ☎ (01225) 448259
RCH Pitchfork; house beer (by Blindmans); 3 changing beers (sourced locally; often Castle Combe, Plain) [H]
A classic, unspoilt pub in a 300-year-old building. The three oak-panelled rooms include a superb northern-style drinking lobby. Although it can get crowded, there is often space in the comfortable back bar. Guest beers are generally from local microbreweries, with a stout or porter usually on offer in the winter months. A local farmhouse cider is also available, along with a range of fine wines and malt whiskies. Sunday hours may be extended in winter. **Q**◐⇌(Spa)🍎🚌

Pig & Fiddle

2 Saracen Street, BA1 5BR
⏲ 11-11.30; 12-10.30 Sun ☎ (01225) 460868
Butcombe Bitter; Fuller's London Pride; 3 changing beers [H]
A large and busy town-centre establishment with a varied clientele and a friendly atmosphere. One end is an old shop front, the other a courtyard with drinking benches and covered heaters. The decor is an esoteric collection of art displays and sports memorabilia. Up to three guest beers come from local breweries. Table football is played, and there are regular live music and open mic nights. The pub is popular with rugby fans and has several large TV screens. 🛋❀◐⇌(Spa)♣🍎🚌📶

Pulteney Arms

37 Daniel Street, BA2 6ND
⏲ 12-3, 5-11 (midnight Thu); 12-midnight Fri & Sat; 12-10.30 Sun ☎ (01225) 463923 🌐 thepulteneyarms.co.uk
Fuller's London Pride; Otter Bitter; Sharp's Doom Bar; Timothy Taylor Landlord; 2 changing beers (sourced nationally; often Exmoor, RCH, Timothy Taylor) [H]
Tucked away near the end of Great Pulteney Street, the Pulteney Arms has been open since 1792. There are five gas light fittings (now sadly condemned) above the bar. The decor has an emphasis on sport, particularly rugby. The cat symbol on the pub sign refers to the Pulteney coat of arms. An extensive and deservedly popular food menu is on offer (no food Sun eves). Two changing guest beers are usually from national breweries.
❀◐◑♣🚌🐾📶

Raven

6-7 Queen Street, BA1 1HE
⏲ 11.30-11 (midnight Fri & Sat); 12-10.30 Sun
☎ (01225) 425045 🌐 theravenofbath.co.uk
House beer (by Blindmans); 4 changing beers (sourced regionally; often Cheddar, Otley) [H]
Busy 18th-century free house in the heart of Bath. The six ales include two brewed exclusively by Blindmans. Guest ales come from far and wide, with several mini beer festivals a year. The main bar and the quieter first-floor bar serve the same range of ales. Famous for its sausages and Pieminister pies, the Raven is one of the few pubs in Bath serving food on Sunday evening. On several bus routes. **Q**◐◑⇌(Spa)♣🍎🍺🚌📶

Royal Oak

Lower Bristol Road, Twerton, BA2 3BW (on A36 at intersection with road to Windsor Bridge)
⏲ 2-midnight; 12-1am Fri & Sat; 12-midnight Sun
☎ (01225) 481409
Butts Jester, Barbus Barbus; Downton IPA; 5 changing beers [H]
Two regulars from Butts Brewery and up to five guest beers from microbreweries near and far are served here alongside an equally interesting range of ciders, perries and bottled British and Belgian beers. There are folk music sessions (alternating Irish and English) on Wednesday evenings and live music plays most weekends. Tuesday is quiz night. Outside is a secluded garden and small on-site car park. A discount of 50p a pint is offered on some of the range to CAMRA members.
❀⇌(Oldfield Park)🍎**P**🚌(5,15,15A)🐾📶

Salamander

3 John Street, BA1 2JL
⏲ 11-midnight (1am Fri & Sat); 11-11.30 Sun
☎ (01225) 428889
Bath Ales Special Pale Ale, Gem, Barnsey, Rare Hare; 2 changing beers (sourced locally; often Bristol Beer Factory, Bath Ales) [H]

This 18th-century building, tucked away in a side street, opened as a coffee bar in 1957 and got a pub licence five years later. Taken over by Bath Ales in around 2000 and revamped in the company's inimitable style, it looks and feels like a pub that has been there for a century or more. Wooden floorboards, wood panelling and subdued lighting add to the ambience of the ground-floor bar, created from several small rooms. A popular restaurant is upstairs. ◑≉(Spa)🍎🚌📶

Star Inn ★

23 Vineyards, BA1 5NA
⌚ 12-2.30, 5.30-midnight; 12-1am Fri & Sat
☎ (01225) 425072 🌐 abbeyales.co.uk/star-inn-bath.co.uk
Abbey Bellringer Ⓗ**; Draught Bass** Ⓖ**; 3 changing beers (sourced nationally; often Adnams, Flipside, Red Squirrel)** Ⓗ
A main outlet for Abbey Ales, this classic town pub was fitted out by Gaskell and Chambers in 1928. Its four small rooms have benches around the walls, wood panelling and roaring fires. The smallest room has a single bench, called Death Row, while the pub itself, which dates from around 1760, is coffin shaped. Bass is served from the cask and complimentary snuff is available. Cheese night is every Thursday and live music features on the first Sunday of each month. Q♣🍎🚌🐾📶

Bishops Lydeard

Bird in Hand L

34 Mount Street, TA4 3LH
⌚ 12-11; 12-10 Sun ☎ (01823) 432090
🌐 thebirdinhand34.com
Cotleigh Tawny Owl; Exmoor Gold; 2 changing beers (sourced locally; often Quantock) Ⓗ
A free house that is very much a community pub at the centre of the village, and 10 minutes' walk from West Somerset Railway. Four ales are served, mainly from local and South-West breweries. The slate-floored bar is warmed by an open fire in winter. Good, locally produced and home-cooked food is served. The skittle alley accommodates functions. Families and dogs are welcome in the large garden. Weekly quiz nights and frequent mini beer festivals are hosted.
Q🐴❀◑≉♣P🚌(18,28)🐾📶

Bishopswood

Candlelight Inn

TA20 3RS (off A303 between Newton and Marsh)
⌚ closed Mon; 12-2.30 (3 Sat & Sun), 6-11
☎ (01460) 234476 🌐 candlelight-inn.co.uk
Otter Bitter; 3 changing beers Ⓖ
Popular and friendly country pub set in a pretty village in the Blackdown Hills. Features include flint walls, wooden floors and open fires, as well as a lovely garden for those warm summer days. Good food is served lunchtimes and evenings using local ingredients wherever possible. Beers come mainly from West Country breweries and there is usually a selection of real ciders. A large dining room is available for private functions and large parties.
Q❀◑🍎P🐾

Bleadon

Queen's Arms

Celtic Way, BS24 0NF (off A370)
⌚ 11.30-11; 12-10.30 Sun ☎ (01934) 812080
Butcombe Bitter; 1 changing beer (often Butcombe) Ⓗ
A 17th-century stone-built pub in the centre of the village. Three rooms converge on the bar; the largest is the main dining area. Food sales are strong, but not at the expense of ale drinkers – the pub is owned by the local Butcombe Brewery. Two real fires and exposed beams add to the cosy atmosphere. There is a garden/patio with a sales hatch. Families are welcome. Regular buses serve the village from Weston. Q❀◑P🚌(83)🐾📶

Bridgwater

Carnival Inn L

37-39 St Mary Street, TA6 3LX
⌚ 8am-midnight (1am Fri & Sat) ☎ (01278) 726180
Greene King Abbot; Ruddles Best Bitter; changing beers (often Exmoor, Otter, Quantock) Ⓗ
A town-centre Wetherspoon pub that takes its name from Bridgwater's famous carnival. Themed food nights include steak night Tuesday, chicken club Wednesday, curry club Thursday and fish on Friday. A cider festival is held in September. There is a large bar area with another room off to one side. A good range of Somerset and Devon ales is available. At the rear is a family section, and outside a courtyard garden with a smokers' area.
🐴❀◑♿🍎🚌📶

Brompton Regis

George Inn L

TA22 9NL
⌚ 12-2.30, 6-11 ☎ (01398) 371273
🌐 thegeorgeonexmoor.co.uk
Exmoor Ale; St Austell Tribute; 2 changing beers (sourced locally) Ⓗ
The George Inn, a 16th-century free house, is in the pretty village of Brompton Regis on the eastern side of Exmoor National Park. The garden has beautiful views over the Exmoor hills. Well-behaved children are made welcome. Food is locally sourced and cooked to order. There is en-suite accommodation. Please note that the pub is closed on Monday October-Easter.
Q🐴❀🛏◑⛺P🐾📶

Buckland Dinham

Bell Inn

High Street, BA11 2QT
⌚ 12-3 (not Mon & Tue), 6-midnight ☎ (01373) 462956
🌐 bellatbuckland.com
Butcombe Bitter; 4 changing beers (sourced nationally; often Wells) Ⓗ
A warm, cosy venue with a community focus – it has produced a village recipe book and local beers feature in the pub's home-prepared dishes. A good range of guest beers is available, many of them locally sourced, plus a couple of real ciders. A three-day summer beer festival with live music is run in August. The pub has its own large rustic campsite with fine countryside views, attracting CAMRA members from all over the UK.
🐴❀◑⛺🍎P🚌(414,424)📶

Burnham on Sea

Dunstan House Inn

8-10 Love Lane, TA8 1EU

11-11 (11.30 Wed; midnight Fri & Sat); 12-11 Sun
(01278) 784343 dunstanhouseinn.co.uk
Courage Directors; St Austell Tribute; Young's Bitter, Special; 2 changing beers (sourced nationally) H
Large refurbished and detached Young's pub next to the hospital, with a flagstone floor in the bar area, a raised dining area, and two open log fires. Outside there is covered decking, a garden and children's play equipment. Most nights feature themed food offers, and there is an extensive menu. A quiz is held on Wednesdays and a music quiz on Sundays. The pub has en-suite accommodation. P

Reed's Arms L

1 Pier Street, TA8 1BT
8am-midnight (01278) 764060
Fuller's London Pride; Greene King Abbot; Ruddles Best Bitter; 7 changing beers (sourced nationally) H
Large seafront corner pub built in the 1850s and formerly known as the Queen's Hotel, reverting back to its original name under Wetherspoon in 2004. The arms which gave the hotel its name are those of George Reed, once Burnham's leading citizen. Multiple seating areas divide up the pub, and there are three outside terraced areas. Dogs are welcome outside only.

Butleigh

Rose & Portcullis

Sub Road, BA6 8TQ
12-2.30, 5.30-11; 12-2.30, 7-10.30 Sun (01458) 850287
rose-and-portcullis.co.uk
Otter Bitter; 4 changing beers (often Butcombe, Cheddar, Hop Back) H
In 1393 Richard II pronounced that all pubs should have signs, but here it is still a work in progress. Inside, old-fashioned banter and camaraderie continue to thrive. A recent addition is the large, airy dining area. The long association with local rugby is preserved, with various memorabilia adorning what was, in a previous life, the public bar. The pub hosts an annual real ale festival and various events throughout the year.
Q **P** (667,8)

Cheddar

Riverside Inn

Cliff Street, BS27 3PX (next to public car park)
9am-11 (midnight Fri & Sat) (01934) 742452
riversidecheddar.co.uk
Cheddar Potholer; Otter Bitter; Sharp's Doom Bar; 2 changing beers H
Large, tastefully decorated pub at the bottom end of the gorge. The public bar has a range of sofas, high stools and TVs offering a choice of sporting events. The lounge leads to a 90-seat restaurant and a huge beer garden bordering the River Yeo, with a heated smoking area and other sheltered areas for abstainers. There is a well-equipped play area for children. Two guest beers, usually of session strength, and Thatchers cider, are served. Food is available all day from 9am breakfast.
Q **P** (126)

Churchill

Crown Inn

The Batch, Skinners Lane, BS25 5PP (off A38)
11-11; 11-10.30 Sun (01934) 852995
Draught Bass; RCH Hewish IPA, PG Steam; St Austell Tribute; 3 changing beers (often Cotleigh, Palmers) G
Long-time Guide regular and winner of many CAMRA awards. It is tucked away down a small lane yet close to the village centre. Several cosy rooms with stone-flagged floors are warmed by two log fires and offer an assortment of seating. Excellent food is provided at lunchtimes made with local ingredients. Up to eight beers, usually local, are served on gravity. Outside drinking areas are to the front and rear. A classic unchanged old pub; cash only, no cards. **Q** **P** (121)

Clevedon

Royal Oak

35 Copse Road, BS21 7QN (near pier)
12-11 (midnight Fri & Sat) (01275) 563879
Butcombe Bitter; Fuller's London Pride; Sharp's Doom Bar; 1 changing beer H
Lively, friendly, mid-terrace pub close to the seafront and connected via an alley. Under new management as of October 2014, it has a large front window and a Tardis-like interior of many rooms. This community hub is home to cribbage and cricket teams. The winner of various awards, it hosts many events, including cooking competitions and dancing, ranging from morris men through belly dance to Zulus. There is a quiz on Monday and folk music on Wednesday. Thatchers cider is sold.
Q (X4,X5,X6)

Congresbury

Plough

High Street, BS49 5JA (off A370 at B3133 jct)
11.30-2.30, 4.30-11; 11.30-midnight Fri; 11.30-3, 5-11 Sat; 12-3, 7-11 Sun (01934) 877402 the-plough-inn.net
Butcombe Bitter; St Austell Tribute; Twisted Oak Fallen Tree; 3 changing beers H
Characterful village pub with flagstone floors and many original features, decorated with interesting local artefacts. Three guest beers are delivered from a row of old cask heads behind the bar, sourced mainly from local breweries. Thatchers cider is also stocked. Food is served lunchtimes and evenings, except Sunday evening, which is quiz night. The pub has real fires and a large garden. Mendip Morris Men meet here. Local CAMRA Pub of the Year 2013, 2014 and 2015.
Q **P** (X1,353)

Corton Denham

Queen's Arms L

DT9 4LR (3 miles S of A303 near Sherborne)
10-11 (midnight Fri & Sat); 11-11 Sun (01963) 220317
thequeensarms.com
Exmoor Ale; Gyle 59 Toujours; 6 changing beers (sourced locally; often Cheddar, Moor Beer, Timothy Taylor) H
Cosy, friendly pub with real fires and an attractive setting. The food ranges from snacks to quality main meals, and many food awards have been won. The accommodation is highly rated, with the garden overlooking rolling countryside. Special events are held. You can ask for a beer in a third-pint glass if you prefer. The pub opens for breakfast at 8am. **Q** **P**

Croscombe

George Inn 🏆

Long Street, BA5 3QH (on A371)
11-3, 6-11 (5-midnight Fri); 11-midnight Sat; 12-11 Sun
☎ (01749) 342306 🌐 thegeorgeinn.co.uk
House beer (by Blindmans) Ⓗ; changing beers (sourced nationally; often Arbor, Cheddar, Three Daggers) Ⓗ/Ⓖ
Attractive 17th-century inn serving at least four guest ales from West Country independents and hosting two beer festivals a year. Blindmans King George and George & Dragon are exclusively brewed for the pub. Four real ciders are on the bar, including Hecks Kingston Black and Thatchers Cheddar Valley. It has a large main bar, a snug with fireplace, a family room and a dining room. Food is home cooked using locally sourced ingredients. A skittle alley/meeting room is to the rear, and there is a large garden with a covered terrace.
Q ❀ ◑ ♿ ♣ ● P 🚌 🐾 ᯤ

Cross

New Inn

Old Coach Road, BS26 2EE (on A38/A361 jct)
12-11 (midnight Fri & Sat) ☎ (01934) 732455
🌐 newinncross.co.uk
Otter Ale; Sharp's Cornish Coaster; 2 changing beers Ⓗ
Roadside inn on the A38, close to the historic medieval town of Axbridge. Popular for its extensive food menu served all day until 9pm (8pm Sun) and beer festivals at Easter and August bank holiday, it usually has three guest beers that can often be adventurous. There is a function room on the first floor. A large hillside garden with children's play facilities offers a fine view of the Mendip Hills and Somerset Levels. Ale is discounted on Thursdays. ❀◑♣P🚌 (126)🐾 ᯤ

Crowcombe

Carew Arms 𝕃

TA4 4AD (village signed off A358)
12-3, 5-11 ☎ (01984) 618631 🌐 thecarewarms.co.uk
Exmoor Ale; Otter Bright; Quantock Wills Neck; 2 changing beers (sourced regionally) Ⓗ
A classic rural pub in a village at the foot of the Quantock Hills. The flagstone public bar has an inglenook, and the large garden looking towards the Brendon Hills makes this popular with locals, walkers and dogs. The bar/restaurant serves locally sourced food. The skittle alley doubles as a function room. A beer festival is held in August. Please note that the pub is open all day in the summer months. Crowcombe Heathfield station on the WSR line is nearby. **Q**❀◑♿⛺♣●P🚌 (18,28)🐾 ᯤ

Dulverton

Bridge Inn 𝕃

20 Bridge Street, TA22 9HJ
12-3, 6-11 (not Mon); 12-11 Fri-Sun ☎ (01398) 324130
🌐 thebridgeinndulverton.com
Exmoor Ale; 3 changing beers (sourced regionally) Ⓗ
Close to the River Barle, this warm, welcoming pub dating from 1845 has a cosy single-room bar with a wood-burning stove and surrounding memorabilia. The Bridge holds a Green Tourism Award in recognition of the environmentally friendly way it is run. An annual beer festival coincides with the local folk festival over the Whitsun holiday. A visit to Dulverton and the bridge is well worth the effort. Opening hours are extended in summer to 12-11pm. **Q**❀◑⛺♣P🚌 (25,198,398)🐾 ᯤ

Dunster

Luttrell Arms Hotel

36 High Street, TA24 6SG
10-11.30 ☎ (01643) 821555 🌐 luttrellarms.co.uk
Exmoor Ale; Otter Amber; 2 changing beers (sourced locally) Ⓗ
The Luttrell Arms occupies the site of three ancient houses dating back to 1443. The back bar with its open log fire is a gem. The garden offers great views of Dunster Castle. This 15th-century inn has 28 unique bedrooms, an à la carte restaurant and private function rooms, with many unusual features in some of the suites. The inn has some of the oldest glass windows in Somerset and examples of fine plasterwork on the lounge ceiling.
Q❀◑⛺♣●🚌 (18,28,198)🐾 ᯤ

East Brent

Brent Knoll Inn

Brent Road, TA9 4JG
12-midnight (2am Fri); 11-2am Sat ☎ (01278) 760335
Fuller's London Pride; Otter Ale; St Austell Tribute; 2 changing beers (sourced nationally) Ⓗ
Large two-roomed traditional pub with a bar with a skittle alley to the side and a lounge bar with dining room. The bar has a logburner, a large-screen TV and pub games. A large garden is to the rear and there is some seating at the front where you can enjoy views of Brent Knoll, a hill that juts out of the Somerset Levels.
Q❀◑♿⛺♣●P🚌 🐾 ᯤ

Emborough

Old Down Inn

BA3 4SA
12-2.30, 6.30-11.30; 12-11 Sun ☎ (01761) 232398
Butcombe Bitter; Draught Bass Ⓖ; 2 changing beers (sourced locally; often Three Daggers) Ⓗ/Ⓖ
A free house first licensed in 1640, this establishment was once an important coaching inn. The spirit of the past lives on in the main bar, where beer is served straight from the cask. Two guests from local breweries are generally available. The bar snacks are excellent value, and likewise the main meals. This friendly and popular hostelry is a classic example of a traditional Somerset inn and is the centre of many local community activities.
Q❀◑♿⛺●P🚌 (173)🐾

Exford

Exmoor White Horse Inn

TA24 7PY (on B3224)
11-11 ☎ (01643) 831229 🌐 exmoor-whitehorse.co.uk
Exmoor Ale, Gold; 3 changing beers (sourced locally) Ⓗ
Set right in the heart of Exmoor, this pub/hotel is a real gem. The long bar furnished with large benches features fine ales alongside a choice of 100 malt whiskies. Outside tables are set on the bank of the River Exe. There are nine walks mapped out for visitors. The restaurant offers local trout, salmon and lobster as well as game dishes.

There are 28 en-suite rooms, some with four-poster beds, as well as a honeymoon suite.
Q❀⊭◑♿♣●P🚌(198)🐾📶

Faulkland

Tucker's Grave ★

BA3 5XF

12-3 (not Mon), 6-11; 12-3, 7-10.30 Sun

☎ (01373) 834230

Butcombe Matthew Pale Ale, Butcombe Bitter Ⓖ

A gem from a bygone age and with a nationally important historic pub interior, this inn was built in the mid-17th century and has changed little since. It was named after Tucker, who hanged himself and was buried at the crossroads outside, and who featured in a song by 1970s punk band the Stranglers. There is no bar, and beers and Thatchers cider are served from an alcove. Shove-ha'penny is played and there is a skittle alley. Camping is available in the grounds. Q❀▲♣●P🐾

Frome

Griffin

Milk Street, BA11 3DB

5-11; 4-1am Fri & Sat; 12-10.30 Sun ☎ (01373) 467766

fromegriffin.co.uk

Milk Street Funky Monkey, The Usual, Beer; 2 changing beers Ⓗ

In the part of Frome known as Trinity or Chinatown, the Griffin is the brewery tap for Milk Street Brewery situated at the back. A wide range of ales is produced along with seasonals and specials. The single bar retains original features such as etched windows, a wooden floor and a stained glass griffin behind the bar. Regular quiz nights and live music are hosted. The small garden is open all year. Food is limited to summer barbecues and Sunday lunches. ❀♣P🚌🐾📶

Glastonbury

George & Pilgrims Hotel

1 High Street, BA6 9DP (near the Market Cross)

11-11 ☎ (01458) 831146 georgeandpilgrimhotel.com

Otter Bitter; St Austell Tribute; 3 changing beers (sourced nationally) Ⓗ

Three-storeyed stone-built gatehouse inn boasting a panelled embattled frontage with mullion windows. Walking through the stout doorway there is a flagstoned corridor leading to the rear patio and several tabled alcoves on the right. The Pilgrims bar on the left retains its old-world charm including medieval artefacts and a ghost. It is worthwhile reading about the history of the hotel over a pint. If you stay the night, choose a room with a four-poster bed. Q❀⊭◑▲●P🚌📶

Green Ore

Ploughboy Inn

BA5 3ET (off A39/B3135 crossroads)

closed Mon; 11-2.30, 5.30-10 (7-11 Sat); 12-3, 7-10.30 Sun

☎ (01761) 241375 ploughboyinn.com

Butcombe Bitter; Otter Ale Ⓗ

In the same safe hands for over 25 years, this substantial stone free house to the north of Wells occupies a corner plot by the traffic lights in the hamlet of Green Ore. The 376 Wells-to-Bristol bus runs nearby and there is a pleasant beer garden to the rear. A single good-sized L-shaped bar with a real fire provides reasonably priced, excellent food, lunchtimes and evenings. No dogs allowed indoors. Q❀◑P🚌(376)

Hallatrow

Old Station

Wells Road, BS39 6EN

12-3, 5-11; 12-11 Fri & Sat; 12-10.30 Sun

☎ (01761) 452228 theoldstationandcarriage.co.uk

Brains The Rev James; Butcombe Bitter; 1 changing beer Ⓗ

Unusual eclectic pub noted for its high-quality food at reasonable prices and its totally eccentric décor. A bewildering array of unexpected items appears throughout. An old GWR railway carriage forms a dining room with a difference and the pub has a crazy golf course. Owned by SA Brains, it sometimes serves its small batch one-off beers. Book ahead to dine at weekends. Children are welcome, as are dogs in the bar only. Five ground floor en-suite rooms are available.
Q❀⊭◑♣P🚌(376)🐾📶

Henstridge

Bird in Hand

Ash Walk, BA8 0QD

11-2.30, 5.30-11; 11-11 Sat; 12-10.30 Sun

☎ (01963) 362255

Butcombe Bitter; 2 changing beers Ⓗ

Old stone village pub with low ceilings, beams, a fireplace at each end of an attractive long bar, and a games room with a TV. There is an adjoining skittle alley. Excellent quality ales and good-value snacks make a visit to this friendly hostelry well worthwhile. At the heart of most village activities, this really is a true community inn.
Q❀◑♣●P🚌(58)📶

Horsington

Half Moon Inn

Duck Lane, BA8 0EF

12-2.30, 6-11; 12-4 Sun ☎ (01963) 370140

Fuller's London Pride; Wadworth 6X; 4 changing beers Ⓗ

Owned and run by the same couple for over 20 years, this pub is the focal point of a lovely village. There are up to three guest ales, and over 1,000 different beers have been served so far. There are gardens to the front and rear, a separate skittle alley, a large function room, an ample car park and 10 letting rooms. Reasonably priced food is available at all sessions. The annual beer festival is well worth a visit. Closed Monday and Tuesday in winter. Q❀⊭◑♣P🚌(58)🐾

Huish Episcopi

Rose & Crown ★ L

TA10 9QT (on A372)

11.30-3 (not Mon), 5.30-11.30; 11.30-midnight Fri & Sat; 12-11 Sun ☎ (01458) 250494

Teignworthy Reel Ale; 2 changing beers (sourced regionally; often Cotleigh, Cottage, Plain) Ⓗ

Grade II-listed 17th-century thatched free house with a nationally important historic interior. Known locally as Eli's, the name of a former landlord, the pub has been in the same family for over 150 years and is locally revered. This quaint inn is unusual in having no bar counter in the flagstoned taproom –

one of the few left in the country. Small drinking areas enable the enjoyment of a relaxed atmosphere almost unheard of in more modern pubs.

Hutton

Old Inn

Main Road, BS24 9QQ
11.30-11 (midnight Fri & Sat); 12-11 Sun
(01934) 812336
Butcombe Gold; Fuller's London Pride; St Austell Tribute; 1 changing beer H
Genuine free house owned by a long-standing Guide landlord, and now a thriving local right at the heart of the local community. The pub is extremely popular for its excellent and great-value food, so booking is advised. Dogs are welcome in the bar. The car park behind the pub is accessed by narrow one-way lanes either side. Food is served lunchtimes and evenings except Sunday, which is quiz night. Up to two guest beers are on the bar.
(4)

Keynsham

Lock Keeper

Keynsham Road, BS31 2DD (on A4175)
11-midnight; 12-11 Sun (0117) 986 2383
lockkeeperbristol.com
Bath Ales Gem; Young's Bitter, Special; 1 changing beer (often Young's) H
Multi-roomed Young's pub, noted for its food, by Keynsham lock on the River Avon. The original 17th-century cottage once brewed its own beer and was named the White Hart. It divides into two parts, with the older bar facing the canal, while the large conservatory and heated veranda overlook the river, pétanque pitches and the popular garden. Families are welcome. Occasional live music features in summer. The pub may stay open later when busy. A guest ale is occasionally on offer.
Q

Old Bank

20 High Street, BS31 1DQ
10-11.30 (1am Fri & Sat); 11.30-10.30 Sun
(0117) 904 6356
Otter Ale; Timothy Taylor Landlord; 2 changing beers H
A free house right in the centre of Keynsham, it has one large room for drinking in, with a function room upstairs and an outdoor drinking area at the rear where the smokers go. Old pictures of Keynsham adorn the walls. There is a small car park to the rear of the pub reached through a narrow archway. The landlord tries to have at least one dark beer on at all times. It can sometimes get lively on late weekend openings.
(39,649)

Kilve

Hood Arms

TA5 1EA (on A39)
11-11 (01278) 741210 thehoodarms.com
Exmoor Gold; Otter Head; 1 changing beer H
Seventeenth-century former coaching inn set beside the main road, near a beach frequented by fossil hunters. It has oak beams and an open fireplace, a comfortable bar and a separate restaurant. Outside is a walled garden where boules is played in the summer. There are 12 en-suite rooms and a lodge available to rent. It is an ideal base for walkers, with easy access to the Quantock Hills and the Coleridge Way. It offers good food and wines and welcomes dogs.
Q (16,24)

Kingsbury Episcopi

Wyndham Arms

Folly Road, TA12 6AT
12-midnight (1am Sat & Sun) (01935) 823239
wyndhamarms.com
Butcombe Bitter; Cheddar Potholer; 2 changing beers (sourced regionally; often Bays, Cotleigh, Teignworthy) H
On the edge of the Somerset Levels, the village is just a few feet above danger level when flooding occurs, so this delightful country pub can provide a welcome haven in the winter months. The pub is around 400 years old and features log fires in the bar and a comfy dining room. Outside is a skittle alley that doubles as a function room, and possibly the fanciest smoking area in the county.
Q

Lower Godney

Sheppey Inn

Glastonbury, BA5 1RZ
closed Mon; 12-3, 5.30-11; 12-midnight Sat; 12-8 Sun
(01458) 831594 thesheppey.co.uk
4 changing beers (sourced regionally; often Glastonbury, Plain) H
Entering this extraordinary pub with a barn-like interior is like coming into a trendy city bar but set in the Somerset Levels. It has a good range of varying real ales, and up to seven ciders on gravity. Outside is a lovely terrace overlooking the eponymous River Sheppey. The food is highly recommended.

Lydford on Fosse

Cross Keys Inn

TA11 7HA (next to A37)
11.30-3, 5-11; 11.30-midnight Fri; 11.30-3, 5-midnight Sat; 12-4, 7-11 Sun (01963) 240473 crosskeysinn.info
4 changing beers (sourced regionally; often Cheddar, Hop Back, Milk Street) G
First mentioned by name in 1759 when it was a tavern, the pub expanded over the years but was eventually in need of complete renovation. After being closed for some time, it reopened in 2013 and has quickly established itself as a real ale venue, with excellent food and accommodation in comfortable surroundings. The owners stage live music, a beer festival and other events, often for charity. There is camping on site.
Q (667)

Martock

White Hart Hotel

East Street, TA12 6JQ
12-3 (not Mon), 5.30-11; 12-3 Sun (01935) 822005
whitehartholtelmartock.co.uk
3 changing beers (sourced regionally; often Otter, Sharp's) H
This Grade II-listed hamstone coaching inn dating from 1735 is a warm and welcoming local. It serves great chef-cooked food, and three real ales are on

handpulls from a rotating choice of 10 often local breweries. Local groups such as music and film clubs use the pub as a meeting place. There is a main bar for drinks and a cosy restaurant for table service. Ten letting rooms are available.
Q🐴❀🛏◐◑♿♣P🚌(N9,N9A,N10)🐾📶

Middlezoy

George Inn 🄻
42 Main Road, TA7 0NN (off A372, 1 mile NW of Othery)
🕒 closed Mon; 12-3, 7-midnight; 12-4, 7-10 Sun
☎ (01823) 698215 🌐 thegeorgeinnmiddlezoy.co.uk
Otter Bright; St Austell Tribute; Slater's Western; 3 changing beers (sourced regionally) 🄷
Friendly 17th-century free house with stone-flagged floors and exposed beams. Beers are mainly from the South-West, and two to three local ciders are always available. Excellent locally sourced food is served Wednesday to Saturday only. The landlord keeps his beers in top condition and runs an annual beer festival over the Easter weekend. This village pub may be a little remote but it is well worth finding.
Q🐴◐◑Ä♣●P🚌(16)🐾📶

Minehead

Kildare Lodge
Townend Road, TA24 5RQ (2 mins from town centre)
🕒 11-3, 6.30-11; 12-5 Sun ☎ (01643) 702009
🌐 kildarelodge.co.uk
St Austell 1913 Cornish Stout; 3 changing beers (sourced regionally) 🄷
Close to Minehead town centre, this Grade II-listed building in the Arts & Crafts style retains many interesting features. There is a small bar, two separate lounges and a dining room. It offers quality ales at low prices. Accommodation includes 12 en-suite rooms and a bridal suite with a four-poster bed. The pub is in the local boules and quiz leagues. An ideal base for exploring Exmoor and nearby Dunster, the West Somerset Railway is nearby. Q❀🛏◐◑♿♣●P🚌(18,28,198)🐾

Old Ship Aground
Quay Street, TA24 5UL (beside Minehead harbour)
🕒 11-11 (midnight Fri & Sat) ☎ (01643) 703516
🌐 oldshipaground.com
Ringwood Best Bitter, Boondoggle; Wychwood Hobgoblin; 2 changing beers 🄷
A 1906 pub with accommodation and a function room, set in a picturesque part of Minehead between the harbour and lifeboat station, with fantastic views over the Bristol Channel. This hostelry offers local and national beers. There is locally sourced food, with a Sunday carvery, curry on Tuesday, pie and mash on Thursday and other food-themed evenings. The West Somerset Railway is a short walk away, and Exmoor National Park a 20-minute drive.
🐴❀🛏◐◑♿Ä♣P🚌(15,28,198)🐾📶

Mudford

Half Moon Inn
Main Street, BA21 5TF (on A359)
🕒 12-11; 12-10.30 Sun ☎ (01935) 850289
🌐 thehalfmooninn.co.uk
3 changing beers (sourced regionally; often RCH) 🄶
Popular 17th-century village roadside inn. It has nine tastefully converted and furnished en-suite rooms in the old skittle alley and log store, and five more in the pub. The real ales are served from a stillage behind the bar. An outside cobbled courtyard is pleasant on warm days. No dogs except guide dogs, please. The extensive menu is displayed on a blackboard, plus daily specials.
Q❀🛏◐◑♿●P🚌(1)🐾📶

Oakhill

Oakhill Inn
Fosse Road, BA3 5HU (on A367)
🕒 12-2.30, 5-11; 12-1.30, 5-midnight Fri; 12-midnight Sat; 12-11 Sun ☎ (01749) 840442 🌐 theoakhillinn.com
Butcombe Bitter; 3 changing beers (sourced regionally; often Castle Combe, Cotleigh) 🄷
This large village centre pub is both a popular local and a family-friendly gastro-pub, with a strong emphasis on organic and locally sourced food. The bar serves two areas and has an open feel. Regular quiz nights are held. Up to three changing guest ales, normally sourced from local and regional micros, are on offer. There is a garden at the rear and the car park is 20 yards up the road in the Shepton Mallet direction. Accommodation is in five 4-star rooms. ❀🛏◐◑●P🚌🐾📶

Pitney

Halfway House 🏆 🄻
Pitney Hill, TA10 9AB (on B3153)
🕒 11.30-3, 4.30-11 (midnight Fri); 11.30-midnight Sat; 12-11 Sun ☎ (01458) 252513 🌐 thehalfwayhouse.co.uk
Butcombe Adam Henson's Rare Breed; Hop Back Summer Lightning; Otter Bright; Teignworthy Reel Ale 🄶**; 6 changing beers (often Butcombe, Hop Back, Teignworthy)** 🄷
An outstanding pub serving eight to 10 local ales on gravity alongside many international bottled beers. This basic but buzzing pub deserves its many accolades. It has flagstone floors, a simple assortment of tables, chairs and benches and three real fires. Superb home-cooked food is based on local produce, and a roast lunch is served on Sundays (no food Sun eves). It is not surprising that, given the beer selection and the reasonable prices, the pub gets very busy.
Q❀◐◑♣●P🚌(54)🐾

Porlock

Ship Inn 🄻
High Street, TA24 8QD
🕒 11-midnight; 12-midnight Sun ☎ (01643) 862507
🌐 shipinnporlock.co.uk
Exmoor Beast; Otter Bitter; 6 changing beers 🄷
At the bottom of the notorious Porlock Hill, this pub is known locally as the Top Ship. Dating from the 13th century, it featured in RD Blackmore's novel Lorna Doone. It still has flagstone floors and an inglenook fireplace. In the summer up to eight real ales are served, plus local cider. This CAMRA award-winning pub has a three-tiered patio garden, skittle alley and en-suite rooms. Beer festivals are held. Well-behaved children and dogs are welcome.
Q🐴❀🛏◐◑♿Ä♣●P🚌(10)🐾

Porlock Weir

Ship Inn 🄻
TA24 8PB (take B3225 from Porlock)

⏲ 11-11; 12-10.30 Sun ☎ (01643) 863288
🌐 thebottomship.co.uk
Exmoor Ale, Stag; St Austell Tribute, Proper Job; 2 changing beers Ⓗ
A 400-year-old inn in Exmoor National Park next to the old harbour, with possibly some of the best views of any Somerset pub, overlooking the Bristol Channel towards south Wales. It is well known for good food served by friendly staff. Busy in the holiday periods, it is ideal for walkers and near Porlock village. A beer festival is held in July, with up to 50 ales to choose from. A large car park is opposite. Q❀◐◑♿⛺♣🍎P🚌(10)🐾

Portishead

Windmill Inn

58 Nore Road, BS20 6JZ (next to municipal golf course)
⏲ 11-11; 12-10.30 Sun ☎ (01275) 818483
Butcombe Bitter, Gold; Fuller's London Pride, ESB; 2 changing beers Ⓗ
Large split-level pub with a spacious patio to the rear, plus an extension enjoying panoramic views. It is above the coastal path on the edge of town, and the Severn Estuary and both Severn bridges can be seen on clear days. A varied menu is served all day and is enormously popular. One large area is set aside for families. The pub was recently acquired by Fuller's and the two guest ales are usually from Butcombe (seasonal) and Fuller's. Thatchers cider is stocked.
Q👪❀◐◑♿🍎P🚌(X2,X3)🐾📶

Priddy

Hunters Lodge

Hillgrove Road, BA5 3AR (isolated crossroads 1 mile from A39 close to TV mast) ST549500
⏲ 11.30-2.30, 6.30-11; 12-2, 7-11 Sun ☎ (01749) 672275
Butcombe Bitter; Cheddar Potholer; 1 changing beer Ⓖ
Timeless, classic roadside inn near Priddy, the highest village in Somerset, popular with cavers and walkers. The landlord has been in charge for well over 40 years. Three rooms include one with a flagged floor, and all beer is served direct from casks behind the bar. Local cider is stocked. The simple home-cooked food is excellent and exceptional value. A folk musicians' drop-in session is held on Tuesday evening. The garden is pleasant and secluded, and mobile phones are not welcome. Q👪❀◐◑♿🍎P🐾

Queen Victoria Inn

Pelting Drove, BA5 3BA
⏲ 12-11 ☎ (01749) 676385
Butcombe Bitter; Fuller's London Pride; 2 changing beers (often Butcombe) Ⓗ
Creeper-clad inn, a pub since 1851, with four rooms that feature low ceilings, flagged floors and log fires. A wonderfully warm and relaxing haven on cold winter nights, it is popular during the Priddy Folk Festival in July and the annual fair in August. Reasonably priced, home-cooked food is a speciality. Children are welcome and there is a play area by the car park. Cheddar Valley and Ashton Still ciders are sold. May close briefly on some afternoons. Q👪❀◐◑♿⛺♣🍎P🐾📶

Puriton

37 Club 🄻

1 West Approach Road, Woolavington Road, TA7 8AD
⏲ 6 (5 Fri)-11.30; 12-midnight Sat; 12-10.30 Sun
☎ (01278) 685190 🌐 37club.co.uk
Butcombe Gold; Quantock Ale; 1 changing beer (often RCH) Ⓗ
Formerly the social club of The Royal Ordnance Factory whose allocated number was 37, this large club offers a great many facilities to members and visitors. It has two bars, a large function room with a stage, two skittle alleys, five snooker tables and a football pitch. Food is served Wednesday-Saturday evenings and there is a Sunday carvery (book ahead). Members are able to use the fishing club lake. 👪❀◐◑⛺♣🍎P🚌(37,375)

Radstock

Fromeway

Frome Road, BA3 3LG
⏲ closed Mon; 12-3, 6-11; 12-11 Sun ☎ (01761) 432116
🌐 fromeway.co.uk
Butcombe Bitter; Wadworth 6X Ⓗ**; 2 changing beers (sourced nationally; often Timothy Taylor, Yeovil)** Ⓗ/Ⓐ
This friendly free house has been in the same family for five generations. The present landlord has been in charge for more than 36 years and produces his own sausages, faggots and home-cured hams for the excellent bar and restaurant meals. Popular with locals, the Fromeway has a warm and relaxing atmosphere. A single bar serves three regular ales, and there are weekly guest beers. The pub organises many functions, quizzes and walks for charity. Three charming bedrooms are available. Q👪❀🛏◐◑🍎P🚌(768,178)🐾📶

Rickford

Plume of Feathers

Leg Lane, BS40 7AH (off A368, 2 miles from A38)
⏲ 12-11 ☎ (01761) 462682 🌐 theplumeoffeathers.com
Butcombe Bitter; Cheddar Potholer; 2 changing beers Ⓗ
A 17th-century building that has been a pub since the 1800s. The interior is divided into several areas including a restaurant with a real fire. The venue provides a pleasant and convenient base from which to walk, fish or explore the Mendips. It has a garden at the rear and a stream running along the front, leading to a ford. Parking is limited. Butcombe seasonal beers often feature among the two guests. A popular charity duck race takes place in July. Q👪❀🛏◐◑♣P🚌(791)🐾📶

Rode

Cross Keys

20 High Street, BA11 6NZ
⏲ 11.30-3, 6-11.30; 11.30-11.30 Sat; 11.30-10.30 Sun
☎ (01373) 830900
Butcombe Bitter; 2 changing beers (sourced regionally; often Butcombe) Ⓗ
Reopened in 2004 after 10 years of closure, this was originally the brewery tap for the long-closed Fussell's Brewery, and more latterly a Bass depot. Sympathetically restored, it has succeeded in bringing back a strong village trade. A passageway featuring a deep well links two bars. There is also a large restaurant. The two guest beers can come

from almost anywhere and encompass major brands, like London Pride, but equally breweries otherwise unknown in the area (eg Red Squirrel). Q P (234,267,767)

Rowberrow

Swan Inn

Rowberrow Lane, BS25 1QL

12-11 summer; 12-3, 6-11; 12-11 Sat winter; 12-10.30 Sun
(01934) 852371

Butcombe Bitter; 3 changing beers (often Butcombe)

Believed to date from around the late 17th century, this Butcombe Brewery-owned country pub enjoys an attractive setting, nestling beneath the Dolebury Iron Age hill fort. A convenient stop for walkers on the Mendip Hills, the emphasis is on home-cooked food with unusual specials, but customers who just want a drink are welcome. There is a collection of artefacts around the walls and a grandfather clock. The large, attractive beer garden and car park are opposite.
Q P

St Georges

Woolpack

Shepherds Way, BS22 7XE (close to M5 jct 21)

11-11; 12-10.30 Sun (01934) 521670

Butcombe Bitter, Gold; Fuller's London Pride; 1 changing beer

This 17th-century coaching house was once a packing station that baled wool for local farmers. Owned by Butcombe since 2006, it has two bar areas, a conservatory and a separate carvery. The pub is in the much-expanded St Georges area just off the M5 at junction 21, and within walking distance of Worle station. It has an extensive menu and daily specials. P (32,X1,85)

Saltford

Bird in Hand

58 High Street, BS31 3EJ

11-11 (01225) 873335 birdinhandsaltford.co.uk

Butcombe Bitter; Sharp's Doom Bar; 2 changing beers

Characterful and smart traditional country inn dating from 1869, 400 yards from the A4 and close to the Bristol to Bath cycle path and the River Avon. There is a long L-shaped bar and a pleasant conservatory with fine views across the garden to the hills beyond. Old photographs feature and there is a small family area. Food is served lunchtimes and evenings, all day at weekends, and there is a gluten-free menu. It has a pétanque piste. P (A4,X39,38)

Shepton Beauchamp

Duke of York

North Street, TA19 0LW

12 (5.30 Mon; 3.30 Tue & Wed)-midnight; 12-11 Sun
(01460) 240314 thedukeshepton.co.uk

Otter Bright; Teignworthy Reel Ale; 1 changing beer (sourced regionally; often Bays, Cheddar, Sharp's)

Charming village centred around the school, church, shop and pub. The latter's slightly raised position on a high pavement enables a voyeuristic view of Somerset life. Split levels in this 17th-century free house help to create an interesting interior, while the quite recent letting rooms to the rear are increasingly popular with touring visitors. Very much a family-run establishment, it seems naturally to attract families with children, and dogs are welcomed. P (81)

South Cadbury

Camelot

Chapel Road, BA22 7EX (just off A303)

11-3, 5-midnight; 11-midnight Fri & Sat; 12-10.30 Sun
(01963) 441685 camelotpub.com

Sharp's Doom Bar; Yeovil Summerset; 2 changing beers (sourced regionally; often Cotleigh, Exmoor, Otter)

A large, attractive pub in the centre of this pleasant village, with flagstoned floors throughout and a log fire at both ends. A display case contains information about the nearby Cadbury Castle (reputed to be King Arthur's Camelot) and artefacts found in various excavations. Excellent home-cooked food is served and friendly staff make for a pleasant visit. The pub is open all day Monday-Thursday in summer. Q P

South Petherton

Brewers Arms

18-20 St James Street, TA13 5BW (½ mile off A303)

11.30-2.30, 6-11; 11.30-midnight Fri & Sat; 12-11 Sun
(01460) 241887 the-brewersarms.com

Otter Bitter; 4 changing beers (often Butcombe, Otter, RCH)

The current landlord has been running the establishment and supporting local charities and organisations for 21 years. In the process he has put some 2,400 ales on offer and makes sure that his staff are knowledgeable about the cellar and the delights of the kitchen. Prospective visitors to either of the two annual beer festivals may wish to book the pleasant accommodation. A regular finalist for CAMRA Somerset Pub of the Year. (81)

Stogumber

White Horse Inn

High Street, TA4 3TA (turn left off A358 at Crowcombe)

12-11 (01984) 656277 whitehorsestogumber.co.uk

Otter Bitter; St Austell Proper Job; 2 changing beers

Traditional free house opposite the church in this picturesque village lying between the Quantock and Brendon Hills. It is popular with railway buffs (the West Somerset Railway is nearby), ramblers and locals alike. The pub has a skittle alley which doubles as a music venue; a music festival is held in September. Locally produced food is served in the lounge and restaurant. Most of the real ales are from West Country breweries. Pétanque is played in summer. P

Taunton

Racehorse Inn

East Reach, TA1 3HT

12-4, 6-11 (midnight Thu); 12-12.30am Fri & Sat; 12-11 Sun (01823) 327513

St Austell Trelawny, Tribute, Proper Job; 1 changing beer

Friendly, popular hostelry close to the town centre at the top of East Reach. The multi-room interior includes front and rear bars, a small lounge with comfortable armchairs and two further drinking areas; outside is a large walled beer garden. A popular meeting point, this is the place to go for good conversation and atmosphere, and there is regular live music. The walls are adorned with various pieces of memorabilia such as old tin signs and musical instruments. No food is served. ❀♿♣🍎🚌🐾📶

Ring of Bells

16-17 St James Street, TA1 1JS
⏲ 12-10 Mon; 11-11; 12-6 Sun ☎ (01823) 259480
🌐 theringofbellstaunton.co.uk
4 changing beers Ⓗ
This town centre free house has gone from strength to strength, and was Somerset CAMRA Pub of the Year 2014. There are two wood-floored bar areas, a downstairs dining section, an upstairs restaurant and a large outside courtyard. Four handpumps serve local, South-West and national microbrewery beers, and regular beer festivals are hosted. Excellent locally produced food is served from light snacks to full meals. Next door to Somerset cricket ground and a short walk from Taunton station. Q🐴❀◑◗≠🚌🐾📶

Trull

Winchester Arms

8 Church Road, TA3 7LG
⏲ 12-3, 6.30-11 (10.30 Sun) ☎ (01823) 284723
🌐 winchesterarmstrull.co.uk
House beer (by Lyme Regis); 2 changing beers (often Dartmoor, Exmoor, St Austell) Ⓗ
Thriving family-run community pub on the outskirts of Taunton near the Blackdown Hills. The comfortable bar is separated from the long dining area by an impressive coal-effect fireplace. Three ales are mainly from south-west breweries. Real cider is served in summer only. Locally sourced home-cooked food is excellent (booking advised at popular times). The stream-side gardens, perfect for family and dogs, host entertainment and barbecues. Q❀🛏◑◗♿♣P🚌(97)🐾📶

Wanstrow

Pub at Wanstrow

Station Road, BA4 4SZ
⏲ 6 (6.30 Mon)-11; 12-2.30, 6-11 Sat & Sun
☎ (01749) 850455 🌐 thepubatwanstrow.co.uk
Blindmans Golden Spring; Cheddar Crown and Glory; 2 changing beers (sourced regionally; often Church End, Twisted, Yeovil) Ⓗ
An absolute gem, this friendly village local has a lounge bar with open fire and flagstone floors that leads to a small restaurant. It serves two regular and two (sometimes three) guest beers, sourced from almost anywhere, along with ciders from Thatchers and Rich's. Games include skittles, bar billiards and ring the bull. A small but imaginative menu is offered and all food is home cooked (meals are by prior arrangement). Closed weekday lunchtimes. Q❀◑◗♣🍎P🐾

Washford

White Horse Inn Ⓛ

Abbey Road, TA23 0JZ (off A39)
⏲ 12-11 ☎ (01984) 640415 🌐 exmoorpubs.co.uk
3 changing beers Ⓗ
Only 500 yards from the ruins of Cleve Abbey, and close to the Torre Cider Farm, this riverside free house is an ideal base for visits to the coast, Exmoor National Park, the Quantock Hills and the West Somerset Railway. You can relax on the riverside balcony in summer, or by the fire in winter. The food includes locally sourced produce when possible. Q❀🛏◑◗♿♣🍎P🚌(18,28)🐾

Watchet

Esplanade Club Ⓛ

5 The Esplanade, TA23 0AJ (opp marina)
⏲ 12-3 (Sun only), 7-midnight ☎ (01984) 634518
4 changing beers (sourced regionally; often Exmoor, Quantock) Ⓗ
Four-times CAMRA Somerset Club of the Year, this major music venue has great views over the marina and the Bristol Channel to south Wales. Built in the 1860s as a sailmaking factory, it became a club in the 1930s. It displays old photographs and memorabilia. There are folk and busker nights in the week and live music every weekend. It is home to the Boat Owners' Club and a short walk to the West Somerset Railway.
🐴❀♿⛺≠♣🍎🚌(16,18,28)🐾

Pebbles Tavern Ⓛ

24 Market Street, TA23 0AN (near museum)
⏲ 10.30-11; 12-10.30 Sun ☎ (01984) 634737
🌐 pebblestavern.co.uk
3 changing beers (often Stowey, Moles, Otter) Ⓖ
This small tavern has won CAMRA branch and regional awards for Cider Pub of the Year. In addition to 20 draught ciders, malt whiskies and cider brandy, there are three real ales, with the rotating guest usually from a small microbrewery. The tavern has close links with the headquarters of national folk music, Halsway Manor. Music nights with folk, sea shanty, acoustic and trad jazz are held regularly. 🐴≠♣🍎🗑🚌(16,18,28)🐾📶

Star Inn Ⓛ

Mill Lane, TA23 0BZ
⏲ 12-3.30, 6.30-midnight; 12-4, 7-midnight Sun
☎ (01984) 631367
4 changing beers Ⓗ
Friendly local offering four different real ales, close to the marina and West Somerset Railway. Twice winner of Somerset CAMRA Pub of the Year, it has darts, quiz and boules teams, and is home to the Sunday night Bad Boys Club. It also hosts port and cheese nights, and has run over 60 beer trips. Festivals and music nights are held in the marquee in summer. Good local food, including seafood, is served. Well-behaved children are made welcome; dogs should be kept on leads.
🐴❀◑◗♿⛺≠♣🍎🐾📶

Wedmore

New Inn Ⓛ

Combe Batch, BS28 4DU (bus stop is 50yds away)
⏲ 12-2.30 (not Mon), 5-midnight; 12-2am Fri; 12-1am Sat; 12-10.30 Sun ☎ (01934) 712099
3 changing beers (sourced nationally; often Exmoor, Otter, Timothy Taylor) Ⓗ
A traditional village inn famous for many local events including the annual turnip prize, conkers, spoof and penny chuffin. The public bar, lounge and dining areas are complemented by beer gardens to the front and back. Forthcoming ales are

listed on a chalkboard and are mainly from South-West micros. There is a skittle alley/function room. Food is home cooked and good value, with food theme nights and a takeaway menu.
Q❀◐▶⚠♣●P🚌(668,670)🐾

Wellington

Dolphin 𝕃

37 Waterloo Road, TA21 8JQ
12 (4 Mon & Tue)-11; 12-10 Sun ☎ (01823) 665889
thedolphinwellington.co.uk
Bath Ales Gem; Otter Amber; 2 changing beers Ⓗ
This traditional town pub has taken on a new lease of life, with new staff, great ales and home-cooked food. The pub frontage is an unusual mural, Under the Sea. Customers are encouraged to request the guest ales they would like to see on the bar. A CAMRA discount of 5 per cent off a pint operates, except on Tuesday when all real ales are £3 from 4pm to closing. Q❀◐▶♿♣●🚌(12,22A)🐾

West Chinnock

Muddled Man 𝕃

Lower Street, TA18 7PT
11-2.30, 7-11; 11-midnight Fri & Sat; 12-11 Sun
☎ (01935) 881235
3 changing beers (often Cheddar, Quantock, Yeovil) Ⓗ
A family-run, popular and traditional free house in a picturesque village. The beer garden at the rear catches the sun throughout the day, while the hanging baskets and troughs are a sight to be seen. A warm welcome is afforded to visitors and locals. Good home-cooked food is served in a happy and jovial way by this family team. Sunday lunch must be pre-booked. Many lager drinkers have been converted to real ale here. Q❀◐▶♿♣●🐾

West Huntspill

Crossways Inn 𝕃

Withy Road, TA9 3RA (on A38)
12-midnight (1am Fri & Sat); 12-11 Sun
☎ (01278) 783756 crosswaysinn.com
Cheddar Potholer; RCH PG Steam; 4 changing beers (sourced regionally; often Exmoor, Otter, St Austell) Ⓗ
This 17th-century inn is a former winner of Somerset CAMRA Pub of the Year. With six real ales on offer, it has several bar areas, two fireplaces with log fires in winter, and an outside fireplace to keep smokers warm. There is a dining room and a skittle alley that doubles as a function room. The food menu is complemented by a specials board. Breakfast is served 7.30-11am, but check first as it may depend whether the letting rooms are occupied. ❀◐▶♿⚠♣●P🚌(15,21)🐾

Weston-super-Mare

Brit Bar

118 High Street, BS23 1HP
12-1am ☎ (01934) 632629
3 changing beers Ⓗ
Town centre pub that has been given a bright, modern makeover while retaining the important traditional elements. Mondays to Wednesdays are gaming nights, with live music at weekends. Two or three changing beers are offered and it is not unusual for all to be dark beers, including stouts and porters. A beer festival is usually held on the May Day weekend and a cider festival on the August bank holiday weekend. Families are welcome in the covered and heated courtyard.
❀🚌🐾

Cabot Court Hotel

Knightstone Road, BS23 2AH (on seafront)
7am-midnight (1am Fri; 2am Sat) ☎ (01934) 427930
Greene King Abbot; Ruddles Best Bitter; changing beers Ⓗ
Large Wetherspoon conversion on the seafront between the Grand Pier and the Winter Gardens. On four levels, each has a distinctive style. There are bars on the ground and second floors with different guest ales in each. The first-floor room is particularly comfortable, with sofas and a real fire in winter – a haven from the TVs and speakers in the other rooms. Local breweries are supported, with Exmoor and GWB often featured. It has 21 letting rooms. Q❀◐▶♿●🚌

Regency

22-24 Lower Church Road, BS23 2AG
10-11.30 (midnight Fri & Sat); 10.45-11.30 Sun
☎ (01934) 633406 theregencyinn.co.uk
Butcombe Bitter; Courage Best Bitter; Draught Bass; Wells Bombardier; 1 changing beer Ⓗ
Comfortable, friendly, town centre local, attracting a mixed clientele including students at lunchtime. The pub has pool, skittles and crib teams, but also offers a quiet refuge for conversation. The pool room with TV and jukebox is separate from the main bar area, and children are welcome here. Keenly priced home-cooked food is offered lunchtimes, plus Wednesday curry and Thursday grill evenings. There are patios to the front and rear. Mini beer festivals feature monthly and occasional live bands. ❀◐▶♣🚌(4,5,7)

Waverley

69 Severn Road, BS23 1DR
12-11 (1am Sat)
Greene King Abbot; St Austell Tribute; 2 changing beers Ⓗ
Genuine old-fashioned community free house in an area with few pubs, to the south of the town centre but walkable from the station. Two guest beers are normally on, often unusual ales. Thatchers ciders are served. A weekly quiz features, as does live music some weekends in the Brig, a former air raid shelter to the rear rumoured to have once been a chapel of rest. It also stages a regular farmers' market. Food is limited to basic snacks. ❀≉●🚌(7)🐾

Wheddon Cross

Rest & Be Thankful Inn 𝕃

TA24 7DR
11.30-2, 6-midnight ☎ (01643) 841222
restandbethankful.co.uk
Exmoor Ale; St Austell Tribute; 2 changing beers Ⓗ
This 19th-century coaching inn, at the heart of Exmoor National Park, is situated at the crossroads of Exmoor's highest village and near to the highest point, Dunkery Beacon, and the renowned Snowdrop Valley. It has its own skittle alley, pool table and darts, and a private function room. A carvery is served on Sundays and Wednesdays. It is also a lively music venue and a favourite place to stay with cyclists and ramblers.
Q❀◐▶♿⚠♣●P🚌(198)🐾

Williton

Mason's Arms 𝕃

2 North Road, TA4 4SN

⏲ 11-2.30, 6-11; 12-3, 7-10.30 Sun ☎ (01984) 639200
🌐 themasonsarms.com

Sharp's Doom Bar; Skinner's Betty Stogs; 2 changing beers 🄷

Beautiful thatched 16th-century inn with oak beams throughout and offering five en-suite rooms in the adjoining annexe. The pub hosts quiz teams and is in the local boules league. It has a pleasant beer garden where locals and visitors alike sit and relax. It has a good reputation for its food and the quality of its ales. Rich's cider is always available. Close to the Quantock Hills, West Somerset Railway and a short drive to Exmoor National Park.
Q❀🛏◑♿♣🍎P🚌(18,28)

Wincanton

Nog Inn

South Street, BA9 9DL

⏲ 10.30-11 (midnight Fri & Sat); 12-11 Sun
☎ (01963) 32998 🌐 thenoginn.com

Otter Bitter; Sharp's Own; 2 changing beers 🄷

Attractive listed pub with a striking Georgian façade fronting a long, narrow building with parts dating back to the 16th century. A secluded sunny garden with covered seating can be found at the far end of the property. The guest ales are often seasonal and an extensive range of continental draught beers is always available, as are real ciders. Regular events on Thursday evenings include comedy night, open mic, quiz night and whisky club. 🐎❀◑♣🍎P🚌(58)🐾📶

Winsford

Royal Oak Inn 𝕃

Halse Lane, TA24 7JE

⏲ 11-3, 6-11; 11-11 Sat & Sun ☎ (01643) 851455
🌐 royaloakexmoor.co.uk

Exmoor Ale, Gold; Otter Amber 🄷

Originally a 12th-century farmhouse, this beautiful thatched inn is in a wonderful location in Exmoor National Park. It has eight en-suite rooms and features in many guides to places to stay. Well-behaved children and dogs are made welcome in the bar. The Winn Brook runs past the pub and over the ford that leads up to Exmoor and Tarr Steps.
Q🐎❀🛏◑♿⛺♣P🚌(198)🐾📶

Winsham

Bell Inn 𝕃

Church Street, TA20 4HU

⏲ 12-2.30 (not Mon), 7-11; 12-3, 7-11 Sat & Sun
☎ (01460) 30677 🌐 thebellwinsham.co.uk

Branscombe Vale Branoc; 3 changing beers (often Cottage, Exmoor, Yeovil) 🄷

Popular village free house with an L-shaped bar and a separate bar/function room where darts, skittles and pool are played. There is a strong commitment to real ale, with up to three rotating guest beers from the West Country. Many village activities are hosted on the patio. Good-value food is served, including a popular Sunday roast and a pensioners' special every Tuesday and Friday lunchtime. Children are made welcome. For walkers the pub is on the Liberty Trail.
🐎❀◑♿♣P🚌(99)🐾

Witham Friary

Seymour Arms ★

BA11 5HF

⏲ 11-11 ☎ (01749) 850742

Cheddar Potholer; 1 changing beer 🄶

This pub with a nationally important historic interior is a hidden rural gem, which has probably changed very little over the past 60-70 years. Built in the 1860s, it was part of the Duke of Somerset's farming estate for his workers. The beer and cider is served from a glass-panelled hatch in the hallway, either side of which are separate rooms for sitting and drinking, one with a bar billiards table. Outside there is a lovely garden.
Q🐎❀♣🍎P🐾

Withypool

Royal Oak Inn 𝕃

TA24 7QP (W of B3223 between Dulverton and Exford)

⏲ 12-3 (not Mon), 6-11 ☎ (01643) 831506
🌐 royaloakwithypool.co.uk

Exmoor Ale, Gold; 2 changing beers (sourced regionally) 🄷

For over 300 years the Royal Oak, set in the heart of Exmoor in this tiny remote village, has been providing great local ale and food. It has two bars, a dining room and eight en-suite rooms. It offers shooting, riding and fishing. Only four miles from Tarr Steps, this is a must-visit when in the area.
Q🐎❀🛏◑⛺♣🍎P🐾📶

Yeovil

Great Western

47 Camborne Grove, BA21 5DG (signed off Lyde Rd)

⏲ 5-midnight; 12-midnight Sat & Sun ☎ (01935) 329272
🌐 thegreatwesternyeovil.co.uk

Wadworth Henry's IPA, 6X; 2 changing beers (sourced nationally; often Wadworth) 🄷

Friendly community local in a residential area recently revitalised by enthusiastic licensees after two periods of closure. The single room contains an interesting collection of memorabilia mostly related to GWR which built the nearby station. There is a pool table and skittle alley and an upstairs function room. The regular and seasonal Wadworth beers are joined by a weekly changing guest beer. Good-value food is served. Regular beer festivals are planned for the future.
🐎❀◑♿⇌(Pen Mill)♣🍎🚌(68)🐾📶

Quicksilver Mail

168 Hendford Hill, BA20 2RG (at jct of A30 and A37)

⏲ 10.30-midnight (1am Sat); 12-11 Sun ☎ (01935) 424721
🌐 quicksilvermail.com

Butcombe Bitter; Dartmoor Jail Ale; Sharp's Doom Bar; 2 changing beers (sourced regionally) 🄷

Friendly, popular pub in the west of the town. The pub's name commemorates a high-speed mail coach service from Exeter to London which used to call here. There is a bar and lower-level restaurant area. Historic photos of the pub and other interesting pictures adorn the walls. Many local societies meet here. A skittles alley doubles as a function room, where there is live music of all types. Good-value food is served; try the excellent Sunday lunch. ❀🛏◑♣P🚌(40,99)🐾📶

STAFFORDSHIRE

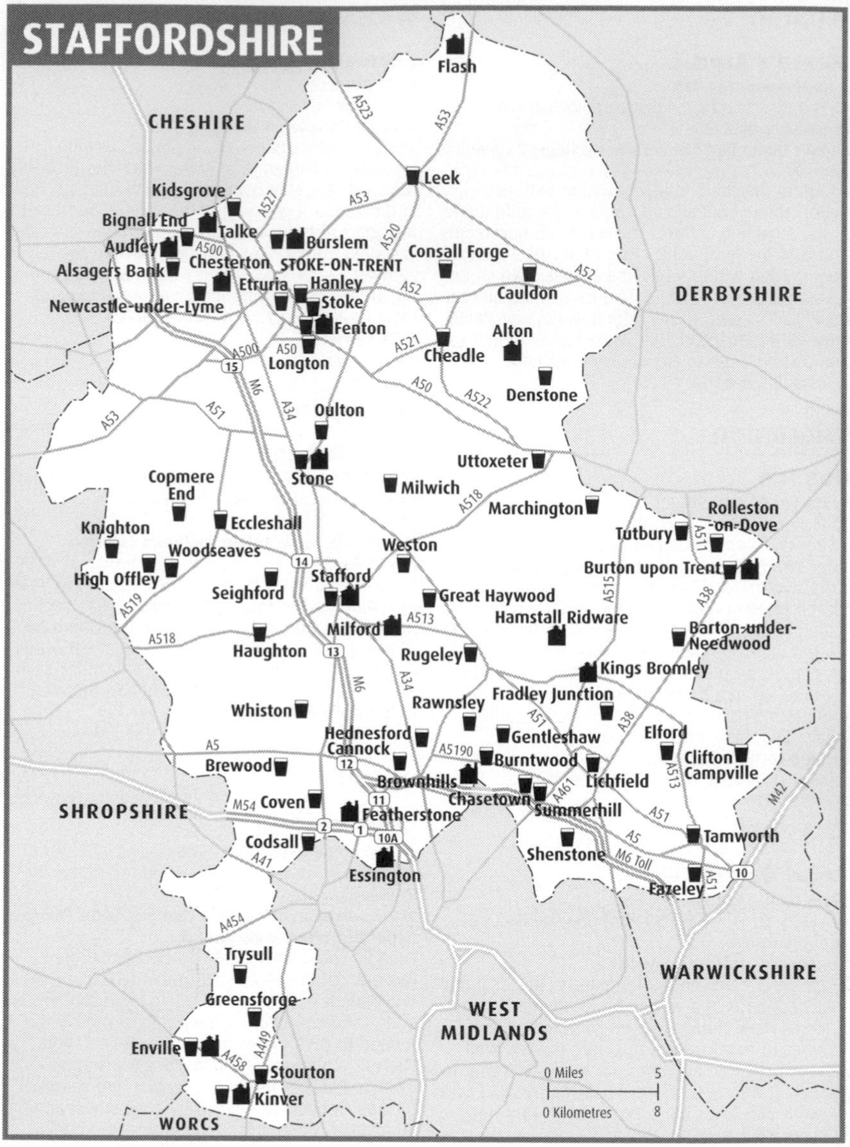

Alsagers Bank

Gresley Arms

High Street, ST7 8BQ (on B5367 4 miles N of Newcastle-under-Lyme)
12 (3 Mon-Wed)-11 ☎ (01782) 722469
10 changing beers (sourced nationally; often Abbeydale, Marston's, Townhouse) Ⓗ
Sitting at a height of 700 feet above sea level, the Gresley Arms commands views over Cheshire, Shropshire and the Wirral. The pub is also close to two country parks. Ten varied real ales are on offer, plus four real ciders and a huge range of imported bottled beers. Good-value meals are served four nights a week, plus Sunday lunch. A regular folk and blues festival, including a beer festival, takes place in May every year. A gem.
P (94,94A)

Barton-under-Needwood

Royal Oak

74 The Green, DE13 8JD (take Wales Lane off B5016)
12-11.30 (12.30am Fri & Sat); 12-11 Sun
☎ (01283) 713852
Marston's Pedigree; 2 changing beers (sourced nationally; often Banks's, Ringwood, Wychwood) Ⓗ/Ⓖ
Bustling community local on the southern edge of the village, home to traditional pub games and an over-40s football team. While parts of the building date back to the 16th century, the pub has only existed since the mid-1800s. Public bar and lounge customers are served from a central sunken bar. Beers are available on handpump or by gravity, direct from the cask, on request.
Q P (7)

Bignall End

Bignall End Cricket Club

Boon Hill, ST7 8LA (400yds from B5500)
7-midnight; 12-midnight Fri-Sun ☎ (01782) 720514
bignallend.play-cricket.com
Draught Bass; 3 changing beers (sourced nationally; often Abbeydale, Little Ale Cart, Mallinson's) H
Popular club now run as a pub, with great views over the Cheshire Plain. Summer and winter beer festivals take place in the upstairs function room. There is also a snooker room and the busy bar caters for sports fans, with TV. Three or four beers are on draught – the Bass and guests from smaller breweries. Covered outside seating is by the cricket pitch, where it is lovely to sit in good weather and watch the sun go down. &P (4)

Swan

58 Chapel Street, ST7 8QD (off B5500 E of Audley)
12-11 (midnight Fri-Sun) ☎ (01782) 720622
theswaninn-stoke.co.uk
Draught Bass; Oakham Citra; 5 changing beers (sourced nationally; often Adnams, North Yorkshire, St Austell) H
A popular community street-corner pub, affectionately known to locals as The Duck. It comprises a large traditional public bar and a smaller comfortable lounge, both with log fires. Outside is a pleasant beer garden with flowers and even fresh vegetables grown for the community. An excellent and varied selection of seven cask beers including darks, milds and pales is served alongside a choice of four traditional ciders and a perry on handpull. (4)

Brewood

Swan Hotel

15 Market Place, ST19 9BS
12-midnight ☎ (01902) 850330
Caledonian Deuchars IPA; Courage Directors; Theakston Black Bull Bitter; Wye Valley HPA; 2 changing beers (sourced locally; often Bathams, Broughs, Three Tuns) H
Characterful old coaching inn with low beamed ceilings and seasonal log fires. Its village-centre location makes it convenient for the Shropshire Union Canal and the Staffordshire Way. Cosy snugs displaying early prints of the area flank the central bar and there is a traditional skittle alley upstairs, which can be hired for private events. There is a fun quiz on Sunday evenings and a TV shows major sporting events. Cheese and ham baguettes are available weekdays. Q&P

Burntwood

Drill Inn

33 Springlestyche Lane, WS7 9HD SK061101
12-midnight (10.30 Sun) ☎ (01543) 675799
drillinnburntwood.co.uk
Fuller's London Pride; 3 changing beers (sourced nationally; often Adnams, Backyard, Wells) H
Vibrant and friendly pub tucked away down a country lane. The homely, sprawling main room is partnered by a quiet snug. Three constantly changing ales are offered, plus occasional beer festivals. There is a large elevated beer garden to the rear and a children's play area. Good food is a draw here, including themed dining nights (no food Mon). There is clay pigeon shooting on alternate Sunday mornings. QP

Burton upon Trent

Burton Bridge Inn

24 Bridge Street, DE14 1SY (on A511)
12-2.30, 5-11; 11.30-11.30 Fri & Sat; 12-3, 7-11 Sun
☎ (01283) 536596 burtonbridgeinn.co.uk
Burton Bridge Golden Delicious, Sovereign Gold, Bridge Bitter, Burton Porter, Stairway to Heaven, Festival Ale; 1 changing beer (sourced regionally; often Everards, Morton, Oakham) H
This 17th-century pub is the flagship of the Burton Bridge Brewery estate and fronts the brewery itself. Two rooms are served from a central bar – a smaller front room with wooden pews, brewery memorabilia, many awards and framed old maps of Burton, and a back room featuring oak beams and panels. The beer range is supplemented by a choice of malt whiskies and fruit wines. A dining room and skittle alley are upstairs. No lunches Sunday-Tuesday. Q

Coopers Tavern ★

43 Cross Street, DE14 1EG (off Station St)
5 (3 Tue & Wed; 12 Thu)-11; 12-11.30 Fri & Sat; 12-11 Sun
☎ (01283) 532551 cooperstavern.co.uk
Draught Bass G**; Joule's Blonde, Pale Ale, Slumbering Monk** H**; 5 changing beers (sourced regionally; often Castle Rock, Holden's, Thornbridge)** H/G
Classic, unspoilt 19th-century ale house, once the Bass Brewery tap and now part of the Joule's estate. The intimate inner tap room has barrel tables and bench seating – the beer is served from a small counter by the cask stillage. The more comfortable lounge leads to a small third room. Up to four varying ciders/perries plus fruit wines are also available. Local folk musicians meet here on Tuesday evenings and live music features on Sunday afternoons. Q

Devonshire Arms

86 Station Street, DE14 1BT
4-11; 12-11 Fri & Sat; 6-11 Sun ☎ (01283) 562392
thedevonshire.co.uk
Burton Bridge Golden Delicious, Bridge Bitter, Damson Porter, Stairway to Heaven, Festival Ale H
Popular old pub dating from the 19th century, Grade II-listed and one of five Burton Bridge

REAL ALE BREWERIES

Beowulf Brownhills
Black Hole Burton upon Trent
Blythe Hamstall Ridware
Burton Bridge Burton upon Trent
Burton Old Cottage Burton upon Trent
Enville Enville
Flash Flash
Gates Burton Burton upon Trent
Grey Friars Featherstone (NEW)
Kinver Kinver
Lymestone Stone
Marston's Burton upon Trent
Morton Essington
Peakstones Rock Alton
Quartz Kings Bromley
RAN Stoke-on-Trent: Fenton (NEW)
Shugborough Milford
Slater's Stafford
Talke O' Th' Hill Talke
Titanic Stoke-on-Trent: Burslem
Tower Burton upon Trent
Townhouse Audley
Weal Chesterton (NEW)

Brewery hostelries in the area. It comprises a public bar at the front, and a larger, more comfortable, split-level lounge to the rear. Note the 1853 map of Burton, old local photographs, and the unusual arched wooden ceilings. An enclosed rear patio features flower borders and hanging baskets. Real cider (provider varies), continental bottled beers and English fruit wines are also stocked. Quiz night is Monday. P

Elms Inn

36 Stapenhill Road, DE15 9AE (on A444)
12-11.30 (midnight Fri & Sat); 12-11 Sun
(01283) 535505 the-elms-burton.co.uk
Draught Bass; Marston's Pedigree; 2 changing beers (sourced nationally; often Everards, Holden's, Thwaites) [H]
Lively local on the opposite bank of the River Trent from the town centre. Built as a private house in the late 19th century, this is one of Burton's original parlour pubs. With sensitive renovation, the small public bar and snug on either side of the bar, plus a side room served through a hatch, are largely unchanged. In contrast, the lounge to the rear has been extended and refurbished in a more modern style. Meals are available until 7pm (3pm Sun).

Old Cottage Tavern

36 Byrkley Street, DE14 2EG (behind town hall)
12-11; 11.30-11 Sun (01283) 511615
Burton Old Cottage Oak Ale, Stout, Halcyon Daze; 3 changing beers (sourced nationally; often Coastal, Milestone, Wentworth) [H]
No longer owned by the brewery but leased from the Tadcaster Pub Company, this traditional local continues to operate as the Burton Old Cottage Brewery tap. The public bar at the front, with a cosy snug to one side, and the wood-panelled lounge to the rear, are served from a central bar. There is also a games/function room (with demountable skittle alley) upstairs. Guest beers usually come from other SIBA members. It hosts the Brewtown Folk Club and Spoken Word events. Q

Roebuck Inn

101 Station Street, DE14 1BT (on jct with Mosley St)
12-midnight (1am Fri & Sat) (01283) 511213
roe-buck-inn.co.uk
Draught Bass; Greene King Abbot; Marston's Pedigree; 2 changing beers (sourced regionally; often Burton Old Cottage, Quartz, Theakston) [H]
Friendly Victorian corner-terrace pub near the railway station, once the Ind Coope Brewery tap, opposite the former brewery. The recently axed classic Draught Burton Ale was launched here in 1976. Inside, there is a long, narrow single room with dark wood panelling and the bar counter down one side. A small patio is available for outdoor drinking, plus a few tables and chairs at the front in summer. Live music plays early Sunday evenings.

Waterloo Inn

50 Ashby Road, DE15 0LQ (on A511)
4-11.30; 3-midnight Fri; 12-midnight Sat; 12-11 Sun 07835 174908
Draught Bass; Marston's Pedigree; 1 changing beer (sourced locally; often Gates Burton, Leatherbritches, Tower) [H]
Traditional two-roomed local in the suburb of Winshill, east of the River Trent – probably Victorian, although there may have been a pub on the site since the 1700s. It was reputedly a halfway point for changing horses on brewery drays delivering to south Derbyshire. There is decking at the front accessed from the public bar via patio doors, providing an alfresco area for warm weather. Pork pies are available at all times, plus sandwiches at weekends. Quiz night is Sunday.
P (8,9)

Cannock

Crystal Fountain ★

35 St Johns Road, WS11 0AL (jct of Avon Rd)
12-11 (midnight Fri & Sat) (01543) 574812
Black Country Bradley's Finest Golden, Pig on the Wall, Fireside; 3 changing beers (sourced nationally; often Exmoor, Mallinson's, Salopian) [H]
Part of the Black Country Ales group, this traditional alehouse built in 1937 has a nationally important historic interior and serves as a local community pub. It has four separate rooms and a secure family garden, plus open fires in bar areas. Bar snacks and rolls are served at all times. Six ales and two ciders feature regularly. Slightly out of the town centre, it is well worth the 10-minute walk. P

Linford Arms

79 High Green, WS11 1BN
8-midnight (1am Fri & Sat) (01543) 469360
Greene King Abbot; Ruddles Best Bitter; 6 changing beers (sourced nationally; often Backyard, Beowulf, Salopian) [H]
Established town-centre Wetherspoon pub serving eight real ales and ciders. The pub name originates from the builders' merchants that formerly occupied the premises. There are good bus and rail links. Food is served daily 8am-11pm. It has seating areas on two floors, with quieter alcoves and a separate snug. Two ale festivals are held each year and local breweries feature regularly. A frequent local CAMRA Pub of the Year finalist, it is not to be missed if visiting Cannock.

Cauldon

Yew Tree Inn L

ST10 3EJ
12-3, 6-11; 12-midnight Sat & Sun (01538) 309876
yewtreeinncauldon.co.uk
Burton Bridge Bridge Bitter; Rudgate Ruby Mild; 2 changing beers (sourced nationally; often Burton Bridge, Draught Bass, McMullen) [H]
Award-winning 17th-century Grade II-listed pub, owned by same family since 1961. A must-visit for anyone in the area, it is truly a living, working piece of history, packed with antiques and items of historical interest. Beer is dispensed from 1920s brass fittings. A selection of foreign bottled beer is also on offer. Light meals and snacks are served, and table skittles, shove-ha'penny, darts, dominoes and cribbage are played. Folk night is the first Tuesday of the month. Note that the postcode is not always reliable for sat nav.
Q P (108)

Chasetown

Uxbridge Arms

2 Church Street, WS7 3QL SK045080
12-midnight (1am Sat); 2-1am Fri (01543) 677852
5 changing beers (sourced nationally; often Ashover, Church End, Derby) [H]

The five ales are forever changing in this deservedly long-standing Guide entry. A wide range of country wines and malt whiskies is available, plus a varying real cider. Sport is popular here, with bowls, darts and football teams. Chasewater Country Park and the associated heritage railway are close by. Good food is available in the lounge and upstairs restaurant (no food Sun eve). Children are allowed until 9pm. P (60,10)

Cheadle

Huntsman

The Green, ST10 1XS

11-11; 12-11 Sun (01538) 750502

thehuntsmancheadle.com

Castle Rock Harvest Pale; Joule's Slumbering Monk; Marston's Pedigree; 3 changing beers (sourced nationally; often Geeves, Peakstones Rock, Slater's)

A family-friendly pub on the edge of the town of Cheadle, ideal for visitors to Alton Towers, the Churnet Valley and the Peak District. It is run by two brothers who pride themselves on a warm welcome for everyone and the quality of their changing real ale selection. A beer festival is held over the Whitsun bank holiday weekend. The food is locally sourced and of a good standard. P (X51)

Clifton Campville

Green Man

Main Street, B79 0AX

12-2.30, 5.30-11; 12-11 Sat; 12-10.30 Sun

(01827) 373262

Marston's Pedigree; 3 changing beers

Friendly community-spirited village inn dating from the 18th century. The right side of the pub offers a lounge-cum-restaurant, while the main entrance takes you into a low-beamed bar warmed by a coal fire. The guest ales, up to three, always change. There is a pool table to the rear plus a devil among the tailors board in the bar, a function room, and outside a terrace at the front and garden at the rear. Daytime-only bus service.

Codsall

Codsall Station

Chapel Lane, WV8 2EJ

11.30-11 (11.30 Fri & Sat); 12-10.30 Sun

(01902) 847061

Holden's Black Country Mild, Black Country Bitter, Golden Glow, Special; 2 changing beers

Sensitively converted from the waiting room, offices and stationmaster's house, the Grade II-listed building comprises a bar, lounge, snug and conservatory and displays worldwide railway memorabilia. Steps lead to the outside drinking area with tables and benches overlooking the working platforms. Bar meals are served all week except Sunday, with home-made curry available on Thursday evenings. Beer festivals are held in May and the weekend after the August bank holiday. Q P (5,10B)

Firs Club

Station Road, WV8 1BX

7.30-11 (midnight Fri); 12-midnight Sat; 12-11 Sun

(01902) 844674 thefirscodsall.com

Banks's Mild, Bitter; 3 changing beers (sourced nationally; often Greene King, Hobsons, Wye Valley)

The Wolverhampton CAMRA Club of the Year 2015 contains a bar area, quiet lounge and sports lounge with pool table, dartboard and card table. There are also snooker tables upstairs. Up to three guest ales, some sourced locally, are served, and a beer festival is held in November. The large function room is available to hire. Show this Guide or a CAMRA membership card to be signed in. The rear entrance in Wood Road is handy for the bus stop. Q P (5,10B)

Consall Forge

Black Lion

Wetley Rocks, ST9 0AJ

12-11; 12-10.30 Sun (01782) 550294

blacklionpub.co.uk

Peakstones Rock Black Hole; 4 changing beers (sourced nationally; often Cottage, Joule's, Kelham Island)

Located at the bottom of Consall Nature Park, next to the Churnet Valley Railway Line and the Cauldon Canal, this free house serves beer from breweries close to home and all around the country. Ciders and perries are also available. Beer festivals are held in December, February and July, in conjunction with the Churnet Valley Railways Ale Trail. Food is available all day in large portions. It is close to Alton Towers and the Peak District. (Churnet Valley Railway) P

Copmere End

Star Inn

ST21 6EW

closed Mon; 12-3, 6-11; 12-11 Sat; 12-10.30 Sun

(01785) 850279 thestarinn-eccleshall.co.uk

Draught Bass; Titanic Anchor Bitter; Wells Bombardier; 2 changing beers (often Cottage, Exmoor, Hop Back)

A thriving 100-year-old pub in the heart of the beautiful Staffordshire countryside and adjacent to Copmere Lake. The pub has become an integral part of this rural community, holding charity auctions and events. The extensive garden with play area is ideal for families. An excellent selection of bar meals and an à la carte menu are offered lunchtimes and evenings. The beer complements the award-winning, locally sourced food. A Titanic Brewery Blue Riband Inn of Excellence. Q P (436)

Coven

Harrows Inn

School Lane, WV9 5AW

12-11 (midnight Fri & Sat) (01902) 790055

theharrowsinn.co.uk

Three Tuns XXX; 5 changing beers (sourced regionally; often Broughs, Marston's, Salopian)

Privately owned, this attractive pub has been a free house since 2012. A central counter serves two refurbished rooms; one is for dining and the other is a public bar with old beams, piano, dartboard and pool table. Home-cooked meals are served all day (until 4pm Sun). Six real ales and up to 10 real ciders and perries are usually stocked. There is a large beer garden and children's play area. P (76)

Denstone

Tavern 𝕃
College Road, ST14 5HR
⌚ 6-11 Mon; 12-2, 5.30-11; 12-midnight Fri-Sun
☎ (01889) 590847 🌐 thetaverndenstone.co.uk
Marston's Burton Bitter, Pedigree; house beer (by Ringwood); 1 changing beer (sourced nationally) Ⓗ
The Tavern is a 17th-century village inn offering fine food and good beers in comfortable surroundings. There is a bar area with darts, a comfortable lounge area and a conservatory for dining. Quiz night is Monday when there is no food. Fresh wood-fired, stone-baked pizzas are served Friday and Saturday evenings, eat in or take away. Guest beers come from the Marston's range. Marston's Western Area Pub Restaurant of the Year 2013. **Q**🐎❀◑▲♣**P**🚌(32A)🐾📶

Eccleshall

Bell Inn 𝕃
16 High Street, ST21 6BZ
⌚ 11-midnight; 12-11.30 Sun ☎ (01785) 850378
🌐 thebelleccleshall.com
Greene King Abbot; Holden's Black Country Bitter, Golden Glow; 3 changing beers Ⓗ
A busy high-street local and former coaching inn in the centre of this small market town. The pub website provides a history of the pub as well as details of ongoing social activities. The Bell has four separate rooms. There are chairs and tables on the pavement area outside for sunny days and smokers. It can get busy with diners at lunchtimes. 🐎❀◐♣**P**🚌(432,23)🐾📶

Elford

Crown Inn 𝕃
The Square, B79 9DB (600yds E of A513) SK189106
⌚ 6-11; 12-midnight Fri & Sat; 12-11 Sun ☎ (01827) 383602
Burton Bridge Sovereign Gold, XL Mild; Draught Bass; 1 changing beer Ⓗ
Welcoming, cosy village pub, with a bar, lounge, dining room and separate pool room. In the 18th century the upstairs rooms were used as a courthouse, and today's dining room once served as the cells. Beamed ceilings feature throughout, with real fires in the bar and lounge. Sovereign Gold is occasionally replaced by Golden Delicious. Food is served until 9pm Wednesday-Saturday, and until 4pm on Sunday. Bar snacks are available at all times. No evening bus service. ◑♣**P**🚌🐾📶

Enville

Cat Inn 🏆 𝕃
Bridgnorth Road, DY7 5HA (on A458)
⌚ 12-2.30 (not Mon), 5-11; 12-11 Fri & Sat; 12-6 Sun
☎ (01384) 872209 🌐 thecatinn.com
Enville Ale, Ginger Beer; 5 changing beers Ⓗ
Parts of this traditional country pub date back to the 16th century. It has three oak-beamed rooms, all with real fires, and a function room upstairs. Hanging baskets adorn the beer garden and courtyard in summer. Enville beers are the regulars plus three guests, usually from local breweries. Home-made dishes and daily specials, using local produce whenever possible, are served. Joint CAMRA branch Pub of the Year 2014, and South Staffordshire Pub of the Year 2013 and 2015. **Q**🐎❀◑🍎**P**🐾📶

Fazeley

Three Horseshoes
New Street, B78 3RD (near jct of A4091 and B5404)
⌚ 12-3, 6.30-11; 12-11 Fri-Sun ☎ (01827) 289754
Draught Bass; Marston's Pedigree; Sharp's Doom Bar Ⓗ
Situated close to a major canal junction and Drayton Manor Theme Park, this is very much a locals' pub, although visitors are assured of a friendly welcome. Renowned for serving a quality pint, the popular landlady has been at the helm for over 20 years. The single main room features a central bar of wood and tiles. A secluded garden to the rear proves popular in the summer. There is a public car park at the nearby town hall.
❀♣🚌(110)🐾📶

Fradley Junction

Swan Inn
DE13 7DN SK140140
⌚ 11-11 (midnight Sat); 12-10.30 Sun ☎ (01283) 790330
Greene King Abbot; Marston's Pedigree; 4 changing beers (sourced regionally; often Derby, Holden's, Purple Moose) Ⓗ
Known locally as the Mucky Duck, this late 18th-century, Grade II-listed, mid-terrace pub overlooks the Trent & Mersey/Coventry canal junction. The cosy public bar, which retains an old-fashioned charm, and a smaller lounge, are on opposite sides of a central serving area. There is a cellar room with vaulted brick ceiling beyond the lounge. Guest beers come mainly from Midlands microbreweries. Real cider (Holden's Summat Else) is served in summer only. Folk night is Thursday, open mic night Sunday. Walkers and boaters welcome.
Q🐎❀◑♣🍎**P**🐾

Gentleshaw

Olde Windmill
Windmill Lane, WS15 4NF SK051118
⌚ 12-midnight ☎ (01543) 682468 🌐 yeoldewindmill.co.uk
Draught Bass; 3 changing beers (sourced regionally; often Burton Bridge, Castle Rock, Springhead) Ⓗ
Welcoming 400-year-old country pub, with smartly attired staff and equally sharp food and drink offerings. Free of tie, the guest ales are usually interesting microbrews. The cosy bar is dog-friendly, while the wood-panelled lounge offers freshly cooked meals including interesting specials. Both rooms feature old-looking beams (some cleverly fake) and open fires. A number of teams use the crown bowling green. The pub is 100 yards from the stump of an old disused windmill.
Q🐎❀◑♿🍎**P**🚌🐾📶

Great Haywood

Clifford Arms
Main Road, ST18 0SR
⌚ 12-11.30 (midnight Fri & Sat); 12-11 Sun
☎ (01889) 881321 🌐 cliffordarms.co.uk
Adnams Broadside; Draught Bass; Morland Old Speckled Hen; 3 changing beers (often Backyard, Everards, Sunny Republic) Ⓗ
Village-centre inn with a large bar providing plenty of seating and a restaurant adorned with past photos of the pub. A popular local, it is home to cribbage, dominoes and quiz teams, as well as a tug o' war team. It is also popular with walkers,

cyclists, boaters and visitors to the nearby Shugborough Estate (National Trust). The Staffordshire Way, and bridge 73 of the Trent & Mersey Canal, are 200 yards along Trent Lane. Q❀◐▲♣●P🚌(841)🐾📶

Greensforge

Navigation

Greensforge Lane, DY6 0AH

12-midnight ☎(01384) 273721

Enville Ale; 3 changing beers Ⓗ

A former Simpkiss pub that is popular with locals and walkers alike due to its position adjacent to the Staffordshire & Worcestershire Canal. There is an interesting collection of heritage canal photo prints on the walls. Up to four real ales are served, which are predominantly local, and a traditional cider. Good food is on offer at reasonable prices. Q❀◐●P🐾📶

Haughton

Bell Inn 𝕃

Newport Road, ST18 9EX (on A518)

12-3, 5-midnight; 12-midnight Fri-Sun ☎(01785) 780301

thebellhaughton.co.uk

Marston's EPA, Pedigree; Timothy Taylor Landlord; 1 changing beer (sourced locally) Ⓗ

The L-shaped interior has a restaurant at the rear that serves really good, locally sourced food. At the front is a small, well-run, friendly bar, with bar snacks on offer. As well as running charity events the pub has six dominoes teams. The guest beer comes from the SIBA list and changes regularly, often from a local brewer. A beer and music festival is held at the end of August. Book ahead for dining. ❀◐♿▲♣P🚌(481,877)🐾📶

Hednesford

Cross Keys Hotel 𝕃

42 Hill Street, WS12 2DN

12-midnight ☎(01543) 879534

Brains Rev James; Draught Bass; Holden's Golden Glow; Morland Old Speckled Hen; Salopian Oracle; changing beers (sourced nationally; often Beowulf, Skinner's, Thwaites) Ⓗ

Up to eight real ales, including several guests, are served at this former coaching inn that dates back to 1746. Hednesford Town Football Club was originally based behind the pub; the licensee is an ex-player and now assistant manager. Sporting and historic photographs decorate the walls and monthly quiz nights are held. It is rumoured that the infamous highwayman Dick Turpin stopped here on his famous ride to York. Local CAMRA Pub of the Year. ❀🛏♣P🚌(33A,60,62)

High Offley

Anchor Inn ★

Peggs Lane, Old Lea, ST20 0NG SJ775256

12-3, 7-11 ☎(01785) 284569

Wadworth 6X Ⓗ

On the Shropshire Union Canal, this Victorian two-bar inn is a rare example of an unspoilt country pub. It has been run by the same family since 1870, when it was called the Sebastopol. It has a lovely award-winning garden. About two miles from the A519, the pub is not easily found, but is well worth the journey. In winter it may only open weekends, and Monday to Thursday lunchtime opening can vary, so it is advisable to check with the venue in advance. Q❀▲♣●P🐾

Kidsgrove

Blue Bell 𝕃

25 Hardingswood, ST7 1EG (off A50 near Tesco)

closed Mon; 1-4 (not Tue-Fri), 7.30-11; 12-10.30 Sun

☎(01782) 774052 bluebellkidsgrove.co.uk

6 changing beers (sourced nationally; often Acorn, Beowulf, Whim) Ⓗ

Genuine free house with the same owners for 17 years and in every Guide since 2000. There are no TVs or games machines, just friendly conversation. The pub attracts customers from a wide area – the Blue Bell Ramblers walk on the second Sunday of the month. It is easily reached by bus, train or boat on the Trent & Mersey and Macclesfield canals, which meet nearby. Six handpumps offer beers from microbreweries plus Belgian and German ales, and real cider and perry. Q❀⇌●P🚌(3,4A)🐾

Kinver

Kinver Constitutional Club 𝕃

119 High Street, DY7 6HL

5 (12 Wed & Thu)-11; 12-midnight Fri; 11.30-midnight Sat; 12-10.30 Sun ☎(01384) 872044

kinverconstitutionalclub.co.uk

Enville Ale; Hobsons Best Bitter, Town Crier; Olde Swan Bumble Hole Bitter; Wye Valley HPA; 5 changing beers Ⓗ

Built in 1902 on the site of an old pub, this converted hotel has three main areas and the bar always dispenses up to 18 real ales. The club enjoys an enviable sporting reputation. Card-carrying CAMRA members are welcome but must be signed in; groups should book ahead. Buses run from Stourbridge, but there is no service after 7pm or on Sunday. It has been local branch CAMRA Club of the Year every year since 2007, and most recently West Midlands Regional Club of the Year in 2013. ❀◐♿♣●P🚌(228)

Knighton

Haberdashers Arms 𝕃

ST20 0QH (between Adbaston and Knighton) SJ753275

12.30 (7 Wed & Thu)-midnight; 12.30-1am Fri & Sat

☎(01785) 280650 haberdashersarms.com

Banks's Mild; Rowton Bitter; 1 changing beer (sourced locally) Ⓗ

Built in about 1840, this traditional country pub offers a warm and friendly welcome. The four compact rooms are served from a central bar. The pub hosts a range of events in its large garden, including the annual Potato Club Show and music festivals. The collection of oil lamps is not just for decoration – on Lamp Nights electric lights are switched off and the lamps are lit, creating a relaxed ambience. Q❀▲♣P🐾

Leek

Fountain Inn 𝕃

14 Fountain Street, ST13 6JR

12-midnight (1am Fri & Sat) ☎(01538) 387205

Draught Bass; Greene King IPA; St Austell Tribute; 4 changing beers (sourced nationally; often Burton Bridge, Buxton, Sunny Republic) Ⓗ

Well-deserved new entry to complement the great pub town of Leek. Close to the town centre and bus station, it is a true free house, totally refurbished in 2013 after a period of closure, with an experienced and knowledgeable landlord. Eight handpulls serve a constantly changing range, plus real cider. Themed food night is Tuesday, and live music plays on Sunday evenings. It has real fires, heated outdoor seating and a small meeting/function room. It stocks an interesting collection of old Good Beer and pub guides. 🕭❀🛏◐♣●🚌🐾📶

Wilkes Head 🏆 Ⓛ

15 St Edward Street, ST13 5DS

⏲ 12 (3 Mon)-midnight; 12-11 Sun ☎ 07976 592787

Whim Arbor Light, Hartington Bitter, Hartington IPA, Flower Power; 2 changing beers (sourced nationally; often Broughton, Burton Bridge, Leadmill) Ⓗ

Well-established entry, said to be the oldest pub in town, with origins dating back to the 13th century. Seven handpulls serve regular ales from the nearby Whim Brewery plus some interesting guests, often stronger than average. A good range of real cider is always available. Regular music festivals are held in the large open-air suntrap yard. A live music jam is hosted on Monday when the musical landlord often entertains. Well-behaved dogs are welcome on a lead. Local CAMRA Pub of the Year 2014.
Q❀♣●P🚌🐾

Lichfield

Duke of Wellington Ⓛ

Birmingham Road, WS14 9BJ

⏲ 4-11; 12-midnight Sat; 12-10.30 Sun ☎ (01543) 256584

Fuller's London Pride; Holden's Golden Glow; Marston's Pedigree; 2 changing beers Ⓗ

Sitting beside a now disused canal, this three-storey pub is easily spotted next to the canal bridge. Well worth the 15-minute stroll from the city centre, it offers two changing guest ales. The split-level, open-plan interior comprises three distinct drinking areas, one with a real fire. Live sport is shown. During the summer months the large garden is popular. A bar snack menu including locally produced pork pies is on offer at all sessions. ❀♣P🚌(X12)🐾📶

Horse & Jockey Ⓛ

8-10 Sandford Street, WS13 6QA

⏲ 11.30-11 ☎ (01543) 410033

Fuller's London Pride; Holden's Golden Glow; Marston's Pedigree; Timothy Taylor Landlord; Wye Valley HPA; 3 changing beers Ⓗ

Deservedly one of the most popular pubs on Lichfield's real ale circuit, this free house complements the regular ales with up to three guests, mainly from microbreweries. There is a cosy snug and a separate games room at the back of the large open-plan bar. Hot food is served Wednesday to Saturday lunchtimes, and a pork pie/cheeseboard selection is always available. Sport is shown on muted TV screens. Over-21s only.
❀◐⇌(City)♣P🚌🐾📶

Whippet Inn 🏆 Ⓛ

21 Tamworth Street, WS13 6JP

⏲ closed Mon & Tue; 12-2.30, 4.30-10; 12-10 Fri & Sat; 12-5 Sun ☎ 07858 753653

4 changing beers Ⓗ

Formerly a dress shop, this micropub opened in 2014. Named after a cheeky boozer in a Carry On film, this tiny place holds true to micropub principles – just real ale, real cider, wines and soft drinks. Four interesting ales are offered, often local, and two ever-changing handpulled ciders. Food is simple snacks like pork pies and Scotch eggs. With seating for around 25 and a maximum capacity of around 40, be prepared to make friends.
Q🕭⇌(City)●🚌🐾

Marchington

Dog & Partridge 🏆

Church Lane, ST14 8LJ

⏲ 12-3, 6-11 (midnight Sat); 12-3, 5-midnight Fri; 12-11 Sun ☎ (01283) 820394 🌐 dogandpartridgemarchington.co.uk

Draught Bass; 3 changing beers (sourced locally) Ⓗ

A gem of a village pub always serving Bass beer and with several handpumps providing constantly changing local guest ales. Formerly a restaurant, the pub is split into four main indoor areas with open fires. Food is served lunchtimes and evenings. A pleasant beer garden to the rear is popular in the summer months. It is renowned locally for its weekly live music sessions and the hosting of regular beer festivals. Parking is available to the side of the building. Children are welcome. Q🕭❀◐▲P🚌(402)📶

Milwich

Green Man

Sandon Lane, ST18 0EG (on B5027)

⏲ 12-2.30 (not Mon-Wed), 5-11; 12-11 Fri & Sat; 12-10.30 Sun ☎ (01889) 505310 🌐 greenmanmilwich.com

Castle Rock Harvest Pale; Draught Bass; Sharp's Doom Bar; 3 changing beers (often Courage, Ludlow) Ⓗ

An inn since 1775, and known as the Green Man since at least 1815, this free house offers guest beers from regional and local brewers. It is popular with walkers and cyclists visiting the area. Home-cooked food is served in the bar and small dining area (no food Mon-Wed). The bar has a real fire and well-behaved dogs are welcome. Outside is an extensive garden area. Ciders are from various sources. 🕭❀◐♣●P🐾📶

Newcastle-under-Lyme

Castle Mona

4 Victoria Street, ST5 1NT

⏲ 4 (12 Sat)-midnight; 12-11 Sun ☎ 07895 555598

Castle Rock Harvest Pale; Oakham Citra; Wells Bombardier; 6 changing beers (sourced nationally; often Greene King, RAN, Springhead) Ⓗ

Only five minutes' walk along the A34 from Newcastle town centre, this hostelry has a wood-panelled lounge with a woodburner, and a traditional bar area where the regulars provide their own entertainment, with hours of chatter, banter and games of bar skittles and pool. Outside is a lovely well-kept beer garden for the summer evenings. Eight real ciders are available. A real traditional English pub with a warm welcome and a sense of community spirit. ❀♣●🚌(3,101,41)📶

Freebird

96 Liverpool Road, ST5 2AX

⏲ 5-midnight (1am Fri); 2-1am Sat; 2-11.30 Sun

Changing beers (sourced nationally; often Falstaff, Ilkley, Salopian) Ⓗ

A biker-friendly pub sporting up to 12 rotating ales of excellent quality from across the whole of the UK as well as a minimum of two real ciders. The main bar has a pool table and a unique display of album artwork, while the gig room plays host to live bands on weekend nights. Five minutes' walk from the town centre, this is well worth a visit. A beer festival is held on the May bank holiday weekend. ♿♣🍎P🚌(4,4A,17)🐾

Hopinn

102 Albert Street, ST5 1JR

⏲ 4-11.30; 12-midnight Sat; 12-11 Sun ☎ (01782) 711121

Black Sheep Best Bitter; Draught Bass; 6 changing beers (sourced nationally; often Mallinson's, Northern Monk, Oakham) Ⓗ

Comfortable and friendly family-owned pub on the edge of the town centre, comprising a front bar, lounge and snug, all with well-preserved original Art Deco features including wood panelling and a rare stained-glass skylight. Up to six guest beers are sourced from a wide variety of breweries – Mallinsons, Oakham and Hopcraft are usually represented and, as the pub name suggests, many are hoppy beers. Real cider is also available. ♣🚌

Lymestone Vaults 𝕃

Pepper Street, ST5 1PR

⏲ 10-11 (midnight Fri & Sat); 12-10.30 Sun

☎ (01782) 615801

Lymestone Stone Cutter, Stone Faced, Foundation Stone, Ein Stein, Stone the Crows; 4 changing beers (sourced nationally; often Derventio, Lymestone, Springhead) Ⓗ

The first pub owned by the Lymestone Brewery of Stone, the Vaults opened at the end of 2012 and was an immediate success with the real ale-drinking populace. Modern and traditional at the same time, the interior is open plan but divided into two rooms due to its L-shaped structure. Nine ales are usually available including seasonal beers and guests from other breweries. Good-value food is available until 3.20pm; last entry to the pub is half an hour before closing. 🐴◐♿♣🍎🚌🐾📶

Victoria

62 King Street, ST5 1HX

⏲ 2-midnight (11 Mon & Wed); 12-11 Sun

☎ (01782) 631505

Draught Bass; Salopian Shropshire Gold; 4 changing beers (sourced nationally; often Greene King, Penpont, Raw) Ⓗ

Closed for five years, this pub was reopened in 2012 and has risen like a phoenix from the ashes. It was hugely successful in its first year, winning the local CAMRA branch Pub of the Year merit award due to the outstanding quality and selection of beers served and the warm and friendly atmosphere. A traditional pub with Victorian-style decoration, it has an amazing wooden bar, a beautiful open fire and a drinking area outside. Q🛏♣🚌

Oulton

Brushmakers Arms

8 Kibblestone Road, ST15 8UW

⏲ 12-midnight (1am Fri & Sat) ☎ (01785) 812062

Thwaites Original, Lancaster Bomber; 1 changing beer (often Skinner's) Ⓗ

Named after a local cottage industry, the Brush is a pub where time stands still. It has many original and traditional features, with local pictures and postcards adorning the walls, reflecting a bygone and more sedate way of life. The small rear paved garden is a real suntrap and doubles as a smoking area. Conversation rules in this jukebox- and gaming machine-free zone. An excellent village local. Q❀▲♣P🚌(4)🐾📶

Rawnsley

Rag

Ironstone Road, WS12 0QD

⏲ 11-11; 12-10.45 Sun ☎ (01543) 277491

🌐 theragatrawnsley.co.uk

Fuller's London Pride; Greene King IPA; Salopian Oracle; 2 changing beers (sourced nationally; often Salopian, Thwaites) Ⓗ

A free house set in three acres of grounds with an award-winning 100-seat restaurant and seven en-suite rooms. There is a bowling green at the rear of the building along with six recently installed camping pods. Regular beer festivals and summer barbecues are held. It is an ideal base to visit local attractions such as Lichfield Cathedral, Trentham Village and Monkey Forest, also Chasewater Light Railway. Q❀🛏◐◑♿▲P🚌(62,62a)

Rolleston-on-Dove

Jinnie Inn

177 Station Road, DE13 9AB (E side of village)

⏲ 11.30-11.30 (midnight Fri & Sat); 12-10.30 Sun

☎ (01283) 812155 🌐 thejinnie.co.uk

Jennings Cocker Hoop; Marston's Pedigree; 2 changing beers (sourced nationally; often Banks's, Ringwood, Wychwood) Ⓗ

Set back from the road, this attractive village pub was converted from a farmhouse in 1991, although it served briefly as an alehouse in the mid-19th century to benefit the builders of the Burton-Tutbury railway, nicknamed the Tutbury Jinnie, hence the pub name. The comfortable lounge bar and the plainer dining room feature beamed ceilings and exposed timber-framed walls. The unusual bar counter top is inlaid with 4,600 1p coins (plus three hidden foreign ones). Quiz night is Monday. 🐴❀◐◑♿♣P🚌(V1)🐾📶

Spread Eagle

Church Road, DE13 9BE (near jct with Burnside)

⏲ 12-midnight; 12-11 Sun ☎ (01283) 813004

🌐 vintageinn.co.uk/thespreadeaglerolleston

Draught Bass; Everards Tiger; Marston's Pedigree; Sharp's Doom Bar; 2 changing beers (sourced nationally; often Brakspear, Purity, Theakston) Ⓗ

Imposing, attractive village pub, parts of which date back to the 16th century. The interior is open plan, with several linked rooms around a central bar. The mixture of high and low ceilings, some with beams, together with slate, quarry tile, wooden and carpeted floors, plus dim lighting, provide some old world charm in a convivial atmosphere. Bar snacks are available (not Sun eves), with an à la carte menu plus specials. Vintage pie day is Wednesday, fish day is Friday, and quiz night Tuesday. 🐴❀◐◑♿P🚌(1,V1)📶

Rugeley

Plaza 𝕃

Horsefair, WS15 2EJ

⏲ 9am-12.30am (1am Fri & Sat); 9am-midnight Sun

☎ (01889) 586831

Adnams Broadside; Greene King Abbot; Ruddles Best Bitter; Sharp's Doom Bar; 3 changing beers (sourced locally; often Backyard, Salopian, Slater's) Ⓗ

Previously a cinema dating from the 1930s, this spacious Wetherspoon pub retains much of the cinematic atmosphere and Art Deco flourishes of the period. The light and airy interior allows for three separate levels including a large window area where the cinema screen once was – this leads to an outside drinking area, with balcony, terrace and lawned garden. Around seven ales are offered, with micros such as Salopian, Slater's and Backyard proving popular. Q ☽ ⌚ ① & ≠ ● 🚃 🚌 ☎

Seighford

Hollybush Inn ℄

Main Road, ST18 9PQ

✪ 12-3, 5-11; 12-11.30 Fri-Sun ☎ (01785) 281644

⊕ hollybushseighford.co.uk

Everards Tiger; Titanic Steerage, Plum Porter; 1 changing beer (sourced nationally; often Batemans) ℍ

Traditional-style village inn resurrected by a community purchase following a period of closure and time served as an Indian restaurant. Managed on behalf of the community by Titanic Brewery, it is its first such venture and first rural pub. There are small, cosy drinking areas within the original half-timbered building, together with dining space in several sections. The outside drinking area at the rear is a real suntrap even in the winter. Q ☽ ⌚ ① ♣ P 🚃 (490) ☺ ☎

Shenstone

Plough

2 Pinfold Hill, WS14 0JN

✪ 12-11 (midnight Fri & Sat) ☎ (01543) 481800

⊕ theploughatshenstone.co.uk

Holden's Golden Glow; St Austell Tribute; 3 changing beers ℍ

Closed for four years, the Plough reopened in 2013 after a major refurbishment. The bar is furnished in a comfortable contemporary fashion. Heading towards the rear takes you past an open-view kitchen and into a series of ever more elegant dining rooms. Upstairs is a stylish dining room. At the front is a tidy beer terrace for summertime tippling. Children are welcome until 7pm, and dogs in the bar only. ☽ ⌚ ① & ≠ P 🚃 ☺ ☎

Stafford

Greyhound ℄

12 County Road, ST16 2PU (off A34, opp jail)

✪ 4-11.30 (midnight Fri); 12-midnight Sat; 12-11 Sun

☎ (01785) 222432 ⊕ greyhoundfreehousestafford.co.uk

Wells Bombardier; 7 changing beers (sourced nationally; often Abbeydale, Bradfield, Kelham Island) ℍ

Less than five-minutes' walk from the centre of Stafford, this two-room free house is well worth a visit. The pub dates from 1831 and a newspaper article from the day it opened can be seen above the bar. Today the pub offers a changing range of seven ales, often from breweries in Yorkshire. If you arrive during opening hours and the front door is closed, walk around the back to Sash Street for entry. Q ⌚ & ♣ P 🚃 ☺

Market Vaults ℄

4 St Martin's Place, ST16 2LA

✪ 12-midnight; 3-11 Sun ☎ (01785) 256126

⊕ themarketvaults.com

Banks's Sunbeam; Jennings Cumberland Ale; Wychwood Hobgoblin; 3 changing beers (often Adnams, Purity, Slater's) ℍ

A welcoming pub in the corner of Stafford's Market Square. A series of rooms and distinct areas ramble around a central bar. Live music features on Saturday nights, open mic on Thursdays, and a folk session 5-8pm on Sundays. Beers vary, mostly from the Marston's range – see the pub's Facebook page for what's on. The food includes steakburgers, sandwiches and soup. ① & ≠ 🚃 ☺ ☎

Olde Rose & Crown 🏆 ℄

10 Market Street, ST16 2JZ

✪ 12-11 (midnight Fri & Sat); 12-10.30 Sun

☎ (01785) 251343

Joule's Blonde, Pale Ale, Slumbering Monk; 1 changing beer (sourced locally; often Joule's) ℍ

A comfortable Joule's house right in the heart of Stafford and much larger than it looks from the outside. Four handpumps serve Joule's ales alongside a cider. Situated next to the Gatehouse Theatre, the pub is a favourite of theatregoers and is frequented by cast members enjoying an after-show pint. An acoustic night is held every Wednesday, and the fourth Tuesday of the month is a storytelling night. Q ☽ ⌚ ① & ≠ ● 🚃 ☺ ☎

Spittal Brook ℄

106 Lichfield Road, ST17 4LP

✪ 12-3, 5-11; 12-11 Fri; 9am-11 Sat & Sun

☎ (01785) 245268

Draught Bass; Ludlow Gold; Sharp's Doom Bar; 3 changing beers (often Castle Rock, Church End, Dark Star) ℍ

A thriving, traditional two-roomed alehouse within walking distance of the town centre. Entertainment includes a folk night on Tuesday, a quiz on Wednesday and a cheese night on the last Sunday of the month - bring your own cheeses to share with others. The pub holds beer and cider festivals in July and October and a guest real cider is always available. Breakfast is served until noon Saturday and Sunday. Food is locally sourced wherever possible. Q ☽ ⌚ ① A ♣ ● 🚃 ☺ ☎

Sun ℄

7 Lichfield Road, ST17 4JX

✪ 12-11 (midnight Fri & Sat) ☎ (01785) 248361

⊕ thesunstafford.co.uk

Everards Tiger; Titanic Steerage, Anchor Bitter, Iceberg, White Star, Captain Smith's; 5 changing beers (sourced nationally; often Boggart Hole Clough, Flipside, Great Heck) ℍ

Titanic Brewery acquired this closed pub in 2010 and reopened it following refurbishment. Twelve handpumps dispense a choice of Titanic beers and changing guests. At least one cider is available, usually from Westons. Food is served throughout the day, using ingredients sourced as locally to the pub as possible. Beer festivals are held in spring and late summer in a large marquee at the rear of the pub. Q ☽ ⌚ ≠ ♣ ● P 🚃 ☺ ☎

Stoke-on-Trent: Burslem

Bull's Head ℄

14 St John's Square, ST6 3AJ

✪ 3-11 (11.30 Wed & Thu); 12-midnight Fri & Sat; 12-11 Sun

☎ (01782) 834153

Titanic Steerage, Iceberg, White Star, Plum Porter; 6 changing beers (sourced nationally; often Ashover, Dancing Duck, Holden's) ℍ

Titanic's brewery tap in the centre of Burslem. It is 10 minutes' walk from Port Vale's ground, and opens at 11am on Vale home Saturdays, welcoming all supporters, home and away. The island bar serves up to 10 real ales on tap plus seven or more real ciders and perries straight from the cellar, alongside draught and bottled Belgian beers. Bar billiards, table skittles and an old jukebox can be found in the public bar. Local CAMRA Potteries Cider Pub of the Year 2014.
Q❀♣ (3,29,98)

Duke William

2 St Johns Square, ST6 3AJ
11.30-11 (midnight Fri & Sat); 12-10.30 Sun
☎ (01782) 814809 dukewilliamburslem.com
Joule's Slumbering Monk; Oakham Citra; Sarah Hughes Dark Ruby Mild; Springhead Roaring Meg; 3 changing beers (sourced nationally; often Abbeydale, Acorn, Salopian) H
An imposing Victorian building in the heart of the Potteries' mother town with a friendly and relaxed atmosphere. The family-run pub is a popular haunt for drinkers and diners since reopening in 2010 following extensive refurbishment. Original features including the horseshoe-shaped bar and heated foot rail have been preserved. The ground floor holds a lounge/bar spanning two rooms and a large public bar. The restaurant is on the first floor and there is a conference room on the second floor. ♿ (3,29,98)

Stoke-on-Trent: Etruria

Holy Inadequate

67 Etruria Old Road, ST1 5PE
4-11 (midnight Thu); 12-midnight Fri-Sun ☎ 07771 358238
Joule's Pale Ale; changing beers H
Winner of local CAMRA branch Pub of the Year for three consecutive years, and County Pub of the Year twice, the Holy is now firmly established as one of the best pubs in the region. It continues to support quality brewers with a choice of six ales, four real ciders and a growing range of bottled beers. Beer festivals are held every bank holiday, when up to 26 beers are served from the stillage room. Bar snacks are available.
Q❀P (4,4A,22)

Stoke-on-Trent: Fenton

Bench & Bar

93 Christchurch Street, ST4 3AJ
12-11.30 (midnight Fri & Sat); 11-11.30 Sun
☎ (01782) 922995
Draught Bass; Hancock's HB; 3 changing beers (sourced nationally; often Lymestone, Offbeat, Peakstones Rock) H
A worthy new entry to this Guide, the Bench has quickly established itself on the real ale scene after becoming a free house in 2013, gaining awards from the local CAMRA branch within its first 18 months. Recently refurbished to a high standard, with a comfortable but contemporary feel, it has two distinct areas and features a fireplace with a local Minton tile hearth. It gets lively on football days due to its proximity to the Britannia Stadium. A beer festival takes place every Easter weekend. ♣ (1,23)

Stoke-on-Trent: Hanley

Coachmakers Arms ★

65 Lichfield Street, ST1 3EA (off A5008)
4 (12 Thu-Sat)-midnight; 12-11 Sun ☎ (01782) 860438
Draught Bass; 4 changing beers H
The Coach, as it is known locally, is a regular and deserved entry in this Guide. A Victorian corridor pub (one of few left in the country), it has for years traded under the shadow of demolition despite having a nationally important historic interior. TV-free, with a roaring fire in a beautiful cast-iron grate, this unique gem offers a traditional drinking ambience that is disappearing elsewhere. A must-see pub when visiting the Potteries. Q♣P

Smithfield

Lower Bethsesda Street, ST1 3DE
12-11 (midnight Fri); 11-midnight Sat ☎ (01782) 280811
thesmithfieldrealale.co.uk
Castle Rock Black Gold, Harvest Pale; Joule's Pale Ale; Oakham Citra; 2 changing beers (sourced nationally; often Abbeydale, Falstaff, Froth Blowers) H
Located opposite Hanley fire station, the Smithfield was built in the 1870s. It offers a warm welcome to all and boasts 10 handpulls serving four regular beers and two rotating guests. There is a pool table in the bar area, plenty of comfortable seating in the lounge and a function room upstairs. Run by the team behind the award-winning Wellington in Birmingham, this is a must-see pub when visiting Stoke. ♣

Victoria Lounge Bar

5 Adventure Place, ST1 3AF (next to bus station)
11-11 ☎ (01782) 273530 thereardon.com
Draught Bass; 5 changing beers (sourced nationally; often Blue Monkey, Brains, Cottage) H
A repeat entry in the Guide for this established city-centre watering hole, known locally as Reardon's as it is part of Reardon's Snooker club. It offers a smart, modern and comfortable interior, with six handpulls serving a varied range of ales, some from local, smaller brewers, and locals can suggest their favourite beers. There is a busy lunchtime carvery and light snacks at other times. A function room is available for hire. ♿P

Stoke-on-Trent: Longton

Congress Inn

14 Sutherland Road, ST3 1HJ (opp police station)
12-midnight ☎ (01782) 763667 thecongressinn.co.uk
Castle Rock Sheriff's Tipple; 6 changing beers (sourced nationally; often Acorn, Brains, Welbeck Abbey) H
Spacious two-roomed pub likened to Dr Who's Tardis; with so much going on, it must be bigger on the inside. Drawing a loyal clientele from a wide area, the pub has won many awards including local and Staffordshire CAMRA Pub of the Year. Up to nine beers are on handpump plus four real ciders, and a large selection of bottled Belgian beers. A beer festival is held every May, with 30 beers plus ciders on gravity. Traditional pub games include table skittles. ♣ (1,2,6)

Stoke-on-Trent: Stoke

Glebe

35 Glebe Street, ST4 1HG
12-midnight (11 Mon & Wed); 12-10.30 Sun
☎ (01782) 860670

Joule's Blonde, Pale Ale, Slumbering Monk; 1 changing beer Ⓗ
A short walk from the rail station, this superb Joule's establishment has justifiably become one of the must-visit pubs in the city. The impressive features, including the beautifully restored stained-glass windows and candlelit tables, all add to the welcoming atmosphere. The three mainstay Joule's beers are supplemented by one handpulled cider. Home-made meals, served lunchtimes and early evenings, are of a high standard.
❀◐◑⇌●🚌(1,3,23)🐾

Wheatsheaf 𝕃
84-92 Church Street, ST4 1BU
✪ 8am-midnight (1am Fri & Sat) ☎ (01782) 747462
Greene King Abbot; Ruddles Best Bitter; changing beers (sourced nationally; often Lymestone, Summerskills, Titanic) Ⓗ
This Stoke town-centre Wetherspoon, a regular Guide entry and highly regarded as one of the best in the local chain, is popular with regulars and visitors alike. Proud of its strong community links, it is often customer-led in its choice of beers. As well as the Wetherspoon regulars, five rotating guest ales are to be found on the bar, with house beer Stookers Ashlar – exclusively brewed by Lymestone – always available. Food is served 8am-11pm.
Q🐴◐◑♿⇌♣●🚌(1,3,31)📶

White Star 𝕃
63 Kingsway, ST4 1JB (off Church St)
✪ 11-midnight; 12-11 Sun ☎ (01782) 848732
Everards Tiger; Titanic Steerage, Iceberg, White Star, Plum Porter, Captain Smith's; 4 changing beers (sourced nationally; often Everards, Titanic, Wharfe Bank) Ⓗ
In the town centre, with a spacious and well-furnished split-level interior, this multi award-winning Titanic Brewery pub is a popular and busy establishment. It serves Titanic's excellent range of beers supplemented by Everards Tiger and four rotating guest ales. An extensive menu of quality home-cooked food is available until 9pm. The décor comprises pictures and newspaper stories of the Titanic and its crew. Q◐◑♿⇌♣🚌(1,3,23)📶

Stone

Pheasant Inn
Old Road, ST15 8HS
✪ 12-11 (midnight Fri & Sat) ☎ 07735 463002
Banks's Mild; Draught Bass; Marston's Pedigree; 1 changing beer (often Castle Rock, Purity, Robinsons) Ⓗ
An old-fashioned corner pub with three separate rooms. The front room is a pleasant, traditional public bar with a logburner, and there are two separate comfy rooms to the rear. The pub is a real community focus hosting numerous local activities as well as offering more traditional pub games. Occasional Sunday lunches are served; it is best to ring beforehand. 🐴❀⇌♣🚌(101,250)🐾📶

Royal Exchange 𝕃
Radford Street, ST15 8DA (on corner of Northesk St)
✪ 12-11 (midnight Fri & Sat) ☎ (01785) 812685
Everards Tiger; Titanic Steerage, Iceberg, White Star, Captain Smith's; 5 changing beers Ⓗ
A one-roomed pub with four distinct drinking areas and real fires at both ends. Ten real ales and one real cider are available including three changing guests, mainly from micros. There are no TVs or piped music, just good craic. Acoustic music nights and quiz nights are hosted and many clubs, including backgammon, knitting, gaming, reading and photography, meet here. Light snacks are available all day, with lunches 12-3pm Friday and Saturday, all featuring local ingredients.
Q🐴❀◐♿⇌♣●🗑🚌(101,250,400)🐾📶

Swan Inn 𝕃
18 Stafford Street, ST15 8QW (on A520)
✪ 12-1am (11 Mon; midnight Tue & Wed); 12-11 Sun
☎ (01785) 815570 🌐 swaninnstone.co.uk
House beer (by Coach House); 8 changing beers (sourced nationally; often Abbeydale, Blythe) Ⓗ
A thriving free house in a carefully renovated Grade II-listed building with nine handpulls, serving anything from anywhere – the beer range can change daily. Four real ciders and bottled varieties are always available. An annual beer festival is held each July, with up to 80 beers on offer. Live music plays twice a week. Over-18s only.
❀♣●🚌(101,250,490)🐾📶

Stourton

Fox
Bridgnorth Road, DY7 5BL (on the main A458)
✪ 11.30-11; 11.30-9 Sun ☎ (01384) 872614
Bathams Best Bitter; 1 changing beer (sourced locally; often Holden's, Wye Valley) Ⓗ
Set in the picturesque Staffordshire countryside between Stourbridge and Kinver. The interior has a new layout, now with three rooms and a large function room. There is also a conservatory area and a spacious garden. Two beers are normally served. An extensive menu and a specials board give plenty of food choice. 🐴❀◐◑P

Summerhill

Boat
Walsall Road, WS14 0BU
✪ 12-3, 6-11; 12-11 Sun ☎ (01543) 361692
🌐 oddfellowsintheboat.com
3 changing beers (sourced nationally; often Cottage) Ⓗ
A free house for real ale and a heaven for lovers of gourmet food. Relax in the reception area and peruse the extensive chalkboard menu while watching the cooking. A Cottage beer is generally featured, plus two ever-changing ales which are usually interesting and frequently local. There is a large enclosed garden area adjacent to the car park. Q❀◐◑♿P🚌🐾📶

Tamworth

King's Ditch 𝕃
51 Lower Gungate, B79 7AS
✪ closed Mon; 4 (12 Fri & Sat)-10.30; 12-7 Sun ☎ 07989 805828 🌐 kingsditch.co.uk
4 changing beers Ⓖ
Specialising mostly in local ales, this is Tamworth's first micropub. Four gravity-served ales are complemented by a wide range of real ciders. Formerly a cycle shop, it has a single ground-floor room plus a small drinking area upstairs, with room for around 40 people. Bare brick and wood characterise the simple, modern style of the decor. Children are welcome until 7pm.
Q🐴⇌●🗑🚌🐾📶

Market Vaults

7 Market Street, B79 7LU
⏲ 12 (2 Tue)-11 ☎ (01827) 66552
🌐 marketvaults-tamworth.co.uk
Joule's Pale Ale, Slumbering Monk; 5 changing beers 🄷
This historic town-centre pub, close to the attractive town hall and Norman castle, is a real local hidden gem. The lower bar at the front and the raised lounge at the rear have a traditional feel, warmed in winter by wood-burning stoves. A picturesque garden provides sanctuary on fine days. Hot food is served until 6pm (not Mon or Wed), including a roast on Sunday. The regular ales are joined by four to five changing guests.
❀◐⇌●🚌🐾📶

Sir Robert Peel 🄻

13-15 Lower Gungate, B79 7BA
⏲ 2 (4 Tue)-11; 12-11 Sat & Sun ☎ (01827) 300910
5 changing beers 🄷
The Peel free house is a well-established town centre ale stronghold, and frequent winner of the CAMRA branch Pub of the Year, including for 2014. It is twinned with a German alehouse and attracts regular exchange visits. Friendly and attentive staff dispense up to five changing ales including Oakham and the Church End house beer Apeeling. The ales are complemented by two real ciders and a large selection of foreign bottled beers. The up-to-date jukebox ensures a lively atmosphere at the weekend. ⇌●🚌🐾📶

Trysull

Bell Inn 🄻

Bell Road, WV5 7JB SO852940
⏲ 11.30-3, 5-11 (midnight Fri); 11.30-midnight Sat; 12-11 Sun ☎ (01902) 892871
Bathams Best Bitter; Holden's Black Country Bitter, Golden Glow; 2 changing beers 🄷
A fine 18th-century building next to the village church, comprising a smallish but cosy bar, pleasant lounge and a large restaurant/dining room. As well as the Holden's range, Bathams Best Bitter is a regular, together with a changing guest, often from a microbrewery. A patio area is to the front of the pub. Popular with walkers, the Staffordshire & Worcestershire Canal is a 15-minute walk away. Q🐴❀◐◑♿P🐾

Tutbury

Cask & Pottle

2 High Street, DE13 9LP
⏲ closed Mon; 12-2, 5-9 (10 Fri); 1-10 Sat; 1-4 Sun ☎ 07595 423614
4 changing beers (sourced locally; often Burton Bridge, Dancing Duck, Nene Valley) 🄶
East Staffordshire's first micropub, opened in October 2013 in a former sweet shop. The small, bright single room on the ground floor of a Victorian terrace features pine benches and tables, but no bar counter. One wall is decorated with an aphorism, a mural and a table of ale measures (a pottle is an archaic name for a half-gallon measure). A window at the rear offers a view of the stillage. Q🐴♿●🚌(1,402/402X)🐾

Uttoxeter

Old Swan 🄻

Market Place, ST14 8HN
⏲ 8am-midnight (1am Fri & Sat) ☎ (01889) 598650
Greene King Abbot; Ruddles Best Bitter; Sharp's Doom Bar; 4 changing beers (sourced locally; often Backyard, Hawkshead, Lymestone) 🄷
Centrally located close to the town's marketplace, this Wetherspoon pub attracts a varied clientele throughout the day. Up to six handpumps are in use at any one time, offering a choice of frequently changing local and national ales. A large open-plan seating area downstairs is supplemented with a quieter upper level to the back. There is also a small rear outdoor patio and separate smoking area. Food is served all day. Very busy on race days.
Q🐴❀◐◑♿⛺⇌●🚌(841,402,32)📶

Weston

Woolpack Inn 🄻

The Green, ST18 0JH (off A518)
⏲ 11-11 (midnight Fri & Sat) ☎ (01889) 270238
🌐 woolpackpubweston.co.uk
Banks's Bitter; Marston's Pedigree; Ringwood Boondoggle; 3 changing beers (often Banks's, Marston's, Ringwood) 🄷
A beautiful village pub set on a tranquil village green in the centre of Weston. Refurbished in 2014, it has plenty of character, with a low ceiling, oak beams and cosy fireplaces. Four bays inside reflect the pub's origins as a row of cottages and blacksmith's shop. Outside there is a big, attractive beer garden. The property is recorded as being owned by the Bagot family in the 1730s.
Q🐴❀◐◑⛺♣●P🚌(825,435,842)🐾📶

Whiston

Swan Inn 🄻

ST19 5QH SJ895144
⏲ 12-3 (not Mon), 5-11; 12-11 Sat; 12-10.30 Sun
☎ (01785) 716200 🌐 swanwhiston.co.uk
Holden's Black Country Bitter; 4 changing beers (sourced nationally; often Ludlow, Sharp's, Three Tuns) 🄷
Although remotely situated, high-quality, well-kept ales and superb food make this a thriving pub. Built in 1593, burned down and rebuilt in 1711, the oldest part today is the small bar housing an inglenook fireplace. The lounge features an intriguing double-sided log fire. Six acres of grounds include a children's obstacle course, aviary and rabbits. Q🐴❀◐◑♿♣●P🚌(878,76)🐾📶

Woodseaves

Cock Inn 🄻

Newport Road, ST20 0NP
⏲ 4-11; 12-11 Fri-Sun ☎ (01785) 284343
Banks's Mild, Bitter; Holden's Golden Glow; Marston's Pedigree; 1 changing beer 🄷
The Cock was originally a farmhouse, with a brewhouse added in the 19th century. The large, comfortable, single-room interior has two fires. The pub is home to darts and dominoes teams, but no TV or gaming machines. As well as a good selection of ales it offers a wide range of malt whiskies. The Shropshire Union Canal is within walking distance. A restaurant has been added to the rear of the pub.
🐴❀◐⛺♣P🚌(432,433)🐾📶

SUFFOLK

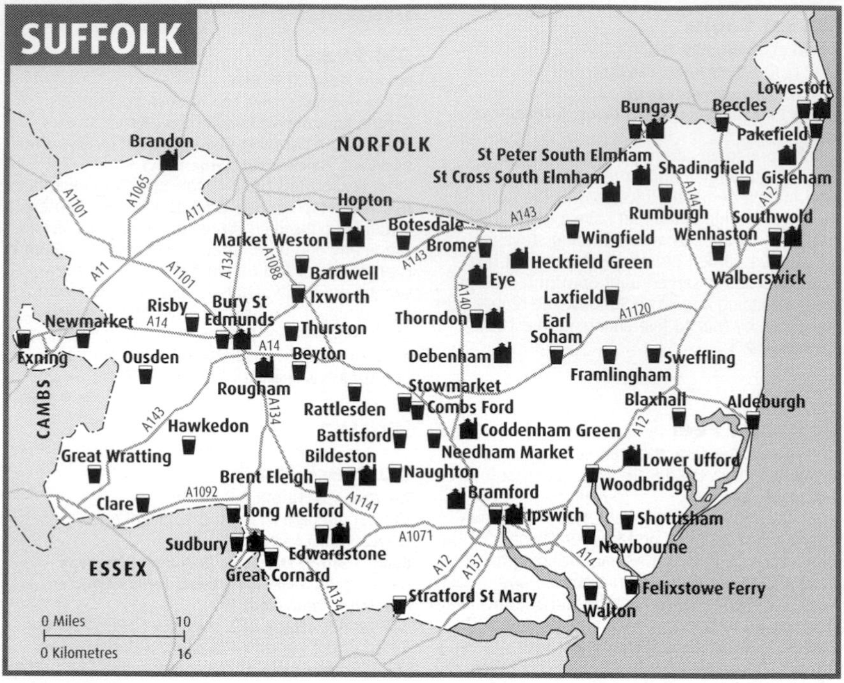

Aldeburgh

White Hart ⓛ

222 High Street, IP15 5AJ

🕏 11.30-11; 12-10.30 Sun ☎ (01728) 453205

Adnams Southwold Bitter, Broadside, Ghost Ship; 2 changing beers Ⓗ

Large, lively and friendly establishment close to the town's renowned chippie. Drinkers can buy fish and chips from next door and eat them in the garden in fine weather. The single-room bar was formerly a public reading room. Occasional live music is hosted. There is covered seating outside, with barbecues and pizzas cooked in a wood-fired oven available Easter until mid-September. Families are welcome in the garden in summer.

🕏❀🚍(64,165,321)❀

Bardwell

Dun Cow

Up Street, IP31 1AA (approx 1 mile off A143 at Stanton)

🕏 11.30-2.30, 5-midnight; 12-midnight Sat; 12-10.30 Sun ☎ (01359) 250806

Greene King IPA; 3 changing beers Ⓗ

A traditional pub in a pleasant village set in the Suffolk countryside. The pub has two bars and offers speciality food nights. Six real ales are available at weekends. Outside is a covered smoking area and large family space in the garden. Party bookings and coaches are welcome if booked in advance. The picturesque restored village windmill is worth a visit and has occasional threshing open days. 🕏❀◑♣P🚍❀

Battisford

Punch Bowl

Straight Road, IP14 2LQ

🕏 6-10.30 Mon & Tue; 12-2.30, 6-11 Wed & Thu; 12-2.30, 6-11.30 Fri & Sat; 12-4, 6.30-10.30 Sun ☎ (01449) 771646

🌐 punchbowlbattisford.co.uk

Adnams Southwold Bitter, Broadside; 1 changing beer Ⓗ

Reopened in 2011 after much refurbishment work, this is Suffolk's first local community-operated inn. The building comprises a large timber-framed bar and a separate restaurant. It now offers a rotating range of guest beers, a wide food menu and a summer beer festival. Acoustic music, vinyl nights and a quiz evening are held monthly. Darts and various pub games are played. The pub is at the far western edge of the village, almost in Little Finborough. 🕏❀◑♣P🚍(462)❀ 🤖

Beccles

Caxton Club ⓛ

Gaol Lane, NR34 9SJ

🕏 12-1.30 (not Tue), 7-11; 12-2, 6.30-11 Fri; 12-11 Sat; 12-10.30 Sun ☎ (01502) 712829

Theakston Black Bull Bitter; 3 changing beers (sourced locally; often Green Jack, Woodforde's) Ⓗ

Spacious club conveniently situated a short walk from train and bus stations and close to the town centre. All members and guests are warmly welcomed (a small charge is made to cover entertainment on Saturday evenings). It has a central bar, TV and darts room and snooker room. There is also a large function room, garden with children's play area and a bowling green. Four real ales and a choice of real ciders are available. Guide dogs only are allowed. 🕏❀&⇌♣●🚍

Beyton

Bear

Tostock Road, IP30 9AG

⌚ 12-2 (not Tue), 5-11; 12-4, 7-10.30 Sun
☎ (01359) 270249 🌐 thebearinnbeyton.co.uk
Woodforde's Wherry; 3 changing beers (sourced regionally) Ⓗ
Rebuilt in 1900 after the original thatched premises perished by fire during a July thunderstorm – a full account of this traumatic event can be found in the bar. The pub has been run by the same family since 1922. It has a traditional interior with a public bar with an open fire and a separate bar with a restaurant serving excellent food (Fri-Sun lunchtimes, Thu-Sat eves). A separate function room is available. Children are welcome in the beer garden. Q🐴❀◐◑♣P🚌(384)🐾

Bildeston

King's Head 𝕃
132 High Street, IP7 7ED
⌚ closed Mon & Tue; 6-midnight Wed (11 Thu); 4 (12 Sat)-midnight Fri; 12-10.30 Sun ☎ (01449) 741434
🌐 bildestonkingshead.co.uk
Kings Head Bildeston Best; 2 changing beers (sourced locally; often Kings Head) Ⓗ
Home of the Kings Head Brewery since 1996, the building's carved timbers indicate its history as part of a larger complex dating from around 1530. Now a single bar with an inglenook fireplace, a friendly ale house atmosphere has evolved, with food available at the weekends only. There is a fully enclosed rear garden with a covered patio area, lawns and play equipment for children. The late May bank holiday beer festival is well-established and popular. 🐴❀◐◑♿♣🍎🚌🐾📶

Blaxhall

Ship 𝕃
School Road, IP12 2DY
⌚ 12-3, 6-11.30; 12-midnight Fri & Sat; 12-10.30 Sun
☎ (01728) 688316 🌐 blaxhallshipinn.co.uk
Adnams Southwold Bitter; Woodforde's Wherry; 3 changing beers Ⓗ
A cosy two-roomed 16th-century pub with a reputation for traditional singing in the bar. The menu offers a wide choice of home-made dishes and daily specials using locally sourced ingredients, with various German options (book for breakfast from 10.30am during the summer months). Live music is hosted at least once a week including folk sessions, and story-telling often on bank holiday weekends. Letting chalets are available beside the pub and camping at the nearby village hall is by arrangement. 🐴❀🛏◐◑♿⛺♣P🚌🐾📶

Botesdale

Greyhound
The Street, IP22 1BS
⌚ 5 (12 Sun)-midnight ☎ (01379) 898003
🌐 greyhoundbotesdale.co.uk
Woodforde's Wherry Ⓗ**; 2 changing beers (often Elmtree, Nethergate)** Ⓖ
Once a coaching inn on the main London-Norwich road, this no-frills pub has lots of character and a loyal following of regulars. The interior comprises a busy bar, quieter lounge and a pool room. Bare floorboards, old furniture, old photos and taxidermy exhibits add to the atmosphere. Good home-made burger nights, curry nights and steak nights are popular. Hog rolls and wedges are served on Sundays. 🐴❀◐◑♣P🚌(304)🐾

Brent Eleigh

Cock ★
CO10 9PB
⌚ 12-4, 6-11; 12-11 Fri & Sat; 12-10.30 Sun
☎ (01787) 247371
Adnams Southwold Bitter; Greene King Abbot; 1 changing beer Ⓗ
The Cock remains a real gem and has been identified by CAMRA as having a nationally important historic interior. It has two bars, the smaller one ideal for families. Landlady Deborah provides good food throughout opening times which keeps visiting walkers and cyclists more than happy. There is outside seating from which to watch the world go by. Castling's Heath supplies the cider. The pub has cats but well-behaved dogs are always welcome. Q❀🛏◐◑♣🍎P🚌(111)🐾📶

Brome

Swan
Norwich Road, IP23 8AP
⌚ 11-2.30, 5 (6 Sat)-11; 12-3, 7-10.30 Sun
☎ (01379) 870749 🌐 bromeswan.com
Adnams Southwold Bitter, Broadside; 1 changing beer (sourced locally; often Buffy's, Elgood, Nethergate) Ⓗ
Heavily timbered 17th-century pub with later additions, set on the main A140 equidistant from Norwich and Ipswich. It has had the same owners for 32 years. Pictures on the wall in the bar show how close a WWII bomber came to demolishing the pub in 1944. The spacious restaurant offers an extensive menu and curry specialities on Saturday evenings. The large beer garden has a children's play area. The local cycling club is based here.
Q🐴❀◐◑♿P🚌(113,114)

Bungay

Chequers 𝕃
23 Bridge Street, NR35 1HD
⌚ 11-midnight ☎ (01986) 893579

REAL ALE BREWERIES

Adnams Southwold
Barrell & Sellers St Cross South Elmham (NEW)
Bartrams Rougham
Brandon Brandon
Brewshed Bury St Edmunds
Briarbank Ipswich
Calvors Coddenham Green
Cliff Quay Debenham
Dove Street Ipswich
Earl Soham Debenham
Green Dragon Bungay
Green Jack Lowestoft
Greene King Bury St Edmunds
Hellhound Bramford
Hoxne Heckfield Green
Kings Head Bildeston
Mauldons Sudbury
Mill Green Edwardstone
Old Cannon Bury St Edmunds
Old Chimneys Market Weston
Shortts Farm Thorndon
St Peter's St Peter South Elmham
Station 119 Eye (NEW)
Trinity Gisleham
Uffa Lower Ufford

Green Jack Golden Best; 4 changing beers (sourced locally; often Grain, Wolf, Woodforde's) Ⓗ
Situated close to the town centre, this inn dates from the 17th-century. It has been decorated to a high standard but retains its original timber frame, wood panelling and doors. Its two rooms are separated by an archway with TV screens in both for sporting events. There is an array of water jugs above the bar. Ample parking is available adjacent to a partially covered area leading to a paved beer garden. Real ales are sourced from local breweries. ❀◐♿⛺♣P🚌(80,88)🐾

Green Dragon 🄻

29 Broad Street, NR35 1EE
11 (12 Sat)-midnight; 12-5 Sun ☎ (01986) 892681
greendragonbungay.co.uk
Green Dragon Chaucer Ale, Gold, Bridge Street Bitter Ⓗ**, Strong Mild** Ⓖ
Bungay's only brewpub is located on the edge of town and is a regular entry in the Guide. Ales are brewed in the outbuildings next to the car park at the rear – brewery tours are available by appointment. There is a public bar, a separate spacious lounge and a side room where families are welcome leading to the garden. Bottle-conditioned and seasonal ales are often on sale. ❀♿⛺♣P🚌(80,88)🐾

Bury St Edmunds

Beerhouse 🄻

1 Tayfen Road, IP32 6BH
5 (12 Sat)-11; 12-10 Sun ☎ (01284) 766415
burybeerhouse.co.uk
Brewshed Best; 7 changing beers (sourced nationally) Ⓗ
Traditional beer house set in an unusual semi-circular Victorian building (previously called the Ipswich Arms), handy for the railway station, and refurbished with a modern feel. Seven beer engines provide an ever-changing selection of real ales. It serves its own beers from the Brewshed Brewery which is located in the back yard and also supplies three other local pubs. Three real ciders are also available. Regular beer festivals and an annual cider festival are hosted. Major sporting events are shown on a big screen.
❀⇌●P🚌🐾ᯤ

Dove 🏆 🄻

68 Hospital Road, IP33 3JU
5-11; 12-3, 6-11 Sat; 12-3, 6-10.30 Sun ☎ (01284) 702787
thedovepub.co.uk
Woodforde's Wherry Ⓗ**; changing beers** Ⓗ/Ⓖ
A former East Anglian CAMRA Regional Pub of the Year, set in a back street just five minutes from the town centre. This community venue has six handpumps and a good selection of real ciders, and staff are knowledgeable about the ever-changing range of ales. The venue is traditionally basic, with a main bar of scrubbed floorboards and a parlour, with no lager, TVs or gaming machines. How pubs used to be. Q❀♣●P🚌🐾

Oakes Barn 🏆

St Andrews Street South, IP33 3PH (opp Waitrose car park)
11-11.30; 12-5 Sun ☎ (01284) 761592 oakesbarn.co.uk
Adnams Southwold Bitter; Crouch Vale Brewers Gold; 4 changing beers Ⓗ
A popular, modern real ale free house with some period features and historic links to the medieval town. Just five minutes from the town centre, it is also a social hub and has a friendly, welcoming atmosphere. Six real ales are always available including one dark beer alongside craft cider, a selection of lagers and wines. Home-made snacks using locally sourced ingredients are served all day. There is a covered smoking area outside and an open courtyard with seating. Regular events are held in the bar and function room which is available for hire. Q❀◐◑♿♣●🚌🐾ᯤ

Old Cannon 🄻

86 Cannon Street, IP33 1JR
12-11 (10.30 Sun) ☎ (01284) 768769
oldcannonbrewery.co.uk
Adnams Southwold Bitter; Old Cannon Best Bitter, Gunner's Daughter; 3 changing beers (sourced nationally; often Mauldons, Old Cannon, Timothy Taylor) Ⓗ
Formerly the St Edmund's Head, this brewpub is on the site of the original Cannon Brewery. An interesting bar area also houses the brewing vessels – it does not brew when the bar is open to customers. As well as its own real ales and guest beers, a wide range of foreign beer is offered. Good food is always available, featuring locally sourced fare. There is accommodation but parking is limited. ❀🛏◐◑⇌P🚌ᯤ

Rose & Crown

48 Whiting Street, IP33 1NP
11.30-11.30; 11.30-3, 7-11.30 Sat; 12-2.30, 8-11.30 Sun
☎ (01284) 755934
Greene King XX Mild, IPA, Abbot; 3 changing beers (often Greene King) Ⓗ
In sight of Greene King's Westgate Brewery, this is a traditional pub with two bars and a separate off-sales hatch. The present tenants have run this house for over 25 years and it has been in the same family for 40 years. Good-value wholesome food is served lunchtimes Monday to Saturday. Children are not allowed in the bars but are welcome in the garden. The pub is a listed building located within the conservation area of Bury St Edmunds, and has a regionally important historic interior. Q❀◐♣🚌🐾ᯤ

Clare

Globe

10 Callis Street, CO10 8PX
5 (4 Fri)-11.30; 11-11.30 Sat; 12-11.30 Sun
☎ (01787) 278122
Young's Bitter; 3 changing beers Ⓗ
A phoenix risen from the ashes, the Globe reopened in 2013 after a two-year closure. Serving one well-kept regular beer and up to three changing guests, it is now a thriving local where beer and conversation dominate. Live music plays every second weekend. It has a separate pool room at the rear and a newly refurbished garden for summer drinking. No food is served. A CAMRA award winner in 2014. Q❀P🚌🐾

Combs Ford

Gladstone Arms

2 Combs Road, IP14 2AP
12-midnight (11 Sun) ☎ (01449) 771608
gladstonearms.co.uk
Adnams Southwold Bitter, Broadside; Crouch Vale Brewers Gold Ⓗ**; 11 changing beers** Ⓗ/Ⓖ

This pub has been recently refurbished and reopened by new owners who also own and run the Dove Street Inn in Ipswich. The two pubs now share a similar beer range including house beers brewed in Ipswich. It also offers four or five ciders and a wide range of lagers and malt whiskies. Monthly live music is hosted and board games are available. A beer festival features over the Easter weekend. The garden at the rear leads to the river. Q☆☺◑&♣♠P♬(87,88)❀☞

Magpie
Combs Road, IP14 2AP
☼ 12 (4.30 Tue)-11; 12-midnight Fri & Sat; 12-10.30 Sun
☎ (01449) 612727
Greene King IPA; Sharp's Doom Bar; 5 changing beers Ⓗ
Large historic two-bar free house serving at least six real ales. The previously run-down pub has now been fully refurbished and offers a good food menu including a traditional roast carvery every Sunday (booking advisable). Live entertainment features on Friday evenings, including jazz, soul, Motown, reggae and rock, as well as Saturday evening sessions and occasional Sunday afternoon jazz. No food on Tuesdays. ☆☺◑&♣P♬(87,88)

Earl Soham

Victoria Ⓛ
The Street, IP13 7RL
☼ 11.30-3, 5.30-11.30; 12-3, 7-10.30 Sun ☎ (01728) 685758
Earl Soham Victoria Bitter, Sir Roger's Porter, Albert Ale, Brandeston Gold, Jolabrug Ⓗ
Popular, traditional Victorian pub with two small bars and an open fire in winter months, which has changed little over the years – it still has an outside toilet. An ever-changing food menu with daily specials is offered lunchtimes and evenings, all home cooked. The pub gets busy at weekends, especially on sunny days when even a seat in the garden can be hard to find. Dogs and children are welcome. The Earl Soham Brewery was originally located behind the pub. Q☆☺◑♠P♬❀

Edwardstone

White Horse Inn Ⓛ
Mill Green, CO10 5PX
☼ 12-3, 5-11; 12-midnight Fri & Sat; 12-11 Sun
☎ (01787) 211211 ⊕ edwardstonewhitehorse.co.uk
Mill Green Mawkin Mild, White Horse Bitter, Green Goose; 3 changing beers (sourced locally; often Mill Green) Ⓗ
Off the beaten track in rural countryside, this is a traditional Suffolk free house with its own Mill Green microbrewery. Six or seven beers are available plus three or four ciders. The pub and brewery are eco-friendly, using solar and wind power, and burning local coppice wood for heating. Home-prepared food uses mainly locally sourced and home-grown ingredients. Three beer festivals with live music are held each year. Two small holiday cottages and a campsite are within the grounds. Q☆☺≠◑Å♣♠P⊟❀☞

Exning

White Horse
23 Church Street, CB8 7EH
☼ 12-midnight ☎ (01638) 577323
Changing beers Ⓗ

Mentioned in the Domesday Book, this fine free house has been run by the same family since 1923. It comprises a public bar, cosy lounge and separate restaurant offering a good choice of home-cooked food. Beers vary from week to week but often include Bass, Doom Bar and Directors. Happy hour is 5.30-6.30pm, extended to 7pm on Friday. A private room can be hired. Q☆◑♣P♬(10,10a)❀

Felixstowe Ferry

Ferry Boat Inn
Ferry Road, IP11 9RZ
☼ 11-3, 5.30-11; 11-11 Sat; 12-10.30 Sun ☎ (01394) 284203
⊕ ferryboatinn.org.uk
Adnams Southwold Bitter; Woodforde's Wherry; 2 changing beers Ⓗ
Popular coastal pub set in a small hamlet one mile north of the main town. The split-level bar has old stone-flagged flooring and traditional seating around a large fireplace with a woodburner. Food is mostly locally sourced and freshly prepared on the premises, including fish from nearby fishermen's huts. Daily specials, gluten-free dishes and vegetarian options are available lunchtimes and evenings. A room to the rear can cater for private functions, while the large garden to the front is busy in summer months.
☆☺◑&♣P♬(76,173,174)❀

Framlingham

Station Hotel Ⓛ
Station Road, IP13 9EE
☼ 12-2.30, 5-11; 12-11 Sat; 11-2.30, 7-10.30 Sun
☎ (01728) 723455 ⊕ thestationhotel.net
Earl Soham Gannet Mild, Victoria Bitter, Brandeston Gold; 2 changing beers (often Earl Soham) Ⓗ
Cosy three-bar pub set in a former station buffet (the branch line closed in 1963). It enjoys a good reputation for food, made with locally sourced ingredients and prepared on the premises. An ever-changing menu is displayed on chalkboards. On Sundays, brunch and beers are available from 10am. Beers and a guest cider are dispensed from a set of Edwardian German silver handpumps. A beer festival is held over the third weekend in July. The garden bar has a wood-fired pizza oven. Children and dogs welcome. Q☆☺◑♣P♬❀☞

Great Cornard

Five Bells
63 Bures Road, CO10 0HU
☼ 11 (12 Sun)-midnight ☎ (01787) 379016
Adnams Southwold Bitter; Greene King XX Mild, IPA; 1 changing beer (sourced regionally) Ⓗ
A friendly community free house situated near the church (home of the five bells) on the main Sudbury to Bures road. The main bar is decorated with philosophical signs and has a library and a piano. There is a separate smaller rear bar. An unusual combination of pub games is available including bar billiards and table football. An open mic session is hosted every third Wednesday as well as other live music. The pies are legendary. A rare outlet for Greene King XX Mild. Q☆☺◑&♣P♠☞

Great Wratting

Red Lion

School Road, CB9 7HA
11-2.30, 5-11; 11-1.30am Sat; 12-3, 7-10 Sun
(01440) 783237
Adnams Southwold Bitter, Broadside; 1 changing beer (often Adnams) H
A whale's jawbones frame the doorway to this village local dating from the 17th or 18th century, making an unusual and amusing entrance. Now a free house, this ex-Adnams pub offers good beer, good food and conversation as its mainstay. Locals love this hostelry and are passionate supporters of the activities overseen by an enthusiastic landlord of long experience. Quiz nights and a darts league thrive here. QP

Hawkedon

Queen's Head

Rede Road, IP29 4NN
5 (12 Fri-Sun)-11 (01284) 789218
hawkedonqueen.co.uk
Adnams Southwold Bitter; Woodforde's Wherry; 4 changing beers H
Up to six ales, a cider and a perry are available at this 15th-century hidden gem. A huge fireplace keeps the bar cosy in winter, the large garden and patio are ideal for summer. High-quality home-made food is available Wednesday and Thursday evenings and lunchtimes and evenings Friday to Sunday. Special food events take place throughout the year and a popular beer festival is held in July. Classic car clubs meet here and numerous other events are held. QP

Hopton

Vine

High Street, IP22 2QX
3-11; 12-midnight Sat; 12-10.30 Sun (01953) 688581
Adnams Southwold Bitter, Broadside; Greene King IPA; 5 changing beers (sourced locally; often Beeston, Colchester) H
On the main road near the church, this village local has been revitalised by an enthusiastic landlord and friendly staff since it was taken over in 2013. Eight ales including a selection of local and regional guests are currently offered at reasonable prices, with Adnams Southwold, Broadside and Greene King IPA as regulars. The pub has a pool table in one of its three separate areas. Outside is a large play area for children. A welcoming inn, popular with locals and visitors. P(100)

Ipswich

Brewery Tap L

Cliff Road, IP3 0AT
11-3, 6-11; 11-11 Sat; 11-10.30 Sun (01473) 225501
thebrewerytap.org
Cliff Quay Anchor Bitter, Tolly Roger; Earl Soham Victoria Bitter; 3 changing beers (often Cliff Quay) H
Old brewer's house located close to the former historic Tolly Cobbold brewery with a large main bar area and various drinking and dining spaces. Alongside mainly locally brewed beers is an extensive food menu with home-produced fare. Themed food nights, home-made pickled eggs and bar snacks are offered. There are fine views of the River Orwell through a bay window in the bar, despite new sea defences being added. Live music is a regular feature. Three private function rooms are available and a secluded garden.
P(1,3,6)

Briarbank Tap

70 Fore Street, IP4 1LB
12-11 (01473) 284000
Briarbank Spice the Main Brace, Samuel Harvey VC, Perpendicular, Old Spiteful; 2 changing beers (sourced locally; often Briarbank) H
This smart, modern, first-floor drinking bar opened in 2013 above the Briarbank Brewery. At one time serving as a bank, the building had been derelict for many years. Many beers from the brewery are also available as keg. The bar operates a membership scheme but offers free entry to CAMRA members and drinkers carrying a copy of this Guide – buzz at the door for attention.

Cricketers

51 Crown Street, IP1 3JA
8am-midnight (12.30am Fri & Sat) (01473) 225910
Greene King IPA, Abbot; 4 changing beers H
Situated opposite the Tower Ramparts bus station, this large 1930s town-centre pub was once a 'Tolly Folly'. Now run by Wetherspoon, it has various seating areas set around a central bar and kitchen. Popular at most times of day, it offers a choice of 12 ever-changing beers on handpump. Regular beer festivals add to the range. The patio area to the side includes a heated smoking area.
QP

Dove Street Inn L

76 St Helen's Street, IP4 2LA
12-midnight (10.30 Sun) (01473) 211270
dovestreetinn.co.uk
Adnams Broadside; Crouch Vale Brewers Gold; Fuller's London Pride; Greene King Abbot H**; changing beers (often Dove Street)** H/G
Popular multi-roomed pub with a large selection of real ales including milds, plus ciders and continental beers. Some ales are from the adjacent brewery, and there is a brew shop next door. Home-cooked food and bar snacks are served at all times. A large covered and heated seating area outside is available for events and private hire. Well-behaved dogs and children are welcome. Three beer festivals are held annually. There are letting rooms above the brewery. Last admission is 10.45pm. (5,66,75)

Fat Cat

288 Spring Road, IP4 5NL
12-11 (midnight Fri & Sat) (01473) 726524
fatcatipswich.co.uk
Adnams Southwold Bitter H**; Crouch Vale Brewers Gold; Fuller's London Pride; Woodforde's Wherry; changing beers** G
Enamel signs, posters and brewery artefacts adorn the walls in this cosy drinking pub, with no background music or games machines. Up to 16 gravity beers are dispensed from the taproom behind the bar, and one or two ciders. The secluded garden and patio provide extra space on sunny afternoons, and barbecues feature occasionally. Meals and snacks are available at lunchtimes, and in the evenings customers are welcome to order in takeaways (not Fri or Sat eve). No children, but well-behaved dogs are allowed. Many local CAMRA Pub of the Year awards.
Q

Mulberry Tree
5 Woodbridge Road, IP4 2EA
🕒 12-11 (1am Fri & Sat) ☎ (01473) 225776
Adnams Southwold Bitter Ⓗ**; changing beers (often Green Jack, Nethergate)** Ⓗ/Ⓖ
This large, imposing pub was bought in 2012 by the current owner and refurbished as a free house after many years of neglect. It now has a large open fire in the main bar, a new kitchen and outdoor seating providing alfresco dining and drinking. Beers are served in oversized glasses. Live music features regularly on Friday and Saturday evenings, with excellent folk sessions on Sunday evenings. Dogs and children are welcome. Local CAMRA Cider Pub of the Year 2013 and 2014.
❀♿●P🚏🚌(11,66)🐾📶

St Jude's Brewery Tavern 🄻
69 St Matthew's Street, IP1 1EW
🕒 4-11; 12-midnight Thu-Sat; 4-10.30 Sun
☎ (01473) 413334 🌐 stjudestavern.com
Changing beers Ⓖ
Small, friendly, Gothic-themed bar close to the town centre with sawdust on the floor and quirky artefacts. Formerly a photographic studio, it opened in 2011 as a tribute to 19th-century back-street beer houses. It is the only pub owned by the former St Jude's Brewery (to be resurrected summer 2015). Up to 20 changing beers and four ciders are served from a gravity stillage alongside five imported lagers. Snacks are served. Live acoustic music plays occasionally and sport is screened on TV. Themed nights include Gothic fancy dress, Halloween and pirate nights.
◐♿♣●🚌🐾

Thomas Wolsey
9-13 St Peters Street, IP1 1XF (300yds from bus station)
🕒 4.30-11 (midnight Fri & Sat); closed Sun
☎ (01473) 210055
Adnams Ghost Ship; Crouch Vale Brewers Gold; Woodforde's Wherry; 1 changing beer Ⓗ
Large single-room lounge bar set in a historic Grade II-listed building. It has a patio area to the side and two nicely furnished function rooms upstairs, used for a wide variety of events including story-telling nights, charity quizzes and meetings. Jazz and R&B feature twice a month on Thursday evenings. Over 40 quality wines are stocked (20 sold by the glass). Games are available including darts. Home supporters only on football match days.
❀≢♣🚌📶

Ixworth

Greyhound
49 High Street, IP31 2HJ
🕒 11.30-2.30, 6 (5 Fri & Sat)-11; 12-3, 7-11 Sun
☎ (01359) 230887
Greene King XX Mild, IPA, Abbot; 2 changing beers (sourced nationally) Ⓗ
Situated on the town's pretty high street, this traditional inn has three bars, one a lovely central snug, and families are welcome. The heart of the building dates back to Tudor times. The pub is a rare outlet for XX Mild. Good-value lunches and early evening meals are served in the restaurant. Dominoes, crib, darts and pool are played in leagues and for charity fundraising.
Q🐴❀◐◑⛺♣P🚌🐾

Laxfield

Royal Oak
High Street, IP13 8DH
🕒 10.30-11.30; 10.30-10.30 Sun ☎ (01986) 798666
Adnams Southwold Bitter, Broadside; Earl Soham Victoria Bitter; Wooforde's Wherry; 2 changing beers Ⓗ
A large, prominent multi-roomed pub close to the church and the magnificent medieval Guildhall (now used as a museum) in this pretty village. Food is served lunchtimes and evenings. It has a small patio seating area to front. Games include pool and cards. The main part of the building dates from the 16th century, with many extensions and alterations subsequently. Occasional live music.
🐴❀◐◑♣P🚌(482,483)📶

Long Melford

Crown Inn
Hall Street, CO10 9JL
🕒 11.30-11; 12-10.30 Sun ☎ (01787) 377666
🌐 thecrownhotelmelford.co.uk
Adnams Southwold Bitter, Ghost Ship; Greene King IPA; 2 changing beers (often Wolf) Ⓗ
Set in the antiques centre of Long Melford, this is a popular family-run free house and cosy hotel. Three regular ales and one changing guest, together with real cider, are on handpump. A high-quality home-cooked menu is served in the large bar or separate restaurant. There is a large attractive patio garden for summer dining and drinking. Twelve comfortable bedrooms are available for those wishing to stay and explore this picturesque area. Q❀🛏◐◑♿●P🚌🐾

Lowestoft

Norman Warrior 🄻
Fir Lane, NR32 2RB
🕒 11-11.30 (12.30am Fri & Sat); 12-11.30 Sun
☎ (01502) 561982 🌐 thenormanwarrior.co.uk
Greene King IPA; Morland Old Speckled Hen; Sharp's Doom Bar; house beer (by Tetley); 1 changing beer (sourced locally; often Green Jack, Lacons, Wolf) Ⓗ
Popular twin-bar local with ample parking, close to the bus stop and a 20-minute walk from Oulton Broad North railway station. It comprises a public bar where pool and darts are played and a comfortable lounge leading to a spacious restaurant serving home-cooked food daily. Outside there is a garden and terrace where a well-attended beer festival is held over the August bank holiday weekend. The guest ale is locally sourced.
🐴❀◐◑♿♣P🚌(102)🐾📶

Stanford Arms 🄻
Stanford Street, NR32 2DD
🕒 4-midnight (10 Mon); 3-1am Fri; 12-1am Sat; 12-midnight Sun ☎ (01502) 587444 🌐 stanfordarms.co.uk
12 changing beers (sourced locally; often Golden Triangle, Grain, Wolf) Ⓗ
This quality free house is a short walk from Lowestoft train and bus stations. The spacious open-plan bar has a large array of handpumps serving mainly local beers. To the rear is a large courtyard garden with its own wood-fired pizza oven (Friday is pizza night). A dish of the day is available late Saturday afternoon. Quiz and food nights are held on Wednesday evenings. A fine collection of trays adorns the walls. Live music features on Sunday afternoons. 🐴❀≢♣●🚌🐾📶

Triangle Tavern [L]

29 St Peters Street, NR32 1QA

11-11 (midnight Thu; 1am Fri & Sat); 12-10.30 Sun
☎ (01502) 582711 green-jack.com

Green Jack Golden Best, Orange Wheat Beer, Trawlerboys Best Bitter, Lurcher Stout, Gone Fishing ESB [H], Ripper Tripel; 2 changing beers (sourced locally; often Crouch Vale, Oakham) [G]

This lively town tavern serves as the Green Jack brewery tap. The characterful front bar is decorated with many brewery and pub awards and is home to live music every Friday evening. A corridor leads to an open-plan back bar with pool table and jukebox. Alongside the full range of Green Jack beers are guest ales, real ciders and continental beers. Quarterly beer festivals are held. Customers are welcome to bring in their own food.
≥♣●🚌🐾

Lowestoft: Pakefield

Oddfellows [L]

6 Nightingale Road, NR33 7AU

11-11; 12-10.30 Sun ☎ (01502) 538415

Adnams Southwold Bitter; Woodforde's Wherry; house beer (by Green Jack); 2 changing beers (sourced locally; often Green Jack, Wolf) [H]

Situated close to the cliff top, the pub is popular with local drinkers, holidaymakers and walkers on the heritage coastal path. The pub comprises three open-plan areas including one for diners and has wooden flooring and panelling throughout. Sporting events are shown on TV screens. Up to five ales are available from local breweries. In summer, a popular beer festival is hosted on the green opposite the pub, and in January a small winter festival is held with the Old Glory Molly dancers performing. ❀()♿🚌🐾

Market Weston

Mill

Bury Road, IP22 2PD

11-3 (not Mon), 5-11; 12-3, 7-11 Sun ☎ (01359) 221018

Adnams Southwold Bitter; Greene King IPA; Old Chimneys Military Mild; 3 changing beers (sourced nationally; often Harveys, Old Chimneys, Wychwood) [H]

Striking white brick and flint-faced inn standing at a crossroads. It is the closest outlet to the Old Chimneys Brewery, located on the other side of the village. The landlady celebrated 20 years at the Mill in 2015. The pub offers an excellent choice of beers, always including a selection from Old Chimneys, complemented by a good menu of home-cooked meals. Q❀()♿♣P🚌(338)🐾

Naughton

Wheelhouse

Whatfield Road, IP7 7BS (450yds off B1078 close to former airbase)

closed Tue; 5-11 (9 Mon); 6-11 Sat; 12-10.30 Sun
☎ (01449) 740496 thewheelhouseatnaughton.co.uk

3 changing beers [H]

A picturesque thatched pub with a low ceiling. The building is reputed to have been an inn since the 12th century and many ancient timbers are in evidence. The main bar is warmed by a traditional open fire and the more spacious public bar has a pool table. A varied and changing selection of ales makes this pub always well worth a visit. The garden to the rear is a pleasant place to relax on sunny days. The bus stop is on the main road.
Q❀♿♣P🚌(111)🐾

Needham Market

Rampant Horse

Coddenham Road, IP6 8AU

12-3, 5-11; 12-11 Sat & Sun ☎ (01449) 722044
therampanthorse.co.uk

Calvors Lodestar Festival Ale, Smooth Hoperator; Woodforde's Wherry [H]

Calvors Brewery purchased and reopened this pub in 2012, selling a wide range of locally sourced food and drink including its own high-quality lagers and, more recently, real ale. Beer festivals feature occasionally and live music is hosted. The pub is close to the railway station which was built in an area previously known as 'camping land', the local pitch for an ancient ball game called Campball – a precursor to football dating back to at least the 17th century. ❀()≥♣P🚌(87,88)🐾

Newbourne

Fox Inn

The Street, IP12 4NY

11-11; 12-10.30 Sun ☎ (01473) 736307
debeninns.co.uk/fox

Adnams Southwold Bitter; 3 changing beers [H]

Picturesque timber-framed, two-bar village local with a large garden, popular with ramblers and cyclists. A wide range of local food is home cooked and served every day, with an à la carte menu, gluten-free options and daily specials. The garden has a large pond and a shed housing an old skittle alley – the only one currently active in Suffolk.
Q❀()♿▲♣P🚌(179)🐾

Newmarket

Golden Lion

44 High Street, CB8 8LB

8am-11 ☎ (01638) 672040

Adnams Ghost Ship; Greene King Abbot; Ruddles Best Bitter; 4 changing beers [H]

This venue is one of Wetherspoon's finest – a large, bustling, 18th-century town pub, situated on the main High Street. Up to seven real ales are available at any one time, including up to four guests, and served by knowledgeable and efficient staff. Real cider is also available. The pub's name is thought to have originated from King Henry I – it is also known as the Lion of Justice. Children are welcome until 9pm in the family area. The pub is popular with the local horse racing community.
❀()♿≥●P🚌🐾

Ousden

Fox

Front Street, CB8 8TR

11-11; 12-5 Sun ☎ (01638) 500740
theousdenfox.co.uk

Greene King IPA; Woodforde's Wherry; 2 changing beers (sourced regionally) [H]

Three distinct areas – public bar with a piano, dining space and seating area with comfy sofas – are all warmed by logburners in winter. Four real ales are available with plans for more, and a changing menu of quality seasonal Anglo-French food is served. Local produce for sale includes

home-made cider. A monthly quiz and car rallies are hosted here. If you wish to camp there is space but no facilities. All the clocks show different times for historic reasons – just ask!
Q🐴❀◖◗♿♣🍎P🚌(312,310)🐾📶

Rattlesden

Five Bells

High Street, IP30 0RA
⌚ 12-midnight (11 Sun) ☎ (01449) 737373
3 changing beers [H]
Set on the high road through a picturesque village, here is a good old Suffolk drinking house – few of its kind still survive. Three well-chosen ales on the bar are usually sourced direct from the breweries. The cosy single-room interior has a games area on a lower level and there is occasional live music. Pub games include shut-the-box and shove-ha'penny plus pétanque in the garden in summer. A motorcycle show is hosted in May. Q❀♣🚌🐾

Risby

Crown & Castle

South Street, IP28 6QU
⌚ 12-3, 5 (6.30 Sat)-11; 12-3, 7-10.30 Sun
☎ (01284) 810393
Adnams Southwold Bitter; 2 changing beers (sourced nationally) [H]
This attractive flint-faced building opened as a pub and shop in the late 1800s and was sold by Greene King in 2014. A 120ft deep unrecorded well was discovered during alterations in recent times and is now a feature beneath a grille in the entrance lobby. The pub has classic back and front bars, with food served in both. The back bar is the public, with games and conversation dominating – well-behaved dogs are allowed in here.
Q🐴❀◖◗♣P🚌🐾

Rumburgh

Buck [L]

Mill Road, IP19 0NT
⌚ 11.45-3, 6.30-11; 12-3, 7-10.30 Sun ☎ (01986) 785257
Adnams Southwold Bitter; 4 changing beers (sourced locally; often Green Jack, Lacons, Mauldons) [H]
Full of character and charm, this splendid pub was originally a guest house for a medieval priory. It has a long, narrow front bar with a games room extension. The original bar is timber framed with a flagstone floor. The back rooms are used for dining, offering good food made with local ingredients. Quiz nights and music events are held regularly and the pub is home to both the Old Glory Molly and Rumburgh morris dancers.
Q🐴❀◖◗⛺♣🍎P🐾📶

Shadingfield

Fox [L]

London Road, NR34 8DD
⌚ closed Mon; 12-3, 6-11; 12-11.30 Fri-Sun
☎ (01502) 575100 🌐 shadingfieldfox.co.uk
Young's London Gold; 6 changing beers (sourced locally; often Green Jack, Lacons, Wolf) [H]
Situated in a tiny village on the edge of Sotterley Park, this inn dates back to the 16th century. The original arched doors and carved fox heads have been retained. The interior comprises a bar with comfortable seating leading to a conservatory and a separate restaurant area. Outside, a patio and small garden are popular in the summer months. Beer festivals are held twice yearly – one over the Father's Day weekend and the other close to Halloween. Live music features every Friday evening. Q🐴❀◖◗♿P🚌(89)🐾📶

Shottisham

Sorrel Horse

Hollesley Road, IP12 3HD
⌚ 12-3, 6-11 (5-midnight Fri); 12-midnight Sat; 10-10.30 Sun
☎ (01394) 411617 🌐 thesorrelhorse-shottisham.co.uk
Adnams Ghost Ship; Earl Soham Victoria Bitter; Woodforde's Wherry; 3 changing beers [G]
A former smugglers' inn dating back to the 15th century, this picturesque thatched two-bar pub retains a gravity stillage for beers. Local villagers helped raise funds to keep the pub open by buying shares in it a few years ago. Acoustic music nights are held monthly and a quiz on Wednesday evenings. The food menu includes various locally sourced dishes prepared on the premises. Special themed evenings often feature and breakfast is served Sundays 9-11am. The main bar has a bar billiards table. Seats in the garden are popular on sunny days. Q🐴❀◖◗♿⛺♣P🚌🐾📶

Southwold

Lord Nelson [L]

42 East Street, IP18 6EJ
⌚ 10.30-11; 12-10.30 Sun ☎ (01502) 722079
🌐 thelordnelsonsouthwold.co.uk
Adnams Lighthouse, Southwold Bitter, Explorer, Ghost Ship, Broadside; 1 changing beer (sourced locally; often Adnams) [H]
There is no shortage of pubs selling Adnams in Southwold and they all have their merits, but the Lord Nelson is a special place in which to drink the full range of Adnams ales, including their seasonal beers. A stone's throw from the sea and Southwold Sailors' Reading Room museum, it is always busy and lively. The central bar has a flagstone floor and open fireplace and is decorated with naval and seafaring memorabilia. Children are welcome in a side room and there is a heated patio area to the rear. 🐴❀◖◗♿⛺🚌🐾

Stowmarket

King's Arms

Station Road, IP14 1RQ
⌚ 11-11; 10.30-11 Sun ☎ 07852 497412
Woodforde's Wherry; 4 changing beers (often Adnams) [H]
Multi-roomed hostelry, just a short walk from the historic railway station and town centre. Pub games are popular, and occasional live music and barbecues are hosted. Food is available until 4pm including snacks, stews, hotpots, chilli and omelettes. The patio to the rear leads to a smoking room and various other spaces used for live music and private parties. There is a children's play area and dogs are welcome when the pub is not busy. Two or three beer festivals are held each year. Cider is also available, usually Old Rosie.
❀◖⇄♣🍎P📺🚌🐾

Royal William

53 Union Street East, IP14 1HP
⌚ 11 (12 Sun)-11 ☎ (01449) 674553

Greene King IPA; Woodforde's Wherry; changing beers Ⓖ
Tucked away down a narrow side street, just a short walk from the town centre, this is a real gem. An end-of-terrace back-street bar, it is well supported by locals and visitors alike. All ales are served by gravity dispense from the cellar behind the bar, with up to eight guest beers. Sport is shown on TV in the bar. There is a games room, home to regular dominoes, darts and crib matches, and a smoking area in the enclosed garden. Traditional music features once a month. Various home-made bar snacks are offered.
🐎❀♿⇌♣●🚌(87,88)🐾📶

Stratford St Mary

Swan
Lower Street, CO7 6JR
⏲ closed Mon & Tue; 11-11; 11-10.30 Sun
☎ (01206) 321244 🌐 stratfordswan.com
3 changing beers Ⓗ
The building is part of a historic former coaching inn dating from about 1520. The original medieval inn was at least three times larger than the remaining structure and included a second wing located on the far side of the car park, since destroyed by fire. The pub has a small, friendly bar retaining many historic features, several other wood-panelled rooms mainly used for dining, and a spacious garden. A free house, it offers a choice of ales as well as a wide range of bottled beers. An on-site brewery was installed spring 2015.
🐎❀◐◑♣●P

Sudbury

Brewery Tap Ⓛ
21-23 East Street, CO10 2TP (200yds from marketplace)
⏲ 11-11 (midnight Fri & Sat); 12-10.30 Sun
☎ (01787) 370876 🌐 blackaddertap.co.uk
Mauldons Moletrap Bitter, Silver Adder, Suffolk Pride Ⓗ**; 3 changing beers (often Mauldons)** Ⓖ
A mecca for real ale drinkers, the Mauldons brewery tap is a comfortable, friendly pub in the old traditional style. Soup, rolls, filled baps, occasional chillies, stews and locally made pies are available and takeaways can be ordered in. Events include a Sunday breakfast club, quiz nights, live music and beer festivals in April and October. The pub is home to golf, darts, crib and bar billiards clubs. A must for beer and pub lovers.
Q❀◐◑♿⇌♣●🥛🚌🐾

Waggon & Horses
Church Walk, Acton Square, CO10 1HJ
⏲ 11-11 (midnight Fri & Sat) ☎ (01787) 312147
🌐 thesudburywaggon.co.uk
Nethergate Growler Bitter; 3 changing beers (often Nethergate) Ⓗ
Following refurbishment by the Growler (now Nethergate) Brewery, the pub was passed on to new independent owners and is now once again a popular feature on the Sudbury pub scene. One regular and three changing guest beers complement the home-cooked high-quality food available. The interior comprises a long main bar with real fire, a small dining area and a snug with a glass floor looking down into the cellar. Beer festivals and live music are planned.
Q🐎❀◐◑♿⇌♣🚌(51,55,111)🐾

Sweffling

White Horse Ⓛ
Low Road, IP17 2BB
⏲ 7-11; closed Tue-Thu; 12-3 Sun ☎ (01728) 664178
🌐 swefflingwhitehorse.co.uk
3 changing beers Ⓖ
The current owners have refurbished this building in a green and environmentally friendly manner. A cosy, traditional two-room pub, it is now warmed by a woodburner and wood-fired range. Gravity-dispensed beers from local brewers are served through the taproom door. Fair-trade, organic and locally produced bottled beers are also available. Hot and cold bar snacks are sold. Various pub games including bar billiards, darts, crib and board games are played, and live music features twice a month. Local CAMRA branch Pub of the Year 2015.
🐎❀🛏⛺♣●P🐾📶

Thorndon

Black Horse
The Street, IP23 7JR
⏲ 12-3, 5 (6 Sat)-11; 12-9 Sun ☎ (01379) 678523
🌐 theblackhorsethorndon.co.uk
Adnams Southwold Bitter; Shortts Farm Strummer; 2 changing beers (sourced regionally; often Grain, Nethergate) Ⓗ
A traditional country pub located in the heart of a pretty village. Dating back to the 1600s and full of character, it has many historic photos of the village on display. The central bar has a log fire and two adjoining restaurant areas. Two guest ales are usually on offer, typically local and often from Brandon, Grain or Woodforde's breweries. At lunchtime there is a carvery, and evening meals are served daily. Dogs on leads are welcome in the main bar area. 🐎❀◐◑♿P🚌(114)🐾📶

Thurston

Fox & Hounds
Barton Road, IP31 3QT
⏲ 12-2.30, 5-11; 12-midnight Fri & Sat; 12-10.30 Sun
☎ (01359) 232228 🌐 thurstonfoxandhounds.co.uk
Adnams Southwold Bitter; Greene King IPA; 4 changing beers (sourced nationally) Ⓗ
A listed building, this popular village local sits in the middle of the village a short walk from the railway station. The restaurant, serving good home-cooked food, is within the public bar area but separated by uplights from an original wall. There is a separate bar for pool and darts. On bank holidays and special occasions live music is performed. Regular quiz nights and bingo also feature. A conker competition is held in the autumn. B&B accommodation is available.
❀🛏◐◑⛺⇌P🚌🐾📶

Walberswick

Anchor Ⓛ
The Street, IP18 6UA
⏲ 11-4, 6-11; 11-11 Sat; 12-11 Sun ☎ (01502) 722112
🌐 anchoratwalberswick.com
Adnams Southwold Bitter, Ghost Ship, Broadside Ⓗ
Rebuilt in the 1920s, this hotel is a classic example of Brewers' Tudor. Situated in a picturesque coastal village accessible from Southwold via footbridge or ferry, it has two cosy alcove areas heated by a real fire on both sides. There is a side room for families

and a spacious restaurant committed to serving seasonal local produce. Accommodation is available in the main building or in chalets in the large garden. Walkers and dogs welcome.
Q🐎❀🛏◐◑♿ΛP🐾

Walton

Half Moon

303 High Street, IP11 9QL
⌚ 12-3 (not Mon), 5-11; 12-11 Sat; 12-3, 7-11 Sun
☎ (01394) 285586
Adnams Lighthouse, Southwold Bitter, Broadside; 2 changing beers (often Adnams) Ⓗ
An excellent traditional, two-bar local community pub with wood panelling and an open fire in the public bar in winter. A meeting place for local groups of all kinds, it has quiz nights, darts matches and a selection of books for customers to read. There are no gaming machines or music. The secure garden has a new children's play area which has proved popular with families. Food is available lunchtimes only. Monthly folk nights are hosted as well as other live music on occasion.
🐎❀◐♿♣P🚌(75,76,77)🐾📶

Wenhaston

Star Inn 𝕃

Hall Road, IP19 9HF
⌚ 12-3, 6-11; 12-11 Sun ☎ (01502) 478240
🌐 wenhastonstar.co.uk
Adnams Southwold Bitter; 3 changing beers (sourced locally; often Green Jack, Humpty Dumpty, Wolf) Ⓗ
This free house is situated on the outskirts of the village with fine views of the Blyth Valley. The interior comprises three small public rooms overlooking a large lawn and garden. The front bar is characterful with old enamel advertising signs plus open fires in winter. Good food is all home cooked using local produce where possible. The pub is popular with walkers and cyclists, accessible by bus and has a large car park to the rear. A beer festival is held over the August bank holiday.
Q🐎❀◐◑♣P🚌(62,88A)🐾

Wingfield

De La Pole Arms

Church Road, IP21 5RA (follow brown tourist signs to Wingfield Barns)
⌚ 12-3, 5-11; 12-11 Sat; 12-10.30 Sun ☎ (01379) 384545
Adnams Southwold Bitter; 2 changing beers (sourced locally; often Black Sheep, Woodforde's) Ⓗ
Traditional village pub in a lovely setting opposite the church where Elizabeth of York is buried. Wingfield College stands next to the church, with Wingfield Barns arts centre alongside. Extensively and lovingly restored in the mid-1990s, the pub is full of character, with oak beams and log fires in the bars. Dogs are welcome in the public bar and food is served in both saloon bar and the restaurant area with its vaulted ceiling.
Q🐎❀◐◑♿♣P📶

Woodbridge

Angel

2 Theatre Street, IP12 4NE
⌚ 12-3, 5-11 (midnight Fri); 12-midnight Sat; 12-10.30 Sun
☎ (01394) 383808 🌐 theangelwoodbridge.co.uk
Adnams Southwold Bitter; 5 changing beers Ⓗ
Five changing beers and over 250 different gins are stocked at this popular and lively 16th-century inn, just off the market square. One bar is used for dining or occasional private hire (by arrangement), serving up home-made food and themed food evenings. Bar areas are furnished in a homely style with additional outside covered seating areas. Live music features regularly and open mic nights twice a month. 🐎❀◐◑≋♣P🐾📶

Cherry Tree

73 Cumberland Street, IP12 4AG
⌚ 10.30-11 ☎ (01394) 384627 🌐 thecherrytreepub.co.uk
Adnams Southwold Bitter, Ghost Ship, Broadside; Elgood Black Dog; 5 changing beers (often Adnams) Ⓗ
Spacious lounge bar/diner with a large central counter and several distinct seating areas. Eight beers are usually on tap and an annual summer beer festival is hosted. Food is served all day, all locally sourced and home cooked, including some gluten-free options. Board games and cards are available to play and a quiz is held on Thursdays. The large recently refurbished garden has children's play equipment. Accommodation is offered in a converted barn. Wheelchair-, child- and dog-friendly. Breakfast is available 8-11am on Sundays. 🐎❀🛏◐◑≋♣P🐾📶

Old Mariner

26 New Street, IP12 1DX
⌚ 11-11; 12-10.30 Sun ☎ (01394) 382679
🌐 theoldmariner.co.uk
Fuller's London Pride; Woodforde's Wherry; Young's Bitter; 2 changing beers Ⓗ
Traditional two-roomed bar serving food (often gluten-free) including tapas, sandwiches and a popular Sunday roast. The front bar with scrubbed tables and a low ceiling is lively, while the rear bar is usually quieter and leads to a separate seating area, garden with smoking area and car park (off Castle Street). The back room can be booked for private parties. A quiz features every other week, story-telling every other month and there is regular live music. 🐎❀◐◑≋♣P🚌🐾📶

Olde Bell & Steelyard

103 New Street, IP12 1DZ
⌚ 12-3, 6-11.30 (12.30am Fri & Sat); 12-3, 7-11 Sun
☎ (01394) 382933 🌐 yeoldebellandsteelyard.co.uk
Greene King IPA, Abbot; 3 changing beers (often Greene King) Ⓗ
Large multi-roomed pub with oak beams in two bars and a separate function room. The steelyard – a former cart weighbridge that dates from 1650 and still works – was on show at the Great Exhibition in 1851. Traditional games include bar billiards, chess and bar skittles. Live rugby is shown on TVs in the side-bar area. Good home-cooked food is served. To the rear of the building is a large heated and covered patio area and disabled access.
🐎❀◐◑♿≋♣🚌🐾📶

> Give my people plenty of beer, good beer and cheap beer, and you will have no revolution among them. **Queen Victoria**

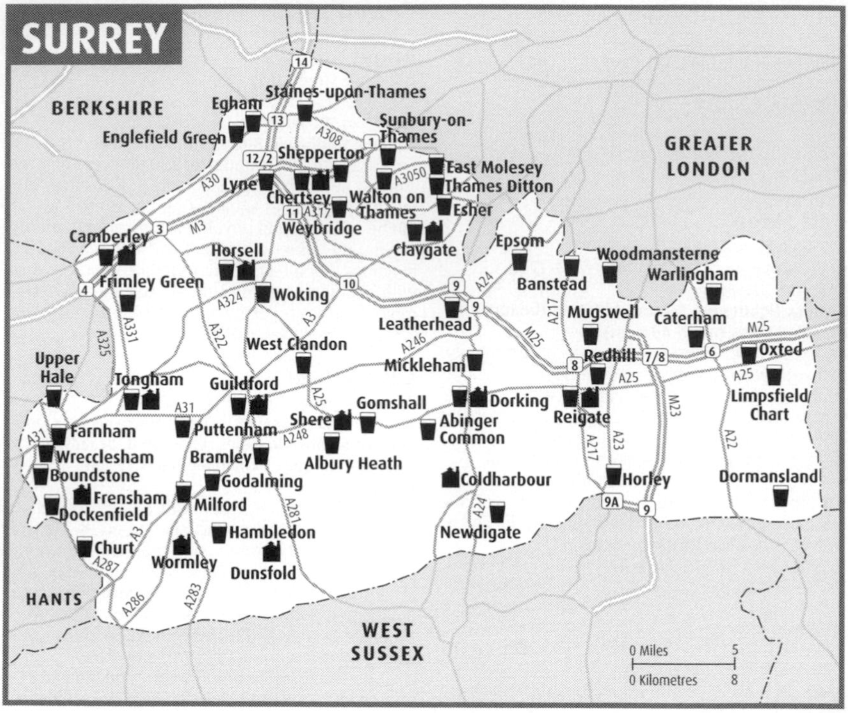

Abinger Common

Abinger Hatch [L]

Abinger Lane, RH5 6HZ (off A25) TQ115459
⏲ 11-11.30; 12-10.30 Sun ☎ (01306) 730737
🌐 theabingerhatch.com
Ringwood Best Bitter; 3 changing beers [H]
The interior of this attractive 17th-century inn, situated opposite a church in the lovely Surrey Hills, rambles over three levels. The lowest part has large flagstones on the floor, with the other areas having bare boards. There are four or five beers served from the beautiful English oak bar, mainly from regional brewers, usually including Ringwood, and often a local ale, usually Tillingbourne. Excellent food, served all day, is a feature, with a varied menu on offer. Outside are large gardens. Q⛭❀◐◑P🚌(22)🐾📶

Albury Heath

William IV [L]

Little London, GU5 9DG TQ065467
⏲ 11-3, 5.30-11; 11-11 Sat; 12-11 Sun ☎ (01483) 202685
🌐 williamivalbury.com
Surrey Hills Ranmore, Shere Drop; Young's Bitter; 1 changing beer [H]
Set on a quiet lane adjoining extensive woodland and popular with walkers, this old-fashioned part-16th-century building features beams, flagstones and a large fireplace where a welcoming wood fire burns brightly in winter. There are two traditional bars and a dining room where excellent home-made meals are served (no food Sun eve). Dishes include Gloucester Old Spot pork from the pigs kept in the field behind the pub. Shove-ha'penny can be played. Q❀◐◑♣P🐾

Banstead

Woolpack

186 High Street, SM7 2NZ
⏲ 11-11; 12-10.30 Sun ☎ (01737) 354560
🌐 thewoolpackbanstead.co.uk
Shepherd Neame Master Brew, Spitfire, Bishops Finger; 2 changing beers [H]
A brick and tile building with a front patio and lawned rear garden. Although a Shepherd Neame pub it offers two true guest beers which almost always come from smaller breweries in the South-East. There is an annual beer festival over the August bank holiday. Good food, using local ingredients whenever possible, is served all day (no food Sun eve), and children are welcome when dining. A jazz afternoon is held on the first Tuesday of the month. ❀◐◑♿P🚌🐾📶

Boundstone

Bat & Ball [L]

15 Bat & Ball Lane, Upper Bourne Lane, GU10 4SA (off Sandrock Hill Rd) SU833444
⏲ 11-11; 12-10.30 Sun ☎ (01252) 792108
🌐 thebatandball.co.uk
Bowman Swift One; Hogs Back TEA; 4 changing beers [H]
Popular family-owned free house offering six interesting beers, mainly from adjoining counties, alongside excellent reasonably priced food. The beer range is clearly displayed with strengths and prices. A family-friendly front room complements the beamed, panelled and log-fired bar which is a cosy inner sanctum for adults. The garden, with children's playground, hosts an annual beer festival. Quiz night is Tuesday and the last Thursday in the month is open mic night, with other live music occasionally. Q⛭❀◐◑♿P🚌(16,17)🐾📶

Bramley

Jolly Farmer

High Street, GU5 0HB

✪ 11 (12 Sun)-11 ☎ (01483) 893355 ⊕ jollyfarmer.co.uk

Bowman Swift One; Young's Bitter; 5 changing beers (sourced nationally; often Cottage, Hammerpot, Long Man) Ⓗ

Privately owned traditional free house in the village centre, with oak beams and a quirky decor adding to the cosy, welcoming atmosphere. High-quality food is served with a children's menu and a popular Sunday lunchtime carvery (booking essential). The changing beers are sourced from a rota of 12 small breweries, several in Sussex, with a dark beer usually among them. Cider is available during the summer months only. Dogs are welcome in the bar but not the restaurant. ⑤⊕🛏️◑♣️🐾P🖥️🐾🛜

Camberley

Claude du Vall Ⓛ

77-81 High Street, GU15 3RB

✪ 8am-midnight (1am Fri & Sat) ☎ (01276) 672910

Greene King Abbot; Ruddles Best Bitter; 4 changing beers Ⓗ

A large, modern Wetherspoon pub strategically placed at the station (and bus stops) end of the High Street. The competitive prices of both food and drinks make this a popular pub at any time of day, with breakfast from 8am. The seating space is imaginatively divided into various large and small areas, some with lounge furniture. The TVs are muted, and generally show news programmes. ⊕◑&≠♠️🖥️🛜

Caterham

King & Queen Ⓛ

34 High Street, CR3 5UA (on B2030)

✪ 11-11 (midnight Fri & Sat); 12-11 Sun ☎ (01883) 345438
⊕ kingandqueencaterham.co.uk

Fuller's Chiswick Bitter, London Pride, ESB; 2 changing beers Ⓗ

This 400-year-old building was one of Caterham's original alehouses. It evolved in the 1840s from three cottages, one a bakery, and still retains three distinct areas. The front bar has the character of a public bar, in the middle is a beamed room with an inglenook fireplace, then there is a lower-level bar which leads to a covered patio. Portraits of King William and Queen Mary, after whom the pub is named, adorn the walls. ⑤⊕◑♣️P🖥️🐾🛜

Chertsey

Thyme at the Tavern Ⓛ

20 London Street, KT16 8AA (jct of London St and Heriot Rd)

✪ 12 (5 Mon)-midnight; 12-1am Fri & Sat ☎ (01932) 429667
⊕ thymeatthetavern.co.uk

Courage Best Bitter; 5 changing beers (sourced locally; often Ascot, Binghams, Thurstons) Ⓗ

This genuine free house was local CAMRA Pub of the Year in 2014. Alongside the regular cask beers, five guests – three or more from local microbreweries – are available. Occasional beer festivals are held. The pub is heavily involved in local charity fundraising. Live music is a regular feature on Friday evenings. Diners have to fit in with drinkers – it can be a squeeze for the well-

regarded Sunday lunches. Outside is a comfortable smokers' refuge in a marquee. ⑤⊕🛏️◑&≠♣️🖥️🐾🛜

Churt

Crossways Inn Ⓛ

Churt Road, GU10 2JS

✪ 11-3, 5-11; 11-11 Fri & Sat; 12-4, 7-10.30 Sun
☎ (01428) 714323 ⊕ weydonian.net/crossways

Arundel Sussex IPA; Courage Best Bitter; Hop Back Crop Circle Ⓗ**; 4 changing beers** Ⓖ

A friendly, welcoming community hostelry with traditional decor and furniture. The current beers are displayed on a blackboard – guest ales are dispensed direct from the cask in the cellar. Good-value, home-made, locally sourced pub food is served at lunchtimes (no food Sun). Wednesday is fish and chips night. The pub has a lovely village-local ambience and is popular with ramblers and cyclists. ⑤⊕◑▲♣️🖥️P🖥️(19)🐾

Claygate

Hare & Hounds

The Green, KT10 0JL

✪ 11-11 ☎ (01372) 465149
⊕ thehareandhounds-claygate.co.uk

6 changing beers (sourced nationally; often Brightwater, Butcombe, St Austell) Ⓗ

At the heart of the community, the pub supports many local sports clubs including rugby, football and cricket. It boasts a regularly changing range of beers from local, regional and larger breweries around the country, including some from the village brewery. Both English and French cuisine is on offer using ingredients from local and sustainable suppliers where possible. A real log fire, terrace and child-friendly garden area add to the pub's appeal. ⑤⊕◑&≠P🖥️(K3)🐾🛜

Dockenfield

Bluebell Ⓛ

Batts Corner, GU10 4EX (½ mile N of village) SU820410

✪ 12-3, 5.30-11; 12-11 Fri & Sat; 12-7 Sun
☎ (01252) 792801 ⊕ bluebell-dockenfield.com

Frensham Rambler; Hogs Back TEA; Triple fff Moondance; 1 changing beer Ⓗ

This rural pub with a cosy fireplace and four real ales is the perfect place after a walk in Alice Holt forest. A good range of food is available from bar snacks to an à la carte menu. Outside is ample parking and a garden with a children's play area for the warmer weather. ⑤⊕◑&▲♣️🐾🐾🛜

REAL ALE BREWERIES

Abbey Ford Chertsey
Ascot Camberley
Brightwater Claygate
Crafty Brewing Dunsfold (NEW)
Dorking Dorking
Frensham Frensham
Hogs Back Tongham
Hoptimists Wormley
Leith Hill Coldharbour
Little Beer Guildford
Pilgrim Reigate
Surrey Hills Dorking
Thurstons Horsell
Tillingbourne Shere

Dorking

Cobbett's Real Ales Ⓛ

23 West Street, RH4 1BY (on A25 one-way system eastbound)
⏲ 12 (10 Fri & Sat)-8; 12-6 Sun ☎ (01306) 879877
🌐 cobbettsrealales.com
3 changing beers Ⓖ
This excellent off-licence and micropub is a must-visit when in the area. The pub is situated in a tiny back room and even has a garden. Two cask beers are usually available at the beginning of the week, with five at weekends including at least one hop-monster on Fridays. Two draught ciders are available plus, in summer, perry. A large number of interesting bottled beers and ciders are also stocked. A 10 per cent discount is offered on Tuesdays. Q🎠❀≋(West)🍎🚌🐾📶

Cricketers Ⓛ

81 South Street, RH4 2JU (on A25 one-way system westbound)
⏲ 12-11 (midnight Thu & Sat; 12.30am Fri)
☎ (01306) 889938 🌐 cricketersdorking.co.uk
Fuller's Chiswick Bitter, London Pride, ESB; 1 changing beer Ⓗ
Small bare-brick pub with a good mix of customers. The walls in the single L-shaped room are covered with old photographs and adverts. Rugby is popular and when England are playing it is standing-room only with customers watching the terrestrial TV. Out back there is a walled Georgian garden – this is the scene of the pub's May bank holiday and autumn beer festivals. Basic lunches are available weekdays. 🎠❀◐♣🚌📶

Red Bar & Lounge Ⓛ

45 Dene Street, RH4 2DW (off A25 opp post office)
⏲ 12-11 (midnight Fri & Sat); 12-10.30 Sun
☎ (01306) 882222
Surrey Hills Ranmore, Shere Drop; 2 changing beers Ⓗ
This smart and comfortable bar, just off the High Street, attracts a good variety of customers. Excellent food is available (no food Sun eve). A comedy night is hosted on the last Wednesday of alternate months (for which a charge is made) and there are music nights two or three times a month, mainly Saturdays. The guest beers are usually from local microbreweries, and the cider tends to be from one of the larger producers. The garden is closed in winter. 🎠❀◐◑🍎P🚌🐾📶

Dormansland

Old House at Home

63 West Street, RH7 6QP
⏲ 12-midnight (1am Fri & Sat) ☎ (01342) 836828
🌐 theoldhousedormansland.com
Shepherd Neame Master Brew Ⓖ**, Kent's Best, Spitfire; 1 changing beer** Ⓗ
A friendly old local hidden away on the west side of the village, but signposted from adjoining roads. The pub was originally a pair of Victorian cottages and is now essentially one bar room. Darts is played in a small room to the left. The upper part of the pub houses a restaurant serving home-cooked meals lunchtimes and evenings, with pizzas available at all times. Some beers are sold direct from casks behind the bar. There is music once a month. Q🎠❀◐◑♿♣P🚌🐾📶

East Molesey

Albion

34-36 Bridge Road, KT8 9HA (off B3379)
⏲ 11-midnight (11 Sun) ☎ (020) 979 1035
Brakspear Bitter; Fuller's London Pride; 4 changing beers Ⓗ
About 400 years old, this is a popular pub and can get busy at times. It has a central bar serving separate drinking and dining areas, with comfortable seating throughout, and a restaurant (booking advised for meals). There is also a seating area outside at the front. The pub is a short walk from Hampton Court Palace and the River Thames. The four changing beers are sourced from throughout the UK and constantly vary. Westons Old Rosie cider is sold.
🎠❀◐◑♿≋(Hampton Court)🍎🚌🐾📶

Bell Inn

4 Bell Road, KT8 0SS (off B369)
⏲ 12-11 (midnight Fri & Sat); 12-10.30 Sun
☎ (020) 8941 0400 🌐 bell-pub.co.uk
Courage Best Bitter, Directors; Fuller's London Pride; Sharp's Doom Bar; house beer (by Twickenham); 1 changing beer Ⓗ
This building dates from 1460 and was later East Molesey's first post office. The historic coaching inn is known locally as the Crooked House – it has many nooks and crannies, one of which houses the dartboard. The 18th-century highwayman Claude Duvalier hid from the Bow Street Runners here and now has a bar named after him. The large garden has a children's play area. Sport is shown on three TVs. 🎠❀◐◑♣P🚌(411,514)🐾📶

Prince of Wales Ⓛ

23 Bridge Road, KT8 9EU (off B369)
⏲ 11-11 (midnight Fri); 10-midnight Sat; 12-11 Sun
☎ (020) 8979 5561 🌐 princeofwaleskt8.co.uk
Greene King IPA; house beer (by Greene King); 3 changing beers Ⓗ
Bustling pub with a fair-sized central bar serving bright, modern drinking and dining areas, with a few comfortable armchairs in the window. The area to the rear is set out for dining, but the tables can be used by drinkers if not reserved. Outside is a front terrace and a pleasant rear courtyard and large garden next to the car park. The changing beers are generally sourced locally. Board games are available. Hampton Court and the River Thames are close by. 🎠❀◐◑♿≋(Hampton Court)P🚌🐾📶

Egham

United Services Club Ⓛ

111 Spring Rise, TW20 9PE (close to A30 Egham Hill)
⏲ 12-11 (midnight Fri & Sat) ☎ (01784) 435120
🌐 eusc.co.uk
Rebellion IPA; Surrey Hills Ranmore; 3 changing beers Ⓗ
A regular winner of CAMRA branch Club of the Year including in 2015. The ever-changing range of guest ales always includes something dark and a good choice of real ciders is served from the cellar. Three beer festivals a year attract visitors from far and wide to enjoy the eclectic range of ales, mostly from some of the newest micros around. Satellite TV and free Wi-Fi are available and live music is hosted on most Saturday evenings. Show a copy of this Guide or CAMRA membership card for entry.
❀♿≋♣🍎P🚉🚌(71,441)📶

Englefield Green

Beehive L

34 Middle Hill, TW20 0JQ (200yds N of A30 Egham Hill)
☼ 12-11 (midnight Fri & Sat); 12-10.30 Sun
☎ (01784) 431621 ⊕ beehiveegham.co.uk
Fuller's Chiswick Bitter, London Pride; Gale's HSB; 1 changing beer (sourced locally; often Fuller's) ⊞
This small pub dating from the 1870s is now open plan with a light and airy feel. It passed through the hands of a number of breweries including Ashby's before becoming an outlier of the Gale's estate and is now owned by Fuller's. It showcases an interesting variety of Fuller's ales including those under the Gale's badge and occasionally a single guest from elsewhere. Freshly cooked food is available throughout the day. Events include regular quiz nights and occasional live music. ❀◐◑P🚌(71,441)🐾📶

Happy Man 🏆 L

12 Harvest Road, TW20 0QS (off A30)
☼ 12-11.30 (midnight Fri & Sat); 12-10.30 Sun
☎ (01784) 433265 ⊕ thehappyman1.weebly.com/index.html
Hop Back Summer Lightning; 3 changing beers ⊞
Originally two Victorian cottages, the building was converted to a pub serving workers building Royal Holloway College. Recently refurbished but virtually unchanged, it is now a popular haunt both for students and locals. Four handpumps dispense a rapidly changing range of guest ales and sometimes additional beers on gravity from the cellar. Darts and quiz nights are hosted and food is available all day. The attractive rear garden has a heated smokers' refuge. Local CAMRA Pub of the Year for 2015. ❀◐◑♣●🚌(71,441)

Epsom

Barley Mow L

12 Pikes Hill, KT17 4EA (off A2022)
☼ 12-11.30 (12.30am Fri & Sat); 12-10.30 Sun
☎ (01372) 721044 ⊕ barley-mow-epsom.co.uk
Fuller's London Pride, ESB; 2 changing beers (sourced nationally; often Fuller's) ⊞
A pleasant old inn, hidden off Upper High Street. It was converted from three cottages some years ago and is now a highly regarded locals' pub. One bar serves many alcoves and other seating areas, with traditional wooden furnishings and leaded windows giving a rustic feel. The garden room is available to hire. A secluded garden at the rear has access from the nearby public car park. The changing beers can be from Fuller's or another brewer. 🐎❀◐◑♿♣🚌(166)🐾📶

Esher

Albert Arms 🏆

82 High Street, KT10 9QS (on A307)
☼ 10-midnight ☎ (01372) 465290 ⊕ albertarms.com
Fuller's London Pride; 5 changing beers (sourced regionally; often Dorking, Frensham, Windsor & Eton) ⊞
Small corner pub with a wooden U-shaped bar at the front and a long and narrow restaurant to the rear. The decor features bare wooden floorboards, wood panelling and framed rugby shirts on the walls. Furnishings include high tables and chairs. Beers come from a mixture of regional and micro breweries, sometimes including LocAles. The pub opens early for breakfast and can get busy on race days. Monthly comedy and quiz nights are hosted. Sky TV shows sporting events. A function room is available to hire. 🐎❀🛏◐◑🚌📶

Farnham

Hop Blossom

50 Long Garden Walk, GU9 7HX (between Waitrose and Castle St) SU838469
☼ 12-11.30 (12.30am Fri & Sat); 12-11 Sun
☎ (01252) 710770 ⊕ hopblossom.co.uk
Fuller's Chiswick Bitter, London Pride, ESB; 1 changing beer (often Fuller's) ⊞
A Victorian corner pub with traditional furniture and decor, bare wooden floorboards and an open log fire in winter. The dried hops above the bar are renewed yearly and release a pleasant aroma when fresh. The staff are friendly and welcoming. The good-sized back room can be used for private functions. There is a bench outside where customers can sit in summer. The pub can be busy on Friday nights and during special events in the town. Q🐎◐♣🚌🐾📶

Jolly Sailor 🏆 L

64 West Street, GU9 7EH
☼ 12-11 (1am Fri & Sat); 12-10 Sun ☎ (01252) 719139
⊕ jollysailorfarnham.com
Greene King IPA; 5 changing beers (sourced locally; often Hogs Back, Tillingbourne, Triple fff) ⊞
This welcoming community pub has been refurbished with a subtle nautical theme. The single bar, which is always pleasantly warm in cold weather, is divided into two sections with a bay window area providing a quieter space. There is a map of Farnham from the 1890s on the ceiling. The outside terrace is comfortable and a perfect place to chill out on a warm summer's evening. Food is served weekday lunchtimes. Local CAMRA branch Pub of the Year 2015. 🐎❀🛏◐♣P🚌(65)🐾📶

Nelson Arms L

50-52 Castle Street, GU9 7JQ
☼ 12-11 (midnight Fri & Sat); 12-10.30 Sun
☎ (01252) 712554 ⊕ nelson-arms.co.uk
Andwells Gold Muddler; Hogs Back TEA; Timothy Taylor Landlord; 1 changing beer ⊞
Originally three farm cottages belonging to the Bishop of Winchester's Estate, this pub has plenty of history. It is named after Admiral Horatio Nelson, who is reputed to have stayed here while visiting Lady Hamilton, who lived nearby. Nowadays, a friendly welcome awaits in traditional surroundings, with an open fireplace and original wooden beams. Good food is served as well as good beer, and there are regular quiz nights, pudding nights, and even a gin night. ❀◐◑🚌🐾

Frimley Green

Rose & Thistle

1 Sturt Road, GU16 6HT
☼ 12-11 (midnight Thu; 12.30am Fri & Sat); 12-10.30 Sun
☎ (01252) 834942 ⊕ theroseandthistlefrimleygreen.co.uk
Fuller's London Pride; Sharp's Doom Bar; 2 changing beers ⊞
A large open-plan pub, subdivided into separate areas with a more secluded conservatory dining space. The regular beer alternates between London Pride and Doom Bar. Up to three guest ales are available at any time, often from distant microbreweries. Food is served throughout the day

until 9pm weekdays, 10pm at weekends, and includes both pub classics and more inventive dishes. The pub aims to be the hub of the local community with live music and an enthusiastic darts scene. Q P (3,11)

Godalming

Jack Phillips

48-56 High Street, GU7 1DY

8am-11 (midnight Thu; 1am Fri & Sat) (01483) 521750

Fuller's London Pride; Greene King IPA, Abbot; Sharp's Doom Bar; 6 changing beers (sourced nationally; often Hogs Back)

Wetherspoon pub, converted from a shop, with a light, airy interior styled to look like an Art Deco ocean liner passenger saloon. It is named after local hero Jack Phillips who was the radio operator on the Titanic. There is a small patio area to the front, overlooking the pavement. Up to seven guest beers supplement the regulars, usually including at least one from a local brewery. A minimum of two real ciders are available. Licensed from 9am. Q

Star Inn

17 Church Street, GU7 1EL

12-11 Mon; 11-11 (11.30 Thu; midnight Fri & Sat); 12-11 Sun (01483) 417717

8 changing beers (sourced nationally; often Greene King)

Dating from the 1830s or earlier, the Star has a small public bar at the front and the main rooms to the side, leading to a patio with smoking area and a separate lounge. Up to eight real ales are stocked, some from the Greene King range, with beer festivals at Easter and Halloween. The pub regularly wins local and regional CAMRA cider awards, with five or six ciders and perries available on the bar.

Gomshall

Compasses

50 Station Road, GU5 9LA (on A25)

11-11; 12-8 Sun (01483) 202506

thecompasses-gomshall.co.uk

Surrey Hills Ranmore, Shere Drop; 1 changing beer (sourced locally; often Surrey Hills)

This 19th-century roadside pub stands between the A25 and River Tillingbourne. The traditional bar is decorated with old farming implements and other tools on its wooden pillars and beams. There is a garden and seating beside the stream. Home-made meals are served in the bar and separate dining room. The guest beer will be from Surrey Hills. Live music plays every Friday, with a music festival over the August bank holiday. Accommodation is in two en-suite rooms. A post office, open each day, is run from the pub.
P (25,32)

Gomshall Mill

52 Station Road, GU5 9LB (on A25)

11-11; 12-10.30 Sun (01483) 203060

gomshallmill.hcpr.co.uk

4 changing beers (often Tillingbourne)

Spanning the River Tillingbourne, the pub sits within a 17th-century timber-framed, timber-clad watermill. The emphasis is on excellent dining, with food available all day. The comfortable bar, with real fire, serves four constantly changing brews, usually including two LocAles, one from Tillingbourne. Dining areas are split across several levels around two waterwheels, formerly used to produce flour – these may be viewed as the stream races beneath your feet. There is a pleasant garden by the mill pond. P (25,32)

Guildford

King's Head

27 King's Road, GU1 4JW (on A320 Stoke Road)

11-11 (1am Fri & Sat); 12-10.30 Sun (01483) 568957

kingsheadguildford.co.uk

Fuller's London Pride, Bengal Lancer, ESB; 3 changing beers (sourced locally; often Fuller's, Surrey Hills, Tillingbourne)

A mid-Victorian street-corner pub with many different drinking and dining areas served from a central bar. The subtle Alice in Wonderland theme celebrates Charles Dodgson's association with the town. Alongside Fuller's seasonal beer, the guest ale is from a local brewery, most commonly Surrey Hills or Tillingbourne. A range of Belgian bottled beers is also available. Food is served from opening until 10pm (9pm Sun). Acoustic music features on Tuesdays and open mic on Thursdays.
(London Rd) P (3,34,35)

Robin Hood

Sydenham Road, GU1 3RH

12-11 (midnight Fri & Sat); 12-9 Sun (01483) 826044

5 changing beers

One of the few traditional pubs remaining in the centre of Guildford. It offers five changing beers – two pumps dispense national or regional brands and the others showcase local beers typically brewed within 30 miles. A sixth handpump has a real cider. Good-value food is served daily lunchtimes and evenings (not Sun eve) with popular steaks available every day.
(London Rd)

Rodboro Buildings

1-10 Bridge Street, GU1 4SB (opp Friary Centre)

8am-midnight (1am Mon; 1.45am Fri & Sat); 9am-10.30 Sun (01483) 306366

Fuller's London Pride; Greene King IPA; Hogs Back TEA; Sharp's Doom Bar; 4 changing beers

This JD Wetherspoon pub is spread over three levels in a Grade II-listed former industrial building that was the original home of the Dennis car, and later truck, company. Branded as a Lloyds No.1, it changes character in the evening, with bouncers on the doors and the downstairs dance floor in use, often with live DJs at the weekend. Choose from a range of up to 10 real ales, often from local breweries.

Row Barge

7 Riverside, GU1 1LW

12-11 (midnight Fri & Sat) (01483) 570242

Ascot On the Rails, Alligator Ale; Dartmoor Jail Ale; St Austell Tribute; Surrey Hills Shere Drop; 1 changing beer

Built in 1856 and extended for the post-war Bellfields Estate, this two-bar pub with pool room is 1½ miles along the River Wey towpath from the town centre, close to the A320 Woking Road. Day and night moorings are available to customers and a cycle rack is provided. Poker nights are Thursdays and live music is hosted on Fridays and Saturdays. Food is served until 7pm (5pm Sun).
P (3,34,35)

Hambledon

Merry Harriers 🄻

Hambledon Road, GU8 4DR SU967391

⏲ 11-2.30, 5.30-11; 11-11 Sat; 11-8 Sun ☎ (01428) 682883

🌐 merryharriers.com

Dark Star Hophead; Surrey Hills Shere Drop; 2 changing beers (sourced regionally; often Firebird, Ringwood) Ⓗ

A stylish yet traditional establishment with a main bar with inglenook fireplace, a small quiet side room and a restaurant/function room. All food (except fish) is sourced from within a 15-mile radius. Llamas can be admired from the large garden or even walked – see website for details. Live music features monthly on a Saturday. Accommodation is available either in a converted barn or the camping field. Closed Monday lunchtimes in winter. Q🚼❀🛏◑◐⛺🍎P🐾📶

Horley

Jack Fairman

30 Victoria Road, RH6 7PZ

⏲ 8am-midnight (1am Fri & Sat) ☎ (01293) 827910

Greene King Abbot; Ruddles Best Bitter; Sharp's Doom Bar; 4 changing beers Ⓗ

Conveniently situated close to the station and the town centre, this Wetherspoon pub occupies a former Kwik-Fit tyre centre built in the 1930s as Fairman's Garage. Jack Fairman was an early racing driver who partnered Stirling Moss in many endurance events and his history and posters are displayed inside. The bar has an industrial look to it with large pipes coming from the ceiling. Three large screens show televised sport. Food is available all day. 🚼❀◑◐♿⇌🚌📶

Horsell

Crown 🄻

104 High Street, GU21 4ST

⏲ 12-11 (midnight Fri); 11-midnight Sat ☎ (01483) 771719

🌐 thecrownhorsell.co.uk

3 changing beers (sourced nationally; often Thurstons) Ⓗ

A rare find in the area, this is a traditional 'wet' pub – the only food on offer is pizza. Three or four beers are available, one often from Thurstons Brewery next door. At other times a local micro is usually represented. An annual beer festival is held at Easter. The large garden has a pétanque piste. Live music features occasionally. 🚼❀♣P🚌(48)🐾📶

Leatherhead

Edmund Tylney

30-34 High Street, KT22 8AW

⏲ 8am-midnight (1am Fri & Sat) ☎ (01372) 362715

Greene King Abbot; Ruddles Best Bitter; Surrey Hills Shere Drop; 6 changing beers Ⓗ

This Wetherspoon pub, a former Woolworths store, lies in the heart of the town, a stone's throw from where the defunct Swan Brewery once stood. Named after a local man who was Master of the Revels to Queen Elizabeth I, the pub is typically open plan though a number of glass partitions create a more intimate ambience. The changing beers frequently include offerings from local suppliers such as Tillingbourne, Dark Star, Twickenham and Sambrook's. A fair range of ciders is also sold. Q🚼❀◑◐♿⇌🍎🚌📶

Running Horse 🄻

38 Bridge Street, KT22 8BZ (off B2122)

⏲ 12-11.30 (10.30 Sun) ☎ (01372) 372081

Shepherd Neame Master Brew, Kent's Best, Spitfire; Surrey Hills Ranmore; 2 changing beers Ⓗ

Overlooking the River Mole, this Grade II*-listed two-room pub, dating from 1403, features a real log fire, home-made food and an outside play area for children. The public bar has TV, a pool table and dartboard, and the rear dining area has a patio. Live blues/rock music sessions are hosted once a month on Saturdays, and live jazz plays Sunday lunchtimes. Quiz night is every Tuesday. The changing beers can be either seasonal offerings from Shepherd Neame or from other brewers. Q🚼❀◑◐♿⇌♣P🚌

Limpsfield Chart

Carpenters Arms 🄻

12 Tally Road, RH8 0TG (off B269) TQ424518

⏲ 12-11 Mon; 11-midnight; 12-10 Sun ☎ (01883) 722209

🌐 carpenterslimpsfield.co.uk

Westerham Finchcocks Original, Spirit of Kent, 1965 Special Bitter Ale; 2 changing beers Ⓗ

This Westerham Brewery tied house features the full range of its beers. The L-shaped bar has parquet flooring and provides ample room for drinkers and diners. Good home-made food is served daily (no food Sun eve). One side of the bar retains a dartboard and the monthly quiz is very popular. The pub is located adjacent to National Trust land, attracting walkers and horse-riders. The locals take great pride in this friendly pub. 🚼❀◑◐♣P🚌(594)🐾📶

Lyne

Royal Marine

Lyne Lane, KT16 0AN

⏲ 12-2.30, 5.30-11; closed Sat; 12-3 Sun ☎ (01932) 873900

🌐 royalmarinelyne.co.uk

Ruddles Best Bitter; Sharp's Doom Bar; 1 changing beer (sourced nationally; often Cotleigh, Goff's) Ⓗ

The name of this former beer house opened in the mid-1800s commemorates Queen Victoria's review of her troops nearby on Chobham Common in 1853. Royal Marines memorabilila, a large collection of drinking jugs and other bric-a-brac are on display. The guest beer may come from far and wide. Generous portions of home-cooked food are served lunchtimes and Monday to Friday evenings (no chips!). Sharp's Atlantic may alternate with Doom Bar. Q🚼❀◑◐P🐾📶

Mickleham

King William IV 🄻

4 Byttom Hill, RH5 6EL

⏲ 11-11; 12-10.30 Sun ☎ (01372) 372590

🌐 thekingwilliamiv.com

Hogs Back TEA; Surrey Hills Shere Drop; 2 changing beers (sourced locally; often Fuller's) Ⓗ

A friendly 18th-century free house clinging to a hillside and overlooking the Mole Valley and Norbury Park. It is quiet during the winter months, but the splendid terraced garden can be packed in summer. An old-fashioned main bar includes a large grandfather clock and an open fire. There is also a small lounge bar. An extensive home-cooked menu offers traditional pub food in addition to more exotic dishes, with vegetarian options.

Steep steps can make access difficult for some. The shared car park is on the A24 southbound.
Q ☸ ❀ ◑ **P** 🚌 (465) 🐾

Milford

Refectory 𝕃

Old Portsmouth Road, GU8 5HJ
⌚ 10.30-11 (10.30 Sun) ☎ (01483) 421234
Dark Star Hophead; Hogs Back TEA; Phoenix Arizona; 3 changing beers 🄷
A fascinating old building, this is a large open establishment with plenty of exposed beams and different drinking areas. There is a pretty fireplace with a roaring log fire in winter. Farming paraphernalia adorn the walls. The three guest beers are generally from independents and microbreweries. Food is served noon-10pm (9.30pm Sun). **Q** ☸ ❀ ◑ ♿ **P** 🚌 (70,71)

Mugswell

Well House Inn 𝕃

Chipstead Lane, CR5 3SQ (off A217) TQ258552
⌚ 12-11 (10.30 Sun) ☎ (01737) 830640
🌐 wellhouseinn.co.uk
Adnams Southwold Bitter; Fuller's London Pride; Surrey Hills Shere Drop; 2 changing beers (sourced locally) 🄷
Grade II-listed building dating from at least the 16th century. In the garden is St Margaret's Well or Mag's Well, mentioned in the Domesday Book, which gives the area its name. There are three bars, all with their own fires, and a conservatory. The main bar has a number of tankards hanging from the beams. The two guest beers change frequently and are usually from local microbreweries. Dogs are welcome in two of the bars. No food Sunday and Monday evenings.
☸ ❀ ◑ ♣ ● **P** 🐾 ᯤ

Newdigate

Surrey Oaks 🏆 𝕃

Parkgate Road, Parkgate, RH5 5DZ (between Newdigate and Leigh) TQ20524363
⌚ 11.30-2.30, 5.30-11; 11.30-11 Sat; 12-9 Sun
☎ (01306) 631200 🌐 surreyoaks.co.uk
Surrey Hills Ranmore, Shere Drop; 3 changing beers 🄷
This attractive 16th-century inn is renowned for its commitment to real ale and has been awarded local CAMRA Pub of the Year every year from 2003 onwards. Hoppy beers are particularly popular and a dark beer is always on sale, plus four ciders and a perry – third-pint glasses are available to help you choose. The main bar features low beams, flagstones and an inglenook fireplace with a wood-burning stove. Beer festivals are held over the late spring and August bank holidays. Excellent food is served from the open kitchen with its wood-fired oven (not Sun eve). ☸ ❀ ◑ ♣ ● **P** 🚌 (22,50) 🐾

Oxted

Oxted Inn 𝕃

Units 1-4 Hoskins Walk, Station Road West, RH8 9HR
⌚ 8am-11 ☎ (01883) 723440
Adnams Broadside; Fuller's London Pride; Greene King IPA; Sharp's Doom Bar; 4 changing beers 🄷
This small purpose-built Wetherspoon pub is just a one-minute walk from the station. Oxted is on the Greenwich Meridian and the interior is decorated with more than 20 working clocks showing the time in various parts of the world. This is the only pub in new Oxted – local historians will find the many photos dating from the early 1900s, including those of pubs that are now closed, of much interest. Food is served all day.
Q ☸ ❀ ◑ ♿ ⇌ 🚌 ᯤ

Puttenham

Good Intent

60-62 The Street, GU3 1AR
⌚ 12-3, 6-11.30 (11 Mon); 12-11.30 Sat; 12-10.30 Sun
☎ (01483) 810387 🌐 thegoodintentpub.co.uk
Otter Bitter; Sharp's Doom Bar; Timothy Taylor Landlord; 3 changing beers 🄷
A 16th-century inn situated in an attractive village nestled under the Hogs Back. The cosy bar with oak beams and an inglenook fireplace is decorated with hops and hop-growing equipment, which serves as a reminder that the largest remaining hop field in Surrey is just 500 yards along The Street. Three guest beers are normally available. Food is served daily except Sunday and Monday evenings – pie night is Tuesday, and fish and chips night is Wednesday. **Q** ☸ ❀ ◑ ⛺ **P** 🐾

Redhill

Garland

5 Brighton Road, RH1 6PP (on A23 S of town)
⌚ 12-11; 12.30-12.30am Fri & Sat ☎ (01737) 764612
Harveys IPA, Sussex Best Bitter, Armada Ale; 3 changing beers 🄷
Located just south of the town centre, and Harveys' only tied house in Surrey, the Garland is a classic Victorian street-corner local. Alongside the beers listed there are usually another two or three seasonal beers. Darts is popular here, with two boards, and there is a bar billiards table. Good-value food is sold lunchtimes and Friday evenings.
☸ ❀ ◑ ⇌ ♣ **P** 🚌 🐾

Sun 𝕃

17-21 London Road, RH1 1LY
⌚ 8am-midnight (1am Fri & Sat) ☎ (01737) 766886
Fuller's London Pride; Greene King Abbot; Ruddles Best Bitter; 6 changing beers 🄷
When the Sun opened on 14 August 1996, it was Wetherspoon's 150th pub and is named to commemorate local astronomer Richard Carrington who wrote Spots on the Sun in 1861. It is a huge brick-built pub with a long bar serving one vast open space. A raised dining area is to be found on the left hand side of the bar and food is served all day until 11pm. There are usually a couple of LocAle beers on sale. ☸ ❀ ◑ ♿ ⇌ ● 🚌 ᯤ

Reigate

Bell 𝕃

21 Bell Street, RH2 7AD (on A217)
⌚ 11-11 (midnight Thu-Sat); 11-10 Sun ☎ (01737) 244438
🌐 thebellreigate.co.uk
Greene King IPA, Abbot; 4 changing beers 🄷
Beyond the tiny frontage of this town-centre pub is a long and narrow bar with wooden flooring and comfortable seating. Six beers are usually available, three from Greene King and the others from local microbreweries, with the guest beers changing frequently. The menu features a number of different burgers supplied from a local butcher

(available lunchtimes and evenings each day). Note the large old Ordnance Survey map on the ceiling. ⏃☺❶⏆≷🖵🐾🛜

Shepperton

Barley Mow Ⓛ
67 Watersplash Road, TW17 0EE (off B376 in Shepperton Green)
✪ 12-11 (10.30 Sun) ☎ (01932) 225326
Hogs Back TEA; Hop Back Summer Lightning; 3 changing beers Ⓗ
Friendly side street community local in Shepperton Green to the west of the main village centre. Five handpumps serve regular ales from Hogs Back and Hop Back, plus local offerings from the likes of Portobello, Twickenham and Sambrook's. Many pumpclips adorn the bar and beams. Entertainment includes live rock or blues bands on Friday and Saturday nights, jazz on Wednesdays, quiz night on Thursdays and charity meat raffles on Sunday afternoons. Outside is a covered and heated patio area for smokers. ☺♣●P🖵(438,458)🐾🛜

Staines-upon-Thames

Bells
124 Church Street, TW18 4ZB (off B376)
✪ 12-4, 5-11; 12-midnight Fri & Sat; 12-11 Sun
☎ (01784) 454240 ⊕ thebellspub.co.uk
St Austell Tribute; Young's Bitter, Special; 1 changing beer (sourced nationally; often Young's) Ⓗ
Friendly, comfortable, 18th-century pub opposite St Mary's Church close to the Thames Path and within easy walking distance of the town centre. Regular beers and seasonals from Young's are available plus up to two guests from microbreweries around the country. Noted locally for the quality of its food, it is often busy in the evenings. The pleasant rear patio garden, with a large heated smokers' canopy, is especially popular in summer, attracting local workers and shoppers. Q☺❶⏆🖵(305)

George
2-8 High Street, TW18 4EE (opp town hall)
✪ 9am-midnight (1am Fri & Sat) ☎ (01784) 462181
Courage Best Bitter; Greene King Abbot; Ruddles Best Bitter; 5 changing beers Ⓗ
Ever-popular, two-storey, town-centre Wetherspoon pub built in the 1990s. The spacious downstairs bar with its mixture of tables and intimate booths is always busy but a quieter bar can be reached via a spiral staircase. Up to six guest ales are dispensed from one bank of handpumps, with the national brands and two real ciders from Westons on the rear bank. A varied selection of foreign bottled beers and ciders is also stocked. Value-for-money pub food is served all day. ❶⏆≷●🖵🛜

Wheatsheaf & Pigeon Ⓛ
Penton Road, TW18 2LL
✪ 12-11 (10.30 Sun) ☎ (01784) 452922
⊕ thewheatsheafandpigeon.co.uk
Fuller's London Pride; Otter Ale; Sharp's Doom Bar; 2 changing beers (sourced nationally; often St Austell, Windsor & Eton) Ⓗ
Welcoming and friendly community local between Staines and Laleham, a short walk signposted from the Thames Path and Staines Town FC. The pub is particularly busy on football match days. Ales often include local micro or West Country guests and

good-value food is served every day (no food Mon and Sun eve). Families are welcome and there is outside seating for the warmer months plus a covered smoking area. Quiz night is Sunday. Beer festivals are regular events. The bus stops in Laleham Road. ⏃☺❶⏆⏆♣P🖵(458)🐾🛜

Sunbury-on-Thames

Hare & Hounds Ⓛ
132 Vicarage Road, TW16 7QX
✪ 11 (12 Sat)-11; 12-10.30 Sun ☎ (01932) 761478
⊕ hareandhoundssunbury.co.uk
Fuller's London Pride, ESB; 1 changing beer (sourced locally; often Fuller's) Ⓗ
Traditional spotless Fuller's local, with separate areas featuring TV sport and pub games. The enthusiastic landlord is keen to extend the real ale choice and a wide range of Fuller's bottled beers is available. There is a separate dining area (which also hosts the Monday night quiz) and the Sunday carvery lunch is particularly popular. The pub is handy for nearby Sunbury Cross shops, and close to junction 1 of the M3. The 235 bus stops outside, with many more from around the Cross. ⏃☺❶⏆≷♣P🖵🐾🛜

Magpie Ⓛ
64 Thames Street, TW16 6AF
✪ 12 (11 Fri & Sat)-11; 12-10.30 Sun ☎ (01932) 782024
⊕ magpiesunbury.com
Greene King IPA; 5 changing beers (sourced locally; often Sambrook's, Truman's, Twickenham) Ⓗ
Recently refurbished rambling old pub on two levels with a Greene King seasonal ale and up to five regularly changing real ales, usually from London or other local microbreweries, available in the downstairs bar along with draught Budvar and other exotics. There is an extensive food menu and the outside drinking area overlooks the Thames. The name relates to a horse called Magpie belonging to a member of the Grand Order of Water Rats, described as 'looking like a drowned water rat'. Children and dogs with well-behaved owners are welcome. ⏃☺❶⏆♣🖵(216)🐾🛜

Thames Ditton

Olde Swan
Summer Road, KT7 0QQ
✪ 11-11 (10.30 Sun) ☎ (020) 8398 1814
⊕ yeoldeswan-thames-ditton.co.uk
3 changing beers Ⓗ
Although much altered, this large pub beside the Thames can trace its history back to the 13th century and the building was once used as a hunting lodge by Henry VIII. Some beers are supplied by Greene King but many are from other brewers both local and further afield. The multi-roomed interior has a stylish but traditional feel with black flagstones around the bar. Quiz nights, comedy nights and discos are held. Access is from the river side of the pub. Q⏃☺❶⏆🖵(514,515)🐾🛜

Red Lion
85 High Street, KT7 0SF
✪ 11-11 (midnight Fri); 10-midnight Sat; 10-10.30 Sun
☎ (020) 8398 8662
2 changing beers (sourced locally; often Brightwater, Surrey Hills, Twickenham) Ⓗ

In the same hands for several years, this quirkily decorated pub, divided into distinct areas, is situated close to the river and just out of the village centre. Old doors, some retaining their locks, make up the front of the bar. The two handpumps dispense mainly locally brewed beers. Food is served all day. ⛾❀◑▶P🚌(514,515)🐾📶

Tongham

White Hart 𝕃

76 The Street, GU10 1DH

🕗 11-11.30 (midnight Fri & Sat); 12-10.30 Sun

☎ (01252) 782419 🌐 thewhitehartttongham.co.uk

Hogs Back TEA; 5 changing beers Ⓗ

A friendly, partially Grade II-listed inn at the heart of village life, with a lounge bar with real fire, saloon bar and sports bar. The pub has a preference for local ales. Tongham-brewed Hogs Back TEA is a permanent beer, with four or five other real ales and real cider also available. Porters and milds frequently appear in winter, with a dark beer the norm all year. Live music features on some weekends. There is no food on Monday.
Q⛾❀◑▶♣🍎**P**🚌(3,20)🐾📶

Upper Hale

Alfred Free House

9 Bishops Road, GU9 0JA

🕗 10-11 (10.30 Sun) ☎ (01252) 820385

🌐 thealfredfreehouse.co.uk

Bowman Wallops Wood Ⓗ**; 3 changing beers (sourced nationally; often B&T)** Ⓗ/Ⓖ

A friendly local tucked away down a narrow road in a residential area, popular with its regulars. An unusual and welcome selection of ales from the B&T Brewery is always available plus three other ales. The pub is now open all day and fresh home-made meals, made with locally sourced ingredients, are served. Two beer festivals are held a year, often with a themed selection of ales, and there is live music every month.
Q⛾◑▶♿♣🍎**P**🚌(4,5)🐾📶

Walton on Thames

Regent 𝕃

19 Church Street, KT12 2QP (on A3050)

🕗 8am-midnight (1am Fri & Sat) ☎ (01932) 243980

Greene King Abbot; Ruddles Best Bitter; 8 changing beers (sourced nationally; often Surrey Hills, Thornbridge, Twickenham) Ⓗ

Characterful Wetherspoon's conversion of the former Regent cinema, decorated in Art Deco style with wood-surround panelling under the curved ceiling and period lighting. At the far end, steps lead up to a small seating area for customers seeking a more secluded spot. The walls are decorated with photos of old Walton plus relics of local connections with the film industry. The pub gets busy at weekends. Gwynt y Ddraig and Westons cider are supplemented by guests. Alcohol is served from 9am. **Q**⛾❀◑▶♿🍎🚌(461,564)📶

Warlingham

White Lion

3 Farleigh Road, CR6 9EG (on B269)

🕗 11.30-midnight ☎ (01883) 625085

Brakspear Bitter; Harveys Sussex Best Bitter; Ringwood Best Bitter; 4 changing beers Ⓗ

The interior of this Ember Inn is a warren of rooms, both modern and ancient, with the oldest section, the middle, believed to date from 1467, when it was a farmhouse. Watch your head while walking around as there are some very low beams. Food is served all day and four guest beers are sold, usually including two from smaller breweries.
❀◑▶♿♣**P**🚌(357,403,409)🐾📶

West Clandon

Onslow Arms

The Street, GU4 7TE

🕗 11-11 (11.30 Fri & Sat); 12-10.30 Sun ☎ (01483) 222447

🌐 onslowarmsclandon.co.uk

Sharp's Cornish Coaster; Surrey Hills Shere Drop; 2 changing beers Ⓗ

Former coaching inn named after local landowners the Earls of Onslow. It has a brick façade with mock-Tudor features and attractive tiling. Inside there are a number of interconnecting areas, predominantly set out for dining but drinkers are welcome, with a guest beer often from a local brewery. Sports events are shown on TV in the garden room, and acoustic music is played on Sundays, bank holidays and some Wednesdays. The house beer is brewed by Caledonian.
⛾❀◑▶♿⇌(Clandon)**P**🚌(463)🐾📶

Weybridge

Old Crown

83 Thames Street, KT13 8LP (off A317)

🕗 10-11; 12-10.30 Sun ☎ (01932) 842844

🌐 theoldcrownweybridge.co.uk

Courage Best Bitter, Directors; Young's Bitter; 1 changing beer Ⓗ

This Grade II-listed pub with a weatherboarded façade dates back to at least 1729. It has several bar and lounge areas to meet the needs of drinkers and diners. The two gardens are popular in summer and mooring for small boats is provided at the waterside, which is at the confluence of the River Wey with the Thames. The changing beer varies in source and can be from a micro. Food is available lunchtimes daily and evenings Wednesday-Saturday. **Q**⛾❀◑▶♣**P**🚌🐾📶

Woking

Herbert Wells 𝕃

51-57 Chertsey Road, GU21 5AJ

🕗 8am-midnight (1am Fri & Sat) ☎ (01483) 722818

Courage Best Bitter; Fuller's London Pride; Greene King Abbot; Hogs Back TEA; Sharp's Doom Bar; 7 changing beers Ⓗ

Six guest beers are usually available at this popular town-centre Wetherspoon pub. Eight real ciders are also on offer along with an interesting selection of bottled beers. Note the novel nod to the pub's namesake dotted around the walls and ceiling. Alcohol is served from 9am and children are welcome when dining until 6pm.
Q⛾◑▶♿⇌🍎🚌📶

Sovereigns

Guildford Road, GU22 7QQ

🕗 11.30-midnight ☎ (01483) 751426

Adnams Broadside; Brakspear Bitter; Ringwood Best Bitter; Sharp's Doom Bar; 4 changing beers Ⓗ

One of Woking's older pubs, this large split-level Ember Inn has several areas including one for family dining (children welcome until 9pm). Four guest beers are served alongside the four regulars. There are frequent food-themed nights and real ales are discounted on Mondays. A charge is made for the car park which is partially refunded on purchases at the bar. ➼❀◑♿⇌P🚌ᯤ

Woking Railway Athletic Club

Goldsworth Road, GU21 6JT (behind offices at E end of Goldsworth Rd) TQ003585

✪ 10.30-11 (11.30 Fri & Sat); 12-10.30 Sun

☎ (01483) 598499

2 changing beers Ⓗ

Lively social club tucked away near Victoria Arch. On entering there is an area devoted to pool (free to play), darts and Sky Sports, while further along the bar is a quieter space plus a large function room. Two reasonably priced guest beers are constantly changing. Children are welcome at all times. Food is limited to rolls on Saturday lunchtimes. For entry show a CAMRA membership card or copy of this Guide. Local CAMRA branch Club of the Year 2015. ➼⇌♣🚌ᯤ

Woodmansterne

Woodman

Woodmansterne Street, SM7 3NL (on B278)

✪ 12-11 (midnight Fri); 10-midnight Sat; 10-10.30 Sun

☎ (01737) 371841 🌐 thewoodmanbanstead.co.uk

Sharp's Doom Bar; 3 changing beers Ⓗ

This attractive brick, flint and tile building also has some late-Gothic flourishes on show. Food is served all day with breakfasts available at weekends. Guest beers come from the Stonegate list and change frequently, including ales from both microbreweries and regional brewers. Local cricket can be viewed from both rear and front gardens, and there is a sandpit for children to play in. ➼❀◑♣P🚌(166)🐾ᯤ

Wrecclesham

Sandrock

Sandrock Hill Road, GU10 4NS

✪ 3.45-11; 12-11 Sat; 12-10.30 Sun ☎ (01252) 715865

🌐 thesandrock.com

Bowman Swift One; Exmoor Gold; Fuller's London Pride; Hop Back Summer Lightning; Sharp's Cornish Coaster; Triple fff Moondance; 1 changing beer Ⓗ

The Sandrock has a contemporary feel, with heavy wooden furnishings and a comfy corner with softer seating. Children are admitted to the small side bar which leads to the attractive and partially covered patio garden. The well-kept beer cellar is complemented by a small but carefully chosen selection of wine. On weekdays the pub opens evenings only. Q➼❀♿P🚌(16,17)🐾ᯤ

Albert Arms, Esher (Photo: John Norman)

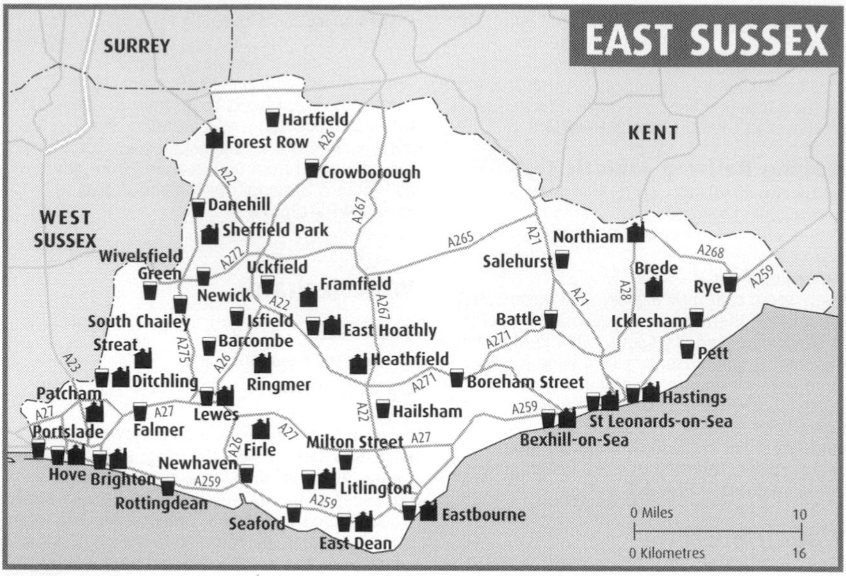

SUSSEX (EAST)

Barcombe

Royal Oak Ⓛ

High Street, BN8 5BA
⏲ 10-11; 12-11 Sun ☎ (01273) 400418
🌐 royaloakbarcombe.co.uk
Harveys Sussex XX Mild Ale, Sussex Best Bitter; 1 changing beer (often Harveys) Ⓗ
Situated in the centre of the small village of Barcombe, north of Lewes, the pub offers two regular ales supplemented by other beers from Harveys such as the relatively new Sussex Wild Hop. Old Ale is usually available in winter. There is a small car park in front, a garden at the rear and it has a skittle alley. The main bar has a real fire. Good-value food is served lunchtimes and evenings. Q🐎❀◐◑♿♣🚌(125)🐾

Battle

Bull Inn Ⓛ

27 High Street, TN33 0EA
⏲ 11-11.30 (12.30am Fri & Sat); 11-10.30 Sun
☎ (01424) 775171 🌐 thebullinnbattle.co.uk
Harveys Sussex Best Bitter; house beer (by Old Dairy); 1 changing beer Ⓗ
A 17th-century pub in the centre of Battle High Street, featuring two inglenook fireplaces, one still in use. The house beer is Top Bull, brewed by Old Dairy, the changing beer varies between local and national ales. The pub is divided into two areas, front and back, either may be used for dining. Accommodation consists of five en-suite rooms, and live music is regularly performed. Food is home cooked and locally sourced where possible. Q🐎❀🛏◐◑♣🚌(95,304,305)🐾📶

Bexhill-on-Sea

Albatross Club (RAFA) Ⓛ

15 Marina Arcade, TN40 1JS (on seafront 200yds E of De La Warr Pavilion)
⏲ 11.30-2.30, 7 (5 Thu)-11; 12-2.30 Sun ☎ (01424) 212916
🌐 bexhillrafa.co.uk
4 changing beers Ⓗ
This friendly club welcomes CAMRA members. It hosts popular beer festivals in April and September in its large function room and has a full diary of regular social events, including jazz, folk and quiz nights. Beers are nationally and locally sourced, often from Rother Valley, Weltons and Dark Star. The club boasts an interesting collection of RAF memorabilia. Regional CAMRA Club of the Year in 2013 and branch Club of the Year in 2014/2015. Q🐎◐≉🍎🚌(98,99)📶

Boreham Street

Bull's Head Ⓛ

Boreham Hill, BN27 4SG
⏲ 12-11; 12-8 Sun ☎ (01323) 831981
🌐 bullsheadborehamstreet.co.uk
Harveys Sussex Best Bitter; house beer (by Harveys); 1 changing beer (sourced nationally; often Harveys) Ⓗ
This 18th-century pub was the first ever Harveys tied house. Welcoming, with its simple wooden furniture and floors, the beer range includes house beer Bull's Head Bitter, Harveys Best and one or two seasonal Harveys ales. A wide selection of home-cooked meals at lunch and dinner sessions are offered. There is garden seating and a large car park to the rear. It has its own campsite with a shepherd's hut complete with shower and toilet. Q🐎❀◐◑♿⛺♣P🚌(98)🐾📶

Brighton

Barley Mow

92 St George's Road, Kemp Town, BN2 1EE
⏲ 12-midnight ☎ (01273) 567680
Changing beers (sourced locally) Ⓗ
In the Kemp Town area of the city close to the seafront and Volks railway station, the pub is reputed to be one of the oldest in this area. The five changing beers come mainly from Sussex micros and the surrounding region. Thatchers

Heritage Cider is also available on handpump. Home-made pies and burgers together with sausages from a local butcher feature on the menu, and there is a selection of tuck shop sweets behind the bar. (37)

Basketmakers Arms

12 Gloucester Road, BN1 4AD
12-midnight (01273) 689006
basket-makers-brighton.co.uk
Butcombe Bitter; Fuller's London Pride, ESB; Gales Seafarers Ale, HSB; 3 changing beers (sourced nationally; often Fuller's) H
Busy two-roomed street-corner pub in the North Laines part of the city serving eight beers, mainly from the Fuller's range, popular with office workers and shoppers alike, and close to an array of independent shops and cafés. Good food is served until 9pm. The meat is free range, the fish locally caught, and vegetarian options are available.

Brighton Beer Dispensary

38 Dean Street, BN1 3EG
12-11 (midnight Fri & Sat) (01273) 710624
brightonbier.com
Changing beers (sourced regionally; often Brighton Bier Co, Late Knights) G
A small pub just off the main shopping area, serving up to 10 real ales and three or four ciders. It is a joint venture between London brewery Late Knights and Brighton Bier Co, so beers from these breweries are usually found here. Guest beers from all over the country are served by gravity. The friendly bar staff will happily help you choose your ale. Good food is served lunchtimes and evenings weekdays and all day weekends. It does a good range of bottled beers.

Craft Beer Co

22-23 Upper North Street, BN1 3FG (short walk from Churchill Square shopping centre)
4-12.30am (1.30am Fri); 12.30-1.30am Sat; 12.30-11 Sun
(01273) 723736
Kent Pale; changing beers (sourced locally) H
Corner pub a block away from the busy Western Road selling a variety of at least seven real ales. Friendly and knowledgeable staff are happy to advise on beer styles. Bottled beers are also available together with locally made bar snacks. The bright and airy interior makes this place popular with drinkers of all ages, and it can get busy lunchtimes and early evenings. The welcome use of oversized, lined glasses ensures full measures are always guaranteed.

Evening Star L

55-56 Surrey Street, BN1 3PB (200yds S of station)
12-11; 11.30-midnight Fri & Sat (01273) 328931
Dark Star The Art of Darkness, Hophead, Dark Star Original; 4 changing beers (sourced regionally; often Dark Star) H
A well-run Guide regular and favourite with ale drinkers of all ages, close to Brighton station. Somewhat spartan furnishings simply enhance the great beer flavours on offer. As a flagship of the Dark Star Brewery, four of its beers are usually on tap, as well as three from other micros. You can also enjoy real cider and a varied selection of European bottled beers. Occasional beer festivals and live music nights feature too.

Hanover L

242 Queens Park Road, Hanover, BN2 9ZB
12-midnight (1am Fri & Sat) (01273) 679902
hanoverbrighton.co.uk
Changing beers (sourced locally) H
An estate pub from circa 1927, since opened out but retaining its well-used function/meeting room. Although the pub is quite large there are discrete areas with a variety of seating and tables. Part of the Indigo chain, it gives you up to five varied Sussex ales plus a local cider on handpump. A premium is charged on halves. Food is served 12.30-10pm, a feature of the bar area being the pizza oven. Sunday roasts are served until 9pm. Quiz night is Tuesday and there is occasional live music. (20,23)

Mitre Tavern

13 Baker Street, BN1 4JN
10.30-11.30 (midnight Fri & Sat); 12-10.30 Sun
(01273) 683173 mitretavern.co.uk
Harveys Sussex XX Mild Ale, Sussex Best Bitter, Armada Ale; 1 changing beer (often Harveys) H
A small back-street pub close to London Road shops and the recently refurbished Open Market. The long, narrow main bar with a real fire has a lost-in-time feel, with a cosy snug leading off. Basic but good-value food is served at lunchtimes. The pub always stocks the rarely found Harveys XX Mild Ale and the monthly Harveys seasonal ales. Real cider is also on offer. There is a small garden courtyard to the rear.

Prestonville Arms

64 Hamilton Road, BN1 5DN (in back street E of Seven Dials)
5-11; 12-midnight Fri & Sat; 12-11 Sun (01273) 736390
theprestonvillearms.co.uk
3 changing beers (sourced nationally; often Fuller's) H
It can be a bit hard to find, but a sign at the road end points you up Hamilton Road to this excellent

REAL ALE BREWERIES

1648 East Hoathly
360° Sheffield Park
Bartleby's Brighton (NEW)
Beachy Head East Dean
Beer Me Eastbourne (NEW)
Black Cat Framfield
Brick House Patcham (NEW)
Brighton Bier Brighton
Burning Sky Firle
FILO Hastings
Franklins Bexhill-on-Sea
Goldstone Ditchling
Gun Heathfield (NEW)
Harveys Lewes
Hastings St Leonards-on-Sea
Hop Yard Forest Row (NEW)
Isfield Framfield
Kemptown Brighton
Kitchen Garden Sheffield Park (brewing suspended)
Laine Brighton
Long Man Litlington
Old Tree Brighton (NEW)
Rectory Streat
Rother Valley Northiam
Three Legs Brede (NEW)
Turners Ringmer
UnBarred Hove (NEW)

back-street pub serving the full Fuller's range. Works by local artists are displayed on the mezzanine level. Watch out for at least two beer festivals a year. The nearest buses are at Seven Dials or Preston Circus.

Prince Albert

48 Trafalgar Street, BN1 4ED

12-midnight (12.30am Fri & Sat) (01273) 730499

Harveys Sussex Best Bitter; changing beers (sourced locally) H

Large Victorian free house with a number of rooms off the main bar and an outside seating area to the front. The six handpumps serve guest ales largely from Sussex breweries. Real cider is also available. Good-quality food is offered 12-9pm (3pm Fri). It serves office workers during the day and a mixed, younger clientele in the evenings, when there is a live band or a DJ. Families are welcome until 6pm.

Southover

58 Southover Street, Hanover, BN2 9UF

3-midnight (1am Fri); 12-1am Sat; 12-midnight Sun
(01273) 601419 thesouthoverbrighton.co.uk

Changing beers (sourced locally) H

The Southover is at the top of the steep hill of the same name and anyone less than fit is advised to use the bus. Survivors of the climb will find a friendly, roomy pub offering a range of bottled beers in addition to those on the five pumps. The ales sold are mostly local. Prices are reasonable for the area but a premium is charged on halves. Food is served evenings with roasts on Sundays.
(18,23)

Crowborough

Coopers Arms

Coopers Lane, TN6 1SN

12-2.30 (not Mon), 5-11; 12-11 Sat & Sun
(01892) 654796

Dark Star Partridge Best Bitter; 2 changing beers H

A late-Victorian traditional community local which has superb views of Ashdown Forest from the beer garden. There is one long bar with a side room for games. Two changing guest beers are on offer, with Sussex breweries usually well represented in this excellent free house. Regular beer festivals are held during the year. A selection of bottled beers is also kept and home-prepared food is available.
Q P (29,29B)

Wheatsheaf

Mount Pleasant, Jarvis Brook, TN6 2NF

12-11; 12-10.30 Sun (01892) 663756
wheatsheafcrowborough.co.uk

Harveys Sussex XX Mild Ale, IPA, Sussex Best Bitter; 1 changing beer (sourced nationally; often Harveys) H

A distinctly rural feel remains within this fine weatherboarded building which first became a pub in 1853. A Harveys tied house since 1998, it offers all the brewery's seasonal beers. Three drinking areas surround a central bar. An interesting history of the pub can be found on the wall in the middle bar. Westons cider is served periodically, and beer festivals are usually held in May and October. The pub recently received an award for its 10th consecutive appearance in this Guide.
Q P (100)

Danehill

Coach & Horses

School Lane, RH17 7JF

12-3, 5.30-11; 12-11 Sat; 12-10.30 Sun (01825) 740369
coachandhorses.danehill.biz

Harveys Sussex Best Bitter; 2 changing beers (sourced locally) H

A traditional country pub built in 1847 and retaining many original features. The former adjoining stables have been converted to a restaurant serving high-quality, locally sourced food. There are separate public and saloon bars with real fires and simple farmhouse-style furniture. It has a large garden to the front with a children's play area, and a rear patio with extensive farmland views. Black Pig cider is seasonally sold, as well as a perry from the same source. Q P (270)

Ditchling

White Horse

16 West Street, BN6 8TS

11-11 (01273) 842006 whitehorseditchling.com

Dark Star Hophead; Harveys Sussex Best Bitter; 3 changing beers (sourced regionally) H

Built in the early 12th-century, the White Horse was a favoured resting point for travellers and smugglers alike. A warren of interconnecting tunnels in the pub's cellar suggests that these may have been used for smuggling goods arriving from overseas and connecting with various networks across the area. The wood-floored split-level main area features a timber-panelled peninsula bar, with five handpumps serving a changing range of beers from mainly smaller brewers, together with the two regular beers. P (824,33)

East Dean

Tiger Inn

The Green, BN20 0DA

11-11 (01323) 423209 beachyhead.org.uk/the_tiger_inn

Beachy Head Original, Legless Rambler; Fuller's Bengal Lancer; Harveys Sussex Best Bitter; Long Man Brewery Long Blonde H

An idyllic 15th-century smugglers' and wreckers' inn, situated at the heart of the village. Set within the South Downs, making it popular with walkers and cyclists, it is the brewery tap for the nearby Beachy Head Brewery. The interior is full of charm and character, with low beams and log fires. Freshly cooked meals are served daily. The inn also offers luxury accommodation. There is outside seating facing the pretty village green. Breakfast is served 8.30-10am.
Q P (12,12A,13X)

East Hoathly

Foresters Arms

6 South Street, BN8 6DS

6-10 Mon; 11.30-3, 6-11; 11.30-11 Sat; 12-10 Sun
(01825) 840208 theforesterseasthoathly.co.uk

Harveys Sussex Best Bitter, Old Ale; 1 changing beer (sourced nationally; often Harveys) H

A warm welcome awaits at this delightful village pub. Originally cottages, it has been a pub since Victorian times. There is a spacious L-shaped bar with a restaurant and dining areas. Outside is a beer garden equipped with a children's play area. Three Harveys beers feature, including seasonal brews, and in summer a real cider. Quality food from a changing menu is offered, made from Sussex ingredients (no food Mon or Tue lunchtime). Darts and toad in the hole are played here. Q P (54)

King's Head

1 High Street, BN8 6DR
11-11; 11-midnight Fri & Sat; 12-11 Sun
(01825) 840238 thekingshead.org
1648 Triple Champion, Signature; Harveys Sussex Best Bitter; 1 changing beer (sourced nationally; often 1648) [H]
This characterful free house, Grade II-listed, was originally the village schoolhouse but has been an inn since 1765. As the tap for the adjacent 1648 Brewing Company, one of Sussex's first microbreweries established in 2003, the handpumps primarily serve its beers, including seasonals, but occasionally feature guest ales along with Harveys Best Bitter. Quality home-made, locally sourced, reasonably priced dishes are served every lunchtime and evening – the bangers and mash and Sunday roasts are noteworthy. Q P (54)

Eastbourne

Crown

22 Crown Street, Old Town, BN21 1PB
11-11 (midnight Fri & Sat); 12-11 Sun (01323) 724654
Harveys Sussex Best Bitter; Shepherd Neame Spitfire; Wadworth 6X [H]**; Young's Special** [H]/[G]**; 2 changing beers** [G]
Friendly community pub in the heart of the old town with two bars, one with a log fire, and a separate pool room at the back. The large enclosed rear garden has children's play equipment and hosts barbecues throughout the summer. Weekly guest beers are offered and there are regular beer festivals. Excellent traditional bar meals are served, with complimentary bar snacks, ale discounts and a meat raffle Sunday lunchtimes. The monthly quiz night includes a complimentary hot buffet. Occasional live music features.

Dew Drop Inn

37-39 South Street, BN21 4UP
12-midnight (1am Fri & Sat) (01323) 723313
3 changing beers (sourced nationally; often Greene King) [H]
Popular town-centre Greene King pub which attracts drinkers of all ages, with a mainly younger crowd in the evenings. The horseshoe-shaped bar area is divided into two, with comfortable seating, and a small garden to the rear. Four beers are usually on offer with two guests; seasonal beer and cider festivals are held. Good-quality food, including speciality burgers, is served until 10pm. DJ nights and live bands sometimes feature at weekends. A discount is offered to CAMRA members. (3,3A)

Dolphin

14 South Street, BN21 4XF
11-11 (midnight Fri & Sat); 12-10.30 Sun
(01323) 746622
Brakspear Oxford Gold; Harveys Sussex Best Bitter; 3 changing beers [H]
Situated in the Little Chelsea area, convenient for Saffrons sports ground, this popular Brakspear town-centre pub has five ales, one Brakspear and, usually, Sussex guests. Featuring an open fire, the front bar attracts drinkers of all ages with its friendly atmosphere; there is also a smaller bar to the rear plus a larger room mainly used by diners, with an outside patio area. Good-quality food, cooked to order, is available. Beer club meetings are held monthly. Q

Eagle

57 South Street, BN21 4UT
11-11 (12.30am Fri & Sat) (01323) 417799
Harveys Sussex Best Bitter; 4 changing beers [H]
Well-decorated pub with a dining area, bar, games room and small roof terrace. Five well-priced real ales are usually on tap: one regular, two local and two nationals. A further handpump usually has a real cider. Regular beer festivals are held. Good food is served all day until 9pm, with an excellent range of home-cooked pies. Several TVs can be found around the pub showing sporting events, with a large projector used for big games.

London & County

46 Terminus Road, BN21 3LX
8am-midnight (1am Fri & Sat) (01323) 746310
Adnams Broadside; Greene King Abbot; Ruddles Best Bitter; changing beers [H]
A Wetherspoon Lloyds No.1 Bar occupying the original 1880 London and County Bank building, centrally located opposite the railway station and convenient for local and county-wide bus routes. It comprises a large ground floor bar with an upper room also available for functions. Three regular ales are always on tap, with four changing beers and Old Rosie cider. Good-value food is served all day. Muted TV screens provide news displays; music is played in the evenings, with a DJ at weekends.

Victoria Hotel

27 Latimer Road, BN22 7BU (behind TAVR Centre)
11-11 (midnight Fri & Sat); 12-10.30 Sun
(01323) 722673 victoriaeastbourne.co.uk
Harveys Sussex Best Bitter, Armada Ale; 1 changing beer (sourced nationally; often Harveys) [H]
The Vic is a classic Victorian London-style rugby-supporting pub (and other sports too). The interior oozes character, with Victoriana in abundance. A large curved front bar welcomes you, while there is a smaller back room with pool, toad in the hole (a peculiarly Sussex game) and other games, and a bijou patio area. Harveys beers, Best and Armada, are regulars and all seasonals appear. Old Rosie cider is also available. There is good food too, Thursday-Saturday daytimes and evenings, plus Sunday lunchtime.

Falmer

Swan Inn

Middle Street, BN1 9PD (just off A27 in N of village)
12-11 (4 Mon); 12-10.30 Sun (01273) 681842
theswanfalmer.co.uk
Palmers Best Bitter, Tally Ho!; 3 changing beers (sourced locally) [H]
Traditional family-run free house near the universities. It has three bar areas – a German model railway runs above the bar in the narrow middle room. Good-value food is served lunchtimes and Thursday and Friday evenings. It gets busy when Brighton & Hove Albion play at

home; the pub opens at 11am on Saturday match days. A small courtyard area sits to the rear of the pub. Q❀◖◗♿≠♣P🚌(28,29)🐾ᯤ

Hailsham

George Hotel 𝕃

1 George Street, BN27 1AD

✪ 8am-11 (midnight Fri & Sat) ☎ (01323) 445120

Greene King Abbot; Ruddles Best Bitter; 3 changing beers Ⓗ

Conveniently located in the town centre opposite the restored picture palace, the Hailsham Pavilion. A spacious area with an L-shaped bar leads to a small raised alcove, plus a beer garden to the rear, and outside seating on the terrace by the side entrance. A selection of reasonably priced guest beers is served, including at least one from a local Sussex microbrewery. Customers have an opportunity to suggest beers from the Wetherspoon's list and vote on those to be stocked. Q🐴❀◖◗♿●🚌ᯤ

King's Head 𝕃

146 South Road, Cacklebury, BN27 3NJ

✪ 12-11 (midnight Fri & Sat) ☎ (01323) 440447

Harveys Sussex Best Bitter; 1 changing beer (sourced nationally; often Harveys) Ⓗ

A tied Harveys house since 1841, the pub dates from 1700. There are two separate bars, exposed beams, open fireplaces, a quiet snug and a large beer garden. A friendly welcome awaits at this community local which has several darts teams, a pool team, knitting club, a weekly Sunday quiz and an annual summer beer festival. Traditional pub games include toad in the hole and shove-ha'penny. Home-made classic pub food is cooked to order. Under new management since May 2014. Q🐴❀◖◗♣●P▯🚌🐾ᯤ

Hartfield

Anchor Inn 𝕃

Church Street, TN7 4AG

✪ 11-11; 12-10.30 Sun ☎ (01892) 770424

🌐 anchorhartfield.com

Black Cat Black Cat; Burning Sky Plateau; Harveys Armada Ale; Larkins Traditional Ale; 2 changing beers Ⓗ

The Anchor was built in 1465 as a manor house. By the 1800s it was a workhouse but changed to selling beer in the 1860s. It is in the centre of this Ashdown Forest village, close to the church. The interior has two bars – the wooden-beamed front bar is decorated with an interesting selection of old pictures and the rear bar features an inglenook. The restaurant is used during busy periods. Food is served all day at weekends in summer. Q🐴❀🛏◖◗♿♣●P🚌(291)🐾ᯤ

Hastings

Crown 𝕃

64-66 All Saints Street, Old Town, TN34 3BN

✪ 11-11; 12-10.30 Sun ☎ (01424) 465100

🌐 thecrownhastings.co.uk

4 changing beers Ⓗ

This establishment has added a different dimension to the Hastings Old Town real ale scene. It has been tastefully refurbished by local craftsmen and serves food mainly sourced locally; clipboards detail available food and where it has come from. Local real ales are common and a good selection of continental beers is offered. It is a relatively small building and its popularity means that space is often at a premium at peak times. At the front is a small outdoor seating area. Q🐴◖◗♣●🚌🐾ᯤ

Dolphin

11-12 Rock-A-Nore Road, Old Town, TN34 3DW

✪ 11-11 (midnight Sat) ☎ (01424) 431197

Dark Star Hophead; Harveys Sussex Best Bitter; Young's Special; 3 changing beers Ⓗ

Opposite the historic fishing huts, this Old Town pub attracts locals and visitors alike. Decorated with fishing memorabilia and serving speciality seafood platters at lunchtimes all week (and on Mon eves) this cosy pub was local CAMRA branch Pub of the Year 2013/2014. There are six beers on handpump including three different guests. Live music is a feature on Tuesdays, Fridays and Saturdays, and a quiz night on Thursdays – outside seating will allow you to take advantage of the views at any time. Q❀◖◗▯🚌(20,100)🐾

First In Last Out 𝕃

14-15 High Street, Old Town, TN34 3EY (near Stables Theatre)

✪ 12-11 (midnight Fri & Sat) ☎ (01424) 425079

🌐 thefilo.co.uk

FILO Brewery Mike's Mild, Crofters, Churches Pale Ale, Old Town Tom, Cardinal; 2 changing beers Ⓗ

Birthplace of the FILO Brewery, this popular Old Town pub has a large bar, a central open fire and a restaurant to the rear. Generally there are six cask beers on tap plus real cider. Good home-cooked food is served (no food Sun and Mon lunchtime). Monday is tapas night and Thursday is Thali. Beer festivals feature most bank holiday weekends. Live blues, jazz or folk music play on most Thursdays and some Sundays. Ore station is nearer than Hastings but a more difficult walk with a less frequent service. Q🐴◖◗♣●▯🚌🐾ᯤ

Jenny Lind 𝕃

69 High Street, Old Town, TN34 3EW

✪ 12-11 (midnight Fri & Sat) ☎ (01424) 421392

🌐 jennylindhastings.co.uk

Theakston Old Peculier; 8 changing beers (sourced nationally; often Franklins, Hastings) Ⓗ

With nine handpumps for ale and one for cider, this pub serves local beers and a range from across the country. Live music is performed at weekends and the pub operates a loyalty scheme. The front bar is long and roomy while a smaller back bar is warmer and more intimate. An upstairs function room hosts a range of events from blues to slot car racing. A terraced garden above and behind the pub is delightful in warm weather. Q🐴❀🛏♿♣●🚌🐾ᯤ

White Rock Hotel 𝕃

White Rock, TN34 1JU (opp pier)

✪ 10-11; 12-11 Sun ☎ (01424) 422240

🌐 thewhiterockhotel.com

4 changing beers Ⓗ

A modern, spacious bar with plenty of seating, and a terrace overlooking the seafront and the newly reopened pier, are the main attractions for non-residents at this large, friendly hotel next to the White Rock Theatre. Four beers are on offer from various independent Sussex breweries. A good range of freshly prepared hot and cold food is available until 10pm. Many of the en-suite guest

rooms have sea views – the best are on the first floor, complete with balconies.
Q🍽🐾🚪◐➊♣♠➡🐾🛏🐕📶

Hove

Neptune Inn Ⓛ

10 Victoria Terrace, BN3 2WB (on coast road E of King Alfred leisure complex)
🕐 12-1am (2am Fri & Sat); 12-midnight Sun
☎ (01273) 736390 ⊕ theneptunelivemusicbar.co.uk
Dark Star Hophead; Greene King Abbot; Harveys Sussex Best Bitter; 2 changing beers (sourced locally) Ⓗ
Five handpumps serve regular favourites plus frequently changing guest ales, always in good condition. This traditional single-bar pub is frequented by a regular local clientele. Live music is strongly supported, with blues and rock every Friday and jazz on Sunday, together with monthly open mic and vinyl nights on the second and fourth Mondays. The decor features music-related pictures, posters and other memorabilia. The inn is on the Brighton to Shoreham coast road near central Hove. 🚌(700)

Westbourne

90 Portland Road, BN3 5DN
🕐 12-11 (midnight Fri & Sat) ☎ (01273) 823633
⊕ thewestbournehove.co.uk
4 changing beers (sourced locally) Ⓗ
Formerly the Aldrington, this large Victorian two-bar pub is at the corner of Portland Road and Westbourne Road. There is covered external seating along the Westbourne Road frontage, together with a patio seating area at the rear. The main bar serves a changing range of local Sussex beers from four handpumps, and there are usually at least six real ciders available from the Cider Shack. Food is cooked to order from the menu, with burgers a speciality. 🐾◐➊≈(Aldrington)➡🚌

Icklesham

Queen's Head

Parsonage Lane, TN36 4BL (opp village hall)
🕐 11-11; 12-10.30 Sun ☎ (01424) 814552
⊕ queenshead.com
Greene King IPA, Abbot; Harveys Sussex Best Bitter; 2 changing beers Ⓗ
An early 17th-century inn in its fourth consecutive decade in this Guide. It stocks five beers – often eight to 10 at weekends – and a real cider. Guest beers are from local breweries and from further afield. In winter three log fires warm the five interior areas. A spacious garden containing a children's play area offers fine views towards Winchelsea and Rye. Good home-made affordable food is served. An autumn beer festival includes Sussex and Kent beers.
Q🍽🐾🐕◐♣➡P🍴🚌(100)🐾📶

Robin Hood Ⓛ

Main Road, TN36 4BD (on A259 at W end of village)
🕐 11-3, 6-11; 11-11 Fri & Sat; 12-10.30 Sun
☎ (01424) 814277 ⊕ robinhoodicklesham.co.uk
Changing beers Ⓗ
Local CAMRA branch Community Pub of the Year 2014, this 17th-century pub offers six or seven beers, always including a low-strength beer and some from local brewers. At least two ciders are also served. Each July a successful village beer

festival is held in an adjacent field. A separate dining area serves up home-cooked food. There is a pool table and the large rear garden has a pétanque piste and a large play area.
Q🍽🐾🐕◐♿♣➡P🚌(100)🐾📶

Isfield

Laughing Fish Ⓛ

Station Road, TN22 5XB (off A26 between Lewes and Uckfield)
🕐 11.30-11 ☎ (01825) 750349 ⊕ laughingfishonline.co.uk
Greene King IPA; Hardys & Hansons Olde Trip; Morland Old Golden Hen; 4 changing beers (sourced nationally; often Greene King, Isfield) Ⓗ
Village pub popular with locals and visitors alike. Two guest beers are always from the Isfield Brewing Company. Traditional home-made food is served, using local suppliers, and a special food evening is hosted on the last Thursday of the month. A quiz night is held on the first Sunday of the month (book in advance) and a folk night on the second Sunday. The pub caters well for families and there is an outdoor play area for children.
🐾🐕◐♿▲♣➡P🚌(29)🐾📶

Lewes

Black Horse

55 Western Road, BN7 1RS
🕐 12-11; 12-10.30 Sun ☎ (01273) 473653
⊕ theblackhorselewes.co.uk
Burning Sky Plateau; Greene King Abbot; 5 changing beers (sourced regionally; often Greene King) Ⓗ
Given a welcome refit two years back, this pub now offers at least seven real ales together with Biddenden cider. A porter or stout is usually on tap during the winter months. Locally sourced food is served seven days a week and the pub boasts an impressive selection of unusual gins. The traditional Sussex game of toad in the hole is played and there is also a bar billiards table. A log fire welcomes you during the cold months.
🐾🐕◐♿♣➡🚌(28,29)🐾📶

Brewers Arms ♀ Ⓛ

91 High Street, BN7 1XN (near Lewes Castle)
🕐 10-11; 12-10.30 Sun ☎ (01273) 475524
⊕ brewersarmslewes.co.uk
Harveys Sussex Best Bitter; 3 changing beers (sourced regionally) Ⓗ
Genuine family-run free house catering for most tastes in its two bars. At the front, the comfortable saloon offers a range of seating and books and games. The rear bar has a pool table and two TVs showing sporting events. The pub is popular on match days with Lewes FC, Brighton & Hove Albion and away fans. Food, including traditional breakfasts, is served until 7pm. The exterior proclaims the former owners, Page and Overton's, Brewers of Croydon. Q🐕◐➊≈♣➡🚌(28,29)📶

Elephant & Castle Ⓛ

White Hill, BN7 2DJ (off Fisher St)
🕐 11.30-11 (midnight Fri & Sat); 12-11 Sun
☎ (01273) 473797 ⊕ elephantandcastlelewes.com
Harveys Sussex Best Bitter; 2 changing beers (sourced locally) Ⓗ
Built in 1838 to provide accommodation and stabling for a new road into the town, the Ellie is a spacious community-based pub, home to one of the famous Lewes Bonfire Societies and a Saturday

folk club. Major sporting events, including the Rugby Six Nations, are shown on a large-screen TV. The pub has a large function room for hire. The changing guest beers are usually from a Sussex brewer and the food is locally sourced.
(127)

Gardener's Arms

46 Cliffe High Street, BN7 2AN
11-11; 12-10.30 Sun (01273) 474808
Harveys Sussex Best Bitter; 4 changing beers (sourced regionally) H
Small, genuine free house in the heart of Lewes, near Harveys brewery. Five constantly changing guest ales are delivered, generally from small breweries all over the country. Harveys seasonal ales and one-off brews often feature. Bottled and draught cider is also available. Food consists of locally made pies and pasties. A Guide and ale trail regular, it is popular with Brighton and Lewes FC fans on match days. No children are allowed. CAMRA local branch and cider Pub of the Year 2014. (28,29)

John Harvey Tavern

Bear Yard, BN7 2AS (opp Harveys brewery)
11-11; 12-10.30 Sun (01273) 479880
johnharveytavern.co.uk
Harveys Sussex Best Bitter H/G**, Armada Ale** H**; 1 changing beer (often Harveys)** H/G
Harveys tied house opposite the brewery shop dispensing beers on handpump and gravity. A warm welcome is assured at this modern pub built in a former stable block beside the River Ouse. The venue has three separate areas: a main bar, a quieter room on the same level and an upstairs restaurant/function room. There is folk music on the second Tuesday of each month. Children are only allowed in the restaurant. The pub is dog-friendly (on leads please). Q (28,29)

Lewes Arms

1 Mount Place, BN7 1YH
11-11 (midnight Fri & Sat); 12-11 Sun (01273) 473152
lewesarms.co.uk
Fuller's London Pride; Gales HSB; Harveys Sussex Best Bitter; 2 changing beers (sourced regionally; often Fuller's) H
In the heart of the county town, this is a traditional ale house popular with visitors and locals alike. Fuller's beers are served plus Harveys Best and a guest. It is home to the world pea-throwing championship, dwyle flunking, spaniel racing and other unusual events. A three-day music festival is hosted in August and an annual pantomime in March in the upstairs function room, in aid of a local charity. Home-made food is available every day. Q (28,29)

Snowdrop Inn

119 South Street, BN7 2BU
12-midnight; 12-11 Sun (01273) 471018
thesnowdropinn.com
Burning Sky Plateau; Harveys Sussex Best Bitter; 4 changing beers (sourced locally; often Burning Sky, Dark Star) H
On the outer edge of the Cliffe area of this historic town, the Snowdrop is a welcoming free house serving six cask ales, one cider and a selection of bottled beers. With UK and continental beers on tap, the pub has a central bar plus an additional upstairs seating area where darts and toad in the hole can be played. Good food is served, and it is family-friendly, with retro sweets for the kids. There are two outside drinking areas.
(28,29)

Litlington

Plough & Harrow

The Street, BN26 5RE
11-11; 12-11 Sun (01323) 870632 thepandh.co.uk
Harveys Sussex Best Bitter; Long Man Long Blonde, Best Bitter; 3 changing beers (sourced nationally; often Long Man) H
The pub is the tap for the Long Man Brewery, which is a few hundred yards down the road. This village free house has an unusual curved bar, more reminiscent of a hotel than a pub. At the front is a secluded snug with an inglenook fireplace. Food is served in all areas of the pub including very attractive garden. Above the bar area various banknotes adorn the wall, presumably from satisfied customers. QP

Milton Street

Sussex Ox

BN26 5RL
11.30-3, 6-11; 11.30-11 Sat; 12-10.30 Sun
(01323) 870840 thesussexox.co.uk
Harveys Sussex Best Bitter; 2 changing beers H
A welcome return to the Guide for this popular free house, under new ownership since April 2014. It has wonderful stretching views of the Cuckmere Valley from the large rear garden and decking area. Catering for drinkers and food lovers alike, the beamed and stone-floored bar has an adjoining dining area and there is a large separate restaurant. The menu includes meat and seasonal vegetables from its own farm nearby. Local cider from South Downs is on tap alongside the real ales.
QP

Newhaven

Hope Inn

West Pier, BN9 9DN (close to Newhaven Fort)
11-11; 11-10.30 Sun (01273) 515389
Harveys Sussex Best Bitter; 2 changing beers (sourced regionally) H
Spacious pub at the far end of Newhaven with a covered balcony overlooking the harbour entrance. The interior has a timber-panelled beamed ceiling, bar and walls, and polished timber floors. Look out for the stained-glass panels, the multitude of nautical themed pictures, and the flag signals on the ceiling beams. Heed the sign warning you against feeding the pub dog. Quiz night is Wednesday. Home-cooked food is available every day. It has a raised patio smoking area at the front.
P

Newick

Crown Inn

22 Church Road, BN8 4JX
11-11.30; 11-10.30 Sun (01825) 723293
thecrownatnewick.co.uk
Harveys Sussex Best Bitter; 2 changing beers (sourced regionally) H
Family-run free house at the southern end of the village near the post office. The 121 bus stops just round the corner. There is a central bar with two smaller rooms off to either side and a very pleasant

garden to the rear. Good-value meals are served using local produce. With two other pubs on the village green, Newick is well worth a whole afternoon's stay, but don't miss the last bus.
❀◑♣●P🚌(31,121)🐾📶

Pett

Royal Oak

Pett Road, TN35 4HG
11-11; 12-10.30 Sun ☎ (01424) 812515
royaloakpett.com
Harveys Sussex Best Bitter; 3 changing beers H
Refurbished in 2011, this village free house serves up to four real ales, often local, together with excellent food, usually locally sourced, as well as meal deals Monday-Thursday. The Oak is popular with locals and visitors alike and has a selection of traditional pub games, including an antique bagatelle board, the forerunner of modern bar billiards. Events include quizzes and occasional live music. Warmed by two open fires, the pub has real character, with friendly staff, and is very welcoming. Q❀◑♣P🚌(347)🐾📶

Two Sawyers

Pett Road, TN35 4HB
12-midnight (1am Fri & Sat) ☎ (01424) 812255
twosawyers.co.uk
Ringwood Fortyniner; 2 changing beers H
A 17th-century village pub with two main bars and a separate restaurant together with smaller, individual dining areas. Four ales are normally on offer, with guest beers frequently from local breweries. The open fires and friendly staff make the pub welcoming. With good locally sourced food served from an extensive menu every day, dining is popular and reservations are recommended. A collection of antique saws decorates the interior of the pub, while outside there are tables and pétanque. Q❀◑♣●P🚌(347)🐾📶

Portslade

Stanley Arms

47 Wolseley Road, BN41 1SS (corner of Wolseley Rd and Stanley Rd)
3 (4 Mon & Tue; 12 Sat)-11; 12-10.30 Sun
☎ (01273) 430234 thestanley.com
Changing beers (sourced regionally; often Downlands, Hop Back, St Austell) H
Family-run free house where beer festivals are held in spring, summer and autumn. Reduced price cellar nights with free nibbles take place every second Monday, 7-9pm. A changing range of UK beers is served from seven handpumps, plus UK and imported bottled and real ciders on draught. It has a football team, sports on HD TV, weekly quiz and crib evenings, occasional live music and talks by sports personalities. A stained glass tiled canopy is over the bar. The pub is named after Henry Morton Stanley, the man who tracked down Doctor Livingstone.
Q❀≠(Fishersgate)♣●🚌(2,2A,46)🐾📶

Rottingdean

Queen Victoria L

54 High Street, BN2 7HF
12-11 (midnight Fri & Sat) ☎ (01273) 302121
thequeenvic.co.uk
Harveys Sussex Best Bitter; Long Man Long Blonde; 3 changing beers (sourced regionally) H
An atmospheric and welcoming pub which greets punters with jazz music and 1930s décor. Chandeliers, big tables, a real fire, a piano and a portrait of Queen Victoria add to the air of grandeur. There are regularly three ciders – Westons Old Rosie and Country Perry and a guest. The pub has also gained a reputation for its gins, and stocks nearly 20 of these. It serves traditional home-made food, and on Saturday afternoons hosts a regular live jazz and brunch event.
❀◑♣●🚌🐾📶

Rye

Globe Inn Marsh

10 Military Road, TN31 7NX
9am-11 ☎ (01797) 225220 globeinnmarshrye.com
House beer (by Tonbridge); 4 changing beers H
A fantastic open fire is the centrepiece of this small food-oriented pub, built about 1834. Creatively designed and furnished, it has a unique open-plan bar delivering mainly local beers from five handpumps, plus a cider in the summer. Good-quality meals are served, including pizzas and quiches cooked on a chestnut-wood-fired oven. Breakfasts are available from 9am. There are unisex toilets and a covered outdoor area, decorated with lobster pots and fishing nets.
❀◑♿≠●🚌(100,344)🐾📶

Ypres Castle Inn

Gun Gardens, TN31 7HH
12-11 (midnight Fri); 12-10.30 Sun; closed Mon winter
☎ (01797) 223248 yprescastleinn.co.uk
Harveys Sussex Best Bitter; 4 changing beers H
Known locally as The Wipers, this attractive weatherboarded pub built in 1640 is accessible from the steps adjacent to the ramparts of the Ypres Tower. It has fantastic views across Romney Marsh and a large garden where music events are held, and there is also an outdoor bar during Wipers Weekends in August. Inside, there is one large bar with an open fire and six handpumps for the beers and a regular cider. The excellent menu includes locally sourced seafood.
❀◑≠●🚌(100,344)🐾📶

St Leonards on Sea

Tower 🏆

251 London Road, TN37 6NB
11-11.30 (12.30am Fri & Sat); 11-11 Sun
☎ (01424) 721773
Dark Star Hophead, American Pale Ale; 4 changing beers H
The Tower is a traditional pub, showing football and other live sporting events on HD TV. It has six handpumps dispensing reasonably priced real ales, including four changing guests, at least one usually a dark beer. Other attractions include a well-stocked jukebox, monthly meat raffle, the odd themed night and occasional pub trips. Friendly staff provide a warm welcome for all, making this local well worth a visit. Local CAMRA Pub of the Year and Cider Pub of the Year 2015.
≠(Warrior Square)♣●🚌🐾📶

Salehurst

Salehurst Halt Ⓛ

Church Lane, TN32 5PH (by church)
closed Mon; 12-11 ☎ (01580) 880620
salehursthalt.co.uk
Harveys Sussex Best Bitter; 2 changing beers Ⓗ
A friendly, traditional, family-run pub, popular with walkers and locals. Guest beers are often from nearby microbreweries and up to three ciders are served in the summer. Good-quality, locally sourced food features strongly. The pretty garden has views over the hop fields in the Rother Valley. Inside, there is a selection of board games, and live music features every second Sunday of the month. On Wednesday evenings in the summer the outdoor pizza oven is popular. Q❀◑♿🍎🐾

Seaford

Wellington Hotel Ⓛ

33 Steyne Road, BN25 1HT
12-11 (midnight Fri & Sat) ☎ (01323) 899517
thewellington-hotel.com
Changing beers (sourced nationally; often Dark Star, Greene King, Long Man Brewery) Ⓗ
Although Greene King supplies the beers for this impressive pub and hotel, the range is amazing and up to 10 can be available, with LocAle and national brewers well represented. Imaginative food deals and accommodation add to the appeal. Situated towards the seafront, it has three rooms – a small sports/TV bar, a big comfortable main bar and another room across the corridor, slightly food-biased. The station, main shops and frequent Brighton-Eastbourne buses are a gentle walk uphill. Q🛏◑⇌🚌

South Chailey

Horns Lodge Ⓛ

South Street, BN8 4BD (on A275)
11.30-2.30 (not Tue), 5.30-11; 11.30-11 Sat; 12-10.30 Sun
☎ (01273) 400422 hornslodge.com
Harveys Sussex Best Bitter; 4 changing beers (sourced regionally) Ⓗ
On the A275 north of Lewes, this pub is popular with locals and visitors alike. Guest beers come from breweries anywhere in the country and at least one cider is always available. The pub has won Country Pub of the Year and Cider Pub of the Year awards from the local CAMRA branch. Various pub games are played including bar billiards and toad in the hole. Food is served daily except Tuesdays. Annual beer, cider and sausage festivals are held. ❀◑♣🍎P🚌(121)🐾

Uckfield

Alma Arms Ⓛ

65 Framfield Road, TN22 5AJ (on B2102)
11-11 (11.30 Fri & Sat); 12-10.30 Sun ☎ (01825) 762232
alma-arms.co.uk
Harveys Sussex XX Mild Ale, Sussex Best Bitter; 1 changing beer (often Harveys) Ⓗ
Harveys pub about five minutes' walk from the town centre, station and buses. The large main bar has smaller seating areas and there are independent meeting/function rooms. A separate area houses a number of traditional games including toad in the hole. While no food is served Monday or Tuesday, Saturday evening has Thai food and Sunday has a selection of roasts 12-4pm. XX Mild is served all year round and the cider is Thatchers Heritage. Q❀◑♿⇌♣🍎P🚌(318,31)🐾

Wivelsfield Green

Cock Inn Ⓛ

North Common Road, RH17 7RH (900yds E of B2112)
12-11; 12-10.30 Sun ☎ (01444) 471668
cockinn-wivelsfield.co.uk
Harveys Sussex Best Bitter; 2 changing beers (sourced locally; often Harveys) Ⓗ
A two-bar pub on the eastern edge of the village, popular with walkers, cyclists and locals alike. A more frequent bus service is available at the other end of the village on routes 40/40X. Two guest beers supplement the Harveys. In summer real cider is available. There is a large garden/seating area to the front and a smaller outdoor area to the side. The recently refurbished lounge bar has a timber-panelled bar counter. Look out for the cow bell. Q❀◑♣P🚌(166,824)🐾

SUSSEX (WEST)

Amberley

Bridge Inn Ⓛ

Houghton Bridge, BN18 9LR (on B2139 just W of railway bridge at Amberley station)
11-11; 12-9 Sun ☎ (01798) 831619
bridgeinnamberley.com
Harveys Sussex Best Bitter; Skinner's Betty Stogs; 1 changing beer (often Langham) Ⓗ
Close to Amberley railway station, Amberley Museum and the South Downs Way, this is a Grade II-listed riverside inn. There is a patio at the front and an attractive gated garden to the side. Inside is a single bar and a large dining area to the rear serving mainly locally sourced produce. The 11th-century church at North Stoke is a pleasant one-mile walk along the riverbank. West Sussex Gazette Pub of the Year 2015.
Q❀◑⇌P🚌(73)🐾

Sportsman Ⓛ

Rackham Road, BN18 9NR (½ mile E of village; signed off B2139)
11-11; 12-10.30 Sun ☎ (01798) 831787
thesportsmanamberley.com
Harveys Sussex Best Bitter; 2 changing beers (sourced locally) Ⓗ
A regular CAMRA branch Pub of the Year winner, the Sportsman is a bracing but rewarding 1½-mile walk along the Arun Valley from Amberley station. An L-shaped bar serves three drinking areas, with at least two the guest beers sourced from local breweries. The modern conservatory restaurant and the outside terrace afford wonderful vistas across the wild brooks. The pub is a popular stop-off for birdwatchers and walkers. The bus serves the pub only on Monday and Friday.
Q❀🛏◑P🚌(73)🐾

Angmering

Spotted Cow Ⓛ

1 The High Street, BN16 4AW (E from village centre along B2225; where B2225 turns S, bear E along unclassified road for about 100yds)
11-3, 5.30-11; 11-11 Fri & Sat; 12-10.30 Sun
☎ (01903) 783919 spottedcowangmering.co.uk

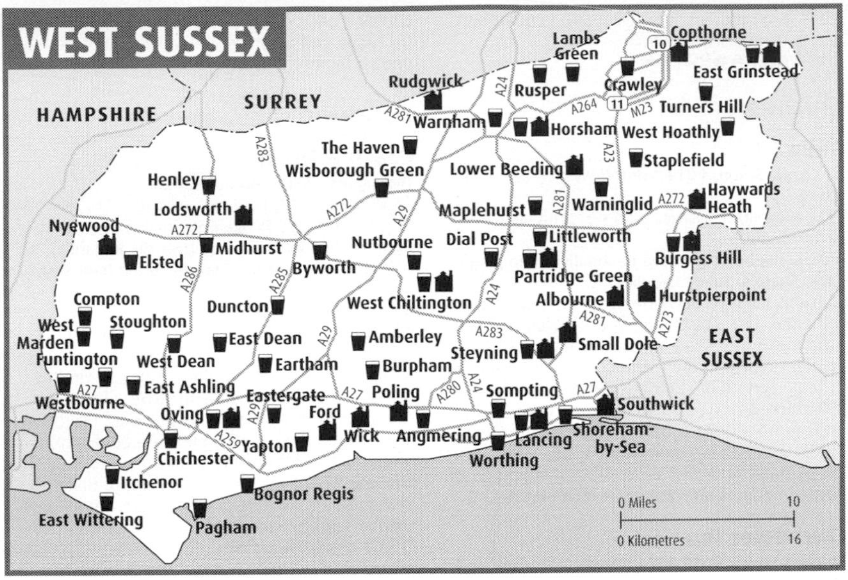

Harveys Sussex Best Bitter; Sharp's Doom Bar; Timothy Taylor Landlord; 3 changing beers H
An 18th-century pub at the end of a country lane away from the centre of Angmering. It has a cosy traditional bar, with a spinning jenny hanging from the ceiling. This was used to divide up contraband between smugglers who used to meet here. There is a large restaurant area including a conservatory for diners. Paintings of cows adorn the walls. The pub has a wonderful garden which offers views of the South Downs. Q A P (9)

Bognor Regis

Hatters L

2-10 Queensway, PO21 1QT (at W end of High St opp Iceland)
8am-midnight (1am Fri & Sat) ☎ (01243) 840206
Greene King Abbot; Ruddles Best Bitter; changing beers (sourced locally; often Goldmark, Irving, Langham) H
This large town-centre Wetherspoon was formerly a Sainsbury's store, part of a concrete '60s retail development at one end of the main shopping street. The usual Wetherspoon beer range of regulars plus changing guests (usually from local micros) can be found, plus good-value food all day. It has an outside drinking and smoking area in a small patio garden at the rear. Public parking is available in Queensway car park or the adjacent multi-storey.

Burgess Hill

Quench Bar & Kitchen L

2-4 Church Road, RH15 9AE
9am-11 (12.30am Thu & Fri; 1am Sat); 11-10.30 Sun
☎ (01444) 253332 quenchbar.co.uk
Harveys Sussex Best Bitter; 2 changing beers (sourced locally; often Dark Star, Downlands) H
Former corner-shop conversion with lounge bar-style décor. The walls are adorned with old postcards of local views alongside more contemporary photographs, also of note is a small display of cameras. Bottled beers from local breweries Kiln and Top-Notch are also featured. Open mic nights are Thursdays from 8.30pm. A limited number of tables and chairs is provided outside. All buses that serve Burgess Hill pass the door.

Burpham

George at Burpham L

Main Street, BN18 9RR
12-3, 6-11; 12-11 Sat; 12-10.30 (5 winter) Sun
☎ (01903) 883131 georgeatburpham.co.uk
Arundel Sussex Gold; Hammerpot Red Hunter; Harveys Sussex Best Bitter; King Beer Horsham Best Bitter H
Formerly the George & Dragon, this attractive village inn was saved from possible closure by local residents and, following tasteful renovation, reopened in 2013. A small single bar with four handpumps offers local ales. The restaurant features an innovative menu (booking is advised in the evening). The car park behind the pub, shared with the recreation ground, affords great views across the Arun Valley and is the starting point for a network of local walks. Walkers are welcome.
Q A P

Byworth

Black Horse Inn L

GU28 0HL (head E from Petworth on the A283 for about 1 mile, then left into The Street)
12-11; 12-8.30 Sun ☎ (01798) 342424
theblackhorseatbyworth.com
Flowerpots Bitter; Fuller's London Pride; 2 changing beers H
Friendly, welcoming, old-style village pub, dating from the 16th century. The cosy bar area has a large open log fire, wooden floors, large beams and wattle and daub walls displaying original photographs and prints. Good real ales are always on tap and guest ales are LocAle. Excellent, locally sourced seasonal food is served. Secluded dining areas overlook the large steeply terraced garden at the back offering stunning views. An iron staircase

leads to an upstairs function room. Regular darts and quiz nights take place.
Q❀♣P (1)

Chichester

Belle Isle

32 Chapel Street, PO19 1AB (off West St, behind post office)
11-midnight; 10-midnight Sat & Sun ☎ (01243) 781085
thebelleisle.co.uk
4 changing beers (sourced nationally; often Magic Rock, Sharp's, Sunny Republic)
Spacious US-style bar/cafe/restaurant close to the cathedral. The atmosphere is of relaxed and retro Americana, attracting families by day and a younger crowd in the evening. Food from the bar or table service area includes nachos, paella and jerk chicken curry. Ales include one from Sharp's and often Sunny Republic Belle Isle Pacific Ale, plus others usually from innovative micros such as First Chop, Magic Rock or Tiny Rebel. A large range of bottled beers is also available. ❀♿

Chichester Inn

38 West Street, PO19 1RP (at Westgate roundabout)
12-11.30 (midnight Fri & Sat); 12-10.30 Sun
☎ (01243) 783185 chichesterinn.co.uk
3 changing beers (sourced locally; often Dark Star, Harveys, Langham)
Pleasant two-bar pub with a real fire, comfy chairs and a mix of seating and table types in the front lounge. The larger public bar to the rear features live music on Wednesday, Friday and Saturday evenings. Outside there is an attractive walled garden with a heated and covered smoking area. Two changing beers, local or otherwise, are added at weekends. Food includes Sunday lunches. Four B&B rooms are available. Between January and March the pub closes 2.30-5.30pm Monday-Thursday and 7pm Sunday. ❀♣P

Dolphin & Anchor

5 West Street, PO19 1QF (opp cathedral)
8am-midnight (1am Fri & Sat) ☎ (01243) 790280
Dark Star Revelation; Greene King Abbot; Sharp's Doom Bar; 5 changing beers (sourced locally; often Arundel, Dark Star, Langham)
The pub is a conversion of part of a historic city centre hotel opposite the cathedral, once two separate hotels that were combined in 1910. it occupies the lower floors of what was the Anchor, and has improved remarkably since the current manager arrived in 2013. The venue is now always popular with young and old alike, and it can be crowded at the bar on weekend evenings. It champions local microbreweries and hosts monthly Meet the Brewer evenings. ❀♿

Eastgate

4 The Hornet, PO19 7JG (500yds E of Market Cross)
12 (11 Wed)-11; 10-12.30am Sat; 12-11.30 Sun
☎ (01243) 774877 theeastgate.co.uk
Fuller's London Pride; Gales Seafarers Ale, HSB; 2 changing beers (sourced nationally; often Adnams, Fuller's, Ossett)
Welcoming town pub with an open-plan bar and tables for diners. Good-quality traditional pub meals are served daily. There is a heated patio garden to the rear, the venue for a beer festival in July. The pub attracts locals, holidaymakers and shoppers from the nearby market with its warm welcome and traditional pub games such as darts, cribbage and pool. Music is turned up late evening on Friday and Saturday, while live bands perform once a month. ❀♣ (51,700)

Compton

Coach & Horses

The Square, PO18 9HA (on B2146)
closed Mon; 12-3, 6-11; 12-3, 7-10 Sun
☎ (023) 9263 1228 coachandhorsescompton.com
Burning Sky Plateau; house beer (by Ballard's); 3 changing beers (sourced locally; often Dark Star, Hammerpot, Langham)
A 16th-century pub in a remote but lovely downland village, popular with walkers and cyclists. The front bar is warm and welcoming with an open fire. A wooden floor, internal window shutters and a wood-burning stove all add character to this excellent village pub. Up to five beers are on tap at weekends. An adventurous menu offers high-quality locally sourced food. The house beer is a dry-hopped version of Ballard's Best Bitter. David and Christiane are the longest serving landlord and landlady in the area.
Q❀♣ (54)

Crawley

Brewery Shades

85 High Street, RH10 1BA
10-11.30 (1am Fri & Sat); 10-10.30 Sun ☎ (01293) 514105
Greene King Abbot; Morland Old Speckled Hen; 4 changing beers
Arguably the oldest building in Crawley High Street, dating back to the 1400s and complete with two active ghosts. The pub is beer-led. The licensee has a true passion for the trade, demonstrated by the inspired range of guest ales and ciders. The haunted upstairs room is now available for meetings. Good food is served during the day and evening – check the specials board or try the mixed grill. ❀

REAL ALE BREWERIES

Adur Steyning
Anchor Springs Wick
Arundel Ford
Ballard's Nyewood
Baseline Small Dole
Bedlam Albourne
Crooked Brook Copthorne (NEW)
Dark Star Partridge Green
Downlands Small Dole
Firebird Rudgwick
Goldmark Poling
Greyhound West Chiltington (NEW)
Gribble Oving
Hammerpot Poling
Heathen Haywards Heath (NEW)
Hepworth Horsham
High Weald East Grinstead
Hurst Hurstpierpoint
Kiln Burgess Hill (NEW)
King Beer Horsham
Kissingate Lower Beeding
Langham Lodsworth
Lister's Ford
Naked Lancing
Pin-Up Southwick
Top-Notch Haywards Heath
Weltons Horsham

Swan 𝕃
1 Horsham Road, West Green, RH11 7AY
⏲ 12-11 (1am Fri & Sat) ☎ (01293) 527447
🌐 theswanpubcrawley.co.uk
Fuller's London Pride; Sharp's Doom Bar; 4 changing beers [H]
A superb example of a street-corner local, this bustling pub is conveniently close to the town centre and on a bus route. No food is served – this is a drinkers' pub, but you are free to bring your own grub. The varied beers frequently include strong brews. Two to three beer festivals are held a year and the pub supports CAMRA's Mild Day in May, serving up to 12 milds. Regular live music is hosted. ♘❀♿⇌♣🍎▯🚌(23)🐾

Dial Post

Crown Inn
Worthing Road, RH13 8NH
⏲ 12-3, 6-11; 12-3 Sun ☎ (01403) 710902
🌐 floatingcrown.co.uk
Harveys Sussex Best Bitter; 2 changing beers [H]
Charming family-run 16th-century pub keen to support local breweries. Its superb home-cooked food is also sourced locally wherever possible. The cosy bar area has kept its traditional style, with oak beams and a woodburner. There is a choice of three dining areas – the conservatory, restaurant and snug – each with a different feel. Walkers and their dogs are welcome. No food Sunday evening. Q♘❀🛏◐◑♿⛺🍎P🚌(23,108)🐾

Duncton

Cricketers 𝕃
High Street, GU28 0LB (on A285 about 5 miles S of Petworth)
⏲ 11-11; 12-10.30 Sun ☎ (01798) 342473
🌐 thecricketersduncton.co.uk
Dark Star Partridge Best Bitter; Triple fff Moondance; 2 changing beers [H]
Family-run 16th-century coaching inn, set in the heart of the West Sussex countryside and close to Goodwood racecourse. Wooden beams run throughout, with a solid oak bar and a large haunted inglenook fireplace, creating an old-fashioned ambience. Good real ales, including LocAles and draught cider, are on tap. Excellent locally sourced home-cooked food, featuring fish and game whenever possible, is on the menu. A function room is available for hire. A large garden is to the rear and families are welcome. Q♘❀◐◑🍎P🚌(99)🐾

Eartham

George 𝕃
PO18 0LT
⏲ closed Mon; 11.30-11; 12-7 Sun ☎ (01243) 814340
🌐 thegeorgeeartham.com
Langham Hip Hop; house beer (by Otter); 2 changing beers (sourced locally; often Bedlam, Downlands, Goldmark) [H]
A spacious old village pub whose landlord's passion for the best of English, and especially Sussex, extends to the entire drinks and food menu. All changing beers are from West Sussex microbreweries. Usually one is a hoppy golden ale while the other is a porter, old ale or mild. The food menu features locally sourced ingredients. Popular with walkers and cyclists, the pub holds a beer festival in its garden each April showcasing 21 West Sussex ales and live music.
Q♘❀◐◑♿P🚌(99)🐾📶

East Ashling

Horse & Groom 𝕃
PO18 9AX (on B2178 in village) SU820077
⏲ 12-11; 12-6 Sun ☎ (01243) 575339
🌐 thehorseandgroomchichester.co.uk
Dark Star Hophead; Hop Back Summer Lightning; Sharp's Doom Bar; Young's Bitter; 1 changing beer (sourced regionally; often Burning Sky) [H]
Between the South Downs and the sea, this fine country free house has been an inn for over 200 years, with a compact bar featuring flagstones, settles, half-panelled walls and a lovely old range. Sympathetically extended, it remains unspoilt. The beers are meticulously presented and sold at consistently good-value prices. A blackboard reveals the diverse, high-quality menu of home-made dishes, all sourced locally (no food Sun eve). En-suite accommodation is dog-friendly, some in a converted 17th-century oak-beamed flint barn.
Q❀🛏◐◑♿⛺♣P▯🚌(54)🐾📶

East Dean

Star & Garter
PO18 0JG (overlooking pond)
⏲ 12-3, 6-11; 11-11 Sat; 12-11 Sun ☎ (01243) 811318
🌐 thestarandgarter.co.uk
Arundel Black Stallion, Castle, Sussex Gold [G]
Nestled opposite the duckpond in this charming downland village, this is an 18th-century free house. Wooden floors and a log fire make the large bar/restaurant most welcoming. It is renowned for good food, using local seasonal produce, with fresh local fish a speciality (booking essential Sun lunchtime). Local Arundel beer is poured straight from the cask from a cold room behind the bar. There is a large walled garden to the rear with several tables and benches. Draught cider is Westons 1st Quality. ♘❀🛏◐◑♿♣🍎

East Grinstead

Ounce & Ivy Bush 𝕃
Little King Street, RH19 3DJ
⏲ 8am-11.30; 8am-10 Sun ☎ (01342) 335130
Adnams Broadside; Greene King Abbot; Ruddles Best Bitter; changing beers [H]
A former bowling alley conveniently situated in the town centre with a name reflecting one of the town's former inns. A local landowning family had a coat of arms featuring the ounce, a wild cat, and an ivy bush, connected with Bacchus, was used to denote a high-class inn. This spacious and family-friendly pub serves food all day and is LocAle accredited, showcasing a local brewery each month. Q♘◐◑♿⇌🚌📶

East Wittering

Shore 𝕃
Shore Road, PO20 8DZ (50yds from sea)
⏲ 11-11; 11-10.30 Sun ☎ (01243) 674454
🌐 theshorepub.co.uk
Dark Star Hophead, American Pale Ale; Palmers Copper Ale; Sharp's Doom Bar, Atlantic; 1 changing beer (sourced regionally; often St Austell) [H]

Friendly beach-side town pub popular with the locals (particularly dog owners) and the many summer visitors. There are two main bars, a children's room and a fair-sized decked area for outside drinking and smoking. The good-quality lunchtime menu can be enjoyed either in the bar or restaurant. Evening meals are only served Thursday (locals night) and Friday (fish night), when extremely inviting menus are on offer at fair prices. Live music features occasionally.
Q🐴❀◐◑♿♣P⊟🚌(52,53)🐾📶

Eastergate

Wilkes Head 🄻

Church Lane, PO20 3UT (off A29 in old village, 350yds S of B2233 roundabout, 1⅓ miles W of Barnham Station) SU943053
✪ 12-11 ☎ (01243) 543380 🌐 wilkesheadeastergate.co.uk
Adnams Southwold Bitter; 5 changing beers (sourced regionally; often Langham, Long Man Brewery, Oakleaf) 🄷
Small Grade II-listed red-brick pub, built in 1803 and named after the 18th-century radical John Wilkes. There is a cosy lounge left of the central bar and to the right a larger room with an inglenook fireplace, flagstones and low beams, plus a separate restaurant. At the rear is a permanent marquee with seating plus a heated smokers' shelter and a large garden. There are five well-chosen changing beers, and regular beer festivals are held. Local CAMRA Pub of the Year 2014.
Q🐴❀◐◑♿♣🍎P🚌(66,85)🐾📶

Elsted

Three Horseshoes

Elsted, GU29 0JY (at E end of village)
✪ 11-2.30, 6-11; 12-3, 7-10.30 Sun ☎ (01730) 825746
Bowman Wallops Wood; Flowerpots Bitter; Young's Bitter; 2 changing beers (sourced locally; often Ballard's, Langham) 🄶
Old and cosy rural inn divided into small rooms, including one reserved for dining and one with a blazing log fire in winter. Outside, the large, pleasant garden enjoys superb views of the South Downs. In summer there are five beers, mainly from local micros, and three in winter, all served by gravity from a stillage alongside the bar. Meals are substantial and of high quality. This is a popular and homely pub, which you will be reluctant to leave.
Q❀◐◑♣P🐾

Funtington

Fox & Hounds

PO18 9LL (on B2146)
✪ 10 (9am Sat)-11; 9am-10.30 Sun ☎ (01243) 575246
🌐 foxandhoundsfuntington.co.uk
Dark Star Hophead; Timothy Taylor Landlord; 2 changing beers (sourced regionally; often Bowman, Long Man, Otter) 🄷
Tastefully modernised roadside village inn on the fringe of the South Downs with a comfortable single bar and rear dining area. Two changing beers are usually from local breweries while the high-quality meals include breakfast from 9am on Saturdays and Sundays, and a carvery served noon-8pm on Sundays. The pub is popular with cyclists and walkers. There is an attractive rear garden plus a front patio, and bank holiday beer festivals are held twice a year. 🐴❀◐◑⛺♣🍎P🚌(54)🐾📶

Henley

Duke of Cumberland 🄻

GU27 3HQ (off A286, 3 miles N of Midhurst) SU894258
✪ 11-11; 12-10.30 Sun ☎ (01428) 652280
🌐 dukeofcumberland.com
Harveys Sussex Best Bitter; Langham Hip Hop, Best; 1 changing beer (sourced locally; often Langham) 🄶
Stunning 15th-century inn nestling against the hillside in over three acres of terraced gardens with extensive views. The rustic front bar has scrubbed-top tables and benches, plus log fires at both ends, while to the rear is a dining extension that blends in perfectly with the original pub and offers much-needed additional space. Outside is a smokers' shelter with its own woodburner. A former local CAMRA Pub of the Year, this is a rural gem. May close winter Sunday evenings. Q❀◐◑♣P🚌(70)🐾

Horsham

Anchor Hotel 🄻

3 Market Square, RH12 1EU
✪ 11-11 (1am Fri & Sat); 12-10.30 Sun ☎ (01403) 250640
Harveys Sussex Best Bitter; 3 changing beers 🄷
This Taylor Walker pub is an impressive Victorian building in the heart of the town, comprising a large ground floor room and balcony room, plus a heated courtyard to the rear. Freshly prepared great British pub food is served daily. There is an emphasis on local ales, complemented by the occasional festival featuring beers from around the country. CAMRA members receive a 10 per cent discount on ales. The Anchor hosts a variety of entertainment including live music, comedy, DJs and quizzes. 🐴❀◐◑♿⇌🚌📶

Beer Essentials 🄻

30a East Street, RH12 1HL
✪ closed Mon; 10-6 (7 Fri & Sat); closed Sun
☎ (01403) 218890 🌐 thebeeressentials.co.uk
Arundel Sussex Gold; changing beers 🄶
A mecca for the connoisseur, this shop opened in Horsham following the demise of King & Barnes in 2000. Up to seven cask ales are served on gravity to take away in two-, four- and eight-pint containers, along with JB medium cider and occasionally perry. The shop also stocks over 150 bottled beers from near and far. A popular beer festival is organised each September in the nearby Drill Hall. Every town should have a shop like this!
Q♿⇌🍎🚌🐾

Lynd Cross 🄻

1 Springfield Road, RH12 2PJ
✪ 8am-11 (midnight Fri & Sat); 8am-10.30 Sun
☎ (01403) 272393
Greene King Abbot; Ruddles Best Bitter; Shepherd Neame Spitfire; changing beers (sourced locally) 🄷
At the end of West Street opposite Shelley's Fountain, the large, popular and unpretentious Lynd Cross occupies premises that were formerly the Horsham Pine Shop. It is a family-friendly open-plan town pub. The local ale is usually sourced from WJ King. The pub hosts Meet the Brewer sessions and several beer festivals throughout the year. Q🐴❀◐◑♿⛺⇌🍎🚌📶

Malt Shovel 🄻

15 Springfield Road, RH12 2PG
✪ 11-11 (1am Fri & Sat); 12-midnight Sun ☎ (01403) 252302
Robinsons Trooper; Timothy Taylor Landlord; changing beers 🄷

Near to the town centre, the pub has a pleasant, warm, bright interior. There are normally up to six real ales and one cider on draught. Ales come from the Enterprise list, but with one guest. The pub usually has live music on Friday and Saturday nights and hosts open mic evenings.
❀♿♣🍎P🚌🐾📶

Piries Bar Ⓛ

15 Piries Place, RH12 1NY
⏲ 11-midnight (2am Fri & Sat); 11-1am Sun
☎ (01403) 267846 🌐 piriesbar.co.uk
Dark Star Hophead Ⓗ
In a building dating from the 15th century with exposed original timber beams, the pub is tucked away down a narrow alley adjoining Horsham's Carfax. It comprises a small downstairs room, an upstairs lounge bar, and a small modern extension in character with the building. Regular charity events are organised. Evenings here can be lively, with karaoke on Sundays, quiz night on Tuesdays and occasional live music. With two cask ales always on offer, this bar is well worth a visit.
🐴◑⇄🚌

Itchenor

Ship

The Street, PO20 7AH (on main street, 100yds from waterfront)
⏲ 11-11; 11-10.30 Sun ☎ (01243) 512284
🌐 theshipinnitchenor.co.uk
Arundel Castle; Ballard's Best Bitter; King Beer Horsham Best Bitter; Langham Hip Hop; 1 changing beer (sourced locally) Ⓗ
Popular pub in an attractive village on the shore of picturesque Chichester harbour. A cosy bar decorated with yachting memorabilia adds to the pub's character, complemented by a pleasant patio, a suntrap in summer. A separate restaurant area offers a wide range of traditional meals including locally landed fish. Accommodation includes a self-contained three-bed cottage and B&B rooms. Buses 52 and 53 stop on the B2179 over a mile away, but the 150 makes occasional stops opposite the pub. Q❀🛏◑◐♿♣P🐾📶

Lambs Green

Lamb Inn Ⓛ

RH12 4RG (2 miles N of A264)
⏲ 11.30-3, 5.30-11; 11-11 Fri & Sat; 12-10.30 Sun
☎ (01293) 871336
Dark Star Hophead; 3 changing beers Ⓗ
Lovely old inn with a mixture of flagstones and wood floors interspersed with wrought-iron work, low-beamed ceilings and exposed brick walls. Furnishings include high-backed settles and soft sofas, and a real fire adds warmth in winter. This welcoming pub with a friendly landlord and staff is committed to LocAle – all beers come from within 25 miles and customers elect the guest beer. Lunchtime and evening meals are served daily using quality home-made locally sourced ingredients, and breakfast is available at weekends. Q🐴❀◑◐♿♣🍎P🚌(52)🐾📶

Lancing

Crabtree Inn

140 Crabtree Lane, BN15 9NQ (head N from Lancing station and turn left at Crabtree Parade of shops; pub is about ½ mile further on)
⏲ 11-11 (12.30am Fri & Sat) ☎ (01903) 755514
Fuller's London Pride; 3 changing beers Ⓗ
A 1930s red-brick community local, of traditional Kemptown Brewery house design, offering three rotating guest ales. The large public bar has darts and pool. The recently refurbished lounge bar offers a quieter, more relaxed experience, and can also be booked for functions. Live music is featured monthly. The garden is spacious, child- and dog-friendly, and includes a covered smoking area. The menu features home-made pies and a Sunday carvery. Recent investment has modernised the pub without sacrificing its traditional ambience.
🐴❀◑◐⇄♣P🚌🐾

Littleworth

Windmill

Littleworth Lane, RH13 8EJ (from A24 or A272 follow signs to Partridge Green along B2135)
⏲ 11.30-11 (midnight Sat); 12-10.30 Sun ☎ (01403) 710308
🌐 windmilllittleworth.com
Harveys Sussex Best Bitter; 2 changing beers Ⓗ
A quiet, independently owned country pub with friendly staff and locals. It has recently undergone a refurbishment but retains many original features including the stone-flagged floor between the two bars. There is an open inglenook fire in the lounge, and the public bar ceiling is decorated with old farming implements. Darts and bar billiards can be played here. A range of second-hand books is for sale in the lobby. Guest ales come from throughout the country. Q❀🛏◑◐♿♣P🎯🚌(17)🐾📶

Maplehurst

White Horse 🏆 Ⓛ

Park Lane, RH13 6LL
⏲ 12-2.30 (not Mon), 6-11; 12-2.30, 6-11.30 Fri & Sat; 12-3, 7.30-11 Sun ☎ (01403) 891208
Harveys Sussex Best Bitter; Weltons Pride 'n' Joy; 3 changing beers Ⓗ
Under the same ownership for over 30 years, this splendid and welcoming country pub has featured in the Guide 29 times. Popular with locals, cyclists and walkers, the cosy interior, with its unusually large wooden bar, boasts real fires and many interesting artefacts and bric-a-brac. While good honest pub fare is provided, the emphasis is on beer and conversation. Many local beers feature, including a good selection of dark ales. Local JB cider is also stocked. Q🐴❀◑◐♣🍎P🐾📶

Midhurst

Swan Ⓛ

Red Lion Street, GU29 9PB (opp church in old town)
⏲ 12-11 (midnight Fri & Sat); 12-11.30 Sun
☎ (01730) 812853
Harveys Sussex Best Bitter; 2 changing beers (often Harveys) Ⓗ
Historic split-level town pub with a boisterous lower section featuring a dartboard and TVs showing sport. Modern decor and wooden flooring feature throughout but the upper section is quieter and cosier, with armchairs and a woodburner,

wooden beams and TVs in silent mode. There is a small area used mainly for dining. Harveys seasonal beers are served alongside one of its regulars and the mainstay Sussex Best. Accommodation is in three en-suite rooms. Limited public parking nearby. Q⚇❀🛏◐◑♣🚌(1,60)🐾📶

Nutbourne

Rising Sun 🄻

The Street, RH20 2HE (turn left off A283 just before bridge over River Chilt)

⏲ 11-3, 6-11; 12-4 Sun ☎ (01798) 812191

🌐 therisingsunnutbourne.co.uk

Draught Bass; Fuller's London Pride; Young's Bitter; 3 changing beers 🄷

This attractive, welcoming, 16th-century village hostelry has been in the Howard family since 1981. It is the centre of village activity, even serving as the local polling station. Excellent food is available in the cosy restaurant and bar area and a good choice of beers, including LocAles. It is a proper pub, with an open log fire and a distinct rural appeal. The garden has chickens and a fine example of a listed outside privy.
Q❀◐◑♣🍎🚌(1)🐾📶

Oving

Gribble Inn 🄻

Gribble Lane, PO20 2BP (at W end of village)

⏲ 11-11; 12-11 Sun ☎ (01243) 786893 🌐 gribbleinn.co.uk

Gribble Ale, Fuzzy Duck, Reg's Tipple, Plucking Pheasant, Pig's Ear 🄷

Once home to a Miss Gribble, this attractive thatched cottage has been a traditional village pub for over 30 years and is home to the Gribble Brewery. It also now houses the village shop. A wide range of Gribble regulars complemented by seasonals are permanently on tap. It is always cosy, with log fires in winter, and home-made food is served in the bar/restaurant. In summer a large attractive garden offers occasional weekend barbecues and the skittle alley is also available for functions. Q⚇❀◐◑♿♣P🚌(85,85A)🐾📶

Pagham

Inglenook 🏆

255 Pagham Road, PO21 3QB

⏲ 11-11 (midnight Fri & Sat) ☎ (01243) 262495

🌐 the-inglenook.com

Fuller's London Pride; Young's Special; 4 changing beers (sourced nationally; often Dark Star, Magic Rock, Thornbridge) 🄷

A 16th-century Grade II-listed hotel, restaurant and free house, owned and run by the Honour family for over 40 years. The hotel is open to non-residents and has facilities for conferences, functions and wedding receptions. There is always a selection of excellent real ales from highly regarded microbreweries, which can be enjoyed in the bar areas, restaurant and front or back gardens. Changing beers tend to be on the strong side. Local CAMRA Pub of the Year 2015.
⚇❀🛏◐◑P🚌(60)🐾📶

Partridge Green

Partridge 🄻

Church Road, RH13 8JS (on B2135 at jct of High St and Church Rd)

⏲ 12-11; 12-10.30 Sun ☎ (01403) 710391

Dark Star Hophead, Partridge Best Bitter; 3 changing beers (often Dark Star) 🄷

A spacious village-centre pub (a former railway hotel) and the Dark Star Brewery tap. It offers great quality ales from the Dark Star range, plus a changing choice of interesting guest ales. Wood-panelled floors run throughout. There are two bars and a separate restaurant area to the rear, with a varied menu offering excellent food. Darts is played in the public bar. There is easily accessible off-street parking.
Q⚇❀◐◑♿♣🍎P🚌(17,108)🐾📶

Rusper

Royal Oak 🄻

Friday Street, RH12 4QA (on Langhurstwood Rd off A264 N of Horsham)

⏲ 12-2.30, 5-9; 12-9 Sat; 12-4 Sun ☎ (01293) 871393

🌐 theroyaloakrusper.webs.com

Surrey Hills Ranmore; 5 changing beers (sourced locally) 🄷

The pub is on a back road between Rusper and Horsham. Seven handpumps dispense real ale from a variety of sources, and two ciders and two perries are usually available. No lager, keg beer or Guinness is served. The Royal Oak raises considerable sums for charity through hosting community events including pantomime horse racing, chicken and snail races, and weed shows. Children are not allowed in the pub.
Q❀🛏◐◑⛺♣🍎P🐾📶

Shoreham-by-Sea

Duke of Wellington 🄻

368 Brighton Road, BN43 6RE (on A259)

⏲ 12-11 (1am Fri & Sat) ☎ (01273) 441297

🌐 dukeofwellingtonbrewhouse.co.uk/home

Dark Star Hophead, American Pale Ale; 4 changing beers (sourced regionally) 🄷

On the eastern side of town, the Welly has plenty of guest beers and always a real cider, together with a good selection of continental bottled beers. There is often live music, especially at the weekend. The planned microbrewery will be the first in the town for nearly 80 years. The leaded windows show that this was once a Kemptown Brewery pub. Cold pies are now available.
❀⥭♣🍎🚌(2,2A,700)🐾📶

Sompting

Gardeners Arms 🄻

West Street, BN15 0AR (on B2222, just S of A27)

⏲ 11-11 (midnight Fri & Sat); 12-11 Sun ☎ (01903) 233666

Harveys Sussex Best Bitter; Hurst Founders Best Bitter; Sharp's Doom Bar; 2 changing beers 🄷

The pub with the train, as it has been referred to, is a friendly free house, located on the original village main street, with a 1962 BR passenger carriage built onto the side. The name of the pub has remained unchanged since 1858. Prints of old Sompting adorn the walls. There is a golf society based here and cribbage is played. One of the guest beers is usually a Harveys dark ale. Home-cooked food is served daily. Q⚇◐◑P🚌(7,16)🐾

Staplefield

Jolly Tanners 🄻
Handcross Road, RH17 6EF
⏲ 11-3, 5.30-11; 11-11 Fri & Sat; 12-10.30 Sun
☎ (01444) 400335 🌐 jollytanners.com
Fuller's London Pride; Harveys Sussex Best Bitter; changing beers 🄷
Independently run free house on the north corner of the cricket green which takes a great pride in providing a wide selection of real ale and cider, as well as tasty food made using local ingredients where possible. This is a friendly place and well worth a visit. A roaring fire welcomes you in winter and there are open mic evenings on Tuesdays. Beer festivals are held regularly during the year, with an excellent range of ales to be enjoyed. CAMRA branch Pub of the Year 2013.
Q🐎❀◐◑♿⛺♣●P🚌(271)🐾📶

Steyning

Chequer Inn 🄻
41 High Street, BN44 3RE
⏲ 10-11 (midnight Fri & Sat) ☎ (01903) 814437
🌐 chequerinnsteyning.co.uk
Dark Star Hophead; Gales HSB; 3 changing beers 🄷
A 15th-century coaching inn retaining many original design features. It has several drinking areas including a covered courtyard garden and a cosy saloon bar with an open log fire. Along with large plasma TVs in the public bar is a 100-year-old three-quarter-size snooker table. Guest ales come from a changing local and regional SIBA list. Home-cooked traditional and speciality food utilises locally sourced ingredients, with the breakfasts ever popular. An hourly bus service operates from Shoreham-by-Sea.
Q🐎❀🛏◐◑♣🚌(2,100,106)🐾📶

Norfolk Arms Hotel
13 Church Street, BN44 3YB (E of village centre, two mins' walk N from White Horse roundabout)
⏲ 12-2, 6-11 (midnight Fri & Sat); 12-2, 7-10.30 Sun
☎ (01903) 812215
Goldmark Hop Idol; Harveys Sussex Best Bitter; Long Man Best Bitter; 1 changing beer 🄷
A traditional beer drinkers' pub, set back off the main high street, with an ambience that is welcoming and friendly. It is a real gem and will take you back in time. An alehouse since at least 1880, parts of the building date from 1668 – original beams are evident and there are real open fires. The pub is home to both cricket and rugby teams. It offers a regularly changing selection of mostly local ales. **Q🐎❀🚌**(2,100,106)🐾

Stoughton

Hare & Hounds 🄻
PO18 9JQ (off B2146, through Walderton) SU803115
⏲ 11-3, 6-11; 11-11 Fri & Sat; 12-10.30 Sun
☎ (02392) 631433 🌐 hareandhoundspub.co.uk
Dark Star Hophead; Flack Manor Double Drop; Harveys Sussex Best Bitter; Otter Amber; 1 changing beer (sourced locally) 🄷
An ideal base for walking, this is a traditional country pub in a beautiful setting. A large dining room serves fresh local produce while the public bar, with racing car pictures and its own fire, is the locals' choice. Two open fires, stone-flagged floors and simple furniture create a wonderful atmosphere. Outside is a paved drinking area and a garden at the back. The 54 bus stops on the B2146, a mile away. The cider is Westons Family Reserve.
Q❀◐◑⛺♣●P📶

The Haven

Blue Ship ★
RH14 9BS (opp Okehurst Road North)
⏲ closed Mon; 11.30-3, 6-11; 11-3, 6-10.30 Thu; 11-3, 6-11 Fri & Sat; 12-4 Sun ☎ (01403) 822709 🌐 theblueship.co.uk
Badger K&B Sussex Bitter; 1 changing beer (often Badger) 🄶
The Blue Ship dates from the 15th/16th centuries. It has four separate rooms retaining many original features, with log fires and a coal-burning stove. Beer is served from two hatches and is on stillage. Excellent pub food is available, with Sunday lunches particularly popular. The pub hosts a gun club and in July the Newfoundland Dog Show. Included in CAMRA's National Inventory of Historic Pub Interiors. **Q🐎❀◐◑♿⛺♣P🐾**

Turners Hill

Red Lion 🄻
Lion Lane, RH10 4NU
⏲ 11-3, 5-11; 11-11 Sat; 12-10.30 Sun ☎ (01342) 715416
🌐 redlionturnershill.com
Harveys Sussex XX Mild Ale, IPA, Sussex Best Bitter, Armada Ale; 2 changing beers (often Harveys) 🄷
Still very much a village local, offering a warm welcome to all who enter. It is a split-level pub with a large inglenook fireplace. Good-value and high-quality lunchtime food is served. The pub has recently had a tasteful extension to the dining area. Children and dogs are welcome and there is a fortnightly quiz. North Sussex CAMRA hosted its first meeting here in 1974 and a beer festival was held to celebrate its 40th anniversary in March 2014. **Q🐎❀◐♿♣●P🚌**(82,84)🐾📶

Warnham

Sussex Oak 🄻
2 Church Street, RH12 3QW
⏲ 11-11; 11-10.30 Sun ☎ (01403) 265028
🌐 thesussexoak.co.uk
Fuller's London Pride; Harveys Sussex Best Bitter; Timothy Taylor Landlord; 3 changing beers 🄷
Popular village pub with a separate dining area. Six handpumps deliver three regular beers and up to three guests. LocAle is actively supported. In the summer months two handpumps dispense real cider and perry. An extensive menu of high-quality, reasonably priced food is available. There is a large garden and dogs are welcome. Quiz nights are held fortnightly, jazz nights on the last Thursday of the month, and beer festivals on bank holidays.
Q🐎❀◐◑♿♣●P🚌🐾📶

Warninglid

Half Moon 🄻
The Street, RH17 5TR
⏲ 11.30-3, 5.30-11; 12-8 Sun ☎ (01444) 461227
🌐 thehalfmoonwarninglid.co.uk
Harveys Sussex Best Bitter; Hurst Founders Best Bitter; Young's Bitter; 1 changing beer 🄷
Large village pub dating back in parts to the 16th century. The entrance leads straight into the bar with oak beams, wooden floors and an open fire. To the right are two further rooms with fires and a

large smartly furnished restaurant featuring a covered and illuminated well flush with the floor. The cellar was upgraded in 2014 with auto-tilt stillage. Regular events take place including a cheesecake charity fundraiser each June.
Q ☸ ❀ ▭ ◐ ♿ P 🚌 (89) 🐾 ᯤ

West Chiltington

Five Bells L

Smock Alley, RH20 2QX (S of West Chiltington)
⏲ 12-3, 6-11; 12-3, 7-10.30 Sun ☎ (01798) 812143
🌐 thefivebellsinn.com
Harveys Sussex Best Bitter; Long Man Best Bitter; 3 changing beers H
Friendly village free house dating from 1935 and run by the same couple since 1983. It offers excellent ales including local brews. A mild is usually on tap, along with Kentish cider. The spacious bar has probably the longest copper top counter in Sussex, and there is a large copper-hooded open fire. Locally sourced home-cooked food is served in the bar and large conservatory dining area, daily except Sunday evening. The accommodation is dog-friendly.
Q ☸ ❀ ▭ ◐ ● P 🚌 (1,74) 🐾 ᯤ

West Dean

Dean Ale & Cider House

Midhurst Road, PO18 0QX (on A286 just S of West Dean College)
⏲ 11-11 (midnight Fri & Sat); 12-10.30 Sun
☎ (01243) 811465 🌐 thedeaninn.co.uk
House beer (by Downlands); 3 changing beers (sourced nationally; often Adnams, Downlands, Tiny Rebel) H
Traditional roadside village pub close to the South Downs and Centurion Way cycle route with an allocated parking area for bicycles. The decor is modern with a stylish beamed bar and spaciously arranged comfortable seating areas, some with sofas. The adjoining high-ceilinged restaurant area is similarly styled, with a large conservatory extension. Outside is a rear garden with both decked and grassed areas. The pub may close on Monday in winter and may only have two changing beers. Q ☸ ❀ ▭ ◐ ♿ ▲ ♣ ● P 🚌 (60) 🐾 ᯤ

West Hoathly

Cat

North Lane, RH19 4PP (next to church)
⏲ 12-11; 12-4 Sun ☎ (01342) 810369 🌐 catinn.co.uk
Harveys Sussex Best Bitter; Larkins Best; 2 changing beers H
A 16th-century free house with four bedrooms in the hilltop village of West Hoathly, ideally situated for walkers. Food is prepared using seasonal vegetables locally sourced where possible. This is a privately owned pub which concentrates on local breweries. Real cider is sometimes available. The main part of the building features a number of timber-beamed rooms with inglenook fireplaces and a well. Q ☸ ❀ ▭ ◐ ♿ ▲ P 🚌 🐾 ᯤ

West Marden

Victoria

PO18 9EN (just W of B2146)
⏲ closed Mon; 12-2.30, 6-10.30 (11 Fri); 12-11 Sat; 12-10 Sun
☎ (023) 9263 1330 🌐 victoriainnwestmarden.co.uk
3 changing beers (sourced locally; often Bowman, Langham) H
Comfortable old rural inn at the heart of its tiny downland community. Cricket and bar billiards teams plus a golf society help maintain its local involvement, and all kinds of country pursuits including walking, riding and shooting are supported. Inside there are several intimate spaces in which to drink and dine, with a log-burning stove for cold evenings. The front garden has splendid views of the surrounding hills. Changing beers usually come from local breweries and occasional beer festivals celebrate local ales.
Q ❀ ◐ P 🚌 (54) 🐾 ᯤ

Westbourne

Stag's Head L

The Square, PO10 8UE (on B2147)
⏲ 12-midnight; 12-11 Sun ☎ (01243) 372393
Bowman Yumi; Greene King IPA; Irving Invincible; Oakleaf Hole Hearted; 1 changing beer (sourced locally; often Flowerpots) H
Early 19th-century pub built on the site of the village market and subsequently extended into a neighbouring shop. The newer area is mainly used for dining (no food Sun eves or Mon Sept-Apr), leaving the remainder of the L-shaped bar with its real fire for drinkers. There is an outside bar in the yard which comes into its own during beer festivals, when the list can feature ales from far and wide. Occasional cider festivals are also held.
☸ ❀ ◐ ♣ ● ▯ 🚌 (36,54) 🐾 ᯤ

Wisborough Green

Three Crowns

Billingshurst Road, RH14 0DX
⏲ 11-11; 12-10.30 Sun ☎ (01403) 700239
🌐 thethreecrownsinn.com
Bedlam Hoppy Golden Ale; Hogs Back TEA; 2 changing beers (often Downlands) H
A warm welcome awaits at this cosy village pub adjacent to the cricket green. A fireplace with a woodburner creates an inviting atmosphere. The pub serves a selection of handpicked local ales including Three Crowns Crowning Glory Ale by Downland. Food is home-cooked using local produce within a 20-mile radius. Regular live music is hosted on a Tuesday night and a seven-course food and beer matching evening was introduced in 2013. Well worth a visit. Q ☸ ❀ ◐ ♿ ♣ P 🚌 🐾 ᯤ

Worthing

Anchored in Worthing L

27 West Buildings, BN11 3BS (close to seafront)
⏲ closed Mon; 12-9.30; 12-5.30 Sun ☎ (01903) 529100
🌐 anchoredinworthing.co.uk
3 changing beers (sourced locally) G
Anchored was the first micropub to open in Sussex. It is between the seafront and the western end of the shopping precinct. On offer is a varied choice of three ales, three ciders, bottled beers, wines and cheeses. All come from across the county. At lunchtimes food can be purchased from the café next door. Among the eclectic range of furniture in this cosy bar is a seat from a B-17 bomber.
Q ● 🚌 (700) ᯤ

Castle Tavern 🄻

1 Newlands Road, BN11 1JR (just E of roundabout on A24 at S foot of railway bridge)

5-11 (midnight Fri); 6-midnight Sat; closed Sun

☎ (01903) 230888

Dark Star Hophead; Harveys Sussex Best Bitter; 3 changing beers Ⓗ

A short walk from Worthing town centre or railway station will take you to this genuine free house. It was built in the 1870s and has an L-shaped bar. On one side is a comfortable candlelit area in which to relax. A changing range of three ales, along with a menu of proper pub food, is here for you to enjoy. On some Saturday evenings there is live music. Darts can be played. Q✿▶≠●🚌🐾

Parsonage Bar & Restaurant 🏆 🄻

10 High Street, Tarring, BN14 7NN (at S end of Tarring High Street)

12-9 Sun & Mon; 11-11 (midnight Fri & Sat)

☎ (01903) 820140 🌐 theparsonage.co.uk

Burning Sky Plateau; Dark Star Hophead; Harveys Sussex Best Bitter Ⓗ**; 2 changing beers (sourced locally)** Ⓗ/Ⓖ

This 15th-century establishment was originally three cottages, saved from demolition in 1927 when bought by a local resident for £900. Once the Museum of Sussex Folklore, this Grade II-listed building has been a restaurant since 1987, serving high-quality food and now offering beers of similar distinction. At least two guest LocAles are always on tap, served by gravity from an outside cold store. In the warmer weather the courtyard garden offers a great opportunity to drink outside.
Q✿◖▶≠(West)🚌(6,16)

Selden Arms

41 Lyndhurst Road, BN11 2DB (about 5 mins from town centre and 2 mins from Worthing Hospital on Lyndhurst Road, opp gasometer by Waitrose)

11-11 (11.30 Fri); 12-11.30 Sat; 12-10.30 Sun

Kent Pale; 5 changing beers Ⓗ

This genuine free house is a Guide regular. The 19th-century inn has a small, single bar with six handpumps, at least one of which dispenses a dark ale. Belgian and German draught and bottled beers are also available. A beer festival is held at the end of January and there is occasional live music. The pub supports a darts team. Photographs of old Worthing hostelries adorn the walls. Friday night is curry night (no food Sun). Q◖♿🚌(106)🐾📶

Yapton

Maypole 🄻

Maypole Lane, BN18 0DP (off B2132 1 mile N of village; pedestrian access across railway from Lake Lane, 1¼ miles E of Barnham stn) SU978042

11.30-11 (midnight Fri & Sat); 12-11 Sun

☎ (01243) 551417

Dark Star Hophead; house beer (by Wessex); 3 changing beers (sourced nationally; often Arundel, Dark Star, Long Man) Ⓗ

Small flint-built free house hidden away from the village centre, down a narrow lane ending in a pedestrian crossing over the railway. The cosy lounge boasts two open fires and a row of eight handpumps, dispensing up to three changing beers and real cider. There is a traditional public bar and a skittle alley/function room. Fresh rolls are served lunchtimes. It now has a new outside seating area.
Q🐴✿♿⛺♣●P🚌(66,700)🐾

Sussex Ox, Milton Street

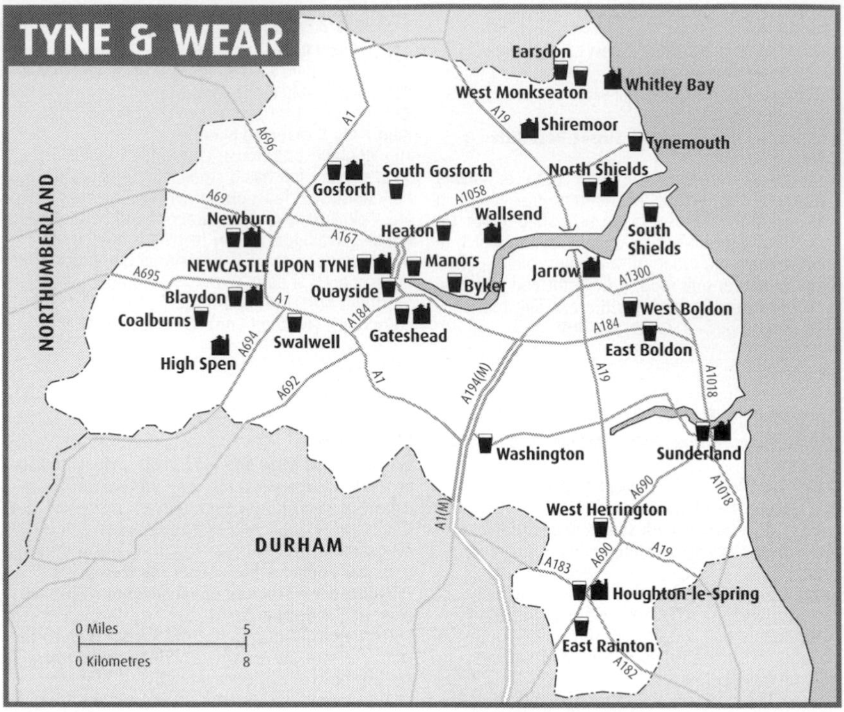

Blaydon

Black Bull

Bridge Street, NE21 4JJ

2-11; 12-midnight Fri & Sat; 12-11 Sun ☎ (0191) 414 2846

blackbull-blaydon.co.uk

Black Sheep Best Bitter; Caledonian Deuchars IPA; 1 changing beer H

Two-roomed pub with traditional values – 'no pool table, no jukebox, no bandit' boasts the proud landlord. Entertainment includes two folk nights weekly, buskers' night, quiz night and live bands once a month. Barbecues are held in the superb rear beer garden during the summer months. The pub enjoys excellent views of the River Tyne and Tyne Valley. Blaydon has benefited from a much-improved rail service and there are now 10 trains a day in each direction calling at Blaydon Station.

Q P (10,10A,10C)

Coalburns

Fox & Hounds

NE40 4JN

4.30-9 Mon; 4-11; 11.30-10.30 Sun ☎ (0191) 413 2549

coalies.co.uk

Hadrian Border Tyneside Blonde; Harviestoun Bitter & Twisted; 4 changing beers H

Welcoming, traditional pub with friendly management and bar staff on the outskirts of Greenside. Dating from 1795, the walls and ceilings are decorated with memorabilia from the local industries of centuries ago, and there is a log-burning stove. The pub has been running an annual leek show since 1979 and also hosts a folk club on Sunday, quiz night on Wednesday and live music on Saturday. Sunday lunches are served noon-4pm. There is a superb beer garden at the rear.

Q P

Earsdon

Beehive L

Hartley Lane, NE25 0SZ

12-11 (10.30 Sun) ☎ (0191) 252 9352

beehiveearsdon.co.uk

Hadrian Border Tyneside Blonde; Mordue Workie Ticket; 1 changing beer H

This 18th-century Grade II-listed building has been an inn since 1896. The superb three-room country pub is now back to its best and the new owners take great pride in the quality of the real ale. A range of blonde, pale and dark beers is usually available. Excellent food is served, made with ingredients sourced from local suppliers. The car park has now been extended and there is a mini goat area, children's secret garden, a picnic site and extra seating. P

East Boldon

Grey Horse

Front Street, NE36 0SJ

12-11 (midnight Fri) ☎ (0191) 519 1796

6 changing beers H

Distinctive mock-Tudor building with separate lounge and bar areas. There are large-screen TVs in the bar for football and other sports. A folk club meets on the first Tuesday of the month and the Boldon History Society on the last Tuesday. There is a separate first-floor function room. Guest beers are mainly from larger independent brewers.

Q P (9,30)

East Rainton

Old Ships Inn

Durham Road, DH5 9QT

12-11 (0191) 584 0944
3 changing beers
Traditional, family-friendly pub with a welcoming atmosphere, popular with locals and visitors alike. The large open-plan L-shaped room has a nautical theme with walls covered in marine charts and many framed photographs of Sunderland shipbuilding. There are no gaming machines or jukebox, just unobtrusive background music. The pub hosts a local cricket team and book club and is a regular stop for local walkers. Quiz night is Tuesday. Freshly cooked, traditional pub food is served until 9pm (4pm Sun). P (20,20A)

Gateshead

Central ★

Half Moon Lane, NE8 2AN
10-11 (10.30 Sun) (0191) 478 2543
Anarchy Blonde Star; 7 changing beers
Marvellous mid 19th-century, Grade II-listed, four-storey wedge-shaped building. It now comprises a revamped public bar, two function rooms and a rooftop terrace. However the Central's main attraction is the quite magnificently restored Buffet Bar (closed when quiet, ask to view), and the reason the pub has been designated by CAMRA as having an historic interior of national importance. It is as fitted out circa 1900 with a carved U-shaped counter and bar back, plasterwork frieze and panelling. The pub is home to regular live music.

Schooner

South Shore Road, NE8 3AF (just down from jct between Saltmeadows Rd and Neilson Rd. Vehicular access is from E end of South Shore Rd)
12-11 (10.30 Sun) (0191) 477 7404
theschooner.co.uk
6 changing beers
Following the purchase of the Schooner, husband and wife team David and Julie have breathed new life into the pub on South Shore Road. There are currently six handpulls for cask ales and one for cask cider – the beer range changes regularly, showcasing the best local and national ales and ciders. Great-value home-cooked food is available throughout the week with a traditional roast on Sundays. Local and touring bands feature at least twice weekly and buskers' afternoon is the first Sunday of the month.
P (93,94)

Wheat Sheaf

26 Carlisle Street, Felling, NE10 0HQ
5 (3 Thu; 12 Fri & Sat)-11; 12-10.30 Sun
(0191) 597 2981
Big Lamp Bitter, Prince Bishop Ale, Sunny Daze; house beer (by Big Lamp); 1 changing beer (sourced locally)
Welcoming street corner pub owned by Big Lamp Brewery and popular with a loyal band of regulars who often travel quite a distance to drink here. The pub features some original details, mismatched furniture and, when needed, real coal fires. The outdoor toilets have original Victorian urinals. There is a fortnightly Monday night quiz, traditional folk music featuring keen local musicians on Tuesday nights and dominoes on Wednesday nights. An original CAMRA clock keeps time behind the bar. Snacks are available.
(Heworth) (27,93,94)

Houghton-le-Spring

Copt Hill

Seaham Road, DH5 8LU (on B1404)
11-11.30 (0191) 584 4485 thecopthill.co.uk
6 changing beers
With a spectacular vista over the Houghton countryside, this former Vaux pub has six handpulls offering a changing selection of ales, half local and half from a wider area. Excellent food including breakfast is served all day from an extensive menu – booking for the recently refurbished restaurant is advisable as it can get busy at evenings and weekends. A variety of party nights is held in the function room. Q P (20)

Newburn

Keelman's Lodge

Grange Road, NE15 8NL
11-11; 12-10.30 Sun (0191) 267 1689
keelmanslodge.co.uk
Big Lamp Sunny Daze, Bitter, Summerhill Stout, Prince Bishop Ale; 1 changing beer
This tastefully converted Grade II-listed former pumping station is now home to the Big Lamp Brewery and the Keelman Pub serves as the brewery tap. A conservatory restaurant offers excellent food and quality accommodation is provided in the adjacent Keelman's Lodge and Salmon Cottage. Attractively situated by Tyne Riverside Country Park, the Coast-to-Coast cycleway and Hadrian's Wall National Trail.
P (22)

Newcastle upon Tyne: Byker

Cluny

36 Lime Street, NE1 2PQ
12-11 (10.30 Sun) (0191) 230 4474
7 changing beers
Large, former industrial building converted into a pub, art gallery and live music venue. The pub runs frequent themed beer festivals and always has a good selection of British and foreign draught and

REAL ALE BREWERIES

Almasty Shiremoor (NEW)
Big Lamp Newburn
Cullercoats Wallsend
Darwin Sunderland
Delavals Whitley Bay (brewing suspended)
Firebrick Blaydon
George N Porter Whitley Bay (brewing suspended)
Hadrian Border Newburn
Hop & Cleaver Newcastle upon Tyne (NEW)
Jarrow Jarrow
Leazes Lane Newcastle upon Tyne
Maxim Houghton-le-Spring
Mordue North Shields
Northern Alchemy Newcastle upon Tyne (NEW)
Northern FC Newcastle upon Tyne: Gosforth
Olde Potting Shed High Spen
Ouseburn Valley Newcastle upon Tyne: Gosforth
Out There Newcastle upon Tyne
Rail Ale Gateshead (brewing suspended)
Tavernale Newcastle upon Tyne
Temptation Houghton-le-Spring
Three Kings North Shields
Two by Two Wallsend (NEW)
Tyne Bank Newcastle upon Tyne

bottled products available. The art gallery shows work of all kinds ranging from final degree shows to local independent established artists in all media, with the displays changing monthly. Live music sessions are held most evenings and feature a wide range of British, European and American musicians. Q◐◑♿🎯🍎🚌📶

Cumberland Arms 𝕃

James Place Street, NE6 1LD (off Byker Bank)
🕒 3-11 (midnight Fri); 12-midnight Sat; 12-11 Sun
☎ (0191) 265 1725 🌐 thecumberlandarms.co.uk
6 changing beers Ⓗ
Three-storey venue rebuilt over 100 years ago and relatively little changed since. It stands in a prominent position overlooking the lower Ouseburn Valley. The pub is home to dance and music groups and its house beer, Rapper from Wylam Brewery, is named after the traditional rapper sword dance. A multiple winner of CAMRA regional Cider Pub of the Year awards, it generally offers up to six ciders or perries. Winter and summer beer festivals are held each year. Closing time may vary. Q🐴❀🛏🎯♣🍎P🐾📶

Free Trade Inn 𝕃

St Lawrence Road, NE6 1AP
🕒 11-11 (midnight Fri & Sat); 12-10.30 Sun
☎ (0191) 265 5764
7 changing beers Ⓗ
This unique former S&N pub was CAMRA Tyneside Pub of the Year in 2013. It has wonderful views of the bridges over the Tyne, and the Newcastle and Gateshead quaysides. A range of up to nine interesting beers from far and wide, as well as two ciders, is available on the bar, with cellar runs willingly offered. An extensive range of foreign bottled beers is also stocked. Service is with a smile, friendly and knowledgeable. Tasty sandwiches are supplied by a local delicatessen. The jukebox is classic and free. The beer garden is excellent. Q🐴❀🎯♣🍎🚌(Q2,106)🐾📶

Newcastle upon Tyne: City Centre

Bacchus 𝕃

42-48 High Bridge, NE1 6BX
🕒 11.30-midnight; 12-11 Sun ☎ (0191) 261 1008
🌐 thebacchusnewcastle.co.uk
6 changing beers Ⓗ
CAMRA Tyneside Pub of the Year four years running, this smart city-centre pub boasts nine handpumps offering a range of changing guest beers, with one pump dedicated to cider and another to beer from Orkney's Highland Brewing Company. A seasonal house beer is brewed by Yorkshire Dales, and a large range of draught and bottled foreign beers is available. Photographs and posters on the walls show the industries in which this region used to lead the world.
🐴◐♿⇌(Central)🎯🍎📶

Bodega 🏆 𝕃

125 Westgate Road, NE1 4AG
🕒 12-11 (midnight Fri); 11-midnight Sat; 12-10.30 Sun
☎ (0191) 221 1552 🌐 thebodeganewcastle.co.uk
Big Lamp Prince Bishop Ale; Durham Magus; 6 changing beers Ⓗ
Two fine stained-glass domes are the architectural highlights of the pub, which is popular with football and music fans. TVs show sporting events and the pub can be busy on match days. The interior offers a number of standing and seating areas with separate booths for more intimate drinking. Several old brewery mirrors adorn the walls. Eight handpumps include beers from Oakham and Fyne Ales, and a good selection of foreign bottled beers is available.
⇌(Central)🎯🍎🐾📶

Fitzgeralds

60 Grey Street, NE1 6AF
🕒 11-midnight; 4-11 Sun ☎ (0191) 230 1350
🌐 fitzgeraldsnewcastle.co.uk
6 changing beers Ⓗ
Large, open-plan, friendly Sir John Fitzgerald-chain pub, recently refurbished with six handpulls serving local and national beers. The pub is much bigger inside than it appears from the outside owing to its depth, with the bar situated towards the back. There is plenty of seating in various areas as well as a large standing area in front of the bar. The experienced landlord likes to offer an ale selection not found elsewhere locally, including an extensive range of bottled beers.
◐⇌(Central)🎯🚌(Q1,Q2)📶

Five Swans

14 St Mary's Place, NE1 7PG
🕒 8-midnight; 8-1am Fri & Sat ☎ (0191) 232 3893
🌐 jdwetherspoon.co.uk/home/pubs/the-five-swans
Adnams Broadside; Fuller's London Pride; Greene King Abbot; Ruddles Best Bitter; 6 changing beers Ⓗ
Multi-roomed Wetherspoon's opposite Newcastle Civic Centre and close to main shopping areas. The beer range includes guests from all the local brewers and from further afield. Food is served all day. Outside there is a drinking area to the front and a 'secret' courtyard through the maze of rooms. Children are welcome until 9pm. The pub area can be booked for private function(s).
Q🐴❀◐◑♿⇌(Manors)🎯♣🚌📶

Hotspur

103 Percy Street, NE1 7RY
🕒 11-11 (1am Tue; midnight Fri & Sat); 12-10.30 Sun
☎ (0191) 232 4352
6 changing beers Ⓗ
Traditional double-fronted city-centre pub opposite Haymarket bus station and Eldon Square, with the universities close by. The Hotspur is a popular pub and especially busy on match days. Quiz night is Monday and Newcastle University Folk Club plays on Tuesday nights. The interior has been refurbished and is much enhanced without losing character. Eight handpulls adorn the bar, six serving guest beers and two serving real cider.
⇌(Central)🎯🍎🐾📶

Lady Grey's 𝕃

20 Shakespeare Street, NE1 6AQ
🕒 11-2am ☎ (0191) 232 3606 🌐 ladygreys.co.uk
Mordue Northumbrian Blonde; 7 changing beers Ⓗ
Close to the historic Theatre Royal and busy shopping areas, this pub, formerly the Adelphi, is a welcome addition to the city-centre real ale scene. Beers are mainly from local brewers Mordue, Hadrian & Border, Allendale and Wylam, with guests from all over the country. A refurbishment has added two more handpumps for beer and two for real cider. Food is served all day.
◐◑⇌(Central)🎯🍎📶

Old George Inn

Old George Yard, NE1 1EZ

11-11 (1am Thu; 2am Fri & Sat); 12-midnight Sun
☎ (0191) 269 3061 oldgeorgeinnnewcastle.co.uk

Draught Bass; 6 changing beers

Built 1582 this historic pub alleged to have been frequented by King Charles I, is a welcoming watering hole for customers who like a piece of Olde England. The corridors and stairs creak and the ambience is mostly original. A cabinet of five handpulls complements the traditional bar area. Smaller bar has additional three handpulls. In summer bands play regularly in the outside yard. Buskers nights Thursdays and Sundays from 7pm
(Newcastle Central)

Pleased To Meet You

High Bridge, NE1 1EW

11-1am (2am Fri & Sat) ☎ (0191) 241 4395
ptmy-newcastle.co.uk

Mordue Five Bridges; 6 changing beers

Totally refurbished to a high standard and serving a multitude of drinks, this gin and real ale eatery has a busy mixed clientele. Situated on Newcastle's premier real ale street, it offers six handpulls serving a variety of brews, both local and national, with a trend towards the out of the ordinary. The front of the building features full-height windows which fold away in summer. To the rear are the smoking cabins. (Central)

Trent House

1-2 Leazes Lane, NE1 4QT

12-11 ☎ (0191) 261 2154

6 changing beers

The world-famous Trent House is situated by Leazes Park, Newcastle University and the RVI. Friendly and laid-back, it is home to the best jukebox in town, featuring an eclectic mix of classic rock, jazz and electronica. The pub has a nightly happy hour 8-9pm, with cask ales priced at £2 per pint, and on the first Sunday of the month ales are just £1 5-10pm. (32,32A)

Newcastle upon Tyne: Gosforth

County

High Street, NE3 1HB

12-11 (10.30 Sun) ☎ (0191) 285 6919

Caledonian Deuchars IPA; Fuller's London Pride; Jarrow Rivet Catcher; Wells Bombardier; Wylam Bitter; 6 changing beers

This large L-shaped bar with pleasant stained-glass windows on the main road frontage attracts a variety of visitors, from office workers to students, and can get busy, especially at weekends. A separate quiet room at the back offers respite from the hustle and bustle of the main bar, and also doubles as a small meeting or function room. Several guest beers are available.

Gosforth Hotel

High Street, NE3 1HQ

11-11 (midnight Fri & Sat) ☎ (0191) 285 6617
gosforthhotelnewcastle.co.uk

Adnams Broadside; Anarchy Blonde Star; Big Lamp Prince Bishop Ale; 3 changing beers

On the corner of a busy junction at the top of the High Street, this is a stalwart of the Gosforth pub scene. Popular with a wide clientele, from nearby office workers to locals and students, the pub often gets busy. Three ales are regularly available along with the occasional guest beer. A quieter adjoining bar opens occasionally at busier times and also serves as a function room. Another function room is available upstairs.

Job Bulman

St Nicholas Avenue, NE3 1AA

8am-11 ☎ (0191) 223 6230

Greene King Abbot; Mordue IPA; Ruddles Best Bitter; 6 changing beers

Popular Wetherspoon pub located just off the High Street, which strives to serve a wide range of real ales at all times. Aside from the two core beers, up to six guests may be available, often from local established breweries or micros. There is a raised area to the right set aside for families and diners.

Newcastle upon Tyne: Heaton

Chillingham

Chillingham Road, NE6 5XN

11-11 (midnight Fri & Sat); 12-11 Sun ☎ (0191) 265 3992
thechillinghamnewcastle.co.uk

Black Sheep Best Bitter; Jarrow Rivet Catcher; Mordue Workie Ticket; 4 changing beers

A large two-roomed pub with contrasting styles appealing to the widest possible customer base – the public bar in traditional dark wood with panelling and a historic mirror recalling the past glories of nearby Wallsend, and the lounge with a contemporary feel, flat-screen TVs for sport and excellent artwork depicting the sights of Newcastle. It offers a good choice of local microbrewery beers, as well as bottled beer, whisky and wine. There is a function room upstairs.
P (62,63)

Northumberland Hussar

Sackville Road, NE6 5SY (off Chillingham Road)

12-11 (11.30 Mon & Tue); 12-midnight Fri & Sat
☎ (0191) 265 0275

5 changing beers

Purpose-built in 1955 and named after a local regiment, a major investment in 2013 transformed the pub, with a stylish horseshoe bar and many interesting artefacts on display. Food is made from scratch in the open kitchen. Two banks of five handpulls serve a range of cask-conditioned ales from both local and national microbreweries. A sixth handpull is dedicated to real cider. Beer is available in third-pint measures if required. Quiz night is Thursday. Children are welcome until 7pm.
P (62,63)

Newcastle upon Tyne: Manors

New Bridge

2-4 Argyle Street, NE1 6PF

11-11 (11.30 Thu & Fri); 12-10.30 Sun ☎ (0191) 232 1020
thenewbridgenewcastle.co.uk

Anarchy Blonde Star; 4 changing beers

Just east of Newcastle city centre, well served by buses and the metro, this pub has no regular beers but offers an ever-changing choice from independent brewers. It is very much a locals' venue, but all are made welcome. The building is next to a business park and facing a large new extension to Northumbria University, so attracts a mixed lunchtime and early-evening crowd enjoying the beer and home-made food.

Newcastle upon Tyne: Quayside

Bridge Tavern 𝕃
7 Akenside Hill, NE1 3UF
12-midnight (1am Fri & Sat); 12-11 Sun
☎ (0191) 261 9966 thebridgetavern.com
7 changing beers Ⓗ
A trendy Newcastle pub with its own microbrewery – the Bridge Tavern's one-barrel plant brews a range of beers under the Tavernale name. Food ranging from bar snacks to buffets and full meals is prepared and cooked by a professional chef. There has been an ale house on this site for over 200 years – the original building was demolished in 1925 and a new premises built following the construction of the town's most famous landmark, the Tyne Bridge. Children are welcome until 7pm. 🐴❀◐◑♿⇌(Central)📺🍎🚌(Q1,Q2)🐾📶

Broad Chare 𝕃
25 Broad Chare, NE1 3DQ
11-11 (10 Mon) ☎ (0191) 211 2144
thebroadchare.co.uk
Wylam Writer's Block; 3 changing beers Ⓗ
A warm welcome awaits in this cosy bar just off Newcastle's historic, bustling Quayside. Stripped floors and exposed brickwork make this a comfortable, quiet bar to relax in and enjoy a pint. Bar food is served all day and there is a restaurant upstairs if you wish to dine in style. The house beer is Writer's Block from Wylam.
◐◑⇌(Manors)📺🍎🚌(Q2)📶

Crown Posada 𝕃
33 Side, NE1 3JE
12 (11 Thu)-11; 11-midnight Fri; 12-midnight Sat; 12-10.30 Sun ☎ (0191) 232 1269 crownposadanewcastle.co.uk
Hadrian Border Tyneside Blonde; Wylam Gold Tankard; 3 changing beers Ⓗ
An architecturally fine pub, identified by CAMRA's as having a regionally important historic interior. Behind the narrow street frontage with two impressive stained-glass windows lie a small snug, bar counter and a longer seating area. There is an interesting coffered ceiling, as well as local photographs and cartoons of long-gone customers and staff on the walls. Small brewers are enthusiastically supported, with three regular local ales. **Q**⇌(Central)📺🚌(Q1,Q2)📶

Hop & Cleaver 𝕃
40 Sandhill, NE1 3JF
12-1am ☎ (0191) 261 0921 hopandcleaver.com
6 changing beers Ⓗ
Interestingly renovated former trendy pub now stripped back to brickwork throughout. It has its own microbrewery in a room that leads through to the Red House next door. The food majors on smoked American-style meats and burgers, while the Red House features specialist pies, peas and mash. A good range of real ales is served from a bar with an open front. You can also access the Red House via the courtyard, which has covered seating and a smoking area. ◐◑♿⇌(Central)📺🚌(Q1,Q2)

Newcastle upon Tyne: South Gosforth

Brandling Villa
Haddricks Mill Road, NE3 1QL
12-11 (midnight Fri & Sat) ☎ (0191) 284 0490
brandlingvilla.co.uk
Harviestoun Bitter & Twisted; Timothy Taylor Landlord; 7 changing beers Ⓗ
Large double-fronted establishment with keen, enthusiastic staff. It offers a constantly changing selection of 10 beers – available in third-pint tasting glasses if you cannot make up your mind – plus two ciders on handpump. The imaginative manager organises various well-attended, beer-related events, including brewery takeovers, local sausage and pie festivals, music, cinema and beer festivals. The house beer, Frank & Bird, is from Hadrian Border Brewery and is a special brew, not a rebadge. 🐴❀◐◑♿📺♣**P**🐾📶

Millstone 𝕃
Haddricks Mill Road, NE3 1QL
12-11 (midnight Fri & Sat) ☎ (0191) 285 3429
Anarchy Blonde Star; Draught Bass; Jarrow Rivet Catcher; Sharp's Doom Bar; 1 changing beer Ⓗ
Refurbished by a new entrepreneurial pub group, this is a modern, stylish, two-roomed pub with the lounge to the front and a small public bar to the rear. The enthusiastic licensee sources beers from local microbreweries as well as offering national favourites. Bass has been the regulars' top choice for many years. The function room upstairs, also renovated, hosts CAMRA events. The house beer, Millstone Ale, is brewed by Camerons of Hartlepool. 🐴❀◐◑📺**P**🚌(55)

North Shields

Low Lights Tavern 𝕃
Brewhouse Bank, NE30 1LL
10-2.30am ☎ (0191) 257 6038
Draught Bass; 3 changing beers Ⓗ
Believed to have been an ale house for over 400 years, this is possibly the oldest pub in the area. The Grade II-listed tavern is now a free house offering a range of guest ales. Three rooms make up the public area, with the bar in the central room. Monday is buskers' night, Thursday acoustic music, and more ad-hoc live music is hosted over the weekend. A genuine community pub where the locals get involved in events including am-dram and craft evenings. 🐴◐◑♿♣🚌(333)🐾📶

Oddfellows 𝕃
7 Albion Road, NE30 2RJ
11 (12 Sun)-11 ☎ (0191) 435 8450
oddfellowspub.co.uk
Jarrow Bitter; 2 changing beers Ⓗ
Small, friendly single-room pub adorned with historic maps and photographs of pre-war North Shields. Three handpulls offer the regular Jarrow Bitter plus two guest ales, and up to six real ciders and perries are available. The pub is home to active football, darts and cricket teams, and hosts regular folk and blues nights and poker nights. A beer festival is held annually outside on the patio. Free soup is served in the winter months.
Q🐴❀◐◑♿📺♣🍎🚌(306)🐾📶

South Shields

Alum Ale House
Ferry Street, NE33 1JR (next to ferry landing)
11-11 (midnight Fri & Sat); 12-11.30 Sun
☎ (0191) 427 7245
Banks's Bitter; Jennings Cumberland Ale, Cocker Hoop; Marston's Pedigree; Wychwood Hobgoblin; 7 changing beers Ⓗ

Small, traditional pub adjacent to the Market Square, River Tyne and ferry landing. It is popular with local ale drinkers as a haven of good beer. Twelve handpumps offer five permanent beers and seven guests from the Marston's range. The pub has three rooms including a cellar bar with low ceilings throughout. There is a lively Irish folk session on the first Sunday of each month.

Maltings

9 Claypath Lane, NE33 4PG (off Westoe Rd)
12-11.30 (midnight Fri & Sat) (0191) 427 7147
Jarrow Rivet Catcher; 3 changing beers H
The Maltings is situated on the first floor of the former Co-op Dairy which became the second home of the Jarrow Brewery in 2008. Take the staircase or lift to a partitioned room with a large central bar and plenty of seating. The full range of Jarrow ales is available but only Rivet Catcher is always on. Thai food is served Tuesday to Saturday and there are quizzes on Wednesday and Sunday.
Q P

Steamboat

Mill Dam, NE33 1EQ (follow signs for Customs House)
12-11 (midnight Thu-Sat); 12-11.30 Sun
(0191) 454 0134
6 changing beers H
Under the same management for the past 25 years, the Steamboat has one of the largest selections of cask ales in South Shields. Eight handpumps dispense a range of beers from small and family brewers across the country, and Meet the Brewer events and beer festivals take place throughout the year. The split-level bar is decorated with a nautical theme. The pub is a short walk from the Shields Ferry and Customs House Theatre.

Sunderland

Avenue

Zetland Street, Roker, SR6 0EQ (just off Roker Avenue)
12.30-11.30; 11-midnight Fri & Sat; 11-11 Sun
(0191) 567 7412
2 changing beers H
Close to the Stadium of Light and Roker seafront, this is a popular local hosting entertainment such as live music, quiz nights and bingo evenings. With a ground-floor lounge and bar, and a games room with a full-size snooker table upstairs, there are plenty of options for relaxing with a handpulled ale. A function room provides extra space during busier periods and is available to hire.
(E1,E6)

Butcher's Arms

143 High Street East, East End, SR1 2BL
11-11; 12-10.30 Sun (0191) 510 3200
4 changing beers H
Emerging after 18 months of closure from the ashes of the late-lamented Clarendon, the new name reflects the trade of the new owner. The pub retains its single-room bar and its friendly atmosphere, with excellent views across the River Wear. Four handpumps dispense local beers with Stables of Beamish featuring heavily. (5,5A)

Chesters

Chester Road, SR4 7DR
10-11 (midnight Fri & Sat); 12-10.30 Sun
(0191) 565 9952
2 changing beers H
This popular pub just outside the city centre was recently refurbished and has a smart yet comfortable interior, with a large main bar and a more intimate area at the back. There is always at least one ale from Maxim Brewery as well as guest ales from other brewers. Outside is ample car parking and a large beer garden. A function room with private bar is also available. P

Dun Cow ★

High Street West, SR1 3HA
12-12.30am (11.30 Sun) (0191) 567 2984
Camerons Strongarm; 6 changing beers H
This Grade II-listed building is an architectural gem and features on CAMRA's National Inventory of Historic Pub Interiors. A three-month refurbishment in 2014 included an impressive restoration of one of the most stunning bar-backs in Britain. The range of six beers is sourced from north-east microbreweries. The pub is next to the Empire Theatre and can get busy around performance times.

Fitzgeralds

12-14 Green Terrace, SR1 3PZ
11-11 (1am Fri & Sat); 12-10.30 Sun (0191) 567 0852
Fyne Ales Jarl; Timothy Taylor Boltmaker; Titanic Plum Porter; 5 changing beers H
Sunderland outpost of the Sir John Fitzgerald chain. This former local and regional CAMRA Pub of the Year has three regular beers complemented by eight guests. There are two separate rooms offering a choice of seating areas, with the smaller nautically themed Chart Room quieter than the main bar. Meet the Brewer evenings are regular events and live music is hosted on Sunday and Tuesday evenings. Q P

Harbour View

Harbour View, SR6 0NU
10.30-11.30 (midnight Fri & Sat) (0191) 567 3878
6 changing beers H
A modern, open-plan lounge bar close to Roker beach. The first floor restaurant offers fine views over the River Wear and marina. Six handpumps dispense two regular ales alongside a choice of guests from near and far. The pub can get busy when Sunderland AFC are at home.
(E1,18,19)

Isis

26 Silksworth Row, SR1 3QJ
12-11 (11.30 Fri & Sat) (0191) 514 7684
Jarrow Rivet Catcher, American IPA; 7 changing beers H
Originally dating back to 1885, the pub was tastefully and extensively renovated and reopened in 2011, after lying dormant for more than two years. A long and narrow wood, chrome and glass bar holds 12 handpulls serving two regular beers and up to seven guests, plus two ciders and a perry. There is a long, narrow lounge to the side of the main bar. Pub photographs abound throughout the building, upstairs and downstairs. Live music plays on Sunday afternoons.
P (10,11)

Ivy House

Ashbrooke, SR2 7AW
11-11; 12-10.30 Sun (0191) 567 3399
5 changing beers H

Tucked away but close to the bus and metro interchange, the Ivy House is well worth seeking out. Five ever-changing guest ales are on offer as well as a guest cider. An extensive range of bottled Belgian beers is also kept. Home-made pizzas and burgers are freshly prepared in an open kitchen next to the bar. Quiz night is Wednesday. Note the stag-horn lights. ❀◑♿⇌☊●P📶

King's Arms

Beach Street, Deptford, SR4 6BU

4.30 (4 Wed & Thu)-11; 12-midnight Fri & Sat; 12-11 Sun
☎ (0191) 567 9804

Timothy Taylor Landlord; 6 changing beers Ⓗ

Established in 1834, the King's Arms is a traditional pub with an L-shaped bar featuring eight handpulls, one regularly dispensing Timothy Taylor Landlord and another a real cider. The remaining beers are sourced from local breweries and beyond. There is a small snug and a marquee outside where live music is hosted. A quiz is held every Sunday and curry night is Thursday. Bar snacks are available. ❀☊●P🚌(10,11)🐾📶

Museum Vaults

33 Silksworth Row, SR1 3QJ

4 (3 Tue & Thu)-11; 12-midnight Fri & Sat; 12-10.30 Sun
☎ (0191) 565 9443

3 changing beers Ⓗ

This small former beer house on the edge of the town centre has been run by the same family for over 40 years. The single room is divided in two, both sides with an open fire. Three cask beers are on offer, sourced from local breweries, as well as student brews from Brewlab. The real ale is complemented by a small range of bottled beers and a real cider. ❀⇌☊●P🚌(10,11)🐾📶

R Bar

Roker Terrace, Roker, SR6 9ND

11-11 (1am Fri & Sat) ☎ (0191) 577 6767

Sonnet 43 Steam Beer, Blonde Beer, Bourbon Milk Stout, India Pale Ale, American Pale Ale Ⓗ

The R Bar is part of the Roker Hotel, with fine views of the mouth of the River Wear and seashore. All six of the Sonnet 43 core beers are on offer, served in tall glasses. The decor is a blend of modern and traditional, and there are separate areas for dining with wood-panelled ceilings and comfortable seating. Meal deals are offered Monday to Friday. Disabled access is to the left of the hotel reception. 🛏◑♿♣P🚌(18,19,E1)📶

Swalwell

Sun Inn

Market Lane, NE16 3AL (just off roundabout at end of Front St)

11 (12 Sun)-11 ☎ (0191) 488 7783

Marston's Pedigree; 2 changing beers Ⓗ

Situated in the heart of the historic village that spawned many internationally renowned engineers and industrialists, and of course the famous Swalwell cabbage. This truly no-nonsense community pub provides good company for locals and strangers alike. Sword dancers, darts, domino handicaps, a monthly pie competition and Saturday buskers' nights all feature. Bar food and snacks are available and are free on Sundays. There is a regular bus service here from Newcastle. ❀♣●🚌🐾

> Good ale is the true and proper drink of Englishmen. He is not deserving of the name of Englishman who speaketh against ale, that is good ale.
> **George Borrow, Lavengro**

Tynemouth

Hugo's at the Coast

29 Front Street, NE30 4DZ

11-11 (midnight Fri & Sat); 11-10.30 Sun
☎ (0191) 257 8956 🌐 hugostynemouth.co.uk

3 changing beers Ⓗ

A tasteful conversion of a former restaurant with pleasing décor – the walls are adorned with local photographs of yesteryear, Tynemouth beach and pony rides. Popular with locals and tourists, the weekends are extremely busy. The men's darts team plays on Tuesday night, quiz night is Wednesday and live music features on the last Thursday of the month. A constantly changing range of guest ales usually includes a Three Kings beer. ◐☊♣🚌(306)📶

Tynemouth Lodge Hotel

Tynemouth Road, NE30 4AA

11-11; 12-10.30 Sun ☎ (0191) 257 7565
🌐 tynemouthlodgehotel.co.uk

Caledonian Deuchars IPA; Draught Bass; Mordue Northumbrian Blonde; 1 changing beer Ⓗ

This attractive externally tiled 1799 free house, situated next to a former house of correction, has featured in every issue of the Guide since 1983. The comfortable pub has a U-shaped lounge with the bar on one side and a serving hatch on the other, and is noted in the area for the quality of its Draught Bass. A popular stopping-off point for those completing the Coast-to-Coast cycle route. Q❀☊P🚌(1,306)📶

Washington

Courtyard

Biddick Lane, NE38 8AB

11-11 (midnight Fri & Sat); 12-11 Sun ☎ (0191) 417 0445
🌐 artscentrewashington.co.uk/courtyard.aspx

Leamside Adventure, Five quarter; Timothy Taylor Landlord; 4 changing beers Ⓗ

Located within the lively arts centre, this light and airy café/bar offers a warm welcome to drinkers and food lovers alike. Eight handpumped beers, one real cider, one perry and a range of bottled Belgian beers are available. An extensive range of food is served throughout the day, with early-evening specials. The pub hosts a weekly quiz and buskers' nights. Outdoor seating is within the spacious courtyard. Popular beer festivals are held annually, on the Easter and August bank holidays. Q❀◑⛺●P🚌(2A,4,8)

Sir William de Wessyngton

2-3 Victoria Road, Concord, NE37 2SY

7am-11 ☎ (0191) 418 0100

Greene King Abbot; Ruddles Best Bitter; 4 changing beers Ⓗ

Large open-plan Wetherspoon pub housed in a former snooker hall and ice cream parlour. It is named after a Norman knight and lord of the manor whose descendants later emigrated to the United States. A real ale oasis, it is the only cask beer outlet in Concord and offers good-value beer and the usual well-priced Wetherspoon menu. The regular ales are complemented by up to four guests, and occasional beer festivals are held. Q&P

Steps

47 Spout Lane, NE38 7HP

3.30 (2.30 Fri)-11; 12-11 Sat; 12-10.30 Sun
(0191) 415 0733

5 changing beers H

Opened in 1894 as the Spout Lane Inn, the pub was renamed The Steps in 1976. The small, comfortable, single-room lounge bar is divided into two drinking areas and the walls are decorated with pictures of old Washington. Five beers are on offer, often including ales from local microbreweries. Quiz nights are Wednesday and Thursday. Opening hours may vary. QP (86)

West Boldon

Black Horse

Rectory Bank, NE36 0QQ (off A184)

11-11 (11.30 Sun) (0191) 536 1814

Jennings Cumberland Ale; 1 changing beer H

An old-fashioned pub with unusual bric-a-brac adorning the walls and candles on the tables. The photographs on display are by the talented chef, and prints are available to buy. The pub has one small L-shaped bar and, with a popular restaurant serving high-quality food, can get busy in the evenings and at weekends. Live music features on Sunday night. Q

West Herrington

Stables

DH4 4ND (off B1286)

12-11 (midnight Fri & Sat) (0191) 584 9226

Black Sheep Best Bitter; Timothy Taylor Landlord; 2 changing beers H

The Stables may not look like a pub from the outside but this riding school conversion is well worth a visit. The deceptively large interior retains the original beams, flagstone floor and wooden furniture. You can sit in the main bar/restaurant or the small snug behind the bar. An extensive food menu is available daily, with tapas on Friday and Saturday evenings. &P

West Monkseaton

Beacon Hotel

Earsdon Road, NE25 9PT

11-midnight (0191) 253 6911

Brakspear Bitter; Caledonian Deuchars IPA; Durham White Gold; 6 changing beers H

Superb modern pub set back from the main road, popular with locals. The manager sources a wide range of ales and there is a quick turnover. Customers can order a wooden paddle of three third-pints for variety. The cellar has dedicated lines so the ale is served at the right temperature. The food is excellent – there are themed food nights Monday to Thursday and chef's specials Friday and Saturday. Quiz nights are Sunday and Wednesday. Q&P (51,57,57A)

Bodega, Newcastle upon Tyne: City Centre (Photo: Cat Button)

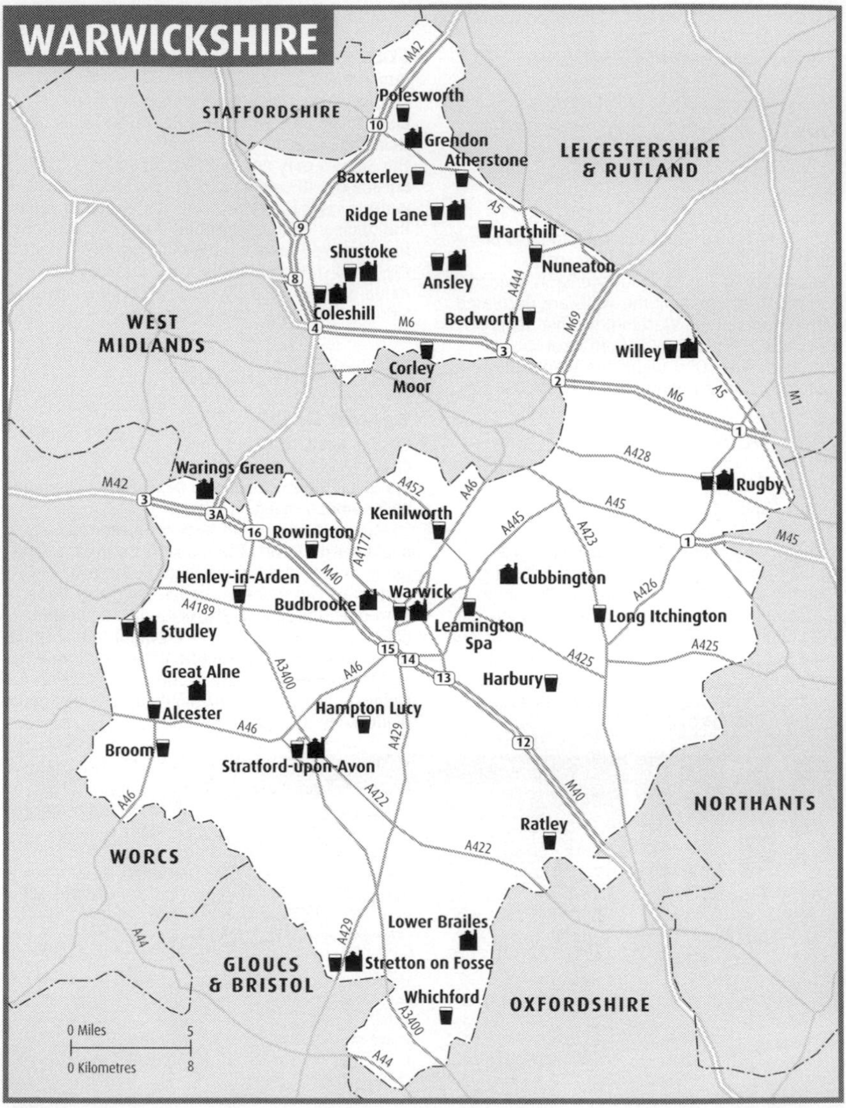

Alcester

Turk's Head

4 High Street, B49 5AD (near church)
12 (10 Sat)-11 (01789) 765948 theturkshead.net
Wye Valley HPA; 3 changing beers (often Otter, Skinner's, Timothy Taylor)
A central location helps make this a popular place. The publican is a cask enthusiast, staging beer festivals during the summer months. Beers are sourced as locally as possible, dispensed from four handpulls. A good range of changing bottled beers is also available, with the most popular ones making it to draught on occasion. The pub is divided into two rooms with real fires and serves traditional pub food – booking is advisable. Regular quiz and open mic nights are hosted. Worth a visit.

Ansley

Lord Nelson Inn

Birmingham Road, CV10 9PQ
12-11 (10.30 Sun) (024) 7639 2305
thelordnelsoninnansley.co.uk
St Austell Tribute; Sperrin Ansley Mild, Head Hunter, Band of Brothers, Third Party, Thick as Thieves; 3 changing beers
This pub has been run by the Sperrin family since 1974 and has featured in the Guide for more than 20 consecutive years. Nine handpulls dispense the family's own Sperrin brews plus ales from other local breweries and some not so local. There is an extensive food menu with many tribute/meal nights. The pub has a nautical theme, and outside is the suntrap courtyard and garden which is a venue for beer festivals and barbecues.

Atherstone

Angel Ale House 🍷 L

24 Church Street, CV9 1RN

☼ 4-11; 12-midnight Sat; 12-10.30 Sun

Blythe Staffie; Oakham Citra; 4 changing beers Ⓗ

Picturesque establishment with a black and white exterior and a bar looking out onto the market square and the church with its unusual octagonal tower. There is a comfortable lounge to the rear. Entry is via the door on the left-hand side. Formerly known as the Angel Inn, up to six real ales are offered, often local and usually including a couple of dark beers. If no parking is available on the market square there is a large free council car park to the rear. ⏰❀♿●🚌(48,765)♣

Baxterley

Rose Inn

Main Road, CV9 2LE (off B4116, W of Atherstone) SP278969

☼ 12-3, 6-11; 12-11 Fri-Sun ☎ (01827) 713939

🌐 roseinnbaxterley.com

Draught Bass; St Austell Tribute; Wells Bombardier; 1 changing beer Ⓗ

Attractive and thriving village inn fronted by a large pond with its duck and moorhen population. While deservedly popular for food, it remains a community drinkers' pub where real ale outsells lager by a factor of three to one. Drinkers are welcome throughout but veer to the dog-friendly bar warmed by an open fire. The intimate split-level lounge is largely frequented by diners, with disabled access to the lower level. There is a separate restaurant with a scenic view plus a skittle alley. ⏰❀🍴♿♣🚌(766)♣🛜

Bedworth

Weavers' Arms

12 Long Street, Bulkington, CV12 9JZ

☼ 3 (1 Wed & Thu)-11; 12-11 Sat & Sun ☎ (024) 7631 4415

Draught Bass; 1 changing beer Ⓗ

This family-owned two-room traditional village pub was converted from weavers' cottages. It has a wood-panelled games room, log-burning fireplace and a slate floor. An extensive well-kept beer garden accommodates barbecues in the summer. Children are welcome, private functions are catered for and the Pork Pie Club, Weavers' Walkers and Hillbilly Golf Society hold regular meetings here. The pub is well-known for the quality of its Bass. Often open after 11pm, but no later than 1am. ⏰❀♣🚌

Broom

Broom Tavern L

32 High Street, B50 4HL

☼ 12-3, 5-midnight; 12-midnight Sat; 12-11 Sun

☎ (01789) 778199 🌐 broomtavern.co.uk

Purity Mad Goose; Sharp's Doom Bar; 3 changing beers (often North Cotswold, Purity, Sharp's) Ⓗ

This lovely brick and timber building has been tastefully restored while retaining a great amount of original character, with many rooms including a cosy snug, and a log fire in winter. It has been reopened by two experienced chefs with a good pedigree in the kitchen, looking to serve local produce. Meals are available lunchtimes and evenings. Local beers are frequently found here

alongside the Cornish contingents and at least one real cider. Outside is a choice of three beer gardens. A local CAMRA award winner.
Q⏰❀🍴●P♣🛜

Coleshill

Green Man

68 High Street, B46 3AH

☼ 11-11; 12-3, 7-10.30 Sun ☎ (01675) 463376

Draught Bass; M&B Brew XI; 2 changing beers Ⓗ

This white-painted three-storey pub sitting on the main town crossroads is hard to miss. The rambling interior features a busy bar and servery area, a comfy lounge to the rear, and a quiet snug to the side. The decor is pleasantly dated, and a display of 1980s beer mats may make older drinkers feel nostalgic. There are TVs throughout but used with discretion. The two guest beers are from the Punch Finest Cask range. ❀♣P🚌♣

Corley Moor

Bull & Butcher 🍷

Common Lane, CV7 8AQ (1 mile W of Corley) SP279850

☼ 9am-midnight (1am Fri-Sun) ☎ (01676) 540241

🌐 bullandbutchercorleymoor.co.uk

Draught Bass; Greene King Abbot; M&B Brew XI; St Austell Tribute; 1 changing beer Ⓗ

Multi-roomed village pub, retaining a traditional village bar with a restaurant at the rear that offers good-value food all day every day. Through the front entrance, there is a wood-beamed flagstone-floored bar which leads to a couple of cosy snugs, warmed by real fires. One varying guest beer accompanies Cask Marque-accredited regulars. Outside, the decking area and garden with imaginative play equipment are popular in summer. Run by the same family and featuring in the Guide for over 10 years, this was the local CAMRA branch's Pub of the Year 2015.
Q⏰❀🍴♿P♣

Hampton Lucy

Boar's Head L

Church Street, CV35 8BE

☼ 12-11 (midnight Fri & Sat); 12-8 (10 summer) Sun

☎ (01789) 840533 🌐 theboarsheadhamptonlucy.co.uk

REAL ALE BREWERIES

Atomic Rugby
Blue Bell Brewhouse Warings Green
Church End Ridge Lane
Church Farm Budbrooke
Clouded Minds Lower Brailes
Griffin Shustoke
Indian Ansley (NEW)
Kendrick's Willey
Merry Miner Grendon
North Cotswold Stretton-on-Fosse
Old Pie Factory Warwick
Purity Great Alne
Red Even Coleshill
Slaughterhouse Warwick
Sperrin Ansley
Stratford Upon Avon Stratford-upon-Avon (NEW)
Warwickshire Cubbington
Weatheroak Studley

Church End Gravediggers Ale; Ringwood Best Bitter; 3 changing beers (sourced locally; often Church End, Church Farm, North Cotswold) H
This former Warwickshire County CAMRA Champion Pub of the Year remains a popular village local and dates back to the 17th century. Situated on a Sustrans route and close to the River Avon, it is frequented by cyclists, walkers and visitors to nearby Charlecote Park. Five or six ales are served including one LocAle. It has a deserved reputation for fresh locally sourced home-made food. A sheltered courtyard proves popular in the summer. An annual themed beer festival is held.
Q P

Harbury

Old New Inn L

Farm Sreet, CV33 9LS (SW of village)
4.30 (12 Fri & Sat)-midnight; 12-11 Sun ☎ (01926) 614023
Church End Goats Milk; Purity Mad Goose; Slaughterhouse Saddleback Best Bitter; 1 changing beer H
Situated on the edge of the village and housed in a former farmhouse and bakery, the building is made of local stone and has two rooms with low ceilings which reflect its age. Outside at the back there is a large family garden. This is a traditional, privately owned village pub where darts, dominoes and pool teams are well-supported and major sporting fixtures are screened on TV.
P (65,66)

Hartshill

Royal Oak L

Oldbury Road, CV10 0TD
4-11; 12-midnight Fri-Sun ☎ (024) 7639 6442
3 changing beers H
Formerly a Charles Wells pub, this is now a free house and has been refurbished to give a village community, old-fashioned, feeling, with many old pictures of Hartshill on display. It offers beers from local breweries as well as those from afar – Little Ale Cart and Tiny Rebel are often represented. A good-sized garden at the rear accommodates live music and beer festivals during the summer months. Q

Henley-in-Arden

Black Swan

23 High Street, B95 5AA
12-11 (midnight Fri & Sat) ☎ (01564) 795338
blackswanhenley.co.uk
Sharp's Doom Bar; Timothy Taylor Landlord; 2 changing beers (often Wells) H
A rambling, multi-room, split-level pub on a classic high street in a lovely old market town. The interior is now semi-open plan, featuring a wealth of beams. The beers are exceptionally well-kept. Traditional pub games include dominoes, crib and darts. Open mic night is the first Wednesday of the month, karaoke features every Friday, a quiz on Thursday, and occasional live music on Saturday. No food Sunday/Monday evenings.
Q P (X20)

Kenilworth

Old Bakery

12 High Street, CV8 1LZ (near A429/A452 jct)
5.30 (5 Fri & Sat)-11; 5.30-10.30 Sun ☎ (01926) 864111
theoldbakery.eu
Wye Valley HPA; house beer (by Wye Valley); 2 changing beers H
A pleasant 15-minute walk from the Castle brings you to this two-roomed hostelry in a picturesque part of Kenilworth near Abbey Fields. There are no games machines or TV, just lively conversation among discerning drinkers. Beams and rustic furniture give the pub a cosy ambience and service is friendly and efficient. Home-made specials are popular on Monday evenings. The house beer is rebadged Wye Valley Bitter. Disabled access is to the rear. Accommodation is offered in 14 en-suite rooms. Q P (11)

Royal Oak

36 New Street, CV8 2EJ (250yds from A429/A452 jct)
4 (12 Sat)-11; 12-10.30 Sun ☎ (01926) 856906
Adnams Southwold Bitter; Sharp's Doom Bar; Timothy Taylor Landlord; 1 changing beer (sourced nationally; often Castle Rock, Robinsons, St Austell) H
This traditional Grade II-listed pub near the heart of old Kenilworth attracts a diverse clientele largely from the local community. There are occasional beer festivals and real cider. Pub games include darts, pool, poker and a chess club. Major sporting events are shown on Sky/BT Sport. There is a south-east facing patio and garden area to the rear. The regular Coventry to Leamington bus service stops nearby. (11)

Virgins & Castle

7 High Street, CV8 1LY (at 429/A452 jct)
11-11 (midnight Fri & Sat) ☎ (01926) 853737
virginsandcastle.co.uk
Everards Beacon Bitter, Sunchaser Blonde, Tiger, Original; 1 changing beer H
Kenilworth's oldest pub is a quality purveyor of Everards beers. With a quaint high-street location near Abbey Fields and Kenilworth Castle, this multi-roomed, split-level pub gets busy with diners enjoying the popular English and Filipino cuisine (no food Sun eve). Two beer festivals are held each year in May and October. Monday is quiz night and traditional acoustic music plays early evening on the last Sunday of the month. There is an outside courtyard. Street parking is limited but a public car park is nearby. Q (11)

Leamington Spa

Cricketers Arms L

Archery Road, CV31 3PT (opp town bowling green)
12-11; 12-10.30 Sun ☎ (01926) 881293
Black Sheep Best Bitter; Slaughterhouse Saddleback Best Bitter; 1 changing beer (often Timothy Taylor) H
A 19th-century town pub on a street corner facing the Royal Leamington Spa bowling club, which holds the Ladies' National Championship each year. The interior of the pub has some timber and oak panelling and is open plan, but each area is distinct, hinting at the original interior design. A secret heated garden is tucked away at the back of the pub. Live music, pub quizzes and darts take place weekly. Food is locally sourced.
Q

Jug & Jester

11 Bath Street, CV31 3AF
8am-midnight (1am Fri & Sat) ☎ (01926) 331820

Adnams Broadside; Greene King Abbot; Ruddles Best Bitter; Sharp's Doom Bar; 5 changing beers (sourced regionally)
Four distinctive drinking areas reflect the original layout of this interesting pub, part of which was once the Regency Royal theatre. Look for the unusual collection of stoneware vats on the high shelf in the middle room. The venue attracts a wide clientele and has a comfortable atmosphere, with an eclectic mix of furniture and pictures depicting the heritage of the town. Old Rosie and Black Dragon ciders are available. Q

Woodland Tavern

3 Regent Street, CV32 5HW
12-midnight (1am Fri & Sat); 12-11.30 Sun
(01926) 425868
Slaughterhouse Saddleback Best Bitter; Wychwood Hobgoblin; 4 changing beers
Landlady Josie has been welcoming locals and visitors to her friendly drinkers' pub for 16 years. Dating back to the early Victorian period, this street-corner hostelry is close to the centre of Leamington Spa and features a traditional public bar and separate lounge, also used as a function room. The unique, partly covered courtyard is decorated with murals depicting local references and jokes.

Long Itchington

Green Man

Church Road, CV47 9PW
5-11.30 (midnight Fri); 12-midnight Sat; 12-10.30 Sun
(01926) 812208 greenmanlongitchington.co.uk
Black Sheep Best Bitter; Fuller's London Pride; Purity Mad Goose; St Austell Tribute; 1 changing beer
Hosts Mark and Sharon run a proper community pub which has earned a regular place in the Guide. The building, which dates back some 300 years, exhibits a number of drinking areas and a function room. With a garden at the rear and patio area at the front, the outside areas are particularly busy in May when the annual beer festival attracts drinkers from miles around. To the rear is a large camping and caravan site. Q P (64)

Harvester

6 Church Road, CV47 9PE (off A423 at village pond, then first left)
12-2.30, 6-11; 12-3, 7-10.30 Sun (01926) 812698
theharvesterinn.co.uk
Hook Norton Hooky; 2 changing beers
This white-fronted building is set 100 yards from the village pond, on the corner of a small square. Simon and Sharon have welcomed drinkers and diners to their unpretentious, friendly village pub since 1984, and it is a regular Guide entry. Various guest ales are supplemented by continental options including a Belgian fruit beer. The pub plays a significant role in the annual village beer festival each May bank holiday. Gruntfuttocks Speciality Pickles can be purchased to take home.
(64)

Nuneaton

Attleborough Arms

Highfield Road, Attleborough, CV11 4PL
11-11 (midnight Fri & Sat); 12-11 Sun (024) 7638 3231
Banks's Bitter; Marston's Pedigree; 4 changing beers
Large open-plan establishment selling a good and often interesting range of beers from the Marston's stable. Many value-for-money meal deals are available and the pub can get busy at times. It is particularly popular with lunchtime diners and football supporters when Nuneaton Town are at home. Buffets can be ordered for special occasions.
P

Crown

10 Bond Street, CV11 4BX (between rail and bus stations)
12-11 (midnight Fri & Sat) (024) 7637 3343
7 changing beers
Close to the railway and bus stations, this regular Guide entry boasts 10 handpulls offering seven real ales including Abbeydale brews, and three ciders or perries. A choice of foreign bottled beers is also stocked as well as a large selection of malt whiskies. Live music features on Saturday nights. There is a large garden to the rear and a function room available for hire. Beer festivals are held in June and December. Sunday lunch is served until 4pm. The pub hosts the Nuneaton Folk Club on the first Wednesday of the month. P

Felix Holt

3 Stratford Street, CV11 5BS
8am-midnight (1am Wed & Thu); 8am-2am Fri & Sat; 8am-11 Sun (024) 7634 7785
Greene King Abbot; Ruddles Best Bitter; Thornbridge Jaipur IPA; changing beers
Large Wetherspoon outlet situated in the town centre. The pub takes its name from the George Eliot novel and the theme is reflected in the décor of books and pictures of local history. There are a further six handpulls providing an interesting range of both local and guest ales. Food is served 8am-10pm. There is a heated area for smokers.
Q

Horseshoes

2 Heath End Road, CV10 7JQ
11-11 (midnight Fri & Sat); 12-11 Sun (024) 7767 5066
Everards Beacon Bitter, Tiger Best Bitter, Original; 2 changing beers
Formerly the Tunnel Brewery tap, this is now an Everards pub. Refurbished in Edwardian style as a traditional English hostelry, with two coal fires, it has a friendly ambience and families are welcome. Ten handpulls dispense the ales. A quiz is held on Wednesday nights and various food theme nights feature regularly. The snug is available to hire for private functions. Close to the George Eliot Hospital and Coventry Canal. Q P

Polesworth

Bull's Head

Tamworth Road, B78 1JH (by canal bridge on B5000)
11-midnight (11.30 Sun) 07796 538415
Sharp's Doom Bar; 2 changing beers
Down-to-earth canalside pub, popular with locals and welcoming to newcomers. The L-shaped bar is usually busy, sometimes showing TV sport. The small lounge through the archway is better for a quiet chat. A variety of teams meets here, including darts, fishing and bowls. There are two guest handpumps, though only one may be in action depending on the time of week. No food, but the independent Indian restaurant upstairs (open every evening) will fetch ale for you from downstairs. P (765,785)

Ratley

Rose & Crown

OX15 6DS

✪ 12-3 (not Mon), 5-11; 12-midnight Fri & Sat; 12-11 Sun
☎ (01295) 678148 ⊕ roseandcrown-ratley.co.uk
Ringwood Best Bitter; St Austell Tribute; Wells Bombardier; 3 changing beers (often Cats, Hook Norton) ⊞

Tucked away at the bottom of an ancient village, this 11th-century pub is a real find for the ale enthusiast, with stone walls, oak beams and open fires ensuring a relaxing and memorable visit. Situated on the northern tip of the Cotswolds, the pub is a welcome stop for dogs and their walkers. Good food includes daily specials, with fish a speciality. The hidden snug is perfect for groups and celebrations. Reputedly haunted by a Roundhead soldier found hiding in the inglenook.
Q ➢ ❀ ⓓ ♪ Å ♣ 🚌 (269) ✿

Ridge Lane

Church End Brewery Tap 🗘

Ridge Lane, CV10 0RD (2 miles SW of Atherstone)
✪ closed Mon-Wed; 6 (12 Fri & Sat)-11; 12-10.30 Sun
☎ (01827) 713080 ⊕ churchendbrewery.co.uk
Church End Poachers Pocket, Gravediggers Ale, What the Fox's Hat, Fallen Angel ⊞

This brewery tap is hidden from the road, with access signposted by a board positioned at the entrance. The brewery can be viewed from the bar area. Eight handpulls serve the bar and vestry. Beers change regularly but always include a mild. The ever-changing ciders are dispensed direct from the cask. Children are not allowed inside but there is a large meadow garden with ample seating. The pub opens on the third Wednesday of the month for Atherstone Folk Club night.
Q ❀ ₺ Å ● P 🚌 (41) ✿ 🕏

Rowington

Rowington Club 🗘

Rowington Green, CV35 7DB (just off B4439 between Rowington and Lapworth; follow signs for Rowington Village Hall) SP1988070150
✪ 2 (12 Sat)-11; 12-10.30 Sun ☎ (01564) 782087
Wye Valley Bitter, HPA; 2 changing beers ⊞

Busy and thriving community club, popular with locals, also open to non-member visitors, with free entry for card-carrying CAMRA members. Frequent entertainment is provided plus seasonal events such as an August beer festival and Marrow Sunday. Three real ales are on offer at all times plus traditional ciders. Bar snacks are available. The large beer garden overlooks the village cricket ground, and the club is handy for local walking and cycling. Always friendly, it is well worth seeking out. ➢ ❀ ₺ ♣ ● P ✿ 🕏

Rugby

Alexandra Arms 🗘

72 James Street, CV21 2SL (next to John Barford car park)
✪ 11.30-11.30 (midnight Fri & Sat); 12-11.30 Sun
☎ (01788) 578660 ⊕ alexandraarms.co.uk
Abbeydale Absolution; Atomic Strike, Half Life; Fuller's London Pride; 4 changing beers ⊞

Bought in 2011 by Atomic Brewery, this town-centre pub has a comfortable newly refurbished

lounge bar where good-value pub food is served at lunchtimes. The large back bar accommodates a pool table, skittles table and the best jukebox in the county. There is a large rear garden which hosts a summer beer festival. The Atomic Brewery is at the back in the garden. Seven times local CAMRA Pub of the Year. Q ➢ ❀ ⓓ ₺ ♣ ♣ ✿ 🕏

Merchants Inn 🗘

5-6 Little Church Street, CV21 3AW (behind Marks & Spencer)
✪ 12-midnight (1am Fri & Sat); 12-11 Sun
☎ (01788) 571119 ⊕ merchantsinn.co.uk
Batemans XB; Oakham Bishops Farewell; Purity Mad Goose; changing beers ⊞

Nine real ales are always available in this flagstoned gem of a pub. Comfortable seating and an open fire help make this a welcoming place to enjoy real ales or a selection of ciders, perries and foreign beers. Excellent home-cooked food is served at lunchtime. The walls are covered in an impressive range of pub and brewery memorabilia. Rugby and cricket feature on the big screen. There are regular beer festivals, theme nights and quizzes. Situated a mile from the railway station. ➢ ❀ ₺ ♣ ♣ ● 🚌 🚌 ✿ 🕏

Raglan Arms

50 Dunchurch Road, CV22 6AD
✪ 4-midnight (1am Fri); 12-1am Sat; 12-midnight Sun
☎ (01788) 544441
Abbeydale Moonshine; Greene King Abbot; Morland Old Golden Hen; house beer (by Greene King); changing beers (sourced nationally; often Belvoir, Newby Wyke, North Cotswold) ⊞

Up to 10 handpumps serving a fine selection of real ales await you at the friendly Raglan Arms. A winner of many CAMRA awards, it was runner-up Rugby Pub of the Year for 2015. The pub has lots of original character, and hosts quiz nights and live music events monthly. It offers tasty locally sourced bar snacks and can cater for corporate and special events. Outside is a heated, covered area. Pop in and see Liz and the team you will not be disappointed with this little gem. ➢ ❀ ♣ P 🚌 ✿

Rugby Tap 🗘

3 St Matthews Street, CV21 3BY
✪ 10-6 (9 Fri & Sat); 12-3 Sun ☎ (01788) 576767
⊕ rugbytap.co.uk
Changing beers (sourced locally; often Byatt's, Church End, Purity) Ⓖ

Opened in 2012, the Rugby Tap off-licence stocks a large selection of LocAles and ciders, both draught and bottled. A large range of imported beers can also be taken home to enjoy. The Rugby Tap Room micropub opened in 2014 in an adjoining space, offering all of the shop's products in an environment that shuns all forms of electronic entertainment. It serves four to five LocAles and ciders and dabbles in traditional pub snacks.
Q ● 🚌 ✿ 🕏

Seven Stars 🍺

40 Albert Street, CV21 2SH
✪ 12-11 (midnight Fri & Sat); 12-10.30 Sun
☎ (01788) 546611
B&T Shefford Bitter, Golden Fox, Dragon Slayer; Everards Tiger; changing beers ⊞

Quintessential back-street local tastefully refurbished in 2012. The pub has plenty of charm and character, offering a warm and friendly welcome. Quiet background music makes conversation a delight. The bar boasts 14 handpumps, with mild and two ciders permanently on offer, and guest beers always available. Live music evenings feature occasionally. CAMRA Rugby Pub of the Year 2014, Warwickshire and West Midlands Pub of the Year and Most Improved Pub 2012. Q ✆ ❀ & ≠ ● 🖪 🛜

Squirrel Inn 🅛
33 Church Street, CV21 3PU
✆ 12-midnight; 4-11 Sun ☎ (01788) 578527
Marston's Pedigree; 4 changing beers (sourced locally; often Dow Bridge, Merry Miner) ⓗ
A small, friendly pub, benefiting from recent subtle improvements, which offers a warm welcome to locals and strangers alike. A real fire creates a cosy atmosphere and adds to the Squirrel's genuine charm. Live music is a big part of the pub's culture, with new talent as welcome as more established artists. Poetry evenings, a book club, darts teams and BT Sport add to the lively mix. Constantly changing guests beers often come from local breweries Merry Miner and Dow Bridge. The station is less than a mile away. ♣ ● 🖪 ❀

Victoria Inn 🅛
1 Lower Hillmorton Road, CV21 3ST
✆ 12 (4 Mon-Wed)-midnight ☎ (01788) 544374
🌐 downthevic.com
Atomic Strike, Fission, Half Life; Hook Norton Hooky; changing beers ⓗ
A traditional Victorian real ale pub owned by the Atomic Brewery with 14 handpumps offering rapidly changing ales. Real cider is also on handpull and a selection of foreign beers is available. Friendly, efficient staff serve in the lively, bustling period lounge and the traditional bar which doubles as a games room for darts and pool. TV sport is screened at weekends. Themed beer festivals are held twice a year. The railway station is less than a mile away. Rugby CAMRA branch Pub of the Year 2013. ✆ ❀ ♣ ● 🖪 ❀ 🛜

Shustoke

Griffin Inn 🅛
Church Road, B46 2LB (on B4116 on sharp bend)
✆ 12-2.30, 7-11; 12-10.30 Sun ☎ (01675) 481205
🌐 griffininnshustoke.co.uk
Marston's Pedigree; RCH Pitchfork; Theakston Old Peculier; changing beers (sourced nationally; often Oakham) ⓗ
Ever-popular family-run Guide regular with its own brewery. The low-beamed interior is blessedly music- and TV-free. It offers seven guest ales, always including a mild and an Oakham beer, and a Griffin Inn ale often features. Up to four real ciders are also available. Winter is superbly cosy when the log-burning stoves are ticking over, while the highlight of summer is a large, busy beer festival. Children are welcome in the conservatory, beer terrace and meadow garden. No food served Sunday. Q ✆ ❀ ◑ Å ● P ❀ 🛜

Plough
The Green, B46 2AN
✆ 12-2.30, 5.30-11; 12-11 Sat; 12-10.30 Sun
☎ (01675) 481557
Draught Bass; 3 changing beers ⓗ
Attractive rural pub that is the focal point of the village, but which also draws much passing trade. Popular for food, the many rooms are often busy with diners. The bar area is compact and cosy, with games hived off to a separate room. Three guest ales are usually on offer, with effort invested to choose the most interesting from the Punch range. Children will like the feathered-and-furry pets area to the rear, while the front has a tidy beer terrace with greenery. ✆ ❀ ◑ & ♣ P 🛜

Stratford-upon-Avon

Bear at the Swan's Nest Hotel 🍺 🅛
Swan's Nest Lane, CV37 7LT (south end of Clopton Bridge)
✆ 12-11 (midnight Fri & Sat) ☎ (01789) 265540
🌐 thebearfreehouse.co.uk
Castle Rock Harvest Pale; Hook Norton Old Hooky; Wye Valley Butty Bach; house beer (by North Cotswold); 4 changing beers (sourced regionally; often Purity, Stratford upon Avon, Wychwood) ⓗ
Historic pub on a waterside location, five minutes' walk from the town centre, serving eight real ales. The focus is on local and regional brewers such as Wye Valley, Hook Norton and Stratford upon Avon, with seasonal beers available. The interior is decked out with wood panelling and a pewter bar; outside, picnic tables are available for riverside drinking. Excellent home-made bar meals are served in a warm, friendly, welcoming atmosphere. Board games and newspapers are available. Local CAMRA branch Pub of the Year 2013 and 2015. ✆ ❀ ◪ ◑ & ♣ P 🖪 ❀ 🛜

New Bull's Head 🅛
9 Bull Street, CV37 6DT (5 mins' walk SW from town centre past council offices)
✆ 11-11; 12-10.30 Sun ☎ (01789) 268832
🌐 thenewbullshead.co.uk
Timothy Taylor Landlord; 3 changing beers (sourced regionally) ⓗ
A family-run community pub located in the heart of Old Town, a short walk from Holy Trinity and the town centre. Four to six beers are always on offer in a wide range of ABVs and a broad spectrum of styles. Food is freshly prepared and Sunday lunch is a highlight, with vegetarian options. Historic pictures and maps are displayed in the dining area and daily newspapers are available. A community shop is open every day in the old snug. Live sport is screened. ✆ ❀ ◑ ♣ 🖪 ❀ 🛜

Stratford Alehouse 🅛
12B Greenhill Street, CV37 6LF
✆ 12-8 (4 Sun) ☎ 07746 807966
🌐 thestratfordalehouse.com
4 changing beers (sourced regionally; often Prescott, Stratford upon Avon, Uley) ⓖ
The only micropub in Stratford-upon-Avon, serving the finest real ale, cider and wine. No music, gaming machines or children distract you, you just get a friendly welcome in a relaxing environment for drinking, chatting, making new friends or reading the newspapers. Snacks are available. Family run, it offers a huge variety of beers from smaller local, regional and national breweries. More than 230 beers from 80 breweries have been dispensed since opening in December 2013. Q & ≠ ● 🖪 ❀

Stretton on Fosse

Plough Inn
GL56 9QX (signed off A429 Fosse Way)
✆ 11-11 ☎ (01608) 661053 🌐 strettonplough.com

Wickwar BOB; 3 changing beers (sourced regionally; often Marston's, North Cotswold, Wye Valley) Ⓗ
A small Cotswold stone-built village pub with parts over 300 years old. The flagstone bar has an inglenook fireplace and there is a further side room for dining. Popular with both villagers and visitors alike, the landlord takes pride in his well-kept ales and quality home-made food. On Sundays the inglenook fire is used to spit roast the beef. The extended garden can cater for outside dining. A friendly family-run establishment that is well worth a visit. Q

Studley

Victoria Works

33 Redditch Road, B80 7AU
12 (4 Mon)-11 ☎ (0121) 445 4411
the-victoria-works.co.uk
Weatheroak St Udley Mild, Weatheroak Ale, Victoria Works, Redwood; 3 changing beers Ⓗ
Formerly the Nag's Head, this pub has become Weatheroak Brewery's tap house. The horseshoe-shaped interior has comfortable seating areas on different levels. The full range of the brewery's superb beers is always available, with a changing guest ale and a real cider. A selection of sandwiches and jacket potatoes is available 12pm-2pm, Tuesday-Saturday. Live music evenings are hosted occasionally while an acoustic artist often plays just for fun. P

Warwick

Cape of Good Hope

66 Lower Cape, CV34 5DP (off Cape Rd)
12-11 (midnight Fri-Sun) ☎ (01926) 498138
thecapeofgoodhopepub.com
Church Farm Harry's Heifer; Hook Norton Hooky; Wye Valley Butty Bach; 3 changing beers Ⓗ
This is a historic 1820s canalside ale house which serves canal users and locals alike. The original building is now the front bar, with a tasteful modern extension to the rear. Internal decorations include much canal memorabilia including interesting maps. The staff are friendly and knowledgeable, and proud to serve local ales and foods. Outside, the seating area and garden are adjacent to the Grand Union Canal and the sometimes busy double lock.
P (G1)

Old Post Office

12 West Street, CV32 6AN
closed Mon; 12-9 (5 Sun) ☎ 07765 896155
Slaughterhouse Saddleback Best Bitter; Young's Special Ⓗ**; 6 changing beers** Ⓗ/Ⓖ
Warwick's first ale house, serving a variety of traditional beers on handpump and straight from the cask, cooled by an ingenious home-made system. Popular with local residents and real ale enthusiasts, this small bar is housed in a former post office just beyond West Gate and near to Warwick Castle. It has been decorated with a large collection of pub memorabilia collected by Tom the landlord which gives it an eclectic look and feel. Real cider is also available.

Punch Bowl

1 The Butts, CV34 4SS
closed Mon; 12-11 (11.30 Thu); 12-10 Sun
☎ (01926) 403846 punchbowlwarwick.co.uk
Changing beers Ⓗ
A real ale pub with five changing guest beers available at all times. A blackboard behind the bar shows the number of different beers sold so far. The building is an old coaching inn with a large open bar area on different levels – a raised area acts as a stage for popular music evenings held every Thursday and other special occasions. International sports events are shown on a large screen. P (X17)

Wild Boar

27 Lakin Road, CV34 5BU
12-11.30 (12.30am Fri & Sat); 12-10.30 Sun
☎ (01926) 499968 thewildboarwarwick.co.uk
Slaughterhouse Saddleback Best Bitter; 10 changing beers (often Everards, Slaughterhouse) Ⓗ
Traditional community pub with a bar and snug, with views into the two-barrel microbrewery. The bar boasts 10 handpumps for ales and two real ciders are also available. A separate function room holds two film and two music evenings a month as well as other events including the popular Hogtober Fest and skittle evenings. There is an attractive patio garden with hop vines. Home-made lunches are served 12-3pm and pies until 9pm, with roast dinners on Sunday.
Q (X17)

Whichford

Norman Knight

CV36 5PE (two miles E of A3400, Long Compton, facing village green)
7-11 Mon; 12-3, 6-11; 12-midnight Sun; 11-11; 12-midnight Sun summer ☎ (01608) 684621
thenormanknight.co.uk
Hook Norton Hooky; Patriot Morris; Purity Pure Ubu; 4 changing beers (often Cats, North Cotswold, Patriot) Ⓗ
A traditional Cotswold pub overlooking the village green serving seven beers and ciders or perries from nine handpumps. The brewery tap for Patriot next door, local ales feature, plus imported draught beers. The pub has a phenomenal local following and welcomes walkers and their dogs. Excellent food is cooked by the award-winning French chef. Music nights are held throughout the year and classic car meets every third Thursday of the month in summer. Q P

Willey

Wood Farm Brewery Tap

Coalpit Lane, CV23 0SL
9am-10; 12-9 Sun ☎ (01788) 833469
woodfarmbrewery.co.uk
Wood Farm 1823 Mild, Webb Ellis, Best Bitter, Victorious, No. 8; changing beers Ⓗ
Set in 35 acres of farmland two miles north-west of Willey, Wood Farm is a barn conversion over two floors with the upstairs doubling as a function room. The ground-floor bar has a logburner and large windows with views through to the brewery; patio doors lead to a large drinking area outside. Breakfast is served 9am-noon, followed by a good home-made lunch and evening menu. A popular carvery features on Sunday. P

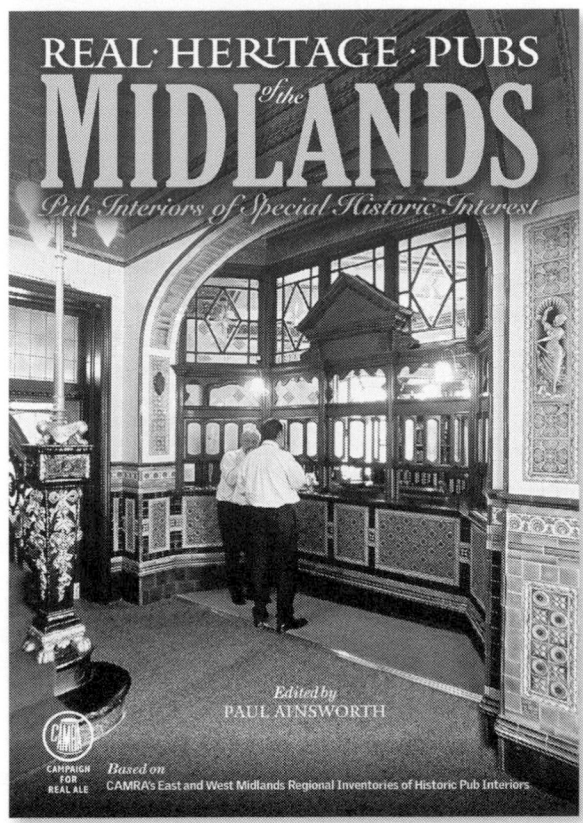

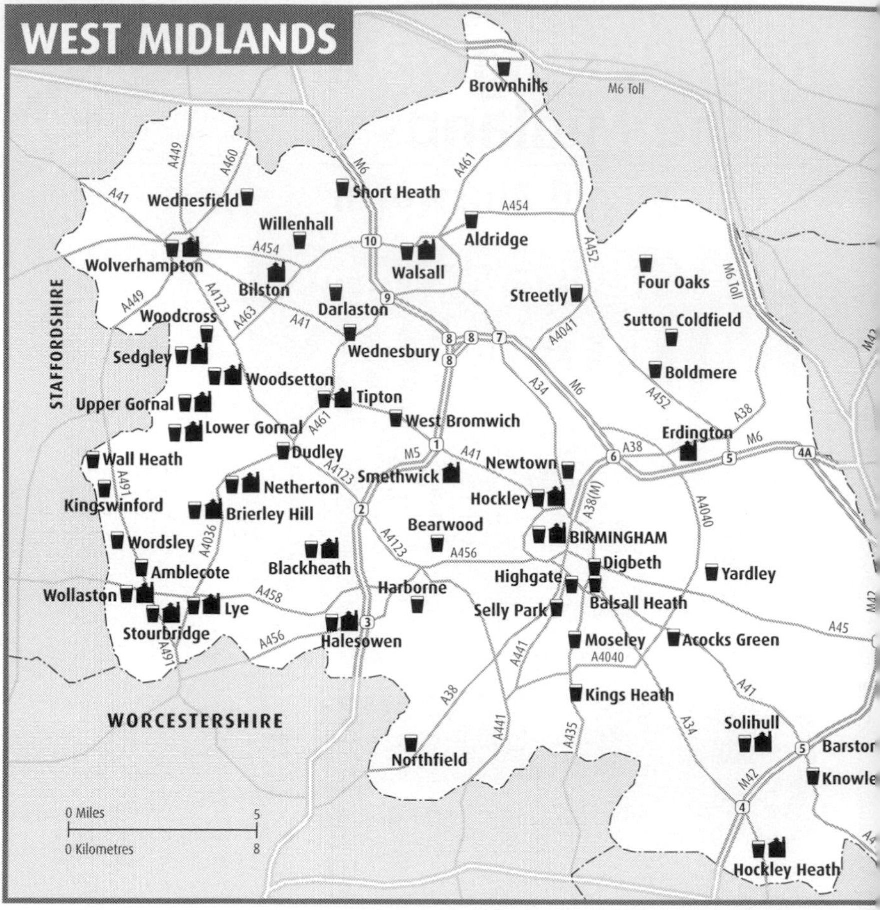

Aldridge

Avion

19 Anchor Road, WS9 8PT

8am-midnight (1am Fri & Sat) (01922) 749810

Greene King Abbot; Ruddles Best Bitter; 8 changing beers (sourced nationally; often Backyard, Beowulf, Lymestone) H

The former Avion cinema (1938-1967) has been successfully converted into a large single-room Wetherspoon outlet with one long bar. It has a great atmosphere and is much loved by families and friends. Some of the original cinema features remain, not least the stained-glass windows. Posters from its former use adorn the walls, many of George Formby, who opened the cinema in 1938. The pub can accommodate parties of up to 12 if pre-booked. Q

Lazy Hill Tavern

196 Walsall Wood Road, WS9 8HB

6-11; 12-2.30, 7-10.30 Sun (01922) 457244

Blythe Staffie; Greene King Abbot; Holden's Black Country Mild, Golden Glow; Morland Old Speckled Hen; Wye Valley Butty Bach; 1 changing beer (sourced nationally) H

Large and welcoming family-run free house with the same licensee for nearly 40 years. The building was originally a farmhouse, then became a country club, and finally a pub in 1986. Four separate rooms are all similarly and comfortably furnished, with a logburner in two. The large function room is used mid-week by local sports and community organisations. There is a car park at the rear and plenty of off-road parking nearby. P

Amblecote

Maverick Drinking House

1 High Street, DY8 4BX (on jct of A491 and A461)

12-11.30 (midnight Wed; 12.30am Fri & Sat); 11.30-11 Sun (01384) 824099

Jennings Cumberland Ale; 3 changing beers H

Large corner establishment and a former CAMRA branch Pub of the Year. The pub has a Wild West theme and is a live music venue for blues, folk, rock and more. Four beers are always on handpump including three guests, two from local breweries. BT Sport, ESPN and the Racing Channel are screened in a separate area when no music is on, and there is a covered, heated smoking area and a small garden. The occasional beer festival is held, locally advertised. Q (256,246,251)

Red Lion

147 Brettell Lane, DY8 4BA

12 (4 Mon & Tue)-midnight (01384) 671743

Olde Swan Entire; Salopian Oracle, Lemon Dream; 2 changing beers (sourced nationally) H

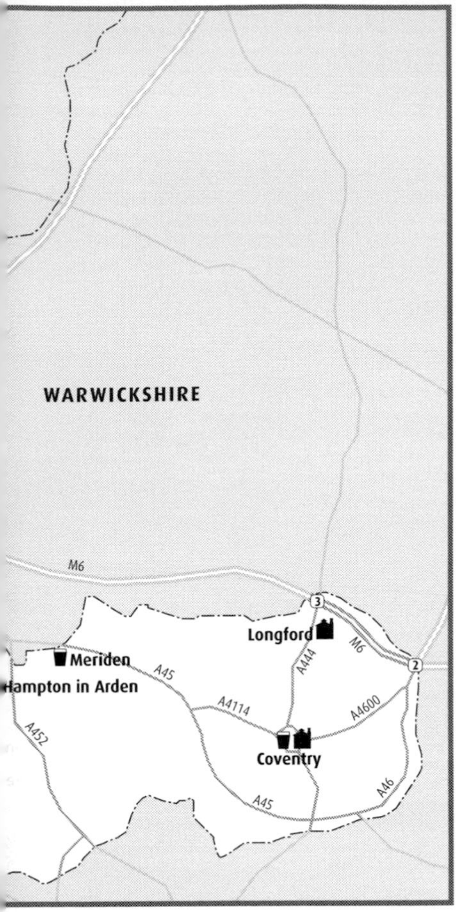

Recently reopened and tastefully refurbished in a modern style, the Red Lion is in an area that has a number of good pubs and is ideal for a pub crawl. With a comfortable, warm atmosphere it is popular, and can get busy on Friday and Saturday nights. A selection of real ales is served, with two changing guests from small breweries sourced nationally. A choice of cobs, pork pies, Scotch eggs and chips is available from the bar.
Q🐴🍎🚌(246,257,256)📶

Robin Hood 🏆 L

196 Collis Street, DY8 4EQ (on A4102 one-way street off Brettell Lane A461)
🕐 12-3 (not Mon & Tue), 5-11; 12-midnight Fri & Sat; 12-11 Sun ☎ (01384) 821120
Bathams Best Bitter; Enville Ginger Beer; Holden's Golden Glow; Olde Swan Bumble Hole Bitter; Wye Valley HPA; 4 changing beers H
A fine traditional Black Country local offering quality ales, good food and a warm welcome. This year sees the pub – current CAMRA branch Pub of the Year – celebrate 160 years as a licensed house. The front rooms house a wonderful beer bottle collection including international and historic brews. The LocAle scheme is emphasised, with beers from local breweries always on offer. The real cider is Thatchers Heritage. A beer and music festival features in October on the rear patio.
Q🐴❀🛏◐◑♿🍎P🚌(246,256,257)📶

Starving Rascal L

1 Brettell Lane, DY8 4BN
🕐 4-11; 12-11 Sat & Sun ☎ 07843 670163
Enville White, Ale; Salopian Oracle; 2 changing beers H
An external restoration has completed the transformation of this friendly local. With five ales and 70 whiskies from around the world on offer, this is a pub for beer and whisky enthusiasts, with bottles and images creatively displayed among the oak features, hanging hops and memorabilia. Sport TV is in the front bar, with a quiet rear lounge and separate pool room. The real cider is Explorer from Orchard Pig. Well-behaved dogs are allowed.
♣🍎P🚌(246)🐾📶

Swan

10 Brettell Lane, DY8 4BN (on A461, ½ mile after A491)
🕐 7-11 Mon-Fri; 12-11 Sat; 12-3, 7-10.30 Sun
☎ (01384) 76932
Sharp's Atlantic; 2 changing beers H
Free house divided into a basic public bar and cosy lounge, with a nice garden to the rear. Two changing beers are offered alongside Sharp's Atlantic, which is now permanently available. If you want to try a beer you have never seen before, this is the place to visit. Cobs are served at lunchtime and there is a varied selection of whiskies to choose from. ❀◐🚌(246)📶

Barston

Bull's Head L

Barston Lane, B92 0JU (on main street, opp church)
SP2073378090
🕐 11-2.30, 5-11; 11-11 Fri & Sat; 12-11 Sun
☎ (01675) 442830 🌐 thebullsheadbarston.co.uk
Adnams Southwold Bitter; Purity Mad Goose; 2 changing beers H

REAL ALE BREWERIES

AJ's Walsall (NEW)
Angel Halesowen
Backyard Walsall
Banks's Wolverhampton
Bathams Brierley Hill
Black Country Lower Gornal
Blue Bear Smethwick
Broughs Wolverhampton
Byatt's Coventry
Craddock's Stourbridge
Fixed Wheel Blackheath (NEW)
Fownes Upper Gornal
Froth Blowers Erdington
Green Duck Stourbridge
Holden's Woodsetton
Lion Heart Longford (NEW)
Newbridge Bilston (NEW)
Olde Swan Netherton
Pig Iron Brierley Hill (NEW)
Rock & Roll Birmingham
Sacre Brew Wolverhampton (NEW)
Sadler's Lye
Sarah Hughes Sedgley
Shed Brewery Hockley Heath
Silhill Solihull
Toll End Tipton
Twisted Barrel Coventry (NEW)
Two Towers Birmingham: Hockley
Websters of Wollaston Wollaston (NEW)

A former 15th-century coaching inn, this is a true country village local, with two comfortable bars plus a small, intimate restaurant. Racing memorabilia is displayed throughout and there are real fires. Seasonal home-cooked food is served plus a standard menu (no food Sun eve). Two regular ales are on the bar plus two guests. Cask Marque and LocAle accredited, the pub has been awarded local CAMRA Pub of the Year six times and has featured in this Guide for over 20 years. The secluded beer garden is popular in summer, especially on the August bank holiday when it hosts the annual village fête. **Q P**

Bearwood

Bear Tavern

500 Bearwood Road, B66 4BX
9am-11 (1am Fri; midnight Sat); 10-11 Sun
☎ (0121) 429 1184
7 changing beers (sourced nationally) H
Situated at the crossroads with Sandon Road and Three Shires Oak Road, this open-plan pub is dominated by numerous sports screens. Competition in the area has led to a marked increase in choice here – up to seven real ales are offered, which can be from local or national brewers. Food is served all day, every day. There is a variety of entertainment at weekends.
(82,120,127)

Midland

526-528 Bearwood Road, B66 4BE
10-11 (midnight Fri & Sat); 12-11 Sun ☎ (0121) 429 6958
Black Country Bradley's Finest Golden, Pig on the Wall, Fireside; changing beers (sourced nationally) H
A former Midland Bank tastefully refurbished by Black Country Ales. The single room serves up to 14 real ales and a traditional cider. The beer cellar is on the same floor and can be viewed through a glass inspection panel. A small selection of continental beers and fruit wines complement the ales. Cobs are available at the bar. Acoustic music is played on Sundays and there is a quiz on Wednesdays. **Q** (120,82)

Birmingham: Acocks Green

Inn on the Green

2 Westley Road, B27 7UH
11-11 (midnight Fri); 10-midnight Sat & Sun
☎ (0121) 708 0108 innonthegreen.pub
Wye Valley HPA; 5 changing beers (sourced nationally; often Church End) H
Big former Mitchells & Butlers roadhouse in the heart of Acocks Green, run by a keen landlord who is an active CAMRA member, with friendly and knowledgeable staff. The ales are always interesting and it is well worth visiting. There are regular karaoke evenings, live sport is shown, and live music plays at the weekend in Route 44. Excellent beer festivals are held four times a year. The pub won the bronze for local CAMRA branch Pub of the Year 2014 and was a finalist for 2013.
(Spring Rd)**P**

Birmingham: Balsall Heath

Old Moseley Arms

53 Tindal Street, B12 9QU (400yds off Moseley Rd)
12-11 (midnight Fri & Sat) ☎ (0121) 440 1954
oldmoseleyarms.co.uk
Enville Ale; Wye Valley Bitter, HPA, Butty Bach; 1 changing beer (sourced nationally) H
Current CAMRA branch Pub of the Year, this is a traditional 19th-century inn. The left bar has an 80in screen for sport, the right bar has a jukebox. Upstairs functions and live entertainment takes place, there is a pool table, and comfy sofas in the covered garden/smoking area. A superb tandoori menu is served Tuesday-Friday 12-2.30pm, Monday-Saturday from 6pm, and all day Sunday. Regular beer festivals showcase 16 ales, cider and perry. Live music featuring local talent is upstairs every Sunday evening. (50)

Birmingham: City Centre

Bacchus

Burlington Arcade, New Street, B2 4JH
11-11 (1am Fri & Sat); 11-10.30 Sun ☎ (0121) 632 5445
Purity Pure Ubu; Sharp's Doom Bar; St Austell Nicholson's Pale Ale; 2 changing beers (sourced nationally) H
Situated below the Burlington Hotel (once known as the Midland Hotel), Bacchus is a part of the Mitchells & Butlers Nicholson's brand. While the beer range is relatively standard for those in the Nicholson's group, the pub is unusually adorned with old-fashioned artwork and relics, and it almost feels as though you are in a cellar. The bar area is small and it can often get busy.
(New St)

Craven Arms

47 Upper Gough Street, B1 1JG (in side street near Mailbox)
12-11 (midnight Fri & Sat) ☎ (0121) 643 2852
Black Country Bradley's Finest Golden, Pig on the Wall, Fireside; 8 changing beers (sourced nationally) H
An early 19th-century former Holden's pub, recently restored by Black Country Ales and sporting an attractive blue-tiled exterior and a cosy interior. In addition to three permanent Black Country beers, between six and eight changing guest casks are on tap from breweries often new to Birmingham. Beer festivals are held regularly and customers are welcome to bring their own food. The pub was awarded silver in local CAMRA branch Pub of the Year 2014 and bronze in 2013.
(New St)

Old Contemptibles

176 Edmund Street, B3 2HB (100yds from Snow Hill station)
11-11 (midnight Fri); 12-midnight Sat; 12-6 Sun
☎ (0121) 200 3310
Purity Pure Ubu; Sharp's Doom Bar; St Austell Nicholson's Pale Ale; 5 changing beers (sourced nationally) H
Red-bricked corner pub, part of the Nicholson's chain, named after the famous World War I soldiers. The pub resembles a Victorian hostelry with chandeliers, a wood-panelled bar and a comfortable snug at the rear. Good-quality food is served, with the guest ales coming from the Nicholson's range; there is also an impressive wine list. The pub is popular with local office workers and has been known to close early if there is not much custom later in the evening.
(Snow Hill/New St)

Post Office Vaults

84 New Street, B2 4BA (entrances are on both New St and Pinfold St)

11-11 (midnight Fri & Sat); 12-11 Sun ☎ (0121) 643 7354
postofficevaults.co.uk

Hobsons Mild; Salopian Oracle; 6 changing beers (sourced nationally)

Only a two-minute walk from the Stephenson Street entrance to New Street station and close to Victoria Square, this subterranean pub offers a range of eight traditional beers in excellent condition. It always keeps at least 350 different bottled beers from all over the world, one of the largest ranges in the country. Serving 14 ciders and perries, the pub was elected West Midlands Cider Pub of the Year 2013 and 2014. The extremely knowledgeable staff will make your visit a pleasure. Q(New St)

Pure Bar & Kitchen

30 Waterloo Street, B2 5TJ (5 mins from New St and Snow Hill stations)

11-11 ☎ (0121) 237 5666 purebarandkitchen.com

Purity Pure Gold, Mad Goose, Pure Ubu; 4 changing beers (sourced nationally; often Kirkstall, Rooster's, Tiny Rebel)

Birmingham's newest real ale outlet, set in a traditional building with an industrial interior on Waterloo Street. Seven cask ales are offered: three from Purity Brewery and four guests. Gourmet food is served – all food is made with beer, and the menu has been matched to the beers available. Landlord James describes the bar as a perfect democratic environment where everyone should be able to find their ideal beer. A large chalkboard behind the bar provides details of which beers are on. (New St/Snow Hill)

Shakespeare

31 Summer Row, B3 1JJ (200yds from city end of Broad St)

10-11 (midnight Fri & Sat) ☎ (0121) 236 8702

Sharp's Doom Bar; St Austell Nicholson's Pale Ale; 4 changing beers (sourced nationally; often Purity)

Glorious red-bricked Victorian local, part of the Nicholson's brand. It is near the Jewellery Quarter and the new Library of Birmingham. The traditional bar has a small hatch to serve the rear snug, which is usually reserved for diners. There is a decorated patio garden to the rear and seating out at the front. It has regularly changing guest ales, an excellent reputation for good food with frequent offers on beer and a burger, and pie and a pint. Families are welcome during food service times which is normally up to 10pm.
(Snow Hill)

Wellington

37 Bennetts Hill, B2 5SN (5 mins from New St and Snow Hill stations)

10-midnight ☎ (0121) 200 3115
thewellingtonrealale.co.uk

Black Country Bradley's Finest Golden, Pig on the Wall, Fireside; Oakham Citra; Purity Mad Goose; Wye Valley HPA; 10 changing beers (sourced nationally; often Froth Blowers Brewing Co, Titanic)

Recently refurbished and extended, with an additional upstairs bar and roof terrace beer garden, this multiple award-winner is a veritable beer festival every day. Sixteen ales and three traditional ciders on handpump, and a wide selection of bottled beers and whiskies, are served to a varied clientele by knowledgeable staff. Regular quizzes, cheese nights and darts competitions are held. Food is not served but you are welcome to bring your own – plates, cutlery and condiments are provided.
Q(New St/Snow Hill)

Birmingham: Digbeth

Anchor ★

308 Bradford Street, B5 6ET (adjacent to Digbeth coach station)

11-midnight (2am Fri & Sat); 12-11.30 Sun
☎ (0121) 622 4516 anchorinndigbeth.co.uk

Hobsons Mild; changing beers (sourced nationally)

Grade II-listed and with a nationally important historic pub interior, a four-times winner of the local CAMRA branch Pub of the Year and a 2013 finalist, the Anchor is a must-visit for the ale enthusiast. Run by the Keane family for over 40 years, it brings the local pub feel to a city centre location. There is a changing beer range, with new breweries often featuring, along with regular beer festivals. The pub is busy when Birmingham City play at home.
Q(New St/Moor Street)

Spotted Dog

104 Warwick Street, B12 0NH

5-11; 3-1am Fri; 12-1am Sat; 12-midnight Sun
☎ (0121) 772 3822 spotteddog.co.uk

Castle Rock Harvest Pale; Holden's Black Country Mild; 3 changing beers (sourced nationally)

A traditional multi-roomed pub with an Irish feel. It is off the beaten track but well worth a trip, with excellent-value Holden's Mild on the bar. The large covered garden/smoking area has heaters and a barbecue area. Live traditional Irish music features on Mondays, jazz on Tuesdays and blues on Thursdays. There is a mixture of sport on the large screen but especially rugby. Excellent Scotch eggs, including vegetarian varieties, are on offer. It can be busy when Birmingham City are at home.
(Bordesley)

White Swan ★

276 Bradford Street, B12 0QY (close to Digbeth bus station)

12-2, 4-11; 12-11 Thu; 11-1am Fri & Sat; 12-11 Sun
☎ (0121) 622 2586

Banks's Mild, Bitter; Jennings Bitter, Cumberland Ale; 1 changing beer

Two-roomed unspoilt Victorian red-bricked pub, identified by CAMRA as having a nationally important historic interior. The main drinking area has a wooden bar with a large bar-back and etched mirrors, and there are stools and bench seating around the walls. An impressive ornately tiled hallway leads to a small lounge and smoking area. It gets busy when sporting events are shown on large pull-down TV screens. Sandwiches, pies and cobs are available. Guest beers are from the Marston's portfolio. (Bordesley)

Woodman ★

New Canal Street, B5 5LG (opp old Curzon St by Millennium Point)

11-11 (midnight Fri & Sat) ☎ (0121) 643 4960
thewoodmanbirmingham.co.uk

Castle Rock Black Gold, Harvest Pale; 6 changing beers (sourced nationally)

Now with an environmentally friendly refurbishment, this pub is Grade II-listed with a nationally important historic interior. It has a red-

bricked tile and terracotta exterior, with an L-shaped bar which is tiled above a wooden dado. A tiled lobby on Albert Street leads to an attractive small drinking area, with a hatch to the servery, and a real fire. The third plain room on the left now makes for a pleasant dividing area. Good food is served daily, and there is an outside seating/dining area. Quiz night is Wednesday.
Q❀◑♿⇌(Moor St)♣●🚌ᯤ

Birmingham: Harborne

Green Man L
2 High Street, B17 9NE
11.30-11 (midnight Fri & Sat) ☎ (0121) 428 3581
Brakspear Bitter; Purity Pure Ubu; Wye Valley Butty Bach; 5 changing beers (sourced nationally) H
A Mitchells & Butlers community pub furnished like other Ember Inns and usually offering the full range of ales. Busy and bustling due to its convenient situation on the High Street, it boasts a good-value food menu served daily until 10pm. There is a heated smoking area in the rear car park area, and the patio at the front can be pleasant in summer. Quiz night is Tuesday. It is ideally placed for the start of a pub crawl.
❀◑♿⇌(University)♣P🚌🐾ᯤ

Junction L
212 High Street, B17 9PT
11-11 (midnight Thu & Fri); 10-midnight Sat
☎ (0121) 428 2635 🌐 thejunctionharborne.co.uk
Purity Mad Goose; Sharp's Doom Bar; Timothy Taylor Landlord; 3 changing beers (sourced nationally; often Adnams, Itchen Valley, Woodforde's) H
This distinctive Edwardian building dominates the High Street. Inside there is a sophisticated feel to the decor with a tiled bar area with seating, leading to a further main dining area. The varied beer range features up to six ales, and quality food is served from an open-plan kitchen, with home-cooked roasts on Sundays. A pleasant, secluded beer garden is at the rear. A quiz takes place every Monday. The pub's original tiles can be viewed in the corridor leading to the toilets.
❀◑♿⇌(University)●🚌🐾ᯤ

White Horse L
2 York Street, B17 0HG
11 (12 Mon)-11.30; 11-12.30am Fri & Sat; 12-11.30 Sun
☎ (0121) 427 8004 🌐 whitehorseharborne.com
Greene King Abbot; 10 changing beers (sourced nationally; often Purity, Sadler's, Three Tuns) H
A much-improved and extended free house just off the busy High Street. There is an island bar with a front snug and a rear heated area. It puts great emphasis on real ale, with an electronic beer board linked to the pub's website. Regular live music nights are held on Fridays and Saturdays, a monthly open mic night on the last Wednesday, and quiz nights every Tuesday. The artwork on the walls is by local artists including the landlord.
❀♿⇌(University)●🚌🐾ᯤ

Birmingham: Highgate

Lamp Tavern L
157 Barford Street, B5 6AH (500yds from A441 Pershore Rd near bottom of Hurst St)
12.30-11 ☎ (0121) 688 1220
Everards Tiger; Hobsons Mild; Rock & Roll Lamplight; Stanway Stanney Bitter; 2 changing beers (sourced nationally; often Abbeydale, Malvern Hills, Rock & Roll) H
A warm welcome awaits from Eddie, the landlord of more than 20 years standing, at this characterful, single-roomed, street-corner local. The Lamp is home to the rooftop Rock & Roll Brewery and its only regular outlet, with one beer from the range always available. It is also the only Birmingham pub to supply Stanway Stanney Bitter. There is a weekly folk club on Friday evenings. A Guide regular, the pub also won silver in the local CAMRA branch Pub of the Year 2013 awards.
♿♣🚌(35,45,47)🐾

Birmingham: Hockley

Black Eagle L
16 Factory Road, B18 5JU (turn right out of Soho Benson Rd metro station, cross road and walk 200yds)
11.30-3, 5.30-11; 11.30-11 Fri; 12-3, 7-11 Sat; 12-3 Sun
☎ (0121) 523 4008 🌐 theblackeaglepub.co.uk
Marston's Pedigree; Sadler's Peaky Blinder; Timothy Taylor Landlord; changing beers (often Dark Star, Holden's, Salopian) H
Traditional award-winning multi-room pub with a restaurant to the rear. While slightly off the beaten track, this real ale oasis is well worth seeking out for its excellent range of ales and good-value food. Three guest beers are always available and annual beer festivals are held in the summer along with occasional barbecues. Real cider and perry usually come from Gwynt y Ddraig or Westons.
❀◑●🚌(74,75,101)🐾ᯤ

Red Lion L
95 Warstone Lane, B18 6NG
10-midnight (2am Fri & Sat) ☎ (0121) 233 9144
🌐 theredlionbirmingham.com
Wye Valley Butty Bach; 3 changing beers (sourced nationally; often Bathams) H
Traditional two-roomed pub that is rich in both local heritage and modern art. It has a lively front bar and a cosy back lounge. A good-sized clubroom is upstairs and there is a sheltered patio and smoking area to the rear. An excellent extensive food menu is served all day, including the popular Cow Club on Mondays. Three changing guest beers are available and two changing ciders. Regular quiz nights are held and large screens show sporting events. ❀◑⇌(Jewellery Quarter)●🚌ᯤ

Birmingham: Kings Heath

Kings Heath Cricket & Sports Club
Charlton House, 247 Alcester Road South, B14 6DT
12-midnight ☎ (0121) 444 1913
Morland Old Speckled Hen; Wye Valley HPA, Butty Bach; 3 changing beers (sourced nationally; often Greene King) H
Welcoming sports club where CAMRA members are permitted entry on production of a membership card (maximum 10 visits per year). The club has two rooms – a comfortable lounge for relaxed drinking and a spacious room for watching sporting events on large screens which also houses two full-size snooker tables. The beer range always includes three rotating guest ales. Varying social events are held throughout the year including live music.
❀◑♿♣P🚌

Birmingham: Moseley

Prince of Wales L

118 Alcester Road, B13 8EE

12-11.30 (1am Fri & Sat) ☎ (0121) 449 4198

theprincemoseley.co.uk

Oakham Citra; Purity Mad Goose; Timothy Taylor Landlord; 3 changing beers (often Castle Rock, Holden's) H

Serving cask ales since 1861, this three-bar pub is a real community local. The front bar boasts an authentic Victorian bar-back and there are two further bars at the back, leading to a beer garden and cigar smoke room boasting the largest collection of Cuban cigars in the country. Two ciders are on sale, alongside a good selection of whiskies and interesting cocktails. There is a TV for sport, a real fire and a quiz night every Tuesday. (1,35,50)

Birmingham: Newtown

Bartons Arms ★

144 High Street, B6 4UP

12-11 (10.30 Sun) ☎ (0121) 333 5988

thebartonsarms.com

Oakham JHB, Inferno, Citra, Bishops Farewell; 2 changing beers (sourced nationally; often Oakham) H

A stunning red-bricked pub run by Oakham Brewery from Peterborough. This 1901 pub is Grade II-listed and has an interior of national historic importance. The Bartons has ornate Minton tiles throughout, including a central tiled staircase, original stained-glass windows and snob screens on the bar. Superb Thai food is served in the lounge. A range of Oakham ales is available, usually including one guest and a cider. Quiz night is Mondays and regular music and beer festivals are held. (Aston)P

Birmingham: Northfield

Black Horse ★ L

Bristol Road South, B31 2QT (opp Sainbury's)

8am-11 (1am Fri & Sat); 8am-midnight Sun

☎ (0121) 477 1800

Greene King Abbot; Ruddles Best Bitter; Sharp's Doom Bar; changing beers (sourced nationally; often Adnams, Fuller's, Purity) H

Large inter-war mock-Tudor road house offering the only extensive real ale choice in this part of the city. It has been transformed from an undesirable local to a popular pub serving consistently good-quality beer. Unusually for Wetherspoon, this pub has a multi-room layout and bars on two levels. It still retains its original Baronial Hall entrance but the bar has been tastefully refurbished with an etched-glass entrance door. There is a bowling green with original outbuildings to the rear. QP

Birmingham: Selly Park

Selly Park Tavern L

592 Pershore Road, B29 7HQ

11.30-11 (midnight Fri & Sat); 12-11 Sun

☎ (0121) 472 4392

Brakspear Bitter; Purity Pure Ubu; 6 changing beers (sourced nationally; often Wye Valley) H

An Ember Inns red-bricked pub dating to 1901, run by the same manager for over 10 years, with a varied clientele. Although it is a large one-roomed pub there are smaller areas so you can still get privacy. The two regular and four guest ales are served by friendly staff. There is an active bowling club and a skittle alley at the rear. Less than one mile from Edgbaston Cricket Ground, it is handy for visiting fans. (Selly Oak)P (45,47)

Birmingham: Yardley

William Tyler

140 Church Street, B25 8UT

8am-11 (midnight Fri & Sat) ☎ (0121) 789 5860

Adnams Broadside; Greene King IPA, Abbot; Sharp's Doom Bar; 4 changing beers (sourced nationally) H

This Wetherspoon pub is a former Woolworth's store, excellently converted. Historic murals adorn the walls and on the ceiling are paintings of Nigel Mansell, Murray Walker and Tony Hancock. There are books for customers to read while enjoying their beer. The light arrangements are made of bottles and wine glasses, a must-see from an architectural point of view. This is a great example of a community local in an area that is sparsely populated by pubs. (Stechford)

Blackheath

Waterfall

132 Waterfall Lane, B64 6RG

12-11 (midnight Fri & Sat) ☎ (0121) 559 9198

Bathams Best Bitter; Enville Ginger Beer; Holden's Golden Glow, Special; 4 changing beers H

Characterful, homely, community-centred pub owned by Holden's. It is close to Blackheath town centre on a steep 10-minute walk uphill from Old Hill station. Basic, good-value food is served from Anne's Kitchen and up to six guest beers, accenting on the strong side, usually from Burton Bridge and Olde Swan breweries. The outside drinking area affords wonderful views during the summer owing to its elevation. It can get crowded at weekends. (Old Hill)P (4M)

Boldmere

Bishop Vesey L

63 Boldmere Road, B73 5UY

8-11 (midnight Fri & Sat) ☎ (0121) 355 5077

Backyard Blonde; Greene King Abbot; Ruddles Best Bitter; Sharp's Doom Bar; changing beers H

Sprawling Wetherspoon pub with an open-plan layout, upstairs seating and an outside patio/smokers area. Boasting 15 consecutive years in the Guide, it is a frequent Pub of the Year for the local CAMRA branch. The loyal local clientele includes a thriving darts team. Children are welcome in the family area until 9pm. Up to eight guest beers, many from local micros, make this a venue not to miss. Real cider features occasionally as well. (Wylde Green)

Brierley Hill

Vine

10 Delph Road, Delph, DY5 2TN

12-11; 12-10.30 Sun ☎ (01384) 78293

Bathams Mild Ale, Best Bitter H

Classic, unspoilt brewery tap with an ornately decorated façade proclaiming the Shakespearean quotation: 'Blessing of your heart, you brew good ale'. Step inside and enter an elongated pub with a labyrinthine feel. The rooms have contrasting characters. The front bar is staunchly traditional while the larger rear bar with its own servery and leather seating houses the dartboard at the far end. On the other side of the central passageway is a homely lounge partly converted from former brewery offices. Q ♣P (X96)

Brownhills

Swan

Pelsall Road, WS8 7DL

4 (2 Fri)-midnight; 12-midnight Sat & Sun

(01543) 820628

Holden's Golden Glow; 2 changing beers

A traditional pub with two rooms served by a central bar. The main drinking area is the bar to the right of the front entrance, with a lounge to the left. Beyond the lounge, a separate area houses the pool table. There is an outside drinking space at the front of the pub. The Swan has been refurbished throughout and is a comfortable and welcoming venue for both locals and visitors. Up to two guest beers supplement the regular beer. Local CAMRA branch Pub of the Year. ♣P

Coventry

Broomfield Tavern

14-16 Broomfield Place, Spon End, CV5 6GY (adjacent to rugby ground but hidden from main road)

4-midnight; 12-1am Fri & Sat; 12-midnight Sun

(024) 7663 0969

8 changing beers (sourced locally; often Church End)

The decor and beer range have improved since this pub became a free house. The small bar is virtually filled with handpumps, and the beer range features many unusual choices. Friday night music sessions often host well-known musicians, and there is live folk/mountain music Mondays and Thursdays. It has twice been local CAMRA branch Cider Pub of the Year. This Victorian inn is in a rural setting but is just behind the main road near Coventry rugby ground. An annual charity fire walk is held in the adjacent park.
♣ (6,6A,10)

City Arms

1 Earlsdon Street, Earlsdon, CV5 6EP (on roundabout at centre of Earlsdon)

8am-midnight (1am Fri & Sat) (024) 7671 8170

Greene King Abbot; Ruddles Best Bitter; changing beers (sourced locally; often Byatt's, Purity)

Named after the Coventry coat of arms, the pub is a large imposing building in the heart of Earlsdon. It has a large open-plan main room with a quieter smaller room at the rear. Part of the Wetherspoon chain since 2000, the pub is an enthusiastic supporter of real ale, allowing customers to assist in the selection of forthcoming beers. The inn has a strong local following but also attracts visitors from further afield, especially at weekends.
P (5,12)

Gatehouse Tavern

46 Hill Street, CV1 4AN (close to Belgrade Theatre and Spon St, nr jct 8 of ring road)

11-11 (11.30 Fri & Sat); 12-10.30 Sun (024) 7663 0140

gatehousetavern.com

7 changing beers

This pub was rebuilt by the landlord from the shell of the former Leigh Mills gatehouse. It is sport-oriented, with stained-glass windows depicting the rugby Six Nations. The garden is the largest within the city centre. Serving a changing range of up to seven real ales, it is popular with shoppers and city-centre workers during the day and hosts a mixed crowd in the evenings.

Greyhound Inn

Sutton Stop, Hawkesbury Junction, CV6 6DF (off Grange Rd at jct of Coventry and Oxford canals)

11-11; 12-10.30 Sun (024) 7636 3046

greyhoundinn.org

Draught Bass; Marston's Pedigree; 2 changing beers

This canalside hostelry is a four-times winner of the local Godiva award for best pub in Coventry and Warwickshire, and local CAMRA Pub of the Year for four consecutive years. The pub dates from the 1830s and the terrace to the front overlooks the bustling junction of two canals. An extensive menu of freshly cooked food is offered. Two major beer festivals take place annually and it is popular with locals and visitors alike. Q ♣P

Nursery Tavern

38-39 Lord Street, Chapelfields, CV5 8DA (1 mile W of city centre, off Allesley Old Rd)

12-11.30 (midnight Fri & Sat); 12-11 Sun

(024) 7667 4530

Courage Best Bitter; Fuller's London Pride; Hook Norton Hooky Mild; 3 changing beers

A classic three-room community pub in the historic watchmaking area and a long-standing entry in this Guide. Each room has a distinct feel, the main bar complemented by a quieter lounge, and a rear room used for live music and quizzes. Roast dinners are served on Sunday lunchtimes. The pub is a supporter of local arts and music, and hosts occasional charity nights in support of local causes.
Q ♣ (6,6A,10)

Old Windmill

22-23 Spon Street, CV1 3BA (in a medieval street, behind IKEA)

12 (3 Mon)-11.30; 12-1am Fri & Sat (024) 7625 1717

RCH Old Slug Porter; Sharp's Doom Bar; Theakston Old Peculier; Timothy Taylor Landlord; Wychwood Hobgoblin; 2 changing beers

A 15th-century building divided into a number of rooms and areas – one was the brewhouse, another has a stove set in a large old fireplace with an adjacent entrance into a priest hole. Two beer festivals are hosted every year. Live music takes place on the first and last Friday of the month, folk on Sunday afternoons and bluegrass once a month. Pork pies are generally available. This city centre pub was local CAMRA Pub of the Year in 2015.
♣

Open Arms

Daventry Road, Cheylesmore, CV3 5DP

11.30-11 (11.30 Wed; midnight Thu-Sat); 11.30-11 Sun

(024) 7650 5129

Brakspear Bitter; Purity Pure Ubu; 4 changing beers (sourced nationally; often Marston's, St Austell)

Post-war family-friendly Ember Inn in an area of the city almost devoid of real ale pubs. It is only about a mile from the city centre, near the War Memorial Park. The LocAle is from Purity. There are often events taking place including live music, especially at weekends, frequently in support of local charities. Although a popular dining pub, food service does not dominate the atmosphere. There is a large garden and car park at the rear. ♿P (9,9A)

Red Lion

Ansty Road, Walsgrave, CV2 2EY
11.30-11 (11.30 Wed; midnight Thu-Sat)
(024) 7661 2168
Brakspear Bitter; M&B Brew XI; Purity Pure Ubu; 5 changing beers Ⓗ
Welcoming modern pub with a single L-shaped bar serving eight real ales including five frequently changing guests. The large garden has plenty of seating and a covered and heated area for smokers. Good food is served all day every day up to 10pm – set menus offer good value for money. The drinks menu contains comprehensive tasting notes including suggested food matches for some of the guest ales. ♿P

Town Crier

Corporation Street, CV1 1PB (next to Ikea)
11-11 (1am Thu-Sat); 12-6 Sun (024) 7663 2317
thetowncriercoventry.com
Marston's Burton Bitter, Pedigree; 3 changing beers Ⓗ
A modern pub built in the late 1980s by Banks's, with a single bar serving one large room. Close to historic Spon Street and the main city-centre shopping areas, it is popular with shoppers and workers, giving it a mixed clientele. There is live music on Saturday evenings and a large screen used occasionally for big sporting events.
♿

Town Wall Tavern

Bond Street, CV1 4AH (behind Belgrade Theatre)
12-11 (midnight Fri & Sat); 12-10 Sun (024) 7622 0963
townwalltavern.co.uk
Adnams Southwold Bitter, Broadside; Draught Bass; 3 changing beers Ⓗ
One of the few remaining traditional locals left in the city centre. Tucked behind the Belgrade Theatre, it is frequented by actors and can become busy during intervals. The bar and lounge are supplemented by the Donkey Box, a small snug at the front which is just big enough to hold a donkey. There is an imaginative food offering including roasts on Sunday lunchtime (no food Sun or Mon eves).

Whitefriars Olde Ale House

114-115 Gosford Street, CV1 5DL
12-midnight (1am Fri & Sat); 12-11 Sun
(024) 7625 1655
5 changing beers Ⓗ
Formerly part of Whitefriars monastery and dating from circa 1335, this atmospheric pub offers two downstairs drinking areas, one with a real fire, and a labyrinth of smaller rooms upstairs. Up to four ciders and five guest beers are on offer. There is a rear garden for fine weather drinking and some music events. Quiz night is Tuesday, open mic is Wednesday and live music plays on Saturday – which can be loud when staged inside the pub.
♿♣ (8,9)

Darlaston

Prince of Wales

74 Walsall Road, WS10 9JJ
2-midnight (1am Fri); 1-1am Sat; 1-midnight Sun
(0121) 568 7317
Holden's Black Country Bitter, Golden Glow; house beer (by Holden's); 1 changing beer (sourced locally) Ⓗ
The lounge has equestrian and maritime prints, with soft bench seats and bar stools. There is a short history of the Darlaston gunlock makers. The long narrow bar has darts played at one end and is decorated with old world bills. There is a conservatory at the rear which is available for functions free of charge. The garden has a bench area with children's slide and two hopscotch tracks. Live entertainment features on Saturday nights and a quiz on Monday nights. Bar snacks are served.
Q♣ (34,39)

Dudley

Court House

30 New Street, DY1 1LP (a short walk from bus station towards police station)
12-11; 12-10.30 Sun (01384) 240062
Black Country Bradley's Finest Golden, Pig on the Wall, Fireside; changing beers Ⓗ
Run by Black Country Traditional Inns as a specialist real ale pub, the regular beers come from the company's own brewery, accompanied by a large selection of guest ales from across the country. The pub has developed a reputation for regularly offering a dark beer. Cider drinkers are well catered for, with a choice of four makes. The small snug and the large upstairs function room complement the facilities. CAMRA Cider Pub of the Year 2013.
Q♿♣ (1,126)

Four Oaks

Butlers Arms

444 Lichfield Road, B74 4BL
12-11 (midnight Fri & Sat); 12-10.30 Sun
(0121) 308 0765 butlersarms.co.uk
4 changing beers Ⓗ
Attractive, family-run suburban pub with a strong local following, but visitors can make use of the nearby bus and rail links. The interior is an eclectic mix of styles with lamps, mirrors and curiosities. The four guest ales vary but usually include a Caledonian beer plus Greene King Abbot. The chalkboard menu is full of fish specials, with meat and vegetarian alternatives. Two small beer terraces to the front allow for alfresco drinking.
Q♿(Butlers Lane)P (X12,902,905)

Mare Pool

297 Lichfield Road, B74 2UG (behind shops on E side of Lichfield Rd)
8am-midnight (1am Fri & Sat) (0121) 323 1070
Greene King Abbot; Ruddles Best Bitter; Sharp's Doom Bar; changing beers Ⓗ
Wetherspoon pub with the chain's usual food offerings and a family-friendly policy attracting a younger clientele during the day. The name refers to one of the many pools that used to surround Sutton, and the watery theme includes hundreds of hanging glass droplets. It has an unusual canopied gas fire and, outside, a suntrap beer terrace. There are occasional showings of big-screen sport. The five guest ales often include Backyard and Purity beers. Q♿P

Halesowen

Hawne Tavern 𝕃

76 Attwood Street, B63 3UG (just off Stourbridge Rd, down Short St opp Tesco Express)
🕔 4.30-11; 12-11 Sat; 12-10.30 Sun ☎ (0121) 602 2601
Bathams Best Bitter; Bob's White Lion; Wye Valley HPA; 6 changing beers Ⓗ
A back-street locals' pub just off the main bus route. It has a large bar with a pool table and a TV showing sport (not Sky), with separate seating areas plus a smaller cosy lounge. There are three regular and up to six guest ales, many from microbreweries, focusing on northern beers. Thatchers Heritage cider is also sold. Baguettes are served in the evenings, hot sandwiches and chips at weekends. The enclosed rear garden is ideal for smokers and sun worshippers.
Q❀♣🍎▯🚌(9,002,004)🐾

Waggon & Horses 𝕃

21 Stourbridge Road, B63 3TU (on main A458, ½ mile from bus station)
🕔 12-11.30 (12.30am Fri & Sat) ☎ (0121) 550 4989
Abbeydale Moonshine; Angel Ales Ale; Bathams Best Bitter; Nottingham Extra Pale Ale; Oakham Inferno; 9 changing beers Ⓗ
Thoroughly welcoming pub with an enviable reputation for its wide selection of expertly kept beers. Fourteen ales are always on the bar, usually including stout or mild, plus real cider and draught Belgian beers. The traditional interior comprises a long bar flanked by quieter seating areas at both ends. Top-quality home-made hot and cold food is served Monday-Saturday until 6.30pm (later on Mon and Wed) with regular steak and curry nights on Mondays. Q◐🍎🚌(9)🐾

Hampton in Arden

White Lion

10 High Street, B92 0AA
🕔 12-11 (midnight Thu-Sat); 12-10.30 Sun
☎ (01675) 442833 🌐 thewhitelioninn.com
Banks's Mild, Sunbeam; Hobsons Best Bitter; M&B Brew XI; Sharp's Doom Bar; Wye Valley Butty Bach Ⓗ
Charming 17th-century timber-framed building with Grade II status, which has been licensed since 1838. It has an L-shaped lounge, a light, airy and open-plan dining area and a separate public bar, with lovely real fires. Quality British pub food with a French accent is served lunchtimes and evenings. The quantity and quality of the real ales here have improved since the current tenant took over in 2010. Q❀🛏◐♿⇌♣P🚌(82)🐾📶

Hockley Heath

Wharf Tavern

2390 Stratford Road, B94 6QT
🕔 12-11 (midnight Fri & Sat) ☎ (01564) 782075
🌐 wharftavern.co.uk
Backyard Blonde; 5 changing beers Ⓗ
As its name suggests, the Wharf Tavern is alongside the Stratford-upon-Avon canal, next to what was a busy wharf. The building dates back to the mid-18th century and has benefited from a sympathetic restoration in 2014. It is a community pub with a darts team and a board game club, and hosts quiz and poker nights. Six real ales are on offer, along with an extensive food menu and home-cooked specials. ❀◐P🚌(S3,X20)🐾📶

Kingswinford

Cottage

534 High Street, DY6 8AW
🕔 11-11; 12-10.30 Sun ☎ (01384) 287133
Enville Ale; St Austell Tribute; 3 changing beers Ⓗ
Interesting cosy former Scottish & Newcastle pub, with food dominating early evening. Large and L-shaped, it is organised into separate areas, serving four real ales with the guests selected from the Punch list. Good-value food is on the menu, with a separate restaurant. It provides a carvery every day and makes it extra special on Sunday. Warm and friendly, well worth a visit. Q◐P🚌(205,255)📶

Park Tavern 𝕃

182 Cot Lane, DY6 9QG (on corner of Cot Lane and Broad St)
🕔 11-11 (midnight Fri & Sat) ☎ (01384) 287178
Bathams Best Bitter; Enville Ale, Ginger Beer; Timothy Taylor Landlord; 2 changing beers Ⓗ
Popular and lively old pub in the back streets of Kingswinford, currently serving six real ales. Opened as the Brickmakers Arms in 1855, it changed to the Park Tavern in 1859. The bar and lounge each have their own feel, but TV does dominate when there are sporting events on. For the peckish try the selection of cobs. There is a patio attached to the rear for smokers and sports enthusiasts alike. ❀♣🍎P🚌(226)🐾📶

Knowle

Vaults

St John's Close, B93 0JU
🕔 12-2.30, 5-11; 12-11.30 Thu-Sat; 12-11 Sun
☎ (01564) 773656
Adnams Lighthouse; Sharp's Doom Bar; St Austell Tribute; Tetley Gold; 2 changing beers Ⓗ
A wide range of quality real ales can be found at this traditional pub as well as real cider from Westons. In recent years it has been a regular winner of the local CAMRA branch Pub of the Year, and is a popular meeting place for those visiting the many local restaurants. Wi-Fi is available and major sporting events are shown on BT Sport TV. Light meals are served 12-2pm, Monday-Saturday. ◖🍎🚌(S2,S3)📶

Lower Gornal

Black Bear

86 Deepdale Lane, DY3 2AE
🕔 5-11; 12-11 Fri & Sat; 12-10.30 Sun ☎ (01384) 253333
6 changing beers Ⓗ
Once a farmhouse, this building has been a pub for over 180 years. Subsidence has taken its toll, there is a distinct slope to the split-level interior, and large buttresses support the downhill exterior walls. The views from the garden are stunning. The house beer Black Bear, from Kinver Brewery, is usually on the bar. There are bus stops close by, or you can walk uphill from the Gornal Wood bus station, or else go downhill from the main number 1 bus route. ❀♣🚌(27,257)🐾

Fountain

8 Temple Street, DY3 2PE (on B4157 5 mins from Gornal Wood bus station)
🕔 12-11; 12-10.30 Sun ☎ (01384) 242777
🌐 fountaininnrealale.co.uk

Greene King Abbot; Hobsons Town Crier; Morland Old Speckled Hen; RCH Pitchfork; 5 changing beers (sourced nationally) H
A serial Guide entry, this excellent free house serves nine real ales accompanied by draught Belgian beers, a real cider and 12 fruit wines. The busy, vibrant bar is complemented by an elevated dining area serving excellent food Monday-Saturday midday-9pm, and Sunday lunches until 5pm. A wide selection of cobs and baguettes is available at lunchtime. During the summer months the rear garden is a suntrap and a pleasant area to while away an hour or two.
P (27,257)

Red Cow L

84 Grosvenor Road, DY3 2PR
4-midnight; 12-midnight Sat & Sun ☎ 07943 189351
Holden's Golden Glow; Wye Valley Butty Bach; changing beers H
A hostelry dating from around the early-19th century, in a cul-de-sac that is part of Grosvenor Road. This community venue supports numerous pub games teams. The narrow bar is to the left, the cosy lounge to the right, divided by a large chimney breast which has openings either side to afford passage between them. A large garden is at the rear. You can get a real cider and six beers here. It is five minutes' walk from the bus stop in Corncrake Road. CAMRA branch and county Pub of the Year 2013. P (257)

Lye

Windsor Castle L

7 Stourbridge Road, DY9 7DG (at Lye Cross)
12-11; 8am-11 Sat ☎ (01384) 897809
Sadler's JPA, Mellow Yellow, Worcester Sorcerer, Thin Ice, Hop Bomb, Mud City Stout; 4 changing beers (sourced locally; often Sadler's) H
Tap house for the family owned Sadler's Ales since 2004, showcasing its range of regular beers along with monthly specials. The modern yet cosy interior creates an atmosphere that is laid-back during the week, livening up at weekends. Home-made food is served daily including breakfast on Saturdays. The adjoining brewery holds various brewing events and accommodation is available. Take-away real ale is offered if you are frequenting one of the many local curry houses for which Lye is famed. Q P (9,276)

Meriden

Queen's Head

Old Road, CV7 7JP
11-11; 11-10.30 Sun ☎ (01676) 522256
Draught Bass; M&B Brew XI; 2 changing beers H
Nestled on the old main road to Coventry, now a single track lane, this is reputed to be Meriden's oldest recorded inn and is popular within the community. This traditional single-roomed pub features two distinct drinking areas. Horse brasses, pictures and memorabilia add to the ambience and reflect a bygone era. Daily lunchtime meals are available while an Indian restaurant upstairs caters for evening diners. Monthly quiz nights are popular. There are two regularly changing guest beers. P

Netherton

Old Swan ★ L

89 Halesowen Road, DY2 9PY (on A459 Dudley-Old Hill road)
11-11; 12-11 Sun ☎ (01384) 253075
Olde Swan Original, Dark Swan, Entire, Bumble Hole Bitter; 1 changing beer (sourced locally; often Olde Swan) H
One of the last four remaining English home-brew pubs from 1974, deservedly on CAMRA's National Inventory of Historic Pub Interiors and home to the Olde Swan Brewery. The bar is an unspoilt treasure and there is a cosy snug. A fifth beer is often available from the on-site brewery. Food is served in the lounge Monday-Saturday lunchtimes and Sunday and Monday evenings (menus vary). There is also an upstairs restaurant which is highly regarded (open Tue-Sat). Booking is essential for Sunday lunches. Q P (243,244,81)

Sedgley

Beacon Hotel ★ L

129 Bilston Street, DY3 1JE (on A463)
12-2.30 (3 Fri), 5.30-11; 12-3, 6-11 Sat; 12-3, 7-10.30 Sun
☎ (01902) 883380 sarahhughesbrewery.co.uk
Sarah Hughes Pale Amber, Sedgley Surprise, Dark Ruby Mild; 3 changing beers H
In the shadow of the ancient Sedgley beacon, this old hotel has sat virtually unchanged for decades. It is a Grade II-listed building and with a nationally important historic pub interior, where time has stood still. At its heart is a central servery with snob screens. There are four rooms including a family room. The Sarah Hughes Brewery lives in a tower at the back and supplies the pub. Joint CAMRA branch Pub of the Year and County Pub of the Year in 2014, and branch Pub of the Year 2015. The Beacon lives up to its name – it shines.
Q P (229,223,224)

Bull's Head

27 Bilston Street, DY3 1JA (on A463)
9.30am-11; 9am-12.30am Fri & Sat ☎ (01902) 671499
Holden's Black Country Bitter, Golden Glow, Special; 1 changing beer H
Not far from the centre of Sedgley village sits this listed building. The bar area extends across the front of the pub and into the two bay windows. More drinking space is found further back in a raised area to the side. Beyond that is now housed a Thai restaurant which also serves takeaways, and English breakfasts at lunchtime. A warm welcome awaits regulars and visitors alike.

White Lion

104 Bilston Street, DY3 1JF
12-3, 6-11; 12-11 Sun ☎ (01902) 685232
Oakham Bishops Farewell; 3 changing beers H
An old pub with a comfortable modern interior. The guest ales are usually pale and hoppy; Dark Star APA features regularly and stronger offerings are available at weekends. The south-facing beer garden makes a lovely suntrap in the right weather. There is a separate dining room where excellent meals, traditionally English in style, are served – you will not leave hungry. Children under eight are welcome only when dining. A five-minute walk from the main number 1 bus route.
P (229,223,224)

Short Heath

Duke of Cambridge 🄻

82 Coltham Road, WV12 5QD

⏲ 12-11 ☎ (01922) 712038

Black Country Bradley's Finest Golden, Pig on the Wall, Fireside; 3 changing beers (sourced nationally) 🄷

A traditional, homely and welcoming pub converted from 17th-century cottages. The public bar has a solid fuel woodburner and the quieter lounge has been tastefully refurbished. The rear room caters for darts and pool and is also used for functions and beer festivals. A quiz is held every other Wednesday. There is a beer garden at the rear of the pub. Q🐴❀♣🍎🚌(341,369)🐾

Solihull

Fieldhouse

10 Knightcote Drive, Monkspath, B91 3JU

⏲ 11.30-midnight; 12-11 Sun ☎ (0121) 703 9209

Brakspear Bitter; 4 changing beers 🄷

Part of the Ember Inns chain, this large, modern pub is tastefully decorated and comfortably furnished, featuring four large fires (one real, three coal-effect) and pleasant patio areas. It usually serves four guest ales from across the country, frequently changing and unusual. Often busy, the pub attracts a wide age range. Regular quiz nights are Sundays and Tuesdays, and on Mondays all cask ales are discounted.
🐴❀◐◑♿⇌(Widney Manor)P🚌📶

Stourbridge

Duke William 🄻

25 Coventry Street, DY8 1EP (corner of Coventry St and Duke St)

⏲ 12-11 (11.30 Fri & Sat) ☎ (01384) 440202
🌐 thedukewilliam.co.uk

Craddock's Saxon Gold, Crazy Sheep, Troll; 6 changing beers (sourced locally; often Craddock's) 🄷

Locally listed Edwardian town-centre pub and home of the Craddock's Brewery. There is a main bar with a real fire, an adjacent snug, and an upstairs function room with a bar. Traditional pie (a choice of eight varieties) and mash is served 12-3pm every day and 5-8pm Monday-Thursday alongside cold snacks. Regular events and brewery tours can be arranged. There is a summer beer and cider festival with a choice of over 15 ales and ciders. Regular ciders are Dogdancer and Thundering Molly. Q❀◐◑♿⇌(Town)🍎🥛🚌🐾📶

Royal Exchange 🄻

75 Enville Street, DY8 1XW (on A458 just off ring road)

⏲ 1 (12 Sat)-11; 12-10.30 Sun ☎ (01384) 396726

Bathams Mild Ale, Best Bitter 🄷

Here you will find a busy traditional bar to the front and a small cosy lounge to the rear accessed through a side passage. The bar is decorated with whisky bottles and boxes, pewter tankards and foreign bank notes. The beer is good value and served in handled glasses on request. The large beer garden to the rear has a covered and heated smoking area. A function room is available upstairs and may be booked for free, and there is a public car park directly opposite. Bathams XXX is on in winter. Q❀♣P🚌(X96,227,228)

Waggon & Horses 🄻

31 Worcester Street, DY8 1AT

⏲ 12 (5 Mon)-11; 12-midnight Thu-Sat ☎ (01384) 395398

Enville Ale, Ginger Beer; Olde Swan Entire; 3 changing beers 🄷

A recent refurbishment has created a comfortable, welcoming alehouse. There is a small bar area to the front with a narrow passageway leading to a larger rear bar. To the side is a long bar with a small serving hatchway. You can usually find two or more real ciders here. Parking can be difficult in the narrow surrounding streets but there is a car park in the town centre, with three hours free parking, which is only a five-minute walk.
❀◐♿⇌(Town)🍎🚌(276,125,251)📶

Streetly

Queslett

Queslett Road East, B74 2EY

⏲ 11.30-11 (midnight Thu-Sat) ☎ (0121) 580 8123

M&B Brew XI; Marston's Pedigree; Purity Pure Ubu; 4 changing beers 🄷

Refurbished Ember Inn that now boasts a large front patio. The open-plan interior is split into a variety of comfortably furnished areas, enhanced by flaming gas fires. Well-presented food is served daily until 10pm. Four guest beers from the Ember seasonal range are offered. Cask Ale Mondays see all real ales offered at a special price. Quizzes are on Tuesdays and Sundays, poker on Mondays and Wednesdays. Live music features occasionally.
🐴❀◐◑♿♣P🚌

Sutton Coldfield

Station

Station Street, B73 6AT (near Sutton station southbound platform)

⏲ 12-11 (midnight Fri & Sat); 12-10.30 Sun
☎ (0121) 362 4961 🌐 thestationsuttoncoldfield.co.uk

Holden's Golden Glow; Timothy Taylor Landlord; house beer (by Holden's); 2 changing beers 🄷

Popular, lively pub with a mixed clientele. Both the bar and lounge are spacious and there is an upstairs function room. Good home-cooked food is served noon-9pm (7pm Sun). Monday is quiz night, Tuesday live music night and the last Thursday in the month is comedy night. The outdoor drinking area plays host to DJs and live music in summertime. Children are welcome until 6pm. The Holden's house beer is called Station Bitter.
🐴❀◐◑⇌🚌📶

Three Tuns

19 High Street, B72 1XS

⏲ 11.30-midnight (11 Mon; 11.30 Tue; 1am Fri & Sat); 11.30-11 Sun ☎ (0121) 355 2996 🌐 threetuns.net

Thwaites Original, Wainwright, Lancaster Bomber; 1 changing beer 🄷

A 16th-century coaching inn, said to be haunted by a Royalist drummer boy. The central coach track is still evident, now a courtyard sheltered by a glazed canopy. There are four rooms, one for quiet contemplation, a bar for chat, a lounge for food and regular live music, and a Sky Sports and games room. Sometimes the guest ale is a special from Thwaites. Food is served noon-9pm (8pm Sun and Mon) and children are welcome until 9pm.
Q🐴◐◑♿⇌♣P🚌🐾📶

Tipton

Fountain

51 Owen Street, DY4 8HE

✪ 11-11 ☎ (0121) 522 3606

Banks's Mild; Wye Valley HPA; 4 changing beers (sourced regionally; often Enville, Hobsons, Wye Valley) Ⓗ

Canalside pub with a central bar and interesting local photos on the walls, serving a good range of six real ales and a traditional cider. Guest beers are sourced through the Punch Taverns Finest Cask Ales scheme. It is family-friendly and serves a range of good-value pub meals and curries lunchtimes and evenings, as well as roasts on Sunday lunchtimes. ⛵❀◖●≉♣●P🖰(311,229,42)🐾 ☎

Rising Sun Ⓛ

116 Horseley Road, DY4 7NH (off B4517)

✪ 12-midnight ☎ (0121) 557 1940

Black Country Bradley's Finest Golden, Pig on the Wall, Fireside; 5 changing beers Ⓗ

A former CAMRA National Pub of the Year, the pub reopened in March 2013 following a superb refurbishment by Black Country Ales. It is an imposing Victorian hostelry with two distinct rooms warmed by open fires. For the summer there is a tidy yard at the back. There are five varying guest beers and one real cider, usually Black Rat. Cobs and snacks are served. It is 10 minutes' walk from Great Bridge bus station, which has frequent services to Dudley, West Bromwich and Birmingham. ❀♣●🖰🐾 ☎

Upper Gornal

Britannia ★ Ⓛ

109 Kent Street, DY3 1UX (on A459)

✪ 12-11; 12-10.30 Sun ☎ (01902) 883253

Bathams Mild Ale, Best Bitter Ⓗ

The Britannia has a nationally important historic pub interior for the taproom at the rear, named after legendary former landlady Sally Perry, which has wall-mounted handpumps. Service can also be obtained from the front bar, itself a comfortable place to be, both areas warmed by a roaring open fire. There is also a family/games room with a TV. Behind the pub is the former brewhouse and a delightful garden. A good selection of bar snacks is available. Bathams XXX is sold in winter. Q⛵❀♣🖰(1)🐾 ☎

Jolly Crispin

25 Clarence Street, DY3 1UL (on A459)

✪ 4-11; 12-11 Fri & Sat; 12-10.30 Sun ☎ (01902) 672220

🌐 thejollycrispin.co.uk

Fownes Crispin's Ommer; 8 changing beers Ⓗ

Lively pub on the main route from Dudley to Sedgley, a former shoemaker's house in the 18th century. It hosts a festival of beer – every day. The pub features regular beers from the on-site Fownes Brewing – the Crispin Ommer is the house beer and up to eight guest pulls are complemented by a real cider. A twice-yearly cider festival is held in the garden and the no.1 bus from Dudley to Wolverhampton stops outside. CAMRA branch Cider Pub of the Year 2014-2015. ❀♣●P🖰(1)🐾 ☎

Wall Heath

Wall Heath Tavern Ⓛ

14 High Street, DY6 0HA (on A449)

✪ 12-midnight (11 Mon); 12-11 Sun ☎ (01384) 287319

Enville Ale, Ginger Beer; Holden's Golden Glow; Sarah Hughes Dark Ruby Mild; Three Tuns XXX; Wye Valley HPA; 2 changing beers Ⓗ

A bustling pub on the A449 approaching Wall Heath village centre. Serving at least eight real ales, with major emphasis on Enville Ales, it can get busy, particularly at weekends with a TV for sport in the bar. The lounge can be predominantly food-oriented, especially in the evenings when tables can be reserved. The menu features good-value cooking. There is a large patio area at the rear which is popular in the summer months. ⛵❀◖●≉P🖰(255,256,257)🐾 ☎

Walsall

Black Country Arms Ⓛ

High Street, WS1 1QW (in market, opp Asda)

✪ 11-11 (midnight Fri); 12-midnight Sat; 12-11 Sun

☎ (01922) 640588 🌐 blackcountryarms.co.uk

Black Country Bradley's Finest Golden, Pig on the Wall, Fireside; changing beers (sourced nationally) Ⓗ

A large, imposing pub on three levels, part of which was originally the Green Dragon Inn, dating back to the 18th century. The pub lay empty for 70 years until extensive refurbishment saw it reopen in 1987. The impressive bar boasts 16 handpumps serving up to 11 guest ales, mainly from microbreweries, with two real ciders always available. Live music features frequently. Booking is recommended for Sunday lunches. ⛵❀◖≉♣●P🖰 ☎

Fountain Inn Ⓛ

49 Lower Forster Street, WS1 1XB (off A4148 ring road)

✪ 12-2.30, 4.30-11; 12-midnight Fri & Sat; 12-11 Sun

☎ (01922) 633307

Backyard The Hoard, Blonde; 5 changing beers (sourced nationally; often Holden's, St Austell) Ⓗ

The brewery tap for Backyard Brewhouse, with up to eight ales on the bar. There are two rooms served by a central bar. This family-run inn has a friendly atmosphere and welcoming staff. Bar snacks include cobs and pork pies. Vinyl night takes place once a month, craft night on a Wednesday, jam night every other Sunday, and a film night every Monday. Q⛵◖≉♣●🖰(10,977,997)

King Arthur

59 Liskeard Road, Park Hall, WS5 3EY (off A34 next to Gillity shopping centre)

✪ 12-11 (midnight Fri & Sat) ☎ (01922) 631400

Greene King Abbot; Hook Norton Hooky; Ruddles Best Bitter; St Austell Tribute; Sharp's Doom Bar; Wye Valley HPA Ⓗ

An urban gem located in Park Hall estate, which is hard to find but definitely worth the effort. It is a two-roomed community pub boasting comprehensive sports viewing and decorated with sporting memorabilia. The front lounge has a separate dining area and is renowned for its selection of steak meals (large parties should book). There is a heated smoking area as well as front and rear beer gardens adjacent to the large car park. ❀◖●P🖰(274)

Longhorn Ⓛ

255 Sutton Road, WS5 3AR

✪ 11-midnight (11 Mon); 11-11 Sun ☎ (01922) 625065

Brakspear Bitter; Purity Pure Ubu; Thwaites Wainwright; 5 changing beers (sourced nationally) Ⓗ

Large 1930s roadside inn with a real community feel. The rear of the pub is given over to diners while drinkers tend to occupy the front section. Many charity events are hosted throughout the year, with quiz nights on Sundays and Wednesdays. Regular food and drinks deals are on offer. There is a function area available free of charge. It will open from 9am for breakfast parties given sufficient notice. ⑤❀⑪&P❖

Lyndon House Hotel ㏑
9-10 Upper Rushall Street, WS1 2HA (between market and St Matthew's church)
❂ 11-11 (1am Fri & Sat); 12-11 Sun ☎ (01922) 612511
⊕ lyndonhousehotel.co.uk
Bathams Best Bitter; Burton Bridge Golden Delicious; Caledonian Deuchars IPA; Greene King Abbot; Holden's Golden Glow; house beer (by Burton Bridge) Ⓗ
Situated at the top of Walsall Market, the Royal Exchange pub was, in 1995, incorporated into an adjoining Salvation Army hostel and leather factory. It now forms the luxurious Lyndon House Hotel. Its comfortable bar has an island counter, cosy corners and an old wood and brick decor. With its function room, downstairs Sally Ann bar and outdoor terraces, the premises have a Tardis quality. Popular with business people, it offers a slice of Walsall life. Occasional entertainment features at weekends. Q❀✦⑪&P⊟(51,377)

Pretty Bricks ㏑
5 John Street, WS2 8AF (near magistrates court, off B4210)
❂ 12-11 (midnight Fri & Sat) ☎ (01922) 612553
Black Country Bradley's Finest Golden, Pig on the Wall, Fireside; 5 changing beers (sourced nationally; often Highland, Salopian, Slater's) Ⓗ
Dating from 1845, the Bricks is a small, friendly and comfortable pub. The bar has a wood fire, lounge, upstairs function room and a small blue brick yard. Actually called the New Inn, its name derives from a part-glazed frontage. This is one of the few pubs from where CAMRA was launched nationally in 1972, driven by early campaigner the late Peter Linley. In that same year Walsall CAMRA was formed with an initial brief to cover the country from here north to John o' Groats.
Q❀⑪➽♣⊕⊟(301)

Walsall Cricket Club
Gorway Road, WS1 3BE (off A34, by university campus)
❂ closed Mon; 8-10.30; 6-11 Fri; 12-11 Sat; 12-10.30 Sun
☎ (01922) 622094 ⊕ walsallcricketclub.com
Castle Rock Harvest Pale; Wye Valley HPA; 1 changing beer (sourced nationally) Ⓗ
On a fine summer evening the click of bat on ball welcomes you to a green oasis in the heart of town. The comfortable club house lounge has a panoramic view of the field, much local cricket memorabilia, and two large sporting screens. There is occasional entertainment and the popular function room is often in use. New building and improvements are planned. Non-members' entry is by CAMRA membership card. Weekend hours are reduced in winter to Saturday 5-11pm, Sunday 12-8.30pm. ⑤❀&♣P⊟(51)❖

Wheatsheaf ㏑
4 Birmingham Road, WS1 2NA
❂ 3-11; 1-midnight Thu; 12.30-1am Fri & Sat; 12-11 Sun
☎ (01922) 636687 ⊕ wheatsheafwalsall.com
Holden's Golden Glow; Salopian Lemon Dream; Wye Valley Dorothy Goodbody's Golden Ale, Butty Bach; 2 changing beers (sourced locally; often Fownes, Holden's, Titanic) Ⓗ
Friendly open-plan community local with live music most weekends. Tuesday is jam night and Thursday is steak night. Traditional lunches are served on Sunday. Up to eight real ales are on tap and a traditional cider. A pub since at least 1801, formerly in the hands of historic brewers Allsopps and then Ansells, it became the Flock & Firkin in the '80s before restoration in 2007.
⑤❀⑪&♣●⊟(51)❖❖

Wednesbury

Cottage Spring ㏑
106 Franchise Street, WS10 9RG
❂ 2-11.30; 12-midnight Fri & Sat; 12-11.30 Sun
☎ (0121) 526 6354
Holden's Black Country Mild, Black Country Bitter; 2 changing beers (sourced locally; often Holden's) Ⓗ
The front bar has old world prints and photos of the pub and owners from yesteryear. Darts is played at one end. The lounge has more of the same prints and old-fashioned manufacturing devices, and a stage area in one corner. The bar features an old red phone box. Friday is quiz night, while live music features on Saturday nights and Sunday afternoons. Sunday lunches are served. Q❀⑪♣P

Olde Leathern Bottel
40 Vicarage Road, WS10 9DW (just off A461, bus 311 from Walsall is a 5-min walk)
❂ 12-2.30 (not Mon), 6-11; 12-3, 6-11.30 Fri; 11-11.30 Sat; 12-4, 7-11 Sun ☎ (0121) 505 0230
3 changing beers (sourced nationally) Ⓗ
The bar and snug of the Bottel are set in cottages dating from 1510, while a later extension contains a comfy lounge. The small snug is often used as a function room. The four rooms have many old photographs and the bar displays a picture of the pub from 1887 and a map of Wednesbury from 1846. At the rear is a pleasant benched patio area with plant pots. There is a quiz on Sunday evenings. Q❀⑪♣P⊟(311)❖

Queen's Head
100 Brunswick Park Road, WS10 9QR
❂ 12-3, 5-11; 12-midnight Fri & Sat; 12-11 Sun
☎ (0121) 448 5535 ⊕ queensheadwednesbury.com
Robinsons Dizzy Blonde; Sharp's Doom Bar; 1 changing beer (often Hobsons, Oakham) Ⓗ
A large brick-built twin-gabled pub, recently refurbished throughout, with two comfortable rooms – a main bar with tables and booths and a side bar with TV and dartboard. A welcoming atmosphere reflects the friendly character of the local punters, who come here to enjoy the good range of ales and food. Occasional beer festivals are held, and a water polo team and Mini enthusiasts club meet here. There is parking to both sides of the pub and a large beer garden to the rear. No food on Sunday evening. ⑤⑪P⊟

Wednesfield

Vine ★ ㏑
35 Lichfield Road, WV11 1TN
❂ 12-11 (midnight Fri & Sat) ☎ (01902) 733529
Black Country Bradley's Finest Golden, Pig on the Wall, Fireside; 6 changing beers Ⓗ
Built in 1938, this Grade II-listed community local is a rare intact example of a simple inter-war working

class pub. It has been identified by CAMRA as having a nationally important historic pub interior for its original bar, lounge and snug. Darts and dominoes are played and there are TVs showing live sport. A covered smokers' shelter and a beer garden provide outdoor drinking areas. Cobs and pork pies are available at all times and Sunday lunches are served until 5pm.
❀◖♣●P🚌(59,89)🐾📶

West Bromwich

Crown & Cushion

2 Lloyd Street, B71 4AT

⏲ 12-midnight; 12-11 Sun ☎ (0121) 553 4493

St Austell Tribute; 2 changing beers (sourced nationally; often Castle Rock) Ⓗ

Family-friendly hostelry with a single-room L-shaped interior, run by a pleasant and welcoming landlady. The pub is popular in summer with visitors to nearby Dartmouth Park. It is only 15 minutes' walk from West Bromwich Albion's football ground and can get busy on match days – away supporters are made welcome.
🐴❀◖♿♣P🚌

Old Hop Pole

474 High Street, B70 9LD

⏲ 12-3, 5-11; 12-1am Fri & Sat; 12-11 Sun ☎ 07946 579957

Wye Valley HPA; 3 changing beers Ⓗ

A friendly and popular local just outside the town centre. The central bar serves a busy front area and a quieter rear room with up to three changing guest ales together with the regular beer, Wye Valley HPA. Cards, darts and dominoes are frequently played at a competitive level. Live music or a disco is staged most Saturday nights. It gets extremely busy when West Bromwich Albion are at home. 🐴❀🚉♣🚌(74,79)

Willenhall

County

7 Walsall Street, WV13 2ES

⏲ 12-11 (midnight Fri-Sun) ☎ (01902) 608283

Wye Valley HPA; 2 changing beers (sourced nationally) Ⓗ

On the main Walsall road, the County is a large street-corner pub dating from 1834 when it was known as the New Inn. The venue includes a comfortable wooden-beamed lounge and a more basic public bar with a pool table and darts. The three handpumps are found in the lounge, where home-cooked food is served daily, including the popular Sunday lunches (booking advised). Children are welcome until 8pm. There is a beer garden at the rear. 🐴❀◖◗♣🚌(529)

Falcon

77 Gomer Street West, WV13 2NR (off B4464 behind flats)

⏲ 12-11; 12-10.30 Sun ☎ (01902) 633378

Exmoor Gold; Salopian Oracle, Golden Thread; 3 changing beers (sourced nationally) Ⓗ

A two-roomed pub with a lively public bar and quieter lounge, a short walk from the town centre. Dating back to 1936, the Falcon has been in the same family for over 30 years. Old pub memorabilia adorn both rooms, where keenly priced beers are served. There is a beer garden at the rear of the pub and plenty of on-street parking nearby. Q🐴❀♣●🍺🚌(525,529)🐾

Malthouse Ⓛ

The Dale, New Road, WV13 2BG

⏲ 8am-midnight (1am Fri & Sat) ☎ (01902) 635273

Greene King Abbot; Ruddles Best Bitter; 5 changing beers (sourced nationally; often Backyard, Sadler's) Ⓗ

A large family-friendly Wetherspoon pub in the centre of the town adjacent to the Dale restaurant. The building was previously used as a cinema and bingo hall, and is built on the site of an old maltings. It has an L-shaped drinking area and an external patio reached via a flight of steps. Although there is no car park, there is plenty of free parking close by. ❀◖◗♿●🚌📶

Wollaston

Graham's Place Ⓛ

73 Bridgnorth Road, DY8 3PZ (on A458 towards Bridgnorth, just before Wollaston island)

⏲ 11-11 ☎ (01384) 440315 🌐 grahams-place.co.uk

Salopian Shropshire Gold, Oracle, Hop Twister; Websters of Wollaston GPA; 3 changing beers Ⓗ

Single-room pub with a modern, clean decor and a variety of feels within the bar area. Freshly prepared meals from locally sourced ingredients are served in the conservatory to the rear, with a more intimate, cosy drinking area to the front and a long bar between the two. Outside is a covered smoking area and patio. Up to seven real ales are on handpull. The microbrewery is now sited to the side of the pub. Tuesday is quiz night.
🐴❀◖◗♿P🚌(227,228,X96)🐾📶

Wolverhampton

Chindit Ⓛ

113 Merridale Road, WV3 9SE

⏲ 4-11 (midnight Fri); 12-midnight Sat; 12-11 Sun ☎ 07986 773487 🌐 thechindit.co.uk

Castle Rock Harvest Pale; Hop Back Summer Lightning; Wye Valley HPA; 2 changing beers (sourced locally; often Burton Bridge, Salopian, Three Tuns) Ⓗ

Originally built in the 1950s as an off-licence and since extended. It is thought that this is the only pub in the country named in honour of Major General Orde Wingate's WWII special forces who served in Burma – their history is displayed on the wall in the lounge. The bar is extensively decorated with music memorabilia and includes a pool table, which is rolled away for the weekly Friday evening music sessions. 🐴❀♿P🚌(3,4)🐾📶

Combermere Arms Ⓛ

90 Chapel Ash, WV3 0TY (on A41 Tettenhall Rd)

⏲ 12-3, 5-11; 12-midnight Fri & Sat; 12-10.30 Sun ☎ (01902) 421880

5 changing beers Ⓗ

Grade II-listed building with original sash windows. The three charming rooms have cosy fireplaces and a wealth of pictures depicting the local football team, classic adverts and a comical Guinness series. A pub favourites menu is available weekday lunchtimes. Cheese, pie and sausage tasting festivals are held annually and there is live entertainment on Saturday evenings in summer. Look for the tree in the Gents and the pub cat. The pub is served by four local buses. Q🐴❀◖P🚌

Dog & Doublet Ⓛ

North Street, WV1 1RE

11-11 (2am Thu & Fri; 3am Sat); 2-10.30 Sun
(01902) 423805 thedoganddoubletinn.co.uk
Ludlow Gold; Purple Moose Ysgawen/Elderflower; 4 changing beers H
This city centre pub near the Civic and Wulfrun Halls is a blend of the traditional and the modern, with real fires and Chesterfield furniture, and a cocktail bar in the outside drinking area. Music features heavily here, with open mic evenings on a Thursday and live bands on a Friday night. No food is served but you are welcome to bring your own – plates and cutlery are provided. Biddenden cider is always available.

Great Western

Sun Street, WV10 0DJ (via subway from high-level station and city centre)
11-11; 11-10.30 Sun (01902) 351090
Bathams Best Bitter; Holden's Black Country Mild, Black Country Bitter, Golden Glow, Special; 2 changing beers H
A previous CAMRA National Pub of the Year near the former low-level railway station. It attracts a varied clientele, and rock climbing, motorbike and railway groups meet here regularly. Plenty of railway and Wolverhampton Wanderers memorabilia is on display and cosy real fires blaze in the winter. Meals are served at lunchtime and snacks are available until 10pm.
P

Hail to the Ale

2 Pendeford Avenue, Claregate, WV6 9EF (on Claregate island)
closed Mon-Wed; 5-10; 12-10 Sat; 12-5 Sun 07846 562910 hailtothealemicropub.co.uk
4 changing beers (sourced regionally; often Morton) H
Welcoming one-room beer-focused pub converted from a vacant shop. The West Midlands' first Micropub Association-accredited pub was opened in 2013 by Morton Brewery. A simple formula is followed with no distractions, just good ale and conversation. Six handpulls deliver at least one Morton ale, different guest beers usually from local microbreweries, a real cider and a perry. Locally sourced fruit wines, pies, cheese, sausage rolls and Scotch eggs are also served. CAMRA branch and county Pub of the Year 2015. QP(5,6)

Hog's Head

186 Stafford Street, WV1 1NA
10-midnight (1am Fri & Sat) (01902) 717955
hogsheadwolverhampton.co.uk
Broughs Springfield; 9 changing beers (sourced nationally; often Holden's) H
A 19th-century city-centre pub with an attractive brick terracotta exterior. A stained-glass window above the entrance still displays the original name, the Vine. The large single room is divided into separate areas, with widescreen TVs showing sport and music videos throughout the building. It serves a broad range of rotating guest ales, many from local microbreweries, and was local CAMRA Pub of the Year in 2013. Popular with all age groups.

Lych Gate Tavern

44 Queen Square, WV1 1TX
11-11 (midnight Fri & Sat) (01902) 399516
lychgatetavern.co.uk
Black Country Bradley's Finest Golden, Pig on the Wall, Fireside; 6 changing beers H
Friendly, traditional, city centre pub opened by Black Country Ales in 2012. One of the oldest timber-framed buildings in Wolverhampton, the Georgian frontage dates from 1726, while the timber-framed part at the rear dates from about 1500. The bar area is reached by a short flight of stairs down from street level and there is a function room for hire upstairs. All floors are accessible via a lift. Local CAMRA Pub of the Year 2014.
Q

Moon under Water

53-55 Lichfield Street, WV1 1EQ (opp Grand Theatre)
7am-midnight (1am Fri & Sat) (01902) 422447
Adnams Broadside; Fuller's London Pride; Greene King Abbot; Ruddles Best Bitter; Sharp's Doom Bar; changing beers (sourced nationally; often Burton Bridge, Morton, Titanic) H
Conveniently located for theatregoers, rail and bus stations. A wide range of food is served from breakfast until 11pm. Wolverhampton memorabilia adorn the walls and the ceiling has some stained glass. It attracts a great variety of customers and can be busy on match days and before or after theatre performances. A well-balanced choice of beers is always available at reasonable prices. A music-free zone, it is great for a chat. News and sports programmes are shown silently.

Newhampton

17 Riches Street, Whitmore Reans, WV6 0DW
11-11 (01902) 680766 thenewhampton.co.uk
Caledonian Deuchars IPA; Courage Best Bitter, Directors; Enville Ale; Three Tuns XXX; Timothy Taylor Landlord; 2 changing beers (sourced nationally; often Wye Valley) H
A Victorian street-corner local catering for a cosmopolitan customer base. Hatches service the (former) smoke room and pool room, which has a jukebox. The bar has an additional handpump for Thatchers Heritage cider. An upstairs function room hosts regular music events including folk and jazz, but has no wheelchair access. The large garden includes a popular seating area, children's small adventure playground, a crown green bowls lawn, occasional pavilion bar and a smoking shelter.

Posada ★

48 Lichfield Street, WV1 1DG (opp art gallery)
12-11; 11.30-1.30am Fri & Sat; 12-10.30 Sun
Hobsons Best Bitter, Town Crier; 4 changing beers (sourced nationally; often Castle Rock, Enville, Sharp's) H
Victorian Grade II-listed city-centre pub with tiled walls, original bar fittings including rare snob screens, and little altered since 1900/1901. It attracts a varied clientele and is quiet during the day but busy in the evenings and at weekends, especially when Wolverhampton Wanderers are at home. There is a courtyard to the rear and a smoking area. Cobs are served and Westons Old Rosie plus one other real cider are on tap.

Royal Oak

70 Compton Road, WV3 9PH (on A454 300yds from Chapel Ash jct)
11.30-11 (midnight Fri & Sat) (01902) 422845
Banks's Mild, Bitter; 5 changing beers (sourced nationally; often Jennings, Ringwood, Wychwood) H

Friendly local a short walk or bus ride from the city centre. It offers a wide range of changing real ales and holds an industry award for its beer quality. A bustling place, it provides good sports coverage, an open mic evening on Wednesday and live bands on Saturday (also Sunday in the summer). Part of the community, the pub raises money for local and national charities and features a book swap library. Fresh cobs are available at the bar.
≿❀♿♣⬤P🚌(10,890)🐾📶

Stile Inn 𝕃

3 Harrow Street, Whitmore Reans, WV1 4PB (off Newhampton Rd East/Fawdry St)
⏲ 11.30-11 (midnight Fri; 1am Sat) ☎ (01902) 425336
🌐 thestileinn.co.uk
Banks's Mild, Bitter, Sunbeam; 1 changing beer (sourced nationally; often Jennings) Ⓗ
A late-Victorian street-corner pub built in 1900, this is a true community local with an emphasis on sport – darts and dominoes feature inside and bowling on the unusual L-shaped crown bowling green outside. Excellent-value food, including Polish dishes, is served all day. Friday is comedy night and Saturday is karaoke night. Situated close to the football ground, the public bar, smoke room and snug are popular with Wolverhampton Wanderers fans on match days. Sky Sports is shown in all rooms. ≿❀◑♣🚌(5,6)🐾📶

Swan 𝕃

Bridgnorth Road, Compton, WV6 8AE (at Compton island, A454)
⏲ 12-11 (midnight Fri & Sat) ☎ (01902) 754736
🌐 swanpubwolverhampton.co.uk
Banks's Mild, Bitter, Sunbeam; Marston's Old Empire; 2 changing beers (sourced nationally; often Brakspear, Jennings, Wychwood) Ⓗ
Built around 1780, this Grade II-listed building is popular with locals and visitors to the area. Close to the Staffordshire & Worcestershire Canal and Smestow Valley Local Nature Reserve, it is an ideal venue for boaters, ramblers and cyclists. It hosts charity dog shows and has a number of beer festivals during the year featuring guest ales from outside the Marston's range. There are three distinct rooms: a games room, a lively bar with local banter, and a more sedate snug.
Q❀♣P🚌(10,890)🐾📶

Woodcross

Horse & Jockey 𝕃

Robert Wynd, WV14 9SB
⏲ 12-11 (11.30 Fri & Sat) ☎ (01902) 662268
🌐 horseandjockeywoodcross.co.uk
Greene King Abbot; Hobsons Twisted Spire, Town Crier; St Austell Tribute; 3 changing beers (sourced locally; often Holden's, Salopian, Three Tuns) Ⓗ
Run by a family of real ale enthusiasts, this friendly and thriving community pub comprises a bar, a large contemporary lounge with seasonal open fire, a rear beer garden and a small smoking shelter at the front. Good-value, home-cooked food, including vegetarian options, is served daily until 8.30pm (4pm Sun) with a pie night Wednesday and grill night Thursday. Tuesday is quiz night. Under-18s are allowed in the lounge area and garden until 8pm.
Q≿❀◑♿♣P🚌(81)🐾

Woodsetton

Park Inn 𝕃

George Street, DY1 4LW (on A457, 200yds from A4123)
⏲ 12-11; 12-10.30 Sun ☎ (01902) 661279
Holden's Black Country Mild, Black Country Bitter, Golden Glow, Special; 1 changing beer Ⓗ
Vibrant suburban brewery tap, under the ownership of the Holden family since 1915. Radiating out from the spacious main bar are a small games room, a raised dining area and a separate conservatory. Functions are catered for and reasonably priced food is served 12-8pm (4.30 Sun). The pub adjoins the brewery, which has been extended and refurbished over the previous year. Note that the new brewery centre is on the right of the car park. ≿❀◑♣P🚌(81,126,229)

Wordsley

New Inn 𝕃

117 High Street, DY8 5QR (on A491)
⏲ 12-11; 12-10.30 Sun ☎ (01384) 295614
Bathams Mild Ale, Best Bitter Ⓗ
On the A491, the building has an imposing three-storey Victorian façade. One of the Bathams 11, it has become very popular and can be extremely busy. An L-shaped bar serves a single room with a small annexe at one end; outside there is a patio area and a newly refurbished garden with a children's play area for the summer. A variety of cobs is served. The pub has the feel of a proper local. Bathams XXX is on the bar in winter. Children are not permitted inside. ≿❀♣P🚌(256,257)🐾

Queen's Head 𝕃

129 High Street, DY8 5QS (on A491)
⏲ 12-11 (midnight Fri & Sat) ☎ (01384) 402967
Black Country Bradley's Finest Golden, Pig on the Wall, Fireside; 6 changing beers Ⓗ
Comfortable roadside watering hole on the main A491 Stourbridge to Wolverhampton road. The layout echoes its multi-roomed past, although most of the original walls have gone. The decor is cosy Victorian/Edwardian in style. Up to nine real ales are on the bar, with three from the parent brewery and a traditional cider. The pub now serves food (book ahead for Sunday dining).
Q❀◑♣⬤P🚌(256,257)🐾📶

Warm beer

It is said that the Maids of Honour of the Tudor Court, who we have seen were ale-ladies, if they cannot be called ale-knights, frequently liked their beer warm, and had it placed upon the hob of the grate 'to take the chill off'. It was therefore natural for their attendants to ask the question, 'From the hob or not from the hob?', which in process of time became 'hob or nob?'
John Bickerdyke, 1889

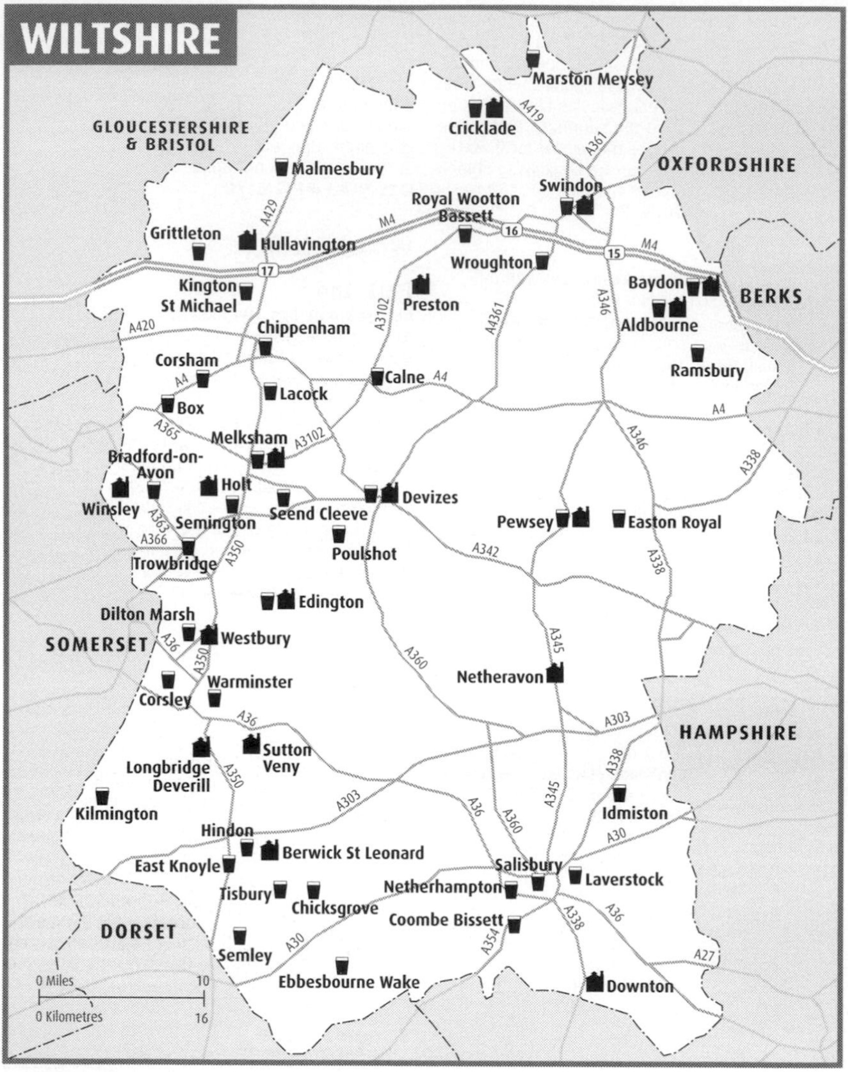

Aldbourne

Crown Hotel

The Square, SN8 2DU

12-midnight (10.30 Sun) ☎ (01672) 540214

thecrownaldbourne.co.uk

Sharp's Doom Bar; Shepherd Neame Amber Ale; 3 changing beers (sourced nationally) Ⓗ

Set in the middle of the village opposite the duck pond, the Crown has a pleasant, relaxed atmosphere. The main bar is stylishly refurbished with a fire during the colder months. A second bar shows films on Monday night. The restaurant serves freshly prepared food with daily specials until 9.30pm. On Sundays there is a carvery until it runs out, then the normal menu. There are four en-suite bedrooms. ❀🛏◐⛺🚌(46,48)🐾📶

Baydon

Red Lion Ⓛ

Ermin Street, SN8 2JP

4-11; 12-midnight Fri & Sat; 12-7 Sun ☎ (01672) 541224

redlionbaydon.weebly.com

Ramsbury Gold; 3 changing beers (sourced regionally; often Hook Norton, Ramsbury) Ⓗ

Mark and Julie celebrated the reopening of the Red Lion as a free house in 2013 with a beer festival. Most of the beers are local, from the likes of Box Steam, Ramsbury and Malmesbury. Three ciders are also available. The Red Lion has established itself as a popular local with quality ales and good home cooking. Live music features once a month. Food is served throughout opening hours.
❀◐🍎P🚌(46,48)🐾📶

Box

Quarrymans Arms Ⓛ

Box Hill, SN13 8HN

8am-11 (midnight Fri & Sat) ☎ (01225) 743569

quarrymans-arms.co.uk

Butcombe Bitter; Moles Best Bitter; Wadworth 6X; 2 changing beers Ⓗ

More than 300 years old, this was originally a miner's dwelling supporting the local Bath Stone mines. The interior comprises three distinct areas – a small snug, the bar and a restaurant area with stunning views towards Bath and across the valley to Colerne. The oak beams are covered in hundreds of pumpclips for beers that have been sold here over the years. Up to two guest beers, Black Rat cider and locally sourced food are served. Four B&B rooms are available. Q P

Bradford-on-Avon

Castle Inn

Mount Pleasant, BA15 1SJ
9am-11; 10-10.30 Sun (01225) 865657
flatcappers.co.uk/thecastle
Three Castles Barbury Castle, Vale Ale; 3 changing beers H
A popular, comfortable pub commanding splendid views across the town towards Salisbury Plain. Refurbishment by Flatcappers earned it a national CAMRA award. A wide range of handpulled real ales is complemented by excellent food, served all day until 10pm. The three guest beers are usually sourced from micros in Wiltshire and east Somerset. In summer a cider, often Broadoak or Honey's, is added to the range. B&B is available, with four luxury double bedrooms.
P

Rising Sun

231 Winsley Road, BA15 1QS
12 (4 Tue)-11; 12-10.30 Sun (01225) 862354
Courage Best Bitter; 2 changing beers H
Popular local with two bars: a small, quiet lounge and a more spacious, livelier saloon with TV screens. Behind is a walled beer garden with patio. The pub is home to darts, quiz, crib, pool and football teams, and hosts regular live music including a Rhythm & Booze beer festival over the August bank holiday. The two guest beers change week by week and the cider is Thatchers Cheddar Valley.

Calne

White Hart Hotel L

London Road, SN11 0AB (on A4 jct with Silver St)
12-11 (1am Fri & Sat) (01249) 812413
whitehartcalne.com
Bath Ales Gem; 3 changing beers (often Castle Combe) H
Built in 1659, and formerly a coaching inn, this hotel has been transformed by the new owners, who are supporters of LocAle. It now attracts locals and visitors alike, who are assured of a friendly welcome in the bar and restaurant, and has an eclectic mix of decoration – from medieval armour and swords to artwork by Banksy. The area behind the fire has a homely feel with sofas and plenty of books to read. The real cider is Black Rat.
P (33)

Woodlands Social Club

Woodland Park, SN11 0JX
6.30-11; 11-midnight Fri & Sat; 12-11 Sun
(01249) 813361
Sharp's Doom Bar; 3 changing beers (sourced regionally; often Castle Combe) H
Historic private members' social club, open to members of CAMRA, just outside the town centre, with a large comfortable bar. The club has built up a great reputation for real ale and was awarded local CAMRA Club of the Year in 2012 and 2014. The steward sources a varied beer range from local and national breweries. An excellent venue for live music, skittles and other pub games.
P (33,55A)

Chicksgrove

Compasses Inn L

SP3 6NB (between Lower Chicksgrove and Sutton Row) ST974294
12-3, 6-11; 12-3, 7-10.30 Sun (01722) 714318
thecompassesinn.com
Butcombe Bitter; 3 changing beers (sourced locally; often Keystone, Plain, Sixpenny) H
Set in the middle of the beautiful Wiltshire countryside, the bar is in the cellar of this 14th-century thatched cottage, with flagstone floors, wooden beams and a large inglenook fireplace. Once a resting place for smugglers between Poole and Warminster, it offers visitors a warm welcome, good ale, excellent food, accommodation, wonderful views and some peace and quiet.
Q P

Chippenham

Buttercross Inn L

Market Place, SN15 3HD (adjacent to the Buttercross)
11-11 (2am Thu-Sat); 12-10 Sun (01249) 460662
Box Steam Piston Broke; Draught Bass; North Cotswold Windrush Ale; 5 changing beers H
Town-centre pub bought from Fuller's and sympathetically refurbished in 2014. Run by an enthusiastic husband and wife team, the pub has three distinct bar areas with plenty of pub memorabilia. Seven real ales and nine real ciders are available as well as Belgian bottled beers. Simple pub food is served including the Pieminister pie range with mash. Regular live music events are held and, although this is not a sports bar, major rugby and some football matches are screened.
Q

REAL ALE BREWERIES

Arkell's Swindon
Box Steam Holt
Castle Combe Preston
Downton Downton
Eastbury Baydon (NEW)
Flying Monk Hullavington
Hop Back Downton
Hop Kettle Cricklade
Kennet & Avon Melksham
Keystone Berwick St Leonard
Moles Melksham
Plain Sutton Veny
Ramsbury Aldbourne
Shed Pewsey
Stonehenge Netheravon
Three Castles Pewsey
Three Daggers Edington
Twisted Westbury
Wadworth Devizes
Weighbridge Swindon
Wessex Longbridge Deverill
Willy Good Ale! Winsley
World's End Pewsey

Three Crowns ⅃

18 The Causeway, SN15 3DB (¼ mile E of town centre)
⊙ 5 (12 Thu)-11; 12-midnight Fri & Sat; 12-11 Sun
☎ (01249) 449029 ⊕ threecrownschippenham.co.uk
7 changing beers (sourced nationally) ⊞
Originally an 18th-century wagon inn on the London to Bath road, this is now a community free house offering seven cask beers from local microbreweries and from further afield. The range always includes two dark beers and one strong brew. CAMRA branch Cider Pub of the Year, it sells three ciders, mainly sourced from Wiltshire producers, and a perry. Four beer festivals are held each year. A popular venue for quiz, poetry and various other ad-hoc theme nights.
Q✿☆♣●P🖥🚃♿

Coombe Bissett

Fox & Goose ⅃

Blandford Road, SP5 4LE
⊙ 11-11; 12-10.30 Sun ☎ (01722) 718437
⊕ foxandgoose-coombebissett.co.uk
Sharp's Doom Bar; 2 changing beers (sourced locally; often Plain, Sixpenny) ⊞
Eighteenth-century coaching inn on the A354 three miles south of Salisbury. A popular community pub, it has a loyal village clientele and a welcoming atmosphere. It is divided into a bar and restaurant, serving an extensive food menu with ever-changing specials. Outside there is a covered smoking area and gardens to the rear. Two regularly changing ales are sourced mostly from local microbreweries. There is a loyalty card scheme for regular diners.
Q✿☆✿🕪♣P🖥(29,184)♿

Corsham

Two Pigs ⅃

Pickwick, SN13 0HY
⊙ 7-11; 12-2.30, 7-10.30 Sun ☎ (01249) 712515
⊕ thetwopigs.co.uk
Stonehenge Pigswill, Danish Dynamite; 2 changing beers (sourced regionally) ⊞
A warm welcome is assured at this former CAMRA branch Pub of the Year, which remains a favourite with an eclectic mix of locals and those drawn to its highly popular blues and rock sessions. Built in the late-18th century, it remains unashamedly traditional, with low lighting, stone-flagged floors and a covered rear courtyard. Regular beers include the aptly named Swill from Stonehenge plus two ever-changing local guests. Q♣🖥(231)

Corsley

Cross Keys Inn

Lye's Green, BA12 7PB
⊙ 12-3, 6-11; 12-11 Sun ☎ (01373) 832406
Wadworth Henry's IPA, 6X; 2 changing beers ⊞
Always worth a visit, this rural gem has a large open fire and a warm, welcoming ambience. It offers a good portfolio of guest beers – often Wadworth seasonals – along with excellent bar food and restaurant meals. There is a function room and an attractive, award-winning garden. The pub actively supports the local cricket team. Situated in good walking country close to Cley Hill and Longleat House and Safari Park.
✿☆🕪♣●P♿🛜

Cricklade

Red Lion ⅃

74 High Street, SN6 6DD
⊙ 12-11 (10.30 Sun) ☎ (01793) 750776
⊕ theredlioncricklade.co.uk
Butcombe Butcombe Bitter; Wadworth 6X; 8 changing beers ⊞
Friendly, popular and comfortable inn, parts of which are quite ancient – the old Saxon town wall passes through the building. It is also home to the Hop Kettle Brewing Co, which started brewing in 2012. Ten real ales – two regular, four from Hop Kettle and four guests – are on handpump, plus real cider. Food is served lunchtimes and evenings Monday-Saturday, lunchtime only on Sunday. There is a large rear garden and five rooms for B&B. A beer festival takes place in June.
Q✿☆🛏🕪◑♿●🚃(51,53)♿🛜

Devizes

British Lion

9 Estcourt Street, SN10 1LQ (on A361 London road opp Kwik Fit)
⊙ 11-11 (midnight Fri & Sat); 12-11 Sun ☎ (01380) 720665
⊕ britishliondevizes.co.uk
Moles Tap Bitter; Plain Innocence; Ramsbury Gold; Stonehenge Pigswill; 4 changing beers (sourced nationally) ⊞
The Lion has featured in the Guide for 20 years. An unpretentious free house with wooden floors, cosy settles and an eclectic group of talkative regulars, it is the essential port of call in town. It offers ales mainly from West Country breweries on its four handpumps, and these change constantly throughout the week. The landlord has a wealth of brewing knowledge and is always pleased to offer his advice. The cider is Cheddar Valley or Black Rat. Not to be missed. ☆●P🖥🚃(49)

Southgate Inn

Potterne Road, SN10 5BY (on jct of Southbroom Rd and Potterne Rd)
⊙ 4-11; 12-midnight Fri & Sat; 12-11 Sun ☎ (01380) 722872
3 changing beers (often Downton, Great Western, Hop Back) ⊞
The five-minute walk from the town centre is well-worth it for the welcome you will receive here. A cosy and friendly pub, it has three separate bar areas and lots of nooks and crannies. The three handpumps feature ales from Hop Back and Downton and a selection of guest ales from the likes of Great Western. Cider may also be available. The pub has a large courtyard area and hosts an annual Easter beer festival, which is always popular. Saturdays often feature live music. Well-behaved dogs are positively encouraged.
✿●P🖥(49)♿🛜

Vaults

28A St John's Street, SN10 1BN (opp town hall)
⊙ 12-9 (6 Sun) ☎ (01380) 721443 ⊕ thevaultsdevizes.com
Kennet & Avon Pillbox, Dundas; 4 changing beers (sourced nationally) ⊞
This is a quirky addition to the town's drinking establishments – a long, galley-style building with fittings and furniture made from reclaimed materials. The bar features up to six real ales on handpump, plus draught cider and a huge selection of bottled beers from around the world. It is the tap for the Kennet & Avon Brewery and offers most of their beers plus many guests. The owner regularly

holds tasting evenings in the vast cellar. Conversation rules here – come early because it fills up quickly. 🍎P🚌(49)🐾

Dilton Marsh

Prince of Wales

94 High Street, BA13 4DZ

⏲ 6 (12 Fri-Sun)-11 ☎ (01373) 865487

🌐 powdiltonmarsh.co.uk

St Austell Cornish Best Bitter, Trelawny, Tribute; 1 changing beer [H]

A smart, friendly locals' pub, refurbished in 2013, with a bar area, separate dining space and a skittle alley doubling as a function room. Outside is a paved area to the side and the beer garden. Traditional pub food is served including Sunday lunches. The guest beer could be from St Austell (HSD or Proper Job) or from elsewhere – often a local micro such as Twisted, Cheddar or Moles, or sometimes a popular national brewery. There is a changing range of ciders from polypins. ❀◑♿⛺♣🍎P🚌🐾📶

East Knoyle

Fox & Hounds

Wise Lane, The Green, SP3 6BN ST87113135

⏲ 11.30-3, 5.30-11 ☎ (01747) 830573

🌐 foxandhounds-eastknoyle.co.uk

3 changing beers [H]

Attractive old thatched black-and-white pub situated high on a hillside with extensive panoramic rural views. Comfortable and cosy inside, the warm welcome is enhanced in winter by a blazing log fire in a huge inglenook fireplace. Three ales are always available encompassing a wide range of strengths and varying continuously, with local beers given prominence. The real cider is Thatchers Cheddar Valley. Food is served at all sessions. An adjacent skittle alley doubles as a function room. Q🐎❀◑🍎P🐾

Easton Royal

Bruce Arms ★ 𝕃

Easton Road, SN9 5LR

⏲ 12-2 (not Mon), 5-11; 12-11 Sat; 12-8 Sun

☎ (01672) 810216 🌐 thebrucearms.net

Stonehenge Pigswill; Wadworth 6X; 2 changing beers (sourced regionally) [H]

This mid 19th-century local is on CAMRA's National Inventory of Historic Pub Interiors and has changed little over time. It has a small bar with furniture that probably goes back to the 1850s and a homely lounge fitted out with easy chairs and a piano. At the back is a larger dining/function room. The pub exists in splendid isolation, so its campsite with full facilities is welcome. It hosts vintage vehicle events and is home to EROS (Easton Royal Onion Society). Q🐎❀◑⛺♣P🚌(96,19)🐾

Ebbesbourne Wake

Horseshoe

The Cross, SP5 5JF

⏲ 12-3 (not Mon), 6.30-11; 12-4 Sun ☎ (01722) 780474

Bowman Wallops Wood; Otter Bitter; Palmers Dorset Gold; 2 changing beers (sourced regionally) [G]

Unspoilt 18th-century pub in a remote rural setting at the foot of an old ox drove. This friendly pub has two small bars that display an impressive collection of old farm implements, tools and lamps, plus a restaurant, conservatory and pleasant garden. Good local food is available Tuesday to Sunday and five beers are served direct from casks stillaged behind the bar. Real cider is also usually on tap. The original serving hatch just inside the front door is still in use. Q🐎❀🛏◑🍎P🚌(29)🐾

Edington

Three Daggers

Westbury Road, BA13 4PG

⏲ 8am-11; 9am-10.30 Sun ☎ (01380) 830940

🌐 threedaggers.co.uk

Three Daggers Daggers Ale; 3 changing beers [H]

This refurbished village pub is now the brewery tap for the eponymous brewery situated in an adjacent farm shop, and has four of their beers on tap. The pub has a main bar with three distinct drinking areas, leading to a seating area and a dining room. Two mirrors hide TV screens that are occasionally used for sporting events. Dogs are welcomed with free biscuits, and accommodation is available. The cider is from Thatchers. Q🐎❀🛏◑♿♣P🚌🐾📶

Grittleton

Neeld Arms

The Street, SN14 6AP

⏲ 12-3, 5.30-11; 12-4, 7-11 Sun ☎ (01249) 782470

🌐 neeldarms.co.uk

St Austell Tribute; Sharp's Doom Bar; 2 changing beers (sourced locally) [H]

Cosy, comfortable 17th-century inn set in a beautiful and unspoilt south-Cotswold village with old prints and photographs adorning the walls and a welcoming log fire in winter. A good selection of home-made food is offered and an ever-changing choice of local beers means there is always something different to try. Popular with locals and visitors, the pub is central to the community. Tourist attractions including Castle Combe, Malmesbury and Bath are close by. Q🐎🛏◑P🐾📶

Hindon

Angel Inn

High Street, SP3 6DJ

⏲ 11-11 (10.30 Sun) ☎ (01747) 820696

🌐 angel-inn-at-hindon.co.uk

Harveys Sussex Best Bitter; Otter Bitter; Timothy Taylor Landlord; 1 changing beer [H]

A beautifully restored 18th-century coaching inn, the Angel was originally known as the Grosvenor Arms. Prior to its construction in 1750 a medieval inn, the Angel, existed on the site. The pub retains many original features including the wooden floors, beams and a huge stone fireplace. Access to the bar is through a pretty south-west-facing walled garden and terrace. Set in an attractive village with a spired church close by. Q🐎❀🛏◑♿P🚌(25)🐾📶

Idmiston

Earl of Normanton 𝕃

Tidworth Road, SP4 0AG

⏲ 12-2.30, 6-11; 12-3, 8-10.30 Sun ☎ (01980) 610251

🌐 earlofnormanton.co.uk

Exmoor Gold; Flowerpots Bitter; Hop Back Summer Lightning; 2 changing beers (sourced locally) [H]

Popular roadside inn with a loyal village clientele and a welcoming atmosphere enhanced by two real fires in winter months. LocAle accredited, it offers two guest ales mostly from nearby breweries. Good-value home-cooked food is served (no food Sun eve). There is a small, pleasant garden on the steep hill behind the pub and a heated, covered smoking area. Live music features occasionally. B&B is available. Local CAMRA Country Pub of the Year 2014. Q🐴❀🛏◐◑P🚌(66,67)🐾📶

Kilmington

Red Lion Inn

B3092, BA12 6RP

⏲ 11-3, 6-11; 11-4, 7-10.30 Sun ☎ (01985) 844263

Butcombe Bitter; Wessex Stourton Pale Ale; 1 changing beer Ⓗ

This 16th-century former farmworker's cottage, located close to Stourhead house and gardens, originally stabled the extra horses needed to climb the steep hill on the adjacent coach road. The single bar is mainly stone flagged with two real fires, and has a dining room leading off the bar. Walkers and dogs are welcome. Real cider is always available. The large garden has a superb smoking space. Q❀◐◑🍎P🐾

Kington St Michael

Jolly Huntsman

SN14 6JB

⏲ 11.30-2.30, 6-11 (midnight Fri & Sat); 12-3, 7-10.30 Sun ☎ (01249) 750305 🌐 jollyhuntsman.com

Moles Gold; Wadworth 6X; 2 changing beers (sourced locally) Ⓗ

A former brewery situated on the village high street, this free house offers a warm and friendly welcome, with a large open fire in the winter. A range of locally brewed real ales and ciders is offered along with an excellent food menu available lunchtimes and evenings, featuring a range of traditional fare and chef's specials. Themed evenings are held on occasion. Accommodation is en suite. Q🐴🛏◐◑♿🍎P🚌(99)

Lacock

Bell Inn 🏆 Ⓛ

The Wharf, SN15 2JP (½ml out of Lacock towards Bowden Hill)

⏲ 11-2.30, 5-11; 12.30-11 Sat; 12-10.30 Sun ☎ (01249) 730308 🌐 thebellatlacock.co.uk

Great Western Maiden Voyage; house beer (by Bath Ales); 3 changing beers Ⓗ

A friendly welcome is assured at this popular free house on the edge of the National Trust village of Lacock, run by the same family since 2000. A regular local CAMRA Pub of the Year, it has an excellent reputation for quality ale and food. Five ales and a real cider are usually available, and two beer festivals are held each year. The house beer, Red Wharf, is brewed to the pub's own recipe by Bath Ales. This place is on National Cycle Network route 403. Q🐴❀◐◑⛺♣🍎P🐾📶

Laverstock

Duck Ⓛ

Duck Lane, SP1 1PU

⏲ 12-midnight ☎ (01722) 327678 🌐 theduckatlaverstock.com

Hop Back Golden Best, Crop Circle, Summer Lightning; 1 changing beer (often Downton) Ⓗ

Large open-plan pub on the edge of Laverstock with patio seating at the front and ample car parking. A full menu is available lunchtimes (not Monday or evenings), plus a popular Sunday roast, regular barbecues and occasional themed dining nights. Live music is hosted at weekends and a quiz on Tuesday. Beer and cider festivals also feature. There is full disabled access and facilities. Ideally located for walkers on the Clarendon Way. Q🐴❀◐♿P🚌(R6,66)🐾📶

Malmesbury

Whole Hog Ⓛ

8 Market Cross, SN16 9AS

⏲ 11-11 (midnight Fri & Sat); 12-11 Sun ☎ (01666) 825845

Flying Monk Elmers; Stonehenge Pigswill; Wadworth 6X; Young's Bitter; 1 changing beer Ⓗ

Located between the 15th-century market cross and the abbey in the oldest borough in England, this is a popular town-centre pub, serving well-kept ales and freshly prepared food. In a commanding position at the top of the high street, the large front window seating area provides the perfect spot to enjoy a pint and watch the world go by. A pub central to the community and equally welcoming to visitors. Q◐◑♣🍎🚌

Marston Meysey

Old Spotted Cow

SN6 6LQ

⏲ 11-11 ☎ (01285) 810264 🌐 theoldspottedcow.co.uk

Butcombe Gold; Otter Bitter; 1 changing beer (sourced nationally) Ⓗ

This welcoming country pub has large gardens and a cosy interior with log fires and beamed ceilings. The pub is popular with locals, who usually congregate around the bar, where three handpumps deliver two regular ales and a guest. Real cider is also available during the summer. There is a strong emphasis on good food. The source of the River Thames is only a few miles away and, with the Thames Path nearby, the pub is attractive to hikers. Q🐴❀◐◑♣🍎P🐾📶

Melksham

Bear

3 Bath Road, SN12 6LL

⏲ 8am-midnight ☎ (01225) 792690

Adnams Broadside; Greene King Abbot; Ruddles Best Bitter; Sharp's Doom Bar; 5 changing beers (sourced nationally; often Box Steam, Moles, Prescott) Ⓗ

A high-specification Wetherspoon pub with a plethora of local history adorning the walls, a real fire and award-winning toilets. Friendly and helpful staff serve a range of four regular ales and five changing guests, often including an American specialist beer. A full range of food is always available, including popular steak, curry and fish nights weekly. Outside is a large paved seating area for drinkers. The bus stop is directly outside. Q🐴❀◐◑♿≠🍎P🚌(272)📶

Netherhampton

Victoria & Albert

SP2 8PU

⏲ 11-3, 5.30-11; 12-3, 7-10.30 Sun ☎ (01722) 743174

3 changing beers 🄷
Classic thatched inn dating from 1540 in a village setting three miles from Salisbury and close to the race course. A log fire provides winter warmth and for summer there is a large garden and covered patio area. A long-standing family-run business, the pub serves quality food ranging from hearty snacks to full meals. The three ever-changing beers are often from small breweries, alongside Black Rat cider. CAMRA local Country Pub of the Year 2015. Quintessentially English – a gem.
Q🐎❀◑●P🐾📶

Pewsey

Crown Inn 🄻
60 Wilcot Road, SN9 5EL
🕐 4 (12 Wed & Thu)-11; 12-11.30 Fri; 12-midnight Sat; 12-10.30 Sun ☎ (01672) 562653
🌐 thecrowninnpewsey.com
Wadworth 6X; World's End Bitterus Magnus, Dark Wonder; 3 changing beers (sourced locally; often Stonehenge, World's End) 🄷
This traditional village local is the brewery tap for World's End and always features at least three of its own beers among the six on offer. The small bar has an attractive stone and brick fireplace in the centre. Chess and poetry nights are regular events and live music features twice a month. Beer festivals are held to mark the summer and winter solstices. Food is served Friday 6-9pm and Sunday lunchtime only unless by prior arrangement.
❀◑⇌♣●🚌(X5)🐾📶

Poulshot

Raven
The Green, SN10 1RW
🕐 closed Mon; 11.30-2.30, 6-11; 12-3 Sun
☎ (01380) 828271 🌐 ravenpoulshot.co.uk
Wadworth Henry's IPA, 6X; 1 changing beer 🄷
A charming village pub with a cosy atmosphere and a large beer garden. Peaceful, friendly and relaxed, it has plenty of wooden chairs and tables. The three Wadworth ales are served from oak casks behind the bar. Food is served throughout the day from an extensive menu which changes regularly. A lovely spot to while away a summer's afternoon, or for the more active the pub is close to Devizes marina and there are many outdoor activities within the area. Opening hours may increase in summer. Q🐎❀◑P🐾

Ramsbury

Crown & Anchor
1 Crowood Lane, SN8 2PT
🕐 8am-11; 9am-10.30 Sun ☎ (01672) 520335
🌐 crownandanchorramsbury.co.uk/index.html
Wickwar Brand Oak Bitter; 3 changing beers (sourced locally; often Ramsbury) 🄷
A quiet and welcoming 19th-century country pub with a small bar surrounded by three rooms, two with fireplaces. Interesting bric-a-brac adorns the low ceiling beams including 200-year-old blacksmith's fixings, and a Victorian beer engine that was used behind the bar is now on display. Thursday is acoustic music night and a quiz is held every Sunday evening. Food includes a carvery on Sunday and fish night on Friday. There is a garden area to the rear. Two en-suite B&B rooms are available. 🐎❀🛏◑P🚌(46,48)🐾📶

Royal Wootton Bassett

Five Bells
Wood Street, SN4 7BD
🕐 12-3, 5-11.30; 12-midnight Fri-Sun ☎ (01793) 849422
Black Sheep Best Bitter; Fuller's London Pride; 4 changing beers (sourced nationally) 🄷
Dating from before 1841, this is a busy and cosy traditional thatched local with a beamed ceiling and open fires. The bar has seven handpumps for two regular beers, four guests and a cider. Food is served lunchtimes and on Wednesday evening themed nights (booking recommended). The pub has darts and crib teams. Special events are held throughout the year. Q❀◑♣●P🚌(55)🐾📶

Salisbury

Duke of York 🄻
34 York Road, SP2 7AS
🕐 6 (4 Sat)-midnight; 4-11 Sun ☎ (01722) 503872
5 changing beers (sourced nationally; often Hop Back, Marston's, Moles) 🄷
Built in 1901 by Ushers and situated down a quiet side street, this small single-bar pub reopened in July 2011 after a long closure. Popular with locals, it has a strong community focus with a regular informal quiz and other events including beer festivals. It is home to the Fisherton History Society. A true free house, it offers a range of beers – the selection may be reduced mid-week – sometimes accompanied by a real cider. ❀⇌♣🚌(R1,R3)📶

King's Head
Bridge Street, SP1 2ND
🕐 7am-midnight (1am Thu-Sat) ☎ (01722) 342050
Greene King Abbot; Ruddles Best Bitter; 7 changing beers (sourced nationally) 🄷
Formerly the County Hotel, this fine stone building sitting alongside the River Avon is now a Wetherspoon Lloyds No. 1 bar. A pub or brewery has occupied this site since 1470. The pub has a spacious interior spread over two levels. The riverside beer garden has recently had new furniture and artificial grass added, allowing alfresco drinking and dining. Music is played Thursday-Saturday evenings.
🐎❀🛏◑♿⇌♣🚌📶

Rai d'Or 🄻
69 Brown Street, SP1 2AS
🕐 5-11; closed Sun ☎ (01722) 327137 🌐 raidor.co.uk
2 changing beers (sourced locally; often Downton, Red Cat, Stonehenge) 🄷
Characterful 13th-century free house with a fascinating history. An inglenook fireplace and low ceilings make for an appealing ambience. Excellent, reasonably priced Thai food is complemented by two ever-changing, usually local, beers. It can be busy at food times, but drinkers are always welcome. There is a discount on food before 6.30pm. A former local CAMRA Pub of the Year. Parking is in the nearby Brown Street car park. 🐎◑⇌♣●🚌🐾

Railway Inn/Dust Hole 🄻
59 Tollgate Road, SP1 2JG
🕐 12-2 (not Wed & Sat), 7-11; 12-3, 6-11 Sun
☎ (01722) 324537 🌐 thedusthole.vpweb.co.uk
Downton Honey Blonde; 2 changing beers (sourced locally; often Andwells, Downton, Plain) 🄷
Friendly local pub close to Salisbury College. This is the only public house in the country to be licensed

under two official names – look at the sign hanging outside. The Railway refers to its proximity to the now-closed goods railway station and the Dust Hole to the coal dust that used to be blown into the bar. No danger of that now. The pub became a free house in 2013. ❀◑♿♣P🚌ᯤ

Village Freehouse 𝕃

33 Wilton Road, SP2 7EF

4 (11 Fri-Sun)-11 ☎ (01722) 329707

Downton Quadhop; 4 changing beers (sourced nationally) Ⓗ

Friendly revitalised local close to the railway station. It offers four changing guest beers, with the focus on local microbreweries and beers unusual for the area – requests welcome. The only regular outlet in Salisbury for dark beers, a dark ale, mild, porter or stout are always on offer. Terrestrial TV and Sky Sports are screened. Popular with rail users, it features rail memorabilia and books. Fresh rolls are available and you are welcome to bring your own food. Local CAMRA Pub of the Year 2014. ⇌🚌(R1,R3)🐾ᯤ

Winchester Gate 𝕃

113-117 Rampart Road, SP1 1JA

3 (12 Thu-Sat)-11; 12-10 Sun ☎ (01722) 322834

winchestergate.co.uk

Hop Back Crop Circle; 3 changing beers (often Downton, Plain, Wessex) Ⓗ

An inn since the 17th century, this free house once provided for travellers at the city's east tollgate. Four handpumps offer ales from across the UK, and a real cider is often alongside. Three beer festivals feature each year, and cider festivals in the spring and autumn. The garden has a pétanque terrain and boules can be played. Live music is hosted every weekend, with an open mic night on the third Wednesday of the month. Filled rolls are sold. LocAle accredited and a former local CAMRA Pub of the Year. ❀♣P🚌ᯤ

Wyndham Arms 🏆 𝕃

27 Estcourt Road, SP1 3AS

4.30-11.30; 12-midnight Thu-Sat; 12-11.30 Sun ☎ (01722) 331026

Hop Back Golden Best, Citra, Crop Circle, Summer Lightning; 2 changing beers (sourced locally; often Downton, Hop Back) Ⓗ

The birthplace of Hop Back Brewery, the Wyndham celebrated 28 consecutive years in the Guide in 2015. A traditional ale house, it has a single bar with six handpumps serving a selection of Hop Back ales, often a Downton seasonal beer and occasionally an ale from further afield. There is also a fine selection of bottled beers and wines. This is a pub for conversation, good-natured banter and fine ales. Local CAMRA Pub of the Year 2015. ♣🚌(R2)🐾

Seend Cleeve

Barge Inn 𝕃

SN12 6QB

11.30-11 (10.30 Sun) ☎ (01380) 828230

bargeinnseend.co.uk/home.php

Wadworth Henry's IPA, Horizon; 2 changing beers Ⓗ

Situated on the picturesque Kennet & Avon Canal, the pub offers excellent food, great Wadworth beers, an extensive wine list and much more. There are many interesting old canal photographs on the walls. A beautiful location to spend lazy afternoons relaxing by the water in summer, and to unwind by cosy log fires in winter – the Barge Inn really is a pub for all seasons. Q❀◑⛺♣●P🚌(49)🐾ᯤ

Semington

Somerset Arms

High Street, BA14 6JR

10-11 (10.30 Sun) ☎ (01380) 870067

somersetarmssemington.co.uk

Box Steam Funnel Blower; Otter Ale; 2 changing beers (sourced locally; often Twisted) Ⓗ

A coaching inn possibly dating back to the 16th century, the pub offers regular beers and guests from micros within 50 miles, complemented by highly regarded food made with local ingredients as far as possible. The village of Semington is now a quiet cul-de-sac after the bypass was built a few years ago and the pub's proximity to the Kennet & Avon Canal makes it popular with boaters, walkers and cyclists. Accommodation is in three luxury en-suite bedrooms. Q❀🛏◑♿♣●P🚌(234)🐾ᯤ

Semley

Benett Arms 🏆

Village Green, SP7 9AS (1 mile E of A350) ST891270

12-3, 5-11 ☎ (01747) 830221 benettarms.co.uk

Ringwood Best Bitter; 2 changing beers Ⓗ

A former Gibbs Mew country pub, this is now a genuine free house sitting by the green and pond in a quiet village. It has a single small bar and separate dining areas. The beer choice varies but there are usually three to choose from, either on handpump or direct from the cellar. Excellent home-cooked food is available at all sessions. A warm welcome is extended to all, including families and dogs, in an area popular with walkers. Q❀◑♿●P🚌(84,247)🐾

Swindon

Beehive

55 Prospect Hill, SN1 3JS

12-midnight (1am Thu-Sat) ☎ (01793) 523187

bee-hive.co.uk

Hardys & Hansons Olde Trip; 5 changing beers Ⓗ

Sympathetically refurbished in 2014, this multi-levelled, bare-boarded pub has retained its charm and four-room layout. It is a Greene King pub, but under its Local Hero initiative the beer range is now wider, with a local focus, and supported by Meet the Brewer evenings. A popular live music venue, it hosts performances on Sunday, Thursday and Friday evenings. The walls are often covered in works of art and posters advertising cultural events. Locally sourced pies are available from lunchtimes to 7.30. ◑♣🚌(12,49)🐾ᯤ

Blunsdon Arms

Lady Lane, SN25 2NA

11-midnight ☎ (01793) 729801

Brakspear Bitter; Wadworth 6X; 4 changing beers (sourced nationally) Ⓗ

This large open-plan Ember Inns pub with plenty of comfortable seating opened in 2006. The four changing beers rotate through a selection of 12, which changes quarterly. Real cider is also on offer. Food is served daily until 10pm. Quiz nights are Wednesday and Sunday and poker nights Monday and Thursday. ❀◑♿♣●P🚌(11A,15)ᯤ

Glue Pot

5 Emlyn Square, SN1 5BP
12 (4.30 Mon)-11; 11.30-11 Fri & Sat; 12-10.30 Sun
(01793) 497420
Downton New Forest Ale; Hop Back Citra, Crop Circle, Entire Stout, Summer Lightning; 3 changing beers (sourced regionally; often Downton, Hop Back) H
The Glue Pot is part of the historic sandstone Railway Village built in the 1840s in Swindon. There are seven Hop Back or Downton ales, one guest, and five real ciders. All real ales are reduced in price on Mondays. This is usually a quiet pub, but it gets quite busy on weekend evenings. There is a pub quiz on Thursday nights. Note the one remaining window with the Allsopp's logo. A winter beer festival features in January or February and another one over the Easter weekend.
(8,14)

Hop Inn L

7 Devizes Road, SN1 4BJ
12-11 (midnight Fri & Sat); 12-10.30 Sun
(01793) 976833 hopinnswindon.co.uk
House beer (by Ramsbury); 4 changing beers (sourced regionally) H
A genuine free house and great example of the trend for micropubs, this former shop has become a popular destination for real ale lovers. It is furnished in an eclectic style with bright plastic chairs and tables made from reclaimed wood. The small bar has five handpumps offering an ever-changing variety of ales sourced from smaller breweries. There are also two real ciders in boxes. Local CAMRA Pub of the Year 2014.
(12,15)

Savoy L

38-40 Regent Street, SN1 1JL
8am-midnight (1am Fri & Sat) (01793) 533970
Adnams Broadside; Greene King Abbot; Ruddles Best Bitter; Wychwood Hobgoblin; 10 changing beers (sourced nationally) H
This lively and welcoming town-centre pub is the oldest Wetherspoon in Swindon, converted from the foyer and ground floor of a 1930s cinema. It has a spacious interior on many different levels, divided into separate areas. Old cinema photographs and memorabilia from the 1930s decorate the walls. There is a TV screen in one corner, mainly silent. A large selection of beers is available and food is served all day until 11pm. Handy for the theatre, cinema, restaurants and shopping. (1,1A)

Weighbridge Brewhouse L

Penzance Drive, SN5 7JL
12-11 (10 Sun) (01793) 881500
weighbridgebrewhouse.co.uk
Weighbridge Brewhouse Brinkworth Village, Weighbridge Best, Pooley's Golden; 3 changing beers H
The Weighbridge Brewhouse is an upmarket brew- and gastro-pub in the former home of Archers brewery. It features a long shiny bar with six handpumps dedicated to the real ales crafted on the premises. Three regular ales are joined by new and seasonal offerings. Seating in the bar is limited, although a terrace is available for the milder season. Live music plays on Thursday, Friday and Saturday evenings. Food is served all day.
P(8,55)

Wheatsheaf L

32 Newport Street, SN1 3DP
12-3, 5-11; 12-midnight Fri & Sat; 12-8 Sun
(01793) 496396
Wadworth Henry's IPA, Horizon, 6X, Swordfish; 2 changing beers (often Wadworth) H
This is a genuine real ale pub with six wooden casks and six handpumps on the bar at the front. However, the wooden casks do not store any beer – the ale is pumped up by air pressure from casks in the cellar. A guest beer comes from the Wadworth list and there is one Wadworth seasonal ale. The front bar is cosy while the back bar opens up into a larger area. Live music plays occasionally, usually on the last Thursday of the month.
Q(12,22)

Yates's L

49-50 Bridge Street, SN1 1BL
10-midnight (1am Fri & Sat); 11-10 Sun
(01793) 484924 weareyates.co.uk/swindon
Greene King IPA; 5 changing beers (sourced nationally) H
Large town-centre chain pub with a better than average turnover of real ales and ciders. It has extended the number of handpumps to six over the past few years and the beers are reasonably priced. The pub can be lively towards the end of the week and at weekends – it is essentially a sports bar with a number of screens showing various sports. Refurbished in the last couple of years, facilities are all on one level.
(1,8)

Tisbury

Benett Arms L

High Street, SP3 6HD
12-midnight (01747) 870428 benetttisbury.co.uk
Keystone Bedrock, Large One; 1 changing beer (sourced regionally) H
A warm welcome and friendly conversation await you at Keystone Brewery's first pub, which reopened in 2012. The front bar is furnished with a range of tables, the rear bar has a pool table, and there are tables outside to the front. Keystone's Large One is badged as Gordon Benett. Hot snacks and light lunches are served daily. Sunday lunches are always popular and curry night is the first Monday of the month. (25,26)

Boot Inn L

High Street, SP3 6PS
11-2.30, 7-11; 12-3 Sun (01747) 870363
3 changing beers (sourced regionally; often Bath Ales, Sixpenny) G
Fine village pub built of Chilmark stone, licensed since 1768. It has a relaxed, friendly atmosphere appealing to locals and visitors alike and conversation thrives. Run by the same landlord since 1976, it became a free house in 2009 and has three or four ales behind the bar. Excellent food is served and there is a spacious garden. A former local CAMRA Pub of the Year.
QP(25,26)

Trowbridge

Sir Isaac Pitman

Market Place, BA14 8AL
8am-midnight (01225) 763287

Adnams Broadside; Ruddles Best Bitter; 4 changing beers Ⓗ
Large and comfortable town-centre Wetherspoon pub with an impressive Victorian stone frontage, set next to Trowbridge old town hall. The usual Wetherspoon regular ales are supplemented by a good selection of ever-changing guests, many of them from local brewers, and beers from further away tend to come from more interesting breweries. Bus stops are directly outside. Less than a minute's walk away is the Albany Palace, another Wetherspoon pub. Q

Warminster

Bath Arms

41 Market Place, BA12 9AZ
7am-midnight (1am Fri & Sat) ☎ (01985) 853920
Adnams Broadside; Greene King Abbot; Ruddles Best Bitter; Sharp's Doom Bar; 5 changing beers Ⓗ
Refurbished and reopened by JD Wetherspoon in April 2014, this large and comfortable Grade II-listed building is one of the town's three remaining 18th-century coaching inns. The beers include the usual Wetherspoon range plus a good selection of guests, many from breweries within 30 or so miles of the town. The upper floors provide accommodation in 10 rooms and the station is just five minutes' walk away.

Fox & Hounds

6 Deverill Road, BA12 9QP
11-11 ☎ (01985) 216711
Wessex Warminster Warrior; house beer (by Wessex); 2 changing beers (sourced regionally; often Sharp's, Twisted) Ⓗ
Friendly two-bar pub that was local CAMRA Rural Pub 2013. The main bar has a pool table and TV for sport at the back; a snug bar is to the right-hand side of the entrance. There is also a large skittle alley and function room. Regular ciders are from Thatchers and Rich's, with up to five guests. Guest real ales are usually from local and regional breweries. Closing time may be later than 11pm. QP

Organ Inn

49 High Street, BA12 9AQ
4 (12 Sat)-midnight; 4-11 Sun ☎ (01985) 211777
theorganinn.co.uk
3 changing beers (sourced regionally; often Cottage, Stonehenge, Twisted) Ⓗ
An inn until 1913, after serving as a butcher's, fishmonger's and greengrocer's, the Organ reopened as a pub in 2006. The welcoming interior comprises three rooms with a traditional feel, plus a snug games room and a skittle alley. The beer range constantly changes but always includes Organ Bitter (the brewery is a secret). A beer festival is held in September. Ciders are mainly Westons and guests. Bar snacks are interesting. There is an art gallery upstairs. Local CAMRA Rural Pub of the Year 2014. Q

Wroughton

Carters Rest

57 High Street, SN4 9JU
5-11; 3-midnight Fri; 12-midnight Sat; 12-11 Sun
☎ (01793) 812288
Cotswold Spring Stunner; Marston's Pedigree New World Pale Ale; Otter Amber; Ramsbury Flint Knapper; Sharp's Doom Bar; 5 changing beers Ⓗ
The pub's name originates from the stables that used to be here, providing extra horses for the journey to Devizes market. The large two bar inn dates from 1904 and is a real ale destination with 10 ales plus one regular and one guest cider/perry. An annual beer festival is held in December. The pub screens live sport and hosts occasional live music. Quiz night is Thursday.
P(49,72)

Compasses, Chicksgrove

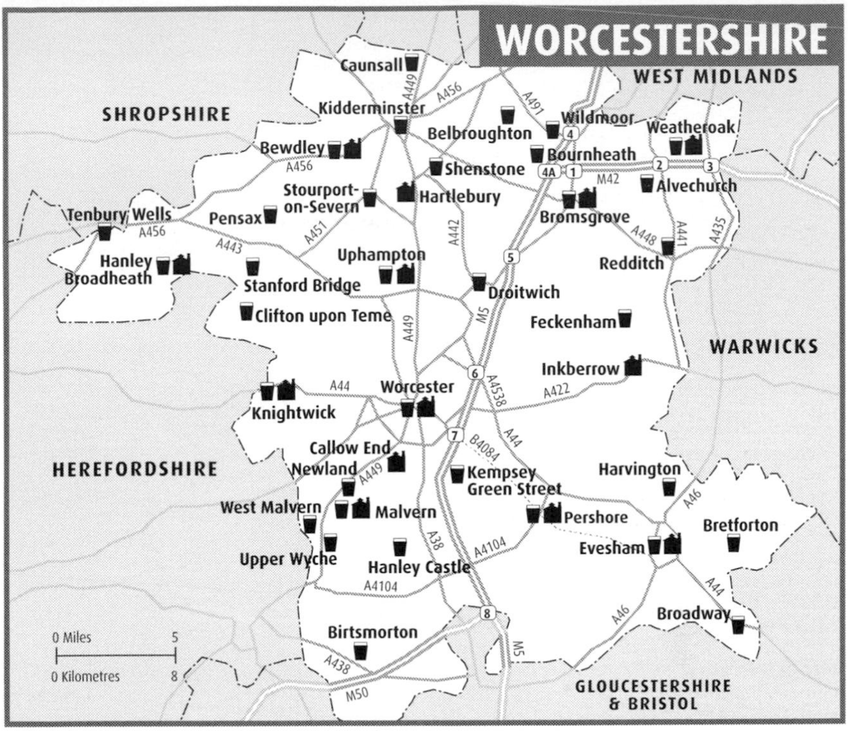

Alvechurch

Weighbridge

Scarfield Wharf, Scarfield Hill, B48 7SQ (follow signs to marina from village) SP022721

12-3, 7-11 (10.30 Sun) (0121) 445 5111

the-weighbridge.co.uk

Weatheroak Tillerman's Tipple; 4 changing beers

This cosy canalside pub is the local CAMRA Pub of the Year. It has two small lounges, a public bar and a pleasant garden. Spring and autumn beer festivals are held. Value home-cooked food is served lunchtimes and evenings (no food Tue & Wed) and excellent Sunday lunches. A covered area outside can be used for functions. House beers are Weatheroak Tillerman's Tipple and Kinver Bargees Bitter. Changing guest beers include a mild, and real cider or perry is available.
Q **P** (146)

Belbroughton

Holly Bush

Stourbridge Road, DY9 9UG (on A491 outside village centre)

11.30-11; 11.30-3, 6-11 Sat; 12-3, 7-10.30 Sun

(01562) 730207

Hobsons Mild, Twisted Spire, Town Crier

A pub since 1845, this was originally a row of terraced cottages. The low-level white building is set back from the A491 dual carriageway between Hagley and the M5 junction 4. Full of character, with low ceilings, it has a single bar serving three separate areas including a dining room. Excellent-value traditional home-made meals are available. A popular pub for Hobsons Mild, and Thatchers cider is on handpump. Near to the Clent Hills (NT). Branch Pub of the Year 2015. **Q** **P**

Bewdley

Great Western

Kidderminster Road, DY12 1BY (near railway bridge and SVR station; walk by signal box and under viaduct)

11.30-11 (01299) 488828

thegreatwesternbewdley.co.uk

Bewdley Worcestershire Way, 2857; Morland Old Golden Hen; 3 changing beers (often Belhaven)

Conveniently located within a short walk of the Severn Valley Railway station, the pub has a simple yet comfortable railway theme reminiscent of an earlier age. Overlooking the bar is an upper level from which to admire the fine glazed decorative wall tiles. Pub snacks such as pork pies and cobs go with the concept of a traditional pub, and on the bar there are six real ales, including regulars from Bewdley Brewery, and a cider.
Q (SVR) **P**

Little Pack Horse

31 High Street, DY12 2DH (300yds from St Anne's Church)

12-3, 6-11 (5-midnight Fri); 11-midnight Sat; 11-10.30 Sun

(01299) 403762 littlepackhorse.co.uk

Bewdley Worcestershire Way; Hobsons Town Crier; 2 changing beers (often St Austell)

Tucked away along the end of the High Street and dating from the 15th century, the pub has a reputation for good beer and food. The cosy interior is an interesting mix of ancient walls and timbers. It specialises in home-cooked meals including the famous Desperate Dan Pie in various sizes, a complete meal in itself. Fish, steak, vegetarian and daily specials are on the chalkboard. Four ales are available including one from the nearby Bewdley Brewery.

Mug House ⓛ

12 Severnside North, DY12 2EE (150yds along Severnside North from river bridge)
☼ 12-11 (11.30 Fri & Sat) ☎ (01299) 402543
⊕ mughousebewdley.co.uk
Bewdley Worcestershire Way; Purity Mad Goose; Timothy Taylor Landlord; Wye Valley HPA; 1 changing beer Ⓗ

Located on the side of the Severn, the Mug House is not to be missed. A friendly pub that welcomes locals and visitors alike, it serves four regular beers, including a brew from Bewdley, plus a guest. There are cosy settles and a log fire in the lounge bar, and to the rear is a sun terrace with a glass-covered patio with grapevines and wisteria. Fine food is served in the restaurant as well as bar meals at lunchtime. Q☼❀☷◑⅄≉(SVR)●🚌😊🔌

Old Waggon & Horses ⓛ

91 Kidderminster Road, DY12 1DG (on Bewdley-Kidderminster road, Catchem's End)
☼ 12-11; 11.30-1am Fri & Sat ☎ (01299) 403170
⊕ waggonbewdley.co.uk
Banks's Mild, Bitter; Bathams Best Bitter; 1 changing beer Ⓗ

Popular locals' and visitors' pub with a central bar that serves three distinct areas. The small wooden-floored snug has settles, tables and a dartboard; the larger room has a roll-down screen for major sporting events, bench seating and a TV. An old kitchen range in the dining area adds to the cottagey feel. Food is available Tuesday and Thursday evenings with a carvery on Sundays. The attractive terraced garden is on many levels. Guest ales come from local independents.
Q❀◑⅄≉(SVR)♣●🅿🚌😊🔌

Birtsmorton

Farmers Arms

Birts Street, WR13 6AP (off B4208) SO790363
☼ 11 (12 Sun)-4, 6-midnight ☎ (01684) 833308
⊕ farmersarmsbirtsmorton.co.uk
Hook Norton Hooky, Old Hooky; 2 changing beers (sourced locally) Ⓗ

Grade II-listed, black and white village pub dating from 1480, found down a quiet country lane. The large bar area features a splendid inglenook fireplace while the cosy lounge has old settles and low beams. Good-value, home-made, traditional food is on offer daily (lunch until 2pm, eve meals until 9.30pm weekdays, 9pm Sun). A beer from a small, local independent brewer is often available. A beer festival is held in August. The safe, spacious garden, with swings, provides fine views of the Malvern Hills. A caravan site is nearby.
Q☼❀◑⅄♣🅿🚌(577)😊🔌

Bournheath

Nailers Arms

62 Doctors Hill, B61 9JE
☼ 12-midnight (1am Fri & Sat); 12-11.30 Sun
☎ (01527) 873045 ⊕ thenailersarms.co.uk
Morland Old Speckled Hen; Wye Valley HPA; 2 changing beers Ⓗ

Dating from the late-18th century, this whitewashed three-gabled building was once a nailmakers' workshop-cum-brewery. The bar has a traditional quarry-tiled floor and a real fire. Two guest ales are usually also on handpump. A reasonably priced food menu is available in the lounge/restaurant; the carvery is a particular favourite. The restaurant closes occasionally for functions such as weddings. A beer festival has become a popular attraction in the pub's calendar in May. ☼❀◑⅄♣🅿😊🔌

Bretforton

Fleece Inn ★ ⓛ

The Cross, WR11 7JE (near church)
☼ 11-3, 6-11; 11-11 Wed-Sat; 12-10.30am Sun winter; 11-11 (10.30am Sun) summer ☎ (01386) 831173
⊕ thefleeceinn.co.uk
Uley Pig's Ear Strong Beer; Wye Valley Bitter; 3 changing beers Ⓗ

Fifteenth-century timber-framed village pub owned by the NT on the edge of the Cotswolds. Recognised by CAMRA as having a nationally important historic pub interior, it is home to a world-famous 17th-century pewter collection. Morris dancers and music feature all year round, with entertainment evenings in the adjacent medieval barn. Two regular beers are complemented by three guests, often from local micros, and up to four ciders, including one produced at the Fleece itself. A pub not to be missed. Q☼❀☷◑⅄♣▲●🚌(554)🔌

Broadway

Crown & Trumpet ⓛ

14 Church Street, WR12 7AE (on road to Snowshill, just off Cotswolds Way)
☼ 11-11 (10.30 Sun) ☎ (01386) 853202
⊕ cotswoldholidays.co.uk
Stanway Broadway Artists Ale; Stroud Tom Long; Timothy Taylor Landlord; 1 changing beer (sourced locally; often Bradfield, Butcombe, Prescott) Ⓗ

Picturesque 17th-century Cotswold stone inn situated on the road to Snowshill, just off the village green. This hostelry has welcoming and friendly staff and an abundance of character, with oak beams and a log fire along with plenty of Flowers Brewery memorabilia. A menu of good, honest, well-cooked pub favourites is offered at reasonable prices. A range of quality ales is always available including Stanway Artist and Timothy Taylor Landlord plus guests along with ciders and perries. Entertainment includes live jazz and blues nights. Q❀☷◑⅄♣●🅿🚌(21)🔌

REAL ALE BREWERIES

Ambridge Inkberrow
Bewdley Bewdley
Bird's Bromsgrove
Brandy Cask Pershore
Cannon Royall Uphampton
Evesham Evesham (brewing suspended)
Firefly Worcester
Friday Beer Malvern
Joseph Herbert Smith Hanley Broadheath
Malvern Hills Malvern
Pope's Worcester
St George's Callow End
Teme Valley Knightwick
Weatheroak Hill Weatheroak Hill, Alvechurch
Winning Post Worcester
Worcester Worcester
Worcestershire Hartlebury

Bromsgrove

Hop Pole

78 Birmingham Road, B61 0DF
4-11 (midnight Fri); 12-midnight Sat; 12-11 Sun
(01527) 870100 hop-pole.com
Sharp's Doom Bar; 2 changing beers (sourced regionally)
The best live music pub in Bromsgrove, various bands play Thursday to Saturday nights and on some Sundays. The bar area gives good views of the stage while there is comfortable seating at the front. At quieter times this is a community-style pub with a brilliant atmosphere. An upstairs games room has two league pool tables. Monday is quiz night. The smoking area is in the beautiful beer garden. Three cask ales are always available.

Ladybird

2 Finstall Road, B60 2DZ (on B4184 on corner of roundabout near station) SO969695
11-11; 12-10.30 Sun (01527) 878014
ladybirdinn.co.uk
Bathams Best Bitter; Wye Valley HPA; 2 changing beers (often Bird's, Sharp's)
This popular local is situated adjacent to the town's railway station. The light, airy lounge, with polished wooden floor, has historic railway photographs and a dartboard in an alcove, in contrast to the busy bar. A function/meeting room is available on the first floor. Pub grub is served every day; however, if your taste is for Italian cuisine try the adjoining privately run restaurant. The attached 45-room Travelodge offers accommodation with breakfast available at the Ladybird. P

Little Ale House

21 Worcester Road, B61 7DL (on corner of Station St)
12-10 (6 Sun) 07773 247179
Ambridge Worcestershire Pale Ale; Bewdley Worcestershire Sway, William Mucklow's Dark Mild; Malvern Hills Black Pear; changing beers
Bromsgrove's first micropub has a friendly and cosy atmosphere. It offers four permanent and four ever-changing ales all served from the cask, including its own house ale, Special Tipple. A selection of real cider and perries is also on offer as well as bottled beers and take-out cartons. The driver is catered for with tea and coffee or soft drinks. A council car park is nearby. Q

Red Lion

73 High Street, B61 8AQ
10-11 (1am Fri & Sat); 12-9 Sun (01527) 758858
Banks's Mild, Bitter; 4 changing beers (often Jennings, Marston's, Ringwood)
Nestled between the busy High Street and the bus station, this cosy and traditional one-roomed pub is popular with the locals. Six real ales feature from an extended range from the Marston's portfolio in the lounge bar, with Banks's Mild and Bitter always available. There is courtyard seating to the rear and a covered and heated smoking area. Fresh rolls are often available. Live sport is shown regularly and a disco takes place on Friday evenings. P

Caunsall

Anchor Inn

DY11 5YL (off A449 Kidderminster-Wolverhampton road)
11-4, 7-11; 11-3, 7-10.30 Sun (01562) 850254
theanchorinncaunsall.co.uk
Hobsons Best Bitter, Town Crier; Wye Valley HPA, Butty Bach; 2 changing beers (often Three Tuns)
Popular village pub run by the same family since 1927. This friendly traditional village local is renowned for its six real ales, ciders and well-filled cobs. A central doorway leads into the barely changing bar with its original 1920s furniture and horse racing memorabilia. The friendly staff welcome an impressive mix of customers and it gets especially busy at lunchtimes. Easily reached from the nearby canal, this gem is well-worth visiting. Local CAMRA Bronze Pub of the Year 2014.
Q P

Clifton upon Teme

New Inn

Old Road, WR6 6DR (signed 200yds off B4204) SO724609
5 (12 Sat & Sun)-midnight (01886) 812226
newinnclifton.com
Wye Valley HPA; 2 changing beers
The pub is located on the old road up the hill and dates back several centuries, as does the imposing yew tree at the front which doubles as a smoking shelter. The building enjoys magnificent views over the Teme and Severn valleys. The large bar area has fireside tables on one side and darts and pool on the other. The adjoining dining room serves home-made meals made with locally sourced produce (food served daily until 9pm, Sunday roast until 4pm). There is a secluded garden to the rear. Frequented by darts teams, bell-ringers, badminton players and young farmers.
Q P (308,310)

Droitwich

Hop Pole

40 Friar Street, WR9 8ED
12-11 (10.30 Sun) (01905) 770155
Enville Ale; Malvern Hills Black Pear; Wye Valley HPA, Butty Bach; 2 changing beers
A warm welcome is always assured at this friendly pub, popular with locals and visitors alike. The 18th-century timber-framed building is in an old part of Droitwich, next to the Norbury Theatre. The multi-roomed interior includes a separate pool room, and outside is a heated patio area for smokers and a garden with seating. Guest beers are mostly from local breweries. Good-value home-cooked food is served at lunchtime. Live music plays some weekends. Close by is the newly restored Droitwich Barge Canal which offers secure moorings.

Evesham

Red Lion

6 Market Place, WR11 4RE
11-11; 12-10 Sun (01386) 761688
Cannon Royall Fruiterers Mild, Blonde Bombshell; 3 changing beers (often Cannon Royall)
Closed for over 100 years, this basic town-centre pub is being sympathetically furbished. Still a work in progress, the small bar, larger seating area and rear snug are full of character. The pub is tucked away in a corner of the market place and with no TV or music it is a great place for people-watching and conversation. There is no food but customers

are welcome to bring their own or order from numerous nearby outlets. Five well-priced Cannon Royall beers and two ciders are available.
Q ♿ (24,28,247)

Feckenham

Rose & Crown

High Street, B96 6HS
11-3, 6-11; 12-11 Sat & Sun ☎ (01527) 892188
roseandcrownfeckenham.co.uk
Banks's Bitter; Brakspear Oxford Gold; 2 changing beers (often Goff's, Marston's) H
A welcoming 19th-century Grade II-listed village pub, owned and run by a family. Up to three real ales are available, and a changing guest beer. An annual beer festival is held over the August bank holiday. The lounge features a real fire, while shove-ha'penny can be played in the bar. Live music sessions are hosted on occasion. There is a large beer garden. Parking is limited, but there is a free car park 200 yards away. Q ♣

Hanley Broadheath

Fox Inn L

WR15 8QS SO671652
5-11; 3-12.30am Fri; 12-12.30am Sat; 12-10 Sun
☎ (01886) 853189
Bathams Best Bitter; Joseph Herbert Smith Foxy Lady; 2 changing beers (often Hogarths) H
The main bar of this 16th-century black-and-white timbered free house is decorated with hops and has a large fireplace with a wood-burning stove. The panelled dining area is separated from the bar by wood beams. Home-made food, including Sunday lunch, is available, with bar snacks at any time. The games room has a pool table, TV and darts. One guest beer is usually from Hogarths Brewery in Bolton. Annual lawnmower racing is held in the adjoining field in August.
Q ♣P

Hanley Castle

Three Kings 🏆 ★ L

Church End, WR8 0BL (signed off B4211) SO838420
12-3, 7-11 (10.30 Sun) ☎ (01684) 592686
Butcombe Bitter; Hobsons Best Bitter; 3 changing beers H
On CAMRA's National Inventory of Historic Pub Interiors, this unspoilt 15th-century country pub on the village green near the church has been run by the Roberts family since 1911. The three-room interior comprises a small snug with large inglenook, serving hatch and settle wall, a small side room, and Nell's Lounge with another inglenook, beams and its own entrance. Three guest ales are on offer, often from local breweries, plus Westons Old Rosie draught cider. Live music sessions feature regularly and a popular beer festival is held in November.
Q ♣P (363)

Harvington

Coach & Horses 🏆

Station Road, WR11 8NJ
5 (12 Sat)-midnight; 12-11.30 Sun ☎ (01386) 870249
coachandhorsesharvington.com
Greene King IPA; 3 changing beers H
Traditional village pub with a separate bar and lounge. The bar has a real fire and the lounge has a logburner in the inglenook. Photos of old Harvington adorn the walls. The pub's real ale drinkers select the guest beers from Finest Cask and SIBA lists. Good-value food is served. A local ukulele group plays on Tuesday and a fun quiz is hosted on Sunday nights. The refurbished skittle alley doubles as a function/training room. An annual beer festival is held in September. Local CAMRA Pub of the Year in 2014 and 2015.
♣P (28,248)

Kempsey Green Street

Huntsman Inn

Green Street, WR5 3QB (from A38 at Kempsey via Post Office Lane) SO868490
5 (12 Sat)-11; 12-4, 7-11 Sun ☎ (01905) 820336
Bathams Best Bitter; Greene King IPA, Abbot H
Formerly a 300-year-old farmhouse, this is now a cosy and friendly multi-roomed local with exposed beams and a real fire. The separate restaurant serves reasonably priced home-cooked food. There is also a skittle alley with its own bar, an attractive garden and a large car park. Closed at lunchtimes during the week. Dogs are welcome in the bar and lounge. ♿♣P

Kidderminster

Olde Seven Stars L

13-14 Coventry Street, DY10 2BG (opp Swan Centre)
11-11 (11.30 Fri & Sat); 12-11 Sun ☎ (01562) 755777
Changing beers H
With six ever-changing real ales and one draught cider, this historic town-centre family-friendly pub is well worth visiting. The front and rear bars display many old features from previous ages. It serves cobs and pork pies, and customers can bring their own food (plenty of takeaways nearby), with tableware and condiments provided. It has a quiet rear garden which is popular in summer. The friendly atmosphere and excellent ales won it local CAMRA Gold Pub of the Year 2014.
♿♣

Station Inn L

7 Farfield, DY10 1UG
12-11 ☎ (01562) 569621 stationkidderminster.co.uk
Enville Ale; Wye Valley HPA; 2 changing beers (sourced regionally; often Enville, Wye Valley) H
A friendly community pub just a short walk from the mainline and Severn Valley Railway stations. Two rooms are served from a central bar, warmed by a real fire in winter, and there is a large beer garden to the rear. Up to four ales are available including beers from Enville. Good-value home-cooked food is served during the day, and traditional roast dinners on Sundays. Quiz night is Thursday. Winner of local CAMRA Silver Pub of the Year 2014. Q ♿♣P

Swan L

Vicar Street, DY10 1DE (opp town hall)
10-11 (1am Fri & Sat); 12-7 Sun ☎ (01562) 823008
Bewdley Worcestershire Way; St Austell Tribute; 4 changing beers H
A one-room pub opposite the town hall dating from 1865 and a worthy survivor of town-centre redevelopment. It serves real ciders and up to six real ales, including one from Bewdley Brewery.

The single room has a front bar area that gets lively on rugby match days and quiet tables for dining towards the back. Breakfast is available from 10am and bar food Monday-Saturday throughout the day. A beer festival is held over the August bank holiday. ⌕◐&♿⊟♨♟

Weavers Real Ale House Ⓛ

98 Comberton Hill, DY10 1QH (300yds down hill from railway station)
☼ 3 (1 Fri)-10.30; 12-10.30 Sat; 12-10 Sun
☎ (01562) 229413
Three Tuns XXX; Wye Valley HPA; 4 changing beers (often Bewdley) Ⓗ
The single lounge bar is reminiscent of a traditional pub, with old pictures and posters on the walls and a conversational atmosphere. Six real ales are on tap including a dark, a stout and a mild, plus two ciders and a perry. Inexpensive pub snacks such as pork pies and cobs are always available. Just a short walk from the railway station, this is a place to stop off for a quiet pint and a chat on the way into town. Public parking is a short distance away.
Q&♿●⊟♨♟

Knightwick

Talbot Ⓛ

WR6 5PH (on B4197, 400yds from A44 jct)
☼ 10-11 ☎ (01886) 821235 ∰ the-talbot.co.uk
Hobsons Best Bitter; Teme Valley T'Other, This, That Ⓗ**; changing beers (often Teme Valley)** Ⓖ
Large country pub, originally a 14th-century coaching inn, with a taproom and lounge bar featuring a large fireplace. The attractive conservatory is especially fine in summer. The small wood-panelled restaurant serves an imaginative menu that makes good use of local ingredients. Three or four beers are usually on the bar from the Teme Valley Brewery behind the pub. There is a farmers' market outside on the second Sunday of the month. Beer festivals are held in April, June and early October (for green hop beers). Dog and walker friendly.
Q⌕⇆❀♠◐&▲♣⊟(420)♨♟

Malvern

Great Malvern Hotel Ⓛ

Graham Road, WR14 2HN (by crossroads with Church St)
☼ 10-11; 11-10.30 Sun ☎ (01684) 563411
∰ great-malvern-hotel.co.uk
Malvern Hills Black Pear; Wye Valley HPA; 2 changing beers (often Morland, Timothy Taylor, Friday Beer Co) Ⓗ
Popular hotel public bar a short level walk from the Malvern Theatres complex, ideal for pre- and post-performance refreshment. The beer range usually includes something from Malvern's two breweries. Meals are served in the bar and the adjoining brasserie, including Sunday lunches. There is also a comfortable lounge with lots of sofas, fresh coffee and newspapers. Live music sessions are hosted throughout the week. The Great Shakes cellar bar features TV sport and is available for hire. On-site parking is limited but there is plenty of public parking nearby.
⌕❀♯◐⇆(Great Malvern)P⊟♨♟

Morgan Ⓛ

52 Clarence Road, WR14 3EQ

☼ 12-3.30, 5-11; 12-11 Fri & Sat; 12-10.30 Sun
☎ (01684) 578575
Wye Valley Bitter, HPA, Butty Bach; 2 changing beers (sourced locally) Ⓗ
This Wye Valley Brewery-owned premises is named after the town's Morgan car factory. The open-plan interior is divided into a games area for darts, a drinking area and a slightly raised seating area with comfy settees. The landscaped patio has ample seating, a fish pond and 'Them Organ' gates. Activities include a monthly book club and weekly quizzes. The pub is muzak-free and the TV is only turned on for major sporting events. Up to two guest beers come from the Wye Valley range.
⌕❀♯⇆(Great Malvern)♣⊟(42,43,44)♨♟

Nag's Head

19-21 Bank Street, WR14 2JG (off Graham Rd at Link Top common)
☼ 11-11.15 (11.30 Fri & Sat); 12-11 Sun ☎ (01684) 574373
∰ nagsheadmalvern.co.uk
Banks's Bitter; Bathams Best Bitter; St George's Friar Tuck, Charger, Dragons Blood; Wood Shropshire Lad; 1 changing beer (often Otter) Ⓗ
The permanent beers at this free house, including those from the owner's brewery St George's in nearby Callow End, are joined by up to eight guests, usually including one from Otter, plus two draught ciders. Mismatched furniture, nooks and crannies, newspapers and foliage create a homely environment. Busy throughout the week, the pub serves quality food in the bar and restaurant. Outside is a large heated area to the front and a garden to the rear. The car park is small but there is ample on-street parking. Dogs are welcome and numerous. ❀◐♣●P⊟(44)♨♟

Newland

Swan Inn

WR13 5AY (just off A449 outside Malvern)
☼ 12-11.30 ☎ (01886) 832224 ∰ theswaninnmalvern.co.uk
Purity Mad Goose; Ringwood Fortyniner; St George's Friar Tuck, Dragons Blood Ⓗ**; 2 changing beers** Ⓗ/Ⓖ
Classic country pub dating from the 17th century on the outskirts of Malvern and overlooking common land at the front. A hop-bedecked open-plan bar is complemented by a dining room with a large add-on conservatory complete with opening roof. To the rear is an enclosed garden, a large field and The Shed for traditional pub games. The bar features beers from the owner's brewery – St George's at Callow End. Q⌕❀♯◐&♣●P⊟(44)♨

Pensax

Bell ♟ Ⓛ

WR6 6AE (on B4202 Clows Top-Great Whitley road)
☼ 12-2.30 (not Mon), 5-11; 12-10.30 Sun ☎ (01299) 896677
Bewdley Worcestershire Way; Exmoor Gold; Hobsons Best Bitter; Wye Valley HPA; 3 changing beers Ⓗ
Local CAMRA Pub of the Decade and previous West Midlands Pub of the Year, this family- and dog-friendly pub is not to be missed. Seven beers including three constantly changing ales plus local cider and perry adorn the bar. There is a separate dining room and a snug where families are welcome. Local seasonal ingredients feature on the food menu. Wooden floors, hanging hops, open fires and pew seating give a true country feel. Well-worth making a detour to visit.
Q⌕❀◐&♣P♨

Pershore

Brandy Cask 🄻

25 Bridge Street, WR10 1AJ
✪ 11.30-2.30, 7-11 (11.30 Thu); 11.30-3, 7-11.30 Fri & Sat; 12-3, 7-11 Sun ☎ (01386) 552602
Brandy Cask Whistling Joe, Brandy Snapper, John Baker's Original; 2 changing beers 🄷
The front entrance leads to a small bar with additional rooms either side. At least three ales brewed on the premises are always available as well as a wide range of guest beers from around the country. Cheddar Valley cider is also normally stocked. Food is good and reasonably priced (no food Mon or Tue in winter). The beautifully kept rear garden runs down to the River Avon.
Q🐎✿◐◑🍎🚌

Redditch

Bramley Cottage 🄻

Callow Hill Lane, Walkwood, B97 5QB (at jct of B4504 Windmill Drive and Callow Hill Lane)
✪ 11.30-midnight (11 Mon & Tue; 11.30 Wed & Thu)
☎ (01527) 542215
Brakspear Bitter; Purity Pure Ubu; 3 changing beers 🄷
This modern, comfortable pub is a popular meeting place for locals. The central L-shaped bar serves up to five real ales. Secluded dining and drinking areas and a real fire help create an intimate atmosphere. A food take-away service is available. Quiz nights are Sundays and Wednesdays from 9pm. Three guest ales are always on offer alongside the regulars, discounted in price on Mondays. There is a patio area outside. Q🐎✿◐◑♿P🚌(55,56)📶

Rising Sun 🄻

4 Alcester Street, B98 8AE (opp town hall)
✪ 8am-midnight (1am Fri & Sat) ☎ (01527) 62452
Greene King IPA, Abbot; Sharp's Doom Bar; 9 changing beers 🄷
Busy town-centre Wetherspoon pub with a large open-plan interior with several booths and comfy settees. A pictorial history of the town's needle and hook industry adorns the walls, as well as local links to the Gunpowder Plot. Outside seating offers shelter from the elements. At least one local beer is always available. Real cider is served from the box. Food is available 8am-10pm daily. Local beer festivals feature regularly as well as two national festivals. 🐎◐◑♿🚆🍎P🚌(57,58)📶

Shenstone

Plough 🄻

DY10 4DL (off A450/A448) SO865735
✪ 12.30-3.30, 6-11; 12-11 Fri & Sat; 12-10.30 Sun
☎ (01562) 777340
Bathams Mild Ale, Best Bitter 🄷
A traditional community pub that has been at the heart of the village since 1840. A long single bar serves both the lounge and public room areas, with a real fire in the lounge. The large enclosed courtyard serves as an overflow area in which children are permitted. Cobs and pork pies are available at lunchtimes. Bathams XXX is served in the winter. Local morris sides dance during the summer months. The Elizabethan Harvington Hall is two miles down the road. Q🐎♿♣P🐾📶

Stanford Bridge

Bridge 🄻

WR6 6RU (signed 100yds off B4203)
✪ 12-midnight (1am Fri & Sat) ☎ (01886) 812771
🌐 stanfordbridgepub.co.uk
Hobsons Twisted Spire; Pope's Worcester Gold; Wye Valley HPA; 3 changing beers 🄷
Large black and white pub, once a country hotel. Its many rooms provide space for socialising, games and dining. The games room has a pool table and TV sport, and the pub hosts cricket and rugby teams. The large patio is mostly under cover and also has a TV. Beers from Herefordshire, Shropshire and Worcestershire line up on the bar, alongside several ciders. Beer festivals are held at Easter, July and October, and other events on bank holidays.
🐎✿◐◑♿♣🍎P🐾📶

Stourport-on-Severn

Black Star 🄻

Mitton Street, DY13 8YP (just off top end of High St next to canal)
✪ 12-11 (midnight Fri & Sat) ☎ (01299) 488838
Wye Valley Bitter, HPA, Butty Bach; 1 changing beer (often Wye Valley) 🄷
Overlooking the canal, the pub was refurbished in 2014 and given a light and airy feel. The main bar has a real fire, low ceilings and cosy corners. At the back is the beer garden with shelter, tables and raised flowerbeds by the canal. Moorings are just through the bridge towards the basins. The varied food menu includes everything from doorstep sandwiches and baguettes to ribeye steaks and everything in between. Food requests are encouraged. Beers are from Wye Valley.
🐎✿◐◑♿🍎🚌🐾📶

Hollybush 🄻

Mitton Street, DY13 9AA (off Lion St down Gilgal)
✪ 12-11 (midnight Fri & Sat); 12-10.30 Sun
☎ (01299) 827435 🌐 hollybushrealalespub.co.uk
Black Country Bradley's Finest Golden, Fireside; 4 changing beers 🄷
A welcoming pub with a relaxed atmosphere offering six real ales from independent breweries and real cider. The single bar serves a split-level lounge with a snug, an upstairs function room with dartboard, and a quiet beer garden at the back. Regular weekly events include live music, quizzes and TV sport. Beer festivals are held twice a year in the main lounge. Awarded local CAMRA Gold Pub of the Year 2013 in recognition of its quality ales and community events. Q🐎✿◑♣🍎🚌🐾📶

Tenbury Wells

Pembroke House

Cross Street, WR15 8EQ
✪ 5-midnight Mon; 12-3, 7-11; 12-1.30am Fri & Sat; 12-midnight Sun ☎ (01584) 810301
Hobsons Best Bitter; 1 changing beer (sourced locally) 🄷
Large 16th-century black and white building on the edge of town. The spacious bar is divided into three areas and warmed by a logburner, giving a cosy feel. Two small separate dining rooms are used for fine dining. The games area has a small TV for sport, with a larger one imported for major events. Live bands play monthly. ✿◐◑♣P📶

Uphampton

Fruiterer's Arms

Uphampton Lane, WR9 0JW SO838648
12-11.30 (midnight Fri & Sat); 12-11 Sun
(01905) 620305
Cannon Royall Fruiterers Mild, King's Shilling, Arrowhead Bitter; 1 changing beer
Located 1 mile north of Ombersley, taking a narrow lane off the A449 dual carriageway, alongside the Reindeer Inn. This venue has been in the same family since 1830 and offers ales from the on-site Cannon Royall brewery. The traditional bar and comfortable lounge with logburner offer reasonably priced drinks, seasonal guest Cannon Royall ales and local cider and perry. Filled rolls are available Friday-Sunday. Children under 14 are welcome until 9pm. Q ♣ P

Upper Wyche

Wyche Inn

Wyche Road, WR14 4EQ (on B4218, follow signs from Malvern to Colwall)
12 (11 Sat & Sun)-11 (01684) 575396
thewycheinn.co.uk
Wye Valley HPA; 3 changing beers (sourced regionally)
The highest pub in Worcestershire, this free house has panoramic views towards the Cotswolds. Ideally situated for hill walkers, it offers two bars – one with pool and darts, the other dedicated to drinking and dining. A range of up to five real ales is available, all sourced from small and micro breweries, including some locals. Home-cooked food is served lunchtimes and evenings. Steak nights on Tuesday and Saturday are especially popular. AA 4-star B&B. Q ♣ P

Weatheroak

Coach & Horses

Weatheroak Hill, B48 7EA (on Alvechurch-Wythall road) SP057740
11.30-11; 12-10.30 Sun (01564) 823386
coachandhorsesinn.co.uk
Hobsons Best Bitter; Holden's Golden Glow; Weatheroak Hill Gold, Icknield Pale Ale, King o' the Hill; Wood Shropshire Lad; 3 changing beers (sourced nationally; often Hook Norton, St Austell, Wood)
Award-winning country free house with a traditional bar with a real fire and quarry-tiled floor, a modern lounge-bar and a restaurant. Formerly a coach house, it has been in the same family for over 40 years. It offers up to 10 real ales from breweries across the West Midlands, including the on-site Weatheroak Hill. Fresh rolls are always available. The restaurant can be used as a function room. Q ♣ P

West Malvern

Brewers Arms

Lower Dingle, WR14 4BQ (S end of village, down track by pub sign on B4232)
12-3, 6-midnight; 12-midnight Fri-Sun (01684) 568147
Malvern Hills Black Pear; Marston's Burton Bitter; Wye Valley HPA; changing beers
Traditional pub in the centre of the village community, providing a big welcome and an ideal refreshment stop for visitors to the Malvern Hills. Up to eight real ales and a draught cider, usually Westons, are available. Home-cooked food is served lunchtimes and evenings (no food Sun eve). The cosy bar can get busy but extra space is available in the function room. Do not be surprised by spontaneous music and singing sessions from local bands and choirs. The garden has fine views to the Black Mountains. Q (675)

Wildmoor

Wildmoor Oak

Top Road, B61 0RB SO963756
5-10.30 Mon; 12-11 (midnight Fri & Sat); 12-10.30 Sun
(0121) 453 2696 wildmooroak.com
3 changing beers (sourced nationally; often Timothy Taylor)
This rural inn is situated about a mile from J4 of the M5. The ales change regularly. It has a reputation locally for its Caribbean and British menu, prepared by award-winning chef Lorenzo. A friendly community pub, it hosts Caribbean nights, music nights, regular Tuesday quiz nights, and an annual beer and cider festival. Outside is an attractive patio drinking area. A former local Cider Pub of the Year. ♣ P (007)

Worcester

Bell

35 St Johns, WR2 5AG (W side of Severn off A44)
10-11 (11.30 Fri & Sat); 11-11 Sun (01905) 424570
Fuller's London Pride; 3 changing beers (sourced regionally; often Sharp's, Thwaites, Hobsons)
A community pub dating from the 17th century with a central corridor with two small rooms on one side and the main bar on the other. At the rear is a second bar used at busy times, and a room available for functions. There is also a popular skittle alley. As well as the regular Fuller's beer there can be up to three guests from local independents or sometimes from more distant breweries. Live music often plays at weekends. ♣

Cardinal's Hat

31 Friar Street, WR1 2NA
12 (4 Mon)-11; 12-11.30 Fri & Sat; 12-10.30 Sun
(01905) 724006 the-cardinals-hat.co.uk
4 changing beers (sourced regionally)
A period building set in the heart of the city with a stone-flagged, panelled passageway leading to the small rooms and outdoor patio at the rear. The main bar at the front with its scrubbed wooden floor, beams and leaded windows is full of life. The atmospheric back room features wood panelling, a stone floor, serving hatch and impressive fireplace. A small snug has views of the bustling old street outside. Q (Foregate St) ♣

Chestnut

17 Lansdowne Road, WR1 1SS (off The Tything)
3-11; 12-midnight Fri & Sat; 12-11 Sun 07773 066192
Thwaites Wainwright; Wye Valley HPA; 2 changing beers
Friendly back-street local, full of character, with two rooms decorated with an eclectic mix of art, a vinyl music player, a selection of books available to borrow, plus a pulpit which is used on occasion. Live music plays every weekend, open mic night is every other Thursday and a quiz is held once a month. Steak night is Wednesday, Thursday is curry night, breakfast is served Saturday 10am-1pm and

roasts Sunday until 4pm. Barbecues are hosted in summer. The TV is only in use on big match nights. ❀◑⇌(Foregate St)♣🍎📶

Dragon Inn

51 The Tything, WR1 1JT (on A449, 300yds N of Foregate St station)
⏲ 4.30 (12 Fri & Sat)-11; 1-4, 7-10.30 Sun ☎ (01905) 25845
🌐 dragoninn-worcester.com
Changing beers (often Beowulf, Little Ale Cart, Mighty Oak) Ⓗ
Georgian building on the edge of the city centre, offering an array of six pumps serving ever-changing beers biased towards Yorkshire including the Little Ale Cart brewery in Sheffield, and often something from Mighty Oak. The hand-pulled draught cider is Thatchers Cheddar Valley. Bottle-conditioned Belgian beers are also stocked. There is a large covered seating area out the back. Regular themed beer and food nights are held on Thursdays, monthly quiz nights on Tuesdays. Good-value lunchtime meals are available Friday-Sunday. Well-behaved dogs are welcome.
Q⛑❀⇌(Foregate St)♣🍎🚌🐾

Firefly Ⓛ

54 Lowesmoor, WR1 2SE
⏲ 3 (12 Sat & Sun)-11 winter; 12-midnight (1am Thu & Fri); 11-2am Sat; 12-11 Sun summer ☎ (01905) 616996
Changing beers Ⓗ
Offering period comfort in a regenerated part of the industrial city, the old vinegar works manager's Georgian residence is now a delightful bar with its own on-site microbrewery (brewing Oct-Mar). There are four handpulls for beer, two for cider. The interior has soft furnishings, subtle lighting and an open fire. Set over three floors, downstairs is a cosy snug with bench sofas. The upstairs bar opens at weekends for live music. There is a paved partially covered beer garden. Beer festivals are held throughout the year. ❀◑⇌(Foregate St)🍎🚌

King Charles II

29 New Street, WR1 2DP
⏲ 11.30-11 (11.30 Fri & Sat) ☎ (01905) 726100
🌐 thekingcharleshouse.com
Craddock's Saxon Gold, Crazy Sheep, Goat Herder Stout, Troll; 4 changing beers Ⓗ
A historically important and listed Tudor black and white building featuring a range of beers from Craddock's, Two Thirsty Brewers and Bridgnorth. Barbourne cider on the pumps is occasionally supplemented with its perry. Speciality pies feature large on the menu. Be sure to check out the rollercoaster ride on the first floor and the skeleton in the oubliette. King Charles II escaped from here after the second Battle of Worcester, but the beer range was not so good then.
Q◐◑⇌(Foregate St)♣🍎🚌🐾📶

Paul Pry ★

6 The Butts, WR1 3PA
⏲ closed Mon; 12-7 (11 Thu-Sat); 7-10.30 Sun
☎ (01905) 729290 🌐 thepaulpry.wordpress.com
3 changing beers (sourced regionally) Ⓗ
An old town-centre market tavern with a well-preserved listed interior. The main bar has a splendid ornate bar-back with mahogany and etched glass to the fore. The back room is an airy homage to Victoriana. The tiled passageway has a couple of steps leading to the toilets and yet more tilework. Local Worcester breweries and Little Ale Cart from Sheffield regularly feature as guest beers. Close to the bus station and library complex.
◐⇌(Foregate St)🍎🚌🐾

Plough Ⓛ

23 Fish Street, WR1 2HN (on Deansway)
⏲ 12-11 (11.30 Fri & Sat); 12-10.30 Sun ☎ (01905) 21381
Hobsons Best Bitter; Malvern Hills Black Pear; 4 changing beers (sourced regionally; often Salopian) Ⓗ
Grade II-listed pub, near the cathedral, with a short flight of steps leading to a tiny bar with rooms leading off to either side. The beers come from breweries in Worcestershire, surrounding counties and occasionally from further afield. Draught cider and perry are from Barbourne in the city. There is also an ever-changing range of whiskies for the connoisseur. Outside is a small patio area. Rolls are available at weekends and when cricket is on.
⛑❀⇌(Foregate St)♣🍎🚌🐾

Postal Order

18 Foregate Street, WR1 1DN
⏲ 8am-midnight (1am Fri & Sat) ☎ (01905) 22373
Greene King Abbot; Ruddles Best Bitter; changing beers (sourced nationally; often Pope's) Ⓗ
A classic Wetherspoon pub created from the old Worcester telephone exchange. The Postal Order has one of the largest real ale sales in Wetherspoon's West Midlands region and a wide range of beers is served. Mini festivals often showcase ales from local breweries, and regular beer festivals are held throughout the year. Westons traditional cider is always stocked. Good-value food is served daily 8am-10pm (alcohol from 9am). The volume on the TV may be turned up for important games. Q⛑◐◑♿⇌(Foregate St)🍎🚌📶

Winning Post

Pope Iron Road, WR1 3HB
⏲ 12-midnight (10.30 Sun) ☎ (01905) 21178
Cannon Royall Arrowhead Bitter; Winning Post Ken Porter, Kevin Tully, Tick Tack Tommy Moore, John Mason Ⓗ
A cosy back-street single-room pub to the north of the city centre close to the racecourse, but at the opposite end to the winning post. The pub's own brewery is across the road. TV sport features large, but a bookshelf offers a good read in a quiet corner. Lunchtime snacks are available. There is a heated area outside for smokers. ◐♿♣🚌

Sick note

Me and some of the fellers decided to cook up a batch of home brew and the instructions on the yeast said Add one packet and wait three days so we added three packets and waited one day. Well, we drank all that brew right up the very next day. Never been sicker in my life.
American home brewer during Prohibition

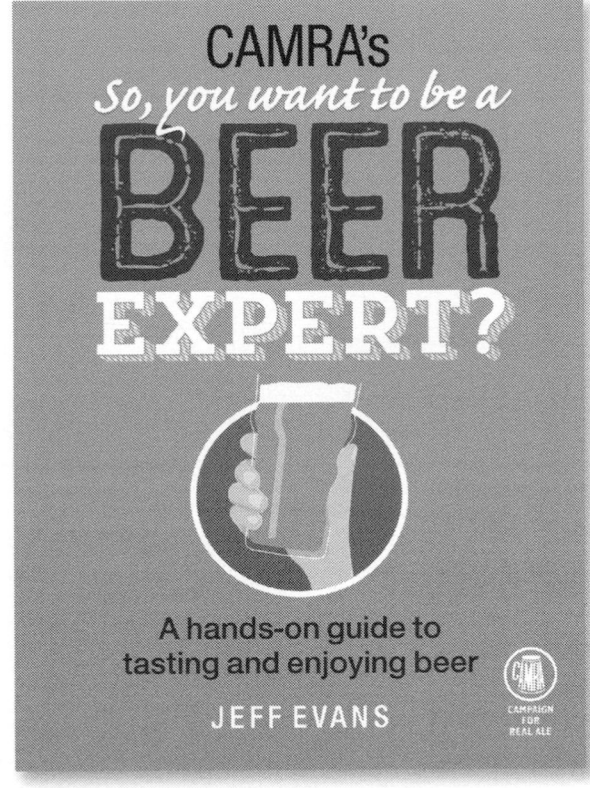

EAST YORKSHIRE

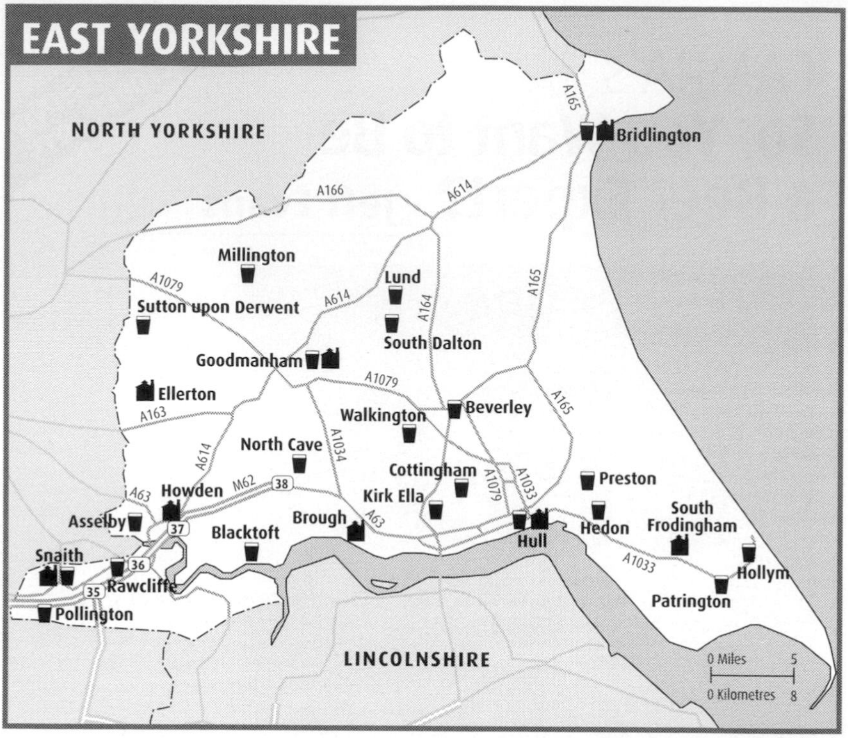

YORKSHIRE (EAST)

Asselby

Whelans Ⓛ
Main Street, DN14 7HE
🕒 6-10; 5-11 Wed-Fri; 12-11 Sat & Sun ☎ (01757) 630409
🌐 whelansofasselby.co.uk
John Smith's Bitter; Timothy Taylor Landlord; 4 changing beers (sourced locally; often All Hallows) Ⓗ
Traditional family-friendly country pub serving four rotating guest beers, mainly from local breweries and often including an ale brewed for the pub by All Hallows. An annual beer festival is held in summer with live music. The pub is actively involved in hosting village community events. Live music, darts matches and quizzes feature on a regular basis. Good-quality food includes local game and produce. 🕿🏠◖♦P♣

Beverley

Chequers Micropub Ⓨ Ⓛ
15 Swaby's Yard, Dyer Lane, HU17 9BZ
🕒 closed Mon; 12-11 (10 Tue & Wed); 12-10
Sun ☎ 07964 227906 🌐 chequersmicropub.co.uk
5 changing beers (sourced regionally; often Atom, Brass Castle, Great Newsome) Ⓗ
Yorkshire's first micropub, in a former baker's and near the bus station. Beers come from local, regional and national microbreweries. Six ciders/perries are sold. The cellar is above the bar. Typically for a micropub, no lager, keg beer or spirits are sold. There is no TV or loud music, making it a place for real conversation, like pubs used to be. Local CAMRA Town Pub of the Year and Cider Pub of the Year 2014. Q🏠≠◖🚽🚍♣

Dog & Duck
33 Ladygate, HU17 8BH (off Saturday Market adjacent to Browns store)
🕒 11-4, 7-midnight; 11-midnight Fri & Sat; 11.30-3, 7-11 Sun
☎ (01482) 862419 🌐 bedandbreakfastbeverley.com
Black Sheep Best Bitter; Copper Dragon Golden Pippin; John Smith's Bitter; Timothy Taylor Golden Best; 2 changing beers (sourced nationally) Ⓗ
Just off the main Saturday Market and close to Beverley bus station, the pub was built in the 1930s and has been run by the same family for over 40 years. It comprises three areas: a bar with a period brick fireplace and bentwood seating, a front lounge and a rear snug. The good-value home-cooked lunches are popular. Guest accommodation is in six purpose-built self-contained rooms to the rear. Lined glasses are used only for Black Sheep beer. 🕿◖≠♠●🚽🚍

Green Dragon
51 Saturday Market, HU17 8AA
🕒 8am-11 (midnight Fri & Sat) ☎ (01482) 889801
🌐 thegreendragonbeverley.co.uk
Greene King IPA; 7 changing beers (sourced nationally; often Adnams, Kirkstall, St Austell) Ⓗ

REAL ALE BREWERIES

All Hallows Goodmanham
Atom Hull
Bird Brain Howden
Bridlington Bridlington
Crystalbrew Brough
Great Newsome South Frodingham
Half Moon Ellerton
Old Mill Snaith
Yorkshire Hull

Brewers' Tudor-fronted inn renamed the Green Dragon in 1765. The entrance is down a side passageway leading to a heated courtyard. The main bar at the rear is long and narrow while the front bar retains some wood panelling and overlooks the market square. Breakfasts are served from 8am (alcohol from 10am) and the extensive menu is available until 10pm. Tuesday and Wednesday are quiz nights.

Tiger Inn

Lairgate, HU17 8JG (near Memorial Hall)
closed Mon; 11-11 (midnight Fri & Sat); 12-11 Sun
(01482) 869040 tiger-inn-beverley.co.uk
Moorhouse's Blond Witch; Timothy Taylor Landlord; Wychwood Hobgoblin; 2 changing beers (sourced regionally)
Attractive 18th-century building given a new front in 1930s Brewers' Tudor style by the now defunct Darley & Co, which once owned several pubs in Beverley. It has a multi-roomed interior with a public bar, snug, dining room/lounge and function room. Many local clubs and societies meet here and folk music sessions are held on Friday evenings. The large car park to the rear was once stables and outbuildings. Meals are served lunchtimes and evenings, with a carvery on Sundays. QP

Woolpack

37 Westwood Road, HU17 8EN (W of Saturday Market via Newbegin)
4.30-10.30 Mon; 12-3, 4.30-11; 12-11 Sat & Sun
(01482) 867095
Banks's Sunbeam; Jennings Bitter, Cocker Hoop, Sneck Lifter; Marston's EPA; Wychwood Hobgoblin; 1 changing beer (sourced nationally)
Located in a Victorian residential street west of the town centre, the Woolpack started life as a pair of cottages and became a public house around 1831, later developing its own brewhouse and stables, and is now owned by Marston's. It retains a quarry-tiled snug from that period and an open fire in winter, and there is a more recent extension to the rear. Meals are served lunchtimes and evenings, 12-7pm on Sundays. Quiz night is Thursday. Q

Blacktoft

Hope & Anchor

Blacktoft Lane, DN14 7YW (3½ miles S of Gilberdyke rail station, follow signs to Blacktoft) SE842242
12 (5 Mon)-11; 12-10.30 Sun (01430) 440441
Marston's Pedigree; Morland Old Speckled Hen; 2 changing beers (sourced regionally; often Copper Dragon, Great Newsome, York)
Thriving village local in a superb location on the bank of the River Ouse – the RSPB's Blacktoft Sands bird sanctuary is visible on the far bank. Laurel and Hardy memorabilia is prominent, as is a collection of jugs suspended from wooden beams. The conservatory offers fine river views. Popular home-cooked meals are served lunchtimes and evenings during the week (no food Mon) and all day at weekends, with booking for Sundays recommended. A mild is often on sale.
P

Bridlington

Marine Bar

North Marine Drive, YO15 2LS (1 mile NE of centre)
11-11 (11.30 Sat) (01262) 675347 marinebar.net
John Smith's Bitter; Timothy Taylor Landlord; Wold Top Bitter; 2 changing beers (sourced regionally; often Daleside, Rooster's)
Large open-plan bar, part of the Expanse Hotel, on the seafront with spectacular sea views from outdoor seating, attracting a good mix of regulars and welcoming to the influx of summer visitors. Home-cooked food, including vegetarian options, is served daily. Twice-weekly quizzes and live music nights are popular. Two regional guest beers are on sale. Ample car parking is available on the promenade and the land train is routed close by during the summer season. A Guide regular.
P(504)

Telegraph Inn

110 Quay Road, YO16 4JB (10 mins from rail station)
12-midnight (1am Fri & Sat) (01262) 674592
Wold Top Anglers Reward; 4 changing beers (sourced regionally; often Acorn, Bradfield, Rudgate)
Welcoming, traditional, family-run free house with an open-plan interior warmed by logburners. Home to Bridlington's only microbrewery, it serves four ales from across Yorkshire, occasionally including Theakston's Old Peculier from the wood. A spacious walled beer garden incorporating the brewery building and encompassing a covered area with a chiminea gives an alfresco feeling. Live music is a feature on Saturdays, and folk music on Tuesdays. Pool and darts teams and a scooter club are hosted throughout the week. A former local CAMRA Town Pub of the Year. P

Cottingham

King William IV

152 Hallgate, HU16 4DB
11-11 (midnight Fri & Sat); 12-11 Sun (01482) 875996
kingwilliamcottingham.co.uk
Banks's Sunbeam; Jennings Cumberland Ale; Marston's Pedigree; 4 changing beers (sourced nationally)
Village centre pub with a quiet, traditional bar and lounge. The pub hosts weekly quiz nights and an annual music festival. At the rear a former brewery has been converted into a function room offering live music and special events. The beer garden and side courtyard have covered smoking areas. Excellent-value meals are served in large and small portions. Up to four guest beers and a cider are on handpump. Local CAMRA Village Pub of the Year 2014. Q(103,105,115)

Railway

11 Thwaite Street, HU16 4QT
12-midnight (12.30am Fri & Sat) (01482) 622980
Black Sheep Best Bitter; Theakston Old Peculier; Timothy Taylor Landlord; 4 changing beers (sourced nationally; often Purity, Robinsons, Wadworth)
This large detached pub has benefited from a tasteful refurbishment. There are deep leather seats in the comfortable lounge where good-value food is served and where bands play at weekends. The separate bar has live sport on TV and is a base for darts, pool and football teams. This is a child-friendly pub which is popular with diners. Four guest beers and two ciders are usually on sale.
P

Goodmanham

Goodmanham Arms Ⓛ

Main Street, YO43 3JA

✪ 11-midnight; 11-11 Sun ☎ (01430) 873849
⊕ goodmanhamarms.co.uk

All Hallows Peg Fyfe Dark Mild, Ragged Robyn; Black Dog Whitby Abbey Ale; Hambleton Stallion; Theakston Best Bitter; house beer (by All Hallows); 3 changing beers (sourced regionally; often Great Newsome, Leeds, Yorkshire) ⓗ

Close to the Wolds Way footpath, with gardens front and back, this brewpub makes an ideal resting place for walkers. You can sample eight ales including three from the on-site brewery and a cider. The two atmospherically lit rooms are separated by a central corridor, with the bar serving both. A large real fire complete with a cooking range and reclaimed farm tools create the ambience of a farmhouse kitchen. Local CAMRA Village Pub of the Year runner-up. Q☼🅮🕭🅮●P🐾

Hedon

Haven Arms Ⓛ

Sheriff Highway, HU12 8HH

✪ 9am-11 (midnight Fri & Sat) ☎ (01482) 897695
⊕ havenarms.co.uk

5 changing beers (sourced regionally; often Great Newsome, Hardys & Hansons, Rudgate) ⓗ

Situated in the historic Haven area of town, once the largest port on the Humber, the pub offers three guest beers, one usually dark and one from a local microbrewery. One real cider increases to two or three from April to September. Reasonably priced pub food, freshly prepared from local ingredients, is served all day from 9am. The venue is licensed for weddings – the large bar, dining room and permanent marquee can accommodate all customer requirements. ☼🅮🕭🅮🍴●P🎪🐾🛈

Shakespeare Inn Ⓛ

9 Baxtergate, HU12 8JN

✪ 12-11 (11.30 Fri & Sat); 12-10.30 Sun ☎ 07547 141412

Tetley Bitter; Timothy Taylor Landlord; 3 changing beers (sourced regionally; often Great Newsome) ⓗ

A 300-year-old pub in the centre of historic Hedon largely unaltered for the past 50 years, featuring original Darley's wall sconces. It is popular with all ages, which makes for a varying clientele. Rugby League memorabilia, reflecting the landlord's previous career, adorn the walls, and a friendly atmosphere encourages the art of conversation. The food menu features freshly cooked local produce with popular changing specials. There are three guest beers, one usually from a local brewery. ☼🅮🕭🅮🍴P🎪🛈

Hollym

Plough Inn Ⓛ

Northside Road, HU19 2RS

✪ closed Mon; 5 (7 winter)-midnight Tue & Wed; 3 (5 winter)-midnight Thu & Fri; 12-midnight Sat; 12-11 Sun
☎ (01964) 612049 ⊕ theploughinnhollym.co.uk

Greene King IPA; 4 changing beers (sourced nationally; often Great Newsome, Greene King) ⓗ

Family-run free house, parts of which date from the 17th-century – note the wattle and daub front wall in the public bar – offering five real ales. Both bars have coal fires bringing warmth and cheer during the winter. Primarily a locals' pub, a base for Withernsea rugby club, Withernsea Harriers and

Withernsea Pigeon Flyers, it is a haven for discerning holiday-makers in the summer. Local CAMRA Village Pub of the Year for 2013. Open bank holiday Mondays.

Q☼🅮🕭🅮🅰♣P🎪🚌(75,76,77)🐾🛈

Hull

Admiral of the Humber

1 Anlaby Road, HU1 2NT

✪ 8am-midnight (1am Fri & Sat) ☎ (01482) 381850

Greene King Abbot; Ruddles Best Bitter; 6 changing beers (sourced nationally) ⓗ

A former paint and wallpaper shop on a site previously connnected to Hull's seafaring past. Now a large single room, mostly on one level, the building is ideally suited to those finding steps or stairs a problem. The pub prides itself on being part of the community, with sport featuring, and is open to away fans when Hull City are at home. A designated area is set aside for diners during the day, and children are welcome until 6pm. Alcohol is served from 9am. ☼🅮🕭🅮🍴≠♣●🚌🛈

Hop & Vine Ⓛ

24 Albion Street, HU1 3TG (250yds from Hull New Theatre)

✪ closed Mon; 11 (4 Tue)-11; 11-11.30 Fri & Sat; closed Sun ☎ 07500 543199 ⊕ hopandvinehull.co.uk

3 changing beers (sourced nationally; often Abbeydale, Acorn, Cottage) ⓗ

Atmospheric basement-bar free house serving three changing guest beers from independent breweries, plus rare farmhouse cider and perry such as local Moorlands Farm Cyder. Oversized lined glasses are used. A select range of Belgian bottled beers plus draught Pilsner Urquell are on the bar. Freshly prepared food including home-baked bread is served until 9pm. Shove-ha'penny, cribbage and shut the box games are available. A former CAMRA National Cider Pub of the Year and four times Yorkshire regional winner. Closed between Christmas and New Year.
🅮≠♣●P🎪🐾🛈

Larkin's Ⓛ

48-52 Newland Avenue, HU5 3AE (near jct of De Grey St)

✪ 12-11.30 (midnight Fri & Sat) ☎ (01482) 440991
⊕ larkinsbar.co.uk

Tom Wood's Best Bitter; Wold Top Wold Gold; 2 changing beers (sourced regionally; often Abbeydale, Cottage, Crystalbrew) ⓗ

Named after poet Philip Larkin, this one-roomed café-bar, previously two shops, can be partitioned for small private functions. A good selection of home-cooked food is served every day, with an excellent Sunday carvery. There is a paved drinking area to the front and an enclosed garden at the rear. Beer festivals, with live music from local acts, are held, usually over bank holiday weekends, in the adjacent car sales yard. ☼🅮🕭🅮🅰🚌

Lion & Key Ⓛ

48 High Street, Old Town, HU1 1QE

✪ 11.30-11 ☎ (01482) 225212

14 changing beers (sourced nationally; often Abbeydale, Milestone, Wentworth) ⓗ

There has been a pub here since 1817 and it reverted to its original name a few years ago. Up to 14 real ales and three ciders are on tap, mostly from microbreweries, and sampling is encouraged. Bottled beers from around the world complement the range. Delicious freshly cooked food made from locally sourced ingredients, especially fish, is served lunchtimes daily and evenings weekdays until 7pm; well-behaved children are welcome during mealtimes. A former local CAMRA Pub of the Year.

Minerva Hotel

Nelson Street, Marina, Old Town, HU1 1XE

11.30-11.30 ☎ (01482) 210025 minerva-hull.co.uk

Tetley Bitter; 5 changing beers (sourced regionally; often Atom, Brass Castle, Yorkshire) H

Overlooking the Humber estuary and Victoria Pier, this famous pub, built in 1829, is a great place to watch the ships go by. Photos and memorabilia are a reminder of the area's maritime past. The central bar serves various rooms including a tiny three-seat snug. The former brewhouse is now home to Hull's smallest theatre (with 40 seats) and is available for functions. The pub is connected to The Deep aquarium by a footbridge at the mouth of the River Hull. (17)

New Adelphi Club

89 De Grey Street, HU5 2RU

8am-11 ☎ (01482) 348216 theadelphi.com

Oakham Citra; 3 changing beers (sourced locally; often Great Newsome) H

Hull's justifiably famous music venue has been the launch pad to many an illustrious career, and has hosted a veritable Who's Who of popular music since opening in 1984. The main music room is complemented by a small front bar that accommodates a pool table and features a cut-off bus front as the bar counter. Access to the small bar is free at all times and no membership restrictions apply. Benefit from a £1 reduction on ale when no musicians are booked. P

Olde Black Boy ★

150 High Street, Old Town, HU1 1PS

12.30 (5 Mon-Wed)-11.30 ☎ (01482) 326516

yeoldeblackboy.weebly.com/index.html

6 changing beers (sourced nationally; often Timothy Taylor, Wychwood) H

Historic pub, licensed since 1729 but which has also been, variously, a wine merchant and a tobacco dealer, traditionally represented by an Indian chief or black boy; note the carved boy's head above the fireplace. First Mondays of the month are for folk music and anyone is welcome to play. Guest beers vary widely and Westons Old Rosie cider is on sale. Bar snacks are now served at all times and an upstairs room may also be available. Q

Olde White Harte ★

25 Silver Street, Old Town, HU1 1JG

11-midnight (1am Fri & Sat); 12-midnight Sun

☎ (01482) 326363 yeoldewhiteharte.com

Caledonian Deuchars IPA, Flying Scotsman; Theakston Best Bitter, Old Peculier; 2 changing beers (sourced nationally) H

Historic pub in a 17th-century merchant's house, with strong connections to the English Civil War. The existing ground floor interior dates back to a major refurbishment in 1881, which was an idealised re-creation of an old English inn, complete with massive inglenook fireplaces and stained-glass windows. The first floor has restaurant facilities, and the Plotting Parlour is available for meetings and functions. There is also a courtyard with heating providing an all-weather outdoor drinking area.

Pave L

16-20 Princes Avenue, HU5 3QA (in the Avenues area)

11-11 (11.30 Fri & Sat) ☎ (01482) 333181

pavebar.co.uk

Tetley Gold; Theakston Best Bitter; 3 changing beers (sourced regionally; often Brass Castle, Saltaire, Yorkshire) H

A continental-style bar that attracts a diverse range of customers. As well as the regular ales there are three guests, usually sourced regionally, and a varied range of European draught and bottled beers. Home-cooked food including vegetarian options is served daily. Free live music features on Tuesday evenings and Sunday afternoons, but the bar closes to the public when ticketed music and comedy nights are held. Westons Rosie's Pig cider is sold.

Sailmakers Arms

Chandlers Court, 159 High Street, HU1 1NQ

12-11 (midnight Wed; 11.30 Thu); 11.30-midnight Fri & Sat; 11.30-11 Sun ☎ (01482) 227437

thesailmakersarms.com

Kelham Island Easy Rider; Sharp's Doom Bar; 4 changing beers (sourced nationally; often Copper Dragon, Moorhouse's) H

A 1980s conversion of a former ship's chandler, set back off a secluded yard at the centre of Hull's historic Old Town, featuring bare brickwork and dark wood fittings. All the food is prepared on-site and locally sourced. A popular acoustic music session takes place every Sunday afternoon, and an open mic night on Wednesdays. Set in the Museum Quarter, the pub is busy during the Easter and Christmas markets and on Heritage weekends.

St John's Hotel

10 Queens Road, HU5 2PY

12-11 (midnight Fri & Sat); 12-11.30 Sun

☎ (01482) 341013

Marston's EPA, Old Empire; 2 changing beers (sourced nationally) H

A Grade II-listed classic street-corner venue boasting one of the least-altered interiors in the city. The welcoming front-corner public bar complements a quiet back room, with original bench seating. A more basic larger room accommodates the pool table and is home to the beer festival bar three times a year. A real community local, it has two darts teams, a football team, and the Oddfellows cricket league which hosts quiz nights in the winter. Tuesday is live music night. Q P

Three John Scotts

Lowgate, Old Town, HU1 1AA

8am-midnight (1am Fri & Sat) ☎ (01482) 381910

Greene King Abbot; Ruddles Best Bitter; 5 changing beers (sourced nationally; often Adnams, Fuller's) H

Originally an Edwardian post office, this open-plan Wetherspoon features modern decor and works of art. The name derives from three successive 19th-century vicars of St Mary's church opposite. The pub has established a broad customer base appealing to a mixed clientele. Up to seven real ales and three real ciders are on sale. Children are welcome up to 7pm. There is a large rear courtyard seating area which is a great suntrap in the summer.

Walters L

21 Scale Lane, Old Town, HU1 1LF

12-11 (11.30 Fri & Sat) ☎ (01482) 224004
8 changing beers (sourced regionally; often Abbeydale, Atom, Saltaire)
The pub's name recalls an 1820s barber shop on the same premises. It is a free house under new ownership since July 2014, and attracts a broad cross-section of drinkers, offering up to eight real ales and two real ciders. Many new microbreweries have been given their Hull debut here, and established local breweries are supported as all beers are from Yorkshire. A selection of continental lagers is offered and take-out containers for cask ales are available.

Whalebone

165 Wincolmlee, HU2 0PA
12-midnight (11 Tue & Wed) ☎ 07506 868461
Copper Dragon Best Bitter; Timothy Taylor Landlord; 5 changing beers (sourced regionally; often Atom, Clark's, Ossett)
A rare gem of a pub in an old industrial area associated with the Greenland whaling trade. Continuously licensed since 1791, the current building dates from 1890 though much altered internally. A free house since 2002, it serves up to five guest beers plus Broadoak Kingston Black and Premium Perry. The walls are adorned with many photos of old Hull pubs and the city's football and Rugby League teams. CAMRA branch City Pub of the Year 2014.

Wm Hawkes

32 Scale Lane, HU1 1LF
12-11 ☎ (01482) 224004 wmhawkes.co.uk
8 changing beers (often Abbeydale, Milestone, Wentworth)
Named after a gunsmith who occupied the premises in the 19th century, this hostelry opened in 2012, although it feels like it has been operating for decades. This is testament to the conversion carried out by the licensees, using fittings reclaimed from other pubs, culminating in it being highly commended in the Pub Design Awards 2013. Eight real ales from a variety of national and local breweries and a changing real cider are on the bar. No keg beer or lager. **Q**

Kirk Ella

Beech Tree

South Ella Way, HU10 7LY
11-11 (midnight Thu-Sat) ☎ (01482) 654350
Black Sheep Best Bitter; Brakspear Bitter; Kirkstall Three Swords; 5 changing beers
Open-plan pub on the western outskirts of Hull, owned by a pub company committed to cask ale. Up to eight real ales are sold, including at least one dark beer, with try-before-you-buy encouraged. Food is served 12-10pm every day, and Monday and Wednesday are quiz nights. Families with children are welcome throughout and a real fire makes for a hospitable winter feel. Buses stop close to the pub until early evening, and later only a 10-minute walk away. **P**(154,180)

Lund

Wellington Inn

19 The Green, YO25 9TE
12-3, 6.30 (7 Mon)-11; 12-10.30 Sun ☎ (01377) 217192
thewellingtoninn.co.uk
John Smith's Bitter; Theakston Best Bitter; Timothy Taylor Landlord; 1 changing beer (sourced locally; often Great Newsome, Hop Studio, Wold Top)
Enjoying a prime location on the green in this award-winning Wolds village, most of the pub's trade comes from the local farming community. Renovated by the present licensee, it features stone-flagged floors, beamed ceilings and three real fires. The multi-roomed interior includes a games room and a candlelit restaurant serving evening meals Tuesday-Saturday. Good food can also be enjoyed at lunchtime from the bar menu and specials board. Guest beers are usually sourced locally. **P**

Millington

Gait

Main Street, YO42 1TX
closed Mon; 12-3 (not Tue-Thu), 6-11; 12-4, 6-11 Sat
☎ (01759) 302045 gait-inn-millington.co.uk
Black Sheep Best Bitter; Tetley Bitter; Theakston Best Bitter; 2 changing beers (sourced locally; often Great Heck, Half Moon, Wold Top)
A pretty pub in the Yorkshire Wolds, three miles from Pocklington, popular with locals, farmers and walkers. The slightly quirky single bar has mismatched tables, knick-knacks on the walls and a wonderful old Yorkshire map on the ceiling. A no-nonsense community pub that is well worth a visit, it hosts an annual beer festival with up to 35 beers. Two guest beers include at least one from a local microbrewery. **P**

North Cave

White Hart

20 Westgate, HU15 2NJ
4-11 (midnight Fri & Sat) ☎ (01430) 470940
whitehartnorthcave.co.uk
3 changing beers (sourced regionally; often Great Newsome, Wold Top)
This welcoming, traditional village pub is a credit to the community it serves. There is a long bar to the side and rear while the quieter front bar has comfortable seating and is where you will find the three real ales. Real fires are lit during winter months, providing further home-from-home comfort. Walkers and dogs are welcome. Local brewery Great Newsome supplies a house beer, White Hart 1776. A popular stopping-off point for visitors to the Beverley races. **Q** **P**(155)

Patrington

Station Hotel

Station Road, HU12 0NE
12-11 ☎ (01964) 630262 stationhotelpatrington.co.uk
Black Sheep Best Bitter; house beer (by Great Newsome); 1 changing beer (sourced regionally)
A family-owned free house on the western edge of the village, this hotel used to service passengers on the Hull to Withernsea railway prior to its closure in the 1960s. The Anglo-German owners have completely refurbished the old building in a welcoming modern-rustic style, and have added a snug and family room. The hotel is renowned locally for the quality of its food, served daily from noon, with steak night on Thursday
P(76)

Pollington

King's Head

Main Street, DN14 0DN

5-11 (midnight Fri); 12-midnight Sat ☎ (01405) 861507

Great Heck Navigator; Tetley Bitter; 2 changing beers (sourced locally; often Great Heck)

Adam and Diane offer a warm welcome at this excellent village pub situated conveniently for the Aire and Calder canal and Transpennine Trail. Popular with regulars, walkers and visitors, the pub is open plan, with a comfortable lounge area featuring a wood-burning stove and another area with a pool table and darts. Quiz night is Friday. Adam is in charge in the kitchen, producing generous portions of excellent traditional pub food. B&B accommodation is available and there is ample parking. Q❀♣P

Preston

Nag's Head

1 Sproatley Road, HU12 8TT

12-3, 5-11; 12-11 Fri-Sun summer ☎ (01482) 897517

nagsheadpreston.co.uk

Morland Old Golden Hen; Timothy Taylor Landlord; 1 changing beer (sourced regionally)

A 400-year-old village pub sympathetically extended over the last 35 years by its current owners. The main lounge bar, separate public bar with a dartboard and comfortable conservatory make this a pub for all. Outside is a large garden with a children's play area and plentiful seating for the summer months. It is community focused, with a monthly charity quiz night and regular charity fun days, and is a base for local darts and domino teams. Q❀♣P (277)

Rawcliffe

Jemmy Hirst at the Rose & Crown

26 Riverside, DN14 8RN (from village green turn N on Chapel Lane)

6 (5 Fri)-midnight; 12-midnight Sat & Sun

☎ (01405) 831038 jemmyhirst.freeservers.com

Timothy Taylor Landlord; 4 changing beers (sourced locally; often Acorn, Hop Studio, York)

An outstanding free house that locals say is the heart of the village. It is well known regionally and has won numerous CAMRA branch awards, including Pub of the Year seven times. There is always a warm, friendly welcome from the owners, locals and Bruno the dog. Book-lined walls and an open fire provide a haven on a cold winter's day. You can sample five real ales and a traditional cider here. The patio and river bank beckon in warmer weather. Q❀♣P (88,400)

Snaith

Brewers Arms Hotel

10 Pontefract Road, DN14 9JS

12-midnight; 12-9.30 Sun ☎ (01405) 862404

Old Mill Traditional Bitter, Blonde Bombshell; 1 changing beer (sourced locally; often Old Mill)

Chris and Chrissie have welcomed real ale drinkers to the Old Mill Brewery's tap and flagship establishment for nearly eight years. A fine example of a large village pub, there are four themed bar areas including a large dining room, three fires, a well (containing a skeleton) and fishing rods. Three real ales are always on handpump – four over most of the summer – plus draught cider. Fresh seafood is a speciality on Fridays and Saturdays. Q❀♣P

South Dalton

Pipe & Glass

West End, HU17 7PN

closed Mon; 12-11; 12-10.30 Sun ☎ (01430) 810246

pipeandglass.co.uk

Black Sheep Best Bitter; house beer (by Great Yorkshire); 3 changing beers (sourced regionally; often John Smith's, Wold Top, York)

Delightful hostelry standing at the site of the original gatehouse to Dalton Hall, featuring exposed beams and custom-made furniture. The owner and chef holds a Michelin star for the sixth consecutive year. Three guest ales come from around Yorkshire, and the real cider is from Moorlands Farm. Five boutique rooms, with views of Dalton Hall, are available. The pub closes for the first two weeks of January but opens on bank holiday Mondays. Q❀P (142)

Sutton upon Derwent

St Vincent Arms

Main Street, YO41 4BN

12-3, 6-11 (10.30 Sun) ☎ (01904) 608349

stvincentarms.co.uk

Fuller's Chiswick Bitter, London Pride, ESB; Timothy Taylor Golden Best, Landlord; York Yorkshire Terrier; 2 changing beers (sourced nationally)

A winner of many York CAMRA awards, this pretty white-painted village free house on a bend in the road has been family owned and well run for many years. A long time supporter of Fuller's beers, it offers a large but consistent range. The bar, featuring a Fuller, Smith & Turner mirror, is popular with locals. Another small bar with a serving hatch leads to the dining rooms. It serves excellent food, catering for a variety of tastes. Q❀P

Walkington

Barrel Inn

35 East End, HU17 8RX

4.30-midnight; 12-1am Sat; 12-midnight Sun ☎ 07550 078833

Thwaites Wainwright, Lancaster Bomber; 3 changing beers (sourced regionally; often Great Newsome, Leeds, Wold Top)

Friendly drinkers' local in a quiet three-pub village, and one of only two Thwaites pubs in East Yorkshire. The interior comprises a front bar with a log fire and beamed ceiling and a connecting lounge, also with a log fire. There is subtle piped music throughout and a TV for sport; occasionally there is live music. Families are welcome. Up to five real ales are sold including one free of tie. A secluded cottage-style beer garden is at the rear. ❀♣ (180,61)

YORKSHIRE (NORTH)

Aldbrough St John

Stanwick

High Green, DL11 7SZ (1 mile from B6275)

closed Mon winter; 12-3, 5.30-11; 12-11 Sat; 12-9 Sun

☎ (01325) 374258 thestanwick.co.uk

NORTH YORKSHIRE

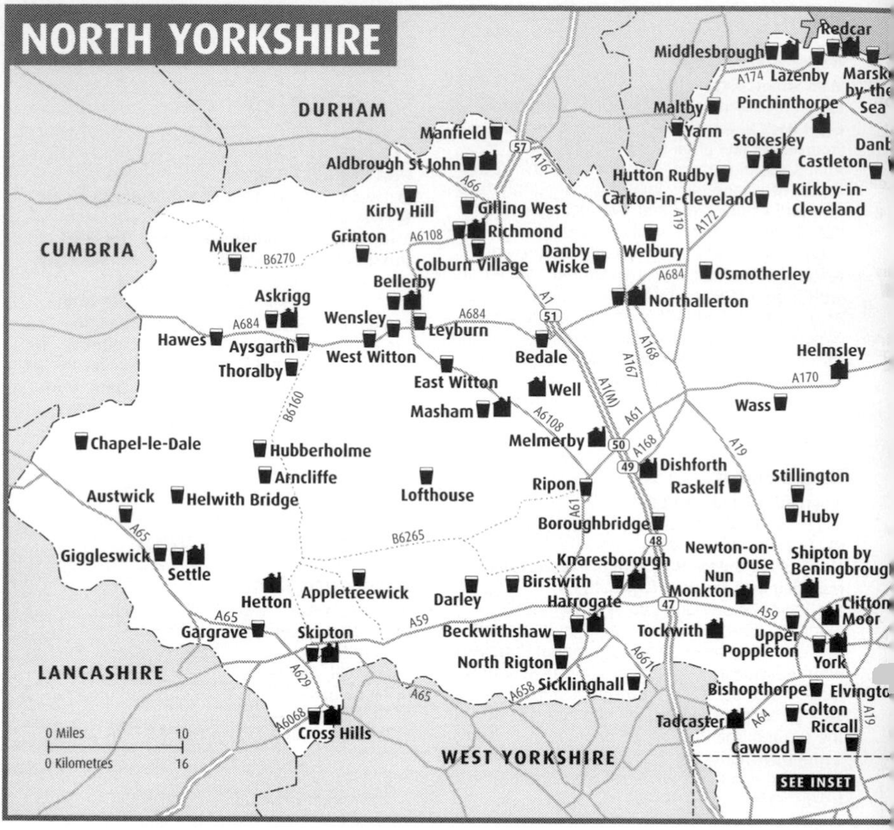

Daleside Bitter; Jarrow Rivet Catcher; 2 changing beers Ⓗ

Located in a picturesque North Yorkshire village on one of the country's largest village greens, this welcoming 19th-century inn has two bars – one for drinkers and one serving the two excellent restaurants. Locally sourced food is available every day. It is the brewery tap for the village's Mithril Ales, with one of its beers always featured. Cricket, quoits, football and darts are supported. Takeaway fish and chips are served on Wednesdays, and roast baguettes on Sundays, 2-5pm.

Q🐴❀◐◑♿P🚌(29)🐾📶

Appletreewick

Craven Arms Ⓛ

BD23 6DA

⏲ 11.30-11; 12-10.30 Sun ☎ (01756) 720270

🌐 craven-cruckbarn.co.uk

Dark Horse Hetton Pale Ale; Moorhouse's Blond Witch; Theakston Old Peculier; Thwaites Original; Wharfedale Blonde; house beer (by Dark Horse); 2 changing beers (sourced regionally; often Moorhouse's, Saltaire) Ⓗ

Dating back to 1548, this multi-roomed Dales free house has stone-flagged floors, oak beams and gas lighting. The main bar features an original Yorkshire range while the cosy taproom has ring the bull. A snug behind the bar leads to the cruck barn, with its minstrels' gallery and large open fireplace, added in 2006 and built using traditional techniques. This can be hired for private functions. Guest beers are served in the summer months and usually include a dark beer.

Q🐴❀◐◑▲♣●P🚌(74)🐾📶

Arncliffe

Falcon Inn Ⓛ

BD23 5QE

⏲ 12-3, 7-11 (closed Tue & Thu eves winter); 12-11 Fri & Sat; 12-10.30 (10 winter) Sun ☎ (01756) 770205

🌐 thefalconinn.com

Timothy Taylor Boltmaker; 1 changing beer Ⓖ

Unspoilt traditional Dales pub-cum-hotel nestled next to the village green, and the original Woolpack in Emmerdale Farm. Eschewing modern gimmickry, the last significant changes to the pub interior occurred in the 1950s. Timothy Taylor Boltmaker is served from the jug or via a recently installed handpump if you wish. A second handpump offers a changing guest beer from a local brewery. Loved by visitors from near and far, the pub is also well supported by Dales folk.

Q🐴❀🛏◐🐾📶

Askrigg

King's Arms Ⓛ

Main Street, DL8 3HQ

⏲ 11-11 (midnight Fri & Sat) ☎ (01969) 650113

🌐 kingsarmsaskrigg.co.uk

Black Sheep Best Bitter; Theakston Best Bitter; house beer (by Yorkshire Dales); 1 changing beer (sourced locally) Ⓗ

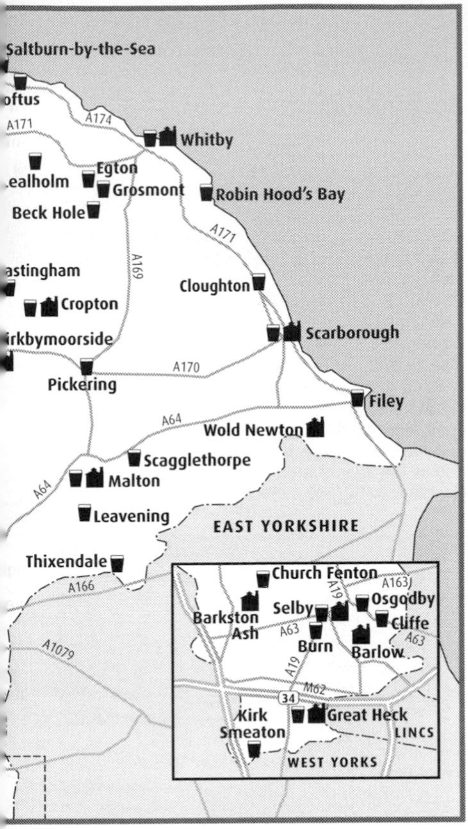

Historic multi-roomed free house of great character, which starred as the Drover's Arms in TV's All Creatures Great and Small. A painting of the local friendly society and a huge open fireplace dominate the stone-flagged bar area, with a separate dining room and restaurant, a vaulted games room to the rear and a small courtyard. No keg beer is sold and the three house beers (one regularly changing) are from the Yorkshire Dales Brewery, a few hundred yards away.
(156)

Austwick

Game Cock

LA2 8BB (on Horton road)
closed Mon; 11.30-11.30 ☎ (015242) 51226
gamecockinn.co.uk
Thwaites Nutty Black, Original, Wainwright; 1 changing beer
Most of the licensed area is a restaurant but there is a lovely little old-fashioned bar at the end of the building. Two small rooms were added to the drinking area in 2010 without spoiling it. Austwick is a quiet and un-touristy village compared with neighbouring Clapham, but there are usually quite a few hikers alongside the locals in the bar. The smoking area is heated and covered. There are weekly specials nights for food – French on Wednesday, steak on Thursday, and fish and chips on Friday. **Q** P (581)

Aysgarth

George & Dragon

DL8 3AD (on main A684 between Hawes and Leyburn)
11-midnight ☎ (01969) 663358
georgeanddragonaysgarth.co.uk
Black Sheep Best Bitter; Theakston Best Bitter; house beer (by Yorkshire Dales); 1 changing beer (sourced regionally)
Situated less than a mile from the famous Aysgarth Falls on the River Ure, this 17th-century coaching inn is set amid stunning Dales countryside. It caters for drinkers in its cosy wood-panelled bar, serving up to five real ales usually including two from the local Yorkshire Dales Brewery. For diners there is a separate restaurant, and en-suite accommodation is offered. An outside drinking area has large thatched umbrellas and great views.
Q P (156)

Beck Hole

Birch Hall Inn ★

YO22 5LE (750yds N of Goathland) NZ821022
11-11 ☎ (01947) 896245
Black Sheep Best Bitter; 2 changing beers
Unspoilt, family-run rural gem, resting in a hamlet of nine cottages, run by the licensee, an accomplished fine artist, for 35 years. A winner of multiple CAMRA awards, including branch 2014 Pub of the Year, it comprises the Big Bar and the Small Bar, sandwiching a sweet shop. Superb outdoor drinking facilities overlook the Murk Esk. The house beer, Beckwatter, is brewed by North Yorkshire. Sandwiches, pies, beer cake and sweets are always available. Opening hours vary during the winter months. **Q**

Beckwithshaw

Smith's Arms

Church Row, HG3 1QW
11-11; 12-10 Sun ☎ (01423) 504871
Black Sheep Best Bitter; Tetley Bitter; 2 changing beers (sourced regionally; often Copper Dragon, Rooster's)
A Chef & Brewer restaurant-cum-pub in an 18th-century inn that was formerly a blacksmith's forge. Set in a quiet hamlet to the south-west of Harrogate, the pub comprises an L-shaped bar area and a separate restaurant. An excellent menu with many seasonal dishes is available throughout the day in both the restaurant and bar. The five handpumps serve two permanent beers and three widely sourced guest ales. **Q** P

Bedale

Green Dragon

16 Market Place, DL8 1EQ
11.30-midnight (1am Fri & Sat); 11.30-11 Sun
☎ (01677) 425246 thedragonbedale.co.uk
Ringwood Best Bitter, Boondoggle; 2 changing beers (sourced nationally; often Marston's, Wychwood)
A comfortable bar on the cobbled High Street of the gateway to the Dales. Up to four beers are on offer, all from the Marston's group. There is live music every Friday night in the front bar, while the quieter lounge is in the conservatory to the rear. The nearby Wensleydale Railway's Bedale station offers regular heritage trains along the picturesque dale.

Bellerby

Cross Keys

DL8 5QS

5-midnight; 12-midnight Sat & Sun ☎ (01969) 624702

crosskeysbellerby.com

John Smith's Bitter; house beer (by Wensleydale); 2 changing beers

The Cross Keys is a community village pub with a strong commitment to real ale, usually including some interesting Yorkshire beers. The landlord always has at least one ale from the nearby Wensleydale Brewery. The main bar has been created by opening out two rooms and has a friendly atmosphere, while there is a pleasant beer garden to the rear.

Q ♣ P (159)

Birstwith

Station Hotel

Station Road, HG3 3AG

10-11 (midnight Fri); 12-11 Sat; 12-10 Sun

☎ (01423) 770254 station-hotel.net

Black Sheep Golden Sheep; Copper Dragon Best Bitter; 3 changing beers (sourced regionally; often Daleside, Ilkley, Rudgate)

This former station hotel has undergone a high-quality refurbishment and is a popular drinking and dining pub. It has three open-plan bar spaces and a separate dining area. There is a large beer garden at the back. Five letting rooms are available, one specially adapted for disabled customers. The pub is noted for its locally sourced food, served all day. The guest beers are usually from local breweries such as Ilkley, Daleside and Rudgate.

P (24)

Bishopthorpe

Ebor

46 Main Street, YO23 2RB

11-midnight; 12-midnight Sun ☎ (01904) 706190

Samuel Smith Old Brewery Bitter

Originally known as the Brown Cow, this 16th-century hotel, located close to the Archbishop's Palace, is officially haunted (Ghost Research Foundation study, 2003). Gordon, the landlord since 1981, makes customers feel welcome. Fresh fish from Whitby is a speciality and vegetarian options are available from an extensive menu, served lunchtimes and evenings (no food Sun eves). There is a large garden to the rear. The pub welcomes children and also features on the Dog-friendly Britain website.

Q ♣ P (11)

Marcia

29 Main Street, YO23 2RA

11-midnight; 12-11 Sun ☎ (01904) 706185

themarciayork.co.uk

Leeds Pale; Rooster's Yankee; Timothy Taylor Landlord; 3 changing beers (sourced locally; often Rudgate, Treboom, York)

Welcoming village inn, popular with locals, benefiting from refurbishment in 2013 and the new landlord's real ale passion. It has six handpumps dispensing mainly LocAles, and hosts a summer beer and cider festival. A good range of food is served every day in the well-laid-out bar and restaurant. It has a relaxed, congenial atmosphere, offering pub games and a quiz night, and is engaged with the community. The conservatory, and, outside, a large garden, tables and a children's play area, make this a popular family pub. Q ♣ P (11)

Boroughbridge

Black Bull Inn

6 St James Square, YO51 9AR

11-midnight; 12-11 Sun ☎ (01423) 322413

blackbullboroughbridge.co.uk

John Smith's Bitter; Timothy Taylor Boltmaker; 1 changing beer (sourced regionally; often Daleside, Partners, Rudgate)

Nestling in a corner of the market square, this 13th-century venue is immaculately kept and comfortably furnished, popular with locals and tourists alike. A Grade II-listed gem, it has a resident ghost. Three drinking and dining areas include a small cosy snug and a larger bar with open fires. A wide range of bar meals is available and there is a separate restaurant. A local CAMRA Pub of the Year and well worth a visit.

Q ♣ P (142,143)

REAL ALE BREWERIES

BAD Dishforth
Barkston Barkston Ash
Black Sheep Masham
Brass Castle Malton
Brown Cow Barlow
Captain Cook Stokesley
Copper Dragon Skipton
Daleside Harrogate
Dark Horse Hetton
Great Heck Great Heck
Great Yorkshire Cropton
Greyhawk Skipton (NEW)
Hambleton Melmerby
Harrogate Harrogate
Helmsley Helmsley (NEW)
Hop Studio Elvington
John Smith's Tadcaster
Jolly Sailor Selby
Knaresborough Knaresborough
Little Brew York
Mithril Aldbrough St John
Moorside Kirkbymoorside (NEW)
Naylor's Cross Hills
North Riding (Brewery) Scarborough (NEW)
North Riding (Brewpub) Scarborough
North Yorkshire Pinchinthorpe
Pennine Well
Redscar Redcar
Richmond Richmond
Rooster's Knaresborough
Rudgate Tockwith
Rydale York
Samuel Smith Tadcaster
Scarborough Scarborough
Settle Settle
Theakston Masham
Three Peaks Settle
Treboom Shipton-by-Beningbrough
Truefitt Middlesbrough
Wainstones Stokesley
Wall's Northallerton
Wensleydale Bellerby
Whitby Whitby
Wold Top Wold Newton
York York
Yorkshire Dales Askrigg
Yorkshire Heart Nun Monkton

Burn

Wheatsheaf L
Main Road, YO8 8LJ
⌚ 12-midnight; 12-11.30 Sun ☎ (01757) 270614
🌐 wheatsheafburn.co.uk
Copper Dragon Best Bitter; Timothy Taylor Boltmaker; 4 changing beers H
Comfortable pub on the A19 serving a varied range of guest beers mainly from Yorkshire breweries. A narrow entrance leads to the bar, separate pool room and spacious lounge with a huge open fire. There is a collection of artefacts from bygone days and memorabilia of 578 Squadron stationed at Burn during World War II. Food is served lunchtimes (Sunday lunch menu only on Sun) and Wednesday-Saturday evenings. Regular beer festivals and a monthly jazz night take place. Q❀◑♣P🚌🐾

Carlton-in-Cleveland

Blackwell Ox Inn
TS9 7DJ (400yds E of A172)
⌚ 11.30-11 ☎ (01642) 712287 🌐 blackwellox.co.uk
Jennings Cumberland Ale; Ringwood Boondoggle; 2 changing beers H
In a beautiful area on the edge of the National Park, and with the same licensee for 27 years, this multi-roomed village inn is renowned equally for its Thai cuisine and its fine beers. Winter Monday evening Thai buffets can easily become habit-forming. Look out also for lunchtime and early doors specials. But you do not have to eat; four handpumps provide an eclectic range of varying beer styles. The garden has an extensive play area.
Q🐴❀◑P🚌(80)

Castleton

Downe Arms
3 High Street, YO21 2EE (500yds S of Castleton Moor railway station)
⌚ 12-11.45 ☎ (01287) 660223 🌐 thedownearms.co.uk
Black Sheep Best Bitter; Camerons Strongarm; 2 changing beers G
Superb family-run and recently refurbished country inn under the stewardship of an enthusiastic CAMRA member who serves two regular beers and two guest beers, one from the SIBA list, and all gravity-fed direct from the cask. Pleasant days are enhanced by the superb views over the North York Moors and the Esk Valley. Lunchtime and early-doors specials are offered from a daily changing menu, and there is a takeaway service. Four letting bedrooms are available. Q🐴❀🛏◑♿≠P🐾📶

Eskdale Inn
Station Road, YO21 2EU (next to Castleton Moor railway station, 500yds N of village centre) NZ684085
⌚ 12-11 ☎ (01287) 660333 🌐 theeskdalecastleton.co.uk
Black Sheep Best Bitter; Copper Dragon Scotts 1816; Tetley Bitter; 1 changing beer H
Wedged between the Esk Valley Railway and the River Esk, this picturesque former station hotel offers a friendly welcome. The casks sit in a cool cellar directly beneath the four handpumps and well away from the roaring fire. The guest beers are often chosen by the locals themselves and are usually something interesting. Two real ciders are also served. A good-value menu is available all day every day. The pub hosts darts and pool teams. There are two letting bedrooms.
Q🐴❀🛏◑≠♣P🍏🐾

Cawood

Ferry L
2 King Street, YO8 3TL
⌚ 4-8 Mon; 12 (4 Tue)-11; 12-1am Fri & Sat; 10-10 Sun
☎ (01757) 268515 🌐 ferryinncawood.com
Leeds Pale; Timothy Taylor Landlord; 3 changing beers (sourced locally) H
Wooden-beamed 16th-century inn with a homely ambience and two open fires to provide a warm welcome on winter days. In summer, a picturesque backdrop of river views, open countryside and the adjacent swing bridge can be enjoyed from the vantage point of the popular outside terrace. Regular quizzes, pub games, live music and extended opening hours ensure this establishment keeps both visitors and the local community well satisfied. 🐴❀◑♿♣P🚌(42)🐾

Chapel-le-Dale

Hill Inn
LA6 3AR (on B6255)
⌚ closed Mon; 12-3, 6-11; 12-11 Sat ☎ (015242) 41256
🌐 oldhillinn.co.uk
Black Sheep Best Bitter; Dent Golden Fleece, Aviator; 1 changing beer H
The inn dates from 1615 and is beloved of generations of hikers and potholers. Well-worn paths run from here to both Whernside (Yorkshire's highest peak) and Ingleborough (its best known). Restored in 2001 with great care, soft furnishings are eschewed in favour of a variety of woodwork and some exposed limestone stonework. It is popular with diners – puddings are a speciality – and there is a sugar sculpture exhibition in an adjoining room (booking advisable for meals). A touring caravan site is attached.
Q❀🛏◑⛺P🍏🚌(831)🐾

Church Fenton

Fenton Flyer L
Main Street, LS24 9RF
⌚ 5-11 (midnight Fri); 12-midnight Sat; 12-10.30 Sun
☎ (01937) 558137 🌐 thefentonflyer.com
Black Sheep Best Bitter; 4 changing beers (sourced locally) H
A cosy, warm, welcoming village pub. The WWII memorabilia and name come from the recently closed airbase nearby. The five LocAles are well kept. Food is served on Friday and Saturday evenings, and a Wednesday-night quiz raises money for local charities. Live music is on the first Friday of each month and there is a monthly Saturday disco and karaoke. Sky Sports TV is screened. 🐴❀◗♿♣P🚌(492)📶

Cliffe

New Inn L
York Road, YO8 6NN
⌚ 2-11; 12-midnight Fri & Sat; 12-10.30 Sun
☎ (01757) 633888 🌐 newinncliffe.co.uk/cms
John Smith's Bitter; 5 changing beers (sourced regionally; often Abbeydale, Half Moon, Brown Cow) H
This welcoming village inn has been transformed from an Enterprise no-hoper into a Yorkshire beer mecca by licensees Ian and Adele. A cosy, two-roomed venue serving five guest beers, almost always local and certainly from Yorkshire, this is a

key stop-off point from the nearby A63. With log fires in winter and a welcoming beer garden in summer, you will always feel at home. Watch out for the August bank holiday beer festival, now an annual fixture, with even more eclectic ales.
❀♿⛺♣P🚌(4)📶

Cloughton

Hayburn Wyke Hotel

Newlands Road, YO13 0AU (off Ravenscar Rd, 1½ miles N of A171 jct)
11-3, 6-midnight (not Mon eve); 11-midnight Sat & Sun winter; 11-midnight summer ☎ (01723) 870202
hayburnwykeinn.co.uk
Black Sheep Ale; 2 changing beers (sourced regionally) Ⓗ
An 18th-century coaching inn in woodland next to the disused Scarborough to Whitby railway, and only minutes away from the Cleveland Way coastal path and rocky beach. It is popular with cyclists and walkers. Home-made food is served lunchtimes and evenings (no food Mon eves) with the Sunday carvery a local favourite. En-suite accommodation is available. Outside is a well-provisioned children's play area and a sizeable heated smoking area. Runner-up local CAMRA Rural Pub of the Year 2014.
❀⛺♣P🚌(115)🐾📶

Colburn Village

Hildyard Arms

Catterick Garrison, DL9 4PD (off A6136 near Catterick Garrison)
12-midnight ☎ (01748) 832353
thehildyardarms.wordpress.com
Black Sheep Best Bitter; 3 changing beers (sourced locally; often Richmond) Ⓗ
Pleasant pub overlooking Colburn Beck, tucked away in a quiet location on the Coast-to-Coast Walk route. Worth seeking out, it features a panelled dining room and a quiet snug bar with bench seating, both with Art Deco fireplaces. Snacks are served 3-6pm in summer, and showers and breakfasts are provided for walkers camping in the garden. There is always one beer from Richmond Station Brewery plus local, regional or national guest ales and Westons Old Rosie cider.
Q❀⛺♣P🐾📶

Colton

Old Sun Inn

Main Street, LS24 8EP
12-3, 6-11; 12-11 Sun ☎ (01904) 744261
yeoldsuninn.co.uk
Timothy Taylor Landlord; 4 changing beers (sourced locally; often Black Sheep, Revolutions) Ⓗ
A 17th-century village pub with an award-winning restaurant featuring locally sourced produce. There are four cosy dining areas together with a drinkers-only bar with five handpumps. It also has an extensive wine list. The interior features traditional low-beamed ceilings and in the winter there are two fires. For the summer there is a patio and a large picnic area. Functions are catered for. A studio barn can sleep up to six on a B&B or self-catering basis. Q❀♿⛺P🚌(21)🐾📶

Cropton

New Inn

YO18 8HH
11-11 (midnight Fri & Sat) ☎ (01751) 417330
newinncropton.co.uk
Great Yorkshire Pale, Classic, Golden; 3 changing beers Ⓗ
Great Yorkshire Brewery's tap, this is a family-run pub on the edge of the North Yorkshire Moors National Park in an attractive stone building. A perfect base for walkers and cyclists, it offers food in the bars, and B&B and camping accommodation. Up to six of its ales are available. A beer festival features in November and a music festival in the summer. Q❀♿⛺♣P🚌🐾📶

Cross Hills

Naylor's Beer Emporium

Midland Mills Station Road, BD20 7DT (in industrial estate on right over railway bridge from Cross Hills)
3 (5 Tue)-11; closed Sun-Wed ☎ (01535) 637451
naylorsbrewery.co.uk
Naylor's Aire Valley Bitter, Pinnacle Blonde; 3 changing beers Ⓗ
In spring 2015 the Emporium, Naylor's brewery tap, expanded upstairs to include the Beer Belly Kitchen serving American diner-style food. In good weather customers spill out into the yard outside. The emphasis is on good company, friendly chatter and the appreciation of good beer. The five Naylor's cask beers are all reasonably priced; the three guests are from the brewery's seasonal range and one is usually dark. Brewery souvenir merchandise and bottled beers can also be purchased. Q❀♿P🚌(66,66A)🐾📶

Danby

Duke of Wellington

West Lane, YO21 2LY (300yds N of railway station)
12-2.30 (not Mon), 7-11; 12-11 Fri & Sat; 12-2.30, 7-10.30 Sun ☎ (01287) 660351 dukeofwellingtondanby.co.uk
Copper Dragon Scotts 1816; Daleside Bitter; 1 changing beer Ⓗ
An 18th-century inn, and recent CAMRA branch Pub of the Year, set in idyllic National Park countryside, close to the popular Visitor Centre and equally popular bakery. It was used as a recruiting post during the Napoleonic Wars. A cast-iron plaque of the first Duke, unearthed during restorations, hangs above the fireplace. All the beers are from Yorkshire while the menu offers traditional British home-cooked meals at their best, using locally sourced produce. Cider and perry are served Easter-October. Q♣🐾

Danby Wiske

White Swan

DL7 0NQ (approx 3 miles N of Northallerton off A167)
7-11; closed Tue; 12-3, 6-11 Sat; 12-3, 7-11 Sun winter; 12-11 (10 Sun) summer ☎ (01609) 775131
thewhiteswandanbywiske.co.uk
Wall's County Town Gun Dog Bitter; 4 changing beers (sourced locally; often Wall's County Town) Ⓗ
A haven for Coast-to-Coast walkers with its accommodation and camping, this CAMRA award-winning village inn champions local beers. The attractive single-room bar has wood-burning stoves and is home to the local sword dancers. Four

changing beers usually include at least one from Wall's of Northallerton, plus Gwynt y Ddraig Happy Daze cider and Westons perry. Lunchtime snacks and evening meals are available April-October, made with locally sourced produce (booking advisable). Hours may vary at quiet times.
Q🐎❀🛏◗⛺♣🍎P🐾📶

Darley

Wellington Inn

Darley Carr, HG3 2QQ (on B6451 W of village)
⏲ 12-11 (midnight Fri & Sat); 12-10.30 Sun
☎ (01423) 780362 🌐 wellington-inn.co.uk
Black Sheep Ale; Copper Dragon Golden Pippin; Tetley Bitter; Timothy Taylor Landlord Ⓗ
Much-extended popular stone-built pub on the edge of Nidderdale. It is food-led but with a range of well-kept ales. The original building houses a comfortable bar with a pool table, and the long extension provides more space, essentially for diners, in a baronial hall-styled room; the fireplace is especially magnificent. Behind is a dining room with spectacular views across Nidderdale.
Q❀🛏◖◗♣P🚌(24)🐾📶

East Witton

Cover Bridge Inn 🄻

DL8 4SQ (½ mile N of village on A6108)
⏲ 11-midnight; 12-11.30 Sun ☎ (01969) 623250
🌐 thecoverbridgeinn.co.uk
Black Sheep Best Bitter; John Smith's Bitter; Theakston Best Bitter, Old Peculier; Timothy Taylor Boltmaker; 3 changing beers (sourced locally) Ⓗ
A splendidly traditional Dales inn where numerous CAMRA awards tell their tale. The River Cover runs along the foot of the attractive garden and play area, near its confluence with the River Ure. Fathom out the door latch and enjoy a warm welcome in the unspoilt public bar with its giant hearth and in the tiny lounge. Eight handpumps dispense locally brewed beers and guests from further afield; there are two real ciders and perry.
Q🐎❀🛏◖◗♿♣🍎P🚭🚌(159)🐾📶

Egton

Wheatsheaf Inn

YO21 1TZ
⏲ closed Mon; 11.30-3, 5.30-11; 11.30-11 Sat & Sun
☎ (01947) 895271 🌐 wheatsheafegton.com
Black Sheep Best Bitter; Timothy Taylor Landlord; 2 changing beers Ⓗ
Winner of many CAMRA awards, this Grade II-listed 19th-century pub serves four Yorkshire beers. It is now in its 16th year in the Guide, and remains under the stewardship of a licensee with 29 years of continuous Guide recognition. Church pews, collectables from auctions and a roaring range add to the ambience. The grassy area to the front and boules to the rear are ideal for summer drinking. The first-class restaurant menu always features local meat, fish and game.
Q❀🛏◖◗♿♣P🚭🚌(99)🐾

Filey

Bonhomme's Bar

Royal Crescent Court, The Crescent, YO14 9JH
⏲ 11-midnight (1am Fri & Sat) ☎ (01723) 515325
5 changing beers (sourced nationally; often Wentworth) Ⓗ
Just off the fine Victorian Royal Crescent Hotel complex, the bar's name celebrates John Paul Jones, father of the American Navy. His ship, the Bonhomme Richard, was involved in a battle off nearby Flamborough Head during the War of Independence. Five handpumps serve rotating guests. Food is served daily (except Mon-Wed winter). A quiz is held on Thursday evening and Saturday afternoon each week. Local CAMRA Rural Pub of the Year runner-up 2014.
🐎◖◗⛺⇌♣🍎🚌(121)🐾📶

Star Inn

23 Mitford Street, YO14 9DX
⏲ 12-midnight (1am Fri & Sat) ☎ (01723) 512031
Black Sheep Best Bitter, Ale; 2 changing beers (sourced nationally) Ⓗ
The Star Inn is just off the town centre and has a large main room and separate restaurant/function room. Two regular beers and two rotating guests are on the bar. Freshly cooked meals are served lunchtimes and evenings (no food Mon). Live entertainment features at weekends, and pub teams participate in a local pool league. Smokers are catered for both front and rear of the building, and parking is provided behind the pub.
🐎❀◖◗♿⇌♣P🚌(121)📶

Gargrave

Masons Arms 🄻

Marton Road, BD23 3NL (on road over River Aire to railway station off A65)
⏲ 12-midnight ☎ (01756) 749304
🌐 masonsarmsgargrave.co.uk
Black Sheep Ale; Tetley Bitter; Timothy Taylor Landlord; 1 changing beer Ⓗ
This attractive, traditional village pub is in a quiet residential location opposite St Andrew's church, close to the railway station and the River Aire. With its low oak-beamed ceilings adorned with horse brasses, it offers a comfortable and relaxing environment both for drinkers and diners. Accommodation is in six en-suite rooms alongside the pub, making it a great base for exploring the Leeds and Liverpool Canal, Malhamdale and the nearby market towns of Skipton and Settle. There is lockable cycle storage for residents.
Q🐎❀🛏◖◗♿⛺⇌♣🍎P🚌(75,210,211)🐾📶

Giggleswick

Hart's Head Hotel 🄻

Belle Hill, BD24 0BA (on B6480 1 mile N of Settle)
⏲ 4 (12 Fri; 11.30 Sat)-11; 12-11 Sun ☎ (01729) 822086
🌐 hartsheadinn.co.uk
Tetley Bitter; 4 changing beers (sourced regionally; often Bowland, Dent, Kirkby Lonsdale) Ⓗ
Open-plan 18th-century coaching inn catering for a wide clientele. The bar separates the comfortable lounge from the area where pub games are played and sport is shown on TV, and there is a full-sized snooker table in the cellar. Freshly prepared meals from a varied menu are served in the adjacent dining room, while the sloping beer garden at the rear is a great place to soak up the sun. A good selection of gins and malt whiskies is available.
🐎❀🛏◖◗♿⛺⇌(Settle)♣P🚌(580,581)🐾📶

Gilling West

White Swan 🄻

51 High Street, DL10 5JG (1 mile W of Scotch Corner, off A66)
10.30-11 ☎ (01748) 82512 thewhiteswan.co
4 changing beers 🄷
A historic coaching inn with open fires, slate floors and a courtyard garden blending the modern with the traditional. Four real ales from local microbreweries, including a house beer from Mithril, are on the bar, and over 40 bottled beers are available. A flagship burger and steak menu showcases the best of the region's produce, featuring 35-day-aged beef, local game, artisan bakers, cheesemakers and a house smokery. Quizzes are fortnightly and music nights monthly. There is also accommodation, in three en-suite rooms. Q P (29)

Great Heck

Bay Horse 🄻

Main Street, DN14 0BE (S of A645 between Pontefract and Snaith)
3-9; 12-midnight Thu-Sat; 12-6 Sun ☎ (01777) 661121
Old Mill Traditional Bitter; 1 changing beer (sourced locally; often Old Mill) 🄷
In a remote country hamlet, this cosy hostelry serves well-kept ales from Old Mill Brewery, whose seasonal beers are featured monthly throughout the year. The pub is divided into three distinct areas – dining rooms at each end and a lounge in the middle. There is a log-burning fire and interesting pictures adorn the walls. Quiz night is Thursday. Opening hours are longer in summer. Q P

Grinton

Bridge Inn

DL11 6HH (on B6270, 1 mile E of Reeth)
12-midnight; 12-11 Sun ☎ (01748) 884224
bridgeinn-grinton.co.uk
Jennings Cumberland Ale; 3 changing beers (often Marston's) 🄷
Friendly and well-run country inn close to the River Swale, set beneath the towering hills of Fremington Edge and Harkerside. Its comfortable lounge, wood-panelled bar and two restaurant rooms are a haven for walkers and cyclists on the Coast-to-Coast and Inn Way walks and Dales Cycle Way. Fresh, home-made food is served all day, along with beers from the Marston's range. Q P (30)

Grosmont

Crossing Club

Co-operative Building, Front Street, YO22 5QE (opp NYMR car park)
8-11 ☎ 07766 197744
5 changing beers 🄷
Set amid beautiful scenery in the Esk Valley, this recent local CAMRA branch Club of the Year stands directly opposite the NYMR/Esk Valley railway stations in what was the village's Co-operative store delivery bay. Converted by dedicated villagers into a railway-themed private members' club 17 years ago, a warm welcome always awaits CAMRA members. For the railway enthusiast, the walls are adorned with both steam and diesel memorabilia. The club's five handpumps have served 1,000 different beers – celebrations are expected soon. Q (99)

Harrogate

Blues Café Bar

4 Montpellier Parade, HG1 2TJ
10-1am; 12-12.30am Sun ☎ (01423) 566881
bluesbar.co.uk
4 changing beers (sourced regionally; often Daleside, Ossett, Rooster's) 🄷
A small single-room music bar modelled on an Amsterdam café bar. There is live music seven evenings a week, with two sessions on a Sunday. Popular with music lovers, it can get busy. Four rotating guest beers are offered, sourced from far and wide. Food is served from 10am until early evening (2pm Sun). Children are permitted until 7pm.

Coach & Horses

16 West Park, HG1 1BJ
11-11; 12-10.30 Sun ☎ (01423) 561802
thecoachandhorses.net
Tetley Bitter; Timothy Taylor Landlord; 4 changing beers (sourced nationally; often Daleside, Rooster's) 🄷
A community pub located by the Stray, filled with snugs and alcoves creating a cosy atmosphere inside. Tables and chairs are provided outside for customers in summer while window boxes create a spectacular display and add year-round colour. The pub offers a guest beer range, serves excellent meals at lunchtimes and has reasonably priced themed evenings; many of these, together with a popular Sunday night quiz, have raised a considerable amount of money for a local children's hospice. Q

Hales Bar 🄻

1-3 Crescent Road, HG1 2RS
12-midnight (1am Thu-Sat); 12-11.30 Sun
☎ (01423) 725570 halesbar.co.uk
Daleside Old Leg Over; Draught Bass; Robinsons Dizzy Blonde; Timothy Taylor Landlord; house beer (by Daleside); 1 changing beer (sourced nationally; often Belhaven, Thwaites, Wells) 🄷
Harrogate's oldest pub and listed on CAMRA's Regional Inventory of Historic Pub Interiors, the Victorian-style lounge has original gas lighting over the bar, and the separate snug is also used as a tearoom. There are six handpumps, two serving a changing range of guest beers. Karaoke and occasional party nights are held. The pub is a rare outlet for Draught Bass and a house beer is supplied by Daleside.

Harrogate Tap

Station Parade, HG1 1TE
11-11; 10-midnight Fri & Sat ☎ (01423) 501644
harrogatetap.co.uk
11 changing beers 🄷
A redundant Victorian station refreshment room, closed for over 30 years, has been given a new lease of life by the owners of the Tap group of station bars. Twelve handpumps serve a changing range of beers from brewers as diverse as Thornbridge, Rooster's and Black Sheep, and there is always a real cider from Thistley Cross. Wood panelling, tiled floors, leather and brass dominate the traditional decor in both the main bar and the small snug at one end. Q

Major Tom's Social

The Ginnel, HG1 2RB
☼ 11-11.30 (1am Fri & Sat)
4 changing beers Ⓗ
An unusual café bar housed upstairs in a former antiques emporium. It provides real ale, pizza, music and art all in one package. Simply furnished and decorated in a mix of styles to suit the eclectic clientele, the artwork on display is for sale. The four handpumps dispense a changing variety of ales, usually including some from Rooster's, Kirkstall and a variety of smaller breweries. There are also interesting bottles from the UK, US and Europe. ◐🖨⇌♣🐾🛜

Old Bell Tavern

6 Royal Parade, HG1 2SZ
☼ 12-11 (midnight Fri & Sat) ☎ (01423) 507930
Hawkshead Windermere Pale; 8 changing beers (sourced regionally; often Black Sheep, Okells, Rooster's) Ⓗ
Formerly Farrar's toffee shop, the building became a pub in 1999 on the site of the Blue Bell Inn. There is a changing range of eight guest beers, usually including a Rooster's, a Taylor's, one from Okells of the Isle of Man, and a dark beer. A real cider and a range of UK and foreign bottled beers complete the choice. The side room has a collection of Farrar's memorabilia and upstairs is a well-regarded restaurant. Q◐🖨⇌🐾🛜

Swan on the Stray

17 Devonshire Place, HG1 4AA
☼ 11-11; 12-10.30 Sun ☎ (01423) 524587
Ilkley Mary Jane; 7 changing beers (sourced nationally; often Black Sheep, Leeds, Okells) Ⓗ
Formerly known as the Black Swan, this pub was extensively refurbished in a modern style, reopening in early 2010. Eight real ales are on handpump with four changing regularly, many from Yorkshire micros. A range of foreign beer is also available on draught plus a real cider and an added selection in bottles. Allied to a good wine choice and excellent bar meals, the pub appeals to all age groups. A beer garden is at the rear and well-behaved children are welcome until 8pm.
🛏🕭◐♿⇌P🛒(104,111)🐾🛜

Winter Gardens

4 Royal Baths, HG1 2RR
☼ 7-midnight (1am Thu; 2am Fri & Sat) ☎ (01423) 877010
Adnams Broadside; Greene King Abbot; Ruddles Best Bitter; Sharp's Doom Bar; 6 changing beers (sourced regionally; often Daleside) Ⓗ
Converted from part of the Royal Baths complex in 2002, this magnificent building has a spacious interior reached from the Parliament Street entrance by a sweeping double stone staircase. Wheelchair access is from the entrance in The Ginnel. In addition to the usual Wetherspoon core range of beers, locally sourced guests are always available across three sets of handpumps. The pub can get very busy due to its location near Harrogate's conference and exhibition centre.
🛏🕭◐♿⇌🐾🛜

Hawes

Crown Inn Ⓛ

Market Place, DL8 3RD
☼ 11-11; 12-11 Sun ☎ (01969) 667212
🌐 crownhawes.co.uk

John Smith's Bitter; Theakston Best Bitter, Lightfoot, XB, Old Peculier; 1 changing beer Ⓗ
A large pub on the main street. Its attractive interior has been opened out to form two main rooms, but it retains a distinct old-fashioned feel with old pictures, brasses and iron artefacts on the walls and ceiling. The lounge at the front has a coal fire at each end, while the bar to the side is partitioned into two distinct drinking areas.
Q🛏🕭🏠♿◐♿♣🛒(156)🐾🛜

White Hart Country Inn ♈

Main Street, DL8 3QL (on one-way system, westbound)
☼ 11-11 ☎ (01969) 667214 🌐 whitehartcountryinn.co.uk
Wensleydale Semerwater; Theakston Best Bitter; 3 changing beers (sourced locally) Ⓗ
Comfortable free house on the town's short one-way system, attractively refurbished in 2015. A large dining room is popular with visitors and a smaller bar features an attractive stone hearth and mock wood panelling. Guest beers are often from the local Yorkshire Dales, Pennine and Wall's breweries. Food is served daily 12-9pm, including beef and lamb from the family farm.
Q🛏🏠◐♿♣🛒(156)🛜

Helwith Bridge

Helwith Bridge Inn Ⓛ

BD24 0EH (off B6479 at Helwith Bridge)
☼ 12-midnight ☎ (01729) 860220 🌐 helwithbridgeinn.co.uk
Three Peaks Ingleborough Gold; Thwaites Original; house beer (by Three Peaks); 3 changing beers Ⓗ
Despite its relative isolation in the tiny hamlet of Helwith Bridge, this is a thriving, no-frills community local where the emphasis is on real ale. The pub has three separate rooms, all reached via the flagged main bar area. Close to Pen-y-Ghent, the pub is the starting point of the Three Peaks cycle race. The house beer, Helwith Bridge Bitter, is Three Peaks Pen-y-Ghent. Self-catering accommodation is available in the adjacent bunk-barn. 🕭🏠◐♿▲♣P🛒(11)🐾🛜

Hubberholme

George Inn Ⓛ

Kirk Gill, BD23 5JE (opp church, 1 mile NW of Buckden)
☼ 12 (4 Mon)-10.30; closed Tue summer; 12-3 (not Mon), 6-10.30; closed Tue; 12-11 Fri & Sat; 12-5 Sun winter
☎ (01756) 760223 🌐 thegeorge-inn.co.uk
Black Sheep Best Bitter; Tetley Bitter; Wharfedale Blonde; 1 changing beer Ⓗ
Supposedly a favourite haunt of JB Priestley, this Grade II-listed whitewashed building dates from the 1600s and boasts mullioned windows, heavy oak beams and flagstone floors. A lighted candle on the bar denotes that it is open and is associated with the Hubberholme Parliament, an annual auction for letting church land. George of the George (the owners' Jack Russell) eagerly greets visitors. The guest beer is often a dark ale. May stay open later on Sunday if busy. Q🕭🏠◐P🐾

Huby

Mended Drum

Tollerton Road, YO61 1HT
☼ 5 (4 Fri)-11; 12-midnight Sat; 12-11 Sun
☎ (01347) 810264 🌐 themendeddrumhuby.blogspot.co.uk

Black Sheep Best Bitter; 2 changing beers (sourced locally; often Hambleton, Little Brew, Wall's County Town) Ⓗ
Formerly known as the Star, the Mended Drum is a community pub at the centre of the village. The landlord has a passion for serving ales brewed within 25 miles of Huby and will be offering beer and music festivals alongside the regular pub quizzes. The pub has a central bar with two seating areas and a separate restaurant.
P (X30)

Hutton Rudby

King's Head

36 North Side, TS15 0DA (W end of village)
4-11.30; 12-midnight Fri-Sun ☎ (01642) 700342
Banks's Sunbeam; Camerons Strongarm; Jennings Cumberland Ale; 1 changing beer Ⓗ
Set in a beautiful village, this previous CAMRA branch award winner is a traditional locals' pub where a friendly welcome is assured. It comprises a comfortable and always busy main bar and a snug where children are welcome. Four handpumps include a guest beer from Marston's. Real fires, a quiz night on Tuesday, a full menu on Wednesday and Friday and live music on Saturday all add to the experience. Outside is a smokers' paradise. Q (80)

Kirby Hill

Shoulder of Mutton

DL11 7JH (2½ miles from A66, 4 miles NW of Richmond)
11-11 ☎ (01748) 822772 shoulderofmutton.net
Daleside Bitter; 3 changing beers Ⓗ
Ivy-fronted country inn in a beautiful hillside setting overlooking Lower Teesdale and the ruins of Ravensworth Castle. The pub has an open-front bar that links the lounge with a cosy restaurant to the rear. Three guest beers (four in summer) are chosen by the regulars. On the edge of the Yorkshire Dales, this is a popular venue for walkers. There are five en-suite bedrooms. Excellent food is served daily, although the bar area remains for drinkers. Q

Kirk Smeaton

Shoulder of Mutton

Main Street, WF8 3JY (follow signs from A1)
12-midnight; 11.30-midnight Sun ☎ (01977) 620348
Black Sheep Best Bitter; 1 changing beer (sourced regionally; often Theakston, Wharfe Bank) Ⓗ
This inn has a relaxed, informal atmosphere, with a roomy lounge and a cosy wood-panelled snug, both with an open fire. It is deep in the heart of Yorkshire close to Brockadale Nature Reserve, the River Went running through. Popular with walkers, the pub is at the heart of the local community. It often has Shoulder of Mutton Ale as a guest beer, brewed by Wharfe Bank Brewery.
P (409)

Kirkby-in-Cleveland

Black Swan

Busby Lane, TS9 7AW (800yds W of B1257) NZ539060
12-midnight ☎ (01642) 712512
Bradfield Farmers Blonde; Copper Dragon Golden Pippin; Timothy Taylor Landlord; 1 changing beer Ⓗ
Nestling at the foot of the North York Moors, and at the crossroads of this ancient village, this warm and cosy free house, comprising a bar, lounge/restaurant and conservatory, affords a friendly and genuine welcome. Three regular beers and a guest beer, always from Yorkshire, are served in a convivial atmosphere where making conversation with the locals seems a must. Bar snacks and a full menu, including daily specials, represent good value. There is a pool table.
Q P (89)

Knaresborough

Blind Jack's

19 Market Place, HG5 8AL
4 (3 Fri; 12 Sat)-11; 12-10.30 Sun ☎ (01423) 869148
Bad Comfortably Numb; Black Sheep Best Bitter; 7 changing beers Ⓗ
A multi-roomed pub with bare brick walls, wooden floorboards and panelling. An award-winning ale house, it provides a focal point for locals and the many visitors who appreciate the excellent selection of ales, cosy ambience and lively banter. The beer range usually includes several from Bad Company Brewery. Listed in this Guide since 1993, Knaresborough Brewery, which was formerly on the premises, has moved to Bad Company's site at Dishforth, and still produces occasional brews.
Q (1)

Cross Keys

17 Cheapside, HG5 8AX
12 (4 Mon & Tue)-11; 12-midnight Fri & Sat
☎ (01423) 863562
Jennings Bitter; Ossett Yorkshire Blonde, Silver King, Excelsior; 2 changing beers Ⓗ
A former Tetley's house, refurbished by Ossett Brewery in its trademark style with stone-flagged floors, bare brick walls and stained glass. This traditional pub serves four regular beers and two guests, one usually a dark beer or stout from either a microbrewery or from one of the other breweries within the Ossett company. Thursday is quiz night and a live band plays on most Saturday nights. Lunches are served on Sundays. (1)

Crown Inn

71-75 High Street, HG5 0HB
8am-midnight (1am Fri & Sat) ☎ (01423) 862122
Greene King Abbot; Ruddles Best Bitter; 9 changing beers Ⓗ
Renovated and extended by Wetherspoon in 2014 from the old Crown and an adjacent building, the decor is crisp and modern with a faint hint of Art Deco. Three main areas provide ample seating and dining space, the area to the back offering more discreet seating. The 12 handpumps serve the usual Wetherspoon mix of standards and beers from smaller breweries, both local and from further afield. There is a small patio area with its own access from the street. (1)

Half Moon

1 Abbey Road, HG5 8HY
5 (12 Sat)-11; 12-10.30 Sun ☎ (01423) 313461
4 changing beers Ⓗ
Small in size but big in atmosphere, this free house has been sympathetically restored to a high standard by its independent owners. Bare brick walls, reclaimed furniture and real fires give the pub a welcoming ambience. Four handpumps dispense a varying range of Yorkshire beers,

usually including one from nearby Rooster's. A grazing menu of meat and cheese platters complements the beers. The pub hosts a team in the annual tug of war across the adjacent River Nidd. ♨❀◑🍎🚌(56,57)🐾📶

Mitre Hotel

4 Station Road, HG5 9AA (opp railway station)
⏲ 12-11 ☎ (01423) 868948 🌐 themitreinn.co.uk
Black Sheep Ale; Okells Manx Pale Ale; 6 changing beers Ⓗ
Ideally placed for the railway station, this Market Town Taverns pub serves eight ales, with several from Yorkshire breweries and one pump dedicated to the town's own Rooster's Brewery. It also offers a good range of speciality bottled beers. Pumpclips adorn the walls of the modern split-level bar. There is a side room and a downstairs function room, and a beer garden with views of the local church. Food is served daily and live music features on Sunday evenings. ♨❀🛏◑♿⇌🍎🚌(1)🐾📶

Lastingham

Blacksmiths Arms

Anserdale lane, YO62 6TN
⏲ 11.30-11.30 ☎ (01751) 417247
🌐 blacksmithslastingham.co.uk
Theakston Best Bitter; 2 changing beers (sourced regionally) Ⓗ
Pretty stone inn in a conservation village opposite St Mary's Church, famous for its 11th-century crypt. The interior comprises a cosy bar with a York range lit in winter, a snug and two dining rooms. Excellent-quality food including local game is served alongside interesting guest beers. A secluded beer garden is to the rear. This remote pub is popular with locals, walkers and shooting parties. Q♨❀🛏◑🐾

Lazenby

Lazenby Social Club

High Street, TS6 8DX (in centre of village, N of A174 bypass)
⏲ 12-11; 12-10.30 Sun ☎ (01642) 453905
Brains Rev James; 1 changing beer Ⓗ
In a pleasant village, wedged between the remnants of Teesside's heavy industries and the Cleveland Hills, this substantial private members' club, and recent award winner, extends a warm welcome to CAMRA members. It comprises a lounge bar, a large bar/games room with pool table, a concert room and a conservatory that houses a full-size snooker table. It was dry for years during Teesside's industrial heyday, but the club has now gained a deserved reputation for selling fine real ales. ♿♣P⊓🚌(63)🐾

Lealholm

Board Inn

Village Geen, YO21 2AJ
⏲ 9am-midnight (2am Fri & Sat) ☎ (01947) 897279
🌐 theboardinn.com
4 changing beers Ⓗ
Overlooking the River Esk, this family-run traditional 17th-century free house is at the centre of village life. Four beers, four real ciders and 60 whiskies are served. It comprises a busy locals' bar, lounge and restaurant, and a riverside patio where an Easter beer festival is held. The superb food is virtually all traceable to within 800 yards of the pub. The licensees air-cure their own hams, keep hens, ducks and livestock, and enjoy local salmon fishing rights. CAMRA branch Community Pub of the Year 2015. Q♨❀🛏◑♿⇌♣🍎P⊓🚌(99)🐾

Leavening

Jolly Farmers Ⓛ

Main Street, YO17 9SA
⏲ 5.30-midnight (1am Fri); 12-1am Sat; 12-midnight Sun
☎ (01653) 658276 🌐 thejollys.co.uk
Timothy Taylor Landlord; York Guzzler; 2 changing beers Ⓗ
Seventeenth-century pub on the edge of the Yorkshire Wolds between York and Malton. The multi-room interior retains old-world cosiness in two small bars, a games/family room and a separate dining room. Community-focused, it stages meetings, charity events, darts and quiz leagues, occasional live music and beer festivals. Varied guest beers from independent breweries make an appearance. The extensive menu of quality food includes locally caught game dishes in season (no food Mon and Tue eves).
Q♨❀◑♿♣P⊓

Leyburn

Golden Lion Ⓛ

Market Place, DL8 5AS
⏲ 11-11 (midnight Fri & Sat) ☎ (01969) 622161
🌐 goldenlionleyburn.co.uk
John Smith's Bitter; Theakston Best Bitter; Wensleydale Coverdale Gamekeeper; 1 changing beer (sourced locally; often Wensleydale) Ⓗ
Traditional market-town pub facing onto the main square of this busy Dales centre, now served by the Wensleydale Railway. The comfortable main bar area is opened out and largely wood panelled, with a real fire at both ends. There is a separate dining room to the rear, particularly busy for the Sunday carvery. The changing beer is from Wensleydale Brewery, either Semerwater or Bitter.
♨🛏◑⛺⇌♣🚌(155,156,159)🐾📶

Lofthouse

Crown Hotel

Thorpe Lane, HG3 5RZ
⏲ 12-3, 6-11; 12-3, 7-10.30 Sun ☎ (01423) 755206
Black Sheep Best Bitter; Theakston Best Bitter; 1 changing beer Ⓗ
A handsome stone building at the far end of beautiful Nidderdale. An unusual panelled entrance corridor leads to a traditionally furnished comfortable bar, with a dining room beyond. Local pictures, maps and lots of brassware decorate the walls. An open fire in winter warms your bones after exploring the surrounding area of outstanding natural beauty, and walking sticks are for sale if needed. In summer there is often a guest from a local brewery. 🛏◑🐾

Loftus

Station Hotel

Station Road, TS13 4QB (100yds S of A174)
⏲ 3-11; 12-11.30 Sat & Sun ☎ (01287) 640373
3 changing beers Ⓗ
This once-bustling railway hotel is now a free house. The last passenger train left in 1960 – the

overgrown platform is still in situ. The licensee, a keen musician and local independent councillor, has served best/premium bitters for 24 years – anything under 4% ABV generally meets with the locals' disapproval. The pub comprises a cosy bar, a lounge and a function room where live music plays Thursday and Saturday. Fans of particularly eccentric railway memorabilia are especially well catered for. ❀♿🍺🚌(4,5)🐾

Maltby

Manor House

High Lane, TS8 0BN (at jct of A1044 and A1045, 2 miles E of Yarm)

⏲ 11-11; 12-10.30 Sun ☎ (01642) 764153

🌐 themanorhouseteesside.co.uk

Black Sheep Best Bitter; 3 changing beers Ⓗ

On the western outskirts of a pretty village, this Sir John Fitzgerald house is now well established following extensive, careful and restrained renovations seven years ago. A recent CAMRA branch award winner, it comes with a welcoming cosiness and warmth, where friendly and enthusiastic staff ensure that the four handpumps provide an interesting mix of differing beer styles. Its Real Ale Club, with significantly discounted prices for all, meets Sunday and Thursday from 6.30pm. Food is served all day every day.

Q🛋❀◐◑♿P🍺📶

Malton

Blue Ball

14 Newbiggin, YO17 7JF

⏲ 12-midnight ☎ (01653) 690692

Tetley Bitter; Timothy Taylor Landlord; 1 changing beer (sourced locally; often Great Yorkshire) Ⓗ

Grade II-listed Yorkshire Heritage pub dating from the 16th century and named the Blue Ball in 1823. The low frontage hides a maze-like interior, with the frontward cosy bar, compact servery and linking corridor retaining most of the pub's historic flavour. A smoking area is located at the rear. Home-cooked food is available daily (but no food Wed). The Blue Ball Folk Club meets on the second Tuesday of each month.

Q🛋◐◑⇌♣P🍺🚌(843)🐾📶

Crown Hotel

12 Wheelgate, YO17 7HP

⏲ 11-11 (11.45 Fri & Sat); 12-11 Sun ☎ (01653) 692038

Jennings Cumberland Ale; house beer (by Leeds); 3 changing beers (sourced nationally) Ⓗ

Grade II-listed market town pub which has been in the same family for 135 years and in the Guide for over 25. Double Chance, brewed by Leeds Brewery, is one of two regular beers offered. Beer festivals are held three times annually. The on-site shop stocks more than 200 beers, specialising in Belgian and British microbreweries. A covered smoking patio is at the rear. Accommodation is available (with discounts for CAMRA members staying two nights or more). Q🛏⇌♣P🚌(843)📶

Spotted Cow

Cattle Market, YO17 7JN

⏲ 4 (11 Tue & Fri; 12 Sat)-midnight; 12-10.30 Sun ☎ (01653) 697568

Marston's Pedigree New World Pale Ale; Tetley Bitter; 1 changing beer (sourced nationally) Ⓗ

Grade II-listed Yorkshire Heritage pub opposite the livestock market and more than 300 years old, with a traditional cruck-framed construction. It has a wonderful tile-floored taproom with wooden seating and a Rose's Brewery mirror, together with a main bar area and separate pool room. A covered smoking area is at the rear. It does bar snacks. This pub has Cask Marque accreditation.

Q🛋⇌♣P🚌(843)🐾📶

Manfield

Crown Inn 🏆

Vicars Lane, DL2 2RF (500yds from B6275)

⏲ 5 (12 Sat)-11.30; 12-11 Sun ☎ (01325) 374243

Village White Boar; 7 changing beers Ⓗ

Local CAMRA Country Pub of the Year 13 times and previously Yorkshire Pub of the Year, this 18th-century inn is in a quiet village. It has two bars and a games room. A mix of locals and visitors creates a friendly atmosphere. Seven guest beers from microbreweries, plus two ciders or perry, are on the bar. A 20-beer festival is held over the May Day weekend and a 14-cider festival in July. There is a monthly quiz on a Tuesday night.

Q🛋❀◑🍎P🍺🚌(29)🐾

Marske-by-the-Sea

Clarendon

88-90 High Street, TS11 7BA

⏲ 11-11 (11.30 Fri-Sun) ☎ (01642) 490005

Black Sheep Best Bitter; Camerons Strongarm; Copper Dragon Golden Pippin; Theakston Best Bitter, Old Peculier; 1 changing beer Ⓗ

A recent CAMRA branch award winner, the Middle House, as it is known, is a family-run, one-room locals' pub, where the walls are adorned with photographs of yesteryear. Six beers are served from a mahogany island bar – a rarity on Teesside. There is no TV or jukebox, no pool table, no children or teenagers – just locals indulging in convivial conversation. There is no catering either, but tea and coffee are available, together with excellent home-made scones at lunchtimes, while a free buffet is provided on Tuesday evenings.

Q❀⇌P🚌(3,X4)

Masham

White Bear

Wellgarth, HG4 4EN

⏲ 11-midnight ☎ (01765) 689319

🌐 thewhitebearhotel.co.uk

Caledonian Deuchars IPA; Theakston Best Bitter, Black Bull Bitter, XB, Old Peculier Ⓗ

The de facto brewery tap for Theakston, the White Bear offers food, drink, accommodation and conference facilities. There is a large dining area to one side and a small cosy taproom to the other serving almost the full range of Theakston beers. The pub hosts a popular three-day beer festival in late June with over 30 beers on offer. This place was a victim of wartime bombing and derelict for many years, before being renovated to a high standard. ❀🛏◐◑♿♣P🚌(159,144)🐾📶

Middlesbrough

Dr Phil's Real Ale House 🏆

10 Pilkington Buildings, Roman Road, Linthorpe, TS5 6DY (100yds N of jct of Roman Rd and The Crescent)

closed Mon; 3-9.30; 1-10 Sat; closed Sun ☎ 07525 337123
drphilsrealalehouse.co.uk
4 changing beers H
Opened in 2013 by a CAMRA member, this pub is in the leafy suburbs of Linthorpe among a terrace of shops, just over a mile south of the town. The five-yards-square micropub manages to accommodate an eclectic mix of drinkers, who have a choice of four changing guest beers as well as cider/perry. Since opening, over 500 different beers have been served. Often, a cask does not even manage to last the day. Winner of CAMRA branch Pub of the Year 2015. Q (11,17)

Swatter's Carr

228-230 Linthorpe Road, TS1 3QW (W side of university, 750 yds S of town centre)
8am-midnight ☎ (01642) 239060
7 changing beers H
Wetherspoon conversion of the Empire and now named after the original 17th-century farmstead, set in the heart of student land and a meeting place for Teesside University Real Ale Society. During the last 300 years it has been a hotel and an opera house, among other incarnations. The nine handpulls deliver the nationally contracted beers and guest beers (usually locally sourced) and there is a real cider. Meet the Brewer events, beer festivals, a January sale and celebrations of various saints' days are all hosted.

Muker

Farmers Arms L

DL11 6QG
11.30-midnight (11 Mon); 11.30-11 Sun
☎ (01748) 886297 farmersarmsmuker.co.uk
Black Sheep Best Bitter; Theakston Old Peculier; Yorkshire Dales Muker Silver; house beer (by Yorkshire Dales); 1 changing beer H
Traditional inn in the centre of a former lead-mining village, set in bleak but beautiful Swaledale countryside. Near both the Coast-to-Coast and Pennine Way routes, it attracts countless visitors. The stone-flagged bar with its open fire is popular with locals and walkers, cyclists and others. As well as a range of local ales there is a guest beer in summer, and home-prepared food is available every day. Q P (30)

Newton-on-Ouse

Dawnay Arms L

Moor Lane, YO30 2BR
closed Mon; 12-2.30, 6-11; 12-11 Sat; 12-10 Sun
☎ (01347) 848345 thedawnayatnewton.co.uk
Black Sheep Best Bitter; 3 changing beers (sourced locally; often Rooster's, Rudgate, Treboom) H
Country gastro-pub with an emphasis on locally sourced food and Yorkshire beer. The modern British menu often includes local game and guest beers are from Yorkshire breweries. The pub features in the Good Food Guide and booking is advisable. The interior is a mix of rustic wooden and upholstered furniture. There are two open fires in winter, and a pleasant garden that leads down to the River Ouse. Handily placed for the bus to and from York. Q P (29)

North Rigton

Square & Compass

Hall Green Hill, LS17 0DJ
10-11 (midnight Thu-Sat); 10-10 Sun ☎ (01423) 733031
thesquareandcompass.com
Leeds Pale; Theakston Best Bitter; Wharfe Bank Washburn Best H
A large, elegant dining pub with multiple spaces – the main bar at the front is pleasant for drinking, furnished with tables and leather armchairs, and there are two more formal dining areas, a more informal part to the side, and a further dining area with a counter at the back. Six handpumps dispense ales from local small breweries and there are well-stocked fridges with a selection of interesting bottled beers.
P (747,X52,X53)

Northallerton

Tickle Toby Inn L

180 High Street, DL7 8JZ
11-11; 12-11 Sun ☎ (01609) 778760
Black Sheep Best Bitter; 3 changing beers (sourced regionally) H
Taking its name from a notorious local highwayman and pickpocket of around the 18th century, this town centre pub has a long, narrow single bar with several drinking areas. Popular with all age groups, it offers a range of guest beers from local and regional breweries. It can be busy during the weekly Wednesday and Saturday markets which take place outside and on weekend evenings.

Tithe Bar

2A Friarage Street, DL6 1DP (just off High St near hospital)
11.30-11 (midnight Fri & Sat) ☎ (01609) 778482
Ilkley Mary Jane; Okells MPA; changing beers H
Cosmopolitan town centre bar just off the busy High Street on the road to the hospital. Part of the Market Town Taverns chain, it has a strong commitment to real ale and also offers numerous continental and speciality bottled beers. The decor is simple, with wooden floors throughout, and there is no music or other electronic entertainment, just conversation. Food is served lunchtimes and early evenings, with a brasserie open upstairs Tuesday-Saturday evenings. Children are welcome during the daytime.
Q

Osgodby

Wadkin Arms L

Cliffe Road, YO8 5HU
12-11 (midnight Fri & Sat) ☎ (01757) 702391
wadkinarms.co.uk/1.html
Brown Cow White Dragon; John Smith's Bitter; 2 changing beers (sourced regionally; often Copper Dragon, Ilkley, Old Mill) H
At the heart of the village and the community, this is a welcoming and cosy pub where the licensee is most sympathetic to CAMRA's aims. There is an emphasis on local beers, and you can expect a couple of mini beer festivals through the summer months. The Wadkin has recently begun to serve meals – look out for a discount for card-carrying CAMRA members. P (4)

Osmotherley

Golden Lion L

6 West End, DL6 3AA (in village centre, 1 mile E of A19)
⏲ 12-2.30 (not Mon & Tue), 6-11; 12-midnight Sat; 12-10.30 Sun ☎ (01609) 883526 🌐 goldenlionosmotherley.co.uk
Timothy Taylor Landlord; 3 changing beers (sourced locally) H
Popular with visitors to the North York Moors, this village on the edge of the National Park is the start of the long-distance Lyke Wake Walk. Hikers and others can enjoy a well-earned rest at the drinking tables outside. Guest beers are from Yorkshire breweries. There is an emphasis on locally sourced food, which has a fine reputation, but there is also a warm welcome for drinkers. Regularly changing beers are from Wall's and other local Yorkshire breweries, and a beer festival is staged each November. Q🛏◑⛺🚌(80,89)🐾📶

Pickering

Sun Inn 🏆

136 Westgate, YO18 8BB (on A171 400yds W of traffic lights in town centre)
⏲ 4-11; 12-midnight Fri & Sat; 12-11 Sun ☎ (01751) 473661 🌐 thesuninn-pickering.co.uk
Leeds Best; Tetley Bitter; 4 changing beers (sourced regionally) H
Friendly local CAMRA Rural Pub of the Year, close to the town and steam railway. Four guest ales are offered (three from Yorkshire micros). A cosy bar with real fire leads to a separate room, ideal for families and special events, opening onto a large enclosed beer garden. Children, walkers and dogs (on leads) are welcome. Regular events include a bi-weekly acoustic music session, community choir, monthly charity quiz and a vinyl night every third Thursday. 🐴❀♿🚆♣🍎🍺🚌🐾

Raskelf

Old Black Bull L

North End, YO61 3LF
⏲ 7-11 Mon; 5-midnight; 12-midnight Sat & Sun ☎ (01347) 821431 🌐 northyorkshotel.co.uk
Theakston Best Bitter, Old Peculier; 1 changing beer H
Enjoy winter visits when the massive central fire will match the warm welcome, or spend summer supping the refreshing ales, but do not miss the chance to appreciate a traditional village pub which has stood the test of time. With accommodation, food and a pool table to boot, if it were not for the convenient buses to either Thirsk or York you might plant roots. 🐴🛏◑♣P🚌(30)

Redcar

Turners Mill

Greenstones Road, TS10 2RA (off B1269, 800yds S of town)
⏲ 11.30-midnight ☎ (01642) 496021
7 changing beers H
This increasingly popular M&B Ember Inn and 2015 CAMRA branch award winner is close to the town's racecourse. Recently refurbished, a cosy, relaxing and welcoming ambience prevails. The ever-enthusiastic staff serve up to eight beers, one of which is usually a stout/porter/old ale, and all on a try-before-you-buy basis. Reasonably priced food is available all day every day. Quiz nights are Wednesday or Sunday. An email newsletter gives details of the pub's latest offers. Cask ale club takes place on Monday.
🐴❀◑♿🚆(Redcar East)P🚌(22,64)📶

Riccall

Greyhound L

82 Main Street, YO19 6TE
⏲ 12-midnight; 3 (12 Sat)-midnight winter; 12-11.30 Sun ☎ (01757) 249101 🌐 thegreyhoundriccall.co.uk
Tetley Mild, Bitter; Theakston Best Bitter; 4 changing beers (sourced nationally; often St Austell, Saltaire, Ossett) H
Busy village pub with seven real ales on the bar at peak times. A member of the OBE club, an Ossett beer can always be found among the regular Theakston and Tetley offerings, while three interesting guests complete the range. The pub boasts successful darts, dominoes and pool teams and is a fine stopping-off point on the York-Selby cycle trail. ❀🛏◑♿♣P🚌(415,416)🐾📶

Richmond

Bishop Blaize Hotel

Market Place, DL10 4QL
⏲ 11-12.30am (1.30am Fri & Sat) ☎ (01748) 518087
Timothy Taylor Landlord; 3 changing beers (sourced nationally) H
CAMRA-commended town-centre pub on the cobbled marketplace. With a strong commitment to cask ale, it offers three changing guest ales from national and regional brewers. Home-cooked traditional pub food is served in two dining areas. A popular upstairs sports bar features pool and live TV sport, while the main bar has music TV and regular folk nights. Richmond's spectacular Norman castle keep forms a backdrop to the beer garden. Accommodation includes an eight-bed dormitory.
🐴❀◑♣🍎🚌🐾📶

Ralph Fitz Randall

6 Queens Road, DL10 4AE (edge of town centre on main Scotch Corner road)
⏲ 9am-midnight (1am Fri & Sat) ☎ (01748) 828080
Greene King Abbot; Ruddles Best Bitter; 8 changing beers (sourced nationally) H
Large single-bar Wetherspoon house converted from Richmond's former post office and telephone exchange on the edge of the town centre. It is set on three levels, with a large family dining area and an outdoor patio to the rear. It offers several cask beers, usually including a locally brewed ale, and has won numerous CAMRA awards. There are several beer festivals each year. Opens at 8am for breakfast. Q🐴❀◑♿🍎🚌📶

Ripon

One-Eyed Rat

51 Allhallowgate, HG4 1LQ
⏲ 5-11; 12-11 Fri & Sat; 12-10.30 Sun ☎ (01765) 607704 🌐 oneeyedrat.com
7 changing beers H
A premier ale house set within a terrace of 200-year-old houses, its narrow frontage leading to a warm and welcoming family-run hostelry. It has seven changing guest beers plus a real cider, and there is always a pump dedicated to a mild or stout/porter, with another for a stronger beer at around 5%, plus a real cider. The pub hosts regular

live music and holds two beer festivals a year. A classic, and continuously in this Guide for over 20 years. Q (36)

Royal Oak

36 Kirkgate, HG4 1PB

11-11 (midnight Fri & Sat) ☎ (01765) 602284

royaloakripon.co.uk

Timothy Taylor Dark Mild, Golden Best, Boltmaker, Landlord; 2 changing beers (sourced regionally; often Saltaire) H

An 18th-century coaching inn in the centre of historic Ripon, beautifully renovated in a modern style, the Royal Oak serves a top-quality range of Timothy Taylor beers alongside regular guests from other Yorkshire breweries. The pub is divided into relaxed dining areas with log-burning stoves and comfortable seating, and has a first-class locally sourced menu. Accommodation is in six stylish and comfortable bedrooms, with a hearty English breakfast included. P (36)

Unicorn Hotel

Market Place East, HG4 1BP

7am-12.30am; 7am-11.30 Sun ☎ (01765) 602202

Adnams Broadside; Greene King Abbot; Ruddles Best Bitter; Sharp's Doom Bar; 3 changing beers H

An old coaching inn renovated and modernised to a high standard by Wetherspoon in 2011, its low ceilings and subdued lighting creating a different ambience to many of the chain's establishments. The rear bar has the standard national beers and a carefully chosen selection from smaller breweries in Yorkshire and beyond. The pictures on the walls celebrate local worthies such as Lewis Carroll, and the medieval splendours of Fountains Abbey. There are 32 letting rooms. P (36)

Robin Hood's Bay

Dolphin

King Street, YO22 4SH (on steep pedestrian-only road, down towards bay, from top car park)

11-11; 12-11 Sun ☎ (01947) 880337

Caledonian Deuchars IPA; Theakston Best Bitter, Old Peculier; 1 changing beer H

Olde-worlde pub, full of memorabilia, popular with locals and visitors alike, where dogs and muddy boots are made equally welcome. It comprises an atmospheric public bar where a real fire burns for most of the year and a large family/dining room. Three regular beers and a guest are served. Quizzes takes place on Sundays, with R&B on Mondays and folk club on Fridays. Access to this part of the village is not that easy for the less able-bodied. (X93)

Victoria Hotel

Station Road, YO22 4RL (at top of cliff by car park)

11.30-11.30; 12-11.30 Sun ☎ (01947) 880205

victoriarhb.com

Camerons Strongarm; Theakston Best Bitter, Lightfoot; 3 changing beers H

A warm welcome awaits at this 19th-century hotel in a superb location on the edge of the cliffs, overlooking the bay of this picturesque resort and providing stunning views from the tea rooms and gardens. The friendly bar serves six beers including two guests, usually from local breweries. Beer bats, holding six third-pints, are available. A good-value, highly regarded menu, including daily specials, is served lunchtimes and evenings. There is a separate room for families. Q P (X93)

Saltburn-by-the-Sea

Saltburn Cricket, Bowls & Tennis Club

Marske Mill Lane, TS12 1HJ (next to leisure centre)

8-midnight (1am Fri & Sat); 11.30-3, 8-midnight Sun

☎ (01287) 622761

2 changing beers H

Visitors are made welcome at this local CAMRA branch multi award-winner. A private sports club, it is run by an enthusiastic steward and is well supported by the local community. It is the watering hole for the local diving club, as well as other sports. The balcony, ideal for lazy summer afternoons, overlooks the cricket field and on match day Saturdays the club opens at 2pm. Two changing beers are served, often not even lasting the night. P (3,X4)

Scagglethorpe

Ham & Cheese Inn

Bull Piece Lane, YO17 8DY

11-11 ☎ (01944) 758249

3 changing beers (sourced regionally; often Brass Castle) H

Village pub 50 yards off the A64 Scarborough to Malton road, three miles east of Malton. There is a spacious single-roomed bar divided into two main areas, together with a separate restaurant which doubles as a function room. Three rotating guest ales, from Yorkshire micros and particularly Brass Castle, are offered. Home-cooked meals are served throughout the day. To the rear is a drinking/smoking area and a large car park. En-suite accommodation is available.
P (843)

Scarborough

Cellars

35-37 Valley Road, YO11 2LY

12-midnight summer; 4-11; 12-midnight Sat winter; 12-11.30 Sun ☎ (01723) 367158

scarborough-brialene.co.uk/cellars.htm

Bradfield Farmers Blonde; Camerons Strongarm; Daleside Monkey Wrench; 3 changing beers (sourced nationally) H

Featuring in the Guide for 17 years, this is Scarborough's longest consecutive entry. A family-run pub converted from the cellars of a Victorian house, it has six handpumps delivering guest beers from nationwide micros. Locally sourced, home-cooked food is served lunchtimes and evenings, with Sunday lunches particularly popular. Quiz night is Tuesday, open mic night is Wednesday, local acoustic acts appear on Thursday, and Saturday is live music night. The patio fronting the pub is an attraction in summer. Children and dogs are welcome and accommodation is available.
P (4)

Indigo Alley L

4 North Marine Road, YO12 7PD

3-11; 12-11 Sat & Sun ☎ (01723) 350599

Wold Top Indigo Ale; 3 changing beers (sourced nationally) H

Recently upgraded into a welcoming open-plan pub retaining a rustic feel and sporting a logburner, this venue has come back on the real ale and traditional cider trail after a few years in the wilderness. It is a true free house, with bare floorboards and the advantages of pool, darts, dominoes and chess. Locally brewed Indigo Ale and draught Gwatkins cider complement specialist lagers. It is dog and child friendly, with live entertainment every Friday.

Lord Rosebery

85-87 Westborough, YO11 1JW

9am-midnight (01723) 361191

Greene King Abbot; Ruddles Best Bitter; 8 changing beers (sourced nationally)

The Lord Rosebery was originally built in 1895 as the Scarborough Liberal Headquarters and then acquired by the Co-operative Society after WWII, who opened a walk-round store in the building. This busy pub is on two levels, with a bar located on both. Changing guest beers are available, food is served all day every day, and there are featured club nights. Q

North Riding Brew Pub

161-163 North Marine Road, YO12 7HU

12-midnight (1am Fri & Sat) (01723) 370004

northridingbrewpub.com

Timothy Taylor Landlord; York Guzzler; 4 changing beers (sourced nationally; often North Riding)

Scarborough's only brewpub and current CAMRA Town Pub of the Year, it serves at least six varying beers from local and microbreweries around the UK. There are always one or more North Riding beers available, complemented by an extensive range of bottled beers. The pub has a public bar, a quiet lounge and an upstairs dining room serving home-cooked food, all with real fires. Quiz night is Thursday. Q (3)

Scholars Bar

6 Somerset Terrace, YO11 2PA

4.30-midnight; 12-midnight Fri-Sun (01723) 372826

House beer (by Wentworth); 6 changing beers (sourced regionally; often North Riding, Ossett)

A warm, friendly atmosphere prevails at this town-centre pub at the rear of the main shopping centre, voted CAMRA runner-up Pub of the Year 2014. It has a large front bar and a games room. A house beer together with six rotating guests sourced from Yorkshire microbreweries are offered plus numerous ciders and perries. Food is served every day except Wednesday. TV screens show major sporting events. Twenty pints are the prize at the Thursday quiz.

Stumble Inn

59 Westborough, YO11 1TS (approx 200yds SW of railway station)

12-11; 12-10.30 Sun 07837 716774

stumbleinnmicropub.weebly.com/home.html

5 changing beers (sourced nationally)

The first micropub in Scarborough, this is a welcome addition to the local real ale scene, located a short walk from the railway station and formerly a solicitors' office. The single-roomed pub offers five rotating guest ales, with local breweries always represented. Up to eight real ciders and perries are also available. A quiet establishment which is ideal for a cosy chat and a chill-out.
Q

Valley Bar

51 Valley Road, YO11 2LX

12-midnight (1am Thu-Sat) (01723) 372593

valleybar.co.uk

Dark Star Hophead; 5 changing beers (sourced nationally; often Scarborough, Theakston)

A cellar bar with six handpumps offering mainly microbrewery beers, usually including one or more from Scarborough Brewery. Up to eight real ciders and perries are also available, Broadoak Perry being a regular, together with over 100 bottles of Belgian beers including Cantillon. Further rooms upstairs, one with a pool table, provide additional seating and can be used for meetings.
(4)

Selby

Giant Bellflower

47a Gowthorpe, YO8 4HF

8am-midnight (1am Fri & Sat) (01757) 293020

Greene King Abbot; Ruddles Best Bitter; changing beers (sourced nationally; often Adnams, Rudgate, Sharp's)

Named in honour of a local 17th-century botanist and converted from a furniture showroom, this modern and spacious pub is completely different from all the others in Selby. Artefacts and pictures from Selby's past complement the light and airy interior; the pub is deceptively large despite its small frontage, with an enormous stainless steel bar taking pride of place. Offering a typical Wetherspoon range of keenly priced beers, real ciders and LocAles, it is an important recent addition to the town's pub scene.

Settle

Lion at Settle

Duke Street, BD24 9DU

11-11.30 (midnight Fri & Sat); 12-11.30 Sun

(01729) 822203 thelionsettle.co.uk

Thwaites Original, Wainwright, Lancaster Bomber; 2 changing beers (sourced locally; often Settle, Thwaites)

Built around 1640, this former coaching inn has two comfortable high-ceilinged rooms for drinking: a main bar with wood panelling, a grand staircase and a huge fireplace, and the refurbished side room, accessed from the bar or via the dwarf door off the street. The separate dining area is light and airy with a modern feel. Outside seating is in the yard to the side of the pub. Tuesdays feature jazz and there are twice-monthly folk sessions on Thursdays. (11,580,581)

Talbot Arms

High Street, BD24 9EX

12-11 (01729) 823924 talbotsettle.co.uk

Theakston Best Bitter; 3 changing beers (sourced regionally; often Settle, Three Peaks)

Just off the square, this family-run free house offers a welcoming and friendly atmosphere. A stove glows in the large stone feature fireplace to the left of the main entrance, with pool table, dartboard and dominoes tables beyond providing a base for teams in local leagues. A pleasant, terraced beer garden is at the rear. The three to five guest beers and cider are usually from Cumbria, Lancashire or Yorkshire. Good-value food is served 12-8pm all week. P (11,580,581)

Sicklinghall

Scotts Arms

Main Street, LS22 4BD (3 miles W of Wetherby)
11-11; 11-10 Sun (01937) 582100 scottsarms.com
Black Sheep Best Bitter; Theakston Old Peculier; Thwaites Wainwright; Timothy Taylor Landlord
Welcoming 17th-century village inn with an excellent reputation for food, served in two large but intimate lounges. An upper-level bar caters for drinkers, while the lower level welcomes diners and drinkers. The garden area is popular with families and walkers in summer as this is good rambling territory. There is a village shop and deli in the pub grounds, with a post office visiting one day a week. P

Skipton

Beer Engine

1 Albert Street, BD23 1JD
closed Mon & Tue; 12-10 (11 Fri & Sat); 12-9 Sun 07834 456134
5 changing beers
Micropub opened in May 2014 in a tiny street close to the town centre and the canal. Offering five ever-changing cask beers, two ciders and an extensive range of bottled beers, owners Steve and Janet have made their mark on the Skipton real ale scene. The beers are stored in refrigerated cabinets behind the bar. The atmosphere is relaxed and friendly, there are books to read or borrow, and local information is available. Well-behaved dogs are welcome.

Bistro des Amis

1 Jerry Croft, BD23 1DX (entrance is from Jerry Croft, next to town hall)
10-11; 11-10.30 Sun (01756) 797919
lebistrodesamis.co.uk
2 changing beers
French-style bistro focusing on quality food and comfortable, relaxed dining. While the emphasis is on dining, the drinker is made welcome in a small bar area. The two handpumps offer an alternating choice: one either Boltmaker or Landlord from Timothy Taylor, the other Ilkley Mary Jane or Bridgehouse Blonde. Food is served all day Sunday. The mezzanine area is suitable for private dining or meetings for up to 10 people.

Narrow Boat

38 Victoria Street, BD23 1JE (alleyway off Coach St nr canal bridge)
12-11 (01756) 797922
Black Sheep Best Bitter; Ilkley Mary Jane; Okells Bitter; Timothy Taylor Landlord; 4 changing beers
On a quiet back street between the High Street and the canal, this civilised beer-drinkers' emporium is worth seeking out. Bare floorboards, old church pews and international breweriana create the atmosphere, with no piped music, jukebox or gaming machines to disturb the conversation. Guest ales, usually including a dark beer, are complemented by continental bottled and draught beers and up to four ciders or perries. There is a quiz on Wednesdays. Well-behaved dogs are welcome. Q

Woolly Sheep

38 Sheep Street, BD23 1HY
10-11 (midnight Thu; 1am Fri & Sat); 12-11 Sun
(01756) 700966 woollysheepinn.co.uk
Timothy Taylor Dark Mild, Golden Best, Boltmaker, Landlord, Ram Tam; 2 changing beers
Timothy Taylor-managed pub, near the bottom of Skipton High Street and handy for the bus station. One long bar serves both the comfortable front room with its real fire and the larger flagstone-floored bar behind. Two areas towards the rear are split level, with priority given to diners. Food is served all day. At the back, the traditional cobbled courtyard has decking with comfortable seating, a canopy and infra-red heaters. Accommodation is in 12 en-suite bedrooms.

Stillington

White Bear

Main Street, YO61 1JU
12-2.30 (not Mon), 5.30-11; 12-2.30, 5.30-midnight Sat; 12-11 Sun (01347) 810338 thewhitebearinn-york.co.uk
Leeds Pale; Samuel Smith Old Brewery Bitter; 3 changing beers (sourced regionally)
Two well-liked permanent beers are complemented by three frequently changing guest ales from local Yorkshire breweries, so there is always something new to try at this traditional free house. It is definitely worth making the effort to visit this country pub if you are not already a lucky regular. P (40)

Stokesley

Spread Eagle

39 High Street, TS9 5AD
11-11; 11-10.30 Sun (01642) 710278
Camerons Strongarm; Marston's Pedigree; 2 changing beers
A small, unspoilt market town pub where friendly regulars drink at one end and diners are warmed by an open fire at the other. Excellent, good-value home-cooked food, complete with details of where the produce has been sourced, is served all day. Two interesting and stronger guest beers from the Marston's stable are always on tap. Families are welcome. A rear garden leads down to the tranquil River Leven, where over-fed ducks amuse children and adults alike. Tuesday is live music night.
Q (29A,89)

White Swan

1 West End, TS9 5BL (at W end of town, 100yds beyond shops)
11-11; 12-10.30 Sun (01642) 710263
thewhiteswanstokesley.co.uk
Captain Cook Red Bay, Slipway, Endeavour, Black Porter, Discovery, Schooner Granville; 1 changing beer
A CAMRA branch multi award-winner and home of Captain Cook Brewery, this superb and traditional one-room 18th-century local is in one of the prettiest areas of this friendly market town. An enthusiastic, hands-on licensee and proud brewery owner serves the brewery's beers together with a locally sourced guest. Quiz night is Wednesday and music nights are held monthly. Beer festivals take place at Easter and in October. Ploughman's lunches are served Wednesday-Saturday. Dogs are welcome but children are not allowed.
Q (29A,89)

Thixendale

Cross Keys
YO17 9TG
⏲ 12-3 (not Mon-Thu), 6-11; 12-3, 7-10.30 Sun
☎ (01377) 288272
Tetley Bitter; 2 changing beers (sourced regionally; often Bradfield, Wold Top) 🄷
Evidence of life in Thixendale has existed for 10,000 years, and this single-room hostelry appears on a map dated 1851. At the heart of five dry valleys, it is popular with walkers, including those on the Wolds Way and, though remote, is well worth seeking out. The two guest beers come from independent breweries and are usually not more than 4% ABV. Children are welcome in the beer garden. Good-value, traditional food is served. Accommodation is in the adjoining converted stable. Q❀🛏◑♣

Thoralby

George Inn
DL8 3SU
⏲ 12-2 (Fri-Sun only), 6.30-11 ☎ (01969) 663256
3 changing beers (sourced locally) 🄷
Small, off-the-beaten-track 18th-century pub that lies tucked away in a small village a few hundred yards from the B6160 Bishopsdale road. The interior has been opened up into a single room but retains two distinct halves and is still cosy and comfortable, with a particularly impressive stone fireplace at one end. Separate apartments offer accommodation. Beers are usually from local Yorkshire brewers. Opens 7pm in winter.
Q🐴🛏◑⛺♣P🚌(156)🐾📶

Upper Poppleton

Lord Collingwood
The Green, YO26 6DP
⏲ closed Mon; 12-3, 5-midnight; 12-midnight Fri-Sun
☎ (01904) 337537 🌐 thelordcollingwood.co.uk
Marston's EPA; Ringwood Best Bitter; Wychwood Hobgoblin; 2 changing beers (sourced nationally; often Jennings, Marston's, Ringwood) 🄷
Fine country pub on the village green set in a lovely 17th-century Grade II-listed building, with friendly, welcoming staff. Up to five ales from the Marston's list are on offer, including seasonals. Good honest food is served lunchtimes and evenings (no food Mon, lunch only Sun). The comfortable interior features timber ceilings and pillars, real fires and a 19th-century carved oak bar. A fairy-lit beer garden, patio and children's play area are to the rear. Accessible from York by bus or rail. 🐴❀◑⇌♣P🚌(10)📶

Wass

Wombwell Arms 🄻
YO61 4BE
⏲ 12-3, 6-11; 12-11 Sat; 12-10.30 Sun ☎ (01347) 868280
🌐 wombwellarms.co.uk
Black Sheep Best Bitter; 2 changing beers 🄷
Cosy stone-clad bar with a dog-friendly front room and plenty of extra dining space, larger than it looks from the outside. The regularly rotating guest beers ensure variety all year round. With accommodation and hearty food to go with the beer, being snowed in could be a treat.
Q🐴❀🛏◑♿🍎P🚌(31X,31,29)🐾

Welbury

Duke of Wellington 🄻
DL6 2SG
⏲ 12-2.30 (not Mon & Tue), 5-11; 12-11 Sat & Sun
☎ (01609) 882464 🌐 thedukeofwellingtonwelbury.com
5 changing beers 🄷
Little gem in a picturesque village. It has a long bar with open fires and offers up to five real ales from local microbreweries. There are several rooms off the main bar serving as dining areas, with reasonably priced food sourced from local farmers and markets. Well known locally for its World Wellie Wanging Championship, it also hosts an annual beer festival in the summer. Stay in one of the five en-suite rooms. Q🐴❀🛏◑♿♣P🐾📶

Wensley

Three Horseshoes 🄻
DL8 4HJ (on A684)
⏲ closed Mon; 12-3, 5.30-11; 12-11 Sat; 12-6 Sun
☎ (01969) 622327
Theakston Best Bitter; Wall's County Town Gun Dog Bitter; house beer (by Yorkshire Dales); 2 changing beers (sourced locally) 🄷
Traditional old country pub on the A684, full of atmosphere, with its small bar and dining room both featuring low beams and real fires. Outside there is a terraced beer garden offering glorious views across Wensleydale, a real suntrap on fine days. Wholesome and reasonably priced lunchtime and evening meals are served daily. Real cider and perry complement the ales on the bar.
Q🐴❀◑♿♣🍎P🚌(156)🐾

West Witton

Fox & Hounds 🄻
DL8 4LP (on A684)
⏲ 12-3, 6-midnight; 12-midnight Sat & Sun
☎ (01969) 623650 🌐 foxwitton.com
Black Sheep Best Bitter; Theakston Best Bitter; 3 changing beers (sourced locally; often Yorkshire Dales) 🄷
Friendly, family-run free house full of character, with a down-to-earth bar and games room popular with locals and visitors alike. Good-value meals are served all week, with a roast on Sunday. The pub was a rest house for Jervaulx Abbey monks in the 1400s, and the dining room boasts an inglenook fireplace with quaint stone oven. A pleasant patio at the rear leads to the quoits pitch. Beware the tight entry to the car park.
Q🐴❀◑♣🍎P🚌(156)🐾📶

Whitby

Black Horse
91 Church Street, YO22 4BH (E side of swing bridge on way to Abbey steps, close to old market square)
⏲ 11-11; 12-10.30 Sun ☎ (01947) 602906
🌐 the-black-horse.com
Adnams Southwold Bitter; Black Dog Rhatas; 3 changing beers 🄷
Former CAMRA branch award winner, this little multi-roomed gem, dating from the 1600s, offers a warm welcome. The frontage, with its frosted glass, together with one of Europe's oldest public serving bars, was built in the 1880s and remains largely unchanged. Beer is served from five handpumps. Snuff, tapas, olives, Yorkshire cheeses

and hot drinks are always available, while hot lunches are served during the winter months. The cider is Westons Rosie's Pig. Accommodation is in four bedrooms. Q (X93,840)

Board Inn

125 Church Street, YO22 4DE (at N end of Church St, by Abbey steps)

11.30-11; 11-11 Sun ☎ (01947) 602884

theboardinnwhitby.co.uk

Caledonian Deuchars IPA; Theakston XB, Old Peculier Ⓗ

The last remaining Board of several that existed during the 1800s on Church Street – traditional shops that sold ale, among other produce, displaying their wares on chalk boards. Today, three beers are served, allowing the drinker, from the front snug, to admire the 199 steps up to the Abbey. There are also fine harbour views to the rear, where the recently refurbished lounge/restaurant serves reasonably priced meals. The famous Fortune's smokehouse can be found nearby. (X93,840)

Granby Hotel

34 Skinner Street, YO21 3AJ (West Cliff, between Flowergate and North Terrace)

11-midnight ☎ (01947) 601747

Camerons Strongarm; Jennings Sneck Lifter; Marston's Pedigree; Wychwood Hobgoblin Ⓗ

Marvellous privately owned free house, attracting both locals and those staying in the West Cliff B&Bs. This busy two-room pub is just off the main tourist drag and is well worth searching out. Though the pub is not tied, three of the regular beers are from Marston's, together with Camerons Strongarm. Particularly noted for its meals, both for value and for size, the Granby is ideally placed for those also requiring a visit to the famous Botham's bakery. (X93,840)

Little Angel Inn

18 Flowergate, YO21 3BA (200yds W of swing bridge, 200yds N of railway/bus station)

11.30-11; 11-11 Sun ☎ (01947) 820475

littleangelwhitby.co.uk

6 changing beers Ⓗ

Just off the main tourist drag and up a slight incline, locals and visitors alike are afforded a genuine friendly welcome at this recently refurbished pub where, it is rumoured, the remains of the Castle form part of the structure. Pub food, large-screen TVs, live music, outside drinking and even a horse mount, for those who require this facility, complement the six beers served in three separate rooms from a central bar. Local CAMRA branch 2015 Best Whitby Pub winner. (X93,840)

Station Inn

New Quay Road, YO21 1DH (opp bus and railway stations)

10-midnight; 10-11.30 Sun ☎ (01947) 603937

stationinnwhitby.co.uk

Black Dog Whitby Abbey Ale; Camerons Strongarm; Copper Dragon IPA; Whitby Platform 3; 4 changing beers Ⓗ

Next to the harbour and marina, this multi-roomed pub and recent CAMRA branch Pub of the Year offers a warm welcome. The enthusiastic licensees ensure that the eight beers, including the house beer, Whitby Platform 3, represent a superb range of varying styles, while cider and fruit wines mean there is something for everyone. Opposite the bus station and NYMR/Esk Valley railway station, the pub has become the discerning travellers' waiting room. Live music features three evenings a week. (X93,840)

Yarm

Black Bull

40-42 High Street, TS15 9BH (E side of High St, by old town hall)

10-midnight (1am Fri & Sat) ☎ (01642) 791251

theblackbullyarm.co.uk

Draught Bass; Sharp's Doom Bar; 3 changing beers Ⓗ

In the centre of a pleasant town, this popular M&B Oaktree pub, which has been under the stewardship of the same licensee for over 20 years, has the best and largest beer garden/heated patio in the area. It has been a favourite haunt for Teesside's 30-somethings for decades. Extended over the years, with two separate bars, there are now five handpumps. The pub is busy during the day, and extremely busy evenings and weekends. Good-value pub food is served all day every day. Q (7,17)

York

Blue Bell ★ L

53 Fossgate, YO1 9TF

11-11; 12-10.30 Sun ☎ (01904) 654904

Bradfield Farmers Bitter, Farmers Blonde; Timothy Taylor Landlord; 4 changing beers (sourced locally; often Brass Castle, Half Moon, Rooster's) Ⓗ

Recognised by CAMRA as having a nationally important historic pub interior for its Edwardian central bar serving two small rooms and side corridor served by a hatch. This is a small venue and it can get busy – there is a strict no-groups policy and entry may be restricted at busy times or on occasions such as race days. The three permanent beers are supplemented by a handpump dedicated to Rooster's ales and three guest beers. Sandwiches are available at lunchtimes. Q

Brigantes L

114 Micklegate, YO1 6JX

12-11 ☎ (01904) 675355

Okells Manx Pale Ale; 9 changing beers (sourced regionally; often Black Sheep, Leeds, Timothy Taylor) Ⓗ

Bright, roomy and welcoming real ale haven just inside the city walls. This Market Town Taverns pub has 10 handpumps that regularly feature local ales from York and Great Heck breweries (in addition to the examples listed above) alongside interesting guests and a range of continental beers and draught cider. The ground floor bar extends to a lounge area at the rear and sideways to a room reserved for diners until 9pm. The Georgian function room upstairs is used for regular social groups and dining. Q

Fox L

169 Holgate Road, Holgate, YO24 4DQ

12-11 (midnight Thu-Sat) ☎ (01904) 787722

Ossett Yorkshire Blonde, Silver King, Excelsior; Tetley Bitter; 5 changing beers (sourced regionally; often Fernandes, Rat, Riverhead) Ⓗ

Set in the Holgate district of York, the Fox is a pub whose history is linked to the golden age of rail. In the spring of 2014, the distinctive Ossett Brewery style was applied, sympathetically restoring this magnificent gem. It has the distinction of being a blue plaque heritage inn, making it a must-visit for anyone seeking out the city's finest watering holes. There is also a large and popular beer garden. P (1,10)

Golden Ball ★

2 Cromwell Road, YO1 6DU

5 (4 Fri; 12 Sat)-11.30; 12-11 Sun (01904) 652211
goldenballyork.co.uk

Everards Tiger; Timothy Taylor Golden Best; Treboom Yorkshire Sparkle; 4 changing beers

Opened as York's first community cooperative pub in 2012, this warm, family-friendly pub is identified by CAMRA as having a nationally important historic pub interior and is Grade II-listed. It has three rooms, a snug and a beer garden. The bar offers seven handpumps including regular Yorkshire beers and guests, along with fresh eggs and bread from local producers. The pub hosts traditional bar billiards games, community group meetings, open mic and quiz nights. Q

Hop

11-12 Fossgate, YO1 9TA

12-11 (midnight Thu-Sat) (01924) 261333
thehopyork.co.uk

Ossett Yorkshire Blonde, Big Red Bitter, Silver King, Excelsior; 5 changing beers (often Fernandes, Rat)

Good beer, pizza and live music sum up the Hop. Owned by Ossett Brewery, beers from its family (Rat, Fernandes and occasionally Riverhead) feature strongly, alongside other guest ales. The front bar area leads to a large open space with long tables at the rear and a stage for regular unplugged music acts. Formerly an Italian restaurant, it features original tiling and exposed brickwork throughout. Pizza, cooked in a wood-fired oven, is served lunchtimes and evenings.

Maltings

Tanners Moat, YO1 6HU

11-11; 12-10.30 Sun (01904) 655387 maltings.co.uk

Black Sheep Best Bitter; York Guzzler; 5 changing beers (sourced locally; often Rooster's)

The beer is the star at this popular pub close to the station. The cask ales change regularly – they are mainly from microbreweries, both local and further afield, with a focus on beers that stand out. There are reclaimed doors covering the ceiling and even a reclaimed toilet acting as a seat in one of the corners. A recent extension has provided more seating and a small area outside, while carefully maintaining the original character.

Pivni

6 Patrick Pool, YO1 8BB

11.30-11.30 (11.45 Fri & Sat) (01904) 635464
pivni.co.uk

5 changing beers (sourced nationally; often Tapped)

Founding bar of the expanding group of Pivovar UK craft beer houses, featuring five regularly changing cask ales from highly regarded breweries throughout the UK. There is also an extensive selection of bottled beers. The beautiful timber-framed building dates back to 1190 and spreads over three floors. Food is restricted to locally sourced artisan pork pies and cheeseboards.

Rook & Gaskill

12 Lawrence Street, YO10 3WP

4-midnight; 12-1am Fri & Sat (01904) 655459
rookandgaskillyork.co.uk

Castle Rock Harvest Pale; 7 changing beers (sourced locally; often Great Heck, Rooster's, Wharfe Bank)

Just outside the ancient city walls, this popular and simply furnished local, with a single split-level bar, keeps a varied clientele happy. A range of rotating guest beers fills eight handpumps, often from local breweries such as Great Heck and Brass Castle, supplementing the two regular beers from Castle Rock and Wharfebank. It was refurbished in 2012 and has a much-improved decked outdoor area. The menu focuses on home-made burgers (including vegetarian).

Slip Inn

Clementhorpe, YO23 1AN

5-11.30; 4-midnight Fri; 12-midnight Sat; 12-11 Sun
(01904) 621793 theslipinnyork.co.uk

Leeds Pale; Rudgate Ruby Mild; Timothy Taylor Boltmaker; Wold Top Wold Gold; 1 changing beer (sourced regionally)

Friendly and traditional community pub, just off York's famous Bishy Road, with two comfy bar rooms and a snug complemented by a rear courtyard. You will find four permanent ales from Yorkshire plus one guest at this independent free house, and many more at its seasonal beer festivals, including an annual festival with the nearby Swan. (11)

Swan ★

16 Bishopgate Street, YO23 1JH

4-11 (11.30 Thu; midnight Fri); 12-midnight Sat; 12-10.30 Sun (01904) 634968

Tetley Bitter; Timothy Taylor Landlord; house beer (by Treboom); 3 changing beers (sourced regionally)

A popular local pub in a traditional West Riding layout, with a bar in a wide passageway and two rooms either end of the bar. It has a nationally important historic pub interior and featured on the cover of Yorkshire's Real Heritage Pubs. The beer garden to the rear has a covered and heated smoking area. It hosts an annual beer festival jointly with the Slip Inn down the road. Three guest beers from around the country and two real ciders/perries are on the bar. (11)

Waggon & Horses

19 Lawrence Street, YO10 3BP

3-11.30; 12-midnight Fri & Sat; 12-11 Sun
(01904) 637478 waggonandhorsesyork.com

Batemans Black & White, XB, Gold; Oakham Citra; 3 changing beers (sourced nationally)

Multi-roomed family-run pub owned by Batemans. The bar area and front room have TVs showing BT sports. The other two rooms at the back are quieter and are used by various local groups to hold meetings. There is a bar billiards table and a selection of board games. Good-value accommodation and food are also offered, and regular live music and poker nights are held.

York Tap

Railway Station, Station Road, YO24 1AB

10-11 (11.45 Fri & Sat); 11-11 Sun (01904) 659009

18 changing beers

Impressive award-winning heritage conversion of the former Victorian tea rooms on York station, now a stunning pub with a circular wooden bar and stained glass in the ceiling domes and windows. There are 20 handpumps selling 18 cask beers plus two ciders or perries. Regularly rotating beers are chosen from a wide selection of Britain's finest breweries, with some of its own Tapped Brewery ales usually available. All styles and strengths of beers are represented. ❀♿⇌🍏🚌🐾

YORKSHIRE (SOUTH)

Arksey

Plough Inn L

2 High Street, DN5 0SF (behind church)
7 (6.30 Thu & Fri)-11; 12-3.30, 6.30-11 Sat; 12-3.30, 8-11 Sun ☎ (01302) 872472 🌐 arkseyplough.co.uk
Old Mill Blonde Bombshell; 1 changing beer (sourced locally; often Wentworth) H
Attractive, multi-roomed community pub where cheerful banter is the order of the day. A free house, this friendly hostelry features beers from small independent local breweries. Brasses and old photographs of the village adorn the lounge, which is heated by a log-burning stove. Reasonably priced bar meals are served Thursday, Friday and Saturday evenings. The excellent Sunday lunch is popular. Quiz nights are held on Thursday and Sunday. This pub is a real gem.
Q❀◑♿♣🚌(64,64A)📶

Armthorpe

Wheatsheaf L

Church Street, DN3 3AE
12 (5 Mon)-11 ☎ (01302) 835868
3 changing beers (sourced nationally; often Dukeries, Jennings, Skinner's) H
The publican is a cask beer enthusiast and holds mini beer festivals throughout the year. With three changing cask ales, chalkboards show what's on now and what's coming next. Family-run, the pub has a separate bar and lounge, serving home-cooked food Tuesday-Sunday, with discounts for CAMRA members. This is a friendly and a fun place to visit, and also provides pub games.
Q❀◑♣🍏P🚌(81,82)🐾📶

Auckley

Eagle & Child

24 Main Street, DN9 3HS
11.30-3, 5-10.30; 11.30-11.30 Fri & Sat; 12-10.30 Sun ☎ (01302) 770406 🌐 eagleandchildauckley.co.uk
Black Sheep Best Bitter; John Smith's Bitter; Timothy Taylor Landlord; 2 changing beers (sourced regionally; often Dukeries, Rudgate) H
A well-known and much-loved pub on the main road in this village. Dating from the early 19th century, it has real character. There are two bars, one with TV sport, the other quieter with tables where bar meals are served. The separate restaurant is decorated with photographs of local historical interest, and the home-cooked meals have a deserved reputation. A winner of numerous CAMRA awards, five handpulls here dispense well-kept real ales. Only one mile from Robin Hood Airport. Q❀◑♿♣P🚌(91)📶

Barnsley

Old No.7 🏆 L

7 Market Hill, S70 2PX
closed Mon; 12-midnight ☎ (01226) 244735
🌐 oldno7barnsley.co.uk
Acorn Barnsley Bitter, Blonde; 6 changing beers H
The No.7, part-owned by Acorn Brewery, has won a number of CAMRA awards including Regional Pub of the Year. The two bars offer eight beers from Acorn and other breweries. A changing range of ciders and perries is supplemented by a wide variety of bottled beers and ciders. Many events are hosted, ranging from Celtic music sessions to open mic nights, there is a popular quiz every Wednesday, and there are frequent beer festivals.
⇌🍏🚌🐾📶

Silkstone Inn L

64 Market Street, S70 1SN
8am-midnight ☎ (01226) 320860
Greene King Abbot; Ruddles Best Bitter; 5 changing beers H
In a busy shopping area, this venue is named after a famous coal seam that stretches under Barnsley. The decor reflects the theme and includes a pit head structure and black light shades with coal-like droplets. The central modern fire creates a warm atmosphere. Popular with families and young groups as well as older couples, a LocAle is available among the many other regional and national guest beers. Food is served until 11pm every day. Q❀⇌🍏📶

Barugh Green

Crown & Anchor L

Barugh Lane, S75 1LL (on B6428)
11.30-11 (midnight Fri & Sat) ☎ (01226) 387200
🌐 thecrownandanchor.com
6 changing beers H
Popular pub offering six real ales and one handpulled cider, with an extensive bottle and draught range from both local and international breweries. It has had a great local following from the start, offering good-quality locally sourced food with attractive daytime price deals. Two quiz nights feature each week. This is a great place to visit, with good bus links from Barnsley. ❀🍏P🚌📶

Bawtry

Ship

Gainsborough Road, DN10 6HT (on A631 near traffic lights)
12-11; 12-10.30 Sun ☎ (01302) 710275
🌐 theship-bawtry.com
4 changing beers (sourced nationally; often Jennings, Marston's, Wychwood) H
One of the local CAMRA area's success stories – the present licensees took over the venue in 2007 and have transformed this once run-down roadside pub. Extensively refurbished inside and out, it offers high-quality meals at reasonable prices. Four cask ales are always available, sourced from the Marston's range. Beer festivals are held twice yearly. This place should please just about everyone. ❀◑♣🍏P🚌(21,25)🐾📶

Birdwell

Cock Inn L

Pilley Hill, off The Walk, S70 5UD
12-10 (midnight Thu-Sat); 12-11.30 Sun
☎ (01226) 744227
Tetley Bitter; 4 changing beers H

SOUTH YORKSHIRE

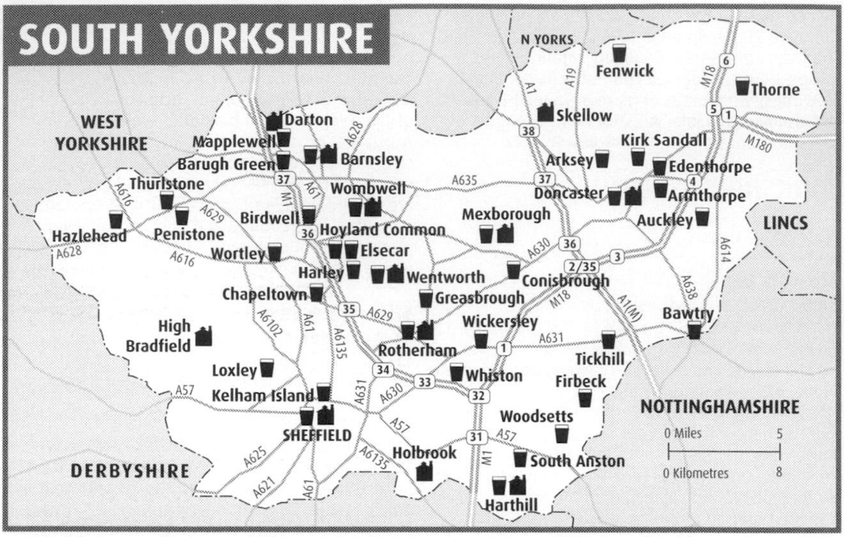

This small stone-built two-room village pub always offers a warm welcome. The larger room has a slate floor and open fire leading to a spacious lounge area with carpeting and plush seating. The smaller room is ideal for parties or meetings. Renowned for its good food, it can be busy for lunchtime and evening meals (booking for Sunday lunch is advised). Five cask ales are on offer including Tetley Bitter, and one real cider.
Q✿◑Å♣●P🚌(7A,67A)

Conisbrough

Hilltop Hotel L

Sheffield Road, DN12 2AY (on A630 at jct of Sheffield Rd and Old Rd)
closed Mon; 5 (4 Fri)-midnight; 12-midnight Sat & Sun
☎ (01709) 868811 thehilltophotel.co.uk
Welbeck Abbey Red Feather; 3 changing beers (sourced locally; often Acorn, Chantry, Concertina) H
A traditional free house serving up to four ales, mainly supplied from local breweries. Situated on the outskirts of Conisbrough, it offers a relaxed and friendly atmosphere. It is split into a public bar and lounge/dining area, the latter serving locally sourced, home-prepared food. The pie shop is open Wednesday to Saturday. Quiz night is on Wednesday (only £1) and includes free supper. Panel games are held on Thursday.
Q✿◑♣P🚌(X78)🐾📶

Doncaster

Corner Pin 🏆 L

145 St Sepulchre Gate West, DN1 3AH (on W side of dual carriageway)
12-11.30; 11.45-10 Sun ☎ (01302) 340670
Stancill Barnsley Bitter; 4 changing beers (sourced locally; often Geeves, Jennings, Theakston) H
Award-winning traditional pub conveniently situated for town and the travel interchange. Beers, in a variety of styles, are mainly from local independent breweries, with a discount for CAMRA members. Beer festivals are held twice-yearly. Food is served weekday afternoons and a popular Sunday lunch until 2.30pm (later if pre-booked). Inside there are lounge and public bar areas, outside there is a decked drinking space to the rear. Local CAMRA Pub of the Year 2015.
✿◑♿⇌♣🚌(71,73A)📶

Doncaster Brewery Tap L

7 Young Street, DN1 3EL
closed Mon; 12 (5 Tue & Wed)-10; 12-4 Sun ☎ 07770 958394
Doncaster Gold Cup; 5 changing beers (sourced locally; often Doncaster, Great Heck) H
Conveniently situated in the town centre, Doncaster Brewery Tap was opened in January 2014. The brewery, originally launched in 2012, was relocated to the rear of the pub in May 2014. This welcoming hostelry offers a range of the brewery's beers, a guest beer and a large variety of real ciders and perries. Green Oak Morris meet on a Wednesday evening, a spoken word evening is held every second Thursday, and a Phantom cinema film screened on the last Friday of the month. Q⇌♣●P🚌🐾📶

Gate House L

Priory Walk, DN1 1TS (off High St, near Mansion House)
8am-midnight (1am Fri & Sat) ☎ (01302) 554540
Adnams Broadside; Greene King Abbot; Ruddles Best Bitter; changing beers (sourced nationally; often Acorn, Caledonian, Elland) H
This purpose-built town-centre Wetherspoon bar becomes busy on race days but at other times provides a refuge of calm, away from traffic and crowds. With a single-floor bar and restaurant area, it caters for all types and ages. It holds regular beer festivals (independent of the national ones) and Meet the Brewer nights. Built on the site of the gatehouse to a medieval priory.
Q✿◑♿⇌●🚌📶

Marketplace Alehouse & Deli L

Market Place, DN1 1ND
closed Mon; 11-11 (6 Tue); closed Sun ☎ 07505 829106
3 changing beers (sourced nationally; often Imperial, Saltaire, Two Roses) H
This beer café opened in December 2013 and is unique in the area. In addition to the three cask ales on offer, visitors can choose from a range of

around 300 bottled beers which are categorised locally, regionally, nationally and internationally. Deli boards, coffee and tea are also available, served by knowledgeable staff. This place has a great buzz at all times and is well worth a visit. Q❀◑≋●⊟(76,77)ᯤ

Plough ★ L

8 West Laith Gate, DN1 1SF (close to Frenchgate shopping centre)

11-11; 11-4, 7-11 Sun ☎ (01302) 738310

thelittleplough.co.uk

Acorn Barnsley Bitter; 2 changing beers (sourced nationally; often Castle Rock) H

Known as the Little Plough, this is a friendly haven for anyone wishing to escape the town centre bustle. CAMRA-friendly, it serves a regular LocAle and holds twice-yearly beer festivals. The interior dates from 1934 and is mentioned in CAMRA's National Inventory of Historic Pub Interiors. There is a public bar at the front and a lounge to the rear, warmed by a real fire, with pictures of old agricultural scenes. Winner of many local CAMRA awards. Q❀≋⊟

Salutation L

14 South Parade, DN1 2DR

12-midnight (10.30 Mon; 11.30 Tue & Wed); 12-10.30 Sun ☎ (01302) 340705 thesalutationdoncaster.co.uk

Black Sheep Best Bitter; Timothy Taylor Landlord; 3 changing beers (sourced nationally; often Ossett, Welbeck Abbey) H

The Salutation is a popular, award-winning former coaching inn dating back to at least the 17th century. It is steeped in Doncaster's history – Doncaster Rovers football club started here using the upstairs room as a changing room, and there are many associations with horse racing. Real fires are a delight in winter. The pub has seven handpumps offering a rotation of well-kept real ales and ciders. Quiz night on Tuesdays is popular. ❀◑●P⊟(55,57,58)🐾

Edenthorpe

Eden Arms

Eden Field Road, DN3 2QR (adjacent to Tesco)

11-11; 11.30-11.30 Wed; 11-midnight Thu-Sat; 11-11 Sun ☎ (01302) 888682

Abbeydale Moonshine; Brakspear Bitter H**; Leeds Pale** H/A**; 2 changing beers (sourced nationally; often Black Sheep, Brains, York)** H

A fine, modern estate pub built in the late 1980s. Attractive and comfortable, it is one of the area's most CAMRA-friendly pubs. A CAMRA discount is always available and on Mondays all cask ales are discounted. Five are on offer, with a display at the entrance informing customers about present and future cask beers. Meet the Brewer evenings are popular, and it is notable for good-quality meals. Q❀◑♿●P⊟(87)ᯤ

Elsecar

Crown Inn L

22 Hill Street, S74 8EL

12-midnight ☎ (01226) 743823

3 changing beers H

Stone community pub a five-minute walk from Elsecar train station, and one of four real ale trail pubs in this picturesque and historic village. It is multi-roomed, with a dining room and new south-facing conservatory that makes an excellent family room. Food is served lunchtimes and evenings, and small functions are catered for. There is a small beer garden to the rear. Local and regional beers are always available from breweries such as Ossett. Buses run every 10 minutes. ❀≋P⊟(66,72)🐾

Market Hotel L

2-4 Wentworth Road, S74 8EP

12-11 ☎ (01226) 742240

Acorn Barnsley Gold; 4 changing beers H

A lovely traditional pub in this historic village. Its ideal location next to the popular heritage centre and proximity to the Trans Pennine Trail make the Market popular with locals and visitors alike. Inside is a multi-room hostelry with a drinking corridor. The walls are adorned with old photographs of the area. Outside, at the front, look above the window for the Horse and Gig for Hire sign. The constantly changing beers are from microbreweries and LocAle is always available. To the rear is an enclosed beer garden. Q❀≋⊟(66,72,227)🐾

Fenwick

Baxter Arms

Fenwick Lane, DN6 0HA (N of road between Askern and Moss)

12 (5.30 Mon)-11 ☎ (01302) 702671

Theakston Best Bitter; 2 changing beers (sourced regionally; often Leeds, Ossett, York) H

This wonderful free house is a rural gem and well worth seeking out. Run by the same family for over 25 years, the welcoming multi-room pub has open fires and a smaller room complete with snooker table. Fresh food, sourced locally, is served all day, and tea and coffee are also available. Beers are from small independent breweries. Outside there is ample parking and seating, with a large garden with a swing and a slide. Wednesday is quiz night. Q❀◑Å♣P🐾ᯤ

REAL ALE BREWERIES

Abbeydale Sheffield
Acorn Wombwell
Blue Bee Sheffield
Bradfield High Bradfield
Chantry Rotherham
Concertina Mexborough
Doncaster Doncaster
Dronfield Sheffield
Exit 33 Sheffield
Fuggle Bunny Holbrook (NEW)
Geeves Barnsley
Glentworth Skellow
Harthill Village Harthill
Imperial Mexborough
Kelham Island Sheffield
Little Ale Cart Sheffield
On the Edge Sheffield
Sheffield Sheffield
Stancill Sheffield
Tapped Sheffield
Toolmakers Sheffield
Two Roses Darton
Wentworth Wentworth
White Rose Sheffield
Wood Street Sheffield

Firbeck

Black Lion 🄻

9 New Road, S81 8JY (opp village hall)
⏲ 11.30-11 Mon; 11.30-3, 5.30-11; 11-11 Sun
☎ (01709) 812575
John Smith's Bitter; 4 changing beers 🄷
This traditional village pub and restaurant has returned to its former glory. It attracts diners, walkers and the local farming community. A free house, it offers four guest beers, usually including ales from local microbrewers. Pictures of old Firbeck adorn the walls of the snug area. It is a former winner of CAMRA Rotherham branch Best Sunday Lunch and other awards. The bus serves the village daytimes only (not Sun). Handy for visiting the ruins of Roche Abbey. **Q❀◐◑♿♣P🚌** (20)🐾

Greasbrough

Prince of Wales

9 Potter Hill, S61 4NU (1½ miles from Rotherham Central, corner of Scrooby St)
⏲ 11-4, 7-11; 12-3, 7-10.30 Sun ☎ (01709) 551358
1 changing beer 🄷
Do not be put off by the shabby exterior of this classic street-corner local – it continues to provide a warm welcome and top-quality cask beer at a fair price from a variety of independent breweries. The guest beer can change up to three times a day, ensuring its quality, and is served in rare oversized glasses. The pub has a traditional layout with a separate taproom and comfortable lounge. It has been run by the same family for over 35 years and has received many local CAMRA awards.
Q❀♣🗑🚌 (39,40,227)

Harley

Horseshoe 🄻

9 Harley Road, S62 7UD (off A6135 on B6090; 1 mile from Wentworth)
⏲ 4-10 Mon; 4 (2 Sat)-11; 12-10.30 Sun ☎ (01226) 742204
🌐 thehorseshoeharley.co.uk
Bradfield Farmers Blonde; 3 changing beers 🄷
Street-corner village local hosting regular events and home to football and pool teams. Guest beers change regularly, ensuring their quality, with ales often coming from local breweries. A carvery is held 12-3pm Sunday (book ahead to avoid disappointment). The Horseshoe has been the hub of the local community for well over a century. Handy for walking around the Wentworth estate and for the Needles Eye and Elsecar Heritage Centre. **❀◐◑♣🚌** (44)

Harthill

Beehive 🏆 🄻

16 Union Street, S26 7YH (opp All Hallows village church)
⏲ closed Mon; 12-2.30, 6-11 (11.30 Fri); 12-3, 6-11.30 Sat; 12-11 Sun ☎ (01909) 770205
🌐 thebeehiveharthill@gmail.com
Harthill Village Ace of Harts, Hart Stopper, Hart's Desire, Dark Hart; Tetley Bitter; 5 changing beers (often Harthill Village) 🄷
The Beehive, named after the beehive-shaped kilns used in lime burning, has been welcoming drinkers since 1833. Excellent home-cooked food and up to 10 real ales are offered. As the brewery tap, the full range of Harthill Village Brewery beers is always available. There is a full-size snooker table and a function room with disabled access. A popular beer and music festival is held in the garden in July. It is home to the Harthill Morris Men and a Friday folk club. Local CAMRA Pub of the Year 2013-2015. **Q❀◐◑♿♣P🚌** (29,74)

Hazlehead

Dog & Partridge 🄻

Bord Hill, Flouch, S36 4HH (on A628 Barnsley-Manchester road near Flouch roundabout)
⏲ 12-11 ☎ (01226) 763173 🌐 dogandpartridgeinn.co.uk
Acorn Barnsley Bitter; 3 changing beers 🄷
Perched high on the approach to Woodhead Pass, this ancient inn, whose history goes back to Elizabethan times, is a beacon of what a great pub should be. It is the perfect place to enjoy a choice of four real ales in front of the roaring open fire, or sample freshly home-cooked food in the cosy corners of the wooden-beamed rooms. This pub is proud to display its many CAMRA accolades.
Q🛏❀P

Hoyland Common

Saville Square 🄻

34 & 36 Sheffield Road, S74 0DQ
⏲ 9am-11 (midnight Fri & Sat) ☎ (01226) 747239
🌐 savillesquarebarnsley.co.uk
3 changing beers 🄷
A modern, warm and inviting bar, with lots of places to chill out, relax and enjoy one of the regular rotating beers from local and national breweries. It has become a popular destination for people to meet up and share a beer and a meal, with a choice of breakfast, main meals and light bites. In the few years this place has been open it has helped increase the footfall to the local pubs around Hoyland Common, and has truly become a great asset to the local community. ❀🚌📶

Kirk Sandall

Glasshouse

1 Doncaster Road, DN3 1HP
⏲ 11.30-11 (midnight Fri & Sat) ☎ (01302) 884268
🌐 glassh.co.uk
5 changing beers (sourced nationally; often Robinsons, Wadworth, Wychwood) 🄷
The Glasshouse has a long historic connection with the glass industry (it is close to the former Pilkington glassworks) and once had a bar made entirely of glass – alas, no more. The open-plan single-room bar has many large-screen TVs showing sport or news. Up to seven years ago, when the present licensee took over, the pub was keg only – since then real ale has become permanent, with five always available on handpull.
🛏❀◐◑♿⇌♣P🚌 (84,84A,84B)📶

Mapplewell

Talbot Inn 🄻

Towngate, S75 6AS
⏲ 12-11 (11.30 Wed); 11.30-midnight Fri & Sat; 11.30-11 Sun
☎ (01226) 385629 🌐 thetalbotmapplewell.co.uk
Two Roses Heron Porter; 3 changing beers 🄷
This friendly and popular pub supports the community through its buy-local policy and serves quality ales from local award-winning brewery Two Roses. A 17th-century coaching inn, it has had

extensive refurbishment exposing attractive stonework to the front of the building. Further work is planned internally. The pub boasts top-quality food both on its bar menu and in its quaint restaurant upstairs. Q P (1,93A)

Mexborough

Concertina Band Club

9a Dolcliffe Road, S64 9AZ (off Bank St, halfway up hill, on left-hand side)

7.45-11; 12-3, 7-11 Fri & Sat; 12-3, 7.45-10.30 Sun

(01709) 580841

Concertina Club Bitter, Old Dark Attic, Bengal Tiger; John Smith's Bitter H

Long-established club and brewery with an interesting history, and a regular in this Guide. The Tina, as it is known locally, was originally home to a concertina band which was formed in 1887. Pictures and memorabilia as well as many CAMRA awards decorate the main room; it also has a small TV and pool room. The cellar brewery provides three regular ales including the award-winning Bengal Tiger. CAMRA members are welcome, just show this Guide or your membership card.

Q

Imperial Brewery Tap

Arcadia Hall, Cliff Street, S64 9HU (opp bus station)

4.30-midnight; closed Tue; 12-midnight Sat & Sun 07428 584000

Imperial Best Bitter, Blonde, Bees Knees, Stout; 2 changing beers (sourced locally; often Great Heck, Steel City) H

Friendly brewery tap with a large main bar and a cosy lounge area, plus a separate games room. Eight handpumps dispense excellent-quality Imperial ales, which may include seasonal specials and one-off brews, as well as guest beers – all served in lined, measured glasses. A real cider is available too. There is entertainment most nights, with live bands on Friday and Saturday evenings. Two annual beer festivals are held, the December event featuring new breweries.

P

Penistone

Royal British Legion Club

14 St Mary's Street, S36 6DT

11-3 (4.45 Thu), 7-11; 11-11.30 Sat; 12-11 Sun

(01226) 766911

2 changing beers H

A well-supported modern British Legion club in this popular market town. It is large, comfortable and well-appointed, with a lounge/concert room and a separate large games/TV room with two snooker tables. Two competitively priced changing guest ales are sold, which are mainly from local breweries. The Trans Pennine Trail runs at the rear of the building. Bingo is played on a Monday evening and regular entertainment on other days. Non-members must be officially signed in (CAMRA members need to show a membership card).

P

Rotherham

Bluecoat

The Crofts, S60 2JD (behind town hall, off Moorgate Rd A618)

8am-midnight (1am Fri & Sat) (01709) 539500

Greene King Abbot; Ruddles Best Bitter; changing beers H

Originally a charity school, opened in 1776, it became a Wetherspoon pub in 2001. The selection of up to 10 beers is listed on a screen at the end of the bar. Local brews feature strongly among the guests. Two changing real ciders or perries are served from boxes behind the bar. The pub commissions a specially brewed beer four times a year from a local brewery. Winner of local CAMRA Pub of the Year five times and numerous other awards. P

Bridge Inn

1 Greasbrough Road, S60 1RB (alongside Chantry Bridge, between bus and rail stations)

12-11 (midnight Fri & Sat); 12-9 Sun (01709) 836818

Old Mill Traditional Bitter, Blonde Bombshell, Yorkshire Porter, Bullion; Timothy Taylor Boltmaker; 4 changing beers (often Old Mill) H

The original home of Rotherham CAMRA, the pub reverted to its former name after a spell as Nellie Denes. It is an Old Mill tied house, built for the nearby Mappin Brewery in 1930 using stone from the original Bridge Inn which dated back to the 1700s. Two guest beers are usually from local microbreweries. There is live music most Fridays and every Saturday, an open mic night every Thursday, and folk and jazz sessions once a month. The food menu is limited but good value.

Cutlers' Arms

29 Westgate, S60 1BQ

12-11 (1am Sat & Sun) (01709) 382581

cutlersarms.co.uk

Chantry New York Pale, Iron & Steel Bitter, Diamond Black Stout; house beer (by Abbeydale); 3 changing beers (often Chantry) H

Originally dated 1825 and rebuilt for Stones Brewery in 1907, the pub was restored to its former Edwardian splendour by Chantry Brewery, reopening in February 2014. It retains some Art Nouveau windows, tiling and the curved bar counter with an elegant dividing screen. It offers a full range of Chantry beers plus guests, and two real ciders are also on tap. Live music plays every Saturday evening, Sunday afternoon and most Fridays. The pub features in CAMRA's National Inventory of Historic Pub Interiors.

Q (69,72,73)

New York Tavern

84 Westgate, S60 1BD

12-midnight (01709) 375596 newyorktavern.co.uk

Chantry New York Pale, Iron & Steel Bitter, Diamond Black Stout; house beer (by Abbeydale); 4 changing beers (sourced locally; often Chantry) H

Listed as a pub since 1856 and reopened by a team from Chantry Brewery in September 2013, it has been fully refurbished as a real ale led venue. Five Chantry beers are on the bar, up to three guests and a real cider or perry, all at competitive prices. A large selection of foreign bottled beers and, unusually, snuff, are also available. The pub bears the old name of the area and a hostelry demolished when the nearby ring road was built. It is near the New York football stadium with Rotherham United memorabilia on display.

(69,72,73)

Sheffield: Central

Bath Hotel ★

66-68 Victoria Street, S3 7QL
12-11 (12.30am Fri & Sat) (0114) 249 5151
beerinthebath.co.uk
4 changing beers (sourced regionally; often Thornbridge)
A careful restoration of the 1930s interior earned this two-roomed pub a conservation award and acknowledgement by CAMRA as having a nationally important historic pub interior. The bar lies between the tiled lounge, a small corridor drinking area, and the cosy well-upholstered snug. There are usually three Thornbridge beers and three guests on tap, plus a good choice of malt whiskies. Live music features regularly and there's a weekly quiz on Thursdays. Q

Devonshire Cat

49 Wellington Street, S1 4HG
11.30-11 (1am Fri & Sat); 12-10.30 Sun
(0114) 279 6700 devonshirecat.co.uk
Abbeydale Moonshine; house beer (by Abbeydale); 9 changing beers
With 12 handpumps adorning the bar and over 100 beers from around the world, the Dev Cat is a great place for the discerning drinker. Now operated by Abbeydale Brewery, who brew the eponymous house beer, there is always a choice of its beers as well as a number of interesting guests. The menu ranges from light snacks through to hearty meals served all day to 8pm (6pm Sun). An excellent stopping-off point for anyone on a brief visit to the city.

Henry's

38 Cambridge Street, S1 4HP
9am-midnight (1am Fri & Sat) 0872 107 7077
House beer (by Clark's); 10 changing beers (sourced regionally; often Sheffield)
Former café/bar reopened as a free house in 2010. Now thriving again after a thorough refurbishment, it offers one of the largest selections of cask ales in the city centre, with up to 11 on tap. The ground floor is open plan, with seating at various levels around the long bar counter. Meals prepared from good locally sourced produce are served daily 11-7pm. Across the beer garden is the in-house Aardvark Brewery with its own bar, the Brewhouse offering a further eight beers.

Old House

113-117 Devonshire Street, S3 7SB
12-1am (2am Fri & Sat) (0114) 276 6002
theoldhousesheffield.com
House beer (by Stancill); 4 changing beers (sourced locally; often Great Newsome, Saltaire)
Unlike many of the trendy bars in the area, the Old House provides a homely atmosphere, giving it a wider appeal. There are seating areas either side of the entrance corridor leading into the main bar. Food, ranging from snacks to hearty mains, is home cooked and available throughout the day. The True North beers are brewed at Stancill and the guest ales are mainly from small Yorkshire breweries.

Old Queen's Head

40 Pond Hill, S1 2BG
10-11 (0114) 327 0704 theoldqueenshead.co.uk
Thwaites Nutty Black, Wainwright, Lancaster Bomber; 2 changing beers (sourced nationally; often Thwaites)
Dating from Tudor times, when it was originally the hunting lodge for the nearby Sheffield Castle, the pub is the oldest surviving domestic building in Sheffield. The central bar serves a U-shaped lounge and adjoins a superb beamed dining room in the oldest part of the building. It is the meeting place for history groups, and is included in popular ghost tours. There are themed food nights, including a Czech night on Mondays.

Red Deer

18 Pitt Street, S1 4DD
12-midnight (1am Fri & Sat); 12-11 Sun
(0114) 272 2890 red-deer-sheffield.co.uk
Kelham Island Easy Rider; Moorhouse's Pride of Pendle; Stancill No.7; 5 changing beers (sourced regionally)
A genuine, traditional local in the heart of the city. The small frontage of the original three-roomed pub hides an open-plan interior extended to the rear with a gallery seating area. As well as the impressive range of cask beers, including up to five guest ales, there is also a selection of continental bottled beers. Meals are served lunchtimes and evenings daily. A popular quiz is held on Tuesday night, and an upstairs function room is available for bookings. Q

Rutland Arms

86 Brown Street, S1 2BS
12-11 (midnight Thu-Sat) (0114) 272 9003
rutlandarmspeople.co.uk
Blue Bee Hillfoot Bitter, Reet Pale; 6 changing beers (sourced regionally)
Occupying a corner site in the Cultural Industries Quarter and near Sheffield's main railway station, the pub has operated as a free house since 2009, under the same ownership as Blue Bee Brewery. The comfortable interior provides ample seating either side of the central entrance, and the walls are decorated with changing displays of work from local artists, as well as photos of old Sheffield pubs. Most of the guest beers come from local and regional microbreweries. Food is served throughout the day until 9pm (6pm Sun).

Sheffield Tap ★

Platform 1b, Sheffield Station, Sheaf Street, S1 2BP
11-11; 10-midnight Fri & Sat (0114) 273 7558
sheffieldtap.com
Tapped Mojo, Rodeo; Thornbridge Jaipur IPA; 7 changing beers
Opened in 2009, this was originally the First Class refreshment room for Sheffield Midland Station, built in 1904. After years of neglect, the main bar area has been the subject of an award-winning restoration and retains many original features. Further seating has been provided in the entrance corridor and to the right of the bar. Usually, three beers are from the on-site Tapped Brewery, which was opened in 2013 in the impressive former dining room. The brewery can be viewed behind a glass screen. Q

Three Tuns

39 Silver Street Head, S1 2DD
11.30-11 (midnight Fri); 12-midnight Sat; 12-11 Sun
(0114) 327 6211 threetunssheffield.co.uk

Blue Bee Reet Pale; Sharp's Doom Bar; 4 changing beers (sourced locally; often Acorn, Blue Bee, Kelham Island) Ⓗ
A triangular-shaped pub on a sharp corner, it has raised seating areas and lots of wooden and brass features. Now operated by Reet Ale Pubs, along with the Closed Shop and the Rutland Arms, it is popular with real ale enthusiasts as well as local office workers. The friendly staff serve six cask beers and provide good-quality traditional pub grub. There is a quiz on Wednesdays at 6pm and occasional live folk music. Q

Sheffield: Chapeltown

Commercial

107 Station Road, S35 2XF
12-11 (midnight Fri & Sat) ☎ (0114) 246 9066
thecommie.co.uk
Wentworth WPA, Bumble Beer; 6 changing beers (sourced nationally; often Durham, Toolmakers, White Rose) Ⓗ
Built in 1890, this friendly, well-established free house is the tap for the nearby Wentworth Brewery. In addition to six guest beers, including a stout or porter, there is at least one real cider. An island bar serves the lounge, games room and snug. Beer festivals are held in May and November. There is an outdoor area to the rear, and an upstairs function room which hosts regular live folk sessions. Monthly tutored whisky tastings take advantage of the extensive range available. Children are welcome. No meals Sunday evening. P(265,31A)

Sheffield: Kelham Island

Fat Cat

23 Alma Street, S3 8SA
12-11 (midnight Fri & Sat) ☎ (0114) 249 4801
thefatcat.co.uk
Kelham Island Best Bitter, Pale Rider; Timothy Taylor Landlord; 8 changing beers (sourced nationally) Ⓗ
Opened in 1981, this is the pub that started the real ale revolution in the Kelham Island area. Beers from around the country are served alongside those from the adjacent Kelham Island Brewery. Vegetarian and gluten-free dishes feature heavily on the menu (evening meals served until 8pm, no food Sun). The walls are covered with many awards presented to the pub and brewery. Beer festivals are held every August and at various other times. Monday is curry and quiz night.
QP

Harlequin

108 Nursery Street, S3 8GG
12-11 (11.30 Thu & Fri; midnight Sat) ☎ (0114) 249 4181
theharlequinpub.co.uk
Exit 33 Blonde, New England Best; 8 changing beers Ⓗ
Operated by Exit 33 Brewing, the Harlequin takes its name from another former Ward's pub just round the corner, now demolished. The large open-plan interior features a central bar with seating on two levels. There are two regular and usually four other beers from Exit 33, as well as guests from far and wide, with the emphasis on microbreweries. A range of boutique bottled beers is also available. Wednesday is quiz night and there is live music at weekends. (47,48,53)

Kelham Island Tavern

62 Russell Street, S3 8RW
12-midnight ☎ (0114) 272 2482 kelhamtavern.co.uk
Acorn Barnsley Bitter; Bradfield Farmers Blonde; Pictish Brewers Gold; Thwaites Nutty Black; 8 changing beers (often Abbeydale) Ⓗ
A former CAMRA National Pub of the Year, this small gem was rescued from dereliction in 2002. Twelve handpumps dispense an impressive range of beers, always including a mild, a porter and a stout. In the warmer months you can relax in the pub's multi award-winning beer garden. Regular folk music features on Sunday evenings and quiz night is Monday. No meals Sunday.
Q

Shakespeare's Ale & Cider House

146-148 Gibraltar Street, S3 8UB
12-midnight (1am Fri & Sat) ☎ (0114) 275 5959
shakespeares-sheffield.co.uk
Abbeydale Deception; 7 changing beers (sourced nationally; often Abbeydale) Ⓗ
Originally built as a coaching inn in 1821, it reopened as a free house in 2011 following a refurbishment including an extension incorporating the archway to the rear yard. The central bar serves three rooms, and there is a further room across the corridor. Up to eight changing guest beers are on tap, together with real cider and over 100 whiskies. There is regular live music in the upstairs Bard's Bar, a quiz is held Thursdays, and beer festivals feature each year. Q

Wellington

1 Henry Street, S3 7EQ
12-11; 12-3.30, 7-10.30 Sun ☎ (0114) 249 2295
5 changing beers (often Beowulf, Millstone, Salamander) Ⓗ
A popular two-roomed street-corner local which champions a range of beers from small independent breweries. The 10 handpumps always offer a stout or porter, a cider and at least three beers from the in-house Little Ale Cart Brewery, which has recently relocated to larger premises, having outgrown the old brewery adjacent to the secluded beer garden. A range of continental bottled beers is also available. Q

Sheffield: Loxley

Nag's Head Inn

Stacey Bank, S6 6SJ
11.30 (10 Sat & Sun)-11.30 ☎ (0114) 285 1202
Bradfield Farmers Bitter, Farmers Blonde, Farmers Brown Cow; 3 changing beers (often Bradfield) Ⓗ
A friendly two-roomed country inn on the main road towards High Bradfield, it's the brewery tap for the nearby Bradfield Brewery. Six beers from the range, including both seasonal beers and one-off specials, are all sold at competitive prices. Good home-cooked food is served (no food Sun eves or Mon and Tues). Excellent views of the Loxley Valley can be enjoyed from the drinking area outside. The games room has a three-quarters-size snooker table. The pub opens at 10am weekends to cater for anglers and walkers. P(61,62)

Sheffield: North

Blake Hotel

53 Blake Street, Walkley, S6 3JQ
12-11.30 (midnight Fri & Sat) ☎ (0114) 233 9336

Acorn Blonde; 5 changing beers Ⓗ
At the top of a steep hill (pedestrian handrails provided), this community pub reopened as a free house in 2010 after seven years of closure. Extensively restored, it has retained many traditional Victorian features including original etched windows and mirrors. A large decked garden has been added at the rear. The five guest beers usually include a stout or porter, the majority from small independent breweries. The pub also provides possibly the most extensive range of whiskies in Sheffield, with over 200 behind the bar. Q❀●🚌(31,31A,95)🐾

Gardeners Rest

105 Neepsend Lane, Neepsend, S3 8AT
3 (12 Thu)-11; 12-midnight Fri & Sat; 12-11 Sun
☎ (0114) 272 4978
Sheffield Crucible Best, Five Rivers, Blanco Blonde, Porter; 8 changing beers (sourced nationally) Ⓗ
Reopened in 2009 after refurbishment following extensive flood damage in June 2007, this friendly, well-run free house acts as the brewery tap for the nearby Sheffield Brewery. The main bar, with its clean, bright interior, houses art exhibitions and a restored bar billiards table. To the rear is a conservatory leading to a beer garden overlooking the River Don. There is live music at weekends. Up to eight guest beers are available, sourced nationwide from small independent breweries, and at least two real ciders. Q❀♿♣●🚌(53)🐾

Hillsborough Hotel L

54-58 Langsett Road, Hillfoot, S6 2UB
12-11 (midnight Fri & Sat) ☎ (0114) 232 2100
hillsborough-hotel.co.uk
Wood Street Larch, Ebony; 5 changing beers (sourced nationally; often Wood Street) Ⓗ
Privately owned 4-star hotel with six en-suite rooms. Wood Street Brewery is located in the cellar and at least four of its beers are always on the bar, together with guest beers from a wide range of independent breweries. There are regular themed events, with folk music on Sunday evenings and a quiz on Tuesdays. The conservatory at the rear offers extensive views over the Don Valley, and a function room is also available. Brewery tours can be arranged. Q❀♣🚌🐾

New Barrack Tavern

601 Penistone Road, Hillsborough, S6 2GA
5 (11 Wed & Thu)-11; 11-midnight Fri & Sat; 12-11 Sun
☎ (0114) 234 9148
Acorn Barnsley Bitter; Bradfield Farmers Bitter; Castle Rock Harvest Pale, Screech Owl; 5 changing beers (often Castle Rock) Ⓗ
Multi-roomed pub with an original 1936 floor plan. It has a Gilmours-branded doorstep and distinctive colourful exterior tiles. There are up to five guest beers, including seasonal ales from Castle Rock. Home-cooked food is served daily. Winner of a 2014 SIBA Best Local award, there is a snug with a local sports theme, and the lounge features live bands at weekends and a comedy club on the first Sunday of the month. Outside is an award-winning heated and covered patio garden. A new function room with its own bar was completed in 2015. Q❀♣●🚌(53)🐾

Walkley Cottage Inn

46 Bole Hill Road, Walkley, S6 5DD
12-11 ☎ (0114) 234 4968
Abbeydale Moonshine; Adnams Broadside; Bradfield Farmers Blonde; Timothy Taylor Landlord; 1 changing beer (sourced nationally) Ⓗ
Originally built for Gilmours, this spacious roadhouse-style suburban local is open plan, with a large L-shaped lounge around a central bar. The extensive sunken beer garden at the rear has spectacular views over the valley. A popular quiz is held Thursdays. There are four regular beers and at least one rotating guest. Good-value meals including OAP specials are available to 7.15pm (5.30pm Sun). ❀P🚌(95)

Sheffield: South

Broadfield

452 Abbeydale Road, Nether Edge, S7 1FR
12-midnight (1am Fri & Sat); 12-11 Sun
☎ (0114) 255 0200
Abbeydale Moonshine; Kelham Island Pale Rider; Stancill Barnsley Bitter; 6 changing beers (sourced regionally; often Abbeydale, Stancill, Summer Wine) Ⓗ
Dating from 1896, the Broadfield became part of the Forum Café Bars Group in 2011. It has established a deserved reputation for quality food with an extensive menu catering for all tastes, including hearty hand-pressed pies and home-made sausages (food served until 10pm). A large range of bottled beers and whiskies supplements the nine cask ales on offer. Situated within the city's antiques quarter, the Broadfield is now a leading player in the Abbeydale social scene.
❀♿●P🚌🐾

Mount Pleasant

293 Derbyshire Lane, Norton Woodseats, S8 8SG
5-midnight (1am Thu); 12-1am Fri & Sat; 12-midnight Sun
☎ (0114) 255 4997
Tetley Gold; 5 changing beers (sourced regionally; often Abbeydale, Milestone, Welbeck Abbey) Ⓗ
Small, welcoming two-roomed pub housed in a former quarryman's cottage built in 1820, and largely unspoilt by progress. Since 1841 there have only been 10 licensees here. The public bar is adorned with a collection of beer bottles from the 1960s and the comfortable quieter lounge features rare whisky bottles consumed by the Whisky Club. There are two quiz nights weekly, and the pub hosts a darts team and a walking club. The annual beer festival is usually in August.
Q❀♣P🚌(20A)🐾

Sheaf View

25 Gleadless Road, Heeley, S2 3AA
11.30-11.30 (12.30am Fri & Sat) ☎ (0114) 249 6455
Acorn Blonde; Kelham Island Easy Rider; 6 changing beers (sourced regionally; often Great Heck, Pictish, Saltaire) Ⓗ
A 19th-century pub near Heeley City Farm, the Sheaf has experienced a chequered history but has become a real ale oasis since reopening as a free house in 2000. The walls and shelves are adorned with beer bottles and assorted breweriana and provide an ideal background for good drinking and conversation. A wide range of Belgian and continental beers, together with malt whiskies, complements the eight real ales. A busy pub, especially on Wednesday quiz nights and Sheffield United match days. Q❀♿♣●P🚌🐾

ENGLAND

Sheffield: West

Closed Shop Ⓛ
52-54 Commonside, S10 1GG
🕐 12-11 (12.30am Fri & Sat) ☎ (0114) 266 0330
🌐 theclosedshopsheffield.co.uk
Blue Bee Reet Pale; 7 changing beers (sourced regionally; often Blue Bee) Ⓗ
Following a significant refurbishment in 2013, there are now eight handpumps dispensing beers from Blue Bee, other local breweries and guests, alongside three real ciders and a perry. The area to the front of the pub has two large bay windows and comfortable seating, and the smaller space at the end of the bar is decorated with historic photos of the local area. There is also a display of eye-catching limited edition prints by a local artist for sale. A further raised area at the rear has a pool table. Q❀◐◑♣●P🚌(95)🐾📶

Greystones Ⓛ
Greystones Road, S11 7BS
🕐 12-11 (11.30 Fri & Sat) ☎ (0114) 266 5599
🌐 mygreystones.co.uk
Thornbridge Wild Swan, Lord Marples, Kipling, Jaipur IPA; 4 changing beers (sourced locally) Ⓗ
A spacious yet homely family-friendly pub, serving as the flagship for Thornbridge Brewery. It boasts eight handpulled real ales showcasing the Thornbridge range, including seasonals and specials. The Backroom hosts some of the finest in contemporary live folk/rock/blues and Americana in the country, along with comedy nights and community projects. Hot food is served daily 12-6pm, along with a range of locally sourced pies made using Thornbridge beer.
Q🐴❀◐♿♣P🚌(84)🐾📶

Princess Royal Ⓛ
43 Slinn Street, Crookes, S10 1NW
🕐 5-midnight; 1-1am Fri; 12-1am Sat; 12-midnight Sun
☎ (0114) 266 0752
Black Sheep Best Bitter; Tetley Bitter; 3 changing beers (sourced locally; often Welbeck Abbey) Ⓗ
This popular local tucked away on the side streets among a row of cottages was once a Victorian beer house. Converted to its present form in the 1920s by Gilmours Brewery, the original etched windows include one for Oatmeal Stouts. The central bar serves the open-plan lounge and a snooker room to the rear. There are quiz nights on Mondays and Thursdays with free sandwiches and chips. The upstairs function room has a pool table and is also used by the Crookes Folk Club on Thursdays.
Q🐴❀◐◑♣🚌(52)🐾📶

Rising Sun
471 Fulwood Road, Nether Green, S10 3QA
🕐 12-11 ☎ (0114) 230 3855
Abbeydale Daily Bread, Brimstone, Moonshine, Absolution; 7 changing beers (often Abbeydale) Ⓗ
Operated by local brewer Abbeydale, this is a large suburban roadhouse in the leafy western side of the city. There are two comfortably furnished rooms, with a raised area to the rear of the main bar. A range of Abbeydale beers is always served, with up to six guests, mainly from micros, dispensed from the impressive bank of 13 handpumps. There is live music on Monday with quizzes on Sunday and Wednesday. The popular Sunfest beer festival is held every July.
Q🐴❀◐◑♣●P🚌(120)🐾📶

University Arms Ⓛ
197 Brook Hill, Broomhall, S3 7HG
🕐 12-11 (midnight Fri & Sat); closed Sun ☎ (0114) 222 8969
Kelham Island Pale Rider; Welbeck Abbey Red Feather; house beer (by Acorn); 4 changing beers (sourced locally) Ⓗ
Owned by the University of Sheffield, this former staff club has an open-plan lounge with a bar at one end adjacent to a small alcove seating area, and a conservatory that leads to the large garden. There is additional seating upstairs with separate rooms for snooker and darts. The guest beers are mostly local and there are regular beer festivals. Entertainment includes a quiz on Tuesday and live blues or jazz some weekends. No food Saturday evening. Q🐴❀◐◑🚆♣🚌(51,52)🐾

York Ⓛ
243-247 Fulwood Road, Broomhill, S10 3BA
🕐 11.30-11.30 (12.30am Fri & Sat) ☎ (0114) 266 4624
🌐 theyorksheffield.co.uk
House beer (by Stancill); 5 changing beers (sourced regionally) Ⓗ
Occupying a prominent site in the centre of Broomhill, the York was built in the 1830s and was originally a blackmith's and alehouse called the Travellers Inn. Extensively refurbished in 2010, with parquet flooring and wood-panelled walls, it offers high-quality dining, with its own bakery and smokery. The house beers are complemented by a range of five local and regional guest ales and two real ciders. Beer and food events feature regularly throughout the year. Q❀◐◑♿●🚌(51,52,120)🐾📶

South Anston

Loyal Trooper
34 Sheffield Road, S25 5DT (off A57, 3 miles from M1 jct 31 heading for Worksop)
🕐 12-11 (midnight Fri & Sat) ☎ (01909) 562203
🌐 loyaltrooperpub.co.uk
Adnams Southwold Bitter; Tetley Bitter; 3 changing beers (often Kelham Island, Sharp's) Ⓗ
Friendly oak-beamed village local, parts of which date back to 1690, selling a range of real ales and good, wholesome locally sourced food at reasonable prices. Guest beers sometimes come from local breweries. Though redecorated recently, the layout is unchanged since the 1960s, with a public bar, snug, lounge and an upstairs function room used by many local groups, including a thriving folk club. Close to St James's Church, it is on the Five Churches walk and handy for Anston Stones Wood and the nearby Butterfly Farm.
Q❀◐◑♿♣P🚌(19,19B)

Thorne

Windmill
19 Queen Street, DN8 5AA
🕐 2-11 (11.30 Fri & Sat); 12-midnight Sun ☎ (01405) 812866
Timothy Taylor Landlord; 2 changing beers (sourced nationally; often Adnams, Black Sheep) Ⓗ
Close to the town centre and convenient for public transport, this friendly community pub has a smart lounge linked by an archway to a larger public bar. Unobtrusive big screens are no deterrent to conversation and cheerful banter. Up to three real ales from independent breweries are on offer. Outside is a large beer garden with play equipment, and ample car parking. Quiz night is Sunday. ❀⇌(North)♣P🚌(87,88)🐾📶

Thurlstone

Huntsman 🄻

136 Manchester Road, S36 9QW (on main A628 through village)
🕓 6 (5 Fri & Sat)-11; 12-10.30 Sun ☎ (01226) 764892
🌐 thehuntsmanthurlstone.co.uk
Black Sheep Best Bitter; Tetley Bitter; Timothy Taylor Landlord; 3 changing beers 🄷
Popular because there is no TV or insistent music, this pub has a fantastic ambience created mainly by a chatty and appreciative clientele. It is a hub for many local activity groups and a strong supporter of local charities. Food is only served on a Sunday lunchtime. Dogs with well-behaved owners are especially welcome. Q🐴✿🚌🐾

Tickhill

Scarbrough Arms 🄻

Sunderland Street, DN11 9QJ (on A631 nr Buttercross)
🕓 12-11; 12-10.30 Sun ☎ (01302) 742977
Greene King Abbot; John Smith's Bitter; Timothy Taylor Boltmaker; Wychwood Hobgoblin; 1 changing beer (sourced locally; often Chantry, Glentworth, Pheasantry) 🄷
A deserving Guide entry since 1990, this three-roomed stone-built pub has won several CAMRA awards over the years. Originally a farmhouse, the building dates back to the 16th century, although it has undergone structural changes since then. The snug is a delight, with its barrel-shaped furniture and real fire, while bar billiards can be played in the bar. An outbuilding doubles as a covered smoking area and an extension for beer festivals which take place in spring and autumn. Real cider is available on tap in summer.
Q🐴✿🛏♣🍎P🚌(22,205)🐾📶

Wentworth

George & Dragon 🄻

85 Main Street, S62 7TN (stands back from road on B6090)
🕓 11-11 (11.30 Thu; midnight Fri & Sat) ☎ (01226) 742440
Changing beers (often Wentworth) 🄷
In a picturesque village, this free house has been licensed since 1804. It offers up to eight ales from local and national brewers, with Wentworth and Chantry breweries regularly featured. The pub has a car park and patio, and a grassed area at the rear with a children's adventure playground and a craft shop. A marquee and function room can be hired. Home-cooked food is popular here. Convenienty located for historic Wentworth Woodhouse, The Needle's Eye and Hoober Stand.
Q🐴✿◐◑P🚌(44,227)🐾

Rockingham Arms 🄻

8 Main Street, S62 7TL
🕓 11-11 (midnight Fri & Sat); 11-10.30 Sun
☎ (01226) 742075
Black Sheep Best Bitter; Theakston Old Peculier; 4 changing beers (sourced regionally; often Wentworth) 🄷
Country inn dating from 1814 with three rooms, a function room and a barn, close to historic Wentworth Woodhouse and the Wentworth Brewery. At least one Wentworth beer is usually available. An ideal stop-off point for walkers, the pub offers accommodation, local entertainment and a range of home-cooked meals. It is a very welcoming venue, warmed by real fires in winter and with a patio and garden for summer drinking. A crown green bowling green is attached.
🐴✿🛏◐◑P🚌(44,227)🐾📶

Whiston

Chequers Inn

Pleasley Road, S60 4HB (on A618, 1½ miles from M1 jct 33)
🕓 12 (4 Mon & Tue)-11; 12-11.30 Fri & Sat
☎ (01709) 325676 🌐 thechequerswhiston.co.uk
Castle Rock Harvest Pale; Sharp's Doom Bar; Shepherd Neame Spitfire; Tetley Bitter; house beer (by Greene King); 1 changing beer 🄷
Standing next to a 13th-century thatched barn, this friendly local replaced an old coaching inn when the road was widened in 1933. One side of the bar acts as a taproom, with a split-level lounge to the right. The large garden features a barbecue area. Situated in the heart of Whiston, the pub is a regular local CAMRA award winner. The food is home-cooked. Features include quiz nights, discos, occasional live music and scooter club meets.
✿◐◑♿♣P🚌(25,27,29)

Hind 🄻

285 East Bawtry Road, S60 4ET (on A631 link road between M1 and M18)
🕓 11.30-midnight ☎ (01709) 532490
Abbeydale Moonshine; Brakspear Bitter; Tetley Bitter; Timothy Taylor Landlord; 2 changing beers (sourced nationally) 🄷
Large pub, built for Mappins Brewery of Rotherham in 1936. Originally the King Edward VIII, it was renamed when the king abdicated. Since refurbishment by Ember Inns the interior has been opened out, creating good disabled access. There are extensive gardens and a patio to the rear, with a snooker table upstairs (membership required to play). Daytime and evening – and now takeaway – food is popular. The pub runs a cask club and offers a 20p per pint discount to CAMRA members, with guest beers cheaper on Mondays.
Q✿◐◑♿P🚌(10,19B)📶

Sitwell Arms 🄻

Pleasley Road, S60 4HQ (on A618, around 1½ miles from M1 jct 33)
🕓 12-11 (midnight Thu-Sat) ☎ (01709) 377003
🌐 thesitwellarms.com
Abbeydale Moonshine; Chantry Iron & Steel Bitter; Greene King Abbot; house beer (by Tetley); 2 changing beers 🄷
Low ceilings and oak beams indicate the age of this building – it was a farm and alehouse before becoming a coaching inn in 1822. The pub has a separate bar and restaurant area and hosts regular quiz nights, karaoke and jam sessions. Outside there is a large garden with children's play area, a big car park and a front patio. The historic Manorial Barn is to the rear. Food includes a Sunday carvery with a choice of joints. An annual brass band festival takes place outside.
🐴✿◐◑♿♣P🚌(25,27,29)

Wickersley

Wickersley Old Village Cricket Club 🄻

Northfield Lane, S66 2HL (opp Wickerley Northfield Primary School, down driveway beside pitch)
🕓 5-10 (11 Wed, Fri & Sat); 12-10 Sun ☎ (01709) 700536

4 changing beers (often Chantry) Ⓗ
Since the club started offering local Chantry Brewery ales, demand for real ale has increased here and there are now four handpumps on the go at this comfortably appointed and friendly venue. The large lounge provides a more peaceful location for a quality beer than the local pubs. CAMRA members are more than welcome for a good-value pint, and of course you can always watch the cricket. Opening hours are likely to be extended when home matches are played. Rotherham CAMRA branch Club of the Year 2014 and 2015.
❀♣P🚌

Wombwell

Anglers' Rest

66 Park Street, S73 0HS
5-11.30 Mon; 5 (7 Wed)-midnight; 12-midnight Sun
☎ (01226) 345747 🌐 anglersrestwombwell.co.uk
Geeves Clear Cut; 5 changing beers Ⓗ
Small, friendly locals' pub on the edge of Wombwell town centre and the Geeves Brewery tap. The beer is excellent, sourced largely from the brewery, and supplemented by ales from other small independent brewers. It is an old-fashioned drinkers' pub. In keeping with this, patrons are expected to join in with the entertainment, including the popular Tuesday night quiz and music night on the second Wednesday of the month. The pub prides itself on being a traditional community local. Q❀●P🚆🚌🐾📶

Woodsetts

Butchers Arms

2 Gildingswell Road, S81 8QA
12-11 (midnight Fri & Sat) ☎ (01909) 567700
🌐 rawbrew.com/butchersarms
Courage Best Bitter; Raw Blonde Pale, JR Best Bitter; 5 changing beers (often Raw) Ⓗ
A joint venture between Raw Pub Co and Enterprise, the Butchers had a complete refurbishment in a contemporary style and reopened in August 2013. Raw ales are prominently featured alongside a number of guest beers across the two bars. A blackboard lists the full range. There is also an interesting range of foreign craft bottled beers to try. Quality home-cooked food is another attraction at this friendly community pub at the heart of an attractive village. Beer festivals and live music feature regularly.
Q❀❀◑♿●P🚌(19A,20)📶

Wortley

Wortley Men's Club

Reading Room Lane, S35 7DB (at back of Wortley Arms public house)
2-11; 12-11 Sat & Sun ☎ (0114) 288 2066
Timothy Taylor Landlord; 2 changing beers Ⓗ
A national award-winning club in the pretty village of Wortley, surrounded by countryside. Originally the estate reading rooms, the opulent interior and exterior feature exposed timber frames, ornate ceilings, wooden panelling and a real fire. Guest ales are from local and national breweries and a guest cider is always on tap. The club runs an annual beer festival in July. Show your CAMRA membership card or a copy of this Guide on entry.
Q❀●P🚌(23,29)

YORKSHIRE (WEST)

Addingham

Swan

106 Main Street, LS29 0NS
5.30 (5 Fri)-11; 12-midnight Sat; 12-10.30 Sun
☎ (01943) 831999 🌐 swan-addingham.co.uk
Ilkley Mary Jane, Black; Timothy Taylor Golden Best; 3 changing beers Ⓗ
This friendly village local retains a four-room layout arranged around a small central bar. The stone-flagged bar, snug and taproom are warmed by real fires in winter. Live bands perform on Saturday evenings and Wednesday is quiz night. Food is served Friday and Saturday evenings and Saturday and Sunday lunchtimes only. Guest beers are from the SIBA and Enterprise lists. Well-behaved dogs welcome. ❀❀◑♣P🚌(X84,762,765)🐾📶

Alverthorpe

Alverthorpe WMC

111 Flanshaw Lane, WF2 9JG (on road from Alverthorpe to Flanshaw; from Wakefield turn left at traffic lights in middle of Alverthorpe)
2 (11.30 Fri & Sat)-11; 12-11 Sun ☎ (01924) 374179
Bob's White Lion; Tetley Bitter; 3 changing beers (sourced locally) Ⓗ
Multi-roomed working men's club with a cosy interior and unusual stained-glass features. A wide selection of guest ales is offered, mainly from local micros. The club is a regular winner of local CAMRA awards. Live entertainment takes place Saturday and Sunday. Snooker and darts are among the traditional games, with wide-screen TV for the armchair enthusiasts. It has sporting teams, and a floodlit bowling green. ❀❀♿♣P🚌(103,114,115)

Baildon

Bull's Head Inn

6 Westgate, BD17 5ES
12-11.30 (midnight Fri & Sat) ☎ (01274) 976416
Saltaire Blonde; Sharp's Doom Bar; Tetley Bitter; 3 changing beers Ⓗ
Two-roomed establishment with log fires and a warming atmosphere. Although it is a locals' pub, visitors are always welcome. There are up to three regularly available real ales and three guests. Pictures of the local area in olden days adorn the walls. There is a quiz on Sunday nights. Occasional music nights are held and piped background music is often played. The pub is welcoming to dogs.
❀♣P🚌🐾📶

Junction

1 Baildon Road, BD17 6AB (on A6038)
12-midnight (1am Fri & Sat) ☎ (01274) 582009
Fuller's ESB; Oakham JHB; Saltaire Blonde; Tetley Bitter; 3 changing beers Ⓗ
Popular three-roomed local comprising a lounge, public bar and a games area. The four regular beers are complemented by three guest ales. Beers from the in-house Junction Brewery usually feature. Real cider and foreign bottled beers are also sold. Food is served weekday lunchtimes and other times by arrangement. A quiz night is held on Thursdays, a jamming session on Sunday nights and pub games during other evenings. A regular beer festival is hosted at the end of July. ❀◑♣●🚌🐾

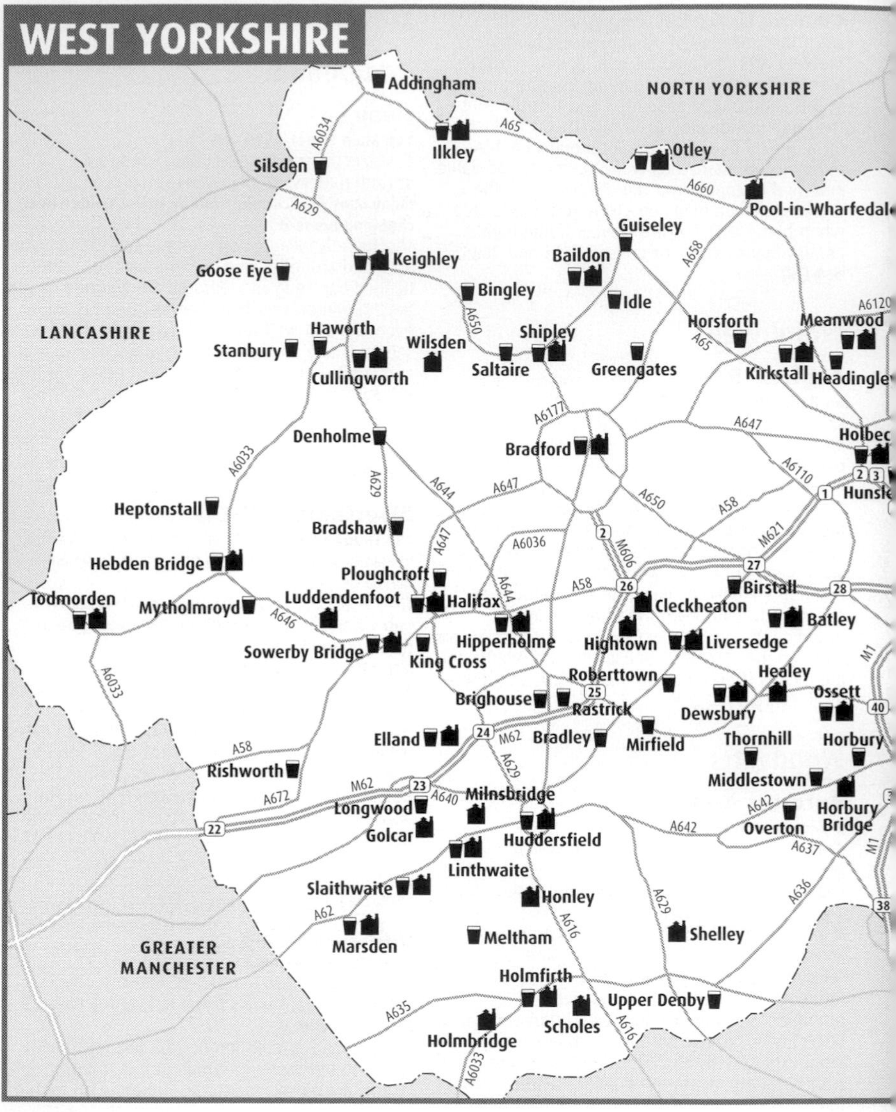

Batley

Taproom

4 Commercial Street, WF17 5HH

4-11; 2-midnight Fri; 12-midnight Sat; 12-11 Sun

(01924) 473223 taproombatley.com

Ossett Yorkshire Blonde; Theakston Old Peculier; 4 changing beers (often Timothy Taylor)

This friendly, vibrant meeting place hosts live music Friday to Sunday nights (free entry). The adjoining Barstow's snug/function room (formerly a greengrocer's) is quieter, decorated with photos of international stars who appeared at the nearby Batley Variety Club, and of local sporting and entertainment celebrities. Keen Batley Rugby League fans meet here. Four guest beers from reputable Yorkshire breweries usually accompany the two regulars. Food is served Thursday-Saturday 4-8pm and Sunday 12-4pm.

Bingley

Foundry Hill

Wellington Street, BD16 2NB (opp railway station)

closed Mon & Tue; 12-midnight (11 Wed); 12-9 Sun

(01274) 566144 foundryhillbar.co.uk

5 changing beers

Modern basement pub comprising a small bar area and an adjacent larger room. A varying range of real ales is sold, often from local breweries but also from further afield, and usually a cider. The pub can get quite busy, especially at weekends, when bookings for dining are advised. Events and entertainment feature occasionally. The pub, or part of it, can be hired for functions.

Off the Tap

Burrage Street, off Chapel Lane, BD16 1GH

closed Mon; 12 (4 Tue)-11.30; 2-11.30 Sun 07960 995267 offthetap.co.uk

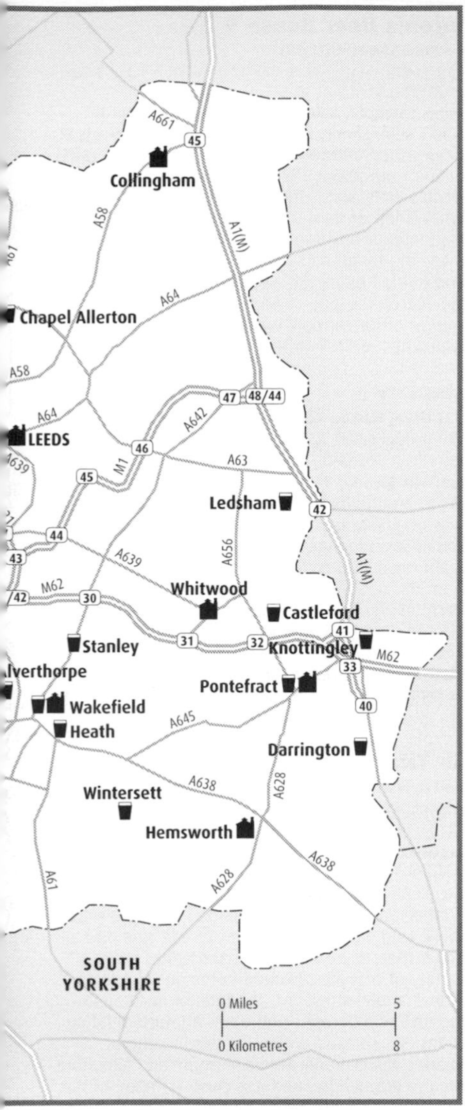

6 changing beers [H]/[G]

Single-room café-style pub offering up to six real ales, with the majority served direct from the cask. A range of beer styles and ales from local breweries are featured. At least one real cider and perry is also sold, as are bottled beers and wines. Live bands often play and there are regular open mic nights mid-week. The pub is closed on Mondays (except bank holidays) and usually the first few weeks in January.

Birstall

Horse & Jockey

97 Low Lane, WF17 9HB (on A643 near village centre)
12 (4 Wed)-midnight; 12-1am Fri & Sat ☎ (01924) 472559
birstalljockey.com

Jennings Cumberland Ale; John Smith's Bitter; Ossett Silver King; 2 changing beers [H]

A country-style pub first licensed in the 1750s, which lies west of the village centre. The open-plan bar is divided into four areas with half-panelled walls and beamed ceilings. Photos show it was once a Kirkstall Brewery house. Darts, dominoes and pool are played, on Thursday there is a music and knowledge quiz, and on Saturday

REAL ALE BREWERIES

Baildon Baildon
Barearts Todmorden
Ben Rhydding Ilkley
Bingley Wilsden (NEW)
Bob's Healey
Bosun's Horbury Bridge
Bradford Bradford (NEW)
Bridestones Hebden Bridge
Bridge Holmbridge (NEW)
Bridgehouse Keighley
Briscoe's Otley
Burley Street Leeds
Cap House Batley
Clark's Wakefield
Collingham Collingham
Elland Elland
Empire Slaithwaite
Fernandes Wakefield
Five Towns Wakefield
Golcar Golcar
Goose Eye Keighley
Halifax Steam Hipperholme
Hamelsworde Hemsworth
Hand Drawn Monkey Huddersfield
Haworth Steam Cleckheaton
Here Be Monsters Scholes (NEW)
Hungry Bear Leeds: Meanwood (NEW)
Ilkley Ilkley
James & Kirkman Pontefract
Junction Baildon
Kirkstall Leeds: Kirkstall
Landlord's Friend Luddendenfoot
Leeds Leeds: Holbeck
Linfit Linthwaite
Little Valley Hebden Bridge
Magic Rock Huddersfield
Mallinson's Huddersfield
Milltown Milnsbridge
New Inn Liversedge
Nook Holmfirth
Northern Monk Holbeck
Oates Halifax
Old Spot Cullingworth
Ossett Ossett
Partners Hightown
Rat Huddersfield
Revolutions Whitwood
Ridgeside Leeds: Meanwood
Riverhead Marsden
Salamander Bradford
Saltaire Shipley
Slighty Foxed Sowerby Bridge
Small World Shelley
Sportsman Huddersfield (brewing suspended)
Stod Fold Halifax
Summer Wine Honley
Sunbeam Leeds
Tapped Leeds
Thirstin Honley
Tigertops Wakefield
Timothy Taylor Keighley
Wharfe Bank Pool-in-Wharfedale
Wharfedale Ilkley

karaoke. Guest beers come mainly from independent breweries. Outside is a paved drinking and smoking patio. Pub policy says no hats, no tracksuit bottoms.
❀♣P🚌(283,229,220)📶

Bradford

Castle 𝕃

20 Grattan Road, BD1 2LU
⏲ 12-11; 1-11 Sun ☎ (01274) 393166
Jennings Cumberland Ale; 3 changing beers Ⓗ
A traditional English pub in an imposing stone building dating from 1898, comprising a large open-plan room with a wraparound bar to one side. Formerly a Webster's house, it now sells a variety of beers of varying strengths in a relaxing atmosphere, and often stocks at least one ale from a local brewery. A dartboard and TV are located to one end. Live folk music plays on a Friday night.
🛋♿⇌(Forster Square)♣🍎🚌🐾

Corn Dolly 𝕃

110 Bolton Road, BD1 4DE
⏲ 11.30-11; 12-10.30 Sun ☎ (01274) 720219
Everards Tiger; Moorhouse's Pride of Pendle; Timothy Taylor Boltmaker; 5 changing beers Ⓗ
Multi award-winning pub a short distance from the city centre and Forster Square railway station. Previously called the Wharf due to its location near the former Bradford Canal, it first opened its doors in 1834. An open-plan layout incorporates a games area to one end. Good-value food is served weekday lunchtimes. It has a friendly atmosphere and is popular before Bradford City matches. A collection of pumpclips adorns the beams.
◐⇌(Forster Square)♣P🚌

Fighting Cock 𝕃

21-23 Preston Street, Listerhills, BD7 1JE (close to Grattans, off Thornton Rd)
⏲ 11.30-11; 12-10.30 Sun ☎ (01274) 726907
Ilkley Mary Jane; Theakston Old Peculier; Timothy Taylor Golden Best, Boltmaker, Landlord; 7 changing beers Ⓗ
A drinkers' paradise in an industrial area, this multi award-winning pub is 20 minutes' walk from the city centre and close to bus routes along Thornton Road and Legrams Lane. It is a popular, unpretentious venue that appeals to a wide variety of people, from loyal locals to well-travelled ale enthusiasts. Twelve real ales are usually on sale, including at least one dark beer. A choice of real ciders and foreign bottled beers is also offered. Good-value lunches are served Monday-Saturday.
◐♣🍎🚌🐾

Haigy's 𝕃

31 Lumb Lane, Manningham, BD8 7QU
⏲ 5-1am (2am Sat); 2-10.30 Sun ☎ (01274) 731644
Tetley Bitter; 4 changing beers Ⓗ
Friendly locals' pub on the edge of the city centre. The guest ales are often of the blonde and golden variety and mainly from local microbreweries. A fine collection of porcelain teapots and an extensive range of pictures is on display in the comfortable lounge. There is a heated smoking area to the rear and a large-screen TV for sport. On Saturdays, when Bradford City FC are playing at home, the pub opens at midday.
❀⇌(Forster Square)♣P🚌🐾📶

Jacob's Beer House 🏆 𝕃

14 Kent Street, BD1 5RL
⏲ 4-11 (10 Mon); 3-11.30 Thu; 12-11.30 Fri & Sat; 3-8 Sun
☎ (01274) 394479
Oates Caragold; Salamander Mudpuppy; Stancill Tom's Mild; Titanic Plum Porter; 5 changing beers Ⓗ
Refurbished and reopened in May 2013, this pub, dating from about 1830, was formerly known as Jacob's Well, and is the only building remaining on what is left of Kent Street. The single-room, open-plan interior has a rustic feel. Nine handpulls offer a varying range and style of real ales. Real cider and bottled beers are also on sale. Menus can be viewed on the pub's Facebook page. The nearby council office car park can be used evenings and weekends. ❀◐◑⇌(Interchange)🍎🚌📶

Monkey 𝕃

931 Great Horton Road, Great Horton, BD7 4AQ
⏲ 3-midnight (1am Fri); 1-1am Sat; 1-midnight Sun
☎ (01797) 596 5991
Junction Blonde; 3 changing beers Ⓗ
Between Bradford and Queensbury, this free house was originally two 17th-century cottages and comprises a lounge and games room. There are real fires during colder periods. The real ales are from the nearby Junction Brewery plus other local microbreweries. Bottled imported beers are also offered. One of the outdoor areas has a barbecue and a covered, seated smoking area. The other is elevated and offers magnificent views over and beyond Bradford. The pool table, jukebox and Wi-Fi are all free. 🛋❀♣🚌(576,610,614)🐾📶

Sir Titus Salt 𝕃

Unit B, Windsor Baths, Morley Street, BD7 1AQ (behind Alhambra theatre)
⏲ 8am-midnight (1am Fri & Sat) ☎ (01274) 732853
Greene King Abbot; Ruddles Best Bitter; 6 changing beers Ⓗ
Excellent conversion of a former public baths by Wetherspoon, comprising a large open-plan main room with an additional room to one side and an upper mezzanine area. Ten handpumps serve a variety of real ales. Named in honour of a local industrial philanthropist, the interior decoration includes photographs and other artefacts relating to his life. Located within Bradford's cultural quarter, the National Media Museum and Alhambra theatre are nearby, and it is close to many of the city's famous curry houses.
Q🛋◐◑♿⇌(Interchange)🍎🚌📶

Sparrow Bar Bier Café 𝕃

32 North Parade, BD1 3HZ
⏲ 11-11 (midnight Thu-Sat); 12-11 Sun ☎ (01274) 270772
🌐 thesparrowbradford.co.uk
4 changing beers Ⓗ
Opened in 2011 by local enthusiasts, this is a simply furnished café-style pub. It offers a main bar area with additional seating in the basement. Four varying cask ales cover a range of beer styles and strengths, while imported Pilsners are served on draught. At least two real ciders are available. No meals are provided but there are deli sandwiches and platters. ♿⇌(Forster Square)🍎🚌🐾📶

Bradley

White Cross

2 Bradley Road, HD2 1XD (on A62, 3 miles from Huddersfield centre, at Leeds Rd/Bradley Rd crossroads)

11.45-11 (midnight Fri & Sat); 12-10.30 Sun
(01484) 425728
Hawkshead Bitter; St Austell Tribute; 3 changing beers H
Standing at a busy crossroads and close to the canal, this award-winning local has featured for over 10 years in the Guide. Its historic roots date from 1806 and it still retains its Bentley Yorkshire Breweries' green-tiled entrance and windows. The dining area and lounge sit either side of the central bar, where two regular beers are supported by up to three varied guests. Home-cooked food is served lunchtimes (but no food Sat).

Bradshaw

Golden Fleece

1 Bradshaw Lane, HX2 9UZ
4-11 (midnight Fri); 12-midnight Sat; 12-10.30 Sun 07522 190990 goldenfleecebradshaw.co.uk
Saltaire Blonde; Theakston Best Bitter; 2 changing beers H
At the heart of Bradshaw, this busy village pub provides the focus for a variety of sports enthusiasts, including pool teams, Sunday footballers and a Sky TV dominoes team. Popular with quiz teams two nights a week, it also has a Saturday disco night, as well as '60s and '70s theme nights. Barbecues are held in the summer to take advantage of the beer garden which enjoys excellent views across nearby countryside. There is a free buffet every Friday night.
P (504,521,539)

Brighouse

Red Rooster

123 Elland Road, Brookfoot, HD6 2QR (on A6025 towards Elland)
4-11; 12-midnight Fri & Sat; 12-10.30 Sun
(01484) 713737
Abbeydale Moonshine; Moorhouse's Blond Witch; Saltaire Blonde; Timothy Taylor Boltmaker, Landlord; 4 changing beers H
Half a mile from Brighouse town centre, it is well worth the walk to this excellent free house. Formerly known as the Wharf, the Rooster was purpose-built around 1900 for the adjacent coal wharf which served much of western Yorkshire. Three wharfmen's cottages still stand alongside the pub by the Red Beck. About 400 yards further on is the Cromwell Bottom nature reserve, from where you can walk along the canal to Elland or Brighouse. Dark beers are always on tap.
P (571,E7,E8)

Richard Oastler

Bethell Street, HD6 1JN
8am-midnight (1am Fri & Sat) (01484) 401756
Greene King Abbot; Ruddles Best Bitter; Sharp's Doom Bar; 7 changing beers H
An interesting Wetherspoon conversion of a Methodist chapel built in 1878. In 2014 it was extended into a later chapel annexe not previously occupied by the pub – this room is available for private functions. The main bar area is lit by two chandeliers hanging from an intriguingly decorated ceiling. Organ pipes, pews and even hymn numbers can still be seen on the upper floor, which is not open to the public. Q

Castleford

Junction

Carlton Street, WF10 1EE (on corner of Carlton St at top of town centre)
2-9 Mon & Tue; 12 (2 Wed & Thu)-11 (01977) 278867
Samuel Smith Old Brewery Bitter; 6 changing beers (often Ridgeside) H
Rejuvenated pub specialising in beers in the landlord's own wooden casks, which are loaned to enterprising local brewers such as Ridgeside, Elland and Wall's. A regular Ridgeside beer, Sam Smith's Old Brewery Bitter and up to six guest beers are dispensed from the wood. It stages an annual Easter Woodfest beer festival. The large horseshoe-shaped bar is kept warm with open fires, and a stove-heated snug is available for functions. Folk night is on the last Sunday of each month, quiz night is Wednesday. Handy for bus and train stations. Q

Cullingworth

George Hotel

Station Road, BD13 5HN
12-11 (midnight Fri & Sat) (01535) 275566
thegeorgecullingworth.co.uk
Old Spot Light But Dark, Spot Light, OSB, Spot o' Bother; 3 changing beers (sourced nationally; often Old Spot) H
Rescued from oblivion in 2011 by local brewery owners, this lovely old-fashioned village pub has a nice setting near the church. The emphasis is primarily on food although there is also a pleasant drinking area. Substantial meals are available from the extensive and imaginative menu, with meal deals offered Mondays and Wednesdays from 5pm. It is the brewery tap for Old Spot Brewery and the beers sold are from its core range as well as specials. Children are welcome until 9pm.
P

Darrington

Spread Eagle

Estcourt Road, WF8 3AP (in centre of village on road linking A1 Darrington exit with Pontefract)
12-3 (not Mon), 5-11; 12-3, 5-midnight Sat; 12-10.30 Sun
(01977) 699698
Leeds Pale; 3 changing beers H
A former coaching inn, this friendly and welcoming community pub is at the heart of the village. Good-quality food is served both in the bar and in a small dining area (no food Sun eve or all day Mon). Monday is quiz night. There is a pleasant function room for hire and a patio outside. It is said that the building is haunted by the ghost of a boy who was shot for horse rustling in 1685.
QP (408,409)

Denholme

New Inn

Denholme Gate, BD13 4JT (on A629)
5-11; 2-11 Sat & Sun 07887 510354
Tetley Bitter; 3 changing beers H
Friendly locals' pub alongside the Keighley to Halifax road, high on the hillside with stunning views. It supports local microbreweries and frequently offers guest ales from further afield, with all beers keenly priced. The interior has an open-plan layout while retaining a multi-room

feel. The conservatory houses a pool table and matches are played on Monday nights. Tuesday is jam night. For the energetic, the Great Northern walking/cycling trail is nearby.

Dewsbury

West Riding Refreshment Rooms

Dewsbury Railway Station, Wellington Road, WF13 1HF

11 (12 Mon)-11; 11-midnight Fri; 10-midnight Sat

(01924) 459193 imissedthetrain.com

Black Sheep Best Bitter; Timothy Taylor Landlord; 6 changing beers H

Set in a listed, tastefully converted railway station building, the West has featured in the Guide for 21 years and has been the local CAMRA Pub of the Year on numerous occasions. Eight handpumps offer an excellent range of beers in many styles. Real cider is sold as well as a range of speciality bottled beers. Live music is performed in the summer on platform 3 in the decked beer garden. A popular Ale Day Breakfast is served on Saturdays.

P

Elland

Barge & Barrel

10-20 Park Road, HX5 9HP (on A6025 NE of town centre)

12-11.30 (01422) 371770

Abbeydale Moonshine; Black Sheep Best Bitter; Milltown Platinum Blonde; Phoenix Wobbly Bob; Timothy Taylor Landlord; 7 changing beers H

A large roadside pub built to serve the former Elland station. A three-sided bar serves the comfortable lounge, with views over the canal and river to Elland town. Opposite, a games area and a snug with an open fire are separated from the bar by partitions of modern stained glass. Up to seven guest beers are dispensed, mainly from microbreweries. The smoking shelter is heated and a decking area provides views of the canal. Thursday is quiz night.

Q P (537,E7,E8)

Drop Inn

12 Elland Lane, HX5 9DU (off link road from A629 to town centre)

4-11; 12-midnight Fri & Sat; 12-11 Sun (01422) 387484

Ossett Pale Gold, Yorkshire Blonde, Silver King; 4 changing beers H

Stone flags and floorboards, and a brick arch between rooms, exhibit the Ossett Brewery pub style. French Renaissance pictures add to the decor along with cigar containers, stone jars and tankards. A stove occupies a large cottage fireplace in the side room. Seven beers in total are served, with four guest beers from Fuller's, other Ossett group breweries and microbreweries. Outside is a heated smoking shelter. A quiz is held every Thursday. Q (278,503)

Goose Eye

Turkey Inn

BD22 0PD

12-11 (midnight Fri & Sat) (01535) 681339

theturkeyinn.com

Goose Eye Bitter, Chinook Blonde; Timothy Taylor Golden Best, Landlord; 4 changing beers (sourced nationally; often Goose Eye) H

Friendly historic pub in a tiny hamlet approached by steep roads or a riverside footpath. It has three snugs, each with a real fire to keep out the winter chill, and is a good base for exploring the surrounding countryside. The stained-glass windows are replicas of the Aaron King originals. It has a pool table, hosts quiz nights on Wednesdays and occasional live music. Food is served all day. Up to four guest beers are usually on tap, one from Goose Eye. P (916,917,918)

Greengates

Albion

25 New Line, BD10 9AS

12-11 (01274) 613211

Acorn Barnsley Bitter; Tetley Bitter; 2 changing beers H

Comfortable, traditional, neighbourhood pub with an L-shaped lounge and a separate public bar where pub games can be played. Previously pubco owned, this establishment became a free house in February 2014. Consistently good ale, including a house beer by the Empire Brewery, is served here by dedicated staff. Real cider is also often available. The venue is popular with the local community and is home to a thriving social club. A regular bus service runs past the building.

P (760)

Guiseley

Guiseley Factory Workers' Club

6 Town Street, LS20 9DT

1-11 (midnight Fri); 11.30-midnight Sat; 11-11 Sun

(01943) 874793 guiseleyfactoryworkersclub.co.uk

Tetley Bitter; 3 changing beers H

Founded over 100 years ago by the Yeadon and Guiseley Factory Workers' Union, this is a friendly club serving three rapidly changing guest ales from micros and independents anywhere in the UK, usually including a dark beer. It is three-roomed, with a small lounge, concert room and snooker room. The club hosts many other local clubs and organisations. An annual beer festival is held in April. CAMRA members are welcome – show this Guide or a membership card.

P (33A,97,737)

Halifax

Cross Keys

3 Whitegate, Siddal, HX3 9AE

3-11; 12-11 Fri-Sun (01422) 300348

6 changing beers H

A true free house with a three-roomed interior and a real fire in the bar area. The six beers always include a dark one. The pub offers pork pies, darts and dominoes, plus live music on Sunday afternoons. Walkers and cyclists are welcome and two letting rooms are available. It is at the southern end of the Halifax Real Ale Mile.

P (542,555)

Dirty Dick's Food & Ale Emporium

1 Clare Road, HX1 2HX

12-11 07887 510354

9 changing beers H

Impressive Grade II-listed building constructed in 1931 using the timbers from HMS Newcastle. The interior comprises three discernible areas – a main bar divided in two and a separate side room. There is also a large function room upstairs. Nine real ales are generally available, eight sourced from a changing range of microbreweries and the pub's own-brand Dirty Dick's. Located close to the town's theatre quarter, this is an ideal place for pre-show drinks. Q◖⇌(Halifax)●P🚌

Three Pigeons 🏆 ★

1 Sun Fold, HX1 2LX

⏲ 4-11; 12-11 Fri-Sun ☎ (01422) 347001

Ossett Pale Gold, Big Red Bitter, Silver King; 4 changing beers Ⓗ

A striking octagonal drinking lobby forms the hub from which five distinctive rooms radiate in this Art Deco pub, built in 1932 by Webster's Brewery. Sensitively refurbished and maintained by Ossett Brewery, this venue attracts a variety of local groups and societies, along with football and Rugby League enthusiasts. Up to four guest beers come from local and regional microbreweries, as well as Ossett's own stable of pub-based microbreweries. Q❀⇌♣●P🚌🐾

Haworth

Fleece Inn 𝕃

67 Main Street, BD22 8DA

⏲ 11-11 (11.30 Fri); 10-11.30 Sat; 10-10.30 Sun ☎ (01535) 642172 🌐 fleeceinnhaworth.co.uk

Timothy Taylor Golden Best, Boltmaker, Landlord, Ram Tam; 1 changing beer Ⓗ

Historic coaching inn on Haworth's famous cobbled Main Street and near the Keighley and Worth Valley Railway. A small room to the right and a dining area offer a quiet alternative to the extremely busy bar. Locally sourced food and accommodation are available. Cyclists are welcome and safe bicycle storage is offered to guests. The beer garden is three storeys up from the bar, on the roof. The Fleece is popular with tourists and locals alike.
❀🛏◖◗♿⛺⇌♣🚌(500,664,665)🐾📶

Heath

Kings Arms ★ 𝕃

Heath Common, WF1 5SL (at edge of Heath Village on Heath Common, off A655 Wakefield-Normanton road)

⏲ 12-11 (midnight Fri & Sat) ☎ (01924) 377527

🌐 thekingsarmsheath.co.uk

Ossett Yorkshire Blonde, Silver King; Tetley Bitter; house beer (by Ossett); 4 changing beers Ⓗ

The Kings Arms, acquired by Clark's Brewery in 1989, is now leased to Ossett Brewery. Built in the early 1700s and converted into a public house in 1841, it consists of three oak-panelled rooms with gas lighting, plus a conservatory and gardens to the rear. In the summer months you can sit outside and relax peacefully amid the acres of common grassland surrounding the area. Quiz night is Tuesday. Time may be called early on quieter evenings. Q❀◖◗♿●P🚌(188)🐾

Hebden Bridge

Fox & Goose 𝕃

7 Heptonstall Road, HX7 6AZ (on A646 at bottom of Heptonstall Rd; on foot walk through Hebden Bridge W along A646 towards Todmorden, pub is on your right)

⏲ 12-midnight (2am Fri & Sat) ☎ (01422) 648052

🌐 foxandgoose.org

6 changing beers Ⓗ

West Yorkshire's first community co-operative pub has been restored to its former glory. All three rooms have gained flagstone floors, and a roaring log fire warms the main bar in winter. The beer range and quality have improved immeasurably and an eclectic clientele ensures a constant buzz of conversation, with visitors welcome to join in. The left-hand room often has live music, and a small-screen TV is used for major sports events. Quiz night is Monday. Q❀♣●P▯🚌🐾📶

Old Gate Bar & Restaurant

1-5 Old Gate, HX7 8JP

⏲ 10-midnight; 10-11 Sun ☎ (01422) 843993

🌐 oldgatehebden.co.uk

Magic Rock Ringmaster; Moorhouse's Pride of Pendle; 7 changing beers Ⓗ

Smart, modern inn and restaurant on two floors with an impressively long copper-topped bar, whose nine handpumps dispense the largest selection of draught ale in town. Quality food is sold all day. Comfortable furniture comprises a mix of tables with chairs or benches and cosy settles. The big picture windows are ideal for watching Hebden's diverse population passing along the main street outside. At least one dark beer is always on sale. ❀◖◗⇌♣●🚌🐾📶

Heptonstall

White Lion

58 Towngate, HX7 7NB

⏲ 12-midnight ☎ (01422) 842027

Goose Eye Chinook Blonde; Thwaites Wainwright; 3 changing beers Ⓗ

Friendly local in the cobbled main street of a historic conservation village. The single bar serves two distinct drinking areas – the left-hand area has a real fire in winter and the space to the right has a piano. Three guest beers and three ciders are sourced from far and wide, and the licensee also runs a beer and cider wholesale company. There is a lovely suntrap beer garden to the rear.
Q❀◖◗♣●🚌(517,596,906)🐾

Hipperholme

Cock o' the North 𝕃

The Conclave, South Edge Works, Brighouse Road, HX3 8EF (on A644)

⏲ 5 (4 Fri)-11; 12-11 Sat & Sun ☎ 07974 544980

🌐 halifax-steam.co.uk

Halifax Steam Aussie Kiss, Jamaican Ginger, Uncle Jon, Cock o' the North; 6 changing beers Ⓗ

Set back from and below the main road in a sectional building, this pub is next to a red-brick industrial unit. The large single room is divided into areas with different types of seating. The atmosphere is relaxed, with a friendly, varied clientele. Three to five rotating ciders are served. Wednesday is quiz night and live music features one weekend a month. Q❀♿⛺●P🚌(548,549)

Holmfirth

Nook (Rose & Crown) 𝕃

7 Victoria Square, HD9 2DN (down alley behind Barclays Bank)

⏲ 11.30-midnight ☎ (01484) 682373

🌐 thenookbrewhouse.co.uk

Nook Yorks, Baby Blond, Rescue Red, Best, Blond, Oat Stout; 2 changing beers Ⓗ

The Nook (properly, the Rose & Crown) dates from 1754 and is a real ale institution. It has appeared more than 30 times in this Guide and continues to evolve. It serves home-cooked food all day, and has been dispensing beers from its own brewhouse since 2009. Guest beers are also available, and Pure North ciders. There is a popular folk club every Sunday evening, and real ale festivals on the weekend before Easter and over the August bank holiday.
(313,314,316)

Horbury

Cricketers Arms

22 Cluntergate, WF4 5AG (Cluntergate is a right fork off High St at its lower end)
4-11; 12-midnight Fri & Sat; 12-11 Sun ☎ (01924) 267032
thecricketershorbury.co.uk
Castle Rock Harvest Pale; Timothy Taylor Landlord; changing beers H
On the edge of the town centre, this former Tetley's house has now reopened as a genuine free house. The pub has had a tasteful refurbishment which has extended the length of the bar. Cheese and meze boards are available at all times. There is a bus stop close by with a frequent service to Wakefield, Ossett and Dewsbury. P

Horbury Bridge

Bingley Arms

221 Bridge Road, WF4 5NL (on A642 by bridge over River Calder, facing viaduct)
12-11; 12-10.30 Sun ☎ (01924) 272838
Ossett Yorkshire Blonde; Rooster's Yankee; Tetley Bitter; Theakston Old Peculier; 2 changing beers H
Built in 1822, this hostelry is bordered by the River Calder and the Aire & Calder Navigation canal, and consists of two rooms, both with open fires. The pub has its own moorings and is named after the Earl of Bingley, who funded the building of the canal. It is reputed to be haunted. The beer garden gets busy on summer evenings and weekends. There is folk music on Thursday evenings.
P (128,231,232)

Horsforth

Town Street Tavern

16-18 Town Street, LS18 4RJ
12-11; 12-10.30 Sun ☎ (0113) 281 9996
Ilkley Mary Jane; Leeds Best; Okells Manx Pale Ale; Timothy Taylor Golden Best; 4 changing beers H
Modern café-style bar on the main shopping street of Horsforth. Eight real ales are served alongside draught and bottled imported beers. Large windows, wooden floors and an absence of piped music create a pleasant ambience. A small patio to the right of the bar area allows some space for outdoor drinking. The upstairs brasserie serves meals from 6pm, while a bar menu is offered at lunchtimes and until 6pm at weekends. Accompanied children are allowed in the main bar until 6pm. Q (50,50A)

Huddersfield

Grove

2 Spring Grove Street, HD1 4BP
12-11 (midnight Thu-Sat) ☎ (01484) 430113
groveinn.co.uk
Magic Rock Ringmaster; Thornbridge Jaipur IPA; Timothy Taylor Landlord; changing beers H
The Grove Inn has a phenomenal choice of 19 cask ales. The three listed above are always available, accompanied by seven rotating ales from Magic Rock, Oakham, Gadds', Buxton, Fuller's, Hawkshead and Durham. The remaining nine beers are sourced from breweries across the UK, with new ones regularly featured. A superb list of over 250 foreign bottled beers is also stocked, as well as real cider. This is a friendly pub with quirky, surreal artwork. Q

HDM Beer Shop

27-30 Wood Street, HD1 1DU
12-11 (1am Thu & Fri); 11-1am Sat; 3-10 Sun
hdmbeershop.co.uk
4 changing beers H
This real ale bar and off-licence is Huddersfield's original micropub and the tap for the Hand Drawn Monkey Brewery. Now extended, it has a quirky, artisan character with its high-level bar, side room with fixed benches and old sofas, suspended ceilings and Jephers the Monkey. Beers include two from HDM and two guests, plus over 200 local and foreign bottled beers and real cider and perry. Tapas-style snacks with vegetarian options are available. Live music features occasionally.
Q

King's Head

St George's Square, HD1 1JF (in station buildings, on left when exiting station)
11 (11.30 Mon)-11; 12-11 Sun ☎ (01484) 511058
Bradfield Farmers Blonde; Magic Rock Ringmaster; Timothy Taylor Golden Best, Landlord; changing beers H
Recently restored popular fixture on Huddersfield's real ale scene, conveniently situated at the listed railway station. A warm and friendly atmosphere makes it a necessary stop for the weary traveller. Ten beers are served (four regular, six guest), all top quality and sold at competitive prices. There are always two dark ales and real cider on handpull. Live bands play on Sunday afternoons. It can get busy at weekends, but is a real local gem to appreciate.

Rat & Ratchet

40 Chapel Hill, HD1 3EB (on A616, just off the ring road)
3-11 Mon; 12 (3 Tue-Thu)-midnight; 12-11 Sun
☎ (01484) 542400
Ossett Yorkshire Blonde, Silver King; Rat White Rat, King Rat; 8 changing beers (often Ossett, Rat) H
The Rat & Ratchet has been part of Huddersfield's real ale scene for many years, regularly winning awards from CAMRA and others. This friendly, recently refurbished pub offers 12 handpulled ales: three from the award-winning on-site Rat Brewery, three from Ossett Brewery and six guest beers, with dedicated mild and stout/porter pumps. A range of ciders and perries is also on sale. There is a popular pub quiz on a Wednesday, and regular beer festivals are held. P

Sportsman

1 St John's Road, HD1 5AY
12-11; 11-midnight Fri & Sat ☎ (01484) 421929
undertheviaduct.com
Timothy Taylor Boltmaker; changing beers H
This restored 1930s pub has won a CAMRA English Heritage Conservation Pub Design award. Eight handpumps include a dedicated pump for a

Mallinsons ale. Guest beers often come from local breweries Empire, Golcar and Magic Rock. A stout/porter is usually on sale, along with two ciders, usually from Pure North. This pub has established itself as a favourite on the Huddersfield drinking scene, and was local CAMRA Pub of the Year in 2013. Food times vary – phone to check.

Star

7 Albert Street, Folly Hall, HD1 3PJ (off A616)
closed Mon; 5 (12 Sat)-11; 12-10.30 Sun
(01484) 545443 thestarinn.info
Pictish Brewers Gold; changing beers (often Mallinsons, Timothy Taylor)
A multi award-winning back-street local which has featured in the Guide for over 10 years. It is a showcase for new breweries, with varying guest ales sourced both nationally and locally, including dedicated pumps for dark beer, Taylor's and Mallinsons breweries. Free from jukebox, pool table or games machine, with lively conversation around the bar and a real fire during winter months, there is always a convivial atmosphere. Three highly rated seasonal beer festivals are held annually in a marquee, featuring all handpulled beers. Q

Vulcan

32 St Peters Street, HD1 1RA
9am-1am (2am Fri & Sat) (01484) 302040
Copper Dragon Golden Pippin; Thwaites Wainwright; 4 changing beers
A traditional town-centre pub with a long-standing licensee and generous opening hours. It has six handpumps – the four guest beers are most commonly from Yorkshire and Lancashire, with Mallinsons and Moorhouse's featuring regularly. Bargain-priced lunches are available every day, and free food is served for regulars Friday teatime. There is a daily happy hour, extended on Wednesday evenings. The pub attracts all age groups, catering for enthusiasts of pool, karaoke and horse racing on Racing UK. Live bands are on stage every Sunday evening.

Idle

Symposium Ale & Wine Bar

7 Albion Road, BD10 9PY (near village green)
5.30 (12 Fri & Sat)-11; 12-10.30 Sun (01274) 616587
Okells Bitter; 5 changing beers
Housed in a Victorian building, formerly a general grocer's and wine merchant's, this is a popular bar/restaurant in the heart of the village. Six real ales are available and it also hosts a beer festival. Draught and bottled beers from around the world are offered. Excellent meals are served from an inventive menu. The rear snug can be used as a small function room and leads to an elevated terrace outside. Q

Ilkley

Bar T'at

7 Cunliffe Road, LS29 9DZ
12-11 (01943) 608888
Black Sheep Best Bitter; Ilkley Mary Jane; Rooster's Wild Mule; Timothy Taylor Landlord; 4 changing beers
Popular side-street pub in the Market Town Taverns group which opened in 1999, following conversion from a china shop. It has a music-free bar area, a basement restaurant and outdoor seating. The pub is renowned for the quality of its beer and food. The guest real ales come in a good, often eclectic, variety of beer styles, many from Yorkshire breweries. A wide range of quality foreign beers is also offered. Home-cooked food is on the menu every day. Q

Crescent Inn

Brook Street, LS29 8DG (within the Crescent Hotel)
12-11 (midnight Thu-Sat) (01943) 811250
Copper Dragon Best Bitter; Leeds Pale; Saltaire Blonde; 5 changing beers
Refurbished in 2011 on the ground floor of a town-centre building that has been a hotel since 1861, the furnishings are smart while the original plasterwork and decorations have been retained. Eight real ales are always on tap. The house ale is produced by Ilkley Brewery and the guests are usually from other local breweries. Bar meals are served, with meal deals during the week, and there is a restaurant adjacent. It has full disabled facilities but the rear door provides best access.

Flying Duck

16 Church Street, LS29 9DS (on A65)
12-11 (midnight Fri & Sat) (01943) 609587
Wharfedale Black, Blonde, Best; 6 changing beers
Originally constructed as a farmhouse in 1709, this is reputed to be Ilkley's oldest pub building. Substantially refurbished and reopened in late 2013, this Grade II-listed building retains many of its original features, such as the York stone and oak flooring, beamed ceilings, internal stonework and mullioned windows. Up to nine real ales and two real ciders are on the bar. Wharfedale Brewery is located to the rear and tours can be arranged. The first-floor function room includes a bar.

Keighley

Boltmakers Arms

117 East Parade, BD21 5HX
11-midnight (11 Mon); 12-11 Sun (01535) 661936
boltmakers.com
Timothy Taylor Dark Mild, Golden Best, Boltmaker, Landlord, Ram Tam; 2 changing beers
Unchanging classic Keighley town-centre pub, the de facto Timothy Taylor Brewery tap and the smallest pub in town. Brewery, whisky and music memorabilia adorn the walls of the single split-level room. The guest beers and handpulled cider are from various sources at the licensee's whim, and there is also a fine selection of single malts. There is a quiz every Tuesday night and live music most Wednesdays.

Brown Cow

5 Cross Leeds Street, BD21 2LQ
4-11; 12-10.30 Sun browncowkeighley.co.uk
Timothy Taylor Golden Best, Boltmaker, Landlord; 4 changing beers
The ethos of this award-winning, family-run, community free house is quality, beer choice and customer comfort. The pub is adorned with local breweriana, including the original sign from the entrance to Bradford's now defunct Trough Brewery. The back room can be booked for meetings. The four guest ales, usually from local micros, always include a dark brew and one higher

strength beer, and the discounted beer on Super Saver Sunday is popular. A no-bad-language policy is in force. P

Cricketers Arms

Coney Lane, BD21 5JE

4-11; 12-midnight Fri; 11.30-midnight Sat; 12-11 Sun
(01535) 669912 cricketersarmskeighley.co.uk

Yates Bitter, Golden Ale; 3 changing beers H

A family-owned free house dating back to the early 1800s, on the edge of the town centre, a short walk from the bus and railway stations. Alongside the regular ales it serves three guest beers from far and wide and a range of bottled beers. Quiz night is Wednesday. (705,720)

King Cross

Big Six

10 Horsfall Street, HX1 3HG (off A646 Skircoat Moor road at King Cross)

4-11; 3.30-midnight Fri; 12-midnight Sat; 12-11 Sun
(01422) 350169 thebig6inn.co.uk

Old Mill Traditional Bitter; 4 changing beers H

A hidden gem in a row of terraces, adjacent to the Free School Lane recreation ground, with a new beer garden. The emphasis at this friendly venue is on good beer and conversation. A through corridor separates the bar and games room from the two lounges. The pub's name derives from a mineral water company that operated here a century ago, whose memorabilia adorn the walls.
Q (577,832)

Knottingley

Steampacket Inn

The Bendles, 2 Racca Green, WF11 8AT (Racca Green is just off A645 at E end of Knottingley; pub is just beyond shops by canal bridge, but can also be reached by canal or by following local roads from Ropewalk at side of town hall)

11-11.30 (12.30am Fri-Sun) (01977) 677266

3 changing beers (sourced regionally) H

On the bank of the Aire & Calder canal, this historic pub was the Commercial until 1986. It is close to the former local shipyard, and a huge anchor from the first screw-steamer, the Message, graces the entrance porch. A decked area overlooks the towpath moorings and secure children's play area. The pub hosts a film night on Tuesday, dance classes on Thursday and a quiz on Thursday nights. Lunches are served Sundays 12-4pm. P

Ledsham

Chequers L

Claypit Lane, LS25 5LP

11-11; 12-6 Sun (01977) 683135
thechequersinn.com

Brown Cow Sessions; Leeds Best; Theakston Best Bitter; Timothy Taylor Landlord; 1 changing beer H

Picture-postcard stone-built village hostelry with a well-kept garden area for the summer and open fires inside for the winter. The Chequers is a historic establishment that can be traced back to 1540 and retains many original features. It is in picturesque countryside and is well used by walkers and their dogs, who are warmly welcomed. The guest beer is from a northern brewery. The place is popular for meals and is quite busy most lunchtimes.
Q P (175,405)

Leeds: Chapel Allerton

Regent L

15-17 Regent Street, LS7 4PE

12-11 (midnight Thu-Sat); 11-11 Sun (0113) 293 9395

Leeds Pale; Tetley Bitter; 6 changing beers H

Two-roomed stone-built pub dating from the 1800s, in the centre of Chapel Allerton. It offers two regular and six changing guest ales chosen from the SIBA list and served by knowledgeable staff. Entertainment is provided by several large-screen TVs showing sport, including one in the beer garden. A general knowledge quiz is held on Mondays and a music and entertainment quiz on Thursdays. Food is served until late. P

Three Hulats L

13 Harrogate Road, LS7 3NB

8am-midnight (1am Fri & Sat) (0113) 262 0524

Greene King IPA, Abbot; 10 changing beers H

Friendly, suburban main-road local in a building that dates from the 1930s. Twelve handpumps offer a changing range of ales from brewers large and small, near and far, with milds, bitters, stouts and speciality beers all making appearances. There is a quiz on Wednesdays and the pub hosts various local groups. Occasionally social trips and brewery visits are arranged. The beer garden is popular on summer days. Families are welcome until 9pm and food is served until 11pm, with takeaways available. P

Leeds: City Centre

Crowd of Favours L

4-12 Harper Street, LS2 7EA

12-11 (midnight Fri & Sat) (0113) 246 9405
crowdoffavours.co.uk

Leeds Pale, Yorkshire Gold, Best, Midnight Bell; 4 changing beers H

Former fish and chip shop with three contemporary yet cosy areas furnished with tables and chairs or sofas. Nowadays the fish batter contains Leeds Brewery ale, as do many other menu items, with food served all day. The brewery's seasonal beer always features alongside three interesting guests from local or regional breweries, always including a dark ale. The downstairs area hosts a cinema night on Tuesdays.

Duck & Drake L

43 Kirkgate, LS2 7DR

11-11; 10-midnight Thu; 10-1am Fri & Sat
(0113) 246 5806 duckndrake.co.uk

Daleside Bitter; Rooster's Yankee; Saltaire Blonde; Theakston Old Peculier; Timothy Taylor Landlord; 10 changing beers (sourced locally; often York, Ossett) H

Victorian corner pub, whose marble door jambs are a fine example of the era. There are a number of original light fittings, and the floorboards in both rooms have survived 200 years of trade. The central bar, with 15 handpumps, sits in between and serves both rooms. A pub noted for the quality of its live music, the front room features a mural on the back wall depicting many blues and rock legends.

Friends of Ham

4 New Station Street, LS1 5DL

12-11 (midnight Thu-Sat); 12-10 Sun (0113) 242 0275
friendsofham.com

4 changing beers H

Cafe bar and charcuterie serving real ales. The ground floor has a U-shaped bar with a small drinking area to one side and a larger seating area to the other. Downstairs is a larger room with bench seating, tables and comfy sofas. There is also a shuffleboard table and a selection of board games. It can get busy on Friday and Saturday nights; if it reaches capacity an entrance policy may apply.

Hop

Granary Wharf, Dark Neville Street, LS1 4BR

12-midnight (0113) 243 9854 thehop-leeds.co.uk

Ossett Pale Gold, Yorkshire Blonde, Big Red Bitter, Silver King, Excelsior; 5 changing beers

Busy, lively pub beneath the arches of platform 17 of Leeds station. Music posters adorn the bare brick walls. Eleven handpumps serve beers from the Ossett family of brewers together with several guest ales and a real cider. The U-shaped bar is surrounded by comfortable seating, and two sets of stairs to either side of the bar lead to an area that hosts live music at weekends. The pie and a pint deal is always good value.

North

24 New Briggate, LS1 6NU

11-2am (1am Mon & Tue); 12-midnight Sun

(0113) 242 4540 northbar.com

5 changing beers

Small venue offering real ales and a huge range of beers from around the world. The bar is along one wall and has five handpumps on it. One of the real ales will always be from a local brewery and there will normally be a dark beer. Regular beer-related events are held. Pictures from local artists are often displayed. Bar food such as pork pies and cheese platters is served.

Palace

Kirkgate, LS2 7DJ

10-11.30 (midnight Fri & Sat); 10-11 Sun

(0113) 244 5882

St Austell Nicholson's Pale Ale; Tetley Bitter; 6 changing beers

Former Melbourne Brewery house in the shadow of Leeds Minster. The building dates from around 1741. The central bar space links two drinking areas to either end of the premises, with plenty of tables available. A good variety of guest beers includes at least one local beer and usually at least one dark beer. There is a heated courtyard bedecked with fairy lights to the rear of the building. Food is served all day.

Reliance

76-78 North Street, LS2 7PN

12-11 (midnight Fri & Sat); 11-10.30 Sun

(0113) 295 6060 the-reliance.co.uk

House beer (by Acorn); 3 changing beers (sourced nationally; often Rooster's)

Modern pub set in a much older building just a few minutes' walk or, for a lot of customers, cycle ride, out of the city centre. Food, including imaginative snacks, is served throughout, but the rear raised area is dedicated to dining. Knowledgeable staff are always willing to be your guide to the range of real ales on the bar, as well as the delights of the bottles in the fridges.

Scarbrough Hotel

Bishopgate Street, LS1 5DY

10-midnight (1am Fri & Sat); 10-10.30 Sun

(0113) 243 4590

St Austell Nicholson's Pale Ale; Tetley Bitter; 6 changing beers

The Scarbrough is a busy ale house and convenient for Leeds railway station. The building dates from 1765 and became a pub in 1826. It is named after Henry Scarbrough, the first owner of the pub, though known then as the King's Arms. At either end of the long bar are comfortable seating areas. The selection of guest ales is sourced from both local breweries and further afield.

Stick or Twist

Podium Buildings, Merrion Way, LS2 8PD

8am-midnight (1am Fri & Sat) (0113) 234 9748

Greene King IPA, Abbot; 10 changing beers

Closest pub to the Leeds Arena and the oldest Wetherspoon in Leeds – the pub's name is a nod to its casino neighbours. Opening hours are extended for arena events. With 12 handpulls, it offers among the largest selection of real ales in the city centre. Food is served 8am-11pm daily. Outdoor seating provides a stunning suntrap in the warmer months. Q

Tapped Leeds

Boar Lane, LS1 5EL

11-11 (midnight Thu; 1am Fri & Sat) (0113) 244 1953

tappedleeds.co.uk

13 changing beers (sourced nationally; often Tapped Sheffield)

American-style brewpub which opened in 2013. The bar is along one wall, with bench seats in the centre of the room and a variety of seating elsewhere. Thirteen cask-conditioned ales are served from the bottom set of beer taps behind the bar. Along the opposite wall is the brewing equipment. The Tapped Brewery cask beer usually comes from Tapped's sister venue in Sheffield. A small pizza kitchen is in one corner.

Templar

2 Templar Street, LS2 7NU

11-11; 12-10.30 Sun (0113) 243 0318

Ridgeside Templar; Tetley Bitter; 6 changing beers

Community local in the city centre, boasting a fine exterior with green and cream glazed Burmantoft tiles. The bowing courtier logo can still be seen in the leaded window panes from when it was a Melbourne Brewery pub. The interior is adorned with wooden panelling, still with the old service bells in place. There are large-screen TVs throughout showing a range of sporting events. Guest beers range from local ales to those from further afield.

Veritas Ale & Wine Bar

43 Great George Street, LS1 3BB

11-11; 12-10.30 Sun (0113) 242 8094

Black Sheep Best Bitter; Ilkley Mary Jane; 6 changing beers (sourced nationally; often Okells, Timothy Taylor)

This busy, modern bar is part of the Market Town Taverns local chain of pubs. Included in the premises is a deli counter featuring local produce, open from 9.30am (10.30am Sun). The single open-plan L-shaped room is on several levels and has four different areas. The six guest beers change regularly and are mainly from local microbreweries. A good range of bottled beers from around the world is also stocked.

Q

Victoria Family & Commercial Hotel

28 Great George Street, LS1 3DL (behind town hall)
11-11 (midnight Fri & Sat); 12-10 Sun ☎ (0113) 245 1386
Leeds Pale; St Austell Nicholson's Pale Ale; Sharp's Doom Bar; Tetley Bitter; 5 changing beers (sourced nationally; often Great Heck, St Austell, Salopian)
The Vic, as it is commonly known, was built in 1865 by the Victoria Hotel Company. At the time it provided accommodation for people attending the newly opened assizes court in Leeds town hall. In 1973 a 1,000-signature petition stopped the building from being destroyed by developers. The Leeds Civic Trust has praised the pub's splendid Victorian features and contribution to city life.

Whitelock's Ale House ★

Turks Head Yard, LS1 6HB (off Briggate)
11-midnight (1am Fri & Sat); 11-11 Sun
☎ (0113) 242 3368 whitelocksleeds.com
Kirkstall Pale Ale; Theakston Best Bitter, Old Peculier; Timothy Taylor Landlord; 6 changing beers (sourced locally; often Acorn, Great Heck, Saltaire)
First licensed as the Turk's Head in 1715, this is the oldest pub in Leeds. The present-day long narrow interior dates from 1895 and is a feast of Victorian mirrors, stained glass and brass. The unusual copper-topped bar, with the bar staff on a higher level than the customers, has a good range of both local and national beers. The sumptuous faience tiling is just one of the many items of historic interest at this must-visit hostelry.
Q

Leeds: Headingley

Arcadia Ale House

34 Arndale Centre, Otley Road, LS6 2UE (corner of Alma Road)
12-11 ☎ (0113) 274 5599 arcadialeeds.co.uk
Black Sheep Best Bitter; Timothy Taylor Boltmaker; 6 changing beers (sourced nationally; often Elland, Ilkley, Rooster's)
This cleverly converted former bank is now a well-established and multi award-winning pub. The bar has ground-floor rooms plus an upstairs mezzanine level, and dogs are welcome. Framed breweriana adorns the walls and some of the light fittings are made from old beer crates. Eight real ales are offered, along with a wide range of draught and bottled foreign beers. Gourmet bar snacks are served. Children, large groups (over six people) and fancy dress are not permitted. Q

Woodies Craft Ale House

104 Otley Road, LS16 5JG
11-11 (midnight Fri & Sat) ☎ (0113) 278 4393
Greene King IPA; Ilkley Black; Leeds Pale; Saltaire Blonde; Timothy Taylor Landlord; 7 changing beers (sourced locally; often Kirkstall, Ridgeside, Rudgate)
Recently refurbished and now with 12 handpumps, over time this pub has been opened out into a single large space with a bar along one wall and drinking areas on three sides. The eclectic décor includes a range of upholstered furniture. Two satellite TV boxes enable different events to be shown at the same time. This is the starting point of the well-known Otley Run pub crawl, and can be busy in the early evening. Quiz nights are Thursday and Sunday. (1,6,28)

Leeds: Holbeck

Cross Keys

107 Water Lane, LS11 5WD
12-11 (midnight Fri & Sat); 12-11.30 Sun
☎ (0113) 243 3711 the-crosskeys.com
4 changing beers (sourced nationally; often Kirkstall, Rooster's)
Despite the unpromising-looking front door, the Cross Keys is a cosy pub with plenty to offer both drinkers and diners. The ground floor has a small, predominantly foodie, area to the left, and a larger traditional-style pub area to the right. Upstairs is a function room. The courtyard drinking yard to the rear is a pleasure in the summer. Kirkstall and Rooster's are frequent visitors to the handpulls, alongside a fridge full of bottles from around the world.

Grove Inn

Back Row, LS11 5PL
12-11 (midnight Fri & Sat) ☎ (0113) 243 6538
8 changing beers (sourced locally; often Daleside, Moorhouse's)
Nestled among modern high-rise buildings, this traditional West Riding-style pub has four rooms off a corridor. Eight ales from local and regional breweries, two guest ciders and Westons Old Rosie are served from the public bar at the front and the corridor. Two small side rooms hold meetings for many organisations. The Concert Room to the rear hosts an eclectic range of music including – every Friday since 1962 – what is reputed to be the oldest folk club in the world.

Midnight Bell

101 Water Lane, LS11 5QN
12-11 (midnight Fri & Sat) ☎ (0113) 244 5044
midnightbell.co.uk
Leeds Pale, Yorkshire Gold, Best, Midnight Bell; 4 changing beers
A Leeds Brewery inn with stone-flagged floors which looks much older than it actually is. This is a pub for all, with intimate dining in the small lounge area to the left and large groups drinking around the bar. The big rear drinking courtyard is ever-popular, and with a serving hatch you do not even need to go inside for a beer. Expect to see guest ales alongside just about the full range of Leeds Brewery beers.

Leeds: Hunslet

Garden Gate ★

3 Whitfield Place, LS10 2QB
12-10 (11 Thu-Sat) ☎ (0113) 277 7705
gardengateleeds.co.uk
Leeds Pale, Best, Midnight Bell; 3 changing beers
A jewel in the crown of Leeds real ale pubs, this Grade II*-listed building remains largely unchanged since it was built in 1903. It offers a glimpse into history with its Edwardian-based interior décor. Since reopening in 2010, this heritage pub, which is on CAMRA's National Inventory of Historic Pub Interiors, has established itself as a community hub and is well worth the short trip out of the city centre to visit.

Leeds: Kirkstall

Kirkstall Bridge Inn

Bridge Road, LS5 3BW

12-11.30 (12.30am Fri & Sat) ☎ (0113) 278 4044
kirkstallbridge.co.uk
Kirkstall Pale Ale, Three Swords, Black Band Porter; 5 changing beers H
Previously known as the Old Bridge Inn, this pub has been tastefully refurbished to a high standard throughout, with plenty of mirrors, photos and breweriana on display. The main bar upstairs has eight handpumps, with four serving beers from the nearby Kirkstall Brewery and the rest dispensing interesting guest ales. The partially stone-flagged downstairs bar has six handpumps and is open during busy periods. The large beer garden overlooks the River Aire. P

West End House L
26 Abbey Road, LS5 3HS
11.30-11 (11.30 Thu; midnight Fri & Sat); 12-11 Sun
☎ (0113) 278 6332 westendleeds.co.uk
4 changing beers H
Popular local next to Kirkstall Leisure Centre with a reputation for good-quality and good-value food – look out for the daily specials. There are six handpumps serving four rotating guest ales and two real ciders or perries. The rear of the central bar is set out mainly for dining. There is an area with comfortable seating to the right of the entrance and the area to the left has high tables and stools.
(Headingley) (33,33A,757)

Leeds: Meanwood

East of Arcadia L
607 Meanwood Road, LS6 4HQ
11-11 (11.30 Fri & Sat); 12-11 Sun ☎ (0113) 275 5488
Black Sheep Best Bitter; Leeds Pale; Okells Bitter; 5 changing beers (sourced nationally; often Ilkley, Ridgeside, Timothy Taylor) H
Modern bar occupying a prominent corner position in the heart of Meanwood. Open plan and on one level, a carpeted area follows the sweep of tall windows curving around the pub. Closer to the bar there is a bare-boarded area with large casks converted to small tables, complete with foot rails. The pale walls display international breweriana. Beers from Ridgeside, Ilkley and Timothy Taylor breweries are normally available. Quiz night is Wednesday.

Linthwaite

Sair L
139 Lane Top, HD7 5SG (top of Hoyle Ing, off A62)
5 (12 Fri & Sat)-11; 12-10.30 Sun ☎ (01484) 842370
Linfit Bitter, Gold Medal, Special, Swift, Autumn Gold, Old Eli H
High on the edge of the Colne Valley, the Sair Inn is home to the famous Linfit Brewery, which recently celebrated over 30 years of brewing. The brewpub, steeped in local history, is a traditional multi-roomed stone building with central bar, real fires and a long-suffering landlord. The beer range is as LocAle as it gets, with eight ales unique to the pub, and real cider from Pure North. It is a welcome refuge for walkers, musicians and visitors alike.
Q (181,183,184)

Liversedge

Black Bull L
37 Halifax Road, WF15 6JR (on A649, close to A62)
12-midnight (1am Fri & Sat) ☎ (01924) 403779
Ossett Pale Gold, Yorkshire Blonde, Big Red Bitter, Silver King, Excelsior; 2 changing beers (often Jennings) H
Ossett Brewery's first pub, refurbished with attention to detail and décor, was acquired in May 2003. The five rooms have their own styles, including one dubbed The Chapel with a mix of stained glass and woodwork and a high ceiling. Nine handpumps always include a mild or dark ale and good guest beers. A regular Guide entry and popular community local with a warm welcome.
P (220,253,254)

Longwood

Dusty Miller Inn L
2 Gilead Road, HD3 4XH
4-11 (midnight Fri); 12-midnight Sat; 12-11 Sun
☎ (01484) 651763 dustymillerlongwood.com
Black Sheep Best Bitter; Milltown Platinum Blonde; Timothy Taylor Landlord; 3 changing beers H
Recently refurbished Punch house, now operated by local brewery Milltown as a brewery tap. Stone floors dominate and local historic photographs adorn the walls in this cosy multi-roomed pub. From its outside benches there are great views of the Colne Valley and it is a haven for walkers. Six real ales are served: two from Milltown, Taylor Landlord, Black Sheep and two guests. You can also get a locally made pie with chutney.
Q (356)

Marsden

Riverhead Brewery Tap L
Peel Street, HD7 6BR
12-midnight ☎ (01484) 844324
theriverheadmarsden.co.uk
Ossett Yorkshire Blonde, Silver King; Riverhead Butterley Bitter, March Haigh, Redbrook Premium; changing beers H
Up to 10 beers are on the bar at this Ossett Brewery pub, including several from the on-site microbrewery. Alongside the permanent and seasonal Riverhead and Ossett beers are several rotating guests, plus real cider. The upstairs restaurant serves excellent food and the brewery is visible from the bar. A popular stop on the real ale rail trail, the pub can be busy on Saturdays. Walkers and dogs are welcome, and alfresco drinking can be enjoyed on the riverside terrace.
Q P (185)

Meltham

Wills o' Nats
Blackmoorfoot Road, HD9 5PS
12-3, 5-11; 11.30-midnight Sat; 11.30-11 Sun
☎ (01484) 850078 willsonats.com
Black Sheep Best Bitter; Bradfield Farmers Blonde; Timothy Taylor Landlord; 3 changing beers H
In 1852 William, son of Nathaniel, took over the Spotted Cow, which gradually became Wills o' Nats. Today it is renowned for locally sourced home-cooked food and six or more ales. Live music events are held on the first Saturday of each summer month, when you can camp behind the pub, which is close to the Peak District and is surrounded by stunning views. A welcome stop for families, walkers and their dogs and a regular in the Guide. P

Middlestown

Little Bull

72 New Road, WF4 4NR (on A642 at crossroads in centre of village)

10-11 (midnight Thu-Sat); 12-11 Sun ☎ (01924) 726142

thelittlebull.co.uk

Bob's White Lion; 3 changing beers

This pub has been established since 1814 and is free of tie. Ales come from local and regional breweries alongside a range of world bottled beers. Real cider is also available. All food is locally sourced and home cooked. A single bar services a number of smaller rooms, one a well-stocked games room, with an open fire in colder weather. There is a car park and large grassed area to the rear. The pub is popular with walkers and visitors to the nearby National Mining Museum.
P (232,128)

Mirfield

Airedale Heifer

53 Stocksbank Road, WF14 9QB (down hill from Nab Lane jct)

4-11 (midnight Thu; 1am Fri); 10-1am Sat; 12-11 Sun
☎ (01924) 689007

Ossett Yorkshire Blonde; 3 changing beers (sourced nationally; often Butcombe, Sharp's, Timothy Taylor)

A family-run pub supporting darts and dominoes teams. Although open plan, there is a cosy feel and a welcoming atmosphere. The guest beers are often from local breweries, or quality brews from further afield. The well-priced home-cooked Sunday lunches are popular, as is the recent introduction of Saturday brunch. The beer garden is well used by families, and dogs are welcome throughout. Frequent bus services stop nearby and the car park is ample.
P (202,203,253)

Flowerpot

65 Calder Road, WF14 8NN (over river, 400yds S of railway station)

12-11.30 (12.30am Fri & Sat); 12-midnight Sun
☎ (01924) 496939

Ossett Yorkshire Blonde, Big Red Bitter, Silver King, Excelsior; 4 changing beers (often Harthill Village, Marston's)

A typically well-refurbished and popular Ossett Brewery house, with a tiled flowerpot in the floor and real fires in several comfortable rooms. An inviting, terraced riverside garden is ideal for summer days. Eight ales from Ossett and independents always include a mild or stout. Haigh's local farm shop pies (with peas) and other pub food are served Monday to Saturday until teatime. Q P (262)

Navigation Tavern

6 Station Road, WF14 8NL (next to Mirfield railway station)

11.30-11; 12-11 Sun ☎ (01924) 492476

Caledonian Deuchars IPA, Flying Scotsman; John Smith's Bitter; Theakston Black Bull Bitter, XB, Old Peculier; 3 changing beers

A canalside free house serving up to eight regular beers plus up to four guests at weekends, and a registered ambassador for Theakston beers at keen prices. The pub features on the Trans Pennine Rail Ale Trail and holds renowned beer festivals three times a year. It hosts Saturday night entertainment and is home to active sports and pool teams. A large function room and an en-suite B&B with stairlift are available. At least two real cider/perries are offered. P

Old Colonial

Dunbottle Lane, WF14 9JJ (off A644 up Church Lane, 1 mile NE of station)

5-11; 12-midnight Fri & Sat; 12-11 Sun ☎ (01924) 496920

Copper Dragon Best Bitter; 5 changing beers

National Pubs in Bloom champion three times, this former club with fascinating memorabilia offers a cosy area with sofas around the fire. There is a Royal British Legion memorial in the garden and local charities are well supported. The spacious conservatory is popular for functions and meetings. Up to six ales from the likes of Thwaites, Lees, the Marston's portfolio and small brewers are on tap. Lunches and evening meals are served Thursday to Saturday and the excellent-value Sunday lunch is recommended. P (202,205)

Mytholmroyd

Robin Hood

Cragg Road, HX7 5SQ (on B6138 1½ miles S of Mytholmroyd)

3-11; 12-11 Fri-Sun ☎ (01422) 885899

Timothy Taylor Landlord; 4 changing beers

Friendly two-roomed split-level local in a beautiful wooded valley popular with walkers and cyclists. On entering, the cosy bar, with a real fire in winter, is to the right while the larger dining room is to the left. Food is served Thursday-Sunday – telephone to check times. There is usually a second beer from Timothy Taylor. Guests are mainly from Yorkshire, such as Abbeydale, Bob's and Ilkley, while Oakham also makes regular appearances. Real cider is sometimes available. Q (900,901)

Ossett

Brewers Pride

Low Mill Road, Healey, WF5 8ND (Healey Rd runs straight down from The Green, by Dimplewell Lodge Hotel, left at Matthews Foods)

12-11; 12-10.30 Sun ☎ (01924) 273865

brewers-pride.co.uk

Bob's White Lion; Rudgate Ruby Mild; 8 changing beers (often Oakham)

An independent free house on the outskirts of Ossett close to the Calder & Hebble canal in the Healey Mills industrial area. Three regular beers plus seven guest ales from microbreweries are on the bar. Food is served Monday-Saturday lunchtimes, and there are themed evenings: Monday pies, Tuesday tapas, Wednesday and Thursday specials. Monday is quiz night. Live music takes place on the first Sunday of each month. Dogs are welcome, and well-behaved children until 8pm. Bus 102 stops 150 yards away.
Q (102,121)

Old Vic

47 Manor Road, South Ossett, WF5 0AU (Manor Rd is a left turn from B6128 at S end of Ossett, or a right turn from The Green near Ossett School)

4-11; 12-midnight Fri & Sat; 12-11 Sun ☎ (01924) 273516

Ossett Pale Gold, Yorkshire Blonde, Big Red Bitter, Silver King; 3 changing beers (often Ossett)

Friendly local pub, previously known as the Victoria, a 10-minute walk from Ossett town centre. Fresh home-cooked food is served. Two varying guest beers and an alternating stout or porter complement the regular well-kept beers. Taken over a couple of years ago by Ossett Brewery, this pub has undergone a renaissance. ⏾❀◖◗&♣◉P🚌(117,126,127)🐾🛜

Otley

Junction Inn L
44 Bondgate, LS21 1AD
✪ 11 (11.30 Thu)-11; 11-midnight Fri & Sat; 12-10.30 Sun
☎ (01943) 463233
St Austell Tribute; Theakston Best Bitter, Old Peculier; Timothy Taylor Boltmaker, Landlord; 6 changing beers Ⓗ
A solid-looking stone-built pub on a prominent street-corner site on the approach from Leeds. Up to 11 ales from around the country are served, along with a real cider and a wide range of malt whiskies. There is a central fireplace, and a collection of leather harnesses and saddles hangs from the ceiling. Pictures of old Otley and some interesting metal beer advertisements and mirrors complete the decor. To the front, roadside tables allow for outdoor drinking. ❀♣◉🚌🐾

Old Cock L
11-13 Crossgate, LS21 1AA
✪ 11-11 ☎ (01943) 464424 🌐 theoldcockotley.co.uk
Ilkley Mary Jane; Theakston Best Bitter; 7 changing beers Ⓗ
Compact and welcoming, this is a genuine free house which opened in 2010 after conversion from a former café, with a traditional pub feel. There are two rooms downstairs with stone-flagged floors and a further room upstairs. The guest ales are mostly from local breweries, and there are at least two real ciders plus a range of foreign beers. No admittance to under-18s. Local CAMRA Pub of the Year 2013. Q&◉🚌🐾🛜

Overton

Reindeer Inn L
204 Old Road, WF4 4RL (signed off A642 near National Coal Mining Museum)
✪ 12 (4 Mon)-midnight; 12-11 Sun ☎ (01924) 848374
6 changing beers (often Cap House) Ⓗ
A traditional, independent free house which was once a coaching inn, now the tap for Cap House brewery, with locally sourced guest beers. Home-cooked food is served in the restaurant and in the conservatory – from there you can proceed into the beer garden that overlooks the National Coal Mining Museum. Quiz night is Wednesday. The games room has a pool table, dartboard, dominoes and games machines. The restaurant is open Tuesday-Saturday lunchtimes, Wednesday-Saturday evenings, and 12-6pm Sunday. ⏾❀◖◗♣◉P🚌(232,128)

Ploughcroft

Sportsman Inn
Bradford Old Road, HX3 6UG (off A647, 1 mile N of Halifax)
✪ 6 (3 Wed & Thu)-11; 3-midnight Fri; 12-midnight Sat; 12-11 Sun ☎ (01422) 367000 🌐 sportsmaninnandleisure.co.uk
6 changing beers Ⓗ
This countryside pub with stunning views is a popular stop-off point for walkers. The changing

beers are from microbreweries, mainly in Yorkshire and Lancashire. Two-pint containers are available for takeaways. A quiz night is staged every Friday and there is free room hire for events. Adjoining is a dry ski slope (signed from the A647) and a children's adventure play centre. Lunches are served at weekends, evening meals Wednesday-Sunday. Q⏾❀◖◗&♣P🚌(576)

Pontefract

Carleton L
Hardwick Road, WF8 3PQ (on A639 1 mile S of town centre)
✪ 11 (12 Fri & Sat)-11 ☎ (01977) 703797
Greene King IPA, Abbot Reserve; Ossett Yorkshire Blonde; house beer (by Greene King); 6 changing beers (often Revolutions, Wharfe Bank) Ⓗ
A popular estate pub which now offers 10 well-kept cask ales, not always from the Greene King stable, although the house beer is brewed by Greene King to the landlady's recipe. There is plenty of outdoor seating round the side and to the rear. It gets busy at weekends, with the locals enjoying sport on the many TV screens. Beer festivals and Meet The Brewer evenings are staged. A carvery is planned following a kitchen refurbishment. ⏾❀◖◗&P🚌🛜

Robin Hood L
4 Wakefield Road, WF8 4HN (at Town End, jct of A645 Wakefield Rd with roads to Barnsley, Doncaster and A1, opp major set of traffic lights)
✪ 5-11; 1-12.30am Fri & Sat; 12-midnight Sun
☎ (01977) 702231
House beer (by Marston's); 4 changing beers (often Phoenix) Ⓗ
Busy locals' pub with a public bar and three other drinking areas. It holds quizzes twice-weekly and has darts and dominoes teams in the local charity league. A winner of several local CAMRA awards including Cider Pub of the Year 2013, it holds a beer festival over the August bank holiday weekend. The James & Kirkman Brewery is behind the pub. Bring your own guitar to the acoustic music sessions on Thursday evenings. Open lunchtimes for private functions.
Q❀&🚃(Tanshelf)♣◉🚌🐾

Rastrick

Roundhill Inn
75 Clough Lane, HD6 3QL (400yds from A643/A6107 jct towards M62 motorway bridge)
✪ 4-11; 12-midnight Sat & Sun ☎ (01484) 713418
🌐 roundhillinn.co.uk
Black Sheep Best Bitter; Timothy Taylor Golden Best, Landlord; 2 changing beers Ⓗ
Two-roomed genuine free house and locals' pub lying on the edge of Rastrick, easily reached by bus from Brighouse or Huddersfield. In daytimes during the week the pub doubles as a private function venue, notably hosting wakes, as the crematorium in neighbouring Kirklees is less than half a mile away. Originally a terrace of three houses, there are plans to extend into an adjoining barn while retaining the two-roomed layout.
Q◖◗&P🚌(547,549)🛜

Rishworth

Booth Wood Inn

Oldham Road, HX6 4QU (short drive from jct 22 of M62) SE034170
12-10 (11 Fri & Sat) (01422) 825600
boothwoodinn.co.uk
Holt Bitter; 5 changing beers H
A traditional country pub and restaurant near the scenic Yorkshire Moors. It is the tap for Oates Brewery and always has one of its beers along with several guest ales. It is open plan, with a large central bar and two restaurant areas featuring beams and a flagstone floor. All food is freshly prepared each day. In addition to the main menu there are daily specials, classic and retro dishes.

Roberttown

New Inn

Roberttown Lane, WF15 7NP
3-11; 12-11.30 Fri & Sat; 12-10.30 Sun (01924) 402069
thenewinnroberttown.com
Abbeydale Moonshine; Leeds Best; house beer (by Mallinsons); 3 changing beers H
A fine example of an old Webster's house, situated at the heart of the village. One of the family's own cellar-brewed beers is always on the bar, together with a seasonal dark beer, as is Bobtown Blonde, brewed exclusively by Mallinsons. There is a snug with comfy chairs and a function room used for occasional live music. The Wednesday night quiz is recommended. An annual beer festival is now well established. P(229,253)

Saltaire

Fanny's Ale & Cider House

63 Saltaire Road, BD18 3JN (on A657, opp fire station)
12 (5 Mon)-11; 12-midnight Fri & Sat (01274) 591419
Timothy Taylor Golden Best, Landlord; 4 changing beers H
Near the World Heritage Site of Saltaire and the historic Salts Mill, this cosy pub was formerly a beer shop. Now a free house, it has three regular ales, up to five guests, and draught ciders. An extension has increased seating capacity downstairs and provided disabled access. Upstairs there is a room with comfortable seating. The gas-lit lounge is adorned with breweriana, and real fires add nicely to the welcome. (675,678,679)

Hop

199 Bingley Road, BD18 4DH
12-midnight (01274) 582111 thehopsaltaire.co.uk
Ossett Yorkshire Blonde, Big Red Bitter, Silver King, Excelsior; 5 changing beers H
The pub is built within an old tram shed (also the pub's former name) which was originally constructed in 1904. It has a large open-plan main room with an upper mezzanine primarily used for dining. A large outdoor seating area is popular in good weather. Many of the real ales are from the Ossett Brewery range or its associated breweries such as Fernandes and Rat. Wood-fired pizzas can be seen being prepared from the main bar area.

Shipley

Fox

41 Briggate, BD17 7BP
10.30-11; 10-midnight Fri & Sat; 12-10.30 Sun
(01274) 594826 thefoxshipley.co.uk
6 changing beers H
Opened in September 2013, this small, friendly and popular single-room, café-style bar is simply but smartly furnished. The six handpulls serve a varying range of real ales, concentrating on microbreweries, especially from the local area. There is also a changing range of continental draught and wheat beers and foreign bottled beers. Real ciders are available, often including one from a local producer. Much of the art on the walls is for sale.

Ring o' Bells

3 Bradford Road, BD18 3PR (on A650)
11-midnight (1am Fri & Sat); 12-11 Sun (01274) 584386
Leeds Pale; Tetley Bitter; 4 changing beers H
Traditional roadhouse pub with an impressive frontage and close to the historic village of Saltaire. Sensitively refurbished in 2014, it retains a comfortable, homely feel. Sports matches are shown on several TV screens, and bands occasionally perform at the pub. Popular poker games and weekly quizzes are held. A small Edwardian smoke room merits a mention in CAMRA's Yorkshire Real Heritage Pubs and is a meeting place for activity groups including writers and anglers. (Saltaire)P

Silsden

King's Arms

Bolton Road, BD20 0JY
12-midnight (01535) 653216
Saltaire Blonde; Theakston Best Bitter; 3 changing beers H
Award-winning, bustling community pub with Tuesday and Thursday music nights, Wednesday quiz nights, a pool table and beer festivals, all combining to make this a great place to visit. Partitions divide the main bar into three distinct areas, each with its own feel. Note the hand-painted designs on the front windows. Westons cider and at least three guest beers from near and far, often including a darker beer, provide something for all tastes. Regular buses between Keighley and Ilkley stop outside.
P(762,765,903)

Slaithwaite

Commercial

1 Carr Lane, HD7 5AN (village centre, off A62)
12-midnight (1am Fri & Sat) (01484) 846258
commercial-slaithwaite.co.uk
Changing beers (often Empire) H
Since reopening in 2009, this village centre free house has enjoyed deserved success. Nine handpumps provide ample variety, with the keenly priced house beers, Commerciale and Moonraker Mild, supplied by Empire Brewery, six rotating guests sourced from far and wide, and one rotating cider. The Commercial is an essential stop for Trans Pennine Rail Ale Trailers and welcomes ramblers and their dogs. An upstairs function room can be used free of charge. Sky Sports and Racing UK are on screen in the bar. Q

Sowerby Bridge

Firehouse 🅛

1 Town Hall Street, HX6 2QD

✪ closed Mon; 4 (12 Sat)-11.30; 12-10.30 Sun

☎ (01422) 832586 ⊕ firehouserestaurant.co.uk

Magic Rock Ringmaster; Moorhouse's Pride of Pendle; 4 changing beers 🅗

Close to the bridge crossing the River Calder in the centre of Sowerby Bridge, this prominent building, dating from 1874, is a popular venue for those who like to eat out with the option of a traditional pint. The family-run outlet has built a good reputation for food and real ale, in particular the pizzas cooked in an open oven and the tapas menu. There are four guest beers with at least one from a local or regional brewer. ◖▣&≉●🖫🛜

Jubilee Refreshment Rooms

Station Road, HX6 3AB (on railway station)

✪ 12-10; 12-9 Sun ☎ (01422) 648285

⊕ jubileerefreshmentrooms.co.uk

3 changing beers 🅗

It took 12 years of patient negotiation for the Wright brothers to change the use of the station buildings to their current use. There is one bar serving three changing beers, offering a pleasant place to while away the time or a stop-off on the real ale trail. Refreshments are available from the early hours to benefit rail users, and alcohol is on sale after noon. A regular feature is the slide and film shows about railway history and other related interests. Trains depart regularly for Leeds and Manchester. Q✿◖≉P

Puzzle Hall

21 Hollins Mill Lane, HX6 2RF (400yds from A58)

✪ 4-midnight (1am Fri); 1-1am Sat; 1-midnight Sun

☎ (01422) 835547 ⊕ puzzlehall.com

Saltaire Blonde; 5 changing beers 🅗

The Puzzle Hall can be found nestling between the canal and the river. The 17th-century building once included a brewery; it now provides a welcoming atmosphere, good beer and a venue for live music. Bands feature on Friday and Saturday nights, and poetry recitals on the first Monday of the month. Thai food is served on Wednesday, Thursday and Sunday 5-9pm. The six varying real ales are from microbreweries. ✿▶≉♣●🖫🛜

Shepherd's Rest

125 Bolton Brow, HX6 2BD (on A58 towards Halifax)

✪ 3-11; 12-11 Fri-Sun ☎ (01422) 831937

Ossett Pale Gold, Silver King; house beer (by Ossett); 5 changing beers 🅗

Built in 1877, this establishment took the name of a previous pub on the other side of the busy main road. A former Whitbread house, it was purchased by Ossett Brewery in 2005, putting the available space to good use. From the entrance steps a triangular area leads to the bar, which faces a cosy lounge with a large brick-arched fireplace. To the left is a comfortable seating area with a flagged floor, leading to an enclosed outside area. Q✿≉♣🖫(560,574,579)❀

Works 🅛

12 Hollins Mill Lane, HX6 2QG

✪ 12-11; 12-10.30 Sun ☎ (01422) 834821

⊕ theworkssowerbybridge.co.uk

Timothy Taylor Golden Best, Boltmaker, Landlord; 6 changing beers 🅗

An award-winning conversion from a former joinery, this is a large open-plan local beside the Rochdale Canal on the western side of the town centre, featuring exposed beams and floorboards. Nine real ales are served, with three from Timothy Taylor and six rotating guests. Food, made with love, is served lunchtime and teatime. On the last Saturday of the month there is a comedy club in the upstairs function room. Q✿❀◖&≉●🖫🛜

Stanbury

Friendly 🅛

54 Main Street, BD22 0HB

✪ 12-11; 12-10.30 Sun ☎ (01535) 645528

3 changing beers (sourced nationally; often Stod Fold, Goose Eye) 🅗

Popular village local which also attracts those walking the Pennine Way or visiting the ruined farmhouse claimed to be Wuthering Heights. The pub is small and retains a traditional layout, with two small lounges either side of a central bar plus a separate games room. Stanbury is only two miles from Haworth but a million miles from its tourist hustle and bustle. At least one beer is usually from Goose Eye Brewery. Tea and coffee can be served on request. ✿&▲♣🖫(664,916,917)❀

Wuthering Heights Inn 🅛

Main Street, BD22 0HB

✪ 12-midnight ☎ (01535) 643332

⊕ thewutheringheights.co.uk

Theakston Best Bitter; Thwaites Wainwright; 2 changing beers 🅗

A popular, friendly local just off the Pennine Way, dating from 1763. Warmed by logburners, the traditional main bar has photographs showing the history of the village and offers an internet terminal for customers' use. The cosy dining room has a Bronte theme. A third room hosts regular folk music gatherings and can be booked for parties and meetings. Extensive outdoor seating provides spectacular views down the Worth Valley. Well-behaved dogs and children are welcome. A quiz takes place every Thursday. ⏴✿◖▲♣🖫(664,916,917)❀🛜

Stanley

Graziers Inn

116 Aberford Road, WF3 4NN (on A642 at bottom of hill after hospitals, near jct with road to Stanley Ferry)

✪ 12-midnight ☎ (01924) 200283

Abbeydale Moonshine; John Smith's Bitter; Theakston Old Peculier; 2 changing beers 🅗

The inn dates from 1890 and is a deserved addition to the Guide. It has served consistently good-quality beers for a number of years. Traditional and welcoming, this pub boasts numerous rooms separated from a central bar. In addition, copper-topped tables and a real fire in winter add to the atmosphere. Pictures of old Stanley adorn the walls. ⏴✿◖&♣🖫❀🛜

Thornhill

Savile Arms

12 Church Lane, WF12 0JZ (on B6117, 2½ miles S of Dewsbury)

✪ 5 (4 Fri)-11; 12-11 Sat & Sun ☎ (01924) 463738

Black Sheep Best Bitter; 2 changing beers (often Copper Dragon, Partners, Saltaire) 🅗

A picturesque village pub and former 18th-century coaching inn popularly known as the Church House. The beamed bar area leads to a colourful mural depicting Thornhill's history. Traditional bar billiards is played in the taproom which stands on the consecrated ground of the parish church. Barbecues are held in a secret garden with picnic tables. Themed meal nights are offered on some Saturdays and a folk club meets on the first Tuesday of the month. Q❀♣P🚌(128,281,283)📶

Todmorden

Staff of Life

550 Burnley Road, Knotts Grove, OL14 8JF

12-3, 5.30-11; 12-midnight Fri-Sun ☎ (01706) 819033

staffoflifeinn.org.uk

Timothy Taylor Golden Best, Landlord; 3 changing beers Ⓗ

Comfortable roadside inn sited in a deep, narrow gorge beneath the local landmark of Eagle's Crag. The three guest ales come from a variety of northern independents, and the high-quality food can be enjoyed at a table in one of several cosy nooks and crannies, or on the outside terrace. Unusual artwork on the walls alludes to the local legend of the White Doe. Ask the licensee to explain the whole unfortunate story.

❀P🚌(589,592)🐾📶

Upper Denby

George Inn

114 Denby Lane, HD8 8UE

5-10.30 (11.30 Fri); 1-11.30 Sat; 11.30-10.30 Sun

☎ (01484) 861347 thegeorgeinn-upperdenby.co.uk

Tetley Bitter; Timothy Taylor Landlord; 1 changing beer (often Great Heck, Ossett, Small World) Ⓗ

Family-run village local which is going from strength to strength since becoming a free house in late 2012. The pub has hosted walk and food days, with home-made pie and peas, along with other functions. Occasional live music and traditional singalongs also take place here. Walkers are welcome, and families until 8.30pm.

❀Ѧ♣P🚌🐾📶

Wakefield

Black Rock

19 Cross Square, WF1 1PQ (between Bull Ring and top of Westgate)

11-11 (midnight Sat); 12-10.30 Sun ☎ (01924) 375550

Tetley Bitter; 4 changing beers Ⓗ

An arched, tiled façade leads into this city-centre local with its small frontage. Inside you will find a warm welcome and a comfy interior including photographs of old Wakefield. The Rock stands as one of the few proper pubs left in the middle of the clubs and bars of Westgate, and is popular with drinkers of all ages looking for a real pint. Patrons are encouraged to suggest beers to try, with four regularly changing guest ales on offer. There is a free function room for private use.

Q⇌(Westgate)🚌

> When you have lost your inns, drown your empty selves, for you will have lost the last of England.
>
> **Hilaire Belloc, The Four Men, 1912**

Bull & Fairhouse

60 George Street, WF1 1DL (turn right out of Westgate station, left at Westgate, then right at traffic lights; bear left at bottom of hill, pub is on left after 200yds)

4-11; 12-midnight Fri & Sat; 12-11 Sun ☎ (01924) 362930

Great Heck Chopper; 4 changing beers Ⓗ

The brewery tap for the Great Heck Brewery, the pub has reverted to an earlier name alluding to the cattle market and fairground in the area. A comfortable multi-roomed premises, it now enjoys a lighter feel, with a new lounge at the front and the toilets relocated to the rear, improving disabled access via a passageway. Play Your Cards Right is held on Thursdays, and live music hosted at weekends. A changing real cider/perry is served on gravity. Q♿⇌(Westgate)♣🚌(443,444)🐾📶

Fernandes Brewery Tap & Bier Keller

5 Avison Yard, Kirkgate, WF1 1UA (turn right approx 100yds S of George St/Kirkgate jct near Scartop Pine)

4-11 (11.30 Thu); 12-midnight Fri & Sat; 12-11 Sun

☎ (01924) 386348

10 changing beers (often Fernandes, Marston's, Ossett) Ⓗ

Owned by Ossett Brewery, Fernandes Brewery operates in the cellar. With 11 handpulls, two are dedicated to dark beers, two are Fernandes beers, two Ossett, one is from the Marston's group, three are guest beers, and one is a draught cider. The Bier Keller, which opens 6pm-midnight Friday and Saturday, has premier foreign beers on draught plus an Ossett beer and a cider on handpump. There is a quiz on Wednesday evenings, folk music on the first Sunday of the month and open mic on the third Sunday. Pets are welcome.

⇌(Kirkgate)🚌🐾

Harry's Bar

107B Westgate, WF1 1EL

5 (4 Fri & Sat)-1am; 12-midnight Sun ☎ (01924) 373773

Bob's White Lion; Moorhouse's Pride of Pendle; house beer (by Five Towns); 5 changing beers Ⓗ

Small one-roomed pub set in an alleyway just off Westgate. A real fire and a bare brick and wood interior plus vintage sporting pictures enhance this small, cosy pub. A selection of bottled Belgian beers adds to the temptation. There is also a fantastic view of Wakefield's famous 99-arch viaduct – if only steam trains were a regular feature. Local CAMRA Pub of the Year 2013.

❀⇌(Westgate)P🚌📶

Hop

19 Bank Street, WF1 1EH (in cobbled street off Westgate almost opp Theatre Royal)

4-midnight (1am Fri); 12-1am Sat ☎ (01924) 367111

Ossett Yorkshire Blonde, Silver King, Excelsior; Rat White Rat; 4 changing beers Ⓗ

Converted into a venue for music, comedy and conversation, this Georgian building retains bare brick walls, fireplaces and other original features, along with new additions including a VW camper van converted into a bar. The main bar has nine handpumps, one reserved for a dark beer and one for a Fernandes or Riverhead beer; a selection of bottled Belgian and American beers is also sold. Open mic night is Monday, a quiz features on Tuesday, and live music on Thursday, Friday and Saturday. Rooms are available for private hire.

❀♿⇌(Westgate)🚌

Wakefield Labour Club 𝕃

18 Vicarage Street, WF1 1QX (at the top of Kirkgate, round corner from Wakey Tavern)

⏲ 7-11 (midnight Fri); 11-midnight Sat; 7-midnight Sun

☎ (01924) 215626 🌐 theredshed.org.uk

5 changing beers Ⓗ

Known as the Red Shed, this is a second-hand army hut which has been extensively refurbished and is home to many union, community and charity groups. Quiz night is Wednesday, occasional live music is staged on the second Saturday of the month and open mic folk music night on the last Saturday. It has three rooms, with two available to hire for functions. There is an extensive collection of union plates and badges over the bar and numerous CAMRA awards adorn the walls. Dogs and well-behaved visitors are welcome.

Q🏇♿⇌(Kirkgate/Westgate)♣🍎**P**🚌🐾

Wintersett

Anglers Retreat 𝕃

Ferrytop Lane, WF4 2EB (between villages of Crofton and Ryhill; follow signs all over district for nearby Anglers Country Park)

⏲ 12-3 (not Tue), 7-11; 12-11 Sat; 12-3.30, 7-11 Sun

☎ (01924) 862370

Acorn Barnsley Bitter; 3 changing beers Ⓗ

This old-fashioned, no frills, rural alehouse is a rare example of a cosy locals' pub, and the owner has just celebrated 20 years in charge. Close to the Anglers Country Park, Haw Wood and the Trans Pennine Trail, it is frequented by twitchers, cyclists, walkers and bikers. There is a beer garden to the side and seats at the front for fine-weather drinking. A large car park is across the road and a frequent bus service stops a three-minute walk away. **Q**🏇❀♿⛺♣**P**🚌(194,195,196)🐾

Fanny's Ale & Cider House, Saltaire (Photo: Bob Steel)

Harp Inn, Old Radnor, Mid-Wales (p595)

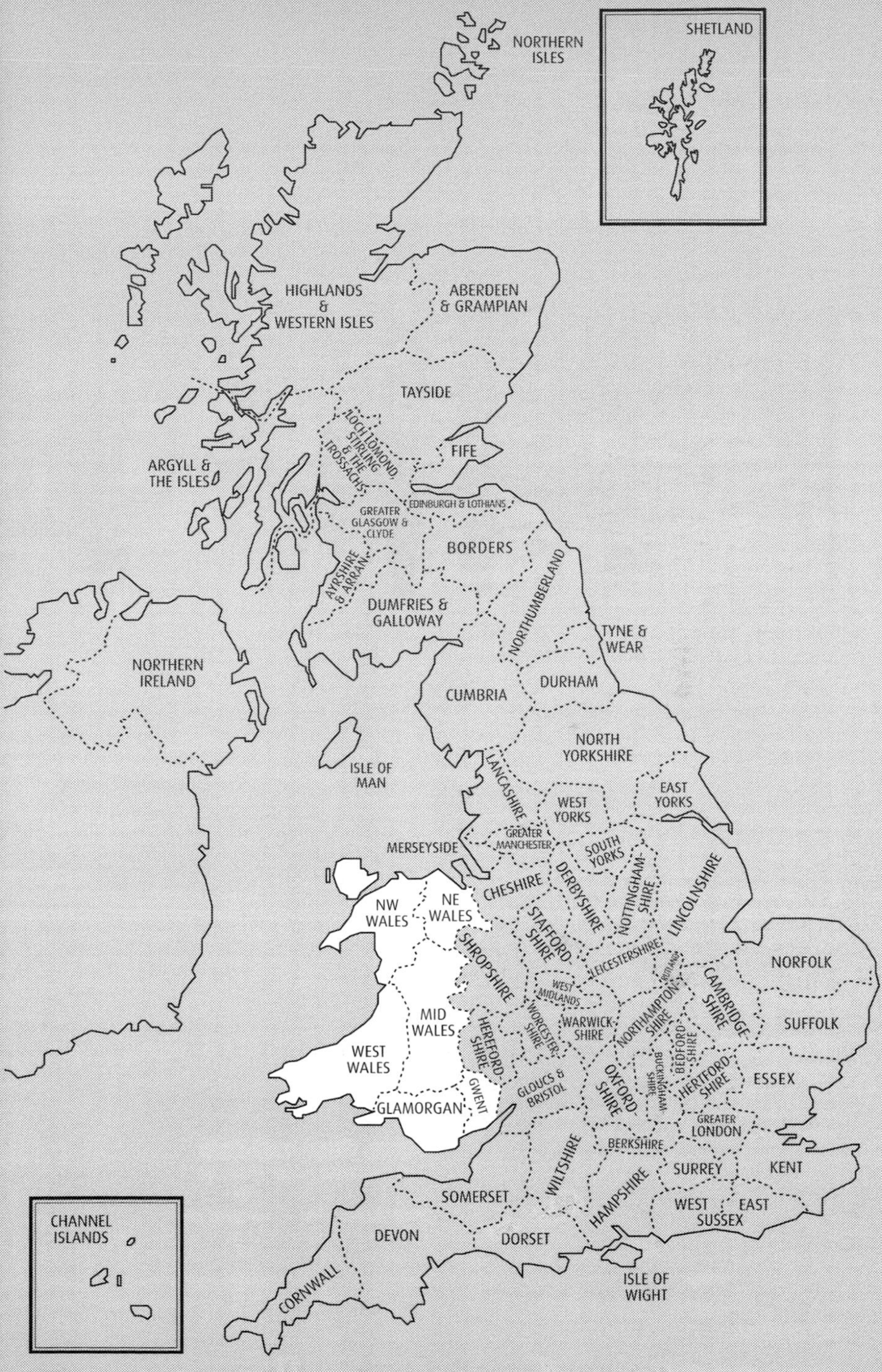
SHETLAND
NORTHERN ISLES
HIGHLANDS & WESTERN ISLES
ABERDEEN & GRAMPIAN
TAYSIDE
LOCH LOMOND, STIRLING & THE TROSSACHS
FIFE
ARGYLL & THE ISLES
EDINBURGH & LOTHIANS
GREATER GLASGOW & CLYDE
BORDERS
AYRSHIRE & ARRAN
DUMFRIES & GALLOWAY
NORTHUMBERLAND
TYNE & WEAR
NORTHERN IRELAND
CUMBRIA
DURHAM
NORTH YORKSHIRE
ISLE OF MAN
LANCASHIRE
WEST YORKS
EAST YORKS
GREATER MANCHESTER
MERSEYSIDE
SOUTH YORKS
CHESHIRE
DERBYSHIRE
NOTTINGHAMSHIRE
LINCOLNSHIRE
NW WALES
NE WALES
STAFFORD SHIRE
SHROPSHIRE
LEICESTERSHIRE
NORFOLK
WEST MIDLANDS
CAMBRIDGE SHIRE
MID WALES
HEREFORD SHIRE
WORCESTER SHIRE
WARWICK SHIRE
NORTHAMPTON SHIRE
SUFFOLK
WEST WALES
BEDFORD SHIRE
BUCKINGHAM SHIRE
OXFORD SHIRE
HERTFORD SHIRE
ESSEX
GWENT
GLOUCS & BRISTOL
GLAMORGAN
GREATER LONDON
BERKSHIRE
WILTSHIRE
SURREY
KENT
SOMERSET
HAMPSHIRE
WEST SUSSEX
EAST SUSSEX
CHANNEL ISLANDS
DEVON
DORSET
ISLE OF WIGHT
CORNWALL

Wales

GLAMORGAN

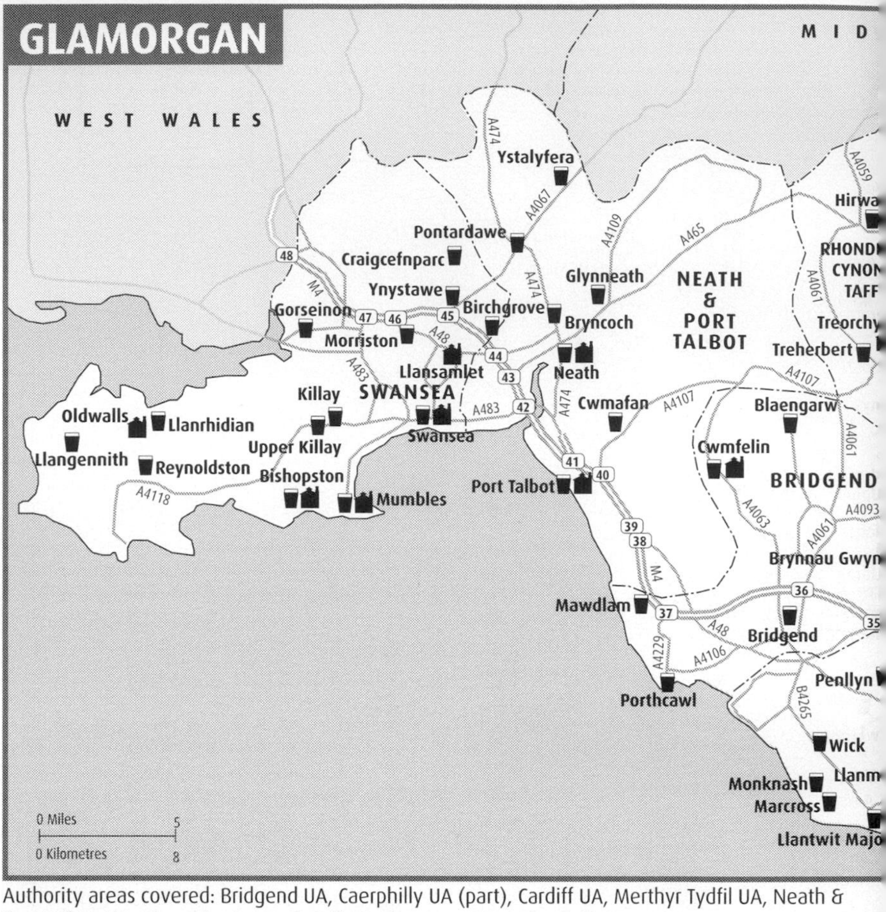

Authority areas covered: Bridgend UA, Caerphilly UA (part), Cardiff UA, Merthyr Tydfil UA, Neath & Port Talbot UA, Rhondda, Cynon & Taff UA, Swansea UA, Vale of Glamorgan UA

Aberdare

Whitcombe Inn

Whitcombe Street, CF44 7DA

12-11.15 ☎ (01685) 875106

Grey Trees Diggers Gold, Drummer Boy; 2 changing beers (sourced locally; often Grey Trees) H

Welcoming and friendly traditional street-corner local, close to the town centre. Local brewery Grey Trees features prominently, and other beers from its range may substitute. The large front bar backs on to a pool room at the rear. Sport is sometimes on TV, but is rarely intrusive. Live music is hosted occasionally. ⇌♣

Aberthin

Hare & Hounds

Aberthin Road, CF71 7LG

12-midnight (1am Fri & Sat) ☎ (01446) 774892

Draught Bass G**; Hancocks HB; Sharp's Atlantic; Wye Valley HPA; 1 changing beer (often Kite)** H

A characterful village pub with stone walls, wooden beams and a log fire. The cosy bar where the locals gather is the focal point but there is also a dining area and a small games room. The south-facing beer garden with its own bar shack is a summer suntrap and live music is occasionally on offer. Traditional pub food is served and there are plans to expand the menu. Occasional beer festivals are held. Q♣P (321)

Barry

Barry West End Club L

54 St Nicholas Road, CF62 6QY

1-midnight; 11-11 Sun ☎ (01446) 735739

Wye Valley HPA; 3 changing beers H

Multiple CAMRA branch Club of the Year winner, the club is housed in a red-brick building overlooking Barry Old Harbour, and features a bar, lounge, function room and snooker room. The steward is devoted to maintaining its reputation for real ale, and holds popular beer festivals during the year. The club welcomes visitors and is a hub of local activity, fielding skittles teams, adult and junior football teams and snooker teams, and is home to fishing and scuba clubs.

Q⇌♣

Birchgrove

Bowen Arms

Birchgrove Road, SA7 9JR (just off M4 jct 44)

12-11 (midnight Fri & Sat) ☎ (01792) 324712

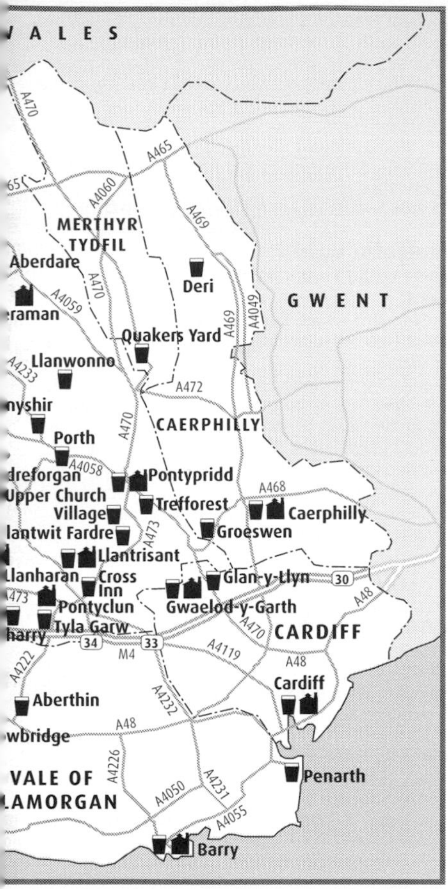

Felinfoel Best Bitter, Double Dragon; 1 changing beer ⊞
Comfortable pub with a single bar and a separate function room. Outside, there is a play area for children and extensive seating. A games room adjoins the main bar, with a pool table, dartboard and TV sport. Live music plays occasionally during holiday periods and some weekends. Good-value food is popular, particularly the home-made chips, and it is advisable to book for the Sunday carvery. ♣P (30,59)

Bishopston

Joiners Arms 𝕃

50 Bishopston Road, SA3 3EJ
3-10.30 Mon & Tue; 11.30-11; 12-10.30 Sun
☎ (01792) 232658
Courage Best Bitter; Marston's Pedigree; Swansea Bishopswood Bitter, Three Cliffs Gold, Original Wood; 2 changing beers ⊞
Situated in the heart of the village, this 1860s free house remains popular with locals and visitors. Home of the Swansea Brewing Company, the pub has two bars and holds beer festivals and occasional music events, usually around public holidays. Good-value food is served lunchtimes and evenings (no food Mon and Sun eve). There is a small car park. A winner of several local CAMRA awards. P (14)

Valley

41 Bishopston Road, SA3 3EJ
12-11 ☎ (01792) 234820
Courage Best Bitter; 3 changing beers ⊞
Traditional country pub set in the heart of the village of Bishopston, Gower. A large porch area (which doubles as a convenient bus shelter) leads to a split-level bar and dining area, with exposed beams, hearth and open fire. Occasional live music and quiz nights are hosted. A wide variety of home-cooked meals made using local ingredients is served daily, with a take-away service available on Sunday lunchtimes. ♣P (14)

Blaengarw

Blaengarw Hotel

The Strand, CF32 8AA
12-11 Mon; 10.30-midnight (11 Tue, Thu & Sun)
☎ (01656) 870287
1 changing beer ⊞
The owners have completed a major refurbishment of this large street-corner local at the heart of the community. The public bar is popular for TV sport and hosts pool and darts league teams, and there is a fine jukebox. Meals are available in the lounge/dining room 12-8pm Tuesday and Thursday, and the Sunday lunches are always an attraction. The famous Welsh hymn Calon Lan was written upstairs. ♣ (12,14,16)

Bridgend

Cabo Roche

Five Bells Road, CF31 3HW
11-11; 12-midnight Sat & Sun ☎ (01656) 663555
Sharp's Doom Bar; 1 changing beer ⊞
Situated at the southern end of the town centre and close to the college, this establishment has continued to thrive since its conversion from a bathroom showroom to a bar in 2007. A mixed clientele uses the three distinct areas – a café, bar, and lounge with comfortable settees. Sports television is available throughout. Real ale is on two handpumps, often including an interesting and well-chosen guest beer. Lunches are served Monday to Friday. ≥P (X2,303)

REAL ALE BREWERIES

Borough Neath (NEW)
Boss Llansamlet (NEW)
Brains Cardiff
Bullmastiff Cardiff
Celt Experience Caerphilly
Cerddin Cwmfelin
Cwm Rhondda Treorchy (NEW)
Glamorgan Llantrisant
Gower Oldwalls
Grey Trees Aberaman
Mountain Hare Brynnau Gwynion
Neath Port Talbot
Otley Pontypridd
Pilot Mumbles (NEW)
Pixie Spring Pontyclun
Surfing Monkey Cardiff (NEW)
Swansea Bishopston
Tomos & Lilford Llantwit Major
Tomos Watkin Swansea
Vale of Glamorgan Barry
Violet Cottage Gwaelod-y-Garth
Zerodegrees Cardiff

Coach Inn

37 Cowbridge Road, CF31 3DH
⏲ 11.30-11; 12-10.30 Sun ☎ None
Wye Valley Butty Bach [H]; changing beers (often Thornbridge, Tiny Rebel) [H]/[G]
Basically furnished free house passionately serving real ale and cider from Wales and beyond. Three guest beers on handpull and two served straight from the cask complement the house ale Butty Bach. Continental beers are available including take-away bottles. Customers enjoy open mic nights, themed nights, brewery trips, a spring beer festival every Easter weekend and a stout and porter festival in November. There is an art wall for the use of local artists. ❀≋♣●🚌(X2,303)🐾ᯤ

Wyndham Arms

Dunraven Place, CF31 1JE
⏲ 9am-midnight (1am Fri & Sat) ☎ (01656) 673571
Greene King Abbot; Sharp's Doom Bar; 4 changing beers [H]
Totally refurbished in 2014, this town-centre Wetherspoon hotel features beers from south Wales breweries. The building dates from 1792, named after a centuries-old local family, and has 25 en-suite bedrooms available. Seating ranges from high stools to comfortable settees in three distinct sections, including areas suited to dining. A conference room is available for hire. The pub opens at 7am for breakfast, the bar opens at 9am. Q🛏◐♿≋●🚌ᯤ

Bryncoch

Dyffryn Arms

Neath Road, SA10 7YF (on A474)
⏲ 12-11 ☎ (01639) 636184 🌐 thedyffrynarms.com
3 changing beers (sourced nationally) [H]
Nestled in beautiful Neath Valley countryside on the A474, this pub has a large car park, garden and children's play area. The inside is modern and well kept, with a real log fire in a central fireplace. Three real ales are served on a changing basis. Food is available in the restaurant and bar until 9pm. ❀◐♿P🚌(122,132)

Brynnau Gwynion

Mountain Hare

Brynna Road, CF35 6PG
⏲ 4 (5 Mon)-11; 12-11 Fri-Sun ☎ (01656) 860453
🌐 mountainhare.co.uk
Mountain Hare Far Shores IPA; Wickwar Brand Oak Bitter; 2 changing beers [H]
This genuine community inn resumed brewing its own beer after many decades in 2013. Along with a Mountain Hare ale on handpump, there is usually a Wickwar beer and interesting guests. A traditional Welsh village local, the pub has been in the same family for over 40 years. There is a lounge, public bar, games room and garden. Sport is often shown on TV in this rugby lovers' pub. Baguettes, pizzas and burgers are available at lunchtimes. ❀◐♿♣●P🚌(44,404)🐾ᯤ

Caerphilly

Green Lady

Pontygwindy Road, CF83 3HF
⏲ 10-11 (midnight Fri & Sat) ☎ (029) 2085 1510
3 changing beers (sourced nationally; often Marston's, Ringwood, Wychwood) [H]
Modern Marston's pub alongside the old main road, north of the town centre. Comfortable and spacious, it has a separate dining/function room. Three handpumps dispense over 32 beers from the Marston's group, including seasonals, on a rotational basis. Good-value meals are available (no food Sun eves). Live music features most Friday and Saturday evenings and there is a quiz night every Sunday.
❀◐♿≋(Energlyn & Churchill Park)P🚌(26,50)

Malcolm Uphill

89-91 Cardiff Road, CF83 1FQ
⏲ 8am-midnight (1am Fri & Sat) ☎ (029) 2076 0720
Greene King Abbot; Ruddles Best Bitter; 5 changing beers (sourced nationally; often Adnams, Kite, Vale of Glamorgan) [H]
Popular Wetherspoon pub, situated at the top of the town, handy for the rail and bus interchange. Up to five guest beers are usually on sale, plus one or two guest ciders. The usual JDW deals and promotions are offered. This pub can be busy at weekends and hosts a popular quiz on Sundays. A separate accessible entrance is available if required. Q❀◐♿≋●🚌ᯤ

Cardiff

Andrew Buchan

29 Albany Road, Roath, CF24 3LH
⏲ 11-11 ☎ None
Rhymney Best, Hobby Horse, Dark, Bitter, Export Ale; 1 changing beer [H]
This converted shop is the brewery tap for Rhymney Brewery and offers the full range of its beers. It features an open fireplace with the brewery moose head hanging above. The pub has developed a good reputation for live music with bands playing several times a week. Changing eclectic exhibitions of modern art are also on display. Happy hour is 5-7pm. An upstairs meeting room is available, free of charge for community groups. ❀≋(Cathays)🚌🐾ᯤ

Chapter Arts Centre

Market Road, Canton, CF5 1QE (off Cowbridge Road East behind Iceland store)
⏲ 12-11 (12.30am Fri; midnight Sat); 12-10.30 Sun
☎ (029) 2030 4400 🌐 chapter.org
Ringwood Best Bitter; 5 changing beers (sourced nationally) [H]
A multi-purpose venue located a good 15-minute walk from the city centre. The contemporary café bar offers up to six beers from both local and nationwide breweries – micro to large. Regular beer festivals are held featuring British and German ales. Behind the bar, the fridges hold an inspiring range of continental bottled beers. Good-quality reasonably priced food is served.
❀◐♿▲●P🚌(17,18)ᯤ

City Arms [L]

10-12 Quay Street, CF10 1EA
⏲ 12-11 (midnight Thu; 2am Fri & Sat); 12-10 Sun
☎ (029) 2064 1913
Brains Dark, Bitter, SA, SA Gold, Rev James [H]; 9 changing beers [H]/[G]
Popular pub in the heart of Cardiff's top beer and cider area. It has two rooms served by a central bar that features many handpumps and a gravity stillage. Though a Brains-managed house, a large range of guest beers from almost anywhere in the UK can be expected. In addition, two handpumps

are set aside for cider or perry. The pub gets extremely busy when events take place at the adjacent Millennium Stadium and Arms Park.
❀♿⛺⇌(Central)♣🍎🚌🐾📶

Cricketers

66 Cathedral Road, Pontcanna, CF11 9LL
🕐 11.30-11 ☎ (029) 2034 5102 🌐 cricketerscardiff.co.uk
Evan Evans Best Bitter, Cwrw, Warrior; 2 changing beers (often Evan Evans) 🄷
A large converted Victorian town house near Glamorgan County Cricket Ground. A long, opened-out interior is divided into comfortable and smartly furnished spaces. There is a well-appointed beer garden at the rear. The only Evan Evans house in Cardiff, its range of beers comes exclusively from the Evan Evans Group. The pub is known for quality food and has won a number of awards.
Q❀◐♿⛺🚌📶

Deri

Heol-y-Deri, Rhiwbina, CF14 6UH
🕐 11.30-midnight ☎ (029) 2062 6237
Brains Bitter; Hancocks HB; Sharp's Doom Bar; 5 changing beers 🄷
This suburban community pub on the northern outskirts of Cardiff has been modernised over the years. Popular and busy, its large lounge is stylishly furnished and divided into distinct areas. Three regular beers are complemented by a changing range of five guest ales from national and local breweries. Quizzes are hosted twice weekly. There is a large car park, outside seating areas and a covered smoking area. Ales are reduced in price on Mondays and a CAMRA discount also applies. The pub is Cask Marque-approved and part of the Perfect Pour campaign.
Q🛋❀◐♿P🚌(21,23)🐾📶

Discovery 🄻

Celyn Avenue, Lakeside, CF23 6EH
🕐 12-11.30 (12.30am Fri & Sat); 12-11 Sun
☎ (029) 2075 5015 🌐 knifeandforkfood.co.uk/discovery
4 changing beers (often Otley) 🄷
A spacious contemporary pub situated close to the north end of Roath Park Lake. The public bar retains a community atmosphere with TV, darts and weekly quiz nights. The larger, quieter lounge/restaurant serves a variety of meals including chef's specials. Outside is a paved, covered patio. An impressive function room is available to hire for weddings and other events. The management has collaborated with Otley Brewery to serve one house beer and three ever-changing guests.
❀◐♿♣P🚌(54)🐾📶

Fox & Hounds

Old Church Road, Whitchurch, CF14 1AD
🕐 11 (12 Sun)-11 ☎ (029) 2069 3377
Brains Dark, Bitter, SA, SA Gold, Rev James; 1 changing beer 🄷
Parts of this old coaching inn date back to the 16th century. Despite being in the suburbs, it has the feel of a country pub. The interior is divided into distinct drinking and dining areas, featuring low beams and flagstone floors. A wide range of reasonably priced food is served, with a curry night on Wednesday. Quiz night is Sunday.
🛋❀◐♿⇌(Llandaff)P🚌(24,25,132)🐾

Gravity Station

6 Barrack Lane, CF10 2FR
🕐 11-7 (11 Fri & Sat); 11-6 Sun ☎ (029) 2024 0252
🌐 thegravitystation.com
4 changing beers (often Hopcraft, Waen) 🄷
Cardiff's first micropub and shop sells a broad spectrum of bottled beers. Unusually, a range of cask ales is kept behind what appear to be kitchen cupboard units and served via screw taps. A central copper-topped table and seating encourage conversation with other customers. The premises provides a relaxing haven from the adjoining busy shopping centre. Acoustic music sessions are hosted on the last Friday of each month.
Q❀♿⇌(Queen St)🍎🚌📶

Lansdowne 🏆

71 Beda Road, Canton, CF5 1LX
🕐 12-11 (11.30 Fri & Sat) ☎ (029) 2022 1312
4 changing beers (often Grey Trees, Tiny Rebel, Waen) 🄷
An impressive red-brick building on a street corner, the exterior features a relief of the beehive trademark of the former Crosswells Cardiff Brewery. The L-shaped interior is divided into distinct drinking areas. This 2014 CAMRA branch Pub of the Year and 2015 joint Pub of the Year features real ales from Welsh and other microbreweries. It hosts an annual beer festival in summer. The pub is popular with locals, young families and discerning football fans on match days. 🛋❀◐⇌(Ninian Park)♣🍎🚌(17,18)🐾📶

Pen & Wig 🄻

1 Park Grove, CF10 3BJ
🕐 11.30-midnight (1am Fri & Sat); 11.30-11.30 Sun
☎ (029) 2037 1217 🌐 penandwigcardiff.co.uk
8 changing beers (sourced nationally; often Brecon Brewing, Celt Experience) 🄷
Just a short distance from the Civic Centre and National Museum of Wales, this Victorian terraced pub is popular with office workers, particularly those in the legal profession, and students. It offers a varied beer range sourced from local, regional and national breweries. Two ciders are also available. The large garden includes a covered section and a smokers' area. ❀◐⇌(Cathays)🍎🚌

Queen's Vaults

29 Westgate Street, CF10 1EH
🕐 10-11 (midnight Fri & Sat); 11-11 Sun ☎ (029) 2022 7966
Felinfoel Double Dragon; 4 changing beers 🄷
Run by local pub company JW Bassett, this great-value pub is usually busy, especially when there are events at the Millennium Stadium or when major sports fixtures are screened on its various TVs. The guest beers can be from local, regional or national breweries – often micros. Cardiff CAMRA Cider Pub of the Year 2014 and 2015, up to six ciders or perries are regularly on offer on gravity dispense. Reasonably priced meals including a Sunday carvery are available.
◐♿⛺⇌(Central)♣🍎🚌

Rummer Tavern

14 Duke Street, CF10 1AY
🕐 11.30-midnight; 12-11 Sun ☎ (029) 2023 5091
🌐 therummertaverncardiff.co.uk
Hancocks HB; Wye Valley HPA; 5 changing beers 🄷
Opposite Cardiff Castle, this claims to be Cardiff's oldest trading pub, with a history spanning back over three centuries. The interior is narrow but long, comprising a series of simply furnished areas, with leaded windows and dark-wood panelling throughout. An upstairs room is available for hire.

The regularly changing guest beers can come from anywhere in the UK. Real cider complements the beer range, and pub food is served until early evening. ◑⅄⇌(Queen St/Central)●🚌≋

Urban Tap House 🏆

26 Westgate Street, CF10 1DD

✪ 12-midnight ☎ (029) 2039 9557 🌐 urbantaphouse.co.uk

8 changing beers (often Tiny Rebel) Ⓗ

The flagship pub for the award-winning Tiny Rebel Brewery. This landmark building is opposite the Millennium Stadium and comprises a number of rooms, upstairs and downstairs, some of which can be hired. It offers an ever-changing range of innovative cask ales, occasional brewery takeovers and a good range of Tiny Rebel's own beers. Real ciders, a comprehensive selection of bottled beers and unusual craft keg products are also on offer. Cardiff CAMRA joint Pub of the Year winner 2015. ♨◑♿⅄⇌(Central)●🚌🐾≋

Zerodegrees

27 Westgate Street, CF10 1DD

✪ 12-11 ☎ (029) 2022 9494 🌐 zerodegrees.co.uk/cardiff

Zerodegrees Mango Wheat Pils, Wheat Ale, India Pale Lager, Black Lager, Pale Ale, Pilsner; 2 changing beers (often Zerodegrees) Ⓐ

Brewpub set in a listed former bus garage. The brewery forms a backdrop to the well-stocked bar. Beer storage tanks rise to one side and are labelled with interesting information about their contents. The decor is contemporary and there are two upstairs areas for diners. Pizzas are a speciality but other food is also served. Happy hour for pints is 4-7pm Monday-Friday. Closing time may extend to midnight. ❀◑♿⅄⇌(Central)🚂🚌≋

Cowbridge

Vale of Glamorgan Inn

51 High Street, CF71 7AE

✪ 12-11 (midnight Fri & Sat) ☎ (01446) 772252

Adnams Broadside; Hancocks HB; Wye Valley HPA, Butty Bach; 1 changing beer Ⓗ

Popular single-roomed pub in the centre of town. The wooden-floored bar area has a warming fire with more seating in the lounge section. Pumpclips hanging over the bar showcase the many guest beers sold. Outside there is an attractive enclosed beer garden with a separate covered and heated smoking area. The annual beer festival coincides with the town's food and drink festival. Good-value home-made food is served lunchtimes (no food Sun). A former CAMRA branch Pub of the Year. Q♨❀◐●🚌(X2)🐾≋

Craigcefnparc

Rock & Fountain

Rhyddwen Road, SA6 5RA

✪ 5 (4 Fri)-11; 3-11 Sat; 12-10.30 Sun ☎ (01792) 843347

Felinfoel Stout; 2 changing beers Ⓗ

Friendly local situated on the side of a steep hill close to the RSPB Cwm Clydach bird sanctuary. There is an outside patio area with seating where you can enjoy the view across the valley. The pub has a comfortable lounge featuring pictures of local interest and pub memorabilia, with a separate games bar for pool, darts, dominoes and sport on TV. ♨❀♣P🚌(121)🐾

Cross Inn

Cross Inn Hotel

Main Road, CF72 8AZ

✪ 12-11 ☎ (01443) 223431

Hancocks HB; Sharp's Doom Bar; Wye Valley HPA; 1 changing beer (sourced nationally) Ⓗ

A warm, welcoming part stone-flagged traditional pub, popular with locals and visitors. The large single room is divided into a bar area with a TV and a spacious lounge/dining area. Beers are excellently kept, and good-value food is served. Wednesday is curry night. Sunday lunches are popular (booking advised). Q❀◑♿♣P🚌≋

Cwmafan

Brit Pub Ⓛ

London Row, SA12 9AH

✪ 11-11 (midnight Fri-Sun) ☎ (01639) 680247

Sharp's Atlantic; 4 changing beers (sourced locally) Ⓗ

Established in 1845, this recently refurbished riverside pub is situated in the picturesque Afan valley, providing a warm welcome for visitors to the area, renowned for its breathtaking scenery and mountain cycling. With its stone floors and open fire, the pub has a relaxed atmosphere and conversation fills the air. Sharp's Atlantic is always available, along with up to four guest ales, mainly sourced locally. Home-made meals are served lunchtime and evenings. Curry night is Tuesday and quiz night on Sunday. Q♨❀🛏◑♿P🚌🐾≋

Cwmfelin

Cross Inn 🏆

Masteg Road, CF34 9LB

✪ 11.45-midnight (1am Fri & Sat); 11-midnight Sun

☎ (01656) 732476 🌐 cerddinbrewery.co.uk

Cerddin Solar, Tubby Chap, Cwrw Tri, Cascade; 1 changing beer (often Cerddin) Ⓗ

Traditional roadside community pub with a brewery behind the beer garden. Home-made curries are served Friday lunchtimes and bar snacks the rest of the week. As well as the Cerddin cask ales, the brewery's bottle-conditioned ales are also stocked, as are three ciders. There are two beer festivals a year – one over the Mayday weekend and the other in the autumn. A book exchange is available. Local CAMRA Pub of the Year 2015. Q❀⇌(Garth)●🚌(32)🐾≋

Deri

Old Club

93 Bailey Street, CF81 9HX

✪ 5 (12 Sat & Sun)-midnight ☎ (01443) 830278

2 changing beers Ⓗ

Independent public house offering a diverse range of widely and locally sourced ales – national brands are rarely seen here. Two beers are always available, occasionally three at weekends. The nearest transport hub is Bargoed, where a bus or taxi to Deri can be found. Alternatively, the former railway path to Deri offers a pleasant 45-minute stroll. Cwm Darran Country Park is nearby. ⅄♣🚌(1)🐾

Glan-y-Llyn

Fagins Ale & Chop House Ⓛ

9 Cardiff Road, CF15 7QD

✪ 11-11 (midnight Thu & Fri); 12-midnight Sat; 12-10.30 Sun
☎ (029) 2081 1800
Dark Star Hophead Ⓗ**; 3 changing beers** Ⓖ
This one-bar free house is popular with all ages. Three gravity-dispensed guest ales change continually, and are regularly modern hoppy brews. Two varying ciders, usually from Gwynt y Ddraig, are also on handpump. A menu of good-value meals is offered in the bar and separate restaurant. Live music features on most Thursdays and some Saturday evenings. The pub is well served by public transport. CAMRA branch Pub of the Year 2014. ⬥✿✪◑●ⵕ(26,132)✿≋

Glynneath

Dinas Rock Hotel Ⓛ
High Street, SA11 5AP
✪ 5-11; 3-midnight Fri; 1-midnight Sat; 12-11 Sun
☎ (01639) 720105
Draught Bass; 3 changing beers (sourced regionally) Ⓗ
This traditional town-centre local has recently been refurbished by the new owners and now has an open-plan layout. The original stone walls remain and two wood-burning stoves make for a cosy atmosphere in winter. The emphasis on real ale is most welcome in an area lacking any choice. Live sport is featured on TV, in particular Six Nations and Ospreys rugby, and live music features at weekends once a month. The location is handy for the famous waterfall walks and information centre just up the road. Pub closed Mondays in winter.
⬥⬥♣●ⵕ(X5,8)✿≋

Gorseinon

Mardy Inn
117 High Street, SA4 4BR
✪ 8am-midnight (1am Fri & Sat) ☎ (01792) 890600
Fuller's London Pride; Greene King Abbot; Ruddles Best Bitter; 4 changing beers Ⓗ
Formerly a traditional high-street pub, this modern Wetherspoon establishment opened in 2013 following a major refurbishment. It has a large single bar with several TVs showing news and sport, and an adjoining airy extension overlooking the furnished patio area. Some interesting pictures of old Gorseinon adorn the walls.
⬥✿◑⬥♣●Pⵕ(400,404)≋

Groeswen

White Cross Inn
CF15 7UT (overlooking Groeswen Chapel)
✪ 4 (12 Fri-Sun)-midnight ☎ (029) 2085 1332
⊕ thewhitecrossinn.co.uk
3 changing beers (sourced regionally) Ⓗ
A little off the beaten track, this traditional gem is well worth finding. Three changing beers are on sale at keen prices, always including a dark, and a real cider is sometimes stocked. Many novel events – often to raise funds for charity – attest to the inclusive and fun nature of the pub. Occasional beer festivals are hosted. Road access is narrow, though the pub is not far from main roads. Local buses stop a mile away. ⬥✿◑♣●P✿≋

Gwaelod-y-Garth

Gwaelod y Garth Inn
Main Road, CF15 9HH

✪ 10-11; 12-10.30 Sun ☎ (029) 2081 0408
⊕ gwaelodinn.co.uk
Wye Valley Bitter; 5 changing beers (often Violet Cottage) Ⓗ
A stone-built multi award-winning village inn. Situated on the slope of Garth Mountain, in the centre of the village, it is popular with locals as well as those who travel some distance to visit. Expect to find at least one beer from the on-site Violet Cottage brewery, complemented by a varying range of real ales which could originate from anywhere across the UK. There is a separate games room and upstairs restaurant.
Q⬥✿⬥◑♣●Pⵕ(26B)

Hendreforgan

Griffin Inn Ⓛ
Gilfach Goch, CF39 8YL (from Tonyrefail on A4093, turn down lane after Gilfach Goch village sign)
✪ 7 (6 Fri)-11; 12-11 Sat & Sun ☎ (01443) 670379
Brains SA; 1 changing beer (sourced locally; often Kite) Ⓗ
Brains SA and one guest beer are usually available at this friendly pub situated at the end of a country lane. Run by the same family for over 60 years, a warm welcome is assured. The interior is adorned with interesting and highly polished artefacts and gleaming brasses. Listed in CAMRA's Real Heritage Pubs of Wales. Q⬥✿⬥♣●Pⵕ(150,172)✿

Hirwaun

Glancynon Inn
Swansea Road, CF44 9PH
✪ 11-11; 12-10.30 Sun ☎ (01685) 811043
1 changing beer (sourced nationally; often Greene King) Ⓗ
A real ale oasis in the village, this imposing pub has a main bar that sprawls over two levels and leads to a well-kept garden. The spacious lounge is popular with diners, offering an attractive menu featuring local organic produce whenever possible. Lunches are served daily (booking is recommended at weekends). A little off the beaten track but easy to find and worth the effort. ✿◑●⬥♣Pⵕ(9)

Killay

Village Inn
5-6 Swan Court, The Precinct, SA2 7BA
✪ 10.30-11 (midnight Thu-Sat); 12-11.30 Sun
☎ (01792) 203311
Fuller's London Pride; Timothy Taylor Landlord; 2 changing beers Ⓗ
Cosy pub with an L-shaped bar and wood panelling, situated in a small shopping precinct. Home-made food is served from a wide-ranging, daily-changing menu, both in the bar and separate restaurant (booking essential). The pub shows selected sport, holds a quiz on Sunday and Tuesday evenings and hosts monthly gatherings of a Song Writers Guild. An annual beer festival is held in April. ◑⬥Pⵕ(20,21)✿≋

Llangennith

King's Head Ⓛ
SA3 1HX
✪ 11-11; 12-10.30 Sun ☎ (01792) 386212
⊕ kingsheadgower.co.uk

Gower Brew 1, Sampson's Jack, Best Bitter, Gold; 1 changing beer Ⓗ
A row of three 16th-century stone-built cottages, the pub has been owned and run by the same family for many years. The full range of ales from nearby Gower Brewery is available plus a cask cider. An impressive variety of home-made food is served all day with dishes inspired by fresh local produce. At the western end of the Gower Peninsula, a short distance from the sandy stretches of Llangennith Beach, the pub offers quality 4-star accommodation.
🚼❀🛏◑♿⛺♣🍎P🚌(116)🐾📶

Llanharan

Turberville
Chapel Road, CF72 9QA
⏲ 12-11.30 (12.30am Fri & Sat) ☎ (01443) 222143
2 changing beers (sourced nationally) Ⓗ
Directly opposite Llanharan railway station, this popular and busy pub offers a changing range of national brand guest beers. It has a plain public bar with traditional pub games and TV sport, and a spacious lounge bar, where meals are served in the evenings. 🚼❀◗♿⇌♣🍎🚌(244)

Llanharry

Fox & Hounds
Llanharan Road, CF72 9LL
⏲ 12-11 (midnight Fri & Sat) ☎ (01443) 222124
🌐 fox-and-hounds-inn-llanhari.co.uk
4 changing beers (sourced locally) Ⓗ
Independent since 2011, this delightful stone pub has rapidly established a reputation as among the best in the area. Sassy modern styling in traditional materials creates a relaxing and comfortable ambience. Up to four guest beers are available, in a range of flavours to suit all tastes, sourced from micro and smaller breweries. Bottled real ciders are also stocked. 🚼❀◑♿♣P🚌(44,244)🐾📶

Llanmaes

Blacksmiths Arms
CF61 2XR
⏲ 12-11.30 (10.30 Sun) ☎ (01446) 795996
🌐 blacksmithsarmsllanmaes.co.uk
Brains Rev James; Hancocks HB; 2 changing beers (often Butcombe) Ⓗ
Deservedly popular pub opposite the village green, which hosts a beer festival each summer as part of the village fair. Highly regarded food includes steak night on Tuesday, and Sunday lunches which change week from week. Charity quiz nights are Wednesday and Sunday. The patio beer garden is fantastic in summer, especially when the barbecue gets fired up. The pub lies very much at the heart of the local community. There is disabled access throughout. Q🚼❀◑♿P🐾📶

Llanrhidian

Dolphin Inn
SA3 1EH (just off B4295 N Gower Road)
⏲ 1 (4.30 Mon-Thu)-11 winter; 1 (4.30 Mon)-11 summer; 12-11 Sun ☎ (01792) 391069
Brains Rev James; Fuller's London Pride; 1 changing beer Ⓗ
Cosy village pub dating from the 18th century on the north side of Gower (look for the yellow dolphin directional signs) next to a 13th-century church, with stunning views of the estuary from the lovely beer gardens. The characterful single room is warmed by a solid fuel stove. There is a children's play area at the rear with a fenced area for rabbits and poultry to roam. Quiz night is Sunday. Check ahead for afternoon opening times.
🚼❀P🚌(115,116)🐾

Greyhound Inn 𝕃
Oldwalls, SA3 1HA (1 mile W of Llanrhidian on B4295)
⏲ 11-11 ☎ (01792) 391027
🌐 thegreyhoundinnoldwalls.co.uk
5 changing beers (sourced locally; often Gower) Ⓗ
Traditional 19th-century inn with a welcoming atmosphere, home to the Gower Brewery, with a varying range of its ales on offer at the bar alongside guests. An extensive home-cooked bar menu is served every day, with Sunday lunches particularly popular. Outside at the rear is a large beer garden with a children's play area and wonderful views over the Gower countryside. Home of the Halfpenny Folk Club every Sunday evening. 🚼❀◑♿♣P🚌(116)🐾📶

Llantrisant

New Inn
Swan Street, CF72 8ED
⏲ 12.30-11 ☎ (01443) 222232
Kite Cwrw Gorslas; 1 changing beer (sourced nationally) Ⓗ
Friendly urban townhouse pub in the heart of Llantrisant Old Town. The traditional and welcoming main bar fronts onto the street and a second room at the back is mainly used for dining. Food is served Wednesday-Sunday. The public car park directly opposite is handy. ❀◑P

Llantwit Fardre

Crown Inn
Main Road, CF38 2HL
⏲ 1 (3 Mon & Tue)-midnight; 12-midnight Sat & Sun
☎ (01443) 218277
3 changing beers Ⓗ
Friendly pub with a large bar and dining area plus a separate function room and games area. Two or three ever-changing beers include local brews much of the time. Live music on Friday and a quiz on Sunday are regular highlights, with other events held throughout the year, often in support of the local community and charities.
🚼❀◑♣P🚌(100,244,400)📶

Llantwit Major

King's Head
East Street, CF61 1XY
⏲ 11.30-11.30 (midnight Fri & Sat); 11.30-11 Sun
☎ (01446) 792697 🌐 sabrain.com/kings-head
Brains Bitter; 1 changing beer (often Clark's) Ⓗ
This family-run town-centre local has been in the Guide for 17 consecutive years. A traditional two-bar pub with a strong local following, the long stone-floored public bar is well used by darts and pool teams. The comfortable wood-panelled lounge leads out to the beer garden. There is a large-screen TV for sport in both bars. Guest beers come from local brewers as well as from afar.
Q🚼❀⇌♣🚌🐾📶

Llantwit Major Rugby Club
Boverton Road, CF61 1XZ
4.30-11 (midnight Fri); 12-midnight Sat; 11-11 Sun
(01446) 792276
Brains Rev James; Sharp's Doom Bar; 1 changing beer (often Black Sheep) H
Friendly community club where non-members are welcome. Two staple beers are always on offer complemented by a guest. The local boxing club shares the facility and there are regular pool and darts league matches. Dogs are welcome in the players' bar, the club's equivalent of a public bar. There is also a cosy lounge bar and a large function room.

Old Swan Inn
Church Street, CF61 1SB
12-11 (10.30 Sun) (01446) 792230
knifeandforkfood.co.uk/swan
4 changing beers H
The oldest pub in town overlooks St Illtyd's Church to the side and the town hall at the front in this historic old part of Llantwit Major. An ever-changing range of ales often showcases Welsh beers. The front bar is popular with drinkers and diners – excellent food is a feature of this attractive and comfortable hostelry – while the popular back bar is somewhat livelier. Beer festivals are hosted in spring and summer. There is free public parking behind the town hall. Q

Llanwonno

Brynffynon Hotel
CF37 3PH (opp church) ST030955
closed Mon; 12-11 (10.30 Sun) (01443) 790272
brynffynonhotel.com
3 changing beers H
Set on top of the ridge between the urban Cynon and Rhondda Fach valleys, this tranquil country inn is a complete contrast. The lounge has a timeless atmosphere with its relaxing leather couches and log-burning fire. The dining room serves food of an excellent standard (booking suggested). Two or three guest beers are available, and beer festivals are held. A patio offers views of the forest and ancient churchyard. P

Marcross

Horseshoe Inn
CF61 1ZG
5.30-11 Mon; 12-2.30, 6-11; 12-11 Sat; 12-10.30 Sun
(01656) 890568 theshoesmarcross.co.uk
Wye Valley Butty Bach; 2 changing beers H
A beautiful 19th-century pub in the tiny village of Marcross. Good food is offered along with regularly changing guest ales often from Welsh breweries. The small interior is cosy on a winter's evening, and on a sunny day the beer garden is a delight. Conveniently situated near the Nash Point car park – from here you can walk along the coastal path or just enjoy the views across the channel.
Q P (303)

Mawdlam

Angel Inn
Marlas Road, CF33 4PG
12-11 (10.30 Sun) (01656) 740456
Gower Gold H**; Sharp's Doom Bar; 2 changing beers (often Kite)** G
Although the majority of the pub's trade is high-quality food – the large car park can fill up at peak times – there is a comfortable bar for drinkers to settle in, which also has a TV for sport. The four ales are all served straight from the cask, kept at perfect temperature out the back. Accommodation is now available. Close to the M4 motorway and Kenfig National Nature Reserve.
Q P (63B)

Monknash

Plough & Harrow
CF71 7QQ
11-11 (midnight Fri & Sat) (01656) 890209
ploughandharrow.org
Draught Bass G**; Hancock's HB** H**; changing beers** G
Renowned, welcoming 14th-century pub, originally a monastic farmhouse for Neath Abbey, with many original features remaining, and large log fires for the winter. Up to eight real ales are available, four on handpump and the others dispensed direct from casks behind the bar, with local breweries well supported, along with real cider and perry. Good home-cooked food is served. The large garden is popular in summer, when beer festivals are also held. A former local CAMRA Cider Pub of the Year winner. Q P (303)

Morriston

Red Lion Hotel
Sway Road, SA6 6JA
8-midnight (1am Fri & Sat) (01792) 761870
Greene King Abbot; Ruddles Best Bitter; 4 changing beers H
Wetherspoon pub with a large dining area featuring an open log fire at the front and high bar stools at the back. On the walls are a number of pictures depicting former local industry, and a community board advertises trips to breweries and events. Outside is a large patio area with tables and chairs and a smoking area. There are good parking facilities and disabled access.
P (4)

Mumbles

Mumbles Ale House
2 Dunns Lane, SA3 4AA
closed Mon & Tue; 5-11 Wed; 12-2, 5-11 Thu; 12-11 Fri & Sat; 12-10.30 Sun 07437 421963
Wye Valley HPA, Butty Bach H/G**; 7 changing beers (sourced nationally; often Butcombe)** G
The latest addition to the thriving real ale offerings in Mumbles, this intimate pub is located on the ground floor of a standard terraced house. Nine real ales are offered – six on gravity dispense, three on handpump – along with ciders, perries, wine, spirits and soft drinks. There is no keg beer. Traditional bar snacks are also available.
(2)

Park Inn L
23 Park Street, SA3 4DA
4 (12 Fri-Sun)-midnight (01792) 366738
5 changing beers (sourced regionally) H
The convivial atmosphere in this small establishment attracts discerning drinkers of all ages, though the games room is particularly popular with younger people. Five handpumps dispense an ever-changing range of beers, with

special emphasis on independent breweries from Wales and the west of England. Alongside a fine display of pumpclips are pictures of old Mumbles and its pioneering railway. A popular quiz is held on Thursday, with occasional music at weekends. ♨❀♣●🚌(2,3)🐾📶

Pilot Inn Ⓛ

726 Mumbles Road, SA3 4EL

⏲ 12-11 (midnight Fri & Sat) ☎ 07897 895511

🌐 thepilotofmumbles.co.uk

Draught Bass; 4 changing beers (sourced nationally; often Pilot) Ⓗ

Welcoming and friendly local on the seafront at Mumbles and home to the Pilot Brewery. This historic pub, built in 1849, is next to the coastal path and popular with lifeboatmen, locals, real ale fans, walkers and cyclists. Six ales are always available plus a wide range of bottled ciders. Hot drinks are also served. Voted Wales CAMRA Pub of the Year 2014. Q♨🚌(2B)🐾📶

Neath

Borough Arms Ⓛ

2 New Henry Street, SA11 1PH (off Briton Ferry road)

⏲ 4.30-9 Mon; 4.30 (4 Thu & Fri; 12 Sat)-11; 12-6 Sun

☎ (01639) 644902 🌐 boroughbreweryneath.com

Draught Bass; 5 changing beers (sourced locally) Ⓗ

This cosy, traditional little gem of a pub is home to the new Borough Brewery and well worth the walk from Neath town centre. The horseshoe-shaped bar features six handpumps which dispense a varying range of mainly local beers, to the delight of the locals. Three of the Borough Brewery ales brewed on the premises are always served, on a changing basis, alongside three guest ales. Winner of local CAMRA Pub of the Year three times, this is probably the best back-street pub in Wales. Q❀♿⇌♣🚌🐾📶

Smiths Arms Ⓛ

New Road, Neath Abbey, SA10 7DG (off A465 on A4320 to Skewen)

⏲ 4 (2 Fri)-11; 12-11 Sat & Sun ☎ (01639) 641770

2 changing beers (sourced locally) Ⓗ

A Grade II-listed building, this traditional pub is close to the ruins of Neath Abbey, a former Cistercian monastery. The interior is attractively decorated and comprises a bar, lounge and function room. The lounge features an open hearth fire. Pool and darts are available in the bar and sport is screened on TV. Live music plays occasionally. Carvery meals are popular on Sundays. A local outlet for the Neath Brewery, two of its ales are served on a changing basis. Q♨❀◐♣🚌🐾

Penarth

Bear's Head

37-39 Windsor Road, CF64 1JD

⏲ 8am-11.30 ☎ (029) 2070 6424

Adnams Broadside; Greene King Abbot; Ruddles Best Bitter; 5 changing beers Ⓗ

A Wetherspoon outlet in the town centre with an extensive open-plan interior including a smaller area upstairs comfortable for families. A clientele of all ages enjoys a variety of up to eight ales, with Welsh breweries making regular appearances alongside the usual range. There is a steady trade most of the week, with good-value food available all day. Bear's Head is a rough translation of Penarth from Welsh – pen meaning head and arth meaning bear. Q♨◑♿⇌(Dingle Rd)●🚌📶

Golden Lion Ⓛ

69 Glebe Street, CF64 1EF

⏲ 10-11; 11-midnight Fri & Sat; 12-10.30 Sun

☎ (029) 2070 1574

3 changing beers (sourced regionally; often Gower, Kite, Otley) Ⓗ

JW Bassett pub situated a short walk from the town centre, towards the Cardiff Bay Barrage. It offers good-value food, including a Sunday carvery, and two or three real ales usually from Welsh breweries. Sports TV is available throughout, even in the small beer garden, and the jukebox has an impressive 20,000 tracks – it can be lively. Regulars include local sports teams, including football and darts sides. ♨❀◑♿⇌(Dingle Rd)♣🚌📶

Pilot

67 Queen's Road, CF64 1DJ

⏲ 12-11 (midnight Fri & Sat); 12-10.30 Sun

☎ (029) 2071 0615 🌐 knifeandforkfood.co.uk/pilot

4 changing beers (often Celt Experience, Otley, Tiny Rebel) Ⓗ

For many years a Brains pub, the Pilot was refurbished in 2012 and is now operated by Knife and Fork Food, with the emphasis on high-quality food, wine and beer. Five handpumps offer quality craft beers and occasional real cider. Ales are chosen from all over the country, and quality Welsh breweries often feature, especially Otley. There is seating outside at the front for warm weather, and a view across Cardiff Bay at the rear. Q♨◑⇌(Dingle Rd)●🚌🐾📶

Penllyn

Red Fox Ⓛ

CF71 7RQ

⏲ 12-11 (10 Sun) ☎ (01446) 772352 🌐 redfoxinn.co.uk

Hancocks HB; Sharp's Doom Bar; 2 changing beers Ⓗ

A warm welcome is guaranteed at this friendly village local. Beyond the thick stone-walled exterior can be found a flagstone-floored main bar area with a log fire and a separate restaurant serving traditional pub favourites. An attractive patio in front of the pub and a large enclosed garden to the rear are perfect places to while away the time in warmer weather with a good pint and a quality meal. Quiz night is the last Thursday of the month. Q♨❀◑♿P🐾📶

Pontardawe

Pontardawe Inn 🏆

123 Herbert Street, SA8 4ED

⏲ 12-midnight ☎ (01792) 447562 🌐 pontardaweinn.co.uk

Banks's Bitter; Marston's Pedigree; 4 changing beers (sourced nationally; often Marston's) Ⓗ

Originally a drovers' pub on the route to Neath mart, and well placed on Route 43 of the National Cycle Network, the Gwachel, as it is known locally, is worth the short walk from the town centre. Live music is prominent every weekend, with Welsh language bands playing on the third Friday of the month. Beer festivals are held in May, August and November. The landscaped garden is a welcome addition in summer. CAMRA branch Pub of the Year in 2014 and 2015. ♨❀◑♿♣P🚌(120,125,132)🐾📶

Travellers Well

76 Commercial Road, Rhydyfro, SA8 4SS
3-11; 12-midnight Fri & Sat; 12-11 Sun ☎ 07757 561568
thetravellerswell.info
2 changing beers (sourced regionally) Ⓗ
Known as the Travs, the pub has a public bar, lounge and games area. Two guest beers are available, usually from Welsh microbreweries. Situated in a good area for walkers between the Baran and Gwrhyd mountains, Carn Llechart Stone Circle, Cwm Ddu Glen and the 1,500 year old Llangiwg Church are worth visiting while in the area. ♣P

Pontypridd

Bunch of Grapes

Ynysangharad Road, CF37 4DA (off A4054)
11-1am (midnight Sun) ☎ (01443) 402934
bunchofgrapes.org.uk
Otley O2 Croeso; 9 changing beers (often Dark Star, Otley, Salopian) Ⓗ
A short stroll from the town centre, this popular pub has distinct areas around a central bar. Six guest beers accompany four from Otley Brewery, plus two ciders/perries. Guest ales are varied and wide ranging. A separate and acclaimed restaurant serves locally sourced food with themed nights a regular feature (booking suggested, especially at weekends). Events include beer, cider and cheese festivals and much more. Winner of many awards including local CAMRA Pub of the Year 2015.
QP

Llanover Arms

Bridge Street, CF37 4PE (opp N entrance to Ynysangharad Park)
11-midnight (11 Sun) ☎ (01443) 403215
Brains Bitter; 2 changing beers Ⓗ
Sensitively refurbished historic gem, retaining much of its old-world charm. Originally a canalside pub with stables, it now stands close to the Pontypridd exit from the A470. Three rooms are linked by a central passageway, each room with its own regulars. Nearby is Ynysangharad Park and the famous town bridge and museum. The Taff Trail passes close by. Q♣P

Patriot Bar

25B Taff Street, CF37 4UA (at N end of main shopping street)
10 (12 Sun)-midnight ☎ (01443) 407915
Rhymney Hobby Horse, Dark, Bevans Bitter, Bitter, Export Ale Ⓗ
Owned by Rhymney Brewery, this no-frills bar serves well-kept and reasonably priced beers to an appreciative and varied clientele. Formerly a shop and known locally as the Wonky Bar, its functional interior was fully refurbished in 2014. Real cider is sometimes available. The pub is situated on the main shopping street and is convenient for the bus and railway stations.

Port Talbot

Lord Caradoc

69-73 Station Road, SA13 1NW
8am-midnight (1am Fri & Sat) ☎ (01639) 896007
Greene King Abbot; Ruddles County; 3 changing beers (sourced nationally) Ⓗ
A typical Wetherspoon pub, situated on the main thoroughfare, close to both the railway and bus stations. The pub attracts a varied clientele, with a family area to the rear where children are welcome. Two regular ales are boosted by an ever-changing choice of guest beers, sourced locally and from further afield. Real draught cider is also available. P

Porth

Rheola

Rheola Road, CF39 0LF
2-midnight; 1-1am Fri; 12-1am Sat; 12-midnight Sun
☎ (01443) 682633
Draught Bass; 1 changing beer (sourced nationally) Ⓗ
This free house is situated where the Rhondda Valley divides and is well served by bus and train. A central bar separates the games room (which can sometimes be loud) and the comfortable lounge. There are quiz nights, whist nights and live music nights. An extra guest beer is added at weekends and all the beers are competitively priced. The outdoor smoking area is sheltered. ♣P

Porthcawl

Lorelei Hotel

36-38 Esplanade Avenue, CF36 3YU
5 (12 Fri-Sun)-11 ☎ (01656) 788342 loreleihotel.co.uk
Draught Bass Ⓖ; Rhymney Export Ale; 2 changing beers (often Tomos Watkin) Ⓗ
Situated close to the seafront and the Grand Pavilion, this seaside hotel has featured in the Guide for the past 17 years. It serves four draught beers and five continental beers, plus cider during the summer, and hosts beer festivals twice a year. Built around the end of the 19th century, during World War I it was two separate buildings – one used as a hospice for injured soldiers. Food is available Tuesday-Friday evenings.
Q♣

Quakers Yard

Glantaff Inn

Cardiff Road, CF46 5AH
11.30-11.30 (1am Fri & Sat) ☎ (01443) 410822
3 changing beers (sourced nationally; often Courage, Rhymney, Wadworth) Ⓗ
Set above the river, this pub is popular with walkers and cyclists on the nearby Taff Trail. Its comfortable bar recalls local history in early photographs and artefacts. Three beers are usually available – two tend to change regularly, the third is often a guest beer back by popular demand. Styles and breweries vary, with a local beer frequently among the range. Good-value, quality food is served. Q(78)

Reynoldston

King Arthur Hotel

Higher Green, SA3 1AD (on village green)
10-11 ☎ (01792) 390775 kingarthurhotel.co.uk
Felinfoel Double Dragon; Sharp's Doom Bar; 3 changing beers (sourced nationally; often Tiny Rebel) Ⓗ
Traditional family-owned hotel and an acclaimed wedding venue. Situated at the foot of Cefn Bryn in beautiful Gower, it overlooks the village green and has a covered seating area outside. The cosy, atmospheric main bar is open to drinkers and diners, offering home-cooked food made with local

produce. Main meals are served lunchtimes and evenings, snacks are available all day. A handpump for a fifth real ale is now on the bar in the Gower Room at the rear of the main bar.
ᕯ⊛⏀◗⅊P🖪(116,118)☎

Swansea

No Sign Bar ♛
56 Wind Street, SA1 1EG
🌣 11-11 (midnight Wed & Thu; 1am Fri & Sat); 12-11 Sun
☎ (01792) 465300 ⊕ nosignwinebar.com
4 changing beers 🖪
Historic narrow bar established in 1690, formerly Mundays Wine Bar and reputedly a regular haunt of Dylan Thomas. Architectural signs from various periods of the pub's past remain, some dividing the interior into separate bar areas. Quality food and wine are available and there are usually four cask ales on sale. Live music features early evenings in the bar on Fridays and Saturdays. Local CAMRA Pub of the Year 2015. ⊛◗⇌●🖪(500)☎

Potters Wheel
85-86 The Kingsway, SA1 5JE
🌣 8am-midnight (1am Thu-Sat) ☎ (01792) 465113
Adnams Broadside; Fuller's London Pride; Ruddles Best Bitter; Sharp's Doom Bar; 3 changing beers (sourced locally) 🖪
A city-centre Wetherspoon outlet with a long sprawling bar area offering various seating arrangements, attracting customers of all ages and backgrounds. An interesting selection of guest beers is available, with a commitment to local breweries. Cask cider is also available. Photographs feature local dignitaries associated with the area's industrial past, particularly the ceramics and pottery industries. ◗⅊⇌●🖪☎

Queen's Hotel
Gloucester Place, SA1 1TY (near Waterfront Museum)
🌣 11-11 (11.30 Sat); 12-10.30 Sun ☎ (01792) 521531
Theakston Best Bitter, Old Peculier; 2 changing beers 🖪
This vibrant free house is near the Dylan Thomas Theatre, City Museum, National Waterfront Museum and marina. The walls display photographs depicting Swansea's rich maritime heritage. The pub enjoys strong local support and home-cooked lunches are popular. Evening entertainment includes a Sunday quiz and live music on Saturday. This is a rare local outlet for Theakston Old Peculier in addition to a seasonal guest beer often from a local microbrewery.
◗⅊🖪☎

Vivian Arms
104 Gower Road, Sketty, SA2 9BZ (Sketty Cross, jct of A4118 and A4216)
🌣 12-11 (midnight Fri & Sat) ☎ (01792) 516194
Brains Bitter, SA, Rev James; 2 changing beers 🖪
Situated on the main crossroads in Sketty, the Vivs is a spacious pub which attracts a wide mix of customers young and old. It has a choice of seating areas including comfortable sofas, and plenty of TV screens throughout showing live sport. Two frequently changing guest beers are available alongside the Brains standards. The pub has a small meeting room and is suitable for family dining. Live music plays on Fridays. ᕯ⊛◗⅊🖪(20,21)☎

Westbourne
1 Brynymor Road, SA1 4JQ
🌣 11-11 Mon (11.30 Tue & Wed; midnight Thu; 12.30am Fri & Sat); 12-11 Sun ☎ (01792) 476637
⊕ westbourneswansea.com
Greene King Abbot; Sharp's Doom Bar; 4 changing beers 🖪
Located on the western fringe of the city centre, this street-corner pub has a single split-level bar and a heated terrace outside. Home to the first self-service beer wall in Wales and iPad tabletop ordering, it is now the place to go for young and old alike. Five or six ales are always available – customers are able to request a particular beer on the pub's website. A popular quiz is held on Tuesday evening. ⊛◗⅊🖪(2,3)☎

Woodman
120 Mumbles Road, Blackpill, SA3 5AS
🌣 11.30-11 (10.30 Sun) ☎ (01792) 402700
4 changing beers 🖪
Local scenes of yesteryear decorate the various rooms and nooks at this spacious establishment situated between the Swansea Bay seafront and the entrance to the beautiful Clyne Gardens. Popular both with families and diners, the pub is also welcoming to those seeking liquid refreshment only. A constantly changing range of guest ales is offered. There are three alfresco seating areas including a small beer garden.
Q ᕯ⊛◗⅊P🖪(2,3,14)☎

Trefforest

Otley Arms ℒ
Forest Road, CF37 1SY (on gyratory system)
🌣 11-midnight (1am Sat); 12-midnight Sun
☎ (01443) 402033 ⊕ otleyltd.co.uk
Otley O1, O2 Croeso; 4 changing beers (often Otley) 🖪
The original Otley family street-corner pub, now much enlarged. Bustling with university students during term time, this establishment is well served by rail and bus. Inside is a multitude of drinking areas and outside a heated and covered smoking area. The four guest beers include one from the Otley range. ◗⇌♣🖪(100,244)⊛

Rickards Arms ℒ
61 Park Street, CF37 1SN
🌣 10-midnight (1am Fri & Sat); 12-11 Sun
☎ (01443) 402305 ⊕ otleyltd.co.uk
Otley O1; 2 changing beers 🖪
Popular with students from the nearby university campus, the cosy atmosphere is enhanced by separate drinking spaces, including a vaulted cellar and upstairs dining area. Famed for its good-value bar food, the breakfasts are a notable feast. Entertainment includes regular quiz nights and music events. Two guest beers are often from the Otley range. ⊛◗⇌♣🖪(100,244)⊛☎

Treherbert

Baglan Hotel ℒ
30 Baglan Street, CF42 5AW
🌣 11-11 ☎ (01443) 776111
Brains SA Gold; 3 changing beers (sourced locally; often Grey Trees, Otley) 🖪
This free house has been in the same family for well over 60 years and the current landlord was born in the pub. Old brewery memorabilia and pictures of visiting celebrities adorn the walls. A large TV and dartboard are provided but conversation often dominates. Three guest beers

from local breweries regularly feature. A comfortable lounge is used mainly for dining. Q🛏◗♣🚌(120,130)

Tyla Garw

Boars Head

Coedcae Lane, CF72 9EZ (600yds from A473 over level crossing)

4-10 Mon; 12-11; 12-10 Sun ☎ (01443) 225400

8 changing beers (often Dark Star, Oakham, Salopian) Ⓗ

This pub has four separate rooms, two set aside for dining, served by a single bar. Up to eight ever-changing beers are available from a wide range of breweries and in all styles from pale to porter. Staff and locals are always happy to advise on choices. One or two beer festivals are held annually, with some beers on gravity. Sunday lunch is popular and booking is advised. The direct walking route from Pontyclun station cuts through a small industrial area. Q❀◑◗⇌(Pontyclun)P

Upper Church Village

Farmers Arms

St Illtyd Road, CF38 1EB

3-11; 12-midnight Thu-Sat; 12-10.30 Sun

☎ (01443) 205766

Brains Rev James; 1 changing beer (sourced nationally) Ⓗ

Single-bar village local with a sizeable and pleasant garden. The guest beers are often unusual for the locality and frequently from smaller brewers. A popular quiz night is hosted on Tuesdays and live music on alternate Thursdays, but beer and conversation are the main attractions, unless there is rugby on TV. ❀P🚌(90)

Upper Killay

Railway Inn

553 Gower Road, SA2 7DS

12-11 (10.30 Sun) ☎ (01792) 203946

Swansea Deep Slade Dark, Bishopswood Bitter, Three Cliffs Gold, Original Wood; 1 changing beer Ⓗ

A classic locals' pub set in woodlands at the top end of Clyne Valley. The adjacent former railway line now forms part of Route 4 of the National Cycle Network. In winter the real fire in the lounge provides welcome warmth and cheer. Traditional cider and at least one guest beer are kept alongside the Swansea Brewing Company beers. A large area outside hosts occasional barbecues, music events and boules tournaments in summer. Q❀♣●P🚌(20,21,118)

Wick

Star Inn

Ewenny Road, CF71 7QA

12 (5 Mon)-11.30; 12-10.30 Sun ☎ (01656) 890080

thestarinnwick.co.uk

Sharp's Doom Bar; 1 changing beer (often Evan Evans) Ⓗ

After a period of closure following disastrous attempts to turn it into a trendy gastro-pub, the Star was totally refurbished by new owners late in 2012, returning it to its former glory as a Guide regular. Originally three farm cottages, the interior has a traditional bar and a lounge/diner and is flagstoned throughout. The friendly staff serve excellent home-cooked meals. Well-behaved dogs on leads are welcome in the bar.
Q❀◑◗♿P🚌(303)🐾

Ynyshir

Ynyshir Hotel

Ynyshir Road, CF39 0EL

5 (4 Fri)-midnight; 12-midnight Sat; 12-10 Sun

☎ (01443) 686791

2 changing beers (sourced locally; often Celt Experience, Grey Trees) Ⓗ

This friendly traditional Valleys pub is situated on the main road through Ynyshir, also the Pontypridd to Maerdy bus route. Two guest ales are served from a variety sourced mainly from Welsh breweries. Several beer festivals are held during the year. The snug, with its wooden bar, is of some historic interest. Other rooms include a plainly furnished public bar and a smaller, comfortable lounge area. At the rear is a modest beer garden. Pub games include pool and darts.
Q❀♣🚌(132,X32)

Ynystawe

Millers Arms

634 Clydach Road, SA6 5AY (on B4603, ½ mile N of M4 jct 45)

11.30-3, 6 (5 Sat)-11; 12-3, 7-10.30 Sun

☎ (01792) 842614 millers-arms.co.uk

Rhymney Hobby Horse; 2 changing beers Ⓗ

Friendly community pub with a highly decorative interior including an extensive teapot collection, a photograph of the landlord with Tom Jones, and artwork by Katherine Jenkins. Busy periods require booking for meals, which are good value and home cooked, served in the bar and separate restaurant. In the spring a garden nesting box is on CCTV for twitchers. The pub is on the main bus routes to Swansea Valley and on cycle path Route 43.
❀◑◗♿P🚌(145,212)

Ystalyfera

Wern Fawr

47 Wern Road, SA9 2LX

2-5, 7 (6.30 Fri)-11; 7-11 Sat; 12-11 Sun

☎ (01639) 843625

Bryncelyn Holly Hop, Buddy Marvellous, Oh Boy; 1 changing beer (sourced locally) Ⓗ

The brewery tap for Bryncelyn Brewery, this is a rare, unspoiled locals' pub with a central bar serving both the bar and lounge. The bar is a step back in time with an interesting display of old mining, industrial and domestic artefacts. It also boasts an old stove that the locals nickname 'the nuclear reactor'. The pub is busy on rugby international days and hosts occasional live music. Opening time on Saturdays may be earlier if there is rugby on. ♣🚌(125)🐾

For we could not now take time for further search (to land our ship) our victuals being much spent especially our beer. **Log of the Mayflower**

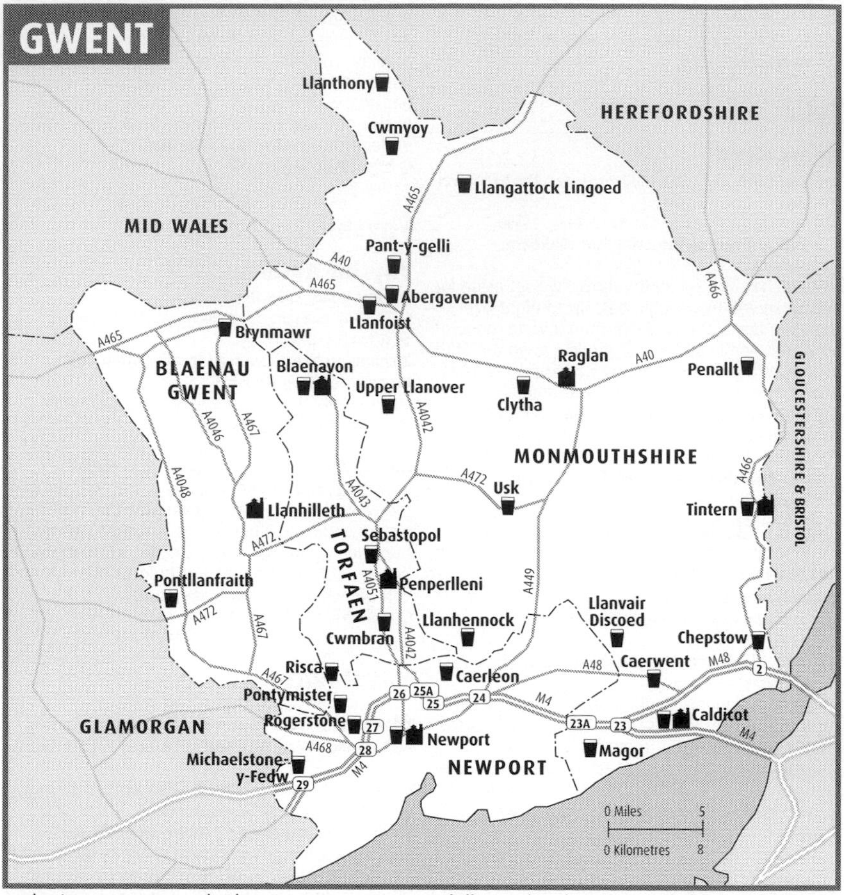

Authority areas covered: Blaenau Gwent UA, Caerphilly UA (part), Monmouthshire UA, Newport UA, Torfaen UA

Abergavenny

Angel Hotel

15 Cross Street, NP7 5EW

10-2.30, 6-11 (11.30 Fri & Sat); 12-2.30, 6-10.30 Sun

(01873) 857121 angelabergavenny.com

Marston's Angel; Sharp's Atlantic; Wye Valley Bitter, HPA; house beer (by Marston's)

This former coaching inn is at the centre of social activity in the town. Always bustling and busy, it offers high-quality food and accommodation and is popular with locals and visitors alike. The main Foxhunter bar is comfortably appointed with an open log fire in the corner, while in the summer the attractive patio area is used for dining. Paintings from local artists adorn the walls.

Q P (X3,X4)

Grofield L

Baker Street, NP7 5BT

5-11 Mon; 11-11.30 (01873) 858939 grofield.com

Rhymney Bitter; Sharp's Doom Bar; 1 changing beer (sourced nationally)

A busy pub opposite the town's cinema and library, just a few yards off the main shopping road through the town. A hugely experienced landlord presides over a fairly large single bar and a surprisingly large and well-maintained garden at the rear, both providing comfortable facilities for drinkers. Good-value lunchtime meals are popular (no food Mon). An inaugural beer festival in June 2014 is now set to become an annual event.

Q (X4,X43)

Blaenavon

Lamb & Fox

The Cottage, Pwll Du, NP4 9SS SO246116

closed Mon-Thu; 7.30 (3 Sat; 12 Sun)-11

Rhymney Bevans Bitter

Remote inn in a glorious setting atop the Blorenge mountain between Abergavenny and Blaenavon, about a mile west of the Keeper's Pond. In the area's industrial heyday it served the village of Pwlldu, which is no more. It only opens at

REAL ALE BREWERIES

Castles Caldicot
Kingstone Tintern
Mad Dog Penperlleni (NEW)
Rhymney Blaenavon
Tiny Rebel Newport
Tudor Llanhilleth
Untapped Raglan

weekends, and only serves one real ale, but is popular with the locals, who probably live some miles away. Food is available, though it would be wise to book beforehand. The pub is set in good walking country, with much to discover of historic interest. ❀◑P🐾

Brynmawr

Hobby Horse

30 Greenland Road, NP23 4DT

11.45-3, 7-11; 11.30-midnight Sat; 11.45-10.30 Sun

☎ (01495) 310996

2 changing beers (sourced regionally) Ⓗ

This family-owned pub is a flagship for real ales in north-western Gwent. Although just two beers are served, they are ever changing – you can expect to discover two fresh beers from two different breweries (often micros) every time you visit. A lounge and dining area leads to a small bar, with a separate restaurant with its own entrance to the right. A large patio at the front is popular in warm weather. ❀◑♿♣P🚌(X4,X15)🐾

Caerleon

Bell Inn

Bulmore Road, NP18 1QQ

12-11 (10.30 Sun) ☎ (01633) 420613

thebellatcaerleon.co.uk

Wye Valley HPA; 2 changing beers (sourced regionally) Ⓗ

This pub maintains a reputation as one of the top gastro-pubs in the area while paying close attention to the provision of good real ale and cider. The promise of dining out on sumptuous food accompanied by tasty ales and ciders brings in customers from far and wide. Thick stone walls enclose a charming low-beamed interior and while some space may be given over to diners at peak times, drinkers still enjoy their ale in the snug near the rear entrance. ❀◑♣●P🚌(27/28,60)

Caerwent

Coach & Horses

Green Lane, NP26 5AX

11-11 ☎ (01291) 420352

caerwent-coachandhorses.co.uk

Brains Rev James; Wye Valley HPA, Dorothy Goodbody's Golden Ale, Butty Bach; 1 changing beer (sourced regionally) Ⓗ

Central village pub renowned for its location near extensive Roman walls – the Roman site has a CADW (Welsh Government historic environment service) visitor centre. The pub has a traditional public bar with tiled floor, comfortable seating, darts and pool. There is also a cosy lounge, restaurant, tea rooms and garden. Food is sourced primarily from local suppliers, with breakfast served from 10am. The large garden has a patio and play area alongside the Roman walls. ❀◑♣P🚌(73)🐾

Caldicot

Castle Inn

64 Church Road, NP26 4HW

closed Mon; 12-11 (midnight Fri & Sat) ☎ (01291) 420509

thecastleinncaldicot.com

2 changing beers (sourced nationally) Ⓗ

In keeping with its name and location near Caldicot Castle & Country Park, some miniature cannons guard the front of this attractive pub. Outside there are extensive gardens and children's play facilities, including a wooden fort which is open at peak times. The internal open-plan layout offers ample room for diners and a small bar area has a welcoming crackling log fire on cold days. Well-known national brands are sold at upmarket prices thanks to Enterprise Inns. ❀◑♿≠P🚌(62,74)

Cross Inn

1 Newport Road, NP26 4BG

11-11 (12.30am Thu-Sat); 12-11 Sun ☎ (01291) 420692

Greene King IPA; Sharp's Doom Bar; 1 changing beer (sourced regionally) Ⓗ

Thriving pub adjacent to Caldicot Cross war memorial, bus stops and shops. The main bar is a place of lively conversation while live music is a big attraction at weekends. A central partition with a wall-mounted TV above a fireplace separates the open-plan drinking area from two seating sections on different levels at the rear. The guest ale is usually sourced from a local Welsh or West Country brewery, and there is often a draught cider on sale. ❀♿≠♣●P🚌(62,74)🐾

Chepstow

Bell Hanger

St Mary's Street, NP16 5EW

8am-midnight ☎ (01291) 637360

Fuller's London Pride; Greene King Abbot; Ruddles Best Bitter; Sharp's Doom Bar; 3 changing beers (sourced regionally) Ⓗ

A converted ironmonger's establishment with the familiar Wetherspoon styling, close to the major tourist attraction of Chepstow Castle. The front entrance leads into a room with a long bar, subdued lighting and semicircular seating areas. A small area with plenty of natural light separates the bar from another spacious section down a flight of stairs. This gives access to the pleasant outdoor area for finer weather, with an entrance from Nelson Street and exit for the railway station. Q❀◑♿≠●🚌(63,74)

Chepstow Athletic Club L

Mathern Road, NP16 5JJ (off Bulwark Rd)

7-11 (11.30 Fri); 12.30-11.30 (midnight summer) Sat

☎ (01291) 622126

Brains SA; Greene King IPA; 2 changing beers (sourced regionally) Ⓗ

A welcoming, convivial and comfortable social club with an emphasis on sport, particularly when rugby is on TV. Two regular ales are supplemented by one frequently changing guest, often from a local brewery. Many local organisations including Chepstow Male Voice Choir use the club for events or for post-practice refreshments. Outside, by the sports field, a patio for soaking up summer sunshine is just within reach of a well-struck cricket ball. Visiting CAMRA members are always welcome – just show your membership card. ❀♿♣P🚌(63,74)

Clytha

Clytha Arms 🏆 L

Groesonen Road, NP7 9BW (on B4598 old road between Abergavenny and Raglan)

WALES

⏲ 12-3 (not Mon), 6-midnight; 12-midnight Fri-Sun
☎ (01873) 840206 🌐 clytha-arms.com
Brecon Three Beacons; Untapped Sundown; Wye Valley Bitter; 3 changing beers Ⓗ
Gwent's Country Pub of the Year 2015 has a landlord dedicated to the art of hospitality. Offering up to seven real ales (always including at least two Welsh beers), a variety of local ciders and perries, and innovative locally sourced food, this is a very popular venue. High-class accommodation and camping facilities make this former dower house an excellent base for the many festivals held throughout the year. Whether you prefer cider, beer, dumplings or traditional pub games, there is a festival for you! Q🐴❀🛏◑♿⛺♣●P🚌(83)🐾

Cwmbran

Bush Inn Ⓛ

Graig Road, NP44 5AN
⏲ 12 (4 Mon-Wed)-11.30 ☎ (01633) 483764
🌐 thebushuppercwmbran.co.uk
2 changing beers (sourced regionally) Ⓗ
Tucked into the mountainside beneath a former mining area, this cosy nook has a homely feel about it – not surprising given that it was once two cottages. Choose from two or three ales, often locally produced, plus a selection of local real ciders. Dining options include popular home-made pizzas and curries. Various weekly entertainment is provided and a good range of indoor games is available. The patio gives panoramic views over Cwmbran and the surrounding countryside towards the Severn Estuary. 🐴❀◑♣●P🚌(1,8)🐾

Mount Pleasant

Wesley Street, NP44 3LX
⏲ 12 (4 Mon)-11; 12-midnight Fri & Sat ☎ (01633) 712176
2 changing beers (sourced regionally) Ⓗ
New licensees took over this, their first pub, in September 2014 and liked it so much they bought it! They then successfully set about revitalising it and attracting back once-loyal former customers. The main bar has two smaller areas on either side – the more secluded area to the left is used mainly for dining. Two ever-changing beers are offered, often including one from the Evan Evans portfolio of beer brands. 🐴❀◑♣P🚌(6)

Queen Inn

Upper Cwmbran Road, NP44 5AX
⏲ 12-11.30 (11 Sun) ☎ (01633) 484252
3 changing beers (sourced regionally) Ⓗ
On the outskirts of Cwmbran in a countryside setting, the Queen is a popular destination for families and has an excellent play area. To the left on entering is the main bar, to the right a lounge. There is also a separate restaurant but meals are served throughout the pub. Two of the three ales on handpump are selected from an approved pub company list, while the licensees have free range with the third. 🐴❀◑♣●P🚌(1,8)🐾

Cwmyoy

Queen's Head

NP7 7NE (in village take the lane signposted Llanthony, pub is about a mile on right) SO311221
⏲ 10.30-2 (not Tue & Fri), 6-11; closed Wed; 11-3, 6-11 Sat; 12-4 Sun ☎ (01873) 890241
Celt Experience Native Storm; 1 changing beer (sourced regionally; often Celt Experience) Ⓗ
This pub stands alone on a quiet lane in the rolling countryside of the Llanthony Valley, yet it is just a couple of miles from the main A465 road and well worth the detour. Heavy beams, low ceilings and flagstoned floors are testimony to the antiquity of the building. Beers from the Celt Experience range are always available. The pub serves not only its own rural community but also the many walkers who enjoy the scenery of this beautiful part of the Brecon Beacons National Park. Q❀◐P

Llanfoist

Bridge Inn

Merthyr Road, NP7 9LH
⏲ 11-11 (midnight Fri-Sat); 12-10.30 Sun ☎ (01873) 854831
🌐 bridgellanfoist.com
Hancock's HB; 2 changing beers (sourced nationally) Ⓗ
Set beside the River Usk, with a large garden overlooking the anglers and views towards Abergavenny Castle, this pub is only a short walk from Abergavenny through the Castle Meadows. Hancock's HB has become the current beer of choice, with a Wye Valley and a Welsh ale usually occupying the two guest pumps. Live music in summer and beer festivals are held on the outdoor stage or in a marquee. The beer festival is usually the first weekend of June.
Q🐴❀🛏◑P🚌(X4)🐾📶

Llangattock Lingoed

Hunter's Moon Inn

NP7 8RR (at road bridge at end of village) SO363201
⏲ 12-11 ☎ (01873) 821499 🌐 hunters-moon-inn.co.uk
Sharp's Doom Bar Ⓗ**; Wye Valley HPA; 1 changing beer (sourced regionally; often Brains Rev James)** Ⓗ/Ⓖ
A 13th-century inn on the Offa's Dyke path next to an interesting church. Run by three generations of the same family, the pub has undoubtedly become the hub of social activity in the village. Visitors are assured of a warm welcome, sustenance and conversation at any time of day. The traditional flagstone-floored bar features an owl who gazes down at you from underneath a hunter's moon. In summer a third beer is available, usually Brains Rev James. Q🐴❀🛏◑♿♣P🐾📶

Llanhennock

Wheatsheaf

NP18 1LT ST353927
⏲ 11-11; 12-4, 8-11 Sun winter; 11 (12 Sun)-11 summer
☎ (01633) 420468
Fuller's London Pride; 2 changing beers (sourced regionally) Ⓗ
With 30 consecutive appearances in the Guide, this is a wonderfully consistent country pub that remains as popular as ever. A very small bar to the left of the entrance and a slightly larger one to the right are both full of memorabilia and old photographs. A small concealed garden outside is a summer suntrap. Two guest beers are offered, often one from a local brewer. Darts is very popular in the evenings. Boules is played in the car park, which has fine surrounding views. 🐴❀◐⛺♣P🐾

Llanthony

Llanthony Priory Hotel

Mill Farm, NP7 7NN (turn left next to Skirrid Mountain Inn and continue for about 6 miles) SO288279
✪ closed Mon; 11-3, 6-11; 11-11 Sat; 11-10.30 Sun
☎ (01873) 890487 ⊕ llanthonyprioryhotel.co.uk
Felinfoel Double Dragon; 1 changing beer (sourced regionally) Ⓗ
A tiny and remarkable bar situated in the one-time cellars of the abbey of this substantial but ultimately doomed monastery. Deserted by the monks even before the Dissolution, the ruins dominate the valley floor between two towering and beautiful ridges. These days few live in the tiny hamlet, or indeed in the whole valley – walkers and trekkers outnumbering locals at weekends and holidays. Between October and Easter the bar opens only at weekends – check times before setting out. Q✿⌀◑ ▲P

Llanvair Discoed

Woodlands Tavern

NP16 6LX
✪ closed Mon; 12-2 (2.30 Sat), 6-11; 12-2 Sun
☎ (01633) 400313
Bath Ales Gem; Felinfoel Best Bitter; Wye Valley Butty Bach; 1 changing beer (sourced locally) Ⓗ
Traditional village inn with many modern touches, owned and run by the same family for many years. Comfortable armchairs and conversation are the order of the day. Three regular ales are on the bar alongside a frequently changing guest ale, usually from a smaller local brewery, plus one ever-changing real cider. The landlord takes equal pride in his food as his ale – he is the chef for the pub's popular restaurant, which serves a range of high-quality meals at real-world prices. ✿◑&♣●P

Magor

Wheatsheaf Ⓛ

The Square, NP26 3HN
✪ 10-11 (midnight Fri & Sat); 12-11 Sun ☎ (01633) 880608
4 changing beers (sourced regionally; often Rhymney) Ⓗ
Large pub with a traditional public bar and a lounge that shares a fireplace with a snug, leading to the spacious restaurant beyond. The ale range is always interesting, usually including one from a local brewery – a log of the ales that pass this way is diligently maintained and displayed by a loyal customer. Diners may choose from a menu with a good choice of dishes. Breakfast is available in Marinello's coffee shop 10am-noon.
❥✿◑&♣●P☲(62,74)✿ ⌖

Michaelstone-y-Fedw

Cefn Mably Arms

CF3 6XS
✪ 12-2.30, 5.30-11 Mon; 12-3.30, 5.30-11.30; 12-3.30, 5.30-midnight Fri & Sat; 12-8.30 Sun ☎ (01633) 680347
⊕ thecefnmablyarms.co.uk
Brains Bitter; Butcombe Gold; 2 changing beers (sourced regionally) Ⓗ
Popular country pub, off the beaten track and inaccessible by public transport, but worth seeking out. The large open-plan interior divides into three distinct areas, one with access to the garden, and is mainly set out for diners. St Michael's Church is

next to the pub, in the traditional rural manner. A 'get you here' service is available, but you will need to arrange your return trip. Q❥✿◑P✿⌖

Newport

Godfrey Morgan Ⓛ

158 Chepstow Road, NP19 8EG
✪ 8am-midnight (1am Fri & Sat) ☎ (01633) 221928
Brains SA; Greene King Abbot; Ruddles Best Bitter; 6 changing beers Ⓗ
This popular Wetherspoon pub at the centre of a shopping precinct was once a cinema, with numerous photos of erstwhile stars with local connections dotted around the walls. As well as the three regular ales, one of JDW's nationwide beers is always available, plus two or more guest ales, all on handpull. Two ciders on gravity are served from the fridge. The main entrance is on the busy Chepstow Road, and there is limited parking at the rear. Q❥✿◑&●P☲⌖

Lamb Ⓨ Ⓛ

6 Bridge Street, NP20 4AL
✪ 10-9 (midnight Wed & Thu; 1.30am Fri & Sat); 1-8 Sun
☎ (01633) 255200 ⊕ thelambnewport.com
Butcombe Bitter; Thwaites Wainwright; 2 changing beers (sourced nationally) Ⓗ
Back in the day this was a two-room boozer – now it is a fully refurbished vibrant open-plan bar. It has a decorative fireplace as its focal point with a large TV screen above it for sport and music channels. The walls at the rear display old prints of yesteryear in Newport. The ale selection nearly always includes one from Newport's own Tiny Rebel brewery. The menu of classic pub food is popular. Quiz night is Wednesday, live music night Friday. ◑⇌●☲⌖

Olde Murenger House

52-53 High Street, NP20 1GA
✪ 12-11; 12-2, 7.30-10.30 Sun ☎ (01633) 263977
Samuel Smith Old Brewery Bitter Ⓗ
Back in the Guide after a brief absence, this town-centre pub remains a quiet haven away from the more rowdy bars that proliferate in the area. It has been run for 20 years by the same manager who maintains his love of real ale and is proud of running the only Sam Smith's outlet in south Wales. The OBB is competitively priced and outsells all other draught products. A warm welcome awaits in one of the oldest buildings in the city. ◑⇌●✿✿

Pen & Wig

22-24 Stow Hill, NP20 1JD
✪ 11-11 (midnight Fri & Sat); 12-10.30 Sun
☎ (01633) 666818
Draught Bass; Felinfoel Double Dragon; Sharp's Doom Bar; 3 changing beers (sourced regionally) Ⓗ
Large pub with an interior partly divided into several sections and levels, creating a spacious feel, all enhanced by much use of dark wood. It attracts a good mix of customers and sells prodigious amounts of its regular beers while also supporting local Welsh breweries and cider makers. The grill menu is popular. The rear decking can get busy in fine weather – it has a TV and hosts occasional live entertainment. Upstairs function rooms are available for hire. ✿◑⇌♣●P☲

St Julian Inn

Caerleon Road, NP18 1QA

11.30-11.30 (midnight Fri & Sat); 12-11 Sun
(01633) 243548 stjulian.co.uk
Wells Bombardier; Young's Bitter; 2 changing beers (sourced regionally; often Bath Ales, Castle Rock) [H]
In a commanding position on a bend in the River Usk, close to historic Caerleon, this pub has been a Guide fixture for over two decades. A central serving area is surrounded by a number of distinct areas. In the basement is a function room with a skittle alley. The two guest beers include a few favourites plus some adventurous ones from micros, often new ventures. There is a fine view from the balcony overlooking the river, especially at sunset. P (27/28,60)

Pant-y-gelli

Crown Inn

Old Hereford Road, NP7 7HR
12-2.30 (not Mon), 6-11; 12-3, 6-11 Sat; 12-3, 6-10.30 Sun
(01873) 853314 thecrownatpantygelli.com
Draught Bass; Rhymney Best; Wye Valley HPA; 1 changing beer (sourced regionally) [H]
A framed certificate at the bar celebrating 10 consecutive years in the Guide reflects the enduring appeal of this popular pub. Although it has built a reputation for excellent food, the lively conversation of local drinkers around the log fire can be heard at any time of the week. Four trophies at the front entrance are testimony to the recent success of the effervescent darts team. The surrounding hills make this a perfect base for a walk. P

Penallt

Boat Inn

Lone Lane, NP25 4AJ SO5350986
12-3, 5-11; closed Tue; 12-11 Sat & Sun winter; 12-11 summer (01600) 712615 theboatpenallt.co.uk
Wye Valley Butty Bach; 2 changing beers (sourced regionally) [G]
Located impressively close to the River Wye and accessed from England by footway alongside an antique former railway bridge, the Boat features a cosy main bar and side room. The cool stillage behind the bar hosts two or three cask ales, though cider sales have now overtaken ale. Many walkers who explore this beautiful valley are fuelled by the pub's generous meals and snacks. Riverside tables and a hillside garden are popular in fine weather. P (69)

Pontllanfraith

Crown Inn

The Bryn, NP12 2HE
4 (2 Fri; 12 Sat)-1am; 12-midnight Sun (01495) 223404
Brains Rev James; 3 changing beers (sourced nationally; often Butcombe, Theakston) [H]
This friendly pub has a small, traditional public bar with a pool table and darts, assorted settles and tables, plus a jukebox. The handpumps can be found on the bar in the spacious lounge which has an attractive coalburner – a welcoming sight on cold days. Up to four ales may be available at any time, always Brains Rev James and frequently Theakston Old Peculier – a local favourite not often seen hereabouts. Telephone ahead for food availability. P (7,26)

Pontymister

Commercial Inn

Commercial Street, NP11 6BA
11 (10 Sat)-11.30; 12-11.30 Sun (01633) 612608
thecommercialpontymister.com
3 changing beers (sourced regionally; often Sharp's Doom Bar, Tiny Rebel) [H]
Thriving pub on the busy main road through town, winner of numerous awards, and succeeding in an area where many have failed. Good-value locally sourced food is available. The handpumps frequently dispense beers from Newport's acclaimed Tiny Rebel Brewery, or sometimes other breweries with which the brewery operates a reciprocal trading arrangement. There is a popular high-quality jukebox plus several large TV screens often showing racing, though these are usually muted.
(Risca & Pontymister) (X15,151)

Risca

Fox & Hounds

Park Road, NP11 6PW
12-midnight (10.30 Sun) (01633) 612937
1 changing beer (sourced regionally) [H]
Popular wet-led pub overlooking the local park. It offers not only traditional indoor games such as darts and pool, but more unusually corks – a local sport. Big sporting events are shown on a drop-down screen. The interior divides into three sections, one large enough to accommodate local bands who entertain on Friday evenings. There is plenty of outdoor seating to make the most of warm weather. Various Wye Valley Brewery ales alternate, with others sourced from all over.
P (X15,151)

Rogerstone

Tredegar Arms

157 Cefn Road, NP10 9AS
12 (4 Mon)-11; 12-10.30 Sun (01633) 547553
Morland Old Speckled Hen [G]**; 2 changing beers (sourced nationally)** [H]
The 'Top TA', as it is often called locally, is back in the Guide under an enthusiastic new licensee after an absence of a few years. The main lounge at the rear has a dining area and a cosy snug running off it. At the front is a small bar where the locals congregate. Morland Old Speckled Hen is the regular beer complemented by two ales that are ever changing, although favourites often return.
P (R1,56)

Sebastopol

Open Hearth

Wern Road, NP4 5DR
11.30-midnight; 12-11.30 Sun (01495) 763752
Kite Welsh Pale Ale; 3 changing beers (sourced regionally; often Rhymney) [H]
Canalside favourite well run by a family who were at the forefront of the Fair Deal For Your Local campaign. Three rooms cater for drinkers and diners while downstairs a function room occasionally hosts live music. The original building – now the bar – was once a cowman's cottage, then a wash house, but it has long since served as a public house, though much expanded over the

years. Towpath seating is popular in warm weather. Last entry is 11pm.
P (X3,X24/24)

Tintern

Anchor Inn

NP16 6TE (off A466 at Tintern Abbey)
9am-11; 12-10.30 Sun (01291) 689582
theanchortintern.com

Wye Valley Butty Bach; 2 changing beers (sourced regionally; often Otter)

This smart, hospitable riverside pub, with its popular café annexe and garden, once housed Tintern Abbey's cider mill. The massive millstone and press in the main bar commemorate the Cistercian monks' labours. Wye Valley beers feature frequently, often alongside one from the nearby Kingstone Brewery. Excellent home-cooked food is available until 9pm. The draught cider is Westons Old Rosie. Local car parks are council run but you can claim the £3 fee as a discount at the bar.
P (69)

Upper Llanover

Goose & Cuckoo

NP7 9ER (turn off A4042 Pontypool-Abergavenny road at sign to Upper Llanover, then follow hand-written signs to the Goose) SO292073
closed Mon; 11.30-3, 7-11; 11.30-11 Fri & Sat; 12-10.30 Sun (01873) 880277 gooseandcuckoo.com

Celt Experience Iron Age; Rhymney Bitter; 1 changing beer (sourced locally)

Just when you think you might be lost after climbing a couple of miles up the twisting lane from the main road at Llanover, the pub suddenly appears, just before the lane becomes a trackway over the mountain. The views over the Usk Valley are extensive and can be enjoyed from the large garden. Inside, the place has barely changed over the last century and offers tremendous rustic charm rather than high levels of comfort. Well worth the effort to get here. Q P

Usk

King's Head Hotel

18 Old Market Street, NP15 1AL
11-11 (10.30 Sun) (01291) 672963
kingsheadusk.com

Fuller's London Pride; Timothy Taylor Landlord; 1 changing beer (sourced nationally)

Here, the ground-floor plan includes the Howard Winstone function room, the Lionel Sweet dining room, plus a cosy bar with loads of olde-worlde charm. Low wood-beamed ceilings, dark decor, an eclectic range of artefacts and a welcoming log fire in cold weather all feature. An appetising range of food can be enjoyed accompanied by a choice of ales – occasionally sourced from a local brewery. With accommodation available this is a good base for visitors. Q P (60,63)

New Court Hotel

62 Maryport Street, NP15 1AD
12-11 (10.30 Sun) (01291) 671319
thenewcourthotel.co.uk

Sharp's Doom Bar; Wye Valley Butty Bach; 3 changing beers (sourced locally)

Comfortable bar-restaurant now firmly back on the map after a major restoration. The easy-on-the-eye decor and cosy seating make the front section and snug attractive to drinkers. Taking centre stage on the bar are seven handpumps offering up to five real ales, including local brews, plus two ciders. Fine mouthwatering cuisine can be enjoyed in the relaxing ambience of the dining room. Highly rated accommodation is available.
Q (60,63)

Bridge Inn, Llanfoist

WALES

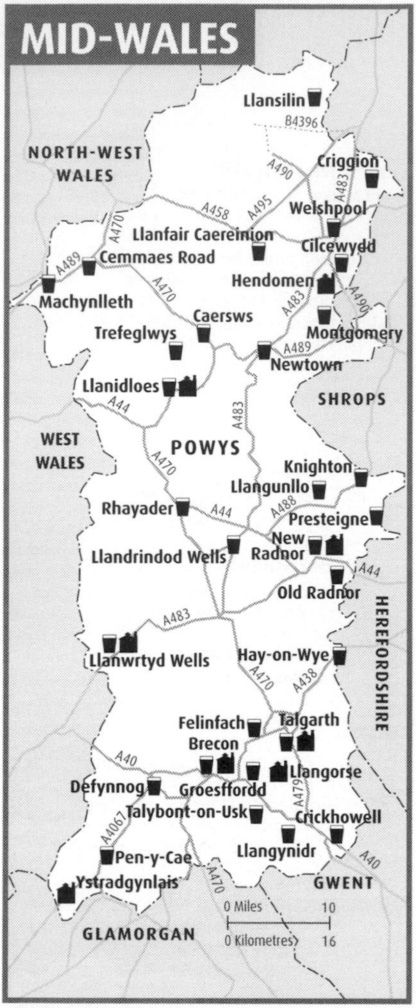

Authority area covered: Powys UA

Brecon

Brecon Rugby Club

63 The Watton, LD3 7EL

5 (11 Sat & Sun)-11 ☎ (01874) 624848 breconrfc.co.uk

3 changing beers Ⓗ

A founder member of the Welsh RFU, this friendly and welcoming club is open to all. A main bar with a separate lounge is towards the front, and there is a spacious function room with a big screen beyond the bar. Outside is a large patio garden and the Brecon Pétanque Club. Beers from local brewers are frequently available plus bottled ciders from Gwynt y Ddraig. The club is often busy during the rugby season, particularly when Wales are playing. Local CAMRA Club of the Year. ♣P

Castle of Brecon Hotel

Castle Square, LD3 9DB

11-11 ☎ (01874) 624611 breconcastlehotel.co.uk

3 changing beers Ⓗ

Formerly an 11th-century Norman castle, then an early coaching inn, the Castle of Brecon retains all the warmth and character of its origins, mixed with the formality of a late-Georgian hotel. Three ales are usually available, often national brands, but occasionally local guests. The large garden boasts stunning views over the Beacons and is immensely popular in the summer. Food is served all day. **Q P**

Caersws

Red Lion

3 Main Street, SY17 5EL (on B4569)

3-11.30 (midnight Fri); 12-midnight Sat; 12-11.30 Sun

☎ (01686) 689378

Monty's MPA; Three Tuns XXX; 1 changing beer Ⓗ

Wood-beamed village locals' pub with two bars, attracting a varied clientele of all ages. Early evenings can be boisterous with the after-work crowd calling in on their way home. A locally produced beer from Monty's Brewery is available and a real cider is also usually on offer. A beer festival is held on the August bank holiday weekend. There is a patio area at the rear for summer drinking. ♣P(X75,X85)

Cemmaes Road

Dovey Valley Hotel ★

SY20 8JZ

6-11 (10.30 Sun) ☎ (01650) 511335

1 changing beer (sourced locally; often Cwrw Cader, Monty's) Ⓗ

Capturing the atmosphere of a bygone age, this gem of a pub is a true survivor and has been recognised by CAMRA as having a nationally important historic interior. Comprising a main bar and a recently opened snug room, it has if anything been enhanced under new ownership, with carpet tiles removed to reveal the original slate floor and fascinating photographs and posters (some rescued from the attic) on the walls. Occasional live music is eclectic in nature – a Galician bagpiper recently made an appearance. **Q P**

Cilcewydd

Square & Compass

SY21 8RU

4.30 (1 Sat)-11; 12-11 Sun ☎ (01938) 580360

Sharp's Doom Bar; 1 changing beer Ⓗ

A rare example of a rural pub that survives on beer sales only, this is a popular community venue situated just off the road and easily missed. It has two rooms – a long main room divided in two by comfortable bench seating with old agricultural photos on the walls, and a second room with wall seating. There are drinking areas outside and gents have the choice of inside or outside toilets. **Q ♣P**

REAL ALE BREWERIES

Brecon Brecon
Bryncelyn Ystradgynlais
Heart of Wales Llanwrtyd Wells
Monty's Hendomen
Radnorshire New Radnor
Redstone Llangorse
Rotters Talgarth
Waen Llanidloes

Crickhowell

Bear Hotel

High Street, NP8 1BW

🕐 11-3, 6 (7 Sun)-11 ☎ (01873) 810408 🌐 bearhotel.co.uk

Brains Rev James; 3 changing beers [H]

Originally a 15th-century coaching inn, this is now an award-winning hotel. The multi-roomed bar enjoys grand surroundings with exposed beams, wood panelling, fine settles and an eclectic selection of furnishings and decorations. There are open fireplaces throughout. Food is high quality with a varied menu featuring much local produce. The hotel is an excellent base for exploring the surrounding Black Mountains and Brecon Beacons National Park. Q🐴✿🛏◐♿⛺P🚌🐾

Criggion

Admiral Rodney Inn

SY5 9AU

🕐 12-10 (11 Fri & Sat) ☎ (01938) 570313

Wye Valley Butty Bach; 1 changing beer [H]

This unspoilt rural inn dates back to the mid-1700s and is named after Admiral Rodney who harvested local oak to build his ships – he is honoured with a pillar on the adjacent hill. The pub is a base for walkers exploring the area. The single-room interior has a fireplace at both ends and a restaurant area to the right as you enter. Posters of Terry Pratchett's Discworld novels decorate the dining space. Q🐴✿◐♿♣P🐾

Defynnog

Tanners Arms

LD3 8SF

🕐 5 (12 Fri-Sun)-midnight ☎ (01874) 638032

🌐 tannersarmspub.com

5 changing beers [H]/[G]

Family-run country pub famous for the warm welcome it offers to locals and tourists alike, set in the delightful village of Defynnog in the Brecon Beacons National Park. Up to five real ales are available as well as a selection of real ciders, mostly from local producers. Home-cooked food is also well worth stopping by for. Several beer and cider festivals are held each year. B&B is offered. A multiple local CAMRA award-winner.
🐴✿🛏◐⛺♣●P🚌🐾📶

Felinfach

Griffin [L]

LD3 0UB (just off A470 3 miles NE of Brecon)

🕐 12-11.30 ☎ (01874) 620111

4 changing beers (sourced locally) [H]

The pub's ethos – the simple things in life done well – says it all. A welcoming country pub, restaurant and rooms, the emphasis here is on good beer and excellent food. The multi-roomed layout allows for discrete areas for drinking and dining. The huge fireplace between the bar and the main dining area dominates in winter, while an Aga lurks in a side room, providing warmth throughout the building. The large garden affords superb views of the surrounding mountains. Beers are sourced from local breweries.
Q🐴✿🛏◐♿P🚌

Groesffordd

Three Horseshoes

LD3 7SN

🕐 12-3 (not Mon), 5-11; 12-11 Fri-Sun ☎ (01874) 665672

🌐 threehorseshoesgroesffordd.co.uk

St Austell Tribute; 2 changing beers [H]

Busy village-centre pub in the heart of the Brecon Beacons, boasting superb views from both the front and rear outdoor seating areas. The pub is only a 10-minute walk from the Brynich Lock on the Monmouthshire & Brecon Canal. Excellent food is on offer and it is worth booking ahead to avoid disappointment. Various events are held throughout the year. 🐴✿◐♿⛺♣●P🐾📶

Hay-on-Wye

Blue Boar

Oxford Road, HR3 5DF

🕐 9am-11 ☎ (01497) 820884

Hook Norton Hooky; Timothy Taylor Landlord; 2 changing beers (sourced regionally) [H]

Comfortable and friendly pub in the centre of the town famed for books, owned and run by the same family for many years. A large central bar dominates, with two separate seating areas around it, each with a log fire. Two regular beers are usually supplemented by one or two guests. Food is available all day in the bar and the separate dining area. Q🐴◐♿🚌🐾📶

Knighton

Horse & Jockey

Wylcwm Place, LD7 1AE

🕐 11-11 ☎ (01547) 520062 🌐 thehorseandjockeyinn.co.uk

2 changing beers (sourced regionally; often Three Tuns, Wood, Wye Valley) [H]

The pub is of late-medieval origins, set around a courtyard, and was once a coaching inn. It has a large restaurant converted from stables. Owned by the same family since 1989, the building is a pleasing mixture of old and new, with a variety of rooms and seating outside in the courtyard. It offers an extensive food menu featuring fresh local produce plus a pizza menu. There are two or three cask beers, usually from Welsh and border breweries. Q🐴✿🛏◐⇌🚌

Llandrindod Wells

Conservative Club

South Crescent, LD1 5DH (opp bandstand)

🕐 11-2, 5.30-11; 11-11.30 Fri & Sat; 11.30-10.30 Sun

☎ (01597) 822126

Brains Bitter; Marston's Pedigree; 1 changing beer [H]

Located in the centre of this historic spa town, the Con Club is a regular Guide entry. It has a large lounge, TV room, games bar, snooker and pool tables and a small front patio/smoking area. Until the early 1970s the building was the Lansdown Hotel. Good-value lunches are served Wednesday-Friday and Sunday. CAMRA members are welcome but visitors must be signed in. Q✿◐♿⇌♣🚌

Hundred House

LD1 5RY

🕐 12-2, 5.30-11 Mon-Fri; 11-11 Sat & Sun ☎ (01982) 570231

Greene King Abbot; Wye Valley Butty Bach; 1 changing beer [H]

In the middle of rolling Welsh hills, the inn takes its name from the Saxon hundred, which was an administrative area. At one time a drovers' inn, it is now a traditional venue, well patronised by the local farming community. There is a lounge, a locals' bar, a pool room with TV (for rugby), a restaurant and beer garden. Welcoming and friendly, the afternoon closing times are flexible, and it usually stays open if there are customers drinking. Abbot is only on in summer.
Q🛋❀🛏◑♿⛺♣P

Llanfair Caereinion

Goat Hotel

High Street, SY21 0QS (off A485)
⏲ 11-11 (midnight Fri & Sat) ☎ (01938) 810428
🌐 thegoathotel.co.uk
3 changing beers (sourced regionally; often Wood) H
Excellent 300-year-old beamed coaching inn with a welcoming atmosphere which attracts both locals and tourists. The plush lounge, dominated by a large inglenook and open fire, has comfortable leather armchairs and sofas. There is a dining room serving home-cooked food and a games room to the rear. The choice of real ale always includes one from the ever-popular Wood Brewery.
Q🛋❀🛏◑♣P🚌🐾

Llangunllo

Greyhound

LD7 1SP (on B4356, off A488)
⏲ closed Mon & Tue; 4.30-11 (2am Fri); 2-2am Sat; 2-11 Sun
☎ (01547) 550400
3 changing beers (sourced nationally; often Broughs, Six Bells, Wrekin) H
This unique 16th-century inn, set in picturesque countryside, is the first stop on the Glyndwr's Way long-distance trail. The beers are usually from Broughs, Six Bells and Wrekin breweries, and the cider is Westons Family Reserve. Beer festivals are held on the May and August bank holidays and regular music sessions are hosted. You are welcome to bring your own food. Opening times are approximate – ring the doorbell any time after midday and with luck you will be served.
❀♣🍎P🍺🐾

Llangynidr

Red Lion

Duffryn Road, NP8 1NT (off B4558)
⏲ 12-11 ☎ (01874) 730223 🌐 theredlionpowys.co.uk
Rhymney Best; 2 changing beers H
Popular village local, away from the main road, which offers a warm welcome to walkers, boaters, families and dogs – the Monmouthshire & Brecon canal is close by. The beer range changes regularly and good-value home-cooked food is served in the bar. A separate games area, outside seating and children's play area make this a pub with something for everyone. Regular quiz nights and live music also feature. 🛋❀🛏◑♣P🚌🐾📶

Llanidloes

Angel Hotel

High Street, SY18 6BY (off A470)
⏲ 12-2.30 (not Wed), 5-11.30; 12-3, 7-11.30 Sun
☎ (01686) 412381
Evan Evans Cwrw; Greene King Abbot; Three Tuns XXX H
Attractive and friendly edge-of-town pub with two comfortable bars. The larger of the two rooms has a stone fireplace and old photographs on the walls. The smaller room has an interesting bar inlaid with old pennies. There is also a spacious restaurant. The building dates from 1748 and local Chartists held meetings here between 1838 and 1839. There is outside seating in front of the pub.
Q🛋◑♿🚌(X75,525)

Stag Inn

15 Great Oak Street, SY18 6BU (off A470)
⏲ 12-11 (1.30am Fri); 11-1.30am Sat ☎ (01686) 414824
🌐 staginnllanidloes.co.uk
Purple Moose Cwrw Eryri/Snowdonia Ale; 1 changing beer (sourced regionally; often Fuller's, Shepherd Neame) H
Friendly town-centre pub offering two real ales and a real cider. The long premises is divided in two – the wooden-floored front area has wall seating and a wood-burning stove, the rear area through an archway has comfortable sofas, a pool table and a piano. There is an outside drinking area to the rear. The pub hosts live music at the weekends. Reasonably priced bar snacks are served and take-away tea and coffee are available.
🛋❀◑♿♣🍎🚌(X75,525)🐾📶

Llansilin

Wynnstay Inn

SY10 7QB
⏲ 5.30-10 (10.30 Tue & Wed; 11 Thu); 2-11 Fri; 1-11 Sat; 12-10.30 Sun ☎ (01691) 791355
🌐 thewynnstayinn.weebly.com
3 changing beers (sourced regionally; often Offa's Dyke) H
Built in 1784, the Grade II-listed Wynnstay is the last of five inns the village once supported. It has a public bar, lounge, pool room and a separate dining room which can be used for small functions. The inn is close to attractions including Pistyll Rhaeadr waterfall, Offa's Dyke Path and the Tanat Valley. The hub of the local community, it is home to various pub teams and hosts regular music nights. Q🛋❀🛏◑♿⛺♣P🐾📶

Llanwrtyd Wells

Neuadd Arms Hotel L

The Square, LD5 4RB
⏲ 11-midnight (2am Fri & Sat) ☎ (01591) 610236
🌐 neuaddarmshotel.co.uk
Felinfoel Double Dragon; Heart of Wales Irfon Valley Bitter, Aur Cymru, Welsh Black, Noble Eden Ale; 4 changing beers (sourced locally) H
This large Victorian hotel serves as the tap for the Heart of Wales Brewery. The Bells Bar features a large fireplace and an eclectic mix of furniture. The bells formerly used to summon servants remain on one wall, along with the winners' boards from some of the town's more unusual competitions. The lounge bar is a little more formal. The hotel takes part in the town's annual events including a major beer festival in November. A good range of real ciders is kept. Q❀🛏◑🚂♣🍎P🐾

Machynlleth

Dyfi Forester

4 Heol y Doll, SY20 8BQ

⏲ 11.45am-1am; 11am-1am Sat & Sun ☎ 07581 025224

Wye Valley Butty Bach; 1 changing beer (sourced regionally; often Evan Evans, Wood) Ⓗ

Halfway between the railway station and town centre, this friendly down-to-earth free house offers a welcoming bar with jukebox, pool, and dartboards – pub games are played with enthusiasm here. The outdoor drinking area is a rear patio with tables. Another Wye Valley beer may replace Butty Bach occasionally. Machynlleth, surprisingly bustling given its small size, is a splendid touring centre with good transport links, and hosts a variety of events including festivals both of comedy and classical music. ❀⇌♣🚌🐾ᯤ

White Horse

42 Heol Maengwyn, SY20 8DT

⏲ closed Mon; 7 (6 Fri)-11; 3-11 Sat; 12-11 Sun

☎ (01654) 702247

2 changing beers (sourced regionally; often Purple Moose) Ⓗ

Opposite Owain Glyndwr's Parliament House on the town's broad main street, this traditional free house has two bars – on one side are a dartboard and jukebox, on the other a pool table and log fire. Bar meals are served (Sunday lunch is very popular) but check ahead for availability. Real cider is often kept in summer. ❀⇌P🚌(T2,X28,X85)🐾

Montgomery

Crown Inn

Castle Street, SY15 6PW

⏲ 11-11 ☎ (01686) 668533

Brains Rev James; Wye Valley Butty Bach; 1 changing beer (sourced regionally; often Three Tuns) Ⓗ

The Crown is the last traditional local in a town that once supported a multitude of hostelries. The pub is home to a large number of local sports teams.The public bar is long and quite narrow with a pool and games area at the rear. A small snug sits opposite with a large array of trophies in it. There are benches for outdoor drinking. Beware of the low beams in the bar area. ❀♿♣

New Radnor

Radnor Arms

Broad Street, LD8 2SP

⏲ 12-2.30 (not Wed), 5-10.30; 12-11 Sat; 12-10.30 Sun

☎ (01544) 350232

3 changing beers (sourced regionally; often Radnorshire, Wood, Wye Valley) Ⓗ

A traditional village pub with two bars in a building that dates from around 1700, situated within the medieval walls and near the castle of this former county town. Several guest beers from the Welsh border area are rotated alongside a range of real ciders. The nearby Radnorshire Brewery at Brookside Farm is Radnorshire's only brewery and its beers feature regularly on the bar. The pub is popular with visitors to the nearby caravan site.
🐎❀◐◑♿⛺♣🍎P🚌(461)🐾ᯤ

Newtown

Railway Tavern

Old Kerry Road, SY16 1BH (off A483)

⏲ 11-2, 7-midnight; 11-midnight Tue & Sun; 11-1am Fri & Sat

☎ (01686) 626156

Hancock's HB; 2 changing beers (sourced regionally; often Salopian, Slater's, Three Tuns) Ⓗ

Another year in the Guide for Dave and Eileen's one-bar local near the station. Two guest beers from regional or small breweries are always on offer. The Railway hosts a number of darts teams and a dominoes team and can get crowded on match nights. The interior is essentially divided in two – a lower bar area and a rear area with wall benches and tables. Note the poster listing over 50 pubs that once operated in Newtown.
Q❀⇌♣🚌(X75)

Sportsman Ⓛ

17 Severn Street, SY16 2AQ (off A483)

⏲ closed Mon; 12-10 (11 Wed & Thu; 11.30 Fri & Sat)

☎ (01686) 623978 🌐 sportsmannewtown.co.uk

Monty's Old Jailhouse, MPA, Sunshine, Masquerade, Mischief; 3 changing beers (sourced nationally; often Monty's, Robinsons, Wychwood) Ⓗ

The Monty's Brewery tap was local CAMRA 2013 Pub and 2014 Welsh Cider Pub of the Year. Five Monty's beers are available plus three guest ales and up to 10 ciders. The pub is divided into three areas – a snug with comfortable wall seating, a main bar area and a rear tiled games area with pool table, TV and darts. The main bar has a muted TV. Outside there is a patio at the rear for summer drinking. Q❀♿⇌♣🍎🚌(X75)ᯤ

Old Radnor

Harp Inn

LD8 2RH (on A44 at Walton follow signs for Harp Inn)

⏲ closed Mon & Tue; 12-3 (not Wed & Thu), 6-11; 12-3, 6-10.30 Sun ☎ (01544) 350655 🌐 harpinnradnor.co.uk

2 changing beers (sourced regionally; often Hobsons, Three Tuns, Wye Valley) Ⓗ

This early-15th-century Welsh longhouse commands a fine view over the Radnor Valley. The building was rescued and restored by the Landmark Trust in 1972 and then sold on in 1983. The interior is a tasteful mix of old and new, including a modern restaurant serving good food made with locally sourced seasonal ingredients. There are occasional steak nights and seasonal tastings. Ales mainly come from regional and local microbreweries and beer festivals are hosted from time to time. Q🐎❀🛏◐◑⛺♣🍎P🐾ᯤ

Pen y Cae

Ancient Briton

Brecon Road, SA9 1YY (on A4067 just S of village)

⏲ 12-midnight ☎ (01639) 730273 🌐 ancientbriton.co.uk

Courage Directors; Wye Valley Butty Bach; house beer (by Wye Valley); 4 changing beers (sourced regionally) Ⓗ

With a spectacular array of 14 handpumps offering a constantly changing choice of beers and ciders, every day is a beer festival at the Ancient. The bar area has a large woodburner – a welcome sight on cold winter days – and a separate comfortable restaurant serves quality home-made food. The pub has Visit Wales 4-star accommodation and a fully equipped camping and caravan site at the rear, making it an ideal base to explore the Brecon Beacons National Park.
🐎❀🛏◐◑♿⛺🍎P🚌(63)🐾ᯤ

Presteigne

Radnorshire Arms Hotel

High Street, LD8 2BE
11-11 ☎ (01544) 267406 radnorshirearmshotel.com
Sharp's Doom Bar; 2 changing beers (sourced nationally; often Adnams, Greene King, Thwaites) Ⓗ
This historic hotel dates back to the 16th century and was the former home of Sir Christopher Hatton, a favourite of Queen Elizabeth I. The pub retains many original features including floorboards and beams, oak panelling and a priest's hole. It offers cosy open fires in winter and a large pleasant garden for the summer. There is an à la carte restaurant, bar food and a pizza menu. Live music features occasionally including Monday evening jam sessions. **P**

Rhayader

Cornhill Inn

West Street, LD6 5AB (400yds west of clock tower on main A470)
4 (12 Sat & Sun)-midnight ☎ (01597) 810029
Sharp's Doom Bar; Waen TWA; 2 changing beers Ⓗ
Sixteenth-century inn providing a pub experience sometimes lost in this modern world. There are two separate rooms and a log fire in winter, and a lively, friendly atmosphere is assured. The beer range usually includes local and regional beers. Outside are a beer garden and covered smoking area. For many years there was a blacksmith's forge at the rear, now converted into a holiday cottage. **Q**

Talgarth

Tower Hotel

The Square, LD3 0BW
4 (11 Fri-Sun)-11 ☎ (01874) 711253
towerhoteltalgarth.co.uk
6 changing beers (sourced locally) Ⓗ
Bright yet cosy modern bar in a small traditional hotel, with a separate restaurant area. Sky Sports is popular for major rugby and football matches. The enthusiastic landlord regularly sources up to six guest beers and a range of real ciders, all from Welsh producers. Local produce is reflected in the food menu. A spring beer festival is hosted alongside a bike festival, and smaller festivals are staged at other times. A multiple local winner of CAMRA awards for beer and cider.
♣**P**

Talybont-on-Usk

Star Inn

LD3 7YX (on B4558 between Brecon and Crickhowell)
11.30-3, 5-11.30; 11-11 Fri-Sun ☎ (01874) 676635
starinntalybont.co.uk
6 changing beers (often Brecon) Ⓗ
Large and lively pub alongside the Monmouthshire & Brecon Canal, with a spacious garden that is extremely popular in summer. The beer range varies constantly, with local ales well represented, served alongside a choice of real ciders. Live music evenings are held regularly, and quiz nights are popular. Excellent food makes good use of local produce. Twice yearly beer festivals are proving extremely successful. The pub has frequently been local CAMRA Pub of the Year.
♣

Trefeglwys

Red Lion

SY17 5PH
5 (2 Fri)-11; 12-midnight Sat; 12-11 Sun
☎ (01686) 430934
Morland Old Speckled Hen; Sharp's Doom Bar; Three Tuns XXX Ⓗ
Friendly beamed village pub with a pleasant view across the valley. The public bar is wood panelled and has an impressive inglenook with a wood-burning stove. A pool room is accessed off the bar down a couple of steps, and the restaurant is to the right as you enter. There are outside drinking areas for warmer weather to the front and rear. The pub attracts a mixed clientele and has a relaxed atmosphere. ♣**P**

Welshpool

Bistro 7

7 Hall Street, SY21 7RY (off A483)
12-11; closed Sun ☎ (01938) 552879 bistroseven.co.uk
3 changing beers (sourced regionally; often Purple Moose, Salopian, Stonehouse) Ⓗ
Formerly the Crown, this friendly town-centre bar and restaurant was local CAMRA Pub of the Year for 2014. Drinkers are welcome and three changing real ales are promoted enthusiastically by the landlord. The bistro has an excellent reputation for its food. There is plenty of seating outside at the front and in the beer garden to the rear of the restaurant, as well as in an outbuilding. A public car park is opposite. (X71,X75)

Ale conner

The official ale-tester wore leather breeches. He would enter an inn without warning, draw a glass of ale, pour it on a wooden bench, and then sit down in the puddle he had made. He would sit for half an hour and would not change his position. At the end of the half hour, he would make as if to rise, and this was the test of the ale; for if the ale was impure, if it had sugar in it, the tester's leather breeches would stick fast to the bench, but if there was no sugar in the liquor, no impression would be present – in other words, the tester would not stick to the seat.

17th-century description of the work of the ale conner, a public official who inspected inns, taverns and ale houses to test the quality of the beer. (William Shakespeare's father was an ale conner.)

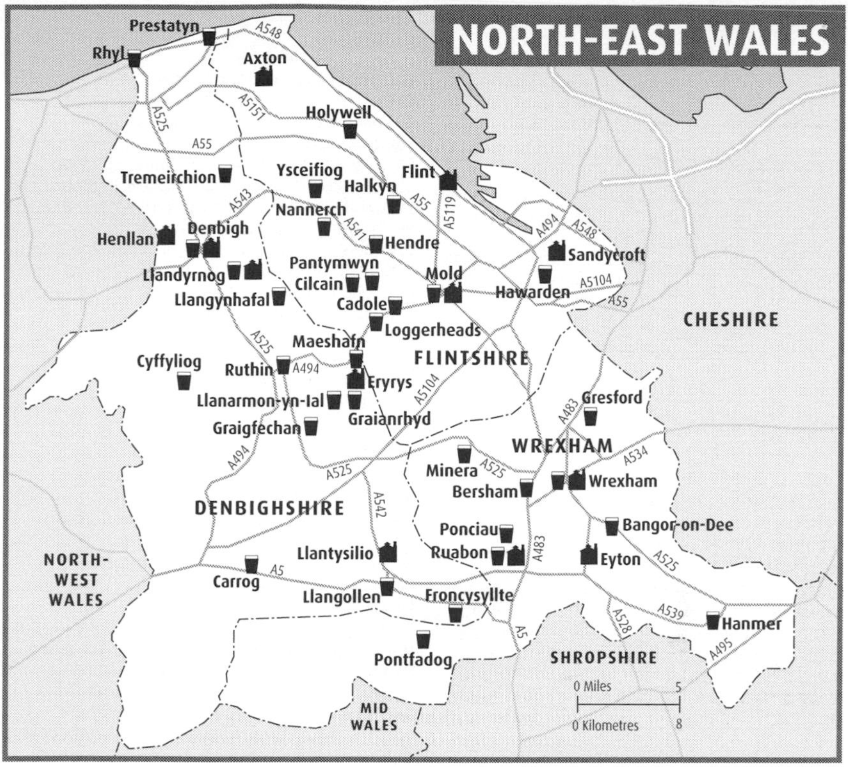

Authority areas covered: Denbighshire UA, Flintshire UA, Wrexham UA

Bangor-on-Dee

Royal Oak

High Street, LL13 0BU

11.30-11 ☎ (01978) 781602

theroyaloakbangorondee.co.uk

Stonehouse Station Bitter; 1 changing beer (sourced locally; often Purple Moose)

Eye-catching mock-Tudor pub nestled on the banks of the River Dee in a picturesque village. Formerly known as the Royal Hotel and the Oak, this food-led pub has been a public house since 1851. Inside is a smart well-decorated open-plan bar and side lounge. Outside is a small patio garden area and further seating overlooking the River Dee, next to the historic bridge and St Dunawd's Church. The guest ale is usually from a local micro.

P (146)

Bersham

Black Lion

Y Ddol, LL14 4HN (off B5099 near Bersham Heritage Centre)

11.30-12.30am (1am Fri & Sat); 11.30-midnight Sun ☎ (01978) 290193 blacklioninnbersham.com

Hydes Original Bitter; 1 changing beer (often Hydes)

Friendly locals' hostelry, also known as the Hole in the Wall, adjacent to the Clywedog industrial trail overlooking the Clywedog River. It is a popular refreshment stop for walkers and visitors to the nearby Bersham Heritage Centre. Three rooms are served by a wood-panelled bar and real fires create a warm, homely atmosphere. There is a beer garden and a play area. Beer and music festivals are hosted in July and October. A second ale comes from Hydes Beer Studio. P (6)

Cadole

Colomendy Arms

Village Road, CH7 5LL (off A494 Mold-Ruthin road)

7 (6 Thu)-11; 4-11 Fri; 2-11 Sat & Sun ☎ (01352) 810217

5 changing beers

A wonderful, basic little pub in the middle of the village, run by the same family for some 27 years and featuring in the Guide for most of that time. It has two cosy rooms warmed by real fires and festooned with local history and photographs. Conversation is king here. Five ever-changing beers

REAL ALE BREWERIES

Axiom Wrexham
Axton Axton (NEW)
Big Hand Wrexham
Buzzard Llandyrnog
Denbigh Denbigh
Deva Craft Sandycroft (NEW)
Erddig Wrexham (NEW)
Facer's Flint
Hafod Mold
Heavy Industry Henllan
Iâl Eryrys
Llangollen Llantysilio
McGivern Ruabon
New Plassey Eyton
Sandstone Wrexham
Wrexham Lager Wrexham

are sourced from far and wide. Be aware that the Black Sheep clock keeps dubious time. The Loggerheads Country Park is close by. Q❀♣P🚌🐾

Carrog

Grouse Inn

B5437, LL21 9AT (on B5437)

🕐 12-midnight ☎ (01490) 430272 🌐 thegrouseinn.co.uk

Lees Bitter, John Willie's; 1 changing beer (often Lees) Ⓗ

Situated alongside the River Dee with spectacular views of the Dee Valley and Berwyn Mountains, the Grouse was originally a farm and brewhouse. The single bar serves JW Lees beers, sometimes from the seasonal range. There are two separate dining rooms off the main bar and a large covered patio area outside overlooking the river. Carrog station on the Llangollen-Corwen Railway is a short walk away. Q❀◐⛺⇌♣P🚌

Cilcain

White Horse

Ffordd Y Llan, CH7 5NN (signed from A451 Mold-Denbigh road)

🕐 12-3, 6-11; 12-11 Sat; 12-10.30 Sun ☎ (01352) 740142

Banks's Bitter; 1 changing beer (sourced locally) Ⓗ

This picturesque country village pub has been a regular in the Guide for over 20 years. It has a traditional layout with a quarry-tiled public bar featuring a set of antique beer engines and a warm, cosy lounge. Situated beside the Clwydian Range, the pub caters for visitors to the nearby Moel Famau and Offa's Dyke.

Q👶❀◐♣P🚌(14C)🐾

Cyffyliog

Red Lion Hotel

LL15 2DN

🕐 closed Mon; 5-10.30 (midnight Fri); 12-midnight Sat; 12-3 Sun ☎ (01824) 710351 🌐 redlionhotel.webs.com

Marston's Burton Bitter, Pedigree; 1 changing beer Ⓗ

Family-run village inn with parts dating back to the 17th century. The focal point is the welcoming lounge with an open fire. There is also a cosy adjacent dining area and a further dining/function room. The public bar includes a pool table and TV. The Gents is bedecked with numerous different wall tiles from a bombed Liverpool factory. Wednesday quiz nights and Thursday curry nights are popular. The pub also serves as the village shop. Q👶◐⛺♣P🐾📶

Denbigh

Brookhouse Mill 🄻

Ruthin Road, LL16 4RD (off A525 S of Denbigh)

🕐 12-3, 6-11.30; 12-11 Sun ☎ (01745) 813377

🌐 brookhousemill.co.uk

Conwy Beachcomber Blonde; 2 changing beers Ⓗ

This plush multi-roomed establishment is situated one mile south east of Denbigh, on the A525 Ruthin road. The 17th-century mill was powered by the River Ystrad and the wheel and workings can still be seen in the restaurant. Local breweries are always represented in the bar. There are function facilities, regularly used by several societies, and a well-appointed garden alongside the river. Buses from Denbigh takes you to the door.

Q👶❀◐♿⛺♣P🚌(55,X50)📶

Froncysyllte

Aqueduct Inn 🄻

Holyhead Road, LL20 7PY (on A5)

🕐 12-11 ☎ (01691) 777118 🌐 theaqueductinn.co.uk

2 changing beers (sourced locally; often Salopian, Stonehouse) Ⓗ

Friendly and welcoming free house standing beside the busy A5 and unmissable in its canary yellow livery. It has a simple three-roomed layout with a small central bar, games room and comfortable lounge with woodburner. The rear verandah offers panoramic views, not least of the Llangollen Canal as it approaches the spectacular and world-famous Pontcysyllte Aqueduct. One Stonehouse ale is always available; two further pumps offer a varying choice. There is limited parking to the side and additional parking down the lane. 👶❀◐♣P🚌(64)🐾📶

Graianrhyd

Rose & Crown

Llanarmon Road, CH7 4QW (on B5430 off A5104)

🕐 4-11; 12-midnight Fri & Sat; 12-10.30 Sun

☎ (01824) 780727 🌐 theroseandcrownpub.co.uk

Black Sheep Best Bitter; 2 changing beers Ⓗ

Cosy, traditional and welcoming village pub, recognised by CAMRA as having an interior of some regional importance. The long bar serves two rooms – one was the original inn and the other was converted in the 1960s from the former living quarters. Guest beers are usually from local breweries – the many badges behind and above the bar testify to the variety. Popular with locals and walkers. Q👶❀◐⛺♣🍏P🚌(2)🐾

Graigfechan

Three Pigeons Inn

LL15 2EU (on B5429 about 3 miles from Ruthin)

🕐 closed Mon; 5-10.30 Tue; 12-3, 5-11 Wed-Fri; 12-11 Sat; 12-10 Sun ☎ (01824) 703178 🌐 threepigeonsinn.co.uk

Sharp's Doom Bar; 3 changing beers Ⓗ

Fine old drovers' inn with parts originating from the 12th century. Original features and open log fires have been retained, the interior tastefully decorated throughout. There is an extensive lounge area with a sports room to one side and a large dining area to the other. Cellars are ideal for keeping the cask ale that is still, on occasion, served direct in jugs. An outdoor area to the rear has great views over the Vale of Clwyd. Regular live music and other special events are hosted. A campsite is adjacent.

👶❀🛏◐⛺♣🍏P🚌(76)🐾📶

Gresford

Griffin Inn

Church Green, LL12 8RG

🕐 4 (7.30 Wed)-11.30; 4-11 Sun ☎ (01978) 855280

Adnams Southwold Bitter; Courage Best Bitter; 1 changing beer (sourced nationally; often Conwy) Ⓗ

The landlady Jean has presided at this friendly community inn since 1973. Listed by CAMRA as a real heritage pub, it has changed little since 1954. Obviously well-cared for, the irregular open-plan interior comprises a comfortable lounge and distinct bar area with interesting pictures adorning the walls. The garden to one side has views of the 15th-century All Saints Church whose bells are one of the Seven Wonders of Wales. Children are welcome in some areas until 8pm. The guest ale is sourced from the Punch List. Q🍴❀♣P🚌(1)📶

Pant-yr-Ochain 🄻

Old Wrexham Road, LL12 8TY (off A5156, E from A483; follow signs to The Flash)
🕐 11.30-11 (10.30 Sun) ☎ (01978) 853525
🌐 pantyrochain-gresford.co.uk
Joule's Slumbering Monk; Purple Moose Cwrw Eryri/ Snowdonia Ale; house beer (by Phoenix); 3 changing beers 🄷
Lovingly restored 16th-century dower house which retains many historic features and sits beside a small lake within extensive gardens. The central room, dominated by a large double-fronted bar, leads to a variety of seating areas including a garden room, a small snug behind the period inglenook fireplace, and the patio and lawn outside. Hugely popular with diners, food is served all day. Three regular beers are supplemented by three guests, often local, and draught cider is usually available. Q🍴❀◐♿♣●P🐾📶

Halkyn

Blue Bell Inn 🏆 🄻

Rhosesmor Road, CH8 8DL (on B5123)
🕐 3 (5 Wed)-11; closed Tue; 5-midnight Fri; 12-midnight Sat; 12-11 Sun ☎ (01352) 780309 🌐 bluebell.uk.eu.org
House beer (by Facer's); 2 changing beers (sourced locally) 🄷
Situated on Halkyn mountain, the Blue Bell is an excellent community pub with weekly events including free guided walks, conversational Welsh classes and trad jazz on Sunday afternoons. In the bar there is a much-needed post office for the village. The licensees normally provide four beers – two house beers, Blue Bell Bitter and Dark Blue Porter, from local brewery Facer's, plus two from other local producers. Ciders feature strongly, with three or four regularly available.
Q🍴❀⛺♣●P🚌(126)🐾📶

Hanmer

Hanmer Arms

SY13 3DE (just off A495 1 mile from A525 jct)
🕐 11-11 (12.30am Fri & Sat) ☎ (01948) 830532
🌐 hanmerarms.co.uk
3 changing beers (sourced regionally; often Hook Norton, Purple Moose, Stonehouse) 🄷
This attractive hotel-restaurant just off the main Wrexham to Whitchurch road makes an ideal base for exploring the north Wales borderlands, Shropshire and Cheshire. The hotel is close to Hanmer Mere and adjacent to the charming 12th-century St Chad's church. Drinkers are welcome in the atmospheric bar with its roaring fire. Lunchtime and evening meals are available from an extensive menu and the beers are often from local micros. Accommodation is available in 12 en-suite bedrooms. Q🍴❀🛏◐♿♣●P🚌(146)🐾📶

Hawarden

Glynne Arms 🄻

3 Glynne Way, CH5 3NS
🕐 11-11 (midnight Fri & Sat) ☎ (01244) 569988
🌐 theglynnearms.co.uk
Facer's This Splendid Ale; 3 changing beers (sourced locally; often Big Hand, Facer's, Heavy Industry) 🄷
Tastefully restored and refurbished 200-year-old village-centre pub and eatery. The interior comprises a simply furnished bar area with semicircular counter and wooden furniture, with separate dining areas and an upstairs function room. The pub has strong links to 19th-century politician and Hawarden resident William Gladstone, whose famous library is in the village. Four mainly locally sourced real ales are always available, and the menu is also strongly focused on local produce. 🍴❀◐♿🚆♣P🚌(4,11)🐾📶

Hendre

Dderwen (Oak) 🄻

Denbigh Road, CH7 5QE (on A541)
🕐 7-midnight (1am Fri; 2am Sat) ☎ (01352) 741466
2 changing beers 🄷
A roadside pub with a central bar serving two rooms, both with ceilings adorned with an impressive collection of pottery. Up to four cask ales are served from north Wales microbreweries including Hafod, Great Orme and Cwrw Llŷn. This 300-year-old pub has a strong community focus, hosting a range of social activities including Welsh singing. It is popular with walkers and visitors to the nearby Clwydian hills.
Q🍴❀♿⛺♣P🚌(14)🐾📶

Holywell

Market Cross

9-11 High Street, CH8 7LA (on main walkway)
🕐 8am-midnight (1am Fri & Sat) ☎ (01352) 717800
Greene King Abbot; Ruddles Best Bitter; 3 changing beers 🄷
Converted in 2011 from a large retail outlet, this small Wetherspoon pub is named after the obelisk of the same name that stood outside. There are many pictures on the walls remembering Holywell and the Greenfield Valley in times gone by. The bar, warmed by a log-burning fire, offers a choice of seating from stools to sofas. St Winefride's Well – the Lourdes of Wales – is near. The Market Cross is a welcome addition to the real ale scene.
Q🍴◐♿●🚌(11)📶

Old Wine Vaults 🄻

Cross Street, CH8 7LP (at jct of High St & Cross St)
🕐 10-midnight (2am Fri & Sat); 12-11 Sun ☎ (01352) 714801
3 changing beers (sourced locally; often Buzzard, Facer's, Heavy Industry) 🄷
A town pub with a large open-plan area and two small rooms served by a single bar. There are several TV screens showing sport, with another screen in the smoking area. Three changing local beers are served. The pub is close to St Winefride's Well, a shrine of unbroken pilgrimage since the 12th century and one of the Seven Wonders of Wales. When local lead mines were still in operation the pub was also the pay office – the safes remain in the bar. ❀♿🚌(11)🐾📶

Llanarmon-yn-Ial

Raven Inn 🄻

Ffordd-Rhew-Ial, CH7 4QE (signed 500yds W of B5430)
🕐 closed Mon; 5-10.30 (11 Fri); 12-11 Sat; 12-9 Sun
☎ (01824) 780833 🌐 raveninn.co.uk
3 changing beers (sourced locally) 🄷
Community-run since 2009, this delightful old pub with a friendly and inviting ambience has gone

WALES

from strength to strength. The bar serves two carpeted areas and a tiled area to one side. Three guest beers are available from local breweries, one usually from the pub's sister enterprise, Cwrw Ial Community Brewing Co. Excellent home-cooked food is served Thursday-Sunday. Three refurbished self-catering rooms are available.
Q♨❀⛟◑♿⛺♣●P🚂🚌(2)🐾📶

Llandyrnog

Kinmel Arms L

Waen, LL16 4HN
✪ 12-3, 5-11; 12-midnight Sat; 12-11 Sun
☎ (01824) 790291 🌐 kinmelarms.com
Thwaites Original, Lancaster Bomber; 2 changing beers H
Warm and friendly traditional pub handy for Offa's Dyke path and Moel Arthur iron age fort. The front bar area features a large fireplace while there are barrel ends from the long-defunct Chester Northgate Brewery displayed to the rear. A large separate dining room is to the right. The guest beer is usually from the local Buzzard or Heavy Industry microbreweries. Q♨❀◑♿⛺P🚌(76)🐾📶

Llangollen

Chainbridge Hotel L

Berwyn, LL20 8BS (off B5103)
✪ 11-11 (10.30 Sun) ☎ (01978) 860215
🌐 chainbridgehotel.com
2 changing beers (sourced locally; often Purple Moose, Stonehouse) H
Historic country hotel in a superb location between the Llangollen Canal and the River Dee, with splendid views of the river and the Llangollen to Corwen Heritage Railway. Travel by bus or steam train to Berwyn then cross the road bridge or pedestrian suspension bridge to the hotel. A pleasant 20-minute walk to Llangollen can be undertaken via the canal towpath. Ales are typically from Stonehouse and Purple Moose breweries. Q♨❀⛟◑⛺⇌(Berwyn)P🚌(T3)🐾📶

Ponsonby Arms L

Mill Street, LL20 8RY (near steam railway)
✪ 12-midnight ☎ (01978) 447985
Bank Top Dark Mild; Bollington Long Hop; Ulverston Flying Elephants; 7 changing beers H
Welcoming independent free house run by the team from the nearby Sun Inn. Regular beers are sourced from Ulverston, Bank Top and Bollington, supplemented by up to seven from micros, along with two real ciders. Lunchtime and evening meals are available. Outside is an extensive beer garden overlooking the river. There is a cask ale promotion every Friday 6-7pm. Quiz night is Tuesday. The pub shares the adjacent council car park (ask at the bar for a free ticket). Q♨❀◑⛺●P🚌(5,T3)🐾📶

Sun Inn L

49 Regent Street, LL20 8HN (400yds E of town centre on A5)
✪ 5-1am (2am Fri & Sat) ☎ (01978) 860079 🌐 sunllan.com
Salopian Shropshire Gold; Ulverston Flying Elephants; 6 changing beers (sourced nationally) H
This characterful free house is a sister pub to the nearby Ponsonby Arms on the other side of the River Dee. The traditional stone-flagged bar room has two open fires and the small raised games area has a pool table and table football. A smaller cosy room can be reached via the walled, covered seating area outside. Live music is hosted Wednesday to Saturday. Up to six guest ales are served, and a cask ale promotion is offered daily 6-7pm. ❀⛺♣●🚌(5,T3)🐾📶

Llangynhafal

Golden Lion Inn

LL16 4LN (at village crossroads)
✪ closed Mon; 4 (6 Tue-Thu)-11; 12-10.30 Sun
☎ (01824) 790451 🌐 thegoldenlioninn.com
Thwaites Original; 1 changing beer (sourced locally; often Buzzard) H
Traditional and welcoming 18th-century village inn at the foothills of the Clwydian Range. The bar serves two distinct areas – the bar room with a pool table and the lounge, which leads down to a dining area. The landlord has been at the helm for 13 years and takes particular pride in his beers and whiskies. The guest beer is often from local Buzzard Brewery. There is a campsite to the rear. A regular participant of the Bus Route 76 Real Ale Festival. Q♨⛟◑⛺♣●P🚂🚌(76)🐾📶

Loggerheads

We Three Loggerheads L

Ruthin Road, CH7 5LH (on A494)
✪ 12-11.30 (9 Sun) ☎ (01352) 810337
🌐 we-three-loggerheads.co.uk
Black Sheep Best Bitter; Hafod Hoppy Extra; 2 changing beers H
Across the A494 from Loggerheads Country Park and within the Clwydian Range AONB, this pub started out as a coaching inn in the 17th century. It has a comfortable bar/lounge and a popular restaurant with wheelchair access. A painting of the Three Loggerheads, reputedly painted by 18th-century artist Richard Wilson to pay his bar bills, hangs at the foot of the stairs. In June, Loggfest, a music and ale festival, is hosted here.
♨❀◑♿⛺P🚌(1,X1)📶

Maeshafn

Miners Arms

Village Road, CH7 5LR
✪ 6-11 Mon & Tue; 12-3, 6-midnight Wed-Fri; 12-11 Sat & Sun
☎ (01352) 810464
Theakston Best Bitter; 2 changing beers (sourced locally) H
Built in the 1820s as part of the development of lead mining in the area, the pub is now popular with hikers visiting local nature reserves. The central bar area has a large wood-burning stove and there is a side room which can accommodate groups. A pleasant area outside at the front of the pub is used for occasional beer and music festivals. The food menu includes daily specials and 'miners mess tin' meals for simpler tastes.
♨❀◑♣P🚌(2)🐾📶

Minera

Tyn-Y-Capel L

Church Road, LL11 3DA
✪ closed Mon & Tue; 5-11 Wed; 12-11 Thu; 12-midnight Fri & Sat; 12-10.30 Sun ☎ (01978) 269347 🌐 tyn-y-capel.com
House beer (by Big Hand); 4 changing beers (sourced locally; often Cwrw LLyn, Heavy Industry) H

This former coaching house reopened in April 2013 as a community venture staffed mainly by volunteers. The bright and airy split-level interior is a focal point for the village, with quizzes and other events regularly taking place. Outside, the impressive terrace affords panoramic views of Esclusham Mountain and the surrounding area. The house beer is complemented by up to four guests, often from local Welsh microbreweries. Real cider is available in the summer months.
Q

Mold

Gold Cape

8-8A Wrexham Street, CH7 1ES (next to Market Square crossroads)
8am-midnight (1am Fri & Sat) (01352) 705920
Greene King Abbot; Ruddles Best Bitter; 10 changing beers H
The Gold Cape is named after a 4,000-year-old gold peytrel found nearby in 1831 – an impression of the ceremonial cape stands in the entrance to this former shop. This Wetherspoon pub has a bar staff with a keen passion for cask beer. The walls display pictures of Mold's past, including local poet Daniel Owen. The pub takes part in a twice-yearly bus-driven beer festival involving up to 10 pubs in the area. Q

Nannerch

Cross Foxes L

Village Road, CH7 5RD
closed Mon; 6-11; 12-2.30, 4-11 Sun (01352) 741293
Buzzard Pale of Clwyd; 2 changing beers H
Set in a charming village close to the church, the Cross Foxes was built by the 18th-century Williams family of Penbedw Estate. It was at one time also a butcher's – the hooks still remain over the bar. The interior has altered very little and divides into four areas – the bar with a large fireplace, where dogs are allowed, a reception bar, lounge and function room. The regular beer is from local brewery Buzzard. Tuesday is curry and a pint night.
P(14)

Pantymwyn

Crown Inn L

Cilcain Road, CH7 5EH
5-11; 12.30-midnight Thu-Sat; 12.30-11 Sun
(01352) 740462
Facer's This Splendid Ale; Wychwood Hobgoblin; house beer (by Facer's); 1 changing beer H
A popular and friendly village local with a good reputation for Welsh beers and locally sourced food. Bay windows overlook the front terrace, and there is a beer garden and extensive children's play area. Crowning Glory is the regular house beer from Facer's. Excellent food is served including ever-popular steaks and generous portions of fish and chips. A favourite with walkers in the area, the pub can get busy, especially at weekends. There is a regular Sunday night quiz.
P(6)

Ponciau

Colliers Arms

Chapel Street, LL14 1SE (off B5426)
7 (4 Fri)-11; 1-11 Sat; 1-10.30 Sun
John Smith's Bitter; Marston's Pedigree New World Pale Ale; 2 changing beers (sourced nationally; often Cheshire Brew Brothers) H
Whitewashed free house on a narrow street of terraced housing. The spick and span front room has slate flooring, comfortable bench seating, small cast-iron tables and multiple screens for TV sport. The décor includes beer posters, breweriana and black and white pithead drawings. There is a tiny snug area and a rear room with a pool table, leading to outside decking and a lawn with trestles. Guest ales are sourced nationally – anything from local micros to the likes of Fuller's and Portobello. (3,3E)

Pontfadog

Swan Inn (Graig)

Llanarmon Road, LL20 7AR (next to post office)
12-2, 4.30-11; 12-3 Sat & Sun (01691) 718273
theswaninnpontfadog.co.uk
1 changing beer (sourced nationally; often Conwy, Felinfoel) H
Welcoming traditional free house in the scenic Ceiriog valley. The cosy red-tiled bar features a central fireplace separating the TV and darts area from the servery, and the Cygnet Restaurant dining room is to one side. One or two real ales are selected from a range of breweries. Themed food nights are hosted. The pub is five miles from Chirk station, with a free taxi service provided. Opening hours vary so please check ahead before visiting.
P(64,65)

Prestatyn

Archies L

151 High Street, LL19 9AS
closed Mon; 12-11 (1.30am Fri & Sat) (01745) 855657
Facer's Flintshire Bitter; 3 changing beers (often Joule's) H
This is a modern, family-run, open-plan pub with doors opening out onto a decking area on the high street. Afternoons are usually quiet but evenings can be lively, with televised sports matches, live music and a weekly quiz. Local brewery Facer's provides the regular beer with three other cask ales also available, usually from local breweries. It is also a regular outlet for beers from the local Axton brewery which has links to the pub.
(11,35,36)

Halcyon Quest Hotel L

17 Gronant Road, LL19 9DT (on A547 just E of town centre)
3-11.30 (12.30am Fri & Sat); 12-11.30 Sun
(01745) 852442 halcyonquest-hotel.com
Facer's Flintshire Bitter; 3 changing beers (sourced locally) H
Known locally as HQ, the Halcyon Quest is located on the southern edge of the town. The open-plan bar features sporting memorabilia throughout, including a rowing boat suspended from the ceiling. There is a garden to the rear complete with a covered area. At least four beers, often local, are usually available, including Facer's Flintshire Bitter. Winner of local CAMRA Pub of the Year in 2014.
P(35,36)

Rhyl

Cob & Pen

143 High Street, LL18 1UF

11-11 (midnight Fri & Sat); 12-11 Sun ☎ (01745) 350446

Banks's Mild; Marston's Burton Bitter, Pedigree; 2 changing beers

Respected and welcoming pub with a central bar and a number of themed seating areas, all decorated imaginatively in recognition of the local heritage. A weekly acoustic night is a popular attraction, as are darts, pool and dominoes. Televised sports events are shown on several large screens. This is one of the few local pubs serving cask-conditioned mild. Located close to the bus and railway station.

Sussex

20-26 Sussex Street, LL18 1SG

8am-midnight (1am Fri & Sat); 8am-11 Sun ☎ (01745) 362910

Greene King Abbot; Ruddles Best Bitter; 3 changing beers

An established Wetherspoon outlet, located in the pedestrianised town centre within a building that has formerly been used as both a Wesleyan Chapel and an Old Comrades' Club. Illustrated panels provide visitors and locals with information about different aspects of the town's history. Alcohol is served from 9am and beers brewed by new microbreweries are sometimes available at the bar. Q

Ruabon

Bridge End Inn

5 Bridge Street, LL14 6DA

5 (4 Fri)-11; 12-11 Sat & Sun ☎ (01978) 810881

mcgivernales.co.uk

8 changing beers (sourced nationally; often Ossett, Salopian, McGivern)

A winner of numerous awards since being taken over and completely revitalised by the McGivern family in 2009, including the ultimate accolade of CAMRA National Pub of the Year in 2011. This welcoming and cosy former coaching inn offers eight changing cask ales, at least one from the on-site McGivern Brewery. Real cider is also available. Families and well-behaved dogs are welcome in the lounge. A beer festival is held over the August bank holiday weekend. The station is nearby. Q P

Ruthin

Castle Hotel

St Peters Square, LL15 1AA

7am-midnight (1am Fri & Sat) ☎ (01824) 709960

Adnams Broadside; Greene King Abbot; Ruddles Best Bitter; changing beers (often Big Hand, Conwy, Purple Moose)

The Castle Hotel stands in St Peter's Square at the highest point in Ruthin. Now a Wetherspoon hotel with 17 rooms, its multi-area interior has different historic themes – Owain Glyndwr, the Myddelton family and Ruthin Castle feature alongside a mention of a long-defunct brewery on the premises. The hotel car park is for residents only. The town itself has many attractions such as the old gaol, craft centre and fascinating old buildings. P

Tremeirchion

Salusbury

LL17 0UN (one mile S of A55 jct 30)

closed Mon & Tue; 4-11; 12-11.30 Fri & Sat; 12-10.30 Sun ☎ (01745) 710262

2 changing beers

Traditional old village inn with parts reputed to date back to the time of Magna Carta. The pub has been reinvigorated over the past five years by the present owners and is divided into different areas including dining rooms, a snug and a meeting room. There is a large outdoor space with a children's play area. Food is locally sourced with pie and fish night on Friday always popular. Beers are often from local microbreweries. P

Wrexham

Elihu Yale

44-46 Regent Street, LL11 1RR

8am-midnight (1am Fri & Sat) ☎ (01978) 366646

Greene King Abbot; Ruddles Best Bitter; 6 changing beers (sourced nationally)

Conveniently located for bus and rail stations and the town centre, this Wetherspoon pub is often bustling with a wide clientele. Formerly the Majestic Cinema, the large room has been divided into discrete areas, including a quieter space near the front. As well as the two regular ales there are usually six guests, typically including one from North Wales, and real cider also features. The usual Wetherspoon food menu is offered with the addition of Welsh dishes. Quiz night is Wednesday. Q (Central/General)

Royal Oak

35 High Street, LL13 8HY

12-midnight ☎ (01978) 358547

Joule's Blonde, Pale Ale, Slumbering Monk; 2 changing beers (sourced locally; often Brimstage, Offbeat, Salopian)

Grade II-listed building with a long, narrow interior in traditional Joule's style, with plenty of wood panelling and etched brewery mirrors. On the chimney breast above the fireplace is displayed the head of an eland antelope. Three regular Joule's ales and a Joule's seasonal are complemented by guests typically from Offbeat, Salopian, Brimstage or Axiom. Real cider is also on handpump. No food is served but you are welcome to bring your own. Darts and traditional board games are available. The small beer garden is open April-September. (Central/General)

Ysceifiog

Fox ★

Ysceifiog Village Road, CH8 8NJ (signed from B5121)

4 (3 Fri)-11; 1-11 Sat & Sun ☎ (01352) 720241

Brimstage Trappers Hat Bitter; Thwaites Original; 2 changing beers (often Great Orme, Hafod, Weetwood)

An 18th-century tavern in a small village off the beaten track, the Fox is a gem worth finding. Open the front door and step back in time to the 1930s. There are four small rooms, two for dining, with food served evenings (not Wed) and Sunday lunchtimes. The bar offers a choice of four beers, mostly from local breweries. Identified by CAMRA as having a nationally important historic interior, this is a rare classic. Q P

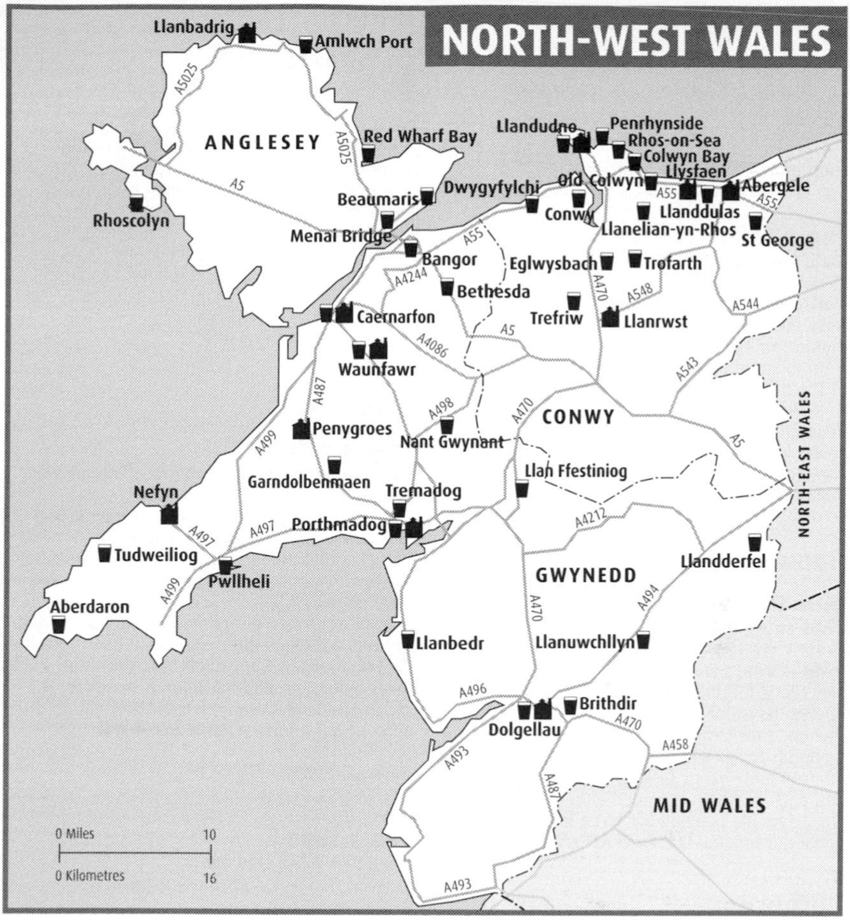

Authority areas covered: Anglesey UA, Conwy UA, Gwynedd UA

Aberdaron

Ty Newydd

LL53 8BE

11-midnight (10.30 Sun) (01758) 760207

gwesty-tynewydd.co.uk

Cwrw Llŷn Brenin Enlli; Purple Moose Calon Lan H

This hotel is situated at the centre of a picturesque and historic village at the end of the Llŷn Peninsula. Beers are from two local breweries. Freshly caught Bardsey lobster and crab are on the menu, as well as afternoon teas. The Wales coastal footpath passes through the village. The en-suite bedrooms offer stunning sea views. Bus services run from Pwllheli. **Q**

Amlwch Port

Adelphi Vaults

Quay Street, LL68 9HD

12-1am (2am Thu-Sat) (01407) 831754

adelphivaults.biz

2 changing beers (sourced locally) G

Built in the 1800s and situated on the Anglesey coastal path, this nautically themed two-room pub is close to the old port. Several museums are nearby that recall the old copper industry. The pub has two ever-changing beers. Locally sourced food is on the menu including seafood from the port, available Easter to late autumn. Check ahead for winter opening hours. **Q**

Bangor

Patricks

59 Holyhead Road, LL57 2HE

11-2am (2.30am Wed & Thu; 3am Fri & Sat)

(01248) 353062

3 changing beers (sourced regionally) G

REAL ALE BREWERIES

Big Bog Waunfawr
Bragdy'r Bwthyn Llanbadrig (NEW)
Cader Dolgellau
Conwy Llysfaen
Great Orme Llandudno
Llŷn Nefyn
Lleu Penygroes
Nant Llanrwst
North Wales Abergele
Old Market Caernarfon (NEW)
Purple Moose Porthmadog
Snowdonia Waunfawr

Situated in upper Bangor, this lively Irish-themed bar is popular both with the locals and students of Bangor University. Numerous TVs display sporting events. There are usually two locally sourced ales and one regional beer on offer. The bar is on the bus route towards the Menai Straits and near the railway station. Note the late opening hours for sport and late-night drinking. ⇌🚌

Tap & Spile

Garth Road, LL57 2SW (off old A5, follow pier signs)
🕔 12-11 (11.30 Tue); 12-11.30 Fri & Sat ☎ (01248) 370835
Marston's Burton Bitter; 6 changing beers 🄷
Busy pub attracting locals, students and visitors to Bangor, with a changing range of up to six real ales from different breweries. It enjoys excellent views of the magnificent pier, the Menai Straits and over to Beaumaris. Good wholesome food including vegetarian options is served at sensible prices, and seven letting rooms are available. A previous winner of local CAMRA branch Pub of the Year.
Q🛏◐🍎🚌🐾

Beaumaris

Olde Bull's Head Inn

Castle Street, LL58 8AA
🕔 11-11 ☎ (01248) 810329 🌐 bullsheadinn.co.uk
Hancock's HB; 2 changing beers 🄷
This Grade II-listed building was the original posting house of the borough. In 1645 General Mytton, a parliamentarian, commandeered the inn while his forces laid siege to the nearby castle. Dr Johnson and Charles Dickens were famous guests and each bedroom is named after a Dickens character. The beamed bar has a large open fire. Parking is limited. Q🐴🛏◐⛺P🚌📶

Bethesda

Douglas Arms Hotel ★

High Street, LL57 3AY
🕔 6-11; 3.30-midnight Sat; 1-3, 7-11 Sun ☎ (01248) 600219
Marston's Burton Bitter, Pedigree; 2 changing beers 🄷
Built in 1820, this was an important coaching inn on the historic Telford post route from London to Holyhead. The Grade II-listed building is recognised by CAMRA as having a a nationally important historic pub interior. The four-room interior has not changed since the 1930s and includes a snug, lounges and a large taproom with a full-size snooker table. Bethesda is convenient for buses to the Ogwen Valley and the surrounding mountains.
Q🐴♿♣🍎🚌

Sior

35-37 Carneddi Road, LL57 3SE
🕔 7-midnight; 5-1am Fri; 1-1am Sat; 1-midnight Sun
☎ (01248) 600072
Jennings Cumberland Ale; 1 changing beer 🄷
A friendly locals' pub in the village of Carneddi just outside Bethesda. A few minutes' drive from the A5, there is plenty of parking nearby. Free of tie, the pub offers a variety of ales from the Marston's range as well as locally brewed beers. There are fine views across the valley to the local slate quarry, which has the longest zip wire in Britain.
Q🚌

Brithdir

Cross Foxes

Dolgellau, LL40 2SG (jct of A470 and A487)
🕔 11-midnight ☎ (01341) 421001
Cwrw Cader Gold; 2 changing beers 🄶
A newly refurbished Grade II-listed building situated near the foot of Cader Idris mountain and four miles from the historic town of Dolgellau. Beers are usually from Cader Ales and other local microbreweries. Breakfast is served from 8am and meals are available all day until 9pm. Dogs are welcome in the bar area. The hotel has Welsh Tourist Board 5-star grading. Bus services T2 pass by, but please check times.
Q🐴❀🛏◐⛺P🚌(T2)🐾📶

Caernarfon

Tafarn Y Porth

5-9 Eastgate Street, LL55 1AG (just off Bangor Rd)
🕔 9am-midnight ☎ (01268) 662920
Big Bog Bog Standard Bitter; Greene King Abbot; Ruddles Best Bitter; 2 changing beers 🄷
Friendly, welcoming Wetherspoon pub opposite the town walls and close to the castle. It has a large open-plan interior and a spacious partly covered courtyard outside with plenty of seating. The real ale range often includes a beer from the Big Bog Brewing Company in Waunfawr, just a few miles away. The pub's location is handy for the Welsh Highland Railway, which takes you to the heart of Snowdonia. Q🐴◐⛺⇌♣🍎🚌

Colwyn Bay

Pen-y-Bryn 🄻

Pen-y-Bryn Road, LL29 6DD
🕔 11-11; 12-10.30 Sun ☎ (01492) 533360
🌐 penybryn-colwynbay.co.uk
Phoenix Brunning & Price Original; Purple Moose Cwrw Eryri/Snowdonia Ale; 4 changing beers 🄷
Open-plan pub popular with all ages, with old furniture, large bookcases and real fires during the winter. The walls are decorated with old photographs and memorabilia from the local area. Panoramic views of Colwyn Bay and the Great Orme can be admired from the terrace and garden. A private function room is available for get-togethers and meetings. Excellent imaginative bar food is served – the menu is updated daily on the website. There are four guest beers, mainly from local and independent breweries. Q❀◐♿🍎P📶

Picture House 🄻

24-26 Prince's Drive, LL29 8LA
🕔 8am-midnight (1am Fri & Sat) ☎ (01492) 535286
Greene King Abbot; Ruddles Best Bitter; 4 changing beers 🄷
A Wetherspoon pub in the former Princess Cinema, now a Grade II-listed building, next to Colwyn Bay railway station. Theatre memorabilia adorn the walls of the three-level building, which also has an upper balcony. There are eight handpumps featuring at least one beer from a local brewery, such as Big Bog, Conwy, Great Orme or Purple Moose, plus guest ciders. Local beer festivals and Meet the Brewer promotions, in addition to Wetherspoon's national events, are held throughout the year. Q◐♿⇌🍎🚌(12,13,14)📶

Conwy

Albion Ale House 🏆 ★ L
Uppergate Street, LL32 8RF
12-11 (midnight Fri & Sat) ☎ (01492) 582484
albionalehouse.weebly.com
8 changing beers (sourced locally) H
Multi-room heritage pub superbly refurbished by the current owners. Each room retains original 1920s features and several have wonderful fireplaces. There is no music or TV, just pleasant conversation. The pub is managed by four local brewers – Conwy, Great Orme, Nant and Purple Moose – and showcases their beers as well as guests. There are two guest Welsh ciders and a good selection of wines and malt whiskies. CAMRA awards include branch and Welsh Pub of the Year.
Q (5,19)

Castle Hotel L
High Street, LL32 8DB
11-11; 11.30-10.30 Sun ☎ (01492) 582800
castlewales.co.uk
Conwy Clogwyn Gold, Welsh Pride; 1 changing beer (often Conwy) H
An old coaching inn dating back to the 15th century, this privately owned hotel is now an upmarket meeting place. Winner of the CAMRA branch Food Pub of the Year 2013, one of the partners is Graham Tinsley, head of the Welsh Culinary Team, and excellent food, made from the finest local produce, is served in the bar and restaurant. A local beer from Conwy Brewery, Dawson's Dark, is only available here. The cider is from Gwynt y Ddraig.
Q P (5,19)

Old White House L
Bangor Road, LL32 8DP
4-11 Mon-Wed; 12-midnight ☎ (01492) 573133
oldwhitehouseconwy.com
Tetley Bitter; 2 changing beers (often Conwy) H
This 17th-century building was once the coach house stable for a now-demolished hotel. The long central bar, featuring a large log-burning stove and a high-beamed roof space, serves the open-plan front lounge and a small rear dining area. The pub hosts a general knowledge quiz on Tuesday, a music quiz on Friday night and live entertainment on Saturday night. Live football is shown on large-screen TVs. Food is available Tuesday to Sunday evening and all day every day in the summer.
P (5,X5)

Dolgellau

Torrent Walk Hotel
Smithfield Street, LL40 1AA
11-midnight ☎ (01341) 422858
Wychwood Hobgoblin; 3 changing beers (sourced locally; often Purple Moose) H
An 18th-century Grade II-listed hotel in the narrow streets of the town centre, retaining most of its multi-roomed interior and old fireplaces, although the bar fittings are from the 1970s. Note the Coffee Room etched in the door from the lobby to the room on the right. A real cider is always served and up to five ales, mostly from local breweries. Dolgellau is an ideal base for walking in the Cader Idris area.

Dwygyfylchi

Gladstone L
Ysgubor Wen Road, LL34 6PS
12-11 (midnight Fri & Sat) ☎ (01492) 623231
thegladstone.co.uk
Black Sheep Best Bitter; 3 changing beers H
Renowned for its magnificent sea views, the pub has been carefully refurbished and retains many of its original features, including the alcoves and traditional decor with wood panelling and old photos. A central bar serves both the dining and drinking areas. Comfortable sofas surround a wood-burning stove, and a galleried balcony with tables and booths overlooks the bar. The restaurant offers imaginative food sourced from local suppliers. There is a function room and accommodation is offered in luxury rooms. The pub also has a wedding licence.
P (5,X5)

Eglwysbach

Bee Inn L
LL28 5UD
closed Mon & Tue; 12-11 Wed-Sat; 12-6 Sun
☎ (01492) 650291
Banks's Bitter; 2 changing beers (sourced regionally) H
This newly refurbished country pub is located in the heart of the Conwy Valley and offers a menu of superb locally sourced home-cooked food. Themed food nights featuring pies or pizzas are also held occasionally and good-value Sunday lunches. The one-roomed bar has a mixture of stone and wood flooring and the walls are adorned with Welsh artwork, Welsh rugby pictures and a selection of musical instruments. Friday is singalong night and open mic nights are sometimes hosted.
P (25)

Garndolbenmaen

Cross Foxes
LL51 9TX (between Caernarfon and Porthmadog off A487)
6-11; 12.30-2.30, 6.30-11 Sun ☎ (01766) 530246
crossfoxesinn.co.uk
3 changing beers H
Two-roomed village inn dating from the 19th century with a central bar. The pub is popular with locals and visitors, attracted by an ever-changing range of beer and good home-cooked food. Meals are served Sunday lunchtimes and every evening. The dining area converts into a popular skittle alley in winter. The local bus stops close by, with regular services Monday-Saturday to Porthmadog and Caernarfon. Q

Llan Ffestiniog

Pengwern
Church Square, LL41 4PB
7-11.30; 5-midnight Fri; 12-midnight Sat & Sun
☎ (01766) 762200 pengwern.org.uk
Purple Moose Cwrw Eryri/Snowdonia Ale; 1 changing beer H
This community-run hostelry was formerly an old drovers' inn. It has one regular beer from Purple Moose and guests from other local breweries such as Big Bog, Cwrw Llŷn and Heavy Industry. The pub holds a beer festival on the August bank holiday

with around 20 beers. An ideal stop-off for walkers in the local area, and there is a bus stop right outside. Q❀🛏◐♿P🚌🐾📶

Llanbedr

Ty Mawr Hotel
LL45 2HH
11-11 ☎ (01341) 241440 🌐 tymawrhotel.com
3 changing beers Ⓗ
Small country hotel set in its own grounds. The modern lounge bar has a slate-flagged floor and cosy wood-burning stove. Unusual flying memorabilia reflect connections with the local airfield. French windows open out onto a veranda and landscaped terrace with seating. A beer festival is held in a marquee on the lawn each year. Popular with locals and walkers, dogs and children are welcome. Meals are served all day. Q🛏◐⛺⇌♣🚌🐾

Llandderfel

Bryntirion Inn
LL23 7RA (on B4401 4 miles E of Bala)
11 (12 Sun)-11 ☎ (01678) 530205 🌐 bryntirioninn.co.uk
Purple Moose Cwrw Eryri/Snowdonia Ale; 1 changing beer (sourced locally; often Big Hand, Conwy) Ⓗ
Former hunting lodge and coaching inn overlooking the River Dee. The single bar services a number of rooms to accommodate diners and families, in addition to the cosy and comfortable bar area with a log fire. There is also a small covered courtyard at the rear. The regular beer is from the Purple Moose Brewery range. A second guest beer varies from other local or national brewers. Good-value accommodation is available. Q❀🛏◐♿♣🍎P🚌(T3)🐾📶

Llanddulas

Valentine
9 Mill Street, LL22 8ES
3-11; 12-midnight Fri & Sat; 12-11 Sun ☎ (01492) 515898
🌐 valentine-inn.co.uk
Marston's Pedigree; 2 changing beers (sourced nationally) Ⓗ
At the centre of this semi-rural seaside village stands this traditional village inn, dating from the 18th century, built on the site of an old clay cottage. To the left is a well-furnished, comfortable lounge and straight ahead is a separate public bar with TV, both with an open fire in winter. Brewery memorabilia and many old framed photographs relating to the Valentine decorate the walls. An attractive drinking area and walled garden for warmer weather may be found to the rear. Q❀⛺♣🚌(12,13)🐾📶

Llandudno

Albert
56 Madoc Street, LL30 2TW
11-11; 12-10.30 Sun ☎ (01492) 877188
🌐 albertllandudno.co.uk
5 changing beers Ⓗ
Just off the town centre and close to the railway station, this popular pub/restaurant offers five handpulled beers from local and independent breweries and a range of tasty meals throughout the day. The beers on offer are clearly displayed on blackboards above and beside the L-shaped bar, with third-pint glasses available. The decor is modern, with a range of interesting photographs and pictures on display. There is covered seating outside at the front. Q❀◐♿⇌🍎📶

Cottage Loaf
Market Street, LL30 2SR
11-11 ☎ (01492) 870762 🌐 the-cottageloaf.co.uk
Conwy Welsh Pride; Courage Directors; 2 changing beers Ⓗ
The building was previously a bakery, hence the name. The interior features stone-flagged floors, an impressive fireplace and a raised timber-floored area – much of the wood came from the Flying Foam, a schooner shipwrecked at Llandudno's West Shore. The Loaf is a popular meeting place for people of all ages, with excellent home-cooked food served all day every day. A major refurbishment and extension took place early in 2014. The guest cider often comes from Gwynt y Ddraig. ❀◐⇌🍎🚌(5,12)📶

King's Head
Old Road, LL30 2NB
12-11 (midnight Fri & Sat) ☎ (01492) 877993
🌐 kingsheadllandudno.co.uk
Greene King IPA, Abbot; 2 changing beers Ⓗ
The 300-year-old King's Head is the oldest inn in Llandudno. It has a traditional split-level bar dominated by a large open fire, and a grill restaurant at the rear serving good-quality food. The pub makes an ideal stop after walking on the Great Orme or riding on Britain's only cable-hauled tramway. Quiz night is Wednesday. ❀◐⛺P🚌

Palladium
7 Gloddaeth Street, LL30 2DD
8am-midnight (1am Fri & Sat) ☎ (01492) 863920
Greene King Abbot; Ruddles Best Bitter; 6 changing beers Ⓗ
A huge Wetherspoon pub converted from a theatre originally built in 1920 on the site of the Market Hall. It opened in 2001 and at the time was the largest pub in the UK. The boxes and upper seating can still be seen, although not used, and the walls are adorned with theatrical memorabilia including original programmes bearing the names of the stars of the day. There are spacious areas on split levels including a family dining room, and a lift is available. ◐♿⇌🍎🚌(5,12)📶

Snowdon
11 Tudno Street, LL30 2HB
12-11 (11.30 Fri & Sat); 12-10.30 Sun ☎ (01492) 872166
🌐 the-snowdonhotel.co.uk
Draught Bass; 3 changing beers (sourced regionally) Ⓗ
Attractively refurbished pub just off the town centre near the tram station, one of the oldest in Llandudno, frequently referred to as the locals' local. Four real ales are usually available, with three thirds on offer for the price of a pint if you cannot make up your mind. The interior comprises a large main drinking area and a small side snug – look for the Snowdon mirror above the fireplace. The garden, with fine views of the Great Orme, won Llandudno in Bloom for its floral display. ❀♣🍎🚌(5,12)🐾

Llanelian-yn-Rhos

White Lion
LL29 8YA

closed Mon; 11.30-3.30, 6 (5 Fri & Sat)-midnight; 12-11 Sun (01492) 515807 whitelioninn.co.uk
Marston's Burton Bitter, Pedigree; 1 changing beer H
A regular in the Guide for more than 20 years, this 16th-century inn situated in the hills above Old Colwyn, next to St Elian's Church, offers a warm welcome. Gracing the entrance are two white stone lions, leading into the bar area with slate-flagged flooring and large comfortable chairs around the log fires. Decorative stained glass is mounted above the bar in the tiny snug. The restaurant serves delicious home-cooked food. Jazz night is Tuesday, quiz night Thursday.
Q P

Llanuwchllyn

Eagles Inn (Tafarn Yr Eryrod)

LL23 7UB
11-11 (midnight Thu-Sat) (01678) 540278
yr-eagles.co.uk
3 changing beers (sourced locally; often Cwrw Cader, Cwrw Llŷn, Purple Moose) H
A friendly welcome awaits at this little gem – an old stone-built village local opposite the church. It retains plenty of historic features including a wonderful stone floor. The bar area also serves as a shop and is open most of the day, although hours may be shorter in winter. The adjacent restaurant serves highly rated locally produced food. The patio garden has good mountain views. It is a 10-minute walk to Llanuwchllyn station on the Bala Lake Railway. P (T3)

Menai Bridge

Anglesey Arms

Mona Road, LL59 5EA (by Menai suspension bridge)
11-11 (midnight Thu-Sat); 12-11 Sun (01248) 712305
anglesey-arms.co.uk
Lees Manchester Pale Ale, The Governor, Bitter H
Dating back more than 200 years, this old coaching house has been completely refurbished. Just over Telford's famous suspension bridge, it is on the main route to Holyhead and ideally situated for Snowdonia, the Llŷn Peninsula, the resorts of Anglesey and the Irish Ferries. Guest beers and seasonal ales are from the JW Lees list and local produce is used in most meals. The large rear rooms are available for functions.
Q P

Liverpool Arms

St George's Pier, LL59 5EY
12-2, 5-11.30; 12-11.30 Fri-Sun (01248) 712453
Facer's Flintshire Bitter; Purple Moose Cwrw Eryri/ Snowdonia Ale H/G**, Ochr Tywyll y Mws/Dark Side of the Moose; 1 changing beer** H
Recently refurbished to a high standard, the Livvy now has four cask ales on offer and serves good-quality home-cooked food.This nautically themed pub is frequented by locals, students in term time and the local sailing fraternity. A short walk takes you beneath the famous suspension bridge and it is close to the quay for local tourist boats. The Anglesey and Welsh Coast footpaths are nearby.

Nant Gwynant

Pen-y-Gwryd

LL55 4NT (at jct of A486 and A4086)
11-11 (01286) 870211 pyg.co.uk
Purple Moose Cwrw Eryri/Snowdonia Ale, Cwrw Madog/Madog's Ale H
Built in 1810 and Grade II-listed, this famous hotel is situated in the heart of Snowdonia. It was used by the team who made the first ascent of Everest. The Everest room has famous signatures on the ceiling, and there are two other small rooms plus a dining room. The hotel features in CAMRA's Real Heritage Pubs of Wales and Great British Pubs. Note that winter opening is restricted but the bar does open for festivities over the New Year.
Q

Old Colwyn

Red Lion

385 Abergele Road, LL29 9PL
5-11; 4-midnight Fri; 12-midnight Sat; 12-11 Sun (01492) 515042
Holden's Black Country Mild; Marston's Burton Bitter; 6 changing beers (sourced nationally) H
This free house serves up to five guest ales from independent and local brewers. It has a cosy L-shaped lounge featuring a real coal fire, antique brewery mirrors and other memorabilia, and a traditional public bar with a pool table, darts and TVs. To the rear is a Victorian-style covered and heated smoking conservatory. The Real Ale Club every Thursday offers nine beers at reduced prices, and guest ciders are available.
Q (12,13,14)

Penrhynside

Penrhyn Arms L

Pendre Road, LL30 3BY
5 (4.30 Thu; 4 Fri; 12 Sat)-11.45; 12-11 Sun 07780 678927 penrhynarms.com
Banks's Bitter; Marston's Pedigree; 4 changing beers (sourced regionally) H
This welcoming local free house has up to four guest beers, concentrating on new breweries and new beers, plus a winter ale on gravity at Christmas. The spacious L-shaped bar has pool, darts and a widescreen TV. The walls are decorated with signed photographs of famous people and numerous awards the pub has won, including local CAMRA Pub of the Year, plus regional, Welsh and national cider awards. Thursday is cheese night.
(12,14,15)

Porthmadog

Spooner's Bar

Harbour Station, LL49 9NF
9am-11; 12-10.30 Sun (01766) 516032
4 changing beers H
The bar's beer range varies, but there are always at least two ales from the local Purple Moose Brewery. Situated in the terminus of the world-famous Ffestiniog Railway and Wesh Highland Railway, steam trains are outside the door most of the year. Food is served every lunchtime, evening meals Tuesday-Saturday, but check first out of season. A former local CAMRA Pub of the Year award winner. Q

Station Inn

LL49 9HT (on mainline station platform)
11-11 (midnight Thu-Sat); 12-11 Sun (01766) 512629

Brains Bitter; Purple Moose Cwrw Eryri/Snowdonia Ale; 1 changing beer 🄷
Situated on the Cambrian Coast railway platform, this pub is popular with locals and visitors alike. It has a large lounge and a smaller public bar, and can get busy at weekends and on nights when live football is shown on TV. A range of pies and sandwiches is available all day. There is a pleasant beer garden at the back. Local buses stop outside the station. ♿▲⇌♣🍎🚌

Pwllheli

Pen Cob

Station Square, LL53 5HG
⏲ 7am-11 ☎ (01758) 704970
Greene King Abbot; Ruddles Best Bitter; 4 changing beers 🄷
This Wetherspoon pub opened in December 2013 opposite the train station at the start (or end) of the scenic Cambrian Line. Formerly a Bon Marche shop, it has been tastefully refurbished and is now a light and airy venue popular with people of all ages. It gets especially busy with locals and tourists at weekends and during the holiday season. The area is popular for sailing. 🐴◑♿⇌🚌

Red Wharf Bay

Ship Inn

LL75 8RJ (off A5025 between Pentraeth and Benllech)
⏲ 11-11 (10.30 Sun) ☎ (01248) 852568
🌐 shipinnredwharfbay.co.uk
Adnams Broadside; Brains SA; 2 changing beers 🄷
Red Wharf Bay was once a busy port exporting coal and fertilisers in the 18th and 19th centuries. Previously known as the Quay, the Ship enjoys an excellent reputation for its bar and restaurant, with meals served lunchtimes and evenings. It gets busy with locals and visitors in the summer. The garden has panoramic views across the bay to south-east Anglesey. The resort town of Benllech is two miles away and the coastal path passes the front door.
Q🐴❀◑♿P

Rhos-on-Sea

Rhos Fynach

Rhos Promenade, LL28 4NG
⏲ 11-midnight ☎ (01492) 548185 🌐 rhosfynach.co.uk
Marston's Pedigree; Tetley Bitter; 1 changing beer (sourced nationally) 🄷
Rebuilt on the site of an old monastery overlooking the promenade and reputedly the oldest building in the area, the Rhos Fynach is an attractively restored pub and restaurant. On the walls are wooden boards featuring interesting historic information about the area. There is a large function room upstairs overlooking the sea for weddings and special occasions. An extensive outdoor drinking and dining area has views of a small local park. Beer is available in third-pint glasses with three for the price of a pint.
🐴❀◑♿P🚌(12,14,15)🐾📶

Rhoscolyn

White Eagle

LL65 2NJ (off B4545 signed Traeth Beach)
⏲ 12-3, 6-11; 12-11 Sat; 12-10.30 Sun ☎ (01407) 860267
🌐 white-eagle.co.uk
Marston's Burton Bitter, Pedigree; Weetwood Eastgate Ale; 2 changing beers 🄷
Saved from closure by new owners, this pub has been renovated and rebuilt with an airy, brasserie-style ambience. It has a fine patio enjoying superb views over Caernarfon Bay and the Llŷn Peninsula to Bardsey Island. The nearby beach offers safe swimming with a warden on duty in the summer months. The pub is also close to the coastal footpath. Excellent food is available lunchtimes and evenings, all day during the school holidays.
Q🐴◑♿▲♣P

St George

Kinmel Arms 🄻

LL22 9BP
⏲ closed Sun & Mon; 12-3, 6-11 (11.30 Fri & Sat)
☎ (01745) 832207 🌐 thekinmelarms.co.uk
Facer's Flintshire Bitter; 2 changing beers (sourced regionally) 🄷
This 17th-century former coaching inn is set on the hillside overlooking the sea. A central bar serves a large combined drinking and dining area with a real log fire in one corner and a spacious conservatory at the rear. Two guest beers come from local breweries, plus a cider from Gwynt y Ddraig. The pub has a reputation for good food, and luxury accommodation is available in four comfortable suites. The owner's art gallery and shop is on site. Q❀🛏◑♿🍎P🐾📶

Trefriw

Old Ship 🄻

LL27 0JH
⏲ closed Mon; 12-3, 6-11; 12-11 Sat & Sun
☎ (01492) 640013 🌐 the-old-ship.co.uk
Banks's Bitter; 2 changing beers 🄷
Dating from the 16th century, this former customs house is now a busy village local. A small central bar serves a cosy L-shaped lounge with an open fire, brass ornaments and pictures of historic and nautical interest. Excellent home-cooked food is available in the dining room, with an inglenook fireplace. This genuine free house offers a good range of guest beers from independent and local breweries such as Conwy, Great Orme and Nant.
Q❀◑P🚌(19)

Tremadog

Union Inn

7 Market Square, LL49 9RB
⏲ 12-2, 5.30-12.30am (11 Sun) ☎ (01766) 512748
🌐 union-inn.com
Big Bog Bog Standard Bitter; Great Orme Atlantis; Purple Moose Cwrw Eryri/Snowdonia Ale 🄷
Friendly village local situated in the village square, with two separate cosy bars and a restaurant at the rear. The pub has a policy of using locally sourced produce, and the ale range mainly features local beers. Children are welcome and there are board games available. Excellent food is served in the bar and restaurant. Tremadog was the birthplace of Lawrence of Arabia. Frequent bus services pass the building Q🐴❀◑♿▲🍎🎲🚌(1A,T2)

Trofarth

Holland Arms 🄻

Llanrwst Road, LL22 8BG

⏲ 12-3, 7 (6 Fri & Sat)-11; closed Wed & Thu; 12-10.30 Sun
☎ (01492) 650777 🌐 thehollandarms.co.uk
3 changing beers (sourced locally) Ⓗ
Family-run pub with a warm welcome for locals and visitors alike, this 18th-century coaching house is set in a country landscape within sight of Snowdonia. It has a pleasantly furnished bar, lounge and restaurant areas. Excellent good-value meals are available daily, with a special themed menu on Mondays. Beers are all local from Conwy, Great Orme and Nant breweries. Live music is hosted on occasion. **Q** ♣**P**

Tudweiliog

Lion Hotel

LL53 8ND (on B4417)
⏲ 11 (11.30 Sat)-11; 11.30-10.30 Sun ☎ (01758) 770244
3 changing beers Ⓗ
The origins of this free house go back more than 300 years. A village inn set on the glorious, quiet north coast of the Llŷn Peninsula, cliffs and beaches are a mile away by footpath, a little further by road. Up to three beers are served depending on the season, with Purple Moose a firm favourite. The pub is accessible by bus from Pwllheli during the day only. Closed Monday lunchtimes in winter. A former local CAMRA Pub of the Year.
Q (8)

Waunfawr

Snowdonia Park 🏆

Beddgelert Road, LL55 4AQ
⏲ 11-11 (10.30 Sun) ☎ (01286) 650409
🌐 snowdonia-park.co.uk
Snowdonia Snowdonia Gold, Carmen Sutra, Cais, Dark and Delicious, Welsh Highland Bitter; 7 changing beers (sourced locally) Ⓗ
Home of the Snowdonia and Big Bog breweries, this is a popular pub for walkers, climbers and families, with children's play areas inside and out. Meals are served all day. The pub adjoins Waunfawr station on the Welsh Highland Railway – stop off here before continuing on one of the most scenic sections of narrow-gauge railway in Britain. There is a large campsite adjacent on the riverside. Local CAMRA Pub of the Year 2012-2015.
Q ♣**P**

Pen-y-Gwryd, Nant Gwynant (Photo: John Whitehead)

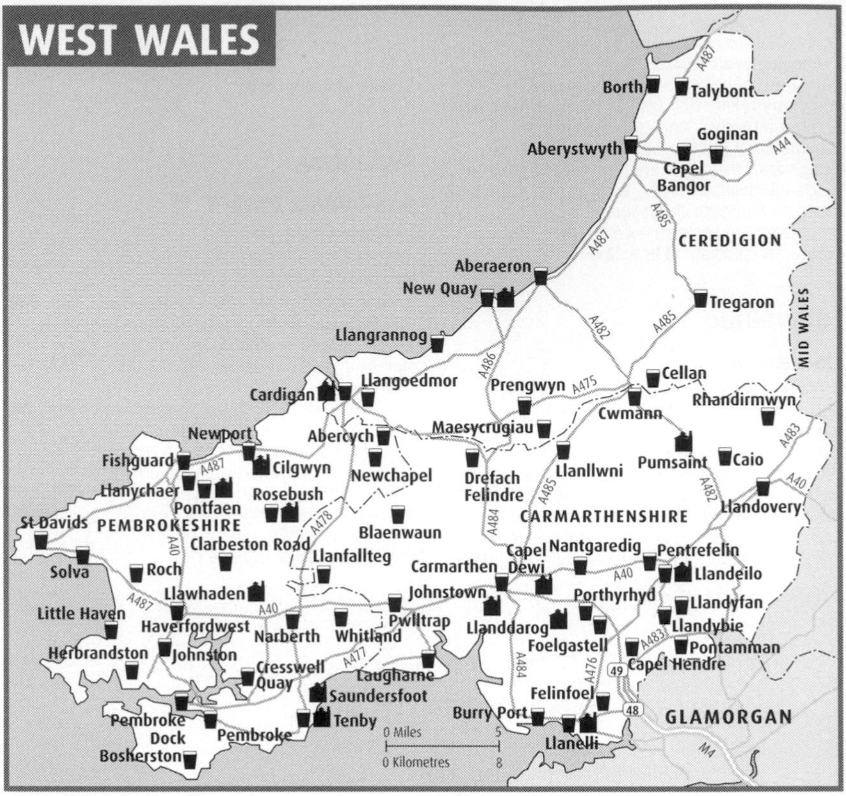

Authority areas covered: Carmarthenshire UA, Ceredigion UA, Pembrokeshire UA

Aberaeron

Harbourmaster

2 Quay Parade, SA46 0BT (off A487 overlooking harbour)

❂ 8am-11.30 ☎ (01545) 570755 🌐 harbour-master.com

Purple Moose Cwrw Glaslyn/Glaslyn Ale; 2 changing beers (sourced regionally; often Otley, Purple Moose) 🄷

A welcome return to the Guide for this light and airy bar forming part of a boutique hotel. The strong Welsh ethos – bilingual signage and staff, many Welsh-speaking customers – extends to beer choice. The guest beer, available Easter to October and Christmas, is always from a Welsh brewery and the house beer, HM, is from Purple Moose. Excellent food is locally sourced. There is an outdoor drinking area at the front overlooking the harbour. Parking is for hotel guests only.

Q❀⊨◑♿Ä🚌(T1,T5)ᯤ

Abercych

Nag's Head 🄻

SA37 0HJ (on B4332 between Cenarth and Eglwyswrw)

❂ 11-3 (not Mon), 6-11; 12-10.30 Sun ☎ (01239) 841200

🌐 nagsheadabercych.co.uk

Mantle Cwrw Teifi; 2 changing beers (sourced nationally; often Coles Family, Jennings) 🄷

This well-restored old smithy boasts a beamed bar, open fires and an attractive riverside garden. The bar area is furnished with collections of old medical instruments, railway memorabilia and timepieces showing the time in various parts of the world. Space is also found for an extensive display of beer bottles. The beer range is local with regional and national guests. Food is sourced locally including trout and lamb, and Sunday roasts are particularly popular. Closed Mondays in winter.

❀⊨◑●Pᯤ

Aberystwyth

Glengower Hotel

3 Victoria Terrace, SY23 2DH (N end of promenade)

❂ 12-11 ☎ (01970) 626191 🌐 glengower.co.uk

Wye Valley Butty Bach; 2 changing beers (sourced regionally; often Brains, Cwrw Cader, Monty's) 🄷

Excellent coastal views can be enjoyed from the suntrap front terrace at this seafront hotel. Inside are a light, airy front bar, quieter dining area, and a large back room with pool and electronic games. Two guest beers (three at busy times) are generally sourced from Wales and the Marches. The cider is from Gwynt y Ddraig. An annual beer festival and raft race are held on the late May bank holiday. Tasty food, locally sourced wherever possible, is served until 8pm (6pm Sun). The hotel closes for a fortnight over Christmas/New Year.

Q❀⊨◑Ä≷♣●🚌(03)🐾ᯤ

Hen Orsaf

26 Alexandra Road, SY23 1LN

❂ 9am-midnight (1am Fri & Sat) ☎ (01970) 636080

Greene King Abbot; Ruddles Best Bitter; Sharp's Doom Bar; 6 changing beers (sourced nationally; often Bluestone, Celt Experience, Mantle) 🄷

An award-winning conversion of Aberystwyth's 1924-built ex-GWR railway station, this excellent Wetherspoon pub offers up to six guest beers with either a Bluestone or a Mantle beer always available. Ciders are from Westons and Gwynt y Ddraig. The usual Wetherspoon policies and promotions apply. Trains, buses and taxis are all adjacent, with a train departure screen in the bar. Outdoor drinking is available on the old station concourse.

Ship & Castle

1 High Street, SY23 1JG

2-midnight (1am Fri); 12-1am Sat 07773 778785

shipandcastle.co.uk

Wye Valley Butty Bach; 4 changing beers (sourced nationally; often Oakham, Tiny Rebel, Wye Valley) H

Aberystwyth's real ale flagship offers microbrewery guests from around the UK and sometimes Ireland, and real cider and perry from Gwynt y Ddraig, alongside small amounts of excellent beer in other formats – craft kegs, bottles (eg Kernel, Tiny Rebel), and even cans. Taste the range with a 'five pump platter' of third-pint measures. Mid-week beer festivals spring and autumn offer extended choice. The well-considered décor reflects the pub's name and history. The venue can be busy for rugby internationals, but is welcoming at all times.

Blaenwaun

Tafarn Yr Oen

SA34 0JD

4-midnight (2am Fri & Sat) (01994) 448899

2 changing beers (sourced regionally) H

This pub, known as the Lamb, is set in an idyllic area and has an original old local ambience with a relaxing atmosphere and welcoming and friendly staff. It offers a range of three or four real ales alongside one or two ciders. A small, quaint pub, darts and pool are played here. There is plenty of parking and a campsite half a mile away.

Q ♣P

Borth

Victoria Inn

High Street, SY24 5HZ

11-2am (01970) 871417

Sharp's Atlantic; Wye Valley HPA; 2 changing beers (sourced nationally; often Hobsons) H

This well-refurbished family-friendly beachside pub has two bars downstairs complemented by an outside decking area, with another bar and restaurant upstairs leading to a terrace with stunning sea views. Logburners add a cosy feel all year round. Live music plays most weekends. Beer is available to take away and real cider is sold in summer. There is an outside grill from Easter to October. Buses from Aberystwyth stop outside (but no Sunday and limited evening services); trains run until late seven days a week.

♣(512)

Bosherston

St Govans Country Inn

SA71 5DN

12-3, 6-11; 12-11 Sat & Sun (01646) 661311

stgovanscountryinn.webeden.co.uk

Evan Evans Cwrw; 3 changing beers (sourced nationally; often Adnams, Elgood's, Navigation) H

With a population of about 300, the village lies just a short walk from the stunning South Pembrokeshire coast and the Bosherston Lily Ponds which are renowned for their beauty in summer and for their varied wildlife. Up to four ales are available from regional and national brewers. The pub has a comfortable interior with exposed beams, horse brasses and a large stone fireplace with logburner giving a cosy feel. It can get busy in the summer months.

Q ♣P(387)

Burry Port

Coasting Pilot Inn

Bridge Street, SA16 0NR

11-11 (10.30 Sun) (01554) 833520

coastingpilothotel.co.uk

2 changing beers (sourced nationally) H

Situated in the harbour town of Burry Port, between Llanelli and Carmarthen, the Coasting Pilot dates from the 1820s and is reputed to be the oldest pub in town. It has a large lounge and dining area where live music often features, alongside an equally spacious bar with pool table, state of the art jukebox, darts and large-screen TVs. It is known locally for good beer, good food and a wonderful friendly atmosphere.

(Pembrey & Burry Port)♣

Cornish Arms

1 Gors Road, SA16 0EL

12-11 (10.30 Sun) (01554) 833224

4 changing beers (sourced regionally) H

Centrally located in a coastal town and conveniently within 100 yards of rail and bus stations, this friendly pub-restaurant is popular with locals and visitors to the area. The bar offers a choice of four real ales, while the restaurant is renowned for its good-quality food, with fish dishes a speciality. Outside, there is a beer garden and smoking area.

Q (Pembrey & Burry Port)

Caio

Brunant Arms

Church Street, SA19 8RD (off A482 near Pumsaint)

11-11 (1am Fri & Sat) (01558) 650483

1 changing beer (sourced locally; often Evan Evans) H

Family-run pub in the centre of the village, and handy for the Dolaucothi Gold Mines. There are plenty of outdoor pursuits nearby including pony

REAL ALE BREWERIES

Bluestone Cilgwyn
Caffle Llawhaden
Coles Family Llanddarog
Evan Evans Llandeilo
Felinfoel Llanelli
Friends Arms Johnstown
Gwaun Valley Pontfaen
Handmade Capel Dewi
Jacobi Pumsaint
Mantle Cardigan
Pembrokeshire Saundersfoot (NEW)
Penlon Cottage New Quay
Seren Rosebush
Tenby Tenby

trekking and walks through the large forest. A legendary Welsh wizard is buried in the church opposite. Good food is served until 9pm every day. One real ale is offered in winter, two in summer, usually supplied by Evan Evans. Q

Capel Bangor

Tynllidiart Arms

SY23 3LR
12-3 (not Mon), 5-midnight; 12-midnight Sun
(01970) 880248 tynllidiartarms.co.uk
Wye Valley Butty Bach; 2 changing beers (sourced nationally; often Purple Moose) H
Situated in the charming village of Capel Bangor on the main A44 leading to Aberystwyth, the Tynllidiart Arms offers a warm welcome to tourists and locals alike. The bar area downstairs is perfect for a cosy pint while the restaurant upstairs serves fine British cuisine, locally sourced wherever possible, including a tasty and flexible children's menu. Dogs are welcome downstairs and on the front terrace outside. The bus service finishes early evening. Q P (X47,525)

Capel Hendre

King's Head Hotel

Waterloo Road, SA18 3SF
4-midnight; 1-10 Sun (01269) 842377
Sharp's Doom Bar; 2 changing beers (sourced regionally) H
Local village pub tucked away just a couple of miles from the former mining town of Ammanford. The main bar has pool and darts, with a sliding door leading to a separate snug. Sharp's Doom Bar is usually on offer alongside a varied choice of guest beers from brewers including Tomos Watkin and Kite. No food is available. There is a large car park. P (128,129)

Cardigan

Grosvenor

Bridge Street, SA43 1HY SN177459
11-11 (01239) 613792
Greene King Abbot; Sharp's Doom Bar; 1 changing beer (sourced nationally) H
Situated on the edge of the town centre next to Cardigan Castle and the River Teifi, this large pub offers a good choice of ales, including a selection of bottled beers. The large open-plan bar/lounge provides various areas to relax, eat and drink, and there is an extra room upstairs for dining and functions. Good-value food is served lunchtimes and evenings every day. An outdoor patio area overlooks the river and the revamped quay area.

Carmarthen

Friends Arms

Old St Clears Road, Johnstown, SA31 3HH
12-11 (midnight Fri); 11-midnight Sat; 11-11 Sun
(01267) 234073
3 changing beers (sourced locally) H
Excellent local hostelry half a mile from Carmarthen town centre, with a cosy and friendly atmosphere and a warm welcome, enhanced by two open fires. Popular with sports fans, it has Sky Sports and ESPN, plus pool and darts. A quiz and bingo are held on alternate Wednesdays in summer. Three real ales are usually offered. A former local CAMRA Pub of the Year, with its own microbrewery. (222,322)

Hen Dderwen

47-48 King Street, SA31 1BH
8am-midnight (1am Sat) (01267) 242050
Greene King Abbot; Ruddles Best Bitter; 3 changing beers (sourced nationally) H
This Wetherspoon pub opened in 2002 and is named after the Carmarthen legend of Merlin and the Old Oak – the story is depicted throughout the premises. Local Welsh ales are always available as well as a good selection of ales from around the UK. There is a Welsh ale festival in March to celebrate St David's Day and two international beer festivals in the spring and autumn – a chance to try something new. A cider festival is held each summer. Food is served all day. Q P

Queen's Hotel

10 Queen Street, SA31 1JR
10-midnight; 11-8 Sun (01267) 231800
5 changing beers (sourced regionally; often Evan Evans) H
Town-centre pub near Carmarthenshire county hall with a bar, lounge and function room used by CAMRA. The public bar is where you will find the locals and it has a TV for sporting events. The patio nestles beneath the castle walls and is a suntrap during the summer months. Beers are sourced mainly from south and west Wales, with some from the west of England.

Cellan

Fishers Arms

SA48 8HU (on B4343) SN596482
4-8 (11 Thu-Fri); 2-11 Sat; 2-8 Sun (01570) 422895
Evan Evans Best Bitter; 1 changing beer (sourced locally; often Evan Evans) H
This friendly pub, dating back to 1580, has a single room divided into a flagstoned and beamed bar area and a lounge area with a large woodburner. There is also a games room with pool and darts and a small rear dining room serving mostly home-made good-value food. Real cider is available during the summer months. The garden has a children's play area and hosts charity barbecues. There is a large TV in the bar mainly for sport. Opening hours may vary. Buses run until early evening Monday to Saturday.
P (585)

Clarbeston Road

Cross Inn

SA63 4UL (N of railway station)
12-midnight (1am Fri & Sat) (01437) 731506
Courage Directors; Greene King Abbot; 1 changing beer (sourced nationally; often Caledonian) H
Multi-roomed village inn, well worth seeking out, with stone and wood floors and original oak beams in abundance. The beer range is regional and national. The large bar area housing pool, TV for sport and jukebox is complemented by two small snugs and a dining room where reasonably priced home-cooked food from a largely grill-based menu is served Thursday to Saturday evenings and Sunday lunchtime. Outside there are more spacious drinking areas. A beer festival is held in summer.
Q P (313,344,432)

Cresswell Quay

Cresselly Arms 🏆 L

SA68 0TE
🕓 12-3, 5-11; 12-11 Sat; 12-3, 5-10.30 Sun
☎ (01646) 651210
Sharp's Doom Bar; Worthington's Bitter Ⓖ; house beer (by Caffle) Ⓗ/Ⓖ; 2 changing beers (sourced locally; often Bluestone, Mantle) Ⓗ
Situated on the Cresswell River, this 250-year-old ivy-covered hostelry is a throwback to the Victorian age. The homely farm kitchen interior, where a roaring fire burns in the hearth, is a haven for locals and visitors alike. Accessible by boat from the Milford Haven estuary at high tide, the pub also lies on a series of interesting walking routes. The house beer from Caffle Brewery and local guests complement the permanent beers dispensed from the cask by jugs. Local CAMRA Pub of the Year 2015. Q🐴❀▲♣●P🚌(361)🐾

Cwmann

Cwmanne Tavern

SA48 8DR (A485/A482 junction) SN582473
🕓 closed Mon; 4 (12 Sun)-11 ☎ (01570) 423861
🌐 cwmannetavern.co.uk
2 changing beers (sourced nationally; often Cottage) Ⓗ
A former coaching inn dating from the 1600s, within easy walking distance of the university town of Lampeter, popular with locals, students and tourists alike. The stone floors and low beams help create a cosy atmosphere. The varied menu (available evenings-only in the week) includes pub favourites, interesting specials and vegetarian options. There is a folk night every Thursday with an ever-changing line-up – bring your own instrument. Cwmann is served by alternate T1 buses only. 🐴❀◗♿♣●P🚌(T1,585)

Drefach Felindre

Red Lion

SA44 5UH SN354388
🕓 4-12.30am (1.30am Fri & Sat); 12-12.30am Sun
☎ (01559) 371677 🌐 redlionwales.co.uk
Mantle Cwrw Teifi; 2 changing beers (sourced nationally; often Marston's) Ⓗ
Located in the small village of Drefach Felindre, near Wales's National Wool Museum, a warm welcome is extended to visitors at this 19th-century pub, which has been renovated in recent years. Now mostly open plan, it has a separate dining room and a large drinking area outside. The original tiled entrance porch is worthy of note. Community focused, it hosts regular fundraising events for charity. A holiday cottage is across the road. The car park is small but on-street parking is also available. Q🐴❀◖◗♿♣P🚌(460)📶

Tafarn John Y Gwas

SA44 5XG SN354383
🕓 5-11; 4-midnight Fri; 12-midnight Sat; 12-11 Sun
☎ (01559) 370469 🌐 johnygwas.co.uk
2 changing beers (sourced regionally; often Bluestone, Purple Moose, Wye Valley) Ⓗ
This early-19th-century village tavern with its striking yellow and black livery attracts locals and tourists alike with snugs, a wood-burning stove, quality beer and cider, and a warm welcome, especially for dogs. Two ales are generally offered, sourced mainly from local Welsh and/or micro breweries. A wide variety of bottled beers and ciders is also available. A beer festival, showcasing more than 10 different ales, is held over the August bank holiday weekend. Basket meals are available every evening, bar meals on Friday and Saturday evenings. 🐴❀◗♣●P🚌(460)🐾📶

Felinfoel

Harry Watkins

2 Millfield Road, SA14 8HY (on A476)
🕓 closed Mon; 12-11 ☎ (01554) 776644
Ringwood Fortyniner; 2 changing beers (sourced nationally) Ⓗ
Renamed after a local rugby hero of yesteryear who features on the pub walls, the pub was originally called the Bear. The open-plan, split-level, family-friendly hostelry has defined dining spaces and a function room, with covered and open drinking areas outside. National cycle and walking paths to the Swiss Valley and beyond are nearby. Quiz nights are Sunday and Wednesday. Good-value food includes a popular carvery. Guest beers are from the Marston's group. No car park, but there is usually ample room on the road.
🐴❀◖◗🚌📶

Fishguard

Pendre Inn

High Street, SA65 9AT (S of town towards Haverfordwest, 300yds from square)
🕓 11 (4 Mon)-midnight; 11-1am Fri & Sat; 12-11.30 Sun
☎ (01348) 874128 🌐 thependreinn.co.uk
Hancock's HB; 2 changing beers (sourced nationally; often Greene King, Ruddles, St Austell) Ⓗ
Friendly traditional pub on the main road south out of town with a good local following and an established reputation for its beer. Two guest ales change regularly and may come from anywhere in the UK. Built around 1790, close to the tollgate on the turnpike road to Haverfordwest, the pub offers pool and darts in the large back bar, while the front bar boasts an inglenook fireplace. Meals, available all day in summer, lunchtimes and evenings in winter (not Mon), include home-made specials.
Q🐴❀◖◗▲♣P🚌(T5)🐾📶

Foelgastell

Smiths Arms

Heol y Foel, SA14 7EL
🕓 12-11 (11.30 Fri & Sat) ☎ (01269) 842213
🌐 thesmithsarms.co.uk
2 changing beers (sourced nationally) Ⓖ
This friendly local pub is a handy stopping-off point from the A48 dual carriageway (follow the brown signs) and a good base for visiting local attractions including the National Botanical Garden of Wales. Meals are served in both the bar and restaurant (no food Sun eve). The beer selection varies, with one or two real ales usually on offer from either local or national breweries. Real cider is often available.
🐴❀🛏◖◗♿●P🚌(166)🐾📶

Goginan

Druid Inn

SY23 3NT (on A44 6 miles E of Aberystwyth)
🕓 12-midnight (1am Fri & Sat) ☎ (01970) 880650

WALES

Wye Valley Bitter, Butty Bach; 1 changing beer (sourced nationally; often Mantle, Purple Moose, Salopian) Ⓗ

This friendly pub, making its 41st entry in the Guide, is the hub of its community and continues to sell excellent beer at reasonable prices. A dining room and pool room flank the L-shaped main bar where dogs are welcome. One guest beer is offered at all times (two at weekends and in summer), and real cider is sometimes available in summer. Occasional music nights (sometimes with acts of more than local renown) and beer festivals are hosted. Food (not served Tuesdays) is popular and high quality. Buses run until early evening Monday-Saturday. ☺⛱◑♣P🚆(X47,525)❀

Haverfordwest

Three Crowns Ⓛ
High Street, SA61 2BW
🌀 11-11.30 (midnight Sat); 12.30-11.30 Sun
☎ (01437) 765931
Courage Directors; Sharp's Doom Bar; 1 changing beer (sourced locally; often Caffle) Ⓗ

A pub since the 17th century, and a Grade II-listed building since 1974, the Three Crowns was refurbished in 2013, retaining original features including the exposed beams and exposed stone walls. Notwithstanding its town-centre location, it offers a welcoming atmosphere, and is handy for both bus and rail stations. The two permanent beers are flanked by a locally sourced guest.
≢♣🚌🚆❀

William Owen Ⓛ
6 Quay Street, SA61 1BG
🌀 9am-midnight (1am Fri & Sat) ☎ (01437) 771900
Caffle Drop Squint; Fuller's London Pride; Greene King Abbot; Ruddles Best Bitter; Sharp's Doom Bar; 2 changing beers (sourced locally; often Bluestone, Mantle) Ⓗ

Pembrokeshire's first and so far only Wetherspoon pub occupies a handsome 19th-century building, formerly a shop, hotel and restaurant, now with a spacious extension to the rear, reputedly built in 1856 for Joseph Thomas, a corn and manure merchant, by local architect William Owen. It has also been a saddler's and more recently the Wilton House Hotel. Beer from one of the county's four breweries is regularly available. The pub offers the chain's standard menu and promotional deals, and is open from 7am for breakfast.
Q☺⛱◑&≢P🚆🚆🛜

Herbrandston

Taberna Inn Ⓛ
SA73 3TD (3 miles W of Milford Haven)
🌀 12-3 (2 Sun), 6-11 ☎ (01646) 693498 🌐 taberna.org.uk
Caffle Drop Squint; Moles Best Bitter; 1 changing beer (sourced nationally) Ⓗ

Designed and built in 1963 by a local carpenter and builder with an eye to the area's then rapidly developing oil and petrochemical industry, the Taberna offers the best real ale choice in the Milford Haven area. Beers are sourced from across Britain, not forgetting Pembrokeshire's own breweries. Real ciders are from Westons and Thatchers (Moles Black Rat). The pub maintains notes of all the guest beers sold throughout the year. A former local CAMRA Pub of the Year.
Q☺⛽◑&▲🍺P🚆🚆(300,315)

Johnston

Vine Inn
Vine Road, SA62 3NY
🌀 11-2, 6-11; 12-11 Sat & Sun ☎ (01437) 890611
Sharp's Doom Bar; Wye Valley Dorothy Goodbody's Golden Ale; 2 changing beers (sourced regionally; often Mantle, Purple Moose) Ⓗ

First licensed in 1810 to Thomas Evans, this pub has been trading successfully ever since, apart from a brief closure a few years ago. A smart, enthusiastically run, black-and-white roadside establishment, it has a good local and countywide following. Local and regional guest ales are available. Inside is a long bar area with exposed beams where many pumpclips tell of past and present beer delights. Local CAMRA Pub of the year for 2014. ☺⛱◑≢🍺P🚆(302,349)

Laugharne

New Three Mariners Inn
Victoria Street, SA33 4SE
🌀 4 (12 summer)-11 ☎ (01994) 427426
Greene King Abbot; 2 changing beers Ⓗ

The building is located in the centre of the historic township of Laugharne and only yards from its early 11th-century castle. Dylan Thomas lived in the town for a number of years and he and his wife Caitlin are laid to rest in the graveyard of St Martin's Church. The pub moved to its current site when the original ale house opposite was converted to a carpentry shop. Popular with locals, it hosts a weekly quiz night.
☺⛱⛲◑&▲P🚆❀🛜

Little Haven

Saint Bride's Inn Ⓛ
St Brides Road, SA62 3UN
🌀 11-midnight ☎ (01437) 781266 🌐 saintbridesinn.co.uk
Brains Rev James; Caffle Darker Side of Pale; Hancock's HB; 2 changing beers (sourced regionally; often Bluestone, Brecon) Ⓗ

Set in a quaint old fishing village in the Pembrokeshire Coast National Park, the St Bride's Inn is a family-run pub in the village centre offering a range of Welsh and Pembrokeshire ales. It is noted for the ancient well in the cellar. The attractive interior includes a separate dining area, and there are heaters on the patio in the pretty suntrap garden for outdoor drinking.
Q☺⛱◑▲P🚆(311,400)🛜

Llandeilo

Angel Hotel
62 Rhosmaen Street, SA19 6EN
🌀 11.30-3, 6-11; closed Sun ☎ (01558) 822765
🌐 angelbistro.co.uk
3 changing beers (sourced locally) Ⓗ

Ideally located in the centre of this picturesque Towy Valley town, the Angel ministers to all needs. The main bar is a U-shaped room providing three real ales, mainly from local breweries, and bar meals. At the back is a bistro dating back to the 1700s, while the first floor offers a beer garden to the rear and a function room boasting a Michelangelo-inspired hand-painted mural. Themed meal nights and music nights are held regularly. ☺⛱⛲◑≢🍺🚆(X13,103)

White Horse
Rhosmaen Street, SA19 6EN
☼ 11-11; 12-10.30 Sun ☎ (01558) 822424
Evan Evans Archers ASB, Cwrw, Warrior; 2 changing beers Ⓗ
Grade II-listed coaching inn dating from the 16th century. The tap for the local Evan Evans Brewery, this multi-roomed hostelry is popular with all ages. There is a small outdoor drinking area to the front and a large council car park to the rear with access down a short flight of steps. A covered area is available for smokers. The pub was local CAMRA Pub of the Year 2014. ◗⇌●🚆🖵(X13,103)

Llandovery

King's Head
1 Market Square, SA20 0AB
☼ 10-11 ☎ (01550) 720393 ⏚ kingsheadcoachinginn.co.uk
Evan Evans Cwrw; 2 changing beers (sourced regionally) Ⓗ
Set in the main square of this historic town and cattle-droving centre on the edge of the Brecon Beacons, this former coaching inn dates from the 1700s. It is a popular base for many organisations including the Rotary Club and cattle breeders. Good food ranges from bar meals to à la carte. Guest beers are predominantly from Wales.
Q🕭🍴◗Å⇌♣🖵(280,281)🐾

Llandybie

Ivy Bush
18 Church Street, SA18 3HZ (100yds from church)
☼ 12-midnight (11 Mon); 11-midnight Sat & Sun
☎ (01269) 850272
Timothy Taylor Landlord; 1 changing beer (sourced regionally) Ⓗ
The oldest pub in the village, this friendly local dates back nearly 300 years. The single-bar room has two comfortable seating areas. Pub games and quizzes are run weekly and a large-screen TV shows sport. The guest beer changes regularly. The local bird-watching group holds its meetings here. Timothy Taylor Landlord plus at least one guest are usually available. The railway station nearby is on the Heart of Wales line. ⇌●P🚆🖵(X13,103)

Llandyfan

Square & Compass
SA18 2UD (between Ammanford and Trapp)
☼ 5 (12 Sat summer)-11; 12-6 Sun ☎ (01269) 850402
Tomos Watkin Old Style Bitter; 2 changing beers Ⓗ
Originally the village blacksmith's, this 18th-century building was converted to a pub in the 1960s. Nestling on the western edge of the Brecon Beacons National Park, it enjoys magnificent local views and plenty of walking opportunities. A traditional family hostelry, it has a wonderful rustic charm and offers a warm, friendly welcome. Usually two, occasionally three, guest beers are available, at least one from a local brewery. Opening hours vary in winter – ring ahead to check.
Q🕭◗Å♣P🖵

Llanelli

York Palace
51 Stepney Street, SA15 3YA (opp Town Hall Square Gardens)
☼ 8am-midnight (1am Fri & Sat) ☎ (01554) 758609
Greene King Abbot; Ruddles Best Bitter; 2 changing beers (sourced nationally) Ⓗ
This former cinema in the town centre is a typical Wetherspoon conversion spread over two levels. The walls are adorned with photographs of local industrial history including Llanelli's famous tin-plate industry. Guest beers are discounted on Sundays and Mondays, and are often sourced locally. There is easy access to the bus station, and the railway station is a 10-minute walk.
Q◗🖶&⇌●🖵🖵🛜

Llanfallteg

Plash
SA34 0UN (off A40 at Llanddewi Velfrey)
☼ 12 (5 Mon & Tue)-11 ☎ (01437) 563472
Wye Valley Butty Bach; 2 changing beers Ⓗ
A terrace-style cottage pub with a garden, and an inn for more than 180 years, the Plash is the centre of village life, with welcoming locals. Quiz night is Tuesday and other events are organised. The guest beers are usually from small, independent breweries. Home-made food, from locally sourced ingredients, is available, with specials on Wednesday, Friday and Saturday. The disabled entrance is to the rear. A small cottage is available to let. A former local CAMRA Pub of the Year.
Q🕭🍴◗Å●

Llangoedmor

Penllwyndu
SA43 2LY (on B4570 E of Cardigan) SN240458
☼ 12-11 ☎ (01239) 682533
Courage Directors; Hancock's HB; 1 changing beer (sourced regionally; often Evan Evans) Ⓗ
Old-fashioned ale house standing at an isolated crossroads where Cardigan's evil-doers were once hanged – the pub sign is worthy of close inspection. The cheerful and welcoming public bar retains its quaintness, with a slate floor and inglenook with wood-burning stove. Good home-cooked food including traditional favourites is available all day in the bar and the separate restaurant. Live music plays on the third Thursday evening of the month.
🕭🏵◗♣P🐾🐾

Llangrannog

Pentre Arms Hotel
SA44 6SP (at seaward end of B4321/B4334)
☼ 12-midnight ☎ (01239) 654345 ⏚ pentrearms.co.uk
Gale's Seafarers Ale; St Austell Tribute; 1 changing beer (sourced regionally; often Mantle) Ⓗ
Set on the Wales Coastal Path in a former seafaring village, this pub commands tremendous sea views (also viewable via beach-facing webcam). The main bar is flanked by the games room – with pool, darts and poker on winter Wednesdays – and dining room. A guest beer is available in summer. Live music plays at weekends. Dogs are welcome in the bar. Bus service is infrequent running daily except Thursdays in summer; Fridays and Saturdays only in winter. 🕭🏵🍴◗Å⇌🖵(552)🐾🛜

Llanllwni

Talardd Arms
SA39 9DX (on A485 N of B4336 jct)
☼ 12-2.30, 6-11 ☎ (01559) 395633 ⏚ talardd.com

1 changing beer (sourced regionally; often Evan Evans) [H]
There are records of this old drovers' inn dating back to 1626, when drovers would stop for refreshments for man and beast before driving their livestock over Llanllwni Mountain on their way to markets over the border. Sympathetically modernised, Tafarn y Talardd continues to offer a traditional warm welcome. Live music, quizzes and film nights are organised most Mondays. Evan Evans Cwrw is usually available, switching to Evan Evans Warrior occasionally. ♘◐♣P🚌(T1)🐾📶

Llanychaer

Bridgend Inn [L]

SA65 9TB (on B4313, 2 miles SW of Fishguard)
⏲ 12-10 ☎ (01348) 872545
Gwaun Valley Blodwen [G]**; house beer (by Gwaun Valley)** [H]**; 2 changing beers (sourced nationally; often Caffle, Mantle)** [H]/[G]
Known locally as the Bont, this friendly country pub, over 150 years old, nestles in the beautiful Gwaun Valley at a bridging point across the river. The cosy bars with log fires serve house beer Bont Ale (brewed by Gwaun Valley) on handpump alongside a range of real ales from local and national breweries. The dining room is housed in the smithy, once run as a complementary business to the inn, and features an external water wheel. Home-made food is served daily, including Sunday lunch. Q♘✿◐⛺♣🍎P🚌(345)🐾📶

Maesycrugiau

Old Railway Inn (Tafarn Llwynann)

SA39 9LL (W off A485 S of Llanybydder) SN474409
⏲ closed Mon-Wed; 6-10.30 Thu-Sat; 12-8 Sun
☎ (01559) 395339
Mantle Cwrw Teifi; 1 changing beer (sourced locally; often Mantle) [H]
Although difficult to find, this quaint, cosy pub is well worth the effort. Previously linked to the long-closed Maesycrugiau GWR railway station, it has a bar, games room and separate dining area. The bar has an open fire and the decor includes bank notes from many different countries hanging from the beams. Sunday lunch is popular – booking is essential. You may wish to phone ahead before visiting to check opening hours. ♘✿◐♣P🐾

Nantgaredig

Railway

Station Road, SA32 7LQ (on B4310 S of village square)
⏲ closed Mon & Tue; 6 (12 Sat)-11; 12-3 Sun
☎ (01267) 290211 🌐 railwaynantgaredig.co.uk
2 changing beers (sourced nationally; often Brains, Marston's) [H]/[G]
A warm welcome awaits at this former hotel which once served Nantgaredig station on the Carmarthen-Llandeilo railway line (closed 1963). The building dates from the 19th century and was tastefully refurbished in 2013. It has three small rooms set around the bar and a separate restaurant where traditional home-cooked food is served. The walls are adorned throughout with local scenes and many mirrors. One beer is available on handpump, an occasional second one on gravity. Buses to the pub are infrequent; more frequent 280/281 buses serve the village square.
♘✿◑♿P🚌(276-279)🐾📶

Narberth

Dingle Inn

Jesse Road, SA67 7DP
⏲ 11-1, 4.30-11; 12-1am Sat; 12-2.30, 4.15-10.30 Sun
☎ (01834) 861806 🌐 dinglecaravanparknarberth.co.uk
Bluestone Bedrock Blonde; 1 changing beer (sourced regionally; often Evan Evans, Mantle) [H]
The Dingle Inn is a friendly local next to a caravan and camping site. There is only one handpump so the real ale changes frequently, with regular customers selecting favourite beers from the local area and further afield. Narberth is a town with a distinctive community spirit, offering a range of specialist shops and facilities such as the award-winning museum that would be the envy of larger places. The railway station is a mile from the town.
♘✿🛏⛺⇌P🚌(381)

New Quay

Sea Horse Inn

Uplands Square, SA45 9QH
⏲ 11-midnight (1am Fri & Sat) ☎ (01545) 560736
2 changing beers (sourced nationally; often Kite, Young's) [H]
This characterful drinkers' hostelry, decorated with fascinating old photographs and cartoons, usually offers two real ales (perhaps just one at the quietest times), with three or more in summer, and runs a beer festival around the August bank holiday. One or two Westons ciders are now available all year round. The pub hosts a quiz night on Thursdays, poker on Sundays and open mic fortnightly. A small patio with benches can catch the sun. The generously filled crusty rolls, available while stocks last, are justly renowned.
♘✿⛺♣🍎🚌(T5)🐾📶

Newchapel

Ffynone Arms

SA37 0EH
⏲ 5-11; 1-1am Sat; 12-11 Sun ☎ (01239) 841800
🌐 ffynnonearms.co.uk
Greene King IPA; St Austell Tribute; 1 changing beer (sourced locally; often Mantle) [H]
A charming traditional 18th-century inn, recently tastefully refurbished. Local ales are often available, with regional and national beers at other times. Welsh cider Gwynt y Ddraig is also sold. The landlady prides herself on the food, offering gluten-free/dairy-free/sugar-free menus made with locally sourced ingredients where possible. Highlights include fish and chips on Wednesday evenings and the Sunday carvery of beef and pork. The Ffynone Arms sits near the borders of three counties – Pembrokeshire, Carmarthenshire and Ceredigion. Welsh and English are spoken.
Q♘✿◐♿♣🍎P🚌

Newport

Castle Inn [L]

Bridge Street, SA42 0TB
⏲ 11-midnight (1am Fri & Sat) ☎ (01239) 820742
🌐 castleinnnewport.co.uk
Felinfoel IPA, Double Dragon; Mantle Cwrw Teifi; Wye Valley Butty Bach; 2 changing beers (sourced regionally; often Mantle) [H]
Friendly, popular local in the characterful small town of Newport, halfway between Cardigan and

Fishguard, with an attractive bar featuring impressive wood panelling. Food is served lunchtimes and evenings in the dining area. Guest beers are local and regional. Beer and cider festivals are held in May and on the August bank holiday. A wealth of prehistoric remains adds interest to the many local walks which include a stretch of the Wales Coastal Path. An off-street car park is situated behind the hotel.
Q P (T5)

Golden Lion

East Street, SA42 0SY (on A487)
12-midnight (11 Sun) (01239) 820321
goldenlionpembrokeshire.co.uk
Bluestone Bedrock Blonde; Sharp's Doom Bar; Worthington's Bitter; 1 changing beer (sourced nationally; often Thwaites) H
Set in the Pembrokeshire Coast National Park and close to the Wales Coastal Path, the Golden Lion is another of Newport's sociable locals and is reputed to have its own resident ghost. A number of internal walls have been removed to create a spacious open-plan bar area, with distinct sections helping to retain a cosy atmosphere. Locally caught fish and Welsh Black beef are specialities, served in the bar and restaurant. Car parking space is available on the opposite side of the road.
Q P (T5)

Pembroke

Old King's Arms

Main Street, SA71 4JS
11-11 (01646) 683611 oldkingsarmshotel.co.uk
Felinfoel Double Dragon; Marston's Old Empire; 2 changing beers (sourced locally; often Bluestone, Evan Evans) H
This former coaching inn is allegedly the oldest in Pembroke, dating back to around 1520. The King's Bar, with four handpumps serving local, regional and national beers, is a small room with exposed stone walls, wood beams and a real fire. There is a separate lounge with a dining area, and a restaurant with space for larger groups. Meat and fish are locally sourced. Q P (349)

Pembroke Dock

First & Last

London Road, SA72 6TX (on A477)
10-1am (1.30am Thu-Sat) (01646) 682687
Brains Rev James; Worthington's Bitter; 1 changing beer (sourced nationally; often Skinner's) H
Friendly single-bar local run by the same family for 50 years. The walls display an eclectic mix of photos and prints. The guest beer can be from anywhere, local or national, and the food is good pub fare. There is a popular quirky Sunday evening quiz. Formerly the Commercial, the pub acquired its new name in 1991 to reflect its edge-of-town location. It is handy for the Cleddau Bridge, giving easy access to Haverfordwest, while Pembroke Dock has a historic naval dockyard and ferry services to Rosslare in Ireland.
Q P (349,356)

Station Inn

Hawkestone Road, SA72 6HN (in station building)
10.30-3, 6.30-11; 12-2.30, 7-11 Sun (01646) 621255
Brains Rev James; Courage Directors; 2 changing beers (sourced nationally; often Otter, Shed) H
Housed in the town's railway station where trains depart for Carmarthen, Swansea and, on summer Saturdays, far-off Paddington, this town-centre pub is close to both the Irish Ferries terminal and Pembrokeshire Coastal Path. Meals are excellent value (no lunches Mon, evening meals Wed-Sat only). Three real ales are generally on sale, with Young's Bitter a frequent visitor and a new beer every Tuesday. The June beer festival offers around 20 beers. Live music is hosted on Saturday evenings. P (349)

Pentrefelin

Cottage Inn

SA19 6SD (on A40, 3 miles W of Llandeilo)
12-11 (01558) 824645 cottageinnbandb.co.uk
Gower Gold; 2 changing beers (sourced locally) H
Warmed by a real fire, this popular family-run local community pub on the A40 dates back to the 1850s – it was formerly a coaching inn and a drovers' hostelry. There is Sky TV in the bar and the pub gets busy when major sporting events are screened. Two or three guest real ales are available. It has a separate restaurant/function room area, and a large covered smoking area at the rear. The large car park has caravanning and camping space. Q P (280,281)

Pontamman

Red Kite Inn

89 Pontamman Road, SA18 2JD (E of Ammanford on A474)
5 (12 Sat & Sun)-11 (01269) 597177
theredkiteinn.co.uk
St Austell Tribute; Wells Bombardier H
Returning to this Guide after more than 20 years, the former Perrivale Inn has reopened as the Red Kite (Barcud Coch), offering a local guest beer alongside its nationally known permanent ales. Live music and quiz nights make for a lively venue most weekends, but there are a number of quiet corners and a separate restaurant.
P (124)

Pontfaen

Dyffryn Arms ★

SA65 9SE (off B4313)
11-11 (01348) 881305
Draught Bass G
This much-loved pub, whose nationally important historic interior is a reminder of how country pubs must once have looked, is the hub of life in a secluded valley whose distinctive cultural traditions include a long history of farmhouse brewing. There is no bar counter – beers are still served by the jug through a sliding serving hatch. Conversation is the main form of entertainment. Featuring in the Guide for many years, this is a timeless gem to be treated with respect. Opening hours may vary depending on custom. Q P

Gwaun Valley Brewery Tap

Kilkiffeth Farm, SA65 9TP (on B4313 between Fishguard and Maenclochog)
11-6; 11-5.45, 7-midnight Fri & Sat; closed Sun
(01348) 881304 gwaunvalleybrewery.co.uk
Gwaun Valley Farmhouse Ale H**, Golden Bitter Ale, King of the Road** H/G

Family-run brewery set in the North Pembrokeshire countryside, with views to the Gwaun Valley and the Preseli Hills. Half the converted farm building that houses the brewery is used as a tasting area, function room and bar, open daytime every weekday and Friday and Saturday evenings. This relaxed and welcoming venue hosts acoustic music sessions every Saturday night. The brewery's full range of draught and bottle-conditioned beers is normally on offer. A holiday cottage has been added to the well-established on-site camping facility. QP

Porthyrhyd

Mansel Arms

Banc y Mansel, SA32 8BS (on B4310 between Porthyrhyd and Drefach)

5-11; 3-midnight Sat; 12-6 Sun ☎ (01267) 275305

2 changing beers (sourced nationally)

Friendly 18th-century former coaching inn with wood fires in each room. The original limestone flags have been broken up and used in the fireplace, and low beams have been added to create atmosphere, with numerous jugs hanging from them in the bar. Pool and darts are played in a room to the rear, which was originally used for slaughtering pigs. Beers are varied, with the Young's range always popular as well as local ales.
QP(129)

Prengwyn

Gwarcefel Arms

SA44 4LU (at A475/B4476 crossroads) SN424442

4-12.30am; 3-1.30am Fri & Sat; 4-8.30 Sun

☎ (01559) 363126 gwarcefel.co.uk

Sharp's Doom Bar; 1 changing beer (sourced nationally; often Evan Evans)

A traditional country inn with a friendly atmosphere, where everyone is welcome, including families and dogs. Situated at the junction of five roads in Prengwyn, three miles north of Llandysul, the pub has a main bar with a wood-burning stove, cosy seating, pool table and dartboard. A separate restaurant area, which caters for functions and parties, offers evening meals Thursdays to Saturdays. The beer garden and ample car park are to the rear. P

Pwlltrap

White Lion

SA33 4AT

12-11; 11-10.30 Sun ☎ (01994) 230370

Courage Directors; Greene King Abbot; Shepherd Neame Bishops Finger; Young's Bitter; 1 changing beer (sourced nationally)

This roadside pub, just outside St Clears on the road to Whitland, is warm and welcoming with a real fire in winter months. It has an old-world charm with oak beams and panelled walls, and boasts a large annexe restaurant with good food. Pool and darts are played and a large TV screen shows sporting fixtures. The pub organises a range of events throughout the year. Two cask beers are available in winter, four in summer.
Q(224,322)

Rhandirmwyn

Royal Oak

SA20 0NY SN80744884

12-2, 6-11 (10.30 Sun) ☎ (01550) 760201

theroyaloakinn.co.uk

3 changing beers

Remote, stone-flagged inn with excellent views of the Tywi Valley and close to an RSPB bird sanctuary. Originally built as a hunting lodge for the local landowner, it is now a focal point for community activities and popular with fans of outdoor pursuits. Two or three guest beers are offered and good wholesome food is served. There are panoramic views from the beer garden at the side of the pub. A four-time local CAMRA Pub of the Year, including in 2015. QP

Roch

Victoria Inn

SA62 6AW (on A487)

12-2.30, 5-11 Mon & Tue; 12-11 ☎ (01437) 710426

thevictoriainnroch.com

Black Sheep Ale; 3 changing beers (sourced nationally; often Evan Evans, Marston's)

Only one mile from the vast expanse of Newgale beach, which can be seen from the pub, this little gem is worth seeking out. Opened in 1851, it was reputedly a stop-off for drovers on their way home from market in Haverfordwest. Its low doorways and beamed ceilings, with a log fire in winter, create a warm atmosphere. A popular quiz night is held on Wednesdays, with curry-and-a-pint deals on Fridays. QP(411)

Rosebush

Tafarn Sinc

SA66 7QU

closed Mon; 12-11 ☎ (01437) 532214 tafarnsinc.co.uk

Worthington's Bitter; 1 changing beer (sourced nationally; often Long Man)

A Victorian hotel first established in 1876 as the Prescelly Hotel when the Clunderwen to Rosebush railway line opened. It closed in 1992 but was bought by a local couple, refurbished and renamed Tafarn Sinc, referring to its corrugated iron ('sinc' in Welsh) construction. Set amidst the scenic beauty of the Preseli mountains, the pub features strongly in the history and social life of the area and is full of old-world character and charm. P

St Davids

Farmers Arms

14-16 Goat Street, SA62 6RF (W of Cross Square, near cathedral)

4 (3 Fri)-midnight; 12-midnight Sat & Sun winter; 11-midnight summer ☎ (01437) 721666

farmersstdavids.co.uk

House beer (by Hancock's); 2 changing beers (sourced nationally; often Evan Evans, Sharp's, Wychwood)

A traditional city pub comprising three rooms – the top bar, mainly for dining, the smaller Coxswains room, which is the social meeting place for the St Davids lifeboat crew, and the Glue Pot bar, where the locals tend to gather around the fire. Outside the south-facing suntrap patio offers views of the cathedral and has a seasonal bar.
Q(411,413)

Solva

Cambrian Inn 𝕃
SA62 6UU (on A487 by bridge)
⏲ 12-3, 5.30-midnight; 12.30-3, 5.30-9.30 winter
☎ (01437) 721210 🌐 thecambrianinn.co.uk
Gwaun Valley King of the Road; 2 changing beers (sourced regionally; often Coles Family, Mantle) [H]
Set in the harbour village of Solva, this trendy modernised pub greets you as you come down the hill into the village from the east. The large bar offers comfortable seating for drinkers and diners. There are paintings from several local artists on the walls. The beers (two in winter and up to four in summer) come mainly from local and regional brewers. Food is locally sourced wherever possible.
Q🛏◑⛺P🚌(411)🐾📶

Talybont

White Lion (Llew Gwyn)
SY24 5ER
⏲ 12-midnight ☎ (01970) 832245
Banks's Mild, Bitter; Marston's Pedigree; 2 changing beers (sourced nationally; often Banks's, Ringwood) [H]
Set on the village green, this friendly community pub is the hub of village life. The main bar with its old slate floor, heated by a small solid-fuel stove, features an interesting local history display and is flanked by a rear bar and games room. Guest beers are from the Marston's group. Curry-and-a-pint deals are available on Thursdays. Evening and Sunday bus services are limited.
🧒❀🛏◑♿P🚌(T2,X28)🐾📶

Tenby

Hope & Anchor 𝕃
St Julian Street, SA70 7AS (between town centre and harbour)
⏲ 11-midnight (10.30 Sun) ☎ (01834) 842131
Sharp's Doom Bar, Atlantic; 4 changing beers (sourced regionally; often Bluestone, Mantle) [H]
Set in the old town on the way down to the harbour, this well-established pub offers a friendly welcome. Food is important here and a range of specials supplements the standard menu. The convivial atmosphere and interesting local décor make it an excellent place to relax over a beer. Up to four guests are sourced mainly from Welsh breweries, and sometimes also Wye Valley. The real ciders include Westons Old Rosie.
🧒❀◑⛺≷🍎P▯🚌(349)📶

Tregaron

Talbot 🏆
The Square, SY25 6JL
⏲ 9am-11 ☎ (01974) 298208 🌐 ytalbot.com
3 changing beers (sourced regionally; often Evan Evans, Mantle, Purple Moose) [H]
This former drovers' inn of immense character offers a public bar at the rear with TV, a small front lounge with an open fire, and a delightful beamed and flagstoned snug with inglenook fireplace. Three real ales in winter, four in summer, always include one from the Mantle Brewery, and a varying selection of cider and perry comes from Gwynt y Ddraig. Excellent locally sourced food includes good vegetarian options. The terrace drinking area has fine views and a memorial to a circus elephant reputedly buried here. Local CAMRA Pub of the Year 2015.
Q🧒❀🛏◑♿♣🍎P🚌(585,588)🐾📶

Whitland

Station House Hotel
St Johns Street, SA34 0AP
⏲ 9am-1am (2am Fri & Sat) ☎ (01994) 240556
Worthington's Bitter; 2 changing beers [H]
A smile and a warm welcome are always on tap at this friendly hostelry. Very much a local pub for all ages, there is something for everyone here, with pool and darts teams and bingo on Sunday evenings. A small separate room is available for people looking for a quiet corner. The pub is only 20 yards from the railway station. The outside drinking area is partly under cover.
❀◑≷♣🍎P🚌🐾📶

Royal Oak, Rhandirmwyn

Stein Inn, Skye, Highlands & Western Isles (p658)

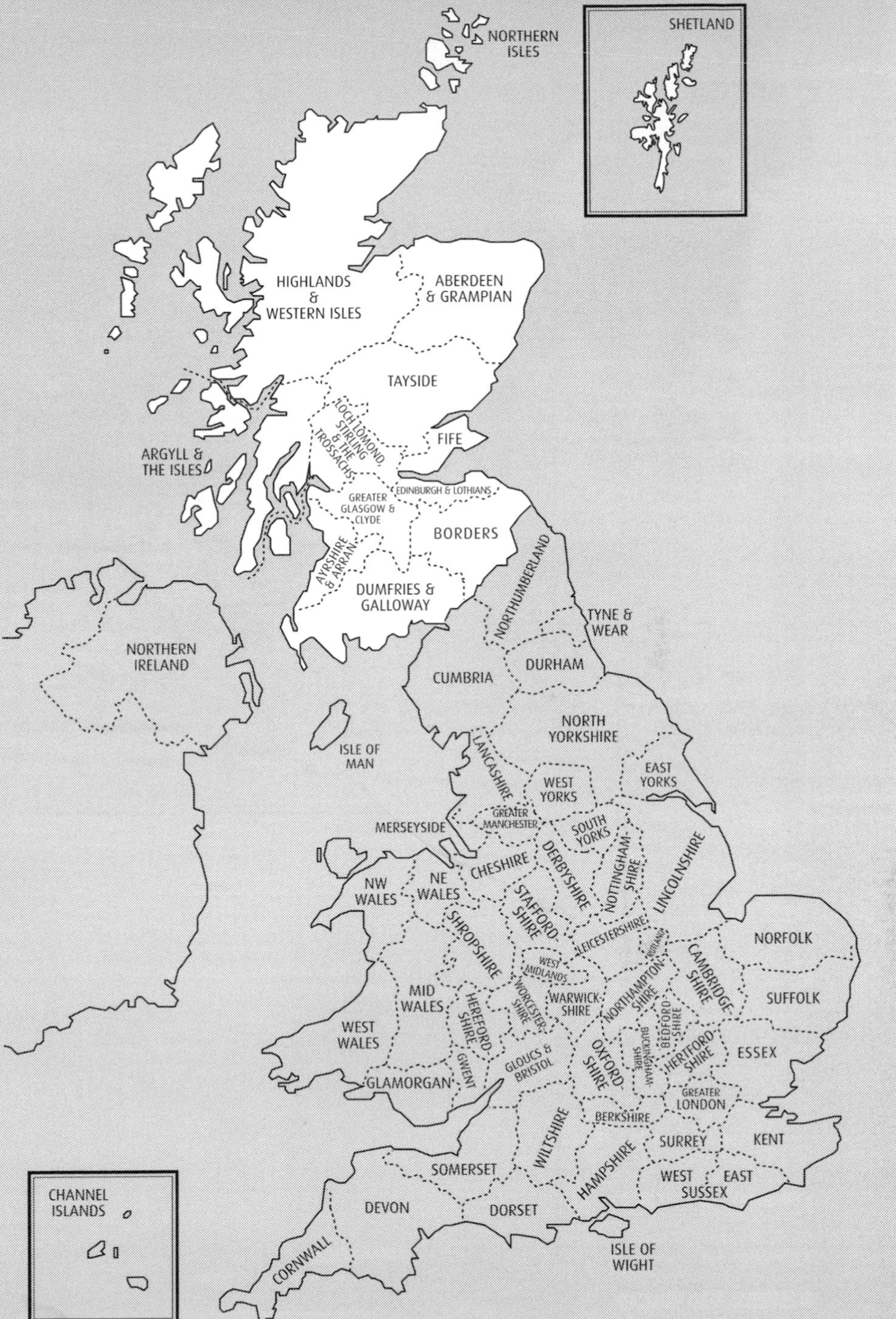
SHETLAND
NORTHERN ISLES
HIGHLANDS & WESTERN ISLES
ABERDEEN & GRAMPIAN
TAYSIDE
LOCH LOMOND, STIRLING & THE TROSSACHS
FIFE
ARGYLL & THE ISLES
EDINBURGH & LOTHIANS
GREATER GLASGOW & CLYDE
BORDERS
AYRSHIRE & ARRAN
DUMFRIES & GALLOWAY
NORTHUMBERLAND
TYNE & WEAR
NORTHERN IRELAND
DURHAM
CUMBRIA
ISLE OF MAN
NORTH YORKSHIRE
LANCASHIRE
WEST YORKS
EAST YORKS
GREATER MANCHESTER
MERSEYSIDE
SOUTH YORKS
CHESHIRE
DERBYSHIRE
NOTTINGHAMSHIRE
LINCOLNSHIRE
NW WALES
NE WALES
STAFFORDSHIRE
SHROPSHIRE
LEICESTERSHIRE
RUTLAND
NORFOLK
WEST MIDLANDS
CAMBRIDGESHIRE
NORTHAMPTONSHIRE
MID WALES
HEREFORDSHIRE
WORCESTERSHIRE
WARWICKSHIRE
SUFFOLK
BEDFORDSHIRE
BUCKINGHAMSHIRE
WEST WALES
GWENT
GLOUCS & BRISTOL
OXFORDSHIRE
HERTFORDSHIRE
ESSEX
GLAMORGAN
GREATER LONDON
BERKSHIRE
WILTSHIRE
SURREY
KENT
SOMERSET
HAMPSHIRE
WEST SUSSEX
EAST SUSSEX
CHANNEL ISLANDS
DEVON
DORSET
ISLE OF WIGHT
CORNWALL

Scotland

ABERDEEN & GRAMPIAN

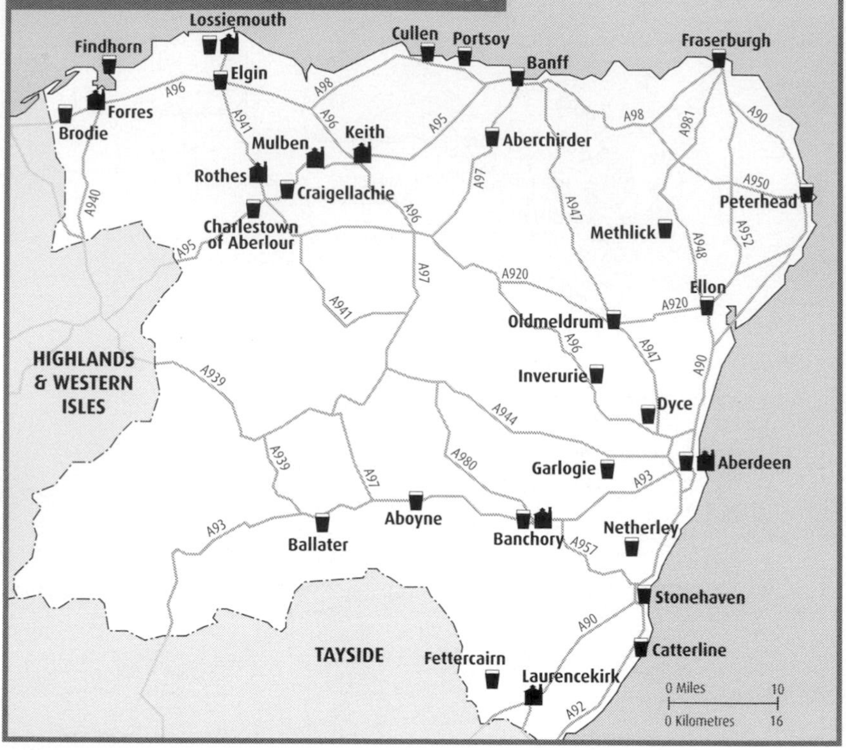

Authority areas covered: Aberdeenshire UA, City of Aberdeen UA, Moray UA

Aberchirder

New Inn

79 Main Street, AB54 7TB

12 (5 Mon)-12.30am; 12-11 Sun ☎ (01466) 780633

newinnaberchirder.co.uk

5 changing beers (sourced nationally; often Camerons, Orkney, Theakston) Ⓗ

The owner of this comfortable inn took over in 2011 and it has since gained a reputation for offering a changing selection of quality ales from UK-wide breweries. It has a cosy bar with different seating areas and a separate dining room and large function room at the rear. Children are welcome in the lounge until 9pm. Food is served Wednesday-Sunday lunchtimes and Tuesday-Sunday evenings. Q P (301)

Aberdeen

Aitchies Ale House

10 Trinity Street, AB11 5LY

8am-10 (11 Fri & Sat); closed Sun ☎ (01224) 575972

McEwan's IPA; Orkney Dark Island Ⓗ

This small corner bar is the closest real ale outlet to the city rail/bus stations and the Union Square shopping complex. Family owned, it retains the flavour of an old-fashioned Scottish pub with bar staff wearing traditional white aprons and service second to none. Bar food is best described as basic Scottish pub grub, including roast beef stovies. A good selection of whiskies includes Bell's special edition decanters. Q

Archibald Simpsons

5 Castle Street, AB11 5BQ (E end of Union St)

8am-midnight (1am Fri & Sat); 9am-11 Sun

☎ (01224) 621365

Caledonian Deuchars IPA; Greene King Abbot; changing beers (sourced regionally) Ⓗ

This Wetherspoon pub is in one of many monumental granite buildings in central Aberdeen designed by local architect Archibald Simpson. The former local headquarters of Clydesdale Bank, it retains many original architectural features. The main room is the high-ceilinged central hall, and there are additional seating areas to the side. The long bar features 12 handpumps offering a variety of beers, frequently from Scottish breweries. There is an outside drinking area on the pavement on Union Street corner.

Carriages

101 Crown Street, AB11 6HH (below Brentwood Hotel)

REAL ALE BREWERIES

Bottle Cap Aberdeen (NEW)
Brewmeister Keith
Burnside Laurencekirk
Deeside Banchory
Quiet Banchory (NEW)
Rothes Rothes (NEW)
six°north Laurencekirk
Spey Valley Mulben
Speyside Craft Forres
Windswept Lossiemouth

11-2.30, 4.30-midnight; 11-midnight Fri & Sat; 5.30-11 Sun
(01224) 595440 brentwood-hotel.co.uk
Caledonian Deuchars IPA; 7 changing beers (sourced regionally; often Highland, Orkney, Windswept) H
Mirrored downstairs bar in the basement of the modernised Brentwood Hotel, with lots of seating areas and comfortable couches. A winner of several local CAMRA awards, it offers eight changing beers, usually a mix of national brands and Scottish micro beers – tasters are offered if undecided. Lunches are available in the bar and the adjoining restaurant serves good food in the evening. Railway and bus stations are easily reached by descending the stairs from nearby Crown Terrace to Bridge Street.

Grill ★

213 Union Street, AB11 6BA
10-midnight (1am Fri & Sat); 12.30-midnight Sun
(01224) 573530 thegrillaberdeen.co.uk
Harviestoun Bitter & Twisted; 3 changing beers (sourced regionally; often Burnside, Fyne Ales, Windswept) H
With an exquisite interior redesigned in 1926 and remaining largely unchanged since, this is the only pub listed in CAMRA's National Inventory of Historic Pub Interiors in the area. For men only until 1975, a ladies' toilet was eventually provided in 1998. Directly opposite the Music Hall, musicians often visit during concert breaks. Guest ales are frequently from a variety of Scottish micros and the large selection of malts has won the pub several awards. Bar snacks are available.

Justice Mill

423 Union Street, AB11 6DA
8-midnight (1am Fri & Sat); 9am-11 Sun
(01224) 252410
Caledonian Deuchars IPA; Greene King Abbot; 2 changing beers (sourced nationally) H
Long, narrow, dark Wetherspoon outlet with raised seating near the bar and booths at both the main entrance and at the rear entrance on Justice Mill Lane. The quiet family-friendly daytime atmosphere changes to a loud maelstrom favoured by a younger clientele in the evenings, with DJs at weekends. The pub has two statement art pieces – a statue of an upside down man and a fire behind glass. Alcohol is available from 11am (12.30pm Sun).

Krakatoa

2 Trinity Quay, AB11 5AA (facing quayside at bottom of Market St)
1-midnight (3am Fri & Sat) (01224) 587602
Windswept Weizen; changing beers (sourced regionally; often Highland, Loch Ness, Windswept) A
Formerly known as the Moorings, this historic harbourside bar, recently refurbished, has a unique interior and a friendly, varied crowd of regulars. A wide selection of beers mainly from Scottish micros is served on up to 12 American-style fonts to the far left of the bar. There are also two similar banks dispensing various beers including Belgian ones. Live music plays every Friday and Saturday night, when there may be a cover charge. Multiple local CAMRA City Pub of the Year winner and current branch Pub of the Year.

Prince of Wales

7 St Nicholas Lane, AB10 1HF (lane opp Marks & Spencer)
10-midnight (1am Fri & Sat); 11-midnight Sun
(01224) 640597 princeofwales-aberdeen.co.uk
House beer (by Inveralmond, Greene King); 8 changing beers (sourced regionally; often Cromarty, Highland, Windswept) H
One of the oldest bars in Aberdeen with possibly the longest bar counter in the city, the Prince of Wales has a friendly atmosphere and a large following of regulars. Tasters are offered of the varied selection of Scottish and English ales, one of the two house beers, and others from the Greene King/Belhaven range. Folk music holds court on Sunday evenings and a prize quiz is hosted on Monday night. Listed in Scotland's True Heritage Pubs, this is a good venue with conversation the only background noise. Food is served until 9pm daily. Q

Six Degrees North

6 Littlejohn Street, AB10 1FF
11-midnight (1am Fri & Sat); 12.30-midnight Sun
(01224) 379192 sixdnorth.co.uk
3 changing beers (sourced regionally; often Cromarty, Six Degrees North) H
A conversion of part of the former college premises, this two-tiered establishment has an industrial décor with exposed granite and modern wooden benches. Upstairs, there is more seating on the balcony. A large blackboard displays the changing range of around 20 Belgian and several locally brewed ales plus a variety of cask beers. A vast range of bottled beers is also stocked. Beers are mostly served in two-third pint glasses. Live music features on the last Sunday afternoon of the month. Bar snacks are available. Q (20)

St Machar Bar

97 High Street, Old Aberdeen, AB24 3EN
11-11 (midnight Fri); 12.30-11 Sun (01224) 483079
themachar.com
Caledonian Deuchars IPA; 3 changing beers (sourced regionally) H
Located in the photogenic and historic Old Aberdeen conservation area amid the university buildings and close by Kings College, the pub is frequented by academia and locals alike. Guest beers, frequently from Scottish micros, are available alongside a comprehensive selection of whiskies. A splendid mirror from the defunct Thomson Marshall Aulton Brewery which was just down the street adorns the wall just inside the front door, and one from the original Devanha Brewery is outside the toilets. CAMRA members, students and OAPs receive a discount.
(20)

Under the Hammer

11 North Silver Street, AB10 1RJ (off Golden Square)
5-midnight (1am Thu); 4-1am Fri; 2-1am Sat; 6-midnight Sun (01224) 640253
Caledonian Deuchars IPA; Inveralmond Ossian; 1 changing beer (sourced regionally) H
Located in a quiet street just minutes off Union Street, this popular pub is in a basement next to an auction house (hence the name), and is convenient for the Music Hall and His Majesty's Theatre. Works by local artists on the walls are for sale if they take your fancy and a large noticeboard has posters advertising forthcoming and past events in town. Guest beers usually come from a wide variety of Scottish breweries including locals. Unobtrusive background music plays.

SCOTLAND

Aboyne

Boat Inn

Charleston Road, AB34 5EL (N bank of River Dee next to Aboyne Bridge)
11-11 (midnight Fri & Sat) (01339) 886137
theboatinnaboyne.co.uk
3 changing beers (sourced regionally) H
Popular riverside inn with a newly redecorated food-oriented lounge. Junior diners (and adults) may request to see the model train, complete with sound effects, traverse the entire pub at picture-rail height upon completion of their meal. The public bar has been extended, with a recess at the back for musicians on live music nights – twice-monthly on Thursday or Friday evenings. A quiz night is hosted monthly. The local Rotary Club regularly meets here. Self-catering accommodation is available including one room with full disabled facilities. Q P

Ballater

Alexandra Hotel

12 Bridge Square, AB35 5QJ
11-2.30, 5-midnight; 11-midnight Fri-Sun
(01339) 755376 alexandrahotelballater.co.uk
Cairngorm Trade Winds; 2 changing beers (sourced regionally; often Cairngorm, Inveralmond, Orkney) H
Originally built as a private home in 1800 and becoming the Alexandra Hotel in 1915, this smart and recently refurbished lounge bar is popular with locals for pub suppers and regular bar drinkers too. Handy for a stop-off on your way to Braemar for the Highland Games or for a visit with the royals at Balmoral, it is easily spotted when entering town from the east side with a prominent display of prior Guide entries. P

Glenaden Hotel

6 Church Square, AB35 5NE
11-1am (midnight Mon-Wed) (01339) 755488
2 changing beers (sourced regionally; often Burnside, Windswept) H
Situated on the far side of the town square, this small hotel displays a prominent external sign for its Barrel Lounge. It serves two beers, always Scottish, with Burnside fairly regular. Darker ales are apparently favoured by the locals and there are plans for more handpumps due to the exceptional demand for real ales from the regulars. An annual beer festival is held in the lounge area to the rear in the autumn. Q P

Banchory

Douglas Arms Hotel

22 High Street, AB31 5SR
11-midnight (1am Fri & Sat); 12-midnight Sun
(01330) 822547 douglasarms.co.uk
Cairngorm Trade Winds; 2 changing beers H
Small hotel with three separate bars and rooms, two of which have plasma TVs where different sports can be watched. The public bar (usually open from 3pm) is a classic Scottish long bar, with etched windows and vintage mirrors, and is featured in CAMRA's Scotland's True Heritage Pubs. The recently refurbished adjacent lounge is a snug area and a separate lounge/diner, and is primarily used for bar suppers. To the rear is a large south-facing decking space, ideal for fair-weather drinking. Q

Ravenswood Club (Royal British Legion)

25 Ramsay Road, AB31 5TS (up Mount St from A93, then second right)
11-11 (midnight Fri & Sat) (01330) 822347
bancharylegion.com
2 changing beers H
Large British Legion club with a comfortable lounge adjoining the pool and TV room and a spacious function room well-used by local clubs and societies as well as members. Darts and snooker are popular and played most evenings. The two handpumps offer excellent value and the beer choice is constantly changing, with ales consistently the best quality in the village. An elevated terrace has fine views of the Deeside hills. Show a copy of this Guide or your CAMRA membership card for entry. P

Banff

Ship Inn

8 Deveronside, AB45 1HP (on seafront near harbour)
12-midnight (1am Fri & Sat) (01261) 812620
Wells Bombardier; 1 changing beer (sourced nationally) H
The interior of this historic nautical-themed inn featured in the film Local Hero. It has a wood-panelled bar and lounge with sea views through the small windows and a fine view across the Deveron mouth to Macduff. A blocked carriage arch hints at the earlier history of the building. Banff Marina, Duff House Gallery (National Gallery of Scotland) and Macduff Aquarium are close by, as are several golf courses. Karaoke and live music feature at weekends. Occasionally the regulars will choose another beer to replace the Bombardier.

Brodie

Old Mill Inn

IV36 2TD (A96 between Forres and Nairn)
11.30-11; 11.45-11 Sun (01309) 641605
oldmillinnbrodie.com
5 changing beers (sourced regionally; often Highland, Speyside Craft, Windswept) H
This gem is a spacious, family-friendly pub-restaurant with a cosy fireside area, smart restaurant, function room and a charming conservatory with views of the old watermill and garden. Up to five ales are available, mainly from Scottish micros including local breweries. An excellent range of meals is offered with specials changing on a daily basis. Live Scottish/Irish instrumental music plays on Sunday evening. Brodie Castle is nearby and the popular Brodie Countryfare is opposite. A beer festival is held in June. A former local CAMRA Country Pub of the Year. Q P (10,11)

Catterline

Creel Inn

AB39 2UL (on coast off A92, five miles south of Stonehaven)
closed Mon Nov-Feb; 12-2, 5.30-midnight (1am Fri); 12-1am Sat; 12-midnight Sun (01569) 750254
thecreelinn.co.uk
4 changing beers (sourced regionally; often Cairngorm, Inveralmond, Stewart Brewing) H

Set in a scenic cliff-top location, the view from the rear garden of this small village inn is not to be missed. Catterline is known as an artists' village, the most famous being Joan Eardley – one of her paintings is on display in the pub along with other artists' work. The Creel is primarily a food venue but the bar area serves as the village local with up to four beers on offer, usually from Scottish micros. Todhead Lighthouse, Crawton Bird Sanctuary and Kinneff Old Church are nearby. Q ♣ P

Charlestown of Aberlour

Mash Tun

8 Broomfield Square, AB38 9QP (signed from village square)
12-12.30am (1am Fri & Sat); 12.30-12.30am Sun
(01340) 881771 mashtun-aberlour.com
2 changing beers (sourced locally; often Cairngorm, Spey Valley) H
Situated near the River Spey and the Speyside Way, this pub is popular with locals and visitors to the area. The owners have a passion for good food and whisky sourced from the many local distilleries. The pub can be busy during local whisky festival events held in the bar. There is a complete collection of Glenfarclas family cask whisky in a glass case. Once the Station Bar, if a train ever arrived at Aberlour Station, its name would revert back to this. P (36)

Craigellachie

Highlander Inn

10 Victoria Street, AB38 9SR (A95, opp Post Office)
12-11 (01340) 881446 whiskyinn.com
Cairngorm Trade Winds; 1 changing beer H
One of the top whisky bars in the world and popular with tourists and lovers of the malt alike, the Highlander can be busy during whisky festivals and the tourist season. An outside decked area with tables and chairs is a delight on a sunny afternoon for dining and drinking. CRAC (Craigellachie Real Ale Club) meets here on the first Wednesday of the month. The bar serves locally sourced food and opens longer hours Easter to September. Q ♣ P (36)

Cullen

Three Kings

17-21 North Castle Street, AB56 4SA
closed Mon & Tue; 5-11 Wed; 12-2, 5-12.30am Thu-Sat; 12-2, 5-11 Sun (01542) 840031
3 changing beers (sourced regionally; often Cairngorm, Orkney, Windswept) H
Situated close to an impressive but now defunct railway viaduct, this small, family-run pub was converted over 40 years ago from 150-year-old railway workers' cottages. A low-beamed roof and real fire help to create a cosy atmosphere on colder days. There is a separate restaurant to the rear and a large outdoor drinking area complete with pétanque courts. Up to three beers are served, mainly from Scottish micros. Q (35)

Dyce

Granite City

Main Terminal, Aberdeen Airport, AB21 7DU
6 (8 Sat)-10; 8-9 Sun (01224) 725711
Sharp's Doom Bar; 4 changing beers (sourced nationally) H
In the main terminal of Aberdeen Airport, close to the entrance, this Wetherspoon bar is popular with airport staff, travellers and offshore workers. The walls display informative framed photographs of local personalities including 'The Scottish Samurai' Thomas Blake Glover – one of the prime movers of Japan's industrialisation in the late 19th century. An extensive outdoor area features the Baby Boar, a sculpture carved from a one-ton boulder of local Kemnay granite. (27,727)

Elgin

Drouthy Cobbler

Shepherd's Close, 48A High Street, IV30 1BU
8am-12.30am (1.30am Fri & Sat) (01343) 553933
thedrouthycobbler.co.uk
3 changing beers (sourced regionally) H
Smart, long and narrow bar opened after extensive refurbishment in 2013. The venue's name is a tribute to John Shanks, who was a shoemaker and an important figure in the conservation of Elgin Cathedral. Sponsored by local gentleman Isaac Forsyth, Shanks was officially appointed Keeper and Watchman in 1826. Food is now available since the recent kitchen refurbishment, and good coffee and cakes are served. Three ales come from Scottish micros and a large and constantly increasing whisky collection is stocked. Alcohol is served from 11am. Q

Muckle Cross

34 High Street, IV30 1BU
8am-midnight (1am Fri) (01343) 559030
Greene King Abbot; 4 changing beers (sourced regionally; often Isle of Skye) H
A small, deservedly popular Wetherspoon pub in a former bicycle repair shop with friendly, efficient staff. The long, pleasant room has ample seating, including a family area. Eight handpumps offer a wide range of beers from national and Scottish micros. The pub also stocks a good choice of malt whiskies from more than 20 local distilleries. An extensive menu features healthy options as well as pub grub. Open from 8am for breakfast, alcohol is served from 11am. Q

Ellon

Tolbooth

21-23 Station Road, AB41 9AE
12-11 (midnight Thu; 12.30am Fri & Sat); 12.30-11.30 Sun
(01358) 721308
Greene King Abbot; 2 changing beers (sourced regionally; often Fyne Ales, Orkney) H
A large pub, popular with all ages, close to the centre of the town and recently refurbished. There are separate seating areas on split levels as well as an airy conservatory. The range of ales depends on availability, but tends to focus on national brands, but not to the exclusion of Scottish micros. Several National Trust Scotland properties are nearby. No food is served. ♣

Fettercairn

Ramsay Arms

Burnside Road, AB30 1XX
12-3, 5.30-11; 12-11.30 Fri & Sat; 12.30-11 Sun
(01561) 340334 ramsayarmshotel.co.uk

SCOTLAND

Inveralmond Ossian, Thrappledouser
In the shadow of the Victoria Commemorative Arch, erected in recognition of the Queen's first trip to the north-east of Scotland, when she spent the night in the hotel, its Victorian heritage lends itself to the cuisine in the open, modern lounge. Close to Fasque Estate, residence of Sir William Gladstone, and near to the visitor centre at the Fettercairn distillery. May close at 10pm in winter if few customers P

Findhorn

Kimberley Inn

94 Findhorn, IV36 3YG
12-midnight (01309) 690492 kimberleyinn.com
2 changing beers (sourced regionally; often Cairngorm, Houston, Orkney)
Self-styled as 'Moray's Seafood Pub', the Kimberley is situated right on the shore of Findhorn Bay in a charming seaside village with a fine stretch of beach. The wood-panelled interior includes a family room, a snug with splendid views of the hills across the Moray Firth, and the bar with an excellent open log fire. Two ales (one in winter) are mainly from Scottish micros. The extensive menu features home-cooked food, especially local seafood, and local ice cream. Q P

Fraserburgh

Elizabethan Bar & Lounge

36 Union Grove, AB43 9PH
9.30am (11 Sun)-1am (01346) 515148
3 changing beers (often Cairngorm, Kelburn)
Set in the middle of a housing estate and near the local Academy, with a mock-Tudor exterior, the large bar and lounge have three distinct sections, with sport on TV in two of them. The bar has featured more than 600 different ales over the past few years, as well as over 200 malts – the largest collection in the area. A former CAMRA Pub of the Year and a recent winner of the SLTN Beer Quality Award.

Garlogie

Garlogie Inn

AB32 6RX
closed Mon winter; 11-2.30, 5-10.30 (11 Fri & Sat); 12.30-9 Sun (01224) 743212 garlogieinn.com
1 changing beer (sourced nationally; often Deeside)
This roadside inn dating from the early-19th century has been run by the Quinn family for nearly 30 years. Numerous extensions have been added to the original building, including a large restaurant area, and the pub has a reputation for excellent food (booking advised). Drinkers are welcome in the small bar area, with a single pump dispensing a beer usually from a Scottish brewery, or occasionally an English one. Drum Castle and Cullerlie Stone Circle are close at hand.
Q P (210)

Inverurie

Gordon Highlander

West High Street, AB51 3QQ
9am-11.30 (1am Fri & Sat) (01462) 626780
Caledonian Deuchars IPA; Greene King Abbot; 3 changing beers (sourced nationally)
A Wetherspoon pub in a splendid Art Deco building which used to be the Victoria Cinema. The name refers to the famous local regiment, and also to a preserved steam engine named after the regiment, which was based at the now defunct Inverurie Locomotive Works nearby. Both historical references are documented in various displays. The books on the shelves are free to read and take home, with donations welcome. The usual Wetherspoon beer festivals feature. Alcohol is served from 11am. (10,37)

Lossiemouth

Skerry Brae Hotel

Stotfield Road, IV31 6QS
12-11 (midnight Fri & Sat) (01343) 812040
skerrybrae.co.uk
Windswept Blonde, APA; 2 changing beers (sourced locally)
Modern hotel and lounge bar, refurbished in 2012 after an uncertain future, with commanding views across the championship golf course, West Beach and the Moray Firth – ideal for sunny days at the coast which can be viewed from the deck and large conservatory. At least two ales from the local Windswept Brewing are usually available alongside a decent selection of malt whiskies. Hearty food is served all day, every day.
Q P (33A,33C)

Methlick

Ythanview Hotel

Main Street, AB41 7DT
11-2.30, 5-11 (1am Fri); 11-12.30am Sat; 12-11 Sun (01651) 806235 ythanviewhotel.co.uk
2 changing beers (sourced regionally; often Fyne Ales, Highland)
Traditional inn in the village centre, home to the Methlick Cricket Club. Log fires warm both the lounge and the friendly sports-themed public bar at the rear. The pub is renowned for the owner Jay's special whole chilli curry, and steak night on Thursday is also popular. Bands play on some Saturdays and quiz nights are hosted. Beers are exclusively from Scottish micros. Haddo House, Tolquhon Castle and Pitmedden Garden are nearby.
P

Netherley

Lairhillock Inn

AB39 3QS (signed off B979, 3 miles S of B9077)
11-11 (midnight Fri & Sat) (01569) 730001
lairhillock.co.uk
Timothy Taylor Landlord; 3 changing beers (sourced regionally)
The INN sign on the roof of this rambling building in attractive open countryside makes it easy to spot from the road. It has a traditional wood-panelled bar warmed by a large log fire in winter, and a lounge with an open fireplace and a large conservatory area, popular for dining. A separate function room, the Crynoch, is also available. Three guest beers (two in winter) are frequently sourced from Scottish breweries. Convenient for the attractions of Stonehaven and Royal Deeside.
Q P

Oldmeldrum

Redgarth Hotel

Kirk Brae, AB51 0DJ (outskirts of village, signpost off A947)
11-3, 5-11 (midnight Fri & Sat); 12-3, 5-11 Sun
(01651) 872353 redgarth.com
3 changing beers (sourced regionally; often Cromarty, Highland, Kelburn) H/G
This renowned local hotel and pub has imposing views over the eastern Grampian mountains. A winner of many local CAMRA awards, it retains a strong reputation for its imaginative choice of beers, sourced from, among others, Timothy Taylor and many Scottish micros. A successful blend of popular family restaurant and marvellous real ale pub, it is appreciated by a dedicated core of regulars. During occasional Brewers in Residence evenings, three handpumped ales may be supplemented by many more on gravity.
Q P

Peterhead

Cross Keys

23-27 Chapel Street, AB42 1TH
8am-11 (midnight Thu; 1am Fri & Sat) (01779) 483500
Caledonian Deuchars IPA; Greene King Abbot; 6 changing beers (sourced nationally) H
A typical Wetherspoon outlet located in the centre of a bustling port, close to the local museum, where you can learn about the town's maritime history. The pub is named after the chapel dedicated to St Peter that previously stood on the site. The long single-room interior has the bar, with eight handpulls, towards the front and a large seating area to the rear. A sheltered and heated area outside caters for hardy souls and smokers. Children are welcome until 8pm if dining.
Q (260,263)

Portsoy

Shore Inn

Church Street, AB45 2QR (overlooking harbour)
11-11 (midnight Thu; 1am Fri & Sat); 1-1am Sun
(01261) 842831
2 changing beers (sourced regionally; often Cairngorm, Windswept) H
This ancient 18th-century coastal inn situated on the oldest harbour on the Moray coast exudes an old-time atmosphere with its low ceilings and dark wooden bar fittings. Up to two ales are stocked (only one off-season). The village hosts an annual boat festival in early July with an outside bar and additional beers on offer. Meal service times vary according to the season – phone ahead to check.

Stonehaven

Marine Hotel

9-10 Shorehead, AB39 2JY (overlooking harbour)
11-midnight (1am Fri & Sat) (01569) 762155
marinehotelstonehaven.co.uk
Six Degrees North Prototype; Timothy Taylor Landlord; 4 changing beers (sourced regionally; often Cromarty, Strathaven, Windswept) H
This small harbourside hotel features a bar with simple wood panelling, a rustic lounge with an open fireplace and an upstairs restaurant. Seating outside offers a splendid view of the harbour. Guest ales are mostly sourced from Scottish breweries, with something from sister brewery Six Degrees North (now relocated to Laurencekirk). Also on sale are several draught Belgian beers and a massive choice of bottled Belgian beers. Historic Dunnottar Castle is one mile south. Multiple winner of CAMRA branch Pub of the Year and Country winner 2014 and 2015.

Ship Inn

5 Shorehead, AB39 2JY (on harbour front)
11-midnight (1am Fri & Sat) (01569) 762617
shipinnstonehaven.com
2 changing beers (sourced regionally; often Cairngorm, Inveralmond) H
Built in 1771, this harbourfront hotel has a maritime-themed, wood-panelled bar and a seating area outside overlooking the water. A mirror from the long defunct Devanha Brewery features prominently. A modern restaurant with panoramic harbour views is adjacent to the bar, with food served all day at the weekend. An extensive range of malt whiskies is stocked. Accommodation is available in 11 guest rooms.

SCOTLAND

Archibald Simpsons, Aberdeen (Photo: David Webb)

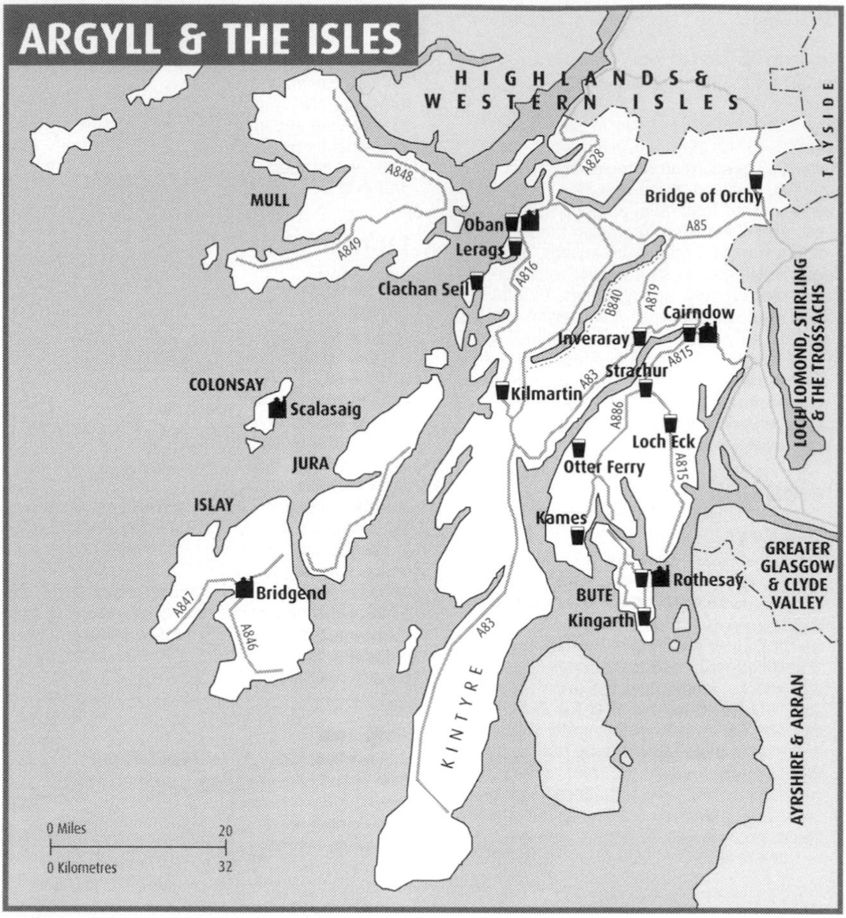

Authority area covered: Argyll & Bute UA

Bridge of Orchy

Bridge of Orchy Hotel

PA36 4AD

11-10.45 (11.45 Fri & Sat) ☎ (01838) 400208
bridgeoforchy.co.uk

Harviestoun Bitter & Twisted; 2 changing beers (sourced regionally) H

Situated on the A82 road to Glencoe and Fort William and with a nearby rail station, this remote hotel is surprisingly accessible. The comfortably furnished bar has three handpumps and the terrace offers impressive views of Glen Orchy and the surrounding mountain scenery. Food and accommodation options are of a high standard. The hotel is just by the West Highland Way which makes it a convenient resting place for walkers. Many other outdoor activities can be found nearby.
P (914)

Cairndow

Fyne Ales Brewery Tap

PA26 8BJ (up side road at head of Loch Fyne)

10-6 ☎ (01499) 600120 fyneales.com/brewery-tap

Fyne Ales Jarl; 4 changing beers (sourced locally; often Fyne Ales) H

The brewery tap and shop opened in 2012 in what was originally a farm building. The bar, with its fine polished granite front, supports five handpumps selling a range of ales from the brewery, along with a full and varied selection of bottled beers. Meat produced on the farm is available to buy and also used to fill the excellent pies. For fine weather there is a courtyard overlooking the brewery.
Q P

Stagecoach Inn L

PA26 8BN (on slip road off A83)

11-11 (1am Fri & Sat); 11-midnight Sun
☎ (01499) 600286 cairndowinn.com

2 changing beers (often Fyne Ales, Loch Lomond) H

Old inn nestling in tall trees beside Loch Fyne at the foot of Glen Kinglas, used as a resting place before the long ascent over the A83 Rest and Be Thankful. The restaurant, converted from stables, enjoys fine views over the loch and leads through an arch to

REAL ALE BREWERIES

Argyll Oban
Bute Isle of Bute: Rothesay (NEW)
Colonsay Scalasaig:Isle of Colonsay
Fyne Cairndow
Islay Bridgend: Isle of Islay

the friendly bar and games room. Two beers are available, one in winter, and good food is served until 9pm. Check for winter opening times.
P (926,976)

Clachan Seil

Tigh an Truish Inn

PA34 4QZ
11 (12 Sun)-11 (01852) 300242 tigh-an-truish.co.uk
3 changing beers (sourced nationally; often Fyne Ales, Orkney)
This attractive rural inn is worth leaving the A816 for en route to visit Seil Island. Twice winner of local CAMRA Argyll Pub of the Year, it has up to three Scottish beers on handpump, often from local Fyne Ales. In summer the sheltered sunny garden and front patio offer pleasant settings and views of Telford's architecturally aesthetic Clachan Bridge. The bar room has rustic wooden furniture and an iron stove. Meals, available only in the summer, are served in the bar and separate dining room.
Q P (418)

Inveraray

George Hotel

Main Street East, PA32 8TT
11 (12 Sun)-midnight (01499) 302111
thegeorgehotel.co.uk
2 changing beers
Located in the charming planned town of Inveraray, which can get busy with tourists, the George has been owned by the same family for six generations. Two beers come mostly from Fyne Ales. The main lounge tends to be popular with visitors while locals prefer the rear public bar. Live blues, folk and rock feature on Friday and Saturday evenings. High-quality bar food and a tempting whisky list are also on offer at this great traditional pub. Q P (926,976)

Kames

Kames Hotel

PA21 2AF
12-midnight (01700) 811489 kames-hotel.com
Fyne Ales Highlander; 1 changing beer (sourced locally; often Fyne Ales)
Historic hotel, full of character, looking down on a small harbour and with stunning views across the Kyles to Bute and beyond. The friendly and lively bar is popular with locals and visitors from both land and sea – 15 moorings are freely available. The meals are freshly prepared and sourced locally where possible, as are the real ales, usually from Fyne Ales. (477,478)

Kilmartin

Kilmartin Hotel

PA31 8RQ (on A816 10 miles N of Lochgilphead)
12 (5 winter)-11; 11-1am Fri; 11-midnight Sat; 12-11 Sun
(01546) 510250 kilmartin-hotel.com
3 changing beers (often Loch Lomond, Orkney)
Whitewashed hotel sitting on a promontory overlooking Kilmartin Glen and many sites of historic and religious significance. The small bar with its fireside nook offers up to three real ales, often from Loch Lomond or Orkney breweries. The games room at the back opens on to a beer garden and leads to a restaurant to one side. Good-quality food from both bar and restaurant menus is available lunchtimes and evenings.
P (423)

Kingarth

Kingarth Hotel

Isle of Bute, PA20 9LU (on A844 at jct for turn-off to Kilchattan)
12-midnight (01700) 831662 kingarthhotel.co.uk
2 changing beers (sourced nationally)
A comfortable, cosy country inn set in a secluded location a short walk from Kilchattan Bay on the lovely isle of Bute. Good food is mostly sourced from local ingredients and can be enjoyed in the Smiddy Bar, converted from a blacksmith's barn, alfresco on the front patio or on the covered verandah at the rear while enjoying the local Bute ale. In winter a woodburner adds to the warm ambience. Always worth the journey.
P (490)

Lerags

Barn

PA34 4SE
12-11; closed Mon-Thu winter (01631) 564618
cologin.co.uk/country-inn
Fyne Ales Highlander; 1 changing beer (sourced regionally)
Lerags Glen offers an escape from the beaten track, with attractive hill walks, fishing and coastal scenery. The family-friendly Barn is an ideal place to stop for refreshments, with a Fyne Ale, usually Highlander, available, and food served all day from a varied menu in the bar/restaurant. There are outside areas for drinking and for children to play. Well worth a detour from the A816 Oban road, but telephone ahead to check opening hours in winter.
Q P

Loch Eck

Coylet Inn

PA23 8SG (on A815 6 miles N of Dunoon)
12-11 (01369) 840426 thecoyletinn.co.uk
2 changing beers (sourced locally)
An attractive 17th-century coaching inn set among trees on the shores of Loch Eck. Situated in Argyll Forest Park, it makes an ideal base for exploring the hills, and fishing permits are available for anglers. After a day outdoors, the small comfortable bar, warmed by a log fire, is a welcome place to enjoy the two real ales which are usually sourced locally. Excellent meals also feature local ingredients. There is a mini beer festival in October. P (484,486)

Oban

Corryvreckan

The Waterfront Centre, Railway Pier, PA34 4LW
11-midnight (1am Fri & Sat); 12-midnight Sun
(01631) 568910
Caledonian Deuchars IPA; Greene King Abbot; house beer (by Strathaven); 9 changing beers
Large, smart, modern Wetherspoon pub situated at the southern end of Oban Bay, conveniently adjacent to the train station and ferry terminal. The single, spacious room has windows offering views over the bay to watch the numerous ferries come and go. The decor has a nautical theme, with wood

used extensively on the walls and ceiling – look for the carved statue of an eagle. Twelve handpumps offer guest beers including some from local breweries and others from further afield.

Otter Ferry

Oystercatcher

PA21 2DH (on B8000 E coast of Loch Fyne)
closed Mon-Fri; 5-11 Sat; 12.30-5 Sun winter; 11-11 summer (01700) 821229 theoystercatcher.co.uk
2 changing beers (sourced nationally)
Attractive pub on the beach by a former ferry dock, forming part of the Argyll Secret Coast on the eastern side of Loch Fyne. The bar and lounge feature real fires, comfortable chairs and two handpumps serving mainly Scottish beers, particularly from Fyne Ales. The quality food menu offers local seafood and other local produce. There are 15 moorings available to motor vessels, RIBS and yachtsmen, who are advised to take note of the mile-long Otter Spit. P

Rothesay

Black Bull Inn

West Princes Street, PA20 9AF (opp harbour)
11-11 (midnight Fri & Sat); 12.30-11 Sun
(01700) 502366
2 changing beers (sourced regionally)
An ever-popular establishment in the centre of town close to the harbour, approached via the splendid Wemyss Bay rail station and the ferry. A fine example of Victorian toilets is close by. This two-bar pub, always popular with yachtsmen, is ideally situated as a meeting point for food and ale for visitors heading to all corners of the island. One of the two real ales comes from the Bute Beer Co nearby.

Strachur

Creggans Inn

PA27 8BX (on A815 at N end of village)
11 (12 Sun)-11 (01369) 860279 creggans-inn.co.uk
2 changing beers (sourced locally; often Fyne Ales)
This historic inn sits on the shores of Loch Fyne. The cosy MacPhunn's bar, warmed by a log fire, is named after a local laird who was hung in Inverary but revived while being rowed home. It is home to the local shinty team. Meals prepared from local produce are served in the dining room and a separate bistro menu is available in the bar. The two real ales are usually from nearby Fyne Ales.
QP(484,486)

George Hotel, Inveraray

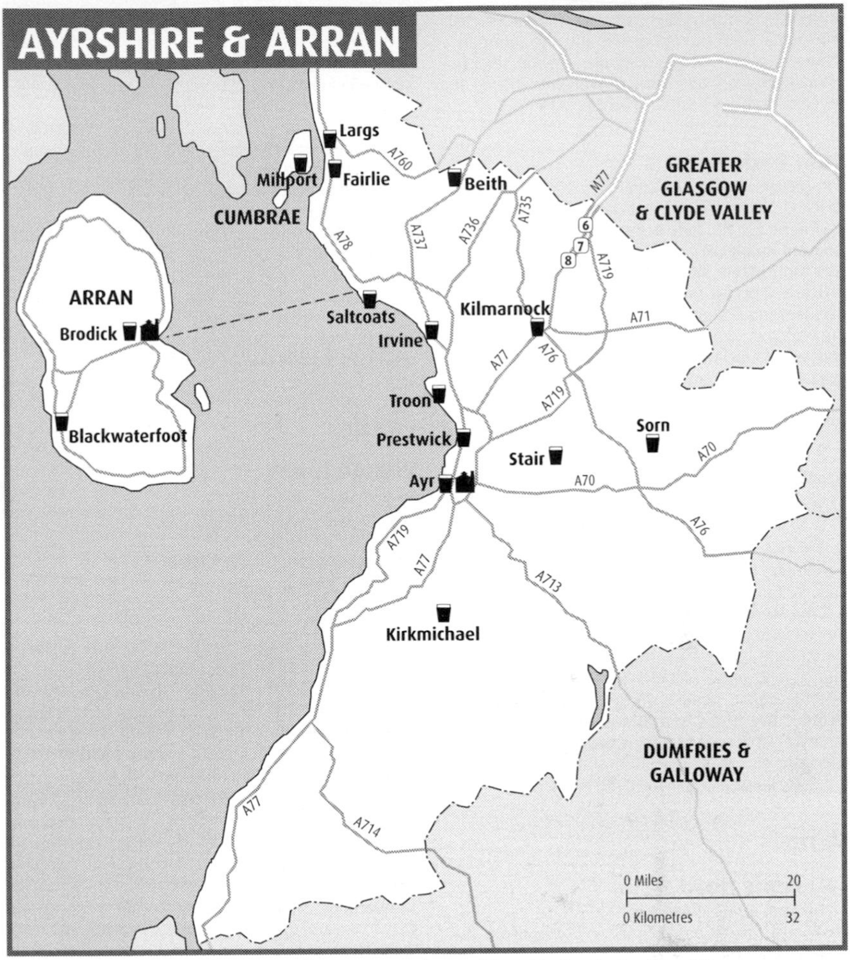

Authority areas covered: East Ayrshire UA, North Ayrshire UA, South Ayrshire UA

Ayr

Abbotsford Hotel

14 Corsehill Road, KA7 2ST

10-12.30am; 12-midnight Sun (01292) 261506

abbotsfordhotel.co.uk

Caledonian Deuchars IPA; 2 changing beers (sourced nationally; often Marston's) H

This family-run hotel, in a residential area south of the town centre, is convenient for the seafront, local golf courses, Burns-related attractions and other delights of the area. Three handpumps dispense the real ales in the aptly named Copper Bar. The guest beers are usually from larger English breweries. Meals are served in both the bar and a separate restaurant area (booking advised). There is also a pool/TV room and a function room/conservatory. P (57,361)

Chestnuts Hotel

52 Racecourse Road, KA7 2UZ (on A719, 1 mile S of centre)

10-11 (12.30am Fri & Sat) (01292) 264393

chestnutshotel.com

3 changing beers (sourced nationally; often Greene King, Kelburn) H

Three changing real ales from both local and larger regional breweries are on offer in The 19th Hole at this well-appointed family-run hotel. The bar itself is a focal point for locals and tourists and features golfing prints and memorabilia, discreet seating around a cosy log fire and a vaulted ceiling that holds a record-breaking collection of whisky water jugs. High-quality meals are served in the bar and the separate restaurant. There is plenty of seating in the garden. P (9)

Geordie's Byre

103 Main Street, KA8 8BU (N of centre, over river towards Prestwick)

11-11 (midnight Thu-Sat); 12.30-11 Sun

(01292) 264925

4 changing beers (sourced nationally; often Fyne Ales, Rooster's) A

This CAMRA award-winning 18th-century pub, located in the Newton area of Ayr, serves up to four guest ales, sourced from far and wide. It is one

REAL ALE BREWERIES

Arran Brodick: Isle of Arran
Ayr Ayr

of the few Scottish pubs using traditional Scottish tall founts. Both the public bar and the lounge feature a wealth of memorabilia. A wide selection of malt whiskies and rums is available. Handy for several local bus routes. Q🖵(2,4,14)🐾

Glen Park Hotel 𝕃

5 Racecourse Road, KA7 2DG
✪ 10 (12 Sun)-midnight ☎ (01292) 263891
Ayr Leezie Lundie, Jolly Beggars; 2 changing beers (sourced locally) ℍ
This comfortable lounge bar, in an attractive 1860s B-Listed Victorian building, is the brewery tap for Ayr Brewing Company which brews in the rear of the building. The guest beers are from Ayr Brewing and usually include a seasonal. Ayr beers are also available to take away. Bar and restaurant meals are available daily except Monday.
🛏🏵🍴◖🕭♿P🚌🖵(9)🐾🐾📶

Wellingtons Bar

17 Wellington Square, KA7 1EZ
✪ 11-12.30am; 12-midnight Sun ☎ (01292) 262794
⊕ welliesbar.weebly.com
3 changing beers (sourced regionally; often Fyne Ales, Kelburn) ℍ
A large Wellington boot advertises the location of this basement bar. Close to the seafront, bus station and local government offices, it attracts tourists and office workers alike. The Wednesday evening quiz is popular and weekend music includes live music or a DJ on Saturdays and an acoustic session on Sunday evenings. The three changing ales usually include at least one from either Kelburn or Fyne Ales. ◖🚲🖵🐾📶

Beith

Saracen's Head Hotel ♟

12 Eglinton Street, KA15 1AQ
✪ 11-11; 10-1am Fri; 9am-1am Sat; 10-midnight Sun
☎ (01505) 502329
2 changing beers (sourced locally; often Kelburn) ℍ
A welcome addition to an area poorly served with real ale, this historic town-centre pub is lively at weekends. Satellite TV caters for the sports enthusiast, along with pool and darts. A varied food menu is always available, prepared at the adjoining takeaway establishment. An outdoor seating area has pleasant views over the Garnock Valley. The pub is accessible by bus from several directions. CAMRA branch Pub of the Year 2014.
🏵🍴◖♿♣🖵(X34,X36,904)📶

Blackwaterfoot: Isle of Arran

Kinloch Hotel

KA27 8ET
✪ 12-midnight ☎ (01770) 860444 ⊕ bw-kinlochhotel.co.uk
House beer (by Ayr); 1 changing beer (sourced nationally; often Caledonian, Theakston) ℍ
This family hotel is a hidden gem on the west coast of the Isle of Arran. Sitting in a quiet rural village, it offers coastal comfort and spectacular scenery. The Kinloch serves fabulous local produce including fish and seafood. It has 37 bedrooms, a restaurant and three refurbished bars. Facilities include a heated indoor swimming pool, children's pool, squash court, snooker room, fitness room and sauna.
🛏🏵🍴◖🕭♿▲♣🖤P🖵(322,323,324)🐾📶

Brodick: Isle of Arran

Ormidale Hotel

Knowe Road, KA27 8BY (off A841 at W end of village)
✪ 12.30-2.30 (not winter), 4-midnight; 12-1am Sat;
12-midnight Sun ☎ (01770) 302293 ⊕ ormidale-hotel.co.uk
Arran Guid Ale; 2 changing beers (sourced nationally; often Caledonian, Houston) Ⓐ
Large red sandstone hotel with a small bar and spacious conservatory set in seven acres of grounds. Beers are served from traditional Scottish tall founts on the boat-shaped bar, with Arran Blonde a regular in summer. Home-cooked meals are recommended. Discos and folk nights are held, and the attractive beer garden has views across Brodick Bay. Accommodation is available all year round. 🛏🏵🍴◖♣P🖵(324)🐾📶

Fairlie

Village Inn 𝕃

46 Bay Street, KA29 0AL
✪ 11-midnight (1am Fri & Sat); 12.30-midnight Sun
☎ (01475) 568432 ⊕ villageinnfairlie.co.uk
3 changing beers (sourced regionally) ℍ
A popular local serving up to three ales, often from local breweries, and hosting an annual beer festival in May. Good-quality reasonably priced meals are available in the public bar and adjacent restaurant which displays sailing pictures commemorating the famous Fyfe boatyard which stood nearby. The pub runs a regular quiz and occasional live music nights. Children are welcome until 10pm in the restaurant but the public bar is a child-free zone. Q🛏🏵◖♿P🖵(585)🐾📶

Irvine

Ship Inn

122 Harbour Street, KA12 8PZ
✪ 12-11 (midnight Fri & Sat) ☎ (01294) 279722
⊕ theshipinnirvine.co.uk
2 changing beers (sourced regionally) ℍ
The Ship is the oldest pub in Irvine, dating back to 1595 and licensed since 1754. Located at Irvine harbour, it is close to the Harbour Arts Centre and Magnum Leisure Centre. There are several dining and drinking areas, all adorned with maritime murals and bric-a-brac. A mast forms part of the main bar structure. The pub has an excellent reputation for food. There is always one ale from Ayr Brewing Company, two during the warmer months. Q🛏🏵◖♿🚲🖵🐾📶

Kilmarnock

Brass & Granite

53 Grange Street, KA1 2DD
✪ 11-midnight (1am Thu-Sat); 12.30-midnight Sun
☎ (01563) 523431
3 changing beers (sourced regionally; often Houston, Inveralmond, Strathaven) ℍ
Open-plan pub near Kilmarnock town centre, close to Rugby Park football ground. Guest beers are usually sourced from local or Cumbrian brewers and there is also a wide range of draught and bottled Belgian beers available. Families are welcome and food is available all day. Several TVs show live sport and regular quizzes are held on Sunday, Monday and Wednesday. ◖♿♣🖵📶

Wheatsheaf Inn

70 Portland Street, KA1 1JG (near bus and rail stations)
8am-midnight (1am Fri) (01563) 572483
Caledonian Deuchars IPA; Greene King Abbot; changing beers (sourced nationally) H
Sizeable town-centre Lloyds No.1 bar, originally the historic Wheatsheaf Hotel, famous for its links to Robert Burns, who was first published in Kilmarnock. The bar is divided into various seating areas, with booths, sofas and a raised dining space. DJs entertain on Fridays and Saturdays, with karaoke early on Friday evening, but otherwise conversation holds sway. Food is standard Wetherspoon fare and nine handpumps dispense a range of ales plus real cider. Licensed from 11am.

Kirkmichael

Kirkmichael Arms

3-5 Straiton Road, KA19 7PH
12-midnight (12.30am Fri & Sat) (01655) 750200
kirkmichaelarms.co.uk
2 changing beers (sourced locally; often Ayr, Houston) H
A friendly country pub at the heart of the community with a lounge bar and separate dining room. Two handpumps serve an Ayr Brewing Co beer plus a guest. Excellent meals are available, with food sourced locally where possible. Walkers and dogs are made welcome, and small functions are catered for. Q (358,361)

Largs

JG Sharps Bar

34-36 Nelson Street, KA30 8LW (turn off seafront at Nardini's)
11-midnight (1am Fri & Sat); 12.30-midnight Sun
(01475) 675515 jgsharps.co.uk
Sharp's Doom Bar; 1 changing beer (sourced nationally) H
Set back from the seafront, Sharps is located on the corner of Nelson Street and Boyd Street. A large traditional pub with many different drinking areas, an open fire warms the bar area. Good-quality pub meals are served at lunchtime and Friday-Sunday evenings. Games and sport on TV are in evidence and there is occasional live music. There is space for smokers in the beer garden outside.
Q

Millport: Isle of Cumbrae

Frasers Bar L

7 Cardiff Street, KA28 0AS
11-midnight (1am Thu-Sat) (01475) 530518
frasersbar.co.uk
2 changing beers (sourced regionally; often Houston, Kelburn) H
Recently refurbished to a high standard, decorated with pictures of historic Clyde steamers, this is a welcoming pub close to the pier and an oasis in an otherwise real ale desert. Two handpumps serve a varied range, usually including a local beer, and good-value pub food is available lunchtimes and early evenings. Children are welcome in the rear lounge until 8pm. Buses meet every ferry from Largs and terminate at the nearby pier.
Q (320)

Prestwick

Prestwick Pioneer

87 Main Street, KA9 1JS
8am-midnight (12.30am Fri & Sat) (01292) 473210
Caledonian Deuchars IPA; Greene King Abbot; changing beers (sourced nationally) H
Modern Wetherspoon outlet in a former Woolworths store, named after the first Scottish Aviation Pioneer built in 1947 at the nearby international airport. It has an airy feel with light-wood decor, and features photos of early Open Golf Championships at Prestwick and of Elvis at the nearby airport – the only place in the UK he stepped foot on. Ten handpumps serve local and national ales and food is available all day. Licensed from 10am.

Saltcoats

Salt Cot

7 Hamilton Street, KA21 5DS
8am-midnight (1am Fri & Sat) (01294) 465924
Greene King Abbot; 4 changing beers (sourced nationally) H
This Wetherspoon conversion, formerly a cinema, is named after the original cottages and salt pans of the old fishing community. The interior features memorabilia relating to the cinema, its entertainers and the community. There are TVs with the sound turned up only for major sporting events. Occasional DJ party nights (for Christmas, Halloween) are hosted. One of the guest beers is usually sourced locally. Food is served daily 8am-11pm with a family dining area and children's menu available. Licensed from 10am.
Q (11,585,X36)

Sorn

Sorn Inn

35 Main Street, KA5 6HU
closed Mon; 12-2.30, 6-10 (midnight Fri); 12-midnight Sat; 12-10 Sun (01290) 551305 sorninn.com
1 changing beer (sourced regionally; often Orkney) H
The inn is the major community hub for the residents of the conservation village of Sorn. The cosy bar has one handpump usually serving ale from Orkney Brewery. The award-winning restaurant features a menu that offers a mix of fine dining and brasserie-style food, much of the ingredients locally sourced. Accommodation is available in four en-suite rooms.
P (X50,X76)

Stair

Stair Inn

KA5 5HW (on B730 7 miles E of Ayr)
12-11 (1am Fri & Sat) (01292) 591650 stairinn.co.uk
1 changing beer (sourced locally; often Strathaven) H
This family-run hotel on the banks of the River Ayr is not accessible by public transport but is well-worth seeking out. The comfortable bar and adjacent restaurant feature bespoke hand-made furniture and the bedrooms are furnished in a similar style. One or two guest ales are available. The food menu relies heavily on local produce and fish from the inn's own smokehouse is a speciality (booking advised at weekends). Q P

Troon

Bruce's Well

91 Portland Street, KA10 6QN

12-midnight; 11-1am Fri & Sat ☎ (01292) 311429

Caledonian Deuchars IPA; 1 changing beer (sourced nationally; often Greene King, Inveralmond) 🄷

A friendly, spacious and comfortable lounge bar, close to Troon town centre and a short walk from the station. A number of TVs show sport with the volume kept down – the bar may open earlier than advertised if there is a big sporting event on. A guest ale comes from the Belhaven list and changes regularly. Unusually, the cellar is situated in a temperature-controlled room off the main bar area. ≹🚌 (10,14,110) 📶

McKay's

69 Portland Street, KA10 6QU

10-12.30am (midnight Sun) ☎ (01292) 737372

3 changing beers (sourced regionally; often Cairngorm, Harviestoun, Inveralmond) 🄷

Attractive town-centre bar with a large beer garden which is popular in summer. The ale range varies, but includes beers from Harviestoun and Inveralmond. Food is served lunchtimes Monday-Thursday and until 8pm Friday-Sunday. The bar hosts an open poker night, usually on Tuesday, and a steak night on Wednesday (booking required). It also holds local dominoes competitions.
≹🚌 (14,10,110) 📶

Scottish beer

Just as monks call their Lenten beers 'liquid bread', it's tempting to call traditional Scottish ales 'liquid porridge'. They are beers brewed for a cold climate, a country in which beer vies with whisky (uisge breatha – water of life) for nourishment and sustenance.

Brewers blend not only darker malts such as black and chocolate with paler grains, but also add oats, that staple of many foodstuffs in the country. In common with the farmer-brewers of the Low Countries and French Flanders in earlier centuries, domestic brewers in Scotland tended to use whatever grains, herbs and plants were available to make beer. The intriguing use of heather in the Fraoch range of ales recalls brewing practice in Scotland from bygone times.

The industrial revolution arrived later in Scotland than in England, and industry tended to concentrate in the Lowland belt around Alloa, Edinburgh and Glasgow. As a result, brewing remained a largely domestic affair for much longer and – as with early Irish ales – made little use of the hop, which could not grow in such inhospitable climes.

Brewing developed on a commercial scale in the Lowlands in the early 19th century at the same time as many French emigres, escaping the revolution, settled in the Scottish capital. They dubbed the rich, warming local ales 'Scottish Burgundy'. Real wine from France, always popular in Scotland as a result of the Auld Alliance, become scarce during the Napoleonic Wars, and commercial brewing grew rapidly to fill the gap and to fuel the needs of a growing class of thirsty industrial workers.

Traditionally, Scottish ales were brewed in a different manner to English ones. Before refrigeration, beer was fermented at ambient temperatures far lower than in England. As a result, not all the sugars turned to alcohol, producing rich, full-bodied ales. As hops had to be imported from England at considerable cost, they were used sparingly. The result was a style of beer markedly different to English ones: vinous, fruity, malty and with only a gentle hop bitterness.

Many of the new breed of ales produced by micro-brewers in Scotland tend to be paler and more bitter than used to be the norm. For the true taste of traditional Scottish ales you will have to sample the products of the likes of Belhaven, Broughton, Caledonian and Traquair.

The language of Scottish beers is different, too. The equivalent to English mild is called Light (even when it's dark in colour), standard bitter is called Heavy premium bitter Export, while strong old ales and barley wines (now rare) are called Wee Heavies.

To add to the complexities of the language differences, many traditional beers incorporate the word Shilling in their names. A Light may be dubbed 60 Shilling, a Heavy 70 Shilling, an Export 80 Shilling, and a Wee Heavy 90 Shilling. The designations stem from a pre-decimalisation method of invoicing beer in Victorian times. The stronger the beer, the higher the number of shillings.

Until recent times, cask-conditioned beer in Scotland was served by air pressure. In the pub cellar a water engine, which looks exactly the same as a lavatory cistern but works in reverse, used water to produce air pressure that drove the beer to the bar. Sadly, these wonderful Victorian devices are rarely seen, and the Sassenach handpump and beer engine dominate the pub scene.

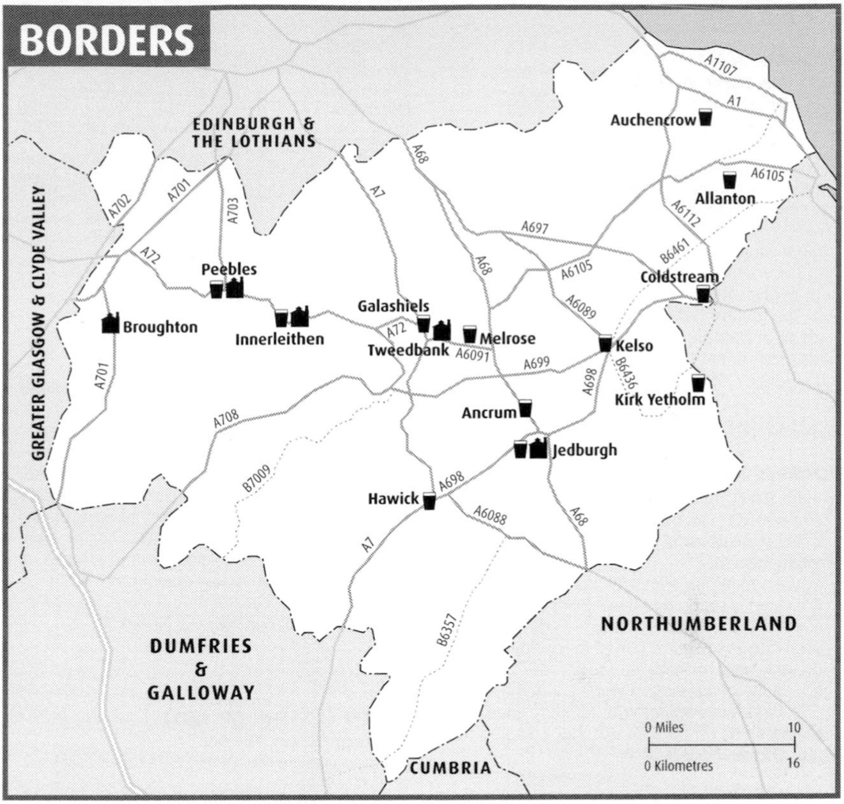

Authority area covered: Scottish Borders UA

Allanton

Allanton Inn

TD11 3JZ

12-11 ☎ (01890) 818260 allantoninn.co.uk

2 changing beers Ⓗ

An old coaching inn with a bright, airy feel which dates back to the 18th century. In the front dining room the emphasis is on serving quality food and the bar area, which looks out over the superb beer garden to the countryside beyond, can also be used by diners when busy. Two real ales are available, often coming from Born in the Borders Brewery or other Scottish micros. With good quality accommodation, this is an ideal base for exploring Berwickshire and north Northumberland.
❀◑♣P (260)

Ancrum

Ancrum Cross Keys

The Green, TD8 6XH (on B6400, off A68)

12 (5 Mon)-11; 12-1am Fri & Sat ☎ (01835) 830242
ancrumcrosskeys.com

4 changing beers Ⓗ

Perched on the Ale Water (yes really!), and recently celebrating its 200th birthday, this village local's front bar has remained largely untouched since 1906, retaining pine panelling throughout and a real fire. There is also a comfortable drinking and dining area and a snug at the front. Owned by Born in the Borders Brewery, food is an intrinsic part of the operation and locally sourced produce (sometimes foraged) is available according to a plough to platter ethos matching the brewery's plough to pint philosophy.
❀◑♿♣P (25,68)

Auchencrow

Craw Inn

TD14 5LS (signed from A1)

12-2.30, 6-11 (midnight Fri); 12-midnight Sat; 12.30-11 Sun ☎ (01890) 761253 thecrawinn.co.uk

2 changing beers Ⓗ

A friendly 18th-century inn where good banter with the locals is assured. The bar has a wood-burning stove and tables for both dining and drinking. Two real ales (three in summer) are usually from smaller breweries, as can be seen from the many pumpclips that festoon the roof beams. Excellent home-cooked food is served in both the bar and the well-appointed restaurant. Beer festivals are held in July and November. Accommodation includes B&B and a self-catering annexe. Q❀◑♣P (34)

REAL ALE BREWERIES

Born in the Borders Jedburgh
Broughton Broughton
Freewheelin' Peebles (NEW)
Tempest Tweedbank
Traquair House Innerleithen

Coldstream

Besom

75-77 High Street, TD12 4AE
11-midnight (1am Fri & Sat); 12.30-midnight Sun
☎ (01890) 882391 besom-inn.co.uk
House beer (by Tetley); 1 changing beer Ⓗ
One of the first and last pubs in Scotland, this three-roomed gem has remained relatively unchanged since it was built in the 1890s and revamped circa 1910. The cosy bar retains its original counter and gantry, while the diverse range of memorabilia, bookshelves and sofa seating gives the feel more of a living room than a pub. The lounge (where families are welcome) leads to a room dedicated to the history of the Coldstream Guards. The house beer Besom Ale is from Tetley. Q♨❀◐♣🚌(67,904)🐾📶

Galashiels

Hunters Hall

56 High Street, TD1 1SE (N side of town centre)
8am-midnight (1am Thu-Sat) ☎ (01896) 759795
Caledonian Deuchars IPA; Greene King Abbot; 3 changing beers Ⓗ
A Wetherspoon pub originally built as a church. The single room is set on two levels with the main area having bare stone walls and some booth seating. Several displays by local artists, many depicting the Gala area, help to make up for the lack of natural light – sadly the previous owners painted out some of the windows. Popular with families, food is available all day from 8am. Alcohol is served from 11am. Q♨❀◐♿▲⇌🚌📶

Hawick

Bourtree

22 Bourtree Place, TD9 9HL (NE edge of centre)
8am-midnight (1am Fri & Sat) ☎ (01450) 360450
Greene King Abbot; 5 changing beers Ⓗ
Built as Hawick Conservative Club in 1897, this listed building has been stunningly transformed into a Wetherspoon pub. The former snooker hall forms the main area, while there are three further areas for quieter or private use. Pictures show a history of Hawick life, including mills, railways, common riding and motorbiking. Regular cask ale and cider promotions and festivals are held. Food is available all day, alcohol is served from 11am.
Q♨❀◐♿P🚌(20,95,120)📶

Exchange Bar (Dalton's)

1 Silver Street, TD9 0AD (off SW end of high street)
11-11 (1am Fri & Sat); 12.30-11 Sun ☎ (01450) 376067
2 changing beers Ⓗ
Hidden away between St Mary's Kirk and the Heart of Hawick Heritage Centre, the pub used to overlook the Corn Exchange, hence the name – however a previous owner was called Dalton and the name has stuck. It is a Victorian gem with original dark-wood panelling and ornate cornice work. The bar is popular with knowledgable locals and there is a comfy lounge used for parties, Friday karaoke and Sunday folk sessions. Children are not admitted. ♣🚌(20,95,120)🐾📶

Innerleithen

St Ronan's Hotel

High Street, EH44 6HF
12-midnight (12.45am Fri & Sat) ☎ (01896) 831487
1 changing beer Ⓗ
This village hotel with a smart blue and white exterior takes its name from a local saint. The public bar is long and thin, with a wood-burning stove. Two alcoves in differing styles offer extra seating and a darts area. A pick-up service is available for Southern Upland Way Walkers and packed lunches can be provided. The single real ale is sourced from a wide variety of brewers, occasionally including the local Traquair.
♨❀🛏▲♣P🚌(X62,62A)🐾📶

Traquair Arms Hotel

Traquair Road, EH44 6PD (b709, off A72)
11-11 (midnight Fri & Sat); 12-11.30 Sun
☎ (01896) 830229 traquairarmshotel.co.uk
Caledonian Deuchars IPA; Timothy Taylor Landlord; Traquair House Stuart Ale Ⓗ
Elegant 18th-century hotel in the scenic Tweed Valley. The comfortable lounge bar features a welcoming real fire in winter. A bistro area and separate restaurant provide plenty of room for diners, with meals served all day at weekends. Visitors including walkers, shooters, anglers and cyclists are all welcome, along with the locals. It is one of the few outlets for draught ales from Traquair House. Bear Ale may replace Stuart Ale at times. ♨❀🛏◐♿▲P🚌(X62,62A)🐾📶

Jedburgh

Canon (Exchange Inn)

8 Exchange Street, TD8 6BH
3-midnight (1am Fri); 12-1am Sat; 12.30-midnight Sun
☎ (01835) 863243
2 changing beers Ⓗ
Compact town-centre locals' pub with a traditional atmosphere, featuring a welcoming real fire, original stone wall and dark-wood beams. The long bar has a small alcove-like area at the end. The real ales are usually from Scotland or northern England. A sports fan's watering hole, the walls are adorned with rugby memorabilia and local history material. Time can easily be whiled away reading the walls or catching up with sporting events on TV. Children are not admitted. ▲♣🚌🐾📶

Kelso

Cobbles Freehouse & Dining

7 Bowmont Street, TD5 7JH (off NE side of town square)
11.30-11; 11-midnight Fri & Sat; 12-11 Sun
☎ (01573) 223548 thecobbleskelso.co.uk
3 changing beers Ⓗ
An award-winning gastro-pub offering an eclectic mix of British classics, Pacific Rim and modern European cuisine. To the right of the main dining area is a lounge bar where beers from Tempest, the pub's microbrewery, are featured. Note that pumpclips are not used – the beers are listed on a blackboard behind the bar. Though the focus is on food (served all day on Sunday), drinkers are welcome here. CAMRA Borders Pub of the Year runner-up 2015. ♨❀◐♿🚌📶

Kirk Yetholm

Border

The Green, TD5 8PQ
11.30 (12 Sun)-11 winter; 11.30-midnight (1am Fri & Sat); 12-midnight Sun summer ☎ (01573) 420237

House beer (by Hadrian Border); 2 changing beers Ⓗ
An attractive 260-year-old coaching inn with bar areas and a conservatory restaurant. Popular with walkers, it is at the confluence of several long-distance footpaths. In a tradition from Wainwright's time, those completing the Pennine Way are awarded a free half of Pennine Pint, the house beer from Hadrian & Border. The inn is noted for its hearty food (served all day on Sunday) and quality real ales from independent breweries on both sides of the border. ⛟♿🛏◑◗Å♣P🚍(81)🐾🛜

Melrose

Burt's Hotel
Market Square, TD6 9PL
🕐 11-2.30, 5-11; 12-2.30, 6-11 Sun ☎ (01896) 822285
🌐 burtshotel.co.uk
Born in the Borders Game Bird; Timothy Taylor Landlord; 1 changing beer Ⓗ
An elegant family-run hotel in the main square, where colourful window boxes provide a striking display in summer. In the lounge bar the décor reflects the country sports interests of many of the clientele. Here the focus is unashamedly on food, which is good – so go on, treat yourself. Those visiting solely for a drink may find space limited. Weather permitting, the beer garden can be an excellent option. Q♿🛏◑◗♿Å♣P🚍🐾🛜

George & Abbotsford Hotel
High Street, TD6 9PD
🕐 11-11 (1am Fri & Sat); 12-11 Sun ☎ (01896) 822308
🌐 georgeandabbotsford.co.uk
3 changing beers Ⓗ
A spacious family-run hotel in the town centre with a comfortable bar and lounges. The owners have carried out much redecoration and refurbishment since their arrival. They are now concentrating on building the real ale portfolio which features interesting beers from both sides of the border, often including Tempest. Meals are served all day on Saturday and Sunday in summer and there are regular music sessions on Wednesdays and weekends. The bar may not open until later Monday-Thursday in January.
Q⛟♿🛏◑Å♣●P🚍🐾🛜

Peebles

Bridge Inn (Trust)
Portbrae, EH45 8AW
🕐 11-midnight (1am Thu-Sat); 12-midnight Sun
☎ (01721) 720589
Caledonian Deuchars IPA; 3 changing beers Ⓗ
Welcoming single-roomed town-centre local, also known as the Trust. The mosaic entrance floor shows it was once the Tweedside Inn. The bright, comfortable bar is decorated with jugs, bottles,

memorabilia of outdoor pursuits and photos of old Peebles. An outdoor heated patio area overlooks the river. The Gents is superb, with well-maintained original Twyford Adamant urinals. There is TV sport and live music on Sunday evening. Children are not admitted. CAMRA Borders Pub of the Year 2015. ♿Å♣🚍(X62,62A)🐾

Cross Keys
Northgate, EH45 8RS
🕐 7am-midnight (1am Fri & Sat) ☎ (01721) 723467
6 changing beers Ⓗ
Old coaching inn, just off the High Street, that reopened as a Wetherspoon pub and hotel in 2014. The large, pleasant, low-ceilinged main bar is on the ground floor. A wide range of real ales is served, sourced from all over the UK, and there is an extensive food menu available all day. A smaller, attractive bar is situated one floor up and allows easy access to an excellent beer garden. Alcohol is served from 11am (noon Sun).
♿🛏◑♿Å●P🚍(X62,62A)🛜

Crown Hotel
High Street, EH45 8SW
🕐 11-midnight (1am Thu-Sat) ☎ (01721) 720239
🌐 crownhotelpeebles.co.uk
1 changing beer Ⓗ
A basic narrow bar that opens out to a seating area with a leather settee and banquettes. There are wooden floors and half-panelled walls throughout. At the back of the bar, down a flight of steps, is a lovely restaurant area with a conservatory. Meals are served all day. The bar is popular with the locals, who make visitors welcome. Live music is hosted occasionally.
⛟♿🛏◑♿Å♣🚍(X62,62A)🐾🛜

Neidpath Inn
27-29 Old Town, EH45 8JF (on A72 W of town centre)
🕐 11-midnight (1am Thu-Sat); 12.30-midnight Sun
☎ (01721) 724306 🌐 neidpathinn.co.uk
Stewart Edinburgh Gold; 1 changing beer Ⓗ
Traditional town pub providing a contrast for drinkers. The front of the L-shaped bar room, with a real fire, is a cosy place to enjoy a relaxing drink, while the back has a pool table and jukebox. Wood, musical instruments and glasswork add to the decor. A separate comfortable lounge leads to an area which in summer spills out onto a decked area outside. Families are welcome in the lounge only.
⛟♿🛏♿Å♣🚍(X62,62A)🐾

Recipe for Buttered Beer

Take a quart of more of Double Beere and put to it a good piece of fresh butter, sugar candie an ounce, or liquerise in powder, or ginger grated, of each a dramme, and if you would have it strong, put in as much long pepper and Greynes, let it boyle in the quart in the maner as you burne wine, and who so will drink it, let him drinke it hot as he may suffer. Some put in the yolke of an egge or two towards the latter end, and so they make it more strength-full.
Thomas Cogan, The Haven of Health, 1584

DUMFRIES & GALLOWAY

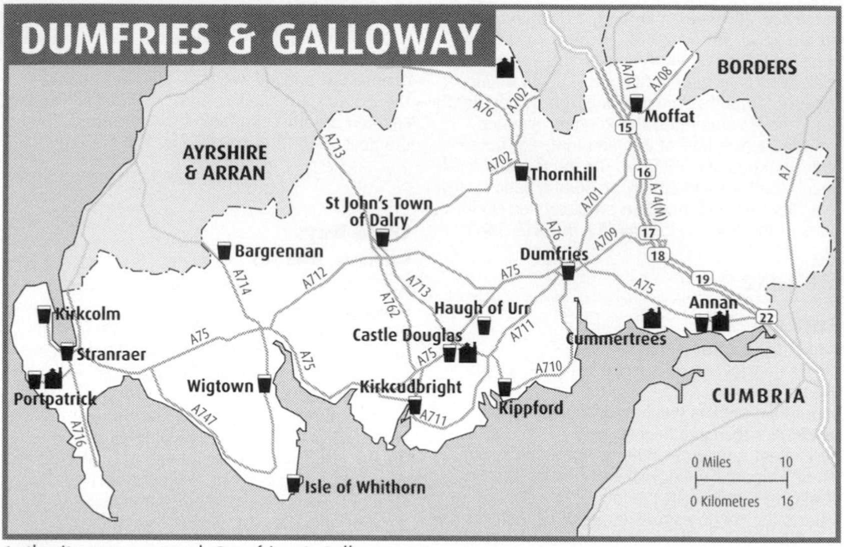

Authority area covered: Dumfries & Galloway UA

Annan

Blue Bell Inn

10 High Street, DG12 6AG

11-11 (midnight Thu-Sat); 12.30-11 Sun

(01461) 202385

Caledonian Deuchars IPA; 3 changing beers H

This former coaching inn dating from 1770, at the western entrance to the town, has won local CAMRA Pub of the Year on several occasions. Four ales are on offer from throughout the UK. A busy, friendly pub, it has a traditional wood-panelled interior featuring quotations, retained from its time as a State Management Scheme pub. A courtyard to the rear provides a pleasant seated area and hosts Cider Sunday in May and Blue Bell Beerfest in August. P

Bargrennan

House o' Hill

DG8 6RN (just off A714 on Glentrool road)

12-11 (01671) 840243 houseohill.co.uk

2 changing beers (sourced regionally; often Fyne Ales, Strathaven, Sulwath) H

Situated in Galloway Forest Park, this small hotel is popular with walkers, climbers, anglers and cyclists. Fully refurbished, it has an attractive interior including a small function room. Two beers are offered, mainly from Scottish microbreweries, and three-day beer festivals with food and live music are held twice a year. The pub specialises in good-value home cooking, using locally sourced supplies and home-grown produce. Regular music events featuring local artists are held throughout the year. Closed early January.
P (359)

Castle Douglas

Sulwath Brewery Tap Room L

209 King Street, DG7 1DT

10-6; closed Sun (01556) 504525

sulwathbrewers.co.uk

8 changing beers H

Sulwath Brewery is the principal brewery in Dumfries & Galloway and its ales have won a number of awards at beer festivals north and south of the border in recent years. The Tap Room is popular with ale lovers in Castle Douglas and surrounds. Sulwath has seven regular brews, with seasonal ales featuring from time to time. The Tap Room sells eight house beers and occasional guest ales from other parts of the country. One draught cider is usually available. Q P

Dumfries

Cavens Arms

20 Buccleuch Street, DG1 2AH

11-11 (midnight Thu-Sat); 12.30-11 Sun

(01387) 252896

Harviestoun Bitter & Twisted; Morland Old Speckled Hen; Phoenix Arizona; Thwaites Wainwright; 4 changing beers H

A busy town-centre pub with a reputation built on the quality of its ales, excellent pub grub and friendly customer service. Four house beers and four guests – and occasionally up to 10 ales – are usually on offer, drawn from a varying range of UK breweries. Regular charity quizzes and other themed nights are hosted. Local CAMRA Pub of the Year 2006-2015.

Coach & Horses

66 Whitesands, DG1 2RS

11 (12.30 Sun)-11 07746 675349

House beer (by Marston's) H

A former coaching inn on the riverside next to the Tourist Information Centre. It has a pleasant large bar area, with a flagstone floor and warming open fire. Handy for local tourist attractions and car parking, it serves one cask ale. Live music events are hosted regularly and attract a crowd. P

New Bazaar

38-39 Whitesands, DG1 2RS

11-11 (01387) 268776

Greene King Abbot; Theakston XB; 2 changing beers H

Former coaching inn beside the River Nith with an airy bar featuring an impressive Victorian gantry and a small lounge with a warming coal fire in winter. Four cask ales are usually on offer – two regulars from Greene King and Theakston and two varying guests. No food is served. The pub is a favourite with football supporters on their way to matches at nearby Palmerston Park, and is ideally situated for car parking and local tourist attractions. There is an area for smoking outside. ♿⇌P🚌🐾

Robert the Bruce

81/83 Buccleuch Street, DG1 2AB

⏲ 10-midnight (1am Fri & Sat); 11-midnight Sun

☎ (01387) 270320

Caledonian Deuchars IPA; Greene King Abbot; changing beers Ⓗ

This former Methodist church, sensitively converted by Wetherspoon, has a relaxed atmosphere and is a popular meeting place in the town centre. It regularly features seven cask ales, and 10 or more during festivals – with up to 50 ales on offer over the period. The standard food menu offers a range of good-value meals served all day, every day. There is a good outside smoking area.

Q🐎◐♿⇌🍎🚌📶

Tam o' Shanter

113/117 Queensberry Street, DG1 1BH

⏲ 11-11 (midnight Fri & Sat); 11-10 Sun ☎ 07855 473933

Broughton Bramling Cross; 3 changing beers Ⓗ

A long-established ale pub, well positioned just off the High Street. This old coaching inn dating back to 1630 has been held in high regard on the Dumfries beer scene for many years. The small, traditional pub has a main bar, a couple of quiet rooms behind, and an upstairs room which hosts live music and other functions. A rotating range of beers includes three from Broughton Brewery and up to two guests. Q⇌P🚌🐾

Haugh of Urr

Laurie Arms Hotel

11-13 Main Street, DG7 3YA

⏲ 12-2, 5-11; 12-midnight Sat & Sun ☎ (01556) 660246

🌐 haugh-of-urr.com

4 changing beers Ⓗ

Welcoming family-run pub and restaurant, popular with locals and visitors for its range of ales and good food, freshly cooked and featuring local produce. The bar has a genuine village-inn atmosphere, enhanced on winter nights by a log fire. Up to four beers are available depending on the season, mainly from small independent breweries. The toilets feature an interesting selection of saucy seaside postcards. Former CAMRA Scottish Pub of the Year and joint branch winner. Q🐎❀◐♣P🚌📶

Isle of Whithorn

Steam Packet Inn

Harbour Row, DG8 8LL (on B7004 from Whithorn)

⏲ 11-11 Mon; 11-3, 6-11 Tue-Thu; 11-midnight Fri & Sat; 12-11 Sun winter; 11-11 (12.30am Fri & Sat) summer

☎ (01988) 500334 🌐 thesteampacketinn.biz

Belhaven IPA; Timothy Taylor Landlord; 4 changing beers (sourced regionally; often Fyne Ales, Orkney, Born in the Borders) Ⓗ

Traditional and historic family-run hotel overlooking the harbour, welcoming to locals and visitors alike, including families and pets. The public bar has stone walls and a multi-fuel stove, and there are pictures of the village and maritime events throughout. Four guest ales from a wide variety of breweries are available in both bars. The extensive food menu features local produce – the Sunday hot buffet is a speciality and there are various themed food nights. Scottish CAMRA Pub of the Year 2014. Q🐎❀🛏◐♣P🚌(415)🐾📶

Kippford

Anchor Hotel

DG5 4LN

⏲ 11-10 ☎ (01556) 620205 🌐 anchorhotelkippford.co.uk

Sulwath Criffel; 2 changing beers Ⓗ

In a picturesque seaside village and sailing centre with fine views over the Urr estuary, this pub offers two cask ales throughout the year and one more during the summer season, usually from the local Sulwath Brewery. Excellent food is available from a varied menu, made with local produce and including good vegetarian options. It has a newly extended dining area and is often busy, so book ahead for the restaurant. When the weather is fine a table outside is the perfect place to watch the world go by. 🐎❀🛏◐♿⛺P🚌🐾📶

Kirkcolm

Blue Peter Hotel

23 Main Street, DG9 0NL (on A718 5 miles N of Stranraer)

⏲ 6 (4 Fri)-11.30; 12-midnight Sat; 12.30-11.30 Sun

☎ (01776) 853221

4 changing beers (sourced nationally) Ⓗ

A small family-run hotel with two bars packed with memorabilia and, outside, a decked patio for viewing the abundant wildlife, including red squirrels. Two handpumps in each bar dispense a constantly changing range of up to four ales, often from Yorkshire breweries. Home-cooked food is made with fresh local produce, also available to take away. Popular with walkers, bird and wildlife watchers and real ale enthusiasts. Good-value B&B is offered. Q🐎❀🛏◐⛺♣🚌(408)🐾📶

Kirkcudbright

Masonic Arms

19 Castle Street, DG6 4JA

⏲ 11-11 ☎ (01557) 330517

2 changing beers Ⓗ

A firm favourite in the town with real ale enthusiasts for many years. It has a sociable main bar, welcoming to both locals and visitors. The tables and bar fronts are made from old malt whisky casks from Islay's Bowmore Distillery. There is a smaller back bar and a garden with a smoking area. Two ales are served throughout the year with perhaps three during the summer. Draught Budvar is also on offer, plus a selection of over 30 bottled beers from around the world, and more than 100 malt whiskies. Q❀♿⛺P🚌🐾

REAL ALE BREWERIES

Andrews Cummertrees
Lola Rose Wanlockhead (NEW)
Madcap Annan
Portpatrick Portpatrick (NEW)
Sulwath Castle Douglas

Selkirk Arms Hotel
High Street, DG6 4JQ
11 (12.30 Sun)-11 (01557) 330402
selkirkarmshotel.co.uk
Sulwath The Grace; 1 changing beer
This traditional hotel has an excellent reputation for accommodation and meals. It serves two cask ales in the lounge and public bars and has a large garden area with tables for the summer months. Kirkcudbright is notable for its artistic heritage and has a number of interesting galleries and museums. Robert Burns is reputed to have written his famous Selkirk Grace while visiting the hotel.
Q P

Moffat

Star Hotel
44 High Street, DG10 9EF
11 (12.30 Sun)-11 (01683) 220156
famousstarhotel.co.uk
Sulwath Criffel; 2 changing beers (often Greene King)
The 'Famous Star Hotel' is recognised by the Guinness Book of Records as the narrowest hotel in Britain. It has been run by the same familiy for over 25 years and offers excellent service. One real ale from the Sulwath Brewery is generally available, with a second guest in the summer months.

Portpatrick

Crown Hotel
9 North Crescent, DG9 8SX (facing harbour)
11-midnight (1am Fri & Sat); 12-midnight Sun
(01776) 810261 crownportpatrick.com
2 changing beers (sourced nationally; often Courage, Thwaites)
This hotel overlooks the picturesque and historic Portpatrick harbour with views on a clear day across to Ireland. The large comfortable bar area at the front is adorned with fine pictures and ornaments and warmed by an open fire. Two regularly changing ales are available from across the UK. Live music plays on Friday and Saturday nights, featuring both local and visiting musicians and groups. (367)

St John's Town of Dalry

Clachan Inn
8-10 Main Street, DG7 3UW
11 (12 Sun)-11 (01644) 430241 theclachaninn.co.uk
2 changing beers
Located in a picturesque village, this inn has established a reputation for excellent food, cosy, well-appointed bedrooms and a welcoming atmosphere. It features an attractive, traditional main bar and a separate restaurant. Two cask ales are always available. The Clachan prides itself on using local produce including organic lamb and venison, and offers a varied menu with daily specials. The inn suits the needs of all those who enjoy country life, and is a convenient stop for walkers on the Southern Upland Way.
Q P

Stranraer

Grapes
4-6 Bridge Street, DG9 7HY
11-11.30 (midnight Thu-Sat); 12.30-11.30 Sun
(01776) 703386 thegrapesbar.co.uk
2 changing beers (sourced nationally; often Orkney, Stewart, Timothy Taylor)
This popular historic public bar, with impressive mirror and gantry, has altered little in over 50 years. It has a separate refurbished snug bar, an upstairs function room with 1930s Art Deco gantry and counter, and a small courtyard with tables and chairs. Regular live music features in the bar on Friday evenings, and occasional music nights in the function room. Two ales are usually on offer, sourced from all over Britain, although there may be just one in winter.

Thornhill

Buccleuch & Queensberry Hotel
112 Drumlanrig Street, DG3 5LU
11 (12.30 Sun)-11 (01848) 330215
buccleuchhotel.co.uk
2 changing beers (often Foxy Blond, Old Speckled Hen)
Built by the Duke of Buccleuch in 1855, the hotel has been recently renovated and the former public bar reopened. An ideal base for exploring the beautiful countryside of Dumfries and Galloway, two cask ales are available to attract visiting anglers and shooters. The main lounge and bar facilities give hotel guests the opportunity to mix with locals and village worthies, who meet in the evening to enjoy a pint or a wee dram.
Q P

Wigtown

Wigtown Ploughman Hotel
30 South Main Street, DG8 9HG
12-10 (midnight Fri & Sat) (01988) 403236
theploughmanhotel.co.uk
Greene King IPA; 3 changing beers (sourced nationally; often Belhaven)
Situated in the centre of Wigtown, Scotland's National Book Town, this is a traditional former coaching inn with an authentic cast-iron pub sign outside. The bar has a country-pub feel about it that appeals to a wide clientele. The hotel has undergone a comprehensive refurbishment – the restaurant has reopened within the past year and the accommodation has been upgraded. It is well-placed to explore local attractions The Machars and the Cradle of Christianity in Whithorn.
Q (415,416)

> How easy can the barley-bree
> Cement the quarrel.
> It's aye the cheapest lawyer's fee
> To taste the barrel.
> **Robert Burns**

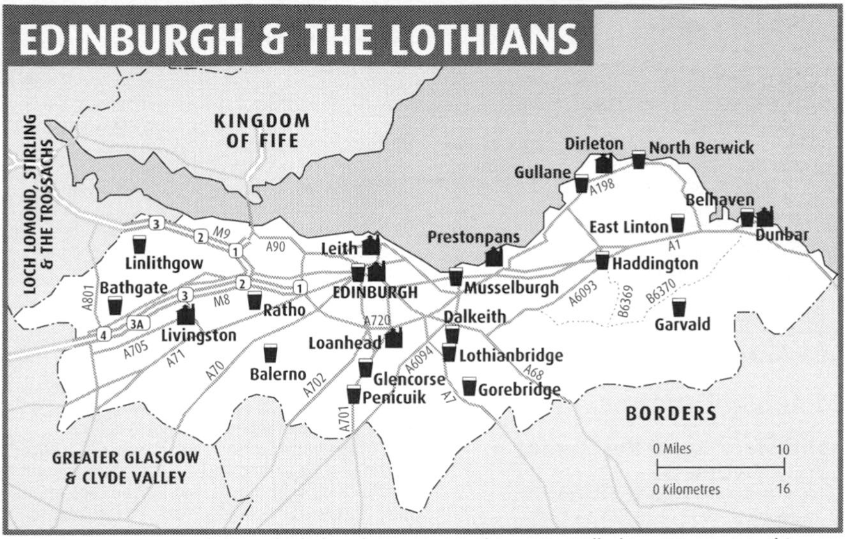

Authority areas covered: City of Edinburgh UA, East Lothian UA, Midlothian UA, West Lothian UA

Balerno

Grey Horse

20 Main Street, EH14 7EH (off A70, in pedestrian area)
11-11 (1am Fri & Sat); 12.30-11 Sun ☎ (0131) 449 2888
greyhorsebalerno.com
5 changing beers Ⓗ

Traditional stone-built village pub, dating from the 18th century. The cosy public bar retains some original features with wood panelling and a fine Bernard's mirror, and the pleasant lounge has green banquette seating. The restaurant next door is part of the pub so you can enjoy a beer with your meal. The menu, available all day April to September, includes Chinese dishes. One folk and one jazz evening are held each month. CAMRA Lothian Pub of the Year runner-up 2015.
Q❀♣(44)

Bathgate

James Young

36-44 Hopetoun Street, EH48 4EU
8am-midnight (1am Thu-Sat) ☎ (01506) 651600
Caledonian Deuchars IPA; Greene King Abbot; 2 changing beers Ⓗ

Wetherspoon pub on two levels named after James Young Simpson, Scottish obstetrician and an important figure in the history of medicine. He was credited with discovering the anaesthetic properties of chloroform and successfully introducing it for general medical use. Major sport is shown on TV, with subtitled news at other times. Music plays on Friday and Saturday evenings. Licensed from 11am (12.30pm Sun), children are welcome until 8pm. ❀♿(4,23,34)

Belhaven

Masons Arms

8 High Street, EH42 1NP
12-2.30, 6-11; 12-midnight Fri & Sat; 12.30-11 Sun
☎ (01368) 864566
2 changing beers Ⓗ

Just a few minutes' walk from Belhaven Brewery, this friendly pub reverted to its original name in 2013. The bright, comfortable bar overlooks the beer garden. One handpump is dedicated to beers from Knops Brewery, while the other occasionally has a beer from Belhaven. In the winter only one beer is usually on. Food is no longer served, the small restaurant area now being used for functions.
❀▲♣(X6,253)

Dalkeith

Blacksmith's Forge

Newmills Road, EH22 1DU
8am-midnight (1am Fri & Sat) ☎ (0131) 561 5100
Caledonian Deuchars IPA; Greene King Abbot; 4 changing beers Ⓗ

Large open-plan Wetherspoon pub divided into several areas with a mix of tables and chairs, high tables and booths with bench seating. The decor includes images of a forge and a large model anvil. The guest beers are often from Scottish breweries. Families are welcome for meals, which are served all day. Licensed from 11am (12.30pm Sun).
Q❀♿

REAL ALE BREWERIES

Alechemy Livingston
Alpha Project Edinburgh (NEW)
Andrew Usher Edinburgh (NEW)
Barney's Edinburgh
Belhaven Dunbar
Bellfield Edinburgh (NEW)
Caledonian Edinburgh
Carbon Smith Edinburgh (NEW)
Edinbrew Livingston (NEW)
Knops Dirleton
Krafty Brew Edinburgh (NEW)
Pilot Leith
Prestonpans Prestonpans
Stewart Loanhead
Top Out Loanhead

East Linton

Linton
3 Bridge End, EH40 3AF
12-11 (midnight Fri & Sat) (01620) 860202
3 changing beers H
Small, welcoming, traditional hotel by the historic brig over the Tyne in a pretty conservation village. There is a quiet, comfortably furnished public bar and a popular restaurant to the rear. Three handpumps usually serve at least one beer from a Scottish microbrewery. The restaurant features good-quality, award-winning, locally-sourced Scottish cuisine (food available all day on Sun). Stained glass windows and a rooftop statue reflect the hotel's former name – the Red Lion.
Q (120,X6)

Edinburgh: Central

Abbotsford Bar & Restaurant ★
3-5 Rose Street, EH2 2PR
11-11 (midnight Fri & Sat) (0131) 225 5276
theabbotsford.com
6 changing beers H/A
A traditional Scottish bar listed on CAMRA's National Inventory of historic pub interiors. The magnificent island bar and gantry in dark mahogany have been a fixture since 1902. The ornate plasterwork and corniced ceiling are outstanding and highlighted by concealed lighting. Six real ales are served, usually from Scottish microbreweries. There is an extensive food menu, available all day in the bar. Diners in the restaurant upstairs can order real ale from downstairs.
Q (Waverley)

Beehive Inn
18-20 Grassmarket, EH1 2JU (old town)
11-midnight (1am Fri & Sat) (0131) 225 7171
5 changing beers H
Large, three-floored, multi-roomed establishment built on the site of a 16th-century inn. Upstairs is the condemned cell door from the old tollbooth. The beer garden has excellent views up to the castle. The pub gets particularly lively on Friday and Saturday evenings, with a DJ providing music and a popular comedy club upstairs. Five real ales are sourced UK-wide with a Scottish bias, and three more are sometimes available upstairs. Meals are served all day. (2)

Blue Blazer
2 Spittal Street, EH3 9DX
11 (12.30 Sun)-1am (0131) 229 5030
Cairngorm Trade Winds A**, Black Gold; Caledonian Deuchars IPA; Harviestoun Schiehallion** H**; 3 changing beers** H/A
Two-roomed pub nestling in the shadow of Edinburgh Castle, with wooden floors, high ceilings and old brewery window panels, and candles in the evening adding to the traditional feel. Named after a local school uniform, a blue blazer is inlaid in tiles on the floor. The pub specialises in beers from Scottish micros. Close to theatres and cinemas, closing time is later during August and December. Toasties are available all day. Children are not admitted.

Bow Bar
80 West Bow, EH1 2HH (old town, off Grassmarket)
12-midnight; 12.30-11.30 Sun (0131) 226 7667
thebowbar.co.uk
Cromarty Happy Chappy; Stewart Brewing Edinburgh No.3; house beer (by Alechemy); 5 changing beers A
One of the first re-creations of a classic Scottish one-roomed ale house, dedicated to traditional Scottish air pressure dispense and upright drinking. The five guest beers can be from anywhere in the UK, and regular beer festivals are held. The walls are festooned with original brewery mirrors and the superb gantry does justice to an award-winning selection of around 290 single malt whiskies and international bottled beers. Pies, soup and bridies are available at lunchtime. Children are not admitted. Q (Waverley) (2)

Cafe Royal ★
19 West Register Street, EH2 2AA (off E end of Princes St)
11-11 (midnight Thu; 1am Fri & Sat); 12.30-11 Sun
(0131) 556 1884 caferoyaledinburgh.co.uk
Broughton Coulsons EPA; 6 changing beers H
One of the finest Victorian pub interiors in Scotland, dominated by an impressive oval island bar with ornate brass light fittings and magnificent ceramic tiled murals of innovators made by Doulton from pictures by John Eyre. The sporting windows of the Oyster Bar were made by the same firm that supplied windows for the House of Lords. Six guest beers are available from regional breweries such as Broughton, Fyne, Harviestoun and Kelburn. Meals are served all day. Q (Waverley)

Guildford Arms
1 West Register Street, EH2 2AA (off E end of Princes St)
11-11 (midnight Fri); 10-midnight Sat; 10-11 Sun
(0131) 556 4312 guildfordarms.com
10 changing beers H
A large venue built in the golden age of Victorian pub design. The high ceiling, cornices and friezes are spectacular, as are the window arches and screens. The restaurant is upstairs in a noteworthy gallery. There is a large standing area around the canopied bar plus extensive seating areas. The diverse range of 10 real ales includes many from Scottish micros, and real cider is occasionally available. Bar snacks are on offer all day Monday-Thursday. Alcohol is served from 11am.
(Waverley)

Halfway House
24 Fleshmarket Close, EH1 1BX (up steps opp Waverley station's Market St entrance)
11-11.30 (midnight Thu; 1am Fri & Sat)
(0131) 225 7101 halfwayhouse-edinburgh.com
4 changing beers H
Cosy, characterful bar hidden halfway down an Old Town close. Railway memorabilia and current timetables adorn the interior of this small, often busy, bar. At the front are tables with window seats and stools. The rear area has more comfortable semi-circular booth seating. There are usually four interesting real ales, mainly from smaller Scottish breweries. Meals and bar snacks are served all day. The bar may stay open until 1am during busy times of year.
(Waverley)

Jolly Judge
7a Lawnmarket, EH1 2PB (in James Court)
12-11 (midnight Fri & Sat); 12.30-11 Sun
(0131) 225 2669 jollyjudge.co.uk
2 changing beers H
Comfortable bar with an attractive painted ceiling hidden down an Old Town close just off the Royal

Mile. There are steps down to the entrance, as was common in the past. The real ales are often from Scottish or Northumbrian micros and a single but varying real cider is available. A welcome spot for refreshment after visiting the castle. Dogs are permitted after 3pm, but no children inside. Q≋(Waverley)

Oxford Bar ★

8 Young Street, EH2 4JB (off Charlotte Sq)
11-midnight (1am Fri & Sat); 12.30-11 Sun
(0131) 539 7119 oxfordbar.co.uk
Caledonian Deuchars IPA; 3 changing beers H
Small, basic, vibrant drinking shop mostly unaltered since the late-19th century. The bar counter nearly fills the small front room but there is more space in the side room. It is renowned as one of the favourite pubs of Rebus and his creator Ian Rankin, and a haunt of many other famous and infamous characters over the years. The three guest beers are usually from Scottish breweries. Children are not admitted. A real taste of New Town past. Q

Teuchters

26 William Street, EH3 7NH
11-1am (0131) 225 2973 aroomin.co.uk/teuchters-2
Caledonian Deuchars IPA; Fyne Ales Jarl; Highland Dark Munro; Timothy Taylor Landlord; 1 changing beer H
A cosy but deceptively roomy bar with a rustic feel, wooden beams and original stone walls. Small place-name plates from Teuchterland act as a frieze along the walls. Seating ranges from chairs around wooden tables to chunky sofas. The gantry has an impressive range of single malt whiskies and an explanation of the pub's name. Snacks are served in the bar while the restaurant downstairs (no disabled access) offers fresh local produce. Food is available all day. Real ales are usually from Scottish micros. (Haymarket)

Thomson's Bar

182-184 Morrison Street, EH3 8EB
12-11.30 (midnight Thu & Sat; 1am Fri); 4-11.30 Sun
(0131) 228 5700 thomsonsbaredinburgh.co.uk
6 changing beers H/A
Superb single-roomed bar modelled on the style of Glasgow architect Alexander 'Greek' Thomson. The hand-made gantry and room panelling are inlaid with scenes from Greek mythology. The walls are decorated with rare mirrors, adverts and point of sale material from long-forgotten breweries. It is a member of Oakham Ales' Oakademy, and up to six, often hoppy, real ales are served from a variety of breweries. No food is served on Sunday and pies only on Saturday. Children are not admitted. Q(Haymarket)

Edinburgh: North

Cask & Barrel

115 Broughton Street, EH1 3RZ
11-12.30am (1am Thu-Sat); 12.30-12.30am Sun
(0131) 556 3132
Caledonian Deuchars IPA, Edinburgh Castle 80/-; Draught Bass; Highland Orkney Best; Young's Special; house beer (by Hadrian Border); 4 changing beers H
Spacious and busy alehouse drawing a varied clientele of all ages, ranging from business people to football fans. The interior features an imposing horseshoe bar, bare floorboards, a splendid cornice and a collection of brewery mirrors. Old barrels serve as tables. The guest beers, often from smaller Scottish breweries, come in a range of strengths and styles. Sparklers can be removed on request. Children are not permitted. (Waverley)

Cumberland Bar

1-3 Cumberland Street, EH3 6RT (new town)
12-midnight (1am Thu-Sat); 11-midnight Sun
(0131) 558 3134 cumberlandbar.co.uk
Caledonian Deuchars IPA; Fyne Ales Jarl; Timothy Taylor Landlord; 4 changing beers H
Elegant, traditional New Town pub with half-wood panelling complemented by dark green leather seating. Exquisite brewery mirrors hang beside framed, decorative and illustrative posters. The corridor between the front drinking area and another cosy drinking area at the back is flanked by a small snug and a side room. Four guest beers are generally from smaller breweries such as Alechemy, Fyne and Highland. Meals are served all day (until 5pm Sun). Q

Malt & Hops

45 The Shore, Leith, EH6 6QU
12-11 (midnight Wed & Thu; 1am Fri & Sat); 12.30-11 Sun
(0131) 555 0083 barcalisa.com
8 changing beers H
Single-roomed, old-fashioned public bar by the Water of Leith dating from 1747. The walls are bedecked with mirrors, prints and beer-related artefacts and memorabilia. A large selection of pumpclips and water jugs, many from long-lost breweries and distilleries, hang from the ceiling along with real hop bines that are renewed every harvest. The wide variety of real ales comes from all over the UK, with an emphasis on smaller breweries. Meals served only on Fridays.

Old Chain Pier

32 Trinity Crescent, EH5 3ED
12-11 (midnight Fri & Sat); 12-11 Sun winter; 12-11 (1am Fri); 11-1am Sat; 11-11 Sun summer (0131) 552 4960
oldchainpier.com
Timothy Taylor Landlord; 3 changing beers H
The only pub in Edinburgh directly on the seafront, with panoramic windows giving superb vistas across the Firth of Forth to Fife and seats to enjoy the view in the summer. Situated in the 1821 booking office of a pier destroyed by a storm in 1898, the building has a colourful history. The conservatory and mezzanine are ideal for meals, served all day, with an emphasis on traditional Scottish pub food. One guest beer is usually from Alechemy.

Stockbridge Tap

2-4 Raeburn Place, Stockbridge, EH4 1HN
12-midnight (1am Fri & Sat); 12.30-midnight Sun
(0131) 343 3000
Alechemy Ritual; Stewart Pentland IPA; 5 changing beers H
Very much a specialist real ale house, offering unusual and interesting beers from all over the UK and holding occasional beer festivals. The L-shaped room, with a bright bar area, boasts mirrors from lost breweries including Murray's and Campbell's. There is plenty of seating and ample space for vertical drinking. A pub food menu is available (no meals all day Mon or Fri-Sun eves). Children are not admitted. CAMRA Edinburgh Pub of the Year 2015. May close early.

SCOTLAND

Teuchters Landing

1c Dock Place, Leith, EH6 6LU

🕘 10.30-1am ☎ (0131) 554 7427 🌐 aroomin.co.uk/teuchters-landing

Caledonian Deuchars IPA; Fyne Ales Jarl; Inveralmond Ossian; Timothy Taylor Landlord; 2 changing beers Ⓗ

Converted from the former waiting room for the Leith to Aberdeen ferry, the attractive bar has a wood-panelled ceiling and tiles featuring random Scottish place names from Teuchterland. There are also some smaller rooms and a large conservatory extension that opens out onto a pontoon floating on the Water of Leith. The food menu, available all day, includes meals served in small or large mugs. An excellent selection of malt whiskies is available. ❀◑♿♣🚌🐾📶

Edinburgh: South

Auld Hoose

23-25 St Leonards Street, EH8 9QN

🕘 12 (12.30 Sun)-12.45am ☎ (0131) 668 2934 🌐 theauldhoose.co.uk

Harviestoun Bitter & Twisted; Wychwood Hobgoblin; 1 changing beer Ⓗ

Traditional pub dating back to the 1860s with a large central horseshoe bar and lots of pictures of old Edinburgh. This is a friendly pub with a broad clientele, including students. The jukebox features metal and punk. A pub quiz is held every Tuesday. Good food is served all day including vegetarian and vegan options (CAMRA members and students receive a 10 per cent discount). The guest beer is usually from a smaller brewery. Newspapers are provided. Children are not admitted. ◑♣🚌(14)🐾📶

Cask & Barrel (Southside)

24-26 West Preston Street, EH8 9PZ

🕘 12-midnight (1am Fri); 11-1am Sat; 12.30-midnight Sun ☎ (0131) 667 0856

Caledonian Deuchars IPA; Highland Orkney Best; Stewart Brewing 80/-; 5 changing beers Ⓗ

Modern re-creation of a Scottish city or tenement bar. The single room, with windows front and back, is divided by a horseshoe bar with a dark-wood gantry adorned with decorative wooden casks. The walls support a fine range of old photos, framed advertisements and historic brewery and distillery mirrors. A good place to try real ales from interesting breweries UK-wide. Children are not admitted. CAMRA Edinburgh Pub of the Year runner-up in 2015. 🚌📶

Cloisters Bar

26 Brougham Street, EH3 9JH

🕘 12-midnight (1am Fri & Sat); 12.30-midnight Sun ☎ (0131) 221 9997 🌐 cloistersbar.com

Stewart Pentland IPA, Holy Grale; 7 changing beers Ⓗ

Established in 1995 in the former All Saints Parsonage, many traditional features have been maintained at this welcoming bar. The wide range of single malt whiskies, gins and rums does justice to the outstanding gantry. Seven guest beers are from breweries UK-wide with Highland and Alechemy brews often among the range. Frequent beer festivals and Meet the Brewer events are held. Meals are freshly prepared and available all day on Saturday (no food Mon or Sun eve). Q◑♣🚌(24)🐾📶

Dagda Bar

93-95 Buccleuch Street, EH8 9NG

🕘 12.30 (1 Sun)-1am ☎ (0131) 667 9773

House beer (by Broughton); 3 changing beers Ⓗ

A really cosy howff situated in the heart of the university area attracting a wide-ranging clientele. The small single room has banquette seating on three sides and a welcoming U-shaped bar. The staff are knowledgable about their beers, which are usually from local breweries, including their own Dagda Ale brewed by Broughton. There is also a good range of whiskies and bottled beers. Children are not admitted. An essential stop on any Southside pub walk. ♣🚌🐾📶

Edinburgh: West

Athletic Arms (Diggers)

1-3 Angle Park Terrace, EH11 2JX

🕘 11-1am ☎ (0131) 337 3822

Caledonian Deuchars IPA, Golden XPA; house beer (by Stewart Brewing) Ⓐ**; 3 changing beers** Ⓗ

Situated between two graveyards, the name Diggers became synonymous with this Edinburgh pub legend, which opened in 1897. Banquette seating lines the walls, and a compass drawing in the floor aids the geographically challenged. A smaller back room has a dartboard and further seating. Quieter now than in its heyday, though packed when Hearts are at home, it continues to extend a warm welcome to locals and visitors alike. The guest beers are sourced from many different breweries. Outstanding pies! ♣🚌🐾📶

Caley Sample Room

56 Angle Park Terrace, EH11 2JR

🕘 12-midnight (1am Fri); 11-1am Sat; 11-midnight Sun ☎ (0131) 337 7204 🌐 thecaleysampleroom.co.uk

Caledonian Deuchars IPA; 7 changing beers Ⓗ

Large one-roomed bar with iron pillars and bare brick walls, divided into dining and drinking areas, which resembles the sample cellar at the nearby Caledonian Brewery. There are seven guest beers, usually from micros, and an interesting range of bottled beers. Popular high-quality food is served all day. The atmosphere is usually relaxed but hots up when Hearts are at home. Dogs are permitted outwith the food area. 🐴◑♿🚌🐾📶

White Lady Hotel

92-98 St John's Road, Corstorphine, EH12 8AT

🕘 7am-midnight (1am Fri & Sat) ☎ (0131) 314 0680

Caledonian Deuchars IPA; Greene King Abbot; 6 changing beers Ⓗ

A Wetherspoon hotel with a comfortable lounge bar separated into multiple sections including a raised area opposite the bar and several alcoves to the rear. The decor includes wood-veneer panelling, Art Deco chandeliers, an open fireplace and a black iron sculpture called The Grim Reaper. Many prints and an engraved stone panel provide historic information about Corstorphine, Edinburgh and Scotland. The rear section has a peaked skylight. The bar can be busy in the evenings, especially at weekends. Alcohol is served from 9am (11am Sun), and food all day. Q🐴❀🛏◑♿P🚌📶

Winstons

20 Kirk Loan, Corstorphine, EH12 7HD (off St Johns Road)

11-11.30 (midnight Thu; 1am Fri & Sat); 12.30-11 Sun
(0131) 539 7077 winstonslounge.co.uk
Caledonian Deuchars IPA; 3 changing beers Ⓗ
A comfortable lounge bar in Corstorphine, just over a mile from Murrayfield Stadium and a half mile from the zoo. Set in a small, modern building, this single-room pub is a warm and welcoming community venue used by old and young alike. The decor features golfing and rugby themes along with historic photos of the area. The guest beers are usually from a variety of Scottish micros. Lunchtime meals include wonderful home-made pies (no food Sun). Children are not admitted.

Garvald

Garvald Inn
EH41 4LN
closed Mon; 12-11 (midnight Fri & Sat); 12.30-7 Sun
(01620) 830311
1 changing beer Ⓗ
A family-run 18th-century pub in a pretty village by the Lammermuir Hills. The bar is cosy and welcoming, with half-panelled walls, a crimson colour scheme and an exposed stone wall with a large wood-burning stove. The single real ale is often from Stewart Brewing. The inn is popular for food, served in both the bar and tiny dining room – the dinner menu is particularly impressive. Live music features occasionally. Q P

Glencorse

Flotterstone Inn
Milton Bridge, EH26 0PP (off A702 by Pentland Hills visitor centre)
11.30-11 (01968) 673717 flotterstoneinn.com
Stewart Pentland IPA; 1 changing beer Ⓗ
This old stone-built inn is a handy place to recover following a day on the Pentland Hills. The lounge bar, warmed by a wood-burning stove, has church pew seating and is decorated with toby jugs and pictures. The attractive dining room has bare stone walls and a wooden ceiling. An extensive range of food is served all day. A modern timber-and-glass extension is available for functions, overlooking the enclosed garden. Guest beers are often from Stewart Brewing. P (101,102)

Gorebridge

Stobsmill Inn (Bruntons)
25 Powdermill Brae, EH23 4HX
11-11.30 Mon & Thu; 12-11 Tue; 11-11 Wed; 11-midnight Fri & Sat; 12.30-11.30 Sun (01875) 820202
1 changing beer Ⓗ
Built in 1866 as a public house, the wooden-floored bar room divides into two areas – one with a long L-shaped counter and bar stools, the other with bench seating, tables and chairs. Wooden panels engraved with sporting scenes hide an intriguingly tiny jug bar. A downstairs lounge is not currently in use. The single real ale is often from a smaller Scottish brewery. Simple bar snacks are available at all times. Over-21s only.
P (29,33)

Gullane

Golf Inn
Main Street, EH31 2AB
11-11 (midnight Thu-Sun) (01620) 843259
golfinn.co.uk
2 changing beers Ⓗ
Modern bar and dining area adjoining the hotel and restaurant. Golfing photos and memorabilia adorn the walls and there is a real fire in winter. Meals are served all day – choose from the bar menu or a three-course set menu in the restaurant. A sports bar/function room leads off the bar. The real ales are usually from the Greene King/Belhaven list.

Haddington

Golf Tavern
5 Bridge Street, EH41 4AU
11-11 (midnight Thu; 1am Fri & Sat); 11-midnight Sun
(01620) 822327 golftavernhaddington.co.uk
1 changing beer Ⓗ
A traditional locals' bar nestling behind the Waterside Bistro on the south-east side of the River Tyne. The public bar, with jugs, bottles and mirrors adorning the walls, has a pool table and dartboard. Only one of the two handpumps is in use, with real ales from Tryst, Broughton and Knops often on tap. The spacious lounge bar acts mainly as a popular restaurant and function room. Food is served all day Saturday and until 7pm on Sunday.

Linlithgow

Platform 3 Ⓛ
1a High Street, EH49 7AB
10.30-midnight (1am Fri & Sat); 12.30-midnight Sun
(01506) 847405 platform3.co.uk
Caledonian Deuchars IPA; 2 changing beers (sourced regionally; often An Teallach, Cairngorm, Harviestoun) Ⓗ
Small, friendly hostelry on the railway station approach, originally the public bar of the hotel next door and renovated in 1998 as a pub in its own right. Look out for the goods train that journeys from the station above the bar, with ducks waiting on a train that never comes. Two changing beers are available, often including Stewart Brewing, with the other from various Scottish breweries. Dogs are welcome, with biscuits 'on tap'.

Star & Garter Hotel
1 High Street, EH49 7AB
11-midnight (1am Fri & Sat); 12.30-1am Sun
(01506) 845647 starandgarterhotel.co.uk
Caledonian Deuchars IPA; Timothy Taylor Landlord; 3 changing beers (sourced regionally; often Fyne Ales, Inveralmond, Tryst) Ⓗ
The Star & Garter was conceived in the same year as was Scotland's national bard, Robert Burns, so the year 2009 marked the 250th anniversary of the poet's birth and also 250 years of Number One, High Street, Linlithgow, affectionately known to local residents as simply The Star. Devastated by fire in 2010, the building rose like a phoenix and was transformed into a fine hotel with public bar and restaurant on the ground floor. Five ales are regularly available. P

Lothianbridge

Sun Inn
EH22 4TR (A7, near Newtongrange)

SCOTLAND

11-11 (midnight Fri & Sat) ☎ (0131) 663 2456
thesuninnedinburgh.co.uk
2 changing beers Ⓗ
A well-appointed award-winning gastro-pub built circa 1870 next to the impressive 23-span Waverley Line viaduct. The tasteful interior has a mixture of exposed stone, papered walls, wooden floors and carpets. Meals are served all day on Sunday until 7pm and afternoon teas are available during the week. Space is limited for drinkers at busy times. The guest beers are usually from local breweries. The bar may close early if quiet.
❀◑♿ΛP (29,39)

Musselburgh

David MacBeth Moir
Bridge Street, EH21 6AG (opp Brunton Theatre)
8am-11 (midnight Thu; 1am Fri & Sat) ☎ (0131) 653 1060
Caledonian Deuchars IPA; Greene King Abbot; 8 changing beers Ⓗ
Wetherspoon pub named after a local physician and writer, set in a former cinema dating back to 1935. The main door and original features have been beautifully restored, and the vast single-room bar is filled with cinema-related Art Deco artefacts. The long bar counter has 10 handpumps offering a good mix of guest ales and a cider, often Westons Old Rosie. Food is served all day. Licensed from 11am (12.30pm Sun). ❀◑♿

Levenhall Arms
10 Ravensheugh Road, EH21 7PP (on B1348 1 mile E of centre)
12-11 (midnight Thu; 1am Fri & Sat); 12.30-midnight Sun
☎ (0131) 665 3220
Inveralmond Ossian Ⓐ**; 3 changing beers** Ⓗ/Ⓐ
A three-roomed hostelry dating from 1830 and close to the racecourse. The lively, cheerfully decorated public bar is half timber-panelled and carpeted. Dominoes is popular here and there is a TV for sporting events. A smaller area leads off, with a dartboard and pictures of old local industries. The pleasant lounge has a hardwood floor and comfortable seating. Expect to find some interesting guest beers from smaller breweries.
❀◐Λ♣P

Volunteer Arms (Staggs)
81 North High Street, EH21 6JE (behind The Brunton)
12-11 (11.30 Thu; midnight Fri); 11-midnight Sat; 12.30-11 Sun ☎ (0131) 665 9654 staggsbar.com
Oakham JHB, Bishops Farewell; 9 changing beers Ⓗ
Superb pub run by the same family since 1858. The bar and snug are traditional, with wooden floors, wood panelling and mirrors from defunct local breweries. The attractive gantry is topped with old casks. The more modern lounge opens at the weekend. Up to nine guest beers, mostly pale and hoppy but often one darker, change regularly. CAMRA Lothian Pub of the Year 2015 and winner of many previous awards – see the bar wall.
❀♣

North Berwick

Nether Abbey Hotel
20 Dirleton Avenue, EH39 4BQ (on A198 ¾ mile W of centre)
11-11 (midnight Thu; 1am Fri & Sat) ☎ (01620) 892802
netherabbey.co.uk
4 changing beers Ⓗ
Busy, family-run, award-winning hotel in a stone-built villa, offering a bright, contemporary interior comprising open-plan rooms including a restaurant. The Fly Half Bar is in a newly expanded split-level glass extension. Real ales are often from Scottish micros, including the local Knops beer – sparklers can be removed on request. The Nethers is famous for its good, freshly cooked and locally-sourced cuisine, served all day Friday-Sunday.
❀◑♿Λ⇌P (X24,124)

Ship Inn
7-9 Quality Street, EH39 4HJ
11-11 (1am Thu-Sat) ☎ (01620) 890676
Harviestoun Schiehallion; 2 changing beers Ⓗ
Spacious, open-plan bar located beneath a tenement block at the leafy east end of town. The bar area has pine floorboards, a mahogany counter and a dark-stained wood gantry. A quieter carpeted area is to the rear. The guest beers often include one with a higher ABV. Sparklers are happily removed on request. The pub is popular for food, with good vegetarian options, served all day until 8pm (6pm winter). ❀◑Λ

Penicuik

Navaar House Hotel
23 Bog Road, EH26 9BY (just W of centre)
12-1am (midnight Sun) ☎ (01968) 672683
navaarhouse.co.uk
Highland Orkney Best; 1 changing beer Ⓗ
A lively pub with a strong community spirit, situated in an old private house, built circa 1895 for Professor James Cossar Ewart and where he conducted his world-famous work on animal hybrids, known as the Pennycuik Experiments. The large bar is open plan, with a log/coal stove and TV screens. The guest beer is usually from Stewart or another Scottish micro. The restaurant serves good locally-sourced food (all day Sat & Sun).
❀◑♣P (37)

Ratho

Bridge Inn
27 Baird Road, EH28 8RA (by Union Canal, bridge 15)
9am-11 (midnight Fri & Sat) ☎ (0131) 333 1320
bridgeinn.com
4 changing beers Ⓗ
Food-oriented old canalside inn with a restaurant and outdoor dining area overlooking the Union Canal. Meals are served all day at weekends. Barge cruises run for lunch, dinner and functions. Dating from 1750, the older part contains a separate bar for drinkers. The real ales are usually from smaller Scottish breweries, with one pump dedicated to Alechemy. The inn was a focal point during the canal restoration campaign. Alcohol is served from 11am (noon Sun). ❀◑♿♣P (20)

Beer is proof that God loves us and wants us to be happy. **Benjamin Franklin**

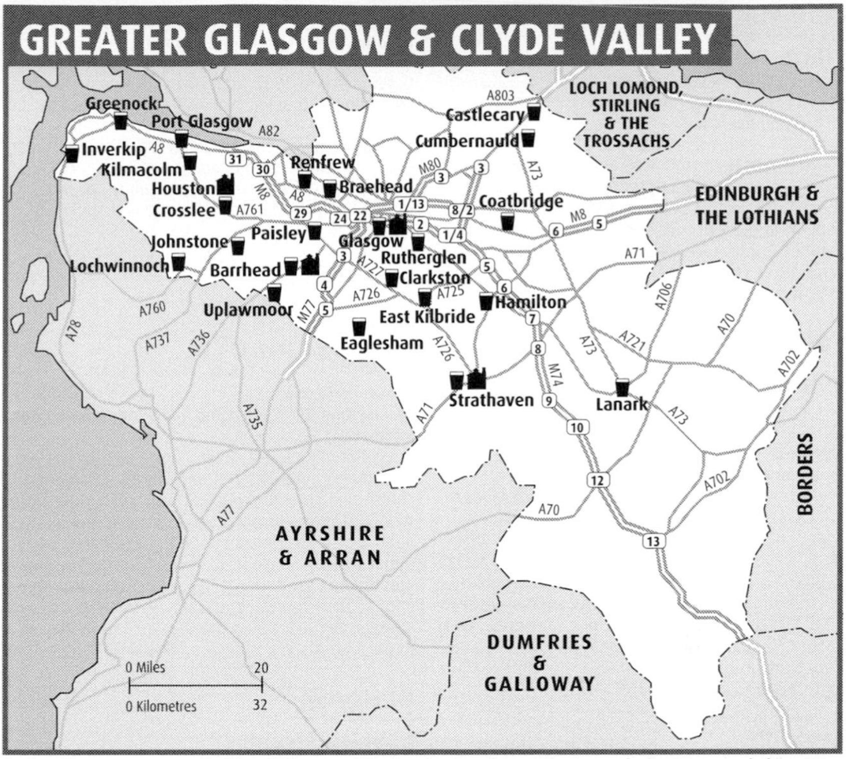

Authority areas covered: City of Glasgow UA, Dunbartonshire UAs, Inverclyde UA, Lanarkshire UAs, Renfrewshire UAs

Barrhead

Cross Stobs Inn

2-6 Grahamston Road, G78 1NS (on B7712)
11-11 (midnight Thu & Sat; 1am Fri); 12.30-11 Sun
(0141) 881 1581
Kelburn Misty Law; 1 changing beer
Eighteenth-century coaching inn on the road to Paisley. The public bar has a real coal fire and retains much of its original charm with antique furniture and service bells. The lounge is spacious and leads out to an enclosed garden to the rear. There is also an outside drinking area at the front of the pub. The public bar leads to a pool room and a function suite. P (51,101)

Waterside Inn

The Hurlet, Glasgow Road, G53 7TH (A736, near Hurlet)
11-11 (midnight Fri & Sat); 12.30-11 Sun
(0141) 881 2822 thewatersideinn.net
1 changing beer (sourced locally; often Kelburn)
A comfortable and friendly bar and restaurant near Levern Water. Food is the main focus here, but there is a cosy area with a real fire for those just wanting a relaxing drink. The decor is clean and traditional, and features old local photographs. Various theme nights are held fairly regularly. There is also a spacious function suite to the rear of the building. The ale is always from the local Kelburn Brewery. Q P (103,X44B)

Braehead

Steam Wheeler

1 Row Avenue, G51 4SY
11-11 (0141) 886 3995
3 changing beers
Modern Marston's family-friendly pub restaurant, situated close to Braehead shopping centre and the King George V Dock. The focus is on dining, with carvery meals served all day, but real ale is not forgotten, with three handpumps serving a selection of English ales primarily from the Marston's range. P

Castlecary

Castlecary House Hotel

Castlecary Road, G68 0HD (just off A80 nr M80 jct 4)
11-11 (11.30 Thu-Sat); 12.30-11 Sun (01324) 840233
castlecaryhotel.com
4 changing beers (sourced nationally; often An Teallach)
A private family-run hotel near the M80 and Glasgow-Edinburgh railway viaduct. Four handpumps can be found in the Wee Bar, but ales can be ordered from any of the three bars. These come mainly from the An Teallach, and from other breweries at busy times. A convenient stop-off for visitors to the Forth & Clyde Canal or the Roman fort on the course of the Antonine Wall.
Q P (X37,X39)

Clarkston

White Cart

61 East Kilbride Road, G76 8HX
11-11; 12-10 Sun ☎ (0141) 644 2711
3 changing beers Ⓗ
A friendly welcome awaits you at this large Chef & Brewer pub. The emphasis here is on food service but there are four handpumps dispensing a changing choice of beers. A patio at the front is popular in the summer and there is an area for families inside. CAMRA members receive a discount of 10 per cent on real ale.
(Busby) P

Coatbridge

Vulcan

181 Main Street, ML5 3HH (jct with Dunbeth Rd)
11-midnight (1am Fri & Sat) ☎ (01236) 437972
Caledonian Deuchars IPA; Greene King Abbot; 4 changing beers (sourced nationally) Ⓗ
Town-centre establishment at the end of Main Street and a rare example of Wetherspoon adapting an existing hostelry. Consequently it is smaller than other pubs in the chain, which helps to give it a cosy, homely and welcoming ambience in an area lacking in real ale. It is popular with a local clientele and those searching for decent beer in North Lanarkshire. The guest ales often come from Scottish breweries.
(Sunnyside)

Crosslee

River Inn

Houston Street, PA6 7AW
9am-11 (midnight Thu; 1am Fri & Sat); 9am-midnight Sun ☎ (01505) 613288 riverinn.co.uk
4 changing beers (sourced regionally) Ⓗ
Opened in 2005, the River Inn is a family-friendly restaurant specialising in locally sourced produce. The warm, welcoming service extends to the Brierie Village Bar, which caters for locals and visitors alike. A quiz night is held every Thursday and several themed food evenings each month, including a family buffet on Tuesday, Wednesday and Thursday, and tapas on the first Monday of the month. P

Cumbernauld

Carrick Stone

52 Teviot Walk, G67 1NG
11-11 (midnight Fri & Sat) ☎ (01236) 850260
Caledonian Deuchars IPA; Fuller's London Pride; Greene King Abbot; 5 changing beers (sourced nationally) Ⓗ
A Wetherspoon pub on two levels at the north-east end of the Cumbernauld shopping centre, taking its name from a standing stone to the north of the town. The two floors have different atmospheres – downstairs there is horse-racing on a screen, upstairs is family- and food-oriented with a 'great outdoors' theme. Convenient for shops, the pub is also close to the leisure centre and a short walk from Cumbernauld House.

Eaglesham

Swan Inn

23 Polnoon Street, G76 0BH
11-11 (midnight Thu-Sat) ☎ (01355) 302673
Timothy Taylor Landlord; 1 changing beer (sourced nationally) Ⓗ
Dating back to 1832, the Swan Inn retains much of its original character, highlighted by a wooden and stained-glass interior. It serves two cask ales – one is Timothy Taylor Landlord and the other a rotating guest. Excellent home-cooked food is served throughout the day in generous portions and reasonably priced – the steak pie is a speciality.

East Kilbride

Hudson's

14-16 Cornwall Way, G74 1JY
11 (12.30 Sun)-midnight ☎ (01355) 581040
hudsonsglasgow.co.uk
Greene King IPA; 2 changing beers (often Broughton, Strathaven) Ⓗ
Busy, handily placed, town-centre pub facing the bus station, near the entrance to the shopping centre and cinema complex, just half a mile from the rail station. Hudsons began serving real ale two years ago and offers two well-priced beers from either nearby Strathaven Ales or Broughton Ales, plus Greene King IPA. It has a long elliptical bar with seating round about and TV screens strategically placed on the walls. The toilets are located up a spiral staircase.

Glasgow

Babbity Bowster

16-18 Blackfriars Street, Merchant City, G1 1PE
11 (12.30 Sun)-midnight ☎ (0141) 552 5055
babbitybowster.com
Caledonian Deuchars IPA; Fyne Ales Jarl; 1 changing beer (sourced regionally; often Inveralmond) Ⓗ
There is a uniquely Scottish flavour to this long-standing Guide favourite, situated in a 1790 building on a pedestrianised street off the High Street. Meals, served in the bar and the restaurant upstairs, feature Scottish ingredients, with some French influences. The comfortable bar has an open fire in winter. Folk musicians entertain on Wednesday and Saturday afternoons. In summer boules is played in the beer garden and patio.
Q (High St)

Blackfriars Ⓛ

36 Bell Street, Merchant City, G1 1LG
11 (12.30 Sun)-midnight ☎ (0141) 552 5924
blackfriarsglasgow.com
5 changing beers (often Alechemy, Kelburn) Ⓗ
Long-standing award-winning real ale outlet in the Merchant City with friendly and efficient staff. It offers five rotating real ales alongside an interesting range of bottled beers, usually including an authentic lambic. The pub hosts bands on Tuesday and Sunday evenings and a comedy club on Saturdays. Good-quality meals are served all

REAL ALE BREWERIES

Clockwork Glasgow
Drygate Glasgow
Houston Houston
Jaw Glasgow (NEW)
Kelburn Barrhead
Strathaven Strathaven
West Glasgow

day. Seating and standing areas are plentiful and although the pub can get busy, it is a must-visit for locals and visitors. (Argyle St)

Bon Accord

153 North Street, Charing Cross, G3 7DA
11 (12.30 Sun)-midnight (0141) 248 4427
bonaccordweb.co.uk
Caledonian Deuchars IPA; Marston's Pedigree; 8 changing beers (sourced nationally) [H]
Traditional hostelry next to the Mitchell Library. One of the first bars in Glasgow to start the revival of cask ale in 1971, nowadays there are 10 handpumps on the bar serving frequently changing guest beers from around Britain. It also hosts several beer festivals annually. In addition, the Bon is one of the best whisky pubs in Scotland, with a selection of over 400 malts and a special house blend. Traditional pub grub is available until 7.45pm. (Charing Cross) (2)

Clockwork Beer Company

Cathcart Road, Mount Florida, G42 9HB
11-midnight; 12.30-11 Sun (0141) 649 0184
Clockwork Original Amber [H], Cartside Red, Lager, Oregon IPA [A]; 5 changing beers (sourced regionally; often Loch Lomond, Stewart) [H]
Ideally located for events at Hampden Park, with great transport links and a car park, this real ale brewpub is not to be missed. Guest ales and strong ales brewed on-site are cask conditioned, while others by Clockwork use a unique tank system for retaining carbon dioxide from fermentation. Good-value food can be enjoyed, with plenty of seating for diners, and there is a mezzanine area available for hire. Several TVs show sport.
(Mount Florida)P

Curlers Rest

256-260 Byres Road, Hillhead, G12 8SH
12-midnight (0141) 341 0737
thecurlersrestglasgow.co.uk
Caledonian Deuchars IPA; Sharp's Doom Bar; Stewart 80/-; 2 changing beers (sourced nationally) [H]
Originally founded in the 17th century beside a pond used for curling, the current pub was constructed from two cottages in the 18th century. A large open-plan bar offers plenty of space for diners and drinkers. Five real ales are available – the guest beers sourced from around the UK – plus a selection of world beers. A bar upstairs provides more seating and an open fire, though the beer range is more limited here.

Drum & Monkey

91-93 St Vincent Street, G2 5TF
11-11 (midnight Fri & Sat) (0141) 221 6636
Caledonian Deuchars IPA; St Austell Nicholson's Pale Ale; 3 changing beers (sourced nationally) [H]
Busy Nicholson's alehouse situated within easy reach of both Central and Queen Street stations. Housed in a former bank dating from 1924, the surroundings are comfortable, with a marble and wood-panelled interior. Three ever-changing guests usually including a dark and a light ale are popular with the varied clientele, particularly the after-work crowd in the early evening. There is a separate dining room to the rear although food is served throughout. The toilets are downstairs via a spiral staircase. (Central)

Edward Wylie

107-109 Bothwell Street, G2 6TS
7am-11.30 (midnight Fri & Sat); 8am-11.30 Sun
(0141) 229 5480
Caledonian Deuchars IPA; Sharp's Doom Bar; 10 changing beers (sourced nationally; often Hawkshead) [H]
A large establishment set in the business district close to Glasgow Central station, offering the standard Wetherspoon fare. The modern bar offers a variety of seating. Given the number of pubs in the chain in Glasgow, the staff work hard to source interesting beers and make this venue distinct in an area not short of competition. The hard work has paid off and customers are offered a superb range of nationally sourced beers in excellent condition. (Central)

Hengler's Circus

351-363 Sauchiehall Street, Charing Cross, G2 3HU
11-midnight (0141) 331 9810
Caledonian Deuchars IPA; Greene King Abbot; 12 changing beers (sourced nationally) [H]
There are 14 handpumps in this Wetherspoon pub to the west of the city centre. Its location on Glasgow's famous Sauchiehall Street means it attracts an eclectic mix of customers. The genial staff are always looking for suggestions for new beers to try. A handy pub whether you are stopping for a short break from shopping or want a longer stay to sample the ever-changing range of well-kept real ales. Q(Charing Cross)

Inn Deep

445 Great Western Road, Hillhead, G12 8HH
12-midnight (11 Sun) (0141) 357 1075 inndeep.com
3 changing beers (sourced nationally; often Williams Bros) [P]
Inn Deep is built into arches along the river walkway beside the former railway station and in the shadow of Kelvin Bridge. Access is from a doorway on the main road or from the walkway. Three real ales include from one from Williams of Alloa and others from newer breweries around Britain, complemented by meals from a good food menu. There is a DJ on Friday and Saturday evenings and a spoken word event on Tuesdays.
(20,6)

Laurieston Bar ★

58 Bridge Street, Tradeston, G5 9HU
11-midnight; 12.30-11 Sun (0141) 429 4528
Fyne Ales Jarl; 2 changing beers (sourced locally; often Fyne Ales) [H]
Identified by CAMRA as having a nationally important historic interior, the Laurieston's original 1960s décor has been retained in superb condition down to the formica-topped mini tables and horseshoe bar. In keeping with its character, the only hot food served comes from a traditional pie warmer. Two Fyne Ales are sometimes joined by a local beer from Jaw. A well-run bar offering a friendly welcome to allcomers, this is a hidden gem. Glasgow CAMRA Pub of the Year 2013.
(Central)

Mulberry St

778 Pollokshaws Road, Strathbungo, G41 2AE
11-11 (midnight Fri & Sat); 12.30-11 Sun
(0141) 424 0858 mulberrystbarbistro.com
Harviestoun Bitter & Twisted; 2 changing beers (sourced locally; often Fyne Ales) [H]
Comfortable community pub in the conservation area of Strathbungo, named after a street in New York's Little Italy to reflect the owner's Italian roots.

SCOTLAND

The bar and restaurant are laid out in a contemporary manner with wooden tables and comfortable chairs. In summer the seating area outside on the pavement quickly fills in fine weather. Good food is served throughout and the guest beers are usually sourced from Fyne Ales.
(Queen's Park)

Pot Still

154 Hope Street, G2 2TH
11-midnight (0141) 333 0980 thepotstill.co.uk
4 changing beers (sourced regionally) H
Conveniently sited city bar in a building that dates back to the early-19th century. It has been a pub since 1870 and was associated with the spirit trade before then. Renowned for its range of whiskies, more than 600 malts are on offer and tasting evenings are hosted. A limited bar menu is available until 6pm and snacks afterwards. The four real ales all come from Scottish micros.
(Queen St)

Sir John Stirling Maxwell

136-140 Kilmarnock Road, Shawlands, G41 3NN
11-midnight (0141) 636 9024
Caledonian Deuchars IPA; Greene King Abbot; 8 changing beers (sourced nationally; often Kelburn) H
A Wetherspoon supermarket conversion in an elevated position at the south end of Shawlands shopping centre. Ten handpumps dispense a wide range of national and regional ales to a largely local clientele. Popular during the day with shoppers and families, the rear area is mainly used for dining. A quiz on the first Sunday of the month and regular Meet the Brewer events help create a friendly community feel. Open from 8am for breakfast every day.
(Pollokshaws East)

State Bar

148 Holland Street, Charing Cross, G2 4NG (just off Sauchiehall St)
11 (12.30 Sun)-midnight (0141) 332 2159
7 changing beers (sourced nationally; often Fyne Ales, Oakham) H
Glasgow CAMRA Pub of the Year in 2015, the State is situated a short distance from Sauchiehall Street – one of Glasgow's main streets. An ever-changing beer range generally includes a number of ales from Peterborough's Oakham Brewery, together with more local beers served from the characterful central island bar. Food is available weekday lunchtimes. The main bar can get busy on Tuesdays for the weekly blues night.
(Charing Cross)

Sweeney's on the Park

962 Pollokshaws Road, Shawlands, G41 2ET
12-midnight (0141) 632 6741
sweeneysonthepark.com
2 changing beers (sourced locally; often Fyne Ales) H
Busy pub situated across from Queens Park close to Shawlands Cross. It has two handpumps in the traditional bar, usually serving beers from Fyne Ales with occasional guests from Jaw. The modern lounge hosts music sessions throughout the week with enough variety to satisfy all tastes. No meals are available but soup and a roll can be served with a drink on Monday-Thursday afternoons and sausage rolls after 4pm on Friday and Saturday.
(Crossmyloof)

Tennent's

191 Byres Road, Hillhead, G12 8TN
11-11 (midnight Thu-Sat) (0141) 339 7203
thetennentsbarglasgow.co.uk
Brains Rev James; Caledonian Deuchars IPA; Fuller's London Pride; Harviestoun Bitter & Twisted; Marston's Pedigree; St Austell Tribute; 3 changing beers (sourced nationally) H
This long-established pub at the heart of the West End has undergone many refurbishments over the years but has retained its original features and kept its character. The rectangular horseshoe bar features 12 handpumps serving nine regular and three guest beers from national breweries. There is a small lounge to one side reached by a short corridor where pictures of the locals are displayed. Good-value meals are served all day.

Three Judges

141 Dumbarton Road, Partick, G11 6PR
11 (12.30 Sun)-midnight (0141) 337 3055
threejudges.co.uk
Caledonian Deuchars IPA; 8 changing beers (sourced nationally) H
A traditional corner tenement pub on a busy junction at the bottom of Byres Road. Locals come to watch the horse-racing or listen to live jazz on Sunday afternoons while real ales fans come from all over for the choice of ales. Eight guest beers are available from both local and national breweries, as well as a guest cider, and an annual cider festival is hosted. Pork pies are served and customers are welcome to bring their own food.
Q (Partick)

Vale

5-7 Dundas Street, G1 2AH
11-midnight (0141) 333 0946
2 changing beers (sourced nationally) H
A long-established pub with a marble frontage, opposite the side entrance to Queen Street station, this busy bar has changed little over recent years. The walls are covered with pictures and displays depicting the history and scenes of Glasgow's past. Screens showing TV sport are a recent addition, as are the two handpumps serving real ales, often from Scottish microbrewers. The function room upstairs hosts occasional music events.
(Queen St)

Greenock

James Watt

80-92 Cathcart Street, PA15 1DD
8-midnight (1am Wed & Thu; 2am Fri & Sat)
(01475) 722640
Caledonian Deuchars IPA; Greene King Abbot; 3 changing beers H
Situated across the road from Greenock Central Station and close to the bus station, this large open-plan Wetherspoon, in a former post office, is named after one of Greenock's famous sons who improved steam engine technology and has the SI unit of power named after him. The chain's standard value-for-money food is available all day and beer festivals are hosted at various times throughout the year. This pub is an oasis in a beer desert. (Central) (X7,X7A)

Hamilton

George Bar
18 Campbell Street, ML3 6AS
⏲ 12-midnight (1am Fri); 12.30-midnight Sun
☎ (01698) 424225
3 changing beers (sourced nationally) Ⓗ
This small family-run community pub has for many years been an oasis in a real ale desert. The stone flooring and wood panel décor give the room a rustic appeal while the seating area outside has a European café feel. The beers are constantly changing although at least one is usually from a Scottish brewery. Meals are served until 6pm (no food Sun). ◐♿⇌(Central)🚌🐾

Inverkip

Inverkip Hotel
Main Street, PA16 0AS
⏲ 11 (12.30 Sun)-11.30 ☎ (01475) 521478 🌐 inverkip.co.uk
Arran Red Squirrel; 1 changing beer Ⓗ
Small family-run hotel just a short walk from the large Inverkip Marina, making it an ideal staging post for those just messing about on the river or passing through on the way to Largs and the Ayrshire coast. This is the only outlet in the area that regularly sells beer from the Arran Brewery, with a second beer usually from another local brewery. ✿🛏◑◐⇌P🚌(578,580)📶

Johnstone

Callum's 🏆 Ⓛ
26 High Street, PA5 8AH
⏲ 11-11.30 (1am Fri & Sat); 12.30-midnight Sun
☎ (01505) 322925 🌐 callums-bar.com
Caledonian Deuchars IPA; Kelburn Pivo Estivo; Orkney Dark Island; 3 changing beers Ⓗ
Popular town-centre pub offering a friendly welcome and a comfortable atmosphere. A large but unobtrusive TV screen features major sporting events. The lounge has an area for formal dining with themed nights including Thursday curry and Friday steak. There is a function room for private parties. Quiz night is Tuesday and live music plays on Saturday. Six real ales are available, mainly from local Kelburn and Houston breweries.
🐴◑◐♿⇌🚌(36,38)📶

Rennies Ⓛ
8 Collier Street, PA5 8AR
⏲ 11-midnight (1am Fri & Sat); 12.30-midnight Sun
☎ (01505) 326486 🌐 renniesbar.co.uk
Greene King Abbot; 1 changing beer (often Kelburn) Ⓗ
Ideally located in the town centre, this is a family-run business with fantastic home cooking, offering value-for-money meals in both the bar and restaurant. The staff are friendly and welcoming, and live music and quiz nights are held regularly. As you would expect from the name, the outlet has a stylish Charles Rennie Mackintosh theme.
🐴◑◐♿⇌🚌(36,38)

Kilmacolm

Pullman Tavern
Elthinstone Court, Lochwinnoch Road, PA13 4LG
⏲ 11-11 (midnight Wed; 1am Fri & Sat); 12.30-11 Sun
☎ (01505) 874501
1 changing beer Ⓗ
This Mitchells & Butlers establishment is the only pub in a small conservation village and was converted from a railway station that once served this beautiful area of the countryside. There is a large seating area outside which is particularly popular in the summer months with families, walkers and cyclists. A Sustrans cycle path from Paisley to Gourock passes by the building.
✿◑◐♿P🚌(X7)🐾📶

Lanark

Clydesdale Inn
15 Bloomgate, ML11 9ET
⏲ 11-midnight (1am Fri & Sat) ☎ (01555) 678740
Caledonian Deuchars IPA; Greene King Abbot; 8 changing beers (sourced nationally) Ⓗ
A Wetherspoon conversion of a former coaching inn that can name Wordsworth and Dickens as former visitors. Today it is a community-friendly pub, popular with locals, but also a convenient hostelry for visitors to New Lanark Village and Falls of Clyde. The central bar hosts eight handpumps serving a selection of beers from all over the UK. There are two rooms to the side and another to the rear which is used at busy times and for functions.
Q🐴◑◐♿⛺⇌P🚌📶

Lochwinnoch

Brown Bull
32 Main Street, PA12 4AH
⏲ 12-11 (midnight Fri & Sat); 12.30-11 Sun
☎ (01505) 843250
Caledonian Deuchars IPA; 3 changing beers (often Kelburn, Stewart, Tryst) Ⓗ
A family-run free house, this village pub is more than 200 years old. Popular with locals and visitors alike, it hosts a quiz night on Tuesday and live music every second Sunday. An ever-changing choice of three guest ales is offered featuring both local and national breweries. There is a quirky seating area outside and the garden to the rear. Bar meals are available and there is a restaurant upstairs serving food made with local produce.
Q🐴✿◑◐♿🍎🚌🐾📶

Paisley

Bull Inn ★ Ⓛ
7 New Street, PA1 1XU
⏲ 11-midnight (1am Fri & Sat); 12.30-midnight Sun
☎ (0141) 849 0472 🌐 bullinnpaisley.co.uk
Caledonian Deuchars IPA; 3 changing beers (sourced regionally; often Arran, Kelburn) Ⓗ
Established in 1901 and identified by CAMRA as having a nationally important historic interior, this is the oldest inn in Paisley. The pub retains many original features including stained-glass windows, three small snugs and a spirit cask gantry, and boasts the only original set of spirit cocks left in Scotland. Guest ales are usually Scottish, with an emphasis on the local Houston and Kelburn breweries. ◑⇌(Gilmour St)🚌🐾📶

Harvies Bar Ⓛ
86 Glasgow Road, PA1 3NU
⏲ 11-11 (1am Fri; midnight Sat); 12.30-midnight Sun
☎ (0141) 889 0911 🌐 harviesbar.co.uk
Kelburn Goldihops; 1 changing beer Ⓗ
Popular tenement-style local situated on the main Paisley to Glasgow road. The spacious open-plan

bar, with raised seating, has three large TV screens showing sport and music videos with the volume turned down low. The pub can get busy during major football matches. Sunday features a quiz night and Monday is poker night. Live music or a DJ play occasionally. ◐♿⇌(Hawkhead)🚌(9,36)📶

Last Post 🄻

2 County Square, PA1 1BN

⏲ 8am-midnight ☎ (0141) 849 6911

Caledonian Deuchars IPA; Greene King Abbot; Ruddles Best Bitter; changing beers 🄷

Large Wetherspoon pub converted from the town's main post office. Open plan in design, there is plenty of seating on two levels. The standard food menu is available. Next to Gilmour Street railway station and close to the bus station, it is handy for a pint between trains or buses. It was the first Wetherspoon pub to hold a Battle of the Brewers competition and continues to run them regularly throughout the year. Six guest ales are usually available. ◐♿⇌(Gilmour St)🚌(9,36)📶

Sandpiper

Glasgow Airport Landside, PA3 2SW

⏲ 3-9.30 ☎ (0141) 842 7858

Greene King Abbot; Sharp's Doom Bar; changing beers 🄷

Positioned on the ground floor, in the public area of the airport, the Sandpiper is ideal if you're looking for an ale before heading through security, waiting for family or friends arriving on an incoming flight or, if you are a plane spotter, in need of refreshment. With six handpumps you are spoiled for choice and can relax watching one of the many TV screens showing 24-hour news or sporting events. ◐♿🚌📶

Wee Howff

53 High Street, PA1 2AN

⏲ 11-midnight (1am Fri & Sat); 12.30-midnight Sun ☎ (0141) 889 2095

3 changing beers 🄷

The Wee Howff has appeared in 25 editions of this Guide and is a little piece of heaven in an otherwise crowded area of cheap drinking establishments. A small, traditional pub with a loyal regular clientele, the Howff offers up to three guest ales from all over Britain selected from a quarterly rotating list. It holds an open mic night on the first Monday of the month and a pub quiz every Thursday. The jukebox caters for the most eclectic of tastes. ⇌(Gilmour St)🚌(9,36)📶

Port Glasgow

Waterwheel

Gallagher Shopping Park, Greenock Road, PA14 5DX

⏲ 9am-11 ☎ (01475) 742167

🌐 waterwheelpubportglasgow.co.uk

Marston's Pedigree; 2 changing beers 🄷

This is a modern family-friendly food-led Marston's pub/restaurant, situated off the A8 on the old East Yard shipbuilding site, with great views of the River Clyde. The focus is on dining, with carvery meals served all day, but real ale fans can enjoy a choice of cask ales on three handpumps from the Marston's family of brewers. 🐴◐⇌P

Renfrew

Lord of the Isles

Unit 21 Xscape, Kings Inch Road, PA4 8XQ

⏲ 8am-midnight (1am Fri & Sat) ☎ (0141) 886 8930

Greene King Abbot; 3 changing beers 🄷

Large, purpose-built Wetherspoon establishment attached to the Soar leisure complex at the Braehead shopping centre. A short stroll allows you to take in the ships docked at Yarrow Shipyard. Throughout the pub the walls display photographs depicting the history of industry on the River Clyde. The outside seating area is south facing and a suntrap on summer days. The standard Wetherspoon food menu is available all day and three ever-changing guest ales are on handpump. ❀◐♿P🚌📶

Rutherglen

An Ruadh Ghlean

40-44 Main Street, G73 2HY

⏲ 11-midnight (1am Fri & Sat) ☎ (0141) 613 2370

Caledonian Deuchars IPA; Greene King Abbot; 6 changing beers 🄷

This is a welcome addition to the former real ale desert of Rutherglen, one of the oldest royal burghs in Scotland. The pub has three distinct seating areas, with views of the pub's cellar and a multi-level garden and smoking area from the windows at the rear. Decorated in typical Wetherspoon style throughout and offering its standard fare, An Ruadh Ghlean is the Gaelic name of the historic royal burgh and translates as 'the red valley'. Q🐴❀◐♿⇌🚌📶

Strathaven

Weavers 🄻

1-3 Green Street, ML10 6LT

⏲ 11.30 (4.30 Tue & Wed)-midnight; 4.30-1am Thu; 11-1am Fri & Sat; 2-1am Sun ☎ 07749 332914

4 changing beers (sourced nationally; often Strathaven) 🄷

This is a one-room pub in the middle of a small town that was once a major centre for the weaving industry. It is a popular meeting place for the local community and famous for its array of large black and white photographs of Hollywood stars. Four handpumps offer an ever-changing range of beers, with one reserved for the nearby Strathaven Ales. Local CAMRA Pub of the Year 2014. ♿🚌(254,256)📶

Uplawmoor

Uplawmoor Hotel 🄻

66 Neilston Road, G78 4AF (off A736)

⏲ 11-11 (10 Mon & Tue); 11-midnight Fri; 11-10 Sun ☎ (01505) 850565 🌐 uplawmoor.co.uk

2 changing beers (sourced locally; often Kelburn) 🄷

Situated in a tranquil village setting just over 10 miles from Glasgow, the building dates back to the 18th century. It was originally a coaching inn used by travellers and customs officers chasing smugglers en-route between Glasgow and the south-west coast of Scotland. Today the hotel continues to offer travellers the opportunity to relax and explore. The interior is rustic and cosy with a public bar, pool room and lounge bar. The beer is always from the local Kelburn Brewing Co. 🐴❀🛏◐♿P📺🚌(395,X44B)🐾📶

Authority areas covered: Highland UA, Western Isles UA

Aviemore

Cairngorm Hotel (Cairn Bar)

77 Grampian Road, PH22 1PE (opp railway station)
11-midnight (1am Fri & Sat); 11.30-midnight Sun
(01479) 810233 cairngorm.com
Cairngorm Stag, Gold
Just across the road from the station, the lounge bar of this privately owned hotel, though large, has a cosy feel. The trade is mainly holidaymakers, but the bar is popular with locals and has a large-screen TV showing sport. Decorated with tartan wall coverings, there is a Scottish theme throughout the hotel, and Scottish entertainment features on many afternoons and evenings.

Old Bridge Inn

Dalfaber Road, PH22 1PU
12-1am (midnight Sun) (01479) 811137
oldbridgeinn.co.uk
Cairngorm Trade Winds; Caledonian Deuchars IPA; 2 changing beers (sourced regionally; often Cairngorm)
Busy pub, popular with outdoor enthusiasts, serving good-quality food made with locally sourced ingredients. Originally a cottage and now greatly enlarged, it lies on the road to the Strathspey Steam Railway overlooking the River Spey. The two guest handpumps dispense the seasonal offering from the local Cairngorm Brewery plus another Scottish ale. Live entertainment is hosted twice weekly, including traditional and modern Scottish music and bands. Children are welcome and there is a bunkhouse attached.

Winking Owl

123 Grampian Road, PH22 1RH
11-midnight (1am Thu-Sat); 12.30-midnight Sun
(01479) 812368 thewinkingowl.co
Cairngorm Stag, Trade Winds, Wildcat; Caledonian Deuchars IPA, Flying Scotsman; 1 changing beer (sourced locally; often Cairngorm)
Legendary Aviemore hostelry, known locally as Winky, now under the stewardship of the nearby Cairngorm Brewery. Reputed to be Aviemore's oldest pub, part of the original inn is where Robert Burns had breakfast during his 1787 Highland tour. The interior has been tastefully redecorated and updated without losing the familiar cosy layout. Beers are from Cairngorm and Caledonian via an innovative brewery tie. The creative all-day menu is designed to please all tastes and appetites, including children.

Carrbridge

Cairn Hotel (Rowanlea Bar)

Main Road, PH23 3AS (just off A9 on B9153 N of Carrbridge)
12-midnight (1am Fri & Sat); 12.30-midnight Sun
(01479) 841212 cairnhotel.co.uk

3 changing beers (sourced regionally; often Cairngorm, Cromarty, Orkney)

Along the road from the Landmark Adventure Park, the Cairn is a traditional Highland inn with seven guest rooms. It is in the Cairngorm National Park and is popular with both locals and visitors. Freshly cooked, seasonal bar meals are available. Three real ales include a local beer from the Cairngorm Brewery, another from Orkney or Cromarty, and the third will be a different Scottish guest ale with every cask. P (15,33,34)

Cawdor

Cawdor Tavern

The Lane, IV12 5XP NH845500

11-3, 5-11 (11-11 summer); 11-midnight Sat; 12.30-11 Sun

(01667) 404777 cawdortavern.co.uk

Orkney Northern Light, Red MacGregor, Dark Island; 1 changing beer (often Atlas, Orkney)

Owned by the same family for nearly 20 years, the pub is at the heart of this conservation village, a short walk from the famous castle and within easy reach of local historic attractions. It has a spacious lounge and cosy public bar, both wood panelled and with log fires, and a large restaurant. Up to four handpumps offer Orkney and Atlas ales – the family also owns the Orkney Brewery at Quoyloo. The Cawdor has a reputation for good food.

Q P (252)

Cluanie

Cluanie Inn

Glenmorriston, IV63 7YW NH076117

8am (12 Sun)-11 (01320) 340238 cluanieinn.com

Loch Ness WilderNESS, HoppyNESS

Cluanie Inn lies next to the A87, the 'Road to the Isles', in the centre of the Highlands surrounded by breathtaking mountain scenery, 20 miles from Loch Ness and 25 from Kyle of Lochalsh. Two Loch Ness ales are available. The hotel is an excellent base for hill walkers and Munro baggers alike, offering a mixture of accommodation from luxury rooms to a club house that sleeps 10. There are no formal camping facilities but 'wild' camping is available locally. Q P (915,916,917)

Dores

Dores Inn

IV2 6TR NH598348

11-11 (midnight Fri & Sat); 12.30-11 Sun

(01463) 751203 thedoresinn.co.uk

4 changing beers (sourced regionally; often Cromarty, Inveralmond, Loch Ness)

On the north-east side of Loch Ness, just eight miles from Inverness, this inn enjoys spectacular views and is ideal for Nessie spotting. The cosy wood-finished bar serves up to four ales, nearly always from Scottish independent breweries such as Cairngorm, Highland and Fyne Ales, with an occasional English ale featured. The welcoming, extended dining room serves good food made with locally sourced ingredients and can get busy at times. Open from 10am for tea, coffee and bakes.

Q P (16,18D,114)

Drumnadrochit

Benleva Hotel

Kilmore Road, IV63 6UH (signed off A82) NH513295

12-midnight (1am Fri); 12.30-11 Sun (01456) 450080

benleva.co.uk

Loch Ness MildNESS; 7 changing beers (sourced regionally; often Loch Ness)

Popular, friendly village inn near Loch Ness, catering for locals and visitors. The sweet chestnut outside this 400-year-old former manse was once a hanging tree. Seven handpumps dispense three Loch Ness Brewery ales accompanied by other Scottish offerings and real cider. Lunches, evening meals and Sunday roasts are available. Entertainment includes poker nights, occasional quiz nights and traditional music. Home of the famous Loch Ness Beer Festival in September and local CAMRA Pub of the Year in 2013.

P

Fort William

Ben Nevis Bar

103 High Street, PH33 6DG

11-1am; 12.30-11.45 Sun (01397) 702295

Caledonian Deuchars IPA; Harviestoun Bitter & Twisted; 1 changing beer (often Harviestoun)

Pleasant two-roomed traditional locals' pub in a building over 300 years old with a ghost in the loft. A decked area at the rear gives splendid views of Loch Linnie. Three handpumps feature Scottish ales from the Mitchells & Butlers list, and over 50 malt whiskies are stocked. A food menu of good honest pub favourites is available all day until around 10pm. Live music plays at weekends.

Ben Nevis Inn

Achintee Road, Claggan, PH33 6TE (signed from N A82 to Inverness) NN125729

12-11; closed Mon-Wed winter (01397) 701227

ben-nevis-inn.co.uk

3 changing beers (sourced locally; often Cairngorm, Isle of Skye)

Popular with outdoor enthusiasts, the inn is housed in a traditional, stone-built barn by the start of the Ben Nevis mountain path. The bar, with long beer hall-style tables and warming stove, is a friendly, informal setting, ideal for the regular live music that plays here. Food is served all day, featuring local produce in a mix of traditional favourites and international dishes, complemented by a choice of three real ales from local breweries. Bunkhouse accommodation sleeps up to 20 people. Check ahead for opening hours in winter. Q P

Cobbs at Nevisport

Airds Crossing, PH33 6EU (beneath Nevisport shop)

11-midnight (1am Fri & Sat); 12.30-midnight Sun

(01397) 704790 cobbs-at-nevisport.co.uk

REAL ALE BREWERIES

An Teallach Dundonell
Black Isle Munlochy
Cairngorm Aviemore
Cromarty Cromarty
Cuillin Sligachan: Isle of Skye
Glenfinnan Glenfinnan
Isle of Skye Uig: Isle of Skye
Loch Ness Drumnadrochit
Old Inn Brewery Gairloch
Plockton Plockton
River Leven Kinlochleven
Wooha Nairn (NEW)

4 changing beers (sourced locally; often Isle of Skye, Orkney) ⊞
At the start/finish of the West Highland and Great Glen ways and close to the Nevis range, this large but cosy bar under the Nevisport shop is a popular meeting place for outdoor enthusiasts. A large fire warms the bar which is adorned with classic mountaineering photographs and outdoor gear. Food is served all day in the bar and upstairs restaurant where children are welcome. Four handpumps dispense a changing range of beers from Highlands and Islands breweries. Live music features regularly. ☕❀⬤①&▲⇌P🖵🛜

Grog & Gruel ⬜
66 High Street, PH33 6AE
✪ 12-11.30 (12.30am Thu-Sat); 5 (12.30 summer)-11.30 Sun
☎ (01397) 705078 ⊕ grogandgruel.co.uk
6 changing beers (sourced locally; often An Teallach, Glenfinnan, Isle of Skye) ⊞
Located at the end of the West Highland Way, halfway along the pedestrianised high street, this award-winning traditional ale house is the perfect place to slake your thirst after the 96-mile hike. Up to six beers are served, fewer in winter, predominantly from Scottish independents. Bar meals and snacks are available all day, and evening meals in the upstairs restaurant. Popular with locals, tourists and outdoor enthusiasts, regular events include live music, open mic nights and beer festivals. ☕①▲⇌⬤🖵🛜

Fortrose

Anderson
Union Street, IV10 8TD (A832)
✪ 4-11.30; closed Mon winter ☎ (01381) 620236
⊕ theanderson.co.uk
3 changing beers (sourced nationally; often Cromarty, Inveralmond) ⊞
Over the past 10 years the bar's three handpumps have offered ales from nearly 400 breweries from all over the UK, with the emphasis on Scottish brews. The shelves groan under the weight of more than 260 malts, 100 Belgian and 30 Mikkeller bottled beers. The restaurant has a well-deserved reputation for excellent meals made with local ingredients. Quiz, music, film and knitting nights all feature regularly. Wood-burning stoves keep the rooms cosy. The pub closes for four weeks in November/December, opening again just before Christmas. Q☕❀🛏①&▲♣⬤P🖵🐾🛜

Foyers

Craigdarroch Inn ⬜
IV2 6XU NH497207
✪ 11-11 ☎ (01456) 486400 ⊕ hotel-loch-ness.co.uk
Loch Ness LightNESS; 1 changing beer (often Loch Ness) ⊞
This AA 4-star inn on the south side of Loch Ness is perched on a hillside with splendid views over the Loch – an ideal base for a spot of monster hunting. Close by are the Falls of Foyers and loch-side/woodland walks. The Am Fuaran Bar (The Well) usually serves LightNESS plus one other brew from the Loch Ness Brewery over the loch. Good seasonal food is available. The hot water and heating are supplied by a biomass wood chip system. Q☕❀🛏①&▲♣P🖵(16)🐾🛜

Glencoe

Clachaig Inn ⬜
PH49 4HX (off A82) NN127567
✪ 11-11 (11.30 Fri; midnight Sat); 12.30-11 Sun
☎ (01855) 811252 ⊕ clachaig.com
10 changing beers (sourced locally; often Orkney, An Teallach, Cairngorm) ⊞
A real ale stronghold for decades, you will be spoilt for choice by the wide range of Scottish brews that feature on up to 15 handpumps. There are three bars to enjoy but the popular Boots bar with its wooden benches and upholstered seating around the walls is the one favoured by the climbers, walkers and tourists who come for the stunning surrounding scenery. Plenty of wood-burning stoves keep the place cosy and there is a hearty food menu to enjoy throughout the day. ☕❀🛏①&♣P🛜

Inverness

Blackfriars ⬜
93-95 Academy Street, IV1 1LU
✪ 11 (3 Mon)-11.30; 11-1am Fri; 11-12.30am Sat; 1-9 Sun
☎ (01463) 233881 ⊕ blackfriarshighlandpub.co.uk
5 changing beers (sourced nationally; often Cromarty, Highland, Inveralmond) ⊞
This popular traditional pub has a spacious single-room interior with a large standing area by the bar and ample seating in comfortable alcoves. The five handpumps deliver a combination of Scottish and English ales, with Scottish beers often from Orkney and Highland breweries, and LocAles from Loch Ness, Cairngorm and Cromarty. The cider is Jaggy Thistle. Good-value home-cooked Scottish fare is served with daily specials including a home-made soup. A welcoming music-oriented venue, bands perform at weekends. ☕①&⇌⬤🖵🛜

Castle Tavern ⬜
1 View Place, IV2 4SA (top of Castle Street)
✪ 11-1am (12.30am Sat); 12-midnight Sun
☎ (01463) 718178 ⊕ castletavern.net
5 changing beers (sourced regionally; often An Teallach, Isle of Skye, Windswept) ⊞
A 73-mile hike along the Great Glen Way or a five-minute stroll from the city centre brings you to this friendly hostelry in a listed building facing the castle and boasting fine views across the River Ness towards the cathedral. Six handpumps dispense a changing range of beers and beer styles, often featuring Scottish independents and LocAle breweries. Bar meals are served all day, and there is a separate restaurant on the first floor. A Victorian-style canopy covers the large beer patio. ☕❀①▲⇌🖵🛜

Clachnaharry Inn ⬜
17-19 High Street, Clachnaharry, IV3 8RB (on A862 Beauly road)
✪ 11-11 (midnight Thu; 1am Fri & Sat); 12-11 Sun
☎ (01463) 239806 ⊕ clachnaharryinn.co.uk
Fyne Ales Jarl; 3 changing beers (often Cairngorm, Greene King, Timothy Taylor) ⊞
Popular with locals and visitors, this friendly 17th-century coaching inn offers high-quality food made with locally sourced ingredients lunchtimes and evenings, and families are welcome. Four handpumps dispense Scottish beers from Inveralmond, Fyne and Cairngorm breweries as well as some from Greene King. The large patio area affords fine views over the Caledonian Canal

sea lock and Beauly Firth toward the Munro, Ben Wyvis. Wednesday is quiz night and Thursday has been a Scottish music jam session night for many years. Q ❀ ◑ ▲ ♣ P 🚌 (28,28A) 🐾 ᯤ

Corriegarth

5-7 Heathmount Road, IV2 3JU (Crown area)
11-midnight (1am Fri & Sat); 12-midnight Sun
☎ (01463) 242730 🌐 corriegarth.com
Caledonian Deuchars IPA; Cromarty Happy Chappy; 2 changing beers
One of the Highland capital's oldest private hotels, constructed around 1840. It is situated in the Crown area of Inverness, a two-minute walk from the city centre, and has six en-suite bedrooms. It has been refurbished to a high standard and is a comfortable, friendly place. In addition to the regular beers, there is a Punch house ale and an occasional guest beer. Q ❀ 🛏 ◑ ♿ ≠ P 🚌 ᯤ

King's Highway

72-74 Church Street, IV1 1EN
11 (12.30 Sun)-1am ☎ (01463) 251830
Adnams Broadside; Caledonian Deuchars IPA; Fuller's London Pride; Greene King Abbot; Sharp's Doom Bar; changing beers (sourced regionally; often An Teallach, Houston)
This former hotel is now a Wetherspoon pub with a 27-room lodge attached which was refurbished in 2013. The vast single-roomed bar is broken up by several pillars and plenty of comfortable seating in alcoves. Up to 10 handpumps serve the regular ales alongside a good mix of guests. Food is standard keenly priced Wetherspoon fare, with breakfast available from 7am. Customers are the typical eclectic mix and the pub gets busy at weekends.
🛏 ◑ ♿ ≠ P 🚌 ᯤ

Number 27

27 Castle Street, IV2 3DU
11-11 (12.30am Fri & Sat); 12.30-11 Sun
☎ (01463) 241999
4 changing beers (sourced regionally; often Inveralmond, Speyside, Windswept)
Alongside the four handpumps, this popular city-centre bar/restaurant offers a large bottle and keg range including continental brews. A good selection of malt whiskies is also stocked. The venue has a reputation for good food – lunches range from sandwiches to light bites while the comprehensive evening menu features traditional main courses made with locally-sourced ingredients including venison and steak. ◑ ≠ 🚌 ᯤ

Phoenix Ale House

106-110 Academy Street, IV1 1LX
11-1am; 12-midnight Sun ☎ (01463) 240300
10 changing beers (sourced nationally; often Houston, Windswept, Cairngorm)
After years of decline, the Phoenix is now a free house and makes a welcome return to the Guide following a 12-year absence. Completely refurbished throughout, the iconic island bar has 10 handpumps offering a wide range of Scottish and English ales, always including a couple of LocAles. The comfortable adjoining lounge is a relaxing place to enjoy a meal from the extensive menu. True to the legend, the Phoenix has risen from the ashes. Q ◑ ♿ ≠ P 🚌

Kincraig

Suie Hotel

PH21 1NA (head of Loch Insh on the B9152, just off A9) NH829057
5-11 (1am Fri & Sat) ☎ (01540) 651344 🌐 suiehotel.com
Cairngorm Trade Winds; 2 changing beers (sourced regionally; often Orkney)
Victorian character hotel located at the south end of the village, run by only the second owner in 108 years. The wooden-floored bar features a large wood-burning stove plus a pool table and jukebox. Three pumps dispense a selection from the local Cairngorm Brewery plus another Scottish guest. Close to the River Spey and Loch Insh, the bar is popular with welcoming locals, hillwalkers, skiers and cyclists. Traditional Scottish music is hosted regularly and good food is served. ❀ 🛏 ♣ P 🚌 🐾 ᯤ

Kinlochewe

Kinlochewe Hotel

IV22 2PA (beside A832 on Gairloch Rd) NH028619
11 (12.30 Sun)-midnight ☎ (01445) 760253
🌐 kinlochewehotel.co.uk
5 changing beers (sourced locally; often Loch Ness, An Teallach, Orkney)
Friendly, family-run 1800s coaching inn. Set in the heart of the magnificent Torridon mountains at the foot of Beinn Eighe, this is an ideal base for exploring the wild scenery of the north-west Highlands. Freshly cooked seasonal dishes are made with high-quality local produce including seafood, game and beef, with an emphasis on simplicity and flavour. Up to five handpumps dispense ales, with a guest in summer, plus Westons Family Reserve cider. A 12-bed bunkhouse is attached.
Q 🛏 ◑ ♿ ▲ ● P 🚌 (700,705,711) 🐾 ᯤ

Munlochy

Allangrange Arms

58 Millbank Road, IV8 8NL
11 (4.45 Mon Oct-Apr)-11; 11-1am Fri & Sat; 11 (12.30 Oct-Apr)-11 Sun ☎ (01463) 819862 🌐 allangrangearms.com
Cromarty Happy Chappy; Orkney Red MacGregor
Modern, lodge-themed, family-friendly pub in the Black Isle village of Munlochy. Quality food made with primarily local produce is served daily (no food Mon Oct-Apr) and a children's menu is available. There is a choice of seating throughout including cosy booths, a small open-plan lounge with a sofa and large-screen TV for sport, and a separate restaurant area. Live music features regularly. Wooden benches outside are pleasant on warmer days. Q ❀ 🛏 ◑ ♿ ♣ P 🚌 🐾 ᯤ

Nairn

Braeval Hotel

Crescent Road, IV12 4NB (E end of town)
12-midnight (12.30am Thu-Sat) ☎ (01667) 452341
🌐 braevalhotel.co.uk
9 changing beers (sourced regionally; often Orkney, Cairngorm, Cromarty)
The family-run Bandstand Bar in the Braeval Hotel has up to nine handpumps offering a good selection of English and Scottish ales. It hosts the largest independent beer festival in the Highlands every spring with around 140 ales and great live music throughout the 10-day event. Quality food is

served in the popular sea-view restaurant. Winner of CAMRA Highland Pub of the Year three times.
Q ❀ ♿ ⛺ ≈ ♣ ● P 🚌 ᯤ

Newtonmore

Glen Hotel

Main Street, PH20 1DD
11 (12.30 Sun)-midnight ☎ (01540) 673203
theglenhotel.co.uk
3 changing beers (sourced regionally; often Cairngorm, Caledonian)
Small, welcoming, family-run Edwardian hotel with the Monadhliath and Cairngorm mountain ranges on its doorstep. It has a good local trade and is also popular with outdoor enthusiasts and tourists. There is a large bar room and separate games and dining rooms, with regular quiz and games nights. Up to three handpumps dispense mainly Scottish beers, plus a Westons cider or perry in the summer. An extensive menu includes a good selection of vegetarian dishes. ♿ ⛺ ≈ ● P 🚌 ᯤ

Plockton

Plockton Hotel

41 Harbour Street, IV52 8TN NG803334
11-midnight; 12.30-11 Sun ☎ (01599) 544274
plocktonhotel.co.uk
House beer (by Inveralmond); 3 changing beers (sourced regionally; often Highland)
Sheltered by mountains and fanned by the warm air of the Gulf Stream, the hotel is at the edge of Loch Carron and boasts breathtaking views across the bay. Seafood is the speciality on an excellent menu that also features locally reared beef and Highland venison. The village has much to offer and is a regular haunt for outdoor enthusiasts. Brews from a variety of Highland and other Scottish micros are regularly on handpump including a house ale. Closed throughout January.
Q ❀ ♿ ≈ P 🚌 (164,620,7100) ᯤ

Roy Bridge

Stronlossit Inn

Main Street, PH31 4AG (3 miles E of A82/A86 jct at Spean Bridge) NN272812
11-11.45 (1am Thu-Sat); 12.30-11.45 Sun
☎ (01397) 712253 stronlossit.co.uk
3 changing beers (sourced regionally; often Orkney, Cairngorm, Fyne Ales)
A roaring log fire warms the cosy bar of this country inn-style hotel, ideally located for enjoying the seemingly endless range of outdoor pursuits on offer in Lochaber. Three regularly changing Scottish beers are available, often from Highlands and Islands breweries, plus an occasional cider. Freshly prepared food is served all day, locally sourced and taking full advantage of Scotland's natural larder. High-quality budget rooms, adjacent to the main hotel, are designed to meet the needs of outdoor enthusiasts.
Q ❀ ♿ ⛺ ≈ ● P 🚌 (19C,41,591) ᯤ

> **The Village Inn**
>
> The village inn, the dear old inn,
> So ancient, clean and free from sin,
> True centre of our rural life.
>
> Where Hodge sits down beside his wife
> And talks of Marx and nuclear fission
> With all a rustic's intuition.
>
> Ah, more than church or school or hall,
> The village inn's the heart of all.
>
> **Sir John Betjeman, 1906-1984, former Poet Laureate**

Thurso

Central Hotel (Top Joe's)

3 Traill Street, KW14 8EJ
11-1am; 12-midnight Sun ☎ (01847) 893129
central-commercial.co.uk
3 changing beers (sourced nationally)
Joe Cardosi came to Thurso in 1910 and established two cafés in Thurso – one on Traill Street, the other at the bottom of town, which became known as the Top and Bottom Joe's. Joe's great grandson Scott Youngson now owns the lively town-centre bar, café and hotel. The horseshoe bar has three handpumps offering varying beers from the Heineken stable, sometimes just one during the quieter winter months. Food can be ordered and served from Caffe Cardosi next door. ⛺ ≈ ♣ P 🚌

Weigh Inn

Burnside, KW14 7UG (N of Thurso on A9 jct to Scrabster)
12-2.30, 4.30-midnight; 12-midnight Fri-Sun
☎ (01847) 893722 weighinn.co.uk
Orkney Corncrake
Overlooking the Pentland Firth with panoramic views of the Orkney Isles, the hotel is close to the Orkney ferry. The Ashes is the main bar, and there are two other bars used for functions. A single real ale is on handpump, alternating between Corncrake and another Orkney beer. There are screens for sport and occasional live entertainment in the bar. Bar meals are served lunchtimes and evenings. Outside is an enclosed children's play area and a patio with tables and seating.
Q ❀ ♿ ⛺ ♣ P 🚌 ᯤ

Ullapool

Argyll Hotel

18 Argyll Street, IV26 2UB
11-1am; 12-midnight Sun ☎ (01854) 612422
theargyllullapool.com
4 changing beers (sourced regionally; often An Teallach)
Busy, small hotel offering breakfast, lunch and dinner all made with locally sourced produce, with good vegetarian and coeliac choices. The beer range includes three changing guest ales plus another from the local An Teallach Ale Co. Live music features on Monday and live bands play on Tuesday and weekends March-October. There are three mini beer festivals including a cider and blues music festival in September. A weekly curry night, quiz and poker keep the bar busy. Ideally located for the ferry to the Hebrides.
❀ ♿ ⛺ ♣ ● P 🚌 🐾 ᯤ

SCOTLAND

Morefield Motel 🄻

North Road, IV26 2TQ (off A835)

⚙ 12-11 ☎ (01854) 612161 🌐 morefieldmotel.co.uk

3 changing beers (sourced regionally; often An Teallach, Cairngorm) 🄷

Locally caught seafood is the speciality on the menu at this family-run, friendly motel. Three ales, fewer in winter, are predominantly from local Highlands breweries. The annual Ullapool Beer Festival is held here in October. The Western Isles ferry terminal in the centre of Ullapool is a short distance away. Winter opening hours can vary. **Q❀🛏◑♿▲P🚌🐾📶**

Waternish: Isle of Skye

Stein Inn 🍷 🄻

MacLeod's Terrace, IV55 8GA (N of Dunvegan, on B886) NG263564

⚙ opening hours vary ☎ (01470) 592362 🌐 steininn.co.uk

3 changing beers (sourced regionally; often Cairngorm, Caledonian, Isle of Skye) 🄷

Dating back to the 18th century, this is the oldest inn on the Isle of Skye, nestling in a row of whitewashed cottages on the shores of Loch Bay, owned and run by the same family for more than 20 years. A large stove warms the cosy low-beamed bar which has fine views over the sea loch to Rubha Maol. Locally caught seafood, landed at the nearby jetty, is served April to October in the bar and restaurant. Guest ales may be from Highland and Loch Ness. For seafarers there are four council moorings. Highlands & Western Isles Pub of the Year 2015. **Q🔥❀🛏◑♿♣P🐾**

Whitebridge

Whitebridge Hotel 🄻

IV2 6UN (SW of Loch Ness on B862) NH487152

⚙ opening hours vary ☎ (01456) 486226

🌐 whitebridgehotel.co.uk

2 changing beers (sourced regionally; often Cairngorm, Cromarty) 🄷

Built in 1899 and located on the 'quiet' side of Loch Ness, this hotel has fishing rights on two local lochs. Inside, the attractive pitch pine-panelled bar, with a welcoming wood-burning stove, has an alcove with a pool table and a separate area used for dining. The traditional pub food is all home cooked. Two ales are usually available, sometimes one in winter. The hotel has a green tourism policy. **Q❀🛏◑♿♣P🚌**(18D,118,301)**🐾📶**

Winking Owl, Aviemore

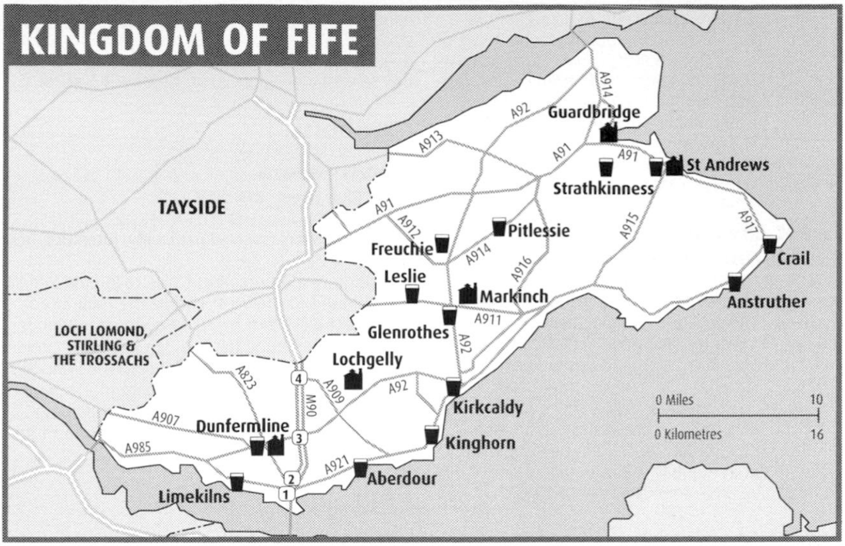

Authority area covered: Fife UA

Aberdour

Foresters Arms

35 High Street, KY3 0SJ

11 (12.30 Sun)-midnight (01383) 860544

forries.co.uk

Caledonian Deuchars IPA; 3 changing beers

A pub at the centre of the community, right in the middle of the village, only minutes away from the railway station. A welcoming retreat for walkers on the Fife coastal path, this family-run inn offers a friendly welcome to all. Live music, quizzes and theme nights are held regularly. Warm yourself by the real coal fire and enjoy a good pub lunch. Kingdom of Fife CAMRA Pub of The Year 2015.

(7)

Anstruther

Boathouse

28 Shore Street, KY10 3AQ

12-11 (midnight Fri & Sat) (01333) 312105

at-the-shore.co.uk

2 changing beers (sourced nationally)

The Boathouse is right in the middle of town by the harbour. It has two handpulls, which offer a variety of beers from local and national breweries. Enjoy a snack in the main bar, or pop into the main restaurant and enjoy fresh, locally prepared meals, while taking in the views of the harbour. At the back of the bar is a games area featuring a pool table. (95,X60)

Ship Tavern

49 Shore Street, KY10 3AQ

11-midnight (1am Fri & Sat); 12.30-midnight Sun

(01333) 310347

2 changing beers (sourced nationally; often Beeches Brewery, Edenmill Brewery St Andrews)

Next door to the famous Anstruther Fish Bar, this traditional pub on the harbour front is a popular meeting place for fishermen, locals and visitors to the museum. The bar has all the character you would expect from a historic fishing village inn. The ever-changing ales are sourced from breweries all over the UK. Take in the views of the harbour or relax in the comfort of the back room.

(X60,95)

Crail

Golf Hotel

4 High Street, KY10 3TD

11-midnight (1am Thu-Sat); 12.30-midnight Sun

(01333) 450206 thegolfhotelcrail.com

3 changing beers

The Golf Hotel is a listed 16th-century coaching inn in a picturesque village in the East Neuk of Fife. The historic bar dates back to 1721, making it one of the oldest in Scotland. The room retains the original low-beamed ceiling, wooden floor and a 16th-century fireplace with a marriage lintel over it bearing the initials of the original owners. Relax with a beer in the garden or enjoy a meal in the restaurant after walking the coastal path.

(95)

Dunfermline

Commercial Inn

13 Douglas Street, KY12 7EB

10-11 (midnight Fri & Sat) (01383) 733876

Caledonian Deuchars IPA, Edinburgh Castle 80/-; Courage Best Bitter; Theakston Old Peculier; 3 changing beers

Cosy town-centre establishment just off the High Street adjacent to the main post office, situated in a historic building dating back to the 1820s. A renowned ale house, it offers seven real ales and a cider. Good food and friendly service attract an eclectic clientele. CAMRA Kingdom of Fife Pub of the Year finalist in 2015 and winner in 2014.

(Town)

Guildhall & Linen Exchange

79-83 High Street, KY12 7DR

8am-midnight (1am Fri & Sat) (01383) 749800

Caledonian Deuchars IPA; Greene King Abbot; changing beers (sourced nationally; often Abbot Brewhouse)

A split-level Wetherspoon pub in a category A listed building, decorated throughout with a mix of modern and Art Deco features. Numerous pictures from years gone by depict Dunfermline's and the Guildhall's past. Among the guest ales are beers from the historic Abbot Brew House, which brews less that 400 yards away. A Kingdom of Fife CAMRA Pub of the Year finalist in 2015 .
(Town)

Sweet Chestnut

Whimbrell Place, KY11 8EX
12-11 (01383) 734103
Marston's Pedigree New World Pale Ale, Pedigree; Wychwood Hobgoblin; 1 changing beer H
The Sweet Chestnut can be found in the Fife Leisure Park, well-served by road and bus links. A typical Marston's outlet, it offers an extensive menu including the popular carvery. A wide range of cask ales from Marston's five breweries can be found on the bar, with two core beers and one guest. This venue is family-friendly, with an indoor and outdoor play area. P(19,19A)

Freuchie

Albert Tavern

2 High Street, KY15 7EX
5 (12 Fri & Sat)-midnight; 12.30-midnight Sun 07876 178863
Changing beers H
A multi award-winner, including former Scottish CAMRA Pub of the Year, Kingdom of Fife Pub of the Year, and a finalist in 2015. A friendly village local, the Albert was reputedly a coaching inn when nearby Falkland Palace was a royal residence. Wainscot panelling and two old brewery mirrors decorate the walls of the bar. A TV in the lounge screens sport. Five handpumps offer weekly changing beers. Q(36,66)

Lomond Hills Hotel

High Street, KY15 7EY
11-2, 5-midnight; 11-midnight Fri & Sat; 12.30-midnight Sun (01337) 857329 lomondhillshotel.com
2 changing beers (sourced nationally; often Beeches) H
Comfortable country hotel, originally a coaching inn established in 1733, with a marvellous view of the Lomond Hills and handy for visiting Falkland Palace. The small, welcoming public bar sports a carved bar top and wood panelling on the walls. A plasma screen shows sport. Two beers are always available. Meals are served in the family lounge and a separate dining room. Outside there is a smoking area and beer garden.
P(36,66)

Glenrothes

Golden Acorn

1 North Street, KY7 5NA
7am-midnight (1am Fri) (01592) 751175
Caledonian Deuchars IPA; Greene King Abbot; changing beers (sourced nationally; often Abbot Brewhouse) H
Wetherspoon establishment with a bar and Wetherlodge, located near the town centre with the bus station only two minutes' walk away. The walls are decorated with scenes of the local area in days gone by. Plasma screens show a number of sporting events. Real ale is offered on seven handpumps alongside a regular cider, and the standard Wetherspoon beer festivals and special deals are available. CAMRA Kingdom of Fife Pub of the Year runner-up in 2014. P

Kinghorn

Crown Tavern

55-57 High Street, KY3 9UW
11 (12.30 Sun)-11.45 (01592) 890340
2 changing beers (sourced nationally; often Beeches, Tryst) H
A bustling two-roomed local, also called the Middle Bar, situated to the west end of the High Street. Two guest ales from microbreweries throughout the UK can be found here, as well as local beers. Attractive stained-glass panels adorn the windows, and the high ceilings feature ornate plaster work. Mainly a sports bar, two TVs screen a wide range of sporting events. A pool table can be found to the side. (7)

Kirkcaldy

Feuars Arms ★

28 Bogies Wynd, KY1 2PH
11.30-midnight (01592) 205577
2 changing beers H
Identified by CAMRA as having a nationally important historic interior with original Edwardian fittings and displays of ceramics. A 59ft-long bar counter is fronted with brown Art Nouveau-style tiles. The large bar area has a mosaic floor, mahogany gantry and long-case clock. Features include stained-glass windows with the arms of Scotland, England and Ireland, lots of etched glass and two mosaic porch floors. The Gents is also well-worth a visit. Q

Harbour Bar

471-475 High Street, KY1 2SN
11-3, 5-midnight; 11-midnight Thu-Sat; 12.30-midnight Sun (01592) 264270
6 changing beers (sourced nationally) H
The building dates from around 1870 and was a ship chandlers' before it became a pub in 1924. It is one of just a few pubs to still have the historic jug bar. The lounge is light and airy with ornate cornices. Six handpumps sell up to 20 different beers a week from micros all over Britain. Kingdom of Fife CAMRA Pub of the Year on numerous occasions, a finalist in 2014 and a previous Scottish Pub of the Year winner. Q

Robert Nairn

2-6 Kirk Wynd, KY1 1EH
8am-midnight (1am Fri & Sat); 8am-11 Sun (01592) 205249
Caledonian Deuchars IPA; Greene King Abbot; 4 changing beers (sourced nationally; often Abbot Brewhouse) H
A Wetherspoon Lloyd's No.1 with a split-level lounge and pictures of old Kirkcaldy on the walls.

REAL ALE BREWERIES

Abbot Dunfermline
Beeches Lochgelly
de bRus Dunfermline (NEW)
Eden St Andrews Guardbridge
Luckie Markinch
St Andrews St Andrews

Six handpulls dispense a variety of beers, local and national, and regular Meet the Brewer evenings are hosted. Set in the city centre, this lively pub attracts a mixed clientele, young and old, who all enjoy the real ales. Big TVs show a range of sporting events and rolling news stories.
ॐ◑♿🕿🚃🚍🔊

Leslie

Burns Tavern
184 High Street, KY6 3DB
☉ 12 (11 Fri & Sat)-midnight; 12.30-midnight Sun
☎ (01592) 741345
Timothy Taylor Landlord; 1 changing beer Ⓗ
Typical Scottish two-room, main-street local in a town once famous for papermaking. The public bar is on two levels, the lower lively and friendly, the upper with a large-screen TV, pool table and football memorabilia on the walls. The lounge bar is quieter and more spacious. Competitions and quizzes are held weekly, and karaoke on Saturday. Leslie Folk Club plays here on a Sunday. Two beers are usually available in this good honest local.
Q♿♣P🚍(38)🐾

Limekilns

Ship Inn
Halketts Hall, KY11 3HJ
☉ 11-11 (midnight Fri & Sat); 12.30-11 Sun
☎ (01383) 872247
3 changing beers (sourced nationally) Ⓗ
Set on the waterfront in a small rural village, this establishment has excellent views across the River Forth. Three guest ales are available, mostly from microbreweries throughout the UK. The bar has a cosy alcove to the left, and a maritime theme features throughout the building. Meals are served lunchtimes with fish and seafood the speciality (booking is essential). A former CAMRA Kingdom of Fife Pub of the Year runner-up. Q♿◑P🚍(6)

Pitlessie

Village Inn
Cupar Road, KY15 7SU
☉ 12-2.30, 5-11 (midnight Thu); 12-midnight Fri (11.30 Sat); 12-11 Sun ☎ (01337) 830595 ● pitlessievillageinn.co.uk
3 changing beers Ⓗ
Old coaching inn decorated with pictures of the maltings that were once opposite. A lovely real fire helps create a cosy atmosphere in the wood-panelled, stone and plaster-walled interior. The room has a corner bar with bar stools and a separate seating area for bar meals or drinks. Three handpulls offer two ever-changing ales and a real cider. There is a large restaurant and separate pool room. High teas are served on Sunday afternoon.
◑🍴P🚍(X24)

St Andrews

Central Bar
77 Market Street, KY16 9NU

☉ 11-11.45 (midnight Fri & Sat); 12.30-11.45 Sun
☎ (01334) 478296
Courage Best Bitter; Fuller's London Pride; Inveralmond Lia Fail; Theakston Old Peculier; 4 changing beers Ⓗ
A characterful city-centre pub on one of St Andrews' main streets, attracting a good mix of students, tourists and locals. The pub has a Victorian-style island bar, large windows and ornate mirrors, creating a late-19th-century feel. Seating outside on the pavement is popular in summer. A former CAMRA Kingdom of Fife Pub of the Year winner. Q♿◑🍴🚍🔊

Criterion
99 South Street, KY16 9QW
☉ 11-midnight (1am Fri & Sat); 12.30-midnight Sun
☎ (01334) 474543
Caledonian Deuchars IPA; 3 changing beers (sourced nationally; often Edenmill) Ⓗ
Lovely local with seating outdoors on the pavement, a big picture window and oak-panelled walls adorned with photographs of St Andrews in days gone by. The pub is renowned for its home-made meals (served until 5pm). Background music plays and a plasma screen shows sport. Open music night on Monday is popular with local artists, and a regular quiz night is hosted during the week.
♿◑🍴🚍

St Andrews Brewing Co
177 South Street, KY16 9EE
☉ 11 (12.30 Sun)-11 ☎ (01334) 471111
● standrewsbrewingcompany.com
Changing beers (sourced locally; often St Andrews) Ⓗ
A new venture for St Andrews Brewing Co, which opened its doors in late 2013, this brewpub showcases a wide range of St Andrews beers in cask, keg and bottles. It has 16 taps, with eight dedicated to cask ales and the rest to specialist cider and beer. Call in for a quick third-pint downstairs by the fireplace or upstairs in the beer hall. A Kingdom of Fife CAMRA Pub Of the Year 2015 finalist. ◑♿🍴🚃🚍🔊

Strathkinness

Tavern
4 High Road, KY16 9RS
☉ 5-11 (midnight Sat & Sun) ☎ (01334) 850085
● strathkinnesstavern.co.uk
3 changing beers Ⓗ
Public bar with seating and a comfortable lounge at one end. There is a separate room with a dartboard, pool table and Sky TV. Three handpulls offer a choice of changing guest ales. Lunches and evening meals are served in the bar and restaurant. Quiz nights are the first and third Tuesday of each month and ceilidh evenings are on Monday. There is a beer garden to the rear and lovely views over the river estuary to the front.
Q♿◑♿♣P🚍(64,64A)🔊

There is nothing which has yet been contrived by man, by which so much happiness is produced as by a good tavern or inn.
In James Boswell, The Life of Samuel Johnson, 1791 [21 March 1776]

LOCH LOMOND, STIRLING & THE TROSSACHS

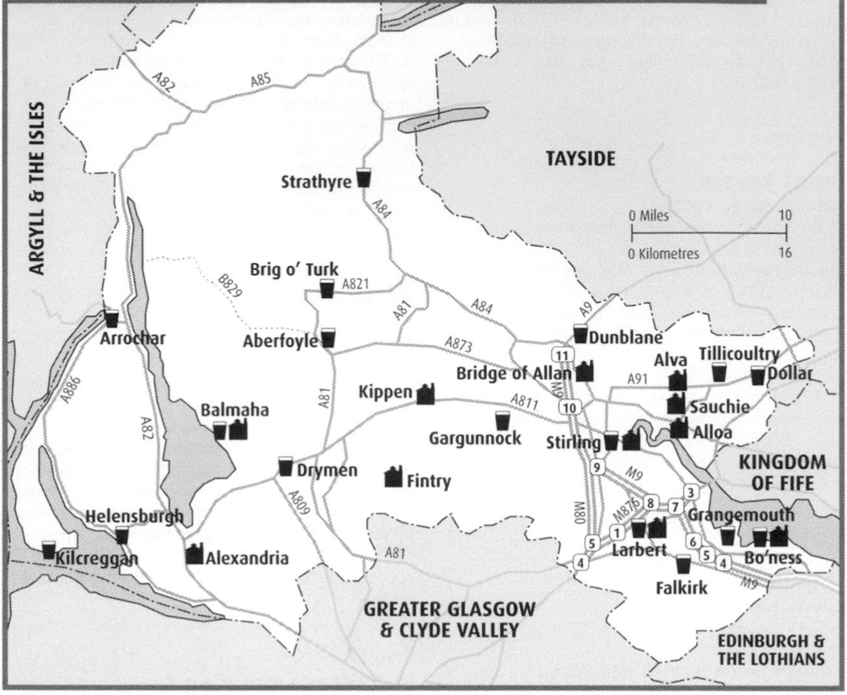

Authority areas covered: Argyll & Bute UA (part), Clackmannanshire UA, Falkirk UA, Stirling UA, West Dumbartonshire UA

Aberfoyle

Forth Inn

Main Street, FK8 3UQ

11-midnight (1am Fri & Sat) ☎ (01877) 382372 forthinn.com

Harviestoun Schiehallion; 4 changing beers (sourced regionally; often Belhaven, Cairngorm, Fallen) Ⓗ

This 100-year-old inn is situated by the River Forth within the Trossachs National Park. The innovative landlord is proud to serve only Scottish ales from up to eight handpumps, with third-pint taster glasses available, and wholesome food featuring locally sourced produce. There is a separate dining room and a 'baronial' dining hall.
Q❀♿▲P (C11)

Arrochar

Village Inn

Shore Road, G83 7AX

11-12.30am (1.30am Fri & Sat); 12-midnight Sun ☎ (01301) 702279 villageinnarrochar.co.uk

Caledonian Deuchars IPA; 3 changing beers (sourced locally; often Loch Lomond) Ⓗ

Hardwood floors and a log fire make for a welcoming ambience here. Popular with walkers and climbers, up to four ales are available and food can be enjoyed in both the bar and restaurant. In summer visitors can enjoy spectacular views of the Cobbler across the loch.
❀♿▲♣P (926,976)

Balmaha

Oak Tree

Main Street, G63 0JQ

8am-midnight ☎ (01360) 870357 theoaktreeinn.co.uk

Balmaha Blonde; 2 changing beers (often Orkney) Ⓗ

An award-winning pub-restaurant in a picturesque village, the Oak Tree now boasts its own Balmaha microbrewery on-site and three handpumps in the bar. Meals are served all day and there is a large outdoor drinking area under the eponymous tree. Licensed from 11am. ❀♿P (309)

Bo'ness

Corbie Inn 🏆

84 Corbiehall, EH51 0AS

12 (12.30 Sun)-11 ☎ (01506) 825307 corbieinn.co.uk

Changing beers (sourced nationally; often Kinneil) Ⓗ

Six ales are usually to be found on handpump, including one from the Kinneil Brew Hoose at the back of the premises. An ideal refreshment stop after a visit to the Bo'ness and Kinneil Railway or the Bo'ness Motor Museum, and also handy for the Hippodrome, Scotland's oldest purpose-built picture house. Very much a community pub and involved in local charity projects.
Q❀P (5C,46)

Brig o' Turk

Byre Inn

FK17 8HT

⏲ 12-11 (midnight Fri & Sat); closed Mon & Tue Dec-Mar
☎ (01877) 376292 🌐 byreinn.co.uk
2 changing beers (sourced locally; often Fallen, Harviestoun, Inveralmond) Ⓗ
Nestled in a tranquil, rural setting, just a few miles from Callander and Aberfoyle, this refurbished old byre in Brig o' Turk is surrounded by rolling countryside and picturesque Trossachs villages. A gastro-pub with a village-inn feel, it serves locally sourced seasonal food, excellent wine sourced from the vineyard and well-kept local microbrewery ales. ❀◐♣P

Dollar

King's Seat
23 Bridge Street, FK14 7DE
⏲ 4-midnight; 12-1am Fri & Sat; 12-midnight Sun
☎ (01259) 742515 🌐 kingsseat.com
Harviestoun Bitter & Twisted; 4 changing beers Ⓗ
Up to six ales and real cider are on offer during the summer, along with bar snacks and restaurant food. Dogs and children are welcome and there are tables and chairs outside for warmer weather. Occasional barbecues and live folk music are hosted. There are many great walks and attractions nearby. Q❀🛏◐♿⛺🍎🚌(23,C69)🐾

Drymen

Clachan
2 Main Street, G63 0BG
⏲ 11-midnight (1am Fri & Sat); 12.30-midnight Sun
☎ (01360) 660824 🌐 clachaninndrymen.co.uk
2 changing beers Ⓗ
The oldest licensed premises in Scotland, dating from 1734, recently sensitively refurbished while preserving many original features. There are two handpumps dispensing an ever-changing selection of excellent local and Scottish beers. Visitors can be sure of a warm welcome, and the pub is a popular stop-off for walkers on the West Highland Way and tourists exploring Loch Lomond National Park. Quality food is served all day in the bar and restaurant. 🔥🛏◐⛺P🚌(309)🐾

Dunblane

Riverside
Stirling Road, FK15 9EP
⏲ 8am-midnight (1am Fri & Sat); 9am-midnight Sun
☎ (01786) 823318 🌐 theriversidedunblane.co.uk
Caledonian Deuchars IPA; 2 changing beers (sourced regionally; often Loch Ness, Orkney, Strathaven) Ⓗ
Stop off here for a hearty breakfast, coffee and home-bakes beside the wood-burning stove, good food in the family-friendly restaurant, or a local beer in the bar or on the riverside terrace. Licensed from 11am. ◐♿⇌🚌

Tappit Hen
Kirk Street, FK15 0AL
⏲ 11-midnight (1am Fri & Sat) ☎ (01786) 825226
🌐 thetappithen-dunblane.co.uk
Belhaven IPA; 4 changing beers Ⓗ
This is a traditional single-room pub with the interior split into different areas by wooden dividers. It hosts a weekly folk music night on a Tuesday and a real ale festival once or twice a year. The locals regularly get together to hold fundraising events in support of local charities.
⇌🚌🐾📶

Falkirk

Behind the Wall
14 Melville Street, FK1 1HZ
⏲ 11-midnight (3am Fri & Sat); 12-midnight Sun
☎ (01324) 633338 🌐 behindthewall.co.uk
Changing beers (often Fyne Ales, Tryst) Ⓗ
This spacious venue for drinking, dining and entertainment was once a bra factory. Popular for watching live sports events, it has plenty of seating and several wide screens. The large room doubles as a live music and comedy venue, hosting bands both local and from many parts of the UK. Eglesbrech is the real ale and whisky bar upstairs, divided into two rooms, with timber furnishings and a wood-burning stove.
🔥❀◐⇌(Grahamston)🚌📶

Wheatsheaf Inn
16 Baxters Wynd, FK1 1PF (off the High Street)
⏲ 11-midnight (1am Fri & Sat); 12.30-midnight Sun
☎ (01324) 638282
Caledonian Deuchars IPA; 3 changing beers (sourced nationally; often Hadrian Border, Ilkley, Knops) Ⓗ
This public house dates from the late-18th century. The wood-panelled bar is furnished in traditional style with plenty of interesting features from the past. Guest beers come from microbreweries in Scotland and England, with two on offer mid-week and three at the weekend. Tea, coffee and snacks are served daily. ❀⇌(Grahamston)🚌

Gargunnock

Gargunnock Inn
Main Street, FK8 3BW
⏲ 12-11; 11-12.30am Fri & Sat; 12.30-11 Sun
☎ (01786) 860333 🌐 gargunnockinn.co.uk
2 changing beers Ⓗ
Dating from the 1700s, this is now a roomy yet cosy pub and restaurant. The bar has two handpumps offering at least one Scottish ale. There are numerous restaurant rooms and seating areas, two wood-burning stoves and exposed original features. An extensive quality food menu is served throughout – chicken with haggis and Aberdeen Angus steaks are notable. Popular local walks abound close by. The annual beer festival is the second Sunday in August. Q🔥❀◐♿♣P🚌(12)📶

Grangemouth

Earl of Zetland
Bo'ness Road, FK3 8AN
⏲ 8am-midnight (1am Fri & Sat); 12.30-midnight Sun
☎ (01324) 499940
Caledonian Deuchars IPA; Greene King Abbot; 2 changing beers (sourced nationally) Ⓗ

REAL ALE BREWERIES

Balmaha Balmaha
Black Wolf Stirling
Devon Sauchie
Fallen Kippen
Fintry Fintry (NEW)
Harviestoun Alva
Kinneil Bo'ness
Loch Lomond Alexandria
Tinpot Bridge of Allan
Tryst Larbert
Williams Alloa

SCOTLAND

Impressive Wetherspoon conversion of a town-centre church, retaining ecclesiastical features such as the organ pipes and stained-glass windows. Two permanent beers are supplemented by up to four regional and national guests. The pub runs regular mini festivals and Meet the Brewer events as well as the usual Wetherspoon festivals. TV screens with subtitles show news and sporting events. Licensed from 9am (12.30pm Sun). (5,15)

Helensburgh

Ashton

West Princes Street, G84 8UG
11-midnight (1am Fri & Sat) (01436) 675900
Belhaven IPA; 2 changing beers (sourced nationally; often Fyne Ales)
This bar features a carved gantry, and during recent work the front of the pub was opened up to reveal a set of ceramic tiles depicting scenes from Scott's Waverley Novels. Live music is a regular Saturday night feature. An ever-changing selection of ales from Scottish micros supported by quality English beers can be found on the bar.
(Central) (1B,316)

Commodore

112-117 West Clyde Street, G84 8ES
11-11; 12.30-10.30 Sun (01436) 676924
Caledonian Deuchars IPA; 2 changing beers (sourced nationally)
Situated on the shores of the Gareloch, the pub has views of the Clyde and passing submarines. A bar area with a variety of seating adjoins the restaurant area. Popular with day trippers, walkers, golfers, fishermen and seafarers, the pub's large garden can be packed in summer and live music features on some nights. It is a short walk from Helensburgh Central and the Glasgow bus service terminates outside. P (1B)

Henry Bell

19-29 James Street, G84 8AS
8am-midnight (01436) 863060
Caledonian Deuchars IPA; Greene King Abbot; changing beers (sourced nationally; often Loch Lomond)
Close to the recently revamped town centre and esplanade, this is an important real ale outlet in the area. The decor is much influenced by Scottish designer Charles Rennie Mackintosh and the walls are adorned with TVs in homage to Helensburgh-born John Logie Baird. A busy and popular venue with both locals and visitors at the heart of the town. Q (Central) (1B,316)

Kilcreggan

Kilcreggan Hotel

Argyll Road, G84 0JP (off Shore Rd at Donaldson's Brae)
12-midnight (1am Fri & Sat) (01436) 842243
kilcregganhotel.com
2 changing beers
Perched on an elevated position above the Clyde, the views are fantastic. Decorated with a nautical theme, the lounge and patio overlook well-established gardens. An ever-changing choice of two ales is sourced mostly from Scottish breweries, particularly Orkney, Strathaven and Fyne Ales. The pub can be approached via the ferry from Gourock or the bus from Helensburgh. Opening hours vary in winter. P (316)

Larbert

Station Hotel

2 Foundry Loan, FK5 4AW
12-11 (midnight Thu; 1am Fri & Sat); 12.30-11 Sun
(01324) 557186 thestationhotellarbert.co.uk
5 changing beers (sourced nationally; often Cairngorm, Greene King, Strathaven)
A popular local, situated next to the railway station and on a regular bus route, this hotel prides itself on the support it gives to a number of community groups. Three to five cask ales are usually on offer and efforts are made to provide a variety of local, regional and national ales. There is a games room and large-screen TVs show sporting events.
P (6,7)

Stirling

Portcullis Hotel

Castle Wynd, FK8 1EG (adjacent to castle esplanade)
11-11; 11.30-midnight Wed-Sat; 11.30-11 Sun
(01786) 472290 theportcullishotel.com
2 changing beers (sourced regionally; often Isle of Skye, Orkney)
Popular pub at the top of the town. Exposed stone walls and an open fireplace with ornate surround create a warm ambience in the heart of old Stirling. The pub is renowned for its food and regularly changing selection of Scottish ales from the far north and west. Always busy, diners are advised to reserve a table. Q P

Strathyre

Inn & Bistro

Main Street, FK18 8NA
12-midnight (1am Fri & Sat); 12.30-midnight Sun
(01877) 384224 innatstrathyre.co.uk
3 changing beers (sourced locally; often Inveralmond, Tryst)
Cosy, popular pub, serving meals in the bar or bistro, all made with local produce. The beers are mainly Scottish during the summer tourist season and from south of the border off season. The beer garden in a raised position enjoys panoramic views. Accommodation is available and dogs and children are permitted in the bar. Opening hours vary in winter. Q P (C60)

Tillicoultry

Woolpack Inn

1-3 Glassford Square, FK13 6AU
11-midnight (1am Fri & Sat) (01259) 750109
thewoolpackinn.net
House beer (by Greene King); 3 changing beers (sourced nationally; often Belhaven, Greene King, Inveralmond)
Originally a drovers' inn, this pub is well-used by friendly locals and hill walkers, and has a comfortable feel. Lively banter dominates rather than TV, muzak or machines. Occasional live music, tasting evenings and quiz nights are hosted. Up to four ales from the Belhaven list change regularly and a good selection of malt whiskies is also available. A former CAMRA Scotland & Northern Ireland Pub of the Year. Q

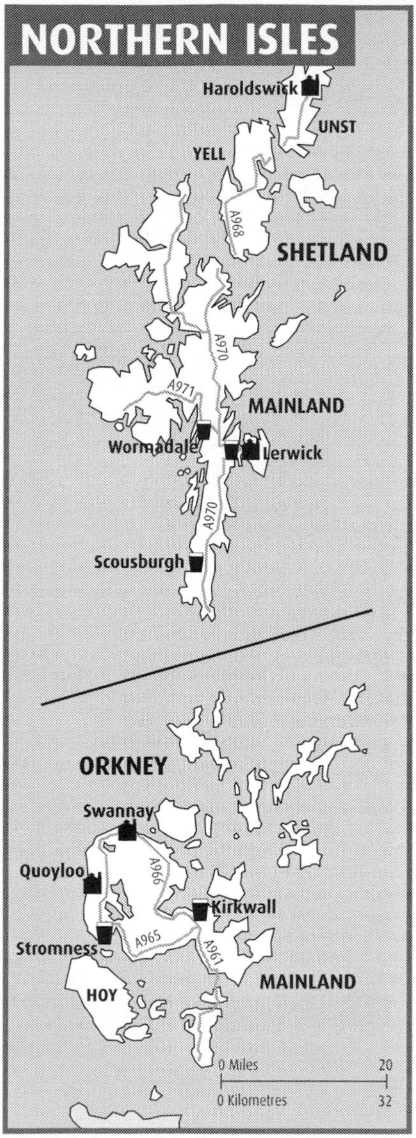

Authority area covered: Highland UA

Kirkwall: Orkney

Ayre Hotel

Ayre Road, KW15 1QX
11-midnight (1am Thu-Sat); 9am-midnight Sun
(01856) 873001 ayrehotel.co.uk
Highland Scapa Special
Overlooking Kirkwall harbour, the oldest part of the Ayre dates back to 1791 – it was a temperance hotel between 1885 and 1938. There are plenty of comfortable seats in the lounge to relax with a pint after a day exploring the many visitor attractions locally. Lunches and evening meals feature Orkney beef, fish and other produce. Close to the bus station and a short walk to ferries to the outer isles of Orkney.

Bothy Bar (Albert Hotel)

Mounthoolie Lane, KW15 1HW
11-midnight (1am Sat); 12-midnight Sun
(01856) 876000 alberthotel.co.uk
Highland Scapa Special; Orkney Red MacGregor; 4 changing beers (sourced locally; often Highland, Orkney)
After reconstruction using much of the original materials following a fire a few years ago, this popular bar in the town centre has more space than previously, with intimate alcoves. Handy for buses, North Isles ferries and the shops, it is frequented by locals and after-work drinkers, and features on the weekend circuit. TVs cater for sports fans and a roaring fire adds warmth in winter. Historic St Magnus Cathedral is close by. A premium is paid for half pints.

Helgi's Bar

14 Harbour Street, KW15 1LE (by harbour)
11-midnight (1am Thu-Sat) (01856) 879293
helgis.co.uk
Highland Dark Munro, Scapa Special, Orkney IPA; 1 changing beer (sourced locally; often Highland)
Converted from a former shipping office, this small, smart bar has the look of a modern café with a local stone floor and wood panelling. Set on the harbour front where seafood is landed daily, it is a handy place to fill in time before island-hopping on the many ferries to outlying parts. Special food nights where food is matched with ales are hosted as well as regular music sessions and Thursday quiz nights. A former CAMRA Northern Isles Pub of the Year. Q

Shore

Shore Street, KW15 1LG (on harbour)
3-11 (midnight Fri); 10-midnight Sat; 10-11 Sun
(01856) 872200 theshore.co.uk
Highland Scapa Special
This smart, modern venue at the pier head may be the first experience of a Scottish bar for passengers disembarking from cruise ships or just a pleasant place to recuperate after a rough ferry crossing from another isle. The main street, with its wide range of shops, is just around the corner, and also St Magnus Cathedral, founded in 1137 by the Viking Earl Rognvald. Cross the road to catch a ferry to other Northern Isles.

St Ola Hotel

Harbour Street, KW15 1LE
11-11.30 (midnight Thu; 1am Fri); 1-1am Sat; 10-midnight Sun (01856) 875090 stolahotel.co.uk
Highland Scapa Special; 2 changing beers (sourced locally; often Highland)
The Ola is on Kirkwall's waterfront with a bar facing the harbour and a larger lounge to the rear, both serving a decent pint plus an extensive range of whiskies. It is a busy, friendly pub with all the major attractions of Kirkwall a short walk away and close to ferries for the northern isles of Orkney.

REAL ALE BREWERIES

Highland Swannay: Orkney
Lerwick Lerwick: Shetland
Orkney Quoyloo: Orkney
Valhalla Haroldswick: Unst

Lerwick: Shetland

Captain Flints

Ellesmere Stores, Esplanade, ZE1 0LL
11-1am ☎ (01595) 692249
Valhalla Simmer Dim; 1 changing beer (sourced regionally) Ⓗ
Two-floored bar situated above Ellesmere Store with a nautical theme and dark-wood panelling. There are excellent views of the small boat harbour and the island of Bressay from seating areas closest to the bar. A small stage area to the rear is used for bands at weekends and the upper floor is a games area. Entry to the bar is via a staircase from a door opposite the Market Cross.

Scousburgh: Shetland

Spiggie Hotel

ZE2 9JE (signed from A970 off B9122)
12-2, 5.30-11; closed Tue; 12-11 Sat; 12-10 Sun
☎ (01950) 460409 thespiggiehotel.co.uk
1 changing beer (sourced nationally) Ⓗ
Small family-run hotel on an elevated site built as the original terminus of the Northern Isles ferries with a small stone-floored bar and adjacent restaurant and various scenic views. The gleaming white Scousburgh Sands are within five minutes' walk, with Sumburgh Head, Jarlshof and Old Scatness a short drive away. Birdwatching and trout fishing on the loch can be arranged. Beers come from Valhalla and Highland breweries, with only one in winter. Phone to check food availability and opening hours in winter. P

Stromness: Orkney

Ferry Inn

10 John Street, KW16 3AD (opp ferry terminal)
4-11 (11.30 Fri); 9am-11.30 Sat; 9.30am-11 Sun winter; 9am-midnight summer ☎ (01856) 850280 ferryinn.com
Highland Scapa Special, Orkney IPA; Orkney Corncrake; 2 changing beers (sourced locally; often Highland, Orkney) Ⓗ
An easy walk from the harbour front, the Ferry is handy for buses to Kirkwall and the ferry from Scrabster. It is popular with locals and visitors, including divers who come to Orkney to explore the sunken German fleet at Scapa Flow. Various attractions nearby include the Ring of Brodgar and Scara Brae village. Annual folk and blues festivals are held, with a marquee erected outside complete with a pump of ale. P

Stromness Hotel

15 Victoria Street, KW16 3AA (opp pier head)
12-midnight (1am Fri & Sat); 12.30-11 Sun; closed Jan-Feb
☎ (01856) 850298 stromnesshotel.com
Highland Scapa Special; Orkney Corncrake; 2 changing beers (sourced locally; often Highland, Orkney) Ⓗ
On the first floor of this imposing hotel you will find the Hamnavoe Lounge, with windows and a small balcony giving commanding views of the harbour. In winter a roaring fire and comfy seating welcome the visitor and there is a separate whisky bar with over 100 bottles to choose from. The Flattie Bar downstairs, open all year round, is complete with a 'flattie' hanging from the ceiling and serves Highland Scapa Special. Jazz, blues and beer festivals are held throughout the year.
P

Wormadale: Shetland

Westings Inn

ZE2 9LJ
12.30-2.30, 5.30-10.30; 6.30-10.30 Sun
☎ (01595) 840242 westings.shetland.co.uk
3 changing beers (sourced nationally; often Fuller's, Timothy Taylor) Ⓗ
Isolated white-painted inn in a stunning location near the summit of Wormadale Hill, two miles west of Tingwall airstrip. There are marvellous sea views from the comfortable lounge area and adjacent games area of Whiteness Voe, Western Shetland and the outlying islands. Three ales are usually available in summer, one in winter, often from Fuller's or Timothy Taylor. Meals are served 7-8pm Monday-Friday by arrangement. The bar may stay open until 1am if busy. Caravans are welcome and camping is available in the pub grounds.
P

Stromness Hotel, Orkney (Photo: George Howie)

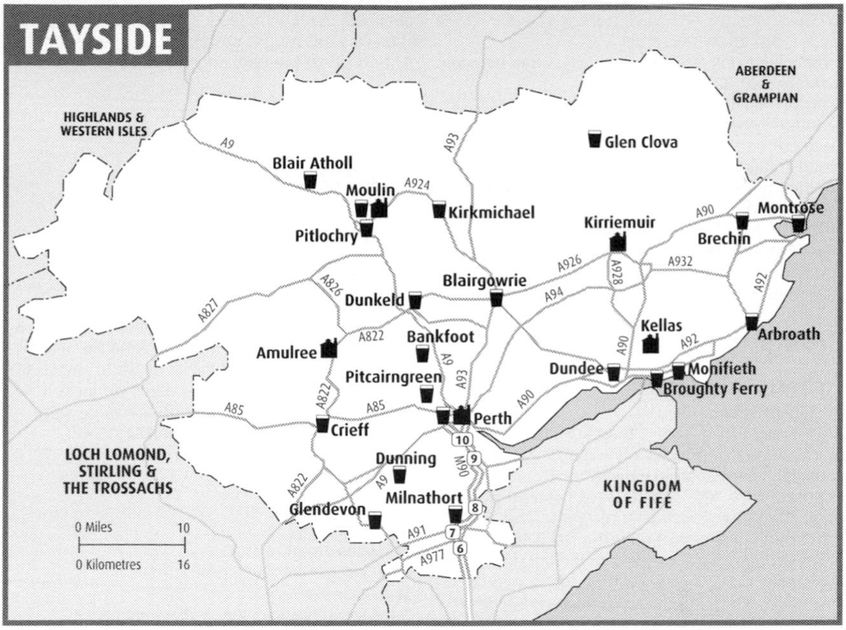

Authority areas covered: Angus UA, City of Dundee UA, Perth & Kinross UA

Arbroath

Corn Exchange

14 Olympic Centre, Market Place, DD11 1HR
⏲ 8am-midnight (1am Fri & Sat) ☎ (01241) 432430
Caledonian Deuchars IPA; Greene King Abbot; Sharp's Doom Bar; 5 changing beers Ⓗ
Located just off the High Street, this Wetherspoon pub occupies a former 19th-century corn exchange. Although largely open plan, there are a number of booths providing some privacy. Boat trips offering fishing or a visit to the 200-year-old Bell Rock lighthouse are available from the nearby harbour. ◑≹🚌📶

Bankfoot

Bankfoot Inn 🏆

Main Street, PH1 4AB
⏲ 12-2 (not Mon & Tue), 6-11; 12-2, 5-12.30am Fri; 12-12.30am Sat; 12-midnight Sun ☎ (01738) 787243
🌐 bankfootinn.co.uk
3 changing beers Ⓗ
Small family-run hotel with a public bar, a cosy lounge bar and an adjoining restaurant, warmed throughout by two real fires in winter. The owners are real ale enthusiasts and strongly committed to local breweries. Two ale fests are held each year. Quality live folk music features every Wednesday evening. Dogs are warmly welcomed. Tayside Pub of the Year 2014. ❀🛏◑♣🚌🐾📶

Blair Atholl

Atholl Arms Hotel

PH18 5SG
⏲ 11-11 ☎ (01796) 481205
Moulin Light, Braveheart, Ale of Atholl, Old Remedial Ⓗ
The Atholl Arms has a grand and imposing façade in the Victorian Highland style. The characterful Highland Bothy Bar offers four ales produced by the local Moulin Brewery, and serves freshly cooked food all day. Blair Atholl and the surrounding area is a popular destination for walking, climbing, biking and sightseeing. There is something for everyone here. 🛏◑≹

Blairgowrie

Ericht Alehouse

13 Wellmeadow, PH10 6ND
⏲ 1-11 ☎ (01250) 872469
Inveralmond Thrappledouser; Stewart Pentland IPA; 4 changing beers Ⓗ
Classic town-centre pub with a friendly atmosphere. There are two seating areas separated by a well-stocked bar. A wide range of ever-changing ales and ciders caters for all tastes. No food is served but customers are welcome to bring their own. A winner of Tayside CAMRA Pub of the Year several times over the past decade. ❀🍺🚌(57,59)

Fair o' Blair

25-29 Allan Street, PH10 6ND
⏲ 11-11 ☎ (01250) 871890
Caledonian Deuchars IPA; Greene King Abbot; 4 changing beers (sourced nationally) Ⓗ
This Wetherspoon venue was opened by the chain in 2013, and still feels fresh and new, with a bright and appealing interior. A great range of beers and real ales is on offer. The typical wide choice of fare is available, expertly presented and served by friendly staff. Good value as ever but the toilets are a hike. ◑📶

Brechin

Caledonian

43 Southesk Street, DD9 6DZ

closed Mon & Tue; 5-10 Wed & Thu; 4.30-11.30 Fri; 3-11.30 Sat; 3-11 Sun (01356) 624345
3 changing beers (sourced regionally; often Houston, Inveralmond)
Named after the privately run railway whose terminus is opposite, the Caledonian features a large bar and dining area. The extensive use of wood creates a warm and inviting interior. In addition to the regular ales, guest beers sourced by the landlord on trips to Hampshire are frequently available. A wide range of continental bottled beers is also offered. Live folk music on the last Friday of the month is popular. Opening hours are extended in summer.

Broughty Ferry

Fisherman's Tavern
10-16 Fort Street, DD5 2AD
11-midnight (1am Thu-Sat) (01382) 775941
fishermanstavern-broughtyferry.co.uk
Changing beers (sourced nationally)
Licensed since 1857, this famous hostelry was originally three fishermen's cottages, later converted into a small hotel. The bar is to the right of the entrance, and a snug is to the left, leading to the dining room/lounge, warmed by a real fire. The lounge to the rear has disabled access from Bell's Lane. Entertainment includes a monthly quiz and an annual beer festival in late May. The ales come from Scottish and English breweries.

Jolly's Hotel
43a Gray Street, DD5 2BJ
7am-midnight (1am Fri & Sat) (01382) 734910
Caledonian Deuchars IPA; Greene King Abbot; 2 changing beers
Closed for several years, this 25-room hotel was bought by Wetherspoon and reopened in early 2014 following a major re-fit. The bar has two large areas, one principally for dining and the other for dining and drinking. A large number of handpulls serve a wide selection of ales. The TVs are usually silent. Outside, there is a patio area with tables. The pub is popular with a mixed clientele of all ages.

Royal Arch
285 Brook Street, DD5 2DS
11-midnight (1am Fri & Sat); 12.30-midnight Sun
(01382) 779741
Caledonian Deuchars IPA; 2 changing beers
A popular locally owned pub in the centre of 'the Ferry'. There are three TVs in the public bar for the many sports fans, and good-quality meals are served in the Art Deco lounge. Three handpulls dispense ales from local brewers as well as from all over Britain. The gantry in the public bar was rescued long ago from the demolished Craigour Bar in Dens Road, and the exterior was refurbished in 2014.

Ship Inn
121 Fisher Street, DD5 2BR
11 (12.30 Sun)-11 (01382) 214235
theshipinn-broughtyferry.co.uk
Timothy Taylor Landlord; 2 changing beers
Traditional free house on the waterfront at Broughty Ferry, with views over the Tay towards Fife. Dating back to 1847, this cosy retreat has some nautical features and is interesting and atmospheric. Three well-kept real ales are usually available. A range of tasty bar meals is on offer and there is a restaurant upstairs. Pavement seating just outside is pleasant in good weather.

Crieff

Tower Gastro Pub
81 East High Street, PH7 3JA
12.30-11; 11-12.30am Fri & Sat; 11-11 Sun
(01738) 650050
Inveralmond Ossian; Strathbraan Head East
This small family-run gastro-pub has been tastefully refurbished by licensees Annie and Bob. The beams and friezes display some interesting and amusing proverbs and quotations. There is a comfortable seating area overlooking the beer garden which has great views south to the Ochil Hills. Two handpumps serve ales from local breweries. Attached to the pub are three self-catering apartments. Q (15,47)

Dundee

Bank Bar
7-9 Union Street, DD1 4BN
11-midnight (10 Mon & Tue); 12.30-7 Sun
(01382) 205037
Caledonian Deuchars IPA; 1 changing beer
A former bank with a collection of themed pictures decorating the walls, it has a bare-boards floor, wooden furnishings and a series of alcoves with tables in the tradition of older Scottish city pubs. Food is served until 7pm every day. Live music performed by skilled musicians features on most Friday and Saturday nights.

Capitol
7-9 Seagate, DD1 2EG
8am-11 (01382) 205950
Caledonian Deuchars IPA; Greene King Abbot; 2 changing beers
Formerly the Capitol cinema, built in 1945, but converted into a Wetherspoon Lloyd's in 2003. A staircase rises to the large upper seating area which is primarily a family and dining area. The pub is popular with shoppers during the day and lively on Friday and Saturday evenings.
(73)

George Orwell
168 Perth Road, DD1 4JS
4-midnight 07958 971847
Edenmill Clock Brew; 1 changing beer (sourced locally)
A good selection of bottled ales is available alongside the single real ale. Lots of George Orwell memorabilia and book covers complement the decor. The bar is the best place in Dundee to watch live sport on TV, with a large drop-down screen, adequate blackout and surround sound. Tayside CAMRA Newcomer Pub of the Year 2014.

Phoenix
103 Nethergate, DD1 4DH

REAL ALE BREWERIES

Inveralmond Perth
Kirrie Kirriemuir (NEW)
MòR Kellas
Moulin Moulin
Strathbraan Amulree

11-midnight ☎ (01382) 200014
Caledonian Deuchars IPA; Timothy Taylor Landlord; 2 changing beers H
A traditional pub with a great atmosphere, a fine range of ales and excellent pub food at conservative prices. Warm and cosy, like all good pubs used to be, it has sturdy wooden seats and tables, green leather benches and a rare Ballingall Brewery mirror. Close to the city centre, it is also handy for the Rep Theatre, Dundee Contemporary Arts and Bonar Hall. Well worth a visit. (73)

Speedwell Bar (Mennies) ★
165-167 Perth Road, DD2 1AS
11 (12.30 Sun)-11 ☎ (01382) 667783
speedwell-bar.co.uk
MòR Brewing MòR Please!; 2 changing beers H
Built in 1903 for James Speed, the bar is known as Mennie's after the family who ran it for more than 50 years. The L-shaped interior is divided by a part-glazed screen and has a magnificent mahogany gantry and counter, dado-panelled walls and an anaglypta Jacobean ceiling. There are two sitting rooms, separated by a glass screen. A selection of 150 malt whiskies is served and bar snacks are often available. (73)

Dunkeld

Royal Dunkeld Hotel
Atholl Street, PH8 0AR
11-11 (12.15am Fri & Sat); 12-11 Sun ☎ (01350) 727322
royaldunkeld.co.uk
Cairngorm Trade Winds; Stewart Brewing 80/-; 1 changing beer H
Located on the main street near the cathedral, this former coaching inn is now a comfortable hotel. It has a restaurant, lounge bar and public bar with an open fire. A pool room with dartboard is adjacent. Three handpulls serve real ale. Good food is available in the bar and restaurant. Outside, the large beer garden is a suntrap in summer. An ideal base for a variety of outdoor activities including walking, fishing and golf.

Taybank Hotel
Tay Terrace, PH8 0AQ
11-11 ☎ (01350) 727340 thetaybank.squarespace.com
Strathbraan Due South, Head East H
'Scotland's musical meeting place' hosts regular organised and impromptu music sessions in an intimate room with an L-shaped bar, attracting locals and tourists. It offers a range of Strathbraan ales and excellent meals, including the Taybank stovies, all highly recommended. Friendly staff make all visitors welcome including children and dogs. The car park and beer garden are opposite, beside the mighty River Tay, and there is a patio for those not nimble enough to cross the road.
P

Dunning

Kirkstyle Inn
Kirkstyle Square, PH2 0RR

> Dost thou think, because thou art virtuous, there shall be no more cakes and ale?
> **William Shakespeare, Twelfth Night**

11-11 ☎ (01764) 684248 kirkstyle-dunning.co.uk
2 changing beers H
Traditional village inn dating from 1760 overshadowed by the impressive Norman steeple of St Serf's Church, home to the ancient Dupplin Cross and other Pictish relics. One or two ales are to be found in the small, cosy public bar, from a variety of Scottish independents as well as English and Welsh regional breweries. There is a separate restaurant. Around a mile west of Dunning village stands a 20ft-high stone cross, a memorial to Maggie Wall who was burned here as a witch in 1657.

Glen Clova

Glen Clova Hotel
DD8 4QS
11-11 (1am Fri & Sat); 12-11 Sun ☎ (01575) 550350
clova.com
2 changing beers (sourced regionally) H
Situated near the head of one of Scotland's most beautiful glens, the hotel is popular with walkers after a day on the hills. The bar has a large log-fired stove and plenty of character. Two handpumps supply the ales, usually from Scottish breweries, and local food, including lamb and venison, is served in both the bar and adjoining restaurant. The hotel has a range of accommodation from bunkhouse and en-suite rooms to self-catering luxury lodges. A summer beer festival is held in the field opposite. P

Glendevon

Tormaukin Hotel
FK14 7JY (A823)
11-11 ☎ (01259) 781252
Harviestoun Bitter & Twisted; 1 changing beer H
This 18th-century former drovers' inn is on the A823 Muckhart to Gleneagles road in a peaceful setting surrounded by the Ochil Hills. It has a comfortable, relaxed atmosphere, with an open fire in winter. The handpulls offer a Harviestoun beer and a choice of other brews. Local venison is a speciality. The landlord previously ran the Bridge of Lochay Hotel at Killin.

Kirkmichael

Strathardle Inn
PH10 7NS (on A924)
11-11 ☎ (01250) 881224 strathardleinn.co.uk
3 changing beers (sourced regionally) H
Small, friendly hotel with a bar room with a coal fire and horse brasses around the mantelpiece. Up to three ales are available from Scottish micros, and good lunches and evening meals are served. The historic coaching inn, dating back to the late 1700s, has a 700-yard fishing beat on the River Ardle which passes in front of the building. The Cateran Trail is also nearby and the Southern Highlands, Glenshee ski slopes, Deeside and Angus Glens are all within reach.

Milnathort

Village Inn
36 Wester Loan, KY13 9YH
2-11 (midnight Fri); 12-midnight Sat; 12.30-11 Sun
☎ (01577) 863293

SCOTLAND

Inveralmond Thrappledouser; 2 changing beers (sourced locally) 🄷
This friendly local has a semi open-plan interior featuring classic brewery mirrors and local historic photographs. The comfortable lounge area has low ceilings, exposed joists and stone walls, and the bar area is warmed by a log fire. At the rear is a games room with a pool table. This pub has been family-owned since 1985 and serves various beers, often locally sourced. Milnathort links some great cycling routes through the Ochils, via Burleigh Castle, to the more leisurely Loch Leven Heritage Trail. ❀♿♣🚌

Monifieth

Milton Inn

Grange Road, DD5 4LU
⏲ closed Mon; 12-2.30, 5-11; 12-midnight Fri & Sat; 12-11 Sun ☎ (01382) 532620 🌐 themiltoninn.co.uk
3 changing beers 🄷
The only premises in Monifieth serving real ale, which this traditional inn does with a passion. Set back from the road, the large gardens and sunny decked area to the rear provide a nice sheltered spot for a pint in the fresh air, or to enjoy a barbecue. Entertainment and events feature regularly. ❀🛏◐◑⇌P🚌ᯤ

Montrose

Market Arms

95 High Street, DD10 8QY
⏲ 11-midnight (1am Thu-Sat) ☎ (01674) 673384
Caledonian Deuchars IPA; 1 changing beer 🄷
Stylishly renovated a few years ago, this busy town-centre pub provides a comfortable retreat for a wide mix of customers. Two handpulls are conveniently sited on a long bar near the entrance in the main area. Several TVs show live sporting events but there is a small snug at the front for those wishing to enjoy a quiet pint. Beers are usually sourced from Scottish brewers. The Montrose Air Station Heritage Centre – the first operational military airfield in the UK – is nearby. ♿▲⇌🚌

Moulin

Moulin Inn

11-13 Kirkmichael Road, PH16 5EH
⏲ 11-11 ☎ (01796) 472196 🌐 moulininn.co.uk
Moulin Light, Braveheart, Ale of Atholl, Old Remedial 🄷
First opened in 1695, the inn is the oldest part of the Moulin Hotel, situated within the village square of an ancient crossroads, just east of Pitlochry. Full of character and charm, it is traditionally furnished and has two log fires. A good choice of home-prepared local fare is available, along with Moulin's own beers, brewed in the old coach house behind the hotel. Outside is an area for dining and drinking in good weather. An ideal base for exploring and outdoor pursuits, with several marked walks nearby. Q🐴❀🛏◐◑♣P

Perth

Cherrybank Inn

210 Glasgow Road, PH2 0NA
⏲ 11-11 (12.30am Thu-Sat); 12-midnight Sun
☎ (01738) 624349 🌐 cherrybankinn.co.uk
Inveralmond Ossian, Duncan's IPA; 4 changing beers (sourced regionally) 🄷
This 250-year-old former drovers' inn is a popular watering hole and stopover for travellers. Ales from Inveralmond and other Scottish independents can be enjoyed in the multi-roomed public bar, or in the larger L-shaped lounge with views up to a woodland walk. Good bar lunches and evening meals are served. The inn has seven well-appointed en-suite rooms, and golf can be arranged for residents. Tayside CAMRA Pub of the Year runner-up 2014. Q🛏◐◑♿▲P🚌🐾ᯤ

Greyfriars

15 South Street, PH2 8PG
⏲ 11-11 (11.45 Fri & Sat); 3-11 Sun ☎ (01738) 633036
🌐 scoop.it/t/greyfriars-bar
Inveralmond Lia Fail; 2 changing beers 🄷
City-centre lounge bar serving up to four ales, often including an Inveralmond beer. Good-value lunches are available in the bar and in a small upstairs area. The pub takes its name from the former Greyfriars monastery. Nearby attractions include a Victorian theatre, art gallery, museum and concert hall. This may well be the smallest lounge bar in the Fair City but it has an enviable reputation among locals and visitors as one of the friendliest. ◐◑🚌

Pitcairngreen

Pitcairngreen inn

PH1 3LP
⏲ 10.30-11 (midnight Fri & Sat) ☎ (01738) 583022
3 changing beers 🄷
A fairly large establishment in a small village, divided into several different areas including a snug warmed by a large open log fire. The landlord and his team have a real enthusiasm for good beer, served on three handpulls. This is the finest place in Tayside to enjoy real ales, ciders and perries, presented professionally and with commitment. Q❀◐◑🍏P🚌(14,15)🐾

Pitlochry

Old Mill Inn

Mill Lane, PH16 5BH
⏲ 11-11 (midnight Sat & Sun) ☎ (01796) 474020
🌐 theoldmillpitlochry.co.uk
Strathbraan Due South, Head East; 2 changing beers 🄷
Built in the 19th century as a mill, with the old mill wheel still in place at the front. This is a family-owned and family-run establishment in the town centre. The bar serves a varied selection of guest ales, as well as the regulars from local Scottish microbreweries including Strathbraan. Winner of Inn of the Year at the 2014 Scottish Hotel Awards. 🐴❀🛏◐◑♿⇌🍏P🚌ᯤ

> Not all chemicals are bad. Without chemicals such as hydrogen and oxygen, for example, there would be no way to make water, a vital ingredient in beer. **Dave Barry**

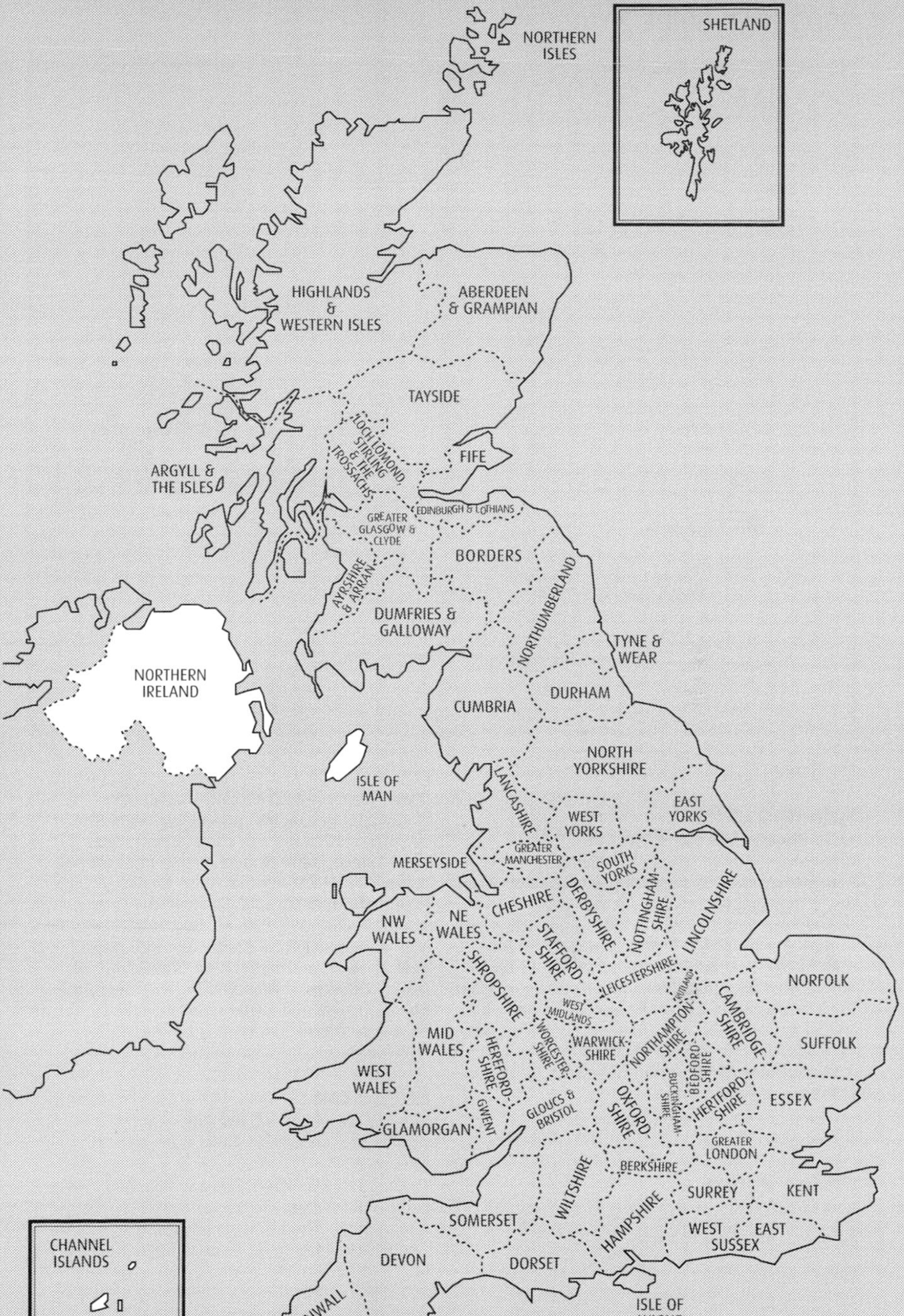
SHETLAND
NORTHERN ISLES
HIGHLANDS & WESTERN ISLES
ABERDEEN & GRAMPIAN
TAYSIDE
LOCH LOMOND, STIRLING & THE TROSSACHS
FIFE
ARGYLL & THE ISLES
EDINBURGH & LOTHIANS
GREATER GLASGOW & CLYDE
BORDERS
AYRSHIRE & ARRAN
DUMFRIES & GALLOWAY
NORTHUMBERLAND
TYNE & WEAR
NORTHERN IRELAND
DURHAM
CUMBRIA
ISLE OF MAN
NORTH YORKSHIRE
LANCASHIRE
WEST YORKS
EAST YORKS
GREATER MANCHESTER
MERSEYSIDE
SOUTH YORKS
CHESHIRE
DERBYSHIRE
NOTTINGHAM-SHIRE
LINCOLNSHIRE
NW WALES
NE WALES
STAFFORD SHIRE
SHROPSHIRE
LEICESTERSHIRE
RUTLAND
NORFOLK
WEST MIDLANDS
CAMBRIDGE-SHIRE
MID WALES
HEREFORD-SHIRE
WORCESTER-SHIRE
WARWICK-SHIRE
NORTHAMPTON-SHIRE
BEDFORD-SHIRE
SUFFOLK
WEST WALES
BUCKINGHAM-SHIRE
HERTFORD-SHIRE
ESSEX
GWENT
GLOUCS & BRISTOL
OXFORD-SHIRE
GLAMORGAN
GREATER LONDON
BERKSHIRE
WILTSHIRE
SURREY
KENT
SOMERSET
HAMPSHIRE
WEST SUSSEX
EAST SUSSEX
CHANNEL ISLANDS
DEVON
DORSET
ISLE OF WIGHT
CORNWALL

Northern Ireland
Channel Islands
Isle of Man

NORTHERN IRELAND

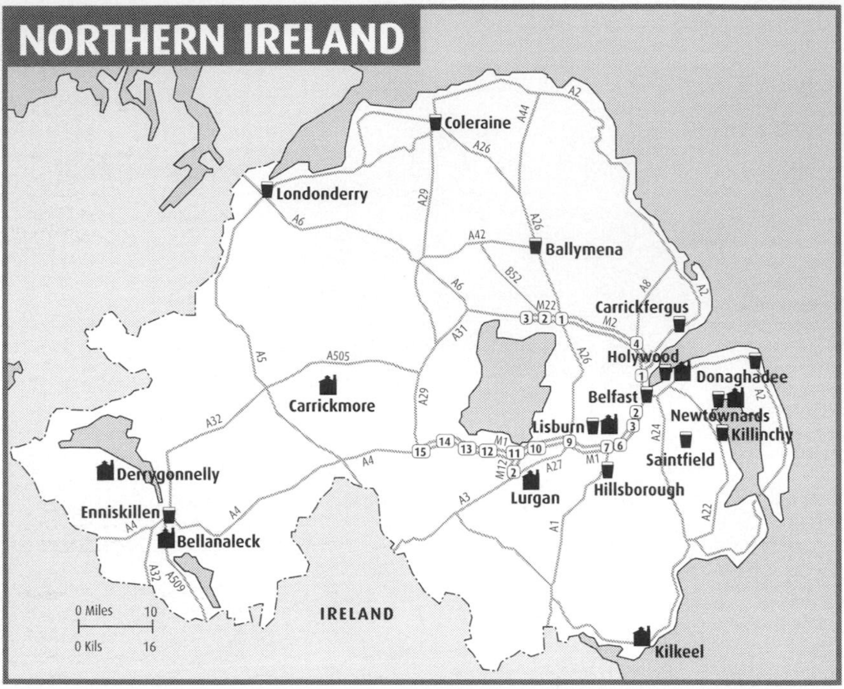

Ballymena

Spinning Mill

17-21 Broughshane Street, BT43 6EB

☉ 8am-midnight (1am Fri & Sat) ☎ (028) 2563 8985

Adnams Broadside; Greene King Abbot; Sharp's Doom Bar; 2 changing beers Ⓗ

Opened in 2000, this was Wetherspoon's first pub in Northern Ireland and is still the only real ale outlet in town. It is a busy venue with bars upstairs and downstairs. There are plenty of pleasing nooks to sit in and up to eight handpumps offering a changing variety of ales. Opens for breakfast from 8am, alcohol served from 11.30am (12.30pm Sun). A former local CAMRA Pub of the Year.

Q◑♿⚠⇌P▯🚌

Belfast

Bridge House

37-43 Bedford Street, BT2 7EJ

☉ 8am-midnight (1am Fri & Sat); 12-midnight Sun ☎ (028) 9072 7890

Fuller's London Pride; Greene King Abbot; Sharp's Doom Bar; changing beers Ⓗ

Large recently renovated Wetherspoon pub – the main bar has been extended and a number of booths added downstairs. Eight handpumps dispense three regular beers and up to six constantly changing guests. The twice-yearly Wetherspoon beer festivals are popular, and the usual good-value Wetherspoon food menu is available. A busy pub, especially at weekends, with friendly, helpful knowledgeable staff. A former local CAMRA Pub of the Year.

Q◐◑♿⇌(Great Victoria St)🍎🚌

Crown ★

46 Great Victoria Street, BT2 7BA (opp Great Victoria St station)

☉ 11.30-midnight; 12.30-11 Sun ☎ (028) 9024 3187

Hilden Ale; St Austell Nicholson's Pale Ale; Whitewater Belfast Ale; 2 changing beers Ⓗ

The Crown is renowned as an architectural masterpiece, with an outstanding interior that dates from 1885. It is now also known as an excellent outlet for real ale, with five handpumps serving Nicholson's Pale Ale and beers from Hilden and Whitewater local breweries. Two guest beers vary, with an occasional beer brewed for the Crown. Good food is served in the Crown Dining Room upstairs and in the downstairs bar. A former CAMRA Northern Ireland Pub Of The Year.

Q◐◑♿⚠⇌(Great Victoria St)🚌

Errigle Inn

312-320 Ormeau Road, BT7 2GE

☉ 11.30-1am; 10-midnight Sun ☎ (028) 9064 1410

🌐 errigle.com

Shepherd Neame Whitstable Bay Pale Ale; Whitewater Belfast Ale Ⓗ

A long-established pub on the south side of the city, situated along the Ormeau Road. Real ale was first sold here many years ago and now there are two handpumps offering a changing variety of Whitewater and Shepherd Neame ales. The venue has five distinct bars ranging from a public bar to a quiet lounge at the back – the ale is to be found in the Tom McGurran bar. TV sport features heavily, along with traditional music and quizzes. Q◐◑♿

John Hewitt

51 Donegal Street, BT1 2FH (100yds from St Anne's Cathedral)

☉ 11.30 (12 Sat)-1am; 7-midnight Sun ☎ (028) 9023 3768

🌐 thejohnhewitt.com

Shepherd Neame Master Brew Ⓗ

Named after the poet, the John Hewitt offers something a little different. It is run by the Belfast Unemployed Resource Centre and profits go to fund the centre's work. It is also a focal point for live music, charity events, art exhibitions and other events. It has been selling Shepherd Neame beers on one handpump for some time now, or an occasional alternative from a brewery in the Republic of Ireland. Q

King's Head
829 Lisburn Road, BT9 7GY (opp Kings Hall at Balmoral)
12-1am (midnight Mon); 12-midnight Sun
(028) 9050 9950 kingsheadbelfast.com
Whitewater Belfast Ale
Converted from a mansion house, the King's Head is a bar, restaurant and music venue. The real ale is available in the public bar, with one handpump serving a variety of Whitewater ales. There are two other drinking areas – a large open-plan space and a comfortable lounge. Food is available in the restaurant upstairs and bar bites are served downstairs. The pub is a little outside Belfast but worth a visit. Bus and rail stops are nearby.
Q(Balmoral)

Sunflower
65 Union Street, BT1 2JG
11.30-midnight (1am Thu-Sat); 5-11 Sun
(028) 9023 2474
Hilden Twisted Hop
This traditional corner pub situated north of the city centre behind Belfast Central Library has been renovated and now serves real ale. The bar downstairs is cosy and has one handpump, offering a variety of ales from Hilden. It is a popular live music venue with bands playing in the bar and in the lounge upstairs. The spacious beer garden is a new addition. Pizza is available Friday and Saturday evenings. A hidden treasure. Q

Carrickfergus

Central Bar
13-15 High Street, BT38 7AN (opp Castle)
8am-midnight (1am Fri & Sat) (028) 9335 7840
Fuller's London Pride; Greene King Abbot; Sharp's Doom Bar; 3 changing beers
Busy town-centre Wetherspoon pub with a choice between the lively downstairs bar and a quieter family dining area upstairs. There are five handpumps on both floors, dispensing the house beers plus up to three guests. The dining area and beer garden enjoy fantastic views which includes Belfast Lough and Carrickfergus Castle. Not far from bus and rail stops. Alcohol is served from 11.30am (12.30pm Sun). Q(563)

Coleraine

Old Courthouse
Castlerock Road, BT51 3HP
8am-midnight (1am Fri & Sat) (028) 7032 5820
Fuller's London Pride; Greene King Abbot; 2 changing beers
One of those Wetherspoon establishments that does not look like a pub at first – it was a courthouse from 1852 to 1985. It is spacious, and some of the original fittings, including the pillars, have been retained. There are five handpumps with up to three guest ales. Food is available downstairs or on the imposing balcony accessed by a grand staircase. Alcohol is served from 11.30am (12.30am Sunday). Q

Donaghadee

Moat Inn
102 Moat Street, BT21 0ED
11.30-11.30; 12.30-10 Sun (028) 9188 3297
moatinn.co.uk
Whitewater Belfast Ale; 1 changing beer (sourced locally; often Whitewater)
The Moat Inn houses a restaurant, lounge and public bar, and has a beer garden. It is situated on the main road that leads into Donaghadee, a popular tourist destination about 20 miles from Belfast. There are two handpumps, both in the public bar. A variety of Whitewater ales is the mainstay, though occasionally there is a guest ale on the second pump. The bar is compact and traditional, a good place to drink and dine in.
Q(7)

Enniskillen

Linen Hall
11-13 Townhall Street, BT74 7BD
8am-11 (midnight Wed-Fri; 1am Sat) (028) 6634 0910
Greene King Abbot; Sharp's Doom Bar; 3 changing beers
This former Vintage Pub has been a busy Wetherspoon outlet for 14 years. The long narrow building has one bar with several drinking areas on different levels. There are five handpumps dispensing the house beers and guests, and real cider is available on gravity. The area, some 80 miles from Belfast, is well worth a visit. Alcohol is served from 11.30am (12.30pm Sun).
QP(261)

Hillsborough

Hillside
21 Main Street, BT26 6AE
12-11.30 (1am Fri & Sat); 12-11 Sun (028) 9268 9233
hillsidehillsborough.co.uk
Hilden Ale, Scullion's Irish, Twisted Hop
An outlet for the Hilden Brewery from the neighbouring city of Lisburn, with three handpumps serving Hilden beers and an occasional guest. The interior has been opened up to make three drinking areas, in addition to a restaurant at the back. Food is also available in the bar. The walls are adorned with pictures of hunting and old Hillsborough. Live music acts play at the weekend and there is a summer beer festival held in the pretty cobblestone beer garden.
Q(38,238)

Holywood

Dirty Duck Ale House
3 Kinnegar Road, BT18 9JN
12-11 (1am Thu-Sat); 12.30-11 Sun (028) 9059 6666
thedirtyduckalehouse.co.uk

REAL ALE BREWERIES

Ards Newtonards
Clanconnel Lurgan
Hercules Holywood (NEW)
Hilden Lisburn
Inishmacsaint Derrygonnelly
Pokertree Carrickmore (NEW)
Sheelin Bellanaleck
Whitewater Kilkeel

NORTHERN IRELAND

3 changing beers (sourced nationally; often Barney's Beer, Inveralmond, Shepherd Neame) Ⓗ
The Duck is a previous CAMRA Northern Ireland Pub of the Year, on the County Down coast, yards from Belfast Lough, with an impressive view. Three ales are usually available including occasional guests. The house beer, Dirty Duck Ale, is brewed by Hilden. Great food is available both downstairs and in the restaurant upstairs. The decor includes a collection of pumpclips and plastic ducks, and a corner celebrating local golfing hero Rory McIlroy. Q❄️❇️◑◐&⇌

Killinchy

Daft Eddy's
Sketrick Island, BT23 6QH (2 miles N of Killinchey at Whiterock Bay)
❇️ 11.30-11.30 (1am Fri); 12-10.30 Sun ☎ (028) 9754 1615
⊕ dafteddys.co.uk
1 changing beer (sourced locally; often Whitewater) Ⓗ
Perhaps Northern Ireland's most picturesque pub, this old favourite has been renovated to include a new log cabin-style public bar within the restaurant area. There is one handpump in the bar with ales available from Whitewater – often Belfast, Copperhead or Bee's Endeavour. The old public bar has been replaced by a coffee bar with a fabulous view. The restaurant continues to serve quality local food, specialising in seafood. Meals can also be enjoyed on the alfresco terrace. Q❄️◑◐&

Lisburn

Tap Room
Hilden Brewery, BT27 4TY (5 mins' walk from Hilden railway halt)
❇️ closed Mon; 12-2.30, 5.30-9; 12-3 Sun ☎ (028) 9266 3863
⊕ taproomhilden.com
Hilden Ale; 1 changing beer (sourced locally; often Hilden) Ⓗ
The best thing about Lisburn is the Hilden Brewery and its Tap Room – the restaurant next to the brewery in the grounds of the Scullion family's Georgian mansion. There are usually two ales from the brewery to accompany the fine locally sourced cuisine. As a licensed restaurant, alcohol is only available with a meal. Functions are also hosted here including an annual beer festival and live music events. Brewery tours can be arranged in advance. Q❄️◑◐⇌(Hilden)🚌(325H)

Tuesday Bell
4 Lisburn Square, BT28 1TS
❇️ 8am-11 ☎ (028) 9262 7390
Adnams Broadside; Fuller's London Pride; Greene King Abbot; Sharp's Doom Bar; 2 changing beers (sourced nationally; often Brains, Sharp's) Ⓗ
Now well into its second decade, the Tuesday Bell continues to serve real ale in the heart of Lisburn. Spread over two floors, it is the focal point of Lisburn Square. There are eight handpumps, five

downstairs and three upstairs. Local ale from Hilden Brewery occasionally appears alongside a selection from the Wetherspoon's list. TV screens show news and background music plays upstairs at the weekend. Alcohol is served from 11.30am (12.30pm Sun). Q❄️❇️◑◐&⇌●P🚌🛜

Londonderry

Ice Wharf
Strand Road, BT48 7AB
❇️ 8am-midnight (1am Thu-Sat) ☎ (028) 7127 6610
Greene King Abbot; Sharp's Doom Bar; 3 changing beers Ⓗ
A wide, spacious hostelry not far from the city's Guildhall Square on the Strand Road. A former hotel, it was Wetherspoon's first Lloyds No.1 bar in Northern Ireland. The large single-floor room has screens dividing the semi-circular bar from the seating area. Real cider is available on gravity alongside the regular and guest ales. Alcohol is served from 11.30am (12.30pm Sun). Q❄️❇️◑◐🚌

Newtownards

Spirit Merchant
54-56 Regent Street, BT23 4LP (next to bus station)
❇️ 8am-midnight ☎ (028) 9182 4270
Fuller's London Pride; Greene King Abbot; Sharp's Doom Bar; 2 changing beers Ⓗ
Wetherspoon venue on the main street near the bus station. Friendly and welcoming, it has the feel of a local pub, with knowledgeable, helpful staff. Five handpumps dispense the regular beers complemented by up to two changing guests. There are three TV screens and a smoking area in the large heated courtyard to the side. The standard good-value Wetherspoon food menu is served, with breakfast from 8am. Alcohol is available from 11.30am (12.30pm Sun). Q❄️❇️◑◐Å🚌(7)

Saintfield

White Horse
49-53 Main Street, BT24 7AB
❇️ 11.30-11.30; 12-10.30 Sun ☎ (028) 9751 1143
⊕ whitehorsesaintfield.com
Whitewater Copperhead, Belfast Ale, Bee's Endeavour; 1 changing beer Ⓗ
One of the few pubs remaining in Saintfield, a historic village some 10 miles from Belfast. Formerly a coaching inn, it is now a modern pub with bar, lounge and bistro areas. A pizza restaurant has recently been added downstairs. Despite the modernisation, part of the building's original walls can still be seen. This is the brewery tap for Whitewater – three or more of its ales are always on handpump. A former CAMRA Northern Ireland Pub of the Year. Q❇️◑◐&🚌(15,215)

By George

It was my Uncle George who discovered that alcohol was a food well in advance of modern medical thought.
P G Wodehouse, The Inimitable Jeeves

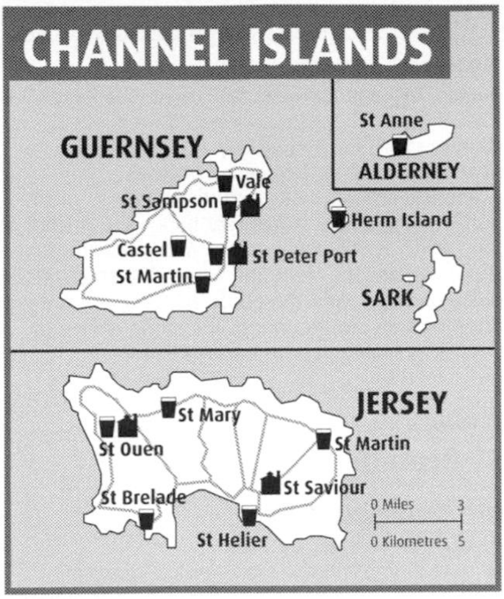

ALDERNEY

St Anne

Georgian House

Victoria Street, GY9 3UF
10-midnight (12.30am Sun) ☎ (01481) 822471
georgianalderney.com
Marston's Old Empire; Ringwood Best Bitter; Wychwood Hobgoblin; 2 changing beers (sourced nationally) Ⓗ
Just up from the town church, the hotel extends a warm welcome to all. There is a pleasant garden with an outside bar and extra casks during the summer months. Live music is occasionally hosted in the garden. Meals are served all day and real cider may be available in the summer. During the winter there are two multi-fuel fires to add to the warm and cosy atmosphere. P

GUERNSEY

Castel

Fleur du Jardin

Kings Mills, GY5 7JT
10.30-11.45 ☎ (01481) 257996 fleurdujardin.com
Sharp's Doom Bar; Wadworth 6X; 1 changing beer (sourced nationally) Ⓗ
A building of unique charm with two bars – one traditional, small and cosy, attached to the restaurant, the other recently renovated in a more contemporary style to create a comfortable, relaxing area to enjoy a beer. A door from this area leads to a large covered patio and out to the garden. Menus in both the bar and restaurant feature fresh local produce. Q P

Grand Mare Hotel & Golf Club

Vazon Bay, GY5 7LL (on Vazon coast road)
10 (12 Sun)-11.45 ☎ (01481) 256576
lagrandemare.com
White Rock Witch Hunter, Wonky Donkey; 2 changing beers (sourced nationally) Ⓗ
The hotel is open all year and welcomes guests and locals alike. It is situated opposite the beach at Vazon, one of the popular west coast bays. The Club bar opens every day and has a large-screen TV showing sport; it has a fire in the winter months. There is also a separate bar with some comfy seats attached to the large restaurant. Children are welcome. P

Herm Island

Mermaid Tavern

GY1 3HR (travel Trident ferry from St Peter Port to Herm, then follow signposts)
11 (12 Sun)-10.30 ☎ (01481) 750050 herm.com/mermaid
3 changing beers (sourced nationally; often Liberation) Ⓗ
A short trip by ferry from Guernsey takes you to Herm. A large courtyard acts as a suntrap in the summer while in winter an open fire creates a cosy atmosphere. Real ale and cider festivals are held twice a year. The house beer, Herm Island Gold, is brewed by Liberation. A trip to Herm to discover the island's peace, tranquillity and outstanding natural beauty is a must for any visitor to Guernsey.

St Martin

Captain's

La Fosse, GY4 6EF
11-11 (midnight Fri & Sat); 12-4 Sun ☎ (01481) 238990
thecaptainshotel.co.uk
Black Sheep Best Bitter; Fuller's London Pride Ⓗ
In a secluded location down a country lane, this is a popular locals' pub with a lively, friendly atmosphere. It has a small raised area in front of the bar furnished with a sofa to make a comfy zone. Good-quality meals can be eaten in the bar or bistro area, or you can take away a pizza. A meat draw is held on Friday. The car park to the rear fills up quickly. P

Douvres Hotel

La Fosse, GY4 6ER
10.30-12.30am ☎ (01481) 238731
lesdouvreshotel.co.uk
2 changing beers Ⓗ
Former 18th-century manor house, set in private gardens in St Martin near the south coast, two-and-a-half miles from St Peter Port, with cliff walks and a tiny fishing harbour. A well-maintained changing range of beers is offered on two handpumps. Excellent meals are served in the bar or restaurant. Live music features on Friday nights and occasional Wednesdays. The venue is popular with locals and visitors. P

St Peter Port

Cock & Bull

Lower Hauteville, GY1 1LL
11-12.45am; closed Sun ☎ (01481) 722660
cockandbullguernsey.com/home
5 changing beers (sourced nationally) Ⓗ
Popular pub, just up the hill from the town church, with five handpumps providing a changing range of beer and cider. Seating is on three levels. Live music features throughout the week, with salsa,

REAL ALE BREWERIES

Liberation St Saviour: Jersey
Pocket St Ouen: Jersey (brewing suspended)
Randalls St Peter Port: Guernsey
White Rock St Sampsons: Guernsey

baroque or jazz on Monday, open mic on Tuesday, jazz on Wednesday, Irish on Thursday and on Saturday a silent set – gentle music that won't hinder good conversation. A meat draw is held on Friday. Open on Sundays only for live rugby. ●🍴🖥️📶

Cornerstone Café Bar 🍷 🅻
2 La Tour Beauregard, GY1 1LQ
🕙 11-11.30; 10-12.30am Fri; 11-12.30am Sat; 12-7 Sun
☎ (01481) 713832 🌐 cornerstoneguernsey.co.uk
4 changing beers (often Liberation, Randalls, White Rock) 🅷
This café has a small bar area to the front and further seating to the rear, and was local CAMRA Pub of the Year 2014. Regular quiz evenings are held and there is a large screen for sporting events. The menu offers a wide range of meals plus daily specials (no food Sun, unless advertised). Ales from Randalls, Liberation and White Rock are among the beers available on four handpumps – check the website for what is on and what is coming. ◑🖥️🖥️📶

Ship & Crown
North Esplanade, GY1 2NB (opp Crown Pier car park on sea front)
🕙 10 (12 Sun)-12.45am ☎ (01481) 728994
Liberation Ale; 3 changing beers 🅷
Traditional local located in the heart of the town, with fantastic views of the harbour, neighbouring islands and Castle Cornet. Friendly and welcoming staff help make it a popular venue with locals, yachtsman and tourists. The walls are decorated with photos of local shipwrecks, Guernsey and the pub under German occupation. All major sports events are shown in a friendly and lively atmosphere. An ideal place to enjoy a pint and a good-value meal, the pub has been in the same family for 35 years. ◑▶●🖥️📶

St Sampson

Fontaine
Vale Road, GY2 4DS
🕙 11 (10 Sat)-midnight; 12-6 Sun ☎ (01481) 247644
1 changing beer (often Randalls) 🅷
The Fontaine is situated on the main road from the Halfway towards L'Ancresse Common and Pembroke Bay. There is a public bar on the road frontage and a large back bar with a serving hatch through to the front. Occasional live music and various social events are hosted, and euchre teams meet once a week. Traditional pub games such as shove-ha'penny, bar billiards and darts are played. With a welcoming host, the pub is popular with locals, particularly for the meat draw on Fridays and Saturdays. 🏵️♣P🖥️📶

Pony Inn
Les Capelles, GY2 4GX (on main road between Guernsey Candles and Oatlands Centre)
🕙 11 (3 Mon)-11; 10-11 Sat; 12-6.30 Sun ☎ (01481) 244374
Sharp's Doom Bar; 1 changing beer
A good pub with well-maintained beer and generous portions of excellent food served in the main bar, conservatory area and separate family dining room (booking advisable, particularly at weekends). The public bar at the side shows televised sports and has a pool table. Ale can be purchased and passed through from the main bar. The staff are friendly and families are welcome. There is disabled access for wheelchair users. 🐶🏵️◑🅖♣P🖥️

Vale

Houmet Tavern
Rousse, GY6 8AR (between Vale Church and Rousse Tower)
🕙 10-12.45am (6 Sun) ☎ (01481) 242214
Greene King Abbot; 2 changing beers 🅷
A popular hostelry with picturesque views of the north of the Island. It has two bars – the Anchor Bar, which is the public bar at the rear with pool and darts, and the Front Bar, where the emphasis is more on food. Only the public bar is open in the afternoon during the week. The same choice of beer is available in both bars. ◑▶P🖥️📶

JERSEY
St Brelade

Old Smugglers Inn
Le Mont du Ouaisne, JE3 8AW
🕙 11-11 ☎ (01534) 741510 🌐 oldsmugglersinn.com
Draught Bass 🅷**; Greene King Abbot** 🅖**; 2 changing beers (often Skinners)** 🅷
Perched on the edge of Ouaisne Bay, the Smugglers has been the jewel of the Jersey real ale scene for many years. Steeped in history, dating back to when pirates were known to enjoy an ale or two here, it is set within granite-built fishermen's cottages with foundations reputedly from the 13th century. Up to four ales are available including one from Skinner's, and mini beer festivals are regularly held. The pub is renowned for its good food and fresh daily specials. Q🐶🖙◑▶●P🖥️(12,15)🐾

St Helier

Forum 🅻
13 Grenville Street, JE2 4UF
🕙 11-11 ☎ (01534) 768105
Liberation Ale; 3 changing beers (often Box Steam) 🅷
On the outskirts of town, the pub is named after the cinema that once stood opposite. It has a modern interior but with a classic feel and includes a number of brass plaques that were taken from the old Royal Court building. Live sport and background music often feature. Three real ales are always available, and a large range of real ciders. A former local CAMRA Pub of the Year. ◑▶🦽♣●🖥️(3)🐾📶

Lamplighter 🍷 🅻
9 Mulcaster Street, JE2 3NJ
🕙 11-11 ☎ (01534) 723119
House beer (by Ringwood); 7 changing beers (often Ringwood, Wells) 🅷
A traditional pub with a modern feel. The gas lamps that gave the pub its name remain, as does the original antique pewter bar top. An excellent range of up to eight real ales is available including one from Skinner's, all served on handpump from the cellar. A choice of real ciders is sometimes also on offer. Local and regional CAMRA Pub of the Year 2014 and local Pub of the Year 2015. ◑▶🖥️🐾📶

Peirson 🅻
17 Royal Square, JE2 4WA
🕙 10 (11 Sun)-11 ☎ (01534) 722726
Draught Bass; Liberation Ale 🅷**; 1 changing beer** 🅖
Nestled in the corner of the Royal Square in the centre of St Helier, the pub is named after Major Francis Peirson and contains historical reminders of

the Battle of Jersey in 1781. Two ales are always on handpump plus an occasional additional ale on gravity. Excellent food is served lunchtimes throughout the year, with evening meals also on offer in summer. The pub has a good reputation with locals and visitors alike. Outside seating is extremely popular in the summer months.
Q⛭◖♿🚌🐾

Post Horn

Hue Street, JE2 3RE
⏲ 10 (11 Sun)-11 ☎ (01534) 872853
Liberation Ale; 3 changing beers (often Butcombe, Liberation) [H]
Busy, friendly pub adjacent to the precinct and five minutes' walk from the Royal Square. Popular at lunchtimes with its own nucleus of regulars, it offers up to four draught ales. The large L-shaped public bar extends into the lounge area with an open fire and TV showing sport. A good selection of freshly cooked food is served. There is a large function room on the first floor, a drinking area outside and a public car park nearby. ❀◖♿🚌🐾📶

St Martin

Royal

La Grande Route de Faldouet, JE3 6UG
⏲ 10 (11 Sun)-11 ☎ (01534) 856289
Draught Bass; Ringwood Best Bitter [H]**; 1 changing beer** [G]
Large, traditional, country-style inn at the centre of St Martin with sizeable public and lounge bars and restaurant area. Owned by Randalls, it has been under the same management for 25 years. The interior features traditional furnishings, cosy corners and a real fire in the colder months. Guest ales are from the Marston's range or Skinner's. Quality food is popular with locals and visitors alike, with a good menu served lunchtimes and evenings until 8.30pm (no food Sun eve).
⛭❀◖◗♿⛺P🚌(3)🐾

Rozel Bar & Restaurant

La Valle de Rozel, JE3 6AJ
⏲ 10 (11 Sun)-11 ☎ (01534) 863478
Draught Bass; Liberation Ale; 1 changing beer (often Ringwood, Skinners) [H]
A charming hostelry tucked away in the north-east corner of the island, under new management as a Liberation Group partner pub. It has a delightful beer garden and an excellent restaurant upstairs. Bar meals are served in the public bar and snug, where there is a real fire in the winter. Locals are friendly if sometimes a little rumbustious.
⛭❀◖◗♿🚌(3)🐾

St Mary

St Mary's Country Inn

La Rue des Buttes, JE3 3DS
⏲ 10 (11 Sun)-11 ☎ (01534) 482897
Liberation Ale; 3 changing beers (often Butcombe) [H]
An archetypal country inn from the outside, this 17th-century farmhouse is opposite the Norman parish church. Following refurbishment in 2009, the interior is contemporary with a main bar and an extensive dining area. Four handpumps serve Liberation and three guest beers, and reasonably priced good food is available daily from an extensive menu. The inn has a comfortable and relaxed atmosphere with seating outside front and rear for when the sun shines. A reasonable walk from the north coast. ⛭❀◖◗♿P🚌(25,27)🐾📶

St Ouen

Farmers Inn

La Grande Route de St Ouen, JE3 2HY
⏲ 10 (11 Sun)-11 ☎ (01534) 485311
Draught Bass; Liberation Ale; 1 changing beer [H]
Situated in the hub of St Ouen, the rustic Farmers Inn is a typical country pub offering up to three ales as well as a locally made cider when available (usually April-July). Traditional pub food is served in generous portions. Best described as a friendly community local, there is a good chance of hearing Jersey French (Jerriais) spoken at the bar.
◗♣P🚌(8,9)

Moulin de Lecq

Le Mont de la Greve de Lecq, JE3 2DT
⏲ 11-11 ☎ (01534) 482818 🌐 moulindelecq.com
4 changing beers (often Liberation, Ringwood, Skinners) [G]
Another free house on the island offering a range of real ales, the Moulin is a converted 12th-century watermill situated in the valley above the beach at Greve de Lecq. The waterwheel is still in place and the turning mechanism can be seen behind the bar. A restaurant adjoins the mill. There is a children's play space and a barbecue area used extensively in the summer. Q⛭❀◖◗♿●P🚌(9)🐾

Fishing for beer

Ah! My beloved brother of the rod, do you know the taste of beer – of bitter beer – cooled in the flowing river? Take your bottle of beer, sink it deep, deep in the shady water, where the cooling springs and fishes are. Then, the day being very hot and bright, and the sun blazing on your devoted head, consider it a matter of duty to have to fish that long, wide stream. An hour or so of good hammering will bring you to the end of it, and then – let me ask you avec impressement – how about that beer? Is it cool? Is it refreshing? Does it gurgle, gurgle and 'go down glug' as they say in Devonshire? Is it heavenly? Is it Paradise and all the Peris to boot? Ah! If you have never tasted beer under these or similar circumstance, you have, believe me, never tasted it at all.
Francis Francis, By Lake and River, 16th century

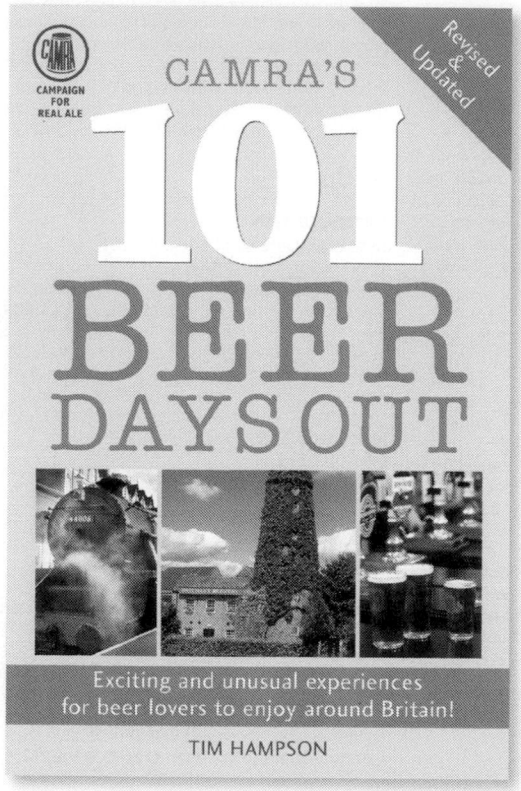

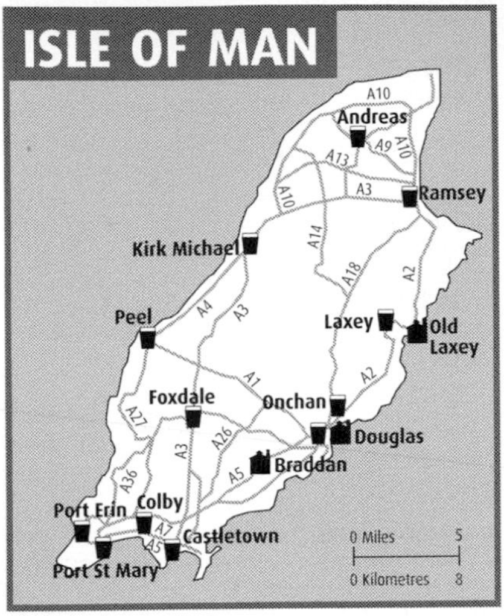

Andreas

Grosvenor

Kirk Andreas, IM7 4HE

⏲ 11-11 ☎ (01624) 888007

Okell's Bitter; 1 changing beer Ⓗ

The Grosvenor has always been an equally popular venue for drinking and dining and has a loyal clientele. The Tap Room is a long-established favourite with locals and patrons from further afield, from families to farmers. It is very much a traditional country bar with a real sense of period charm and character. You can enjoy beers from the Island's largest brewery, Okell's. Quiz night is Sunday and everyone is welcome. **Q🛏◐◑♣P🚌**

Castletown

Castle Arms

The Quay, IM9 1LD

⏲ 12-11 (midnight Fri & Sat) ☎ (01624) 824673

Okell's Bitter; 3 changing beers (often Okell's) Ⓗ

An attractive and historic pub, the Castle Arms is also known as the Glue Pot – presumably due to the difficulty its clientele have in extricating themselves. It is next to Castletown harbour beneath the walls of Castle Rushen and handy for other heritage attractions. Two small ground-floor rooms have nautical and Manx motor racing themes. The patio is ideal for watching quayside vessels and waterfront wildlife. The only pub in the British Isles to feature on a banknote (Manx £5). **❀◐▲⇌♣🚌**(1,2)

Sidings

Victoria Road, IM9 1EF

⏲ 11.30-11.30 (12.30am Fri & Sat) ☎ (01624) 823282

Bushy's Castletown Bitter, Ruby (1874) Mild, Bitter; Okell's Bitter; changing beers (often Copper Dragon) Ⓗ

The Sidings is a favourite with locals and visitors, comprising two large lounges, a pool room and large beer garden at the rear. On entering, the 10 handpumps stretching the length of the bar are an attractive sight. The pub is a popular stop-off for bus and train travellers calling in to enjoy the range of guests and local beers on offer. **❀◐⇌♣P🚌📶**

Colby

Colby Glen Hotel

Main Road, IM9 4LR

⏲ 12-2.30, 5-11.30 (midnight Fri); 12-midnight Sat; 12-11 Sun ☎ (01624) 834853

Okell's Bitter; 2 changing beers (often Okell's) Ⓗ

A new entry in the Guide, this is a refurbished, modernised and tastefully redecorated pub in the heart of the village. A popular and comfortable local, it has two separate main rooms and a games room at the rear. Wholesome food attracts local diners and those from further afield. Quizzes are a regular feature. A function room is available and car parking is opposite. **Q🛏❀◐◑♿▲♣P🚌**(1)

Douglas

Albert Hotel

3 Chapel Row, IM1 2BJ

⏲ 10-11 (11.45 Fri & Sat); 12-11 Sun ☎ (01624) 673632

Okell's Bitter; 3 changing beers (often Bushy's, Hooded Ram, Okell's) Ⓗ

The nearest real ale pub to the sea terminal, the Albert is an unspoilt local with many regulars. It has a traditionally laid-out central bar and dark wood panelling, with a pool table in one room and interesting pictures of Steampacket boats in the other. Sport on TV is a frequent feature but never loud enough to spoil conversation. The drinks are reasonably priced, the three resident beers coming from the likes of Okell's, Bushy's and Hooded Ram. **Q♣🚌**

Cat With No Tail

Hailwood Court, Governors Hill, IM2 7EA

⏲ 12-11 (midnight Fri & Sat) ☎ (01624) 616364

Okell's Bitter; 2 changing beers (often Okell's) Ⓗ

A modern pub serving Governors Hill housing estate, situated two miles from central Douglas. The Cat has a public bar with large-screen Sky Sports, pool and darts. Karaoke night is the last Friday of each month. The large lounge has a conservatory which leads to a spacious outside seating area with patio and play area. The main beer is Okell's Bitter with a seasonal or guest ale usually also on offer. **🛏❀◐◑♿P🚌**(12,22)

Horse & Plough

Isle of Man Business Park, Bradden, IM2 2QZ

⏲ 12-3, 5-11 (midnight Fri); 12-midnight Sat; 12-11 Sun ☎ (01624) 626060

Okell's Bitter; 3 changing beers (often Okell's) Ⓗ

Modern Heron & Brearley pub, serving the IoM Business Park and nearby housing estate. There is ample space for diners, families and drinkers to relax in an informal atmosphere, with a good design of offshoot rooms. The large conservatory is popular for functions, and leads to an outside seating area at the rear. There is a pool table and TV sport. An interesting food menu accompanies up to four real ales. The pub is busy following an excellent refurb. **🛏❀◐◑♿♣P🚌**

REAL ALE BREWERIES

Bushy's Braddan
Hooded Ram Douglas
Okell's Douglas
Old Laxey Old Laxey

ISLANDS

Prospect Hotel
Prospect Hill, IM1 1ET
🕛 12-11 (midnight Fri & Sat); closed Sun ☎ (01624) 616773
Okell's Bitter; changing beers (often Okell's) Ⓗ
Opened in 1857, the pub is in the finance sector of the island's capital. The law courts are in close proximity and the walls feature many pictures relating to the law profession. The bar is busy and popular, especially among office workers. Fourteen handpumps have recently been fitted, with up to six guests often chosen by customers. Wednesday is quiz night. ◐≠●🚌📶

Queen's Hotel
Queens Promenade, IM2 4NL
🕛 12-midnight (1am Fri & Sat) ☎ (01624) 674438
Okell's Bitter; 3 changing beers (often Okell's) Ⓗ
One of just a few remaining pubs on Douglas promenade, the refurbished Queen's is popular with visitors and locals alike. There is a great view of Douglas bay, ferries and trams from the terrace, which has plenty of seating under heated awnings. Inside there are three distinct areas, one with a pool table, two with low-volume TVs featuring sport. Pub grub is served seven days a week and there is live music at weekends.
Q🐎❀◐◑♿≠(Derby Castle)♣●🚌

Rovers Return
11 Church Street, IM1 2AG
🕛 12-11 (midnight Fri & Sat) ☎ (01624) 676459
Bushy's Ruby (1874) Mild, Bitter; 5 changing beers (often Bushy's) Ⓗ
The Rovers is an interesting pub to say the least – handpumps fashioned from fire hoses, a real fire beneath the dartboard and a shrine to Blackburn Rovers FC are just some of its quirks. Then there is its truly eclectic and enthusiastic clientele. Desperate Dan-size portions of food are served at lunchtimes. The building would be a famous landmark if it was not tucked away behind the town hall. ❀◐≠♣●🚌📶

Terminus Tavern
Strathallan Crescent, IM2 4NR
🕛 12-11 (midnight Fri & Sat) ☎ (01624) 624312
Okell's Bitter; 3 changing beers (often Okell's) Ⓗ
Located next to the starting point for the seasonal Manx Electric Railway and horse trams, the Terminus has a comfortable, spacious front bar with alcoves around its large front windows. There is also a side bar for pool and darts, and a large outside seating area with views across Douglas Bay. This friendly pub is popular for dining and can get busy during peak times. Okell's Bitter is offered alongside several changing guests.
🐎❀◐◑♿≠(MER)♣P🚌(25,26,27)

Woodbourne Hotel 🏆
Alexander Drive, IM2 3QF
🕛 3 (12 Sat & Sun)-midnight ☎ (01624) 676754
Okell's Bitter; 5 changing beers (often Okell's) Ⓗ
Large three-bar Victorian local in a residential area within walking distance of Douglas centre. What was once the gents-only bar is now used to promote cask ale, offering a range of Okell's beers alongside four or five guests. The Woody is a popular, friendly pub with a varied clientele, and boasts a genuine community spirit, with a proud record of charity fundraising. A regular pub quiz is held on Sunday evening, and there is a separate games room for pool. Current local CAMRA pub of the year. ❀♣●🚌📶

Foxdale

Baltic Inn
1 Glentramman Terrace, IM4 3EE
🕛 4 (2 Fri & Sat)-midnight ☎ (01624) 801305
Okell's MPA; 1 changing beer (often Okell's) Ⓗ
Quiet, cosy local, with one main room divided into separate seating areas. A roaring real fire in winter adds to the atmosphere. It now has real ale on handpump to supplement the bottled Okell's IPA and Maclir. There are some interesting photos on the walls of Foxdale during the mining boom. The best way to find out about this friendly village pub is to pay it a visit. Q♣

Kirk Michael

Mitre
Main Road, IM6 1AJ
🕛 12-2 (not Mon), 5-11; 12-2, 5-midnight Fri; 12-midnight Sat; 12-11 Sun ☎ (01624) 878244
Okell's Bitter; 1 changing beer (sourced nationally) Ⓗ
This is the oldest pub on the island and has had one of the best refurbs while maintaining a wonderful quaint and cosy atmosphere. The staff are hospitable and all visitors are made to feel welcome. Inside there are open fires, stunning old beams and a wood-panelled pool room with stained-glass windows. Outside there is a fantastic beer garden with breathtaking views. Traditional home-cooked food is served Tuesday-Saturday lunchtimes and early evenings, and a roast with all the trimmings on Sundays. Q❀◐◑♿⛺♣P🚌

Laxey

Bridge Inn
6 New Road, IM4 7BE
🕛 11.30-11 (midnight Fri & Sat) ☎ (01624) 862414
Bushy's Bitter; Morland Old Speckled Hen; 1 changing beer Ⓗ
Popular and lively local pub in the centre of the village. The Bridge has been refurbished but retains its friendly atmosphere and continues to serve an excellent pint. It offers occasional live music, a wide-screen TV and pool table. In 1897, after the Snaefell mining disaster in which 20 men perished, the cellar area was used as a temporary morgue. There are rumours of a resident ghost.
❀◐◑⛺≠♣🚌

Onchan

Manx Arms
Main Road, IM3 1BE
🕛 12-11 (midnight Fri & Sat); 12-midnight Sun ☎ (01624) 675484
Okell's Bitter; 2 changing beers (often Okell's) Ⓗ
Traditional village pub on the main road with a lounge and bar with pub games including pool, darts and dominoes, and a large-screen TV for sport. Live music features most Saturday evenings as well as an occasional karaoke night. There is an attractive heated patio at the front for smokers and another at the rear next to the large car park. The regular beer is from Okell's with a seasonal or guest ale also usually on offer. No food is served. A lively and friendly pub. ❀♿♣P🚌(3,23)📶

Peel

Creek Inn

Station Place, IM5 1AT

☼ 10-11 (midnight Fri & Sat) ☎ (01624) 842216

Okell's Bitter; changing beers ℍ

Traditional harbourside pub popular with locals and tourists, with ample outdoor seating on the edge of the picturesque harbour. The lounge bar has a nautical theme with etched-glass screens featuring sailing ships separating the cosy seating areas. A good selection of ales is on offer to complement the comprehensive food menu. Locally caught Manx queenies (queen scallops) are a speciality, together with locally cured kippers. The pub hosts live music at weekends. ☕♠◑▸▲♣♨☐(5,6)🛜

Marine Hotel

Shore Road, IM5 1AH

☼ 12-midnight ☎ (01624) 842337

Bushy's Bitter; Okell's Bitter; 4 changing beers (often Hooded Ram) ℍ

Popular with all ages, the Marine Hotel overlooks the beach and historic Peel Castle. It has two bar areas, one a traditional drinking corridor, and a large restaurant accessed via a separate entrance, serving excellent meals seven days a week. A much-improved pub in recent years, it offers locally brewed Bushy's and Okell's beers plus guests. Manx cider is available too. ◑♣♨☐(5,6)🛜

White House Hotel

2 Tynwald Road, IM5 1LA

☼ 11-midnight ☎ (01624) 842252

⊕ thewhitehousepeel.com

Bushy's Ruby (1874) Mild, Bitter; Moorhouse's Pride of Pendle; Okell's Bitter; 4 changing beers ℍ

This is a truly classic establishment – cosy, friendly and welcoming. It has a snug, public bar, separate pool room and a larger room for TV sport and live music at the weekends. One of the few pubs on the island to sell local cider, usually Westons, it has the unrivalled distinction of once winning local CAMRA Pub of the Year three times in a row, and again most recently in 2013. Q❀▲♣♨P☐(5,6)

Port Erin

Bay Hotel

Shore Road, IM9 6HL

☼ 12-11 ☎ (01624) 832084

Bushy's Castletown Bitter, Ruby (1874) Mild, Bitter, Old Bushy Tail; 3 changing beers ℍ

Bushy's flagship pub is on one of the best beaches on the island. Beach concerts and and a promenade patio make the Bay a great summertime venue, with local bands playing in the winter. The full range of Bushy's brews is available, and can be sampled by ordering a special tasting tray. The interior comprises four traditional rooms – public bar, quiet room, dining room and band area. Isle of Man Cider Pub of the Year 2015. Q♠❀◑&≋♣♨🛜

Falcon's Nest Hotel

Station Road, IM9 6AF

☼ 10.30-midnight (1am Fri & Sat); 10.30-11 Sun

☎ (01624) 834077 ⊕ falconsnesthotel.co.uk

Bushy's Bitter; 3 changing beers ℍ

The Falcon's Nest Hotel on the south-west coast, overlooking the beautiful crescent-shaped bay, is a free house with two bars. The residents' lounge bar, also open to the public, is in the true tradition of a public house, where visitors can enjoy an ever-changing range of guest beers and local ales while relaxing in front of an open fire. The Victorian-style Gladstone restaurant offers an extensive à la carte menu and an ever-popular Sunday lunch carvery. Q♠◑≋♣☐🛜

Haven

Station Road, IM1 1BS

☼ 12-11 (midnight Fri & Sat) ☎ (01624) 834030

Okell's Bitter ℍ

Refurbished at the end of 2009, this is a well-laid-out venue with a welcoming atmosphere. The front bar is extremely popular with the footie crowd and the back bar is where the locals hang out. Located conveniently next to the train and bus stations, the Haven is a great place to start or finish a tour of Port Erin. ≋(IMR)♣☐

Port St Mary

Albert Hotel

Athol Street, IM9 5DS

☼ 11-midnight; 12-1am Fri & Sat; 12-midnight Sun

☎ (01624) 832118

Bushy's Bitter, Old Bushy Tail; Okell's Bitter; 1 changing beer ℍ

Traditional pub in the heart of the village boasting impressive views over the picturesque harbour. It has three rooms – a large public bar with a games area and a smaller lounge bar, both warmed by real fires, and a seating area with tables used during busier times. Well-decorated and comfortably furnished, with Manx Gaelic language quotations adorning the walls, this is an ideal pub to relax in following a sea fishing trip. Beware the low doorway to the Gents. Q❀♠◑♣P☐(1,2)

Shore Hotel

Shore Road, IM9 5LZ

☼ 12-11.30 (midnight Fri & Sat) ☎ (01624) 832269

Bushy's Old Bushy Tail; Okell's Bitter ℍ

Large sturdy building with stunning views over Gansey Bay. There is a separate bar with a pool table and a popular restaurant, also available for private functions. The outdoor seating area is sheltered from what can be biting winds. A quiz is held on Tuesday nights. This is one of the few outlets that regularly sells Old Bushy Tail. B&B accommodation is available. ♠◑▸P☐

Ramsey

Mitre

16 Parliament Street, IM8 1AP

☼ 11-11 ☎ (01624) 813257

Bushy's Bitter; Okell's Bitter; 2 changing beers (often Hooded Ram, Okell's) ℍ

Large building with views of the quayside. There are distinct and separate bars on three levels; the basement Schooner bar is popular with young revellers at the weekend, while live music is hosted in the upstairs bar. Lunchtime food is available including popular Sunday lunches. The Bushy's and Okell's bitters are regulars, with Okell's Jough also often on tap alongside beers from other local breweries. ◑

Plough

46 Parliament Street, IM8 1AN

☼ 4.30-11 (midnight Fri); 12-midnight Sat; 12-11 Sun

☎ (01624) 813323

ISLANDS

Okell's Bitter; 1 changing beer Ⓗ
Busy pub on Ramsey's main street where, during the day, shoppers taking a break mingle with football fans. In the evening a mixed clientele vies for space in the two small bar areas. This free house has sold Okell's Bitter for several years and more recently has added an ever-changing guest beer. The Plough is a proud sponsor of Shennaghys Jiu, a Manx music festival held in Ramsey in March/April. ◑≠(MER)♣

Stanley

West Quay, IM8 1DW
⏲ 12 (3.30 Wed)-11; 12-midnight Fri & Sat
☎ (01624) 812258
Okell's Bitter; 1 changing beer Ⓗ
If you wander into the Stanley you could be forgiven for thinking you have stepped back in time. This is a small, old, traditional Manx pub and none the worse for it. Settle in next to the beautiful open fire and enjoy a pint of Okell's but be prepared to be interrogated – in the nicest possible way of course! A popular and busy karaoke night is hosted every Friday. Heron & Brearley Cask Ale Pub of the Year 2015. **Q**

Trafalgar Hotel

West Quay, IM8 1DW
⏲ 11-11 (12.15am Fri & Sat); 11.30-11 Sun
☎ (01624) 814601
Bushy's Bitter; Moorhouse's Black Cat; Okell's Bitter; 1 changing beer Ⓗ
Traditional genuine single-room pub situated on the harbour behind the main shopping street. A CAMRA Isle of Man branch Pub of the Year finalist for many years, the real ales including guests are sourced from all over the UK. Friendly, welcoming and always busy, it is particularly popular during TT week and just around the corner from spectacular views of the races. A function room upstairs is available for meetings. The Trafalgar has been under the same ownership for more than 21 years. **Q**⛺≠(MER)♣🚌(3,5,6)

Woodbourne Hotel, Douglas

Green Dragon, Wymondham, Norfolk (p361)

Orkney brewery, Quoyloo, Orkney (p867)

The Breweries

Breweries overview

Global giants may be on merger trail to move into the cask market

The real ale revival seems unstoppable. There are 204 new breweries listed in the Breweries section of this edition and the increase from year to year grows rather than diminishes.

There is however a possible downside to this success. With sales of old-fashioned 'smoothflow' keg beers, such as John Smith's and Tetley's, in free fall and international lager brands also struggling to maintain sales, will the giant global brewers take a long, hard look at the real ale sector and decide to move back into it through acquisitions and takeovers?

The globals

The first stirring of interest in the cask sector came from Molson Coors, the Canadian-American giant based in the former Bass breweries in Burton-on-Trent. In 2011 the group bought the Cornish brewer Sharp's for £20 million and in four years has turned Doom Bar into a national brand.

Other global brewers may follow the Molson Coors' route. Evidence of this came in 2015 when SABMiller, the world's second-biggest brewer, stunned the industry with a £50 million takeover of the London independent Meantime. The takeover was less of a shock to those who believed it was the likely outcome when former Miller Brands managing director Nick Miller moved to become chief executive of Meantime in 2011. Miller Brands is the British subsidiary of SABMiller, a South African and American group whose main beers include Peroni, Miller Lite and the original Czech golden lager, Pilsner Urquell.

Meantime was founded in 1999 by master brewer Alastair Hook, who trained at both Heriot-Watt brewing school in Edinburgh and the world's leading brewing college in Munich. Hook makes no real ale and has mapped out a new route to market with such 'craft beers' as London Pale, London Lager and Yakima Red that are sold to specialist bars and restaurants as well as supermarkets. His main site in Greenwich has a German brewing kit that cost £7 million and has a capacity of 200,000 barrels a year.

In 2015 Meantime was bought by SABMiller

SABMiller says it will turn Meantime into a 'centre of excellence', the base for experimenting with new beers and distributing existing beers to mainland Europe. Alastair Hook believes in using the finest raw materials but he's now employed by a global corporation in which accountants and other bean-counters play a major rule. They will run the slide rule over Meantime's costs and there could be pressure to make savings by using cheaper raw materials, which will lead to less flavoursome beers.

The other global brewers based in the UK will have watched the activities of Molson Coors and SABMiller with keen interest. Heineken UK, Britain's biggest brewer as a result of buying the Scottish & Newcastle breweries in 2008, no longer seems content to rest on the laurels of its Caledonian Brewery in Edinburgh that produces the award-winning Deuchars IPA, now a national brand. In July 2015 it announced it was building a small pilot plant at Caledonian that will test a series of new beers, the most successful of which will become regular brews. It seems unlikely it will expand further into cask beer as it has sold its ownership of the Courage, McEwans's and Younger's brands to Charles Wells and has allowed Newcastle Brown Ale, now brewed at the John Smith's brewery in Tadcaster, Yorkshire, to be overtaken by the likes of Doom Bar and Old Speckled Hen in bottle.

The problem facing AB InBev, Carlsberg and Molson Coors is that their brewing plants are so highly automated and inflexible that they can switch to real ale only by buying smaller breweries with the correct type of equipment. Neither AB InBev nor Carlsberg seems in any hurry to enter the cask beer sector. Carlsberg's lack of interest is demonstrated by the fact that Tetley is no longer part of its corporate title and the Tetley cask beers are now brewed under licence by Marston's. Early in 2015 Carlsberg axed Draught Burton Ale, the only beer produced by a national brewer ever to win CAMRA's Champion Beer of Britain award.

AB InBev's complete lack of interest in the sector can be measured by the fact that it's willing to sell Draught Bass, Boddingtons and Flowers to anyone with £15 million in the piggy bank.

Regional & family brewers

Between the global brewers and the small independent sectors, regional and family brewers range from large breweries such as Fuller's, Greene

King, Marston's and Charles Wells to much smaller producers who feel ground between the upper and lower echelons of the industry.

The problems facing smaller brewers was emphasised in July 2015 when Bateman's in Wainfleet, Lincolnshire, announced it was dramatically reducing its annual production from 18,000 barrels to just 7,000. By cutting production, Bateman's will pay a reduced level of duty on beer under the terms of Progressive Beer Duty. PBD was introduced by the government in 2002 and was designed as a sliding scale that enabled small brewers to pay a much lower level of duty than bigger producers.

But Stuart Bateman, claims PBD penalises breweries of his size as smaller ones can undercut him with savings of around £64 a barrel, which equates to a reduction of 27 pence a pint at the bar. Bateman says he will concentrate on his core brands and may even have to axe his popular dark mild, Black & White. With other family brewers of similar size, he is arguing within the trade body the Independent Family Brewers of Britain for an approach to government to review PBD in order that middle-ranking producers are not penalised.

Batemans is having to axe some popular beers to reduce its duty bill

Further up the pecking order, the Marston's group has kept faith with its Banks's, Brakspear, Jennings, Ringwood and Wychwood breweries and remains a major producer of cask beer.

Greene King, having acquired the Spirit group of pubs for £774 million, is now a mighty force in brewing and retailing, with an estate of more than 3,000 pubs. Its IPA at 3.6% may not be every beer drinkers' idea of a true India Pale Ale but the stronger version, IPA Reserve at 5.4%, is a good interpretation of the style and some excellent beers are emerging from its micro-plant within the main brewery at Bury St Edmunds.

Charles Wells has launched a new series of TV commercials for Bombardier and its paler version, Burning Gold, with comedian and actor Bob Mortimer taking over from the late Rik Mayall. The company owns a range of brands – Courage, McEwan and Younger – bought from Heineken and has had considerable success, on draught and in bottle, with DNA, a beer that's a blend of its own Eagle IPA and a stronger IPA brewed by the Dogfish Head brewery in the U.S. It continues to brew the Young's cask ales for the London-based pub company.

Fuller's invested £5 million in expanding its Chiswick brewery and remains a potent force with a range of cask ales that include the ever-popular London Pride and ESB, the excellent Bengal Lancer IPA, superb bottle-conditioned beers, and a regular series of beers based on recipes culled from recipe books of the 19th and early 20th centuries.

Small independents

'Small' is no longer a word that fits easily with the sector that comes under the umbrella of the Society of Independent Brewers or SIBA. A number of former micros are now brewing more beer that long-established regionals, but the sector is dominated by companies that are happy to stay small.

They argue a different case to Bateman's. They says PBD has worked well, encouraging people to enter the industry, brew good beer and create both jobs and improved choice for consumers.

Without doubt, this sector brings an unprecedented dynamism to beer making. Small brewers are not content to produce tried-and-trusted traditional British beer styles but have innovated with great verve and enthusiasm.

Today, thanks to this fast-growing sector, drinkers can enjoy such styles as sour, oak-aged, fruit, herbs and spiced beers along with ales made with the addition of chocolate, coffee and even chillis. As a result of their size and ability to make short-run beers, the sector is able to produce a range of beers beyond the capability of bigger brewers.

Otter Brewery's Eco Cellar ...one of several breweries committed to aiding the environment

How to use the Breweries section

This section lists breweries operating in the United Kingdom, the Isle of Man and the Channel Islands. Breweries are listed in alphabetical order. They include independent companies (regional, family, micro-brewers and brewpubs), national brewers and global groups. If a brewery owns more than one site, these are cross-referenced. Within each brewery entry, regular beers are listed in increasing order of strength. Websites should be consulted when breweries produce occasional or seasonal beers that are available for less than six months of the year. We mention when breweries produce bottle-conditioned beers but do not list or evaluate them: for further information, see CAMRA's *Good Bottled Beer Guide.*

KEY TO BREWERY ENTRIES

BREWERY SYMBOLS

Brewpub: a pub that brews beer on the premises.

Cyclops: the brewery is affiliated with the Cyclops system for describing beers to consumers.

CAMRA tasting notes, supplied by a trained CAMRA tasting panel. Beer descriptions that do not carry this symbol are based on more limited tastings or have been obtained from other sources.

A CAMRA Beer of the Year in 2014.

One of CAMRA's Beers of the Year 2015: a finalist in the Champion Beer of Britain competition held during the Great British Beer Festival in London in August 2015, or in the Champion Winter Beer of Britain competition held earlier in the year.

Serve with tight sparkler: the brewery's beers can be acceptably served through a 'tight sparkler' attached to the nozzle of the beer pump, designed to give a thick collar of foam on the beer.

Do not serve with tight sparkler: the brewery's beers should NOT be served through a tight sparkler. CAMRA is opposed to the growing tendency to serve southern-brewed beers with the aid of sparklers, which aerate the beer and tend to drive hop aroma and flavour into the head, altering the balance of the beer achieved in the brewery. When neither symbol is used it means the brewery in question has not stated a preference.

Brewery tours available: check with individual breweries for details.

Brewery shop: beer available to take away. Check opening hours in advance.

RAIB **Real Ale in a Bottle:** the brewery produces bottle-conditioned beer (known by CAMRA as Real Ale in a Bottle).

Seasonal beers: the brewery produces seasonal beers in addition to its regular range.

ABBREVIATIONS

OG Stands for Original Gravity, the measure taken before fermentation of the level of 'fermentable material' (malt sugars and added sugars) in the brew. It is only a rough indication of strength and is no longer used for duty purposes.

ABV Stands for Alcohol by Volume, which is a more reliable measure of the percentage of alcohol in finished beer. Many breweries now only disclose ABVs but the Guide lists OGs where available. Often the OG and the ABV of a beer are identical, i.e. 1035 and 3.5 per cent. If the ABV is higher than the OG, i.e. OG 1035, ABV 3.8, this indicates that the beer has been 'well attenuated' with most of the malt sugars turned into alcohol. If the ABV is lower than the OG, this means residual sugars have been left in the beer for fullness of body and flavour: this is rare but can apply to some milds or strong old ales, barley wines and winter beers.

SIBA Indicates a member of the Society of Independent Brewers.

IFBB Indicates a member of the Independent Family Brewers of Britain.

NOTE: The Breweries section was correct at the time of going to press and every effort has been made to ensure that all regularly-available cask-conditioned beers are included.

The Breweries

The breweries listed in this section include micro, small, family, regional, national and global companies. Please use the Beer index (p971) to help locate beers.

1648 SIBA

⊟ Old Stables Brewery, Mill Lane, East Hoathly, East Sussex, BN8 6QB
☎ (01825) 840830 ⊕ 1648brewing.co.uk

⊠ The 1648 brewery, set up in the old stable block at the King's Head pub in 2003, derives its name from the year of the deposition of King Charles I. One pub is owned and more than 40 outlets are supplied. !! ☛ ◆ RAIB

Hop Pocket (OG 1039, ABV 3.7%)

Triple Champion (OG 1041, ABV 4%)
A chestnut-coloured traditional English ale, deeply flavoured and full-bodied.

Signature (OG 1044, ABV 4.4%)
Pale, light, crisply refreshing ale with a bitter aftertaste.

Laughing Frog (OG 1052, ABV 5.2%)
Dark gold-coloured, full-bodied ale, lightly hopped with a full, malty flavour.

3 Brewers SIBA ◉

The Potato Shed, Symonds Hyde Lane, Hatfield, Hertfordshire, AL10 9BB
☎ (01707) 271636 ☎ 07941 854615
⊕ 3brewers.co.uk

⊠ Launched in 2013 by three enthusiastic brewers from St Albans who transformed a former potato shed into an eight-barrel brewery. It is located on a working farm and sources fresh water from the farm borehole. The brewery supplies two permanent beers to pubs in and around the St Albans district and also to local beer festivals. Spent malt is turned into compost for the farm. The brewery shop is located at Cellar Door Wines, Unit 1, Verulam Industrial Estate, St Albans. !! ☛

Golden (OG 1038, ABV 3.8%)
A refreshing, light gold-coloured beer with a subtle citrus flavour and a hint of sweetness.

Classic English Ale (OG 1040, ABV 4%)
Deep amber in colour with a light, hoppy aroma and a rich and rounded malty taste balanced by subtle hoppiness to give a clean, smooth and refreshing ale.

Special English Ale (OG 1048, ABV 4.8%)
A robust and full-bodied premium ale with a deep copper colour. English hops give a hint of berries. Well-balanced and smooth.

360° SIBA ◉

Unit 22, Bluebell Business Estate, Sheffield Park, East Sussex, TN22 3HQ
☎ (01825) 722375 ⊕ 360degreebrewing.com

⊠ Brewing began in 2013 using a six-barrel plant. !! ◆

Pale #39 (ABV 3.9%)

Sussex #42 (ABV 4.2%)

West Coast IPA (ABV 5.6%)

Light-coloured, hoppy and moderately bitter beer. Well-balanced and easy-drinking despite its strength.

4Ts

Unit 15, EBL Centre, Picow Farm Road, Runcorn, Cheshire, WA7 4UA ☎ 07917 730184

Office: 72 Rydal Avenue, Warrington, Cheshire, WA4 6AT ⊕ 4tsbrewery.co.uk

4Ts began brewing in 2010 in Warrington but moved to larger premises in Runcorn using a five-barrel plant in 2012. It offers a core range of four beers plus many themed and special brews. Beers are usually available in the Tavern, Warrington. ◆

Pale Ale (ABV 3.7%)
A pale, refreshing session ale. Spicy notes from European hops help make this ale well balanced throughout.

APA (ABV 4%)
An American-style pale ale with spicy and citrus hints throughout with a hint of bitterness at the end, leaving a citrus burst of flavour.

IPA (ABV 4.6%)
Lots of bitterness and bursts of aroma with hints of citrus and passion fruit.

Stout (ABV 5%)
Well-balanced and smooth with biscuit, chocolate and burnt notes at the start, then English hops break through giving a burst of flowery tones.

8 Sail SIBA

Heckington Windmill, Hale Road, Heckington, Lincolnshire, NG34 9JW
☎ (01529) 469308 ☎ 07866 183479
⊕ 8sailbrewery.co.uk

8 Sail Brewery was established in 2010 and operates on a six-barrel brew plant. The brewery nestles in the shadow of Heckington Windmill, Britain's only eight-sailed windmill, from where the brewery takes its name. The mill is now working and helping to mill malted grain for the brewery. The brewery shop stocks Lincolnshire bottle-conditioned beers alongside local ciders. A Victorian bar and display of pub drinking vessels were due to be installed in 2015. ☛ ◆ RAIB

Millwright Mild (OG 1035, ABV 3.5%)
Rich, dark malt flavours are balanced lightly with hops. The aroma is chocolaty with a dry roast and liquorice flavour.

Ale (OG 1038, ABV 3.8%)
A refreshing traditional English pale ale.

Windmill Bitter (OG 1038, ABV 3.8%)
An amber-coloured session bitter with a blend of malt and hops.

Blonde (OG 1040, ABV 4%)
A blonde beer, gently hopped to create a refreshing taste.

Merry Miller (OG 1041, ABV 4.1%)

A traditional bitter. Mid brown in colour with a nutty, malty flavour.

Flour Power (OG 1042, ABV 4.2%)
A refreshing pale summer beer.

Golden Ale (OG 1044, ABV 4.4%)
A well-balanced pale beer with a citrus and peach aroma and a dry, slightly tart, citrus-dominated flavour

Millstone (OG 1045, ABV 4.5%)
A modern premium bitter with a good balance of malt flavours and hops.

Deacon John Ales After the Gold Rush (OG 1047, ABV 4.6%)
A medium-bodied ale/lager hybrid with a malty character. Mild and fruity with an assertive hop bitterness.

Kibbled (OG 1047, ABV 4.6%)
A well-rounded and balanced red ale with a pleasant malt character.

Windy Miller (OG 1047, ABV 4.6%)
A rich, dark, smooth-flavoured stout brewed with plenty of oat malt.

Damson Porter (OG 1050, ABV 5%)
Damsons are added to give a full-bodied fruitiness to the rich, complex flavours provided by the malts. Aroma is bitter with caramel malt tones. Flavour is malty and slightly fruity with a bitter finish.

Sail Away (OG 1050, ABV 5%)
Brewed in the style of a German Kölsch with a good balance of malt and hops.

Victorian Porter (OG 1050, ABV 5%)
A true porter brewed to a Victorian recipe with an aroma of berries, sour fruits and roasted malts and deep, intense, chocolaty flavours giving this dark beer a rich and full-bodied flavour.

Old Colony (Deacon John Ales) (OG 1053, ABV 5.3%)
An American-style pale ale hopped with a combination of English and American hops.

Black Widow (OG 1055, ABV 5.5%)
A strong, dark ruby mild. Dark malt and liquorice flavours dominate.

John Barleycorn IPA (OG 1055, ABV 5.5%)
Brewed to recreate the taste of an original English IPA using English hops.

Imperial Oat Malt Stout (OG 1067, ABV 6.8%)
A black beer brewed with a generous amount of black and oat malt. Liquorice and linseed have been added to complement the dark malts.

A-B InBev

Porter Tun House, 500 Capability Green, Luton, Bedfordshire, LU1 3LS
☎ (01582) 391166 ⊕ inbev.com

No real ale.

Abbey SIBA ⊙

Abbey Brewery, Camden Row, Bath, BA1 5LB
☎ (01225) 444437 ⊕ abbeyales.co.uk

Founded in 1997, Abbey Ales was the first brewery in Bath for over 50 years. It supplies more than 80 regular outlets within a 20-mile radius. It operates four tied houses. ‼◆

Somerset Ale (OG 1038, ABV 3.8%)

Bath Best (OG 1040, ABV 4%)

Bellringer (OG 1042, ABV 4.2%) ◀
A notably hoppy ale, light to medium-bodied, clean-tasting, refreshingly dry, with a balancing sweetness. Citrus, pale malt aroma and dry, bitter finish.

Abbey Ford

c/o 6 Ford Road, Chertsey, Surrey, KT16 8HD
⊕ abbeyfordbrewery.co.uk

Abbey Ford began brewing in 2013. Beers can be found around the Chertsey area. ◆

Knight on the Tiles (ABV 4%)
A dark amber-coloured session ale. Sweet to start with a subtle hop finish.

AD 666 (ABV 4.8%)
A full-bodied special bitter. Dark amber in colour with a ruby hue. Sweet malt up front turns to a slightly bitter finish.

Abbey Grange

See Llangollen

Abbeydale SIBA ⊙

Unit 8, Aizlewood Road, Sheffield, South Yorkshire, S8 0YX
☎ (0114) 281 2712 ⊕ abbeydalebrewery.co.uk

Since starting in 1996, Abbeydale Brewery has grown steadily; it now produces upwards of 130 barrels a week, and recent investment has enabled further growth. ◆

Matins (OG 1034.9, ABV 3.6%)
Pale and full flavoured; a hoppy session beer.

Brimstone (OG 1039, ABV 3.9%)
A russet-coloured bitter beer with a distinctive hop aroma.

Moonshine (OG 1041.2, ABV 4.3%)
A well-balanced pale ale with a full hop aroma. Pleasant grapefruit traces may be detected.

Absolution (OG 1050, ABV 5.3%)
A fruity pale ale, deceptively drinkable for its strength. Sweetish but not cloying.

Black Mass (OG 1065, ABV 6.7%)
A strong black stout with complex roast flavours and a lasting bitter finish.

Abbot

Maygate, Dunfermline, KY12 7NE
☎ (01383) 733266 ☎ 07790 172708
⊕ abbothouse.co.uk

⊠ Abbot Brewhouse began brewing in 2013 in an outbuilding adjoining the historic Abbot House Heritage Centre and Dunfermline Abbey. The layout of the brewhouse and brewing methods used replicate pre-industrial 17th century brewing of the time. A wide range of beers is produced many of which utilise historic recipes adapted to suit modern tastes. There is a public viewing area with accompanying storyboards for visitors detailing the historic role of ale in Dunfermline. ‼ ⇟ RAIB

Pilgrim (OG 1030, ABV 3%)

A refreshing 'small beer' produced from the second mash of Benedictus – a light session ale with hoppy undertones.

Codebreaker (OG 1035, ABV 3.6%)
A hoppy session beer.

Heritage Mild (OG 1042, ABV 4.2%)
A sweet, dark, full-bodied mild balanced with a lightly hopped bittersweet finish.

Pot Stirrer (OG 1040, ABV 4.2%)
A red-coloured classic Scottish beer with a balance of slightly peppered malt and refreshing New World hops.

Dunfermline Nut Brown (OG 1045, ABV 4.4%)
A dark premium beer using a blend of six different malts balanced by traditional English hops.

Adventuress (OG 1046, ABV 4.5%)
A well-balanced golden ale with a blend of hops.

Scottish Blossom Honey Beer (OG 1047, ABV 4.8%)
A lightly hopped and malted honey beer made with the honey gathered from the Perthshire fruit fields.

Scottish Heather Honey Beer (OG 1047, ABV 4.8%)
A lightly hopped and malted honey beer made with heather honey ensuring the subtle aroma and taste predominates.

Ale Wand (OG 1048, ABV 5%)
A dark, malty brew with liquorice and dark chocolate overtones.

Dunfermline Best (OG 1050, ABV 5.2%)
A traditional best bitter with a well balanced malt and hop flavour and slightly fruity aftertaste.

Dunfermline Pilsner (OG 1050, ABV 5.2%)
A crisp pilsner-type lager made with a floral aroma and hoppiness.

Guild Ale (OG 1050, ABV 5.5%)
A light-coloured IPA using British and New World hops.

Kingdom 10:4 Ale (OG 1052, ABV 5.5%)
A balanced golden brown-coloured beer.

Benedictus (OG 1068, ABV 7%)
A highly aromatic strong beer, rich in flavour.

Acorn SIBA

Unit 3, Aldham Industrial Estate, Mitchell Road, Wombwell, Barnsley, South Yorkshire, S73 8HA
☎ (01226) 270734 acorn-brewery.co.uk

Acorn was set up in 2003 with a 10-barrel expanding to a 20-barrel plant when the brewery moved to larger premises and currently has a 160-barrel a week capacity. All beers are produced using the Barnsley Bitter yeast strain, dating back to the 1850s. ♦RAIB

Yorkshire Pride (OG 1037, ABV 3.7%)
This session beer is golden in colour with pleasing fruit notes. A mouthwatering blend of malt and hops create a fruity taste which leads to a clean bitter finish.

Barnsley Bitter (OG 1038, ABV 3.8%)
A brown bitter with a smooth malty bitterness throughout with notes of chocolate and caramel. Fruity bitter finish.

Barnsley Gold (OG 1041.5, ABV 4%)
This golden ale has fruit in the aroma with a hoppy and fruity flavour throughout. A well-hopped, clean, dry finish.

Blonde (OG 1040.5, ABV 4%)
A clean-tasting, golden-coloured hoppy beer with a refreshing bitter and fruity aftertaste.

1887 Red (OG 1044, ABV 4.4%)

Old Moor Porter (OG 1045, ABV 4.4%)
A rich-tasting porter, smooth throughout with a hint of chocolate and liquorice.

Sovereign (OG 1044, ABV 4.4%)
Brown in colour with malt and fruit aromas, a roast maltiness and fruitiness carry on to the aftertaste.

Gorlovka Imperial Stout (OG 1058, ABV 6%)
This black stout is rich and smooth and full of chocolate and liquorice flavours with a fruity, creamy finish.

Acton

Unit 2, 13b Castle Island Way, North Seaton, Northumberland, NE63 0EL ☎ 07707 703182
actonales1@outlook.com

Formerly known as Gundog, brewing began in 2011 using a 10-barrel plant. Brewing takes place twice a week producing three regular ales throughout the year, with new ales tried periodically. Two other ales are regularly produced by blending.

Pilgrim's Way (OG 1041, ABV 4%)
A pale golden ale, crisp and hoppy with a flush of bitterness at the end.

Golden Cocker (OG 1042, ABV 4.1%)
Dark gold-coloured beer with a good nose and citrus and melon finish.

Seahouses Pale (OG 1043, ABV 4.2%)
A pale ale, hoppy with a clean bitter finish.

Adkin

Correspondence only: c/o 52 Adkin Way, Wantage, Oxfordshire, OX12 9HW ☎ 07709 86149
adkinbrewery.co.uk

Adkin was established on a 0.5-barrel plant in 2007. A new similar-sized plant was installed in 2013. Twelve brews are produced by prior order. The beers are most easily found at regional beer festivals, but are starting to appear in the local free trade. !!RAIB

Adnams SIBA

Sole Bay Brewery, East Green, Southwold, Suffolk, IP18 6JW
☎ (01502) 727200 ☎ 07787 151311
adnams.co.uk

The company was founded by George and Ernest Adnams in 1872. About 70 pubs are owned and there is national distribution. Beers are from a new 300-barrel plant within the confines of the present site. !! ♦

Lighthouse (OG 1037, ABV 3.4%)
A quaffable beer with bitterness predominating.

Southwold Bitter (OG 1037, ABV 3.7%)
Aromas of toffee apple, caramel and sulphur. Taste is a complex mix of malt toffee and roast bitterness

with hops. Malty bitter and apple flavours linger into the aftertaste.

Old Ale (OG 1044, ABV 4.1%) 🍺 ◆
Aromas of malt and soft cheese, leading to malty and sweet flavours with berries and vanilla. Caramel and roast finish.

Explorer (OG 1042, ABV 4.3%) 🍺 ◆
Fruity bitter taste with a delicate sweet aftertaste.

Ghost Ship (OG 1046, ABV 4.5%)

Broadside (OG 1049, ABV 4.7%) ◆
Rich, malty aroma with blackberries and dried fruit. Rich and full flavours of malt and fruit, with roast and caramel notes and subtle hops. Well-balanced, long-lasting aftertaste.

Tally Ho (OG 1075, ABV 7%) 🍺
A strong old ale.

Adur

Brick Barn, Charlton Court, Mouse Lane, Steyning, West Sussex, BN44 3DG
☎ (01903) 867614

Office: 2 Sullington Way, Shoreham-by-Sea, West Sussex, BN43 6PJ ⊕ adurbrewery.com

⊗ Adur Brewery, nestled in the heart of the South Downs, was launched in 2008 on a 5.5-barrel plant, marking the return of brewing to the Adur Valley after an interval of nearly 100 years. The brewery was sold to the Adur Valley Co-Operative Ltd in 2012, including the Adur Brewery name and recipes. A large part of the output is sold as bottle-conditioned beer. ‼ RAIB

Chillinger Gold (OG 1036, ABV 3.7%)
A light golden, refreshing chilli ale with a taste of root ginger. Its initial sweetness is counter-balanced by the hint of chilli and delicate ginger, which continues to a dry finish.

Ropetackle Gold (OG 1036, ABV 3.7%)
A light, golden ale with an initial sweetness and delicate aroma balanced by a dry finish.

Hop Token: Amarillo (OG 1040, ABV 4%)
An amber-coloured bitter. A flowery, spicy and citrus aroma, with hints of peach and grapefruit. The hoppiness carries over into the taste, together with notes of toffee, malt and grapefruit, a good bitterness and a long, dry finish.

Hop Token: Citra (OG 1040, ABV 4%)
An amber-coloured bitter with zest of lime, citrus and tropical fruits giving a long finish.

Hop Token: Summit (OG 1040, ABV 4%)
A bitter beer with hints of tangerine in the aroma and flavour.

Velocity (OG 1044, ABV 4.4%)
Traditional best bitter with a hoppy aroma and a hint of marmalade in the taste.

Black William (OG 1055, ABV 5%)
A rich, black stout with dark chocolate aromas and roasted flavours.

Robbie's Red (OG 1050, ABV 5.2%)
A strong red-brown ale with an aroma of malt and hops. Slight initial sweetness leads into complex flavours including smoky orange peel and a satisfying bitterness which persists into the long finish.

AJ's (NEW) SIBA 👁

Unit 12, Ashmore Industrial Estate, Longacre Street, Walsall, WS2 8QG ☎ 07860 585911 ✉ ajs-ales@hotmail.com

Established in 2015, AJ's uses a five-barrel plant. At present brewing takes place twice a week. Mainly local Black Country pubs are supplied. ◆

Best Bitter (ABV 4%)
An amber-coloured bitter, brewed using English hops.

SPA (ABV 4.2%)
A straw-coloured, easy-drinking ale, brewed using a blend of Australian, New Zealand and English hops.

Ruby Red (ABV 4.4%)
A copper-coloured bitter brewed using American hops.

Alcazar

⬛ Alcazar Brewery, Church Street, Old Basford, Nottingham, NG6 0GA
☎ (0115) 978 2282 ☎ 07886 091769

Office: Turnstone Taverns, c/o Railway Tavern, 188 Station Road, Langley Mill, Derbyshire, NG16 4AE
⊕ turnstonetaverns.co.uk

Alcazar was established in 1999 and is located behind its brewery tap, the Fox & Crown. The brewery is full mash with a 10-barrel brew length. ‼◆

Sheriffs Gold (OG 1036, ABV 3.6%) ◆
Slightly sweet yellow-coloured session bitter.

Ale (OG 1040, ABV 4%) ◆
Flagship golden ale, full of citrus hops with a dry, bitter aftertaste.

New Dawn (OG 1045, ABV 4.5%) ◆
Full-bodied golden ale.

Foxtail (OG 1049, ABV 4.9%) ◆
A strong malty and bitter brown ale. Also known as Brush Bitter.

Vixen's Vice (OG 1052, ABV 5.2%) ◆
A premium strength hoppy pale ale.

Alchemist

See Golden Duck

Alechemy SIBA

Unit 2c, Young Square, Brucefield Industry Park, Livingston, EH54 9BX
☎ (01506) 413634 ☎ 07748 156973
⊕ alechemybrewing.com

Dr James Davies, a keen craft brewer and chemist, started brewing in 2012. A 12-barrel plant is used. New beers are being produced regularly: see website for details. Beers can be found in pubs across the UK. ◆ RAIB

Starlaw (OG 1040, ABV 3.5%)
Session beer with citrus and tropical fruit character.

Rhapsody (OG 1038, ABV 3.8%)
An extra pale ale.

Ritual (OG 1042, ABV 4.1%) ◆

A well-balanced golden ale. A strong hop character is balanced by malt and fruit with a long and dry finish.

Five Sisters (OG 1045, ABV 4.3%) ◈
Flavoursome tawny beer with a good balance of malt, hops and fruit plus hints of roast and caramel. Lingering distinctive finish.

10 Storey Malt Bomb (OG 1049, ABV 4.5%)
A modern take on a traditional 80/- using 10 different malts.

Bad Day At The Office (OG 1047, ABV 4.5%)
A golden ale dry hopped with Australian varieties.

Miss America (ABV 4.5%)

Black Aye PA (OG 1047, ABV 4.6%) ◈
A dark robust beer with substantial malt and a significant hop character. Roast, caramel and fruit add to the complexity.

Citra Burst (OG 1056, ABV 5.4%)
Heavily hopped pale ale bursting with grapefruit and tangerine aromas with a pleasant bitter aftertaste.

AleCraft

c/o Farmers Boy, 134 London Rd, St Albans, Hertfordshire, AL1 1PQ ☎ 07939 634677

Office: c/o 17 Springhill, Nuneaton, Warwickshire, CV10 0NP ⊕ alecraftmanagement.co.uk

AleCraft began brewing in 2012 as a cuckoo brewery utilising the equipment at the Verulam brewery in St Albans. Beers are delivered direct to Yorkshire, the Midlands and the south east. **RAIB**

Simplicity (OG 1038, ABV 3.6%)
A hoppy, straw-coloured session bitter with a hop nose and flavour.

Sauvin So Good (OG 1039, ABV 4%)
A straw-coloured ale with a massive citrus and gooseberry nose and flavour that lingers through to the long bitter finish.

Night on the Tiles (OG 1044, ABV 4.7%)
A gold-coloured American pale ale with a big hop character.

Bartholomew Porter (OG 1048, ABV 4.8%)
A deep ruby, almost pure black ale, overrun with massive chocolate, burnt and roast malt flavours.

Fudgey Porter (OG 1048, ABV 4.8%)
A version of Bartholomew Porter with vanilla fudge added.

High Five (OG 1056, ABV 5.9%)
A combination of five hop varieties gives this IPA a big, generous hop character.

Sonoma (OG 1070, ABV 8%)
An American-style double IPA. Deep golden in colour with a big hop character.

Ales of Scilly SIBA

2b Porthmellon Industrial Estate, St Mary's, Isles of Scilly, Cornwall, TR21 0JY
☎ (01720) 423233 ☎ 07810 816681
⊕ alesofscilly.co.uk

⊠ Opened in 2001, Ales of Scilly is the most south-westerly brewery in Britain. Several island pubs are supplied, with occasional exports to mainland beer festivals. ‼☗◆

Challenger (OG 1039, ABV 4.2%)

Alfred's SIBA

Unit 5B, Scylla Industrial Estate, Winnall Valley Road, Winchester, Hampshire, SO23 0LD
☎ (01962) 859999 ⊕ alfredsbrewery.co.uk

⊠ Alfred's is a 3.5-barrel brewhouse opened by Steve and Isabelle Haigh in 2012. Steve previously brewed for three other renowned Hampshire breweries. Deliveries are made to pubs within 15 miles of Winchester. Production of the mainstay Saxon Bronze is complemented by seasonal and one-off beers. ‼☗◆

Saxon Bronze (OG 1038, ABV 3.8%)
Easy-drinking amber-coloured session beer with a crisp finish.

All Day (NEW)

Salle Brewery Barns 14, 15, 16, Salle Moor Farm, Wood Dalling Road, Salle, Norfolk, NR10 4SB
☎ (01603) 951173 ☎ 07825 604887
⊕ alldaybrewing.co.uk

⊠ Recently established in former farm buildings, the brewery has taken the unusual step of establishing its own hop yard, the first in Norfolk for many years, with a view to being self-sufficient in traditional (tall) English varieties of hop. The beer range is being developed at present.

Drink Me (OG 1053, ABV 5%)
Distinctly hoppy with strong bitterness, but balanced malt and body.

All Hallows

▤ Main Street, Goodmanham, East Yorkshire, YO43 3JA
☎ (01430) 873849 ⊕ goodmanhamarms.co.uk

☺Abbie Logozzi, landlady of the Goodmanham Arms, started brewing in 2012 in outbuildings behind the pub. The ex-Goodmanham Brewery Buildings were purchased and a five-barrel plant installed. The brewery name comes from the adjacent 12th-century All Hallows Church. Local legendary characters are used in the naming of some of the beers. Brews are supplied to the pub, beer festivals when requested, and mainly to local free trade. ◆

Peg Fyfe Dark Mild (OG 1040, ABV 3.6%)

Mischief Maker (OG 1042, ABV 3.8%)
A copper-coloured session bitter.

Gooders Gold (OG 1044, ABV 4%)

Wayward Angel (OG 1044, ABV 4%)

Ragged Robyn (OG 1058, ABV 4.8%)
A traditional ruby-coloured heritage ale.

No Notion Porter (OG 1060, ABV 5.6%)

Allendale SIBA ◉

Allen Mills, Allendale, Northumberland, NE47 9EQ
☎ (01434) 618686 ⊕ allendalebrewery.com

☺Brewing returned to Allendale in 2006 and the business now supplies more than 300 pubs, shops and restaurants across the North of England from its 10-barrel plant. ‼☗◆

Wagtail Best Bitter (OG 1037, ABV 3.8%) ◆
Amber bitter with spicy aromas and a long, bitter finish.

Golden Plover (OG 1039, ABV 4%) ◆
Light, refreshing, easy-drinking blonde beer with a clean finish.

Pennine Pale (OG 1040, ABV 4%)
A light golden ale, brewed with a trio of American hops for a full citrus fruit flavour and a refreshing finish.

APA (OG 1056, ABV 5.5%)
A full-bodied IPA with citrus and tropical aromas, full of flavour and refreshing bitterness.

Wolf (OG 1053, ABV 5.5%) ◆
Full-bodied red ale with bitterness in the taste giving way to a fruity finish.

Red Rye (OG 1060, ABV 6%)

AllGates SIBA 👁

The Old Brewery, Brewery Yard, off Wallgate, Wigan, WN1 1JU
☎ (01942) 234976 ⊕ allgatesbrewery.com

👁AllGates commenced brewing in 2006 in a fully restored Grade II-listed tower brewery at the rear of Wigan's General Post Office. A modern five-barrel plant is used. Beers are principally delivered to its own nine-pub estate. ‼◆

Florida (OG 1036, ABV 3.6%)
A blonde ale, pale and easy drinking.

Tag (OG 1036, ABV 3.6%) ◆
Dark brown beer with a malty, fruity aroma. Creamy and malty in taste, with blackberry fruits and a satisfying aftertaste.

California (OG 1037, ABV 3.8%) ◆
A pale yellow beer with a restrained hoppy and fruity aroma. It is clean and fresh tasting, with hops and fruit in the mouth and a bitter hoppy finish.

Napoleon's Retreat (OG 1038, ABV 3.9%)
A deep golden/copper-coloured traditional session bitter.

Pretoria (OG 1039, ABV 3.9%)
Refreshing golden session ale with distinctive citrus aromas.

Dry Bones (OG 1040, ABV 4%)
Light golden and hoppy with tropical fruits and hints of melon.

Allsaints

c/o Coastal Brewery, Unit 10B, Cardrew Industrial Estate, Redruth, Cornwall, TR15 1SS ☎ 07790 274112

❌ Formerly known as Doghouse Brewery, which closed in 2007, Allsaints recommenced production in 2008 and currently use spare capacity at Coastal Brewery in Redruth. Four regular beers are produced. ◆

St Piran Cornish Best Bitter (OG 1040, ABV 4%) ◆
Red beer with malt aroma. Malt dominates the taste balanced by ripe stone fruit notes. Short malt and caramel finish.

St Arnold (OG 1046, ABV 4.6%)

Almasty (NEW)

Unit 11, Algernon Industrial Estate, New York Road, Shiremoor, NE27 0NB

Opened in 2014, this one-man-operated 10-barrel plant produces unfined, unfiltered beers. The brewery tap is the Free Trade Inn, Byker, and holds twice-yearly open day events in spring and summer. Pumpclips are made from screen-printed, hand-sawn logs. The beer range continuously changes, with monthly output always including heavily hopped pale ales/IPAs plus Saisons, sours, porters and stouts. Outlets are supplied across the UK. A barrel-ageing programme is also in place. ‼◆

Alnwick

Alnwick, Northumberland
✉ info@spiritofnorthumberland.com

Beers are contract brewed by three unnamed northern breweries.

Canny Bevvy (ABV 2.8%)

Scotch Ale (ABV 3.6%)

Amber Ale (ABV 3.8%)

Gold (ABV 4.2%)

IPA (ABV 4.5%)

Stout (ABV 4.5%)

Brown Ale (ABV 4.7%)

Alpha Project (NEW)

133 Lothian Road, Edinburgh, EH3 9AB
☎ (0131) 229 0759 ⊕ thehangingbat.com

❌ Started in 2012, the Alpha Project runs from within the Hanging Bat bar, having produced more than 100+ new beers so far under four different brewers, all with an MSc in Brewing and Distilling. There are plans to open a full-scale brewery by 2016.

Loose Seal (OG 1035, ABV 3%)

Hot Ham Water (OG 1044, ABV 4.6%)
Polish wheat beer, subtly smoky, dry and crisp with a noble hop bitterness and aroma.

Black Heart (OG 1061, ABV 6.2%)
A black IPA with Ethiopian coffee.

Um-Bango (OG 1081, ABV 9.4%)

Alphabet (NEW)

99 Northern Western Street, Ardwick, Manchester, M12 6JL ⊕ alphabetbrewing.co.uk

Alphabet began brewing in 2014 and is situated in Manchester city centre under railway arches. It has a 60-barrel capacity with a five-barrel kit and focuses mainly on keg-style beers. The brewery also bottles its own beers. Cask beers can be supplied for beer festivals.

Amber SIBA

Unit 7, Outram Business Centre, Whiteley Rd, Ripley, Derbyshire, DE5 3QL
☎ (01773) 512864 ⊕ amberales.co.uk

❌ Amber Ales began production in 2006 on a five-barrel plant obtained from the former Firkin brewpub chain. Five core beers and a range of experimental and seasonal ales are produced, all available at the brewery tap, the Talbot Taphouse in Ripley. Around 50 outlets are supplied direct, further afield via distributors. Bottle-conditioned beers are suitable for vegans. !! ♦ RAIB

Chocolate Orange Stout (OG 1040, ABV 4%)

Derbyshire Gold (OG 1039, ABV 4%)
A well-hopped golden ale.

Original Black Stout (OG 1040, ABV 4%)
Traditional stout made with a complex blend of five malts to give a full-flavoured, yet smooth and easy-drinking base with a subtle hop aroma.

Barnes Wallis (OG 1040, ABV 4.1%)
An easy-drinking IPA-style bitter, copper-coloured with a full malt flavour.

Revolution (OG 1047, ABV 4.5%)

Dambuster (OG 1051, ABV 5.5%)

Imperial IPA (OG 1058, ABV 6.5%)
Triple-hopped traditional IPA with a substantial malty base and a big hop profile.

Ambridge

Unit 2a, Priory Piece Business Park, Priory Farm Lane, Inkberrow, Worcestershire, WR7 4HT
☎ (01386) 792233 ☎ 07964 630355
ambridgebrewery.co.uk

Ambridge commenced brewing in 2013, initially for the family pub, the Bulls Head in Inkberrow. Later that year they acquired the Wyre Piddle Brewery. The beers from both breweries continue to be brewed but during 2013 relocated to a single brew house on the outskirts of the village. Further regular and seasonal beers are planned along with bottled beers and a shop. !!

Shires Bitter (OG 1039, ABV 3.8%)

Just Jane (OG 1040, ABV 3.9%)
A refreshing golden session beer. Hops are balanced by malt throughout.

Worcestershire Pale Ale (WPA) (OG 1043, ABV 4.2%)
A premium pale ale with a good balance of hops and malt. Hops carry on from the taste to a bittersweet finish.

Red Zeppelin (OG 1046, ABV 4.5%)
A deep amber/red-coloured ale with a distinctive hop aroma and palate.

Jester (OG 1048, ABV 4.8%)
British Jester single-hopped beer with a punchy aroma of grapefruit and tropical fruits. Pale gold with a delicate bitter finish.

Brewed under the Wyre Piddle name:

Piddle in the Hole (OG 1040, ABV 3.9%)
Copper-coloured and quite dry, with lots of hops and fruitiness throughout.

Piddle in the Dark (OG 1046, ABV 4.5%)
A rich ruby-red bitter with a smooth flavour.

Piddle in the Wind (OG 1046, ABV 4.5%)
A superb mix of flavours. A hoppy nose continues through to a lasting aftertaste, making it a good, all-round beer.

An Teallach SIBA

Camusnagaul, Dundonnell, Garve, IV23 2QT
☎ (01854) 633306 ✉ ataleco1@yahoo.co.uk

An Teallach was formed in 2001 by a husband and wife team, David and Wilma Orr, on the family croft on the shores of Little Loch Broom, Wester Ross. More than 60 pubs are supplied. !! ♦

Beallach Na Ba (ABV 3.8%)
Golden-amber hoppy brew with some background malt.

Ale (OG 1042, ABV 4.2%)
A classic pint in the Scottish 80/- tradition. Plenty of malt in the nicely-balanced bittersweet taste.

Crofters Pale Ale (OG 1042, ABV 4.2%)
A good quaffing, lightly-flavoured golden ale. Citrus hops in the taste and with a slight astringency in the finish.

Suilven (OG 1043, ABV 4.3%)
A refreshing yellow brew with plenty of citrus fruits and hops throughout.

Beinn Dearg Ale (OG 1044, ABV 4.4%)
A well-balanced malty, hoppy, sweetish beer with a long, malty bitter aftertaste.

Kildonan (OG 1044, ABV 4.4%)
Plenty of fruit and a good smack of bitterness in this golden ale.

Anarchy SIBA

Unit 5, Whitehouse Farm Centre, Stannington, Northumberland, NE61 6AW
☎ (01670) 789755 ☎ 07702 810111
anarchybrewco.com

A 10-barrel brewery ran by an enthusiastic team producing a range of hand-crafted beers and lagers with big, bold flavours. Some beers are produced in collaboration with local bands. !! RAIB

Smoke Bomb (OG 1043, ABV 3.9%)
Bitter with a light smoky nose and Bavarian smoked ham and citrus flavours matched with dark, smooth toffee malts.

Blonde Star (OG 1041, ABV 4.1%)
Lemon, grapefruit and passion fruit flavours from the hops combine with pale malts to give a crisp and fresh light-bodied session blonde beer.

Citra Star (OG 1041, ABV 4.1%)
Citrus, grapefruit, lemon, lime and passion fruit flavours come from the hops to give a clean, crisp, light-bodied blonde ale.

Rough Justice (OG 1046, ABV 4.5%)
Resinous pine and orange flavours create a dry and bitter dark red rye beer.

Grin & Bare It (OG 1050, ABV 5%)
A pale wheat beer made with South Pacific hops.

Urban Assault (OG 1050, ABV 5%)
Medium-bodied light red-coloured pale ale with heavy notes of lemon, orange and passion fruit in the flavour, followed by a bitter finish.

Crime Scene (OG 1056, ABV 5.5%)
Fruit-flavoured, medium-bodied amber-coloured beer made using caramel malts that melts into a long-lasting bitter aftertaste.

Quiet Riot (OG 1063, ABV 6.6%)

Kiwi fruit, lime and orange zest flavours combine to give a big bitterness that is balanced with sweet malts.

Sublime Chaos (OG 1075, ABV 7%)
Liquorice, chocolate and caramel-flavoured breakfast stout infused with Ethiopian Guji natural coffee beans backed with dark malts.

Anchor Springs SIBA

Lineside Way, Wick, West Sussex, BN17 7EH
☎ (01903) 719842
✉ debbie@jenkinslittlehampton.co.uk

Kevin Jenkins, owner of the Crown, Littlehampton, established the brewery in 2010 using the five-barrel plant previously at the Dark Star brewery. Main outlets are the brewery tap, the Crown, Littlehampton, and the Spy Glass, Worthing. ♦RAIB

LA Gold (OG 1039.5, ABV 3.7%)
A golden session ale. An initial sweetness leads to a citrus kick and lingering crisp, clean finish.

Mild (OG 1045.5, ABV 3.8%)

Anchors Aweigh (OG 1040, ABV 4%)

Worthing Best (OG 1045, ABV 4%)
A blackberry fruit aroma and sweet initial taste is followed by bitter sharpness. A good malty mouthfeel with more dark berry fruit leads to a lingering, rising bitter finish.

Riptide (OG 1045, ABV 4.1%)
A copper-coloured ale with a malted caramel nose and initial sweetness of milk chocolate leading to a complex palate and lingering bitter finish.

Neptune (OG 1043, ABV 4.3%)

Hornblower (OG 1045, ABV 4.5%)

Liberty (OG 1048, ABV 4.8%)

Mothers Ruin (OG 1063, ABV 6%)
A copper-coloured ale, malty and with spices and orange zest, a complex flavour with a balance of sweetness and bitter finish.

Andrews

1 Railway Cottages, Cummertrees, DG12 5QG
☎ (01461) 700387 ☎ 07785 613321
✉ aemmerson999@googlemail.com

Andrews Ales began brewing in 2011 and is situated at the family home using a one-barrel plant. The brewing capacity has now expanded to three barrels. Cask and bottle-conditioned beers are supplied direct by the brewery to pubs and independent shops. ♦RAIB

Supus Lupus (OG 1036, ABV 3.6%)
A straw-coloured session ale with a light, zesty finish.

Cummertrees Pale Ale (OG 1040, ABV 4%)
A full-bodied beer, refreshingly clean and crisp.

Into The Darkness (OG 1046, ABV 4.3%)
A dark ale hopped with classic British hops to give a full-bodied and quaffable stout.

Andwell SIBA

Andwell Lane, Andwell, Hampshire, RG27 9PA
☎ (01256) 761044 🌐 andwells.com

Brewing commenced in 2008 on a 10-barrel plant. It relocated and expanded in 2011 to an idyllic riverside location with a new bespoke 20-barrel plant and offers tours and direct sales from its brewery shop. Beer is distributed within a 40-mile radius to Hampshire, Surrey, Wiltshire, Berkshire, Greater London and the Isle of Wight. More than 200 outlets are supplied. !! ♦

Resolute Bitter (OG 1038, ABV 3.8%)
An easy drinking session bitter. A malty aroma, leads into an initially malty flavour with some bitterness and sweetish finish.

Gold Muddler (OG 1039, ABV 3.9%)
Light golden standard bitter. Aroma of hops and malt; characteristics carried into the flavour with solid bitterness and dry, biscuity finish.

King John (OG 1042, ABV 4.2%)
Malty best bitter, low in hops with short initial bitterness and underlying sweetness, leading to some dryness in the finish.

Rudy Darter (OG 1047, ABV 4.6%)
A ruby chestnut ale with a hoppy, spicy aroma. The beer has a full-bodied and fruity taste with a dry finish.

Angel SIBA

62a Furlong Lane, Halesowen, West Midlands, B63 2TA ☎ 07847 300350 🌐 angelales.co.uk

Angel Ales began commercial brewing in 2011 and is expanding outlets. The brewery building has been a Chapel of Rest, a coffin makers' workshop and a pattern makers' before becoming a brewhouse. Beers are produced using organic materials where possible, and all stouts are vegan-friendly. ♦RAIB

Ale (OG 1042, ABV 4.1%)
Ultra pale and intensely hopped bitter with a citrus nose and lingering bitter finish.

Ginger Stout (OG 1048, ABV 4.8%)
A summer stout produced using fresh ginger root.

Anglesey (NEW)

Chaen Ddu, Carmel, Isle of Anglesey, LL71 7DE

The brewery began in 2015 producing bottled beers only. Cask-conditioned beers are planned.

Animal

See XT

Anspach & Hobday

118 Druid Street, Bermondsey, London, SE1 2HH
☎ (020) 8617 9510 🌐 anspachandhobday.com

Anspach & Hobday began commercial brewing in 2014 using a one-barrel plant, upgrading to 2.5 barrels later that year. It is based in a railway arch in Bermondsey. There are plans for expansion. Beer is mostly bottled or kegged with some available cask-conditioned. A brewery taproom is open at weekends.

Smoked Brown (ABV 6%)

Porter (ABV 6.7%)
Roasted notes throughout with caramel, fruit and hops in the flavour and finish, which is slightly dry.

Appleby (NEW)

Unit D3, Cross Croft Industrial Estate, Wellhouse Road, Appleby-in-Westmorland, Cumbria, CA16 6HX
☎ (01768) 353846 ⊕ applebybrewery.co.uk

Established by Fred Mills in 2015 using a former Rolls-Royce sotrage unit on the outskirts of the town. The beers are available at selected pubs across Cumbria, but mainly in the Eden Valley area.

Senior Moment (OG 1039, ABV 3.9%)
An old-fashioned bitter

Mid-life Crisis (OG 1042, ABV 4.2%)
An IPA of dark, characteristic hops.

Appleford

Unit 14, Highlands Farm, High Road, Brightwell-cum-Sotwell, Oxfordshire, OX10 0QX
☎ (01235) 848055 ⊕ applefordbrewery.co.uk

Appleford Brewery opened in 2006 when two farm units were converted to house an eight-barrel plant. Deliveries are made to a number of local outlets as well as nationally, via the brewery or wholesalers. ◆RAIB

Brightwell Gold (OG 1041, ABV 4%)

Power Station (OG 1043, ABV 4.2%)
A copper-coloured, slightly malty bitter.

Arbor SIBA ⟨⊙⟩

181 Easton Road, Easton, Bristol, BS5 0HQ
☎ (0117) 329 2711 ⊕ arborales.co.uk

⊗ Arbor Ales began brewing in 2007 and has relocated and expanded several times, the latest being in 2012 and now using a 12-barrel plant. A wide range of beers is brewed, with particular pride taken in darker ales. ☰◆

Oyster Stout (OG 1046.5, ABV 4.6%) ◣
A rich stout with chocolate undertones. Real oysters are added in the copper. Fruity and roast flavours with a creamy mouthfeel.

Yakima Valley (OG 1067, ABV 7%) ◣
A strong, full-bodied IPA. Hoppy and fruity. Sweetness is well balanced with bitterness, lasting into a soft bitter aftertaste.

Archerfield

See Knops

Archers

See Evan Evans

Ards

34b Carrowdore Road, Newtonards, Co Down, BT22 2LX ☎ 07515 558406
✉ ardsbrewing@blackwood34.plus.com

Ards began brewing in 2011 using a 100-litre plant. A five-barrel plant is now in operation, allowing cask production in addition to the increasing range of bottle-conditioned beers. RAIB

Argyll

Cuan Mor, 60 George Street, Oban, PA34 5DS

☎ (01631) 565078

Office: Unit 8a, Baliscate Industrial Estate, Oban, PA34 5SD ☎ (01631) 564492
⊕ obanbaybrewery.co.uk

Argyll Breweries was formed in 2010 following the merger of Oban Bay and Isle of Mull breweries, continuing to trade under those names. Cask production is only at the Oban site. ‼

Kilt Lifter (OG 1039, ABV 3.9%)

Skinny Blonde (OG 1041, ABV 4.1%)

Ginger Jakey (OG 1042, ABV 4.2%)

Skelpt Lug (OG 1042, ABV 4.2%)

Fair Puggled (OG 1045, ABV 4.5%)

Arkell's SIBA IFBB ⟨⊙⟩

Kingsdown, Swindon, Wiltshire, SN2 7RU
☎ (01793) 823026 ⊕ arkells.com

Arkells Brewery was established in 1843 by John Arkell, and the family still brews beer in the original Victorian brewhouse every day. The brewery owns 99 pubs in Berkshire, Gloucestershire, Oxfordshire and Wiltshire. ‼☰◆

Wiltshire Gold (OG 1038, ABV 3.7%)
A light golden-coloured ale with a satisfyingly sweet malty flavour. The use of traditional hops give the beer a mellow floral hop aroma followed by a distinctive hoppy taste.

3B (OG 1040, ABV 4%) ◣
A medium brown beer with a strong, sweetish malt/caramel flavour. The hops come through strongly in the aftertaste, which is lingering and dry.

Bee's Organic (OG 1045, ABV 4.5%)
Organically grown malted barley, hops and organically produced honey give this golden ale a light, fresh taste.

Moonlight (OG 1046, ABV 4.5%)
Golden auburn in colour with a warm, toasty aroma and distinctive citrus hoppy flavour.

Kingsdown (OG 1051, ABV 5%) ◣
A rich, deep russet-coloured beer, a stronger version of 3B. The malty/fruity aroma continues in the taste, which has a hint of pears. Hops come through in the aftertaste.

Arkwright's

c/o The Real Ale Shop, 47 Lovat Road, Preston, Lancashire, PR1 6DQ ☎ 07944 912326
⊕ arkwrightsbrewery.com

Arkwright's began brewing at the rear of the Real Ale Shop on Lovat Road in 2010 using a 2.5-barrel plant. In 2014 the plant was upgraded to a 10-barrel plant previously used by Wolf brewery and moved to a nearby industrial unit. ◆

Arran SIBA

Cladach, Brodick, Isle of Arran, KA27 8DE
☎ (01770) 302353

Office: 100 Wellington Street, Glasgow, G2 6DH
⊕ arranbrewery.com

The brewery opened in 2000 using a 20-barrel plant. 300 outlets are supplied direct. ‼☰◆RAIB

Guid Ale (OG 1038, ABV 3.8%)
A refreshing, golden-coloured session ale with a delicate balance of malt and fruit.

Red Squirrel (OG 1038, ABV 3.9%)
Session beer with a balanced malty and hop blend containing hints of liquorice and burnt toffee with a characteristic nutty aroma.

Dark (OG 1042, ABV 4.3%) ◈
A well-balanced malty beer with plenty of roast and hop in the taste and a dry, bitter finish.

Sunset (OG 1042, ABV 4.4%)
An amber-coloured summer ale with a lightly perfumed aroma, good balance of malt, fruit and hops and a pleasant dry finish.

Clyde Puffer (OG 1045, ABV 4.5%)
A stout with a deep, dark colour. Sweet and mellow with a low hop taste.

Fireside (OG 1044, ABV 4.7%)
A smooth malty brew with a pleasant hop character. Bittersweet finish with a hint of ginger.

Blonde (OG 1048, ABV 5%) ◈
A hoppy beer with substantial fruit balance. The taste is balanced and the finish increasingly bitter. An aromatic strong bitter that drinks below its weight.

Brewery Dug (OG 1055, ABV 5.5%)
An American-style IPA with a good aroma. Dry hopped for extra flavour.

ID (OG 1060, ABV 6%)
A dark, hoppy beer.

Arrow

c/o Wine Vaults, 37 High Street, Kington, Herefordshire, HR5 3BJ
☎ (01544) 230685 ✉ deanewright@yahoo.co.uk

Brewer Deane Wright built this five-barrel brewery at the rear of the Wine Vaults and started brewing in 2005. The Wine Vaults is the only pub outlet for Arrow Bitter.

Bitter (OG 1042, ABV 4%)

Art Brew

Dorset ☎ 07881 783626 🌐 artbrew.co.uk

⊗ Art Brew started brewing in 2008 on a five-barrel plant near the Jurassic Coast, but the brewery plans to relocate to new premises in Devon at the end of 2015. Brewing will continue at Sherfield Village Brewery (qv) until the new site is established. Monkey IPA will continue to be brewed along with a rolling programme of new beers.

Monkey IPA (OG 1058, ABV 6.4%)
Massively hopped IPA.

Artisan

See Evan Evans

Artisan Brewing

See Pipes

Arundel SIBA

Unit C7, Ford Airfield Industrial Estate, Ford, West Sussex, BN18 0HY
☎ (01903) 733111 🌐 arundelbrewery.co.uk

⊗ Founded in 1992, Arundel Brewery is the historic town's first brewery in 70 years. A seasonal beer is alway available, plus occasional brands in selected months. The brewery opened a shop in 2014, at River Road, Arundel, but beer and other merchandise can also be purchased from the brewery office. !! ♦

Black Stallion (OG 1037, ABV 3.7%) ◈
A dark mild with well defined chocolate and roast character. The aftertaste is not powerful but the initial flavours remain in the clean finish.

Castle (OG 1038, ABV 3.8%) ◈
A pale tawny beer with fruit and malt noticeable in the aroma. The flavour has a good balance of malt, fruit and hops, with a dry, hoppy finish.

Sussex Gold (OG 1042, ABV 4.2%) ◈
A golden-coloured best bitter with a strong floral hop aroma. The ale is clean-tasting and bitter for its strength, with a tangy citrus flavour. The initial hop and fruit die to a dry and bitter finish.

Sussex IPA (OG 1045, ABV 4.5%)
Formerly known as Heritage IPA. A special bitter with a complex roast malt flavour leading to a fruity, hoppy, bittersweet finish.

Stronghold (OG 1047, ABV 4.7%) ◈
A smooth, full-flavoured premium bitter. A good balance of malt, fruit and hops comes through in this rich, chestnut-coloured beer.

Trident (OG 1050, ABV 5%)
An amber-coloured strong beer with a citrus, fruity aroma. The taste is clean and refreshing with a hoppy, fruity flavour and a pleasant dry bitter finish.

Wild Heaven (OG 1052, ABV 5.2%)
A hoppy American-style pale ale with strong grapefruit, orange and lime notes and a citrus bitter finish.

Ascot SIBA

Unit 5, Compton Place Business Centre, Surrey Avenue, Camberley, Surrey, GU15 3DX
☎ (01276) 686696 🌐 ascot-ales.co.uk

⊗ Ascot Ales started production in 2007 on a four-barrel plant in a small industrial unit. The brewery has successfully expanded over the years and is now brewing 11 regular beers and many seasonals including a single hop series: see website. Bottle-conditioned beers are suitable for vegetarians and vegans. !! ♦ RAIB

Alley Cat Ale (OG 1038, ABV 3.8%) ◈
A pale brown session bitter with malt flavours present throughout. Dry with a lasting sharp and bitter finish.

On the Rails (OG 1039, ABV 3.8%) ◈
Chocolaty mild with a notable hop character throughout, bittersweet in the taste and aftertaste, with a dry finish.

Aureole Ale (OG 1039, ABV 4%)
Low strength golden ale with lots of citrus flavour.

Posh Pooch (OG 1042, ABV 4.2%) ◈

A best bitter with balancing biscuity malt sweetness. Some citrus fruitiness and a clean hoppy aftertaste.

Penguin Porter (OG 1045, ABV 4.5%)

Alligator Ale (OG 1047, ABV 4.6%) ◆
Some grapefruit in the aroma, with hop and bitterness in the taste and plenty of balancing biscuit in the aroma and aftertaste.

Single Hop (OG 1045, ABV 4.6%)
Copper-coloured IPA brewed each month showcasing a single hop variety.

Anastasia's Exile Stout (OG 1049, ABV 5%) 🍴 🎁 ◆
Burnt coffee aromas lead to a roast malt flavour in this black beer. Notably fruity throughout, with a bittersweet aftertaste.

Rhino Rye (OG 1049, ABV 5%)

Red IPA (OG 1054, ABV 5.5%)
An intensely hopped red IPA, using several varieties of New World hops to give a citrus, grapefruit taste.

Anastasia's Imperial Stout (OG 1078, ABV 8%)

Ash Valley

☰ Prince of Wales, Green Tye, Hertfordshire, SG10 6JP
☎ (01279) 842139 **☎** 07966 474730
⊕ thepow.co.uk/the-brewery

⊠ The brewery is part of the Prince of Wales pub in Green Tye, run by the landlord. Three regular beers and occasional specials are produced. Most of the beer is sold at the pub and occasional CAMRA beer festivals, and a small amount is swapped with other brewers.

Country Bitter (OG 1037, ABV 3.7%)
A brown-coloured session bitter.

Prince of Wales IPA (OG 1039, ABV 3.9%)
A session IPA.

Pale Rider (OG 1047, ABV 4.1%)

Poppy Fields (OG 1044, ABV 4.4%)
A light gold-coloured, easy-drinking ale.

Ashley Down

15 Wathen Road, St Andrews, Bristol, BS6 5BY
☎ (0117) 983 6567 **☎** 07563 751200
✉ ashleydownbrewery@gmail.com

⊠ Ashley Down began brewing in 2011 using a 5.5-barrel plant in the owner's garage. After spending a year sharing a unit with Wiper and True (qv), they are now back in the owner's large, but reconfigured, garage. There are plans for expansion and to relocate to new premises. ◆RAIB

Remedy (OG 1037.5, ABV 4%) ◆
Characteristics of a dark mild and a red. A pronounced aroma of crystal malt precedes a malty astringent taste with hints of toffee and dark fruit. The aftertaste is thin and short.

Landlords Best (OG 1040, ABV 4.2%) ◆
Malty best bitter with balancing hops and astringency in the aftertaste.

Pale Ale (OG 1040.5, ABV 4.3%) ◆
Sweet best bitter balanced with hoppy bitterness which continues to the aftertaste.

Ashleyhay (NEW) SIBA

New Buildings Farm, Taylors Lane, Ashleyhay, Derbyshire, DE4 4AH **☎** 07708 050019
✉ jim@ashleyhaybrewery.co.uk

⊠ The brewery is situated near the market town of Wirksworth, Derbyshire. Its ales are produced using natural spring water, solar energy and, where feasible, with hops grown on site. Traditional methods are combined with modern hopping techniques. The owner has plans to expand the brewery and open a micropub.

Citra Pale (OG 1043, ABV 4.3%)

CJ Porter (OG 1048, ABV 4.8%)

Red Tape IPA (OG 1050, ABV 5%)

Knobstick IPA (OG 1052, ABV 5.3%)

Ned's Big Shed (OG 1054, ABV 5.4%)

Ashover SIBA

☰ Unit 1, Derby Road, Clay Cross, Chesterfield, S45 9AG **☎** 07803 708526 **⊕** ashoverbrewery.com

Ashover Brewery first brewed in 2007 on a 3.5-barrel plant in the garage of the cottage next to the Old Poets' Corner in Ashover. In 2015 it took over the former Brown Ales brewery in nearby Clay Cross, and all regular beers are now brewed there, with the original plant in Ashover being used for special and one-off brews. The brewery caters mainly for the Old Poets' Corner and its sister pub, the Poet and Castle in Codnor. Other local free houses and festivals are also supplied. House beers are also produced for pubs within the Brown Ales group. ‼RAIB

Light Rale (OG 1038, ABV 3.7%) ◆
Light in colour and taste, with initial sweet and malt flavours, leading to a bitter finish and aftertaste.

Poets Tipple (OG 1041, ABV 4%) ◆
Complex, tawny-coloured beer that drinks above its strength. Predominantly malty in flavour, with increasing bitterness towards the end.

Littlemoor Citra (OG 1041, ABV 4.1%)
A pale session beer.

Hydro (OG 1043, ABV 4.2%) 🍴 ◆
Easy to drink golden beer with a predominantly hoppy aroma. Hop and fruit flavours and an initial sweetness lead to a dry, clean finish and aftertaste.

Rainbows End (OG 1045, ABV 4.5%) ◆
Slightly smooth, bitter golden beer with an initial sweetness. Grapefruit and lemon hop flavours come through strongly as the beer gets increasingly dry towards the finish, ending with a bitter, dry aftertaste.

Coffin Lane Stout (OG 1050, ABV 5%) ◆
Excellent example of the style, with a chocolate and coffee flavour, balanced by a little sweetness. Finish is long and quite dry.

Butts Pale Ale (OG 1055, ABV 5.5%) ◆
Pale and strong yet easy to drink golden bitter. Combination of bitter and sweet flavours mingle with an alcoholic kick, leading to a warming yet bitter finish and aftertaste.

Atlantic

Treisaac Farm, Treisaac, Newquay, Cornwall, TR8 4DX

☎ (01637) 880326 🌐 atlanticbrewery.com

Ⓧ Specialist microbrewery producing organic and vegan ales. All ales are unfiltered and finings-free. There are nine core brews including four food-matched Dining Ales developed with Michelin chef Nathan Outlaw. Casks are supplied locally and into London, with bottle-conditioned beers available nationally. RAIB

Ale (OG 1038, ABV 4%) ◆
A pale amber ale, with good body, sweet malt and hints of vanilla. Well-hopped yet balanced.

Azores (OG 1042, ABV 4.2%)
Distinct American hops are complemented by smooth English and Cornish hops to create this hoppy transatlantic pale ale.

Gold (OG 1043, ABV 4.6%) ◆
Refreshing, crisp golden ale lightly spiced with zingy ginger. Dry finish with the lingering light marmalade of First Gold hops.

Pilgrim (OG 1046, ABV 4.6%) ◆
A ruby-brown beer with a malty nose. Malt dominates the creamy taste and finish balanced by bitter and fruity hops.

Bee Keeper (OG 1046, ABV 4.8%)
A smooth, balanced, golden-coloured honey beer.

Blue (OG 1045, ABV 4.8%) ◆
This dark ruby porter floods the palate with sweet malt, roast coffee, dark chocolate, a soft smokiness and orange nose.

Red (OG 1047, ABV 5%) ◆
Malty, smooth red ale with nutty flavours and natural cloudiness. Dryness of the hop finish is balanced by sweet malt.

Fistral (OG 1048, ABV 5.2%) ◆
Full-flavoured copper wheat beer. Sweet, stone-fruit flavours blend with biscuit malt and citrus hops. Malt finish with hops and dryness.

Discovery – Easterly (OG 1050, ABV 5.5%) ◆
A golden pale ale with crisp distinct flavours of lime, chilli and ginger. Sweet malt balances the citrus aroma tones.

Discovery – Northerly (OG 1050, ABV 5.5%) ◆
Rich Cornish porter with blackcurrant and molasses. Full-bodied dark roasted malts, hints of chocolate, ripe blackcurrants and black cherries.

Discovery – Southerly (OG 1050, ABV 5.5%) ◆
Smooth blonde ale with elderflower and lemon. Gentle hops, sweet malt with floral and citrus zest finish.

Discovery – Westerly (OG 1050, ABV 5.5%) ◆
Red Celtic ale with cinnamon and orange. Full-bodied bitter with gentle citrus marmalade and mild nutty spice flavours.

Atlas

See Orkney

Atom SIBA

Unit 4, Food & Tech Park, Malmo Road, Sutton Fields Industrial Estate, Hull, East Yorkshire, HU7 0FY
☎ 07908 737769 🌐 atombeers.com

Atom is a collaboration between Allan Rice and Sarah Thackray, set up in 2013 in a modern industrial unit north-west of Hull city centre. The 10-barrel brewing equipment, which came from Oban Ales, is supplemented by a fermentation capacity of 120 barrels and a conditioning capacity of 120 barrels.

Schrodingers Cat (OG 1035, ABV 3.5%)
A pale ale brewed using different mashing mechanisms creating a full-bodied, low-ABV hop bomb.

Blonde Ale (OG 1040, ABV 4%)
A fresh, smooth, easy-drinking pale beer with citrus notes.

Camomile (OG 1042, ABV 4.2%)
An easy-drinking ale with a fragrant floral aroma created using the camomile from the Blending Rooms in Hull.

Pale Ale (OG 1045, ABV 4.5%)
A malty and hoppy pale ale with bags of flavour.

Dark Alchemy (OG 1049, ABV 4.9%)
A rich, complex malt bill with bitterness and aroma from cardamom and coriander but no hops, creating a porter rich in body, smooth and characterful.

India Pale Ale (OG 1056, ABV 5.6%)
Lots of malt and big juicy hops.

Atomic

c/o Alexandra Arms, 72-73 St James Street, Rugby, Warwickshire, CV21 2SL
☎ (01788) 576194 ☎ 07986 983984

Correspondence: 1 Lower Hillmorton Road, Rugby, Warwickshire, CV21 3ST 🌐 atomicbrewery.com

Atomic Brewery started production in 2006 and is run by CAMRA members Keith Abbis and Nick Pugh. Two pubs are owned, the Victoria Inn and the Alexandra Arms, the latter being where the brew plant resides. !! ◆

Strike (OG 1039, ABV 3.7%)
A pale golden ale with a sharp, fruity aroma and a good bitter finish.

Fission (OG 1040, ABV 3.9%)
An amber-coloured session ale with a good helping of Cascade hops.

Spectrum (ABV 4%)
Pale golden in colour with a huge grapefruit nose and aroma.

Dark Matter (ABV 4.1%)
A dark, well-hopped ale with hints of chocolate and a good bitter finish.

Fusion (OG 1042, ABV 4.1%)
A golden-coloured ale with a citrus, hoppy aroma leading to a good bitter finish.

Half life (OG 1051, ABV 5%)
A premium IPA, golden in colour with a citrus nose to finish.

Attwood

See Worcestershire

Austendyke

The Beeches, Austendyke Road, Weston Hills, Spalding, Lincolnshire, PE12 6BZ ☎ 07866 045778

Austendyke Ales began brewing in 2012 using a seven-barrel plant. The brewery is operated on a part-time basis by brewer Charlie Rawlings and business partner Nathan Marshall, who handles sales. The brewery owns and runs its micropub, the Prior's Oven, Spalding, and serves several locally brewed beers by gravity.

Long Lane (OG 1039, ABV 4%)
A traditional copper-coloured bitter.

Sheep Market (OG 1040, ABV 4%)

Bakestraw (OG 1041, ABV 4.1%)
Pale, hoppy best bitter.

Holbeach High Street (OG 1045, ABV 4.5%)
An old-fashioned dark-coloured best bitter.

Hogsgate (OG 1050, ABV 5%)
A traditional copper-coloured ale.

Axholme SIBA

7 Lakes Country Park, Wharf Road, Crowle, Lincolnshire, DN17 4JS ☎ 07551 910040

Office: 2 Garthorpe Road, Luddington, Lincolnshire, DN17 4QT axholmebrewing.co.uk

Former Thorne brewer Mike Richards commissioned Scunthorpe's first-ever microbrewery in 2012 using a 2.5-barrel plant from Brupaks. In 2013 the company relocated to a brand new four-barrel brewplant in Crowle. Beers are distributed nationwide. ♦RAIB

Best Bitter (OG 1038, ABV 3.8%)

Clearwater Pale Ale (OG 1041, ABV 4.3%)

Special Reserve (OG 1066, ABV 7.2%)
Amber-coloured beer with flavours of brandy and dried fruits.

Axiom

Unit 4a, Wrexham Enterprise Park, Ash Road, North Wrexham Industrial Estate, Wrexham, LL13 9JT ☎ 07544 280353 axiombrewing.co.uk

Axiom commenced brewing in 2014 on a self-built four-barrel plant. A core range of beers is available as well as occasional experimental beers and collaboration brews.

New Dawn (OG 1042, ABV 4.2%)
A session beer, light with a fresh hoppiness.

Red Mist (OG 1045, ABV 4.5%)
American-style rye beer. Subtle spiciness from the rye combines with pine and grapefruit from the hops.

Dusk (OG 1049, ABV 4.9%)
Rich and dark, notes of figs, raisins and dark chocolate. Bittersweet.

Axton (NEW)

Pentre Lane, Axton, nr Trelawnyd, CH8 9DH

Axton began brewing in 2015 on a 1.5-barrel plant mainly supplying Archies bar in Prestatyn with regular specials, experimental brews and re-creations of old brewery recipes.

Aylesbury

Hop Pole, 83 Bicester Road, Aylesbury, Buckinghamshire, HP19 9AZ ☎ (01844) 239237 aylesburybrewhouse.co.uk

Established in 2011 at the Hop Pole as a sister brewery to Vale (qv). Limited edition, one-off beers are brewed on a weekly basis. !!

Pure Gold (OG 1040, ABV 3.8%)
Deep golden in colour with a fruity, citrus aroma, a hoppy bite and a dry, zesty finish.

Ayr SIBA

5 Racecourse Road, Ayr, KA7 2DG ☎ (01292) 263891 ✉ anthony.valenti@btinternet.com

Ayr began brewing in 2009 on a five-barrel plant and is located at the Glenpark Hotel. As well as the hotel around 50 other outlets are supplied throughout Scotland and England. !!♦

Leezie Lundie (OG 1037.5, ABV 3.8%)
A pale golden session ale with hints of grapefruit and a dry, lingering finish.

Jolly Beggars (OG 1041, ABV 4.2%)
A complex best bitter with plenty of character and lingering malty aftertaste.

Rabbie's Porter (OG 1042.5, ABV 4.3%)
A robust full-bodied porter with well-balanced toffee, fruity malt and a slightly smoky finish.

Towzie Tyke (OG 1044.5, ABV 4.6%)
An amber ale with a refreshingly dry long bitter finish.

B&T SIBA

The Brewery, Shefford, Bedfordshire, SG17 5DZ ☎ (01462) 815080 banksandtaylor.com

Banks & Taylor – now just B&T – was founded in 1982. It produces 12 regular beers, plus monthly specials and occasional beers, in an industrial unit close to the town centre. There are six tied houses, all selling B&T beers plus guest beers and real cider. !!♦

Two Brewers Bitter (OG 1036, ABV 3.6%)
Bronze-coloured bitter with citrus hop aroma and taste and a dry finish.

Shefford Bitter (OG 1038, ABV 3.8%)
A pale brown beer with a light hop aroma and a hoppy taste leading to a bitter finish.

Shefford Dark Mild (OG 1038, ABV 3.8%)
A dark beer with a well-balanced taste. Sweetish, roast malt aftertaste.

Golden Fox (OG 1041, ABV 4.1%)
A golden, hoppy ale, dry tasting with a fruity aroma and citrus finish.

Black Dragon Mild (OG 1043, ABV 4.3%)
Black in colour with a toffee and roast malt flavour and a smoky finish.

Dunstable Giant (OG 1044, ABV 4.4%)
Dark tawny-coloured bitter with a subtle blend of malt and hops.

Dragon Slayer (OG 1045, ABV 4.5%)
A golden beer with a malt and hop flavour and a bitter finish. More malty and less hoppy than is usual for a beer of this style.

Edwin Taylor's Extra Stout (OG 1045, ABV 4.5%)
A complex black beer with a bitter coffee and roast malt flavour and a dry bitter finish.

Fruit Bat (OG 1045, ABV 4.5%)

THE BREWERIES

A warming straw-coloured beer with a generous taste of raspberries and a bitter finish.

Shefford Pale Ale (SPA) (OG 1045, ABV 4.5%) ◆
A well-balanced beer with hop, fruit and malt flavours. Dry, bitter aftertaste.

SOD (OG 1050, ABV 5%)
SOS with caramel added for colour.

SOS (OG 1050, ABV 5%) ◆
A rich mixture of fruit, hops and malt is present in the taste and aftertaste of this beer. Predominantly hoppy aroma.

Baby Ox

See Oxfordshire

Bacchus

▤ Bacchus Hotel, 17 High Street, Sutton-on-Sea, Lincolnshire, LN12 2EY
☎ (01507) 441204 ⊕ bacchushotel.co.uk

Bacchus began brewing in 2010 and now has a two-barrel plant supplying the Bacchus Hotel. New equipment and a bottling line were installed in 2013. ‼RAIB

Best Bitter (OG 1043, ABV 4.3%)

Blonde (OG 1045, ABV 4.5%)

Sutton Pride (OG 1045, ABV 4.5%)

Backyard SIBA 👁

Unit 8a, Gatehouse Trading Estate, Lichfield Road, Brownhills, Walsall, West Midlands, WS8 6JZ ☎ 07591 923370 ⊕ thebackyardbrewhouse.com

Backyard began brewing in 2008 and expanded in 2012 to a 12-barrel plant brewing up to 50 barrels a week. Two pubs are owned: the Fountain, Walsall and the Saddlers Arms, Solihull. A 0.5-barrel experimental plant is in operation. ◆

Bitter (OG 1040, ABV 3.8%)
A blonde bitter, slightly sweet with hints of tangerine and fruit salad.

Hoard (OG 1040, ABV 3.9%)

Blonde (OG 1041, ABV 4.1%)

Chinook IPA (OG 1050, ABV 5%)
Single-hopped IPA with spicy, juniper and lavender notes and a smoky element, citrus undertone and aroma.

East Kent Golding IPA (OG 1050, ABV 5%)
Single-hopped IPA with a subtle grapefruit and thyme aroma with a hint of orange to taste.

BAD SIBA

Unit 3, North Hill Road, Dishforth, North Yorkshire, YO7 3DH
☎ (01423) 324005 ⊕ wearebad.co

Brewing commenced in 2014 using a 13-barrel plant producing initially three core beers inspired by both traditional British and modern US styles. A 2.5-barrel plant is used for monthly specials often incorporating seasonal ingredients and also for more experimental and radical brews. A distillery is to be installed hence the name is an acronym for the Brewing & Distilling Company. ‼◆

Comfortably Numb (ABV 3.8%)
Fruity and slightly bitter, hoppy with notes of tangerine, mango, grapefruit and pineapple.

Love Over Gold (ABV 4.1%)
A blonde ale; light, hoppy and well-balanced with grapefruit and grassy notes.

Wild Gravity (ABV 5.2%)
An IPA with a malty backbone and tropical hop flavours.

Dazed and Confused (ABV 5.5%)
Dark rich milk stout with hints of cherry, chocolate, coffee and almond.

Bad Seed SIBA

Unit 6, 6 Rye Close, York Way Industrial Estate, Malton, North Yorkshire, YO17 6YD
⊕ badseedbrewery.co.uk

Started in 2013 by James Broad and Chris Waplington, the four-barrel brewery produces a core range of bottled beers, available across the UK, supplemented by a few specials.

Badger

See Hall & Woodhouse

Baildon SIBA

Unit D, Tong Park Business Centre, Otley Road, Baildon, West Yorkshire, BD17 7QD
⊕ baildonbrewing.co.uk

Brewing began in 2014 using a six-barrel plant. The brewery is run by Leigh Terry, head brewster. ◆RAIB

Blonde (ABV 3.6%)
A refreshing, zesty ale.

Brunette (ABV 3.9%)
A well-rounded ruby ale.

Auburn Flame (ABV 4.2%)
A crisp ale with spicy hops and a hint of soft fruit.

Ballard's SIBA 👁

The Old Sawmill, Nyewood, Petersfield, GU31 5HA
☎ (01730) 821362 ⊕ ballards-brewery.org.uk

Launched in 1980 by Mike and Carola Brown at Cumbers Farm, Trotton, Ballard's has been trading at Nyewood since 1988 and now supplies 70-80 outlets. ‼◼◆RAIB

Midhurst Mild (OG 1034, ABV 3.4%)
Traditional dark mild, well-balanced and refreshing with a biscuity flavour.

Golden Bine (OG 1038, ABV 3.8%) ◆
Amber-coloured, clean-tasting bitter. A roast malt aroma leads to a fruity, slightly sweet taste and a dry finish.

Best Bitter (OG 1042, ABV 4.2%) ◆
A copper-coloured beer with a malty aroma. A good balance of fruit and malt in the flavour gives way to a dry, hoppy aftertaste.

Wild (OG 1047, ABV 4.7%)
A blend of Mild and Wassail.

Nyewood Gold (OG 1050, ABV 5%)

Wassail (OG 1060, ABV 6%) ◆

A strong, full-bodied, tawny-red, fruity beer with a predominance of malt throughout, but also an underlying hoppiness.

Balmaha

Oak Tree Inn, Balmaha, Loch Lomond, G63 0JQ
☎ (01360) 870357 ⊕ oak-tree-inn.co.uk

Balmaha began brewing in 2012 using a one-barrel plant. ‼♦

Bank Top SIBA 👁

The Pavilion, Ashworth Lane, Bolton, BL1 8RA
☎ (01204) 595800 ⊕ banktopbrewery.com

👁Bank Top was established in 1995. Since 2002 the brewery has occupied a Grade II-listed tennis pavilion. In 2007 the brewing capacity was doubled with the installation of a 10-barrel plant and in 2008 David Sweeney became the sole proprietor. Bank Top Brewery Estates was formed in 2010 and now owns two pubs. ‼♦

Barley to Beer (OG 1036, ABV 3.6%)
A pale bitter with a citrus lemon and herbal finish.

Sweeneys (OG 1038, ABV 3.8%)
An amber-coloured bitter with a bold, crisp flavour and a delicate, slightly spicy aroma.

Bad to the Bone (OG 1040, ABV 4%)
A tan-coloured beer with floral qualities and delicate citrus notes.

Dark Mild (OG 1040, ABV 4%) 🍺◆
Dark brown beer with a malt and roast aroma. Smooth mouthfeel, with malt, roast malt and hops prominent throughout.

Flat Cap (OG 1040, ABV 4%) 🍺◆
Amber ale with a modest fruit aroma leading to a beer with citrus fruit, malt and hops. Good finish of fruit, malt and bitterness.

Gold Digger (OG 1040, ABV 4%) ◆
Golden-coloured, with a citrus aroma, grapefruit and a touch of spiciness on the palate; a fresh, hoppy, citrus finish.

Old Slapper (OG 1042, ABV 4.2%)
A quaffable golden-amber beer with citrus, floral and peach notes on the nose. Lightly-hopped with a soft fruity taste.

Pavilion Pale Ale (OG 1045, ABV 4.5%) ◆
A yellow beer with a citrus and hop aroma. Big fruity flavour with a peppery hoppiness; dry, bitter yet fruity finish.

Blonde (OG 1050, ABV 5%)
An pale ale made with New Zealand hops resulting in a pleasant woody flavour and distinct berry aroma.

Port O Call (OG 1050, ABV 5%) ◆
Dark brown beer with a malty, fruity aroma. Malt, roast and dark fruits in the bittersweet taste and finish.

Banks's

Park Brewery, Wolverhampton, West Midlands, WV1 4NY
☎ (01902) 711811 ⊕ bankssbeer.co.uk

Banks's was formed in 1890 by the amalgamation of three local companies. Hanson's was acquired in 1943 but its Dudley brewery was closed in 1991.

Hanson's beers are now brewed in Wolverhampton, though a few of its pubs retain the Hanson's livery. Banks's Mild, the biggest-selling brand, is a fine example of West Midlands mild ale and in 2010 the group decided to return to the traditional name of Mild, rather than Original, to keep pace with growing demand for the style. Marston's, over the past few years, has taken on contract brewing some well-known national beer brands following the closure of the original brewery. The majority of this brewing has been undertaken at the Banks's site. Banks's now brews cask beers for Carlsberg and Thwaites. Part of Marston's PLC. ‼▤

Mild (OG 1036, ABV 3.5%) ◆
An amber-coloured, well-balanced, refreshing session beer.

Bitter (OG 1038, ABV 3.8%) ◆
A pale brown bitter with a pleasant balance of hops and malt. Hops continue from the taste through to a bittersweet aftertaste.

Sunbeam (OG 1042, ABV 4.2%)
Zesty golden blond ale, with citrus and grapefruit overtones. A vibrant hop aroma leads to a long finish.

Brewed for Marston's:

EPA (OG 1036, ABV 3.6%)

Brewed under the Daniel Thwaites brand name:

Wainwright (OG 1042, ABV 4.1%)
A straw-coloured bitter with soft fruit flavours and a hint of malty sweetness.

Lancaster Bomber (OG 1044, ABV 4.4%)
Well-balanced, copper-coloured best bitter with firm malt flavours, a fruity background and a long, dry finish.

Brewed under the Mansfield brand name:

Cask Ale (OG 1038, ABV 3.9%)

Contract brewed for Carlsberg Tetley:

Tetley Gold (OG 1041, ABV 4.1%)

Contract brewed for Carlsberg:

Tetley Mild (OG 1034, ABV 3.3%)

Tetley Bitter (OG 1035, ABV 3.7%)

Contract brewed for Daniel Thwaites:

Original (OG 1036, ABV 3.6%)
Hop-driven, yet well-balanced amber session bitter. Hops continue through to the long finish.

Barearts

Beer Shop & Tasting Room, 108-110 Rochdale Road, Todmorden, West Yorkshire, OL14 7LP
☎ (01706) 839305 ⊕ barearts.com

A four-barrel brewery that began production in 2005 and specialises in strong, bottle-conditioned beers. It is named after an art gallery dedicated to nude artwork. Each brew is unique and helps comprise a changing range of around 20 beers including stouts and barley wines. There is a selection of vintage ales matured for at least one year. ▤RAIB

Barkston

Orchard House, Saw Wells Court, Barkston Ash, North Yorkshire, LS24 9UJ

☎ (0845) 224 6324 ☎ 07764 750959
🌐 barkstonbrewery.com

Barkston Brewery is situated in the picturesque village of Barkston Ash, four miles south of Tadcaster. Production started in 2011 experimenting with different malt and hop combinations before settling on the current range of four beers. New equipment with increased capacity was installed in 2013.

3B (OG 1040, ABV 4%)
A session beer with a creamy head and smooth taste.

Blonde (OG 1040, ABV 4%)
A light golden beer with an intense hoppy flavour and light citrus aroma.

Gold (OG 1040, ABV 4%)
A golden summer ale with an interesting mix of subtle and refreshing hop flavours and aromas.

Belle (OG 1047, ABV 4.7%)
A dark ruby-coloured ale with a biscuit flavour from heavily roasted malt combinations.

Barlick

Greyhound, 61 Manchester Road, Barnoldswick, Lancashire, BB18 5PW
☎ (01282) 850670 🌐 barlick-brewery.co.uk

Barlick began brewing in 2012 at the Greyhound in Barnoldswick, where a beer is always available. A four-barrel plant is used. Barlick is the colloquial name for the town. ♦

Barlicker Bitter (OG 1036, ABV 3.6%)

Hare of the Dog (OG 1038, ABV 3.8%)

40 Steps (OG 1039, ABV 3.9%)

Rag Albert (OG 1040, ABV 4%)

Barlow

Units 5 & 6, Shippen Rural Business Centre, Church Farm, Barlow, Derbyshire, S18 7TR
☎ (0114) 289 1767 🌐 barlowbrewery.co.uk

Brewing started in 2009 on a self-built 2.5-barrel plant. Expansion to five-barrel capacity was completed in 2014. Beers are supplied to the Hare & Hounds in Barlow and other local outlets. The brewery aquired its first pub, the Tap House, in 2014. ♦ RAIB

Heath Robinson (OG 1039, ABV 3.8%)
A traditional dark bitter with a malty background and a balanced, bitter finish.

Betty's Blonde (OG 1042, ABV 4%)
Brewed with a blend of pale malts to give a light golden colour, hopped for subtle citrus and passion fruit flavours with a clean, crisp finish.

Beyond the Pale (OG 1042, ABV 4%)

Carnival Ale (OG 1042, ABV 4%)
A light, golden pale ale with a citrus finish.

Dark Horse (OG 1043, ABV 4.2%)
A dark bitter, brewed with English malts to give its dark colour and coffee aroma. English hopped for a nicely balanced finish.

Three Valleys IPA (OG 1052, ABV 5%)
An American-style IPA bursting with tropical fruit and citrus flavours; clean bitter finish.

Full Monty (OG 1067, ABV 6.5%)
A strong, full-flavoured IPA. Golden in colour with complex passion fruit, citrus and mandarin orange flavours with a warming alcoholic finish.

Anastasia (OG 1076, ABV 7.5%)
Strong, dark and smooth with complex malt flavours, chocolate, coffee and a hint of fruit.

Barnet

Black Horse, Wood Street, High Barnet, EN5 4BW
☎ (020) 8449 2230 🌐 blackhorsebarnet.co.uk/brewery

Brewing began in 2013. One beer is regularly available with additional different brews produced each week.

Palomino (ABV 4%)

Barney's SIBA

Summerhall Brewery, 1 Summerhall, Edinburgh, EH9 1PL ☎ 07512 253660 🌐 barneysbeer.com

The only microbrewery in Edinburgh's city centre, Barney's Beer was founded in 2010 and now brews on the site of the original 1800s Summerhall brewery. Summerhall is Edinburgh's centre for the arts and science. ‼

Good Ordinary Pale Ale (OG 1038, ABV 3.8%)
An English-style bitter, gold-coloured and full-bodied.

Extra Pale (OG 1040, ABV 4%)
Brewed using lager malt and hops. Light and refreshing.

Red Rye (OG 1044, ABV 4.5%)
Copper-coloured with a clean, crisp, dry and fruity taste.

Volcano IPA (OG 1049, ABV 5%)
Light-coloured, hoppy, American-style pale ale.

Barngates SIBA

Barngates, Cumbria, LA22 0NG
☎ (01539) 436575 🌐 barngatesbrewery.co.uk

Barngates was established in 1997 to supply only the Drunken Duck Inn. It became a limited company in 1999. Expansion over the years plus a new purpose-built 10-barrel plant in 2008 means it now supplies more than 150 outlets throughout Cumbria, Lancashire, Yorkshire and Northumberland. ‼

Pale (OG 1036, ABV 3.3%)
A well-balanced, fruity, hoppy bitter with plenty of flavour for its strength.

Tunnellers Dark Mild (OG 1037, ABV 3.4%)
Sweet start builds nicely to a full-bodied fruity mild with roast flavours dominating the finish.

Cat Nap (OG 1037, ABV 3.6%)
Pale beer, unapologetically bitter, with a dry, astringent finish.

Cracker (OG 1038, ABV 3.9%)
A flavoursome malty bitter, fruity but not sweet. Dry in taste rather than finish.

Brathay Gold (OG 1042, ABV 4%)
Attractive sweet and rich aroma is followed by plenty of fruit and hops then a long bitter finish.

Goodhew's Dry Stout (OG 1045, ABV 4.3%)

The inviting roast aroma leads to an easy-drinking, full-bodied and well-balanced roasty stout.

Tag Lag (OG 1044, ABV 4.4%)
A pale amber beer, smooth and sweetly malty to begin but a lasting, bitter finish.

Red Bull Terrier (OG 1048, ABV 4.8%)
Red-coloured beer with full mouthfeel and roast bitterness lingering through to the long finish.

Barnsley

See Wentworth

Barrell & Sellers (NEW) SIBA

Spring Farm, St Cross South Elmham, Harleston, Suffolk, IP20 0NZ
☎ (01986) 783902 ☎ 07788 561455
barrellandsellers.co.uk

Brewing began in 2014, producing easy-drinking classic beers using only English-grown hops and malt. The cask beers are supplied to a small number of local pubs and its bottled-conditioned beers are available direct from the brewery or through selected retail outlets. !! ♦ RAIB

Best Bitter (OG 1041, ABV 4.2%)

Pale Ale (OG 1041, ABV 4.2%)

Brown Ale (OG 1045, ABV 4.7%)

Barrowden

c/o Exeter Arms, 28 Main Street, Barrowden, Rutland, LE15 8EQ
☎ (01572) 747247 exeterarmsrutland.co.uk

The brewery was established in 1998. Martin Allsopp bought the pub and brewery in 2005, which is situated in a barn at the back of the Exeter Arms. ♦

Pilot (OG 1028, ABV 2.6%)

Seventy Lambs (OG 1038, ABV 3.6%)

Beech (OG 1040, ABV 3.8%)

Own Gear (OG 1040, ABV 4%)

Hop Gear (OG 1046, ABV 4.4%)

Bartleby's (NEW)

Coachwerks, 19 Hollingdean Terrace, Brighton, BN1 7HB
☎ (01273) 275012 ☎ 07518 485342
bartlebysbrewery.com

Bartleby's began trading in 2014 in Brighton. Since opening it has expanded its distribution to local pubs and has established an on-site shop with home deliveries by veloelectric tricycle. An on-site venue is used for music, community events and art shows. !!

Beadlespoon (OG 1040, ABV 3.6%)

Preference (OG 1040, ABV 3.6%)

Calico (OG 1044, ABV 4.2%)

Erly Red (OG 1048, ABV 4.8%)

Idle Bo (OG 1048, ABV 4.8%)

Long Nose (OG 1048, ABV 4.8%)

Wooden Boy (OG 1055, ABV 5.6%)

Bartrams

Rougham Estate, Ipswich Road (A14), Rougham, Suffolk, IP30 9LZ
☎ (01449) 737655 ☎ 07768 62581
bartramsbrewery.co.uk

The brewery was set up in 1999. In 2005 the plant was moved to a building on Rougham Airfield, the site of Bartram's Brewery between 1894 and 1902 run by Captain Bill Bartram. His image graces the pump clips. Beers are available in a selection of local pubs and there is a large amount of trade through local farmers' markets. Marld, Beltane Braces and all porters and stouts are suitable for vegetarians and vegans. !! ♦ RAIB

Marld (OG 1033, ABV 3.4%)
A traditional mild. Spicy hops and malt with a hint of chocolate, slightly smoky with a light, roasted finish.

Washing Machine Bitter (ABV 3.6%)
A golden bitter.

Premier Bitter (OG 1038, ABV 3.7%)
A traditional quaffing ale, full-flavoured but light, dry and hoppy.

Rougham Ready (OG 1038, ABV 3.8%)
A light, crisp bitter, surprisingly full bodied for its strength.

Milkmaid (ABV 4%)
A copper-coloured traditional bitter.

Bee's Knees (OG 1042, ABV 4.2%)
An amber-coloured beer with a floral aroma; honey softness on the palate leads to a crisp, bitter finish.

Captain Bill Bartram's Best Bitter (OG 1048, ABV 4.8%)
Modified from a 100-year old recipe, using full malt and traditional Kentish hops.

Captain's Stout (OG 1049, ABV 4.8%)
Biscuity dark malt leads to a lightly smoked aroma, plenty of roasted malt character, coffee notes and a whiff of smoke.

Cherry Stout (OG 1048, ABV 4.8%)
Sensuous hints of chocolate lead to a subtle suggestion of cherries.

Suffolk 'n' Strong (OG 1050, ABV 5%)
A light, smooth and dangerously potable strong bitter, well-balanced malt and hops with an easy finish.

Comrade Bill Bartram's Egalitarian Anti Imperialist Soviet Stout (OG 1070, ABV 6.9%)
A Russian stout by any other name, a luscious easy-drinking example of the style.

Brewed for Cambridge Rock events:

Cambridge Rock (ABV 3.8%)
A golden-coloured bitter with New World hops.

Brewed for the John Peel Centre, Stowmarket:

John Peel Centre (ABV 3.7%)
A copper-coloured bitter using New World hops.

Barum SIBA

c/o Reform Inn, Pilton, Barnstaple, Devon, EX31 1PD
☎ (01271) 329994 barumbrewery.co.uk

Barum was formed in 1996 by Tim Webster and is housed in a conversion attached to the Reform Inn that acts as the brewery tap and main outlet. Distribution is exclusively within Devon. ‼☕♦

Original (OG 1044, ABV 4.4%)
Mid-brown best bitter with a sweet malty palate and bittersweet aftertaste.

EPA (OG 1046, ABV 4.6%)
Very pale golden ale with citrus/grapefruit notes throughout. Clean dry finish.

Breakfast (OG 1048, ABV 5%)
Copper-coloured, malty premium bitter with a floral nose and a bittersweet finish.

Baseline

Golding Barn Industrial Estate, Henfield Road, Small Dole, West Sussex, BN5 9XH
☎ (01903) 915025 ⊕ baselinebrewing.co.uk

⊗ Brewing started in 2012 on a five-barrel plant nestling in the South Downs. The beer is unfined with no Isinglass, making it suitable for vegetarians.

Thunderbolt Bitter (OG 1040, ABV 4%)
A full-flavoured, copper-coloured session bitter with a spicy, earthy and floral flavour.

Dark Matter (OG 1055, ABV 5.5%)
A dark, full-bodied ale. The initial flavour is roasted malt with spicy hops and a fruity but dry bitter finish.

English Electric Lightning (OG 1060, ABV 6%)
A classic English special bitter; burnished orange in colour.

Batemans SIBA IFBB ◉

Salem Bridge Brewery, Mill Lane, Wainfleet, Lincolnshire, PE24 4JE
☎ (01754) 880317 ⊕ bateman.co.uk

◉ Bateman's Brewery was established in 1874 it has been brewing award-winning beers for four generations. All 62 tied houses serve cask-conditioned beer. The beer range may change as a result of a decision in July 2015 to reduce the amount of beer brewed. ‼☕♦

Black & White (OG 1036, ABV 3.6%) ◆
Gentle roast fruity airs preface this red-brown, caramel-infused brew. Malt and a stewed plummy sweetness initially give depth. Caramel dominates the short, simple finish.

XB (OG 1037, ABV 3.7%) ◆
A well-rounded, smooth malty beer with a blackcurrant fruity background. Hops flourish initially before giving way to a bittersweet dryness that enhances the mellow malty ending.

Gold (OG 1039, ABV 3.9%)
A golden-coloured, refreshing beer with a citrus flavour and aroma, which is quite dry.

XXXB (OG 1045, ABV 4.5%) ◆
A brilliant blend of malt, hops and fruit on the nose with a bitter bite over the top of a faintly banana maltiness that stays the course. A russet-tan brown classic.

Salem Porter (OG 1048, ABV 4.7%) ⊡ ◆
A black and complex mix of chocolate, liquorice and cough elixir.

Victory Ale (OG 1062, ABV 5.9%)
A dark amber, strong English ale brimming with biscuity malt and succulent raisin and sultana fruits,

combined with peppery spices producing a full body and a marmalade aroma.

Bath SIBA ◉

Hare House, Southway Drive, Warmley, Bristol, BS30 5LW
☎ (0117) 947 4797 ⊕ bathales.com

⊗ Established in 1995, Bath Ales uses traditional brewing techniques with cutting-edge technology. An experimental brewery produces unusual and fashionable brews under the Beerd brand name. More than 400 regional outlets are supplied. Twelve pubs and sites are operated across the south-west, all serving cask ale, one of which brews its own specials. ‼☕♦RAIB

Special Pale Ale (OG 1039, ABV 3.7%) ◆
Hoppy, pale golden session bitter. Light citrus aroma with bittersweet flavours and a bitter aftertaste. Some samples may have a hint of caramel.

Gem (OG 1042, ABV 4.1%) ◆
Pale brown best bitter with sweet fruit and malt flavours and a hint of caramel. Little aroma but a balanced taste with a short bitter finish.

Barnsey (OG 1045, ABV 4.5%) ◆
A dark brown old ale with a grainy mouthfeel. Malt, dark fruits and toffee flavours combine to provide sweetness before a lingering bitter finish.

Festivity (OG 1050, ABV 5%) ⬚
A wintery beer brewed with floor-malted Maris Otter barley and roasted chocolate malt.

Platform 3 (OG 1055, ABV 5.7%)
An IPA with tropical fruit aromas, hints of citrus honey flavours, and a long bitter finish.

Brewed under the Beerd brand name:

Monterey (OG 1040, ABV 3.9%)

Silver Tip (OG 1046, ABV 4.7%)

Bathams IFBB

Delph Brewery, Delph Road, Brierley Hill, West Midlands, DY5 2TN
☎ (01384) 77229 ⊕ bathams.com

◉ A classic Black Country small brewery established in 1877. Tim and Matthew Batham represent the fifth generation to run the company. The Vine, one of the Black Country's most famous pubs, is also the site of the brewery. The company has 11 tied houses and supplies around 30 other outlets. Batham's Bitter is delivered in 54-gallon hogsheads to meet demand. ◆

Mild Ale (OG 1036.5, ABV 3.5%) ◆
A fruity, dark brown mild with malty sweetness and a roast malt finish.

Best Bitter (OG 1043.5, ABV 4.3%) ◆
A pale yellow, fruity, sweetish bitter, with a dry, hoppy finish. A good, light, refreshing beer.

Battledown SIBA ◉

Keynsham Works, Keynsham Street, Cheltenham, Gloucestershire, GL52 6EJ
☎ (01242) 693409 ☎ 07734 834104
⊕ battledownbrewery.com

⊗ Established in 2005 by Roland and Stephanie Elliott-Berry, and joined in 2006 by Ben Jennison-

Phillips (ex-Whittingtons), Battledown operates an eight-barrel plant from an old engineering works and supplies more than 250 outlets. Visitors are always welcome. There is an online shop for mail order purposes. ‼ ▅ ♦ RAIB

Sunbeam (OG 1037, ABV 3.8%)
A pale ale with a refreshing aroma and sharp but smooth taste, leaving a dry, hoppy aftertaste which lingers on the palate.

Natural Selection (OG 1041, ABV 4.2%)
A deep golden beer, the malt is evident but gives way to the triple hop addition giving a spicy and slightly citrus finish.

Premium (OG 1046, ABV 4.6%)
A rich amber ale. A malty aroma and taste with a deep satisfying, full-bodied fruit and malt texture leaving a well-rounded mellow aftertaste.

Special (OG 1050, ABV 5.2%)
A well-balanced and crisp pale ale.

Black (OG 1070, ABV 7.2%)
A dark, complex, full-bodied stout.

Four Kings (OG 1066, ABV 7.2%)
A strong ale with a heady aroma.

Battlefield SIBA

See Tunnel

Bays SIBA ◉

Aspen Way, Paignton, Devon, TQ4 7QR
☎ (01803) 555004 ⊕ baysbrewery.co.uk

⊗ Bays Brewery opened in 2007 in an old steel fabrication unit in Paignton using a 20-barrel plant. The brewery delivers to many pubs, hotels and restaurants in the south-west and further afield. ‼ ▅ ♦

Topsail (OG 1040, ABV 4%)

Gold (OG 1042, ABV 4.3%)

Devon Dumpling (OG 1048, ABV 5.1%)

Beachy Head SIBA

Seven Sisters Sheep Centre, Birling Manor Farm, Gilberts Drive, East Dean, East Sussex, BN20 0AA
☎ (01323) 423313 ☎ -

Estates Office: The Green, East Dean, East Sussex, BN20 0BS ⊕ beachyhead.org.uk

⊗ The 2.5-barrel brew plant was installed at the rear of the sheep centre in 2006. Beachy Head Brewery produces both cask and bottle-conditioned ales, supplied regularly to around 25 outlets, three of which are local pubs. The full range of ales (including seasonals) can be sampled at the Tiger Inn in East Dean village, which is the brewery tap. ‼ ♦ RAIB

South Downs Ale (OG 1044, ABV 4.4%)

Beachy Original (OG 1045, ABV 4.5%)

Legless Rambler (OG 1050, ABV 5%)

Bear Claw

Unit 3, Meantime Workshops, Spittal, Northumberland, TD15 1RG ☎ 07919 276715
⊕ bearclawbrewery.weebly.com

Bear Claw began brewing in 2012 using a two-barrel plant, producing an ever-changing range of mainly highly-hopped cask-conditioned ales and many bottle-conditioned beers, including continental styles. The most regular outlet is the Barrels Alehouse in Berwick on Tweed. Expansion is planned as demand is high. RAIB

Beartown SIBA ◉

Bromley House, Spindle Street, Congleton, Cheshire, CW12 1QN
☎ (01260) 299964 ⊕ beartownbrewery.co.uk

☺ Congleton's links with brewing can be traced back to 1272. Two of its most senior officers at the time were Ale Taster and Bear Warden, hence the name of the brewery. Beartown began brewing in 1994, a 25-barrel plant is used. Five pubs are owned. Both the brewery's Navigation in Stockport and the Beartown Tap in Congleton have been named CAMRA regional pubs of the year. More than 250 outlets are supplied. ‼ ▅ ♦

Best Bitter (OG 1037, ABV 3.7%)
A copper-coloured session beer with a full palate of malt and crisp hops.

Bear Ass (OG 1040, ABV 4%)
Dark ruby-red, malty bitter with a good hop nose and fruity flavour with dry, bitter, astringent aftertaste.

Ginger Bear (OG 1040, ABV 4%)
The flavours from the malt and hops blend with the added bite from the root ginger to produce a quenching blonde ale.

Kodiak Gold (OG 1040, ABV 4%) ◀
Hops and fruit dominate the taste of this crisp yellow bitter and these follow through to the dryish aftertaste. Biscuity malt also comes through on the aroma and taste.

Bearskinful (OG 1042, ABV 4.2%) ◀
Biscuity malt dominates the flavour of this amber best bitter. There are hops and a hint of sulphur on the aroma. A balance of malt and bitterness follow through to the aftertaste.

Bearly Literate (OG 1045, ABV 4.5%)
Golden pale ale. Floral scented and packed with the flavours of summer fruits and lemon, ending with a smooth dryness.

Polar Eclipse (OG 1048, ABV 4.8%) ◀
Classic black, dry and bitter stout, with roast flavours to the fore. Good hop on the nose follows through the taste into a long, dry finish.

Blackbear (OG 1050, ABV 5%)
A ruby-coloured strong mild. Subtle roast and malt flavours fill the taste complemented by a mellow sweetness.

Bruins Ruin (OG 1050, ABV 5%)
Deep copper-coloured premium ale. Full of malty character and a palate of sweet, smooth, fruity flavours.

Beavertown SIBA

Units 17 & 18, Lockwood Industrial Park, Mill Mead Road, Tottenham Hale, London, N17 9QP
☎ (020) 8525 9884 ☎ 07976 984173
⊕ beavertownbrewery.co.uk

⊗ Beavertown moved into a large industrial unit in 2014 and expanded again in 2015. It is a sizeable craft brewery with six regular beers and many seasonal, one-off and collaboration beers. Most are sold in key-keg, can and keg without filtration or pasteurisation. Real ale is produced on a small plant. ♦ RAIB

Neck Oil (OG 1043, ABV 4.3%)
Pale brown beer with a creamy mouthfeel. Hints of citrus and peach with a dry, biscuity finish.

Smog Rocket Porter (OG 1054, ABV 5.4%)
Treacle, citrus, roast and hops are all present in this slightly smoky black porter. Finish has some burnt bitterness.

Beckstones

Upper Beckstones Mill, The Green, Millom, Cumbria, LA18 5HL ☎ 07780 608906
beckstonesbrewery.co.uk

On the site of an 18th-century mill, with its own water supply, this five-barrel operation continues to win awards. Beer names have connections to the long-closed Millom Iron Works or local characters; the brewer designs the distinctive pump clips. ♦

Barley Juice (OG 1033, ABV 3.4%)
Full-flavoured, beautifully-balanced, emphatically fruity, hoppy beer.

Beer O'Clock (OG 1036, ABV 3.5%)
A fascinating blend of flavours delivering ever-changing mouthfuls of sweet, fruity and hoppy bitterness.

Leat (OG 1036, ABV 3.6%)
A refreshing golden bitter with tangy fruit and a rising hop finish.

Black Dog Freddy Mild (OG 1038, ABV 3.8%)
A full-bodied, beautifully-balanced ruby dark mild, replete with fruit and roast malt.

Iron Town (OG 1038, ABV 3.8%)
Creamy sweet brown ale full of well-balanced fruit and hop.

Border Steeans (OG 1040, ABV 4.1%)
An old-fashioned tawny bitter with a sweet start, some bitter notes and plenty of aftertaste.

Rev Rob (OG 1044, ABV 4.6%)
A golden beer with a pronounced grapefruit aroma and taste. The hoppy bitterness lasts through to the aftertaste.

Bedlam SIBA

Albourne Farm, Shaves Wood Lane, Albourne, West Sussex, BN6 9DX
☎ (01273) 978015 bedlambrewery.co.uk

Brewing takes place in a converted barn on Albourne Farm. Beer is supplied to outlets throughout the south-east and London along with a number of beer festivals. RAIB

Benchmark (ABV 4%)
An amber-coloured best bitter with refreshing bitterness and sweet, fruity notes. The hops are balanced by a rich, malty character with a hint of chocolate.

Golden (ABV 4.2%)
A session bitter with a bright bitterness on the palate.

IPA (OG 1048, ABV 4.8%)
A rich, full-flavoured IPA.

Porter (OG 1050, ABV 5%)
Plenty of roasted malt aromas and flavours. Rich and dark with a full palate and lasting bittersweet finish.

Beeches

39 The Beeches, Lochgelly, KY5 9QB
☎ (01592) 782474 ☎ 07761 752876
thebeechesbrewery@gmail.com

Beeches came into existence from the love of small batch home brewing. Run by a husband and wife team, production started in 2012 using a 10-gallon plant in a small outbuilding at the rear of the family home.

Amazing Ale (OG 1040, ABV 3.6%)
A blonde ale, with a sweetness on the palate and a floral aftertaste.

Amazing Citra (OG 1038, ABV 3.8%)
A light, easy-drinking session ale with a grapefruit character from the hop.

Pale Face (OG 1036, ABV 3.8%)
A light, pale session ale.

Cats IPA (OG 1039, ABV 3.9%)
A pale ale with a floral aroma, slightly spicy with a citrus aftertaste.

Cats Whiskers (OG 1042, ABV 3.9%)
A golden ale, light and crisp with a citrus aftertaste.

Meedies Mash (OG 1046, ABV 3.9%)
Amber-coloured with a malty nose, bitter finish and a slightly spicy aftertaste.

Beech Nut Ale (OG 1044, ABV 4.1%)
Malt on the nose, smooth drinking with chocolate notes and a slight malty taste.

Hop Trial (OG 1046, ABV 4.2%)

Sleeping Giant (OG 1042, ABV 4.2%)

Cats Capers (OG 1046, ABV 4.4%)

Meedies Magic (OG 1040, ABV 4.4%)

One Hundred (OG 1048, ABV 4.7%)
A light, pale golden-coloured ale with a hint of honey and ginger.

Blonde Bi'ere (OG 1052, ABV 4.8%)

Lo'Gelly Happylands (OG 1056, ABV 5.5%)

Beer Engine

Newton St Cyres, Devon, EX5 5AX
☎ (01392) 851282 thebeerengine.co.uk

Beer Engine was developed in 1983 and is the oldest continuously working microbrewery in Devon. The brewery is visible behind glass downstairs in the pub. Several outlets are supplied, as well as all local beer festivals. !! ♦

Rail Ale (OG 1037, ABV 3.8%)
A straw-coloured beer with a fruity aroma and a sweet, fruity finish.

Silver Bullet (OG 1040, ABV 4%)
A light, medium-strength summer beer with a bitter aftertaste.

Piston Bitter (OG 1043, ABV 4.3%)
A mid-brown, sweet-tasting beer with a pleasant, bittersweet aftertaste.

Sleeper Heavy (OG 1052, ABV 5.4%)

A red-coloured beer with a fruity, sweet taste and a bitter finish.

Beer Me (NEW)

The Belgian Café, 11-23 Grand Parade, Eastbourne, East Sussex, BN21 3YN
☎ (01323) 729967 beermebrewery.com

Beer Me was launched in 2014 by the owners of the Belgian Café in Eastbourne, building on 10 years in the catering industry. It uses a 2.5-barrel plant and produces continental-style beers which are served direct from the brewery. ‼

Blonde (OG 1061, ABV 6%)
Malty, but not too sweet, focusing on malt flavour.

Dubbel (OG 1060, ABV 6%)
A medium-bodied, Belgian-style dubbel with pronounced fruitiness (raisin, orange) and chocolate flavours.

Beer Nouveau (NEW)

Dovedale Avenue, Prestwich, M25 0BT
beernouveau.co.uk

Beer Nouveau started in 2014 on a hand-built nine-gallon brew plant. Within three months demand saw a second nine-gallon plant installed. RAIB

M25 (OG 1030, ABV 3.7%)
A slightly sweet nose accompanying a short, sweet and delicately hopped taste with a dry finish.

Prestwich Pale (OG 1038, ABV 3.9%)
A light, hoppy session beer with an underlying hint of malty sweetness.

Body Snatcher (OG 1040, ABV 4.2%)
A rich, copper-coloured session beer. A slightly sweet malt base sits underneath a fresh, spicy hop aroma. Dry, crisp and clean hop flavours linger to produce a balanced, bitter aftertaste.

Manchester Sun (OG 1052, ABV 5.3%)
A golden bitter, light on hops on the nose, but heavy on the palate with a little maltiness.

Satanic Mills (OG 1056, ABV 6%)
Smooth and slightly sweet stout with a traditional malt base and a less conventional hop schedule to produce a light yet still powerful flavour.

Uncle Sam (OG 1057, ABV 6.3%)
Golden amber in colour with a light floral, almost fruity aroma and a massive hop hit on the tongue; dry, slightly biscuity aftertaste.

Beer Refinery (NEW)

Tin Shed, Chapel Court Enterprise Centre, Wervin Road, Wervin, Chester, CH2 4BT ☎ 07939 875308
thebeerrefinery.co.uk

The Beer Refinery is a partnership of 10 engineers, some home brewers, and some just beer lovers. Brewing began in 2014 using a locally built four-barrel plant. 14 outlets are supplied. ‼ ♦

Mischief Pale Ale (ABV 5.1%)

Beer Studio

See Hydes

Beerd

See Bath

Beeston SIBA

Fransham Road Farm, Beeston, Norfolk, PE32 2LZ
☎ (01328) 700844 ☎ 07768 742763
beestonbrewery.co.uk

The brewery was established in 2006 in an old farm building using a five-barrel plant. Brewing water comes from a dedicated borehole and raw ingredients are sourced locally whenever possible. All beers are also available in five-litre mini casks. ‼ RAIB

Squirrels Nuts (OG 1035, ABV 3.5%)
Cherry, chocolate and vanilla aroma. A malt and cherry sweetness comes to the fore but quickly fades. Short finish.

Bloomers (OG 1039, ABV 4%)

Worth the Wait (OG 1041, ABV 4.2%)
Hoppy throughout with a growing dryness. Complex and grainy with fruit notes, malt and understated bitterness.

Stirling (OG 1045, ABV 4.5%)
Rich malty red bitter with toffee notes.

Dry Road (OG 1048, ABV 4.8%)

Village Life (OG 1047, ABV 4.8%)
Copper-coloured with a nutty character. Malty throughout, a bittersweet background gives depth. Strong toffee apple finish.

On the Huh (OG 1048, ABV 5%)
A fruity raisin aroma. A bittersweet maltiness jousts with caramel and roast. A dry hoppiness adds to a strong finale.

Old Stoatwobbler (OG 1065, ABV 6%)

Brewed for Brancaster Brewery:

Best (OG 1038, ABV 3.8%)

Sharpie K12 (ABV 4.3%)

Malthouse Bitter (OG 1044, ABV 4.4%)

Oyster Catcher (OG 1044, ABV 4.4%)

Wreck SS Vina (OG 1049, ABV 4.9%)

Beeston Hop (NEW)

Gwenbrook Avenue, Beeston, Nottingham, NG9 4BA
beestonhop.co.uk

A nano-brewery launched in 2015 producing mainly bottle-conditioned beers. Cask beers are occasionally produced for festivals using capacity at other breweries. The beers are unfined, unfiltered and unpasteurised and are suitable for vegans unless otherwise indicated. RAIB

Belhaven

Brewery Lane, Dunbar, EH42 1PE
☎ (01368) 862734

Office: Spott Road, Dunbar, EH42 1RS
belhaven.co.uk

Belhaven brewery is one of the oldest brewing sites in Scotland. Established in Dunbar in 1719, it brews beers made with water from its own well and local Scottish barley. Part of Greene King PLC. ‼ 🛒

60/- Ale (OG 1030, ABV 2.9%) ◆
A fine example of a Scottish light. This bittersweet, reddish-brown beer is dominated by fruit and malt with a hint of roast and caramel, and increasing bitterness in the aftertaste.

IPA (OG 1038, ABV 3.8%)
A golden ale with refreshing floral and citrus tones produced by a well-balanced fusion of malt and hops giving a clean, crisp flavour.

80/- Ale (OG 1040, ABV 4.2%) ◆
One of the last remaining original Scottish 80 Shillings. Malt is the predominant flavour characteristic, though it is balanced by fruit and a little hop. A complex ale, true to the 80/- style.

Black (OG 1041, ABV 4.2%)
A smooth, balanced stout with malty body and roast notes of dark chocolate and coffee.

St Andrew's Ale (OG 1046, ABV 4.9%)
A bittersweet beer with lots of body. The malt, fruit and roast mingle throughout with hints of hop and caramel.

Bell Street

57-59 Bell Street, Henley-on-Thames, Oxfordshire, RG9 2BA
☎ (01491) 570217 🌐 bellstreetbrewery.co.uk

Bell Street Brewery opened in 2013 at the rear of Brakspear pub company's refurbished Bull on Bell Street. A four-barrel plant is used. The beers are sold at the pub and through the Brakspear estate. ♦

Brakspear Special (OG 1043, ABV 4.3%)
Tawny-coloured beer with a well-balanced aroma and a hint of sweetness. Full bodied, the initial sweetness gives way to a dry hop bitterness.

Belleville SIBA

36 Jaggard Way, Wandsworth Common, London, SW12 8SG ☎ 07712 298273
🌐 bellevillebrewing.co.uk

Belleville began brewing in 2012. It was formed by a group of parents who met in the playground of a local primary school and specialises in American-style beers. ‼ ♦

Calif-Oregon Amber (ABV 4.2%)

Northcote Blonde (OG 1042, ABV 4.2%) ◆
Smooth golden ale with biscuity character and a trace of hoppy bitterness. Fruit is pineapple, orange and mixed citrus.

Balham Black (ABV 4.6%)

Battersea Brownstone (OG 1048, ABV 4.8%) ◆
Complex beer with chocolate and blackcurrant notes on nose and palate coupled with a little malty sweetness. Hoppy bitter finish.

Chestnut Porter (OG 1049, ABV 4.9%) ◆
Brown creamy beer with roast and nutty notes throughout and a little hoppiness and fruit. Faintly bitter. Short dry finish.

Commonside Pale Ale (OG 1050, ABV 5%) ◆
A full-flavoured golden beer with hops and fruit throughout. The initial palate is sweet but then the bitterness develops.

Thames Surfer (OG 1057, ABV 5.7%) ◆
Strong pale brown-coloured IPA with citrus, hops, honey and spicy notes. There is a long-lasting faintly hoppy, bitter finish.

Tie-Dye Rye (OG 1054, ABV 5.8%)

Bellfield (NEW)

6 Logie Mill, Beaverbank Business Park, Edinburgh, EH7 4HG ✉ Info@bellfieldbrewery.com

Bellfield Brewery started in 2015 and produces small batches of naturally gluten-free beers and lagers combining traditional brewing methods and non-traditional ingredients. It supplies only local outlets at present, but there are plans to expand its markets. ♦

Bellinger's SIBA

Station Road, Grove, Oxfordshire, OX12 0DH
☎ (01235) 772255 🌐 bellingersbrewery.co.uk

⊗ The late Mike Bellinger established the brewery as a family partnership in 2011. Currently a five-barrel plant, it supplies cask-conditioned beer to the Plough, West Hanney, and sells bottles and polypins in the garage forecourt shop. ‼ 🛒 ♦ RAIB

Original Bitter (OG 1040, ABV 4.1%)
A light and refreshing easy-drinking beer.

Best Bitter (OG 1046, ABV 4.9%)
Rich tasting with a complex flavour.

Belvoir SIBA

Crown Park, Station Road, Old Dalby, Leicestershire, LE14 3NQ
☎ (01664) 823455 🌐 belvoirbrewery.co.uk

Belvoir (pronounced 'beaver') Brewery was set up in 1995 by former Shipstone's and Theakston's brewer Colin Brown. Long-term expansion has seen the introduction of a 20-barrel plant that can produce 50 barrels a week. There is also a visitor centre incorporating brewery memorabilia, a bar, restaurant and shop (open seven days a week). Around 150 outlets are supplied direct. ‼ ♦ RAIB

Dark Horse (OG 1034, ABV 3.4%)

Whippling (OG 1037, ABV 3.6%)

Star Bitter (OG 1039, ABV 3.9%) ◆
Reminiscent of the long-extinct Shipstone's Bitter, this mid-brown bitter lives up to its name as it is bitter in taste but not unpleasantly so.

Gordon Bennett (OG 1041, ABV 4.1%)
Light chestnut-coloured beer with a biscuity character and a pleasant hop finish.

Beaver Bitter (OG 1043, ABV 4.3%) ◆
A light brown bitter that starts malty in both aroma and taste, but soon develops a hoppy bitterness. Appreciably fruity.

Old Dalby (OG 1050, ABV 5.1%)
A rich, smooth ruby red strong ale with pleasant hop character.

Contract brewed for Hoskins Brothers:

Hob Bitter (OG 1040, ABV 4%)

IPA (OG 1040, ABV 4%)

Contract brewed for Shipstone's Beer Co Ltd:

Bitter (OG 1036, ABV 3.8%)

Amber-coloured, dry, classic Nottingham-style bitter.

Gold Star (OG 1037, ABV 4.2%)
Smooth, well-balanced blonde ale, clean and crisp with a light, subtle hop finish.

Contract brewed for Steamin' Billy Brewing Co:

Tipsy Fisherman (OG 1036, ABV 3.6%)
Traditional light amber-coloured bitter with a mellow, crisp flavour and a hoppy aftertaste.

Bitter (OG 1043, ABV 4.3%)
A golden bitter with a pronounced floral flavour and aroma followed by a lingering hoppy aftertaste.

1485 (OG 1050, ABV 5%)

Skydiver (OG 1050, ABV 5%)
Full strength mahogany-coloured beer, a fine balance of malty sweetness and hop bitterness. Deceivingly drinkable.

Ben Rhydding

Margerison Crescent, Ben Rhydding, Ilkley, West Yorkshire, LS29 8QZ 🌐 benrhyddingbrewery.com

The brewery started in 2013 and specialises in bottle-conditioned beers made in small batches. Occasional casks are produced for local beer festivals or other local events. ♦RAIB

Beowulf SIBA

Forest of Mercia, Chasewater Country Park, Pool Lane, Brownhills, Staffordshire, WS8 7NL
☎ (01543) 454067 ☎ 07714 291226
🌐 beowulfbrewery.com

Beowulf Brewing Company is based at the Chasewater County Park. Its beers appear as guest ales predominantly in the central region, but also across the country. The brewery's dark beers have a particular reputation for excellence. ‼♦RAIB

Beorma (OG 1038, ABV 3.9%)
A perfectly-balanced session ale with a malty hint of fruit giving way to a lingering bitterness. Background spice excites the palate.

Chasewater Bitter (OG 1043, ABV 4.4%)
Golden bitter, hoppy throughout with citrus and hints of malt. Long mouth-watering, bitter finish.

Chase Buster (OG 1045, ABV 4.5%)
A pale golden bitter.

Dark Raven (OG 1048, ABV 4.5%)
Dark with apple and bonfire in the aroma. Sweet and smooth like liquid toffee apples with a sudden bitter finish.

Swordsman (OG 1045, ABV 4.5%)
Pale gold, light fruity aroma, tangy hoppy flavour. Faintly hoppy finish.

Folded Cross (OG 1045, ABV 4.6%)
Malt and caramel aromas and tastes with hints of fruity biscuits are nudged aside by the robust hops which give a lingering bitter edge.

Hurricane (OG 1041, ABV 4.6%)
A copper-coloured bitter.

Dragon Smoke Stout (OG 1048, ABV 4.7%)
Black with a light brown creamy head. Tobacco, chocolate, liquorice and mixed fruity hints on the aroma. Bitterness fights through the sweet and roast flavours and eventually dominates. Hints of a good port emerge.

Finn's Hall Porter (OG 1049, ABV 4.7%)
Dark chocolate aroma, after-dinner mints, coffee and fresh tobacco. Good bitterness with woodland hints of autumn. Long, late bitterness.

Mercian Shine (OG 1048, ABV 5%)
Amber to pale gold with a good bitter and hoppy start. Plenty of caramel and hops with background malt leading to a good bitter finish with caramel and hops lingering in the aftertaste.

IPA (OG 1074, ABV 7.2%)
Malty aroma with plenty of hops. Sweet malty start, malty middle and hoppy finish. Complex tastes abound with fruit, sweetness and hops all combining to produce a fine taste, strong and warming.

Berrow

See Towles'

Bespoke SIBA

Unit 5, The Mews, Mitcheldean, Gloucestershire, GL17 0SL
☎ (01594) 546557 🌐 bespokebrewery.co.uk

Brewing commenced in 2012 on a 5.5-barrel plant on the site of the former Wintles Brewery. In 2014 capacity was increased to 12 barrels. Speciality-labelled bottles are offered for celebratory occasions. An on-site brewery tap opens on Fridays 2-11pm. ‼♦

Raging Ale (OG 1035, ABV 3.4%)
Light golden-coloured session bitter with a zesty finish brewed exclusively with British malt and hops.

Saved by the Bell (OG 1038, ABV 3.8%)
A light, refreshing session bitter with a spicy hop bite and a light floral aroma from the late hop addition.

Running the Gauntlet (OG 1046, ABV 4.4%)
Full malty flavoured bitter with rich roasted undertones balanced with good hop bitterness with spicy blackcurrant aromas from late hopping.

Going Off Half-cocked (OG 1045, ABV 4.6%)
A spicy hopped golden pale ale.

Money for Old Rope (OG 1049, ABV 4.8%)
Classic stout with rich dry flavours of malt and grain with deep hop bitterness.

Over a Barrel (OG 1052, ABV 5%)
A richly-coloured fruity strong ale with generous peppery finish.

Betteridge's (NEW)

Coopers Barn, The Dene, Hurstbourne Tarrant, Hampshire, SP11 0AG ☎ 07771 966058
🌐 betteridgesbrewery.co.uk

Trading since 2014, Betteridge uses a 2.5-barrel plant. Founder and brewer Mark Betteridge brews four core beers using principally English hops and traditional floor-malted barley. Beers are supplied to beer festivals, private events and to a growing number of pubs in the Test Valley area and occasionally further afield. RAIB

Old Chap (ABV 3.8%)

Jenny Wren (ABV 4.2%)
A golden-coloured, single-hopped beer with a distinctive hop flavour and malty notes.

Private Sector (ABV 4.2%)
A full-flavoured amber-coloured ale.

Serious Black (ABV 4.2%)
A complex enriched stout with coffee, chocolate notes and roast flavours but with some underlying sweetness from added lactose.

Bewdley SIBA

Unit 7, Bewdley Craft Centre, Lax Lane, Bewdley, Worcestershire, DY12 2DZ
☎ (01299) 405148 ⊕ bewdleybrewery.co.uk

⊠ Bewdley began brewing in 2008 on a six-barrel plant in an old school. This was upgraded to a 10-barrel plant in 2014. Brewing experience days are offered, please ring for details. Beers are brewed with a railway theme for the nearby Severn Valley Railway. ‼◆ RAIB

Worcestershire Way (OG 1036, ABV 3.6%)
A light beer with citrus notes.

Old School Bitter (OG 1038, ABV 3.8%)
Session bitter with a hoppy finish.

Sir Keith Park (OG 1045, ABV 4.5%)

2857 (OG 1050, ABV 5%)

Worcestershire Sway (OG 1050, ABV 5%)
A stronger version of Worcestershire Way, slightly sweeter with more body.

William Mucklows Dark Mild (OG 1060, ABV 6%)

Bexar County

8 Belgic Square, Padholme Road, Peterborough, Cambridgeshire, PE1 5XF ☎ 07934 722584
⊕ bexarcountybrewery.com

Bexar was established in 2013, brewing American-style beers. There is no regular beer list, as the brewer is constantly innovating new recipes.

Bexley (NEW) SIBA ◉

16a Manford Industrial Estate, Erith, Kent, DA8 2AJ
☎ (01322) 337368 ⊕ bexleybrewery.co.uk

Opened in 2014, the brewery produces regular and seasonal brews from a six-barrel plant with two conical fermenters. The beers are conditioned for at least seven days prior to release. Brewer Cliff Murphy and wife Jane also undertake weekend off-sales of the distinctive 'parakeet'-labelled bottled beers on site. ‼➡◆

Golden Acre (OG 1040, ABV 4%)
A refreshing single-malt golden ale with light fruity aroma and zesty citrus flavour.

Bexley's Own Beer (OG 1042, ABV 4.2%) ◔
A brown-coloured best bitter with apple notes and a trace of hops with strong bitter flavour and finish.

Redhouse Premium (OG 1041, ABV 4.2%)
A rich-flavoured pale ale with a clean finish and late hop bitterness.

Big Bog SIBA

c/o Tafarn Snowdonia Parc, Waunfawr, LL55 4AQ
☎ 07769 110791 ⊕ bigbog.co.uk

Big Bog was established in 2011 by Paul Jefferies of Hydes Brewery. The brewery, which shares its site with the Snowdonia Parc brewpub, underwent rapid expansion in 2013 and now supplies 85 outlets direct. ◆

Bog Standard Bitter (OG 1036, ABV 3.6%)
A light-coloured session ale with medium bitterness and a distinctive hoppy finish.

Hinkypunk (OG 1041, ABV 4.1%)
Hoppy beer with intense citrus notes. Extremely pale in colour.

Welsh Pale Ale (OG 1042, ABV 4.2%)
Tawny-coloured classic British ale with a medium bitterness and dry finish.

Swampy (OG 1044, ABV 4.7%)
Ruby red in colour with a robust bitterness that is offset by a slightly sweet finish owing to the inclusion of muscovado sugar in the recipe.

Quagmire (OG 1058, ABV 6%)
A strong but deceptively easy drinking beer. Mid-brown in colour with a medium to high bitterness.

Bog Super IPA (OG 1068, ABV 7%)
An IPA with a tawny colour, great strength and robust bitterness.

Big Clock

⊟ Grants, 1 Manchester Road, Accrington, Lancashire, BB5 2BQ
☎ (01254) 393938 ⊕ thebigclockbrewery.co.uk

Brewing commenced in 2014. A 6.5-barrel plant is used.

Sunny Boy (ABV 3.8%)
A deep golden hoppy ale with a floral, herbal taste and nose.

100 (ABV 4%)

Pals (ABV 4%)
Easy-drinking light blonde bitter with a floral nose.

Dirty Blonde (ABV 4.2%)
Blonde beer with blackcurrant, lemon and spicy flavours.

Dark Knight (ABV 4.5%)
A velvety stout with a spicy, liquorice taste.

Big Ears

See Ash Valley

Big Hand SIBA

Unit A1, Abbey Close, Redwither Business Park, Wrexham, LL13 9XG
☎ (01978) 660709 ☎ 07946 514238
✉ dave@bighandbrewing.co.uk

◉ Big Hand is a family owned and run brewery that began brewing in 2013 using a 10-barrel plant. It opens on the first Friday of each month for its Weekend Wind Down event where you can enjoy beer served from a bar in the brewery itself. In 2014 its award-winning beer, King's Bane, featured in the Stranger's Bar in the House of Commons. The brewery sponsors the Focus Wales music festival in Wrexham. ‼➡◆

Solaris (OG 1035.9, ABV 3.7%)

King's Bane (OG 1038, ABV 3.9%) ◔

A clean-tasting malty bitter with a fruity aroma and peppery hops evident in the full, smooth mouthfeel.

Seren (OG 1038, ABV 3.9%)

Melyn (OG 1039, ABV 4%) ◆
A malty, hoppy beer with a faint fruit aroma and bittersweet taste. The initial sweet malt flavours combine with hoppy bitterness in the aftertaste.

Bastion (OG 1041, ABV 4.2%)

Tyn-y-Capel Ale (OG 1041, ABV 4.2%)

Domino (OG 1046, ABV 4.4%) ◆
A smooth and fruity stout, quite hoppy and roasty with hints of berries in the initial sweetness leading to a satisfying hoppy finish.

Havok (OG 1049, ABV 5%)

Bad Gorilla (OG 1060, ABV 6%)

Big Lamp

Grange Road, Newburn, Newcastle upon Tyne, NE15 8NL
☎ (0191) 267 1689 ⊕ biglampbrewers.co.uk

⊕Big Lamp started in 1982 and relocated in 1997 to a 55-barrel plant in a former water pumping station. It is the oldest microbrewery in the north-east of England. Around 160 outlets are supplied and two pubs are owned, one of which (the Keelman) is attached to the brewery. ‼ ◆ RAIB

Sunny Daze (OG 1036, ABV 3.6%) ◆
Golden, hoppy session bitter with a clean taste and finish.

Bitter (OG 1039, ABV 3.9%) ◆
A clean-tasting bitter, full of hops and malt. A hint of fruit with a good, hoppy finish.

Lamplight Bitter (OG 1042, ABV 4.2%)
Crisp, light and refreshing ale with a dry aftertaste.

Summerhill Stout (OG 1044, ABV 4.4%) ◆
A rich, tasty stout, dark in colour with a lasting rich roast character. Malty mouthfeel with a lingering finish.

Prince Bishop Ale (OG 1048, ABV 4.8%) ◆
A refreshing, easy-drinking bitter. Golden in colour, full of fruit and hops. Strong bitterness with a spicy, dry finish.

Premium (OG 1052, ABV 5.2%) ◆
Hoppy ale with a good bitter finish.

Keelman Brown (OG 1057, ABV 5.7%)
A full-bodied ale with a hint of toffee.

Big Rabbit (NEW)

Unit 1, Butterleigh Sawmill, Butterleigh, Cullompton, Devon, EX15 1PP
☎ (01884) 308633 ☎ 07926 191089

Office: Olde Mill Ltd, 12 East Street, Suite 101, Epsom, Surrey, KT17 1HX ⊕ oldemill.co.uk

Part of Olde Mill Ltd, of London Cider Company fame, Big Rabbit commenced brewing in 2014 in a former sawmill. There are plans for bottle-conditioned beers during the coming year. The brewery often uses locally sourced ingredients and Herefordshire hops. The company also produces cider and has its own winery. ◆

Unit 1 Red Ale (ABV 4%)

Heavily roasted barley gives this beer a red colour, a bitter note and body. Generous hopping gives added bitterness and aroma.

Wild West Country (ABV 4%)
A light and refreshing session ale with a malty, biscuity flavour.

Black Annie (ABV 4.5%)
A smooth, full-flavoured stout, brewed using West Country chocolate and amber malts, locally sourced barley and oats, and English hops.

Orange Elephant IPA (ABV 4.5%)
A well-hopped Devon IPA. High in bitterness, but balanced by traditional malt sweetness.

Hedgerow Hooligan (ABV 5%)
Pale and amber malts give a subtle malty taste, with bittering and aroma hops, and the addition of wild elderflower to dry hop.

Hop Fodder (ABV 5.1%)
A full-bodied, light amber ale, with a complex hop character and good bitterness and aroma.

Big Shed (NEW)

2 Muckleton Lane, Shawbury, Shrewsbury, SY4 4HF
☎ (01939) 250678 ⊕ bigshedbrewery.co.uk

Big Shed Brewery opened in 2014 on a smallholding in rural North Shropshire using a new 20-barrel plant and brewing in a traditional manner. Three mainstream beers are produced. ◆

Battlefield Gold (ABV 3.8%)
A classic session beer with a touch of darker malts, a dry background and a hint of citrus grapefruit and lemon.

Copper Mine Ale (ABV 3.8%)
A well-rounded Northern best bitter, amber in colour with a hint of chocolate and the earthy flinty/minty flavour of Fuggle hops.

Sentinel Amber Ale (ABV 3.8%)

Engineers Best (ABV 4.2%)
An easy-drinking, golden-coloured pale ale with adequate body and mouthfeel but a restrained malt flavour and a hint of sweetness. The aromatic complex hop flavour has a light lemon/citrus note.

Big Smoke (NEW)

Antelope, 87 Maple Road, Surbiton, Surrey, KT6 4AW
☎ (020) 8339 9721 ☎ 07859 884190
⊕ bigsmokebrew.co.uk

⊠ Big Smoke is a purpose-built brewery established in 2014 in courtyard buildings behind the Antelope pub, Surbiton. The five-barrel brew kit is used twice weekly; a range of core beers and bi-monthly ales are available in the Antelope, the Sussex Arms in Twickenham, the Lyric in Soho, the Express in Brentford and occasionally in other local pubs and at beer festivals. All the ales are unfined and unfiltered, suitable for vegans. ◆

Session Pale Ale (ABV 3.8%)

Dark Wave Porter (ABV 5%)

Electric Eye Pale Ale (ABV 5%)

Underworld Milk Stout (ABV 5%)

Billericay (NEW) SIBA

🏠 Essex Beer Shop, Billericay, Essex, CM12 9LS

☎ (01277) 500121 ☎ 07788 373129
🌐 billericaybrewing.co.uk

Billericay Brewing opened at its present site in 2014, having brewed at Pitfield the previous year. A micropub and beershop are next door. ‼ ⛟

Zeppelin (ABV 3.8%)

Blonde (ABV 4%)

Dickie (ABV 4.2%)

A Mild With No Name (ABV 5.5%)
An easy-drinking strong mild.

Chapel Street Porter (ABV 5.9%)

Mayflower Gold (ABV 6.5%)
A hoppy IPA.

Binghams SIBA

Unit 10, Tavistock Industrial Estate, Ruscombe, Berkshire, RG10 9NJ
☎ (0118) 934 4376 🌐 binghams.co.uk

Binghams began brewing in 2010, producing 40 firkins in each batch. The brewery is situated in an industrial unit on the site of a former brickworks – hence the name of one of the beers. Head brewer Chris Bingham is a member of the local branch of CAMRA and had extensive experience in home-brewing and a local brewery prior to starting up. ‼ ⛟ RAIB

Twyford Tipple (OG 1040, ABV 3.7%)
Tawny-coloured bitter with a good balance of malt and hops in the flavour and a citrus hop finish.

Brickworks Bitter (OG 1047, ABV 4.2%)
Chestnut-coloured best bitter with a sweetish, malty nose. Hops balance the maltiness to give a well-rounded flavour with a slightly nutty hint and a sweet, earthy aftertaste.

Coffee Stout (OG 1056, ABV 5%)
A mellow beer with darks malts that complement the coffee flavour.

Doodle Stout (OG 1056, ABV 5%)
A blend of dark malts provide a complex character. Named after the brewery dog called Stout that happens to be a Labradoodle.

Ginger Doodle Stout (OG 1056, ABV 5%)
A dark stout with a subtle hint of ginger which rounds off the bitterness.

Hot Dog Chilli Stout (OG 1056, ABV 5%)
Doodle Stout with a hint of chilli to provide a warm glow on the aftertaste.

Space Hoppy IPA (OG 1052, ABV 5%)
Pale golden and packed with hops to create a complex flavour and a long citrus finish.

Vanilla Stout (OG 1052, ABV 5%)
Infused with vanilla pods that complement the dark malts to create a smooth-drinking, dark stout.

Bingley (NEW)

Unit 2, Old Mill Yard, Shay Lane, Wilsden, West Yorkshire, BD15 0DR
☎ (01535) 274285 🌐 bingleybrewery.co.uk

Bingley is a small, family-run brewery and opened in 2014 using a six-barrel plant. It is located in a rural setting in the village of Wilsden, part of Bingley Rural Ward. More than 20 outlets are supplied. ‼

Goldy Locks (OG 1039, ABV 4%)

Thirst Brew (OG 1042, ABV 4.3%)

1848 (OG 1046, ABV 4.8%)

3X (OG 1048, ABV 5%)

Blantyre Red (OG 1048, ABV 5%)

Jamestown (OG 1052, ABV 5.4%)

Bird Brain

30 Hailgate, Howden, East Yorkshire, DN14 7SL
☎ (01430) 432166 ☎ 07790 615915
✉ birdbrainbrewery@tiscali.co.uk

Bird Brain began brewing in 2009 on a two-barrel plant expanded to four barrel capacity in 2012. Brewing twice a month, the brewery supplies local pubs and beer festivals. ♦

Shiny (OG 1038, ABV 3.9%)

Howden Bittern (OG 1039, ABV 4%)

Bird's SIBA

Ladybird Barn, Old Burcot Lane, Bromsgrove, Worcestershire, B60 1PH
☎ (01527) 889870 🌐 birdsbrewery.co.uk

Bird's began brewing in 2009, supplying its beers to pubs across the West Midlands. One-off brews are produced for special events. ‼ ⛟ ♦ RAIB

Mild High Club (OG 1037, ABV 3.7%)
A traditional mild. A full malty flavour gives way to a dry finish with a creamy nutty aftertaste with just a hint of dark chocolate.

Natural Blonde? (OG 1040, ABV 4%)
A refreshing blonde beer. Floral on the nose, plenty of fruit and hops in the mouth with just the right amount of malt to balance. A pleasant hoppy aftertaste with a gentle crisp bitter finish.

Nightjar (OG 1040, ABV 4%)
An easy-drinking, well-balanced, smooth malty beer with a hint of sweetness and a distinctive nutty finish.

Amnesia (OG 1045, ABV 4.5%)
A pale straw-coloured ale with a fruity zest, a slight orange citrus undertone combining with a mixture of hops to provide a dry hoppy finish.

Black Widow Stout (OG 1045, ABV 4.5%)
A traditional smooth and satisfying stout. A roasted malt flavour with a bitter edge and overtones of blackcurrant, raisins and liquorice.

Skullduggery (OG 1052, ABV 5.2%)
A strong tawny-coloured ale, well-rounded with an initial sweetness followed by hoppiness provided with tones of molasses.

Bishop Nick SIBA

33 East Street, Braintree, Essex, CM7 3JJ
☎ (01376) 349605 🌐 bishopnick.com

Bishop Nick was launched in 2011 by Nelion Ridley, a member of the family that ran Ridley's brewery near Chelmsford. In 2013 a new brewery was establihsed in Braintree using a 20-barrel plant. Three regular beers are brewed and additional regular seasonal beers. A brewery shop opened in 2014. ⛟ ♦ RAIB

Ridley's Rite (OG 1036, ABV 3.6%)

Heresy (OG 1041, ABV 4%)

1555 (OG 1043, ABV 4.3%)

Bishop's Crook SIBA

51 Woodford Close, Penwortham, Lancashire, PR1 9BX ☎ 07516 478003
bishopscrookbrewery.com

A small brewery based at the home of one of the owners, it started brewing commercially in 2013 and currently has just a handful of regular outlets.

Withy Way (OG 1038, ABV 3.8%)
A light pale ale with floral, citrus and tropical flavours.

Ah Fuggit (OG 1040, ABV 4%)
A copper-coloured ale brewed with traditional English hops with a citrus twist.

Initiate (OG 1040, ABV 4%)
A golden ale with strong citrus and tropical fruit flavours.

Brown Edge (OG 1041, ABV 4.1%)
A chestnut-coloured ale with slight malty tones and a hoppy finish.

Lancashire's Invaders (OG 1042, ABV 4.2%)
A dark golden ale, well hopped and providing a burst of grapefruit, lemon and pine.

Bishop's Stortford

Correspondence: 24 Trinity Street, Bishop's Stortford, Hertfordshire, CM23 3TJ
☎ (01279) 503224
bishopsstortfordbrewery@hotmail.co.uk

Established in 2012, the brewery has produced beer on various other brewer's equipment. Since the start of 2014 the brewery has used spare capacity at Ash Valley Brewery (qv) in Green Tye, Hertfordshire. ♦

SPA (Stortford Pale Ale) (OG 1042, ABV 3.8%)
Burnished gold in colour with a full, fruity hop character and soft bitterness.

American Graffiti (OG 1044, ABV 3.9%)
A dark mild with a tropical flavour.

Stortford Sunrise (OG 1043, ABV 4%)
A gold-coloured session beer with subtle bitterness, a peachy hop aroma and a soft, toffee-like malt character.

BSB (Bishop's Stortford Bitter) (OG 1044, ABV 4.1%)
A traditional English bitter, deep copper in colour with a smooth malt flavour.

Stortford Sunset (OG 1045, ABV 4.2%)
A rich, amber-coloured beer with a pronounced malt flavour and smooth, orangy character.

Stortford Oat Stout (OG 1048, ABV 4.8%)
Smooth stout with a full mouthfeel.

Good Hope IPA (OG 1051, ABV 5.2%)
A modern IPA with a honeyed malt base and tropical New World hops.

TSA (Traditional Strong Ale) (OG 1063, ABV 6.2%)
Deep ruby in colour with a full malt flavour and blackcurrant character.

Bitter End

See Tirril

Black Bear (NEW)

c/o Black Bear Inn, 8-10 North Street, Wiveliscombe, Somerset, TA4 2JY
☎ (01984) 623537 liquidbrighton1@gmail.com

Originally named East Stratton, brewing began in 2014 and was based at the Northbrook Arms in East Stratton, Hampshire. The brewery relocated and was renamed in 2015. Seasonal beers are planned.

Wivey Best (ABV 3.8%)
Copper-coloured bitter, brewed with Cascade and Northdown hops.

Wivey Pure (ABV 3.8%)
A golden version of Wivey Best.

Black Cat SIBA

Unit 12, Knights Business Centre, Squires Farm Industrial Estate, Palehouse Common, Framfield, East Sussex, TN22 5RB blackcat-brewery.com

Black Cat began brewing in 2011 in Groombridge using a 2.5-barrel plant, suppying three to four local pubs. It has now relocated to Framfield, expanded and is owned and run by husband and wife team, Paul and Kate. ♦RAIB

Hopsmack (OG 1040, ABV 4%)
A golden beer, refreshing and hoppy with citrus overtones.

Original (OG 1042, ABV 4.2%)
A hoppy, bitter, amber-coloured beer balanced with malt.

Black Cat (OG 1049, ABV 4.9%)

Black Country SIBA

Rear of Old Bulls Head, 1 Redhall Road, Lower Gornal, West Midlands, DY3 2NU
☎ (01384) 401820

Office: 69 Third Avenue, Pensett Trading Estate, Kingswinford, West Midlands, DY6 7FD
blackcountryinns.co.uk

Originally brewing at the rear of the Old Bulls Head since 2004, the brewery relocated in 2015. Beers are also brewed under the Thomas Guest Brewing Company name. ‼♦

Bradley's Finest Golden (OG 1040, ABV 4.2%)
A straw-coloured quaffing beer with a bold citrus hop aroma, fruity balanced sweetness and a lingering, refreshing aftertaste.

Pig on the Wall (OG 1042, ABV 4.3%)
A refreshing chestnut brown beer with a complex flavour of light hops giving way to a bittersweet blend of roasted malt. Suggestions of chocolate and coffee undertones.

Fireside (OG 1047, ABV 5%)
A well-rounded premium bitter, amber in colour, clean in taste leading to a pleasant, dry finish.

Black Dog

See Hambleton

Black Flag

Unit 4D, Bridge Road Industrial Estate, Goonhavern, Cornwall, TR4 9QL
☎ (01872) 858004 ⊕ blackflagbrewery.com

⊗ Black Flag began brewing in 2013 using an eight-barrel plant. Much use is made of New Zealand and US hops. ◆RAIB

Chameleon (OG 1038, ABV 3.8%) ◣
Golden ale. Grassy and floral hops throughout. Punchy lemon citrus flavour with apricot and peaches. Bitter, dry and crisp finish.

Fang (OG 1040, ABV 4%) ◣
Light amber-coloured best bitter with hop aroma. Orange and tart grapefruit throughout, balanced by light malt. Light hop bitter finish.

Nancarrow Barn Ale (OG 1040, ABV 4%)
Easy-drinking tawny-coloured ale with a balance of nectarine and biscuit tones throughout with a drying aftertaste.

Naughty Pilchard (OG 1040, ABV 4%) ◣
Pale brown best bitter with malt aroma. Malt flavour with a sharp bite of hops. Dry, malty and citrus finish.

Blonde (OG 1042, ABV 4.2%) ◣
Golden beer with hoppy citrus nose. Mainly hop taste with sweet oranges and some roast malt. Bitter and hoppy finish.

White Cross IPA (OG 1057, ABV 5.7%) ◣
Amber beer with fruity and malty aroma. Powerful hop bitterness with fruit sweetness, grapefruit and apple. Dry and bitter finish.

Black Hole SIBA

Unit 63GF, IMEX Business Park, Shobnall Road, Burton upon Trent, Staffordshire, DE14 2AU
☎ (01283) 619943 ☎ 07864 966452
⊕ blackholebrewery.co.uk

⊗ Black Hole was established in 2007 with a purpose-built 10-barrel plant in the former Ind Coope bottling stores. Fermenting capacity was increased in 2012 to enable the production of up to four brews per week. Around 600 outlets, mainly in the Midlands, are supplied direct, and many more via wholesalers. The brewery was bought by the owners of Mr Grundy's Brewery (qv) in 2014. ‼◆

Bitter (OG 1040, ABV 3.8%) ◣
Amber glow and malt and spicy hop aroma. Fresh lively session beer hopped to give a clean, crisp finish of hoppy dryness and a touch of astringency.

Cosmic (OG 1044, ABV 4.2%) ◣
Almost golden with an initial malt aroma. The complex balance of malt and English hops give lingering tastes of nuts, fruit and a dry hoppy bitterness.

Red Dwarf (OG 1045, ABV 4.5%) ◣
Red as named with a sweetshop start of sugary sweet fruits with citrus centres. Malt is elbowed aside by the hops which dominate the tongue-tickling bitter end.

Supernova (OG 1048, ABV 4.8%) ◣
Pure gold. Like marmalade made from Seville oranges and grapefruit, the aroma mimics the sweet start but gives into the hops which deliver a dry, lingering bitter finish.

Cyborg (OG 1055, ABV 5.5%)

A rich golden ale with a citrus aroma and bitter taste.

Milky Way (OG 1059, ABV 6%) ◣
Honey and banana nose advises the sweet taste but not the sweet, dry spicy finish from this wheat beer.

Black Horse SIBA 👁

26 Nottingham Court, Nottingham Road, Louth, Lincolnshire, LN11 0WB
☎ (01507) 354331

Office: Freshwater Cottage, 2 Chapel Brow, Charlesworth, Glossop, Derbyshire, SK13 5HH
⊕ blackhorsebrewing.co.uk

⊗Black Horse began brewing in 2012. A five-barrel plant is currently used. The brewery boasts a retail outlet and a fully licensed bar, where events including tasting sessions and beer festivals are held each year. It trades on local markets and the beers are to be found in various retail outlets. ⌐

Mild Midlander (OG 1034, ABV 3.4%)
A dark, rich and creamy mild with notes of roasted coffee.

Bitter Feud (OG 1038, ABV 3.8%)
Amber-coloured ale with a complex butterscotch taste.

Lincolnshire Traditional Bitter (OG 1038, ABV 3.8%)
A traditional English session bitter with a smooth finish.

Wheres My Fiorucci (OG 1038, ABV 3.8%)
Amber-coloured session beer with delicate malt flavours and a slightly spicy aroma.

Queens (OG 1040, ABV 4%)
A full-bodied golden ale.

Pleasant Blonde (OG 1042, ABV 4.2%)
Refreshing blonde ale with a clean citrus hop flavour and flowery grapefruit aroma.

Saturdays Blonde (OG 1042, ABV 4.2%)
A delicate pale ale bittered with carefully selected citrus hops, leaving a subtle yet refreshing aftertaste.

Black Frog (OG 1044, ABV 4.6%)
Dark English ale with complex malt flavours, nicely bittered with a slight smoky aroma.

Nicholas de Luda (OG 1050, ABV 5.4%)
A rich, dark, old-style English stout, full-bodied and packed with flavour.

Thanks Pa (OG 1057, ABV 6%)
Traditional strength IPA with a floral bouquet and citrus finish.

Black Iris SIBA

Unit 1, Shipstone Street, New Basford, Nottingham, NG7 6GJ
☎ (0115) 979 1936 ✉ blackirisbrewery@gmail.com

Black Iris began brewing in 2011 using a six-barrel plant behind the Flowerpot pub in Derby. It expanded to a brand new 10-barrel plant in 2014 and relocated to premises in Nottingham. ‼◆

Snake Eyes (OG 1038, ABV 3.8%)
An American-hopped pale ale.

Bleeding Heart (OG 1044, ABV 4.5%)

A hoppy red beer with a dry finish from the rye malt.

Better the Devil You Know (OG 1053, ABV 5.5%)
Pale, citrus, Australian-style IPA with big fruity aromas and a lingering bitterness.

Black Isle

Old Allengrange, Munlochy, Ross-shire, IV8 8NZ
☎ (01463) 811871 ⊕ blackislebrewery.com

☺Black Isle Brewery was set up in 1998 in the heart of the Scottish Highlands. It expanded substantially in 2011 with a new brewhouse and bottling line. All beers are organic with Soil Association certification. !! ☞ ♦

Yellowhammer (OG 1038, ABV 3.9%) ◥
A refreshing, hoppy golden ale with light hop and passion fruit throughout. A short bitter finish.

Red Kite (OG 1042, ABV 4.2%) ◥
Tawny ale with light malt on the nose and some fruit on the palate. Slight sweetness in the taste and a short bitter finish.

Heather Honey (OG 1045, ABV 4.6%) ◥
Sweet honey-flavoured brew.

Porter (OG 1046, ABV 4.6%) ◥
A hint of liquorice and burnt chocolate on the nose and a creamy mix of malt and fruit in the taste.

Black Metal (NEW)

Unit 3, 6B Dryden Road, Loanhead, EH20 9LZ
☎ (0131) 623 3411 ☎ 07711 295385
⊕ blackmetalbrewery.com

Black Metal Brewery was established in 2012 by two old friends, originally brewing from home. A 1000-litre plant is now used, sharing equipment at Top Out (qv) brewery. All beers are suitable for vegans. RAIB

Will-o'-the-Wisp (OG 1057, ABV 6%)
A juniper smoked ale. Full-bodied with a slightly smoky flavour and fruity aftertaste.

Blood Revenge (OG 1065, ABV 6.6%)
A rye stout.

Yggdrasil (OG 1056, ABV 6.6%)
A strong, full-bodied pale ale, fruity, aromatic and slightly bitter.

Black Paw SIBA

Unit 4, Westgate Road, Bishop Auckland, County Durham, DL14 7AX
☎ (01388) 602144 ☎ 07557 020664
⊕ blackpawbrewery.co.uk

Black Paw began brewing in 2011 using a 12-barrel plant and now supplies pubs across the north east of England. Occasional open days are held. ♦

Bishop's Best (OG 1038, ABV 3.8%)
Tasty session bitter with a slight hint of chocolate.

Paw's Gold (OG 1040, ABV 4%)
A rich golden bitter with a malt and hop taste developing.

Archbishop's Ale (OG 1041, ABV 4.1%)
Full-flavoured and smooth.

Polar Paw (OG 1044, ABV 4.4%)
Bittersweet dark ale with a pleasant hoppy aroma and aftertaste.

Dark Seam (OG 1050, ABV 5%)
A deliciously dark and full-flavoured beer with chocolate taste and a hint of coffee.

IPA (OG 1050, ABV 5%)
Amber-coloured and brewed to an American recipe, there is a strong complex aroma and a refreshing bitter finish.

Black Rock SIBA

Unit 6c, Empire Way, Tregoniggie Industrial Estate, Falmouth, Cornwall, TR11 4SN
☎ (01326) 379477 ⊕ blackrockbrewing.com

⊗ Black Rock began brewing in 2013. Beers are available in Five Degrees West in Falmouth and a number of other local outlets. Further beers are planned plus a bottling line. RAIB

Pale Ale (OG 1042, ABV 4.2%) ◥
Light-tasting golden best bitter with faint hop aroma. Hops, tropical fruits, honey and earthy malt flavours. Persistent fruity aftertaste.

Deep (OG 1058, ABV 5%) ◥
Earthy, light hop and malt aroma. Strong hop bitterness in the mouth balanced by sweet fruit. Pear flavour aftertaste.

Black IPA (OG 1058, ABV 6%) ◥
Strong black porter with roast malt throughout. Smooth, rich flavours of raisins and cloves. Moderate hop bitterness, fading slowly.

Black Sheep SIBA ◉

Wellgarth, Masham, Ripon, North Yorkshire, HG4 4EN
☎ (01765) 689227 ⊕ blacksheepbrewery.co.uk

☺Established 1992 by Paul Theakston, a member of Masham's famous brewing family, in the former Wellgarth Maltings using the traditional Yorkshire Square fermenting system. The company now supplies around 600 free trade outlets, with national exposure through pubcos and wholesale channels, but owns no pubs. Production is 75% cask with the remainder bottled. Paul has now handed over operations to his sons. !! ☞ ♦

Best Bitter (OG 1038, ABV 3.8%) ◥
A hoppy and fruity beer with strong bitter overtones, leading to a long, dry, bitter finish.

Golden Sheep (OG 1039, ABV 3.9%)
A balanced blonde beer with a dry and refreshing bitterness. Light golden in colour with fresh citrus fruit flavours and a clean, crisp finish.

Ale (OG 1044, ABV 4.4%)
A premium bitter with robust fruit, malt and hops.

Riggwelter (OG 1059, ABV 5.9%) ◥
A fruity bitter, with complex underlying tastes and hints of liquorice and pear drops leading to a long, dry, bitter finish.

Black Tor SIBA

Unit 5, Gidley's Industrial Estate, Christow, Exeter, Devon, EX6 7QB
☎ (01647) 252120 ⊕ blacktorbrewery.co.uk

Brewing began on this site in 1998 under the Scattor Rock name using a five-barrel plant. The brewery changed hands in 2009, trading under the Gidley's name, before another change of hands in 2013 when it became Black Tor. It changed hands again in 2015. The brewery is located in the Teign

Valley in the beautiful East Dartmoor National Park. Outlets are supplied in Devon and on the Cornwall border.

Pride of Dartmoor (OG 1040, ABV 4%)
A mid-brown session bitter with a gentle floral aroma and pleasant taste.

Resolution (OG 1044, ABV 4.4%)
A smooth, full-flavoured malty bitter with a gentle, sweet finish.

Dartmoor Pale Ale (OG 1045, ABV 4.5%)

Tor Ale (OG 1048, ABV 4.8%)
A deep golden brown ale with a hoppy aroma and sweet, malty finish.

Templer's IPA (OG 1056, ABV 5.6%)
Classic IPA flavours with a gentle dark fruit twist.

Black Wolf

VC2 Brands, Unit 7c, Bandeath Industrial Estate, Throsk, Stirling, FK7 7NP
☎ (01786) 817000 🌐 blackwolfbrewery.com

Established in 2005, and now owned by VC2 Brands, the brewery is located in a former torpedo factory on the shores of the River Forth. In 2014 the brewery changed its name from Traditional Scottish Ales to Black Wolf Brewery and rebranded its range of award-winning beers. ♦

Nevis (ABV 4%)
A chestnut-red ale, malty and full-bodied with a lightly-hopped aftertaste.

Glencoe (ABV 4.5%)
A stout with plenty of malt and roast balanced by fruit and finished with a hint of hop.

William Wallace (ABV 4.5%)
A dark ale, hoppy and fruity with a hint of toffee.

Lomond Gold (ABV 5%)
A golden ale, zesty with a floral aroma with a hint of citrus. Light with a sweet taste.

BlackBar

Unit B3, Button End Industrial Estate, Harston, Cambridgeshire, CB22 7GX
☎ (01223) 872131 ☎ 07811 499914
🌐 blackbar.co.uk

BlackBar was established in 2011. Around 10 outlets, mostly in the Cambridge area, are supplied direct. Mini-casks are also available. RAIB

Bitter (ABV 3.6%)
A malty, tawny brown-coloured bitter with a noble hop finish.

Blacklight (ABV 4%)
A blonde beer with hops on the nose.

Porteur (ABV 4%)
A malty brown-coloured porter.

Black Economy (ABV 4.6%)

Blackbeck

Blackbeck Inn, Blackbeck, Egremont, Cumbria, CA22 2NY
☎ (01946) 841661 🌐 blackbeckbrewery.co.uk

A five-barrel brewery, established in 2009 and owned by a father and daughter team, producing hand-crafted ales using English malts and hops. Beers have fairground themed names and are also available in bottles and mini casks. ♦

Belle (OG 1038, ABV 3.8%)
A sweet, tasty, dark mild.

Trial Run (OG 1037, ABV 3.8%)
A fresh and fruity yellow beer with a lasting hoppy finish.

Blackedge SIBA

Shuttle House, Hampson Street, Horwich, BL6 7JH
☎ (01204) 692976 ☎ 07795 654895
🌐 blackedgebrewery.co.uk

Blackedge Brewery, established in 2011, is a traditional five-barrel brewery producing hand-crafted ales using only natural ingredients. No extracts or pellets are used in the brewing process. A core range of ten beers is permanently available with special seasonal ales brewed monthly. The brewery houses a shop selling hand bottled beers and various branded gifts. !! ♦ RAIB

Session (OG 1038, ABV 3.5%)
A golden session bitter, surprisingly full bodied with a grapefruit flavour and aroma.

HoP (OG 1039, ABV 3.8%)
Generously-hopped to give a clean, dry refreshing and hoppy citrus, floral-flavoured session beer.

Black (OG 1047, ABV 4%)
A velvety stout with intense roasted barley flavours and rich undertones of chocolate and coffee with a liquorice finish.

Pike (OG 1042, ABV 4%)
A pale ale with plenty of sweet, citrus hop flavour.

American Pale Ale (OG 1043, ABV 4.2%)
Light hoppy beer made using American hops giving intense citrus aromas.

Platinum (OG 1046, ABV 4.4%)
Blonde ale, light in colour, lightly hopped to give a clean, citrus flavour and sweet citrus aroma.

BLONDe (OG 1046, ABV 4.5%)
Full-flavoured, full-bodied blonde ale, well-hopped to give a clean, crisp fruit-like flavour and aroma.

Dark Rum (OG 1045, ABV 4.6%)
Dark rich porter with roasted coffee and chocolate flavours, hints of liquorice and finished with sweetness from the dark rum.

IPA (OG 1047, ABV 4.7%)
Full-bodied, full-flavoured and well-balanced hoppy and intensely citrus IPA with a grapefruit aroma.

Black Port (OG 1045, ABV 4.9%)
Black beer with malty, fruity aroma. Rich, with chocolate and dark fruits to taste with a slightly drier finish.

Blackhill SIBA

Pontop Business Park, Harelaw Industrial Estate, Stanley, County Durham, DH9 8HN ☎ 07905 788286
🌐 blackhillbrewery.com

Blackhill began brewing in 2012 using spare capacity at Geltsdale Brewery. In 2013 it moved to its own premises using a 10-barrel plant. Beers are named after Durham coal mining seams. Further beers are available on rotation: see website. ♦

70 Fathom (ABV 4%)

Blackjack SIBA

36 Gould Street, Manchester, M4 4RN
☎ (0161) 819 2767 ⊕ blackjack-beers.com

⊕ Blackjack started brewing in 2012 using a 4.5-barrel plant, producing a large range of regular beers, many using Belgian and farmhouse yeasts. Beers are named with a playing card theme, and are widely available in the local free trade as well as further afield. A number of house beers are brewed for selected pubs. Most beers are suitable for vegans.

Pokies (OG 1039, ABV 3.9%)
Extra pale New Zealand-hopped session bitter.

Shuffled Deck (OG 1039, ABV 3.9%)
Aromas are marmalade with pine and grapefruit. Flavours are woody with sweet citrus and bitter grapefruit with a dry finish.

Bramling Cross (OG 1040, ABV 4%)
Single-hopped best bitter.

New Deck (OG 1042, ABV 4.2%)
A crisp hoppy ale with a satisfying finish.

Solitaire (OG 1042, ABV 4.3%)
A pale session ale with a blend of lager malt and Maris Otter, simply hopped with delicate US and German varieties.

First Deal (OG 1044, ABV 4.4%)
A ruby-coloured ale with a dried fruit aroma with flavour of berries, earthy malts and a spicy, bitter finish.

Small Saison (OG 1042, ABV 4.5%)
Spicy and dry.

Double Bluff (OG 1048, ABV 4.8%)
An amber ale with full aroma and bitter notes.

River (OG 1049, ABV 4.8%)
Brown ale with farmhouse yeast.

Beginner's Luck (OG 1050, ABV 5%)
All American Cascade-hopped pale ale. Punchy fruit aroma with a golden IPA bitterness and colour.

Black Maria (OG 1057, ABV 5%)
A dark ale with a hoppy aroma, light body and a stout-like colour.

Stout (OG 1050, ABV 5%)
Aroma is roasted malts and chocolate syrup. Flavour is similar with a hint of maple syrup and light bitter hops. Finish is slightly fruity.

Aces High (OG 1055, ABV 5.5%)
Aroma has some ripe citrus notes of melon and orange. Flavour is sweet with mild grass and pine, along with more ripe tangerine and melon.

Dragon's Tears (OG 1054, ABV 5.8%)

Four of a Kind (OG 1060, ABV 6.2%)
American-style IPA hopped with a blend of four US varieties.

Brewed for the Anchorage, Sheffield:

Anchorage (ABV 3.4%)

Brewed for the Crescent, Salford:

Crescent Ale (ABV 4%)

Brewed for the Jack in the Box, Altrincham

House Pale (OG 1040, ABV 4%)
English-hopped pale ale.

Brewed for the Moorbrook, Preston:

Moorbrook Pale Ale (ABV 3.9%)

A citrusy pale ale.

Blackmore

🏠 Trooper Inn, Golden Hill, Stourton Caundle, Dorset, DT10 2JW
☎ (01963) 362405 ✉ kevinstaunton@aol.com

⊗ This small 0.5-barrel brewpub began brewing in 2011. One beer from the range of two is produced each week.

Ale (OG 1038, ABV 3.8%)

Pale (OG 1042, ABV 4.2%)

Blackwater

See Salopian

Blakemere

Blakemere Craft Centre, Chester Road, Sandiway, Northwich, Cheshire, CW8 2EB
☎ (01606) 301000 ☎ 07768 790300

Formerly known as Northern, brewing began in 2003 on a five-barrel plant in Runcorn. In 2005 the brewery was renamed and relocated to a larger unit at Blakemere Craft Centre. Bottle-conditioned beers are available from the on-site shop. ◆RAIB

Freshly Squeezed (OG 1039, ABV 3.8%)

Bobby Dazzler (OG 1040, ABV 3.9%)

Navajo (OG 1039, ABV 3.9%)

Black Mamba (OG 1040, ABV 4%)

Soul Rider (OG 1042, ABV 4%)

Cherry Baby Mild (OG 1040, ABV 4.1%)

Gold (OG 1046, ABV 4.3%)

Hit & Run (OG 1044, ABV 4.5%)

Jewel IPA (OG 1046, ABV 4.6%)

Chilli Chocolate Stout (OG 1045, ABV 5%)

Fruit Stout (ABV 5%)

Summit Special (OG 1049, ABV 5%)
A fruity premium bitter made from a single hop variety.

Two Tone Special (OG 1049, ABV 5%)

Deep Dark Secret (OG 1050, ABV 5.2%) 🍺

Cosmic IPA (OG 1057, ABV 6%)
A highly-hopped, strong IPA.

Blindmans SIBA

Talbot Farm, Leighton, Frome, Somerset, BA11 4PN
☎ (01749) 880038 ⊕ blindmansbrewery.co.uk

Established in 2002 in a converted milking parlour and purchased by its current owners in 2004, this five-barrel brewery has its own water spring. The range of ales is regularly on tap at the Cornerhouse, Frome. ‼◆

Buff (OG 1036, ABV 3.6%)
Amber-coloured, smooth session beer.

Golden Spring (OG 1040, ABV 4%)
Fresh and aromatic straw-coloured beer, brewed using selected lager malt.

Mine Beer (OG 1042, ABV 4.2%)
Full-bodied, copper-coloured, blended malt ale.

Icarus (OG 1045, ABV 4.5%)
Fruity, rich, mid-dark ruby ale.

Bloomsbury (NEW)

Perseverance, 63 Lamb's Conduit Street, Bloomsbury, London, WC1N 3NB
☎ (020) 7405 8278

Based in the cellar of the Perseverance pub, brewing began in 2015. Three core beers are produced plus a seasonal. ♦

Best Bitter (ABV 4.1%)

Pale Ale (ABV 4.1%)

IPA (ABV 4.2%)

Blue Anchor SIBA

50 Coinagehall Street, Helston, Cornwall, TR13 8EL
☎ (01326) 562821 spingoales.com

15th-century thatched brewpub, the oldest continuously brewing plant in the country. Home of the famous Spingo ales, which are produced from the well water beneath the pub. ‼♦RAIB

Flora Daze (OG 1040, ABV 4%)
A well-hopped bitter with a strong floral/citrus aroma from a late addition of hops. A good hop flavour with a smooth, delicate and dry finish.

Jubilee IPA (OG 1045, ABV 4.6%)
Copper-coloured best bitter with fruity hop aroma. Biscuit malt and fresh hop bitter taste. Long, bitter finish with rising dryness.

Ben's Stout (OG 1048, ABV 4.8%)
A classic stout complemented by the brewery's sweet spring water.

Spingo Middle (OG 1050, ABV 5.1%)
Sweet and creamy, brown, strong bitter. Dried fruit and roast in aroma. Malt flavour throughout with plums, apples and melon.

Spingo Special (OG 1066, ABV 6.7%)
Smooth, red, strong old ale. Red wine aroma. Powerful flavours of sweet stone fruits, malt and hops. Vinous but delicate.

Blue Bear SIBA

Unit 5, Empire House, 11 New Street, Smethwick, West Midlands, B66 2AJ
☎ (0121) 565 5622 info@bluebearbrewery.com

Blue Bear brewery, formerly in Worcestershire, relocated to an industrial unit in Smethwick on the outskirts of Birmingham. The nine-barrel plant produces a selection of beers, most of it under contract for the now defunct Highgate & Davenports brewery of Walsall. Much of the beer is keg but cask-conditioned beers are now being promoted.

Wanderlust (OG 1038.8, ABV 3.8%)

Amarillo Armadillo (OG 1042.8, ABV 4.2%)

Contract brewed under the Highgate & Davenports brand name:

Highgate Dark Mild (OG 1036.8, ABV 3.4%)

Davenports England's Glory (OG 1037.5, ABV 4%)

Davenports Original Bitter (OG 1041.8, ABV 4%)

Blue Bee SIBA

Unit 29-30, Hoyland Road Industrial Estate, Sheffield, South Yorkshire, S3 8AB bluebeebrewery.co.uk

Blue Bee was originally set up in 2010 by award-winning brewer Richard Hough and is now operated by a small local pub company, Reet Ale Pubs, with the beer brewed by Josh Jepson. The beers are available to the free trade across Yorkshire, the Midlands and north west England. ‼♦

Light Blue (OG 1036, ABV 3.6%)
A pleasant floral aroma leads to a full fruity flavour and an intense bitter finish.

Bees Knees Bitter (OG 1040, ABV 4%)
A dark bitter, deep chestnut in colour, a distinctive hop character leads to a lasting bitter finish.

Reet Pale (OG 1040, ABV 4%)
Pale with floral and citrus flavours leading to a dry bitter finish.

Lustin for Stout (OG 1048, ABV 4.8%)
A rich, complex stout, full-bodied and black in colour. Plenty of roast malt flavours.

Yekaterrina Alexeevna Russian Imperial Stout (OG 1075, ABV 7%)

Blue Bell

Cranesgate South, Whaplode St Catherine, Lincolnshire, PE12 6SN
☎ (01406) 701000 ☎ 07813 819746

Office: Sycamore House, Lapwater Lane, Holbeach St Marks, PE12 8EX bluebellbrewery.co.uk

The Blue Bell Brewery was founded in 1998 behind the Blue Bell pub. The brewery operates as a separate business from the pub but the pub acts as the brewery tap. Ingledingle Ale is only available in the Blue Bell. ‼♦RAIB

Frightened Pheasant (OG 1037, ABV 3.7%)
A well-balanced, refreshing golden beer.

Old Honesty (OG 1040, ABV 4.1%)
Traditional brew with a full-bodied rounded bitterness.

Ingledingle Ale (OG 1054, ABV 5.1%)

Blue Bell Brewhouse

Blue Bell Cider House, Warings Green Road, Warings Green, Warwickshire, B94 6BP ☎ 07922 554181

A one-barrel plant set up in 2013 to resurrect on-site brewing at the Blue Bell Cider House (brewing ceased in 1968), expanding to a 2.5-barrel plant in 2014. Operated by the ex-head brewer at Weatheroak Hill and the Old Pie Factory, it brews solely for the Blue Bell and local festivals. Initially brewing an ever-changing range, a regular beer is now available.

Harley Barley (ABV 4.2%)
An American-style pale ale.

Blue Cow

High Street, South Witham, Lincolnshire, NG33 5QB
☎ (01572) 768432 bluecowinn.co.uk

⊕Blue Cow is a traditional 13th-century pub with a brewery. The beer is only available in the pub or at CAMRA beer festivals. ‼

Best Bitter (OG 1038, ABV 3.8%)
Hoppy, golden ale, with fresh initial taste.

Witham Wobbler (OG 1046, ABV 4.5%)
Dark amber in colour with a rich malty aromatic nose which leads to an impressive bitterness.

Blue Monkey SIBA

10 Pentrich Road, Giltbrook Industrial Park, Giltbrook, Nottinghamshire, NG16 2UZ
☎ (0800) 028 0329 ⊕ bluemonkeybrewery.com

⊕Blue Monkey was established in 2008 as a 10-barrel plant but moved in 2010 to a bigger site to meet increasing demand. It now brews around 15,000 pints a week to supply more than 200 local outlets and selected national distributors. The name stems from a nickname for the blue flames that used to rise from the chimneys of Stanton Ironworks, a prominent local foundry. ▰

Marmoset (OG 1038, ABV 3.6%) ◆
Highly hopped, citrus-flavoured golden beer with a dry bitter finish.

BG Sips (OG 1041, ABV 4%) ◆
Pale golden hoppy beer, brewed mainly with Brewers Gold hops. Fruity and bitter.

Sanctuary (OG 1041.8, ABV 4.1%) ▣ ◆
Copper-coloured malty beer with German and American hops.

99 Red Baboons (OG 1042, ABV 4.2%) ◆
Red in colour with a malty fruitiness. Not overly hoppy.

Right Turn Clyde (ABV 4.3%)

Infinity (OG 1045.7, ABV 4.6%) ▣ ◆
Golden ale packed with Citra hops.

Guerrilla (OG 1052, ABV 4.9%) ◆
A creamy stout, full of roast malt flavour and a slightly sweet finish.

Ape Ale (OG 1052, ABV 5.4%) ▢ ◆
Intensely hopped, strong golden ale with a dry bitter finish.

Blueball

Kash 22, 22 Church Street, Frodsham, Cheshire, WA6 6QW
☎ (01928) 733116

⊕Blueball originally started brewing as Bridgewater Brewery in 2010 behind a homebrew shop in Frodsham. The business relocated to Runcorn and expanded later the same year using a five-barrel plant. A bar and restaurant, Kash, opened in Chester in 2011. In 2013 the brewery relocated to a newly opened second bar in Frodsham. ◆ RAIB

Indie Girl (OG 1036, ABV 3.8%)
A pale golden ale with a citrus and tropical fruit aroma. The finish is clean and dry with a long, hoppy aftertaste.

Gold Digger (OG 1038, ABV 4%)
Golden in colour with a subtle malt profile giving way to a tropical fruit explosion from the hops.

Reservation (OG 1050, ABV 5.2%)

Zeppelin (OG 1053, ABV 5.5%)

Spank (Industrial IPA) (OG 1059, ABV 6%)
Sweetish strong ale.

Bluestone (Lancashire) SIBA

Unit 6, Daniel Street Industrial Estate, Whitworth, Lancashire, OL12 8BX
☎ (01706) 853009 ☎ 07802 792536
⊕ bluestonebrewery.co.uk

Bluestone is a small 3.5-barrel brewery using traditional methods including 'double dropping' fermentation. Brewing currently only takes place at the weekend.

Quarrymans Stout (OG 1041, ABV 4%)
A black stout, full of traditional flavour.

EPA (English Pale Ale) (OG 1042, ABV 4.2%)
A traditional dry pale ale with strong malt and hop flavours.

Night Hops Stout (OG 1043, ABV 4.2%)
Dark, dry stout with a good hop flavour through the roasted malt, liquorice and spice.

AKA (Amber Kitchen Ale) (OG 1043, ABV 4.4%)
Based on an old recipe this is a mild/brown ale, lightly hopped with a caramel and liquorice malty flavour.

Spodden Pilsner (OG 1048, ABV 4.4%)
A full-bodied Bohemian-style Pilsner. Hoppy and full-flavoured.

Bluestone (Pembrokeshire) SIBA

Tiriet, Cilgwyn, Pembrokeshire, SA42 0QW
☎ (01239) 820833 ⊕ bluestonebrewing.co.uk

A family-run business established in 2013 on a working organic hill farm in the Preseli Hills within the Pembrokeshire Coast National Park. The 10-barrel brewery has been installed in a renovated 200-year-old stone barn, which also doubles as a cold store and office. The brewery uses water from a private supply which filters down through the Preseli Hills. Numerous local outlets are supplied as well as wholesalers around the UK. ‼♦

Rockhopper (OG 1039, ABV 3.9%)
A classic pale amber-coloured bitter with a light malt base and a spicy fruitiness from the hops.

Bedrock Blonde (OG 1040, ABV 4.5%)
A straw-coloured blonde ale with creamy soft malt flavours.

Elderflower Blonde (OG 1040, ABV 4.5%)
Straw-coloured, delicately hopped, and finished with a hint of elderflower.

Hammerstone IPA (OG 1044, ABV 4.5%)
A modern IPA providing a fruity, effervescent and refreshing taste.

Rocketeer (OG 1046, ABV 4.6%)
A traditional full-bodied bitter with a rich, malty base.

Blythe SIBA

Blythe House Farm, Lichfield Road, Hamstall Ridware, Staffordshire, WS15 3QQ ☎ 07773 747724
⊕ blythebrewery.co.uk

⊗ Blythe began brewing in 2003 using a 2.5-barrel plant in a converted barn. 15 outlets are supplied direct. ‼♦ RAIB

Ridware Pale (OG 1042, ABV 4.3%) ◆
Bright and golden with a bitter floral hop aroma and citrus taste. Good and hop-sharp, bitter and refreshing. Long, lingering bite with ripples of citrus across the tongue.

Chase Bitter (OG 1044, ABV 4.4%) ◆
Fresh fruity aroma touched by malt from this amber beer. Sweet biscuity start with caramel support and fruit hints. Hops emerge to give a satisfyingly bitter finish.

Staffie (OG 1044, ABV 4.4%) ◆
Hoppy and grassy aroma with hints of sweetness from this amber beer. A touch of malt at the start is soon overwhelmed by hops. A full hoppy, mouth-watering finish.

Palmers Poison (OG 1045, ABV 4.5%) ◆
Refreshing dark beer. Tawny but light headed. Coffee truffle aroma, pleasingly sweet to start but with a good hop mouthfeel.

Johnsons (OG 1056, ABV 5.2%) ◆
Black with a thick head. Refreshingly hoppy and full-bodied with lingering bitterness of chocolate, dates, coal smoke and liquorice.

Bob's SIBA

Healey Brewery, Brewers Pride, Low Mill Road, Healey, West Yorkshire, WF5 8ND ☎ 07789 693597

The brewery was founded in 2002 by Bob Hunter in outbuildings behind the Red Lion pub and moved to a new 10-barrel plant, part of the original Ossett brewhouse, in 2009. Production is up to 650 gallons a week and the beers appear regularly in more than 25 freehouses across West Yorkshire and in the West Midlands via wholesalers. !! ♦

White Lion (OG 1043, ABV 4.3%)
Pale, flowery, lager-style beer.

Chardonnayle (OG 1051.5, ABV 5.1%)
Complex strong pale ale with hints of lemongrass and fruits, aroma hops dominating the flavour.

Boggart Hole Clough SIBA

Building 7, Wilsons Park, Monsall Road, Newton Heath, Manchester, M40 8WN
☎ (0161) 277 9666 boggart-brewery.co.uk

A continually growing brewery, now an eight-barrel plant in its third home, with its own distribution arm, working extensively with north-west breweries and outlets. Monthly specials and unique commissions are available. ♦RAIB

Cascade (OG 1040, ABV 4%)
A bitter, hoppy session ale.

Dark Mild (OG 1040, ABV 4%)
A classic dark mild.

Mud Brawler (ABV 4.5%)
A robust porter complemented with fresh vanilla.

Rum Porter (OG 1046, ABV 4.6%)
A classic porter with a smooth roast finish, enhanced by a sweet, spicy hop taste, complemented with a hint of dark rum.

Bollington SIBA

Adlington Road, Bollington, Cheshire, SK10 5JT
☎ (01625) 575380 bollingtonbrewing.co.uk

Bollington began brewing in 2008 with the Vale Inn, Bollington, as the brewery tap. Around 40 outlets are supplied direct. The Park Tavern in Macclesfield and the Cask Tavern in Poynton are also owned. All three pubs serve mainly Bollington beers. !! ♦

Long Hop (OG 1039, ABV 3.9%)
Pale lager-style bitter with fruity, refreshing hops.

Ginger Brew (OG 1041, ABV 4.1%)
A classic ginger bitter with a hoppy, bitter flavour and a smooth taste with fresh root ginger added at the end.

White Nancy (OG 1040, ABV 4.1%)
Pale-coloured light bitter with a good hoppiness and light body.

Best (OG 1041, ABV 4.2%)
A hoppy bitter. Clean and crisp with a light golden colour and a refreshing bitter aftertaste.

Dinner Ale (OG 1042, ABV 4.3%)
Deep copper-coloured beer with a fresh, slightly fruity nose. A traditional-style bitter with a dry, hoppy finish.

Oat Mill Stout (OG 1049, ABV 5%)
An oatmeal stout with a twist. A hoppy bitter taste keeps the sweetness in check and allows for a fine dark beer.

Eastern Nights (OG 1056, ABV 5.6%)
A pale gold-coloured balanced IPA with a modest hop content. Easy-drinking for the strength.

Goldenthal (OG 1068, ABV 7.4%)
Golden-coloured, hoppy, European-style barley wine.

Bondgate

30 Bondgate Close, Hexham, Northumberland, NE46 1DG ☎ 07500 018209
bondgatebrewery.moonfruit.com

Bondgate began brewing in 2013 using a three-barrel plant built from salvaged equipment. Limited edition ales: see website.

Magellan's Fate (OG 1042, ABV 4%)
A light, citrus, easy-drinking pale ale.

Ghost Empire (OG 1043, ABV 4.3%)
A pale ale with a hint of dark toffee, sweet malt and marmalade.

Storm Crow (OG 1050, ABV 5%)
A dark, citrus ale.

Tigerfish IPA (OG 1055, ABV 5.3%)
An IPA of the Victorian era, brewed to a recipe from 1868.

Hexham Riot (OG 1057, ABV 5.5%)

Waterloo (OG 1056, ABV 5.5%)

Bootleg IFBB

Horse & Jockey, 9 The Green, Chorlton-cum-Hardy, M21 9HS
☎ (0161) 860 7794 horseandjockeychorlton.com

Situated in the Horse & Jockey Inn on the Green, the brewery is in a tiny space above the dining room where evidence remains of a historic brewery. !! ♦

Chorlton Pale Ale (OG 1040, ABV 4%)

A refreshing blonde beer with a hint of citrus and a long, dry finish.

Black Widow (OG 1041.3, ABV 4.4%)
A smooth, easy-drinking stout with subtle hints of coffee and chocolate and a long, dry finish.

Contraband (OG 1037.2, ABV 4.5%)
A crisp, dry pale ale, hoppy with a hint of grapefruit.

Lawless (OG 1042.6, ABV 4.7%)
A dry, copper-coloured ale with a hint of spice on the nose and a slight presence of caramel in the after taste.

USA IPA (OG 1062, ABV 5.5%)
An American-style IPA.

Born in the Borders

Lanton Mill, Jedburgh, TD8 6ST
☎ (01835) 830495 ☎ 07802 416494
borninttheborders.com

Born in the Borders Brewery is Scotland's original plough-to-pint brewery, and started brewing as Scottish Borders Brewery in 2011 using barley from its own farm. Beyond its core range of ales, recent projects include the brewery's 'Wild Harvest' initiative, which sources locally foraged ingredients for its ales. Taking their provenance story even further, the brewery has recently launched a visitors' centre, offering brewery tours, a café/ restaurant and retail units featuring Borders beer, produce and food. !! ♦

Foxy Blonde (OG 1037.5, ABV 3.8%)
Brewery-grown barley and a complex mixture of hops combine to create a golden ale bursting with citrus and floral flavours.

Game Bird (OG 1039.5, ABV 4%)
An amber ale with a good balance of malty sweetness and late summer fruit with a long and easy finish.

Holy Cow (OG 1041, ABV 4.2%)
Hints of dark malt combine with a long floral finish.

Gold Dust (OG 1041.5, ABV 4.3%)
A light IPA with a burst of hop aroma.

Dark Horse (OG 1044, ABV 4.5%)
A classic dark ale that has overtones of coffee and chocolate with a surprisingly spicy finish that lingers on the tongue.

Borough (Lancaster) SIBA

3 Dalton Square, Lancaster, LA1 1PP ☎ 07912 679761 theboroughbrewery.co.uk

Borough Brewery is located in the cellar of the Borough, a freehouse in the centre of Lancaster. A 2.5-barrel plant is used to produce vegan beers. ♦

Pale (OG 1038, ABV 3.7%)
Dry, refreshing, hoppy bitter beer.

Bitter (OG 1040, ABV 4%)
Sweet malty bitter with caramel flavours and light hop balance.

Summertime Dark (OG 1040, ABV 4%)

Wintertime Dark (OG 1050, ABV 5%)
Well-balanced, roasty dry stout with full body and lingering finish.

Borough (Neath) (NEW) SIBA

2 New Henry Street, Neath, SA11 1PH
☎ (01639) 644902 ☎ 07577 461915
boroughbreweryneath.com

Opened in 2014, the brewery was built by the landlord Kevin Davies in a converted outbuilding at the rear of the pub. Beers are named primarily after the local coal and steel industry. !! RAIB

Welsh Gold (OG 1038, ABV 3.8%)
Hints of chocolate and nuts to taste with a slightly bitter finish.

Iron Runner (OG 1042, ABV 4.3%)
Bitter with a roasted nutty aftertaste.

Triple Bleeder (OG 1046, ABV 4.3%)
Amber-coloured bitter ale with a dry hoppy taste.

Full Blast (OG 1050, ABV 4.7%)
Golden-coloured, fruity, zesty ale.

Nut Red Coke (OG 1052, ABV 4.8%)
Chestnut-coloured ale with malt overtones accented with hops.

Pithead Porter (OG 1058, ABV 5.4%)
Full-bodied porter with nutty overtones with a hint of chocolate aftertaste.

Borough Arms (Crewe)

33 Earle Street, Crewe, Cheshire, CW1 2BG
☎ (01270) 254999 borougharmscrewe.co.uk

A two-barrel brewery opened in 2005 to supply the pub but with beers occasionally available at festivals. Brewing is currently suspended. !! ♦

Boss (NEW) SIBA

14 Worcester Court, Mannesmann Close, Llansamlet, Swansea, SA7 9FD
☎ (01792) 790726 ☎ 07825 525735
bossbrewing.co.uk

The brewery opened in 2015 by Roy Alkin and Sarah John, using a 10-barrel plant. There are already plans to expand and to provide bottling and casking facilities. 100 outlets are supplied. A brewpub and shop are also planned for the near future. !! RAIB

Blonde (OG 1040, ABV 4%)

Blaze (OG 1045, ABV 4.5%)
Golden ale with a floral, herbal aroma and a zingy citrus, spicy flavour.

Bare (OG 1050, ABV 5%)
A lager-style bitter with a clean, spicy finish.

Black (OG 1050, ABV 5%)
Roasted coffee and chocolate aromas, with flavours of fire-roasted nuts, toffee and chocolate.

Brave (OG 1054, ABV 5.5%)
Tropical fruit, elderflower and rose aromas, with flavours of grapefruit, citrus and pine.

Bosun's SIBA

Unit 20, Wakefield Commercial Park, 97 Bridge Road, Horbury Bridge, West Yorkshire, WF4 5NW ☎ 07703 535735 bosunsbrewery.co.uk

The first brew was produced in 2013 by a father and son team who have both served in the armed forces. The regular beers are produced on a 10-

barrel plant with some given military themed names. ‼◆

Golden Rivet (OG 1037, ABV 3.7%)
Smooth malty golden beer named after the mythical last rivet fixed when a ship is built.

Maiden Voyage (OG 1039, ABV 3.9%)
Chestnut brown-coloured traditional English ale.

Bermuda Triangle (OG 1041, ABV 4.1%)
Fruity golden ale with a soft citrus aroma and flavour.

Bosuns Whistle (OG 1043, ABV 4.3%)
Well-rounded golden best bitter.

Botley SIBA

Botley Mills, Mill Hill, Botley, Hampshire, SO30 2GB
☎ (01489) 784867 ☎ 07909 337212
⊕ botley-brewery.co.uk

⊗ Botley Brewery was established in 2010 and uses a five-barrel plant. ◆RAIB

Mill (OG 1038, ABV 3.8%)
A light session bitter, copper in colour, with a fresh aftertaste.

Bottas (OG 1042, ABV 4.2%)
An amber-coloured best bitter with a hoppy aroma and a good depth of flavour.

Cobbett's (OG 1045, ABV 4.5%)
A light, fruity golden ale with a clean bitter finish.

Bottle Brook

Church Street, Kilburn, Belper, Derbyshire, DE56 0LU
☎ (01332) 880051 ☎ 07971 189915

⊗ A sister brewery to Leadmill (qv), Bottle Brook was established in 2005 using a 2.5-barrel plant on a tower gravity system. New World hops are predominantly used. The core range of beers is supplemented by one-off brews.

Columbus (OG 1040, ABV 4%)

Heanor Pale Ale (OG 1041, ABV 4.2%)

Roadrunner (OG 1047, ABV 4.8%)

Mellow Yellow (OG 1054, ABV 5.7%)

Rapture (OG 1058, ABV 5.9%)

Sand in the Wind (OG 1060, ABV 6.1%)

Bottle Cap (NEW)

🔠 10 Littlejohn Street, Aberdeen, AB10 1FF

Unit 12, North Beach Road, Balmedie, Aberdeen, AB23 8XG ☎ 07850 367911 ⊕ bottlecapbrewery.com

The brewery was launched in 2014 as an on-site microbrewery in the Bottle Cap Bar, Aberdeen. It produces mainly bottle-conditioned and keg beers. In 2015 it acquired new, larger, premises and operates from both sites to meet demand. The beers are supplied to the bar and local outlets. A range of cask-conditioned ales is planned. RAIB

Bournemouth

Unit 6, 4-6 Abingdon Road, Nuffield Industrial Estate, Poole, Dorset, BH17 0UG
☎ (01202) 280405 ⊕ bournemouthbrewery.co.uk

Brewing began in 2013 using a one-barrel plant but has since increased capacity to seven barrels. Most of the beer is sold directly from the brewery and is brewed on demand. A small proportion goes to local pubs and beer festivals, which is increasing as production grows. ‼☗◆

Best (OG 1038, ABV 3.9%)
A session bitter with a slightly malty taste.

Wessex Wobble (OG 1041, ABV 4.3%)
Best bitter with a mildly hoppy taste.

Golden Grains (OG 1044, ABV 4.6%)
This pale golden beer has a mild sweetness and strong hop flavour.

Battleaxe (OG 1057, ABV 6.3%)
Lots of dark malts rounded off with powerful hops.

Bowland SIBA 👁

Holmes Mill, Greenacre Street, Clitheroe, Lancashire, BB7 1EB
☎ (01200) 443592 ⊕ bowlandbrewery.com

☺The brewery opened in 2003 and was taken over in 2014 by the Warburton brothers, who operate several hotels and pubs in the area. It moved to Clitheroe in 2015 and a visitor centre is planned. Around 100 outlets are supplied throughout the north-west of England. ☗◆RAIB

Sawley Tempted (OG 1038, ABV 3.7%)
A copper-coloured fruity session bitter with toffee in the mouth and a spicy finish.

Gold (OG 1039, ABV 3.8%)
A hoppy, golden bitter with intense grapefruit flavours.

Hen Harrier (OG 1040, ABV 4%) ◣
The malty start belies what comes next: fruity, sweet, hoppy bitter with a long-lasting finish comprising all the previous elements.

Dragon (OG 1043, ABV 4.2%)
A golden bitter with rounded fruit in the mouth and a refreshing finish.

Buster (OG 1046, ABV 4.5%)
Well-balanced, medium-bodied and rounded. Generous American hops provide long tropical undertones.

Bowman SIBA 👁

Wallops Wood, Sheardley Lane, Droxford, Hampshire, SO32 3QY
☎ (01489) 878110 ⊕ bowman-ales.com

⊗ Brewing started in 2006 in converted farm buildings. The brewery supplies more than 100 outlets. A new 40-barrel plant came on line in 2013, which is now working alongside the original 20-barrel plant. In addition to the standard beers, a range of seasonal brews and monthly specials is produced. ‼◆RAIB

Elderado (OG 1036, ABV 3.5%) ◣
Straw-coloured beer flavoured with elderflower. Citrus aroma with a fruity, bitter taste. Good hoppiness and background sweetness. Dry bitter finish.

Swift One (OG 1038, ABV 3.8%) ◣
Easy-drinking bitter, well-balanced with sweet maltiness leading to a bittersweet finish and slightly dry, hoppy aftertaste.

Meon Valley Bitter (OG 1040, ABV 3.9%)

Yumi (OG 1039, ABV 3.9%)
A fairly bitter beer, rich amber in colour.

Wallops Wood (OG 1040, ABV 4%) ◆
No particular flavour dominates this well-crafted beer. Malt flavours throughout balanced by toffee notes, sweetness and a slightly dry finish.

Quiver Bitter (OG 1043, ABV 4.5%) ◆
Fruity best bitter, golden in colour with hoppy aroma leading through to a balanced, bittersweet taste and refreshing hoppy finish.

Bowness Bay

Green Lane, Winster, Cumbria, LA23 3NL ☎ 07768 116794 🌐 bownessbaybrewing.co.uk

Brewing began in 2012 using a four-barrel plant bought from the now closed Northcote brewery in Norwich.

Mere Gold (OG 1038, ABV 3.8%)
A smooth, rich, hoppy golden ale with light tropical fruit flavours.

Swan Blonde (OG 1039, ABV 4%) ◆
Fruity aroma, clean balanced beer with lightly hopped finish.

Swift Bitter (OG 1044, ABV 4.5%)
Full and rounded, with a creamy caramel undercurrent.

Teal Tipple (OG 1045, ABV 4.5%)
A copper-coloured session ale, light and refreshing.

Swan Black (OG 1046, ABV 4.6%) ◆
Stout-like beer with a fruity raisiny middle, grainy mouthfeel and roast bitter finish.

Box Steam SIBA

The Midlands, Holt, Wiltshire, BA14 6RU
☎ (01225) 782700 🌐 boxsteambrewery.com

The brewery was founded in 2004 and boasts a Fulton steam-fired copper, hence the name. New ownership since 2006 meant expansion and increased capacity with the brewery moving to larger premises in Holt in 2011. Two Wiltshire pubs are owned and more than 100 outlets supplied. !! ◆

Half Sovereign (OG 1038, ABV 3.4%)
A full-bodied, copper-coloured bitter with a citrus flavour, a tropical fruit aroma and a smooth, rich, malty taste.

Tunnel Vision (OG 1040.5, ABV 4.2%)
A well-rounded light amber-coloured bitter. Clean tasting, with a slight bitterness on the finish.

Piston Broke (OG 1045, ABV 4.5%)
A full-bodied deep golden ale with a refreshing hoppy, citrus palate and a subtle fruit-hop aroma.

Soul Train (OG 1047, ABV 4.7%)
A clean and refreshing blonde beer.

Bradfield SIBA

Watt House Farm, High Bradfield, Sheffield, South Yorkshire, S6 6LG
☎ (0114) 285 1118 🌐 bradfieldbrewery.co.uk

Established in 2005, Bradfield is a family-run business, based on a working farm in the Peak District using pure Milstone Grit springwater. In 2009 the brewery bought its first brewery tap, the Nags Head, Loxley. ◆RAIB

Farmers Bitter (OG 1039, ABV 3.9%)
A traditional copper-coloured malt ale with a floral aroma.

Farmers Blonde (OG 1041, ABV 4%)
Pale, blonde beer with citrus and summer fruits aromas.

Yorkshire Farmer (ABV 4%)
A gold-coloured beer, light on the palate with a smooth, bitter finish.

Farmers Brown Cow (ABV 4.2%)
A rich, deep chestnut-coloured ale with a smooth, creamy head. A citrus aftertaste gives way to a long, dry finish.

Farmers Stout (OG 1045, ABV 4.5%)
A dark stout with roasted malts and flaked oats and a subtle, bitter hop character.

Farmers Pale Ale (ABV 5%)
A distinctive fruity pale ale, well-balanced with a powerful floral bouquet, full-bodied with a dry aftertaste.

Bradford (NEW) SIBA

22 Rawson Road, Westgate, Bradford, BD1 3SQ
☎ (01274) 379054 🌐 bradfordbrewery.com

The brewery was established in 2015, seeing the return of brewing to Bradford city centre for the first time in 60 years. It is based in newly converted, former factory buildings and uses a 10-barrel plant. The beers are available at the on-site Brewfactory pub, where a feature glass wall allows visitors to view the brewery in operation. !!

Hockey Pale (ABV 3.6%)

Razorback (ABV 3.7%)

Northern Soul (ABV 3.8%)

Odsal Top (ABV 4%)

Origin (ABV 4.2%)

Lost in New York (ABV 5.3%)

Death Cookie (ABV 5.7%)

Brains IFBB

Crawshay Street, Cardiff, CF10 1SP
☎ (029) 2040 2060 🌐 sabrain.com

Brains was established in 1882 at the Old Brewery, moving to the former Hancock's brewery site in 1999. The company has remained in family ownership and runs over 270 pubs throughout Wales, the Midlands and the West Country and is heavily involved in sponsoring Welsh sport. A new microbrewery within the existing site has produced an ever-increasing range of new beers, which have proved popular within the Brain's estate. ◆

Dark (OG 1035.5, ABV 3.5%) ◆
A tasty, classic dark brown mild, a mix of malt, roast, caramel with a background of hops. Bittersweet, mellow and with a lasting finish of malt and roast.

Bitter (OG 1036, ABV 3.7%) ◆
Amber-coloured with a gentle aroma of malt and hops. Malt, hops and bitterness combine in an easy-drinking beer with a bitter finish.

SA (OG 1042, ABV 4.2%) ◆

A mellow, full-bodied beer. Gentle malt and hop aroma leads to a malty, hop and fruit mix with a balancing bitterness.

SA Gold (OG 1042, ABV 4.2%) ◆
A golden beer with a hoppy aroma. Well-balanced with a zesty hop, malt, fruit and balancing bitterness; a similar satisfying finish.

Rev James (OG 1045.5, ABV 4.5%) 🍺 🍾 ◆
A faint malt and fruit aroma with malt and fruit flavours in the taste, initially bittersweet. Bitterness balances the flavour and makes this an easy-drinking beer.

Contract brewed for Molson Coors:

M&B Brew XI (OG 1036, ABV 3.6%)

Hancock's HB (OG 1037, ABV 3.7%)

Worthingon's Bitter (OG 1037, ABV 3.7%)

Brakspear 👁

Eagle Maltings, The Crofts, Witney, Oxfordshire, OX28 4DP
☎ (01993) 890800 ⊕ brakspear-beers.co.uk

Brakspear beers have been brewed in Oxfordshire since 1779. They continue to be traditionally crafted at the Wychwood Brewery (qv) in the historic market town of Witney using the original Victorian square fermenters and the renowned 'double drop' fermenting system. Part of Marston's PLC. ‼ ꇛ ◆ RAIB

Bitter (OG 1035, ABV 3.4%)
A classic copper-coloured pale ale with big hop resins, juicy malt and orange fruit aroma, intense hop bitterness in the mouth and finish, and a firm maltiness and tangy fruitiness throughout.

Oxford Gold (OG 1040, ABV 4%)
Zesty aroma, a full fruity flavour and a golden colour.

Brampton SIBA 👁

Units 4 & 5, Chatsworth Business Park, Chatsworth Road, Chesterfield, Derbyshire, S40 2AR
☎ (01246) 221680 ⊕ bramptonbrewery.co.uk

👁The original Brampton Brewery closed in 1955. In 2007 a new brewery was established, and brewing commenced on an eight-barrel plant. Two tied houses are situated close to the brewery. ‼ ꇛ ◆ RAIB

Golden Bud (OG 1037, ABV 3.8%) ◆
Crisp and refreshing golden bitter with a pleasant balance of citrus, sweetness and bitter flavours. Light and easy to drink.

1302 (OG 1039, ABV 4%)
A sweeter pale ale.

Griffin (OG 1040, ABV 4.1%)
A pale, slightly-sweet summer ale.

Best (OG 1041, ABV 4.2%) ◆
Classic, drinkable bitter with a predominantly malty taste, balanced by caramel sweetness and a developing bitterness in the aftertaste.

Impy Dark (OG 1047, ABV 4.3%) ◆
Strong roasted coffee aroma and a rich flavour of vine fruit and chocolate combine to make this a tasty mild ale.

Jerusalem (OG 1046, ABV 4.6%)

The rich and roasted malt notes defy the pale colour in this special bitter.

Tudor Rose (OG 1045, ABV 4.6%)
A well-balanced and creamy pale ale with good hop nose and mouthfeel.

Wasp Nest (OG 1049, ABV 5%) ◆
Strong and complex with malt and hop flavours and a caramel sweetness.

Speciale (OG 1056, ABV 5.8%)
An IPA-style ale, the fruity hoppiness is balanced beautifully by the residual sweetness of such a strong ale.

Brancaster

See Beeston

Brandon

76 High Street, Brandon, Suffolk, IP27 0AU
☎ (01842) 878496 ☎ 07876 234689
⊕ brandonbrewery.co.uk

Brandon started brewing in 2005 on the site of an old dairy situated on the Suffolk-Norfolk border. Beers are based on traditional styles which include unique recipes and incorporate locally sourced ingredients. ‼ ꇛ RAIB

Breckland Gold (OG 1038, ABV 3.8%)
A delicate, smooth, slightly spicy taste and a dry, lingering, malty finish.

Old Rodney (OG 1040, ABV 4%) ◆
Damson jam aroma precedes a flavoursome balance of malt, fruit and hops in this tawny best bitter. Gently fading finish.

Paddys Pride (OG 1040, ABV 4%)
A dark ruby mild, smooth malt flavours ending with a little roast bitterness.

Saxon Gold (OG 1040, ABV 4%)
A pale, golden beer with a subtle aroma of hops. The taste is a clean, crisp mix of spice and bitter fruits with a dry, hoppy finish.

Strawberry Wheat (OG 1040, ABV 4%)
A pale ale, includes torrefied wheat and pulped strawberries.

Waxies Dargle (OG 1040, ABV 4%)
This copper-coloured brew has rich malt flavours and a good hoppiness.

Molly's Secret (OG 1041, ABV 4.1%)
A pale ale based on an old recipe.

Norfolk Poacher (OG 1041, ABV 4.1%) ◆
A rich malty roast aroma that follows through to flavours of malt, hops, fruit and sweetness. Sweetness dominates a long complex finish.

Royal Ginger (OG 1041, ABV 4.1%)
A refreshing summer ale with a distinctive mix of malt and hoppy spice, balanced with a gentle ginger flavour and finish.

Gun Flint (OG 1042, ABV 4.2%)
Roasted malts are used to produce a malty, chocolate flavour. This combines well with spicy, citrus hops to give a dry, bittersweet, roasted malt finish.

Wee Drop of Mischief (OG 1042, ABV 4.2%)
An amber-coloured premium bitter. Gentle malt flavours give way to a hop character and a dry, increasingly bitter aftertaste.

Rusty Bucket (OG 1044, ABV 4.4%) ◆
Aromas of figs and malt with dried fruit, and flavours of malt and hops, leading to a bitter, biscuity aftertaste. A well-balanced traditional best bitter.

Grumpy Bastard (OG 1045, ABV 4.5%)

Slippery Jack (OG 1045, ABV 4.5%)
A dark brown stout. Complex but well-balanced flavours of roasted grain and hop bitterness. Dry with a lingering, pleasantly bitter finish.

'Old on to Your 'at (OG 1047, ABV 4.7%)
Dark amber in colour, big malt flavours overlaid with a tangy fruit bitterness.

Nappertandy (OG 1050, ABV 5%)
A reddish amber beer, full-bodied with a malty aroma. Crisp and spicy with an underlying citrus flavour and a dry, malty, bitter fruit finish.

Brandy Cask

Brandy Cask, 25 Bridge Street, Pershore, Worcestershire, WR10 1AJ
☎ (01386) 552602

Brewing started in 1995 in a refurbished bottle store in the garden of the pub. Brewery and pub now operate under one umbrella, with brewing carried out by the owner/landlord. Beers are supplied only to the pub. ‼◆

Whistling Joe (OG 1036, ABV 3.6%) ◆
A sweet, fruity, copper-coloured beer that has plenty of contrast in the aroma. A malty balance lingers but the aftertaste is not dry.

Brandysnapper (OG 1040, ABV 4%) ◆
Golden brew with low alpha hops. Plenty of fruit and hop aroma leads to a rich taste in the mouth and a lingering aftertaste.

John Baker's Original (OG 1048, ABV 4.8%) ◆
A superb blend of flavours with roasted malt to the fore. The rich hoppy aroma is complemented by a complex aftertaste.

Branscombe Vale SIBA

Branscombe, Devon, EX12 3DP
☎ (01297) 680511 🌐 branscombevalebrewery.co.uk

The brewery was set up in 1992 in cowsheds overlooking the sea owned by the National Trust, the two partners converting the sheds and digging their own well. In 2008 a new 25-barrel plant was shoehorned in through the roof. ◆RAIB

Mild (OG 1036, ABV 3.7%)

Branoc (OG 1038, ABV 3.8%) ◆
Pale brown brew with a malt and fruit aroma and a hint of caramel. Malt and bitter taste with a dry, hoppy finish.

Draymans Best Bitter (OG 1042, ABV 4.2%)

Summa This (OG 1040, ABV 4.2%)

Best Bitter (OG 1045, ABV 4.6%) ◆
Reddy/brown-coloured beer with a fruity aroma and taste, and bitter/astringent finish.

Summa That (OG 1049, ABV 5%)
Light golden beer with a clean and refreshing taste and a long hoppy finish.

Brass Castle SIBA

10a Yorkersgate, Malton, North Yorkshire, YO17 7AB
☎ (01653) 698683 ☎ 07563 579723
🌐 brasscastlebrewery.co.uk

The brewery is based in the centre of Malton with a 12-barrel plant, having begun life on a one-barrel kit in the owner's garage. All beers are unfined and so are suitable for vegetarians and vegans. The brewery welcomes visitors and hosts a bottle/homebrew shop alongside its tap room. ‼◆RAIB

Cliffhanger (OG 1040, ABV 3.8%)
A refreshing hop-laden golden ale infused with citrus notes.

Tail Gunner (OG 1042, ABV 4%)
A dry-hopped rye session ale with a reddish hue.

Hazelnut Mild (OG 1044, ABV 4.2%)
A five-malt nut brown mild with a delicate hazelnut aroma.

Mosaic (OG 1043, ABV 4.3%)

Best Bitter (OG 1046, ABV 4.5%)
A brass-coloured traditional special bitter.

Oatmeal Pale (OG 1046, ABV 4.6%)

Snoweater (OG 1050, ABV 4.8%)

Brass Lager (OG 1053, ABV 5.3%)
A malt-forward Vienna lager.

Bad Kitty (OG 1060.5, ABV 5.5%)
A chewy chocolate vanilla-flavoured a porter.

Eclipse (OG 1061, ABV 5.7%)
A dark variant of Sunshine IPA, a citrus hop punch is followed by a light roasty aftertaste.

Sunshine (OG 1061, ABV 5.7%)
A full-bodied IPA.

Burnout (OG 1062, ABV 5.8%)
A robust peat-smoked porter.

Heretic (OG 1061, ABV 6.1%)

Braunton (NEW)

Unit 9, Chivenor Business Park, Braunton, Devon, EX31 4AY
☎ (01271) 867382 ☎ 07551 870925
🌐 brauntonbrewery.co.uk

After some small-scale brewing, Braunton was established in 2014. Commercial brewing began in early 2015. The brewery has moved to new premises and uses a six-barrel plant. Three beers are currently produced.

#1 Pale (OG 1039, ABV 3.8%)
Clean, crisp, refreshing pale ale with long hop overtones.

#2 Bitter (OG 1041, ABV 4%)
Well-rounded, easy-drinking bitter, with malted caramel leading to a delicate hop aroma.

#3 IPA (OG 1042, ABV 4.2%)
Well-balanced light malts and dry English hops.

Braydon

See Castle Combe

Brecon SIBA

8a Brecon Enterprise Park, Brecon, Powys, LD3 8BT
☎ (01874) 620800 🌐 breconbrewing.co.uk

THE BREWERIES

Brecon was established in 2011 by Buster Grant. Seasonal and special beers are also available including beers from the Genesis Project. !! ♦ RAIB

Three Beacons (OG 1030, ABV 3%)
A low-ABV, American-style pale ale – golden hued, full-bodied and extensively hopped with six different varieties.

Welsh Beacons (OG 1037, ABV 3.7%)
A golden bitter with a gentle floral bitterness and a full flavour.

Copper Beacons (OG 1041, ABV 4.1%)
A copper-coloured best bitter – smooth with well-balanced fruit and hop flavours.

Gold Beacons (OG 1042, ABV 4.2%)
Deep golden ale with soft, well-defined bitterness balancing a blend of malts.

Red Beacons (OG 1050, ABV 5%)
Premium red IPA, smooth and well-hopped.

Brentwood SIBA

Calcott Hall Farm, Ongar Road, Brentwood, Essex, CM14 5RE
☎ (01277) 200483 brentwoodbrewing.co.uk

Since its launch in 2006 Brentwood has steadily increased its capacity and distribution, relocating to a new purpose-built brewery unit in 2013 with a visitor centre. Seasonal and special beers are also available including more unusual beer styles under the Elephant School brand name. !! ♦ RAIB

BBC2 (OG 1030, ABV 2.5%)
Full-bodied mid-brown bitter with a dry tropical citrus flavour.

IPA (OG 1039, ABV 3.7%)
A lightly-hopped, pale session beer.

Marvellous Maple Mild (OG 1038, ABV 3.7%)
Dark brown mild with a hint of maple syrup.

Best (OG 1042, ABV 4.2%)
A traditional, light-coloured best bitter with a well-rounded flavour and aroma.

Gold (OG 1043, ABV 4.3%)
A heavily-hopped golden beer with a fruity taste and bitter finish.

Chockwork Orange (OG 1067, ABV 6.5%)
A deep chocolate malty beer brewed with oranges and matured to provide a classic old ale-style beer.

Brew By Numbers

79 Enid Street, London, SE16 3RA ☎ 07528 684105
brewbynumbers.com

Brew By Numbers is a small brewery established in 2012 with plans to move to larger premises. The vegan-friendly beers are bottled on site, with primary fermentation yeast carried over. Each beer is also sold by number, the first part relating to the style of beer and the second to the recipe within that style. RAIB

Brew Company

See Exit 33

BrewDog

Balmacassie Industrial Estate, Ellon, AB41 8BX
☎ (01358) 724924 brewdog.com

No real ale. Established in 2007 by James Watt and Martin Dickie. Thirteen UK bars and three overseas bars are owned, with more bars and a new warehouse planned for 2015. Most of the output is bottled, with some keg production.

Brewhouse & Kitchen

Bristol (NEW): 31-35 Cotham Hill, Clifton, Bristol, BS6 6JY
☎ (0117) 973 3793

Dorchester: 17 Weymouth Avenue, Dorchester, DY1 1QY ☎ (01305) 265551

Highbury (NEW): 2a Corsica Street, Highbury, London, N5 1JJ ☎ (020) 7226 1026

Islington (NEW): 5 Torrens Street, Islington, London, EC1V 1NQ ☎ (020) 7837 9421

Poole (NEW): 3 Dear Hay Lane, Poole, Dorset, BH15 1NZ ☎ (01202) 771246

Portsmouth: 26 Guildhall Walk, Portsmouth, PO1 2DD ☎ (02392) 891340 brewhouseandkitchen.com

Brewing started in 2013 in Portsmouth, the first in the growing Brewhouse & Kitchen chain. There are now six brewpubs, each producing its own particular range of beers with its brewery on open display in the bar area, following the B&K style. Local freehouses and beer festivals can be supplied. !! ♦

Brewed at Bristol:

Crockers (OG 1038, ABV 3.6%)
A light bitter ale, dry and thirst quenching. Named after Crocker & Sons Brewery & Wine Merchants, who brewed on the site in 1840.

Hornigold (OG 1039, ABV 3.9%)
A straw-coloured ale, packed with American hops for a dry bitter finish with a citrus aroma.

Grantleach (OG 1046, ABV 4.6%)
A copper-coloured British ale, fruity and balanced.

Yankee Cabot (OG 1054, ABV 6%)
An IPA with a malty backbone, and zestiness from its American hops.

Brewed at Dorchester:

Station Masters Ale (OG 1035, ABV 3.2%)
Golden session ale with dry mouthfeel.

Nine Stones (OG 1040, ABV 3.8%)
A golden ale.

Crickmay (OG 1044, ABV 4.2%)
Traditional copper-coloured ale with a good bitter bite and fruitcake sweetness.

CrumbleHolme (ABV 4.3%)
An oatmeal stout.

Judge Jefferies (OG 1045, ABV 4.5%)
Single-hopped blonde ale.

Durnovaria Dark (OG 1046, ABV 4.7%)
Hoppy black ale with rich taste.

Cerne Abbas Giant (OG 1052, ABV 5.2%)
American-style IPA, golden in colour, citrus/pine aroma and a biscuity backbone.

Brewed at Highbury:

Tramshed (ABV 3.6%)

Goalscorer (ABV 4%)

Astronomer (ABV 4.5%)

No. 19 (ABV 4.5%)

Romford Pele (ABV 4.5%)

Illustrator (ABV 5.5%)

Brewed at Islington:

Arc Angel (ABV 3.6%)

Spandau B (ABV 4%)

Myddlton (ABV 4.5%)

Britton (ABV 5%)

Watchmaker (ABV 5.5%)

Chaplin (ABV 6%)

Brewed at Poole:

Brewers House (OG 1036, ABV 3.6%)
Traditional amber bitter that is both malty and bitter with delicate hop flavour and aroma.

Brownsea Boy (OG 1040, ABV 4%)
Caramel and toasted malts give a full-bodied flavour that gives way to a piny, resinous hop finish.

Squirrel Island (OG 1040, ABV 4%)
American-style amber-coloured brown ale. Amber ale with a malty sweetness balanced by a bright citrus hop finish.

Code Name (OG 1045, ABV 4.5%)
A jet black oatmeal stout with a deep, rich roasted flavour and a hint of chocolate.

Rhodes Test (OG 1045, ABV 4.5%)
Bright, hoppy and refreshing. An easy-drinking pale ale.

Telemark Extra (OG 1050, ABV 5%)
Bitter and hoppy. A floral, fruity ale.

Brewed at Portsmouth:

Little Bricky (OG 1035, ABV 3.4%)
A dark brown ale, the flavour focusing more on a blend of malts than hops. A classic southern-style mild.

Mucky Duck (OG 1035, ABV 3.4%)
A light copper-coloured session bitter with a good balance of malt and hops in both flavour and aroma.

Sexton (OG 1040, ABV 4%)
Pale golden-coloured beer with a soft bitterness and a fruity hop flavour and aroma.

Troubleshooter (OG 1040, ABV 4%)
A deep copper-coloured traditional bitter with caramel malt balanced by bitterness from English hops.

Black Swan (OG 1056, ABV 5.7%)
A big, bold, hoppy black ale of American style. A firm bitterness supports a pronounced hop flavour and aroma.

Brewmeister SIBA

Unit R, Isla Bank Mills, Keith, AB55 5DD
☎ (01542) 488006 ☎ 07827 333646
🌐 brewmeister.co.uk

Brewmeister began brewing in 2012 at Kincardine O'Neil, Aberdeenshire, but moved in 2013 to an industrial unit in Keith in Moray and again in 2014 to a bigger unit on the same estate. Beer is mainly available in bottles in selected specialist off-licenses although cask is becoming available in a few outlets. RAIB

Blonde (OG 1050, ABV 4%)
Light and refreshing with a light, hoppy profile.

Kaiser (OG 1044, ABV 4.5%)
A wheat beer with honey notes.

Black Hawk (OG 1051, ABV 5%)
Coffee stout made with chocolate and coffee beans.

Supersonic IPA (OG 1048, ABV 5%)
Extremely hoppy with hints of pineapple and exotic fruits.

Ten (OG 1095, ABV 10.1%)
Slightly sweet but hoppy with a fruity aroma and complex malty character.

Brewshed

1 Tayfen Road, Bury St Edmunds, Suffolk, IP32 6BH
☎ (01284) 848066 🌐 brewshedbrewery.co.uk

⊠ Brewshed began brewing in 2011 using a five-barrel plant in the buildings located behind the Beerhouse, one of its pub outlets.

Pale (OG 1040, ABV 3.9%)

Best (OG 1044, ABV 4.3%)

Rioja Porter (OG 1048, ABV 4.8%)

American Blonde (OG 1055, ABV 5.5%)

Brewshine

4 Littledale, Kendal, Cumbria, LA9 7SG ☎ 07817 873997 🌐 brewshine.co.uk

Brewing began in 2014 using a nine-gallon plant situated in a garage in Kendal. There are plans for expansion.

Silly Billy (OG 1038, ABV 3.8%)
A smooth copper-coloured bitter with balanced flavours and a caramel finish.

Billonde (OG 1040, ABV 4%)
A light citrus fruity flavour. Refreshing.

Billy Goat Ale (OG 1040, ABV 4%)
Dark amber in colour with a rich malty taste. Well-balanced with hops to leave a dry, caramel-chocolate finish.

Billyonaires Gold (OG 1040, ABV 4%)
A light refreshing beer with a citrus fruity flavour.

Brewsmith (NEW) SIBA

Unit 11, Cuba Industrial Estate, Ramsbottom, Lancashire, BL0 0NE
☎ (01706) 829390 🌐 brewsmithbeer.co.uk

Brewsmith was established in 2014 by the Smith family – James, Jennifer and Ted. ‼

Bitter (ABV 3.9%)
A pale session bitter. Moderate bitterness, pronounced floral/citrus hop aromas.

Pale Ale (ABV 4.2%)
A refreshingly bitter and hoppy pale ale.

Anvil Ale (ABV 4.5%)

Oatmeal Stout (ABV 5.2%)
A full-bodied, richly textured stout.

IPA (ABV 6%)
Rich mouthfeel, big hop aromas, long, dry bitter finish.

Brewster's SIBA

Unit 5, Burnside, Turnpike Close, Grantham, Lincolnshire, NG31 7XU
(01476) 566000 brewsters.co.uk

Brewster is the old English term for a female brewer and Sara Barton is a modern example. Originally established in the Vale of Belvoir in 1998 and moving to Grantham in 2006, Brewsters produces a range of traditional and innovative beers with two regularly changing ranges; Wicked Women (4.8%) and WhimsicAles (4.0%). !! ♦

Hophead (OG 1036, ABV 3.6%)
This amber beer has a floral/hoppy character; hops predominate throughout before finally yielding to grapefruit in the lasting dry finish.

Marquis (OG 1038, ABV 3.8%)
A well-balanced and refreshing session bitter with maltiness and a dry, hoppy finish.

Hopticale Illusion (OG 1040, ABV 4%)
A deep red beer with a big hop flavour, balanced with roast malts to give a flavoursome session brew.

Aromantica (OG 1042, ABV 4.2%)
A touch of roast malt for a light amber brew with a slightly sweet nutty flavour. Citra hops to the fore give tropical hop notes and aromas of lime and passion fruit with a refreshingly long, aromatic finish.

Hop A Doodle Doo (OG 1043, ABV 4.3%)
A copper-coloured ale with a rich, full-bodied feel and fruity hop character.

Decadence (OG 1044, ABV 4.4%)
A golden ale with a hint of malt sweetness with passion fruit and grapefruit aromas on the nose. First taste gives a complex zesty hop palate leading on to a fresh herb finish.

Aromatic Porter (OG 1045, ABV 4.5%)
A rich roasty dark porter with citrus and tropical fruit hop flavours.

Stilton Porter (OG 1049, ABV 4.9%)
A rich roast-flavoured porter with spicy, rich hop flavours.

Briarbank SIBA

70 Fore Street, Ipswich, Suffolk, IP4 1LB
(01473) 284000

Office: Quay Street, Ipswich, IP12 1BX
briarbank.org

The Briarbank Brewing Company was established in 2013, and is situated on the site of the old Lloyds Bank on Fore Street. The brewery is a small two-barrel plant. The bar above offers the range of beers. !! ♦

Briar Bitter (ABV 3.7%)
A traditional copper-coloured English bitter.

Brick SIBA

Arch 209, Blenheim Grove, Peckham, London, SE15 4QL brickbrewery.co.uk

Brick began brewing in 2013. A brewery tap room is open on Saturdays from 12-6pm. The beers brewed vary from week to week. Local pubs, bars and restaurants are also supplied.

Brick House (NEW)

Patcham, Brighton, BN1 8HQ 07708 384604
brickhousebrewingco@gmail.com

Brick House has grown organically from humble homebrewing beginnings and plans to continue in this vein. Current output is a single firkin and 24 bottles a week. There are plans to upscale to a 100-litre kit with output of two firkins a week. RAIB

Requiem (ABV 4%)
An easy-drinking, full-flavoured session beer. Hoppy with a malty backbone and lingering aftertaste.

Bridestones SIBA

Smithy Farm, Long Causeway, Blackshaw Head, Hebden Bridge, West Yorkshire, HX7 7JB
(01422) 847104 bridestonesbrewery.co.uk

Bridestones, situated close to a rock outcrop from which it takes its name, started brewing in 2006 and currently supplies more than 60 outlets. Its brewery tap is the New Delight Inn in Blackshaw. ♦RAIB

Indians Head (OG 1037, ABV 3.7%)
Light amber-coloured session bitter with a citrus hop finish.

Sandstone (OG 1039, ABV 3.9%)
Amber-coloured session bitter with equal amounts of malt, fruit and bitterness. Initial balance gives way to a more bitter aftertaste.

Pennine Best (OG 1041, ABV 4%)

Pennine Gold (OG 1043, ABV 4.3%)
Good hop aroma and flavour; fruity, refreshing and easy to drink best bitter.

Pennine Bier (OG 1045, ABV 4.4%)
Aromatic nose with citrus fruits dominating. An initial rounded mouthfeel gives way to strong bitterness.

Dark Mild (OG 1045, ABV 4.5%)
Dark brown strong mild with a complex nose of caramel and roasted malt. Good balance of sweetness and bitterness on the palate. Upfront bitterness in the finish.

American Pale Ale (OG 1050, ABV 5%)
A strong but easy-drinking pale ale.

Pennine Pale Ale (OG 1048, ABV 5%)

Bridge (NEW)

The Bridge, Woodhead Road, Holmbridge, Holmfirth, West Yorkshire, HD9 2NQ
(01484) 687652 07970 779762

Brewing began in 2014 using a 2.5-barrel plant, in premises at the Bridge pub in Holmbridge. It produces beers for the pub and also for its companion pub, Brambles, in Holmfirth.

Blonde (ABV 3.7%)

American Pale Ale (ABV 4%)

Bitter (ABV 4%)

Bridgehouse SIBA

Unit 1, Aireworth Mills, Aireworth Road, Keighley, West Yorkshire, BD21 4DH
(01535) 601222 bridgehousebrewery.co.uk

Bridgehouse began brewing in 2010 using a 10-barrel plant. The brewery purchased the recipes and branding of Old Bear Brewery in 2014 and moved into its premises in Keighley. Relocation is planned in 2015. ‼◆

Blonde (OG 1040, ABV 4%)

Airedale (OG 1042, ABV 4.2%)

Porter (OG 1045, ABV 4.5%)

Brewed under the Old Bear brand name:

Estivator (OG 1037, ABV 3.8%) ◆
This straw-coloured bitter has a grassy hop character in the aroma and taste with marmalade fruitiness. The finish is dry and bitter.

Black Mari'a (OG 1043, ABV 4.2%)
A black stout, smooth on the palate with a strong roast malt flavour and fruity finish.

Yorkshire Ale (OG 1042, ABV 4.2%)

Goldilocks (OG 1047, ABV 4.5%) ◆
A fruity, straw-coloured golden ale, well-hopped and assertively bitter through to the finish.

Hibernator (OG 1055, ABV 5%) ◆
A complex rich dark ale dominated by roast and bitter flavours against a background sweetness. Roast coffee, hints of caramel and dark vine fruit on the nose. The finish is bitter and astringent.

Bridgetown

🏠 Albert Inn, Bridgetown Close, Totnes, Devon, TQ9 5AD
☎ (01803) 863214 ⊕ albertinntotnes.com/bridgetown-brewery

Bridgetown started brewing in 2008 on a 2.5-barrel plant. ◆

Albert Ale (OG 1036, ABV 3.8%)

Totnes Hemp Beer (OG 1042, ABV 4%)

Bitter (OG 1041, ABV 4.2%)

Shark Island Stout (OG 1044, ABV 4.5%)

Bridlington

🏠 110 Quay Road, Bridlington, East Yorkshire, YO16 4JB
☎ (01262) 674592

Bridlington was founded in 2014 and is based in an outhouse in the beer garden of the Telegraph Inn. One regular ale is produced with further beers planned. The Pack Horse in Bridlington is also owned.

Jackdaw (ABV 4.3%)

Briggs

c/o Unit 1, Waterhouse Mill, 65-71 Lockwood Road, Huddersfield, West Yorkshire, HD1 5QU ☎ 07427 668004 ⊕ briggssignatureales.weebly.com

Nick Briggs, a former member of the brewing team at Mallinson's and former head brewer at Elland, has branched out on his own producing his first brew on the Mallinson's plant. Now producing various regular, rotating, modern, hop-forward beers.

Northern Soul (OG 1038, ABV 3.8%)
Pale bitter with a citrus and zesty aroma from an abundance of American hops.

Brightlingsea

🏠 Rosebud, 66-67 Hurst Green, Brightlingsea, Essex, CO7 0EH
☎ (01206) 304571 ⊕ rosebudpub.co.uk

Brightlingsea operates from a 3.5-barrel plant within the Rosebud pub. Beers are brewed on demand and the pub aims to have at least one on sale at any time.

Brighton Bier SIBA

Unit 20, Bell Tower Industrial Estate, Roedean Road, Brighton, East Sussex, BN2 5RU
☎ (01273) 567374 ☎ 07515 956976
⊕ brightonbier.com

Brighton Bier was established in 2012. Originally based at the Hand in Hand pub in Brighton, it moved into new premises in 2014 with the opening of a new 15-barrel brewery. Beers are available throughout the south-east, and increasingly across the country. The brewery also part-owns the Brighton Beer Dispensary pub in Brighton with Late Knights Brewery.

Thirty Three (OG 1035, ABV 3.3%)

Brighton Bier (ABV 4%)

West Pier (OG 1042, ABV 4%)

Underdog (ABV 4.2%)

No Name Stout (ABV 5%)

South Coast IPA (ABV 5%)

Dealer's Choice IPA (ABV 5.1%)
An ever-changing series of IPAs exploring the beer style using different hops and recipes for each brew run.

Grand Porter (ABV 5.2%)

Brightside SIBA

Unit 10, Dale Industrial Estate, Radcliffe, M26 1AD
☎ (0161) 725 9644 ☎ 07870 207442
⊕ brightsidebrewing.co.uk

Brightside is an 18-barrel plant established in 2010 which began commercial production in 2011. It moved from the back room of the family bakery into dedicated industrial premises in 2013. All cask-conditioned beers are suitable for vegetarians and bottle-conditioned beers for vegans. **RAIB**

Odin (OG 1038, ABV 3.8%)
A fresh, light-bodied blonde ale brewed with a blend of American hops to give a fruity, citrus flavour and moderately bitter finish.

Our Town (OG 1040, ABV 4%)
A mid-weight copper-coloured beer. Crystal and amber malts brewed with tropical fruit flavoured hops create a maltiness and depth of flavour.

B-Side (OG 1042, ABV 4.2%)
Light and refreshing, with fruity notes and a gentle malty, lightly bitter finish.

Best Bitter (OG 1044, ABV 4.3%)
A dark amber-coloured traditional English best bitter with a great depth of flavour.

Mancunian (OG 1044, ABV 4.4%)
A blonde ale with the emphasis on hop flavour rather than bitterness. Fresh, light-bodied and hoppy.

Underworld (OG 1049, ABV 4.4%)

A dry, medium-bodied porter. More bitter than you might expect from a traditional porter. Aromas of coffee and dried fruit.

Darkside Stout (OG 1052, ABV 4.6%)
A jet black stout with espresso coffee and dark chocolate flavours, with more than a touch of smoke on the finish.

Manchester Skyline (OG 1044, ABV 4.6%)
Lager malt, wheat and four speciality malts give a deep golden colour and complex flavour.

Maverick IPA (OG 1047, ABV 4.8%)
Light amber in colour but with a weighty rich malt base, and punchy citrus hop character. Refreshingly bitter but not overpowering.

Amarillo (OG 1048, ABV 5%)
A dry, light amber-coloured beer, liberally hopped without being overwhelmingly bitter.

Brightwater SIBA

9 Beaconsfield Road, Claygate, Surrey, KT10 0PN
☎ (01372) 462334 ☎ 07802 316389
⊕ brightbrew.co.uk

⊗ Brightwater is an eco-friendly five-barrel brewery with two six-barrel fermenters, situated at the rear of a domestic property. Established in 2013, it supplies the Brewery Tap outside Claygate station, the Hare & Hounds in Claygate and other local Surrey and South London pubs.

Little Nipper (OG 1033, ABV 3.3%)

Top Notch (OG 1035, ABV 3.5%)
Well-balanced amber-coloured ale with floral hop notes providing a clean bitter finish.

Daisy Gold (OG 1040, ABV 4%) ◆
Golden-coloured ale with a moderate tropical fruit hoppy character and some balancing malt leading to a bittersweet finish.

Wild Orchid (OG 1040, ABV 4%)
Dark, oatmeal porter enhanced with a Madagascan vanilla pod in each cask giving the beer fragrant vanilla undertones.

All Citra (OG 1043, ABV 4.3%)
Bitter with bite, resulting in a distinctly citrus flavour.

Brigstock

7 Park Walk, Brigstock, Kettering, Northamptonshire, NN14 3HH
☎ (01536) 373428 ⊕ brigstockbrewhouse.co.uk

Philip Wilks began brewing in 2012 on a small 52-litre plant using natural spring water from a local limestone aquifer. Six regular beers are brewed. RAIB

Autumn Harvest (OG 1049, ABV 4.2%)
A mellow autumnal beer. The citrus aroma and lingering hoppy taste derive from the use of three different hop varieties.

Gold (OG 1049, ABV 4.2%)
A golden summer ale, with a zesty aroma and refreshing citrus taste.

Liberator (OG 1049, ABV 4.2%)
A refreshing ale with a bitterness along with the subtle flavours of toffee, honey and mead.

Cocoa Special Edition Old Nick's Favourite (OG 1053, ABV 4.8%)

A dark, rich beer. A balanced mixture of black strap molasses, black and chocolate malts and cocoa nibs gives a distinctive flavour of liquorice and toffee with a gentle undertone of chocolate.

Old Nick's Favourite (OG 1053, ABV 4.8%)
A dark, rich beer using English malt and whole hops. A balanced mixture of black strap molasses with black and chocolate malts gives a distinctive flavour of liquorice and toffee.

Potter's Ruin (OG 1053, ABV 4.8%)
A distinctive fruity taste, rounded with a toffee flavour and a pleasant hoppy finish.

Brimstage SIBA

Home Farm, Brimstage, CH63 6HY
☎ (0151) 342 1181 ☎ 07870 968323
⊕ brimstagebrewery.com

Brewing started in 2006 on a 10-barrel plant in a redundant farm dairy in the heart of the Wirral countryside. This is Wirral's first brewery since the closure of the Birkenhead Brewery in the late 1960s. Around 60 outlets are supplied. ‼◆

Sandpiper Light Ale (OG 1036.5, ABV 3.6%)
A session beer; well-balanced, light and refreshing with tropical fruit flavours.

Trappers Hat Bitter (OG 1037.5, ABV 3.8%)
Gold-coloured with a complex bouquet. It provides a mouthful of fruit zest, with hints of orange and grapefruit. A refreshingly hoppy session brew.

Rhode Island Red Bitter (OG 1039, ABV 4%) ◆
Red, smooth and well-balanced malty beer with a good dry aftertaste. Some fruitiness in the taste.

Scarecrow Bitter (OG 1041, ABV 4.2%)
Orange marmalade in colour, this well-balanced session brew has a distinct citrus fruit bouquet and a bitter finish.

Briscoe's

16 Ash Grove, Otley, West Yorkshire, LS21 3EL
☎ (01943) 466515 ✉ briscoe.brewery@virgin.net

☺The brewery was launched in 1998 by microbiologist/chemist Dr Paul Briscoe in the cellar of his house with a one-barrel brew length. Dr Briscoe is currently producing one brew per week on his original plant; several beers are produced on an irregular basis.

Chevin Bitter (OG 1039, ABV 3.8%)
Golden, hoppy bitter.

Otley Gold (OG 1040, ABV 3.9%)

Lighter Shade of Pale (OG 1040, ABV 4%)

Bristol Beer Factory SIBA

Unit A, The Old Brewery, Durnford Street, Ashton, Bristol, BS3 2AW
☎ (0117) 902 6317

Office: c/o Tobacco Factory, Raleigh Road, Southville, Bristol, BS3 1TF ⊕ bristolbeerfactory.co.uk

A 30-barrel microbrewery in a part of the former Ashton Gate Brewing Co, which closed in 1933. 50 outlets are supplied and output and brewing capacity are steadily increasing. ◆RAIB

Nova (OG 1040, ABV 3.8%) ◆

Citrus hop aroma to this straw-coloured, light-bodied and bitter session ale. Hop-led taste with lemon fruit and pale malt following into a bitter hop aftertaste.

Seven (OG 1043, ABV 4.2%) ◈
Mid-brown best bitter with a fruity aroma. Balanced malt and hops with hints of fruit and caramel flavours. Malt and bitterness remain on the aftertaste.

Sunrise (OG 1044, ABV 4.4%) ◈
Refreshing golden ale with grassy hops giving bitter citrus fruit flavours and leading to a bitter finish.

Milk Stout (OG 1049, ABV 4.5%) ◈
Sweet, full-bodied black stout with lactose creaminess. Finishes with smoky roast bitterness.

Independence (OG 1046, ABV 4.6%) ◈
Strong, hoppy aroma and initial flavour. Sweet fruitiness follows, leading to a bitter hoppy finish. Well-balanced with impressive flavour for its strength.

Britannia

Royal Standard of England, Forty Green, Buckinghamshire, HP9 1XS
☎ (01494) 673382 rsoe.co.uk

Britannia began brewing in 2012. The brewery is located in one of the outbuildings at the Royal Standard of England pub in Forty Green, Buckinghamshire. Brewing is currently suspended.

Britman

The Stables, Burton Manor, Burton, Cheshire, CH64 5SJ ☎ 07925 875836
britmanbrewerburtonmanor@gmail.com

Opened in 2014, this 100-litre brewery has been designed, manufactured and installed by the owners and brewers. Located in the old stables of Burton Manor it blends into the character of this listed building. The beers are available in selected local pubs.

London Porter (OG 1043, ABV 4.5%)
Dark, hoppy and slightly bitter with a treacle and coffee aftertaste.

Best Bitter (OG 1044, ABV 4.6%)
Smooth, light and pleasantly bitter.

Golden Ale (OG 1044, ABV 4.6%)
A true golden ale, hoppy and slightly bitter with a mild, sweet aftertaste.

Brixton

Arch 547, Brixton Station Road, Brixton, London, SW9 8PF ☎ 07761 436757 brixtonbrewery.com

Located in a railway arch in central Brixton, the brewery opened in 2013. The bulk of the production is currently bottled, but cask-conditioned ales feature as occasional guests in several pubs in the Brixton area. Beers are generally named after places in Brixton. ♦ RAIB

Reliance Pale Ale (OG 1042, ABV 4.2%) ◈
Grapefruit and hops are present throughout this refreshing golden ale. Dry aftertaste with a hint of bitterness.

Effra Ale (OG 1045, ABV 4.5%) ◈
Dry, copper-coloured best bitter with hops and a trace of citrus in the flavour and finish, which is bitter.

Atlantic APA (OG 1054, ABV 5.4%)

Electric IPA (OG 1065, ABV 6.5%)
Full-bodied IPA; balances malty sweetness and hoppy bitterness with a floral, citrus and tropical fruit hit.

Brockley SIBA

31 Harcourt Road, Brockley, London, SE4 2AJ
☎ 07814 584338 brockleybrewery.co.uk

Established in 2013 by a group of local beer enthusiasts within a converted builder's workshop. The original five-barrel plant has been extended and there are plans to increase capacity further. The brewery concentrates on supplying outlets within a five-mile radius. ♦

Golden Ale (OG 1038, ABV 3.8%) ◈
A hoppy golden ale with some citrus throughout and a bitter finish. Trace of caramelised malt.

Pale Ale (OG 1041, ABV 4.1%) ◈
Well-balanced, dry, hoppy best bitter with some apricot fruit overlaid with biscuit malt.

Porter (OG 1043, ABV 4.3%) ◈
Roast malt with a hint of blackcurrant becoming more hoppy and bitter late in the taste and aftertaste.

Red Ale (OG 1048, ABV 4.8%)
Strong, copper-coloured bitter with a dry finish.

Brodie's SIBA

816a High Road, Leyton, London, E10 6AE ☎ 07828 498733 brodiesbeers.com

Siblings James and Lizzie began commercial brewing in 2008 on a five-barrel plant at the back of the William IV pub in East London. Beers are available at the William IV and their small chain of family-owned pubs as well as other local outlets. !! ♦ RAIB

Citra (OG 1031, ABV 3.1%) ◈
Citrus and tropical fruit in aroma and flavour, which is dry, bitter and faintly sweet. Bitterness grows on drinking.

Kiwi (ABV 3.8%) ◈
A smooth-drinking yellow beer. Flavour is malty sweet overlaid by green fruit, a little hops and a bitter character.

Bethnal Green Bitter (OG 1040, ABV 4%) ◈
A brown-coloured, refreshing but full-bodied bitter with a malty sweetness. Finish is dry with an increasing bitterness.

Old Street Pale Ale (OG 1050, ABV 5%) ◈
Hops and citrus fruit are balanced in this golden beer by the bitterness, a biscuity sweetness and a creamy mouthfeel.

California (OG 1053, ABV 5.3%) ◈
Smooth yellow beer with a citrus fruit aroma. Sweet citrus fruit is balanced with bitterness on the palate and aftertaste.

Broughs

192 Staveley Rd, Wolverhampton, West Midlands, WV1 4RL ☎ 07814 158292
✉ broughsltd@yahoo.co.uk

Broughs is a family-run brewery which began trading in 2008 using spare capacity at several breweries around the West Midlands. In 2011 it moved into rented premises at the former Butlers Springfield brewery (1873-1991). Redevelopment of the site has led Broughs to relocate to more modern premises. It continues to brew three times a week on its four-barrel plant. No pubs are owned, but more than 30 outlets in the West Midlands, Staffordshire and Shropshire are regularly supplied direct. !! RAIB

Springfield (OG 1040, ABV 4%)
A light golden-coloured session ale with a subtle clean taste from the unusual blend of hops.

Blonde (OG 1046, ABV 4.6%)
A contemporary, hoppy and fruity pale yellow-coloured ale.

Pale Ale (OG 1048, ABV 4.8%)
A traditional, strong, pale ale bursting with a sweet hop flavour and a pleasant bitter finish.

Superior (OG 1050, ABV 5%)
A strong, dark mild with a sweet malty finish.

Broughton SIBA

Broughton, ML12 6HQ
☎ (01899) 830345 broughtonales.co.uk

Founded in 1979, Broughton Ales was then one of the first microbreweries. Broughton has developed since then and though more than 60% of production goes into bottle for sale in Britain and abroad, it retains a sizeable range of cask ales. All beers are suitable for vegetarians. !! ♦

Brewer's Gold (OG 1040, ABV 4%)
Using hops from four different countries creating a combination of citrus, orange and pine flavours with subtle hints of spice and plenty of biscuit malt balance.

Clipper IPA (OG 1042, ABV 4.2%)
A light-coloured, crisp, hoppy beer with a clean aftertaste.

Merlin's Ale (OG 1042, ABV 4.2%)
A well-hopped, fruity flavour is balanced by malt in the taste. The finish is bittersweet, light but dry.

Dark 'n' Cloudy Oatmeal Espresso Stout (OG 1044, ABV 4.4%)
A black, medium-bodied stout full of vanilla, espresso and oatmeal flavours.

Exciseman's 80/- (OG 1046, ABV 4.6%)
A traditional 80/- cask ale. A dark, malty brew. Full drinking with a good hop aftertaste.

Dark Dunter (OG 1050, ABV 4.8%)
Bursting with oatmeal and chocolate aromas complemented by dark roasted malts and a rich aftertaste.

Proper IPA (OG 1052, ABV 5%)
Intense spice and biscuit hop flavours.

6.2 IPA (OG 1060, ABV 6.2%)
With quadruple the hops of a typical IPA, this dark chestnut brown example has a bold citrus aroma and a biscuit bitter aftertaste.

Old Jock (OG 1070, ABV 6.7%)
Strong, sweetish and fruity in the finish.

Brown SIBA

See Ashover

Brown Cow

Brown Cow Road, Barlow, North Yorkshire, YO8 8EH
☎ (01757) 618947 browncowbrewery.co.uk

Brewing since 1997, Brown Cow has won awards at many festivals. Keith and Sue Simpson operate a six-barrel plant at its maximum capacity of 17 barrels per week. Handcrafted cask beers brewed using traditional methods are delivered direct from the brewery. Beers are also brewed for Suddaby's. ♦RAIB

Sessions (OG 1033, ABV 3.6%)
A pale, hoppy session beer with a refreshing finish and citrus notes in the aftertaste.

Bitter (OG 1038, ABV 3.8%)
Copper-coloured classic bitter brewed with English hops. Round and full in flavour with a smooth finish.

White Dragon (OG 1039, ABV 4%)
A pale, aromatic beer with a good level of bitterness, citrus undertones and a clean finish.

Scruff's Gold (OG 1041, ABV 4.2%)
Well-balanced golden traditional English ale, round and full-flavoured with a smooth finish.

Captain Oates Mild (OG 1044, ABV 4.5%)
A dark mild with a complex mix of malts and oats. Well-balanced with undertones of coffee and chocolate.

Mrs Simpson's Thriller in Vanilla (OG 1049, ABV 5.1%)
A rich porter brewed with fresh vanilla pods complementing the dark malts.

Broxbourne

Unit 17, Hoddesdon Industrial Estate, Pindar Road, Hoddesdon, Hertfordshire, EN11 0DD
☎ (01438) 940937 broxbournebrewery.co.uk

Broxbourne began brewing in 2013 using a two-barrel plant. Bottle-conditioned beers are also produced under the Fallen Angel brewery name. RAIB

Cowgirl Gold (ABV 4.2%)

Angry Ox Bitter (ABV 4.8%)

Brunning & Price

See Phoenix

Brunswick SIBA

1 Railway Terrace, Derby, DE1 2RU
☎ (01332) 410055 ☎ 07534 401352
brunswickbrewingcompany.co.uk

Derby's oldest brewery, it is a 10-barrel tower plant built as an extension to the Brunswick Inn (qv) in 1991. Bought by Everards in 2002, the brewery is now run separately yet in conjunction with the pub. It supplies the inn, Everards, wholesalers and the free trade, with weekly local deliveries and rotational bi-monthly deliveries to other regions within 100 miles. Brunswick also swaps with other breweries. ‼ ♦ RAIB

White Feather (OG 1038, ABV 3.6%)
Pale yet full-bodied session beer, easy-drinking with a citrus twist.

Triple Hop (OG 1040, ABV 4%)
Straw-coloured ale, three hop varieties used in three stages give a bitter astringency.

Usual (OG 1042, ABV 4.2%)
A traditional English malty best bitter, smooth with hints of toffee.

Railway Porter (OG 1045, ABV 4.3%)
A classic dark porter, lightly hopped with chocolate and coffee notes.

Rocket (OG 1047, ABV 4.7%)
A New World IPA, the use of US and Pacific hops imparts citrus, apricot and mango flavours.

Black Sabbath (OG 1058, ABV 6%)
A strong, dark ale with finely balanced flavours of liquorice, coffee and chocolate.

Bryncelyn

Unit 303, Ystradgynlais Workshops, Trawsffordd Road, Ystradgynlais, SA9 1BS
☎ (01639) 841900
✉ bryncelynbrewery@hotmail.co.uk

Opened in 1999, the brewery relocated to its present premises in 2008 with a six-barrel plant acquired from Webbs Brewery of Ebbw Vale. The owner is fond of Buddy Holly and this is reflected in beer names. ‼ ♦ RAIB

Holly Hop (OG 1039, ABV 3.9%)
Pale amber with a hoppy aroma. A refreshing hoppy, fruity flavour with balancing bitterness; a similar lasting finish. A beer full of flavour for its gravity.

Buddy Marvellous (OG 1040, ABV 4%)
Dark brown with an inviting aroma of malt, roast and fruit. A gentle bitterness mixes roast with malt, hops and fruit, giving a complex, satisfying and lasting finish.

Oh Boy (OG 1045, ABV 4.5%)
An inviting aroma of hops, fruit and malt, and a golden colour. The tasty mix of hops, fruit, bitterness and background malt ends with a long, hoppy, bitter aftertaste.

Bucks Star (NEW) SIBA

23 Twizel Close, Stonebridge, Buckinghamshire, MK13 0DX
☎ (01908) 590054 🌐 facebook.com/BucksStarUK

Possibly the first microbrewery to be solar-powered from panels on the brewery roof, Bucks Star opened in 2015 on a 10-barrel plant. It uses collaborative social media campaigning to help plan future beers. RAIB

No. 1 (OG 1040, ABV 4%)

Bude SIBA

Unit 1, Kings Hill Industrial Estate, Bude, Cornwall, EX23 8QN
☎ (01288) 359937 ☎ 07414 660787
🌐 budebrewery.co.uk

Originally established in 2011 near Launceston as Fry's Brewery, and now relocated to Bude, it started beer production under the Bude Brewery name in 2014. The beer range has also been revamped, with a core range of four brews currently in production.

Neet (OG 1037, ABV 3.7%)

Haven (OG 1042, ABV 4.2%)
Tawny best bitter with hop aroma. Balanced hop and malt character with notes of apple, cranberry, cherry, marmalade and honey.

Summerleaze (OG 1047, ABV 4.7%)
Refreshing pale brown strong bitter. Sweet malt with stone fruit flavours balanced by hops, becoming bitter.

Black Rock (OG 1051, ABV 5.1%)
Red porter with malt aroma. Sweet roast malt and stone fruit flavours with bitterness. Malt, hops and dry bitter finish.

Buffy's SIBA

Rectory Road, Tivetshall St Mary, Norfolk, NR15 2DD
☎ (01379) 676523 🌐 buffys.co.uk

Established in 1993, Buffy's brewing capacity is 20 barrels. The brewery owns two pubs, the Wicklewood Cherry Tree and the Foulden White Hart. Barley for all brewing is grown in Norfolk. Around 100 outlets are supplied. ♦ RAIB

Norwich Terrier (OG 1036, ABV 3.6%)
A peachy aroma introduces this refreshing, gold-coloured bitter. Strong bitter notes, hops and grapefruit produce a long, dry finish.

Bitter (OG 1039, ABV 3.9%)
A strong plummy aroma leads into a sweet malty beginning. Caramel notes add depth to a long fruity finish.

Mild (OG 1042, ABV 4.2%)
Complex with a smooth but grainy feel. Caramel and blackcurrant initially bolster the heavy malt influence. Short malty finish.

Polly's Folly (OG 1043, ABV 4.3%)
Well-balanced with a definitive malty spine. Elderberry notes and a long, dry, bittersweet finale.

Hopleaf (OG 1044.5, ABV 4.5%)
A gentle hop nose. Strawberries mingle with the hops as the malt gently subsides to leave a bittersweet, dry finish.

Mucky Duck (OG 1044, ABV 4.5%)
Roasted malt throughout with a sweet fruitiness giving depth without becoming dominant. Chewy mouthfeel and lingering finish.

Norwegian Blue (OG 1049, ABV 4.9%)
Nutty caramel aroma. A well-balanced mix of malt and bitterness with caramel, hops, and sweetness. Strong, increasingly bitter finish.

Ale (OG 1055, ABV 5.5%)

Bull Lane

See Stables

Bullfinch

☎ 07515 167925 🌐 thebullfinchbrewery.co.uk

Bullfinch began brewing in 2014 using a 2.5-barrel plant. Production is mainly keg but bottle-conditioned beers are available. The brewery formerly used spare capacity at Anspach & Hobday (qv) and is moving to new premises in 2015.

Bullmastiff

14 Bessemer Close, Leckwith, Cardiff, CF11 8DL
☎ (029) 2066 5292 ✉ bob.bullmastiff@live.co.uk

The brewery has recently been purchased following the retirement of the founders, Bob and Paul Jenkins. The new brewer, Ramphai, is believed to be the only Thai brewer currently producing in the UK. The beers are still brewed using the founders' recipes and are available in south-east Wales, with the JD Wetherspoon Bears Head in Penarth serving as the informal brewery tap.

Slobberchops (OG 1046, ABV 4.6%)

Welsh Red (OG 1048, ABV 4.8%)

Olde Snarler (OG 1053, ABV 5.1%)

Son of a Bitch (OG 1062, ABV 6%) ◆
A complex, warming amber ale with a tasty blend of hops, malt and fruit flavours, with increasing bitterness.

Special Reserve (OG 1068, ABV 6.5%)

Bumpmill

The Cottage, Hallfieldgate, Shirland, Derbyshire, DE55 6AG
☎ (01773) 830431 🌐 bumpmillbrewery.co.uk

A four-barrel family brewery located in a converted building overlooking the beautiful Amber Valley. The name comes from the site of an old Bump Mill close by – bump was coarse cotton used to make wicks for candles. Bumpmill has one tied house, Stanley's micro pub in Matlock. ♦

Moonraker (OG 1038, ABV 3.8%)
A quaffable blonde ale.

Drops of Jupiter (OG 1040, ABV 4%)
A blonde pale ale with grapefruit notes leading to a slightly bitter finish.

Heart of Gold (OG 1042, ABV 4.2%)
A golden pale ale.

Thunder Road (OG 1044, ABV 4.4%)
Copper-coloured premium bitter. Full-bodied chocolate and roast malt with a smooth finish.

Glory Daze (OG 1045, ABV 4.5%)
A traditional amber-coloured bitter.

Buntingford SIBA

Greys Brewhouse, Therfield Road, Royston, Hertfordshire, SG8 9NW
☎ (01763) 250749 ☎ 07879 698541
🌐 buntingford-brewery.co.uk

Brewing commenced on the current site in 2005 and has expanded to a capacity of around 60 barrels a week. Two regular beers are brewed year round alongside occasional brews and themed specials. The beers are brewed using water from an on-site well and all liquid waste is treated in a reed bed. The brewery is located on a conservation farm and there is a wide variety of bird life visible from the doors of the brewhouse, often including rare and endangered species. !! ♦

Highwayman (OG 1036, ABV 3.6%)

Twitchell (OG 1038, ABV 3.8%)

Burley Street

Fox & Newt, 7-9 Burley Street, Leeds, LS3 1LD
☎ (0113) 245 4505 ✉ i_bennett.fox@hotmail.co.uk

Burley Street Brewhouse is in the cellar of the Fox & Newt pub where the first brewery was installed by Whitbread in the 1980s. The freehold was purchased by the current owners and brewing recommenced in 2010 and then again, after a two-year break, in 2015 by the team from the Whippet Brewing Company. The Pack Horse at Woodhouse is the only other outlet supplied.

Brickyard (OG 1038.5, ABV 3.7%) ◆
Drinkable session bitter with a good mix of malt and hops, amber-coloured with a lingering bitter finish.

Laguna Seca (OG 1041, ABV 4%) ◆
Golden, blonde beer with a grapefruit flavour. Initial sweetness and full body are balanced by a dry, fruity, citrus finish.

Burning Sky SIBA

Place Barn, The Street, Firle, East Sussex, BN8 6LP
☎ (01273) 858080 🌐 burningskybeer.com

Burning Sky started brewing in 2013 using a 15-barrel plant, based on the Firle Estate in the South Downs. It is owned and run by Mark Tranter (ex-Dark Star head brewer). Brewing takes place four days a week, initially producing five regular beers. The brewery has its own yeast strains suited to the beer styles. It specialises in pale ales and Belgian-inspired farmhouse beers and has an extensive barrel-aging programme. RAIB

Plateau (OG 1035, ABV 3.5%)
Pale gold in colour with a crisp malt edge and sharp bitterness. Full in flavour, zesty and refreshing.

Aurora (OG 1056, ABV 5.6%)
A premium strength pale ale with a blend of malts to provide a juicy backbone and a pale amber colour. Hops give a resinous mouthfeel – big citrus and tropical fruit flavours, which are prominent, yet well balanced.

Devil's Rest IPA (OG 1070, ABV 7%)
A full strength IPA with a burnt orange colour and full flavour.

Burnside SIBA

Laurencekirk Business Park, Laurencekirk, Aberdeenshire, AB30 1EY
☎ (01561) 377316 🌐 burnsidebrewery.co.uk

Burnside began brewing in 2010 using a 2.5-barrel plant. There are plans for an upgrade to a 6.5-barrel plant and a bottling kit. RAIB

Black Katz (OG 1036, ABV 3.6%)

3-BULLZ (OG 1038, ABV 3.8%)

Mad Dogz (OG 1038, ABV 3.8%)

Wild Rhino (OG 1045, ABV 4.5%)

M-PIRE (OG 1052, ABV 5.2%)

Burscough SIBA

c/o Hop Vine, Liverpool Road North, Burscough, Lancashire, L40 4BY
☎ (01704) 893799 ☎ 07831 225656
⊕ burscoughbrewery.co.uk

Burscough commenced brewing in 2010 in old stable buildings in the courtyard to the rear of the Hop Vine, Currently brewing on a four-barrel plant but plans are underway to relocate and to expand.

Flat Rib Mild (OG 1036, ABV 3.6%)
A classic mild; dark and satisfying.

Priory Gold (OG 1038, ABV 3.8%) ◄
A sweet and fruity, lightly bittered, easy-drinking session beer.

Duke of Lancaster (OG 1040, ABV 4%) ◄
Brown beer with a roast bitter finish.

Mere Blonde (OG 1040, ABV 4%) ◄
A pale, full-flavoured, thirst quenching golden ale with a light bitterness and a prominent citrus hop aroma. The malt undertones in the body are complemented by a full hop flavour which gives way to a grapefruit finish.

Ringtail (OG 1042, ABV 4.2%)
A ruby red ale. Full-bodied with a prominent bitterness and a delightful malt character. A noticeable grassy aroma with hints of marmalade and molasses.

Black Canon Stout (OG 1045, ABV 4.5%)
A dark stout, full-flavoured with hints of coffee and liquorice in the finish.

Mug Billy (OG 1045, ABV 4.5%)
A traditional best bitter. Light amber in colour and easy-drinking with a noticeable bitterness.

Wailing Willy (OG 1050, ABV 5%)
A premium pale beer with a slightly fruity taste.

Thorougood (OG 1051, ABV 5.1%)
Golden in colour with a citrus finish.

Sutler's IPA (OG 1055, ABV 5.5%)
A powerful, amber-coloured, heavily-hopped ale. A sharp, prominent bitterness gives way to a massive aroma with hints of grapefruit and other citrus fruits.

Burton Bridge SIBA ⊚

24 Bridge Street, Burton upon Trent, Staffordshire, DE14 1SY
☎ (01283) 510573 ⊕ burtonbridgebrewery.co.uk

⊚The brewery was established in 1982 by Bruce Wilkinson and Geoff Mumford and owns five pubs in the local area, including its CAMRA award-winning brewery tap. More than 300 outlets are supplied direct. ‼️ 🍺 ◆ RAIB

Golden Delicious (OG 1037, ABV 3.8%) ◄
A Burton classic with sulphurous aroma and well-balanced hops and fruit. An apple fruitiness, sharp and refreshing start leads to a lingering mouth-watering bitter finish with a hint of astringency. Light, crisp and refreshing.

Sovereign Gold (OG 1040, ABV 4%) ◄
Sweet caramel aroma with a grassy hop start with malt overtones. Fresh and fruity with a bitterness that emerges and continues to develop.

XL Bitter (OG 1039, ABV 4%) ◄
Another Burton classic with sulphurous aroma. Golden with fruit and hops and a characteristic

lingering aftertaste hinting of toffee apple sweetness.

Bridge Bitter (OG 1041, ABV 4.2%) ◄
Gentle aroma of malt and fruit. Good balanced start finishing with a robust hop mouthfeel.

Burton Porter (OG 1044, ABV 4.5%) ◄
Chocolate aromas and smooth taste of smoky roasted grain and coffee.

Damson Porter (OG 1044, ABV 4.5%)

Stairway to Heaven (OG 1049, ABV 5%) ◄
Golden bitter. A perfectly balanced beer. The malty and hoppy start leads to a hoppy body with a mouthwatering finish.

Top Dog Stout (OG 1049, ABV 5%) ◄
Black and rich with a roast and malty start. Fruity and abundant hops give a fruity, bitter finish with a mouth-watering edge. Also available as Bramble Stout.

Festival Ale (OG 1054, ABV 5.5%) ◄
Caramel aroma with plenty of hop taste balanced by malty sweetness.

Thomas Sykes (OG 1095, ABV 10%) ◄
Kid in a sweetshop aroma. Rich fruity spirited tastes – warming and dangerously drinkable.

Burton Old Cottage

Unit 10, Eccleshall Business Park, Hawkins Lane, Burton upon Trent, Staffordshire, DE14 1PT ☎ 07909 931250 ⊕ oldcottagebeer.co.uk

☺The brewery was originally installed in the old Heritage Brewery. When the site was taken over, it moved to a modern industrial unit. The brewery was sold in 2005, the following year saw heavy investment in new production and storage facilities by the new owners. ‼️◆

Oak Ale (OG 1044, ABV 4%) ◄
Tawny, full-bodied bitter. A sweet start with balanced fruit gives way to a slight roast taste with some caramel for interest. A dry, hoppy finish satisfies the palate.

Chestnut (OG 1042, ABV 4.2%)
A dark session ale with a touch of bitterness and a pleasant, full aftertaste.

Stout (OG 1047, ABV 4.7%) ◄
Roast aroma with background fruit, roast tastes with gentle sweetness. Bitterness develops surprisingly from the sweet start to leave a sharp-edged mouthfeel. Roast throughout with a malt background.

Pastiche (OG 1050, ABV 5.2%)
A smooth, balanced ale with a complex taste and aroma.

Halcyon Daze (OG 1050, ABV 5.3%) ◄
Tawny and creamy with touches of hop, fruit and malt aroma. Fruity taste and finish.

Burtonwood

Bold Lane, Burtonwood, Warrington, Cheshire, WA5 4TH
☎ (01925) 220022 ⊕ thomashardybrewery.co.uk

Thomas Hardy's only brewery was run as a contract operation for Heineken/John Smiths and some smaller breweries. It was taken over by Molson Coors in 2015. Currently producing no real ale.

Bushy's SIBA

Mount Murray Brewery, Mount Murray, Braddan, Isle of Man, IM4 1JE
☎ (01624) 661244 ⊕ bushys.com

⊚Launched in 1986 as a brewpub, Bushys relocated in 1990 when demand outgrew capacity. Bushys goes one step further than the Manx Pure Beer Law preferring the German Reinheitsgebot (Pure Beer Law) that excludes sugar. ‼◆

Castletown Bitter (OG 1035, ABV 3.5%)
A light, golden session beer full of floral and citrus hints.

Ruby (1874) Mild (OG 1035, ABV 3.5%) ◆
Classic full-bodied malty ruby mild with sweet caramel flavours throughout, and well-balanced hops.

Bitter (OG 1038, ABV 3.8%) ◆
A traditional malty and hoppy beer with good balance. The fruit lasts through to the bitter finish.

Old Bushy Tail (OG 1045, ABV 4.5%)
A reddish-brown beer with a pronounced hop and malt aroma, the malt tending towards treacle. Slightly sweet and malty on the palate with distinct orange tones. The full finish is malty and hoppy with a hint of toffee.

Butcombe ⊙

Cox's Green, Wrington, Somerset, BS40 5PA
☎ (01934) 863963 ⊕ butcombe.com

⊠ Butcombe was bought by the Jersey-based Liberation Group for a reported £15m in 2015. Originally established in 1978 by Simon Whitmore and sold to Guy Newell and friends in 2003, Butcombe moved to a new purpose-built brewery with a 150-barrel plant in 2005. It supplies around 500 outlets direct and similar numbers via wholesalers and pub companies. The brewery has an estate of 18 freehouses. ‼🍺◆

Adam Henson's Rare Breed (OG 1038, ABV 3.8%) ◆
Sulphurous aroma with undertones of unripe fruit combine in this thin-bodied ale. Bitterness and astringency dominate and continue into the finish.

Matthew Pale Ale (OG 1038, ABV 3.8%) 🍺
Light amber-coloured, hoppy beer with citrus notes, balanced with a floral aroma and a clean, dry finish.

Bitter (OG 1039, ABV 4%) ◆
Bitter tawny ale. Malt with hops and ripe fruit contribute to a well-balanced flavour. Long, refreshing, bitter aftertaste.

Gold (OG 1045, ABV 4.4%) 🍺 ◆
Amber golden ale with light aroma of fruit and hops, leading to well-balanced flavours of malt, pale fruit and hops. Bitter aftertaste.

Bute (NEW)

15-17 Columshill Street, Rothesay, Isle of Bute, PA20 0DN
☎ (01700) 504260 ☎ 07980 259511
⊕ butebrewco.co.uk

Situated in the centre of Rothesay on the Isle of Bute, brewing began in 2015. Beers are supplied to several local outlets, and further afield. Beer festivals are also supplied. ‼🍺

Scalpsie Blonde (ABV 3.8%)
A good session blonde.

Red (ABV 4.2%)
A caramel beer with some fruitiness from the hops

Maids (ABV 4.3%)
Malty sweetness is balanced wtih bitterness from the hops.

Butts SIBA

Northfield Farm, Wantage Road, Great Shefford, Berkshire, RG17 7BY
☎ (01488) 648133 ⊕ buttsbrewery.com

⊠ The brewery was set up in a converted barn in 1994. In 2002 the brewery took the decision to become dedicated to organic production; all the beers brewed use organic malted barley and organic hops and are certified by the Soil Association. 🍺◆RAIB

Jester (OG 1036, ABV 3.5%) ◆
A pale brown session bitter with a hoppy aroma and a hint of fruit. The taste balances malt, hops, fruit and bitterness with a hoppy aftertaste.

Traditional (OG 1040, ABV 4%) ◆
A pale brown bitter that is quite soft on the tongue with hoppy citrus flavours accompanying a gentle bittersweetness. A long, dry aftertaste is dominated by fruity hops.

Barbus Barbus (OG 1046, ABV 4.6%) ◆
Golden ale with a fruity hoppy aroma and a hint of malt. Hops dominate taste and aftertaste, accompanied by fruitiness and bitterness, with a hint of balancing sweetness.

Buxton SIBA

Unit 4, Staden Business Park, Staden Lane, Buxton, Derbyshire, SK17 9RZ
☎ (01298) 244200 ☎ 07754 015743
⊕ buxtonbrewery.co.uk

Buxton Brewery was set up in 2009 as a five-barrel brewery and now currently operates on a 24-barrel plant. Water is drawn from its own borehole. Its brewery tap is in Buxton and it exports to 25 countries. ◆RAIB

Jacob's Ladder (OG 1027, ABV 2.7%)
Low strength session bitter with a big hop character.

Moor Top (OG 1038, ABV 3.6%)
Heavily-hopped pale ale with a refreshing grapefruit bitterness.

Rednik Stout (OG 1045, ABV 4.1%)
Classic stout with big roast malt character.

SPA (Special Pale Ale) (OG 1041, ABV 4.1%)
A single-hopped beer showcasing Citra hops.

Wild Boar (OG 1057, ABV 5.7%)
IPA with tropical fruit on the palate and nose, with a soft mouthfeel.

Axe Edge (OG 1065, ABV 6.8%)
IPA with big tropical and zesty fruit nose and palate.

Extra Stout (OG 1081, ABV 7.4%)
Big malt, roast character.

Tsar (OG 1096, ABV 9.5%)
Huge, rich stout with notes of dark chocolate, coffee, molasses and dried fruit.

Buzzard

Speddyd Farm, Llandyrnog, LL16 4LE ☎ 07972 202880 ⊕ buzzardbrewery.co.uk

Brewing commenced in 2013 on a 2.5-barrel plant in a former farm building. 30-50 pubs are supplied with a 30-mile radius. There are plans to start bottling beer.

Village Bitter (OG 1039, ABV 3.9%) ◆
A malty session bitter with a dry taste and subtle hop characteristics leading to a bitter finish.

Best Bitter (OG 1042, ABV 4.2%)

Pale of Clwyd (OG 1042, ABV 4.2%) ◆
A light and fruity best bitter with a sweetish initial taste and a hoppy, dry finish.

Vale Ale (OG 1045, ABV 4.5%) ◆
A dark-brown best bitter, smooth and malty with a dry, hoppy finish.

Old Buzzard (OG 1050, ABV 5.3%)

Bwthyn (NEW)

Llanbadrig, Llanbadrig, LL67 0LN

Brewing began in 2014. Initially only bottle-conditioned beers are produced. RAIB

By the Horns SIBA

Unit 25, Summerstown, London, SW17 0BQ
☎ (020) 3417 7338 ⊕ bythehorns.co.uk

⊗ By the Horns began brewing in 2012 using a 5.5-barrel plant. It is located in industrial units near Wimbledon Stadium. The brewery has a licence for on and off sales at its on-site bar, and hold regular comedy evenings. ▰

Stiff Upper Lip (OG 1038, ABV 3.8%) ◆
A classic amber-coloured bitter, well-balanced with hops to the fore and a hint of citrus. Dry bitter finish.

Mayor of Garratt (ABV 4.3%) ◆
Amber best bitter with sweet biscuit and orange fruit flavour. Long dry finish with some bitterness and peppery hop.

Diamond Geezer (OG 1049, ABV 4.9%) ◆
Malty, hoppy red ale with blackcurrant, citrus and faint roast notes. Bitterness develops and builds in the aftertaste.

Lambeth Walk (OG 1051, ABV 5.1%) ◆
Well-balanced black porter with hops and a little fruit throughout. The roasted bitterness is complemented by the malt notes.

Byatt's SIBA

Unit 10, Lythalls Lane Industrial Estate, Lythalls Lane, Coventry, CV6 6FL
☎ (024) 7663 7996 ⊕ byattsbrewery.co.uk

Established in 2011 and located on the north side of Coventry, now supplying the local West Midlands area and expanding into other regions, this was the first commercial brewery in the city for over 80 years. ◆ RAIB

XK Dark (OG 1038, ABV 3.5%) 🗇 📕 ◆
Smoky aromas then a mass of varied tastes ending in diminishing hop and roast.

Coventry Bitter (OG 1039, ABV 3.8%)

Big Cat (OG 1042, ABV 4%)

Phoenix Gold (OG 1043, ABV 4.2%)

Urban Red (OG 1047, ABV 4.5%)

Regal Blond (OG 1053, ABV 5.2%)

C&C Wellpark

Wellpark Brewery, 161 Duke Street, Glasgow, G31 1JD

No real ale. ‼

Cader SIBA

Unit 4, Marian Mawr Enterprise Park, Dolgellau, LL40 1UU ☎ 07931 734655 ⊕ caderales.com

Cader Ales was founded in 2012 by a husband-and-wife team. It was expanded in 2013 to its present five-barrel capacity. It is situated close to the centre of the picturesque market town of Dolgellau. ‼

Cader Gold (OG 1038, ABV 3.8%)
A light, hoppy golden ale with a subtle aroma of honey, lemon and tarragon.

Idris Bitter (OG 1041, ABV 4.1%)
Traditional bitter using a blend of malted barley and Willamette hops to give soft caramel and spicy notes.

Tallyllyn Pale Ale (OG 1044, ABV 4.4%)
A classic IPA using Cascade hops to give refreshingly bitter, citrus floral notes.

Glasdir Copper (OG 1045, ABV 4.5%)
A deep, copper-coloured ale with spicy tones and malty finish with a touch of caramel.

Red Bandit (OG 1050, ABV 5%)
A warm ruby ale based on a traditional recipe with spicy berry aromas.

Caffle SIBA

The Old School, Narberth, SA67 8DS
☎ (01437) 541502 ⊕ cafflebrewery.co.uk

⊗ Caffle began brewing in 2013 using a four-barrel plant producing ale in small batches, mainly for the local market. Further beers are planned. ‼ ▰ RAIB

Quay Ale (OG 1044, ABV 4%)

Sholly Amber (OG 1043, ABV 4.1%)
Amber brown in colour, with liquorice and caramel notes.

Kift Blonde (OG 1044, ABV 4.3%)
Straw-coloured, with citrus and floral notes, flavoured with nettle tips.

Darker Side of Pale (OG 1044.5, ABV 4.4%)
American-style pale ale – medium amber in colour, well-hopped and fruity.

In The Grip (OG 1052, ABV 4.7%)
Ruby-red in colour, malty caramel, slightly sweet, warming.

Skaddly Puck (OG 1048, ABV 4.8%)
An IPA-style best bitter with a hoppy citrus flavour.

Drop Squint (OG 1052, ABV 5.2%)
Light golden in colour, smooth, clean tasting with honey, malt and biscuit flavours.

Cairngorm SIBA

Unit 12, Dalfaber Industrial Estate, Aviemore, PH22 1ST
(01479) 812222 cairngormbrewery.com

Cairngorm produces seven regular cask beers along with seasonal ales on a 20-barrel plant. Now with its own bottling line and a capacity of 140 barrels, the free trade is supplied as far as the central belt, nationaly via wholesalers. !! ♦

Nessies Monster Mash (OG 1040, ABV 4.1%)
A good traditional English-type bitter with plenty of bitterness and strong malt flavour and a fruity background. Lingering bitterness in the aftertaste with diminishing sweetness.

Stag (OG 1040, ABV 4.1%)
A fine best bitter with plenty of roast and hop throughout. This tawny brew also has plenty of malt in the lingering bittersweet aftertaste.

Trade Winds (OG 1043, ABV 4.3%)
A multi-award winning beer. A massive citrus fruit, hop and elderflower nose leads to hints of grapefruit in the mouth. The exceptional bitter sweetness in the taste lasts through the long, lingering aftertaste.

Black Gold (OG 1044, ABV 4.4%)
Roast malt dominates throughout, slight smokiness in aroma leading to a liquorice and blackcurrant taste giving it a background sweetness. Long, dry bitter finish.

Gold / Sheepshaggers Gold (OG 1044, ABV 4.5%)
Fruit and hops to the fore with a hint of caramel in this sweetish brew.

Highland IPA (OG 1049, ABV 5%)
Refreshing light-coloured, citrus-hopped IPA.

Wildcat (OG 1049.5, ABV 5.1%)
A full-bodied warming strong bitter. Malt predominates but there is an underlying hop character through to the well-balanced aftertaste. Drinks dangerously less than its ABV.

Caledonian SIBA

42 Slateford Road, Edinburgh, EH11 1PH
(0131) 337 1286 caledonianbeer.com

The brewery was founded by Lorimer & Clark in 1869 and was sold to Vaux of Sunderland in 1919. In 1987 the brewery was saved from closure by a management buy-out and became independent. The brewery was purchased by S&N in 2004 and became part of Heineken in 2008. Monthly guest beers are produced, as well as a rolling programme of special beers covering each of the seasons. A pilot plant has been installed to make trial beers. !! ♦

Deuchars IPA (OG 1039.5, ABV 3.8%)
Golden session ale with hop aroma and dry bitter finish. Balanced, with malt adding body and fruit a balancing sweetness.

Flying Scotsman (OG 1045.5, ABV 4%)
Well-balanced, malty beer with bittersweet character. Similar to a Scottish 80/-, but dryer and with more hop bitterness.

Edinburgh Castle 80/- (OG 1042.4, ABV 4.1%)
A predominantly malty brown beer with soft roast and caramel throughout. Fruit gives sweetness, typical of a Scottish 80/-.

Golden XPA (OG 1044, ABV 4.3%)
Nicely balanced golden ale with malt and fruit throughout, Hops come to the fore in the increasingly dry, bitter aftertaste.

Calverley's SIBA

23a Hooper Street, Cambridge, CB1 2NZ
(01223) 312370 07769 537342
calverleys.com

Sam Calverley and his brother began brewing in 2013 after many years as home brewers. They are currently supplying local pubs.

Citra Bitter (ABV 3.6%)
Classic British bitter with a modern hop.

Best Bitter (ABV 4.8%)
A smooth amber-coloured ale, with a good balance of malt and subtle bittering hops.

IPA (ABV 5%)

Calvors SIBA

Home Farm, Coddenham Green, Suffolk, IP6 9UN
(01449) 711055 calvors.co.uk

Calvors Brewery was established in 2008 and brews four craft lagers, as well as cask-conditioned beers. All beers are suitable for vegetarians and vegans.

Lodestar Festival Ale (OG 1038, ABV 3.8%)
A rich, golden straw-coloured beer with a gentle sweetness and honey aroma. Lightly hopped, creating a well-balanced ale.

Smooth Hoperator (OG 1040, ABV 4%)
A pale ale combining four different malts to give a copper colour and a background sweetness. Well-rounded and easy-drinking.

Cambridge

1 King Street, Cambridge, CB1 1LH
(01223) 858155 thecambridgebrewhouse.com

Brewing began in 2013. ♦

King's Parade (ABV 3.8%)
A good traditional English bitter with moderate biscuity malt and resiny hop throughout and a hint of caramel. Dry finish.

Misty River (ABV 4.2%)
Golden beer dominated by grapefruit on nose, palate and a lingering dry aftertaste.

Night Porter (ABV 4.4%)
A creamy black/red beer luxuriating in a blend of dark chocolate and coffee, softened by raisins.

Cambrinus

See Liverpool Organic

Camden Town SIBA

55-59 Wilkin Street Mews, Kentish Town, London, NW5 3NN
(020) 7485 1671 camdentownbrewery.com

No real ale. Camden Town is a modern, automated brewhouse situated in five railway arches underneath Kentish Town West railway station, NW5, with two other arches as storage areas, and six conditioning tanks outside. There is a brewery tap on site, in one arch. The majority of its output is in keg form, with one of its beers contract brewed by de Brabandere of Belgium, which has bought a 10% share in Camden. There are plans to build larger premises. ‼

Hood (OG 1043, ABV 4.3%)

Slap Ale (OG 1043, ABV 4.3%)
Pale with a hoppy palate that is not overpowering.

Teddy Bear (OG 1043, ABV 4.3%)
Pale, easy-drinking bitter.

Camerons SIBA

Lion Brewery, Stranton, Hartlepool, County Durham, TS24 7QS
☎ (01429) 852000 cameronsbrewery.com

Founded 1865, Camerons was bought in 2002 by Castle Eden and production moved to Hartlepool. In 2003 the Lions Den, a 10-barrel microbrewery, was set up to produce and bottle small batches of guest ales and undertake contract brewing and bottling. ‼ ♦

Best Bitter (OG 1036, ABV 3.6%)
A light bitter but well-balanced, with hops and malt.

IPA (OG 1038, ABV 3.8%)
A straw-coloured, light IPA.

Strongarm (OG 1041, ABV 4%)
A well-rounded, ruby-red ale with a distinctive, tight creamy head; initially fruity, but with a good balance of malt, hops and moderate bitterness.

Trophy Special (OG 1040, ABV 4%)
An amber ale, slightly sweet and malty, fruity and hoppy.

Gold Bullion (OG 1043, ABV 4.3%)
Gold-coloured, full-bodied ale with a good hop flavour

Contract brewed for Heineken:

John Smith's Bitter (OG 1035, ABV 3.8%)

Cannon Royall SIBA IFBB

Fruiterer's Arms, Uphampton Lane, Uphampton, Worcestershire, WR9 0JW
☎ (01905) 621161 cannonroyall.co.uk

Cannon Royall's first brew was in 1993 in a converted cider house behind the Fruiterer's Arms. The brewery supplies a number of mainly local outlets. ‼ ♦ RAIB

Fruiterers Mild (OG 1037, ABV 3.7%)
This black-hued brew has rich malty aromas that lead to a fruity mix of bitter hops and sweetness, and a short, balanced aftertaste.

Hunny Bear (OG 1038, ABV 3.8%)

King's Shilling (OG 1038, ABV 3.8%)
A golden bitter that packs a citrus hoppy punch throughout.

Arrowhead Bitter (OG 1039, ABV 3.9%)
A powerful punch of hops attacks the nose before the feast of bitterness. The memory of this golden brew fades too soon.

Comfortably Stout (OG 1041, ABV 4%)
Full-flavoured, slightly dry, light stout.

Arrowhead Extra (OG 1043, ABV 4.3%)
A Fuggles hop punch leads to a smooth palate and pleasant finish with a good malt balance.

Blond Bombshell (OG 1043, ABV 4.3%)

Grapeshot (OG 1043, ABV 4.3%)
Gold-coloured with a citrus bite.

Canopy (NEW)

Arch 1127, Bath Factory Estate, 41 Norwood Road, Herne Hill, London, SE24 9AJ ☎ 07792 463386
canopybeer.com

Canopy started brewing in 2014 and opened a tap room in 2015. Its beers are suitable for vegans and vegetarians. ‼ RAIB

Sunray Pale (OG 1041, ABV 4%)

Full Moon Porter (OG 1045, ABV 4.8%)

Ruskin Wheat Beer (OG 1052, ABV 5.2%)

Brockwell IPA (OG 1049, ABV 5.4%)

Milkwood Amber (OG 1058, ABV 7%)

Canterbury Ales SIBA

Unit 7, Stour Valley Business Park, Ashford Road, Chartham, Kent, CT4 7HF
☎ (01227) 732541 ☎ 07944 657978
canterbury-ales.co.uk

Brewing commenced in 2010. The eight-barrel plant was supplied by PBC Brewery Installations. ‼

Wife of Bath's Ale (OG 1038, ABV 3.9%)
A golden beer with strong bitterness and grapefruit hop character, leading to a long, dry finish.

Reeve's Ale (OG 1040, ABV 4.1%)

Miller's Ale (OG 1044, ABV 4.5%)

Canterbury Brewers

Foundry Brew Pub, White Horse Lane, Canterbury, Kent, CT1 2RU
☎ (01227) 455899 thefoundrycanterbury.co.uk

Canterbury Brewers started brewing in 2011, situated in the Foundry brewpub (formerly a Victorian foundry) in the heart of Canterbury. 2013 saw a significant increase in capacity. 16 beers are usually available all year round, with a small core range and many seasonal beers and specials. Several events and festivals are run throughout the year, including the Kent Green Hop Festival. The company also runs the nearby City Arms.

Biggleston's Birdman (OG 1035, ABV 3.6%)
American-style brown ale.

Foundryman's Gold (OG 1040, ABV 4%)

Foundry Torpedo (OG 1044, ABV 4.5%)

Streetlight Porter (OG 1059, ABV 5.8%)

Cap House

444-446 Bradford Road, Batley, West Yorkshire, WF17 5LW
☎ (01924) 479909 ☎ 07981 858270
caphousebrewery.co.uk

Cap House began in 2011 using a 2.5-barrel brew plant as a joint venture between Peter Lister, who has a plastics business at the location, and

THE BREWERIES

Gary Wardman of the Reindeer Inn, Overton, which is the brewery tap. ♦

Miners A Pint (OG 1038, ABV 3.8%)
A tangy session bitter with a smooth mouthfeel balanced by a toffee undertone and deep, dry finish with lingering fruit notes.

Blonde & Beyond (OG 1040, ABV 4%)
A light, hoppy beer brewed to create a well-balanced fruity taste. Refreshing citrus and grapefruit flavours for a bittersweet finish.

Fox Hunter (OG 1040, ABV 4%)
Thick, creamy head, followed by a subtle balance of hoppy, fruity, bittersweet flavours of caramel and a hint of liquorice with a malty fruit aroma. Easy-drinking, full-bodied ale.

Hay Blondie (ABV 4.2%)
A light, golden ale.

Miners a Light (OG 1042, ABV 4.2%)
A smooth, blonde ale releasing light fruity notes with a hint of citrus.

Ruby (OG 1054, ABV 5.6%)
A rich ruby red ale with a smooth finish with fruity nut/toffee aroma and tangy palate.

Captain Cook SIBA

White Swan, 1 West End, Stokesley, North Yorkshire, TS9 5BL
☎ (01642) 710263 captaincookbrewery.com

The Captain Cook Brewery is located within the 18th-century White Swan pub. The brewery, which started in 1999, has a six-barrel plant. ‼♦

Resolution (OG 1037, ABV 3.7%)

Botany Bay (OG 1040, ABV 4%)
A light ale with a hint of grapefruit and spruce.

Red Bay (OG 1040, ABV 4%)
Irish-style, red, hoppy ale.

Sunset (OG 1040, ABV 4%)
A smooth, light ale with a hint of citrus flavours.

Slipway (OG 1042, ABV 4.2%)
A light-coloured, full-flavoured, hoppy ale with a smooth malt aftertaste.

Endeavour (OG 1043, ABV 4.3%)
Brown ale with a bitter finish.

Black Porter (OG 1044, ABV 4.4%)
Chocolate notes and dominant roast flavours lead to a dry, bitter finish.

Carbon Smith (NEW)

69C Mayfield Road, Edinburgh, EH9 3AA ☎ 07518 106487 carbonsmith.co.uk

Carbon Smith started brewing in a fourth-floor tenement flat bedroom in Edinburgh. It now occupies a self-built two-barrel brewery in the Newington area of the city and has plans to expand to a 10-barrel plant.

Carlisle SIBA

Spinners Arms, Cummersdale, Carlisle, Cumbria, CA2 6BD
☎ (01228) 532928 ☎ 07423 595921
thespinnersarms.org.uk

Carlisle is a family-run brewery established in 2013 using a 2.5-barrel plant. Situated behind the owner's freehouse, beer is available in the pub and other local outlets. ‼

Pale Ale (OG 1039, ABV 3.8%)
A traditional pale ale, light and crisp. A session ale with biscuit tastes coming through from the malts and enough bitterness from the hops to make it refreshingly well-balanced.

Spun Gold (OG 1043, ABV 4.2%)
A red/gold-coloured beer with a sweet taste. The hops follow on to build on the flavour and complement the balanced finish.

Flaxen (OG 1042, ABV 4.5%)

Magic Number (OG 1046, ABV 4.5%)
A premium bitter, soft and smooth with caramel and toffee flavours, lightly bittered to give a refreshing, malty beer.

Nut Brown (OG 1048, ABV 4.7%)
A chestnut-coloured beer with a full-flavoured, rounded, nutty taste with hops adding to the overall fruitiness. It builds up a warm, sweet nutty flavour, the hops lingering in the mouth.

Oatmeal Stout (OG 1048, ABV 4.7%)
The oatmeal gives a softness in the mouth, with a creamy head against the darkness of the flavours. Soft and rounded, it gives coffee, chocolate and smoky aromas.

Carlsberg

Jacobsen House, 140 Bridge Street, Northampton, NN1 1PZ
☎ (01604) 668866 carlsberg.co.uk

International lager brewery, which, while brewing no real ales, is a major distributor of real ales. The Tetley-owned real ales are brewed under contract by Marston's.

Castle SIBA

Unit 9a-7, Restormel Industrial Estate, Liddicoat Road, Lostwithiel, Cornwall, PL22 0HG
☎ (01726) 871133 ☎ 07800 635831
castlebrewery.co.uk

Brewing started in 2008 on a two-barrel plant. Only bottle-conditioned ales are produced. RAIB

Castle Combe SIBA

The Brewhouse, Preston West Farm, Preston, Chippenham, Wiltshire, SN15 4DX
☎ (01249) 892900 castlecombebrewery.co.uk

Brewing began on a farm in Wiltshire in 2009 using a five-barrel plant under the Braydon Ales name. A change of ownership in 2014 saw a name change and a new beer range. More than 30 outlets are supplied direct with further outlets via the SIBA direct delivery scheme. ‼♦

Bybrook Bitter (OG 1034, ABV 3.5%)
Pale single malt, single hop, easy-drinking beer with a citrus taste.

Pendulum Pale Ale (OG 1037, ABV 3.8%)
Well-hopped, full-bodied golden bitter.

Doing Little Bitter (OG 1040, ABV 4.1%)
Light copper-coloured ale with a gentle bitter taste from the English hops.

Circuit Bitter (OG 1043, ABV 4.4%)
A well-balanced, chestnut-coloured premium bitter.

Castle Rock SIBA ◉

Queensbridge Road, Nottingham, NG2 1NB
☎ (0115) 985 1615 ⊕ castlerockbrewery.co.uk

☺ Castle Rock was established in 1998. Since then capacity has steadily increased with the largest expansion taking place in 2010 which gave a total capacity of 360 barrels a week. Beers are distributed through its estate of 20 pubs and further afield through wholesalers. A few different beers are brewed each year to support the Nottinghamshire Wildlife Trust and a unique Nottinghamian Celebration beer is brewed quarterly. A visitors' centre opened in 2011. ‼◆RAIB

Sheriff's Tipple (OG 1034, ABV 3.4%) ◄
Tawny-coloured malty beer with Goldings hops.

Black Gold (OG 1037, ABV 3.8%) ⬚ ◄
A dark ruby mild. Full-bodied and fairly bitter.

Harvest Pale (OG 1037, ABV 3.8%) ◄
Pale yellow beer, full of hop aroma and flavour. Refreshing with a mellowing aftertaste.

Red Riding Hood (OG 1042.5, ABV 4.3%) ◄
Reddish brown fruity bitter with initial malt, caramel and hops leading to a lasting malty bitter finish.

Preservation Fine Ale (OG 1044, ABV 4.4%) ◄
A traditional copper-coloured English best bitter with malt predominant. Fairly bitter with a residual sweetness.

Elsie Mo (OG 1045, ABV 4.7%) ◄
A strong golden ale with floral hops evident in the aroma. Citrus hops are mellowed by a slight sweetness.

Midnight Owl (OG 1055, ABV 5.5%) ▣
A rich, warming winter ale with a distinctive hop and caramel finish.

Screech Owl (OG 1055, ABV 5.5%) ◄
A classic golden IPA with an intensely hoppy aroma and bitter taste with a little balancing sweetness.

Castles SIBA ◉

Symondscliffe Way, Caldicot, NP26 5PW
☎ (01291) 422032 ☎ 07825 992604
⊕ castlesbrewery.co.uk

Brewing began in 2014. RAIB

Court Jester (OG 1038, ABV 3.8%)
A refreshing session pale ale.

White Knight (OG 1041, ABV 4.1%)
American-style pale ale with a peach aroma and vibrant taste.

Portcullis (OG 1042, ABV 4.2%)
A russet-brown ale with a vibrant tropical fruit aroma. Full-bodied with a malty yet rounded taste.

Kings Reserve (OG 1043, ABV 4.3%)
Amber ale made with a blend of malts with an orange, dry taste.

Black Smith (OG 1046, ABV 4.6%)
Rich in malt and roasted barley with a hint of liquorice.

Castor SIBA

30 Peterborough Road, Castor, Cambridgeshire, PE5 7AX
☎ (01733) 380337 ⊕ castorales.co.uk

This three-barrel brewery, established in 2009, is located in a specially converted outhouse in the garden of the founder brewer. The Prince of Wales Feathers in Castor village features the beers, as well as the Beehive in Peterborough and other local outlets. ‼◆

Durobrivae (OG 1037, ABV 3.7%)

Hopping Toad (OG 1040, ABV 4.1%)
A light golden bitter, the pale malt balanced by bittering and aroma hops giving a refreshing citrus flowery finish with a fruity aftertaste.

12th Man (OG 1044, ABV 4.5%)
A triple-hopped beer with spicy citrus and floral aromas and taste with an orange finish.

Dark Side of the Comet (OG 1045, ABV 4.5%)
A dark beer featuring six different malts with generous hop additions.

Cathedral Heights SIBA ◉

Unit 12, Churchill Business Park, Bracebridge Heath, Lincoln, LN4 2HD ☎ 07545 090318
⊕ chbrewery.co.uk

Cathedral Heights was established by Steve Marston in 2011, brewing on a nine-gallon plant in his kitchen. In 2013, after a year out of production, the brewery relocated to a business unit in Bracebridge Heath where a 2.5-barrel plant was installed. On and off sales are available and a local delivery service is offered.

Just Married (OG 1037, ABV 3.8%)
A light and refreshing pale ale with a hoppy finish.

Lincoln Pale (OG 1037, ABV 3.8%)
A light and refreshing pale ale with a hoppy finish.

Churchills Pride (OG 1038, ABV 3.9%)
A copper-coloured ale.

Strait IPA (OG 1039, ABV 3.9%)
A pale golden, slightly citrus tasting beer.

BBH Bitter (OG 1042, ABV 4.3%)
A hoppy, refreshing golden bitter.

Devils Nightmare (OG 1042, ABV 4.3%)
A smooth, dark mild; sweet and malty.

Steep Hill (OG 1041, ABV 4.3%)
A dark copper-coloured ale with malty tones and a fruity finish.

Castle Dungeon (OG 1050, ABV 5.4%)
A full-bodied stout, with added chocolate.

Cats SIBA ◉

Unit 18, Sugarswell Business Park, Shenington, Oxfordshire, OX15 6HW ☎ 07557 527789
⊕ catsbrewingco.com

Chris and Tom's brewery (hence Cats), was set up in 2013 using a six-barrel plant. ▰

Tabby (OG 1041, ABV 4.1%)
A fruity, amber-coloured ale.

Mog (OG 1045, ABV 4.5%)

Clouder (OG 1050, ABV 5%)

Caveman

The Cave (below The George & Dragon), 1 London Road, Swanscombe, Kent, DA10 0LQ ☎ 07900 234644 ⊕ cavemanbrewery.co.uk

Caveman began brewing in 2012 and moved to its current site beneath the George & Dragon pub in 2013 using a four-barrel plant. It is named for the local discovery in the 1930s of skull fragments from a Paleolithic human, then the oldest remains found in the UK. Beers can be found nationwide through various wholesalers with direct supply to London, Kent and parts of Sussex. ◆RAIB

Palaeolithic (OG 1038, ABV 3.8%)
A pale ale with Cascade hops and some slight malt sweetness.

Citra (OG 1042, ABV 4.1%)
A hoppy pale ale with a malt character that lets the citrus flavours from hops shine through. A refreshing session beer.

Neanderthal (OG 1044, ABV 4.4%)
An ale full of roast and caramel malt flavours and traditional Kent hops.

Cavedweller Porter (OG 1060, ABV 5.8%)
A porter with a coffee, chocolate and roast malt flavour set against subtle refreshing hops.

Caythorpe SIBA

⊟ c/o Black Horse, 29 Main Street, Caythorpe, Nottinghamshire, NG14 7ED
☎ (0115) 966 4933 ☎ 07807 583724
⊕ caythorpebrewery.co.uk

Established in 1996 using a 2.5-barrel plant in a building at the rear of the Black Horse pub, the brewery upgraded to a six-barrel plant in 2010. ‼

Dark Gem (OG 1033.3, ABV 3.5%)
A subtly hopped dark mild with a hint of chocolate.

One Swallow (OG 1034, ABV 3.6%)
Golden session bitter, crisp and well hopped.

Cocker Beck (OG 1034.7, ABV 3.7%)
Copper-coloured, light-flavoured bitter.

Dover Beck (OG 1037, ABV 4%) ◥
Pale brown-coloured, well-balanced session bitter. Initial malt is offset by a slight hoppy bitterness.

Outlaw (ABV 4%)
Smooth bitterness with a light orangy citrus hop finish.

Stout Fellow (OG 1040, ABV 4.2%)
A dark stout, brewed with roasted barley to give a roast character.

Classic (OG 1042, ABV 4.6%)
Traditional copper-coloured, premium bitter, malty and well-hopped.

Celt Experience SIBA ◉

Unit 2E, Pontygwindy Industrial Estate, Pontygwindy Road, Caerphilly, CF83 3HU
☎ (029) 2086 7707 ☎ 08708 033876
⊕ theceltexperience.co.uk

Established in 2007 as successor to Newmans of Somerset and expanded in 2014, Celt Experience produces a permanent range of beers and the seasonal Shape Shifter range. There are also occasional collaborative brews in conjunction with guest brewers and beer writers. Beers are distributed widely. ‼ ⏄

La Tene (OG 1035, ABV 3.3%)
A dry-hopped bitter, with massive hop presence.

Iron Age (OG 1035, ABV 3.5%)
A red-coloured table ale.

Dark Age (OG 1040, ABV 4%)
A resinous dark ale.

Golden (OG 1045, ABV 4.2%)
Robustly-flavoured, dry-hopped golden ale.

Native Storm (OG 1044, ABV 4.4%)
A dry-hopped IPA.

Silures (OG 1046, ABV 4.6%)
Munich-style pale beer, with massive hop finish.

Lammas Harvest (OG 1055, ABV 5.4%)
Strawberry Berliner Weiss-style beer.

Bleddyn (OG 1056, ABV 5.6%)

Brigid Fire (OG 1065, ABV 6.3%)
A smoked rye IPA.

Halstatt Deity (OG 1068, ABV 6.6%)
Saison-style pomegranate fruit beer.

Cerddin SIBA

⊟ c/o Cross Inn, Maesteg Road, Cwmfelin, CF34 9LB
☎ (01656) 732476 ☎ 07949 652237
⊕ cerddinbrewery.co.uk

Established in 2010 using a 2.5-barrel plant with conditioning and malting rooms in a converted garage. Beer is usually only available from the owner's pub, the Cross Inn in Cwmfelin. ◆RAIB

Solar (OG 1040, ABV 4%)
A red-coloured beer with a good level of bitterness and blackcurrant aftertaste.

Tubby Chap (OG 1043, ABV 4.3%)
A copper-coloured beer, sweet, smooth and full-bodied. Rich and fruity.

Cascade (OG 1047, ABV 4.8%)
A single-hopped, straw-coloured beer with a citrus finish.

Cerne Abbas (NEW) SIBA

North End Farm, Venn Lane, Chideock, Dorset, DT6 6JY
☎ 07506 303407

Office: The Mill House, Mill Lane, Cerne Abbas, Dorset, DT2 7LB ⊕ cerneabbasbrewery.com

⊠ Established in 2014 by Vic Irvine and Jodie Moore using a five-barrel plant. The beers are made as naturally as possible using local, chalk-filtered water. The brewery supplies locally to pubs.

Ale (OG 1040, ABV 3.8%)
Triple-hopped and well-balanced tawny ale with a fuller mouthfeel and refreshing finish.

Blonde (OG 1042, ABV 4.2%)
Single-hopped blonde ale.

Chadwick's (NEW)

Unit 27, Castle Mills, Aynam Road, Kendal, Cumbria, LA9 7DF ☎ 07983 543724 ⊕ chadwicksbrewery.co.uk

☺Chadwick's began brewing in 2014 using the 4.5-barrel plant from the now defunct Great Gable Brewery.

Castle Mills Mild (ABV 3.6%)
A black, full-bodied dark mild, smooth and rounded with a liquorice aftertaste.

Kirkland Blonde (ABV 3.6%)
An easy-drinking session beer with a delicate hop flavour and aroma.

Miller Bridge Bitter (ABV 4%)
A dark mahogany-coloured ale, packed full of malty and caramel flavours.

Castle Pale (ABV 4.2%)
A pale, straw-coloured beer with a citrus taste and aroma from American hops and a pleasant, dry finish.

Chalk Hill

▤ Rosary Road, Norwich, NR1 4DA
☎ (01603) 477078 ⊕ thecoachthorperoad.co.uk

⊠ Chalk Hill began production in 1993 on a 15-barrel plant. It supplies local pubs and festivals. ‼◆

Tap Bitter (OG 1036, ABV 3.6%) ◄
Well-balanced with a light, hoppy character in both aroma and taste. Malt provides contrast. Short, dry and bitter finish.

CHB (OG 1042, ABV 4.2%) ◄
Malty with fruity cooking apple notes, hoppy bittersweet background. A gentle malt aroma and sticky mouthfeel. Long finish.

Gold (OG 1043, ABV 4.3%) ◄
A light hoppy nose. Grapefruit, banana and hops blend in a well-balanced beginning. The finish develops a growing bitterness.

Dreadnought (OG 1049, ABV 4.9%) ◄
A rich, resinous aroma introduces a heavy malty brew. Raisin and plum with a sweet malty backbone. Singularly abrupt ending.

Chantry SIBA

Unit 1, Callum Court, Gateway Industrial Estate, Parkgate, Rotherham, South Yorkshire, S62 6NR
☎ (01709) 711866 ☎ 07815 727285
⊕ chantrybrewery.co.uk

Brewing returned to Rotherham with the opening of Chantry in 2012 using the latest brewing technology in a 20-barrel state of the art plant built by Sheffield-based Moeschle UK. ‼

New York Pale (OG 1039, ABV 3.9%)
A pale session bitter with a refreshing citrus taste and a crisp bitter finish.

Iron & Steel Bitter (OG 1040, ABV 4%)
Chestnut-coloured beer with complex spicy flavours of dark fruits with a clean finish. An easy-drinking Yorkshire session bitter.

Diamond Black Stout (OG 1045, ABV 4.5%)
Full-bodied dry stout with a bitter finish, spicy with hints of liquorice and dark berries.

Chapel

Dinesfield, Chapel Lane, Criftins, Shropshire, SY12 9LZ
☎ (01691) 690412 ☎ 07928 682174
⊕ chapelbrewery.co.uk

Chapel began brewing in 2013 using a one-barrel plant behind the brewer's bungalow. Occasional specials are brewed for festivals.

Angel's Share (OG 1040, ABV 4%)

Miracle (OG 1044, ABV 4.4%)

Last Supper (OG 1046, ABV 4.7%)
A light blonde beer with passion fruit, lychee and grapefruit notes.

Amen (OG 1049, ABV 5%)
A blonde IPA with a balance of malt and citrus, floral and herb notes.

Babylon (OG 1048, ABV 5%)

Chapel Street

▤ Thatched House, Ball Street, Poulton-le-Fylde, Lancashire, FY6 7BG
☎ (01253) 891063 ⊕ thatchedhousepoulton.co.uk

This four-barrel plant is situated in the coach house of the award-winning Thatched House pub in Poulton-le-Fylde and has been brewing almost to capacity since opening in 2014. High local demand means that the whole of production is sold in the pub plus at a few selected beer festivals. ◆

Brewhouse Blonde (OG 1038, ABV 3.8%)
Blonde session ale with aromas of citrus, lemon and pine.

Elderflower Blonde (ABV 4.1%)

Brewhouse Gold (OG 1042, ABV 4.2%)

Boca Espresso Stout (ABV 4.4%)

Charnwood (NEW) SIBA ⊚

22 Jubilee Drive, Loughborough, Leicestershire, LE11 5XS
☎ (01509) 218666 ⊕ charnwoodbrewery.co.uk

☺ Charnwood is a family-run 10-barrel brewery established in 2014 in a former mozzarella factory. Beers are available in many local pubs. The front of the building has been fitted out as a shop and reception area, with large glass windows giving a good view into the brewery. ‼▤◆

Salvation (OG 1038, ABV 3.8%)
A light, refreshing golden beer with tropical fruit, citrus, and floral flavours. American Cascade and Amarillo hops create a citrus aroma, and crisp, clean bitterness on the finish.

Vixen (OG 1040, ABV 4%)
A well-balanced, copper-coloured best bitter with subtle hints of honey, spice and hedgerow fruits. Late added Pacific Gem hops deliver a fruity nose and finish.

Cheddar SIBA ⊚

Winchester Farm, Draycott Road, Cheddar, Somerset, BS27 3RP
☎ (01934) 744193 ⊕ cheddarales.co.uk

⊠ Established in 2006, this 100-barrel brewery has a production split of approximately 85% cask-conditioned beer with the remainder bottle conditioned. Its bottling plant produces around 75,000 bottles annually. Around 450 outlets and 80 pubs are supplied. ‼▤◆RAIB

Bitter Bully (OG 1038.5, ABV 3.8%) ◄

Light session bitter with flowery hops on the nose and a dry, bitter finish.

Gorge Best (OG 1040, ABV 4%) ◈
Malty bitter with caramel and fruit notes followed by a short bittersweet aftertaste.

Potholer (OG 1043.5, ABV 4.3%) ◈
A well-balanced golden ale with fruit and sweetness throughout and some bitterness to finish.

Totty Pot (OG 1044.5, ABV 4.5%) ◈
Roasted malts dominate this smooth, well-flavoured porter. Hints of coffee and rich fruits follow with a well-balanced bitterness.

Cheeky Imp (NEW)

Unit1, 127a Station Road, Waddington, Lincolnshire, LN5 9QT ☎ 07884 022236
✉ yellowbellyale@me.com

😊A part-time brewery established in 2015 after many years in homebrewing. 10 outlets are supplied.

Delta Pale (OG 1038, ABV 3.8%)

Fleur De Lis (OG 1038, ABV 3.8%)

Bombs Away (OG 1040, ABV 4%)

Olde Yeller (OG 1044, ABV 4.6%)

Gorilla Mash (OG 1054, ABV 6%)

Cheshire Brew Brothers SIBA ◉

Unit 6, Stanney Mill Industrial Estate, Dutton Green, Ellesmere Port, Cheshire, CH2 4SA ☎ 07890 567582
⊕ cheshirebrewbrothers.co.uk

Brewing began in 2014. The brewery is run by two friends who call themselves the Brew Bros after being inspired by a beer trip to Belgium.

Chester Gold (ABV 3.6%)
Deep gold-coloured beer with a soft, citrus, honey taste and floral honey aroma.

Earl's Eye Amber (ABV 3.8%)
Dry, hoppy and fruity amber ale with a spicy, malty aroma.

Cheshire Best Bitter (ABV 4%)
A traditional bitter, malty, lightly spicy and dry with a sweetening aftertaste.

Roodee Dark (ABV 4%)
Deep red porter with a hoppy, dry, coffee taste and roasted, malty aroma.

Cheshire Brewhouse SIBA

Units 5 & 6, Daneside Business Park, Riverdane Road, Congleton, Cheshire, CW12 1UN
☎ (01260) 274788 ☎ 07830 304929
⊕ cheshirebrewhouse.co.uk

😊Cheshire Brewhouse was established in 2012 using a five-barrel plant, expanding in 2014 to a 10-barrel one. The business has taken over adjacent premises and the brewery is now capable of producing 160 firkins a week. Bottling is carried out on site. ‼◆

Cheshire Gap (ABV 3.8%)
An English pale ale.

Cheshire Set (ABV 4%)
A pale and refreshing beer with citrus hops.

Engine Vein (ABV 4.2%)
A traditional best bitter.

Lindow (ABV 4.5%)
A lighter take on stout, malty and easy-drinking with a hint of espresso and dark chocolate balanced with vine fruits.

DBA (ABV 4.6%)
A Burton-style bitter. Strong and malty with a peppery hop finish .

Chew Valley (NEW)

Sunningdale, Hillcrest, Pensford, Somerset, BS39 4AS
☎ 07753 686179 ⊕ chewvalleybrewery.co.uk

The brewery opened in 2014 using a one-barrel plant supplying the Chew Valley and surrounding areas. Brewing of cask-conditioned ales is currently suspended while the brewery concentrates on a range of bottled beer, which is contract brewed elsewhere.

Chiltern SIBA ◉

Nash Lee Road, Terrick, Aylesbury, Buckinghamshire, HP17 0TQ
☎ (01296) 613647 ⊕ chilternbrewery.co.uk

⊗ Founded in 1980, Chiltern was one of the first microbreweries in the country and is the oldest independent brewery in Buckinghamshire and the Chiltern Hills, growing from a capacity of five to its present 15-barrel plant. Now run by the second generation of the Jenkinson family, George and Tom, it supplies around 100 outlets including its own brewery tap, the Farmers' Bar, at the historic King's Head in Aylesbury. ‼ ᵬ ◆ RAIB

Pale Ale (OG 1037, ABV 3.7%) ◈
An amber, refreshing beer with a slight fruit aroma, leading to a good malt/bitter balance in the mouth. The aftertaste is bitter and dry.

Black (OG 1040, ABV 3.9%)
Dark treacle tones, hints of roast barley and well-hopped. Rich, smooth flavours abound leading to a light, rewarding finish.

Beechwood Bitter (OG 1043, ABV 4.3%) ◈
This pale brown beer has a balanced butterscotch/toffee aroma, with a slight hop note. The taste balances bitterness and sweetness, leading to a long bitter finish.

Chorlton (NEW)

69 North Western Street, Manchester, M12 6DX
⊕ chorltonbrewingcompany.com

Brewing began in 2014 and, despite the name, lack of available space means that the brewery isn't based in Chorlton. Owner Mike Marcus is passionate about sour beers and yeast experiments inspired by classic European beer styles. A regular IPA is planned and experiments with novel ingredients like woodruff, sarsaparilla and myrrh. RAIB

Julian Church

🏛 Old Dairy, Whitehill Farm, Loddington Road, Cransley, Northamptonshire, NN14 1PY ☎ 07794 289559

Office: 79 Edmond Street, Kettering, Northamptonshire, NN16 0HS
jchurchbrewery.co.uk

Julian Church started brewing in 2009 at the Alexandra Arms in Kettering on Nobby's Brewery's old five-barrel plant when Nobby's expanded and moved. In 2014 the brewery moved to bigger premises in an old dairy at Cransley near Kettering. !!

More Tea Vicar (OG 1037, ABV 3.7%)

Gold Testament (OG 1036, ABV 3.9%)

Lion's Den (OG 1040, ABV 4%)
A red/brown-coloured bitter.

Martyr (OG 1040, ABV 4.1%)
An amber-coloured beer with a caramel flavour and a light, bitter finish.

Freaky Sheep (OG 1045, ABV 4.5%)

Hymn Moosic (ABV 4.5%)

Wonky Spire (ABV 4.7%)

Church End SIBA

Ridge Lane, Warwickshire, CV10 0RD
(01827) 713080 churchendbrewery.co.uk

The brewery started in 1994 in an old coffin shop in Shustoke. It moved to the present site and upgraded to a 10-barrel plant in 2001 with further expansion to a 20-barrel plant in 2008. Many one off specials and old recipe beers are produced. Beers are available at the Brewery Tap, Ridge Lane, and its sister pub, the George & Dragon, Stoke Golding. !! ♦ RAIB

Poachers Pocket (OG 1036, ABV 3.5%)

Cuthberts (OG 1038, ABV 3.8%)
A refreshing, hoppy beer, with hints of malt, fruit and caramel taste. Lingering bitter aftertaste.

Goats Milk (OG 1038, ABV 3.8%)

Gravediggers Ale (OG 1038, ABV 3.8%)

What the Fox's Hat (OG 1044, ABV 4.2%)
A beer with a malty aroma, and a hoppy and malty taste with some caramel flavour.

Vicar's Ruin (OG 1044, ABV 4.4%)
A straw-coloured best bitter with an initially hoppy, bitter flavour, softening to a delicate malt finish.

Stout Coffin (OG 1046, ABV 4.6%)

Fallen Angel (OG 1050, ABV 5%)

Church Farm SIBA

Church Farm, Budbrooke, Warwickshire, CV35 8QL
(01926) 411569 07939 607027
churchfarmbrewery.co.uk

Church Farm was established in 2012 in the farm's former dairy. The plant was converted from the old milk processing equipment and has now expanded to seven-barrel capacity to meet demand. Beers are brewed from local ingredients and the water comes from the farm's own well. ♦ RAIB

Old Pal (OG 1038, ABV 3.6%)
A pale, golden ale. Slight flowery hop aroma and mouthfeel, with a smooth mellow taste and long-lasting finish.

Ren's Pride (OG 1044, ABV 4%)
An amber-coloured best bitter with a slightly sweet taste. The distinctive initial flavour comes from a complex array of malts.

Brown's Porter (OG 1042, ABV 4.2%)
A porter with a smooth coffee taste and a long-lasting, creamy aftertaste.

Harry's Heifer (OG 1044, ABV 4.2%)
A light amber-coloured quaffable best bitter with slight floral notes.

Ciren

Twelve Bells, 12 Lewis Lane, Cirencester, Gloucestershire, GL7 1EA
(01285) 652230 07702 489589
twelvebellscirencester.com/cirencester-ales-brewery.html

Ciren Ales is a small microbrewery at the rear of the Twelve Bells pub in Cirencester established in 2012. The brewer is the owner, Steve. !! ♦

Bells Bitter (OG 1040, ABV 3.8%)
Light brown-coloured bitter with a hoppy taste.

Bellend Blonde (OG 1044, ABV 4.2%)
A light citrus fruity beer.

Bells Best Mate (OG 1044, ABV 4.2%)
A dark, full-flavoured beer.

Clanconnel

Unit 5 , 2 New Line, Gibson's Hill, Lurgan, Co Armagh, BT66 8TA 07711 626770

Office: PO Box 316, Craigavon, BT65 9AZ
clanconnelbrewing.com

Clanconnel started producing bottled beer in 2008. Cask-conditioned beer is occasionally available.

Clark's SIBA

Westgate Brewery, Wakefield, West Yorkshire, WF2 9SW
(01924) 373328 07801 922473 hbclark.co.uk

Founded in 1906, Clark's ceased brewing during the 1960s/70s but resumed cask ale production in 1982 and now delivers to around 220 outlets throughout the Midlands and the north of England using its own wholesale network of depots. Its two pubs serve cask ale. A new range of ales was introduced in 2014 called Merrie City Craft Beers. ♦

Traditional (OG 1038, ABV 3.8%)
Copper-coloured beer with a hoppy aroma and lasting refreshing bitter taste.

Classic Blonde (OG 1039, ABV 3.9%)
Pale straw-coloured beer with a fruity aroma and light, spicy taste.

Atlantic Hop (OG 1040, ABV 4%)
A pale amber-coloured session ale with a fresh citrus aroma and a tropical fruit taste. The unique blend of hops leave a bittersweet aftertaste.

Westgate Gold (OG 1042, ABV 4.2%)
Golden beer with a creamy, malty aroma and a sharp, dry finish.

Clarkshaws SIBA

Arch 283, Belinda Road, off Coldharbour Lane, Loughborough Junction, London, SW9 7DT 07989 402687 clarkshaws.co.uk

Clarkshaws is a small brewery established in 2013 focusing on using ingredients sourced in the UK and on reducing beer miles. The beers are vegetarian and are accredited by the Vegetarian Society.

Gorgon's Alive (OG 1040, ABV 4%) ◆
An amber-coloured unfined beer with spicy hop in the aroma, flavour and dry finish, balanced by a hint of honey.

Phoenix Rising (OG 1040, ABV 4%)
An easy-drinking session ale with hints of spice and chocolate. Ruby in colour, it is well-balanced with a fusion of hops and mellow malt in the mouth.

Strange Brew No. 1 (OG 1040, ABV 4%)

Hellhound IPA (OG 1056, ABV 5.5%) ◆
Spiced and citrus notes in this unfined amber beer with a bitterness in the flavour and finish, which is dry.

Clearwater SIBA

Unit 1, Little Court, Manteo Way, Gammaton Road, Bideford, Devon, EX39 4FG
☎ (01237) 420492 ⊕ clearwaterbrewery.co.uk

⊠ Clearwater began brewing in 1999 using a 10-barrel brewery, relocating from Great Torrington to Bideford in 2014. It regularly supplies more than 250 outlets across the south west and increasingly supplies national wholesalers with its Devon's Own labelled beers. !! ◆ RAIB

Best Bitter (OG 1037.3, ABV 3.5%)
A traditional-style brown ale with hints of blackcurrant; well-balanced and hoppy with a bitter finish.

Real Smiler (OG 1037, ABV 3.7%)
A golden. crisp and hoppy ale.

Devon Dympsy (OG 1039, ABV 4%)
This smoky, smooth chestnut-coloured ale has a lemon aroma and a citrus edge.

Proper Ansome (OG 1041, ABV 4.2%)
Full-flavoured dark beer; full of malt.

Devon Darter (OG 1043, ABV 4.5%)
A fruity, copper-coloured beer with an aroma of grapes, a nutty taste and a light bitterness.

Cliff Quay

Unit 1, Meadow Works, Kenton Road, Debenham, Suffolk, IP14 6RT
☎ (01728) 861213 ⊕ cliffquay.co.uk

Cliff Quay was established in 2008 by former Wychwood brewer Jeremy Moss and John Bjornson (owner of the Earl Soham Brewery) in part of the historic Tolly Cobbold brewery in Ipswich. In 2012 the brewery relocated to Debenham, a small, picturesque market town, due to redevelopment of the former brewery site. Now re-established alongside Earl Soham brewery, with shared shop and offices. !! 🍺 ◆

Bitter (OG 1034, ABV 3.4%) ◆
Pleasantly drinkable, well-balanced malty sweet bitter with a hint of caramel, followed by a sweet/malty aftertaste. A good flavour for such a low gravity beer.

Anchor Bitter (OG 1040, ABV 4%)

Black Jack Porter (OG 1042, ABV 4.2%) ◆

Unusual dark porter with a strong aniseed aroma and rich liquorice and aniseed flavours, reminiscent of old-fashioned sweets. The aftertaste is long and increasingly sweet.

Tolly Roger (OG 1042, ABV 4.2%) ◆
Well-balanced, highly drinkable, mid-gold summer beer with a bittersweet hoppiness, some biscuity flavours and hints of summer fruit.

Tumblehome (OG 1047, ABV 4.7%)

Sea Dog (OG 1053, ABV 5.5%)
A sack full of malted wheat and a blend of fragrant punchy hops. Bursting with the flavours of lemon and grapefruit with a full maltiness in contrast.

Clipper

≣ Bell & Talbot, 2 Salop Street, Bridgnorth, Shropshire, WV16 4QU
☎ (01746) 763233 ⊕ bellandtalbotbridgnorth.co.uk

⊙ Clipper began brewing in 2014 using a two-barrel plant in an old two-storey brewhouse at the rear of the Bell & Talbot in Bridgnorth. Two beers are produced and are available only in the pub. Brewing was temporarily suspended in 2015.

Clockwork

≣ 1153-1155 Cathcart Road, Glasgow, G42 9HB
☎ (0141) 649 0184 ⊕ clockworkbeercompany.co.uk

⊙ Established in 1997, Clockwork is owned by Thistle Pub Company III. The beers are stored in cellar tanks where fermentation gases from the conditioning vessel blanket the beers (but not under pressure). A wide range of ales, lagers and specials is produced. Most beers are naturally gassed while the Craft Lager is pressurised. The establishment has parted ways with its previous managing company, Maclays, and in mid 2014, the pub underwent a full refurbishment. !! 🍺 ◆

Original Amber (OG 1038, ABV 3.8%)

Cascade Parade (OG 1042, ABV 4.2%)

Pacific Pale Ale (OG 1042, ABV 4.2%)
Fresh, easy-drinking pale ale with tropical fruit flavours and hints of melon and grape.

Cartside Red (OG 1044, ABV 4.4%)
Classic red ale with brewed with German malts and American hops giving a deep, berry finish.

Lager (OG 1048, ABV 4.8%)
Classic lager with a crisp, almost sweet taste.

RunAbout Stout (OG 1050, ABV 4.9%)
Intense roasted flavours are balanced with a silky smooth finish. Freshly ground coffee and oats add depth.

Seriously Ginger (OG 1050, ABV 5%)

Oregon IPA (OG 1059, ABV 5.5%)
American-style IPA with a big citrus bite.

Hampden Roar (OG 1064, ABV 6%)
Complex dark ale. Five different malts are fused, creating an elaborate bittersweet undertone.

Clouded Minds SIBA ⊚

Unit 5B, Brailes Industrial Estate, Winderton Road, Lower Brailes, Warwickshire, OX15 5JW ☎ 07530 998149 ⊕ cloudedminds.co.uk

Brewing began in 2013, using spare capacity at various breweries around London and Derbyshire. In 2014 the brewery moved to its own site near Banbury using a 10-barrel plant. The London area is mainly supplied but also some outlets in Birmingham, Nottinghamshire, Derbyshire and some national pub chains. Wholesalers also distribute the beers more widely. RAIB

Catholic's Choice (OG 1028, ABV 2.8%)
Hints of grapefruit through a citrus flavour and aroma. Herbal and moderately dry.

N29 (OG 1036, ABV 3.7%)
Light, citrus pale ale brewed with a small percentage of rye malt.

N253 (OG 1037, ABV 3.9%)
Medium-bodied oatmeal American-style pale ale. Fruity and resiny.

N18 (OG 1038, ABV 4%)
A pale ale. Mild citrus, pine and resin.

Luppol (OG 1040, ABV 4.2%)
A drinkable and refreshing beer with a good bitter finish.

Clout Stout (OG 1048, ABV 4.5%)
Velvet mouthfeel with an aroma of roasted malts, cocoa, dried fruits and figs. Mildly sweet and sour with a smoky and bitter finish.

Hazelnutter (OG 1048, ABV 5%)
Well-balanced, smooth American-style brown ale brewed with organic Italian hazelnuts.

Elisir (OG 1052, ABV 5.3%)
Caramel and biscuit taste from the malts balanced by a generous amount of American hops. Fruity.

Black Pike (OG 1057, ABV 6.1%)
Medium-bodied, highly-hopped black IPA.

Dolce Vita (OG 1058, ABV 6.2%)
A West Coast American-style IPA. Fruity and mildly spicy with a dry finish.

Double Clout Stout (OG 1064, ABV 6.6%)
A rich and smooth coffee stout.

Cloudwater (NEW)

Units 7-8, Piccadilly Trading Estate, Manchester, M1 2NP
☎ (0161) 661 5943 ⊕ cloudwaterbrew.co

Set up in 2015 in the former Ancoats goods depot, Cloudwater specialises in modern, seasonal beers with four distinct line-ups each year using local or seasonally available ingredients. ◆

Clun SIBA

▤ White Horse Inn, The Square, Clun, Shropshire, SY7 8JA
☎ (01588) 640305 ⊕ whi-clun.co.uk

Formerly a tiny brewery, capacity was increased to 2.5 barrels in 2010. Established behind the White Horse in Clun, beers are produced for the pub and increasingly the local trade. ◆

Loophole (OG 1035, ABV 3.5%)
A dry, hoppy, light-coloured beer with a crisp, hoppy flavour.

Pale (OG 1040, ABV 4.1%)
A pale, clean-tasting, bitter beer.

Citadel (OG 1065, ABV 5.9%)

A strong ale, golden in colour with rich and fruity malt flavours met head on by intense hop bitterness and aroma which give rise to a long-lasting dry finish.

Coach House SIBA ◉

Wharf Street, Howley, Warrington, Cheshire, WA1 2DQ
☎ (01925) 232800 ⊕ coach-house-brewing.co.uk

☺ Coach House was established in 1991 by three former employees of Greenall Whitley Brewery, which had had a presence in Warrington since 1786. The 40-barrel plant produces up to 240 barrels a week. ◆

Coachman's Best Bitter (OG 1037, ABV 3.7%) ◣
A well-hopped, malty bitter, moderately fruity with a hint of sweetness and a peppery nose.

Gunpowder Mild (OG 1037, ABV 3.8%) ◣
Biscuity dark mild with a blackcurrant sweetness. Bitterness and fruit dominate with some hints of caramel and a slightly stronger roast flavour.

Honeypot Bitter (OG 1037, ABV 3.8%)
A medium-bodied golden bitter, lightly hopped. Brewed with Cheshire honey.

Farrier's Best Bitter (OG 1038, ABV 3.9%)
A smooth, tawny-coloured beer, slightly sweet but with rich hop flavours developed in the mouth.

Cromwells Best Bitter (OG 1040, ABV 4%)
Amber-coloured, well-balanced beer with a smooth, clean-hopped finish.

Cheshire Gold (OG 1042, ABV 4.1%)
A pale golden beer hopped with a pine lemon crispness.

Dick Turpin (OG 1042, ABV 4.2%) ◣
Malty, hoppy pale brown beer with some initial sweetish flavours leading to a short, bitter aftertaste. Sold under other names as a pub house beer.

Flintlock Pale Ale (OG 1044, ABV 4.4%)
A pale golden beer, light on the palate with a touch of sweetness in the finish.

Innkeeper's Special Reserve (OG 1045, ABV 4.5%) ◣
A darkish, full-flavoured bitter. Quite fruity, with a strong, bitter aftertaste.

Postlethwaite (OG 1045, ABV 4.6%)
A distinctive dry and fruity pale ale. Traditionally dry-hopped to give a fine hop aroma.

Posthorn Premium (OG 1050, ABV 5%)
A rich, straw-coloured smooth premium ale. The beer has a robust malty palate and well-balanced bitterness with a complexity of flavours.

Coastal SIBA

Unit 10B, Cardrew Industrial Estate, Redruth, Cornwall, TR15 1SS
☎ (01209) 212613 ☎ 07875 405407
⊕ coastalbrewery.co.uk

⊠ Established in 2006, Coastal operates from a five-barrel plant. An adjacent bottle shop and micropub sells a selection of its beers. ☛◆RAIB

Cornish Bronze (OG 1037, ABV 3.7%)
A traditional session bitter.

Hop Monster (OG 1038, ABV 3.7%)

A thirst-quenching, hoppy session bitter, with a citrus fruit finish.

Handliner (OG 1040, ABV 4%)
A session bitter with a malty, fruity finish and moderate bitterness.

Merry Maidens Mild (OG 1040, ABV 4%) ◆
A black mild. Smooth and creamy with roasted malt, charcoal and liquorice sweetness fading slowly to a refreshing, dry finish.

Angelina (OG 1042, ABV 4.1%) ◆
Golden ale with delicate floral aroma. Grassy, citrus hops with sweet grapefruit, marmalade and apricot throughout. Crisp, dry, fruity finish.

Golden Hinde (OG 1044, ABV 4.3%)
Hopped with Brewer's Gold to give a lingering, sweetish mouthfeel, it is pleasantly bitter with a clean, sparkling finish.

Pier Porter (OG 1043, ABV 4.3%)
A wholesome, full-bodied porter. Heavy malt flavour gives way to a malt character.

Poseidon Extra (OG 1046, ABV 4.5%)
A pale gold ale packed with citrus hop and fruit flavours, rounded off by a fresh citrus blast. There are pronounced citrus hop aromas throughout.

Cornish Cascade (OG 1050, ABV 5%) ◆
Golden ale with hoppy aroma. Strong citrus hop taste, bitter and fruity with sweet malt. Long, bitter and dry finish.

Cornish Porter (OG 1050, ABV 5%)
Dark and smooth, with a full roast flavour that belies its strength.

St Pirans Porter (OG 1060, ABV 6%)
A traditional, full-bodied porter using seven different malts. Roasty, toasty malt notes mix with abundant hops.

Erosion (OG 1077, ABV 7.5%) ◆
After an aroma promising roast caramel this powerful, warming dark old ale bursts with molasses and roast malt. Liquorice adds to the finish.

Kernow Imperial Stout (OG 1090, ABV 9%)
This full-flavoured, warming dark stout bursts with molasses and roast malts. Roast caramel adds to the dry stout finish.

Colchester SIBA

Viaduct Brewhouse, Unit 16, Wakes Hall Business Centre, Wakes Colne, Essex, CO6 2DY
☎ (01787) 829422 ⊕ colchesterbrewery.com

⊗ Set up in 2012 by three friends, Tom Knox, Roger Clark and Andy Bone, using the 'double drop' fermentation process. Popular during the early 20th century this process requires additional brewing vessels in a two-tier system resulting in clean beer with pronounced flavours. ‼ ⬛ ◆ RAIB

Diesel (OG 1037, ABV 3.6%)
A session bitter, rich amber in colour.

AK Pale (OG 1038, ABV 3.7%)
1900s-style pale ale, mildly hopped. Fresh and fruity.

Metropolis (OG 1039, ABV 3.9%)
A golden hoppy beer with depth of flavour and a long, spicy finish.

Braggot (OG 1042, ABV 4%)
An easy-drinking honey beer.

Jack Spitty's Smuggler's Ale (OG 1042.7, ABV 4%)

No. 88 (OG 1042, ABV 4%)
A dark amber-coloured malty bitter.

No. 1 (OG 1042, ABV 4.1%) 🍺
A classic English best bitter, copper in colour.

Pontisbright (OG 1041, ABV 4.1%)
American-hopped mahogany-coloured ale, with hops providing fruit on the palate and a long, lingering bitter finish.

Drizzle (OG 1044, ABV 4.2%)

Red Diesel (OG 1042, ABV 4.2%)
Red-coloured best bitter, well-balanced with a long, rich finish.

Romani Ite Domum (OG 1045, ABV 4.3%)
A hoppy golden ale.

Trinovantes Gold (OG 1044, ABV 4.3%)

Anne Downes (OG 1045, ABV 4.4%)
Dark brown bitter, full and fruity with a lingering hoppy finish.

Mild Ale (OG 1047, ABV 4.5%)
Dark ruby mild. Sweet and fruity.

Brazilian Coffee & Vanilla Porter (OG 1048, ABV 4.6%)

Double Brown Ale (OG 1047.5, ABV 4.6%)
Dark brown beer, malty, sweetish and balanced.

Old King Coel London Porter (OG 1052.5, ABV 5%)

Coles Family

⬛ **White Hart Thatched Inn & Brewery, Llanddarog, Carmarthen, SA32 8NT**
☎ (01267) 275395 ⊕ thebestpubinwales.co.uk

The brewery is based at the ancient White Hart Inn, built in 1371, which historically had a brewery on site. Brewing started again in 1999 on a nine-gallon plant. A one-barrel plant was fitted in 2000 and in 2012 the brewery was opened to the public. Many unique ales are brewed throughout the year with cider also produced.

Merlins (OG 1040, ABV 4%)
A rich, creamy stout.

Swn Y Dail (OG 1040, ABV 4%)

Golden Ale (OG 1042, ABV 4.2%)

Llanddarog (OG 1042, ABV 4.2%)

Cwrw Blasus (OG 1044, ABV 4.4%)

Collingham SIBA

Brooklands, Leeds Road, Collingham, Leeds, West Yorkshire, LS22 5AA
☎ (01937) 573096 ☎ 07538 431921
⊕ collinghamales.co.uk

⊛ Microbrewery based in the village of Collingham, brewing handcrafted ales for the local community. The owner was formerly head brewer at one of Yorkshire's most prestigious, regional family breweries. ◆

Blonde (OG 1038, ABV 3.8%)
Crisp, refreshing blonde ale with a fruity, citrus kick.

Journeyman (OG 1039, ABV 3.9%)
A malty, hoppy beer.

Artisan's Choice (OG 1043, ABV 4.4%)

Smooth-drinking golden ale with a pronounced fruity, citrus hop character.

Colonsay

The Brewery, Scalasaig, Isle of Colonsay, PA61 7YT
☎ (01951) 200190 🌐 colonsaybrewery.co.uk

Colonsay began brewing in 2007 on a five-barrel plant. Beer is mainly bottled or brewery conditioned for the local trade. RAIB

Combined Brewers (NEW)

The Brewery, Totworth Business Park, Falfield, Gloucestershire, GL12 8HQ
☎ (01454) 323088 🌐 springbrewing.com; severnvalebrewing.co.uk

⊗ In 2014 Cotswold Spring Brewing Co merged with Severn Vale Brewing Co, both originally established in 2005, to form Combined Brewers Ltd. The breweries relocated to new, purpose-built premises in 2015 – a 30-barrel plant with water supplied from its own borehole. The Cotswold Spring and Severn Vale brands will still be brewed separately. !! ♦ RAIB

Brewed under the Cotswold Spring brand name:

Ambler (OG 1040, ABV 3.8%)
A smooth session beer with a long palate. A good malty start is complemented with a well-rounded, hoppy finish.

OSM (OG 1039, ABV 3.9%)
A complex seven-grain mild, initially dry with a bitter sweetness. Chocolate notes and a long finish.

Stunner (OG 1041, ABV 4%)
Spicy biscuit aromas blend into hoppy and pale fruit flavours. Refreshing, hoppy and slightly astringent finish.

Codger (OG 1042, ABV 4.2%)
Quite bitter with a slightly malty background. Hops throughout give lasting bitterness which complements the hints of dark fruit flavour.

Brewed under the Severn Vale brand name:

Nibley Ale (OG 1039, ABV 3.8%)
A light and refreshing ale.

Dursley Steam Bitter (OG 1043, ABV 4.2%)
A refreshing golden ale full of flowery hops.

Freeride (OG 1043, ABV 4.2%)
A golden best bitter using New Zealand hops, producing a soft, fruity flavour.

Luverley Jub'lee (OG 1043, ABV 4.2%)
A well-balanced golden best bitter with bold fruity hops in the finish.

Severn Sins (OG 1053, ABV 5.2%)
A jet-black stout with a dry roast malt flavour with hints of chocolate and liquorice.

TSB (Thornbury Special Bitter) (OG 1060, ABV 6.3%)
Rich and powerful IPA with a robust bitterness followed by a fruity marmalade finish.

Compass SIBA

7 Clare Terrace, Carterton, Oxfordshire, OX18 3ES
☎ (01993) 846846 🌐 compassbrewery.com

⊗ Compass began brewing in 2009 using spare capacity at other breweries. Brewing still takes place at North Cotswold Brewery (qv), although Compass owns its own site at Carterton, used for bottling, casking and kegging the beer. It is run by Matthias Sjoberg, who takes brewing ideas from around the world to create experimental and interesting recipes. Beers are hard to find as there are only two local outlets. ♦ RAIB

Isis Pale Ale (OG 1041, ABV 4.1%)
Malty aromas on a backdrop of hops. Sweet malt with some fruity esters and a gentle bitterness that lingers.

Baltic Night Stout (OG 1048, ABV 4.8%)
Well-balanced roasted bitterness with a hoppy, floral aroma. Roasted barley gives it a hint of coffee and a long, dry cocoa finish.

King's Shipment IPA (OG 1060, ABV 6%)
A strong IPA with hoppy bitterness balanced with malty sweetness. Dry-hopped with oak chips. Based on East London Bow Brewery's IPA brewed in the 1790s for shipment to India.

Concertina SIBA

9a Dolcliffe Road, Mexborough, South Yorkshire, S64 9AZ
☎ (01709) 580841 ✉ concertina@btconnect.com

Concertina started in 1992 in the cellar of a club once famous as the home of a long-gone concertina band. The plant produces up to eight barrels a week for the club and other occasional direct outlets and the wider trade, via beer wholesalers. !! ♦

Concrete Cow SIBA

59 Alston Drive, Bradwell Abbey, Milton Keynes, Buckinghamshire, MK13 9HB
☎ (01908) 316794 ☎ 07889 665745
🌐 concretecowbrewery.weebly.com

⊗ Concrete Cow opened in 2007 on a 5.5-barrel plant. The beers are named after aspects of local history. The brewery supplies pubs, farmers' markets, local shops and restaurants. English single malt also available. !! ♦ RAIB

Bit o' Bully (OG 1035, ABV 3.5%)
A golden bitter full of biscuit, malt, grain and toast flavours.

Pail Ale (OG 1036, ABV 3.7%)
A light-coloured ale brewed using lager malt.

Fenny Popper (OG 1039, ABV 4%)
A light-coloured, zesty ale.

Cock 'n' Bull Story (OG 1041, ABV 4.1%)
A dark amber-coloured, malty beer.

Cloven Hoof (OG 1045, ABV 4.5%)
A dark vanilla stout flavoured with natural vanilla pods.

Coniston SIBA

Coppermines Road, Coniston, Cumbria, LA21 8HL
☎ (01539) 441133 🌐 conistonbrewery.com

A 10-barrel plant started in 1995 behind the Black Bull Inn in Coniston, it now brews 40 barrels a week and supplies numerous outlets locally and nationally. Some bottle-conditioned Coniston beers are brewed using Hepworth's Horsham plant, others are bottled on site. !! RAIB

THE BREWERIES

Oliver's Light Ale (OG 1035, ABV 3.4%) ◈
A fruity, hoppy, straw-coloured bitter with plenty of flavour for its strength.

Bluebird Bitter (OG 1036, ABV 3.6%) ◈
A yellow-gold, predominantly hoppy and fruity beer, well-balanced with some sweetness and a rising bitter finish.

Asrai (OG 1039, ABV 4%) ◈
Crisp on the palate, a gently hopped beer with a full-bodied finish.

Bluebird Premium XB (OG 1040.5, ABV 4.2%) ◈
Well-balanced, hoppy and fruity golden bitter. Bittersweet in the mouth with dryness building.

Old Man Ale (OG 1040.5, ABV 4.2%) ◈
Delicious fruity, winey beer with a complex, well-balanced richness.

Special Oatmeal Stout (OG 1045, ABV 4.5%) ◈
A well-balanced, easy-drinking stout, fruity with a balanced ratio of malt to hop bitterness. A good starting point for novice stout drinkers.

K7 (OG 1045, ABV 4.7%) ▤ ◈
Balanced fruity hoppy bitter, plenty of body and a long, hoppy, bitter finish.

Thurstein Pilsner (OG 1044.5, ABV 4.8%) ◈
True to style; mild but unusually sweet, with a hoppy fruitiness.

Blacksmiths Ale (OG 1047.5, ABV 5%)
A well-balanced strong bitter with hints of Christmas pudding.

Infinity IPA (OG 1055, ABV 6%) ◈
High-impact strong bitter. Fruity aromas persist in the powerful but well-balanced hoppiness and sweetness with nothing being lost in the finish.

No. 9 Barley Wine (OG 1087.5, ABV 8.5%) ◈
Hops and alcohol dominate with appropriate sweetness and fruit on the tongue. A full-bodied and beautifully balanced beer.

Connoisseur (NEW)

(Rear of) Wolverhampton House, 121-125 Church Street, St Helens, Merseyside, WA9 1JS ☎ 07921 838831 ✉ connoisseur-ales@outlook.com

Connoisseur Ales launched in 2014, but is built on many years' brewing experience. The team behind the brewery, Mark, Gillian and Kevin Yates, formerly ran Liverpool's Baltic Fleet and the Albion in Warrington.

Bloody Mild (ABV 3.7%)
Complex malt flavours and a hint of chocolate combined with hops added more for their aroma and flavour than for bitterness.

Usual (ABV 3.8%)
A traditional ale with characteristic hop bitterness.

Ruby Ruby Ruby Ruby (ABV 4.1%)
A balance of hops and malt provides a rich, ruby base over which Columbus and Junga hops have been overlaid to preserve the ale's malty character.

Lucem Light Ale (ABV 4.3%)
Hoppy brew with a distinctive nose and floral citrus taste.

Hempen (ABV 4.6%)

Raven Street Porter (ABV 4.9%)
A black beer with a crisp yet full mouthfeel.

Bôte Noir Dry Stout (ABV 5%)

Full-flavoured dry stout with coffee, chocolate and a hint of smoke. A creamy, oatmeal-like body complements the complex multi-grain grist and provides a delicate molasses and spice nose.

Ex Terra Lupus IPA (ABV 5.6%)
A strong, clean and crisp pale ale with a pronounced and well-balanced hop profile.

Conquest

See Whitby

Consett Ale Works SIBA ◉

▤ **Grey Horse Inn, 115 Sherburn Terrace, Consett, County Durham, DH8 6NE**
☎ **(01207) 591540** ⊕ **consettaleworks.co.uk**

The brewery opened in 2006 in the stables of a former coaching inn at the rear of the Grey Horse, Consett's oldest pub. The name commemorates the historic Consett Steel Works that closed in 1980. The brewery expanded in 2007 to cope with demand. Over 100 outlets are supplied direct. Recent investment includes new barrel stock. ‼️ ➤◆

Steel Town Bitter (OG 1039, ABV 3.8%)

White Hot (OG 1040, ABV 4%)

Cast Iron (OG 1040, ABV 4.1%)

Consett Stout (OG 1045, ABV 4.3%)

Men of Steel (OG 1045, ABV 4.3%)

Red Dust (OG 1045, ABV 4.5%)

Conwy SIBA

Unit 2, Ty Mawr Enterprise Park, Tan y Graig Road, Llysfaen, LL29 8UE
☎ **(01492) 514305** ⊕ **conwybrewery.co.uk**

⊚ Conwy started brewing in 2003, relocating to its present address in 2013. Around 50 outlets are supplied. ‼️ ➤◆RAIB

Clogwyn Gold (OG 1037, ABV 3.6%) ◈
A full-flavoured golden ale featuring strong citrus fruit flavours throughout. Hoppy bitterness dominates the full mouthfeel and lasting finish.

Infusion (OG 1039, ABV 3.9%)
Light, refreshing pale ale with a long hoppy finish from infusion of hops.

Minera Mountain Ale (OG 1040, ABV 4%)
Copper-coloured, light and crisp ale with a hint of heather.

Welsh Pride (OG 1040, ABV 4%)
A clean-tasting malty bitter. Fruit in aroma and taste with a crisp, grainy mouthfeel and a lingering, hoppy, bitter aftertaste.

Honey Fayre (OG 1044, ABV 4.5%)
Golden best bitter with a hint of honey sweetness balanced by an increasingly hoppy, bitter finish. Slightly thin mouthfeel for a beer of this strength.

Rampart (OG 1046, ABV 4.5%) ◈
A dark, fruity beer with a sweetish initial taste. Fruit flavours accompanied by the underlying hoppiness continue into the bittersweet aftertaste.

Copper Dragon IFBB

Units 3 & 4, Enterprise Way, Airedale Business Park, Skipton, North Yorkshire, BD23 2TZ
☎ (01756) 701289 🌐 greyhawkbrewery.co.uk

Copper Dragon was established in 2003 and relocated to its present address in 2015. The 30-barrel plant is of a twin-vessel, Bavarian design. The brewery now has its own bore-hole water supply. Bottling and canning facilities are planned. The brewery went in to administration in 2015. See Greyhawk ♦

Black Gold (OG 1036, ABV 3.7%)
This smooth dark ale has a malty, roast character throughout with dark vine fruit notes and a bitter roast finish.

Best Bitter (OG 1036, ABV 3.8%)
A traditional Yorkshire bitter with a malty aroma and a hoppy bitter taste with hints of fruit and a bitter finish.

Golden Pippin (OG 1037, ABV 3.9%)
A golden ale with a citrus aroma and flavour. The dry, bitter astringency increases in the aftertaste.

Scotts 1816 (OG 1041, ABV 4.1%)
This best bitter is fruity and malty with a bitter finish. Look for hints of nuts, tropical fruits and vanilla in the aroma and taste.

Copper Kettle

Bencroft Grange, Bedford Road, Rushden, Northamptonshire, NN10 0SE ☎ 07883 833687
🌐 ckcb.webs.com

Originally established in 2012 by three former soldiers turned brewers who set up a 3.5-barrel plant on a historic farm and former site of an alehouse, it is now run by one of the original brewers. The beers can be found at a number of local pubs and clubs including the award-winning Rushden Historical Transport Society. RAIB

UXB (OG 1037, ABV 3.6%)
A light, refreshing bitter.

Vann's Cross (OG 1039, ABV 3.8%)
A tawny-coloured bitter with a light but bitter taste and a bitter finish.

Cornucopia (OG 1041, ABV 4%)
A golden best bitter with a balanced malt and bitter taste and a long bitter finish.

Bencroft Best Bitter (OG 1042, ABV 4.1%)

Coppice Side

Unit 3, Heanor Small Business Centre, Adams Close, Heanor, Derbyshire, DE75 7FW ☎ 07790 305682

A five-barrel plant, Coppice Side was established in 2010. The site is shared with Leadmill Brewery (qv), although the two breweries are separate enterprises. Traditional English hops are used wherever possible. The brewery tap is the Butchers Arms, Langley. ♦

Nottingham Blonde (OG 1040, ABV 4%)
Crisp and hoppy with a fruity aroma.

Owd Miner (OG 1040, ABV 4%)
Traditional copper-coloured ale with good hop characteristics.

XOB (OG 1043, ABV 4.4%)

Coppice Light (OG 1044, ABV 4.5%)

Ninkasi (OG 1045, ABV 4.6%)

Scary Crow (OG 1052, ABV 5%)
Flagship premium pale ale. Full mellow flavour with citrus and floral notes.

Copthorne

Majors Farm, Woodcotes Lane, Darlton, Nottinghamshire, NG22 0TL ☎ 07523 340989
✉ copthornebrewery@gmail.com

Former Milestones brewer Dean Penney started production in 2010 in converted outbuildings at the Nags Head, Sutton-on-Trent. The 3.5-barrel plant was previously installed at the former Cathedral Brewery in Lincoln. The brewery relocated to larger premises in 2011. ♦

Gold (OG 1037, ABV 3.6%)
A hoppy golden ale with a bitter finish.

Classic (OG 1038.2, ABV 3.8%)
A light, hoppy session ale.

Comanchie (OG 1040, ABV 4%)
Copper in colour with caramel overtones.

Cossack (OG 1042.6, ABV 4.3%)
Bronze-coloured ale with a hint of toffee.

Coquetdale

Unit 4c, Rothbury Industrial Estate, Rothbury, Northumberland, NE65 7QJ
☎ (01669) 621411 ✉ owen.jackson@btconnect.com

Coquetdale brews on a five-barrel plant, originally from Geltsdale brewery, where the owner/brewer also received brewing training. The brewery has an expanding portfolio of locally named beers.

Snitter (OG 1038, ABV 3.8%)
A malty traditional bitter.

Coquet Ale (OG 1041, ABV 4.1%)
A refreshing pale ale.

Thrum (OG 1043, ABV 4.3%)
A fruity and spicy pale ale.

Corfe Castle

Bucknowle Farm, Corfe Castle, Dorset, BH20 9BP
☎ (01929) 480730 🌐 corfecastlebrewery.co.uk

Corfe Castle is a family-owned brewery established in 2012, brewing in the beautiful Corfe Valley in Dorset. The range of four cask ales is brewed in limited quantities, being supplied to local pubs and festivals in and around Dorset. A larger facility is being developed. ♦

Corinium

Cirencester, Gloucestershire, GL7 2HB ☎ 07716 826467 🌐 coriniumales.co.uk

Corinium Ales was launched in 2012. Brewing takes place on a recently expanded one-barrel plant in a converted garage. The award-winning beers are mainly available bottle-conditioned and make up the brewer's 'Roman Collection' but cask-conditioned production of the beers is increasing. ♦ RAIB

Gold (OG 1043, ABV 4.2%)

THE BREWERIES

An easy-drinking fruity ale with a mellow blend of malt and hops and a soft bitter finish.

Bodicacia (OG 1045, ABV 4.7%)
A full-bodied pale ale brewed with English hops to give a long-lasting citrus finish.

Centurion (OG 1051, ABV 4.7%)
A rich, malty stout with chocolate undertones. Lightly hopped leaving a well-rounded aftertaste.

Ale Caesar (OG 1050, ABV 5%)
A well-hopped IPA with a tropical fruit aroma balanced with a pleasing bitterness.

Cornish Chough SIBA

Trethvas Farm, Lizard, Cornwall, TR12 7AR
☎ (01326) 290908

⊗ Cornish Chough, the most southerly brewery on the UK mainland, commenced brewing in 2011 at its present location on Trethvas Farm, Lizard village. The brewery has its own borehole and draws water from between two seams of serpentine rock. ‼ RAIB

Serpentine (OG 1042, ABV 4%) ◆
Light-bodied tawny best bitter with gentle malt and ripe fruit aroma. Strongly malty in taste with sweetness and a delicious bitterness plus a hint of grapefruit that lingers into a dry finish.

Kynance Blonde (OG 1039, ABV 4.2%) ◆
Refreshing golden ale with crisp, hop taste and light bitterness. Lemon, peach and honey flavours and a hoppy finish.

Cadgwith Crabber (OG 1043, ABV 4.3%) ◆
Smooth, copper-coloured best bitter. Biscuit malt balanced with citrus hop character, apples, toffee and vanilla. Gentle fruity and astringent finish.

Fire Raven (OG 1047, ABV 4.7%) ◆
Black porter with hop aroma. Velvety roasted barley with bitter chocolate and liquorice. Faint sweet malt and hops. Short finish.

Lizard Storm (OG 1048, ABV 4.8%) ◆
Smooth, red strong bitter with malty fruitiness in the taste. Apples and hops balance the malt. Lingering sweet, fruity finish.

Cornish Crown SIBA

End Unit, Badger's Cross Farm, Badger's Cross, Penzance, Cornwall, TR20 8XE
☎ (01736) 449029 ☎ 07870 998986
⊕ cornishcrown.co.uk

⊗ Cornish Crown began brewing in 2012 on a six-barrel plant and is based on a farm high above Mounts Bay. It was established by the brewer and landlord of the Crown Inn in Penzance, which acts as the brewery tap. Beer is available in local outlets and can be found as far away as the Southampton Arms in London. RAIB

Mousehole (OG 1039, ABV 3.9%)
A slightly maltier and less hoppy beer than the bitter.

St Michaels (OG 1040, ABV 4%) ◆
Copper-coloured best bitter with a dry bitter aftertaste. Flavours of apple and tropical fruits with moderate hop bitterness and malt.

Causeway (OG 1041, ABV 4.1%) ◆
Copper-coloured best bitter with light fragrant nose. Biscuit malt and hops with damson and rum butter flavours. Bitter, dry finish.

One Hop One Grain (OG 1041, ABV 4.1%) ◆
Amber-coloured best bitter with hops dominant from aroma to finish. Taste balanced by malt, marmalade, caramel. Refreshing dry, bitter finish.

Honeyfuggle (OG 1043, ABV 4.5%) ◆
Yellow-coloured hoppy beer with sweet honey and malt in the mouth. Hop aroma and a bitter finish with some dryness.

SPA (OG 1048, ABV 4.8%) ◆
Heavily-hopped, refreshing golden strong bitter with biscuit malt and stone fruits in the mouth. Finish is bitter, hoppy and dry.

Porter (OG 1053, ABV 5.2%) ◆
Black vanilla porter with roast malt aroma. Smooth chocolate, liquorice, deep plum and black cherry, laced with cream. Burnt coffee aftertaste.

IPA (OG 1055, ABV 5.5%) ◆
Amber-coloured strong bitter with hop nose. Powerful hop bitter taste, persistent malt. Orange marmalade, lemon and peach. Bitter, dry finish.

Red IPA (OG 1057, ABV 5.9%) ◆
Strong brown beer with hops, vine fruit and honey aroma. Rich, sweet malt and fruit cake. Long bitter, dry finish.

Corvedale SIBA ◉

▤ Sun Inn, Corfton, Shropshire, SY7 9DF
☎ (01584) 861239 ⊕ corvedalebrewery.co.uk

☺Brewing started in 1999 behind the pub. Landlord Norman Pearce is also the brewer and uses only British malt and hops, with water from a local borehole. Bottle-conditioned beers are suitable for vegetarians and vegans. ‼ ◆ RAIB

Dale Ale (OG 1040, ABV 4%)
Aromas of smoky molasses and dates with fruity, nutty toffee tastes.

Fuggles Gold (OG 1042, ABV 4.2%)

Golden Dale (OG 1043, ABV 4.2%)

Katie's Pride (OG 1040, ABV 4.3%)

Norman's Pride (OG 1043, ABV 4.3%)
A golden amber beer with a refreshing, slightly hoppy taste and a bitter finish.

Farmer Rays Ale (OG 1045, ABV 4.5%)
A clear, ruby bitter with a smooth malty taste.

Pax Ale (OG 1045, ABV 4.5%)

St George's Stout (OG 1045, ABV 4.5%)

Dark & Delicious (OG 1045, ABV 4.6%)
A dark ruby beer with hops on the aroma and palate, and a sweet aftertaste.

Cotleigh SIBA

Ford Road, Wiveliscombe, Somerset, TA4 2RE
☎ (01984) 624086 ⊕ cotleighbrewery.com

Established in 1979, Cotleigh is based in the historic brewing town of Wiveliscombe. It supplies direct to 750 pubs, 200 retailers and selected wholesalers. ‼ ☞ ◆ RAIB

Harrier (OG 1035, ABV 3.5%)
A light, golden ale with a delicate floral and fruity aroma for a refreshing sweet and slightly hoppy finish.

Tawny Owl (OG 1038, ABV 3.8%) ◆

Well-balanced, tawny-coloured bitter with plenty of malt and fruitiness on the nose, and malt to the fore in the taste, followed by hop fruit, developing to a satisfying, bitter finish.

25 (OG 1040, ABV 4%)
A pale golden beer with a fresh aroma and fruit-filled finish.

Commando Hoofing (OG 1040, ABV 4%)
A pale-golden beer, refreshing and slightly sparkling.

Golden Seahawk (OG 1042, ABV 4.2%) ◆
A gold, well-hopped premium bitter with a flowery hop aroma and fruity hop flavour, clean mouthfeel, leading to a dry, hoppy finish.

Barn Owl (OG 1045, ABV 4.5%) ◆
A pale to mid-brown beer with a good balance of malt and hops on the nose; a smooth, full-bodied taste where hops dominate, but balanced by malt, following through to the finish.

Honey Buzzard (OG 1045, ABV 4.5%)
Uses pure honey from David Pearce Honey Farm. A smooth creamy and chocolate palate with a subtle bittersweet finish.

Old Buzzard (OG 1048, ABV 4.8%)
A traditional dark ale, deep copper-red in colour with the roasted chocolate malt giving a dry, nutty flavour with hints of biscuit. The finish in the mouth is dry, smoky and smooth.

Cotswold SIBA

College Farm, Stow Road, Bourton-on-the-Water, Gloucestershire, GL54 2HN
☎ (01451) 824488 ☎ 07760 889100
cotswoldlager.com

An independent producer of lager and speciality beers. The brewery was established in 2005 and moved to its current location in 2010. More than 60 outlets are supplied. !! ◆

Cask (ABV 4%)
Copper-coloured, well-hopped, easy-drinking ale.

Cotswold Lion SIBA

Grain Store 5, Dowmans Farm, Coberley, Gloucestershire, GL53 9QY
☎ (01242) 870164 cotswoldlionbrewery.co.uk

Brewing began in 2012 using a 10-barrel plant located in a grain store on a farm in the Cotswolds. Established by John Kemp, former head brewer of Nailsworth Brewery, and Andy Forbes, formerly of Festival Brewery. RAIB

Shepherd's Delight (OG 1036, ABV 3.6%)
A light session ale, crisp and full of citrus flavours.

Best in Show (OG 1042, ABV 4.2%)
Plenty of blackberry fruit with a hint of honey.

Golden Fleece (OG 1044, ABV 4.4%)
A twist on an IPA, filled with Jamaican fruit.

Cotswold Spring SIBA

See Combined Brewers

Cottage SIBA

The Old Cheese Dairy, Hornblotton Road, Lovington, Somerset, BA7 7PS
☎ (01963) 240551 cottagebrewing.co.uk

The brewery was established in 1993 in West Lydford and moved to larger premises in 1996, doubling brewing capacity at the same time. In 2001 a 30-barrel plant was installed. Around 1,500 outlets are supplied. A visitor centre and shop are planned. !! ◆

Southern Bitter (OG 1039, ABV 3.7%)
Gold-coloured beer with malt and fruity hops on the nose. Malt and hops in the mouth with a long, fruity bitter finish.

Pacific (OG 1040, ABV 4%)
A gold-coloured ale with a vibrant hop aroma and finish.

Duchess (OG 1042, ABV 4.2%)
A tawny-coloured ale with a balanced bitter finish and distinctive spicy aroma.

Tornado (OG 1042, ABV 4.2%)
A tawny-coloured ale, well-hopped for a light, crisp finish on the palate.

Somerset & Dorset (S&D) (OG 1045, ABV 4.4%)
A traditional best bitter with a deep red colour. Well-hopped with a rich, malty flavour.

Golden Arrow (OG 1045, ABV 4.5%)
A hoppy golden bitter with a powerful floral bouquet, a fruity, full-bodied taste and a lingering dry, bitter finish.

Goldrush (OG 1051, ABV 5%)
A deep golden premium ale. Well-balanced with a distinctive and vibrant aroma.

Norman's Conquest MM (OG 1050, ABV 5%)
A dark, mature, smooth ale. Full-bodied with hints of chocolate, bitter orange and vine fruits.

Cotton End (NEW)

Pomfret Arms, 10 Cotton End, Northampton, NN4 8BS
☎ (01604) 765544

Brewing began in 2014 on a small brewplant located in outhouse behind the Pomfret Arms, focusing on experimental and specialist beer styles for sale in the pub and at local beer festivals. Customers are invited to suggest beers for brewing.

Country Life SIBA

The Big Sheep, Abbotsham, Bideford, Devon, EX39 5AP
☎ (01237) 420808 ☎ 07971 267790
countrylifebrewery.co.uk

Country Life is based at the Big Sheep tourist attraction. The brewery offers a beer show and free samples in the shop during the peak season (Apr-Oct). A 15.5-barrel plant was installed in 2005, making Country Life the biggest brewery in north Devon. Around 100 outlets are supplied. !! ◆ RAIB

Old Appledore (OG 1037, ABV 3.7%)
A classic session beer with a real depth of taste.

Reef Break (OG 1039, ABV 4%)
A gentle sweet, malty taste.

Shore Break (OG 1042, ABV 4.4%)
A light, easy-drinking, refreshing ale.

Black Boar/Board Break (OG 1044, ABV 4.5%)

An easy-drinking porter. Smoky and rich on the nose with coffee and toffee notes.

Golden Pig (OG 1046, ABV 4.7%)

Country Bumpkin (OG 1058, ABV 6%)
A malty, full-flavoured, smooth-tasting ale.

CrackleRock

The Old Cooperage, High Street, Botley, Hampshire, SO30 2EA ☎ 07733 232806 ⊕ cracklerock.co.uk

⊠ Experienced head brewer Andy Ingram began brewing in 2014 at the Old Cooperage in the centre of Botley using refurbished equipment. Further beers are planned. !! ☞♦

Crackerjack (OG 1039, ABV 3.8%)
Clean-tasting, light, hoppy ale.

Barleycorn (OG 1043, ABV 4.2%)
Well-balanced traditional English bitter.

Gold Rush (OG 1046, ABV 4.5%)
A premium golden ale with a full, deep, malty flavour and good hop balance.

Craddock's

▤ Duke William, 25 Coventry Street, Stourbridge, West Mdlands, DY8 1EP
☎ (01384) 440202 ⊕ craddocksbrewery.com

⊠ Craddock's is located to the rear of the award-winning pub the Duke William. It is a four-barrel plant selling exclusively to its three pubs; the Duke William, the Plough & Harrow, Stourbridge and the King Charles, Worcester. !! ♦ RAIB

Saxon Gold (OG 1041, ABV 4%)

Crazy Sheep (ABV 4.5%)

Troll (OG 1052, ABV 5.4%)
A deceptively strong golden ale, with a bittersweet taste, and dry hop finish.

Crafty Beers

▤ Carpenters Arms, 10 High Street, Great Wilbraham, Cambridgeshire, CB21 5JD
☎ (01223) 813938 ⊕ craftybeers.co.uk

⊠ Crafty Beers are brewed by Robert Beardsmore in the old stables at the Carpenters Arms. This small 1.5-barrel brewpub started production in 2012. Beer is available in the Carpenter Arms and can also be found at a number of local pubs and beer festivals. RAIB

Mild Mannered (OG 1040, ABV 3.5%)
A smooth, dark mild, packed with malt flavours and a hint of sweetness.

Sixteen Strides (OG 1037, ABV 3.8%)
A generously-hopped pale ale with plenty of citrus aroma.

Carpenter's Cask (OG 1042, ABV 4.2%) ◆
A well-balanced amber brew with biscuit malt character giving way to hops on the palate and long finish.

Sauvignon Blonde (OG 1044, ABV 4.4%)
An aromatic golden ale.

Crafty Brewing (NEW) SIBA ◉

Thatched House Farm, Loxhill, Dunsfold, Surrey, GU8 4BW

☎ (01483) 271814 ⊕ craftybrewing.co.uk

⊠ Situated behind Dunsfold aerodrome, Crafty's base at Thatched House Farm has a historic connection with the Canadian troop presence during WW2. In early 2015 Crafty installed a new five-barrel plant with four core beers being produced. These are supplied to nearby pubs in cask and to local stores in bottle. There are plans for a wider range of beers in the future, including seasonal offerings. RAIB

Loxhill Biscuit (OG 1038, ABV 3.8%)
Well-balanced session golden ale with floral notes.

Dark Session (OG 1040, ABV 4%)
An amber-coloured best bitter.

Heady Steady Go (OG 1045, ABV 4.5%)
An American-style pale ale.

IPA (OG 1047, ABV 4.7%)
An amber-coloured IPA.

Crafty Devil

27 Loftus Street, Cardiff, CF5 1HL
⊕ craftydevilbrewing.co.uk

Brewing commenced in 2014 initially producing keg and bottled beers only with a view to producing cask-conditioned beers in the future.

Crafty Pint

▤ Half Moon, 130 Northgate, Darlington, County Durham, DL1 1QS
☎ (01325) 469965 ☎ 07804 305175
⊕ thecraftypint.co.uk

The Crafty Pint Brewery was established n 2013 in the cellar of the Half Moon, bringing commercial brewing back to Darlington for the first time since 1934. The brew length is only 10 gallons, making it a nanobrewery. Occasional one-off beers are brewed solely for the pub and there are also collaborations with Just A Minute Brewery (qv) in Spennymoor. ◆

Tawny Mild (OG 1040, ABV 4%)

Porter (OG 1045, ABV 4.5%)

Cranky Cobbler (NEW)

Unit 7, Bondfield Avenue, Kingsthorpe, Northampton, NN2 7RD ☎ 07914 092606
✉ crankycobbler@outlook.com

⊠ A family-run microbrewery, established in 2014 by two brothers after making homemade wine and beer for several years. Production began in 2015 using a 0.5-barrel plant. There are plans to expand. RAIB

English Pale Ale (ABV 4.5%)

Amber Ale (ABV 5.0%)

Stout (ABV 5.2%)

Crate

Unit 7, White Building, Queens Yard, Hackney Wick, London, E9 5EN ☎ 07834 275687
⊕ cratebrewery.com

Crate is a brewery and pizzeria opened in 2012 and situated in a canalside former print factory. RAIB

Best Bitter (OG 1045, ABV 4.3%) ◆

Brown beer with roast and berry fruitiness. Sweetness and biscuit character is offset by bitterness that lingers with roast notes.

Stout (OG 1057, ABV 5.7%) ◆
Slightly smoky nose with blackcurrant fruit. Caramelised toffee and liquorice flavour that lingers. A little black roast notes throughout.

Cromarty SIBA

Davidston, Cromarty, IV11 8XD
☎ (01381) 600440 🌐 cromartybrewing.co.uk

Cromarty began brewing in 2011 in a purpose-built brewhouse. Additional fermenters were installed in 2014 and again in 2015 to meet demand. Nine regular ales are brewed. !!

Atlantic Drift (OG 1035, ABV 3.5%) ◆
Good citrus hop flavour throughout.

Hit the Lip (OG 1037, ABV 3.8%) ◆
A good mouth-puckering grapefruit hoppy brew with a dry finish.

Happy Chappy (OG 1040, ABV 4.1%) ◆
A golden ale with plenty of hop character. Floral citrus hop aroma with a bitter taste which increases in the aftertaste.

Kowabunga (OG 1046, ABV 4.6%) ◆
A golden hoppy brew.

Brewed Awakening (OG 1048, ABV 4.7%) ◆
A roasted malty brew with added coffee, making for a dry bitter finish.

Red Rocker (OG 1048.5, ABV 5%) ◆
Red-coloured bitter using rye.

Rogue Wave (OG 1052, ABV 5.7%) ◆
Strong citrus hoppy bitter.

Ghost Town (OG 1058, ABV 5.8%) ◆
Dark malty brew with a blackcurrant and liquorice background.

AKA IPA (OG 1067, ABV 6.7%) ◆
Strong IPA with a smooth, citrus, hoppy taste.

Cronx SIBA

Unit 6, Vulcan Business Centre, Vulcan Way, New Addington, CR0 9UG
☎ (01689) 809093 ☎ 07793 974395
🌐 thecronx.com

Cronx began brewing in 2012 and is the first commercial brewery in the area since 1954. ♦

Standard (ABV 3.8%) ◆
Easy-drinking brown bitter with sweetish fudge and spicy hoppiness notes throughout. A malty bitter finish with a dryness that remains.

Kotchin (ABV 3.9%) ◆
Grapefruity beer with pleasant hoppy notes. A little sweetness is balanced by a crisp bitter finish that grows on drinking.

Entire (ABV 5.2%) ◆
Dark brown porter with chocolate roast notes in the aroma, flavour and finish. The fruit character is of caramelised raisins.

Crooked Brook (NEW)

Unit 5, Woodside Service Station, Copthorne Road, Copthorne, West Sussex, RH10 3PD ☎ 07462 523013
✉ info@crookedbrook.co.uk

Established in 2014 as a traditional cask brewery.

Carnival (OG 1041, ABV 4.1%)

Smugglers (OG 1045, ABV 4.3%)

Cropton

See Great Yorkshire

Cross Bay SIBA

White Lund Industrial Estate, Morecambe, Lancashire, LA3 3PT
☎ (01524) 39481 🌐 crossbaybrewery.co.uk

Cross Bay commenced brewing in 2011 on a 28-barrel brew plant and has a brewing capacity of 168 barrels a week. !! ♦

Halo (OG 1037, ABV 3.6%) ◆
A crisp and hoppy pale bitter.

Nightfall Pale Bitter (OG 1038, ABV 3.8%) ◆
A sweet, malty, gently-hopped bitter with some fruit.

Dusk Ruby Ale (OG 1040, ABV 4%)
A ruby ale, kicking in with a strong fruity nose, bursting onto the palate with a roasted but fruity bitter body with hints of cocoa, following through with a floral/blackcurrant aroma.

Sunset Blonde (OG 1043, ABV 4.2%) ◆
Sweet and fruity best bitter with a rising bitter finish.

Zenith (OG 1050, ABV 5%) ◆
Gentle bitterness and fruity sweetness with some astringency in the finish.

Crouch Vale SIBA

23 Haltwhistle Road, South Woodham Ferrers, Essex, CM3 5ZA
☎ (01245) 322744 🌐 crouchvale.co.uk

Founded in 1981 by two CAMRA enthusiasts, Crouch Vale is now well established as a major player in Essex brewing, having moved to larger premises in 2006. The company is also a major wholesaler of cask ale from other independent breweries, which it supplies to more than 100 outlets as well as beer festivals throughout the region. One tied house, the Queen's Head in Chelmsford, is owned. !! ♦ RAIB

Blackwater Mild (OG 1037, ABV 3.7%) ◆
A dark bitter rather than a true mild. Roasty and bitter towards the end.

Essex Boys Best Bitter (OG 1038, ABV 3.8%)
Full-bodied and malty with hops shining through; a classic session beer.

Brewers Gold (OG 1040, ABV 4%) ◆
Pale golden ale with a striking citrus nose. Sweet fruit and bitter hops are well matched throughout.

Yakima Gold (OG 1042, ABV 4.2%)
Pale ale, earthily aromatic and highly drinkable.

Amarillo (OG 1050, ABV 5%)
A strong golden ale with a spicy aroma, juicy malt mouthfeel and an extremely long and bitter hop finish.

Crown

See Wood Street

Cryptic (NEW) SIBA

3 Carrington Field Street, Heaviley, Stockport, SK1 3JN
☎ (0161) 222 8840 ☎ 07932 545939
crypticales.co.uk

Cryptic Ales was founded in 2014 using a 10-barrel plant after discussion between four quiz team members. Further ales are planned. A one-barrel plant is used for experimental and speciality beers under the Cryptic Labs brand name.

Tip Of The Tongue (OG 1048, ABV 5%)
Chestnut-coloured strong bitter with a roasted malt profile.

Crystalbrew SIBA

Building 40, British Aerospace Business Park, Saltgrounds Road, Brough, East Yorkshire, HU15 1EQ
☎ 07773 938380

Office: 88 Highfields, South Cave, Brough, HU15 2AJ
crystalbrew.co.uk/beerfinder

Brewing began in 2014 using an eight-barrel plant. The brewery is named in honour of Hull University's world famous Crystal Group in Chemistry, the first group to successfully make the liquid crystals that are an essential part of modern life. !!

Crystal Limonite Bitter (OG 1035, ABV 3.8%)
Good body, malty and hoppy with a smooth finish with caramel hints.

Crystal Jade (OG 1035, ABV 4%)
Hoppy, citrus and refreshing blonde beer with a citrus flavour and dry bitterness.

Crystal Blond (OG 1039, ABV 4.5%)
Thirst-quenching and well-hopped beer with complex citrus hints.

Cuillin

Sligachan Hotel, Sligachan, Carbost, Isle of Skye, IV47 8SW
☎ (01478) 650204 ☎ 07795 250808
sligachan.co.uk

The five-barrel brewery opened in 2004 and is situated in central Skye at the foot of the Cuillin mountains. The water from the Cuillins provides a distinctive colour and taste to the ales. The brewery is closed in winter. !!♦

Cullercoats SIBA

Westfield Court, 19 Maurice Road Industrial Estate, Wallsend, Tyne & Wear, NE28 6BY
☎ (0191) 252 8765 ☎ 07895 692881

Office: 17 St Oswins Avenue, Cullercoats, Tyne & Wear, NE30 4PH cullercoatsbrewery.co.uk

Ex-solicitor Bill Scantlebury established Cullercoats in 2011 and brews at least once a week producing about 18 barrels with the help of brewer's mate Doug. Wife Anna looks after the paperwork. ♦

Shuggy Boat Blonde (OG 1039, ABV 3.8%)
A refreshing blonde beer, smooth and fresh.

Lovely Nelly (OG 1039, ABV 3.9%)
A full-bodied, bronze-coloured session beer with a biscuit malt flavour balanced with a smooth bitterness from the hops.

Jack the Devil (OG 1045, ABV 4.5%)
Delicious and rich, a dark chestnut-coloured ale. Perfect balance of malty nuttiness and a fresh, hoppy aroma.

Shuggy Boat Blonde Special (OG 1050, ABV 5%)

Watch House Winter Warmer (OG 1050, ABV 5%)
Warming, dark-coloured English ale, malty with spicy/berry flavours.

Cumberland

The Forge, Great Corby, Cumbria, CA4 8LR
☎ (01228) 560899 ☎ 07747 841671
cumberlandbreweries.co.uk

Cumberland was established in 2009 with a bespoke 10-barrel brewing plant and situated in a building at the heart of the village, previously the farriers shop from 1833. !!

Corby Ale (OG 1038, ABV 3.8%)
A fruity session beer with sweetness leading to gentle bitterness in the aftertaste.

Corby Amber (ABV 4%)
A gentle brown ale; mild, fruity and sweet.

Corby Blonde (OG 1042, ABV 4.2%)
Melon fruity hoppiness gives a light, refreshing drink.

Corby Noir (OG 1044, ABV 4.5%)
Fruity aroma, sweet roast middle and dry finish.

Corby Fox (OG 1048, ABV 4.7%)
Full-bodied deep red-brown ale. Smooth, with lots of soft fruit flavours.

Cumbrian Legendary SIBA

Old Hall Brewery, Hawkshead, Cumbria, LA22 0QF
☎ (01539) 436436 cumbrianlegendaryales.com

First established in 2003, the brewery is located in an idyllic position in a renovated barn on the shores of Esthwaite Water. The success of Loweswater Gold has meant the brewery is thriving. !!♦

Esthwaite Bitter (OG 1038.5, ABV 3.8%)
Amber session ale with sweetness, fruit and hoppiness in fine balance.

Langdale (OG 1040, ABV 4%)
Fresh grapefruit aromas with hoppy fruity flavours and crisp hop finish, make for a well-balanced beer.

Grasmoor Dark Ale (OG 1043, ABV 4.3%)
Dark fruity beer with complex character and roast nutty tones leading to a short, refreshing finish.

Loweswater Gold (OG 1041, ABV 4.3%)
A dominant fruity body develops into a light bitter finish. A beer that belies its strength.

American Invasion (OG 1047, ABV 5%)
Well-balanced, gold-coloured beer with big hop impact and long, fruity finish.

Cwm Rhondda Ales (NEW)

Fforch Farm Cemetry Road, Treorchy, Glamorgan, CF42 6TF

☎ (01443) 777491 🌐 CwmRhonddaAles.co.uk

Situated on a farm in the Rhondda valley and brewing on a 2.5-barrel plant using water from its own well. Limited trial production started in 2015 with a 4.5% pale ale called Boyo. There are plans to increase the range to six ales once the brewery building is completed and the bio-mass boiler installed.

Daleside SIBA

Camwal Road, Starbeck, Harrogate, North Yorkshire, HG1 4PT
☎ (01423) 880022 🌐 dalesidebrewery.com

Opened in 1991 in Harrogate with a 20-barrel plant, the brewery delivers direct to a range of outlets including pubs, restaurants and farm shops from Newcastle to Chesterfield as well as nationally via wholesalers. ♦

Bitter (OG 1039, ABV 3.7%)
Pale brown in colour, this well-balanced, hoppy beer is complemented by fruity bitterness and a hint of sweetness, leading to a long, bitter finish.

Blonde (OG 1040, ABV 3.9%)
A pale golden beer with a predominantly hoppy aroma and taste, leading to a refreshing, hoppy, bitter but short finish.

Old Leg Over (OG 1043, ABV 4.1%)
Well-balanced, mid-brown refreshing beer that leads to an equally well-balanced fruity bitter aftertaste.

Special Bitter (OG 1043, ABV 4.1%)
A mid-amber beer with a malty nose and a hint of fruitiness. Hops and malt carry over to leave a clean, hoppy aftertaste.

Monkey Wrench (OG 1055, ABV 5.3%)
Premium deep chestnut-coloured beer with a spicy fruit aroma and warming spicy flavour.

Morocco Ale (OG 1057, ABV 5.5%)
A rich, dark spiced ale.

Dancing Duck SIBA

1 John Cooper Buildings, Payne Street, Derby, DE22 3AZ
☎ (01332) 205582 ☎ 07581 122122
🌐 dancingduckbrewery.com

Dancing Duck was established in 2010 by Rachel Mathews using a 10-barrel brew plant. Its name comes from the local greeting 'ay up me duck'. The brewery operates two local pubs, the Exeter Arms and the New Zealand Arms in Derby.

Ay Up (OG 1040.5, ABV 3.9%)
A pale ale session bitter. Subtle malt and floral notes are matched with citrus hop, rounded off with a slightly dry finish.

Waitangi (OG 1041.3, ABV 4%)
An easy-drinking, crisp, clean pale ale, subtle malt character is balanced with zesty lemon and lime hops.

Nice Weather (OG 1042, ABV 4.1%)
Copper-coloured fruity ale packed full of flavour. Blackberry, strawberry and floral rose notes in perfect balance with just the right amount of malt character.

22 (OG 1044.1, ABV 4.3%)
A well-balanced best bitter with good malty flavour and dark fruit notes offset by a strong hop with a clean finish.

DCUK (OG 1042, ABV 4.3%)
A pale ale with a fruity aroma. A juicy citrus flavour with hints of orange, mango, lemon and pine.

Dark Drake (OG 1051, ABV 4.5%)
Malty, caramel and liquorice flavours combine in a smooth-drinking velvety oatmeal stout with a freshly roasted coffee and tea finish.

Gold (OG 1046.5, ABV 4.7%)
A modern IPA with powerful hoppy bitterness and aroma balanced with strong malt notes. English hops give peppery, plum-like and orange zest flavours.

Amberillo (OG 1047.2, ABV 4.8%)
An easy-drinking amber ale. Earthy aromatic American hops are balanced with biscuit malt flavours leading to a spicy, peppery finish.

Duck's Courage (OG 1048.8, ABV 5%)

Indian Porter (OG 1051.8, ABV 5%)
Smoky bonfire flavours with a spicy hop and pleasant warming afterglow.

Seduction (OG 1051.3, ABV 5.2%)
A malt-led beer, dark fruity flavours are followed by a lingering, powerful American hop.

Abduction (OG 1053, ABV 5.5%)
A myriad of tropical flavours in harmonious balance with an enjoyable level of hoppy bitterness, a good malt character and clean finish.

Dancing Man

Wool House, Town Quay, Southampton, SO14 2AR
☎ (023) 8033 7232 🌐 dancingmanbrewery.co.uk

Dancing Man began brewing in 2011 in the Platform Tavern. In 2015 the brewery moved to the historic Wool House in order to expand and include an onsite bar and restaurant. One-off and rare brews are available throughout the year. ♦RAIB

Pilgrim's Pale Ale (OG 1039, ABV 3.9%)
A pale golden ale with tropical fruit aromas, a smooth, bitter flavour and a clean and crisp finish.

Congo Driftwood (OG 1042, ABV 4.2%)
A modern pale ale with the addition of fresh mango and papaya in the fermenter which delivers unique tropical flavours.

Jack O' Diamonds (OG 1045, ABV 4.5%)
Complex malty red ale. Lots of American hops play off the malt body to give a fruity, rich beer.

Fiddler's Jig (OG 1047, ABV 4.8%)
A rich malt body, with fruity hop flavours.

Big Casino (OG 1049, ABV 5%)
Pine and citrus fruit aroma with a warming malt body and a smooth bitterness with juicy hop flavours.

Last Waltz (OG 1052, ABV 5.3%)
A black IPA with an intense hoppy nose with tropical fruit notes, a smoky roasted malt flavour and a dry bitter finish.

Dancing Men (NEW)

Hill House Inn, The Hill, Happisburgh, Norfolk, NR12 0PW
☎ (01692) 650004 🌐 hillhouseinn.co.uk

THE BREWERIES

⊗ Brewing began in 2014 at the 16th-century Hill House Inn on Happisburgh's fast-eroding clifftop. The microbrewery is named in honour of a famous Sherlock Holmes story written by Sir Arthur Conan Doyle after he visited the pub in 1903. ‼

Deerstalker (OG 1034, ABV 3.5%)
A single-hopped session ale with a bitter finish and a hint of liquorice.

After the Storm (OG 1039, ABV 3.8%)
An easy-drinking session beer with a slightly peaty finish.

Soggy Seagull (OG 1043, ABV 4.2%)
Refreshing, clean-tasting beer with well-balanced fruit.

Knight's Noffin (OG 1046, ABV 4.8%)
A dark porter-style beer with toasted toffee malt flavours.

Cliffhanger (OG 1049, ABV 5.1%)
An easy-drinking, pale, single-hopped ale with a smooth honey finish.

Dark Horse SIBA

Coonlands Laithe, Hetton, North Yorkshire, BD23 6LY
☎ (01756) 730555 ⊕ darkhorsebrewery.co.uk

☺Dark Horse began brewing in 2008. The brewery is based in an old hay barn within the Yorkshire Dales National Park. More than 30 outlets are supplied direct. ‼

Craven Bitter (OG 1038, ABV 3.8%) ◆
Well-balanced bitter with biscuity malt and fruit on the nose continuing into the taste. Bitterness increases in the finish.

Hetton Pale Ale (OG 1041, ABV 4.2%) ◆
Golden, well-balanced, full-bodied, with hoppy bitterness on the palate overlaying a malty base and a spicy citrus character.

Dark Star SIBA ◉

22 Star Road, Partridge Green, West Sussex, RH13 8RA
☎ (01403) 713085 ⊕ darkstarbrewing.co.uk

⊗ Dark Star started in the cellar of the Evening Star in Brighton and in 2010 moved to its current premises using a 45-barrel plant. Copies of classic European, American or old English beer styles are regularly produced. ‼ 〓 ◆RAIB

Art of Darkness (OG 1040, ABV 3.5%)
A low-gravity beer with classic roast flavours and a hint of sweetness.

Hophead (OG 1040, ABV 3.8%) 🍺 ◆
A golden-coloured bitter with a fruity/hoppy aroma and a citrus/bitter taste and aftertaste. Flavours remain strong to the end.

Partridge Best Bitter (OG 1041, ABV 4%)
Traditional Sussex-style best bitter.

Espresso (OG 1043, ABV 4.2%)
Freshly ground Arabica coffee beans are added to the copper for a few minutes after the boil of this rich, black beer.

American Pale Ale (OG 1048, ABV 4.7%)
American-style pale ale. Full of the aroma of hops.

Festival (OG 1051, ABV 5%)
A chestnut/bronze-coloured bitter with a smooth mouthfeel and freshness.

Original (OG 1051, ABV 5%) 🍺
A dark, strong and bitter beer.

Winter Meltdown (OG 1051, ABV 5%)
A deep bronze-coloured beer, cask-conditioned with Chinese stem ginger and other spices to produce an aromatic warmth.

Revelation (OG 1056, ABV 5.7%) 🍺

DarkTribe

🍺 **Dog & Gun, High Street, East Butterwick, Lincolnshire, DN17 3AJ**
☎ (01724) 782324 ⊕ darktribe.co.uk

☺A small brewery was built during the summer of 1996 in a workshop at the bottom of his garden by Dave 'Dixie' Dean. In 2005 Dixie bought the Dog & Gun pub and moved the 2.5-barrel brewing equipment there. The beers generally follow a marine theme, recalling Dixie's days as an engineer in the Merchant Navy and his enthusiasm for sailing. Local outlets are supplied. ‼♦

Dixie's Mild (OG 1034, ABV 3.6%)

Honey Mild (OG 1032, ABV 3.6%)

Pieces of 8 (OG 1033, ABV 3.6%)

Three Point Six (OG 1033, ABV 3.6%)

Full Ahead (OG 1034, ABV 3.8%) ◆
A malty smoothness is backed by a slightly fruity hop that gives a good bitterness to this amber-brown bitter.

Captain Floyd (OG 1035, ABV 3.9%)

Ruddy L (OG 1035, ABV 3.9%)

Albacore (OG 1036, ABV 4%)

Sternwheeler (OG 1037, ABV 4.2%)

Old Gaffer (OG 1038, ABV 4.5%)

Dartmoor SIBA ◉

The Brewery, Station Road, Princetown, Devon, PL20 6QX
☎ (01822) 890789 ⊕ dartmoorbrewery.co.uk

⊗ Formerly named Princetown, Dartmoor Brewery was established in 1994 and is the highest brewery in England at 1,465 feet above sea level. In 2012 the capacity was increased to 360 barrels a week by the addition of another 60-barrel fermenter with a further increase in 2013. All beer is brewed using Dartmoor and Devon-grown barley. ‼RAIB

Best (OG 1037, ABV 3.7%)
An amber-coloured ale with a citrus fruit character.

IPA (OG 1039.5, ABV 4%) ◆
There is a flowery hop aroma and taste with a bitter aftertaste to this full-bodied, amber-coloured beer.

Dragon's Breath (OG 1044, ABV 4.4%)
A unique winter warmer flavoured with black treacle. Deep ruby brown in colour, rich and full-bodied with an aftertaste of Morello cherries.

Legend (OG 1043.5, ABV 4.4%)
A classic, smooth, full-flavoured and well-balanced beer with a crisp malt fruit finish. Golden brown in colour with an aroma of fresh baked bread with a hint of spice.

Jail Ale (OG 1047.5, ABV 4.8%) ◆

Hops and fruit predominate in the flavour of this mid-brown beer, which has a slightly sweet aftertaste.

Darwin SIBA

1 West Quay Court, Sunderland Enterprise Park, Sunderland, Tyne & Wear, SR5 2TE
☎ (0191) 549 9450 ⊕ darwinbrewery.com

☺Established in 1994, Darwin Brewery is now based in purpose-built premises in Sunderland with a 3.5-barrel brew plant. The brewery supports students on Brewlab brewing courses at the university, who produce many unique specialist and international beers, often available locally. A range of established Darwin beers are also produced, some based on analysis of historic recipes or student initiatives. ‼◆RAIB

Evolution (OG 1039, ABV 4%)

Beagle Blonde (OG 1039, ABV 4.1%)
A bitter and hoppy blonde ale with a spicy citrus aftertaste.

Rolling Hitch (OG 1051, ABV 5.2%)
A traditional IPA with citrus fruit character balanced with a dry, crisp finish.

Extinction Ale (OG 1084, ABV 8.3%) 🍷

Dawkins SIBA

The Now Thus Brewery, Unit 7, Timsbury Workshop Estate, Hayeswood Road, Timsbury, Bath, BA2 0HQ
☎ (01761) 472242 ⊕ dawkinsales.com

The established Dawkins Taverns group of independent Bristol pubs bought the former Matthews Brewery in 2009. Five pubs are owned and around 80 outlets are supplied direct. A core range of five ales is produced plus around 12 specials a year. The brewery plans to move all of its production during 2015 to new premises in Easton, Bristol, where test brewing is already underway. ‼🍺◆

Bristol Blonde (ABV 3.8%)
Pale gold beer with citrus aroma and flavour with tones of vanilla.

Bristol Best (OG 1041, ABV 4%)
Copper-coloured with a malty aroma. Malt flavour with biscuity tones and bitter finish.

Miners Gold (OG 1040, ABV 4%)
Golden ale with a slightly spicy fruit aroma and flavour.

Green Barrel (ABV 4.2%)

Resolution IPA (OG 1053, ABV 5.3%)
An amber-gold IPA with a mango/grapefruit flavour.

de bRus (NEW)

≣ The Bruery, 25 Canmore Street, Dunfermline, KY12 7NU
☎ (01383) 747757 ⊕ debrusbrewery.com

Located near Dunfermline's city centre and just along the road from the renowned Alhambra Theatre, the brewery opened in 2013.

IPA (ABV 4.2%)

Nut Brown (ABV 4.5%)

Blonde (ABV 5%)

Deeply Vale

Unit 24, Peel Industrial Estate, Chamberhall Street, Bury, BL9 0LU
☎ (0161) 761 7334 ☎ 07736 936973
⊕ deeplyvalebrewery.com

☺Deeply Vale is a family-run business established in 2012 using a 2.5-barrel plant. The brewery's name immortalises the Deeply Vale area near Bury, famed for legendary 1970s music festivals.

Still Walking (OG 1036, ABV 3.8%)
A light, well-balanced, easy-drinking session ale, with a fruity aroma and a velvety smooth feel.

Golden Vale (OG 1041, ABV 4.2%)
A deep golden ale. The flavour is refreshing, robust and satisfyingly malty. A complex bitterness with a smooth, caramel finish.

DV8 (OG 1050, ABV 4.8%)
A thick and creamy breakfast stout.

Deeside

Lochton of Leys, Banchory, AB31 5QB
☎ (01330) 825598 ☎ 07765 124162

Office: Escape Business Technologies, 5 Carden Place, Aberdeen, AB10 1UT ⊕ deesidebrewery.co.uk

Originally established as Hillside Brewery in 2005, it quickly expanded and was renamed Deeside Brewery in 2006. The company was sold in 2012 and moved to new premises in 2013.

Swift (OG 1038, ABV 3.8%)
Light session pale ale.

Macbeth (OG 1042, ABV 4.1%)

Rye (ABV 4.8%)

IPA (ABV 5.2%)

Degrees Plato (NEW)

Netil Market, 23 Westgate Street, London, E8
☎ 07460 693206 ⊕ dplato.com

No real ale. Beers produced are mainly keg and available from the brewery to drink in the market. The range varies, and includes some bottled beers. Saturday is the main market day but the brewery is open also at other times.

Delavals 👁

26 Windsor Gardens, Whitley Bay, Tyne & Wear, NE26 3BG ☎ 0844 504 2214 ⊕ delavals.com

Delavals started brewing in 2010 using a two-barrel plant, reviving an 18th century ale for Seaton Delaval Hall in partnership with the National Trust. It continues to work closely to create a range of fine ales that help to promote and preserve regional landmarks. Brewing is currently suspended.

Souter Lighthouse Best Bitter (OG 1037.5, ABV 3.8%)
A traditional copper-coloured English bitter. Well-rounded, bittersweet with a little malt and rich fruity aromas.

Lindisfarne Castle Dark Ale (OG 1039, ABV 4%)
An old Scottish ale with a twist, an amber/stout fusion. Light and easy-drinking for a dark ale. Sweet and malty, made with Hyssop to give a silky finish.

Seaton Delaval Hall Pale Ale (OG 1040.6, ABV 4.2%)
A golden-coloured classic English pale ale, crisp and refreshing with a hoppy aroma and a dry finish.

Washington Old Hall Honey Beer (OG 1045.4, ABV 4.6%)
A golden ale with honey, not sweet as you might expect, but a tantalising blend of biscuity malt, light floral aromas and warming honey.

Denbigh

Crown Workshop, Crown Lane, Denbigh, LL16 3SY
☎ (01745) 817021 🌐 bragdydinbych.co.uk

Brewing commenced in 2012 at the rear of the Hope & Anchor pub. The brewery relocated in 2015 to a dedicated brewhouse in the town. Beers are mainly bottle-conditioned for markets and fairs but also supplied cask-conditioned to the pub. ♦RAIB

Earls Folly (OG 1042, ABV 3.6%)

Cadlas Ceiliogod (Cock Pit) (OG 1045, ABV 4.5%)
A tawny-coloured bitter. Well-hopped, with caramel and malt highlights.

Cwrw Du'nbych (Denbigh Black) (OG 1050, ABV 5%)
A traditional Celtic black porter with a rich, roasted flavour and hints of Muscovado.

No X (OG 1044, ABV 5.3%)
A cask-conditioned lager.

Dent SIBA

Hollins, Cowgill, Dent, Cumbria, LA10 5TQ
☎ (01539) 625326 🌐 dentbrewery.co.uk

Dent was set up in 1990 in a converted barn next to a former farmhouse in the Yorkshire Dales National Park. In 2005 the brewery was completely refurbished and capacity expanded. One pub is owned. More than 150 outlets are supplied direct. ‼

Fellranger (OG 1035, ABV 3.7%)

Golden Fleece (OG 1035, ABV 3.7%)
Light, hoppy and fruity, with a bitter aftertaste.

Station Porter (OG 1042, ABV 3.8%)
A veritable malt feast for the beer's strength. A complex porter ending with roast highlights.

Aviator (OG 1039, ABV 4%)
This amber ale is characterised by citrus, caramel and hop flavours that evolve into a bitter finish.

Rambrau (OG 1042, ABV 4.5%)
A cask-conditioned lager brewed using lager malt and Hallertauer hops. It is a clean, crisp and refreshing lager-style beer.

Ramsbottom Strong Ale (OG 1042, ABV 4.5%)
This complex, mid-brown beer has a warming, dry, bitter finish to follow its unusual combination of roast, bitter, fruity and sweet flavours.

Kamikaze (OG 1047, ABV 5%)
Hops and fruit dominate this full-bodied, golden strong bitter, with a dry bitterness growing in the aftertaste.

T'owd Tup (OG 1056, ABV 6%)
A rich, full-flavoured, strong stout with a coffee aroma. The dominant roast character is balanced by a warming sweetness and a raisiny, fruitcake taste that lingers on into the finish.

Derby SIBA

Masons Place Business Park, Nottingham Road, Derby, DE21 6AQ
☎ (01332) 242888 ☎ 07887 556788
🌐 derbybrewing.co.uk

A family-run microbrewery, established in 2004 in the old Masons Paintworks Varnish Shed by head brewer Trevor Harris, founder and former brewer at the Brunswick Inn, Derby (qv). The business has grown over the years and four pubs are now owned around Derby. More than 400 outlets are supplied including major retailers. In addition to the core range there are at least four new beers each month which includes the new monthly Craft Collection range of beers. ‼♦

Hop Till You Drop (OG 1039, ABV 3.9%)
A blonde brew with fruity overtones and dry finish.

Triple Hop (OG 1041, ABV 4.1%)
A classic pale ale, well-balanced with a combination of hop varieties.

Business As Usual (OG 1044, ABV 4.4%)
An easy-drinking, flavoursome copper-coloured beer, perfectly balanced, smooth and malty with a satisfying finish.

Double Mash (OG 1046, ABV 4.6%)
A balanced ruby brew, crafted using the double mash brewing process.

Penny's Porter (OG 1046, ABV 4.6%)
A rich, dark, robust brew, with a fine hop balance.

Old Friend (OG 1047, ABV 4.7%)
A classic well-rounded brew, balanced and full-bodied.

Dashingly Dark (OG 1048, ABV 4.8%)
A smooth, dark brew with complex flavours and a chocolate roasted finish.

Mercia IPA (OG 1050, ABV 5%)
An IPA with a modern twist.

Old Intentional (OG 1050, ABV 5%)
A full-bodied, malty premium beer, rich chestnut in colour and perfectly balanced with a delicate sweet aroma and a smooth finish.

Quintessential (OG 1058, ABV 5.8%)
Complex and well-rounded with fruit and citrus flavours.

Derventio SIBA

The Brew Shed, Darley Abbey Mills, Darley Abbey, Derbyshire, DE22 1DZ
☎ (01332) 380199 ☎ 07975 944242
🌐 derventiobrewery.co.uk

Derventio Brewery was established in 2005 and first brewed in 2006 at Trusley Brook Farm. In 2011 the six-barrel brewery relocated to the Grade I-listed Mill Complex, which is part of the Derwent Valley Mills World Heritage Site. The brewery tap can be hired for private parties. A popular 'Day with the Brewer' is available, by prior arrangement. The brewery is one of the founding members of the Derbyshire Brewers Collective. ‼♦

Minerva (OG 1036.8, ABV 3.8%)
An amber-coloured bitter.

Cupid (OG 1039.7, ABV 4.1%)
Golden beer made with honey. A delicate sweetness is balanced with bitterness from the hops.

Emperors Whim (OG 1040.7, ABV 4.2%)
Golden hoppy ale with a long, bitter finish.

Centurion (OG 1041.7, ABV 4.3%)
Amber-coloured bitter with a hoppy aftertaste.

King Arthur (OG 1041.7, ABV 4.3%)
Brown-coloured bitter with sweet biscuit malt flavours and a smooth, balanced hop bitterness.

Et tu Brutus (OG 1043.6, ABV 4.5%)
Dark ale demonstrating a suprising smoothness, but with a long, bitter finish.

Feast (OG 1046.5, ABV 4.8%)
IPA giving a dry and fruity aftertaste.

Cleopatra (OG 1048.4, ABV 5%)
A complex beer rounded off with First Gold hops and a hint of apricot.

Venus (OG 1048.4, ABV 5%)
A light-coloured, well-balanced, smooth premium ale with a light fragrant hop finish.

Barbarian (OG 1053.3, ABV 5.5%)
A dark beer; smooth with a lingering finish of a subtle hop character.

Derwent SIBA

Units 2a-2c, Station Road Industrial Estate, Silloth, Cumbria, CA7 4AG
☎ (01697) 331522 ⊕ derwentbrewery.co.uk

Derwent was set up in 1996 in Cockermouth and moved to Silloth in 1998. A large range of ales is produced, available throughout the north of England. ♦

Cote Light (OG 1034, ABV 3.6%)

Carlisle State Bitter (OG 1036, ABV 3.7%)
Malty, biscuity, hoppy beer with a gold colour.

W&M Mild (OG 1036, ABV 3.7%)

Parsons Pledge (OG 1039, ABV 4%)
Amber ale with a biscuity tang and a slightly fruity finish.

Reaper (OG 1042, ABV 4.3%)

Mutineer (OG 1043, ABV 4.4%)

W&M Pale Ale (OG 1042, ABV 4.4%)
A sweet, fruity, hoppy beer with a bitter finish.

Deva Craft (NEW)

Unit 14, Engineer Park, Babbage Road, Sandycroft, CH5 2QD ☎ 07841 384143 ⊕ devacraftbeer.co.uk

Deva Craft was set up in 2014 by father-and-son team Ade and Nick Gilbody. Brewing started in 2015 on a five-barrel plant. Beers are available in many outlets throughout North Wales and Cheshire. !!

Nemesis (OG 1040, ABV 4%)

Gladius (OG 1042, ABV 4.1%)

Equinox (OG 1045, ABV 4.7%)

Brewed for the Cellar Bar, Chester:

Cellarium (OG 1040, ABV 4%)

Deverell's

Unit 16, Globe Industrial Estate, Grays, Essex, RM17 6ST ☎ 07843 627791 ⊕ deverellsbrewery.com

Established in 2012 using a 2.5-barrel plant, Deverell's was the first commercial brewer in Thurrock since Charringtons acquired and closed Seabrooks Brewery more than 80 years ago. The brewery operates its own pub, the Traitors Gate, Grays. Special monthly brews are available exclusively for the pub. It also contract brews for a Chelmsford-based company selling beers under its own brand names. A move is planned to new premises, which have been obtained and are being renovated, which will increase capacity to six-barrels. ♦RAIB

Rock n Rolla (OG 1040, ABV 4%)

Redemption (ABV 4.5%)
Full-flavoured amber ale based on an American red ale, sweet with caramel, well-balanced hop profile, brewed with all American hops.

Devon

Mansfield Arms, 7 Main Street, Sauchie, Clackmannanshire, FK10 3JR
☎ (01259) 722020 ⊕ devonales.com

Established in 1992 to produce cask ales for the Mansfield Arms, Sauchie, Devon is the oldest operating brewery in the county. A second pub, the Inn at Muckhart, was purchased in 1994 and the only beers sold there are from the Devon Ales brewery. The brewery is now selling beer to the open market. !!

Original (70/-) (OG 1038, ABV 3.8%)
A full-bodied session ale with a prominent malty flavour and a distinct hoppiness.

Thick Black (OG 1042, ABV 4.2%)

Pride (OG 1046, ABV 4.8%)

Devon Earth SIBA

Buckfastleigh, Devon ☎ 07927 397871

Office: 7 Fernham Terrace, Torquay Road, Paignton, Devon, TQ3 2AQ ✉ info@devonearthbrewery.co.uk

Devon Earth was launched in 2008 on a 2.5-barrel plant located on the banks of the River Dart on the edge of Dartmoor and is run on a part-time basis. It supplies beer festivals and pubs mainly in the Torbay area. ♦

Devon Earth (OG 1042, ABV 4.2%)
A light, refreshing summer ale with a satisfying bitter finish.

Grounded (OG 1047, ABV 4.7%)
A well-rounded traditional session ale.

Lost in the Woods (OG 1052, ABV 5.2%)
A dark, full-flavoured porter with roasted malt flavours and a touch of liquorice.

Dickens (NEW)

Great Expectations, 33 London Street, Reading, RG1 4PS
☎ (0118) 9503925
✉ greatexpectations@thechapmansgroup.co.uk

A microbrewery situated in the Great Expectations pub, Reading, it went into full production in 2015. Its beers are named after Dickens' characters.

Dickensian 👁

Roden Nurseries, Roden Lane, Roden, Shropshire, TF6 6BP ☎ 07752 331633
⊕ dickensianbrewery.co.uk

Dickensian is now using a 12-barrel brewing kit in an old vehicle storage shed, its smaller kettle being unable to keep up with demand; the beers are named around Dickens' novels and characters, and are given volume numbers. ♦

Ale of Two Cities (ABV 3.8%)
Light amber-coloured session bitter, triple-hopped.

David Hopperfield (ABV 4%)
A pale ale, hoppy, dry and refreshing.

Martin Guzzlewit (ABV 4.2%)
A blonde ale with a light, crisp finish.

Nicholas Nicklebeer (ABV 4.4%)

Great Fermentations (ABV 4.6%)
A traditional cloudy Belgian wheat beer, sweet and deceptively strong.

Digfield SIBA

Lilford Lodge Farm, Barnwell, Northamptonshire, PE8 5SA
☎ (01832) 273954 ⊕ digfield-ales.co.uk

⊠ Digfield Ales started brewing in 2005 on a five-barrel plant, which was later expanded to seven barrels. Increased demand led to a move to larger premises in 2012, still in the Barnwell area. A reed bed effluent system has been installed and brewing capacity increased to 15 barrels with new equipment. More than 40 free houses are supplied. ♦

Fools Nook (OG 1037, ABV 3.8%) ◆
The floral aroma, dominated by lavender and honey, belies the hoppy bitterness that comes through in the taste of this golden ale. A fruity balance lasts.

Chiffchaff (OG 1038, ABV 3.9%)
An amber-gold pale ale with a distinct hoppy aroma.

Barnwell Bitter (OG 1039, ABV 4%) ◆
A fruity aroma introduces a beer in which sharp bitterness is balanced by dry, biscuity malt.

Shacklebush (OG 1044, ABV 4.5%) ◆
This amber brew begins with a balance of malt and hop on the nose which develops on the palate, complemented by a mounting bitterness. Good dry finish with lingering malt notes.

Mad Monk (OG 1047, ABV 4.8%) ◆
Fruity beer with bitter, earthy hops in evidence.

Dominion

Unit 2a, New House Farm, Little Laver Road, Moreton, Essex, CM5 0JE
☎ (01277) 890580 ☎ 07931 120806
⊕ dominionbrewerycompany.com

⊠ Dominion was established in 2012 by Andy Skene, renting the premises and Pitfield brand names from the founder of Pitfield, Martin Kemp. ●● RAIB

Woodbine Racer (OG 1042, ABV 4.2%)
A golden beer using only American hops.

Canada (ABV 6%)

Deep red ale with rich malt flavours, hints of caramel, with tropical fruit flavours and aroma.

Woodbine Racer Turbo (ABV 6.2%)
An ale with the aroma of oranges, malty sweet with a juicy bitterness.

Yukon Gold (OG 1090, ABV 9.7%)

Brewed under the Pitfield Brewery brand name:

Pure Gold (OG 1039, ABV 3.9%)
Golden ale, initially malty with a complex bitter finish.

Chococino Dark Beer (OG 1038, ABV 4%)

Eco Warrior (OG 1043, ABV 4.5%) ◆
Golden ale with a vivid, citrus hop aroma. The hop character is balanced with a delicate sweetness in the taste, followed by an increasingly bitter finish.

Red Ale (OG 1046, ABV 4.8%) ◆
Complex beer with a full, malty body and strong hop character.

1850 London Porter (OG 1048, ABV 5%) ◆
Big-tasting dark ale dominated by coffee and forest fruits. The finish is dry but not acrid.

N1 Wheat Beer (OG 1048, ABV 5%)
Brewed with a high percentage of malted wheat. Classic Belgian wheat beer flavours.

1837 India Pale Ale (OG 1065, ABV 7%)
A true IPA, strong in alcohol, with lots of hops. A light copper-coloured beer with floral aroma.

Sovereign IPA (OG 1066, ABV 7%)
An IPA aged in Cognac casks.

Imperial Chocolate Stout (OG 1070, ABV 7.3%)
A traditional stout with overtones of chocolate.

Doncaster

7 Young Street, Doncaster, South Yorkshire, DN1 3EL
☎ (01302) 376436 ☎ 07770 958394
⊕ doncasterbrewery.co.uk

Established in 2012 and initially based at an industrial unit in Kirk Sandall, Doncaster, the brewery moved to new premises in the centre of Doncaster in 2014 and opened a micropub tap room. ♦

Sand House (OG 1038, ABV 3.8%)

Cheswold (OG 1042, ABV 4.2%)

Gold Cup (OG 1045, ABV 4.5%)

First Aviation (OG 1050, ABV 5%)

Donnington 👁

Upper Swell, Stow-on-the-Wold, Gloucestershire, GL54 1EP
☎ (01451) 830603 ⊕ donnington-brewery.com

Thomas Arkell bought a 13th-century watermill in 1827 and began brewing on the site in 1865; the waterwheel is still in use. Thomas's descendant Claude owned and ran the brewery until his death in 2007, supplying 20 outlets direct. It has now passed to Claude's cousin, James Arkell, also of Arkells Brewery, Swindon (qv). ☛RAIB

BB (OG 1035, ABV 3.6%) ◆
A pleasant amber bitter with a slight hop aroma, good balance of malt and hops in the mouth and a bitter aftertaste.

Gold (OG 1041, ABV 4%)

A golden ale with a citrus flavour followed by a rounded malt finish.

SBA (OG 1045, ABV 4.4%) ◆
Malt dominates over bitterness in the subtle flavour of this premium bitter, which has a hint of fruit and a dry, malty finish.

Dorking SIBA

Engine Shed, Dorking West Station Yard, Station Road, Dorking, Surrey, RH4 1HF
☎ (01306) 877988 ∰ dorkingbrewery.com

⊠ Dorking started brewing in 2008 and supplies an increasing number of local pubs and clubs. New fermenters were purchased in 2013 and brewing takes place at least twice a week. ‼️🍺◆

Black (ABV 3.5%)
An aroma and taste of sweet roasted malt, coffee and lightly burnt caramel. A creamy mouthfeel, it is lightly-hopped for a smooth, dry bitter, toffee finish.

Gold (OG 1042, ABV 3.8%)
A light golden bitter full of hoppy flavour and aroma.

Smokestack Lightnin' (ABV 4%)
A robust, subtly-hopped red ale infused with smoky notes.

DB Number One (OG 1045, ABV 4.2%) ◆
Hoppy best bitter with underlying orange fruit notes. Some balancing malt sweetness in the taste leads to a dry bitter finish.

Oatmeal Stout (ABV 4.5%)
A dark stout with a smooth finish. Coffee and caramel tastes are complemented by a hint of blackcurrant.

Ceres (ABV 4.6%)
A cloudy, hazy, amber-coloured ale with a touch of banana and tropical fruit aromas.

Red India Ale (OG 1051, ABV 5%)
A strong, hoppy red beer with hints of fruit cake, a malty, caramel finish and a pleasing bitterness.

Ruby (ABV 5.2%)
A strong dark ale with a smooth, rich, toffee and caramel flavour laced with a hint of banana on the nose.

Northdowns Bel (ABV 5.5%)
A smooth, strong Belgian-style ale. Complex flavours of malt, caramel, raisins, dates and biscuit. A light bitterness with a smooth mouthfeel.

Dorset SIBA 👁

Unit 7, Hybris Business Park, Warmwell Road, Crossways, Dorset, DT2 8BF
☎ (01305) 777515 ∰ dbcales.com

⊠ Founded in 1996, Dorset Brewing Company relocated from Hope Square, Weymouth, once the old Devenish and Groves breweries site, to new purpose-built premises in 2010. In 2008 it took over the running of Dorchester's brewpub, Tom Brown's (Goldfinch Brewery). Beers are available in local pubs and selected outlets throughout the south west. ‼️◆

Dorset Knob (OG 1039, ABV 3.9%) ◆
Complex bitter ale with strong malt and fruit flavours despite its light gravity.

Tom Brown's (OG 1039, ABV 4%)

A pale bitter with a fruity nose. The taste is bittersweet with malt, fruit and some hop. Complex aftertaste.

Jurassic (OG 1040, ABV 4.2%) ◆
Clean-tasting, easy-drinking bitter. Well-balanced with lingering bitterness after moderate sweetness.

Yachtsman (OG 1048, ABV 4.7%)
A pale golden bitter-tasting beer with hints of vanilla and honey in the aroma and aftertaste.

Durdle Door (OG 1046, ABV 5%) ◆
A tawny hue and fruity aroma with a hint of pear drops and good malty undertone, joined by hops and a little roast malt in the taste. Lingering bittersweet finish.

Brewed under the Goldfinch Brewery name:

Flashman's Clout (OG 1045, ABV 4.5%)

Dorset Piddle

See Piddle

Double Top SIBA

Unit 4, Kilton Terrace, Worksop, Nottinghamshire, S80 2DQ ☎ 07973 521824

Office: Mallard, Station Approach, Carlton Road, Worksop, Nottinghamshire, S81 7AG

☺ Double Top procured a 2.5-barrel plant in 2012, with fermenting capacity for 7.5 barrels a week. This was expanded to a five-barrel plant in 2015 with a fermenting capacity of 20 barrels. It caters for its brewery tap, the Mallard on Platform 1 of Worksop railway station, and for regional beer festivals and free houses. ‼️◆

Nelson Mild (OG 1037, ABV 3.5%) 🍺
A traditional-style dark mild with a delicate blend of six malts.

Golden Arrow (OG 1038, ABV 3.9%)
A golden ale with citrus notes.

Shanghai Bitter (OG 1041, ABV 4.2%)
Light, hoppy session ale.

Adonis (OG 1042, ABV 4.3%)
A pale bitter with a dry, biscuity finish.

Treble 20 (OG 1043, ABV 4.5%)
Straw-coloured ale, hoppy and bitter.

Madhouse (OG 1055, ABV 5.2%)
A modern-style porter.

IPA (OG 1055, ABV 5.5%)
Deep golden and strong traditional IPA.

Dove Street SIBA

82 St Helens Street, Ipswich, Suffolk, IP4 2LB
☎ (01473) 211270 ☎ 07880 707077
∰ dovestreetbrewery.co.uk

⊠ Dove Street began brewing in 2011 using a 2.5-barrel plant in a garage opposite the Dove Street Inn. The pub and beer festivals are supplied. ‼️🍺

Underwood Mild (OG 1033, ABV 3.2%)
A dark, traditional, thirst-quenching mild, packed with flavour and aroma, with freshness and spice.

Bitter (OG 1038, ABV 3.7%)
A traditional bitter with a dryish finish.

**Incredible Taste Fantastic Clarity
(OG 1041, ABV 4%)**
Golden hoppy session beer; clean, clear and crisp.

Dove Elder (OG 1042, ABV 4.1%)
Traditionally brewed speciality beer. Late hopped with Brewers Gold and the wort percolated over dried elderflowers.

Thirsty Walker (OG 1047, ABV 4.6%)
Strong, well-balanced and thirst-quenching beer.

Summer Light Evening (OG 1051, ABV 5%)
Light with a bitter finish and underlying flavour of caramel.

Old Ipswich Liquor (OG 1055, ABV 5.5%)
Aged for deep complex flavours. Chocolate and liquorice notes with a long, well-rounded finish.

Dow Bridge SIBA 👁

2-3 Rugby Road, Catthorpe, Leicestershire, LE17 6DA
☎ (01788) 869121 ⊕ dowbridgebrewery.co.uk

Dow Bridge commenced brewing in 2001 and takes its name from a local bridge where Watling Street spans the River Avon. The brewery uses English whole hops and malt with no adjuncts or additives. More than 50 outlets are supplied direct.
‼ ⬛ ◆ RAIB

Bonum Mild (OG 1035, ABV 3.5%) 🍺
Complex dark brown, full-flavoured mild, with strong malt and roast flavours to the fore and continuing into the aftertaste, leading to a long, satisfying finish.

Acris (OG 1037, ABV 3.8%)
Classic full-flavoured session bitter.

Centurion (OG 1039, ABV 4%)
Copper-coloured, well-rounded best bitter. Good balance of malt and hops in the flavour.

Legion (OG 1041, ABV 4.1%)
Golden hoppy ale. A good balance of malt and fruity hop on the nose and palate.

Ratae'd (OG 1041, ABV 4.3%) 🍺
Tawny-coloured, full-bodied beer with bitter hop flavours against a grainy background, leading to a long, bitter and dry aftertaste.

Dow Bridge Dark (OG 1042, ABV 4.4%)
A strong, dark, full-bodied ale with roast malt giving hints of chocolate.

Gladiator (OG 1046, ABV 4.5%)
Ruby chestnut-coloured, well-balanced beer. Smooth and malty, but with a bitter, dry finish. Some fruit aroma and slight toffee sweetness.

Fosse Ale (OG 1046, ABV 4.8%)
Well-balanced premium beer with caramel and burnt toffee flavours leading to a hoppy, dry finish.

Praetorian Porter (OG 1048, ABV 5%)
Dark, rich, full-bodied porter. Slightly sweet with hoppy undertones.

Onslaught (OG 1049, ABV 5.2%)
A deep ruby-coloured strong ale. A good balance of fruit and hops with rich flavours and aroma.

Downlands SIBA 👁

Unit Z (2a), Mackley Industrial Estate, Small Dole, West Sussex, BN5 9XE
☎ (01273) 495596 ⊕ downlandsbrewery.com

⊠ A 10-barrel brewery set up in 2012 distributing beers across the south-east of England. Six core beers are produced in addition to an ever-changing range of specials and one-offs. ‼◆

Root Thirteen (OG 1036, ABV 3.6%)
A crisp, light golden ale with floral, zesty aromas and grapefruit and citrus flavours.

Best (OG 1041, ABV 4.1%)
A traditional, malty and fruity best bitter.

Dark (OG 1041, ABV 4.1%)
A smooth, mahogany-coloured session stout, smoky and vanilla.

Pale (OG 1040, ABV 4.1%)
Bold, rounded, fruity hop build.

Bramber (OG 1047, ABV 4.5%)
A well-hopped American-style amber ale.

Devils Dyke Porter (OG 1050, ABV 5%)
Toffee, chocolate and smoky flavours are complemented by a subtle hint of marmalade.

Downton SIBA

Unit 11, Batten Road, Downton Industrial Estate, Downton, Wiltshire, SP5 3HU
☎ (01725) 513313 ⊕ downtonbrewery.com

⊠ Downton was set up in 2003. The brewery has a 20-barrel brew length and produces around 1,500 barrels a year. Around 100 outlets are supplied direct. ⬛ RAIB

New Forest Ale (OG 1037, ABV 3.8%) 🍺
An amber-coloured bitter with subtle aromas leading to good hopping on the palate. Some fruit and predominate hoppiness in the aftertaste.

Quadhop (OG 1038, ABV 3.9%) 🍺
Pale golden session beer, initially hoppy on the palate with some fruit and a strong hoppiness in the aftertaste.

Elderquad (OG 1039, ABV 4%) 🍺
Golden yellow bitter with a floral fruity aroma leading to a good well-hopped taste with hints of elderflower. Dryish finish with good fruit and hop balance.

Honey Blonde (OG 1041, ABV 4.3%) 🍺
Straw-coloured golden ale, easy-drinking with initial bitterness giving way to slight sweetness and a lingering, balanced aftertaste.

Nelson's Delight (OG 1044, ABV 4.5%)
An amber bitter full of hoppy character and a rich resinous aroma. Underlying sweetness and strength provided by the addition of navy rum.

Dark Delight (OG 1053, ABV 5.5%) 🍺
A strong, dark brown best bitter, malt and roast in the aroma and on the palate initially, giving way to a balanced, lingering aftertaste with noticeable hoppiness.

Chocolate Orange Delight (OG 1052, ABV 5.8%)
A speciality old ale with pronounced chocolate flavours. A pleasant orange addition combines perfectly.

IPA (OG 1063, ABV 6.8%) 🍺
Golden yellow strong bitter with good balance of hops and fruit, slight sweetness and some malt notes, all through to the aftertaste.

Dragonfly SIBA

George & Dragon, 183 High Street, Acton, London, W3 9DJ
(020) 8992 3712 07788 859450
dragonflybrewery.co.uk

Brewing began in 2014 with a Chinese-built brewing kit installed in the back bar of the George & Dragon. The pub is supplied along with other outlets in the same pub group. Occasional specials are brewed.

2 O'Clock Ordinary (OG 1043, ABV 4%)
Pale brown best bitter with hops and fruit aroma and flavour, with a bitterness that is present in the finish.

Dark Matter (OG 1047, ABV 4.3%)
Stout with mocha roast aroma and flavour with berry fruits and sweet treacle. Dry, clean, roast aftertaste. Easy to drink.

Early Doors (OG 1044, ABV 4.3%)
Dark golden best bitter with grapefruit and hops building and lingering in the dry bitter finish, balanced by some malty sweetness.

Draycott (Cambridgeshire)

Low Farm, 30 Mill Road, Buckden, Cambridgeshire, PE19 5SS
(01480) 812404 07740 374710
draycottbrewery.co.uk

The brewery is located in an old farm complex and was set up by Jon and Jane Draycott in 2009. Only one-pint bottle-conditioned beers are produced. RAIB

Draycott (Derbyshire) (NEW)

73 Aston Lane, Shardlow, Derbyshire, DE72 2GX
07834 728540
draycottbrewingcompany@yahoo.co.uk

Small microbrewery established in 2014, supplying local pubs and beer festivals. Expansion is planned following relocation to new premises in 2015. It aims to brew beers using different world hop varieties. Five core beers have been developed over the past year.

Gold Nugget (ABV 3.8%)
Light-coloured, lager-style beer. Refreshing citrus taste.

Butcher's Bitter (ABV 4.2%)
Traditional bitter with caramel notes and a hint of nut.

California Steam Beer (ABV 4.2%)
American-style red beer. Dry and refreshing, with a hint of citrus.

Kentucky Common Ale (ABV 4.2%)
American-style amber bitter with big flavours, brewed with rye, maize and other grains native to Kentucky.

Miller's Beer (ABV 4.2%)
Medium dark bitter with complex flavours.

Driftwood SIBA

Driftwood Spars Hotel, Trevaunance Cove, St Agnes, Cornwall, TR5 0RT
(01872) 552591 driftwoodsparsbrewery.co.uk

Brewing since 2000 on a custom-built five-barrel plant, the brewery has since expanded to incorporate additional fermentation and conditioning capacity plus a brewery shop and visitor centre with annual production now standing at 1,300 barrels. Monthly specials are produced for selected circulation only. Besides the pub, other outlets and beer festivals are supplied. !! ♦RAIB

Bawden Rocks (OG 1037, ABV 3.8%)
Smooth copper-coloured bitter, aromatic hops and refreshing biscuit malt and bitterness with Seville orange and plum fruit. Dry, crisp finish.

Dek (OG 1038, ABV 3.8%)
Bitter, dry golden ale with light citrus aroma. Orange and lemon flavours with hop bitterness rising towards the finish, fading slowly.

Lewsey Lou's (OG 1038, ABV 3.8%)

Blue Hills Bitter (OG 1039, ABV 4%)
Medium-bodied refreshing bitter with a hoppy aroma. Flowery, grassy hops dominate the flavour to the end with gentle biscuity malt.

Booskor (OG 1043, ABV 4.2%)

Forest Blond (OG 1044, ABV 4.4%)
A golden best bitter, with a light malt flavour and a hint of caramel and blackberry hop notes.

Badlands Bitter (OG 1047, ABV 4.8%)
Red winter warmer, rich in sweet malt, figs and raisins balanced by hoppiness, finishing with fruit esters, bitterness and dryness.

Lou's Brew (OG 1049, ABV 5%)
Golden beer with strong lemon and grapefruit flavours, bitterness and dryness throughout. Long, tangy finish with hop bitterness fading.

Alfie's Revenge (OG 1060, ABV 6.5%)
Brown old ale with malt, sweet fruit aroma and flavours, balanced by spicy hop bitterness. Fruity finish with rising astringency.

Dronfield

c/o Wood Street Brewery, Hillsborough Hotel, Wood Street, Sheffield, South Yorkshire, S6 2UB 07966 143420

Dronfield began brewing in 2013 using spare capacity at Wood Street Brewery (qv). Different beers are brewed each month. Local pubs and beer festivals are supplied.

Citra (OG 1038, ABV 3.8%)

Amber (OG 1042, ABV 4.2%)

Topaz Pale (OG 1043, ABV 4.3%)

Drygate SIBA

85 Drygate, Glasgow, G4 0UT
(0141) 212 8810 drygate.com

Restaurant, bar and microbrewery, Drygate is a joint venture of Tennent's and Williams Bros, though operationally independent. The on-site brewery began production in 2014. A core range of keg and bottled beers has been launched. The brewery is also committed to cask-conditioned ale, at least one permanent cask is on at all times.

Forelsket (OG 1044, ABV 4.5%)

THE BREWERIES

DT

🍺 Royal Standard Inn, 700 Dorchester Road, Upwey, Dorset, DT3 5LA
☎ (01305) 812558 ⊕ theroyalstandardupwey.co.uk

DT Ales began brewing in 2010 to supply the pub using a one-barrel plant. No other outlets are supplied.

dt3 (ABV 3.5%)
A pale summer ale.

dt4 (ABV 4.5%)
A hoppy beer.

Dukeries SIBA

Carlton Forest Distribution Centre, Unit 6, Blyth Road, Worksop, Nottinghamshire, S81 0TP ☎ 07584 305027 ✉ phil.owen@dukeriesbrewery.co.uk

☺Founded in 2012 and located in the heart of the Dukeries in Nottinghamshire using a five-barrel plant. ◆

Blonde (OG 1038, ABV 3.8%)
Blonde ale with citrus notes and low bitterness ensuring a clean, crisp feel throughout.

Baronet (OG 1039, ABV 3.9%)
Traditional chestnut bitter with slight nutty flavour mixed with hints of fruit leading to a dry bitter finish.

Pale Ale (OG 1040, ABV 4%)
Citrus pale ale with passion fruit overtones and a hoppy finish.

A Ray of Sunshine (OG 1041, ABV 4.2%)
A fruity beer, full of character and flavour. Tropical fruits throughout with a clean, fresh feel on the palate.

De Lovetot (OG 1041, ABV 4.2%)
Golden pale ale. Well-balanced with citrus fruit aroma and mouthfeel leading to a bitter finish.

Lady Matilda (OG 1044, ABV 4.5%)
American-style pale ale brewed with three American hops. Citrus notes with medium bitterness.

Mining Stout (OG 1044, ABV 4.5%)
A dark ale full of deep, strong character. Bursting with robust rich flavours leading to a well-balanced, dry finish.

IPA (OG 1046, ABV 4.9%)
A traditional English IPA, full of complex hop character. The flavours from the malts blend perfectly to create a full, long-lasting experience.

Lord Furnival (OG 1049, ABV 5.3%)
Strong ale with lemon citrus notes and a dry finish.

Gunsmoke (OG 1050, ABV 5.5%)
Russet-brown beer with hints of chocolate and liquorice with a soft, dry finish.

Dunham Massey

100 Oldfield Lane, Dunham Massey, WA14 4PE
☎ (0161) 929 0663 ⊕ dunhammasseybrewing.co.uk

☺Opened in 2007, Dunham Massey brews traditional north-western ales using only English ingredients. The beer range is also available bottle conditioned. Around 30 outlets are supplied direct, along with the brewery tap, Costello's Bar, Altrincham. A sister brewery, Lymm (qv), opened in 2013 with Costello's Bar in Stockton Heath tied to both breweries. 🍺◆RAIB

Little Bollington Bitter (OG 1037, ABV 3.7%) ◆
Straw-coloured light ale with malt and citrus fruit taste and a dry, bitter finish.

Chocolate Cherry Mild (OG 1040, ABV 3.8%)
A multi-award winning speciality beer. It has the all dark chocolate, coffee and liquorice flavours of a dark mild blended with a dry, bittersweet cherry flavour.

Dunham Dark (OG 1040, ABV 3.8%) ◆
Dark brown beer with malty aroma. Fairly sweet, with malt, some roast, hop and fruit in the taste and finish.

Dunham Light (OG 1040, ABV 3.8%)
A creamy, malty, easy-drinking light mild.

Big Tree Bitter (OG 1041, ABV 3.9%)
A session bitter, golden in colour, full-bodied, with a good balance of hops and malt.

Obelisk (OG 1040, ABV 3.9%)
Light and hoppy, but not too bitter, with hints of citrus and grapefruit.

Dunham Milk Stout (OG 1051, ABV 4%)
A classic, full-bodied, sweet stout with a creamy, roast malt character.

Landlady (OG 1040, ABV 4%)
A light, refreshing, biscuity, dry ale, with a spicy hop finish.

Dunham Stout (OG 1046, ABV 4.2%)
A creamy, full-bodied dry stout, with a classic bitter, burnt, dark roast flavour.

Stamford Bitter (OG 1045, ABV 4.2%)
A golden, full-bodied bitter, with a complex blend of hops giving a slightly dry finish.

Deer Beer (OG 1047, ABV 4.5%)
A clean, full-bodied, malty English ale, with a hint of toffee, and a distinct hop finish.

Cheshire IPA (OG 1047, ABV 4.7%)
A fairly strong pale, hoppy and bitter IPA.

Dunham Porter (OG 1056, ABV 5.2%) 🍺
A classic old-style English porter, creamy, full bodied and packed with flavour.

East India Pale Ale (OG 1062, ABV 6%)
A stronger IPA brewed in the traditional East India style, using all English ingredients. Light and hoppy.

Dunham Gold (OG 1070, ABV 7.2%)
A Belgian-style English ale. Strong, light and fruity, with a hoppy finish.

Dunscar Bridge SIBA

Unit 13a, Dunscar Bridge Business Park, Blackburn Road, Bolton, BL7 9PQ
☎ (01204) 600713 ⊕ dunscarbridge.co.uk

☺ Dunscar Bridge began brewing in 2009 on a 4.5-barrel plant in the Brewhouse pub in Eagley. An additional 25-barrel plant was added in 2012 in the former Dunscar bleach works, a stone's throw from the Brewhouse. The brewery supplies the group's own pubs plus Wetherspoon outlets in the north-west. ‼

Dunscar Blonde (ABV 3.8%)

Dunscar Gold (ABV 4%)

Lancashire Stout (ABV 4%)

A full-bodied flavour with biscuity aromas and a dry bitter, roasted taste.

Dunscar Best Bitter (ABV 4.1%)
A smooth beer, lightly caramelised and distinctly hoppy with a slightly dry finish. A generous collection of aromas from wood and pine to soft fruits and roasted coffee.

Dunscar Amber Ale (ABV 4.5%)

Durham SIBA

Unit 6a, Bowburn North Industrial Estate, Bowburn, County Durham, DH6 5PF
☎ (0191) 377 1991 ⊕ durhambrewery.co.uk

☺ Established in 1994, Durham has a portfolio of around 40 beers, some permanent, some on rotation with new beers appearing regularly. Five litre mini-casks can be purchased in the shop or online. Bottle-conditioned beers are available and suitable for vegans. Beers are available in Newcastle and Durham pubs. ‼ ☞ RAIB

Magus (OG 1036, ABV 3.8%) ◣
Pale malt gives this brew its straw colour but the hops define its character, with a fruity aroma, a clean bitter mouthfeel, and a lingering dry, citrus-like finish.

Citra Nova (OG 1039, ABV 3.9%)
Massive hop bouquet with a lively, fresh grapefruit bitterness.

Pale Ice (OG 1039, ABV 3.9%)
A refreshing and bitter pale beer with a clean bitterness and floral aroma.

Apollo (OG 1040, ABV 4%)
Pale and aromatic, hoppy American-style IPA. Full-bodied, grapefruity and refreshing.

Black Velvet (OG 1040, ABV 4%)
Dark malts and English hops hark back to the rich coffee and roast flavours of the 18th century.

White Gold (OG 1040, ABV 4%)
Satisfying floral hop aroma and grapefruit body.

White Amarillo (OG 1041, ABV 4.1%)
Easy-drinking, clean and satisfying beer.

Columbus IPA (OG 1042, ABV 4.2%)
Full-bodied, hoppy American-style IPA. Peachy aroma with a full grapefruit body.

Evensong (OG 1050, ABV 5%)
Goldings and Fuggles hops combine with darker malts to give a traditional English character.

White Stout (OG 1072, ABV 7.2%)
A modern pale stout, full-bodied and strong. American Columbus hops are used throughout to give a massive floral and resinous character.

Earl Soham SIBA

Meadow Works, Cross Green, Debenham, Suffolk, IP14 6RP
☎ (01728) 861213 ⊕ earlsohambrewery.co.uk

☒ Earl Soham was set up behind the Victoria pub in Earl Soham in 1984 and continued there until 2001, when the brewery relocated, moving again in 2013 to Debenham. The Victoria and the Station in Framlingham both sell the beers on a regular basis, as does the Brewery Tap in Ipswich. When there is spare stock, beer is supplied to local free houses and as many beer festivals as possible. 30 outlets are supplied and two pubs are owned. ‼ ☞ ◆ RAIB

Gannet Mild (OG 1034, ABV 3.3%) ◣
A beautifully-balanced mild, sweet and fruity flavour with a lingering, coffee aftertaste.

Victoria Bitter (OG 1037, ABV 3.6%) ◣
A light, fruity, amber session beer with a clean taste and a long, lingering hoppy aftertaste.

Elizabeth Ale (OG 1040, ABV 4.2%)
A clean, bitter premium beer.

Sir Roger's Porter (OG 1042, ABV 4.2%) ◣
Roast/coffee aroma and berry fruit introduce a full-bodied porter with roast/coffee flavours. Dry roast finish.

Albert Ale (OG 1045, ABV 4.4%)
Hops dominate every aspect of this beer, but especially the finish. A fruity, astringent beer.

Brandeston Gold (OG 1045, ABV 4.5%) ◣
Popular beer brewed with local ingredients. A sharp clean flavour, malty/hoppy and heavily laden with citrus fruit. Malty finish.

East London SIBA

Unit 45, Fairways Business Centre, Lammas Road, London, E10 7QB ☎ 07900 288873
⊕ eastlondonbrewing.com

☒ The East London Brewing Company is a 10-barrel microbrewery run by a husband-and-wife team. It has been producing ales for pubs, bars, restaurants and off-licences since 2011. ◆ RAIB

Orchid (OG 1040, ABV 3.6%) ◣
Black mild with traces of vanilla in the aroma and flavour with dark roast notes and a little fruitiness.

Pale Ale (OG 1042, ABV 4%) ◣
Dark gold beer with a fruity aroma and a slightly citrus marmalade character in the flavour. Lingering bitter finish.

Foundation Bitter (OG 1044, ABV 4.2%) ◣
Hoppy brown best bitter with pronounced bitterness. It is balanced by a little fudge maltiness and a touch of blackcurrant.

Nightwatchman (OG 1046, ABV 4.5%) ◣
Sweet caramelised fruit diminishes in this brown beer's aftertaste, which is complex with a hint of treacle and some dryness.

Jamboree (OG 1048, ABV 4.8%) ◣
Golden beer with lychee and caramelised orange and some peppery hop in the flavour. The finish is bitter and slightly dry.

Quadrant Oatmeal Stout (OG 1063, ABV 5.8%)
A smooth stout with a silky mouthfeel, rich dark fruit flavour and hints of coffee.

East Stratton

See Black Bear

Eastbury (NEW)

New Finches, Baydon, Marlborough, Wiltshire, SN8 2XA ⊕ eastburybrewingcompany.co.uk

☺ A microbrewery and bottling plant established by two Berkshire-based entrepreneurs in 2014, in the heart of the Valley of the Racehorse in the Wiltshire/Berkshire/Oxfordshire borders area. Three ales and a porter are currently brewed. ‼ ☞ RAIB

Golden Valley (ABV 3.8%)
A crisp and refreshing summer ale.

Sarsen (ABV 3.9%)
Traditional British amber-coloured bitter.

Red Kite (ABV 4.2%)
A full-bodied beer with aromas of lemongrass and citrus fruits.

Old Forge (ABV 4.7%)
A deep brown porter with a malty aroma and chocolate notes. Deep sweetness with light fruitiness of malt and raisins.

Eccleshall SIBA

See Slater's

Eden SIBA

Brougham Hall, Brougham, Cumbria, CA10 2DE
☎ (01768) 210565 ☎ 07729 677692
⊕ edenbrewery.com

Set up in 2011, Eden Brewery is now run by Jason Hill, assisted by Linda and Chris. The five-barrel brewery is located in the Old Brewery at historic Brougham Hall and has the capacity to brew 45 barrels a week. ◆

Best (OG 1039, ABV 3.8%)
A well-balanced traditional ale using classic English hops. Light chestnut in colour with subtle character and flavour.

Fuggle (OG 1039, ABV 3.8%)
Initially sweet, a gently hopped pale beer with a more bitter finish.

Dynamite (OG 1040, ABV 4%)
Distinctive American-style pale ale with good flavour and aroma.

Atomic Blonde (OG 1041, ABV 4.1%)
A hoppy, thirst-quenching session ale.

Gold (OG 1042, ABV 4.2%)
Gentle fruity and honey aromas to start leading to a well-balanced sweet beer with a lasting hoppy finish.

First Emperor (OG 1046, ABV 4.6%)
Fascinatingly fruity beer with balanced malt and hops and a hint of butterscotch combining to a rich bitter finish.

Eden St Andrews SIBA

Main Street, Guardbridge, KY16 0UU ☎ 07786 060013 ⊕ edenbrewerystandrews.com

⊛ The brewery was established in 2012 using a five-barrel plant in part of the former Guardbridge paper mills. In 2014 a new 20-barrel plant and distillery was installed. ‼ ☛ RAIB

St Andrews Blonde (OG 1040, ABV 3.8%)

19th (OG 1041, ABV 3.9%)

Clock Brew (OG 1045, ABV 4.3%)

1882 Lager (OG 1048, ABV 4.5%)

Seggie Porter (OG 1053, ABV 5.5%)

Edenfield (NEW)

▤ Rostron Arms, 1 Market Place, Edenfield, Lancashire, BL0 0JZ

☎ (01706) 821756
Edenfield commenced brewing in 2014.

Old Red Dog (ABV 3.9%)
An amber-coloured bitter with a slightly dry aftertaste.

Edinbrew (NEW) SIBA

Unit 5, Knightsbridge East Industrial Estate, Livingston, West Lothian, EH54 8RA
☎ (01506) 422136 ⊕ edinbrew.beer

Edinbrew opened in 2015 within a small industrial estate in the Knightsridge area of Livingston. The brewery, operated by Ross Hamilton, who trained at the Milestone Brewery, uses a 5.5-barrel plant. Four cask ales are produced and supplied to outlets across Edinburgh. ‼

Divided City (OG 1043, ABV 3.8%)

Friendly Fire (ABV 4.3%)

85 Shilling (ABV 4.6%)

Industrial Pale Ale (OG 1054, ABV 5%)

Eight Arch (NEW) SIBA

Unit 3A, Stone Lane Industrial Estate, Wimborne Minster, Dorset, BH21 1HB
☎ (01202) 889254 ☎ 07554 445647
⊕ 8archbrewing.co.uk

Brewing commenced in 2015 on a five-barrel plant situated in a unit on a small industrial estate on the outskirts of Wimborne Minster. Local pubs and clubs are supplied. ☛

Bowstring Bitter (ABV 3.8%)

Parabolic Pale Ale (ABV 4.5%)

Elephant School

See Brentwood

Elgood's SIBA IFBB ◉

North Brink Brewery, Wisbech, Cambridgeshire, PE13 1LW
☎ (01945) 583160 ⊕ elgoods-brewery.co.uk

⊗ The North Brink brewery was established in 1795. Owned by the Elgood family since 1878, the fifth generation are now involved in running the business. Elgood's has approximately 30 tied pubs within a 50-mile radius of the brewery and a substantial free trade. Lambic style beers have been produced recently using the breweries old open cooling trays as fermenting vessels. Off sales are available all year round from the brewery office when the visitor centre is closed. ‼☛◆

Black Dog (OG 1036.8, ABV 3.6%) ▱ ✎
Black/red mild with liquorice and chocolate. Dry roasty finish.

Cambridge Bitter (OG 1037.8, ABV 3.8%) ✎
Fruit and malt on the nose with increasing hops and balancing malt on the palate. Dry finish.

Golden Newt (OG 1041.5, ABV 4.1%) ✎
Golden ale with floral hops and sulphur aroma. Floral hops and a fruity presence on a bittersweet background lead to a short, muted hoppy and fruity finish.

EP (OG 1043.8, ABV 4.3%)
A premium robust ale with a good aroma of hops and malt.

Black Eagle Imperial Stout (OG 1087, ABV 8.7%) ◆
Raisins and soft fruit complement roast malt in this warming dark ruby stout. Bittersweet conclusion.

Elixir

c/o Alechemy Brewing Ltd, Unit 2c, Young Square, Brucefield Industrial Estate, Livingston, EH54 9BX
☎ 07760 330122 ⊕ elixirbrew.com

Elixir Brew Company is an award-winning experimental brewery that produces beers using New World hops, unusual ingredients and novel techniques. Established in 2012, Elixir beers are now produced at a variety of breweries throughout the UK, including frequent collaborations with the host brewers.

Elland SIBA ◎

Units 3-5, Heathfield Industrial Estate, Heathfield Street, Elland, West Yorkshire, HX5 9AE
☎ (01422) 377677 ⊕ ellandbrewery.co.uk

☺Orginally formed in 2002 as Eastwood & Sanders by the amalgamation of the Barge & Barrel and West Yorkshire Breweries, the company was renamed Elland in 2006 to reinforce its links with the town. The brewery has a capacity of 50 barrels (200 firkins) a week. ‼◆RAIB

Ellium (ABV 3.8%) ◆
Light straw-coloured, smooth and rounded with sweet fruit aromas and dry finish.

Pale (OG 1041, ABV 4%) ◆
Creamy yellow-coloured, hoppy ale with hints of citrus fruits. Pleasantly strong bitter aftertaste.

Beyond the Pale (OG 1042, ABV 4.2%) ▯ ◆
Gold-coloured robust, creamy beer with ripe aromas of hops and fruit. Bitterness predominates in the mouth and leads to a dry, fruity and hoppy aftertaste.

Nettlethrasher (OG 1044, ABV 4.4%) ◆
Grainy amber-coloured beer. A rounded nose with some fragrant hop notes followed by a mellow nutty and fruity taste and a dry finish.

1872 Porter (OG 1065, ABV 6.5%) ▯ ◆
Creamy, full-flavoured porter. Rich liquorice flavours with a hint of chocolate from roast malt. A soft but satisfying aftertaste of bittersweet roast and malt.

Elliswood SIBA ◎

Unit 3, Southways Industrial Estate, Coventry Road, Hinckley, Leicestershire, LE10 0NJ ☎ 07717 662139

Office: 123 Wykin Road, Hinckley, Leicestershire, LE10 0NJ ⊕ theelliswoodbrewery.co.uk

Tracy Ellis and Phil Woodward began brewing in 2013 using a David Porter 5.5-barrel system with a capacity to brew twice weekly. Housed in a spacious modern unit but with a desire to produce old values.

Best of Both (OG 1040, ABV 4%)
A clean, refreshing pale ale with mild floral aroma.

Conny Quaffer (OG 1041, ABV 4.1%)

A deep golden-coloured ale with a crisp, clean biscuit taste.

Barrel of Laughs (OG 1042, ABV 4.2%)
Copper-coloured ale with a fine balance of hops, giving a spicy vanilla undertone. Slight bitterness all the way through with a sweet, pleasant aftertaste.

Just One More (OG 1042, ABV 4.2%)
A citrus beer with blackberry and grapefruit undertones.

Jolly Jack Tar (OG 1047, ABV 4.3%)
A rich, creamy milk stout using English hops giving a smooth chocolate aftertaste.

Nelson's Right Arm (OG 1044, ABV 4.5%)
A deep dark red/mahogany-coloured autumn beer with heavy hints of autumn fruits.

Legless (OG 1048, ABV 4.9%)
A full-bodied beer, gold in colour and easy on the palate with undertones of blackberry and spice.

Last Porter Call (OG 1051, ABV 5.1%)
A modern robust porter with a malty palate. A spicy, earthy aroma giving a subtle almond taste, which gives the beer depth and complexity.

Shipwrecked (OG 1054, ABV 5.4%)
Bronze-coloured beer, crisp and dry with a smooth, clean hoppy taste with a slight aroma of lemons.

Elmtree SIBA

Snetterton Brewery, Unit 10, Oakwood Industrial Estate, Harling Road, Snetterton, Norfolk, NR16 2JU
☎ (01953) 887065 ☎ 07939 549241
⊕ elmtreebeers.co.uk

Elmtree was established in 2007 using a five-barrel plant and moved in 2008 to new premises. 120 outlets are supplied direct. All beers are available in bottle-conditioned form suitable for vegans. 🍴◆RAIB

Burston's Cuckoo (OG 1038, ABV 3.8%)
A glorious nasal feast of floral hops with a tantalising hint of citrus, rounding off into a refreshingly long dry finish. Wonderful with spicy food.

Bitter (OG 1041, ABV 4.2%)
A well-balanced copper coloured crisp beer, the early malt notes give way to a distinctively complex Goldings hop finish.

Mad Maudie (OG 1044, ABV 4.5%)
A clear fresh ale perfect for the sizzling days of summer. The unusual hop combination imparts a light hint of white wine.

Norfolk's 80 Shilling Ale (OG 1044, ABV 4.5%) ◆
Roast malt and caramel provide balance to an inherent hoppy bitterness. A mix of well-balanced flavours. Finish becomes chewy

Dark Horse (OG 1050, ABV 5%) ◆
Jet black with roast dominating both aroma and taste. A fruity, prune-like background gives depth. Increasingly malty finish.

Golden Pale Ale (OG 1048, ABV 5%)
A pale ale in the traditional style that is initially malty and delicately bittered. The long dry biscuit finish is enhanced by the subtle citrus aromas.

Nightlight Mild (OG 1057, ABV 5.7%) ◆
A heavy mix of liquorice, roast and malt infuses aroma and first taste. A sweet spiciness slowly develops.

Empire SIBA

The Old Boiler House, Unit 33, Upper Mills, Slaithwaite, Huddersfield, West Yorkshire, HD7 5HA
☎ (01484) 847343 ☎ 07966 592276
⊕ empirebrewing.com

Empire Brewing was set up 2006 in a mill on the bank of the scenic Huddersfield Narrow Canal, close to the centre of Slaithwaite. In 2011 the brewery upgraded from a five-barrel to a 10-barrel plant. Beers are supplied to local free houses and through independent specialist beer agencies and wholesalers. ◆ RAIB

Golden Warrior (OG 1039.5, ABV 3.8%)
Pale bitter, quite fruity with a sherbet aftertaste, moderate bitterness.

Strikes Back (OG 1041, ABV 4%)
Pale golden bitter with a hoppy aroma and good hop and malt balance with a citrus flavour, light on the palate. Good session beer.

Valour (OG 1042.5, ABV 4.2%)

Longbow (OG 1043, ABV 4.3%)

Imperium (OG 1050, ABV 5.1%)

Emsworth

Rear of 16 West Street, Emsworth, Hampshire, PO10 7DY ☎ 07717 510294
⊕ theemsworthbrewery.co.uk

Michael and Hilary Bolt began their family-run brewery in 2012 on a 2.5-barrel plant, obtained from Oban Ales, in a shed behind an antiques shop in Emsworth. Brewing is currently suspended. ◆

Slipper (OG 1039, ABV 3.9%)

Fairfield (OG 1041, ABV 4.1%)

Wayfarer (OG 1041, ABV 4.1%)

Ennerdale SIBA

Croasdale Farm Barn, Ennerdale, Cumbria, CA23 3AT
☎ (01946) 861755 ☎ 07918 626652
⊕ ennerdalebrewery.co.uk

⊛Ennerdale began brewing in 2010. This 10-barrel brewery is situated in a converted barn in the village of Croasdale overlooking the Ennerdale Valley. All the beers are produced using the brewery's own source of spring water. Beers are distributed largely in West Cumbria but also into the Lake District more widely. ‼◆

Blonde (OG 1039, ABV 3.8%) ◣
A sweet, fruity, light-coloured beer with gentle bitterness.

Black Sail Bitter (OG 1040, ABV 3.9%) ◣
The roasted malt underpins this tawny, drying, hoppy bitter

Darkest (OG 1044, ABV 4.2%) ◣
Sweet, roasty, black mild with a fruity, hoppy flavour.

Wild Ennerdale (OG 1043, ABV 4.2%)
Golden amber in colour, with a good hop aroma and well-rounded bitterness.

Enville SIBA

Coxgreen, Hollies Lane, Enville, DY7 5LG
☎ (01384) 873728 ⊕ envilleales.com

⊠ Enville Brewery is sited on a picturesque Victorian, Grade II-listed farm complex, using natural well water, traditional steam brewing and a reed and willow effluent plant. Enville Ale is infused with honey and is from a 19th-century recipe for beekeeper's ale passed down from the former proprietor's great-great aunt. ‼🛒◆

LPA (Light Pale Ale) (OG 1039, ABV 4%)
Traditional session bitter; dry and golden with a mellow, hoppy flavour.

Nailmaker Mild (OG 1041, ABV 4%)
A well-defined hop aroma and underlying sweetness give way to a dry finish.

Simpkiss (OG 1039, ABV 4%)

Cherry Blonde (OG 1042, ABV 4.2%)
A light blonde bitter, delicately infused with essence of cherry to produce a Belgian-style fruit beer, which has a bitter finish and is dry, hoppy and refreshing.

Saaz (OG 1042, ABV 4.2%) ◣
Golden lager-style beer. Lager bite but with more taste and lasting bitterness. The malty aroma is late arriving but the bitter finish, balanced by fruit and hops, compensates.

White (OG 1041, ABV 4.2%) ◣
Yellow with a malt, hops and fruit aroma. Hoppy but sweet finish.

Ale (OG 1044, ABV 4.5%) ◣
Sweet malty aroma and taste, honey becomes apparent before bitterness finally dominates.

Old Porter (OG 1044, ABV 4.5%) 🍷 ◣
Black with a creamy head and sulphurous aroma. Sweet and fruity start with touches of spice. Good balance between sweet and bitter, but hops dominate the finish.

Ginger Beer (OG 1045, ABV 4.6%) ◣
Golden bright with gently gingered tangs. A drinkable beer with no acute flavours but a satisfying aftertaste of sweet hoppiness.

Gothic (OG 1051, ABV 5.2%) 🍷
A dark winter ale made from black malt and specialised sugars, with hints of honey adding to the rounded flavour.

Epping

See Dominion

Erddig (NEW) SIBA 👁

▤ **Unit 56, Clywedog Road, North Wrexham Industrial Estate, Wrexham, LL13 9XN**
☎ (01978) 664478 ☎ 07967 585514
⊕ erddigbrewery.co.uk

⊛Erddig began brewing in 2014 using equipment from the Llangollen Brewery.

Penny Farthing (OG 1039, ABV 3.9%)

Squires Best (OG 1042, ABV 4.2%)

Essex Street (NEW)

▤ **46 Essex Street, London, WC2R 3JF**
☎ (020) 7936 2536 ⊕ templebrewhouse.com

⊛Opened in 2014 within the Temple Brew House pub. At present there are two regular beers plus seasonal and one-off brews. The City Pub Co also operates brewpubs in Bath and in Cambridge. ‼

TemPAle (ABV 3.8%)

Gavel (ABV 4.3%)

Evan Evans SIBA

The New Brewery, 1 Rhosmaen Street, Llandeilo, Carmarthenshire, SA19 6LU
☎ (01558) 824455 🌐 evan-evans.com

Evan Evans opened in 2004. Brewing capacity is now 8,000 barrels per annum. Eight pubs are owned. It is Wales' first Soil Association organic-approved brewery. In 2009 the brewery bought Archers Brewery of Swindon's brands and now brew all of Archer's regular and seasonal ales. However, the Archer's range may soon be contracted out to be brewed at Wessex Brewery. Other seasonal beers under the Artisan, WH Buckley and Porter Street brands are also brewed, the latter brand in anticipation of setting up a new brewery on the eastern outskirts of London. ‼ ♦

BB (Best Bitter) (OG 1036, ABV 3.6%)
An easy-drinking best bitter. Malty with a clean hop palate.

Cwrw (OG 1043, ABV 4.2%)
A rich, malty flavour with a distinct fruity palate.

Warrior (OG 1046, ABV 4.6%)
A distinctive and full-bodied premium ale. Malty and fruity, dry hop finish.

Brewed under the Archers brand name:

Golden Ale (OG 1040, ABV 4%)

ASB (OG 1041, ABV 4.1%)

Empire (OG 1047, ABV 4.7%)

Everards SIBA IFBB

Castle Acres, Narborough, Leicestershire, LE19 1BY
☎ (0116) 201 4100 🌐 everards.co.uk

Established by William Everard in 1849, Everards brewery remains an independent family-owned company. Four core ales are brewed as well as a range of monthly beers. Everards owns a pub estate of more than 170 tenanted houses throughout the Midlands. ‼ ♦

Beacon Bitter (OG 1036, ABV 3.8%)
Light, refreshing, well-balanced pale amber bitter in the Burton style.

Sunchaser Blonde (OG 1038, ABV 4%)
A golden brew with a sweet, lightly hopped character. Some citrus notes to the fore in a quick finish that becomes increasingly bitter.

Tiger Best Bitter (OG 1041, ABV 4.2%)
A mid-brown, well-balanced best bitter crafted for broad appeal, benefiting from a long, bittersweet finish.

Original (OG 1050, ABV 5.2%)
Full-bodied, mid-brown strong bitter with a pleasant rich, grainy mouthfeel. Well-balanced flavours, with malt slightly to the fore, merging into a long, satisfying finish.

Evesham

17 Oat Street, Evesham, Worcestershire, WR11 4PJ
☎ (01386) 443628 ✉ eveshambrewery@aol.com

Evesham Brewery is located in the former Green Dragon pub. Beer is produced as required by demand from the brewery's own pub. Other outlets are supplied. Brewing is currently suspended.

Exe Valley SIBA

Land Farm, Silverton, Exeter, Devon, EX5 4HF
☎ (01392) 860406 🌐 exevalleybrewery.co.uk

Exe Valley was established as Barron's Brewery in 1984. The brewery is located in a converted barn overlooking the Exe Valley and Dartmoor hills. Locally sourced malt and English hops are used, along with the brewery's own spring water. Around 100 outlets are supplied within a 45-mile radius of the brewery. Beers are also available nationally via wholesalers. ♦RAIB

Bitter (OG 1036, ABV 3.7%)
Mid-brown bitter, pleasantly fruity with underlying malt through the aroma, taste and finish.

Barron's Hopsit (OG 1040, ABV 4.1%)
Straw-coloured beer with strong hop aroma, hop and fruit flavour and a bitter hop finish.

Dob's Best Bitter (OG 1040, ABV 4.1%)
Light brown bitter. Malt and fruit predominate in the aroma and taste with a dry, bitter, fruity finish.

Devon Glory (OG 1046, ABV 4.7%)
Mid-brown, fruity-tasting beer with a sweet, fruity finish.

Mr Sheppard's Crook (OG 1046, ABV 4.7%)
Smooth, full-bodied, mid-brown beer with a malty-fruit nose and a sweetish palate leading to a bitter, dry finish.

Exeter Old Bitter (OG 1046, ABV 4.8%)
Mid-brown old ale with a rich fruity taste and slightly earthy aroma and bitter finish.

It's Phil's Ale (OG 1046, ABV 4.8%)
A deep golden-coloured, hoppy beer.

Exeter SIBA

Unit 1, Cowley Bridge Road, Exeter, Devon, EX4 4NX
☎ (01392) 823013 🌐 exeterbrewery.co.uk

Exeter Brewery, formerly Topsham & Exminster, began brewing in 2003. In 2012 the brewery moved to a larger site in Exeter and is now the only brewery in the city.

Lighterman (OG 1036, ABV 3.5%)
A light copper-coloured ale with a fruity malt flavour and traditional bitter finish.

Avocet (OG 1038.5, ABV 3.9%)
An organic beer. Straw-coloured with a refreshing, slightly citrus taste and hoppy aroma.

'fraidNot (OG 1040, ABV 4%)
A golden hoppy beer with a distinct clean citrus bitterness and lasting dry finish.

Ferryman (OG 1041, ABV 4.2%)
Classic copper-coloured session ale with a well-balanced, sweet, warm malt flavour and crisp bitter finish.

County Best (OG 1045, ABV 4.6%)
Premium strength best bitter with a rich malt fruity flavour and smooth, bittersweet finish.

Darkness (OG 1050, ABV 5.1%)

Beautifully-balanced stout with complex chocolate and coffee flavours.

Exit 33

Unit 7, 107 Fitzwalter Road, Sheffield, South Yorkshire, S2 2SP
☎ (0114) 270 9991 ✉ thebrewcompany@gmail.com

Formerly known as Brew Company, brewer Pete Roberts set up this eight-barrel plant in part of a former factory in Sheffield's industrial east end in 2008. House beers are brewed for the nearby Harlequin and Riverside pubs. ♦

Simcoe (OG 1037, ABV 3.8%)
A pale session bitter wth passion fruit, apricot and pine aroma from the hops and a sharp, juicy flavour.

Blonde (OG 1039, ABV 4%)
A light-coloured, easy-drinking session beer brewed with German lager hops.

Liquid Gold (OG 1039, ABV 4%)
A deep golden orange beer with sweet malt overtones balanced by refreshing fruity and spicy hop characteristics.

Blonde Ambition (OG 1041, ABV 4.2%)
Blonde ale with a malty taste combining with a zesty character and fruity bite, a gentle bitter taste and clean, refreshing finish.

New England Best (OG 1041, ABV 4.2%)
Rich, smooth beer with a distinctive malty base, a rich flavour and dark colouring.

Hop Ripper IPA (OG 1041.7, ABV 4.3%)
A pale IPA, bitter and hoppy.

Oat Stout (OG 1042, ABV 4.3%)
Dark, full-bodied traditional stout.

Hop Monster (OG 1043.6, ABV 4.5%)
Golden ale with resinous pink grapefruit, biting citrus and soft floral characters and a long bitter finish. Very hoppy.

Yellow Rose (OG 1044, ABV 4.5%)
Golden ale with a floral and fruity character.

Kiwi Pale Ale (OG 1045, ABV 4.6%)
New Zealand-style pale ale with floral characters of pine needles, tropical fruits and citrus notes.

Frontier IPA (OG 1045.5, ABV 4.7%)
Straw-coloured, crisp and dry with a bitter aftertaste.

Crazy Horse IPA (OG 1049, ABV 5.1%)
Full-flavoured IPA with a clean, sharp, pine-like aroma complemented by a hint of citrus and tropical fruit characters.

Exmoor SIBA

Golden Hill Brewery, Old Brewery Road, Wiveliscombe, Somerset, TA4 2PW
☎ (01984) 623798 🌐 exmoorales.co.uk

Somerset's largest brewery was founded in 1980 in the old Hancock's brewery, which closed in 1959. In 2015 Exmoor moved to new and larger premises within 100 yards of the original site, thus doubling brewing capacity. Around 250 outlets in the south-west are supplied and others nationwide via wholesalers and pub chains. !! ♦

Ale (OG 1039, ABV 3.8%)
A pale to mid-brown, medium-bodied session bitter. A mixture of malt and hops in the aroma and taste lead to a hoppy, bitter aftertaste.

Fox (OG 1043, ABV 4.2%)
A mid-brown beer. The slight maltiness on the tongue is followed by a burst of hops with a lingering bittersweet aftertaste.

Gold (OG 1045, ABV 4.5%)
A yellow/golden best bitter with a good balance of malt and fruity hop on the nose and the palate. The sweetness follows through an ultimately more bitter finish.

Stag (OG 1050, ABV 5.2%)
A pale brown beer, with a malty taste and aroma, and a bitter finish.

Beast (OG 1066, ABV 6.6%)
A dark-coloured brew with the characteristics of a strong porter and a complex, long aftertaste.

Facer's

A8-9, Ashmount Enterprise Park, Aber Road, Flint, CH6 5QT ☎ 07713 566370 🌐 facers.co.uk

Facer's is the oldest existing brewery in Flintshire. Ex-Boddington head brewer Dave Facer ran the brewery single handed from its launch in 2003 until he took on his first employee in 2008 and expanded to twice the floor space. Around 100 outlets are supplied. !! ♦

Mountain Mild (OG 1035, ABV 3.3%)
A fruity dark mild, not too sweet, with underlying roast malt flavours and a full palate for its low ABV.

Clwyd Gold (OG 1034, ABV 3.5%)
Clean tasting session bitter, mid-brown in colour with a full mouthfeel. The malty flavours are accompanied by increasing hoppiness in the bitter finish.

Flintshire Bitter (OG 1035, ABV 3.7%)
Well-balanced session bitter with a full palate. Some fruitiness in aroma and taste with increasing hoppy bitterness in the dry finish.

Abbey Original (OG 1038, ABV 4%)
A sweetish golden beer with a good hop and fruit aroma, juicy taste and a dry hoppy finish.

Abbey Red (OG 1038, ABV 4%)
A darker version of Abbey Original, copper-coloured with a sweet, malty taste and a bittersweet aftertaste.

North Star Porter (OG 1042, ABV 4%)
Dark, smooth, porter-style beer with good roast notes and hints of coffee and chocolate. Some initial sweetness and caramel flavours followed by a hoppy, bitter aftertaste.

Sunny Bitter (OG 1040, ABV 4.2%)
An amber beer with a dry taste. The hop aroma continues into the taste where some faint fruit notes are also present. Lasting dry finish.

DHB (Dave's Hoppy Beer) (OG 1041, ABV 4.3%)
A dry-hopped version of Splendid Ale with some sweet flavours also coming through in the mainly hoppy, bitter taste.

This Splendid Ale (OG 1041, ABV 4.3%)
Refreshing tangy best bitter, yellow in colour with a sharp hoppy, bitter taste. Good citrus fruit undertones with hints of grapefruit throughout.

Landslide (OG 1047, ABV 4.9%)

Full-flavoured, complex premium bitter with tangy orange marmalade fruitiness in aroma and taste. Long-lasting hoppy flavours throughout.

Fakir

c/o 30 Harford Street, Norwich, NR1 3AY ☎ 07713 789085 🌐 fakirbrewery.com

⊗ Fakir began brewing in 2010 using spare capacity at several breweries based in Norfolk. Cask beer is supplied to local pubs and Indian restaurants. Further beers are planned. RAIB

Old Fakir's Gold (OG 1048, ABV 5.1%)
A golden ale with a delicate citrus grapefruit aroma without compromising the lasting bitterness needed for a dry, satisfying finish.

Fallen

Station House, Kippen, Stirlingshire, FK8 3JA ☎ 07507 862167 🌐 fallenbrewing.co.uk

Fallen began brewing in 2014 using a 10-barrel plant. ♦RAIB

Odyssey (ABV 4.1%)
An easy-drinking, lager-style beer with a fruity aroma and slightly spicy, citrus flavour.

Dragonfly (ABV 4.6%)
Sweet floral and citrus hop aromas give way to resinous, citrus and pine hop flavours balanced by rich biscuit and caramel malts.

Blackhouse (ABV 5%)
A complex, deep brown, smoky beer with a subtle fruity hop flavour.

Grapevine (ABV 5.4%)
Big tropical and citrus fruit flavours and aromas develop into a lasting bitterness.

Fallen Angel

See Broxbourne

Falstaff SIBA

24 Society Place, Normanton, Derby, DE23 6UH ☎ 07947 242710 🌐 falstaffbrewery.co.uk

⊗ Attached to the Falstaff freehouse, the brewery dates from 1999 but was refurbished and re-opened in 2003 under new management. Themed special beers are produced all year round, including exclusive specials for the Babington Arms, Derby. ♦

3 Faze (OG 1040, ABV 3.8%)
Light gold in colour with a malt and honey nose. Smooth malt flavours lead to a clean, balanced malt and hop finish.

Fist Full of Hops (OG 1044, ABV 4.5%)
Golden amber in colour, powerful hop aromas with citrus undertones. Complex mouth-filling hop flavours and a long, hop-filled aftertaste.

Phoenix (OG 1045, ABV 4.7%)
A smooth, tawny ale with fruit and hop, joined by plenty of malt in the mouth. A subtle sweetness produces a drinkable ale.

Smiling Assassin (OG 1050, ABV 5.2%)
Dark amber in colour with a fruity malt nose. Fruity malt flavours and a fruity finish with hops coming through at the end.

Faringdon

1 Park Road, Faringdon, Oxfordshire, SN7 7BP ☎ (01367) 241480 ✉ swanfaringdon@yahoo.co.uk

⊗ Faringdon opened in 2010 using a one-barrel plant; brewing on a larger-scale began in 2011. The beers are brewed by Stuart Bruton and supplied to the brewery tap, the Swan. !!♦RAIB

Folly Ale (OG 1039.5, ABV 4%)
A traditional English bitter, copper coloured, fruity and sweet with late bitterness from the Goldings and Challenger hops.

PGA (OG 1039, ABV 4%)
Mid-amber in colour with sweet undertones and a hoppy aftertaste.

Farmer's SIBA

See Maldon

Farriers Arms

The Forstal, Mersham, Kent, TN25 6NU ☎ (01233) 720444 🌐 thefarriersarms.com

Brewing commenced in 2010 in this brewpub owned by a consortium of villagers. !!♦

Farriers 1606 (OG 1038, ABV 3.7%)

Fat Cat

Fat Cat Brewery Tap, 98-100 Lawson Road, Norwich, NR3 4LF ☎ (01603) 788508 ☎ 07795 633368 🌐 fatcatbrewery.co.uk

⊗ Fat Cat Brewery was founded by the owner of the Fat Cat free house in Norwich. Brewing started in 2005 at the Fat Cat's sister pub, the Fat Cat Brewery Tap, under the supervision of former Woodforde's owner Ray Ashworth. !!♦RAIB

Bitter (OG 1038, ABV 3.8%)
Gold-coloured with a grapefruit and sulphur aroma. A mix of malt, citrus and hop with a dry, bitter ending.

Hell Cat (OG 1040, ABV 4.1%)
Clementines and hops anchor this lively but full-bodied brew. A strong bittersweet but satisfying finale.

Top Cat (OG 1047, ABV 4.7%)
A complex malt, caramel, and blackberry aroma leads into a similarly creamy beginning which continues to a richly satisfying finish.

Marmalade Cat (OG 1055, ABV 5.5%)
Rich and complex with malt and marmalade dominating every corner. Copper-coloured and grainy with a solid bitter finale.

Fat Pig SIBA

2 John Street, Exeter, Devon, EX1 1BL ☎ (01392) 437217 🌐 fatpig-exeter.co.uk

⊗ Brewing commenced in 2013 using a 2.5-barrel plant to supply the Fat Pig and its sister pub the Rusty Bike in Exeter. ♦

Pigasus Brown Ale (OG 1039, ABV 3.9%)

Pigmalion Bitter (OG 1042, ABV 4.2%)

John Street Ale (OG 1043, ABV 4.3%)

Ham 69 ESB (OG 1048, ABV 4.8%)

Phat Nancys IPA (OG 1051, ABV 4.8%)

Felinfoel SIBA

Farmers Row, Felinfoel, Llanelli, SA14 8LB
☎ (01554) 773357 ⊕ felinfoel-brewery.com

Founded in the 1830s, the company is still family-owned and is now the oldest brewery in Wales. The present buildings are Grade II*-listed and were built in the 1870s. It supplies cask ale to half its 84 houses, though some use top pressure dispense, and to approximately 350 free trade outlets. ‼ ➛ ♦

IPA (OG 1036, ABV 3.6%)

Celtic Pride (OG 1045, ABV 3.9%)
A light, golden premium ale with a bright, clean flavour and citrus overtones.

Double Dragon (OG 1042, ABV 4.2%) ◆
This pale brown beer has a malty, fruity aroma. The taste is also malt and fruit with a background hop presence throughout. A malty and fruity finish.

Stout (OG 1048, ABV 5%)
A Welsh stout created with a subtle blend of chocolate malt giving a predominantly roast barley flavour and a rich, creamy head.

Fell

Unit 27, Moor Lane Business Park, Flookburgh, Cumbria, LA11 7NG
☎ (01539) 558980 ☎ 07967 503689
⊕ fellbrewery.co.uk

⊠ Fell Brewery was founded in 2012 by homebrewer Tim Bloomer and friend Andrew Carter, brewing beers inspired by their travels in the US and Belgium.

Progressive Pale Lite (OG 1032, ABV 3.5%)
A lower alcohol, less bitter version of its big brother.

YOLO (OG 1035, ABV 3.7%)
An easy-drinking, hoppy golden ale.

AAA (OG 1041, ABV 4.4%)
An amber-coloured ale with American influences.

Patriot Wheat (OG 1043, ABV 4.5%)
A wheat beer brewed with the addition of orange peel and elderflowers to keep things fresh, floral and fruity.

Robust Porter (OG 1051, ABV 4.8%) ◆
Roast dominates throughout; fruit comes through on drinking, with a dry and bitter finish.

Smoked Porter (OG 1045, ABV 4.8%)

Progressive Pale (OG 1051, ABV 5.1%)
A light-bodied, balanced pale ale with a generous helping of hops.

Tinder Box IPA (OG 1059, ABV 6.3%)
A strongly-hopped IPA with an initial sweetness leading to a lingering bitter aftertaste.

Fellows

2 Leopold Walk, Cottenham, Cambridgeshire, CB24 8XS
☎ (01954) 250262 ⊕ fellowsbrewery.co.uk

⊠ Fellows began production in 2010 though brewer Mark Burton had been developing recipes for a year or so before. Five regular beers are

available with plans for a series of special ales. Beers are increasingly visible in the local free trade.

Cambridge Fellow (OG 1038, ABV 3.8%)
A golden session ale, light and clean-tasting.

Gulping Fellow (OG 1042, ABV 4.2%)
A dry bitter finish complements the spicy hop character of this well-balanced best bitter.

Burton Snatch (OG 1048, ABV 4.8%)
Blonde ale with a citrus aroma and refreshing palate. A hint of wet leather completes the finish.

Jolly Fellows (OG 1050, ABV 5%)
Full-bodied, clean-tasting premium bitter.

Clever Fellow (OG 1052, ABV 5.2%)
Malt loaf and toffee flavours combine with back of the tongue bitterness to achieve a balanced richness.

Felstar

Felsted Vineyards, Crix Green, Felsted, Essex, CM6 3JT
☎ (01245) 361504 ☎ 07546 096374
⊕ felstarbrewery.co.uk

⊠ Felstar Brewery opened in 2001 with a five-barrel plant based in the old bonded warehouse of the Felsted Vineyard. A small number of outlets are supplied. ‼ ➛ ♦ RAIB

Felstar (OG 1036, ABV 3.6%)
Amber-coloured session bitter with an aroma of traditional English hops and a long, bitter finish.

Summer Light (OG 1038, ABV 3.8%)

Old Essex (OG 1039, ABV 3.9%)

Crix Forest (OG 1040, ABV 4%)
A toasty dark mild with hints of berries, a hoppy nose and a bitter finish.

Lightburst (OG 1040, ABV 4%)

Witchcraft (OG 1044, ABV 4.4%)

Good Knight (OG 1050, ABV 5%)
A dark porter with gentle smoky and spicy flavours balancing the bitter hoppiness.

Hoppy Hen (OG 1050, ABV 5%)
An old ale with rich malty and spicy flavours and strong hoppy nose and bitter finish from American hops.

Pecking Order (OG 1050, ABV 5%)

Fernandes

⊟ 5 Avison Yard, Kirkgate, Wakefield, West Yorkshire, WF1 1UA
☎ (01924) 291709 ⊕ ossett-brewery.co.uk

☺ Opened in 1997 and housed in a 19th-century malthouse, Ossett Brewing Company purchased the brewery and tap in 2007 but independent brewing continues. Around 90 different beers are brewed each year. The tap sells Fernandes and Ossett beers as well as guest ales; the former are more widely available through Ossett's supply chain. ‼ ♦

Malt Shovel Mild (OG 1038, ABV 3.8%)
A dark, full-bodied, malty mild with roast malt and chocolate flavours, leading to a lingering, dry, malty finish.

Ale to the Tsar (OG 1042, ABV 4.1%)

A pale, smooth, well-balanced beer with some sweetness leading to a nutty, malty and satisfying aftertaste.

Centaur (OG 1045, ABV 4.5%)
A dry pale ale with balanced notes of orange zest, coriander and pine.

Black Voodoo (OG 1050, ABV 5.1%)
Smooth, full-bodied black stout with chocolate, orange and vanilla flavours coming through.

Double Six (OG 1062, ABV 6%)
A powerful, dark and rich strong beer with an array of malt, roast malt and chocolate flavours and a strong, lasting malty finish, with some hoppiness.

FILO SIBA

The Old Town Brewery, Torfield Cottage, 8 Old London Road, Hastings, East Sussex, TN34 3HA
☎ (01424) 420212 filobrewing.co.uk

The brewery at the First In Last Out public house was established in 1985, with the current owners taking over in 1988. In 2011 the brewery relocated two minutes' walk away, remaining in the Old Town. The First In Last Out (FILO) is still supplied direct together with pubs throughout Sussex and Kent. ‼♦

Mike's Mild (OG 1035, ABV 3.4%)

Crofters (OG 1037, ABV 3.8%)

Bourne Blonde (OG 1040, ABV 4%)

Churches Pale Ale (OG 1042, ABV 4.2%)

Old Town Tom (OG 1044, ABV 4.5%)

Cardinal (OG 1046, ABV 4.6%)

Gold (OG 1050, ABV 4.8%)

Fintry (NEW)

23 Main Street, Fintry, Stirlingshire, G63 0XA
☎ (01360) 860224 ☎ 07833 662820

Fintry Brewing was established in 2013 in premises at the Fintry Inn. After expansion in 2015, it now uses an eight-barrel plant with a capacity of 2,600 litres a week. The beers are named after local hills and streams, though distribution is far beyond the Endrick Valley. There are also plans to bottle-condition a range of beers. ‼♦

Cringate Gold (ABV 3.7%)
A refreshing, golden-coloured session ale.

Clachertyfarlie (ABV 3.9%)
Mellow pale ale; fresh, grassy, with a dry bitter finish.

Stronend (ABV 3.9%)
Dark, easy-drinking ale with blueberry notes.

Knockbuckle (ABV 4.1%)
A hoppy, amber-coloured ale with a bitter finish.

Meikle Bin (ABV 4.1%)
A dark red, malty 70 shilling-style ale with a balanced, bitter finish.

Firebird SIBA

Old Rudgwick Brickworks, Lynwick Street, Rudgwick, West Sussex, RH12 3UW
☎ (01403) 823180 firebirdbrewing.co.uk

Firebird began brewing in 2013 and has grown rapidly with new beers, new vessels, and extended warehouse and an expanded team of five people. Brewing beer styles from around the world, it now has six cask and eight bottled beers available at any one time. ‼ ♦ RAIB

Heritage XX (OG 1041, ABV 4%)
A fresh, hoppy, full-bodied best bitter.

Pacific Gem (OG 1042, ABV 4.2%)
A pale straw-coloured beer with a pronounced bitterness, oaken flavours and a blackberry aroma.

No 79 (OG 1043, ABV 4.3%)
A full and fruity pale golden ale.

Old Ale XXXX (OG 1045, ABV 4.5%)
A smooth, bittersweet dark ale with hints of roasted chocolate.

Paleface APA (OG 1053, ABV 5.2%)
A zesty, aromatic American-style pale ale.

Firebrick SIBA

Units 10 & 11, Blaydon Business Centre, Cowen Road, Blaydon, Tyne & Wear, NE21 5TW
☎ (0191) 447 6543 firebrickbrewery.com

Firebrick began brewing in 2013 on a 2.5-barrel plant from the former Bull Lane Brewery in Sunderland. Expansion in 2014 saw a new 12-barrel plant installed with the original plant being used for specials. Beers are available at selected pubs between North Yorkshire and the Scottish Borders plus nationally via wholesalers. ♦

Blaydon Brick (OG 1038, ABV 3.8%)

Coalface (OG 1040, ABV 3.9%)

Tyne 9 (OG 1040, ABV 3.9%)

Trade Star (OG 1041, ABV 4.2%)

Stella Spark (OG 1043, ABV 4.4%)

Elder Statesman (OG 1045, ABV 4.5%)

Firefly

Firefly, 54 Lowesmoor, Worcester, WR1 2SE
☎ (01905) 616996 ☎ 07525 445988
thefirefly@hotmail.co.uk

A pub microbrewery, Firefly started brewing in 2012 using a 0.5-barrel plant. ♦

Firehouse

Unit 8a, Harrison Way, Dowland Business Park, Manby, Lincolnshire, LN11 8UX ☎ 07956 405089
firehouse-brewery.co.uk

Firehouse began brewing in 2014 and uses a one-barrel plant, with plans to expand to five barrels.

Mainwaring's Mild (ABV 3.4%)

Woodman Pale Ale (ABV 4.4%)

Wobbly Weasel (ABV 4.9%)

Lincolnshire Country Bitter (ABV 5.1%)

First Chop

Unit 3, Trinity Row, Trinity Way, Salford, M3 5EN
☎ 07970 241398 firstchopbrewingarm.com

First Chop Brewing Arm was established in 2012 at the Outstanding Brewery in Bury. Production was transferred to Salford in 2013 and the brewery now uses an eight-barrel plant situated in a railway arch, which also contains a secret garden and reggae sound system.

AVA (OG 1034, ABV 3.5%)
A hoppy blonde ale.

MIA (OG 1035, ABV 3.5%)
A session ale with good malt and hop character.

DOC (OG 1038, ABV 4.1%)
A pale ale with big hoppy flavours and a pleasant, lingering bitterness.

HOP (OG 1038, ABV 4.1%)
A session pale ale with massive hop flavours.

TEA (OG 1048, ABV 5%)
A full-bodied pale ale.

SIP (OG 1052, ABV 5.4%)
A full-bodied strong pale ale with tropical fruit flavours.

SYL (OG 1064, ABV 6.4%)
A black IPA.

Fisher

Lower Farm, Noke, Oxfordshire, OX3 9TX
☎ (01865) 246611

⊗ Brewing commenced in 2012 on a five-barrel plant. Limited production of the four core beers is available at the James Street Tavern in Oxford, the Rock of Gibraltar in Enslow Bridge and beer festivals. A bottling line is planned. ♦

Vicar's Daughter (OG 1036, ABV 3.7%)
Light and hoppy session bitter.

Piper at the Gates Of Dawn (OG 1038, ABV 3.9%)
A light bitter with malty overtones.

Solicitors (OG 1042, ABV 4.2%)
Dark, full-bodied smoky bitter.

Confessor (OG 1043, ABV 4.4%)
A well-hopped, spicy golden beer.

Five Oh (NEW)

83 Agecroft Road West, Prestwich, M25 9RF ☎ 07772 243089 ✉ fiveohbrewco@sky.com

Five Oh began brewing in 2014 on a small scale focusing on bottled beers, which are based on international styles or have some unusual ingredients. Some of its range is suitable for vegans. RAIB

Five Points SIBA

3 Institute Place, Hackney Downs, London, E8 1JE
☎ (020) 8533 7746 🌐 fivepointsbrewing.co.uk

Five Points commenced brewing in 2013 on a 10-barrel plant in the heart of Hackney. Based in a railway arch under Hackney Downs Railway Station, the brewery takes its name from the five-way junction where Dalston Lane, Amhurst Road and Pembury Road meet, the Five Points. Beers are available unfiltered in bottles.

Pale (OG 1044, ABV 4.4%)
A fresh, zesty, aromatic pale ale.

Railway Porter (OG 1053, ABV 4.8%)
A classic London-style porter with a twist. Aromas of chocolate and coffee with hints of caramel.

Hook Island Red (OG 1058, ABV 6%)
A full-bodied, aromatic red rye ale with some dryness and spice and some pine and passion fruit hoppiness.

Five Towns

651 Leeds Road, Outwood, Wakefield, West Yorkshire, WF1 2LU
☎ (01924) 781887
✉ malcolmbastow@googlemail.com

Five Towns began production on a 2.5-barrel plant in 2008 and mostly supplies outlets in Yorkshire. ♦RAIB

Outwood Bound (OG 1040, ABV 4.2%)
A chestnut-coloured beer with a toffee nose and strong, dry, bitter finish.

Callum's Best (OG 1041, ABV 4.6%)
A dark-coloured bitter with a full flavour and bitter finish.

Ponte Carlo Stout (OG 1048.7, ABV 4.6%)
Bitter chocolate and malt aromas, smooth malt and chocolate with a hint of liquorice in the mouth and a dry, bittersweet finish.

Niamh's Nemesis (OG 1053, ABV 5.7%)
A full-bodied IPA with hints of grapefruit before a dry finish.

Fixed Wheel (NEW) SIBA

Unit 9, Long Lane Trading Estate, Long Lane, Blackheath, West Midlands, B62 9LD ☎ 07766 162794 🌐 fixedwheelbrewery.co.uk

⊗ Set up in 2014 by cycling and brewing enthusiasts Scott Povey and Sharon Bryant, this full mash brewery is situated on a trading estate on the Blackheath/Halesowen border. It brews twice a week using an eight-barrel plant. ♦RAIB

Chain Reaction Pale Ale (ABV 4.2%)
American-style pale ale brewed with English malt and US hops giving orange and citrus flavours.

Blackheath Stout (ABV 5%)
A full-bodied fruity stout with an oaky bitterness and a smooth, creamy, dark fruits finish.

No Brakes IPA (ABV 5.9%)
An American-style IPA with fruity, citrus flavours and a touch of sweetness.

Carbon Black IPA (ABV 6%)
Light and intensely hoppy on the palate with big tropical fruit aroma and flavours.

Flack Manor SIBA

8 Romsey Industrial Estate, Greatbridge Road, Romsey, Hampshire, SO51 0HR
☎ (01794) 518520 🌐 flackmanor.co.uk

⊗ Flack Manor commenced brewing in 2010 using a 20-barrel plant purchased from Canada. The brewery employs the 'double drop' method of fermentation. Beers are supplied to local outlets within approximately 30 miles of Romsey.
!! ♦RAIB

Flack's Double Drop (OG 1037, ABV 3.7%)
Brown session bitter. Hops and some bitterness in the taste with more hoppiness and some malt in a long finish.

Flack Catcher (OG 1045, ABV 4.4%)

Well-balanced best bitter with malty nose and citrus hints. Hoppy taste balanced with fruity sweetness and a lingering finish.

Hedge Hop (OG 1050, ABV 4.9%)
Deep, biscuity maltiness balanced with exotic fruit and spicy flavours. Brewed with five types of malt and three varieties of hops.

Flash

Moss Top Farm, Moss Top Lane, Flash, Staffordshire, SK17 0TA ✉ flashbrewery@hotmail.com

The brewery is located high in the Peak District and was founded by two friends who brew on a part-time basis. All natural ingredients are used including spring water and seaweed finings, which make the beer suitable for vegans. Due to the altitude a brick boiler was found and is used in the brewing process rather than electrical equipment. Three bottle-conditioned beers are produced and are sold at Leek market, which is the only sales outlet. RAIB

Flipside SIBA

The Brewhouse, Private Road No. 2, Colwick, Nottinghamshire, NG4 2JR
☎ (0115) 987 7500 ☎ 07958 752334
flipsidebrewery.co.uk

Andrew and Maggie Dunkin established their six-barrel brewery in an industrial unit in Colwick in 2010. With production at full capacity the brewery expanded to 12 barrels in 2013 and relocated to a larger adjacent unit. In 2012 the Flipping Good Beer Shop opened, which also operates online. In 2014 Flipside's brewery tap opened, the Volunteer in nearby Carlton. !! ♦ RAIB

Sterling Pale (OG 1039, ABV 3.9%)
A fairly hoppy session pale ale. Easy-drinking with a bitter, spicy hop flavour.

Dark Denomination (OG 1041, ABV 4%)
Well-rounded, mildly hopped beer. Chocolate and caramel malt flavours combine delicately with blackcurrant hop flavours.

Copper Penny (OG 1043, ABV 4.2%)
An easy-drinking session bitter. Light brown, moderately bitter but with good hop flavours, ending with a hint of tangerine.

Golden Sovereign (OG 1043, ABV 4.2%)
A golden session ale. Refreshingly bitter with dry biscuit flavours, American hops are added to produce a pleasant citrus and grapefruit flavour in the finish.

Franc in Stein (OG 1043, ABV 4.3%)
A quaffable ale with strong floral flavours with hints of lemon grass and Earl Grey tea.

Random Toss (OG 1044, ABV 4.4%)
A refreshing pale ale with lemon and lime tropical fruit flavours.

Kopek Stout (OG 1046, ABV 4.5%)
Rich chocolate and malt flavours. Brewed using traditional English hops.

Flipping Best (OG 1046, ABV 4.6%)
A traditional dark brown best bitter. Strong malt flavours complemented with good bitterness and gentle hop flavours.

Dusty Penny (OG 1052, ABV 5%)
A full-bodied porter. Bursting with chocolate and caramel malt flavours, rounded off with bitterness provided by traditional English Hops.

Clippings IPA (OG 1062, ABV 6.5%)
A traditional IPA, golden in colour with crushed gooseberry and bitter white wine hop flavours.

Russian Rouble (OG 1072, ABV 7.3%)
A strong dark Imperial stout with rich chocolate and malt flavours. Brewed using traditional English hops

Florence

Capital Pub Co PLC, 131-133 Dulwich Road, Herne Hill, London, SE24 0NG
☎ (020) 7326 4987 ☎ 07973 465081
florencehernehill.com

The Florence has been brewing since opening in 2007 and uses a five-barrel plant. Purchased by beer historian Peter Haydon from Greene King following the acquisition of Capital Pubs, it brews for Capital Pub Co pubs and produces 'A Head in a Hat' beers, specialising in London beer recipes, for the London free trade. In 2013 extra fermentation and maturation vessels were added. ♦

Bonobo (OG 1045, ABV 4.5%)
A well-balanced brown beer with a strong citrus hop character, some butterscotch and a dry aftertaste.

Weasel (OG 1045, ABV 4.5%)
Citrus hops dominate this light-drinking, straw-coloured beer, including in the finish, which is dry and bitter.

Beaver (OG 1048, ABV 4.8%)
Naturally cloudy beer with orange essence and wheat. Citrus notes throughout but fading in the dry, slightly bitter finish.

Brewed under the 'A Head in a Hat' brand name:

Titfer (OG 1037.3, ABV 3.5%)
Easy-drinking pale brown bitter with some peppery hop character and some fruit that fades in the dry bitter finish.

Trilby (OG 1044, ABV 4%)
Tawny brown beer based on a Barclay Perkins recipe. Lemon and biscuit flavours with a little spicy hop and dryness throughout.

Tommy (OG 1047, ABV 4.2%)
Sweet, slightly fruity nose, a smooth mouthfeel. Honeyed orange fruit and bitter hops with a little dryness balancing the beer.

Topper (OG 1047.6, ABV 4.8%)
Roasted coffee/cocoa nose and palate mixed with bitter dry roast notes lingering in the finish. Rich and complex.

Flowerpots SIBA

Brandy Mount, Cheriton, Hampshire, SO24 0QQ
☎ (01962) 771534 flowerpots-inn.co.uk

Flowerpots began production in 2006. Brewster Catherine Bate heads the brewing team. Many local outlets are supplied direct. ♦

Perridge Pale (OG 1035.5, ABV 3.6%)
Pale, easy-drinking golden ale. Honey-scented with hops, grapefruit and bitterness throughout. Crisp with some citrus notes.

Bitter (OG 1038, ABV 3.8%)

THE BREWERIES

Dry, earthy hop flavours balanced by malt. Good bitterness with some hop in aroma and sharp, bitter finish. Refreshing bitter.

Goodens Gold (OG 1046, ABV 4.8%) ◆
Complex full-bodied golden ale, bursting with hops and citrus fruit and a snatch of sweetness, leading to long dry finish.

Flying Monk SIBA

Bradfield Manor Farm, Hullavington, Wiltshire, SN14 6EU
☎ (01666) 838415 ☎ 07896 600901

Brewery founded in 2014 by four friends who used to play at Minety Rugby Club, but who have access to significant brewing expertise. Two regular ales are produced.

Elmers (OG 1040, ABV 3.8%)

Habit (OG 1045, ABV 4.2%)
A traditional English best bitter.

Fool Hardy SIBA

Hope Inn, 118 Wellington Road North, Heaton Norris, Stockport, SK4 2LL
☎ (0161) 637 6191 foolhardyales.co.uk

Martin and Samantha Wood bought the Hope Inn in 2012 and installed the brewery in the cellar. The beers first went on sale in 2013. In 2014 the brew kit was upgraded almost doubling capacity to 4.5 barrels. The brewery currently supplies the pub, beer festivals and the free trade. !! RAIB

Jack's Ripper (OG 1034, ABV 3.4%)
An oatmeal stout; smooth, complex and dark.

Rhidonkulous (OG 1037, ABV 3.7%)
A pale, triple-hopped session ale with zesty citrus notes.

Rash Dash (OG 1038, ABV 3.8%)
A rich copper-coloured beer with a light floral aroma. Initial toffee flavour immediately gives way to a bombardment of hops that linger for a long aftertaste.

Ravenous Romp (OG 1038, ABV 3.8%)
A contemporary twist on the traditional bitter – brewed with New World hops.

Rival Blond (OG 1039, ABV 4%)
A pale blonde session ale, hoppy and zesty. Distinct fruit flavours from the New Zealand hops.

Rou Shou (OG 1042.4, ABV 4.3%)
A clean-drinking, sweet, refreshing pale ale with a strong floral aroma and elderflower notes from the Cascade hops.

Risky Blond (OG 1042, ABV 4.4%)
An easy-drinking golden ale with a good balance of hops, subtle hints of citrus and a well-rounded finish.

Reckless Danger (OG 1054, ABV 5%)
A sweet-tasting beer with bitterness poking through. A clean hoppy finish and moderate aftertaste.

Russian Roulette (OG 1049, ABV 5%)
A crisp, hoppy, distinctive and bitter IPA, brewed with four different hops.

Force

Unit 2, Global Business Park, Wilkinson Road, Cirencester, Gloucestershire, GL7 1YZ ☎ 07532 097050 forcebrewery.com

Force Brewery was established in 2014 using a four-barrel gravity-fed brew plant. Carry-out ales are available direct from the brewery, which hosts regular tours and is a licensed venue for events. Further beers are planned. !!

Chasing Leather (OG 1041, ABV 4%)
An aromatic pale ale packed with grapefruit notes.

Yankee Zulu (OG 1039, ABV 4%)
A golden bitter with subtle, spicy bitterness and mellow, floral aromas.

Ephemeral Tan (OG 1046, ABV 4.5%)
A bronze-coloured ale with a touch of caramel and a spiciness on the palate.

Thunderball (OG 1051, ABV 5%)
A robust stout enriched with deep, roasty flavours met with a gentle smoothness from the aroma of the Phoenix hop.

Forge SIBA

Ford Hill Forge, Hartland, Devon, EX39 6EE
☎ (01237) 440015 ☎ 07837 487800
forgebrewery.co.uk

This multi award-winning brewery was set up near Bideford in Devon by Dave Lang, who commenced brewing in 2008 using a five-barrel plant. ◆RAIB

Discovery (OG 1039, ABV 3.8%)
A golden, hoppy ale.

Devon Maid (OG 1040, ABV 4%)

Hartland Blonde (OG 1040, ABV 4%)
A light, hoppy beer with citrus notes.

Lite House (OG 1042, ABV 4.3%)
Golden in colour with hints of elderflower and a citrus bite.

IPA (OG 1044, ABV 4.5%)
A light, hoppy beer with grapefruit and citrus notes.

Ascension (OG 1046, ABV 4.6%)
Amber-coloured beer with complex hop flavours.

Rev Hawker (OG 1046, ABV 4.6%)

Dreckly (OG 1046, ABV 4.8%)
A warm, ruby-coloured strong premium ale fortified with gorse and heather, rich in malt with a spicy aroma and a malty aftertaste.

Handsome (OG 1048, ABV 5.1%)
A light brown-coloured, well-balanced, hoppy beer.

Foundry

See Canterbury Brewers

Four Candles (NEW)

1 Sowell Street, St Peters, Kent, CT10 2AT ☎ 07947 062063 thefourcandles.co.uk

Based in the cellar of the micropub of the same name, Four Candles uses a 2.5-barrel plant and produces up to 10 nine-gallon casks with each brew. Brewing takes place at least once a week, supplying the micropub, which is named after the well-known Two Ronnies sketch.

Fourpure SIBA

22 Bermondsey Trading Estate, Rotherhithe New Road, London, SE16 3LL
☎ (020) 3744 2141 🌐 fourpure.com

Fourpure began brewing in 2013. Beers are available in cans and kegs, unfiltered, unpasteurised and unfined. Special bottle-conditioned beers are also available. RAIB

Fownes

25 Clarence Street, Upper Gornal, West Midlands, DY3 1UL ☎ 07790 766844

Office: 42 The Ridgeway, Sedgley, Dudley, DY3 3UR 🌐 fownesbrewing.co.uk

The brewery was established in 2012 by James and Tom Fownes in premises to the rear of the Jolly Crispin in Upper Gornal. It expanded to a three-barrel plant in 2014. Beers are available in the Jolly Crispin and local free houses. !! RAIB

Elephant Riders (OG 1039, ABV 3.9%)

Gunhild (OG 1041, ABV 4%)
A honey ale, made with blossom honey.

Origin (OG 1040, ABV 4%)

Crispin's Ommer (OG 1038, ABV 4.1%)

Frost Hammer (OG 1047, ABV 4.6%)
A pale ale with a bitter dryness punctuated by a strong grapefruit aroma.

Ulfsberg Cross (OG 1045, ABV 4.8%)
A traditional bitter made using only British Bramling Cross hops.

Firebeard's Old Favourite No. 5 Ruby Ale (OG 1051, ABV 5%)
A rich ruby-coloured mild ale full of malty flavour with fruity notes.

Prophets of Doom (OG 1049, ABV 5%)

Troll Hunter (OG 1051, ABV 5.3%)

King Korvak's Saga (OG 1058, ABV 5.4%)
A traditional porter with roast, chocolaty flavours.

Fox

22 Station Road, Heacham, Norfolk, PE31 7EX
☎ (01485) 570345 🌐 foxbrewery.co.uk

Based in an old cottage adjacent to the Fox & Hounds pub, Fox Brewery was established in 2002 and now supplies around 30 outlets as well as the pub. All the Branthill beers are brewed from barley grown on Branthill Farm and malted at Crisps in Great Ryburgh. A hop garden next to the brewery, trialled during 2009, has been enlarged. !! ♦ RAIB

Branthill Best (OG 1037, ABV 3.9%)

Red Knocker (OG 1037, ABV 3.9%)
Copper-coloured and malty.

LJB (OG 1040, ABV 4%)
A well-balanced malty brew with a hoppy, bitter background. Long finish with a growing sultana-like fruitiness.

Bullet (OG 1042, ABV 4.2%)
Pale golden yellow beer with resinous hop aroma and tropical fruit flavours.

Branthill Norfolk Nectar (OG 1043, ABV 4.3%)
Slightly sweet. Brewed only with Maris Otter pale malt.

Warrior (OG 1043, ABV 4.4%)

Cascade (OG 1051, ABV 5%)
A light beer with a hoppy flavour.

Nelson's Blood (OG 1049, ABV 5.1%)
A liquor of beers. Red, full-bodied. Made with Nelson's Blood rum.

IPA (OG 1051, ABV 5.2%)
Based on a 19th-century recipe. Easy-drinking for its strength.

Foxfield SIBA

Prince of Wales, Foxfield, Cumbria, LA20 6BX
☎ (01229) 716238 🌐 princeofwalesfoxfield.co.uk

Foxfield is a 4.5-barrel plant in old stables attached to the Prince of Wales. Several other outlets are supplied. Tiger Tops in Wakefield is also owned. The beer range constantly changes. Dark Mild is suitable for vegans. !! ♦

Dark Mild (OG 1040, ABV 3.7%)
Traditional dark mild, low hop bitterness is compensated for with sweetness and roast malts.

Franklins SIBA

1066 Country Brewery, Pebsham Farm Industrial Estate, Pebsham Lane, Bexhill-on-Sea, East Sussex, TN40 2RZ
☎ (01424) 731066 🌐 franklinsbrewery.co.uk

Franklins is now brewing on a 10-barrel kit in a converted milking barn in the Sussex countryside. Steve Medniuk is sole owner. Beers are supplied throughout the south east, London and beyond. There are plans for expansion to a 15-barrel kit, and bottle-conditioned beers will soon be available. !!

English Garden (OG 1042, ABV 3.8%)
A hoppy, golden session ale.

Mumma Knows Best (OG 1043, ABV 4.1%)
A refreshing traditional English best bitter rich in mango, lemon and earthy pine flavours.

Citra IPA (OG 1056, ABV 5.5%)
Single-hopped IPA for serious beer lovers, bursting in citrus and lychee flavours and aroma.

Smoked Porter (OG 1052, ABV 5.5%)
A rich, intense, satisfying porter made with oatmeal. Added chipotle chillies accentuate the smokiness and provide a touch of heat.

Freedom SIBA

1 Park Lodge House, Bagots Park, Abbots Bromley, Staffordshire, WS15 3ES
☎ (01283) 840721 🌐 freedomlager.com

No real ale. Freedom specialises in producing hand-crafted English lagers, all brewed in accordance with the German Reinheitsgebot purity law. Six beers are currently produced. !!

Freeminer SIBA

Whimsey Road, Steam Mills, Cinderford, Gloucestershire, GL14 3JA
☎ (01594) 827989 🌐 freeminerbrewery.co.uk

Founded by Don Burgess in 1992, Freeminer – previously Freeminer Brewery – changed hands in 2006 but Don Burgess remained in post. Bottle-conditioned beers are available (brewed for the Co-op). Co-op beers are now brewed with barley grown on Co-op farms and malted at Warminster. Fairtrade and organic beers are also produced, with limited edition cask versions available for Fairtrade fortnight. ◆ RAIB

Freeminer (OG 1038, ABV 4%) ◆
A light, hoppy session bitter with an intense hop aroma and a dry, hoppy finish.

Slaughter Porter (OG 1047, ABV 4.8%)
Dark, but not a stout; well-defined aroma of Fuggles hops and hints of the lighter side of this complex hop.

Speculation (OG 1047, ABV 4.8%) ◆
An aromatic, chestnut-brown, full-bodied beer with a smooth, well-balanced mix of malt and hops, and a predominately hoppy aftertaste.

Freewheelin' (NEW)

Shed 3, South Park, Peebles, EH45 9ED ☎ 07802 175826 ⊕ freewheelinbrewery.co.uk

Freewheelin' began brewing in 2013. ◆

Blonde on Blonde (ABV 3.8%)
A modern IPA with citrus notes, sharp hoppy flavours and character.

Ruby Tuesday (ABV 4.3%)
A dark, refreshing beer.

Crossroads IPA (ABV 4.4%)
A traditional, well-rounded IPA.

Crossroads XXX IPA (ABV 5.2%)
A stronger version of Crossroads IPA.

Frensham SIBA

The Old Dairy, Pierrepont Home Farm, The Reeds, Frensham, Surrey, GU10 3BS
☎ (01252) 793956 ☎ 07825 220698
⊕ frenshambrewery.co.uk

Set in the Surrey countryside, Frensham is a microbrewery situated in a 17th-century restored barn on a working dairy farm. Regular open days are held. The brewery is fully licensed. ◆

Soul of the Shoes (ABV 3.8%)
A light, floral session beer with biscuit orange notes.

Rambler (ABV 3.9%)
A golden-coloured, refreshing session ale with well-rounded floral and hop aromas. Fruity hops with an oak edge give rise to a satisfying bitterness.

Forager (ABV 4.5%)
Rich copper-coloured ale. A complex floral aroma with subtle oak/vanilla notes, offset with a caramel/spicy hop balance. Lingering bitter finish.

Friends Arms

≣ Old St Clears Road, Johnstown, SA31 3HH
☎ (01267) 234073 ⊕ thefriendsarms.co.uk

⊠ Friends Arms Brewery opened in 2011 on the premises of the Friends Arms, a traditional local community pub, which acts as the brewery tap.

Friday Beer

Unit 4, Link Business Centre, Malvern, Worcestershire, WR14 1UQ
☎ (01684) 572648 ⊕ thefridaybeer.com

Founded in 2011, the Friday Beer Co primarily produces bottle-conditioned ales, selling across the Three Counties. Available cask-conditioned in a small number of local pubs. !! ☛ RAIB

Jubilee (OG 1034, ABV 3.1%)
A medium dark session ale good on its own or with food.

Friday Light (OG 1037, ABV 4.2%)
A straw-coloured ale, with generous malt flavours from rye.

Pinnacle (OG 1046, ABV 4.5%)
The recipe combines a variety of hops with grain to produce ale with a touch of rye.

Black Hill Stout (OG 1052, ABV 4.7%)
This smooth, sweet version of the old classic is full of complex malty flavours.

Friday Gold (OG 1054, ABV 5.6%)
This refreshing golden ale is made with a combination of English and American hops which helps to create a smooth beer with a slight taste of citrus.

Frodsham SIBA

Lady Heyes Craft Centre, Kingsley Road, Frodsham, Cheshire, WA6 6SU
☎ (01928) 787917 ☎ 07776 391196
⊕ frodshambrewery.co.uk

☺ Frodsham has been brewing since 2005 (initially as Stationhouse Brewery in Ellesmere Port). Bottle-conditioned beers are suitable for vegans. A labelling service is provided for bottles to enable them to be personalised for commemorative occasions or as gifts. !! ☛ ◆ RAIB

Flaxen Jade (OG 1037, ABV 3.7%)
Blonde ale with citrus notes and a black pepper kick.

Devil's Garden (OG 1037, ABV 3.9%)
An amber-coloured beer with traditional biscuit flavour and raisin aftertaste.

Splash! (OG 1038, ABV 3.9%)
A blonde, refreshing, summer beer. Crisp and citrus with hoppy flavours.

Danny (OG 1038, ABV 4%)
Golden-coloured, floral, hoppy ale specially brewed to help restore the Daniel Adamson steamer.

Dark Ark Ale (OG 1039.6, ABV 4%)
A dark malty beer with rich raisin and fruit flavours.

Gold (OG 1037.9, ABV 4.1%)
Gold-coloured ale, rich hoppy flavours with a spicy tang.

Porter (ABV 4.1%)
A traditional porter with coffee and toffee.

Froda's Ale (OG 1040, ABV 4.2%)
A traditional tawny bitter, with hoppy and slight liquorice taste.

Buzzin' (OG 1042, ABV 4.3%) ◆
Golden fruity bitter dominated by a honey sweetness. Good hop flavours in initial taste and a long, lasting dry finish.

Iron Man (OG 1043, ABV 4.5%)

Chestnut brown ale, nutty with a full hop flavour.

800 Ale (OG 1045.5, ABV 4.7%)
A golden-coloured bitter beer. Floral with late wine flavours.

Aonach (OG 1049, ABV 4.9%)
A typical Scottish-style 80/- beer. Dark amber in colour, late hopped with New Zealand varieties.

Lammastide (OG 1052, ABV 5%)
An English wheat beer with distinct elderflower aromas.

Frog Island SIBA

The Maltings, Westbridge, St James Road, Northampton, NN5 5HS
☎ (01604) 587772 ⊕ frogislandbrewery.co.uk

Established in 1994, Frog Island specialises in beers with personalised bottle labels, available by mail order. The brewery changed hands in 2013 and is now run by husband-and-wife team Paul Burchell and Zoe Cushnie plus Philip Burchell. Around 40 free trade outlets are supplied as well as some Everards pubs. ‼◆RAIB

Best Bitter (OG 1038, ABV 3.8%) ◄
Blackcurrant and gooseberry enhance the full malty aroma with pineapple and papaya joining on the tongue. Bitterness develops in the fairly long hop finish.

Lock Stock & Barrel (OG 1040, ABV 4%)
A rounded bittersweet malt taste is complemented by a refreshing bitter finish.

Shoemaker (OG 1043, ABV 4.2%) ◄
An orangy aroma of fruity hops is balanced by malt. Citrus and hoppy bitterness last into a long, dry finish. Amber in colour.

That Old Chestnut (OG 1044, ABV 4.4%)
A smooth, easy-drinking beer with subtle roasted notes. Cascade hops bring a sweet, spiciness to the beer while Target hops contribute bitterness to the dry, malty finish.

Natterjack (OG 1048, ABV 4.8%) ◄
Deceptively robust, golden and smooth. Fruit and hop aromas fight for dominance before the grainy astringency and floral palate give way to a long, dry aftertaste.

Fire-Bellied Toad (OG 1048, ABV 5%) ◄
Amber-gold brew with an extraordinary long bitter/fruity finish. Huge malt and Phoenix hop flavours have a hint of apples.

Croak & Stagger (OG 1054, ABV 5.6%) ◄
The initial honey/fruit aroma is quickly overpowered by roast malt then bitter chocolate and pale malt sweetness on the tongue. Gentle, bittersweet finish.

Front Row SIBA

Unit 1, Hopkins Close, Greenfield Farm Industrial Estate, Congleton, Cheshire, CW12 4TR
☎ (01260) 289055 ☎ 07861 718673
⊕ frontrowbrewing.co.uk

After starting operations on a 2.5-barrel plant in 2012, Front Row expanded to an eight-barrel plant in 2014 to meet demand. ‼◆

Crouch (OG 1039, ABV 3.8%)

Touch (OG 1038, ABV 4%)

Pause (OG 1049, ABV 4.5%)

Engage (OG 1047, ABV 4.8%)

Collapsed (OG 1052, ABV 5.6%)

Frontier (NEW)

Flower Pot, 23-25 King Street, Derby, DE1 3DZ
☎ 0333 003 5008

Office: 3 Saddlers Gate, Radcliff-on-Trent, Nottingham, NG12 2NU ⊕ frontierbrewing.co.uk

Brewing began in 2014 after taking over the brewing plant at the Flower Pot pub in Derby. Frontier is a separate business to the pub but its beers are usually available there. ◆

Gold Rush (OG 1037, ABV 4%)
A golden ale, single hopped with Cascade.

Pioneer (OG 1040, ABV 4.3%)
A golden, crisp, hoppy pale ale with a dry finish.

Ramification (OG 1042, ABV 4.5%)
A traditional bitter. Official beer of the Derby County FC Supporters' Club.

Atlas Stout (OG 1046, ABV 5%)
A full-bodied, rich, dry stout. Coffee and chocolate notes give way to a dry finish.

Froth Blowers SIBA

Unit W34, Hastingwood Industrial Park, Wood Lane, Erdington, West Midlands, B24 9QR ☎ 07908 056009 ⊕ frothblowers.co.uk

Froth Blowers began brewing in 2013 using a six-barrel plant. Five core beers are brewed, predominantly blonde. ◆

Piffle Snonker (ABV 3.8%)
A light blonde beer with a floral nose and sweet start but a bitter finish.

Bar-King Mad (ABV 4.2%)
A light blonde single-hop Citra beer.

Wellingtonian (ABV 4.3%)
A pale ale made with two New Zealand hop varieties.

Gollop With Zest (ABV 4.5%)
A blonde beer with a floral start and a citrus finish.

Hornswoggle (ABV 5%)
A full-bodied blonde beer with a floral nose and sweetish start, soon replaced by a dry and satisfying bitterness.

Fugelestou

See Fulstow

Fuggle Bunny (NEW) SIBA ◉

Unit 1, Meadowbrook Park Industrial Estate, Station Road, Holbrook, South Yorkshire, S20 3PJ
☎ (0114) 248 4541 ☎ 07813 763347
⊕ fugglebunnybrewhouse.co.uk

This husband-and-wife team commenced brewing in 2014. The brewery name arose from a combination of an English hop (Fuggle) and the image of a rabbit (synonymous with rebirth and resurrection). ‼

Chapter 5 Oh Crumbs (OG 1038, ABV 3.8%)

Amber-coloured with hints of spice, cedar and pine. Sweet caramel and biscuity flavours give a distinctive finish.

Chapter 2 Cotton Tail (OG 1040, ABV 4%)
Fruity aromas of lychees and citrus with a dry, hoppy finish due to the five varieties of hops.

Chapter 6 Hazy Summer Daze (OG 1042, ABV 4.2%)
Tropical flavours with mango, lime, apricot, melon, lychees and grapefruit with fresh floral aromas.

Chapter 1 New Beginnings (OG 1049, ABV 4.9%)
Amber-coloured classic bitter with a sweet edge of honey and spice leading to a dry, hoppy aftertaste.

Chapter 3 Orchard Gold (OG 1050, ABV 5%)
Golden ale with hints of spice and honey and an earthy undertone.

Chapter 7 Russian Rare-Bit (OG 1050, ABV 5%)
Dark, malty and complex ale with an intriguing twist of chocolate, coffee and liquorice aromas. British hops lend bittering qualities.

Chapter 4 24 Carrot (OG 1060, ABV 6%)
Smooth aromas of citrus and blackberry with a spicy, malt-flavoured hoppiness.

Fulflood Arms

28 Cheriton Road, Winchester, Hampshire, SO22 5EF
☎ (01962) 842996
✉ thefulfloodarms@hotmail.co.uk

Established in 2012 in a Greene King pub using a one-barrel plant, the brewery now uses a 1.5-barrel plant. It brews only occasionally (since 2015), as and when time permits. The beer is supplied to the Fulflood Arms pub or its sister pub, the Queen Inn (also brewing occasionally).

Full Mash SIBA

17 Lower Park Street, Stapleford, Nottinghamshire, NG9 8EW
☎ (0115) 949 9262 fullmash.net

Brewing commenced in 2003, and since then the brewery has grown steadily, with a gradual expansion in outlets and capacity. ♦

Horse & Jockey (OG 1039, ABV 3.8%)

Séance (OG 1041, ABV 4%)
Predominantly hoppy golden beer, with a refreshing bitter finish.

Illuminati (OG 1043, ABV 4.2%)
Well-balanced pale ale with a full-bodied hop flavour and a refreshing zesty finish.

Wheat Ear (OG 1043, ABV 4.2%)
Pale, clear wheat beer, fruity and aromatic.

Warlord (OG 1045, ABV 4.4%)
Amber-coloured beer with an initial malt taste leading to a dry bitter finish.

Apparition (OG 1046, ABV 4.5%)
A pale hoppy bitter brewed with Brewers Gold hops.

Nevermore (OG 1047, ABV 4.6%)
Well-rounded stout with soft roast chocolate flavours.

Manhaton Pale?? (OG 1053, ABV 5.2%)
Refreshing, pale, American-style IPA with a complex citrus aroma and big hop finish.

Bhisti (OG 1063, ABV 6.2%)
Strong IPA with a warning kick of bitterness.

Fuller's SIBA

Griffin Brewery, Chiswick Lane South, London, W4 2QB
☎ (020) 8996 2000 fullers.co.uk

Fuller, Smith and Turner's Griffin Brewery has stood on the same site in Chiswick for more than 350 years. The partnership from which the company now takes its name was formed in 1845 and members of the founding families are still involved in running the company today. Three different Fuller's beers have won the Champion Beer of Britain title, Chiswick Bitter, London Pride and ESB. At the end of 2005 Fuller's announced an agreed acquisition of Hampshire brewer George Gale. The company now operates 362 pubs and hotels. Fuller's stopped brewing at the Gale's Horndean site in 2006 and all the brands, including some seasonals, are now brewed at Chiswick.
!! ♦ RAIB

Chiswick Bitter (OG 1034.5, ABV 3.5%)
Refreshing pale brown bitter with some citrus notes on the palate fading in the aftertaste, which is hoppy and slightly dry. Aroma is of hops with a trace of biscuit.

Oliver's Island (OG 1039, ABV 3.8%)
A smooth and refreshing golden ale with delicate floral and citrus aromas, biscuity, grapefruit flavours, tropical notes and a crisp, malty finish.

London Pride (OG 1040.5, ABV 4.1%)
Well-balanced, smooth best bitter with orange citrus fruit, malt and hops in aroma and flavour, which linger into a slightly bitter aftertaste. Honey and toffee develop as the beer matures.

Bengal Lancer (OG 1049.5, ABV 5%)
Rich, creamy and well-balanced pale brown IPA with a gold hue. Hops with a dryish bitterness harmonise with the fruit and malty sweetness that linger into the aftertaste.

London Porter (OG 1056.8, ABV 5.4%)
The dark roast malt gives bitter and slightly dry characteristics to this smooth black porter, which has caramelised fruit notes that are more pronounced in the flavour and finish.

ESB (OG 1054, ABV 5.5%)
Bitter orange marmalade with hops, creamy toffee and some raisins are all present in this multifaceted strong brown bitter. A satisfying long, bitter, dry finish balanced by a malty sweetness.

Brewed under the Gale's brand name:

Seafarers Ale (OG 1036.8, ABV 3.6%)
A pale brown bitter, predominantly malty, with a refreshing balance of fruit and hops that lingers into the aftertaste where a dry bitterness unfolds.

HSB (OG 1050, ABV 4.8%)
Dates and dried fruit with some spicy hops in the nose adding to the caramelised orange and treacle in the flavour of this smooth brown beer. Malty throughout with a bittersweet finish.

Fulstow

13 Thames Street, Louth, Lincolnshire, LN11 7AD
☎ (01507) 608202 fulstowbrewery.com

Fulstow operates on a 2.5-barrel plant and started brewing in Fulstow in 2004, before moving to Louth in 2006. 'Fugelestou Ales' are one-off beers produced along with the regular range, all only available at the brewery tap, the Gas Lamp Lounge in Louth. ‼ ⬛ RAIB

Fulstow Common (OG 1038, ABV 3.8%)
A copper-coloured, medium-bodied beer with a strong hop character and malt discernible in the taste.

Marsh Mild (OG 1039, ABV 3.8%)
Traditional mild with a malty aroma. Chocolate malt on the palate with toffee and caramel overtones.

Northway IPA (OG 1042, ABV 4.2%)
A clean, crisp ale with a citrus aroma; hoppy with a dry finish.

Pride of Fulstow (OG 1045, ABV 4.5%)
Copper-coloured bitter with a ripe malt taste in the mouth and a good hop balance. A dry finish with blackcurrant fruit notes.

Sledgehammer Stout (OG 1077, ABV 8%)
A strong, dark stout with raisin and liquorice and roast barley notes balanced by a strong hop flavour

Funfair SIBA

⬛ Chequers Inn, Toad Lane, Elston, Nottinghamshire, NG23 5NS
☎ (01636) 525257 ☎ 07971 540186
⬜ funfairbrewingcompany.co.uk

Funfair was launched in 2004 in Holbrook, relocated to Ilkeston, Derbyshire and then relocated again in 2012 to the Chequers Inn in Elston, where a new 10-barrel plant is used. The Chequers also serves as the brewery tap. More than 40 outlets are supplied. ‼ ◆ RAIB

Gallopers (OG 1037, ABV 3.8%)
Well-hopped, pale session bitter.

Teacups (OG 1040, ABV 4%)
A traditional ginger beer.

Waltzer (OG 1044, ABV 4.5%)
Copper-coloured, easy-drinking bitter.

Brandy Snap (OG 1046, ABV 4.7%)
Golden ale containing root ginger.

Dive Bomber (OG 1047, ABV 4.7%)
Refreshing straw-coloured premium ale.

Dodgem (OG 1047, ABV 4.7%)
Golden premium pale ale with a unique blend of hops.

Fuzzy Duck SIBA

18 Wood Street, Poulton Industrial Estate, Poulton-le-Fylde, Lancashire, FY6 8JY ☎ 07904 343729
⬜ fuzzyduckbrewery.co.uk

Fuzzy Duck was established in 2006 as a commercial home-based brewery. It relocated to Poulton-le-Fylde later that year, expanding capacity to an eight-barrel plant. The brewery delivers over a wide area of the north west. ‼ ◆

Golden Cascade (OG 1038, ABV 3.8%)
Golden-coloured ale brewed with Cascade hops for a citrus flavour and a floral aroma.

Mucky Duck (OG 1042, ABV 4%)

Dark stout, slightly sweet with chocolate and coffee notes from the roasted malt.

Pheasant Plucker (OG 1042, ABV 4.2%)
Amber beer with a slightly spicy taste and a citrus finish.

Cunning Stunt (OG 1044, ABV 4.3%)
Amber-coloured beer with a blackcurrant and herbal aroma.

Ruby Duck (OG 1053, ABV 5.3%)
Dark ruby-coloured beer with a rich full body and complex fruit flavours.

Fyne SIBA

Achadunan, Cairndow, PA26 8BJ
☎ (01499) 600120 ⬜ fyneales.com

☺ Fyne Ales has been brewing since 2001 and is situated at the head of Loch Fyne. In 2012 an on-site brewery tap was added. Expansion has allowed for the production of experimental brews. FyneFest runs annually, celebrating local fare and showcasing other breweries. ‼ ⬛ ◆ RAIB

Jarl (OG 1038, ABV 3.8%) ⬜
A light, golden ale with strong citrus notes.

Piper's Gold (OG 1037.5, ABV 3.8%) ◆
Fresh, golden session ale. Well bittered but balanced with fruit and malt. Long, dry, bitter finish.

Maverick (OG 1040.5, ABV 4.2%) ◆
Full-bodied, roasty, tawny best bitter. Well-balanced, fruity and well-hopped.

Hurricane Jack (OG 1042.5, ABV 4.4%)
Smooth golden ale with deep citrus flavours that mellow to a lingering citrus bitter finish.

Vital Spark (OG 1042.5, ABV 4.4%)
A rich, dark beer. The taste is clean and slightly sharp with a hint of blackcurrant.

Avalanche (OG 1043.5, ABV 4.5%) ◆
This true golden ale starts with citrus hops on the nose. Well-balanced with good body and fruit balancing a refreshing hoppy taste, it finishes with a long bittersweet aftertaste.

Highlander (OG 1046, ABV 4.8%) ◆
Full-bodied, bittersweet ale with a good dry hop finish. In the style of a Heavy although the malt is less pronounced and the sweetness ebbs away to leave a bitter, hoppy finish.

Sublime Stout (OG 1067, ABV 6.8%)
A stout with a hint of liquorice on the aftertaste.

Superior IPA (OG 1070, ABV 7.1%)
With aromas of apricot and pine resin this IPA has a dusty, hoppy bitterness with a dry, fruity and hoppy aftertaste and a medium to full body with an oily mouthfeel.

G2 SIBA ☺

Unit 5, Ashford Works, Brunswick Road, Cobbs Wood, Ashford, Kent, TN23 1EH ☎ 07772 080777
⬜ g2brewing.com

Formerly known as Spencer's, the brewery was set up in 2012 by Brian Spencer, a retired space rocket fuel engineer. The brewery came under new ownership in 2014 when its name was changed to G2 Brewing. The brewery was upgraded and commercial production recommenced in 2015.

Vela Blonde (OG 1042, ABV 4.2%)

Octava IPA (OG 1044, ABV 4.4%)

Gadds'

See Ramsgate

Gale's

See Fuller's

Gambling Man

61 Low Willington, Willington, County Durham, DL15 9AB ☎ 07977 154675
✉ brewery@gamblingmanbrewco.com

Gambling Man was established in 2011 by avid home brewers Paul Armstrong and Dave Walls. The brewery name was thought up by the brewers during a game of five card draw and all the regular ales have gambling/casino-related names. ♦

Croupier (ABV 3.4%)

Pit Boss (ABV 4.4%)

Jack of Clubs (ABV 4.7%)

Gargoyles

See Isca

Gas Dog

Noel's Arms, 31 Burton Street, Melton Mowbray, Leicestershire, LE13 1AE ☎ 07921 260063

9 Westview, Somerby, Leicestershire, LE14 2QH
gasdogbrewery.co.uk

Gas Dog began brewing in 2013 at the same premises as Parish Brewery, but using a separate 0.5-barrel plant. In 2014 it relocated to an outbuilding at the rear of the Noel's Arms in Melton Mowbray and a bottling plant was added. Three regular beers are produced along with special brews under the title 'Leicester Legends'. ♦

Ginger Whinger (OG 1050, ABV 3.8%)
Pale, golden ale infused with honey and ginger.

Hello Dolly (OG 1040, ABV 3.8%)
Old-fashioned amber-coloured session bitter.

Bitter (OG 1040, ABV 4%)
Hoppy, golden ale.

Gates Burton

Reservoir Road, Burton upon Trent, Staffordshire, DE14 2BP
☎ (01283) 532567
✉ gatesburtonbrewery@talktalk.net

The Gates Burton Brewery was established in 2011 using a one-barrel plant. Additional beers are planned. ‼

Reservoir (OG 1046, ABV 4.6%)
Full-bodied, amber-coloured ale with a finely balanced malt and hop character giving a smooth finish. Hops arrive late on the palate.

Damn (OG 1050, ABV 5%)
Smooth-drinking ruby ale with chocolate malt tones and delicately hopped with a subtle sweet finish.

Geeves SIBA

Unit 12 Grange Lane Industrial Estate, Carrwood Road, Stairfoot, Barnsley, South Yorkshire, S71 5AS
☎ 07859 039259 geevesbrewery.co.uk

Geeves began brewing in 2011 using a 5.5-barrel plant with recipes developed when the owners lived on a narrow boat. Its original branding was themed around the waterways to reflect this unusual heritage, but 2015 has seen a rebranding of both its regular and seasonal beers. ‼ ♦RAIB

No. 1 (OG 1038, ABV 3.8%)
Traditional bitter, with a well-rounded malty base and a hoppy finish.

Renaissance (OG 1040, ABV 4.1%)

Aurelian (OG 1043, ABV 4.2%)
A pale ale with a dry, citrus bitterness and a zingy aftertaste and aroma.

Captain Gingerbread (OG 1043, ABV 4.3%)
A naturally hazy wheat beer infused with ginger. Spicy, refreshing and with a hint of citrus.

Clear Cut (OG 1044, ABV 4.4%)
An extra pale ale with a citrus kick.

Smokey Joe Stout (OG 1050, ABV 5%)
A strong stout, rich and robust.

Fully Laden (OG 1060, ABV 6%)
An strong IPA with a juicy, citrus, sweet floral taste and aroma with a satisfying bitterness.

Geipel SIBA

Pantglas Llangwm, Corwen, LL21 0RN
☎ (01490) 420838 ☎ 07549 526287 geipel.co.uk

Geipel commenced brewing in 2013 producing classic German-style, unpasteurised and unfiltered beers in keg and bottle form only, mainly supplying bars and off-licences in North Wales and Greater Manchester.

George N Porter

See under Porter

George Samuel

Spennymoor, Co Durham
☎ (01609) 882464
georgesamuelbrewingcompany.co.uk

A small, two-barrel brewery originally set up at the Duke of Wellington pub in the small village of Welbury near Northallerton, and named after the brewer's two sons. It has now moved to a private address in Spennymoor.

By George She's Got It (OG 1036, ABV 3.6%)
Blonde session ale brewed with three hops, giving it a good hoppy punch.

Brew It Again Sam (OG 1042, ABV 4.2%)

Golden Wellingtons (OG 1050, ABV 5%)
Golden premium ale combining three malts and two hops to give a bittersweet character.

George Wright SIBA

See under Wright

George's SIBA

Common Road, Great Wakering, Essex, SS3 0AG
☎ (01702) 826755 ☎ 07771 871255
🌐 georgesbrewery.com

George's Brewery and Hop Monster Brewing Company are owned by the same brewer, using the same plant. George's concentrates on traditional styles and Hop Monster on the more unusual. Special brews are available every month. ‼ ♦

Wallasea Wench (OG 1037.5, ABV 3.6%)
A pale copper-coloured, easy-drinking beer with low bitterness and a smooth mouthfeel.

Wakering Gold (OG 1039.5, ABV 3.8%)
Bursting with fresh hop aroma.

Best (OG 1041, ABV 4%)
Copper-coloured, finely crafted session bitter.

Cockleboats (OG 1039, ABV 4%)
Deep copper-coloured beer, brewed using five malts.

Broadsword (OG 1046, ABV 4.7%)
Ruby/copper-coloured with a malty smooth start and a well-balanced, dry finish.

Excalibur (OG 1051.5, ABV 5.4%)
Brewed in collaboration with Russ Barnes of Red Fox Brewery.

Merry Gentlemen (OG 1058, ABV 6%)
A warming winter ale. Dark chocolate, black cherries and old port flavours dominate this velvety old ale.

Excalibur Reserve (OG 1067, ABV 7.2%)
Full on citrus rush with fruit overtones and the warmth of ancient Armagnac.

Brewed for the Trout Tavern, Southend:

Trout Ale (OG 1037.5, ABV 3.6%)

Gertie Sweet

See New Plassey

Gipsy Hill SIBA

Unit 11, Hamilton Road Industrial Estate, 160 Hamilton Road, West Norwood, London, SE27 9SF
☎ (020) 8761 9061 🌐 gipsyhillbrewing.com

Gipsy Hill was founded in 2014 by Sam and Charlie using a 15-barrel plant. It produces session-strength cask and bottled beers mainly for the local market in London. ♦RAIB

Beatnik (ABV 3.8%)

Southpaw (ABV 4.2%)

Dissident (ABV 4.8%)

Glamorgan

Unit J, Llantrisant Business Park, Llantrisant, CF72 8LF
☎ (01443) 406080 🌐 thekitebrewery.com

Formerly known as the Kite Brewery, this 30-barrel plant is now well established since its move to Llantrisant in 2013. The brewing team produces a well-developed range of year-round and seasonal ales with additional special brews to mark notable events. Distribution across South, West and Mid Wales is undertaken by sister company Glamorgan Beer Company and further afield by selected wholesalers. ♦

Cwrw Gorslas/Bluestone Bitter (OG 1040, ABV 4%)
A well-rounded bitter delivering softly roasted undertones to a malty body complemented by a smooth and robust hoppiness from nose to finish.

Welsh Pale Ale (OG 1042, ABV 4.1%)
A crisp pale ale, light gold in colour, and full of bright citrus aromas and flavours. Finishes dry, fruity and hoppy.

Jemima's Pitchfork (ABV 4.4%)

Bull Ring Porter (OG 1047, ABV 4.7%)
A traditional porter with a complex combination of several malts and hops to produce a rich and smooth dark chocolate character with a herbal bitterness.

Glastonbury SIBA

Unit 11, Wessex Park, Somerton Business Park, Somerton, Somerset, TA11 6SB
☎ (01458) 272244 🌐 glastonburyales.com

Glastonbury Ales was established in 2002 on a five-barrel plant. In 2006 the brewery changed ownership and has now expanded to a 20-barrel plant. ‼ ♦

Mystery Tor (OG 1040, ABV 3.8%)
A golden bitter with plenty of floral hop and fruit on the nose and palate, the sweetness giving way to a bitter hop finish. Full-bodied for a session bitter.

Lady of the Lake (OG 1042, ABV 4.2%)
A full-bodied amber best bitter with plenty of hops to the fore, balanced by a fruity malt flavour and a subtle hint of vanilla, leading to a clean, bitter hop aftertaste.

Love Monkey (OG 1042, ABV 4.2%)
Golden ale loaded with zesty fruity hops and a variety of delicious malts. Refreshing fruity notes finally succumb to a robust full on body.

Black As Yer 'At (OG 1043, ABV 4.3%)
A richly roasted stout.

Hedge Monkey (OG 1048, ABV 4.6%)
A well-rounded, deep amber-coloured bitter. Malty, rich and hoppy.

Golden Chalice (OG 1048, ABV 4.8%)
Light, golden-coloured best bitter with a robust malt character.

Thriller Cappuccino Porter (OG 1050, ABV 5%)

Glenfinnan

Sruth A Mhuilinn, Glenfinnan, PH37 4LT
☎ (01397) 704309 ☎ 07999 261010
🌐 glenfinnanbrewery.co.uk

Glenfinnan opened in 2007 and operates on a four-barrel plant. It produces around 600 litres per week during the tourist season. Further expansion is planned. ♦

Gold Ale (OG 1040, ABV 3.8%)

Standard Ale (OG 1044, ABV 4.2%)

Glentworth

Glentworth House, Crossfield Lane, Skellow, Doncaster, South Yorkshire, DN6 8PL
☎ (01302) 725555

⊚The brewery was founded in 1996 and is housed in former dairy buildings. The five-barrel plant supplies more than 80 pubs. Production is concentrated on mainly light-coloured, hoppy ales. ◆

Globe

目 144 High Street West, Glossop, Derbyshire, SK13 8HJ
☎ (01457) 852417 ⊕ globepub.co.uk

Globe was established in 2006 by Ron Brookes on a 2.5-barrel plant in an old stable behind the Globe pub. Grandson Toby now has a major role in the brewery under the watchful eye of Ron. The beers are mainly for the pub but special one-off brews are produced for beer festivals. ◆

Amber (OG 1040, ABV 3.9%)

Blondie (OG 1039, ABV 3.9%)

Stout (OG 1040, ABV 3.9%)

Comet (OG 1043, ABV 4.3%)

Gloucester SIBA

Fox's Kiln, West Quay, The Docks, Gloucester, GL1 2LG
☎ (01452) 668043 ☎ 07503 152749
⊕ gloucesterbrewery.co.uk

⊗ Situated in the historic and iconic Gloucester Docks, brewing began in 2011. The brewery has recently expanded into larger premises in the Dock area to cope with increased demand while retaining and sympathetically restoring their original converted stables site for experimental brews and a bar named Tank. The full range of beers is regularly available in pubs throughout Gloucestershire and further afield, notably Bristol. A new beer is brewed on a bi-monthly basis as part of a craft ale range. !! ☛ ◆ RAIB

Priory Pale (OG 1037, ABV 3.7%)
A refreshing hoppy ale with citrus and tropical notes.

Gold (OG 1040, ABV 3.9%)
A crisp, hoppy golden ale.

Cascade (OG 1042, ABV 4.2%)
Big malty backbone with bold Cascade hops.

Galaxy (OG 1052, ABV 5.2%)
A golden ale bursting with hop character.

Goacher's

Unit 8, Tovil Green Business Park, Burial Ground Lane, Tovil, Maidstone, Kent, ME13 6TA
☎ (01622) 682112 ⊕ goachers.com

A traditional brewery that uses only malt and Kentish hops for all its beers. Phil and Debbie Goacher have concentrated on brewing good wholesome beers without gimmicks. Two tied houses and around 30 free trade outlets in the mid-Kent area are supplied. Special is brewed for sale under house names. !! ◆

Real Mild Ale (OG 1033, ABV 3.4%) ◣

A rich, flavourful mild with moderate roast barley and a generous helping of chocolate malt.

Fine Light Ale (OG 1036, ABV 3.7%) ◣
A pale, golden-brown bitter with a strong, floral, hoppy aroma and aftertaste. A hoppy and moderately malty session beer.

Special/House Ale (OG 1037, ABV 3.8%)

Best Dark Ale (OG 1040, ABV 4.1%) ◣
Dark in colour but light and quaffable in body, this ale features hints of caramel and chocolate malt throughout.

Crown Imperial Stout (OG 1044, ABV 4.5%) ◣
A good, well-balanced roasty stout, dark and bitter with just a hint of caramel and a lingering creamy head.

Gold Star Strong Ale (OG 1050, ABV 5.1%) ◣
A strong pale ale brewed from 100% Maris Otter malt and East Kent Goldings hops.

Goddards SIBA ⊚

Barnsley Farm, Bullen Road, Ryde, Isle of Wight, PO33 1QF
☎ (01983) 611011 ⊕ goddardsbrewery.com

⊗ Anthony Goddard established what is now the oldest active brewery on the Isle of Wight in 1993. Originally occupying an 18th-century barn, a new brewery was built in 2008, quadrupling its capacity, which has since been further increased. Goddard's remain a locally-focused business distributing ales on the Isle of Wight and the easily accessible counties of southern England. ☛ ◆

Ale of Wight (OG 1037, ABV 3.7%)
An aromatic, fresh and zesty pale beer.

Scrumdiggity (OG 1039, ABV 4%) ◣
Well-balanced session beer that maintains its flavour and bite with compelling drinkability.

Wight Squirrel (OG 1042.5, ABV 4.3%)
A russet-coloured best bitter with an initial dry taste on the palate.

Fuggle-Dee-Dum (OG 1047, ABV 4.8%) ◣
Brown-coloured strong ale with plenty of malt and hops.

Goff's SIBA

9 Isbourne Way, Winchcombe, Gloucestershire, GL54 5NS
☎ (01242) 603383 ⊕ goffsbrewery.com

⊗ Goff's is a family concern that has been brewing cask-conditioned ales since 1994. The ales are available regionally in more than 200 outlets and nationally through wholesalers. ☛ ◆

Jouster (OG 1040, ABV 4%) ◣
A tawny-coloured ale, with a light hoppiness in the aroma. It has a good balance of malt and bitterness in the mouth, underscored by fruitiness, with a clean, hoppy aftertaste.

Tournament (OG 1038, ABV 4%) ◣
Dark golden in colour, with a pleasant hop aroma. A clean, light and refreshing session bitter with a pleasant hop aftertaste.

White Knight (OG 1046, ABV 4.7%) ◣
A well-hopped bitter with a light colour and full-bodied taste. Bitterness predominates in the mouth and leads to a dry, hoppy aftertaste.

Golcar

60a Swallow Lane, Golcar, West Yorkshire, HD7 4NB
☎ (01484) 644241 ☎ 07970 267555
⊕ golcarbrewery.co.uk

☺Golcar started brewing in 2001 and production has increased from 2.5 barrels to five barrels a week. The brewery owns one pub, the Rose & Crown at Golcar, and supplies other outlets in the local area. ‼

Dark Mild (OG 1035, ABV 3.6%) ◈
Dark mild with a light roasted malt and liquorice taste. Smooth and satisfying.

Pennine Gold (OG 1038, ABV 4%)
A hoppy and fruity session beer.

Town End Bitter (OG 1038, ABV 4%) ◈
Amber bitter with a hoppy, citrus taste, with fruity overtones and a bitter finish.

Guthlac's Porter (OG 1047, ABV 5%)
A robust all-grain and malty working man's porter.

Golden Duck SIBA

Unit 2, Redhill Farm, Top Street, Appleby Magna, Leicestershire, DE12 7AH ☎ 07846 295179
⊕ goldenduckbrewery.com

Golden Duck began brewing in 2012 using a five-barrel plant. It is run by the father-and-son team of Andrew and Harry Lunn. Beers have a cricket-related theme and are always available in Mushroom Hall, Albert Village. ◆

LFB (Lunns First Brew) (OG 1043, ABV 4.3%)
Traditional golden-coloured hoppy session ale with citrus overtones.

Wristy Fitzy (OG 1046, ABV 4.6%)
Smooth, rich chestnut ale, hoppy with slight malty overtones.

Lunnys No. 8 (OG 1048, ABV 4.8%)
Hoppy bitter with a fruity and lasting aroma.

Bodies Bottom Lip (OG 1052, ABV 5.2%)
Strong porter with chocolate overtones.

Contract brewed for Alchemist Brewery:

Firestarter (ABV 3.9%)

Golden Triangle SIBA

Unit 9, Watton Road, Norwich, NR9 4BG
☎ (01603) 757763 ☎ 07976 281132
⊕ goldentrianglebrewery.co.uk

⊠ Golden Triangle, named after an area of Norwich, has been brewing modern, hop-forward ales on a 10-barrel plant since 2011. The brewery moved to the current premises in 2012, and continue to add new beers to their range. Beers are mainly found in pubs across Norwich.

City Gold (OG 1038, ABV 3.8%) ◈
A lemony hop aroma introduces a smoky mix of citrus, hop and bitterness. Finish develops a dry astringency.

Mosaic City (OG 1037, ABV 3.8%)
A full-bodied, light golden ale with a distinctive flavour.

Citropolis (OG 1039, ABV 3.9%)
A light, refreshing and zesty golden ale with citrus hop notes and a fruity aroma.

Bonny's Gold (OG 1040, ABV 4%)
A golden citrus hoppy ale with a American hop profile. The two hops work well with a good malt backbone.

Black Hops IBA (OG 1047, ABV 4.6%) ◈
Intense hop and cherry aroma. Complex mix of malt, cherry and bitterness dominated by hops. Challenging, increasingly bitter ending.

Red Square (OG 1046, ABV 4.6%)
A red ale brewed with a balanced, complex flavour that develops into a strong hoppy finish.

Hop Lobster (OG 1051, ABV 5.5%)
A strong golden ale with citrus hop character.

Golden Valley (NEW)

Moorhampton Farm, Abbeydore, Herefordshire, HR2 0AL ☎ 07828 935675

Office: Unit 7, Three Elms Trading Estate, Hereford, HR4 9PU

Golden Valley Brewery uses a one-barrel plant and produces eight to twelve firkins a month.

DPA (Dore Pale Ale) (ABV 4%)

Knock 'em Back (ABV 4.4%)

Goldmark SIBA ◉

Unit 23, The Vinery, Arundel Road, Poling, West Sussex, BN18 9PY
☎ (01903) 297838 ☎ 07900 555415
⊕ goldmarks.co.uk

⊠ Ex-biochemist and home brewer Mark Lehmann began commercial brewing in 2013 using an 11-barrel plant. Beers are available in many outlets nationwide. ‼RAIB

Ebony Mild (OG 1035, ABV 3.5%)
Black spicy mild with hints of chocolate, coffee and toffee.

Liquid Gold (OG 1040, ABV 4%)
A refreshing, full-bodied golden beer with bursts of fruit and citrus.

Phoenix (OG 1041, ABV 4.1%)
A brown ale with hints of toffee and caramel and a smooth hop finish.

Red IPA (OG 1043, ABV 4.3%)
A triple-hopped red ale using caramelised red German malt.

American Hop Idol (OG 1040, ABV 4.4%)
A pale ale using six American hop varieties balanced with roasted malt.

Warrior (OG 1046, ABV 4.6%)
A brown ale with hints of honey and caramel, finishing with a smooth hop note.

Black Lion Porter (OG 1048, ABV 4.8%)
A rich, smooth, satisfying black porter with chocolate hints and a coffee end note.

Vertigo Craft Lager (OG 1048, ABV 4.8%)
A Helles-style recipe, aged for 12 weeks.

Goldstone SIBA ◉

The Forge, Ditchling Common Industrial Estate, Streat Lane, Ditchling, East Sussex, BN6 8SG
☎ (01444) 257053

257 Dyke Road, Hove, East Sussex, BN3 6PA
⊕ goldstonebrewery.co.uk

⊠ Located in an old forge in the South Downs, Goldstone is the brainchild of Mark Francis, who, while running a bar in Brussels, fell in love with the vast selection of Belgian beers. The team consists of Mark, his wife Alison and award-winning consultant brewer Richard Venour. The brewery is named after a 20-ton rock found in Sussex, believed to have been used by druids for worship.

Old Charmer (OG 1041, ABV 4.1%)
A light, thirst-quenching ale with an assertive bitterness and tropical fruit and spicy aroma.

Ruddy Duck (OG 1041, ABV 4.1%)
Medium-bodied dark ale with notes of caramel, chocolate and coffee and a dry finish.

Beacon Best Bitter (OG 1042, ABV 4.2%)
A well-balanced amber ale in the style of a traditional best bitter; there is maltiness on the palate with a dry, bitter finish.

Cascade (OG 1044, ABV 4.4%)
An American-style, single-hopped ale with strong aromas of citrus fruit.

East Slope Ale (OG 1044, ABV 4.4%)
Golden ale with a smooth, light and hoppy flavour.

Amarillo (OG 1045, ABV 4.5%)
Golden-coloured, single-hopped American-style ale with strong aromas of grapefruit and gooseberry and a dry bitter finish.

Goodall's

⊟ The Lodge, 88 Crewe Road, Alsager, Staffordshire, ST7 2JA
☎ (01270) 873669
✉ goodalls.brewery@hotmail.co.uk

Goodall's began brewing in 2010 at the Lodge in Alsager using a 2.5-barrel plant. ‼◆

Goody SIBA

Bleangate Brewery, Braggs Lane, Herne, Kent, CT6 7NP
☎ (01227) 361555 ⊕ goodyales.co.uk

Goody began brewing in 2012 using a 10-barrel plant. Only locally grown Kent hops are used and a wood-burning boiler is used to heat the water for the brews using wood from its copse, thereby minimising the use of non-renewable fuel. 🍺◆RAIB

Genesis (OG 1035, ABV 3.5%)
A dark ruby-coloured, single-hopped ale with a full flavour and lasting bitter finish.

Good Health (OG 1038, ABV 3.6%)
A honey-coloured, golden ale with a fresh hoppy finish and undertone of zesty orange.

Good Life (OG 1040, ABV 3.9%)
Fresh-tasting pale ale, bursting with citrus flavours and golden hops.

Good Heavens (OG 1042, ABV 4.1%)
An amber-coloured, hoppy ale.

Good Sheppard (OG 1045, ABV 4.5%)
Deep amber ale with a warm vanilla twist on the palate and a soft feel on the tongue.

Good Lord (OG 1047, ABV 5%)
A rich porter with a smooth roasted coffee tinge and a silky bitter finish.

Goose Eye SIBA

Ingrow Bridge, South Street, Keighley, West Yorkshire, BD21 5AX
☎ (01535) 605807 ⊕ goose-eye-brewery.co.uk

⊚Goose Eye is a family-run brewery supplying 60-70 regular outlets, mainly in Yorkshire and Lancashire. The beer are available through national wholesalers and pub chains. ◆

Springwell (OG 1036, ABV 3.6%)

Barm Pot Bitter (OG 1038, ABV 3.8%) ◄
Bitter, hop and fruit flavours dominate this golden session bitter over a malty base. Increasingly dry and bitter finish.

Goose Eye Bitter (OG 1038, ABV 3.9%) ◄
Traditional Yorkshire brown session bitter, with well-balanced malt and hops and a pleasingly bitter finish.

Blackmoor (OG 1040, ABV 4%)
A dark beer session beer.

Chinook Blonde (OG 1042, ABV 4.2%) ◄
An increasingly tart, bitter finish follows assertive grapefruit hoppiness in the aroma and tropical fruit flavours in this satisfying brew.

Golden Goose (OG 1045, ABV 4.5%)
A straw-coloured beer light on the palate with a smooth and refreshing hoppy finish.

Over and Stout (OG 1052, ABV 5.2%) ◄
A full-bodied stout with roast and malt flavours mingling with hops, dark fruit and liquorice on the palate. Look also for tart fruit on the nose and a growing bitter finish.

Pommies Revenge (OG 1052, ABV 5.2%) ◄
Golden strong bitter combining grassy hops, a cocktail of fruit flavours, a peppery hint and a hoppy, bitter finish.

Goosnargh SIBA

⊟ Horns Inn, Horns Lane, Goosnargh, Lancashire, PR3 2FJ
☎ (01772) 864382 ⊕ yehornsinn.co.uk

Brewing began in 2013 using a five-barrel plant in a tiny outbuilding at Ye Horns Inn. Most of the equipment came from the Grindleton Brewery, which closed in 2010. The beer is served at the pub and in local free houses. ‼◆

Truckle (OG 1035, ABV 3.7%)
A dark malty beer with a slight nutty taste and a hint of sweetness.

Bit o' Blonde (OG 1038, ABV 4%)
A light ale, crisp and clean.

Gold (OG 1037, ABV 4%)
A golden beer, light but hoppy with a zesty finish.

**RGB (Real Goosnargh Bitter)
(OG 1040, ABV 4.3%)**
A copper-coloured beer with an earthy, fruity flavour. Nicknamed Reet Gradley Bitter.

Gower SIBA ◉

⊟ Greyhound Inn, Oldwalls, Llanrhidian, SA3 1HA
☎ 07967 484356 ⊕ gowerbrewery.com

⊠ Established in 2011 by master brewer Dave Campbell, who has more than 24 years of brewing knowledge and experience. ◆

Brew 1 (OG 1039, ABV 3.8%)
Honey-coloured ale with a pronounced floral aroma.

Black Diamond (OG 1042, ABV 4.2%)
A full-bodied Welsh porter, smoky, with chocolate and liquorice flavours, and subtle spicy, bittering hops.

Sampson's Jack (OG 1042, ABV 4.2%)
A classic copper-coloured traditional British ale.

Best Bitter (OG 1045, ABV 4.5%)
A traditional honey-coloured ale with a full-bodied, balanced malty flavour and crisp lingering bite of hop.

Gold (OG 1045, ABV 4.5%)
Thirst-quenching golden ale, refreshing citrus flavours and the lovely aroma of Cascade hops.

Lighthouse (OG 1046, ABV 4.5%)
A light, thirst-quenching continental-style lager.

IPA (OG 1049, ABV 4.8%)
A full-flavoured hoppy IPA.

Rumour (OG 1050, ABV 5%)
Strong ruby red ale, with complex tastes and aromas, produced from a delicate mix of malts and hops.

Power (OG 1052, ABV 5.5%)
A powerful IPA.

Grafters SIBA

Half Moon, 23 High Street, Willingham by Stow, Lincolnshire, DN21 5JZ
☎ (01427) 788340 🌐 graftersbrewery.com

Brewing started on a 2.5-barrel plant in 2007 in a converted garage adjacent to the owner's freehouse, the Half Moon. 2013 saw an upgrade to a 10-barrel plant. !! ♦

Moonlight (OG 1038, ABV 3.6%)
A light, citrus beer.

Traditional (OG 1040, ABV 3.7%)
A traditional beer, fairly light in colour but with a light, hoppy finish.

Over the Moon (OG 1041.5, ABV 4%)

Darker Side of the Moon (OG 1043, ABV 4.2%)
A dark, strong mild with a smooth, chocolaty taste.

Wobble Gob (OG 1048, ABV 4.9%)
A deep ruby-coloured beer with a slightly floral and roasted taste.

Grafton SIBA

Walters Yard, Unit 4, Claylands Industrial Estate, Worksop, Nottinghamshire, S81 7DW
☎ (01909) 476121 ☎ 07436 282779

Office: Oak Close, Crabtree Park Estate, Worksop, Nottinghamshire, S80 1BH
✉ susanhale1865@gmail.com

Grafton is a 12-barrel brewery established in 2007. The brewery tap is the Grafton Hotel, Worksop. A new brewery, visitor centre and shop opened in 2014. !! ♦

Framboise (OG 1038, ABV 4%)
A pale yellow-coloured ale, with a raspberry aroma leading to raspberry sweetness coming through on the palate and a smooth bitter finish.

Silhouette (OG 1038, ABV 4%)
A pale beer. The addition of vanilla pods gives a unique vanilla flavour.

Lady Julia (OG 1041, ABV 4.3%)
A golden ale. Wheat and barley produce a crisp beer with a floral hop aroma.

Bananalicious (OG 1043, ABV 4.5%)
Mid brown ale with a banana and toffee aftertaste.

Lady Ruby (OG 1043, ABV 4.5%)
A dark ruby-coloured ale made with cherries. Hint of cherries on the nose, on the palate a bitter start which then finishes with a cherry bomb on the back of the tongue. An easy-drinking beer.

Apricot Jungle (OG 1046, ABV 4.8%)
A fruity, golden beer with honey, apricot and almond notes. The sweetness is balanced by hop bitterness.

Blondie (OG 1046, ABV 4.8%)
A strong golden-coloured beer whose aroma is dominated by characteristic citrus notes. Hops and fruit on the palate are balanced by malt, leading to a hoppy finish with soft fruit flavours.

Coco Loco (OG 1048, ABV 5%)
This dark/black-coloured beer is rich with caramel flavours. Full-bodied and well-balanced, coconut oil is added giving sweetness on the palate. An enjoyable, quirky beer.

Charioteer (OG 1063, ABV 6.5%)
An easy-drinking, strong beer. Subtle, with citrus flavours, giving a berry aroma and fruity flavour with a hint of malty sweetness, leading to a smooth, long finish.

Grain SIBA

South Farm, Tunbeck Road, Alburgh, Harleston, Norfolk, IP20 0BS
☎ (01986) 788884 🌐 grainbrewery.co.uk

Grain Brewery was launched in 2006 by Geoff Wright and Phil Halls in a converted dairy in the Waveney Valley. It upgraded to a 15-barrel plant in 2012. Two bars are owned, the Plough, Norwich, and the Corn Hall Bar, Diss. !! RAIB

Oak (OG 1038, ABV 3.8%) ◆
A balanced mix of malt and hops with marmalade overtones. A hint of molasses in the short sharp ending.

3.1.6. (OG 1039, ABV 3.9%) ◆
Hops mingle with a citrus marmalade bite in both aroma and taste. Long strong finish with growing malty bitterness.

Blonde Ash Wheat Beer (OG 1040, ABV 4%) ◆
Banana notes flow through this sweet smoky brew. Yellow-hued with a grainy mouthfeel and a quick fruity finale.

Best Bitter (OG 1042, ABV 4.2%) ◆
A well-balanced, complex bitter. A mix of flavours with malt and hops ably supported by caramel and bitterness.

Redwood (OG 1048, ABV 4.8%) ◆
Heavy blackcurrant airs give way to a rich fruity bitterness with malt overtones. Copper-coloured, crisp and satisfying.

Black IPA (ABV 5%)

Blackwood Stout (OG 1050, ABV 5%) ◆

THE BREWERIES

Roast dominates from the initial aroma to the long, lingering ending. A bittersweet chocolate undercurrent adds depth.

India Pale Ale (OG 1065, ABV 6.5%) 🍴 ◆
Powerful complex and rich throughout. Malt and hops vie with tropical fruit and bitterness for dominance. Challenging and rewarding.

Grainstore SIBA 👁

🏚 **Station Approach, Oakham, Rutland, LE15 6RE**
☎ (01572) 770065 ⊕ grainstorebrewery.com

☺ Grainstore, the smallest county's largest brewery, has been in production since 1995, founded by Tony Davis and Mike Davies. After 30 years in the industry Tony decided to set up his own business after finding a derelict Victorian railway grainstore building. Now retired, he has handed the reins to his son, William. 80 outlets are supplied. ‼ 🍴◆

Rutland Bitter (OG 1032, ABV 3.4%)
A light, well-balanced session beer. One of the few beers that are registered PGI (Protected Geographical Indication).

Rutland Panther (OG 1034, ABV 3.4%) ◆
This reddish-black mild punches above its weight with malt and roast flavours combining to deliver a brew that can match the average stout for intensity of flavour.

Cooking (OG 1036, ABV 3.6%) ◆
Tawny-coloured beer with malt and hops on the nose and a pleasant grainy mouthfeel. Hops and fruit flavours combine to give a bitterness that continues into a long finish.

Red Kite (OG 1038, ABV 3.8%)
Made with the traditional mild ale malt variety that was a staple of Midlands bitters and milds in the 1950s, giving a maltier/sweeter beer with greater body than today's bitters and with a darker hue.

Steelback IPA (OG 1042, ABV 4.2%)
A full-bodied, golden-coloured IPA.

Triple B (OG 1042, ABV 4.2%) ◆
Initially hops dominate over malt in both the aroma and taste, but fruit is there, too. All three linger in varying degrees in the sweetish aftertaste of this brown brew.

GB Best (OG 1043, ABV 4.3%)
A smooth, light ale with a pronounced floral aroma and flavour.

Gold (OG 1045, ABV 4.5%)
A refreshing, light-golden brew, with a mellow malt sweetness finely balanced by the smooth bitterness, subtle flavours and floral aromas.

Ten Fifty (OG 1050, ABV 5%) ◆
Pungent banana and malt notes on the nose. On the palate, rich malt and fruit are joined by subtle hop on a bittersweet base. Dry malt aftertaste with some fruit.

Rutland Beast (OG 1053, ABV 5.3%) 🍴
A unique, strong mild ale. Complex flavours with chocolate and coffee notes as well as raisins and autumn fruits.

Nip (OG 1073, ABV 7.3%) 🍴
A well-balanced barley wine with a blend of sweetness and hop bitterness. Smooth and warming with raisins and winter fruit as the dominant flavour notes.

Grampus (NEW)

🏚 **Grampus Inn, Lee Bay, Ilfracombe, Devon, EX34 8LR**
☎ (01271) 862906 ⊕ thegrampus-inn.co.uk

⊗ Grampus was opened in 2014 at the back of the Grampus Inn by Bill Harvey, the owner. It is a small plant using traditional brewing methods, but combining some unique and unusual ingredients. At present, most production is sold though the pub, with just a few casks going to local pubs. Beers also available in cask and takeaway five-pint boxes. ◆

Bitter (OG 1039, ABV 4%)

Ale (OG 1042, ABV 4.4%)

Granite Rock

Unit 19, Kernick Road Industrial Estate, Penryn, Cornwall, TR10 9EP
☎ (01326) 379251 ☎ 07436 817974
⊕ graniterockbrewery.co.uk

⊗ Granite Rock was established in 2013 as a brewery and home brew shop. Located on an industrial estate in Penryn, the two-barrel plant currently supplies the free trade in west Cornwall. ‼ 🍴◆ RAIB

Penryn Company Pale Ale (OG 1040, ABV 4%)
A light hoppy session beer.

Bronescombe's Vision (OG 1048, ABV 5.2%)
Deep-coloured hearty bitter with a malty, fruity aroma and a dry pleasant bitter finish.

Glasney College Porter (OG 1050, ABV 5.4%) ◆
Black porter with roast malt aroma. Full-bodied taste of creamy coffee and dark chocolate, liquorice and pear drops. Light finish.

Great Heck SIBA

Harwinn House, Main Street, Great Heck, North Yorkshire, DN14 0BQ
☎ (01977) 661430 ☎ 07723 381002
⊕ greatheckbrewery.co.uk

☺ Great Heck began production in 2008 in a converted slaughterhouse. The brewery moved across the road to a converted cottage in 2012 and now produces its regular beers on a 15-barrel plant with capacity for 45 barrels per week. ‼◆

Chopper (OG 1037, ABV 3.8%)
A pale session beer.

Angel (OG 1037, ABV 3.9%)
A clean, dry, moderately bittered pale ale.

Dave (OG 1038, ABV 3.9%)
A dark session bitter with a satisfying roasty taste.

Navigator (OG 1039, ABV 3.9%)
Traditional mahogany-coloured session bitter with subtle yet exotic hop aromas.

Blonde (OG 1043, ABV 4.3%)
A richly balanced blonde beer with a zesty finish.

Voodoo Mild (OG 1043, ABV 4.3%)
Rich, black mild bursting with flavour from the roasted malts.

Citra (OG 1043, ABV 4.5%)
A refreshing golden ale with tropical fruit flavours and aroma.

Simcoe (OG 1043, ABV 4.5%)
Refreshing golden ale with tropical fruit flavours and aroma balanced by light gold malts.

Amish Mash (ABV 4.7%)
A cloudy wheat beer with notes of banana and clove.

Treasure IPA (OG 1045, ABV 4.8%)
Smooth golden IPA with moderate bitterness and distinctive tropical fruit notes.

Treason Stout (OG 1054, ABV 5.4%)
An unfined wheat stout.

Vanilla Wheat Stout (OG 1054, ABV 5.4%)
An unfined, far from traditional stout with English hops and vanilla pods giving a subtle balance of flavours. Smooth and satisfying.

Shankar IPA (OG 1055, ABV 5.9%)
A pale, hoppy, fruity beer with a clean zesty finish. Named after sitar player Ravi Shankar.

Black Jesus (OG 1060, ABV 6.5%)
A black IPA brewed with large quantities of premium American hops and special dehusked German roasted malt.

Yakima IPA (OG 1070, ABV 7.4%)
Deep golden in colour, low in bitterness. The alcohol balances the fruity hop flavours and aromas.

Great Newsome SIBA ◉

Great Newsome Farm, South Frodingham, Winestead, East Yorkshire, HU12 0NR
☎ (01964) 612201 ⊕ greatnewsomebrewery.co.uk

☺ Nestled in the Holderness countryside, Great Newsome began brewing in 2007 in renovated farm buildings. A range of beers are now brewed using barley from the farm and brewing can be seen from a newly-built viewing area. Beer is distributed throughout the UK and overseas. ‼☞♦

Sleck Dust (OG 1037, ABV 3.8%)
Straw-coloured, refreshingly bitter session beer with floral aroma and subtle dry finish.

Ploughman's Pride (OG 1042, ABV 4.2%)
A dark rich malty ale with liquorice tones.

Pricky Back Otchan (OG 1042, ABV 4.2%)
Hoppy golden bitter with fresh citrus aroma.

Frothingham Best (OG 1042, ABV 4.3%)
Dark amber best bitter with subtle dry finish.

Holderness Dark (OG 1042, ABV 4.3%)
Dark, strong mild. Malty notes with a hint of sweetness.

Jem's Stout (OG 1044, ABV 4.3%)
Dark, smooth beer with smoky, roasted malt flavours and aroma.

Great Oakley SIBA ◉

Ark Farm, High Street South, Tiffield, Northamptonshire, NN12 8AB
☎ (01327) 351759 ☎ 07850 327658
⊕ greatoakleybrewery.co.uk

The brewery commenced production in 2005 in Great Oakley and relocated to Tiffield in 2012. It is run by husband-and-wife team Phil and Hazel Greenway. More than 60 outlets are supplied, including the George, Tiffield, which is the brewery tap. ‼☞♦RAIB

Welland Valley Mild (OG 1037, ABV 3.6%)
A dark, traditional mild. Full of flavour.

Wagtail (OG 1040, ABV 3.9%)

Light coloured with a unique bitterness derived from New Zealand hops.

Wot's Occurring (OG 1040, ABV 3.9%)
A mid-golden session bitter with a subtle hop finish.

Marching In (OG 1041, ABV 4.1%)
A golden, clean-tasting beer.

Tiffield Thunderbolt (OG 1043, ABV 4.2%)
A pale beer brewed with two different New Zealand hops.

Harpers (OG 1044, ABV 4.3%)
Traditional mid-brown bitter with a malty taste and slight hints of chocolate and citrus in the finish.

Gobble (OG 1045, ABV 4.5%)
Straw-coloured with a pleasant hop aftertaste.

Delapre Dark (OG 1047, ABV 4.6%)
A dark, full-bodied ale made from five different malts.

Abbey Stout (OG 1051, ABV 5%)
A dark rich stout.

Tailshaker (OG 1051, ABV 5%)
A complex golden ale with a great depth of flavour.

Great Orme SIBA

Builder Street, Llandudno, LL30 1DR
☎ (01492) 330680 ⊕ greatormebrewery.co.uk

☺ Great Orme began in 2005 as a five-barrel plant, situated in the Conwy Valley. It has recently moved to larger premises in the Victorian seaside town of Llandudno, within sight of the Great Orme from which the microbrewery takes its name. It now brews on an 18-barrel plant. Around 50 outlets are supplied. ♦

Welsh Gold (OG 1036, ABV 3.6%) ◕
A pale brown malty session bitter with a dry taste. Some hoppy flavours develop in the bitter aftertaste.

Welsh Black (OG 1042, ABV 4%) ▮◕
Smooth-tasting dark beer with roast coffee notes in aroma and taste. Sweetish in flavour and having some characteristics of a mild ale with hoppiness also present in the aftertaste.

Orme (OG 1042, ABV 4.2%) ◕
Malty best bitter with a dry finish. Faint hop and fruit notes in aroma and taste, but malt dominates throughout.

Celtica (OG 1045, ABV 4.5%) ◕
Yellow in colour with a zesty taste full of citrus fruit flavours. Some initial sweetness followed by peppery hops and a bitter finish.

Red Dragon (OG 1045, ABV 4.5%) ◕
A light-brown best bitter with a sweet malty taste accompanied by faint fruit notes and peppery hops in the finish.

Ynys Mon (OG 1045, ABV 4.5%)
Deep copper with chocolate malts. Sweet aftertaste.

Great Western SIBA ◉

Stream Bakery, Bristol Road, Hambrook, Bristol, BS16 1RF
☎ (0117) 957 2842
⊕ greatwesternbrewingcompany.co.uk

⊗ Great Western is a 12-barrel brewery set up in 2008 by Kevin Stone in a former bakery. The property has been renovated resulting in a bespoke showpiece brewery retaining many of the building's original features. 200 outlets are supplied and one pub is owned. ‼ ♦

HPA (OG 1040, ABV 4%)
Hoppy yellow bitter with clean citrus flavours leading to a lingering astringent finish.

Maiden Voyage (OG 1040, ABV 4%)
An amber bitter with a light aroma of malt and fruit which continues to the palate before leading to a strong bitter finish.

Bees Knees (OG 1041, ABV 4.2%)
Golden-coloured beer, bitter with malt nose and flavour and some honey. Lasting astringent bitter aftertaste.

Exhibitionist (OG 1044, ABV 4.5%)

Classic Gold (OG 1044, ABV 4.6%)
Golden ale with subtle aromas of pale malt and fruits. Citrus fruits with balanced hop and malt character with a lingering bitter finish.

Old Higby (OG 1045, ABV 4.8%)
Full-bodied malty bitter with roast notes on the nose. Hints of fruit flavour give way to a bitter hop finish with some astringency throughout.

Bristol Belle (OG 1047, ABV 5%)

Moose River (OG 1047, ABV 5%)

Great Yorkshire

Cropton, North Yorkshire, YO18 8HH
☎ (01751) 417330
thegreatyorkshirebrewery.co.uk

Great Yorkshire took over the Cropton Brewery in 2012 concentrating on the production of keg Yorkshire Lager and Yorkshire Blackout. Check the website for limited edition and other cask ales. ‼ ♦ RAIB

Yorkshire Pale (OG 1038, ABV 3.8%)
A New World-style pale ale, light and smooth with the flavours of mango and pineapple.

Yorkshire Classic (OG 1043.5, ABV 4%)
Light chestnut-coloured beer with a smooth malty taste balanced with complex biscuity flavours.

Yorkshire Golden (OG 1045, ABV 4.2%)
A refreshing golden beer with hints of caramel and a honey-like sweetness.

Yorkshire Blackout (OG 1051, ABV 5%)

Green Dragon

Green Dragon, 29 Broad Street, Bungay, Suffolk, NR35 1EF
☎ (01986) 892681

The Green Dragon pub was purchased in 1991 and the rear converted to a brewery. In 1994 the plant was expanded and moved to a converted barn. The doubling of capacity allowed the production of a larger range of ales, including seasonals. ‼ ♦

Chaucer Ale (OG 1037, ABV 3.8%)

Gold (OG 1045, ABV 4.4%)

Bridge Street Bitter (OG 1045, ABV 4.5%)

Strong Mild (OG 1054, ABV 5.5%)
A dark, ruby-coloured ale. Plum and dark chocolate on the nose with a rich and smooth taste full of dark malt notes.

Green Duck

Unit 13, Gainsborough Trading Estate, Rufford Road, Stourbridge, West Midlands, DY9 7ND
☎ (01384) 377666

Unit 2b, Gainsborough Trading Estate, Rufford Road, Stourbridge, DY9 7ND greenduckbrewery.co.uk

Green Duck began brewing in 2012 and relocated to its present site in Stourbridge in 2013. Experimental beers are brewed alongside a core range. The brewery has an onsite brewery tap, the Badelynge Bar, where the brewing equipment can be viewed through a glass partition. Private paries and quarterly beer festivals are hosted. ‼ ♦

Drunken Duck (ABV 3.9%)
Straw-coloured ale, with a lemon and lime edge.

Sitting Duck (ABV 4%)
A true pale ale, hoppy and grainy.

Duck Blonde (ABV 4.2%)
English pale ale, brewed using passion fruit.

Duck & Dive (ABV 5.9%)
Floral IPA with strong grapefruit notes.

Green Jack SIBA

Argyle Place, Love Road, Lowestoft, Suffolk, NR32 2NZ
☎ (01502) 562863 ☎ 07895 089150
green-jack.com

⊗ After 10 years at Oulton Broad, Green Jack moved to the Triangle Tavern, Lowestoft, in 2003 and then to a nearby 35-barrel plant in 2009. Three pubs are owned and more than 150 outlets supplied. ‼ ♦ RAIB

Golden Best (OG 1038, ABV 3.8%)
Cut grass hop aroma deepens on the palate of this golden bitter. Initially bitter, the aftertaste is fairly short and hoppy.

Orange Wheat Beer (OG 1041, ABV 4.2%)
Marmalade aroma with a hint of hops, leading to a well-balanced blend of sweetness, hops and citrus with a malt background. Mixed fruit flavours in the aftertaste.

Trawlerboys Best Bitter (OG 1045, ABV 4.6%)
Tawny beer with aroma of apple, sultana and malt plus hints of caramel and hops. Rich fig and plum base with malt and roast overtones. Strong finish with a sticky mouthfeel.

Lurcher Stout (OG 1046, ABV 4.8%)
Pleasant malt, roast and fruit aromas. Blackberry, raisin and port flavours. Long dry bitter roast finish.

Mahseer IPA (OG 1048, ABV 5%)

Rising Sun (OG 1048, ABV 5%)
Golden ale.

Red Herring (OG 1048, ABV 5.1%)

Gone Fishing ESB (OG 1052, ABV 5.5%)

Ripper Tripel (OG 1074, ABV 8.5%)

Baltic Trader Export Stout (OG 1092, ABV 10.5%)

Green Mill SIBA

▤ Harewood Arms, 2 Market Street, Broadbottom, SK14 6AX ☎ 07967 656887
⊕ greenmillbrewery.co.uk

☺ Green Mill started brewing in 2007 on a 2.5-barrel plant and moved in 2010 to the Cask & Feather in Rochdale. The brewery relocated again in 2013 to the Harewood Arms in Broadbottom. A number of occasional beers are brewed. Around 40 outlets are supplied. ◆

Gold (OG 1035, ABV 3.6%)
A quaffable golden session bitter.

Chief (OG 1041, ABV 4.2%)
A smooth pale bitter with American hop varieties.

Citrus Snap (OG 1040, ABV 4.2%)
A copper-coloured bitter with lots of citrus notes.

Old Git (OG 1040, ABV 4.2%)
A refreshing golden ale, complex and well-hopped.

Talisman (OG 1040, ABV 4.2%)
A straw-coloured golden ale with tropical fruit notes.

Pot Black Porter (ABV 4.4%)

Smokey Joe (ABV 4.4%)
A porter with a strong, smoky taste.

Flavia (OG 1042, ABV 4.5%)
A blonde beer with a fresh hop aroma brewed with lager malt, leading to a clean dry finish.

Northern Lights (OG 1045, ABV 4.5%)
A pale premium bitter, well-hopped.

Big Chief (OG 1052, ABV 5.5%)
A hoppy premium bitter.

Greene King ☺

Westgate Brewery, Westgate Street, Bury St Edmunds, Suffolk, IP33 1QT
☎ (01284) 763222 ⊕ greeneking.co.uk

☒ Greene King has been brewing in the market town of Bury St Edmunds since 1799. It brews its beers using water drawn from artesian chalk wells below its brewhouse as well as local East Anglia malt. Part of Greene King PLC. ‼ ☛ ◆ RAIB

XX Mild (OG 1035, ABV 3%)
A dark mild with a sweet and roast flavour.

IPA (OG 1036, ABV 3.6%) ◄
Hop-infused fruit cake aromas. Complex flavours of malt, caramel and hop with both sweetness and bitterness. A lingering mellow aftertaste with blackberries.

London Glory (OG 1041.1, ABV 4%)
Rich, fruity and full of flavour.

IPA Gold (OG 1041, ABV 4.1%)
A deep golden ale with a blend of tropical fruits, mango and spicy notes.

Abbot (OG 1049, ABV 5%) 🍷 ◄
Strong malt, toffee and caramel aromas. Rich malty caramel flavours with vine fruit and a little hop bite. Heavy sweet finish with a subtle hint of bitterness in the aftertaste.

IPA Reserve (OG 1055.5, ABV 5.4%)
A full-bodied amber ale. Grapefruit and orange citrus tones combine with the floral and herbal notes from the hops and lead to a dry bitter finish.

Brewed under the Hardys & Hansons brand name:

Bitter (OG 1038, ABV 3.9%)
A balance of sweetness and bitterness that combines with a subtle hop character. A distinctive beer with a full finish.

Olde Trip (OG 1043, ABV 4.3%)
A rich toffee flavoured beer with a fruity character and a clean, bitter finish.

Brewed under the Morland brand name:

Original Bitter (OG 1039, ABV 4%)
A subtle malt and fruit character and a pronounced bitter finish.

Old Golden Hen (OG 1038.6, ABV 4.1%)
Light golden beer brewed using the Galaxy hop to give tropical fruit notes.

Old Speckled Hen (OG 1045, ABV 4.5%) ◄
Smooth, malty and fruity, with a short finish.

Brewed under the Ruddles brand name:

Best Bitter (OG 1037, ABV 3.7%) ◄
An amber/brown beer, strong on bitterness but with some initial sweetness, fruit and subtle, distinctive Bramling Cross hop. Dryness lingers in the aftertaste.

County (OG 1043, ABV 4.3%) ◄
Sweet, malty and bitter, with a dry and bitter aftertaste.

Brewed under the Tolly Cobbold brand name:

English Ale (OG 1033.6, ABV 2.8%)
Amber ale brewed using a complex mix of hops to offer balanced bitterness with strong tropical notes.

Greenfield SIBA ☺

Unit 8, Waterside Mills, Greenfield, Saddleworth, OL3 7NH
☎ (01457) 879789 ⊕ greenfieldbrewery.co.uk

☺ Greenfield was launched in 2002 and is situated in an old spinning mill next to the River Chew on the edge of the Peak District National Park. Spring water from the National Park is used for brewing. It is open to the public and supplies beer to them and to more than 200 outlets. ‼ ☛ ◆

Silver Owl (OG 1042, ABV 4%)
A golden-amber beer with an aroma of citrus fruits and hints of vanilla – oranges, dryness and lightly hopped taste.

Thirst Born (OG 1041, ABV 4.1%)
Floral citrus aroma with malt and hops. Taste of citrus, peach, floral malt.

Dobcross Bitter (OG 1041, ABV 4.2%)
An amber beer with lemon flavours and a dry finish.

Copper Caskade (OG 1042, ABV 4.3%)
Full-bodied, copper-coloured beer made with Cascade hops. A medium bitterness with a hoppy finish revealing both citrus and fruit tones.

Vanilla Stout (OG 1048, ABV 5.2%)
A true black stout. Initial flavours of both chocolate and coffee are revealed before the roasted malts give way to a natural vanilla finish, created by the use of real vanilla pods during the cask maturation stage.

Greenodd

⊟ Ship Inn, Main Street, Greenodd, Cumbria, LA12 7QZ ☎ 07782 655294

✉ greenoddbrewery@yahoo.co.uk

⊕ Established in 2010 at the Ship Inn on a two-barrel plant. The majority of production goes to the Ship with the remainder going to local free trade. ‼♦

Kiln (OG 1038, ABV 3.8%)

Blonde (OG 1040, ABV 4%)

Best Bitter (OG 1041, ABV 4.1%)

Roundabout (OG 1043, ABV 4.3%)

Brunette (OG 1045, ABV 4.5%)

Greg's SIBA

⊟ Dambusters Inn, 23 High Street, Scampton, Lincolnshire, LN1 2SD

☎ (01522) 730123 ⊕ gregsbrewery.com

Greg's is a microbrewery launched in 2013 on the premises of the Dambusters Inn. Following recent expansion, head brewer Greg Algar, landlord of the pub, has been joined by Joe Asplin. ♦

Navigator (OG 1040, ABV 3.6%)
A fresh, hoppy pale ale with plenty of fruit and a floral aroma producing light bitterness.

Aviator (OG 1042, ABV 3.8%)
A golden ale with moderate bitterness and floral and citrus characteristics.

Final Approach (OG 1045, ABV 4.2%)
A rich, smooth best bitter with an autumn fruit and caramel aroma and satisfying finish.

Grey Friars (NEW) SIBA

Featherstone Hall Farm, New Road, Featherstone, Staffordshire, WV10 7NW
☎ (01785) 840093 ☎ 07966 361443

17 Cranbrooks, Wheaton Aston, Staffordshire, ST19 9PZ ⊕ greyfriarsbrewery.co.uk

Established in 2014 and using equipment originally from Upham Brewery, Hampshire, the three-barrel plant is installed in a barn, formerly used as a snooker room and which still contains the original wood panelling.

Bobby (ABV 4%)

Auld Jock (ABV 4.7%)
A golden ale with a sweet initial taste, a hint of citrus and clean finish on the palate.

Grey Trees SIBA ◉

Unit 5-6, Gasworks Road, Aberaman, CF44 6RS
☎ (01685) 267077 ⊕ greytreesbrewery.com

Grey Trees began brewing at the Red Cow Inn in 2011 on the outskirts of Aberdare and relocated to its present location in 2013, upgrading to a 10-barrel plant originally used by Breconshire, with five fermentation vessels. It supplies an increasing number of local outlets, as well as in other parts of South Wales. There are a number of open nights throughout the year (see website for details). ‼RAIB

Caradog's Bitter (OG 1038, ABV 3.9%)

A copper-coloured ale with a crisp flavour and a dry finish.

Black Road Stout (OG 1040, ABV 4%)
A dark, smooth stout with delicate roasted flavours and a bittersweet aftertaste.

Diggers Gold (OG 1040, ABV 4%)
A golden ale with fresh citrus aromas and a subtle bitterness.

Drummer Boy (OG 1042, ABV 4.2%)

Valley Porter (OG 1046, ABV 4.6%)
Warming and rich, with notes of dark fruits, coffee, chocolate and hazelnuts.

JPR Pale (OG 1046, ABV 4.7%)
A traditional British pale ale, well-balanced with a citrus aroma and taste.

Afghan Pale Ale (OG 1054, ABV 5.4%)
Brewed in the style of an American pale ale. Full-flavoured, crisp and thirst quenching.

Greyhawk (NEW)

Units 3 & 4, Enterprise Way, Airedale Business Centre, Skipton, North Yorkshire, BD23 2TZ
☎ (01756) 701289 ⊕ greyhawkbrewery.co.uk

Beers are brewed on a five-barrel, artisanal plant of Bavarian design. Two regular beers are currently available, shortly to be supplemented by a limited-edition range. There are plans to offer specially tailored 'brewer for the day' courses. ‼🍽

Blonde Obsession (OG 1040, ABV 4%)
A full-flavoured blonde ale.

Nirvana Pale (ABV 4.3%)
A well-balanced pale beer with a hoppy aroma and increasing bitterness.

Brewed for Copper Dragon (qv):

Black Gold (OG 1036, ABV 3.7%)

Best Bitter (OG 1036, ABV 3.8%)

Golden Pippin (OG 1037, ABV 3.9%)

Scotts 1816 (OG 1041, ABV 4.1%)

Greyhound (NEW) SIBA

Watershed, Smock Alley, West Chiltington, RH20 2QX
☎ 07973 625510 ⊕ greyhoundbrewery.co.uk

Brewing began in 2012 in the kitchen of the brewers' home, moving to the garage as production increased. The first commercial brew was in 2015. The brewery now uses a five-barrel plant, producing up to 2000 litres a month. Cask-conditioned beers are supplied to local pubs and beer festivals; bottle-conditioned beers are supplied both to local and London-based restaurants. RAIB

Good Ordinary Bitter (ABV 3.8%)

Special Blonde (ABV 3.9%)

Amber Eyes (ABV 4.2%)

Special B46 (ABV 4.6%)

Rainbow Eyes (ABV 4.8%)

Gribble

⊟ Gribble Inn, Oving, West Sussex, PO20 2BP
☎ (01243) 786893 ⊕ gribbleinn.co.uk

⊠ Established in 1980 using a five-barrel plant, the Gribble Brewery is the longest-serving brewpub in the Sussex area. Independently owned and run by the licensees. A number of local outlets are supplied. ☛♦

CHI P A (OG 1040, ABV 3.8%)

Gribble Ale (OG 1041, ABV 4.1%)

Fuzzy Duck (OG 1045, ABV 4.3%)

Reg's Tipple (OG 1050, ABV 4.8%)
Named after a customer from the early days of the brewery. It has a smooth nutty flavour with a pleasant afterbite.

Plucking Pheasant (OG 1052, ABV 5%)

Pig's Ear (OG 1058, ABV 6%)

Wobbler (OG 1058, ABV 7.2%)

Griffin

⬚ Church Road, Shustoke, Warwickshire, B46 2LB
☎ (01675) 481205 ⊕ griffininnshustoke.co.uk

Brewing started in 2008 in the old coffin shop premises adjacent to the Griffin Inn. The five-barrel brewery is a venture between Griffin licensee Mick Pugh and his son Oliver. Most output goes to the pub, but free trade presence is increasing. ‼♦

Dark Mild (OG 1028, ABV 2.8%)
Dry, assertive mild with a good roasty character.

Pale (OG 1044, ABV 4.4%)

Yeti (OG 1047, ABV 4.7%)
A light-coloured pale ale, with a grapefruit aftertaste.

Black Magic Woman (OG 1050, ABV 5%)

GT

Unit 5, The Old Aerodrome, Chivenor Business Park, Braunton, Devon, EX31 4AY ☎ 07909 515170
⊕ gtales.co.uk

⊠ GT Ales started in Barnstaple in 2013, producing only bottle-conditioned beers, before relocating to larger premises in Braunton in 2015. It now also brews cask ale. A brand new five-barrel plant purchased from Oban Ales has been installed. More than 20 local outlets are supplied. ♦RAIB

Thirst of Many (OG 1043, ABV 4.2%)
An amber-coloured best bitter with a fruity taste and hint of caramel. Good medium hop finish and a slight malty taste.

Natural Blonde (OG 1044, ABV 4.5%)
A refreshing, pale golden-coloured ale with hop and citrus/gooseberry notes and a floral aroma.

Gun (NEW) SIBA ◉

Hawthbush Farm, Gun Hill, Heathfield, East Sussex, TN21 0JY
☎ (01323) 700200 ☎ 07900 683355
⊕ gunbrewery.co.uk

⊠ Gun Brewery is located on a beautiful 140-acre organic mixed farm in the Sussex Weald. It generates much of its own power from a 15-kW solar array and heating comes from a wood-powered boiler. Spent grains keep the local livestock happy and all the water used for brewing comes from the brewery's own spring. The beers (except Parabellum) are suitable for vegans and are supplied to more than 20 outlets.
RAIB

Scaramanga Pale Ale (OG 1038, ABV 3.8%)

Parabellum Milk Stout (OG 1057, ABV 4.1%)
A well-balanced stout with chocolate flavours in the finish.

Project Babylon Pale Ale (OG 1049, ABV 5%)
A full-flavoured, pale beer with strong citrus notes.

Zamzama IPA (OG 1060, ABV 6.5%)

Gun Dog Ales SIBA

Unit 5b, Great Central Way, Woodford Halse, Northamptonshire, NN11 3PZ
☎ (01327) 264095 ⊕ gundogales.co.uk

Gun Dog began brewing in 2012 using a six-barrel plant. All beers are also available bottle conditioned. ‼☛♦RAIB

Jack's Spaniels (OG 1038, ABV 3.8%)
A floral, refreshing blonde ale made with a blend of malt and Cascade hops.

Booze Hound (OG 1042, ABV 4.2%)
A copper-coloured IPA with a slightly sweet taste and a bitter finish.

Lord Barker (OG 1042, ABV 4.2%)
A rich, dark, smooth and well-balanced stout with a chocolate aroma, rounded flavour and a clean finish.

Bad to the Bone (OG 1045, ABV 4.5%)
A light brown English-style bitter with biscuit undertones and a fruity hop finish.

Gundog

See Acton

Gwaun Valley

Kilkiffeth Farm, Pontfaen, SA65 9TP
☎ (01348) 881304 ⊕ gwaunvalleybrewery.co.uk

Gwaun Valley began brewing in 2009 on a four-barrel plant in a converted granary. The brewery offers views of the Presel Hills and has a camp site, a holiday cottage and pitches for five caravans. ‼☛

Bitter Ale (OG 1040, ABV 4%)

Farmhouse Ale (OG 1040, ABV 4%)
A malty ale with a smooth, balanced character.

Golden Bitter Ale (OG 1040, ABV 4%)
A smooth bitter ale with a strong hoppy flavour and a crisp finish.

Light Ale (OG 1040, ABV 4%)
Refreshing and easy drinking with citrus undertones and a clean finish.

St Davids Special (OG 1040, ABV 4%)
A light, fruity beer with a refreshing citrus flavour.

Blodwen (OG 1041, ABV 4.1%)
Creamy, full-bodied bitter, ruby red in colour with a hint of caramel.

Pembrokeshire Best (OG 1045, ABV 4.5%)
A full-flavoured, malty bitter ale with a hoppy finish.

Calon Lan (OG 1048, ABV 4.8%)

Malty with a medium body and a bittersweet aftertaste.

Gyle 59 SIBA

The Brewery, Sadborrow Estate Yard, Thorncombe, Dorset, TA20 4PW
☎ (01297) 678990 ☎ 07833 204543 🌐 gyle59.co.uk

⊗ Gyle 59 is a 10-barrel brewery that began commercial production in 2014. All beers are unfined and available cask and bottle-conditioned. Bottling takes place on site with bottles being available by mail order. Beer can be bought at the brewery and a shop is planned. !! ♦ RAIB

Freedom Hiker (OG 1038, ABV 3.7%)
Session bitter.

Happy Daze (OG 1040, ABV 4%)
A wheat beer with a hint of banana and coriander.

Toujours (OG 1042, ABV 4%)
A Saison-style beer.

Halcyon Daze (OG 1046.5, ABV 5%)

Pale & Bitter (OG 1046, ABV 5%)
A strong pale ale.

IPA (OG 1050, ABV 5.3%)

Dorset Gipa (OG 1050, ABV 5.4%)
A ginger-infused IPA.

Dark & Bitter (OG 1054, ABV 5.8%)
A black IPA.

Favourite (OG 1060, ABV 6.6%)
A smooth, rich porter.

Starstruck (OG 1060, ABV 6.6%)
A fruity porter enhanced by the addition of star anise.

IPA Strong (OG 1063, ABV 7.2%)

Hackney SIBA

Arch 358, Laburnum Street, Hackney, London, E2 8BB
☎ (020) 3489 9595 🌐 hackneybrewery.co.uk

⊗ Having met eight years ago while working at the Eagle on Farringdon Road, home brewers and good friends Jon Swain and Peter Hills decided to turn their pastime in to a profession and brew beer in the heart of Hackney. They are committed to supporting local charities. RAIB

Golden Ale (OG 1041, ABV 4%) ◆
A light fruity ale with a malty biscuit quality. A touch of dryness and a pleasant bitterness in the finish.

Best Bitter (OG 1044, ABV 4.4%) ◆
Malty sweetness is present with trace of toffee. Hop notes and a fruit-cocktail flavour diminish in the dry aftertaste.

American Pale Ale (OG 1045, ABV 4.5%) ◆
Copper brown beer with a sweet citrus aroma and full, smooth mouthfeel. Citrus and floral hops on the palate .

New Zealand Pale Ale (OG 1045, ABV 4.5%)
Pale ale with a fruity hop aroma. Residual sweetness and fruity hop on the taste.

Hadrian Border

Unit 5, The Preserving Works, Newburn Industrial Estate, Shelley Road, Newburn, Newcastle upon Tyne, NE15 9RT
☎ (0191) 264 9000 🌐 hadrian-border-brewery.co.uk

Originally based at the Four Rivers site in Newcastle, the brewery relocated to Newburn in 2011 with a new 30-barrel brew plant to meet increased demand. Core brands, available nationally via wholesalers, are popular throughout Tyneside, Northumberland, Edinburgh, Glasgow and Yorkshire. !! ♦ RAIB

Tyneside Blonde (OG 1037, ABV 3.9%) ◆
Refreshing blonde ale with zesty notes and a clean, fruity finish.

Farne Island Pale Ale (OG 1038, ABV 4%) ◆
A copper-coloured bitter with a refreshing malt/hop balance.

Flotsam (OG 1038, ABV 4%)
Bronze-coloured with a citrus bitterness and a distinctive floral aroma.

Newburn No.1 (OG 1041, ABV 4.1%) ◆
Light amber ale, well-hopped with only Pioneer to give a light spicy/fruity finish.

Needles and Pins (OG 1041.5, ABV 4.2%)
Dark amber-coloured beer, fruity and well-bodied.

Secret Kingdom (OG 1042, ABV 4.3%)
Dark, rich and full-bodied, slightly roasted with a malty palate ending with a pleasant bitterness.

Coast to Coast (OG 1041.5, ABV 4.4%)
Light amber and hoppy beer with a good malt balance.

Reiver's IPA (OG 1042, ABV 4.4%)
Golden bitter with a clean citrus palate and aroma with subtle malt flavours breaking through at the end.

Jetsam (OG 1043, ABV 4.5%)

Northumbrian Gold (OG 1044, ABV 4.5%)

Grainger Ale (OG 1045, ABV 4.6%)
Brewed using a single malt, and hopped with a selection of three varieties giving a well-balanced, refreshingly bitter finish.

Hafod

Old Gas Works, Gas Lane, Mold, CH7 1UR ☎ 07901 386638 🌐 welshbeer.com

◎Hafod began brewing in 2011 on a small scale and moved to new premises in 2014 to provide additional capacity. A number of speciality beers using ingredients from the local upland areas and heathlands are also produced on a limited basis. ♦ RAIB

Taverns Tipple (OG 1034.5, ABV 3.5%)

Classic (OG 1036.5, ABV 3.8%) ◆
Copper-coloured, smooth and full-bodied. Juicy malt taste with some initial toffee flavours and hops developing in the aftertaste.

Moel Famau Ale (OG 1039, ABV 4.1%) ◆
A speciality dark ale brewed using local heather giving a dry, roasty taste with underlying sweet malt flavours.

H:E (OG 1040.5, ABV 4.3%) ◆
A clean-tasting best bitter, pale and hoppy with hints of vanilla in the dry taste.

Hopper (OG 1040.5, ABV 4.3%) ◀
A full-flavoured session bitter with a mouthwatering taste of peppery hops and a lasting dry finish.

Moel Fenlli (OG 1045, ABV 4.4%)
A speciality golden ale made with heather honey.

Moel Arthur (OG 1046, ABV 4.5%)
Seasonal fruity favourite crafted with Clwydian Range bilberries.

Hammer (OG 1059, ABV 6.6%) ◀
A sweet, strong bitter full of tropical fruits in aroma and taste, balanced by a powerful hoppy finish.

Hale's (NEW)

Walters Yard, Unit 3, Claylands Industrial Estate, Worksop, Nottinghamshire, S81 7DW ☎ 07436 282779 ✉ susanhale1865@gmail.com

Owners Suzi and Richard Hale founded the brewery in 2013, initially producing small test brews sold at the Grafton Hotel, Worksop. A bottling plant enables contract bottling for other microbreweries. ◆

Sacred Heart (OG 1034, ABV 3.6%)
Golden-coloured session ale, low in strength but with bags of flavour.

Fallen Heart (OG 1041, ABV 4.3%)
Easy-drinking, mid-brown traditional bitter.

Fire Heart (OG 1046, ABV 4.8%)
An orange/red-coloured ale with spicy overtones on the palate.

Ice Heart (OG 1046, ABV 4.8%)
An extra pale ale with a well-balanced taste and citrus overtones.

Black Heart (OG 1048, ABV 5%)
A black IPA. The combination of German malts allow the flavours of the hops to come through with a little roast flavour.

Half Moon SIBA ◉

Forge House, Main Street, Ellerton, East Yorkshire, YO42 4PB
☎ (01757) 288977 ☎ 07741 400508
⊕ halfmoonbrewery.co.uk

Established in 2013 by Tony and Jackie Rogers, the brewery is based in the original blacksmith's forge next to their house. A five-barrel plant produces three core beers and a monthly special. Ales are available in the local and surrounding areas. ◆

Dark Masquerade (OG 1039, ABV 3.6%)
A rich ruby-coloured ale packed with dark chocolate and liquorice flavours.

Galileo (OG 1039, ABV 3.8%)
A bright, blonde ale with refreshing citrus notes and a crisp finish.

Old Forge Bitter (OG 1039, ABV 3.8%)
A bright, amber-coloured ale with a soft spiced lemon and honeyed flavour.

Halfpenny

▤ **Crown Inn, High Street, Lechlade, Gloucestershire, GL7 3AE**
☎ (01367) 252198 ☎ 07585 440369
⊕ halfpennybrewery.co.uk

⊠ Halfpenny was established in 2008 on a four-barrel plant at the Crown at Lechlade, visible in a glazed outbuilding, and has since expanded to a third fermentation vessel. Currently brewing only for the pub. !! ⇛RAIB

Thames Tickler (OG 1040, ABV 4%)

Old Lech (OG 1045, ABV 4.5%)

Halifax Steam

▤ **The Conclave, Southedge Works, Brighouse Road, Hipperholme, West Yorkshire, HX3 8EF** ☎ 07974 544980 ⊕ halifax-steam.co.uk

☺Brewing since 1999, the five-barrel plant supplies only the brewery tap, the Cock o' the North. A range of permanent beers and around 200 different rotating beers are brewed, including the only rice beers in the country. 10-12 Halifax Steam beers are available in the pub at any one time, plus occasional guests on a fair trade basis. ◆

Aussie Kiss (OG 1038, ABV 3.8%)
Light beer with a hoppy flavour and finish.

Uncle Jon (OG 1043, ABV 4.3%) ◀
Roast predominates in this creamy, dark brown stout. The finish is smooth with no harsh edges.

Childcatcher (OG 1048, ABV 4.8%)
Pale-coloured, smooth-drinking beer with a citrus hop aroma and flavour.

Hall & Woodhouse (Badger) IFBB ◉

Bournemouth Road, Blandford St Mary, Blandford Forum, Dorset, DT11 9LS
☎ (01258) 452141 ⊕ hall-woodhouse.co.uk

⊠ Hall & Woodhouse has been brewing in the heart of the Dorset countryside since 1777. As one of the leading independent brewers in the UK, Hall & Woodhouse is well known for its range of award-winning ales brewed under the Badger brand and its estate of more than 200 pubs across the south of England. The brewery, owned and run by the seventh generation of the Woodhouse family, brews with Dorset spring water filtered through the Cretaceous chalk downs and drawn-up 120 feet from the its own wells. Badger cask ales are available exclusively in Hall & Woodhouse public houses. !! ⇛ ◆

K&B Sussex Bitter (OG 1036, ABV 3.5%) ◀
Traditional, lightly-hopped, easy-drinking session bitter with hints of malt and caramel and the traditional Badger fruit flavour predominating in the lingering bitter aftertaste.

Badger First Call (OG 1041, ABV 4%) ◀
Fine example of a best bitter with good, but not over-powering, hop aromas and flavours and a good bittersweet aftertaste.

Tanglefoot (OG 1047, ABV 4.9%) ◀
Relatively sweet-tasting and deceptive, given its strength. Pale malt provides caramel overtones and a bittersweet finish.

Hambleton SIBA ◉

Melmerby Green Road, Melmerby, North Yorkshire, HG4 5NB
☎ (01765) 640108 ⊕ hambletonales.co.uk

☺Established in 1991 on the banks of the River Swale in the Vale of York, after several moves

Hambleton now occupies purpose-built premises. Capacity is 100 barrels a week with a monthly special supplementing the core range. Village Brewer and Black Dog beers are contract brewed and a bottling line handles more than 50 brands for other brewers. ‼◆

Bitter (OG 1038.5, ABV 3.8%)
A golden bitter with a good balance of malty and refreshing citrus notes leading to a mellow, tangy finish.

Stallion (OG 1041, ABV 4.2%) ◗
A premium bitter, moderately hoppy throughout and richly balanced in malt and fruit, developing a sound and robust bitterness, with earthy hops drying the aftertaste.

Stud (OG 1042.5, ABV 4.3%) ◗
A strongly bitter beer, with rich hop and fruit. It ends dry and spicy.

Nightmare (OG 1050, ABV 5%) ▱ ◗
This impressively flavoured beer satisfies all parts of the palate. Strong roast malts dominate, but hoppiness rears out of this complex blend.

Contract brewed for Black Dog Brewery, Whitby:

Whitby Abbey Ale (OG 1037.5, ABV 3.8%)

Schooner (OG 1041.5, ABV 4.2%)

Rhatas (OG 1045, ABV 4.6%)

Contract brewed for Village Brewer:

White Boar (OG 1037.5, ABV 3.8%)

Bull (OG 1039, ABV 4%)

Hamelsworde

16 Longworth Road, Hemsworth, West Yorkshire, WF9 4SZ ☎ 07530 669332 ⊕ hamelsworde.co.uk

The brainchild of enthusiastic home brewer Dan Jones, his beers were originally brewed using a 50-litre boiler in a converted garage. A one-barrel plant was installed in 2013. RAIB

Spanish Stout (OG 1045, ABV 4.2%)
A traditional stout with strong roasted flavours and a sweet liquorice taste complemented by aniseed.

Haley's Comet (OG 1047, ABV 4.5%)
A fresh, light summery ale with a citrus aroma and taste.

Jumping Pirate (OG 1051, ABV 4.9%)
A light golden ale in a Bavarian style, brewed with German Hallertau and Tettnanger hops, it has floral, pine and citrus notes which makes this a complex beer, smooth on the finish.

Colin Brown Ale (OG 1054, ABV 5.2%)
A fruity hop aroma leads to a malty, nutty bittersweet flavour with a long, dry aftertaste while the late addition of Cascade hops creates a citrus burst.

Scalded Shoulder (OG 1054, ABV 5.2%)
A refreshing golden wheat beer, single-hopped with Saaz hops and finished with coriander and orange.

Cherokee America IPA (OG 1063, ABV 6%)
A copper-coloured IPA with a strong, fruity hop aroma.

Hammerpot SIBA

Unit 30, The Vinery, Arundel Road, Poling, West Sussex, BN18 9PY ☎ (01903) 883338 ⊕ hammerpot-brewery.co.uk

⊗ Hammerpot started brewing in 2005 using a five-barrel plant, which was upgraded to 10 barrels in 2011. The brewery supplies as far as London and Southampton. ◆RAIB

Shooting Star (OG 1038, ABV 3.8%)

HPA (OG 1044, ABV 4.1%)
A light, golden-coloured, tangy pale ale with a full, fresh hop flavour.

Red Hunter (OG 1046, ABV 4.3%)
A ruby red bitter with a full-bodied, rich character. A premium bitter that drinks smoothly, leaving a fine lace in the glass.

Woodcote (OG 1047, ABV 4.5%)
A tangy amber-coloured bitter with a pleasant dry finish.

Brighton Belle (ABV 4.6%)
Pale amber-coloured bitter. Fresh floral hops notes, spicy orange, crisp grapefruit and a hint of caramel.

Bottle Wreck Porter (OG 1047, ABV 4.7%)
A traditional pitch black porter with coffee, chocolate and rich roast malt flavours.

Madgwick Gold (OG 1050, ABV 5%)
A refreshing golden ale with a fresh citrus spice hop aroma.

Hammerton SIBA ◉

Unit 8 & 9, Roman Way Industrial Estate, 149 Roman Way, Barnsbury, London, N7 8XH ☎ (020) 3302 5880 ⊕ hammertonbrewery.co.uk

Hammerton Brewery began brewing in London in 1868. It ceased to brew in the late 1950s and the brewery was later demolished. In 2014, a member of the Hammerton family decided to resurrect the family name in brewing. A 15-barrel plant is used. RAIB

Oyster Stout (ABV 4.2%) ◗
Liquorice and fruit on the palate. Dry finish with a little dark roast character and a touch of caramelised fruit.

Hand Drawn Monkey

Plover Road Garage, Plover Road, Lindley, Huddersfield, West Yorkshire, HD3 3HS ☎ (01484) 655262 ☎ 07739 754816 ⊕ hdmbeer.com

Hand Drawn Monkey commenced brewing on the Mallinson's Brewery plant during 2012 and took over the plant after Mallinson's moved premises.

Malpa (OG 1039, ABV 3.9%)

Pale Ale (OG 1040, ABV 4%)

Monkeys Love Hops (OG 1042, ABV 4.2%)

What Would Jephers Do (OG 1045, ABV 4.5%)

Porter (OG 1048, ABV 4.8%)

IPA (OG 1050, ABV 5%)

Double Belgium (OG 1060, ABV 6%)

Handley's

🍺 Willow Tree, Front Street, Barnby in the Willows, Nottinghamshire, NG24 2SA
☎ (01636) 629003 ⊕ willowtreebarnby.co.uk

Handley's began brewing in 2011 on a 0.5-barrel plant installed behind the Willow Tree pub by owner Brett Handley. Beer is mostly sold in the pub but can be found at beer festivals and in other outlets if stocks permit.

Handmade SIBA

Ffos Y Ffin Fawr, Capel Dewi, SA32 8AG
☎ (01559) 371784 ☎ 07896 690020
⊕ handmadebeer.co.uk

Brewing began in 2013. The brewery is situated in a farm shed off the beaten track. The plant and site were previously used by the Ffos y Ffin Brewery.
◆ RAIB

Cwrw Sir Gar (OG 1040, ABV 4%)

Pale Ale (OG 1042, ABV 4.2%)

Welsh Gold (OG 1042, ABV 4.2%)

Special Bitter (OG 1045, ABV 4.5%)

Hanlons SIBA 👁

Hill Farm, Half Moon Village, Newton St Cyres, Devon, EX5 5AE
☎ (01392) 851160 ⊕ hanlonsbrewery.com

Formerly known as O'Hanlons, the brewery moved to Half Moon, near Exeter, in 2013. More than 400 outlets are supplied nationwide. The building comprises a shop and a bar/restaurant. ‼ 🍺

Firefly (OG 1035, ABV 3.7%) ◄
Malty and fruity light bitter. Hints of orange in the taste.

Copper Glow (OG 1042, ABV 4.2%)
Copper-coloured ale with a hint of toffee, light bitterness and aroma. Malty, fruity tastes combine with the definite perfume of rich roast barley.

Dry Stout (OG 1043, ABV 4.2%) ◄
A dark malty, well-balanced stout with a dry, bitter finish and plenty of roast and fruit flavours up front.

Yellowhammer (OG 1041, ABV 4.2%) ◄
A well-balanced, smooth pale yellow beer with a predominant hop and fruit nose and taste, leading to a dry, bitter finish.

Port Stout (OG 1041, ABV 4.8%) ▦ ◄
A black beer with roast malt in the aroma that remains in the taste but gives way to hoppy bitterness in the aftertaste.

Stormstay (OG 1048, ABV 5%)
Amber-coloured ale with a toffee and floral hop nose and hints of tangerine. Malt, caramel and biscuit nestle with the three aroma hops.

Happy Valley

8 Hazelhurst Drive, Bollington, Cheshire, SK10 5QT
☎ 07758 512080 ⊕ happyvalleybrewery.co.uk

⊠ Happy Valley was established in 2010 by David and Nicola Hughes using a 2.5-barrel plant. Pubs are supplied in Cheshire, Derbyshire, Greater Manchester and Staffordshire. ‼◆

Old Mill Town (OG 1036, ABV 3.6%)

A traditional dark mild.

Small & Mighty (OG 1036, ABV 3.6%)
A clean, crisp and refreshing ale. A lasting, floral, citrus aroma with a hint of lemon.

Sworn Secret (OG 1038, ABV 3.8%)
Pale straw-coloured ale with a strong hop character. It has a pleasant hoppy nose with a citrus aftertaste.

Little Rascal (OG 1039, ABV 3.9%)
A golden session ale, well-balanced with a lingering citrus and grapefruit aftertaste.

Five Rings (OG 1040, ABV 4%)
Crisp, clean tasting ale.

Lazy Daze (OG 1042, ABV 4.2%)
Golden-coloured ale with a hoppy finish.

Black Out XO Rum Porter (OG 1044, ABV 4.4%)
A dark, full-bodied porter with a deep, intense malty flavour. Dark roasted and chocolate malts with a lingering aroma of Barbadian oak-aged rum.

Black Magic (OG 1046, ABV 4.6%)
A full-bodied stout.

Tie the Knot (OG 1050, ABV 5%)
A straw-coloured strong bitter with malt tastes and big hop character.

Dangerously Dark (OG 1056, ABV 5.6%)
A black IPA-style beer.

Bollywood IPA (OG 1058, ABV 5.9%)
A full-bodied, straw-coloured strong bitter with rounded malt flavours blended with bitterness and a big hop character. Deep and intensely rich taste.

Harbour SIBA

Trekillick Farm, Kirland, Bodmin, Cornwall, PL30 5BB
☎ (01208) 832131 ☎ 07870 305063
⊕ harbourbrewing.com

⊠ Harbour is an innovative 10-barrel brewery founded on the outskirts of Bodmin in 2011. Brewed using local spring water, the regular beers are established in an increasing number of outlets.

Light (OG 1037, ABV 3.7%) ◄
Light, golden ale with hop aroma. Hops dominate the taste with some pineapple, citrus and pear drops. Hoppy, dry finish.

Amber (OG 1037.5, ABV 4%) ◄
Pale brown bitter with a floral hop aroma. Peach and citrus flavours with biscuit malt. Quite sweet taste and finish.

IPA (OG 1048.5, ABV 5%) ◄
Amber-coloured strong bitter-cum-golden ale with heady citrus hop aroma. Hoppy, bitter taste and finish with citrus fruits but subdued malt.

Porter (OG 1055, ABV 5.5%) ◄
Smooth, creamy, black porter with roast malt aroma. Malty, smoky and sweet followed by a bitter tang. Sweet finish.

Harbour Pale (OG 1059, ABV 6%) ◄
Amber strong bitter with powerful citrus hop aroma. Intense citrus hop flavour with marmalade, orange and bitterness. Hoppy, dry finish.

Hardhead SIBA

Unit 26, Pensilva Industrial Estate, Pensilva, Cornwall, PL14 5RE

☎ (01208) 590707 ☎ 07763 766106
⏚ hardheadbrewery.co.uk

⊠ Hardhead is a three-barrel brewery situated on the southern edge of Bodmin Moor, established in 2014. Brewing is currently suspended. ◆

Hardknott SIBA

Unit 10, Devonshire Road Industrial Estate, Millom, Cumbria, LA18 4JS
☎ (01229) 779309 ⏚ hardknott.com

☺Hardknott began brewing in 2005 at the Woolpack Inn in Boot. The brewery relocated to Millom and expanded in 2010. It supplies beers both nationally and internationally, in a variety of formats. The 16-hectolitre brewhouse is complemented with modern multi-purpose fermentation tanks and a bottling line. !! ◆ RAIB

Katalyst (OG 1040, ABV 3.8%) ◄
An assertively hoppy, bitter beer, with a sweet fruity taste which diminishes in the finish.

Lux Borealis (OG 1038, ABV 3.8%) ◄
Fruity, hoppy aromas lead to a well-balanced middle with hops increasing in the finish.

Continuum (OG 1042, ABV 4%) ◄
An amber-coloured beer with pronounced hops and bitterness right through to the aftertaste. Some maltiness in the aroma and taste.

Cool Fusion (OG 1044, ABV 4.4%) ◄
A well-balanced, mild sweet beer with ginger. The ginger bite builds in the finish.

Duality (OG 1044, ABV 4.5%)

Dark Energy (OG 1052, ABV 4.9%) ◄
A hoppy aroma leads to a dry hoppy beer with plenty of roast.

Code Black (OG 1056, ABV 5.6%) ◄
High impact hops and roast malt leave a lasting impression.

Azimuth (OG 1057, ABV 5.8%) ◄
Floral and fruity esters and lots of interesting hops and some complex bitterness create a fascinating tasting experience.

Infra Red (OG 1065, ABV 6.2%)
Hints of toffee and popcorn. Citrus fruits dominate.

Hardys & Hansons

See Greene King

Haresfoot SIBA ◉

2 River Park Industrial Estate, Billet Lane, Berkhamsted, Hertfordshire, HP4 1HL
☎ (01442) 862878 ⏚ haresfoot.com

⊠ Brewing returned to the heart of Berkhamsted in 2014 after an absence of 100 years. The brewery, established by a consortium of eight local businessmen, is situated in an industrial unit close to the Grand Union Canal. Four core beers are produced on the dual channel 12 and 2.5-barrel plant. !! ☛

Sundial Golden Ale (OG 1038, ABV 3.8%)
A refreshing light golden ale with generous late hopping leading to an undercurrent of exotic fruits.

Lock Keeper's Launch Ale (OG 1039, ABV 3.9%)

A complex blend of malts with a hoppy edge and delicate fruit notes, leading to a long bittersweet aftertaste.

Conqueror's Premium Bitter (OG 1043, ABV 4.4%)
A full-bodied bitter with roasted barley creating a chestnut-coloured ale with a lingering malty taste and rounded bitter finish.

Totem American IPA (OG 1042, ABV 4.5%)
American-style IPA which explodes with citrus flavours and hop aromas all balanced by subtle malt character.

Harrogate SIBA

41 Claro Court Business Centre, Harrogate, North Yorkshire, HG1 4BA ☎ 07774 891664
⏚ harrogatebrewery.co.uk

Started in 2013, the brewery also uses the name Spa Town Ales on the pumpclips for its range of ales.

Tewit Well Ale (OG 1041, ABV 4.1%)
Copper-coloured traditional Yorkshire bitter tasting of malt, spices and orange peel.

Stray Ale (OG 1042, ABV 4.2%)
Golden ale with a spicy flavour and lingering hop finish.

Pinewoods Pale Ale (OG 1044, ABV 4.4%)
Pale beer with citrus hoppy flavours.

Hornbeam (OG 1045, ABV 4.5%)
A copper-coloured beer, fruity and hoppy.

No. 5 Porter (OG 1053, ABV 5.1%)
A rich, fruity dark beer, ruby brown in colour with roasted malt, fruit and spice.

Pump Room (OG 1055, ABV 5.4%)
Ruby-coloured, rich, dark and fruity beer.

Kursaal Porter (OG 1069, ABV 6.9%)
A rich, bittersweet example of the style tasting of espresso, liquorice and chocolate.

Hart Family SIBA

The 1833 Brewery, 21 Nene Court, The Embankment, Wellingborough, Northamptonshire, NN8 1LD
☎ (01933) 228324 ☎ 07891 212476
⏚ hartfamilybrewers.com

⊠ Hart Family Brewers was established in 2012 using an eight-barrel plant. It is owned and operated by Rob and Sarah Hart, who are indulging their passion after a combined 25 years in the drinks industry. Recent expansion including a third fermenter gives weekly production of up to 38 barrels a week. !! ☛ RAIB

House Beer (OG 1036, ABV 3.6%)
A classic country bitter with straightforward flavours of British malt and English hops.

Harts No 1 (OG 1043, ABV 4.1%)
A tawny-coloured premium bitter with fruity, malty aromas and grassy, citrus notes. Fresh and fruity on the palate with spicy bitterness and citrus, hay-like aromas on the refreshing finish.

Harts No 9 (OG 1044, ABV 4.3%)
A golden beer, light and refreshing with spicy grapefruit aromas. Fresh and light on the palate with pithy grapefruit flavours supported by biscuity malt.

Harts No 3 (OG 1047, ABV 4.7%)

A fruity ruby-coloured beer with full malty, spicy aromas. Full on the palate with rounded, rich malty flavours supported by gentle spicy hoppiness.

Harts No 8 (OG 1052, ABV 5%)
A dark beer with bold toasted fruit aromas and hints of espresso. Full and warming roasted fruit and molasses flavours balanced by bitter coffee, chocolate and spice aromas over a long finish.

Pale (OG 1052, ABV 5%)
Strong bitter beer. Biscuity malt complemented by a marked orange-scented bitterness.

Hart of Preston SIBA

Unit 5, Oxhey Trading Estate, Greenbank Street, Preston, Lancashire, PR1 7PH
☎ (01772) 437651 ⊕ hartbreweryltd.co.uk

☺Hart opened in 1995 behind the Cartford Hotel in Little Eccleston. In 2010 the brewery relocated to Preston. It supplies a number of local outlets.
‼◆RAIB

Pale Ale (OG 1039, ABV 3.8%)
An easy-drinking beer with a hoppy finish.

Lancashire Best Bitter (OG 1039, ABV 3.9%)
A premium golden ale.

Ice Maiden (OG 1040, ABV 4%) ◄
Hoppy, crisp, straw-coloured bitter with floral notes and a dry finish.

Lord of the Glen (ABV 4.2%)

EPA (ABV 4.5%)

Victorian Oyster Stout (ABV 5.5%)

Hart of Stebbing

▤ White Hart, High Street, Stebbing, Essex, CM6 3SQ
☎ (01371) 856383 ⊕ hartofstebbingbrewery.co.uk

☒ The brewery was established in 2007 by Bob Dovey and Nick Eldred, who is also the owner of the White Hart pub where the brewery is based. At present only the White Hart and local beer festivals are supplied. ◆

Hart IPA (OG 1035, ABV 3.5%)

Harthill Village SIBA

Union Street, Harthill, South Yorkshire, S26 7YH
☎ 07736 246474 ⊕ harthillbrewery.co.uk

Brewing began in 2013 using a five-barrel plant supplying local pubs, clubs and shops. ◆

Ace of Harts (OG 1039, ABV 3.9%)
A traditional, well-balanced amber bitter with a subtle malty sweetness and spicy, fruity aroma.

Hart Stopper (OG 1040, ABV 4%)
Hoppy blonde ale with a fresh aroma of citrus and berry fruits with hints of zest and spice.

Hart's Desire (OG 1044, ABV 4.4%)
An amber-coloured premium ale with a fresh aroma of citrus with floral and spicy notes balanced with biscuity, malty, sweet flavours.

Dark Hart (OG 1050, ABV 4.8%)
A rich, smooth, full-bodied dark ale with a toffee, malty sweetness and a dry, biscuity fullness complemented by the spicy, blackcurrant aroma.

Hart of Steel (OG 1056, ABV 5.5%)

A refreshing golden ale with vibrant aromas of pine and citrus. A sweet, malty flavour complements the hops.

Dark Hart Festival Reserve (OG 1068, ABV 6.5%)
Premium version of Dark Hart with an increased intensity of flavour and hoppy finish.

Hartshorns

Unit 4, Tomlinsons Industrial Estate, Alfreton Road, Derby, DE21 4ED ☎ 07830 367125
⊕ hartshornsbrewery.com

☒ Hartshorns began brewing in 2012 using a six-barrel plant installed by brothers Darren and Lindsey Hartshorn. ▰

Highgate (OG 1044, ABV 4.3%)
Smooth, easy-drinking pale copper-coloured ale. Balanced malt sweetness with fruity hop flavour and a well-rounded bitterness.

Stormin Auburn (OG 1045, ABV 4.5%)
A mild bitterness and crystal malt flavour characterise this amber ale, complemented by distinctive American hop flavour and aroma.

Floss the Boss (OG 1046, ABV 4.6%)
This thirst-quenching pale golden ale has three separate hop additions during the brewing process to give a distinct flavour, balanced with a rich, malty sweetness.

Brooklyn Nights (OG 1052, ABV 5.4%)
An American-style brown ale with a complex malt base. A blend of American hops provide abundant flavour and aroma, with an assertive bitterness, while a specially selected American yeast produces a clean, dry finish.

Shakademus (OG 1052, ABV 5.4%)
Full-bodied with a citrus hop bite; a satisfying premium golden ale.

Apocalypse (OG 1055, ABV 6.2%)
Easy-drinking golden ale with a clean bitter finish. Refreshingly crisp and packed with hop character.

Harveys IFBB ◉

Bridge Wharf Brewery, 6 Cliffe High Street, Lewes, East Sussex, BN7 2AH
☎ (01273) 480209 ⊕ harveys.org.uk

☒ Established in 1790, this independent family brewery operates from the banks of the River Ouse in Lewes. A major development in 1985 doubled the brewhouse capacity and subsequent additional fermenting capacity has seen production rise to more than 38,000 barrels a year. There is also a microbrewery on site used to brew special beers including replicating old Lewes Brewery recipes using the County Town Beers name. Harveys supplies real ale to all its 48 pubs and 550 free trade outlets in the south-east. ‼▰◆RAIB

R (ABV 2.8%)

Sussex XX Mild Ale (OG 1030, ABV 3%) ⬒ ◄
A dark copper-brown colour. Roast malt dominates the aroma and palate leading to a sweet, caramel finish.

IPA (OG 1033, ABV 3.5%)
Formerly Sussex Pale Ale.

Sussex Wild Hop (OG 1037, ABV 3.7%)

Sussex Best Bitter (OG 1040, ABV 4%) ⬒ ◄

Full-bodied brown bitter. A hoppy aroma leads to a good malt and hop balance, and a dry aftertaste.

Old Ale (OG 1043, ABV 4.3%)

Olympia (OG 1042, ABV 4.3%)

Armada Ale (OG 1045, ABV 4.5%) ◆
Hoppy amber best bitter. Well-balanced fruit and hops dominate throughout with a fruity palate.

Harviestoun SIBA

Harviestoun Brewery, Alva, FK12 5DQ
☎ (01259) 769100 harviestoun.com

Harviestoun has grown from one-man brewing in a bucket in the back of a shed in 1983 to a 60-barrel, multi-award-winning brewery today. With a reputation for experimentation, the brewery adds around eight to ten short-run seasonals to its core range of two ales. !! ◆ RAIB

Bitter & Twisted (OG 1036, ABV 3.8%) ◆
Refreshingly hoppy beer with fruit throughout. A bittersweet taste with a long bitter finish. A golden session beer.

Schiehallion (OG 1048, ABV 4.8%) ◆
A Scottish cask lager, brewed using a lager yeast and Hersbrucker hops. A hoppy aroma, with fruit and malt, leads to a malty, bitter taste with floral hoppiness and a bitter finish.

Harwich Town

Station Approach, Harwich, Essex, CO12 3NA
☎ (01255) 551155 harwichtown.co.uk

Brewing started in 2007 on a five-barrel plant next to Harwich Town railway station. The brewer is a CAMRA member and former customs officer. Beers are named after local landmarks, characters or events. 50 outlets are supplied. The brewery holds a beer festival in July and a festival special is brewed for the Harwich and Dovercourt Bay Winter Ale Festival in December. !! ◆ RAIB

Bay Bitter (OG 1036, ABV 3.6%)

Ha'penny Mild (OG 1036, ABV 3.6%)

EPA 100 (OG 1038, ABV 3.8%)

Leading Lights (OG 1038, ABV 3.8%)

Ganges (OG 1040, ABV 4%)

Misleading Lights (OG 1040, ABV 4%)

Bathside Battery Bitter (OG 1042, ABV 4.2%)

Redoubt Stout (OG 1042, ABV 4.2%)

Parkeston Porter (OG 1045, ABV 4.5%)

Lighthouse Bitter (OG 1048, ABV 4.8%)

Phoenix APA (OG 1052, ABV 5%)

Hastings SIBA

Unit 12, Conqueror Industrial Estate, Moorhurst Road, St Leonards-on-Sea, East Sussex, TN38 9NB
☎ (01424) 572050 hastingsbrewery.co.uk

Hastings is a small brewery established in 2010, exclusively producing unfined beers suitable for vegetarians and vegans. It currently operates on a five-barrel plant. Beers are available to the trade in cask and online in polypins and bottles. RAIB

Session Pale (OG 1040, ABV 3.8%)

Mosaic Pale (OG 1049.5, ABV 4.8%)

Four Cees (OG 1050, ABV 5.5%)

Slovenian Brown (OG 1057, ABV 6%)

Havant SIBA

Unit 25, The Tanneries, Brockhampton Lane, Havant, Hampshire, PO9 1JB
☎ (023) 9247 6067 thehavantbrewery.co.uk

Havant began brewing in 2009 on a one-barrel plant, upgraded in 2011 and moved to new premises in 2013, where it increased capacity again to five barrels. !! ◆ RAIB

Decided (OG 1035, ABV 3.8%)

Dropped (OG 1039, ABV 3.8%)

Started (OG 1039, ABV 4%)

Herd (OG 1045, ABV 4.2%)

Stopped Dancing (OG 1042, ABV 4.4%) ◆
Golden-coloured best bitter. Biscuity aroma and taste. Fruit and hops dominate but not overpower, leading to a pleasant bittersweet finish.

Finished (OG 1049, ABV 5%)

Hawkshead SIBA

Mill Yard, Staveley, Cumbria, LA8 9LR
☎ (01539) 822644 hawksheadbrewery.co.uk

Hawkshead Brewery was established in 2002 by former BBC journalist Alex Brodie. The brewery outgrew its original premises (a barn at Hawkshead) and moved to its present site at Staveley in 2006 where a purpose-built 20-barrel plant was installed. Further expansion in 2010 added a second bar to the Beer Hall, which is the visitor centre and brewery tap. A kitchen serves 'beer tapas' to complement the beer and the open-plan layout means visitors can see the brewery at work. Pubs are supplied throughout the north-west. !! ◆ RAIB

Iti (OG 1036, ABV 3.5%)

Windermere Pale (OG 1036, ABV 3.5%) ◆
Crisp and fruity yellow beer with hints of melon and grapefruit and a strong bitter aftertaste.

Bitter (OG 1037, ABV 3.7%) ◆
Well-balanced, thirst-quenching beer with fruit and hops aroma, leading to a lasting bitter finish.

Red (OG 1042, ABV 4.2%) ◆
An impressive colour for this richly flavoured beer; lots of fruitiness and good hop flavour with a lingering aftertaste.

Lakeland Gold (OG 1043, ABV 4.4%) ◆
Fresh, well-balanced fruity, hoppy beer with a clean bitter aftertaste.

Dry Stone Stout (OG 1044, ABV 4.5%) ◆
Black, dry, bitter stout with an astringent, roast finish.

Great White (OG 1048, ABV 4.8%)
Great White is a spiced wheat beer. It is brewed with coriander seeds, Seville orange peel and Motueka hops from New Zealand.

Brodie's Prime (OG 1048, ABV 4.9%) ◆
Complex, dark brown beer with plenty of malt, fruit and roast taste. Satisfying full body with a clean finish.

Cumbrian Five Hop (OG 1050, ABV 5%)
A robust hoppy bitter with citrus hops and fruity middle.

Lakeland Lager (OG 1045, ABV 5%)
A cask-conditioned lager.

NZPA (OG 1056, ABV 6%)
A hoppy bitter with a sweet, fruity taste and a resounding dry bitter finish.

IPA (OG 1065, ABV 7%)
A modern IPA, amber in colour, with huge hop flavours.

Haworth Steam

Rose & Crown, 2 Westgate, Cleckheaton, West Yorkshire, BD19 5ET
☎ (01535) 646059 ☎ 07974 483310
haworthsteambrewery.co.uk

Established in 2011 using a five-barrel plant, the brewery now has online sales and a café, bar and bistro in Haworth acting as the brewery tap. There are plans to increase both beer range and production.

True Tyke (OG 1038, ABV 3.8%)
Amber-coloured Yorkshire bitter with creamy biscuit notes and a distinctive breadiness.

WD Austerity (OG 1038, ABV 3.8%)
Blonde ale with plenty of cereal and digestive biscuit on the nose. Creamy malt body gives a floral finish.

Ironclad 957 (OG 1043, ABV 4.3%)
Stout with caramel and raisin in the nose and a little drying smoke on the finish.

Fallwood XXXX (OG 1052, ABV 5.2%)
Full-bodied ale full of roasted barley and First Gold hops giving a toffee-apple red colour with a hint of fruit.

Hay Rake

Blackstone Edge Old Road, Littleborough, OL15 0JX
☎ (01706) 379689 ☎ 07775 792684
hayrakebrewery.info

Mark Wickham, the landlord of the Rake Tapas Restaurant, resurrected the Hay Rake microbrewery in 2013. The Rake brewed its own beer during the reign of Queen Victoria but stopped in 1901. Mark is keen to revive the tradition of locally-brewed ale.

Dawn's Hopping Mad (OG 1038, ABV 3.8%)
A blend of five hops with a hint of chilli and ginger.

Dawn's Called Thyme (OG 1040, ABV 4%)
Citrus with a blend of thyme and fresh peaches.

Early Dawn (OG 1041, ABV 4.1%)
An IPA using a blend of four hops with a hint of honey and lemongrass.

Dawn's Dark Side (OG 1044, ABV 4.4%)
A blend of four hops with molasses and coriander.

Dawn's Autumn Gold (OG 1045, ABV 4.5%)
A blend of four hops with a hint of liquorice and golden syrup.

Haywood Bad Ram SIBA

Callow Top Holiday Park, Buxton Road, Sandybrook, Ashbourne, Derbyshire, DE6 2AQ
☎ (01335) 344020 ☎ 07974 948427
callowtop.co.uk/callow-top-brewery

Established in 2003, the brewery was based in a converted barn but a new brewery and bottling plant became operational in 2012. One pub is owned (on site) and several other outlets are supplied. !! RAIB

Thoroughbred Bad Ram (OG 1038, ABV 3.8%)
A refreshing straw-coloured ale with a crisp bite and spice and flowery notes.

Dr Samuel Johnson (OG 1044, ABV 4.5%)
A slightly fruity and refined spicy flavour.

Callow Top Imperial IPA (OG 1050, ABV 5.2%)
A full-bodied, rich ale with a fruity and slightly citrus aftertaste.

Head in a Hat

See Florence

Healey's

Wellington Inn, Main Street, Loppergarth, Cumbria, LA12 0JL
☎ (01229) 582388

Healey's began brewing in the Wellington in 2012 using a custom-made 2.5-barrel stainless steel plant, which can be viewed through full-length windows in the pub.

Golden (OG 1037, ABV 3.6%)
A well-hopped light golden bitter with a smooth finish.

True Brit (OG 1037, ABV 3.6%)
A golden-coloured bitter made with all English hops and a hint of roasted malt.

Dark Mild (OG 1038, ABV 3.7%)
Dark mild with a reddish hue. Roast flavours at the outset mingle with fruit and sweetness in the middle. A drier finish completes the beer.

Blonde (OG 1040, ABV 4%)
Aromatic bitter, sweet and tasty from the start with increasing hops and a dry bitter finish.

Best (OG 1042, ABV 4.2%)
Traditional-style best bitter with developing good hop bitterness. Fruity middle and a touch of roast bitterness balance the underlying sweetness.

Loppergarth Pale Ale (OG 1048, ABV 5%)
A well-hopped strong bitter in the style of the original India Pale Ale. Late hopped for added aroma.

Heart of Wales

Stables Yard, Zion Street, Llanwrtyd Wells, LD5 4RD
☎ (01591) 610236 heartofwalesbrewery.co.uk

The brewery was set up with a six-barrel plant in 2006 in old stables at the rear of the Neuadd Arms Hotel. Beers are brewed using water from the brewery's own borehole. Seasonal brews celebrate local events such as the World Bogsnorkelling Championships. All bottle-conditioned beers are suitable for vegetarians and vegans. Cambrian Heart Ale was commissioned by and is brewed for the Cambrian Mountains Initiative, inspired by the Prince of Wales, which aims to promote and support rural producers and communities in the region. !! ♦ RAIB

Irfon Valley Bitter (OG 1038, ABV 3.6%)

Aur Cymru (OG 1040, ABV 3.8%)

Bitter (OG 1042, ABV 4.1%)
A light chestnut bitter in the Northern style, it has a fine smooth balance between malt and hop.

Big Red Chopper (OG 1043, ABV 4.3%)

Welsh Black (OG 1045, ABV 4.4%)
A full-flavoured, complex and smooth stout.

Cambrian Heart Ale (OG 1045, ABV 4.5%)
Light golden brown ale with a refreshing fruity body and a hoppy finish.

Noble Eden Ale (OG 1046, ABV 4.6%)
A dark brown premium ale bursting with fruit and malt, with just a hint of chocolate. A full-bodied, satisfying pint.

Inn-stable (OG 1065, ABV 6.8%)
A powerful ale with a warming malty body and a smooth finish.

Heath Village

Owlcotes Farm, Shire Lane, Heath, Derbyshire, S44 5SQ ☎ 07799 608356
heathvillagebrewery.co.uk

Small 0.5-barrel plant established in 2014 on a farm in Heath Village. The brewery is run by a consortium of six people from the village. It is intended to expand the capacity in the future.

Heath Gold (ABV 4.4%)
Dual-hopped English IPA.

Heathen's Ale (ABV 4.8%)
Full-bodied with a hint of spice.

Heathen (NEW)

Grape & Grain, 51 The Broadway, Haywards Heath, West Sussex, RH16 3AS
☎ (01444) 456217 ☎ 07825 429428
heathenbrewers.co.uk

Located in the basement of the Grape & Grain off-licence and delicatessen, brewing began in 2014 using a full mash, two-barrel plant. A small range of cask-conitioned beers is produced, with plans for bottling in the future. Local outlets and beer festivals are supplied.

Rhubarb (OG 1044, ABV 4.5%)
A best bitter brewed with honey and rhubarb.

Porter (OG 1055, ABV 5%)

Chemistry (OG 1050, ABV 5.5%)
A Belgian-style wheat beer.

Honey (OG 1049, ABV 5.5%)
A honeyed West Coast-style IPA.

Iceni Genie (OG 1057, ABV 5.5%)
An English pale ale.

Heathton

c/o Old Gate, Heathton, Shropshire, WV5 7EB

This brewery is planned to be resurrected at the Old Gate pub, but its three beers are produced at present in three different breweries, and served only in the Old Gate.

Heavy Industry SIBA

The Old Slaughterhouse, Denbigh Street, Henllan, LL16 5AR
☎ (01745) 816316 ☎ 07812 346466
heavyindustrybrewing.com

Established in 2012, Heavy Industry brews with a 10-barrel plant situated in an old slaughterhouse in the village of Henllan. ♦

Diawl Bach (OG 1036.5, ABV 3.8%)
Citrus fruit flavours feature strongly in this uncompromising, hoppy bitter. The tart taste continues long into the aftertaste.

Electric Mountain (OG 1036.5, ABV 3.8%)
A full-bodied session bitter, dry and well-balanced with a satisfying hoppy finish.

Freak Chick (OG 1042, ABV 4.5%)
A red malty beer given an earthy, spicy and zesty character by a complex blend of five hops, balanced by the sweetness of the malts.

High Voltage (OG 1042, ABV 4.5%)
A dry, bitter beer full of citrus fruit, hoppy flavours which dominate the taste and lasting bitter finish.

Nelsons Eye (OG 1042, ABV 4.5%)
Heavily hopped with a strong, sharp bitter taste. Citrus fruit notes, mainly grapefruit, in the aroma and palate continue into the hoppy, bitter aftertaste.

Nos Smoked Porter (OG 1045, ABV 4.5%)

77 (OG 1046, ABV 4.9%)
A strong bitter with a powerful smack of fruit and hops. Tangy fruit flavours and hoppy bitterness feature strongly in the aroma, taste and finish.

Collaborator (OG 1046, ABV 5%)
A smooth and satisfying dark, hoppy beer. The juicy malty taste is quite roasty and leads to a dry, hoppy aftertaste.

Pigeon Toed Orange Peel (OG 1048.5, ABV 5.2%)
A wheat beer, citrus notes complemented by a tangy, hoppy aftertaste.

Heineken Royal Trafford

Royal Brewery, 201 Denmark Road, Manchester, M15 6LD

No real ale.

Hellhound

Sycamore Farm, Somersham Road, Bramford, Suffolk, IP8 4NN
☎ (01473) 831200 ☎ 07850 076202
hellhoundbrewery.co.uk

Hellhound was established in 2009, initially producing bottled beers. In 2014 the brewery relocated to its current site, a farm in Bramford with its own private water supply. Around 100 outlets are supplied across East Anglia. ♦

Dirty Blond (OG 1039, ABV 3.9%)
A New Zealand hopped blonde ale with a citrus finish.

Helmsley (NEW)

18 Bridge Street, Helmsley, North Yorkshire, YO62 5DX
☎ (01439) 771014 ☎ 07525 434268

Located within the North York Moors National Park, brewing began in 2014. The brewery has a viewing gallery, tasting room and brewery tap. Local pubs are supplied. RAIB

Yorkshire Legend (ABV 3.8%)

Striding the Riding (ABV 4%)

Howardian Gold (ABV 4.2%)

IPA (ABV 5.5%)

Hen House

The Old Dairy, Walliscote Farm, High Street, Whitchurch-on-Thames, Oxfordshire, RG8 7EP
henhousebrewery.co.uk

Hen House began brewing in 2012 on a 30-litre plant. Only bottle-conditioned beers are produced, available from the brewery shop. ♦ RAIB

Hepworth SIBA

Beer Station, Railway Yard, Horsham, West Sussex, RH12 2NW
(01403) 269696 hepworthbrewery.co.uk

Hepworth's was established in 2001, initially bottling beer only. In 2003 draught beer brewing was started with Sussex malt and hops. 274 outlets are supplied. !! ♦

Traditional Sussex Bitter (OG 1035, ABV 3.5%)
A fine, clean-tasting amber session beer. A bitter beer with a pleasant fruity and hoppy aroma that leads to a crisp, tangy taste. A long, dry finish.

Dark Horse (OG 1038, ABV 3.8%)
Nutty and roasted malt characters with a complementary bitterness.

Summer Ale (OG 1038, ABV 3.8%)

Pullman First Class Ale (OG 1041, ABV 4.2%)
A sweet, nutty maltiness and fruitiness are balanced by hops and bitterness in this easy-drinking, pale brown best bitter. A subtle bitter aftertaste.

Prospect Organic (OG 1045, ABV 4.5%)
A well-balanced and traditional brew.

Classic Old Ale (OG 1046, ABV 4.8%)
A traditional winter brew, rich with a variety of roasted malts balanced with sweetness and the bitterness of Admiral hops.

Iron Horse (OG 1048, ABV 4.8%)
There's a fruity, toffee aroma to this light brown, full-bodied bitter. A citrus flavour balanced by caramel and malt leads to a clean, dry finish.

Hercules (NEW)

Hercules House, 5 Harbour Court, Heron Road, Holywood, Belfast, BT3 9HB
(028) 9036 4516 niall@herculesbrewery.com

The original Hercules Brewing Company, founded in the 19th century, was one of 13 breweries in Belfast at the time. The company has been re-established to produce small batch brews using old brewing traditions. Its output is all under the Yardsman brand name.

Belfast Pale Ale (ABV 4%)
Floral aroma with rich caramel; well-balanced fruity palate leading to a dry, full-bodied citrus finish.

IPA (ABV 4.3%)
Easy-drinking American-style IPA. Full-bodied with citrus hoppiness and a fruity finish.

Here Be Monsters (NEW)

22 Paris Road, Scholes, West Yorkshire, HD9 1UA
07792 174863 herebemonstersbrewery.co.uk

A small brewery producing only bottle-conditioned beers from a one-barrel plant. RAIB

Hereford SIBA

88 St Owen Street, Hereford, HR1 2QD
(01432) 342125 jfkenyon@aol.com

From its inception in 2000, the brewery has steadily increased production. In 2010 its name changed from the Spinning Dog to the Hereford Brewery. Around 50 outlets are supplied. !! ♦ RAIB

Herefordshire Owd Bull (OG 1039, ABV 3.9%)
A good session beer with an abundance of hops and bitterness. Dry, with citrus aftertaste.

Dark (OG 1040, ABV 4%)
A dark, malty mild with a hint of bitterness and a touch of roast caramel. A smooth drinkable ale.

Herefordshire Light Ale (HLA) (OG 1040, ABV 4%)
A crisp, light, refreshing ale made with Herefordshire hops.

Best Bitter (OG 1042, ABV 4.2%)

Gamekeepers Bitter (OG 1042, ABV 4.2%)

Celtic Gold (OG 1045, ABV 4.5%)
A bright gold-coloured best bitter, full of fruit and blackcurrant flavours.

Mutley's Revenge (OG 1048, ABV 4.8%)
A strong, smooth, hoppy beer, amber in colour. Full-bodied with a dry, citrus aftertaste.

Mutts Nuts (OG 1050, ABV 5%)
A dark, strong ale, full-bodied with a hint of a chocolate aftertaste.

Hermitage

Heathwaite, Slanting Hill, Hermitage, Berkshire, RG18 9QG
(01635) 200907 07980 019484
hermitagebrewery.co.uk

Brewing began in 2013 in the village of Hermitage, West Berkshire, using a 0.5-barrel plant. The owner, Richard Marshall, taught food science at degree level and has been brewing his own beers for more than 40 years. Bottle-conditioned beers are sold in local shops and post offices. Some cask-conditioned beer is also available. RAIB

Tom Herrick's (NEW)

The Stable House, Main Street, Carlton on Trent, Nottinghamshire, NG23 6NW 07877 542331
tomherricksbrewery@hotmail.com

Tom Herrick installed his bespoke 2.5-barrel stainless steel brewery at the front of his premises during 2014 and began small-scale commercial brewing in 2015. The brewery is operated only on a part-time basis with output going to festivals and supporting local pubs.

Bomber Command (OG 1045, ABV 4.2%)

A pale copper-coloured ale, full bodied and malty with a delicate, well-balanced hop profile.

Hesket Newmarket SIBA

Old Crown Barn, Back Green, Hesket Newmarket, Cumbria, CA7 8JG
☎ (01697) 478066 ⊕ hesketbrewery.co.uk

☺ Founded in 1988, and bought by a co-operative in 1999 to preserve a community amenity. All the beers are named after local fells, except for Doris' 90th Birthday Ale. ‼☗♦

Blencathra Bitter (OG 1035, ABV 3.2%) ◄
A malty, tawny ale, mild and mellow for a bitter, with a dominant caramel flavour.

Haystacks (OG 1037, ABV 3.7%) ◄
Light, easy-drinking, thirst-quenching blond beer; pleasant for its strength.

Skiddaw Special Bitter (OG 1037, ABV 3.7%)
An amber session beer, malty throughout, well-balanced with a dryish finish.

Black Sail (OG 1042.1, ABV 4%) ◄
A sweet stout with roast flavours.

Helvellyn Gold (OG 1039, ABV 4%) ◄
Complex hoppy and fruity beer with malt presence and refreshing finish.

High Pike (OG 1042, ABV 4.2%) ◄
A traditional style bitter; fruity with a dry finish.

Doris' 90th Birthday Ale (OG 1045, ABV 4.3%) ◄
A fruity premium beer.

Scafell Blonde (OG 1043, ABV 4.4%) ◄
A hoppy, sweet, fruity, pale-coloured bitter.

Brim Fell (OG 1047, ABV 4.5%)
A light copper-coloured IPA, generously, but not overly hopped. Enough body to back up the hop bitterness, and a little residual sweetness from the malt balances the beer well. A light malt giving way to floral and citrus hops.

Catbells Pale Ale (OG 1050, ABV 5%) ◄
Golden ale with a nice balance of fruity sweetness and bitterness, almost syrupy but with an unexpectedly dry finish.

Old Carrock Strong Ale (OG 1060, ABV 6%) ◄
Reddy brown strong ale, vine-fruity in flavour with a slightly astringent finish.

Hewitt's

c/o Brentwood Brewery, Calcott Hall Farm, Ongar Road, Brentwood, Essex, CM15 9HS ☎ 07949 565424

Correspondence: 40 Marconi Road, Chelmsford, Essex, CM1 1QD ⊕ hewittsbrewery.co.uk

Hewitt's was founded in 2010, using spare capacity at Brentwood Brewery (qv). Brewing is currently suspended.

Hexhamshire SIBA ◉

Leafields, Ordley, Northumberland, NE46 1SX
☎ (01434) 606577 ⊕ hexhamshire.co.uk

Hexhamshire was founded in 1993 and is run by one of the founding partners and his family. 30 outlets are supplied direct and many others through the SIBA direct delivery scheme.

Devil's Elbow (OG 1036, ABV 3.6%) ◄

Amber brew full of hops and fruit, leading to a bitter finish.

Shire Bitter (OG 1037, ABV 3.8%) ◄
A good balance of hops with fruity overtones, this amber beer makes an easy-drinking session bitter.

Blackhall English Stout (OG 1040, ABV 4%) ◄
A pleasant bitter beer with a strong roast malt flavour.

Devil's Water (OG 1041, ABV 4.1%) ◄
Copper-coloured best bitter, well-balanced with a slightly fruity, hoppy finish.

Whapweasel (OG 1048, ABV 4.8%) ◄
An interesting smooth, hoppy beer with a fruity flavour. Amber in colour, the bitter finish brings out the fruit and hops.

Old Humbug (OG 1055, ABV 5.5%)

High House Farm SIBA

Matfen, Newcastle upon Tyne, NE20 0RG
☎ (01661) 886192 ⊕ highhousefarmbrewery.co.uk

The brewery was founded in 2003 by a Brewlab graduate on a working farm with a visitor centre, brewery shop and function room. This has now expanded to include a successful restaurant and a wedding venue. More than 350 regional outlets are supplied with beers made using many ingredients from the farm. ‼☗♦

Sundancer (OG 1036, ABV 3.6%)

Pullet Please (OG 1037, ABV 3.7%)
A gold-coloured refreshing ale with a delicate grapefruit nose and a crisp, dry finish. An easy-drinking bitter.

Auld Hemp (OG 1038, ABV 3.8%) ◄
Tawny-coloured ale with hop, malt and fruit flavours and a good bitter finish.

Nel's Best (OG 1041, ABV 4.2%) ◄
Golden hoppy ale full of flavour with a clean, bitter finish.

Matfen Magic (OG 1046.5, ABV 4.8%) ◄
Well-hopped brown ale with a fruity aroma. Malt and chocolate overtones with a rich, bitter finish.

High Weald SIBA

Bulrushes Business Park, Coombe Hill Road, East Grinstead, West Sussex, RH19 4LZ ☎ 07836 291430

Office: 23 Hermitage Road, East Grinstead, West Sussex, RH19 2BP ⊕ highwealdbrewery.co.uk

⊠ Established in 2013, High Weald Brewery has grown to a four-barrel plant size. The brewery produces both cask- and bottle-conditioned ales, supplying local free houses, shops and festivals and is increasing direct sales at farmers' and community markets. Further expansion of both the beer range and brewing and bottling capacity is planned. RAIB

Best (OG 1038, ABV 3.8%)
A fine session ale.

Greenstede Gold (OG 1040, ABV 4%)
A refreshing golden ale.

Charcoal Burner (OG 1043, ABV 4.3%)
A traditional English stout. Roasted malts bring a rich, satisfying flavour, combined with the velvety smoothness from generous quantities of oats.

Highland SIBA

Swannay Brewery, Swannay by Evie, Orkney, KW17 2NP
☎ (01856) 721700 highlandbrewco.com

Brewing began in 2005 at the redundant Swannay dairy. A bigger plant was soon required and installed to meet demand. Around 300 outlets are supplied throughout Scotland and the north of England, as well as in the London area. ‼♦

Orkney Best (OG 1038, ABV 3.6%)
A refreshing, light-bodied, low-gravity golden beer bursting with hop, peach and sweet malt flavours. The long, hoppy finish leaves a dry bitterness.

Island Hopping (OG 1039, ABV 3.9%)
Fruity hoppiness with some caramel with a lasting bitter aftertaste.

Dark Munro (OG 1040, ABV 4%)
The nose presents an intense roast hit which is followed by summer fruits in the mouth. The strong roast malt continues into the aftertaste.

Scapa Special (OG 1042, ABV 4.2%)
A good copy of a typical Lancashire bitter, full of bitterness and background hops, leaving your mouth tingling in the lingering aftertaste.

Sneeky Wee Orkney Stout (OG 1044, ABV 4.2%)
Plenty of malt and roast with a mixed fruit berry background. Dry bitter finish.

Orkney IPA (OG 1048, ABV 4.8%)
A traditional bitter, with light hop and fruit flavour throughout.

St Magnus Ale (OG 1049, ABV 5.2%)
A complex, tawny bitter with a stunning balance of malt and hop and some soft roast. Full-bodied.

Orkney Blast (OG 1058, ABV 6%)
Plenty of alcohol in this warming strong bitter/ barley wine. A mushroom and woody aroma blossoms into a well-balanced smack of malt and hop in the taste.

Highwood SIBA

See Tom Wood's

Hilden SIBA

Hilden House, Hilden, Lisburn, Co Antrim, BT27 4TY
☎ (028) 9266 0800 hildenbrewery.co.uk

Established 1981, Hilden is Ireland's oldest independent brewery. Now in the second generation of family ownership, the beers are widely distributed across the UK. The beers are regularly available in Wetherspoon outlets in Northern Ireland. ‼♦

Ale (OG 1038, ABV 4%)
An amber-coloured beer with an aroma of malt, hops and fruit. The balanced taste is slightly slanted towards hops, and hops are also prominent in the full, malty finish.

Silver (OG 1042, ABV 4.2%)
A pale ale, light and refreshing on the palate but with a satisfying mellow hop character derived from a judicious blend of aromatic Saaz hops.

Headless Dog (OG 1042, ABV 4.3%)
A well-hopped bright amber-coloured ale.

Molly Malone (OG 1045, ABV 4.6%)
Dark ruby-red porter with complex flavours of hop bitterness and chocolate malt.

Scullion's Irish (OG 1045, ABV 4.6%)
A bright amber ale, initially smooth with a slight taste of honey that is balanced by a long, dry aftertaste that lingers on the palate.

Halt (OG 1058, ABV 6.1%)
A premium traditional Irish red ale with a malty, mild hop flavour.

Hill Island SIBA

Unit 7, Fowlers Yard, Back Silver Street, Durham, DH1 3RA ☎ 07740 932584
mike@hillisland.freeserve.co.uk

Established in 2002, the brewery name is a literal translation of Dunholme from which Durham is derived. It is situated in the Fowlers Yard complex by the banks of the Wear in the heart of Durham City. Beers can be crafted exclusively for individual pubs. Beer festivals take place at the brewery each month. ‼♦

Peninsula Pint (OG 1036.5, ABV 3.7%)
Blonde and hoppy with a zesty aroma.

Bitter (OG 1039, ABV 3.9%)
A red/gold-coloured bitter with pronounced caramel flavour and zesty bitterness.

Stout for the Count (OG 1040, ABV 4%)
A traditional full-bodied stout. Almost black in colour with roast coffee flavours from the dark malt used and a clean hop bitterness.

Neptune's Gold (OG 1042, ABV 4.2%)
Subtle bitterness balanced with hop flavours and hint of tropical fruit.

Cathedral Ale (OG 1042, ABV 4.3%)
Ruby red in colour with hints of roast malts and crisp bitterness.

Thai Red (OG 1043, ABV 4.3%)

THAIPA (OG 1043, ABV 4.3%)
A speciality beer with added lemon grass.

Griffin's Irish Stout (OG 1045, ABV 4.5%)
A black and bitter traditional Irish-style stout.

Hillside SIBA

Holly Bush Farm, Ross Road, Longhope, Gloucestershire, GL17 0NG
☎ (01452) 830222 ☎ 07905 246189
hillsidebrewery.com

A six-barrel plant in a reconstructed farm dairy that started in 2011. A 200-foot bore hole produces pure water rich in minerals ideally suited to brewing. The regular beers are supplemented by limited run specials that explore different styles and flavours. ‼♦

Over the Hill (OG 1042, ABV 3.5%)
Single-hopped malty dark mild.

Pinnacle (OG 1039, ABV 3.8%)
A fruity pale ale.

Legless Cow (OG 1044, ABV 4.2%)
A well-balanced and full-flavoured best bitter.

Legend of Hillside (OG 1047, ABV 4.7%)
A rich pale ale with a strong hop finish.

Hobsons SIBA 👁

Newhouse Farm, Tenbury Road, Cleobury Mortimer, Shropshire, DY14 8RD
☎ (01299) 270837 ☎ 07506 155551
⊕ hobsons-brewery.co.uk

Established in 1993 in a former sawmill, Hobsons relocated to a farm site with more space in 1995. A second brewery, bottling plant and a warehouse have been added along with significant expansion to the first brewery. Beers are supplied within a 50-mile radius. The brewery has an onsite wind turbine and utilises environmental sustainable technologies where possible. ‼ 🍺 RAIB

Mild (OG 1034, ABV 3.2%) ◆
A classic mild. Complex layers of taste come from roasted malts that predominate and give lots of flavour.

Twisted Spire (OG 1036, ABV 3.6%)
Vibrant blonde beer with a light fizz and sweet floral aroma bringing bursts of refreshing flavour and a crisp dry finish.

Best Bitter (OG 1038.5, ABV 3.8%) ◆
A pale brown to amber, medium-bodied beer with strong hop character throughout. It is consequently bitter, but with malt discernible in the taste.

Old Prickly (OG 1042, ABV 4.2%)
Pale ale full of hops giving a complex flavour of floral and citrus notes with a lingering but subtle bitterness.

Town Crier (OG 1044, ABV 4.5%)
A full-flavoured crisp golden ale with a big voice, the elegant straw-coloured bitter has a hint of sweetness which is complemented by subtle hop flavours, leading to a dry finish.

Hogarths (NEW)

🍺 Hogarths, 37-41 Churchgate, Bolton, BL1 1HU
☎ (01204) 386964

Microbrewery located in the old kitchen of a Bolton pub of the same name.

Beer Street (ABV 3.8%)
A session ale with good hop balance.

Liberty (ABV 3.8%)
A light, fruity bitter.

Hoggleys

See Phipps

Hogs Back SIBA 👁

Manor Farm, The Street, Tongham, Surrey, GU10 1DE
☎ (01252) 783008 ⊕ hogsback.co.uk

⊗ This traditionally-styled brewery, established in 1992, boasts an extensive range of award-winning ales, brewed from the finest malted barley and whole English hops. The shop sells all the brewery's beers and related merchandise plus over 400 beers and ciders from around the world. Fully guided tours with tastings are available. In 2014 the brewery planted hops on neighbouring farmland, restoring the ancient Farnham White Bine variety. ‼ 🍺 ◆ RAIB

HBB (OG 1039, ABV 3.7%) ◆

Biscuity aroma with some hops and lemon notes. Well-balanced, plenty of hop in the mouth with a long-lasting, dry bitter aftertaste.

TEA (OG 1044, ABV 4.2%) 🍺 ◆
A tawny-coloured best bitter with toffee and malt present in the nose. A well-rounded flavour with malt and a fruity sweetness.

Hop Garden Gold (OG 1048, ABV 4.4%) ◆
Full-bodied with an aroma of malt, hops and fruit. Hoppy bitterness grows in an increasingly dry aftertaste with a hint of sweetness.

A over T (OG 1094, ABV 9%) ◆
Full-bodied, tawny-coloured barley wine. The malty aroma with hints of vanilla lead to a well-balanced taste where the hops cut through the underlying sweetness and dominate in the finish.

Holden's SIBA IFBB 👁

George Street, Woodsetton, Dudley, West Midlands, DY1 4LW
☎ (01902) 880051 ⊕ holdensbrewery.co.uk

⊛A family brewery spanning four generations, Holden's began life as a brewpub in 1915. Continued recent expansion sees 20 tied pubs, a new brewhouse and a shop. 🍺 ◆

Black Country Mild (OG 1037, ABV 3.7%) ◆
A good red/brown mild; a refreshing, light blend of roast malt, hops and fruit, dominated by malt throughout.

Black Country Bitter (OG 1039, ABV 3.9%) 🍺 ◆
A medium-bodied, golden ale; a light, well-balanced bitter with a subtle, dry, hoppy finish.

Golden Glow (OG 1045, ABV 4.4%)
A pale golden beer with a subtle hop aroma plus gentle sweetness and a light hoppiness.

Special (OG 1052, ABV 5.1%) ◆
A sweet, malty, full-bodied amber ale with hops to balance in the taste and in the good, bittersweet finish.

Holsworthy

Unit 5, Circuit Business Park, Clawton, Devon, EX22 6RR
☎ (01566) 783678 ☎ 07879 401073
⊕ holsworthyales.co.uk

Holsworthy Ales began brewing in 2011 using a six-barrel plant, serving the local rural community. ‼ 🍺 RAIB

Mine's a Mild (OG 1035, ABV 3.5%)
A traditional English mild with a rich malty taste. Lightly-hopped to give a good balance and finish.

Original (OG 1038, ABV 3.8%)

Sunshine (OG 1040, ABV 4%)

Muck 'n' Straw (OG 1044, ABV 4.4%)

Make Me Hoppy (OG 1046, ABV 4.7%)

Tamar Black (OG 1048, ABV 4.8%)
A rich, deep-roasted stout with a traditional taste but with enough bitterness to produce a balanced beer with a pleasant finish.

Hop on the Run (OG 1048, ABV 5%)

Old Market Monk (OG 1059, ABV 6.1%)

Holt SIBA IFBB 👁

The Brewery, Empire Street, Cheetham, Manchester, M3 1JD
☎ (0161) 834 3285 ⊕ joseph-holt.com

☺The brewery, established in 1849 by Joseph and Catherine Holt, is still a family-run business and is now in the hands of the great, great-grandson of the founder. It supplies approximately 130 free trade outlets as well as its own estate of 130 tied pubs. ⌐

Mild (OG 1033, ABV 3.2%) ◆
A dark brown/red beer with a fruity, malty nose. Roast, malt, fruit and hops in the taste, with strong bitterness for a mild, and a dry malt and hops finish.

IPA (OG 1038, ABV 3.8%) ◆
Golden bitter with biscuity malt, hops and restrained lemony notes. Dry, bitter finish.

Bitter (OG 1040, ABV 4%) ◆
Copper-coloured beer with malt and hops in the aroma. Malt, hops and fruit in the taste with a bitter and hoppy finish.

Two Hoots (OG 1043.8, ABV 4.2%)
A light, crisp and refreshing ale with a hint of citrus that is beautifully balanced.

Holy Well (NEW)

4 Barnfield Close, Egerton, Bolton, BL7 9UP ☎ 07949 179338 ⊕ holywellbrewing.com

Holy Well is a nanobrewery and the brewing sister to the Crafty Ales company, which sells beer from Lancashire microbreweries at local farmers' markets and online. RAIB

The Imp (OG 1060, ABV 4.7%)

The VIC (OG 1065, ABV 6.1%)

The Midge (OG 1066, ABV 6.3%)

The BBBBlonde!! (OG 1066, ABV 6.5%)

Honest Brew

c/o Late Knights Brewery, 21 Southey Street, Penge, London, SE20 7JD

Brewing takes place using spare capacity at Late Knights (qv).

Hooded Ram SIBA

Hills Meadow, Douglas, Isle of Man, IM3 1LE
☎ (01624) 612464 ⊕ hoodedram.com

☺ Brewing began in 2013 on a 2.5-barrel plant. Expansion in 2014 saw an increase to a 10-barrel plant. Beers are available cask-conditioned throughout the island and bottle-conditioned beers are sold directly through the brewery shop and in some local off-licences and restaurants/bars. ‼ ⌐ RAIB

Rams Head Bitter (OG 1037, ABV 3.7%)

Sovereign Ram Single Hop (OG 1037, ABV 4.1%)

Amber Ram (OG 1038, ABV 4.3%)

Fat Ram Colonial Not So Pale Ale (OG 1044, ABV 4.5%)

Jack The Ram Stout (OG 1044, ABV 4.7%)

Little King Louis IPA (OG 1054, ABV 6%)

Hook Norton SIBA IFBB 👁

The Brewery, Brewery Lane, Scotland End, Hook Norton, Oxfordshire, OX15 5NY
☎ (01608) 737210 ⊕ hooky.co.uk

☒ Hook Norton was founded in 1849 by John Harris, a farmer and maltster. The current premises were built in 1900 and Hook Norton is one of the finest examples of a Victorian tower brewery. It is the oldest independent brewery in Oxfordshire, still housing much of the original machinery including a 25hp steam engine, which operates occasionally. ‼ ⌐ ◆ RAIB

Hooky Mild (OG 1033, ABV 2.8%) ◆
A chestnut brown, easy-drinking mild. A complex malt and hop aroma give way to a well-balanced taste, leading to a long, hoppy finish that is unusual for a mild.

Hooky (OG 1036, ABV 3.5%) ◆
A classic golden session bitter. Hoppy and fruity aroma followed by a malt and hops taste and a continuing hoppy finish.

Lion (OG 1043, ABV 4%)
Brewed with a blend of four malts and four varieties of hops to give a complex fruity nose and bittersweet finish.

Old Hooky (OG 1048, ABV 4.6%) ◆
A strong bitter, tawny in colour. A well-rounded fruity taste with a balanced bitter finish.

Hop & Cleaver (NEW)

⊟ 44 Sandhill, Newcastle upon Tyne, NE1 3JF
☎ (0191) 261 1037 ⊕ hopandcleaver.com

Established in 2014 the brewery is situated in the Hop & Cleaver pub, where the brewing equipment is on view. Its constantly changing beer range is cask conditioned and supplied solely to the pub. It plans to supply other locations in the future. ◆

Hop & Stagger SIBA

⊟ 3 West Castle Street, Bridgnorth, Shropshire, WV16 4AB
☎ (01746) 763962 ⊕ hopandstaggerbrewery.co.uk

Hop & Stagger began brewing in 2012 having set up a 2.5-barrel plant at the White Lion Inn, Bridgnorth, initially brewing a range of bitters and occasional seasonal ales exclusively for the pub. ◆

Simpson's Original (OG 1038, ABV 3.6%)
A light mild.

Golden Wander (OG 1042, ABV 4.1%)
A crisp, pale golden ale with fruity notes and a lightly hopped finish.

Pure Amber (OG 1045, ABV 4.5%)
A zesty, light-coloured ale.

Hop Art (NEW) 👁

The Brewery, Blacknest Industrial Park, Blacknest Road, Blacknest, Hampshire, GU34 4PX
☎ (01252) 364436

Office: Newtown House, 38 Newtown Road, Liphook, Surrey, GU30 7DX ⊕ hopartbrewery.com

☒ Hop Art was established in 2014 with a brand new, custom-built 10-barrel plant. There is capacity to brew three times a week at present, with plans to increase do daily production. Eighty outlets are supplied. !! ▶

Hoppy Blonde (OG 1044, ABV 4.3%)

Rood (OG 1046, ABV 4.4%)

Golden IPA (OG 1057, ABV 5.2%)

Nero (OG 1057, ABV 5.2%)

US Amber (OG 1057, ABV 5.6%)

Hoppist (OG 1064, ABV 6.1%)

Hop Back SIBA

Units 22-24, Batten Road Industrial Estate, Downton, Salisbury, Wiltshire, SP5 3HU
☎ (01725) 510986 ⊕ hopback.co.uk

Founded in 1987, Hop Back owns 10 pubs and distributes nationally. The flagship beer, Summer Lightning, has won numerous CAMRA awards. Bottled Crop Circle is accredited gluten-free and Entire Stout is suitable for vegans. !! ♦ RAIB

Golden Best (OG 1035, ABV 3.5%)
A light gold, refreshing session bitter. The hoppy aroma leads to bitterness initially, leading through to the finish with some fruit.

Citra (OG 1044, ABV 4%)
A golden-coloured, thirst-quenching ale with a lemony, grapefruity aftertaste and a crisp, dry bitterness.

Crop Circle (OG 1041, ABV 4.2%)
A pale yellow best bitter with a fragrant hop aroma, complex hop, fruit and citrus flavours with a balanced hoppy, bittersweet aftertaste.

Spring Zing (OG 1041, ABV 4.2%)
A pale, aromatic and dry-hopped beer.

Taiphoon (OG 1041, ABV 4.2%)
A clean tasting light fruity beer with hops and fruit on the aroma, complex hop character and lemongrass notes in the taste, slight sweetness balanced with some astringency in the aftertaste.

Entire Stout (OG 1044, ABV 4.5%)
A smooth, rich, ruby-black stout with strong roast and malt aromas and flavours, with a long bitter sweet and malty aftertaste.

Summer Lightning (OG 1048, ABV 5%)
Golden-coloured strong bitter with a hoppy aroma and slightly astringent bitterness in the taste, balanced with some fruit sweetness, in the dry aftertaste.

Hop Fuzz SIBA

Unit 8, Riverside Industrial Estate, West Hythe, Kent, CT21 4NB ☎ 07730 768881 ⊕ hopfuzz.co.uk

Hop Fuzz was started by two friends in 2011 and is situated on an industrial estate next to the Royal Military Canal (and a main cycle route) at West Hythe. The brewery is environmentally friendly, using solar power, recovering and re-using heat, and supplying feed to the local animal park. Major expansion took place in 2014. ♦

Yellow Zinger (OG 1038, ABV 3.7%)

Martello (OG 1038, ABV 3.8%)

English (OG 1044, ABV 4%)

Old American Pale (OG 1042, ABV 4.2%)

Hop Kettle SIBA

Red Lion, 74 High Street, Cricklade, Wiltshire, SN6 6DD
☎ (01793) 750776 ⊕ hopkettlebrewery.co.uk

Brewing began in 2012 using a four-barrel plant. The brewery is situated in a stone barn behind the Red Lion Inn, Cricklade. Many beer styles are brewed with some being barrel-aged in whisky and rum casks on site. There are plans to introduce an area that will allow people to dine among the brewing equipment. ♦

Pair by Comparison (OG 1040, ABV 3.8%)

Tricerahops (OG 1042, ABV 4.1%)

North Wall (OG 1043, ABV 4.2%)

Hop King (NEW)

Eastern Avenue, Reading, Berkshire, RG1 5SF
✉ hopkingbrewingcompany@gmail.com

Brewing began in 2014. The initial capacity is approximately half a barrel, with plans to expand to a four or five-barrel plant. Four core beers are produced, all bottle-conditioned. They can sometimes be found at the Grumpy Goat, Harris Arcade, Reading. RAIB

Hop Monster

See George's

Hop Studio SIBA

3 Handley Park, Elvington Industrial Estate, York Road, Elvington, North Yorkshire, YO41 4AR
☎ (01904) 608029 ⊕ thehopstudio.co.uk

Brewing began in 2012 using a 10-barrel plant situated in an industrial unit just outside York. Seven regular ales are produced. Bottle-conditioned, seasonal and experimental beers are also produced, some conditioned in wooden casks, and some brewed with partners. Outlets in Yorkshire are supplied direct and the rest of the UK via wholesalers. ♦ RAIB

Blonde (OG 1037, ABV 3.5%)
A citrus and gooseberry driven pale blonde session ale.

York Quaffing Ale (OG 1041, ABV 3.8%)
Complex malt underpins blackberry and orange flavours. There's a hint of tangerine in the aroma.

XP – Extra Pale (OG 1043, ABV 4%)
Balanced light citrus fruit and hop flavours, with an intense creamy bitter finish.

Gold (OG 1048, ABV 4.5%)
A full-flavoured, easy-drinking ale, with soft, rounded bitterness and citrus and tropical fruit flavours.

Obsidian (OG 1052, ABV 5%)
A well-structured black IPA with notes of grapefruit, balanced by powerful pine scent hops. Dark but unexpectedly refreshing.

XS – Extra Special (OG 1061, ABV 5.5%)
Strong and complex, this ale is driven by its slightly spicy dark fruit base. Malty and bitter, floral and citrus aromatics add depth.

Vindhya (OG 1058, ABV 6%)

A contemporary strong IPA-style beer, full of powerful citrus and spicy hops with a bittersweet finish.

Hop Stuff SIBA

Unit 7, Gunnery Terrace, Cornwallis Road, Woolwich, London, SE18 6SW
☎ (020) 8854 9509 ☎ 07850 086461
⊕ hopstuffbrewery.com

Hop Stuff began brewing in 2013. ◆

Fusilier (OG 1041, ABV 4.3%) ◣
Biscuity malty best bitter with spicy hop notes. Finish is sweetish, slightly dry with a faint bitterness. Rich, smooth mouthfeel.

Pale (OG 1045, ABV 4.5%) ◣
Slightly dry amber bitter with a complex hop character throughout. Citrus notes in the flavour and finish, which is bitter.

Renegade IPA (OG 1056, ABV 5.6%) ◣
Smooth dark-gold IPA with grapefruit and spiced hops aroma and flavour. Warm lingering finish that is bitter and dry.

Hop Yard (NEW)

The Yard, Hartfield Road, Forest Row, East Sussex, RH18 5AA ☎ 07769 313410 ⊕ hopyardbrewing.co.uk

⊠ Hop Yard began brewing in 2014 using a 100-litre brew length. It has a brewery bar and supplies local outlets. ⊨RAIB

Desert Chrome (OG 1043, ABV 4.6%)

Golden Ale (OG 1046, ABV 5%)

Hopcraft

See Pixie Spring-Hopcraft

Hopdaemon SIBA

Unit 1, Parsonage Farm, Seed Road, Newnham, Kent, ME9 0NA
☎ (01795) 892078 ⊕ hopdaemon.com

Tonie Prins originally started brewing in Tyler Hill near Canterbury in 2000 and moved to a new site in Newnham in 2005. The brewery currently supplies more than 100 outlets and is working at full capacity. ‼RAIB

Golden Braid (OG 1039, ABV 3.7%) ◣
A refreshing golden session bitter with a good blend of bittering and aroma hops underpinned by pale malt.

Incubus (OG 1041, ABV 4%) ◣
A well-balanced, copper-hued best bitter. Pale malt and a hint of crystal malt are blended with bitter and slightly floral hops to give a lingering hoppy finish.

Skrimshander IPA (OG 1045, ABV 4.5%)
An aromatic copper-coloured pale ale with a refreshing taste and a fruity finish.

Green Daemon (OG 1048, ABV 5%)
A golden beer with tropical fruit aromas and a crisp, clean finish. Brewed in the style of a Bavarian Helles (light lager).

Leviathan (OG 1057, ABV 6%)

A strong ruby-coloured ale with spicy hop aromas and a rich, malty finish.

Hope

76 Corringham Road, Stanford-le-Hope, Essex, SS17 0AE ☎ 07903 793223 ⊕ hopebrewery.co.uk

⊠ Hope was founded in 2013 using a 0.25-barrel plant, expanding to 2.5-barrels in 2014 using the old kit as a pilot plant. There are plans for relocation and further expansion. ◆RAIB

SX Pale (OG 1040, ABV 3.9%)

Strangely SX (OG 1041, ABV 4%)

SX Dark (OG 1042, ABV 4.2%)

SX Gold (OG 1042, ABV 4.2%)

SX Delight (OG 1044, ABV 4.4%)

SX Demon (OG 1044, ABV 4.4%)

SX Porter (OG 1049, ABV 4.6%)

SX Dragon (OG 1049, ABV 5%)

Hope Valley

Losehill Hall Youth Hostel, Castleton, Derbyshire, S33 8WB

Brewing started in 2009 in the former Castleton Youth Hostel but moved to its present location in 2012 when this closed. The two-barrel plant was formerly used by Edale. Only limited supplies are brewed and these are sold exclusively on the bar in the youth hostel when available.

Hophurst (NEW) SIBA

Unit 8, Hindley Business Centre, Platt Lane, Hindley, WN2 3PA
☎ (01942) 522333 ⊕ hophurstbrewery.co.uk

☺ Hophurst Brewery was started in 2014 by Stuart Hurst, whose passion for producing craft ales combined with 20 years of supporting businesses and re-skilling unemployed people created a unique social enterprise brewery that employs people over the age of 50 and guides them through their training programme in the Wigan area. Six core beers are produced. ◆

Flaxen (ABV 3.7%)
An easy-drinking pale golden session ale with a fresh, earthy hoppy aroma with hints of honey and a long, refreshing finish.

Campfire (ABV 3.9%)
A dark mild with a smoky, malty taste and aromas of roasted coffee and chocolate.

Joust (ABV 4%)
A well-rounded and refreshing pale ale, with flavours of spice, citrus and zesty orange.

Twisted Vine (ABV 4.1%)
A golden bitter with citrus hoppy aromas of grapefruit and passion fruit.

Cosmati (ABV 4.2%)
A hoppy golden ale with flavours of blueberry, citrus and tropical fruit.

Debonair (ABV 4.9%)
A robust stout with flavours of roasted coffee and liquorice and a pleasant bitter aftertaste.

Hops & Glory

See Solvay Society

Hopshackle SIBA

Unit F, Bentley Business Park, Blenheim Way, Northfields Industrial Estate, Market Deeping, Lincolnshire, Lincolnshire
☎ (01778) 348542 hopshacklebrewery.co.uk

Hopshackle was established in 2006 using a five-barrel plant. A 10-barrel plant was installed in 2015. More than 40 outlets are supplied direct. ♦ RAIB

Simarillo (OG 1037, ABV 3.8%)
Gold-coloured beer with an aroma of citrus and soft fruits. The taste is tangy fruit with blackberry, plum and pineapple.

Zen (OG 1037, ABV 3.8%)
Traditional, full-flavoured and full-bodied bitter; malty and fruity with a bittersweet finish.

American Pale Ale (OG 1042, ABV 4.3%)
An amber-coloured ale with a fruity, zesty aroma. The taste is citrus hop with a background of gooseberry and lychees and a dry bitter finish.

Hopnosis (OG 1050, ABV 5.2%)
Golden beer with a strong aroma of sweet malt and fruit. The taste is of strong citrus and tropical fruits with a dry finish.

Hopstar SIBA

Unit 9, Rinus Business Park, Grimshaw Street, Darwen, Lancashire, BB3 2QX ☎ 07933 590159
hopstarbrewery.co.uk

Hopstar first brewed in 2004 on a 2.5-barrel plant and expanded in 2010 to a new unit with a six-barrel plant. More than 100 outlets are supplied around Lancashire and the Greater Manchester area. The brewery tap is Number 39 in Darwen. !! ♦ RAIB

Chilli (OG 1039, ABV 3.8%)

Dizzy Danny Ale (OG 1039, ABV 3.8%)

Dark Knight (OG 1041, ABV 4%)

JC (OG 1041, ABV 4%)

Lancashire Gold (OG 1041, ABV 4%)

Lush (OG 1041, ABV 4%)

Smokey Joe's Black Beer (OG 1041, ABV 4%)

Hoptimists SIBA

Unit 6, Ground Floor, Coopers Place, Combe Lane, Wormley, Surrey, GU8 5SZ
☎ (01428) 684121 hoptimists.co.uk

Hoptimists began brewing in 2013 using a six-barrel plant.

Golden Dawn (ABV 3.8%)
An amber-coloured ale; fruity and aromatic.

Glass Half Full (ABV 4%)
A copper-coloured best bitter with a bitter aftertaste and floral hop aroma.

Hornbeam SIBA

1-1c Grey Street, Denton, Manchester, M34 3RU
☎ (0161) 320 5627 ☎ 07984 443383
hornbeambrewery.com

Hornbeam began brewing in 2007 on an eight-barrel plant. Regular monthly special beers are brewed. !! ♦ RAIB

Orange Blossom (OG 1038, ABV 3.8%)
Zesty golden pale ale.

Top Hop Best Bitter (OG 1041, ABV 4.2%)
Full-bodied with malt appeal and ample bitterness.

Black Coral Stout (OG 1043, ABV 4.5%)
A smooth, dry roast malt stout. Dark and full-bodied with a rich, creamy head. Satisfying with a subtle bitterness.

Horncastle (NEW)

Old Nicks Tavern, Horncastle, Lincolnshire, LN9 5DX
☎ (01507) 526862 horncastleales.co.uk

Brewing began in 2014 using a 3.75-barrel plant. The brewery is situated in Old Nicks Tavern with beer being available in the pub plus other Lincolnshire outlets. !!

Midnight Tempter (OG 1036.5, ABV 3.6%)
Smooth roasted flavours with a hoppy edge.

Damned Deceiver (OG 1038, ABV 3.8%)
Smooth rich chestnut-coloured beer with a full body.

Angel of Light (OG 1039.5, ABV 4%)
Light and malty beer with a nutty aftertaste.

Lilith's Lust (OG 1040.5, ABV 4.1%)
Traditional red-coloured bitter, malty and full-bodied.

Satan's Fury (OG 1040.5, ABV 4.1%)
Full-bodied, fruity IPA with a dark golden colour.

Sacrificed Soul (OG 1042, ABV 4.3%)
Chestnut-coloured, full-bodied bitter with caramel flavours and a slighty sweet edge.

Lucifer's Desire (OG 1046, ABV 4.8%)
Deep golden beer with citrus flavours and hoppy aftertaste.

Hoskins Brothers

See Belvoir

Houston

South Street, Houston, PA6 7EN
☎ (01505) 612620 houstonbrewery.co.uk

Established in 1997, the brewery is attached to the Fox & Hounds pub and restaurant. Beers are delivered throughout Britain either direct or via a network of distributors. !! ♦

Killellan Bitter (OG 1037, ABV 3.7%)
A light session ale with a floral hop and fruity taste. The finish of this amber beer is dry and quenching.

APA (OG 1039, ABV 3.9%)
A pale, refreshing citrus ale. Zingy and packed full of hop aroma, with an intense fruit taste.

Blonde Bombshell (OG 1040, ABV 4%)
A gold-coloured ale with a fresh hop aroma and rounded maltiness.

Peter's Well (OG 1042, ABV 4.2%)
Well-balanced fruity taste with sweet hop, leading to an increasingly bittersweet finish.

Slainte (OG 1043, ABV 4.3%)
Challenger hops explode on the nose leaving an aroma of malt and hops. The taste is long and deep with mature fruit notes that linger.

Tartan Terror (OG 1045, ABV 4.5%)

Howard Town SIBA

Hawkshead Mill, Hope Street, Glossop, Derbyshire, SK13 7SS
☎ (01457) 869800 ⊕ howardtownbrewery.co.uk

Established in 2005, this eight-barrel, award-winning brewery moved to its current location in 2007. An on-site bar caters for members evenings and open days. Bottle-conditioned beers are suitable for vegetarians. ‼ ☒ ♦RAIB

Mill Town Mild (OG 1038, ABV 3.5%)
Dark and lightly hopped with hints of toffee and coffee.

Longdendale Lights (OG 1039, ABV 3.9%)
A light-bodied, blonde refreshing ale.

Monk's Gold (OG 1040, ABV 4%)
A golden session ale with subtle orange notes.

Wren's Nest (OG 1041, ABV 4.2%)
Citrus, floral hops dominate this uncompromising bitter.

Super Fortress (OG 1044, ABV 4.4%)
Tasty, well-balanced premium chestnut bitter with malty caramel notes and fruity hops.

Dinting Arches (OG 1045, ABV 4.5%)
A light copper-coloured bitter with a hint of blackcurrant.

Glott's Hop (OG 1050, ABV 5%)
A strong and assertively bitter, straw-coloured ale with citrus notes.

Dark Peak (OG 1064, ABV 6%)
Strong and dark with a hint of liquorice and a warming rum kick.

Howling Hops

⊟ Unit 9a, Queen's Yard, White Post Lane, Hackney Wick, London, E9 5EN
☎ (020) 3583 8262

Cock Tavern, 315 Mare Street, Hackney, London, E8 1EJ ⊕ howlinghops.co.uk

☒ Brewing began in 2012. A wide range of cask and bottle-conditioned beers is produced, with four cask beers usually available at any one time. A new plant opened in 2015 in Hackney Wick, serving a couple of real ales along side 10 large tank beers. The original brewery at the Cock operates as a boutique brewery, brewing one-off speciality beers and beers using new hop varieties. RAIB

Mild (ABV 3.3%)

Pale Ale (ABV 3.8%)

Light Ale (ABV 4.2%)

Pale XX (ABV 5%)

Ruby Red (ABV 5%)

Smoked Porter (ABV 5.2%)

IPA (ABV 6%)

Old London Stout (ABV 6%)

Hoxne SIBA

Larch Barn, Heckfield Green, Suffolk, IP21 5AA
☎ 07563 558889 ⊕ hoxnebrewery.co.uk

Hoxne Brewery was an idea conceived in 2013 with brewing commencing in 2014. It is a member of the East Anglian Brewers Co-operative and the Barley to Beer Project. ♦RAIB

Heritage (ABV 5%)

Brakey Wood (ABV 5.4%)
Made from the finest Maris Otter barley from Branthill Farm, Wells-next-the-Sea, this deep coloured IPA has been created using masses of US hops both in the copper during the initial brewing phase and again later once conditioning has begun to deliver a classic IPA taste.

Sarah Hughes

⊟ Beacon Hotel, 129 Bilston Street, Sedgley, West Midlands, DY3 1JE
☎ (01902) 883381 ⊕ sarahhughesbrewery.co.uk

Traditional Black Country Victorian tower brewery, taken over by Sarah Hughes in 1921. Brewing ceased in the 1950s and recommenced in 1987. The original grist case and rare open-topped copper give a unique character to the brews. The Beacon Hotel is the brewery tap. ‼♦

Pale Amber (OG 1038, ABV 4%)
A well-balanced beer, initially slightly sweet but with hops close behind.

Sedgley Surprise (OG 1048, ABV 5%) ◥
A bittersweet, medium-bodied, hoppy ale with some malt.

Dark Ruby Mild (OG 1058, ABV 6%) ◥
A dark ruby strong ale with a good balance of fruit and hops, leading to a pleasant, lingering hops and malt finish.

Humpty Dumpty SIBA

Church Road, Reedham, Norfolk, NR13 3TZ
☎ (01493) 701818 ☎ 07843 248865
⊕ humptydumptybrewery.co.uk

⊠ Established in 1998, this 11-barrel, award-winning brewery continues to grow and expand its range of beers. The on-site shop sells bottled beer from the brewery and local cider. ‼ ☒ ♦RAIB

Little Sharpie (OG 1039, ABV 3.8%) ◥
Aroma redolent with fresh peach and apricot. Hoppy character with a bitter backlash and biscuity undertones. Long, dry, hoppy finish.

Lemon & Ginger (OG 1041, ABV 4%)
An amber-coloured, crisp ale with a ginger and lemon tang.

Swallowtail (OG 1041, ABV 4%) ◥
Fruity airs introduce this amber-gold ale. Hops reinforce the citrus backbone and grainy mouthfeel. A pleasant, slowly drying finish.

Ale (OG 1043, ABV 4.1%) ◥
A hoppy vanilla fudge edge in both nose and taste. Malt provides balance as a gentle bitterness quickly recedes. Lengthy finish.

Broadland Sunrise (OG 1044, ABV 4.2%) ◥
Hoppy throughout with a strong malt and bitter background. A grainy mouthfeel, hoppy aroma and long, strong finale.

Red Mill (OG 1045, ABV 4.3%)
A crisp, hoppy red-coloured ale with caramel and fruit notes.

Reedcutter (OG 1045, ABV 4.4%) ◆
A sweet, malty beer, golden hued with a gentle malt background. Smooth and full-bodied with a quick, gentle finish.

Cheltenham Flyer (OG 1046, ABV 4.6%) ◆
A full-flavoured golden, earthy bitter with a long, grainy finish. A strong hop bitterness dominates throughout. Little evidence of malt.

EAPA (East Anglian Pale Ale) (OG 1046, ABV 4.6%) ◆
Amber gold-coloured with an orange marmalade nose. A bittersweet caramel beginning slowly dries out as malty notes fade away.

Norfolk Nectar (OG 1046, ABV 4.6%) ◆
Honey notes wrap around all other flavours and aromas. Hops and caramel give a counterpoint to the rich, sweet base.

Hungry Bear (NEW)

10-14 Stonegate Road, Meanwood, Leeds, LS6 4HY
☎ (0113) 274 0241 🌐 thehungrybear.co.uk

Hungry Bear began brewing in 2013 in the upstairs rooms of the Hungry Bear restaurant. A wide range of ales is produced in batches of about 70 litres, which are bottled and conditioned on site and supplied to the restaurant. All beers are suitable for vegans. There are plans to increase production to supply other local outlets. ‼ RAIB

Hunsbury Craft

23 Limefields Way, East Hunsbury, Northamptonshire, NN4 0SA
☎ (01604) 766228 ☎ 07798 907242
✉ johngeorgemargetts@tiscali.co.uk

Hunsbury Craft was established in 2010 using a 0.5-barrel plant, increasing to 2.25-barrel plant to meet demand.

Best Bitter (OG 1040, ABV 3.9%)

Copper (OG 1041, ABV 4.2%)

JD's Robust Porter (OG 1051, ABV 5.4%)

Mel's Mild (OG 1054, ABV 5.4%)

Magic (OG 1058, ABV 5.6%)

Young Chick (OG 1060, ABV 6%)

Old Rooster (ABV 7.1%)

Hunters SIBA

Bulleigh Barton Farm, Ipplepen, Devon, TQ12 5UE
☎ (01803) 814399 ☎ 07540 657115
🌐 thehuntersbrewery.co.uk

Hunters began brewing in 2008. The award-winning brewery has a 60-barrel brew length and 4,000 gallon fermenting capacity. A bottling, labelling and packing plant means it can turn out 3,000 bottle-conditioned beers per hour; this coupled with a dedicated conditioning room is enabling Hunters to bottle for others as well as itself. Fruit beers are also brewed. ‼ ◆

Crack Shot (OG 1038, ABV 3.8%)
Good malt feel in the mouth with a dry, tangy, bitter finish.

Best (OG 1040, ABV 4%)
A smooth amber-coloured pint.

Crispy Pig (OG 1042, ABV 4%)
A speciality beer with a hint of apples.

Half Bore (OG 1040, ABV 4%)
Brewed with Devon honey for a full, malty flavour.

Devon Dreamer (OG 1042, ABV 4.1%)
A smooth, refreshing session ale.

Pheasant Plucker (OG 1044, ABV 4.3%)
Full-flavoured with a bittersweet finish.

Royal Hunt (OG 1055, ABV 5.5%)
A premium ale.

Black Jack (OG 1062, ABV 6%)
A strong but light-tasting triple-hopped stout made with Devon honey.

Full Bore (OG 1070, ABV 6.8%)
Malt flavours, made with Devon honey.

Hurns

See Tomos Watkin (under W)

Hurst SIBA

Western Road, Hurstpierpoint, West Sussex, BN6 9SP ☎ 07866 438953
✉ hurstbrewery@hotmail.co.uk

Hurst is a four-barrel microbrewery based at the White Horse, Hurstpierpoint, founded in 2012 but reviving a name dating back to 1862. More than 100 outlets are supplied between south London and Brighton. ‼ ◆

Founders Best Bitter (ABV 4.2%)
A nutty brown in colour with a rounded malty taste, suffused with subtle caramel.

Watchtower (ABV 5.5%)
A strong, dark porter with a distinctive bitterness created by highly roasted malts, with a rich, creamy head.

Hydes

The Beer Studio, 30 Kansas Avenue, Salford, M50 2GL
☎ (0161) 226 1317 🌐 hydesbrewery.com

Hydes has been a regional brewer since 1863 with its focus on cask ales to be supplied to their own tied estate of more than 70 pubs, as well as to the wholesale and free trade. Four main ranges of beer are produced: Hydes (including their bi-monthly Celebration ales); the Beer Studio – a monthly changing beer using rare and unusual hops and malts; the Lowry Collection – a bi-monthly changing beer celebrating the Salford artist L.S. Lowry; and Provenance, a changing bi-monthly world beer. ◆

Light Mild/1863 (OG 1033.5, ABV 3.5%) ◆
Lightly hopped, pale brown session beer with some hops, malt and fruit in the taste and a short, dry finish.

Owd Oak (OG 1033.5, ABV 3.5%) ◆
Dark brown/red in colour, with a fruit and malt nose. Taste includes biscuity malt and green fruits, with a satisfying aftertaste.

Original Bitter (OG 1036.5, ABV 3.8%) ◆

Pale brown beer with a malty nose, malt and an earthy hoppiness in the taste, and a good bitterness through to the finish.

Finest (OG 1044, ABV 4.5%)
A full-bodied and slightly sweet beer.

Iâl SIBA

Pant Du Rd, Eryrys, CH7 4DD ☎ 07956 440402
cwrwial.com

Cwrw Iâl Community Brewery is run as a social enterprise assisted by EU funding with all profits used for local community projects. The 10-barrel plant is situated in a former truck maintenance workshop and first brewed in 2014. It supplies outlets along the North Wales coast, Borders, Cheshire and Manchester.

Volunteer (OG 1037, ABV 3.8%)
A light copper-coloured session ale

Haul Gwyn Extra Pale Ale (OG 1040, ABV 4%)
A pale ale made with lager malts and wheat.

Kia Kaha! (OG 1043, ABV 4.3%)
Pale ale, late and dry-hopped.

Limestone Cowboy (OG 1045, ABV 4.5%)
Hop-forward, robust, deep copper-coloured ale.

Pothole Porter (OG 1054, ABV 5.1%)
Black and roasted with the addition of Golding hops.

Iceni SIBA

Foulden Road, Ickburgh, Norfolk, IP26 5HB
☎ (01842) 878922 ☎ 07949 488113
icenibrewery.co.uk

Iceni was launched in 1995 by Brendan Moore. The brewery is also the headquarters of the East Anglian Brewers Co-op (EAB). ‼ ♦ RAIB

Fine Soft Day (OG 1038, ABV 4%)
Golden hued with toffee notes throughout. A creamy, lightly-hopped backdrop softly sinks into a pleasant sweetness.

Idle

White Hart Inn, Main Street, West Stockwith, Nottinghamshire, DN10 4EY
☎ (01427) 753226 ☎ 07949 137174
theidlebrewery.co.uk

The brewery began production in 2007 and is situated in a converted stable at the back of the White Hart Inn, which Brian Cooper, the brewer, now owns, alongside the River Idle. Since acquiring the pub, Brian has no plans for expansion. ‼♦

Golden Crown (OG 1038, ABV 3.8%)
Golden beer with taste and body.

Idle Dog (OG 1041, ABV 4.2%)
A copper-coloured ale, moderately hoppy with a good balance of malt and hops leading to a bitter finish.

Idle Sod (OG 1041, ABV 4.2%)
Light golden ale with a deep, fruity aroma and a well-balanced bittering.

Idle Tongue (OG 1041, ABV 4.2%)

Black & Tan (OG 1042, ABV 4.3%)

Black Abbot (OG 1044, ABV 4.6%)
Strong, robust and hefty. A dark black ale with deep roasted notes.

Idle Landlord (OG 1044, ABV 4.6%)
A dark brown ale with plenty of body, a malty flavour and a caramel/coffee finish.

Idle Valley (NEW) SIBA

Barham House, Aurillac Way, Hallcroft Industrial Estate, Retford, Nottinghamshire, DN22 7PX ☎ 07850 228383 idlevalleybrewing.com

Idle Valley began brewing in 2014 using a 1.46-barrel/240 litre plant, housed within Barham House on the Hallcroft Trading Estate, Retford. The custom-built plant was constructed based on the head brewer's homebrew equipment. Brewing takes place twice a week. Beers are supplied to Christmas markets, local bottle shops, restaurants and selected beer festivals. RAIB

Ilkley SIBA

The New Brewery, Ashlands Road, Ilkley, West Yorkshire, LS29 8JT
☎ (01943) 604604 ilkleybrewery.co.uk

Ilkley Brewery was founded in 2009 and since moving to larger premises in 2011, using a 20-barrel plant, now produces up to 160 barrels a week. In July 2015, Ilkley was bought by the Half Full Beer Co, which plans to expand production. ‼♦RAIB

Mary Jane (OG 1036, ABV 3.5%)
A crisp, pale ale with citrus aromas.

Black (OG 1041, ABV 3.7%)
Dark session beer with a blend of five malts to give a smooth, mellow, easy-to-drink malt flavour with a hint of liquorice in the finish.

Joshua Jane (OG 1040, ABV 3.7%)
A traditional nut-brown Yorkshire bitter with a strong hoppy finish.

Gold (OG 1040, ABV 3.9%)
An easy-drinking, golden-coloured ale with a light floral aroma leading to a soft citrus fruit flavour and a gentle bitter aftertaste.

Ruby Jane (OG 1043, ABV 4%)
Soft, smooth ruby mild with subtle bitterness and a creamy mouthfeel.

Lotus IPA (OG 1054, ABV 5.6%)
Golden-coloured IPA with strong aromas and flavours of mango, grapefruit and all-round citrus.

Imperial

Arcadia Hall, Cliff Street, Mexborough, South Yorkshire, S64 9HU
☎ (01709) 584000 ☎ 0742 8422703
imperialclub@hotmail.co.uk

Brewing began in 2010 using a six-barrel tower brewery system located in the basement of the Imperial Club, Mexborough. Beer is available in the club as well as local outlets. ‼♦RAIB

Bitter (OG 1039, ABV 3.9%)

Blonde (OG 1040, ABV 4%)

Darkness (OG 1040, ABV 4%)

Bees Knees (OG 1043, ABV 4.2%)

Hop Bomb (OG 1042, ABV 4.2%)

IPA (OG 1052, ABV 5.5%)

Stout (OG 1054, ABV 5.8%)

Incredible (NEW) SIBA

214-224 Broomhill Road, Brislington, Bristol, BS4 5RG
☎ 07780 977073 🌐 incrediblebrewingcompany.com

Incredible Brewing specialises in producing small batches of craft beer using traditional methods. The three core beers are supplemented by several speciality beers, seasonal specials and occasional brews. ♦RAIB

Pale Ale (ABV 4.2%)

Amber Ale (ABV 5%)

Indian Pale Ale (ABV 5.6%)

Independent Lakeland Breweries

See Strands and Yates

Indian (NEW)

Old Stable Block, Red House Farm, Nuneaton Road, Ansley, Warwickshire, CV10 0QU
☎ (024) 7639 4386 🌐 indianbrewery.com

This six-barrel brewery, established in 2005 as the Tunnel Brewery at the Lord Nelson Inn, relocated to the picturesque stable block at Red House Farm in 2011. In 2015 the owners of Tunnel Brewery went their separate ways, with Mike Walsh retaining the brewery and renaming it the Indian Brewery. !!

Indian Summer (ABV 4%)
Golden orange bitter.

IPA (ABV 4.9%)

Peacock (ABV 5%)
Ruby old English ale.

Bombay Honey (ABV 5.6%)
A deep golden-coloured honey beer.

Indigenous (NEW)

Peacock Cottage, Main Street, Chaddleworth, Berkshire, RG20 7EH
☎ (01488) 505060 🌐 indigenousbrewery.co.uk

⊗ An occasional and informal microbrewer for many years, Kevin Brady established Indigenous in 2014, increasing production using a 2.5-barrel plant. Beers are supplied to local pubs and a growing number of regional beer festivals. !!

Summer Solstice (OG 1042, ABV 4.1%)
A straw-coloured pale ale with a fresh, hoppy aroma, a subtle bitterness and a long, dry finish.

Old Cadger (OG 1046, ABV 4.5%)
Rich malts and fruity hops combine to produce a balanced, full-flavoured beer.

Monocle (OG 1049, ABV 4.6%)
A smooth stout with a malty aroma and a slightly dry finish.

Nosey Parker (OG 1058, ABV 5.5%)
A strong ruby-red mild with a sweet malty base and a hint of hops.

Inishmacsaint

7 Drumadown Road, Drumskimly, Derrygonnelly, Co Fermanagh, BT93 6DN
☎ (028) 6864 1031 ✉ gordyfallis@hotmail.com

Inishmacsaint is small-scale brewery that has been in production since mid-2009. A larger brew plant is now in use producing a range of bottle-conditioned beers. RAIB

INNformal (NEW)

Five Bells, Baydon Road, Wickham, RG20 8HH
☎ (01488) 657300 🌐 fivebellswickham.co.uk

⊗ INNformal was established in 2015 in a purpose-built building behind the Five Bells pub in Wickham. A bore hole in the pub garden supplies water for the 2.5-barrel plant. A secondary 0.5-barrel kit is used for experimental brews. Beers are supplied mainly to the Five Bells and the John O'Gaunt, Hungerford. !!

San FrINNcisco (OG 1059, ABV 6.1%)
West Coast-style IPA.

INNDeep (OG 1062, ABV 7.2%)
A chocolate stout.

Innis & Gunn

Canning Street, Edinburgh, EH3 8EG
☎ (0131) 272 2782 🌐 innisandgunn.com

Innis & Gunn does not brew but Tennents produces one regular bottled (not bottle-conditioned) beer for the company, Oak Aged Beer (ABV 6.6%). There are three further beers in the permanent range: Original (ABV 6.6%), Blonde (ABV 6%) and Rum Cask (ABV 7.4%). A range of limited edition beers is also produced each year.

Instant Karma

4 John St, Clay Cross, Derbyshire, S45 9NQ
☎ (01246) 250366 🌐 instantkarmabrewery.co.uk

Instant Karma began brewing in 2012 using a five-barrel plant with a brew length of 15 barrels per week. The brewery is part of the Rykneld Turnpyke brewpub.

Test Brew Number One! (OG 1039, ABV 3.9%)

Test Brew Number Two! (OG 1045, ABV 4.5%)

Sutra (OG 1053, ABV 5.5%)

Interbrew Magor

Magor Brewery, Magor, NP26 3DA

UK subsidiary of AB InBev. No real ale.

Interbrew Samlesbury

Cuerdale Lane, Samlesbury, Lancashire, PR5 0XD

UK subsidiary of AB InBev. No real ale.

Interbrew UK

Porter Tun House, Capability Green, Luton, Bedforshire, LU1 3LS
☎ (01582) 391166

No real ale.

Intrepid (NEW) SIBA 👁

Unit 12, Vincent Works, Brough, Bradwell, Derbyshire, S33 9HG
☎ (01433) 621851 ☎ 07941 995368
⊕ intrepidbrew.co.uk

☺Brewing commenced in 2014 using an eight-barrel plant. ‼

Explorer (OG 1038, ABV 4%)
A refreshing blonde beer with fruity aromas and a crisp dry finish.

St Bernard (OG 1044, ABV 4.4%)
A malty ale with oak and vanilla aromas, and caramel and biscuit flavours.

Porter (OG 1049, ABV 4.8%)
A traditional East India porter but with a less bitter finish.

Traveller (OG 1049, ABV 5.4%)
American-style IPA with a fruity flavour and bitter finish.

Inveralmond SIBA 👁

22 Inveralmond Place, Inveralmond, Perth, PH1 3TS
☎ (01738) 449448 ⊕ inveralmond-brewery.co.uk

☺Established in 1997, Inveralmond was the first brewery in Perth for more than 30 years. The brewery has expanded from a 10-barrel to a 30-barrel plant and there are plans for further growth. Around 250 outlets are supplied. ‼🍺♦

Fair Maid (OG 1036, ABV 3.6%) ◆
A well-balanced Scottish ale with fruit and malt tones. Hops provide an increasing bitterness in the finish.

Ossian (OG 1042, ABV 4.1%) ◆
Well-balanced best bitter with a dry finish. This full-bodied amber ale is dominated by fruit and hop with a bittersweet character although excessive caramel can distract from this.

Thrappledouser (OG 1043, ABV 4.3%) ◆
A refreshing amber beer with reddish hues. The crisp, hoppy aroma is finely balanced with a tangy but quenching taste.

Lia Fail (OG 1048, ABV 4.7%) ◆
The Gaelic name means Stone of Destiny. A dark, robust, full-bodied beer with a deep malty taste. Smooth texture and balanced finish.

Rascal London Porter (OG 1056, ABV 5.6%)

Ironbridge

See Wrekin

Irving SIBA 👁

Unit G1, Railway Triangle, Walton Road, Portsmouth, Hampshire, PO6 1TQ
☎ (023) 9238 9988 ⊕ irvingbrewers.co.uk

⊗ Established in 2007 by former Gale's brewer Malcolm Irving using a 15-barrel plant. Around 120 outlets are supplied in Hampshire, Sussex and Surrey with beers available further afield through beer swaps with other breweries. ‼🍺♦

Frigate (OG 1039, ABV 3.8%)
Golden bitter with a citrus hop flavour complemented by a background sweetness.

Type 42 (OG 1042, ABV 4.2%)
A robust best bitter with a deep ruby red hue balancing sweet hedgerow berry notes with a long, roasted malt finish and a deep bitterness.

Admiral Stout (OG 1042.5, ABV 4.3%)
A classic dark oatmeal stout, deep black in colour with a smooth, rounded malt flavour balanced with a strong bitterness.

Invincible (OG 1048, ABV 4.6%) ◆
Tawny-coloured strong bitter. Sweet and fruity with underlying maltiness throughout and gradually increasing dryness, contrasting with the sweet finish.

Iron Duke (OG 1053, ABV 5.3%)
A refreshing, well-balanced strong IPA. Hoppy – but not overly so.

Irwell Works SIBA

Irwell Street, Ramsbottom, BL0 9YQ
☎ (01706) 825019 ⊕ irwellworksbrewery.co.uk

☺ Irwell Works started brewing in 2010 in a building dating from 1888 that once housed the Irwell Works Steam, Tin, Copper & Iron Works. It now houses a six-barrel plant. A bar opened on the first floor in 2011. ‼

Lightweights & Gentlemen (OG 1031, ABV 3.2%) ◆
Light, refreshing pale ale with some fruitiness and a hoppy, bitter finish.

Tin Plate (OG 1033, ABV 3.6%)
Brewed as a traditional dark mild, low in strength and a rich creamy flavour but with a slight bitterness to contrast.

Copper Plate (OG 1036, ABV 3.8%) ◆
Traditional northern bitter. Copper-coloured with satisfying blend of malt and hops and good bitterness.

Richard Mason 1888 (OG 1039, ABV 4%)
Richard Mason built Irwell Works in 1888. A mid-strength, single-hopped beer with a mild bitterness and pleasant mildly hopped aftertaste.

Costa Del Salford (OG 1039, ABV 4.1%)
A hoppy summer ale, this beer is light in colour with bags of flavour.

Steam Plate (OG 1042, ABV 4.3%)
A golden best bitter with medium bitterness balanced with a slight sweetness and a slightly nutty flavour.

Iron Plate (OG 1043, ABV 4.4%) ◆
Roast malt in the aroma is joined by hop and a toasty bitterness in the taste and finish.

Mad Dogs & Englishmen (OG 1052, ABV 5.5%)
Export-style pale ale hopped in the style of an IPA. Little sweetness for its strength and a strong hop character make this a smooth, easy-drinking beer.

Isca SIBA

Court Farm, Holcombe, Dawlish, Devon, EX7 0JT
☎ 07773 444501 ⊕ iscaales.co.uk

Isca Ales has developed a niche market by bottling a lot of production and supplying beer festivals outside their region. All bottle-conditioned beers are suitable for vegans. 🍺RAIB

Citra (OG 1038, ABV 3.8%)

Light, refreshing beer with grapefruit aroma leading to a dry bitter finish.

Dawlish Summer (OG 1038, ABV 3.8%)
A light beer with a hoppy aroma.

Golden Ale (OG 1038, ABV 3.8%)
A golden bitter with a hoppy aroma.

Dawlish Bittter (OG 1042, ABV 4.2%)
Classic English bitter full of English hops and West Country malt.

Glorious Devon (OG 1044, ABV 4.4%)
The combination of three hops gives a grassy hop aroma with hoppy aftertaste.

Holcombe Gold (OG 1045, ABV 4.5%)
Golden beer full of English and American hops leading to a dry bitter finish.

Dawlish Pale (OG 1050, ABV 5%)
Grassy hop aroma with intense hoppy aftertaste.

Achilles Ale (OG 1054, ABV 5.4%)
Dark, strong, malty ale.

Isfield SIBA

Unit 16, New Place Farm, New Place Farm, Framfield, East Sussex, TN22 5RH
☎ (01825) 750633 ☎ 07803 716758

Imperial Cottage Station Road, Isfield, TN22 5UJ
✉ enquiries@isfieldbrewing.co.uk

⊗ Isfield began brewing in 2012 using a five-barrel plant. ♦

Bitter (OG 1040, ABV 3.7%)
A chestnut-coloured session bitter with a fruity and malty aroma with a biscuity sweet taste.

Straw Blond (OG 1043, ABV 4.1%)
Straw-coloured with a tropical fruit aroma, citrus taste and a dry finish.

Toad in the Ale (OG 1050, ABV 4.8%)
A dark premium bitter with a roasted, smoky aroma with a liquorice and chocolate taste.

Flapjack (OG 1055, ABV 5.3%)
Oatmeal stout with a roast coffee aroma and a rich, full, oaty taste with hints of berries.

Isla Vale (NEW)

17 Westbrook Gardens, Margate, Kent, CT9 5DJ
☎ (01843) 292451 ☎ 07980 174616
islavalealesmiths.co.uk

⊗ Established in 2014 from a residential address in Westbrook (Margate) using a 100-litre brew length. At present 10 local micropubs are supplied. There are plans to expand the brewery, number of outlets, production and range of ales. ♦

Golding Delicious (OG 1040, ABV 3.8%)
A light copper-coloured, hoppy session ale, with a slight malty sweetness.

Hopping Mad (OG 1042, ABV 4%)
A traditional session bitter with a variety of hops, complex aromas and malty flavours.

Cock a Snook (ABV 4.6%)
A dark golden, short session ale with good hop aroma and hints of fruit.

Natural Blonde (ABV 4.7%)
A refreshing blonde ale with initial floral notes and a lasting hoppy bitterness throughout and citrus finish.

Befuggled (OG 1052, ABV 5.2%)
A rich, malty ESB-style ale.

Portly Pig Porter (OG 1053, ABV 5.2%)
A rich, dark porter-style ale with hints of coffee and caramel.

IPA (OG 1058, ABV 5.5%)
A modern take on a traditional IPA using a variety of New World hops. A hint of fruit with an intense hoppy aroma and flavour.

Brewed for the Wheel House pub, Birchington:

Bosun's Best (OG 1044, ABV 4.2%)

Island SIBA

Dinglers Farm, Yarmouth Road, Newport, Isle of Wight, PO30 4LZ
☎ (01983) 821731 isleofwightbrewery.com

⊗ Island Brewery is the realisation of Tom Minshull's ambition to brew real ales to complement the existing family-owned drinks distribution business. Brewing commenced in 2010 using a 12-barrel brewery. More than 100 outlets are supplied direct. ‼♦

Nipper Bitter (OG 1038, ABV 3.8%)
Straw-coloured, light and refreshing with a distinguishable balance of malt and hops and a satisfying afterbite.

Wight Gold (OG 1040, ABV 4%)
Golden brown in colour with rounded malt and hops throughout.

Yachtsmans Ale (OG 1042, ABV 4.2%)
Chestnut-coloured ale with a rich, malty mouthfeel and hop aroma.

Wight Diamond (OG 1046, ABV 4.4%)

Wight Knight (OG 1045, ABV 4.5%)
Strong, full-bodied beer.

Vectis Venom (OG 1048, ABV 4.8%)
Easy-drinking with an underlying smoothness.

Earls RDA (OG 1052, ABV 5%)
Rich yet understated stout, with a strong espresso aftertaste.

Islay SIBA

The Brewery, Islay House Square, Bridgend, Isle of Islay, PA44 7NZ
☎ (01496) 810014 islayales.com

Brewing started on a four-barrel plant in a converted tractor shed in 2004. The brewery shop is next door. The island is more famous for its whisky, but the brewery has established itself as a must-see place for those visiting the eight working distilleries. ‼ ♦ RAIB

Isle of Mull

See Argyll

Isle of Purbeck SIBA

Manor Road, Studland, Dorset, BH19 3AU
☎ (01929) 450227 isleofpurbeckbrewery.com

⊗ Founded in 2003, the brewery is situated in the grounds of the Bankes Arms Hotel, overlooking Studland Bay on the Jurassic Coast. The 10-barrel plant produces six core beers plus seasonals and an annually brewed cold-filtered Pilsner lager called Purbex. The core beers are available nationwide via exchange swaps with other microbrewers. Bottle-conditioned beer is available direct from the brewery and from retailers throughout Hampshire and Dorset. ◆RAIB

Purbeck Best Bitter (OG 1036, ABV 3.6%) ◥
A classic malty best bitter with rich malt aroma and taste and smooth malty bitter finish.

Harry's (OG 1040, ABV 4%)
A well-balanced beer with sweet and malty flavours and a hint of spicy hops.

Fossil Fuel (OG 1040, ABV 4.1%) ◥
Amber bitter with complex aroma with a hint of pepper; rich malt dominates the taste, leading to a smooth dry finish.

Solar Power (OG 1043, ABV 4.3%) ◥
Tawny-coloured mid-range ale brewed using Continental hops. Well-balanced flavours combine to provide a strong bitter taste but short, dry finish.

Studland Bay Wrecked (OG 1044, ABV 4.5%) ◥
Deep red ale with slightly sweet aroma reflecting a mixture of caramel, malt and hops that lead to a dry, malty finish.

Purbeck IPA (OG 1047, ABV 4.8%) ◥
Mid-brown beer with hop/malt balance in the flavour and a long dry aftertaste

Isle of Skye SIBA

The Pier, Uig, Isle of Skye, IV51 9XP
☎ (01470) 542477 ⊕ skyebrewery.co.uk

☺The Isle of Skye Brewery was established in 1995. Originally a 10-barrel plant, it was upgraded to 20 barrels in 2004. Angus MacRuary has sold the majority share holding to IOSB Holdings Ltd, but will continue to run the brewery side. The brewery underwent rebranding in 2014. Further expansion is planned. ‼▆◆

Skye Light (OG 1038, ABV 3.8%) ◥
A slightly hoppy nose leads to a powerful hop and fruit taste and a sharp finish.

Skye Otter Ale (OG 1041, ABV 4%)

Tarasgeir (OG 1040, ABV 4%) ◥
The peat-roasted barley dominates giving a mellow peaty whisky taste.

Thistle and the Fern (OG 1041, ABV 4%) ◥
Good mix of hops and malt with a bitter earthy background.

Young Pretender (OG 1039, ABV 4%) ⬡ ◥
A fruity, full-bodied golden ale, predominantly hoppy and fruity. The bitterness in the mouth is also balanced by summer fruits and hops, continuing into the lingering bitter finish.

Red (OG 1041, ABV 4.2%) ⬡ ◥
A light, fruity nose with a hint of caramel leads to a hoppy, malty, fruity flavour and a dry, bittersweet finish.

Gold (OG 1041.5, ABV 4.3%) ◥
Porridge oats are used to produce this delicious speciality beer. Nicely balanced, it has a refreshingly soft fruity, bitter flavour with an oaty background.

Black (OG 1044, ABV 4.5%) ⬡ ◥
A complex, tasty brew worthy of its many awards. Full-bodied with a malty richness. Malt holds sway

but there are plenty of hops and fruit to be discovered in its varied character. A delicious Scottish old ale.

IPA (OG 1046, ABV 4.5%) ◥
Well balanced with a good malty background and complemented with flavoursome Sorachi Ace hops.

Blaven (OG 1047, ABV 5%) ◥
A well-balanced strong amber bitter with kiwi fruit and caramel in the nose and a lingering sharp bitterness.

Cuillin Beast (OG 1066, ABV 7%) ◥
A winter warmer; sweet and fruity, and much more drinkable than the strength would suggest. Plenty of caramel throughout with a variety of fruit on the nose.

Itchen Valley SIBA

Unit 4, Prospect Commercial Park, Prospect Road, New Alresford, Hampshire, SO24 9QF
☎ (01962) 735111 ⊕ itchenvalley.com

⊗ Established in 1997, Itchen Valley moved to new premises in 2006 with a 20-barrel plant. The brewery has a gift shop and offers brewery tours and mini conferencing facilities. More than 350 pubs are supplied, with wholesalers used for further distribution. ‼▆◆RAIB

Belgarum (ABV 3.9%)
A hoppy bitter sweetened with Hampshire honey and offset by the addition of elderflower.

Q.E.D. (OG 1041, ABV 4.1%) ◥
Copper-coloured best bitter with a hint of crystal malt and a pleasant bitter aftertaste.

Hampshire Rose (OG 1042, ABV 4.2%)
A golden amber ale. Fruit and hops dominate the taste throughout, with a good mouthfeel.

Pure Gold (OG 1046, ABV 4.8%) ◥
Aromatic hoppy, strong bitter. Golden-coloured, with initial maltiness and grapefruit counterbalanced with some sweetness, leading to a dry finish.

Jacobi SIBA

Penlanwen Farm, Pumsaint, Carmarthenshire, SA19 8RR
☎ (01558) 650605 ⊕ jacobibrewery.co.uk

Brewing started in 2006 in a converted barn. There is no brewery tap, but regular outlets for the beers are Dolaucothi in Pumpsaint and the Blue Bell in Llandovery. Former beers named Light, Beekeepers, and Dark have been re-named. ◆

Gold Miner (OG 1038, ABV 3.9%)
Golden light ale with floral flavours reminiscent of elderflower, and a clean bitter finish.

Red Squirrel (OG 1044, ABV 4.3%)
Chestnut-coloured bitter with fruit undertones and a dry bitter finish.

Dr Harries Dark Magic (OG 1050, ABV 4.7%)
Dark, rich, old-style ale; smooth with a chocolate bitter finish.

James & Kirkman

4 Wakefield Road, Pontefract, West Yorkshire, WF8 4HN

☎ (01977) 702231
✉ eastcoastbrewing@hotmail.co.uk

Brewing began in 2013 behind the Robin Hood pub using a 2.5-barrel plant. Beers were previously brewed at East Coast Brewing (qv), owned by the same brewers.

Little John (ABV 3.6%)

James Street

≣ City Pub Company, 14 James Street West, Bath, BA1 2BX
☎ (01225) 805609 ⊕ thebathbrewhouse.com

⊠ The James Street Brewery opened in 2013 and is owned by the City Pub Company (West), which owns several other pubs, including brewpubs in Cambridge and in Henley, London. The compact plant is on the ground floor of the Bath Brewhouse, with the conditioning tanks on the first floor. Occasional special ales are brewed. The company's other pub, the Cork in Bath, is also supplied. ‼▼◆

Gladiator (OG 1040, ABV 3.8%) ◀
Hazy, pale brown beer with little aroma. Thin, sweetish flavour with some malt. Dry aftertaste.

Emperor (OG 1044, ABV 4.4%) ◀
Golden-coloured beer with little aroma. A little caramel and fruit in the flavour, but dryness and bitterness is dominant. Dry astringent aftertaste.

Jarrow SIBA ◉

≣ 54 Aidan Court, Jarrow, Tyne & Wear, NE32 3EF
☎ (0191) 483 6792 ⊕ jarrowbrewery.co.uk

☺ Brewing commenced at the Robin Hood, Jarrow in 2002, moving to South Shields in 2008. In 2013 brewing returned to Jarrow using a 40-barrel plant. In 2015 former Vaux brewery managing director, Frank Nicholson, was appointed as new chairman. ‼◆

Bitter (OG 1037.5, ABV 3.8%)
A classic session ale.

Rivet Catcher (OG 1039, ABV 4%) ◀
A light, smooth, satisfying golden bitter. Subtle fruity hops give the taste profile on the tongue and nose.

Joblings Swinging Gibbet (OG 1041, ABV 4.1%)
A copper-coloured, well-balanced beer with a good hop aroma and a fruity finish.

Caulker (OG 1040.5, ABV 4.2%)
A light, smooth, satisfying golden hoppy ale, with a lingering grapefruit zest finish.

Red Ellen (OG 1042.5, ABV 4.4%)
A rich, ruby red, full-bodied ale with a citrus hop aroma.

McConnells Irish Stout (OG 1045, ABV 4.6%) ◀
A rich, creamy stout with a long, lingering liquorice and pale chocolate finish.

Westoe IPA (OG 1044.5, ABV 4.6%)
A pale golden ale with a soft malt character and refreshingly complex hop aroma – easy-drinking premium ale.

Isis (OG 1049, ABV 5%)
A well-balanced golden premium ale with a full hop aroma and grapefruit presence on the palate.

American IPA (OG 1051, ABV 5.5%)

A full-bodied golden IPA with orange and pink grapefruit hop flavours.

Jaw (NEW) SIBA ◉

Unit 9, The Centre Point, 67b Montrose Avenue, Hillington Industrial Estate, Glasgow, G52 4LA
☎ (0141) 237 5840 ⊕ jawbrew.co.uk

Brewing began in 2014. RAIB

Fathom (ABV 4%)
A tasty dark ale.

Drop (ABV 4.2%)
An easy-drinking pale ale with good bitterness and a full hop character.

Drift (ABV 4.6%)
A full-bodied golden ale.

Jennings ◉

Castle Brewery, Cockermouth, Cumbria, CA13 9NE
☎ (01900) 820362 ⊕ jenningsbrewery.co.uk

◉Jennings Brewery was established as a family concern in 1828 in the village of Lorton. The company moved to its present location in 1874. Pure Lakeland water is still used for brewing, drawn from the brewery's own well. Part of Marston's PLC. ‼▼◆

Dark Mild (OG 1031, ABV 3.1%) ◀
A well-balanced, dark brown mild with a malty aroma, strong roast taste, not over-sweet, with some hops and a slightly bitter finish.

Bitter (OG 1035, ABV 3.5%) ◀
A malty beer with a good mouthfeel that combines with roast flavour and a hoppy finish.

Cumberland Ale (OG 1038, ABV 4%) ◀
A tawny, hoppy beer with a dry aftertaste.

Cocker Hoop (OG 1044, ABV 4.6%) ◀
Full-bodied complex bitter beer with plenty of hops and a rising bitter finish.

Sneck Lifter (OG 1051, ABV 5.1%) ◀
A strong, dark brown ale with a complex balance of fruit, malt, sweet and roast flavours through to the finish.

Jo C's SIBA

The Old Store, Walsingham Road, West Barsham, Norfolk, NR21 9NP
☎ (01328) 863854 ⊕ jocsnorfolkale.co.uk

⊠ Starting in 2010, Jo Coubrough (the county's only brewster) established a 10-barrel brewery in a former farm building in Norfolk. The beers are available in Flying Kiwi Inns, other free trade outlets, and at the brewery. Mini-casks and bottles are also available. ‼▼

Norfolk Kiwi (OG 1038.5, ABV 3.8%) ◀
Yellow-coloured, hop dominated bitter. Citrus notes vie with bitterness to add depth. Quick, slightly astringent finish.

Bitter Old Bustard (OG 1045, ABV 4.3%) ◀
A mixture of malt and caramel on the nose is joined by a dark fruitiness in the flavour. Quick finish.

Knot Just Another IPA (OG 1052, ABV 5%)

A light amber-coloured, well-balanced, strong bitter. Well-hopped with both traditional and modern varieties of English hop.

Jolly Sailor SIBA

Olympia Hotel, 77 Barlby Road, Selby, North Yorkshire, YO8 5AB
☎ (01757) 268918 ☎ 07923 635755
⊕ jolly-sailor-brewery.webplus.net

Jolly Sailor began brewing in 2012 at Ricall Business Park, a former mine site near York. Production was moved to the Olympia Hotel, Selby, in 2013, where the regular beers are always available and increasingly in other local pubs. ♦

Bullseye Bitter (OG 1039, ABV 3.8%)

Jolly Blonde (OG 1036.5, ABV 3.8%)

Jolly Scotsman's Bitter (OG 1038, ABV 3.8%)
A fruity amber-coloured ale with citrus notes.

Yellow Jersey (OG 1036, ABV 3.8%)
A pale ale brewed with English hops.

Cue Brew (OG 1040, ABV 4%)
A dark mild.

Jollyboat SIBA

Coach House, Buttgarden Street, Bideford, Devon, EX39 2AU
☎ (01237) 424343

⊠ Established in 1995, the brewery is named after a sailor's leave vessel and all the beers have a nautical theme. Most outlets supplied are in Devon. ‼♦

Grenville's Renown (OG 1038, ABV 3.8%)
Mid-brown bitter with a full flavour.

Mainbrace (OG 1042, ABV 4.2%) ◥
Pale brown brew with a rich, fruity aroma and a bitter taste and aftertaste.

Plunder (OG 1049, ABV 4.8%)
Red/brown beer with an aromatic nose, a good balance of malt, hops and fruit present throughout leading to a bitter finish.

Contraband (OG 1056, ABV 5.8%)
Dark brown-coloured beer with chocolate, roasted malts, raisins and some spiciness in the aroma. Cinnamon and nutmeg spiciness melds with chocolate and fruity flavours with strong roasty bitterness in the finish.

Jones the Brewer

Unit 2, The Old Garage, Whitney-on-Wye, Herefordshire, HR3 6ER
☎ (01497) 831220 ☎ 07010 717232
⊕ jonesthebrewer.co.uk

Damian Jones started this five-barrel brewery in 2013. It supplies to more than a dozen local outlets and also direct from the brewery and website. New beers are introduced to the regular range via the Epicurious series, a limited run used to judge popularity. ‼ RAIB

Abigail's Party (OG 1036, ABV 3.8%)
A light golden-coloured, easy-drinking pale ale. A zesty aroma leads to small fruit/malt sweetness, overlaid with dominant grapefruit and lemon citrus flavours.

Malty Python (OG 1049, ABV 4.2%)
A dark copper-coloured brown ale with a caramel malt and a subtle wheat aroma. Soft malty toffee flavours and caramel undertones with a mild dry bitterness in a short finish.

Creature (OG 1046, ABV 4.5%)
A golden honey-coloured bitter, with a pine resin aroma, and pine/cedar flavours that mix with an emerging burst of citrus fruit, tropical high notes and caramel undertones.

Dennis Hopper (OG 1045, ABV 4.7%)
An American-style pale ale with a full but crisp malt body that is complemented by a refined bitterness and a full hop flavour.

Rechtifier (OG 1052, ABV 5.7%)
A traditionally unfined and unfiltered German-style Weissbier (wheat beer). A clean, flavoursome sweet banana fruitiness leads to a subtle lemon tartness and just a trace of bitterness.

Wheat Stone Bridge (OG 1052, ABV 5.7%)
A yellow-coloured Belgian-style wheat beer with a spicy fruit aroma. An orange fruit sweetness combines with warming coriander spice and a bready wheat body.

Jean Paul Citra (OG 1061, ABV 6.6%)
A honey-coloured IPA, rich fruity aroma that follows into the taste, intense citrus fruits and grapefruit flavours, rich and lasting into a long, bitter finish.

Joule's SIBA ◉

The Brewery, Great Hales Street, Market Drayton, Shropshire, TF9 1JP
☎ (01630) 654400 ⊕ joulesbrewery.co.uk

Re-established in 2010, following a break of 40 years, Joule's is situated in Market Drayton and uses its own mineral water. It concentrates on three core beers and in 2013 launched a seasonal ale portfolio, experimenting with unusual beer styles. ‼♦

Blonde (OG 1038, ABV 3.8%)
Light, refreshing and subtle, a well-balanced blonde beer. Hops deliver a citrus and hoppy aroma characteristic of this continental style.

Pale Ale (OG 1042, ABV 4.1%)
Made from the original Joule's recipe from 1779. A crisp beer with initial impact, giving way to a pleasant bitter finish.

Slumbering Monk (OG 1045, ABV 4.5%)
Full-bodied with deep, malty and nutty fullness. Hints of caramel give a round, soft, satisfying smoothness in this bright copper ale, cut with light, hoppy bitterness.

Junction

1 Baildon Road, Baildon, West Yorkshire, BD16 6AB

Junction is a small microbrewery established in 2012 in the cellar of the Junction pub in Baildon, brewing about 300 gallons a week. Beer is sold in the pub and other local outlets. RAIB

Tommy's Tipple (OG 1037, ABV 3.7%)
A chestnut-coloured session bitter; smooth-tasting with a hoppy finish.

Blonde (OG 1040, ABV 4%)
A blonde session bitter, offering a big flavour and a dry finish.

Dark Thoughts (OG 1046, ABV 4.6%)
Porter with roasted, nutty flavours and hops which give a bitter edge.

Just A Minute

Coulson Street, Spennymoor, County Durham, DL16 7RS ☎ 07586 896091
⊕ justaminutebrewery.co.uk

Established by two friends in 2010, a 2.5 barrel plant was commissioned in 2011 and was refurbished in 2014. Seasonal beers and one-off brews are produced alongside regulars. The brewery has also recently started a contract brewing arrangement with the Half Moon in Darlington, producing two seasonal ales. ◆

Ruby Tuesday (OG 1039, ABV 3.9%)

Tyme Tunnel (OG 1041, ABV 4.1%)

Stoppy Back (OG 1042, ABV 4.2%)

Golden Dawn (OG 1043, ABV 4.3%)

IPA (OG 1046, ABV 4.6%)

Time 'n' 'Arf (OG 1050, ABV 5%)

Kelburn SIBA ◉

10 Muriel Lane, Barrhead, G78 1QB
☎ (0141) 881 2138 ⊕ kelburnbrewery.com

⊠ Kelburn is an award-winning family business established in 2002. Beers are available bottled, cask-conditioned and to take away in polypins. ‼◆

Goldihops (OG 1038, ABV 3.8%) ◕
Well-hopped session ale with a fruity taste and a bitter finish.

Pivo Estivo (OG 1038, ABV 3.9%)

Misty Law (OG 1040, ABV 4%)
A dry, hoppy amber-coloured ale with a long-lasting bitter finish.

Red Smiddy (OG 1040, ABV 4.1%) ◕
This bittersweet ale predominantly features an intense citrus hop character that assaults the nose and continues into the flavour, balanced perfectly with fruity malt.

Regnitz (OG 1042, ABV 4.4%)

Dark Moor (OG 1044, ABV 4.5%) ▣
A dark, fruity ale with undertones of liquorice and blackcurrant.

Jaguar (OG 1043, ABV 4.5%) ▣

Cart Noir (OG 1046, ABV 4.8%)

Cart Blanche (OG 1048, ABV 5%) ◕
A golden, full-bodied ale. The assault of fruit and hop camouflages the strength of this easy-drinking ale.

Kelham Island SIBA

23 Alma Street, Sheffield, South Yorkshire, S3 8SA
☎ (0114) 249 4804

Office: Prospect House, 17 Alma Street, Sheffield, S3 8RY ⊕ kelhambrewery.co.uk

☺Opened in 1990 behind the Fat Cat pub, the brewery moved to new purpose-built premises in 1999. The old building is used as a visitor centre. A brewery shop is housed with new offices in nearby Prospect House. ‼ ⟱ ◆ RAIB

Best Bitter (OG 1038, ABV 3.8%)
Classic amber-coloured Yorkshire bitter with spicy, earthy aromas and a sweet, refreshing, malty finish.

Pride of Sheffield (OG 1040.5, ABV 4%)
A full-flavoured amber-coloured bitter.

Easy Rider (OG 1041.8, ABV 4.3%) ◕
A pale, straw-coloured beer with a sweetish flavour and delicate hints of citrus fruits. A beer with hints of flavour rather than full-bodied.

Riders on the Storm (OG 1045, ABV 4.5%)
A robust golden pale ale with berry notes and slight roasted notes.

Pale Rider (OG 1050, ABV 5.2%) ▣ ◕
A full-bodied, straw-coloured pale ale, with a good fruity aroma and a strong fruit and hop taste. Its well-balanced sweetness and bitterness continue in the finish.

Keltek SIBA ◉

Candela House, Cardrew Way, Redruth, Cornwall, TR15 1SS
☎ (01209) 313620 ⊕ keltekbrewery.co.uk

⊠ Keltek has undergone a number of expansions in recent years and is now a major force in Cornwall and further afield. Bottling is carried out for several other Cornish breweries. ⟱ ◆ RAIB

Even Keel (OG 1034, ABV 3.4%) ◕
Copper-coloured session bitter with a floral hop nose. Malt and hops dominate the taste with apple fruit notes. Bitter, dry finish.

Golden Lance (OG 1038, ABV 4%) ◕
Gold-coloured bitter with peaty, smoky malt and strong hop flavour. Hops in the aroma. Dryness rises to dominate the finish.

Magik (OG 1040, ABV 4.2%) ◕
Tawny best bitter with gentle malt and hops aroma. Malt dominates, balanced by dry, hop bitterness. Dry, bitter hop finish.

King (OG 1049, ABV 5.1%) ◕
Copper-coloured strong bitter with a hop aroma. Citrus hop and dry, malt taste. Bitter hop finish with sweet malt.

Contract brewed for Roseland:

Cornish Shag (OG 1037, ABV 3.8%)
Copper-coloured session bitter.

Kemptown

🏠 33 Upper St James's Street, Kemptown, Brighton, East Sussex, BN2 1JN ☎ 07967 681203

☺Founded in 1989, the brewery is the smallest commercially operating tower brewery in the world. The beers are exclusively available on site at the Hand in Hand brewpub and are brewed by the team behind Brighton Bier. ‼

Kemptown (OG 1040, ABV 4%)
A light session ale. Crisp and hoppy.

Ye Olde Trout (OG 1045, ABV 4.5%)
A golden brown-coloured beer with fruity aromas and a dry finish.

Kendal

🏠 19 Lowther Street, Kendal, Cumbria, LA9 4DH

☎ (01539) 733803 🌐 burgundyswinebar.co.uk

Kendal began brewing in 2011. Beer is now produced every week and the brewery is at full production. ‼

Helga's Dunkel Bier (OG 1037, ABV 3.7%)
Brewed to the style of a traditional German Dunkel (dark) beer with a smooth and malty taste.

Mountain Medicine (ABV 3.7%)
A blonde session ale with a well-balanced flavour.

Webster's (OG 1037, ABV 3.7%)
A traditional bitter.

Eleven Bells (OG 1039, ABV 3.9%)
A light, well-hopped beer with a citrus finish.

Pale Ale (OG 1042, ABV 4.2%)
Straw-coloured ale using all American hops.

Gold (OG 1043, ABV 4.3%)
A golden beer with a strong bitter finish.

Silver Tanner (OG 1044, ABV 4.4%)
Copper-coloured bitter, malty with a lasting bitter finish.

Grisleymires Stout (OG 1047, ABV 4.7%)
A dark chocolate taste with a hint of bitterness.

Kendrick's SIBA

Coalpit Lane, Willey, Warwickshire, CV23 0SL
☎ (01788) 833469 ☎ 07912 481250
🌐 kendricksbrewing.co.uk

The brewery, formerly Wood Farm Brewery, opened in 2011 and was taken over and renamed by Linden and Jane Kendricks in 2015. The brewery can be viewed from the bar of the visitor centre, which has an outside patio area with tables, and is set in 36 acres of Warwickshire countryside. Food is available. ‼ ♦ RAIB

1823 Mild (OG 1035, ABV 3.5%)

Webb Ellis Bitter (OG 1038, ABV 3.8%)

Playon (OG 1040, ABV 4%)

Scrum (OG 1040, ABV 4%)

Best Bitter (OG 1042, ABV 4.2%)

Victorious (OG 1042, ABV 4.2%)

No. 8 (OG 1050, ABV 5%)

Kennet & Avon

34 Old Broughton Road, Melksham, Wiltshire, SN12 8BX ☎ 07917 272482
🌐 kennetandavonbrewery.co.uk

Kennet & Avon began brewing in 2014, with the beers originally being brewed by Wessex Brewery (qv) while the plant was under construction. The brewery relocated to its present site in 2015. The beers are available at the owner's micropub, the Vaults in Devizes, and in outlets throughout the West Country.

Pillbox (OG 1039, ABV 4%)
A light, refreshing ale with a hoppy bite.

Dundas (OG 1041, ABV 4.2%)
A copper-coloured best bitter with a pleasant bitterness and citrus hoppy aroma.

Rusty Lane (OG 1044, ABV 4.4%)
A rusty-coloured Irish-style red ale with rounded toffee malt flavour and floral hop finish.

Caen Hill Hop (OG 1050, ABV 5%)
An American-style IPA with a powerful floral hop flavour.

Savernake (OG 1053, ABV 5.3%)
Full-bodied, black beer with aromas of liquorice, roast coffee and chocolate, with a delicate aftertaste. This barley and oat brewed beer is certified gluten-free.

Kent SIBA

The Long Barn, Birling Place Farm, Stangate Road, Birling, Kent, ME19 5JN
☎ (01634) 780037 🌐 kentbrewery.com

Kent Brewery was founded in 2010 by Toby Simmonds (ex-brewer from Dark Star) and Paul Herbert. Originally brewed at Larkins, a 10-barrel plant has been in operation at the Birling site since 2011. More than 150 outlets are supplied direct, mainly throughout Kent, Sussex and London. ♦ RAIB

Session Pale (OG 1037, ABV 3.7%)

Black Gold (OG 1040, ABV 4%)

Pale (OG 1040, ABV 4%)

Cobnut (OG 1041, ABV 4.1%)

KGB (Kent Golding Bitter) (OG 1041, ABV 4.1%)

Zingiber (OG 1041, ABV 4.1%)

Brewers Reserve (OG 1050, ABV 5%)

Beyond The Pale (OG 1054, ABV 5.4%)

Enigma (OG 1055, ABV 5.5%)

Kernel SIBA

Arch 11, Dockley Road Industrial Estate, London, SE16 3SF
☎ (020) 7231 4516

Registered Office: 01 Spa Business Park, Spa Road, London, SE16 4QT 🌐 thekernelbrewery.com

Kernel was established in 2010 by Evin O'Riordain and moved to larger premises in 2012 to keep up with demand. The brewery produces bottle-conditioned beers, as well as the occasional cask, and has won many awards for its wide, ever-changing range of pale and dark beers. Beers are available from the brewery on a Saturday as well as an exclusive selection of pubs around the country. RAIB

Table Beer (OG 1037, ABV 3%)

Pale Ale (OG 1050, ABV 5.3%)

Export India Porter (OG 1062, ABV 5.8%)

India Pale Ale (OG 1065, ABV 7%)

London 1890 Export Stout (OG 1078, ABV 7.3%)

Imperial Brown Stout (OG 1098, ABV 10%)

Keswick SIBA

The Old Brewery, Brewery Lane, Keswick, Cumbria, CA12 5BY
☎ (01768) 780700 🌐 keswickbrewery.co.uk

Keswick, run by Sue Harrison, began brewing in 2006 using a 10-barrel plant. It is located on the site of a brewery that closed in 1897. Outlets include Middle Ruddings Hotel, Braithwaite and Dog & Gun, Keswick, with many other Lakeland pubs supplied. ‼ ♦

THE BREWERIES

Thirst Gold (OG 1035, ABV 3.6%)
Golden in colour and full of flavour.

Thirst Session (OG 1036, ABV 3.7%) ◄
A sweet start with a hint of roast gives way to a dry, bitter finish.

Pale Ale (ABV 4.2%)
A pale golden ale.

Thirst Run (OG 1041, ABV 4.2%) ◄
A well-balanced golden beer that maintains its fruitiness from start to finish.

Thirst Fall (OG 1047, ABV 4.8%) ◄
Sweet with vinous fruitiness. Astringency dominates the finish.

Kew (NEW)

477 Upper Richmond Road West, Richmond, SW14 7PU
☎ (020) 8878 9415 ⊕ kewbrewery.co.uk

⊠ Established in 2015, Kew Brewery is a family-run, independent brewery situated less than a mile from the world-famous Royal Botanic Gardens at Kew. It uses a six-barrel brew length. ‼ ☰ ◆ RAIB

Botanic (ABV 3.8%)
An amber-coloured session ale with tangerine and peach aromas giving way to biscuit and caramel in the body, and a soft, long bitterness.

Chocolate Milk Stout (ABV 3.9%)
A complex, full-flavoured low-ABV stout made with real organic chocolate and milk sugar. The blend of four malts, oats and wheat with a 'dry hop' of cacao nibs add a rich, bittersweet chocolate flavour.

Petersham Porter (ABV 4.3%)
Rich and complex, with flavours of toffee, chocolate, coffee, plums and liquorice with a touch of smokiness. Gently dry-hopped, to add a fresh, floral note to the earthy, malty aroma.

Sandycombe Gold (ABV 4.4%)
A pale golden ale. Crisp, hoppy and refreshing, with a lingering bitterness and big fruit and spice aroma.

Pagoda Pale (ABV 4.5%)
Brewed with a full-bodied pale malt base, with the addition each time of a different English hop.

Richmond Rye (ABV 4.5%)
A spicy and refreshing beer with a subtle dryness coming from the rye.

Keystone SIBA

Old Carpenters Workshop, Berwick St Leonard, Wiltshire, SP3 5SN
☎ (01747) 820426 ⊕ keystonebrewery.co.uk

⊠ Set up in 2006 with a 10-barrel plant, the brewer aims to be as sustainable and efficient as possible, brewing traditional southern English-style beers using local ingredients. The beers are available in the brewery-run Benett Arms, Tisbury. Around 150 other outlets are also supplied. ‼ ☰ ◆

Bedrock (OG 1035, ABV 3.6%) ◄
Copper-coloured bitter, hops and malt in the aroma, followed by fruit and bitterness in the taste. Long, lingering aftertaste.

Gold Hill (OG 1039, ABV 4%) ◄
Amber-coloured bitter with a floral/citrus aroma, clean-tasting with balanced bittersweet taste right through to the aftertaste, which has a slightly hoppy astringency.

Large One (OG 1041, ABV 4.2%) ◄
Copper-coloured malty best bitter, fruit and bitterness to the fore initially, long fruit and bitter hop flavours to the finish.

Kiln (NEW)

4 Alexandra Road, Burgess Hill, West Sussex, RH15 0EW ☎ 07800 556729 ⊕ thekilnbrewery.co.uk

Kiln Brewery was set up by two friends in 2014. It produces two beers at present, with more planned. The beers are available mainly at local outlets.

Boardwalk (OG 1045, ABV 4.5%)

Brewlin Rouge (OG 1050, ABV 5.1%)

King Alfred

11 Mill Rise, Bourton, Dorset, SP8 5DH
☎ (01747) 840967 ✉ kingalfredales@aol.com

⊠ King Alfred is a 0.5-barrel garage brewery that started production in 2012. It currently brews about once a month. A few local pubs and beer festivals are supplied.

871 (OG 1043, ABV 4.3%)
Mid brown-coloured malty bitter with balanced hop flavours.

Saxon Gold (OG 1048, ABV 4.8%)
Mid gold-coloured bitter with prominent hop flavours and aroma.

King Beer SIBA ◉

3-5 Jubilee Estate, Foundry Lane, Horsham, West Sussex, RH13 5UE
☎ (01403) 272102 ⊕ kingbeer.co.uk

⊠ Launched in 2001, the brewery was purchased by Niki and Justin Deighton in 2013, along with existing head brewer Ian Burgess. It is now brewing up to 110 barrels a week under the Kings Heritage and Kings Evolution brands. ‼ ☰ ◆ RAIB

Horsham Best Bitter (OG 1038, ABV 3.8%) ◄
A predominantly malty best bitter, brown in colour. The nutty flavours have some sweetness with a little bitterness that grows in the aftertaste.

Brighton Blonde (OG 1039, ABV 3.9%)

Kings Best (OG 1040, ABV 4%)

Poachers Moon (OG 1040, ABV 4.1%)

Northern Lights (OG 1042, ABV 4.2%)

Lost Kingdom (OG 1052, ABV 5.2%)

King's Cliffe

Unit 10, Kingsmead, Station Road, King?s Cliffe, Northamptonshire, PE8 6YH ☎ 07843 288088
⊕ kcbales.co.uk

⊠ In 2014, exactly 100 years after the last brewery in King's Cliffe ceased brewing, village resident Jeremy O'Neill set up this new venture. It currently produces five barrels a week. ‼ ◆

5C (OG 1038, ABV 3.8%)

No. 10 (OG 1040, ABV 4%)

60 Degrees (OG 1046, ABV 4.6%)

K2 (OG 1055, ABV 5.5%)

Kings Clipstone

Keepers Bothy, Kings Clipstone, Nottinghamshire, NG21 9BT
☎ (01623) 823589 ☎ 07790 190020
kingsclipstonebrewery.co.uk

Located in the heart of Sherwood Forest, Kings Clipstone began brewing in 2012 using a five-barrel plant. The owners, David and Daryl Maguire, brew a range of core beers plus one-off brews and seasonals. Beers are available nationwide to freehouses, festivals and wholesale markets. !! ♦

Palace Pale (ABV 3.6%)
A light and crisp golden ale with a refreshing taste.

Hop On (OG 1039, ABV 3.8%)
A pale and refreshing session beer with fruity Cascade aroma hops.

Moonbeam (ABV 4.2%)
A mid-strength chestnut-coloured bitter with a full flavour and well-rounded finish.

Sire (OG 1043, ABV 4.2%)
A well-rounded beer with a clean bitter finish.

Queen Bee (ABV 5.1%)
A ruby red strong ale, classically rich and smooth.

Kings Head

Kings Head, 132 High Street, Bildeston, Suffolk, IP7 7ED
☎ (01449) 741434 bildestonkingshead.co.uk

Kings Head has been brewing since 1996 in an old cart lodge at the back of the pub. Under new ownership since 2008, the three-barrel plant brews fortnightly. !! ♦

Bildeston Best (OG 1036, ABV 3.6%)
Traditional best. Well-hopped with a malty sweetness and dry finish.

Brettvale Gold (ABV 3.6%)

Kingstone SIBA

Tintern, NP16 7NX
☎ (01291) 680111 kingstonebrewery.co.uk

Kingstone Brewery is located in the Wye Valley close to the famous Tintern Abbey. Brewing began on a four-barrel plant in 2005. Special brews are marketed under the Hapax Brewing Co label. !! RAIB

Tewdric's Tipple (OG 1038, ABV 3.8%)
An ale with a dry, bitter character and a tangy core.

Challenger (OG 1040, ABV 4%)
A smooth, richly hopped, well-balanced ale with a malty nose and toffee undertones.

Gold (OG 1040, ABV 4%)
A straw-coloured smooth ale with citrus notes and a balanced, hoppy finish.

Premium Stout (OG 1044, ABV 4.4%)
A smooth, rich stout with bitter finish.

Classic (OG 1045, ABV 4.5%)
A distinctly hoppy, dry ale with a floral nose and a smooth finish.

1503 (OG 1048, ABV 4.8%)
A deep chestnut-coloured, lightly-hopped ale bursting with complex rich flavours.

Abbey Ale (OG 1051, ABV 5.1%)
An amber-coloured, full flavoured ale. The hoppy edge is balanced by a smooth, malty richness.

Humpty (OG 1058, ABV 5.8%)
An IPA with a slightly sweet, floral nose, a balanced level of malt supporting the hops and finally a subtle but slightly citrus finish.

Kinneil

84 Corbiehall, Bo'ness, EH51 0AS ☎ 07789 204008
kinneilbrew.co.uk

Kinneil began brewing in 2011 using a 2.5-barrel plant. The brewery is adjacent to the Corbie Inn but separately owned.

Wonderfu' Jake (OG 1037, ABV 3.6%)

Katie Wearie's (OG 1039, ABV 3.8%)

Wayfinder (OG 1038, ABV 3.8%)

Pennvael Amber (OG 1042, ABV 4%)

Kincardine Sunset (OG 1042, ABV 4.1%)

Caer Edin Dark (OG 1044, ABV 4.2%)

Kinver SIBA

Unit 1, Britch Farm, Rocky Wall, Kinver, Staffordshire, DY7 5NW ☎ 07715 842676 kinverbrewery.co.uk

Established in 2004, Kinver produces a wide range of different beer styles including one-off specials. The brewery relocated in 2012 to a new 10-barrel plant on the edge of Kinver due to increased demand. Around 30 outlets are supplied direct including several in Kinver. ♦ RAIB

Light Railway (OG 1038, ABV 3.8%)
Straw-coloured session beer. A fruity and malty start quickly gives way to well-hopped bitterness and lingering hoppy aftertaste.

Cavegirl Bitter (OG 1040, ABV 4%)

Edge (OG 1041, ABV 4.2%)
Amber with a malty aroma. Sweet fruity start with a hint of citrus marmalade in the spicy-edged malt; lasting hoppy finish that is satisfyingly bitter.

Noble (OG 1043, ABV 4.5%)
Fruity hop aroma. A fruity start then the grassy hops give a sharp, bitter finish with malt support.

Maybug (OG 1045, ABV 4.8%)
Cask-conditioned lager-style beer brewed with Tettnang hops.

Half Centurion (OG 1047, ABV 5%)
A golden best bitter; malty before the American Chinook hop takes command to give a balanced hoppy finish and provide the great aftertaste.

Khyber (OG 1054, ABV 5.8%)
Golden strong bitter with a Centennial hop bite that overwhelms the fleeting malty sweetness and drives through to the long, dry finish.

Over the Edge (OG 1068, ABV 7.5%)
Complex, strong, golden winter ale.

Kirkby Lonsdale SIBA

Unit 2F, Old Station Yard, Kirkby Lonsdale, LA6 2HP
☎ (01524) 272221 ☎ 07793 149999
kirkbylonsdalebrewery.com

Kirkby Lonsdale is a family-run business established in 2009 on a six-barrel plant. ♦

Tiffin Gold (OG 1036, ABV 3.6%) ◆
A full-flavoured grapefruit, hoppy and bitter beer with a dry finish.

Stanley's Pale Ale (OG 1038, ABV 3.8%) ◆
Hops dominate this sweet and fruity, well-balanced beer.

Ruskins Bitter (OG 1039, ABV 3.9%) ◆
A tawny bitter with a distinctive aroma of fruit and malt. The clean, hoppy flavour is well-balanced with fruity sweetness leading to a sustained bittersweet finish.

Singletrack (OG 1040, ABV 4%) ◆
Crisp citrus hops predominate in a well-balanced beer with a pleasant bitter finish.

Radical Red (OG 1042, ABV 4.2%) ◆
Malty beer with a caramel sweetness that is balanced by a bitter finish.

Monumental Blonde (OG 1045, ABV 4.5%) ◆
Distinctly hoppy, a fruity, sweet, pale-coloured, full-bodied bitter.

Jubilee Stout (OG 1055, ABV 5.5%) ◆
Rich, well-balanced stout with malt. A long aftertaste retains this complexity and is surprisingly refreshing.

Kirkstall SIBA

Unit 6, Canal Wharf, Wyther Lane, Kirkstall, Leeds, West Yorkshire, LS5 3BT
☎ (0113) 345 8835 ⊕ kirkstallbrewerycompany.com

Brewing began in 2011 at a site within yards of the original Kirkstall Brewery beside the Leeds-Liverpool canal with nearby Kirkstall Abbey and lost local industries providing inspiration for the beer names. There are plans to move to a new site in 2015. The beer range can always be found at the Kirkstall Bridge Inn nearby. ◆

**BYB (Best Yorkshire Bitter)
(OG 1036, ABV 3.5%)** ◆
Gentle but bitter beer, with some citrus fruits making this an easy-drinking session pale ale.

Pale Ale (OG 1040, ABV 4%) ◆
A refreshing golden-coloured bitter beer with citrus hop flavours and zesty bitterness, especially in the finish which is lingering.

Three Swords (OG 1045, ABV 4.5%) ◆
Good quantities of hops and juicy fruit define this yellow beer, a bittersweet taste and a tenacious pithy marmalade finish.

Dissolution IPA (OG 1050, ABV 5%)

Black Band Porter (OG 1055, ABV 5.5%) ◆
Dark, smooth and rich with a full aroma and even bigger flavour. Generous fruity taste, hints of chocolate and liquorice.

Generous George (OG 1060, ABV 6%)

Kirrie (NEW)

Bon Scott Brewery, 8 Bon Scott Place, Kirriemuir, Angus, DD8 4LD ☎ 07855 808975 ⊕ kirrie-ales.co.nf

Kirrie Ales is a microbrewery situated in the picturesque town of Kirriemuir, birthplace in 1860 of J. M. Barrie, creator of Peter Pan, and gateway to the Angus Glens. The brewery space measures only 8 by 9 feet. 70-80 litres a day are produced. RAIB

Kissingate

Pole Barn, Church Lane Farm Estate, Church Lane, Lower Beeding, West Sussex, RH13 6LU
☎ (01403) 891335 ☎ 07909 975664
⊕ kissingate.co.uk

⊠ Kissingate was founded in 2010 by husband and wife team Gary and Bunny Lucas using an eight-barrel plant. In 2012 the brewery moved into a new purpose-built barn conversion. Many events are held throughout the year catering for beer enthusiasts and special interest groups. ‼ ☛ ◆

Storyteller (OG 1036, ABV 3.5%)

Sussex (OG 1040, ABV 4%)

Black Cherry Mild (OG 1042, ABV 4.2%) ▣
Subtle rounded flavours from black and amber malts, with hints of fruitiness from black cherries and a lasting but mild bitterness from the hops.

Moon (OG 1045, ABV 4.5%)
A golden ale with a lightly roasted malt taste, late autumn apples and the lingering bitterness of Challenger hops.

Old Tale Porter (OG 1045, ABV 4.5%)
A classic full-flavoured London porter.

Mandarina Red (OG 1048, ABV 4.8%)
A complex red-coloured IPA with multiple flavour layers of malt and prominent citrus fruits. Piny and citrus bitter finish.

Chennai Premium IPA (OG 1050, ABV 5%)

Smelter's Stout (OG 1052, ABV 5.1%)

Mary's Ruby Mild (OG 1064, ABV 6.5%)
Deep ruby in colour with gentle aromas of port. Intense and rounded malt flavours. Light and floral hop aftertaste.

Kitchen Garden

Old Walled Garden, Sheffield Park, East Sussex, TN22 3QX
☎ (01825) 790775 ⊕ kitchengardenbrewery.co.uk

Kitchen Garden is a small one-barrel plant producing only bottle-conditioned ales, all suitable for vegetarians. It is situated in a Victorian walled kitchen garden at Sheffield Park. The beers are available from the brewery shop and at several outlets in Sussex including Middle Farm, Firle. Brewing is currently suspended. ☛ ◆ RAIB

Kite SIBA ◉

See Glamorgan

Knaresborough

🗐 **19 Market Place, Knaresborough, North Yorkshire, HG5 8AL**
☎ (01423) 869148

Established in 2012 above Blind Jacks pub in Knaresborough, the 0.5-barrel brewery specialises in stronger, sometimes experimental beers inspired by US craft brewing. BAD Co brewery at Dishforth has the same ownership.

Knops SIBA

The Walled Garden, Archerfield Estate, Dirleton, North Berwick, EH39 5HQ ☎ 07949 879147
⊕ knopsbeer.co.uk

⊛Knops began brewing in 2010 under contract. In 2013 it moved to new premises on the Archerfield Estate at Dirleton on the East Lothian coastline with an 11-barrel plant. Beers are based on modern interpretations of traditional styles and are bottled in-house. Cask-conditioned beers are available widely in Eastern Scotland and the Glasgow area. !! RAIB

East Coast Pale (OG 1039, ABV 3.8%)
A light aromatic session beer with malt and hops in the nose and some citrus notes.

Musselburgh Broke (OG 1045, ABV 4.5%)
Modern interpretation of a 19th-century style. Has a chestnut colour and a malty sweetness, with some hops for balance.

California Common (OG 1048, ABV 4.6%)
A deep golden ale with a clean hop finish and light toffee notes followed by a lingering bitterness.

India Pale Ale (OG 1047, ABV 5%)
Light golden ale with a citrus and apricot aroma. Well-balanced by a smooth honeyed malt backbone.

Black Cork (OG 1066, ABV 6.5%)
An intensely dark beer with a prominent chocolate/coffee bitterness and hop aroma.

Contract brewed for Archerfield Fine Ales:

Golden Ale (OG 1039, ABV 3.8%)

Dark Ale (OG 1046, ABV 4.7%)

India Pale Ale (OG 1047, ABV 5%)

Krafty Brew (NEW) SIBA

11 Stewartfield, Edinburgh, EH6 5RQ
☎ (0131) 555 7189 ⊕ kraftybrew.com

Krafty Ales is a small brewery specialising in 'brew-it-yourself' and 'own-label' products. A range of bottle-conditioned beers is also sold under the Krafty brand name. RAIB

Kubla

The Source Building, Tower Farm, Dean's Cross, Lydeard St Lawrence, Somerset, TA4 3QN ☎ 07855 342208 ⊕ kubla.co.uk

The five-barrel plant was established in 2012 on Tower Farm in the Brendon Hills, Exmoor. Part of the farm was a former cheese factory. Beers are available in local pubs and clubs. RAIB

Rise: Pale Ale (OG 1042, ABV 4.2%)

Rock: Saison (OG 1042, ABV 4.2%)

Paradise: Stout (OG 1048, ABV 4.8%)

Lacons SIBA ⊙

The Courtyard, Main Cross Road, Great Yarmouth, Norfolk, NR30 3NZ
☎ (01493) 850578 ⊕ lacons.co.uk

⊠ Lacons has a rich history dating back to 1760. The brewery was closed by Whitbread in the 1960s. In 2010 a beer distributor, J.V. Trading, looked into the possibility of reopening the brewery, and acquired its trading name and yeast strains. The new brewery opened in 2013. Beers are available through free trade outlets across East Anglia. !! ⟺ ◆ RAIB

Encore (ABV 3.8%)
Pale amber in colour, with delicate fruit aromas. A golden session beer with a balance of dry pine and citrus followed by a long, dry finish.

Falcon Ale (ABV 4.2%)
A classic dark bitter, well-balanced with complex, lightly spiced flavours. The finish is balanced between fruitiness and bitterness.

Legacy (ABV 4.4%)
Blonde ale with a citrus aroma and a long, mellowing bitter finish.

Audit (ABV 8%)
A dark, copper-coloured barley wine with flavours of berry fruit and spice. The finish is warming, smooth and sweet.

Laine

⬛ **Brighton: North Laine Bar & Brewhouse, 27 Gloucester Place, Brighton, East Sussex, BN1 4AA ☎ (01273) 683666**

Acton: Aeronaut, 264 Acton High Street, Acton, London, W3 9BH ☎ (020) 8993 4242

Battersea (NEW): Four Thieves, 51 Lavender Gardens, London, SW11 1DJ ☎ (020) 7223 6927

Hackney: People's Park Tavern, 360 Victoria Park Road, Hackney, London, E9 7BT ☎ (020) 8533 0040
✉ northlainepub@drinkinbrighton.co.uk; aeronaut@drinkinlondon.co.uk; hello@peoplesparktavern.pub

Laine launched its first brewery in 2012, in Brighton, using a five-barrel plant based within the North Laine pub, which is owned by the drinkinbrighton pub group. The brewing equipment and process can be viewed from the bar. In 2013 a sister brewery was opened in Acton, London, with the brewing equipment - three fermenters producing 60 firkins of beer a week - visible behind the left-hand bar. Since then two more Laine breweries have been established in London, in Hackney (2014) and Battersea (2015). !! ⟺

Acton Ale (OG 1039, ABV 3.7%) ✎
Easy-drinking brown bitter with hops and some caramelised orange fading in the finish, which is a little bitter and dry.

Oatmeal Stout (OG 1045, ABV 4.5%)

Random Pale Ale (OG 1046, ABV 4.6%) ✎
A refreshing pale golden ale with a developing hop bitterness and notes of lemon grass.

IPA (OG 1050, ABV 5%)

Porter (OG 1053, ABV 5.3%)

LAM (NEW)

9 River View, Sandford-on-Thames, Oxfordshire, OX4 4YF ☎ 07913 061025 ⊕ lambrewing.com

LAM began brewing in 2014 on a 50-litre plant. It's operated on a part-time basis at present but plans to expand. Only bottle-conditioned beers are produced, available at farmers' markets and the brewery. RAIB

Lancaster SIBA

Lancaster Leisure Park, Wyresdale Road, Lancaster, LA1 3LA
☎ (01524) 848537 🌐 lancasterbrewery.co.uk

Lancaster began brewing in 2005. The brewery moved to new premises in 2010 and installed a larger 60-barrel brewing plant. As well as the regular beers, seasonal beers are brewed under the T'ales from the Brewhouse name. Four pubs are owned in Lancashire and the south lakes. !! ♦

Amber (OG 1037, ABV 3.6%)
Amber malt flavours lead to an increasingly astringent bitter finish.

Blonde (OG 1041, ABV 4%)
A pale, gently-hopped, easy-drinking, mild bitter with an astringent finish.

Black (OG 1045, ABV 4.5%)
A satisfying and robust, roast bitter beer with hints of sweet fruitiness.

Red (OG 1047, ABV 4.8%)
Sweet start with lasting roast malts leads to a satisfying bitter finish.

Landlocked (NEW)

Beehive, 151 Peasehill, Ripley, Derbyshire, DE5 3JN
☎ 07845 609585 ✉ brewhousemike@gmail.com

Landlocked began brewing in 2014 using a five-barrel plant in outbuildings behind the Beehive Inn in Ripley. The beers can be found in the Beehive, the Honeypot bar, the Five Lamps and other local freehouses. ♦RAIB

Honeypot Pale (OG 1036, ABV 4%)
Pale golden ale brewed with a touch of honey.

Bernard's Chisel (OG 1040, ABV 4.3%)
Chestnut-coloured English best bitter.

Island IPA (OG 1044, ABV 4.7%)
A golden IPA, powerfully hopped with New Zealand hops.

A & E (OG 1064, ABV 7.4%)
An amber IPA., strong and powerful.

Landlord's Friend

Kershaw House Inn, Luddenden Lane, Luddendenfoot, West Yorkshire, HX2 6NW
☎ (01422) 882222 ✉ landfriendbeers@aol.co.uk

Landlord's Friend began brewing in 2010 using a 2.5-barrel plant. Around 30 outlets are supplied direct. ♦

Langham SIBA

Old Granary, Langham Lane, Lodsworth, West Sussex, GU28 9BU
☎ (01798) 860861 🌐 langhambrewery.co.uk

Langham was established in 2006 in an 18th-century granary barn and is set in the heart of West Sussex with fine views of the rolling South Downs. It is owned by Lesley Foulkes and James Berrow who brew and run the business. The brewery is a 10-barrel steam-heated plant and more than 200 outlets are supplied. !!

Halfway to Heaven (OG 1035, ABV 3.5%)
A chestnut-coloured beer with a balanced biscuit maltiness and citrus and fruit hop character with a hint of spice.

Hip Hop (OG 1038, ABV 4%)
A blonde beer; clean and crisp. The nose is loaded with floral hop aroma while the pale malt flavour is overtaken by a dry and bitter finish.

Sundowner (OG 1042, ABV 4.2%)
A deep golden beer. The nose has tropical fruit, pineapple and citrus notes with a smooth maltiness in the background. There is a balanced dry and bitter finish with floral hop aroma.

Best (OG 1043, ABV 4.5%)
A tawny-coloured classic best with well-balanced malt flavours and bitterness.

Arapaho (OG 1046, ABV 4.9%)
An American-style pale ale.

LSD (Langham Special Draught) (OG 1049, ABV 5.2%)
An auburn beer with rich, complex flavours and a deep red glow. The sweet maltiness is balanced with spicy hop aromas and a dry finish.

Black Swallow (OG 1055, ABV 6%)
A black IPA.

Langton SIBA

Grange Farm, Welham Road, Thorpe Langton, Leicestershire, LE16 7TU
☎ (01858) 540116 ☎ 07840 532826
🌐 langtonbrewery.co.uk

Established in 1999 in outbuildings behind the Bell Inn, East Langton, the brewery relocated in 2005 to a converted barn at Thorpe Langton, where a four-barrel plant was installed. Further expansion in 2010 significantly increased capacity. !! ♦RAIB

Caudle Bitter (OG 1039, ABV 3.9%)
Copper-coloured session bitter that is close to a pale ale in style. Flavours are relatively well-balanced throughout with hops slightly to the fore.

Inclined Plane Bitter (OG 1042, ABV 4.2%)
A straw-coloured bitter with a citrus nose and long, hoppy finish.

Hop On (OG 1044, ABV 4.4%)
A premium bitter, deep chestnut in colour with a good balance of flavours and aroma.

Scarecrow (OG 1044, ABV 4.4%)
Smooth, well-balanced, slightly fruity and sweet.

Bowler Strong Ale (OG 1048, ABV 4.8%)
A strong traditional ale with a deep red colour and a hoppy nose.

Bullseye (OG 1050, ABV 4.8%)
Intensely dark stout with flavours of liquorice and chocolate.

Larkins SIBA

Larkins Farm, Hampkins Hill Road, Chiddingstone, Kent, TN8 7BB
☎ (01892) 870328

It's been over 25 years since the farming and hop growing Dockerty family bought the original Royal Tunbridge Wells Brewery and moved it to Larkins Farm where Bob Dockerty started brewing in 1987. Production of its three main brews and two seasonal ales has steadily increased. All beers now include hops grown on Larkins Farm itself. All ales are delivered direct to around 70 freehouses within a 20-mile radius of the brewery. !!♦

Traditional Ale (OG 1035, ABV 3.4%)
Tawny in colour, a full-tasting hoppy ale with plenty of character for its strength.

Best (OG 1045, ABV 4.4%) ◆
Full-bodied, slightly fruity and unusually bitter for its gravity.

Late Knights

21 Southey Street, Penge, London, SE20 7JD ☎ 07786 830368 🌐 lateknightsbrewery.co.uk

⊗ Originally using spare capacity at Truefitt Brewery in Middlesbrough in 2012, Late Knights began brewing using a six-barrel plant in an old converted slaughterhouse in London in 2013. ♦

Crack of Dawn (ABV 3.7%) ◆
Amber hoppy beer with strong citrus notes. The flavour has a faint maltiness and bitterness. The aftertaste is bitter and fractionally dry.

Dawn's Early Light (ABV 4%)

Hop o' the Morning (ABV 4.2%) ◆
Strong black roast bitter character in the aroma and flavour with some coffee notes and fruit. Long, bitter, dry finish.

Morning Glory (ABV 4.4%)

Old Red Eyes (ABV 4.5%) ◆
Reddish brown beer with a clean hop flavour and hints of citrus and butterscotch. The finish is hoppy and dryish.

Worm Catcher (ABV 5%) ◆
Amber-coloured beer with a honey marmalade sweetness and a bitterness that builds and lingers in the slightly dry finish.

Latimer ◎

13 South Folds Road, Oakley Hay, Northamptonshire, NN18 9EU ☎ 07812 450988

Office: 11 Meadway Close, Kettering, Northamptonshire, NN15 6QG 🌐 latimerales.com

No real ale. Latimer is a small two-barrel brewery, established in 2012, that shares the Tom Smith brewing plant but uses separate fermenters.

Leadmill

Unit 3, Heanor Small Business Centre, Adams Close, Heanor, Derbyshire, DE75 7SW ☎ 07971 189915 ✉ leadmill@fsmail.net

⊗ Set up in Selston in 1999, Leadmill moved to Denby in 2001 and again in 2010 to Heanor, where it shares a site with Coppice Side Brewery (qv). A sister brewery to Bottle Brook (qv), the brewery tap is at the Old Oak, Horsley Woodhouse. ♦

Langley Best (OG 1036, ABV 3.6%)

Mash Tun Bitter (OG 1036, ABV 3.6%)

Old Oak Bitter (OG 1037, ABV 3.7%)

B52 (OG 1050, ABV 5.2%)

Slumdog (OG 1058, ABV 5.9%)

Leamside SIBA

Three Horseshoes, Pit House Lane, Leamside, County Durham, DH4 6QQ
☎ (0191) 584 2394
🌐 threehorseshoesleamside.co.uk

Brewing began in 2012 using a 2.5-barrel plant. Beers are available at the Three Horseshoes as well as its three sister pubs.

Adventure (OG 1038, ABV 3.8%)
A deep golden-coloured session bitter. Soft fruit flavours and well-balanced medium bitterness.

Alexandrina (OG 1041, ABV 4.2%)
Light gold in colour. Initial bitterness gives way to citrus fruit flavours.

Brockwell (OG 1042, ABV 4.2%)
A straw-coloured pale ale with tropical fruit flavours from New World hops.

Five Quarter (OG 1052, ABV 4.5%)
A silky smooth mouthfeel with berry fruit flavours and hints of coffee and chocolate.

Resolution (OG 1052, ABV 4.5%)
Premium pale ale brewed with a blend of American hops. Well-balanced bitterness and subtle fruit flavours.

Leatherbritches

Brewery Yard, Tap House, Annwell, Smisby, Derbyshire, LE65 2TA ☎ 07976 279253
🌐 leatherbritches.co.uk

⊙ The brewery, founded in 1993 in Fenny Bentley, has relocated and expanded over the years, moving to its current address in 2011. Both the Tap House Brewery (qv) and Leatherbritches brew on the same plant but the two businesses are separate. !!♦ RAIB

Goldings (OG 1036, ABV 3.6%)
A light golden beer with a flowery hoppy aroma and a bitter finish.

Lemongrass & Ginger (OG 1036, ABV 3.8%)
Pale and hoppy ale infused with lemon grass and ginger. Crisp and refreshing.

Ashbourne Ale (OG 1040, ABV 4%)
A pale bitter brewed with Goldings hops for a crisp, lasting taste.

Doctor Johnsons (OG 1040, ABV 4%)
A mid-brown ale, not heavily hopped but full-bodied with some caramel flavour.

Scoundrel (OG 1040, ABV 4.1%)
Full-bodied porter, with a well-rounded, sweet finish.

Dovedale (OG 1044, ABV 4.4%)
A copper-coloured bitter with a crisp finish.

Ginger Helmet (OG 1047, ABV 4.7%)
As for Hairy Helmet but with a hint of ginger.

Hairy Helmet (OG 1047, ABV 4.7%)
A pale bitter, well-hopped but with a sweet finish.

Bespoke (OG 1050, ABV 5%)
Full-bodied, well-rounded premium bitter.

Porter (OG 1055, ABV 5.5%)
Complex yet satisfying porter.

Scary Hairy (OG 1059, ABV 5.9%)
Pale and hoppy, a stronger version of Hairy Helmet.

Scary Hairy Export (OG 1064, ABV 7.2%)

Extremely strong pale bitter produced with New World hops creating a bitter, dry finish.

Leazes Lane

▤ Trent House, 1-2 Leazes Lane, Newcastle upon Tyne, NE1 4QT
☎ (0191) 261 2154

Leazes Lane began brewing in 2013 using a one-barrel plant. Beer is only available in the pub.

Ledbury SIBA

Gazerdine House, Hereford Road, Ledbury, Herefordshire, HR8 2PZ
☎ (01531) 671184 ☎ 07957 428070
⊕ ledburyrealales.co.uk

☺Brewing began in 2012. Beers are produced using locally-sourced ingredients whenever possible. Distribution is generally within a 15-mile radius of the brewery. ‼

Bitter (OG 1038, ABV 3.8%)
A traditional copper colour with a noticeably bitter start and an enjoyable finish with hints of spice and citrus.

Dark (OG 1039, ABV 3.9%)
It has a chocolate and coffee start with a smooth, mellow finish with notes of spice, marmalade and honey.

Gold (OG 1040, ABV 4%)
A golden bitter, well-balanced with a honey and fruit finish.

Leeds SIBA ◉

▤ 3 Sydenham Road, Leeds, West Yorkshire, LS11 9RU
☎ (0113) 244 5866 ⊕ leedsbrewery.co.uk

☺Production began in 2007 using a 20-barrel plant. The largest independent brewer in the city, it uses a unique strain of yeast originally used by a defunct West Yorkshire brewery. Seven pubs are owned and around 300 outlets are supplied direct. ◆

Pale (OG 1037.5, ABV 3.8%) ◄
Hops and fruit, sometimes citrus, mix with a caramel sweetness through to the bitter, hoppy finish. Light gold in colour.

Yorkshire Gold (OG 1040, ABV 4%) ⌂ ◄
Plenty of zesty citrus flavours, a wallop of hops and a long-lasting bitter finish make this a refreshing beer.

Best (OG 1041, ABV 4.3%) ⌂ ◄
A pleasing mix of malt and hops makes this smooth copper-coloured bittersweet beer complex and refreshing.

Midnight Bell (OG 1047.5, ABV 4.8%) ⌂ ▦ ◄
A full-bodied strong mild, deep red/brown in colour. Malty caramel character with chocolate present throughout.

Leek

See Staffordshire

Lees IFBB ◉

Greengate Brewery, Middleton Junction, Manchester, M24 2AX
☎ (0161) 643 2487 ⊕ jwlees.co.uk

☺Family-owned since its foundation by John Lees in 1828, the brewery has a tied estate of around 170 pubs, mostly in north Manchester, Cheshire, Lancashire and North Wales. The vast majority serve cask beer. The current head brewer is a family member. ‼

Brewer's Dark (OG 1032, ABV 3.5%) ◄
Formerly GB Mild, this is a dark brown beer with a malt and caramel aroma. Creamy mouthfeel, with malt, caramel and fruit flavours and a malty finish. Becoming rare.

Manchester Pale Ale (OG 1038, ABV 3.7%)
A golden ale, clean, crisp and refreshing with hop bitterness and citrus aroma.

Governor (OG 1038, ABV 3.8%)
Malty auburn/amber beer with floral and citrus notes and a clean, dry finish.

Bitter (OG 1037, ABV 4%) ◄
Copper-coloured beer with malt and fruit in the aroma, taste and finish.

John Willie's (OG 1041, ABV 4.5%)
A well-balanced, full-bodied premium bitter.

Moonraker (OG 1073, ABV 6.5%) ⌂ ▦ ◄
A reddish-brown beer with a strong, malty, fruity aroma. The flavour is rich and sweet, with roast malt, and the finish is fruity yet dry. Available only in a handful of outlets.

Left Bank (NEW)

Blackhorse Workshop, 1-2 Sutherland Road Path, Walthamstow, London, E17 6BX ☎ 07815 849523
⊕ leftbankbrewery.co.uk

⊗ Brewing began in 2013 under the name of Wilcumestowe Brewery at the Hornbeam Café. It moved to the Blackhouse Workshop in 2014 on a 0.5-barrel plant, and now supplies the workshop and local events. Expansion is planned. ‼ ▤ ◆ RAIB

Pale Ale (ABV 4.5%)

Milk Stout (ABV 5.1%)

Sorachi Saison (ABV 5.4%)

Left Handed Giant (NEW)

Unit 9, Wadehurst Industrial Park, St Phillips Road, Bristol, BS2 0JE
☎ (0117) 318 2102 ⊕ lefthandedgiant.com

Launched in 2015, Left Handed Giant is a four-man cuckoo brewery with three core beers: a pale, a porter and a USPA. It brews regular collaborations with other leading breweries from the area.

Leighton Buzzard (NEW) SIBA ◉

Unit 23, Harmill Industrial Estate, Grovebury Road, Leighton Buzzard, Bedfordshire, LU7 4FF ☎ 07538 903753 ⊕ leightonbuzzardbrewingcompany.co.uk

The first brewery to operate in Leighton Buzzard for over 100 years. Established in 2014 by local CAMRA member and home brew enthusiast Jon d'Este-Hoare, the first beers are upscaled versions of his home brews. ‼ ▤ ◆

Narrow Gauge (OG 1040, ABV 3.9%)
A golden ale, light and refreshing with a dry bitter taste and crisp citrus finish.

Restoration Ale (OG 1049, ABV 4.6%)
A mid-brown best bitter; fruity and refreshing.

Rebel Yell (OG 1053, ABV 5%)
A black IPA with smooth, rich malt followed by sharp, dry hops.

Leila Cottage SIBA

▤ Countryman, Chapel Road, Ingoldmells, Skegness, Lincolnshire, PE25 1ND
☎ (01754) 872268 ⊕ home2.btconnect.com/countryman-ingoldmells

Leila Cottage started brewing in 2007 is now using a 2.5-barrel plant. The brewery is situated at the Countryman pub – Leila Cottage was the original name of the building before it became a licensed club and more recently a pub. The history of the Countryman and the brewery is on display in the pub. ‼ ☞ RAIB

Leila's Lazy Days (OG 1040, ABV 3.6%)
An easy-drinking, light IPA-style beer with a slightly citrus taste and a hint of caramel.

Ace Ale (OG 1040, ABV 3.8%)
A session bitter with a roast malt body and a gentle hop bitterness.

Lincolnshire Life (OG 1040, ABV 4.2%)
A dark, full-bodied, malty bitter with a toffee aroma and taste using a blend of three hop varieties and three malts.

Leila's One Off (OG 1045, ABV 5.1%)
A strong-flavoured, dark, full-bodied bitter brewed with two varieties of hops and four malts.

Leith Hill

▤ c/o Plough Inn, Coldharbour Lane, Coldharbour, Surrey, RH5 6HD
☎ (01306) 711793 ⊕ ploughinn.com

⊠ Leith Hill was established in 1996 at the Plough Inn using home-made equipment and was moved to converted storerooms at the rear in 2001, increasing capacity to 2.5 barrels in 2005. All beers brewed are sold only on the premises. ‼ RAIB

Beautiful South (OG 1036, ABV 3.6%)
Yellowish in colour, a hoppy session beer with a little malt character.

Crooked Furrow (OG 1040, ABV 4%) ◕
Malty beer, with some balancing hop bitterness. Pale brown with an earthy, malty aroma and a long, dry and bittersweet aftertaste.

Tallywhacker (OG 1048, ABV 4.8%) ◕
Dark, sweet and fruity old ale with good roast malt character.

Lerwick SIBA

Staneyhill, North Road, Lerwick, Shetland, ZE1 0QA
⊕ lerwickbrewery.co.uk

Lerwick Brewery was established in 2011 using a 12-barrel plant and sits at the very edge of the North Atlantic. It brewed only keg and bottled beer from its inception, but in 2015 launched a cask ale range that will be exported to the Scottish mainland. More beers are planned.

Shetland Pale Ale (ABV 3.8%)

IPA (ABV 5%)

Leyden

▤ Lord Raglan, Walmersley Old Road, Nangreaves, BL9 6SP
☎ (0161) 764 6680 ⊕ lordraglannangreaves.co.uk

☺Leyden was established in 1999. In addition to the permanent range a number of seasonal and occasional beers are brewed. ‼♦

Black Pudding (OG 1040, ABV 3.8%)
A dark brown, creamy mild with a malty flavour, followed by a balanced finish.

Nanny Flyer (OG 1040, ABV 3.8%)
A drinkable session bitter with an initial dryness, and a hint of citrus, followed by a strong, malty finish.

Balaclava (OG 1040, ABV 4.2%)
A brown-coloured session bitter with malty and hoppy flavours.

Light Brigade (OG 1042, ABV 4.2%) ◕
Copper in colour with a citrus aroma. The flavour is a balance of malt, hops and fruit, with a bitter finish.

Rammy Rocket (OG 1042, ABV 4.2%)
A smooth, straw-coloured ale.

Forever Bury (OG 1047, ABV 4.5%)
This dark brown bitter has a distinct fruity aroma with a smooth, malty finish.

Raglan Sleeve (OG 1047, ABV 4.6%) ◕
Dark red/brown beer with a hoppy aroma and a dry, roasty, hoppy taste and finish.

Crowning Glory (OG 1068, ABV 6.8%)
A surprisingly smooth-tasting beer for its strength.

Liberation SIBA ◉

Tregear House, Longueville Road, St Saviour, Jersey, JE2 7WF
☎ (01534) 764089 ⊕ liberationgroup.com

⊠ The Liberation Brewery is located at Longueville, just outside St Helier using a 40-barrel and an 8-barrel plant. Its multi-award-winning flagship beer, Liberation Ale, is now regularly seen on the mainland, as well as on the other Channel islands. 68 pubs are owned with around two-thirds of these serving cask ale. ‼♦

Ale (OG 1039, ABV 4%)
Golden beer with a hint of citrus on the nose.

IPA (OG 1047, ABV 4.8%)
Traditional IPA. A coriander-style citrus hop flavour is derived from the finest New Zealand hops, leaving a crisp, balanced finish.

Lincoln Green SIBA ◉

Unit 5, Enterprise Park, Wigwam Lane, Hucknall, Nottingham, NG15 7SZ
☎ (0115) 963 4233 ☎ 07748 111457
⊕ lincolngreenbrewing.co.uk

☺Anthony Hughes established the Lincoln Green Brewing Company in 2012 using a 10-barrel plant. Locally-sourced ingredients are used to create five regular beers and, in addition, seasonal and special brews are available that link to local and national events. The brewery takes its name from the colour of dyed woollen cloth associated with the legend of Robin Hood. ♦RAIB

Marion (OG 1038, ABV 3.8%)
Full-bodied pale ale, packed with citrus hop and a hint of grapefruit.

Hood (OG 1042, ABV 4.2%)
Best bitter in a classic English style, giving a full-rounded bitterness with a gentle floral aroma.

Sherwood (OG 1044, ABV 4.4%)
An extra pale ale with orange citrus aroma and biscuit malt.

Tuck (OG 1047, ABV 4.7%)
A well-rounded porter with a hint of dark chocolate and a blackcurrant aroma.

Sheriff (OG 1055, ABV 5.5%)
A true English pale ale with strong bitterness and orange citrus hop.

Lincolnshire (NEW) SIBA

Unit 3, 39 Monks Way, Lincoln, LN2 5LN ☎ 07508 554890 lincolnshirebrewingco.co.uk

An events company that operates mobile bars, in 2014 it started brewing for its own bars and has since expanded into the free trade. A three-barrel plant brews both cask and bottle-conditioned beers, with bottling carried out in-house. Beers can be found at local fairs, shows and markets. RAIB

Great Tom (ABV 3.7%)
A dark ale with elements of chocolate and coffee in the nose. A fruity and dark malt mouthfeel with a long but soft bitter finish.

Spicy Sausage (ABV 4.1%)
A Lincolnshire amber ale, with a sharp bitterness and dry finish.

Friendly Rottweiler (ABV 4.5%)
A light, crisp ale with a subtle hoppy taste.

Cheeky Imp (ABV 4.6%)
A malty ale with caramel notes and hoppy aromas. A good mouthfeel and slightly sweet taste.

Linfit

Sair Inn, 139 Lane Top, Linthwaite, Huddersfield, West Yorkshire, HD7 5SG
☎ (01484) 842370

A 19th-century brewpub that started brewing again in 1982. The beer is only available at the Sair Inn.

Lion Heart (NEW) SIBA

14a Hales Industrial Estate, Rowleys Green Lane, Longford, Coventry, CV6 6AL
☎ (024) 7666 7413 lionheartbrewery.com

Opened in 2014 in an industrial unit near the Ricoh Arena, using a 2.5-barrel kit. Three core beers are produced, which are available both cask and bottle conditioned. Occasional specials are also brewed. RAIB

IPA (ABV 3.8%)

Amber (ABV 4.8%)

Dark Ruby (ABV 5.5%)

Lion's Tale SIBA

Red Lion, High Street, Cheswardine, Shropshire, TF9 2RS
☎ (01630) 661234 cheslion96@yahoo.co.uk

The brewery building was purpose-built in 2005 and houses a 2.5-barrel plant. Jon Morris and his wife Shiela have owned the Red Lion since 1996. ♦RAIB

Blooming Blonde (OG 1041, ABV 4.1%)

Lionbru (OG 1041, ABV 4.1%)

Chesbrewnette (OG 1045, ABV 4.5%)

Lister's SIBA

The Old Dairy, Ford Lane, Ford, West Sussex, BN18 0DF
☎ (01903) 739117 ☎ 07775 853412
listersbrewery.com

Brewing began in 2012 using a 0.25-barrel kit. The brewery relocated in 2014 and expanded to a five-barrel plant.

Best Bitter (ABV 3.9%)

Special Ale (ABV 4.6%)

Little Ale Cart SIBA

c/o The Wellington, 1 Henry Street, Sheffield, South Yorkshire, S3 7EQ
☎ (0114) 249 2295

Brewing started in 2001, as Port Mahon, in a purpose-built brewery behind the Cask & Cutler. In 2007 the brewery and pub were taken over and the names of both changed to Little Ale Cart Brewing and the Wellington. Beer is brewed only for the Wellington and the Dragon pub in Worcester. The beer range varies as the brewer trials new recipes, but tends to include a 4%, 4.3% and a 5% ABV beer.

Little Beer SIBA

Building 3, 14-15 Midleton Road, Guildford, Surrey, GU2 8XW
☎ (01483) 497201 littlebeer.co.uk

Little Beer Corporation is a Guildford-based 10-barrel brewery that produces premium bottled, cask-conditioned and keg beers. It is run by Jim Taylor, who is also majority owner, alongside around 300 local shareholders. A monthly beer club (including beer, food and music) is for paid membership only. See website for details. !!

Little Haka (OG 1035, ABV 4.5%)
A light-bodied, full-flavoured, thirst-quenching ale, with passion fruit and gooseberry aromas.

Little Smooth (OG 1045, ABV 4.5%)
A full-flavoured milk stout.

Little Slow (OG 1050, ABV 5%)

Little Vienna (OG 1051, ABV 5%)

Little Snug (OG 1060, ABV 5.4%)
A traditional mellow pale ale, with a hint of nuts from the sweet chestnuts added in the mash.

Little Tenderness (OG 1054, ABV 5.4%)
An American-style amber ale with light biscuit and caramel sweetness.

Little Rosy (OG 1053, ABV 5.5%)

Naturally cloudy wheat beer with raspberries added during secondary fermentation, giving a dry bitterness, complementing the tartness of the fruit.

Little Wild (OG 1058, ABV 5.9%) ◆
A red IPA, rich and full flavoured with strong hop character balanced with solid maltiness and a dry bitter finish.

Little Icarus (OG 1052, ABV 6%)
A Belgian-style Wit beer, brewed with some unmalted wheat, and spiced with coriander, kiwi fruit and honey.

Little Harvest (OG 1065, ABV 6.4%)

Little Brew SIBA

15-16 Auster Road, Clifton Moor, York, YO30 4XA
littlebrew.co.uk

Brewing began in 2012 using a one-barrel plant in the Camden area of London. In 2014 the brewery relocated to Clifton Moor, York.

Gold (OG 1047, ABV 4.2%)

Ruby (OG 1050, ABV 4.6%)

Porter (OG 1054, ABV 5%)

IPA (OG 1058, ABV 5.5%)

Extra Porter (OG 1060, ABV 5.7%)

Little Bush (NEW)

51 Brook Lane, Marehay, Ripley, Derbyshire, DE5 8JA
(01773) 570830 hollybushmarehay.co.uk

A four-barrel plant, located in the cellar of the Hollybush pub in the village of Marehay, Little Bush commenced brewing in 2015.

D-Light (ABV 4.2%)

Fuggler (ABV 5.3%)

One for the Ditch (ABV 7.3%)

Little Valley SIBA

Unit 3, Turkey Lodge Farm, New Road, Cragg Vale, Hebden Bridge, West Yorkshire, HX7 5TT
(01422) 883888 littlevalleybrewery.co.uk

Little Valley began brewing in 2005 on a 10-barrel plant. All beers are organic and vegan, and Ginger Pale Ale uses Fairtrade ingredients. Around 100 outlets are supplied. Several beers are contract brewed for Suma Wholefoods and in 2012 the brewery was contracted by the Benedictine Order of Ampleforth Abbey to brew and bottle their Ampleforth Abbey Beer (ABV 7%). ♦RAIB

Ginger Pale Ale (OG 1037, ABV 4%) ◆
Full-bodied speciality ale. Ginger predominates in the aroma and taste. It has a pleasantly powerful, fiery and spicy finish.

Cragg Vale Bitter (OG 1039, ABV 4.2%) ◆
Grainy, pale brown session bitter, light on the palate with a delicate flavour of malt and fruit and a bitter finish.

Hebden's Wheat (OG 1043, ABV 4.5%) ◆
A pale yellow, creamy wheat beer with a good balance of bitterness and fruit, a hint of sweetness but with a lasting, dry finish.

Vanilla Porter (ABV 4.5%) ◆
Dark and complex speciality beer. Fresh vanilla dominates both the aroma and taste. Smooth, mellow finish.

Stoodley Stout (OG 1044, ABV 4.8%) ◆
Dark brown creamy stout with a rich roast aroma and fruity, chocolate, roast flavours. Well-balanced with a clean bitter finish.

Tod's Blonde (OG 1045, ABV 5%) ◆
Bright yellow, grainy, speciality beer with a citrus hop start and a dry finish. Fruity, with a hint of spice. Similar in style to a Belgian blonde beer.

Python IPA (OG 1055, ABV 6%) ◆
Amber-coloured grainy beer with a complex bitter fruit palate subtly balance by a malty sweetness, leading to a strong, lingering bitter aftertaste.

Liverpool Craft SIBA

62-64 Bridgewater Street, Liverpool, L1 0AY
(0151) 236 9400 liverpoolcraftbeer.com

Liverpool Craft began brewing in 2011 using a 10-barrel plant, relocating to the other side of the city centre in 2015. A visitor centre is planned. The brewery regularly supplies arts and music venues as well as local pubs. Swaps with other breweries make the beers available further afield. ♦RAIB

Quokka (OG 1038, ABV 3.9%)
An Australian-style session IPA; floral, hoppy and refreshing.

Toast (OG 1042, ABV 4.2%)
A biscuity, hoppy amber ale.

Love Lane Pale (ABV 4.5%)
A pale ale. The biscuit malt balances the whole leaf citrus hops for a refreshing, lasting taste.

American Red (OG 1047, ABV 5%)
A classic American-style red ale.

IPA (OG 1047, ABV 5%)
This single-hop IPA uses Columbus hops to bring out a pine and citrus aroma against a backdrop of Maris Otter and a touch of crystal malt for balance.

Brew #56 (OG 1049, ABV 5.4%)
A single-hopped, strong pale bitter with a balanced palatable finish.

Rye Pale Ale (OG 1050, ABV 5.6%)
A crisp pale ale.

West Coast Pale (OG 1058, ABV 6.2%)
A hoppy pale ale.

Liverpool Organic SIBA

39 Brasenose Road, Liverpool, L20 8HL
(0151) 933 9660 liverpoolorganicbrewery.com

Liverpool Organic started brewing in 2009. Outlets are supplied around the extended Merseyside area with its cask and bottle-conditioned beers. The brewery also supports many local beer festivals and also run festivals of its own including the largest beer event in Liverpool. Beers are also brewed under the name of the now defunct Cambrinus brewery. !!♦RAIB

Cascade (OG 1038, ABV 3.8%)
An intensely-hopped light session bitter.

Joseph Williamson (OG 1039, ABV 4%)
Traditional malty bitter flavours with floral elements building to a smooth, satisfying finish.

Liverpool Pale Ale (OG 1039, ABV 4%)

Dry hoppy notes with floral complexity giving way to spicy tones and a slightly creamy malt finish.

Bier Head (OG 1040, ABV 4.1%)
Sharp, hoppy foretaste with complex spice and crisp malt tones, building to a rich, mellow aftertaste.

24 Carat Gold (OG 1041, ABV 4.2%)
Generously hopped with a bitterness that builds steadily towards a lingering finish with spicy orange notes.

Best Bitter (OG 1042, ABV 4.2%)
Good, hoppy bitterness balanced with pale malts. A crisp, refreshing finish with a hint of citrus fruit.

Liverpool Stout (OG 1048, ABV 4.3%)
Strong, dark and dry stout with a smooth, spicy finish.

William Roscoe (OG 1042, ABV 4.3%)
Hoppy and fruity with a hint of dryness and bitterness building to a crisp and slightly earthy malt finish.

Honey Blond (OG 1043, ABV 4.5%)
A subtle and not cloyingly sweet honey aftertaste married to a solid malt backbone and a good hoppy character.

Josephine Butler (OG 1043, ABV 4.5%)
Initial citrus hops followed by elderflower fruit and pale, biscuity malt with a refreshing, sharp finish.

Kitty Wilkinson (OG 1047, ABV 4.5%)
Vanilla, butterscotch and chocolate combine in the roasted malty taste with a fairly dry finish and a generous cocoa bitterness.

Empire Ale (OG 1056, ABV 5.3%)
A strong ruby ale with slightly sweet finish.

Brewed under the Cambrinus Brewery name:

Deliverance (OG 1042, ABV 4.2%)
Pale gold beer with a sharp, hoppy taste.

Endurance (OG 1044, ABV 4.3%)
A beer with vanilla notes made with English malt and hops.

Lizard

The Old Nuclear Bunker, Pednavounder, Pednavounder, Cornwall, TR12 6SE
☎ (01326) 281135 ⊕ lizardales.co.uk

⊗ Launched in 2004, Lizard Ales is now based at former RAF Treleaver, a massive disused nuclear bunker in the countryside near Coverack on the Lizard Peninsula. Specialising in bottle-conditioned ales, it mainly supplies west Cornwall. ‼ RAIB

Kernow Gold (OG 1037, ABV 3.7%)

Bitter (OG 1041, ABV 4.2%) ◈
Pale brown beer with aroma of ripe apples. Roast malt with fruit esters balanced by bitterness. Bitter finish with dryness.

Frenchman's Creek (OG 1042, ABV 4.8%)

An Gof (OG 1049, ABV 5.2%) ◈
Robust and smooth tawny ale dominated by malt in the mouth with a hint of smoke. Fruity hops follow on into the bitter finish.

Llangollen SIBA

Abbey Grange Brewing Ltd, Abbey Grange Hotel, Horseshoe Pass Road, Llantysilio, LL20 8DD
☎ (01978) 861916 ⊕ llangollenbrewery.com

Brewing began in 2010 on a 2.5-barrel plant. RAIB

Grange No.1 (OG 1032, ABV 3.2%)
A pale ale with a fruity taste and aroma and a slight hoppy finish.

Wrexham Borders Bitter (OG 1039, ABV 3.9%)
A pale ale with fruity notes. Haylike and distinctively hoppy.

Bitter (OG 1042, ABV 4.2%)
A pale ale with a fruity aroma and distinctive hoppy finish.

Holy Grail (OG 1043, ABV 4.3%)
A light citrus pale ale.

Welsh Black (OG 1055, ABV 5.5%)
Chocolate and toffee notes with a hoppy finish.

Lleu

Unit A9, Penygroes Industrial Estate, Penygroes, LL54 6DB ☎ 07756 547650 ⊕ bragdylleu.co.uk

Brewing began in 2014 using a 1.25-barrel plant. The beer reflects the Welsh folklore tales of the Mabinogi in both name and character.

Lleu (OG 1040, ABV 4%)
Full-bodied ale with a good mouthfeel and a lasting and satisfying hoppy aftertaste. Good, easy-drinking session bitter.

Llŷn

Unit 6, Ffordd Dewi Sant, Nefyn, Gwynedd, LL53 6EG
☎ 07792 050134 ⊕ cwrwllyn.com

◎ The brewery is a co-operative of 12 friends that began brewing in 2011 producing 44 barrels per week. There are firm plans for a new brewery, incorporating a gas combustion system. ‼

Y Brawd Houdini (OG 1036, ABV 3.8%)
A summer ale, citrus and flowery.

Brenin Enlli (OG 1038, ABV 4%)
Classic copper-coloured, hoppy bitter.

Seithenyn (OG 1040, ABV 4.2%)
Golden ale with continental character.

Cochyn (OG 1043, ABV 4.5%)
Ruby Welsh ale.

Loch Lomond SIBA

Block 1, Unit 5, Lomond Industrial Estate, Alexandria, G83 0TL
☎ (01389) 755698 ☎ 07891 920213
⊕ lochlomondbrewery.com

Established in 2011 by Fiona and Euan MacEachern, it is the only brewery around Loch Lomond. ‼ ♦

Bonnie 'n' Bitter (OG 1036, ABV 3.6%)
A blonde, easy-drinking bitter with citrus flavours and a full, rounded bitterness.

West Highland Way (OG 1038, ABV 3.8%)
A light ale with fruity flavours.

Bonnie 'n' Blonde (OG 1040, ABV 4%)
A light, refreshing ale with a well-rounded citrus flavour.

Ale of Leven (OG 1045, ABV 4.5%)
An amber-coloured beer, easy-drinking with a slight sweetness and spicy bitterness.

Silkie Stout (OG 1050, ABV 5%)
A black stout with chocolate orange spicy notes.

Kessog Dark Ale (OG 1052, ABV 5.2%)
A dark beer with warm, spicy flavours.

Loch Ness SIBA

🍺 Blarmor, Drumnadrochit, IV63 6UG
☎ (01456) 450726 ⊕ lochnessbrewery.com

☺ Brewing began in 2011 using a two-barrel plant in the grounds of the Benleva Hotel. The brewery moved in 2012 to nearby premises using an eight-barrel plant. Beers are available in the local area, central Scotland and northern England plus exports to Italy, Russia and Singapore. There are plans for expansion. ‼🍺◆

MildNESS (OG 1040, ABV 3.5%) ◀
Roasted malt aroma gradually dies away leaving a soft caramel roasted bitterness.

LightNESS (OG 1039, ABV 3.9%) ◀
Golden refreshing hoppy bitter with a hint of peaches.

WilderNESS (OG 1039, ABV 3.9%) ◀
Fruity, hoppy brew with a slight malt background. Bittersweet turning to a more bitter finish.

CaithNESS (OG 1044, ABV 4%) ◀
Golden amber citrus, hoppy bittersweet taste with a sweeter finish.

MadNESS (OG 1042, ABV 4%) ◀
A brown-coloured, hoppy bitter.

SaaziNESS (OG 1042, ABV 4%) ◀
Refreshing golden ale, light citrus and hop flavoured using Saaz hops.

RedNESS (OG 1042, ABV 4.2%) ◀
Reddy brown in colour with a good mix of malt and hops with a raspberry background in this bittersweet brew.

LochNESS (OG 1044, ABV 4.4%) ◀
A malty, fruity, sweetish brew in the 80/- style. Hints of chocolate and blackcurrant.

DarkNESS (OG 1052, ABV 4.5%) ◀
Roasted chocolate malt with a slight blackcurrant background. Thick brown head all the way to the bottom.

InverNESS (OG 1042, ABV 4.5%) ◀
Golden hoppy brew with a slight sweetness in the background.

HoppyNESS (OG 1050, ABV 5%) 🍺 ◀
Golden smooth citrus, hoppy brew. The initial sweetness turns to a bitter finish. Does not drink its strength.

Prince of DarkNESS (OG 1095, ABV 10%) ◀
Creamy, heavy on malt with roast, chocolate and liquorice flavours coming through.

Loddon SIBA 👁

Dunsden Green Farm, Church Lane, Dunsden, Oxfordshire, RG4 9QD
☎ (0118) 948 1111 ⊕ loddonbrewery.com

☒ This family-run brewery was established in 2002, in a brick-and-flint barn that was originally a grain store. The custom-built 17-barrel plant typically produces 120 barrels a week, and supplies more than 500 outlets far and wide. Popular open evenings are held quarterly. ‼🍺◆

Hoppit (OG 1036.2, ABV 3.5%) ◀
Hops dominate the aroma of this drinkable, light-coloured session beer. Malt and hops create a balanced taste and a pleasant bitterness carries through to the aftertaste.

Hullabaloo (OG 1043.8, ABV 4.2%) ◀
A hint of fruit in the initial taste develops into a balance of hops and malt in this well-rounded, medium-bodied bitter with a bitter aftertaste.

Ferryman's Gold (OG 1045.8, ABV 4.4%) ◀
Golden-coloured with a strong hoppy character throughout, accompanied by fruit in the taste and aftertaste.

Bamboozle (OG 1049.5, ABV 4.8%) ◀
Full-bodied and well-balanced. Distinctive bittersweet flavour with hop and caramel to accompany.

Forbury Lion (OG 1056.5, ABV 5.5%)
A malty IPA with a strong complex hop finish.

Lola Rose (NEW)

🍺 Wanlockhead Inn, Wanlockhead, ML12 6UZ
☎ (01659) 74535 ⊕ lola-rose-brewery.co.uk

Lola Rose is based in the family-run Wanlockhead Inn, situated in the scenic Lowther Hills of the Scottish Lowlands. Two core beers are produced. Local outlets only are supplied at present. RAIB

1531 Red (ABV 4.3%)

1531 Blonde (ABV 4.4%)

London Beer Factory SIBA 👁

Unit 4, 160 Hamilton Road, West Norwood, London, SE27 9SF ☎ 07760 290489
⊕ thelondonbeerfactory.com

The London Beer Factory started brewing in 2014 using a 20-barrel plant. Local outlets are supplied. A tap room is open to the public at weekends.

London Session (ABV 3.8%)

Chelsea Blonde (ABV 4.3%) ◀
Golden ale with grapefruit and hoppy notes throughout. Finish is dry and refreshing.

Paxton Pale Ale (ABV 5%)

London Brewing

🍺 Bull, 13 North Hill, Highgate, London, N6 4AB
☎ (020) 8341 0510 ⊕ londonbrewing.com

☒ London Brewing Co began brewing in 2011 at the Bull in Highgate using a 2.5-barrel plant. In 2014 it acquired its second pub, the Bohemia in North Finchley, at which brewing began in 2015 in a new 6.5-barrel brewhouse. ◆

Highrise (OG 1040, ABV 3.9%) ◀
A fruity, yellow-coloured ale with a bitter character balanced by a fudge sweetness and a touch of lemon/lime peel.

Beer Street (OG 1042, ABV 4%) ◀
Well-balanced copper brown best bitter with hoppy bitterness underpinned by a caramelised malt character. Fruit is present throughout.

Vista (OG 1047, ABV 4.7%) ◀
Smooth brown best bitter. Some nutty notes with hints of chocolate balanced by fruit. Lingering, dry bitter finish.

Skyline (OG 1053, ABV 5.3%) ◆
Pale brown beer with a honey sweetness and a some soft fruit notes. Sweetness is balanced by a bitter dryness.

Long Arm (NEW)

🍴 Ealing Park Tavern, 222 South Ealing Road, Ealing, W5 4RL
☎ (020) 8758 0878 ⊕ ealingparktavern.com

A microbrewery located in a gastropub on the Brentford/Ealing border, producing three regular ales. Birdie Flipper, a red ale, is particularly noteworthy as unusual for the region. The beers are available across London at the ETM chain of bars and restaurants. ‼

Lucky Penny (OG 1041, ABV 4%)

Birdie Flipper (OG 1045, ABV 4.5%)

IPA OK (OG 1051, ABV 5.5%)

Long Lane

Correspondence: Unit 2, Redhill Farm, Top Street, Appleby Magna, Leicestershire, DE12 7AH
☎ (01530) 813800

Opened in 2010 at the Matchless Homebrew shop, with beers brewed by passionate brewster Ann Saunders. In 2014 the brewery was closed and beers are now brewed at Golden Duck. All beers are available bottle-conditioned; however cask-conditioned beers can be produced to order.

Long Man SIBA 👁

Church Farm, Litlington, East Sussex, BN26 5RA
☎ (01323) 871850 ☎ 07976 777992
⊕ longmanbrewery.com

⊠ Long Man began brewing in 2012 using a 20-barrel stainless steel plant. Hops and grain are sourced locally with a view to using barley currently being grown on the farm, as well as a traditional strain of Sussex yeast. ‼

Long Blonde (OG 1039, ABV 3.8%)
A light-coloured golden ale with a distinctive hoppy aroma and crisp, clean bitterness on the finish. Smooth, light and refreshing.

Best Bitter (OG 1040, ABV 4%)
Well-balanced with a complex bittersweet malty taste, fragrant hops and a characteristic long deep finish. A traditional Sussex-style best bitter.

Copper Hop (ABV 4.2%)

Old Man (OG 1048, ABV 4.3%)
Dark beer with soft malt notes of coffee and chocolate combined with a pleasant light hoppiness creating a rich, full-tasting old ale.

Sussex Pride (OG 1045, ABV 4.5%)
A classic strong pale ale. Bronze-coloured with a fruity nose and full round flavours. A perfect balance between malt and hops.

American Pale Ale (OG 1046, ABV 4.8%)
A triple-hopped APA has a pleasant citrus fruit aroma and characteristic robust bitterness.

Longden SIBA 👁

Red Lion, Longden Common, Shropshire, SY5 8AE
☎ 07958 007551 ⊕ longdenbrewing.co.uk

👁Longden Brewing Company has been brewing since 2013 using a five-barrel plant. Beer names are inspired by local legends. The regular beers are usually available at the Red Lion (the brewery tap) and in a number of free houses in Shropshire, including several in Shrewsbury town centre. ◆

Golden Arrow (OG 1038, ABV 3.8%)
A pale ale with an abundance of hop character.

Sawn Off (OG 1042, ABV 4%)
A copper-coloured, flavoursome best bitter, balancing a rich blend of malts with gentle bitterness from a mix of traditional British hops.

Spire Dancer (OG 1044, ABV 4.2%)

Longdog SIBA

Unit A1, Moniton Trading Estate, West Ham Lane, Worting, Hampshire, RG22 6NQ
☎ (01256) 324286 ☎ 07827 618733
⊕ longdogbrewery.co.uk

⊠ Longdog was established in 2011 using a six-barrel plant. The name is inspired by the owner's greyhound. ‼🍽◆

Bunny Chaser (OG 1036, ABV 3.6%)
A dark copper-coloured session bitter with plenty of malt in the mouth and a good whack of bitterness.

Golden Poacher (OG 1038, ABV 3.9%) ◆
A fruity nose with plenty of hops, balanced by a malty sweetness in the flavour. The hops build to a faint astringent finish.

Brindle Bitter (OG 1041, ABV 4.2%) ◆
Well-crafted best bitter. Malt nose with caramel hints and berry fruits. Maltiness leads into moderate hop flavour with bitter aftertaste.

Kismet (OG 1045, ABV 4.5%)

Lamplight Porter (OG 1048, ABV 5%) ◆
Splendid porter, smoky and drier than many, with strong roast flavours giving way to a blackberry taste and slightly vinous finish.

Longhill

Longhill Cottage, Whitstone, Cornwall, EX22 6UG
☎ (01288) 341466

⊠ Longhill began brewing in 2011 using a 0.5-barrel plant, upgraded in 2012 to a four-barrel plant to meet demand. The beers are named with a wind theme. Eight outlets are supplied direct.

Whistler (OG 1038, ABV 3.8%)

Westerly (OG 1040, ABV 4%) ◆
Copper-coloured best bitter with a malt and toffee aroma. Mainly malt and caramel flavour. Light finish with malt, fruit and bitterness.

Gale Force (OG 1048, ABV 4.8%) ◆
Copper-coloured strong bitter. Malt and almonds aroma. Malty flavours with toffee and nuts. Short, malty, dry finish with stone fruit.

Hurricane (OG 1048, ABV 4.8%)

Loose Cannon SIBA

Unit 6, Suffolk Way, Abingdon, Oxfordshire, OX14 5JX
☎ (01235) 531141 ⊕ lcbeers.co.uk

Loose Cannon began production in 2010 using a 15-barrel brew plant, reviving Abingdon's brewing history after the Morland Brewery closed in 2000. Beers can be found in an increasing number of local pubs, with the Chester in Oxford acting as the brewery tap. There are plans for expansion. Popular brewery evenings take place on the first Tuesday of the month. ‼️🍴♦

Gunners Gold (OG 1034.5, ABV 3.5%)
Golden, easy-drinking session ale with a subtle peach flavour.

Abingdon Bridge (OG 1041, ABV 4.1%)
Full flavoured and smooth, with well-rounded bitterness from Fuggles hops. Amarillo hops give the beer a light citrus and floral finish.

Bandwagon (OG 1041.5, ABV 4.2%)
Full-flavoured, copper-coloured bitter. Rounded malty body. Mixed berry finish.

Dark Horse (OG 1042, ABV 4.3%)
Dark beer with a fruity hop aroma.

Lord Conrad's

Unit 21, Dry Drayton Industrial Estate, Scotland Road, Dry Drayton, Cambridgeshire, CB23 8AT ☎ 07736 739700 ⊕ lordconradsbrewery.co.uk

Lord Conrad's was established in 2007 and moved to Dry Drayton in 2011 using a 2.5-barrel plant. One permanent outlet is supplied, the Abbot's Elm in Abbots Ripton, along with other local free houses and beer festivals. The brewery adheres strongly to 'green' principles, using low energy systems, recycled materials and local ingredients.

Stoat Warbler (OG 1035, ABV 3.4%)

Zulu Dawn (OG 1037, ABV 3.5%)

Hedgerow Hop (OG 1039, ABV 3.7%)
A wild amber-coloured ale made with locally-picked hops and supporting the RSPB.

Lickety Split (OG 1038, ABV 3.8%)
Sweet, malty brown ale, light but not overly hoppy.

Conkerwood (OG 1044, ABV 4%)
A dark porter with hints of liquorice.

Gubbins (OG 1040, ABV 4%)
A real mixed bag, much like its name, with a hint of spice.

Slap n' Tickle (OG 1042, ABV 4.3%)
A summer blonde with a big slap of bitterness and just a tickle of hops.

Zulu (OG 1047, ABV 4.5%)
A strong black bitter.

Pheasant's Rise (OG 1050, ABV 5%)
Smoky, woody traditional strong ale.

Stubble Burner (OG 1050, ABV 5%)
A straw-like beer with a good earthy nose and a well-balanced fruity bitterness.

Lovebeer (NEW)

95 High Street, Milton, Oxfordshire, OX14 4EJ ☎ 07889 455845

Jim Southey has been brewing ale since 2013 and became licensed to sell to the public in 2014.

Molly's Malt (ABV 4%)
A standard bitter with a good balance of malt and hops.

Purdy Peculiar (ABV 4.3%)

An amber-coloured beer with a hoppy citrus flavour.

Luckie

Haig Business Park, Balgonie Road, Markinch, KY7 6AQ ☎ (01333) 352801 ⊕ luckie-ales.com

Luckie Ales was established by Stuart McLuckie in 2009. Brewing moved to Haigs Business Park in 2012 using a one-barrel plant. The brewery specialises in handcrafted Scottish beers and historic British ales. Beers are brewed on demand.

Ludlow SIBA ◉

The Railway Shed, Station Drive, Ludlow, Shropshire, SY8 2PQ ☎ (01584) 873291 ⊕ theludlowbrewingcompany.co.uk

Established in 2006, the brewery, now in its 10th year, occupies a converted railway sidings shed. Brews are produced using a 20-barrel brewing plant. The premises also function as a brewery tap, visitor centre and events area. ‼️🍴

Best (OG 1037, ABV 3.7%)
A golden amber-coloured, well-balanced session beer with a banana, pineapple and toffee aroma and a resinous, dry finish.

Blonde (OG 1040, ABV 4%)
A pale golden ale with a lemon citrus aroma and a balanced, crisp citrus taste.

Gold (OG 1041, ABV 4.2%)
A golden ale with a papaya, pineapple and lemon aroma and a soft, full-bodied, creamy taste.

Black Knight (OG 1045, ABV 4.5%)
A ruby black stout with a smoky, liquorice aroma and sweet, roasted nutty flavour.

Boiling Well (OG 1045.5, ABV 4.7%)
An auburn-coloured beer with a grassy aroma of autumn fruit with a full-bodied sweet then dry taste.

Stairway (OG 1047, ABV 5%)
A grassy, citrus floral aroma with a sharp, sweet, full-bodied taste.

LWC

Beers brewed under the Gray's brand. See Marston's

Lyme Regis SIBA

Mill Lane, Lyme Regis, Dorset, DT7 3PU ☎ (01297) 444354 ⊕ lymeregisbrewery.com

⊗ Lyme Regis Brewery, formerly known as Town Mill, began brewing in 2010 using a four-barrel plant in a part of the mill that at one time housed the Lyme Regis electricity generator, although historic use of the building was as a brewer's malthouse. The outside area is now licensed and is proving popular. Contract brewing is carried out for other breweries. ‼️🍴 RAIB

Cobb (OG 1041, ABV 3.9%)
An amber/brown bitter with a full flavour and traditional-tasting fruity hop finish.

Lyme Gold (OG 1042, ABV 4.2%)

THE BREWERIES

A pale summer ale, easy-drinking with a refreshing citrus aroma.

Town Mill Best (OG 1045, ABV 4.5%)
A reddish brown bitter with a fruit and nut flavour.

Black Ven (OG 1050, ABV 5%)
A dark brown porter with a pronounced depth of flavour, enhanced with the blackcurrant fruitiness of the hops.

Revenge (OG 1052, ABV 5.3%)
A traditional IPA with a well-balanced hop and spiced fruit flavour.

Lymestone SIBA

The Brewery, Mount Road, Stone, Staffordshire, ST15 8LL
☎ (01785) 817796 ☎ 07891 782652
lymestonebrewery.co.uk

Lymestone commenced brewing in 2008. Rapid growth has seen the beers supplied direct to 300 outlets, with beer also being available via wholesalers. The brewery opened its first pub in 2012, the Lymestone Vaults, Newcastle-under-Lyme. !! ♦

Stone Cutter (OG 1037, ABV 3.7%)
Hoppy and grassy aroma, clean, sharp and refreshing. A hint of caramel then intense bitterness emerges with a good bitter aftertaste and touch of astringency.

Stone Faced (OG 1040, ABV 4%)
Subtle citrus and toffee flavours balanced by a hoppy aroma and bitter finish.

Foundation Stone (OG 1047, ABV 4.5%)
An IPA-style beer with pale and crystal malts. Faint biscuit and chewy, juicy fruits burst on to the palate then spicy Boadicea and Pilot hops pepper the taste buds to leave a dry, bitter finish.

Ein Stein (OG 1052, ABV 5%)
A pale, citrus, hoppy ale.

Stone the Crows (OG 1056, ABV 5.4%)
A rich dark beer from chocolate malts. Fruit, roasts and hops abound to leave a deep lingering bitterness from Styrian Goldings and Millennium hop mix.

Abdominal Stoneman (OG 1072, ABV 7%)
An American-style pale ale with a massive hoppy finish.

Lymm

18 Bridgewater Street, Lymm, Cheshire, WA13 0AB
☎ (0161) 929 0663 ✉ info@lymmbrewing.co.uk

Lymm is a small, family-run brewery, launched in 2013. Located in an old post office, the brewing equipment is downstairs in what used to be the mess rooms with a brewery tap upstairs in what was the sorting office/post office counter. A sister brewery to Dunham Massey (qv), a joint bar opened in 2013, Costello's Bar, Stockton Heath. ♦

Bitter (OG 1040, ABV 3.8%)
A light, refreshing, medium-bodied session bitter, with a good balance of malt and hops.

Bridgewater Blonde (OG 1041, ABV 4%)
Light, delicate, hoppy, subtle and refreshing.

Heritage Trail Ale (OG 1046, ABV 4.5%)
An easy-drinking, well-balanced best bitter, fruity with a light, crisp hop.

Dam Strong Ale (OG 1071, ABV 7.2%)
Belgian-style English ale; strong, malty and fruity with a dry finish.

Lytham SIBA

8 Cambell's Court, Lord Street, St Annes, Lancashire, FY8 2DF
☎ (01253) 725440 lythambrewery.co.uk

Lytham is a well-established, family-run brewery that began brewing in 2007. !! ♦

Amber (OG 1037, ABV 3.6%)
A traditional malty beer using English hops.

Blonde (OG 1038, ABV 3.8%)
A pale golden beer with a subtle hop aroma and a smooth, dry finish.

Gold (OG 1042, ABV 4.2%)
A golden beer with a fruity aroma and lasting bitter finish.

Royal (OG 1044, ABV 4.4%)
A full-bodied English ale with a crisp, fruity aroma and a smooth, dry finish.

Stout (OG 1046, ABV 4.6%)
Dark, rich, roasty, full-bodied stout.

IPA (OG 1054, ABV 5.6%)
A pale bitter with a fresh, sweet, hoppy flavour leading to a long, dry finish.

McGivern

c/o Bridge End Inn, 5 Bridge Street, Ruabon, LL14 6DA
☎ (01978) 810881 ☎ 07891 676614
mcgivernales.co.uk

The brewery was established in 2008 and was originally based at the brewer's home in Wrexham but moved in 2011 to the award-winning Bridge End Inn in Ruabon using a 2.5-barrel plant. ♦

Bridge Bitter (OG 1039, ABV 3.9%)

Bridge Pale (OG 1039, ABV 3.9%)

Pyramid Porter (OG 1045, ABV 4.5%)
A hoppy porter with chocolate undertones.

Gambit (OG 1047, ABV 4.7%)

Enigma (OG 1050, ABV 5%)

McMullen SIBA/IFBB

26 Old Cross, Hertford, SG14 1RD
☎ (01992) 584911 mcmullens.co.uk

McMullen, Hertfordshire's oldest independent brewery, was founded in 1827. Under the banner of the Whole Hop Brewery (the name emphasising the company's continuing policy of using only traditional brewing materials) eight or more seasonal beers are produced a year. All 135 pubs, now spread across south-east England, serve cask beer. !! ♦

AK (OG 1035, ABV 3.7%)
A pleasant mix of malt and hops leads to a distinctive, dry aftertaste that isn't always as pronounced as it used to be.

Cask Ale (OG 1039, ABV 3.8%)
Subtle biscuity flavour and citrus hops create a light and refreshing ale.

Country Bitter (OG 1042, ABV 4.3%)

A full-bodied beer with a well-balanced mix of malt, hops and fruit throughout.

IPA (OG 1047, ABV 4.8%)
A strong bitter with deep rich flavours created with specially kilned amber malts.

Maclay

See Clockwork

Mad Cat SIBA

Brogdale Farm, Brogdale Road, Faversham, Kent, ME13 8XZ
☎ (01795) 597743 ☎ 07960 263615
madcatbrewery.co.uk

Mad Cat was established in 2012 by Peter Meaney in a refurbished cold store using an eight-barrel plant.

Auburn Copper Ale (ABV 4.2%)

Platinum Blonde (ABV 4.2%)

Golden IPA (ABV 4.6%)

Jet Black Stout (ABV 4.6%)

Mad Dog (NEW)

Unit L1b, Park Farm, Plough Road, Penperlleni, NP4 0AL ☎ 07703 731197

Office: 75 Brynhyfryd, Croesyceiliog, NP44 2LN
maddogbrew.co.uk

Brewing began in 2014 based at the brewer's home in Cwmbran. The brewery moved to its current premises in 2015 expanding to a brewlength of five barrels. Another relocation, back to Cwmbran, to larger premsises and a 10-barrel plant is planned.

Afternoon Sunshine (OG 1042, ABV 4.2%)
Golden in colour with the aroma of citrus and tangerine, tropical fruits to taste and finishing with a subtle spicy note.

Dirty Dog (OG 1045, ABV 4.5%)
Copper-coloured ale with flavours of chocolate, orange and grapes.

Bark Like A Bird (OG 1052, ABV 5.2%)
Deep red in colour with bitterness and sweet chocolate followed by tropical fruits and citrus.

Mad Hatter

8 Watkinson Street, Liverpool, L1 0BE
☎ (0151) 739 1702 ☎ 07474 797450
madhatterbrewing.co.uk

Mad Hatter began brewing in 2013 combining traditional techniques with new flavours and approaches to brewing. Most of the output is bottled or keg with cask-conditioned beers making an occasional appearance around Merseyside. In 2014 the brewery relocated to Baltic Triangle.

Penny Lane (ABV 3.9%)
Easy-drinking beer packed full of flavour with a tropical fruit aroma and refreshing bitterness.

Nightmare on Bold Street (ABV 5.3%)
Rich milk stout with fresh beans from Bold Street coffee. Roasted flavours of chocolate and coffee are softened by a gentle sweetness.

Toxteth IPA (ABV 6.5%)
Hops are perfectly balanced against a rich malt backbone.

Madcap SIBA

Greenknowe Avenue, Annan, DG12 6ER
☎ (01461) 203495 ☎ 07801 699161
madcapbrewery.com

Madcap began brewing in 2009. It concentrates on the production of bottle-conditioned beers.

Madrigal (NEW)

Upper Glen, King Street, Combe Martin, Devon, EX34 0DB ☎ 07857 560677
madrigalbrewery.co.uk

The brewery was established in 2014. The beers are supplied only locally. RAIB

Wheatear (OG 1037, ABV 3.4%)
Wheat beer made with fresh ginger and coriander.

Garland (OG 1036, ABV 3.5%)
A wheat beer with hints of tropical fruits.

Surfer Rosa (OG 1036, ABV 3.6%)
A unique ale, made with English hops and a spicy red rye malt.

Fossil (OG 1043, ABV 4%)
A well-rounded amber ale.

Severed Hand (OG 1041, ABV 4.1%)
A velvety porter.

Hanged Man (OG 1042, ABV 4.2%)
A stout, named after the hills surrounding Combe Martin.

Magic Rock SIBA

Units 1-4, Willow Lane, Huddersfield, West Yorkshire, HD1 5EB
☎ (01484) 649823 magicrockbrewing.com

Magic Rock began brewing in 2011 in the Old Bed Factory attached to the Rockshop Wholesale Company in Huddersfield. In 2015 the brewery relocated to its present address. ♦RAIB

Ringmaster (OG 1038, ABV 3.9%)
Pale ale with a floral/grassy aroma and citrus hops.

Rapture (OG 1044.5, ABV 4.6%)
Full-bodied red ale, with grapefruit and pine aromas, with pithy orange, and a rich malty body.

High Wire (OG 1051, ABV 5.5%)
West Coast-style pale ale, with mango, lychee and grapefruit flavours.

Dark Arts (OG 1057, ABV 6%)
Chocolate, liquorice, blackberry and fig flavours with a long, roasted bitter finish.

Magpie SIBA

Unit 4, Ashling Court, Ashling Street, Nottingham, NG2 3JA ☎ 07738 762897 magpiebrewery.com

Launched in 2006, this six-barrel plant only uses British hops and malt. The brewery maintains a large core range, plus seasonal and one-off beers. ♦RAIB

Hoppily Ever After (OG 1035, ABV 3.8%)
Blonde refreshing beer with distinct hop flavour.

Angry Bird (OG 1039, ABV 4%)
Heavily-hopped ruby ale.

Flyer (OG 1038.8, ABV 4.1%)
Single-hopped with Flyer hops giving a fruity and slightly spicy flavour to this light golden ale.

Best (OG 1040.7, ABV 4.2%) ◆
A malty traditional pale brown best bitter, with balancing hops giving a bitter finish.

Raven Stout (OG 1044, ABV 4.4%)
Rich and full-bodied, roast and smoky-flavoured smooth dark stout.

Thieving Rogue (OG 1042, ABV 4.5%) ◆
A hoppy golden ale with a long-lasting, bitter finish.

Midnight Porter (OG 1049.4, ABV 5%)
Rich and creamy dark porter with coffee, raisins and chocolate flavours.

JPA (OG 1048.6, ABV 5.2%)
Mature hops, citrus fruit nose with a balance of hops and malt in the mouth with a smooth, hoppy aftertaste.

Maidstone

Unit 11, The Old Brewery, Rocky Hill, London Road, Maidstone, Kent, ME16 0DZ
☎ (01622) 757705

A four-barrel brewery situated in the former stable block of the old Style & Winch brewery in Maidstone. Test brewing commenced in 2013 and the first beer went on sale in 2015. Further beers are planned across a range of styles to be made available locally, particularly at the Flower Pot pub.

Eight (OG 1052, ABV 4.5%)
A smooth, dark ale with gentle bitterness, a hint of chocolate and medium aroma based on Kentish hops.

Maldon

Stable Brewery, Silver Street, Maldon, Essex, CM9 4QE
☎ (01621) 851000 ⊕ maldonbrewing.co.uk

⊗ Established in 2002, this family-run brewery is tucked away behind the 14th-century Blue Boar Hotel. The eight-barrel plant is at full production serving over 50 outlets including many Gray & Sons houses. ♦ RAIB

Farmer's IPA (OG 1036, ABV 3.6%)
A crisp IPA based on an old Ridley's recipe.

Drop of Nelson's Blood (OG 1038, ABV 3.8%)
An easy-drinking bitter originally brewed for Trafalgar Day. Brandy is added to each cask.

Hotel Porter (OG 1041, ABV 4.1%)
A classic stout with a smoky tang produced by a good amount of roast barley.

Pucks Folly (OG 1038, ABV 4.2%)
A pale golden ale with a spicy character and pineapple in the aroma and taste.

Farmer's Golden Boar (OG 1050, ABV 5%)
An amber-coloured ale with a hoppy aroma.

Dark Horse (OG 1064, ABV 6.6%)
A chestnut-coloured bitter, smooth but with spice in the finish.

Wallet (OG 1070, ABV 7.4%)
A pale, aromatic strong ale.

Mallard SIBA

Unit A, Maythorne, Nottinghamshire, NG25 0RS
☎ 07811 193930

The 2.25-barrel plant occupies the land that in past times was used to grow North Clay hops. Brewer Steve Hussey took over the brewery in 2010 from Phil Mallard, who began the brewery in 1995, and moved it to its current address. There are plans for expansion and to produce bottle-conditioned beers. !! ♦

Duck 'n' Dive (OG 1039, ABV 3.7%) ◆
A bitter, pale golden beer, with a dry finish.

Greet Ale (OG 1037, ABV 3.7%)

Golden Duck (OG 1039, ABV 3.9%)

Quacker Jack (OG 1040, ABV 4%)

Feather Light (OG 1040, ABV 4.1%) ◆
A straw-coloured lager-style beer with a hoppy taste and aroma.

Duckling (OG 1041, ABV 4.2%) ◆
A dry-hopped, golden ale. Extremely bitter; hops dominate in the aroma and aftertaste.

Specduckular (OG 1042, ABV 4.2%)

Mallinson's

Unit 1, Waterhouse Mill, 65-71 Lockwood Road, Huddersfield, West Yorkshire, HD1 3QU
☎ (01484) 654301 ☎ 07850 446571
⊕ drinkmallinsons.co.uk

⊚ The brewery was originally set up in 2008 on a six-barrel plant by CAMRA members Tara Mallinson and Elaine Yendall. The company moved to new premises in 2012 after trial brewing its core beers on a new 15-barrel plant for several weeks. For beer range, including seasonal and special beers: see website. !! ♦ RAIB

Malt SIBA

Collings Hanger Farm, 100 Wycombe Road, Prestwood, Buckinghamshire, HP16 0HP
☎ (01494) 865063 ☎ 07815 187113
⊕ maltthebrewery.co.uk

⊗ Opened in 2012 in a converted dairy, the 10-barrel brewery has conservation at its heart; from the use of local ingredients, to spent grain sent to the local farm. The ales are also used in pies and sausages. !! ♦

Missenden Pale Ale (OG 1035, ABV 3.6%)
An easy-drinking session ale, light amber in colour.

Dark Ale (OG 1038, ABV 3.9%)
Smooth, mild and drinkable. Full of deep malt tones.

Golden Ale (OG 1038, ABV 3.9%)
Light and refreshing with a citrus finish.

Prestwood's Best (OG 1043, ABV 4.4%)
Classic-style bitter with a dry finish. Made with a blend of traditional British hops.

IPA (OG 1048, ABV 5%)
Aromatic with a bitter finish.

Malvern Hills SIBA

15 West Malvern Road, Malvern, Worcestershire, WR14 4ND

☎ (01684) 560165 ⊕ malvernhillsbrewery.co.uk

Founded in 1998 in an old quarrying dynamite store and now an established presence in the Three Counties, Birmingham and the Black Country. The core brews are supplemented by a rolling programme of monthly specials. !! ♦

Beacon Gold (OG 1037, ABV 3.7%)

Feelgood (OG 1037, ABV 3.8%)

Priessnitz Plzen (OG 1040, ABV 4.3%) ◣
A mix of soft fruit and citrus give this straw-coloured brew its quaffability, making it ideal for quenching summer thirsts.

Black Pear (OG 1042, ABV 4.4%) ◣
A sharp citrus hoppiness is the main constituent of this golden brew that has a long, dry aftertaste.

Mantle SIBA ⊚

Unit 16, Pentood Industrial Estate, Cardigan, SA43 3AG
☎ (01239) 623898 ☎ 07552 609909
⊕ mantlebrewery.com

Mantle began brewing in 2013 using a 10-barrel plant. Honing their skills brewing traditional beers for the local market, Ian and Dominique Kimber have now branched out into New World hops to extend their portfolio. Pubs throughout South and West Wales are supplied direct, select wholesalers delivering further afield. !! ☒ ♦

Rock Steady (OG 1038, ABV 3.8%)
Golden session ale with great depth of flavour. Satisfying and refreshing.

MOHO (OG 1041.5, ABV 4.3%)
Robust and aromatic Welsh pale ale, finely balanced and full-flavoured.

Cwrw Teifi (OG 1045, ABV 4.5%)
Full-bodied malt-driven best bitter with a well-balanced and pleasant hop finish.

Dark Heart (OG 1052, ABV 5.2%)
Rich, dark and smooth porter with a hint of spice.

Marble SIBA

41 Williamson Street, Manchester, M4 4JS
☎ (0161) 819 2694 ⊕ marblebeers.com

⊚Marble began brewing in 1997 at the Marble Arch Inn in Manchester but now brews at a larger 12-barrel plant in a nearby unit, producing vegan beers. It supplies its own three pubs and more than 70 other outlets. !! ♦ RAIB

Pint (OG 1038.5, ABV 3.9%)
A dry session bitter with notes of citrus and grapefruit.

Manchester Bitter (OG 1040.5, ABV 4.2%) ◣
Yellow beer with a fruity and hoppy aroma. Hops, fruit and bitterness on the palate and in the finish.

Lagonda IPA (OG 1047, ABV 5%) ◣
Golden yellow beer with a spicy, fruity nose. Fruit, hops and malt in the mouth, with a dry fruitiness continuing into the bitter aftertaste.

Ginger 5.1 (OG 1047.5, ABV 5.1%)
This full-bodied, copper-coloured beer displays a delicate blend of cloves, coriander and heaps of fiery ginger.

Chocolate Marble (OG 1054.5, ABV 5.5%)

Brewed with an emphasis on chocolate malts; tasting of coffee, cocoa and liquorice with a quenching bitter finish.

Dobber (OG 1056.5, ABV 5.9%) ⬚
A dark golden IPA with pronounced New Zealand hop character and smooth biscuit base offset by fruit aroma.

Earl Grey IPA (OG 1065, ABV 6.8%)
With timed additions of Earl Grey during fermentation, heavy infused hopping and traditional cask maturing, the result is a citrus fruit aroma and smooth sleek texture; hop notes are complemented by Bergamot and a light tannic finish.

Marlpool

5 Breach Road, Marlpool, Heanor, Derbyshire, DE75 7NJ
☎ (01773) 711285 ☎ 07963 511855
⊕ marlpoolbrewing.co.uk

Marlpool was set up by brothers Andy and Chris McAuley in 2010 using a 2.5-barrel plant situated in an old slaughterhouse. The majority of the beer is sold through its own micro pub built into the old butcher's shop attached to the brewery. The remainder is sold to local outlets. !! ♦ RAIB

Blind Boris (OG 1038, ABV 3.5%)
Traditional dark mild.

Otters Pocket (OG 1040, ABV 4%)
Easy-drinking, smooth amber-coloured ale.

Scratty Ratty (OG 1044, ABV 4.4%)
Pale ale lightly hopped with a bitter, dry finish.

Derbyshire Classic (OG 1048, ABV 4.8%)
A premium amber-coloured bitter.

Owd Sowj (OG 1050, ABV 5%)
Full-bodied traditional dark bitter.

Marston's SIBA ⊚

Shobnall Road, Burton upon Trent, Staffordshire, DE14 2BW
☎ (01283) 531131 ⊕ marstons.co.uk

⊚Marston's, formerly Wolverhampton & Dudley, has grown with spectacular speed over the last 10 years. It became a super-regional in 1999 when it bought both Mansfield and Marston's breweries, though it quickly closed Mansfield. In 2005 it bought Jennings of Cockermouth and has invested £250,000 in Cumbria to expand fermenting and cask racking capacity. In total, Marston's owns 1,500 pubs and supplies some 3,000 free trade pubs and clubs throughout the country. It added a further 70 pubs in 2006 when it bought Celtic Inns for £43.6 million. In 2007 it paid £155 million for the 158-strong Eldridge Pope pub estate. In the same year it bought Ringwood in Hampshire and also added Brakspear and Wychwood in Witney, Oxfordshire. In 2015 it bought the brewing division of Daniel Thwaites and now has a 10-year supply agreement with Thwaites's 350 pubs. Marston's has been brewing cask beer in Burton since 1834 and the current site is the home of the only working Burton Union fermenters, housed in rooms known as the Cathedral of Brewing. Burton Unions were developed in the 19th century to cleanse the new style of pale ale yeast. Only Pedigree is fermented in the unions but yeast from the system is used to ferment the other beers. Marston's

THE BREWERIES

continues to take contract brewing. In 2014 InBev renewed the contract to brew the iconic cask beer Draught Bass. **!! ↝ RAIB**

Burton Bitter (OG 1037, ABV 3.8%) ↝
Overwhelming sulphurous aroma supports a scattering of hops and fruit with an easy-drinking sweetness. The taste develops from the sweet middle to a satisfyingly hoppy finish.

**Pedigree New World Pale Ale
(OG 1038, ABV 3.8%)**
Hops impart a mellow, understated bitterness, complemented by a blast of tropical fruit flavours – peach, apricot, melon and passion fruit. A light citrus tingle follows, leading to a fragrant and refreshing finish.

Pedigree (OG 1043, ABV 4.5%) ↝
Pale brown with a sweet hoppy aroma. Malt with a dash of hop flavours give a satisfying tasty finish.

Old Empire (OG 1057, ABV 5.7%) ↝
Sulphur dominates the gentle malt aroma. Malty and sweet to start but developing bitterness with fruit and a touch of sweetness. A balanced aftertaste of hops and fruit leads to a lingering bitterness.

For AB InBev:

Draught Bass (OG 1043, ABV 4.4%) ↝
Hints of caramel aroma and taste, lightly hopped for a short bitter finish.

Martland Mill (NEW) SIBA

Unit 5, Otterwood Square, Martland Mill, Wigan, WN5 0LF
☎ (01942) 665656 ⊕ martlandmillbrewery.co.uk

☺Brewing began in 2014. The brewery is located a stone's throw from the town centre in the busy area of Martland Mill Park.

Spinner's Gold (ABV 3.8%)
An easy-drinking golden ale. Created with a well-balanced hoppiness and a pleasant citrus taste with a hint of spiciness.

Clogmaker (ABV 4%)
A rich, golden, full-bodied ale with a refreshing fruity flavour and an inkling of cedar and honey.

Lancashire Loom (ABV 4%)
A light golden ale bursting with a real fruit punch of grapefruit, lychees and lemon with a slight floral note.

MASH SIBA ◉

Middle Barn, Burcot Farm, East Stratton, Hampshire, SO21 3DZ
☎ (01962) 795023 ⊕ mashbrewery.com

⊗ MASH began brewing in 2013 using a one-barrel plant. A new 10-barrel plant was installed in 2014. **RAIB**

Pale (OG 1035, ABV 3.8%)
A pale ale with a subtle aroma and long bitter finish.

Bitter (OG 1037, ABV 3.9%)
A copper-coloured beer with a fruity, peachy aroma and a dry bitter flavour.

Gold (OG 1039, ABV 4%)
A refreshing beer with zesty citrus flavours.

Amber (OG 1042, ABV 4.3%)

A well-balanced beer with floral aromas.

Chocolate Stout (OG 1047, ABV 5%)
A rich, black stout with roasted malt and burnt coffee flavours. Dark chocolate is added during the brew.

Masters

⊟ Unit 8, Greenham Business Park, Greenham, Somerset, TA21 0LR
☎ (01823) 674444 ⊕ mastersbrewery.co.uk

The brewery was established in 2006 but had to close in 2009. In 2011 it was reopened using a 2.5-barrel plant. Brewing is currently suspended. **!!**

Matlock Wolds Farm (NEW)

South Barn, Cavendish Road, Farm Lane, Matlock, Derbyshire, DE4 3GZ ☎ 07852 263263
⊕ woldsfarm.co.uk

Brewing began in 2014 on a 50-litre kit. Production is mostly bottle-conditioned and available locally. Cask-conditioned beers are available by arrangement. There are plans for expansion to a 250-litre kit. **RAIB**

Mauldons SIBA ◉

Black Adder Brewery, 13 Church Field Road, Sudbury, Suffolk, CO10 2YA
☎ (01787) 311055 ⊕ mauldons.co.uk

The Mauldon family started brewing in Sudbury in 1795. The brewery with 26 pubs was bought by Greene King in the 1960s. The current business, established in 1982, was bought by Steve and Alison Sims in 2000. They relocated to a new brewery in 2005, with a 30-barrel plant that has doubled production. One pub is owned and around 150 outlets are supplied. **!! ↝ ♦**

Micawber's Mild (OG 1035, ABV 3.5%) ↝
Light, easy-drinking mild. Malty smoothness with a rich roast flavour turns into a caramel liquorice aftertaste.

Moletrap Bitter (OG 1038, ABV 3.8%) ↝
Pleasant fulfilling ale, with a dark fruity aroma, sticky toffee mouthfeel and a sweetness that gives depth to the flavour.

Silver Adder (OG 1042, ABV 4.2%) ↝
Light fruity aroma, dry hoppiness and citrus fruit with rich honey in the taste, and a long, fruity, sweet aftertaste. Refreshing and well-balanced.

Suffolk Pride (OG 1048, ABV 4.8%) ↝
A full-bodied, copper-coloured beer with a good balance of malt, hops and fruit in the taste.

Suffolk Punch (OG 1048, ABV 4.8%)

Black Adder (OG 1053, ABV 5.3%) ↝
Malty, roasty aroma leads to a well-balanced full-bodied beer, malty with roast and dark soft fruit overtones.

Maule (NEW)

42 Rothersthorpe Avenue, Northampton, NN4 8JH
⊕ maulebrewing.com

Brewing began in 2014 on a self-built plant. Production is mainly unfiltered keg and bottle-conditioned beers, but cask-conditioned ales are occasionally produced for festivals. Most output is supplied to London outlets. RAIB

Refreshing blonde ale with citrus flavours on the nose and aftertaste.

Maxim

1 Gadwall Road, Rainton Bridge South, Houghton-le-Spring, DH4 5NL
☎ (0191) 584 8844 maximbrewery.co.uk

Rising from the ashes of Sunderland brewer Vaux, Maxim was set up with a 20-barrel plant in Houghton-le-Spring in 2007. More than 100 outlets are supplied direct and four pubs are owned. ‼ ♦

Lambtons (OG 1039, ABV 3.8%)
Smooth golden ale, with citrus and hoppy flavours.

Samson (OG 1040, ABV 4%)
Traditional best bitter, chestnut brown in colour, with a caramel taste and a balance of bitterness.

Ward's Best Bitter (OG 1040, ABV 4%)
Brewed to a traditional process, a tawny copper-coloured best bitter with a sweet, toasted biscuit flavour. Slightly hoppy and fruity.

Swedish Blonde (OG 1042, ABV 4.2%)
This smooth beer is light in colour and has refreshing hoppy and complex grapefruit flavours on the palate.

Double Maxim (OG 1048, ABV 4.7%)
A brown ale with a fruity, caramel, malty, nutty taste and a hint of sweetness. Smooth and well-balanced.

American Pride IPA (OG 1055, ABV 5.2%)
A hoppy American-style IPA.

Maximus (OG 1062, ABV 6%)
Dark ruby-coloured, full-bodied premium ale. Sweet with a liquorice flavour, caramel and dark fruits.

Maypole

North Laithes Farm, Wellow Road, Eakring, Newark, Nottinghamshire, NG22 0AN ☎ 07971 277598
maypolebrewery.co.uk

The brewery opened in 1995 in a converted 18th-century farm building. After changing hands in 2001 it was bought by the former head brewer, Rob Neil, in 2005. Seasonal beers can be ordered at any time for beer festivals: see website for details and list. ♦

Midge (OG 1035, ABV 3.5%)
A pale beer, brewed with bags of American hops; lasting bitter finish.

Little Weed (OG 1037, ABV 3.8%)
Deep golden in colour, subtle bitterness from a blend of hops.

Celebration (OG 1038, ABV 4%)
Amber-coloured traditional English ale, slightly nutty overtones.

Gate Hopper (OG 1040, ABV 4%)
Cascade hops give this golden ale a floral aroma and lingering hoppy bitterness.

Hop Fusion (OG 1040, ABV 4.2%)
A pale golden ale.

Major Oak (OG 1042, ABV 4.4%)
A well-balanced red/brown, full-bodied bitter, hints of fruit and burnt malt.

Wellow Gold (OG 1044, ABV 4.6%)

Meantime SIBA

Units 4 & 5, Lawrence Trading Estate, Blackwall Lane, London, SE10 0AR
☎ (020) 8293 1111

Head Office: Norman House, 110-114 Norman Road, London, SE10 9EH meantimebrewing.com

No real ale. Founded in 2000, Meantime brews a wide range of continental-style beer and traditional English bottled ales. Two pubs are owned. In 2010 the brewery relocated to larger premises in Greenwich. A six-barrel brewery is also owned at the Old Brewery, the Old Royal Naval College in Greenwich, and is used to brew limited-edition beers. Taken over by SABMiller in 2015. ‼

Medieval

Home Farm, New Road, Colston Bassett, Nottinghamshire, NG12 3FQ ☎ 07884 151945
medievalbeers@gmail.com

Medieval started production in 2012 in Nottingham and moved to its current site at Colston Bassett later that year using a 10-barrel plant. Production is currently suspended pending relocation. ♦

Chivalry (OG 1038, ABV 3.8%)
Pale session ale with a balanced combination of malt and hop.

Knight Hood (OG 1042, ABV 4.2%)
Amber-coloured ale with a deep hoppy taste.

Crusader (OG 1044, ABV 4.4%)
Pale ale that is slightly sweet with a refreshing citrus finish.

Melbourn

All Saints Brewery, All Saints Street, Stamford, Lincolnshire, PE9 2PA
☎ (01780) 752186

A famous Stamford brewery that opened in 1825 and closed in 1974. It re-opened in 1994 and is owned by Samuel Smith of Tadcaster (qv). Melbourn brews four handcrafted, organic fruit beers (Cherry, Strawberry, Apricot and Raspberry) using the antique steam-driven brewing equipment. The beers are all suitable for vegans and are organic, sold in bottles only. They are not bottle conditioned. ‼

Melwood SIBA

7 Stanley Grange, Knowsley Park, Merseyside, L34 4AR
☎ (0151) 214 3340 ☎ 07545 265283
melwoodbeer.co.uk

Melwood began brewing in 2013 using a five-barrel plant in an old dairy that used to house the Cambrinus Brewery. Seasonal beers are available as well as monthly specials in the Icons of Rock series. ♦

Lovelight (OG 1038, ABV 3.8%)
Light, hoppy blonde beer. Bold yet refreshing with a big hop aroma and crisp, biting flavour.

THE BREWERIES

Equinox (OG 1040, ABV 4%)
English pale session bitter.

Deadhead (OG 1041, ABV 4.1%)
A hazy, hoppy beer with a robust yet fruity flavour and aroma.

Citradelic (OG 1051, ABV 5.1%)
A light pale ale with grapefruit, lychee and gooseberry aromas.

Mercian

50 Berwick Road, Buxton, Derbyshire, SK17 9PE
☎ (01298) 71551 ✉ info@mercianbreweryltd.co.uk

Established in 2013, Mercian is a small scale brewery producing creative, modern ales. Originally based in Llanbydder, it relocated to Buxton in 2015. The range of beers is in development.

Merlin SIBA

3 Spring Bank Farm, Congleton Road, Arclid, Cheshire, CW11 2UD
☎ (01477) 500893 ☎ 07812 352590
merlinbrewing.co.uk

Established in 2010 using an eight-barrel plant in a farm unit just outside Sandbach, Merlin is a family-run concern. The beers are principally supplied to outlets within a 30-mile radius. The plant has capacity for expansion, and helps its environment by disposing of spent grain and water on the farm. !! RAIB

King's Ale (OG 1036, ABV 3.6%)
A light brown, easy-drinking bitter, with a slightly floral and spicy aroma.

Merlin's Gold (OG 1038, ABV 3.8%)
Light golden ale with rounded floral citrus flavours.

Excalibur (OG 1039, ABV 3.9%)
A light-coloured session ale. Bitter, hoppy flavours are accompanied by a faint sweetness.

Morgana (OG 1040, ABV 4%)
A smooth mid-brown bitter.

Spellbound (OG 1040, ABV 4%)
A full-flavoured bitter, light chestnut in colour with a dry finish.

Wizard (OG 1042, ABV 4.2%)
A hoppy, bitter, golden-coloured ale with generous hints of grapefruit flavour.

Dragonslayer (OG 1056, ABV 5.6%)
A dark brew with complex flavours. Easy-drinking, belying its strength.

Merrimen SIBA

Unit 12, Litchborough Industrial Estate, Northampton Road, Litchborough, Northamptonshire, NN12 8JB
☎ (01327) 831308 ☎ 07414 007999
merrimen.co.uk

Merrimen commenced brewing on an eight-barrel plant in Litchborough in 2013. All beers are named on a 'Merri' theme. During 2014 the brewery underwent refurbishment, and a young apprentice brewer, Oliver, joined the team. Outlets include pubs and off-licences in Northampton, Coventry and surrounding areas. Merrimen now has a mobile bar available for hire, including six hand pumps, and racking and cellar cooling for 12 casks. RAIB

Merri Gold (OG 1034, ABV 3.5%)
A pale golden ale with grapefruit and gentle malt aroma, with a light spice and citrus taste.

Merri One (OG 1033, ABV 3.6%)
A light amber ale with medium bitterness, combining three spicy hops.

Hail Merri (ABV 3.8%)
Deep amber in colour with a fruity, floral and malty aroma, a biscuity, bitter taste and a dry finish.

Merri Weather (OG 1038, ABV 4%)
Rich golden-coloured beer with a refreshing flavour.

Be Merri (OG 1042, ABV 4.5%)
Premium amber-coloured bitter with roasted chocolate malt and a smooth rounded taste.

Merry Miner

Unit 20-21, Grendon House Farm, Grendon, Warwickshire, CV9 3DT ☎ 07811 932721
merryminerbrewery.com

Merry Miner commenced brewing in 2010. The brewery is based in farm buildings on the outskirts of the village of Grendon, near Atherstone. The brewery and beers are named after the brewer's former occupation. Also brews under the name of Morgans. !! ♦

Miner's Best Bitter (OG 1035, ABV 3.7%)
A pale, smooth traditional best bitter with a crisp bitter aftertaste.

Warwickshire's Finest (OG 1036, ABV 3.8%)
Light amber-coloured session bitter.

Self Rescuer (OG 1039, ABV 3.9%)
Deep golden in colour with a pleasing bitterness and a smooth malty aftertaste.

Davy's Lamp (OG 1038, ABV 4%)
A pale, full-flavoured bitter.

Bevin Boys (OG 1039, ABV 4.1%)
An American-style IPA full of character and aromas with a pleasant finish.

Cap Lamp (OG 1039, ABV 4.2%)
Mid-gold in colour with a refreshing crisp bitterness.

Deputy Drop (OG 1040, ABV 4.3%)

Going Underground (OG 1041, ABV 4.4%)
A refreshing amber beer.

Pit Pony (OG 1041, ABV 4.5%)
Deep golden smooth bitter.

Methane (OG 1045, ABV 5%)
A light golden bitter with a citrus bitter finish.

Brewed under the Morgans brand name:

Chedhams Ale (OG 1036, ABV 3.8%)
Dark golden. Tangy with a bitter/fruit taste and a tart, hoppy aftertaste. Finishes dry.

Mersea Island

Rewsalls Lane, East Mersea, Essex, CO5 8SX ☎ 07970 070399 merseabrewery.co.uk

⊗ The brewery was established at Mersea Island Vineyard in 2005, producing cask and bottle-conditioned beers. The brewery supplies several local pubs on a guest beer basis as well as most local beer festivals. The brewery holds its own festival of Essex-produced ales over the four-day Easter weekend. ☕RAIB

Mersea Mud (OG 1036, ABV 3.8%)
An easy-drinking mild ale with a refreshingly malty flavour.

Yo Boy! (OG 1038, ABV 3.8%)
A session bitter with a long-lasting bitterness on the finish.

Lion Bitter (OG 1038, ABV 3.9%)
A pale amber bitter with nutty and caramel flavours and a smooth finish.

Gold (OG 1043, ABV 4.4%)
A refreshing golden ale.

Skippers (OG 1047, ABV 4.8%)
A best bitter, dark amber in colour with a good malty flavour and a smooth bitterness.

Oyster Stout (OG 1048, ABV 5%)
A traditional oyster stout with local Mersea Island oysters added, giving a distinct flavour.

Middle Earth

Rowditch Inn, 246 Uttoxeter Road, Derby, DE22 3LL
☎ 07504 304564

Office: 53 Springfield Road, Etwall, Derbyshire, DE65 6JZ ⊕ mebrewco.com

Set up in 2011, Middle Earth uses the 3.75-barrel plant based at the Rowditch Inn in Derby (also used by the Rowditch Brewery, qv). Steve Twells (the Rowditch brewer) established Middle Earth as a separate venture to utilise spare plant capacity to produce different brews for free trade sale. Following the successful start of its first micropub, the brewery will concentrate on house ales and one stout, with all other products to be brewed periodically.

Prancing Pony (OG 1039, ABV 3.9%)
Golden session bitter. Extremely bitter with large amounts of hops giving a sharp grapefruit flavour and a pepper aroma.

Rivendale (OG 1044, ABV 4.3%)
A well-balanced golden bitter.

Honey Dragon (OG 1044, ABV 4.5%)
A well-balanced golden bitter with subtle honey notes.

Black Rose (OG 1048, ABV 4.6%)
Complex malt flavours, chocolate predominates, combined with subtle ginger.

Mighty Oak

14b West Station Yard, Spital Road, Maldon, Essex, CM9 6TW
☎ (01621) 843713 ⊕ mightyoakbrewing.co.uk

⊠ Mighty Oak was formed in 1996 and has expanded considerably following a move to Maldon in 2001. Current capacity is 8,000 barrels a year following the acquisition of an adjacent building and enlarged plant. 350 outlets are supplied. Twelve monthly ales are brewed based on a theme, which for 2016 is motorcycles. ‼☕♦

IPA (OG 1031.5, ABV 3.5%) ◣
Light-bodied, pale session bitter. Hop notes are initially suppressed by a delicate sweetness but the aftertaste is more assertive.

Oscar Wilde (OG 1039.5, ABV 3.7%) ◣
Roasty dark mild with suggestions of forest fruits and dark chocolate. A sweet taste yields to a more bitter finish.

Captain Bob (OG 1039.5, ABV 3.8%) ⏢
A traditional deep amber bitter with a fruity and hoppy aroma. There is a slight sweet maltiness that balances an easy-going bitterness, followed by hints of gooseberry, elderflower and grape in the finish.

Maldon Gold (OG 1039.5, ABV 3.8%) ◣
Pale golden ale with a sharp citrus note moderated by honey and biscuity malt.

Kings (OG 1042.6, ABV 4.2%)
A deep golden beer bursting with hoppy fruitiness. The orange, nectarine and passion fruit flavours last long into the finish.

English Oak (OG 1047.9, ABV 4.8%) ◣
Strong, tawny-coloured, fruity bitter with caramel, butterscotch and vanilla. A gentle hop character is present throughout.

Saxon Strong (OG 1062, ABV 6.5%)
An amber ale with malt flavours balanced by a strong hop finish. The flavour is caramel and dark berry with hints of wood and toffee.

Mile Tree SIBA

Mile Tree Lane, Wisbech, Cambridgeshire, PE13 4TR
☎ 07858 930363 ⊕ miletreebrewery.co.uk

Mile Tree began brewing in 2012 using a five-barrel plant. Local outlets and beer festivals are supplied. ♦RAIB

Milestone SIBA ◉

Great North Road, Cromwell, Newark, Nottinghamshire, NG23 6JE
☎ (01636) 822255 ⊕ milestonebrewery.co.uk

☺Established in 2005, Milestone currently brew on a 12-barrel plant. More than 150 outlets are supplied. ‼☕♦RAIB

Lion's Pride (OG 1038, ABV 3.8%)
Copper-coloured session ale.

Sherwood Pale Ale (OG 1039, ABV 3.9%)

Shine On (OG 1039, ABV 4%)
Straw-coloured session ale with floral and citrus notes.

Loxley Ale (OG 1042, ABV 4.2%)
Golden brew with a subtle hint of honey.

Black Pearl (OG 1043, ABV 4.3%)
A traditional Irish-style stout.

Crusader (OG 1044, ABV 4.4%)

Rich Ruby (OG 1044, ABV 4.5%)
Rich, smooth, creamy Celtic red ale.

American Pale Ale (OG 1046, ABV 4.6%)
A blond, hoppy citrus ale.

Olde English (OG 1049, ABV 4.9%)
Full-bodied winter warmer with a pleasing nutty finish.

Anniversary Ale (OG 1050, ABV 5%)
Amber-coloured ale.

Magna Carta Ale (OG 1050, ABV 5%)
Light golden ale.

Game Keeper (OG 1052, ABV 5.2%)

Raspberry Wheat Beer (OG 1055, ABV 5.6%)
Continental-style ale infused with fresh fruit.

Milk Street SIBA 👁

🏠 Griffin, 25 Milk Street, Frome, Somerset, BA11 3DB
☎ (01373) 467766 ⊕ milkstreetbrewery.co.uk

⊗ Milk Street was established in 1999 in a former 'private' cinema situated behind the Griffin pub. The cinema is long gone and now houses the brewery, which expanded in 2005 and is capable of producing 30 barrels a week. It mainly produces for its own estate of three outlets with direct delivery to pubs in a 30-mile radius. Wholesalers are used to distribute the beers further afield. ‼◆

Funky Monkey (OG 1040, ABV 4%)
Copper-coloured summer ale with fruity flavours and aromas. A dry finish with developing bitterness and an undertone of citrus fruit.

The Usual (OG 1045, ABV 4.4%)

Zig-Zag Stout (OG 1046, ABV 4.5%)
A dark ruby stout with characteristic roastiness and dryness with bitter chocolate and citrus fruit in the background.

Beer (OG 1049, ABV 5%)
A blonde beer with musky hoppiness and citrus fruit on the nose, while more fruit surges through on the palate before the bittersweet finish.

Mill Green SIBA

🏠 White Horse, Edwardstone, Suffolk, CO10 5PX
☎ (01787) 211118 ⊕ millgreenbrewery.co.uk

⊗ Mill Green started brewing in 2008 in a new complex behind the White Horse pub in Edwardstone. It has won awards for environmental innovation. The brewing liquor is heated by solar panels and a wood-fired boiler while a wind turbine supplements power on site. A 10-barrel fermentation run is used to produce a number of seasonal and one-off brews in addition to the regular range. ◆

Mawkin Mild (OG 1028, ABV 2.9%) 🍺
A complex mild, with a strong aroma and flavour for such a low gravity beer. Bitter coffee notes in the taste and aftertaste.

White Horse Bitter (OG 1036, ABV 3.6%)
A traditional session bitter with a spicy, bitter, lasting finish.

Golden Fleece (ABV 4%)
Single-hop pale ale.

Boxford Best (ABV 4.3%)

Millis SIBA 👁

St Margaret's Farm, St Margaret's Road, South Darenth, Kent, DA4 9LB
☎ (01322) 866233 ⊕ millisbrewing.com

☺ John and Miriam Millis started with a 0.5-barrel plant at their home in Gravesend. Demand outstripped the facility and Millis moved in 2003 to its current location – a former farm cold store – using a 10-barrel plant. They now supply around 40 outlets within a 50-mile radius. ◆ RAIB

Gravesend Guzzler (OG 1037, ABV 3.7%)
Pale, easy-drinking, fruity session beer.

Guinea Guzzler (OG 1037, ABV 3.7%)
Pale, easy-drinking, fruity session beer.

Golden Wobbler (OG 1041, ABV 4.1%)
A pale gold beer with a hoppy citrus aroma and grapefruit and light spice flavours.

Dartford Wobbler (OG 1043, ABV 4.3%)
A tawny-coloured, full-bodied best bitter with complex malt and hop flavours and a long, clean, slightly roasted finish.

Millstone SIBA 👁

Unit 4, Vale Mill, Micklehurst Road, Mossley, OL5 9JL
☎ (01457) 835835 ⊕ millstonebrewery.co.uk

Established in 2003 by Nick Boughton and Jon Hunt, the brewery is located in an 18th-century textile mill. The eight-barrel plant produces a range of pale, hoppy beers and a traditional stout. More than 40 regular outlets are supplied. ◆

Vale Mill (OG 1039, ABV 3.9%)
A pale gold session bitter with a floral and spicy aroma building upon a crisp and refreshing taste.

Three Shires Bitter (OG 1040, ABV 4%) 🍺
Yellow beer with hop and fruit aroma. Fresh citrus fruit, hops and bitterness in the taste and aftertaste.

Tiger Rut (OG 1040, ABV 4%)
A pale, hoppy ale with a distinctive citrus/grapefruit aroma.

Stout (OG 1045, ABV 4.5%)
A traditional dry stout; pale chocolate malt, roasted barley, and a hint of sweetness to the aroma.

True Grit (OG 1050, ABV 5%)
A well-hopped strong ale with a mellow bitterness and a citrus/grapefruit aroma.

Brewed for the Rising Sun, Mossley:

Rising Sunsation (OG 1047, ABV 4.7%)
A pale, dry bitter with hints of pine.

Milltown SIBA

The Brewery, The Old Railway Goods Yard, Scar Lane, Milnsbridge, West Yorkshire, HD3 4PE ☎ 07946 589645 ⊕ milltownbrewing.co.uk

☺ Milltown began brewing in 2011 using a four-barrel plant. ‼◆

Golden Hop (OG 1037, ABV 3.8%)

Slubbers Gold (OG 1040, ABV 4.2%)

Milton SIBA

Pegasus House, Pembroke, Waterbeach, Cambridgeshire, CB25 9PY
☎ (01223) 862067 ⊕ miltonbrewery.co.uk

⊗ The brewery has grown steadily since it was founded in 1999 and now operates pubs in Cambridge, London, Peterborough and Norwich through a sister company. In 2012 the brewery moved to larger premises in the village of Waterbeach. ‼

Minotaur (OG 1035, ABV 3.3%) 🍺
A dark ruby mild with liquorice and raisin fruit throughout. Light, dry finish.

Dionysus (OG 1037, ABV 3.6%) 🍺

Yellow bitter with good balance of biscuity malt and citrus hop. Some malt and hops linger on the long, dry aftertaste.

Tiki (OG 1038, ABV 3.8%) ◆
Straw-coloured golden ale with passion fruit, grapefruit and lemon hop character. Dry, slightly astringent aftertaste.

Justinian (OG 1039, ABV 3.9%) ◆
Straw-coloured bitter with pink grapefruit hop character and light malt softness. Dry finish.

Pegasus (OG 1043, ABV 4.1%) ◆
Malty amber-coloured, medium-bodied bitter with faint hops. Bittersweet aftertaste.

Sparta (OG 1043, ABV 4.3%) ◆
A yellow/gold best bitter with floral hops, kiwi fruit and balancing malt softness which fades to leave a long, dry finish.

Nero (OG 1050, ABV 5%) 🗓 ◆
A complex black beer comprising a blend of milk chocolate, raisins and liquorice. Roast malt and fruit complete the experience.

Cyclops (OG 1055, ABV 5.3%)
Deep copper-coloured ale, with a rich hoppy aroma and full body; fruit and malt notes develop in the finish.

Marcus Aurelius (OG 1075, ABV 7.4%) ◆
A powerful black brew brimming with raisins and liquorice. Big balanced finish.

Mitchell Krause

See Tractor Shed

Mithril

Mithril, Aldbrough St John, North Yorkshire, DL11 7TL
☎ (01325) 374817 ☎ 07889 167128
⊕ mithrilales.co.uk

⊙Mithril started brewing in 2010 in old stables opposite the brewer's house on a 2.5-barrel plant. Owner/brewer Pete Fenwick, a well-known craft brewer, brews twice a week to supply the local area of Darlington and Richmond. A new beer is brewed every week. ◆

Dere Street (OG 1039, ABV 3.8%)
Amber-coloured bitter with a fruity, malty sweetness and a smooth, hoppy finish.

White Swan Bitter (ABV 3.8%)
A light brown-coloured beer, malt to start with a hoppy finish.

A66 (OG 1041, ABV 4%)
A crisp, refreshing, satisfying golden beer. A dry bitterness, with a lingering citrus and spicy hop taste and aroma.

Flower Power (OG 1043, ABV 4.3%)
This pale ale packs massive citrus, fruity hop flavour. Hints of grapefruit and floral notes on the tongue from the late addition of elderflower.

Mix

3 Cemmaes Court Road, Hemel Hempstead, Hertfordshire, HP1 1ST ⊕ mixbrewery.co.uk

A small brewery established in 2013 and based in a domestic garage. Beer is produced in small batches allowing for an ever-changing range.

Mobberley SIBA

Dairy Farm, Church Lane, Mobberley, Cheshire, WA16 7RA
☎ (01565) 873601 ☎ 07879 771209
⊕ mobberleyfineales.co.uk

⊠ Mobberley began brewing in 2011 in an old milking parlour on a working farm in the heart of the Cheshire countryside. ◆

CropCutter (OG 1026, ABV 2.6%)
A fruity, golden ale with a lingering aftertaste. A low ABV, the careful selection of malts and high alpha hops ensures a deep fruity yet citrus taste to savour. Rich and bright gold in colour, with a citrus aroma, deep fruity flavour and long, lingering aftertaste.

HedgeHopper (OG 1039, ABV 3.8%)
A golden, refreshing ale, light and aromatic.

RoadRunner (OG 1039, ABV 3.8%)
A light-coloured pale ale with a delicate, lightly spicy finish. Rich in flavours, sweet to the taste and smooth. Good head retention and sweet, delicate, refreshing hop aroma from a combination of English hops.

WhirlyBird (OG 1040, ABV 4%)
Pale ale, sweet yet full-bodied, light yet complex with a smooth, subtle, zesty finish.

BarnBuster (OG 1042, ABV 4.2%)
A rich, amber-coloured ale, full-bodied yet smooth. A hint of spiciness and a malty, mildly bitter, yet slightly spicy/citrus finish.

Moles SIBA 👁

5 Merlin Way, Bowerhill, Melksham, Wiltshire, SN12 6TJ
☎ (01225) 708842 ⊕ molesbrewery.com

Moles was established in 1982 by Roger Catte, a former Ushers brewer, using his nickname for the brewery. 10 pubs are owned, all serving cask beer. More than 200 outlets are supplied direct. ‼ ☛ ◆

Tap Bitter (OG 1035, ABV 3.5%)
A session bitter with a smooth, malty flavour and clean bitter finish.

Gold (OG 1038, ABV 3.8%)
Golden, refreshingly hoppy beer with a citrus zest flavour and tropical fruit aroma.

Best Bitter (OG 1040, ABV 4%)
A well-balanced, amber-coloured bitter; clean, dry and malty with some bitterness, and delicate floral hop flavour.

Elmo's Fire (OG 1044, ABV 4.4%)
Medium-bodied pale ale. Refreshingly bitter with a fruity, spicy aroma and long bitter finish.

Landlords Choice (OG 1045, ABV 4.5%)
A dark, strong, smooth porter, with a rich fruity palate and malty finish.

Rucking Mole (OG 1045, ABV 4.5%)
A chestnut-coloured premium ale, fruity and malty with a smooth bitter finish.

Mole Catcher (OG 1050, ABV 5%)
A copper-coloured ale with a spicy hop aroma and taste, and a long bitter finish.

Molson Coors SIBA

Molson Coors (Burton): 137 High Street, Burton upon Trent, Staffordshire, DE14 1JZ
☎ (01283) 511000

Molson Coors (Alton): Manor Park Brewery, Alton, Hampshire, GU34 2PS

Molson Coors (Tadcaster): Tower Brewery, Wetherby Road, Tadcaster, North Yorkshire, LS24 9SD
molsoncoorsbrewers.com

Molson Coors is the result of a merger between Molson of Canada and Coors of Colorado, US. Coors established itself in Europe in 2002 by buying part of the former Bass brewing empire, when Interbrew (now AB InBev) was instructed by the British government to divest itself of some of its interests in Bass. Coors owns several cask ale brands. It brews 110,000 barrels of cask beer a year (under licensing arrangements with other brewers) and also provides a further 50,000 barrels of cask beer from other breweries. In 2011 Molson Coors bought Sharp's brewery in Cornwall (qv) in a bid to increase its stake in the cask beer sector. No cask ale is produced in Burton. Home of the multi-award-winning Worthington White Shield bottle-conditioned IPA.

Moncada SIBA

Unit 1, Buspace Studios, Conlan Street, London, W10 5AT
☎ (020) 8964 0829 moncadabrewery.co.uk

Moncada began brewing in 2011 using a six-barrel plant. ♦RAIB

Notting Hill Bitter (ABV 3.7%)
Brown bitter with a good balance of hops and sweetness and a pleasant finish.

Notting Hill Blonde (ABV 4.2%)
Continental style golden beer with a smooth mouthfeel, sweetish with a touch of honey and fruity hops. Short, crisp finish.

Notting Hill Amber (ABV 4.7%)
Full-bodied, creamy, amber-coloured beer with a citrus aroma and flavour, well-balanced by the sweet biscuit character.

Notting Hill Porter (ABV 5%)
Rich black porter with dark roast bitterness and black treacle, which linger in the finish. Some faint hoppy notes .

Notting Hill Stout (ABV 5%)
A dry malty beer with roast, caramel and a little malty sweetness. The pleasant aftertaste is long and lingering.

Notting Hill Ruby Rye (ABV 5.2%)
Sweetish ruby red beer with a full fruity aroma, a creamy mouthfeel and a little roast throughout.

Mondo (NEW)

86-92 Stewarts Road, London, SW8 4UG
☎ (020) 7720 0782 ☎ 07453 312170
mondobrewingcompany.com

The brewery opened in 2015 using a 10-hectolitre brew kit. A taphouse has recently been added. !!

Rider Pale Ale (OG 1046, ABV 4.8%)

James Brown Ale (OG 1050, ABV 5%)

Kemosabe IPA (OG 1060, ABV 6.4%)

Monkey Chews (NEW)

Montague Arms, 289 Queens Road, Peckham, London, SE15 2PA
☎ (020) 7635 9880 montaguearms@gmail.com

Monkey Chews is the name of the brewing operation at the Monatgue Arms in Peckham. The beers became available in 2015 at the Montague Arms and its sister pub, the Brown Derby, Kennington. It is named after the owner's previous bar in Chalk Farm, which was demolished.

Chronic Hip Hop (ABV 3.8%)

Darktown (ABV 4.2%)

Gator Blood (ABV 4.6%)

Monty's SIBA

Unit 1, Castle Works, Hendomen, Montgomery, SY15 6HA
☎ (01686) 668933 montysbrewery.co.uk

Monty's began brewing in 2009 and was the first brewery in Montgomeryshire since the Eagle brewery in Newtown closed in 1990. Three pubs are leased by the brewery's sister company, Hophouse Inns: Sportsman in Newtown, Powis Arms in Lydbury North and the Cottage Inn in Montgomery. The Cottage also acts as Monty's visitor centre. ♦RAIB

Old Jailhouse (OG 1039.5, ABV 3.9%)
Copper-coloured bitter with a good blend of malt and hops.

Midnight (OG 1040, ABV 4%)
A dark, smooth, creamy stout.

Moonrise (OG 1040, ABV 4%)
A copper-coloured, gently malty, well-balanced traditional brew.

MPA (OG 1040.5, ABV 4%)
Pale ale with a good bitter character.

Sunshine (OG 1041, ABV 4.2%)
A golden, hoppy, floral/citrus ale with a pleasantly dry finish.

Masquerade (OG 1046, ABV 4.6%)
A gluten-free premium golden bitter with tropical fruit flavour and Citra hop aroma.

Mischief (OG 1050, ABV 5%)
Strong golden ale with a good balance of malt and hop bitterness.

Magnitude (OG 1075.5, ABV 7.5%)
A premium strong golden ale. Smooth with a hint of sweetness in the finish.

Moonshine

Hill Farm, Shelford Road, Fulbourn, Cambridgeshire, CB21 5EQ ☎ 07906 066794

Office: 28 Radegund Road, Cambridge, CB1 3RS
moonshinebrewery.co.uk

Established in 2004, the brewery produces up to 20 barrels a week. Locally produced ingredients are used including water from the brewery's own well and barley grown on the farm where the brewery is based. CAMRA beer festivals are supplied throughout the country, with 30 local outlets supplied direct. ♦RAIB

Trumpington Tipple (OG 1038, ABV 3.6%)

Cambridge Pale Ale (OG 1038, ABV 3.8%)
Golden beer, light to the palate with a dry, citrus finish.

Shelford Crier (OG 1038, ABV 3.8%)

Harvest Moon Mild (OG 1040, ABV 3.9%)

Barton Bitter (OG 1040, ABV 4%) ◆
Pale brown with red and amber highlights, balanced malt and hops and a fruity backdrop on both nose and palate. A bittersweet flavour dries as fruit and sweetness diminish.

Reach For The Moon (OG 1040, ABV 4.1%)
Deep ruby-coloured bitter with a hoppy aroma and aftertaste.

Cambridge Best Bitter (OG 1041, ABV 4.2%)

Red Watch Blueberry Ale (OG 1040, ABV 4.2%)

Reel Ale (OG 1041, ABV 4.2%)

Budding Moon (OG 1043, ABV 4.5%)

Nightwatch Porter (OG 1043, ABV 4.5%) ⬚

Black Hole Stout (OG 1048, ABV 5%)

Hot Numbers Coffee Stout (OG 1057, ABV 5.5%)
Dark roasted malt with balanced coffee and hops. The addition of lactose adds sweetness to the flavour.

Chocolate Orange Stout (OG 1068, ABV 6.7%) ⬚

Ison (OG 1074, ABV 8%)

Wheat Wine Ale (OG 1091, ABV 10.5%)
A barley wine produced using wheat instead of barley.

Moonstone

▤ Ministry of Ale, 9 Trafalgar Street, Burnley, Lancashire, BB11 1TQ
☎ (01282) 830909 ⊕ moonstonebrewery.co.uk

☺A small, three-barrel brewery, based in the front room of the Ministry of Ale pub. Brewing started in 2001 and beer is only available in the pub. ‼

Black Star Dark (OG 1037, ABV 3.4%)

Pale Ale (OG 1036, ABV 3.6%)

Moor SIBA

Days Road, Bristol, BS2 0QS ☎ 0117 ☎ (941 4460)
⊕ moorbeer.co.uk

⊗ Moor Beer was founded in 1996, originally brewing in Ashcott. Since being relaunched in 2007 in Long Sutton the brewery has gone through a steady expansion programme, resulting in the relocation to larger premises in central Bristol featuring a shop and brewery tap. All beers are produced without isinglass finings and are naturally hazy. ‼ ☲ ◆RAIB

Revival (OG 1038, ABV 3.8%)
An immensely hoppy and refreshing pale ale.

Nor Hop (OG 1041, ABV 4.3%)

Raw (OG 1043, ABV 4.3%) ◆
Pale brown best bitter with a powerful aroma. Bitter orange fruit with a hint of tropical lychee on the tongue. Sweetish background and a bitter finish.

So'Hop (OG 1041, ABV 4.3%)

Amoor (OG 1045, ABV 4.5%)

Dark Alliance (OG 1045, ABV 4.5%)
A hoppy coffee stout.

Illusion (OG 1045, ABV 4.5%)
Session strength version of a black IPA, powerfully hopped.

Confidence (OG 1046, ABV 4.6%)
A hoppy American-style red ale.

Ported Amoor (OG 1047, ABV 4.7%)
Amoor with added reserve port.

Radiance (OG 1048, ABV 5%)

Smokey Horyzon (OG 1050, ABV 5%) ◆
A speciality beer made using smoked rye. Hoppy, pale brown strong ale with plenty of body, balanced by the sweetness of unfermented, rich, dry rye malt, and very smoky.

Hoppiness (OG 1065, ABV 6.5%)

Moorhouse's SIBA ◉

The Brewery, Moorhouse Street, Burnley, Lancashire, BB11 5EN
☎ (01282) 422864 ⊕ moorhouses.co.uk

Established in 1865 as a soft drinks manufacturer, the brewery started producing cask-conditioned ale in 1978. A new brewhouse and visitor centre opened in 2012. The company owns three pubs. ‼◆

Black Cat (OG 1036, ABV 3.4%) ◆
A dark mild-style beer with delicate chocolate and coffee roast flavours and a crisp, bitter finish.

Premier Bitter (OG 1036, ABV 3.7%) ◆
A clean and satisfying bitter aftertaste rounds off this well-balanced hoppy, amber session bitter.

Pride of Pendle (OG 1040, ABV 4.1%) ◆
Well-balanced amber best bitter with a fresh initial hoppiness and a mellow, malt-driven body.

Blond Witch (OG 1045, ABV 4.5%) ◆
A light ale, fruity with lasting finish.

Pendle Witches Brew (OG 1050, ABV 5.1%) ◆
Well-balanced, full-bodied, malty beer with a long, complex finish.

Moorside (NEW)

34 Dove Way, Kirkby Mills Industrial Estate, Kirkbymoorside, North Yorkshire, YO62 6QR
☎ (01751) 433335 ☎ 07745 311626
⊕ moorsidebrewery.com

Retired from Joseph Holt Ltd, where he was head brewer, Keith Sheard founded Moorside in 2014. The brewery has separate 10-barrel and one-barrel plants with the latter used for brewing experience days and experimental brews. Water is drawn from an artesian well. There is also a brewery bar. ‼

MòR SIBA

Old Mill, Kellas, DD5 3PD ☎ 07884 346351
⊕ morbrewing.co.uk

Retired lifeboat coxswain Jim Hughan teamed up with family friend Ross Niven to establish the 2.5-barrel brewery in 2012. Just over a year later it expanded to a 4.3-barrel plant with six fermenters. ‼◆RAIB

MòR-Calm and Wise! (OG 1034, ABV 3.4%)

A yellow-coloured ale bursting with zingy hops. A pepper and lemon flavour with a smooth aftertaste.

MòR Tea Vicar? (OG 1038, ABV 3.8%)
A pale amber bitter with a pleasant balance of malt and hops. With a malty, fruity aroma and a pronounced bitter finish, this is a well-balanced, refreshing session ale.

MòR-Bidly Dark! (OG 1039, ABV 3.9%)
A dark chocolate, malty mild, lightly-hopped with an aromatic, coffee/vanilla aftertaste.

MòR-Scode! (OG 1040, ABV 4%)
A light citrus session ale with overtones of grapefruit and a smooth finish.

MòR-Ish! (OG 1042, ABV 4.2%)
A bright amber ale with a malty, fruity aroma and a well-balanced and controlled bitter finish.

MòR Please! (OG 1045, ABV 4.5%)
A clean-tasting, full-bodied golden session bitter, bursting with malt and hops. There's just a hint of honey with a good hoppy finish.

MòR-Ticia! (OG 1045, ABV 4.5%)
A full-bodied stout with a hint of Vimto and a dark chocolate aftertaste.

Mordue SIBA

Units D1 & D2, Narvic Way, Tyne Tunnel Estate, North Shields, Tyne & Wear, NE29 7XJ
☎ (0191) 296 1879 mordue brewery.com

In 1995 the Fawson brothers revived the Mordue Brewery name (the original closed in 1879). High demand required moves to larger premises and replacing the original five-barrel plant with a 20-barrel one. The beers are distributed nationally and 300 outlets are supplied direct. !! ♦ RAIB

Five Bridges (OG 1038, ABV 3.6%)
Crisp, golden beer with a good hint of hops, the bitterness carries on in the finish. A good session bitter.

Northumbrian Blonde (OG 1040, ABV 4%)
A blonde beer with a citrus aroma and hoppy finish.

Workie Ticket (OG 1045, ABV 4.5%)
Complex tasty bitter with plenty of malt and hops, and a long, satisfying bitter finish.

Radgie Gadgie (OG 1048, ABV 4.8%)
Strong, easy-drinking bitter with plenty of fruit and hops.

IPA (OG 1051, ABV 5.1%)
Easy-drinking golden ale with plenty of hops, the bitterness carries on in the finish.

Morland

See Greene King

Morton

Unit 10, Essington Light Industrial Estate, Essington, Staffordshire, WV11 2BH ☎ 07988 69647

Office: 96 Brewood Road, Coven, WV9 5EF
mortonbrewery.co.uk

Morton was established in 2007 on a three-barrel plant. 20 outlets are supplied direct plus various beer festivals, and a selection is always available at the brewery's own micropub, Hail to the Ale.
!! ♦ RAIB

Essington Dark Mild (OG 1036, ABV 3.6%)

Essington Bitter (OG 1037, ABV 3.8%)
A fruity, hoppy session ale.

Merry Mount (OG 1037, ABV 3.8%)
A traditional bitter.

Essington Blonde (OG 1039, ABV 4%)
A thirst-quenching pale ale made with American hops.

Essington Ale (OG 1041, ABV 4.2%)
A refreshing golden session ale.

Jelly Roll (OG 1041, ABV 4.2%)
A dry-hopped best bitter.

Essington Gold (OG 1044, ABV 4.4%)
A refreshing golden ale.

Essington Supreme (OG 1046, ABV 4.6%)
Premium brown ale, dark and sweet

Scottish Maiden (OG 1045, ABV 4.6%)
A malty premium bitter.

Essington IPA (OG 1046, ABV 4.8%)
A pale, hoppy IPA.

Moulin

2 Baledmund Road, Moulin, Pitlochry, PH16 5EL
☎ (01796) 472196

Office: Moulin Hotel, 11-13 Kirkmicheal Road, Moulin, Pitlochry, PH16 5EH moulinhotel.co.uk

The brewery opened in 1995 to celebrate the Moulin Hotel's 300th anniversary. Two pubs are owned and four outlets are supplied. !! RAIB

Light (OG 1036, ABV 3.7%)
Thirst-quenching, straw-coloured session beer, with a light, hoppy, fruity balance, ending with a gentle, hoppy sweetness.

Braveheart (OG 1039, ABV 4%)
An amber bitter, with a delicate balance of malt and fruit and a Scottish-style sweetness.

Ale of Atholl (OG 1043.5, ABV 4.5%)
A reddish, quaffable, malty ale, with a solid body and a mellow finish.

Old Remedial (OG 1050.5, ABV 5.2%)
A distinctive and satisfying dark brown old ale, with roast malt to the fore and tannin in a robust taste.

Mountain Hare

Mountain Hare Inn, Brynna Road, Brynnau Gwynion, CF35 6PG
☎ (01656) 860453 mountainhare.co.uk

Paul Jones, licensee of the Mountain Hare, finally realised his ambition of installing a brewery in his family-owned pub. A 1.5-barrel custom-built brewing plant was installed in the pub and the beer first went on sale in 2013, supplying only the pub itself. There are plans for expansion to meet demand.

Far Shores IPA (OG 1039, ABV 3.9%)
A pale brown hoppy ale.

First Gold (OG 1041, ABV 4.1%)

A golden, well-hopped bitter. The blend of three hops provides initial citrus in the mouth giving way to a satisfying bitter finish.

Mouselow Farm

3 Mouselow Farm, Dinting, Derbyshire, SK13 7QQ
☎ 07920 048252 ✉ glossopowl@btinternet.com

Mouselow Farm began brewing in 2013 using a 2.5-barrel plant housed in a converted barn. Brewing is on a part-time basis. Local free houses and beer festivals are supplied. ◆

Golden Gosling (OG 1037, ABV 3.6%)
Light, delicately-hopped bitter.

Udder the Influence (OG 1041, ABV 4%)
Medium-hopped session bitter.

Hair of the Horse (OG 1043, ABV 4.3%)
A premium copper-coloured bitter.

Mr Grundy's SIBA

▤ Georgian House Hotel, 34 Ashbourne Road, Derby, DE22 3AD
☎ (01332) 349806 ⊕ mrgrundysbrewery.co.uk

The brewery opened in 2010 using a four-barrel plant constructed from made-to-measure vessels to fit into a converted bedroom. Beers are produced for the company's own tavern (Mr Grundy's) and hotels.

Trench Foot (OG 1038, ABV 3.8%)
Darkish in colour with strong malt flavours with some bittering using traditional hops.

Passchendaele (OG 1039, ABV 3.9%)
An English, straw-coloured, pale, sharp bitter with citrus overtones.

Bullet (OG 1043, ABV 4.3%)
Dark ale with a treacle aroma and a smooth rounded taste.

Red Baron (OG 1043, ABV 4.3%)
A rich, malty, dark red-coloured bitter with strong caramel overtones, lightly hopped to allow the malt flavours to permeate.

No Man's Land (OG 1045, ABV 4.5%)
Dark in colour, yet hoppy, retaining the soft malty flavours of a traditional bitter.

Mr Majolica (NEW)

Units 7a & 15, Thurrock Enterprise Centre, Maidstone Road, Grays, Essex, RM17 6NF ☎ 07834 539761
⊕ mrmajolica.co.uk

⊠ A family-run microbrewery situated in Grays town centre, Mr Majolica began brewing in 2014 on a 2.5-barrel plant. Pubs and clubs are supplied around Essex, north Kent and east London. Bottling is planned.

Chuckaboo (OG 1036, ABV 3.8%)
Refreshing amber-coloured session beer.

Excelsior (OG 1040, ABV 4%)
An easy-drinking golden ale.

Neck Oil (OG 1040, ABV 4.1%)
A hoppy light-brown ale with English and American hops.

Enterprise (OG 1043, ABV 4.5%)
A pale ale.

Evolution (OG 1046, ABV 4.8%)

A rich, brown, strong bitter.

Muirhouse

Unit 1, Enterprise Court, Manners Avenue, Manners Industrial Estate, Ilkeston, Derbyshire, DE7 8EW
☎ 07916 590525 ⊕ muirhousebrewery.co.uk

Muirhouse was established in 2009 in a domestic garage in Long Eaton, it expanded in 2011 to an industrial unit in Ilkeston where brewing takes place up to four times a week. The brewery tap is in Ilkeston. ‼ ◆ RAIB

Not on the Buses (OG 1039, ABV 3.8%)
Pale golden session beer made with a blend of American and English hops.

Shunters Pole (OG 1040, ABV 3.8%)
A pale, refreshing, hoppy bitter.

Ruby Jewel (OG 1040, ABV 3.9%)
A ruby-coloured malty beer with tastes of toffee.

Shopping for Hops (OG 1040, ABV 3.9%)
Pale session beer with a citrus bitterness.

Buzzard Bitter (OG 1040, ABV 4%)

Fully Fitted Freight (OG 1041, ABV 4%)
A premium bitter with a fine blend of malt and hops and a distinctive finish.

Tick Tock (OG 1041, ABV 4%)

Magnum Mild (OG 1045, ABV 4.5%)
Dark, smooth, strong mild.

Pirate's Gold (OG 1045, ABV 4.5%)
Pale to golden beer with a hint of caramel.

Tractor Spotter (OG 1045, ABV 4.5%)

Lurch's Liquor (OG 1050, ABV 5%)
Sweet, smooth stout packed with dark malts.

Ilkeston Giant (OG 1052, ABV 5.1%)
Strong pale ale with a fruity bitterness from Cascade and Columbus hops.

Foundries IPA (OG 1052, ABV 5.2%)
Deceptive in strength, a blend of English and American hops.

Hat Trick IPA (OG 1052, ABV 5.2%)
Bittered with a citrus hop and finished with a hat trick of American hops.

Stumbling Around (OG 1050, ABV 5.2%)
A dark red strong malty beer.

Mulberry Duck

Elan Portway, Burghill, Herefordshire, HR4 8NF
☎ 07740 468675 ⊕ mulberryduck.co.uk

Mulberry Duck opened in 2012 in a former dairy using a 3.75-barrel plant. Three beers are brewed, supplied to the local free trade.

Golden Sparkle (ABV 3.8%)

Amber Sparkle (ABV 4.1%)

Wildfowler (ABV 4.1%)

Mumbles SIBA

Office: 23 Oakland Road, Mumbles, Swansea, SA3 4Q
☎ 07757 109938 ⊕ mumblesbrewery.co.uk

Mumbles was established in 2011 and began brewing in 2013. The beers are supplied to numerous pubs in South Wales and the Bristol area.

Since 2014 brewing has taken place using spare capacity at other local breweries while new, larger, premises are sought. Director/brewer Rob Turner has initiated collaborative projects with other breweries, including Hopcraft and Grey Trees, with more planned. ♦

Mile (OG 1039, ABV 4%)
Light in colour but big on Chinook hop flavours, which linger well for a session bitter.

RevoLver (OG 1040, ABV 4%)
A hoppy pale ale with ever-changing hops.

Gold (OG 1042, ABV 4.3%)
A light, refreshing, thirst-quenching pale ale, golden in colour. Well-hopped, the lemon and lime flavours linger well.

Gold (OG 1044, ABV 4.4%)
Classic refreshing golden beer.

Oystermouth Stout (OG 1043, ABV 4.4%)
A rich, creamy head and dark roasted malt flavours distinguish this classic stout, with the slightest hint of the sea due to the addition of real oysters.

Black Storm (OG 1045, ABV 4.5%)
A complex-tasting stout.

Lifesaver Strong Bitter (OG 1048, ABV 4.9%)
A smooth, malty, bronze-coloured ale. Deceptively easy-drinking, with a clean hop finish.

Wrecker (OG 1050, ABV 5%)
Dark strong bitter, initial chocolate taste developing into clean, refreshing maltiness.

India Pale Ale (OG 1052, ABV 5.3%)
A traditional IPA, light gold in colour. The beer is rounded and full-bodied and easy-drinking.

Musket SIBA

Unit 7, Loddington Farm, Loddington Lane, Linton, Kent, ME17 4AG ☎ 07967 127278
musketbrewery.co.uk

Musket began production in 2013 in refurbished mushroom sheds at Loddington Farm, in the heart of the Kent countryside. In the 1700s the local area was used for military training camps for what seemed like the inevitable invasion from France, hence the brewery and beer names. ♦

Trigger (OG 1032, ABV 3.6%)
A hoppy, easy-drinking session ale.

Fife & Drum (OG 1034, ABV 3.8%)
A golden ale with tastes and aromas of spice, honey, marmalade, floral and a hint of wild blackcurrant.

Flintlock (OG 1037, ABV 4.2%)
A best bitter with spicy orange undertones and just a hint of marmalade.

Muzzleloader (OG 1044, ABV 4.5%)
Smoky and dark with a faint spicy aroma of orange.

Powder Burn (OG 1039, ABV 4.5%)
A session porter with earthy and sweet aromas.

Nailsworth

Village Inn, The Cross, Nailsworth, Gloucestershire, GL6 0HH ☎ 07963 200768
nailsworth-brewery.co.uk

After 96 years commercial brewing returned to Nailsworth in 2004 in the form of a six-barrel microbrewery. Beers are sold mainly at the Village Inn above the brewery and at the Star Inn, in Fishponds, Bristol. ‼♦RAIB

Alestock (OG 1036, ABV 3.6%)
A light-coloured ale full of elderflower notes.

Mayor's Bitter (OG 1042, ABV 4.3%)
A best bitter with malt textures complemented by a long-lasting taste of blackcurrant.

Old Rocky (OG 1044, ABV 4.4%)
Light IPA-style beer with a big grapefruit flavour.

Town Crier (OG 1046, ABV 4.5%)
A premium ale with delicate grassy and floral overtones.

Red October (OG 1049, ABV 4.9%)
A ruby-coloured, rich and malty, well-balanced strong bitter.

Naked SIBA

Unit F, MMBC, 2-3 Commerce Way, Lancing, West Sussex, BN15 8TA
☎ (01903) 791230 nakedbeerco.com

Established by Robert Thomas in 2013, Naked Beer began brewing in 2014 using a five-barrel plant. The brewery has undergone much development in its first year. New beers are planned. RAIB

Streaker (OG 1042, ABV 4%)
A session IPA with a dry, crisp finish.

Indecent Exposure (OG 1046, ABV 4.5%)
A surprisingly hoppy, dark porter, with a flavour profile of dark roasted fruits and a slightly chocolate bitter finish.

Biscoteque (OG 1050, ABV 5%)
A milk stout made from a blend of German and Belgian malts and Lotus Bakery Biscoff cookies. Dark, sweet and milky with rich caramel, chocolate and cinnamon biscuit flavours.

Get Lucky (OG 1055, ABV 5.5%)
A well-balanced American-style pale ale with tropical fruit flavours.

Freudian Slip (OG 1068, ABV 6.5%)
A dark crimson-coloured beer, sweet and nutty.

Naked Brewer

Corner Pin, Palmerston Street, Westwood, Nottinghamshire, NG16 5HY ☎ 07908 531901
cornerpinwestwood@hotmail.co.uk

The brewery was set up in 2010 in a skittle alley behind the Corner Pin pub and can be viewed from the function room. Due to demand the skittle alley may need to be moved to allow for increased production. Beer is mainly brewed for the pub but is occasionally supplied to beer festivals or for swaps with other brewpubs. ‼♦

Hopsession (OG 1038, ABV 3.8%)
A light amber bitter retaining a smooth creamy head, with a malty/straw-like aroma and crisp bitter finish.

Blush (OG 1045, ABV 4.5%)
A dark ruby bitter with caramel undertones and a mid bitter finish.

Palindrome (OG 1048, ABV 4.7%)
Smooth creamy porter with a mellow bitter finish.

Nant

Penrhwylfa, Maenan, Llanrwst, LL26 0UF ☎ 07723 036862 🌐 bragdynant.co.uk

⊠ Nant commenced brewing in 2007 with a plant purchased from the Yorkshire Dales Brewery. Capacity is currently 10-15 nine gallon firkins a week. ♦RAIB

Brenin (OG 1038, ABV 3.8%)
A light golden session ale with balanced hops and malt.

Cwrw Chwarel (OG 1036, ABV 3.8%)
Pale gold session ale.

Cennin (OG 1039, ABV 3.9%)
A pale gold bitter brewed with fennel infusion.

Cwrw Coryn (OG 1042, ABV 4.2%)
Traditional amber-coloured beer. Slightly malty with good bitter overtones.

Chwaden Aur (OG 1043, ABV 4.3%)
Gold-coloured ale with a citrus aroma and full mouthfeel. Grapefruit and lemon citrus taste balance with biscuity malt for a long, fruity finish.

Rwster (OG 1046, ABV 4.6%)
Deep copper-coloured sweet and malty ale.

Mwnci Nel (OG 1055, ABV 5.5%)
A special dark ale not excessively sweet but dominated by burnt chocolate flavours, balanced with hops.

Navigation SIBA

Trent Navigation Inn, 17 Meadow Lane, Nottingham, NG2 3HS
☎ (0115) 986 9877 🌐 navigationbrewery.com

Brewing began in 2012 in the old stable block of the Trent Navigation Inn. The brewery is owned by sister company Great Northern Inns and supplies cask beers to the pubs in its estate. ‼

Britannia (OG 1038, ABV 3.8%)
Tawny-coloured malty bitter.

New Dawn Pale (OG 1039, ABV 3.9%)
Golden-coloured ale with initial fruit and hops and a bitter finish.

Golden Anchor (OG 1041.8, ABV 4.3%)
Golden best bitter.

Eclipse (OG 1043.5, ABV 4.4%)
Dark roast stout aroma and aftertaste with bitterness and some sweetness.

Viceroy IPA (OG 1050, ABV 5.2%)
Golden IPA, hoppy and bitter throughout.

Apus (OG 1054, ABV 5.5%)
American-style IPA brewed with lager malts and balanced with a full American hop, deceptively drinkable with a lasting aftertaste.

Naylor's SIBA

Midland Mills, Station Road, Cross Hills, North Yorkshire, BD20 7DT
☎ (01535) 637451 🌐 naylorsbrewery.com

Naylors started brewing in 2005 at the Old White Bear pub in Cross Hills. Expansion required a move to the current site in 2006 and included a rebranding of the beers. Further expansion in 2009 gave bigger facilities for brewing as well as a shop and bar. Around 400 outlets are supplied. Bottle-conditioned ales are available on request, suitable for vegetarians. Annual community cider pressing and fermentation is undertaken. ‼ RAIB

Aire Valley Bitter (OG 1037, ABV 3.8%)
Predominantly malty traditional mid-brown bitter with subtle fruit and hops in the nose and taste and a growing bitter finish.

Velvet (OG 1039, ABV 3.9%)
Chocolate and roast aromas and flavours predominate in this dark brown mild which has an increasingly roast bitter finish.

1641 (OG 1039, ABV 4%)

Pinnacle Blonde (OG 1041.5, ABV 4.3%)
Hoppy, fruity aroma followed by grassy hop and tropical fruit flavours. The finish remains hoppy with a bitter, fruity edge.

Black & Tan (OG 1042, ABV 4.4%)

Old Ale (OG 1054, ABV 5.9%)

Neath

Endeavour Close, Port Talbot, SA12 7PT ☎ 07772 468436 🌐 neathales.co.uk

Neath Ales was established in 2009 and produces a range of single hop variety cask and bottle-conditioned beers (the latter suitable for vegans). Specials beers and one-off brews are also available with some beers being released under the Black Falls brand name. ♦RAIB

Firebrick (OG 1042, ABV 4.2%)
Amber-coloured best bitter with British hop flavour and aroma.

Witch Hunter (OG 1042, ABV 4.2%)
Well-balanced ruby ale with roasted malt and hop fruit flavours.

Deliverance (OG 1045, ABV 4.5%)
Smooth bronze-coloured beer.

Dewi Sant (OG 1048, ABV 4.8%)
A pale ale with a nicely balanced hop fruit flavour.

Gold (OG 1050, ABV 5%)
Citrus/grapefruit hop aroma and flavour dominate this golden ale.

Black (OG 1055, ABV 5.5%)
Dark malt flavours are balanced by aggressive hopping rates making this strong black ale dangerously drinkable.

Green Bullet (OG 1060, ABV 6%)
IPA with massive hop aroma and flavour.

Nelson SIBA

Unit 2, Building 64, The Historic Dockyard, Chatham, Kent, ME4 4TE
☎ (01634) 832828 🌐 nelsonbrewery.co.uk

Based in Chatham's Historic Dockyard and brewing on a nautical theme, the brewery supplies award-winning ales direct to more than 330 outlets. ‼ ♦RAIB

Pieces of Eight (OG 1040, ABV 3.8%)
A light, refreshing ale with full-flavoured hops and a hint of chocolate aftertaste.

Admiral IPA (OG 1040, ABV 4%)
A traditional IPA with a combination of citrus flavours on the palate.

Midshipman Dark Mild (OG 1040, ABV 4%)

A dark mild, leaving a roasted aftertaste on the palate.

Trafalgar Bitter (OG 1040, ABV 4.1%)

Powder Monkey (OG 1043, ABV 4.3%)
A golden ale with a smooth aftertaste which leaves sweetness on the palate.

Pressgang Pale Ale (OG 1044, ABV 4.3%)
A straw-coloured ale, smooth but hoppy.

Friggin' in the Riggin' (OG 1046, ABV 4.5%)
Premium bitter with smooth malt flavour and bittersweet aftertaste.

Pursers Pussy Porter (OG 1051, ABV 4.8%)
A traditional porter.

Nelson's Blood (OG 1062, ABV 6%)
A strong malty ale with mellow roast tones, slightly nutty and fruity with a warm aftertaste.

Nene Valley SIBA

Oundle Wharf, Station Road, Oundle, Northamptonshire, PE8 4DE
☎ (01832) 272776 🌐 nenevalleybrewery.com

⊗ Established in 2011, a bespoke 15-barrel plant was installed in former Water Board premises on expansion in 2012. Around 175 outlets are supplied in Cambridgeshire, Lincolnshire, Northamptonshire and Rutland, with a few satellite outlets in Staffordshire and Warwickshire. A brewery tap, Tap & Kitchen, opened on the same site in 2014.
!! ♦ RAIB

Simple Pleasures Ale (OG 1036, ABV 3.6%)
A light, clean and refreshing beer with a pleasing citrus hop aroma and flavour.

Blonde Session Ale (OG 1037, ABV 3.8%)

Dark Horse (OG 1054, ABV 3.8%)
A dark ruby mild with roasted grains giving hints of chocolate, coffee and liquorice.

Jim's Little Brother (OG 1038, ABV 3.8%)
A session-strength IPA, golden with pleasant passion fruit and grapefruit hop flavours.

Bitter (OG 1040, ABV 4.1%)
Floral hop and malt aroma introduces a full clean biscuit malt taste balanced by bitterness and some fruit, ending with a long malt and bitter finish

Starless Stout (OG 1042, ABV 4.2%)
Smooth oat stout, refreshing dark grain flavours with a slight hop bite to finish.

Australian Pale (OG 1044, ABV 4.4%)
A rich golden ale with a floral aroma preceding citrus and tropical fruit flavour from the hops.

DXB Special Bitter (OG 1046, ABV 4.6%)
Chestnut in colour with plenty of maltiness. Balanced with late-hopped spicy character.

Big Bang Theory (OG 1051, ABV 5.3%)
Well-balanced pale ale with a big hop aroma giving way to malty sweetness and a gentle bitter finish.

Jim Irving Pale (OG 1056, ABV 5.6%)
Full bodied, with a big malty taste backed with heaps of zesty hop flavour.

Bible Black (OG 1067, ABV 6.5%)
Initial rich and fruity flavours give way to a chocolate and roasted finish.

Fenland Farmhouse Saison (OG 1057, ABV 7.2%)
Refreshing Belgian-style ale with a hint of spice.

Nethergate SIBA

Growler Brewery, The Street, Pentlow, Essex, CO10 7JJ
☎ (01787) 283220 🌐 nethergatebrewery.co.uk

⊗ Starting at Clare in 1986 the brewery moved to Pentlow, Essex in 2005, where after large growth there is still room to expand. The brewery name, under new owners, was changed to Growler but in 2014 original owner Dick Burge returned and restored Nethergate. !! ♦

IPA (OG 1036, ABV 3.5%)
Bitter-tasting session beer with some fruit and malt balancing the predominate hop character. Dry aftertaste.

Priory Mild (OG 1036, ABV 3.5%)
A black bitter rather than a true mild. Strong roast and bitter tastes dominate throughout.

Umbel Ale (OG 1039, ABV 3.8%)
Pleasant, easy-drinking bitter, infused with coriander, which dominates.

Growler Bitter (OG 1040, ABV 3.9%)
Light tasting, sweetish and fruity session beer.

Lemon Head (OG 1041, ABV 4%)
A tantalising union of lemon and ginger creates an unmistakable thirst-quenching beer.

Hound Dog (OG 1043, ABV 4.2%)
Light golden beer, smooth and refreshing at the start with a well-rounded bitterness before the hop explosion leaves a slightly fruity taste at the end.

Essex Border (OG 1049, ABV 4.8%)
A pale golden summer ale, fruity and spicy with a pleasant malty finish; an easy-drinking beer.

Old Growler (OG 1051, ABV 5%)
Well-balanced porter in which roast grain is complemented by fruit and bubblegum.

Umbel Magna (OG 1051, ABV 5%)
Old Growler flavoured with coriander. The spice is less dominant than in Umbel Ale, with some of the weight and body of the beer coming through.

Essex Beast (OG 1063, ABV 6.2%)
Strong, dark, complex and robust ale with chocolate and rich toffee flavours.

New Bristol

20a Wilson Street, Bristol, BS2 9HH ☎ 07837 976871
🌐 newbristolbrewery.co.uk

⊗ Brothers Tom and Noel commenced brewing on a five-barrel plant in 2013. Three beers are brewed regularly, along with a selection of stouts and IPAs.
♦ RAIB

365 (OG 1041, ABV 4%)
A session bitter with plenty of upfront malt and toffee.

Oohlala (OG 1040, ABV 4.2%)
An amber-coloured beer balanced by sweet, spicy notes with hints of citrus and herbs from the French hop Aramis and the zest of 60 lemons.

Beer Du Jour (OG 1046, ABV 4.6%)
A bittersweet, strong bitter with citrus fruit aromas and flavours which continue in the aftertaste. Unfined so may be hazy.

New Inn

New Inn, 112 Roberttown Lane, Roberttown, Liversedge, West Yorkshire, WF15 7NP
☎ (01924) 402069 ⊕ thenewinnroberttown.com

Brewing commenced in 2012 using a half-barrel brew plant located in the cellar of the New Inn, Liversedge. The beer is produced in wood-clad vessels by Joe Kenyon, the ex-brewer at Riverhead Brewery and his son, Andrew. ♦

Pale Bob (OG 1038, ABV 3.8%)

Golden Bob (OG 1040, ABV 4%)
A golden beer flavoured with European hops with a refreshing aftertaste.

Rusty Bob (OG 1045, ABV 4.5%)
A smooth, malty traditional Yorkshire bitter packed with flavour and a slightly bitter aftertaste.

Bobcastle Brown (OG 1046, ABV 4.6%)
A dark brown bitter, smooth and easy-drinking, with a pleasant bitter aftertaste.

Bobmeister (OG 1049, ABV 4.9%)
Lager-based golden ale with German hops for a full flavour.

Bombay Bob (OG 1060, ABV 6%)
A strong, pale beer full of flavours with ginger, cardamom and mint to the fore.

New Lion SIBA

Station Road, Totnes, Devon, TQ9 5JR
☎ (01803) 226277 ⊕ lioncraftbrewery.com

The original Lion Brewery closed in 1926 and was restarted in 2013 by four local business people. The only memorabilia found for the old brewery is a mirror for the 'Celebrated Totnes Stout', which the brewery recently revived. Experimental brews are tested through customers in the Bay Horse, Totnes. There is a commitment to providing apprenticeship opportunities and work experience for people with learning difficulties. ♦

Mane Event (OG 1039, ABV 3.8%)
A golden-coloured, drinkable modern session bitter.

Totnes Stout (OG 1045, ABV 4.4%)
Silky and smooth due to the addition of oats, this stout offers a good mouthfeel coupled with deep roasted and coffee notes. Unfined.

Pandit IPA (OG 1046, ABV 4.9%)
A citrus and floral nose complemented on the palate by a well-defined, biscuity malt character.

New Plassey

Eyton, LL13 0SP ☎ 07769 155874
✉ plassey.brewery@gmail.com

Plassey brewery was founded in 1985 on the 250-acre Plassey Estate. Following the merger of Plassey and the Gertie Sweet Brewery in 2012, the New Plassey Brewery was formed.

New World Pale (OG 1039, ABV 3.9%)
A pale beer, well-balanced with a hoppy bite.

Plassey Bitter (OG 1040, ABV 4%) ◆
Smooth and malty best bitter, reddish brown in colour, with a good hop and fruit balance and a dry finish.

Midnight Mild (OG 1042, ABV 4.2%)
A medium strength mild with a real fullness of character and flavour. Dark and subtle.

Offa's Dyke (OG 1043, ABV 4.3%)
Pale, crisp and refreshing bitter brewed with the finest quality malt and hops.

Dusky Maiden Stout (OG 1044, ABV 4.4%)
A dark, complex-flavoured stout.

Deep Porter (OG 1045, ABV 4.5%)
A smooth, deep brown porter.

Cherry Diva (OG 1047, ABV 4.7%)
A pale beer with a subtle flavour of Maraschino cherry.

Cwrw Tudno (OG 1050, ABV 5%)
A pale strong bitter.

Dragons Breath (OG 1060, ABV 6%) ◆
A well-balanced strong bitter. Plum fruit in aroma with the initial sweetness followed by a powerful smack of hops and fruit.

Newark SIBA

77 William Street, Newark, Nottinghamshire, NG24 1QU ☎ 07908 550249 ⊕ newarkbrewery.co.uk

Newark Brewery was established in 2012 on the site of a former maltings using an eight-barrel plant. The bulk of production is supplied to local pubs. Its brewery tap is the Ram in Castle Gate, Newark.

Best (OG 1038, ABV 3.8%)
Deep copper-coloured ale with a biscuity malt nose. Sweet toffee dominates the palate with a long, fruity finish.

NPA (Newark Pale Ale) (OG 1039, ABV 3.8%)
Pale gold in colour, citrus lemon on the nose, leading to a fruity finish.

BLH4 (OG 1040, ABV 4%)
Brewed with very pale malts and plenty of Amarillo and Willamette hops.

Norwegian Blue (ABV 4%)
Deep gold in colour. Grapefruit and citrus orange on the nose. Malty lemon on the palate with a long finish.

Pure Gold (ABV 4.5%)
A rich gold in colour with biscuit and burnt orange on the nose, leading to a soft biscuit finish.

Summer Gold (OG 1045, ABV 4.5%)
Deep gold in colour with a strong, sweet citrus nose. The lime character and light malt balance produce a lasting finish.

Phoenix (ABV 4.8%)
Russet brown in colour, slight spice and roasted malt on the nose, with a fruity treacle, full-bodied finish.

5.5 (ABV 5.5%)
Deep gold-coloured strong ale, strong honey on the nose with sweet soft fruits on the finish.

Newbridge (NEW)

Unit 3, Tudor House, Moseley Road, Bilston, West Midlands, WV14 6JD ☎ 07970 456052
⊕ newbridgebrewery.co.uk

Established in 2014 using a five-barrel plant.

Little Fox (ABV 4.2%)
A Black Country-style bitter.

Solaris (ABV 4.5%)

Indian Empire (ABV 5.1%)

Newby Wyke SIBA

Unit 24, Limesquare Business Park, Alma Park Road, Grantham, Lincolnshire, NG31 9SN
☎ (01476) 565682 ⊕ newbywyke.co.uk

⊠ The brewery is named after a Hull trawler skippered by brewer Rob March's grandfather. It started life in 1998 as a 2.5-barrel plant in a converted garage then moved to premises behind the Willoughby Arms, Little Bytham. In 2009 it moved back to Grantham with a brew length of 10 barrels. !! ◆

Banquo (OG 1036, ABV 3.8%)
Pale blonde in colour with a full hoppy taste and a long, fruity finish.

Orsino (OG 1037, ABV 4%)
A blonde ale with a bright, fruity citrus and mango taste moving to a soft citrus hop finish.

Kingston Topaz (OG 1039, ABV 4.2%)
A single-hopped ale with floral undertones.

Bear Island (OG 1043, ABV 4.6%)
A blonde beer with a hoppy aroma and a crisp, dry finish.

White Squall (OG 1044, ABV 4.8%) ◆
Blonde-hued with a hoppy aroma. Generous amounts of hop are well-supported by a solid malty undercurrent. An increasingly bittersweet tang makes itself known towards the finish.

Newmans

See Celt Experience

Nine Standards

See Settle

Nobby's SIBA

▤ Unit 2, Cottingham Way, Thrapston, Northamptonshire, NN14 4PL
☎ (01832) 730800 ⊕ nobbysbrewery.co.uk

Paul 'Nobby' Mulliner started commercial brewing in 2004 on a 2.5-barrel plant at the rear of the Alexandra Arms, Kettering. The brewery relocated to the Ward Arms, Guilsborough, in 2007 where a 14-barrel plant was installed at the rear and subsequently expanded. The full range of beers are bottled in-house. 2014 saw another move to larger premises in Thrapston. !! ╤ ◆ RAIB

Claridges Crystal (OG 1036, ABV 3.6%)
Ultra pale summer ale, crisp and fresh with a slightly citrus hop finish.

Guilsborough Guzzler (OG 1036, ABV 3.6%)
An easy-drinking malty auburn ale with a gentle hop finish.

Best (OG 1037, ABV 3.8%)
A fine session ale with an excellent hop finish.

Guilsborough Gold (OG 1041, ABV 4%)
Golden ale with full-bodied, balanced traditional hop finish.

Wild West (OG 1046, ABV 4.6%)
Mahogany-coloured beer, full and flavoursome.

Tow'd Navigation (OG 1067, ABV 6.1%)
Dark strong ale from years gone by. Rich malt and hops and wonderfully warming.

Nook SIBA

▤ Riverside, 7b Victoria Square, Holmfirth, West Yorkshire, HD9 2DN
☎ (01484) 682373 ⊕ thenookbrewhouse.co.uk

☺ The Nook Brewhouse is built on the foundations of a previous brewhouse dating back to 1754, next to the River Ribble. Two brewery taps are supplied, one with a restaurant whose dishes are matched with the beer brewed on site. A history room with renovated archives dating back to the 1700s and a brewery shop are also planned. !!

Yorks (OG 1037, ABV 3.7%) ◆
A well-balanced bitter with light malt and hop aroma and hop and fruit in the taste, developing in strength. A good session beer.

Baby Blond (OG 1038, ABV 3.8%)
A pale ale packed with hop flavours and citrus notes for a refreshing finish.

Rescue Red (OG 1038, ABV 3.8%)
A deep red ale, subtly hopped to give a floral aroma and finish, balanced with a rich malt base.

Best (OG 1040.5, ABV 4.2%) ◆
An easy-drinking best bitter with hints of malt and floral hops in the aroma. The taste has an abundance of hops and fruit and a pleasant, crisp, malty aftertaste.

Blond (OG 1042.5, ABV 4.5%) ◆
A golden ale with intense fruit and hop tastes, which lessen in the aftertaste.

Oat Stout (OG 1052, ABV 5.2%)
A distinctive stout with a rich flavour and full body, imparting dark chocolate and liquorice notes.

Norfolk SIBA ◉

Moon Gazer Barn, Harvest Lane, Hindringham, Norfolk, NR21 0PW
☎ (01328) 878495 ⊕ norfolkbrewhouse.co.uk

⊠ Brewing began in 2012 using a 10-barrel plant. The brewery is owned and run by Rachel and David Holliday. Chalk-filtered water is used from the brewery's own well. !!

Dewhopper Cask Lager (OG 1038, ABV 3.8%)

Moon Gazer Amber Ale (OG 1040, ABV 4%)
This amber ale combines a full-bodied bitterness with fruity overtones, creating an impressive flavour and a smooth, lasting finish.

Moon Gazer Golden Ale (OG 1040, ABV 4%)
This golden ale has a fresh, citrus aroma and a well-hopped character, with fruit and hop flavour carrying through to the refreshing, crisp, dry finish.

Moon Gazer Ruby Ale (OG 1040, ABV 4%)
A ruby-coloured bitter with a rich, spicy, roasted aroma and a full malty body, resulting in a full-bodied mouthfeel.

Moongazer Dark Mild (OG 1051, ABV 4.9%)
This strong dark mild has a subtle blackcurrant aroma, full-bodied with a rich, fruity, sweet finish.

Stubblestag Cask Lager (OG 1049, ABV 5%)

Norland (NEW)

c/o 4c Ladyship Business Park, Mill Lane, Halifax, West Yorkshire, HX3 6TA ☎ 07475 085385
✉ norlandbeersltd@outlook.com

Founded in 2014, Norland brews on a six-barrel plant using spare capacity at Oates Brewery.

Barnstormers (OG 1040, ABV 3.8%) ◆
Amber-coloured refreshing session bitter. Mellow fruity flavour with hints of caramel that lingers into the aftertaste where a dry bitterness unfolds.

Moorish Mild (OG 1042, ABV 4%) ◆
Malty, caramel and fruit flavours combine wonderfully in a smooth-drinking, refreshing , tawny-coloured mild with a lingering toffee finish.

Showcase (ABV 4.2%) ◆
A full-bodied and well-rounded red ale. The hoppy taste is balanced by smooth malt and mellow fruit, leading to a long, dry finish.

Best Bitter (OG 1045, ABV 4.3%) ◆
An amber-coloured beer infused with the flavour of malt, hops and fruit. Hoppy bitterness remains assertive in the aftertaste. A classic example of a traditional northern ale.

North Cotswold SIBA

Unit 3, Ditchford Farm, Stretton-on-Fosse, Warwickshire, GL56 9RD
☎ (01608) 663947 ⊕ northcotswoldbrewery.co.uk

◉North Cotswold started in 1999 as a 2.5-barrel plant, which was upgraded in 2000 to 10 barrels.
🛒◆RAIB

Windrush Ale (OG 1036, ABV 3.6%)
A thirst-quenching amber-coloured session bitter, brewed with finest English hops for a traditional taste. A malty, slightly sweeter palate.

Moreton Mild (OG 1038, ABV 3.8%)
A classic dark mild with a nutty palate.

Cotswold Best (OG 1040, ABV 4%)
An easy-drinking straw-coloured best bitter.

Shagweaver (OG 1045, ABV 4.5%)
A pale, hoppy bitter made with a trio of New Zealand hops.

Hung, Drawn 'n' Portered (OG 1050, ABV 5%)
Strong, dark-coloured porter with a malty finish.

North Curry SIBA

The Old Coach House, Gwyon House, Church Road, North Curry, Somerset, TA3 6LH ☎ 07928 815053
⊕ thenorthcurrybrewerycouk.com

⊠ The brewery opened in 2006 and is attached to one of the oldest properties in North Curry, where brewing last took place in the village in the 1920s. Beers are available at farmers markets in Taunton and Minehead and in local shops. ◆RAIB

Howzat (OG 1036, ABV 3.7%)
A refreshing golden ale with fruity hops and a smooth aftertaste.

Curry Gold (OG 1038, ABV 3.9%)
A gold-coloured beer with a fruity aroma and a smooth sweetness contrasting with the bitter hops.

Red Heron (OG 1041, ABV 4.3%)
A full-bodied, malty ale, balanced by the bitterness of Golding hops.

Withyman (OG 1042, ABV 4.6%)
The malty flavour has a bitterness and punch from Pacific Gem hops.

Level Headed (OG 1043, ABV 4.7%)
A traditional old English ale made with chocolate malt. It has a dark ruby colour making it rich and full of flavour.

Alfred's Stout (OG 1047, ABV 5.1%)
A black, dry stout with a good, robust flavour.

North Riding (Brewery) (NEW)

Unit 9, Betton Business Park, Racecourse Road, East Ayton, Scarborough, YO13 9HD
☎ (01723) 864845 ☎ 07930 843868
⊕ northridingbrewery.com

Brewing commenced in 2015 on a 10-barrel plant with four core beers and monthly specials being produced.

Bramling Gold (OG 1039, ABV 3.8%)
A golden copper-coloured session bitter.

Cascade Pale Ale (OG 1042, ABV 4%)
A US-hopped pale ale with citrus qualities.

Mosaic Pale Ale (OG 1044, ABV 4.3%)
A US-hopped ale with blueberry and citrus flavours.

Citra Pale Ale (OG 1045, ABV 4.5%)
Easy-drinking premium pale ale with a grapefruit and lemon taste and aroma.

North Riding (Brewpub)

🏠 North Marine Road, Scarborough, North Yorkshire, YO12 7HU
☎ (01723) 370004 ⊕ northridingbrewpub.com

Brewing commenced in 2011 using a two-barrel plant situated in the cellar of the pub, which is now brewing to capacity with three fermenting vessels.
◆RAIB

Peasholm Pale Ale (OG 1042, ABV 4.3%)
Pale and hoppy. Single-hopped with Citra giving a citrus bitterness and a long, smooth finish.

North Star SIBA ◉

Unit 6, Gallows Industrial Park, off Furnace Road, Ilkeston, Derbyshire, DE7 5EP ☎ 07521 961881
⊕ northstarbrewery.co.uk

◉North Star was established in 2012 by a long-term home brewer using a purpose-built 10-barrel plant. Now supplying numerous local outlets and distributing widely through wholesalers, production has increased to a level where several family members are now involved in the process.
‼◆RAIB

Sentinel (OG 1039, ABV 3.8%)
A pale, American-style ale with citrus undertones.

Helmsman (OG 1041, ABV 4.2%)
A pale ale with a full malt flavour and a delicate hop balance with a satisfying fruit finish.

Pathfinder (OG 1045, ABV 4.5%)
A special bitter with full roast malt and rich orange peel overtones. The malt is balanced by four hop varieties.

Trailblazer (OG 1044, ABV 4.5%)

Astronomer (OG 1048, ABV 4.8%)

A stout with rich roast malt flavour and dark chocolate overtones which lead to a dry biscuit finish.

Polaris (OG 1049, ABV 5%)
A dark ruby porter with chocolate, liquorice and coffee aromas. The flavours lead to a hop and bitter finish.

Endeavour (OG 1053, ABV 5.4%)
A dark beer with complex fruit flavours and notes of pepper, culminating in full malt flavouring and a toffee and wine-like finish.

North Wales

Tan-y-Mynydd, Moelfre, Abergele, LL22 9RF ☎ 0800 083 4100 🌐 northwalesbrewery.net

John Wood established his brewery in 2007. In 2012 a bore hole was drilled to supply water for brewing. Mead and soft drinks are also produced. RAIB

Bodelwyddan Bitter (OG 1038, ABV 3.8%)

Chilli Beer (OG 1040, ABV 4%)

Dandelion & Burdock (OG 1040, ABV 4%)
Alcoholic dandelion & burdock, brewed with single lager malt.

Abergele Ale (OG 1050, ABV 5%)

Welsh Stout (OG 1052, ABV 5.2%)

North Yorkshire SIBA

Pinchinthorpe Hall, Pinchinthorpe, North Yorkshire, TS14 8HG
☎ (01287) 630200 🌐 nybrewery.co.uk

Founded in Middlesbrough in 1989 the brewery moved to Pinchinthorpe Hall, a moated, listed medieval estate near Guisborough in 1998. Its own spring water produces a distinctive flavour. More than 100 trade outlets are supplied. Most cask beers are organic with some occasional beers not so. ‼ ♦ RAIB

Best Bitter (OG 1036, ABV 3.6%)
Refreshing session beer. Clean-tasting, well-hopped, copper-coloured.

Golden Ginseng (OG 1036, ABV 3.6%)
Clean-tasting, well-hopped traditional beer with ginseng.

Prior's Ale (OG 1036, ABV 3.6%)
Light, refreshing and surprisingly full-flavoured for a pale, low gravity beer, with a complex, bittersweet mixture of malt, hops and fruit carrying through into the aftertaste.

Archbishop Lee's Ruby Ale (OG 1040, ABV 4%)
Maltiness is predominant with some hops in the taste.

Boro Best (OG 1040, ABV 4%)
Mid brown in colour with a malty aroma. A full-bodied beer.

Crystal Tips (OG 1040, ABV 4%)
Full-bodied, malt-flavoured ruby bitter.

Love Muscle (OG 1040, ABV 4%)
Thirst-quenching. Crisp and golden.

Honey Bunny (OG 1042, ABV 4.2%)
Golden bitter with a hoppy finish and a hint of honey.

Mayhem (OG 1043, ABV 4.3%)
Refreshing, clean-tasting, well-hopped pale ale.

Cereal Killer (OG 1045, ABV 4.5%)
Light-coloured clear wheat bitter with a distinctive hop nose.

Fools Gold (OG 1046, ABV 4.6%)
Pale, refreshingly complex golden ale. Fruity aroma with a bittersweet flavour

Golden Ale (OG 1046, ABV 4.6%)
A well-hopped, lightly-malted, golden premium bitter, using Styrian Goldings and Goldings hops.

Flying Herbert (OG 1047, ABV 4.7%)
Smooth, full-flavoured premium bitter with a malty, fruity and dry finish.

Lord Lee's (OG 1047, ABV 4.7%)
A refreshing, red/brown beer with a hoppy aroma. The flavour is a pleasant balance of roast malt and sweetness that predominates over hops. The malty, bitter finish develops slowly.

White Lady (OG 1047, ABV 4.7%)
A hoppy, strong, pale-coloured beer.

Dizzy Dick (OG 1048, ABV 4.8%)
Strong, smooth, dark ale with plenty of hops.

Rocket Fuel (OG 1050, ABV 5%)
A strong golden ale.

Valhalla (OG 1055, ABV 5.5%)
Strong traditional bitter with plenty of hops and a subtle hint of malt.

Northern SIBA

See Blakemere

Northern Alchemy (NEW)

The Lab, Cumberland Arms, St James Street, Newcastle upon Tyne, NE6 1LD ☎ 07834 386333 🌐 wearenorthernalchemy.com

Brewing began in 2014. Production is mostly keg but some cask-conditioned beer is available.

Northern FC

McCracken Park, Great North Road, Gosforth, Newcastle upon Tyne, NE3 2DT 🌐 northernfootballclub.co.uk

Established in 2012 to supply the clubhouse for the Northern RUFC. The range is developing.

Northern Monk SIBA

The Old Flax Store, Marshalls Mill, Holbeck, Leeds, LS11 9YJ
☎ (0113) 243 6430 🌐 northernmonkbrewco.com

Based in a Grade II-listed mill building in the centre of Leeds, Northern Monk started brewing as cuckoo brewers in 2013 and set up at the new site in 2014 using a 10-barrel plant.

True North (OG 1037, ABV 3.7%)
Hops dominate this light yellow beer, but there is a bitterness which builds in strength then lingers in the finish.

Monacus NZ Pale Ale (OG 1045, ABV 4.5%)

Northumberland SIBA

Accessory House, Barrington Road, Bedlington, Northumberland, NE22 7AP
☎ (01670) 822112 northumberlandbrewery.co.uk

Brewing began in 1996 in Ashington using a five-barrel plant. Relocation and expansion mean that the brewery now uses a 10-barrel plant and has an on-site brewery tap, Fuggles. 30-40 barrels are brewed each week of a wide range of ales. !! ♦

Pit Pony (OG 1039, ABV 3.8%)

Fog on the Tyne (OG 1040.5, ABV 4.1%)

Norton

Norton Priory, Tudor Road, Manor Park, Runcorn, Cheshire, WA7 1SX
☎ (01928) 716971 ☎ 07767 354674
nortonbrewing.com

Situated within the grounds of Norton Priory, the brewery was created as a social enterprise by Halton Borough Council to provide employment opportunities for people with learning disabilities, autism and other disabilities. It opened in 2011 with a 2.5-barrel plant and began bottling in 2012.

Priory Gold (ABV 4.2%)
A refreshingly crisp, traditional-style, amber-coloured ale.

Priory Velvet (ABV 4.3%)
A smooth, dark ruby ale brewed using chocolate malt.

Priory Ale (OG 1045, ABV 4.5%)
A smooth, golden-coloured ale with a hint of orange.

Noss Beer Works SIBA

Unit 6, Ash Court, Pennant Way, Lee Mill, Devon, PL21 9GE ☎ 07977 479634 nossbeerworks.co.uk

Noss Beer Works, based in Lee Mill, was formed in 2012 using a six-barrel plant. The beers are made from only the finest locally sourced hops and malts. !! RAIB

Church Ledge (OG 1040, ABV 4%)
A late-hopped blonde IPA, light, hoppy and zesty.

Gara Point (ABV 4.2%)

Mew Stone (OG 1043, ABV 4.3%)
A copper-coloured, well-balanced and refreshing ale.

Ebb Rock (OG 1049, ABV 4.9%)
A dark copper-coloured, full-bodied beer.

Brewed for the Nowhere Inn, Plymouth:

Likely Bitter (ABV 4.2%)

Nottingham SIBA

Plough Inn, 17 St Peter's Street, Radford, Nottingham, NG7 3EN
☎ (0115) 942 2649 ☎ 07815 073447
nottinghambrewery.co.uk

The former owners of the Bramcote and Castle Rock Breweries re-established the Nottingham Brewery in 2000 in a purpose-built brewhouse behind the Plough Inn. Philip Darby and Niven Balfour set out to revive the brands of the original Nottingham Brewery, closed by Whitbread in the 1950s, with a view to supplying local outlets within the LocAle ethos. !!

Rock Ale Bitter Beer (OG 1038, ABV 3.8%)
A pale and bitter, thirst-quenching hoppy beer with a dry finish.

Rock Ale Mild Beer (OG 1038, ABV 3.8%)
A reddish-black malty mild with some refreshing bitterness in the finish.

Legend (OG 1040, ABV 4%)
A fruity and malty pale brown bitter with a touch of sweetness and bitterness.

Extra Pale Ale (OG 1042, ABV 4.2%)
A hoppy and fruity golden ale with a hint of sweetness and a long-lasting bitter finish.

Dreadnought (OG 1045, ABV 4.5%)
Well-balanced best bitter. Blend of malt and hops give a rounded, fruity finish.

Bullion (OG 1047, ABV 4.7%)
A refreshing premium golden ale. Brewed with a single malt variety, it is triple-hopped and exceptionally bitter.

Supreme (OG 1052, ABV 5.2%)
A strong, amber-coloured, fruity ale. A touch of malt in the taste is followed by a sweet and slightly hoppy finish.

Brewed for the Broadway Cinema Café Bar, Nottingham:

Broadway Reel Ale (OG 1044, ABV 4.4%)
Hoppy, amber-coloured best bitter.

Brewed for the Trent Bridge Inn, West Bridgford:

Trent Bridge Inn Ale (OG 1038, ABV 3.8%)
Tawny, traditionally-hopped bitter.

Nutbrook SIBA

6 Hallam Way, West Hallam, Derbyshire, DE7 6LA
☎ 0800 458 2460 nutbrookbrewery.com

Nutbrook was established in 2007 on a one-barrel brewery in the owners' garage. This was supplemented in 2010 with a six-barrel plant at Oakfield Farm, Stanley Common. Beers are brewed to order for domestic and corporate clients, and customers can design their own recipes. !! RAIB

Responsibly (OG 1041, ABV 4%)
A light bronze-coloured, crisp beer with a fruity flavour.

Banter (OG 1040.8, ABV 4.5%)
A light golden-coloured beer, New World hops give a traditional hoppy taste and floral notes.

More (OG 1047, ABV 4.8%)
Dark beer with a subtle red tint, burnt roasted barley taste and sweet bitterness.

Black Beauty (OG 1054, ABV 5%)
A traditional milk stout with a secret ingredient giving undertones of chocolate, honey and nuts.

Perfect Fifth (OG 1047.8, ABV 5%)
A strong pale ale with honey tones. Brewed with a combination of traditional English hops and fresh and fruity American varieties.

O'Hanlon's

See Hanlons

THE BREWERIES

Oakham SIBA

2 Maxwell Road, Woodston, Peterborough, Cambridgeshire, PE2 7JB
(01733) 370500 oakhamales.com

The brewery started in 1993 in Oakham, Rutland, and moved to Peterborough in 1998. The brewery's main production site is a 75-barrel plant. An additional six-barrel plant is located at its city-centre brewpub, which makes special and one-off brews. Around 350 outlets are supplied and four pubs are owned. !! ♦ RAIB

JHB (OG 1038, ABV 3.8%)
Straw-coloured golden ale dominated by citrus hop character throughout. Long, dry, slightly astringent finish.

Inferno (OG 1039, ABV 4%)
The citrus hop character of this straw-coloured brew begins on the nose and builds in intensity on the palate. Clean dry citrus finish.

Citra (OG 1042, ABV 4.2%)
Refreshing grapefruit and peach aroma and flavour characterise this golden ale. Bittersweet palate gives way to a long dry aftertaste.

Scarlet Macaw (OG 1043, ABV 4.4%)
Tart gooseberry and soft peach on the nose and intense bitter finish.

Bishops Farewell (OG 1046, ABV 4.6%)
Powerfully citrusy, the hops and fruit on the aroma of this golden/yellow beer become bittersweet on the palate. Zesty citrus aftertaste.

Oakleaf SIBA

Unit 7, Clarence Wharf Industrial Estate, Mumby Road, Gosport, Hampshire, PO12 1AJ
(023) 9251 3222 oakleafbrewing.co.uk

Ed Anderson set up Oakleaf with his father-in-law, Dave Pickersgill, in 2000. The brewery stands on the side of Portsmouth harbour. Some 350 outlets are supplied direct with national deliveries via wholesalers. !! ♦ RAIB

Heart of Gold (OG 1038, ABV 3.8%)
An easy-drinking golden ale with a hint of spices and balanced sweetness.

Quercus Folium (OG 1040, ABV 4%)
A traditional mid-brown bitter with an initial malty flavour leading to a long hoppy finish.

Nuptu'ale (OG 1042, ABV 4.2%)
An intense spicy, floral aroma leads to a complex hoppy taste. Well-balanced with malts and citrus flavours and a hint of sweetness.

Hole Hearted (OG 1048, ABV 4.7%)
Amber-coloured with a strong floral hop aroma continuing into the flavour, with some malt, leading to a long, bittersweet finish.

I Can't Believe It's Not Bitter (OG 1048, ABV 4.9%)
Clean and crisp with a fruity aftertaste and a lingering citrus finish.

India Pale Ale (OG 1053, ABV 5.5%)
Initially dry and bitter. Full-flavoured and complex marmalade/aniseed notes to follow, leaving a lingering bitterness on the palate.

Blake's Heaven (OG 1065, ABV 7%)

Brewed for Suthwyk Ales:

Old Dick (OG 1038, ABV 3.8%)
Pleasant, clean-tasting pale brown bitter. Easy-drinking and well-balanced. Brewed using ingredients grown on the farm.

Liberation (OG 1042, ABV 4.2%)
Light-coloured with a soft berry fruit flavour.

Skew Sunshine Ale (OG 1046, ABV 4.6%)
An amber-coloured beer. Initial hoppiness leads to a fruity taste and finish with a slightly cloying mouthfeel.

Palmerston's Folly (OG 1050, ABV 5%)
A clear wheat and barley beer. Slightly dry with a hint of honey in the aftertaste.

Oates SIBA

4 Ladyship Business Park, Mill Lane, Halifax, West Yorkshire, HX3 6TA
(01422) 320100 07770 572055
oatesbrewing.co.uk

Oates was founded in 2011 by former landlord Mark Oates and brewer Richard Munro using a six-barrel plant. ♦

O.M.T. (OG 1038, ABV 3.8%)
A light straw-coloured beer with a hoppy nose and light fruity flavour followed by a strong bitter aftertaste.

Caragold (OG 1041, ABV 4.1%)
Gold-coloured refreshingly light ale. Honey-scented with a clean and fresh fruity taste. Hints of astringency in the finish.

Golden Oates (OG 1041, ABV 4.1%)
A golden, honey-coloured beer which oozes caramel and honey on the nose, with a long bitter finish.

Wild Oates (OG 1043, ABV 4.3%)
Rich malty beer with complex fruit and bitter notes followed by a clean, light, satisfying finish.

Summit (OG 1045, ABV 4.5%)
Full-bodied amber best bitter. Fruity caramel nose. Hoppy with bitterness mellowed by a fruity aftertaste.

Oban Bay SIBA

See Argyll

Occasional (NEW)

Roosters of Babylon, Babylon Lane, Silverton, Devon, EX5 4DT 07506 355318 occasionalbrewing.co.uk

Established in 2014. Currently only bottle-conditioned beers are produced and are sold through local retailers, farmers' markets and other events. RAIB

Odcombe

Masons Arms, 41 Lower Odcombe, Odcombe, Somerset, BA22 8TX
(01935) 862591 masonsarmsodcombe.co.uk

Oscombe opened in 2000, but closed a few years later. It re-opened in 2005 with assistance from Shepherd Neame (qv). Brewing takes place once a week and beers are available only in the Masons Arms. !! ♦

No 1 (OG 1040, ABV 4%)

Traditional best bitter flavoured with East Kent Golding hops.

Spring (OG 1042, ABV 4.1%)
Amber ale, light and hoppy with floral notes.

Roly Poly (OG 1042, ABV 4.3%)
Autumn ruby-coloured beer with juniper berries and star anise. A slightly stronger tasting beer.

Odyssey (NEW)

Brockhampton Brewery, Oast House Barn, Whitbourne, Bromyard, Herefordshire, WR6 5SH
⊕ odysseybrewco.com

This six-barrel brewery was bought in 2014 by Alison and Mitchell Evans, who also own the Beer in Hand in Hereford. The original building, a restored barn on a National Trust estate, has been retained.

Syren (ABV 3.9%)

Evil Empire (ABV 4.2%)

Little India Pale Ale (ABV 4.5%)

Crowd Control (ABV 6%)

Offa's Dyke SIBA

🯄 Chapel Lane, Trefonen, Shropshire, SY10 9DX
☎ (01691) 656889

☺ Established in 2007, the brewery and adjoining pub straddle the old England/Wales border, Offa's Dyke. The owner has small-scale hop cultivation. The Olde Vaults and adjacent Ironworks in Oswestry serve as alternative brewery taps. ‼🛒◆RAIB

Barley Gold (OG 1038, ABV 3.6%)
A full-bodied session bitter. Bitterness with hops and fruit. Lingering bitterness.

Offa's Pride (OG 1040, ABV 3.8%)
A well-rounded bitter with a fruity finish.

Thirst Brew (OG 1042, ABV 4%)
A malty premium bitter with a bitter finish.

Grim Reaper (OG 1050, ABV 5%)
Dark and smooth with a rich flavour. Roast and chocolate dominate in the aroma. Not too sweet for its gravity.

Offbeat SIBA

Unit 6, Thomas Street, Crewe, CW1 2BD ☎ 07502 096438 ⊕ offbeatbrewery.com

☺Offbeat began brewing in 2010, quickly expanding to a six-barrel plant. Brewery open nights (usually first Friday of the month) are a regular occurence. Beers are available at many local outlets and around the north-west. ‼◆RAIB

Outlandish Pale (OG 1037.8, ABV 3.9%)
A pale ale with a fresh burst of lemon hoppiness.

Kooky Gold (ABV 4.1%)
Light, golden session ale, easy-drinking and with low bitterness.

Odd Ball Red (OG 1040.4, ABV 4.2%)
A bold, fruity ruby red ale with a spicy flavour and finish.

Way Out Wheat (OG 1043.6, ABV 4.5%) 🗍
A naturally cloudy wheat beer with oranges and coriander.

Disfunctional Functional IPA (ABV 4.8%)

San Diego-inspired, heavily hopped IPA.

Okell's SIBA ◉

Kewaigue, Douglas, Isle of Man, IM2 1QG
☎ (01624) 699400 ⊕ okells.co.uk

☺Founded in 1874 by Dr Okell, this is the main brewery on the island and moved in 1994 to a new, purpose-built plant at Kewaigue. All the beers are produced under the Manx Brewers' Act. ‼◆

MPA (Manx Pale Ale) (OG 1036, ABV 3.6%)
Pale gold and fruity with a dry finish.

Bitter (OG 1035, ABV 3.7%) 🍺
A golden beer, malty and hoppy in aroma, with a hint of honey. Rich and malty on the tongue, it has a dry, malt and hop finish. A complex but rewarding beer.

Olaf (OG 1040, ABV 3.9%)
Deep black in colour with aromas of coffee and liquorice.

Dr Okell's IPA (OG 1044, ABV 4.5%)
A light-coloured beer with a full-bodied taste. The sweetness is offset by strong hopping that gives the beer an overall roundness with spicy lemon notes and a fine dry finish.

Alt (OG 1050, ABV 4.9%)
A copper-coloured beer with a crisp, elegant and fresh flavour, with hints of gooseberry and citrus.

Steam (OG 1052, ABV 5%)
A dark gold beer with a citrus, herb, sherbet and resin aroma. Drying with a spicy bitter palate.

Old

See Meantime

Old Bear SIBA

See Bridgehouse

Old Bog

🯄 Masons Arms, 2 Quarry School Place, Oxford, OX3 8LH
☎ (01865) 764579 ✉ theoldbog@hotmail.co.uk

Established in 2005 on a one-barrel plant behind the Masons Arms, brewing only takes place at weekends. The beers, when available, are sold at the pub (generally at weekends) and occasionally at local beer festivals. A number of one-off brews appear throughout the year. ◆

Quarry Gold (OG 1041, ABV 4.1%)
Clean-tasting golden bitter with well-balanced sweet and bitter characteristics.

Half Wit (ABV 4.5%)
A malty, dark amber wheat beer.

Quarry Goldish (ABV 4.6%)
Golden ale with mild fruit notes and a sweet finish.

Wheat Beer (ABV 5%)
Pale gold-coloured ale with a light citrus hoppiness.

Monstrous Mild (ABV 5.6%)
Strong, smooth, dark mild with fruity and malty tastes.

Old Cross

▤ Old Cross Tavern, 8 St Andrew Street, Hertford, SG14 1JA
☎ (01992) 583133

⊗ The microbrewery was set up in 2008 and is located within the pub. Owner Nigel Beviss brews solely for the Old Cross Tavern. There are two regularly available beers plus special single-hop brewed ales, with one always available at the bar.

Laugh and Titter (OG 1037, ABV 3.7%)

Gertcha! (OG 1039, ABV 3.9%)

Old Dairy SIBA ◉

Units 2 & 3, Tenterden Station Estate, Station Road, Tenterden, Kent, TN30 6HE
☎ (01580) 763867 ⊕ olddairybrewery.com

Old Dairy was founded in 2009. It relocated from Rolvenden in 2014 to larger premises near the Kent & East Sussex Railway in Tenterden in order to increase brewing capacity. There is a brewery shop offering discounts to CAMRA members along with a loyalty card scheme. ‼ ⬛ ◆ RAIB

Red Top (OG 1038, ABV 3.8%) ◥
A sweetish copper-coloured bitter with hints of caramel and a subtle hop character.

AK 1911 (OG 1041, ABV 4.1%)

Copper Top (OG 1041, ABV 4.1%)
Dark, full-flavoured best bitter.

Gold Top (OG 1043, ABV 4.3%) ◥
A well-balanced golden ale with a good blend of malt and hops followed by a long, bittersweet finish.

Silver Top (OG 1046, ABV 4.5%) ◥
A well-crafted complex stout with a good balance of dark malts, roast barley and caramel, and a long finish.

Blue Top (OG 1048, ABV 4.8%) ◥
Rich and full-bodied, this pale brown ale has a long bittersweet finish and a hint of aroma hop.

Old Forge

▤ Radnor Arms, 32 Coleshill, Coleshill, Oxfordshire, SN6 7PR
☎ (01793) 873915 ☎ 07771 613556
⊕ oldforgebrewery.co.uk

⊗ Old Forge began brewing in a converted outbuilding at the Radnor Arms in 2010 using a four-barrel plant. Brewing ceased for a few months but started again in 2015 with Andy Meeson (from Old Bog) as head brewer. Brewing takes place at weekends. The core range and some Old Bog and Halfpenny beers are produced. ‼ ◆ RAIB

Anvil Ale (OG 1037, ABV 3.8%)
Light, amber-coloured session ale with traditional bitterness.

Blacksmiths Gold (OG 1042, ABV 4%)
Refreshing straw-coloured ale with citrus notes and a hoppy floral finish.

Hammer & Tongs (OG 1043, ABV 4.2%)
Ruby in colour, bitter yet mellow in taste.

Sledgehammer (OG 1048, ABV 5%)
Deep red, full-bodied premium ale with hints of chocolate and caramel.

Old Inn Brewery

▤ Old Inn, Flowerdale Glen, Gairloch, IV21 2BD
☎ (01445) 712006 ⊕ theoldinn.net

Brewing began in 2010 using a 150-litre plant. ◆

Erradale IPA (OG 1041, ABV 4.2%)

Blind Piper (OG 1046, ABV 4.6%)

Old Laxey

▤ Shore Hotel Brew Pub, Old Laxey, Isle of Man, IM4 7DA
☎ (01624) 863214 ✉ shore@manx.net

Beer brewed on the Isle of Man is brewed to a strict Beer Purity Act. Additives are not permitted to extend shelf life, nor are chemicals allowed to assist with head retention. Old Laxey's beer is sold mostly through the adjacent Shore Hotel. ‼

Bosun Bitter (OG 1038, ABV 3.8%)
Crisp and fresh with a hoppy aftertaste.

Old Luxters

Chiltern Valley Vineyard, Hambledon, Henley-on-Thames, RG9 6JW
☎ (01491) 638330 ⊕ chilternvalley.co.uk

Situated in a 17th-century barn beside the Chiltern Valley Vineyard. Old Luxters is a traditional brewery established in 1990 and was awarded a Royal Warrant of Appointment in 2007. The core range is bottle-conditioned beers. ‼ ⬛ ◆ RAIB

Old Market (NEW)

Old Market Hall, Palace Street, Caernarfon, LL55 1RR

Situated in a 19th-century former market hall building, close to Caernarvon Castle. The beer is usually available in the Old Market Hall bar, but may also be found in other local outlets.

A55 (OG 1042, ABV 4.2%)

Old Mill SIBA

Mill Street, Snaith, East Yorkshire, DN14 9HU
☎ (01405) 861813 ⊕ oldmillbrewery.co.uk

Opened in 1983 in a 200-year-old former malt kiln and corn mill, the brew-length is 60 barrels. The brewery is building a tied estate, now standing at 19 houses. Beers can be found nationwide through wholesalers and around 80 free trade outlets are supplied direct. ‼ ◆

Traditional Mild (OG 1034, ABV 3.4%) ◥
A satisfying roast malt flavour dominates this easy-drinking, quality dark mild.

Traditional Bitter (OG 1038.5, ABV 3.8%) ◥
A malty nose is carried through to the initial flavour. Bitterness runs throughout.

Blonde Bombshell (OG 1042, ABV 4%)
An easy-drinking, straw-coloured beer with delicate and refreshing fruity flavours.

Red Goose (OG 1042, ABV 4.2%)
A rich, ruby-coloured, malty beer.

Old Curiosity (OG 1044.5, ABV 4.5%) ◥
Slightly sweet amber brew, malty to start with. Malt flavours all the way through.

Bullion (OG 1047.5, ABV 4.7%) ◥

The malty and hoppy aroma is followed by a neat mix of hop and fruit tastes within an enveloping maltiness. Dark brown/amber in colour.

Old Pie Factory SIBA 👁

Montague Road, Warwick, CV34 5LW
☎ (01926) 402100 ⊕ oldpiefactorybrewery.co.uk

Old Pie Factory began brewing in 2011 using a 5.5-barrel plant. The brewery is located at Underwood Wines and is a joint venture between Underwood Wines, the Old Fourpenny Shop Hotel in Warwick and the Case is Altered in Five Ways.

Bitter (OG 1038.5, ABV 3.9%)
Classic English session bitter with only English ingredients.

Pale (OG 1040, ABV 4.1%)
Light and refreshing straw-coloured ale with pleasing hoppy notes.

Old Sawley SIBA

⊟ White Lion, 352 Tamworth Road, Sawley, Derbyshire, NG10 3AT ☎ 07722 311209

Office: 22 Park Street, Long Eaton, Derbyshire, NG10 4AN
✉ oldsawleybrewingcompany@gmail.com

Old Sawley Brewing Company was established in 2013. Brewing takes place on a half-barrel plant upstairs at the White Lion pub in Sawley, but a 10-barrel brew plant at the rear of the pub is expected to be in operation during 2016. The brewery supplies Midland beer festivals and two local pubs. ◆

Tollbridge Porter (OG 1049, ABV 4.5%)

Old School SIBA

Holly Bank Barn, Crag Road, Warton, Lancashire, LA5 9PL
☎ (01524) 740888 ☎ 07515 376700
⊕ oldschoolbrewery.co.uk

A 12-barrel brewery, founded in 2012, located in a renovated 400-year-old former school outbuilding overlooking the picturesque village of Warton. Beer is mainly sold to free houses within a 40-mile radius. Regular open nights are held: see website. Five-litre mini casks are available direct from the brewery. ‼⊠◆

Hopscotch (OG 1037, ABV 3.7%) 🍺
Initially hoppy, astringency builds in this satisfying beer, ending with a bitter finish.

Textbook (OG 1039, ABV 3.9%)

Detention (OG 1041, ABV 4.1%) 🍺
Light, malty bitter, sweetish middle with a gentle finish.

Headmaster (OG 1045, ABV 4.5%)
A dark, strong best bitter. It mixes a complex malty flavour with a blackcurrant aroma, leaving a subtle sweet nutty aftertaste.

Old Spot

Manor Farm, Station Road, Cullingworth, Bradford, West Yorkshire, BD13 5HN
☎ (01535) 691144 ⊕ oldspotbrewery.co.uk

Old Spot, named after the owner's sheepdog, started brewing in 2005. The beers are available locally, with the George Hotel, Cullingworth, being the main outlet and de facto brewery tap. ‼◆

Light But Dark (OG 1043, ABV 4%)
Chestnut-coloured bitter with a slight malty taste and pleasant bitter finish. An ideal session beer.

Spot Light (OG 1040, ABV 4.2%) 🍺
This smooth-drinking golden ale has a slightly fruity, hoppy aroma leading to a well-balanced fruit, hop flavour with hints of pineapple and a long bittersweet finish.

Inn-Spired (OG 1043, ABV 4.3%)
Light-coloured bitter with a light, hoppy taste and a slight, fruity finish.

OSB (OG 1042, ABV 4.5%)
A golden-coloured, full-bodied bitter.

Spot O'Bother (OG 1060, ABV 5.5%)
Porter with a chocolate ice cream taste and slight liquorice bitterness to finish. A complex brew.

Old Tree (NEW)

SILO Restaurant, 39 Upper Gardener Street, Brighton, BN1 4AN ☎ 07413 064346 ⊕ oldtreebrewery.com

Old Tree Brewery, part of the Old Tree Co-operative, is based in the zero-waste Silo restaurant in Brighton. As brewers, makers and gardeners the group has envisioned a production process for drinks making that contributes to land regeneration, to reverse its depletion. Old Tree produces an IPA in addition to a spiced plum cider, elderberry bubbly and soft drinks.

Old Worthy (NEW) SIBA

Office: 24a Ainslie Place, Edinburgh, EH3 6AJ ☎ 07955 113083 ⊕ oldworthybeer.co.uk

Brewing takes place on a 10-barrel plant. The beers are designed to be drunk as a 'half 'n' half', a beer served with a dram of whisky on the side. The malt used is sourced from Scottish whisky distilleries. 200 outlets are supplied.

Wild Bill's Aces Eights (OG 1050, ABV 5%)
Salted chocolate stout.

Worthy Cause (OG 1050, ABV 5%)

Cure for Scurvy (OG 1050, ABV 5.5%)
A whisky-infused marmalade pale ale.

Midnight Caper (ABV 5.5%)
A smoked amber ale.

De'ils Awa' (ABV 6.5%)
Red IPA.

Lost in the Dark (OG 1050, ABV 7.6%)
Barrel-aged Scottish pale ale.

Old Cannon 👁

⊟ 86 Cannon Street, Bury St Edmunds, Suffolk, IP33 1JR
☎ (01284) 768769 ⊕ oldcannonbrewery.co.uk

⊠ The St Edmunds Head pub opened in 1845 with its own brewery. Brewing ceased in 1917, and Greene King closed the pub in 1995. It re-opened in 1999 as the Old Cannon Brewery complete with a unique state-of-the-art brewery housed in the bar area. A growing number of local outlets are supplied. ‼◆

Best Bitter (OG 1037, ABV 3.8%) ◆
Traditional East Anglian bitter. Rich hoppy aroma and bitterness dominate throughout with just a hint of sweetness in the aftertaste.

Hornblower (OG 1038, ABV 4%)
Light in colour with an IPA hoppiness.

Gunner's Daughter (OG 1052, ABV 5.5%) ◆
A well-balanced strong ale with a complexity of hop, fruit, sweetness and bitterness in the flavour, and a lingering hoppy, bitter aftertaste.

Olde Potting Shed

Collingdon Buildings, Collingdon Road, High Spen, Tyne & Wear, NE39 2EQ
☎ (01207) 545577

Brewing began in 2013 using a five-barrel plant.

Midas Touch (ABV 3.9%)

Swannee River (ABV 4.5%)

Hero (ABV 5%)

Olde Swan

▤ 89 Halesowen Road, Netherton, Dudley, West Midlands, DY2 9PY
☎ (01384) 253075

☺ A famous brewpub best known as Ma Pardoe's after the matriarch who ruled it for years. The pub has been licensed since 1835 and the present brewery and pub were built in 1863. Brewing continued until 1988 and restarted in 2001. ‼◆

Original (OG 1034, ABV 3.5%) ◆
Straw-coloured light mild, smooth but tangy, and sweetly refreshing with a faint hoppiness.

Dark Swan (OG 1041, ABV 4.2%) ◆
Smooth, sweet dark mild with late roast malt in the finish.

Entire (OG 1044, ABV 4.4%) ◆
Faintly hoppy, amber premium bitter with sweetness persistent throughout.

NPA (Netherton Pale Ale) (OG 1048, ABV 4.8%)
First brewed as a one-off celebratory drink in mid-2014, this is a pale and hoppy ale.

Bumble Hole Bitter (OG 1052, ABV 5.2%) ◆
Sweet, smooth amber ale with hints of astringency in the finish.

Old Chimneys

Hopton End Farm, Church Road, Market Weston, Diss, Suffolk, IP22 2NX
☎ (01359) 221411/221013
⊕ oldchimneysbrewery.com

Old Chimneys opened in 1995, moving to a converted farm building in 2001. Most of the beers are named after rare species found nearby.
‼ ▤ ◆ RAIB

Military Mild (OG 1035, ABV 3.3%) ◆
A rich, dark mild with good body for its gravity. Sweetish toffee and light roast bitterness dominate, leading to a dry aftertaste.

Great Raft Bitter (OG 1040, ABV 4%)
Pale copper-coloured bitter bursting with fruit. Malt and hops add to the sweetish fruity flavour, which

is rounded off with hoppy bitterness in the aftertaste.

Black Rat Stout (OG 1048, ABV 4.4%)
Roast malt and coffee flavours with body and sweetness from added lactose.

Golden Pheasant (OG 1044, ABV 4.5%)
Pale, dry bitter with citrus, apple and malt balanced with robust hop bitterness.

Arrowhead (OG 1047, ABV 4.8%)
A premium dark, ruby ale with smooth, malty tones.

Oldershaw SIBA ⊚

Heath Lane, Barkston Heath, Grantham, Lincolnshire, NG32 2DE
☎ (01476) 572135 ⊕ oldershawbrewery.com

⊗ Oldershaw Brewery has been brewing since 1997. Owned and run by brewster Kathy Britton, it is a nine-barrel plant and brews in the region of 300,000 pints a year. The brewery produces around 25 different beers of varying styles. ‼ ▤ ◆

Barkston Bitter (OG 1036, ABV 3.6%)
A mellow amber session bitter, softly spiced citrus and a smooth malt base.

Mowbray's Mash (OG 1037, ABV 3.7%)
A gold-tinted amber ale with a zesty character. The hops add a fruity edge to a softly nutty base.

Heavenly Blonde (OG 1038, ABV 3.8%)
Best-selling pale blonde session beer, packed with refreshing tropical fruits with a crisp dry finish.

Newton's Drop (OG 1041, ABV 4.1%) ◆
Balanced malt and hops but with a strong bitter, lingering taste in this mid-brown beer.

Caskade (OG 1042, ABV 4.2%) ◆
A gentle blend of flavours combine into a smooth, undemanding pint. Malt vies with a hoppy bitterness for initial recognition. Traces of caramel and sulphur appear before the short, sharp finish.

Great Expectations (OG 1040, ABV 4.2%)
A pale gold beer incorporating citrus-rich Galaxy and Cascade hops.

Grantham Stout (OG 1043, ABV 4.3%)
Dark brown and smooth with a rich roast malt flavour, warming fruity, complex flavours. A long, moderately dry finish.

Mosaic Blonde (OG 1041, ABV 4.3%)
Satisfying lager-style beer featuring three hop varieties. Powerfully citrus and tropical.

Posh Blonde (OG 1041, ABV 4.3%)
Crisp lager-style beer, enhanced by fruity, floral and citrus-infused notes.

Regal Blonde (OG 1042, ABV 4.4%) ◆
Straw-coloured, lager-style beer with a good malt/hop balance throughout; strong bitterness on the taste lingers.

Old Boy (OG 1047, ABV 4.8%) ◆
A full-bodied amber ale, fruity and bitter with a hop/fruit aroma. The malt that backs the taste dies in the long finish.

Blonde Volupta (OG 1050, ABV 5%)
Straw-coloured zesty premium beer packed with complexity and intense tropical fruit flavours leading to a crisp dry finish.

Alchemy (OG 1052, ABV 5.3%)

A premium golden bitter, easy-drinking and well-balanced with tropical citrus notes and subtle French toast malts.

On the Edge

Nether Edge, Sheffield, South Yorkshire ☎ 07975 989654 ✉ ontheedgebrew@gmail.com

On the Edge started brewing commercially in 2012 using a 0.5-barrel plant in the brewer's home. Brewing takes place once a week. Three local pubs are supplied as well as beer festivals. There is no regular beer list as new brews are constantly being tried.

One Mile End

⚑ **White Hart Brew Pub, 1-3 Mile End Road, London, E1 4TP**
☎ (020) 7790 2894 ☎ 07912 411147
⊕ the-white-hart.co.uk/microbrewery

⊠ Previously known as Mulligans, Simon McCabe took over as head brewer in 2014 and relaunched the brewery as One Mile End Brew Co. Capacity is 2,500 litres per week. The beers are available at the White Hart and its sister pub, the Alma, in Pentonville. ◆ RAIB

Temperance (ABV 3.5%)
A light ale with pine and fruits of the forest hop aromas, and a hint of caramel.

Salvation Pale Ale (ABV 4.4%)
A pale ale with grapefruit and orange aromas, balanced bitterness and a slightly sweet finish.

Hospital Porter (ABV 5.2%)
A London brown porter with rye adding a savouriness to the roasted malt flavour.

Snakecharmer IPA (ABV 5.7%)
A full-bodied, fruity IPA with an intense aroma of sweet lemon, blueberries and tropical fruits, and a slight caramel finish.

Ancho Cocoa Stout (ABV 6.4%)
Chilli chocolate stout.

Opa Hay's

Glencot, Wood Lane, Aldeby, Norfolk, NR34 0DA
☎ (01502) 679144 ☎ 07916 282729
⊕ engelfineales.com

Opa Hay's began brewing in late 2008. It is a small, family-run microbrewery, taking its name from the brewer's great grandfather. Only traditional brewing methods are used, with ingredients that are, where possible, sourced locally. ◆ RAIB

Engels Fruity Little Number (ABV 3.6%) ◀
Powerful citrus/grapefruit aroma with malt and hops. Smoky sweetish flavours with fruit notes, and a fruity, hoppy aftertaste.

Engel's Best Bitter (ABV 4%)
A triple-hopped aromatic beer, an old-fashioned traditional English ale.

Matilda's Revenge (ABV 4.3%)
Golden ale originally brewed to commemorate the resident ghost that haunts the Kings's Head Hotel.

Samuel Engels Meister Pils (SEMP) (ABV 4.8%)
A Pilsner-style beer, light in colour with a hoppy aroma.

Liquid Bread (ABV 5.2%)

Bavarian-style wheat beer, naturally cloudy, with a distinct aroma of cloves and banana.

Orbit (NEW) SIBA

Arches 225 & 228, Fielding Street, Walworth, London, SE17 3HD
☎ (020) 7703 9092 ☎ 07885 663842
⊕ orbitbeers.com

Brewing began in 2014 on a 10-barrel kit. European-style bottle-conditioned and keg beers are produced with three core beers and quarterly seasonals making up the range. RAIB

Orkney ◉

Quoyloo, Stromness, Orkney, KW16 3LT
☎ (01667) 404555 ☎ 07721 013227

Office: Sinclair Breweries Ltd, Cawdor, IV12 5XP
⊕ sinclairbreweries.co.uk

☺ Orkney was established in 1988 in an old village school building. Having incorporated sister brewery Atlas (qv), it moved next door in 2010 to enable an increase in capacity and the completion of an award-winning visitor centre in 2012. ‼ ☛ ◆

Raven (OG 1038, ABV 3.8%) ◀
A well-balanced quaffable bitter. Malty fruitiness and bitter hops last through to the long, dry aftertaste.

Dragonhead (OG 1040, ABV 4%) ◀
A strong, dark malt aroma flows into the taste in this superb Scottish stout. The roast malt continues to dominate the aftertaste, and blends with chocolate to develop a strong, dry finish.

Northern Light (OG 1040, ABV 4%) ◀
A well-balanced golden ale with a real smack of fruit and hops in the taste and an increasing bitter aftertaste.

Red MacGregor (OG 1040, ABV 4%) ◀
This tawny red ale has a powerful smack of fruit and a clean, fresh mouthfeel. Generally a well-balanced bitter.

Corncrake (OG 1042, ABV 4.1%) ◀
A straw-coloured beer with soft citrus fruits and a floral aroma.

Dark Island (OG 1045, ABV 4.6%) ◀
The roast malt and chocolate character varies, making the beer hard to categorise as a stout or an old ale. A sweetish roast malt taste leads to a long-lasting roasted, slightly bitter, dry finish.

Skull Splitter (OG 1080, ABV 8.5%) 🍴 ◀
An intense velvet malt nose with hints of apple, prune and plum. The hoppy taste is balanced by satiny smooth malt with fruity spicy edges, leading to a long, dry finish with a hint of nut.

For Atlas Brewery:

Wayfarer (OG 1044, ABV 4.4%) ◀
Full of citrus fruits and hops.

Golden Amber (OG 1045, ABV 4.5%) ◀
Refreshing hops, honey, marmalade and grapefruit to the fore with a dry, hoppy finish.

Blizzard (OG 1047, ABV 4.7%) ◀
Light on malts and hops with ginger and spices coming through.

Ossett SIBA 👁

Kings Yard, Low Mill Road, Ossett, WF5 8ND
☎ (01924) 261333 ⊕ ossett-brewery.co.uk

☺ Ossett began brewing in 1998, moving to a new site in 2005. An extra 40-barrel fermenter was added in 2014, increasing total brewing capacity to 280 barrels a week. The brewery owns 23 pubs, five of which are 'Hop'-branded bars – larger city centre venues with real ale and live music – in Wakefield, Leeds, Sheffield, York and Saltaire. ‼ 🍽 ◆

Pale Gold (OG 1038, ABV 3.8%)
A light, refreshing pale ale with a light, hoppy aroma.

Big Red Bitter (OG 1042, ABV 4%)
Deep red, malty Yorkshire bitter.

Inception (OG 1043, ABV 4%)
A deep golden, full-bodied ale, moderately bitter but with a powerful hop aroma.

Silver King (OG 1041, ABV 4.3%)
A lager-style beer with a crisp, dry flavour and citrus fruity aroma.

Treacle Stout (OG 1050, ABV 5%)
A rich and robust stout. The addition of black treacle gives intense depth and roasted malts impart a coffee flavour. Generous amounts of hops add a dry citrus finish to this complex black ale.

Excelsior (OG 1051, ABV 5.2%)
A strong pale ale with a full, mellow flavour and a fresh, hoppy aroma with citrus/floral characteristics.

Otherton (NEW)

c/o Offbeat Brewery, Unit 6, Thomas Street, Crewe, Cheshire, CW1 2BD ☎ 07921 717154

Office: Corner Cottage, Boscomoor Lane, Penkridge, ST19 5NU ⊕ othertonales.co.uk

Otherton Ales started life in Penkridge, Staffordshire, on the edge of Cannock Chase, with the forest and its resident deer population inspiring what is now the brewery logo. Since 2014 production has moved to spare capacity at Offbeat Brewery, Crewe.

Otley SIBA 👁

Unit 39, Albion Industrial Estate, Pontypridd, Mid Glamorgan, CF37 4NX
☎ (01443) 480555 ⊕ otleybrewing.co.uk

☺ Otley Brewing was established in 2005 and since then the brewery has almost tripled in size, taking over adjacent industrial units. There is now an on-site shop. The beers are supplied to many outlets across South Wales and in the London area. ‼ 🍽 ◆ RAIB

01 (OG 1038, ABV 4%) 🍺 🌢
A pale golden beer with a hoppy aroma. The taste has hops, malt, fruit and a thirst-quenching bitterness. A satisfying finish completes this beer.

02 Croeso (OG 1040, ABV 4%)
Light golden ale full of citrus hop aromas.

04 Colombo (OG 1038, ABV 4%)
A golden, hoppy beer.

03 Boss (OG 1042, ABV 4.4%)

Chestnut red bitter using American hops for bitterness and aroma.

12 Thai Bo (OG 1045, ABV 4.6%)
Clear wheat beer with lemongrass, lime leaf and galangal.

05 Hop Angeles (OG 1047, ABV 4.8%)
An American-style red ale.

09 Blonde (OG 1047, ABV 4.8%)
Clear wheat beer flavoured with roasted orange peel, corriander and cloves.

07 Weissen (OG 1048, ABV 5%)
Cloudy, German-style wheat beer.

10 Oxymoron (OG 1047, ABV 5.5%)
A black IPA-style bitter.

06 Porter (OG 1063, ABV 6.6%)

11 Motley Brew (OG 1072, ABV 7.5%)
Double IPA with big hop aromas and high bitterness, giving a classic IPA mouthfeel.

Otter SIBA 👁

Mathayes, Luppitt, Honiton, Devon, EX14 4SA
☎ (01404) 891285 ⊕ otterbrewery.com

⊠ Otter Brewery is a family-run brewery set high up in the Blackdown Hills. Environmental responsibility lies at the heart of the brewery's ethos. Otter's eco cellar has been built underground and is naturally chilled. The beers are made from the brewery's own springs and locally sourced ingredients. ‼ ◆

Bitter (OG 1036, ABV 3.6%) 🍺 🍢 🌢
Well-balanced, amber session bitter with a fruity nose and bitter taste and aftertaste.

Amber (OG 1038.5, ABV 4%) 🍺
A well-balanced bitter with hints of tropical fruit and spice – sometimes with an impression of ginger.

Bright (OG 1039, ABV 4.3%) 🌢
Pale yellow/golden ale with a strong fruit aroma, sweet fruity taste and a bittersweet finish.

Ale (OG 1043, ABV 4.5%) 🌢
A full-bodied best bitter. A malty aroma predominates with a fruity taste and finish.

Head (OG 1054, ABV 5.8%)
Fruity aroma and taste with a pleasant bitter finish. Dark brown and full-bodied.

Ouseburn Valley

11 Dilston Terrace, Gosforth, Tyne & Wear, NE3 1XX
☎ 07932 677899 ⊕ ouseburnvalleybrewery.co.uk

Ouseburn Valley started in the owner's garage in 2010, and in 2011 the plant was moved to the cellar of the Brandling Villa pub where both capacity and beer range were increased. After a flood in 2012, brewing is back in the owner's garage. ◆

Armstrong Bitter (OG 1042, ABV 4.1%)
Pleasant rich yellow colour, light spicy aroma with soft caramel overtones and a long bitter finish.

Golden Ale (OG 1044, ABV 4.4%)
Dark gold in colour with light hop aroma, sweet malty taste with a smooth finish.

India Pale Ale (OG 1047, ABV 4.7%)

Pale gold in colour with a strong hop aroma and a long dry finish.

Milk Stout (OG 1047, ABV 4.7%)
Traditionally dark in colour with a liquorice aroma, sweet liquorice and slightly coffee taste.

American Honey (OG 1049, ABV 5%)
Rich dark gold in colour with sweet honey taste and strong dry hop aroma.

Out There SIBA

Unit 4, Foundry Lane Industrial Estate, Newcastle upon Tyne, NE6 1LH ☎ 07946 579 534
⊕ outtherebrewing.com

Out There was established in 2012 by Steve Pickthall. Branding and beer names are themed around the 1950s space race.

Space is the Place (OG 1034, ABV 3.5%)
An amber-coloured table beer with a cream head. The aroma is digestive biscuits and brown bread with a sweet malt flavour and floral notes.

Laika (OG 1049, ABV 4.8%)
A straw-coloured cloudy beer. The aroma is citrus with a hint of custard cream biscuits and the flavour of orange peel and spices liven the pale malt base.

Celestial Love (OG 1051, ABV 5.1%)
A rich red beer. The aroma is caramel with a hint of malt loaf and the taste is sweet malt with floral and grapefruit hop flavours.

Outlaw

See Rooster's

Outstanding SIBA ◉

Britannia Mill, Cobden Street, Bury, Lancashire, BL9 6AW
☎ (0161) 764 7723 ⊕ outstandingbeers.com

Born of an aspiration to create outstanding beers and established in 2008, the brewery operates a dual system, brewing on a 15-barrel plant and using a 2.5-barrel plant for special and experimental brews. Selective free trade accounts are supplied nationally. ◆

3.9 (OG 1036, ABV 3.9%)
Pale, light and hoppy.

UltraPale (OG 1041, ABV 4.1%)
Aromatic golden ale. Not too bitter.

Red (OG 1045, ABV 4.4%)
Copper-coloured, mellow, biscuity.

Blond (OG 1044, ABV 4.5%)
Pale, citrus and refreshing.

IPA (OG 1058, ABV 5.5%)
Golden, dry and bitter.

Stout (OG 1061, ABV 5.5%)
Jet black and roasty with liquorice notes.

Imperial IPA (OG 1065, ABV 7.4%)
Golden and strong.

Oxfordshire Ales ◉

12 Pear Tree Farm Industrial Units, Bicester Road, Marsh Gibbon, Bicester, Buckinghamshire, OX27 0GB
☎ (01869) 278765 ⊕ oxfordshireales.co.uk

The company first brewed in 2005 and now supplies over 100 outlets as well as several wholesalers from its 15-barrel plant. There is a bottling line onsite. The Baby Ox Brewery produces interesting one-off ales. ‼◆

Triple B (OG 1037, ABV 3.7%) ◆
This pale amber beer has a huge caramel aroma. The caramel diminishes in the initial taste, which changes to a fruit/bitter balance. This in turn leads to a long, refreshing, bitter aftertaste.

Oxford Best (OG 1039, ABV 3.9%)
A multi-hopped, chestnut-coloured traditional bitter with a caramel finish.

Blenheim (OG 1042, ABV 4.2%)
A refreshing golden ale with a fresh, zesty, spicy hop aroma, biscuity malt taste and pleasant dry finish.

Pride of Oxford (OG 1042, ABV 4.2%) ◆
An amber beer, the aroma is butterscotch/caramel, which carries on into the initial taste. The taste then becomes bitter with sweetish/malty overtones. There is a long, dry, bitter finish.

Marshmellow (OG 1047, ABV 4.7%) ◆
The slightly fruity aroma in this golden-amber beer leads to a hoppy but thin taste, with slight caramel notes. The aftertaste is short and bitter.

Padstow SIBA

The Brewery, Unit 4a, Trecerus Industrial Estate, Padstow, Cornwall, PL28 8RW
☎ (01841) 532169 ☎ 07834 924312
⊕ padstowbrewing.co.uk

⊗ The brewery started commercially in 2013 using a 0.5-barrel plant. Owners Des and Caron Archer, Caron being the brewster, have since installed a custom-built 10-barrel plant. Beer festivals and local outlets are supplied. ‼⌖RAIB

Pale Ale (OG 1037, ABV 3.6%) ◆
Golden beer with assertive hop aroma. Citrus hops dominate the taste with bitterness and dryness. Hoppy, refreshing and crisp finish.

Pilot (OG 1040, ABV 4%) ◆
Tawny-coloured best bitter with malt aroma. Biscuit malt dominates the taste with apple fruit and liquorice notes. Malty, bitter finish.

Windjammer (OG 1042, ABV 4.3%)

Stormrunner (OG 1042, ABV 4.4%)

Pride (OG 1044, ABV 4.5%)
Amber-coloured best bitter with a touch of honey.

IPA (OG 1046, ABV 4.8%) ◆
Amber-coloured strong bitter. Fully hopped on nose and taste with orange bitterness. Sweet finish with citrus hops and faintly dry.

Padstow May Day (OG 1048, ABV 5%) ◆
Yellow-coloured golden ale with powerful citrus hop aroma and flavour. Grapefruit and moderate bitterness. Strong grassy hop finish with dryness.

Sundowner (OG 1060, ABV 6.8%)

Palmers SIBA IFBB ◉

The Old Brewery, West Bay Road, Bridport, Dorset, DT6 4JA
☎ (01308) 422396 ⊕ palmersbrewery.com

Palmers is Britain's only thatched brewery and dates from 1794. It is situated in Bridport, the heart of the Jurassic Coast in south-west Dorset. The company continues to make substantial investment in its 54 tenanted pubs, all serving cask ale. An additional 400 outlets are supplied to the free trade.

Copper Ale (OG 1036, ABV 3.7%)
Beautifully balanced, copper-coloured light bitter with a hoppy aroma.

Best Bitter (OG 1040, ABV 4.2%)
Hop aroma and bitterness stay in the background in this predominately malty best bitter, with some fruit on the aroma.

Dorset Gold (OG 1046, ABV 4.5%)
More complex than many golden ales thanks to a pleasant banana and mango fruitiness on the aroma that carries on into the taste and aftertaste.

200 (OG 1052, ABV 5%)
This is a big beer with a touch of caramel sweetness adding to a complex hoppy, fruit taste that lasts from the aroma well into the aftertaste.

Tally Ho! (OG 1057, ABV 5.5%)
A complex dark old ale. Roast malts and treacle toffee on the palate lead in to a long, lingering finish with more than a hint of coffee.

Panther

Unit 1, Collers Way, Reepham, Norfolk, NR10 4SW
☎ 07766 558215 pantherbrewery.co.uk

Panther began brewing in 2010 on an industrial estate near the old railway station, formerly the home of Reepham Brewery. Beer and other merchandise can be purchased direct from the brewery or online from the brewery website. ♦ RAIB

Mild Panther (OG 1035, ABV 3.3%)
A smooth malty character and notes of chocolate which gives this beer plenty of flavour and aroma.

Ginger Panther (OG 1037, ABV 3.7%)
Refreshingly clean ginger wheat beer with a distinct fiery kick.

Golden Panther (OG 1039, ABV 3.7%)
A golden-coloured ale with a citrus flavour and floral aroma. A light and refreshing ale with bite.

Pink Panther (OG 1039, ABV 3.8%)
A pink, fruity wheat beer, refreshingly balanced with a bittersweet fruity finish.

Honey Panther (OG 1044, ABV 4%)
A gentle flowing brew with honey and malt throughout. Malt, caramel and hop. Amber-coloured with a tapering bittersweet finale.

Red Panther (OG 1041, ABV 4.1%)
Full-flavoured brew. Solidly malty in both aroma and taste. Hops, and a residual sweetness, provide balance.

Black Panther (OG 1050, ABV 4.5%)
This dark ale is full flavoured, smooth and complex. It has a bittersweet balance that leads to a dry finish.

Beast of the East (OG 1052, ABV 5.5%)
An amber-coloured IPA, refreshing, with floral and grapefruit notes from New Zealand hops.

Paradigm (NEW)

4d Green End Farm, 93a Church Lane, Sarratt, WD3 6HH
☎ (01923) 291215 paradigmbrewery.com

Founded by two friends, Neil Hodges and Rob Atkinson, Paradigm went into production in 2015. Their five-barrel plant is located in an industrial unit on a farm. One-off beers are also brewed. ♦

Low Hanging Fruit (OG 1036, ABV 3.7%)
A refreshing pale ale with citrus flavours of tangerine and grapefruit.

Win-Win (OG 1044, ABV 4.2%)
A best bitter made with five malts and a blend of Kent and US hops.

Paradise

Bird in Hand, Trelissick Road, Hayle, Cornwall, TR27 4HY
☎ (01736) 753974
birdinhand@paradisepark.org.uk

Brewing first started in 1981 under the name Paradise Brewery, named after its location, the Paradise Bird Park. The name was changed to Wheal Ale in 1995. Brewing ceased in 2004 but re-started in 2009 under the original Paradise Brewery name. ♦

Paradise Bitter (OG 1043, ABV 4.3%)
Copper-coloured best bitter with malty and fruity aroma. Malty and sweet body, heavy fruity flavour with toffee. Apple finish.

Oscars Alchemy (OG 1048, ABV 4.8%)
Light ale with Fuggles and Cascade hops, Maris Otter malt and some gorse flowers.

Artist (OG 1055, ABV 5.2%)
Full-bodied tawny ale with faint aroma of malt. Heavy sweet malt and bubblegum esters in the mouth with a balance of hops. Dryness and bitterness in the finish.

Parish

6 Main Street, Burrough on the Hill, LE14 2JQ
☎ (01664) 454801 ☎ 07715 369410
bazbrewery@gmail.com

Parish began in 1983 and now operates on a 20-barrel plant, with capacity to brew a further 12 barrels. The brewery is located in a 400-year-old building next to Grants Freehouse, which stocks the full range of beers. Other local outlets are also supplied and one-off brews are produced for beer festivals. RAIB

PSB (OG 1038, ABV 3.8%)
Hoppy session beer with malty aftertaste.

Burrough Bitter (OG 1047, ABV 4.8%)
Darker version of PSB with good balance of malt and hops. Reddish brown in colour.

Poachers Ale (ABV 6%)
Deep ruby red, full-bodied, malty blended beer. Not to be underestimated in strength.

Baz's Bonce Blower (OG 1098, ABV 12%)
Strong, dark beer with a rich, malty character. A Christmas pudding ale.

Park (NEW) SIBA ⊚

**95 Elm Road, Kingston-upon-Thames, Surrey,
KT2 6HX ☎ 07932 624395/07949 574618**

**Office: 38 St Georges Road, Kingston-upon-Thames,
Surrey, KT2 6DN ⊕ theparkbrewery.com**

⊗ The Park Brewery was founded in 2014 in a former greengrocer's premises, using a one-barrel plant. Focus is on a range of bottle-conditioned beers, named after sites in the adjacent Richmond Park, and which are available through the local off trade. Cask beer is supplied to beer festivals and local pubs. There are plans to expand to a four-barrel kit in 2015. ‼◆RAIB

Gallows Gold (ABV 5%) ◕
Hoppy golden ale with citrus notes. Bitterness comes through later in the taste and finish.

Spankers IPA (ABV 6%)

Two Storms Ruby (ABV 7.1%)

Parker

**Unit 3, Gravel Lane, Banks, Lancashire, PR9 8BY
☎ (01704) 620718 ☎ 07949 797889
⊕ theparkerbrewery.co.uk**

⊚Parker was established in 2014 using a 25-litre plant, and has since expanded to a five-barrel plant producing both cask-conditioned ales and bottled beers. ‼RAIB

Centurion Pale Ale (OG 1040, ABV 3.9%)
A light, refreshing pale ale with zesty fruit flavours and a crisp, dry and hoppy finish.

Barbarian Bitter (OG 1040, ABV 4.1%)
Golden, amber-coloured traditional ale with notes of caramel. Smooth and well-balanced, an easy-drinking ale.

Viking Blonde (OG 1042, ABV 4.5%)
A blonde ale with subtle hints of blackcurrant and summer berry fruit flavours with a refreshing, full crisp finish.

Dark Spartan Stout (OG 1052, ABV 5%)
Silky smooth beer with hints of chocolate and coffee.

Partizan SIBA

**8 Almond Road, South Bermondsey, London,
SE16 3LR
☎ (020) 8127 5053 ☎ 07708 263931
⊕ partizanbrewing.co.uk**

Partizan began brewing in 2012. Each brew is different, but they are based on a variety of international styles and all are vegan-friendly and bottled by hand on site. RAIB

Partners SIBA ⊚

**The Brew House, 589 Halifax Road, Hightown,
Liversedge, West Yorkshire, WF15 8HQ
☎ (01924) 457772 ⊕ partnersbrewery.co.uk**

Partners was formed in May 2011 following the purchase of the long-established Anglo Dutch Brewery by Richard Sharp. The brewery moved into newly renovated premises in 2015 and has invested in a new, 15-barrel, state-of-the-art brewery to meet increased demand for its beers. Partners owns three pubs, the Brew House in

Hightown, Halfway House in Morley and the Shant in Halifax. ‼◆

J.Y.B. (OG 1035, ABV 3.5%)
An easy-drinking session beer brewed with four different malts creating a complex character.

Working Class Hero (OG 1038, ABV 3.8%)
A bitter-tasting session beer with a strong, hoppy aftertaste.

Blond (OG 1039, ABV 3.9%)
A blonde, crisp, aromatic session beer. Brewed using layered malts and finished with Gem and Challenger hops.

Cascade (OG 1040, ABV 4%)
A light, refreshing beer with citrus and blackcurrant notes.

Triple Hop (OG 1042, ABV 4.2%)
A triple-hopped APA using Willamette, Cascade and Cluster hops to produce a refreshing brew with high bitterness and a hoppy aftertaste.

Ghost (OG 1043, ABV 4.5%)
A pale, full-bodied bitter with a fresh, gentle nose, taken over by a smooth hop and citrus finish.

Tabatha (OG 1054, ABV 6%) ◕
Golden-coloured Belgian-style Tripel with a strong fruity, hoppy and bitter character. Powerful and warming, slightly thinnish, with a bitter, dry finish.

Peak SIBA

**Barn Brewery, Chatsworth, Bakewell, Derbyshire,
DE45 1EX
☎ (01246) 583737 ⊕ peakales.co.uk**

⊚Peak Ales opened in 2005 in former derelict farm buildings on the Chatsworth estate aided by a DEFRA Rural Enterprise Scheme grant and support from trustees of Chatsworth Settlement. Main beer production moved to a new facility at Ashford in the Water in 2014 to increase capacity. Beers are available throughout the Peak District and beyond. ‼◆

Swift Nick (OG 1038, ABV 3.8%) ◕
Easy-drinking, copper-coloured bitter with balanced malt and hops and a gentle, hoppy, bitter finish.

Bakewell Best Bitter (OG 1041, ABV 4.2%) ◕
Full-bodied tawny bitter with a hoppy bitterness against a malty background, leading to a hoppy, dry aftertaste.

Chatsworth Gold (OG 1045, ABV 4.6%) ⬚ ◕
Speciality beer made with honey, which gives a pleasant sweetness leading to a hop and malt finish.

Peakstones Rock SIBA ⊚

**Peakstones Farm, Cheadle Road, Alton, Staffordshire,
ST10 4DH ☎ 07891 350908 ⊕ peakstonesrock.co.uk**

⊗ Peakstones Rock was established in 2005 with a five-barrel brewery located on a farm in the Peak District Park. The plant was expanded to 10-barrel capacity in 2009. The brewery supplies an expanding free trade market in the North Midlands and surrounding areas. ‼◆RAIB

Nemesis (OG 1042, ABV 3.8%) ◕
Biscuity aroma with some hop background. Sweet start, sweetish body, then hops emerge to give a

fruity middle. Bitterness develops slowly to a tongue-tingling finish.

Pugin's Gold (OG 1043, ABV 4%)
A light golden-coloured beer with a citrus bite and aroma and a dry finish.

Chained Oak (OG 1045, ABV 4.2%)
A copper-coloured beer with a smooth flavour and good aroma.

Alton Abbey (OG 1051, ABV 4.5%)
A ruby-coloured beer with a smooth, fruity flavour.

Black Hole (OG 1048, ABV 4.8%)
Grassy aroma with a malt background. Hops hit the mouth and intensify. Bitterness lingers with some mouth-watering astringency.

Oblivion (OG 1055, ABV 5.5%)
A golden-coloured beer with plenty of body and a strong flavour and aroma. Easy-drinking despite its strength.

Peerless SIBA

The Brewery, 8 Pool Street, Birkenhead, Merseyside, CH41 3NL
(0151) 647 7688 peerlessbrewing.co.uk

Peerless began brewing in 2009 and is under the directorship of Steve Briscoe. Beers are sold through festivals, local pubs and the free trade. !! ♦

Pale (OG 1036, ABV 3.8%)
Pale session ale. Good initial bitterness and a hint of grapefruit on the finish.

Jinja Ninja (OG 1040, ABV 4%)
Ginger beer made with fresh root ginger, chilli and lemon. Before tasting there is an aroma of fresh ginger followed by a kick from the ginger aftertaste.

Paxtons Peculiar (ABV 4.1%)
This copper-coloured ale is a complex array of malt, hints of chocolate and fruity citrus overtones.

Triple Blonde (OG 1040, ABV 4.1%)
A blonde beer with a fruity citrus finish.

Crystal Maze (ABV 4.4%)
A ruby ale. Good bitterness and a hint of fruit on the finish.

Viking Gold (OG 1044, ABV 4.6%)
A well-balanced golden ale with initial hop bitterness and a citrus finish. The distinct citrus fruit and hop aroma leads to a crisp, dry finish.

Oatmeal Stout (OG 1050, ABV 5%)
Full-bodied black stout with a good mouthfeel and toffee and caramel tones. An element of sweetness balances the bitterness from the roast malts.

Red Rocks (OG 1047, ABV 5%)
Well-bodied ruby ale. Rich malt flavours combine with hops for a beer with fruity overtones.

Knee-Buckler IPA (ABV 5.2%)
A strong bitter with initial hop bitterness which is matched by sweetness from the malts. The aftertaste and aroma comes from a blend of hops which gives a distinct fruity finish.

Full Whack (OG 1054, ABV 6%)
The high level of alcohol is complemented by increased bitterness and a fruity hop finish.

Pembrokeshire (NEW)

The Ridgeway, Saundersfoot, SA69 9JU
(01834) 813574
pembrokeshirebrewingco.co.uk

Opened in 2014 with a 2.5-barrel, full-mash plant, the brewery plans to install a Burton Union system by 2016, making it the second of only two in the country and one of three in the world. Beer fests are held every month.

Cariad (OG 1039, ABV 3.9%)
Copper-coloured beer, full-bodied with a citrus aroma.

Daft Bass (OG 1041, ABV 4.1%)
A flagship beer with a balanced mixture of malt and hops.

Pembrokeshire Pale Ale (OG 1041, ABV 4.1%)
A refreshingly hoppy, full-bodied pale ale with a subtle character.

Black Bart (OG 1045, ABV 4.5%)
A rich stout brewed to the original Champion Beer of Wales 1998 recipe. With a balanced blend of roasted barleys and robust hops.

Saundersfoot Supreme Ale (OG 1045, ABV 4.5%)
A full-bodied premium bitter that glides across the palate.

Knocker (OG 1050, ABV 5%)

IPA (OG 1060, ABV 6%)

Penlon Cottage

Panteg Farm, New Quay, SA45 9TL
(01545) 561492 penlon.biz

After 10 years' operation, Penlon Cottage, strongly focussed on an ethos of sustainability, changed hands in 2014 and in early 2015 moved to new premises nearby, where re-equipment and facilities for visitors are planned. Mainly bottle-conditioned beers, but cask being trialled. RAIB

Pennine SIBA

Well Hall Farm, Well, North Yorkshire, DL8 2PX
(01677) 470111 pennine-brewery.co.uk

Pennine began brewing in Batley in 2012 using an 18-barrel lager plant complete with lauter [filtration] tun. In 2013 the brewery relocated to Well, near Masham, and now produces four core beers plus seasonals. A visitor centre opened in 2014. !! ♦

Amber Necker (OG 1039, ABV 3.9%)
A session beer with a smooth and creamy texture and a hoppy aftertaste.

Best Bitter (OG 1040, ABV 3.9%)

Real Blonde (OG 1041, ABV 4%)
Finely balanced blonde ale with a fruity aftertaste.

Natural Gold (OG 1043, ABV 4.2%)

Penpont

Inner Trenarrett, Altarnun, Launceston, Cornwall, PL15 7SY
(01566) 86069 penpontbrewery.co.uk

Penpont opened in 2008 and has steadily increased the range and production since then. The brewery has also won a number of awards. Its beers are available in pubs across Cornwall. ‼♬◆

St Nonna's (OG 1037, ABV 3.7%) ◢

Tawny session bitter with floral nose and balanced malt and hop bitterness throughout with roast and sweet notes. Bitter finish.

Cornish Arvor (OG 1040, ABV 4%) ◢

Well-balanced tawny best bitter. Principally bitter with fruity sweetness and some malt. Bitter hop-fruit finish.

Creation Pale Ale (OG 1039.2, ABV 4.2%) ◢

Gold-coloured bitter with hop aroma. Hoppy taste with sweet peach, citrus zing and roast malt. Bitter, slightly dry finish.

Shipwreck Coast (OG 1044, ABV 4.4%) ◢

Golden ale with citrus aroma. Powerful lemon citrus hop dominates the taste and finish with bitterness and fruits. Faint dryness.

Roughtor (OG 1047, ABV 4.7%) ◢

Copper-coloured strong bitter with malt and citrus hop aroma. Hop bitterness balanced by malt, plum and marmalade. Bitter, dry finish.

Beast of Bodmin (OG 1046.5, ABV 5%) ◢

Brown strong bitter with malt aroma. Smooth roast malt, chestnuts and complex fruits in the mouth. Refreshing malty, bitter finish.

Stormer IPA (OG 1046.7, ABV 5.2%)

Pentrich (NEW)

Pease Hill, Ripley, Derbyshire, DE5 3JN ☎ 07787 420875 ✉ pentrichbrewingco@gmail.com

Two former home brewers began producing beer for sale in their garage in Pentrich, before moving to share the plant of the Landlocked Brewing Co at the Beehive Inn, Ripley in 2014. Pentrich produces a variety of cask and bottled beers with ingredients from all over the globe. Beers can be purchased direct from the brewer.

1817 (ABV 4.5%)

A full-bodied amber ale with a dry fruit aroma and a bitter finish.

Cut Your Teeth (ABV 5%)

Bright golden-coloured, hoppy session IPA.

Three Graves (ABV 6%)

A strong, dark porter, made using only British ingredients.

Thousand Suns (ABV 7%)

Double red ale with a bright red hue derived from speciality Belgian and German malts, with an abundance of American hops for bitterness and strong fruit and pine aromas.

Penzance

🍺 Star Inn, Crowlas, Penzance, Cornwall, TR20 8DX ☎ (01736) 740375 ⊕ penzancebrewing.wordpress.com

⊗ Owner Peter Elvin began brewing in 2008 on a self-built five-barrel plant in the old stable block of the Star Inn. The fermentation capacity has since been expanded, increasing the volume and range of beers produced. Production is now at full capacity of 1,400 barrels a year. Besides the pub, selected outlets and beer festivals are supplied. ‼◆

Mild (OG 1042, ABV 3.6%)

Crowlas Bitter (OG 1037, ABV 3.8%) ◢

Refreshing, copper-coloured session bitter with light malt aroma. Light biscuit maltiness and hops. Lingering finish of malty bitterness with dryness.

Potion No 9 (OG 1039, ABV 4%) ◢

Golden ale with floral, grapefruit hops dominating nose and taste. Big bitter taste grows into a complex grapefruit, apricot finish.

Brisons Bitter (OG 1043, ABV 4.5%) ◢

Tawny best bitter with malt aroma. Malt dominates the taste with sweetness, fruits and bitterness. Malt finish with sweet toffee.

Thirty Summit (OG 1043, ABV 4.5%) ◢

Golden ale with resinous hop and fruit aroma. Lemon hops dominate the flavour with sharp bitterness. Bitter with dry finish.

Trink (OG 1048, ABV 5.2%) ◢

Golden ale with grapefruit nose. Powerful, punchy and astringent hop flavours with grapefruit marmalade and peaches. Bittersweet and hoppy finish.

Mellow (OG 1050, ABV 5.5%) ◢

Powerful citrus hop and malt in aroma and taste, leading to an astringent finish balanced by subtle lemon fruitiness.

IPA (OG 1058, ABV 6%)

A strong, traditional style IPA.

Scilly Stout (OG 1067, ABV 7%) ◢

Dark brown, full-bodied and creamy stout. Burnt malt, liquorice, chicory and prunes taste. Long, bittersweet finish with strong roast malt.

People's (NEW)

Mill House, Mill Lane, Thorpe-next-Haddiscoe, Norwich, NR14 6PA ☎ (01508) 548706 ⊕ thurlton-queenshead.co.uk/ QHPeoples_Brewery.html

⊠ A tiny one-barrel brewery associated with the Queen's Head pub in Thurlton, which takes most of its output. Also supplies small quantities to pubs in the Raveningham area. The brewer was previously with Blackfriars in Great Yarmouth.

Northdown Bitter (ABV 3.8%)

Named after the hop used to give it the bitterness and character of beers of the past.

Pheasant Plucker (ABV 4.2%)

Cascade (ABV 4.5%)

Brewed with a variety of malts including rye, and dry hopped with Cascade to give a dry, fruity finish.

Pheasantry SIBA ⊙

🍺 High Brecks Farm, Lincoln Road, East Markham, Nottinghamshire, NG22 0SN ☎ (01777) 872728 ☎ 07948 976749 ⊕ pheasantrybrewery.co.uk

⊙ Pheasantry began brewing in 2012 using a new 10-barrel plant from Canada. Situated in a listed barn on a farm, the brewery and visitor centre incorporate a restaurant, tearooms and bar, with the brewery visible through glass partitions. It supplied some 200 pubs and retail outlets in Nottinghamshire, Lincolnshire and South Yorkshire. ‼♬

Best Bitter (OG 1038, ABV 3.8%) 🍺

Smooth-tasting, copper-coloured beer with medium bitterness and low to medium sweetness. It has a light spicy aroma.

Pale Ale (OG 1040, ABV 4%)
A pale-coloured, smooth-tasting beer brewed from Maris Otter malt.The blend of hops added during the brewing process gives floral and citrusy notes with a dry finish.

Ringneck Amber Ale (OG 1041, ABV 4.1%)
Well-hopped English beer, well-rounded with a low to medium sweetness.

Dark Ale (OG 1042, ABV 4.2%)
A smooth, soft, satisfying dark ale with malty flavours, balanced bitterness and a velvety texture.

Lincoln Tank Ale (OG 1042, ABV 4.2%)
Amber-coloured, well-hopped brew. Designed to raise money for the Lincoln Tank Memoria.

Dancing Dragonfly (OG 1050, ABV 5%)
Refreshing blonde beer with exotic fruit flavours.

Phipps SIBA

The Albion Brewery, 54 Kingswell Street, Northampton, NN1 1PR
☎ (01604) 946606 ☎ 07717 078402
phipps-nbc.co.uk

Originally founded in Towcester in 1801, Phipps had been brewing in Northampton since 1817 until taken over by Watney Mann, which closed the brewery in 1974. The company name and recipes were acquired and in 2008 the first Phipps draught beer reappeared after 40 years, brewed to the original recipe at Grainstore Brewery (qv) in Oakham. The Albion Brewery site, once owned by Phipps, was acquired and a new 15-barrel brewing plant installed in 2014 to enable Phipps beers to be once again brewed in the town. Hoggleys brewery, which was established in 2002, merged with Phipps NBC at the end of 2013 and all Hoggleys beers are now brewed on the Phipps plant, with the former Hoggleys plant sold to Merrimen Brewing (qv). All Hoggleys beers are suitable for vegans as is Ratliffes Celebrated Stout. !! ♦ RAIB

Diamond Ale (OG 1037, ABV 3.7%)
A light amber-coloured harvest ale.

India Pale Ale (OG 1043, ABV 4.3%)
A pale amber-coloured best bitter recreated from an old Phipps recipe. A residual malt sweetness and the grapefruit note from the hops gives a fine, fresh, crisp finish.

Steam Roller (ABV 4.4%)
A dark, malty beer with smoky notes.

Gold Star (OG 1050, ABV 5.2%)
An export pale ale.

Brewed for Hoggleys Brewery:

Mill Lane Mild (OG 1040, ABV 4%)
Brewed from mild, black and crystal malts.

Northamptonshire Bitter (OG 1040, ABV 4%)
A straw-coloured bitter brewed with pale malt only.

Reservoir Hogs (OG 1042, ABV 4.3%)
Mid golden, hoppy and refreshing.

Pump Fiction (OG 1045, ABV 4.5%)
Light copper-coloured beer, complex but easy-drinking.

India Pale Ale (OG 1050, ABV 5%)
A hoppy, full-bodied IPA.

Solstice Stout (OG 1050, ABV 5%)
A rich, full-flavoured stout made with a wide range of malts.

Brewed under NBC brand name:

Red Star (OG 1038, ABV 3.8%)
A pre-WW2-style session beer; maltier, sweeter, darker and fuller-bodied than present-day versions.

Brewed under Ratliffes brand name:

Celebrated Stout (OG 1043, ABV 4.3%)
A creamy, well-balanced stout with just a hint of bitterness.

Phoenix SIBA

Green Lane, Heywood, OL10 2EP
☎ (01706) 627009 ✉ tony@phoenixbrewery.co.uk

Established in Ellesmere Port in 1982, Oak Brewery moved to the old Phoenix Brewery in Heywood and adopted the name in 1991. It now supplies 400-500 outlets plus wholesalers. Restoration of the old brewery, built in 1897, is ongoing. ♦

Hopsack (OG 1038, ABV 3.8%)
A light-drinking, hoppy session beer.

Navvy (OG 1039, ABV 3.8%)
Amber-coloured beer with a citrus fruit and malt nose. Good balance of citrus fruit, malt and hops with bitterness coming through in the aftertaste.

Monkeytown Mild (OG 1039, ABV 3.9%)
Dark-coloured mild with fruitiness, bitterness and a smooth full malt finish.

Arizona (OG 1040, ABV 4.1%)
Yellow in colour with a fruity and hoppy aroma. A refreshing beer with citrus, hops and good bitterness, and a shortish dry aftertaste.

Spotland Gold (OG 1041, ABV 4.1%)
A pale, hoppy beer with a lingering bitter finish.

Pale Moonlight (OG 1042, ABV 4.2%)
Quite bitter with lingering grassy hop finish.

Black Bee (OG 1045, ABV 4.5%)
Brewed with honey, this porter has a malty aroma, which tastes of dark fruit, honey and a hint of coffee.

White Monk (OG 1045, ABV 4.5%)
Yellow-coloured beer with a citrus fruit aroma, plenty of fruit, hops and bitterness in the taste, and a hoppy, bitter finish.

Thirsty Moon (OG 1046, ABV 4.6%)
Tawny beer with a fresh citrus aroma. Hoppy, fruity and malty with a dry, hoppy finish.

West Coast IPA (OG 1046, ABV 4.6%)
Golden in colour with a hoppy, fruity nose. Strong hoppy and fruity taste and aftertaste with good bitterness throughout.

Double Gold (OG 1050, ABV 5%)
Full-bodied, premium bitter.

Wobbly Bob (OG 1060, ABV 6%)
A red/brown beer with malty, fruity aroma and creamy mouthfeel. Strongly malty and fruity in flavour, with hops and a hint of herbs. Both sweetness and bitterness are evident throughout.

Brewed for Brunning & Price Pub Co

Original (ABV 3.8%)

Pictish

Unit 9, Canalside Industrial Estate, Rochdale, OL16 5LB
☎ (01706) 522227 🌐 pictish-brewing.co.uk

The brewery was established in 2000 and supplies around 60 free trade outlets in the north-west and West Yorkshire. ♦

Brewers Gold (OG 1038, ABV 3.8%)
Yellow in colour, with a hoppy, fruity nose. Soft maltiness and a strong hop/citrus flavour lead to a dry, bitter finish.

Alchemists Ale (OG 1043, ABV 4.3%)
Yellow beer with generous hop and fruit on the nose and palate. Good bitter hop finish.

Piddle SIBA

Unit 7, Enterprise Park, Piddlehinton, Dorset, DT2 7UA
☎ (01305) 849336 ☎ 07730 436343
🌐 piddlebrewery.co.uk

Piddle began brewing in 2007 and in 2011 moved to larger adjacent premises, where it now brews on a 30-barrel plant. The brewery supplies pubs and other outlets across Dorset and beyond. ♦

Jimmy (OG 1040, ABV 3.7%)
Pale brown session beer with a good depth of malty flavours for its strength.

Piddle (OG 1043, ABV 4.1%)
An amber-coloured, full-bodied beer that is slightly sweet but malty with a fruity nose leading to a resinous hoppy flavour with a twist of citrus fruit, giving way to a dry bitter finish.

Slasher (OG 1053, ABV 5.1%)
Blonde, lager-style beer brewed with extra pale malt and wheat. Deceptively light, with hops chosen for their floral aroma and flavour. Slightly sweet with a refreshing, dry bitter finish.

Pied Bull

Pied Bull Hotel, 57 Northgate Street, Chester, CH1 2HQ
☎ (01244) 325829 🌐 piedbull.co.uk

Pied Bull began brewing in 2011 using a one-barrel plant. Beer is mainly for in-house consumption, but local beer festivals are supplied and occasional brewery swaps occur. ♦

Sensibull (OG 1039, ABV 3.8%)
Session ale brewed with a British-style rounded malt base balanced against a light hop profile.

Gullabull (OG 1040, ABV 3.9%)
A pale ale with a strong pink-grapefruit aroma.

Pied Eyed (OG 1040, ABV 4%)
A well-balanced session bitter with a good malty foretaste and a hoppy aftertaste.

Quaffabull (OG 1039, ABV 4%)
A refreshing, light pale ale with hints of citrus notes.

Bulls Hit (OG 1055, ABV 4.3%)
A refreshing, light golden-coloured ale with an abundance of American and New Zealand hops.

Matador (OG 1049, ABV 5%)
A rich, malt-driven ale with an aromatic hop profile. 2012 Champion Beer of Cheshire.

Sitting Bull (OG 1050, ABV 5%)
An American-style IPA.

Black Bull Porter (OG 1060, ABV 5.2%)
A classic porter brewed to a local recipe dating from 1865, using a blend of six malts and English hops to give a dry coffee flavour.

Redbull (OG 1057, ABV 5.5%)
A rich, deep red ale with a chocolate undertone. Dry hopped for a fruity finish.

Pig & Porter

18h Chapman Way, Tunbridge Wells, Kent, TN2 3EF
☎ (01424) 893519 🌐 pigandporter.co.uk

Originally brewing at several microbreweries in Sussex and Kent, brewing has taken place on its own plant in Tunbridge Wells since 2013 using a 10-barrel plant. ♦

Ashburnham Pale Ale (ABV 3.8%)
Classic English pale ale.

Red Spider Rye (ABV 5.5%)
Red rye beer, dry hopped in the cask.

Pig Iron (NEW)

Unit 3, Venture Way, Brierley Hill, West Midlands, DY5 1RQ 🌐 pigironbrewingco.co.uk

Set up in 2015, this three-barrel plant is situated on the edge of the Merry Hill shopping centre. The brewer, from a former baking family, acquired the kit from Brewmeister in Northern Scotland. The brewery supplies free trade outlets within five miles of the brewery and the brewer's home.

Blonde (OG 1037, ABV 3.8%)
Smooth, light blonde beer.

Hog Ore Best Bitter (OG 1041, ABV 4%)
A smooth traditional best bitter.

Pig Pub

Pig in Muck, Manor Road, Claybrooke Magna, Leicestershire, LE17 5AY
☎ (01455) 202859 🌐 piginmuck.com/brewery

Brewing began in 2013 using a two-barrel plant. Beers are available in the Pig in Muck and the Criterion in Leicester. Special beers are brewed for the pub by customers.

Weiner Bitter (ABV 3.8%)
A straw-coloured session bitter. Hoppy and fruity throughout with a compounding bitterness culminating on a a distinct dryness at the finish.

Pig Out (ABV 3.9%)
Dark amber-coloured beer with a pleasant bitterness and a fruity citrus finish.

Claybrooke Bitter (ABV 4.2%)
A full-bodied, dark amber-coloured beer with a malty aroma. Bitter at the start with a hint of fruit in the middle of the palate and a soft hop flavour to finish.

Pigs Best Bitter (ABV 4.2%)
A golden brown beer with a hint of citrus. The fresh hoppiness comes through at the end with a malt finish.

Pigeon Fishers

Unit B1 & B2, Devonshire Buildings, Works Road, Hollingwood, Derbyshire, S43 2PE ☎ 07506 000989 🌐 pigeonfishers.com

Pigeon Fishers was founded by managing director Ade Cole in 2014 with the help of co-directors Neil Turner and Kathy Chadwick. Originally using a one-barrel plant donated by Thornbridge Brewery, it upgraded to a 2.5-barrel plant from Barlow Brewery later in the year. ♦

Poacher's Thirst (ABV 4%)
An easy-drinking amber-coloured ale, full of malt and hops.

Cynosure (ABV 4.6%)
A smooth-drinking floral and citrus beer with a strawberry and cherry finish.

Pikefields (OG 1052, ABV 5.2%)
An American-style pale ale, hoppy with malty middle notes and a citrus finish.

Pilgrim SIBA

11 West Street, Reigate, RH2 9BL ☎ (01737) 222651 🌐 pilgrim.co.uk

⊗ Pilgrim was set up in 1982 in Woldingham, Surrey, and moved to Reigate in 1985. The original owner, Dave Roberts, is still in charge. Beers are sold to around 40 local outlets. ‼♦

Quench (OG 1037, ABV 3.6%)

Surrey Bitter (OG 1038, ABV 3.7%)
Pineapple, grapefruit and spicy aromas. Biscuity maltiness with a hint of vanilla balanced by a hoppy bitterness and refreshing bittersweet finish.

Progress (OG 1041.5, ABV 4%)
Well-rounded, tawny-coloured bitter. Predominantly sweet and malty with an underlying fruitiness and hint of toffee, balanced with a subdued bitterness.

Quest (OG 1043, ABV 4.3%)

Pilot (NEW)

726 Mumbles Road, Mumbles, Swansea, SA3 4EL ☎ 07897 895511 🌐 thepilotbrewery.co.uk

Pilot began production on its 2.5-barrel plant in 2013, located at the rear of the Pilot Inn on the Mumbles seafront. The output is mainly for the Pilot Inn but can also be found at festivals and other select outlets.

Revolver (OG 1040, ABV 4%)
Pale ale brewed with a changing hop variety.

GOLD (OG 1044, ABV 4.4%)
Refreshing, golden-coloured ale.

Black Storm (OG 1045, ABV 4.5%)
Stout with a complex taste.

Wrecker (OG 1049, ABV 5%)
A dark, strong bitter with a unique flavour. An initial chocolate taste develops into a clean, refreshing maltiness.

Pilot Beer

22 Jane Street, Leith, EH6 5HD ☎ (0131) 561 4267 ☎ 07805 760018 🌐 pilotbeer.co.uk

Pilot started brewing in 2013 in an industrial unit in Leith using a salvaged five-barrel plant. Graduates of the Heriot-Watt University Brewing degree course, the owners infuse a number of flavours in their hop-forward beers. Distribution is to the Edinburgh area at present but is becoming more widespread.

Blond (OG 1047, ABV 4%)
A modern, fresh and zesty pale ale made with a smooth full body. Generously hopped for a huge tropical fruit hit.

Vienna Pale (OG 1043, ABV 4.6%)
Light and dry with a delicate yet earthy, herbal flavour, followed up with an easy, rounded bitterness.

Iced Tea Ale (OG 1048, ABV 5%)
A refreshing, amber-coloured beer brewed with a uniquely produced tea blend. Orange and peach tones to the tea and malt base are lifted by crisp, bright hops and fresh lemongrass.

Mochaccino Stout (OG 1069, ABV 5.5%)
A rich, dark milk stout infused with an exclusive coffee roast, organic cocoa nibs and Madagascan vanilla. Lactose gives a sweet silkiness and enormous body to this opulent beer.

India Pale (OG 1060, ABV 6.4%)
Toasted fenugreek and unrefined jaggery sugar add complex spice, maple and caramel flavours to huge floral, pine and grassy notes, finished off with a powerful yet smooth bitterness.

Pin-Up SIBA

Unit 3, Block 3, Chalex Industrial Estate, Manor Hall Road, Southwick, Brighton, West Sussex, BN42 4NH ☎ (01273) 411127 🌐 pinupbeers.com

⊗ Pin-Up began brewing in 2011. The brewery moved from Crowborough to Southwick, near Brighton, in 2014 and uses a five-barrel plant. ♦RAIB

Natural Blonde (OG 1037, ABV 3.8%)

Honey Brown (OG 1039, ABV 4%)

Red Head (OG 1041, ABV 4.2%)

Milk Stout (OG 1044, ABV 4.5%)

Pipes

183a Kings Road, Cardiff, CF11 9DF ☎ 07776 382244 🌐 pipesbeer.co.uk

Formery known as Artisan, the brewery was established in 2008. All beers are unfiltered, without additives or preservatives and suitable for vegans. The main output is bottled and keg beers, although cask-conditioned beers are occasionally produced. The brewery has monthly open days - please contact brewery for details. ‼♦

Pitfield SIBA

See Dominion

Pixie Spring-Hopcraft

Unit C1, Coed Cae Lane Industrial Estate, Pontyclun, CF72 9HG ☎ 07814 255943 🌐 pixiespring.com; fb.hopcraftbrewing.co.uk

Pixie Spring began brewing in 2011 in the cellar of the Wheatsheaf, Llantrisant. In 2012 there was a joining of forces with Gazza Prescott of Steel City Brewery to form the trading name Pixie Spring-Hopcraft and a move followed to the present premises with a new 12-barrel plant. Output under the Pixie Spring banner is restricted to a few regular beers, whereas Hopcraft badged beers are mostly one-off, well-hopped recipes. A separate 0.75-barrel plant is used for specials.

Plain SIBA

17c Deverill Trading Estate, Sutton Veny, Wiltshire, BA12 7BZ
☎ (01985) 841481 ⊕ plainales.co.uk

Plain Ales started production in 2008 on a 2.5-barrel plant in a garage, and expanded to a 20-barrel plant in 2011. ‼◆

Sheep Dip (OG 1040, ABV 3.8%)

Wife's Bitter (OG 1041, ABV 3.8%)

Arty Farty (OG 1039, ABV 3.9%)

Innocence (OG 1042, ABV 4%)
A straw-coloured, fragrant bitter.

Innspiration (OG 1042, ABV 4%) 🍺
A traditional, copper-coloured, easy-drinking bitter.

Inntrigue (OG 1044, ABV 4.2%)

Inndulgence (OG 1055, ABV 4.5%)
A dark ruby porter with coffee, chocolate and a hint of smoke.

Inncognito (OG 1053, ABV 4.8%) 🍺

Plain India Pale Ale (OG 1052, ABV 5.2%)

Plassey

See New Plassey

Platform 5 SIBA

🍺 Railway Brewhouse, 197 Queen Street, Newton Abbot, Devon, TQ12 2BS
☎ (01626) 437140 ⊕ platform5brewing.co.uk

Platform 5 is a family-run microbrewery established in 2013 using a six-barrel plant. The Railway Inn is supplied along with Molloys in Teignmouth and Torquay. The brewery is situated in part of an enclosed alley under the disused Platform 5 of Newton Abbot station, with the other part housing the pub's skittle alley.

Coaster (OG 1040, ABV 4.0%)
A light, refreshing session ale.

Antelope (OG 1043, ABV 4.3%)
A hoppy pale ale.

Whistleblower (OG 1046, ABV 4.6%)
An English-hopped premium ale.

Western Gold (OG 1048, ABV 4.8%)
A citrus hopped golden ale.

IPA (OG 1058, ABV 5.8%)
Brewed with English and American hops.

Plockton

5 Bank Street, Plockton, Ross-shire, IV52 8TP
☎ (01599) 544276 ☎ 07823 322043
⊕ theplocktonbrewery.com

The brewery started trading in 2007 and expanded to a 2.5-barrel plant in 2009. Bottle-conditioned beers are available and are suitable for vegetarians. ‼◆RAIB

Ciste Dhubh (OG 1040, ABV 3.9%) 🍺
Excellent mix of malts and hops in this dark brew. Initial bitter turning bittersweet.

Fiddlers Fancy (OG 1046, ABV 4.6%) 🍺
Refreshing, grapefruit aroma and taste turning to a more malty finish.

Plockton Bay (OG 1047, ABV 4.6%) 🍺
A well-balanced, tawny-coloured best bitter with plenty of hops and malt which give a bittersweet fruity flavour.

Poachers

439 Newark Road, North Hykeham, Lincolnshire, LN6 9SP
☎ (01522) 807404 ☎ 07954 131972
⊕ poachersbrewery.co.uk

☺Brewing started in 2001 on a five-barrel plant. In 2006 it was downsized to 2.5-barrel and relocated to outbuildings at the rear of the brewer's home. 2011 saw capacity returned to five barrels. Regular outlets in Lincolnshire and surrounding counties are supplied direct; outlets further afield via wholesalers. ‼◆

Trembling Rabbit Mild (OG 1034, ABV 3.4%)
Rich, dark and mild with a smooth malty flavour and a slightly bitter finish. Local honey used.

Shy Talk Bitter (OG 1037, ABV 3.7%)
A pale golden-coloured, crisp-tasting session beer; refreshing with citrus overtones.

Rock Ape (OG 1038, ABV 3.8%)
A traditional brown session bitter produced from purely English ingredients.

Poachers Pride (OG 1040, ABV 4%)
An amber-coloured bitter with a fine flavour and an aroma that lingers.

Bog Trotter (OG 1042, ABV 4.2%)
An amber-coloured, full-flavoured, malty beer with a delicious bitter aftertaste.

Lincoln Best (OG 1042, ABV 4.2%)
A flowery, hop-nosed, brown beer with a well-balanced but bitter taste that stays with the malt, becoming more apparent in the drying finish.

Billy Boy (OG 1044, ABV 4.4%)
A rich, full-flavoured brown beer. Named after the brewery dog, a Border Collie.

Imp Ale (OG 1044, ABV 4.4%)
Copper-coloured ale, fruity and floral with a bitter finish.

Black Crow Stout (OG 1045, ABV 4.5%)
A delicious, full-bodied stout that has an aftertaste that lingers. Burnt toffee and caramel flavours come to the fore.

Hykeham Gold (OG 1045, ABV 4.5%)
A cask-conditioned lager that has both flavour and taste.

Monkey Hanger (OG 1045, ABV 4.5%)
A ruby-red bitter. Smooth, fruity flavour balanced by the bitterness of the hops.

Jock's Trap (OG 1050, ABV 5%)
A strong, pale brown bitter with a hoppy flavour and aroma with a slightly dry fruit finish.

Trout Tickler (OG 1055, ABV 5.5%)
A strong ruby bitter with intense flavour and character, and sweet undertones with a hint of chocolate. A rich, malty beer.

Pocket

La Croix Farm, La Rue de la Croix, St Ouen, Jersey, JE3 2HA ☎ 07797 771931
✉ jerseybeer@jerseymail.co.uk

⊗ As the name implies, Pocket Brewery began in 2011 on a small scale. Brewing was undertaken occasionally on demand with the beers available locally in bottle-conditioned form and sometimes in cask at local freehouses and beer festivals. Brewing is currently suspended. RAIB

Pokertree (NEW)

The Brewhouse, 357b Drumnakilly Road, Carrickmore, Co Tyrone, BT79 9JY
☎ (028) 8076 1923 ⊕ pokertreebrewing.co.uk

Opened in 2014, Pokertree brews small batch beers using all natural and, where possible, local ingredients. It is planning a range of four ales —all bottle-conditioned and open-fermented using traditional techniques. RAIB

Pope's

73a Blackpole Trading Estate West, Worcester, WR3 8TJ
☎ (01905) 755016 ✉ popesbrew@btconnect.com

Pope's is a family-run brewery established in 2012. A 4.5-barrel brew plant is used with brewing taking place twice a week, supplying the local free trade and further afield. Beer names are influenced by the local area. ‼ ▰ ◆ RAIB

Cavalier (OG 1036, ABV 3.6%)

Hop Market (OG 1038, ABV 3.8%)

Worcester Gold (OG 1040, ABV 4%)

Hope & Glory (OG 1046, ABV 4.6%)

Pope's Yard

477-479 Whippendell Road, Watford, Hertfordshire, WD18 7PU
☎ (01923) 224182 ⊕ popesyard.co.uk

Pope's Yard began commercial brewing in 2012 using a one-barrel plant. Cask and bottle-conditioned beers are available but no regular beers are produced. RAIB

Poppyland

46 West Street, Cromer, Norfolk, NR27 9DS
☎ (01263) 513992 ☎ 07887 389804
⊕ poppylandbeer.com

Established in 2012 by museum curator and geologist Martin Warren as a working retirement project, Poppyland brews and bottle-conditions small batches of beer, especially saisons, IPAs, porters and fruit beers. Beers are unfiltered, vegan-friendly and gluten free RAIB

George N Porter

Whitley Bay, Tyne & Wear, NE26 1AP

☎ (0191) 290 2134 ☎ 07980 842087
✉ gnporterbrewing@gmail.com

George N Porter is a 2.5-barrel microbrewery established in 2012. Brewing is currently suspended.

Porter Street

See Evan Evans

Portobello SIBA

Unit 6, Mitre Bridge Industrial Estate, Mitre Way, Kensington, London, W10 6AU
☎ (020) 8969 2269 ⊕ portobellobrewing.com

⊗ Portobello began brewing in 2012 using a 10-barrel plant. ◆

Pale (OG 1040, ABV 4%) ◈
Golden, well-balanced best bitter with a citrus character, some spiced hops and some malty sweetness that fades.

Star (OG 1044, ABV 4.3%) ◈
Pale brown, malty best bitter with a sweetish nose and a strong bitter finish. Hints of nut on the palate.

APA (OG 1050, ABV 5%) ◈
Full-bodied, straw-coloured strong ale. Honey sweetness and soft citrus fruit are balanced by bitter hops. Dry aftertaste.

Portpatrick (NEW)

The Neuk, Portpatrick, Stranraer, DG9 9EF ☎ 07826 542149 ⊕ portpatrick-brewery.co.uk

☺ The brewery opened in 2015 using a 1.5-barrel brew length in converted space in outbuildings. ◆ RAIB

Dorn Rock (OG 1044, ABV 4.3%)

Fog Horn (OG 1050, ABV 4.8%)

Potbelly SIBA ◉

Sydney Street Entrance, Kettering, Northamptonshire, NN16 0JA
☎ (01536) 410818 ☎ 07834 867825
⊕ potbelly-brewery.co.uk

Potbelly started brewing in 2005 on a 10-barrel plant and supplies some 200 outlets. The brewery has won numerous awards for its beers. ‼ ▰ ◆ RAIB

Pig Tales (OG 1036, ABV 3.6%)

Best (OG 1036.9, ABV 3.8%)
A traditional, chestnut-coloured bitter.

Hop Trotter (OG 1041, ABV 4.1%)
A golden-coloured beer with spicy aromas and citric notes.

Beijing Black (OG 1045, ABV 4.4%)
A strong dark mild.

Pigs Do Fly (OG 1041, ABV 4.4%)
A light, single-hopped golden ale.

Bellowhead Hedonism (OG 1045, ABV 4.5%)
A light-coloured bitter with a citrus hoppy finish. Brewed with the help of Bellowhead, a local band.

Captain Pigwash (OG 1050, ABV 5%)
An easy-drinking dark porter.

Crazy Daze (OG 1050, ABV 5.5%)

A light golden bitter with hidden strength.

Potton 👁

10 Shannon Place, Potton, Bedfordshire, SG19 2SP
☎ (01767) 261042 ∰ pottonbrewery.co.uk

Bedfordshire Breweries took over the ownership and management of the Potton brewery in 2013. The core beers from the Potton range are still available. Around 140 outlets are supplied direct. ◆ RAIB

Shannon IPA (OG 1034, ABV 3.6%)
A well-balanced, session bitter with good bitterness and fruity late-hop character.

Phoenix (OG 1036, ABV 3.8%)
A soft, smooth beer with an aromatic hop character.

Penny Bitter (OG 1038, ABV 4%)
A dark red, malty, traditional-style bitter with a light hop character.

Shambles Bitter (OG 1043, ABV 4.3%)
A robust, pale and heavily hopped beer with a subtle dry hop character.

Village Bike (OG 1043, ABV 4.3%) ◣
Classic English premium bitter, amber in colour, heavily late-hopped.

Prescott SIBA

Unit 1, The Bramery Business Park, Alstone Lane, Cheltenham, Gloucestershire, GL51 8HE ☎ 07526 934866 ∰ prescottales.co.uk

Prescott Ales was established in 2008, and brews on a 25-barrel plant. It takes its name from the famous Prescott Hill Climb, which is also the home of the Bugatti Owners Club UK. Beer names are inspired by the golden age of motoring. ‼◆

Hill Climb (OG 1039.5, ABV 3.8%)
A late-hopped, pale straw-coloured IPA-style session beer with a refreshing, fruity finish.

Chequered Flag (OG 1042, ABV 4.1%)
A generously hopped amber-coloured ale with a malty finish.

Track Record (OG 1044, ABV 4.4%)
A light copper-coloured, fruity best bitter with a full-bodied, slightly sweet finish.

Grand Prix (OG 1050, ABV 5.2%)
A dark amber-coloured strong ale with a rich, smooth finish.

Preseli

See Tenby

Pressure Drop

Unit 19, Bohemia Place, Hackney, London, E8 1DU
☎ (020) 8533 0614 ∰ pressuredropbrewing.co.uk

Pressure Drop is run by three partners who were home brewers but began commercial brewing in 2013 using a five-barrel plant and a small pilot kit. RAIB

Prestonpans

🛢 227-229 High Street, Prestonpans, East Lothian, EH32 9BE
☎ (01875) 819922 ∰ thegoth.co.uk

A microbrewery was installed at the award-winning pub, the Prestoungrange Gothenburg, in 2004. Originally trading as Fowler's Ales, the brewery is now under new management. Beers are supplied to the pub.

Fowler's 80/- (ABV 4.2%)

Gothenburg Porter (ABV 4.4%)

Private Brewery of Bob

c/o Farmers Boy, 134 London Road, St Albans, Hertfordshire, AL1 1PQ ☎ 07880 743357
∰ bob-brewery.co.uk

The Private Brewery of Bob run by Martin Slaughter who produces a range of bottle-conditioned beers for the off-trade and some local pubs. Four regular bottle-conditioned beers are brewed as well as several seasonals and specials. ◆ RAIB

Privateer

Unit 75, Temperance Street, Ardwick, Manchester, M12 6HU
☎ (0161) 273 7077 ☎ 07969 771102
∰ privateerbeers.com

Privateer began brewing in 2012 using a 6.5-barrel plant. Only American hops are used and all beers are brewed under 5% ABV. ◆

Problem Child

🛢 Wayfarer Inn, Alder Lane, Parbold, Lancashire, WN8 7NL
☎ (01257) 464600 ☎ 07588 736926
∰ problemchildbrewing.co.uk

Problem Child began brewing in 2013, at the Wayfarer Inn, Parbold, owned by Johnny and Rachel Birkett. The brewery name originates from the family history of the Wayfarer. Once a problem child, prodigal daughter Rachel is now home and happily married to Johnny, the head brewer. Obi, aged seven, is apprentice brewer and problem child.

Scallywag (OG 1037, ABV 3.7%)

Rascal (ABV 3.8%)

Rapscallion (ABV 4.2%)

Good Spankin' (ABV 4.4%)

Little Punk (ABV 4.5%)

Scoundrel (OG 1046, ABV 4.6%)

Prospect SIBA 👁

Unit 11, Bradley Hall Trading Estate, Bradley Lane, Standish, Wigan, WN6 0XQ
☎ (01257) 421329 ∰ prospectbrewery.com

Prospect Brewery was founded in 2007 and relocated to its present premises in 2010, expanding to a 12-barrel plant. The brewery owns two local pubs where the beers are available alongside guest ales. One pub, the Silver Tally, Standish, is jointly owned with Daniel Thwaites. A cask ale and cider bar, Wigan Central, owned solely by the brewery, opened in 2014. ♦

Silver Tally (OG 1037, ABV 3.7%)
A clean, pale golden-coloured bitter with citrus aromas and a full hop flavour with a dry bitter finish.

Golden Prospects (OG 1040, ABV 3.8%)
A golden-coloured session bitter, packed with hop flavours of citrus and passion fruit.

Whatever! (OG 1040, ABV 3.8%)
Pale bitter packed with hop flavour and aroma.

Nutty Slack (OG 1039, ABV 3.9%) ◆
Dark brown mild ale with malt and fruit in the aroma. Creamy and chocolaty on the palate, with both malt and fruit in evidence. Malty and moderately bitter finish.

Hopper (OG 1040, ABV 4%)
A pale golden beer with citrus hops and a satisfying sweet balance.

Pioneer (OG 1040, ABV 4%)
A light-bodied amber-coloured beer with aromas of dry pale malt and earthy hops.

Cascade Blonde (OG 1039, ABV 4.1%)
A yellow/gold beer with zesty citrus notes; clean and refreshing lemon taste.

Blinding Light (OG 1042, ABV 4.2%)
A pale, refreshing beer with citrus and spicy notes.

Gold Rush (OG 1045, ABV 4.5%)
A deep golden ale with hoppy and bitter flavours, light fruity notes and a grassy floral finish.

Big John (OG 1047, ABV 4.8%)
A dark stout bursting with smoky liquorice flavour with a satisfying bitter aftertaste.

Purity SIBA

The Brewery, Upper Spernal Farm, Spernal Lane, Great Alne, Warwickshire, B49 6JF
☎ (01789) 488007 🌐 puritybrewing.com

Brewing began in 2005 in a purpose-designed plant housed in converted barns. The brewery incorporates an environmentally-friendly effluent treatment system. It supplies the free trade within a 70-mile radius and delivers to more than 500 outlets. ‼ ♦

Pure Gold (OG 1039.5, ABV 3.8%)
An easy-drinking beer with a dry and bitter finish.

Mad Goose (OG 1042.5, ABV 4.2%)
Light copper in colour with a zesty hop character with citrus overtone.

Pure Ubu (OG 1044.8, ABV 4.5%)
A premium amber-coloured beer with a balanced, full-flavoured beer.

Longhorn IPA (ABV 5%)
A copper-coloured beer with citrus and tropical fruit tones.

Saddle Black (ABV 5.1%)
A black beer with a smoky and citrus aroma.

Purple Moose SIBA

Madoc Street, Porthmadog, LL49 9DB
☎ (01766) 515571 🌐 purplemoose.co.uk

Purple Moose opened in 2005 using a 10-barrel plant in a former iron works in the coastal town of Porthmadog. In 2013 a new 40-barrel plant was installed, significantly increasing production. The names of the beers reflect local history and geography. ‼ ♦

Cwrw Eryri/Snowdonia Ale
(OG 1035.3, ABV 3.6%) ◆
Golden-coloured, refreshing bitter with citrus fruit hoppiness in aroma and taste. The full mouthfeel leads to a long-lasting, dry, bitter finish.

Cwrw Madog/Madog's Ale
(OG 1037, ABV 3.7%) ◆
Full-bodied session bitter. Malty nose and an initial nutty flavour but bitterness dominates. Well-balanced and refreshing with a dry roastiness on the taste and a good dry finish.

Cwrw Ysgawen/Elderflower
(OG 1039, ABV 4%) ◆
A pale and refreshing elderflower beer with a good citrus fruit aroma, bittersweet taste, and a zesty, hoppy, mouthwatering finish.

Cwrw Glaslyn/Glaslyn Ale
(OG 1040.5, ABV 4.2%) ◆
Refreshing, light and malty amber-coloured ale. Plenty of hop in the aroma and taste. Good smooth mouthfeel leading to a slightly chewy finish.

Ochr Tywyll y Mws/Dark Side of the Moose
(OG 1045, ABV 4.6%) ◆
A dark, complex beer, quite hoppy and bitter with roast undertones. Malt and fruit flavours also feature in the smooth taste and dry finish.

Q (NEW)

16 The Ringway, Queniborough, Leicestershire, LE7 3DL ☎ 07762 300240 🌐 qbrewery.co.uk

Q is a microbrewery based in Queniborough in a converted building behind the house of head brewer Tim Lowe, and officially launched at the Queniborough beer festival in 2014. It uses a 0.5-barrel brew kit, producing a firkin and a pin from each batch brewed.

Quantock SIBA

Westridge Way, Broadgauge Business Park, Bishops Lydeard, Somerset, TA4 3RU
☎ (01823) 433812 🌐 quantockbrewery.co.uk

Quantock is a family-run brewery that started trading in 2008 on an eight-barrel plant. The brewery supplies beers to outlets throughout the south-west and further afield via wholesalers. Beers are available to the public direct from the brewery and via online sales from the website. ♦ RAIB

Ale (OG 1036, ABV 3.8%)
An amber-coloured beer with a fruity, full-bodied flavour with a dry finish to the palate. The blend of English hops creates a balanced, fruity character with a delicate spicy aroma.

Ginger Cockney (OG 1037, ABV 4%)
A copper-coloured ale, generously hopped with American hops with a hint of fresh ginger.

Rorke's Drift (OG 1039, ABV 4.2%)
A light, refreshing lager-style beer, a fruit-filled experience with a delicate citrus aroma. Brewed in support of the Royal Engineers Association (REA) with five pence from every pint being donated to the association.

Sunraker (OG 1039, ABV 4.2%)
A pale straw-coloured beer, light and refreshing with a delicate, clean grassy hop finish.

Wills Neck (OG 1040, ABV 4.3%)
A bright golden ale with a rich malty flavour. Late-hopped to produce a prominent aroma with hints of grapefruit and cherries and a lasting bitterness on the palate.

White Hind (OG 1042, ABV 4.5%)
A chestnut-coloured best bitter brewed from a blend of three malts to give a full-bodied, malty flavour with the roast malt coming through and a dry finish. The beer is generously hopped with a blend of English varieties producing a spicy aroma.

Royal Stag IPA (OG 1056, ABV 6%)
A copper-coloured beer with a malty and fruity flavour, generously hopped with a blend of the finest English hops. The beer has a smoky aroma with hints of banana and toffee.

UXB (OG 1088, ABV 9%)
A strong beer, slightly sweet with a full malty flavour.

Quantum

Unit 4, Victoria Works, Hempshaw Lane, Stockport, SK1 4LG ☎ 07976 032465
quantumbrewingcompany.co.uk

The brewery was established in 2011 using a five-barrel plant on the site of the former Shaws Brewery. It brews short-run beers and one-off specials mainly for the local free trade and Wetherspoon outlets. ‼

Quartz SIBA

Archers, Alrewas Road, Kings Bromley, Staffordshire, DE13 7HW
☎ (01543) 473965 quartzbrewing.co.uk

Quartz was established in 2005 by Scott and Julia Barnett. There are five regular beers produced in cask, bottle and mini-cask, supplemented with seasonal specials. Around 50 outlets are supplied direct. ‼ ♦

Blonde (OG 1038, ABV 3.8%)
Little aroma, gentle hop and background malt. Sweet with unsophisticated sweetshop tastes.

Crystal (OG 1040, ABV 4.2%)
Sweet aroma with some fruit and yeasty Marmite hints. Hoppiness begins but dwindles to a bittersweet finish.

Extra Blonde (OG 1042, ABV 4.4%)
Sweet malty aroma with a touch of fruit. Sweet start, smooth with a hint of hops in the sugary finish.

Heart (OG 1045, ABV 4.6%)
Pale brown with some aroma of fruit and malt. Gentle tastes of fruit and hops eventually appear to leave a bitter finish.

Cracker (OG 1050, ABV 5%)
Chestnut in colour with a slight roasted aroma, smooth fruit notes leaving a dry hop finish.

Queen Inn SIBA

28 Kingsgate Road, Winchester, Hampshire, SO23 9PG
☎ (01962) 853898 thequeeninnwinchester.com

Brewing began in 2014 using a 1.5-barrel brew plant. At present beers are only brewed for the pub.

St Cross Ale (ABV 4.1%)

Queen's Head (NEW)

Queen's Head, 66 Acton Street, London, WC1X 9NB
☎ (020) 7713 5772

Situated in the basement of the Queen's Head pub, brewing began in 2014. Beer is mainly keg and supplied direct to the pub. Bottle-conditioned ales are planned.

Quercus SIBA

Unit 2M, South Hams Business Park, Churchstow, Devon, TQ7 3QH
☎ (01548) 854888 quercusdevonales.com

Quercus began trading in 2007, using an eight-barrel brew plant. The brewery was sold in 2012 by the founder Peter Walker to local residents John Tiner and Mike George. Beers are available in local pubs and shops. ♦

Best Bitter (OG 1040, ABV 4%)
An amber-coloured bitter with balanced malt and bitterness.

Prospect (OG 1040, ABV 4%)
Subtle bitterness and a sweet malt flavour with a rich aroma and colour.

Shingle Bay (OG 1042, ABV 4.2%)
A light, golden, easy-drinking ale with fruity citrus aroma and taste giving a subtle, crisp bite to refresh the palate.

Harry's (OG 1046, ABV 4.6%)
A rich, dark ale, with sweet malty chocolate aromas leading on to a complex finish of sweet malt and lingering hops.

Quiet (NEW)

Buchanan's Bistro, Woodend Barn, Burn O'Bennie, Banchory, Aberdeenshire, AB31 5QA
☎ (01330) 826530 buchananfood.com

Quiet Brewery is situated at Buchanan's Bistro, whose owners came to brewing through an interest in ferments of the kitchen: bread, yogurt, cheese. Beers are available bottle-conditoned only and are supplied exclusively to the bistro. ♦RAIB

Radnorshire SIBA

Timberworks, Brookside Farm, New Radnor, LD8 2SU
☎ (01544) 350456 ☎ 07789 909748
radnorhillsholidaycottages.com

Radnorshire is a microbrewery set up in 2012 in a barn on the grounds of a farm offering holiday cottage accommodation. It uses its own spring water. Drinkers staying at the cottages are supplied as well as a few local pubs. ‼

Whimble Gold (OG 1038, ABV 3.8%)
Light and hoppy golden ale.

Four Stones (OG 1040, ABV 4%)
A light amber ale with a subtle maltiness.

Smatcher Tawny (OG 1042, ABV 4.2%)
Mellow, tawny-coloured best bitter.

Water-Break-Its-Neck (ABV 5.7%)

Rail Ale

Schooner, South Shore Road, Gateshead, Tyne & Wear, NE8 3AF ☎ 07758 653510

Established in 2013, and based at the Schooner pub, Rail Ale is the first microbrewery in Gateshead. Beers are available at the Schooner and other local outlets, and are named with a railway theme. Brewing is currently suspended.

Amber Aspect (OG 1039, ABV 3.8%)
A traditional, refreshing, amber-coloured bitter.

Night Train (OG 1040, ABV 4%)
A dark beer, dry-hopped giving a smooth velvet taste.

Railway Tavern

58 Station Road, Brightlingsea, Essex, CO7 0DT

The brewery started life as a kitchen-sink affair in 1998. In 2012 the brewery was completely refurbished; a two-barrel plant is used to create a selection of dark beers suitable for vegetarians. ‼

Crab & Winkle Mild (OG 1036, ABV 3.6%)
Thin-bodied mild with a pear drop aroma and a roasty taste. The aftertaste is slightly ash-like with suggestions of bitter chocolate.

Bladderwrack Stout (OG 1047, ABV 4.7%)
Full-bodied stout with an intense roast grain character that is initially underpinned by subtle sweetness, which subsides to leave a drier finish.

Ramsbottom Craft SIBA

1 Heapworth Avenue, Ramsbottom, BL0 9EH ☎ 07976 263344 rammycraft.com

Brewing began in 2011 from a microbrewery in owner Matt Holmes's converted garage. 2014 saw production go full-time and the bottling side of the business moved to a bespoke unit, creating more room to expand the brewery. Larger premises are now being sought due to increased demand. The bottle conditioned ales are suitable for vegetarians and vegans. ♦RAIB

Stellar IPA (OG 1040, ABV 3.7%)
Refreshing medium-bodied ale with intensely fruity finish.

Bumble's Honeyed Ale (OG 1039, ABV 4%)
Elderflower and honey-based EPA.

Rammy Ale (OG 1041, ABV 4%)
A session bitter using Styrian and Goldings hops.

Flaori Maori (OG 1042, ABV 4.1%)
Balanced session ale, initial light malt gives way to an increasingly red fruit finish.

Chocolate Porter (OG 1043, ABV 4.2%)
Cocoa steep giving mocha notes.

Fat Lady Stout (OG 1043, ABV 4.3%)
Dark brown, almost black stout with a hint of roast in the aroma and a smooth taste.

Gift o' Gold (OG 1046, ABV 4.5%)
Copper/golden ale with a floral aroma and flavour notes of honey, spice and vanilla.

Oh Sunny Day (OG 1046, ABV 4.5%)
A pale yellow-coloured mellow ale with balanced malt sweetness and fruitiness.

Mango Beach (OG 1054, ABV 5.5%)
American pale ale using Amarillo hops.

Ramsbury SIBA

Stockclose Farm, Aldbourne, Wiltshire, SN8 2NN ☎ (01672) 541407 ☎ 07843 289527 ramsburybrewery.com

Ramsbury started brewing in 2004 using a 10-barrel plant and is situated high on the Marlborough Downs in Wiltshire. The brewery uses home-grown barley from the Ramsbury Estate. Expansion in 2014 saw an upgrade to a 30-barrel plant with a visitor centre and a well to provide the water. A distillery that uses grains grown on the estate became operational in 2015. ‼♦

Bitter (OG 1036, ABV 3.6%)
Amber-coloured beer with a smooth, delicate aroma and flavour.

Deerstalker (OG 1040, ABV 4%)
Amber-coloured best bitter with smooth, bitter finish.

Kennet Valley (OG 1041, ABV 4.1%)
A light amber-coloured, hoppy bitter with a long, dry finish.

Flint Knapper (OG 1042, ABV 4.2%)
Rich amber in colour with a malty taste.

Gold (OG 1045, ABV 4.5%)
A rich golden-coloured beer with a light hoppy aroma and taste.

Silver Pig Stout (OG 1047, ABV 4.7%)
A full-flavoured stout with a coffee chocolate finish.

Deerhunter (OG 1050, ABV 5%)
Rich ruby red in colour; a well-balanced winter ale.

Belapur IPA (OG 1055, ABV 5.5%)
A five-hop IPA.

Ramsgate SIBA

1 Hornet Close, Pyson's Road Industrial Estate, Broadstairs, Kent, CT10 2YD ☎ (01843) 868453 ramsgatebrewery.co.uk

Ramsgate was established in 2002 at the back of a Ramsgate pub. In 2006 the brewery moved to its current location, allowing for increased capacity and bottling. ‼♦RAIB

Gadds' No. 7 Bitter Ale (OG 1037, ABV 3.8%)

Gadds' Seasider (OG 1042, ABV 4.3%)

Gadds' No. 5 Best Bitter Ale (OG 1043, ABV 4.4%)

Gadds' No. 3 Kent Pale Ale (OG 1047, ABV 5%)

Gadds Faithful Dogbolter Porter (OG 1054, ABV 5.6%)

Randalls SIBA

La Piette Brewery, St Georges Esplanade, St Peter Port, Guernsey, GY1 3JG ☎ (01481) 720134 randallsbrewery.com

Randalls has been brewing since 1868 and until recently was the only brewery on Guernsey (White Rock being the other one). The company was bought out in 2006 and moved into a modern, purpose-built 60-hectolitre brewhouse in 2008. 17 pubs are owned and a further 70 outlets are supplied. ‼♦

Patois (OG 1045, ABV 4.5%)

RAN (NEW) SIBA

Unit 8, Ormonde Street, Fenton, Stoke-on-Trent, Staffordshire, ST4 3NP ☎ 07843 092620
🌐 ranales.co.uk

RAN Ales microbrewery began brewing in 2014 using a one-barrel kit in the garage to the rear of the owners' house. It relocated in 2015 to larger, purpose-built premises nearby, increasing capacity to 2.5 barrels.

Flya (ABV 4.5%)
Amber-coloured, easy-drinking session ale with a malty bitterness.

Hedge Hopper (ABV 4.5%)
A light golden-coloured bitter with refreshing fruity notes.

Coppa Flya (ABV 5%)
A copper-coloured bitter with a dry finish and a complementary caramel aftertaste.

Owd Flya (ABV 5%)
A rich dark ale with a bittersweet finish and a chocolaty finish on the tongue.

Stout (ABV 5.3%)
Rich and flavoursome dark ale with hints of coffee and chocolate.

Rat

Rat & Ratchet, 40 Chapel Hill, Huddersfield, West Yorkshire, HD1 3EB
☎ (01484) 542400 ☎ 07906 279038
✉ ratandratchet@ossett-brewery.co.uk

The Rat & Ratchet was originally established as a brewpub in 1994. Brewing ceased and it was purchased by Ossett Brewery (qv) in 2004. Brewing re-started in 2011 with a capacity of 30 barrels per week. A wide range of occasional beers with Rat themed names supplements the regular ales. ♦

Rat Attack (OG 1038, ABV 3.8%)
A pale golden session beer. Generous dry hopping gives a powerful citrus aroma.

White Rat (OG 1040, ABV 4%)
A pale hoppy ale with an intensely aromatic and resinous finish.

Black Rat (OG 1047, ABV 4.5%)
Porter with burnt, coffee and chocolate malt character. Slightly sweet on the palate, but moderate bitterness and a fruity/spicy aroma.

King Rat (OG 1050, ABV 5%)
A white wine aroma. Bitterness is high, but balanced by a residual malty sweetness.

Rat Against the Machine (OG 1071, ABV 7%)
A well-hopped IPA.

Raw SIBA

Units 3 & 4, Silver House, Adelphi Way, Staveley, Derbyshire, S43 3LJ
☎ (01246) 475445 🌐 rawbrew.com

Raw began brewing in 2010 using a five-barrel plant from Prospect Brewery of Wigan. Six core beers and a seasonal special are always available. !!♦

Baby Ghost IPA (OG 1039, ABV 3.9%)
Powerful, citrus-hopped session IPA.

Blonde Pale (OG 1039, ABV 3.9%)
Refreshing pale ale with German hops for a dry lager style.

JR Best Bitter (OG 1042, ABV 4.2%)
Traditional brown bitter with sweet biscuit malt flavours. Smooth, balanced bitterness.

Dark Peak Stout (OG 1045, ABV 4.5%)
Easy-drinking stout with plenty of malt flavours. English hopped for a smooth bitter finish.

Edge Pale Ale (OG 1045, ABV 4.5%)
Pale ale with balanced bitterness and a citrus aroma.

Anubis Porter (OG 1051, ABV 5.2%)
Smooth roast malt and mild coffee flavours with a lingering bitterness and gentle hop aroma.

Grey Ghost IPA (OG 1056, ABV 5.9%)
Powerful IPA with citrus and grapefruit flavours. Smooth and deceptively easy to drink

RCH SIBA

West Hewish, Somerset, BS24 6RR
☎ (01934) 834447 🌐 rchbrewery.com

The brewery was originally installed in the early 1980s behind the Royal Clarence Hotel, Burnham-on-Sea. Since 1993 brewing has taken place in a former cider mill at West Hewish. A 30-barrel plant was installed in 2000. RCH supplies 150 outlets and the award-winning beers are available nationwide through its own wholesaling company, which also distributes beers from other small independent breweries. ♦RAIB

Hewish IPA (OG 1036, ABV 3.6%)
Thinnish session bitter with plenty of malt, hops and pale fruit on the nose and palate. An astringent finish. Pitchfork's little brother.

Hewish Mild (OG 1036, ABV 3.6%)
Black mild with light roast nose. Hints of roast malt and slight apple taste with an astringent finish.

PG Steam (OG 1039, ABV 3.9%)
A tawny beer with a hint of unripe fruit and some malt in the flavour. Bitterness and astringency throughout.

Pitchfork (OG 1043, ABV 4.3%)
Some citrus aroma is followed by a bitter, hoppy taste with grapefruit notes. Finishes with an astringent and bitter aftertaste.

Old Slug Porter (OG 1046, ABV 4.5%)
Powerful aroma of roast and dark fruit which continues into the roast malt flavours. Bitter, slightly astringent finish.

East Street Cream (OG 1050, ABV 5%)
Brown beer which is low in flavour for the ABV, with an astringent finish.

Double Header (OG 1053, ABV 5.3%)
A strong, full-bodied golden bitter with a citrus taste and fruity hop nose. A bitter, astringent finish.

Firebox (OG 1060, ABV 6%)
Strong golden bitter with complex hoppy and fruity aroma. Sweet apple flavours give way to a lingering bitter aftertaste.

Reality

127 High Road, Chilwell, Nottingham, NG9 4AT
☎ 07801 539523
✉ alandenismonaghan@hotmail.com

THE BREWERIES

Reality began brewing in 2010 in the unused space of an IT business, hence the pun on Real-ITy. Beers are mainly themed around the brewery name and are available in select local outlets and nationally at beer festivals.

Virtuale Reality (OG 1039, ABV 3.8%)
A pale session brew.

No Escape (OG 1043, ABV 4.2%)

Bitter Reality (OG 1044, ABV 4.3%)
A copper-coloured bitter.

Stark Reality (OG 1046, ABV 4.5%)
Amber-coloured bitter with a hint of rum.

Reality Czech (OG 1047, ABV 4.6%)

Rebel SIBA

Century House, Kernick Industrial Estate, Penryn, Cornwall, TR10 9EP
☎ (01326) 617780 ⊕ rebelbrewing.co.uk

⊗ Rebel began brewing in 2011. It expanded to a nine-barrel plant with a shop and bar in 2012, supplying local pubs. In 2015 an 18-barrel plant was installed to meet local and national demand. !! ♦ RAIB

Surfbum IPA (OG 1034, ABV 3.5%)
Crisp and fragrant golden-coloured ale with plenty of citrus hoppiness.

Gold (OG 1038, ABV 3.8%) ◆
Refreshing golden ale with a light hop and fruit nose. Sweet grapefruit and citrus marmalade throughout. Bitter and slight dry finish.

Bal Maiden (OG 1041, ABV 4%) ◆
Pale brown best bitter with malt aroma. Full malt and bitter ale with apple and lemon flavours. Lingering bittersweet finish.

Sail Ale Golden Ale (OG 1041, ABV 4%)
Golden-coloured, crisp session ale with balanced malt and citrus tones.

Penryn Pale Ale (OG 1043, ABV 4.3%) ◆
Amber best bitter with hop and mango nose. Bitter taste, fruit, biscuit malt and toffee. Short, fresh hop bitter finish.

Bullhorn Black Lager (OG 1049, ABV 4.9%)

80/- Scotch Ale (OG 1051, ABV 5%) ◆
A dark brown porter with roast malt aroma. Roast and biscuit malt balanced by sweet plum and bitterness. Long finish.

Oyster Stout (OG 1051, ABV 5.1%) ◆
A smooth, black stout with oysters. Chocolate roast malt flavour with smoky and creamy texture lasting into long, malty finish.

Mexi-Cocoa Choc-Vanilla Stout (OG 1085, ABV 8.5%)
Smooth, robust chocolate and vanilla flavours throughout.

Rebellion SIBA

Marlow Brewery, Bencombe Farm, Marlow Bottom, Buckinghamshire, SL7 3LT
☎ (01628) 476594 ⊕ rebellionbeer.co.uk

⊗ Established in 1993, Rebellion has grown steadily with one site move and several expansion projects, including a new on-site shop. The brewery currently brews approximately 70,000 pints per week, supplying more than 400 local pubs and clubs within a 30-mile radius of Marlow. The shop provides customers with fresh real ale, bottled beers, merchandise and local produce and the ever-popular membership club now has over 3,700 active members. !! ♦

IPA (OG 1039, ABV 3.7%) ◆
Copper-coloured bitter, sweet and malty, with resinous and red apple flavours. Caramel and fruit decline to leave a dry, bitter and malty finish.

Smuggler (OG 1042, ABV 4.1%) ◆
A red-brown beer, well-bodied and bitter with an uncompromisingly dry, bitter finish.

Mutiny (OG 1046, ABV 4.5%) ◆
Tawny in colour, this full-bodied best bitter is predominantly fruity and moderately bitter with crystal malt continuing to a dry finish.

Rectory SIBA

Streat Hill Farm, Streat Hill, Streat, Hassocks, East Sussex, BN6 8RP
☎ (01273) 890570 ✉ rectoryales@hotmail.com

⊗ Rectory was founded in 1995 by the Rev Godfrey Broster to generate funds for the maintenance of his three parish churches. 107 parishioners are shareholders. Production is split between the Streat Hill Farm, where seasonal and specials beers are brewed, and the micro-plant at Harvey's brewery (qv). !! ♦

Rector's Light Relief (OG 1045, ABV 4.5%)
Golden ale with a fresh, floral aroma and distinctly hoppy, bitter characteristics.

Rector's Revenge (OG 1050, ABV 5%)
Traditional-style mid-brown-coloured strong bitter with good balance of malt and hops and a long bitter finish.

Red SIBA

Unit 1, The Orchard, Garden Farm, The Town, Great Staughton, Cambridgeshire, PE19 5BE ☎ 07827 294229 ⊕ redbrewery.com

Red Brewery was established using a four-barrel plant in 2012 in a converted farm building in the village of Great Staughton. ♦ RAIB

Sundial Gold (OG 1041, ABV 4.1%)
Golden ale, with balanced, deep hop character. Citrus with a light hop finish.

Pathfinder (OG 1045, ABV 4.8%)
Amber-coloured ale with orange and grapefruit citrus notes.

White Duck (OG 1045, ABV 4.8%)
Pale, highly-hopped ale with grapefruit flavours.

All Saints Porter (OG 1051, ABV 5.2%)
Smooth, dark porter with a hint of chocolate and blackcurrant.

Staughton Bitter (ABV 5.2%)
Copper-coloured hoppy bitter. Light fruit.

Valhalla (OG 1053, ABV 5.5%)
Bronze-coloured strong beer. Highly-hopped with rounded fruit.

Juggernaut (OG 1063, ABV 6.7%)
Garnet-coloured winter ale. Floral and slightly sweet.

Red Cat SIBA 👁

Unit 10, Sun Valley Business Park, Winnall Close, Winchester, Hampshire, SO23 0LB
☎ (01962) 863423 ☎ 07824 876489
⊕ redcatbrewing.co.uk

Red Cat was established in 2014 by Andy Mansell and Iain McIntosh using an 11-barrel plant. It supplies Hampshire and bordering counties. A small bar in the brewery sells a range of products. 🛒

Prowler Pale (OG 1034.5, ABV 3.6%)
A light straw-coloured session bitter, slightly fruity, with hints of hops.

Bitter (OG 1037, ABV 3.7%)
Light brown bitter with a burst of fruit on the nose and a slight dryness on the palate.

Best (OG 1042.3, ABV 4.2%)
A traditional, bronze-coloured best bitter with a rounded malty flavour and not too much bitterness or hop notes.

Mr M's Porter (OG 1050, ABV 4.5%)
A complex beer with aromas of chocolate, vanilla and soft Greek coffee. Low levels of hops allow the malts to shine through. Full in the mouth yet easy-drinking.

TomCat (OG 1044.4, ABV 4.7%)
A golden premium ale with a full hop flavour that is not overly bitter.

MaCavity (OG 1055.5, ABV 5.3%)

Red Even

Unit 53, Coleshill Industrial Estate, Station Road, Coleshill, Warwickshire, B46 1JT
☎ (01675) 464762 ✉ redeven@hotmail.co.uk

Red Even began brewing in 2013. It currently produces cask-conditioned beers plus beers bottled on its own facility.

Shooting Dice (OG 1042, ABV 4.2%)
An American-style pale ale with a firm malt base and biscuit notes leading to a light hop finish.

Red Fox SIBA

The Chicken Sheds, Upp Hall Farm, Salmons Lane, Coggeshall, Essex, CO6 1RY
☎ (01376) 563123 ⊕ redfoxbrewery.co.uk

Red Fox began brewing in 2008 and has continued to expand in line with increasing demand. Around 35 outlets are supplied direct. Several local pubs now stock the beers. Mini-pins and pins can be purchased direct from the brewery. ‼◆RAIB

Mild (OG 1037, ABV 3.6%)
A classic dark, full-flavoured mild with hints of chocolate and a deep roast barley flavour.

IPA (OG 1038, ABV 3.7%)
An East Anglian-style copper-coloured beer with a delicate flavour.

Bitter (OG 1039, ABV 3.8%)
A traditional-style bitter which perfectly balances malt and fruit flavours.

Hunter's Gold (OG 1040, ABV 3.9%)
A golden beer with a delicate citrus aroma.

Best Bitter (OG 1040, ABV 4%)
A light brown bitter with a full flavour and malty backbone.

Coggeshall Gold (OG 1041, ABV 4%)
An aromatic golden beer, packed full of citrus and exotic fruit flavours. Unusually for a beer of this style it does not have a bitter finish.

Surrex Gold (OG 1041, ABV 4.1%)
A highly-hopped, aromatic beer. Pink grapefruit and peach aromas abound leading to a slightly bitter finish.

Black Fox Porter (OG 1046, ABV 4.8%) 🍺
A rich-flavoured black beer packed with malty flavour and undertones of chocolate.

Wily Ol' Fox (OG 1050, ABV 5.2%)
An aromatic amber-coloured ale made from English hops and malt, with a soft, fruity palate.

Red Ink (NEW) SIBA 👁

Unit 8, Greenham Business Park, Greenham, Somerset, TA21 0LR
☎ (01823) 765015 ☎ 07957 213743
⊕ redinkbrewing.com

A 2.5-barrel plant established in 2014. Brewing is currently suspended.

Red Rock SIBA

Higher Humber Farm, Bishopsteignton, Devon, TQ14 9TD
☎ (01626) 879738 ☎ 07894 35094
⊕ redrockbrewery.co.uk

Red Rock first started brewing in 2006 with a four-barrel plant and upgraded in 2011 to a 7.5-barrel one. It is based in a converted barn on a working farm using locally-sourced malt, fresh hops and the farm's own spring water. It has a bar and can accommodate private functions. ‼🛒◆RAIB

Red Rock (OG 1041, ABV 4.2%)

Red Shoot

🍺 Toms Lane, Linwood, Ringwood, Hampshire, BH24 3QT
☎ (01425) 475792 ⊕ redshoot.co.uk

⊗ The 2.5-barrel brewery was commissioned in 1998. About half the output is sold in the pub, the remainder to other local outlets distributed by Wadworth (qv).

New Forest Gold (OG 1038, ABV 3.8%)
A refreshing golden ale with a light, floral, citrus taste, moving towards a burnt toffee finish.

Muddy Boot (OG 1042, ABV 4.2%)
A dark mild brewed with Golding hops, molasses and some chocolate malt.

Tom's Tipple (OG 1048, ABV 4.8%)
A copper-coloured, strong, malty bitter with some citrus balance to the toffee and malt flavours.

Red Squirrel SIBA 👁

Unit 24 Boxted Farm, Berkhamsted Road, Potten End, Hertfordshire, HP1 2SQ
☎ (01442) 256970 ⊕ redsquirrelbrewery.co.uk

⊗ Red Squirrel started brewing in Hertford in 2004 using a 10-barrel plant. In 2011 it moved to Potten End near Hemel Hempstead to brand new premises and has subsequently expanded production. ‼◆

Red Dawn Mild (OG 1037.7, ABV 3.7%)

Dark red in colour with mellow and nutty overtones and a smooth and rounded palate.

Hopfest (OG 1037, ABV 3.8%)
Pale, golden ale with a floral/citrus aroma and elderflower notes.

Legally Blonde (OG 1040, ABV 4%)
Hops give a fresh, citrus flavour with herbal, floral and buttery notes.

Conservation Bitter (OG 1040, ABV 4.1%)
A chestnut brown traditional bitter with a hoppy, fruity bitterness and biscuit flavours with a hint of spice and chocolate.

Mr Squirrel (OG 1042.9, ABV 4.3%)
A chestnut red-coloured bitter, lightly hopped with a creamy texture. Hints of caramel and vanilla complement the slightly hoppy and malty overtones.

Jack Black (OG 1047.7, ABV 4.8%)
A black IPA featuring the hop profile of an IPA and the dark colour of a porter.

London Porter (OG 1048, ABV 5%)
Dark brown/black porter with a good balance of chocolate and roasted barley. Full-bodied on the palate with bittersweet liquorice, rich chocolate flavours and a creamy finish.

Redwood American IPA (OG 1051, ABV 5.4%)
Based on a secret Michigan recipe, golden orange in colour, with complex hoppy aromas, floral/citrus tones and a long, lingering finish.

Redball

Kash Bar, 121 Brook Street, Chester, CH1 3DU
☎ (01244) 401777 ☎ 07807 444625
✉ redballbrewery@gmail.com

Redball was started at Alex Haycraft's Kash Bar in Chester early in 2014. A sister brewery to Blueball (qv), the purpose was to brew strong premium beers for consumption both at the Kash Bar in Chester and at Kash 22 bar in Frodsham. ‼

Redchurch

275-276 Poyser Street, Bethnal Green, London, E2 9RF
☎ (020) 3487 0255 ☎ 07968 173097
theredchurchbrewery.com

Redchurch was established in 2011 by Gary Ward using an eight-barrel plant and is situated in a unit under the railway arches in Bethnal Green. The brewery produces seven beers at present, in key casks and bottles, for both the domestic and export markets. There are ongoing plans for expansion. ♦ RAIB

Redemption SIBA

Unit 2, Compass West Industrial Estate, 33 West Road, Tottenham, London, N17 0XL
☎ (020) 8885 5227 redemptionbrewing.co.uk

Redemption began brewing in 2010 on a 12-barrel plant. Most of the beer is supplied in casks to pubs in north and central London and to beer festivals. Beers are available bottle-conditioned and in polypins from the brewery. ‼ ♦ RAIB

Trinity (OG 1036.6, ABV 3%)
Refreshing golden beer with strong citrus notes throughout. The strong bitterness is softened by a little sweet malt character.

Pale Ale (OG 1037.5, ABV 3.8%)
Well-balanced amber bitter with hops and citrus orange throughout. The sweet maltiness fades leaving a slightly dry, bitter finish.

Hopspur (OG 1044.5, ABV 4.5%)
Hoppy bitter notes are present in this tawny brown best bitter which has a hint of coffee roast throughout and some caramelised citrus notes.

Urban Dusk (OG 1044.5, ABV 4.6%)
Full-bodied brown best bitter; chocolate and fudge in the aroma and flavour overlaid with citrus. Lingering, dry bitter finish.

Friendship Porter (OG 1051.5, ABV 5.1%)
Sweetish smooth porter with a mix of liquorice, caramel and roast notes. A pleasant burnt roast gives dry, bitter overtones.

Big Chief (OG 1052.5, ABV 5.5%)
Golden ale with a smooth mouthfeel and a strong fruity aroma, flavour and finish, which is also dry and bitter.

Redscar SIBA

c/o Cleveland Hotel, 9-11 High Street West, Redcar, North Yorkshire, TS10 1SQ
☎ (01642) 513727 ☎ 07828 855146
redscar-brewery.co.uk

Redscar first brewed in 2008. In 2014 it increased its capacity to a five-barrel plant. The brewery supplies the hotel, local pubs and beer festivals. ‼ ♦

Jazz (OG 1040, ABV 4%)
Light-coloured session beer delicately hopped with three varieties.

Poison (OG 1040, ABV 4%)
A dark, full-bodied ale.

Sands (OG 1043, ABV 4.2%)
A hoppy golden ale.

Pier (OG 1046, ABV 4.5%)
A dark, full-bodied ale with a rich, fruity flavour.

Rocks (OG 1045, ABV 4.5%)

Beach (OG 1050, ABV 5%)

Redstone

Tynwllyd Farm, Llangorse, LD3 7UA ☎ 07581 878604
redstone-brewery.com

Redstone started brewing in 2012 using the remnants of the Tudor Brewery, formerly based in Abergavenny. A four-barrel plant has been installed in a converted Edwardian granary to supply the local area. ‼ ♦

Gorsey (OG 1045, ABV 4.2%)
Light blonde ale with citrus aroma and grapefruit flavour.

Exile (OG 1048, ABV 4.8%)
A dark beer, with a smoky aroma.

Redwell SIBA

7 The Arches, Bracondale, Trowse Millgate, Norwich, NR1 2EF
☎ (01603) 624072 redwellbrewing.com

Redwell began brewing in 2013 using a 10-barrel plant. Production is mostly keg or bottled but occasional cask-conditioned ales are produced for beer festivals or by special request for local outlets.

RedWillow SIBA

Sutton Mill, Gunco Lane, Macclesfield, Cheshire, SK11 7JL
☎ (01625) 502315 ⊕ redwillowbrewery.com

☺ Toby McKenzie and his wife Caroline began brewing in 2010 from a unit within Sutton Mill. The award-winning beers are distributed nationwide. Experimental brews are branded under the Faithless label: see website. One bar is owned, the RedWillow Bar in Macclesfield. ◆RAIB

Seamless (OG 1034, ABV 3.6%)
A light and hoppy pale ale.

Headless (OG 1037, ABV 3.9%) ⏳
Refreshingly floral pale ale with a restrained orange-led bitterness.

Mirthless (OG 1037, ABV 3.9%)
A refreshing, easy-drinking pale ale with a smooth finish.

Feckless (OG 1040, ABV 4.1%)
A classic best bitter, rich toffee and malt balanced with the subtle hop flavours.

Directionless (OG 1041, ABV 4.2%) ⏳
A balanced and easy-drinking session ale, warm amber in colour, with a subtle candied orange fruitiness.

Wreckless (OG 1046, ABV 4.8%)
A pale ale with massive amounts of tropical fruit flavour and a clean finish.

Heartless (OG 1048, ABV 4.9%)
A bold and complex beer with a dry, balanced bitterness and a long espresso finish.

Sleepless (OG 1052, ABV 5.4%)
An American-style amber ale. Rich toffee malt flavours are followed by juicy hops with a long, clean bitter finish.

Smokeless (OG 1055, ABV 5.7%) 🍺
A smooth smoky porter infused with chipotles.

Shameless (OG 1057, ABV 5.9%)
An American-style IPA.

Soulless (OG 1059, ABV 6.5%)
A black IPA.

Ageless (OG 1065, ABV 7.2%)
An American-style IPA with a huge hit of mango, lychee and pineapple, with a long, clean bitter finish.

Reedley Hallows SIBA

Unit B3, Farrington Close, Farrington Road Industrial Estate, Burnley, Lancashire, BB11 5SH ☎ 07963 038220 ⊕ reedley-hallows-brewery.co.uk

☺Brewing started on this four-barrel plant in 2012. Having moved to larger premises the brewery now has nine fermenters to cope with the production of its six core beers, one of which contributes £3 per firkin to the local Pendleside Hospice. ‼

Old Laund Bitter (OG 1038, ABV 3.6%)
A good session beer, smooth and creamy with a distinctive hoppy aftertaste.

Filly Close Blonde (OG 1040, ABV 3.9%)

A well-balanced ale, bitter and spicy with a good fruity finish.

Pendleside (OG 1042, ABV 4%)
A light-coloured beer with hints of tropical fruits and a spicy aftertaste.

Monkholme Premium (OG 1042, ABV 4.2%)
A premium golden ale, smooth with a hoppy taste throughout.

New Laund Dark (OG 1044, ABV 4.4%)
A dark stout, sweet with a smoky, bitter finish.

Nook of Pendle (OG 1050, ABV 5%)
An amber, warming ale with a dried fruit and malty aroma. Tropical fruits in the taste with a bittersweet finish.

Revolutions SIBA

Unit B7, Whitwood Enterprise Park, Speedwell Road, Whitwood, Castleford, West Yorkshire, WF10 5PX
☎ (01977) 552649 ☎ 07801 701089
⊕ revolutionsbrewing.co.uk

Revolutions began brewing in 2010. All beers are musically inspired, reflecting formats from the analogue era mainly brewed to 3.3% (33 rpm), 3.9% (EP), 4.5% (45 rpm) and 6.0% (C60). The Rewind 33 series of monthly specials references music from 33 years ago. ‼◆

Cocker (OG 1040, ABV 3.9%)
Pale brown/golden, English-hopped ale; fruity with moderate levels of bitterness.

EP Session Pale (OG 1040, ABV 3.9%)
A pale ale with balanced levels of sweetness and bitterness with a crisp, lemony hop finish.

Clash London Porter (OG 1045, ABV 4.5%)
A complex dark malty beer rounded off with a smooth hop finish.

Go-Go American Pale (OG 1045, ABV 4.5%)
A golden pale ale hopped with three American citrus-floral hops.

Pretender Blonde (OG 1045, ABV 4.5%)
A blonde ale with medium levels of bitterness and with pine, lemon and lime hop notes.

Debaser (OG 1059, ABV 6%)
Full-flavoured, light-coloured IPA using Australian and American hop varieties.

Manifesto (OG 1059, ABV 6%)
A rich, dark stout.

Rhymney SIBA

Gilchrist Thomas Industrial Estate, Blaenavon, Torfaen, NP4 9RL
☎ (01685) 722253 ⊕ rhymneybreweryltd.com

☺Rhymney first brewed in 2005. The 75-hl plant was sourced from Canada. Around 220 outlets are supplied. In 2012 the brewery relocated to Blaenavon with a new brewing centre and visitor facility. ‼🍴RAIB

Best (OG 1037, ABV 3.7%)

Hobby Horse (OG 1038, ABV 3.8%)

Dark (OG 1040, ABV 4%) ⏳

Bevans Bitter (OG 1042, ABV 4.2%)

Bitter (OG 1043, ABV 4.3%)

Export Ale (OG 1050, ABV 5%)

Richmond SIBA

Station Brewery, Station Yard, Richmond, North Yorkshire, DL10 4LD
☎ (01748) 828266 ⊕ richmondbrewing.co.uk

Richmond opened in 2008 in the Victorian station complex beside the River Swale. The brewery's output is split between cask-conditioned (60%) and bottled ales (40%). Beers are available in the local area in the Hildyard Arms in Colburn, Bolton Arms in Leyburn and the Castle Tavern in Richmond. Ownership changed in 2013. !! ♦RAIB

SwAle (OG 1035, ABV 3.7%)
Dark mild brewed using chocolate malt with slightly more bitterness than a traditional mild.

Station Ale (OG 1039, ABV 4%)
Light golden bitter brewed using hedgerow hops.

Dale Strider (OG 1043, ABV 4.5%)

Stump Cross Ale (OG 1046, ABV 4.7%)

Ridgeside SIBA

Unit 24, Penraevon 2 Industrial Estate, Meanwood, Leeds, West Yorkshire, LS7 2AW ☎ 07595 380568
⊕ ridgesidebrewery.co.uk

Ridgeside began brewing in 2010 using a four-barrel plant, which is set to expand. Special brews are produced monthly alongside an extensive core range. Regular outlets are supplied around Leeds. In July 2015 the brewery was sold to the brewing team of Matt Lovell and Juan Carlos Mendoza. ♦

Jailbreak (OG 1038, ABV 3.8%)
A pale session beer.

Eldorado (OG 1039, ABV 3.9%)
Bitterness dominates this hoppy beer, gold in colour with much grapefruit in evidence from start to finish.

Cascade (OG 1041, ABV 4.1%)
A single-hop pale ale.

Templar (OG 1042, ABV 4.2%)

Rushmore (OG 1043, ABV 4.3%)
A pale ale brewed using American hops.

Innuendo (OG 1045, ABV 4.5%)
A mid-strength pale amber ale.

Eclipse (OG 1046, ABV 4.6%)
A refreshing pale ale packed with American and Australian hops.

Legacy (OG 1047, ABV 4.7%)
An easy-drinking pale amber beer.

Desert Aire (OG 1048, ABV 4.8%)
An American-hopped pale ale.

Stargazer (OG 1049, ABV 4.9%)
Pleasant golden beer with some malt. Hops are present throughout, particularly in the finish where they are spicy and linger.

Black Night (OG 1050, ABV 5%)
Complex, rich black beer with an intriguing smoked malt, bitter coffee yet fruity flavour, finishing with strong roasty bitterness.

Long Way From Home (OG 1050, ABV 5%)

Shot in the Dark (OG 1050, ABV 5%)
A premium oatmeal stout infused with fresh North Star coffee.

Coda (OG 1057, ABV 5.7%)
A refreshing strong, hoppy and bitter golden ale with an onslaught of citrus.

Eliminator (OG 1060, ABV 6%)

Ridgeway

Beer Counter Ltd, South Stoke, Oxfordshire, RG8 0JW
☎ (01491) 873474 ⊕ ridgewaybrewery.co.uk

Set up by ex-Brakspear head brewer Peter Scholey, Ridgeway specialises in bottle-conditioned beers, although cask beers are occasionally offered locally. At present the beers are brewed by Peter using his own ingredients on the plant at Hepworth's Brewery (qv) and Cotswold Brewery (qv).

Ringwood

Christchurch Road, Ringwood, Hampshire, BH24 3AP
☎ (01425) 471177 ⊕ ringwoodbrewery.co.uk

Ringwood was bought in 2007 by Marstons for £19 million. Production has been increased to 50,000 barrels a year. Some 750 outlets are supplied. Ringwood beers are now available in Marston's pubs throughout the country. Part of Marston's PLC. !! ♦

Best Bitter (OG 1038, ABV 3.8%)
A malty session bitter with strong toffee notes in the aroma, leading to a short, bittersweet finish. Malt tends to dominate throughout.

Boondoggle (ABV 4.2%)

Fortyniner (OG 1049, ABV 4.9%)
A caramel, biscuity aroma, with hints of damson, lead to a sweet but well-balanced taste with malt, fruit and hop flavours.

Old Thumper (OG 1055, ABV 5.1%)
A powerful, sweet, copper-coloured beer. A fruity aroma preludes a sweet, malty taste with fruit and caramel and a bittersweet aftertaste.

Ripple Steam SIBA

Parsonage Farm, Vale Road, Sutton, Kent, CT15 5DH
☎ 07917 037611 ⊕ ripplesteambrewery.co.uk

Ripple Steam began brewing commercially on a farm in Kent in 2012. ♦

Milk Stout (ABV 3.5%)

Best Bitter (ABV 4.1%)

Green Hopped IPA (ABV 4.5%)

IPA (ABV 4.5%)

River Leven

Lab Road, Kinlochleven, PH50 4SG ☎ 07901 873273
⊕ riverlevenales.co.uk

River Leven was established 2011 in the former carbon bunker of the aluminium smelter factory in Kinlochleven. Only pure malt cask-conditioned ale is produced.

Blonde (OG 1040, ABV 4%)
A clean-tasting, pale golden beer with hints of citrus.

Traditional IPA (OG 1040, ABV 4%)
The distinctive, traditional British bittering hops combine with the nutty flavour of the malt to produce this copper-coloured ale.

Riverhead

2 Peel Street, Marsden, Huddersfield, West Yorkshire, HD7 6BR
☎ (01484) 841270 (Pub) ossett-brewery.co.uk

Riverhead is a brewpub that opened in 1995. Ossett Brewing (qv) purchased the site in 2006 but runs it as a separate brewery. It has since opened the Dining Room on the first floor, which uses Riverhead beers in its dishes. There are many rotating beers produced as well as seasonals. ‼♦

Legger's Lite (OG 1037, ABV 3.6%)
A refreshing session bitter with a powerful citrus aroma.

Butterley Bitter (OG 1038, ABV 3.8%)
A light and refreshing traditional Yorkshire bitter.

Black Moss Stout (OG 1044, ABV 4.3%)
A rich, full-bodied and roasty black stout, moderately bitter and delicately hopped.

White Cloud (OG 1044, ABV 4.5%)
A dry, refreshing and fairly bitter premium ale with intense citrus aromas.

March Haigh (OG 1046, ABV 4.6%)
Malty and full-bodied mid-brown traditional premium ale with moderate bitterness and spicy hop aroma.

Redbrook Premium (OG 1055, ABV 5.5%)
A malty, full-bodied strong ale with a mellow palate and gentle spicy aroma.

Riverside

Bee's Farm, Wainfleet, Lincolnshire, PE24 4LX
☎ (01754) 881288 ☎ 07779 280996

Riverside started brewing in 2003 on a five-barrel plant, moving to its present site in 2008. Since 2014 the brewery has operated on a part-time basis, mainly at weekends, with a reduced level of production. It supplies a small number of regular local outlets. ♦

Robin Hood SIBA

Unit 3, Northgate Place, High Church Street, New Basford, Nottingham, NG7 7JT ☎ 07804 499462
robinhoodbrewery.com

Robin Hood began brewing in 2012, originally using spare capacity at another brewery. It moved to its own premises in 2013 using a 5.5-barrel plant. ♦

Maid Marian Extra Pale (OG 1039, ABV 3.9%)
Pale straw-coloured ale with overtones of honey, balanced with a hint of hop aroma and bitterness.

Robin Hood (OG 1040, ABV 4%)
A traditional English ale, light brown in colour with the distinctive aroma and taste of English hops and malt, with a smooth, dry finish.

Golden Archer (ABV 4.2%)
Deep golden ale, hints of orange in the aroma with a fruity hop taste and bitter edge for balance.

Will Scarlet (OG 1042, ABV 4.2%)
Red-coloured ale with spicy hop overtones and port-like flavours.

Friar Tuck Stout (OG 1044, ABV 4.4%)
Dark and malty, with coffee and chocolate flavours balanced out with a hint of hop background.

Outlaw (OG 1044, ABV 4.4%)
Golden ale with floral citrus hop aroma and crisp hop finish.

Sheriff of Nottingham (OG 1046, ABV 4.6%)
A tawny-coloured special ale, initial fruity hop flavour developing into a satisfying bitterness to finish.

Little John Strong (OG 1050, ABV 5%)
Deep gold-coloured strong ale. Full-bodied with an aroma and taste of barley wine to start, then developing a bitter, hoppy but balanced finish.

Robinsons SIBA IFBB

Unicorn Brewery, Lower Hillgate, Stockport, Cheshire, SK1 1JJ
☎ (0161) 612 4061 robinsonsbrewery.com

Robinsons has been brewing since 1838 and the business is still owned and run by the family. It has an estate of around 300 pubs stretching from Cheshire to Cumbria and out to North Wales. 2015 saw 1892 Mild discontinued and the introduction of Wizard, a new session bitter. The brewery is investing £23 million in its pub estate and reported record beer production in 2015. ‼♦

Wizard (OG 1037, ABV 3.7%)
A mid-brown session beer, well-balanced, crisp and refreshing.

Dizzy Blonde (OG 1037, ABV 3.8%)
A straw-coloured summer ale with a distinctive hop aroma.

Hartleys XB (OG 1040, ABV 4%)
An overly sweet and malty bitter with a bitter citrus peel fruitiness and a hint of liquorice in the finish.

Cumbria Way (OG 1040, ABV 4.1%)
A pronounced malt aroma with rich fruit notes. Rounded malt and hops in the mouth, long dry finish with citrus fruit notes.

Cwrw'r Ddraig Aur (OG 1041, ABV 4.1%)

Unicorn (OG 1041, ABV 4.2%)
Amber beer with a fruity aroma. Malt, hops and fruit in the taste with a bitter, malty finish.

Trooper (OG 1048, ABV 4.8%)
Dark golden-coloured hoppy beer brewed in conjunction with Iron Maiden's Bruce Dickinson.

Double Hop (OG 1050, ABV 5%)
Pale brown beer with malt and fruit on the nose. Full hoppy taste with malt and fruit, leading to a hoppy, bitter finish.

Old Tom (OG 1079, ABV 8.5%)
A full-bodied, dark beer with malt, fruit and chocolate on the aroma. A complex range of flavours includes dark chocolate, full maltiness, port and fruits and lead to a long, bittersweet aftertaste.

Rock & Roll SIBA

Lamp Tavern, 157 Barford Street, Birmingham, B5 6AH
☎ (0121) 688 1220 ☎ 07922 554181
markwshepherd@btinternet.com

Owned and operated by Mark Shepherd, former head brewer at Weatheroak Hill and the Old Pie Factory, Rock & Roll is Birmingham's only rooftop pub brewery. The two-barrel plant was hand-crafted in Birmingham to fit into the limited space available. Due to the brewery's compact size, specials beers are regularly available. Unfined and vegan ales are also available in the pub as well as the local free trade and regional beer festivals. !! ♦

Lamplight (OG 1039, ABV 3.9%)

Instant Calmer (OG 1040, ABV 4%)

Brew Springsteen (OG 1042, ABV 4.2%)

Rocket Science

73 Firgrove Crescent, Yate, BS37 7AJ ☎ 07759 271993 ⊕ rocketscienceales.co.uk

Rocket Science is a nanobrewery, which commenced brewing in 2013. The range is currently only available bottle conditioned. RAIB

Rockin' Robin SIBA ◉

Campfield Farm, Haste Hill Road, Boughton Monchelsea, Kent, ME17 4LR ☎ (01622) 747106 ☎ 07787 416110 ⊕ rockinrobinbrewery.co.uk

Brewing began in 2011 using a one-barrel plant in a garden shed. It moved to its current location in 2014. Outlets throughout north Kent and the south-east London borders are supplied, including several micropubs. !! ♦

Reliant Robin (OG 1035, ABV 3.6%)
An auburn-coloured classic session bitter. Rich with traditional hop notes on the palate and a fresh, spicy finish.

Hoppin' Robin (OG 1036, ABV 3.7%)
A traditional English session bitter. A complex ale with full malt, fruit in the mouth and Kentish hops on the tongue.

RPA (OG 1038, ABV 3.9%)
A light but refreshing pale ale.

Robin Redbest (OG 1041, ABV 4%)
Light amber in colour with initial good hop flavour moving to a pleasant malty finish.

Rocka Hula (OG 1039, ABV 4%)
A pale ale with English malt and a variety of American hops, giving a fruity and slightly spicy taste.

Reckless Robin (OG 1044, ABV 4.5%)
A strong bitter that delivers a fresh hoppy punch, well-balanced with soft fruit malt.

Rockingham SIBA

Blatherwycke, Northamptonshire ☎ (01832) 280722

Office: 25 Wansford Road, Elton, Cambridgeshire, PE8 6RZ ⊕ rockinghamales.co.uk

⊠ Rockingham is a small brewery established in 1997 that operates from a converted farm building near Blatherwycke, Northamptonshire, with a two-barrel plant producing a prolific range of beers. It supplies half a dozen local outlets. ♦

Forest Gold (OG 1039, ABV 3.9%)
A hoppy blonde ale with citrus flavours. Well-balanced and clean finishing.

Hop Devil (OG 1040, ABV 3.9%)
Six hop varieties give this golden ale a bitter start and fruity finish.

White Rabbit (OG 1040, ABV 4%)

Light golden ale brewed with Australian and New Zealand hops. Bitter start and a tropical fruit finish.

Saxon Cross (OG 1041, ABV 4.1%)
A golden red ale with a coffee aroma and fruit and blackcurrant undertones.

Fruits of the Forest (OG 1043, ABV 4.3%)
A multi-layered beer in which summer fruits and several spices compete with a big hop presence.

Dark Forest (OG 1050, ABV 5%)
A dark and complex beer with malty/smoky flavours that give way to a fruity, bitter finish.

Rocky Head

Unit 16, Glenville Mews, Kimber Road, Southfields, London, SW18 4NJ ☎ (020) 8875 9917 ⊕ sites.google.com/site/ rockyheadbrewery

Rocky Head is a microbrewery set up in 2012 by a group of friends inspired by the American craft brewing scene. A range of vegan-friendly bottle-conditioned beers is brewed on a five-barrel plant. RAIB

Romney Marsh (NEW)

Unit 7, Jacks Park, Cinque Ports Road, New Romney, Kent, TN28 8AN ☎ (01797) 362333 ☎ 07796 176011 ⊕ romneymarshbrewery.com

⊠ A 12-barrel, family-run brewery founded in 2015 by former Come Dine with Me executive producer Matt Calais. Cask beer is supplied to outlets throughout South East Kent and East Sussex. There are plans to open a brewery shop. !! RAIB

Romney Golden Ale (OG 1038, ABV 3.9%)

Romney Best (OG 1040, ABV 4.2%)

Romney Amber Ale (OG 1041, ABV 4.4%)

Rooster's SIBA ◉

Unit 3, Grimbald Park, Wetherby Road, Knaresborough, North Yorkshire, HG5 8LJ ☎ (01423) 865959 ⊕ roosters.co.uk

◉Rooster's was founded in 1993 by Sean and Alison Franklin. The brewery was acquired by the Fozard family in 2011 when Sean and Alison retired. One-off and occasional experimental brews are also brewed under the Outlaw Brewing Co name. !! ♦

Buckeye (OG 1035.5, ABV 3.5%)
An easy-drinking, well-hopped pale ale, producing an orange, citrus fruit aroma and a refreshing level of bitterness.

Blind Jack (OG 1036.5, ABV 3.7%)
A quaffable red ale with citrus fruit aromas and a light, spicy finish.

Wild Mule (OG 1037, ABV 3.9%)
A session-strength pale ale, brewed using New Zealand's Nelson Sauvin hop, which creates a white wine fruitiness that's backed up by a lasting grapefruit bitterness.

YPA (Yorkshire Pale Ale) (OG 1039.5, ABV 4.1%)
A pale, aromatic, summer ale that offers up delicate peach and berry fruit flavours.

Yankee (OG 1041, ABV 4.3%) ◆

A straw-coloured beer with a delicate, fruity aroma leading to a well-balanced taste of malt and hops with a slight evidence of sweetness, followed by a refreshing, fruity/bitter finish.

Fort Smith (OG 1048, ABV 5%)
A bold IPA with tropical and passion fruit aromas and a lasting, bitter finish.

Londinium (OG 1054, ABV 5.5%)
A dark beer with a hint of coffee on the finish, brewed with the addition of Taylors of Harrogate After Dark coffee.

Baby-Faced Assassin (OG 1058, ABV 6.1%)
An IPA with hoppy aromas of mango, apricot, grapefruit and mandarin orange, along with a lasting, juicy, tropical fruit bitterness.

Roseland

目 c/o Roseland Inn, Philleigh, St Mawes, Truro, Cornwall, TR2 5NB
☎ (01872) 580254 ☎ 07977 472484
⊕ roselandinn.co.uk

Established in 2009 by its owner/brewer at the Roseland Inn, St Mawes, with the beers mostly named after local birds and available in the pub. See Keltek

Rossendale

目 Griffin Inn, 84 Hud Rake, Haslingden, Lancashire, BB4 5AF
☎ (01706) 214021 ⊕ rossendalebrewery.co.uk

☺Formerly known as Pennine Ales, the brewery acquired the brew plant previously used by Porter Brewing Co in 2007 and is based in the cellar of the Griffin Inn in Haslingden. It produces seven regular cask ales.

Floral Dance (OG 1040, ABV 3.8%)
A pale and fruity session beer.

Hameldon Bitter (OG 1040, ABV 3.8%)
A dark traditional bitter with a dry and assertive character that develops in the finish.

Ale (OG 1045, ABV 4%)
A malty aroma leads to a complex, malt dominated flavour, supported by a dry, increasingly bitter finish.

Glen Top Bitter (OG 1040.5, ABV 4%)
A citrus, full-bodied, pale beer with a dry aftertaste.

Halo Pale (OG 1045, ABV 4.5%)
A citrus, pale ale, finishing with a slightly bitter aftertaste.

Pitch Porter (OG 1050, ABV 5%)
A full-bodied, rich beer with a slightly sweet, malty start, counter balanced with sharp bitterness and a roast barley dominance.

Sunshine (OG 1055, ABV 5.3%)
A hoppy and bitter golden beer with a citrus character. The lingering finish is dry and spicy.

Rother Valley SIBA

Gate Court Farm, Station Road, Northiam, East Sussex, TN31 6QT
☎ (01797) 252922 ☎ 07798 877551

⊗ Rother Valley Brewing Co was established in Northiam in 1993, overlooking the Rother Levels

and the Kent & East Sussex Railway. Established and new hop varieties are grown on the farm and also sourced locally. Brewing is split between cask and an ever-increasing range of filtered bottled beers. Around 100 outlets are supplied direct and through wholesalers. ‼◆

Honeyfuzz (OG 1038, ABV 3.8%)
A pale bitter flavoured with Sussex honey, subtle but not sweet with a citrus twang on the finish.

Smild (OG 1038, ABV 3.8%)
A full-bodied, dark, creamy mild with hints of chocolate.

Level Best (OG 1040, ABV 4%) ◥
Full-bodied tawny session bitter with a malt and fruit aroma, malty taste and a dry, hoppy finish.

Copper Ale (OG 1041, ABV 4.1%)
A copper-coloured ale with a good balance of malt and hops.

Hoppers Ale (OG 1044, ABV 4.4%)
A copper-coloured ale. The initial burst of hop is followed by a pleasant caramel taste.

Boadicea (OG 1045, ABV 4.5%)
A straw-coloured beer with a delicate, fruity flavour.

Blues (OG 1050, ABV 5%)
A dark, winter-style old ale.

Rothes (NEW)

77 New Street, Rothes, Aberlour, AB38 7BJ ☎ 07736 233634 ✉ therothesbrewery@sky.com

⊠ Situated in the heart of the Spey Valley, Rothes began producing commercially in 2014. Initially producing only bottle-conditioned beers, cask ales are now also brewed, with an output of up to 800 litres a week. RAIB

Rotters

目 Tower Hotel, Talgarth, LD3 0BW
☎ (01874) 711253 ⊕ rottersbrewery.co.uk

☺Rotters Brewery opened in 2010. ‼◆

Utter Rotter (OG 1040, ABV 3.9%)

Grounds For Divorce (OG 1048, ABV 4.7%)
A premium ruby ale.

Round Tower SIBA

Unit 11a, Robjohns House, Navigation Road, Chelmsford, Essex, CM2 6ND
☎ (01245) 807343 ☎ 07905 255909
⊕ roundtowerbrewery.co.uk

Round Tower began brewing in 2013, the first brewery in Chelmsford since Grays & Sons ceased brewing in 1974. Former home brewer Simon Tippler started on a small scale but has now expanded to a brew length of five barrels. Several local pubs are supplied and the beers can also be found in the Grays & Sons estate and other selected free houses. RAIB

Stout (OG 1043, ABV 4.2%)
A rich and complex stout.

Slipstream (OG 1053.5, ABV 6%)
A black IPA.

Rowditch

Rowditch Inn, 246 Uttoxeter New Road, Derby, DE22 3LL
☎ (01332) 343123

The Rowditch Brewery was established in 2010 and is a 3.75-barrel plant situated on the premises of the Rowditch pub. Various one-off and seasonal ales are periodically available. ♦

St Stephens (OG 1038, ABV 3.6%)
Citrus-flavoured, golden, bitter ale.

Eruption (OG 1038, ABV 3.8%)

Full Flower Moon (OG 1045, ABV 4.5%)
A well-balanced premium bitter.

More Beer (OG 1045, ABV 4.5%)

RPA (OG 1047, ABV 4.7%)
A balanced golden bitter.

Rowett (NEW)

Storrs Cottage, North Thoresby, Lincolnshire, DN36 5QL
☎ (01472) 841080 rowettbrewing.com

Founded in 2014 as a commercial 0.5-barrel nanobrewery, Rowett Brewing supply their flagship whisky-barrel-aged beer to pubs in Grimsby and the Lincolnshire Wolds. ♦

Oak Barrel Stout (OG 1056, ABV 5.2%)
A rich oatmeal stout, aged in oak whisky barrels.

Rowton SIBA

Stone House, Rowton, Telford, Shropshire, TF6 6QX
☎ 07746 290995 rowtonbrewery.com

Rowton was established in 2008 on a four-barrel plant in an old cow shed on the owner's farm. Water is drawn from a borehole on site. ♦

Moonstruck Mild (OG 1033, ABV 3.8%)

Pure Gold (OG 1038, ABV 3.8%)

Bitter (OG 1040, ABV 3.9%)

Galaxy (OG 1044, ABV 4.3%)

Dark Side Stout (OG 1045, ABV 4.5%)

Rtwo Dtoo

Steamhouse, Station Road, Urmston, M41 9SB
☎ (0161) 748 6487 thesteamhouse.co.uk

The unusual name of this brewery comes from the triumvirate who run it – Rob, Ron and Danny (two 'R's and a 'D' too). Established in 2013 and located at the Steamhouse pub in Urmston.

Ruddles

See Greene King

Rudgate SIBA

2 Centre Park, Marston Moor Business Park, Tockwith, York, North Yorkshire, YO26 7QF
☎ (01423) 358382 rudgatebrewery.co.uk

Rudgate began brewing in 1992 on a disused WWII airfield that was chosen because of its water suitability. The original brewery was in a former ammunition building, expanding into a modern facility in 2011. Traditional methods are followed using a full mash infusion system and fermentation is achieved using its own strain of Yorkshire brewing yeast. ♦

Jorvik Blonde (OG 1036, ABV 3.8%)
Blonde ale with a balanced hoppy bitterness and a crisp, fruity finish.

Viking (OG 1036, ABV 3.8%)
An initially warming and malty, full-bodied beer, with hops and fruit lingering into the aftertaste.

Battleaxe (OG 1040, ABV 4.2%)
A well-hopped bitter with slightly sweet initial taste and light bitterness. Complex fruit character gives a memorable aftertaste.

Ruby Mild (OG 1041, ABV 4.4%)
Nutty, rich ruby ale, stronger than usual for a mild.

Volsung (OG 1046, ABV 5%)
A premium bitter, golden-coloured with distinctive lemon on the nose.

York Chocolate Stout (OG 1049, ABV 5%)
Deep rich stout with complex balanced flavours and a subtle chocolate finish.

IPA (OG 1053, ABV 5.2%)
Initially bittersweet, well-balanced complex fruit, hints of citrus and a bitter, hoppy finish.

Runaway

Unit 4, Millgate, Dantzic Street, Manchester, M4 4JW
☎ (0161) 832 2628 ☎ 07505 237078
therunawaybrewery.com

Runaway began brewing in 2014 using a 5.5-barrel plant producing bottle-conditioned beers. RAIB

Rusty Prop (NEW)

Unit 10, Abbey Enterprise Centre, Premier Way, Romsey, Hampshire, SO51 9AQ ☎ 07791 966095
rustypropbrewing.co.uk

Brewing began in 2014 to create full-flavoured, environmentally-conscious beers. RAIB

Airhead (OG 1041, ABV 4%)
American-style pale ale, slightly sweet and fruity with a hoppy afternote.

Flugtag (OG 1047, ABV 4.7%)
A traditional English pale ale brewed with Bavarian yeast. Full-bodied caramel and nutty flavours but light on the palate.

Rydale SIBA

Evergreen, Malton Road, York, North Yorkshire, YO32 9TN
☎ (01904) 400303

Rydale began brewing in 2013 using a four-barrel plant, supplying pubs in the local area. Further beers and a bottling line are planned.

Angler (OG 1038, ABV 3.8%)

Gold (ABV 3.8%)

Pale (ABV 3.8%)

Rambler (OG 1038, ABV 3.8%)

Bitter (ABV 4%)

Stout (ABV 4.3%)

S&P

Homestead, Drayton Lane, Horsford, Norfolk, NR10 3AN ☎ 07552 300768 ⊕ spbrewery.co.uk

☒ Production commenced in 2013 using a 10-barrel plant constructed upon land once owned by prominent Norfolk brewers Steward & Patteson (1800-1965), hence the name. Locally produced malts are used as is water from the brewery's own borehole. ‼

Topaz Blonde (OG 1038, ABV 3.7%)
A golden-coloured beer with a citrus aroma and grapefruit taste. A crisp, bitter finish.

Barrack Street Bitter (OG 1041, ABV 4%) ◀
A refreshing amber ale. A gentle hop aroma sits comfortably with the malty biscuit flavour. An increasingly bitter finish.

First Light (OG 1042, ABV 4.1%) ◀
A light golden beer. A strong citrus aroma and deep hoppy flavour is complemented by a lingering bitter finish.

Dennis (OG 1042, ABV 4.2%)
A rich amber bitter with a well-balanced malty sweetness.

Eve's Drop (OG 1046, ABV 4.3%) ◀
A well-balanced golden ale. Hops and malts dominate with a peppery mouth feel giving way to lingering sweetness.

Darkest Hour (OG 1047, ABV 4.4%)
Roasted barley gives a faint coffee aroma and taste to this full-bodied Irish stout.

NASHA IPA (OG 1050, ABV 5%)
A persistent head sits atop a rich amber ale with well-balanced malty sweetness.

Sacre Brew (NEW)

Unit 13, Monmore Road, Wolverhampton, WV1 2TZ ☎ 07413 432120

Sacre Brew is a small, artisanal 1.2-barrel microbrewery based at the Hungry Bistro in Wolverhampton. Beers are supplied to pubs across the West Midlands as well as to the bistro. All Sacre Brew beers are suitable for vegans. RAIB

Saddleworth

⊟ Church Inn, Church Lane, Uppermill, Oldham, OL3 6LW
☎ (01457) 820902 ⊕ churchinnsaddleworth.co.uk

☺Saddleworth started brewing in 1997 in a 120-year old brewhouse at the Church Inn. Brewery and inn are set above a valley overlooking Saddleworth Moor. Brewing capacity was significantly expanded in 2011 with a new 13-barrel plant. ♦

More (OG 1038, ABV 3.8%)

St George's Bitter (OG 1038, ABV 3.8%)
Quite dry and bitter, with some citrus and nutty notes.

Honey Smacker (OG 1042, ABV 4.1%)
Hoppy and slightly sharp, with citrus notes.

Hop Smacker (OG 1042, ABV 4.1%)
A hoppy golden ale.

Slap & Tickle (OG 1045, ABV 4.3%)

Shaftbender (OG 1060, ABV 5.4%)

Aroma and flavours of liquorice, roast malt, chocolate and coffee.

Sadler's SIBA ◉

⊟ Unit 2, Conyers Trading Estate, Station Drive, Lye, West Midlands, DY9 2RE
☎ (01384) 895230 ⊕ sadlersales.co.uk

☺Third and fourth generation brewers John and Chris Sadler re-opened this historic brewery in 2004. The brewery tap house was built and opened in 2006 next to the brewery. Around 250 outlets are supplied. A new 30-barrel plant, visitor centre, shop and tasting room opened in 2015. ‼ 🍺

JPA (OG 1038, ABV 3.8%)
A pale, hoppy bitter with a crisp and zesty lemon undertone.

Mellow Yellow (OG 1041, ABV 4.1%)
A pale ale brewed with plenty of hop and honey.

Worcester Sorcerer (OG 1043, ABV 4.3%)
Brewed with English hops and barley with hints of mint and lemon, creating a floral aroma and crisp bitterness.

Thin Ice (OG 1045, ABV 4.5%)
A pale ale. Bitter but with an orange and lemon finish.

Peaky Blinder (OG 1046, ABV 4.6%)
A refreshing and hoppy black IPA.

Boris Citrov (OG 1047, ABV 4.7%)
A punchy orange marmalade ale with a sweet, crisp and fruity finish.

Hop Bomb (OG 1050, ABV 5%)
A powerful IPA, balanced malt sweetness supports the hop aroma and flavour explosion.

Red IPA (OG 1057, ABV 5.7%)

Mud City Stout (OG 1066, ABV 6.6%)
Rich, full-bodied strong stout brewed with raw cocoa, fresh vanilla pods, oats, wheat and dark malts.

Saffron SIBA

The Cartshed, Parsonage Farm, Henham, Essex, CM22 6AN
☎ (01279) 850923 ☎ 07980 972067
⊕ saffronbrewery.co.uk

☒ Founded in 2005, the brewery was upgraded to a 15-barrel plant in early 2008 and re-located to a converted barn at Parsonage Farm, with a purpose-built reed bed for environmentally-friendly disposal of waste products. 40 outlets are supplied direct. ‼ ♦ RAIB

IPA (OG 1036, ABV 3.6%)

Ramblers Tipple (OG 1040, ABV 3.9%)
A rich, copper-coloured bitter with toffee and caramel flavours.

Brewhouse Bell (OG 1041, ABV 4%)
Golden amber in colour with citrus and hop flavours balancing well for a clean, fresh finish.

Littlebury Lighthouse (OG 1043, ABV 4.2%)

Blonde (OG 1044, ABV 4.3%)
A light golden ale with a delicate balance of citrus and smooth, malty flavours and a crisp finish.

Squires Gamble (OG 1044, ABV 4.3%)

Traditional-style copper ale; soft, mellow, full-flavoured and hoppy with citrus and biscuit hints.

Flying Serpent (OG 1046, ABV 4.5%)

Henham Honey (OG 1047, ABV 4.6%)

Tiddly Vicar (OG 1051, ABV 5%)
Dark copper-coloured nutty beer with a light, spicy finish.

Silent Night (OG 1053, ABV 5.2%)

St Andrews

Unit 7, Bassaguard Business Park, St Andrews,
KY16 8AL ☎ 07879 399441
⊕ standrewsbrewingcompany.com

Established in 2012, St Andrews Brewing Company produces bottle-conditioned beers that are available across Fife and Scotland. Beers are brewed in small batches of just 750 bottles. Seven regular beers are supplemented with monthly guest ales. Cask beers are supplied to a number of local outlets including the brewery tap in St Andrews, opened in 2013. The brewery relocated to new premises in St Andrews in 2014. **RAIB**

Wee Blonde (OG 1035, ABV 3.7%)
Gentle blonde ale with light citrus hops, hints of fruit, and a floral aroma.

Seventy Bob (OG 1037, ABV 3.8%)
A traditional 70/- brown ale with toffee and malt aromas leading to nutty chocolate, toast and caramel flavours, rounded off with a subtle and balanced bitter finish.

Fife Gold (OG 1040, ABV 4.2%)
Straw yellow in colour with a fresh floral aroma backed up with a citrus punch of lemon, lime and grapefruit coming through from a blend of North-West American hops.

Crail Ale (OG 1043, ABV 4.5%)
A bright golden ale with long-lasting citrus and floral flavours.

Oatmeal Stout (OG 1043, ABV 4.5%)
A smooth, full-bodied Scottish oatmeal stout. Strong coffee, chocolate and dark fruit flavours balanced against a blend of hops to create a rich, silky aftertaste.

Neuk Ale (OG 1046, ABV 4.6%)
Dark mahogany in colour with rich dark fruit, chocolate and roast coffee flavours. A long-lasting bitter aftertaste ties together with a fresh finish.

Eighty Bob (OG 1046, ABV 4.8%)
A traditional Scottish 80/- ale. Complex malt flavours dominate.

India Pale Ale (OG 1048, ABV 5%)
Bold IPA with a hop kick and a depth of orange and tropical fruit flavours that are both refreshing and complex.

St Austell SIBA ◉

63 Trevarthian Road, St Austell, Cornwall, PL25 4BY
☎ (01726) 74444 ⊕ staustellbrewery.co.uk

⊠ Founded in 1851, St Austell Brewery remains family owned. Its cask beers are available in all its pubs, and throughout the UK. The brewery hosts its own Celtic beer festival in November each year.
‼ ⛉ ◆ RAIB

Cornish Best Bitter (OG 1035, ABV 3.5%) ◆

Light, refreshing copper-coloured bitter with malt aroma. Gentle biscuit malt and hops flavour with low bitterness. Bitter, dry finish.

Trelawny (OG 1039, ABV 3.8%) ◆
Tawny bitter with aroma of hops and stone fruits. Hop bitterness and some citrus develop into caramel-malt sweetness. Refreshing, crisp finish.

Tribute (OG 1043, ABV 4.2%) ⬚ ◆
Pale brown best bitter with malt and hop aroma. Dominant hop bitterness with biscuit malt, ending refreshingly bitter and dry.

Proper Job (OG 1046, ABV 4.5%) ◆
Golden ale with resinous hop aroma. Copious citrus fruits with bitterness and crisp hop bitter and grapefruit finish, becoming dry.

HSD (OG 1052, ABV 5%) ▤ ◆
Malt and stone fruit aroma leads into rich, balanced fruit, caramel, bitterness and malt which last into the long finish.

1913 Cornish Stout (OG 1052, ABV 5.2%) ◆
Velvet black stout with roast coffee aroma. Powerful roast malt with vine fruit and esters. Roast, dry and bitter finish.

Brewed for the Nicholson's Pub Company:

Nicholson's Pale Ale (OG 1040, ABV 4.1%)

St George's SIBA

The Old Bakery, Bush Lane, Callow End,
Worcestershire, WR2 4TF
☎ (01905) 831316 ⊕ stgeorgesbrewery.co.uk

The brewery was established in 1998 in old village bakery premises and acquired in 2006 by Duncan Ironmonger, who owns three nearby pubs. The brewery supplies local free houses and wholesalers for a wider distribution. ‼ ◆

By George (OG 1036, ABV 3.6%)
A clean-drinking pale golden ale with a strong floral aroma and citrus hop notes. This beer is full-bodied and full-flavoured yet gentle enough to make it a session beer.

Friar Tuck (OG 1040, ABV 4%)
A golden bitter with a smooth, refreshing bitter and citrus character.

Worcester Sauce (OG 1043, ABV 4.3%)
A chestnut-coloured ale with a hoppy aroma and a strong bitter finish.

Dream Weaver (OG 1045, ABV 4.5%)

Charger (OG 1046, ABV 4.6%)
A light golden beer with a citrus blast and a hint of grapefruit.

Dragons Blood (OG 1048, ABV 4.8%)
A ruby red-coloured beer with a hint of chocolate and an earthy and slightly spicy aroma.

St Peter's SIBA ◉

St Peter's Hall, St Peter South Elmham, Suffolk,
NR35 1NQ
☎ (01986) 782322 ⊕ stpetersbrewery.co.uk

⊠ St Peter's Brewery is based adjacent to a moated medieval hall near Bungay, Suffolk. Established in 1996 it concentrates in the main on bottled beer/keg (85% of capacity) but has a rapidly increasing cask market. Two pubs are owned. 45% of production is exported to 32 countries worldwide. ‼☎♦

Best Bitter (OG 1038, ABV 3.7%) ◈
A complex but well-balanced hoppy brew. A gentle hop nose introduces a singular hoppiness with supporting malt notes and underlying bitterness. Other flavours fade to leave a long, dry, hoppy finish.

Mild (OG 1037, ABV 3.7%) ◈
Heady aroma of caramelised blackberries and black toffee. Excellent complex flavours with caramel, blackberries, hops and an astringent bitterness. Long, sustained finish with a roast coffee bitterness; increasingly dry.

Organic Best (OG 1041, ABV 4.1%) ◈
A dry and bitter beer with a growing astringency. Pale brown in colour, it has a gentle hop aroma which makes the definitive bitterness surprising.

G-Free (OG 1048, ABV 4.2%)
A pale golden, gluten-free ale with citrus and mandarin aromas. Suitable for coeliacs.

Ruby Red (OG 1043, ABV 4.3%)
A tawny red ale with subtle malt undertones and a distinctive spicy hop aroma.

Organic Ale (OG 1045, ABV 4.5%) ◈
A rich toffee apple aroma and a smooth grainy feel. Malt and caramel initially match the dry hoppy bitterness. As the flavours mature, liquorice dryness develops. Full-bodied.

Golden Ale (OG 1047, ABV 4.7%) ◈
Amber-coloured, full-bodied, robust ale. A strong hop bouquet leads to a mix of malt and hops combined with a dry, fruity hoppiness. The malt quickly subsides, leaving creamy bitterness.

Grapefruit Beer (OG 1047, ABV 4.7%) ◈
With a strong aroma and taste of grapefruit, this refreshing beer is exactly what it says on the tin. A superb example of a fruit beer.

IPA (OG 1055, ABV 5.5%)
A full-bodied, highly-hopped pale ale with a zesty character.

Salamander SIBA

22 Harry Street, Dudley Hill, Bradford, West Yorkshire, BD4 9PH
☎ (01274) 652323
⊕ salamanderbrewingcompany.co.uk

⊠ Salamander first brewed in 2000 in a former pork pie factory. An expansion in 2004 increased capacity to 40 barrels per week. Direct deliveries are made to around 100 outlets in Yorkshire, Cumbria, Lancashire, Manchester, Derbyshire, Leicestershire and Lincoln. ‼♦

Blondie (ABV 4%)
A refreshing pale ale, malty with a gentle hop aroma.

Mudpuppy (OG 1042, ABV 4.2%) ◈
A well-balanced, copper-coloured best bitter with a fruity, hoppy nose and a bitter finish.

Golden Salamander (OG 1045, ABV 4.5%) ◈
Citrus hops characterise the aroma and taste of this golden premium bitter, which has malt undertones throughout. The aftertaste is dry, hoppy and bitter.

Spectre Stout (ABV 4.5%)
A deep black/red-coloured ale with a coffee aroma and a robust roast malt flavour.

Bright Black Porter (ABV 4.8%)
An intense porter with a hint of rum and caramel.

Salopian SIBA ◉

The Old Station Yard, Station Road, Hadnall, Shropshire, SY4 3DD
☎ (01743) 248414 ⊕ salopianbrewery.co.uk

☺The brewery was established in 1995 in an old dairy on the outskirts of Shrewsbury but moved in 2014 to its new location in an industrial unit in the village of Hadnall, where is now produces more than 150 barrels a week. Salopian also brews under the Blackwater Brewery name. ‼☎♦RAIB

Shropshire Gold (OG 1037, ABV 3.8%) 🍶🍺
A light, copper-coloured ale with an unusual blend of body and dryness.

Oracle (OG 1040, ABV 4%) 🍺
A crisp golden ale with a striking hop profile. Dry and refreshing with a long aromatic finish.

Darwins Origin (OG 1042, ABV 4.3%) 🍶🍺
A light copper ale with a striking hop profile which is balanced by a refined malt finish.

Hop Twister (OG 1044, ABV 4.5%) 🍶
A premium bitter with a citrus flavour and complex hop finish. Refreshing and crisp.

Lemon Dream (OG 1043.5, ABV 4.5%) 🍶
A light gold ale brewed with wheat malt and subtly flavoured with fresh lemons.

Golden Thread (OG 1048, ABV 5%) 🍺
A bright gold ale. Strong and quite bitter but well-balanced.

Saltaire SIBA ◉

Unit 6, County Works, Dockfield Road, Shipley, West Yorkshire, BD17 7AR
☎ (01274) 594959 ⊕ saltairebrewery.co.uk

☺ Launched in 2006, Saltaire is an award-winning brewery based in a former Victorian power station. A mezzanine bar gives visitors views of the brewing plant and the chance to taste the beers. A brewery tap and shop opened in 2014. More than 600 pubs are supplied across West Yorkshire and the north of England. ‼☎♦

Blonde (OG 1040, ABV 4%) 🍺 ◈
Thirst quenching and quaffable, this straw-coloured beer is slightly sweet and well-rounded with fruit, malt and hops in the taste and a fruity, hoppy finish.

Elderflower Blonde (OG 1040, ABV 4%) ◈
An easy-drinking, smooth, golden-coloured ale with subtle elderflower aroma leading to a pleasant elderflower fruit taste and a long, refreshing finish.

Raspberry Blonde (OG 1040, ABV 4%)
Refreshing blonde ale infused with a hint of raspberries.

Amarillo Gold (OG 1044, ABV 4.4%)
A straw-coloured bright wheat beer with a light biscuit base, a distinct orange bouquet and an intense citrus flavour.

Cascade Pale Ale (OG 1046, ABV 4.8%) ◈
A well-balanced golden bitter with smooth mouthfeel, floral hop aromas and pronounced bitterness, culminating in a long, dry finish and dry aftertaste.

Triple Chocoholic (OG 1048.5, ABV 4.8%) 🍷 ▣ ◆
A creamy, dark brown, roast, chocolate stout with a dry bitter finish and a rich chocolate aroma.

Stateside IPA (OG 1059, ABV 6%)
American-style IPA with a rich gold base a hoppy balancing bitterness and fruity, citrus flavours.

Sambrook's SIBA ◉

Units 1-3, Yelverton Road, Battersea, London, SW11 3QG
☎ (020) 7228 0598 ⊕ sambrooksbrewery.co.uk

⊠ Sambrook's was founded by Duncan Sambrook and David Welsh in 2008, supplying its award-winning ales throughout London. The brewery bar hosts regular events and is open for members on the first Friday of every month. ‼ 🍽 ◆RAIB

Wandle Ale (OG 1038.5, ABV 3.8%) 🍷 ◆
Dryness balances the rounded sweetish malt flavour of this fruity, quaffable pale brown bitter. Some peach and citrus notes.

Pumphouse Pale Ale (OG 1041.5, ABV 4.2%) ◆
Refreshing golden beer with a hint of citrus aroma becoming more pronounced on the palate, lingering into the bitter finish.

Junction Ale (OG 1045.5, ABV 4.5%) ◆
Well-balanced best bitter with soft fruit and figs aroma. The flavour is a little more blackcurrant plus creamy toffee.

Powerhouse Porter (OG 1050, ABV 4.9%) ◆
Dark brown porter with a pleasant roasted malt nose with some sultana, blackcurrant and treacle character. Dry roasted finish.

Sandstone SIBA

Unit 5, Wrexham Enterprise Park, Preston Road, off Ash Road, North Wrexham Industrial Estate, Wrexham, LL13 9JT
☎ (01978) 664805 ☎ 07851 001118
⊕ sandstonebrewery.co.uk

Sandstone Brewery was established as a four-barrel plant in 2008. More than 60 outlets in north Wales and north-west England are supplied. The brewery was taken over by new owners in 2013 with the existing portfolio retained and a number of new beers added. ◆

Sandstone Edge (OG 1039, ABV 3.8%) ◆
A satisfying session ale, this pale, dry, bitter beer has a full mouthfeel and a lingering hoppy finish that belies its modest strength.

Onyx Dragon (OG 1040, ABV 4%)
Black in colour with hints of chocolate, toffee and caramel.

Post Mistress (OG 1046, ABV 4.4%) ◆
A full-bodied, smooth premium bitter, ruby-red in colour, with a rich, mellow taste. Good combination of malt, hops and fruit in aroma and initial taste leading to a lasting, satisfying finish.

Racing Dragon (OG 1044, ABV 4.4%)

Twisted Dragon (OG 1058, ABV 5.8%)

Sawbridgeworth SIBA

▤ **81 London Road, Sawbridgeworth, Hertfordshire, CM21 9JJ**

☎ (01279) 722313 ☎ 07446 960409
⊕ thegatepub.net

⊠ Set up in 2000 by owners Tom and Gary Barnett, the brewery is situated behind the Gate Inn. Tom is a former professional footballer whose clubs included Crystal Palace. Brewing is carried out by ex-Nethergate brewer Bob Renvoise. Special or one-off beers are regularly brewed. ‼◆

Manor Mild (OG 1034, ABV 3.4%)

IPA (OG 1038, ABV 3.8%)

Selhurst Park Flyer (OG 1038, ABV 3.8%)

Gold (OG 1040, ABV 4%)

Is It Yourself (OG 1042, ABV 4.2%)

Dragon's Blood (OG 1043, ABV 4.3%)

Saxon City

Glebe Farm Industrial Estate, Stoke Edith, Hereford, HR1 4HG
☎ (01432) 890688 ⊕ herefordcasks.co.uk

☺ Brewing began in 2010 in a vacant unit adjoining a cask factory using a six-barrel plant by PBC Brewery Installations. Three beers are produced on demand and are available in pins and firkins. Brewing is currently suspended.

Scarborough SIBA

Unit 1B, Stadium Works, Barry's Lane, Scarborough, North Yorkshire, YO12 4HA
☎ (01723) 367506 ⊕ scarboroughbrewery.co.uk

Scarborough Brewery was established in 2010 using a one-barrel plant. In 2011 commercial brewing began using a 10-barrel plant from Wold Top Brewery. Beers can be found at its brewery tap, the Valley Bar in Scarborough, and nationwide via wholesalers. ◆

Blonde (OG 1038, ABV 3.8%)
Easy-drinking pale session beer with a subtle citrus flavour and hoppy aroma.

Cascades (OG 1041, ABV 4.1%)
Pale straw-coloured beer with a zesty citrus flavour and floral hoppy aroma.

Chinook (OG 1041, ABV 4.1%)
Straw-coloured pale beer with spicy bitter flavours and a fruity hoppy aroma.

Citra (OG 1042, ABV 4.2%)
Refreshing and light pale golden beer with light citrus aromas.

Sealord (OG 1043, ABV 4.3%)
Golden ale brewed with a combination of hops that give subtle hints of lime, grapefruit and melon.

Stout (OG 1046, ABV 4.6%)
Full-bodied dark stout brewed using five malts giving depth of flavour and a bitter chocolate aroma.

American Pale (OG 1050, ABV 5%)
American-style golden beer with a crisp, hoppy taste and floral aroma.

Schoolhouse (NEW) SIBA

Unit 1, Cleveland Industrial Estate, Darlington, Co Durham, DL1 2PB
☎ (01325) 461812
⊠ gannaway@schoolhousebrewery.co.uk

⊕ Formed in 2013, Schoolhouse Brewery is the first six-barrel brewery to be based in Darlington for more than 70 years. 20 outlets are supplied. Developments for the coming year include Wedding Favour brew days for groom and best man. ‼

Tuck Shop (OG 1033, ABV 3.7%)

100 Lines (OG 1032, ABV 3.8%)

Abacus (OG 1035, ABV 3.9%)

Master's Study (OG 1042, ABV 4.6%)

Terminus (OG 1048, ABV 6%)

Scottish Borders SIBA ◉

See Born in the Borders

Scribbler's SIBA ◉

7 Lime Grove, Stapleford, Nottinghamshire, NG9 7GF
☎ (0115) 875 1759 ☎ 07780 662244
⊕ scribblers-ales.com

Scribbler's was established in 2014 by Richard Nettleton, an author (hence the name) and Roger Frost. The 4.5-barrel plant was constructed by the owners, the fermentation and mash tun converted from old ice cream vessels. The copper came from Grafton Brewing Co (qv). Beer names are based on classic book titles.

Beerfest at Tiffanys (OG 1046, ABV 3.8%)
Traditional English session bitter with a slightly spicy aftertaste.

Hoppy Potter & the Goblet of Ale (OG 1048, ABV 4.2%)
Light-coloured ale with hoppy citrus aromas.

Masher in the Rye (OG 1053, ABV 4.8%)
Golden-coloured, American-style ale with delicate hop aromas.

Rubecca (OG 1053, ABV 4.8%)
Smooth ruby-coloured beer with hints of chocolate.

One Brew Over the Cuckoo's Nest (OG 1058, ABV 5.3%)
A premium ale, not too dark, but with a distinctive mouthfeel and smooth, sweet traditional hop flavours.

Beyond Reasonable Stout (OG 1068, ABV 6%)

Seren SIBA

Syfnau House, Rosebush, SA66 7QY
☎ (01437) 532098 ⊕ serenbrewing.com

⊗ Seren is an award-winning nanobrewery on the edge of the Preseli mountains in North Pembrokeshire. Beers are crafted on a small scale.

Bluestone IPA (OG 1042, ABV 4.2%)
Gold-coloured beer with citrus and tropical hop aromas and flavours.

Blackstone Stout (OG 1045, ABV 4.5%)

Factory Steam (OG 1045, ABV 4.5%)
A steam-brewed, full-bodied, copper-coloured best bitter. Fruity, with a firm bitterness and biscuity malt notes.

Browncoat (OG 1047, ABV 4.7%)
An American-style brown ale. Grapefruit aroma and flavour, with a malty backbone with hints of chocolate.

Ink Spot (OG 1050, ABV 5%)
A session version of Indian Ink. Citrus and pine plays over roast.

Indian Ink (OG 1062, ABV 6.5%)
A black IPA. Citrus and pine plays over a touch of roast.

West Wales IPA (OG 1062, ABV 6.5%)
Full-strength American-style IPA. Gold-coloured with citrus and tropical hop aroma and flavour.

Settle SIBA

Unit 8, The Sidings, The Sidings, Settle, North Yorkshire, BD24 9RP
☎ (01729) 824936 ⊕ settlebrewery.co.uk

⊕ Settle Brewery is located in a small industrial unit adjacent to Settle railway station. Brewing started in 2013 using a new 12-barrel kit. Brewer Ian Simkins originally brewed at Nine Standards Brewery in Kirkby Stephen. More than 40 outlets across Cumbria, Yorkshire and Lancashire are supplied. The beers are also available through wholesalers. ‼♦

Light (OG 1036, ABV 3.6%)
A delicate straw-coloured beer with a subtle blend of fruit and spice flavours and citrus overtones.

Mainline (OG 1037.5, ABV 3.8%)
A refreshing, delicately fruity golden IPA-style beer with a hint of sweetness.

Classic (OG 1039, ABV 4%)
A rich, floral, one-hop bitter.

Contract brewed for Nine Standards Brewery:

No. 4 Amber Ale (OG 1037, ABV 3.7%)
A dark amber-coloured bitter with a fruity, spicy nose.

No. 1 Golden Ale (OG 1040, ABV 4.1%)
A flavoursome golden ale with a hint of blackcurrant.

No. 2 Pale Ale (OG 1042, ABV 4.3%)
A classic pale ale with a strong hoppy aroma.

No. 3 Porter (OG 1048, ABV 4.7%)
A robust porter with caramel and coffee notes and smoky undertones.

Seven Bro7hers (NEW) SIBA ◉

33 Waybridge Enterprise Centre, Daniel Adamson Road, Salford, M50 1DS
☎ (0161) 637 9929 ☎ 07849 612737
⊕ sevenbro7hers.com

Brewing began in 2014 using a 10-barrel plant.

Session (ABV 3.8%)
A thirst-quenching session ale with citrus aromas, tropical fruit flavours and a light malt base giving way to strawberry and elderflower undertones.

EPA (ABV 4.8%)
An English pale ale, golden in colour with a floral tropical fruit aroma. The flavour is sweet with tropical fruit notes and a sweet caramel finish.

IPA (ABV 5%)
A classic American-style IPA that is bitter rather than sweet. Grapefruit and floral undertones and intense citrus aroma.

Stout (ABV 5.2%)
A smooth, dark stout with roasted coffee and chocolate, and fruity undertones from the hops.

The addition of star anise gives a distinctive yet subtle liquorice character.

Severn Vale SIBA 👁

See Combined Brewers

Shalford SIBA 👁

PO Box 10411, Braintree, Essex, CM7 5WP
☎ (01371) 850925 ☎ 07749 658512
🌐 shalfordbrewery.co.uk

Shalford began brewing in 2007 on a five-barrel plant at Hyde Farm in the Pant Valley in Essex. More than 50 outlets are supplied direct. ◆RAIB

1319 Mild (OG 1037, ABV 3.7%)
Roast malt and chocolate sweetness with a slight bitter finish.

Barnfield Pale Ale (OG 1038, ABV 3.8%) 🍺
Pale-coloured but full-flavoured, this is a traditional, hoppy bitter rather than a golden ale. Malt persists throughout, with bitterness becoming more dominant towards the end.

Braintree Market Ale (OG 1040, ABV 4%)
Traditional, easy-drinking session ale with a hoppy, lingering, dry finish.

Levelly Gold (OG 1040, ABV 4%)
Golden, summery bitter with a pleasant finish.

Stoneley Bitter (OG 1042, ABV 4.2%) 🍺
Dark amber session beer whose vivid hop character is supported by a juicy, malty body. A dry finish makes this beer very drinkable.

Hyde Bitter (OG 1047, ABV 4.7%) 🍺
Stronger version of Barnfield, with a similar but more assertive character.

Levelly Black (OG 1048, ABV 4.8%)
A dark, heavy, well-hopped ale with grainy toffee taste topped with a thick creamy head.

Rotten End (OG 1065, ABV 6.5%)
Strong beer with slightly sweet, nutty undertones and a bitter edge to finish.

Shardlow 👁

The Old Brewery Stables, British Waterways Yard, Cavendish Bridge, Leicestershire, DE72 2HL
☎ (01332) 799188 ✉ nev@shardlowbrewery.co.uk

👁On a site associated with brewing since 1819, Shardlow delivers to more than 100 outlets throughout the East Midlands and is also one of the largest UK cider distributors. Reverend Eaton is named after a scion of the Eaton brewing family, Rector of Shardlow for 40 years. The brewery tap is the Blue Bell Inn at Melbourne, Derbyshire. Prolific supplier of beers to local beer festivals. ‼◆RAIB

Chancellors Revenge (OG 1036, ABV 3.6%)
A light-coloured, refreshing, full-flavoured and well-hopped session bitter.

Cavendish Dark (OG 1037, ABV 3.7%)
A mild, well-balanced beer with a hoppy aftertaste.

Golden Hop (OG 1041, ABV 4.1%)
Golden, sweet-tasting beer.

Kiln House (OG 1041, ABV 4.1%)
A refreshing golden ale with a lingering bitter finish.

Narrow Boat (OG 1043, ABV 4.3%)

A pale amber bitter, with a short, crisp, hoppy aftertaste.

Cavendish Bridge (OG 1045, ABV 4.5%)
Pale amber premium bitter. Refreshing, clean and fruity with a pleasing bitter finish.

Cavendish Gold (OG 1045, ABV 4.5%)
Pale gold in colour, bright and clean-tasting. A full-bodied ale with pronounced bitterness and complexity.

Reverend Eaton (OG 1045, ABV 4.5%)
A smooth, medium-strong bitter, full of malt and hop flavours with a sweet aftertaste.

Mayfly (OG 1048, ABV 4.8%)
Fruit notes predominate together with a pronounced malty aroma. Easy-drinking but strong.

Five Bells (OG 1050, ABV 5%)
Dark, rich, ruby-coloured ale, powerful and bittersweet to the palate. Coffee notes complete the profile.

Whistlestop (OG 1050, ABV 5%)
A smooth and surprisingly strong pale beer.

Sharp's 👁

Pityme Business Centre, Rock, Cornwall, PL27 6NU
☎ (01208) 862121 🌐 sharpsbrewery.co.uk

⊗ Sharp's was bought for £20 million by Molson Coors in 2011. The brewery was founded in 1994 and within 15 years had grown from producing 1,500 barrels a year to 60,000. £7.5 million of investment from Molson Coors has brought the capacity up to 200,000 barrels a year. The company delivers beer to more than 1,200 outlets across the south of England via temperature-controlled depots in Bristol and London. Molson Coors has stressed that it will maintain production in Cornwall. Part of Molson Coors PLC. 🚚◆RAIB

Cornish Coaster (OG 1035.2, ABV 3.6%) 🍺
Refreshing copper bitter. Gentle balance of biscuit malt, fruit and sweetness. Fruit in the finish with bitterness and faint dryness.

Doom Bar (OG 1038.5, ABV 4%) 🍺
Tawny brown bitter with gentle fruit aroma. Balanced taste of biscuit malt, resinous hops with apple, strawberry and plum fruits.

Atlantic (OG 1043, ABV 4.2%) 🍺
Gold-coloured best bitter with fragrant hop aroma. Orange citrus with caramel sweetness balanced by malt and bitterness. Tropical fruit hints.

Own (OG 1042.5, ABV 4.4%) 🍺
Brown best bitter with English hop and malt aroma. Fruity, hoppy taste with malt and bitter roasted biscuit, finishing dry.

Special (OG 1048.5, ABV 5%) 🍺
A tawny strong bitter with hops and caramel aroma. Sweet malty taste, with fruit and light roast throughout, becoming dry.

Shed Ales

Broadfields, Pewsey, Wiltshire, SN9 5DT
☎ (01672) 564533 ☎ 07769 812643
🌐 shed-ales.com

Shed Ales was launched in 2012 operating from a one-barrel plant in a converted garden shed. The brewery currently produces four core ales and several bespoke ales, available at selected local outlets. A house beer is produced for the Royal Oak, Great Wishford. ♦

Dig It (OG 1037.5, ABV 3.7%)
A light amber session ale.

Patrick's Best (OG 1039, ABV 3.8%)
Copper-coloured easy-drinking session ale.

Shed Some Light (OG 1041, ABV 3.8%)
A refreshing blonde beer with a light, earthy hop aroma and flavour.

Dibber (OG 1042.5, ABV 4.2%)
Light amber with a biscuit malt and citrus hop aroma. Easy-drinking with a good balance of malt and fruity hop notes and a dry finish.

Shed Brewery

2232 Stratford Road, Hockley Heath, West Midlands, B94 6NU ☎ 07910 004041
✉ perryclarke1961@gmail.com

⊗ Beers are available at several pubs and clubs in Solihull and Birmingham, and some outlets further afield. Production is 140 bottles per week plus single casks for specific outlets and local beer festivals. There are eight beers in the range plus a seasonal porter. All beers are suitable for vegetarians and vegans. ♦

Session Bitter (OG 1039, ABV 3.8%)
A copper-coloured session bitter with a long hoppy taste.

Archers Ale (OG 1040, ABV 4%)
A blonde ale with a creamy malt taste with a burst of hops in the mouth followed by a long hoppy finish.

Hemlingford Ale (OG 1040, ABV 4%)
Copper-coloured hoppy ale with a malty, creamy taste.

Hockley Citrus (OG 1020, ABV 4%)
A blonde ale, full of citrus hops and bitter in the mouth with a lingering hoppy taste.

Warwick Bear (OG 1040, ABV 4%)
Refreshing, light and hoppy with a lingering hop taste.

Executioners Porter (OG 1048, ABV 4.6%)
Dark, creamy, smooth and dry with a late roast malt character and nutty finish.

Shed Gold (OG 1048, ABV 5%)
A golden beer with a smooth, easy taste and caramel notes.

Spotted Cock (OG 1050, ABV 5%)
A strong copper-coloured beer, malty in the mouth.

Dark Knight (OG 1058, ABV 5.8%)
Dark ruby in colour with a mild bitterness and chocolate taste.

Sheelin Brewery

178 Derrylin Road, Bellanaleck, County Fermanagh, BT92 2BA ☎ 07730 432232 ⊕ sheelin.com

Sheelin was established by brewer and chemist Dr George Cathcart in 2013. Beer is mainly available in bottles.

Sheffield SIBA

Unit 111, JC Albyn Complex, Burton Road, Sheffield, South Yorkshire, S3 8BT

☎ (0114) 272 7256 ⊕ sheffieldbrewery.com

⊛Sheffield began brewing in 2007 in the former Blanco polish works using a 10-barrel plant. The brewery operates on the tower principal in premises which also are also used as a venue for corporate or social gatherings. More than 50 outlets are supplied direct. ‼

Crucible Best (OG 1038, ABV 3.8%)
Session best bitter brewed with a complex blend of malts. Two bittering hops provides a perfect balance.

Five Rivers (OG 1038, ABV 3.8%)
Easy-drinking, straw-coloured session ale. The hoppy aroma carries through to the finish.

Blanco Blonde (OG 1042, ABV 4.2%)
Continental lager-style beer.

Seven Hills (OG 1041, ABV 4.2%)
A premium bitter.

Porter (OG 1045, ABV 4.4%)
A porter with rich chocolate, malty and caramel flavours.

Forgemasters (OG 1038, ABV 4.8%)
A robust, straw-coloured pale ale.

Shepherd Neame IFBB ◉

17 Court Street, Faversham, Kent, ME13 7AX ☎ (01795) 532206 ⊕ shepherdneame.co.uk

⊗ Shepherd Neame traces its history back to 1698, making it the oldest continuous brewer in the country, though brewing probably began even earlier. The 1914 oak mash tuns are still operational. The company has 350 tied houses in the south east, nearly all selling cask ale. More than 2,000 other outlets are also supplied. The cask beers are made with Kentish hops, barley and water from their own artesian well. The company also brew cask ales under the Faversham Steam Brewery and No. 18 Yard Brewhouse names. ‼ 🚚 ♦ RAIB

Master Brew (OG 1032, ABV 3.7%) 🍂
A distinctive bitter, mid-brown in colour, with a hoppy aroma. Well-balanced, with a nicely aggressive bitter taste from its hops, it leaves a hoppy/bitter finish, tinged with sweetness.

Whitstable Bay Pale Ale (OG 1038, ABV 3.9%)
A full-bodied, fruity ale with a subtle bitterness and grapefruit and pine aromas.

Kent's Best (OG 1036, ABV 4.1%)
A robust bitter which merges the biscuity sweetness of English malt with the fruity, floral bitterness of locally grown hops.

Spitfire (OG 1036, ABV 4.2%)
A commemorative Battle of Britain brew for the RAF Benevolent Fund's appeal, now the brewery's flagship ale.

Bishops Finger (OG 1046, ABV 5%)
A strong ale with a complex hop aroma reminiscent of lemons, oranges and bananas combined with malt, molasses and toffee. Refreshing with a good malt character tinged with a lingering bitterness.

Sherfield Village SIBA

Goddards Farm, Goddards Lane, Sherfield on Loddon, Hampshire, RG27 0EL ☎ 07906 060429
🌐 sherfieldvillagebrewery.co.uk

Sherfield Village started brewing in 2011, based in a converted barn on a working dairy farm. The brewery uses a five-barrel plant, supplying local pubs and regional festivals. As well as its regular beers, numerous seasonal and one-off specials are available. Extensive use is made of New World hops, particularly those from New Zealand. Dry-hopped versions of single-hop beers are usually available. ♦RAIB

Threesome (OG 1030, ABV 3%)
Copper-coloured session beer with a long, hoppy finish.

SOLO Southern Gold (OG 1040, ABV 4%)
A golden beer with a citrus flavour and a floral nose.

SOLO Green Bullet (OG 1042, ABV 4.3%) ◆
A strong lemony nose, with hops dominating the taste building to a strong aftertaste with a big astringent hit at the end.

SOLO Single Hop (OG 1042, ABV 4.3%)
A golden ale which uses a single hop variety that changes every month, therby subtly changing the beer characteristics.

Hoppy Harrington (OG 1046, ABV 4.7%)
A mid-brown strong bitter using five different hops. It has a complex, sweetish flavour and a satisfying hoppy finish.

Pioneer Stout (OG 1048, ABV 5%)
A black stout, packed with chocolate malt and Pioneer hops, and a hint of vanilla.

ShinDigger

Office: 170 Vie Building, 185 Water Street, Manchester, M3 4JU 🌐 shindiggerbrewing.co

ShinDigger was established in 2013, and uses spare capacity at other breweries. A project of two former Manchester University students, their output is predominantly keg but occasionally cask ales make an appearance.

Shiny SIBA

Furnace Inn, 9 Duke Street, Derby, DE1 3BX
☎ (01332) 385981

Brewing commenced in 2012 using a six-barrel plant sited in the beer garden of the Furnace Inn. After initially brewing solely for the pub, 2014 saw an increase in scale and output, with beers distributed across most of the country. A second pub was acquired in 2014. ♦RAIB

New World (OG 1039, ABV 3.7%)
Golden in colour with powerful citrus hop flavours.

Silver Man (OG 1040, ABV 4%)
A light, refreshing cloudy wheat beer.

Bank Vault (OG 1045, ABV 4.3%)
A golden ale.

Wrench (OG 1045, ABV 4.4%)
A full-bodied stout. Vegan-friendly.

4 Wood (OG 1045, ABV 4.5%)
Traditional, well-balanced light chestnut-coloured ale with a delicate hop finish.

Affinity (OG 1046, ABV 4.6%)
Strong golden bitter with lots of fruity hops.

Tomahawk (OG 1058, ABV 6%)
A refreshing IPA with citrus flavour and aromas.

Ship Inn

Ship Inn, Newton Square, Low Newton-by-the-Sea, Northumberland, NE66 3EL
☎ (01665) 576262 🌐 shipinnnewton.co.uk

Brewing commenced in 2008 on a 2.5-barrel plant; the brewery now produces 7.5 barrels per week. All regular beers are brewed in rotation but are only available on the premises. A special beer (4.2% ABV) is brewed for every 100 brews. ♦RAIB

Sandcastles at Dawn (OG 1038, ABV 3.8%)
A pale session beer, light and crisp with a delicate floral finish.

Sea Coal (OG 1040, ABV 4%)
A dark wheat beer, mild coffee, bittersweet chocolate, berry fruit finish.

Sea Wheat (OG 1040, ABV 4%)
A pale crisp, sharp English-style wheat beer, citrus burst, strong grapefruit.

Ship Hop Ale (OG 1042, ABV 4.2%)
A light copper-coloured ale, dry with hints of orange and marmalade, balanced and rounded.

Dolly Daydream (OG 1043, ABV 4.3%)
A classic premium bitter, slight toffee edge, subtle vine fruit finish.

Shipstones

See Belvoir

Shoes SIBA

Three Horseshoes Inn, Norton Canon, Hereford, HR4 7BH
☎ (01544) 318375

Established in 1994. The beers are brewed from malt extract and are normally only available at the Three Horseshoes. Each September Canon Bitter is brewed with green hops fresh from the harvest. !! RAIB

Norton Ale (OG 1038, ABV 3.6%)

Canon Bitter (OG 1040, ABV 4.1%)

Peploe's Tipple (OG 1060, ABV 6%)

Farrier's Ale (OG 1114, ABV 15%)

Shortts Farm SIBA

Shortts Farm, Thorndon, Suffolk, IP23 7LS ☎ 07900 268100 🌐 shorttsfarmbrewery.com

Shortts Farm Brewery was established in 2012 by Matt Hammond on what has been the family farm for over a century. A five-barrel brewing plant is used. All of the beers are based around a musical theme inspired by a love of real ale and music. RAIB

Strummer (OG 1038, ABV 3.8%)
An amber ale. Easy-drinking, light and hoppy bitter with a good malty character.

Blondie (OG 1040, ABV 4%)
A well-balanced blonde beer with refreshing fruity hops and biscuity malt flavours.

Skiffle (OG 1047, ABV 4.5%)
Chestnut in colour. A complex and malty rich bitter with a great balance of hops over malt, creating a full-flavoured premium ale.

Indie (OG 1048, ABV 4.8%)
A golden IPA. Subtle but refreshing citrus fruit followed by a spicy and almost honey-like lingering bitter finish.

Shotover SIBA

Coopers Yard, Manor Farm Road, Horspath, Oxfordshire, OX33 1SD
☎ (01865) 876770 ☎ 07801 570444
shotoverbrewing.com

A family-owned and -run brewery four miles from Oxford city centre. It began brewing in 2009 and supplies outlets in the Oxford area. Bottle-conditioned beers are available and suitable for vegetarians. Cask ale suitable for vegetarians can also be supplied. !! ♦ RAIB

Prospect (OG 1040, ABV 3.7%)
Big flavour local bitter.

Trinity (OG 1040, ABV 4.2%)
Pale gold in colour with an intense grapefruit hop character.

Scholar (OG 1047, ABV 4.5%)
Deep copper-coloured premium bitter combining a silky malt base with a mixture of oranges, grapefruit and spiciness and a satisfying bitter finish.

Shottle Farm

School House Farm, Lodge Lane, Shottle, Derbyshire, DE56 2DS
☎ (01773) 550056 ☎ 07877 723075
shottlefarmbrewery.co.uk

Located in the hills above Belper, the Grade II-listed farm is part of the Chatsworth Estate. Family-run, Shottle Farm Brewery has been in production since 2011 with a 10-barrel plant and uses its own natural spring water and local honey. One-off and occasional beers are available. Its brewery tap is the nearby Bulls Head, Belper Lane End, and the George & Dragon, Belper, is regularly supplied along with several other outlets. ♦ RAIB

Shottlecock (OG 1034.9, ABV 3.6%)
Single malt beer with Fuggles hops and local honey. In the summer the honey is replaced with home-made elderflower syrup.

Black Peggy (OG 1037.8, ABV 3.9%)
Smooth, easy-drinking brew with chocolate malt and oatmeal giving pleasing hints of liquorice.

Shottle Pale Ale (OG 1037.8, ABV 4%)
Pale ale with a hint of citrus, brewed with local honey.

BOB (Best of Both) (OG 1038.8, ABV 4.1%)
A full-flavoured real lager.

Eight Shilling (OG 1038.8, ABV 4.1%)
A rich, dark beer. Smooth and malty. Full-bodied, pleasant aftertaste with undertones of treacle and caramel.

Belper Bitter (OG 1038.8, ABV 4.2%)

Shottle Gold (OG 1041.7, ABV 4.3%)
A golden ale with a floral aroma with a fruity hint of citrus lemon. Crisp and easy on the palate.

Dilks (OG 1048.4, ABV 5%)
Smooth, well-balanced amber-coloured ale with a slight sweetness and a hint of citrus.

Shoulder of Mutton (NEW)

12 Chapel Rd, Weldon, Northamptonshire, NN17 3HP
☎ (01536) 601016
shoulderofmuttonweldon@hotmail.com

Brewing began in 2014 using a two-barrel plant. Beers are currently only available in the pub.

Dragline (OG 1040, ABV 3.9%)
Golden ale, light and crisp with delicate fruit and floral notes.

Rosie's Sweatbox (OG 1042, ABV 4.2%)
A rich and tasty dark ale.

Weldon Windmill (OG 1042, ABV 4.2%)
A smooth best bitter.

Shugborough SIBA

Shugborough Estate, Milford, Staffordshire, ST17 0XB
☎ (01782) 823447 shugborough.org.uk

Brewing in the original brewhouse at Shugborough, home of the Earls of Lichfield, restarted in 1990 but a lack of expertise led to the brewery being a static museum piece until Titanic Brewery of Stoke-on-Trent (qv) began helping in 1996. !!

Miladys Fancy (OG 1048, ABV 4.6%)

Lordships Own (OG 1052, ABV 5%)

Signature Brew (NEW)

Unit 25, Leyton Business Centre, Etloe Road, London, E10 7BT
☎ (020) 7684 4664

Office: Workshop 45, Hackney Downs Studios, Hackney Downs, London, E8 2BT
signaturebrew.co.uk

Signature Brew was established in 2011 using spare capacity at a number of breweries, originally brewing beers in collaboration with music artists. In 2014 it launched a range named Signature Brew Originals. Beers are available cask-conditioned, in bottles (including bottle-conditioned ales) and keg. For the full range of beers including collaborations, see website. ♦ RAIB

Silhill SIBA

Oak Farm, Hampton Lane, Catherine-de-Barnes, Solihull, West Midlands, B92 0JB
☎ (0845) 519 5101 ☎ 07977 444564

Office: PO Box 15739, Solihull, West Midlands, B93 3FW silhillbrewery.co.uk

Established in 2010, Silhill is a small independent brewery now based in premises just outside Solihull town centre using a 10-barrel plant. !! RAIB

Stars & Stripes (OG 1039, ABV 3.9%)
An American-style pale ale with a grapefruit aroma, silky smooth, leading to a dry finish.

Gold Star (OG 1041, ABV 4.1%)
A golden amber ale. Malty and smooth, finishing with a delicate honey note.

Blonde Star (OG 1043, ABV 4.3%)
A refreshing, sweet citrus pale ale.

Dark Star (OG 1045, ABV 4.5%)
A chestnut ale, warm and well-balanced, with a hint of chocolate.

North Star (OG 1047, ABV 4.5%)
An American raspberry oatmeal stout.

Silver Street

Clarence Hotel, 2 Silver Street, Bury, BL9 0EX
☎ (0161) 763 9399 ⊕ theclarence.co.uk

Silver Street began brewing in 2014 at the Clarence Hotel in Bury.

Session (OG 1039, ABV 3.7%)
Well-balanced session ale with an interesting blend of hops; tangerine and blackcurrant notes.

One (OG 1040, ABV 4%)
Pale ale with plenty of hop.

Ruby, Ruby, Ruby, Ruby (OG 1047, ABV 4.7%)
Deep ruby ale with plenty of malty, biscuity goodness and jammy, plummy notes with a fruity nose.

Porter (OG 1053, ABV 5%)
A deceptively easy-drinking robust porter with a hint of liquorice and a floral, orange peel aroma.

Driftwood IPA (OG 1056, ABV 5.7%)
English-hopped IPA.

Silverstone

Kingshill Farm, Syresham, nr Silverstone, Northamptonshire, NN13 5TH
☎ (01280) 850629
⊕ silverstonebrewingcompany.com

The brewery, which is located near the celebrated motor racing circuit, opened in 2008. With a change of hands in 2013 the brewery has expanded its products and services. ‼

Pitstop Bitter (OG 1038, ABV 3.8%)

Pole Position (OG 1041, ABV 4.1%)

Skidmark (ABV 4.2%)

Chequered Flag (OG 1043, ABV 4.5%)

Simpsons

White Swan, Eardisland, Herefordshire, HR6 9BD
☎ (01544) 388635 ⊕ simpsonsfineales.co.uk

Tim Simpson acquired the White Swan in 2011 and set up the brewery at the rear of the pub in 2013. Beers are currently served in the White Swan, and locally to the free trade. A bottling facility is now in operation to supply local county shows. ♦

Golden Cock (OG 1037, ABV 3.7%)

Red Leg (OG 1043, ABV 4.3%)

Black Grouse (OG 1045, ABV 4.5%)

Old English (OG 1047, ABV 4.7%)

Sinclair

See Orkney

Siren Craft SIBA

Unit 1, Hogwood Industrial Estate, Weller Drive, Finchampstead, Berkshire, RG40 4QZ
☎ (0118) 973 0929 ⊕ sirencraftbrew.com

Siren Craft is a 40-barrel brewery, established in 2013 and extended in 2014 with a new bottling facility. The brewery is influenced by the US and European craft brewing movement. An extensive barrel-aging programme commenced in 2013 with many interesting beers produced. The brewery boasts an eight-tap tasting room. A balance of cask, keg and bottles are distributed throughout Europe. ‼ ♦ RAIB

Undercurrent Oatmeal Pale Ale (OG 1042, ABV 4.5%)
A pale ale with spicy, grassy aromas and a taste of grapefruit and apricot.

Soundwave IPA (OG 1056, ABV 5.6%)
An American-style West Coast IPA; golden, immensely hoppy and with grapefruit, peach and mango flavours.

Liquid Mistress Red IPA (OG 1061, ABV 5.8%)
An American-style West Coast red ale: burnt raisins and crackers balanced by a citrus grapefruit and peach spark.

Broken Dream Breakfast Stout (OG 1072, ABV 6.5%)
A breakfast stout with a gentle touch of smoke, coffee and chocolate. Deep and complex.

Six Bells

Church Street, Bishop's Castle, Shropshire, SY9 5AA
☎ (01588) 638930 ⊕ sixbellsbrewery.co.uk

Six Bells started in 1997 with a five-barrel plant. It supplies customers both within Shropshire and over the border in Wales. A new 12-barrel plant opened in 2010. In addition to the three core beers, an ale of the month is also brewed. ‼ ♦

Noggin' (OG 1037, ABV 3.8%)
A pale, fairly hoppy bitter.

Ow Do! (OG 1040, ABV 4%)
Rich amber-coloured beer full of spicy, fruity character.

Cloud Nine (OG 1043, ABV 4.2%)
Well-hopped golden ale with citrus notes throughout.

six°north

Reekie House, Aberdeen Road, Laurencekirk, AB30 1AG
☎ (01561) 377047 ☎ 07840 678243
⊕ sixdnorth.co.uk

⊗ The brewery brews beers in the Belgian tradition, using a purpose-built 20-hectolitre (approx 12.5-barrel) plant. Depending on beer style, the beers are supplied as cask or keg as appropriate. Brewing started in 2013. ‼

Prototype (ABV 4.2%)

Maes (ABV 4.6%)

66 IBU (ABV 6.6%)

Scotch (ABV 7%)

Chopper Stout (ABV 8%)

Six O'Clock

Gould Street, Manchester, M4 4RN
⊕ sixoclockbeer.co.uk

Six O'Clock Beer began brewing in 2013. Three core beers are available. ‼

Overtime (OG 1042, ABV 4.2%)
A light, hoppy pale ale.

Union (OG 1048, ABV 5%)
A robust IPA with a unique flavour.

Bolt (OG 1054, ABV 5.6%)
A balance between the body of a dark beer and the hoppiness of an IPA.

Sixpenny SIBA

The Dairy Building, Manor Farm, Sixpenny Handley, Dorset, SP5 5NU
☎ (01725) 762006 ⊕ sixpennybrewery.co.uk

⊗ Established in 2007, Sixpenny relocated to Dorset from Surrey in 2009 and now operates from a 20-barrel brewery on a farm site close to the village of Sixpenny Handley. It has its own onsite shop and bar, the Sixpenny Tap. More than 50 outlets are supplied including house beers to local Wetherspoon pubs. ‼🍴♦

6D Best Bitter (OG 1042, ABV 3.8%)
A well-balanced ale with a rounded malt flavour that leads to a pleasantly bitter and hoppy finish.

Addlestone Ale (OG 1044.5, ABV 4.2%)
Copper-coloured premium best bitter with a good balance of malt and hops.

Gold (OG 1044, ABV 4.2%)
A golden ale, slightly citrus flavoured with a distinct hoppy floral aroma.

SAM fm Ale (OG 1043.5, ABV 4.2%)
A well-balanced, amber-coloured best bitter.

IPA (OG 1053, ABV 5.2%)
Traditional IPA with a powerful hop character and a long, rounded malt finish.

Skinner's SIBA ◉

Riverside, Newham Road, Truro, Cornwall, TR1 2DP
☎ (01872) 271885 ⊕ skinnersbrewery.com

⊗ Award-winning brewery established in 1997. The brewery moved to bigger premises in 2003, opening a shop and visitor centre. The 25-barrel plant produces 25,000 hectolitres a year. Some speciality beers are brewed and marketed under the Cornish Beer & Surf Co brand. ‼🍴♦

Cornish Trawler (OG 1038, ABV 3.8%)
Light golden hoppy bitter. Well-balanced with a smooth bitter finish.

Ginger Tosser (OG 1038, ABV 3.8%) 🍴◆
Amber beer with fruit and spicy hop aroma. Initial malt followed by sweet spice tingle and orange citrus. Short finish.

Betty Stogs (OG 1040, ABV 4%) ◆
Copper best bitter with gentle hop aroma. Balance of light citrus hops and apple, sweet malt and bitterness. Long finish.

Heligan Honey (OG 1040, ABV 4%) ◆
A pale brown beer containing Cornish honey. Citrus hop zing balanced by sweet honey and bitterness. Lingering bittersweet, dry aftertaste.

River Cottage EPA (OG 1040, ABV 4%) ◆
Gold-coloured best bitter with floral hop aroma. Robust hops, sweet fruit, bitterness and malt flavours. Hoppy, rising bitter, dry finish.

Lushingtons (OG 1041, ABV 4.2%) ◆
Golden ale with citrus hop aroma. Strong citrus hops dominate. Bitter with sweetness, tropical fruits. Long, dry, citrus finish.

Cornish Knocker (OG 1044, ABV 4.5%) ◆
Refreshing golden ale with fragrant apple and hop aroma. Citrus hops, malt and summer fruit flavours. Bitter and astringent finish.

Porthleven (OG 1048, ABV 4.8%) 🍴◆
Golden ale with elderflower nose. Smooth citrus hop taste with bitter grapefruit and honey tones. Bitter, dry, citrus hop finish.

Slater's IFBB ◉

St Albans Road, Common Road Industrial Estate, Stafford, ST16 3DR
☎ (01785) 257976 ⊕ slatersales.co.uk

☺ The brewery was opened in 1995 and in 2006 moved to new, larger premises. It has won numerous awards from CAMRA and SIBA and supplies a large number of outlets. 2015 saw Slater's celebrate its 20th anniversary. ‼🍴

Rye IPA (OG 1038.5, ABV 3.8%)

Top Totty (OG 1039, ABV 4%) ◆
Great yellow colour with a fruit and hop nose. Hop and fruit balanced taste leads to citrus hints with mouth-watering edges. Dry finish with tangs of lemon.

Premium (OG 1042.5, ABV 4.4%) ◆
Pale brown bitter with malt and caramel aroma. Malt and caramel taste supported by hops and some fruit provide a warming descent and satisfyingly bitter mouthfeel.

Smoked Porter (OG 1046, ABV 4.8%)

Western (OG 1048, ABV 4.9%)
A heavily-hopped pale ale with a heady hop aroma and a chewy aromatic finish.

Haka (OG 1049, ABV 5.2%) ◆
New Zealand hops give a distinctive aroma and taste to this beer.

Slaughterhouse SIBA

🏚 Bridge Street, Warwick, CV34 5PD
☎ (01926) 490986 ⊕ slaughterhousebrewery.com

Production began in 2003 on a four-barrel plant in a former slaughterhouse. Around 30 outlets are supplied. The brewery premises are licensed for off-sales direct to the public. In 2010 Slaughterhouse opened its first pub, the Wild Boar in Warwick. ‼

Saddleback Best Bitter (OG 1038, ABV 3.8%)
Amber-coloured session bitter with a distinctive hop flavour.

Pale Ale (OG 1041, ABV 4.1%)
A classic English pale ale with a dry, quenching balance of malt and hops, and a long finish with light fruit notes.

Extra Stout Snout (OG 1044, ABV 4.4%)

Boar D'eau (OG 1045, ABV 4.5%)

Wild Boar (OG 1052, ABV 5.2%)

A robust dark beer.

Sleaford

21 Pride Court, Enterprise Park, Sleaford, Lincolnshire, NG34 8GL ☎ 07530 559322
sleafordbrewery@gmail.com

Sleaford was established in 2010 and came under new ownership in 2013. It is a family-run brewery creating small batch craft beers on a one-barrel plant. The brewery produces a wide range of styles and is constantly looking to expand its range.
♦ RAIB

Tropico (OG 1036, ABV 3.5%)
A low strength golden beer with tropical fruit aromas and a bitter tropical fruit taste.

Pale Partridge (OG 1041, ABV 3.9%)
A pale yellow beer with a light and spicy aroma and an easy-drinking balanced flavour.

Hedgerow Silver (OG 1042, ABV 4%)
A pale beer with floral and elderflower aroma leading to a spicy finish.

Pleasant Pheasant (OG 1043, ABV 4.2%)
A copper-coloured best bitter. Earthy and spicy aroma with a malty, caramel, bitter finish.

Hedgerow Gold (OG 1045, ABV 4.4%)
A pale golden beer with honey and spices giving a spicy aroma leading to a smooth and sweet, spicy finish.

Screaming Eagle Stout (OG 1050, ABV 4.8%)
A complex deep red stout with coffee, sweet chocolate and roasted aroma and taste.

Old Albert ESB (OG 1051, ABV 5%)
Copper brown-coloured ESB with a toffee aroma and a bittersweet caramel finish.

Midnight Runner (OG 1053, ABV 5.2%)
Dark old ale with a complex spicy hop and roasted aroma and a deep roasted taste.

Slighty Foxed SIBA

Unit 25, Asquith Bottom Mill, Sowerby Bridge, West Yorkshire, HX6 3BS ☎ 07412 008221
slightlyfoxedbrewery.co.uk

Slightly Foxed launched in 2011 as a venture between an award-winning landlord and a local businessman. Originally using spare capacity at Brass Monkey Brewery, Slightly Foxed bought the brewery in 2012. ♦

Howlin Fox (OG 1035, ABV 3.5%)
Easy-drinking, crisp and refreshing session beer. Hoppy with a light fruity citrus palate followed by a mellow finish.

Slightly Foxed (OG 1038, ABV 3.8%)
Pale golden, light and refreshing beer with a spicy, grapefruit flavour, a light, fruity floral aroma and a clean, dry finish.

Flying Fox (OG 1043, ABV 4.3%)
Pale and hoppy bitter with a touch of apricot flavour.

Fox Glove (OG 1043, ABV 4.3%)
A golden-coloured premium best bitter with a full-bodied, fruity flavour and fruit aromas.

Urban Fox (OG 1048, ABV 4.8%)
Well-balanced, dark-coloured London porter. Chocolate nose with a rich, fruity, roast flavour and a mild aftertaste.

Bengal Fox (OG 1052, ABV 5.2%)
A bright golden beer with a complex combination of pine, citrus and vanilla flavours.

Prairie Fox (OG 1052, ABV 5.2%)
An American-style pale ale. Plenty of hops on the nose. It has a mildly spicy and predominately citrus palate followed by a mellow and dry aftertaste.

Small Paul's

27 Briar Close, Gillingham, Dorset, SP8 4SS
☎ (01747) 823574 smallbrewer@btinternet.com

Launched in 2006, this half-barrel brewery is located in the owner's garage. There are usually two brews a month. A small number of local pubs and clubs are supplied direct and beers can be designed and brewed to order. ♦

Gylla's Gold (OG 1039, ABV 3.8%)
Easy-drinking session ale. Mild fruit hop aromas lead to bitter hop flavours and a lingering dry hop aftertaste.

Amber Nectar (OG 1042, ABV 4.2%)
Amber full-bodied best bitter. Slight citrus aroma with balanced malt and spicy hop flavours and a bitter finish.

Invicta (OG 1042, ABV 4.2%)
Pale, aromatic and hoppy with a long bitter finish.

Challenger II (OG 1044, ABV 4.3%)
A copper-coloured, slightly sweet, malty bitter.

Wyvern (OG 1044, ABV 4.4%)
Red/brown-coloured, well-balanced best bitter with malt and caramel flavours and short, bittersweet finish.

Gillingham Pale (OG 1045, ABV 4.5%)
Fruity, caramel aromas lead to complex bitter flavours and short, dry finish.

Small World SIBA

Unit 10, Barncliffe Business Park, Near Bank, Shelley, West Yorkshire, HD8 8LU
☎ (01484) 602805 ☎ 07540 319326
smallworldbeers.com

The brewery is situated in the picturesque Barncliffe valley in rural Shelley. The beers are brewed on a 20-barrel plant using spring water from an on-site bore hole. There is a small bar on site and brewery tours and tastings are available on request. ‼

Barncliffe Bitter (OG 1037, ABV 3.7%)
Pleasant, light-drinking bitter with fruit and citrus notes and a lasting bitterness through the finish.

Long Moor Pale (OG 1039, ABV 3.9%)
Pale ale with grapefruit and citrus notes, and a light bitter finish.

Spike's Gold (OG 1043, ABV 4.4%)
Smooth, well-balanced golden ale with fruit and hop flavours through to the finish.

Thunderbridge Stout (OG 1051, ABV 5.2%)
Traditional dry stout with roast flavours giving way to smooth coffee undertones and a sharp, dry finish.

Twin Falls (OG 1051, ABV 5.2%)

Full-bodied pale ale with fruity aroma, strong tropical fruit and hop taste.

Joseph Herbert Smith

Fox Inn, Hanley Broadheath, Worcestershire, WR15 8QS
☎ (01886) 853189 ☎ 07527 066474
⊕ jhstraditionalbrewery.com

☺The brewery was established in Staffordshire in 2007 by Jonathan Smith. In 2008 it relocated to barns adjacent to the Fox Inn. All equipment is gas fired and ingredients are sourced locally where possible. ‼◆

Amy's Rose (OG 1040, ABV 4%)
A traditionally-brewed mild ale.

Snooty Fox (OG 1042, ABV 4.1%)
A copper-coloured, English-style best bitter.

Foxy Lady (OG 1043, ABV 4.3%)
A premium light bitter.

Teddy's Tipple (OG 1044, ABV 4.4%)
A sweetish bitter.

Samuel Smith

High Street, Tadcaster, North Yorkshire, LS24 9SB
☎ (01937) 832225 ⊕ samuelsmithsbrewery.co.uk

☺Fiercely independent, family-owned company. Tradition, quality and value are important, resulting in brewing without any artificial additives. All real ale is supplied in wooden casks. A bottle-conditioned beer (Yorkshire Stingo, ABV 8%) is only available in specialist off-licences. **RAIB**

OBB (Old Brewery Bitter) (OG 1040, ABV 4%) ◈
Malt dominates the aroma, with an initial burst of malt, hops and fruit in the taste, which is sustained in the aftertaste.

Tom Smith

13 South Folds Road, Oakley Hay, Northamptonshire, NN18 9EU
☎ (01536) 399859 ☎ 07956 051922
✉ mark@tomsmithales.co.uk

Tom Smith Brewery was established in 2012 by Mark Smith in an industrial unit in the back streets of Kettering. In 2013 the brewery moved to the site of Latimer Ales (qv) in Oakley Hay to share brewing facilities. Brewing was suspended during 2014 but resumed in 2015.

John Smith's

The Brewery, Tadcaster, North Yorkshire, LS24 9SA
☎ (01937) 832091 ⊕ heineken.com

The brewery was built in 1879 by a relative of Samuel Smith (qv). John Smith's became part of the Courage group in 1970 before being taken over by S&N and now Heineken UK. Major expansion has taken place, with 11 new fermenting vessels installed. Traditional Yorkshire Square fermenters have been replaced by conical vessels. John Smith's cask Magnet has been discontinued. John Smith's Bitter in cask form is brewed under contract by Cameron's Brewery (qv) in Hartlepool.

Snaggletooth

Rear of 11 Pole Lane, Darwen, Lancashire, BB3 3LD
☎ 07810 365701 ⊕ snaggletoothbrewing.com

Snaggletooth was established in 2012 by three beer geeks with a passion for crafting ales. A 2.5-barrel plant is used at the Hopstar Brewery (qv) in Darwen, Lancashire.

Allotropic Pale Ale (ABV 3.8%)
A pale ale with floral and citrus notes using New Zealand hops.

Déjà Brewed (OG 1040, ABV 4%)
Refreshing ale with floral, spicy and citrus flavours.

'Cos I'm a Lobster (OG 1044, ABV 4.2%)
Summery red-coloured ale with subtle roasted malts.

Snowdonia

Snowdonia Parc Brewpub & Campsite, Waunfawr, Caernarfon, LL55 4AQ
☎ (01286) 650409 ⊕ snowdonia-park.co.uk

Snowdonia started brewing in 1998 in a two-barrel brewhouse. The brewing is now carried out by the owner, Carmen Pierce. The beer is brewed solely for the Snowdonia Park pub and campsite.

Gwyrfai (OG 1037, ABV 3.8%)
A tawny-coloured ale with bitterness from traditional hop varieties.

Trithro (OG 1038, ABV 3.8%)

Gold (OG 1040, ABV 4%)
A pale and hoppy beer with citrus notes.

Theodore Stout (OG 1040, ABV 4.1%)
A robust roast flavour is complemented by a full-bodied and smooth mouthfeel. The hops lends a tart bitterness to the dry, espresso-like finish. The complex coffee aromas mingle with light liquorice notes.

Carmen Sutra (OG 1043, ABV 4.4%)

Cais (OG 1045, ABV 4.8%)
A dark beer with rich flavours and balanced bitterness.

Dark & Delicious (OG 1046, ABV 5%)
Rich, dark and complex with a real depth of flavour.

Welsh Highland Bitter (OG 1048, ABV 5.2%)
A traditional premium strong ale that is malty and full. A slight sweetness extends into the finish of this mid-brown, balanced beer.

Solvay Society (NEW)

Hops & Glory, 382 Essex Road, London, N1 3PF
☎ (020) 7226 2277

Set up by head brewer Roman Hochuli and busines partner JP Hussey, Solvay Society began brewing in 2014 in the cellar of a Walthamstow pub using a small 0.5-hectolitre kit. In 2015 it transferred the equipment to the Hops & Glory pub, in north London. Keg beer only is produced at present. Hops & Glory staff occasionally use the brew kit to supply the bar.

Son of Sid

Chequers, 71 Main Road, Little Gransden, Cambridgeshire, SG19 3DW

☎ **(01767) 677348** ⊕ **sonofsid.co.uk**

⊗ Son of Sid was established in 2007. The three-barrel plant is situated in a separate room at the back of the pub and can be viewed from a window in the lounge bar. It is named after the father of the current landlord, who ran the pub for 42 years. His son has carried the business on for the past 23 years as a family-run enterprise. Beer is sold in the pub and at local beer festivals. **!! ☞ RAIB**

English Ale (OG 1035, ABV 3.5%)
Traditional ale with a clean, malty taste and a good hop character.

Muck Cart Mild (OG 1035, ABV 3.5%) ◆
Black mild with a resounding roast malt presence and a caramel background in aroma and taste. There is some sweetness but the balance is predominantly dry and bitter, with increasing bitterness in the aftertaste.

Golden Shower (OG 1039, ABV 3.9%)
Full-bodied golden beer with a light hop character and a defined maltiness.

Songbird

Stumble Inn, 37 Tamworth Rd, Long Eaton, Derbyshire, NG10 1JF
☎ **(0115) 972 4529** ☎ **07912 601475**
⊕ **songbirdbrewery.co.uk**

Songbird was founded in 2013 by father and daughter, Martin and Samantha Dodsworth, using a two-barrel plant situated at the rear of the Stumble Inn. Production commenced in 2014.

Bitter Sweet Symphony (OG 1040, ABV 4%)
Light, bittersweet ale.

Double Bass (OG 1042, ABV 4.2%)
Malty, brown-coloured traditional bitter.

Mild Thing (OG 1042, ABV 4.2%)
Dark, rich, full-bodied malty ale.

Melody Pale (OG 1044, ABV 4.5%)
Light in colour, a sweet, hoppy ale.

Ale House Rock (OG 1047, ABV 4.8%)
A traditional porter. Rich and dark with an outstanding depth of flavour.

Sonnet 43 SIBA ☜

Durham Road, Coxhoe, County Durham, DH6 4HX
☎ **(0191) 377 3039** ⊕ **sonnet43.com**

☺ Sonnet 43 began brewing in 2013. The name and brewing ethos is inspired by the most famous work of poet Elizabeth Barratt Browning. Five core beers are available as well as specials. The brewery has six tied outlets and supplies extensively to the free trade. ☞

Steam Beer (OG 1038, ABV 3.8%)
A medium-bodied, refreshing amber ale with a slightly bitter aftertaste.

Blonde Beer (OG 1041, ABV 4.1%)
A straw coloured wheat-style beer with a sweet, delicate, floral hop aroma.

Bourbon Milk Stout (OG 1046, ABV 4.3%)
Bourbon, cocoa and oats give this dark beer a rich, full-bodied, chocolaty bitterness.

India Pale Ale (OG 1044, ABV 4.4%)

Classic strong pale ale with a light gold appearance, a complex hoppy aroma and delicate fruity malt taste.

American Pale Ale (OG 1055, ABV 5.4%)
Pale bronze in colour and full-bodied with a complex character and spicy, peppery aroma. A fragrant bouquet with a fruity, malty and spicy flavour.

South Hams SIBA

Stokeley Barton Farm, Stokenham, Devon, TQ7 2SE
☎ **(01548) 581151** ⊕ **southhamsbrewery.co.uk**

The brewery moved to its present site, a milking parlour, in 2003, with a 10-barrel plant and plenty of room to expand. It supplies more than 60 outlets in south Devon. Wholesalers are used to distribute to other areas. Three pubs (one being the brewery tap) are owned. **!! ♦ RAIB**

Devon Pride (OG 1039, ABV 3.8%)
A dark amber-coloured beer, smooth to drink with a malty palate.

Wild Blonde (OG 1044, ABV 4.4%)
A refreshing golden-coloured beer.

Hopnosis (OG 1046, ABV 4.5%)

Eddystone (OG 1050, ABV 4.8%)
A golden IPA with a distinct fruity aroma and fruity palate.

Pandemonium (OG 1054, ABV 5%)

Southbourne

c/o 26 Boreham Road, Bournemouth, Dorset, BH6 5BW
☎ **(01202) 421190** ☎ **07845 795464**
⊕ **southbourneales.co.uk**

⊗ Southbourne started brewing in 2014 using spare capacity at the Town Mill Brewery (qv), until it has sufficient funding to establish its own brewhouse. It currently brews two or three times a month. ♦

Paddlers (ABV 3.6%)
A light but balanced session bitter with only moderate hop characteristics.

Sunbather (ABV 4%)
A red-coloured ale with moderate hop bitterness and flavour but with toffee notes in the distinctive malt flavour.

Headlander (ABV 4.2%)
Floral aroma and full bitterness from the hops balanced with malt.

Beachcomber (ABV 5.7%)
A full-flavoured 1920s-style brown ale with a good malt and hop balance.

SouthDowns

See Downlands

Southport SIBA

Unit 3, Enterprise Business Park, Russell Road, Southport, Merseyside, PR9 7RF ☎ **07748 387652**
⊕ **southportbrewery.co.uk**

⊚Southport Brewery was established in 2004 on a five-barrel plant. Outlets are supplied in Southport, north-west England and nationally. ♦

Cyclone (OG 1039.5, ABV 3.8%)
A bronze-coloured bitter with a fruity blackcurrant aftertaste.

Sandgrounder Bitter (OG 1039.5, ABV 3.8%)
Pale, hoppy session bitter with a floral character.

Dark Night (OG 1040.5, ABV 3.9%)
A dark traditional mild.

Carousel (OG 1041.5, ABV 4%)
A refreshing, floral, hoppy best bitter.

Golden Sands (OG 1041.5, ABV 4%)
A golden-coloured, triple-hopped bitter with citrus flavour.

Natterjack (OG 1043.5, ABV 4.3%)
A premium bitter with fruit notes and a hint of coffee.

Southwark (NEW) SIBA ⊙

46 Druid Street, London, SE1 2EZ
☎ (020) 3302 4190 ⊕ southwarkbrewing.co.uk

⊠ Another addition to the burgeoning Bermondsey brewing scene, Southwark Brewing Company opened in 2014 focussing on cask ales. A tap room is open on a Friday evening and Saturday offering the brewery's three regular real ales plus seasonal brews. Further beers are planned. 🛒♦

LPA (London Pale Ale) (ABV 4%)

Bermondsey Best (ABV 4.4%) ◆
A well-balanced best bitter with the fruity notes developing in the finish, which is bitter. Some malty notes on the palate.

Gold (ABV 5.2%)

Spa Town

See Harrogate

Spencer's

See G2

Sperrin SIBA

▤ Birmingham Road, Ansley, Warwickshire, CV10 9PQ
☎ (024) 7639 2305 ☎ 07917 772208
⊕ sperrinbrewery.co.uk

Sperrin began brewing in 2012 and is situated by the side of the Lord Nelson Inn. A brewery was first established there in 1868. Beers are also available at its sister pub, the Blue Boar in Mancetter. ‼♦RAIB

Ansley Mild (OG 1035, ABV 3.5%)
A traditional recipe giving a rich, roast, malty-flavoured mild.

Head Hunter (OG 1038, ABV 3.8%)
Triple-hopped amber ale with slight fruity hints and a pleasant, dry finish.

Band of Brothers (OG 1042, ABV 4.2%)
Hoppy and full-flavoured golden ale with long-lasting, smooth, citrus and refreshing overtones.

Third Party (OG 1048, ABV 4.8%)
Malty ruby ale with a floral aroma and hints of fruit and spice.

Thick as Thieves (OG 1068, ABV 6.8%)
Strong stout, rich in hops with an array of roasted chocolate malts giving a smooth, liquorice, well-balanced finish.

Spey Valley

Mains of Mulben, Mulben, Keith, AB55 6YH ☎ 07780 655199 ⊕ speyvalleybrewery.co.uk

David Macdonald began brewing in 2007. A two-barrel plant is used, sourced from the Loch Ness Brewery. Beers are available in 20 outlets locally. ♦

David's Not So Bitter (OG 1046, ABV 4.4%) ◆
Light brown with a good mix of malts, hops and red fruits.

Stillman's IPA (OG 1047.6, ABV 4.6%) ◆
A light, hoppy bitter.

Spey Stout (OG 1055, ABV 5.4%) ◆
A good, thick, dark malty stout with a smoky background.

Speyside Craft SIBA

2 Greshop Road, Forres, IV36 2GU
☎ (01309) 358082 ☎ 07854 053277
⊕ speysidecraftbrewery.com

Based in a traditional whisky-producing area, Speyside Brewery uses the same water that goes into the production of Scottish whiskies. A number of local outlets are supplied. A donation from sales of Bottlenose Bitter goes to help support the work of the Whale & Dolphin Conservation Society. ♦

Bow Fiddle Blonde (OG 1038, ABV 3.8%)

Bottlenose Bitter (OG 1041, ABV 4.1%)

Randolph's Leap (OG 1049, ABV 4.9%)

Moray IPA (OG 1055, ABV 5.5%)

Findhorn Killer Red IPA (OG 1056, ABV 5.6%)

Spire SIBA

Bull Paddock Farm, Sutton Lane, Sutton Scarsdale, Derbyshire, S44 5UW
☎ (01246) 807940 ⊕ spirebrewing.co.uk

⊚ Originally set up in 2006, the Spire brand came under the ownership of a long-standing CAMRA member in 2014 and the new-look brewery relocated to Sutton Scarsdale. The old 10-barrel plant has been replaced with a new 15-barrel British kit. ♦RAIB

Whiter Shade (OG 1039, ABV 4%)
Pale straw-coloured session bitter with a subtle lemon hop finish. It is refreshingly smooth with a well-balanced malt flavour.

Chesterfield Best Bitter (OG 1043, ABV 4.5%) ◆
Classic brown strong bitter with malt and fruit flavours and a hint of caramel and chocolate in the finish. There is a little bitterness in the aftertaste.

Spitting Feathers SIBA ⊙

Common Farm, Waverton, Cheshire, CH3 7QT
☎ (01244) 332052 ☎ 07974 348325
⊕ spittingfeathers.org

⊚Spitting Feathers was established in 2005. The brewery is located in a sandstone building set around a cobbled yard. Around 200 local outlets are supplied. A range of occasional beers are brewed to old recipes under the Heritage Ales brand. ‼♦

Session Beer (OG 1035, ABV 3.6%)
A golden session bitter. Traditional English malts and hops combine to make this a well-balanced and satisfying beer.

Thirstquencher (OG 1038, ABV 3.9%) ◀
Powerful hop aroma leads into the taste. Bitterness and a fruity citrus hop flavour fight for attention. A sharp, clean golden beer with a long, dry, bitter aftertaste.

Special Ale (OG 1041, ABV 4.2%) ◀
Complex tawny-coloured beer with a sharp, grainy mouthfeel. Malty with good hop coming through in the aroma and taste. Hints of nuttiness and a touch of acidity. Dry, astringent finish.

Old Wavertonian (OG 1043, ABV 4.4%) ◀
Creamy and smooth stout. Full-flavoured with coffee notes in aroma and taste. Roast and nut flavours throughout, leading to a hoppy, bitter finish.

Sportsman

⌷ 1-3 St John's Road, Huddersfield, West Yorkshire, HD1 5AY ☎ 07903 040873
✉ info@sportsmanbrewingcompany.co.uk

☺ The brewery opened in 2011 in the cellars of the Sportsman pub on a two-barrel plant Owing to restricted capacity, brewing was later split between the brewpub and Golcar Brewery (qv) to meet demand. Brewing is currently suspended while new premises are sought.

Springhead SIBA ◉

Robin Hood Site, Main Street, Laneham, Nottinghamshire, DN22 0NA
☎ (01777) 228080 ☎ 07720 461655
⊕ springhead.co.uk

☺ Springhead Brewery opened in 1990, and relocated to its current address in 2011. Around 500 outlets are supplied direct and the brewery owns five pubs. Drop p' the Black Stuff is suitable for vegans. Brewery tours start and finish at Meg's Bar, which is part of the brewery building, where you can also watch the brewery in operation. The Bees Knees pub is adjacent to the brewery, where the core beers plus the current seasonal brew are always available. ‼ ⛟♦

Outlawed (OG 1040, ABV 3.8%)
A triple-hopped, easy-drinking American-style pale ale, with a citrus aroma.

Drop o' the Black Stuff (OG 1041, ABV 4%)
A smooth, dark, easy-drinking porter.

Robin Hood (OG 1041, ABV 4%)
A chestnut brown traditional bitter with a good head and plenty of hops.

Maid Marian (OG 1045, ABV 4.5%)
A pale golden beer with a fruity orange aroma and a dry finish.

Leveller (OG 1047, ABV 4.8%)
A dark, smoky, intense flavour with a toffee finish. Brewed in the style of Belgian Trappist ale.

Roaring Meg (OG 1052, ABV 5.5%)
A smooth, classic IPA. Golden, with a citrus honey aroma and a dry finish.

Squawk (NEW)

Unit 4, Tonge Street, Ardwick, Manchester, M12 6LY
☎ 07590 387559 ⊕ squawkbrewingco.com

Squawk initially cuckoo-brewed on the Hand Drawn Monkey plant in Huddersfield in 2013, with the first brew from the Manchester site being in 2014. The eight-barrel plant is located in a railway arch in Ardwick. The beer range varies but includes a pale ale, an IPA, a stout and a porter. RAIB

Stables

⌷ Beamish Hall Country House Hotel, Beamish, County Durham, DH9 0YB
☎ (01207) 288750 ⊕ beamish-hall.co.uk/stables

Stables was established as part of a £1 million development of an old stable block of Beamish Hall, converting a disused building to a restaurant and eight-barrel microbrewery. The hotel is supplied plus the Sun Inn at Beamish Museum. The brewery also brews under the Bull Lane Brewing Co name. ‼♦

Beamish Hall Best Bitter (OG 1038, ABV 3.8%)

Old Miner Tommy (OG 1037, ABV 3.8%)

Bobby Dazzler (OG 1042, ABV 4.2%)

Coppy Lane (OG 1043, ABV 4.2%)

Silver Buckles (OG 1044, ABV 4.4%)

Beamish Burn (OG 1045, ABV 4.5%)

Bell Tower (OG 1052, ABV 5%)

Brewed under the Bull Lane Brewing Co name:

SOL (Stadium of Light) (ABV 3.8%)

Stampede (ABV 4.2%)

Butcher's Brew (ABV 4.4%)

Double Barrel (ABV 5%)
All brewed for the Butchers Arms in Sunderland.

Staffordshire

12 Churnet Court, Cheddleton, Staffordshire, ST13 7EF
☎ (01538) 361919 ☎ 07971 808370
⊕ staffordshirebrewery.co.uk

No real ale. Brewing started in 2002 and the brewery has steadily increased in capacity since. A 20-barrel brew plant was completed in 2011. The brewery was renamed from Leek Brewery in 2013 at which time cask production ceased, being replaced by filtered, pasteurised bottled beers only. Cask-conditioned ales are brewed for Wicked Hathern Brewery Ltd using a six-barrel plant. ‼

Brewed for Wicked Hathern Brewery:

Albion Special (OG 1042, ABV 4%)
Light copper in colour with a nutty aroma and a smoky malty taste, the hops leading through.

Hawthorn Gold (OG 1045, ABV 4.6%)
A light golden, easy-drinking beer with a good balance of hops and malt.

Staggeringly Good (NEW)

Office: Flat 1, 46 Clarence Parade, Southsea, PO5 2FH
☎ 07881 943452 ⊕ staggeringlygood.com

⊗ Currently using brewery equipment at the Brewhouse & Kitchen (Portsmouth) (qv) while an independent site is sought within the Portsmouth area. There are plans to expand the beer range over the next year. ♦RAIB

Staggersaurus (OG 1039, ABV 4%)
A deep golden ale with summer fruit aromas with grapefruit on the palate. A light bitterness softens to give a refreshing finish.

ThaiRannoCitrus (OG 1048, ABV 5%)
A pale ale with brewed with kaffir lime and American hops. Lime and peach flavours and aromas are balanced with hoppy bitterness.

Post Impact Porter (OG 1057, ABV 5.4%)
A rich, dark porter with roasted malt and chocolate flavours.

VelociRapture (OG 1060, ABV 6.5%)
A well-rounded, crisp and refreshing American-style IPA with a strong fruit character and bitterness.

Stamps

The Basement, 17 Boundary Street, Everton, Liverpool, L5 9UB ☎ 07779 000094
🌐 stampsbrewery.co.uk

Brewing began in 2012 on an environmentally-friendly brew plant: power for brewing comes from 52 solar panels and a biomass boiler, used grain is sent to a local city farm for animal feed and rainwater is recycled and used for floor cleaning. The beers are named after famous world postage stamps. ‼

Blonde Moment (OG 1037, ABV 3.6%)
A pale-coloured beer with a smooth floral and citrus aroma and flavour. A good session beer.

Bondi Blonde (OG 1037, ABV 3.7%)
A pale, full-flavoured blonde beer, floral notes and citrus evident.

Mail Train (OG 1042, ABV 4.2%)
Traditional bitter, an abundance of hops leaves a noticeable bitterness with a malt character.

Russian (OG 1040, ABV 4.2%)
A copper-coloured ale with a hoppy finish.

Swedish Blonde (OG 1041, ABV 4.3%)
A generous amount of hops with a strong hint of citrus.

Inverted Jenny (OG 1046, ABV 4.6%)
Golden in colour, a grassy and floral bouquet with a noticeable tinge of caramel.

Flying Cloud (OG 1052, ABV 5.2%)
A dry, pale, lager-style session beer.

Stancill SIBA

Unit 2, Oakham Drive, off Rutland Road, Sheffield, South Yorkshire, S3 9QX
☎ (0114) 275 2788 ☎ 07809 427716

Stancill began brewing in 2014 and is named after the head brewer and co-owner. It is situated on the doorstep of the late Cannon Brewery, taking advantage of the soft Yorkshire water. ‼

Tom's Mild (OG 1036.5, ABV 3.4%)

Barnsley Bitter (OG 1037.5, ABV 3.8%)

Blonde (OG 1038.5, ABV 3.9%)

Ginger (OG 1039.5, ABV 4%)

No. 7 (OG 1042, ABV 4.3%)

Porter (OG 1042.5, ABV 4.4%)

Stanway

Stanway House, Stanway, Gloucestershire, GL54 5PQ
☎ (01386) 584320 🌐 stanwaybrewery.co.uk

Stanway is a small brewery founded in 1993 with a five-barrel plant that confines its sales to the Cotswolds area (15 to 20 outlets). The brewery is the only known plant in the country to use wood-fired coppers for all its production. ♦

Stanney Bitter (OG 1042, ABV 4.5%)
A light, refreshing, amber-coloured beer, dominated by hops in the aroma, with a bitter taste and a hoppy, bitter finish.

Star SIBA

Unit D, Bentley Business Park, Northfields Industrial Estate, Market Deeping, Lincolnshire, PE6 8LD
☎ (01778) 380480 ☎ 07885 666836
✉ starbrewco@gmail.com

Star commenced production in 2014 using a 10-barrel brew plant. It has since expanded capacity to 20 barrels, producing a core range of three beers plus rotating seasonal ales. Outlets throughout the UK are supplied. Star beers are now available in the JD Wetherspoons chain. ‼♦

Comet (OG 1038.5, ABV 3.8%)
Well-hopped blonde ale.

Meteor (OG 1040, ABV 4%)
Traditional amber ale, brewed with English malt and hops.

Galaxy (OG 1044, ABV 4.4%)
Crisp, golden best bitter.

Star Inn Community

Star Inn, 2 Back Hope Street, The Cliff, Higher Broughton, M7 2PD ☎ 07713 325306
✉ lee.renforth@hvpd.co.uk

The former Star Inn Brewery was renamed Star Inn Community by new brewer David Bogie, who took over in 2015. David, who is also the brewer at Brinkburn Street Brewery in Newcastle upon Tyne, runs the brewery together with Lee Renforth using the original four-barrel plant in the small on-site brewhouse at the picturesque 19th-century Star Inn, owned and run as a cooperative by its customers.

Station 119 (NEW)

Rokeby Old Hall, Wilby, Eye, Suffolk, IP21 5LF
☎ 07766 701440 🌐 station119.co.uk

Brewing started in 2014 with three beers produced on a two-barrel plant. The beers are available locally from Snape Maltings, Marlesford Farm Shop/cafe and Sweffling White Horse. RAIB

Steamin' Billy

See Belvoir

Steel City

c/o Toolmakers Brewery, 6-8 Botsford Street,
Sheffield, South Yorkshire, S3 9PF
⊕ steelcitybrewing.co.uk

⊠ Steel City was established in 2009 and brews once or twice a month. Brewing activity was originally based at the Brew Company before moving on to Little Ale Cart's premises for three years. It currently uses spare capacity at Toolmakers Brewery (qv).

Stewart SIBA

26a Dryden Road, Bilston Glen Industrial Estate,
Loanhead, EH20 9LZ
☎ (0131) 440 2442 ⊕ stewartbrewing.co.uk

☺ Established in 2004 by Steve Stewart, a qualified master brewer. The brewery moved to a larger, custom-built brewery in 2013 with a brand new 50-hectolitre plant from Bavarian Brewing Technologies. Seasonal and bottle-conditioned beers supplement the regular range along with Natural Selection beers brewed by Herriot Watt students. Beers are distributed throughout the UK, although they are mainly sold in south-east Scotland. !! ▭ ♦ RAIB

Pentland IPA (OG 1040, ABV 3.9%) ◀
A pleasing, hoppy, golden session ale. The dry bitter taste is well-balanced by sweetness from the malt, and fruit flavours. The aftertaste is dry with a lingering bitterness.

Cascade (OG 1041, ABV 4.1%) ◀
This tawny-coloured beer is born from American hops and Scottish malt. The hop character overlays a solid malt base. Hints of roast and substantial fruitiness give a complex character. A bittersweet taste leads to a dry bitter finish.

Edinburgh No.3 (OG 1043, ABV 4.3%) ◀
An excellent example of a Scottish heavy ale. Full-bodied and dark with a predominantly malt character, fruit notes and a gentle infusion of hop. A bittersweet beer with a dry finish.

80/- (OG 1044, ABV 4.4%) ◀
Traditional Scottish heavy. The complex profile is dominated by malt with fruit flavours giving the sweetish character typical of this beer style. Hops provide a gentle balancing bitterness that intensifies in the dry finish.

Edinburgh Gold (OG 1048, ABV 4.8%) ◀
A full-bodied but easy-drinking Continental-style golden ale. Bitterness from the hop character is strong in the finish and complemented in the taste by a little sweetness from malt and fruit flavours.

Sticklegs

Unit 7, Old Forge Court, Colchester Road, Elmstead
Market, Essex, CO7 7EA ☎ 07971 138038
⊕ sticklegs.co.uk

⊠ Sticklegs was established in 2008 at the Cross Inn, Great Bromley. It has since moved and expanded and is now based on a two-barrel and six-barrel plant in Elmstead. !! ▭

Malt Shovel Mild (OG 1032, ABV 3.4%)

Old Forge Bitter (OG 1038, ABV 3.8%)

Stour Gold (OG 1040, ABV 3.8%)

Tendring 100 (OG 1041, ABV 4%)

Elmstead Stout (OG 1046, ABV 4.8%)

Nemesis (OG 1048, ABV 5%)

Stocklinch

Unit 3, Manor Farm, Stocklinch, Somerset, TA19 9JG
☎ 07711 479917 ⊕ stocklinchales.co.uk

⊠ Established in 2012 in a converted farm building, Stocklinch uses a five-barrel plant supplying a number of local outlets. The brewery is licensed to open for a few days each month, mainly at weekends, which compensates for the lack of a village pub. !! ▭ ♦

Ramblers Gold (OG 1038, ABV 3.8%)
Refreshing light golden beer with a slight aftertaste of grapefruit.

Jakes (OG 1040, ABV 4%)

Gunner Boyce (OG 1042, ABV 4.2%)

Jakes Special (OG 1045, ABV 4.5%)

Rusty Boiler (OG 1045, ABV 4.5%)
Mid brown best bitter, strong fruity flavours with a lick of caramel.

Black Smock (OG 1050, ABV 5%)
Dark beer with a strong rich taste of chocolate liquorice and coffee with a hint of blackcurrant.

Ramblers Gold Extra (OG 1050, ABV 5%)

Stockport (NEW) SIBA ◉

Arch 14, Heaton Lane, Stockport, SK4 1AQ
☎ (0161) 477 1084 ☎ 07442 530728
⊕ stockportbrewingcompany.com

☺ Previously sharing equipment at another local brewery, Stockport Brewing Co installed its own eight-barrel plant in 2014. HMRC accreditation was gained and brewing commenced in the same year. The brewery now has a regular brewing capacity of 100 firkins a week, producing more than 15 different ales. The beers are available at over 100 pubs across the north-west. !! ▭ ♦

Bitter Lemon (ABV 4.2%)
A straw-coloured hoppy beer with a bitter lemon finish.

Crown Best Bitter (ABV 4.2%)
Amber-coloured ale with a smooth, hoppy taste. Double hopped with a dry finish.

Stock Porter (ABV 4.8%)
Liquorice and malty nose with coffee and chocolate notes.

Stockton (NEW)

28 Light Pipe Hall Road, Stockton on Tees, Co Durham,
TS18 4AH
☎ (01642) 678334
⊕ stocktonbrewingcompany.co.uk

Stockton Brewing Co started production in 2015 based in an industrial unit. It uses a 2.5-barrel plant. RAIB

Black Swann Oatmeal Stout (OG 1049, ABV 5%)

New World Order IPA (OG 1062, ABV 6.2%)

Stod Fold SIBA 👁

Stod Fold Farm, Hays Lane, Halifax, West Yorkshire, HX8 2UL
☎ (01224) 245951 ☎ 07870 498324
⊕ stodfoldbrewing.com

Stod Fold was founded by childhood friends Paul Harris and Angus Wood. They designed and built the brewery themselves and the result is a fully integrated, bespoke, computer-controlled, state of the art 10-barrel plant. The brewery is not open to the public but once a month is open to trade partners only.

Gold (OG 1038, ABV 3.8%) ◄
A refreshing, hoppy and fruity session ale. It has a crisp bitter aftertaste.

Amber (OG 1042, ABV 4.2%) ◄
Well-balanced best bitter. Overtones of fruit and hops. Easy-drinking with a mild bitter finish.

Blonde (OG 1045, ABV 4.5%) ◄
Smooth-tasting, easy-drinking fruity beer with a lingering dry finish.

Pils (OG 1048, ABV 4.8%) ◄
Smooth-tasting specialist beer with light hoppy yet mild aftertaste. A light mellow ale with a mouth-filling flavour.

Stokesley SIBA

See Wainstones

Stonehenge SIBA 👁

The Old Mill, Mill Road, Netheravon, Salisbury, Wiltshire, SP4 9QB
☎ (01980) 670631 ⊕ stonehengeales.co.uk

The brewery was founded in 1984 in what was originally a water-driven mill built in 1914. In 1993 the company was bought by Danish master brewer Stig Andersen and now supplies more than 300 outlets. From 2013 a new borehole, accessing the Salisbury Plain aquifer, has been supplying the brewery's water. It is of such pristine quality that the brewery now bottles and sells it under the Stonehenge name. ‼◆

Spire Ale (OG 1037, ABV 3.8%) ◄
A pale golden-coloured session bitter with an initial bitterness giving way to a well-rounded bitter aftertaste with discernible fruit balance.

Pigswill (OG 1039, ABV 4%) ◄
A tawny-coloured session bitter with an initial pleasant hop aroma and slight bitterness to the initial taste moving to a well-rounded bitter finish with slight malt and fruit in the finish.

Heel Stone (OG 1042, ABV 4.3%) ◄
A copper-coloured best bitter with some malt and fruit in the aroma continuing into the initial taste along with pleasant hoppiness. Medium-bodied with plenty of flavour in the aftertaste with noticeable malt, fruit and hops.

Great Bustard (OG 1046, ABV 4.8%) ◄
A copper-brown coloured strong bitter. Complex malt and fruit flavours at first with a long fruit and bitter aftertaste.

Danish Dynamite (OG 1048, ABV 5%) ◄
Golden-coloured strong bitter with good hop and fruit aromas. Complex flavours in the initial taste

with a beautifully balanced full-bodied aftertaste with hops and fruit to the fore.

Stonehouse SIBA

Stonehouse, Weston, Oswestry, Shropshire, SY10 9ES
☎ (01691) 676457 ⊕ stonehousebrewery.co.uk

Stonehouse was established in 2007 on a 15-barrel plant. The brewery was based in former chicken sheds and is next to the old Cambrian railway line. A new building has expanded brewing capacity to 22 barrels and includes a visitor centre. More than 200 local outlets are supplied direct. ‼🍺RAIB

Sunlander (OG 1037, ABV 3.7%)
Pale with a balance of citrus and floral hops from Australia.

Station Bitter (OG 1041, ABV 3.9%)
A traditional, amber-coloured bitter. A full-bodied session beer with a perfect balance of fruity hops and roasted malt.

Cambrian Gold (OG 1042, ABV 4.2%)
A deep golden fruity beer with a subtle dry finish.

Wheeltapper's Wheatbeer (OG 1043, ABV 4.5%)
A refreshing, golden wheat beer with hints of coriander and lemon zest.

KPA (OG 1047, ABV 4.6%)
A crisp pale ale with a herby, floral note.

Off the Rails (OG 1048, ABV 4.8%)
A rich and malty premium bitter, with a classic British hop flavour.

Storm SIBA

2 Waterside, Macclesfield, Cheshire, SK11 7HJ
☎ (01625) 431234 ⊕ stormbrewing.co.uk

☺Storm Brewing was founded in 1998, operating from an old ICI boiler room. In 2001 it moved to its current location, which until 1937 was a pub called the Mechanics Arms. More than 60 outlets are supplied. ◆RAIB

Beauforts Ale (OG 1038, ABV 3.8%)
Golden brown, full-flavoured session bitter with a lingering hoppy taste.

Desert Storm (OG 1040, ABV 3.9%)
Amber-coloured beer with a smoky flavour of fruit and malt.

Bosley Cloud (OG 1041, ABV 4.1%) ◄
Dry, golden bitter with peppery hop notes throughout. Some initial sweetness and a mainly bitter aftertaste. Soft, well-balanced and quaffable.

Ale Force (OG 1042, ABV 4.2%) ◄
Amber, smooth-tasting, complex beer that balances malt, hop and fruit on the taste, leading to a roasty, slightly sweet aftertaste.

Downpour (OG 1043, ABV 4.3%)
A pale ale with a full, fruity flavour with a hint of apple and sightly hoppy aftertaste.

PGA (OG 1044, ABV 4.4%) ◄
Light, crisp, lager-style beer with a balance of malt, hops and fruit. Moderately bitter and slight dry aftertaste.

Hurricane Hubert (OG 1045, ABV 4.5%)
A dark beer with a refreshing full, fruity hop aroma and a subtle bitter aftertaste.

Silk of Amnesia (OG 1047, ABV 4.7%) ◄

Smooth, premium, easy-drinking bitter. Fruit and hops dominate throughout. Not too sweet, with a good lasting finish.

Red Mist (OG 1049, ABV 4.8%)
A dark red/black porter with fruity notes and a hoppy finish.

Stowey

Old Cider House, 25 Castle Street, Nether Stowey, Somerset, TA5 1LN
☎ (01278) 732228 ⊕ stoweybrewery.co.uk

Stowey was established in 2006, primarily to supply the owners' guesthouse and to provide beer to participants on 'real ale walks' run from the accommodation. The brewery also runs brewery workshop courses and supplies seasonal brews to the village pubs on a guest beer basis. ‼♦

Nether Ending (OG 1044, ABV 4.2%)

Strands

Strands Inn, Nether Wasdale, Cumbria, CA20 1ET
☎ (01946) 726237 ⊕ strandshotel.com

Strands Brewery is a six-barrel plant with a 30-barrel fermentation capacity. The majority of beers are available bottle conditioned, and the brewery plans to sell them online. Six of the beers are available on the bar of the Strands Inn at all times. ‼♦ RAIB

Pied Piper (OG 1030, ABV 2.7%)
Lots of traditional mild characteristics: malty, caramel, roast, sweet and fruity.

Green Bullet (OG 1037, ABV 3.5%)
A light and creamy wheat beer.

Responsibly (OG 1038, ABV 3.7%)
Clean-tasting, heavily-hopped and lightly smoked beer.

Brown Bitter (OG 1039, ABV 3.8%)
A complex tasting brown beer with a lingering bitter aftertaste

Errmmm... (OG 1039, ABV 3.8%)
A complex, traditional bitter.

Red Screes (OG 1047, ABV 4.5%)
A rich-tasting, smooth, strong bitter; full-flavoured with plenty of roast and malt tastes.

T'errmmm-inator (OG 1050, ABV 5%)
A smooth, dark brown, roast-led beer. Full-bodied and well-balanced.

Brewed for Independent Lakeland Breweries:

Gold Wing (OG 1040, ABV 4%)
A clean, crisp and dry golden ale with delicate citrus aromas and a tasty finish.

Dark Knight (OG 1050, ABV 5%)
A deep, dark, well-balanced ale.

Stratford Upon Avon (NEW) SIBA

Warwick Road, Stratford-upon-Avon, Warwickshire, CV37 0NT ☎ 07866 495232 ⊕ sua-brewery.co.uk

Stratford Upon Avon Brewery is the first brewery in Stratford since Flowers in the 1960s. It was established by Richard Williams in 2014 on his family farm, which lies on the River Avon. The brewery has been developed around an environmentally-friendly approach, using the farm's own small solar farm, wind turbine and bore hole, with an electric van for local deliveries. ♦

Stratford Gold (ABV 3.8%)
A golden-coloured refreshing ale.

Stratford IPA (ABV 4%)
A full-bodied ale with hints of honey and citrus fruits.

Malty Pig Bitter (ABV 4.4%)
A malty but well-hopped ale with biscuity flavours.

Dark Star Porter (ABV 4.6%)
A full-bodied ale with hints of coffee and chocolate.

Strathaven SIBA

Craigmill Brewery, Sandford Road, Strathaven, ML10 6PB
☎ (01357) 520419 ⊕ strathavenales.com

Strathaven Ales is a 10-barrel brewery on the River Avon close to Strathaven and was converted from the remains of a 16th-century mill. The range is distributed throughout Scotland and the north of England. ‼♦

Clydesdale (OG 1038, ABV 3.8%)

Avondale (OG 1048, ABV 4%)

Old Mortality (OG 1046, ABV 4.2%)

Claverhouse (OG 1046, ABV 4.5%)

Strathbraan SIBA

Deanshaugh, Amulree, PH8 0EB
☎ (01350) 725264 ☎ 07747 857908
✉ strathbraan.bry@btinternet.com

Strathbraan began brewing in 2012 using a 10-barrel plant.

Due South (OG 1038, ABV 3.8%)

Head East (OG 1042, ABV 4.2%)

Strawman

Arch 75, 876 Old Kent Road, Peckham, London, SE15 1NQ
☎ (020) 7112 9102 ⊕ strawmanbrewery.com

Strawman began brewing in 2013. Brewing is currently suspended.

Stringers SIBA

Unit 3, Low Mill Business Park, Ulverston, Cumbria, LA12 9EE
☎ (01229) 581387 ⊕ stringersbeer.co.uk

Stringers is a small family-run brewery. Brewing started in 2008 on a five-barrel plant run on 100% renewable energy. No. 2 Stout and Dark Country are suitable for vegans. Plan B is gluten free. ♦ RAIB

Plan B (OG 1036, ABV 3.7%)
An easy-drinking, zingy and pale thirst quencher.

No. 2 Stout (OG 1042, ABV 4%)
A robust drying stout full of roast and hop bitterness.

Yellow Lorry (OG 1039, ABV 4%)

West Coast Blond (OG 1042, ABV 4.4%)

A golden beer with a hoppy, fruity aroma and taste, with bitterness and a little astringency in the aftertaste.

Victoria IPA (OG 1053, ABV 5.5%)
Spicy, tropical fruit from the hops, then some bitter marmalade, with a definite bitter finish.

Brewed for Independent Lakeland Breweries:

Wolf Warrior (OG 1035, ABV 3.5%) ◆
A hoppy aroma and a fruity, full-bodied taste of hops, finishes with a drying bitterness.

Stroud SIBA

Unit 11, Phoenix Works, London Road, Thrupp, Gloucestershire, GL5 2BU
☎ (01453) 887122 stroudbrewery.co.uk

Established in 2006, Stroud Brewery supports the local economy and does not sell its organic bottled beers through supermarkets. The ales are sold in 40-50 pubs, independent retailers and the brewery shop. ♦RAIB

Tom Long (OG 1039, ABV 3.8%)
Amber-coloured session beer with a spicy citrus aroma.

Organic Ale (OG 1041, ABV 4%)
A refreshing, golden organic ale with a delicate apple aroma.

Budding (OG 1045, ABV 4.5%)
A pale ale with a grassy bitterness, sweet malt and floral aroma.

Stumptail

North Street, Great Dunham, Norfolk, PE32 2LR
☎ (01328) 701042 stumptail@btinternet.com

Stumptail began commercial home-brewing in 2011 using a 100-litre plant. Bottle-conditioned beers are produced with cask-conditioned versions brewed to order. Only the west Norfolk area is supplied. RAIB

Stumpy's

See Yates'

Suddaby's

See Brown Cow

Sultan (NEW)

78 Norman Road, Wimbledon, SW19 1BT
☎ (020) 8544 9323 ☎ 07951 201240
hopback.co.uk

Brewing occurs only occasionally (monthly) at present while the brewery commissions the equipment. 'One-off' brews are planned to complement the regular range of Hop Back/ Downton beers in the pub.

Sulwath SIBA

The Brewery, 209 King Street, Castle Douglas, DG7 1DT
☎ (01556) 504525 sulwathbrewers.co.uk

Sulwath started brewing in 1995. The beers are supplied to markets as far away as Devon in the south and Aberdeen in the north. The brewery has a fully licensed brewery tap. Cask ales are sold to around 100 outlets and four wholesalers. !! ♦RAIB

Cuil Hill (OG 1039, ABV 3.6%) ◆
Distinctively fruity session ale with malt and hop undertones. The taste is bittersweet with a long-lasting dry finish.

Tri-ball (OG 1039, ABV 3.9%)
A fresh, crisp and blonde session ale.

Grace (OG 1044, ABV 4.3%)
A refreshing, rich ale with a full-bodied flavour that balances the caramel undertones.

Black Galloway (OG 1046, ABV 4.4%)
A robust porter/stout.

Criffel (OG 1044, ABV 4.6%) ◆
Full-bodied beer with a distinctive bitterness. Fruit is to the fore of the taste with hops becoming increasingly dominant in the taste and finish.

Galloway Gold (OG 1049, ABV 5%) ◆
A cask-conditioned lager that will be too sweet for many despite being heavily hopped.

Knockendoch (OG 1047, ABV 5%) ◆
Dark, copper-coloured, reflecting a roast malt content, with bitterness from Challenger hops.

Solway Mist (OG 1052, ABV 5.5%)
A naturally cloudy wheat beer. Sweetish and fruity.

Summer Wine

The Old Furnace, Unit 15 Crossley Mills, New Mill Road, Honley, West Yorkshire, HD9 6QB
☎ (01484) 665466 summerwinebrewery.co.uk

Brewing commenced in 2006 on a 10-gallon kit with an emphasis on bottle-conditioned beer. A 2007 upgrade saw a 0.5-barrel plant installed and in 2008 the brewery expanded to a six-barrel plant. Over 500 outlets are supplied direct. Two differing specials are available each month.

Resistance (OG 1037, ABV 3.7%)
Dark ruby mild with a malty body and hints of caramel, cocoa and bitter roasted barley combined with a light fruity hop character.

Zenith (OG 1040, ABV 4%)
Pale golden beer with floral aroma and a crisp bitter finish.

Barista (OG 1048, ABV 4.8%)
A rich coffee-flavoured stout which gets its flavour from ground Arabica added at the end of the boil.

Teleporter (OG 1050, ABV 5%)
A porter with a creamy body and cocoa, caramel and vanilla flavours.

Oregon (OG 1055, ABV 5.5%)
American-style pale ale with grapefruit, sherbet, spicy and floral aroma, malty body and hop finish.

Rogue Red Hop Ale (OG 1058, ABV 5.8%)
Deep ruby red with good body, and tasty flavour and finish.

Diablo (OG 1060, ABV 6%)
A strong IPA with tropical fruit aroma and flavours.

Summerskills SIBA

15 Pomphlett Farm Industrial Estate, Broxton Drive, Billacombe, Plymouth, Devon, PL9 7BG
☎ (01752) 481283 summerskills.co.uk

⊠ Established in a vineyard in 1983 at Bigbury-on-Sea, Summerskills moved to its present site in 1985 and is the oldest brewery in Plymouth. Wholesalers and pub companies perform national distribution and the beers regularly appear in a selection of local outlets. ♦ RAIB

Start Point (OG 1036, ABV 3.7%)
Golden ale with a clean and fresh nose. Sweet upfront with a delicate bitter finish.

Westward Ho! (OG 1040, ABV 4.1%)
Amber-coloured beer with an initial light fruity taste, followed by a zesty and fruity finish.

Best Bitter (OG 1042, ABV 4.3%) ◆
A mid-brown beer, with plenty of malt and hops through the aroma, taste and finish. A good session beer.

Tamar (OG 1042, ABV 4.3%)
A tawny-coloured bitter with a fruity aroma and a hop taste and finish.

Devon Dew (OG 1044, ABV 4.5%)
Honey yellow in colour with a floral, clean malty aroma. Sweet lemon upfront, with a long grapefruit finish. Mildly hopped.

Menacing Dennis (OG 1045, ABV 4.5%)
Golden amber in colour, with aromas of dark malt and hops, and a slight hint of liquorice.

Bolt Head (OG 1046, ABV 4.7%)
Ruby red premium beer. Sweet rum-like aroma, full fruit taste, followed by a citrus orange finish.

Whistle Belly Vengeance (OG 1047, ABV 4.7%)
Russet brown-coloured with a smoky, caramel aroma and a rich, sharp chocolate taste.

First Light (OG 1054, ABV 5.5%)
Bright amber-coloured strong summer ale. Initial toffee taste, followed by an orange and sherbet finish.

Indiana's Bones (OG 1055, ABV 5.6%)
Russet brown in colour, with a smoky fresh-hop aroma. Full-bodied, with a roast burnt and slightly sweet taste.

Sunbeam

Leeds, West Yorkshire ☎ 07772 002437
⊕ sunbeamales.co.uk

Sunbeam Ales was established in a back-to-back house in Leeds in 2009. Brewing began commercially in 2011, with only bottled beers being produced. Capacity has increased since the brewer moved and the brewery now offers both cask and bottle-conditioned beers. RAIB

Sunny Republic SIBA 👁

The Old Grain Barn, North West Farm, West Street, Winterborne Kingston, Dorset, DT11 9AT
☎ (01929) 471600 ⊕ sunnyrepublic.com

⊠ Located just outside the village of Winterbourne Kingston on a barley farm in two converted Georgian grain barns. Brewing began in 2012 using a state-of-the-art 30-barrel custom-built plant. Beers are available nationally and exported to six countries. ‼ ☷

Guardian Angel (OG 1040, ABV 4%)
Traditional copper-coloured best bitter.

Ram Raddle (OG 1041, ABV 4%)

Classic best bitter with hints of caramel balanced by slightly orange floral hops.

Full English (OG 1041, ABV 4.1%)
Classic English best bitter with aromas of hopsacks, mowed lawns and orange marmalade.

Beach Blonde (OG 1043, ABV 4.4%)
Blonde ale with tropical aroma of mango, grapefruit and lychee. Upfront bitterness yields to a light malt body.

Shark Head (OG 1047, ABV 4.4%)
A modern take on a rare Pils variant, with a clean bitterness and a citrusy-pepper bite.

Black Swan Stout (OG 1045, ABV 4.5%)
Classic English stout with hints of roastiness.

Red Bus (OG 1049, ABV 4.8%)
Big, hoppy and resinous, an easy-drinking, full-flavoured beer.

Dune Raider (OG 1051, ABV 5%)
A blend of sweet malts and bitter hops.

Hop Dog IPA (OG 1055, ABV 5.5%)
Citrus-dominated IPA with an enduring bitter finish yet surprisingly easy drinking.

Rotovator (OG 1056, ABV 5.5%)
IPA with a solid malt body balanced by fruity and floral esters from the hops.

Surfing Monkey (NEW)

31 Fairwater Grove West, Cardiff, CF5 2JN ☎ 07412 365789 ⊕ surfingmonkeybrewery.com

Brewing began in 2014 utilising a large garage at the rear of a private house. Further beers are planned.

Blown-out Baboon (OG 1038, ABV 3.8%)
Pale session ale, finished with Citra hops, to add late bitterness on the tongue.

Offshore Howler (OG 1040, ABV 4%)
Cloudy wheat beer with orange and coriander.

Surrey Hills SIBA

Denbies Wine Estate, London Road, Dorking, Surrey, RH5 6AA
☎ (01306) 883603 ⊕ surreyhills.co.uk

⊠ Surrey Hills began brewing in 2005 near Shere, moving to Dorking in 2011. Nearly 95% of production is sold within 15 miles of the brewery. The beers have won several local and national awards. ‼ ☷ ♦

Ranmore (OG 1039, ABV 3.8%) ▮ ◆
A light, flavoursome session beer. An earthy hoppy nose leads into a grapefruit and hoppy taste and a clean, bitter finish.

Shere Drop (OG 1043, ABV 4.2%) ⬠ ▮ ◆
A hoppy ale with some balancing malt. A pleasant citrus aroma and a noticeable fruitiness in the taste, with some sweetness.

Gilt Complex (OG 1047, ABV 4.6%)

Greensand IPA (OG 1047, ABV 4.6%) ◆
A strong-flavoured and easy-drinking IPA, with intense grapefruit and hops in the aroma and taste and soft citrus finish.

Suthwyk

See Oakleaf

Swan

▤ Swan on the Green, West Peckham, Kent, ME18 5JW
☎ (01622) 812271 ⊕ swan-on-the-green.co.uk

The brewery was established in 2000 in an old coal shed behind the Swan on the Green pub using a two-barrel plant. ‼◆

Fuggles Pale (OG 1037, ABV 3.6%)

Trumpeter Best (OG 1041, ABV 4%)

Cygnet (OG 1048, ABV 4.2%)

Bewick Swan (OG 1052, ABV 5.3%)

Swansea SIBA

▤ Joiners Arms, 50 Bishopston Road, Bishopston, Swansea, SA3 3EJ
☎ (01792) 232658

☺Opened in 1996, Swansea was the first commercial brewery in the area for almost 30 years. Two regular outlets are supplied along with other pubs in the South Wales area. ‼◆

Deep Slade Dark (OG 1034, ABV 4%)
A dark brown-coloured beer with a reddish hue with a nutty, malty taste. The aroma is malty with a little roast.

Bishopswood Bitter (OG 1043, ABV 4.3%) ◈
A delicate aroma of hops and malt in this pale brown colour. The taste is a balanced mix of hops and malt with a growing hoppy bitterness ending in a lasting bitter finish.

Three Cliffs Gold (OG 1042, ABV 4.7%) ◈
A golden beer with a hoppy and fruity aroma, a hoppy taste with fruit and malt, and a quenching bitterness. The pleasant finish has a good hop flavour and bitterness.

Original Wood (OG 1046, ABV 5.2%) ◈
A full-bodied, pale brown beer with an aroma of hops, fruit and malt. A complex blend of these flavours with a firm bitterness ends with increasing bitterness.

Taddington

Blackwell Hall, Blackwell, Buxton, Derbyshire, SK17 9TQ
☎ (01298) 85734

No real ale. Taddington started brewing in 2007, and brews one Czech-style unpasteurised lager in two different strengths: Moravka (ABV 4.4% and 5%), which is available on draught. Taddington also supplies an unfiltered version of Moravka called Moravka Kvasnicove.

Talke O' Th' Hill

Merelake Road, Talke, Staffordshire, ST7 1UE
☎ 07875 951399 ⊕ talkeothhill.co.uk

Talke O' Th' Hill began brewing in 2011 using a two-barrel plant on a family farm on the Staffordshire border. The brewery is based on two floors in old farm buildings. ◆

Citrade (OG 1043, ABV 4.4%)

Potter's Porter (OG 1044, ABV 4.4%)

First Porter Call (OG 1045, ABV 4.5%)

Tally Ho! (NEW)

14 Market Street, Hatherleigh, Devon, EX20 3JN
☎ (01837) 810306 ☎ 07532 105871
⊕ tallyhobrewery.co.uk

The Tally Ho! brewery was recommissioned in 2015 after a number of years lying dormant. The brewery is situated in the Tally Ho! pub. One beer is currently produced.

Ukulale (OG 1042, ABV 4.2%)

Tap East SIBA

▤ 7 International Square, Montficet Road, Westfield Stratford City, Stratford, London, E20 1EE
☎ (020) 8555 4467 ⊕ tapeast.co.uk

⊠ Tap East began brewing in 2011 and is located in the Westfield shopping centre next to the Olympic Park. ₪◆

Tonic Ale (OG 1032, ABV 3%) ◈
A refreshing golden ale with strong citrus throughout. Faint biscuit notes and a bitter, dry aftertaste.

East End Mild (OG 1037, ABV 3.5%) ◈
Dark mild that has roast and a little fruit and treacle on the palate fading in the shortish dry finish.

JWB (OG 1040, ABV 3.8%)
Bitter, malty backbone with a good dose of hops.

APA (OG 1046, ABV 4.4%) ◈
Yellow-coloured beer with citrus throughout and a dash of pineapple. Bitterness grows on drinking, balanced by a little sweetness.

Coffee in the Morning (OG 1059, ABV 5.3%) ◈
Black porter with coffee dominating the aroma and flavour and lingering in the dry bitter finish. Trace of liquorice.

IPA (OG 1054, ABV 5.3%)
Series of IPAs with different hops used each time.

Tap House

▤ Tap House, Annwell Lane, Smisby, Derbyshire, LE65 2TA
☎ (01530) 413604 ☎ 07528 145217
⊕ taphouse-smisby.co.uk

⊠ Established in 2010, this purpose-built brewery supplies beers to its two pubs, the Tap House, Smisby, and the Kings Arms, Coleorton, as well as to pubs across Derbyshire and Leicestershire. Tap House and Leatherbritches share the same brewery plant and brewer, but the two businesses are run independently.

Ashby Pride (OG 1038, ABV 3.8%)
A light, quaffable session beer.

Gold (OG 1042, ABV 4%)
A light, hoppy golden ale.

Kingdom (OG 1046, ABV 4.5%)
A chestnut-coloured beer with a hint of caramel.

Malt Teaser (OG 1046, ABV 4.6%)
A rich crimson beer full of malt flavours with a light toffee aftertaste.

Dark & Dangerous (OG 1048, ABV 5%)

A delicious dark and complex porter with subtle chocolate flavours.

Tapped

Sheffield: Sheffield Tap, Platform 1b, Sheffield Station, Sheaf Street, Sheffield, South Yorkshire, S1 2BP
☎ (0114) 273 7558

Leeds: Tapped Leeds, 51 Boar Lane, Leeds, West Yorkshire, LS1 5EL ☎ (0113) 244 1953
tappedbrewco.com

Brewing began in 2013 after the old Edwardian dining rooms were converted into an onsite brewery with a viewing gallery at the Sheffield Tap pub. The beer is also supplied to the Euston Tap, Harrogate Tap, York Tap, and Pivni, York. A further on-site brewery opened at Tapped Leeds in 2014.

Ale (OG 1035, ABV 3.5%)
A session bitter.

Mojo (OG 1036, ABV 3.6%)
A clear, crisp, light pale ale.

Rodeo (OG 1039, ABV 4%)
An American-hopped session pale ale.

Stogie (OG 1041, ABV 4%)
An English dry stout with a bitter, slightly sour finish.

Bramling (OG 1042, ABV 4.2%)
Golden best bitter.

Liberty (OG 1052, ABV 5.2%)
Rich, dark treacle stout with subtle bitterness and hop aroma.

Miami Weisse (OG 1055, ABV 5.5%)
Fresh-tasting Hefeweiss-style beer with banana and clove aromas.

Bullet (OG 1059, ABV 5.9%)
Strong IPA with fruit candy aroma.

Tapstone (NEW)

11 Bartlett Park, Millfield, Chard, Somerset, TA20 2BB
☎ (01460) 929156 ☎ 07969 651998
tapstone.co.uk

Founded in 2015, Tapstone is a modern brewery focusing on hop-forward beers. The brewery was custom-built around a unique brewing process that preserves delicate hop oils – making beers with a saturated hop flavour. It is a green brewery using renewable energy.

Barn Storm (OG 1040, ABV 4%)
Herb garden flavours with a crisp lemon aroma, balanced by a strong and wholesome malt backbone.

Wild Woods (OG 1040, ABV 4%)
An IPA with pine and grapefruit aromas, and a sweet, hoppy, resin mouthfeel.

Sea Monster (OG 1042, ABV 4.2%)
A fresh and fruity pale ale with heady tropical flavours over a crisp citrus base, with gooseberry and lime.

Voodoo Juice (OG 1048, ABV 4.8%)
An IPA with heady stone-fruit aromas and vibrant orange flavour.

Tarn Hows (NEW) SIBA

Low Bield, Knipe Fold, Outgate, Ambleside, Cumbria, LA22 0PU
☎ (01539) 436409 ☎ 07935 789581
tarnhowsbrewery.com

A small microbrewery near Hawkshead specialising in traditional British ales using oak casks, which provide an additional dimension to the beer flavour.

Beertrix Porter (ABV 4%)
A traditional porter-style beer with liquorice and vanilla flavours from the whisky-barrel oak casks.

Grized Ale (OG 1041, ABV 4.2%)
A moderately dark, old ale-style beer with a hint of smoked malts, with warming notes of wood, wine and pine.

Puddled Duck (OG 1051, ABV 5.2%)
Dark golden IPA.

Tatton SIBA

Unit 7, Longridge Trading Estate, Longridge Trading Estate, Knutsford, Cheshire, WA16 8PR
☎ (01565) 750747 ☎ 07738 150898
tattonbrewery.co.uk

Tatton is a family-run business based in the heart of Cheshire. Brewing commenced in 2010 using a steam-fired, custom-built, 15-barrel brewhouse. It supplies pubs throughout Cheshire and the north-west. !! ♦

Ale (OG 1036, ABV 3.7%)
An easy-drinking session ale with a rich copper colour. It has a full malty/toffee flavour balanced by a soft bitterness and hoppy, fruity taste and aroma.

Blonde (OG 1039, ABV 4%)
A clean-tasting, smooth pale ale with a New World hop aroma.

Best (OG 1040.5, ABV 4.2%)
A classic, light amber-coloured best bitter with a clean malt flavour and fine hop character.

Gold (OG 1046, ABV 4.8%)
A golden special ale with a maltiness backed by a robust hoppiness.

Tavernale

Bridge Tavern, 7 Akenside Hill, Newcastle upon Tyne, NE1 3UF
☎ (0191) 232 1122 thebridgetavern.com

Brewing since 2013 in association with the Wylam Brewery (qv), a two-barrel plant supplies beers to the Bridge Tavern with the in-house brewer creating bespoke 360-pint batches of ale. ♦

Tavy SIBA

Unit 9, Porsham Close, Beliver Industrial Estate, Roborough, Devon, PL6 7DB ☎ 07966 522266

Tavy Ales Ltd Jasmine Cottage, Peter Tavy, Tavistock, PL19 9NN tavyales.co.uk

Tavy Ales is a family-run brewery. It formed in 2012, and is located in Roborough, on the outskirts of Plymouth, with a six-barrel plant. !! ♦

Best Bitter (OG 1043, ABV 4.3%)

A full-bodied chestnut brown beer with a well-rounded, complex malt flavour and early bitterness.

Ideal Pale Ale (OG 1048, ABV 4.8%)
A pale golden beer loaded with citrus flavour, balanced bitterness and body with a strong floral and hoppy aroma.

Porter (OG 1052, ABV 5.2%)
A dark stout with a roasted, bittersweet flavour and an intense chocolate finish.

Timothy Taylor SIBA IFBB

Knowle Spring Brewery, Keighley, West Yorkshire, BD21 1AW
☎ (01535) 603139 timothy-taylor.co.uk

An independent, family-owned company established in 1858, Timothy Taylor has occupied the Knowle Spring site since 1863. Pennine spring water is used to brew its award-winning ales which are served in 18 tied pubs as well as more than 300 directly delivered outlets. Expanded brewing facilities opened on the main site in 2011.

Dark Mild (OG 1034, ABV 3.5%)
Malt and caramel dominate throughout in this sweetish beer with background hop and fruit notes.

Golden Best (OG 1033, ABV 3.5%)
Refreshing, amber-coloured traditional Pennine light mild. Malty throughout. Fruit in the nose increases to complement the delicate hoppy taste.

Boltmaker (OG 1038, ABV 4%)
Tawny bitter combining hops, fruit and nutty malt. Lingering, increasingly bitter aftertaste. Formerly, and sometimes still, sold as Best Bitter.

Landlord (OG 1042, ABV 4.3%)
A fine-tasting best bitter combining citrus peel aromas, rich malt, spicy hops, an underlying marmalade sweetness and long bitter finish.

Ram Tam (OG 1043, ABV 4.3%)
A black beer with red highlights topped by a coffee coloured head. Roast coffee bitterness is balanced by fruit and malt with burnt caramel coming through in the dry and bitter finish.

Taylors

London Tavern, Church Street, Attleborough, Norfolk, NR17 2AH
☎ (01953) 457415 ☎ 07789 133851
taylorsbrewery@gmail.com

Brewing began in 2014, primarily to supply the owner's two pubs in Attleborough; the London Tavern and Ry's Bar (formerly the Bear). Beers are now also supplied to local free houses.

Number One (ABV 3.9%)
A hoppy bitter.

Second Coming (ABV 3.9%)
A well-balanced traditional English session bitter.

Remember Me (OG 1044, ABV 4.4%)
Cara malt beer with a caramel note and a dry finish.

Stitched Up (ABV 4.7%)
Premium bitter.

Teignworthy SIBA

The Maltings, Teign Road, Newton Abbot, Devon, TQ12 4AA
☎ (01626) 332066 teignworthybrewery.com

Teignworthy Brewery opened in 1994 within Tuckers historic maltings building. The 20-barrel plant produces 50 barrels a week using malt from Tuckers and supplies around 300 outlets in Devon and Somerset. !! ♦ RAIB

Neap Tide (OG 1038, ABV 3.8%)
A pale fruity bitter.

Reel Ale (OG 1039.5, ABV 4%)
Clean, sharp-tasting bitter with lasting hoppiness; predominantly malty aroma.

Gun Dog (OG 1043.5, ABV 4.3%)
A light bronze-coloured ale with a flowery, fruity aromatic finish.

Spring Tide (OG 1043.5, ABV 4.3%)
An excellent, full and well-rounded, mid-brown beer with a dry, bitter taste and aftertaste.

Old Moggie (OG 1044.5, ABV 4.4%)
A golden-coloured, hoppy, fruity ale.

Beachcomber (OG 1045.5, ABV 4.5%)
A pale brown beer with a light, refreshing fruit and hop nose, grapefruit taste and a dry, hoppy finish.

Teme Valley SIBA

Talbot, Bromyard Road, Knightwick, Worcestershire, WR6 5PH
☎ (01886) 821235 ☎ 07792 394151
temevalleybrewery.co.uk

Established in 1997 to brew beer for the Talbot, Knightwick. Only hops grown in Herefordshire and Worcestershire are used in brewing. Some 30 outlets are supplied throughout the Marches and West Midlands. !! ♦ RAIB

T'Other (OG 1035, ABV 3.5%)
Refreshing amber beer offering an abundance of flavour in the fruity aroma, followed by a short, dry bitterness.

This (OG 1037, ABV 3.7%)
Dark gold brew with a mellow array of flavours in a malty balance.

That (OG 1041, ABV 4.1%)
A rich fruity nose and a wide range of hoppy and malty flavours in this copper-coloured best bitter.

Talbot Blond (OG 1042, ABV 4.4%)
A smooth, well-hopped, rich pale beer.

Tempest

Block 11, Units 1 & 2, Tweedbank Industrial Estate, Tweedbank, TD1 3RS
☎ (01896) 759500 ☎ 07590 834017
tempestbrewingco.com

Based in a former dairy, Tempest was set up in 2010 by Gavin Meiklejohn, brewer and co-proprietor of the Cobbles Inn in Kelso, which is the brewery tap. In 2015 the brewery moved from Kelso to new premises at Tweedbank (near Galashiels). Gavin's focus is on bold flavours and ingredients to produce interesting styles based on classic and New World beers. !! ♦ RAIB

Armadillo (ABV 3.8%)

A session ale with a fresh hop assault of citrus and tropical fruits.

Temptation

18D Cherry Way, Dubmire Indistrial Estate, Houghton-le-Spring, Tyne & Wear, DH4 5RJ ☎ 07932 774745
temptationbrewingcompany.co.uk

Temptation began brewing in 2011 using a 2.5-barrel plant upgrading to six barrels in 2013. A core range of five American-inspired beers is regularly available. Local outlets are supplied in a 20-mile radius of the brewery. The installation of a small brewery tap is planned.

Belgian Wheat (ABV 4.3%)

New Zealand Pale Ale (ABV 4.3%)

Sorachi Ace (ABV 4.3%)

Vanilla Bourbon Porter (ABV 4.8%)

Cascadian Dark (ABV 5%)

Extra IPA (ABV 5.2%)

Red Rye IPA (ABV 5.5%)

Tenby

Unit 15, The Salterns, Tenby, Pembrokeshire, SA70 8EQ
☎ (01834) 218090 ☎ 07410 169447
tenbybrewingco.com

Tenby uses a six-barrel plant, formerly the Preseli Brewery. The two new, young brewers have introduced an interesting new range of beers. Cask and bottled beers are supplied to outlets in Pembrokeshire, neighbouring counties and further afield. Spent grain is fed to animals at a local ecofarm, and through energy savings the brewery plans to become carbon neutral accredited this year. RAIB

West Coast Rocks (OG 1040, ABV 3.8%)
A malty body with a hint of spiced blackberry.

Pembrokeshire Promise (OG 1046, ABV 4.5%)
An ESB with hints of caramel, complex grain and mellow bitter hops.

Barefoot Blonde (OG 1041, ABV 4.6%)
A refreshing, clean and crisp blonde ale, infused with kafir lime leaves.

Black Flag Porter (OG 1055, ABV 5.2%)
Full of character, with coffee and chocolate and a hint of vanilla spiced rum.

Terrace

Sandford Terrace, Aylburton, Lydney, Gloucestershire, GL15 6DW
☎ (01594) 840100 ☎ 07942 205947
web@terracebrewery.co.uk

Temptation was established in 2012 in a shed in the brewer's garden, producing bottle-conditioned beers from a 0.5-barrel plant. The range has now increased to six beers, which are available in local farm shops. RAIB

Thame

East Street, Thame, Oxfordshire, OX9 3JS
☎ (01844) 218202
thamebrewery@btinternet.com

This one-barrel brewery was set up in 2009 by Peter Lambert and Oak Taverns in the old stables at the Cross Keys. Beer is produced for the Cross Keys and beer festivals, and includes many one-off brews.

Mr Splodge's Mild (OG 1037, ABV 3.8%)
A dark mild named after the pub cat.

Windy Indy (OG 1038, ABV 4%)
Malty ruby ale, named after the landlady's horse.

Hoppiness (OG 1042, ABV 4.2%)
A golden ale.

That Little Brewery

c/o Farmer's Boy, 134 London Road, St Albans, Hertfordshire, AL1 1PQ
☎ (01582) 768925

That Little Brewery, 5 Station Road, Harpenden, Hertfordshire, AL5 4SN ☎ (01582) 768925
thatlittleplace.co.uk

That Little Brewery produces two bottle-conditioned beers available at That Little Place restaurant in Harpenden. Cask-conditioned beer is available at the Farmer's Boy in St Albans, and at beer festivals. RAIB

Theakston

The Brewery, Masham, North Yorkshire, HG4 4YD
☎ (01765) 680000 theakstons.co.uk

After several years under the control of other companies, Theakston is now owned by four brothers, grandsons of Thomas Theakston, the son of the company's founder, who built the brewery in 1875. A new fermentation room was built in 2004 to provide additional flexibility and capacity, and further capacity was added in 2006. !! ♦

Best Bitter (OG 1038, ABV 3.8%)
A golden-coloured beer with a full flavour that lingers pleasantly on the palate. With a good bitter/sweet balance, this beer has a robust hop character, citrus and spicy.

Black Bull Bitter (OG 1037, ABV 3.9%)
A distinctively hoppy aroma leads to a bitter, hoppy taste with some fruitiness and a short bitter finish.

Lightfoot (OG 1041, ABV 4.1%)

XB (OG 1044, ABV 4.5%)
A sweet-tasting bitter with background fruit and spicy hop. Some caramel character gives this ale a malty dominance.

Old Peculier (OG 1057, ABV 5.6%)
A full-bodied, dark brown, strong ale. Slightly malty but with hints of roast coffee and liquorice. A smooth caramel overlay and a complex fruitiness leads to a bitter chocolate finish.

Thirst Class (NEW)

Unit 16, Station Road Industrial Estate, Reddish, Stockport, SK5 6ND
☎ (0161) 431 3998 thirstclassale.co.uk

Thirst Class opened in 2014 in the centre of Stockport using a purpose-built two-barrel plant, constructed by award-winning brewer Richard Conway. The brewery relocated to larger premises in 2015 enabling production on a full-time basis. It produces four core beers, along with a number of speciality one-off brews. All the beers are available as both cask and bottle-conditioned. ◆RAIB

Pale and Interesting (OG 1043, ABV 3.4%)
English bitter with a rich, malty body and a clean, bitter finish.

Stockport Common Beer (OG 1053, ABV 4.9%)
A California-style common/steam beer with grapefruit and pine flavours and a crisp, clean finish.

Stocky Oatmeal Stout (OG 1057, ABV 5.5%)
Smooth, full-bodied oatmeal stout with notes of coffee and chocolate.

Hoppy Couple IPA (OG 1060, ABV 6.3%)
American-style IPA. Rich copper in colour with a big citrus hop aroma and flavour.

Thirstin

60 Thirstin Road, Holney, West Yorkshire, HD9 6JR
⊕ thirstinbrewhouse.wordpress.com

Thirstin is a small 2.5-barrel brewery situated in the Holme valley, set up by Stewart Horn.

Mild Thirst (OG 1036, ABV 3.6%)
A dark mild.

Thirstin Four (OG 1040, ABV 4%)
A pale session bitter.

Thirst Quencher (OG 1050, ABV 5%)
A strong pale ale.

Thomas Guest

See Black Country

Abraham Thompson

Flass Lane, Barrow-in-Furness, Cumbria, LA13 0AD
☎ 07708 191437
✉ abraham.thompson@btinternet.com

☺The half-barrel plant was set up in 2005 to return Barrow-brewed beers to local pubs. Distribution is limited to a few outlets in the Low Furness area but beer can usually be found at Ulverston Beer Festival. ◆

John Thompson

▤ Ingleby, Melbourne, Derbyshire, DE73 7HW
☎ (01332) 862469 ⊕ johnthompsoninn.com

▧ The brewery was established by John Thompson in 1977 as an addition to the John Thompson Inn, which he converted from a 15th-century farmhouse in 1968. It is now run by his son Nick. JTS XXX is Derbyshire's longest continuously brewed ale. ‼◆

JTS XXX (OG 1041, ABV 4.1%)

Gold (OG 1045, ABV 4.5%)

Thornbridge SIBA ◉

Riverside Business Park, Buxton Road, Bakewell, Derbyshire, DE45 1GS
☎ (01629) 815999 ⊕ thornbridgebrewery.co.uk

☺ The first Thornbridge beers were produced in 2005 using a 10-barrel brewery, housed in the grounds of Thornbridge Hall. The beers have gained considerable success with over 300 consumer and industry awards being won. A 30-barrel brewery opened in Bakewell in 2009. The original site continues to develop new, seasonal and speciality beers. 200 outlets are supplied direct. 12 pubs are managed and owned. ‼▤◆RAIB

Wild Swan (OG 1035, ABV 3.5%) ◣
Pale yet flavoursome and refreshing beer. Plenty of lemony citrus hop flavour, becoming increasingly dry and bitter in the finish and aftertaste.

Brother Rabbit (OG 1035, ABV 4%)
Yellow in colour with a clean, hoppy aroma, a resinous finish and some bitterness.

Lord Marples (OG 1041, ABV 4%) ◣
Smooth, traditional, easy-drinking bitter. Caramel, malt and coffee flavours fall away to leave a long, bitter finish.

Ashford (OG 1043, ABV 4.2%)
A brown ale with a floral hoppiness, a smooth, malty kick and a delicate coffee finish.

Kipling (OG 1050, ABV 5.2%) ◣
Golden pale bitter with aromas of grapefruit and passion fruit. Intense fruit flavours continue throughout, leading to a long bitter aftertaste.

Jaipur IPA (OG 1055, ABV 5.9%) ◣
Flavoursome IPA packed with citrus hoppiness that's nicely counter-balanced by malt and underlying sweetness and robust fruit flavours.

Saint Petersburg Imperial Russian Stout (OG 1073, ABV 7.4%) ◣
Good example of an imperial stout. Smooth and easy to drink with raisins, bitter chocolate and hops throughout, leading to a lingering coffee and chocolate aftertaste.

Three B's SIBA ◉

▤ Black Bull, Brokenstone Road, Tockholes, Blackburn, Lancashire, BB3 0LL
☎ (01254) 581381 ⊕ threebsbrewery.co.uk

Robert Bell acquired the Black Bull in 2011 and the brewpub now supplies 50 outlets. A bottling plant has been installed and bottle-conditioned beers are now available. ‼◆RAIB

Bee Thrifty (OG 1036, ABV 3.4%)
A light and refreshing amber-coloured beer.

Stoker's Slake (OG 1038, ABV 3.6%) ◣
Lightly roasted coffee flavours are in the aroma and the initial taste. A well-rounded, dark brown mild with dried fruit flavours in the long finish.

Honey Bee (OG 1039, ABV 3.7%)
A golden beer with honey apparent in both aroma and taste.

Bobbin's Bitter (OG 1038, ABV 3.8%)
A golden bitter with warm aromas of nutty grain and a full, fruity flavour with a light, dry finish.

Bee Blonde (OG 1041, ABV 4%)
A distinctive, pale bitter with a light, dry, balance of grain and hops and a delicate finish with citrus fruits.

Black Bull (OG 1042, ABV 4%)
A dark ruby red bitter. Rich in character with a hint of chocolate.

Weaver's Brew (ABV 4%)
A pale blonde beer with a hop flavour.

Fettler's Choice (ABV 4.2%)
An amber-coloured beer with a smooth, light taste.

Tackler's Tipple (OG 1044, ABV 4.3%)
A dark best bitter with full hop flavour, biscuit tones on the tongue and a deep, dry finish.

Doff Cocker (OG 1045, ABV 4.5%) ◆
Yellow with a hoppy aroma and initial taste giving way to subtle malt notes and orchard fruit flavours. Crisp, dry finish.

Pinch Noggin (OG 1046, ABV 4.6%)
A dark, strong best bitter with full hop flavour and a long aftertaste.

Knocker Up (OG 1047, ABV 4.8%) ◆
A smooth, rich, creamy porter. The roast flavour is foremost without dominating and is balanced by fruit and hop notes.

Shuttle Ale (OG 1050, ABV 5.2%)
A rustic-coloured traditional strong pale ale.

Three Blind Mice

Unit W10, Black Bank Business Park, Black Bank Road, Little Downham, Cambridgeshire, CB62UA
☎ 07912 875825

Three Blind Mice began brewing in 2014 using a five-barrel plant, supplying outlets in Cambridgeshire. An ever-changing range of beers is brewed throughout the year. ♦

Table Liquor (ABV 2.8%)
A dry, light and bitter pale ale with a big hop punch.

Faintest Idea (ABV 3.5%)
A touch of caramel brings a little sweetness and body to this well-balanced quaffable pale beer.

Lonely Snake (ABV 3.5%)
A golden-coloured, hoppy session ale.

Corumbo (ABV 4.2%)

Yankee Kangaroo (ABV 4.3%)
A copper-coloured ale.

Generation Red (ABV 4.5%)
A ruby-coloured beer with a subtle roasted malt character, nicely balanced with both fruity and resinous hop flavours.

Number One (ABV 4.5%)
Well balanced and hoppy with citrus notes.

Pale Ale No. 1 (ABV 4.5%)
Well balanced and hoppy with citrus notes.

Black Bank Porter (ABV 4.7%)
Roasted malt, coffee and chocolate with a nice bitter finish.

Odds & Sods (ABV 5.2%)
A hoppy IPA.

Dirty Goulash (ABV 8.2%)
A rum-infused beer, easy-drinking for its strength. Rum flavours balance nicely with the sweet, roasted malt backbone.

Three Castles

Unit 12, Salisbury Road Business Park, Pewsey, Wiltshire, SN9 5PZ
☎ (01672) 564433 ☎ 07725 148671
threecastlesbrewery.co.uk

Three Castles is an independent, family-run brewery established in 2006. !! ♦ RAIB

Barbury Castle (OG 1039, ABV 3.9%)
A balanced, easy-drinking pale ale with a hoppy, spicy palate.

Saxon Archer (OG 1040, ABV 4%)

Vale Ale (OG 1043, ABV 4.3%)
Golden-coloured with a fruity palate and strong floral aroma.

Corn Dolly (OG 1047, ABV 4.7%)

Three Daggers SIBA

Westbury Road, Edington, Wiltshire, BA13 4PG
☎ (01380) 830940 threedaggersbrewery.com

Three Daggers Brewery was established in 2013 using a 2.5-barrel brew plant in a farm shop next to the pub. Malt is sourced locally from Warminster Maltings and hops from Charles Faram in Herefordshire. Beer is available in the pub and selected other local outlets. Bottled beers are available in the farm shop. !! ♦ RAIB

Daggers Blonde (OG 1037, ABV 3.6%)

Daggers Ale (OG 1041, ABV 4.1%)

Daggers Edge (OG 1047, ABV 4.7%)

Three Kings SIBA

14 Prospect Terrace, North Shields, Tyne & Wear, NE30 1DX ☎ 07580 004565
threekingsbrewery.co.uk

Three Kings started in 2012 using a 2.5-barrel plant, upgrading to a five-barrel one in 2013. A core range of beers is now available with previous occasional beers being brewed again on request. ♦

Billy Mill (OG 1040, ABV 4%)

Gallowgate Raw (OG 1045, ABV 4.4%)

Ring of Fire (OG 1048, ABV 4.5%)

Three Legs (NEW)

Burnt House Farm, Udimore Road, Brede, East Sussex, TN31 6BX ☎ 07783 973161 thethreelegs.co.uk

Three Legs was started by three friends who met studying wine-making and viticulture at university. After working in the wine industry for nine years, they turned to real ale and opened a small batch nanobrewery. There are plans to increase to four-barrel capacity. !! RAIB

Amber (OG 1044, ABV 4.5%)

IPA (OG 1044, ABV 4.5%)

Three Peaks

Scar Top Brewery, Buck Haw Brow, Settle, North Yorkshire, BD24 0DJ
☎ (01729) 822939 ☎ 07795 358932

Office: 7 Craven Terrace, Settle, BD24 9DB
threepeaksbrewery.co.uk

⊗ Formed in 2006 using a five-barrel plant, Three Peaks is run by husband-and-wife team Colin and Susan Ashwell, assisted by Andrew Murphy. The brewery is located on Buck Haw Brow, Settle. Three regular beers are brewed along with an occasional beer. ♦

Pen-y-Ghent Bitter (OG 1040, ABV 3.8%) ◆

The malty character of this mid-brown session bitter is balanced by fruit in the aroma and taste. The finish is malty and hoppy.

Ingleborough Gold (OG 1041, ABV 4%) ◆
This golden-coloured best bitter is hoppy throughout with fruit in the aroma and taste and a hoppy bitter finish.

Whernside Pale Ale (OG 1042, ABV 4.2%)

Three Sods (NEW)

Bethnal Green Working Men's Club, 42 Pollard Row, Bethnal Green, E2 6NB ☎ 07544 422236
threesodsbrewery.com

Based in a working men's club in East London, Three Sods specialise in small batch beers produced using a range of malts and hops from around the world.

Same Again (ABV 4.4%)

Mud Puddler Black IPA (ABV 4.8%)

Three Tuns SIBA

16 Market Square, Bishop's Castle, Shropshire, SY9 5BN
☎ (01588) 638392 threetunsbrewery.co.uk

Brewing on this site started in the 16th century and was licensed in 1642. A small-scale tower brewery from the late 19th century survives as one of the Famous Four pub breweries still running in 1970s. !! ◆ RAIB

Mild (OG 1040, ABV 3.4%)
Tawny coloured winter beer of rich maltiness with burnt and roasted flavours.

1642 Bitter (OG 1042, ABV 3.8%)
A golden ale with a light, nutty maltiness and spicy bitterness.

XXX (OG 1046, ABV 4.3%) ◆
A pale, sweetish bitter with a light hop aftertaste that has a honey finish.

Stout (OG 1048, ABV 4.4%)
Old-fashioned-style stout.

Cleric's Cure (OG 1059, ABV 5%)
A light tan-coloured ale with a malty sweetness. Strong and spicy with a floral bitterness.

Steampunk (OG 1065, ABV 6.5%)
Rich dark and fiery, smooth barley wine with flavours of liquorice, ginger, caramel and roasted malts lasting through into a strong bitter finish.

Thurstons (Horsell) SIBA

The Courtyard, 102c High Street, Horsell, Surrey, GU21 4ST
☎ (01483) 729555 ☎ 7789936784
thurstonsbrewery.co.uk

Originally based in the Crown, Horsell, Thurstons moved next door in 2014 when the brewery upgraded to a 4.5-barrel plant. The beer range has developed over the first full year of production so that Malt Way and Festival are now brewed on an occasional basis.

Horsell Best (OG 1040, ABV 3.8%)
A balanced, full-bodied session ale.

Horsell Gold (OG 1040, ABV 3.8%)
A golden beer with a rounded bitterness, caramel and spice on the palate, and a hoppy aroma.

Stedmans Ale (OG 1042, ABV 4.1%)
A refreshing, balanced golden ale with a crisp citrus taste.

Milk Stout (OG 1055, ABV 4.5%) ◆
Smooth, sweet stout, with a chocolaty flavour. A sweet malty flavour with a pleasant sharpness and a slightly dry finish.

Thwaites SIBA IFBB

Star Brewery, PO Box 50, Blackburn, Lancashire, BB1 5BU
☎ (01254) 686868 danielthwaites.com

In April 2015, Thwaites sold its brewing division to Marston's for £25.1 million. The Blackburn brewery, founded in 1807, closed in February 2014 with production of 100,000 barrels a year transferred to Marston's Wolverhampton plant. Thwaites said in 2014 it planned to build a new greenfield brewery near Blackburn, but it has now signed a 10-year deal with Marston's to supply its 350 pubs. Marston's beers will also be made available to Thwaites's licensees. Thwaites's 100-barrel pilot brewery will be retained at Blackburn: it makes short-run specialist beers in cask, keg and bottled versions. See Banks's !! ◆ RAIB

Nutty Black (OG 1036, ABV 3.6%)

Ticketybrew SIBA

16 Waterloo Court, Stalybridge, SK15 2AU ☎ 07970 093665 ticketybrew.co.uk

Ticketybrew is a husband-and-wife-run brewery that opened in 2013 and focuses on vegan-friendly bottled beers. RAIB

Jasmine Green Tea (OG 1038, ABV 3.8%)
The addition of jasmine green tea, phoenix pearls and lemon peel create a light and refreshing ale, with hop bitterness complemented by fresh lemon rind.

Munchner (ABV 4.3%)
A traditional beer that mixes malty caramel sweetness with a distinctive German hop aroma and the spicy flavours of Belgian yeast.

Rose and Ginger Wheat Beer (OG 1044, ABV 4.5%)
A wheat beer with an aroma of roses, balanced by a subtle kick of fresh ginger.

Pale Ale (OG 1050, ABV 5.3%)
American bittering and aroma hops balanced with a sweetness provided by Belgian yeast.

Blonde (OG 1047, ABV 5.6%)
Soft floral and fruit on the nose with a spicy, fruity and yeasty flavour.

Tigertops

22 Oakes Street, Flanshaw, Wakefield, West Yorkshire, WF2 9LN
☎ (01229) 716238 ☎ 07951 812986
tigertopsbrewery@hotmail.com

Tigertops was established in 1995 by Stuart Johnson and his wife, Lynda, who, as well as owning the brewery, run the Foxfield brewpub in Cumbria (qv). The brewery is run on their behalf by Barry Smith, supplying five regular outlets. Beers

THE BREWERIES

are brewed on demand with seasonal and experimental beers also available. ♦

Tiley's (NEW)

Ham Green, Ham, Gloucestershire, GL13 9QH
☎ (01453) 810284 🌐 the-sally-at-ham.com

A microbrewery established in 2015 in an outbuilding of the Salutation Inn, Ham. The brewery holds open evenings.

Tillingbourne SIBA

Old Scotland Farm, Staple Lane, Shere, Surrey, GU5 9TE
☎ (01483) 222228 🌐 tillybeer.co.uk

⊗ Tillingbourne began brewing in 2011 on a farm site previously used by Surrey Hills Brewery using its old 17-barrel plant. Around 25 local outlets are supplied. !! ♦

Source (OG 1033, ABV 3.3%)

Black Troll (OG 1035, ABV 3.7%) ◆
A black bitter in which initial roast notes are eventually overpowered by citrus hop through to the finish.

AONB (OG 1036, ABV 4%) ◆
Golden ale in which citrus hop dominates throughout. Some balancing malt in the aroma and taste, however.

Falls Gold (OG 1037, ABV 4.2%) ◆
While hops dominate, balancing malt is evident throughout. Hints of grapefruit in the aroma and taste lead to a dry finish.

Hop Troll (OG 1045, ABV 4.8%)
American-style IPA with plenty of hops

Summit (ABV 6%)

Time and Tide

Office: 10 Herschell Road, East Walmer, Kent, CT14 7SQ ☎ 07739 868256
🌐 timeandtidebrewing.co.uk

Time and Tide began brewing in 2013 using spare capacity at Ripple Steam Brewery (qv). ♦RAIB

Tindall

Toad Lane, Seething, Norfolk, NR35 2EQ

Tindall Ales began brewing in 1998. The brewery was originally based in Ditchingham but moved to its current location towards the end of 2001. ♦

Best Bitter (OG 1037, ABV 3.7%)

Fuggled Up (OG 1037, ABV 3.7%)

Mild (OG 1037, ABV 3.7%)

Liberator (OG 1038, ABV 3.8%)

Alltime (OG 1040, ABV 4%)

Mundham Mild (OG 1040, ABV 4%)

Ditchingham Dam (OG 1042, ABV 4.2%)

Seething Pint (OG 1043, ABV 4.3%)

Norwich Dragon (OG 1046, ABV 4.6%)

Honeydo (OG 1050, ABV 5%)

Tinpot

Allanwater Brewhouse, Queens Lane, Bridge of Allan, Stirlingshire, FK9 4NY
☎ (01786) 834555 ✉ tinpot@bridgeofallan.co.uk

Tinpot opened in 2009 using a one-barrel plant designed to brew speciality beers and started supplying CAMRA beer festivals in 2010. The beer range varies depending on season and demand and is expanding each year. !! ♦RAIB

Gold Pot 70/- (OG 1042, ABV 3.9%)
A pale golden best bitter.

Beetroot & Black Pepper (OG 1043, ABV 4%)

Lavender Pot (OG 1043, ABV 4%)

Nettle Pot (OG 1044, ABV 4%)
A hoppy IPA brewed by the Stirling University Craft Beer Society.

Prune Pot (OG 1042, ABV 4%)

Tea Pot (Earl Grey) (OG 1042, ABV 4%)

Tea Pot (Lapsang Souchong) (OG 1042, ABV 4%)

Wit Pot (OG 1043, ABV 4%)
Wheat beer flavoured with orange peel, coriander and liquorice.

Banana Pot (OG 1044, ABV 4.2%)

75/- Pot (OG 1044, ABV 4.3%)
A copper-coloured beer, malty, lightly hopped and satisfying.

Marmalade Pot (OG 1046, ABV 4.4%)

Rhubarb & Ginger Pot (OG 1046, ABV 4.4%)

Thai Pot (OG 1046, ABV 4.4%)

Chilli Pot (OG 1046, ABV 4.5%)

Choc Pot 80/- (OG 1046, ABV 4.5%)
A brown best bitter.

Honey (OG 1056, ABV 4.5%)

Honey Gluten Free (OG 1056, ABV 4.5%)
Brewed from Sorghum grass and flavoured with Scottish heather honey.

Mango Pot (OG 1047, ABV 4.5%)

Raspberry Pot (OG 1048, ABV 4.5%)

Treacle (OG 1052, ABV 4.5%)

Treacle Gluten Free (OG 1052, ABV 4.5%)
Brewed from Sorghum grass and flavoured with Scottish black treacle.

5 Spice Pot (OG 1046, ABV 4.6%)

Curry Pot (OG 1046, ABV 4.6%)

Game Pot (OG 1046, ABV 4.6%)

Bramble Pot (OG 1052, ABV 5%)

Pot Black (OG 1052, ABV 5%)

Pot of Gold (OG 1052, ABV 5%)

Wheat Pot (OG 1053, ABV 5%)

Procrastination (OG 1060, ABV 6%)
A hoppy IPA brewed by the Stirling University Craft Beer Society.

Tinshed (NEW)

Justice Close Farm, Tilbrook Road, Kimbolton, Cambridgeshire, PE28 0JW ☎ 07585 551499

Correspondence: 52 Main Road, Stonely, St Neots, Cambridgeshire, PE19 5EP 🌐 tinshedbrewery.com

Tinshed Brewery was established in 2014 using a home-made four-barrel set-up. The brewery is run by three close friends from the village of Kimbolton and produces three core beers and seasonal specials, supplying local pubs, clubs and beer festivals. Bottles of seasonal specials will be produced throughout the year. !! ♦ RAIB

Skinny Pig (OG 1039, ABV 3.8%)
Burnished gold in colour with a light hoppy aroma; balanced malt and hops produce a complex spiced flavour, complemented by a sweet, long, dry finish.

Golden Weasel (OG 1040, ABV 4%)
A full-flavoured, refreshing, light bitter with a clean, fresh finish.

Old Smokey (OG 1041, ABV 4.1%)
A copper-coloured beer with an initial hint of malt followed by a hop aroma and a long, dry, nutty finish.

Tintagel SIBA

Condolden Farm, Tintagel, Cornwall, PL34 0HJ
☎ (01840) 213371 🌐 tintagelbrewery.co.uk

This 7.5-barrel brewery was established in 2009 in a redundant milking parlour on the highest farm in Cornwall. Some 80 outlets are now supplied direct. ♦ RAIB

Castle Gold (OG 1038, ABV 3.8%)
Heavily hopped golden ale. Citrus hops and noticeable malt taste. Bitterness throughout with citrus and stone fruits. Lingering dry finish.

Cornwall's Pride (OG 1040, ABV 4%)
Tawny-coloured best bitter with peaty malt aroma. Nutty malt then hop bitterness with complex flavours. Bitterness and rising dry finish.

Arthur's Ale (OG 1044, ABV 4.4%)
Copper-coloured best bitter with malt aroma. Best bitter and golden ale combined. Malt, stone-fruit sweetness and citrus hop bitterness.

Harbour Special (OG 1048.9, ABV 4.8%)
Brown strong bitter with ripe, fruity, malty aroma. Rich, nutty malt, stone fruits and esters to taste, finishing bitter and dry.

Tiny Rebel SIBA

Unit 12 & 12a, Maes Glas Industrial Estate, Greenwich Road, Newport, NP20 2NN
☎ (01633) 547378 ☎ 07980 798268
🌐 tinyrebel.co.uk

Tiny Rebel opened in 2012. It operates on a 12-barrel brew plant consisting of 10 fermentation and two conditioning tanks. ♦

1 Inch Punch (OG 1039, ABV 3.9%)
Golden-coloured American-style session beer brewed using Mosaic hops.

Flux (OG 1039, ABV 4%)
Black pale ale.

Hank (OG 1038, ABV 4%)
American-style pale ale.

Fubar (OG 1041, ABV 4.4%)
Floral hoppy flavours upfront, leading to a dry, spicy bitterness.

Loki (OG 1042, ABV 4.5%)
A black IPA.

Loki Lite (OG 1044, ABV 4.5%)
An IPA with citrus aromas, tropical fruit punch flavours and bitterness. Refreshing on the palate.

XLPA (OG 1042, ABV 4.5%)
Extra light pale malt is balanced with American hops.

Billabong (OG 1045, ABV 4.6%)
Australian-style summer pale ale.

Cwtch (OG 1045, ABV 4.6%)
A Welsh red ale made with six malts and two American hops.

Full Nelson (OG 1046, ABV 4.8%)
Maori pale ale using only New Zealand hops.

Zool (OG 1046, ABV 4.8%)
American-style pale ale.

Dirty Stopout (OG 1052, ABV 5%)
A complex smoked oak stout.

Urban IPA (OG 1051, ABV 5.5%)

Rebel Alliance (OG 1055, ABV 6.5%)
A collaboration brew with Dark Star. New Zealand Saison-style beer with big grapefruit and spice flavours and piny, resinous aromas.

Hadouken (OG 1069, ABV 7.4%)
Hefty IPA brewed with a variety of American hops.

Tipples

Unit 3, The Mill, Wood Green, Salhouse, Norfolk, NR13 6NY
☎ (01603) 721310 🌐 tipplesbrewery.com

Tipples was established in 2004 on a six-barrel brew plant. In addition to a full range of cask ales, an extensive range of bottled beers is produced, which can be found in some farmers markets and supermarkets in Norfolk. ♦ RAIB

Hanged Monk (OG 1038, ABV 3.8%)
Strong roast and malt notes dominate the aroma and taste. A grainy mouthfeel with caramel and a growing vinous finish.

Sundown (OG 1040, ABV 3.9%)
Berries and malt introduce this smooth creamy bitter. Bitterness gives depth to the fruity malt core as it slowly sweetens.

Redhead (OG 1042, ABV 4.2%)
Malt and hops in both nose and palate. Toffee in the initial taste gives way to an increasing bitterness.

Brewers Progress (OG 1046, ABV 4.6%)
Solid and malty with strong caramel and vanilla support. Smooth and creamy with added depth by a bitter blackcurrant fruitiness.

Moonrocket (OG 1050, ABV 5%)
A complex golden brew. Malt, hop, bitterness and a fruity sweetness swirl round in an ever-changing kaleidoscope of flavours.

Tipsy Angel

Lower Angel, 27 Buttermarket Street, Warrington, Cheshire, WA1 2LY
☎ (01925) 653326 ☎ 07909 893912
✉ andycharlie1@hotmail.co.uk

Tipsy Angel began brewing in 2011 using a one-barrel plant. The brewery was founded to recreate the brews from the original recipes of Walker's of Warrington. Beers are mainly produced for the

THE BREWERIES

Lower Angel pub, but are also occasionally available at beer festivals. ‼◆

Angelic Mild (OG 1038, ABV 3.8%)
Dark mild, faithfully brewed from the old Walker's recipes.

Angelic Blonde (OG 1044, ABV 4.4%)
A modern blonde bitter, using traditional British ingredients.

Angel's Folly (OG 1052, ABV 5.2%)
Flagship beer from the old Walker's recipes; strong, dark and complex, rich in texture, with an aroma of strong malted barley and a subtle mouthfeel with a lingering finish.

Tír Dhá Ghlas

▤ Cullins Yard, 11 Cambridge Road, Dover, Kent, CT17 9BY
☎ (01304) 211666 ⊕ cullinsyard.co.uk/brewery/

⊗ Brewing began in 2012 using a two-barrel plant. Beers are available only in Cullins Yard bar/restaurant and occasionally at the nearby Royal Cinque Ports Yacht Club, particularly when they are holding beer festivals.

Tirril SIBA

Red House, Long Marton, Cumbria, CA16 6BN
☎ (01768) 361846 ⊕ tirrilbrewery.co.uk

☺Established in 1999, Tirril Brewery has twice outgrown its premises. Capacity has grown to 60 barrels. More than 170 outlets are supplied, 100 of which regularly stock the beer. One pub is owned. ‼◆

Original Bitter (OG 1038.5, ABV 3.8%)
Lightly hopped, golden-brown session beer.

Ullswater Blonde (OG 1038.5, ABV 3.8%)
Pale golden, easy-drinking session beer.

Grasmere Gold (OG 1039, ABV 3.9%)
Gently hopped golden amber beer.

Eden Valley (OG 1040, ABV 4%)
A pale session bitter with a fresh taste.

Old Faithful (OG 1040, ABV 4%) ◀
Initially bitter, gold-coloured ale with a hoppy finish.

1823 (OG 1041, ABV 4.1%)
A full-bodied session bitter with a gentle bitterness.

Academy Ale (OG 1041.5, ABV 4.2%)
A dark, full-bodied, traditional rich and malty ale.

Borrowdale Bitter (OG 1041.5, ABV 4.2%)
An amber ale with a nice bite.

Red Barn Ale (OG 1043, ABV 4.4%)
A ruby red ale with a strong hop character.

Contract brewed for Bitter End:

Lakeland Golden (ABV 4.3%)

Titan

▤ Golden Eagle, 6 St Katherine's Court (off Agard Street), Derby, Derbyshire, DE22 3AY
☎ (01332) 298465 ☎ 07749 556837
⊕ titanbrewery.co.uk

⊗ Set-up by former Mr Grundy's brewers in 2014 with plans to install the brewery in a commercial

unit. At present the beers are being brewed on the Mr Grundy's (qv) plant. They own a nearby pub, the Golden Eagle (formerly the Graduate).

Bitter (OG 1036.8, ABV 3.8%)
Dark, malty and smooth.

Pale (OG 1038.7, ABV 4%)
Light and fruity.

Gold (OG 1043.5, ABV 4.5%)

Stout (OG 1047, ABV 4.8%)
Dark, oaty and caramel.

IPA (OG 1048.5, ABV 5%)
Golden, full-flavoured and hoppy.

Titanic SIBA ⊚

Unit 5, Callender Place, Burslem, Stoke-on-Trent, Staffordshire, ST6 1JL
☎ (01782) 823447 ⊕ titanicbrewery.co.uk

☺ Founded in 1985 and named after Captain Smith, a Potteries man and the captain of the Titanic. One of the earliest microbreweries, Titanic has grown into a local brewer with a small, constantly expanding tied pub estate and supplies free trade customers across the Midlands and the North West. 2014 saw a major investment in the brewery and brewhouse creating a brewery shop and sample room. ‼ ☰◆ RAIB

Mild (OG 1036, ABV 3.5%) ◀
Fresh fruity hop aroma leads to a caramel start then a rush of bitter hoppiness ending with a lingering dry finish.

Steerage (OG 1036, ABV 3.5%) ◀
Pale yellow bitter. Flavours start with hops and fruit but become zesty and refreshing in this light session beer with a long, dry finish.

Lifeboat (OG 1040, ABV 4%) ◀
Dark brown with fruit, malt and caramel aromas. Sweet start, malty and caramel middle with hoppiness developing into a fruity and dry lingering finish.

Anchor Bitter (OG 1042, ABV 4.1%) ◀
Amber beer with a spicy hint to the fruity start that is followed by a rush of hops in the dry bitter finish.

Iceberg (OG 1042, ABV 4.1%) ◀
Yellow gold sparkling wheat beer with a flowery start leading to a massively hoppy, zesty finish.

Titanic Cherry Dark (OG 1045, ABV 4.4%)

Chocolate and Vanilla Stout (OG 1047, ABV 4.5%) ◀
Chocoholic paradise with real coffee and vanilla support. Cocoa, sherry and almonds lend depth to this creamy, drinkable 'heaven in a glass' stout.

Stout (OG 1046, ABV 4.5%) ◀
Roasty, toasty with tobacco, autumn bonfires, chocolate and hints of liquorice; perfectly balanced with a bitter, dry finish reminiscent of real coffee.

Titanic Cappuccino Stout (OG 1046, ABV 4.5%)

White Star (OG 1050, ABV 4.8%) ◀
Hints of cinnamon apple pie are found before the hops take over to give a bitter edge to this well-balanced, refreshing fruity beer.

Plum Porter (OG 1051, ABV 4.9%) ▮ ◀
Dark brown with a powerful fruity aroma. A sweet plum fruitiness gives way to a gentle bitter finish.

Captain Smith's Strong Ale
(OG 1054, ABV 5.2%) ◆
Red brown and full bodied, lots of malt and roast with a hint of honey but a strong bittersweet finish.

Toll End

▤ c/o Waggon and Horses, 131 Toll End Road, Tipton, West Midlands, DY4 0ET ☎ 07903 725574

The four-barrel brewery opened in 2004. With the exception of Phoebe's Ale, named after the brewer's daughter, all brews commemorate local landmarks, events and people. ‼RAIB

William Perry (OG 1043, ABV 4.3%)

Black Bridge (OG 1044, ABV 4.4%)

Phoebe's Ale (PA) (OG 1047, ABV 4.7%)

Power Station (OG 1049, ABV 4.9%)
Cask-conditioned lager.

Charlie Blackout Stout (OG 1054, ABV 5.4%)

Tollgate SIBA

Unit 1, Southwood House Farm, Staunton Lane, Calke, Leicestershire, LE65 1RG
☎ (01283) 229194 ⊕ tollgatebrewery.com

⊠ This family-run six-barrel brewery was founded in 2005 on the site of the old Brunt & Bucknall Brewery in nearby Woodville, but relocated to new premises on the National Trust's Calke Park estate in 2012. Around 150 outlets are supplied direct. Bottle-conditioned beer constitutes nearly 40% of production and is available suitable for vegans.
‼◆RAIB

Viking Gold (OG 1039, ABV 4.1%)
A light, bright golden ale with a citrus aroma.

California Steam (OG 1041, ABV 4.2%)
Brewed in the style of a US West Coast beer to produce a pale golden colour.

Bitter (OG 1041, ABV 4.3%)
A smooth, easy-drinking bitter.

Darkwood Bitter (OG 1042, ABV 4.4%)
A traditional dark amber bitter brewed using English hops.

Ashby Pale (OG 1043, ABV 4.5%)
A light, refreshing beer with a citrus finish.

Red Star IPA (OG 1043, ABV 4.5%)
A classic hoppy IPA.

Billy's Best Bitter (OG 1044, ABV 4.6%)
Dark amber best bitter.

Red McAdy (OG 1043, ABV 5%)
Whisky-conditioned northern ale.

Tolly Cobbold

See Greene King

Tom Herrick's

See under H

Tombstone SIBA

20 Estcourt Road, Great Yarmouth, Norfolk, NR30 4JQ
☎ 07584 504444 ⊕ tombstonebrewery.co.uk

⊠ Tombstone was established in 2013 and is run by former home brewer Paul Hodgson. It is named after the town cemetery which backs onto it. All the beers have a Wild West theme. 20 outlets are supplied in and around Yarmouth and several in Norwich.

Arizona (OG 1040, ABV 3.9%)
Light amber ale, malty, hoppy with a touch of citrus.

Gunslinger (OG 1044, ABV 4.3%)
Golden with a caramel, nutty finish.

Lone Rider (OG 1044, ABV 4.3%)
A deep ruby-coloured, hoppy ale.

Stagecoach (OG 1044, ABV 4.4%)
A smooth, dark, malty ale with a hit of liquorice.

Texas Jack (OG 1050, ABV 4.8%)
Ruby-coloured ale with full-on flavour and a twist of plums.

Big Nose Kate (OG 1054, ABV 5.3%)
Ruby-coloured ale. Malty and fruity with a subtle passion fruit taste.

Tomos & Lilford

Unit 14, Heritage Business Park, Wick Road, Llantwit Major, CF61 1YU
☎ (01446) 796905 ☎ 07779 132647

Office: 117 Boverton Road, Llantwit Major, CF61 1YA
✉ tomos.lilford@gmail.com

⊠ Launched in 2013 by keen experimental home brewers Rolant Tomos and brothers Rob and James Lilford. The brewery supplies pubs and clubs across the Vale and further afield; all point of sale material is bilingual. ◆

Triple Hop (OG 1040, ABV 4%)
American-style session bitter.

Personal Best (ABV 4.5%)
Malty session beer with creamy, nutty notes.

Gaucho (OG 1050, ABV 5%)
Brewed to commemorate 150 years since the Welsh arrived in Patagonia. An IPA with a long, smooth finish based on an old recipe using 40% wheat and a South American herb tea.

O.P.A. (OG 1050, ABV 5%)
American-style IPA. Hoppy, refreshing and satisfying.

Rosemary Ale (ABV 5%)
Very pale, refreshing ale, bursting with the flavours of honey and rosemary.

Hay (OG 1052, ABV 5.2%)
An English-style IPA with the addition of hay for sweetness and aroma.

Tonbridge SIBA

Unit 19, Branbridges Industrial Estate, East Peckham, Kent, TN12 5HF
☎ (01622) 871239 ⊕ tonbridgebrewery.co.uk

⊠ Tonbridge Brewery was launched in 2010 using a four-barrel brew kit, expanding in 2013 to a 12-barrel plant. Owned and run jointly by Paul Bournazian and Mark Gardner, it produces cask-conditioned ales using predominantly Kent-grown hops. The full range of ales is available in five-litre mini casks. Pubs and shops are supplied throughout

Kent as well as parts of Surrey, Sussex, Essex and south-east London. ‼

Traditional Ale (OG 1038, ABV 3.6%)
Easy-drinking and refreshing ale with a light, fruity taste and hop aroma.

Copper Nob (OG 1039.5, ABV 3.8%)
A fairly dry, rich copper-coloured ale with taste in depth. Robust fruity flavour from the hops.

Alsace Gold (OG 1041.5, ABV 4%)
Golden ale with a light caramel maltiness balanced with a delicate floral hoppiness.

Rustic (OG 1041.5, ABV 4%)
Deep bronze-coloured, rich-tasting country ale. Lightly hopped giving a delicate spicy taste and aroma.

Blonde Ambition (OG 1043.5, ABV 4.2%)
A crisp, refreshing, full-flavoured blonde ale with spicy and citrus notes.

Ebony Moon (OG 1044, ABV 4.2%)
A rich porter with a pronounced maltiness balanced with a light bitterness.

Union Pale (OG 1047, ABV 4.7%)
An American-style pale ale with rich malt flavours balanced by citrus and tropical fruit aromas.

Toolmakers SIBA

6-8 Botsford Street, Sheffield, South Yorkshire, S3 9PF
☎ 07956 235332 🌐 toolmakersbrewery.com

Toolmakers is a family-run brewery established in 2013 in an old tool-making factory. Beers are brewed on a five-barrel plant and are available in local pubs. Brewing takes place once a week and the beers are available in the Forest freehouse next door. ‼

G Philips Driver (OG 1042, ABV 4.2%)
A well-flavoured hoppy ale.

Razmataz (OG 1042, ABV 4.2%)
Smooth with a light colour, floral aroma and citrus taste.

Fine Finish (OG 1043, ABV 4.3%)
Well-balanced, full-bodied blonde ale with a good hoppy flavour.

Pin Hammer (OG 1043, ABV 4.3%)
A well-balanced traditional beer made with pale chocolate and caramel with a soft finish.

Toffee Hammer (OG 1043, ABV 4.3%)
Well-balanced beer with caramel hints of chocolate and liquorice.

Flange Noire (OG 1048, ABV 4.8%)
A dark ale made with Vienna and pale chocolate malts for a light taste and lots of flavour.

Black Edge (OG 1052, ABV 5.2%)
A dark chocolate-flavoured beer.

Top-Notch

Haywards Heath, West Sussex, RH16 1UQ ☎ 07963 829368 🌐 topnotchbrewing.co.uk

The 0.5-barrel brewery is situated in a converted residential outbuilding in Haywards Heath. RAIB

Hop Festival (OG 1038, ABV 3.9%)

Royal Fanfare (OG 1044, ABV 4.6%)

Flare-Path (OG 1052, ABV 5.5%)

Top Out

Unit 3, 6b Dryden Road, Loanhead, EH20 9LZ
☎ (0131) 440 0270 ☎ 07742 234970
🌐 topoutbrewery.com

Brewing began in 2013 using a six-barrel plant. Initially focusing on mostly bottle-conditioned output, the brewery has expanded into brewing cask beer for the on-trade. The beer range is currently being developed and additional fermentation capacity is being installed. Branding has a topographical theme. Top Out is a host for cuckoo brewery Black Metal and also contract brews for Secret Herb Garden. ♦RAIB

Staple (OG 1037, ABV 4%)

Smoked Porter (OG 1060, ABV 5.6%)

Cone (OG 1058, ABV 6.8%)

Topsham SIBA

Globe Hotel, Fore Street, Topsham, Devon, EX3 0DP
☎ (01392) 874818 🌐 topsham-ales.co.uk

⊠ Topsham Ales has operated since 2010 in premises within the Globe Hotel. It is run solely by volunteers, and is one of only a handful of co-operatively owned breweries in the UK. Brewing takes place once a fortnight and also some bottling. The beer is sold locally. ‼

Totally Brewed SIBA

Units 8 & 9, Meadow Lane Fruit and Veg Market, Clarke Road, Nottingham, NG2 3JJ ☎ 07702 800639
🌐 totallybrewed.com

◎ Totally Brewed began brewing in 2014 using a seven-barrel plant previously used at White Dog Brewery. A diverse range of hop-forward beers are produced including seasonal and one-off brews. ♦

Slap in the Face (OG 1040, ABV 4%)
A hoppy, blonde session ale.

Papa Jangle's Voodoo Stout (OG 1046, ABV 4.5%)
A complex, flavoursome, dark stout.

Punch in the Face (OG 1047, ABV 4.8%)
A hoppy IPA brewed with American hops.

Four Hopmen of the Apocalypse (OG 1047, ABV 5.2%)
A hoppy IPA with four hop varieties.

Captain Hopbeard (OG 1050, ABV 5.5%)
A Pacific-style IPA made with Australian and New Zealand hops.

Totem (NEW)

11 Cleaveland Rise, Ogwell, Newton Abbot, Devon, TQ12 6FF
☎ (01626) 330358 ✉ totembrewing@gmail.com

No real ale. Totem currently brews one beer, Tropical Storm, producing a 20-litre keg every one to two weeks. The beer is available at Teign Cellars, Newton Abbot. Expansion is planned.

Totnes (NEW)

59A High Street, Totnes, Devon, TQ9 5PB
☎ (01803) 849290 ☎ 07974 828971
✉ richard.kidd@idnet.net.uk

The brewery is situated at the rear of a bistro/bar in Totnes. It has a portfolio of four main ales plus additional specials.

Seven Seas (OG 1039, ABV 3.8%)
An American-style IPA hopped with seven varieties.

Golden Brown (OG 1046, ABV 4.4%)
A smooth, creamy, American-style amber ale with caramel notes.

Ink (OG 1050, ABV 5.2%)
A chocolate-malted porter with burnt toffee notes.

Spanner Hand (OG 1052, ABV 5.2%)
A sweet, strong English pale ale.

Towcester Mill SIBA

The Mill, Chantry Lane, Towcester, Northamptonshire, NN12 6AD
☎ (01327) 437060 ☎ 07812 366369
⊕ towcestermillbrewery.co.uk

⊠ A five-barrel brew plant situated at the Old Mill in Towcester, brewing a range of Towcester Mill beers. There is a brewery tap and shop on site. ‼️🍽◆

Crooked Hooker (OG 1040, ABV 3.8%)
Amber-coloured session ale with a satisfying bitter finish.

Mill Race (OG 1040, ABV 3.9%)
A blonde beer with a herbal and grapefruit finish.

Bell Ringer (OG 1044, ABV 4.4%)
A golden-coloured ale with subtle malt tones, and orange and citrus notes from the hops.

Black Fire (OG 1050, ABV 5.2%)
Brewed using selected malts, adding only colour, allowing the dark fruit aromas of the hops to come through.

Tower SIBA

Old Water Tower, Walsitch Maltings, Glensyl Way, Burton upon Trent, Staffordshire, DE14 1PZ
☎ (01283) 562888 ⊕ towerbrewery.co.uk

☺ Tower was established in 2001 by John Mills, formerly a brewer at Burton Bridge, in a converted derelict water tower of Thomas Salt's Brewery. The conversion was given a Civic Society award for the restoration of a historic building in 2001. Tower has 20 regular outlets. ‼️🍽◆

Thomas Salt's Burton Ale (OG 1035, ABV 3.5%)

Bitter (OG 1042, ABV 4.2%) ◆
Gold-coloured with a malty, caramel and hoppy aroma. A full hop and fruit taste with the fruit lingering. A bitter and astringent finish.

Malty Towers (OG 1044, ABV 4.4%)

Gone for a Burton (OG 1046, ABV 4.6%)

Imperial Pale Ale (OG 1050, ABV 5%)

Towles' SIBA

Unit 11, Circuit 32, Easton Road, Easton, Bristol, BS5 0DB ☎ 321 3188 ⊕ towlesfineales.co.uk

Towles' is a 10-barrel brewery built in the tower style and run by Andrew and Anna Towle. The equipment was purchased from Berrow Brewery in 2011 and brewing commenced on the site in Easton in 2012. The Berrow beers continue to be brewed. The brewery includes a shop and tasting room. ‼️🍽◆RAIB

Old Smiler (OG 1041, ABV 4.1%) ◆
Slight aroma of malt. Taste is malty with a little pale fruit. Malty aftertaste.

Berrow Copper Leaf (OG 1042, ABV 4.2%) ◆
A malty beer with a malty aroma and malty taste. Some dark fruit. Malty aftertaste.

For Whom the Bell (OG 1043, ABV 4.5%)
A malty taste with a hoppy aroma.

Ma Beese's Chocolate Stout (OG 1065, ABV 6.9%)

Town Mill

See Lyme Regis

Townes

🛢 **Speedwell Inn, Lowgates, Staveley, Derbyshire, S43 3TT**
☎ (01246) 472252 ✉ townesbrew@gmail.com

Townes Brewery started in 1994 and has been situated at the rear of the Speedwell Inn, Staveley, since 1997. After the retirement of brewer Alan Wood in 2013, Lawrie and Nicoleta Evans have continued brewing to the same recipes on the five-barrel plant. ◆

Speedwell Bitter (OG 1039, ABV 3.9%) ◆
Straw-coloured session bitter with little aroma. Initially quite sweet leading to a bitterness developing in the long, slightly astringent aftertaste.

Staveley Cross (OG 1043, ABV 4.3%) ◆
Amber-gold best bitter with a faint banana aroma. Hoppy with bitterness present throughout, culminating in a short, dry, slightly astringent aftertaste.

Pynot Porter (OG 1045, ABV 4.5%) ◆
Red-brown porter with a faint malt and roast coffee aroma. Roast malt flavours combine with vine fruit, becoming increasingly bitter towards the finish.

Double Bagger (OG 1049, ABV 5%)

Townhouse

Units 1-4, Townhouse Studios, Townhouse Farm, Alsager Road, Audley, Staffordshire, ST7 8JQ ☎ 07976 209437 ✉ j.nixon2@btinternet.com

Townhouse was set up in 2002 with a 2.5-barrel plant. In 2004 the brewery scaled up to five barrels. Demand is growing rapidly and in 2006 two additional fermenting vessels were added. Bottling is planned. ‼️🍽◆

Track (NEW)

5 Sheffield Street, Manchester, M1 2ND
☎ (0161) 273 4832 ☎ 07725 692096
⊕ trackbrewing.co

Track Brewing Co is a microbrewery based in the heart of Manchester. Brewing began in 2014 using a nine-barrel plant producing a varied beer range and seasonals. ‼️🍽◆

Sonoma (OG 1040, ABV 3.8%)
A light pale with citrus and fruit aromas.

Ozark (ABV 4.4%)
An easy-drinking, well-balanced and refreshing American-style pale ale. Dry hopped with a pale malt backbone.

Mazama (ABV 5.5%)
Smooth, citrus IPA with spicy notes from the hops.

Toba (OG 1054, ABV 5.6%)

Tractor Shed SIBA

The Tractor Shed, Calva Brow, Workington, Cumbria, CA14 1DB
☎ (01900) 68860 🌐 tractor-shed.co.uk

Set up in 2009, as Mitchell Krause, beers were originally contract brewed. A new brewery opened in 2013 in an old tractor shed on the family farm. A cold store was fitted in 2014. Although initial focus was on bottled and kegged continental-style beers, its first cask-conditioned beer was produced in 2014. Hefe Weiss is also available bottle-conditioned. The brewery was renamed in 2014. Tractor Shed now contract brews various beers for Shindigger, mostly for bottle and keg. !! RAIB

Traditional Scottish Ales SIBA

See Black Wolf

Traquair House SIBA

Traquair House, Innerleithen, EH44 6PW
☎ (01896) 830323 🌐 traquair.co.uk/brewery

The 18th-century brewhouse is based in one of the wings of the 1,000-year-old Traquair House, Scotland's oldest inhabited house. All the beers are oak-fermented and 60% of production is exported. !! ♦

Bear Ale (OG 1050, ABV 5%)

Treboom SIBA

Millstone Yard, Main Street, Shipton-by-Beningbrough, North Yorkshire, YO30 1AA
☎ (01904) 471569 ☎ 07761 608662

Office: c/o Nova Scotia Cottage, Acaster Malbis, YO23 2PY 🌐 treboom.co.uk

Treboom began in 2011 using a 10-barrel plant with production going mainly to pubs within a 50-mile radius ♦

Tambourine Man (OG 1038.5, ABV 3.9%)
A deep golden-coloured ale with a hint of maltiness complemented by fruit flavours from the hops.

Yorkshire Sparkle (OG 1039, ABV 4%)
Pale ale with a fresh citrus taste.

Kettle Drum (OG 1042, ABV 4.3%)
Copper-coloured with a distinct fruitiness and robust hop flavours leading to a clean finish.

Hop Britannia (OG 1050, ABV 5%)
A hoppy strong pale ale brewed using only British hops. Honey in colour with intense citrus fruit and spice notes.

Très Bien (NEW)

36b The Manor, Main Street, Tur Langton, Leicestershire, LE8 0PJ ☎ 07976 310860
🌐 tresbienbrewery.com

Très Bien Brewery opened in 2014, supplying a small selection of pubs throughout Leicestershire. What began as a fictional brewery for the labels of home-brew Christmas presents now exists in a small, real, one-man brewery in a corner of Tur Langton.

Ponytail Pale Ale (OG 1034, ABV 3.4%)
A light and hoppy golden ale with a strong citrus aroma.

Killer Whale (OG 1040, ABV 3.8%)
An easy-drinking, light and hoppy session pale ale. Citrus and floral aromas with a delicate bitterness.

Cascade (OG 1048, ABV 4.5%)
A single-hopped pale ale, light and golden in colour with pronounced floral aromas.

Chinook (OG 1048, ABV 4.5%)
A golden, single-hopped pale ale with citrus and pine aromas.

Citra Special Pale Ale (OG 1046, ABV 4.5%)
A citrusy, single-hopped golden ale with tropical and mango flavours.

Simcoe Special Pale Ale (OG 1046, ABV 4.5%)
A straw-coloured, single-hopped golden ale with a pronounced tropical aroma.

Porter (OG 1052, ABV 5%)
A smoky, chocolaty porter.

Tring SIBA

Dunsley Farm, London Road, Tring, Hertfordshire, HP23 6HA
☎ (01442) 890721 🌐 tringbrewery.co.uk

Founded in 1992, Tring Brewery moved to its present site in 2010. It brews more than 130 barrels a week, producing a core range of nine beers augmented by monthly and seasonal specials, most taking their names from local myths and legends. The brewery continues its practice of using international hop varieties in its monthly specials. !! ♦ RAIB

Side Pocket for a Toad (OG 1035, ABV 3.6%)
A straw-coloured ale with citrus notes and floral aroma with a crisp, dry finish.

Brock Bitter (OG 1036, ABV 3.7%)
A mid-brown quaffing ale with a hint of sweetness and caramel.

Mansion Mild (OG 1036, ABV 3.7%)
Smooth and creamy dark ruby mild with a fruity palate and gentle late hop.

Kotuku (OG 1039, ABV 4%)
A straw-coloured ale using New Zealand Waimea hops.

Ridgeway (OG 1039, ABV 4%)
Balanced malt and hop flavours with a dry, flowery hop aftertaste.

Moongazing (OG 1042, ABV 4.2%)
Amber, red-hued with a rounded bitterness and hoppy aftertaste.

Tea Kettle Stout (OG 1047, ABV 4.7%)
Rich and complex traditional stout with a hint of liquorice and moderate bitterness.

Colley's Dog (OG 1051, ABV 5.2%)
Dark but not over-rich, strong yet drinkable, this premium ale has a long dry finish with overtones of malt and walnuts.

Death or Glory (OG 1074, ABV 7.2%)
A strong, dark, aromatic barley wine.

Trinity Ales

Church Road, Gisleham, Suffolk, NR33 8DS
☎ (01502) 743121 ⊕ trinityales.co.uk

⊠ Trinity Ales was launched in 2009 using a four-barrel plant. It uses pure spring water from its own ancient well along with locally sourced ingredients. Pubs, restaurants, retail outlets and festivals are supplied throughout Suffolk, and beyond. RAIB

Wishing Well (OG 1039, ABV 3.8%)

Church Key (OG 1040, ABV 4.0%)

High Light (OG 1040, ABV 4%)

Black Street Smithy (OG 1045, ABV 4.5%)

Gisleham Gold (OG 1045, ABV 4.5%)

Triple fff SIBA 👁

Magpie Works, Station Approach, Four Marks, Alton, Hampshire, GU34 5HN
☎ (01420) 561422 ⊕ triplefff.com

⊠ Established in 1997 close to a stop on the Watercress Line, the brewery and all the beers except Alton's Pride are named following a musical theme. The fff refers to fortissimo, meaning louder or stronger. Brewing on a 50-barrel plant since 2006, multiple CAMRA awards have been won, including Supreme Champion Beer of Britain in 2008 for Alton's Pride. Two pubs are owned: the Railway Arms, Alton, and the White Lion, Aldershot. ‼🍴◆RAIB

Alton's Pride (OG 1039, ABV 3.8%) 🍺 ◄
Full-bodied session bitter. An initially malty flavour fades as citrus notes and hoppiness take over, leading to a lasting hoppy/bitter finish.

Pressed Rat & Warthog (OG 1039, ABV 3.8%) 🍺 ◄
Toffee aroma with hints of blackcurrant and chocolate lead to a well-balanced flavour with roast, fruit and malt vying with the hoppy bitterness.

Moondance (OG 1042, ABV 4.2%) ◄
An aromatic citrus hop nose, balanced by bitterness and sweetness in the mouth. Bitterness increases in the finish as fruit declines.

Trossachs Craft

See Tryst

Truefitt

3 Carcut Road, Lawson Industrial Estate, Middlesbrough, TS3 6QL ☎ 07883 072389
⊕ truefittbrewing.co.uk

☺ Truefitt began brewing in 2012 using a four-barrel plant producing up to 16 barrels a week. Vegan beers are available to order. ◆RAIB

Willow Beck Pale (OG 1039.5, ABV 3.7%)

Erimus Pale Ale (OG 1041, ABV 3.9%)

A pale session beer with a crisp aroma, floral and citrus notes and a bitter finish.

North Riding Bitter (OG 1042, ABV 4%)
A traditional bitter, loaded with hops, giving the beer an earthy nuttiness.

Ironopolis Stout (OG 1051, ABV 4.7%)
A bold stout packed full of chocolate and roast malt.

Mydilsburgh IPA (OG 1052, ABV 5%)
A well-hopped IPA with a spicy dry finish.

Truman's SIBA

The Eyrie, 2-4 Stour Road, London, E3 2NT
☎ (020) 8533 3575 ⊕ trumansbeer.co.uk

The legendary East London brewery, Truman's was reborn in 2013, 24 years after the original Brick Lane brewery's closure in 1989. The new brewery is a 40-barrel plant in Hackney Wick, just a stroll down the Roman Road from the original site. The original Truman's yeast, recovered from the National Collection of Yeast Cultures, is used. ◆RAIB

Swift (OG 1040.5, ABV 3.9%) ◄
Well-balanced golden bitter with hops and a trace of grapefruit on the nose and palate and a bitter finish.

Runner (OG 1040, ABV 4%) ◄
Traditional brown best bitter with spicy hoppy aroma and flavour fading in the dry aftertaste. Some marmalade fruity notes.

Tryst SIBA

Lorne Road, Larbert, Stirlingshire, FK5 4AT
☎ (01324) 554 000 ⊕ trystbrewery.co.uk

Tryst started production in 2003. A large range of beers is produced, all available in cask and bottles. Supermarkets across the UK are supplied. ‼🍴◆RAIB

Brockville Dark (OG 1039, ABV 3.8%)
A full-tasting session ale with hints of liquorice and roasted grains.

Brockville Pale (OG 1039, ABV 3.9%)
A pale golden session ale, smooth on the palate.

Hop Trial (OG 1040, ABV 3.9%)
Lager malt with a variable hop profile.

Bla'than (OG 1041, ABV 4%)
A strong floral nose and refreshing taste enhanced with elderflower and pale malts.

Drovers 80/- (OG 1041, ABV 4%)
A traditional, well-malted 80/- with an element of sweetness. A gentle nose complements a smooth finish.

Carronade Pale Ale (OG 1043, ABV 4.2%)
A pale ale bursting with citrus flavours.

Sherpa Porter (OG 1044, ABV 4.4%)

German Hops Pils (OG 1045, ABV 4.5%)

V.I.P. (OG 1046, ABV 4.5%)
Light brown best bitter, deep hop taste and floral nose

Zetland Wheatbier (OG 1046, ABV 4.5%)
Refreshing with a distinctive banana nose, a typical European cloudy wheat beer.

RAJ IPA (OG 1055, ABV 5.5%)
Exclusively English hopped with balanced flavours, with a hoppy aroma and palate.

Tudor SIBA

Unit 1, Llanhilleth Industrial Estate, Llanhilleth, Gwent, NP13 2RX
☎ (01495) 441308 ☎ 07775 684569
tudorbrewery.co.uk

Tudor is a family-run, four-barrel plant that began brewing in 2012. Several pubs are supplied locally, with others further afield. RAIB

Blorenge (OG 1038, ABV 3.8%)
A light, pale ale with a fresh citrus undertone.

Black Mountain Stout (OG 1039, ABV 4%)
A traditional stout brewed using malts and roasted barley.

IPA (OG 1039, ABV 4%)
A classic IPA with a sharp, hoppy, grapefruit finish.

Skirrid (OG 1040, ABV 4.2%)
A full-flavoured dark beer.

Sugarloaf (OG 1044, ABV 4.7%)
A medium dry beer, rounded and full-bodied with smooth caramelised undertones.

Winter Cheer (OG 1046, ABV 5%)
A dark ale infused with ground ginger, lemon rind, honey, cinnamon and nutmeg.

Black Rock (OG 1050, ABV 5.6%)
Bordering on a porter, this dark ale has a rich aroma and dark appearance with a smooth chocolate-coffee aftertaste.

Tunnel SIBA

c/o Unit 3, Southways Industrial Estate, Coventry Road, Hinckley, Leicestershire, LE10 0NJ ☎ 07765 223110 tunnelbrewery.co.uk

Tunnel was established in 2005 using a six-barrel plant. It relocated to new premises at Red House Farm, Ansley, Warwickshire in 2011. Following another move in 2015, it now brews using spare capacity at Elliswood (qv) in Hinckley, Leicestershire. !! ♦ RAIB

Percheron (OG 1037, ABV 3.7%)
Refreshing citrus pale golden ale.

Late Ott (OG 1040, ABV 4%)
Dark golden session bitter with a fruity nose and perfumed hop edge. The finish is dry and bitter.

Meadowlands (OG 1040, ABV 4%)
Pale golden in colour with a fruity, citrus taste and light hoppy aroma.

Trade Winds (OG 1045, ABV 4.6%)
An aromatic, copper-coloured beer with an aroma of Cascade hops and a clean, crisp hint of citrus, followed by fruity malts and a dry finish full of scented hops.

Parish Ale (OG 1047, ABV 4.7%)
A reddish-amber, malty ale with a slight chocolate aroma enhanced by citrus notes. It becomes increasingly fruity as the English hops kick in. Smooth, gentle hop bitterness in the finish.

Shadow Weaver (OG 1046, ABV 4.7%)
A dark stout starting with chocolate and roasted coffee on the tongue, developing through slight fruit into a dry, mellow, bitter finish.

Fields of Gold (OG 1048, ABV 5%)
Pale in colour with a hoppy taste and floral nose.

Nelson's Column (OG 1051, ABV 5.2%)
A ruby red, strong old English ale.

East India Pale Ale (OG 1058, ABV 5.9%)
Robust in flavour with a good hit of hops.

Turners SIBA

Highfield Farm, The Broyle, Ringmer, East Sussex, BN8 5AR
☎ (08456) 892689 ☎ 07896 598172
turnersbrewery.com

Turners began brewing in 2012, initially as a guest brewery in Hampshire, but moving to its own premises in Ringmer 2013.

Golden Ale (OG 1035, ABV 3.5%)
A floral, fruity and hoppy beer with a pleasant aftertaste.

Blonde (ABV 3.8%)
A refreshing fruity beer with a crisp dry finish. Full of subtle malty flavours.

East Sussex Bitter (OG 1039, ABV 3.9%)
A light, refreshing beer with a floral nose and a fruity and hoppy palate.

Best (OG 1041, ABV 4.1%)
A caramel-coloured traditional best bitter with a smooth yet complex flavour profile and a fruity aroma.

Ruby Mild (OG 1046, ABV 4.6%)
A fruity body with a smooth and subtle chocolaty finish.

American Pale Ale (ABV 4.7%)
A light-coloured, strongly hopped and bitter-tasting pale ale.

Porter (ABV 4.9%)
A silky body with rich malty flavours.

IPA (ABV 5.1%)
A smooth and hoppy IPA with a balanced flavour,

Turnstone (NEW)

20 West Cliff, Whitstable, CT5 1DN ☎ 07807 262662
turnstoneales@outlook.com

Turnstone Ales is a small, home-based brewery. Both cask-conditioned and bottle-conditioned beers are produced. The beers are supplied in cask to two local pubs while the bottle-conditioned versions are available at local outlets and on the brewers bottle stall at Faversham market. All the beers are suitable for vegetarians and vegans. RAIB

Three Seas Pale Ale (OG 1042, ABV 4.2%)

Columbine Pale Ale (OG 1044, ABV 4.4%)

Dolphin Ale (OG 1050, ABV 5%)

Ruby Porter (OG 1052, ABV 5%)

Turpin SIBA

Turpins Lodge, Lodge Farm, Tadmarton Heath Road, Hook Norton, Oxfordshire, OX15 5DQ
☎ (01608) 737033
turpinbrewery@btconnect.com

Brewing started in 2013. A number of local pubs are supplied regularly, as well as a few pubs further afield in Rugby and Birmingham. ♦

Golden Citrus (OG 1042, ABV 4.2%)

Tweed (NEW) SIBA 👁

Unit D1C, Newton Business Park, Talbot Road, Newton, Hyde, Greater Manchester, SK14 4UQ
☎ (0161) 368 8608 ⊕ tweedbrewing.com

Tweed began brewing in 2014 on a five- to six-barrel plant in a small unit on an industrial business park. ◆

Six Points (ABV 3.7%)
Amber-coloured ale packed with a delicate spice and pleasant bitterness.

Tweed Pale Ale (ABV 3.8%)
A straw-coloured pale ale with early pine and cedar notes making way for a subtle honey finish.

Twickenham SIBA 👁

Unit 6, 18 Mereway Road, Twickenham, TW2 6RG
☎ (020) 8241 1825 ⊕ twickenham-fine-ales.co.uk

⊠ The brewery was set up in 2004 using a 10-barrel brew kit and was the first brewery in Twickenham since the 1920s. It expanded to a 25-barrel plant in larger premises in 2012. Pubs and clubs are supplied within 25 miles of the brewery, including central London. ‼️ 🍴◆

Sundancer (OG 1037, ABV 3.7%) 🍺
Light, zesty, golden ale with citrus notes dominating from beginning to end. Finish is bitter but balanced by biscuity sweetness.

Grandstand Bitter (OG 1037, ABV 3.8%) 🍺
Pale brown beer with peach, citrus and malt on the palate, fading in the bitter, slightly dry finish.

Redhead (OG 1040, ABV 4.1%) 🍺
A creamy chestnut brown best bitter with interesting sweet caramel hints with a mild, short, roasted bitter finish

Naked Ladies (OG 1044, ABV 4.4%) 🍺
Refreshing dark golden ale with a touch of spicy hop in the flavour, but fruit dominates with a lasting bitterness.

Twisted SIBA 👁

Unit 8, Commerce Business Centre, Commerce Close, Westbury, Wiltshire, BA13 4LS
☎ (01373) 864441 ☎ 07512 261914
⊕ twisted-brewing.com

⊠ Twisted began brewing in 2014 using a new six-barrel plant. Outlets in west Wiltshire and north Somerset are supplied. ◆

Gaucho (OG 1038, ABV 3.6%)

Rider (OG 1041, ABV 4%)

Conscript (OG 1043, ABV 4.2%)

Pirate (OG 1043, ABV 4.2%)

Twisted Barrel (NEW)

▤ Unit 5, Fargo Village, Far Gosford Street, Coventry, CV1 5ED
☎ (024) 7610 1701 ⊕ twistedbarrelale.co.uk

⊠ Commencing commercial production as a pico-brewery in 2013 using a brew length of 60 litres, Twisted Barrel expanded to a six-barrel brewery and moved to its new location in Fargo Village in 2015. A brewery tap house opened to the public in summer 2015. All beers are suitable for vegans. ‼️ 🍴 RAIB

Beast of a Midland Mild (OG 1041, ABV 3.4%)

Sine Qua Non (OG 1046, ABV 4.6%)

Inspired (OG 1050, ABV 5%)

Saison from Another Place (OG 1052, ABV 5.2%)

Gods Twisted Sister (OG 1056, ABV 5.7%)

Call of Korriban (OG 1056, ABV 6%)

In Amber Clad (OG 1059, ABV 6%)

Twisted Oak SIBA 👁

Yeowood Farm, Iwood Lane, Wrington, Somerset, BS40 5NU ☎ 07917 457797
⊕ twistedoakbrewery.co.uk

⊠ Twisted Oak began brewing in 2012 using a five-barrel plant. ◆RAIB

Fallen Tree (OG 1038, ABV 3.8%) 🍺
Superb bittersweet session bitter. Aroma and flavour of hops and ripe fruit. Complex and satisfying bitter, astringent finish.

Wild Wood (OG 1040, ABV 4%) 🍺
Little aroma. Very smooth, with flavours of hops and fruit and a little malt. Minimal aftertaste.

Old Barn (OG 1045, ABV 4.5%) 🍺
Fruity red ale. Well-balanced flavour with a long bitter finish.

Spun Gold (OG 1045, ABV 4.5%) 🍺
Classic golden ale with a soft mouthfeel. Spicy notes balance the fruity malt aroma and flavour. Hops in the aroma develop into a bitter finish.

Two Beach SIBA

Ness Cove, Shaldon, Devon, TQ14 0HP
☎ (01626) 873427 ⊕ odetruefood.com/brewery

Two Beach began brewing in 2013 using the plant previously used at Ringmore Craft Brewery. They now produce three regular ales, with the occasional seasonal beer available. ◆

Ode Ale (ABV 4.2%)
A light amber ale with a citrus twist. Lots of hops but finely balanced with strong hints of elderflower.

Shaldon Shag Ale (ABV 4.2%)
A fruity, hoppy beer with a light malt and summer fruits aroma, with a hint of caramel. Zesty taste and a well-balanced finish.

Oarsome Ale (ABV 4.7%)
A dark amber ale with flavoursome hoppy tones. Aroma full of hops and barley, with a hint of sweet fruit. Smooth and easy on the palate with deep caramel flavours.

Two by Two (NEW) SIBA

Unit 19, Point Pleasant Industrial Estate, Wallsend, Tyne & Wear, NE28 6HA ☎ 07723 959168

Office: 14 Albany Gardens, Whitley Bay, Tyne & Wear, NE26 2DY ✉ twobytwobrewing@gmail.com

Brewing began in 2014 using a five-barrel plant. Three core beers are produced plus a different one-off special brewed every two weeks. Bottle-conditioned ales are planned. ◆RAIB

LeapFrog (ABV 4.1%)

Flying Rhino (ABV 5.2%)

Monkey Puzzle (ABV 5.4%)

Two Cocks SIBA

Church Lane, Enborne, Berkshire, RG20 0HB
☎ (01635) 47351 ☎ 07876 594501
⊕ twococksbrewery.com

⊗ The brewery was established in 2011 after wild hops were found growing in the farm's hedgerows. A 180-feet deep borehole supplies water for the brewery. Many local and regional outlets are regularly supplied. Most beer names refer to the 1st Battle of Newbury in the English Civil War. ☛

Diamond Lil (OG 1035, ABV 3.2%)
A light and fruity golden ale.

1643 Cavalier (OG 1039, ABV 3.8%)
A light, refreshing, thirst-quenching golden ale with a combination of hops.

1643 Leveller (OG 1040, ABV 3.8%)
A malty session bitter brewed with a single variety of old English hop.

1643 Roundhead (OG 1042, ABV 4.2%)
A full-bodied, smooth best bitter.

1643 Puritan (OG 1049, ABV 4.5%)
A dark stout with notes of caramel and chocolate.

1643 Viscount (OG 1054, ABV 5.6%)
An unusually fruity strong beer.

Two Rivers SIBA

2 Sluice Bank, Denver, Downham Market, Norfolk, PE38 0EQ
☎ (01366) 380131 ☎ 07518 099868
✉ denverbrewco@hotmail.com

Two Rivers was established in 2012 by John Nash. Bottle-conditioned ale has been available since establishment of the brewery and cask ales have been produced since 2013. All beers are suitable for vegans and vegetarians. ‼♦RAIB

Miners Mild (OG 1032, ABV 3.1%)
Easy-drinking tawny-coloured mild, with a good malt character, light finish and chocolate notes.

Hares Hopping (OG 1041, ABV 4.1%)
Refreshing, clean-flavoured bitter with a distinctive late bitterness and dry finish.

Kiwi Kick (ABV 4.1%)
A golden-coloured bitter with a pleasant hop aroma and zesty hop finish.

Denver Diamond (OG 1047, ABV 4.5%)
Bitter in colour with a fuller-bodied malty finish. A rounded bitter and malt taste with a grassy, slightly floral aromatic character.

Porters Pride (OG 1050, ABV 5%)
A full-bodied and well-balanced porter. Rich, with a slight sweetness cutting through the smooth malt. Coffee and chocolate aromas and taste, with a liquorice/vanilla finish.

Norfolk Stoat (OG 1050, ABV 5.8%)
A full-bodied, silky and well-balanced oatmeal stout with a subtle burnt edge.

Brewed for the Liberty Belle, Ely:

Penguin Golden Ale (OG 1043, ABV 4.4%)

Happy Hopper (OG 1047, ABV 4.5%)
Straw-coloured bitter with a fresh, green hop aroma and finish.

Brewed for the Wellington public house, Feltwell:

Almost Home (OG 1043, ABV 4.3%)

Feltwellington Golden Ale (OG 1046, ABV 4.7%)

Two Roses SIBA

Unit 9, Darton Business Park, Barnsley Road, Darton, South Yorkshire, S75 5QX ☎ 07780 701254
⊕ tworosesbrewery.co.uk

⊗ Two Roses started brewing in 2011 using an eight-barrel plant installed in a former carpet factory. Four core beers are brewed, supplemented during the year with special brews. ‼☛♦

Full Nelson (OG 1040, ABV 3.8%)

Chinook (ABV 4%)

Galaxy (OG 1040, ABV 4%)

Heron Porter (OG 1040, ABV 4.2%)

Two Towers SIBA

Unit 1, Mott Street Industrial Estate, 51 Mott Street, Hockley, Birmingham, B19 3HE
☎ (0121) 439 7253 ☎ 07795 247059
⊕ twotowersbrewery.co.uk

Established in 2010, the 10-barrel brewery has recently expanded into an adjacent premises. Most of the production is bottle-conditioned with cask making up about 40%. Seven regular ales are supplemented by six rotating specials. The brewery also undertakes bespoke brewing for special events, mainly local. ‼☛♦RAIB

Baskerville Bitter (OG 1038, ABV 3.8%)
Full-bodied bitter with a blend of four hops, providing a complex, but well-balanced ale.

Complete Muppetry (OG 1043, ABV 4.3%)

Chamberlain Pale Ale (OG 1042, ABV 4.5%)
A crisp light ale loaded with grapefruit flavours with a long hoppy finish.

Jewellery Porter (OG 1049, ABV 5%)
A full-bodied wholesome stout with a thick and slightly chocolate texture underlined with English hops.

Birmingham Special Ale (OG 1043, ABV 5.4%)
Maltly strong bitter with a full body, reflecting the flavours and characteristics of traditional English ales.

Tydd Steam SIBA

Manor Barn, Kirkgate, Tydd Saint Giles, Cambridgeshire, PE13 5NE
☎ (01945) 871020 ☎ 07932 726552
⊕ tyddsteam.co.uk

⊗ Tydd Steam Brewery opened in 2007 in a converted agricultural barn, using a 15-barrel plant since 2011. The brewery is named after two farm steam engines. Around 70 outlets are supplied direct. ‼♦RAIB

Barn Ale (OG 1038, ABV 3.9%) ⊡ ◆
A golden bitter that has good biscuity malt aroma and flavour, balanced by spicy hops. Long, dry, fairly astringent finish.

Piston Bob (OG 1044, ABV 4.6%) ◆
Malt and faint hops on the aroma progress through to a malty flavour complemented by a balance of

hops and fruit. A long, dry finish rounds off this amber strong bitter.

Tyne Bank SIBA

Unit 11, Hawick Crescent Industrial Estate, St Lawrence Road, Newcastle upon Tyne, NE6 1AS
☎ (0191) 265 2828 ☎ 07989 426604
⊕ tynebankbrewery.co.uk

⊗ Tyne Bank began brewing in 2011. In addition to its core range, monthly specials and seasonal beers are available. ‼️🍴◆

Single Blonde (OG 1037, ABV 3.5%)
Light ale, slightly dry bitterness with hints of vanilla.

Pacifica (OG 1040, ABV 4%)
A well-hopped pale ale which uses four varieties of hops from countries bordering the Pacific ocean.

Monument Bitter (OG 1041, ABV 4.1%)
Smooth, balanced bitter with a berry fruit character.

Dark Brown Ale (OG 1042, ABV 4.2%)
Newcastle-brewed dark brown ale.

Silver Dollar (OG 1050, ABV 4.9%)
Hoppy American-style ale with lasting bitterness and a citrus kick.

Southern Star (OG 1051, ABV 5%)
A New Zealand-style IPA with a bold fruity aroma and crushed grapefruit flavour.

Uffa

White Lion Inn, Lower Street, Lower Ufford, Suffolk, IP13 6DW
☎ (01394) 460770 ⊕ uffordwhitelion.co.uk/brewery

Uffa began brewing in 2011 using a 2.5-barrel plant. It is situated next to the White Lion pub in a converted coach house. ◆

Fox (OG 1037, ABV 3.7%)

Golden Hoard (OG 1038, ABV 3.7%)
A golden-coloured ale with a spicy taste and earthy aromas.

Rædwald (OG 1037, ABV 3.7%)
A bitter, golden-coloured pale ale with a crisp refreshing citrus flavour.

Longboat (OG 1051, ABV 4.7%)
A light-brown, hoppy ale, bursting with citrus and caramel flavours.

Uley

The Old Brewery, 31 The Street, Uley, Gloucestershire, GL11 5TB
☎ (01453) 860120 ⊕ uleybrewery.com

⊗ Brewing at Uley began in 1833 as Price's Brewery. After a long gap, the premises were restored and Uley Brewery opened in 1985. It has its own spring water, which is used to mash Tucker's Maris Otter malt, and boiled with Herefordshire hops. Uley delivers to 40-50 outlets in the Cotswold area while brewing to capacity. ◆

**Hogshead Cotswold Pale Ale
(OG 1035, ABV 3.5%)** ◣

A pale-coloured, hoppy session bitter with a good hop aroma and a full flavour for its strength, ending in a bittersweet aftertaste.

Bitter (OG 1040, ABV 4%) ◣
A copper-coloured beer with hops and fruit in the aroma and a malty, fruity taste, underscored by a hoppy bitterness. The finish is dry, with a balance of hops and malt.

Laurie Lee's Bitter (OG 1045, ABV 4.5%)
A copper-coloured, full-flavoured, hoppy bitter with some fruitiness and a smooth, long, balanced finish.

Old Ric (OG 1045, ABV 4.5%) ◣
A full-flavoured, hoppy bitter with some fruitiness and a smooth, balanced finish. Distinctively copper-coloured, this is the house beer for the Old Spot Inn, Dursley.

Old Spot Prize Strong Ale (OG 1050, ABV 5%) ◣
A distinctive, full-bodied, ruby-coloured ale with a fruity aroma, a malty, fruity taste with a hoppy bitterness, and a strong, balanced aftertaste.

Pig's Ear Strong Beer (OG 1050, ABV 5%) ◣
A deceptively strong, pale-coloured beer with a light hop balance leads to a hoppy, fruity aroma and a smooth bitter finish.

Ulverston

Lightburn Road, Ulverston, Cumbria, LA12 0AU
☎ (01229) 586870 ☎ 07840 192022
⊕ ulverstonbrewingcompany.co.uk

☺The brewery occupies the octagonal bullring of the old livestock market. There is a bar that overlooks the brew-plant which opens by prior arrangement and during some local festivals. ‼️🍴◆

Flying Elephants (OG 1037, ABV 3.7%) ◣
Clean, refreshing yellow-coloured bitter, sweet and fruity with a dry citrus finish.

Celebration Ale (OG 1039, ABV 3.9%) ◣
Yellow-coloured fruity bitter with hints of tangerine and a notably sustained dry finish.

Harvest Moon (OG 1039, ABV 3.9%) ◣
A well-balanced, pale, hoppy bitter.

Another Fine Mess (OG 1040, ABV 4%) ◣
A refreshing, gold-coloured bitter. Initially fruity but with a rising bitterness.

Laughing Gravy (OG 1040, ABV 4%) ◣
Smooth and grainy brown bitter with a good mix of flavours.

Lonesome Pine (OG 1042, ABV 4.2%) ◣
A fresh and fruity pale gold beer; honeyed, lemony and resiny with an increasingly bitter finish.

Fra Diavolo (OG 1043, ABV 4.3%) 🍾

UnBarred (NEW)

33 Bolsover Road, Hove, East Sussex, BN3 5HQ
☎ 07850 070471 ⊕ unbarredbrewery.com

⊗ UnBarred uses a purpose-built brewery in the owner's garden. It produces beers in limited small batches, with some collaborations with other brewers and the local community including beekeepers and coffee shops. Six outlets are supplied. ‼️RAIB

Benchmark (OG 1047, ABV 4.7%)

Unsworth's Yard SIBA

4 Unsworth's Yard, Ford Road, Cartmel, Cumbria,
LA11 6PG ☎ 07810 461313 ⊕ unsworthsyard.co.uk

☺Opened in 2011, the 1.5-barrel plant was
upgraded in 2014 to a five-barrel one. The brewery
produces beers named after historic figures and
legends. Beers are available in Cartmel pubs and
other local outlets as well as the brewery's own
tasting room and fully-licensed bar. ‼🍴

Freedom Under Law (OG 1037, ABV 3.5%)
A light but full-flavoured amber-coloured ale with a
bitter finish.

**J.C. Dickinson's – Land of Cartmel
(OG 1038, ABV 3.7%)** ◆
Fruity and hoppy with a bitter finish.

Cartmel Peninsula (OG 1039, ABV 3.8%)
A mellow and sweet English bitter brewed with
100% Kent hops.

Crusader Gold (OG 1041, ABV 4.1%)
A crisp and refreshing golden ale with subtle citrus
finish.

**Cartmel Wharf Sandpiper Cask
(OG 1038, ABV 4.3%)**
A crisp, light blonde beer from lager malt and
delicately flavoured German hops.

**Sir Edgar Harrington's Last Wolf
(OG 1045, ABV 4.5%)**
A rich, malty bitter with red fruit and chocolate
flavours.

Untapped SIBA ⊚

Unit 6, Little Castle Farm Business Park, Raglan,
Monmouthshire, NP15 2BX
☎ (01291) 690074 ⊕ untappedbrew.com

Untapped was established in 2009. Beers were
intitally brewed at Whittingtons Brewery in
Newent, Gloucestershire, but in 2013 they moved
to their own plant in Raglan. The Whittingtons
range of bottled beers are also brewed here.
Untapped has developed its own core range of ales
and also experimental brews created primarily for
the bottled market. ‼🍴◆RAIB

Border Bitter (OG 1036.8, ABV 3.8%)

Sundown (OG 1038.8, ABV 4%)

Moonow (OG 1038.3, ABV 4.2%)

U.P.A. (OG 1043.6, ABV 4.5%)

Triple S (OG 1048.4, ABV 4.9%)

Crystal (OG 1052.3, ABV 6%)

Upham SIBA ⊚

Stakes Farm, Cross Lane, Upham, Hampshire,
SO32 1FL
☎ (01489) 861383 ⊕ uphambrewery.co.uk

⊗ Upham began brewing in 2009 and expanded to
a 30-barrel plant in 2013. It owns 12 pubs and
supplies more than 450 other outlets. 🍴◆RAIB

Tipster (OG 1036, ABV 3.6%) ◆
An easy-drinking and light golden ale. Initial
hoppiness and fruit is balanced by maltiness that
lasts into the finish.

Punter (OG 1039, ABV 4%)

Light amber-coloured ale with sweet and floral hop
aroma. A balanced flavour of refreshing bitterness
and maltiness with a dry, fruity finish.

Stakes (OG 1045, ABV 4.8%)
A full-bodied ale with striking bitterness, tastes of
grapefruit and toffee, and a hoppy finish.

Andrew Usher (NEW)

📃 32b West Nicolson Street, Edinburgh, EH8 9DD
☎ (0131) 662 1757 ⊕ andrewushers.co.uk

Formerly Usher's of Edinburgh, the renamed
Andrew Usher & Co started brewing in 2015 and is
based in a bar of the same name.

Happy Cycling 80/- (ABV 4.8%)

Usher's IPA (ABV 6%)

Vagrant (NEW)

Correspondence: Gould Street, Manchester, M4 4RN
☎ 07939 032080 ⊕ vagrantbrewing.com

A cuckoo brewery, established in 2014, using spare
capacity at other breweries based around
Manchester.

Vale SIBA ⊚

Tramway Business Park, Ludgershall Road, Brill,
Buckinghamshire, HP18 9TY
☎ (01844) 239237 ⊕ valebrewery.co.uk

⊗ Established in 1995 and initially based in
Haddenham, Vale moved to Brill in 2007. In 2010 it
expanded to 20-barrel brew plant. Five pubs are
owned, including the Hop Pole where sister
brewery the Aylesbury Brewhouse (qv) opened in
2011. ‼🍴◆RAIB

Brill Gold (OG 1035, ABV 3.5%)
Golden session ale with a full malt flavour, well-
balanced with fruity, slightly citrus hop aromas and
a soft bitterness.

Best IPA (OG 1036, ABV 3.7%) ◆
This pale amber beer starts with a slight fruit
aroma. This leads to a clean, bitter taste where
hops and fruit dominate. The finish is long and
bitter with a slight hop note.

Black Swan Mild (OG 1038, ABV 3.9%)
Dark and smooth with hints of chocolate and coffee
on the nose and a malty, dry finish.

Wychert Ale (OG 1038, ABV 3.9%)
A traditional Thames Valley beer. Woody flavours
are notable in this malty beer with a finish of port
and berries on the nose.

VPA (Vale Pale Ale) (OG 1042, ABV 4.2%)
An assertive, dry, hoppy ale with a citrus nose,
combined with a pronounced malt background.

Red Kite (OG 1043, ABV 4.3%)
Refreshing, chestnut-coloured beer with a bitter
finish.

Black Beauty Porter (OG 1044, ABV 4.4%) ◆
A dark ale, the initial aroma is malty. Roast malt
dominates initially and is followed by a rich
fruitiness, with some sweetness. The finish is
increasingly hoppy and dry.

Gravitas (OG 1047, ABV 4.8%)

A strong pale ale packed with hop and citrus flavours, rounded off by a dry, malty, biscuit finish. A pronounced hop aroma throughout.

Vale of Glamorgan SIBA

Unit 8a, Atlantic Trading Estate, Barry, CF63 3RF
☎ (01446) 730757 ⊕ vogbrewery.co.uk

☺ Founded in 2005 using a 10-barrel plant, Vale of Glamorgan has developed a reputation locally for its range of high-quality beers. Local pubs and clubs are supplied, and the beers are available nationwide via swap deals with other brewers. A recent overhaul of the beer range has seen some new additions to the portfolio. There are plans for the brewery to be sold to a small local pub chain, including all its beers and recipes, and free trade accounts. The core range of Vale of Glamorgan beers will remain available. ◆RAIB

Light Headed (OG 1040, ABV 4%)
A light, easy-drinking ale.

Original No. 1 (OG 1042, ABV 4.2%)
Classic-style best bitter, thirst quenching and tasty.

Grog-y-Vog (OG 1042, ABV 4.3%)
A typical Welsh-style bitter.

Nugget (OG 1043, ABV 4.3%)
A hoppy, refreshing golden ale.

Dark Matter (OG 1044, ABV 4.4%)
A deeply satisfying, complex, robust, blackcurrant stout with a fruity aftertaste balanced with liquorice, chocolate and coffee.

Dakota Red (OG 1045, ABV 4.5%)
American-style red ale, bitter and well-balanced with good hop flavours.

Rorke's Draught (OG 1046, ABV 4.6%)
A traditional best bitter, hops dominate but a good maltiness sits in the background.

Cwrw Dewi (OG 1050, ABV 5%)
Strong and satisfying with initial malt flavours balanced with powerful hoppiness to follow.

Valhalla

Valhalla Brewery, Haroldswick, Unst, Shetland, ZE2 9TJ
☎ (01957) 711658 ⊕ valhallabrewery.co.uk

The brewery started production in 1997, set up by husband and wife team Sonny and Sylvia Priest. A bottling plant was installed in 1999. A new brewery building was opened in 2012, converted from part of the former RAF SaxaVoord camp at Haroldswick. ◆

White Wife (OG 1038, ABV 3.8%) ◈
Predominantly malty aroma with hop and fruit, which remain on the palate. The aftertaste is increasingly bitter.

Old Scatness (OG 1038, ABV 4%)
A light bitter.

Simmer Dim (OG 1039, ABV 4%) ◈
A light golden ale. The sulphur features do not mask the fruits and hops of this well-balanced beer.

Auld Rock (OG 1043, ABV 4.5%) ◈
A full-bodied, dark Scottish-style best bitter, it has a rich malty nose but does not lack bitterness in the long, dry finish.

Sjolmet Stout (OG 1048, ABV 5%) ◈
Full of malt and roast barley, especially in the taste. Smooth, creamy, fruity finish, not as dry as some stouts.

Verulam

🏠 Farmers Boy, 134 London Road, St Albans, Hertfordshire, AL1 1PQ
☎ (01727) 860535 ⊕ farmersboy.co.uk

⊗ Established in 1997, Verulam is situated at the rear of the Farmer's Boy and produces beers for the pub, where a selection is always available. Beer is supplied locally and to CAMRA festivals. It also brews for the free trade under the Ale Craft name. The brewery is home to two 'cuckoo' breweries: the Private Brewery of Bob and That Little Brewery (qv). ‼RAIB

Half Nelson (OG 1029, ABV 2.8%)
A straw-coloured, low gravity beer with a big hop flavour and character.

Black Mild (OG 1033, ABV 3.3%)
Easy-drinking dark mild with rich dark malt tones.

Farmer's Delight (OG 1036, ABV 3.9%)
Straw-coloured beer with distinct hop aroma and flavour.

Run o' t' Mill (OG 1041, ABV 3.9%)
Copper-coloured session beer with a balanced flavour.

Farmers Joy (OG 1043, ABV 4.5%)
Ruby, almost black beer, with a combination of dark malt roast and citrus hop flavours.

Citra Hit (OG 1046, ABV 4.6%)
Pale ale with big hop character throughout.

Vibrant Forest SIBA

Unit 3, Gordleton Business Park, Bowling Green, Lymington, Hampshire, SO41 8JD
☎ (023) 8066 9204 ☎ 07921 753109
⊕ vibrantforest.co.uk

⊗ Located in the New Forest, Vibrant Forest began brewing commercially in 2011 using a one-barrel plant. This award-winning brewery has progressed to a 10-barrel capacity and now produces bottle-conditioned ales as well as cask ales. 🍺◆RAIB

Nova Foresta (OG 1038, ABV 3.8%)
An amber-coloured, hoppy bitter.

Flying Saucer (OG 1041, ABV 4.3%)
A full-flavoured golden ale with fruity, floral and citrus-like flavours. Fresh and hoppy with a long bitter finish.

Cydonia (OG 1046, ABV 4.7%)

Farmhouse Ale (OG 1043, ABV 5%)
A light golden ale with slightly peppery and spicy aromas, subtle bitter and fruity flavours and a dry finish.

Pale Ale (OG 1047, ABV 5%)
A bitter and crisp blonde ale, with tropical hop notes of lychee, mango and passion fruit.

Metropolis (OG 1100, ABV 6%)

Kaleidoscope (OG 1060, ABV 6.5%)

Village Brewer 👁

See Hambleton

Village Brewer: Brew Twenty2 (NEW)

c/o 22 Coniscliffe Road, Darlington, County Durham, DL3 7RG
☎ (01325) 354590 🌐 villagebrewer.co.uk

Part of the long-established Village Brewer (qv), this one-barrel microbrewery was established in 2015 in the old kitchen area at the multi-award-winning alehouse Number Twenty2, in Darlington. Its beers supply the pub. A nanodistillery is also at the premises.

Violet Cottage

Gwaelod-y-Garth Inn, Main Road, Gwaelod-y-Garth, CF15 9HH
☎ (029) 2081 0408

The brewery was established in 2012 in a converted outbuilding at the rear of the Gwaelod-y-Garth Inn, within the grounds of the licensee's private house. All brews are subject to availability as the brewer decides, rather than during a particular season. Most of the output is sold within the pub. ♦

VIP SIBA

Unit E, Hawkshill Business Park, Lesbury, Northumberland, NE66 3PG ☎ 07545 885352
🌐 thevillageinnpub.co.uk

Brewing began in 2012 using a five-barrel plant to serve the owner's pub, the Village Inn in Longframlington, and the local free trade. Around 150 outlets are supplied.

Village Bike (OG 1040, ABV 4%)

Village Copper (OG 1042, ABV 4.2%)

Village Ghost (OG 1045, ABV 4.5%)

Volden

35a Neville Road, Croydon, CR0 2DS

Antic acquired the former Clarence & Fredericks brewery in Croydon in 2015 and established a new brewery, Volden, to produce an exclusive beer for the company's estate of pubs in the London area.

VIM (ABV 3.8%)

Wadworth SIBAIFBB

Northgate Brewery, Devizes, Wiltshire, SN10 1JW
☎ (01380) 723361 🌐 wadworth.co.uk

Established in 1885 by Henry Wadworth, this impressive Victorian red-brick brewery dominates the market town. Traditional Shire horse-drawn drays deliver beer locally around Devizes. Wadworth has 250 pubs throughout southern England. !! ♦ RAIB

Henry's IPA (OG 1035, ABV 3.6%)
A classic session beer with malt-led flavours.

Horizon (OG 1039, ABV 4%)
A pale gold beer with zesty citrus and hop aromas and a crisp, tangy finish on the palate.

6X (OG 1040.5, ABV 4.1%)
Copper-coloured ale with a malty and fruity nose, and some balancing hop character. The flavour is similar, with some bitterness and a lingering malty, but bitter finish.

Bishop's Tipple (OG 1048, ABV 5%)
A golden-coloured brew giving well-balanced hop bitterness and a clean finish.

Swordfish (OG 1049, ABV 5%)
A full-bodied, deep copper-coloured ale flavoured with Pussers Rum.

Waen SIBA

Unit 7, Maesyllan Industrial Estate, Llanidloes, Powys, SY18 6YU
☎ (01686) 627042 🌐 thewaenbrewery.co.uk

Waen began brewing in 2009 on a five-barrel plant in Penstrowed. Increased demand saw the brewery relocate to its present address. Outlets across the UK and Europe are supplied, both direct and via wholesalers. The beers are available at the Old Mill bar, Llanidloes, and at the brewery's outlet, the Gravity Station, Cardiff. !! ♦ RAIB

TWA (OG 1030, ABV 3.7%)
British hops and malt give a complex, yet balanced, pale ale

Festival Gold (OG 1042, ABV 4.2%)
A well-hopped beer.

Pamplemousse (OG 1040, ABV 4.2%)
Pale ale full of American and New Zealand hops, fresh and zingy with a lingering finish.

Landmark (OG 1048, ABV 5.5%)
An IPA with full-on hop bitterness with a crisp citrus bite.

Chili Plum Porter (OG 1067, ABV 6.1%)
A sumptuous and fruity porter with rich dark fruit flavours and warm chilli tingle.

Snowball (OG 1073, ABV 7%)
A stout with dark chocolate, vanilla and coconut flavours. A teacake in a bottle.

Wagtail

New Barn Farm, Wilby Warrens, Old Buckenham, Norfolk, NR17 1PF
☎ (01953) 887133 🌐 wagtailbrewery.com

Wagtail Brewery went into full-time production in 2006. All beers are now only available bottle-conditioned and all are suitable for vegetarians and vegans. RAIB

Wainstones

Unit 9, Terry Dicken Industrial Estate, Station Road, Stokesley, North Yorkshire, TS9 7AE ☎ 07885 240226
🌐 stokesleybrewing.co.uk

Wainstones began brewing in 2010 using a 2.5-barrel plant set up in a small industrial unit in Stokesley, trading as the Stokesley Brewing Company.

Amber (OG 1038, ABV 3.8%)
Distinctive light golden-coloured ale with moderate bitterness and a pleasant floral nose.

Sandstone (OG 1040, ABV 4%)
Traditional brown-coloured ale with moderate bitterness and a pleasant aftertaste.

Ironstone (OG 1042, ABV 4.2%)

A classic rich and full-flavoured ale made with English malts and complex hops giving a smooth aftertaste.

Copper (OG 1043, ABV 4.3%)
A copper-coloured ale hopped with Cascade and Galena varieties.

Steel River (OG 1043, ABV 4.3%)
Traditional chestnut-coloured ale with medium bitterness, full of flavour from American hops.

Jet (OG 1045, ABV 4.5%)
An unusual black ale full of flavour with a hoppy aftertaste.

Transporter (OG 1045, ABV 4.5%)
A dark porter with a creamy head and a deep malty taste.

Wall's County Town

2 Binks Close, Standard Way Business Park, Northallerton, North Yorkshire, DL6 2YB
☎ (01609) 258226 ☎ 07810 123084
✉ Info@wallsbrewery.co.uk

Brewing began in 2011 on a 5.5-barrel plant. Beers can be found in more than 100 local outlets.
‼ ◆ RAIB

County Best (OG 1034, ABV 3.2%)

Summer Gold (OG 1036, ABV 3.6%)

Gun Dog Bitter (OG 1039, ABV 3.8%)

Keepers Gold (OG 1039, ABV 3.9%)

Brewers Gold (OG 1039, ABV 4%)
A malty-flavoured, golden session beer.

Darkside (OG 1040, ABV 4.4%)
A milk stout, creamy with a soft, sweet taste followed by a light bitterness.

Longevity (OG 1040, ABV 4.4%)
A dark ale brewed with chocolate malt and First Gold hops for an orange finish.

Beaters Choice (OG 1050, ABV 4.6%)

Explorer IPA (OG 1050, ABV 4.7%)

Wantsum SIBA

Units 22 & 23, Sparrow Way, Lakesview International Business Park, Hersden, Kent, CT3 4AL
☎ (0845) 040 5980 ⊕ wantsumbrewery.co.uk

⊗ Wantsum was established in 2009 by James Sandy and takes its name from the nearby Wantsum Channel. In 2012 a new plant was installed, increasing brewing capacity to 12 barrels. A new fermenter was delivered in 2015. Outlets are supplied throughout Kent and south-east London. ‼ ◆ RAIB

More's Head (OG 1034, ABV 3.5%)
A chestnut-coloured bitter with malt and roasted grains balanced against fruit and floral hops with a hint of citrus.

1381 (OG 1036, ABV 3.8%)
A light amber-coloured IPA combining pale and crystal malts with hops to give delicate citrus and herbal aromas.

Black Prince (OG 1036.5, ABV 3.9%)
A rich, full-bodied Kent mild, smooth on the palate with subtle hop notes.

Imperium (OG 1037, ABV 4%)

A deep amber-coloured best bitter; smooth biscuit malts and rich hoppy nose give balance.

Fortitude (OG 1039, ABV 4.2%)
This bitter combines four types of malt to give depth of body and has a pronounced hop finish.

Miller's Mirth (OG 1039, ABV 4.2%)
A copper-coloured floral and spicy bitter with a smooth hop finish.

One Hop (OG 1042, ABV 4.5%)
Wantsum's recent venture is to brew a one-hop beer; the hop will be changed every couple of months.

One Hop Amarillo (OG 1042, ABV 4.5%)

Dynamo (OG 1043, ABV 4.6%)
A crisp, light, golden-coloured ale; fruity and floral with an orange citrus twist.

Black Pig (OG 1044, ABV 4.8%)
A smooth beer with burnt chocolate and smoky malt notes mixed with delicate hop bitterness and floral notes; adapted from a Russian Imperial porter recipe.

Golgotha (OG 1047, ABV 5.5%)
A rich, deep and broad malt base gives this stout a long smooth finish. Hops are prominent on the nose with blackcurrant, liquorice and cedar.

Ravening Wolf (OG 1052, ABV 5.9%)
A light amber-coloured strong pale ale; toasted biscuit and rye malt flavours support a pine lemon hop crispness with a hint of vanilla.

Wapping

🏛 **Baltic Fleet, 33a Wapping, Liverpool, L1 8DQ**
☎ (0151) 709 3116 ⊕ balticfleetpubliverpool.com

☺Wapping brewery was established in 2002 in the cellars of the pub on the waterfront in Liverpool using the old Passageway Brewery plant. Stan Shaw, the brewer since inception, stood down in 2014. His assistant Angus Morrison stepped into the role and has introduced a new range of beers based around his native Scottish heritage. ◆ RAIB

70/- (Seventy Shilling) (OG 1038, ABV 3.7%)
Scottish-style heavy.

Baltic Gold (OG 1039, ABV 3.9%) 🍺
Hoppy golden-coloured ale with plenty of citrus hop flavour. Refreshing with good body and mouthfeel.

Baltic Pale (OG 1040, ABV 4%)
Pale hoppy bitter.

Summer Ale (OG 1042, ABV 4.2%) 🍺
Refreshing, golden-coloured beer with floral hops dominating the nose and taste. Some fruit also on the aroma and in the taste. Good bitterness throughout, leading to a dry, bitter aftertaste.

Stout (OG 1050, ABV 5%) 🍺
Roast coffee and bitter chocolate dominate the flavour.

Warwickshire SIBA 👁

Bakehouse Brewery, Queen Street, Cubbington, Warwickshire, CV32 7NA
☎ (01926) 450747 ⊕ warwickshirebeer.co.uk

A six-barrel brewery in a former village bakery which has been in operation since 1998. Beers are available from local farm shops, garden centres, wine specialists and supermarkets, and from the brewery's four pubs. ☒♦RAIB

Shakespeare County (OG 1034, ABV 3.4%)
A refreshing, low-gravity, deep copper-coloured ale with a fruity, spicy and floral aroma. Full bodied, soft and hoppy to taste.

Fusilier (OG 1039, ABV 3.9%)
A commemorative bitter to celebrate the homecoming of the 1st Battalion Royal Regiment of Fusiliers. A traditional classic bitter with a fruity, hoppy, malty aroma and sharp, light and malty taste.

Darling Buds (OG 1041, ABV 4%)
A refreshing, pale beer brewed with lager malt.

Duck Soup (OG 1043, ABV 4.2%)

Lady Godiva (OG 1042, ABV 4.2%)
An aromatic, golden-coloured ale, with honey and malt on the nose. A slightly sweet, biscuity maltiness is balanced by the rounded bitterness of the hops. The honeyed sweetness of the palate surrenders to a lingering bitterness in the finish.

Golden Bear (OG 1049, ABV 4.9%)
An assertive, golden-brown beer characterised by a long-lasting, slightly resiny bitterness, with a fruity, warming finish with hints of spice and orange.

Ball Stitcher (OG 1051, ABV 5%)
A proper IPA with good strength, but an easy-drinking golden bitter.

Kingmaker (OG 1055, ABV 5.5%)
A rich, fruity amber-coloured beer; easy-drinking considering the strength. A fruity, malty, toffee aroma leads onto a palate with overtones of spice and caramel. A warming alcoholic dry finish.

Watermill SIBA 👁

☒ Watermill Inn, Ings, Cumbria, LA8 9PY
☎ (01539) 821309 ☎ 07831 873300
⊕ lakelandpub.co.uk

☺Watermill was established in 2006 in a purpose-built extension to the inn. The beers have a doggie theme, dogs being welcome in the pub. The brewery was extended in 2008 with a new plant planned within the grounds. Beers are also sold under the Windermere Brewing Co name. ‼♦

Collie Wobbles (OG 1037.5, ABV 3.7%)
A pale gold bitter with a slight citrus taste. A good hop and malt balance gives way to a dry finish.

Black Beard (OG 1038, ABV 3.8%) ♠
Full-bodied, fruity, dark mild with hints of chocolate.

A Bit'er Ruff (OG 1041.5, ABV 4.1%) ♠
Hops dominate this beer. There is some fruit and sweetness but the bitter flavours take charge.

Ruff Justice (OG 1041, ABV 4.2%)
A malty, golden-coloured ale, well-balanced with caramel, light floral hops and a fresh, dry finish.

Windermere Blonde (OG 1041.5, ABV 4.2%) ♠
Light and creamy, fruity and sweet with good hop balance.

Isle of Dogs (OG 1044, ABV 4.5%) ♠
A complex fruity bitter with lasting flavours in the finish.

W'Ruff Night (OG 1047.5, ABV 5%) ♠
Straw-coloured, sweet and fruity, uncomplicated beer with bitterness in a short-lived aftertaste.

Dog'th Vader (OG 1050, ABV 5.1%) ♠
Intensely flavoursome porter: malt, caramel, roast, fruit and hops all vie for attention.

Tomos Watkin SIBA

Unit 3, Alberto Road, Century Park, Valley Way, Swansea Enterprise Park, Swansea, SA6 8RP
☎ (01792) 797300 ⊕ tomoswatkin.com

Brewing started in 1995 in converted garages in Llandeilo using a 10-barrel plant. The brewery moved to bigger premises in Swansea in 2000 and the plant increased to a 50-barrel capacity. Over 60% of production is bottled beers (not bottle conditioned). More than 600 outlets are currently supplied. ‼☒♦

Cwrw Braf (OG 1038, ABV 3.7%)
A clean-drinking, amber-coloured ale with a light bitterness and gentle hop aroma.

Blodwens Beer (OG 1045, ABV 4.5%)
Light blonde beer with delicate creamy finish with a hint of citrus.

Old Style Bitter/OSB (OG 1045, ABV 4.5%) ♠
Amber-coloured with an inviting aroma of hops and malt. Full bodied; hops, fruit, malt and bitterness combine to give a balanced flavour continuing into the finish.

Watts Brewing? (NEW)

☒ Magnet Freehouse, 51 Wellington Road North, Stockport, SK4 1HJ
☎ (0161) 429 6287 ⊕ themagnetfreehouse.co.uk

☺ Brewing began in 2014 initially producing three beers. Although some repeats are possible, a regular range is not planned. Beers are brewed to suit the season using the newest malts and hops available. ♦

Waveney

☒ Queen's Head, Station Road, Earsham, Norfolk, NR35 2TS
☎ (01986) 892623 ✉ lyndahamps@aol.com

⊠ Established at the Queen's Head in 2004, the five-barrel brewery produces three beers, regularly available at the pub along with other free trade outlets. ♦

East Coast Mild (OG 1037, ABV 3.8%) ♠
A traditional mild with distinctive roast malt aroma and red-brown colouring. A sweet, plummy malt beginning quickly fades as a dry roasted bitterness begins to make its presence felt.

Lightweight (OG 1039, ABV 3.9%) ♠
A gentle beer with a light but well-balanced hop and malt character. A light body is reflected in the quick, bitter finish. Golden hued with a distinctive strawberry and cream nose.

Welterweight (OG 1042, ABV 4.2%)

Weal (NEW)

Unit 6, Newpark Business Park, London Road, Chesterton, Staffordshire, ST5 7HT
☎ (01782) 565635 ⊕ wealales.co.uk

A small microbrewery established in 2014 on a one-barrel plant. It expanded to a six-barrel plant in 2015 and has plans to open a small bottling operation.

Sqweal (ABV 3.9%)

Wealy Hopper (ABV 4.2%)

Weals in Motion (ABV 4.6%)

Weal Noir (ABV 4.8%)

Unweal Stout (ABV 5%)

Potters Weal (ABV 5.5%)

Weard'ALE

▤ Hare & Hounds, 24 Front Street, Westgate, County Durham, DL13 1RX
☎ (01388) 517212

Brewing commenced in the Hare & Hounds in 2010. The beers are mainly sold on the premises but some have found their way to nearby beer festivals and other local pubs.

Challenger (OG 1038, ABV 3.8%)
Named after the hops, and with taste to match. A sharp and tasty bitter.

Gold (OG 1038, ABV 3.8%)
Refreshing, with light appearance but surprising body.

Fell Over (ABV 4%)
A mellow and refreshing session bitter.

Dark Nights (ABV 4.4%)
Dark and full-flavoured.

Weatheroak SIBA

Unit 7, Victoria Works, Birmingham Road, Studley, Warwickshire, B80 7AP
☎ (0121) 445 4411 (eve) ☎ 07798 773894

Office: Victoria Works, 33 Redditch Rd, Studley, B80 7AU ⊕ weatheroakbrewery.co.uk

⊠ The brewery was set up in 1997 at Weatheroak Hill. It is now in a spacious factory unit in Studley. Weatheroak supplies 40 outlets and its brewery tap is the nearby Victoria Works pub. ‼

St Udley Mild (OG 1034, ABV 3.4%)

Light Oak (OG 1036, ABV 3.6%) ◗
This straw-coloured quaffing ale has lots of hoppy notes on the tongue and nose, and a fleetingly sweet aftertaste.

Tillerman's Tipple (OG 1039, ABV 3.9%)

Weatheroak Ale (OG 1041, ABV 4.1%) ◗
The aroma is dominated by hops in this golden-coloured brew. Hops also feature in the mouth and there is a rapidly fading dry aftertaste.

Victoria Works (OG 1043, ABV 4.3%)
A pale, hoppy bitter with a citrus finish.

Redwood (OG 1047, ABV 4.7%)
A rich, tawny-coloured, strong but mellow beer with a short-lived sweet fruit and malt balance.

Keystone Hops (OG 1050, ABV 5%) ◗
A golden yellow-coloured beer that is surprisingly easy to quaff given the strength. Fruity hops are the dominant flavour without the commonly associated astringency.

Weatheroak Hill SIBA

▤ Coach & Horses, Weatheroak Hill, Worcestershire, B48 7EA
☎ (01564) 823386 (pub)

Weatheroak Hill brews at the busy Coach & Horses pub and restaurant near Alvechurch. The range has increased significantly over the past two years and currently includes about ten beers in a wide variety of styles. The beers are brewed mainly for the pub (which usually stocks five), although there are plans to make the beers available more widely. ‼◆

Weatheroak Hill Gold (OG 1035, ABV 3.5%)

Icknield Pale Ale (OG 1038, ABV 3.8%)

Radford Ale (OG 1040, ABV 4%)

Indian Summer (OG 1042, ABV 4.2%)

WHB (Weatheroak Hill Bitter) (OG 1042, ABV 4.2%)

Dark Horse (OG 1046, ABV 4.6%)

King O' the Hill (OG 1054, ABV 5.4%)

Websters (NEW)

▤ 73 Bridgnorth Road, Wollaston, West Midlands, DY8 3PZ
☎ (01384) 440315 ✉ grahams.place@yahoo.com

☺ Websters microbrewery set up adjacent to the Graham's Place pub, in Wollaston, in 2014. Beers are currently sold through the pub, with plans to supply the local free trade in due course.

GPA (OG 1045, ABV 4.5%)

Tarty Sara (OG 1051, ABV 5.1%)

Weetwood SIBA

The Brewery, Common Lane, Kelsall, Cheshire, CW6 0PY
☎ (01829) 752377 ⊕ weetwoodales.co.uk

☺Weetwood Ales began brewing in 1992 in a barn in the tiny hamlet of Weetwood and moved to a new 30-barrel plant in 2011. Since new ownership in 2014 there are plans to increase capacity and broaden the beer range. More than 300 outlets are supplied regularly.

Best Bitter (OG 1038.5, ABV 3.8%) ◗
Pale brown beer with an assertive bitterness and a lingering dry finish. Despite initial sweetness, peppery hops dominate throughout.

Mad Hatter (OG 1038.5, ABV 3.9%)
A red-brown beer with fruity and malty flavours throughout and spicy and floral notes.

Cheshire Cat (OG 1040, ABV 4%) ◗
Pale, dry bitter with a spritzy lemon zest and a grape aroma. Hoppy aroma leads through to the initial taste before fruitiness takes over. Smooth, creamy mouthfeel and a short, dry finish.

Eastgate Ale (OG 1043.5, ABV 4.2%) ◗
Well-balanced and refreshing clean amber beer. Citrus fruit flavours predominate in the taste and there is a short, dry aftertaste.

Old Dog Bitter (OG 1045, ABV 4.5%) ◗
Robust, well-balanced amber beer with a slightly fruity aroma. Rich malt and fruit flavours are balanced by bitterness. Some sweetness and a hint of sulphur on nose and taste.

Ambush Ale (OG 1047.5, ABV 4.8%) ◀
Full-bodied malty, premium bitter with initial
sweetness balanced by bitterness and leading to a
long-lasting dry finish. Blackberries and bitterness
predominate alongside the hops.

Oasthouse Gold (OG 1050, ABV 5%) ◀
Straw-coloured, crisp, full-bodied and fruity golden
ale with a good dry finish.

Weighbridge SIBA

▪ Penzance Drive, Swindon, Wiltshire, SN5 7JL
☎ (01793) 881500 ⊕ weighbridgebrewhouse.co.uk

⊠ The Weighbridge Brewery forms part of the
Weighbridge Brewhouse restaurant and bar, based
in the former home of Archer's brewery and once
part of Swindon Railway Works. Established in 2011
under the ownership of Anthony and Allyson
Windle and with the brewing skills of Mark
Wallington, formerly of Archers Brewery, and his
assistant Tim Sherod, this microbrewery continues
to offer an increasing diverse mix of ales to
supplement its core range. Take outs are available.
‼◆

Brinkworth Village (OG 1038, ABV 3.6%)
A light, hoppy refreshing ale with a floral, spicy
aroma. Easy-drinking session beer.

Best (OG 1044, ABV 4.3%)
Pale with a spicy aroma. A good bitter ale but with
a malty aftertaste.

Pooley's Golden (OG 1048, ABV 4.7%)
A robust, full-bodied, golden-coloured ale with
plenty of bitterness and with an unusual
gooseberry aroma. The aftertaste is an excellent
balance of malt and hop.

Weird Beard SIBA

Unit 5, Boston Business Park, Trumpers Way, Hanwell,
London, W7 2QA
☎ (020) 3645 2711 ⊕ weirdbeardbrewco.com

⊠ Brewing began in 2013 on an industrial estate
in Hanwell. The plant has since expanded and has
two new 20-barrel fermenters in addition to its six
10-barrel ones. Beer is mostly bottled, but some is
available cask conditioned. RAIB

Dark Hopfler (OG 1043, ABV 2.5%)
A hoppy, dark beer boasting pine and chocolate on
the nose. Roasted malt and sweet cocoa flavours
carry into the taste, which is balanced with
resinous hop bitterness.

Black Perle (OG 1053, ABV 3.8%) ◀
Coffee milk stout with roast notes throughout this
full-favoured, sweetish black beer. Finish has some
black roast bitter dryness.

Mariana Trench (OG 1048, ABV 5.3%) ◀
Passion fruit and citrus are noticeable throughout
this malty, sweet, golden beer. Bitterness builds
and lingers overlaid by dryness.

Decadence Stout (OG 1062, ABV 5.5%)
Cocoa and coffee play a key role, with a roasted
malt bill and smooth body.

Hive Mind (OG 1052, ABV 5.5%)
A hoppy red ale with a subtle honey aroma and
sweetness. A dry biscuit finish complements the
caramel flavours of the malts.

K*ntish Town Beard (OG 1054, ABV 5.5%)

An American wheat ale with bold US hop flavours
and a rich body and spiciness.

Hit The Lights (OG 1056, ABV 5.8%)
A clean, bitter IPA with plenty of fruity hop
character.

Fade to Black (OG 1063, ABV 6.5%) ◀
Balanced black IPA with some fruitiness. The beer
contains crystal rye and chocolate malt, which give
roast coffee notes throughout.

Welbeck Abbey SIBA 👁

Brewery Yard, Welbeck, Nottinghamshire, S80 3LT
☎ (01909) 512539 ☎ 07921 066274
⊕ welbeckabbeybrewery.co.uk

The microbrewery is housed in a listed barn at the
centre of the Welbeck country estate, and the brew
plant was previously used at Kelham Island. The
brewery, which opened in 2011, produces a range
of different styles of beer. Head brewer Claire
Monk trained at the Kelham Island Brewery after
studying microbiology at Sheffield University. ‼

Henrietta (OG 1035, ABV 3.6%)
Full of hop character with bitter notes balanced by
a citrus and grassy nose.

Red Feather (OG 1040, ABV 3.9%)
A traditional dark amber ale brewed with crystal
malt for subtle notes of caramel and toffee.

Harley (OG 1038, ABV 4.3%)
Lightly citrus pale ale brewed with American and
German hops.

Portland Black (OG 1043, ABV 4.5%) 🍷
A rich and smooth black beer, smooth with smoke,
liquorice and burnt toffee flavours and a distinctly
vanilla nose.

Cavendish (OG 1046, ABV 5%)
A blonde beer laced with zesty notes of grapefruit.

Wellcross

123 Tower Hill Road, Upholland, Lancashire, WN8 0DS

Brewing began in 2012 using a 2.5-barrel plant.
Brewing only takes place three or four times a year
with limited output and distribution.

Charles Wells IFBB 👁

Bedford Brewery, Havelock Street, Bedford,
MK40 4LU
☎ (01234) 272766 ⊕ charleswells.co.uk

☺ Charles Wells has been brewing in Bedford since
1876 when the founder built a brewery on the
banks of the Ouse River. It relocated to a new site
in Havelock Street in 1976. In 2006 Wells merged
its brewing and brands division with Young's of
Wandsworth when the London brewery closed and
the company became known as Wells & Young's.
Both run their own pub estates under their family
names. In 2014, however, the brands became
wholly owned by Charles Wells, which has restored
its original company name. It runs an estate of 200
pubs and brews beers for the Young's pub
company. In 2007, Wells bought the Courage
brands from Scottish & Newcastle (now Heineken
UK) and added the former McEwan's and Younger's
brands in 2011. ‼🍺◆RAIB

Eagle IPA (OG 1035, ABV 3.6%) ◀

A refreshing, amber session bitter with pronounced citrus hop aroma and palate, faint malt in the mouth, and a lasting, dry, bitter finish.

Bombardier (OG 1041, ABV 4.1%) ◆
A heavy aroma of malt and raspberry jam. Traces of hops and bitterness are quickly submerged under a smooth, malty sweetness. A solid, rich finish.

Burning Gold (OG 1041, ABV 4.1%)
A golden version of Bombardier.

Brewed under the Courage brand name:

Best Bitter (OG 1038, ABV 4%)
Good fullness mixed with a bitter/fruity palate, finished off with a fine mouthfeel.

Director's (OG 1043, ABV 4.8%)
A rich, fruity and full-bodied, chestnut-coloured classic ale.

Brewed under the McEwan's brand name:

IPA (ABV 4%)
A full-bodied, hoppy ale that delivers a citrus fruit aroma and a dry, refreshing finish.

Amber (OG 1037.2, ABV 4.1%)

Signature (OG 1043, ABV 4.8%)

Brewed under the Young's brand name:

Bitter (OG 1034, ABV 3.7%) ◆
This light-drinking amber bitter has citrus initially on the palate with sweet malt and a hint of hops that linger into a slightly dry and bitter finish.

London Gold (OG 1037, ABV 4%) ◆
A dark gold beer with a smooth mouthfeel. Citrus and malt in the low aroma, coming through more strongly on the palate and aftertaste with a little peach. Dry finish.

Special (OG 1043, ABV 4.5%) ◆
Pale brown in colour, this rounded best bitter has citrus throughout plus some slight creamy toffee, which balances the bitterness that grows in the aftertaste.

Weltons SIBA

1 Mulberry Trading Estate, Foundry Lane, Horsham, West Sussex, RH13 5PX
☎ (01403) 242901/251873 ⊕ weltonsbeer.co.uk

⊠ Ray Welton moved the brewery into a factory unit in 2003. More than 70 different beers are brewed every year. Pubs throughout the south-east and London are supplied. Bottle-conditioned beers are available and are suitable for vegetarians and vegans. ‼◆RAIB

Pride 'n' Joy (ABV 2.8%) ◆
A light brown bitter with a slight malty and hoppy aroma. Fruity with a pleasant hoppiness and some sweetness in the flavour, leading to a short malty finish.

Horsham Pale (ABV 3.7%)

Sussex Pride (ABV 4%)
A copper-coloured malty ale with berry fruit and nutty flavours and spiced rum aroma.

Old Cocky (ABV 4.3%)

Old Harry (ABV 5.2%)
Deep red-coloured beer with a malty but nutty flavour.

Churchillian (ABV 6.6%)

Burnt charcoal flavours with hints of treacle toffee and toast and berry fruit aromas.

Wensleydale SIBA

Manor Farm, Bellerby, North Yorkshire, DL8 5QH
☎ (01969) 622463 ☎ 07765 596666
⊕ wensleydalebrewery.co.uk

☺Wensleydale Brewery was set up in 2003 and currently operates on a five-barrel plant. It was taken over by Geoff Southgate and Carl Gehrman in 2013. Around 100 outlets are supplied direct.
‼ ⬛◆RAIB

Lidstone's Rowley Mild (OG 1032, ABV 3.2%) ◆
Chocolate and toffee aromas lead into what, for its strength, is an impressively rich and flavoursome taste. The finish is pleasantly bittersweet.

Bitter (OG 1036, ABV 3.7%) ◆
Intensely aromatic, straw-coloured ale offering a superb balance of malt and hops on the tongue.

Falconer Session Bitter (OG 1038, ABV 3.9%)
A fruity, malt-based session ale, copper in colour, with a long, bitter, dry finish.

Semerwater Summer Ale (OG 1040, ABV 4.1%)
Pale ale with citrus aromas. The clean, hoppy nose is balanced by a light, malty sweetness.

Stuka (OG 1045, ABV 4.2%)
An amber-coloured ale.

Coverdale Gamekeeper (OG 1042, ABV 4.3%)
A copper-coloured best bitter, with huge spicy hop flavours and a juicy malt flavour.

Black Dub Oat Stout (OG 1043, ABV 4.4%)
Black, silky and nourishing with a rich concentration of four different malts and oats.

Gold (OG 1044, ABV 4.5%)
Aromatic and spicy hop flavours, combine with the lightest of kilned malts to make a highly quaffable, light golden best bitter

Coverdale Poacher IPA (OG 1048, ABV 5%) ◆
Citrus flavours dominate both aroma and taste in this pale, smooth, refreshing beer; the aftertaste is quite dry.

Wentwell

Unit 16, Perkins Industrial Estate, Mansfield Road, Derby, DE21 4AW ☎ 07900 475755
⊕ wentwellbrewery.com

Wentwell Brewery was established in 2011 and began commercial brewing on a one-barrel set-up in the owner's garage, before moving to a three-barrel plant in a new commercial premises. Eight regular beers are produced with occasional seasonals and one-off brews. Several local outlets are supplied, with beers regularly available at Wentwell's two pubs, Derby micropub the Little Chester Ale House and the Last Post in Burton upon Trent. ◆RAIB

Jeremiah Mild (OG 1035, ABV 3.3%)
Smooth, dark and malty, with a lot of body.

Derby Pale Ale (OG 1039, ABV 3.8%)
A pale straw-coloured hoppy bitter.

Derbyshire Gold (OG 1039, ABV 3.9%)
A light, refreshingly hoppy and zesty session beer.

Justice for Gingers (OG 1040, ABV 4%)
A pale bitter infused with ginger.

Little Tick (OG 1040, ABV 4%)
Straw-coloured bitter, triple hopped for a fuller flavour.

Farm Hands' Bitter (OG 1042, ABV 4.1%)
A rich copper-coloured best bitter with a smooth rounded flavour and balanced bitterness.

Barrel Organ Blues (OG 1046, ABV 4.5%)
Golden brown, full-bodied premium bitter with a rich, malty flavour and aroma.

Nellie's Best (OG 1050, ABV 5.3%)
A full-flavoured strong bitter brewed with molasses.

Wentworth SIBA

Power House, Gun Park, Wentworth, South Yorkshire, S62 7TF
☎ (01226) 747070 ⊕ wentworthbrewery.co.uk

☺ Founded in 1999 in the power house in the grounds of Wentworth Woodhouse, a custom-built 30-barrel brewery was commissioned in 2006, now producing about 4,300 barrels a year. Bottled beers are brewed under the Wentworth and Barnsley Beer Company brands. ‼◆RAIB

Brewers Blonde (ABV 3.8%)

Imperial Ale (OG 1038, ABV 3.8%)
A tawny, bitter beer with a floral aroma and a hint of sweetness in the aftertaste.

WPA (OG 1039.5, ABV 4%) ◣
A well-hopped IPA-style beer that leads to some astringency. A very bitter beer.

Best Bitter (OG 1040, ABV 4.3%) ◣
A hoppy, bitter beer with hints of citrus fruits. A bitter note dominates the aftertaste.

Bumble Beer (OG 1043, ABV 4.3%)
A pale golden beer made with local honey.

Black Zac (OG 1046, ABV 4.6%)
A mellow, dark ruby-red ale with chocolate and pale malts leading to a bitter taste, with a coffee finish.

Oyster Stout (ABV 4.8%)

Gold (ABV 5%)

Wessex

Rye Hill Farm, Longbridge Deverill, Wiltshire, BA12 7DE
☎ (01985) 844532
✉ wessexbrewery@tinyworld.co.uk

⊠ The brewery went into production in 2001 and moved to its current location in 2004. 15 local outlets are supplied. Beers are also available through selected wholesalers. Beers are occasionally contract brewed when capacity permits. ◆

Stourton Pale Ale (OG 1038, ABV 3.5%)
A very pale, hoppy session beer with plenty of character.

Longleat Pride (OG 1040, ABV 4%)
A pale, hoppy bitter.

White Dwarf (OG 1040, ABV 4%)

Merrie Mink (OG 1041, ABV 4.2%)
A full-flavoured best with a strong hop aroma.

Warminster Warrior (OG 1045, ABV 4.5%)
Full-flavoured premium bitter.

Golden Apostle (OG 1048, ABV 4.8%)

Galaxy (OG 1050, ABV 5%)

Beast of Zeals (OG 1066, ABV 6.6%) 🍾

Russian Stoat (OG 1080, ABV 9%)
Dark and strong.

WEST

⬚ Binnie Place, Glasgow Green, Glasgow, G40 1AW
☎ (0141) 550 0135 ⊕ westbeer.com

No real ale. Brewery-bar and restaurant, producing German-style beer to the Bavarian Purity Law. Beers are usually served under pressure, but not pasteurised. Four regular beers are produced. ‼◆

West Berkshire SIBA ◉

The Flour Barn, Frilsham Home Farm Units, Yattendon, Berkshire, RG18 0XT
☎ (01635) 202968 ⊕ wbbrew.com

⊠ Established in Frilsham in 1995 and now based on the edge of Yattendon, having moved to a new 50-barrel brewhouse, with office and shop, in 2011. Expanding following investment, brewing is carried out in a sustainable way, with an emphasis on British ingredients. A core range of cask ales supplies the south of England. In 2014, David Bruce, founder of the Firkin brewpub chain and then Slug & Lettuce bars, took over as chairman. ‼🍺◆RAIB

Mr Chubb's Lunchtime Bitter (OG 1041, ABV 3.7%) ◣
A drinkable, balanced, session bitter. A malty caramel note dominates aroma and taste and is accompanied by a nutty bittersweetness and a hoppy aftertaste.

Maggs' Magnificent Mild (OG 1041, ABV 3.8%) ◣
Silky, full-bodied, dark mild with a creamy head. Roast malt aroma is joined in the taste by caramel, sweetness and mild, fruity hoppiness. Aftertaste of roast malt with balancing bitterness.

Good Old Boy (OG 1043, ABV 4%) ◣
Well-rounded, tawny bitter with malt and hops dominating throughout. A balancing bitterness accompanies the taste and aftertaste.

Mr Swift's Pale Ale (OG 1043, ABV 4%)
A golden, fruity bitter made from a mixture of Fuggles and Goldings over a pale malt base, producing a very drinkable session ale.

Dr Hexter's Healer (OG 1051, ABV 5%) ◣
An amber-coloured strong bitter with malt, caramel and hops in the aroma. Taste is a balance of malt, caramel, fruit, hops and bittersweetness. Caramel, fruit and bittersweetness dominate the aftertaste.

Westerham SIBA ◉

Grange Farm, Pootings Road, Crockham Hill, Kent, TN8 6SA
☎ (01732) 864427 ⊕ westerhambrewery.co.uk

The brewery was established in 2004 at the National Trust's Grange Farm, and is housed in a former dairy. More than 500 outlets are supplied in Kent, Surrey, Sussex and London. ◆RAIB

Finchcocks Original (OG 1036.2, ABV 3.5%)

Mid-gold session beer. Citrus notes on the palate with a hint of biscuit and resiny hoppiness.

Grasshopper (OG 1039, ABV 3.8%)
A dark, malty bitter with nutty, roasted notes from the chocolate malt.

Spirit of Kent (OG 1039.5, ABV 4%)
Crisp golden ale with floral and fruity notes. Complex tropical fruit and citrus flavours blend with the sweet malt. Assertive dry hop notes on the finish.

British Bulldog (OG 1043.5, ABV 4.3%)
A rich, full-bodied best bitter with a massive aroma and palate of jammy fruit, biscuity malt and bitter hop resins.

1965 (OG 1047.5, ABV 4.8%)
A clean, refreshing bitter with a full-bodied flavour.

Hop Rocket (OG 1047, ABV 4.8%)
Traditional IPA with plum jam and blackcurrant aroma and palate, balanced by sappy malt and a long, lingering, bitter, fruity finish.

Audit Ale (OG 1061, ABV 6.2%)
Wonderful, hoppy, strong and bitter.

Brewed for the Spirit Pub Company:

Taylor Walker 1730 Special Pale Ale (OG 1040, ABV 4%)
Flavours of lemon balm, honey and blackcurrant, merged with grassy, earthy and botanical tones to create a well-balanced ale.

WH Buckley

See Evan Evans

Whaley Bridge

Elnor Avenue, Whaley Bridge, Derbyshire, SK23 7JR
☎ 07890 455279
✉ whaleybridgebrewery@gmail.com

Whaley Bridge Brewery was set up by a former home brewer and launched commerically in 2012. A one-barrel, purpose-built plant was installed in a workshop at the rear of the owner's premises supplying local free houses and eateries. Relocation to larger premises is planned for 2015. RAIB

Hockerley Ruby Ale (OG 1040, ABV 4%)
A fruity ruby ale with a hoppy aroma and a hint of treacle.

Anakena (OG 1042, ABV 4.2%)
A summer ale, pale and tropical.

Buxworth Ale (OG 1042, ABV 4.2%)
Fruity and flowery, with a hint of spice and a hoppy finish.

Goyt Valley (OG 1044, ABV 4.4%)
An earthy, golden-coloured ale with spicy notes.

Stoneheads (OG 1047, ABV 4.8%)
American and Slovenian hops and a blend of malt and wheat give a taste of citrus, a honey finish and a hoppy aroma. Complex.

Rapa Nui (OG 1047, ABV 4.9%)
A pale amber ale with subtle spice and a hint of orange.

Wharfe Bank SIBA 👁

Unit 4, Pool Business Park, Pool Road, Pool-in-Wharfedale, West Yorkshire, LS21 1EG
☎ (0113) 284 2392 ⊕ wharfebankbrewery.co.uk

Wharfe Bank commenced brewing in 2010 using a 20-barrel plant in a converted paper mill on the banks of the River Wharfe. The regular range of beers is complemented by two distinct series of monthly specials often featuring unusual ingredients or rare beer styles. ‼◆

Washburn Best (OG 1036, ABV 3.7%) 🔩
Easy-drinking malty session beer, more sweet than bitter, pale brown in colour.

Tether Blond (OG 1039, ABV 3.8%) 🔩
A moderately hopped, smooth, fruity light ale, with some lemon flavours which continue to the gentle finish.

Ro Sham Bo (OG 1043, ABV 4.2%)
Golden session IPA with a tropical fruit aroma and a crisp, refreshing finish.

Black Hawk (OG 1046, ABV 4.5%)
Black IPA that balances subtle malt flavour with a citrus-led aroma and long finish.

Yorkshire IPA (OG 1052, ABV 5.1%)
Powerful, amber-coloured IPA combining a robust malt profile with juicy, citrus bitterness in the finish.

Wharfedale SIBA 👁

🏠 Back Barn, 16 Church Street, Ilkley, West Yorkshire, LS29 9DS
☎ (01943) 609587 ⊕ wharfedalebrewery.com

Wharfedale began brewing in 2012 using spare capacity at Five Towns Brewery in Wakefield. Brewing moved to Ilkley in 2013 using a 2.5-barrel plant located at the rear of the Flying Duck pub. Special 'one-off' beers are brewed in addition to the core range.

Black (OG 1037, ABV 3.7%)
A smooth, well-balanced beer with lasting flavour. Subtle hints of chocolate, coffee and liquorice come together in this rich, dark mild.

Blonde (OG 1039, ABV 3.9%)
A straw-coloured session blonde ale with lingering citrus/grapefruit flavours and a fresh, satisfying bitter finish.

Best (OG 1040, ABV 4%)
A traditional chestnut-coloured Yorkshire bitter. Subtle malt flavours give way to a floral, spicy hoppiness and a mild bitter finish.

Whim SIBA

Whim Farm, Hartington, Derbyshire, SK17 0AX
☎ (01298) 84991 ⊕ whimales.co.uk

Whim opened in 1993 in outbuildings at Whim Farm. The beers are available in 50-70 outlets and the brewery's tied house, Wilkes Head in Leek. ◆

Arbor Light (OG 1035, ABV 3.6%)
Light-coloured bitter, sharp and clean with lots of hop character and a delicate light aroma.

Hartington Bitter (OG 1039, ABV 4%) ⬚
A light, golden-coloured, well-hopped session beer. A dry finish with a spicy, floral aroma.

Hartington IPA (OG 1045, ABV 4.5%)

Pale and light-coloured, smooth on the palate allowing malt to predominate. Slightly sweet finish combined with distinctive light hop bitterness. Well rounded.

Flower Power (OG 1053, ABV 5.3%)
Light, golden-coloured beer with a flowery hop aroma, citrus with mild spice on the palate and a dry, bitter finish.

Whistling Kite SIBA

35a Buccleuch Street, Kettering, Northamptonshire, NN16 9EE ☎ 07891 956055

Office: 23 New Road, Geddington, Northamptonshire, NN14 1AT ✉ phillipsjez@aol.com

⊗ Located in a former shoe factory, this six-barrel plant was established in 2013 by Jez Phillips. ♦

Starry Kite (OG 1038, ABV 3.6%)
Dark ruby beer with roast and biscuit notes.

Jai Ho (OG 1038, ABV 3.8%)
A light IPA with a tangy finish.

Wet Your Whistle (OG 1040, ABV 3.8%)
A well-rounded, mahogany-coloured session bitter.

Little Squirt (OG 1039, ABV 3.9%)
A copper-coloured bitter with a tangy bitterness.

Honeymoon (OG 1041, ABV 4%)
A golden-coloured ale with mellow honey tones.

Eleanor's Ise (OG 1041, ABV 4.2%)
A pale golden ale.

Whitby SIBA

Abbey Farm, East Cliff, Whitby, North Yorkshire, YO22 4JR ☎ 07516 116377 🌐 whitby-brewery.com

Whitby Brewery was established in 2012 under the Conquest name. It relocated in 2015 and is situated only a stone's throw from Whitby Abbey on the beautiful Cleveland Way. Events are held regularly at the brewery's Great Hall visitor centre. ‼

Abbey Blonde (OG 1036, ABV 3.6%)
A golden blonde ale with a zesty finish and strong notes of toffee.

Whaler (OG 1040, ABV 4%)
A fruity pale ale with a malty, citrus flavour and a bitter finish.

Saltwick Nab (OG 1044, ABV 4.2%)
A full-bodied ruby red ale with a pleasantly fruity finish.

Jet Black (OG 1047, ABV 4.5%)
A well-balanced porter packed with liquorice, coffee and sweet toffee.

Black Death (OG 1050, ABV 5%)
A stout porter full of liquorice with hints of chocolate.

IPA (OG 1054, ABV 5.1%)
A hoppy IPA with a floral aroma and grapefruit undertones.

Brewed for the Station Inn, Whitby:

Platform 3 (OG 1038, ABV 3.6%)
Nutty pale ale with a smooth citrus finish.

White Horse SIBA

3 Ware Road, White Horse Business Park, Stanford-in-the-Vale, Oxfordshire, SN7 8NY
☎ (01367) 718700 🌐 breweryoxfordshire.co.uk

⊗ White Horse was founded in 2004. The brewery now has its own pub in Oxford as well as supplying outlets nationally. Five regular beers plus specials are brewed. ‼ ♦

Bitter (OG 1038.7, ABV 3.7%)
Golden-coloured bitter, well-hopped with a clean, fruity finish.

Black Beauty (OG 1043.2, ABV 3.9%)
A rich, deep ruby mild.

Village Idiot (OG 1041.8, ABV 4.1%)
A blonde ale with a complex hop aroma and taste.

Dark Blue Oxford University Ale (OG 1045, ABV 4.3%)
A dark chestnut-coloured beer made using crystal and roast malts.

Wayland Smithy (OG 1047.1, ABV 4.4%)
A red-brown ale with a nice biscuit flavour that is balanced with a spicy hop finish.

White Park SIBA

Perry Hill Farm, Bourne End Road, Cranfield, Bedfordshire, MK43 0BA
☎ (01223) 911357 🌐 whiteparkbrewery.co.uk

⊗ White Park is a family business established in 2007 on a five-barrel plant. Spent malt is recycled as feed for rare breed cattle. 60 outlets are supplied direct. In 2009 the brewery began bottling and supplies pubs and local stores including Budgens. ♦

First Flight (OG 1036, ABV 3.7%)

White Gold (OG 1037, ABV 3.8%)

Bedford Best (OG 1040.5, ABV 4.1%)
Traditional best bitter, smooth and slightly biscuity witih a balanced bitterness.

Cranfield Bitter (OG 1042.5, ABV 4.4%)
Amber-coloured, malty, full-flavoured bitter.

Kellyhopter (ABV 4.8%)
Light yellow-coloured, malt-based ale with four varieties of hop.

GB (OG 1047, ABV 5%)

Moonshine (OG 1050, ABV 5.2%)

White Rock SIBA

Units 6 & 7, Dysons Complex, Southside, St Sampsons, Guernsey, GY2 4QJ
☎ (01481) 249920 ☎ 07911 760302
🌐 whiterockbrewery.gg

White Rock began brewing in 2013 in a modern industrial unit in the north of the island. It is gaining a foothold in the free trade on an island that is dominated by tied houses. ‼

Wonky Donkey (OG 1047, ABV 4.7%)
A distinctive, hoppy bitter with hints of citrus. Quite bitter on the tongue initially, this ale then settles nicely at the finish.

Lost Tourist (OG 1050, ABV 5.3%)
A full-strength IPA with a hoppy, citrusy and slightly caramel flavour. Refreshing, summer drinking, though not a session beer.

White Rose SIBA

119 Chapel Road, Burncross, Chapeltown, Sheffield, South Yorkshire, S35 1QL
☎ (0114) 297 6150
✉ whiterose.brewery@btinternet.com

☺Gary Sheriff, former head brewer at Wentworth brewery, set up White Rose in 2007. It shares the Little Ale Cart Brewery's premises behind the Wellington in Sheffield. Some equipment is used jointly but White Rose uses its own fermenters. ‼◆

Original Blonde (OG 1040, ABV 4%)

Stairway to Heaven (OG 1044, ABV 4.3%)

Raven (ABV 4.6%)

Whitewater

40 Tullyframe Road, Kilkeel, Co Down, Northern Ireland, BT34 4RZ
☎ (028) 4176 9449 ⊕ whitewaterbrewery.com

Set up in 1996, Whitewater is now the biggest brewery in Northern Ireland. One pub is owned, the White Horse in Saintfield, Co. Down. ‼◆

Copperhead (OG 1037, ABV 3.7%)

Crown and Glory (OG 1038, ABV 3.8%)

Belfast Black (OG 1042, ABV 4.2%)

Belfast Ale (OG 1046, ABV 4.5%)

Clotworthy Dobbin (OG 1050, ABV 5%)

Whitstable SIBA

Little Telpits Farm, Woodcock Lane, Grafty Green, Kent, ME17 2AY
☎ (01622) 851007 ⊕ whitstablebrewery.co.uk

Whitstable Brewery was founded in 2003. It currently provides all the beer for the Whitstable Oyster Company's three restaurants and hotel as well as a brewery tap, plus supplying pubs in Kent, London and Surrey. ◆

Native Bitter (OG 1036, ABV 3.7%) ◁
A classic copper-coloured Kentish session bitter with hoppy aroma and a long, dry bitter hop finish.

Renaissance Ruby Mild (OG 1038, ABV 3.7%)
Deep ruby in colour, this classic mild has a nutty taste with a gentle roast malt aroma.

East India Pale Ale (OG 1040, ABV 4.1%) ◁
A well-hopped golden IPA with good grapefruit aroma hop character and lingering bitter finish.

Oyster Stout (OG 1045, ABV 4.5%)
Rich, dry, deep chocolate and mocha flavours.

Pearl of Kent (OG 1043, ABV 4.5%)
A light-coloured, well-rounded premium golden ale with tropical fruit flavours.

Winkle Picker (OG 1042, ABV 4.5%)
A well-balanced amber best bitter. Pleasant maltiness offset by a firm but not overpowering bitterness and orange flavours.

Kentish Reserve (OG 1047, ABV 5%)
Reddish amber-coloured premium bitter. Malty notes with flavours of peaches and plums, ending on a note of rich ruby port.

Whittingtons SIBA ◉

Three Choirs Vineyards Ltd, Newent, Gloucestershire, GL18 1LS
☎ (01531) 890555 ⊕ three-choirs-vineyards.co.uk/wine/beers

⊠ Whittingtons started in 2003 using a purpose-built, five-barrel plant producing 20 barrels a week. The legendary Dick Whittington came from nearby Pauntley, hence the name and feline theme. ‼🚚◆RAIB

Whittlebury

See Towcester Mill

Why Not

27 Redfern Road, Norwich, NR7 9RB
☎ (01603) 300786 ⊕ thewhynotbrewery.co.uk

Why Not opened in 2006 with equipment located in a custom-built wooden unit. The brewery can produce up to two barrels per brew. All beers are available in bottle-conditioned form and are occasionally put into casks to order. RAIB

Wally's Revenge (OG 1040, ABV 4%) ◁
A bitter beer with a hoppy background. The bitterness holds on to the end as an increasing astringent dryness develops.

Roundhead Porter (OG 1045, ABV 4.5%)
A traditional old-style London porter.

Cavalier Red (OG 1047, ABV 4.7%) ◁
Explosive fruity nose belies the gentleness of the taste. The summer fruit aroma dominates this red-gold brew. A sweet, fruity start disappears under a quick, bitter ending.

Norfolk Honey Ale (OG 1050, ABV 5%)
A golden beer with a honey nose. A definite hop edge leaves a honey aftertaste.

Chocolate Nutter (OG 1056, ABV 5.5%)

Wibblers SIBA

Joyces Farm, Southminster Road, Mayland, Essex, CM3 6EB
☎ (01621) 772044 ⊕ wibblersbrewery.org.uk

⊠ Wibblers was established in 2007 and expanded to a 20-barrel plant in 2009. Production is currently 45 barrels per week. More than 100 outlets are supplied including many of the Gray & Sons pubs. ‼🚚◆RAIB

Dengie IPA (OG 1037, ABV 3.6%)
Malty and full-flavoured with gentle bitterness and balanced sweetness.

Apprentice (OG 1039, ABV 3.9%)
Amber session beer with a hoppy aroma and light, malty taste.

Dengie Dark (OG 1039, ABV 4%)
Smooth, light malty beer with subtle bitterness and balancing sweetness.

Dengie Gold (OG 1040, ABV 4%)
Golden with a refreshing hop punch providing a citrus aroma and balanced bitterness.

Hop Black (OG 1041, ABV 4%)
A dark bitter that tastes light and hoppy.

Dengie Best (OG 1041, ABV 4.1%)

A pale ale with a balance of malty mouthfeel and peppery bitterness.

Crafty Stoat (OG 1056, ABV 5.3%)

Wicked Hathern

See Staffordshire

Wickwar SIBA ◉

Old Brewery, Station Road, Wickwar, Gloucestershire, GL12 8NB
☎ (01454) 292000 ⊕ wickwarbrewing.co.uk

Wickwar was established as a 10-barrel brewery in 1990, expanding to 40 barrels in 2004. 350 outlets are supplied on a regular basis and the beers are available nationally through most distributors and SIBA. ‼🍴🍺◆

BOB (OG 1040, ABV 4%) 🍺
Amber-coloured with a distinctive blend of hop, malt and apple/pear citrus fruits. The slightly sweet taste turns into a fine, dry bitterness, with a similar malty-lasting finish.

Cotswold Way (OG 1042, ABV 4.2%) 🍺
Amber-coloured, it has a pleasant aroma of pale malt, hop and fruit. Good dry bitterness in the taste with some sweetness. Similar though less sweet in the finish, with good hop content.

Falling Star (OG 1043, ABV 4.2%)
A golden premium beer brewed with Warminster's Maris Otter malt and a blend of American and German hops giving a floral aroma and a light malty finish.

Wild Beer SIBA

Lower Westcombe Farm, Evercreech, Somerset, BA4 6ER
☎ (01749) 838742 ☎ 07968 721841
⊕ wildbeerco.com

Brewing began in 2012 using a 24-hectolitre plant. Cask, keg and bottle-conditioned beers are available. ◆RAIB

Bibble (ABV 4.2%)
Pale ale with tropical fruits and mangoes. Unfined, so is naturally hazy.

Scarlet Fever (ABV 4.8%)
A classic British-style ale. New World hops balance the caramel and bready sweetness of English malts.

Fresh (ABV 5.5%)
Fragrant pale ale made with both northern and southern hemisphere hops.

Madness IPA (ABV 6.8%)
Highly-hopped American-style pale ale.

Wild Boar SIBA

🍴 Wild Boar, Crook Road, Bowness-on-Windermere, Cumbria, LA23 3NF
☎ (08458) 504604 ⊕ englishlakes.co.uk/the-wild-boar-inn-brewhouse

⊗ Large, traditional Lakeland Inn in a luxury hotel style with its own microbrewery, on which brewing began in 2013. ◆

Blonde Boar (OG 1037, ABV 3.7%)

A light, refreshing ale with a zesty, fruity aroma and a light, clean body. Low in bitterness with an abundance of New World hops.

Mad Pig Ale (OG 1039, ABV 4%)
A classic, well-balanced session ale with a dry body.

Hogsheads 54 (OG 1054, ABV 5.5%)
A hoppy IPA with flavours of citrus and pine giving way to a bitter but clean finish.

Wild Card

Unit 7, Ravenswood Industrial Estate, Shernhall Street, Walthamstow, London, E17 9HQ
☎ 7982402650 ⊕ wildcardbrewery.co.uk

⊗ Wild Card began brewing in 2013, initially using spare capacity at several breweries in and around London. It now has its own six-barrel plant in Walthamstow. 🍺

Wild Card Pale (ABV 3.8%)

Jack of Clubs (ABV 4.5%) 🍺
Initially malty but the hops and bitter flavours develop on drinking in the red-coloured beer. Traces of blackberries.

King of Hearts (ABV 4.5%)

Queen of Diamonds (ABV 5%)

Wild Horse (NEW) SIBA

Unit 4, Cae Bach Builder St, Llandudno, LL30 1DR
☎ (01492) 868292 ⊕ wildhorsebrewing.co.uk

No real ale. Small craft brewery concentrating on supplying keg and bottled beers to local bars and off-licences. Brewery tours and a visitor centre are planned.

Wild Weather SIBA ◉

Unit 19, Easter Park, Benyon Road, Silchester, Hampshire, RG7 2PQ
☎ (0118) 970 1837 ⊕ wildweatherales.com

Wild Weather was established in 2013 on the Hampshire/Berkshire border. American and New World hops are used to create distinctive ales. 🍺◆RAIB

Sundowner (OG 1035, ABV 3.4%)
A light golden beer with subtle floral and fruity notes.

Big Muddy (OG 1038, ABV 3.8%)
Tawny session beer where smooth malty bitterness combines with floral spicy and mild citrus hoppy overtones.

Black Night (OG 1039, ABV 3.9%)
A dark mild, with a light taste that rapidly develops into a complex blend of rich malt and hop flavours and a hint of caramel. The aftertaste is long, dry, hoppy and toasty.

Little Wind (OG 1042, ABV 4.2%)
A deep amber-coloured ale with a touch of copper.

Stormbringer (OG 1044, ABV 4.5%)
Malty and hoppy.

Shepherd's Warning (OG 1056, ABV 5.6%)
A smooth, rich IPA with a hit of hoppy grapefruit, peach and mango flavours.

Williams

New Alloa Brewery, Kelliebank, Alloa, FK10 1NT
☎ (01259) 725511 🌐 williamsbrosbrew.com

Brothers Bruce and Scott Williams started brewing Heather Ale in 1993. A range of indigenous, historic ales has since been added. Hundreds of cask ale outlets are supplied worldwide.

Gold (OG 1040, ABV 3.9%)
Golden session beer with a crisp mouthfeel and lemony hop aromas.

Harvest Sun (OG 1041, ABV 3.9%)
A straw-coloured beer with a citrus aroma that gives way to a balanced and satisfyingly bitter finish.

Fraoch Heather Ale (OG 1041, ABV 4.1%)
The unique taste of heather flowers is noticeable in this beer. A fine floral aroma and spicy taste give character to this drinkable speciality beer.

80/- (OG 1046, ABV 4.2%)
A rich mahogany ale, with malt and butter aroma, biscuit texture, orange peel infusion, and a clean, satisfyingly sweet finish.

Black (OG 1042, ABV 4.2%)
A light-bodied, rich dark ale in the style of Czech dark lagers. Aromatic and full-flavoured with coffee and chocolate undertones and a blackcurrant aroma.

Roisin-Tayberry (OG 1040, ABV 4.2%)
A sweetish, fruity light pink beer with a distinct soft fruity aroma and flavour.

Birds & Bees (OG 1044, ABV 4.3%)
A bright, golden ale with a late infusion of fresh elderflowers and lemon zest. Fruity, aromatic and deliciously refreshing.

Cock o' the Walk (OG 1042, ABV 4.3%)
A classic red ale brewed with large amounts of crystal malt and hops from around the world.

Kelpie (OG 1045, ABV 4.4%)
A rich, dark chocolate-coloured ale, which has the aroma of a fresh Scottish sea breeze and a distinctive malty texture.

Red (OG 1045, ABV 4.5%)
A rich amber-coloured beer with a bouquet of caramel, amber malts and sweet berries giving way to a palate of biscuit malts, woody and fruity hops that deliver a medium dry finish. Toffee flavours and citrus hop aromas.

Good Times (OG 1050, ABV 5%)
Golden yellow in colour with a refreshing botanical aroma. Refreshing, fruity malty and aromatic.

Grozet (OG 1050, ABV 5%)
Lagered gooseberry beer. Crisp, fresh and clean tasting.

Joker IPA (OG 1050, ABV 5%)
A well-balanced, full-flavoured IPA with a complex layer of malts and blended hops. Golden in the colour, bittersweet and fruity on the nose with hints of cedar.

Seven Giraffes (OG 1051, ABV 5.1%)
Classic IPA with late infusion of elderflower. Gold-coloured with aromas of elderflower and citrus hops, followed by sweet caramel. On the tongue the biscuity malts are well balanced with the bitterness of the hops, freshness of the lemon and lingering floral elderflower aftertaste.

Midnight Sun (OG 1058, ABV 5.6%)
A rich, black, smooth porter with an afterbite of fresh root ginger.

Ebulum (OG 1062, ABV 6.5%)
Rich and dark, brewed with hops and bog myrtle then cold conditioned with fresh elderberries from a recipe taken from a 16th-century historic record in the Scottish Highlands. A dark, rich, fruity beer with a strong hop aroma and satisfying bitter conclusion.

Profanity Stout (OG 1068, ABV 7%)
Black in colour with full, floral, fruity aromas and a huge roasted malt character that gives way to a dry hopped bitter finish.

Alba Scots Pine Ale (OG 1075, ABV 7.5%)
A traditional Highland recipe spiced with spruce and pine with a complex wood flavour and a lingering finish. Rich-tawny coloured.

Willy Good Ale!

The Old Forge, Hartley Farm, Winsley, Wiltshire, BA15 2JB ☎ 07711 364202 🌐 willygoodale.com

Award-winning Willy Good Ale was set up by head brewer Will Southward in 2010 inspired by the hoppy, often strong beers he discovered during a trip to the US. The brewery upgraded to a six-barrel plant in 2011 due to demand. Shops, pubs, cafés and restaurants are supplied in the local area as well as beer festivals, parties and wedding around the country.

Willy Hop (OG 1040, ABV 4%)
Pale ale, dry hopped providing a fuller-flavoured beer.

Beerier Beer (OG 1042, ABV 4.2%)
An English single-hop amber ale.

High Fives (OG 1048, ABV 5%)
A strong IPA.

Hopadelic (OG 1048, ABV 5%)
Dry hopped pale ale with a floral aroma and hints of passion fruit.

Willy Brown (OG 1048, ABV 5%)
A nut-brown ale dedicated to the legendary blues singer Robert Johnson.

Wheat a Second (OG 1050, ABV 5.2%)
A refreshing wheat beer with a hint of orange and coriander.

Willy's

17 High Cliff Road, Cleethorpes, Lincolnshire, DN35 8RQ
☎ (01472) 602145

The brewery opened in 1989 to provide beer mainly for its in-house pub in Cleethorpes, although some beer is sold in the free trade. It has a five-barrel plant with maximum capacity of 15 barrels a week. The brewery can be viewed at any time from pub or street. ‼♦

Original (OG 1039, ABV 3.9%)
A light brown 'sea air' beer with a fruity, tangy hop on the nose and taste, giving a strong bitterness tempered by the underlying malt.

Wilson Potter SIBA

Unit E2 Hanson Close, Middleton, M24 2QZ

THE BREWERIES

☎ (0161) 654 6446 ☎ 07761 055567
🌐 wilsonpotterbrewery.co.uk

Wilson Potter was established in 2011 by two former home brewers, Kathryn Harrison and Amanda Seddon. RAIB

Cascale (OG 1038, ABV 3.7%)
Pale and hoppy beer.

Don't Fall (OG 1039, ABV 3.9%)
A light, hoppy pale ale made using lager malt.

Tandle Hill (OG 1040, ABV 3.9%)
A blonde beer with strong citrus flavours and aroma.

Triple Gem (OG 1040, ABV 3.9%)
A pale ale with oaken flavours and distinct notes of fresh blackberry.

Bon Don Doon (OG 1042, ABV 4.2%)
A refreshing pale ale with hints of lemon.

In the Black (OG 1048, ABV 4.2%)
Fruity, with roast malt and liquorice notes, with a sweet liquorice and roast finish.

Ruby Red (OG 1047, ABV 4.4%)
An easy-drinking rich ruby ale with a full-bodied malty berry taste and a floral hop finish.

In Shreds (OG 1047, ABV 4.7%)
A pale ale with notes of lemon and pine.

Wimbledon (NEW)

8 College Fields, Prince George's Road, Colliers Wood, London, SW19 2PT
☎ (020) 3674 9786 🌐 wimbledonbrewery.com

Set up by Mark Gordon after a 23-year career in the City, Wimbledon began production in summer 2015 with former Young's brewer Derek Prentice at the helm of a brand new 30-barrel plant. The initial range is focused on the finest English ingredients with additional seasonal brews and a range of more experimental 'New World' beers to come. !! ♦ RAIB

Common Pale Ale (ABV 3.7%)
Golden-coloured session bitter.

Tower SPA (ABV 4.6%)
Amber-coloured best bitter; floral and citrus aromas with a well-balanced finish.

Quartermaine IPA (ABV 5.8%)
English-style IPA; rich and punchy.

Wincle SIBA

Tolls Farm Barn, Dane Bridge, Wincle, Cheshire, SK11 0QE
☎ (01260) 227777 ☎ 07701 075368
🌐 winclebeer.co.uk

Wincle was set up in 2008 in a redundant milking parlour on a working farm set within the Peak District National Park. In 2011 it relocated to a new 15-barrel plant in Wincle. !! ♦ RAIB

Waller (OG 1038, ABV 3.8%)
A pale and refreshing beer with a distinctive hop character.

Rambler (ABV 4%)
A well-balanced beer with malt and autumn fruit hoppiness.

Life of Riley (ABV 4.2%)
Golden, straw-coloured blonde ale that is zesty and refreshing.

Sir Philip (OG 1041, ABV 4.2%)
Amber in colour, this premium bitter has light malty overtones, balanced with the classic pairing of Fuggles and Target hops.

Wibbly Wallaby (OG 1043, ABV 4.4%)
A full-bodied golden beer with fruity, hoppy overtones and a dry, slightly biscuity finish.

Windermere

See Watermill

Windsor & Eton SIBA

Unit 1, Vansittart Estate, Duke Street, Windsor, Berkshire, SL4 1SE
☎ (01753) 854075 🌐 webrew.co.uk

Four friends, including two fully-qualified brewers, set up the brewery in 2010 though their brewing experience goes back to the original Courage Brewery. The purpose-built plant is 18 barrels, which produces cask, keg and bottled beers for around 250 outlets in London and the Thames Valley area. !! ♦ RAIB

ParkLife (OG 1037, ABV 3.2%)
A full-flavoured light ale with a citrus aroma and taste.

Knight of the Garter (OG 1036.5, ABV 3.8%)
A straw-coloured golden ale with a distinctive fresh citrus hop aroma.

Windsor Knot (OG 1039, ABV 4%)
Amber ale with a grapefruit aroma. An initially sweet malt and fruit taste followed by a mild, bitter finish.

Guardsman (OG 1041, ABV 4.2%)
A tangy best bitter, tawny in colour, with a fresh hoppy finish mellowed with the use of oak during conditioning.

Conqueror (OG 1049, ABV 5%)
A complex black IPA, with a full roasted taste and intense hop aroma and flavour.

Windswept SIBA

Unit B, 13 Coulardbank Industrial Estate, Lossiemouth Moray, Lossiemouth, IV31 6NG
☎ (01343) 814310 ☎ 07896 897 944
🌐 windsweptbrewing.co.uk

Windswept began brewing in 2012 using a 10-barrel plant installed by John Trow of Oban Ales. It is situated near the gates of RAF Lossiemouth and run by two former Tornado pilots who are CAMRA members. !! RAIB

Blonde (OG 1039, ABV 4%)
A smooth, golden, citrus hoppy brew.

APA (OG 1046, ABV 5%)
A well-balanced maltiness leads to a long, tangy finish.

Weizen (OG 1052, ABV 5.2%)
Cloudy wheat beer with banana and pear drop flavours and a hint of spice.

Wolf (OG 1064, ABV 6%)
Dark, strong-tasting, roasted malty brew with coffee background.

Typhoon (OG 1062, ABV 6.2%)

Windy SIBA

Volunteer Inn, New Road, Seavington St Michael, Somerset, TA19 0QE
☎ (01460) 240126 thevolly.co.uk

Windy Brewery was established in 2011. The name of the brewery stems from the time when alterations were carried out to the back of the pub and the workmen suffered extremes of varying weather conditions. ♦

Tornado (OG 1039, ABV 3.9%)
Traditional brown bitter.

Southerly (OG 1042, ABV 4%)

Flurry (OG 1042, ABV 4.1%)

Fresh Breeze (OG 1043, ABV 4.1%)
Made for Burns night.

Hurricane (OG 1043, ABV 4.2%)
American-style IPA.

Northerly (OG 1050, ABV 4.8%)

Winning Post

Winning Post Pub, 6 Pope Iron Road, Worcester, WR1 3HB
☎ (01905) 21178

A small pub brewery established in 2014.

Ken Porter (ABV 3.7%)

Kevin Tully (ABV 3.9%)

Tick Tack Tommy Moore (ABV 4%)

John Mason (ABV 4.2%)

Winster Valley

Brown Horse Inn, Winster, Cumbria, LA23 3NR
☎ (01539) 443443 winstervalleybrewery.co.uk

Winster Valley was established in 2009 using a 2.5-barrel plant at the Brown Horse Inn in Winster. !!

Dark Horse (OG 1035, ABV 3.5%)
A dark, warming mild with soft mouthfeel and roasted malt aromas.

Hurdler (OG 1035, ABV 3.5%)
A golden ale with a hint of sweetness on the nose tilted towards the hops and soft malty flavour.

Best Bitter (OG 1036, ABV 3.7%)
Smooth and full-bodied, with a roasted malt flavour and a hint of caramel.

Lakes Blonde (OG 1037, ABV 3.7%)
An uncomplicated fruity, hoppy bitter.

Old School (OG 1037, ABV 3.9%)
Full-tasting pale ale, with floral aroma on the finish.

Chaser (OG 1041, ABV 4.1%)
Smooth, chestnut-coloured red ale, with caramel and toffee notes and a sweet bitter finish.

Winter's

8 Keelan Close, Norwich, NR6 6QZ
☎ (01603) 787820 wintersbrewery.co.uk

Winter's was established in 2001 by David Winter, who had previous award-winning success as brewer for both Woodforde's and Chalk Hill breweries. Winter's ales have won many awards, with David now passing his brewing knowledge to his son, Mark, an award-winning brewer in his own right. ♦

Mild (OG 1036.5, ABV 3.6%)
Classic red-brown mild with a nutty roast character. A well-balanced mix of malt caramel, and roast. Lingering bitter finish.

Cloudburst (OG 1037.5, ABV 3.7%)
Copper-coloured with a malty nose. A bitter beginning with malt and hop notes ends in a long, dry, finale.

Bitter (OG 1038.5, ABV 3.8%)
A well-balanced amber bitter. Hops and malt are balanced by a crisp citrus fruitiness. A pleasant hoppy nose with a hint of grapefruit. Long, sustained, dry, grapefruit finish.

Genius (OG 1041.5, ABV 4.1%)
A dark brown stout that has a smooth mouthfeel with a grainy edge. Roast dominates throughout but is balanced by a mix of malt, a bittersweet fruitiness and an increasingly nutty finish.

Golden (OG 1041.9, ABV 4.1%)
Just a hint of hops in the aroma. The initial taste combines a dry bitterness with a fruity apple buttress. The finish slowly subsides into a long, dry bitterness.

Revenge (OG 1047.9, ABV 4.7%)
Blackcurrant notes give depth to the inherent maltiness of this pale brown beer. A bittersweet background becomes more pronounced as the fruitiness gently wanes.

Storm Force (OG 1053, ABV 5.3%)
A well-defined, sweetish brew. Hops and vine fruit give depth to the malty backbone of this pale brown strong beer. All flavours hold up well as the finish develops a warming softness.

Wiper and True

2-8 York Street, St Werburghs, Bristol, BS2 9XT
☎ (0117) 941 2501 wiperandtrue.com

Launched in 2012 and originally using spare capacity at other breweries, it shared premises during 2014 with Ashley Down Brewery (qv). Since 2015 it has operated from its own 15-barrel plant. Most of its production is bottled or keg with a small amount going into casks.

Wizard SIBA

Unit 4, Lundy View, Mullacott Cross Industrial Estate, Ilfracombe, Devon, EX34 8PY
☎ (01271) 867260 bruce@wizardbrewery.co.uk

Established in 2003 in Warwickshire and moving to Devon in 2007, the brewery was taken over by Bruce Hutton and his team. They have revamped pumpclips and bottle labels, introduced new beers and taken on the Pier Brewery Tap & Grill in Ilfracombe to promote them. At present the beers are supplied only to the brewery tap. !! ♦

Young Apprentice (OG 1038, ABV 3.6%)

Lundy's Gold (OG 1042, ABV 4.1%)

Phoenix (ABV 4.2%)

Druid's Fluid (OG 1048.5, ABV 5%)

Thirst Borne (ABV 5%)

Wobbly SIBA

Unit 22c, Beech Business Park, Tillington Road, Hereford, HR4 9QJ
☎ (01432) 355496 ☎ 07702 739357
wobblybrewing.co.uk

Wobbly began brewing in 2013 using a 2.5-barrel plant and is an off-shoot of AJP Process Pipework. Four core beers are produced in addition to its 'Hop Headed' range of special brews. ♦RAIB

Wobbly Wabbit (ABV 4%)

Gold (OG 1036.5, ABV 4.2%)
A lightly hopped 3.8% traditional golden brown bitter.

Wobbly Welder (OG 1046.5, ABV 4.8%)
A golden-coloured strong bitter.

Wold Top SIBA

Hunmanby Grange, Wold Newton, Driffield, East Yorkshire, YO25 3HS
☎ (01723) 892222 woldtopbrewery.co.uk

An integral part of Hunmanby Grange Farm, Wold Top brewed its first ale in 2003 and uses home and Wolds-grown malting barley and chalk filtered water from the farm's own borehole. The beer range includes special edition cask and bottled beers plus a gluten free beer, Against the Grain. The brewery installed a bottling line in 2008 and contract bottles for other breweries. ♦RAIB

Bitter (OG 1036, ABV 3.7%)
A crisp, clean, aromatic session bitter. Full-flavoured with a long, hoppy finish.

Indigo Ale (OG 1037, ABV 3.7%)
An easy-drinking, crisp, single-hopped bitter. Only available at the Indigo Alley, Scarborough.

Anglers Reward (OG 1039, ABV 4%)
A refreshing, golden pale ale with a fruity bitterness and lingering aftertaste.

Headland Red (OG 1042, ABV 4.3%)
A mellow, malty red ale.

North Bay Premium (OG 1043, ABV 4.3%)
A smooth, malty-flavoured premium beer. Only available at the Old Scalby Mills, Scarborough.

Against the Grain (OG 1045, ABV 4.5%)
Made from lager malt, maize, hops and yeast, a full-flavoured bitter beer with refreshing bitterness and citrus aftertaste. The gluten content is certified to be well below the required codex standard of 20 ppm.

Wold Gold (OG 1046, ABV 4.8%)
A light-coloured summer beer with a soft, fruity flavour with a hint of spice.

Scarborough Fair IPA (OG 1060, ABV 6%)
Strong and well hopped.

Wolf SIBA

Decoy Farm, Norwich Road, Besthorpe, Attleborough, Norfolk, NR17 2LA
☎ (01953) 457775 wolfbrewery.com

The brewery was founded in 1996 on a 20-barrel plant, which was upgraded to a 25-barrel one in 2006. The brewery also has a bottling plant with an output capability of 2,000 bottles an hour. More than 300 outlets are supplied. ♦

Edith Cavell (OG 1037, ABV 3.7%)
A hoppy, thirst-quenching beer with a fruity finish.

Golden Jackal (OG 1039, ABV 3.7%)
A hoppy, citrus nose and first taste. Increasingly dry bitter ending as citrus notes fade.

Lavender Honey (OG 1037, ABV 3.7%)
Malty caramel aroma leads into a bittersweet beginning with background honey notes. A long drying finish.

Wolf in Sheep's Clothing (OG 1039, ABV 3.7%)
A malty, dark berry bouquet. Malt, with a bitter background, is the dominant flavour of this clean-tasting beer.

RAF Collection Battle of Britain (OG 1039, ABV 3.9%)
Signally malty throughout, a complex brew with caramel, vine fruit and an initial sweetness. Dramatic, quick bitter finale.

Wolf Ale (OG 1039, ABV 3.9%)
A copper-coloured, full-bodied ale.

Lupus Lupus (OG 1042, ABV 4.2%)
Hops, with a citrus edge, dominate both aroma and taste. A biscuity background disappears quickly in a short sharp finish.

Sirius Dog Star (OG 1044, ABV 4.4%)
Unique-flavoured, lightly hopped red ale. Smooth, with a soft, fruity finish.

Straw Dog (OG 1045, ABV 4.5%)
Delicately flavoured with a fruity character. A redcurrant aroma gives way to marmalade and hops. A strong increasingly bitter finale.

Silver Fox (OG 1045, ABV 4.6%)
Refreshingly zesty pale beer.

Mad Wolf (OG 1048, ABV 4.7%)
Smooth, dark and malty ale.

Granny Wouldn't Like It (OG 1049, ABV 4.8%)
Complex, with a malty bouquet. Increasing bitterness is softened by malt as a gentle, fruity sweetness adds depth.

Woild Moild (OG 1048, ABV 4.8%)
Heavy and complex with malt, vine fruit, bitterness and roast notes vying for dominance. Increasingly dry finish.

Grandma's Rich Porter (OG 1050, ABV 5%)
Pale and chocolate malts infused with English hops and spicy cloves give this beer a warming, smooth mellowness.

Contract brewed for City of Cambridge Brewery:

Boathouse (OG 1037, ABV 3.7%)
A light copper-coloured session bitter with a pleasant aroma.

Hobson's Choice (OG 1041, ABV 4.2%)
A pale-coloured ale with a refreshing, hoppy aftertaste.

Atom Splitter (OG 1045, ABV 4.5%)
A golden ale bursting with hoppy flavours.

Parkers Piece (OG 1050, ABV 5%)
A chestnut-coloured fruity beer with the long-lasting bitterness of Goldings hops.

Wollaton

Unit 4, Balloon Woods Industrial Estate, Coventry Lane, Wollaton, Nottinghamshire, NG9 3GJ ☎ 07879 664 702

Lenton Business Centre, Nottingham, NG7 2BY
⊕ thewollatonbreweryco.co.uk

Wollaton is a 1,000 litre brewery that started production in 2013 initially producing just bottled beers. Brewing is currently suspended.

Wood SIBA ◉

Wistanstow, Craven Arms, Shropshire, SY7 8DG
☎ (01588) 672523 ⊕ woodbrewery.co.uk

The brewery opened in 1980 in buildings next to the Plough Inn, still the brewery's only tied house. Steady growth over the years included the acquisition of the Sam Powell Brewery and its beers in 1991. Around 200 outlets are supplied. ‼◆

Parish (OG 1038, ABV 3.8%) ◣
A blend of malt and hops with a bitter aftertaste. Pale brown in colour.

Shropshire Lass (OG 1040, ABV 4%)
A golden ale with zesty bitterness.

Beauty (OG 1042, ABV 4.2%)
Mid amber colour. A fusion of fruity hops give a lingering bitter aftertaste together with a well-rounded maltiness.

Shropshire Lad (OG 1045, ABV 4.5%)
A strong, well-rounded bitter.

Wood Farm

See Kendrick's

Wood Street SIBA

▤ Hillsborough Hotel, 54-58 Langsett Road, Sheffield, South Yorkshire, S6 2UB
☎ (0114) 234 8307
✉ info@woodstreetbrewery.co.uk

Formally the Crown Brewery, Wood Street opened in 2012 under new ownership at the re-named Hillsborough Hotel in Sheffield. The brewery uses a four-barrel plant and has doubled output since it began. ‼RAIB

Elm (OG 1039, ABV 3.9%)
A session beer with citrus notes, a fresh and hoppy taste with a crisp refreshing aftertaste.

Hazel (OG 1040, ABV 4%)
A traditional amber-coloured bitter, very smooth on the palate.

Larch (OG 1045, ABV 4.5%)
A full-bodied, well-rounded golden ale with a crisp fruitiness.

Maple (OG 1045, ABV 4.6%)
A golden-coloured, mild honey beer with local honey added to give a well-balanced ale with a touch of sweetness.

Ebony (OG 1051, ABV 5%)
Dark stout with a ruby edge,with coffee and chocolate undertones and a big deep aroma.

Birch (OG 1051, ABV 5.1%)
A well-balanced strong pale bitter, smooth tasting with a distinct hoppy flavour with a long refreshing finish.

Tom Wood's SIBA ◉

Melton High Wood Farm, Melton High Wood, Melton Ross, Lincolnshire, DN38 6AA
☎ (01652) 680001 ⊕ tom-wood.com

The Tom Wood range of beers is brewed in the 60-barrel Highwood plant. The range consists of three permanent beers and quarterly seasonal beers. ◆

Best Bitter (OG 1035.5, ABV 3.5%) ◣
A good citrus, passion fruit hop dominates the nose and taste, with background malt. A lingering hoppy and bitter finish.

Lincoln Gold (OG 1041, ABV 4%)
Pale bitter with a fruity aroma and slightly zesty flavour but retaining malt characteristics.

Bomber County (OG 1046, ABV 4.8%) ◣
An earthy malt aroma but with a complex underlying mix of coffee, hops, caramel and apple fruit. The beer starts bitter and intensifies to the end.

Wooden Hand ◉

Unit 3, Grampound Road Industrial Estate, Grampound Road, Truro, Cornwall, TR2 4TB
☎ (01726) 884596 ⊕ woodenhand.co.uk

⊗ Wooden Hand was founded in 2004, and changed hands in 2015. The brewery supplies around 50 outlets with a high percentage of production being sold further afield via wholesalers. A bottling line was installed in 2005, which also contract-bottles for other breweries.

Pirate's Gold (OG 1040.6, ABV 4%) ◣
Yellow best bitter with hop aroma. Burst of hops with malt and bitterness, with caramel and fruit. Dry, bitter finish.

Cornish Gribben (OG 1041.6, ABV 4.1%)
A distinctive, well-hopped beer, with citrus and fruit notes. Well-balanced, bittersweet finish.

Cornish Buccaneer (OG 1043.6, ABV 4.3%)
A golden beer with full-flavoured hop character, good fruit and hop balance and a long, dry finish.

Black Pearl (OG 1050.6, ABV 4.5%)
A rich, nutty stout with good hop balance and dry chocolate finish.

Cornish Mutiny (OG 1048.6, ABV 4.8%) ◣
Tawny strong bitter with malt aroma. Sweet, biscuit malt and bitterness dominate the taste with fruit and dryness. Short finish.

Woodforde's SIBA ◉

Broadland Brewery, Woodbastwick, Norfolk, NR13 6SW
☎ (01603) 720353 ⊕ woodfordes.co.uk

⊗ Founded in 1981 in Drayton, Woodforde's moved to Erpingham in 1982, and then to a converted farm complex in Woodbastwick, with greatly increased production capacity, in 1989. Major expansion in 2001 saw a further increase in fermentation capacity and a new brewery shop and visitor centre. In 2008 a new Briggs's brewhouse, complete with hopback, was added. Woodforde's runs two tied houses, with around 600 outlets supplied on a regular basis. ‼☗◆RAIB

Mardler's (OG 1036, ABV 3.5%) ◣

Chocolate and roast aromas introduce this well-balanced dark mild. Vanilla, caramel and malt boost the dominant roast and chocolate flavours.

Wherry (OG 1037.5, ABV 3.8%) ◈
Amber-coloured with an orange citrus nose. A swirling mix of malt, hops, citrus and bitterness combine into a tangy marmalade dryness.

Once Bittern (OG 1040, ABV 4%) ◈
A light malty nose. A dark marmalade tang gives an edge to the dominant malt character. Long bittersweet ending.

Sundew (OG 1039, ABV 4.1%) ◈
Hops emerge from a mix of malt, fruit and bitterness to provide a cutting edge to both taste and aroma.

Bure Gold (OG 1043, ABV 4.3%)
A well-balanced blend of malt and hop with significant citrus and bitter contributions. Crisp and easy drinking.

Nelson's Revenge (OG 1045, ABV 4.5%) ◈
An infusion of vine fruit, malt and hops provide a rich, rewarding experience. A sweet, Madeira-like finale.

Woodlands SIBA

Unit 3, Meadow Lane Farm, London Road, Stapeley, Cheshire, CW5 7JU
☎ (01270) 841511 🌐 woodlandsbrewery.co.uk

◎ The brewery opened in 2004 and moved to larger premises in 2008. An extension in 2010 allowed for increased production. The beers are brewed using water from a spring that surfaces on a nearby peat field at Woodlands Farm. More than 100 outlets are supplied including the brewery's tied houses. ‼ ♦ RAIB

Mild (OG 1035, ABV 3.5%)
A dark mild ale.

Old Faithful (OG 1036, ABV 3.6%)
A pale session bitter.

Red Squirrel (OG 1038, ABV 3.8%)
A session bitter with a hint of blackcurrant

Hop as Hell (OG 1040, ABV 4%)
A pale beer with a long-lasting bitter finish.

Ash Blonde (ABV 4.1%)
A blonde, fruity ale with a lingering crisp aftertaste.

Oak Beauty (OG 1042, ABV 4.2%) ◈
Malty, sweetish copper-coloured bitter with toffee and caramel flavours. Long-lasting and satisfying bitter finish.

APA American Pale Ale (OG 1043, ABV 4.3%)
Hoppy pale ale with citrus flavours

Witch Prime (ABV 4.3%)
A pale hoppy ale with citrus aftertaste.

Best Bitter (OG 1044, ABV 4.4%)

Midnight Stout (OG 1044, ABV 4.4%) ◈
Classic creamy dry stout with roast flavours to the fore. Well-balanced with bitterness and good hops on the taste and a good dry, roasty aftertaste. Some sweetness.

New Leaf (OG 1046, ABV 4.6%)
A deep, rich, malty refreshing beer

Generals Tipple (OG 1055, ABV 5.5%)
A refreshing, medium-hopped IPA.

Wooha (NEW)

Unit 8A1, Balmakeith Business Park, Nairn, IV12 5QR
☎ (01667) 459929 ☎ 07811 260732
🌐 woohabrewing.com

Wooha opened in 2015 using a 10-barrel plant. It specialises in producing bottle-conditioned ales. Cask-conditioned beers are brewed on demand for beer festivals. Pubs and retail outlets are supplied locally, in Nairn, and across Scotland. RAIB

Worcester

Arch 49, Cherry Tree Walk, Worcester, WR1 3AU
☎ 07906 432049 🌐 worcesterbrewingco.co.uk

A six-barrel brewery in the heart of Worcester. The brewer is keen to use only traditional British hops.

Gyle 2 (OG 1040, ABV 4%)
Pale gold bitter packing a hop punch.

Gyle 1 (OG 1045, ABV 4.5%)
Light amber-coloured, fruity ale.

Worcestershire SIBA 👁

Hartlebury Brewery, Station Road, Hartlebury, Worcestershire, DY11 7YJ
☎ (01299) 253617
🌐 worcestershirebrewingcompany.co.uk

◎ Worcestershire Brewing Co was established in 2011 as Attwood Ales on a new 10-barrel plant to the rear of the Tap House, a conversion of the original Hartlebury station ticket office. It has five tied pubs. Beers are sold direct to free houses, clubs and pub companies in the Worcestershire and West Midlands areas. ‼♦

Gold (OG 1038, ABV 3.8%)
A refreshing golden beer that uses the Golding hop to its best. Packed with fruity, hoppy flavours, it has a malty, herbal aroma with a hint of orange.

Attwood's Pale Ale (OG 1039, ABV 4%)
A crisp, light and refreshing IPA, traditionally brewed, with a clean bitterness and hoppy aroma.

Farmers Dark Ale (OG 1043, ABV 4.2%)
A smooth, slightly smoky, dark session ale with a caramel finish.

Nectar Bitter (OG 1043, ABV 4.2%)
A well-balanced, light golden bitter with a gentle sweetness that counters the hops.

Attwood's Bitter (OG 1049, ABV 5%)
A tawny copper premium bitter with dried fruit aromas, rich and warming on the palate with a bite.

World's End

Crown Inn, 60 Wilcot Road, Pewsey, Wiltshire, SN9 5EL
☎ (01672) 562653 🌐 thecrowninnpewsey.com

⊠ World's End Ales was established in 2009 on a one-barrel plant at the rear of the Crown Inn in Pewsey. World's End is the 18th-century name for the area in which the brewery is located. ‼♦

Marilyn (ABV 3.7%)

Diana (ABV 3.9%)

Mercian Incursion (OG 1039, ABV 4%)
A golden-coloured ale.

Bitterus Magnus (OG 1041, ABV 4.1%)
A well-balanced, chestnut-coloured ale with a good malt, low bitter flavour with a sweet finish.

Pewsey Mild (OG 1048, ABV 4.8%)
A dark-coloured mild full of roasted malt flavours with a sweet finish.

Worsthorne SIBA

Unit 11, Siberia Mill, Holgate Street, Briercliffe, Burnley, Lancashire, BB10 2HQ
☎ (01282) 422588 ☎ 07815 708289
worsthornebrewingcompany.co.uk

Worsthorne began brewing in 2011 using a 5.5-barrel plant. More than 100 outlets are supplied direct. The brewery moved to a larger premises in 2014, behind the original building. ♦

Gold (OG 1036, ABV 3.6%)
Lightly bittered golden ale with a spicy aroma.

Packhorse (OG 1037, ABV 3.7%)
Pale amber ale with subtle earthy bitterness and floral spicy finish.

Foxstones (OG 1039, ABV 3.9%)
Traditional-style amber bitter with well-balanced hoppy aroma and lingering floral aftertaste.

Some Like It Blond (OG 1039, ABV 3.9%)
A blonde beer with a lingering dry aftertaste.

Redman (OG 1042, ABV 4.2%)
Smooth, well-flavoured light bitter. Overtones of honey and citrus with satisfying aftertaste and subtle lingering bitterness.

Old Trout (OG 1045, ABV 4.5%)
Well-flavoured red/brown ale.

Blackthorn Stout (OG 1049, ABV 4.9%)
Rich dark stout with distinct chocolate and liquorice flavours, a hint of ripe berries and a smooth bitter aftertaste.

Colliers Clog (OG 1055, ABV 5.5%)
A strong pale ale, lightly bittered with spicy overtones and a citrus finish.

Worthington's

See Brains

Wrekin

Pheasant, 54 Market Street, Wellington, Telford, Shropshire, TF1 1DT
☎ (01952) 260683 ☎ 07795 517903
ironbridgebrewery.co.uk

Wrekin Brewing Company (formerly Ironbridge Brewery) was established in 2014 at the Pheasant in Wellington, having relocated from Ironbridge, where it was first established in 2008. A 12-barrel plant is used with the majority of production supplying the brewery's two pubs. Wenlock Stout is on limited supply and is stored for four weeks and supplied in oak casks. Experience days are available.

Blond (OG 1037, ABV 3.6%)

Best Bitter (OG 1039, ABV 3.9%)

Pale Ale (OG 1040, ABV 4%)

Ironbridge Gold (OG 1045, ABV 4.4%)

Wenlock Stout (OG 1052, ABV 5.1%)

Wrexham Lager

43a St Georges Crescent, Wrexham, LL13 8DB

No real ale. Lager was first brewed in Wrexham in 1882 and returned to the town in 2011 following the closure in 2000 of the original Wrexham Lager brewery. This new, German-built, 50-hectolitre brewery produces keg and bottled lagers but no cask beers.

Wriggle Valley (NEW)

Wriggle Valley Brewery, Ryme Intrinseca, Sherbourne, Dorset, DT9 6JT ☎ 07952 198777
wrigglevalleybrewery.co.uk

Wriggle Valley began brewing in 2014 in a converted garage at the owner's home using a three-barrel plant. Brewing takes place twice a week. Beers are supplied mainly in pins to local outlets. ♦ RAIB

Ryme Rambler (OG 1040, ABV 4%)
A tawny-coloured ale.

Copper Hoppa (OG 1047, ABV 4.5%)
A full-bodied dark copper ale with big fruit aromas and flavour.

Valley Gold (ABV 4.5%)
A refreshing golden ale using English and American hops.

George Wright SIBA

Unit 11, Diamond Business Park, Sandwash Close, Rainford, Merseyside, WA11 8LY
☎ (01744) 886686 georgewrightbrewing.co.uk

George Wright started production in 2003. The original 2.5-barrel plant was replaced by a five-barrel one, which has since been upgraded again to 25 barrels with production of 200 casks a week. !! ♦

Drunken Duck (OG 1040, ABV 3.9%)
Fruity gold-coloured bitter beer with good hop and a dry aftertaste. Some acidity.

Long Boat (OG 1040, ABV 3.9%)
Good hoppy bitter with grapefruit and an almost tart bitterness throughout. Some astringency in the aftertaste. Well-balanced, light and refreshing with a good mouthfeel and long, dry finish.

Blonde Moment (OG 1040, ABV 4%)
A premium blonde beer. Light in colour, herbal nose with a sweet aftertaste.

Mild (OG 1042, ABV 4%)
A dark, creamy mild.

Pipe Dream (OG 1044, ABV 4.3%)
Refreshing, hoppy best bitter with a fruity nose and grapefruit to the fore in the taste. Lasting dry, bitter finish.

Pure Blonde (OG 1045, ABV 4.6%)
A premium blonde ale, light and hoppy with an earthy hop flavour.

Cheeky Pheasant (OG 1047, ABV 4.7%)
Light amber in colour, distinctive fruit, malty taste with a sweet aftertaste.

Roman Black (OG 1047, ABV 4.8%)
A dark premium ale, smooth and creamy leaving a long, malty, sweet taste.

Blue Moon (OG 1048, ABV 5%)

Easy-drinking, strong, gold-coloured beer. Good malt/bitter balance and well-hopped.

Mocne Piwo (OG 1051, ABV 5.1%)
Strong ale, light amber in colour with a hoppy aftertaste.

Northern Lights (OG 1049, ABV 5.1%)
Strong ale, amber in colour. A strong citrus taste is balanced by the bitter hop.

Wychwood ◉

Eagle Maltings, The Crofts, Witney, Oxfordshire, OX28 4DP
☎ (01993) 890800 ⊕ wychwood.co.uk

Wychwood brewery is located in the Cotswold market town of Witney. The brewers take inspiration from the myths and legends associated with the ancient medieval Wychwood forest to create a range of award-winning, characterful ales. Part of Marston's PLC. ‼ ➤ ◆ RAIB

Hobgoblin Gold (OG 1042, ABV 4.2%)

Piledriver (OG 1043, ABV 4.3%)

Hobgoblin (OG 1045, ABV 4.5%)
A well-balanced blend of smooth, rich and satisfying flavours combined with a crisp, refreshing bitterness.

Wye Valley SIBA ◉

Stoke Lacy, Herefordshire, HR7 4HG
☎ (01885) 490505 ☎ 07970 597937
⊕ wyevalleybrewery.co.uk

☺ Founded in 1985 in Canon Pyon, the award-winning brewery is now situated in Stoke Lacy. Regarded as a successful regional brewery, a new brewhouse was commissioned in 2013 and is now operational. ‼ ➤ RAIB

Bitter (OG 1037, ABV 3.7%) ◈
A beer whose aroma gives little hint of the bitter hoppiness that follows right through to the aftertaste.

HPA (OG 1040, ABV 4%) ◈
A pale, hoppy, malty brew with a hint of sweetness before a dry finish.

**Dorothy Goodbody's Golden Ale
(OG 1042, ABV 4.2%)**
A light, gold-coloured ale with a good hop character throughout.

Butty Bach (OG 1046, ABV 4.5%)
A burnished gold, full-bodied premium ale.

**Dorothy Goodbody's Wholesome Stout
(OG 1046, ABV 4.6%)** ◈
A smooth and satisfying stout with a bitter edge to its roast flavours. The finish combines roast grain and malt.

Wylam SIBA

South Houghton Farm, Heddon on the Wall, Northumberland, NE15 0EZ
☎ (01661) 853377 ⊕ wylambrewery.co.uk

☺ Wylam started in 2000 on a 4.5-barrel plant. New premises and a 20-barrel plant were built on the same site in 2006 which now has a visitor area and shop, with further expansion planned. The brewery delivers to more than 200 local outlets. ‼ ➤ ◆

Bitter (OG 1039, ABV 3.8%) ◈
A refreshing, copper-coloured, hoppy bitter with a clean, bitter finish.

Gold Tankard (OG 1040, ABV 4%) ◈
Fresh clean flavour, full of hops. This golden ale has a hint of citrus in the finish.

Collingwood (OG 1041, ABV 4.1%)
Honey-coloured with a sweet tangerine aroma. Light and soft-bodied with a citrus zest/fresh pinewood flavour and a dry, bitter finish.

Writer's Block (OG 1041, ABV 4.1%)
Pale gold beer with a citrus nose. Full of hops with a bitter finish

Angel (OG 1044, ABV 4.3%)
A pale copper-coloured, well-balanced bitter ale with a citrus aroma.

Red Kite (OG 1046.5, ABV 4.5%)
A ruby ale in the style of a traditional Scotch. Hops are balanced by residual maltiness to give subtle hop character and a rich palate.

Haugh Porter (OG 1046, ABV 4.6%) ◈
A dark, satisfying porter, smooth, full of character and complex flavours – hints of chocolate, liquorice and malt.

Wyre Piddle ◉

See Ambridge

XT SIBA

Notley Farm, Chearsley Road, Long Crendon, Buckinghamshire, HP18 9ER
☎ (01844) 208310 ⊕ xtbrewing.com

⊗ XT started brewing in 2011 with a British-built 18-barrel plant. It supplies direct to pubs in Buckinghamshire, Oxfordshire and the Midlands. The brewery shop sells its bottle-conditioned beers and locally-made cider. The brewery also produces a range of limited edition, one-off brews under the Animal Brewing Co name. ‼ ➤ ◆ RAIB

Four (OG 1037, ABV 3.8%)
A balanced, mellow session amber ale with pine and citrus hop notes.

One (OG 1041, ABV 4.2%)
Pale blonde beer with dry citrus, lemon and spice notes.

Three (OG 1041, ABV 4.2%)
An American-style pale ale with citrus and pine flavours, light biscuit malt character.

Two (OG 1041, ABV 4.2%)
Golden ale with chewy, juicy malts and mellow, balanced hop character.

Eight (OG 1045, ABV 4.5%)
A full-bodied dark porter with roast malt, coffee and bitter chocolate notes.

Fifteen (OG 1044, ABV 4.5%)
English-hopped IPA, pale amber with caramel malt notes and a lasting floral, grassy hop character.

Six (OG 1045, ABV 4.5%)
A rich, ruby red beer with a strong malt character and soft citrus hop finish.

Thirteen (OG 1044, ABV 4.5%)
A red ale, brewed with a range of citrus aromatic hops.

Five (OG 1052, ABV 5.5%)
An amber-coloured ale with intense hop character on a full-bodied malt base.

XPA (OG 1055, ABV 5.9%)
A pale, golden American-style IPA with a clean malt character and an intense mix of aromatic fruity hops.

Xtreme

67 Red Barn, Turves, Cambridgeshire, PE7 2DZ
☎ 07427 661839 ⊕ xtremeales.com

⊠ Run by a father and son, Xtreme began brewing in 2013 using a one-barrel plant supplying local outlets and beer festivals. ‼♦

Pigeon Ale (OG 1043, ABV 4.3%)

Chocolate Stout (OG 1050, ABV 5%)

Yard of Ale SIBA

☰ Surtees Arms, Chilton Lane, Ferryhill, County Durham, DL17 0DH
☎ (01740) 655724 ☎ 07540 733513
⊕ thesurteesarms.co.uk

Established in 2008, the 2.5-barrel microbrewery supplies ales to its brewery tap, the Surtees Arms, beer festivals and to a growing number of pubs from North Tyne to South Tees. ‼♦RAIB

One Foot In The Yard (OG 1044, ABV 4.5%)
Premium golden ale. Fruity on the nose and palate with a sweet finish.

Yates SIBA

Ghyll Farm, Westnewton, Cumbria, CA7 3NX
☎ (01697) 321081 ⊕ yatesbrewery.co.uk

☺The first of Cumbria's new generation of breweries, established in 1986 and bought by Graeme and Caroline Baxter in 1998. It brews using a 20-barrel brewhouse and reed bed effluent system, and utilises a limited number of site-grown hops in its beers. ‼♦

Bitter (OG 1036, ABV 3.7%) ▣ ♦
A well-balanced, full-bodied bitter, golden in colour with complex hop bitterness. Good aroma and distinctive flavour.

Golden Ale (OG 1038, ABV 3.9%) ♦
Skilful use of lager malt and hops results in a pale beer with a light bitterness; melon fruit and a clean, refreshing finish.

Sun Goddess (OG 1041, ABV 4.2%) ♦
A complex, full-bodied beer, packed with tropical fruit.

Contract brewed for Independent Lakeland Breweries:

Aurora (ABV 3.9%)
Smooth and zesty bitter.

Entente Cordiale (ABV 3.9%)

Yates' SIBA

Unit 4C, Langbridge Business Centre, Newchurch, Isle of Wight, PO36 0NP
☎ (01983) 867878 ⊕ yates-brewery.co.uk

Brewing started in 2000 on a five-barrel plant at the Inn at St Lawrence. In 2009 the brewery moved to Newchurch and upgraded to a 10-barrel plant. Stumpy's Brewery was bought out by Yates' in 2009 and Old Stumpy (ABV 4.5%) and Tumbledown (ABV 5%) are produced on request. ‼♦RAIB

Best Bitter (OG 1039, ABV 3.8%)

Golden Bitter (OG 1040, ABV 4%)

Undercliff Experience (OG 1040, ABV 4.1%)
An amber ale with a bittersweet malt and hop taste with a dry, lemon edge that dominates the bitter finish.

Sunfire (OG 1042, ABV 4.3%)
A full-bodied bitter with strong citrus aroma and bitter taste.

Blonde Ale (OG 1045, ABV 4.5%)

Holy Joe (OG 1050, ABV 4.9%)

Dark Side of the Wight (OG 1049, ABV 5%)
Malty milk chocolate at first in the nose, then plenty of orange fruit. It is bitter, malty and toasted to taste, with perfumed bitter orange notes always present. Bitter, roasted, perfumed finish.

TropicAle (OG 1050, ABV 5%)
Beer brewed using hops grown at the Ventnor Botanic Gardens on the Isle of Wight.

Special Draught (OG 1056, ABV 5.5%)

YSD (OG 1056, ABV 5.5%)
Golden in colour, with a tart fruit nose, this strong beer has a dry, hoppy, bitter taste that belies its strength. Fruit notes emerge and linger in the dry, bitter, hoppy aftertaste.

Wight Old Ale (OG 1060, ABV 6%)
A deep ruby ale with a smooth taste.

Yule Be Sorry (OG 1072, ABV 7.2%)
A rich, full-bodied, dark beer.

Yelland Manor

Lower Yelland Farm, Yelland, Devon, EX31 3EN
☎ (01271) 860355 ☎ 07770 267592
✉ yellandmanor@gmail.com

Yelland Manor began brewing in 2013 using a five-barrel plant situated in a converted milking parlour. Around a dozen local pubs and hotels are supplied.

Standard (OG 1043, ABV 4.2%)

Classic (OG 1045, ABV 4.4%)
Traditional English best bitter.

Yeovil SIBA ◉

Unit 5, Bofors Park, Artillery Road, Lufton Trading Estate, Yeovil, Somerset, BA22 8YH
☎ (01935) 414888 ⊕ yeovilales.com

Yeovil Ales was established in 2006 using an 18-barrel plant. ♦RAIB

Glory (OG 1039, ABV 3.8%)
A well-balanced bitter with citrus hop notes.

Star Gazer (OG 1042, ABV 4%)
Dark copper-coloured bitter with a late-hopped floral bouquet.

Summerset (OG 1043, ABV 4.1%)
Blonde ale with a fruity hop finish.

Lynx Wildcat (OG 1044, ABV 4.3%)

Stout Hearted (OG 1048, ABV 4.3%)

Ruby (OG 1047, ABV 4.5%)
A red-coloured bitter with rich malt depth.

POSH (OG 1054, ABV 5.4%)
A strong IPA with a fruity body and hoppy finish.

Yetman's

Bayfield Farm Barns, Bayfield Brecks Farm, Bayfield, Norfolk, NR25 7DZ ☎ 07774 809016 ⊕ yetmans.net

A 2.5-barrel plant built by Moss Brew was installed in restored medieval barns in 2005. The brewery supplies local free trade outlets. RAIB

Red (OG 1036, ABV 3.8%)

York SIBA ◉

12 Toft Green, York, North Yorkshire, YO1 6JT ☎ (01904) 621162 ⊕ york-brewery.co.uk

York started production in 1996, it was the first brewery in the city for 40 years and was acquired by Mitchell's of Lancaster in 2008. Five pubs are owned in York and Leeds. The brewery is open for guided tours: the 20-barrel plant has a viewing platform overlooking the conditioning and fermenting rooms. ‼ ⏚ ♦

Guzzler (OG 1036, ABV 3.6%) ◗
Refreshing golden ale with dominant hop and fruit flavours developing throughout.

Yorkshire Terrier (OG 1041, ABV 4.2%) ◗
Refreshing and distinctive amber/gold brew where fruit and hops dominate the aroma and taste. Hoppy bitterness remains assertive in the aftertaste.

Centurion's Ghost Ale (OG 1051, ABV 5.4%) ◗
Dark ruby in colour, full-tasting with mellow roast malt character balanced by light bitterness and autumn fruit flavours that linger into the aftertaste.

Yorkshire SIBA

Brewery Wharf, The Old Fruit Market, 70 Humber Street, Kingston upon Hull, HU1 1TU ☎ (01482) 618000 ☎ 07850 494990 ✉ guy@yorkshirebrewing.co.uk

⊕ Brewing started in 2012 in the Old Fruit Market quarter of Hull using a six-barrel plant. Two of the beers are named in honour of the Holy Trinity Church in Hull. A bottling plant, tours and a retail outlet are established. Festivals and local outlets are supplied. ‼ ⏚ ♦ RAIB

Mutiny (OG 1036, ABV 3.6%)
Based on a 1760 London Porter recipe. An easy-drinking ale with rich coffee and chocolate characteristics.

Tyger Tyger (OG 1036, ABV 3.6%)
A light, refreshing session bitter with a fruit twist aftertaste.

Supernatural Blonde (OG 1041, ABV 4.1%)
A refreshing pale ale with a citrus taste.

True North (OG 1041, ABV 4.1%)
A classic Yorkshire bitter.

Moondance (OG 1045, ABV 4.5%)
A golden blonde ale infused with passion fruit for a refreshing taste.

Oregon Gold (OG 1045, ABV 4.5%)

A traditionally cloudy Belgian-style wheat beer, brewed with coriander and Curacao oranges.

Passion (OG 1045, ABV 4.5%)
A golden ale with a hint of passion fruit.

Honeymoon (OG 1048, ABV 4.8%)
A traditionally cloudy Belgian-style wheat beer, infused with English honey.

Raspberry Tipple (OG 1048, ABV 4.8%)
A traditionally cloudy Belgian-style wheat beer, infused with raspberries.

Strawberry Blonde (OG 1048, ABV 4.8%)
A traditionally cloudy Belgian-style wheat beer, infused with strawberries.

Waver Ryder (OG 1052, ABV 5.2%)
A complex West Coast-style IPA.

Yorkshire Dales

Seata Barn, Elm Hill, Askrigg, North Yorkshire, DL8 3HG ☎ (01969) 622027 ☎ 07818 35592 ⊕ yorkshiredalesbrewery.com

☺Situated in the heart of the Yorkshire Dales, brewing started in a converted milking parlour in 2005. Installation of a five-barrel plant increased capacity to 20 barrels a week. More than 150 pubs are supplied throughout the North of England. ♦ RAIB

Butter Tubs (OG 1037, ABV 3.7%)
A pale golden beer with a dry bitterness complemented by strong citrus flavours and aroma.

Askrigg Bitter (OG 1038, ABV 3.8%)

Leyburn Shawl (OG 1038, ABV 3.8%)
A crisp, dry, pale ale with an underlying sharpness.

Buckden Pike (OG 1040, ABV 3.9%)
A refreshing blonde beer with a crisp, fruity finish.

Nappa Scarr (OG 1041, ABV 4%)
A golden ale brewed with a trio of American hops for citrus and peach flavours throughout.

Muker Silver (OG 1041, ABV 4.1%)
A blonde lager-style ale, crisp with a sharp, hoppy finish.

Askrigg Ale (OG 1043, ABV 4.3%)
A pale golden ale with intense aroma that generates a crisp, dry flavour with a long, bitter finish.

Garsdale Smokebox (OG 1057, ABV 5.6%)
A complex ale created by smoked and dark malts. Deep, rich chocolate and coffee flavours are complemented by the smokiness.

Yorkshire Heart SIBA

The Vineyard, Pool Lane, Nun Monkton, YO26 8EL ☎ (01423) 330716 ☎ 07838 030067 ⊕ yorkshireheart.com

☺Yorkshire Heart has been brewing since 2011 and is situated adjacent to the Yorkshire Heart vineyard and winery, not far from York. Six regular ales are produced. ‼ ♦

Lightheart (OG 1033, ABV 3.3%)
A pale ale full of fresh citrus flavours.

Hearty Bitter (OG 1037, ABV 3.7%)
A sparkling amber brown bitter full of the aromas of roasted malt.

Hearty Mild (OG 1039, ABV 4%)

A rich-flavoured mild with hints of nuts and chocolate with a natural residual sweetness.

SilverHeart IPA (OG 1039, ABV 4%)
An IPA with a slight citrus taste.

JRT Best Bitter (OG 1041, ABV 4.2%)
Golden ale with a refreshing taste and flavour.

Blackheart Stout (OG 1047, ABV 4.8%)
Stout with a chocolate, liquorice flavour.

Heartger Lager (OG 1047, ABV 5%)
Brewed using lager malts and citrus hops.

Young's

See Charles Wells (under W)

Zerodegrees SIBA

Blackheath: 29-31 Montpelier Vale, Blackheath, London, SE3 0TJ
☎ (020) 8852 5619

Bristol: 53 Colston Street, Bristol, BS1 5BA ☎ (0117) 925 2706

Cardiff: 27 Westgate Street, Cardiff, CF10 1DD ☎ (029) 2022 9494

Reading: 9 Bridge Street, Reading, Berkshire, RG1 2LR ☎ (0118) 959 7959 🌐 zerodegrees.co.uk

Brewing started in 2000 in Greenwich, London, and now four brewpubs are owned, each incorporating a state-of-the-art, computer-controlled, German plant producing unfiltered and unfined ales and lagers. All beers use natural ingredients and are suitable for vegetarians, and are served from tanks using air pressure (not CO2). There are regular seasonal specials including fruit beers: see website. !!♦

Mango Wheat Ale (OG 1040, ABV 4%)
Hazy yellow wheat beer. Syrupy sweet mango texture and flavour with a short aftertaste.

Wheat Ale (OG 1045, ABV 4.2%)

Black Lager (OG 1048, ABV 4.6%)
Dark roast aromas and flavour. Hint of sweetness with a light body and a bitter finish.

Pale Ale (OG 1046, ABV 4.6%)
Amber ale with dry hop and spiciness on the nose and palate and a bitter finish.

Pilsner (OG 1048, ABV 4.8%)
Sweet-tasting golden lager with a short, bittersweet finish.

Zymurgorium (NEW)

Unit 19, Irlam Business Centre, Soapstone Way, Irlam, M44 6RA

Office: 8 Tours Avenue, Northern Moor, Manchester, M23 0LQ 🌐 zymurgorium.com

A combined meadery and brewery established in 2014, with most of its output in bottled form.

THE BREWERIES

SIBA's Beerflex scheme

In 2002, the Society of Independent Brewers (SIBA) launched a direct delivery scheme, now renamed Beerflex, which enables its members to deliver beer to individual pubs rather than to the warehouses of pub companies. Before the scheme came into operation, small craft brewers could only sell beer to the national pubcos if they delivered beer to their depots. In one case, a brewer in Sheffield was told by Punch Taverns that the pubco would only take his beer if he delivered it to a warehouse in Liverpool and then returned to pick up the empty casks. In the time between delivery and pick-up, some of the beer would have been delivered by Punch to ... Sheffield.
The scheme has been such a success that Beerflex is now a separate but wholly owned subsidiary of SIBA. See: **www.siba.co.uk/dds_site**

Closed breweries

The following breweries have closed, gone out of business or suspended operations since the 2015 Guide was published:

2 & Nine, Warrington, Cheshire
Barge & Barrel, Elland, West Yorkshire
Beer Geek, Aston, West Midlands
Betjeman, Wantage, Oxfordshire
Big Beer, Bristol, Gloucestershire & Bristol
Brown, Clay Cross, Derbyshire
Buckingham, Buckingham, Buckinghamshire
Carters, Machen, Glamorgan
Clarence & Fredericks, Croydon, Surrey
Coach & Horses, Chepstow, Gwent
Complete Pig, Britwell Salome, Oxfordshire
Cox & Holbrook, Buxhall, Suffolk
Craftsman, Manchester, Greater Manchester
Cych Valley, Abercych, West Wales
Dem Bones, Leicester, Leicestershire
DemonBrew, Larbert, Edinburgh & the Lothians
Doghouse, Jurby, Isle of Man
Earls, N1: Islington, Greater London
Eastwood, Elland, West Yorkshire
Elveden, Elveden, Norfolk
Evening Star, St Helens, Merseyside
Four Alls, Ovington, Durham
Four Thorns, Heslington, North Yorkshire
Garage, Plympton St Maurice, Devon
Geltsdale, Brampton, Cumbria
Gwynant, Capel Bangor, West Wales
Ha'penny, Ilford, Essex
Hearsall, Coventry, West Midlands
Hektor's, Southwold, Suffolk
Henley, Henley on Thames, Oxford
Highwood (Chelmsford), Highwood, Essex
Indian Summer, Saffron Walden, Essex
Jubilee Tower, Darwen, Lancashire
Liquid, Leith, Edinburgh & the Lothians
Liverpool One, Liverpool, Merseyside
Loch Leven, Blairadam, Kingdom of Fife
Long Itch, Offchurch, Warwickshire
Malmesbury, Royal Wootton Bassett, Wiltshire
Mayfields, Leominster, Herefordshire
Minster, Kidderminster, Worcestershire
Norfolk Square, Stokesby, Norfolk
Norwich Bear, Norwich, Norfolk
Ole Slewfoot, North Walsham, Norfolk
Ordnance City, Ashcott, Somerset
Owenshaw, Sowerby Bridge, West Yorkshire
Patriot, Whichford, Warwickshire
Plymouth, Plymouth, Devon
Prior's Well, Hardwick Village, Nottinghamshire
Publisher, Ludlow, Shropshire
Ringway, Reddish, Greater Manchester
Shamblemoose, SE20: Penge, Greater London
Sherborne, Sherborne, Dorset
Shires, Madeley, Shropshire
Tunnfield, Hope Valley, Shropshire
Two Bridges, Caversham, Berkshire
Uncle Stuarts, Blofield, Norfolk
Warcop, St Brides Wentlooge, Gwent
Whale, Brailes, Warwickshire
Whalebone, Hull, East Yorkshire
Whitworth, Shirley, West Midlands
Wirksworth, Wirksworth, Derbyshire
Wissey Valley, Downham Market, Norfolk
Witham, Witham, Essex
Worth, Poynton, Cheshire
William Worthington's, Burton-upon-Trent, Staffordshire

Future breweries

The following new breweries have been notified to the Guide and will start to produce beer during 2015/2016. In a few cases, they were in production during the summer of 2015 but were too late for a full listing:

12 Bar, Marden, Kent
4Four, Llanfallteg, Carmarthenshire
Aardvark, Sheffield, South Yorkshire
Ainsty, Malton, North Yorkshire
Alehouse & Kitchen, Worthing, West Sussex
Ampthill, Ampthill, Bedfordshire
Attwell's, St Nicholas at Wade, Kent
Bakers Dozen, Ketton, Leicestershire
Black Tap, Stafford, Staffordshire
Box Social, Newcastle upon Tyne, Tyne & Wear
Bridgnorth, Bridgnorth, Shropshire
Bragdy Twt Lol, Pontypridd, Glamorgan
Broadway, Shifnal, Shropshire
Burton Town, Burton upon Trent, Staffordshire
Calderdale, Wainstalls, West Yorkshire
Campervan, Edinburgh, Edinburgh & the Lothians
Consall Forge, Consall Forge, Staffordshire
Delaneys, Norwich, Norfolk
Drink Up, Horwich, Greater Manchester
Dynamite Valley, Ponsanooth, Cornwall
Electric Bear, Bath, Somerset
Elusive, Farnborough, Surrey
Farr, Harpenden, Hertfordshire
Farmageddon, Comber, Northern Ireland
Fat Brewer, Crook, Co Durham
Five Kingdoms, Isle of Whithorn, Dumfries & Galloway
Fleetwood, Fleetwood, Lancashire
Forth Bridge, Edinburgh, Edinburgh & the Lothians
Furnace, Derby, Derbyshire
Godstone, South Godstone, Surrey
Grasshopper, Nuthall, Nottinghamshire
Great Central, Leicester, Leicestershire
Harborough, Market Harborough, Leicestershire
Hop Forge, Lledrod, West Wales
Hornes, Milton Keynes, Buckinghamshire
Inkspot, Greater London
Karrock, Brampton, Cumbria
Kettledrum, Burham, Kent
Mad Dog, Southampton, Hampshire
Med, Cambridge, Cambridgeshire
Neatishead, Neatishead, Norfolk
Pumphouse, Toppesfield, Essex
Red Hand, Donaghmore, Northern Ireland
Red Star, Formby, Merseyside
Rivington, Chorley, Lancashire
St Ives, St Ives, Cornwall
St Judes, Ipswich, Suffolk
Salisbury, Bournemouth, Dorset
Secret Herb Garden, Loanhead, Edinburgh & the Lothians
Snowhill, Scorton, Lancashire
Stanley, Portslade, East Sussex
Stratford St Mary Swan, Stratford St Mary, Suffolk
Stubborn Mule, Timperley, Greater Manchester
Tarn 51, Altofts, West Yorkshire
Trinity, Outwood, West Yorkshire
Virtuoso, Norwich, Norfolk
Woodcote Manor, Dodford, Worcestershire

Indexes & Further Information

Places index

C

N

O

P

Q

R

S

U

V

W

Y

Beers index

These beers refer to those in bold type in the breweries section (beers in regular production) and so therefore do not include seasonal, special or occasional beers that may be mentioned elsewhere in the text.

A

C

D

BEERS INDEX

E

G

H

J

N

BEERS INDEX

O

P

BEERS INDEX

Q

R

S

T

U

V

X

Y

Z

Award winning pubs
Local CAMRA Pubs of the Year

The Pub of the Year competition is judged by CAMRA members. Each of the CAMRA branches votes for its favourite pub: criteria include the quality and choice of real ale, atmosphere, customer service and value. The pubs listed below are current winners of the title; look out for the 🏆 symbol next to the entries in the Guide.

England

🏆 Bedfordshire
Sun, Felmersham
Engineers Arms, Henlow
Black Lion, Leighton Buzzard

🏆 Berkshire
Six Bells, Beenham
Fox & Hounds, Caversham
Queen's Head, Wokingham

🏆 Buckinghamshire
Mitre, Buckingham
White Horse, Hedgerley
Royal Standard, Wooburn Common

🏆 Cambridgeshire
Mill, Cambridge
Prince Albert, Ely
Hand & Heart, Peterborough

🏆 Cheshire
Cellar, Chester
Hops, Crewe
White Lion, Disley
Swan with Two Nicks, Little Bollington
Lion Hotel, Moulton
Prospect, Runcorn

🏆 Cornwall
Hole in the Wall, Bodmin

🏆 Derbyshire
Smith's Tavern, Ashbourne
Old Poets' Corner, Ashover
Druid Inn, Birchover
Black Horse, Coton-in-the-Elms
Alexandra Hotel, Derby
Dewdrop, Ilkeston
Holly Bush, Makeney
Angler's Rest, Millers Dale
Devonshire Arms, South Normanton
Old Hall Inn, Whitehough

🏆 Devon
Bridford Inn, Bridford
Red Lion, Exbourne
Fortescue Hotel, Plymouth
Tom Cobley Tavern, Spreyton

🏆 Dorset
Royal Oak, Weymouth
Taphouse, Wimborne Minster

🏆 Durham
Quakerhouse, Darlington
Old Elm Tree, Durham
Surtees Arms, Ferryhill Station
Rat Race Ale House, Hartlepool

🏆 Essex
Orange Tree, Chelmsford
Victoria Inn, Colchester
Horse & Groom, Cornish Hall End
White Hart, Grays
Mayflower, Leigh-on-Sea
Carpenters' Arms, Maldon
Woodbine Inn, Waltham Abbey
White Hart, Weeley Heath

🏆 Gloucestershire
Sandford Park Alehouse, Cheltenham
Plough Inn, Cold Aston
Salutation Inn, Ham

🏆 Hampshire
George, Alton
Flowerpots Inn, Cheriton
Plough Inn, Little London
Hole in the Wall, Portsmouth

🏆 Herefordshire
Beer in Hand, Hereford

🏆 Hertfordshire
Orange Tree, Baldock
Rising Sun, Berkhamsted
Sportsman, Croxley Green
Crooked Billet, Ware

🏆 Isle of Wight
Railway, Ryde

🏆 Kent
Yard of Ale, Broadstairs
Carpenters Arms, Coldred
Bell & Jorrocks, Frittenden
Cock Inn, Luddesdown
Windmill, Sevenoaks Weald
Paper Mill, Sittingbourne
Red Lion, Snargate
King's Arms, Upper Upnor
Ship Centurion, Whitstable

🏆 Lancashire
Admiral Lord Rodney, Colne
Borough, Lancaster
Taps, Lytham
Cricketers, Ormskirk
Ale Emporium, Preston

🏆 Leicestershire
Wheel, Branston
Halfway House, Donisthorpe
Queen's Head, Hinckley
King's Head, Leicester
Stilton Cheese, Somerby

🏆 Lincolnshire
Nottingham House, Cleethorpes
Eight Jolly Brewers, Gainsborough
Dog & Bone, Lincoln
White Hart, Ludford
Royal Oak, Snitterby

🏆 Greater London
Hope, Carshalton
Craft Beer Co, EC1: Hatton Garden
Olde Mitre Inne, High Barnet
Woodies, New Malden
Tapping the Admiral, NW1: Camden Town
One Inn The Wood, Petts Wood
Blythe Hill Tavern, SE23: Forest Hill
Eagle Ale House, SW11: Clapham Junction
Rifleman, Twickenham
Mad Bishop & Bear, W2: Paddington
Grosvenor, W7: Hanwell
Travellers Friend, Woodford Green

🏆 Greater Manchester
Pendle Witch, Atherton
Harewood Arms, Broadbottom
Victoria & Albert, Horwich
Crown & Kettle, Manchester: City Centre
Knott Bar, Manchester: City Centre
Baum, Rochdale
Magnet, Stockport: Heaton Norris
John Bull Chophouse, Wigan

🏆 Merseyside
Gallagher's Pub & Barber's Shop, Birkenhead
Liverpool Pigeon, Crosby
Freshfield, Freshfield
Cricketers Arms, St Helens

Norfolk
Coach & Horses, Dersingham
Queen's Head, Earsham

Northampton
Head of Steam, Lilbourne
Queen Adelaide, Northampton

Northumberland
John Bull Inn, Alnwick

Nottinghamshire
Robin Hood & Little John, Arnold
Marquis of Granby, Granby
Railway Inn, Mansfield
Final Whistle, Southwell

Oxfordshire
Red Lion, Horley
Plum Pudding, Milton
Masons Arms, Oxford
Royal Oak, Wantage

Rutland
Green Dragon, Ryhall

Shropshire
Black Boy, Bridgnorth
Prince of Wales, Shrewsbury

Somerset
Plough, Congresbury
George Inn, Croscombe
Halfway House, Pitney

Staffordshire
Coopers Tavern, Burton upon Trent
Harrows Inn, Coven
Cat Inn, Enville
Cross Keys Hotel, Hednesford
Wilkes Head, Leek
Whippet Inn, Lichfield
Dog & Partridge, Marchington
Olde Rose & Crown, Stafford
Holy Inadequate, Stoke-on-Trent: Etruria

Suffolk
Dove, Bury St Edmunds
Oakes Barn, Bury St Edmunds

Surrey
Happy Man, Englefield Green
Albert Arms, Esher
Jolly Sailor, Farnham
Surrey Oaks, Newdigate

East Sussex
Brewers Arms, Lewes
Tower, St Leonards on Sea

West Sussex
White Horse, Maplehurst
Inglenook, Pagham
Parsonage Bar & Restaurant, Worthing

Tyne & Wear
Bodega, Newcastle upon Tyne: City Centre
Steamboat, South Shields

Warwickshire
Lord Nelson Inn, Ansley
Angel Ale House, Atherstone
Bull & Butcher, Corley Moor
Seven Stars, Rugby
Bear at the Swan's Nest Hotel, Stratford-upon-Avon
Victoria Works, Studley
Wild Boar, Warwick

West Midlands
Robin Hood, Amblecote
Old Moseley Arms, Birmingham: Balsall Heath
Bishop Vesey, Boldmere
Swan, Brownhills
Old Windmill, Coventry
Beacon Hotel, Sedgley
Hail to the Ale, Wolverhampton

Wiltshire
Bell Inn, Lacock
Wyndham Arms, Salisbury
Benett Arms, Semley
Carters Rest, Wroughton

Worcestershire
Holly Bush, Belbroughton
Three Kings, Hanley Castle
Coach & Horses, Harvington
Bell, Pensax

East Yorkshire
Chequers Micropub, Beverley

North Yorkshire
Harrogate Tap, Harrogate
White Hart Country Inn, Hawes
Crown Inn, Manfield
Dr Phil's Real Ale House, Middlesbrough
Sun Inn, Pickering
Maltings, York

South Yorkshire
Old No.7, Barnsley
Corner Pin, Doncaster
Beehive, Harthill
Kelham Island Tavern, Sheffield: Kelham Island

West Yorkshire
Jacob's Beer House, Bradford
Junction, Castleford
Three Pigeons, Halifax
Grove, Huddersfield
Brown Cow, Keighley
Kirkstall Bridge Inn, Leeds: Kirkstall
Flowerpot, Mirfield

Wales

Glamorgan
Lansdowne, Cardiff
Urban Tap House, Cardiff
Cross Inn, Cwmfelin
Pontardawe Inn, Pontardawe
Bunch of Grapes, Pontypridd
No Sign Bar, Swansea

Gwent
Clytha Arms, Clytha
Lamb, Newport

Mid-Wales
Star Inn, Talybont-on-Usk

North-East Wales
Blue Bell Inn, Halkyn
Bridge End Inn, Ruabon

North-West Wales
Albion Ale House, Conwy
Snowdonia Park, Waunfawr

West Wales
Cresselly Arms, Cresswell Quay
Royal Oak, Rhandirmwyn
Talbot, Tregaron

Scotland

Aberdeen & Grampian
Krakatoa, Aberdeen

Ayrshire & Arran
Saracen's Head Hotel, Beith

Dumfries & Galloway
Cavens Arms, Dumfries

Edinburgh & the Lothians
Stockbridge TapEdinburgh: North

Greater Glasgow & Clyde Valley
State Bar, Glasgow
Callum's, Johnstone

Highlands & Western Isles
Stein Inn, Waternish, Isle of Skye

Kingdom of Fife
Foresters Arms, Aberdour
Loch Lomond, Stirling & the Trossachs
Corbie Inn, Bo'ness

Tayside
Bankfoot Inn, Bankfoot

Channel Islands

Guernsey
Cornerstone Café Bar, St Peter Port

Jersey
Lamplighter, St Helier

Isle of Man

Woodbourne Hotel, Douglas

Readers' recommendations

Suggestions for pubs to be included or excluded

All pubs are regularly surveyed by local branches of the Campaign for Real Ale to ensure they meet the standards required by the *Good Beer Guide*. If you would like to comment on a pub already featured, or on any you think should be featured, please fill in the form below (or a copy of it), and send it to the address indicated. Alternatively, email **gbgeditor@camra.org.uk**. Your views will be passed on to the branch concerned. Please mark your envelope/email with the county where the pub is, which will help us to direct your comments efficiently.

Pub name:

Address:

Reason for recommendation/criticism:

Pub name:

Address:

Reason for recommendation/criticism:

Pub name:

Address:

Reason for recommendation/criticism:

Your name and address:

Please send to: [Name of county] Section, Good Beer Guide,
230 Hatfield Road, St Albans, Hertfordshire AL1 4LW

Have your say

Feedback on the Good Beer Guide

We are always trying to improve the *Good Beer Guide* for our readers and we welcome your feedback. If you have any suggestions for how the *Good Beer Guide*, Good Beer Guide Mobile Edition or sat-nav POI could be improved, please let us know. Simply fill out the form below (or a copy of it) and send it to the address indicated, or make your comments on our website at: **www.camra.org.uk/gbgfeedback**. Thank you.

Colour sections:

Pubs section:

Brewery section:

Good Beer Guide e-book:

Good Beer Guide Mobile:

Good Beer Guide sat-nav POI:

What other suggestions do you have?

Please send to: Good Beer Guide – Have your say,
230 Hatfield Road, St Albans, Hertfordshire AL1 4LW

Outside influences

Beer for all seasons

The dynamic, fast-changing British beer scene is bursting with an array of new styles. Brewers are no longer content to remain with a limited range of beers based solely on British styles but are scouring the world to find new flavoursome drinks.

The 'buzz beer' of the moment is a Belgian style called saison. It was once confined to the French-speaking area of Belgium but it's been taken up with great enthusiasm by not only British brewers but also by beer makers in Australia and the United States.

Saison, as the name suggests, was originally a seasonal beer, brewed by farmers to refresh themselves and their labourers during the harvest period. The classic producer of saison is Dupont at Tourpes, which started life on a farm that produced beer from the 1840s. It's now completely dedicated to brewing. Its main beer is called simply Saison, is 6.5% alcohol, and is brewed with Pilsner malt and English and Styrian Goldings hops.

It's the nearby Brasserie à Vapeur – the Steam Brewery – that has caught the imagination of a number of British brewers. Owner Jean-Louis Dits has a passion for 'botanicals' and uses such herbs and spices as anis, black pepper, orange peel and medicinal lichen in his interpretations of saison.

A further excellent example comes from the Silly Brewery, which is not a joke but is based in a village called Silly. As with Dupont, brewing started on a farm in the 19th century. Silly's 5% Saison is notably fruity owing to the use of some darker caramalt alongside pale malt, and the beer is hopped with English Challenger and German Hallertauer varieties.

British brewers now trying their hands at saison include Brew by Numbers, By the Horns, Ilkley, Partizan, Poppyland and Wild Beer. Ilkley has a rhubarb saison while Martin Warren at Poppyland in Cromer, Norfolk, has several versions, including damson and crab – Cromer is famous for its seafood as well as poppies.

Martin has also created interest in an almost forgotten German beer known as Gose. The beer is an ancient style from the town of Goslar in the Leipzig region and it has links to the 'wild fermentation' lambic beers of Belgium and the sour wheat beers of Berlin. Gose is made from a 50:50 blend of malted barley and wheat, is lightly hopped and its signature flavour comes from the addition of salt as a flavour enhancer. Martin follows the correct procedure by removing a portion of the mash of grain and allowing it to sour from the action of wild yeasts in the atmosphere and then returning it to the rest of the mash.

Sour beer has become a fashionable style in Britain, with the main inspiration coming from Belgian lambic beer. Lambic and its blended version called gueuze are made entirely by spontaneous fermentation, allowing wild yeasts in the atmosphere to begin the process of

Poppyland Brewery in Norfolk makes several saisons

transforming malt sugars into alcohol. Most British brewers of the style lack the equipment to make lambic in the true fashion and sour the beer by adding the main wild yeast, *Brettanomyces*, to their beers: samples of 'Brett' as it's known for short, can be bought commercially.

One British brewer who makes lambic in the authentic fashion is Elgood's in Wisbech, Cambridgeshire, which has the open cooling trays, known as 'cool ships', where the sugary malt extract or wort is inoculated by wild yeasts. Following fermentation, the beer is stored for several months in oak casks bought from the French wine industry. As a result of strict *appellations* imposed by both the Belgian and European governments, the terms lambic and gueuze can be used only in Belgium, hence the term 'sour' in other countries.

Elgood's Coolship lambic-style beer

Other brewers producing sour beer include Buxton, Chorlton, Kernel, Siren and Wild Beer. Belgian lambic brewers don't like the term sour: they say their beers are acidic, in the manner of Brut Champagne, but the term 'acidic beer' is unlikely to find favour in overseas markets.

Belgium is also famous for its ales brewed in monasteries by Trappist monks. The *Good Beer Guide* reported in 2015 on the abbey beer brewed by the Little Valley brewery in North Yorkshire for Benedictine monks at Ampleforth Abbey. This has been joined by Quarr Abbey Ale, brewed by Goddards on the Isle of Wight for Cistercian monks at Quarr Abbey. The abbey dates from 1132 and was wrecked during the dissolution of Henry VIII but was rebuilt early in the 20th century. The 6.5% bottled beer has an addition of sweet gale and coriander, grown in the abbey gardens, alongside malt and hops, to give the beer an authentic medieval character.

A number of British brewers have taken up the challenge of producing another Belgium abby tradition: Dubbel or dark ales and strong golden Triples. Another Belgian tradition of adding fruit to beer has been taken up by a large number of British brewers. In Belgium, there are two types of fruit lambic, made with the addition of cherries and raspberries, but many other brewers there also add fruit to beers made by conventional fermentation. The addition of fruit, as well as herbs, spices, chocolate and coffee, is now widespread in Britain.

Wheat beers, in both the German and Belgian styles, are equally popular here. A typical Bavarian-style wheat beer, if brewed with the correct yeast culture, will have a quenching character with pleasing flavours of bubblegum, bananas and cloves. Belgian-style wheat beer is equally refreshing and often features the addition of milled coriander seeds and orange peel.

For several years, British brewers have followed the American trend of producing pale ales and IPAs with a massive bittersweet citrus character due to the use of American hops. But American brewers are now moving away from 'extreme beers' and are making 'session' pale ales that, while rich in hop character, are more easily drinkable and less challenging. A number of British-brewed 'American Pale Ales' are now following this welcome trend. As the castle guard says in Hamlet: 'For this relief, much thanks.'

Quarr Abbey on the Isle of Wight is run by Cistercian monks and a local brewery makes beer for them using sweet gale and coriander from the monastery gardens

Books for beer lovers

CAMRA's **So, You Want to Be a Beer Expert?**

Jeff Evans

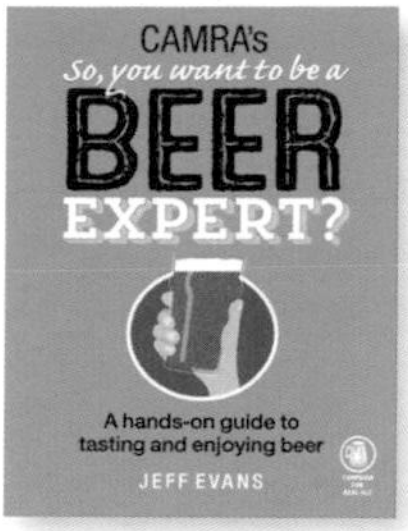

More people than ever are searching for an understanding of what makes a great beer, and this book meets that demand by presenting a hands-on course in beer appreciation, with sections on understanding the beer styles of the world, beer flavours, how beer is made, the ingredients, and more. Uniquely, *So, You Want to Be a Beer Expert?* doesn't just relate the facts, but helps readers reach conclusions for themselves. Key to this are the interactive tastings that show readers, through their own taste buds, what beer is all about. CAMRA's *So, You Want to Be a Beer Expert?* is the ideal book for anyone who wants to further their knowledge and enjoyment of beer.

£12.99 ISBN 978-1-85249-322-6 CAMRA members' price £10.99 Publishes October 2015

Good Bottled Beer Guide

Jeff Evans

A pocket-sized guide for discerning drinkers looking to buy bottled real ales and enjoy a fresh glass of their favourite beers at home. The new eighth edition of the *Good Bottled Beer Guide* is completely revised, updated and redesigned to showcase the very best bottled British real ales now being produced, and detail where they can be bought. Everything you need to know about bottled beers; tasting notes, ingredients, brewery details, and a glossary to help the reader understand more about them.

£12.99 ISBN 978-1-85249-309-7 CAMRA members' price £10.99

The CAMRA Guide to **London's Best Beer, Pubs & Bars** - 2nd Edition

Des de Moor

The essential guide to London beer, completely revised for 2015. *London's Best Beer, Pubs & Bars* is packed with detailed maps and easy-to-use listings to help you find the best places to enjoy perfect pints in the capital. Laid out by area, the book will be your companion in exploring the best pubs serving the best British and world beers. Additional features include descriptions of London's rich history of brewing and the city's vibrant modern brewing scene, where brewery numbers have more than doubled in the last three years. The venue listings are fully illustrated with colour photographs and include a variety of real ale pubs, bars and other outlets, with detailed information to make planning any excursion quick and easy.

'...meticulously researched and open-minded' Will Hawkes, *The Independent*

£12.99 ISBN 978-1-85249-323-36 CAMRA members' price £10.99

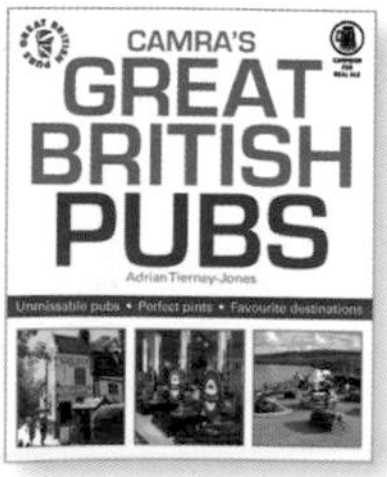

Great British Pubs

Adrian Tierney-Jones

Great British Pubs is a practical guide that takes you around the very best public houses in Britain and celebrates the pub as a national institution. Every kind of pub is represented in these pages with categorised listings featuring full-colour photography illustrating a host of excellent pubs from the seaside to the city and from the historic to the ultra-modern. Articles on beer brewing, cider making, classic pub food recipes and traditional pub games are included to help the reader fully understand what makes a pub 'great'.

£14.99 ISBN 987-1-85249-265-6 CAMRA members' price £12.99

Brew Your Own British Real Ale

Graham Wheeler

The perennial favourite of home-brewers, *Brew Your Own British Real Ale* is a CAMRA classic. This new edition is enhanced and illustrated. Written by homebrewing authority Graham Wheeler, *Brew Your Own British Real Ale* includes detailed brewing instructions for both novice and more advanced home-brewers, as well as comprehensive recipes for recreating some of Britain's best-loved beers at home.

£14.99 ISBN 978-1-85249-319-6 CAMRA members' price £12.99

The Beer Select-O-Pedia

Michael Larson

The Beer Select-O-Pedia is a an enthusiast's guide through the delicious world of beer, demystifying scores of traditional and innovative new styles from Britain & Ireland, Continental Europe and America. Organised in families of beer styles according to their origins, it is easy to look up the style of beer you are drinking and discover more. Much more than a list of recommended brews and breweries, this book gives beer lovers all the information they need to navigate the ever-expanding world of beer and find new brews to excite their tastebuds.

£12.99 ISBN 978-1-85249-318-9 CAMRA members' price £10.99

CAMRA's **101 Beer Days Out**

Tim Hampson

Revised and updated for 2015, *101 Beer Days Out* is the perfect handbook for the beer tourist wanting to explore beer, pubs and brewing in the UK. From brewery tours to rail-ale trails, beer festivals to hop farms, brewing courses to historic pubs, Britain has a huge variety of beer experiences to explore and enjoy. *101 Beer Days Out* is ordered geographically, so you can easily find a beer day out wherever you are in Britain, and includes full visitor information, maps and colour photography, with detailed information on opening hours, local landmarks and public transport links to make planning any excursion quick and easy.

£12.99 ISBN 978-1-85249-328-8 CAMRA members' price £10.99 Publishes October 2015

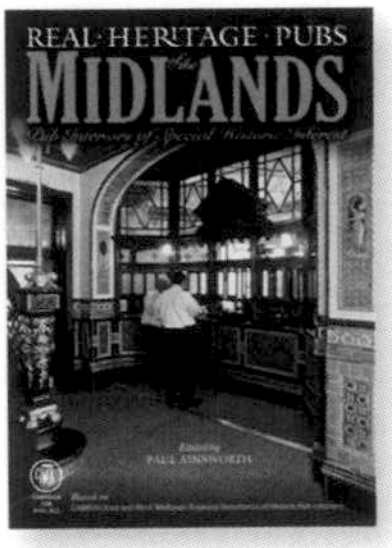

Real Heritage Pubs of the Midlands

Edited by **Paul Ainsworth**

This guide will lead you to the pubs throughout the Midlands that still have interiors or internal features of real historic significance. They range from rural time-warp pubs to ornate drinking palaces, and include some unsung interiors from the inter-war period. This is the first guide of its kind for the Midlands and it champions the need to celebrate, understand and protect the genuine pub heritage remaining to us.

'...a superbly-illustrated tome' *Derby Telegraph*

£5.99 ISBN 978-1-85249-324-0 CAMRA members' price £4.99

Britain's Beer Revolution

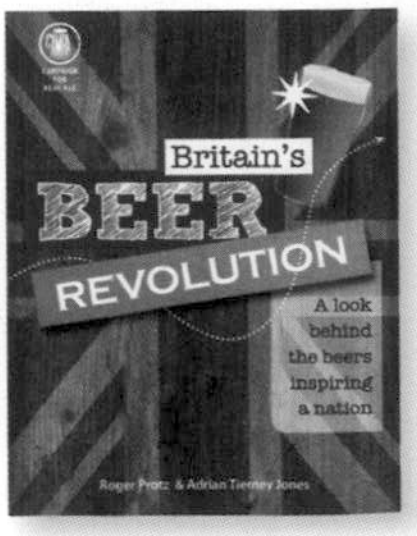

Roger Protz & Adrian Tierney-Jones

UK brewing has seen unprecedented growth in the last decade. Breweries of all shapes and sizes are flourishing. Established brewers applying generations of tradition in new ways rub shoulders at the bar with new micro-brewers. Headed by real ale, a 'craft' beer revolution is sweeping the country. In *Britain's Beer Revolution* Roger Protz and Adrian Tierney-Jones look behind the beer labels and shine a spotlight on what makes British beer so good.

£14.99 ISBN 978-1-85249-265-6 CAMRA members' price £12.99

Order these and other CAMRA books online at **www.camra.org.uk/books**, ask your local bookstore, or contact: CAMRA, 230 Hatfield Road, St Albans, AL1 4LW. Tel: 01727 867201.

Good Beer Guide digital editions

The *Good Beer Guide* is also available in digital formats, including an e-book, mobile app and sat-nav download. Together, these offer the perfect solution to pub-finding on the move. To discover more, scan the QR code or visit **www.camra.org.uk/gbgdigital**.

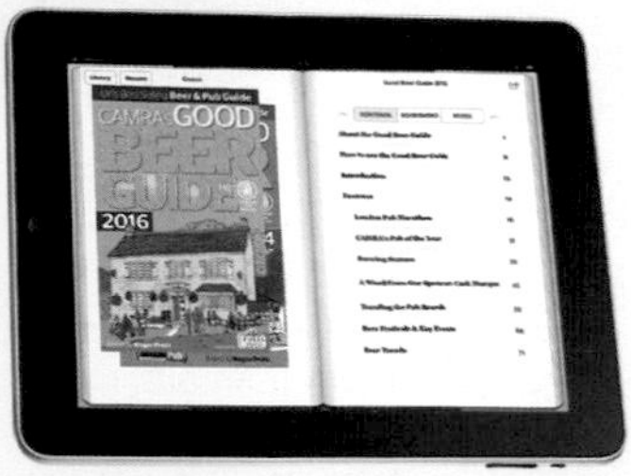

Good Beer Guide e-book

The *Good Beer Guide 2016* e-book will be available from autumn 2015 in the widely compatible ePUB and Kindle formats. The e-book provides all the benefits of portable, searchable and adaptable digital content while also making the Guide fully interactive, taking advantage of GPS, mobile and Internet connectivity to bring exciting new features.

- Portable, electronic version of the printed Guide
- Fully interactive, searchable content in ePUB and Kindle formats, compatible with iPad, Kindle and many other e-readers
- Includes full-colour features and images from the printed book, as well as complete pubs and breweries listings*
- Active e-mail and web links within entries*
- Postcode links to Google maps to help you navigate*

ePUB

Available on the iBookstore

amazonkindle

Visit **www.camra.org.uk/gbg** for further information and for details of where to buy.

*Where e-reader allows

Good Beer Guide Mobile

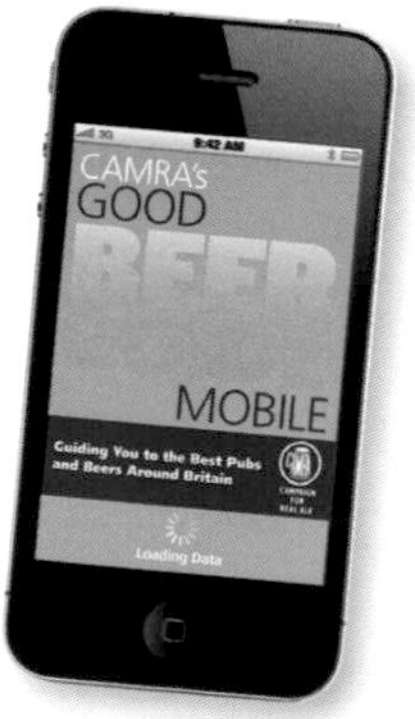

The Good Beer Guide Mobile app for Apple and Android™ devices provides detailed information on local *Good Beer Guide* pubs, breweries and beers wherever you are or wherever you are going. Features include:†

- Search results with full pub descriptions and detailed visitor information
- Detailed information on all UK real-ale breweries and their beers
- CAMRA tasting notes for hundreds of regular beers
- Interactive maps to help you find your way
- Search by postcode, pub or place name, or auto-locate
- Custom functions that allow you to mark your favourite pubs and write your own personal reviews

To download, visit the Apple **App Store** or **Google Play** store.
For more information visit: **www.camra.org.uk/gbgmobile**

Available on the App Store

Google play

†App is free to download with an in-app subscription required for full features. Subscription-free use allows for sinlge, auto-locate search results only. NOTE: Standard network charges apply when using the app.

Good Beer Guide sat-nav download

Priced at just £2.99, the Good Beer Guide POI (Points of Interest) file allows users of TomTom, Garmin and Navman sat-nav systems to see the locations of all the 4,500 current *Good Beer Guide* pubs and all the UK's real-ale breweries and plan routes to them. So, no more wasting time getting lost down country lanes – now, wherever you are, there is no excuse for not finding your nearest *Good Beer Guide* pub.

For more information and to download visit: **http://www.camra.org.uk/gbg-sat-nav**

An offer for CAMRA members

Good Beer Guide annual subscription

Being a CAMRA member brings many benefits, not least a big discount on the *Good Beer Guide*. Now you can take advantage of an even bigger discount on the Guide by taking out an annual subscription.

Simply fill in the form below and the Direct Debit form on p1015 (photocopies will do if you don't want to spoil your book), and send them to CAMRA at 230 Hatfield Road, St Albans, Hertfordshire AL1 4LW. You will then **receive the Good Beer Guide automatically every year**. It will be posted to you before the official publication date and before any other postal sales are processed. You won't have to bother with filling in cheques every year and you will receive the book at a lower price than other CAMRA members (for instance, the **2015** Guide was sold to annual subscribers **for just £10** including postage & packing). So sign up now and be sure of receiving your copy early every year.

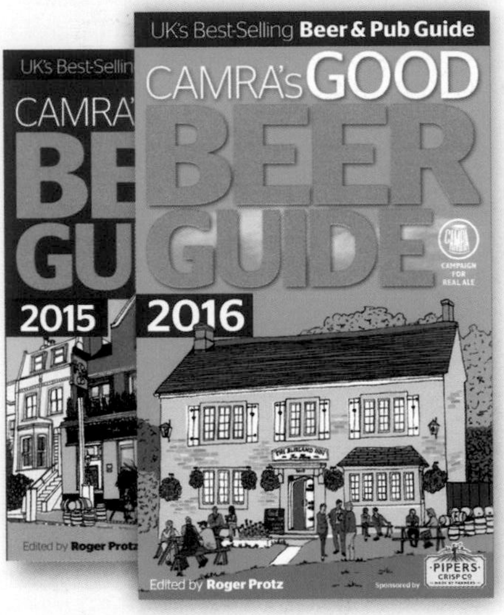

Note: This offer is open only to CAMRA members and is only available through using a Direct Debit instruction to a UK bank. This offer applies to the **Good Beer Guide 2017** onwards.

CAMRA's GOOD BEER GUIDE

Name ______________________

CAMRA Membership No. ______________________

Address and Postcode ______________________

____

____

____

____

I wish to purchase the *Good Beer Guide* annually by Direct Debit and I have completed the Direct Debit instructions to my bank which are enclosed.

Signature ______________________ Date ______________________

CAMPAIGN FOR REAL ALE

Instruction to your Bank or Building Society to pay by Direct Debit

DIRECT Debit

Please fill in the form and send to: Campaign for Real Ale Ltd, 230 Hatfield Road, St. Albans, Herts. AL1 4LW

Name and full postal address of your Bank or Building Society

To The Manager — Bank or Building Society

Address

Postcode

Name (s) of Account Holder (s)

Bank or Building Society account number

Branch Sort Code

Reference Number

Originator's Identification Number

9	2	6	1	2	9

FOR CAMRA OFFICIAL USE ONLY

This is not part of the instruction to your Bank or Building Society

Membership Number

Name

Postcode

Instruction to your Bank or Building Society

Please pay CAMRA Direct Debits from the account detailed on this Instruction subject to the safeguards assured by the Direct Debit Guarantee. I understand that this instruction may remain with CAMRA and, if so, will be passed electronically to my Bank/Building Society

Signature(s)

Date

Banks and Building Societies may not accept Direct Debit Instructions for some types of account

detached and retained this section

DIRECT Debit

This Guarantee should be detached and retained by the payer.

The Direct Debit Guarantee

- This Guarantee is offered by all Banks and Building Societies that take part in the Direct Debit Scheme. The efficiency and security of the Scheme is monitored and protected by your own Bank or Building Society.
- If the amounts to be paid or the payment dates change, CAMRA will notify you 10 working days in advance of your account being debited or as otherwise agreed.
- If an error is made by CAMRA or your Bank or Building Society, you are guaranteed a full and immediate refund from your branch of the amount paid.
- You can cancel a Direct Debit at any time by writing to your Bank or Building Society. Please also send a copy of your letter to us.

Join the Campaign!

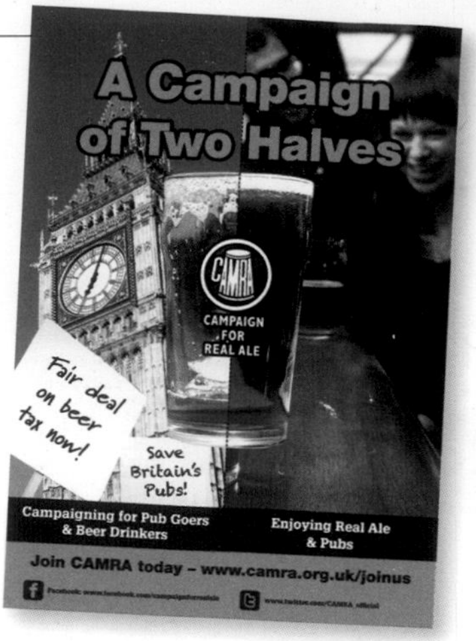

CAMRA, the Campaign for Real Ale, is an independent not-for-profit, volunteer-led consumer group. We promote good-quality real ale and pubs, as well as lobbying government to champion drinkers' rights and protect local pubs as centres of community life.

CAMRA has over 175,000 members from all ages and backgrounds, brought together by a common belief in the issues that CAMRA deals with and their love of good-quality British beer. From just £24 a year – that's less than a pint a month – you can join CAMRA and enjoy the following benefits:

- A monthly colour newspaper and quarterly magazine informing you about beer and pub news and detailing events and beer festivals around the country.
- Free or reduced entry to over 160 national, regional and local beer festivals.
- Money off many of our publications including the *Good Beer Guide* and the *Good Bottled Beer Guide*.
- A 10% discount on all holidays booked with Cottages4you and Hoseasons, a 10% discount with Beer Hawk, plus much more.
- £20 worth of J D Wetherspoon real ale vouchers* (40 x 50 pence off a pint).

For more details please visit **www.camra.org.uk/benefits**.

If you feel passionately about your pint, here is how to join us...

Just fill in the application form below (or a photocopy of it) and the Direct Debit form on the previous page to receive 15 months membership for the price of 12!**

(If you wish to join but do not want to pay by Direct Debit, please fill in the application form and send along with a cheque, payable to CAMRA. Please note than non-Direct Debit payments will incur a £2 surcharge.)

Please send applications to: CAMRA, 230 Hatfield Road, St Albans, Hertfordshire AL1 4LW

Please tick appropriate box	**Direct Debit**		**Non-Direct Debit**	
Single membership (UK & EU)	£24.00	☐	£26.00	☐
Concessionary membership (under 26 or 60 and over)	£16.50	☐	£18.50	☐
Joint membership	£29.50	☐	£31.50	☐
Concessionary joint membership	£19.50	☐	£21.50	☐

Life membership information is available on request.

Title ____ Forename(s) ______________________ Surname ______________________

Address ____

____ Postcode ______________

Date of Birth ______________ Email address ______________________________

Signature ____

Partner's details (for Joint Membership)

Title ____ Forename(s) ______________________ Surname ______________________

Date of Birth ______________ Email address ______________________________

CAMRA will occasionally send you e-mails related to your membership. We will also allow your local branch access to your email. If you would like to opt-out of contact from your local branch please tick here ☐ (at no point will your details be released to a third party).

Find out more at **www.camra.org.uk/join** or telephone **01727 867201**

*Joint members receive £20 worth of J D Wetherspoon vouchers to share.
**15 months membership for the price of 12 is only available the first time a member pays by Direct Debit.
NOTE: Membership prices and benefits are subject to change. REF: GBG2016